March 14–18, 2015
Vancouver, BC, Canada

Association for Computing Machinery

Advancing Computing as a Science & Profession

CSCW'15

Proceedings of the 2015 ACM International Conference on Computer-Supported Cooperative Work and Social Computing

Sponsored by:

ACM SIGCHI

Supported by:

NSF, Facebook, GRAND, Microsoft Research, Bloomberg, Northwestern University School of Communication, IBM Research, Google and Simon Fraser University

Vol. 1 of 2

Association for
Computing Machinery

Advancing Computing as a Science & Profession

The Association for Computing Machinery
2 Penn Plaza, Suite 701
New York, New York 10121-0701

Notice to Past Authors of ACM-Published Articles
ACM intends to create a complete electronic archive of all articles and/or other material previously published by ACM. If you have written a work that has been previously published by ACM in any journal or conference proceedings prior to 1978, or any SIG Newsletter at any time, and you do NOT want this work to appear in the ACM Digital Library, please inform permissions@acm.org, stating the title of the work, the author(s), and where and when published.

ISBN: 978-1-4503-2922-4 (Digital)

ISBN: 978-1-4503-3766-3 (Print)

Additional copies may be ordered prepaid from:

ACM Order Department
PO Box 30777
New York, NY 10087-0777, USA

Phone: 1-800-342-6626 (USA and Canada)
+1-212-626-0500 (Global)
Fax: +1-212-944-1318
E-mail: acmhelp@acm.org
Hours of Operation: 8:30 am – 4:30 pm ET

Printed in the USA

Welcome from the General Chairs

We are excited to welcome the CSCW community to Vancouver, British Columbia, Canada, for the 2015 ACM Conference on Computer Supported Cooperative Work and Social Computing!

CSCW is the premier venue for research on computer-mediated collaboration, social computing, and social media, from the design of technical systems for collaboration to ethnographic studies of systems in the wild. The mission of the conference is to share research that advances the state of human knowledge and improves both the design of systems and the ways they are used. The diversity of work in our conference program reflects the diversity of technology use in people's work, social, and civic lives as well as the geographic and cultural diversity of contributors.

This diversity and quality is reflected in CSCW's submissions, which have once again surpassed prior years. Technical chairs David McDonald and Luigina Ciolfi have continued to refine our revise and resubmit process for papers, with 161 of 575 submissions accepted. In addition, we will feature 11 workshops, 32 posters, 18 demos, and 5 panels.

Our featured speakers also testify to the quality and varied interests of CSCW. Jeff Hancock of Cornell University will open the conference, speaking on "The Facebook Study: A Personal Account of Data Science, Ethics and Change." Our closing plenary will feature Zeynep Tufekci, University of North Carolina, Chapel Hill, speaking on "Algorithms in our Midst: Information, Power and Choice when Software is Everywhere."

We are also honored to welcome Wanda Orlikowski of MIT as the recipient of this year's CSCW Lasting Impact award for her influential 1992 paper, "Learning from Notes: organizational issues in groupware implementation."

This year, CSCW has some unique new features. One of our innovations was the institution of a reviewer mentorship program, organized by Pernille Bjørn, to help increase the number of well-trained reviewers and keep pace with our growth. We are also excited to be co-located with ACM's Learning at Scale (L@S) conference. We invite L@S conference goers to attend our opening keynote on Monday morning and encourage our attendees to attend the L@S closing keynote (Peter Norvig, Director of Research at Google) on Sunday. L@S will take place during our preconference and there will be plenty of opportunities for attendees to mingle during breaks and evening hours.

Every year, putting together CSCW is a massive collaborative effort. We especially thank all the CSCW authors for contributing the intellectual and technical innovation at the core of our excellent program this year. We are grateful to the program committee and reviewers, who worked hard in providing detailed feedback for authors and improving the quality of the program. We thank our entire hard-working conference committee, an amazing group of people who volunteered many hours of their time and every one of whom helped innovate, solve problems, and bring together the scientific content and social experience of CSCW 2015. We also thank Lisa Tolles at Sheridan Communications, Yvonne Lopez at Executive Events, and Ashley Cozzi and Stephanie Sabal from ACM for all of their assistance with arrangements, registration, and publications. Special thanks go out to John and Joanne Lateulere for their invaluable help with conference planning and management. Finally, we thank our sponsors ACM and SIGCHI, as well as our early sponsors Facebook, National Science Foundation, Microsoft Research, GRAND, Bloomberg, IBM Research, Northwestern University, Simon Fraser University and SFU School of Interactive Arts & Technology, and Google for their generosity.

Finally, thank you, conference goers, for your part in making CSCW what it is today. We hope you will enjoy not only the conference, but everything the beautiful city of Vancouver has to offer in spring.

Dan Cosley
CSCW'15 General Chair
Cornell University, USA

Andrea Forte
CSCW'15 General Chair
Drexel University, USA

From the Papers & Notes Co-Chairs

CSCW 2015

The CSCW community continues to grow. This year we received 575 papers which represents a 13% increase over the total submissions for the prior year. We had submissions from 24 countries covering all continents.

This year was the fourth year of the "Revise and Resubmit" (R&R) process. Over the last four years the CSCW conference community has been conducting the review process in two rounds. In the first round reviewers are encouraged to review papers with an eye to improving the intellectual strength and contributions of the paper, making it clear which changes would be helpful and which are likely required to make the paper acceptable. In the second round, the same reviewers see the same paper and review to understand whether or not the revised paper now meets the standards of the CSCW community as acceptable. This two-round review model, with encouraging and intellectual give-and-take, is designed to improve papers of good quality but in need of work that might otherwise slip just below the bar in the more common one-shot reviewing conferences. As the Papers Co-Chairs we received numerous email commenting on the high quality of the reviewing, even from some authors whose work was not accepted.

Of all the submissions, 262 were offered the opportunity to R&R, representing a little over 45% of the original submissions. A very small number of authors either withdrew their papers or otherwise declined to resubmit their papers. The Program Committee accepted 161 papers for an acceptance rate of 28% of the total.

The R&R process would not have been possible without the work of 96 Program Committee (PC) members, making up the largest ever PC for a CSCW conference (a 50% increase in committee members over 2014). This represents the substantial increase in the number of CSCW researchers actively involved in the intellectual decision making for the community. Our work to expand the PC included reaching out to more junior researchers, industry researchers, as well as our more established colleagues. This year's PC is one of the most diverse to date and is testament to the richness within the CSCW community in terms of countries, institutions and areas of expertise.

We also wish to acknowledge the 720 external reviewers that have generously volunteered their time and expertise to ensure the quality of the CSCW 2015 program.

We hope you enjoy!

Luigina Ciolfi
Sheffield Hallam University

David W. McDonald
University of Washington

Table of Contents

Mood and Emotion

Framing Collaboration: Systems and Analysis

Understanding Deviance in Collaboration

Urban Environments

All in the Family

Trust & Anonymity

Computer Supported Happiness

Annotation Systems and Approaches

Scientific Domains

Leveraging the Crowd

Mobile Collaboration

Studies of Coordination

Young Adults and Online Behavior

Crowd Work and Crowd Process

Volunteerism

Teamwork Challenges

Politics and Social Networks

Motivating Peer Production

My Mobile, My Friends

Is There a Doctor in the Room?

Leveraging Language

Collaboration in a Globalised World

Technologies in the Workplace

Creative Collaborating

Collaborating Around Crisis

Location, Location, Location

Communities for Individual Behavior Change

Wikipedia: Structure & Function

Collaboration in the Open Classroom

Journalism and Politics

Gender and Sexual Identity

Social Dynamics and My Phone

Recommender Systems

The Powers of Co-location

Collaborative Design Approaches

Collaborating Under Constraints

Civic Participation

Experiencing Social Media

Children and Families

Motivating Crowdwork

There's Just Something About Hands

Games and Virtual Worlds

Motivation and Dynamics of the Open Classroom

Closing Keynote

CSCW 2015 Conference Organization

General Co-Chairs:	Dan Cosley *(Cornell University, USA)* Andrea Forte *(Drexel University, USA)*
Papers Co-Chairs:	Luigina Ciolfi *(Sheffield Hallam University, UK)* David McDonald *(University of Washington, USA)*
Posters Co-Chairs:	Karyn Moffat *(McGill University, Canada)* Aleksandra Sarcevic *(Drexel University, USA)*
Panels Co-Chairs:	Louise Barkhuus *(Stockholm University, Sweden)* Anatoliy Gruzd *(Ryerson University, Canada)*
Workshops Co-Chairs:	Laura Dabbish *(Carnegie Mellon University, USA)* Jenn Thom *(Amazon.com, USA)*
Demos Co-Chairs:	Tomoo Inoue *(University of Tsukuba, Japan)* Tony Tang *(University of Calgary, Canada)*
Publicity Co-Chairs:	Moira Burke *(Facebook, USA)* Elizabeth Gerber *(Northwestern University, USA)* Andrés Monroy-Hernandez *(Microsoft Research & University of Washington, USA)* Dario Taraborelli *(Wikimedia Foundation, USA)*
Doctoral Consortium Co-Chairs:	Carl Gutwin *(University of Saskatchewan, Canada)* Abigail Sellen *(Microsoft Research Cambridge, USA)*
Student Volunteer Co-Chairs:	Erin Brady *(University of Rochester, USA)* Syavash Nobarany *(University of British Columbia, Canada)*
Treasurer:	Jeremy Birnholtz *(Northwestern University, USA)*
Proceedings Co-Chairs:	Jacqueline Pike *(Duquesne University, USA)* Andrea Wiggins *(University of Maryland, USA)*
Local Arrangements & Accessibiity Co-Chairs:	Serena Hillman *(Simon Fraser University, Canada)* Carman Neustaedter *(Simon Fraser University, Canada)*
Sponsorship Co-Chairs:	Sean Goggins *(University of Missouri, USA)* Steven Poltrock *(USA)*
Graphic Design & Webmastering:	Xiaohui Eva Luo *(Georgia Institute of Technology, USA)* Elizabeth Murnane *(Cornell University, USA)*

Best of CSCW Committee:
Loren Terveen *(University of Minnesota, USA)*
Danyel Fisher *(Microsoft Research, USA)*
Myriam Lewkowicz *(Troyes University of Technology, France)*
Jeremy Birnholtz *(Northwestern University, USA)*
Jacki O'Neill *(Microsoft Research India, India)*
Aleksandra Sarcevic *(Drexel University, USA)*
Carla Simone *(University of Milano-Bicocca, Italy)*
Josh Introne *(Michigan State University, USA)*

CSCW Lasting Impact Award Committee:
Jakob Bardram *(IT University of Copenhagen, Denmark)*
Susan Fussell *(Cornell University, USA)*
Elizabeth Churchill *(Google, USA)*
John Tang *(Microsoft Research, USA)*
Luigina Ciolfi *(Sheffield Hallam University, UK)*
David McDonald *(University of Washington, USA)*

CSCW Reviewer Mentors:
Pernille Bjørn, Chair *(IT University of Copenhagen, Denmark)*
Morgan Ames *(University of California, Irvine, USA)*
Tone Bratteteig *(University of Oslo, Norway)*
John M. Carroll *(The Pennsylvania State University, USA)*
Dan Cosley *(Cornell University, USA)*
Giorgio De Michelis *(University of Milan-Bicocca, Italy)*
Paul Dourish *(University of California, Irvine, USA)*
Rosta Farzan *(University of Pittsburgh, USA)*
Fernando Figueira Filho *(Federal University of Rio Grande do Norte, Brazil)*
Joel Fischer *(University of Nottingham, UK)*
Morten Fjeld *(Chalmers University of Technology, Sweden)*
Benjamim Fonseca *(University of Trás-os-Montes e Alto Douro, Portugal)*
Andrea Forte *(Drexel University, USA)*
Wai-Tat Fu *(University of Illinois, Urbana-Champaign, USA)*
Joanne Hinds *(University of Bath, UK)*
Gary Hsieh *(University of Washington, USA)*
Jina Huh *(Michigan State University, USA)*
James Howison *(University of Texas, Austin, USA)*
Adriana Iamnitchi *(University of South Florida, USA)*
Pertti Järvinen *(University of Tampere, Finland)*
Jofish Kaye *(Yahoo!, USA)*
Rajiv Krishnamurthy *(Facebook, USA)*
Wayne Lutters *(University of Maryland, Baltimore County, USA)*
Winter Mason *(Stevens Institute of Technology, USA)*
Victoria Pammer-Schindler *(Graz University of Technology, Austria)*
Dave Randall *(University of Siegen, Germany)*
Lionel P. Robert, Jr. *(University of Michigan, USA)*
Duncan Sanderson *(Téléuniversité Montréal, Canada)*
Sarita Yardi Schoenebeck *(University of Michigan, USA)*
Gunnar Stevens *(University of Siegen, Germany)*

CSCW Reviewer Mentors (continued):

Deborah Tatar *(Virginia Institute of Technology, USA)*
Jamie Teevan *(Microsoft Research, USA)*
Loren Terveen *(University of Minnesota, USA)*

CSCW Reviewer Mentees:

Elena Agapie *(University of Washington, USA)*
Karin Ahlin *(Mid Sweden University, Sweden)*
Syed Ishtiaque Ahmed *(Cornell University, USA)*
Tawfiq Ammari *(University of Michigan, USA)*
Nazanin Andalibi *(Drexel University, USA)*
Milena Araujo *(Federal University of Campina Grande, Brazil)*
Mariam Asad *(Georgia Institute of Technology, USA)*
Amir Azarbakht *(Oregon State University, USA)*
Andrea Barbarin *(University of Michigan, USA)*
Nils Bornoe *(Aalborg University, Denmark)*
Amira Chalbi *(University of Paris-Sud, France)*
Shuo Chang *(University of Minnesota, USA)*
Nan-Chen Chen *(University of Washington, USA)*
Stella Christodoulaki *(University of Paris-Sud, France)*
António Correia *(University of Trás-os-Montes e Alto Douro, Portugal)*
Anahita Davoudi *(University of Central Florida, USA)*
Wenfei Don *(Uppsala University, Sweden)*
Alison E. Doub *(The Pennsylvania State University, USA)*
Toni Ferro *(University of Washington, USA)*
Cédric Foucault *(University of Paris-Sud & ENS Cachan, France)*
Anita Marie Gilbert *(University of California, Irvine, USA)*
Francisco J. Gutierrez *(University of Chile, Chile)*
Oliver Haimson *(University of California, Irvine, USA)*
Susanna Heyman *(KTH Royal Institute of Technology, Sweden)*
Syed Ali Hussain *(Michigan State University, USA)*
Maia Jacobs *(Georgia Institute of Technology, USA)*
Rasmus Eskild Jensen *(IT University of Copenhagen, Denmark)*
Imrul Kayes *(University of South Florida, USA)*
Elizabeth Kaziunas *(University of Michigan, USA)*
Na Li *(The Pennsylvania State University, USA)*
Katherine Lo *(University of California, Irvine, USA)*
Angela Locoro *(University of Milan-Bicocca, Italy)*
Claudia López *(University of Pittsburgh, USA)*
Haley MacLeod *(Indiana University, USA)*
Jamie Mahoney *(University of Lincoln, UK)*
Jennifer Marlow *(Carnegie Mellon University, USA)*
Stina Matthiessen *(IT University of Copenhagen, Denmark)*
Tien T. Nguyen *(University of Minnesota, USA)*
Nigini Abilio Oliveira *(Federal University of Campina Grande, Brazil)*
Pinar Ozturk *(Stevens Institute of Technology, USA)*
Yushan Pan *(University of Oslo, Norway)*
Michelle Purcell *(Drexel University, USA)*

CSCW Reviewer Mentees (continued):

Katherine Ringland *(University of California, Irvine, USA)*
Thijs Roumen *(National University of Singapore, Singapore)*
Saiph Savage *(University of California, Santa Barbara, USA & National Autonomous University of Mexico, Mexico)*
Sophie KyoungHee Son *(Korea Advanced Institute of Science and Technology, South Korea)*
Oliver Stickel *(University of Siegen, Germany)*
Minhyang Suh *(University of Washington, USA)*
Athanasios Taousakos *(University of Paris-Sud, France)*
Jimmy Ti *(Queensland University of Technology, Australia)*
Luis Contreras Toledo *(University of Bristol, UK)*
Emma Tonkin *(University of Bristol, UK)*
Stela Valchovska *(University of Nottingham, UK)*
Hanna Vrzakova *(University of Eastern Finland, Finland)*
Joanne White *(University of Colorado, Boulder, USA)*
Christine Wolf *(University of California, Irvine, USA)*
Pawel Woźniak *(Chalmers University of Technology, USA)*
Yu Wu *(The Pennsylvania State University, USA)*
Sangseok You *(University of Michigan, USA)*
Alyson Young *(University of Maryland, Baltimore County, USA)*
Amy X. Zhang *(Massachusetts Institute of Technology, USA)*
Saijing Zheng *(The Pennsylvania State University, USA)*

CSCW 2015 Program Committee Members

*Committee members whose names appear in **bold** are being recognized by fellow Associate Chairs for one or more excellent reviews*

Joanna Abraham, *University of Illinois,* USA
Judd Antin, *Yahoo! Research,* USA
Daniel Avrahami, *FXPAL,* USA
Louise Barkhuus, *Stockholm University,* Sweden
Jacob Biehl, *FX Palo Alto Laboratory,* USA
Jeffrey Bigham, *Carnegie Mellon University,* USA
Jeremy Birnholtz, *Northwestern University,* USA
Pernille Bjørn, *IT University of Copenhagen,* Denmark
Alexander Boden, *Fraunhofer Institute for Applied Information Technology (FIT)*, Germany
Claus Bossen, *Aarhus University,* Denmark
Nina Boulus, *IT University of Copenhagen,* Denmark
Tone Bratteteig, *University of Oslo,* Norway
Barry Brown, *University of California, San Diego,* USA
Amy Bruckman, *Georgia Institute of Technology,* USA
Moira Burke, *Facebook,* USA
Alan Chamberlain, *The University of Nottingham,* UK
Yunan Chen, *University of California, Irvine,* USA
Coye Cheshire, *University of California, Berkeley,* USA
Lars Rune Christensen, *IT University of Copenhagen,* Denmark
Gregorio Convertino, *Xerox Research Center Europe,* France
Dan Cosley, *Cornell University,* USA
Edward Cutrell, *Microsoft Research India,* India
Antonella De Angeli, *University of Trento,* Italy
Cleidson de Souza, *Universidade Federal do Pará,* Brazil
Xianghua Ding, *Fudan University,* China
Steven Dow, *Carnegie Mellon University,* USA
Arvid Engström, *Mobile Life at Interactive Institute,* Sweden
Ingrid Erickson, *Rutgers University,* USA
Rosta Farzan, *University of Pittsburgh,* USA
Andrew Fiore, *Facebook,* USA
Danyel Fisher, *Microsoft Research,* USA
Morten Fjeld, *Chalmers University of Technology,* Sweden
Benjamim Fonseca, *University of Trás-os-Montes e Alto Douro (UTAD)*, Portugal
Susan Fussell, *Cornell University,* USA
Elizabeth Gerber, *Northwestern University,* USA
Alain GIBOIN, *INRIA,* France
Eric Gilbert, *Georgia Institute of Technology,* USA
Sukeshini Grandhi, *Eastern Connecticut State University,* USA
Antonietta Grasso, *Xerox Research Centre Europe,* France
Carl Gutwin, *University of Saskatchewan,* Canada
Ido Guy, *Yahoo! Labs,* Israel
Aaron Halfaker, *University of Minnesota,* USA
Christine Halverson, *IBM T.J. Watson Research Center,* USA
Mark Handel, *The Boeing Company,* USA
Jina Huh, *Michigan State University,* USA
Claudia-Lavinia Ignat, *INRIA Lorraine,* France
Joshua Introne, *Michigan State University,* USA
Michal Jacovi, *IBM Research Lab in Haifa,* Israel
Brian Keegan, *Northwestern University,* USA
Wendy Kellogg, *IBM T.J. Watson Research Center,* USA
Cliff Lampe, *University of Michigan,* USA
Edith Law, *Harvard University,* USA
Gilly Leshed, *Cornell University,* USA
Myriam Lewkowicz, *UTT,* France
Kurt Luther, *Virginia Tech,* USA
Wayne Lutters, *University of Maryland, Baltimore County,* USA
Gloria Mark, *University of California, Irvine,* USA
Andres Monroy-Hernandez, *Massachusetts Institute of Technology,* USA
Michael Muller, *IBM Research*, USA
Maria Normark, *Södertörn University,* Sweden
Jacki O'Neill, *Microsoft Research India*, India
Volkmar Pipek, *University of Siegen,* Germany
Anne Marie Piper, *Northwestern University,* USA
Erika Poole, *Penn State University,* USA
Michael Prilla, *Institute for Applied Work Science Bochum,* Germany
Emilee Rader, *Michigan State University,* USA
David Randall, *University of Siegen*, Germany
Madhu Reddy, *Pennsylvania State University,* USA
David Redmiles, *University of California, Irvine,* USA
David Ribes, *Georgetown University,* USA
Lionel Robert, *University of Michigan,* USA
Daniela Rosner, *University of Washington,* USA
Aleksandra Sarcevic, *Drexel University,* USA
Steve Sawyer, *Syracuse University,* USA

m.c. schraefel, *University of Southampton*, UK
Bryan Semaan, *Syracuse University,* USA
David A. Shamma, *Yahoo!,* USA
Aaron Shaw, *Northwestern University,* USA
Patrick Shih, *The Pennsylvania State University,* USA
Irina Shklovski, *IT University of Copenhagen,* Denmark
Carla Simone, *DISCO-Universita' di Milano-Bicocca -Italy,* Italy
Gunnar Stevens, *Institute of Information Systems / University of Siegen,* Germany
Norman Su, *Indiana University*, USA
John Tang, *Microsoft Research,* USA
Hilda Tellioglu, *Vienna University of Technology,* Austria
Loren Terveen, *University of Minnesota,* USA
Jennifer Thom, *Amazon,* USA
Zachary Toups, *New Mexico State University,* USA
Sarah Vieweg, *Qatar Computing Research Institute,* Qatar
Jessica Vitak, *University of Maryland,* USA
Hao-Chuan Wang, *National Tsing Hua University,* Taiwan
Yang Wang, *Syracuse University,* USA
Rick Wash, *Michigan State University,* USA
Svetlana Yarosh, *University of Minnesota,* USA
Xiaomu Zhou, *Rutgers University,* USA

CSCW 2015 Paper Reviewers

*Reviewers whose names appear in **bold** are being recognized by the Associate Chairs for one or more excellent reviews*

Margunn Aanestad
Lada Adamic
Phil Adams
Elena Agapie
Karin Ahlin
Syed Ishtiaque Ahmed
June Ahn
Warren Allen
Jens Allwood
Peter Alston
Morgan Ames
Tawfiq Ammari
Nazanin Andalibi
Lars Bo Andersen
Paul André
Craig Anslow
Panayotis Antoniadis
Milena Araujo
Rosa Arriaga
Henrik Artman
Mattias Arvola
Mariam Asad
Marcos Baez
Naveen Bagalkot
Brian Bailey
Saeideh Bakhshi
Eytan Bakshy
Elizabeth Bales
Dawna Ballard
Stinne Ballegaard
Liam Bannon
Andrea Barbarin
Flore Barcellini
Jakob Bardram
Jeffrey Bardzell
Jordan Barlow
Scott Bateman
Eric Baumer
Natalie Bazarova
Roman Bednarik
Andrew Begel
Bo Begole
Marek Bell
Aurélien Bénel
Frank Bentley
Laura Benton
Michael Bernstein
Nadia Bianchi-Berthouze
Matthew Bietz
Dorrit Billman
Igor Bilogrevic
Jan Boehmer
Elizabeth Bonsignore
Silvia Bordin
Alan Borning
Nis Bornoe
Nathan Bos
Guillaume Bouchard
Kristy Boyer
Alessandro Bozzon
Erin Brady
Robin Brewer
Pam Briggs
Christopher Brooks
Jed Brubaker
Elizabeth Buie
Jean-marie Burkhardt
Jenna Burrell
Richard Byrne
Federico Cabitza
Béatrice Cahour
Stefan Carmien
Stefania Castellani
Marcelo Cataldo
Teresa Cerratto Pargman
Meeyoung Cha
Abdelberi Chaabane
Y.-L. Betty Chang
Chen Chen
Francine Chen
Mike Chen
Nan-Chen Chen
Nicholas Chen
Xiang 'Anthony' Chen
Shiwei Cheng
Marshini Chetty
Ed Chi
Parmit Chilana
Eun Kyoung Choe
Ming Ki Chong
Tanzeem Choudhury
Stella Christodoulaki
Hao-Hua Chu
Tyng-Ruey Chuang
Chia-Fang Chung
Giovanni Luca Ciampaglia
Adrian Clear
D Coetzee
Benjamin Collier
Tommaso Colombino
Rob Comber
Bernard Conein
António Correia
Lynne Coventry
Henriette Cramer
Justin Cranshaw
Alma Leora Culen
Aron Culotta
Chandrika Cycil
Mary Czerwinski
Laura Dabbish
Peter Danholt
Sauvik Das
Anahita Davoudi
Munmun De Choudhury
Fiorella De Cindio
Giorgio De Michelis
Laura Devendorf
Nicholas Diakopoulos
Tawanna Dillahunt
Jill Dimond
Yvonne Dittrich
Wenfei Dong
Brian Dorn
Honglu Du
Nicolas Ducheneaut
Paul Dunphy
Serge Egelman
Kate Ehrlich
Michael Ekstrand
Yasmine El-Glaly
Nicole Ellison
Niklas Elmqvist
Jennifer Englert
Sheena Erete

Thomas Erickson
David Evans
Robert Farrell
Toni Ferro
Oliver Ferschke
Bruce Ferwerda
Casey Fiesler
Fernando Figueira Filho
Flavio Figueiredo
Ailbhe Finnerty
Joel Fischer
Colin Fitzpatrick
Heather Ford
Cédric Foucault
Amy Franklin
Guo Freeman
Samantha Fried
Wai-Tat Fu
Ge Gao
Jayden Garner
Daniel Gatica-Perez
R.Stuart Geiger
Bluma Gelley
Darren Gergle
Kathrin Gerling
Marco Gerosa
Werner Geyer
Anita Gilbert
Mareike Glöss
Gerard Goggin
Sean Goggins
Jennifer Golbeck
Richard Gomer
Amy Gonzales
Joseph Gonzales
Elizabeth Goodman
Mary Gray
Rebecca Gray
Anders Green
William Green
Michael Greenberg
Christian Greiffenhagen
Catherine Grevet
Nir Grinberg
Miria Grisot
Erik Grönvall
Kristina Groth
Dan Gruen
Ning Gu
Shion Guha
Julien Guibourdenche
Philip Guo
Francisco Gutierrez
Joshua Hailpern
Oliver Haimson
Julia Haines
Maria Håkansson
Megan Halpern
William Hamilton
Jessica Hammer
Kyungsik (Keith) Han
Jeff Hancock
Mark Hancock
Benjamin Hanrahan
Emily Harburg
Ellie Harmon
Franklin Harper
Richard Harper
Christopher Harris
Drew Harry
Björn Hartmann
Mark Hartswood
Andrea Hartzler
Ari Hautasaari
Gillian Hayes
Brent Hecht
Tomi Heimonen
Libby Hemphill
David Hendry
Thomas Herrmann
Morten Hertzum
Susanna Heyman
Benjamin Mako Hill
Brian Hilligoss
Serena Hillman
Jon Hindmarsh
Chaya Hiruncharoenvate
Christopher Hoadley
Bernie Hogan
Naja Holten Møller
Hwajung Hong
Jason Hong
Lichan Hong
Juan Pablo Hourcade
Aaron Houssian
James Howison
Gary Hsieh
Jochen Huber
David Huffaker
Amanda Hughes
Julie Hui
Jessica Hullman
Syed Hussain
Alice Hutchings
Helge Hüttenrauch
Inseok Hwang
Kori Inkpen
Shamsi Iqbal
Lilly Irani
Petra Isenberg
Corey Jackson
Steven Jackson
Abigail Jacobs
Maia Jacobs
Mattias Jacobsson
Mohammad Hossein Jarrahi
Tom Jenkins
Rasmus Jensen
Haiyan Jia
Lian Jian
Hongxia Jin
Christopher Jones
Jasmine Jones
Fatima Jonsson
Anirudha Joshi
Suhas Govind Joshi
David Joyner
Wendy Ju
Oskar Juhlin
Malte Jung
Yumi Jung
Sasa Junuzovic
Sanjay Kairam
Yoram Kalman
Santosh Kalwar
Noreen Kamal
Bridget Kane
Ruogu Kang
Thomas Kannampallil
Anne Marie Kanstrup
Karrie Karahalios
David Kaufman
Andrea Kavanaugh
Joseph 'Jofish' Kaye
Elizabeth Kaziunas
Lyndon Kennedy
M. Laeeq Khan
Donnie Kim
Jeeeun Kim
Juho Kim
Sung-Hee Kim
Sunyoung Kim
Taemie Kim

David Kirk
Reuben Kirkham
Spyros Kitsiou
Funda Kivran-Swaine
Styliani Kleanthous
Mark Klein
Scott Klemmer
Kristina Knaving
Benjamin Koehne
Joseph Konstan
Matthias Korn
Yubo Kou
Yong Ming Kow
Sven Kratz
Robert Kraut
Pavel Kucherbaev
Katie Kuksenok
Anand Kulkarni
Chinmay Kulkarni
Neha Kumar
Diana Kusunoki
Harris Kyriakou
Jarmo Laaksolahti
Ben Lafreniere
Nicolas LaLone
Shyong Lam
Airi Lampinen
James Landay
Monica Landoni
Walter Lasecki
Thomas LaToza
Yann Laurillau
Christopher Le Dantec
Alex Leavitt
Charlotte Lee
Seungyon Claire Lee
Benedikt Ley
Jia Li
Na Li
Daniel Liebling
Michael Liegl
Christopher Lima
Rhema Linder
Siân Lindley
Conor Linehan
Wang Ling
Jessica Lingel
Lars Lischke
Eden Litt
Leslie Liu
Sophia Liu
Angela Locoro
Thomas Lodato
Claudia López
Zhihan Lu
Thomas Ludwig
Johan Lundin
zhihan lv
Christopher MacLellan
Haley MacLeod
Rachel Magee
Jamie Mahoney
Lena Mamykina
Nicolas Mangano
Jennifer Mankoff
Sampada Marathe
Gabriela Marcu
Drew Margolin
Annette Markham
Jennifer Marlow
David Martin
Paulo Martins
Misa Maruyama
Christopher Mascaro
Jorge Matias
Tara Matthews
Stina Matthiesen
Hanna Maurin
Matthieu Mazzega
Victoria McArthur
Joe McCarthy
David McDonald
Poppy McLeod
Donald McMillan
Richard Medland
Yevgeniy Medynskiy
David Mellis
Maria Menendez
Amanda Menking
Samantha Merritt
Enza Messina
Solomon Messing
Ronald Metoyer
Tommi Mikkonen
David Millen
Andrew Miller
Gregor Miller
Robert Miller
Tanushree Mitra
Manas Mittal
Wendy Moncur
Peter Mooney
Jonathan Morgan
Jonathan Morgan
Meredith Morris
Robert Morris
Dan Morrow
Gabriel Mugar
Claudia Müller
Sean Munson
David Murakami Wood
Elizabeth Murnane
Alison Murphy
Brad Myers
Mor Naaman
Lennart Nacke
Mathieu Nancel
Bonnie Nardi
Carman Neustaedter
Duyen Nguyen
Tien Nguyen
Syavash Nobarany
Sylvie Noël
Oded Nov
Francisco Nunes
Mohammad Obaid
Brendan O'Connor
Erick Oduor
Anne Oeldorf-Hirsch
Alice Oh
Nigini Oliveira
Gary Olson
Judith Olson
Thomas Olsson
Robert On
Babajide Osatuyi
Myle Ott
Pinar Ozturk
Stefano Padilla
Xinru Page
Drew Paine
Chankyung Pak
Joyojeet Pal
Leysia Palen
Yushan Pan
Katherine Panciera
Hugo Paredes
Daniel Pargman
Albert Park
Souneil Park
Kayur Patel
Jessica Pater
Sharoda Paul

Joslenne Pena
Wei Peng
Adam Perer
Simon Perrault
Mark Perry
Tamara Peyton
Antonio Piccinno
Hannah Pileggi
Tamar Pincus
Kathleen Pino
Valerie Polichar
Andreas Poller
Wanda Pratt
Nuno Preguica
Reid Priedhorsky
Jason Procyk
Michelle Purcell
Yin Qu
Alexander Quinn
Irene Rae
David Randall
Matt Ratto
Ilaria Redaelli
Daniel Rees Lewis
Stuart Reeves
Katharina Reinecke
Christian Reuter
Corinne Ribert-Van De Weerdt
Alexander Richter
Scott Robertson
Tom Rodden
John Rooksby
Asta Roseway
Luca Rossi
Chiara Rossitto
Mary Beth Rosson
Thijs Roumen
Mark Rouncefield
Jeffrey Rzeszotarski
Alan Said
Pascal Salembier
Mohamed Sarwat
Saiph Savage
Florian Schaub
Chris Schmandt
Jodi Schneider
Raz Schwartz
Tobias Schwartz
Lauren Scissors
Jeremy Scott
Mark Selby
Shilad Sen
Bernard Senach
Leslie Setlock
Burr Settles
N. Sadat Shami
Nikhil Sharma
Sarika Sharma
Wes Sharrock
Scott Sherwood
Frank Shipman
Liz Sillence
Leif Singer
Petr Slovák
Madeline Smith
Jaime Snyder
Jacob Solomon
Eduardo Solteiro Pires
KyoungHee Son
Vladimir Soroka
Tasos Spiliotopoulos
Emma Spiro
Janaki Srinivasan
Kevin Stanley
Kate Starbird
Luke Stark
Bogdan State
Martin Stein
Stephanie Steinhardt
Igor Steinmacher
Erik Stolterman
Simone Stumpf
Masanori Sugimoto
Minhyang (Mia) Suh
Maoyuan Sun
Alistair Sutcliffe
Anthony Tang
Charlotte Tang
Athanasios Taousakos
Dario Taraborelli
Yla Tausczik
Rannie Teodoro
Elizabeth Thiry
Jakob Tholander
John Thomas
Bart Thomee
Jimmy Ti
Matthieu Tixier
Peter Tolmie
Catalina Toma
Stephanie Tong
Erik Trainer
Stefano Tranquillini
Khai Truong
Hsin-yi Tsai
Jason Tsay
Zeynep Tufekci
Michael Twidale
Heli Väätäjä
Rajan Vaish
Stela Valchovska
Kami Vaniea
Julita Vassileva
Tiffany Veinot
Gina Venolia
Nervo Verdezoto
Guri Verne
Chris Vincent
John Vines
Gianluigi Viscusi
Tatiana Vlahovic
Juergen Vogel
Dirk Vom Lehn
Hana Vrzakova
Ina Wagner
Judy Wajcman
James Wallace
Jillian Wallis
William Yang Wang
Yi-Chia Wang
Yiran Wang
Peter Wardrip
Morten Warncke-Wang
Nic Weber
Carolyn Wei
Nadir Weibel
Joanne White
Kevin White
Andrea Wiggins
Lauren Wilcox
Hiroko Wilensky
Jutta Willamowski
Wesley Willett
Michele Williams
Matt Willis
Max Wilson
Fredrik Winberg
Susan Winter
Pamela Wisniewski
Donghee Yvette Wohn
Christine Wolf
Anita Woll
Paweł Woźniak

Yu Wu
Volker Wulf
Susan Wyche
Lu Xiao
Bin Xu
Naomi Yamashita
Huahai Yang
Jiang Yang
Sarita Yardi Schoenebeck
Ming Yin
Chuang-wen You

Sangseok You
Alyson Young
Lixiu Yu
Chien Wen Yuan
Hideto Yuzawa
Mark Zachry
Gabriela Zago
Amy Zhang
Haoqi Zhang
Dejin Zhao
Saijing Zheng

Haiyi Zhu
Mengxiao Zhu
Ann Zimmerman
John Zimmerman
Philippe Zimmermann
Moustafa Zouinar
Arkaitz Zubiaga
Kathryn Zyskowski
Douglas Zytko

CSCW 2015 Sponsor & Supporters

Sponsor: SIGCHI

Champions: NSF, facebook

Benefactors: Graphisme, animation et nouveaux médias GRAND Graphics, Animation and New Media; Microsoft Research; Bloomberg

Contributors: Northwestern University School of Communication; IBM Research

Friends: Google™; SFU SIMON FRASER UNIVERSITY ENGAGING THE WORLD

The Facebook Study: A Personal Account of Data Science, Ethics and Change

Jeff Hancock
Cornell University

Abstract

Big social data, such as that produced by Facebook and Twitter, have the potential to transform the social sciences and lead to advances in understanding human behavior. At the same time, novel large-scale methods and forms of collaboration between academia and industry raise new and important ethical questions.

In this talk I will discuss the Facebook Emotion study and step through several aspects of the study that involve important ethical decision points, and provide some insights on why the study generated such massive attention and criticism. I will also discuss the experience of an Internet-scale controversy, from the personal costs to the gift of criticism, and the potential opportunities to move the discussion forward.

ACM Classification

K.4.1 [Public Policy Issues]—Ethics; J.4 [SOCIAL AND BEHAVIORAL SCIENCES]; H.4.3 [Communications Applications]

Author Keywords: emotional contagion, research ethics, academia-industry collaboration, computational social science

Short Bio

Jeff Hancock is a Professor in the Departments of Communication and Information Science at Cornell University. He is currently the Chair of the Information Science Department and the co-Director of Cognitive Science. At the Cornell Social Media Lab Professor Hancock and his group work on questions concerned with psychological and interpersonal processes that take place online. The team specializes in using computational linguistic analysis to understand how the words we use can reveal psychological and social dynamics, such as deception and credibility, emotional dynamics, intimacy and relationships, and social support. Recently Professor Hancock has begun work examining how people understand and reason about algorithms. Funding from the National Science Foundation and the Department of Defense supports his research, which has been frequently featured in the popular media, including the New York Times, CNN, NPR, and the BBC. Dr. Hancock earned his PhD in psychology at Dalhousie University, Canada, and joined Cornell in 2002.

CSCW 2015, March 14–18, 2015, Vancouver, BC, Canada.
ACM 978-1-4503-2922-4/15/03.
http://dx.doi.org/10.1145/2675133.2697078

Understanding the Effects of Crowdfunding on Entrepreneurial Self-Efficacy

Emily Harburg, Julie Hui, Mike Greenberg, Elizabeth M. Gerber
Segal Design Institute
Northwestern University
Evanston, IL 60208
{eharburg, juliehui, mdgreenb}@u.northwestern.edu, {egeber}@northwestern.edu

ABSTRACT
Crowdfunding is emerging as a new socio-technical system that is changing how entrepreneurs interact with their community of financial supporters. While computer supported cooperative work (CSCW) researchers have begun to explore how this new type of system influences entrepreneurial work, less is understood about how the system influences their psychological experience—specifically self-efficacy, or belief in one's own ability to succeed at a task, which affects persistence, learning, and performance. Drawing on Bandura's Social Cognitive Theory, we conducted a qualitative study of 53 entrepreneurs using crowdfunding and found that crowdfunding can influence self-efficacy through (1) social validation, (2) role modeling, (3) mastery, and (4) physiological states supported by socio-technical features, such as displaying a concrete goal, examples of other's work, or public feedback. Results suggest how socio-technical systems can be designed to help entrepreneurs perform to enhance our economic and social prosperity.

Author Keywords
Crowdfunding, Self-Efficacy, Social Cognitive Theory, entrepreneurship, public validation, modeling, mastery

ACM Classification Keywords
H.5.3 [Group & Organization Interfaces]: Computer-supported cooperative work, Web-based interaction

INTRODUCTION
Crowdfunding—raising funds from online crowds typically in exchange for an award [11]—has been particularly attractive to entrepreneurs who lack equity and access to traditional sources of funding [12]. Rather than asking for funds from venture capitalists, banks, or foundations, entrepreneurs can seek contributions from thousands of people through crowdfunding platforms, like Kickstarter [21] (see Figure 1). Crowdfunding platforms have raised more than 1 billion dollars for thousands of entrepreneurs in the past five years [44]. As CSCW researchers investigate the crowdfunding ecosystem as a new form of computer supported cooperative work, we are learning how the tools in the crowdfunding ecosystem support not just the exchange of funds, but also the exchange of ideas and instruction ranging from programming and manufacturing to marketing and project management [31][12]. For example, entrepreneurs share instructional YouTube videos and use Facebook and Twitter to spread their ideas.

Figure 1: An entrepreneur from Wisconsin showcases his oven controller product on Kickstarter, a crowdfunding platform.

While we are coming to understand how the socio-technical system supports the work of an entrepreneur, we know little about how people feel when engaged in this work. Understanding what work is accomplished using socio-technical systems and how workers feel about the work is critical for societies that rely on motivated entrepreneurs to start new ventures and create new jobs [16,17]. The psychological experience of entrepreneurs – particularly novice entrepreneurs – is critical as it influences their motivation to overcome the inevitable obstacles associated with entrepreneurship, such as doubt in their idea, lack of role models, or uncertainty about next steps [36].

Entrepreneurial self-efficacy (ESE) describes the belief one has in their ability to succeed at tasks critical for entrepreneurship [4]. Higher levels of self-efficacy are associated with greater levels of success and motivation in entrepreneurs [36].

CSCW 2015, March 14–18, 2015, Vancouver, BC, Canada.

http://dx.doi.org/10.1145/2675133.2675142.

Recent CSCW research suggests that online communities, such as Wikipedia or Dribble, may be particularly well suited to support increased levels of self-efficacy through providing a community of support, role models, and feedback to participants. While researchers understand that online communities can be effective in helping users feel supported, little has been explored regarding how the crowdfunding experience specifically influences the self-efficacy of entrepreneurs [19]. Crowdfunding provides a unique avenue to study entrepreneurial self-efficacy given its role as a space for entrepreneurs – often novices— to seek financial and emotional backing for their work. Through this research, we seek to answer:

- *How does the community and public aspect of crowdfunding affect entrepreneurial self-efficacy?*
- *How do the socio-technical features of crowdfunding systems affect entrepreneurial self-efficacy?*

By understanding these questions, we can identify opportunities to refine and redesign crowdfunding platforms to improve the user psychological experience and ultimately learning and performance [24].

RELATED WORK

We ground our study in research on entrepreneurship, social cognitive theory, and online communities in order to better understand how performing entrepreneurship publicly and in an online community develop self-efficacy in entrepreneurs.

Entrepreneurial Self-efficacy

The uncertain nature of entrepreneurial work, defined as the discovery and creation of a new venture [36], requires that entrepreneurs believe in their own abilities sufficiently to take action [29]. Entrepreneurial self-efficacy, or belief in one's own abilities to succeed at entrepreneurial tasks, positively influences performance as well as the goals entrepreneurs set [8]. Tasks include networking, marketing, managing, and risk-taking. Further, ESE influences persistence in working towards these goals, creativity, and the ability to recover from failure [14]. In this way, self-efficacy can significantly influence entrepreneurial intentions and performance. An entrepreneur who lacks self-efficacy is unlikely to pursue new ventures and believe in their own abilities [8].

Bandura's Social Cognitive Theory suggests that self-efficacy can be developed in four ways: experience of mastery (seeing oneself succeed at tasks), modeling (seeing examples of similar others succeeding at tasks), social persuasion (getting feedback and encouragement from others), and physiological states (physical and emotional response to various situations) [4]. While we understand how self-efficacy develops in face-to-face contexts, we know less about how entrepreneurial self-efficacy develops in a computer-mediated experience, specifically through crowdfunding. The purpose of this research is to explore how crowdfunding platforms and experiences influence self-efficacy development in entrepreneurs so that we can create better socio-technical interfaces to support entrepreneurs as they engage in their work.

Computer-Supported Entrepreneurship

CSCW researchers have begun to explore the role of computer-supported tools in entrepreneurial development. For example, research suggests that entrepreneurs use social media to communicate ideas to potential consumers [13], websites to request and manage resources among collaborators [31], and networking tools to reach out to peers [18]. Online communities of practice, or groups bounded together by a shared passion or expertise, have been shown to help develop user's sense of professional identity [37]. Online platforms, like Dribble, were shown to help users build their reputation in a transparent setting, as well as to draw inspiration from others' work [28]. Research on the online Do-It-Yourself (DIY) craft community found that skill development increased motivation for users to participate in communities, as well as the opportunity to getting project feedback [27]. In addition, online communities like GitHub encourage transparency, which has been shown to increase collaboration and learning among users doing complex activities [9].

Crowdfunding offers a platform where entrepreneurs can display their work to a global community [12]. Research suggests that entrepreneurs report finding value in aspects of crowdfunding beyond financial support, such as the community that forms around them during the process of a campaign [19]. Research also suggests that crowdfunding can lead entrepreneurs to develop new professional connections with their colleagues through sharing their crowdfunding work [31]. In addition, crowdfunding can be used as a way to help entrepreneurs reach new business markets that they could not access offline [1], as well to better understand their market [41], and how much potential customers would be willing to pay [5]. Furthermore, research demonstrates that even when crowdfunding campaigns fail, entrepreneurs still find it to be a positive experience and can pick themselves back up, as 43% of those who relaunch their projects went on to succeed [15]. This suggests that crowdfunding may influence not just the way entrepreneurs work but also how they feel about their own abilities and the way they react to failure.

Self-Efficacy Development in Online Communities

Research in online communities has begun to examine ways that these spaces can be used motivate and develop self-efficacy in users. For example, signals of social support or approval, such as personal tokens of appreciation, were shown to increase user participation on Wikipedia by 60% [34]. In addition, 78% of Wikipedians agreed that "having others compliment you on your edits/articles" is the primary reason why people decide to make more edits on Wikipedia [45]. Participating in such community supportive platforms has shown to help confirm one's self-image of being an efficacious person [33]. As such, the simple act of participating on a platform can improve user's sense of self-efficacy around their ability to perform and contribute [23]. Participation in social media communities, such as Facebook or MySpace, has also been shown to heighten user self-efficacy. Research suggests that some users go on Facebook to find greater purpose, to affiliate with others, to receive social support, to feel less uncertain about oneself, and to find a greater sense of self-efficacy [11]. In addition, research suggests that MySpace and Facebook support sociability as they allow youth to connect with others who are unable to connect in offline spaces [7].

Online learning communities have also been shown to heighten self-efficacy around task performance [38]. For instance, studies have shown that online learning communities increased student participation and provided a space where users felt less intimidated and pressured [42]. Online learning communities also offer users the ability to collaborate with a large number of people that might be typically inaccessible offline [35]. Large online community size has been shown to have a positive association with user self-efficacy and motivation to contribute [23]. Crowdfunding communities are in part effective because they allow users to draw from a large collective group with similar interests to receive feedback and pool resources [19].

While online communities may often be effective at building self-efficacy and drawing from the strength of a crowd, they also have the potential to negatively impact self-efficacy. One's self-efficacy has been shown to decrease when people fail publicly or engage in upward social comparison [4]. For instance, when users within online communities, like Kickstarter, make mistakes, their errors are more visible which can lead to more embarrassment than when mistakes are made privately [19]. Research suggests that competition with large audiences can make it harder for users – particularly novices – to stand out as they compete with others in the community [28]. In addition, users report feeling more intimidated when they see a competitive landscape online or that their domain is full of others [24].

Building from this research, we are interested in how social cognitive theory applies to crowdfunding communities. We know little about how participating in crowdfunding influences the psychological experience of entrepreneurs and the impact that this process has on self-efficacy. The crowdfunding platform provides an ideal context for us to better understand what does and doesn't work in an online environment. By doing so, we will be able to better design interactive systems that support engagement as well as performance.

METHODS

Interview Participants

To understand how participation in the crowdfunding community affects self-efficacy, we conducted a qualitative study of 53 entrepreneurs on crowdfunding over three years, interviewing them about their experiences during the crowdfunding process. Interviews followed a semi-structured protocol, focusing on the project creators' experience with their campaign. Like previous CSCW researchers interested in developing an initial understanding of an emerging phenomenon [32], we chose this method of semi-structured interviews because it allowed us the opportunity to ask questions directly of entrepreneurs and to evaluate what key themes arose. In addition, previous CSCW researchers [19] used this methodology to study self-efficacy and found this to be an accurate measure of assessment[1]. This data has been used to inform previous studies on the role of community in crowdfunding [19], motivations and deterrents to crowdfund [12], the affect of public failure [15], and the role of social networks in campaign publicity [18]. In this study, we focus on a previously uncovered emergent theme of how project creators build entrepreneurial self-efficacy.

Participants used three different platforms—Kickstarter, IndieGoGo, and Rockethub—the most popular and successful platforms in the US [2]. Project types varied including Art (7), Comics (3), Dance (1), Design (16), Education (1), Fashion (2), Film & Video (8), Food (4), Games (10), Music (3), Photography (3), Publishing (7), Science (4), Technology (3), and Theater (3). Approximately 50% of project creators met their fundraising goal on at least one of their projects, which is similar to the success rate of Kickstarter, the largest crowdfunding platform [44]. Most creators maintained full time day jobs – spending between 30 minutes and 7 hours a day on weeknights or weekends working on their crowdfunding project. Three informants relied on crowdfunding as their primary source of income. Participant ages ranged from 20 to 65 years old and raised between $41 and $433,365. Fourteen creators launched more than one campaign, ranging between one to nine campaigns per creator interviewed. Interviewees were not compensated for their participation.

Procedure

We recruited interview participants through random and snowball sampling, which allowed us to identify typical and atypical participants from the crowdfunding population. We divided our semi-structured interview protocol into two sections. In the first section, we asked participants about their professional background and how they learned about and became engaged in crowdfunding. During the second phase, we asked participants to describe the work involved—both collaborative and independent. Average interview length was 30 minutes. Interviews were conducted over video conferencing, phone, and in person. Interviews were conducted during and after the creators' campaigns. Advantages of this research approach include collecting both reflective and in situ data. Disadvantages include biases from self-report [39].

Analysis

In this study, we used structured quantitative analysis [32] to examine the role of self-efficacy in crowdfunding. We based our initial coding protocol on Social Cognitive Theory [5] to identify instances of public validation, modeling, mastery, and physiological states in the socio-technical system. We then collected each instance in an excel spreadsheet and studied how these instances did or did not build self-efficacy. The theme of

[1] See Future Work section to see limitations of this methodology and possible avenues to move to in future research

Mechanisms	Socio-technical Features	Self-Efficacy Effects & Examples
1. Public Validation	- Public and permanent display of contributions - Project pages accessible to global online audience	**Positive Self-Efficacy**: Entrepreneurs feel validated, connected, and encouraged by support. (Ex: *"It felt good to know that people wanted my product.")* **Negative Self-Efficacy**: Entrepreneurs feel lack of support and validation from others. (Ex: "*No one was supportive… It brings up all kinds of doubts, you think – is this project any good, is there a market out there for it?*")
2. Modeling	- Project pages capture entrepreneurs' project themes, goals, success, and failures - Search tool affords shadowing of similar others	**Positive Self-Efficacy**: Entrepreneurs feel encouraged by seeing examples of others succeeding; learn from failure examples. (Ex: "*Seeing projects was really helpful and it was cool to see that people buy things—it doesn't have to be professional.*") **Negative Self-Efficacy**: Entrepreneurs feel discouraged by seeing examples of others failing; overwhelmed by pressure of seeing what it takes to succeed. (Ex: "*I don't do well modeling off other people.*")
3. Mastery	- Project pages show funds raised and progress toward goal - Video and site showing skills and number of page views	**Positive Self-Efficacy**: Entrepreneurs feel like they've gained skills through visible progress (*Ex: "I think that this [crowdfunding] is a really doable way to really practice and hone those [business] skills.")* **Negative Self-Efficacy**: Entrepreneurs feel down after seeing selves not achieve set goal. (Ex: "*It was a little depressing. I was defeated.*")
4. Physiological States	- Project pages show regular updates, days remaining, and funding goals - Project pages display to public success or failure of project	**Positive Self-Efficacy:** Entrepreneurs feel physically and emotionally energized by crowdfunding process. *(Ex: "I was so excited when results came in. I reached a goal and then I was like 'okay, keep going!')* **Negative Self-Efficacy:** Entrepreneurs feel physically and emotionally exhausted by crowdfunding process. (Ex: "*15 days of hell—I couldn't sleep it was awful. It'd get little dings thinking it was a donation, but it was not. It was torture.*")

Table 1. Mechanisms and Socio-Technical System Features of Crowdfunding Influencing Entrepreneurial Self-efficacy

self-efficacy originally surfaced along with other themes such as collaboration [21] and networking [20] during a prior longitudinal grounded theory [42] study of crowdfunding.

RESULTS

Our findings suggest that crowdfunding communities can both increase and decrease self-efficacy levels in entrepreneurs through socio-technical features on the site. Supporting Bandura's Social Cognitive Theory, we found that crowdfunding sites influenced helped build self-efficacy through facilitating (1) public validation, (2) modeling, (3) mastery experiences, and (4) physiological states [4]. Entrepreneurs expressed gains in self-efficacy through the following platform features: the ability to receive feedback and the number of backers supporting their work, seeing examples of others succeeding on crowdfunding to serve as role models, or having their percent funded and financial progress publicly showcased. However, our results also suggest that self-efficacy can be decreased when entrepreneurs lack public validation for their work, when they feel daunted by their work, and when their failed project is publicly visible to others. We summarize the key mechanisms and socio-technical features that influence entrepreneurial self-efficacy in Table 1. The following sections will go through these findings in greater detail, with quotes from our interviews with entrepreneurs to support each claim.

1. Public Validation

Entrepreneurs report building self-efficacy through public validation, or the process of a group verifying their work which in turn shapes their own opinions about themselves [3]. The crowdfunding process allows entrepreneurs to be able to receive support from a wide audience of strangers and offers others a tangible way to support them in their work.

1.1 Public Validation Legitimizes Work

By receiving positive feedback, encouragement, and financial support, entrepreneurs report feeling their ideas are valued and legitimate. One entrepreneur crowdfunding his scientific research explained that having others express interest in his work and offer financial support boosted his self-efficacy in his own abilities to pursue his work:

"For any project you sort of wonder if people are going to like you and like your [work]...so I definitely got more confident once people were clearly interested in it, and clearly engaging in the dialogue and supporting me financially."

Entrepreneurs report that public validation through crowdfunding, via platform features such as comments and dollars pledged, makes them feel more confident that their work is something that others desire. One entrepreneur of a board game project explained that after his successful crowdfunding campaign, he felt that he could demonstrate to a publisher that he has a strong audience of support for his work. In turn, this allowed him to confidently show that he could be successful professionally and it legitimized his product to others:

"Now there's actually real hard numbers showing, 'Hey, there's an interested audience in this enough to get this number of orders um, now are you interested?' ... So I can go in there [to speak with a publisher] with much more confidence ... I can license that game to a publisher, which I've done twice...actually three times now."

1.2 Public Validation Motivates Effort

Entrepreneurs also report feeling more motivated and excited about their work through engaging with the public online. Crowdfunding comment boards allow entrepreneurs to receive feedback on their ideas. As an entrepreneur working on a photography project explained:

"People talking about and people helping you get your ideas together and.... commenting kind of inspires you to add more and more to the idea and make it more successful."

Receiving feedback and support from the public motivated this entrepreneur to pursue and improve upon his photography work. In addition, positive feedback can motivate users to feel like their work is desired.

Another entrepreneur building a consumer product venture reported that the process of going through crowdfunding helped him confirm that he could be successful if he tried and that he should follow his intuition, as he stated:

"It was awesome. It was 100% confirming. It gave me tons of confidence. That's part of why I asked for so little. There wasn't a sense that I was a surefire winner. It was hugely helpful to my confidence and it encouraged me to follow my instincts."

Though he had at first doubted his abilities to raise money and asked for little at the start to protect himself and have a higher chance of winning, he felt a renewed sense of confidence about his decisions after seeing the support of others through the crowdfunding process.

1.3 Public Validation Helps Entrepreneurs Overcome Obstacles

The supportive relationship developed between entrepreneurs and funders can also lead them to seek new opportunities after crowdfunding. For example, one entrepreneur expressed how, after failing his crowdfunding campaign, his team went on to sell their product on eBay because of the encouragement of their Kickstarter backers. This suggests that supportive relationships developed with their funders through crowdfunding can lead them to effectively sell their work on other online platforms. One entrepreneur went on to sell over 7,000 copies of his game on Amazon, thus making the leap into the mainstream product market [46].

Entrepreneurs express that the support of others helps them believe that they can do their work. This can influence what entrepreneurs tell themselves about their performance abilities. For example, a photographer who raised $2,000 to finance a community venture to raise awareness of homelessness discussed how the feeling of having many people supporting his work made him feel that he had to have more optimistic self-talk. He explained:

"You have to tell yourself the entire time, 'Hey, this is going to happen, this is going to get funded, and this is going to be an awesome project because you have all these people backing you up the entire way.'"

This entrepreneur shows how having the support of a crowd backing up his work throughout the 30 day campaign made him feel that he needed to push himself and change his beliefs about the project. Thus, crowdfunding platforms offer a unique setting where entrepreneurs can put their work out to the public for recognition, comments, and financial support. If the support is there, this validation can help entrepreneurs change their perception of self-efficacy.

When crowdfunding entrepreneurs fail to reach their funding goals, continued validation of their work by the public encourages them to persevere. For example, one independent comic book artist expressed how after failing his first campaign, he and his team cut all communication with their supporters for two weeks. Yet their supporters still checked in to ask how things were going and to offer their support. In turn he expressed that the process of failing helped to strengthen him as an entrepreneur as learned many lessons from his first failure:

"I don't want to be cheesy but [failing] made me stronger... I mean, by going dark for two weeks, people literally wrote me 'Hey are you guys still around? ... Then if you saw the latest Kickstarter [campaign], ... first thing we said is we failed, we didn't do it, we wanted to raise seven grand, now we're back, we're smarter, and we're redoing it."

By showing their interest in the entrepreneurs' work even after a failed campaign, public validation helped the entrepreneur to recover quickly and return to work.

1.4 Public Validation from Strangers Creates Feeling of Impact

Participants also gained confidence in their abilities to succeed at their projects through receiving the support of people outside of their personal network. One entrepreneur of a photography franchise explained:

"Some of my biggest pledges are from people that I've never known, so it's really cool to see that other people are inspired by it... There is one woman who's pledged on my project and we constantly talk... she kind of helps me with coming up with new things and she's been sharing the page and she's been contacting news outlets around here to kind of tell them about the project."

This entrepreneur found it motivating and surprising that his supporters came from all over the globe and were willing to offer their suggestions and financial support. The crowdfunding process allows for the chance to seek support from a wider audience and motivation from outside of the typical network they can access offline. He was unsure that his project would have been possible without a crowdfunding platform, like Kickstarter:

"It would have been a lot tougher [without Kickstarter] and it would have been more selective of people, a more select group of funders. It's just cool that people from California have pledged for my project and I'm in Detroit. And it's just like a whole different experience that Kickstarter offers."

Being able to receive validation from a geographically diverse audience online allows them to see the positive impact of their work on a larger scale. As one entrepreneur seeking funding for a DNA project explained:

"I've gotten dozens of emails from people around the world who are really interested in the project, and who want to help on the scientific end or telling their friends and family, or a documentary TV producer contacted me, so I mean these are things that don't normally happen if you just have a grant proposal... so putting it out the public has been really great for me."

Many entrepreneurs reported being encouraged by the inflow of support and positive attention that was drawn to their projects through the crowfunding process.

1.5 A New Avenue for Public Validation

Crowdfunding also provides a unique community where the public can offer support through an easier-to-access medium. For example, on Kickstarter, supporters can quickly donate through Amazon payments. Given that the crowdfunding process takes place online, funders from around the world can easily offer their support and funding. An owner of a dance studio described how the dance community was more likely to donate money to support her dance shows through Kickstarter than through traditional donation methods, such as in person:

"I have people that have been fans of mine for a long time who had never donated and when we did it on Kickstarter they did."

This entrepreneur suggests that the set-up of crowdfunding platforms made it more feasible or appealing for the public (and "long-time" fans) to actually be able to support her financially.

Entrepreneurs also expressed that crowdfunding allowed them to give others a technological platform to support their work:

"And it turns out that there were a lot of friends and family that wanted to support what I was doing and didn't have an avenue to do so. And [crowdfunding] provided an avenue."

Crowdfunding allows a communal space for entrepreneurs to have new opportunities for gaining public awareness and receive funding for their work. In addition, entrepreneurs reported that crowdfunding provides a unique (and unparalleled) space for them to actually see "followers turn into real dollars" and provides a way to "monetize social media".

1.6 Visualization of Feedback Boosts Self-Efficacy

Crowdfunding platforms also offer the unique ability of viewing the validation of others in a public setting. Entrepreneurs can receive quantitative data through number of comments, e-mail notifications, numbers of funders, and financial support. These features can help to increase the self-efficacy of entrepreneurs.

Many entrepreneurs expressed how much they enjoyed seeing "likes" for their crowdfunding projects and doing so helped them understand the number of people they are reaching and the quantity of people who recognize their work. This visual demonstration of public support can increase their self-efficacy and belief in their ability to succeed at their work.

"It's absolutely amazing that you can come up with an idea and have the whole world sit there and pledge for your idea to actually happen, you know? And all that excitement that I get every day that I see so and so pledged $20 so and so pledged $200, all that excitement I owe to everybody else, and...it kind of gives you a lot of faith in the world and faith in you know the project itself because it's not just you that is so excited about it...You have people on a daily basis pledging for your project and commenting and messaging, and it's an ego boost."

The visualization of success for an entrepreneur through e-mails, likes, commenting, messaging, and financial pledges can help boost their sense of efficacy and make them feel that others are excited about the work that they are doing.

1.7 Negative Self-Efficacy through Public Validation

While some entrepreneurs felt highly supported through their campaign, others expressed that the lack of support in crowdfunding led them to feel unvalued in their work. Some entrepreneurs expressed that they received little to no support throughout the entirety of their campaigns. For example, one entrepreneur working on a video project spent over $200 advertising for his project and still received no support or financial backers. As he stated:

"Support? Not at all. I didn't receive any contact from anyone in those 10 days. Went in without any expectations as it was my first attempt. People have such low attention spans that they probably don't read the text... I have done enough sales, I am tired of selling myself."

This entrepreneur decided after the campaign that moving forward he would not turn to the crowd for help, but keep things more private.

Another entrepreneur hoping to publish her first book described her shift in self-efficacy after people didn't support her work:

"Oh my god, I lost confidence in myself...I was hurt by some of the people who didn't kick in, it was ... harmful to my ego."

Entrepreneurs expressed the challenge of having people they thought would support them not do so. One entrepreneur reported that she expected her friends to contribute, but their lack of support made her feel less confident in her ability to succeed and made her discount the support of others who have already backed her project. She continued:

"So that was hard, you know, 'cause I do have a lot of friends, and I do a lot of stuff for my friends, and when I was in the black, believe me they were all getting stuff from me. And it's kinda hard when the shoes on the other foot and you hope people will support you, and they don't."

The lack of public support made the entrepreneur feel abandoned and she realized that she had less support for her work than anticipated. Another entrepreneur expressed a similar sentiment after not receiving the expected support from friends:

"I networked on Facebook and on social media but there has been no interest or support for it yet- closest friends are the least supportive when you try to do something different."

In addition, some entrepreneurs struggled with getting feedback that they disagreed with or was negative from the public. This was particularly offensive as it was from people they did not know and thus seemed more critical. As one entrepreneur working on selling hooks explained after receiving critical design feedback on crowdfunding:

"It's a little bit of an insult for people to say you know you can do this better. There were also some moderately negative [points of feedback]. When someone criticizes, it's hard."

The lack of support from others or negative feedback led some entrepreneurs to feel depressed and more critical of their work. Entrepreneur's perspective can change as they realize that there might be less support for their idea than they expected, given the expansive nature of the Internet and the large number of projects that are available for funders to support. This is consistent with research suggesting that users can become disillusioned when they see the competitive space they are entering [24].

2. Modeling

Our interviews suggest that crowdfunding platforms provide a unique opportunity for role modeling, or seeing examples of similar others as motivation for self, which can boost self-efficacy [4]. This is done through entrepreneurs being able to view others' project profiles via the crowdfunding platform. For example, a film director described that after seeing one of his peers raise money for a film through crowdfunding, he started using social media to build an audience to finance his own short film. He eventually raised over $15,000 from 314 people:

"I was baffled by the idea that the guy just, in like a 24-hour period, used Twitter to raise like thousands of...And it really flipped a switch for me, and I realized social networking and stuff is really going to change the way creative people can get things done... I can get on Twitter today and raise money for a movie tomorrow. Like I've been cultivating my Twitter circle, my twitter network for like 5 years now."

This entrepreneur saw the benefits of using a social media tool, like Twitter, to raise support for his idea. Seeing this example motivated him to begin building his network for his own campaign.

2.1 Learning From the Lessons of Others

In addition, entrepreneurs report learning from others, which can shape their own behavior. As one entrepreneur said,

"I tried to read what some of the other people had done and pay attention to the people who were successful and tried to learn from them because I think some of the things about it were potentially counter intuitive. For example, ... my initial inclination was to make the time frame as long as possible, thinking that that would help me to raise more money. But, the advice I seem to get from reading about other people's experience was that having a shorter campaign was actually more beneficial."

This entrepreneur succeeded his funding goal and raised $4,741 for his photography program. Seeing examples of others gives entrepreneurs the confidence to try it themselves. For example, a 40-year-old man described how he was motivated to pursue his long-time dream of starting a food truck business after seeing other novice entrepreneurs succeed through crowdfunding:

"The guy that did one on Kickstarter two weeks ago ... it was essentially a little frame that you would sit a cell phone on top of... This is essentially a cardboard box with a hole in it! [laugh] It is! ... It was just unbelievable how much money he raised."

By seeing the example of others with similar skill levels succeeding, he said he realized that he was capable of doing the same. Entrepreneurs find role models by browsing crowdfunding project pages and learning from how others presented and approached their work. In addition they report using the way others manage their projects to help guide how theirs are managed. Entrepreneurs express learning from others on crowdfunding platforms regarding organization about deliverables and using social media to market their products.

2.2 Learning From Others' Mistakes & Failures

Entrepreneurs also report learning from the mistakes of others and hope to avoid the same pitfalls themselves. One game designer explained how he noticed that many projects would show a similar pattern where they would generate a lot of enthusiasm on Kickstarter and then show no activity for months after the campaign, causing much of the enthusiasm to burn off. He described how he did not want to make the same mistake:

"I wanted to do ... an instant gratification thing... with the first novel as quickly as possible, which is why we didn't start a Kickstarter until we actually [were] well under way, editing and layout was happening."

Surprisingly entrepreneurs did not report being frustrated by seeing the failures of others, but encouraged and inspired to not make the same mistakes.

2.3 Learning From Apprenticeship Model

Entrepreneurs expressed how working beside others helped them learn and gain confidence in running their own crowdfunding project. One entrepreneur working in the tabletop gaming community explained his process of shadowing a fellow entrepreneur on their crowdfunding campaign before trying it out for himself:

"I rode shotgun on a couple of Kickstarters ... so I kind of got to see someone else running a Kickstarter, but with the ultimate thing being a product that got added in my catalogue... [laugh] that was a nice dip the toe in way of approaching it."

This entrepreneur highlights the benefits of learning through apprenticeship, which is a crucial element within communities of practice [25]. He went on to lead four successful crowdfunding campaigns selling his board games after this experience. Another entrepreneur shadowed a friend who was also raising funds for a game design:

"I kind of rode on [a fellow entrepreneur's] coattails a bit when he was developing a little matrix game ... and that was what initially exposed me to kind of the versatility of crowdfunding, that you can actually get small print runs done for a committed and really strong fan base."

The crowdfunding platform provides a unique place for entrepreneurs to draw inspiration from others through seeing sample projects or serving as an apprentice. In turn, many entrepreneurs reported feeling greater belief in their own abilities.

2.4 Negative Self-Efficacy through Modeling

While some entrepreneurs found inspiration looking at entrepreneur examples online, others found this process to be demotivating and stifling. Some entrepreneurs expressed that seeing examples made them feel that all of the good ideas had already been taken or that only people with an established reputation succeed. One entrepreneur working on selling CD's explained:

"I spent about a week reading the Kickstarter website -- I looked at projects and what kinds of things had gotten sold and action. It seem that the best things have already gotten a following..."

Seeing that others were ahead of where they were or had a seemingly unfair advantage was demotivating to some entrepreneurs. This is consistent with Bandura's theory that even the mere sight of a formidable looking opponent can lower self-efficacy more than when someone is faced with an opponent that looks less impressive [4]. Several entrepreneurs also commented that with so much content on the Internet they felt that people could not see their projects and that their ideas were more hidden online.

Entrepreneurs also expressed frustration by the misconception that crowdfunding was easy. Many saw examples of crowdfunding projects online and anticipated that they would be able to mirror their success, only to find that it was more difficult that they thought, consistent with CSCW research on the role of community in crowdfunding [19]. One entrepreneur who worked on a CD campaign explained this realization:

"I've noticed that it's a lot more competitive to get your idea out there than it sounds... it sounds really easy to be like, "Ok, I'm going to come up with this project and post it all over the internet, and people are going to love it!" and it's not that easy because... the internet is full of endless possibilities and...They're so overwhelmed by everything else that you see and hear and watch on a daily basis."

Other entrepreneurs expressed that it was a lot more difficult than it had seemed, as one voiced: *"I've realized that it's not as easy as Kickstarter would say that it is."*

Another entrepreneur expressed how he looked at examples of other projects and tried to model his after theirs, but was unsuccessful.

"I wrote mine in the same format of someone who raised a couple thousands. People said to lower the amount you are asking for, now asking for more specific things, but haven't been successful yet. Even though I advertised everywhere-every group or social media."

Although the entrepreneur modeled the behavior of others, they didn't find the same level of success. Our research demonstrated that some entrepreneurs draw great inspiration from others within the community, yet some can develop unrealistic expectations or fail to pursue their own strategies as they attempt to follow the example of others.

3. Mastery

The crowdfunding experience can also influence entrepreneur's sense of mastery, or seeing oneself succeed or fail at a task [4]. The platform allows entrepreneurs to gain concrete skills and observe their success as well as their failures displayed in a public setting. This can both increase and decrease self-efficacy. The entrepreneurs we interviewed reported gaining skills in things like management, communication and marketing, as well as social networking to advance their work.

3.1 Project Management Skills

Entrepreneurs reported that working on crowdfunding projects helped them improve their management of large-scale projects. As one entrepreneur working on an art crowdfunding project reported:

"It was a very sort of complicated thing to pull off and doing it really gave me a lot of confidence in myself and my team on how we can pull off large-scale projects."

This entrepreneur showed that her confidence in herself and her team was strengthened through feeling a sense of mastery after succeeding at the task. Many entrepreneurs expressed feeling a sense of accomplishment and mastery as they succeeded what they had set out to do.

3.2 Communication Skills

Crowdfunding platforms provide a space where entrepreneurs can jump into their work and take risks. It also provides the chance for entrepreneurs to practice communicating their work to others. One entrepreneur described how she had to learn how to explain her work in a way that would inspire others who knew little about the subject:

"To be able to communicate with people who aren't scientifically minded takes a skill and a realm of comfort, so making the video was key. And being able to come up with something inspiring and understandable to the general public... definitely requires a set of skills that writing a grant to NSF would never call upon."

By learning how to communicate their work to a broader audience on crowdfunding platforms, participants found that they were able to reach many more people than they would typically reach offline. In turn, this process pushed them to become skilled at different communication styles. Entrepreneurs also report learning how to communicate different messages to different audiences depending on what they need to hear:

"It's very different to pitch your project to the public than it is to pitch it to a grant organization and you know it may seem like there's two divergent streams, like two very different ways of presenting your project... and trying to convince the public that I'm not just this person in my ivory tower, and thinking thoughts that don't mean anything to anyone but myself and so it's really sort of pairing those two together is what I'm learning how to do."

Entrepreneurs build skills in communicating to new audiences and presenting their work in a way that makes sense to novices in order to garner their support. Entrepreneurs also reported learning how to make a convincing video for their project that others would want to watch:

"I've been surprised by some of the stuff I've learned about the utility of the video in the project, but also about it's length, like you lose most of your viewers of the video by the 90 second mark, unless you've really hooked them. And many don't watch past the first 30 seconds, so like you have to really up front deliver the reason to buy."

3.3 Social Networking Skills

Entrepreneurs reported improving their social networking skills through publicizing their work on crowdfunding platforms. As one entrepreneur pursuing a photography crowdfunding campaign remarked:

"*I've gotten better at probably you know, being more confident in the way that I social network, and knowing that I'm not looking as terrible as I think I look.*"

Crowdfunding provides a space where entrepreneurs can get noticed by a large crowd of people from around the world and develop a reputation for their work that is not feasible offline. This allows entrepreneurs who may not have been known before, to develop a sense of professionalism for their work. As one game designer described how he built a stronger following with each successive crowdfunding project he launched:

"I had built up enough of an audience that people were interested in my first commercial game, and then my second commercial game, and then my third commercial game. And so gradually I found myself becoming a professional game designer, totally by this totally weird roundabout way that's sort of a new model compared to what used to be the norm."

Entrepreneurs reported that opportunities arose through the crowdfunding process that helped build up their professional reputation. This is consistent with Weick's theory of "small wins," suggesting that in order to accomplish a larger task, they need to first have a smaller accomplishment [43]. One entrepreneur explained some of the new opportunities that arose from her crowdfunding campaign:

"Well, I got a book deal, that was the biggest thing. My book... is coming out at the end of March. I also got to be on CNN, which was great. I spoke about the project at the Museum of Contemporary Art in Chicago...Having $25,000, a chunk of capital, that gave me a lot more financial security than I've ever really had."

3.4 Professional Development Skills

Through developing their reputation as experts on crowdfunding platforms, entrepreneurs reported that they felt like they could mentor and support others in developing their work. Entrepreneurs explained that after going through the crowdfunding process they felt confident sharing their lessons learned with others. As one entrepreneur described:

"I still am learning it...it's a fun experience, um, and now I feel much more confident in offering advice to people [compared to] where I was five years ago."

Entrepreneurs reported that as they went through the crowdfunding process, they found themselves being able to speak in conferences and public platforms about their expertise. One entrepreneur who was new to business explained how after participating in crowdfunding, someone asked him to speak on a panel about his experience

"Suddenly I found myself like talking for 5 minutes straight about like the business elements going into it and why you want to try to launch your project on a Tuesday because you know marketing research has shown people tend to interact more with social media and read blog posts and maybe hop over to Kickstarter page on Tuesdays."

The entrepreneur surprised himself by how articulate he was on this issue and how he was able to teach others after going through the process himself. He also reported feeling able to more confidently speak on the topic, via blogs and other platforms, like Pinterest:

"I think have culled you know that... advice down to a few links of interest that I've put on a Pinterest board that I try to share out to people when people come to me now and ask, "How do, how do I do a Kickstarter?" I'm like well go read all these first, and then come back... I've ended up being a guy who knows a lot about Kickstarter."

Entrepreneurs explained that they were able to offer insights and their developed expertise with others after working on crowdfunding platforms. An entrepreneur explained how he mentored a couple dozen people on crowdfunding platforms after going through the experience himself. The crowdfunding process allows entrepreneurs to develop their expertise in the field and develop themselves as professionals.

3.5 Negative Self-Efficacy through Mastery

While many entrepreneurs expressed feeling a positive sense of mastery through crowdfunding, others expressed that not achieving their goal led them to doubt their work and belief in themselves. As one entrepreneur working on selling his music said,

"It was very hard [when I didn't make the goal], it brings up all kinds of doubts, you think -- is this project any good, is there a market out there for it?"

Others expressed that in the process of the campaign they realized their weaknesses as entrepreneurs or lack of skills. One entrepreneur said that he wished he had the skills to put up a video and felt that it negatively influenced his project not having one on his project page. Another entrepreneur working on raising funds for a building expressed: *"[I gained] no skills, but it highlighted a shortcoming that I lack which is clarity and communication."*

Other entrepreneurs expressed that the process of not accomplishing the goal they set for themselves was defeating. The nature of their failure being so public and obvious from the website caused additional grief. As one filmmaker entrepreneur remarked:

"It was a little depressing. It was obvious that it was going to fail. I was defeated but trying to find other ways to get it funded."

Having campaign failure publicly displayed permanently on the crowdfunding website also negatively impacted entrepreneurs. One entrepreneur working on a crowdfunding project raising money to remodel a home ended up deactivating his Facebook account and not wanting to go on the Internet after his project failed.

Failing at a personal goal can be defeating, yet having this failure publicly displayed for the world to see can lead some entrepreneurs to retreat and decrease self-efficacy.

4. Physiological States

Our results also demonstrated that some entrepreneurs found the process of running a crowdfunding campaign physically and emotionally exhilarating. Many expressed the thrill of having a specific time pressure on themselves to raise the funds and that this energy pushed them forward. One entrepreneur working on developing a game for female scientists described how the process was similar to the exhilaration of running in a marathon. As she described:

"The emotional involvement was like running in a race and having people cheer for you. Relying on so many people made it seem realistic for me... It was so cool because we set a goal, and to see us actually hit it,.. It gives you confidence to see that it actually happened and if you did it then you'd do it again. It gives you a feeling of "Damn!"

Entrepreneurs expressed the excitement of getting to watch their product be released to the world and the emotional thrill of seeing how people responded to their work. As entrepreneur described:

"To me, it wasn't so much the amount of money, it was more of just the fun of seeing my product in the world."

Many expressed that it was much more the funding and more so about the emotional energy that they received. One entrepreneur working on publicizing his music told about the calls and e-mails he received during the campaign, which gave him greater meaning and value to his work. As he said,

"Anyone that I met or saw knew about it [my crowdfunding project] and it was all they talked about.... To see how many people responded and engaged in the process was really exciting and made me appreciate what I do. I realized that there is a place for what I do."

Many entrepreneurs found great energy and exhilaration from the crowdfunding campaign and from the short process of asking for funds from others. One entrepreneur described the enthusiasm he feels when receiving emails from those who support his projects:

"My favorite thing is waking up in the morning and looking at my email saying, "So-and-so pledged!" You know and it's like you get those Kickstarter emails and I'm just like, "Ooh!" like all excited and I'm constantly refreshing it."

E-mail notifications as well as social media "likes" and "comments" about one's crowdfunding project uplifted the spirits of entrepreneurs and boosted their self-efficacy.

4.1 Negative Self-Efficacy through Physiological States

Yet while some found the crowdfunding project exciting and exhilarating, others found it incredibly demanding and emotionally stressful. As one entrepreneur working on selling a rap CD stated about the campaign,

"It was 15 days of hell -- I couldn't sleep it was awful. I'd get little dings thinking it was a donation, but it was torture. Really stressful because you're trying with everything you have to raise money and spending everything you did. If money's not coming in, you're trying to think about what you are doing wrong."

Another said how the campaign changed while they were working on it, but tried to brush things off after failing to get the funding they had requested:

"I started out really confident, I just wanted to get a sense of how much people connected with the music and if the quality was better and if they felt more confident in donating.. I was really excited putting it up, but I was really down..."

Some entrepreneurs mentioned how the process affected them physically and emotionally and the stress that was involved with pushing an idea forward and not receiving the support they expected. This negative physiological response led to decreased levels of self-efficacy in entrepreneurs.

Entrepreneurs expressed how the process of asking for money was physically and emotionally daunting for them. As one entrepreneur working on a music campaign said:

"It's a scary thing asking everyone for all of that and to be honest it still weighs on me because I still have to give back the rewards, even $20 is a lot to ask. Now I make a concerted effort to help and I understand how hard it is to raise money, and it

was scary. And it walks this fine line of remembering that you're raising money for a good thing and being conscious."

The entrepreneur demonstrates the physical and emotional weight that the process can have on entrepreneurs. Others report of the endurance needed for this type of emotionally exhausting task. One entrepreneur reported the process of sticking with their goal and the physical trials of the process and making oneself vulnerable:

"When I launched the campaign, I remember pressing "Launch!" and feeling so good... But really it was just beginning... it was like an endurance task – how many people we can get... It was the worst feeling, like check your pride at the door. Even going back looking at Facebook I want to go back to people and say "oh god, I'm so sorry that I asked money of you"... This is a bit ridiculous."

Entrepreneurs mention the "endurance" and the effort needed to do this type of work and the physical and emotional exhaustion that the trying process of a campaign can have on entrepreneurs that can decrease self-efficacy.

DISCUSSION

Through a qualitative study of 53 entrepreneurs, we find that crowdfunding can provide a highly unique opportunity to influence the self-efficacy of entrepreneurs as they pursue their work. Our results suggest that crowdfunding platforms have the potential to support interpersonal interactions that motivate entrepreneurial work more efficiently and at a large scale. For example, users report gaining confidence in their work through features such as: positive affirmation and visual support from the crowd; seeing successful examples or shadowing others; mastering skills such as learning to communicate their projects; and gaining motivation to succeed through having a timeline for their project during the campaign. Yet we find that the same principles that can build self-efficacy in entrepreneurs can also sometimes make it weaker. Several socio-technical features of the crowdfunding interface that were shown to negatively influence self-efficacy included: negative feedback from backers, permanent public display of failed projects, the misconception around the ease of crowdfunding, and the time intensive nature of campaigns which left some entrepreneurs exhausted and stressed. These features played a role in developing negative self-efficacy in some entrepreneurs.

Contributions to Social Cognitive Theory

This work builds on social cognitive theory in several key ways. At a high level, it suggests that self-efficacy can be developed in crowdfunding spaces through public validation, modeling, mastery, and physiological states, four features that support self-efficacy based on social cognitive theory [4].

Public Validation

Our results suggest that audience size and social anonymity can impact self-efficacy on crowdfunding platforms. Entrepreneurs reported feeling increased confidence after receiving feedback from those they did not know as it felt as though their work was more valid. In addition, the large audience size made entrepreneurs feel like a large crowd was watching them, which is not always as accessible in offline environments. While research argues that online communities can offer a safe space for users [42], our data demonstrates that crowdfunding platforms can be risky, challenging spaces where users receive harsh criticism, praise, or both, from the public. Thus our research demonstrated that entrepreneurs can both increase or decrease self-efficacy quite severely given the validation (or lack there of) of their online audience.

Modeling

This research adds complexity to social cognitive theory around modeling by suggesting that even when entrepreneurs see examples of others failing, they can still develop self-efficacy for their work. Though past research argued that self-efficacy can be decreased through social comparison [4], our results suggest that social comparison and watching the failures or successes of others on crowdfunding can increase ones learning and self-efficacy towards their work. This points to the value of entrepreneurs shadowing others and learning from their experiences to gain heightened self-efficacy for their work.

Mastery

This work also builds on social cognitive theory through demonstrating how mastery in an online setting can impact self-efficacy, particularly given the audience size. Crowdfunding platforms create a space where it is very obvious if entrepreneur achieve or fail to reach their goal. Our results suggest that this public display of mastery or failure can influence an entrepreneur's perceptions of their own abilities. Given the large audience size online, entrepreneurs can feel higher or lower levels of mastery depending on their results, which can influence their entrepreneurial self-efficacy.

Physiological State

Furthermore, this research builds on social cognitive theory around physiological factors through demonstrating that with an emotionally taxing process like crowdfunding—where stakes are high, deadlines are short, and members feel accountable, vulnerable to their supporters – higher stress can be deduced. Entrepreneurs who were most successful were those who had a plan ahead of time and knew what to expect. Thus, greater counseling of entrepreneurs before entering the process could be helpful.

Contributions to Computer-Supported Entrepreneurship

This research builds on previous computer-supported entrepreneurship research by showing how crowdfunding experiences online support or hinder self-efficacy in entrepreneurs. While entrepreneurs reported gaining skills and boosts in their confidence through using crowdfunding sites, our results also showed that even experience failure in crowdfunding could sometimes build self-efficacy. This boost came from online social support, people continuing to encourage them in their work, which put the entrepreneurs on track to try again. Previous research pointed at how some sites have used badging to motivate and reward users [26]. Our research suggests that that social support for entrepreneurs on crowdfunding platforms may be stronger than financial benefits alone. Many respondents reported that this social support was more important than the money and why they did it. However, while the public experience of crowdfunding engaged more people in social support, it also exposed entrepreneurs to public experiences of criticism. While receiving feedback can support improved work quality [40], excess criticism and failure can be detrimental for one's self-efficacy [4].

Opportunities for Entrepreneurs in Online Communities

Our findings suggest that crowdfunding has the potential to change how novice entrepreneurs view their work and build their careers moving forward after the campaign. Currently opportunities for novice entrepreneurs to build self-efficacy are often competitive and limited to a few selected entrepreneurs, such as Tech Stars [47]. In addition, novices typically don't have an established following to provide support [28]. Yet crowdfunding allows them to not only get financial support, but also the psychological support needed to perform their work. In addition, it provides an opportunity for any entrepreneur to submit their idea and call on a large audience of people from around the world to support them.

More entrepreneurs are now beginning their careers through crowdfunding because working on these platforms provides them with possible support, mentoring, and training that are less available offline. Some design instructors have already begun to teach students to crowdfund as part of their course projects [10]. Since anyone with Internet access can crowdfund, entrepreneurs from underserved communities or with few connections to angel investors or venture capitalists have the same opportunities as those surrounded by traditional funding opportunities. This empowering experience can allow people of all ages, ethnicities, and genders to initiate and make progress on their projects at a speed and scale that is not available to all offline [22].

DESIGN IMPLICATIONS

This study points to several design principles that we recommend for future systems including: (1) the importance of providing public validation to entrepreneurs throughout the crowdfunding process, (2) showcasing mastery and skills gained on the site rather than failure, and (3) providing ways for entrepreneurs to learn from the failures and successes of others through the crowdfunding process and combat fatigue.

To begin, we recommend that crowdfunding platforms provide an online space where entrepreneurs can receive positive support and encouragement from others in the community. This is consistent with empirical research of online communities that rely on reputation systems and badges [26] to promote participation and better work. For example, Wikipedia started WikiLove, which allows users to get notes and images of encouragement from fellow users in the community. Providing tools for entrepreneurs to receive positive affirmation, such as "barnstars" on Wikipedia or "likes" on Facebook, could be helpful in building self-efficacy [6]. We also recommend providing more ways to see the level of public support or people who have viewed their page. Currently crowdfunding platforms provide badges for supporters every time they fund a new type of project, but there is no equivalent badge system for entrepreneurs. Allowing entrepreneurs to see their funding progress in ways other than the dollar amount could help to boost self-efficacy.

It can be helpful to facilitate the realization of skill mastery by entrepreneurs, as well as encouraging them to gain more skills. This might be done through a badge system that depicts different skills learned, such as a communication badge if you send a certain number of updates or a funding badge when you hit a certain target financial goal by an early period of time. For example, Codeacademy depicts user success on user pages with stars and checks of success. This allows users to feel a sense of pride for what they have accomplished thus far. Displaying these badges will also allow others to identify experts with certain skills, thus promoting the culture of mentorship in crowdfunding communities.

However, we also find that for those who don't reach their financial goals, the visual display of their failure can be quite demotivating. We recommend providing a way for those to manage the failure experience [15]. For example, entrepreneurs could pick what data is shown depending on how their campaign is progressing or have the option to remove failed crowdfunding projects to reduce feelings of failure. In addition, we recommend a way to notify others in the community if you are struggling and need support. Building on Bandura's theory of public validation and our findings, we suggest providing ways for people to feel supported despite failure. For example, crowdfunding platforms could encourage supporters of failed projects to send encouraging notes to entrepreneurs post-failure to boost self-efficacy and help people bounce back.

Entrepreneurs can discover new ways to conduct their work, as well as how to avoid common mistakes through seeing the examples of others. Thus, we recommend providing a tool to allow people to shadow others doing crowdfunding projects in similar spaces. For example, entrepreneurs could list the skills that they need help with and be matched with other entrepreneurs who have experience with these skills. We learned that it is helpful to "ride shotgun" with others through an apprenticeship model, building on research in communities of practices describing the importance of apprenticeships in learning new skills. For example, IndieGoGo labels each crowdfunding team member with a "user role," [20] which could help novice entrepreneurs to identify who to ask for help. We recommend allowing a user resource exchange [15] that helps find role models depending on what specific skills are needed (ex: combatting failure, advertising, etc.). Building on social cognitive theory of role modeling and our findings, we also recommend showing some role models of people failing and coming back to succeed at a crowdfunding campaign [4].

FUTURE WORK

Entrepreneurial work can be daunting [36]. Understanding how to best support entrepreneurs as they work via online tools could shape the way people pursue their work. Future work will involve developing our understanding of what specific parts of the campaign affect self-efficacy most and how to enhance these features to build self-confidence. We plan to conduct greater experimental work to measure the impact of crowdfunding on entrepreneurial self-efficacy [8] in order to better disaggregate specific platform features from entrepreneur experiences.

For instance, we could use self-efficacy survey to measure changes before and after running a crowdfunding campaign. While our qualitative methodology was effective for identifying early patterns and creating a baseline understanding what is occurring within the development of self-efficacy in crowdfunding, this methodology had its limits in allowing us to pull apart specific effects on entrepreneurial self-efficacy. In the future we will run a regression analysis of what factors are most impactful in entrepreneurs with higher levels of self-efficacy, comparing features such as age, business experience, and product type. This study will illuminate individual characteristics and the experience of social technical systems. Additionally, we plan to run a controlled experiment where a set of entrepreneurs are given self-efficacy enhancing socio-technical features while working on their crowdfunding project (ex: being sent positive feedback and being shown examples of positive role models throughout their work on the project) and compare the self-efficacy levels and results of those not using the tool. The control would allow us to understand the impact of self-efficacy tools on performance and retention.

CONCLUSION

Crowdfunding provides a new avenue for entrepreneurs to increase their self-efficacy through (1) public validation, via public financial and emotional support from an audience, (2) modeling, via entrepreneurs access to examples and lessons of other entrepreneurs, (3) mastery, via the development of concrete new skills as a result of publishing on the site, and (4) physiological states, via the way entrepreneurs can feel energized during crowdfunding campaigns. Yet not everyone receives these benefits. Our results demonstrate that crowdfunding can also decrease entrepreneurial self-efficacy from these very same features. These results point to ways socio-technical systems can be improved to develop the self-efficacy of entrepreneurs. Crowdfunding provides hope for a future where entrepreneurs can go to crowdfunding platforms to receive support and boost their self-efficacy for their work. In doing so, we can broaden participation in entrepreneurial work by emphasizing the supportive aspects of crowdfunding.

ACKNOWLEDGEMENTS

Thanks to Claire McCloskey and Nicole Zhu for their help with interviews and data analysis for this research. Thanks also to our participants for their thoughtful insights.

REFERENCES

[1] Agrawal, A., Catalini, C., and Goldfarb, A. *Offline Relationships, Distance, and the Internet: The Geography of Crowdfunding*. National Bureau of Economic Research,, Cambridge, MA, 2011.

[2] Alexa.com. 2011. http://www.alexa.com/.

[3] Asch, S. Opinions and Social Pressure. *Scientific American 193*, 5 (1955), 31–35.

[4] Bandura, A. *Self-efficacy: The exercise of control*. W. H. Freeman and Company, 1997.

[5] Belleflamme, P., Lambert, T., and Schwienbacher, A. Crowdfunding: An Industrial Organization Perspective. *Prepare for the workshop on Digital Business Models: Understanding Strategies*, (2010).

[6] Benkler, Y., Shaw, A., and Hill, B.M. Peer Production: A Modality of Collective Intelligence. In *The Collective Intelligence Handbook*. (in preparation).

[7] Boyd, N.G. and Vozikis, G.S. The influence of self-efficacy on the development of entrepreneurial intentions and actions. *Entrepreneurship Theory and Practice 18*, (1994), 63–63.

[8] Chen, C., Greene, P.G., and Crick, A. Does entrepreneurial self-efficacy distinguish entrepreneurs from managers. *Journal of Business Venturing` 13*, (1998), 295–316.

[9] Dabbish, L., Stuart, C., Tsay, J., and Herbsleb, J. Social coding in GitHub: Transparency and collaboration in an open software repository. *Proc. of CSCW*, ACM (2012), 1277–1286.

[10] Dow, S., Gerber, E., and Wong, A. A pilot study of using crowds in the classroom. *Proc. of CHI*, (2013), 227–236.

[11] Gangadharbatla, H. Facebook me: Collective self-esteem, need to belong, and internet self-efficacy as predictors of the iGeneration's attitudes toward social networking sites. *Journal of Interactive Advertising 8*, 2 (2008), 5–15.

[12] Gerber, E.M. and Hui, J. Crowdfunding: Motivations and Deterrents for Participation. *ACM Transactions on Computer-Human Interaction 20*, 6 (2013), 34:1–34:32.

[13] Gilbert, E. Designing social translucence over social networks. *Proc. of CHI*, (2012), 2731–2740.

[14] Gist, M.E. Self-efficacy: Implications for organizational behavior and human resource management. *Academy of Management Review 12*, 3 (1987), 472–485.

[15] Greenberg, M. Learning to Fail: Experiencing Public Failure Online Through Crowdfunding. *Proc. of CHI*, (2014).

[16] Grudin, J. and Poltrock, S.E. Computer-supported cooperative work and groupware. *Advances in Computers 45*, (1997), 269–320.

[17] Hackman, J.R. and Oldham, G.R. *Work redesign*. Addison-Wesley, Reading, Mass, 1980.

[18] Hui, J., Gerber, E., and Gergle, D. Understanding and Leveraging Social Networks for Crowdfunding: Opportunities and Challenges. *Proc. of DIS*, (2014).

[19] Hui, J.S., Greenberg, M.D., and Gerber, E.M. Understanding the Role of Community in Crowdfunding Work. *Proc. of CSCW*, (2014), 62–74.

[20] IndieGoGo.com. 2011.

[21] Kickstarter.com. 2013. http://www.kickstarter.com/.

[22] Kittur, N., Nickerson, J., Bernstein, M., et al. The Future of Crowd Work. *Proc. of CSCW*, (2013), 1301–1318.

[23] Kollock, P. The economies of online cooperation. *Communities in cyberspace*, (1999), 220.

[24] Kraut, R.E. and Resnick, P. *Building successful online communities*. The MIT Press, 2012.

[25] Lave, J. and Wenger, E. *Situated Learning: Legitimate peripheral participation*. University of Cambridge Press, Cambridge, 1991.

[26] Liang, C.-Y., Chen, C.-H., and Hsu, Y.-L. The Participation Motivation and Work Styles of the Administrators for Chinese Wikipedia (Article written in Chinese). *Journal of Educational Media and Library Sciences 46*, 1 (2008), 81–109.

[27] Luther, K., Caine, K., Ziegler, K., and Bruckman, A. Why it works (when it works): success factors in online creative collaboration. *Proc. of GROUP*, ACM (2010), 1–10.

[28] Marlow, J. and Dabbish, L. From rookie to all-star: professional development in a graphic design social networking site. *Proc. of CSCW*, ACM (2014), 922–933.

[29] McMullen, J.S. and Shepherd, D.A. Entrepreneurial action and the role of uncertainty in the theory of the entrepreneur. *Academy of Management Review 31*, 1 (2006), 132–152.

[30] Mintzberg, H. An Emerging Strategy of "Direct" Research. *Administrative Science Quarterly 24*, (1979), 580–589.

[31] Muller, M., Geyer, W., Soule, T., Daniels, S., and Cheng, L.-T. Crowdfunding inside the enterprise: employee-initiatives for innovation and collaboration. *Proc. of CHI*, (2013), 503–512.

[32] Panovich, K., Miller, R., and Karger, D. Tie strength in question & answer on social network sites. *Proc. of CSCW*, ACM (2012), 1057–1066.

[33] Rafaeli, S. and Ariel, Y. 11 Online Motivational Factors: Incentives for Participation and Contribution in Wikipedia. (2008).

[34] Restivo, M. and van de Rijt, A. Experimental study of informal rewards in peer production. *PloS one 7*, 3 (2012), e34358.

[35] Rosen, Y. and Rimor, R. Using a collaborative database to enhance students' knowledge construction. *Interdisciplinary Journal of E-Learning and Learning Objects 5*, 1 (2009), 187–195.

[36] Shane, S. *A General Theory of Entrepreneurship: The Individual-Opportunity Nexus*. Edward Elgar Publishing Limited, Northampton, MA, 2003.

[37] Sharratt, M. and Usoro, A. Understanding knowledge-sharing in online communities of practice. *Electronic Journal on Knowledge Management 1*, 2 (2003), 187–196.

[38] Shea, P. and Bidjerano, T. Learning presence: Towards a theory of self-efficacy, self-regulation, and the development of a communities of inquiry in online and blended learning environments. *Computers & Education 55*, 4 (2010), 1721–1731.

[39] Spradley, J.P. *Participant Observation*. Rinehart and Winston, New York, 1980.

[40] Vygotsky, L.S. *The collected works of L. S. Vygotsky*. Plenum, New York, 1987.

[41] Ward, C. and Ramachandran, V. Crowdfunding the next hit: Microfunding online experience goods. *Proc. of NIPS, Workshop on Computational Social Science and the Wisdom of Crowds*, (2010).

[42] Warschauer, M. Computer-mediated collaborative learning: theory and practice. *The Modern Language Journal 81*, 4 (1997), 470–481.

[43] Weick, K.E. Sensemaking in Organizations: Small Structures with Large Consequences. In *Social Psychology in Organizations: Advances in Theory and Research*. Simon & Schuster, Englewood Cliffs, NJ, 1993, 10–37.

[44] Kickstarter Stats. *Kickstarter*. http://www.kickstarter.com/help/stats.

[45] Wikipedia editor survey: Top-line data released — Wikimedia blog. http://blog.wikimedia.org/2011/06/17/wikipedia-editor-survey-top-line-data-released/.

[46] *Cards Against Humanity*.

[47] Techstars. *Techstars*. http://www.techstars.com/.

Crowds on Wall Street: Extracting Value from Collaborative Investing Platforms

Gang Wang[†], **Tianyi Wang**[†‡], **Bolun Wang**[†], **Divya Sambasivan**[†], **Zengbin Zhang**[†]
Haitao Zheng[†] **and Ben Y. Zhao**[†]
[†]Department of Computer Science, UC Santa Barbara
[‡]Department of Electronic Engineering, Tsinghua University
{gangw, tianyi, bolunwang, divya_sambasivan, zengbin, htzheng, ravenben}@cs.ucsb.edu

ABSTRACT
In crowdsourced systems, it is often difficult to separate the highly capable "experts" from the average worker. In this paper, we study the problem of evaluating and identifying experts in the context of SeekingAlpha and StockTwits, two crowdsourced investment services that are encroaching on a space dominated for decades by large investment banks. We seek to understand the quality and impact of content on collaborative investment platforms, by empirically analyzing complete datasets of SeekingAlpha articles (9 years) and StockTwits messages (4 years). We develop sentiment analysis tools and correlate contributed content to the historical performance of relevant stocks. While SeekingAlpha articles and StockTwits messages provide minimal correlation to stock performance in aggregate, a subset of experts contribute more valuable (predictive) content. We show that these authors can be easily identified by user interactions, and investments using their analysis significantly outperform broader markets. Finally, we conduct a user survey that sheds light on users views of SeekingAlpha content and stock manipulation.

ACM Classification Keywords
H.3.5 Information Storage and Retrieval: Online Information Services; J.4 Computer Applications: Social and Behavioral Sciences

General Terms
Measurement; Management; Design

Author Keywords
Crowdsourcing; Stock Market; Sentiment Analysis

INTRODUCTION
The "wisdom of the crowd" phenomenon has revolutionized content generation, discovery and curation in the Internet age. User-contributed content now dominate restaurant views (Yelp), travel and hospitality (TripAdvisor), encyclopedias (Wikipedia), general Q&A (Quora, Yahoo Answers), and even photography (Flickr). Even as content proliferates on these platforms, content curation, *e.g.* identifying high quality content and the "experts" who generate such content, is a growing challenge [4, 19, 48].

CSCW 2015, March 14–18, 2015, Vancouver, BC, Canada.

http://dx.doi.org/10.1145/2675133.2675144

This problem is especially critical in the rapidly growing area of collaborative investment analysis, *i.e.* user-contributed analysis on value and investment strategies of stocks, bonds and commodities. For over 150 years, personal investment advice has been the exclusive domain of investment banks and wealth advisors such as Goldman Sachs and Lehman Brothers. Over the last decade, however, networks like CNBC and Bloomberg established roles as independent sources of financial news, and the financial crisis of 2008 led to the collapse of several of the oldest investment banks (Bear Stearns, Lehman Brothers). Filling in the void were rapidly growing services such as SeekingAlpha and StockTwits, where independent analysts and retail investors could contribute and share analysis for free. SeekingAlpha now reports more than 3 million users and 9 million unique monthly visits. This represents a significant portion of the US investment market, where more than 50 million estimated households own mutual funds or equities [20].

In this paper, we seek to understand the quality and impact of analysis shared on collaborative investment platforms, and how to distinguish high quality analysis from biased or uninformed opinions. We target the two primary yet quite different social investment platforms, SeekingAlpha and StockTwits, and analyze the potential for investment returns following their recommendations versus the market baseline, the S&P 500 stock market index. We seek to understand how expertise of contributors can affect the quality and utility of contributed content, using SeekingAlpha as an "expert" model (all content is contributed by less than 0.27% of users) and StockTwits as a "peer" model (any user can contribute).

Our work has three goals. First, we assess the quality of content in these platforms to determine if how much value, if any, these collaborative platforms provide to individual investors. Second, we contrast two platforms using an "expert" based model and a "peer" based model, to explore the design principles and lessons for building collaborative social investing systems. Finally, we wish to evaluate techniques to identify the most effective "expert contributors" in the crowd.

We summarize our contributions below.

First, we gather longitudinal datasets from both platforms since their inception (9 years for SeekingAlpha, 4 years for StockTwits). We develop sentiment analyzers on each dataset, using a mixture of keyword processing and machine learning classifiers. Validation shows our methods achieve high accuracy in extracting sentiments towards individual stocks (85.5% for SeekingAlpha, 76.2% for StockTwits).

Second, we analyze correlation between content sentiments from both services with stock returns at different time scales. We show that content from both SeekingAlpha and StockTwits provide minimal forward correlation with stock performance. While the average article provides little value, we find that a subset of "top authors" in SeekingAlpha contribute content that shows significantly higher correlation with future stock performance.

Third, we evaluate the hypothetical performance of simple investment strategies following top authors from both platforms. We show that strategies based on sentiment from top SeekingAlpha authors perform exceptionally well, and significantly outperform broader markets. More importantly, we show that these experts can be easily identified without historical stock market data, using only user interactions with their articles as a guide. This suggests the design of a "meta-reputation" system for users that can serve to both curate content and simplify its discovery.

Fourth, we conduct a large scale survey of SeekingAlpha users and contributors to understand their usage, reliance, and trust in the SeekingAlpha service. Results show that despite seeing potentially intentionally misleading or manipulative articles, most users still rely heavily on the site content for investment advice. Most consider SeekingAlpha unique, and would not use a competing alternative in its absence.

A recent article in a financial journal also studied SeekingAlpha and showed statistical correlation between its content and earning surprises [9]. In contrast, our work contrasts the performance of expert (SeekingAlpha) versus peer-based (StockTwits) systems, evaluates the performance of realistic and simple trading strategies, and reports user views of SeekingAlpha through detailed surveys.

In summary, the rise of collaborative investment analysis has significantly changed how retail investors manage their investments. Our analysis shows that even on curated sites such as SeekingAlpha, most articles are poor indicators of market performance. However, a subset of SeekingAlpha authors provide valuable content that can be leveraged to build trading strategies that significantly outperform the broader markets. More importantly, these authors can be identified not only by their statistical performance, but more easily by the feedback their articles generate from other users. This shows that even for a complex and domain-specific such as stock trading, broader input from the crowd can help identify high quality content in a sea of data. Finally, results from our user survey confirm that most SeekingAlpha users have seen and have learned to distinguish biased or manipulative articles from useful articles.

BACKGROUND: SEEKINGALPHA AND STOCKTWITS

Seeking Alpha. Launched in 2004, SeekingAlpha (SA) is the most popular platform today for independent stock analysis. As of early 2014, SA has more than 8 million unique monthly viewers and 3 million registered users [47]. SA's content is mainly contributed by roughly 8000 registered *contributors* [1], and articles are vetted by an editorial board before publication on the site. Users can subscribe to stocks of interest to receive related articles and news summaries, *follow* contributors to receive their articles, and interact with contributors and other users through *comments* on articles. SA contributors include independent investors, portfolio managers, professional investors and investment firms. Roughly 400 out of 8000 contributors self-identify as investment firms. SA pays each contributor $10 per 1000 page views on articles.

StockTwits. StockTwits (ST) started in 2009 as a financial social network for sharing ideas among traders. Anyone on StockTwits can contribute content – short messages limited to 140 characters that cover ideas on specific investments, and post their messages to a public stream visible to all. There's no editorial board or content curation, and users are not compensated for their messages. Like Twitter, ST users *follow* others to build directional social links; and also follow the stock symbols they are interested in. Unlike SeekingAlpha, StockTwits provides real-time streaming of investor sentiment towards individual stocks. As of the end of 2013, StockTwits has over 300K registered users and its content reaches an audience of 40 million across the Internet [2].

METHODOLOGY

Seeking Alpha and StockTwits represent the largest and most representative sites in expert and peer-based investment analysis. In this study, we seek to quantify correlation between sentiment in user-contributed investment analysis to real movements in stock equities, how and if such correlations can be leveraged for investment gain, and how users view and utilize platforms such as SeekingAlpha in their investments. Our methodology is as follows:

- First, we gather complete datasets of contributed articles from SeekingAlpha and "twits" from StockTwits. We then develop sentiment analyzers for both datasets and evaluate their accuracy.
- Second, we compute statistical correlation between sentiment of contributed content to the performance of stocks they discuss. We do so for different time scales and both individual stocks and the aggregate market. We also sort authors by their performance to identify authors whose content consistently correlate with stock performance.
- Third, we propose strategies for identifying and trading stocks using sentiments from top authors in both platforms, and evaluate them against baseline market indices. We explore the efficacy of strategies that identify top authors by historical performance and by interactions with other users.
- Finally, we use a large user survey of SeekingAlpha users and contributors to understand how they utilize social investing platforms and their views on stock manipulation. Stock "pump-and-dump" scams have been discovered on SA in the past [13, 24].

Site	Data Since	Total Posts	Posts w/ Stocks	Active Users (Authors)	Covered Stocks
SeekingAlpha	2004	410K	163K	228K (8783)	10.4K
StockTwits	2009	12.7M	8.5M	86K (86K)	9.3K

Table 1. Basic statistics of collected data.

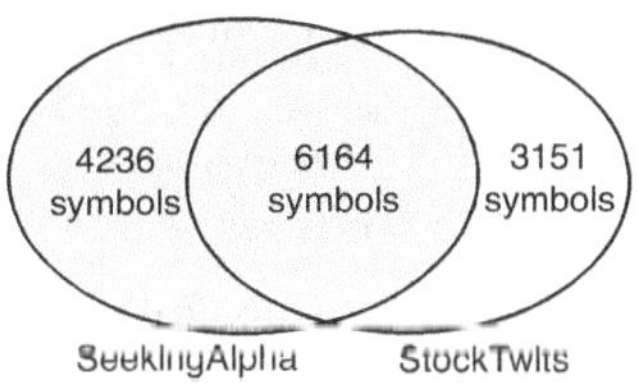

Figure 1. Stock symbols extracted from SA and ST.

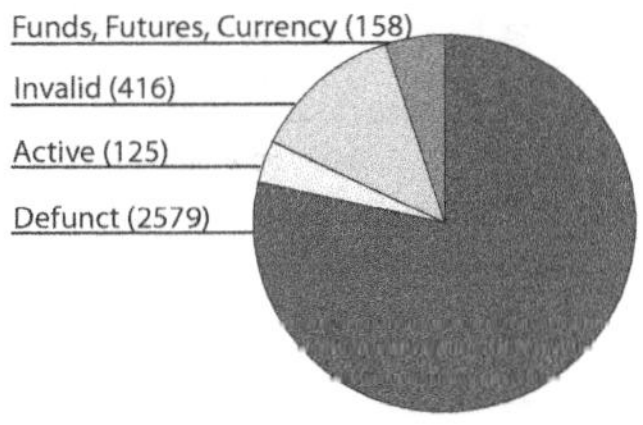

Figure 2. Breakdown of symbols without history price.

DATA COLLECTION

SeekingAlpha. In April 2014, we crawled the complete list of historical articles published on SeekingAlpha since its launch in 2004. This produced 410,290 articles written by 8,783 authors, 2,237 news and conference transcripts[1]. Our analyses focus on articles and do not include news in the form of SA "market currents" or transcripts. Our crawl also produced 4,115,719 total comments, of which 75% were written by 227,641 non-contributing users. The remaining 25% are from authors themselves. We crawl profiles of all authors and active users for their brief bio and number of followers and followees.

Each SeekingAlpha article has an "about" field that lists what stock(s) the article discusses. 163,410 (about 40%) of our articles have at least one stock symbol in their about field. Articles without stock symbols usually discuss overall market trends or sectors of stocks. From our entire dataset of SeekingAlpha articles, we were able to extract 10,400 unique stock symbols.

StockTwits. We are fortunate to receive permission from StockTwits Inc. to access their historical message archive, including all messages posted from 2009 (initial launch) to February 2014. The dataset contains 12,740,423 messages posted by 86,497 users. Each message includes a messageID, author's userID, author's number of followers (followees), timestamp, and message text. Each message is limited to 140 characters, and stock symbols are preceded by a "CashTag" ($). In our dataset, about 67% of StockTwits messages have at least one CashTag. From these messages, we extract 9,315 unique stock symbols.

StockTwits messages can also be labeled "bullish" or "bearish"[2] by the author to label their sentiments towards the mentioned stocks. 10% of messages (1.3 million) have this label. We use these labeled messages later as ground-truth to build and evaluate sentiment analysis tools.

Stock Historical Price Data. Our two datasets include a total of 13,551 *unique* stock symbols. Symbols from two sites do not completely overlap (Figure 1): 6,164 symbols appear in both datasets, most represent stocks on the NASDAQ and NYSE exchanges. SeekingAlpha-only symbols (4,236) are mostly small stocks sold on Over-The-Counter Bulletin Board (OTCBB), while StockTwits-only symbols (3,151) are mostly from the Toronto Stock Exchange.

We use the Yahoo! Finance open API [3] to crawl historical prices for all stock symbols. For each stock, we obtain its historical *daily* opening and closing prices, volume, and intraday price range. Of our 13,551 symbols, we found data for 10273 symbols. We track down the 3278 missing symbols using both Yahoo Finance and Bloomberg (see Figure 2). First, 2579 missing symbols are defunct, *i.e.* symbols made invalid due to corporate breakups, merge/acquisitions, or bankruptcy. Second, 125 are active stocks, either on foreign exchanges or OTC stocks not covered by Yahoo. Third, 158 symbols are ETF or mutual Funds, Futures contracts, and Currencies. Finally, we manually inspect the remaining 416 symbols, and find they are often user-defined symbols such as `$CRASH`, or non-listed companies such as `$QUORA`. Missing symbols account for 7% of SeekingAlpha articles and 6% of StockTwits messages, thus we believe it would not impact our overall conclusion. We summarize our final datasets used in our analysis in Table 1.

PRELIMINARY DATA ANALYSIS

Here, we briefly analyze our datasets to understand the structure of user communities and content in these two systems. The two systems are quite different. SeekingAlpha focuses on detailed, blog-like contributions by a small group of "experts" further curated by editors, and the large majority of users consume and comment on articles. In contrast, StockTwits encourages short, terse contributions by all users. We compare and contrast the platforms on growth over time, skew of author contributions, distribution of stocks covered, and the structure of social connections in the community.

User Growth. Figure 3 plots the growth of users over time for both systems. Recall our SeekingAlpha data includes all users who have contributed or commented on at least 1 article. At both sites, active users are growing at a stable rate, but only make up a small portion of all registered accounts (236,000 active versus 3.4 million accounts in SeekingAlpha, and 86,000 active versus 300K accounts for StockTwits).

Distribution of content over authors and stocks. Author's contribution to the platform is measured by the number of articles from the author. For both SeekingAlpha and StockTwits, we find the contribution per authors is highly skewed (Figure 4(a)). On SeekingAlpha, 20% of the most active users contributed 80% of articles, while on StockTwits, 20% of active users contributed 90% of the messages. Even though StockTwits tries to leverage the power of the crowd, it has an even higher skewness in content contribution than SeekingAlpha. This sheds concerns that the wisdom of the crowd is likely to be dominated by the most active authors.

Content posted on both sites is also highly skewed to a small portion of "popular" stocks (Figure 4(b)). More than 70% of SeekingAlpha articles cover top 10% of the most popular

[1] Transcripts cover board meetings and conference calls.

[2] Bullish (bearish) means investors believe the stock price will increase (decline).

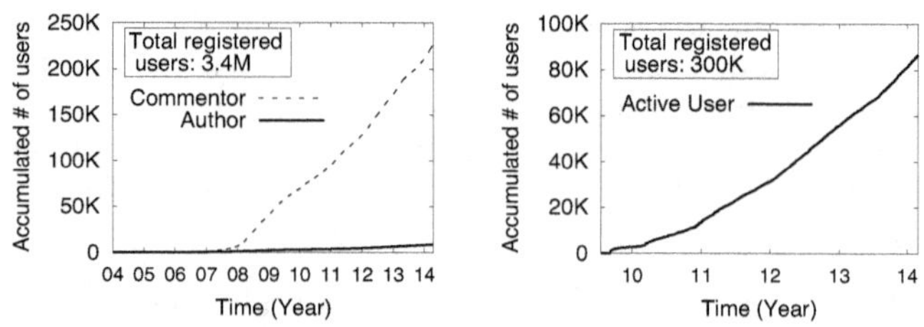

(a) SeekingAlpha (b) StockTwits

Figure 3. Total number of authors and active users over time. The number of active users is only a small portion of all registered users.

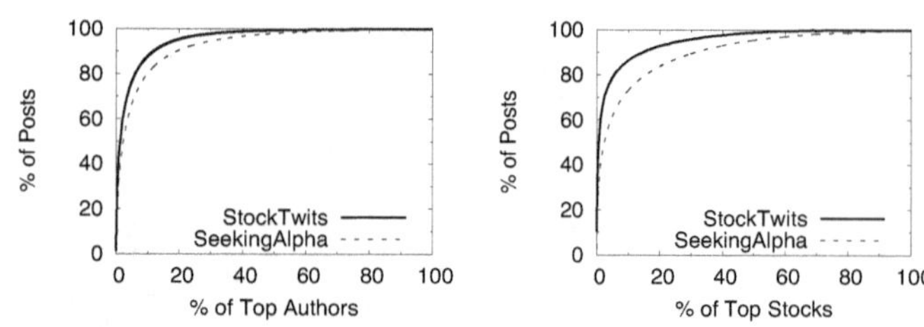

(a) Posts by authors. (b) Posts per stock.

Figure 4. Distribution of articles over authors and individual stocks.

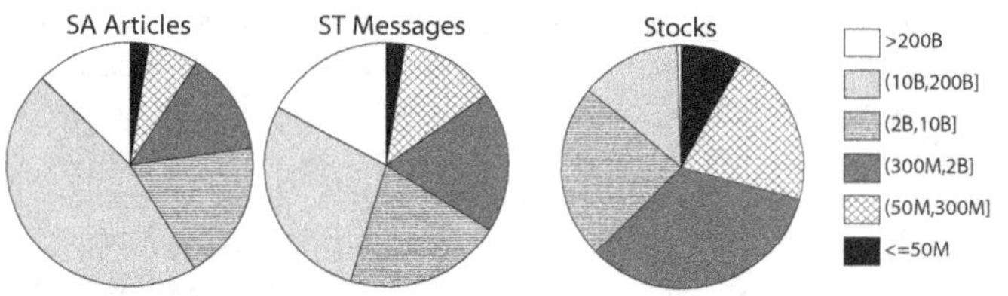

(a) Breakdown of Posts (b) Breakdown of Stocks

Figure 5. % of posts/stocks in different market cap. categories.

Graph	Nodes	Edges	Avg. Degree	Cluster. Coef.	Avg. Path	Assort.
SeekingAlpha	386K	3.9M	19.91	0.150	3.09	-0.428
Facebook [52]	1.22M	121M	199.6	0.175	5.13	0.17
Flickr [32]	1.85M	22.6M	24.5	0.313	5.67	0.202
Quora [48]	790K	14.5M	36.8	0.139	3.92	-0.039

Table 2. Comparing the structure of social graphs from SeekingAlpha and more traditional social networks.

stocks. The skew is even stronger in StockTwits, with 90% of messages focusing on 10% most popular stocks.

Figure 5 shows the heavy emphasis of articles on large capitalization companies. 47% of SeekingAlpha articles and 28% of StockTwits messages cover stocks of companies between $10 Billion and $200 Billion in market cap, which account for only 14% of all stocks. The emphasis is stronger for the largest companies (market cap >$200 Billion). They account for only 0.3% of all stocks, but are covered by 10-15% of the content on both platforms.

Social Connections and Graphs. We analyze social connections in SeekingAlpha to understand the structure of the network (similar data was not available for StockTwits). We crawled a full snapshot of the SeekingAlpha network in October 2013, using contributors as seeds and crawling all reachable users. The result graph has 386K nodes and 3.9M edges.

We compute key graph metrics and compare them against those of popular social networks in Table 2. The Facebook graph is from the Australia regional network in the reference paper [52]. First, SeekingAlpha has a similar clustering coefficient to other social networks, indicating that SeekingAlpha has a similar level of local connectivity. Second, SeekingAlpha has a dramatically different (negative) assortativity value compared to other networks. Assortativity measures how strongly users tend to connect to others with similar degree of connectivity. Positive assortativity indicates a preference to link to users with similar degree, while negative assortativity indicates a preference to link to users with different degree. SeekingAlpha's extremely negative assortativity (-0.428) indicates that SeekingAlpha exhibits a highly bi-partite structure, where most connections are between users following contributors, but with fewer connections amongst accounts of the same type. Finally, the very low average path length in SeekingAlpha is indicative of networks where super nodes produce short connections between users.

SENTIMENT EXTRACTION

Our analysis on the value of user-contributed investment analysis hinges on our interpretation of sentiment in SeekingAlpha articles and StockTwits messages. The first step in this process is developing reliable tools to extract sentiment (positive or negative opinion) on stocks from posted articles and messages. We discuss our sentiment analysis techniques here, and rely on them in later sections to compute stock performance correlation and to drive trading strategies.

Our approaches to extract sentiment from SeekingAlpha and StockTwits are quite different. More specifically, SeekingAlpha articles are sufficiently long to apply an approach using a keyword dictionary, while we applied a supervised machine learning approach for the short messages in StockTwits, using messages with "bullish" or "bearish" labels as training data. Our validation results show we achieve an accuracy of 85.5% for SeekingAlpha and 76.2% for StockTwits. We note that these accuracy results are on par or significantly better than existing sentiment analysis techniques [9, 18].

Sentiment Analysis: Seeking Alpha

We develop a dictionary based method to extract sentiment from SeekingAlpha articles. At a high level, we measure author sentiment (towards a stock) based on the ratio of positive and negative keywords in the article. We rely on a widely used financial sentiment dictionary [30] to identify positive and negative keywords in the article, and calculate the sentiment score as $S = log\frac{1+\sum P_i}{1+\sum N_i}$, where P_i (N_i) is the number of positive (negative) words or phrases in sentence i. The sentiment score is a decimal value with high positive value indicating strong and positive sentiment, and vice versa. For example, an extremely positive article with 100 positive words and 0 negative words gets a score of 4.6; an extremely negative article with 100 negative words gets -4.6.

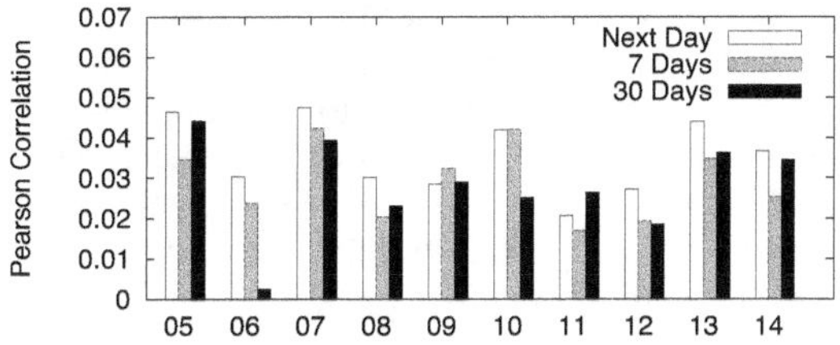

(a) SeekingAlpha (2005-2014)

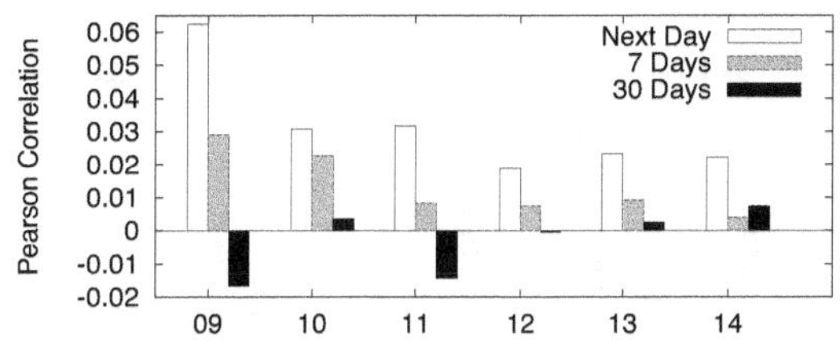

(b) StockTwits (2009-2014)

Figure 6. Pearson correlation coefficient between article sentiment and near term stock price movement (in 1, 7, 30 days).

However, there are problems with applying this method naively to SeekingAlpha articles. First, many articles discuss multiple stocks, and sentiments may be quite different for each discussed stock. Generating one sentiment score for all stocks is clearly oversimplifying. Second, simple keyword counting can easily make mistakes. For instance, "low risk" contains negative keyword "risk" but the overall sentiment is positive. Also negation usually changes the sentiment of words, such as "not good," or "no benefits."

We make several refinements to our method to address these challenges. First, we partition multi-stock articles and assign individual sentences to each stock symbol[3]. Our method is a simple distance-based slicing: we consider stock symbols (and its company names) as landmarks, and we assign each sentence to the closest landmark in the article. Next, we make two adjustments to basic keyword counts. First, we identify the sentiment of noun phrases such as "higher revenue," "low return," "low risk." We extract frequent noun phrases that occur in more than 1% of articles, and manually label their sentiment. Second, we reverse the sentiment of words or phrases affected by negation words [39].

To validate our method, we sample 300 articles from our article collection and manually label their sentiment as positive or negative. We have three graduate students read each article and vote for the final label. Then we run our sentiment extraction method on these articles to generate sentiment scores. The result shows our method achieves 85.5% accuracy. Note that this accuracy only considers the polarity of the scores, *i.e.* whether an article is positive or negative.

Sentiment Analysis: StockTwits

Roughly 10% of StockTwits messages already have sentiment labels, either "bullish" or "bearish." Our goal is to extract sentiment for the remaining 90%. We choose to use supervised Machine Learning, since messages are too short for dictionary-based approaches (confirmed with experiments).

To build a machine learning classifier, we follow prior work [38] to use the existence of unigrams (*i.e.* unique words) as features. To reduce noise in the machine learning model, we exclude infrequent unigrams that occur less than 300 times over all messages, and remove stopwords, stock symbols and company names from messages. We use the ground-truth messages as training data, and empirically test multiple machine learning models, including Naive Bayes, Supported Vector machine (SVM) and Decision Trees. We randomly sample 50K messages labeled as "bearish" and 50K labeled as "bullish," and run 10-fold cross validation. We find the SVM model produces the highest accuracy (76.2%), and use SVM to build the final classifier used on all messages.

The sentiment score of StockTwits messages is binary: 1 indicates positive sentiment and -1 indicates negative sentiment. For rare messages with multiple symbols, we attribute the same sentiment score to all symbols in the message (messages are too short to slice).

PREDICTING STOCK PRICE CHANGES

Using our sentiment analysis tools, we can now quantify the value of SeekingAlpha and StockTwits content, by measuring statistical correlation between their sentiment towards individual stocks, and each stock's near-term price performance. Our goal is to study such correlation for different time periods after the content was published, for both platforms and over different historical periods (to account for bull/bear cycles in the stock market).

Per-article Sentiment and Stock Performance

We start by studying how well each article predicts the future price trends of the stocks it discusses. We compute the Pearson correlation coefficient [40] between article's sentiment (positive or negative) and stock's future price change. For simplicity, we ignore magnitude of price movements and strength of sentiments, and reduce both metrics to binary (positive/negative) values. Pearson correlation coefficient is widely used to measure the linear correlation between two variables[4]. Its value ranges from -1 to 1, where 1 means perfect positive correlation, 0 means no correlation, and -1 means perfect negative correlation. In this context, the Pearson coefficient is 1 if a stock always increases in value after it is discussed positively by an article.

We compute the Pearson coefficient between two variables S and P. S is 1 (-1) if the article's sentiment is positive (negative); and P is 1 or -1 depending on whether the discussed stock goes higher or lower in price. We study stock price changes in different time windows after a relevant article is published, including the next day, the next week and the next month. For articles with multiple stock symbols, we count each stock as one data point. We also group articles in each

[3]Stock symbols are easily recognized as hyperlinks in each article.

[4]For two variables X and Y, the Pearson correlation coefficient $\rho_{X,Y} = \frac{E[(X-\mu_X)(Y-\mu_Y)]}{\sigma_X \sigma_Y}$, where μ_X and σ_X is the mean and standard deviation of X and E is the expectation.

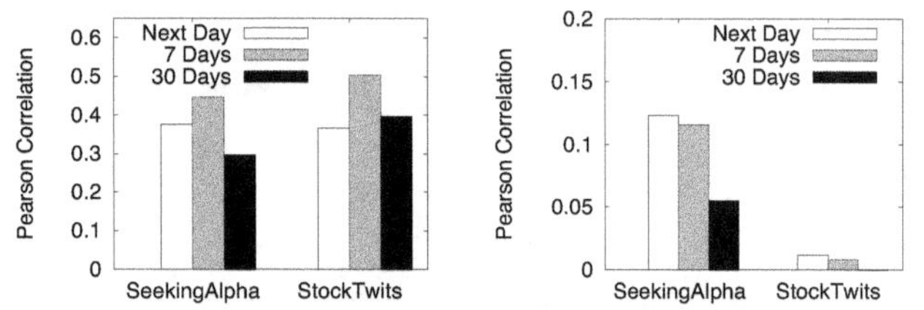

(a) Top authors ranked by 2013. (b) Top authors ranked by 2012.

Figure 7. Correlation analysis of stock performance in 2013 by top authors. We consider two sets of authors, top authors based on performance in 2013 (left) and based on performance in 2012 (right).

year and compute the per-year Pearson correlation coefficient to understand the consistency of correlation across different years. Results are shown in Figure 6.

First, we observe that correlation is extremely low across different time windows and different market years for both systems. To better understand the Pearson values, consider that a prediction history of 75% correlation would produce a Pearson coefficient of 0.4. The most significant correlation in our results is 0.05, which translates to a prediction accuracy of 53%, 3% better than a random guess. This means that taken as an aggregate, SeekingAlpha articles and StockTwits messages provide minimal value for investors.

Looking closer, SeekingAlpha generally does a bit better than random, while StockTwits has weaker, sometimes negative correlations. Clearly StockTwits is better as a gauge of instantaneous market sentiment, and a poor predictor of even near-term performance. In contrast, SeekingAlpha is a bit more consistent over different time windows, and still has some value for predicting price movements in the following month. We note that SeekingAlpha accuracy is a bit lower for market years with high volatility (2008–2009, 2011–2012).

Predicting price changes between two time points can be challenging given the high volatility of individual stock prices. Here, we simplify the metric by only predicting the up and down of *average* price within certain time window before and after the article. For a simple experiment, we use 2013 data to compute Pearson correlation between article sentiment and the average price of one week before and after the article. We find the correlation scores are slightly improved (0.067 for SA and 0.035 for ST), but are still very weak correlations.

The natural followup question is: is the weak correlation consistent across all authors, or are there authors whose contributions provide consistently good predictors of stock performance but are buried in the noise? Here, we perform a simple test to determine if more accurate authors exist. We rank authors based on how well their articles predict stock returns in a single year, *e.g.* 2013. For each author, we measure the average hypothetical return per article for all her articles as a percentage after a time window W. If $P(x)$ is the stock closing price of a given day x, and the article is posted on day d, then return R from a positive article is $R = \frac{P(d+W)-P(d)}{P(d)}$, and return on a negative article is $R = -\frac{P(d+W)-P(d)}{P(d)}$.

For our experiment, we set W to one week, and compute the average return per article to rank authors in 2013. We then take a closer look at correlations of 500 stocks discussed by the top ranking authors. Figure 7(a) clearly shows that correlation scores for top authors in SeekingAlpha and StockTwits are both very high (around 0.4), *i.e.* top authors can predict stock movement within a week with $\sim 75\%$ accuracy.

In practice, we cannot use data from the current year (*e.g.* 2013) to identify top authors for that year. We can only rely on past performance to guide us. Thus we repeat the experiment: using 2012 data to rank authors, and then we study the performance of their 2013 stock recommendations. As expected, correlation results for those authors' stocks in 2013 (see Figure 7(b)) are much lower. Top SeekingAlpha authors show a significant correlation score around 0.12, which is still significantly better than the average. This confirms our intuition, that filtering out the "noise" does indeed reveal more accurate contributors in the crowd. Note that this does not hold for StockTwits, *i.e.* no StockTwits authors can consistently predict stock performance over different time periods.

Aggregated Sentiment for Market Prediction

Since the correlation between articles and individual stocks is weak, we consider aggregated sentiment of all articles as a possible predictor for the market as a whole. Here we use the S&P 500 index[5] as a metric for overall market performance. Here, we treat the S&P 500 index as a single stock and trade it based on the *aggregated* sentiment over time. In practice, this can be done using SPY, an Exchange Traded Fund (ETF) that tracks the S&P 500.

The process is intuitive: we start by holding a position in the S&P 500. After every K days, we check the aggregated sentiment of articles posted in the past K days, and choose to either buy or sell the S&P 500. Sentiment over a window of K days is computed by first computing the average sentiment of all articles for each day, then setting the overall sentiment to positive if there are more net-positive days than net-negative days. If the sentiment for a window is negative, we sell our entire position (if any) in the S&P 500. If the sentiment is positive, we buy back our full position if we have none, or hold it if we already have a position.

Long-term Performance. We simulate this trading strategy using data from SeekingAlpha (January 2005 to March 2014) and StockTwits (September 2009 to February 2014)[6]. We set time window K to *one week* (we evaluate K's impact later). On each dataset, we run two configurations, one using "all" sentiment from the entire network, and the other only taking sentiment specifically about the 500 stocks listed in S&P 500 index[7]. As a baseline, we run a "buy-and-hold" strategy on S&P 500 index, that is, holding the stock for the entire duration of the simulation.

[5] S&P 500 is a widely-accepted market index based on the market capitalizations of 500 large companies.

[6] SeekingAlpha only had 3 total articles in 2004. Thus we start our SeekingAlpha simulations from 2005.

[7] The stocklist of S&P 500 index changes periodically, and we adapt the list in our evaluation accordingly.

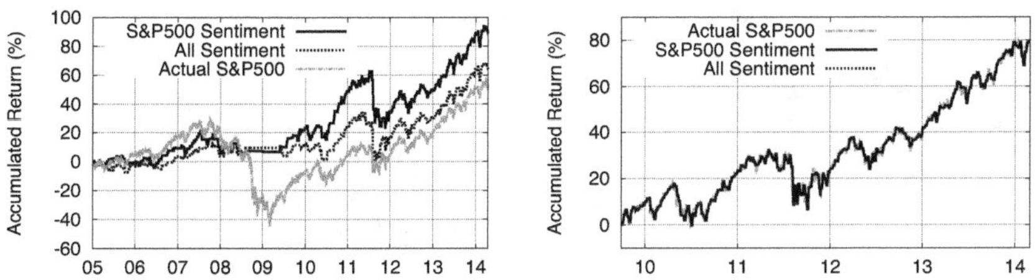

(a) SeekingAlpha (2005-2014) (b) StockTwits (2009-2014)

Figure 8. Predicting S&P 500 index using aggregated sentiment of whole site versus only using sentiment related to the indexed 500 stocks.

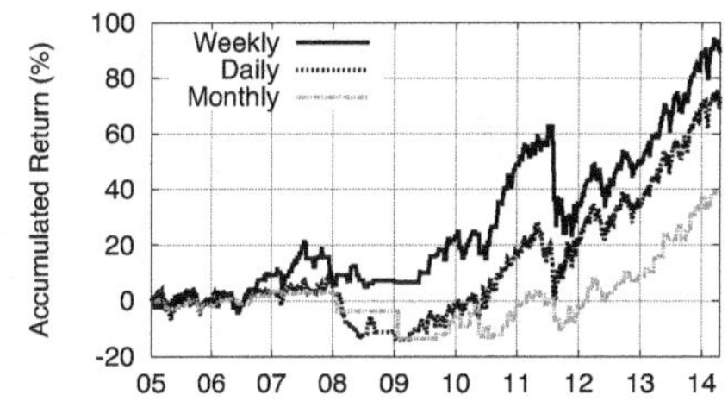

Figure 9. Impact of trading time window (SA).

Figure 8 plots the total return (normalized by initial investment) accumulated over time. For SeekingAlpha (Figure 8(a)), we find both configurations outperform the actual S&P 500. Aggregated sentiment can generally predict market trends. Not surprisingly, sentiment specifically about the 500 stocks in the index produces more accurate results. A closer look shows that our strategy significantly outperforms the real market during 2008–2010, when the financial crisis caused the stock market (and the S&P 500) to lose more than half of its value. Given the overall negative sentiment in SeekingAlpha, our strategy held no positions and avoided much of the market losses. For StockTwits (Figure 8(b)), we find that all three lines completely overlap. In fact, after we aggregate the sentiment of the whole network, StockTwits's overall opinion towards the market is almost always positive. Our sentiment-driven trading is equivalent to buy-and-hold.

Impact of Time Window K. To understand the time frame K for aggregating sentiment that optimizes accuracy, we test 1-day, 1-week and 1-month respectively and run the trading method only with sentiment related to the 500 stocks in the index. The results are shown in Figure 9-10. For SeekingAlpha, acting on weekly sentiment is clearly the sweet spot. Acting on daily sentiment over-reacts, while acting on monthly sentiment is too slow to respond to market changes. For StockTwits, different K values have minimal impact, but daily outperforms weekly by a narrow margin. We use weekly sentiment aggregation in our later trading strategies.

In summary, our analysis shows that sentiment to performance correlation is quite low for both SeekingAlpha and StockTwits. However, there are authors who consistently provide high-correlation analysis in their articles. The challenge is to identify them efficiently. Next, we address this challenge and develop practical sentiment-driven strategies for stock trading that can significantly outperform the market.

PRACTICAL SENTIMENT-BASED TRADING

Thus far, we have determined that while correlation to stock performance is low over all articles as a whole, certain subsets of the user population contribute content with much stronger correlation to stock performance. Two key questions remain. First, can these "valuable" authors be identified easily? Second, once identified, can their content be analyzed to form the basis of real stock trading strategies, and how well would such strategies perform?

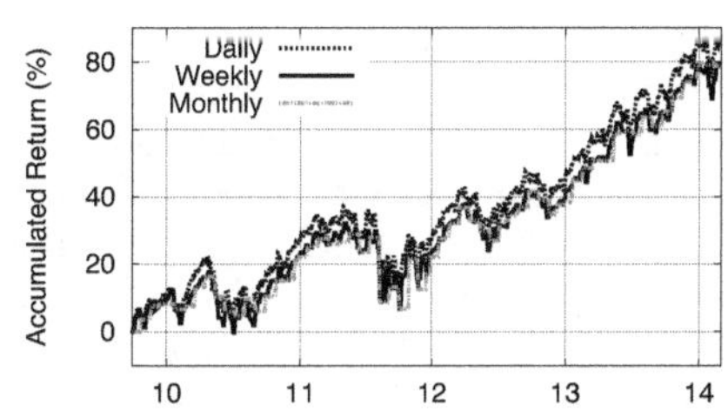

Figure 10. Impact of trading time window (ST).

We address these questions in three parts. First, we explore several possible ranking heuristics for identifying the valuable authors (and their analysis contributions) from both SeekingAlpha and StockTwits. Second, we consider possible stock trading strategies based on sentiment analysis of these contributions. Finally, we use historical stock data to drive simulations of these trading strategies, and use empirical results to draw conclusions about the value of these top authors, and the efficacy of our mechanisms to identify them.

Ranking Authors

To identify the (possibly small) subset of top authors in our systems, we explore two different sets of heuristics. First, we consider using empirical past performance, *i.e.* correlation between sentiment and stock performance, as a gauge to rank authors. While this is likely the most direct way to rank authors by performance, its computation requires access to significant resources, including past stock data and sentiment analysis tools. Second, we consider a simpler alternative based on user interactions (comments). The intuition is that user feedback and engagement with content provides a good indicator of valuable content.

Ranking Authors by Prediction Accuracy. Our first ranking heuristic is purely empirical: we rank authors based on how well their previous articles predict stock returns. For a given author and historical time period (*e.g.* a year), we compute average hypothetical return of her articles posted during that given period. Recall that we used this in previous section as a metric of an author's prediction ability. A variant of this ranking metric is an author's average hypothetical return *per stock*. Compared to the *per article* metric, this highlights authors who have consistently good performance over a range of stocks over those who write numerous articles on a small set of stocks. We consider both metrics in our experiments.

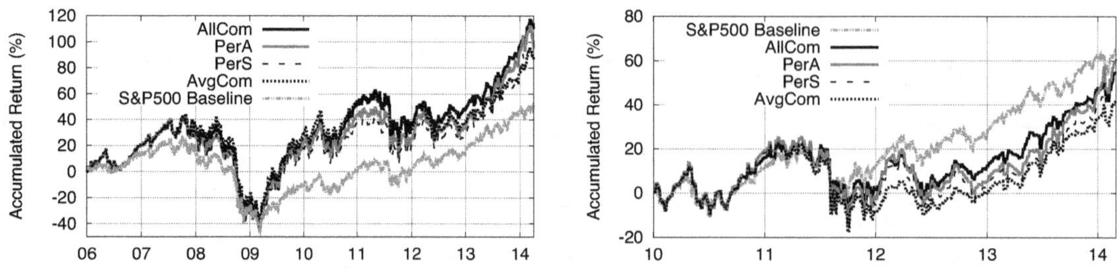

(a) SeekingAlpha (2006-2014) (b) StockTwits (2010-2014)

Figure 11. Investing results on 500 stocks recommended by top authors over the years.

Ranking Authors by Received Comments. The challenge with empirical performance-based metrics is that it requires significant resources in historical data and computation. Here, we also consider the value of a simpler approximation based on reader engagement. The intuition is that the audience in these systems is a valuable asset, and we can observe reader responses to contributed content and indirectly infer the value of the content. More specifically, we use two heuristics that rank authors based on either total number of comments or comments per-article. Without semantic analysis of comments, we use the number of comments over a prior period (*e.g.* a year) as an approximate indicator of user agreement.

Sentiment-based Stock Trading Strategies

Given a ranking of top authors, the next step is to formulate a stock trading strategy that takes advantage of (hopefully) valuable and predictive sentiment on individual stocks. Our strategies select a group of stocks to trade each year, from stocks mentioned by articles from top authors from the prior year (sorted by either correlation or comments). For simplicity, we build a portfolio for our simulations from the 500 stocks mentioned by the top-ranked authors. Experiments with smaller portfolios show highly consistent results, and are omitted for brevity.

In terms of trading strategies, we implement two simple strategies: a basic "long" strategy (buy or sell based on sentiment) similar to the one used to trade the `SPY` in last section, and a more aggressive "long/short" strategy that allows investors to short stocks. For both strategies, we trade stocks on a weekly basis based on earlier results (Figures 9–10).

Long Strategy. Our long strategy builds a portfolio by initially spreading funds evenly to purchase N stocks, $N = 500$ in our examples. We make trading decisions on each stock independently on a weekly basis, using weekly sentiment from the same top authors identified from the prior year, *i.e.* the same top authors used to select the 500 stocks. For each stock in the portfolio, we sell our entire position in the stock if the sentiment about this stock in the past week is negative. Otherwise, we hold the stock (or buy it back if we sold it earlier). If the stock was not covered by a "top author" in the past week, no action is taken. We use the same sentiment aggregation method as before, but only consider the top author's sentiment on each stock. The return of the portfolio is the sum of returns over all stocks.

Long/Short Strategy. A more aggressive "long/short" strategy not only buys stocks with positive sentiment, but also proactively "shorts" stocks with negative sentiments. Shorting is the practice of borrowing a stock to sell at the current price and buying it back at a lower price [11]. Investors target stocks they believe will drop in value, and profit from the drop between their sell price and repurchase price. Shorting is generally considered to be very risky, because the price of a stock can go up without limit, thus there is no limit to the size of potential losses on a short position.

In our short strategy, if the aggregated sentiment on a stock is negative in previous week, we not only sell any shares of the stock in our portfolio, but we also short the stock for a week (and buy shares back at the end of the week). We short a number of shares equal to value to $\frac{1}{N}$ of our total portfolio. If and when we have lost 100% of the value initially allocated to a stock, then we close our position on that stock permanently.

Empirical Evaluation

We evaluate trading strategies generated using a combination of author ranking heuristics and long vs. long/short trading strategies. For our author ranking heuristics, we use average return per article (*PerA*), average return per stock (*PerS*), number of total comments (*AllCom*), and average comments per article (*AvgCom*). As described above, we choose 500 stocks mentioned by the top ranked authors, and split the funds of a hypothetical portfolio evenly among them. Each week, we trade them based on aggregated sentiment from our chosen top authors (the same authors used to select the 500 stocks) in the previous week. By default, we regard one year as a cycle, and rerank authors and reset the list of stocks for the portfolio at the beginning of each year (using the heuristics of previous year).

Q1: Do our strategies outperform the broader markets?

We simulate our strategies using historical stock price data and compare them to a baseline following a "buy-and-hold" strategy on the S&P 500 index. We ignore transaction fees in our simulations and initially focus on the long-only strategy. We plot results in Figure 11.

The first takeaway is that SeekingAlpha clearly out-performs the baseline market under all settings. For example, our "all comment" strategy produces a normalized total return of 108% at the end of the 8-year period, compared to 47.8% of

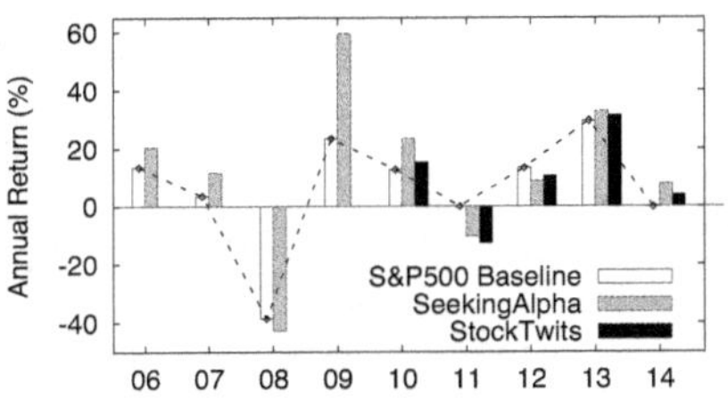

Figure 12. Breakdown of returns in each year, with "All comment" strategy.

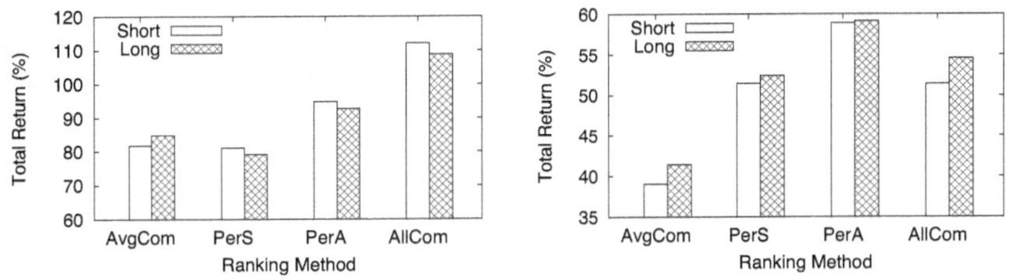

(a) SeekingAlpha (2006–2014) (b) StockTwits (2010–2014)

Figure 13. The total return with long strategy versus short strategy.

the S&P 500. This represents more than 10% annual compounded return, during a time period that includes two market crashes (2008, 2011), and *not including dividends*. Since StockTwits only started in 2009, its simulations ran on only 4 years of historical data. The same strategy on StockTwits produced a total return of around 54.5% from 2010 to 2014. This is a good return in absolute terms, but significantly below the baseline S&P 500 (64.1%) during the same timeframe. We further breakdown the returns of each year in Figure 12 ("all comment" strategy). Results show that SeekingAlpha consistently generates higher annual returns than StockTwits.

Implications. This result is *significant*, because it means we can in fact use empirical methods to identify the articles of value from SeekingAlpha. More importantly, we *significantly* outperform the S&P 500 using a very simple trading strategy that ignores semantic meaning of the articles and uses only binary sentiment values. As context, we consider hedge funds, which manage money for large investors, and charge annually 2% of assets managed and 20% commission on all gains. The 2.5 *trillion* dollar hedge fund industry has underperformed the S&P 500 for 5 years in a row, and has fallen behind the S&P by 97% since 2008 [25]. Significantly outperforming the S&P over a period of 10 years would be considered excellent performance for a managed hedge fund. Achieving this result by mining an open community like SeekingAlpha is ample evidence of the very high quality of analysis by the small set of expert authors.

Q2: What ranking method identifies experts most effectively?

The next big question is can we validate a simple methodology for identifying the top performing authors. Among a number of author ranking heuristics, we find the all-comment metric (*R-allC*) to obtain the highest level of investment returns in our SeekingAlpha simulations (see Figure 11). Similarly, the same strategy also performs the best for StockTwits, outperforming other metrics in most years.

Implications. This result implies that not only does something as simple as comment count do a great job of identifying top authors in SeekingAlpha, but it does even better than heuristics based on prior-year performance. Note that we are not leveraging sentiment analysis on comments, only the number of comments. This implies that the majority of comments are supportive notes that validate the article's analysis and insights. More importantly, this highlights the value of the SeekingAlpha user population as a filter to identify the best analysts among the authors. Even for a subject as complex and domain specific as stock analysis, a reasonably knowledgeable crowd can serve to pinpoint valuable content in an otherwise mixed collection of content.

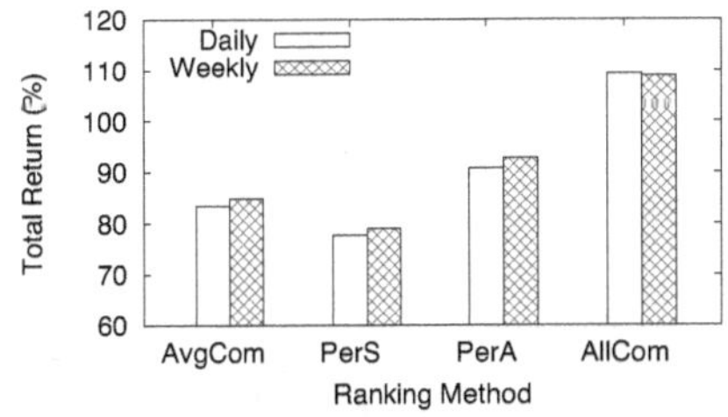

(a) SeekingAlpha (2006–2014)

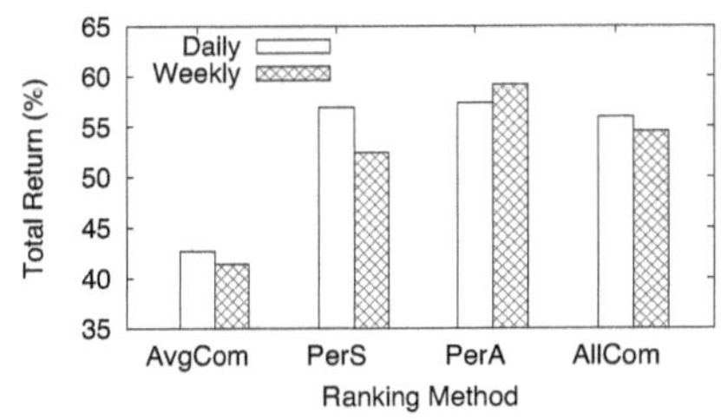

(b) StockTwits (2010–2014)

Figure 14. The total return with daily trading and weekly trading.

Q3: Do more aggressive strategies improve performance?

We also study the impact of allowing shorts of stocks along with traditional long positions. Shorting stocks is a typical strategy used by hedge funds, but rarely used by individual investors because of its potential for unbounded loss. We repeat the same experiment as above, but add a long/short strategy in addition to the long strategy. The results are plotted in Figure 13 (note the different time frames in the two subfigures). The high level observation is that adding shorts improves performance for strategies based on SeekingAlpha, but not significantly enough to justify the added risk.

Implications. Shorting stocks is a highly valued tool for hedge funds, who are expected to use it to produce positive returns even in negative markets. Yet our results show that the majority of user-contributed short strategies do not produce significant gains over long-only strategies. Given the significant added risk, this suggests that sentiment-based trading strategies should focus on long-only strategies to minimize risk while achieving the gains of a long/short strategy.

Q4: Does this approach support "real-time" trading?

Finally, we evaluate the impact of smaller time window to aggregate sentiment and trade, especially given the real-time nature of StockTwits. We perform experiments using one-day time windows, and show the results (long-only strategy) in Figure 14. For StockTwits, daily trading leads to incrementally higher returns compared to those using weekly windows. The opposite is true on SeekingAlpha, where the lower frequency of articles mean that weekly trading outperforms daily trading strategies.

Implications. This again confirms the real-time nature of StockTwits messages. In practice, transactions fees will play a role in determining the trading frequency that maximizes gains. Optimizing that tradeoff would require more complex models beyond the scope of this paper.

Discussion and Limitations. Given the complexities of financial investments, our models are clearly an over-simplification of the possible trading strategies. We ignore strength of sentiments, and reduce strategies to a binary "buy all in" or "sell all shares." Our goal is to understand the lower bound performance from extracting only the higher order bits of analysis. Weighing sentiment from articles and more nuanced strategies like "dollar-cost averaging" or "cost-basis averaging" are likely to improve performance further, but we leave the confirmation of those strategies to future work.

One possible concern is whether our system will impact the overall health of the market — by allowing end-users to access the same "optimized" information for trading. We believe this is very unlikely. Intuitively, movements on the stock market are dominated by large hedge funds and pension funds. Even perfectly synchronized, retail investors following SeekingAlpha would not produce meaningful price movements for the vast majority of individual equities.

Intuitively, our results suggest the wisdom of a "smaller, smarter crowd" can outperform a larger, more general crowd, especially for crowdsourcing tasks that require specific domain knowledge (financial knowledge in our case). Moreover, the larger crowd is still helpful as members collaboratively discover domain experts through their interactions. We hope future work will explore how to apply this insight to other domain-specific crowdsourcing applications. Most importantly, our results demonstrate that even when the overall crowd produces low quality results, the crowd itself can help us identify the top experts amongst them. In other words, the crowd can *identify* good work even when it is incapable of producing it directly. This suggests the design of an interaction-based "meta-reputation" system that would greatly assist users in their discovery of high quality content.

The implications on collaborative work systems are significant. It is often the case that the crowd as a whole produces suboptimal results, but subsets amongst them produce exceptionally good results. In some contexts, it is possible to identify these top experts using ground truth "tests" [49]. More often, however, there is no ground truth data, or there is no way of testing workers without inadvertently influencing them. Our work suggests that in certain contexts, workers' meta-evaluation of each other's results could provide a robust way to identify the most capable workers in a population.

ID	Question	Tester
1	How many years of experience do you have in investing in the stock market?	Author & User
2	How often do you trade stocks based on opinions and information gathered from reading SeekingAlpha articles?	User
3	Do you think you can trust the authors on SeekingAlpha?	User
4	How often have you seen articles on SeekingAlpha that looked like they were heavily biased, written with the intent to manipulate a particular stock (to move its price up or down)?	Author & User
5	If and when you did see what looked like an article intent on stock manipulation, what is your general reaction?	User
6	Do you think SeekingAlpha articles can impact the future movement of stocks they focus on?	Author
7	If SeekingAlpha did not exist, where would you post your investment ideas?	Author

Table 3. Survey questions to SeekingAlpha authors and normal users. We limit the number of questions to improve our chances of getting responses.

SEEKINGALPHA USER SURVEY

The final component of our study deploys a user survey on SeekingAlpha to better understand users' levels of investment experience, and how they feel about the utility and reliability of SeekingAlpha articles. These responses will help us understand the level of impact articles have on SA users, and how they deal with any potentially manipulative articles.

Survey Setup

In May 2014, we sent out a user survey via private messages in SeekingAlpha to 500 authors and 500 non-contributing users. We received 199 responses (95 from authors and 104 from normal users). We chose authors and users to ensure we captured a full range of activity levels. We sorted authors into buckets by the number of articles written and users into buckets by the number of comments, and randomly sampled from each bucket to choose our targets.

We asked normal users 5 questions and authors 4 questions (see the full questions in Table 3). First, to measure demographics, we ask both authors and users about their levels of investing experience (Q1). Second, to understand user's perceived value of the platform, we ask whether normal users trade stocks based on SA articles (Q2) and whether they trust authors (Q3). For authors, we ask which platforms if any they would use to disseminate investing ideas if SeekingAlpha were no longer available (Q7). Third, in terms of risks in the platform, we ask both authors and users whether they have seen heavily biased (potentially manipulative) articles (Q4). Finally, we ask normal users for their reaction to stock manipulation (Q5), and authors whether they believe articles can actually impact stock price (Q6).

User Responses

We first look at demographics of the survey respondents. We plot responses to Q1 in Figure 15(a). The large majority of respondents have over 10 years of investing experience. Surprisingly, we find that the portion of experienced investors (*i.e.* >10 years) is higher in normal users than in authors.

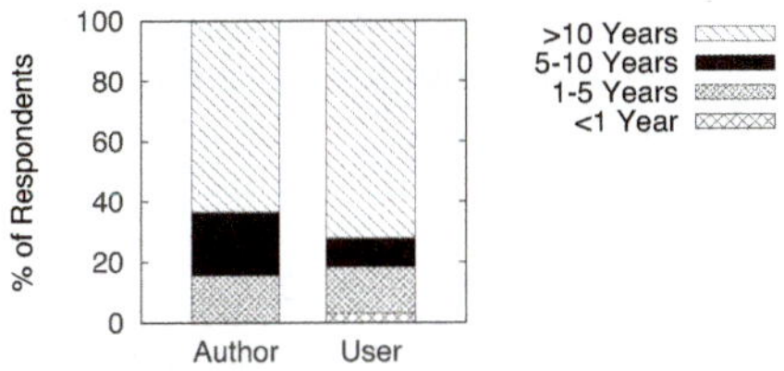

(a) Investing experience (Yrs)

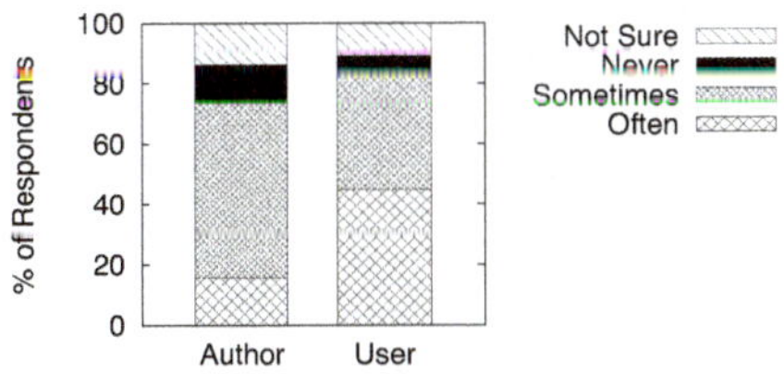

(b) Seen manipulation?

Figure 15. Results of two questions for both authors and users.

Perceived Value. First, in response to Q2, 70% of users stated that they "sometimes" or "very often" traded stocks following opinions from SeekingAlpha. 5% of users stated they "always" relied on information from SA articles. The remaining 25% "never" followed views from articles. Two respondents added clarifying comments that they treated SeekingAlpha as an important information source for research, but did not follow opinions blindly. As a whole, it is clear that SeekingAlpha articles play an important role in most users' investment decisions.

In response to Q3, 83% of users stated they trusted "some" or "most" SeekingAlpha authors, and 1% stated they fully trusted authors. 16% did not trust authors at all. This suggests that while SeekingAlpha users generally acknowledge the value of the platform, hesitations and concerns remain.

Q7 asked authors where they would disseminate their ideas if SeekingAlpha were no longer available. Surprisingly, only 6% of authors chose StockTwits, and more chose Twitter (7%), Yahoo! Finance Message Board (9%) and Motley Fool (22%). Still, the majority of authors (56%) did not choose any existing platform, but preferred a personal website or nothing at all. Clearly, SeekingAlpha provides a unique and valuable platform for its contributors.

Biased Articles and Stock Manipulation. SeekingAlpha's nature makes it possible for companies or individuals to profit by influencing users and manipulating stock prices. Some of these efforts were identified and publicly documented [13, 24]. Surprisingly, both authors and users (80%) stated that they have seen manipulative articles on SA (Figure 15(b)). More normal users reported frequently seeing manipulative articles. When asked about their response to manipulative articles (Q5), 42% stated that they would dispute the conclusions using comments on the article, 3% would report to SeekingAlpha admins, while 25% "do nothing." 20 users added further detailed comments to explain: 15 respondents stated biased articles are to be expected and ignored; 2 people said they would blacklist the author and never read their articles again; 2 stated they could still extract value from dissenting comments on the article. Finally, one user stated that it was very difficult to distinguish between real stock manipulations from authors with strong personal preferences.

Impact. We ask if authors believe their articles have the power to impact stock prices (Q6). More than 62% of authors believed this was true; 14% said no, and the rest were unsure. One author commented that SeekingAlpha articles typically cannot impact large cap stocks like Apple (AAPL), but could affect small and micro cap stocks.

Finally, we also received unsolicited anecdotal feedback from past authors on additional types of author misbehavior. They identified some authors who generated large volumes of articles solely for the purpose of soliciting users to subscribe to their investment website memberships. They also identified others who produced detailed articles at extremely high volumes, too high to be produced even by a full time professional. The assertion is these accounts are managed by teams of writers who generate numerous articles to increase in reputation and ranking, only to then profit by manipulating one or two stocks they own in large volume. While we cannot confirm or disprove these assertions, they are consistent with other survey responses, and could account for the apparent disconnect between poor average correlation of articles and high correlation of articles by top authors.

RELATED WORK

Stock Market Prediction. Stock market prediction via data mining has been explored in a variety of contexts, including Google trends [41], Wikipedia [33], online blogs [10, 16], financial news [15, 43], and social content from Twitter [7, 8, 42, 44] and Facebook [22]. Some have studied stock-centered social networks, *i.e.* StockTwits [35, 36] and SeekingAlpha [9]. Most of these draw their conclusions based on short-term data of less than a year, despite the highly cyclical nature of bull and bear markets that lasts multiple years. In contrast, our data covers up to 9 years, long enough to cover both crashes (2008–2009) as well as strong bull markets (2013). In addition, our comparative analysis between StockTwits and SeekingAlpha helps us understand the impact of leveraging experts as contributors versus average users.

Sentiment-based Investing and Analysis. There are a few works on sentiment based investment strategy. Most papers focus on the prediction and investment on several selected stocks [36]. Other work [31] invests on all possible stocks in the market. Prior works [5, 28] use small datasets from Twitter/StockTwits to quantify the noisiness in overall sentiment, and to motivate the need for contributions from experts. This is consistent with our results that show the best performance is achieved from identifying and relying on top experts.

Existing sentiment extraction methods vary widely from dictionary based methods [12, 17, 30] to supervised machine learning algorithms [29, 39, 6]. Dictionary based methods require domain specific dictionaries [30], and do not work well with short texts like tweets [6] and reviews [39]. Researchers have applied supervised machine learning algorithms to sentiment classification, with common features such as term frequency, parts of speech, and negations [29].

Crowd-based Stock Prediction. Estimize[8] is an open financial platform that aggregates estimates of company earnings reports from the opinions of independent, buy-side, and sell-side analysts, along with private investors. Estimize has contributions from 4628 analysts covering over 900 stocks. Note that Estimize focuses on predictions of quarterly earnings results, not stock performance.

Crowdsourcing and Collaborative Work. Researchers have studied crowdsourcing and collaborative works under contexts ranging from translation and labeling [45], to answering questions [34, 48, 46], to gathering opinions [53], and even performing creative collaboration tasks [23]. One of the key challenges in collaborative work is the uneven expertise and low quality of contributions from large crowds [26]. Recent works have explored different directions to design better crowdsourcing systems, including quality control on contributors and content [45, 37], identifying domain experts [21, 27], and applying weighted methods to integrate crowd results [14]. In the application context of collaborative investment analysis, our work demonstrates that more "skilled" experts can be identified in collaborative crowds through interactions with the broader crowd. Even crowds who cannot generate valuable content can identify those who can.

Finally, crowdsourcing platforms are making a significant impact on the security of online communities. While they can be used as effective tools for detecting fake accounts on online social networks [49], they can also provide willing labor for performing tasks to bypass traditional security mechanisms [51]. While recent works are making progress against these malicious crowdsourcing systems [50], they remain one of the biggest challenges facing online systems today.

CONCLUSIONS AND FUTURE WORK

In this paper, we analyze the correlation between stock performance and user contributed content sentiment over a period of 4–9 years. Our analysis shows that while expert-contributed stock analysis in SeekingAlpha provides more positive correlation than user-generated content from StockTwits, the correlation is very weak. We show that valuable content can be extracted using well designed filters based on user comments, and can lead to strategies that significantly outperform the broader stock market. Future work lies in better identification of biased or manipulative content on SeekingAlpha, as well as further analysis of how to extend such methods to other platforms.

Our work suggests that even complex, domain specific tasks such as stock analysis can benefit from collaboratively generated content. Even when only a small portion of users is capable of generating valuable content, others in the crowd help by indirectly identifying the valuable content through their interactions. This suggests a possible design for "meta-reputation" systems that highlight quality content by tracking user interactions in the crowd.

[8] `http://www.estimize.com`

ACKNOWLEDGMENTS

We would like to thank Chris Corriveau for providing access to their StockTwits dataset, and the anonymous reviewers for their helpful comments. This project was supported in part by NSF grants IIS-1321083, CNS-1224100, by the DARPA GRAPHS program (BAA-12-01), and by the Department of State. Any opinions, findings, and conclusions or recommendations expressed in this material are those of the authors and do not necessarily reflect the views of any funding agencies.

REFERENCES

1. About seekingalpha. `http://seekingalpha.com/page/about_us`.
2. About stocktwits. `http://stocktwits.com/about`.
3. Yahoo finance api. `https://code.google.com/p/yahoo-finance-managed/wiki/csvHistQuotesDownload`.
4. Adamic, L. A., Zhang, J., Bakshy, E., and Ackerman, M. S. Knowledge sharing and yahoo answers: everyone knows something. In *Proc. of WWW* (2008).
5. Bar-Haim, R., Dinur, E., Feldman, R., Fresko, M., and Goldstein, G. Identifying and following expert investors in stock microblogs. In *Proceedings of the Conference on Empirical Methods in Natural Language Processing (EMNLP)* (2011).
6. Barbosa, L., and Feng, J. Robust sentiment detection on twitter from biased and noisy data. In *Proc. of COLING* (2010).
7. Bollen, J., Mao, H., and Zeng, X. Twitter mood predicts the stock market. *Journal of Computational Science 2*, 1 (2011), 1–8.
8. Brown, E. D. Will twitter make you a better investor? a look at sentiment, user reputation and their effect on the stock market. In *Proc. of SAIS* (2012).
9. Chen, H., De, P., Hu, J., and Hwang, B.-H. Wisdom of crowds: The value of stock opinions transmitted through social media. *Review of Financial Studies 27*, 5 (2014), 1367–1403.
10. De Choudhury, M., et al. Can blog communication dynamics be correlated with stock market activity? In *Proc. of HyperText* (2008).
11. Diamond, D. W., and Verrecchia, R. E. Constraints on short-selling and asset price adjustment to private information. *Journal of Financial Economics 18*, 2 (1987), 277 – 311.
12. Esuli, A., and Sebastiani, F. Pageranking wordnet synsets: An application to opinion mining. In *Proc. of ACL* (2007).

13. Feuerstein, A. Galena biopharma pays for stock-touting campaign while insiders cash out millions. TheStreet News, February 2014.

14. Forlines, C., Miller, S., Guelcher, L., and Bruzzi, R. Crowdsourcing the future: predictions made with a social network. In *Proc. of CHI* (2014).

15. Fung, G. P. C., Yu, J. X., and Lam, W. Stock prediction: Integrating text mining approach using real-time news. In *Proc. of CIFER* (2003).

16. Gilbert, E., and Karahalios, K. Widespread worry and the stock market. In *Proc. of ICWSM* (2010).

17. Godbole, N., Srinivasaiah, M., and Skiena, S. Large-scale sentiment analysis for news and blogs. In *Proc. of ICWSM* (2007).

18. Gonçalves, P., Araújo, M., Benevenuto, F., and Cha, M. Comparing and combining sentiment analysis methods. In *Proc. of COSN* (2013).

19. Harper, F. M., Raban, D., Rafaeli, S., and Konstan, J. A. Predictors of answer quality in online Q&A sites. In *Proc. of CHI* (2008).

20. 2013 investment company fact book. Tech. rep., Investment Company Institute, 2013. `http://www.ici.org/pdf/2013_factbook.pdf`.

21. Jacovi, M., Guy, I., Kremer-Davidson, S., Porat, S., and Aizenbud-Reshef, N. The perception of others: inferring reputation from social media in the enterprise. In *Proc. of CSCW* (2014).

22. Karabulut, Y. Can facebook predict stock market activity? *SSRN eLibrary* (2011).

23. Kim, J., Cheng, J., and Bernstein, M. S. Ensemble: exploring complementary strengths of leaders and crowds in creative collaboration. In *Proc. of CSCW* (2014).

24. Kimelman, J. An insider's tale of a stock promotion plan. Barrons News, March 2014.

25. Kishan, S., and Bit, K. Hedge funds trail stocks by the widest margin since 2005. Bloomberg News, December 2013.

26. Kittur, A., Nickerson, J. V., Bernstein, M., Gerber, E., Shaw, A., Zimmerman, J., Lease, M., and Horton, J. The future of crowd work. In *Proc. of CSCW* (2013).

27. Liao, Q. V., Wagner, C., Pirolli, P., and Fu, W.-T. Understanding experts' and novices' expertise judgment of twitter users. In *Proc. of CHI* (2012).

28. Liao, W., Shah, S., and Makrehchi, M. Winning by following the winners: Mining the behaviour of stock market experts in social media. In *SBP*. 2014.

29. Liu, B. Sentiment analysis and opinion mining. *Synthesis Lectures on Human Language Technologies 5*, 1 (2012), 1–167.

30. Loughran, T., and McDonald, B. When is a liability not a liability? textual analysis, dictionaries, and 10-ks. *The Journal of Finance 66*, 1 (2011), 35–65.

31. Makrehchi, M., Shah, S., and Liao, W. Stock prediction using event-based sentiment analysis. In *Proc. of WI-IAT* (2013).

32. Mislove, A., Marcon, M., Gummadi, K. P., Druschel, P., and Bhattacharje, B. Measurement and analysis of online social networks. In *Proc. of IMC* (2007).

33. Moat, H. S., Curme, C., Avakian, A., Kenett, D. Y., Stanley, H. E., and Preis, T. Quantifying wikipedia usage patterns before stock market moves. *Scientific Reports 3* (2013).

34. Nichols, J., Zhou, M., Yang, H., Kang, J.-H., and Sun, X. H. Analyzing the quality of information solicited from targeted strangers on social media. In *Proc. of CSCW* (2013).

35. Oh, C., and Sheng, O. Investigating predictive power of stock micro blog sentiment in forecasting future stock price directional movement. In *Proc. of ICIS* (2011).

36. Oliveira, N., Cortez, P., and Areal, N. On the predictability of stock market behavior using stocktwits sentiment and posting volume. In *Progress in AI*. 2013.

37. Otterbacher, J. 'helpfulness' in online communities: A measure of message quality. In *Proc. of CHI* (2009).

38. Pang, B., and Lee, L. Opinion mining and sentiment analysis. *FTIR 2*, 1-2 (2008), 1–135.

39. Pang, B., Lee, L., and Vaithyanathan, S. Thumbs up?: sentiment classification using machine learning techniques. In *Proc. of ACL* (2002).

40. Pearson, K. Contributions to the mathematical theory of evolution. II. skew variation in homogeneous material. *Phil. Trans. R. Soc. A 186* (1895), 343–414.

41. Preis, T., Moat, H. S., and Stanley, H. E. Quantifying trading behavior in financial markets using google trends. *Scientific Reports 3* (2013).

42. Rao, T., and Srivastava, S. Analyzing stock market movements using twitter sentiment analysis. In *Proc. of ASONAM* (2012).

43. Schumaker, R. P., and Chen, H. Textual analysis of stock market prediction using breaking financial news: The azfin text system. *ACM TOIS 27*, 2 (2009), 12.

44. Sprenger, T. O., Tumasjan, A., Sandner, P. G., and Welpe, I. M. Tweets and trades: The information content of stock microblogs. *European Financial Management* (2013).

45. Sun, Y.-A., and Dance, C. R. When majority voting fails: comparing quality assurance methods for noisy human computation environment. In *Proc. of Collective Intelligence* (2012).

46. Tausczik, Y. R., Kittur, A., and Kraut, R. E. Collaborative problem solving: a study of mathoverflow. In *Proc. of CSCW* (2014).

47. Tweney, D. Seeking alpha: Who needs an acquisition when we're doing so well? VentureBeat News, October 2013.

48. Wang, G., Gill, K., Mohanlal, M., Zheng, H., and Zhao, B. Y. Wisdom in the social crowd: An analysis of quora. In *Proc. of WWW* (2013).

49. Wang, G., Mohanlal, M., Wilson, C., Wang, X., Metzger, M., Zheng, H., and Zhao, B. Y. Social turing tests: Crowdsourcing sybil detection. In *Proc. of NDSS* (2013).

50. Wang, G., Wang, T., Zheng, H., and Zhao, B. Y. Man vs. machine: Practical adversarial detection of malicious crowdsourcing workers. In *Proc. of USENIX Security* (2014).

51. Wang, G., Wilson, C., Zhao, X., Zhu, Y., Mohanlal, M., Zheng, H., and Zhao, B. Y. Serf and turf: crowdturfing for fun and profit. In *Proc. of WWW* (2012).

52. Wilson, C., Boe, B., Sala, A., Puttaswamy, K. P. N., and Zhao, B. Y. User interactions in social networks and their implications. In *Proc. of EuroSys* (2009).

53. Xu, A., Huang, S.-W., and Bailey, B. Voyant: generating structured feedback on visual designs using a crowd of non-experts. In *Proc. of CSCW* (2014).

Crowdfunding Science: Sharing Research with an Extended Audience

Julie S. Hui
Segal Design Institute
Northwestern University
2133 Sheridan Rd., Evanston, IL 60208
juliehui@u.northwestern.edu

Elizabeth M. Gerber
Segal Design Institute
Northwestern University
2133 Sheridan Rd., Evanston, IL 60208
egerber@northwestern.edu

ABSTRACT

Crowdfunding is changing how, why, and which research projects are pursued. With the increasing number of crowdfunded research projects, it is important to understand what drives scientists to launch crowdfunding campaigns and how it affects their work. To better understand this recent phenomenon, we present a grounded theory of how and why scientists crowdfund. Through 27 semi-structured interviews, we find that scientists are motivated to crowdfund in order to share their work and engage the public in the research process in ways traditional science work has not offered. Scientists also perceive crowdfunding as a more accessible way to get funds quickly compared to existing fundraising mechanisms, such as grant applications. However, they must learn to use more accessible language to successfully communicate their research through social media to a broad audience of non-scientists and professional peers. Based on these findings, we discuss design implications to inform future crowdfunding platforms and support tools.

Author Keywords

Crowdfunding; Citizen Science; Computer Mediated Communication; Design

ACM Classification Keywords

H.5.3 [Group and Organization Interfaces]: Design

General Terms

Crowdsourcing, Design

INTRODUCTION

The Internet has radically changed how scientists work, from data collection to academic publishing [6]. Scientists archive data online to share with colleagues [4], use video chat to connect with collaborators across the globe [1,4], organize the crowd in online citizen science platforms to analyze data [48,49,57], and update their lab webpages to distribute recent publications to colleagues. Now, the Internet is changing how scientists interact not just with collaborators, but also with funders. Crowdfunding has become an increasingly popular way for scientists to solicit funds [55], and by running a crowdfunding campaign online, scientists can also communicate and connect with an extended network that they otherwise may not have reached.

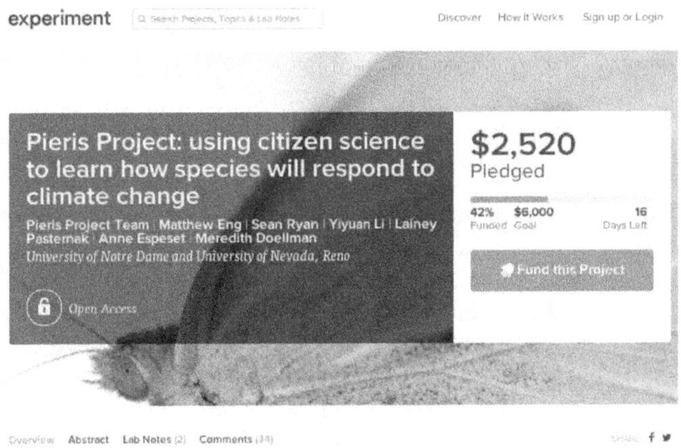

Figure 1: A crowdfunding science project page on a the crowdfunding platform, Experiment.

As the US continues to recover from research budget cuts [28], scientists search for new ways to fund their work. Crowdfunding science is the process of requesting financial resources from the crowd to support scientific research projects, often in exchange for a reward. Crowdfunding science differs from traditional science funding sources, such as grants and fellowships, because it 1) provides a way for scientists to share current research in an easy to understand format with the general public and 2) allows the public to influence future research directions by directly providing funds and ideas. In a mutually beneficial relationship, the public provides financial support, and in exchange, scientists participate in online discussions and share their work in a public-friendly manner, often through video and blog posts rather than journal articles and technical presentations.

CSCW '15, March 14 - 18, 2015, Vancouver, BC, Canada.
Copyright 2014 ACM 978-1-4503-2922-4/15/03…$15.00.
http://dx.doi.org/10.1145/2675133.2675188

For instance, one researcher raised over $10,000 to sequence DNA from ancient Roman skeletons. She posted a three-minute video explaining her research interests, goals, and funding request on a dedicated page within Rockethub, one of the top crowdfunding science platforms [60], and received donations from over 150 supporters. She used social media, such as Facebook and Twitter, to share the link to the crowdfunding page with her extended network. Shortly thereafter, a popular news blog noticed and disseminated the project video, helping surpass her funding goal by almost 70%. Like many others who crowdfund [30], she found that her supporters gave more than money: they sent messages of support through email, shared the project with their own social network, and asked her questions to learn more about her research. These interactions extend beyond science work in a way that the typical research grant writing process does not offer.

Crowdfunding science offers a novel area of study for CSCW researchers interested in designing tools to increase public engagement and broaden dissemination of scientific research. We initiate research in this emergent area with a qualitative study of 27 scientists who chose to crowdfund their research in order to understand how and why scientists use crowdfunding. Findings inform design principles to create and improve existing support tools.

BACKGROUND: CROWDFUNDING SCIENCE

Crowdfunding is defined as the online request for resources from a distributed audience to pursue a project [3,21]. Currently, the majority of science crowdfunding[1] is taking place on crowdfunding science-specific platforms rather than as a separate category on general crowdfunding platforms like Kickstarter. This may be due to the different nature of scientific research as compared to creating consumer products and services. Unlike with many traditional crowdfunding projects, crowdfunding scientists are raising funds with the end goal of furthering scientific knowledge, for which they must follow a specific process to collect data and validate their findings.

Crowdfunding could change how science work is performed by directly connecting fundraising with the need to interact with an extended audience of supporters outside their field of research. For these reasons, we focus specifically on scientists who use platforms where they maintain their own project page and interact directly with the public. We can then better understand how crowdfunding scientists are communicating and engaging with a wide range of people.

Scientists Who Crowdfund

The majority of scientists using crowdfunding may be novice rather than expert researchers, suggesting implications for supporting researchers with limited professional experience. While few people have published demographics on the crowdfunding science community, Experiment, one of the most popular crowdfunding science platforms, shared that the majority (58%) of their participants are post-doc, graduate and undergraduate researchers [31,61], most of whom have limited experience writing and producing research-related content for a general audience. The remaining 42% are made up of professors and industry professionals. Similar to other online populations, scientists' fluency with the Internet, social media, and multimedia technologies varies widely [26,38].

Platform Models

There are various types of crowdfunding platforms, such as using sites that specifically focus on research (i.e. Experiment [61]), sites run by universities (i.e. UCLA SPARK [63]), sites that host a variety of projects (i.e. Rockethub [60]), sites that broker the relationship between researchers and funders (i.e. Benefunder [64]), and sites that offer funder equity in the final product (i.e. MicroVentures [65]). Platforms follow an *all-or-nothing* or *keep-what-you-raise* funding model, or allow the project creator to choose between either. The former only lets scientists keep the funds if they meet their funding goal, while the later allows scientists to keep however much they raise whether or not they meet their goal.

Crowdfunding Work

As described in previous research [30], running a crowdfunding campaign includes activity not only on the crowdfunding platform, but also elsewhere such as on social and news media. Crowdfunding scientists prepare the campaign by choosing the duration of their campaign – typically between one and three months [61,66] and creating the campaign material, which includes a written description, short video, and often additional blogs and social media pages for visibility [30]. When supporters visit the live project page, they choose to pledge dollar amounts based on rewards specified by the crowdfunding scientist. After the campaign, scientists deliver the promised rewards as well as updates on the progress of their research.

RELATED WORK

Science crowdfunding combines elements of public engagement in science, peer collaboration in science, and crowdfunding. We examine related research to frame our theoretical expectations for *how* and *why* scientists crowdfund.

Public Engagement in Science

Public engagement in science is concerned with the ways scientific activities and research can be shared with the non-scientists [7]. The Internet is changing the way scientists do this through how they communicate and collaborate with the public [8,54].

[1] Science crowdfunding platforms [61,62] use a variety of terms to describe participants and their projects including "science," "research," "project," "backers," "funders," and "creators." For consistency, we refer to *crowdfunding scientists* as the people who request funds through crowdfunding platforms, *supporters* as people who donate funds to projects through crowdfunding platforms, and *campaign* as the organization of online activity to achieve a the crowdfunding financial goal.

Communicating Science to the Public

Traditionally, scientific work has been shared with the public through popular press articles or shows, which "translate" scientific terminology to more easily understandable language. Now, the Internet is allowing more scientists to engage directly with the public through written and video blogs, personal websites, and public online speeches like Ted Talks [67]. These new avenues of communication not only allow scientists to reach people outside their field [46], but also provides a way for scientists to grow an interested audience who can now receive online updates about their work, such as through YouTube or blogs.

Researchers studying public engagement in science find that scientists communicate with the public through one- and two-way interactions [8,53]. This could include open access journals [54] (one-way), or online discussion boards (two-way), which have allowed scientists and the public to work together to inform a research agenda and assist with the research process [44].

Consistent with motivational theory, scientists are motivated to connect with others as part of their work process [50]. Recent CSCW research found that science majors were motivated to share their knowledge on Wikipedia because it connected them with a large online audience [15]. Similarly, previous research on crowdfunding describes people's desire to share their work in order to connect with like-minded people [21]. Crowdfunding science builds on existing models of public engagement by allowing scientists an easy and direct way to communicate with the public in addition to collecting financial resources for their work. Inspired by motivational theory, we expect that sharing one's work publicly also builds a sense of mastery and competency, which supports self-confidence and desire to create high quality and more creative work [2,50].

Collaborating With the Public Through Citizen Science

Citizen science is an increasingly popular avenue for public engagement in science and demonstrates a trend to engage the public as research helpers. Rather than simply sharing information with the public, citizen science allows for research collaborations where members of the public participate in the scientific investigation [10,56], such as data collection and analysis.

Motivations to participate for scientists include desire to enhance their own research, collaborate with volunteers, educate others, and participate in open science, while motivations for citizen participants are more often intrinsic, such as desire to inform and be a part of the research agenda [43,47,49]. Deterrents for citizen science include variability in data quality [11,18], difficulty managing the hundreds or thousands of volunteers [57], and costs of running a citizen science platform [5].

CSCW researchers have identified design implications and built tools to improve participation and data quality on citizen science platforms. Sheppard and Terveen argue for including interactive tutorials and videos that teach data collection processes, applications that provide instant in situ feedback, and tools to allow citizens to explore data themselves [51]. Wiggins describes how improving information and communication technologies can support better project management [57]. Others describe ways platform features can support participant intrinsic motivation [43] as well as ways to increase project awareness and recruitment through social media strategies [48]. To help more scientists participate in citizen science, researchers have built mobile [34] and web [36] platforms to ease the onboarding process for mass data collection.

However, unlike citizen science, the focal contribution of science crowdfunding is money, not labor. Because funding is involved, scientists who crowdfund may feel more motivated than scientists of citizen science projects to take into consideration their supporters' opinions and suggestions.

Peer Collaboration in Science

While research has shown that scientists tend to collaborate with people who are physically close, email and other forms of online communication have made it easier to reach out and establish fruitful collaborations among distant research groups [17,58]. By working with others, scientists have been able to share large datasets [4] and gain access to financial resources, equipment and knowledge that they would otherwise not have been able to acquire easily [6]. Having access to the right tools supports a sense of autonomy [50], allowing people to work on projects that they are intrinsically motivated to pursue.

Furthermore, public partnerships, such as co-authoring papers [32], allow scientists to formally associate themselves with established researchers, thus building social capital [22] and a sense of relatedness with like-minded others [50]. Those who choose not to take advantage of their scientific network may be at risk of performing redundant research or having to spend more money on personal equipment [17]. Crowdfunding scientists have already begun to form such relationships with other crowdfunding scientists, which is why it is important to view crowdfunding science not only as a funding mechanism, but also as a peer collaboration support tool. Similar to research on crowdfunding motivations [21], we expect to see scientists motivated to connect with other scientists who could provide interesting ideas and new perspectives on their work.

Crowdfunding Science

Much of the discussion around crowdfunding science is still based in popular press [16,45], as few researchers have performed empirical studies of crowdfunding specifically in the context of science. Scientists speculate that a large audience, accessible and persuasive language, and outreach efforts are key factors to successfully raising funds [55]. These expectations are consistent with existing crowdfunding research, which describe the importance of building a support network [29,30], and using social media [40] and persuasive language [39].

From an initial qualitative study of 47 crowdfunding project creators, Hui et al. [30] found evidence that certain types of crowdfunding creators, such as visual artists or musicians, struggled less to communicate their message through social media compared to scientists and engineers. This suggests that scientists may overcome different communication barriers than non-scientists in order to explain their work effectively.

Muller et al. found that in crowdfunding within the enterprise, where employees crowdfund each other's projects, there was an increase in inter-departmental collaboration [41]. Because employees were given an opportunity to share their work with others, they were able to foster new professional connections. We expect to see similar motivations to connect with peers in crowdfunding science where the increased visibility of one's research will help scientists form collaborations and share ideas with people outside their immediate field of research.

However, no researchers have performed a qualitative study of this community of scientists who crowdfund to better understand why they are turning to crowdfunding and how these new practices could inform science work and crowdfunding overall.

METHODS

We took a grounded theory approach [52] to understand how and why scientists interact with their extended network during their crowdfunding campaign. We perform open qualitative data collection so as not to unnecessarily constrain the emergent framework.

Participants

In this study, we interviewed 27 (7 female) participants from Rockethub, Experiment, Petridish, and FundaGeek, over a yearlong period. We examined a diverse yet representative set of participants including scientists who were conducting research in biology (6), computer science (2), entomology (3), electrical engineering (2), anthropology (2), education (2), public health (1), neuroscience (1), ecology (3), applied science (1), nanotechnology (1), energy (1), bioengineering (1), and physics (1). 24 participants crowdfunded on science-specific platforms whereas the remainder used general platforms that supported science-related projects. Participants raised between $1,120 and $33,795. While some exceeded their fundraising goal, others just met a fraction of their goal. No informants relied on crowdfunding as their primary source of income, and all participants were US-based. Participants' employment statuses included high school student (1), undergraduate student (4), graduate student (13), professor (3), and researcher (6). We recruited participants through email and platform message systems aiming for a diverse range of participants. To understand if motivations or deterrents change over time, we interviewed scientists who were both currently crowdfunding and had finished crowdfunding. Scientists were not compensated for their participation.

Data Collection

We used semi-structured interviews to collect qualitative data. We began each interview with a description of our research method and explanation of our research interests in crowdfunding. We expressed our interest in understanding how scientists who crowdfund engage with an extended network and why they chose to crowdfunded in the first place. We concluded the interview with reassurance of anonymity of the data collection.

The average length of the interview was 30 minutes. All interviews were conducted over Skype, Google Hangouts, or phone because of the geographic distribution of participants. All interviews were audio-recorded and transcribed for analysis immediately following the interviews. We guaranteed anonymity by disguising informant's names, positions, and project titles.

Analysis

We employed selective coding and analysis [52] to understand 1) how scientists share their work with an extended audience through crowdfunding, and 2) why they are motivated to participate [21]. This framing allowed particular themes about scientific communication and engagement [8,37,42,54], scientific peer collaboration [17], and motivation [13,21] to emerge. As more data was gathered and analyzed, we simultaneously researched pertinent literature to understand existing theory related to these themes. Three coders began the process of selective coding by flagging each instance where participants communicated interacting with people outside their immediate academic circle. Instances were recorded using private Google Sheets. We identified 23 different themes, abandoning those for which there was insufficient data and clustered the remaining into groups based on frequency counts.

FINDINGS

The data describe three ways that scientists who crowdfund connect with an extended network of non-scientists and peer researchers. We then expand on initial motivations to crowdfund science research. Furthermore, we provide examples throughout of how existing online platforms and tools support this work and motivations to participate.

Engage Non-Experts Through the Research Process

The data show that scientists are motivated to achieve broader impact in line with the goals of the National Science Foundation of "promoting teaching, training, and learning" and "disseminating research broadly to enhance scientific and technological understanding" [68]. Crowdfunding scientists do this by describing their work in public forums and webpages, answering questions about their research area, and giving them an opportunity to impact the advancement of research through financial support. For instance, a professor studying cancer treatments described how he liked that crowdfunding allowed the public to see the research that goes into the project:

"It allows a form for people to engage in science...going through that product lifecycle, one gets to see where ideas come from, who's behind them and how do they plan to change the world with it."

Crowdfunding provides a way for people who are interested in science research to contribute and learn, motivations consistent with general crowdfunding supporters [21] and in citizen science [43,47]. A zoology PhD student described how her supporters not only funded her work, but also asked about how to perform data collection:

"I have been asked about the equipment I used to date my site. I've posted pictures of the equipment...and more information on the lab itself... Most of the times I get questions like that, they're from people who funded me, who are actually interested in paleo, but not working in the field."

By engaging non-scientists in the research endeavor, scientists see the process of crowdfunding as a more "direct" way to connect with the public and teach them about their research practices. The crowd aspect of crowdfunding allows scientists to reach a much wider audience compared to traditional funding where your application is only read by a handful of people. An entomologist described this difference:

"The fact that you're getting 1,000 views is 1,000 that you're touching and they're watching, and there are people that actually fund you, and they become part of your audience. They stick with you...You're able to blog just to those people and keep them in the loop, and communicate with them, so they can participate not just by funding, but you can actually bring them along for your research endeavor.

Similar to findings on crowdfunding work in general, the process of crowdfunding science also encompasses not just maintaining a crowdfunding project page, but also other forms of public engagement, such as creating a blog, writing popular press articles, and communicating with fans on social media [30]. Participants describe using a suite of social media platforms, including their personal Facebook Feed, creating a Facebook Group, Twitter, Google+, personal blogs, personal websites, and Reddit. The wide variety of outlets allows scientists to share their interests with a range of supporters outside of academia. An ecologist described how his job as a researcher did not require him to share his research in public avenues the way that running a crowdfunding project did:

"I view crowdfunding as a way to kind of share some of my passion about the work that I'm doing. There's a reason that I'm interested in the question that I'm asking. There's a reason that I keep studying the oceans and what's going on as they're confronted with climate change and all sorts of other impacts. I have very few opportunities to communicate that [in my job]."

Figure 2: A crowdfunding scientist publicizes his project through Twitter.

Furthermore, in running their campaigns, crowdfunding scientists see themselves as science mentors to the general public:

"I would answer their questions about parasites...or they'd like ask about books that they like could read to follow up on something, and I would tell them about books... Hopefully they'll think of me in the future if they have a question."

Crowdfunding not only educates the public on research, but also allows the public to inform the research agenda as well. In the process of disseminating knowledge, a PhD student described how interacting with the crowd *"stimulated [her] thinking"* and *"sparked[ed] new ideas"* for future studies on parasites. Another crowdfunder described ideas exchanged between her and other crowdfunding scientists as *"cross pollination."* Sharing work with someone outside one's project team has been shown to support creativity and new ways of tackling problem solving [24,25].

By running a crowdfunding campaign, scientists are given the opportunity to not only receive funds, but also share what it's like to perform research from study design to field work. Crowdfunding scientists achieve this work using social technologies, such as maintaining public webpages and engaging in direct conversations on their crowdfunding project page. These public relationships last over time, which sets it apart from traditional funding transactions where scientists may receive funds from a grant officer who privately checks in once a year.

Communicate Research Using Accessible Language

Scientists also learn how to communicate their research using language that resonates with a broad audience. This stands in contrast to how scientists typically communicate – through lengthy written grants, papers or presentations to an expert scientific audience. Many participants describe how they were not initially skilled at communicating their work to non-scientists. A PhD student studying marine biology described how crowdfunding required a completely different skillset from his everyday research:

"As students, we are trained to research issues, write papers and submit grant proposals. But we are not trained to make videos and to reach out to the public."

Crowdfunding provides an avenue to build these skills, which participants describe as being useful when "go[ing] to an event" and "talking to every single person". An ecologist described how the crowdfunding process of making a video and writing a description helped him learn to explain his research succinctly:

"[Crowdfunding] helped me tremendously in putting together a message, my elevator speech if you will. It's helped me put together that 5 minute pitch of 'What do you do? Oh, well, I do x, y, and z.'"

Another PhD student in computer science said he learned to use *"shorter sentences that sound interesting"* in order to be more *"appealing to the outside world."*

In communicating with non-scientists, participants expressed their hope to still communicate the "deeper scientific purpose". Scholars who study science communication describe how converting scientific publications into public-friendly articles follows a process of removing complicated language and subtleties in order to reduce it to a simple set of facts [8]. However, some researchers find that scientists purposefully do not want to do this because they worry it may misrepresent their work [12].

In addition, they also learn to communicate through different media, such as video, blog articles (see Figure 3), and in-person. They see these as "cool ways" to describe their work outside of journal articles and conference presentations. One of the most difficult tasks of a crowdfunding campaign is creating a video [30]. While many participants had trouble with this aspect of the crowdfunding process, those that were able to learn video-making felt it was a valuable skill. A researcher of an anthropology project described her experience with videography:

"I've never made a video before for my research, and sort of trying to put that together in the style of you know History Channel documentary...it was really a lot of fun, so I really enjoyed that. It's definitely not something you would do for a grant like the National Science Foundation."

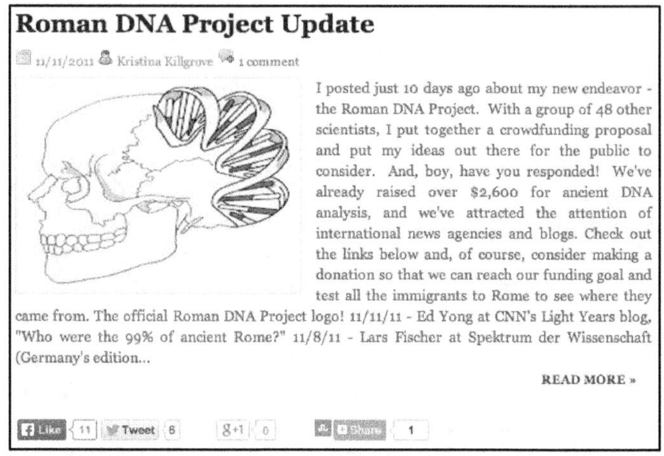

Roman DNA Project Update

11/11/2011 Kristina Killgrove 1 comment

I posted just 10 days ago about my new endeavor - the Roman DNA Project. With a group of 48 other scientists, I put together a crowdfunding proposal and put my ideas out there for the public to consider. And, boy, have you responded! We've already raised over $2,600 for ancient DNA analysis, and we've attracted the attention of international news agencies and blogs. Check out the links below and, of course, consider making a donation so that we can reach our funding goal and test all the immigrants to Rome to see where they came from. The official Roman DNA Project logo! 11/11/11 - Ed Yong at CNN's Light Years blog, "Who were the 99% of ancient Rome?" 11/8/11 - Lars Fischer at Spektrum der Wissenschaft (Germany's edition...

READ MORE »

Like 11 Tweet 6 g+1 0 Share 1

Figure 3: A crowdfunding scientist posts a blog entry on her research progress.

Participants also expressed improving their communication skills by soliciting and receiving feedback from peers and supporters. Being able to point to an online video and description of their project allowed scientists to easily communicate with other scientists about their work. Rockethub and Experiment scaffolded these interactions by setting up online communities where scientists could discuss topics and help each other before they went public with their campaign. A participant using Rockethub described how she found it useful to get feedback from other scientists launching projects:

"We had a wiki. We all put up our projects, and people would comment on them, so I got a lot of good feedback from the other people who were also putting up projects, and I commented on their projects."

The public process of communicating one's work forced participants to practice and receive feedback. A PhD student explained how the iterative process improved his communication skills:

"I got comments on the video and the kind of questions that people would ask in those comments or would ask when they sent me emails helped me figure out what I was explaining well and what I was explaining not well. And so I feel like I've been able to hone my explanation a bit because of that."

Participants see the benefits of learning to communicate with the public in more easy to understand terms because it increases public interest in science and improves their ability to succinctly explain the importance of their work, a skill necessary to succeed as a researcher. Participants learn to better communicate through frequent interaction and feedback in online community platforms like forums and social media sites.

Find Academic Peers through Campaign Publicity

Regular interactions in online forums and sharing work publicly help scientists who crowdfund create a community with other scientists. Scientists describe crowdfunding as a "public space" for making "connections" with other researchers.

Creating a crowdfunding page increases visibility for one's work, making it easier for other scientists to find researchers in the same field. A new assistant professor described how crowdfunding drew people interested in her research:

"Other scientists have seen [my campaign], and they've contacted me and talked to me about [research]."

They also use their project as a way to network with other scientists whom they have not met through traditional ways of connecting, such as through conferences:

"I've found them online through their Petri Dish [crowdfunding page] and gone, I didn't know you were doing that! That's really cool!"

Scientists use research connections to find people who can provide help on their research, such as feedback on an experimental setup or access to expensive equipment. A researcher described how the review process typically involves "hardcore physicists" giving feedback that is "very harsh." Therefore, he sees crowdfunding as a great way to meet others that may be able to provide their professional opinion in a more supportive rather than competitive atmosphere:

"Being crowdfunded, you expose yourself to a lot of other scientists. They really help us move forward and we really are craving for their feedback."

In addition to feedback, crowdfunding could support increased collaboration between scientists, which has shown to foster data [4] and idea [23] sharing for scientific progress:

"Another SciFund participant I got in touch with later...we actually ended up submitting a symposium proposal for a meeting."

Novice scientists see it as a great opportunity to locate mentors who are critical for professional development. A biology PhD student described how having a crowdfunding campaign gave her a reason to reach out to more experienced researchers:

"One of the great things about the SciFund Challenge was that I had an excuse to contact people that I wanted to contact for a while, but didn't really have an excuse to contact."

Similar to previous research on how expert crowdfunders contribute back to the community by giving advice on how to run a campaign [30], we find the similar interactions in the science space. One PhD studying parasites described how many professors approached him asking for advice on how to fund their own projects:

"Once I was funded...I've had a lot of people in my department of all ranges, from grad student to professors, just come and talk to me about advice and how they can do a crowdsourcing campaign."

Learning crowdfunding skills gives a way for novices in their scientific field to act as mentors to more senior researchers. Another participant described how crowdfunding "enlarged [her] community and overall interested group." Similarly, a high school student described how she looks forward to maintaining the relationships she made through crowdfunding in her future college research experiences

Participants described how their crowdfunding campaign served as conversation starter with peers and mentors in order to build useful, long lasting relationships in the future.

Motivations and Deterrents to Crowdfund Science

In addition to understanding how crowdfunding scientists connected with an extended audience, we also explored why they initially chose to crowdfund.

Motivations

Compared to traditional grantsmanship, scientists perceive that crowdfunding can help raise funds relatively quickly and that it provides a space to support riskier ideas that may not appeal to traditional funding agencies. While the work required to raise funds is considered difficult for scientists in terms of the skills, time, and attitude required to publicize on social media, scientists with an existing support network perceive the work as a monetization of their connections.

The immediacy of crowdfunding provides support when other funding sources are limited. Scientists explain that they may need extra funds in the middle of their study to buy laboratory materials or pay for data collection travel expenses. Many of these actions are time sensitive and running a month long campaign to raise funds for an immediate need is more desirable than writing a grant or fellowship application that may take months to process. A PhD student studying marine biology used crowdfunding to buy diving equipment for his upcoming research trip when his advisor was unable to provide him with the needed funds.

"With crowdfunding, it's been really cool to see all of this happening now, and to know that come January, I will be able to start this project. I don't have to wait six months to get my funding."

Scientists also like seeing funds trickle in every day as opposed to waiting to hear back months after submitting a grant proposal. They describe receiving news about supporter activity as "fun" and "exciting." A biology re

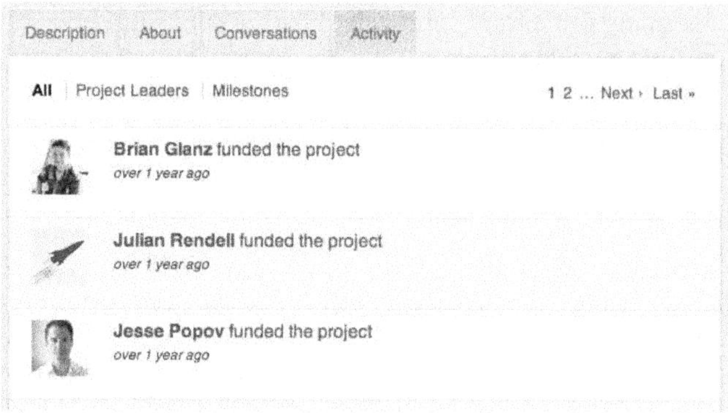

Figure 4: Rockethub provides a list of supporters as well as milestone notifications for when certain funding levels are reached.

searcher studying crustaceans described the emotional rush from getting notifications each day:

"It was highly emotional because you get the highs, you get the little rush when you actually see you know, 'So-and-so has funded your project,' and that comes into your email, it's like, 'Yay!' And that's a great feeling."

Involving the crowd in research funding has allowed scientists to see the people who support their work through the online list of supporters (see Figure 4). This stands in contrast to getting grant reviews back from a small panel of researchers through private communication channels. An undergraduate researcher of a computer science project described how she preferred being supported by the crowd compared to anonymous people in a funding agency:

"I haven't personally met most of the donors, but you know, being able to see a list of exactly who's contributing is a nifty change from just getting unmarked well, marked...with government dollars."

Scientists see crowdfunding as a way to encourage the work of novice scientists and the pursuit of unique research ideas. One participant studying zoology described how her work did not qualify for other forms of funding:

"Because of my status in a different program, I don't qualify for many of the same kinds of funding as a traditional paleontologist would...[My research] is not inexpensive, and I am a graduate student with tuition and all. [Crowdfunding] provided these means of funding my project and my research that I would otherwise not have access to."

With crowdfunding, scientists are judged less on their reputation and more on how their work appeals to the public. An entomologist who raised over $10,000 described his previous frustration with the NSF:

"It's getting so competitive. [The NSF] is becoming more conservative. It's not funding wild ideas that may be very good because they're too risky."

Some scientists are concerned projects will primarily be judged on scientists' salesmanship rather than research abilities [55]. However, this is not significantly different from grant applications, which also need to be written clearly and persuasively.

Participants also describe their desire to "bring democracy to the world of fundraising" in order to remove the "mysterious nature" of what and how research is funded. One participant lamented how there was no research version of the Grameen Bank, an organization that provides the ability to microfinance individuals in third world countries.

Deterrents

In addition to the outlined motivations to crowdfund science, scientists still identified many reasons why crowdfunding is not ideal, including overcoming institutional red tape, time and skills needed to publicize effectively online, risk of idea theft, and attitudes of asking for money online. For instance, because crowdfunding science has only recently started gaining attention, most research institutions lack infrastructure to foster crowdfunding easily.

Participants describe how their institutions are confused about opening an account for researchers to receive public donations and have been asked to contact every individual supporter with necessary paperwork. A participant described how her financial office had trouble understanding the nature of crowdfunding donations:

"Does it count as one large donation or does it count as many small donations? Each individual contributor needs to be contacted by the university and confirm with the university that they know that the donation was not tax deductible...Accounting offices at universities are not set up yet for this kind of funding structure."

Similar to other ways of securing funding, it still requires hard work. For people who have full time jobs as researchers—writing papers, taking or teaching classes, and performing studies—running a crowdfunding campaign can be overwhelming. A PhD student at a midwestern university described the stress of running a crowdfunding campaign:

"The fundraising should have been a fulltime job...and web development, as well, was a fulltime job. So, I was basically doing three fulltime jobs at the same time. And I'm also doing a PhD and I'm also teaching at a university, so I have like basically, 5 official titles. So that was definitely hard."

Despite the workload, novice researchers have expressed feeling more secure about their ability to crowdfund compared to getting a research grant. Another participant thought the crowdfunding was "much less stressful" because she didn't have to fill out "all the applications." An anthropologist studying breastfeeding described how she felt the work more likely would pay off:

"It was a lot of work, but I felt like all of the work was worthwhile, whereas when you write a normal grant, you can maybe put a ton of effort in, and then all you hear back is no."

However, while crowdfunding a certain amount seems more certain, scientists who choose to use an All-or-Nothing platform express worries that their network is not strong enough to meet the funding goal. One participant described how her advice to a friend considering crowdfunding deterred her from the experience:

"I told her my experience and she did not decide to pursue [crowdfunding] because, as she put it, 'If it's mostly people you know, no one I know has that kind of money to give me.'"

Furthermore, although participants were motivated to engage a broader audience, they also take into consideration the risk of sharing their research openly. While sharing one's research with other scientists can help with research collaborations or mentorship relationships, it also puts one at risk of idea theft. Although none of the scientists that we interviewed reported having their ideas stolen, many expressed concerns. For instance, a university professor of an applied science project explained how crowdfunding may not be ideal for beginning researchers:

"Early stage people that have new findings, and they haven't protected it, should stay away [from crowdfunding]...If you make it public, you can't patent it or you have a very limited amount of time to file a provisional [patent]...The ideal time to do crowdfunding is when the technology is in a mature enough stage."

However, data from beginning researchers with limited capital suggest that they are willing to put up with this risk in order to receive immediate funds because they have few other choices.

In addition, while creators appreciate interacting with people to receive feedback, they feel uncomfortable asking for monetary help. The persistent and ongoing face-to-face and computer mediated communication is critical to achieving funding success, but can feel uncomfortable because it breaks certain social norms. One scientist described it as *"hounding."* Another participant who reached his funding goal expressed his extreme discomfort:

"[Requesting funds] was the biggest challenge because you have to do it. You have to send emails to your friends... you feel like a beggar, a glorified beggar."

Overall, scientists are motivated to seek funds through crowdfunding for a variety of reasons including speed, freedom from large funding agencies, being more democratic, and being funded by many people. However, they are deterred because of the time commitment, bureaucratic red tape, possible idea theft, and discomfort asking for money.

DISCUSSION

Crowdfunding allows scientists to share their work with the public, connect with research peers, and solicit resources outside traditional funding mechanisms. These opportunities allow scientists to feel *competence* in their work through acting as an expert in their field, *relatedness* with others by establishing connections to people with similar interests, and *autonomy* by having access to financial resources without having to apply to traditional funding sources that can take months of effort with no reward. The combination of competence, relatedness, and autonomy, form the groundwork of self-determination theory, which describes how people are more likely to be self-motivated and produce higher quality work [50].

Competence through Public Engagement and Communication

As crowdfunding becomes a more popular and accepted way to fund scientific research [55], it shows how the Internet is changing established work practices and what is needed to build professional expertise. Unlike other popular crowdfunding categories, such as art or product design, showing or explaining one's work to a general audience has not been a common form of fundraising for individual scientists. Science foundations and societies have long sought donations for research, but until crowdfunding, scientists have rarely taken it upon themselves to solicit resources by publicizing their work to a extended network of friends, family, and beyond. Other forms of promoting public awareness of science, such as through popular press, have involved hiring a science journalist to translate research.

Crowdfunding builds on the more recent ways scientists are engaging with the public, such as through blogs and social media [44,46], by providing an opportunity to use these to both seek needed resources and build a sense of competence. Our data gave examples of how scientists are viewed as experts and mentors to people interested in their work. Participants describe sharing information with supporters on how to perform research at home and what tools they used in their research process. Currently, the value of scientific work is mainly judged through publications and grant funding. While these methods of peer review within the scientific community ensure scientists are following proper standards and methods, the practice of crowdfunding introduces a new model of how the public could play a role in the research ecosystem.

While many participants described sharing their work with people outside their field as one of the most rewarding aspects of crowdfunding, they also faced challenges learning to communicate with non-scientists. As such, learning how to create a project pitch might be even more difficult for crowdfunding scientists compared to general crowdfunding project creators. Related work on cognitive science and learning sciences describe how scientists have trouble distilling their work in a way that is easily understandable by the public [37] because they often become so knowledgeable about their subject that they develop an "expert blind spot" [12,42]. Others describe how some scientists feel that simplifying their work to a point where the public can understand would misrepresent their findings [12].

While sharing one's work publicly has shown to build competence and support motivation to participate, scientists also need to learn the skills to share their work effectively so that they can evolve with how science may be performed and evaluated as crowdfunding becomes more popular.

Relatedness through Peer Collaboration and Crowdfunding Communities

Similar to findings on research collaborations [17] and motivations to crowdfund in general, scientists are also motivated to build professional connections. Compared to general crowdfunding platforms, Kickstarter having launched over 160,000 projects, crowdfunding science platforms are still very much in the nascent stage with about 150 projects launched on Experiment [31] and Rockethub's SciFund Challenge [9] each. This small community benefits crowdfunding scientists because platforms can hold close-knit online wikis and forums where project creators come to know each other's work in order to give feedback. Traditionally, scientists give feedback during peer review for publications or in established work contexts [17]. Crowdfunding provides a new context for these relationships to happen, which could increase the strength and innovation of science work by involving more diverse perspectives [24,25] and increased opportunities for feedback [27].

Scholars who study collaboration in science find that working with other scientists improves access to resources and equipment [33], information [6], and authorship status [22]. We found that scientists who made collaborations through crowdfunding engaged with other scientists by submitting project proposals with people they met in the crowdfunding community.

However, compared to general crowdfunding project creators where there are thousands of existing projects, crowdfunding scientists do not have the same level of access to mentors or role models from which to draw inspiration [19,20]. Unlike many creative-type crowdfunding projects, the outcome of science crowdfunding is not a product or form of entertainment (e.g. iPad accessory, film), but artifacts of the research process, such as copies of the crowdfunder's research articles [61] or naming rights for a research specimen. Because these rewards may not be as enticing as a commercial product, crowdfunding scientists face greater challenges with building a community of supporters and fans. Thus it is more imperative to build tools that provide access to other more expert crowdfunders who may be able to provide help or advice.

Autonomy through Crowdfunding as a New Funding Model

Scientists are acutely aware of the importance of funding on their research agenda. Studies on scientific work reveal that researchers often spend 40% of their time on bureaucratic duties like grant writing [59]. Our data suggests that scientists, particularly novices who have a limited track record, found that they have a higher chance acquiring funds through crowdfunding than through applying for a grant. Others described how crowdfunding allowed them to overcome small obstacles in their research process, such as quickly soliciting small amount of funds for a last minute round of data collection, which applying for a research grant would have taken months to accomplish.

However, even though crowdfunding may provide funds quicker and to people with limited research reputation, many crowdfunders do not realize the amount of work it takes to create and sustain a crowdfunding project [9,30]. Unfortunately, crowdfunding is more than just creating a project page with video and written description. It requires crowdfunders to publicize their work constantly on social media, learn new communication skills, and manage hundreds of supporters [30]. While research on crowdfunding has shown that people have turned to community support tools and resources to achieve these tasks [30], project creators of both science and non-science campaigns agree that crowdfunding takes a concerted effort.

Summary

While we found scientists to be motivated to experience a sense of competence through acting as a field expert, relatedness by connecting with other scientists, and autonomy by being able to seek resources quickly, we also found that scientists were not used to communicating their work to a new audience and felt overwhelmed by the responsibilities of crowdfunding work. Furthermore, we find that crowdfunding science is different from crowdfunding creative-type projects for two main reasons:

1) Scientists have traditionally not had to rely on communicating their work to an extended network of friends, family, and the general public in order to fund their science research, which may make learning the process of crowdfunding science more difficult.

2) Unlike general crowdfunding projects, which typically involve creating a product or service that supporters can have or experience, such as a video game, the outcome of science research is furthering scientific knowledge. This more ambiguous end goal may make it more difficult for scientists to reach the same level of Internet popularity as other types of crowdfunding projects creating consumer products.

While crowdfunding platforms have succeeded at using the Internet to remove many of the barriers needed to collect financial resources from a large number of people, CSCW researchers must continue to better understand what about this new model of fundraising can motivate increased communication and collaboration between scientists and a wider extended audience.

IMPLICATIONS FOR DESIGN

We suggest design implications for tools supporting 1) a wider range data sharing and visualization, 2) building science communication strategies with non-scientists, 3) interactions between crowdfunding scientists for feedback and collaborations, and 4) financial on-boarding strategies for large research institutions and universities. By designing crowdfunding tools and platforms, we can help more scientists involve the public in a variety of research efforts.

Currently, crowdfunding science platforms look very similar to general crowdfunding platforms. Project pages include a video, project description, funding goal and rewards. However, because crowdfunding science projects focus less on producing a consumer product and more on furthering knowledge, these forms of public engagement may not be enough. Although most platforms include forums where scientists and supporters can converse, they offer few other capabilities to support dissemination of in-depth research material. In order to provide easier avenues for engagement, platforms could create interactive galleries to share images of data or mechanisms for scientists to solicit feedback before launching the campaign. Following research in public engagement in science, such tools would support knowledge transfer, active discussion, and collaborative shaping of the research agenda [7,53].

Many scientists don't have the technical skills to create a custom platform themselves [36]. Unlike citizen science, which requires much more work by the scientists to set up a custom system for mass data collection or analysis, crowdfunding platforms are able to streamline certain platform features like providing video uploading features or a comment feed. Some platforms like Experiment help scientists communicate their work effectively through one-on-one support with platform staff and requiring crowdfunding scientists to answer three basic questions on their campaign page: "What is the context of this research?", "What is the significance of this project?", and "What are the goals of the project? " Including more mentorship support and structured presentation formats in other platforms could ease the communication process for new crowdfunding scientists.

Furthermore, as described earlier, crowdfunding science is still relatively new and has a much smaller community of participants than general crowdfunding platforms like Kickstarter. Some platforms, such as Rockethub and Experiment, have taken advantage of the smaller community size and incorporate forums where scientists can comment and send messages to other crowdfunding scientists. However, only three of the six platforms that we studied reported having an online forum just for project creators.

In addition, we find that crowdfunding is particularly attractive to novice researchers who have difficulty getting grants from more prestigious funding sources. Economic research on the effects of decreasing government funding in research find that federal funding does not crowd out private funding of researchers [14]. Our results suggest that crowdfunding may be particularly valuable to people who have trouble getting traditional funding, such as novice researchers. In order to better support novices, crowdfunding platforms may need to design better onboarding interfaces for universities. Already, some platforms [61,69] have started setting up official relationships with universities, and some universities have started their own crowdfunding platforms [63,70].

LIMITATIONS

Our participants used four of the most popular crowdfunding science platforms. However, there are additional crowdfunding platforms and it is possible that participants on other platforms are motivated to participate for different reasons. It is also possible that platforms motivate participants differently [35]. We also do not discuss motivations for donating to crowdfunding science projects, as what scientists may find valuable may not be what supporters find valuable. Further, we suspect that motivations for participation may vary slightly as platforms are redesigned, more people are aware of the phenomenon, and expectations for participation in crowdfunding are altered.

FUTURE WORK

Learning how to interact with the public effectively takes an entire new skillset that scientists may not have, and acquiring this skillset is time and effort intensive. Future work will focus on designing support tools for crowdfunding platforms that are informed by scientist's needs to alleviate the strain of onboarding for scientists who may want to crowdfund their research. We also plan to perform a study of supporter motivations in order to better understand what type of people support and whether crowdfunding science is targeting a representative sample of the public.

CONCLUSION

Science research is crucial for the advancement of society. Yet the struggle continues to overcome obstacles that broaden participation and funding of innovative work. As CSCW researchers, we are called to study and design emerging systems that fundamentally reduce the barriers to participation. By realizing new opportunities for funding and communicating science, crowdfunding can provide new ways for scientists to engage the public and scientific peers in their research process.

ACKNOWLEDGEMENTS

We thank Amy Laurin, Lauren Tindal, and Cassie Coravos for helping with data collection, coding, and insights. We also thank Michael Greenberg for his feedback.

REFERENCES

1. Aragon, C.R., Poon, S., and Silva, C.T. The changing face of digital science: new practices in scientific collaborations. *Proc. of CHI*, (2009), 4819–4822.
2. Bandura, A. *Self-efficacy: The exercise of control*. W. H. Freeman and Company, 1997.
3. Belleflamme, P., Lambert, T., and Schwienbacher, A. Crowdfunding: tapping the right crowd. *Journal of Business Venturing*, (2013).
4. Birnholtz, J.P. and Bietz, M.J. Data at work: supporting sharing in science and engineering. *Proc. of GROUP*, (2003), 339–348.

5. Bonney, R., Cooper, C.B., Dickinson, J., et al. Citizen science: a developing tool for expanding science knowledge and scientific literacy. *BioScience 59*, 11 (2009), 977–984.
6. Bozeman, B. and Corley, E. Scientists' collaboration strategies: implications for scientific and technical human capital. *Research Policy 33*, 4 (2004), 599–616.
7. Bucchi, M. Of deficits, deviations and dialogues: Theories of public communication of science. *Handbook of public communication of science and technology*, (2008), 57–76.
8. Bucchi, M. *Science and the media: alternative routes to scientific communications*. Routledge, 2013.
9. Byrnes, J.E., Ranganathan, J., Walker, B.L.E., and Faulkes, Z. To Crowdfund Research, Scientists Must Build An Audience For Their Work. *PeerJ PrePrints*, (in press).
10. Cohn, J.P. Citizen science: Can volunteers do real research? *BioScience 58*, 3 (2008), 192–197.
11. Crowston, K. and Prestopnik, N.R. Motivation and data quality in a citizen science game: A design science evaluation. *Proc. of HICSS*, (2013), 450–459.
12. Davis, P.R., Horn, M.S., and Sherin, B.L. The Right Kind of Wrong: A "Knowledge in Pieces" Approach to Science Learning in Museums. *Curator: The Museum Journal 56*, 1 (2013), 31–46.
13. Deci, E.L. and Ryan, R.M. *Intrinsic Motivation and Self-determination in Human Behavior*. Plenum Press, New York, 1985.
14. Diamond, A.M. Does Federal Funding "Crowd In" Private Funding of Science? *Contemporary Economic Policy 17*, 4 (1999), 423–431.
15. Farzan, R. and Kraut, R.E. Wikipedia classroom experiment: bidirectional benefits of students' engagement in online production communities. *Proc. of CHI*, (2013), 783–792.
16. Feder, T. Scientists Experiment with Crowdfunding. *Physics Today 66*, 4 (2013), 23–24.
17. Finholt, T.A. Collaboratories. *Annual review of information science and technology 36*, 1 (2002), 73–107.
18. Galloway, A.W., Tudor, M.T., and HAEGEN, W.M.V. The reliability of citizen science: a case study of Oregon white oak stand surveys. *Wildlife Society Bulletin 34*, 5 (2006), 1425–1429.
19. Gentner, D., Loewenstein, J., and Thompson, L. Learning and transfer: A general role for analogical encoding. *Journal of Educational Psychology 95*, 2 (2003), 393.
20. Gentner, D. The mechanisms of analogical learning. *Similarity and analogical reasoning 199*, (1989), 241.
21. Gerber, E.M. and Hui, J. Crowdfunding: Motivations and Deterrents for Participation. *ACM Transactions on Computer-Human Interaction 20*, 6 (2013), 34:1–34:32.
22. Hagstrom, W.O. *The scientific community*. Southern Illinois University Press Carbondale, 1975.
23. Hara, N., Solomon, P., Kim, S.-L., and Sonnenwald, D.H. An emerging view of scientific collaboration: scientists' perspectives on collaboration and factors that impact collaboration. *Journal of the American Society for Information Science and Technology 54*, 10 (2003), 952–965.
24. Hargadon, A. and Bechky, B. When collectives of creatives become creative collectives: A field study of problem solving at work. *Organization Science 17*, (2006), 484–500.
25. Hargadon, A. and Sutton, R.I. Technology Brokering and Innovation in a Product Development Firm. *Administrative Science Quarterly 42*, (1997), 716–749.
26. Hargittai, E. Digital Na(t)ives? Variation in Internet Skills and Uses among Members of the "Net Generation."*Sociological Inquiry 80*, 1 (2010), 92–113.
27. Hattie, J. and Timperley, H. The power of feedback. *Review of Educational Research 77*, 1 (2007), 81–112.
28. Hourihan, M. *AAAS Report XXXVIII: Research and Development FY 2014*. 2013.
29. Hui, J., Gerber, E., and Gergle, D. Understanding and Leveraging Social Networks for Crowdfunding: Opportunities and Challenges. *Proc. of DIS*, (2014).
30. Hui, J.S., Greenberg, M.D., and Gerber, E.M. Understanding the Role of Community in Crowdfunding Work. *Proc. of CSCW*, (2014), 62–74.
31. Jasklowski, O. Project people distribution (from chat). 2014.
32. Katz, J.S. and Martin, B.R. What is research collaboration? *Research policy 26*, 1 (1997), 1–18.
33. Kevles, D.J. *The physicists: The history of a scientific community in modern America*. Harvard University Press, 1995.
34. Kim, S., Mankoff, J., and Paulos, E. Sensr: evaluating a flexible framework for authoring mobile data-collection tools for citizen science. *Proc. of CSCW*, (2013), 1453–1462.
35. Kraut, R. and Resnick, P. *Building Successful Online Communities: Evidence-Based Social Design*. MIT Press, Cambridge, 2012.
36. Law, E., Dalton, C., Merrill, N., Young, A., and Gajos, K.Z. Curio: A Platform for Supporting Mixed-Expertise Crowdsourcing. *Proc. of HCOMP*, (2013).
37. Lemke, J.L. *Talking science: Language, learning, and values*. ERIC, 1990.
38. Litt, E. Measuring users' internet skills: A review of past assessments and a look toward the future. *New Media & Society 15*, 4 (2013), 612–630.
39. Mitra, T. and Gilbert, E. The language that gets people to give: Phrases that predict success on kickstarter. *Proc. of CSCW*, ACM (2014), 49–61.

40. Mollick, E.R. The Dynamics of Crowdfunding: An Exploratory Study. *Journal of Business Venturing 29*, 1 (2013), 1–16.

41. Muller, M., Geyer, W., Soule, T., Daniels, S., and Cheng, L.-T. Crowdfunding inside the enterprise: employee-initiatives for innovation and collaboration. *Proc. of CHI*, (2013), 503–512.

42. Nathan, M.J., Koedinger, K.R., and Alibali, M.W. Expert blind spot: When content knowledge eclipses pedagogical content knowledge. *Proceedings of the Third International Conference on Cognitive Science*, (2001), 644–648.

43. Nov, O., Arazy, O., Lotts, K., and Naberhaus, T. Motivation-targeted personalized UI design: a novel approach to enhancing citizen science participation. *Proc. of ECSCW*, (2013), 287–297.

44. Nowotny, H., Scott, P., and Gibbons, M. *Re-thinking science: knowledge and the public in an age of uncertainty*. SciELO Argentina, 2001.

45. Orelli, B. Biotech crowdfunding paves way for angels. *Nature Biotechnology 30*, 11 (2012), 1020–1020.

46. Peterson, I. Touring the scientific web. *Science Communication 22*, 3 (2001), 246–255.

47. Raddick, M.J., Bracey, G., Gay, P.L., et al. Galaxy zoo: Exploring the motivations of citizen science volunteers. *Astronomy Education Review 9*, 1 (2010), 010103.

48. Robson, C., Hearst, M., Kau, C., and Pierce, J. Comparing the use of social networking and traditional media channels for promoting citizen science. *Proc. of CSCW*, (2013), 1463–1468.

49. Rotman, D., Preece, J., Hammock, J., et al. Dynamic changes in motivation in collaborative citizen-science projects. *Proc. of CSCW*, (2012), 217–226.

50. Ryan, R. and Deci, E. Self-determination theory and the facilitation of intrinsic motivation, social development, and well-being. *American Psychologist, 55 55*, (2000), 68–78.

51. Sheppard, S.A. and Terveen, L. Quality is a verb: The operationalization of data quality in a citizen science community. *Proceedings of the 7th International Symposium on Wikis and Open Collaboration*, ACM (2011), 29–38.

52. Strauss, A. and Corbin, J. *Basics of Qualitative Research: Grounded Theory Procedures and Techniques*. Sage Publications, London, 1990.

53. Trench, B. Science Communication and Citizen Science: How Dead is the Deficit Model. *IX International Conference on Public Comunication of Science and Technology (PCST), Seoul, Korea*, (2006).

54. Trench, B. Internet: turning science communication inside-out? In *Bucchi, Massimiano and Trench, Brian, (eds.) Handbook of Public Communication of Science and Technology*. Routledge, London and New York, 2008.

55. Wheat, R.E., Wang, Y., Byrnes, J.E., and Ranganathan, J. Raising money for scientific research through crowdfunding. *Trends in ecology & evolution*, (2012).

56. Wiggins, A. and Crowston, K. From conservation to crowdsourcing: A typology of citizen science. *Proc. of HICSS*, (2011), 1–10.

57. Wiggins, A. Free as in puppies: compensating for ict constraints in citizen science. *Proceedings of the 2013 conference on Computer supported cooperative work*, (2013), 1469–1480.

58. Wulf, W.A. The national collaboratory–a white paper. *Towards a national collaboratory*, (1989), 17–18.

59. Dr. No Money: The Broken Science Funding System. *Scientific American*, 2011. http://www.scientificamerican.com/article/dr-no-money/.

60. Rockethub. 2011. http://www.rockethub.com/.

61. Experiment. https://experiment.com/.

62. SciFund Challenge. http://scifundchallenge.org/.

63. UCLA Spark. https://spark.ucla.edu/.

64. Benefunder. http://benefunder.org/.

65. MicroVentures. https://microventures.com.

66. Petri Dish. http://www.petridish.org/.

67. TED: Ideas worth spreading. http://www.ted.com/.

68. Merit Review Criterion: Broader Impacts. *National Science Foundation.* http://www.nsf.gov/funding/pgm_summ.jsp?pims_id=13626.

69. Launcht. http://www.launcht.com/.

70. Crowdfund MIT. https://crowdfund.mit.edu/.

Reliving the Past & Making a Harmonious Society Today: A Study of Elderly Electronic Hackers in China

Yuling Sun, Silvia Lindtner, Xianghua Ding, Tun Lu, Ning Gu
School of Computer Science, Fudan University, Shanghai 201203, China
Shanghai Key Laboratory of Data Science, Fudan University, Shanghai 201203, China
{yulingsun.lv, silvia.lindtner}@gmail.com, {dingx, lutun, ninggu}@fudan.edu.cn

ABSTRACT
This paper tells a story of DIY (do it yourself) making that does not neatly fit more familiar narratives of making: as individual empowerment, as a democratizing force, and as technoscientific innovation. Drawing on ethnographic research with a collective of elderly electronic hackers in China, we provide insights into the socio-technical and politico-economic processes of hacking and making. This paper examines how the activity of making functioned for elderly DIY enthusiasts as way of remaking and reliving the past and as a means for expressing class belonging and citizenship. We show that making and hacking is not practiced in a void independent of social, political or economic forces. Rather, making unfolds in relation to, and is contingent on, societal norms and specific techno-cultural histories. As much as hacking empowers certain people, it excludes others and functions as a site for the exercise of power and social distinction making.

Author Keywords
DIY; elders; maker; hacker; China; values; culture; communities; collectives; politics; amateur expert.

ACM Classification Keywords
H.5.m. Information interfaces and presentation (e.g., HCI): Miscellaneous.

INTRODUCTION
Imagine a tiny apartment of a large high-rise building in Shanghai: the hallways and most of its rooms are filled with stacks of old analog radios, some with their cases open and wires sticking out, while others are seemingly untouched and function as devices of nostalgia, ranging from pocket radios to Wurlitzer type play stations, many dating back to post-world-war-II Europe. Amidst the stacks of devices one finds a workstation – a table filled with boxes, wires, an oscillator next to a soldering iron and voltmeter. A little further in, in the bedroom, a self-made bedside lamp fills the stuffed room with a warm and cozy light that automatically turns on and off depending on the time of the day (see Figure 1).

Figure 1. The home of an elderly radio hacker: Repair, collecting, and custom-made appliances.

This scenario is typical of many of the home workshops of elderly electronic hackers (age 55 and older) we frequented on a regular basis as part of an ethnographic study we conducted in Shanghai, China over 1.5 years. Whether they repaired broken radios or modified an existing lamp to fit their needs, the elderly makers we worked with evidenced a familiarity with the tools and processes of "making" not dissimilar from the recent and growing academic and popular interest in DIY (do it yourself) making, hacking, tinkering, repair, customization, and so on.

In the fields of CSCW and HCI, DIY making and hacking are typically described as a multitude of creative practices including but not limited to building, repurposing and repairing artifacts without the aid of experts or professionals [18, 38]. Makers show off their creations at maker-related events such as the Maker Faire and come together at shared community spaces such as maker labs and hackerspaces. Prior work has shown that across these efforts, making has transformed from a hobbyist movement driven by geeks hacking away on the weekends into a nascent professional field that emerges in parallel to academic and industry research labs [30].

What pervades much of this prior work on making, hacking, repair and DIY culture, however, is a fairly utopian narrative [4, 38]. For instance, making is rendered as a new form of learning [23], savior of broken economies [10] and driver of innovation [9]. Often inexplicitly, DIY making is understood as something that young people do – or at least as something driven by a younger to middle-aged white collar working class society. With the notable exceptions of [19, 38], little prior work has explored sites of making that

CSCW '15, March 14 - 18, 2015, Vancouver, BC, Canada.
Copyright 2015 ACM 978-1-4503-2922-4/15/03...$15.00.
http://dx.doi.org/10.1145/2675133.2675195

do not neatly fit popular stories of making as technological progress and creative expression. Our work fills this gap by providing insights into the making practices, visions, and aspirations of a collective of elderly electronic hackers in China.

While the so-called maker movement attracts a fairly affluent class of people in their thirties and forties [41], many of its proponents invoke their parent's generation, their fathers in particular, admired for their "authentic" engagement with making – a making with one's hands that's in touch with the affordances of physical materials, tools and machines. For instance, notorious figures in the so called "maker movement" such as Chris Anderson (former editor in chief of Wired magazine, now CEO of the DIY Drone company "3DRobotics"), Dale Dougherty (founder of Make Magazine), or Eric Pan (founder and CEO of Seeed Studio) all have articulated that their work is in part motivated by the wish to return to earlier modes of technology production. While prior research has allowed us to understand more deeply the visions, motivations and practices of these members of contemporary maker culture, we know relatively little about other generations of technology enthusiasts and what motivated them. Turner and Douglas, based on historical analysis, have shown that the roots of contemporary hacker culture in the United States go back to the 1960s and 70s counterculture [40, 46]. In contrast, we explore, here, making and hacking motivated by necessity and making rather than a countercultural spirit.

What are the visions and practices of technology producers, who hack technologies out of necessity rather than out of a countercultural drive? What histories of hacking, other than those of US post-cold war technological innovation, can we trace?

In this paper, we provide an alternative story of technology production, grounded in our work with elderly electronic hackers in China, one that doesn't inherently equate making and hacking with values of individual empowerment, counterculture and democratization as heavily promoted by contemporary maker initiatives [6, 41]. For the elders we worked with, values and practices of making, hacking, tinkering with electronics and broadly adopting a DIY approach to life were rooted in childhood memories and personal histories of coming of age in China in the 1940s, 50s and 60s. During their coming of age, political slogans such as "finding a way to technology" [1] and "If you want something done right, do it yourself" [31] were common in China, encouraging people to explore technology and design by themselves. Similarly, during the period of the Cultural Revolution in the 1960s and 1970s, many educated urban youth in China were forced to move to the countryside to engage in physical labor, an experience that many of the elderly hackers we worked with shared and that significantly shaped their early encounter with and take on the role of technology in their lives. At the same time, their tinkering and hacking work was motivated by their concerns for and engagement with contemporary Chinese society.

For the purposes of this paper, we refer to their practices variously as hacking and making, by which we neither wish to connote the at times negative meaning of hacking (as in: hacking illegally into a system) nor to suggest that the elderly self-identified as members of the contemporary maker movement as in Make magazine's use of the term. When we speak of our interlocutors as hackers, makers or DIY enthusiasts, we wish to highlight their commitment to principles of reuse and resourcefulness, a deep material engagement with electronic devices, and tinkering and play with electronics. These values and practices are not dissimilar from self-identified makers and hackers today.

Terms like 'hacking' and 'making' are often used interchangeably, although some associate a commercial interest with the term making [32]. Our own prior research as well as an emerging body of literature on these activities has shown that terms like hacking and making vary depending on the context in which they are invoked [26, 30, 32]. For instance, the term 'making' might be used to promote one's work to a wider audience, such as schools and governments, while 'hacking' often connotes a commitment to produce technology by opening up and building on top of pre-existing devices and artifacts rather than building from scratch. Often, both terms are used interchangeably. While some individuals identify more strongly with one or the other label (hacker or maker), there is no unified agreement of what counts as making but not as hacking and vice versa.

Our goal, here, then is to take seriously the kinds of hacking, making, tinkering, and repair work that the elderly perform and that unfold in parallel to and largely unnoticed by more popular self-identified makers and hackers. Throughout the paper, we shed light on the confluence of the technological, social and historical dimensions of hacking. We will explore the following three questions: What motivates elderly individuals to tinker with, make, hack, repair, and open up technology? How do their practices differ and/or relate to the global maker movement? What is the relationship between elders' electronic hacking projects and contemporary social and technological transformations in China?

This paper contributes to prior work on DIY, hacking, repair, and making in CSCW and adjacent field, in three specific ways. First, this research demonstrates that making practices are multiple, rooted in people's specific social, historical, and economic backdrops. In other words, our research demonstrates that making and hacking practices are imbued with meaning that is socially, historically and culturally situated. Just as visions of a contemporary maker movement in the United States are rooted in a growing interest in revitalizing the American economy and bring back the "made in America" brand [30], making, hacking, repair, and DIY practices of Chinese elders are tied to specific social and economic concerns unique to China. Second, we show that making and hacking in elderly populations is not necessarily disassociated from the digital. Instead, digital artifacts were front and center in the making and hacking activities of the elderly population that we studied. For example, participants in our fieldsites set up their own web forums to facilitate the emergence of a larger collective of like-minded electronic hackers. Thus, this research demonstrates that making and hacking in an elderly population does not exist outside or independent of information technology and software programming as is commonly expected of this population, but is instead deeply rooted and sustained through digital practices. Third and finally, we argue that CSCW researchers and practitioners must engage deeply and critically with contemporary promotions of making and hacking as a democratizing force and site of individual empowerment [34]. As much as hacking empowers certain people, it simultaneously excludes others and can function as a site through which social distinctions of class are enacted, playing into broader socio-cultural and socio-economic power dynamics.

In what follows, we first present a brief literature review of prior work on making, DIY, hacking and tinkering, followed by a detailed account of our research methods. We then present our main findings, with a particular focus on making practices as a site of collective social identity, memory practice, and engagement with the Chinese nation and society. We found that the motivation for elder making practices stems from their engagement with aspects of their childhood and coming of age, self-reflection and identity making practices, as well as China's modernization processes, politico-economic context. As we will show in this paper, the elders strongly believed that their hacking practice helps improve contemporary society and well being in China. Finally, in the discussion, we lay out the contributions of this work to CSCW by analyzing in depth the socio-cultural, socio-economic, technological and infrastructural aspects of making. We demonstrate how elderly hackers came together as a larger collective through their shared passion in electronic hacking and through their online communication practices.

RELATED WORK

DIY making practices have been broadly studied in CSCW, HCI, and related fields over the last decade. This scholarship revels that many who identify with making, hacking, and DIY activities and movements more broadly are committed to resourcefulness, creativity, and a desire to build their own tools and devices rather than accepting those provided to consumers by large corporations. Across prior work, DIY, making, and hacking have been analyzed as a site of novel forms of engagement with diverse materials [8, 39] and community formation around lay expertise and open sharing [24, 25]. Diverse making practices have been explored, including dissembling [37], repairing [38], and the Chinese open manufacturing culture *shanzhai* [27]. Researchers have highlighted the social and technological impact of making on design [24, 44, 45], education [12, 23], and well as entrepreneurship [10]. Kolko *et al.* [23], for instance, stress the educational value of hands-on and interdisciplinary engagement provided by making practices. Similarly, Tanenbaum *et al.* [43] describe these activities as a form of *democratizing technology*, focusing on the playfulness, utility and expressiveness in DIY making practice. It is important not to undervalue the quality and impact of artifacts produced via these modes of production. Past work has shown that technologies and products produced by DIY makers are often similar or even competitive to professional designers and research labs, particularly in fields such as open source 3D printing [17] and robotics [11].

While much of the early work on making and hacking has focused on its impact on education, the economy, and innovation, more recently a body of critical scholarship has emerged [4, 38, 41, 54]. This work has highlighted how making and hacking cultures, despite their narratives of open-ness and inclusiveness, are often exclusive in practice. For instance, participation of women and other minority populations remains low [38, 41, 54]. In addition, the increasing participation of corporations, venture capitalists and governments, has begun to shape making and hacking collectives, increasingly giving such institutions external to the maker community large sway over access to tools and other resources [26]. As a point of example, take the sponsorship of Maker Faires by companies and organizations such as Intel, Ford, Disney, and DARPA, to name just a few.

Our approach in the research presented here is aligned with the growing body of work that draws attention to sites of making outside of hackerspaces, Maker Faires, and other fairly recent and popular avenues of making and tinkering. In this paper, we explore an idiosyncratic site of hacking and making, elderly hacking cultures, to help us understand making and hacking practices in new ways. In particular, we build on prior work by [4, 16, 19, 38] that has begun to draw attention to the kinds of making and hacking practices usually rendered invisible to stories of technological progress and innovation. Jackson et al. for instance, highlight, that practices such as maintenance and repair are to a large extent "rendered invisible under our normal modes of picturing and theorizing technology" and are marginal activities to "a Western and productivist imagination" [18]. At the same time, as [38] demonstrate, repair and maintenance have also become the site of first-world intervention in the Global South, rooted in an idealization of repair promoted as site of empowerment and sustainability amidst a culture of planned obsolescence and passive consumption. Studies such as [38] on the one laptop per child program in South America found that repair work is branded as a solution to localizing technology and educating underprivileged populations about technology. Specifics of local contingencies such as shortages of resources as well as pre-existing repair and making cultures are rarely taken into account.

Building on this prior work, we wish to draw attention to practices of repairing, fixing, hacking, collecting, and redesigning of existing or even outdated technology. Although the elders in our study aligned in their values of sustainability and resourcefulness with a broader innovation and creativity discourse, their work remained invisible to the sources of funding that enable projects such One Laptop Per Child [51] or hackerspaces as innovation houses [30]. We also extend from this prior research by tracing historical roots of contemporary hacking and making practices other than more familiar stories of US counterculture and IT innovation. Repairing, reusing and redesigning of old and malfunctioning technologies was a common virtue the Chinese government heavily promoted in the 1950s, 60s, and 70s. For the elders we worked with, a DIY approach towards life and technology production, hence, provides a site not just for material production but also a means to relate to the past and to make sense of contemporary social and technological transformations in China. Thus, this case study of elderly electronic hackers gives a glimpse into a much larger technological and cultural practice of making-do and DIY out of necessity that shapes Chinese society and economy from the past through present-day [15, 26]. Members of China's contemporary hackerspace and maker culture, for instance, invoke China's unique history of technology production, making-do and manufacturing as a form of "hacking with Chinese characteristics [26]. By tracing some of these alternative histories of making and hacking and the experiences of those who have lived through them, we hope to avoid mapping onto our fieldsites in China a global narrative of hacker and DIY maker culture that inevitably equates it – as common in both popular journalism and academic scholarship – with the history of the US counterculture movement.

RESEARCH SITES AND METHODS

We draw from long-term ethnographic research conducted over 1.5 years, spanning both online and offline sites traversed by elderly electronic hackers in China. We employed a range of qualitative methods, including semi-structure interviews, participant-observations of online and offline gatherings and at home workshops and studios. Our research began when we came across a series of online forums populated by a collective of passionate radio hackers. These included: 1) the "Radio Forum;" founded in the 1990s, it has today more than three hundred thousand users and is also known as the "worldwide group of Chinese radio network amateurs." 2) The "New World Wireless Forum;" founded in 2007, it has over three thousand users, whose majority are elderly electronic hackers from Shanghai. 3) The "Crystal Radio Forum;" founded in 2000, it has around 186 thousand users and draws in specifically those who hack and repurpose old electronics and radios. These three forums provided platforms for people to show off their creations, communicate with others about collecting and repair work, provide advice for others or receive answers to technical questions, and so forth.

By engaging with the members of these forums, the first author, a native Mandarin speaker, began to establish rapport with the founders and organizers of the websites, subsequently being invited to a series of offline gatherings and events. Throughout our ethnographic research, we interacted and observed more than 100 elderly electronic hackers. Over time, we began following more closely the work of 22 hackers, including, for instance, radio hackers, radio collectors, the software developer of the "Radio Forum," the organizers and participants in a regular offline gathering, and the employees of TECSUN Co. Ltd., a factory that manufactures radio network infrastructures in China.

Our 22 interlocutors were all male, with their age ranging from 46-78. 18 were more than 57 years old and 15 had already retired. They had worked/were working in a range of occupations including academia, education, civil service, journalism, management, as factory workers and service staff. Their educational backgrounds were diverse: while some had only primary school training others had university degrees.

All but two of our participants interacted with us regularly face-to-face in their homes, in their home studios, or in coffee houses. This format worked well for our study as it allowed us to observe first hand their technology productions, the materials and websites they used for repair work and hacking. They also shared with us the images and videos they had produced about their work over the last years. We conducted a series of semi-structured interviews, where we asked details about how they had first begin working with electronics, the specifics of their practice, tools and technologies they produced, as well as the kinds of online resources they relied upon. All interviews were conducted in Mandarin Chinese and later transcribed into Chinese and English for open and axial coding.

In addition to interviews and participant observation online and offline, we also followed two groups that had formed on Chinese instant message clients, focused on DIY making and radio hacking. We attended a series of informal meetings and offline gatherings: we hung out regularly at four elderly home studios, following their journeys to local electronics markets and TECSUN Co. Ltd., as well as their visits to the Xinghai Radio Network Museum (a museum about the history of radios, founded in 2012 by one of our interlocutors). Throughout our research, we used a grounded theory approach [42] to conduct analysis as we collected data. As themes began to emerge, we iteratively posed more questions around these themes in subsequent interviews and focus groups. When themes began to repeat themselves, we stopped the data collection process. The quotes used in this paper were translated from Chinese into

English by the first author, with the support by the second author. All of the names used are pseudonyms.

FINDINGS

It was common amongst our interlocutors to work with a diverse set of materials including but not limited to electronics, wood, plastic, and more. A central focus of production that many shared was the making of electronic equipment, crystal radios and television sets in particular. Many had begun to develop a passion for these technologies during their adolescence, when they often lacked access and financial means to these technologies. In what follows, we demonstrate how the elders' contemporary hacking and making practices are deeply rooted in their personal experiences of coming of age during a politico-economic climate of local shortages, political promotions of resourcefulness and a making-do mentality.

Histories of National DIY

In the 1950s, the Chinese government began promote what one might describe as a technoscientific maker ethos. A series of political slogans such as "finding a way to technology (向科技进军)" [1] and "if you want something done right, do it yourself (自己动手 丰衣足食)" [31] had become increasingly common. Across political discourse and economic reforms, technology was promoted as the crucial path to improve the strength and independence of the Chinese nation state.

Within this specific historical political climate, citizens were encouraged to build and implement their own technologies. Many of our interlocutors expressed that these political interventions had a strong influence on them. Childhood dreams of becoming a scientist or engineer were common. They had learned, early on, that their participation in the production of electronic technology was considered essential in furthering the economic development and independence of the Chinese nation state. During the periods of the Cultural Revolution in the 1960s and 70s, many urban youth were required to move to the countryside and make a living off of physical labor. Political propaganda during this time actively encouraged citizens to be self-reliant and to make and produce their own machines, infrastructures and resources needed for daily life and work. In addition, a pervasive lack of basic resources, brought with it a certain do it yourself mentality (or 自力更生 in Chinese), a hacking out of necessity or making-do, which – as our interlocutors told us – was understood as central in instilling a sense of individual and collective well-being. All of this, ranging from the political promotions of self-reliance to the lack of resources, had significantly impacted the elders' coming of age. Making and hacking of electronics was simultaneously source of income, site of socializing, and political propaganda.

Promotions of this DIY ethos remained, in altered form, also after the Cultural Revolution. Deng Xiaoping's economic reforms of opening up in the 1970s and 80s, for instance, were ripe with promotions of a making-do mentality aimed at developing a scientific and technological force. Chinese citizens were encouraged to acquire technical ingenuity and a basic understanding of a variety of technological artifacts including but not limited to sound equipment, television, audio amplifiers, circuit structures and factory machineries.

Take 59-year old hacker Fang, for instance, whose knowledge in electronics had helped him get a significant promotion in his job. He was working at a famous landmark hotel in Shanghai at that time, and had noticed that an unusually high percentage of light bulbs burned out every month. He began to investigate the cause and redesigned the hotel's electronic circuitry, which not only reduced the overall power consumption of the hotel by 5%, but also – in his words *"greatly improved the customer experience!"* And, he proudly continued: "*on top of it, because of the improvements I made, I got a promotion at work.*"

Many of the other elderly hackers, similar to Fang, had made a living off of their ingenuity of working with materials, tools and electronics. After retirement, they continued to make and fix electronics, but as retirees began to think of it more as a "lifestyle" choice and as something they did "just for fun". While DIY making continued to be a predominant mode of living, it had turned into a leisure activity and a way of connecting to other like-minded elderly. Some made their own home appliances or electronic devices, which they preferred over purchasing the latest state-of-the-art products.

Although many told us with pride about their accomplishments, regardless of whether it was a materials-based solution to a problem encountered in a former job or a novel repair created in their homes, they distinguished their work from contemporary promotions of technological innovation. 52-year old Dan, for instance, who owns a home workshop, emphasized that the kinds of making practices he and his elderly peers conducted was different from the ways in which technology innovation is typically promoted in mainstream culture in China. He further elaborated that his work was not focused on a particular end goal, but on playfulness and tinkering: *Our form of DIY, from circuit board design to packaging, every process is designed based on how we like it. These DIY objects are treasures to me. I often buy old components from the flea markets, and then play with them. Making is a spiritual practice. I usually communicate about what I make with my peers, with other elders, and design with them, together. The whole process makes me happy and fulfilled."*

Tinkering with elctronics, here, functioned as a means to socialize with other like-minded peers and provided a sense of fulfillment. Others in our study reflected that their engagement with electronics today granted them the fulfillment of an old *"childhood dream."* Many agreed it constituted a particular *"lifestyle"* that they shared with people of the same age, or even a *"valuable art."* To hack, remake, and repair old electronics, practices reminiscent of their coming of age, provided satisfaction, happiness, a sense of accomplishment and pride. Jin, 64, explained to us that the satisfaction he felt was *"not about the end result of having a physical artifact, but about every part of the process of making it."* A particular prominent device that embodied this sense of reliving an old childhood dream was the 2P3 radio, a DIY radio kit that was sold in the 1950s and 60s to schools and individual households that could afford it. The kit contained the plastic casing of a portable pocket radio as well as the schematics of the electronic circuitry and components needed to make your own (see figure 2).

As children, only a few of the elderly could afford the components that went into building the radio. And so many shared a mutual passion to rebuild today the device that they had so much aspired during their coming of age. Many conducted weeks of tedious search for original components at electronic and flea markets throughout the city as well as online. Others began to design new features and add-ons to the old 2P3 radio, which – once accomplished – they showed off during the frequent offline gatherings. Hacking of electronics, here, functioned as a way to re-engage with and relive a particular aspect of the past, which we will examine in more detail next.

Figure 2. The image of the 2P3 radio, the schematics and the rebuilt version

Hacking as Memory Practice

A hacker ethos and DIY approach to technology production is often envisioned as a way to challenge passive models of consumption and produce alternative and potentially more resourceful technological innovations [30, 33, 52]. In contrast, for the elderly electronic hackers, making functioned less as a way to promote or imagine an alternative technological future, but as a memory practice aimed at making and remaking both China's past and present [7]. For instance, what many in our study shared was the passion to repair and rework old and outdated technology including components such as electronic tubes, power amplifiers, transistors, and so on. To deeply understand and bring back to life what was old and discarded was considered in and of itself a valuable endeavor. The old was not something to overcome, but something to remobilize today.

A particular emphasis was put on preserving technologies of the past, including collecting, reusing and repairing electronic materials and equipment. For example, most of our interlocutors had accumulated a large variety of diverse materials through scavenging surplus stores and flea markets and exchanging components and tools with peers. For many, these practices of collecting and reusing old discarded materials were articulated as a crucial way to "save" and record China's history of technological development for the younger generations. Yu, for instance, had amassed an extensive collection of original electronics components, which he used to re-create exact copies of classic radio brands. He also improved and redesigned some of these devices into new and more advanced versions. Here, reuse, copy and redesign together constituted the means to both relive and remake the past.

Yu, and many others, expressed a concern that with the contemporary focus on "newness" important aspects of the past would be lost: *"Technology is becoming more developed today, and these old things will be eliminated. Young people in China, they like new things, and don't care about these old things anymore. But for us, these old technologies are the most precious. I am very happy when I repair a classic radio. Of course, I know of high-end technology brands such as iPhone and iPad. I have them, but I rarely use them. They can be bought at any time and any place. But this old art of DIY making, people forget how to do it, and don't know how to do anymore."*

Many believed that this "old art of DIY making" was worth preserving as it functioned as a lens into China's cultural heritage and history. Gang, 67, the founder and organizer of the "New World Wireless Forum", told us, *"We are all amateurs. What we do can't be compared to professional engineers. But nevertheless, you can learn about China's history, culture, custom and even national characteristics from our DIY practice"*. Zhang, 72, a well-known radio collector in Shanghai, spent most of his retirement income to collect and repair classical radios from both China and abroad. He frequently invited visitors to his home to show off his collections and self-made creations. He dreams to have his collection featured in a museum with the goal to preserve, as he put it, a precious part of history: "*Once, a person wanted to use 5 million RMB* [Chinese renminbi – Chinese currency] *to buy my radios, but I refused. I want to denote my collection to our country and use it to remember and preserves this history, and let more people know, this is the Chinese radio culture and our technological history.*"

Some indeed managed to receive significant attention of their physical collections and creations, being reported in local media and news magazines [2, 3]. Others shared things online, including their creations, materials and step-by-step instructions. Yet others produced carefully crafted video records of their own repair and remake practices, many of which functioned as how-to tutorials, and shared them on Chinese video sharing platforms such as Youku and Tudou. Sharing practices were aimed at connecting to other like-minded collectors and hackers, but also at promoting an aspect of China's techno-cultural past and preserve it for future generations.

Taken together, what see here is how making, hacking, reuse, and repair functioned as a site of constructing a techno-cultural national and cultural identity for China by remembering a particular aspect of the past: a commitment to DIY making, resourcefulness and reuse, which many considered crucial for China's further development, however also feared being increasingly lost.

Building Your Own Smart Home: Mundane Forms of Innovation

Many believed that a commitment to reuse and resourcefulness was increasingly rare. What had become the norm, they elaborated, was conspicuous consumption and a loss of China's culture and tradition of sustainable living. A DIY approach had been an essential tactic of survival during their coming of age, but was something that young people today did not need or care about. While many of our interlocutors did not think of themselves as innovators, their attitudes and practices reflected many facets of contemporary maker and hackerspace culture. For instance, many elders believed that making was a site of empowerment and that one could only truly "own" technology if it was hacked and made by themselves: *"the iPhone or iPad, and the likes, are all designed for you by others. Those are really nice, but you don't own this technology."*

Many also built technological solutions quite similar to those currently promoted as the next generation of Internet enabled devices such as smart home applications. Take, for instance, Fang, who began to advance his own home with ubiquitous smart technology after he retired about 5 years ago (see figure 3). His apartment is enhanced with a series of add-ons and electronic improvements, which he described as follows: *"when we grew up, we shared an interest and ability in designing everything by ourselves. This is something that we are proud of. Take, for instance, my apartment. I designed the whole place by myself. A person who is into DIY can really apply this knowledge to every aspect of daily life. For instance, I design crystal radios as well as my apartment and repair all my household appliances."* Fang's approach to creating a smart home was focused predominantly on making small improvements – mundane forms of ingenuity aimed at improving his day-to-day living situation. For instance, he enhanced a bedside lamp with a sensor that replaced the standard switch and turned the light on and off based on motion and touch. For elders like him, he explained to us, the standard on-and-off switch was too small and not user friendly. He also added a safety light to his bathroom that automatically turned on and off based on people entering and leaving the room. He showed us how he had further improved an energy-saving light and redesigned a music player (see Figure 3).

While Fang did not attempt to turn his creations into actual products, some of the other elders had filed patents for their

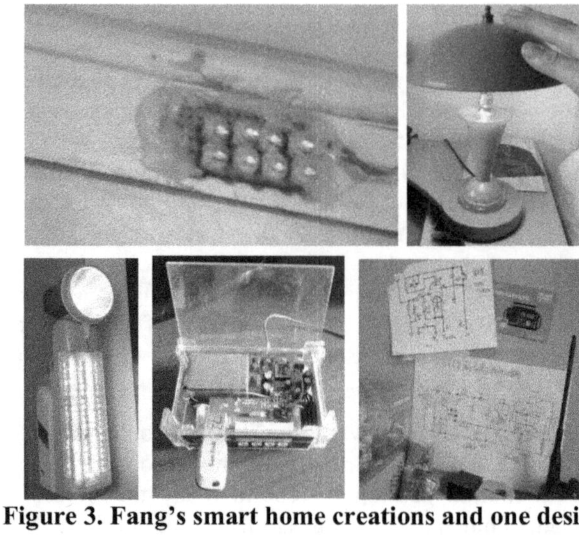

Figure 3. Fang's smart home creations and one design drawing

inventions (see Figure 4) or even published articles and books on the topic [48, 49]. Regardless of whether or not their hobbyist practice was specifically aimed at the advancement of scientific knowledge, all of the elders understood their creations as unique contributions to Chinese society. They strongly believed that their DIY practices made them members of a collective of elders that constituted a productive force in society, which many emphasized was of particular importance as they transitioned into retirement. In the next section, we will discuss in greater detail how making and hacking gave elders a sense of contributing back to society and to the nation's future development.

Collective Identity Practice: "We are a High-quality Population"

Many of our interlocutors thought of themselves as members of a larger collective, who shared a cultural mindset, upbringing, and approach towards life, technology, and society. A sense of collective identity was continuously reinforced through both online and offline interaction. By collective, here, we refer to prior work from media studies that has demonstrated how people, who do not necessarily personally know one another, identify as members of a larger like-minded collective [29, 47, 50]. Prior work has examined how the *use and consumption* of analog media such as newspapers [50] and digital media [47] can forge the formation of larger collectives. Here, we focus on the ways in which the *production* of technological artifacts can also function as site of cultural production and collective

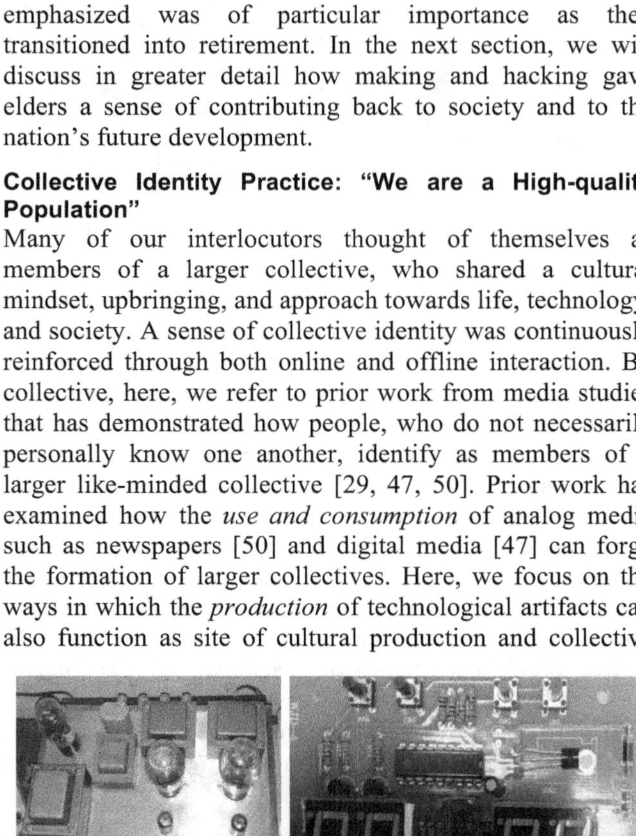

Figure 4. Dian's patented products

identity formation.

Across our interactions and conversations, many agreed that they belonged to a population of *"higher quality.*" They believed that those with technological skills were of a "*social elite*," contributing to China's social and economic development. They emphasized that people "like them" would not be driven to hack out of economic interest or to make a huge profit, but out of curiosity and a genuine interest for the inner workings of technology. Amongst their peers, they openly shared designs, sources, and schematics of the kinds of devices they made. This was something, they agreed, not everyone would readily do, but only people of a *"certain personality"* would practice. Reputation and social recognition by others were central aspects.

Many believed that DIY making was particularly apt to help bond people and allow them to develop trust to one another, something many considered very difficult and rare in China. Many told us that prior to their engagement with the online radio and electronics community, they had often felt isolated. Few had stayed in touch with acquaintances from work and expressed that generally they believed it was hard to trust and build friendships to strangers in China, or as Liu emphasized: *"The radio group is very important for me. You know, having a sincere friend is very hard to find in this society."* The founder of the online Radio Forum, similarly, told us that his main motivation for setting up an online platform for passionate radio hackers was less so driven by his technological interest, but by the goal to connect to other like-minded people.

Some also began collaborations with the aforementioned TECSUN Company, testing its products and improving electronic equipment. We interviewed an employee at TECSUN, who expressed how much his company valued the collective of elders: "*Communication with this group of elderly is very useful to our company. When we design a new radio, their suggestions and user experience tests are helpful for us to improve our product. We usually ask them for advice in the form of questionnaire or through the online forum.*"

Many shared the belief that these online sharing practices did not only provide people with personal fulfillment and important social connections at an older age, but could also improve society as a whole. They distinguished their work in particular from other elders, who would spend their time playing games, drinking, and watching TV, activities which they regarded as harmful to the healthy and harmonious development of Chinese society. In contrast, DIY making, they argued, was a *healthy* activity and *valuable* to society that could improve people's well-being and social stability. Take for instance 59-year old Chang, the organizer of the online Radio Network community, when he argued that: "*DIY making is very healthy for elderly people. We get to meet many people through this. We are not alone. We are high quality people, in comparison with others who like to smoke and drink. DIY making gives us something to do and can avoid that elders become a burden for society. I believe that we are helpful to social stability and harmony."*

These notions of a quality workforce and its connections to social harmony, as anthropologist Aihwa Ong [35] observed, are laden with meaning. As a narrative of Chinese modernity, the notion of harmonious society gained force under Deng Xiaoping, being promoted as a moral force. The notion has been used ever since to justify a series of regulatory measurements, including Internet censorship, promoted as the necessary means to avoid Internet addiction and "unhealthy" development of China's youth [28]. This notion of constructing a harmonious and healthy Chinese society is taken up by the elders and applied to their DIY making practices. DIY making and hacking becomes a marker of social status and class, rendering people engaged in electronic reuse, repair and production as socially distinct.

Open Source Sharing: the Role of Software & Hardware

All of our interlocutors were involved in both online and offline collaborative practices. Online practices included the sourcing of components (*e.g.* on Taobao or eBay), but also the sharing of how-to instructions, self-made devices, repair work as well as news articles, general advice and writings (e.g. on forums and social networking sites). People also networked offline, for instance, during their tours of flea and electronic markets in the search for components and materials, offline gatherings, and group visits to local museums. Friendships were fostered across both offline and online interactions, constituting together a peer-based open source environment that enabled collaborative tinkering and knowledge exchange.

Over time, these interactions lead to the exchange of information beyond engagement with electronics. The elderly shared worries about their families and children, politics as well as age-related concerns. Many emphasized that the collective was unique, because it was made of people who were committed to life-long learning, or as one person once posted online: *"we are never too old to learn."* DIY making was considered a particularly effective way to learn, because it required knowledge exchange and collaboration. The elderly, so to say, were producers of their own smart homes and learning platforms. They installed software systems, retrieved information online, created and edited digital photos and videos, shopped online, and set up web services. Reflecting on these practices, they often told us humorously us that their drive for learning came from peer pressure, accompanied by a practice of exchanging favors and support.

We would like to emphasize, here, is the central role that software plays in making and hacking practices. Maker culture is often celebrated for its return to an engagement with physical materials, often thought of as more authentic and intuitive than an engagement with software code and digital materials. However, making and hacking practices are often contingent on the writing of software code (*e.g.* to program the system that runs on a chip or microntroller platform) and the use of online platforms (*e.g.* online repositories and file sharing platforms). Although our interlocutors did not write software for their electronic hacks, they did for the set up of online platforms and forums, crucial to the social organization of their hacking and sharing work.

DISCUSSION

Through our ethnographic research with elderly electronic hackers in China, we have drawn attention to the contingent aspects of making and hacking. We have shown that a deep engagement with technology production is not limited to the value systems, techniques and platforms of those who promote a contemporary maker movement rooted in US Internet counterculture. We have shed light on the particulars of a culture of technology producers, whose work is entangled with histories of production, cultural and socio-economic development in China. We have also shown how the elders' commitment to re-use of old and discarded technologies was wrapped up in a much larger politico-economic project dating back to periods of the Cultural Revolution that promoted self-reliance and resourcefulness as a virtue for Chinese citizens.

While electronic hacking constituted a site of open collaboration, individual fulfillment and social networking, it simultaneously functioned as a site of distinction making, whilst peers not engaged in technology production were rendered of lower quality and as contributing less to the healthy and harmonious development of Chinese society. In what follows, we discuss in more detail these sociotechnical and politico-economic processes of hacking we observed. Hacking is by no means void of politics or a practice that is inherently outside of or removed from wider systems of power. We also discuss the importance of understanding contemporary making and hacking cultures in relation to local histories of making. We believe that these findings have important implications for how CSCW approaches questions of making, hacking, tinkering, and materiality.

Histories of Hacking

We have demonstrated in this paper that making cultures are rooted in specific local histories of techno-cultural, political and economic processes. Making and hacking is often thought of as a global practice that spans across and connects geeks across multiple regions [20]. Recently, the vision of a rising global maker movement has instilled a particular kind of imaginary of what counts as hacking, DIY and making and who counts as a maker or hacker. For instance, the hacking of electronics, and the hacking of radio technology in particular, is often associated with a countercultural ethos, *i.e.* a commitment to the creation and spread of information that challenges top-down state broadcasting media. When people promote hacking and making today, they often invoke earlier generations of tinkers. Think, for instance, of how radio hackers such as the "Hams," as Kristen Haring [14] documents so well, figure in a wider public imaginary about technological ingenuity and creative expression.

We have documented, in this paper, the values and practices of a hacking culture that emerged independently from better-known stories of open-source geeks, countercultural hackers and hardware enthusiasts in the West. In doing so, we have also shown how making and hacking proliferates beyond familiar sites of technology production. At the same time, we have demonstrated that making and hacking, counter to a common rhetoric of empowerment, inclusivity and open-ness, is an exclusive practice and site of distinction making. For our interlocutors, repairing of old radios and tinkering with electronics was a means to position themselves as a productive force in contemporary Chinese society. Hacking, here, was the site to express and enact citizenship that rested on one's social *and* technological abilities.

In this sense, hacking for our interlocutors was a site of empowerment in low-resource workplaces situated in a specific political and cultural moment of Chinese history. Thus, hacking has figured prominently into their understanding of their individual worth over the life course, and this sense of technologically-based self worth remains after retirement. Further, through their hacking practices, the elders in our study found a like-minded collective of peers, enabling them to discuss personal concerns and worries and reflect on ongoing changes in Chinese society and the economy. They did not think of themselves as isolated from society nor did they think of themselves as weak or in need of new technologies. On the contrary, they strongly believed that their DIY approach towards technology production and life more broadly has value to society. Their hacking, repair and making practices were oriented in parts towards sustaining a particular aspect of Chinese history and Chinese cultural tradition – a DIY ethos that they experienced as central to Chinese society during their coming of age.

CSCW researchers have long been concerned with the interweaving of technological and social processes. They have shown that technologies are neither fixed in a particular point in time nor isolated from the people, who develop, use, and shape technology, *e.g.* [13, 21, 22, 36]. Our study of the social, historical, and technological processes of DIY hacking and making contributes to this sociotechnical systems research. What we would like to emphasize, here, in particular is the importance of engaging with historical processes of design and technology production. Thus, we wish to re-open the question of sociotechnical systems by investigating how the social and technological come together with regards to people's varying social and economic positions over time. Technologies, their use and their design, are contingent on specific historical moments and processes. Individual life stories, memories and experiences are wrapped up in these technological changes over time, and impact technology production and use today. As we have shown in this paper, hacking and repairing constituted for the elders an act of reliving and re-evaluating their past as Chinese tradition. Further, the elders used hacking and making to urge others, particularly younger generations, to take participation in a shared cultural heritage seriously as a virtue. Technology production, here, is not only socially and culturally contingent, but tied up with deeply personal and emotional re-engagements with the past.

Politics of Making

Those who promote the rise of a contemporary maker movement often portray making as a democratizing force and site of individual empowerment amidst a pervasive passive consumer culture and corporate control [5]. These values of individual empowerment are inscribed into the technologies produced: for instance, open source hardware kits are designed to help proliferate making and hacking and enable many to design their own systems.

With the notable exceptions of [4, 18, 38], there is little reflective engagement amongst practitioners and scholars, who promote making and hacking as a new educational or economic force, with the kinds of values and ideologies they themselves inscribe in the products or open hardware solutions they design. In this paper, we have shown that hacking and making has politics – today as much as in the past. A multitude of stakeholders, ranging from technology producers such as the elderly electronic hackers we worked with, all the way to governments and corporations, all meddle with and shape infrastructures of technology production. Beyond the immediate confines of our fieldsite, prior research has shown that making and hacking has drawn significant attention and investment from governments (e.g. both the US and China) as well as corporations such as Intel and Foxconn [26]. As researchers and designers of technological systems, we have to consider these many other players involved in designing and shaping technologies, their value systems and agendas.

Winner [53] once argued that technologies are deeply interwoven in the conditions of modern politics, shaping and being shaped by the exercise of power and the experience of citizenship. Our research draws attention specifically to how processes of technology production – not just things but the *making of things* – are expressions of citizenship, power and class. DIY making and hacking, as such, is neither solely a democratizing force [43] in and of itself, nor is it necessarily a site of (democratized) individual empowerment [34]. Rather, as much as it empowers certain people, hacking and making also functions as a practice of exclusion, a site through which power is exercised via enactment and preservation of social-cultural and socio-economic class distinctions.

CONCLUSION

As practices of making and hacking receive increasing interest from scholars, politicians, investors, and corporations alike, it becomes increasingly important to understand cultures of making in practice. In this paper, we report findings from ethnographic research with elderly electronic hackers in China. We document their motivations, aspirations and technological creations, with a particular focus on the historical and politico-economic processes that shaped their work. The paper challenges more common narratives of making as a global democratizing force and site of individual empowerment across regions, socio-economic class, gender, and so on. We ground our investigation in an analysis of the history and politics of DIY in China, relating our ethnographic findings to historical and discourse analysis. We also draw from prior work in media studies in order to show how hacking emerged as a productive force for the elderly we worked with, enabling them to exercise social status, trust and collective identity. We end the paper with a call for CSCW practitioners and researchers to ground future work on making and hacking in a deep engagement with both the histories and politics of making.

ACKNOWLEDGMENTS

We thank all our participants and collaborators in this research. We also thank Katie Pine, David Li, Anna Greenspan, and Paul Dourish for their valuable input and feedback. The research is supported in part by the National Natural Science Foundation of China (NSFC) under the awards 61332008, 61272533 and 61300201, Shanghai Science & Technology Committee Project under the award 13ZR1401900, the US National Science Foundation under the award 1321065, and the ISTC-Social (Intel Science and Technology Center for Social Computing).

REFERENCES

1. New China's scientific & technological achievements. http://scitech.people.com.cn/GB/10143296.html.
2. The story of Radio King. http://news.xinhuanet.com/collection/2004-09/02/content_1937483.htm.
3. Minglv Zhang: the sound of classic radio. http://fashion.ifeng.com/news/detail_2012_11/19/19288296_0.shtml.
4. Ame, M., Bardzell, J., Bardzell, S., Lindtner, S., Mellis, D. and Rosner, D. Making Cultures: Empowerment, Participation, and Democracy - or Not? *In Proc. Panel at CHI 2014*, ACM Press (2014).
5. Anderson, C. *Makers: the new industrial revolution*. Random House, 2012.
6. Bardzell, J., Bardzell, S. and Toombs, A. "now that's definitely a proper hack": self-made tools in hackerspaces. *In Proc. the 32nd annual ACM conference on Human factors in computing systems (CHI 2014)*, ACM Press (2014), 473-476.
7. Bowker, G.C. *Memory practices in the sciences*. MIT Press Cambridge, MA, 2005.
8. Buechley, L. and Perner-Wilson, H. Crafting technology: Reimagining the processes, materials, and cultures of electronics. *ACM Transactions on Computer-Human*

Interaction (TOCHI) 19, 3 (2012), 21.

9. Buechley, L., Rosner, D.K., Paulos, E. and Williams, A. DIY for CHI: methods, communities, and values of reuse and customization. *In Proc. CHI Extended Abstracts on Human Factors in Computing Systems* (2009), 4823-4826.
10. Cervantes, R. and Nardi, B. Building a Mexican startup culture over the weekends. *In Proc. the 4th international conference on Intercultural Collaboration*, ACM Press (2012), 11-20.
11. Drury, J.L., Scholtz, J. and Yanco, H.A. Awareness in human-robot interactions. *In Proc. IEEE International Conference on Systems, Man and Cybernetics* (2003), 912-918.
12. Eisenberg, M. Pervasive fabrication: Making construction ubiquitous in education. *In Proc. Fifth Annual IEEE International Conference onPervasive Computing and Communications Workshops (PerCom Workshops 2007)*, 193-198.
13. Grudin, J. Why CSCW applications fail: problems in the design and evaluationof organizational interfaces. *In Proc. the 1988 ACM conference on Computer-supported cooperative work (CSCW 1988)*, ACM Press (1988), 85-93.
14. Haring, K. *Ham radio's technical culture*. MIT Press, 2007.
15. Ho, J. Shanzhai: Economic/Cultural Production through the Cracks of Globalization. Crossroads: Cultural Studies Conference (2010).
16. Houston, L. Inventive Infrastructure: An Exploration of Mobile Phone, *Lancaster University*, 2014.
17. Hudson, S.E. Printing teddy bears: a technique for 3D printing of soft interactive objects. *In Proc. the 32nd annual ACM conference on Human factors in computing systems (CHI 2014)*, ACM Press (2014), 459-468.
18. Jackson, S.J. and Kang, L. Breakdown, obsolescence and reuse: HCI and the art of repair. *In Proc. the 32nd annual ACM conference on Human factors in computing systems (CHI 2014)*, ACM Press (2014), 449-458.
19. Jackson, S.J., Pompe, A. and Krieshok, G. Repair worlds: maintenance, repair, and ICT for development in rural Namibia. *In Proc. the ACM 2012 conference on Computer Supported Cooperative Work (CSCW 2012)*, ACM Press (2012), 107-116.
20. Kelty, C.M. *Two bits: The cultural significance of free software*. Duke University Press, 2008.
21. Kling, R. Social informatics: A new perspective on social research about information and communication technologies. *Prometheus 18*, 3 (2000), 245-264.
22. Kling, R. Social informatics. *Information Technology & People 1*, 17 (2004), 1-20.
23. Kolko, B., Hope, A., Sattler, B., MacCorkle, K. and Sirjani, B. Hackademia: building functional rather than accredited engineers. *In Proc. the 12th Participatory Design Conference: Research Papers-Volume 1* (2012), 129-138.
24. Kuznetsov, S. and Paulos, E. Rise of the expert amateur: DIY projects, communities, and cultures. *In Proc. the 6th Nordic Conference on Human-Computer Interaction: Extending Boundaries*, ACM Press (2010), 295-304.
25. Kuznetsov, S., Taylor, A.S., Regan, T., Villar, N. and Paulos, E. At the seams: DIYbio and opportunities for HCI. *In Proc. the Designing Interactive Systems Conference (DIS 2012)*, ACM Press (2012), 258-267.
26. Lindtner, S. Hackerspaces and the Internet of Things in China: How makers are reinventing industrial production, innovation, and the self. *China Information 28*, 2 (2014), 145-167.
27. Lindtner, S. and Li, D. Created in China: the makings of China's hackerspace community. *Interactions 19*, 6 (2012), 18-22.
28. Lindtner, S. and Szablewicz, M. China's many Internets: Participation and digital game play across a changing technology landscape. *Online Society in China: Creating, Celebrating, and Instrumentalising the Online Carnival, ed. David Herold and Peter Marolt. New York: Routledge* (2011), 89-105.
29. Lindtner, S., Chen, J., Hayes, G.R. and Dourish, P. Towards a framework of publics: Re-encountering media sharing and its user. *ACM Transactions on Computer-Human Interaction (TOCHI) 18*, 2 (2011), 5.
30. Lindtner, S., Hertz, G. and Dourish, P. Emerging Sites of HCI Innovation: Hackerspaces, Hardware Startups & Incubators. *In Proc. the SIGCHI conference on Human factors in computing systems (CHI 2014)*, ACM Press (2014).
31. Mao, Z. *Quotations from Chairman Mao*.
32. Maxigas. Hacklabs and Hackersapces – Tracing two genealogies. *Journal of Peer Production*, Issue 2: Bio/Hardware hacking (2012).
33. Mellis, D., Follmer, S., Hartmann, B., Buechley, L. and Gross, M. FAB at CHI: digital fabrication tools, design, and community. *In Proc. Extended Abstracts on Human Factors in Computing Systems*, ACM Press (2013), 3307-3310.
34. Mellis, D.A. and Buechley, L. Do-it-yourself cellphones: an investigation into the possibilities and limits of high-tech diy. *In Proc. the 32nd annual ACM conference on Human factors in computing systems (CHI 2014)*, ACM Press (2014), 1723-1732.
35. Ong, A. *Flexible citizenship: The cultural logics of transnationality*. Duke University Press, 1999.
36. Orlikowski, W.J. Sociomaterial practices: Exploring technology at work. *Organization studies 28*, 9 (2007), 1435-1448.
37. Rosner, D. Making Citizens, Reassembling Devices: On Gender and the Development of Contemporary Public Sites of Repair in Northern California. *Public Culture 26*, 1 72 (2014), 51-77.
38. Rosner, D. and Ames, M. Designing for repair?: infrastructures and materialities of breakdown. *In Proc. the 17th ACM conference on Computer supported*

cooperative work and social computing (CSCW 2014), ACM Press (2014), 319-331.

39. Rosner, D. and Taylor, A.S. Antiquarian answers: book restoration as a resource for design. *In Proc. the SIGCHI Conference on Human Factors in Computing Systems (CHI 2011)*, ACM Press (2011), 2665-2668.
40. Rossinow, D. The New Left in the Counterculture: Hypotheses and Evidence. *Radical History Review 1997*, 67 (1997), 79-120.
41. Sivek, S.C. "We Need a Showing of All Hands" Technological Utopianism in MAKE Magazine. *Journal of Communication Inquiry 35*, 3 (2011), 187-209.
42. Strauss, A.L., Corbin, J. and Others *Basics of qualitative research*. Sage Newbury Park, CA, 1990.
43. Tanenbaum, J.G., Williams, A.M., Desjardins, A. and Tanenbaum, K. Democratizing technology: pleasure, utility and expressiveness in DIY and maker practice. *In Proc. the SIGCHI Conference on Human Factors in Computing Systems (CHI 2013)*, ACM Press (2013), 2603-2612.
44. Taylor, A.S. and Swan, L. Artful systems in the home. *In Proc. the SIGCHI conference on Human factors in computing systems (CHI 2005)*, ACM Press (2005), 641-650.
45. Torrey, C., McDonald, D.W., Schilit, B.N. and Bly, S. How-To pages: Informal systems of expertise sharing. *ECSCW 2007*, Springer (2007), 391-410.
46. Turner, F. *From counterculture to cyberculture: Stewart Brand, the Whole Earth Network, and the rise of digital utopianism*. University Of Chicago Press, 2010.
47. Varnelis, K. *Networked publics*. The MIT Press, 2012.
48. Wang, X. Forty years between radio and me. http://www.tecsun.com.cn/article/2003/04.htm.
49. Wang, X. (ed.), *Simulation and design of Class-D APA(audio power amplifier)*. PTPRESS, 2012.
50. Warner, M. Publics and counterpublics. *Public culture 14*, 1 (2002), 49-90.
51. Warschauer, M. and Ames, M. Can One Laptop per Child save the world's poor? *Journal of International Affairs 64*, 1 (2010).
52. Watson, M. and Shove, E. Product, Competence, Project and Practice DIY and the dynamics of craft consumption. *Journal of Consumer Culture 8*, 1 (2008), 69-89.
53. Winner, L. Technological euphoria and contemporary citizenship. (2005).
54. Wuschitz, S. Feminist Hackerspaces: A Research on Feminist Space Collectives in Open Culture, *Fakultaet fuer Architektur and Raumplanung, Technical University of Vienna*, 2014.

Hacking Culture, Not Devices: Access and Recognition in Feminist Hackerspaces

Sarah Fox, Rachel Rose Ulgado, and Daniela K. Rosner
Human Centered Design & Engineering
University of Washington
sefox, rulgado, dkrosner@uw.edu

ABSTRACT

This paper examines the motivations, activities, and ideals of people organizing feminist hackerspaces: collaborative workspaces developed to support women's creative and professional pursuits. Drawing on interviews, participant observation and archival data collected across the Pacific Northwest over nine months, we show how members of these spaces use small-scale collaborative design and acts of making to work out their place in society in ways that contest widely accepted understandings of hacking, technology, and collaboration. In designing how the space should look, feel, and run, members reframe activities seldom associated with technical work (e.g., weaving, identity workshops) as forms of hacking. In so doing, they shift concerns for women in technology from questions of access (who is included) to questions of recognition (who is visible) while grappling with productive ambiguities in between. We describe lessons these tension present for examining women's relations with technology in CSCW.

Author Keywords

Hacking; making; craft, hackerspaces; feminism; STS.

ACM Classification Keywords

K.4.0. Computers in Society: general.

INTRODUCTION

Over the last ten years, makerspaces and hackerspaces have cropped up far and wide, from San Francisco to Abu Dhabi. These practices have become of increasing concern to the field of computer-supported cooperative work (CSCW) as it reaches beyond design implications to policy and industrial change. CSCW and human-computer interaction research following these trends explores hacking as grassroots entrepreneurial and technological innovation [4,25,26,34,36].

In this paper, we focus on emerging forms of hacking in *feminist hackerspaces* — workspaces that support the creative and professional pursuits of women. Feminist hackerspaces developed in 2012, most prominently in the Pacific Northwestern United States, to make room for different values, goals and practices. We examine the feminist ideals that develop in these spaces as both discursive and material phenomena that shed new light on what counts as hacking, technology and collaboration. More specifically, by tracing the often-explicit interweaving of hacking things with hacking the self, we show how feminist hackerspaces reorient our concern for women in technology from ideas of access to an ongoing working through of definitions, acknowledging the breadth of technical work that women already do. Hacking thus becomes a technological imaginary, a set of deeply held ideas and norms subject to failures and partial readings that shape the work of technology cultures.

To arrive at this argument, we draw on interview data and ethnographic fieldwork conducted in women-oriented hackerspaces over nine months as well as research in science and technology studies (STS) and gender studies that seeks to challenge perceptions of technology and innovation as stable or fixed categories [44]. In focusing on feminist forms of collaborative work, this paper follows a renewed interest in the role feminist epistemologies and methods might play in research on social and collaborative systems, a trend most evident in recent conversations within the CSCW community [13,22]. In particular, we adopt a reflexive position in which we examine the workings of not only our participants but also ourselves. Rather than emphasize a feminist research agenda, however, we sought to engage those who have already adopted and adapted feminism for their purposes: to build and maintain community, to articulate difference and subvert oppression, and to catalyze (and help fulfill) personal and professional goals. In particular, we pose the following questions: (1) What does it mean to gain access to these spaces? What forms of participation and collective practice emerge? (2) What makes these spaces sites of hacking? What kinds of work and tools do these spaces encourage or make possible? (3) What makes these spaces 'feminist'? How is feminism enacted?

In addressing these questions, we offer three contributions to CSCW. First, we extend CSCW's discussions of feminist theory and Johanna Sefyrin's argument, in particular, that "to find women who participate in the design of IT, [...we might] analyze the practices behind the professional catego

CSCW 2015, March 14–18, 2015, Vancouver, BC, Canada.

ACM 978-1-4503-2922-4/15/03...$15.00.
http://dx.doi.org/10.1145/2675133.2675223

ries that are involved in IT design" [40:708]. Rather than professional IT design, we examine forms of hobbyist innovation and technology development that remain variously overlooked, such as sensibilities of craft and concerns for identity work. Second, we contribute a new perspective on emerging do-it-yourself collaborative work practices that surfaces some of the tensions and ambiguities around inclusivity and control, particularly concerning women's place in those activities. Lastly, by revealing the frictions within, we show how hacking becomes a site for working out women's relations with technology in productive ways, ultimately enabling us to reimagine women's engagements with collaborative systems and how those relations might be done differently.

Related Work

Before we discuss how feminist approaches have informed CSCW scholarship, we wish to briefly consider the historical forces at work behind the scenes. According to historian Ruth Oldenziel, long before hackerspaces and technology startups, Victorian era women authors used the literary genre to develop stories around engineering, a typically male genre: "deliberately choosing the engineer as the protagonist for her novel, she chose to display her competence in a male genre for the purpose of casting it aside, thereby signaling a new relationship with her readers" [32:140]. American Progressive era women, historian Steven Gelber [14] explains, similarly took pride in being able to perform a 'man's job' in home improvement [14:99], undermining do-it-yourself manuals' portrayals of women as generally unwilling to use heavy tools. Feminists of this period in Britain and the United States welcomed machines that carried out strenuous domestic work as part of a "grand domestic revolution," according to urban historian Dolores Hayden [20]. These women actively debated the influence of technology, identifying economic exploitation by men as the root of their inequality.

More recently, feminist designers and critics have pointed to important disconnects between the stereotypes circulated about women and the changing ways women see themselves. Members of the 1980s feminist architectural collective Matrix, for example, have critiqued the 'idealized' pattern of women's place in suburban homes in the United Kingdom, correlating the isolation of domestic life with women's subordinate position in society [28]. A decade later, the Riot Grrrl movement, spearheaded by members of the punk scene in Olympia, Washington and Washington D.C., challenged the masculine culture of punk rock through the exchange of craft-based knowledge and the formation of spaces to practice and record music. They broadcast their motto 'Revolution Girl Style Now' through a series of *zines*, handmade publications with limited distribution [51]. Today, several of the feminist hackerspace members we will describe similarly foreground craft-based knowledge and have contributed to the publication of *Model View Culture*, an online publication with an accompanying print quarterly, tackling topics such as 'sex and sexuality' and surveillance.

Though the emergence of feminist hackerspaces is fairly recent, the driving forces behind them are not new. Next we consider how these legacies of opposition reemerge within recent work within (and just outside) CSCW on hobbyist and small-scale creative activities, and discuss their recent uptake within design and engineering communities.

Hacking, Craft and Collaborative Work

Over the last decade, research in CSCW and human-computer interaction (HCI) has focused new attention on cultures of hacking, making, crafting and do-it-yourself (DIY) practice. This work has positioned hacking as a necessary facet of livelihood work [24], a pleasurable mode of technical engagement [19,37,41], a 'grassroots' model for innovation and entrepreneurism [26,47], and a form of resistance to mainstream culture [4,25,47]. This last strand of research has emphasized the social and cultural transformations hacking can bring about, troubling definitions of access, openness and transparency [8:514].

Put into practice, this perspective has prompted Buechley and colleagues to develop hardware and software tool kits to help people, especially girls, develop engineering skills through craft activities such as sewing [7]. The hackademia project by Kolko and colleagues similarly provides pedagogical infrastructure for supporting 'non-experts' in gaining technical literacy [25]. Through hacking, technologies may make space for new values and gender dynamics [37].

However, highlighting limitations to these social transformations, Dawn Nafus examines open source software developers to suggest a "broader problem of socio-technical construction, where both the material aspects of computing and the social identities that people create for themselves [...] are cultures made by and for men" [31:671]. Others have traced women's roles in hobbyist computing cultures, showing how hacking affords opportunities to reaffirm masculine imagery through 'healthy rebellion' associated with electronics disassembly [36, 38]. As we will see, the spaces we visited challenged masculine claims to computing by broadening categories of socio-technical production.

Feminism and CSCW

CSCW research so far has used feminist approaches and frameworks to make sense of new collaborative social systems, examining the role of gender in digitally-mediated peer production [13], investigating differences in attitude and engagement among men and women in online reviewing communities [20], and exploring the use of reflexivity as a feminist approach to studying and supporting the organization of social movements [10].

Resurfacing some of these trends, Bardzell and Bardzell have outlined information technology research methods that rely on feminist epistemologies that reflect "a core value of feminism: critiquing and resisting the status quo" [5:675]. Most recently, a 2013 CSCW workshop on feminist approaches to social media research [22] sought to help researchers learn from each other, reflect on their work through questions of gender representation and inclusion, and explore how a feminist agenda might refigure definitions and research programs in CSCW. In general, these activities emphasize the need for studies of CSCW to investigate how forms of cultural production reaffirm or challenge the oppression of women through economic, political, social, and psychological means.

Our work directly builds on these efforts by examining the emergence of self-defined feminist hackers and how they have used the term *feminism* in defining their goals, collective activities, and to some extent the things they create. In doing so, we also point to opportunities for developing a design discourse within CSCW that not only helps us imagine fresh roles for design within social systems research, but also integrates contemporary feminist approaches currently underexplored by the field. Rommes and colleagues contend that IT development has benefited little from feminist studies and vice versa, concluding, "*it is still an open question how feminist theory and gender analysis of ICTs translate into a 'feminist' design of computational artifacts*" [35:656]. It is this question we seek to explore by investigating the social organization of feminist hackerspaces.

Just outside CSCW, a different and somewhat more radical body of feminist scholarship has engaged with design and technology development through the lens of new materialism [2,23,46] often proceeding from the field of Science and Technology Studies. This approach has invited a critique of conventional technology and gender studies in which scholars treat technology as 'open to interpretation' but gender as stable [28]. Some of this thinking arises from 'deconstructive feminist theory' which, according to Doris Allhutter, "disavows 'femininity' and 'masculinity' as ontologically coherent identities" [1:685]. Using a form of 'deconstructive' memory work wherein people recognize and describe memories using clichéd language, Allhutter calls for direct intervention into the ways software developers forge their social relations. In doing so, she seeks to draw attention to normative sense-making strategies involved in memory work. By reflecting on their language, developers may make decisions that reflect their recognition of a-priori assumptions.

Despite the promise of such interventions, other scholars identify important hurdles to adopting feminist approaches in IT development. For Suchman [44], for example, the categories of "designer" and "user" obscure the complexities and contingencies of the social life they describe. Johanna Sefyrin [40] builds on this argument by exploring the practices behind our accounts of IT development, suggesting that women get systematically excluded from these accounts. By following women participating in an IT design project in a Swedish government agency, Sefyrin shows how the substantive contributions women make go unacknowledged: "*the question of whether women can be considered insiders or outsiders of IT design also has to do with how 'IT design' is defined*" [40:709].

It is how this definitional work informs our analysis of collaborative systems that we consider next. Just as Allhutter, Sefyrin, and others use their investigations of the mutual-construction of gender and technology as an intervention into social studies of IT, we offer our analysis of feminist hackerspaces as interventions into CSCW design and development methods. As we will describe, our work as interviewers, observers, and participants enabled us to better understand and also interject new questions into these worlds, fostering reflection among our research subjects and ourselves.

EXAMINING FEMINIST HACKERSPACES

Since their inception in 2012, women-oriented hackerspaces have offered local residents a place to gather, share ideas, learn creative techniques, and grow professional partnerships in what some term an "emerging DIY culture" [30]. According to our interviewees, the Berkeley-based Mothership Hackermoms — a community workshop dedicated to the needs of "mothers of all genders" [30] — were first to introduce such projects to the 'hacker' scene. Their funding campaign on kickstarter.com and a panel at the San Jose DIY festival *Maker Faire* sparked a flurry of interest, particularly among participants at women-oriented IT conferences like AdaCamp and women-in-tech mailing lists. Soon after Hackermoms opened its doors, organizers of the Seattle Attic launched what they called a "feminist hackerspace," a material response to the male-dominated technology community of which many of the members were professionally affiliated. Inspired by subsequent conversations at the *2013 AdaCamp* in San Francisco, participants began feminist hackerspaces later that year in Portland (Flux) and San Francisco (Double Union). Organizers of the sites remain connected through what a Seattle Attic member called an "informal network." They maintain a Google Group featuring continued threads of conversation about their respective hackerspaces and shared resources like example planning documents. They are also connected to other non-feminist spaces by personal relationships like roommates (in the case of Double Union and Noisebridge), or marital partners (who were members of Mothership Hackermoms and Ace Monster Toys respectively).

From their inception, the Seattle Attic and Portland Flux have allowed members of any gender (roughly 12 of 18 identify as female at the Attic; 2 of 13 in Flux) while San Francisco Double Union has not allowed members who identify as male. Upstart costs for each of the sites was provided largely by one or at most core set of a few organizing members. Continued funding was collected from membership fees and, in the cases of Seattle Attic and Double Union, successful crowdfunding campaigns.

In our conversations with leaders of these spaces, we learned that their original motivations focused on concerns for safety and shared values, often materialized in the physical design of the space. One organizer explained:

> *As a woman in technology, it's like, I'm already part of a like a 10, 20 percent group so it doesn't really take a lot to turn me off. So I think like I'm just more sensitive to like things like the space sucking and being dark and gloomy.*

Becoming "more sensitive" to the design of the space seemed to come, in part, from feeling marginal to technology cultures. Other members noted discomfort and even vulnerability in their interactions within existing hackerspaces, often declining to share personal experiences in favor of recounting the experiences of others:

> *I would almost rather share the experiences that I've heard from other women in town [... A woman] was working on something and this kid next to her was like bragging to her about how he had gotten a woman online to show him her breasts by threatening to hurt a kid. And she was like "What is going on here? Why are you telling me this?" And she looked at the guy who runs the space and pays the rent here and was like "Are you going to do anything about this?" And then, like, he didn't.*

Accounts like this one point to the moral character of such retellings, asking us to consider how third-person reports implicate others (a "kid," a "guy") in the accomplishment of value-laden practices such as sexual harassment. By describing the lone woman in the space and the man's detached disposition (in a place of authority but doing nothing to resolve the matter), this member suggests a kind of moral imperative to reveal rather than conceal unethical practices.

Similar stories of harassment circulated widely in the spaces we visited, reinforcing members' desire for both awareness and acknowledgement of oppression. They became implicative of the kinds of reflexive practices not normally considered integral to high-tech environments within large corporations or academic institutions. Yet not all members made investments in learning and practicing technology development. While most Seattle Attic members worked within information technology (IT) industries, several of these professions fell under customer service. In Portland's Flux, seven of twelve members identified as professional programmers. As our work unfolded, we found these affiliations with IT industry shaped how members participated in (and pushed back on) hacking and engineering.

Methods

To investigate our questions we took a qualitative, ethnographic approach. In October of 2012, the third author began ethnographic interviews with Mothership Hackermoms, a women-organized site dedicated to helping mothers feel more fulfilled by their creative and professional pursuits. She observed members' practices in their own environments and documented them through a combination of photos and field notes from December 2012 to July 2013. All three authors subsequently followed up this fieldwork with ethnographic interviews conducted between January 2013 and February 2014 with 13 maker and hackerspace members who engaged in processes of redefining the role of marginalized groups, primarily women, in technology production and hacking. This included computer programmers, fine artists, and authors as well as leaders of four feminist and women-operated hackerspaces and a male member of a 'traditional' hackerspace who began a feminist book club. Thc third author additionally interviewed ten organizers of related technology development endeavors such as Survival Research Labs and the Flaming Lotus Girls in Northern California. Lastly, we conducted research in the members' online archives and in individual participants' collections of artifacts and writings.

We identified interviewees based on recommendations from close contacts and other hackerspace members, our prior knowledge of their work, and public listings of their activities in hackerspaces or online. Interviews followed a semi-structured format organized around questions of identity, goals, and practices, the members' experiences in the spaces and their motivations for joining. Most interviews lasted between one and two hours, and we conducted all but one interview in person. Whenever possible, we combined interviews with hackerspace visits and observations of events and workshops in and around three feminist hackerspaces: Double Union in San Francisco, CA, Flux in Portland, OR, and Seattle Attic Community Workshop in Seattle, WA. To the best of our knowledge, these collectives represent the first of five in the United States to call their spaces "feminist hackerspaces."

Our approach draws on interpretivist perspectives in which researchers aim to translate rather than transcribe social phenomena. Instead of seeking an objective, transparent view of these settings, we used our own subjective experiences — often closely tied to the subjects we studied — to generate *intersubjective* knowledge. In particular, we considered how our status as upper-middle class researchers presiding as faculty or pursuing postgraduate education at a public institution in the United States might influence our accounts. Additionally, each of us identifies as female and is similar in age (24-34) and race (white and Asian) to the members we observed in each of the spaces. We have also worked professionally in the technology industry and identify in some way as feminist. While studying members' 'social justification of belief' [26], we considered the extent to which we resembled our subjects in background and ideology.

In conducting our analysis, we sought to deepen discussions of feminist approaches in CSCW by reflecting on the activities of both our research subjects and ourselves in line with interpretivist and inductive approaches [26]. This entailed a close reading of our data while 'dwelling in' new materialist scholarship encouraging forms of reflexive intervention within design and engineering cultures [2,23,46]. The research team met frequently to iteratively code our field notes, interview transcripts, and archival data and identify emergent themes. Alongside weekly meetings, we met regularly with a member of the social science faculty at our home institution to discuss our subjective perceptions and improve the accuracy of our interpretations. Early rounds of coding guided subsequent data collection, such as a tighter focus on issues of access and recognition that emerged as key themes in our fieldwork. When disagreements arose, such as the scope of the term 'access'—which ranged in understandings from the physical means of entry into the spaces to membership application processes—we revisited our first-hand reflections on the organizational setting and external theories to interrogate differences of interpretation. The following sections draw out aspects of our fieldwork and interviews directly related to the questions of participation, hacking, and feminism explored in this analysis.

What does it mean to gain access to these spaces?

To begin thinking about the forms of access and participation that emerge in these spaces, we wish to visit an excerpt from the field notes where we entered Seattle Attic for the first time.

> *I found the main entrance to the building closed and only accessible through a side door protected by a callbox. When scrolling through the names in the callbox I found half of the space's title along with the first name of its original organizer. I pushed the button to request entry and was sent to a computer generated automated message that triggered the system to buzz me in. I made a few turns and found my way to a set of two traction elevators, loud and slow. I could see the gears and pulleys working. When I arrived on the correct floor I found the space by following the only light. I knocked lightly on the glass of the door and I was told to come in.*

Even from these early interactions we observe some of the features of the space that hint at wider concerns for who may engage with and within it. To begin, the partially-visible name on the callbox label and concealed entrance suggest an intentional obscuring of the hackerspace project. In an interview, the founder described the name of the space, Seattle Attic Community Workshop, as a "*completely neutral like new term that I just pulled it off [sic] my ass.*" She made no direct reference to a way of working or a community of practice and, instead, located her thinking in Marxist scholarship calling for a "non-repressive inclusion of all the groups marginalized by a bourgeois society" [15]. For her, this meant rethinking how people who may not currently consider themselves hackers and makers might build a hackerspace — "*both the name of the Attic and also the imagery and design,*" she explained. Another member pointed out that the Seattle Attic remained, as far as she knew, the only wheelchair accessible hackerspace in Seattle "*and that was not accidental.*" Participation in the space meant not only dissolving certain barriers to entry, but also actively extending who gets access inside.

The location of the hackerspace itself enabled another form of participation, one that emphasized members' interests in controlling access. Like the pulleys that revealed the inner workings of the elevator, the door of the hackerspace remained visible to a searching eye but otherwise hidden from the street. This tension between visibility and refuge unfolded in other spaces we visited. Two authors got lost during fieldwork in a less-trafficked area of Oakland, discovering that their mobile mapping application incorrectly positioned the space. They ultimately called the hackerspace member they planned to meet, who subsequently drove them to her space. We later learned that she and other organizers of the space purposefully chose not to locate their hackerspace adjacent to San Francisco serving transit in order to better serve their immediate, local community (instead of interested outsiders like us). This experience of struggling to find our way and relying on a hackerspace member for guidance prompted us to reflect our variable positions in the spaces and communities we were visiting. To some we were guest researchers and workshop facilitators, but to others we were conspicuous outsiders and perhaps even interlopers. Whatever the case, we depended on the organizers and members to let us in and sometimes even pick us up down the street.

A feminist hackerspace in San Francisco similarly chooses not to disclose their address online and instructed us not to share its exact location in our reports. Only visitors already familiar with the space or determined to find it might make their way inside. At the Attic, the age of the elevator and quality of light in the space prevented us from catching an immediate glimpse. Ambiguity and obscurity, in this way, became modes of selective recognition, a notion that contrasts with declarations of openness touted by members of many other community organizations and hackerspaces [4,26]. Rather than open to all, the space became available to people who knew how and where to look. This method of coming into contact with members prefigures an uncertainty around inclusion in the hackerspace, as demonstrated by codes of conduct.

Moral Accountability

Organizers developed codes of conduct to provide institutional safeguards against harassment and opportunities for those marginalized in high-tech contexts to feel supported. One founder described her willingness to apply such codes:

> *If it were to turn out that key people in our organization were acting abusively then [...] we would be aware of the defensive dynamic that often happens and try to divert that.*

By enforcing codes of conduct, this member hoped to support open conversation about shared values and topics such as gender, identity, inequality, and inclusion while 'diverting' other kinds of social dynamics. As Sophie Toupin, a feminist scholar and member of a feminist hackerspace in Montreal recently wrote, "*When feminist and anti-oppression politics are not explicitly part of the ethos of a space whether virtual or physical, the burden of education will often be placed upon the people who are living these oppressions*" [48]. Without these codes, members faced having to explain their viewpoints again and again, as opposed to doing the work that they came to the space to do. One member spoke about her first impression upon reading her feminist hackerspace's anti-harassment policy:

> "*[E]ven] before I knew anyone here, [...] I didn't need to be anything other than myself because I totally cleared everything on the list.*

'Clearing' the list meant getting through an initial filter that allowed members show up to the space feeling confident they would be treated ethically. Members of each space described vetting potential new members through nomination, voting and, in some cases, in person meetings during an open house. This process raised concerns for whether the group might become a clique, one member noted. Leigh, a founding member of Seattle Attic described codes developing in response to prior experiences with what she called "shit-testing." When asked to elaborate, she explained:

> *I think of [shit testing] like in security, there's this idea of failing open versus failing close. If there's a failure condition, do you let anything through or do you stop letting anything through? Shit testing is like failing closed. It's like making people justify their presence, like are they really hacking or whatever all of these different ways that people sort of police who can and can't be in the space. Whereas like requiring the people operate from a fundamental position of respect is like failing open.*

Reflecting her technical background, Leigh drew parallels between her space's membership policy and security code. As an example of 'failing closed,' shit-testing serves as a policing mechanism that does not make its rules apparent. 'Failing open,' on the other hand, implies acting respectfully toward other members, regardless of their technical skill, with the expectation that they have agreed to the same fundamental rules and possess similar values — whether or not they program or align with a specific definition of hacking. In addition to illustrating differences in the ways members manage the space, the metaphor also reinforces this member's own background in internet security, simultaneously legitimating her right to use hackerspace discourse and opening it up to critique. Just as the ambiguous signage, the locked, somewhat obscured entrance and the computer-generated message point to a means of selectively limiting physical access to the space, the process of engaging with members and becoming a member reveal an equally important emphasis on controlling participation. In this way, the rights to admission that get materialized by the space get set up against a conceptual framework of openness and sharing to which the members appeal (exemplified, as we will soon see, by tools such as the 'documentation station'). Enabling participation, therefore, become less about admissibility and access than moral accountability.

Collective Practice as Companionship

Before turning to specific modes of hacking, we wish to highlight one last aspect of members' participation: what one member described as being "companionable." By this she meant a sense of cohesion enhanced by diverging activities: "*working on typing, and then have someone over there reading in the library, and then flipping through books, and another person -- two more people on the couch having a conversation.*" The language of companionship came to define and support the development of feelings of confidence. For example, when one space needed new tables, a member with expertise held a 'table-building workshop,' showing people how to assemble durable and aesthetic tables, enabling collective investment in the space, and strengthening her belief in her own abilities as a maker. The experience left her feeling "*less of a member and more of a partner.*" Working alongside one another as companions meant collectively struggling with questions of independence and professionalization. Another member referred to this as "*computering together,*" or "*having a space where you can come into your own but also watch other people learn and grow.*" We witnessed this kind of cooperation as a powerful yet silent alliance between members, foreshadowing the hacking practices that develop across these sites.

What makes these spaces sites of hacking?

Hacking, as documented in prior scholarship [4,8], implies multiple sensibilities, from rebellion to technical prowess, to 'dilettantism,' engaging in engineering activities as an amateur rather than professional. Within the three feminist hackerspaces we studied, notably different definitional work came into view, most clearly through the tools members put to use. In this section, we uncover hacking as forms of crafting and identity work, noting the contested nature of these transformations. We then describe difficulties members experienced in assuming a hacker identity and the ideological shifts they hope to bring about.

Hacking as Crafting

On the face of it, many tools within these sites seem at home in a conventional hackerspace. We observed resources for hardware hacking such as soldering irons, laptops, and what one member called a "documentation station," a tripod-mounted webcam with a microscope and light positioned over an electronics workbench for digitally capturing and sharing video of microelectronics tinkering. As in other recent accounts [4], analogue tools sat next to these devices. For instance, during workshops in Seattle Attic we saw knitting and crocheting tools, a variety of looms, button making supplies, a 19th century, industrial sewing machine, and associated restoration materials. Such juxtapositions to call into question the kinds of activity identified as 'technology' in line with common definitions of do-it-yourself culture that contest mainstream technology development (e.g., [4,26,36]).

In addition to challenging technology conventions, we found the notion of hacking as dabbling or tinkering trumped by the seriousness and care with which members approached their non-digital work. At one fiber-arts workshop, for example, an organizer passed around samples of her materials, some in their raw form and others that she had spun by hand. She explained the differences between synthetic and protein fibers, the strengths of these fibers before and after weaving, and what happens to them when met with water. Her close study of the material make up recalled her doctoral training in a chemistry lab. This merging of hackerspace activities with careful craftwork suggests an intentional entanglement of hacking and practices traditionally associated with women.

Hacking and the Aesthetics of Domesticity

Stepping back from organized activities, we find the layout of these spaces offers another picture of hacking within these worlds. During off-hours, members tended to work alongside one another on couches or other comfortable furniture under soft lighting. The incorporation of domestic furniture and an aesthetic of coziness — the close proximity of chairs and tables, accent colors like orange on the Attic's trim or teal in Portland's tables, small areas for refreshments (tea making, in particular) — distinguished the spaces from their office-building neighbors.

During our conversations, a number of members expressed an interest in creating spaces with clean and 'open' features. This can be seen with the removal of an office door bisecting the Seattle Attic. In a similar adaption, several members of the San Francisco space felt the roof of the rented office space felt too low. In response, they took out the ceiling tiles, revealing natural light through rooftop windows, and installed a set of paper lanterns. They described this as a cheap solution to opening up the space as well as creating more natural, soft lighting as opposed to the artificial, fluorescent lighting that was originally in the space. Another member noted, "*...we tried to make this as physically inviting as possible. This is also a cleaner space than a lot of hackerspaces [...] you see something dirty, you clean it up...clutter can also be an accessibility thing.*" Members from San Francisco Double Union also indicated a desire for organization in the space, noting that "*developing more labels ...will help.*" In this sense, members began to hack not only their existing spaces, but also a dirty and chaotic garage aesthetic long associated with masculine do-it-yourself culture [14].

The Ambiguity of Hacker-Identity

When it came to defining hacking, several members recalled the film *Hackers* and its mid-1990s portrayal of the young white male breaking into computers and using them for unintended purposes. Others characterized the activity in contradictory or uncertain terms. For example, one organizer who initially described *hacker* as a "compliment," noting, *"It'll be like calling yourself a genius,"* later explained:

> *I think the term can kind of really be pretentious, you're just working on your iOS app all day, like your hackerspace, [...] but then that comes back into this policing of what is hacking. So, I have like mixed feels about that.*

In this way, hacking entailed certain ambiguities, critiqued for its self-importance or its encoding of individualism and technological utopianism (as in [41]), and prompting members to wrestle with their discomfort with such critiques.

"Intersectional feminist" hackerspace founder Jen Mai Wu felt that the terms hacker and maker lacked representation for people of color and low-income residents, those unable to 'take advantage' of the maker movement. She explained:

> *[Hacking is] like a rebranding of stuff that has been going on for a long time [...] You make your jams, whatever. You grow your own food. Now people are doing that, and they're kind of like boutique, expensive stuff. [...] I noticed that a lot of the people who were benefiting from the maker movement who kind of were able to liberate themselves from the job that they didn't like and were able to do something like take a hobby and turn it into something they really loved.*

Growing up canning as part of a routine activity, she found projects associated with the so-called maker movement oddly familiar. The fact that they celebrated such domestic labor as a "boutique" leisure experience further highlighted their privilege. This privilege entailed not only an ability to learn new skills, but also a capacity to frame such learnings as sources of empowerment, opposition to the conventional "job." Resisting mainstream culture requires an advantaged position in society, as Coleman explains: "those geeks and hackers who channel their labor politically represent one type of privileged actor" [8:515]. This perspective — brought into the territory of domestic work — begins to further undo and destabilize the cultural project of hacking and making. Pointing to the maker movement as a catch all for the counterculture invites new contestations of hacking.

Hacking as Identity Work

Alongside such ambiguities, we observed practices of looking inward – a kind of hacking of the self – become valued but often misunderstood forms of innovation within these spaces. We spoke with an organizer who explained how she decided to leave her graduate studies after observing sexism, racism, and emotionally abusive management techniques from her male supervisors. As female academics working primarily in male dominated fields of technology design and computer science, we were able to relate to her experiences with a fairly high degree familiarity, even to the extent that we knew some of the same researchers. In many ways though our differences, namely her departure from the academy versus our choosing to stay, became the more important aspect of our conversations. Referring to her choice of leaving her program as "leaning out," she contrasts these experiences with her leadership experience in the feminist hackerspace:

> *I never put myself down as a leader, what have you, but I'm getting compliments on how I'm running the meetings and on my leadership - it's amazing. It's like, where did that come from?*

While building confidence in these new skills, this member wrestled with redefining herself as a leader. She reflected on this issue in a daylong, women-only hackerspaces workshop dealing with 'impostor syndrome,' what one member described as "the inability to own one's accomplishments."

Before we discuss this workshop in more detail below, we wish to point out how this attention to self-definition resurfaced in additional workshops catered to the process of building and maintaining one's sense of purpose and role in society. These tendencies to examine the self as a site of hacking extended to events at other women-organized spaces, including "identity workshops" and a weekly meeting called "Failure Club." For participants in Failure Club, failure meant not playing by the rules and getting yourself at least part of the way toward your goal. One women who sought to write a memoir without prior writing experience finished one chapter by the end of failure club — a massive feat that involved challenging bouts with childcare. "The only true failure is not showing up," the club founder explained. Breakdown implied innovation; productive changes in one's life plan.

Importantly, these breakdowns surfaced in our own fieldwork experiences as well, particularly as we sought to relate to issues of motherhood, race and socioeconomic privilege. As middle-class women belonging to different racial and ethnic groups, we found such interactions unsettle our own roles as outsiders, participants, colleagues, and friends. During our analyses, for example, one author became a mother, creating recurring moments for reflection on dissolving definitions of self and new opportunities for analysis. Taking a cue from Jackson's recent writing on breakdown and repair [24], we find our own standing within these spaces constructed different moments for a productive reimagining of conventional forms of innovation. As we look to the role of feminism in these spaces, we more closely examine this attention to fracture and failure.

What makes these spaces feminist?

To understand how members describe these spaces as feminist, we first look to their strategies for differentiating various strands of feminist thought, particularly the feminist ideas promoted within the hackerspace and those circulated by popular accounts of IT development. In our informal conversations, several members expressed overt criticism of popular views on feminism, especially those of Facebook COO Sheryl Sandberg, author of the best selling autobiography *Lean In* [39]. At the time of writing, for example, we learned of a campaign underway at Double Union to edit, correct, and provide inline commentary on a copy of Sandberg's book that had been facetiously donated by a fellow women-centered technology organization. During multiple meetings, we observed members denounce Sandberg's message that women should take on stronger leadership roles as putting the onus on women to move toward gender equity. Such discussion extended to other women-oriented sites. For instance, after concluding our interview with Oakland LOLSpace member and organizer, Jen-Mai Wu, she asked what the members of the feminist hackerspaces thought of *Lean In*. When the first author told her that many of them expressed criticisms, she nodded, offered a slight smile, and said, "Good." Attitudes toward the book became a gauge by which people could assess each other.

However, differentiating Sandberg's feminist ideas from those of the hackerspace became more difficult. At a daylong 'impostor syndrome' workshop hosted at the Seattle Attic, we found that much of the conversation focused on popular accounts of the "syndrome," also cited in Sandberg's book. For instance, the facilitators discussed a quantitative study measuring how individuals interpret their "locus of control" that found women more often felt that they did not have power over their circumstances, a dilemma Sandberg seeks to unseat. The facilitators also led an exercise based on the work of Amy Cuddy wherein participates assumed a series of "power poses" for several minutes. This portion of the workshop focused on recognizing and combating feelings of inadequacy, mostly in professional settings, in much the same way that Sandberg discusses.

Where we began to see differences between the feminist messages in *Lean In* and those of the hackerspace were in subsequent conversations highlighting structural barriers women confronted in a more adversarial or even slightly fraudulent manner. One approach by Pyladies of Portland, a women-only Python meetup, involved first teaching novice members to become fluent with the core competencies of git, an open source version control system. The idea, the workshop facilitator explained, was that when these women code in public they appear highly skilled to those around, bypassing some of the potential "shit-testing" they might normally endure. Similarly, during the workshop, one organizer spoke of Adria Richards, a technology consultant who identified technological work as being her "ticket out of poverty." According to the organizer, Richard's stated tactic for dealing with people who were trying to test her knowledge was to "steamroll them." Stemming from this conversation, the organizer told the story of her recent highly publicized firing from a development job. She recounted that while at a technology conference Richards overheard lewd comments about "big dongles" from male conference goers. Richards' response was to publicly shame them by posting their photos on Twitter. Richards was subsequently fired from her job because her company found the violation of privacy more offensive than the original comments.

Through telling these stories, members distanced themselves from a rhetoric of participation implicit in *Lean In* and other popular feminist accounts. Rather than expecting that women should be able to 'sit at the table' with men, these hackerspace members surfaced many of the same contradictions within hacking cultures. In asking for a more equal treatment of women, they faced difficulties finding safety and support for difference. As we next describe, members used feminist framings to continually question their ability and responsibility to change those worlds.

Feminism as a Filter

Some members spoke of taking up a feminist label to cultivate a shared language and a shared set of ideals. A president of one of the feminist hackerspaces put this succinctly: '*Feminist' is a nice scary word...So it makes it easier to find people who agree with [our] values.*" Another interviewee and space organizer recalled the decision process for explicitly naming theirs a feminist hackerspace: *"...you'll keep away a lot of people you don't want. It creates a very explicit filter which will push people away which will be very nice."* In calling these spaces feminist hackerspaces, these organizers and members set up a social mechanism for keeping out those who might have fundamentally different worldviews.

One feminist hackerspace president also recognized the potential for the term 'feminist' to deter people they might hope to invite into the space: *"...Where I hesitate around calling it a feminist hackerspace is a feminist has a lot of nice white lady baggage around it...So we try to make it clear with the rest of the way that we put ourselves forward that that's not we're going for."* To offset what she termed "negative" filtering, she spoke of using the term "intersectional feminist," a phrase featured on the front page of all three feminist hackerspaces websites during the time of our observation (2 of the 3 at the time of writing). According to prominent critical race theorist Kimberlé Crenshaw, whom this member cited, intersectional feminism recognizes that there are a multiplicity of factors that influence social prejudice and injustice and these factors interact with each other resulting in oppression that varies in degree and intensity. Such factors include, but are not limited to, race, class, gender, ability, and sexual orientation. Other members cited work by Lisa Nakamura and Virginia Eubanks, both of whom interweave questions of social justice surrounding race and gender with analyses of IT cultures. The president spoke of using the term to disassociate from past feminist movements and to represent the group's interest having a membership that is "diverse" or "inclusive."

> *"[A] lot of us are nice white ladies and we try not to be jerks about it and we really - try - we try to look at history and try not to do the same damn [thing...]. And since the feminist movement keeps on doing that. [...] I would feel weird being all yes, we're an antiracist hackerspace when most of our members are white. So I guess there's kind of that sort of aspect of not quite knowing how to talk about it."*

In this excerpt we see feminism portrayed as partially aspirational. The present member base (mostly white, mostly well-educated, and mostly well paid) did not necessarily represent the group's desired membership or set of ideals (emphasizing ethnic and socioeconomic diversity). Members described attempting to cope with this discrepancy by acknowledging legacies of marginalization embedded in efforts to promote women's values.

Feminism as Framing Device

Consider a specific case of collaborative technology development entitled "Plastic Fantastics." discussed by two members of Portland Flux as inspired by what one called "critiques of technology development" in feminist writing, such as the article by Sophie Toupin [48]. Specifically interested in aiding projects that did not use computers in the manipulation of the material, this member described providing support for creative work using plastic. During the event, he helped two local hot sauce makers create a funnel that they could use to adapt an industrial food processor to better receive the thousands of peppers they handle during a job. He recalled getting pressure from another visitor to use computer-based technology during the process. In defense of their low-fi approach, he enumerated the amount of time and new knowledge it would take for the famers to develop a solution with computational technology: *"10 hours...to learn CAD...3 hours to build his first model...this is a large object so it'd take 8-10 [hours]...to print it."* Even with all of that time the problem still would not be solved because the plastics that come out of 3D printers are not food grade.

Reflecting on this interaction, the interviewee and open house facilitator deemed this man's continued push for 3D printing "technological chauvinism," in that the 3D printer would not solve his problem – i.e. in addition to the cost and speed, none of the plastics that would have come out of the 3D printers would have been food grade. His colleague's sense of superiority, he explained, was the result of "*computer people, because they earn a lot of money, [assuming] that their skills are therefore inherently valuable.*"

Here we witness on a small scale how, in Judy Wajcman's words, "technological change is a process subject to struggles for control by different groups" [49]. The member questioned the underlying assumptions made by that "technological chauvinist," that learning CAD and 3d printing would be valuable to the farmers, and rejected them based on alternative values. Rather than requiring the hot sauce makers conform to trends in DIY manufacturing, he advocated for the development of a solution that he felt would get them back to hot sauce making most quickly and easily. By restricting the open night to only include development without digital technologies, the hosting member and the space privileged a type of knowledge that is marginalized in other technical, but non-feminist contexts.

Moves like these helped members call attention to themselves as knowledge producers not only within hacker communities but also beyond. A member from the Portland Flux hackerspace, for example, told us that members received frequent requests for interviews from various media outlets every other week since their inception. Industry also focused attention on these and similar groups. During the spring of 2014, Intel sponsored two small conferences related to hacker and maker culture, both of which hosted a panel on women and hacking.

Feminism, in this way, symbolized not a conventional plea for equality as expressed by popular books such as Sheryl Sandberg's *Lean In* (often dismissed or admonished by members), but an attempt to trouble gender categories, draw attention to reflexivity and, in some cases, introduce a filter through which only certain people might approach members of attempt to join the group. The term also contested a static gender identity, enabling members to both justify and inspire their attempts to redefine technology design.

DISCUSSION

So far we have seen a variety of collaborative forms emerge in the feminist hackerspaces we studied. In some ways, these spaces operate much like other hackerspaces. Usually full of tools for making and modifying, they attract people interested in learning engineering competencies, meeting like-minded people, and building artifacts in their spare time [4,26,47]. However, as we have seen, these spaces also differ in some notable ways from more conventional sites of hacking and hobbyist technology development. For one, organizers grapple with their relative privilege and desires for 'openness.' Even as they advocate for diversity, members create physical and organizational mechanisms for selectively limiting entry such as codes of conduct. While they use the term *hacking* to describe their work, they hesitate in embracing a hacker identity. And though they often voice distain for popular accounts of feminism within IT development, their interests sometimes closely resemble strategies promoted by many of those accounts (impostor syndrome workshops, scholarships for membership, for example).

Despite these apparent inconsistencies — and partly in response to their continued reappearance — members find ways of promoting their own practices and ideals. To call these spaces *hackerspaces* or sites of *hacking*, members deliberately subverted and reframed the extant language of DIY, innovation, and selfhood within computing engineering cultures. As technology scholars have noted, the rise of hackerspaces has followed the emergence of hackers as particular kinds of people: the 'amateur expert' [34], the open innovator [26], and the curious tinkerer [4]. By aligning their work with these technical profiles, feminist hackerspace members aimed to legitimate their experiences within cultures of engineering. In the use of looms they hacked technology legacies: purposefully incorporating alternative histories of female labor into technology innovation. By carving out a space for identity work, they hacked the self: revealing subtle and intimate forms of innovation in their reflexive analyses. These realignments were not merely linguistic, broadening definitions of hacking. They also assumed different bounds to hacking and technological innovation through the new experiences they brought about.

Returning to Johanna Sefyrin's question raised above, how women could be considered insiders in IT design, hacking, or engineering cultures, more broadly had to do with not only how they defined these concepts, but how they propagated the definitions to others outside their hackerspaces (media pundits, other hackerspace members), using narratives of production to reaffirm them.

The sections that follow consider how these practices reinvigorate questions of access and recognition in CSCW and for two core concepts, in particular: (1) *invisible work*, and (2) the *space-place* distinction. The first concerns issues of access and legibility, a theme connected to our first and third research questions; the second concerns what makes these sites places and spaces of hacking, a debate linked to our second research question.

Invisible Work and Partiality

In *Making Work Visible*, Lucy Suchman outlined the tradeoffs of rendering certain aspects of work practices visible to others within organizations [45]. Star and Strauss [42] expanded this argument, elaborating the circumstances surrounding different labor conditions. They highlighted the taken-for-granted nature of workers, their acts of working, and their products of work across varied domains from domestic service to nursing interventions. Further distinguishing these modes of visibility, Nardi and Engeström [32] identified four categories of invisible work: (1) work done 'behind-the-scenes,' (2) routine or mundane work that necessitates considerable competence and knowledge, (3) work done by people out of view, and (4) ad hoc work crucial to an organization's functioning.

In some ways, the activities we observed among feminist hackerspace members fit comfortably within this framework. The work that once appeared routinized, undocumented, or otherwise removed from engineering cultures — child rearing, craftwork or identity — became freshly visible under the rubric of hacking and tinkering. Members called attention to different skillsets, such as the proficient use of looms, in validating their acts of making. Still, as Star and Strauss [42] warn, exposing these skills also meant creating potential burdens of communication and opportunities for surveillance, as demonstrated by the emergence of 'hate mail' and members' wishes to remain anonymous during the course of our study. Rending work visible meant weighing invisibility against exploitation.

However, in other ways, the feminist hackerspace members we studied had their own ideas of visibility. In constructing their sites, they (more or less intentionally) made the space available to some people and not others — providing wheelchair accessibility with limited access to public transportation, for example. In doing so, they learned what kinds of visibly they hoped to engender, what Donna Haraway would call *partial perspectives*. A scholar known for her defining feminist critiques of science and technology, Haraway [16] describes such partiality as limited comprehension of the differences between ourselves and others –

"even when the other is our own machine" [16:583]. According to anthropologist Marilyn Strathern, influential for her studies of gender relations in Melanesia, "partiality is the position of being heard and making claims;" it is fully engaged and yet highly specific [43].

In the course of exposing invisible work, the members we visited made partiality a condition of being seen – whether by potential members, the media, or inquiring design-researchers like us. Understanding their practices as necessarily limited and located, they embraced the dual meaning of partiality. They recognized the *power* and *appeal* of hacker cultures while carefully *limiting access* to their space based on time, location, and social circumstance. In aligning themselves with hacking cultures, members made themselves, their work and their products known and accountable to engineering worlds while challenging the "view from nowhere" [16], the essential, fixed position from which they may be perceived. Acknowledging this partiality helped members not only declare no form of work inherently visible or invisible (in line with Star and Strauss [42]), but also recognize all forms of visibility inherently partial, as Haraway would have us believe [16].

For CSCW, this suggests understanding the act of making visible (or invisible) as necessarily moral and political – always raising questions around who or what has the *power to see*. Like members of the spaces we visited, CSCW might explore the possibility for a richer relationship between women and technology. For example, alongside studies of mobile dating applications such as Tinder, we could study feminist alternatives such as Siren (http://siren.mobi), a recent mobile dating platform designed to allow women to specify their visibility within a certain distance for a limited duration of time. Seeking out and investigating feminist designs already in place invites opportunities for recognizing partiality in CSCW design.

Dis-placing Space

When Harrison and Dourish [17] first drew attention to the difference between space and place for CSCW, the promise of 'virtual collaborative systems' helped catalyze a growing interest in digital space. The space/place distinction offered a framework for recognizing the interpretive dimensions of these developments. It suggested looking beyond the structural features of virtual sites to the rich cultural understandings of interaction embedded within them.

Ten years on, Dourish re-examined this distinction, highlighting space, not just place, as a social product. He discouraged a "layer-cake" reading of space and place, in which place might be understood to exist on top of a semi-stable space. Instead, he claimed "the social runs right through any 'foundational' account of space" and that "spatialities are relative to the different constituencies, populations, and agencies at work" [11]. This reconsideration echoes feminist critiques within the fields of architecture and planning that have argued that space perpetuates inequity and have expressed the revolutionary potential of appropriating and reorganizing space [28,50].

Our analysis of feminist hackerspaces suggests we might fruitfully revisit the place/space distinction as part of a feminist critique of design. The people we studied described themselves as members of hacker-*spaces*, highlighting the form of their work environments over the practices within them. Members were highly aware of this sited-ness, often pointing to their relationship with the surrounding neighborhood. For example, organizers of LOLSpace, the Oakland collective, rented space in an ethnically and socially diverse enclave of East Oakland, next to particular activist and outreach community-service organizations such as Eastside Arts Alliance and the Bikery, a not-for-profit community bike repair shop. Organizers of Double Union, the San Francisco feminist hackerspace, similarly located their room adjacent to a women's health collective. A feminist concern for spatiality involved choosing a location with care: selectively aligning their site with others developing within and around them.

Moreover, the *spaces* created within the hackerspace (documentation stations, mailing lists) — and the *places* they housed (sites of identity management or failure) — helped members move their understandings of access from abstract and authoritative positions to more vulnerable and embodied ones. Warning of such abstractions, Leslie Weisman's [50] feminist critique of built space illustrates the multitude of discriminatory forms architecture can take: whether separating out the sitting room (for women) from the billiards room (for men) or placing the (mostly male) executives in offices overlooking the city while their (mostly female) staff sit in crunched communal spaces below. She shows us how the design of both space and place can contribute to the sites that oppress women as well as enable their liberation – producing homes, for example, that support different experiences of women's life cycle, from childhood to widowhood. The members we visited acknowledged these cultural and historical contingencies while trying to establish a proportionate commitment to gender equality in space *and* place design.

As CSCW continues to wrestle with notions of space and place, this work points to possibilities for a productive feminist encounter with new forms of mobile and collective practice. Embracing partiality, studies of mobile collaborative media such as Twitter or Skype might call attention to the limited perspectives produced by the routine spaces they reveal and the places they inhabit, such those enabled by the design of car interiors. As one hackerspace member redesigning these features explained to us, "*with minor infrastructure changes such as the disappearance of an ashtray, nothing's changed since 1950 [...Cars are] designed by men [...]And women and mothers are super users...*" Much of what members considered in designing space was built on their partial and reflexive understandings of place.

CONCLUSION

In *Designing Culture*, feminist media scholar Anne Balsamo argues for understanding technology innovation as not only the development of gadgets, media forms, and networked communication platforms, but also the range of human practices it makes possible. "The *real* business of technological innovation," she explains, "is the reproduction of technocultures over time" [2:4-5]. If designing devices entails designing culture, a similar argument surfaces within the hackerspaces we visited. The technological innovation encoded in hacking practice becomes less about the resulting products (micro electronics, woven garments, reflexive subjects) than the cultural shifts they engender. By making their activities visible to wider engineering cultures (in blog posts, panels, conferences, press inquiries), members call for popular media, industry and academia—those who consistently disregard the cultural consequences of technology innovation—to attend to the moral implications of hacking: who gets recognized, who recognition effects, and why. Hacking refigures culture, not only technology.

However, in the sites we visited, practices of hacking call forth something more — what Harrison, Sengers and Tatar have described as 'epistemological trouble' in their reflections on 'third paradigm HCI' [17]. Harrison and colleagues rely on feminist science studies to formulate unified alternatives to established conceptual frameworks within HCI like claims to universal objectivity. In the communities we entered, this surfaced through inclusive forms of exclusion and inclusive form of exclusion. By troubling the boundaries between inclusion and exclusion, members entangled the dominant discourse on accessibility: showing us how no technological relation is inherently so, but that they are constitutively and productively intertwined [3].

This argument has implications for not only hacking research, but also how CSCW treats categories such as *women* and *technology*. If a dominant paradigm projects women as unfit for, or uninterested in technology development, feminist hackerspace members presented a compelling alternative: women as ideal agents of technological change. By wrestling with definitions and rules for membership, they called attention to the productivity of materializing difference within a conventional technological paradigm around women and technology.

In this sense, we find a compelling parallel between the forms of hacking at play in the feminist hackerspaces we investigated and women's relations to technology development more broadly. Efforts to increase the participation of women in design and engineering fields involve circumventing a naïve belief in biological (or sexual, or racial) essentialism. Like our feminist hackerspace members, the practices of women in relation to social systems and media are "not the expression of essential feminine insight" [2:33]. Instead this case highlights the importance of recognizing the diverse gendered forms and modes of technology development already underway. From "failing open" to "failure club," these breakages and ambiguities enable us to reconsider how women's relations with technology might be actively changed.

ACKNOWLEDGEMENTS

We greatly appreciate the generosity of feminist hackerspace members who welcomed us in and spoke with us. We also thank Angela Ginorio, Beth Kolko, members of the TAT Lab and our anonymous reviewers for their invaluable comments on drafts of this paper.

REFERENCES

1. Allhutter, D. "Mind Scripting A Method for Deconstructive Design." *Science, Technology & Human Values* 37, no. 6 (2012): 684-707.
2. Balsamo, A. *Designing culture: The technological imagination at work*. Duke University Press, 2011.
3. Barad, K. (2003). Posthumanist Performativity: Toward an Understanding of How Matter Comes to Matter. *Signs: Journal of Women in Culture and Society*, 28(3), 801–831.
4. Bardzell, J., S. Bardzell, and A. Toombs. 2014. "now that's definitely a proper hack": self-made tools in hackerspaces. In *Proc. of CHI '14*. (2014): 473-476.
5. Bardzell, S., and J. Bardzell. "Towards a feminist HCI methodology: social science, feminism, and HCI." In *Proc. of CHI'11*, (2011): 675-684.
6. Bowker, G. C., and S. L. Star. *Sorting things out: Classification and its consequences*. MIT press, 1999.
7. Buechley, L., and B. M. Hill. "LilyPad in the wild: how hardware's long tail is supporting new engineering and design communities." In *Proc. of DIS* (2010): 199–207.
8. Coleman, G. *Coding freedom: the ethics and aesthetics of hacking*. Princeton University Press, 2012.
9. Dawkins, N. "Do-It-Yourself: The Precarious Work and Postfeminist Politics of Handmaking (in) Detroit." *Utopian Studies* 22, no. 2 (2011): 261-284.
10. Dimond, J. P., Michaelanne Dye, Daphne Larose, and Amy S. Bruckman. "Hollaback!: the role of storytelling online in a social movement organization." In *Proc. of CSCW'13*, (2013): 477-490.
11. Dourish, P. Re-space-ing place: "place" and "space" ten years on. In *Proc. of CSCW '06*, (2006): 299-308.
12. Dunbar-Hester, C. "Geeks, Meta-Geeks, and Gender Trouble Activism, Identity, and Low-power FM Radio." *Social Studies of Science* 38, no.2 (2008): 201-232.
13. Forte, A., J. Antin, S. Bardzell, L. Honeywell, J. Riedl, and S. Stierch. "Some of all human knowledge: gender and participation in peer production." In *Proc. of CSCW'12*, (2012): 33-36.
14. Gelber, S. M. *Hobbies: Leisure and the culture of work in America*. Columbia University Press, 1999.
15. Grenzfurthner, J. and F. A. Schneider. "Hacking the Spaces." *Monochrom. monochrom.at/hacking-the-spaces*
16. Haraway, Donna. "Situated knowledges: The science question in feminism and the privilege of partial perspective." *Feminist studies* (1988): 575-599.

17. Harrison, S., and P. Dourish. "Re-place-ing space: the roles of place and space in collaborative systems." In *Proc. of CSCW'96 (1996)*: 67-76.

18. Harrison, S., P. Sengers, and D. Tatar. "Making epistemological trouble: Third-paradigm HCI as successor science." *Interacting with Computers* 23, no. 5 (2011): 385-392.

19. Hartmann, B, S. Doorley, and S. R. Klemmer. "Hacking, mashing, gluing: Understanding opportunistic design." Pervasive Computing, IEEE 7, no. 3 (2008): 46-54.

20. Hayden, Dolores. *The grand domestic revolution: A history of feminist designs for American homes, neighborhoods, and cities*. MIT Press, 1982.

21. Hemphill, L., and J. Otterbacher. "Learning the lingo?: gender, prestige and linguistic adaptation in review communities." In *Proceedings of the ACM 2012 conference on Computer Supported Cooperative Work*, (2012).

22. Hemphill, L, I. Erickson, D. Ribes, and I. Mergel. "Feminism and social media research." In *Proc. of the conference on Computer supported cooperative work & social computing*, (2014): 319-322.

23. Hird, M J. "Feminist Matters New Materialist Considerations of Sexual Difference." *Feminist Theory* 5, no. 2 (2004): 223-232.

24. Jackson, S. J., A. Pompe, and G. Krieshok. "Repair worlds: maintenance, repair, and ICT for development in rural Namibia." In *Proc. CSCW'12*, (2012): 107-116.

25. Kolko, B., A. Hope, B. Sattler, K. MacCorkle, and Behzod Sirjani. "Hackademia: building functional rather than accredited engineers." In *Proc. of the 12th PDC: Research Papers-Volume 1*, (2012): 129-138.

26. Kvale, S. (1996). *InterViews: An Introduction to Qualitative Research Interviewing*. London: SAGE Pub.

27. Lindtner, S., G. Hertz, and P. Dourish. "Emerging sites of HCI innovation: hackerspaces, hardware startups & incubators." In *Proc. of CHI'14*: (2014) 439-448.

28. Matrix (Organization), ed. *Making space: women and the man-made environment*. Pluto Press (UK), 1984.

29. Mellström, U. "The intersection of gender, race and cultural boundaries, or why is computer science in Malaysia dominated by women?." *Social Studies of Science* 39, no. 6 (2009): 885-907.

30. Mothership Hackermoms mothership.hackermoms.org

31. Nafus, D. "'Patches don't have gender': What is not open in open source software." *new media & society* 14, no. 4 (2012): 669-683.

32. Nardi, B. A., and Y. Engeström. "A web on the wind: The structure of invisible work." Computer Supported Cooperative Work (CSCW) 8, no. 1 (1999): 1-8.

33. Oldenziel, R. *Making technology masculine: men, women and modern machines in America*, 1870-1945. Amsterdam University Press, 1999.

34. Paulos, E. "The rise of the expert amateur: DIY culture and citizen science." In Proceedings of the 22nd annual ACM symposium on User interface software and technology, pp. 181-182. ACM, 2009.

35. Rommes, E., C. Bath, and S. Maass. "Methods for intervention: gender analysis and feminist design of ICT." *Science, technology, & human values* 37, no. 6 (2012): 653-662.

36. Rosner, D K., and M. Ames. "Designing for repair?: infrastructures and materialities of breakdown." In Proc. of CSCW'14, pp. 319-331. ACM, 2014.

37. Rosner, D., and J. Bean. "Learning from IKEA hacking: i'm not one to decoupage a tabletop and call it a day." In Proc. of the SIGCHI Conference on Human Factors in Computing Systems (2000): 419-422.

38. Rosner, D. K. "Making Citizens, Reassembling Devices: On Gender and the Development of Contemporary Public Sites of Repair in Northern California." Public Culture 26, no. 1 72 (2014): 51-77.

39. Sandberg, S. *Lean in*. AW Bruna LeV., 2013.

40. Sefyrin, J. "Entanglements of participation, gender, power and knowledge in IT design." In *Proc. of Participatory Design Conference* (2010): 111-120.

41. Sivek, S. C. "“We Need a Showing of All Hands” Technological Utopianism in MAKE Magazine." *Journal of Communication Inquiry* 35, no. 3 (2011): 187-209.

42. Star, S L, and Anselm Strauss. "Layers of silence, arenas of voice: The ecology of visible and invisible work." Computer supported cooperative work (CSCW) 8, no. 1-2 (1999): 9-30.

43. Strathern, M. *Partial connections*. Rowman Alt., 2005.

44. Suchman, L. "Do categories have politics? The language/action perspective reconsidered." In *Proc. of ECSCW'93*, pp. 1-14. Springer Netherlands, 1993.

45. Suchman, L. "Making work visible." Communications of the ACM 38, no. 9 (1995): 56-ff.

46. Suchman, L. "Located accountabilities in technology production."*Scandinavian Journal of Information Systems* 14, no. 2 (2002): 91-106.

47. Tanenbaum, J. G., A. M. Williams, A. Desjardins, and K. Tanenbaum. "Democratizing technology: pleasure, utility and expressiveness in DIY and maker practice." In *Proc of CHI'13*, pp. 2603-2612. ACM, 2013.

48. Toupin, S. “Feminist Hackerspaces as Safer Spaces?” dpi.studioxx.org/en/feminist-hackerspaces-safer-spaces

49. Wajcman, J. *Feminism Confronts Technology*. Pennsylvania: Penn State U. Press, 1991.

50. Weisman, L. K. *Discrimination by design: A feminist critique of the man-made environment*. UI Press, 1994.

51. White, E. *“Revolution Girl Style Now.” Rock She Wrote: Women Write About Rock, Pop and Rap*. Ed. Evelyn McDonnell and Ann Powers. New York: Dell Publishers, 1995. 396–408.

Worship, Faith, and Evangelism: Religion as an Ideological Lens for Engineering Worlds

Morgan G. Ames
Intel Science and Technology Center for Social Computing
University of California, Irvine
ideology@morganya.org

Daniela K. Rosner
Department of Human-Centered Design and Engineering
University of Washington
dkrosner@uw.edu

Ingrid Erickson
School of Communication and Information
Rutgers University
ingrid.erickson@rutgers.edu

ABSTRACT
While some in the CSCW community have researched the *values* in technology design and engineering practices, the underlying *ideologies* that reinforce and protect those values remain under-explored. This paper seeks to address this gap by identifying a common ideological framework that appears across four engineering endeavors: the OLPC Project, the National Day of Civic Hacking, the Fixit Clinic, and the Stanford d.school. We found that all four of these communities utilized elements of religious practice to affirm their membership and shared vision. We describe the forms of *worship* we saw in these engineering worlds, their practices of *evangelism*, and the ways in which they *addressed doubt*. We also demonstrate the role mythologies play as ideologically charged narratives. Our discussion of these parallels illuminates the extent and consequences of quasi-religious practices in engineering worlds and illustrates the utility of using religion as a 'lens' for understanding ideological commitments in engineering culture.

Author Keywords
Design; doubt; engineering worlds; evangelism; faith; fixing; hackathons; ideology; ideological work; mythology; OLPC; practice; quasi-religious behaviors; religion; values; worship.

ACM Classification Keywords
K.4.0. Computers in Society: general.

INTRODUCTION
Engineers often narrate their activities as empirically grounded, pragmatic, and solidly secular. The worlds that these developers, designers, and analysts create and inhabit through their common practices identify a cutting-edge, scientific, and rational worldview, not one steeped in tradition and focused on faith. A similar emphasis on the primacy of empirical evidence imbues the computer-supported cooperative work (CSCW) community, as it does in many other scientific communities.

CSCW '15, March 14 – 18, 2015, Vancouver, BC, Canada.

ACM 978-1-4503-2922-4/15/03...$15.00
http://dx.doi.org/10.1145/2675133.2675282

Even researchers who design for spiritual experiences and expose progressive views of automation in religious ritual (e.g. morning prayer, Shabbat) [46,47] use empirically-driven methodologies to develop their claims [6,48].

Empirical evidence suggests, however, that religious metaphors are more entwined with technology than may be generally acknowledged. Scholars in science and technology studies and related fields have explored how technologies become 'salvific' or 'sublime' [33,36]. Apple Inc. has been a particularly fruitful target of this kind of analysis, given the religious overtones of its marketing and the zealotry of its users [10,25,32,34,41,42]. Campbell and La Pastina, for instance, show how popular discourse adopted religious terms to frame and define the reception of the Apple iPhone, such as the phrase 'Jesus Phone' [10:1192]. Their analysis traces various kinds of narratives linking technological artifacts with redemption, divinity, spirituality, and religious experience [10:1194].

Here, we examine the religious language that animates not just *technologies*, but the *practices* of the engineering worlds that produce these technologies. Though we did not enter our research sites looking for religious parallels – i.e., we did not raise questions about religion in our interviews or observations – we discovered that the engineering and design practices we encountered in our data were steeped in what we call *quasi-religious* behaviors. We define 'quasi-religious' as enacting faith-like practices without necessarily following established religious tenets. We understand 'religion' moreover to refer to a coherent system of faith outside of the auspices of 'evidence' in which certain objects and practices take on symbolic import [17,44]. We found quasi-religious parallels across all four of our field sites: the National Day of Civic Hacking, in which computer programmers volunteer an afternoon or weekend to write code for civically-minded projects; the Fixit Clinic, where volunteer 'coaches' help people repair broken devices; the Institute of Design at Stanford (d.school), in which students are trained in design thinking and practice; and the One Laptop per Child (OLPC) project, which designed a laptop meant to overhaul education across the Global South.

In this paper, we describe how the practices and discourses we found within these engineering communities surfaced three quasi-religious behaviors. First, we found that individual and collective practices of *worship* were a central element of performing group membership. Second, we observed the communities engage in various forms of *evangelism* to convert people to their worldviews. Third, we noted various strategies to *address doubt* among the faithful.

Why does this matter? We assert that recognizing and interrogating the vernacular religiosity within our field sites advances how the CSCW community theoretically engages with engineering worlds in three ways. First, it meaningfully expands how we understand and examine motivations to participate in engineering communities, both for longtime participants and potential newcomers, even in the face of daunting obstacles or counterevidence. Second, it highlights some of the blind spots that particular ideological commitments can raise, which can render these communities less inclusive, less impartial, less evidence-driven, and more hostile to constructive criticism than their ideals often suggest. Third, it demonstrates some of the merits of extending beyond an analysis of 'values' to attend to the ideologies (described below) that undergird these values, a point we return to at length in our discussion. Overall, we argue that understanding the ideological frameworks of sociotechnical production could help our field account for the extant faith-based motivations behind our own design and engineering practices, potentially avoiding the pitfalls associated with them or even problematizing the ideological frameworks that are less just or inclusive than the ideals of our profession would suggest.

BACKGROUND AND THEORETICAL DEVELOPMENT

Several concepts from social theory are central to our analysis. In this section, we develop what we mean by 'religion,' detail the role that mythologies play in the connection between religion and engineering worlds, and discuss how this is an example of an ideological framework.

Durkheim defines religion as any unified system of beliefs and practices relative to objects considered 'sacred' [17]. In our analysis, we contend that both technologies and the processes that create them (e.g. 'design thinking') become sacred. 'Religion' further refers to a system of faith that is maintained and strengthened outside of the auspices of 'evidence', in which ritualized collective practices take on symbolic import [17,44]. While we recognize the diversity of worldwide practices that may fall under the scope of 'religion,' we limit the term herein to the scope it generally inhabits in the United States (also the location of all of the engineering communities we studied), which is dominated by Judeo-Christian religious frameworks.

As also discussed in the introduction, scholars of science and technology have uncovered deep-seated connections between technological *objects* and religion, for example pointing to the prevalence of religious language within branding discourse [32,34,41,42] or showing how specific technologies are rhetorically connected to divinity and redemption in use [10,23,25,33]. These scholars have found that technologies can evoke what cultural historian Vincent Mosco refers to as 'the sublime,' or feelings of awe, transcendence, and connection to a greater purpose – feelings that, not coincidentally, are also central to religious experience [33].

We further saw that quasi-religious practices and discourses were often enacted with *mythologies* [33], or foundational narratives that were ritualistically circulated within the community and told to outsiders to reinforce collective beliefs. Considering the role of mythologies in the connection between ubiquitous computing and religious experience, Dourish and Bell use Mosco's formulation of mythologies as narratives that make certain futures appear at once magical and inevitable, straightforward and 'divine' [16]. They juxtapose these divine mythologies against the 'messiness' and contested nature of everyday life, concluding, like Mosco, that mythologies are much more than simple falsehoods; they "animate individuals and societies by providing paths to transcendence … [and] the promise of the sublime" [16:4].

Similarly implicating religion in his analysis of techno-utopian mythologies, religion scholar William Stahl shows how the mythologies present in popular accounts of technology's role in society both reveal and conceal its social influence [42]. Describing these stories as technological utopias and dystopias, Stahl illustrates the salvation, liberation and fear that emerge through technological myth-making, concluding that "our language about technology is implicitly religious" [42:3]. On the other hand, he also identifies counter-narratives that "break the spell of the present," exposing the ideological stakes that underpin commonly circulated mythologies and suggest concrete alternatives to existing technology practice (a theme that will surface in our discussion of doubt). In doing so, he underscores the ethical dimensions of technological myth-making.

These collective beliefs, in turn, make up what social theorists refer to as an *ideology*: a framework of norms, whether conscious or unconscious, that shape thoughts and actions. Cultural theorist Stuart Hall describes an ideology or ideological framework (we use the two interchangeably) as a "system for coding reality" that "becomes autonomous in relation to the consciousness or intention of its agents" [20:71]. Many possible ideologies may be present in engineering communities at the same time – capitalist, libertarian, and individualist ideologies, for example. Hall notes that this concept has been useful in social theory as "a way of representing the order of things which endowed its limited perspectives with that natural or divine inevitability which makes them appear universal, natural and coterminous with 'reality' itself" [20:65]. What is important in this definition is the way that ideology fades into the background: an ideology "works" because it "represses any recognition of the contingency of the historical conditions on which all social relations depend. It represents them, instead, as outside of history: unchangeable, inevitable and natural" [20:76]. In this light, the three quasi-religious behaviors we witnessed and mythologies we saw circulating helped establish, negotiate, and reinforce the ideological tenets of the communities we studied. Mythologies furthermore served as a specific mode of reifying and naturalizing these ideological norms through ritualized telling and re-telling of narratives.

A final term that will be useful in the analysis that follows is that of an *engineering world*, of which each of these communities is a part. Strauss [43] describes 'worlds' as sets of shared activities connected by a "network of communication," including creating and negotiating common boundaries, standards, ideas of 'worth,' and modes of judgment. Further fleshing out the idea of 'worlds,' Becker describes art worlds as "the network[s] of people whose cooperative activity, organized via their joint knowledge of conventional means of doing things, produces the kind of art works that the art world is noted for" [5]. These worlds may be at times ad hoc, temporary, or inter-organizational, but they are ideologically 'legible' to one another and recognized from both inside and out as belonging to a culture; to paraphrase Gertrude Stein, there's a 'there' there.

Under the umbrella of 'engineering worlds', we include various disciplines involved with the design and development of new information and communication technologies in the larger network of communication, including computer science/engineering, mechanical engineering, and various forms of design. Within these worlds, we argue that designers and engineers understand themselves as ethical agents who assume a responsibility to protect their group's mission and cohesion, and they consequently propagate practices and mythologies that are in line with the group's underlying ideological framework. We suggest that these findings are not unique to the groups we studied, but are instances of a quasi-religious orientation across engineering worlds (and possibly beyond) more generally.

DATA SOURCES AND METHODS

Four sites of observation and analysis

We focus here on the practices of four engineering worlds. The first is the National Day of Civic Hacking, in which computer programmers volunteer an afternoon or weekend to write code for civically-minded projects. The second is the Fixit Clinic, where volunteer 'coaches' help people repair and re-use broken devices. The third is the Institute of Design at Stanford (d.school), in which students are trained in design thinking and practice. The fourth is the One Laptop per Child (OLPC) project, which designed a laptop meant to overhaul education across the Global South. All four sites we examined involved participants who were drawn to the project because of a conviction that its approach will affect the world in a way that they support. These common elements of *passion* and *conviction* further highlight the religious aspects of their practices. While parallels to religious thought and practice are not unique to volunteer-based communities focused on social change, the communities we studied make such practices more apparent.

We do not use these sites as 'case studies' in the traditional sense, but rather empirical and historical materials through which we find commonalities. In the following sections, we instead integrate our findings thematically.

One Laptop per Child Project

MIT professor and Media Lab co-founder Nicholas Negroponte announced the One Laptop per Child project in 2005. He described a 'mission' to build a $100 laptop (a benchmark that proved to be infeasible), with open-source educational material based on the tenets of 'constructionist' learning [39,40], for children in developing countries. In practice, there are about 2.5 million in use around the world today, 85% of them in Latin America [3]. The ideas behind the project had been circulating among MIT's computer science and design faculty and students for at least 35 years before OLPC's unveiling, starting with a 1971 NSF research grant that MIT professor Seymour Papert received to design computers for education.

The first author has been researching the OLPC project since 2008. Her work includes seven months of ethnographic fieldwork of an OLPC project in Latin America, as well as ongoing archival research on the development of OLPC and the ideas behind it. The latter contributes to the arguments in this paper, focusing exclusively on the Boston-based founding group involved with design and development of OLPC's XO laptops.

National Day of Civic Hacking

The first National Day of Civic Hacking (hackforchange.org) took place at 95 different locations across the United States on June 1-2, 2013. Local groups affiliated with the national movement independently organized events at each location. They designed the events to gather 'hackers' who were interested in applying their programming expertise to civic problems and issues. The event was endorsed by the White House and involved 26 government agencies or institutions that often provided access to datasets.

The third author collected online promotional and post-facto summary materials from events around the country and also conducted ethnographic observations at the 'Hack the Rock' event in Rockaway Beach, New York, a Queens neighborhood that was particularly hard hit by Hurricane Sandy. Much of the civic hacking going on that day in the Rockaways involved the design and development of tools to prepare for, survive, or recover from a future natural disaster.

Fixit Clinic

Since 2009, the East Bay Fixit Clinic has hosted 'pop-up' events dedicated to "the guided disassembly of your broken stuff," as their tagline states. Roughly once a month, small groups of tech-savvy volunteers gather at local libraries, museums, and hackerspaces (community-operated workspaces most often dedicated to electronics tinkering) in the San Francisco Bay Area to help residents take apart and learn to fix their broken products.

The second author conducted participant observation at seven repair events hosted by two repair collectives in the Bay Area and spoke with approximately 60 participants. She complemented her ethnographic work with extensive formal interviews with 20 participants, including leaders, organizers, activists, and attendees, whose repair activities critically informed the development and maintenance of contemporary repair movements. Lastly, she conducted in-depth research in the Fixit Clinic and Repair Café's online archives and in individual participants' collections of artifacts and writings.

Stanford d.school

The Hasso Plattner Institute of Design at Stanford (or "d.school") is an interdisciplinary hub for Stanford students, industry executives, and design professionals to take classes in entrepreneurship and engineering. Affiliated faculty promote principles of 'design thinking,' a human-centered design methodology with origins in mechanical engineering and product design. While the institute itself does not grant degrees or hire tenure-track faculty, its affiliations with the Departments of Engineering and Art enable enrolled graduate students to receive Masters Degrees in design through the Joint Program in Design.

The second author conducted participant observation from December 2012 through June 2013 of a capstone course at the d.school called *d.garage,* and spoke with roughly 50 participants at the Institute. She carried out interviews with 11 program affiliates, including leaders and students of the d.school and the Joint Program in Design.

Methodology

Collectively, this paper draws on archival research, discourse analysis, interviews, and ethnographic observations. The first author analyzed the forty-year development of the ideas behind OLPC's 'Children's Machine' via its documented history, the third author conducted observations and a discourse analysis of the events and media surrounding the National Day of Civic Hacking, and the second author made ethnographic observations of and interviews with participants and hobbyist fixers at the Fixit Clinic and teachers and students at the Stanford d.school. All observations were recorded as handwritten fieldnotes and interviews were audio recorded and transcribed.

To analyze these data, we adopted an iterative, inductive approach common in anthropology and cultural studies, namely to combine a thorough understanding of participants' worldviews with a more critical-theoretical interpretation of these worldviews as 'texts' able to expand or contest broader theoretical questions. This systematic approach is in keeping with the theory-building described in Michael Burawoy's Extended Case Method [8], which outlines a rigorous reflexive alternative to the demands of positivist research. Instead of striving for reactivity, reliability, replicability and representativeness, all of which introduce highly problematic 'context effects' (especially in qualitative research), the Extended Case Method acknowledges the inevitability of the researcher's *intervention*, accounts for the *process* of interpretation given participants' contexts and histories, works toward identifying the underlying forces that structure everyday life ('*structuration*'), and iteratively *reconstructs* social theory given one's findings. Burawoy demonstrates that this reflexive approach "also seeks generalizable and falsifiable explanations … but true to its own principles, arises from a critical engagement with positive science" [8:11]. This orientation allowed us to begin reaching beyond a participant's articulated values to identify mechanisms by which the groups commonly deployed ideas to defend the legitimacy of their practices and discourses.

We employed the Extended Case Method over the course of several months in person and via a series of Google Hangout sessions, due to the distributed nature of our team. In early discussions, we analyzed our own and each other's field data and jointly identified a host of common themes that had independently emerged in our projects. We also conducted an extensive literature review drawing in research from many different fields including HCI, media studies, anthropology, religious studies, communication, and sociology. Collectively reflecting on common themes and emergent syntheses, we hypothesized that the existence of these commonalities was due to the shared social context in which all of our field sites operate: American engineering culture. We then turned back to our data, where we iteratively discussed and further identified several forms of quasi-religious practices that appeared in each of our sites – practices, it is worth noting again, that occurred without prompting or intervention from us.

QUASI-RELIGIOUSITY IN ENGINEERING WORLDS

Our inductive process of synthesis and theorization resulted in the identification of three common themes across our data: practices of *worship*, practices of *evangelism*, and practices of *addressing doubt.* Collectively, these themes indicate a set of quasi-religious practices that extend across engineering worlds. Below, we show how the motivations and practices of the four engineering worlds we studied, though they may be framed by the participants themselves as 'rational' and evidence-based, resemble religious practice.

Worship: the practices and rituals of faith

Those who participate in the engineering worlds we studied confirm and renew their faith in technological practices via specific forms of worship. By *worship* we mean ritualized practices of homage to particular beliefs important in the community, through either individual or collective rites [44]. In this section, we show how these practices create, reinforce, and highlight the shared experiences in each community, its reason for existence, and the individual reasons community members have for continuing their membership [19]. We also show how the narratives that structure and justify these practices become mythological in stature, doing work to maintain the group's shared ideological framework.

We will further see that by way of continued reproduction, these activities became legitimated and, at times, reified to the point of social exclusion or interactional difficulties with other groups. On the other hand, it is through this collective form of practice that a group comes to define, understand and enact its values and beliefs, which is an essential antecedent to maintaining a shared ideological framework and ultimately ensuring the sustainability of the group.

Individual forms of worship

Our first example of worship in engineering worlds involves the ritualized articulation of belief by individual members of engineering worlds. Among those involved with the One Laptop per Child (OLPC) project, it is commonly held that computers offer children unique opportunities for passionate play, enlightenment, and a connection to the sublime. This belief, formalized in OLPC's mission statement [37], is legitimated by those in the community through providing ritualized examples of the centrality of computers in their *own* childhoods. This is framed by the community as rational evidence justifying their project (despite its anecdotal and idiosyncratic nature [2]). However, telling the story of a childhood passion (often defiant [2]) for computers – whether on personal blogs, public OLPC mailing lists, or elsewhere – signals participants' motivation for joining the project and the legitimacy of their membership in the congregation. By connecting themselves to a shared mythology that is so central to the community, clearly they belong.

OLPC co-founder Seymour Papert, acknowledged by other founders as the intellectual father of the project, originated the form and substance of this cosmological myth in describing his close relationship with gears as an engineering-focused 'object-to-think-with,' his childhood substitute for the not-yet-widespread computer. "*I fell in love with the gears,*" Papert explains, italics his, in his 1980 book *Mindstorms*. He continues,

> "This is something that cannot be reduced to purely 'cognitive' terms. Something very personal happened. … This book is the result of my own attempts over the past decade to turn computers into instruments flexible enough so that many children can each create for themselves something like what gears were for me." [39:viii]

Though Papert's story does not involve computers, his entire career focused on applying his experience with gears to the computer, which he called "the Proteus of machines … [that] can appeal to a thousand tastes" [39:viii]. In a later book, *The Children's Machine* (a direct reference to what would later become OLPC's laptop), Papert explains that he came to believe that computers could fulfill this role in his experiences with the nascent MIT hacker community in the late 1960s. This community's passionate play with computers, itself a kind of worship (and described in more detail in [28]), had a profound effect on Papert:

> "I had my first experience of the excitement and the holding power that keeps people working all night with their computers. I realized that children might be able to enjoy the same advantages – a thought that changed my life." [40:13]

The continued popularity of Papert's ideas – within OLPC and beyond – attest to the power of the mythology that (some) children's passionate play with computers is a path to the sublime. Indeed, Papert's book *Mindstorms* could be regarded as a kind of 'bible' for the movement as it continues to circulate among those in the community and to be assigned in design and engineering classes, spreading the group's mythology of finding oneself and connecting to like-minded others through the machine and the ideology underlying it along the way. (The text, in fact, is given to all incoming students at the MIT Media Lab, and one required assignment for first-year students is to write about what object served as their own personal 'gears' in their childhood.) This mythology served to link the passions of many of those involved with the project, as well as many of its greatest admirers.

Technical practice as a form of worship is made even more overt at the Stanford Institute of Design (d.school) – and in these examples, the participants even stray from the 'rational' commitments to evidence in their unprompted use of religious language, though they continued to justify their passions with language of rationality. Teachers enthusiastically talk about how students "flip" – become converts to design thinking – in what one staff member and graduate of the d.school called a "hallelujah moment," noting the number of people who have described the d.school philosophy as "cultish." The founder of the d.school, David Kelley, himself admits that his belief in *design thinking*, the philosophy undergirding his pedagogical goals at the institute, is religious in nature – a parallel that was entirely unprompted:

> "This [design thinking] is my only organized religion in that way. … It's like whatever religions do for you – whether it's a crutch, whether it makes you feel good, or whether it just gets you through the day, view of afterlife, or whatever else – [for me it's about] this whole notion of helping people through unlocking their creative ability. I mean, it's got *chemical* with me."

'Getting chemical' for Kelley was like falling in love with gears or the engrossing play with MIT's mainframes for Papert: it involved a highly personal passion rooted in a sense of possibility that their object of worship provided them. And just as Papert shared this experience with others, Kelley sought to instill in students a faith that they too could 'unlock their creative ability' through design thinking, and moreover that these creative abilities could change the world. Kelley identified this feeling as his 'only organized religion,' recognizing the role of his faith in design thinking as a source of his motivation.

A third example of worship comes from Chris Witt, a volunteer at the Fixit Clinic who took particular pleasure in reusing and repairing old bikes. He described his attachment to repair work as a kind of religious experience – though with a different kind of motivation. He explained (again, unprompted):

> "It took me a long time to realize that I don't have any particular regard for any organized religion, but for me [repair work] has become, in a way, a kind of religious practice that I evolved without ever thinking of it that way. So there's an amorphous mass of earth worshippers out there, and that's not what I would call [repair work], but it's as close as it gets."

Here, Witt admits that his repair work involved expressing adoration for the earth and the environment – he does not see himself as the same as 'earth worshippers,' but still, his devotion to repair is 'as close as it gets.' As a volunteer at the Fixit Clinic, he enacted this passion both with other volunteer 'coaches' and with the visitors that he was there to help. This process enabled him to publicly sanctify his respect for the environment as a kind of religious practice. Though Witt's interests lay resolutely outside organized religion, like Kelley he saw commonalities between his volunteer repair work and more traditional forms of faith-based worship.

Communal forms of worship

While some devotional practices – like Papert's gears or Witt's repair-work – are expressed individually or asynchronously, worshippers often value collective religious practice, whether expressed in thoughtful collective silence like the Quakers or exuberant songs like the Baptists. Thus, while worship is an individual religious expression, it is often enacted, strengthened, and shaped in the company of others [44].

Collective practices of worship occurred at a spring 2013 Fixit Clinic meeting at the Albany Community Center, which found the Clinic's founder and lead organizer, Peter Mui, standing on a chair, his arms raised. "Ladies and gentlemen, start your repairs!" he called out after introducing the afternoon's activities. The cacophony of repair activities fell to a hush during Mui's introduction, and all eyes turned toward him. A similar speech marked the official beginning of each event, ritualistically transforming the crowd into a congregation with a common purpose. Mui later said he consciously used these introductions to set a particular tone for the meeting.

Meeting together was similarly a critical part of the National Day of Civic Hacking. Organizers spoke of the need for "citizens" (primarily software developers) to be co-located in the ritualized practice of the hackathon as they strove to pound out viable and innovative solutions together. In Palo Alto, the convening was organized to not only to bring people together but to celebrate the city as well. Their hackathon took place outdoors in the beautiful California weather and was accompanied by family-friendly activities, a stage for TED-like talks from local technological dignitaries, and a techie 'farmer's market' where developers wandered among the stalls to exchange ideas or receive feedback from technologists rather than buying local produce. The ritualized forms of worship at work here were quintessentially Californian, bucking centralized and formal worship for outdoor marketplaces and egalitarian collaboration.

Worship within engineering worlds thus takes place both at the individual and the community level. Engaging in shared rituals such as hacking, tinkering, designing or fixing together collectively motivates participation in the world, reinforces beliefs, and expresses devotion to the group. These moments also allow stories to circulate that can take on the form of mythologies, expressing on-the-surface values as well as tapping the underlying ideological framework of these groups. For programmers, a day of hacking with fellow coders is simultaneously a time for reinforcing a mythology about the power of technical problem solving and the virtue of civic-mindedness. Papert and his colleagues celebrated their devotion to computers together and younger contributors ritualistically connected their ecstatic childhood computer experiences to this culture, many of them wanting to give those same experiences to children around the world via OLPC, as we will see in the next section [28,40]. And at Stanford's d.school, the communal practice of design, in and of itself a powerful example of worship, was further sanctified by its location in two highly ritualized spaces at the school, the classroom and design studio. These classes and studio spaces served to gather and connect students from across campus (through class enrollment) and across the world (through the design master's program). Yet, given the high demand for design training, they also excluded individuals and groups that did not fit the school's idea of a promising design student.

We turn next to understanding how these individual and collective practices of devotion also produced tactics for spreading messages of faith beyond the bounds of these communities.

Evangelism: bringing more people into the fold

Members of engineering worlds are often ready evangelists with a zeal for converting non-believers to their worldviews. These practices are one of the normative aspects of an ideology [20]. The four engineering worlds we analyzed each engaged in practices of evangelism, including education, recruiting, and publicity, making this a goal within their respective communities. In contrast to faith, which is a personal, inward-facing and sometimes exclusionary way of adhering to a set of beliefs, evangelism orients communal beliefs outward with an eye toward propagating the ideology through associated practices. Understood this way, our analysis of evangelism bears resemblance to sociological studies of social movements (e.g., see [11,13]).

Fixit Clinic founder Peter Mui explained some of his more evangelistic techniques in an interview. He said,

> "We also do that celebratory thing when people fix stuff. Okay? Because we want, we want to give this affirmation. This sort of 'come to Jesus' moment [laughs]."

For Mui, coming to the Fixit Clinic meant learning to embrace an ideology of economic empowerment in which one could feel confident taking apart devices, figuring out how they were produced, and maybe even suggesting alternatives. He wanted participants' experience of tightening a screw in a toaster that no longer heated, adding a bead of solder to a Bluetooth device without signal, or sewing a new buckle to a tattered leather boot to enable them to think differently about their consumption practices. If a person came away from the Clinic with additional technical skills as well, all the better. Using a triumphant disposition, Mui wanted to inspire a "moment" of change in people's thinking that promoted a particular set of countercultural beliefs – an ideology – around consumption and engineering.

A second example showcases the thin line between evangelism and worship. Stanford d.school founder David Kelley's desire to see students "flip" into being design thinkers is at once an act of worship – tied to rituals of the classroom and design studio – and one of evangelism. He further explained the evangelistic aspect by discussing the magic of that conversion moment:

> "When students come up and I see their eyes sparkle and they say, 'Oh my god. You know, when I came to Stanford I didn't think this way at all and now I think this way…and I'm making better decisions and I'm going to change my job […]' And they cry and whatever. That's what I'm after. That's the selfish part of this religion. It's that I get to witness this kind of 'flipping' to feeling positively about themselves. So, if it's not a religion, then it's this kind of selfish gratification thing of as many people flip[ping] as possible."

More explicitly discussing his evangelistic ambitions, Kelley explained that he wanted to teach as many people as possible about design thinking because he considered it to be a powerful tool, again bringing up religious parallels without prompting:

> "I really believe that this can help people and so I want them to know that it exists. It is not religious in that it is forced – that this is the right one compared to any other. […] It's religious in the sense I want everybody to know about it."

The blurred boundaries of evangelistic worship at Stanford can be contrasted with the case of the all-night programming sessions that Papert and others in OLPC shared at MIT. There the practices of worship had no evangelizing function; they were comprehensible only those who were already steeped in the ideological framework of the community.

Evangelism at the National Day of Civic Hacking was less overt than with Mui or Kelley, but the mythologies at play there still affected the tone of the whole event. Invitations to participate encouraged all citizens to get involved, irrespective of their technological abilities. At the same time, organizations with names such as Code for Good and Rally for Impact sponsored the events, and these names influenced participants' interpretations toward a mythology central to hackathons that code ideated and (at least partially) developed in an afternoon *could* have a lasting impact, perhaps even more impact than the incremental results of long-standing nonprofits or advocacy groups. Altogether, this branding had a proselytizing influence promoting code as salvific, and moreover encouraged the involvement of a crowd self-selected to believe in such a mission.

During observations at the Rockaways hackathon in Queens, New York, a steady stream of tech-sympathetic community members, like missionaries, came into the school to share their stories of devastation from Hurricane Sandy and to promote their latest ideas about what technological services might have been useful at the time. Their appeals helped to dissuade skeptical voices and set the tone for a charismatic afternoon. During the coding spree itself, the tenor of activity celebrated the value of efficient production, not deliberation. The motto set from the organizers -- "less yack, more hack" – kept people on the right path and dissuaded critical views or ongoing discussion. In this way, the timed and goal-driven structure of a hackathon helped to symbolize the tenets of this faith as ordered and rational – something driven by passion but kept in line by constraints. Nothing here was too unfamiliar, critical, or disruptive, which was meant as a welcome invitation to tech-curious neophytes.

In the case of One Laptop per Child, the project's central mission was one of evangelism. However, this proselytic drive ended up doing more than recruiting new members to the cause. Rather, some in the project allowed their zeal to make them less evidence-driven and more hostile to constructive criticism. After the OLPC project was announced in 2005, a number of journalists and academics (e.g. [4,29,45]) questioned whether money would be better spent on ensuring adequate food, sanitation, or other basic necessities instead of buying laptops for children. Responding with the same kind of "disruptive" rhetoric that portrays new technologies as being a "radical break from history" that many techno-utopian projects use in legitimating themselves [33], many of those leading or involved with OLPC talked about how their laptop was uniquely qualified to change the world by remaking children across the Global South in their own image [24,30,35]. Their laptop would let children learn how to program computers, which would naturally facilitate their becoming the same kind of 'hackers' as the developers themselves – a subject position they considered powerful, freeing, and altogether desirable to have, as we saw in the ideology undergirding their faith. This, in turn, would naturally lead to economic growth, no matter how disadvantaged or infrastructure-poor the area started. OLPC co-founder and leading evangelist Nicholas Negroponte articulated this view succinctly in a 2008 video OLPC posted on YouTube (http://youtube.com/watch?v=o97UD78s6iM):

> "[The XO laptop] is probably the only hope. I don't want to place too much on OLPC, but if I really had to look at how to eliminate poverty, create peace, and work on the environment, I can't think of a better way to do it."

Project co-founder and then-software director Walter Bender explained in a 2007 Radio Open Source interview how the machine could have these world-changing effects simply by children "be[ing] able to reach inside the machine … and touch it, and transform it, and explore it as deeply as they want to" [30]. What lay behind the evangelistic (not to mention technologically determinist) mythology that ameliorating issues of economic, cultural, and environmental import can be achieved by giving children open-source laptops is less a rational examination and more a highly personal, quasi-religious set of worship practices between developers and their computers that they sought to spread.

That spreading this worldview would also be a *shortcut* to cultural and economic change was another notable feature of

OLPC's evangelistic beliefs [24,30,35]. In the same 2007 Radio Open Source interview, Bender explained that OLPC was an "end-run around the status quo [to] move a little bit quicker to reaching more children" [30]. Both Bender and Negroponte referred to the project as a "Trojan Horse" [30,35], Bender elaborating that it was "a backdoor into overhauling the entire education system of a lot of the countries that we are talking about" [30], and Negroponte further explaining, "We need to reach the most children possible and leverage them as the agents of change" [35]. Here, again, we see this rhetoric framing a technological solution as radically breaking the rules that governed and constrained previous interventions, even when in reality it differed from other development projects only in hubris. This blind spot – the mythology that simply reaching children with OLPC's laptops would overhaul national economies – anchors an ideology of technological determinism with a specific idea of how learning (or fixing or hacking) should be accomplished: in a very personal relationship between an individual and a computer, just as Papert, Negroponte, and others wrote about experiencing themselves in their practices of worship.

Whether the ideologies in these communities reflected the belief that design thinking or programming can effectively solve problems that other approaches have not been able to, that fast action is preferable over careful deliberation, or that tinkering with electronics can usher in new worldviews, each group used some form of evangelism to celebrate the power of their engineering practices. Each of the communities we examined sought to spread their faith and practices of worship to new members, from community participants to university students to children in the Global South. Their zeal often led them to overstate the power of their solutions and ignore challenges or complications, even when their claims lacked evidence. Indeed, a common theme across these worlds, and in engineering worlds more generally, is that computer technologies represent such a radical break from the past and from other approaches that historical or comparative data provide nothing useful in understanding them. On the contrary, exploring the limits and ideological commitments of these groups serve to reconnect them to history and contextualize their "disruptive" rhetoric [33].

Both worship and evangelistic practices can be challenged or internally rejected, however. We next turn to examine the origin and nature of these challenges and to document the reparative practices these communities took on in response.

The ideological work of addressing doubt

Practices of worship and evangelism were not always met with complete acceptance, and sometimes particular events shook the faith of the group. While doubt was sometimes part of the ideological framework of the community itself – in other words, certain kinds of doubt were 'orthodox' – there were other instances where neophytes or even long-time acolytes lost their faith and challenged the ideological underpinnings that motivated the community, even asserting that the community was based more on faith than fact.

Doubt highlights the translation-work that must occur between ideologies and the 'messiness' of everyday life, which may not always conform to ideological norms [16]. Cultural historian Bennett Berger develops the idea of *ideological work* to describe this process. Ideological work can take the form of "selling out" (adjusting one's beliefs to match circumstances) or "realizing" (adjusting circumstances to match one's beliefs), but more often is instantiated as "accommodating," or meeting in the middle [7:18–22]. In this section, we focus on the ideological work that doubt created, describing the responses the faithful made to shore up or reconcile their beliefs. This analysis also reveals that the responses of both doubters and the faithful lay bare additional blind spots around inclusivity and partiality in these engineering worlds.

At the National Day of Civic Hacking, one kind of doubt was very much part of the fabric of the events themselves: doubt in the efficacy of government institutions. The hackers involved were, however, not cynical about state of affairs: they optimistically saw themselves as saviors for the perceived failures of today's government structures, and their solutions as a path to civic redemption. They viewed an ability to hack as not only an opportunistic way to 'act,' but really the only way to have agency in civic matters. As with OLPC, technological solutionism was more akin to finding faith after having been tested in the wilderness: here, finally, is the way to move mountains; here, finally is a more direct channel to the sublime.

Some voices, however, questioned this techno-fetishistic zeal, allowing us to observe how doubt and disbelief unfolded and was attended to. In a blog post entitled "Hacking for Good" (http://homecookedtheory.com/archives/2013/06/07/hacking-for-good), Melissa Gregg, a scholar at Intel Research, challenged the premise behind the National Civic Day of Hacking event she attended, wondering what made hacking in concert with government agencies and community members necessarily good. The larger community behind the event chose to simply ignore these critiques – likely something possible only because of the distributed nature of this engineering world and not a viable long-term form of ideological work – organizing a second event around the same ideological message (i.e., hacking as a civic virtue) for the summer of 2014.

Like Gregg's doubt of civic hacking, one of David Kelley's students expressed doubt about the value that design thinking may actually provide at the Stanford d.school. While admitting that design thinking was 'fun and interesting,' he questioned whether it could have the amount of impact in the world that d.school teachers promised to their students. Bringing in religious language – again, without prompting – by comparing his teachers to preachers and their message to proselytizing, this student raised the heretical thought that their religious devotion to design thinking might be obscuring its limitations:

> "[Design thinking,] it's preaching. It's creating a religion that needs followers. It already has leaders but the leaders need people to follow them. So that I think [design

> thinking] does carry well [to other contexts] and it does do that, but it also doesn't necessarily recognize how difficult it is to be good at it. … It seems like it's not nearly that hard to be a priest. You stand in front of a group of people. You read a gospel. You have a book that tells you what to do. But there's a lot to it I guess. Not just preaching, but doing the work. There's a lot of design out there where people think they can do it, try to do it and it seems fun and interesting but it doesn't really work as well… And to some degree I think the proselytizing may be masking that fact."

While this student's doubt arose in the normal course of his studies, a community's faith can also be shaken in response to a particular event, as was the case for OLPC. A defining moment for the OLPC community, one that tested the conviction of many involved, occurred in spring 2008. Negroponte had announced the '$100 Laptop' three years earlier and the project had garnered gushing praise from engineering communities and the press [4], if not the rush of country-scale orders that were expected. Still, the project's commitment to open-source software, their focus on passionate learning with computers [40], and their bold rhetoric about overhauling education worldwide attracted a large and loyal following of employees, volunteers, and corporate contributors.

Then, in a stunning reversal, Negroponte announced in spring 2008 that he was in negotiations with Microsoft to put Windows on the XO laptop instead of Sugar, the in-house open-source platform built on Red Hat Linux. This unexpected move towards proprietary software undercut the faith in open-source that had inspired many participants' involvement in the project. Some participants fought back, publicly re-affirming their motivations for joining the project, while others quit the project altogether. Collective sentiments were summed up on the Free Software Foundation website (http://fsf.org/blogs/rms/can-we-rescue-olpc-from-windows) by technology pundit and self-styled open-source 'evangelist' Richard Stallman, who had previously been a vocal supporter of OLPC:

> "Since the OLPC was first announced we have envisioned it as a way to lead millions of children around the world to a life in which they do computing in freedom. … Proprietary software keeps users divided and helpless. … You might as well introduce the children to an addictive drug. If the XO turns out to be a platform for spreading the use of proprietary software, its overall effect on the world will be negative."

Stallman's statements – equating proprietary software with an addictive drug – may seem extreme, and he was in fact ridiculed by some in the press for it. However, many others in the engineering worlds that had been supporting OLPC agreed with his statement. OLPC co-founder Walter Bender echoed Stallman in a post on the OLPC News blog (independent and often critical of the project; http:// olpcnews. com/ software/ sugar/confessions_of_a_fundamentalist.html), articulating what OLPC should represent with a distinctly religious tone. Bender pushed back on a statement from Negroponte that the project was too full of open-source 'fundamentalists' by claiming that he was only a 'fundamentalist' about learning – but that the learning they wanted to enable was only possible with open-source software:

> "I am a fundamentalist – but in regard to what? Not software. I am a fundamentalist about learning! That is not to say I am not passionate about FOSS [free and open source software], but as the means, not the end, towards a 'constructionist' learning model."

Bender echoes the religious language of 'fundamentalism' that Negroponte used as critique, but appropriates it as a positive trait, simultaneously drawing a boundary around what he understood as OLPC's mission. After all, who could argue with being a 'fundamentalist' about learning?

Here, Stallman and Bender both demonstrate the kind of ideological work faithful community members felt compelled to perform in order to defend their views of the OLPC project against challenges to the community's ideologies. While some were puzzled by their urgency and vehemence, these statements, if interpreted with a religious lens, make sense: not only was the project under attack, but so too were the mythologies, the ideologies, the very faith of its true believers.

Around the same time, one early and previously evangelistic employee [24] left OLPC. In a blog post (http://radian.org/notebook/sic-transit-gloria-laptopi), he publicly questioned not only Negroponte but the whole premise of the project. This man's crisis of faith resulted in the need for a different type of ideological work – work that ultimately rejected OLPC's mission in light of the project's new reality. He said,

> "My theory is that technical people, especially when younger, get a particular thrill out of dicking around with their software. Much like case modders, these folks see it as a badge of honor that they spent countless hours compiling and configuring their software to oblivion. Hey, I was there too. And the older I get, the more I want things to work out of the box."

These examples showcase how faith in the engineering worlds we studied was repaired, adapted, and even abandoned in response to challenges from without and within. The role of and response to doubt in these communities highlight the quasi-religious fervor that doubters can both uncover in their questioning and elicit in response. The ideological work that took place around incidents of doubt further enriches our understanding of how engineering worlds enforce mythologies that are used to motivate and reinforce their central ideologies.

DISCUSSION

These themes illustrate the ways in which quasi-religious practices substantively inform and facilitate many of the ideologies of engineering worlds. We have illustrated how our subjects inform their goals and discourses through practices of worship, evangelism and the ideological work of addressing doubt. Our data show that volunteer participants in fixing events and hackathons promote evangelistic messages extolling the virtues of rapid action and praising the ways that exploratory electronics tinkering can uncover new ways of seeing the world. In parallel, One Laptop per Child (OLPC) project adherents articulate their approach as the "one true path," believing that programming and computer use is capable of solving problems that other approaches cannot. Finally, we note how Stanford Institute of Design educators are enraptured by the moments of conversion that their design thinking myths produced in their students, even as some in their flock questioned how zealous proselytizing might be concealing the limits of the method.

These findings suggest not only evidence of quasi-religious behaviors and mythologies but also a rationale for seeking this evidence out. Understanding how forms of worship, evangelism and faith operate in engineering cultures can help scholars unpack the sociality, organization and praxis of engineering worlds in new ways. Identifying ideologies, in particular, which may otherwise be as invisible to those familiar with those worlds as water is to the proverbial fish [15:123], is especially important. Our intention is not to advocate for an eradication of ideologies; just as it is impossible to escape the bounds of our own subjective points of view, so too is it impossible to operate entirely outside of the frameworks of ideologies. However, a large body of Marxist theory (e.g. see [20]) notes that becoming cognizant of the ideological frameworks in which we operate allow us to evaluate whether they are really serving the purposes we hope or assume they are. Only by way of this cognizance can we shift them if they are not.

So what have we learned about engineering worlds? Our religious framework surfaced faith-like practices that link aspects of technology innovation to worship, evangelism and ideological work. While the volunteers and contributors we studied may discount or overlook these insights, we contend that these practices reveal an understudied but *necessary* part of technical work, namely the need within engineering worlds – particularly those building new tools and services – to establish foundational mythologies and modes of worship, influence anticipated beneficiaries, and test and reinforce values against doubt.

The role of quasi-religious practice in engineering worlds

Throughout our findings, we saw examples of how quasi-religious practices (worship, faith, evangelism) provided benefits to the communities in which they were enacted. For students at the Stanford d.school, for example, Kelley's formulation of design thinking marked an evangelistic turn to user-centered product development. Contributors to the OLPC project used evangelism to affirm their belief in the power of computers in childhood and to push back against doubters, even in the face of what might otherwise feel like overwhelming odds. The use of quasi-religious behaviors not only contributed to community-building and other world-changing activities, it also imposed coherence on situations that helped people persevere in the face of doubt and tackle seemingly impossible issues. In the groups we studied, this faith-based coherence played a positive role and demonstrated a unique generative power *vis-à-vis* organizers' beliefs.

On the other hand, we saw that these behaviors could also restrict and narrow group membership, goals, and design possibilities, delimiting what engineers viewed as accomplishable and/or important. The same utopian zeal for design thinking, learning with computers, or democratizing technology that inspired our participants had a blinding effect when it prevented them from recognizing or appreciating ideological diversity, much less constructively confronting problems of socio-economic disparity, racial and gender bias, or other issues of social justice beyond most of their everyday experiences.

Such limitations were most noticeable in the trenches of technology development. There, engineers who were largely male and upper or middle class envisioned cultural programs that reflected their own worldviews and ultimately served their own interests. In the groups we studied, this entailed helping those who already had leisure time and environmental convictions repair their own devices, building applications that reflected the civic identities of an entrepreneurial middle class, or trying to remake students at Stanford or children around the world in their own image. Echoing work by Oudshoorn, Rommes, and Stienstra [38], we found that the engineers involved in each of the projects we discussed adhered most passionately to tenets that mirrored their own ideologies, that echoed their own mythologies. These proclivities shaped the design of subsequent events, laptops, and software, but failed to account for the needs and diversity of 'users' who may have different views.

It may appear that our findings apply primarily to zealous, volunteer-centric engineering communities, since three of our four field sites were such (with the exception of the d.school). We disagree. Based on ongoing interactions with a number of other engineering worlds, we posit that these practices can be found across American engineering culture more broadly. Indeed, given that the CSCW community is itself an engineering world, we wonder what this framework can tell us about ourselves as researchers and designers. To address this question, we turn next to the ways in which these quasi-religious practices can extend CSCW's analytical possibilities.

The case for attending to ideologies in CSCW

A number of frameworks within CSCW examine the values or practices of organizations, such as Values in Design (VID), discourse analysis, and Actor-Network Theory (ANT). While each of these approaches enables us to identify and reflexively account for the kinds of practices we have explored here, even collectively they overlook part of our story.

For example, Value Sensitive Design (VSD) [18] and value discovery [12] have helped expose the articulated values and commitments extant in many engineering worlds. The VSD approach generally focuses on human values of "moral import" as classified by deontological and consequentialist moral philosophy [18:13], such as privacy, informed consent, human welfare, sustainability, and justice. Within this work, researchers have tended to interpret the concept of values (cognitive, moral, aesthetic) as deep or sacred properties of one's humanity. However, we find that the ideological commitments that undergird these values often remain taken-for-granted and underexposed. Furthermore, these frameworks have trouble explaining the processes of value production and maintenance – values in collective praxis.

Our perspective augments the core work of attending to values in design by recognizing the importance of focusing on how such values emerge from practice. Rather than values-in-*design(ed) objects*, the notion of values-in-*(design) practice* helps explicate the ideological norms that make certain cultural values natural, commonsense, or even invisible – just as the 'Protestant Ethic' makes certain values-in-practice such as industriousness seem natural and inevitable in American culture more broadly. As with attending to the underlying 'design ethos' that drives (certain kinds of) innovation in engineering worlds [22], a values-in-practice perspective regarding technology design and development yields insights even when values do not clearly make it "into" designers' and developers' products. In fact, our approach attends to values even when they may not even be clearly articulated as 'values.'

Discourse analysis likewise exposes how actors discursively construct a particular reality to reify common ideals, influence outcomes, and shape shared ideological structures [14]. Though this approach accounts for the deployment of ideology in discourse, it largely overlooks the explicit connections between discourse and ideology-*in-action* – in our case, how ideologically-motivated practices co-constitute modes of innovation and social organization, as well as social cognition [14]. Though our analysis often draws on the rhetoric of leaders and other highly visible members of the engineering worlds we studied, this rhetoric illuminates practices of these individuals and groups, such as the passionate computer play or 'fundamentalist' re-appropriation in OLPC, or the 'come to Jesus' moments in the design classroom or repair clinic.

Conversely, engagements with ANT often emphasize the mobilization and enrollment of actors (both human and nonhuman/technological) in the form of actor-networks, but here too the beliefs, values and mythologies that underlie these networks often go neglected, especially if these ideas do not take material form [27:2]. Indeed, Callon's ethnomethodological turn to advocate the use of actors' own categorizations of the world to structure research [9] may obscure these actors' ideological commitments via categorizations they may not realize they are making, just as VID favored explicitly recognized over implicit values. Finally, while an ANT framework provides constructive tools for analyzing the 'scripts' that designers build into technologies [1], it falls short of providing the means to account for how these ideological frameworks animate or inhabit these practices or products, making this aspect of the actor-network easily overlooked and thus uncritically assumed.

In contrast, our work reveals not only how illustrative but important it is, especially politically, to expose the ideologies in play in engineering worlds. This is a subject that Maher, a scholar of the open-source software community, claims "is all too often limited to impoverished discussions that emphasize instrumental efficacy at the expense of critical and rhetorical awareness" [31:369]. The kinds of ideologies we have detailed in this paper not only expose our participants' beliefs and related practices, but they also help make sense of them within broader ideological movements in which they are situated – oftentimes movements that participants may not actively articulate or even be aware of. In other words, we show that our subjects are embedded in the wider ideological space of American engineering culture, which informs the local ideological space instantiated within disparate engineering communities. The common quasi-religious behavior across all four of our otherwise quite different 'congregations' serves to illustrate the existence and organizational reach of this shared ideological creed.

While it may seem difficult to identify ideological frameworks when our subjects and participants are themselves not aware of them, we believe that it is strategically possible to do so. Indeed, we have some tips for interested researchers. Attending to points in the data where participants fall back on ritualized stories or behaviors that cannot quite be explained 'rationally' – instances that might be considered types of worship, evangelism, or ideological work/faith repair – provides a fruitful avenue to start. In particular, we suggest that researchers zero in on points of friction or doubt within a community (as well as the concomitant response) as a way of bringing ideological commitments to the surface.

It is also wise to follow where the data take you. To our surprise, some participants (e.g. Kelley of the d.school, Witt of the Fixit Clinic) drew their own direct parallels between their work and religious practice, whereas others made use of religious metaphors to explain their goals (e.g. Mui of the Fixit Clinic), especially when their belief systems were challenged (e.g. Bender of OLPC). While these participants may or may not recognize the norms undergirding their statements as ideological in nature (recall Hall's emphasis that ideologies often appear natural and inevitable to those immersed in them), their unprompted words gave us clues for what to attend to in our analysis. Moreover, their religious statements could be interpreted as themselves assertions of the faithful in the face of (potential) doubt – from us as researchers. We drew connections between these empirical results and the sociological and critical scholarship on ideologies and engineering worlds to surface the ideological undercurrents at play in these communities.

Our attention to the *mythologies* that circulated in the communities we studied – of the computer-obsessed child or the empowered designer – also showed us how communities strengthened and spread their belief systems through narratives. We could then follow these threads throughout our fieldwork, interviews, and archival research to uncover broader ideological frameworks. Attending to these mythologies is thus another strategy for examining the ideologies of engineering worlds.

Within CSCW, attending to ideologies can help researchers identify important mechanisms through which groups cohere and validate themselves or disband and dissolve, as it has in the social sciences. Emerging social movements increasingly draw on engineering discourses to legitimate their claims, so understanding these ideologies is particularly important. Still, the tacit nature of many ideologies can make them more difficult to 'harness' productively: the jump from these identifications to productive suggestions can be especially difficult, and something with which social science has wrestled for decades [20].

Future work could explore this avenue, along with other questions such as: what fosters greater commitment among participants in a 'hackathon' and how might the event's branding undermine or reinforce participants' own experience of their work? Or how might the ritual display of ideological commitments help support the growth and maintenance of social movements? Are there more direct parallels between the strategies of organized religion and social organization, and if so, what might we learn from those parallels?

Overall, we hope that our results can serve to 'make the familiar strange,' as Stuart Hall would say [20], for researchers in CSCW to address these and other questions raised by attending to ideologies. While concrete design suggestions are not the goal of this paper, we also hope that this work helps designers – who often hope to 'do good' through technological intervention in ways similar to those in the communities studied here – identify their own ideological commitments.

CONCLUSION

A central goal of this work has been to investigate, articulate and demystify the ideologies of engineering worlds, as demonstrated through common quasi-religious behaviors and mythologies. With this lens, we interpreted the empirical data from four research sites to identify the beliefs and meanings espoused by our participants. Analysis of each project revealed that religious sentiments such as passion, conviction, and belief serve as forces that help participants express core convictions, recruit followers and maintain motivation in the face of great odds, critique, or conflicting evidence. Our point in this exposition is not to reduce ideology to an 'objective' religious formulation or undervalue its cultural power, nor is it to suggest that with quasi-religious behaviors these communities are somehow 'wrong' or 'non-modern' [26]. After all, Berger writes, "religion is perhaps the strongest example of symbolic meanings exercising causal force in private and public life" [7:151–152]. Rather, we have looked to religion as an important, culturally salient framework too often overlooked in the attempt to discuss the ideologies inherent in the seemingly neutral tenets and practices of engineering and design.

If we were to turn our gaze to our own field of CSCW, might these kinds of religious inclinations be equally prevalent? Might the analysis of those tendencies enable us to recognize the prioritization of particular populations or identify central blind spots within our field? If we were to follow Donna Haraway – a scholar known for her defining feminist critiques of science and technology – we might answer yes. "All Western cultural narratives about objectivity," she writes, "are allegories of the ideologies governing the relations of what we call mind and body, distance and responsibility" [21:583]. While we chose to examine other engineering groups in this paper, understanding the ramifications of quasi-religious practices within the engineering worlds *we* inhabit could shed further light on the underlying ideologies at stake, such as how design practices privilege and prioritize certain types of users. To do this, we might take into account not only the identity [38] of community members and their professed values but also their often taken-for-granted systems of belief, foundational myths, strategies for keeping their faith, and motivations for evangelizing their views – in other words, their ideologies-in-practice. While this discussion could be very important to our field, it is beyond the scope of our analysis here and we leave it to future work.

ACKNOWLEDGMENTS

This work is indebted to the friends, colleagues, and anonymous reviewers who pushed us to develop and clarify our ideas, including Megan Finn, Pernille Bjorn, and Lilly Irani. Thanks also to Katie Shilton for helping with NDoCH data collection. And as always, we thank our participants, without whom this work would not have been possible.

REFERENCES

[1] Akrich, M. The De-Scription of Technical Objects. In W.E. Bijker & J. Law, eds., *Shaping Technology*. MIT Press, 1992.

[2] Ames, M.G., Rosner, D.K. From Drills to Laptops: Designing modern childhood imaginaries. *Information, Communication & Society 17*, 3 (2014), 357–370.

[3] Ames, M.G. Translating Magic: The Charisma of OLPC's XO Laptop in Paraguay. In E. Medina, I. da C. Marques, and C. Holmes, eds., *Beyond Imported Magic: Essays on Science, Technology, and Society in Latin America.* MIT Press, 2014.

[4] Ananny, M. The $100 Laptop: Trojan Horse, Piñata or Social Movement? *Europe*, (2005), 1–16.

[5] Becker, H.S. *Art Worlds.* U. California Press, 1982.

[6] Bell, G. No More SMS from Jesus: Ubicomp, Religion and Techno-spiritual Practices. *Proc. Ubicomp 2006*, ACM Press, 141–158.

[7] Berger, B. *The Survival of a Counterculture: Ideological Work and Everyday Life Among Rural Communards.* Transaction Publishers, 1981.

[8] Burawoy, M. The Extended Case Method. *Sociological Theory* 16, 1 (1998), 4–33.

[9] Callon, M. Some Elements of a Sociology of Translation: Domestication of the Scallops and the Fishermen of St Brieuc Bay. In J. Law, ed., *Power, Action and Belief: A New Sociology of Knowledge?*

Routledge, 1986, 196–233.

[10] Campbell, H.A., La Pastina, A.C. How the iPhone Became Divine: New media, religion and the intertextual circulation of meaning. *New Media & Society* 12, 7 (2010), 1191–1207.

[11] Cohen, R., Rai, S.M. *Global Social Movements: Towards a cosmopolitan politics. In Global Social Movements.* Athlone Press, 2000, 1–17.

[12] Le Dantec, C.A., Poole, E.S., Wyche, S.P. Values as lived experience. *Proc. CHI 2009,* ACM Press, (2009), 1141.

[13] Dearden, A. and Walker, S. Designing for Civil Society. *Proc. HCI 2003*, 157–158.

[14] Van Dijk, T.A. Discourse Analysis as Ideology Analysis. In C. Schäffner and A. Wenden, eds., *Language and Peace.* Dartmouth Publishing, 1995, 17–33.

[15] Dobrin, S.I. *Constructing Knowledges: The Politics of Theory-Building and Pedagogy in Composition.* SUNY Press, 1997.

[16] Dourish, P., Bell, G. *Divining a Digital Future: Mess and Mythology in Ubiquitous Computing.* MIT Press, 2011.

[17] Durkheim, E. Elementary *Forms of Religious Life.* George Allen & Unwin Ltd, 1915.

[18] Friedman, B., Kahn, P.H., Borning, A. Value-Sensitive Design and Information Systems. In P. Zhang and D. Galletta, eds., *Human-Computer Interaction in Management Information Systems: Foundations.* M.E. Sharpe, Inc., 2006.

[19] Gerber, E. *Devotion to an Innovation Process: The Case of Human Centered Design.* Unpublished doctoral dissertation, 2007.

[20] Hall, S. The Rediscovery of 'Ideology': The Return of the Repressed in Media Studies. In M. Gurevitch, T. Bennett, J. Curran and J. Woollacott, eds., *Culture, Society, and the Media.* Methuen, 1982, 56 –90.

[21] Haraway, D. Situated Knowledges: The Science Question in Feminism and the Privilege of Partial Perspective. *Feminist Studies* 14, 3 (1988), 575–599.

[22] Irani, L. *Designing Citizens in Transnational India.* Unpublished doctoral dissertation, 2013.

[23] Kelly, K. Nerd theology. *Technology in Society* 21, 4 (1999), 387–392.

[24] Krstic, I. Google EngEDU Tech Talk: Ivan Krstić. 2007.

[25] Lam, P.-Y. May the Force of the Operating System be with You: Macintosh Devotion as Implicit Religion. *Sociology of Religion* 62, 2 (2001), 243–262.

[26] Latour, B. *We Have Never Been Modern.* Harvard University Press, 1993.

[27] Law, J. Notes on the Theory of the Actor Network: Ordering, Strategy and Heterogeneity. *Systems Practice* 5, 4 (1992), 379–393.

[28] Levy, S. *Hackers: Heroes of the Computer Revolution.* Anchor Press Doubleday, 1984.

[29] Luyt, B. The One Laptop per Child project and the Negotiation of Technological Meaning. *First Monday* 13, 6 (2008).

[30] Lydon, C. One Laptop Per Child? 2007. http://radioopensource.org/one-laptop-per-child/.

[31] Maher, J.H. The Technical Communicator as Evangelist: Toward Critical and Rhetorical Literacies of Software Documentation. *Journal of Technical Writing and Communication* 41, 4 (2011), 367–401.

[32] Mickey, S.F. *Constructing The Prophet: Steve Jobs and the Messianic Myth of Apple.* 2013.

[33] Mosco, V. *The Digital Sublime: Myth, Power, and Cyberspace.* MIT Press, 2005.

[34] Muniz Jr., A.M., Schau, H.J. Religiosity in the Abandoned Apple Newton. *Journal of Consumer Research* 31, (2005), 737–747.

[35] Negroponte, N. Email attachment. devel, sugar, community-news mailing lists, 2008. http://lwn.net/Articles/279288/.

[36] Noble, D.F. *The Religion of Technology: The Divinity of Man and the Spirit of Invention.* Penguin, 1999.

[37] OLPC staff. OLPC Mission: Frequently Asked Questions. OLPC Website, 2012. http://laptop.org/en/vision/mission/faq. shtml#faq5.

[38] Oudshoorn, N., Rommes, E., Stienstra, M. Configuring the User as Everybody: Gender and Design Cultures in Information and Communication Technologies. *Science, Technology & Human Values* 29, 1 (2004), 30–63.

[39] Papert, S. *Mindstorms: Children, Computers, and Powerful Ideas.* Basic Books, 1980.

[40] Papert, S. *The Children's Machine: Rethinking school in the age of the computer.* Basic Books, 1993.

[41] Robinson, B. Apple and the religious roots of technological devotion. *LA Times*, 2013.

[42] Stahl, W.A. *God and the Chip: Religion and the Culture of Technology.* Wilfrid Laurier University Press, 1999.

[43] Strauss, A. A Social World Perspective. *Studies in Symbolic Interaction* 1, (1978), 119–128.

[44] Weber, M. *The Sociology of Religion.* Beacon Press, 1993.

[45] Winters, N. and Ananny, M. Development Ideologies of the One Laptop Per Child (OLPC) Programme. 2007.

[46] Woodruff, A., Augustin, S., Foucault, B. Sabbath Day Home Automation: "It's Like Mixing Technology and Religion." *Proc. CHI 2007*, ACM Press, 527–536.

[47] Wyche, S.P., Aoki, P.M., Grinter, R.E. Re-placing faith: Reconsidering the Secular-Religious Use Divide in the United States and Kenya. *Proc. CHI 2008,* ACM Press, 11–20.

[48] Wyche, S.P., Grinter, R.E. Extraordinary Computing: Religion as a Lens for Reconsidering the Home. *Proc. CHI 2009,* ACM Press, 749–758.

Authenticity, Relatability and Collaborative Approaches to Sharing Knowledge about Assistive Living Technology

John Vines[1], Peter Wright[1], David Silver[2], Maggie Winchcombe[2] and Patrick Olivier[1]

[1]Culture Lab,
School of Computing Science,
Newcastle University, UK
{john.vines; p.c.wright; patrick.olivier}@ncl.ac.uk

[2]Years Ahead Partnership,
London, UK
{david.silver; maggie.winchcombe}
@yearsahead.co.uk

ABSTRACT

Health and care providers are increasingly looking to online and peer-to-peer services to supplement existing channels of assistive living technology (ALTs) provision and assessment. We describe the findings from 12 co-design workshops with 28 people from the UK representing a range of older people with and without health conditions, users of ALT and carers for people using such devices. The workshops were conducted to explore issues related to finding reliable information about ALT with the goal of gathering requirements for the design of a peer-to-peer knowledge sharing platform. Our analysis highlights how a current reliance on peers and informal networks relates to a desire to establish the authenticity and relatability of another person's experience to one's own circumstances. This connects to a perceived mistrust in information where provenance and authenticity is not clear. We use these to critique the wisdom of taking an e-marketplace and recommendation service approach to ALT provision and assessment, and offer alternatives based on our findings.

Author Keywords

Assistive technology; peer-to-peer healthcare; online health communities; older people; ageing; co-design.

ACM Classification Keywords

H.5.m. Information interfaces and presentation (e.g., HCI): Miscellaneous.

INTRODUCTION

The study of collaborative and peer-to-peer communities around issues to do with personal health is an important area of CSCW research [15,16,20,22]. Forums, message boards and online information resources, that are often collectively contributed to by members of the public, have been demonstrated to be a useful means for bringing people together who have similar conditions and health needs [30], providing a shared understanding of what it means to live with specific conditions [22], and support a widened awareness of how to live healthily [16]. Such collaborative approaches to healthcare have been particularly influential in the UK, where patients are encouraged to review and rate the public health services they have used [1], to contribute their knowledge and experience to online resources [17] or share advice with peers via online communities [14].

CSCW '15, March 14-18, 2015, Vancouver, BC, Canada.
Copyright is held by the owner/author(s). Publication rights licensed to ACM.
ACM 978-1-4503-2922-4/15/03...$15.00
http://dx.doi.org/10.1145/2675133.2675222

We extend current CSCW research on collaborative approaches to personal health by exploring the applicability of existing approaches to peer knowledge sharing in the context of searching for expertise and information around assistive living technology (ALT). ALT is a broadly defined category of products or devices that enable older people or those with disabilities to live more independently than would otherwise be possible [49]. Our research was undertaken in the UK, where historically most ALT assessment and provision has been state-provided by local government authorities as part of social care services. As with much social care provision in the UK, ALT is an increasingly mixed-economy (private and state funded) and market-oriented domain. This comes with a shift in policy towards supporting patient and consumer choice—suggesting those who require ALT have a greater autonomy in deciding what they use and buy. However, there are well-known issues such as a lack of public awareness of what is available, inappropriate selling, and a large proportion of ALT abandonment by owners shortly after first use [37]. This is problematized further in the UK as the ALT market is mostly formed of small and relatively unknown companies.

In line with the UK Government's 'digital by default' strategy [11], local authorities are looking to online services as a way to resolve some of these challenges. This has led to a range of online information portals and marketplaces for ALT being piloted by different authorities (e.g. [24, 39]), while there are moves to incorporate peer-to-peer elements through user-generated feedback on ALT products and retailers [33]. In our research, we set out to understand the information, advice and expertise seeking needs of people who are purchasing or in receipt of ALT. Our aim was to explore the ways in which online services and digital platforms—including those being piloted by local authorities—may meet these needs. We conducted a series of 12 design workshops with groups of existing users of ALT, family caregivers and older people who considered themselves potential future users of ALT. Our workshops set out to explore the problems that people faced in finding information about ALT that is relevant to their needs. Through discussion and design activities we explored the formal and informal sources of advice and guidance participants already accessed and the barriers faced in relating advice to individual circumstances. We offer two main contributions to CSCW discourse on collaborative approaches to healthcare. First, we highlight the ways in which the trustworthiness of advice and expertise in this context is tightly related to the perceived relatedness of content and access to local resources to assess this advice. Second, we highlight how the practical but highly personalized nature of the information requirements for users of ALT raise implications for the ways in which online communities that support the collaborative exchange of information are designed. In response, we contribute a series of design considerations for collaborative information sharing, focusing on how online communities may be enhanced to support the informational needs of ALT users and how future infrastructuring [29] work is needed to enhance cooperative work between public and private stakeholders and the public.

THE CONTEXT: ALT PROVISION IN THE UK

ALT covers a wide range of potential devices ranging from small aids (e.g. jam-jar openers or grabbers to help pick up objects) to home adaptations (e.g. stair lifts and bath steps) and electronic aids (e.g. fall alarms and pill dispensers). Up to 13m people in the United States currently use some form of ALT to help them everyday [47], while in the UK it is claimed up to 3m people would benefit from digital ALT services [10]. While there has been substantial growth in the range of ALTs available in recent years, there is a widely acknowledged lack of public awareness about its benefits and the relative quality between devices [13].

Our research was conducted with the eventual goal of developing tools and platforms that help existing and future users of ALT to access and share relevant information resources with each other. The research was conducted in the UK, and there are further particularities to ALT provision here that impact on potential use and access. Historically, aids and adaptations have been provided by local government authorities. This typically involves Occupational Therapists (OTs) visiting people in their homes to assess their physical and cognitive requirements in relation to their daily living activities—although more recently assessments may be made over the phone by an OT's assistant who follows a decision tree. From these assessments OTs provide recommendations for what equipment and adaptations should be provided, which are then delivered and installed by the local authority or its appointed contractors. However, this is only done when the ALT required meets a need that the Local Authority has a duty to provide for, e.g. bathing. Changes to social care in the UK however mean that people are now being provided with 'personal budgets' by their local authority, with a view to tailoring assessments and allowing individuals to spend their budgets as they see fit [8]. As a way of supporting people in making decisions about how, where and what to spend these budgets on, local authorities have started to commission online services and portals. Some are developing information gateways that provide links to products, service providers and charities specifically focused on the needs of older people (e.g. [24]). Many more have purchased generic online marketplaces that have lightweight self-assessment tools that then list a catalogue of products and services recommended by that local authority that may meet that person's needs (e.g. [39]). There is wide acceptance within authorities, however, that these online resources are somewhat limited in their value as they still require significant management and updating (which invariably means they are out-dated quickly). Furthermore, they offer few opportunities for members of the public to contribute their own knowledge and expertise, or provide ways for them to articulate whether a recommended vendor or information source was of any value to them. As such, there are calls from some authorities, charities and ALT service providers for recommendation services that integrate catalogues with the everyday expertise and contributions of citizens [33].

Collaborative and peer-to-peer healthcare

In many respects, the above debate surrounding ALT information and provision in the UK is representative of wider changes to the delivery and experience of health care resulting from greater access to the Internet and collaborative information sharing. Over the last decade there has been a huge growth in interest in the role that collaborative approaches to healthcare can play in providing new models of patient-centred and peer-produced health information and advice. A significant body of research has investigated how online health communities (message boards, email lists, blogging platforms and forums) provide valuable resources for people living with specific conditions [4, 30, 36]. It has been argued that involvement in such communities can empower patients by offering them new channels to understanding their condition and understanding why decisions about treatment have been made [4]. Maloney-Krichmar and Preece's [30] seminal work highlights some of the core qualities that online communities may offer people experiencing specific health conditions. This includes providing a channel to communicate anxieties and concerns to supportive others [30]. Online communities also enable community members to participate in a myriad of ways, such as being able to provide data and facts to others, to proactively and subtly request information and support, or just provide praise to others [30]. The literature on online health communities highlights a number of qualities that typically support active participation, including their increased anonymity which supports greater disclosure [23], confronting people with experiences that are similar or opposed to their own [31], and as a way of finding experience-rich information that is hard to find through formal channels [15].

HCI research on online health communities in HCI has thus far focused primarily on their emotional support qualities (e.g. [23, 30]) or on ways to increase participation [31]. This has included studies of such communities for older adults [27, 36] and family caregivers [46]. However, there has been relatively little work on exploring the ways in which people identify expertise relevant to their needs. Exceptions to this include [6, 7] which highlighted the strategies that women with breast cancer take when trying to identify 'everyday' experts. We expand this work but deal with a context where there is no established common ground between individuals whose needs (and their understanding of these needs) are in flux and where access to local ALT resources is of greater concern than social support.

Recommender systems and online marketplaces

A further area relevant here is the growing literature on recommendation services and online marketplaces, both of which have grown enormously in popularity over the last decade. Websites such as TripAdvisor, Urbanspoon and Yelp provide the public with a wealth of reviews of local hotels, restaurants and bars. A significant amount of research on recommendation services has focused on improving the algorithms underlying recommendations (e.g. [19]) or developing tools and visual cues to support making sense of reviews on these sites (e.g. [51]). Brown's [5] ethnographic work of review site users, however, highlights some of the motivational factors for use of these sites in the first place instead. It was noted that such sites allowed people to pre-visit locations and establishments, arming them with information in preparation for a visit.

Review and recommendation services have also become an integral component of online commerce and marketplaces. Online commerce research has highlighted how negative reviews of products have a greater impact on subsequent sales than positive reviews [9], and reviews are particularly influential when products are new and less well known [21]. Furthermore, reviews on sites like Amazon become more influential in the context of 'experience products' [38]—i.e., those products that require use or consumption in order to judge their quality or worth [28]. In a similar vein, it has been noted that on Amazon those reviews considered 'helpful' are typically those including experiential insights based on the context of using a product and advice on how to best use it [42].

The reliability of online reviews has often been debated. It is not uncommon to see news stories of how business owners place false reviews [43] on TripAdvisor. In 2012, Amazon deleted several thousand 'fake' reviews after public complaints [44]. Similar concerns have been raised about the reliability of user-generated reviews as they have started to become influential in the domain of healthcare. In 2009 the UK's NHS opened a rating and review function on their Choices website allowing patients and their families to rate NHS services and write short reviews backing up their score. Proponents have argued that this enables doctors and staff to better understand patient experiences and improve services in the future [1]. Those challenging the idea have questioned the impact overtly negative and positive reviews may have on trusted relationships between patients and health professionals [32]. Clearly, the perceived reliability of such information becomes even more critical when moving from leisure to health.

As noted already, the popularity of review sites across a number of domains has lead to calls that user-based recommendation services could increase the wider public awareness of ALT and the purchasing of more appropriate devices by users [41]. Indeed, ALT recommendation sites already exist (such as GadgetGateway [53]), and it is possible to purchase and review ALT and mobility aids from Amazon.com and affiliated merchants. But these sites are notable for their absence of reviews and poorly updated content. Furthermore, there is not yet a sense of how appropriate such resources may be to existing or future ALT users. In our work we examined the reasons existing resources may fail to attract reviews, and what critical factors related to the experience of ALT use need to be accounted for in the design of such online services.

DESIGNING THE RESEARCH

In designing our study, we worked closely with a social enterprise set-up whose aim is to improve choice and independence for older people in the UK. In developing our approach, we explicitly drew on insights from the literature on peer-to-peer health and online health communities as well as the experiences of our collaborators. We focused the study around exploring three interrelated issues.

First, while there is a widely acknowledged lack of knowledge and awareness around ALT, there is an equal lack of research into precisely how people go about looking for information and advice on it in the first place. Therefore, a primary focal point of our study was to *explore the information seeking strategies and the local resources and strategies* that participants draw upon when trying to find advice and guidance on ALT.

Second, we wished to understand the perceived differences between accessing and using advice and recommendations online as compared to advice received in person. That ALT has historically been supplied and funded by the state involving in-person assessments may mean participants may place different levels of expectation on interactions occurring online or offline in this domain. Furthermore, given the noted recent publicity in the UK press around the fallibility of online review sites, we felt it important to understand if participants *trusted certain sources of information related to ALT more than others* and what implication these may have for online service provision.

Third, we were not just interested in understanding how people might find information, advice and resources related to ALT but *designing new resources that help them in finding out about the right ALT*—i.e, ones that met their particular needs and came from reputable sources. The self-assessment of need in the context of ALT is particularly challenging as individuals will likely be going through significant personal or familial changes. Furthermore, in many instances it may be a family member or friend acting as a carer who is informally assessing needs, adding further layers of complexity.

The overall goal of exploring these three interrelated issues was to identify the requirements for new collaborative and peer-to-peer online services that support the public in locating expertise in ALT relevant to their needs.

Participants

We undertook a series of design workshops with people representing a diverse range of beneficiaries and users of ALT. In recruiting participants we explicitly aimed to work with older people who either had experienced living with a range of ALT devices or helped others in acquiring them. In total we met with 28 participants, with a mean age of 70 years. Our oldest participant was 84 years old, with our youngest being 43. 19 (68%) of our participants were female. Of those participants older than 65, 66% considered themselves frequent users of the Internet from their home through personal computers, tablets and smartphones. This is above the UK average for this age range (47%) [35]. At the same time, our participants reported generally low-use or knowledge of online communities, social networking and recommendation services (two participants used Facebook, and 4 had used TripAdvisor). None were aware of the online services provided by their LAs or any local ALT charities.

The range of experiences among our participants and their motivations for taking part in the research were diverse. 8 identified themselves primarily as frequent users of ALTs. Of these, only 1 participant had not directly purchased their own aids or adaptations, having received theirs primarily through their local authority. The remaining 7 ALT users had used a mixture of products purchased by themselves, provided by the state or given to them by friends and family members. 10 further participants self-identified as carers for their partners or parents who had chronic conditions and disabilities. They configured their participation in the research in reference to their experiences of purchasing, installing and maintaining ALTs on behalf of those they cared for. Their motivations for taking part ranged from wanting to find out about new gadgets to a desire to share their frustrations of struggling to find information about ALT. The remaining 10 participants did not self-identify as either users of ALT nor carers but as individuals that were concerned about their own future welfare. They drew upon the narratives of friends and family members to motivate their participation in this research—highlighting the problems that significant others in their lives had faced in finding reliable information around ALT, and the problems they had with both state provided and privately purchased aids.

It is important to note that while the above distinctions are useful to illustrate the diversity of the participants, individuals would often sit between group boundaries. For example, one participant came to the workshops with the intention of discussing his experiences of searching for equipment and devices for his Mother who was living with dementia. But he was also a wheelchair user, and frequently drew upon his personal experiences of assessing his own needs. Similarly, individuals who identified themselves as 'users' of ALT also acted as carers for spouses, brothers and sisters, who themselves had gone through similar experiences.

Co-Design workshops

We met the participants in 6 separate groups. In arranging the groups, we did not aim to separate participants into distinct categories. Rather, we wished to place their experiences and views 'in dialogue' [50] with one-another. We met each of the 6 groups twice in a series of 2 design workshops (12 workshops in total). The aim of these workshops was to elicit rich discussions and undertake co-design activities related to the three core issues we wished to explore. We carefully constructed our methods to reflect the challenge of supporting participants in imagining the role technology may play in a context where it is yet to intervene greatly, and also to engage them in dialogue with each other around their potentially diverse experiences and needs. In the following sections we describe the methods used in these workshops.

Workshop 1: Introductions and Invisible Design

The first workshop opened with participants introducing themselves to one-another and being invited to explain their interest in the topic of the workshops. This was structured through asking each participant to start with 'I'm here because…' and then detailing their motivations for participating in the research. Following this, participants were invited to recall their experiences of ALT—including how they had come into contact with it, where they had accessed or purchased it from, and how they ended up with the equipment and devices that they or their family members owned. This provided opportunities to explore a wide range of commonalities and differences between participants in relation to our first issue of concern: *the information seeking strategies and the local*

Figure 1. A still from the 'Cucumber' invisible design film with Stan explaining to Billy the service he has signed up to.

resources drawn upon when making decisions around ALT. During this discussion-based activity—which lasted between 60 and 90 minutes—the researcher visually documented the different resources (organisations, retailers, publications, people) participants referred to as a map for all to see.

This activity was followed by a presentation of an Invisible Design film [3] called *Cucumber*. In Invisible Design films the focus is on the dialogues between characters who discuss a technology that is in the scene but never seen. This technique has been highlighted as particularly useful in undertaking co-design with older people in the early stages of a design process [3]. We developed our Invisible Design Film with a view to engaging participants in speculations around the relationship between the characters and issues to do with online information exchange and sharing advice and tips with peers. The aim here was to explore the second focal point of whether participants *trusted certain sources of information related to ALT more than others* about ALT and the differences between receiving advice from strangers and friends.

The *Cucumber* film opens with an older gentleman—Billy—sat in his armchair watching TV. A *"knock knock"* is heard followed by a male voice: *"it's only me!"*. Another older gentlemen—Stan—enters the room holding a bag of shopping. Upon closing the door a picture falls off the wall behind Billy. As a result, what ensues is a back and forth between the two with Stan talking about a new service he uses to get advice and tips from people to fix problems like this. But Billy refuses to accept Stan's advice. He questions whether those giving tips would be *"cowboys"*. When Stan explains *"he bought a knife sharpener, based on a recommendation"*, Billy replies with *"Aye, from a guy who makes knife sharpeners"*. After some more discussion, Billy starts to come round to the idea, but Stan says: *"You've got to sign up. I can ask for you, but if you want one you've got to sign up. You should. You'd be good man."* Billy sits back in his chair: *"Ah well. Maybe"* he sighs. As with prior Invisible Design films humour plays an important role, emphasized by the film's ending of Stan giving Billy a cucumber, the reason for him visiting in the first place.

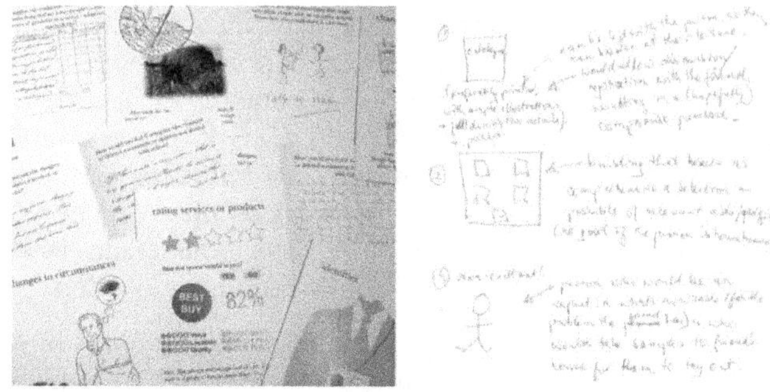

Figure 2. A collection of Topic Cards with written responses (left) and an example of participant drawing in response to design activity on rear of card (right).

After watching the film, participants were asked to comment on the film and then to address the 'invisible design' (the imagined online peer-to-peer ALT community) associated with it. This discussion would last anywhere between 30 to 60 minutes. In their entirety, the workshops lasted up to 3 hours in length.

Workshops 2: Participant-led topic cards

At the end of the first workshops each participant was provided with a pack of 8 prompt cards (Figure 2). Inspired by the Questionable Concept technique [48], the prompt cards were designed to gather further reflection on issues touched upon in the Cucumber film. Each card had an illustration on the front with a title and a quote from the film. Inside, there were two open-ended questions and a small design activity for participants to respond to. The cards were intended to provoke deeper discussion and reflections on the design of the peer-to-peer platform. For example, the 'membership' card posed questions related to the provenance of information and whether participants would feel differently if people providing recommendations were recognisable members of a community. The design activity here asked participants to 'write or draw what you would like to know about other members of the community'. It was explained to participants that they did not have to respond to all of the cards and that the second workshop will be based on discussing the cards that they had completed.

The second workshops were structured around each participant selecting a prompt card to discuss and allowing them to lead discussion around this issue. Participants took it in turns to talk about the card they had chosen, why they had chosen it, and what their responses were. The researcher would invite the other participants to talk about their own responses to the same card (if they had done so) with a view to drawing out further overlaps and contrasting views around the design of the platform.

Data analysis

Each workshop was audio recorded, resulting in approximately 28 hours of data. These recordings, along with written responses on the cards, were transcribed. Combined with the visual material, this was treated as a data corpus on which an inductive thematic analysis [2] was performed. The analysis proceeded through the development of single-word codes that summarised textual excerpts at the sentence level for text and an artefact level for visual material. Codes were grouped together to generate 4 themes from the data: (1) *expertise and advice,* (2) *authenticity and transparency*, (3) *family, friend and peers as a resource,* (4) and *relatability and testability*.

EXPERTISE AND ADVICE

The opening 'I'm here because' discussions provided a structure for participants to discuss their existing strategies and challenges for finding information about ALT. As noted, none of the participants were aware of existing online resources provided either by their local authority or by charities and non-profits. Indeed, a lack of awareness of any sort of information or support was common:

> *"If I wanted to go and buy some fruit, in 15-20 minutes I could've visited 6 shops and bought some. If I want to see somebody about the arthritis in my wrist, I haven't the faintest idea who I would go and see."* – M2

In making sense of this situation, M2 was aware that at some level that as his challenge was related to his arthritis then it may be seen as a medical issue. But at the same time he was aware that it was not a concern with the medical condition itself but the impact that it has upon his life. He was not seeking advice on how to remedy his discomfort but rather how to alter the environment around him to make conducting activities as comfortable as possible. It was difficult for participants to make sense of this complex relationship however. There was still an expectation among a large majority (n=15) of participants that their doctor would be able to advise them. M4, for example, spoke at length about how he visited his doctor on a number of occasions and asked about *"things to help him around the home"* following being diagnosed with polymyalgia rheumatica. All that his doctor provided after several visits was suggestions on what Internet search engines and search terms to use to find information. This raised further challenges for M4, as he did not consider himself *"very good at operating the home computer"*. He had a view, shared by others, that his doctor had the credibility and qualifications to provide informed advice. In reality, however, there is little interaction between doctors and local authorities in assessing the needs of an individual.

M4's experience also illustrates how participants felt comfortable visiting their doctor to ask for advice, but did not feel at ease with the idea of having an Occupational Therapist visit their home and *"assess"* them. In M4's case this was partly a result of not wanting to be *"bothersome"*, to *"escalate the situation"* and be seen to be *"making more out of it than I need to"*. While a trip to the doctor's surgery for advice was acceptable, there was clear discomfort at the idea of someone visiting his home to assess him. This also illustrated a desire across participants that while advice and guidance was desired, so was a feeling of dealing with and managing it individually or within the family: *"My husband had a bypass on the damaged nerves in his hands and arms, and I'd never thought about getting help. We just got on with it."* (F14).

To a small number of participants (n=4), however, it was surprising that the issue of information and advice seeking around ALT was worthy of investigation. F3 for example had used a number of aids at home since she had surgery 10 years ago: *"I have a lot of gadgets, help and all sorts of things. It surprises me that some people don't know where to go."* F3, along with two of the family carers (F12 and F17), had received all of their aids from their local authority—however, none of these participants were aware of the upcoming changes to state provision that meant how they accessed and used this service would change. M1 was also surprised at others' lack of knowledge of how to seek advice. Having lost his sight 10 years ago, he has since received monthly newsletters from the Royal National Institute for the Blind: *"I get a product newsletter* [...] *They send their stuff out to blind persons to be tested, and ask them at the end for a review on it"* (M1). He trusted this because it came as a recommendation from a charity he trusted and as he had been a *"reviewer"* himself a number of times.

AUTHENTICITY AND TRANSPARENCY

It was clear that ALT was a particularly problematic topic when it came to trusting sources of information. While there was a lack of awareness at three levels—that ALT exists, what its potential benefits are and where to go for advice—there was a great awareness of sources of advice that should not be trusted or were lacking in authenticity. All but 3 participants recalled stories of door-to-door salesmen who appeared to target their or their older family members' homes to sell expensive adaptable furniture and equipment. Two participants explained how they had purchased a large number of electronic aids for themselves (M4) and for their mother (F14) based on adverts in newspapers and catalogues received in the mail. Adverts for products would come with grandiose claims and quotes from customers about how the gadget had changed their lives, yet it was common for gadgets to break within weeks of purchase. The sharing of these negative experiences was combined with a general sense across all the groups that older people and carers in emotionally distressing situations had heightened vulnerabilities, and a prime target of rogue traders and salesmen *"hard selling"* (F11) inappropriate products: *"I think we are aware that there are many people trying to talk us into agreements that are not true and people who try to gain from other people's lack of knowledge."* (F7). This reinforced a reliance on state services, as they were seen to be more trusted and independent in their advice.

The deep sense of distrust surrounding ALT was particularly evident during the invisible design activity when participants speculated about the relationship between the characters in the *Cucumber* film. First, some participants raised concerns about the unstated motivations of people providing *"seemingly unbiased advice"*. The

Figure 3. Topic card responses from F10 (left) and F18 (right) highlighting preferences for in-person and hands-on experiences of sharing advice with others.

scriptwriter had intended Stan to come across as trying to help his friend Billy by giving him advice on how to adapt based on what he had seen online through the device *"in his bag"*. Approximately half of the participants (n=12) deemed that Stan had hidden motivations however. They specifically latched onto a part of the script where Stan reiterated to Billy the need to 'sign up' to this service in order to receive information. A number of participants reacted angrily and felt *"uneasy"* (F3) at this point. This was in part because there was an expectation that the 'free' aspects of the service would be temporary: *"the first month would be free and then you have to pay for it afterwards"* (F2). Furthermore, there was a view that even if Stan was acting in the best interests of Billy, then there was too much ambiguity on: *"who it is exactly that is providing the recommendations in the first place"* (F6).

The lack of transparency of whom was providing a particular recommendation or piece of advice was seen as a particular problem with existing review sites. During the Invisible Design activity, participants picked up on the qualities that Stan's service shared with services such as TripAdvisor. Those participants who had used such sites felt that people providing reviews would be doing so for underhand reasons: *"How true are they? Are these reviews put together by Amazon?"* (M1); *"I tend not to look at those sorts of things, because you get just rants."* (M2); "[I'm] *never sure if the "put downs" have been posted by competitors."* (M5). Others spoke about the *"unsettling"* experiences of receiving emails from sites such as Amazon making suggestions about what other products might meet their needs: *"It's like, "We noticed you bought this." So, it's as if they're keeping tabs on everything that you do."* (F1). Such emails were seen as invasive rather than helpful and participants felt companies were only interested in selling products rather than genuinely finding something that was of interest or relevance to them. Based on these comparisons it was clear that having viewed the film the majority of participants did not consider Stan a friend or an ally, but a deceptive individual trying to influence Billy.

FAMILY, FRIENDS AND PEERS AS A RESOURCE

Given that most of our participants did not rely on their local authority for assessments around their needs—and visiting their doctor or trusting commercial advertising was not a viable option—there was often a reliance on family members, friends and people in similar circumstances as sources of advice and guidance. For example, 4 of the older participants relied on their adult children to perform lengthy searches on the Internet to find information on their behalf: *"I'll just ask him* [her son] *to have a look for me now"* (F15). It was notable however that those who stated having the most success identifying and purchasing new equipment were those who had had chance conversations and meetings with friends and peers. Returning to M4's experience, the resolution to his information challenge was through a chance meeting with an old friend he was visiting for an unrelated reason: *"She found out I had got PMR. She produced four pages of information on it, with ways to change your home and bits of equipment to do small things in the kitchen and bathroom."* (M4). In a similar vein, in the topic card discussions in the second workshop 12 participants chose the 'sharing solutions' card to discuss with the group. In these discussions they recalled chance exchanges of information and knowledge related to ALT between friends. F2 explained how she met an old friend at the bus stop recently after a long period of not seeing her:

> *"She needed her walking stick but she kept dropping it,* [...] *she had to stop going into town. Somebody had told her about this thing* [it] *goes round your wrist, and the other on the stick* [...] *such a little thing has made all the difference to her life, she's independent again."*

F2 was so impressed with this adaptation that she made a note of its design for future reference, and shared it with everyone in the workshop. She explained how she knew of other people with similar problems, and would share this tip with them (Figure 3). Relatedly, 5 female participants explained how they would regularly go to coffee and tea mornings with friends. At these get-togethers they would allow *"only 10 minutes for ailments!"* (F8) and use this as an opportunity to talk about their problems and exchange ideas about changes they had made to their homes to make their lives easier. Such exchanges of information and advice also frequently occurred during our workshops. At the first workshops more experienced participants would offer suggestions to others on gadgets to help with specific activities and routines in their homes. At the second workshops, participants brought catalogues or print-outs of products they had spoken about previously. M1 proudly demonstrated his 'pen friend', which allowed him to record and recall messages from barcodes stuck onto objects. As he had very limited eyesight, this *"gadget"* was perfect in helping him find items around the home and not have to rely on his wife all the time. The other participants in this group were engrossed in his demonstration, exclaiming: *"That would be handy on my prescriptions"* (F6); *"I need one of them now!"* (F4). Indeed, several participants suggested that one way of resolving the issue of a lack of knowledge about ALT would be to provide spaces for informal get-togethers at community facilities, mimicking our workshops (Figure 3).

RELATABILITY AND TESTABILITY

Friends and peers were also influential due to the commonalities (or not) that they had with one-another. As such, their accounts, advice and experience were more easily 'relatable' to a participant's own situation than people whose background and provenance was unclear. For example, F4 explained how she valued the opinions of her female friends in particular *"because what a man might find easy to use, I with little, rotten grip might find very difficult to use. I think only my older lady friends understand this".* Participants who already used various forms of ALT found that the *"best recommendations"* they had received tended to be from people with very similar disabilities, conditions and life experiences to their own. F8 and F9, who both suffered from rheumatoid arthritis, found meeting people of a similar age with symptoms of a similar severity on a social level provided them with a great amount of advice in relation to useful aids to buy for their home. Friends were also important "recommenders" due to the social and cultural commonalities people felt they had with one-another. A small number of participants relied heavily on age-related or condition specific charities for any advice in relation to ALT. While in some cases this was motivated because they were seen to be trusted and independent organisations, in others the motivation was they felt the people making recommendations could more easily relate to their own circumstances. Participants found comfort in knowing advice would be coming from someone whose life experiences may not be far removed from theirs: *"It is re-assuring that they have had 'hands on' experience of needs similar to your own"* (F4). Suggestions from friends in particular came with a contextual understanding of that person's values, tastes and life experiences.

Relatability was also important in supporting reflection upon one's own circumstances and needs. Participants who were active users or seekers of ALT all spoke of the trial and error approach they had to take to the purchase and use of aids and adaptations. This was not just a limitation on available information on products, but also a limitation on their understanding of their or their family member's needs. Returning to M4's experience, he spoke candidly about his experiences of being diagnosed with polymyalgia rheumatica:

> *"I'd never even heard of it until it hit me. I was travelling up from London, got to Durham, started to get my thing ready, and found I couldn't get out of the chair and I couldn't reach my case above my head or anything. A young lady in her thirties got my bag down for me and stood me up, and opened the door at Newcastle so I could fall out, because it only stops for three minutes. For the next five weeks when I went to bed, my wife had to turn me in bed, this sort of thing."* – M4

M4's situation was not unusual among the older participants. The onset of his condition was dramatic and fast. He had no time to prepare for or adjust to the situation and was immediately confronted with the fact that he could no longer do even the simplest of activities he could before. But through relating his experiences to that of his friend in a similar circumstance, M4 began to come to a realisation of how he needed to "approach" everyday activities. Others explained how situations such as this were alike to a personal *"crisis"* where their lives or the lives of the person they cared for changed dramatically in a short space of time. During these periods of great transition, individuals felt as though they were continually playing catch-up with their changing needs and understanding of how daily activities needed to be adjusted or adapted. As such, it makes it impossible to know what to look for in order to help, as the reference point (the body) continually changes. These concerns were not just limited to those experiencing the onset of a condition or returning home following surgery—carers also commented on the great challenge of making quick decisions on someone else's behalf: *"you have to make decisions about adaptations very quickly, because the hospital is going to chuck her out."* (M8). In both M4's and M8's circumstances, the search for items to adapt the home was a process of continually asking questions about their or their Mother's needs—and indeed, the failure for M4 in finding suitable equipment to make his life easier continually allowed him to understand what his needs were not if nothing else.

Finally, even if shared knowledge was relatable at some level, then some form of physical access to locations where these items could be tested was of utmost importance. There were two reasons for the apparent need to visit locations nearby to see potential purchases. First, participants valued the people and organizations surrounding products as much as the product itself. They would carefully choose not just what they wished to purchase but also whom they would buy them from. Second, and perhaps more challenging in practice, was the view that ALTs are a type of 'experience product' [34] that require holding and experiencing prior to purchase in order to assess that they meet one's needs. One of the great challenges here is that not only is there great diversity in the range of devices available but also in the needs of potential purchasers, users and their homes. F12 had cared for her Mother for 15 years and had a great amount of experience buying small aids or investing in larger adaptations to support her mobility. As a result of not knowing where to source certain devices locally, she often relied on purchasing adaptations online or over the phone based on advice she had seen on online message boards. Frequently what was delivered was not appropriate for her Mother's specific physical needs or for the space requirements in her home: *"You think, What an absolute waste. If only we'd had the chance to go somewhere and try out a prototype, it would have saved all of that money"* (F12).

DISCUSSION

Our findings highlighted that our participants appreciated the opportunity to make informed decisions around the types of ALT that they purchase and use. At the same time, they frequently struggled in identifying sources of information that were reliable, authentic and relevant to their own needs. While online information resources and catalogues are being introduced, none of our participants were aware of these. There was a reliance on perceived ALT experts—such as doctors. But an equal lack of awareness of what is available by these experts, along with a lack of co-ordination between health providers, local authorities, and charitable organisations, introduces barriers to accessing informed advice. The lack of such resources and experts to draw upon further complicated periods in life where time is of a virtue and individuals have to quickly adapt or make quick decisions on the behalf of others. Therefore, rash decisions can be made, inappropriate equipment purchased or installed, and ALT thus become disused and abandoned in people's homes.

As was expected at the outset, there were also issues to do with the trustworthiness of ALT information sources. There was a lack of trust in online reviews and advice. While this was generally expected given wide scepticism around the authenticity of content on review services such as TripAdvisor, there were concerns very specific to the domain of practical ALT advice that problematized online content further. The lack of context and transparency on who may be providing advice and recommendations impacted not just on its credibility but also its relatability. There was a deep sense that such content would be inappropriate for decisions that may significantly impact on a person's life. Yet at the same time it was clear that making decisions was a highly collaborative activity, and participants had great trust in advice and recommendations from friends and peers they personally knew. Furthermore, we saw how the interactions between participants—most of whom never met each other prior to this research—promoted dialogues and the sharing of tips, advice and knowledge around ALT. Friends, peers and fellow participants were trusted for the same reasons that online content was not: they knew these people well in social circles; or they regularly saw them in their community; or they knew enough about their friends' lives to assess how relatable a recommendation may be to their own needs; or their peers were aware of accessible locations to buy, request or even test out these devices; or through in-person dialogue and rich descriptions they were able to assess whether one person's suggestion was immediately relevant to their own needs.

The existing agenda of the UK Government and its local authorities around information portals, online marketplaces and recommendation services currently fails to account for complex and subtle needs of individuals searching for advice and recommendations for ALT. However, while there was a great amount of mistrust and reservation about the role of digital technology in the sharing of relevant knowledge and advice, this was not necessarily a blanket suspicion or disregard of online content. Indeed there were clear opportunities for developing online communities and resources that are collectively and collaboratively contributed to. Our findings can inform the design of the growing number of technologies addressing issues of trust in peer-to-peer healthcare and bridge online communities with locally relevant and community developed information resources. The following sections discuss these areas to develop and offer general reflections on our findings and approach.

Supporting collaborative contributions and legibility

Our findings highlighted how the trustworthiness of advice was related to the capability for individuals to relate these to one's own circumstances. Prior work has explored the issue of trustworthiness among peer-produced health content, noting for example overtly emotional accounts [18], an inability to see similarities between a stated situation and one's own context [52], and commercial overtones of websites [41] all being barriers to trust. A popular response has been to develop interface cues that communicate the trustworthiness of content to a user—for example, through ranking content based on network analyses [12], by highlighting the expertise of a contributor [29] or by using 'bandwagon' cues to visualise the popularity of content to other community members [26]. While these types of cues may provide an immediate sense of the value of contributions, they assume a critical mass of users and also a community that is coherent in being able to assess the value of content. As we have highlighted, our specific context deals with a situation where there is no existing online user base and, even if there were, users would be diverse in ways that makes such cues redundant.

A potentially more fruitful approach here might be to support deepened and more contingently sensitive engagement from and between contributors and readers. Insight can be gleaned here from discourse analyses of online health communities that have highlighted the ways in which users negotiate the trustworthiness of content. For example, Sillence [40] noted how members of an online community for men with prostate cancer would negotiate the applicability of requests for advice to their own experiences through the careful curation and reading of profile content. Requests for advice were met with requests for greater detail, with members providing examples of their own experiences at the same time to illustrate the types of insight needed to meaningfully respond. As such, the trustworthiness of content was facilitated through threading advice with examples of personal experiences and linking to external resources that acted as evidence. These observations come from an online community in practice—however, they raise three opportunities for design in regards to the ways in which such interactions between members could be supported by interface cues.

First, carefully worded ***contribution cues*** could act as prompts and suggestions for the type of language used and detail to add when posting content (e.g., an experience of ALT). For example, it was clear from our workshops that the great potential of ALT is that it can enable people to continue independently performing routine activities they value. Contributors may be prompted to focus on their personal story as a journey—what had changed in their life, what impact this had on their everyday routines, and how a device improved this situation (or not). A similar story-based approach could be taken for those requesting support or advice. Through conveying their experience in this way, community members would increase opportunities for others to identify how relatable their experience is to their own circumstances.

Second, working alongside contribution cues we might imagine those reading the content are provided with ***legibility cues***. We saw in our workshops that a core quality of understanding the relatedness of accounts was dialogue between participants. Here, polite questioning of experiences was used as a way to explore the relatedness of another participant's experiences to their own. However, what was an atmosphere of polite scrutiny in a workshop can all too easily become more toxic online (e.g. [45]). As such, we suggest here that legibility cues are simple prompts that are offered to a reader to promote their engagement with contributions and to offer questions to support them in reflecting on post content in relation to their own needs. These questions may be generated by other readers and contributors, highlighting the ways that contributions and requests for information could be read or interpreted to support legibility. The aim here would be to engender a level of personal scrutiny valued in workshops without necessarily promoting an atmosphere of conflict around the validity of a contribution.

Third, online ALT services would benefit from ***enriched profiles and contributions*** that embrace multiple forms of content creation. One benefit of our topic card approach was that some participants were able to express anxieties and frustrations better through visual imagery and drawings than they could in text or in person. It also supported the expression of practical information in a more coherent manner—such as F2's sketch of an adaptation. We also saw opportunities for video and photo sharing to act as a conduit to making experiences and advice more relatable as well. Visually documenting equipment in use in 'real' home environments would be crucial to helping others envision its relatedness to one's own circumstances. But furthermore, user-contributed content in this form would support a greater amount of authenticity and the evidencing of ALT experiences. This would be particularly important given the wide mistrust of promotional material around ALT.

Infrastructuring localised resources

The success of taking a peer-to-peer approach to sharing experiences related to ALT is not just dependent on contributions being relatable, but also having awareness of the local availability of ALT in the first place and being able to test them. Information and advice can only help so much in a context where people's circumstances can be so different—from their physical capabilities through to what they value aesthetically and the environment they live in. Therefore, any peer-to-peer service must integrate online content with signposts to locations where gadgets and technology can be touched, seen and tested.

While technically the development of signposts within an online community to trusted locations is very feasible (for example, using locative media and mapping systems), there are a number of reasons to doubt the efficacy of a primarily technical response. ALT retailers and service providers and disability centres do exist in the UK, but they are still highly distributed, reflecting their publically funded heritage. That means facilities and resources available to people in certain locations may not be reflected in others—even across the same city, depending on authority boundaries. Instead, we suggest a more appropriate response would be to explore opportunities for infrastructuring—the alignment of social (i.e. people and practices) and material (i.e. artefacts and technology) resources [25,28]. In CSCW, the notion of infrastructuring has been used as a focal point of studying the ways that people and organisations cooperate in order to facilitate the operation and integration of collectively shared resources, knowledge and technical systems (e.g. [25]). However, it is rarely considered how infrastructuring may be proactively supported and the ways in which socio-technical platforms may be supported in developing over time (notable exception being [28]). We can envisage infrastructuring in the domain of ALT occurring at two levels.

A primary infrastructuring activity would be to develop greater coordination and information sharing between existing public, privately and voluntarily provided ALT services. In regards to seeking expertise and advice, we saw how there is a need to engage health providers to act as trusted intermediaries for any online resource and support those seeking advice in facilitating its access and use. But there is also a need to ensure that those resources already in development (information portals and online commerce) provided by local authorities signpost one-another and are updated with accurate and relatable listings of products and services available in the local area. This requires further work around who exactly is contributing and updating information on such sites, their ongoing governance, and whether communities or user advocates themselves might contribute content when new local facilities and resources become identified.

Secondly, infrastructuring activities could orient around resource mapping and identifying gaps in resource and service provision. Building on Grimes et al's [15] notion of 'deeply local' online communities, the ambition here should be to use local knowledge to map what ALT relevant facilities and resources are accessible within a specific locality. At one level, it could be imagined that this would lead to the mapping of resources and expertise beyond retailers and disability centres, to include local advocates and 'lead users' that are willing to act as demonstrators and 'show and tell' their own equipment to those who are requesting help. Furthermore, through mapping, imbalances in ALT availability and provision across localities might be highlighted. Thus providing opportunities for further engagements with public and private bodies to improve local ALT provision and the availability of facilities and, thus, awareness of ALT in specific geographical communities.

Reflections on our study and findings

As a final point, it is worth us reflecting a little on the findings of our study and our methodological approach, given the exploratory nature of our work and our atypical methods. First, it's important to note that we did not set out to build an online platform and study its use. Rather our work set out to study a context where there is great societal change and no existing reference point for online peer-to-peer exchange. Our methodology responded to this by providing structure and activities to support participants in expressing their experiences and imagining how these may be altered in the future. Although developing an online platform and deploying it in a field trial could be the subject of future work, our findings suggest that further infrastructural work is required before this would be fruitful and meaningful.

A further point to reflect on is our decision to explore this context through workshops where relevant parties were brought together to engage in activities and discussion relevant to this understudied domain. The workshops were successful in as much as they revealed a myriad of issues and design opportunities for online services and technologies in this domain. However, future ethnographically informed research in this domain is required that targets in more detail some of the core issues identified in this study.

It is also worth reflecting on the methods that we used to engage our participants in discussion, especially as they may seem non-trivial. As noted by Briggs et al. [3], Invisible Design films in particular are challenging to produce and require great care in balancing the narrative context of characters, emphasising a technological intervention (the design) but being explicitly non-committal about what its form or function is. Briggs et al. [3] highlighted how these films can be frustrating to participants—and indeed we had reactions from some participants who just *"wanted to know what was in the bag"* (F3) or felt *"if it had told us what was in his bag then it would have been much better"* (F12). One of the main purposes of these types of films however—and especially so in *Cucumber*—is to avoid discussion that focuses on form and promote debate around the experiences of the characters in screen. As such, the film succeeded at this, albeit in a way not imagined by the research team. Rather than focusing on Stan and Billy's relationships with the unseen individuals that were offering advice and recommendations to Stan, participants focused on the relationship between these two on-screen characters. Interestingly, what was scripted as two 'mates' having a catch-up was frequently taken to be one more active individual enforcing his way of doing things on his 'friend'. These insights were still useful however, as they highlighted immediate challenges to trusting advice from others in this context—challenges that are further emphasised when taken to online environments.

CONCLUSION

In this paper, we have focused on exploring the challenges and opportunities that are facing the use of peer-to-peer approaches to knowledge sharing in the context of ALT provision in the UK. We noted that peer-to-peer exchanges may have the potential to widen awareness of ALT to those who may need it. Yet to make any online community or service in this space meaningful and relatable, content and contributions must communicate rich insights about the context that the advice comes from. Yet perhaps of most importance is the need for supporting the testability of others' experiences and signposting physical locations to try ALT in one's own community. As it stands, such facilities are few and far between. Therefore, future design activity may focus on the development of tools and platforms that support the sharing of these locations, and encourage peers to meet and share their experiences with each other in person. This raises great implications for the ways in which governments in nations such as the UK are replacing public services that have relied on interactions between people with digital alternatives. Rather than taking a 'build and they will come approach'—as is the case with the existing tactic of developing information portals and online marketplaces—we have argued that this is a context that requires infrastructuring and the development of tools to support this process.

ACKNOWLEDGEMENTS

This research was performed as part of the Technology Strategy Board project 'SALT' (2377-25137). We would like to thank our participants for their time, and Selina Sutton, Rob Comber and the anonymous reviewers for their helpful comments on earlier versions of this paper.

REFERENCES

1. Bacon, N. Will doctor rating sites improve standards of care? Yes. *British Medical Journal*, 2009, (338), 688-689.
2. Braun, V., and Clarke, V. Using thematic analysis in psychology. *Qualitative research in psychology*, 3(2), 77-101.

3. Briggs, P. et al. Invisible design: exploring insights and ideas through ambiguous film scenarios. In: *Proc. DIS '12*. ACM, 534-543.
4. Broom, A. Virtually he@lthy: The impact of internet use on disease experience and the doctor-patient relationship. *Qualitative Health Research*, 15 (3), 325-345.
5. Brown, B. Beyond recommendations: Local review websites and their impact. *TOCHI*, 19 (4), article 27.
6. Civian, A., McDonald, D., Unruh, K., and Pratt, W. Locating patient expertise in everyday life. In: *Proc. GROUP '09*, ACM (2009), 291-300.
7. Civian-Hartzler, A., McDonald, D., Powell, C., Skeels, M., Mukai, M., and Pratt, W. Bringing the Field into Focus: User-centered Design of a Patient Expertise Locator. In: *Proc. CHI '10*, ACM (2010), 1675-1684.
8. Coulter, A. Do patients want a choice and does it work? *British Medical Journal*, 2010 (341), c4989.
9. Cui, G., Lui, H., and Guo, X. The effect of online consumer reviews on new product sales. *Int. J. Electronic Commerce*, 17 (1), 39-58.
10. Department of Health. *Whole system demonstrator programme*. UK Government, London, 2011.
11. Department of Work and Pensions. *Digital by default: high quality digital services, focused on users, and clear support for those who are not yet online*. UK Government, London, 2012.
12. Fenandez-Luque, L., Karlsen, R., and Melton, G. HealthTrust: A social network approach for retrieving online health videos. *J. Medical Internet Research*, 14 (1), e22.
13. Field, M., and Jette, A (Eds.). *The future of disability in America*. The National Academies Press, Washington D.C., 2007.
14. GB Doc. http://www.gbdoc.co.uk/
15. Grimes, A., Bednar, M., Bolter, J., and Grinter, R. EatWell: sharing nutrition-related memories in a low-income community. In: Proc. *CSCW '08*, ACM (2008), 87-96.
16. Grimes, A., Landry, B., and Grinter, R. Characteristics of shared health reflections in a local community. In: *Proc. CSCW '10*, ACM, 435-444.
17. Health Talk Online. http://www.healthtalkonline.org/
18. Hinton, L., Kurinczuk, J., and Ziebland, S. Infertility; isolation and the Internet: A qualitative interview study. *Patient Educ Couns*, 81 (3), 436-441.
19. Herlocker, J., Konstan, J., Terveen, L., and Riedl, J. Evaluating collaborative filtering recommender systems. *TOIS*, 22 (1), 5-54.
20. Hong, H., Kim, J., Abowd, G., and Arriaga, R. Designing a social network to support the independence of young adults with autism. In: *Proc. CSCW '12*, ACM, 627-636.
21. Hu, N., Liu, L., and Zhang, J. Do online reviews affect product sales? The role of reviewer characteristics and temporal effects. *Inf Technol Manage*, 9, 201-214.
22. Huh, J., and Ackerman, M. Collaborative help in chronic disease management: supporting individualized problems. In: *Proc. CSCW '12*, ACM, 853-862.
23. Hwang, K., Ottenbacher, A., Green, A., Cannon-Diehl, M., Richardson, O., Bernstram, E., and Thomas, E. Social support in an internet weight loss community. *Int. J. Med. Inform.*, 79 (1), 5-13.
24. Information Now. http://informationnow.org.uk/
25. Jackson, S., Pompe, A., and Krieshok, G Repair worlds: Maintenance, repair, and ICT for development in rural Namibia. In: Proc. CSCW '12, ACM, 107-116.
26. Kim, H., and Sundar, S. Using interface cues in online health community boards to change impressions and encourage user contribution. In: *Proc. CHI '11*, ACM Press (2010), 599-608.
27. Klooster, J., Beijnum, B., Pawar, P., Sikkel, K., Meertens, L., and Hermens, H. Virtual communities for elderly healthcare: User-based requirements elicitation. *Int. J. Networking and Virtual Organizations*, 9 (3), 214-232.
28. Le Dantec, C. Participation and publics: Supporting community engagement. In: *Proc. CHI '12*, ACM, 1351-1360.
29. Liao, Q., and Fu, W. Expert Voices in Echo Chambers: Effects of Source Expertise Indicators on Exposure to Diverse Opinions. In: *Proc. CHI '14*, ACM (2014), 2745-2754.
30. Maloney-Krichmar, D., and Preece, J. A multilevel analysis of sociability, usability and community dynamics in an online health community. *TOCHI*, 12 (2), 201-232.
31. Massimi, M., Bender, J., Witteman, H., and Ahmed, O. Life transitions and online health communities: Reflecting on adoption, use and disengagement. In: *Proc. CSCW '14, ACM* (2014), 1491-1501.
32. McCartney, M. Will doctor rating sites improve standards of care? No. *British Medical Journal*, 2009, (338), 688-689.
33. Moran, A. *Raising the standard: The final report of a feasibility scheme to rate, approve or accredit assistive technology*. Years Ahead Partnership, London, 2011.
34. Nelson, P. Information and consumer behaviour. *J. of Political Economy*, 78 (2), 311-329.
35. OFCOM. *Accessing the internet at home: A quantitative and qualitative study among people with the internet at home*. OFCOM, London, 2009.
36. Pfeil, U., Zaphiris, P., and Wilson, S. Older adults' perceptions and experiences of online social support. *Interacting with Computers*, 21, 159-172.
37. Phillips, B. and Zhao, H. Predictors of assistive technology abandonment. *Assistive Technology*, 5, (1), 36–45.

38. Senecal, S., and Nantel, J. The influence of online product recommendations on consumers' online choices. *Journal of Retailing*, 80 (2), 159-169.
39. Shop4Support. https://www.shop4support.com/
40. Sillence, E. Seeking out very like-minded others: Exploring trust and advice issues in an online heath support group. *Int. J. of Web Based Communities*, 6 (4), 376-394.
41. Sillence, E., Hardy, C., and Briggs, P. Why don't we trust health websites that help us help each other? An analysis of online peer-to-peer healthcare. In: *Proc. WebSci '13*, ACM, 396-404.
42. Skalicky, S. Was this analysis helpful? A genre analysis of the amazon.com discourse community and its "most helpful;" product reviews. *Discourse, Context and Media*, 2, 84-93.
43. Smith, O. TripAdvisor reviewer exposed as hotel executive. http://www.telegraph.co.uk/travel/travelnews/10076753/TripAdvisor-reviewer-exposed-as-hotel-executive.html
44. Streitfeld, D. Giving Mom's book five stars? Amazon may cull your review. http://www.nytimes.com/2012/12/23/technology/amazon-book-reviews-deleted-in-a-purge-aimed-at-manipulation.html
45. Suler, J. The online disinhibition effect. *CyberPsychology & Behaviour*, 7 (3), 321-326.
46. Tixier, M., Gaglio, G., and Lewkowicz, M. Translating social support practices into online services for family caregivers. In: *Proc. GROUP '09*, ACM (2009), 71-80.
47. US Census Bureau Newsroom: Facts for Features & Special Editions: Facts for Features: 20th Anniversary of Americans with Disabilities Act. http://www.census.gov
48. Vines, J. et al. Questionable concepts: Critique as a resource for designing with eighty somethings. In: *Proc. CHI '12*, ACM, 1169-1178.
49. World Health Organization. *World report on disability*. Geneva, Switzerland, 2011.
50. Wright, P., and McCarthy, J. *Experience-centered design: Designers, users, and communities in dialogue*. Morgan & Claypool, New York, 2010.
51. Zanker, M. The Influence of Knowledgeable Explanations on Users' Perception of a Recommender System. In: *Proc. RecSys '12*, ACM, 269-272.
52. Ziebland, S. and Wyke, S. Health and illness in a connected world: How might sharing experiences on the Internet affect people's health? *Millbank Quarterly* 90 (2), 219-249.
53. UK Gadget Gateway. http://www.gadgetgateway.org.uk

To Risk or Not to Risk? Improving Financial Risk-Taking of Older Adults by Online Social Information

Jason Chen Zhao
Keio-Nus CUTE Center
Singapore
zhaoch21@gmail.com

Wai-Tat Fu
Department of Computer Science
University of Illinois at Urbana-Champaign
wfu@illinois.edu

Hanzhe Zhang
Department of Economics
University of Chicago
hanzhe@uchicago.edu

Shengdong Zhao
NUS-HCI lab
National University of Singapore
zhaosd@comp.nus.edu.sg

Henry Been-Lirn Duh
HIT Lab AU
University of Tasmania
Henry.Duh@utas.edu.au

ABSTRACT

Increasing number of older adults manage their retirement savings online. A crucial element of better management is to take rational financial risk – to strike a reasonable balance between expected gain and loss under uncertainty. With the emergence of Web 2.0 technologies, social trading networks can help individuals make better financial decisions by providing information about others' actions. It is, however, unclear whether these resources is beneficial to older adult's own financial decisions, especially because older adults are vulnerable to poor risk management. To address this question, we devise an experiment that improves upon an existing experimental economic task. We find that both peer information (detailed choices by a few individuals) and majority information (aggregated choices of the crowd) help older adults make more risk-neutral decisions. Furthermore, the combination of peer and majority information corrects more mistakes of more risk-averse older adults.

Author Keywords

Social information; decision-making; risk-taking; older adults; experience-based task.

ACM Classification Keywords

H.5.m. Information interfaces and presentation (e.g., HCI): Miscellaneous.

INTRODUCTION

Older adults represent an increasing proportion of the global population and hold a disproportionately large share of total personal wealth [39]. By 2020, adults aged 65 and over are expected to own one-third of all publicly held stocks in America [2]. To accommodate the growing "silver industry", the financial industry offers a variety of retirement investment plans and investment vehicles. Product variety and complexity inevitably require older adults to make better financial decisions. Although popular stereotypes suggest that older adults are more risk-averse than younger adults, economic and psychological studies show that older people generally make less optimal decisions than younger adults in financial situations and take risks in situations that require risk-averse behaviors (e.g., retirement saving management) [24, 30].

Older adults transition from information receivers to potential information contributors under emerging Web 2.0 technologies [4]. Social information (e.g. rating, comments, polls) can be more easily accessed by aging adults, and has great potential in helping older adults make better financial decisions by learning from others' experience.

Figure 1 Screenshot of ZuluTrade, a social trading website. Member's investment portfolios can be shared and followed.

Two types of social information are commonly found on the Web: (1) peer information – detailed choices by a few individuals, and (2) majority information – aggregated statistics about the choices of the crowd. For example, when people shop online, users can share their purchasing activities via social networking websites such as Twitter or Facebook, which provide other people with detailed

CSCW '15, March 14-18, 2015, Vancouver, BC, Canada.
Copyright 2015 ACM 978-1-4503-2922-4/15/03 $15.00
http://dx.doi.org/10.1145/2675133.2685033

individual choices. Some websites provide users with majority information, such as average ratings or total number of buyers of different products. In the finance domain, social trading networks, a type of online financial platforms, integrate social features to help users make decisions. For example, eToro and ZuluTrade let members share their investment decisions with explicit trading information and provide details beyond traditional financial forums that discuss only users' ideas (Figure 1). Geezeo and Wesabe allow users track their financial details. Two million households used these sites in 2008, and according to a Wall Street Journal report [19], that number is expected to jump to 16 million households within 10 years. As more older adults use the Internet to manage their financial assets [11], social information may also make aging adults feel vulnerable to risky investment options and fraudulent marketing practices [40]. Although important, there is still a general lack of research on how the online social systems influence financial decision-making behaviors. While it is usually difficult if not impossible to inform "correct" decisions (as they are either unknown in advance or hard to define), one reasonable and crucial objective for designers of online financial websites should be to help older adults manage risks better. As researchers of Computer Supported Cooperative Work (CSCW), we aim in this paper to understand whether the majority information and peer information, the social cues used in social trading networks can encourage rational risk-taking behavior among older adults.

Financial decision-making is a complex process that involves diverse variables, such as the domain knowledge or the personal financial condition of users. To clearly identify the sources of potential social influence, we conducted a lab-controlled study as the first step. Moreover, financial risk-taking is an experience-based decision-making process, in which the risk must be gauged empirically through the past experiences. Beyond the decision-making by users' own experiences, social trading networks encourage social learning by allowing the user to learn from the successes and failures of others, continually and gradually [27]. In recent years, several HCI and CSCW studies have investigated the influence of social cues on younger users' choice making [15, 22, 31, 32, 41], but the tasks used in these studies are description-based tasks, in which people make the decisions simply based on the descriptions of different options. This cannot represent the scenarios commonly encountered by older adults' risk management as they make continuous, long-term financial decisions such as retirement investment. Instead, our study builds on Knutson and Kuhnen's Behavioral Investment Allocation Strategy (BIAS) task and its subsequent modifications.

BIAS task is an experimental, experience-based task that investigates risk-taking behavior by minimizing the influence of participants' real-world financial knowledge [21, 29]. Furthermore, the BIAS task was designed to have a clear definition of rational risk-neutral choice, which helps us to investigate and highlight the irrational aspects of financial decisions.

Through the study, we are interested in understanding how social information commonly found on the social trading networks may influence risk-taking behavior. In particular, we are interested in whether providing older adults with peer information, majority information, and the combination of the two types of information, are effective in encouraging older adults to better manage risk.

SOCIAL TRADING NETWORKS

Financial trading was centered on the relationship between customers and brokers. Now with the surveillance of Web 2.0 technologies, it becomes possible to gather user-generated financial contents and provide users a new way of analyzing financial decisions by integrating other decision-makers' real-time trading data feed. Social trading networks have emerged in recent years, through the social networking websites. Users of social trading networks can easily look up other users' trading performance as well as the descriptive data of the crowd.

Figure 2. Screenshot of Stocktwits, where users can view the popularity and crowd sentiment towards an asset.

Social trading networks have several advantages over the traditional trading channels. Enabling transparent trading information flow, social trading networks make financial information of specific customer segments accessible to users according to users' own interest. For example, older adults can use the platform to understand the investment decisions of their peers with a similar financial situation and comparable risk management needs. Second, through information sharing, social trading offers investors the opportunity to work collaboratively with others on financial decisions. Moreover, financial systems could generate wisdom of the crowd [34], since cash incentive is the key driving force behind optimal rational crowd intelligence.

Although a variety of social trading networks platforms are rapidly emerging, there are mainly two categories: integrate social information of (1) other users of the platforms, and (2) users' existing social network. For example, eToro allows users to view other users' portfolios and to place a trade exactly like theirs. Other applications such as Stocktwits or Likefolio enable users to connect existing social networks, including Facebook and Twitter, to collect crowd opinions towards a specific asset (Figure 2).

RELATED WORK

Online financial decision-making in the social trading networks is collaborative and collective in nature. The HCI and CSCW communities have put increasing research efforts into understanding and measuring online social dynamic systems that investigate how users consume social networks content [25], share knowledge among social networks [14], and make choices based on social cues [31, 32]. Brief summaries of two relevant research areas follow.

Preferential Choice

People use the information on the web to help them make daily decisions, such as choosing movies, picking out clothes, or buying stock. To make these decisions, people collect information about options and engage in a process of comparison that ends with a choice. Understanding and facilitating consumers' choice-making process has received increased attention from the CSCW and HCI communities [22]. Jameson defined the term "preferential choice" to distinguish from "non-preferential choice" that exist only in terms of the correct solutions – for example, "which button needs to be clicked to send the email" [17]. For instance, in online shopping platforms or cultural markets (e.g. movie-booking systems), the social information gathered is subject to personal interest and preference. To investigate the preferential choice-making process, researchers commonly use the description-based decision-making tasks that provide complete information about probabilities and outcomes of each choice. Some studies used this type of experimental task to examine the influence of different kinds of information on people's online decision-making behaviors [31, 32]. By adding different interface cues (e.g. credibility of the information source, narrative of the information, and social cues), these studies identify people's preferential choices towards the descriptions of options with respect to the cues.

However, preferential choice making is not common in financial settings. Of particular concern to financial decisions is the phenomenon that people usually make decisions from experience, based on trends of recent payoffs from the investments of specific financial assets, because it is usually easier to judge the quality of a decision based on direct, perceived consequences. Although participants have their preferential choices based on their preferred risk-taking strategy, there often exists an optimal choice based on economic theories. Thus, decisions resulting from experience-based tasks, such as the Iowa Gambling Task and BIAS (refer to [24] for a complete review), have been extensively studied for these situations. In these tasks, explicit information about probabilities and outcomes is not shown and participants must rely on task experience acquired through task feedback. Thus, to better understand how online social information can influence older adults' financial decision-making behaviors, our current study adopts the BIAS task, which allows us to directly measure whether subjects are making better risk management in an experience-based task setting.

Social Influence

In a nutshell, social influence takes place when people adjust their beliefs and behaviors with respect to others whom they feel similar, in accordance with psychological principles or the majority of an individual's referent social group [8]. A number of empirical studies have considered effects of social influence in various settings, including education, beliefs, preferences, and financial decision making within physical groups [5, 20]. Recent research extends this investigation with the deployment of social media [12]. Kim explored common social cues used in the health domain and found that these cues had a strong influence on decision preference among young people, further revealing more influence between cues in which bandwagon effects were shown [31]. A similar finding was reported in [41]. By using tasks deployed on Mechanical Turk, Zeinab et al. found the information from the crowd had a greater effect than a friend's recommendation on the willingness of an individual to choose an option. This implies that majority information may have a stronger influence than peer information on people's online decisions. While generating social information or enabling social interaction among users provides a valuable reference source for people, biased social information can have a negative impact in settings that have optimal choice. In a social visualization study, Hullman et al. [15] found that unbiased social signals lead to fewer visual perception errors than those resulting from non-social settings and biased signals, which have converse effects.

Although the above studies show the importance of social influence on people's judgments, they have not addressed the current focus on financial risk-taking behaviors. Unlike the social influence in preferential choice making, the social influence in financial decision-making is actually a social learning process, as people need to make continuous decisions by combining own judgments with ideas from others. Social learning was found effective in improving the quality of online collaborative knowledge sharing [36] and crowdsourcing tasks [23]. In the finance domain, Wei Pan etc. has conducted the first study with social trading networks [37]. By analyzing the dataset from eToro, they found that social influence plays a significant role in users' trades, especially when the trading information consists of higher uncertainty. Furthermore, in his newly published book *Social Physics* [27], Alex Pentland summarizes Wei Pan's findings as the effects of social learning and idea flow through the social network, where the traders who have the right balance and diversity of peer ideas gain more than individual traders. However, the monetary gain doesn't necessary be equal to rational decisions or better risk management. In a certain period, active risk-seeking investors (or gamblers) may have better profits than rational investors, but this trading strategy may not be suitable for older adults in managing their retirement investment. Also, in [37], they did not tease apart majority information and peer information. Furthermore, the real-world data from eToro may not be ideal for understanding the rational aspects of the influence of social information, since the investment choices could be influenced by other confounding variables such as the user's financial domain knowledge and motivation of investment. As online interface designers, we would like to further understand the influence of specific types of social information on older adults' decisions.

OLDER ADULTS' RISK-TAKING AND DECISION BIASES

Risk is usually associated with uncertainty in outcomes when people make decisions [28]. If the provided information is complex and uncertain, individuals tend to use heuristics to make decisions [35]. For example, in the context of financial decision-making, people may estimate good investment vehicle merely relying on its short-term performance. As Gilbert pointed out, when there is little detailed information about the future, people tend to use their affect in the moment as a proxy for what the future will be [13]. This strategy simplifies cognitive workload, but results in sub-optimal decisions, that is, decisions that do not maximize monetary payoffs on average. While such affective forecasting errors may influence decisions for everyone, the limits of older adults' recollections of the past and lack of up-to-date domain knowledge make this forecasting error especially impactful [38]. In addition, from the developmental perspective, Socioemotional Selectivity Theory [6] suggests that older adults tend to optimize emotional experience when growing old, which involves reducing negative arousal during anticipation of negative events. Although these affective regulations may be healthy for balancing emotional experience and optimizing well-being, they may have negative effects on financial planning such as blunted loss anticipation.

In the decision-from-experience scenarios, the influence of decision bias has a significant effect on older adults. In a meta-review of aging risk-taking research, Mata [24] concluded that aging adults made more sub-optimal choices than younger individuals in an experience-based task, while no such difference was observed in a description-based task because learning deficits have stronger effects on decision-making from experience.

However, we postulate that the social information aggregated in the social trading platforms could modulate the decision bias for two reasons. First, the transparent information sharing can serve as the reinforcement and correction of older adults' own memory thereby decreasing the uncertainty of information and the influence of older adults' recollections limits. Second, the continuous and gradual information from peers and crowd creates an ideal environment to encourage social learning. In such situation, older adults can improve their investment strategies through the interaction between social learning with individual learning. By allowing the ideas flow, the social information provided may benefit older adults to make more risk-neutral decisions by modulating the influence of the learning deficits as well as the influence of affective regulation on proneness for financial decision mistakes.

Hence, the current study proposes the following hypotheses:

H1: Majority information can improve older adults' financial risk management.

H2: Peer information can improve older adults' financial risk management.

As reported in [31] and [41], the majority information has a stronger influence than peer information when users make decisions. We expect similar result in the experience-based decision-making settings, as the bandwagon effect is associated with this type of information:

H3: Majority information has a larger effect than peer information.

Aging adults have a more salient age identity and influence among their peer age group than younger adults [9], as previous studies have shown that social effects play an important role in seniors' purchasing behaviors and retirement savings decisions [10]. This finding strongly indicates that social influence could affect risk-taking behaviors.

H4: Peer information and majority information CAN modulate older adults' risk-taking attitude.

By a large-scale survey on older adults' technology use, the Internet usage among aged 65+ has increased to 40%, but only around 5% of those aged 85+ were Internet users [7]. Therefore, we choose the population group aged 65 on average as the "older adults" investigated in our study.

METHODOLOGY

We conducted a laboratory experiment modified from the BIAS task to incorporate social information. The risk-taking behaviors defined in the BIAS task are consistent with the anticipatory neural activity using event-related fMRI [21]. Moreover, although the BIAS task is an abstract version of real-world financial decision-making, it was demonstrated to have ecological validity: subjects who made more risk-neutral choices in the experiment also possessed more assets in the real world settings [29].

BIAS Task

In the BIAS task, subjects were required to allocate their money among three options: two stocks that yield variable returns, and one bond that yields a constant return of $1 per trial. One stock is "good" and generates a higher expected payoff (+$10 with 50% probability, $0 with 25% probability, -$10 with 25% probability), and the other is "bad" and generates a lower expected payoff (-$10 with 50% probability, $0 with 25% probability, +$10 with 25% probability). For each trial, earnings were drawn independently from these distributions. In each block of trials, the computer randomly selected one to be the "good" stock and the other one to be "bad" stock, but the subject remained unaware and can only infer which one was good from previous gains and losses of the stocks' performances.

During each trial, subjects first saw the three options (Anticipation) and then selected one of three assets on the next page (Choose). After the selection, their earnings for that trial, total earnings, and the outcomes of all assets were displayed and followed by the page of a fixations cross (Fixation) (Figure 3). The participants were asked to perform the task at their own pace and were not allowed to take notes.

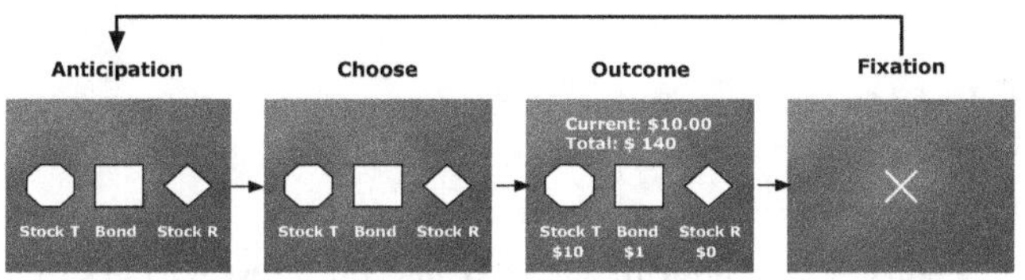

Figure 3. The conceptual workflow of each trial of BIAS task

Given that the actual monetary amounts at stake in each trial were small (−$1 to $1, since one-tenth of the task earning was given as the final reimbursement), the task defined the rational choice as the choice a risk-neutral, perfect Bayesian updater would make to maximize expected monetary return [27].

This risk-neutral actor updates the possibility of each option that generates the highest expected payoff based on Bayes' rule. To be specific, he or she would pick a stock i if the dividend D_k^i of this stock is at least as large as the bond earnings ($1) during trial k, that is, if: $E\left[D_k^i \middle| I_{K-1}\right] \geq 1$, where the I_{K-1} is the set of information up to trial k-1. Outcomes of stocks in each block were randomly generated from the probability distributions. From multiple sets of five blocks of outcomes, we selected the sets that the risk-neutral model earned $75 in each to control the difficulty across conditions.

For each trial, any choice that departs from the rational choice belongs to one of the three types of mistakes. When the rational choice is a riskless option (i.e., a bond) but the subject chooses a risky option (i.e., a stock), it is categorized as a **risk-seeking mistake (RSM)**. When the rational choice is a risky option (i.e., a stock) with the optimal expected payoff, but the subject chooses a riskless option (i.e., a bond), it is categorized as a **risk-averse mistake (RAM)**. If the subject chooses the other stock, then it is categorized as a **confusion mistake (CM)**, which the study does not analyze.

Social Information Modeling

Majority information

In his book *The Wisdom of Crowds,* Surowiecki suggests that aggregating the imperfect, distributed knowledge of a large group of people would yield better intelligence [34]. Alternatively, as proposed in theory of information cascade, if a group of people in a population exerts a stronger influence on others, the "herding" effect may cause others in the same population to abandon their own information in favor of following others [3]. Similarly, in the social media community, Sundar defines the behavior of blindly relying on the collective opinion of others as the "bandwagon effect" [33]. However, in a recent journal paper [1], Acemoglu demonstrates through social network analysis that "as networks of people grow larger, they'll usually tend to converge on an accurate understanding of information distributed among them, even if individual members of the network can observe only their nearby neighbors."

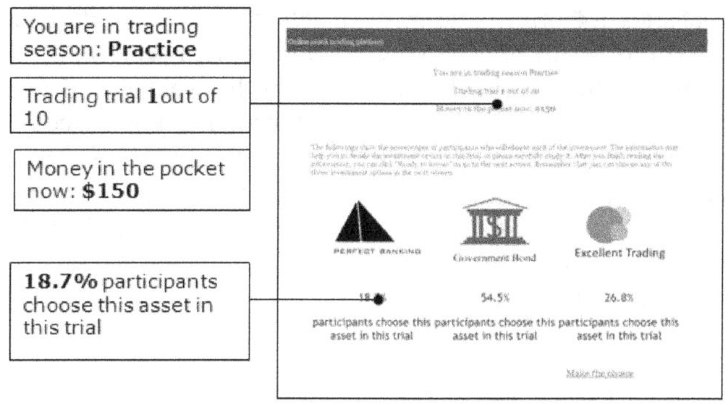

Figure 4. Majority information interface

To what extent of the majority information consists of the rational decision is a sophisticated economic question that involves many contextual factors and ongoing debates of the representative modeling of the real world, and is beyond the scope of this current paper. In our study, we modeled the majority information based on classic economics theory to maximize expected utilities [16]. We assumed that most of the decision-makers would behave rationally in our experiment. Thus, we generated the proportion based on the expected payoff. For example, the option with the highest expected payoff has the largest reported proportion, which is also the choice of a perfectly rational agent. The majority information assumption was proved by our experimental result. In the 1-5 blocks (the blocks without social information), participants made the average number of 4.51 rational choices in each block, which meant that around forty-five percent of people made the rational choice in each trial that consisted of the largest proportion among the three choices.

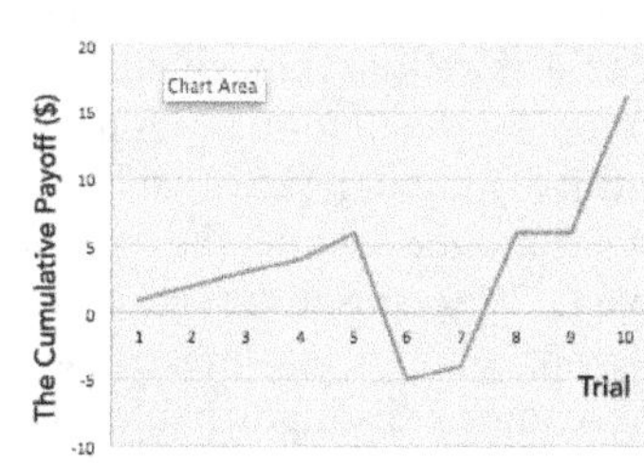

Figure 5. Example of payoff distribution within one block

Notably, in the experiment, the benefit of simply following the majority information was not obvious. Since the risk neutral agent chose the options with the highest *expected* payoff, not the options with *actual* payoff, the payoff of a risk-neutral choice at a certain period may be less than the risk-seeking or risk-averse strategy. We selected the distribution of stocks' outcomes that the risk-neutral actor earned $75 in each of five blocks, which was an average of $15 in each ten trials. Figure 5 shows an example of payoff distribution of a risk neutral agent's choice in a block of ten trials.

Peer information

Although according to classic economics theory we assumed that most of the people are risk-neutral in a transparent information environment, the individuals' decisions could be varied based on people's preferred risk-taking attitudes [25]. For example, in the webpage of most followed users in eToro (Figure 6), user 1 is a risk-seeking investor while user 2 is a risk-averse investor. Thus, in the attempt to simulate real world scenarios, we modeled peer information as the different attitudes of people risk-taking behaviors, from absolute risk-averse (the people who don't invest at all), risk-averse, risk neutral to risk-seeking.

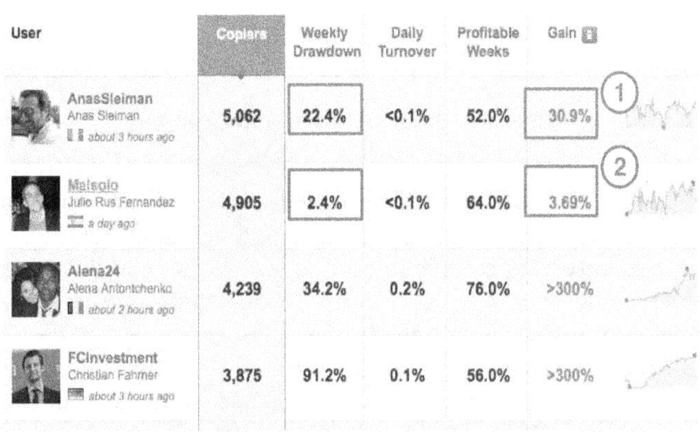

Figure 6. Screenshot of eToro Openbook's most followed users

The four virtual peers' choices are the choices made by four "ideal" agents with different utility functions that exhibit different levels of risk aversion, ideally to simulate the risk-taking attitudes present in a real-world population. Peer 1 is a risk-neutral, linear utility maximizer who always makes rational choices according to definition. Peers 2 and 3 make the choices as if they are risk-averse agents with the constant absolute risk averse (CARA) utility function: $1 - \exp(-a\ (10 + x))$ with a=0.5 for Peer 2 and a=0.0002 for Peer 3. Peer 4 is risk seeking with the agent's choices generated by the risk-seeking utility function $(150 + x)^2$. . The CARA utility function [25] can be only risk-averse with a concave function, while the risk-seeking function must be convex. We chose the parameters of the two functions different enough to make the distribution of virtual agents' choices distinguishable. The interfaces of majority information and peer information (Figure 4 and 7) are designed to be similar to the relevant webpages shown in the social trading networks platforms, that is, majority information with the crowd choice's indicator (Figure 2) and peer information with the performance of the selected individuals in the form of investment preference, current investment outcome, and line graph of the payoff trend (Figure 6).

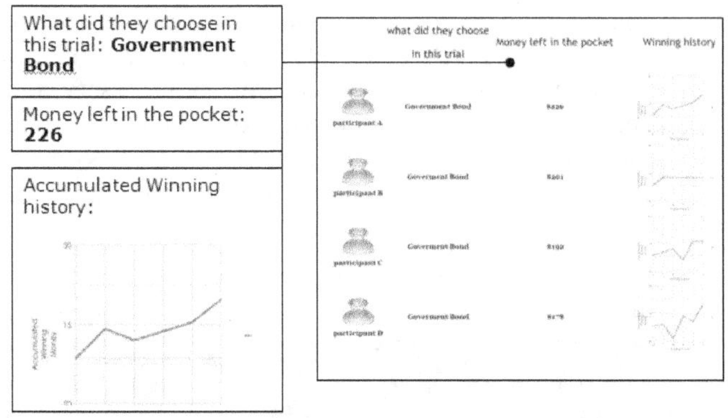

Figure 7. Peer information interface, the upper part of this interface same as figure 4, except the majority information

Experimental Manipulations

In order to involve the social signal in the experiment, we told the participants in the social conditions that our system had already collected other participants' data and would extract the relevant information to help them play the task. Also, we specifically designed the task interface. In the login page of the experiment task, we randomized a number between 200 and 250 to inform participants of their user status: "Welcome to our online stock trading task. You are the XXX participant!" This number was required for participants to take notes to get the final reimbursement at the end of the experiment.

To avoid information sharing, participants were assigned to sit far apart and were not allowed to communicate.

Experiment Design

The study followed a between-subjects design with four conditions: 1) baseline condition; 2) with peer information; 3) with majority information; 4) with both peer information and majority information. Forty-eight participants (M= 62.08, SD = 5.59) were recruited from an aging volunteer organization in Singapore. All participants had basic computer skills and Internet experience (they had taken part in local senior computer classes). Before the study, we tested participants' knowledge of possibility. Only participants who understood the relevant concept were enrolled in our experiment.

The information a subject faced was different across the four conditions. In Condition 1 (baseline condition), each person observed only the realization of each stock and bond after each of the choices. In addition to information available in Condition 1, Group 2 participants had access to peer information and Group 3 participants had access to the majority information. In Group 4, all types of information available to Groups 2 and 3 were simultaneously shown to the participants, and the realization of the stock was shown after each choice was made.

Procedure

The participants were asked to read the instructions of the experiment upon arriving the experiment room. In the instructions, we showed participants the possibility of stocks' performance and reminded them, "Please use your best judgment to make the decision and the final reimbursement for your participation will be ten percent of your task earning." Before the start of the formal study, they had three blocks to practice the baseline task organized by the experimenters, during which the experimenters would answer any questions related to the interface and task rule to minimize adapting effects. After the formal study, the experimenters debriefed the participants and conducted an interview with them. The whole experiment took approximately two hours.

Each participant began with $150 virtual money. At the end of the experiment, one-tenth of the virtual money left was given as a reimbursement. The whole experiment consisted of 10 blocks, with 10 trials in each block. All participants performed baseline task in the first stage, comprised of five blocks, and then were randomly assigned to four groups for the second stage, which was comprised of another five blocks.

DATA ANALYSIS

Social Information on Risk-neutral Choice-Making

At first, to understand the effects of social information on older adults' risk-neutral financial decisions, we conducted a three-way ANOVA on the number of risk-neutral choice as dependent variable, with stages (blocks 1-5 vs. blocks 6-10), majority (with or without), and peer (with or without) information as independent variables. The two-way interaction between stage and majority information is significant $(F(1,44)=5.23, p<0.05, \eta^2=0.11)$.

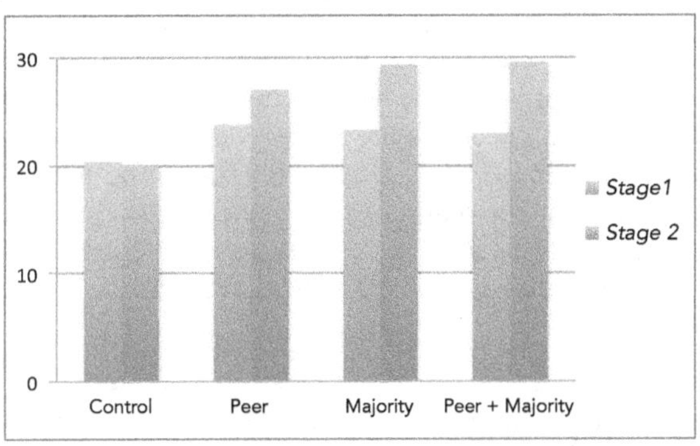

Figure 8. Average number of risk-neutral choices

To understand this two-way interaction, we first performed an ANOVA with the number of the risk-neutral choice as dependent variable in the baseline condition (first 5 blocks), which yielded a non-significant risk-neutral choice * group interaction, $(F(3,44)=0.72\ p=0.545, \eta^2=0.05)$, indicating that there was no individual difference on the ability to perform task among the participants of four groups. We then performed a repeated ANOVA on risk-neutral choice with stages as independent variable, and found that, except for group 1, which showed a non-significant result, the difference between stages (first and last 5 blocks) was significant in all three groups $((F(1, 11)=5.616, p<0.05, \eta^2=0.34)$ in group 4 (with peer information and majority information), $(F(1, 11)=5.965, p<0.05, \eta^2=0.35)$ in group 3 (with majority information), and $(F(1, 11)=4.804, p=0.05, \eta^2=0.30)$ in group 2 (with peer information)). The results suggested that after controlling individual differences, participants had made more risk-neutral choices. These indicated that both peer information and majority information helped them to correct some amounts of heuristic forecasting bias in the decision-making process. Therefore, H1 and H2 were supported (Figure 8).

To further explore the differences between effects of majority information and peer information, we conducted a two-way ANOVA on risk-neutral choice in only stage 2 (the last 5 blocks). The results showed that there was no significant interaction between the effects of w/without peer and w/without majority on number of risk-neutral choice, $(F(1, 44)=2.48, p=0.123, \eta^2=0.05)$ and no significant difference in risk-neutral choice between w/without peer $(p=0.098, \eta^2=0.06)$ but there was a significant difference between w/without *majority* $(p<0.01, \eta^2=0.15, d=0.748)$. The Cohen's d indicated that the result had a large effect size. Simple effects analysis showed that there were significantly more risk-neutral choices with the majority information than without the majority information $(p<.05)$. This result was consistent with the previous studies on social cues [31, 41], which indicated that majority information had a larger effect on people's decisions than information from individuals. Thus, H3 was supported by the main effect.

Effect of Social Information on Risk Attitude

We defined "corrections" of each type of mistake (RSM and RAM) as the difference between the number of mistakes in the experimental condition (stage 2) and number of mistakes in the baseline condition (stage 1). We then calculated the correlation between the number of RAMs the participants made in the baseline condition (which reflected their risk attitude, i.e., how risk-averse they were) with the number of corrections of each type of mistake in order to study to what extent the effects of social information depended on participants' risk attitude. We found that the correlation was significant in only group 4 (with both peer and majority information provided), in which we found that participants who were more risk-averse tended to have more corrections of risk-averse mistakes $(r=-0.622, p<0.05)$ *and* fewer corrections of risk-seeking mistakes $(r=0.869, p<0.001)$. In other words, the social information helped to correct the most mistakes of the same risk-taking type. Specifically, risk-averse participants corrected more RAMs than RSMs, while risk-seeking participants corrected more RSMs than RAMs. In summary, H4 was partly supported by the findings that social information could be effective in nudging participants towards making more risk-neutral decisions and adjusting their own biased risk-taking attitudes.

Strategies used in performing the task

After the formal experiment, the researchers debriefed the participants and then conducted a short interview regarding the investment strategies applied to the task and in real life.

Attitudes towards the BIAS task

Although the BIAS task is a shorter and simpler version than the financial decision-making in real world scenarios, participants still expressed that it was relatively difficult to make decisions: "*The task is a little complex to me. I forget the deep mathematics already, but I can still make decisions by memorizing the good stock.*" When this participant was asked about the way to define "good stock," his answer was a simpler decision-making strategy confounded with using heuristics: *"The one shows $10 dollar more often.*" The participants made risk-taking mistakes with respect to their particular risk-taking attitudes: "*When I gather enough money, I will continually buy bonds,*" or "*I will always choose the good stock, because in the long run it will make profits.*"

Attitudes towards social information

Before the experiment debriefing, the participants in the social information condition (groups 2, 3, 4) did not express concerns about the authenticity of the social information. They also shared their strategies with us, which were similar to the real world social effects. In the majority information condition: "*When I get confused by the stock price, I will listen to the others' opinion,*" "*I don't have enough financial knowledge, thus I just follow the majority choice, which is a safer way not to lose the game,*" or "*I think I am better with financial decisions, so I make decisions on my own. However, I will refer to others' choices when I forget something.*" In the peer information condition, the situation was more complex, as the participants had to identify "which peer made better financial decisions": "*I keep an eye on their performance, and try to pick the best one to follow*"; "*Like real life, I consult my friend's opinion, but I do not totally believe their decisions. So I choose to compare the opinion leader's choice with my choice, then make the final decision.*"

Strategies in real life

There were a surprisingly high proportion of participants investing in the stock market. In their experience, the social factors played an important role: "*My sister invests in the stock market, so I just follow her,*" "*I pay attention to the company fame and its recent stock payoff. I do not believe in experts' opinions, because they make profits from my decisions and may cheat me. However, I believe my friends' opinions,*" and "*Currently, most of our older people put our savings in the bank. It's much safer and I don't have enough money to make risky choices.*" Our participants showed strong interest in asset management but relied on limited information sources (friends, intuition about majority).

DISCUSSION AND IMPLICATION

The findings in this work support that social information improves older adults' financial risk-taking. Through the social learning, older adults can modulate the negative influence of decision bias caused by heuristic forecasting and learning deficits. As a starting point, our study investigates the social information used in social trading networks. The next step of our research should consider the effects of tie strengths of older adults' existing social networks. Although there is little existing implementations of utilizing users' social ties in current social trading platforms, the potential implications may be promising. A recent study on social ties in teams' collaborative problem solving suggests that the strongest ties have an effect on the final performance [26]. We would like to know whether the strongest social tie of older adults has a larger effect than majority information. However, as noted by Alex Pentland [27], if the social networks of user's circle are too tight while with the similar characteristics, it will limit the payoff of social learning. Thus, the implications of tuning down effects of social tie should be investigated.

Our study examines the rational aspect of financial risk-taking. It is not equivalent to the "correct" decision with respect to the particular individual's situation. The "correct" decision for an individual is hard to define without knowing his or her contextual information. For example, the purchase of an asset may be a rational decision in the absolute sense, but it could impede the older adult's ability to pay for a hospital visit, which is more important to the older adult's well-being. Thus, requiring older users to report additional information such as health conditions, personal assets, and daily expenses, the social trading platforms can selectively present the social information gathered from people with similar backgrounds, in order to help older adults to make more potentially "correct" decisions. Our current study focuses on the financial context. We expect that the same results also apply to other situations where decisions are made under uncertainty and by prior experience, such as choosing an online education service, online labor market (e.g., Elance.com, Guru.com), or online storefronts (e.g., Zaarly.com). Future studies should investigate whether the same effects can be found in these settings.

Our results have important implications for designers of online financial platforms. Presenting social information from others or crowd can sway older users' decisions and modulate their risk-taking attitudes, thereby influencing factors up to the quality of risk management, such as participation and long-term adoption. The results also imply that designs of financial websites should more clearly visualize both descriptive information of risk and experience-based information of risk in forms that help older adults improve the effectiveness of social learning thereby nudging them toward more risk-neutral behavior. Future research is needed to further test what/how both types of information should be presented to convey risk information, especially in a way that is effective for older investors. Given that experience-based learning is more effective for presenting rational risk-taking behavior, it may be beneficial to allow older adults to perform virtual investments and share this information with others, thus promoting the understanding of the risk involved. It is possible, for example, to allow older adults to engage in some form of a social game in which they share and compete with each other using virtual money. This approach would allow older adults to experience and learn the outcomes of different types of investment options, before they perform real world investment.

The contributions we make to online financial platforms design are based on a lab experiment that focuses on a limited environment and limited options. Clearly, actual financial decisions are more complex and involve more options. However, the *categories* of options of the real world asset allocation are often similar to the ones we used in the study –i.e., safe but less rewarding versus risky but more rewarding. Additionally, the same categories of investment assets are also commonly used to educate investors on how they should allocate their assets.

LIMITATIONS

There are several concerns worth discussing. First, the majority information was constructed based on the classical economics viewpoint that most people are rational in the open information environment. We acknowledge that it is possible that the majority decisions of users could be irrational in some specific scenarios. For example, a "bad information cascade" happened in a restricted information exchange environment (e.g. unbalanced information sharing between senior investors and common users). The current experiment therefore did not allow us to tease apart effects of social influence and rational decisions. In the next experiment, we plan to create conditions in which the majority information would lead participants further away from rational choices. We will then be able to test to what extent people "blindly" follow others, choose rationally instead of following others, or pursue a decision that is mixed between the two effects.

In addition, although we obtained significant results from the experiment indicating that social information had a strong effect on older adults' financial risk-taking behaviors, the sample size was still too small for us to induce more detailed explanations. Future research should conduct this study on a larger scale. This will allow us to analyze the actual dynamics of social influence on choice behavior. For example, an individual is possibly using a weighted average of his/her own and others' information to make investment decisions, and the weights may be heterogeneous across participants. Future research could also conduct analysis based on existing online corpus in situations with or without social information.

Lastly, since we conducted the experiment in Singapore, it was possible that cultural issues impacted the extent to how social information was interpreted and how risk was perceived. Future studies should consider replicating the studies in other countries.

CONCLUSION

In this paper, we have provided evidence suggesting that social information has an effect on older adults' financial decision-making behavior. Expanding an experience-based decision task, we found the unbiased aggregated social signal or individuals' choices could nudge older adults towards making better risk management in online financial decisions. The bandwagon effect was stronger than the peer effect. In addition, we found that the more risk-averse an older adult, the more influential the aggregates of social information. While social information is widely utilized in Web 2.0 platforms, to the best of our knowledge, our research is the first to embrace an experience-based task to investigate its influence on people's risk-taking behaviors. We argue that future online financial systems should consider incorporating this type of information as a design factor in improving people's financial well-being.

ACKNOWLEDGMENTS

We thank the AC and anonymous reviewers for their constructive comments and feedback. This research is supported by NUS DPRT grant R-263-000-626-133.

REFERENCES

1. Acemoglu, D., Dahleh, M.A., Lobel, I., and Ozdaglar, A. Bayesian learning in social networks. *Review of Economic Studies 78*, 4 (2011), 1201-1236.
2. Bertoni, D. *Identity Theft: Governments Have Acted to Protect Personally Identifiable Information, But Vulnerabilities Remain: Congressional Testimony*. GAO, 2009.
3. Bikhchandani, S., Hirshleifer, D., and Welch, I. A theory of fads, fashions, customs, and cultural change as information cascades. *Journal of Political Economics 100*, 5 (1992), 992-1026.
4. Burmeister, O.K. What seniors value about online community. *Community Informatics 8*, 1 (2012).
5. Bursztyn, L., Ederer, F., Ferman, B., and Yuchtman, N. Understanding peer effects in financial decisions: Evidence from a field experiment. *NBER Working Papers 18241*, (2012).
6. Carstensen, L.L., Isaacowitz, D.M., and Charles, S.T. Taking time seriously: A theory of socioemotional selectivity. *American Psychologist 54*, (1999), 165–181.
7. Charness, N., Fox, M.C., and Mitchum, A.L. Lifespan cognition and information technology. *Handbook of lifespan psychology*. Springer, New York, 2010.
8. Cialdini, R. *Influence: The psychology of persuasion*. Collins, New York, 2007.

9. Coupland, J., Coupland, N., Giles, H., and Henwood, K. Formulating age: Dimensions of age identity in elderly talk. *Discourse Processes 14*, (1991), 87-106.

10. Duflo, E., and Saez, E. Participation and investment decisions in a retirement plan: The influence of colleagues' choices. *Journal of Public Economics 85* (2002), 121-148.

11. Garg, V., Camp, L.J., Lorenzen-Huber, L.M., Connelly, K. Risk communication design for older adults. *Gerontechnology 11,* 2 (2012).

12. Gerard, B., Kimberly, L., Xiaoqing, W., Klarissa, C., Dan, F., Paul, R., and Robert, E.K. Using social psychology to motivate contributions to online communities. In *Proc. CSCW '05*, 212-221.

13. Gilbert, D.T., and Wilson, T.D. Why the brain talks to itself: sources of error in emotional prediction. *Philosophical Transactions of the Royal Society B*, 364 (2009), 1335-1341.

14. Gray, R., et al. Who Wants to Know? Question Asking and Answering Practices Among Facebook Users. In *Proc. CSCW '13*, 1213-1224.

15. Hullman, J., Adar, E., and Shah, P. The impact of social information on visual judgments. In *Proc. CHI '11*, 1461–1470.

16. Markowitz, H. Portfolio selection. *Journal of Finance*, (1952), 77–91.

17. Jameson, A. Choices and decisions of computer users. *The Human-Computer Interaction Handbook: Fundamentals, Evolving Technologies and Emerging Applications.* CRC, 2012.

18. Kenneth, J.A., Robert, E.F., et al. The promise of prediction market. *Science 320*, (2008), 877-878.

19. Kim, J.J. A Slew of New Web Sites Are Trying to Attract Young People By Combining Social Networking With Personal Finance. *Wall Street Journal.*

http://online.wsj.com/article/SB118177906703834565.html

20. Kim, Y., Kang, J., and Kim, M. The Relationships among Family and Social Interaction, Loneliness, Mall Shopping Motivation, and Mall Spending of Older Consumers. *Psychology & Marketing 22*, 12 (2005), 995-1015.

21. Kuhnen, C.M., and Knutson, B. The neural basis of financial risk taking. *Neuron 47*, (2005), 763–770.

22. Lelis, S., and Howes, A. Informing decisions: how people use online rating information to make choices. In *Proc. CHI '11*, 2285-2294.

23. Lixiu, Y., Paul, A., Aniket, K., and Robert, K.A. Comparison of Social, Learning, and Financial Strategies on Crowd Engagement and Output Quality. In *Proc. CSCW '14*, 967-978.

24. Mata, R., Josef, A.K., Samanez-Larkin, G.R., and Hertwig, R. Age differences in risky choice: a meta- analysis. *Annals of the New York Academy of Sciences 1235*, 1 (2011), 18-29.

25. Morgan, J.S., Lampe, C., and Shafiq, M.Z. Is news sharing on Twitter ideologically biased? In *Proc. CSCW '13*, 887–896.

26. Montjoye, Y.A., Stopczynski, A., Pentland, A., et al. The strength of the strongest ties in collaborative problem solving. *Nature Scientific reports*, 4 (2014).

27. Pentland, A. *Social Physics: How Good Ideas Spread-The Lessons from a New Science.* Penguin Press, 2014.

28. Rabin, M. Risk aversion and expected-utility theory: A calibration theorem. *Econometrica*, (2000).

29. Samanez-Larkin G.R., Kuhnen C.K., Yoo D.J., and Knutson, B. Variability in nucleus accumbens activity mediates age-related suboptimal financial risk-taking. *Journal of Neuroscience 30*, 4 (2010), 1426-1434.

30. Samanez-Larkin, G.R., Wagner A.D., and Knutson, B. Expected value information improves financial risk taking across the adult life span. *Social Cognitive and Affective Neuroscience 6*, 2 (2011), 207-217.

31. Sook- Kim, H., and Sundar, S,S. Using interface cues in online health community boards to change impressions and encourage user contribution. *In Proc. CHI '11*, 599-608.

32. Sundar, S. S., Oeldorf-Hirsch, A., and Xu, Q. The bandwagon effect of collaborative filtering technology. *Ext. Abstracts CHI '08*.

33. Sundar, S. S. The MAIN Model: A heuristic approach to understandin technology effects on credibility. *Digital media, youth, and credibility.* MIT (2007), 73-100.

34. Surowiecki, J. *The wisdom of crowds.* Doubleday, 2004.

35. Tversky, A., and Kahneman, D. Judgment under uncertainty: Heuristics and biases. *Science 185*, (1974), 1124–31.

36. Wai-Tat F., and Wei, D. Collaborative Indexing and Knowledge Exploration: A Social Learning Model. *IEEE Intelligent Systems 27*, 1 (2012), 39-46.

37. Wei, P., Altshuler, Y., and Pentland, A. Decoding Social Influence and the Wisdom of the Crowd in Financial Trading Network. *In IEEE Social Computing*, 2012.

38. Weierich, M.R., et al. Older and wiser? An affective science perspective on age-related challenges in financial decision making. *Social Cognitive and Affective Neuroscience*, 6 (2011), 195- 206.

39. World Population Ageing 1950-2050. http://www.un.org/esa/population/publications/worldageing 19502050.

40. Yoon, C., et al. Cognition, Persuasion and Decision Making in Older Consumers. *Marketing Letters 16*, 3-4 (2005), 429-441.

41. Zeinab, A., Christina, A., and Bernardo, A.H. Swayed by Friends or by the Crowd? *Social Informatics* 7710, (2012), 365-378.

Wireless Visions: Infrastructure, Imagination, and U.S. Spectrum Policy

Richmond Y. Wong
School of Information
UC Berkeley
richmond@ischool.berkeley.edu

Steven J. Jackson
Dept. of Information Science
Cornell University
sjj54@cornell.edu

ABSTRACT

Effective use of spectrum is essential to the forms of mobile, ubiquitous, and social computing that increasingly shape and define CSCW research. This paper calls attention to the key policy processes by which the future of wireless spectrum – and the forms of technology design and use that depend on it – is being imagined, shaped, and contested. We review CSCW and HCI scholarship arguing for infrastructure and policy as important but neglected sites of CSCW analysis, and separate lines of work arguing for 'sociotechnical imaginaries' as key sites and outcomes of technology policy and design. We then turn to histories of U.S. spectrum regulation, before analyzing ongoing FCC policy actions around incentive auctions and unlicensed spectrum use. We argue that such processes are central to the imagination and future of mobile computing; and that CSCW can benefit from adding such policy concerns to its traditional repertoires of design and use.

Author Keywords

Spectrum; policy; infrastructure; sociotechnical imaginaries; imagination

ACM Classification

K.4.1 Public Policy Issues; K.5.2 Government Issues

INTRODUCTION

In 2010, President Barack Obama issued a memorandum [44] requiring 500 MHz of spectrum – invisible electromagnetic waves that allow wireless devices to transmit and receive signals – to be made available for broadband use, touting the need for "expanded wireless broadband access [that] will trigger the creation of innovative new businesses, provide cost-effective connections in rural areas, increase productivity, improve public safety, and allow for the development of mobile telemedicine, telework, distance learning, and other new applications that will transform Americans' lives." Two years later, Federal Communications Commission (FCC) Chairman Julius Genachowski addressed the same general vision [22], but in more urgent terms: "Just as we must pursue future-oriented energy technologies and policies, we have no choice on our airwaves: we must make better, more efficient use of spectrum...Before long, almost every device we can imagine - from our dishwashers to our cars - will have embedded Internet-connected sensors, and video and other high-data uses will be part of this picture." The alternative, claimed Genachowski, would be dire: "If we don't take the necessary steps, the spectrum crunch will become a spectrum crisis. This would threaten a uniquely powerful opportunity for U.S. innovation and economic growth - wireless broadband - and potentially cede leadership to our global competitors."

As the above passages make clear, wireless spectrum and the policies that govern it are increasingly central to the visions of broad-scale change and growth that define scholarship and practice in the contemporary social computing environment. As wireless technologies (and the collaborative and social computing applications that run on them) become more pervasive in everyday life, the basic processes by which wireless futures are imagined and enacted through policy become increasingly central to CSCW itself, providing (or failing to) the core infrastructure on which CSCW practice and design efforts rely. Stable, accessible, affordable, and appropriately managed spectrum is increasingly a *sine qua non* of collaborative and social computing systems (or at very least the rapidly growing number of these that operate on a mobile or wireless basis). At the same time, the apparently technical and legal processes of spectrum policy turn out to be social to the core, caught up in the broader cultural (and contested!) processes by which new social computing forms are imagined, practiced, and designed. Contemporary debates around spectrum policy are at once debates about the future of computing, its changing shape and needs, and its broader role and contributions to social life. Current debates in spectrum policy help set the conditions of possibility against which the design, practice, and imagination of emergent collaborative and social computing tools unfolds. They are also shaped by the same broad scale and open-ended (re)imaginations of technology and social life that feed into CSCW work in its moments of research and design.

This paper analyzes core regulatory and policy processes through which new spectrum futures are being built: in law,

CSCW 2015, March 14–18, 2015, Vancouver, BC, Canada.

ACM 978-1-4503-2922-4/15/03…$15.00
http://dx.doi.org/10.1145/2675133.2675229

in code, and in the visions of a networked life that underlie each. It makes three basic contributions to CSCW research. First, it casts light on spectrum infrastructures and policy processes crucial to the success of the field. Traditional CSCW concerns about collaborative tools and practices, and a more recent set of concerns around the shape and nature of mobile and ubiquitous computing, increasingly have to contend with the ways in which wireless technologies interact with – and may be limited by – the spectrum environments in which they live. Second, this paper extends recent CSCW work that seeks to restore policy as a necessary and appropriate site of CSCW analysis. Third, we introduce the concept of sociotechnical imaginaries to cast new light on how social and cultural meanings and visions of the good life may become embedded in technological practices at moments of policy formation. This joins a growing body of CSCW work that has sought to operationalize vision and imagination as a formative influence on the design and cultural appropriation of new computing tools. At the highest level, we argue that wireless infrastructures and the forms of computing design and use which run on them may be deeply if subtly shaped by the policy and regulatory processes that surround them (and vice versa); and that better understanding of such processes can deepen our understanding and potentially help shape the landscape in which CSCW operates.

The paper that follows advances these claims though four basic steps. We first review current literatures around infrastructure and policy in CSCW and introduce the concept of sociotechnical imaginaries. We then turn to the contested history of U.S. spectrum regulation, showing the wider forces and imaginaries that have shaped this regulatory history over time. We then follow two current instances of spectrum controversy – around the proper shape and form of incentive auctions, and unlicensed spectrum use, respectively – revealing the wider processes, visions, and imaginaries they embed. We conclude by discussing key findings around spectrum policy and the work of imagination, and drawing lessons for CSCW practice and scholarship.

RELATED WORK & BACKGROUND

CSCW is undergoing a moment of expansion. Mapping changes in the sites and scales of computing and collaboration itself, recent CSCW scholars have encouraged CSCW researchers to look beyond the moment of design, and above the level of the artifact. Monteiro et al. [33] advocate the study of information infrastructures and the entanglements of seemingly unrelated technologies across multiple times and contexts, arguing that CSCW's tendency to focus on localized system implementation and use neglects a wider and important range of actors and factors in the shaping of a technology. Edwards et al. [13] have urged CSCW and HCI designers to look deeper into the stack of computing, to understand how interfaces, artifacts, and systems sit atop and are profoundly shaped by standards and infrastructures that go typically unaddressed in traditional user-centered design processes. Jackson et al. [26, 27] have urged CSCW researchers to (re)engage technology policy, offering the field's expertise around collaboration and social computing to a growing range of questions and controversies defining public and corporate policies in the collaboration and social computing environment.

Other lines of work have sought to extend CSCW attention to collective processes of imagination, and their role in the design, development, and use of emergent computing forms and tools. This includes work that has approached imagination as a quality or resource of the designer or user. Design artifacts such as prototypes [31], scenarios, and design workbooks [21], represent ways in which designers and developers imagine users, systems, practices, or contexts of use, inscribing notions of the future into the built forms of computational artifacts. Lindtner et al. [32] have examined the role of imagination in the transnational adoption of technologies, and Sengers and Gaver [42] have discussed imagination as a resource for users to interpret design. Still other work has extended the concept of imagination in a cultural direction, exploring how imaginations of ubiquitous computing are embedded, expressed, and reinforced through the actions and products of researchers and practitioners in the field [12] and through sociotechnical visions expressed in the media [23].

But as a largely separate line of work in the STS and science policy space has argued, imagination is no less present or consequential in moments of technology policy formation, including in its technical and regulatory guise. As Jasanoff and Kim [28] explain, sociotechnical imaginaries emerge as "collectively imagined forms of social life and social order reflected in the design and fulfillment of nation-specific scientific and/or technological projects." These imaginaries represent futures that are both feasible and worthy of collective hope and effort, building projections of "what is good, desirable, and worth attaining" [28]. Building on a wider body of social theory (including seminal work on social imaginaries by political theorist Charles Taylor [43]), sociotechnical imaginaries call attention to the role of the nation state in defining the purposes of technology by tying national visions of culture and identity to concrete policy or funding decisions. They also call out the ways in which science and technology projects and apparently neutral technical decision-making can come to encode, reinforce, or stand in for collective visions of identity or the 'good life' [19, 28].

Sociotechnical imaginaries represent an important addition to other recent approaches to technology policy that have sought to extend understanding beyond simple instrumental and interest-based analyses. Analysts of policy networks [39] have emphasized the fundamentally networked quality of technical decision-making, arguing for the role of interrelated networks, relationships, and linkages among policymaking and other stakeholder communities in creating policies. Analysts of advocacy coalition frameworks [40] have called attention to the ways in which heterogeneous stakeholders interact and coordinate to enact policies. Neo-institutional approaches [20, 36, 37] have explored the role of institutions and wider institutional 'fields' in setting the terrain of policy action, establishing distinct constraints and affordances that draw out certain forms of action and organization while precluding others. Collectively, these approaches speak to the determinants of policymaking, the roles of group ideologies, determining who stakeholders are and how they interact, and the nature of social and power structures. Theories of sociotechnical imaginaries encompass and build on these concerns, while incorporating the role of broader cultural beliefs and values that are not as easily accounted for through network, discourse, or institutional analysis. They also direct attention to the specific instantiations of broad-scale imaginaries within the practices and materialities of technology artifacts themselves.

From the standpoint of the spectrum policy concerns tackled here and CSCW more generally, the concept of sociotechnical imaginaries does important work. Sociotechnical imaginaries allow us to view technological projects and developments within a larger societal context, and analyze their interaction with social life. By reorienting policy as a process of imagination, sociotechnical imaginaries allow CSCW to approach and engage policy in news ways. Sociotechnical imaginaries shape and are shaped by the practices and processes of technology designers and researchers, policymakers, and other policy stakeholders. They show how cultural and social imaginations are mutually constituted with the goals, priorities, and benefits of technology, outlining the extent to which technological choice and form may be caught up in winder, and sometimes contested, cultural and social arrangements.

Spectrum infrastructure is vital to the operation of wireless devices and to emergent forms of mobile and ubiquitous computing. Recent work in CSCW has discussed cases and contexts including mobile health context-aware computing [1], the role of Bluetooth-using sensors or smartphones in crowdsourcing and citizen science [29], ubiquitous sensor networks in urban areas [18], and new forms of high-bandwidth-using communication such as collaborative live video [14]. Currently contested FCC decisions will set the stage for new designs and practices related to wireless technologies. The choice of what spectrum frequencies to allocate for internet access affects whether signals can penetrate through buildings in urban areas, or transmit across long distances in rural areas, influencing the development of mobile and geolocation based systems. The way in which frequencies are allocated can enable (or prevent) the adoption of higher bandwidth Wi-Fi standards. Spectrum usage rules may create restrictions on wireless transmissions indoors, near hospitals, or in other locations. Debates over spectrum regulatory regimes often translate into a choice between increasing capacity of cellular networks, or Wi-Fi and Bluetooth networks, affecting what types of mobile devices and sensors can be used in an area. These regulatory regimes are also associated with competing views between limited and open access to technological systems. Cultural meanings of technology are not just influenced by the imaginations of designers and users, but also by the imaginations expressed (explicitly or implicitly) through regulations, proposals, and other processes of policymaking.

Investigating spectrum extends CSCW analysis both practically and theoretically. Practically, spectrum infrastructure is crucial to the wireless systems on which CSCW increasingly relies. Theoretically, our analysis extends work understanding how broader cultural processes affect the imagination, practice, and design of technology, particularly contributing to a growing body of CSCW work that attends to the policy processes and conditions around technological development. The following sections apply these concepts to problems of contemporary U.S. spectrum policy. We begin by reviewing historical and contemporary technological and policy developments and debates in spectrum. We then explain and analyze two contemporary spectrum debates – around license auctions and unlicensed spectrum, respectively – before turning to a discussion of the significance of spectrum policy and sociotechnical imaginaries for CSCW research more generally.

CONTESTING SPECTRUM: HISTORY AND CONTEMPORARY DEVELOPMENTS

Over the past century of radio spectrum history in the United States, shifts in basic understandings and practices around electromagnetic spectrum parallel considerable technological, regulatory, and social change. Spectrum has long been historically contested, and conflicting social visions and imaginations have always been at the heart of the core policy processes that govern it. This contestation is particularly prominent in policy debates in response to (and in anticipation of) emerging wireless technologies, representing the working out of new sociotechnical imaginaries. Understanding the historical policy responses to emerging technologies and the contexts for those responses can help us understand the policy concerns that shape contemporary forms of computing and communication. Both historical and current technical and policy debates have significant cultural dimensions that are wrapped up in broader social visions.

This constitutive principle can be witnessed at multiple moments of wireless policy history. When wireless radio was introduced to the U.S. in 1899, three groups fought to be the main users of radio, each representing a different vision about the future of radio and who would control it [11]. The press framed radio as a way to disseminate news to the public at faster speeds and lower prices than the telegraph or telephone. The Navy considered military or government promotion and control of radio as a sign of international prestige and strength. Hobbyists envisioned radio belonging to "the people," where individuals would communicate with each other through amateur clubs. The Radio Act of 1912 responded to increasing spectrum congestion and addressed the question "Who has the right to transmit?" [11]. Congress felt that government stewardship over spectrum would best serve "the people," while they felt that hobbyists created wasteful and dangerous interference. Subsequent actions established private corporations and commercial broadcasters as the main stakeholders and users of radio, diminishing the role of amateur users. The 1912 Act established a centralized government licensing system, later incorporated into the Federal Communications Commission (FCC) in 1927, whose impact is still felt, as today, much of the spectrum is licensed to private corporations and commercial entities. The FCC continues to allocate spectrum for various uses, determining the size of bands and the technical rules of use, and assigns those allocations to users through a variety of licensing regimes.

The emergence of wireless television in the 1940's shows a similar story of conflicting sociotechnical visions [25]. Radio companies heavily invested in developing television technology, so their previous ideals of a commercially supported network-based broadcast system translated from radio to television. However, the FCC envisioned local broadcasters, not national networks, as the center of the broadcast system, believing that local broadcasters would respond to local community needs, create diversity, and represent the "public good." In 1941 the FCC began television service but authorized commercial operation to allow operators to recoup development costs. The FCC distributed television spectrum licenses equally across the nation by geographic area to implement their vision of local broadcasters. But because it was based on geography, not population, most stations did not have the economies of scale that network television stations would have, and could not support themselves in the commercial system. This system allowed the rise of the three network oligopoly, reinforcing the commercial vision of broadcasting.

The broadcast reform movement of the 1960's [24], occurring simultaneously as other activist movements in American civil society, was largely concerned about broadening the range of actors involved in spectrum debates and changing the conception of "the public good." Prior to the 1960's, there was no way for citizens to publicly challenge broadcast licenses, as predominantly only other licensees had legal standing before the FCC. Broadcasters had a narrow view of what constituted legitimate actors, arguing that the public interest was already represented by the FCC. Reform groups believed that the FCC alone was not sufficient in protecting and promoting the public interest. Tensions surrounding who should be allowed to have a voice in these debates came to the surface in the 1966 case *Office of Communication of the United Church of Christ v. FCC*, which ruled in favor of the reformers, expanding the definition of who has legal standing to argue before the FCC, allowing citizens to challenge the licensing of commercial stations, and widening the number of legitimate stakeholders involved in spectrum.

Contemporary approaches to spectrum build from this technical and regulatory history and tend to follow either a policy- or technology- centered path. Policy-centered approaches seek to reform the mechanisms by which spectrum is awarded and used, encouraging efficient, optimal, and high-value uses, and generally fall into one of three approaches. First, advocates of market-based licensed approaches have argued for salable property or quasi-property rights as a way of ensuring efficient spectrum distribution, and looked towards market mechanisms like auctions as means of awarding new spectrum made available through redistribution. A property-like license grants a licensee exclusive use of certain frequencies in a particular geographic area. Second, others argue for commons-based unlicensed approaches, analogizing spectrum as a common resource, allowing anyone following a few basic operating rules to access and use the spectrum without purchasing a license. This would lower barriers to entry and allow more users to access the same frequencies of spectrum. While these two policy approaches have existed in some form for decades, a growing third group broadly proposes creating spectrum "sharing" environments [38] in response to the spectrum crunch, as most spectrum has already been allocated and assigned; there is no "new" spectrum to be found. Sharing environments have primary and secondary users: the primary user has greater protection rights from interference while secondary users can use the same frequencies as long as they do not interfere with the primary users. However, questions persist [35] as to how the primary and secondary users should be regulated.

Technology-centered approaches tend to make more efficient and "opportunistic uses" [15] of spectrum by helping devices transmit on frequencies otherwise not being used in a certain location at a particular time. One such solution is white space databases, first tested in 2008. White space is spectrum that has been allocated for a use, but is not being used or is unassigned in a specific geographic location. This spectrum can be used for other purposes without impact on the primary user. The databases provide centralized management and organization, communicating with devices to see where, when, and on what frequencies it is safe to transmit without interfering with primary users. Cognitive radio is similar. A cognitive device can itself sense if other devices are transmitting on the same frequency and in the same location, determining when it is opportune to transmit signals. With dynamic frequency selection technology, cognitive radios can sense several frequencies for primary users, and reallocate signals accordingly. Both white space databases and cognitive radio work well with unlicensed and spectrum sharing policies, more easily allowing users to transmit on multiple frequencies in crowded environments.

Outcomes of regulatory debates directly affect technology design and use (including the social computing tools and practices regularly studied by CSCW researchers). Cellular internet services are built on licensed spectrum because cellular carriers can afford to pay for licenses. Wi-Fi networks and Bluetooth technologies were developed and operate on unlicensed spectrum, in part due to the openness and lower barriers to entry in the unlicensed environment. The choice to regulate a band of spectrum as licensed or unlicensed affects how users can access spectrum reliant services, such as what types of wireless devices they have to purchase or organizations they may have to work with in order to access spectrum, like mobile phone companies. The geographic availability of both licensed and unlicensed spectrum also affects where and how users can use internet-connected devices. Furthermore, there is also debate as to whether or not more spectrum should be devoted to wireless broadband versus other uses like emergency communication networks or local television stations. Spectrum management technologies that allow sharing environments often envision a non-internet service like radar communication as the primary user and internet service as the secondary user, whether licensed cellular or unlicensed Wi-Fi based. Other views of sharing environments envision the primary user as licensed cellular service and the secondary user as unlicensed Wi-Fi service.

This brief overview of U.S. spectrum policy reveals several notable features. One of these concerns the deep interweaving (or 'knots' [26]) which connect design, practice, and policy over time. This is particularly visible during the emergence of new technologies and regulations, such as television. Over time, the uses of spectrum have grown, from radio broadcasting to television, cellular phones, Wi-Fi, Bluetooth, and more. Correspondingly, the class of claimants on spectrum spaces has grown, incorporating a new class of engineers, businesses, designers, and users creating, deploying, or adopting these technologies. Although conceptions of the "user" in spectrum policy often differs from CSCW conceptions of the user – users are generally considered in broader terms such as consumers, viewers, or the general public – the way that users are envisioned by policymakers expresses a social vision associated with the technologies. Spectrum debates around technical standards and regulations are wrapped up in broader social visions regarding the public good and the role of wireless technologies in society. Whether through institutional, political, or economic muscle, incumbent stakeholders have often played a large (some would say too large) role in defining and sometimes limiting spectrum debates. Concurrently, spectrum debates are embedded in broader shifts in regulatory and political philosophy, such as social reform movements in the 1960's. Imagination has been a force through which spectrum debates and controversies take form and are managed. These imagined visions have shifted over time, but are of fundamental importance to spectrum debate. Imagination is both social and technical, envisioning particular users, uses of spectrum, and views of the "public good," as well as envisioning future devices, systems, and standards.

The sections that follow extend this analysis by considering two pending policy actions in the spectrum space. The first concerns the introduction of a policy tool called an 'incentive auction' in order to expand licensed spectrum use for broadband but also asks how licensed users might share spectrum with unlicensed secondary users. The second describes the expansion of unlicensed spectrum for broadband and also raises concerns about incumbent services located in the same bands. These two policy and technical debates are also implicitly debates over the cultural dimensions and social visions of spectrum. We then turn to a more general discussion of patterns and tensions in contemporary spectrum policy and their implications for CSCW research.

CONTEMPORARY SPECTRUM DEBATES

The FCC Incentive Auction

While the FCC has used auctions to assign spectrum since 1993, the idea of an "incentive auction" was first described in the 2010 National Broadband Plan. In 2012, the FCC proposed rules [16] for an incentive auction to reallocate television spectrum for internet usage, consisting of three parts. The first part is a reverse auction, allowing broadcast television licensees in the 600 MHz range to submit bids to relinquish spectrum in exchange for payments, funded by the later forward auction of new licenses. The second part is a repacking of the newly obtained spectrum for wireless internet, and creating the new rules of use for these bands. The last part is the forward auction of new licenses for wireless internet uses, mostly to telecommunications companies to expand cellular networks. A successful auction requires the interplay between all three components.

Most stakeholders tend to fall into one of three competing groups: those who want to increase licensed spectrum for internet via cellular networks such as telecommunications companies, those who want to increase unlicensed spectrum for internet via Wi-Fi such as software companies and Wi-Fi device manufacturers, and incumbent low-power broadcasters who want to preserve spectrum for low-power television broadcasting. The FCC proposes repacking the 600 MHz band into 5 MHz blocks. They envision the use of Frequency Division Duplex (FDD) standards, such as 3G and 4G network standards, as FDD standards require a pair of 5 MHz blocks, one for uplink signals, and one for downlink signals [9]. The FCC also proposes creating guard bands (unassigned frequencies to help prevent interference) to protect continuing TV channels from interference. The FCC's plan is shown in Figure 1. It may be possible to instead use the guard band frequencies for unlicensed uses, by using white spaces databases or cognitive radio to make sure that their signals do not interfere with licensed operators. The FCC frames this proposal by linking it to

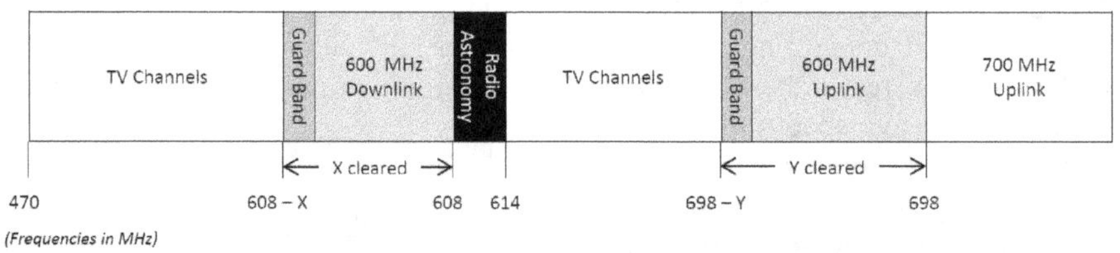

Figure 1. A possible band plan of the 600 MHz band as proposed by the FCC [16]. The areas "X cleared" and "Y cleared" are proposed to be auctioned off in 5 MHz block licenses. The variables X and Y indicate that the FCC is not yet sure how much TV spectrum will be cleared in the reverse auction. The appropriate size for the guard bands is currently contested.

economic growth and a narrative of American exceptionalism, saying "Meeting this [spectrum shortage] challenge is essential to continuing U.S. leadership in technological innovation, growing our economy, and maintaining our global competitiveness" [16].

At the heart of this debate is the form and nature of the public good, seen through contestation over the appropriate form and mechanism of efficiency, concerns about public access and competition, and beliefs about the reliability of new technologies. Regarding the most efficient use of spectrum, licensed regime supporters advocate shrinking guard band sizes to free more spectrum for licensed auctions, stating that these bands are "prime spectrum for the provision of mobile broadband services, so the guard bands should be limited in size to what is necessary to mitigate harmful interference, rather than attempting to maximize unlicensed spectrum use" [6]. Unlicensed spectrum advocates cite the potential for transformative innovations in unlicensed spectrum such as Wi-Fi and Bluetooth, and argue for larger guard band sizes to support unlicensed devices operating on wider band white space standards. They also cite the economic efficiency of unlicensed spectrum as "a complement and cost saving to both commercial wireless carriers and to wireline ISPs" [9]. Technical arguments about efficiency represent broader cultural claims about the relative importance and envisioned future roles of cellular and Wi-Fi based services.

Furthermore, some groups argue for using Time Division Duplex (TDD) standards instead of FDD, which requires a different, simpler organization of uplink and downlink bands. TDD could also benefit newer market entrants or those with fewer spectrum holdings like Sprint, while FDD is likely to benefit current operators such as AT&T and Verizon, who already have existing FDD infrastructure. Arguments for TDD are also based in certain hopes and representations of TDD standards and technologies. Referring to TDD as the "global solution for unpaired spectrum," and citing its use by other countries [10], Sprint frames TDD as the standard of the future. Yet FDD is embedded into current policies, regulations, and technological device designs. These debates help explain why a standard that may be the most efficient in one aspect, such as the technically efficient TDD, may not be adopted. Many groups associate the public good with the most efficient use of spectrum (even considering the difficulty of defining efficiency). But others associate the public good with other qualities, such as increasing public access to broadband internet connections through Wi-Fi, maintaining public access to television, or creating a more competitive environment for wireless carriers. Eventual regulatory choices in the 600 MHz band will embrace certain definitions and visions of the public good and efficiency at the expense of other competing definitions, embedding those values in the wireless infrastructure.

Contestation occurs over meanings of new spectrum management technologies that allow unlicensed devices to share spectrum with licensed devices, like white spaces databases or cognitive radios and their associated standards. Fears about their reliability are raised as opponents state [4] that band sizes "should be sized consistent with today's filter technology, not for future, aspirational technologies." Implicitly, this is a fear of an expanded unlicensed spectrum environment exploding with multitudes of new wireless devices. Supporters portray the these technologies as safe and tested, citing the FCC's resources devoted to white spaces deployment, including "testing and approving database administrators for commercial use, and certifying white spaces equipment" [5]. This debate is reflected in the development of regulatory rules for these bands which will favor the use of certain technological systems over others, implicitly favoring their associated values and narratives.

The physical properties of the 600 MHz band easily allow the transmission of information across long distances, making it valuable for deploying large wireless networks in open areas. The auctioning of 600 MHz spectrum provides the opportunity to greatly increase the capacity of wireless broadband networks, whether based on licensed spectrum for mobile broadband, or unlicensed spectrum for Wi-Fi. This is also likely the last auction of spectrum in this range for the foreseeable future, raising the stakes of these debates as there may be few future chances to change the rules and organization of this band once a proposal is adopted.

A number of more general features stand out in this debate. First, there are different conceptions of which stakeholders are legitimate and which should hold more influence, particularly between cellular network supporters and Wi-Fi supporters, while both tend to marginalize the role of low-power television broadcasters. Second, users are broadly conceived of as consumers who need more broadband access to accommodate higher bandwidth-using services and a greater ubiquity of wireless devices, though how broadband will be accessed (via cellular networks or Wi-Fi) is contested. Third, defining the "public interest" is contested, with different implications for what type of technical and regulatory environments would best serve that public interest. Fourth, current debates about the 600 MHz broadcast spectrum build upon past actions, technologies, and regulations, such as the legacy of the broadcast TV system, and the embeddedness of prior standards such as FDD. Lastly, this case is placed within a larger debate over how to best manage spectrum, mostly contested between unlicensed and licensed management regimes. Any lasting solution will not be purely one or the other, but will combine both management regimes. However, questions still exist regarding the extent to which they should coexist, and if one management regime should be valued more than the other. These technical and regulatory debates are also debates about what types of sociotechnical futures we will enact and what cultural values we will promote.

Expanding Unlicensed Spectrum

In February 2013, the FCC issued an NPRM regarding "Revision of Part 15 of the Commission's Rules to Permit Unlicensed National Information Infrastructure (U-NII) Devices in the 5 GHz Band" [17]. The FCC intended to revisit the rules governing unlicensed devices in the 5 GHz bands, which were written in 1997. Part 15 Rules govern the operation of unlicensed devices: wireless devices can operate without obtaining licenses as long as they follow rules intended to prevent interference for licensed devices operating within and adjacent to U-NII bands. Thus unlicensed devices are generally required to operate at low power over relatively short distances. Wi-Fi devices are an example of an application operating under these rules. Currently, there are several U-NII bands, seen in Figure 2, each with different operating rules.

The rules of existing U-NII bands vary. While they all allow for the operation of unlicensed devices, some have different restrictions on indoor and outdoor usage, different power limits, and different rules about what measures unlicensed devices need to take in order to avoid interference with legacy licensed services like radar or satellite communications. One section is governed by Part 15.247 and U-NII-3 rules, where manufacturers can decide which of these rules make more sense for them when building devices. The FCC proposes to expand U-NII rules into two new bands, designated U-NII-2B and U-NII-4, increasing the amount of contiguous U-NII spectrum.

Expanding U-NII carries potential issues. Incumbent services in the U-NII-2B and U-NII-4 bands include satellite services, weather radar, services used by local TV stations to provide weather warnings to viewers, and Dedicated Short Range Communications Service (DSRC) systems. DSRC is for automobile safety systems, such as vehicle-to-vehicle wireless communications that may warn drivers of impending dangerous conditions, or help make the vehicle take evasive action. These incumbent users operate within a licensed regulatory regime. Some form of spectrum sharing and mitigation of interference between licensed incumbent users and unlicensed U-NII devices in these bands is proposed to protect incumbent services.

The main opportunity of unifying the U-NII rules is the possible adoption of the IEEE 802.11ac Wi-Fi standard, which uses wider bandwidth, up to 160 MHz, for up to 1 Gigabit per second services. However, each of the U-NII bands has different policies of use, so if the 160 MHz-wide Wi-Fi channel was spread across two or more U-NII bands, it could fall under multiple sets of operating rules. Reconciling differences like power or location limits would create larger swaths of contiguous spectrum regulated in the same way allowing multiple 160 MHz-wide channels.

The FCC also identifies an increase in U-NII interference incidents "caused by users unlawfully modifying and operating unlicensed devices that have not been certified" [17]. Many manufacturers create devices that can work all the U-NII bands, but use software to operate on a specific band. If users edit the software, they may cause a device to operate in bands where the device causes harmful interference. The proposal envisions users as consumers whose interaction these devices does not include editing device software.

Central to this debate are varying portrayals and perceptions of stability, risks, and benefits of spectrum sharing management technologies. The push to increase unlicensed spectrum in the U-NII-2B and -4 bands is in part predicated on the development and trust of new technologies such as dynamic frequency selection and geolocation databases that allow spectrum sharing between new unlicensed devices and prior licensed incumbent devices. DSRC and Doppler licensees argue that these new tools are risky and pose potential threats to public safety if interference occurs. This represents a fear of a broadened unlicensed spectrum environment exploding with new wireless devices. While it is generally agreed that incumbents deserve protection from interference, there is debate over how much interference constitutes *harmful* interference and how well new technologies can mitigate that interference. Automobile manufacturers of DSRC devices and Doppler radar operators argue that their services protect public safety, writing "DSRC holds great promise for saving lives…these

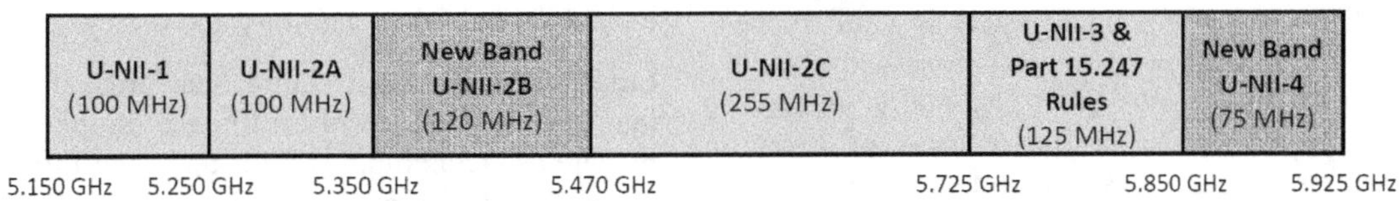

Figure 2. Current U-NII Bands and new bands proposed by the FCC in the NPRM [17].

enhanced safety features contain stringent communication requirements that must be protected" [3] and that "accurate weather data that can be rapidly delivered to local communities is a critical public safety priority" [8]. Thus they argue that they should have greater and preferential access to spectrum, priority to transmit, and greater levels of protection from interference from unlicensed devices.

The values of economic growth and innovation underlie most stakeholders' arguments: effective spectrum management is seen as a way to grow the U.S. economy and promote technological innovation. The FCC states that these changes "would continue to foster the development of new and innovative unlicensed devices, and increase wireless broadband access and investment" [17]. Yet the value of economic growth can be interpreted in conflicting ways. Unlicensed spectrum and Wi-Fi advocates argue that access to a harmonized unlicensed spectrum presents an environment with low barriers and easier access to entry, promoting innovation and meeting growing consumer demand. They envision a future of more unlicensed devices with more uses, writing "A more unified and streamlined regulatory structure will...promote the growth of the U-NII market...Technologies will have myriad uses that are vastly different from what reasonably could have been predicted when the U-NII-1 rules were first adopted in 1997" [7]. Meanwhile, incumbent licensed users argue that more unlicensed devices will present unknown factors, decreasing the spectrum's value; guarantees of stability and interference protection are needed for companies to invest money into building and innovating new technologies.

The debates in this case exhibit several general features as well. First, questions and contentions once again exist about who the legitimate stakeholders in creating spectrum policy are, and how much influence they should have. This is seen in disagreements between Wi-Fi advocates (including Wi-Fi and spectrum sharing device manufacturers, public interest groups, and software and internet companies) and incumbent spectrum users. Second, users are envisioned in several ways. Unlicensed spectrum advocates envision users as consumers who will use mobile internet services that require more data and content to be sent faster among more devices. The FCC and many manufacturers envision users as consumers of content who should not directly interact with device software. Third, the public interest is alluded to by many of the commenters, if not directly described. One view equates the public interest with the consumer's interest – the benefits of competition, lower prices, and marketplace innovation stem from an unlicensed spectrum regime. Another view is centered on public safety: widespread adoption of services that protect public safety during disasters or prevent disasters is vital to the public interest. Yet another view envisions expanding broadband connectivity via Wi-Fi as the public interest. Fourth, the FCC is operating in the context of legacy incumbent operators and devices built for the existing U-NII regulatory environment. Lastly, these debates are exploring how the regulatory environment can support the possibility of mutual coexistence of licensed-, unlicensed-, and sharing-based spectrum management regimes. Working out the technical and regulatory coexistence of these regimes relies on sorting out and ultimately embracing certain sociotechnical visions and cultural values.

DISCUSSION

This paper has sought to reveal the complexities and intricacies of spectrum debates, in both their historical and contemporary variants. It has introduced the concept of sociotechnical imaginaries as a way of understanding the mutual relationships between policy and technology design and practice. It has demonstrated the deep contestation of spectrum and the role of imagination in spectrum debates, both historically and in two contemporary cases that address the spectrum crunch. Here we discuss the importance of new attention to spectrum infrastructure and spectrum policy, supplementing CSCW's traditional orientations towards design and practice at the level of individual artifacts and systems.

Evaluating U.S. spectrum policies reveals several dimensions of sociotechnical imaginaries that emerge repeatedly over the history and contemporary practice of policy making around spectrum. The first concerns the debate over which actors should be allowed to participate in spectrum debates, both in terms of which groups' imaginaries are deemed legitimate and in terms of what groups are envisioned as legitimate policy actors. The second dimension is a contested imagined view of who the *users* of spectrum are (which are not always the same as the answer to question one). The third dimension consists of the debated definition and interpretation of the "public interest" at the heart of spectrum debates. The fourth dimension is that sociotechnical imaginaries are shaped by prior and existing technologies and regulations. They are built upon and constrained by the technical, regulatory, and cultural legacies of the past. The last dimension reveals the direct and real consequences sociotechnical imaginaries have on immediate questions surrounding spectrum management policies and techniques. Imaginaries are not merely theoretical, but affect real policy debates and actions.

Sociotechnical imaginaries reframe policy as imaginative and cultural processes. Using this to understand and engage policy and infrastructure, especially spectrum, can contribute to CSCW scholarship in three ways: understanding how infrastructures imagine and shape social and technological development, presenting a policy-centered resource for design, and analyzing how imagined futures and cultural values are mutually reflected and embedded in both technology and policy.

First, spectrum infrastructure, standards, and the regulations that govern them deeply influence the practice and design of wireless technologies built upon the infrastructure. At a deeper level, sociotechnical imaginaries help imagine and create future social and technological worlds and environments in which CSCW operates in. The resolution of current spectrum debates will shape the environment in which wireless devices will operate in. In the incentive auction case, the dominance of cellular or Wi-Fi based internet services will affect the types of technologies CSCW researchers can study, design, or implement, such as the ability to use mobile sensors or smartphone services. In the U-NII case, adoption of the 802.11ac Wi-Fi standard could increase the locations and contexts in which users use video and other high bandwidth forms of communication. Constraints on power or indoor usage affect the locations and ways that wireless devices and sensors can be designed and deployed. Limits on unlicensed spectrum near legacy licensed users such as DSRC vehicles or radar stations could affect the design and use of mobile and location-based systems. Debate over legitimate stakeholders, legitimate users, and legitimate user actions can affect how users access and interact with spectrum-using devices, such as the ability or inability to edit device software. Current spectrum debates represent the emergence of new technological and regulatory opportunities, sparking contestation and debate. These debates will eventually stabilize and coalesce around a new sociotechnical imaginary around spectrum embracing certain sociotechnical visions.

Second, sociotechnical imaginaries provide a policy-centered resource for design to create and explore imagined futures of technologies, society, and configurations of users. Used to supplement traditional user-centered design, policy-centered analysis and design can contribute alternative views of users and provide insight into social values and sociotechnical infrastructures underlying current design and practice. A focus on policy broadens the design space by considering design opportunities presented (or inhibited) by alternate policies and infrastructures. How would a wireless device or service be designed if wireless broadband was only offered via cellular providers, or only via Wi-Fi? How would users interact with sensors that could only be used indoors, or only outdoors? Furthermore, understanding the debate and contention around spectrum policy and regulation can help us understand gaps that users may face, such as differences between indoor and outdoor operation of devices, switching between cellular and Wi-Fi networks, or the limits of wireless device use in sensitive locations such as near vehicle safety systems. These understandings of policy can be leveraged as a resource by designers and practitioners for seamful design [2, 42], allowing users to be aware of, interpret, and engage the uncertainties and conflicts present in wireless policies and infrastructure. CSCW can likewise contribute to the policy domain. In particular, there is space for CSCW to contribute an understanding containing more concrete notions of users and designers that have been largely missing from policy debates. This can be done through direct engagement with the policy making process or by shaping these notions through processes of imagination, building narratives through conversation, publication, and design.

Third, as an analytic tool for CSCW, sociotechnical imaginaries help us understand how broader cultural beliefs and visions become embedded and reflected in policies, regulations, sociotechnical systems, and technical artifacts. Values in Design work in the CSCW and CHI communities has investigated the human values promoted by or embedded in technologies. Some work has also investigated connections between values and broader cultural dynamics and norms. Sociotechnical imaginaries and the policy processes that in part frame them are a key mechanism by which values get built into the systems and infrastructures that CSCW relies on. The licensed versus unlicensed regulatory debate in the incentive auction weighs the values of closed versus open access, mirroring questions about closed and open technological systems. Conflicting notions of the public good in the U-NII case debate what values are deemed legitimate: broadening internet access and speed, increasing economic growth, or protecting public safety. Understanding these dynamics opens a space for researchers and designers to investigate how the values embedded in or promoted by technologies interact with the values and norms expressed through policymaking processes. By placing these broader processes and institutions, including policy, as a central part of CSCW analysis, we are better able to move beyond statements of technological or social causality and investigate sites of mutual sociotechnical shaping that may have long-term effects on the nature, shape, and impact of CSCW and social computing tools and practices.

Some of this sociotechnical shaping occurs at the level of metaphor. Metaphors, such as those underlying spectrum policy and technology policy, contain implicit cultural assumptions. Metaphors also provide tangible ways to describe invisible spectrum and provide common terminology for a wide variety of stakeholders [34]. Land is often used as a spectrum metaphor. In the land metaphor, licensed spectrum is analogized as private property, while unlicensed spectrum is represented as a commons. However, land-based metaphors imply one regulatory regime per one section of spectrum; spectrum sharing regimes do not translate well in this metaphor. The land metaphor also tends to focus on policy-centered solutions over technology-centered solutions. Despite their shortcomings, metaphors are cognitive constructs that help shape human thought and reasoning [30]. These metaphors become so deeply embedded that they become "real" and assumed true, shaping our expectations and outlook of spectrum along technical, social, and regulatory dimensions. Attention to sociotechnical imaginaries helps us reveal, understand, and question these assumptions. Making metaphors visible through sociotechnical imaginaries allows us to better understand social values and assumptions in the design space by embracing, questioning, or inverting dominant metaphors, similar to critical and reflective design techniques [41]. Harmon and Mazmanian [23] discuss how cultural meanings of personal technologies are affected by cultural narratives in advertisements and news articles. Similarly, policy has the ability to shape technologies' cultural meanings through metaphor. Metaphors can be shaped and changed, however, providing an opportunity for CSCW to leverage its knowledge and experience by helping to form or contest the underlying metaphors that shape the sociotechnical imaginaries involved in policymaking. Conversations, publications, and design work are ways to engage in creating cultural meanings [23]. Through processes of imagination, CSCW researchers and practitioners can affect metaphors and narratives about wireless technologies.

CONCLUSION

At the time of writing, spectrum policy in the U.S remains fundamentally unsettled. As regulators try to allocate more spectrum for cellular broadband networks and/or unlicensed use, opportunities and risks for new and incumbent stakeholders are growing. In both cases, technical questions regarding standards and band sizes are linked with social questions regarding access and legitimate stakeholders. Competing definitions of efficiency and the public good, perceptions of benefits and risk of new technologies, and broader sociotechnical values and priorities must be negotiated. These debates are framed against the backdrop of the uncertainties posed by a looming spectrum crunch, which threatens an imagined future of Americans leveraging ubiquitous wireless broadband for innovation, health care, media content, social interaction, and many of the other claims and visions around the future of ubiquitous and mobile forms of computing.

Within this unsettled environment, attention to the sociotechnical imaginaries that frame and construct such debates is crucial. Sociotechnical imaginaries provide a tool for analyzing technology policies and can be leveraged as a resource and inspiration for design. They embed visions of stakeholders, users, and the public good that are central to the collective choices and accommodations being made around spectrum (and on which future innovations in design and use will rest). Per prior CSCW work on policy knots [26], they help us understand the interactions that occur at the intersection of design, practice, and policy. At the same time, wireless technologies (and the collaborative and social computing applications they support) are increasingly becoming central to CSCW work. Practically, maintaining a steady, stable, and accessible spectrum infrastructure is essential for creating a future of wireless and mobile devices, services, and applications. Furthermore, investigation of the dynamics of spectrum policy extends our understanding of how broader cultural processes interact with the imagination, practice, and design of technology. Better understanding of spectrum policy and the sociotechnical imaginaries that guide it can help enrich both the theoretical and practical reach of CSCW research.

REFERENCES

1. Baumer, E.P.S., Katz, S.J., Freeman, J., Adams, P., Gonzales, A.L., Pollak, J., Retelny, D., Niederdeppe, J., Olson, C.M., & Gay, G.K. Prescriptive persuasion and open-ended social awareness: expanding the design space of mobile health. In *Proc. CSCW 2012*, ACM Press (2012). 475-484
2. Chalmers, M., and Galani, A. Seamful interweaving: heterogeneity in the theory and design of interactive systems. In *Proc. DIS 2004*, ACM Press (2004). 243-252.
3. Comments of the American Association of State Highway & Transportation Officials. (2013). http://apps.fcc.gov/ecfs/document/view?id=7022418817
4. Comments of the Consumer Electronics Association (2013). http://apps.fcc.gov/ecfs/document/view?id=7022111851
5. Comments of Google Inc. and Microsoft Corp. (2013). http://apps.fcc.gov/ecfs/document/view?id=7022112070
6. Comments of Mobile Future (2013). http://apps.fcc.gov/ecfs/document/view?id=7022111797
7. Comments of Motorola Mobility LLC. (2013). http://apps.fcc.gov/ecfs/document/view?id=7022418844
8. Comments of the National Association of Broadcasters (2013). http://apps.fcc.gov/ecfs/document/view?id=7022418770
9. Comments of Public Interest Spectrum Coalition (2013). http://apps.fcc.gov/ecfs/document/view?id=7022112381
10. Comments of Sprint Nextel Corporation (2013). http://apps.fcc.gov/ecfs/document/view?id=7022112071
11. Douglas, S. *Inventing American Broadcasting, 1899-1922.* Johns Hopkins University Press, 1987.
12. Dourish, P. & Bell, G. *Divining a Digital Future: Mess and Mythology in Ubiquitous Computing.* The MIT Press, 2011.
13. Edwards, W.K., Newman, M.W., and Poole, E.S. The infrastructure problem in HCI. In *Proc. CHI 2010*, ACM Press (2002), 423-432.
14. Engstrom, A., Perry, M., and Juhlin, O. Amateur vision and recreation orientation: creating live video together. In *Proc. CSCW 2012*. ACM Press (2012), 651-660.
15. FCC. Connecting America: The National Broadband Plan. (2010). http://broadband.gov/plan/
16. FCC. Expanding the Economic and Innovation Opportunities of Spectrum through Incentive Auctions. (2012). http://www.fcc.gov/document/broadcast-television-spectrum-incentive-auction-nprm

17. FCC. Revision of Part 15 of the Commission's Rules to Permit Unlicensed National Information Infrastructure (U-NII) Devices in the 5 GHz Band. (2013). http://www.fcc.gov/document/5-ghz-unlicensed-spectrum-unii

18. Foth, M., Choi, J.H., and Satchell, C. Urban Informatics. In *Proc. CSCW 2011*, ACM Press (2011). 1-8.

19. Fujimura, J. Scientists as Sociocultural Entrepreneurs. *Genetic Nature/Culture: Anthropology and Science Beyond the Two-culture Divide*. University of California Press, 2003.

20. Galperin, H. Beyond Interests, Ideas, and Technology: An Institutional Approach to Communication and Information Policy. *The Information Society 20,* 3 (2004), 159-168.

21. Gaver, W. Making spaces: how design workbooks work. In *Proc. CHI 2011*, ACM Press (2011), 1551-1560.

22. Genachowski, J. Winning the Global Bandwidth Race: Opportunities and Challenges for Mobile Broadband. (2012). http://www.fcc.gov/document/chairman-genachowski-winning-global-bandwidth-race

23. Harmon, E. and Mazmanian, M. Stories of the Smartphone in everyday discourse: conflict, tension & instability. In *Proc. CHI 2013*, ACM Press (2013), 1051-1060.

24. Horwitz, R.B. Broadcast reform revisited: Reverend Everett C. Parker and the "standing" case (office of communication of the United church of Christ v. Federal Communications Commission). *The Communication Review 2*, 3 (1997), 311-348.

25. Horwitz, R.B. *The Irony of Regulatory Reform: The Deregulation of American Telecommunications.* Oxford University Press, 1989.

26. Jackson, S.J., Gillespie, T., and Payette, S. The Policy Knot: Re-integrating Policy, Practice and Design in CSCW Studies of Social Computing. In *Proc. CSCW 2014*, ACM Press (2014). 588-602.

27. Jackson, S.J., Steinhardt, S.B., and Buyuktur, A. Why CSCW Needs Science Policy (and Vice Versa). In *Proc. CSCW 2013*, ACM Press (2013). 1113-1124.

28. Jasanoff, S. and Kim, S.H. Containing the atom: sociotechnical imaginaries and nuclear power in the United States and South Korea. *Minerva 47*, 2 (2009), 119-146.

29. Kim, Sunyoung, Mankoff, J., and Paulos, E. Sensr: evaluating a flexible framework for authoring mobile data-collection tools for citizen science. In *Proc. CSCW 2013*, ACM Press (2013). 1453-1462.

30. Lakoff, G., and Johnson, M. *Metaphors We Live By.* University of Chicago Press, 1980.

31. Lim, Y.K., Stolterman, E., and Tenenberg, J. The anatomy of prototypes: Prototypes as filters, prototypes as manifestations of design ideas. *ACM ToCHI 15,* 2 (2008).

32. Lindtner, S., Anderson, K., and Dourish, P. Cultural appropriation: Information technologies as sites of transnational imagination. In *Proc. CSCW 2012*, ACM Press (2012), 77-86.

33. Monteiro, E., Pollock, N., Hanseth, O., and Williams, R. From Artefacts to Infrastructures. *Computer Supported Cooperative Work* 22 (2013), 575-607.

34. Osenga, K. The Internet is not a Super Highway: Using Metaphors to Communicate Information and Communications Policy. *Journal of Information Policy* 3 (2013).

35. Peha, J. M. Sharing Spectrum Through Spectrum Policy Reform and Cognitive Radio. *Proceedings of the IEEE* 97, 4(2009), 708-719.

36. Powell, W.W. and DiMaggio, P.J. The Iron Cage Revisited: Institutional Isomorphism and Collective Rationality in Organization Fields. *The New Institutionalism in Organizational Analysis.* University of Chicago Press, 1991.

37. Powell, W.W. and DiMaggio, P.J. Introduction. *The New Institutionalism in Organizational Analysis.* University of Chicago Press, 1991.

38. President's Council of Advisors on Science and Technology. *Realizing the Full Potential of Government-Held Spectrum to Spur Economic Growth.* (2012).

39. Rhodes, R.A.W. and Marsh, D. New directions in the study of policy networks. *European Journal of Political Research 21*, 1-2 (1992), 181-205.

40. Sabatier, P. An Advocacy Coalition Framework of Policy Change and the Role of Policy-Oriented Learning Therein. *Policy Sciences 21,* 2-3 (1988), 129-168.

41. Sengers, P., Boehner, K., David, S., & Kaye, J.J. Reflective Design. In *Proc. CC 2005*. ACM Press (2005), 49-58.

42. Sengers, P. and Gaver, B. Staying open to interpretation: engaging multiple meanings in design and evaluation. In *Proc. DIS 2006*, ACM Press (2006), 99-108.

43. Taylor, C. *Modern Social Imaginaries.* Duke University Press, 2004.

44. The White House. Presidential Memorandum: Unleashing the Wireless Broadband Revolution. (2010). http://www.whitehouse.gov/the-press-office/presidential-memorandum-unleashing-wireless-broadband-revolution

Understanding Copyright Law in Online Creative Communities

Casey Fiesler, Jessica L. Feuston, Amy S. Bruckman
GVU Center
Georgia Institute of Technology
85 5th St. NW, Atlanta, GA 30332 USA
casey.fiesler; jfeuston; asb @cc.gatech.edu

ABSTRACT

Copyright law is increasingly relevant to everyday interactions online, from social media status updates to artists showcasing their work. This is especially true in creative spaces where rules about reuse and remix are notoriously gray. Based on a content analysis of public forum postings in eight different online communities featuring different media types (music, video, art, and writing), we found that copyright is a frequent topic of conversation and that much of this discourse stems from problems that copyright causes for creative activities. We identify the major types of problems encountered, including chilling effects that negatively impact technology use. We find that many challenges can be explained by lack of knowledge about legal or policy rules, including breakdowns in user expectations for the sites they use. We argue that lack of clarity is a pervasive usability problem that should be considered more carefully in the design of user-generated content platforms.

Author Keywords

Copyright; Creativity; Fanworks; Intellectual property; Law; Online communities; Policy; Remix; User-generated content

ACM Classification Keywords

K.4.1 **[Computers and Society]:** Public Policy Issues --- *Intellectual property rights*

INTRODUCTION

Copyright law, once primarily the domain of publishers and lawyers, is now relevant to anyone with an Internet connection and a "share" button. Whereas four decades ago when the Copyright Act was passed infringement typically involved printing presses or Xerox machines, today unauthorized copying is an everyday activity for many people—to the point where, as Lawrence Lessig famously put it, perhaps we are raising an entire generation to think that they are criminals [25]. Likewise, with user-generated content taking over the web, *protecting* a copyright is something that concerns a growing number of people who are showcasing their creative work online. Multiple stakeholders with often competing interests make this a complicated design space. These stakeholders include not only copyright holders and content creators, but also technology designers.

However, just because copyright is relevant to more people does not mean that the law surrounding it is any less complex. Indeed, it is even more so, since technological advances tend to exacerbate existing confusions in the law as new policies struggle to keep up with developing technology and practices. Therefore it is unsurprising that misunderstandings, misconceptions, and confusion about the law are commonplace among many different types of content creators and consumers [1,13,17,19,23,27].

This potential confusion is particularly striking for legal gray areas such as remix. Along with distribution and sharing, technological advances have made content reuse an easy task for the ordinary Internet user—from remix videos created with software that now comes on every computer to simple image macros generated by any number of websites. Whereas the average person may know enough about copyright to recognize that sharing a downloaded song is not acceptable, the question of whether they are permitted to use part of a song in a remix video is more difficult to answer because the law does allow for some uses of copyrighted content. Otherwise, *Saturday Night Live* could not parody films and journalists could not quote from books in book reviews. This same copyright exception potentially covers creative works such as music sampling, remix videos, and fan fiction.

In the United States, the legal doctrine that governs when it is permissible to appropriate copyrighted material is called *fair use*,[1] and even before widespread use of the Internet,

ACM 978-1-4503-2922-4/15/03...$15.00.
http://dx.doi.org/10.1145/2675133.2675234

[1] Fair use in U.S. law (though there are similar concepts for other countries) is a codified exception to copyright law. It covers, for example, parody and news reporting. It can also allow for creative re-uses such as remix. Though a judge determines whether a situation is fair use on a case-by-case basis, the Copyright Act of 1976 provides four factors to be weighed in making the determination:

(1) the purpose and character of the use, including whether such use is of a commercial nature or is for nonprofit educational purposes;

the Supreme Court in *Campbell v. Acuff-Rose* (1992) referred to it as the "most troublesome" part of all of copyright law. Prior work has shown that for online creators who work with appropriated material, there is indeed confusion about relevant law and that community norms sometimes fill in these gaps in understanding [13].

An additional source of confusion for amateur content creators showcasing their work online can be their own rights in their work. Whereas in most countries copyright vests at the time of creation and therefore automatically exists as soon as someone creates something original, it is a common misconception that making something available on the web puts it into the public domain,[2] or that registration is required for having a copyright in a work.[3] Additionally, Terms of Service governing copyright terms for the websites used for sharing are often long and difficult to understand [12]. Therefore, creators are sometimes unsure about their own rights, including how to deal with plagiarism and—going back to fair use—how other people can use parts of their work.

Despite the lack of bright line rules for some of these copyright concepts, many Internet users make decisions every day about what is permissible and what is not. In doing so, they must negotiate multiple sources of rules, including the letter of the law, website policies, community norms, and ethical standards. It is therefore unsurprising that copyright law is a frequent topic of conversation in the online communities where content creators gather.

In this study, we use these conversations as a starting point to understand the challenges that these creators face in an uncertain legal environment. By analyzing public forum postings in online creative communities, we discern how the law is understood (and—most importantly—not understood), discussed, and engaged with, and its effects on creative activities and online interaction. Focusing primarily on U.S. law, we identify five types of problems related to copyright encountered by creators in these communities, and discuss how community policies and incomplete information contribute to these problems. We also discuss how these problems impact interaction and technology use, which could have design implications for technology and online community designers.

RELATED WORKS

CSCW research often emphasizes the importance of designing with the entire socio-technical system in mind. With respect to online content creation, we know that creativity does not exist in a vacuum, but rather is influenced by context such as the connection between the artist and broader cultural and technological factors [7]. In previous studies of remixers, there has been a necessary backdrop of copyright in discussions of issues such as distribution, sharing, or commercialization [6,18].

In other studies of amateur content creation, copyright has been a more central part of the discussion. Two different studies examining attitudes about content reuse concluded that behavior does not track completely to either the law or to website policy and guidelines, but relies heavily on social norms as well [13,27]. In communities of video mash-up artists [9], fanworks creators[4] [13], or even knitters [19], behavior and attitudes are often guided by intuitions and norms about appropriation. For example, conflicts that have erupted over the years in fan communities reveal a number of strongly entrenched social norms related to copyright: norms about plagiarism, attribution, what constitutes commercialization, and "filing the serial numbers" off fan fiction (i.e., changing the names of characters and then publishing it) [21]. Remixers such as fan fiction writers represent a group struggling to understand and locate the law within these cultural norms [29]. In some communities, these norms and ethical standards have been formalized into codes of best practices [2].

Part of the reason that norms can be particularly complex in these communities is that interpretations of relevant laws can vary substantially. Not only in copyright, but for realms such as privacy as well, the law is often context-dependent, which can be frustrating for designers and researchers [20]. Fair use in particular is decided on a case-by-case basis. Designed purposefully as a heuristic rather than a bright line rule, this flexibility is desirable in a legal context (particularly since the law can be slow to catch up to technology), but essentially impossible to model computationally [2,11]. Even though years of case precedent have clarified many areas of fair use, amateur creative content has been less frequently litigated. Therefore, some communities' uses cut through both the clear and unclear areas of the law.

---

(2) the nature of the copyrighted work;
(3) the amount and substantiality of the portion used in relation to the copyrighted work as a whole; and
(4) the effect of the use upon the potential market for or value of the copyrighted work (17 U.S.C. § 107)

[2] Creative works in the public domain have no copyright and therefore are freely available for anyone to use. There are typically three ways this can happen: (1) the copyright has expired (e.g., the works of Jane Austen or Mozart); (2) the copyright has been forfeited (e.g., dedicating a work to the public domain with a license) or (3) copyright is inapplicable for that work (e.g., works from the U.S. government are excluded from copyright). Simply making something available for other people to consume does not forfeit any intellectual property rights or put it into the public domain.

[3] The standard of copyright applying at creation was established internationally by the Berne Convention in 1886. The United States did require registration of copyrighted works before joining this treaty in 1989. Though in the United States there are legal advantages to registration, such as statutory damages for infringement, since 1989 neither a mark nor registration is required for a work to be considered copyrighted.

[4] "Fanworks" refer to art, writing, music, video, or other media that is based on media properties such as television shows or books. For example, a fan fiction story might involve the continuing adventures of the characters from *Harry Potter*. Practices dating back to Sherlock Holmes and Jane Austen makes the "fandom" community some of the very earliest remixers [8].

Unsurprisingly, prior work reveals misconceptions about copyright law among those who inevitably engage with it—including remix video creators [1], documentary filmmakers [23], and librarians [17]. However, even without the knowledge to back it up, intricate intuitions about the law can form, which we have specifically seen in communities of online content creators [13,14,27,28,29].

Though policy-relevant themes such as these have been addressed in recent CSCW work, they are rarely prioritized [20], and discussions of privacy and security are more common than discussions of intellectual property. Jackson et al. have cautioned against a model of policy within CSCW research as static, irrelevant, or merely an external backdrop, and suggested instead that it be considered a key third factor alongside design and practice [20]. They present these factors as intertwined in CSCW systems: technology can have consequences for proceeding social and policy arrangements; policy can impact how tools are used and understood; and unanticipated uses can impact both design and policy. One purpose of the current work is to better understand the role of copyright policy alongside design and practice within the context of online creativity.

METHODS

For this study we wanted to focus on activities for which the relevant law can be particularly complicated (such as fair use), and therefore sought out online communities where creative appropriation is common. Based on the creative activities reported by participants in a previous study about remix and fanworks [13], we identified four major media types associated with this type of creativity: art, music, video, and writing. In determining which communities to study, we used Alexa search engine rankings as a proxy for popularity, choosing search terms for each media type that specified remix or appropriation: "fan art" (art), "music remix" (music), and "fan fiction" (writing). For video, due to difficulty finding online communities in a search for "remix video," we chose to examine one site with a broader focus (keyword "video") and one with a narrower focus (keyword "machimina" as an example of a specific type of remix video).

	Description	Approximate Total Public Posts	Approximate Posts Scraped	Posts in Data Set	Estimated Copyright Percentage
DeviantArt Art c. 2000 forum.deviantart.com	One of the largest social networks on the web, a popular space for artists both amateur and professional to showcase their work	15,800,000	49,464	50	3%
Fanart Central Art c. 2004 forums.fanart-central.net	An online art gallery that hosts primarily fandom-based art and fiction, but also allows original submissions	278,000	20,875	50	11%
Remix64 Music c. 2002 remix64.com/board	A Commodore 64 and Amiga music remix community, containing news and reviews as well as a place for users to upload their work	73,000	1,099	50	5%
OverClocked Remix Music c. 2003 ocremix.org/forums	A video game music community featuring fan-made remixes and information	636, 000	7,642	50	5%
YouTube Video c. 2005 productforums.google.com/forum/#!forum/youtube	The largest user-generated content video site on the web; though it does not have a general forum for discussion, it does have a very large help forum in a Google Group	500 per day	17,546	50	13%
MMORPG Forum Video c. 1999 mmorpgforum.com	A site for discussion of massively multiplayer online roleplaying games; the largest sub-forums are dedicated to machinima, Warcraft movies and Warhammer movies	113,000	364	23	3%
HarryPotterFanFiction.com Writing c. 2009 harrypotterfanfiction.com/forums	The oldest fan fiction site on the web dedicated to the *Harry Potter* novels, housing over 78,000 stories	70,000	1,211	16	2%
Twisting the Hellmouth Writing c. 2008 forum.tthfanfic.org	A fan fiction archive with over 15,000 stories based on the *Buffy the Vampire Slayer* and *Angel* television shows	54,000	1,590	50	7%

Table 1. Website information and statistics

For each of these keyword searches, we chose the top sites under the search results that: (a) were online communities; (b) featured user-generated content of the appropriate media type; (c) had active *public* forums with more than 100 posts; and (d) were primarily in English. We chose two sites for each media type (see Table 1).

In the spring of 2013, we scraped public forum posts (only those posts viewable to anyone on the web without creating an account or logging in) associated with these online communities. A "post" includes the initial post along with all the comments that follow. We collected the content as well as header information (title, author, date/time) for each post and corresponding comments. In narrowing down the data set of all forum posts to only conversations about copyright, we had to go beyond the obvious method of doing a keyword search for "copyright." Using only this keyword would leave out relevant conversations that did not include the word—perhaps systematically so, as some posters may not know enough about copyright to use that term. Using a sample of 200 posts from these online communities, we pulled out common related terms in order to create a comprehensive set of keywords to search for conversations about copyright. We used an inter-rater reliability measure to validate this manual judgment by having two additional coders judge a random sample of 10% of these posts, resulting in 100% agreement with the original coder. We also validated the sufficiency of the keywords by testing them on another sample of posts and then comparing the search results to another set of manually judged posts. Though there were a number of false positives, there were no false negatives. The final list of keywords used included: attorney, copyright, copy, copying, illegal, infringement, lawyer, legal, license, permission, plagiarism, plagiarist, rights, steal, stole, and trademark.

We completed a scrape based on these keywords, resulting in nearly 100,000 total posts across our eight different forums (see Table 1). Because there were false positives in this data (e.g., a post that might contain the word "legal" but discuss privacy rather than copyright), one coder (whose judgment was validated using the inter-rater reliability measure noted above) used a random number generator to sample posts from this group, adding posts to our final data set only if they included some discussion of copyright. We collected a maximum of 50 posts from each site, though some had less than 50 as their total number of posts about copyright. Because some sites had a much smaller number of posts, keeping this number small allowed us to have a fairly stratified sample. In sum, we began with a set of millions of forum posts across eight different communities, narrowed this down to approximately 100,000 posts that might be about copyright, and then narrowed this to a tractable number of posts *only* about copyright based on a random sample. Our final data set has a total of 339 forum posts.

In analyzing our resulting data set, we looked to grounded theory, a method for collecting and analyzing qualitative data in order to generate theories that are "grounded" in that data from the beginning [5]. It provides a set of systematic guidelines for analysis while maintaining flexibility to fit the given set of data. This approach is particularly useful for sifting through large amounts of unstructured data, and makes its greatest contribution in areas where there has been little research [24]. When using this method for extant texts such as Internet discussions, it is important to situate the texts in their contexts and incorporate that context into the generated theory [5]. Grounded theory beginning with open coding is a technique used often in online forum content analysis [16,31].

Using this approach, we began with inductive, open coding in which we coded the data for emergent phenomena [32]. Two coders, including the first author who is a law school graduate and copyright expert, coded subsets of the data independently, meeting periodically to discuss the codes and synthesizing them into a single set. Refining the codes was an iterative process until we had a total of 87 open codes that were grouped into 8 higher-level categories. We considered our codes finalized when the categories were "saturated"—that is, we found no new insights or new properties to these categories in the remainder of our data set [5]. Using these finalized categories, we coded the data again, including an overlap of 10% which we used to calculate inter-rater reliability with a percent agreement of 94% and Cohen's Kappa of .77 [26].

Data Set Limitations

Likely because the forums we studied are all English language and most of the sites based in the United States, most legal discussion focused on U.S. law. In our data set, only 5 posts out of 339 made any specific reference to the law of another country—for example, fair use equivalents in other countries such as Canada's fair dealing. Though many core copyright concepts discussed are largely universal due to the Berne Convention,[5] it is also true that international law complicates issues of copyright and that social norms about copyright can vary wildly from culture to culture.

Since we do not have demographic information for the online communities we studied beyond the posting statistics noted in Table 1, we cannot make statements about the representativeness of these users for content creators generally. Additionally, the sites represent a range of different internal copyright policies and related technologies. For example, YouTube uses an automated

[5] The Berne Convention (created in 1886) is an international agreement that governs copyright, requiring signed countries to recognize the copyrights of authors in the other countries. It contains some universal provisions, such as a minimum copyright term and allowances for fair use. As of 2013, 167 states are parties to this agreement. The United States signed on in 1989.

content ID system to assist in removing copyrighted content and includes pages of copyright policy explanations, whereas Remix64 has no Terms of Service posted at all. Though we also know that based on readability levels that even if users did read site policies (which most do not) that they might not understand them [12]. Because these eight sites are quite different in terms of user base and copyright enforcement, the issues discussed in our results unless stated otherwise appeared for at least two of these sites in our dataset. We saw evidence that social norms and copyright literacy among users varies across sites; however, it was not within the scope of the current study to compare and contrast these sites.

It should also be noted that though all of our data comes from information publicly viewable online, we still opted for "light disguise" as suggested for studies of amateur artists online [3]. Therefore, we omit usernames from our results as well as any quotations that might address blatantly illegal activity or reveal personally identifying information.

RESULTS

Though our final data set consists of 339 randomly sampled posts, these were not the only copyright-related posts in the hundreds of thousands of forum posts available to us. Due to false positives, the initial results of our keyword search does not give us an accurate count of how many copyright-related posts there were on these sites. Therefore, in order to estimate the prevalence of this topic of conversation, we also took a random sample of 100 posts from each of the eight sites. We noted how many copyright-related posts there were in these samples, resulting in a basic estimate for the prevalence of copyright as a conversation topic on each site (see Table 1). Though these percentages might seem small, three percent of DeviantArt's 15 million posts, for example, is still hundreds of thousands of conversations.

None of the online communities that we studied have any focus on copyright issues or any features in the sites themselves to lead creators towards these discussions. It appears that the topic simply comes up organically, conversations taking place most commonly within "General" or "Off-Topic" sub-forums.

When categorizing each overall post by type, we found that by far the most common type of conversation occurring, (beyond even unrelated conversations that veered off-topic to copyright) were those in which someone was asking a question about copyright. In both DeviantArt and YouTube, the two largest sites, question-and-answer posts made up more than half of the copyright-related posts for those sites. The vast majority of these asked questions were answered by at least one person.

The iterative codes from our data set converged on topics such as legal concepts, ethical judgments, enforcement, and attitudes. However, one clear theme that emerged was the prevalence of *problems* related to copyright expressed by creators in these conversations. Most of the posts in our data set could be labeled as expressing some sort of problem. We identified five major types:

(1) avoiding trouble,

(2) dealing with consequences,

(3) fear of infringement,

(4) dealing with infringement, and

(5) incomplete information.

The final category is an overarching problem, and the others focus on either the point of view of creators who are appropriating work, or the point of view of creators who are concerned about protecting their own work. We use these five problem types as a framework for discussing this data.

Avoiding Trouble

A common problem directly expressed by these creators is worry over whether something they are doing might be infringing someone else's copyright. Many of the posts are essentially asking "Is this going to get me into trouble?" or "How can I avoid getting into trouble?" Out of all of the question-and-answer posts, these types of questions are the most prevalent. Many of these questions are quite nuanced, without simple yes-or-no answers.

For example, two questions with potentially complex answers come from Overclocked, a music remix site: "Is it legal to use extracted vocals in a remix of a commercial song?" and "Is it copyright infringement to use chiptune SFX on an album designed to generate revenue as a donation to a religious entity?"

The advice that the posters receive in return varies in quality, but interestingly, tends to veer towards stricter interpretations of copyright. It is more common to see "No you can't do that" than "Yes you can" or even "Yes you can if you follow these guidelines." Of course, not all copyright interpretations are strict; when we do see "Yes you can," it is often followed by "... because no one will notice."

[Site: MMORPG Forum] *It's not like the RIAA goes around youtube and puts a big lawsuit on them for using their music. Do you REALLY think that every single movie maker has taken the time to buy the rights of the music they used? Get some common sense, imo.* [6]

However, particularly keeping in mind that the other community members answering the questions are likely *not* copyright experts, the "better safe than sorry" flavor of advice makes sense.

[6] The Recording Industry Association of America is the trade organization that represents record labels in the United States, a large part of their mission being to protect the intellectual property of these labels. They have brought a number of high-profile lawsuits for copyright infringements against individuals engaged in file-sharing.

One of the responses to the religious donation question above was: "The best thing you can do I would think is to phone and/or email the companies own the sounds." This is not bad advice, and in fact "ask permission" is a common refrain. However, it is also the case that an amateur remixer contacting a large copyright holder to ask for permission to use something is unlikely to get a helpful result. Nearly every time someone in one of our posts mentioned contacting a copyright holder, it went something like this comment on a Remix64 post: "I tried to contact the legal owner of the music but the Liverpool studio didn't take time to answer my question." Advice to ask for permission was also the response to the following two questions from worried creators.

[DeviantArt] *Let's say that I want to use a photo of a celebrity in a piece of digital artwork. The photo would not be the entire piece...just a small part of it. (The vast majority of the piece would be my own work.) Unfortunately, I realized (belatedly) that pictures of celebrities are generally copyrighted. I'm not planning to sell my work... just display it online. Is there any possible way to use celebrity pictures WITHOUT committing copyright infringement?*

[YouTube] *I made a remix for a song by artist Linkin park and have no intentions to sell or use the video for commercial purposes. how do I remove copyright flags???*

In both of these examples, the original poster is asking about a remix activity that based on the descriptions here could very likely be fair use. In our data there are a number of cases of fair use not being discussed as an option. For example, one answer is: "You need a LICENSE in writing from the copyright owner or his agent spelling out in nauseating detail just what you can and cannot do with the audio. Nothing else matters." The original poster's response was to thank the respondent profusely for the advice, implying that they will likely follow it. However, as noted above, contacting copyright owners rarely has a positive result. One might speculate that given this advice the remixer might simply decide not to post their video after all. This is a solution to their problem of how to avoid infringing copyright, though arguably not the ideal one.

This category is also where we see the most examples of what could be considered legal advice—such as asking a copyright holder for a license. Though we sometimes see an IANAL ("I am not a lawyer") disclaimer, more often we simply see advice provided with complete confidence but no credentials. In contrast, in every rare instance of *actual* expertise, we see an "I am a lawyer, but" disclaimer stating that they are not providing actual legal advice (which is dangerous for lawyers to do outside of an attorney-client relationship). Sometimes posters will provide links to actual legal resources, though this is somewhat uncommon. Of course, we also see a lot of "you should consult a lawyer" as advice—which like the suggestion to ask permission is not *bad* advice, but impractical. Lawyers are expensive, perhaps a reason why these creators are asking advice from strangers on the Internet in the first place.

Many of the posters also note that they researched the issue first themselves and were confused by the law or unable to find satisfactory answers. This is one place where we see a potential failure of site policies or copyright explanations, when posters note that they were unable to find the information that they need.

Dealing with Consequences

Also from the perspective of those creators who are appropriating content, a related problem to avoiding trouble is dealing with consequences after the fact. Many of the posts in our data set were creators asking for advice about what they should do (or simply complaining) after they have been accused or officially sanctioned for copyright violations—whether or not that accusation or sanction was legitimate.

[YouTube] *So I posted a video and used some music, I then got an e-mail from youtube saying it was copyrighted by SME (who ever they are) and I wanted to know, will I go to jail or [lose] my channel?*[7]

[FanArt Central] *I did not 'edit' the images to my desire, I DREW them, with my mouse. I am not trying to hide the fact that I used heavy references on this piece... If this is against the rules, I will be glad to remove it. If not, is there any way to proclaim that this is my work, and for people to stop accusing me?*

A lack of knowledge also contributes to this problem. Frequently the posters do not understand why they were sanctioned, either because of confusion about copyright law or confusion about site policies. Responses tend to cite these policies rather than the law, though the two are typically linked. In response to the YouTube question above, someone simply states "If you get three copyright strikes your account will be terminated" while another response briefly explains the Automated Content ID system that seeks out copyrighted content on YouTube (though no one assures the original poster that jail time is not a potential consequence for a YouTube copyright strike).

This problem is more frequent on YouTube than on the other sites studied, likely due to the Content ID system that automates taking down videos when there are copyright claims. Of course, this automation also means that there are false positives, when content is taken down erroneously

---

[7] Under the Digital Millennium Copyright Act, third-party content providers such as YouTube are required to take actions on copyright claims by removing the content accused of infringing. This "takedown notice" procedure notifies the person who uploaded the content, providing options for filing a "counter-claim" if the content is not infringing. The DMCA also makes it a criminal act to circumvent technological copyright protection measures. Because remixing often requires gathering source material, the DMCA often hits hardest at transformative uses by people who are attempting to conform with the law [35].

[30]. There have been some well-publicized examples of YouTube removing remix videos that are almost certainly fair use, for example [15]. Unfortunately, though fair use's flexibility makes it valuable as a legal doctrine, this same flexibility makes it a nightmare for computational models [11]. Previous research has uncovered that fear of work being taken down can affect technology or site choice [13], and here we also see examples of creators deciding to stop using YouTube due to disagreement with their copyright policies.

[YouTube] *These guys are making fools of themselves claiming they have rights to Handel, Bach, and Mozart. It's just an excuse to put advertising on the screen when the video runs. I signed up on Vimeo.*[8]

[YouTube] *As long as this problem continues unsolved, and YT staff does not fix it, there's no point in being a partner (unless I can get full immunity)... a few seconds from some random WMG music was heard inside those files. This can be easily classified as a fair use in the copyright laws.*

[YouTube] *Iv'e looked all over Youtube. There is no place to report People Continually false copyrighting, and people who threaten to take channels down by False flagging. Am I supposed to sit here and watch my channel get taken down for lies? When you search through the report section, there is no option for these things. YOUTUBE, DO SOMETHING!*

In our data set, references to legal consequences were scarce. Typically the worst consequence would be the removal of work or of a user account. However, outside official sanctions, accusations within the community, fueled by social norms, can have consequences as well. This is discussed in more detail from the opposing point of view in terms of dealing with cases of infringement. However, it is notable that in the current category, the posters do not tend to receive a lot of sympathy in response to their problems. There are few examples of other community members coming to their defense or noting that they may have been wrongly sanctioned. There appears to be a default assumption that site sanctions are typically correct.

Fear of Infringement

In the previous two categories, we see the point of view of mostly artists who are appropriating existing work, either in legitimate remixes or actual infringement, and the problems caused by unclear law or policy surrounding content reuse. In these next two categories we get the point of view of copyright holders—when artists are trying to protect their work from infringement.

Though there are examples of this problem across all studied sites, it appears to be most frequent among digital artists, especially on DeviantArt. This makes sense, as DeviantArt hosts a number of professional artists for whom protecting the monetary value of their work is a real concern. Plagiarism is a much more common complaint than remixing, and there is a great deal of discussion about the role of credit and permission.

[DeviantArt] *I would like to make it so that I can display my art work but not allow others to copy it. How do I do that?*

[Harry Potter Fan Fiction] *I was thinking about posting my stories online and I'm wondering how safe it really is. Even if I put a copyright on it and say 'Everything you don't recognize is property of me' there is still a chance that someone will take it, right? Is there any way I can protect my work more? Thanks.*

Posters often express frustration that there isn't more that they can do to protect their work—for example, that the site moderators aren't doing enough or that the site's policies aren't effective, sometimes making suggestions for policy or workflow changes.

[DeviantArt] *I've reported it to dA a few times over the last couple of months, but no action seems to be taken. One report even came back "invalid" (she stole the photo from the girls private Facebook for Christ's sake)*

[DeviantArt] *I'd like to suggest if at all possible for DA staff to make it to where deviations that are submitted in must be manually approved or denied. The reason I say this is because there are people who have been treating DA like it's myspace, photobucket, facebook, etc in which completely goes against the copyright policy*

This demonstrates something of a reversal from remixers deciding not to use a particular site for fear of their work being flagged for infringement and removed. Instead, we see creators deciding not to use a site because of fear their work will be infringed upon.

[DeviantArt] *I just finished a play but nobody wants to look at it because they're busy. Of course I got it done really quickly, it's the FIRST DRAFT and I need you to look at it, mom! :< And I'm not posting it here for fear of Copyright Infringement*

We also see incomplete or incorrect information contributing to this problem, as many creators have some fundamental misunderstandings about the way that copyright works. The advice for "how can I protect my work?" can be as bad as some of the advice for "how can I avoid infringing?" For example, copyright registration is not necessary—copyright vests at the time of creation. A common misconception is that you have to *do* something to have rights in your work (such as register it with the Copyright Office).

[DeviantArt] *there are several different ways to copyright. the "automatic" copyright actually only protects you to a*

[8] Handel, Bach, and Mozart compositions would certainly be in the public domain—though sound recordings may not be.

certain extent. while other forms such as trademarking would further protect you through copyrighting names, figures, symbols, words, etc that are contained within an image. "all rights reserved" is another one.

It is also worth noting that for creators who might be interested in more permissive uses of their work, there is little information available on the sites or in the forums about things like open licenses. In the very few instances in which Creative Commons[9] was mentioned, posters did not seem very knowledgeable about how it functions.

Dealing with Infringement

With respect to possible infringement that has already taken place, we do see some "someone stole my work, so what do I do now?" sorts of questions. However, the more common interactions here are calls for action or public shaming. Though there are occasional threats for legal action, mostly these posts include requests for other community members to report someone for a Terms of Service violation, or simply calling them out publicly. This is a form of community social norm policing.

[Overclocked] *Why exactly does it say [username] and have a link to [username]'s (old?) webpage by it? Explain that to me and then I'll be happy to comment on your ALLEGED remix. Otherwise, nice try, genius. Don't let the door hit you on the way out, music thief.*

[Twisting the Hellmouth] *it does smack of plagiarism, though at least he's up-front about saying he didn't write it. Not naming the real author is VERY bad, and I'm about to write a review saying so.*

Here we see strong evidence of social norms against plagiarism within these communities. These instances of public shaming can arguably be more effective than official sanctions in these kinds of situations, particularly when the community members are unclear on the law or do not have faith in the site itself to properly enforce it. Some legal scholars have noted that particularly in realms in which the law is gray, social norms can carry more weight than written law [10,14]. Fan communities in particular have been described as "hypervigilant" when it comes to policing plagiarism, with one fan fiction community going so far as to maintain a list of known plagiarizers [4].

As far as the outcomes of these posts, sometimes they work exactly as intended:

[Remix64] *well it's all sorted now. Got an apology from him, so the matter is resolved as far as I'm concerned. Happy for this thread to be deleted.*

Other times, they can backfire. This is also an example of a social norm—a norm about what kinds of behavior needs policing and how to go about it.

[Twisting the Hellmouth] *I've looked the forum over and you show an astonishing lack of common sense when it comes to "problems", especially when it involves moderators. There's nearly a half dozen occasions I've located on here where you could have easily contacted a site moderator and/or administrator regarding your perceived "problem", but have decided to air it publicly to try and stir up other members so you don't have to stick your neck out by yourself.*

Additionally, sometimes social norms or even community policies do not actually track to the law. We have seen evidence of this previously with respect to understandings of fair use among remixers [13]. One striking example of this is the policy from the Twisting the Hellmouth fan fiction community about appropriation of elements in the work posted there. In an initial discussion of this topic, a writer asked if this was permissible, and another poster explained why they considered it unethical.

[Twisting the Hellmouth] *I'd expect you (and we would double check) to obtain permission to do fanfic based off [a fanwork]. It'd be like you reading one of [username]'s fics and then deciding to make a "sequel" out of the blue. I wouldn't like it, no other author here would like it.*

This is actually a common norm within fanworks communities, when the same guidelines for re-use do not apply to other fanworks as they do for media properties. In other words, it's not okay to remix the remixes. Though fan creators recognize that this is not a legal or economic argument, the stance revolves around community norms and established etiquette [4]. The original poster here noted the potential hypocrisy in this stance, but then stated an intention to follow the community norm.

[Twisting the Hellmouth] *how does this differ from taking a story written by any established author? have we gained the permission of every writer and director of every single Book, TV show and Flim that the site covers? don't understand how someone who writes a story based on someone else?s work without getting permission from the original writer can complain about someone writing a story based on their work. It just smacks of double standards to me. But that is just my opinion and I'm more than happy to follow the general fanfic rule that it's taboo.*

In a later post in the forum, the site moderators came to the community for input on an official policy on this exact issue, and put forth this policy:

[Twisting the Hellmouth] *I came up with this as a potential solution for authors who want to write stories based on the*

[9] Creative Commons licenses are a method for content creators to share their work more freely by communicating that it is "some rights reserved" rather than "all rights reserved" [25]. For example, a DeviantArt artist could put a Creative Commons Attribution No-Derivatives Non-Commercial license on their artwork, meaning that someone else could copy and use it, but they would have to credit the creator, could not modify the piece, and could not make any money from it.

stories of other authors. Quote 1. If you want to base your story on another author's work you must contact them and ask permission and attribute them if they give it. Ideally, this should be before you start writing so you don't waste your time if someone responds negatively. 2. If you do not get a response within two weeks, you can post the story but must still attribute their work. 3. The original author can ask to have your story removed from the site at any time, even if they have given their permission in the past. They have the right to change their mind.

Interestingly, this policy also goes beyond the requirements of the law. Assuming that fan fiction is fair use, then permission is not required. However, Twisting the Hellmouth already has a policy in place that prohibits posting fan fiction that is based on the property of copyright owners who have expressly stated that they do not want fan fiction written about their work (for example, author Anne Rice saying that it "upsets [her] terribly" and George R.R. Martin stating that he doesn't want people "making off with" his characters [4]). This request does not actually hold any legal weight in cases of fair use, but is instead an ethical norm. Unsurprisingly, there were community members who felt that the policy of non-response indicating permission was also too lenient, however.

[Twisting the Hellmouth] *I do not know of any fanfiction archives that allow or even support authors playing in other authors' verses without their permission. I don't think that this site should become the first. I do not want authors on this site to feel that their hard work is not protected. I do not want authors to feel that their stories, their ideas, are up for grabs by whoever wants them.*

The excerpt above provides an example of a situation in which the law is less strict than a website policy (based on an ethical judgment rather than a legal one) which is less strict than a social norm. Similarly, Twisting the Hellmouth requires disclaimers ("I do not own the characters in this story"), which carry no legal weight, but follow social norms among fanworks creators regarding credit. Negotiating multiple sources of rules seems to be one cause of confusion in these spaces.

Incomplete Information

Though a lack of understanding of the law or site policies is an overarching problem throughout our other categories as well, there are many instances of information seeking behavior outside of discussions of specific cases. Sometimes these are simply expressions of confusion about copyright law in general. Perhaps they choose to post about it in these communities because they have seen other discussions of copyright. For example, this poster on Overclocked asked a very basic question about copyright law that did not directly relate to the content of the website:

[Overclocked] *If downloading copyrighted music for free is illegal, then why can we listen to a music video on youtube or some amv of it. That's how I listen to music that I don't own.*

In these general discussions as well as in specific instances arising from the problems previous discussed, we see both correct and incorrect explanations of the law in response. Some posters (though IANAL seems to apply) are actually very knowledgeable about the law and appear to seek out these discussions specifically to answer questions. One poster in the Remix64 music remix community appears in 35 out of 50 copyright-related posts, almost always answering questions.

Of course, the danger is that there is no simple way to tell the good from the bad when it comes to legal information and advice. For example, the following is an explanation of fair use provided by a poster, and though it contains some elements of truth, it is not quite right, since it suggests that only educational or news purposes constitute fair use.

[Twisting the Hellmouth] *Actually under copyright law, the copyright owner doesn't have to prove a person made a profit OR caused damage. They just have to prove someone else used their copyright material in an illegal way. And almost any use is illegal. Unless that someone else is using the work as a reference in a non-fiction educational work or a news article, they will lose the law suit.*

In a more troubling example, this was a response to a post about a YouTube takedown in which the original poster stated that they thought their remix video was fair use.

[YouTube] *There is really no such thing as fair use. If you use someone else property without permission it's still called stealing.*

When the original poster then cited the fair use provision in the Copyright Act, this was the response:

[YouTube] *You might want to look into that law you posted the Copyright Act 1976 because since 1976 to 2010 it's been updated to take in this little thing called the internet. That's like me bring up a law from 1853 trying to defend my right to drive without pants.*[10]

Sometimes legal explanations aren't blatantly wrong, but just simplistic.

[YouTube] *There's nothing particularly mind-boggling about copyright law: only the original owner has the "right", literally, to make "copies."*

At least occasionally, community members will point out that it might not be the best idea to trust strangers on the Internet with legal advice. In one exchange on DeviantArt, one poster argued "I'd tried looking up on the net, but I find

[10] Even though the Copyright Act is decades old, it is still the law of the land. This is one reason that it is desirable for laws like fair use to be somewhat vague and flexible, because they can be interpreted in light of new technology [2].

it easier to get a straightforward answer from a person's personal point-of-view than to try to make sense of miles and miles to text," to which the response was, "Someone's point of view could be wrong, though."

Though these question-and-answer posts are the most common in our data set, there are also examples of higher-level discussions about copyright, often containing nuanced understandings of the issues involved even if not representing completely correct interpretations of the law.

[Twisting the Hellmouth] *I imagine most people here have read about the book series "50 Shades of Grey", a recently published erotic novel trilogy that was originally posted as "Master of the Universe" – a Twilight fanfiction story posted on fanfiction.net. I thought it would be appropriate here to discuss the morality – perhaps even the legality – of fanfiction writers publishing their works with a few changes.*

Sometimes these discussions do not even relate to the content of the community—for example, a discussion about software piracy on a music remixing site—which suggests that for these types of content creators copyright is something that is of general interest to them even outside of the immediate challenges they face.

[Overclocked] *I find that more and more people around me have no scruples with illegally downloading software. I would love, believe me, to own some of these programs, but I know that it is stealing. I feel you are no less a criminal for pirating programs than for shoplifting or pickpocketing. Is it easier to justify because you won't ever see the guy who's losing money, often thousands of dollars, because of your whim? Someone want to explain your reasoning behind doing this? You know you do it.*

A side effect of these discussions and information-seeking is that some community members are doing legal research and learning things that they wouldn't otherwise, due to their engagement with these communities and this type of content creation.

[Twisting the Hellmouth] *I write fan fiction of a limited sort (BtVS or Crossovers with BtVS) so I'm not exactly unbiased. When I first started writing it I did some basic research on the legal issues. My understanding is that there haven't been any actual court cases involving fan fiction (In the US anyway).*

[Overclocked] *Let me just say I'm really enjoying this conversation. I went to school for music business and I like honing my knowledge with this kind of academic discussion, especially when the result of the exchange can potentially help someone!*

Therefore, these copyright discussions maintain a precarious position of both advancing and contributing to knowledge, and potentially spreading misinformation.

DISCUSSION

We have described five emergent themes in our data as *problems* or *challenges* faced by creators in these online communities—but what are the consequences of these problems? Based on our data set, we saw little evidence of legal consequences beyond those handled directly by the website (such as DMCA takedown notices). Though lawsuits from content owners are not outside the realm of possibility, in practice they are more likely to go through the website itself to have content removed.

Therefore, setting aside that more unlikely consequence, there are four primary potential bad outcomes for content creators: (1) their work is removed from the site due to a policy violation or takedown notice; (2) their work is copied or distributed by someone else without their permission; (3) they decide not to upload their work to the site because of fear of getting into trouble or fear of someone else copying it; or (4) they violate a rule or norm and are shamed or ostracized by the community.

The secondary outcome of most of these, besides the distress of the creators themselves, is less creative work in these communities. Arguably this is a poor outcome for both the websites and the creators, as well as outside consumers of that content. Fair use, in addition to being context-dependent, tends to be value-laden as well, and not every lawyer or judge will see remix as a valuable form of art (while many others would disagree) [36]. However, "less creativity" as an outcome also goes against the spirit of intellectual property in general—which as provided for in the Constitution exists to incentivize invention.

In legal terms, a *chilling effect* is when someone doesn't do something that they should be able to do because of a fear of legal consequences. Though traditionally examined in terms of the suppression of speech, this is something that can happen with creativity as well. As legal scholar Rebecca Tushnet points out, even though the law at its core values creativity, not everyone has the same tolerance to risk and so it is still susceptible to being suppressed by copyright expansionism [34]. Our data set showed specific instances of chilling effects within these communities (e.g., decisions not to upload work onto YouTube due to improper takedown notices), and we could extrapolate to more (e.g., creators being told that their work would definitely be infringing if they don't get permission from the copyright holder). Additionally, content creators not trusting in the site to protect their work from copyright infringement is a kind of reverse chilling effect that has the same outcome. Choosing to not use a technology for fear of copyright infringement is similar to evidence of technology non-use due to fear of privacy invasion [22]; both represent a lack of faith in the website to protect their interests.

Accepting these as problems that should be addressed, where do we begin in thinking about solutions? In our descriptions of the five copyright-related challenges observed in these communities, we see two major recurring *causes*. The first is a lack of information—misunderstanding, confusion, or ignorance of the law or site policy, and difficulty finding answers when sought. The second is some perceived failing of the site or technology itself—not providing needed information, policy or enforcement inadequacies, and imperfect or overreaching enforcement tools.

When it comes to the first problem of lack of information, though simple lack of knowledge and lack of research can explain much of it, unclear law and unclear community policies are contributors as well. This lack of clarity is also exacerbated by the spread of misinformation in the very conversations that we studied. Though some of the community members are well informed about copyright law and do a service to their community by answering questions, there are also many instances of incorrect information or simple bad advice. We could argue for better copyright education for people in general, but when misinformation and confusion is affecting user experience on these websites, then it becomes a usability problem appropriate for site designers to address.

From a design point of view, this is an incredibly complex space. Prior work has shown that when it comes to copyright, there are instances in which what the law says, what people think the law says, what people think is ethical, community norms, and what people actually do are completely different [13]. The discrepancy between law, site policy, and norms on Twisting the Hellmouth is a telling example of this kind of complexity. There we see a legal rule (fair use for transformative work) that is less strict than a site policy (seek permission when possible for re-use of fan fiction elements) that is less strict than a community norm (never re-use fan fiction elements without permission). Piling onto the problem of the law itself being gray, creators may also have to deal with multiple sources of rules that sometimes contradict each other.

IMPLICATIONS FOR DESIGN

In thinking about potential solutions from the point of view of online community designers and maintainers, our findings point to some specific recommendations: (1) providing plain language explanations of copyright policies; (2) monitoring user concerns and questions about copyright; (3) providing dedicated spaces for legal conversations and questions; (4) considering existing social norms in the creation of policies; and (5) scaffolding copyright knowledge in the design of content uploading tools.

First, it is important to consider the clarity, readability, and comprehensiveness of copyright-related site policies. Unfortunately, Terms of Service in these online creative communities tend to be long and at a high reading level [12]. YouTube and DeviantArt, the largest of the sites we studied by far, both have pages dedicated to copyright policies, which include some plain language explanations of copyright law. YouTube even has a "Copyright School" video where the explanations are provided by cheerful cartoon characters. Though both sites should be commended for plain language copyright policies, and in fact for mentioning fair use in them at all (rare among these types of sites), their explanations present fair use as something confusing and scary that should only be attempted with the help of an attorney. To quote DeviantArt's section on fair use:

[Fair use is] very limited, complex to analyze under the law and require[s] the help of expert advice from a lawyer. We recommend you talk to your own lawyer if you want to know more about fair use as it applies to the work you are doing. If it turns out that it isn't fair use, you may be liable for very serious money damages.

In other words, as stated in YouTube's Copyright School: "You could get in a lot of trouble. That's how the law works." Presenting fair use in this manner could arguably contribute to chilling effects. Similar to if advice is "ask for permission," if advice is "hire a lawyer," then the better-safe-than-sorry response would likely just be to not post the work. Policies like these could contribute to the "climate of fear" that exists among remixers, the cloud of legal uncertainty formed due to a lack of legal precedent [36].

Part of the problem here is that though ideally we might like to suggest that these sites rewrite their policies to be friendlier to fair use, there are competing interests at stake. In terms of lowering both cost and legal risk, it is likely not in the sites' best interest to adjudicate fair use themselves. The flexibility of fair use as a doctrine means that there are examples of fair use being construed strictly, which also accounts for risk averse behavior. Meanwhile, the sites also have to consider the interests of both users who are appropriating and users who are in fear of others appropriating their work. This is a difficult balance to strike, but simply providing copyright policies in readable language helps with the user information deficit.

Additionally, even if policy or Terms of Service re-writes are an impractical solution (consider as well the cost of attorneys!), these websites have a valuable resource at hand. It is the same one that we have for this study: information about what their users do and do not understand about copyright law and policy. Even something as simple as the construction of an FAQ that covers recurring questions in these communities would be a step in the right direction.

Additionally, none of these communities have a dedicated space for questions or conversations about copyright. We do see knowledgeable community members appearing in these posts to answer questions, and they might do so even more frequently if the relevant posts were easily accessible. Encouraging critical thinking about copyright among community members could also have positive policy outcomes. Aufderheide and Jaszi argue in their book *Reclaiming Fair Use* that it would be in the best interest of creative communities to articulate their own understandings of fair use, because judges sometimes consult patterns of use when making fair use determinations [2]. For example, the documentary film community has benefited from a document of best practices.

Also, the Organization for Transformative Works (OTW), a non-profit dedicated to preserving and defending fanworks as legitimate cultural objects, has had an influential seat at the table in U.S. copyright policymaking [36]. This organization formed following online discussions about disillusionment in the fan community about the policies of existing online communities and a desire to create a space of their own [21]. Additionally, the fan fiction archive created by OTW volunteers, Archive Of Our Own, has both copyright policies and design features derived from the existing social norms of the community. Legal scholars have suggested that copyright law could benefit (and indeed, be more frequently followed) if it more closely resembled emerging copyright norms [14,33]. Though the law is slow to change, websites have more control over their own policies and can take into account the norms of their user base.

In terms of potential technological solutions, unfortunately automated copyright infringement detection is imperfect [30], and the flexibility of fair use exacerbates the problem even further [11]. However, there may be simpler solutions for small positive changes. Consider this idea put forth by a poster in the DeviantArt forums:

[M]y suggestion would be: make a big fat explanation in the poems-upload-centre under the "submit preview picture" upload, that only pictures may be uploaded, that were created by the artist himself. And that neither pictures found in the internet, e.g. by google, nor pictures that you own (e.g. that hangs on your wall) may be submitted as long as you are not the artist and owner of the copyright.

The idea here is essentially a copyright reminder at the time of upload. Of course, this specific poster's solution does not account for fair use. However, one example of an existing solution is the process for uploading an image onto Wikipedia, which functions as something of a fair use wizard [15]. Wikipedia requires information about the origin of the image, and if the user chooses "I believe this is fair use," there are options for common fair use rationale to choose from, such as "the object of discussion in an article" or "excerpt from a copyrighted work." This essentially scaffolds an understanding of fair use for the user. If YouTube, for example, had a similar wizard that prompted for fair use rationale if they indicate that the video contains third-party content, then this would not only similarly scaffold knowledge, but the information could be passed on to copyright holders before they can issue a takedown notice. Decreasing the knowledge gap here would also shift some balance of power to the content creator.

Future Work

Because intellectual property is not an area that has been extensively studied within CSCW or HCI, there is a great deal of opportunity for future work in this space. As noted in discussing the limitations of this data set, the current study is confined to specific websites with a purposeful skew towards amateur remix and appropriation. There are a number of other contexts in which discussions of intellectual property are prevalent online—for example, file sharing communities, Wikimedia Commons, and commercial sites such as Etsy. There is also opportunity to look more closely at cultural differences in norms, as well as issues specifically related to international law. Ongoing work includes comparisons of social norms across different types of communities, as well as a closer look at the different stakeholders, such as the people crafting copyright policies.

Other data sources as well could provide more insight into this subject. One observation from our data is the prevalence of copyright disclaimers. Though they carry no legal weight, they are commonplace in fanworks [4,33], and also appear frequently accompanying YouTube videos (e.g., "no copyright infringement intended"). This is an example of information about copyright that could be gleaned from the artifacts themselves rather than explicit conversations among users. Moreover, the Wikipedia upload wizard described above essentially provides thousand and thousands of examples of fair use rationale given by Wikipedia users.

CONCLUSION

Unfortunately, copyright will continue to be a hard problem in online creative communities. There are many stakeholders with competing interests—lawmakers, copyright holders, online content creators, content consumers. However, technologies and websites that facilitate creation and sharing are also part of this environment and should be considering these issues in terms of both usability and design. It is important, then, for designers and researchers in the CSCW community to have some understanding of copyright law as well. As Jackson et al. point on in their discussion of the role of policy in CSCW systems, it should not be the case that consideration of policy comes only *after* design and practice [20]. Copyright policy is deeply intertwined with any kind of creative activity, especially in the context of sharing and collaboration. This study reveals that it is an important aspect of interactions between creators in these online communities, and therefore should be an important part of the user model in design decisions. We should not only be thinking of ways to help creators better understand copyright, but also considering the implications of the ways they currently understand it as well.

ACKNOWLEDGMENTS
Thanks to Gabriel Perez for his assistance on this research project, as well as to the reviewers for their valuable feedback. This work is supported by NSF IIS-1216347.

REFERENCES

1. Aufderheide, P., Jaszi, P., and Brown, E.N. The Good, The Bad, and The Confusing: User-Generated Video Creators on Copyright. *American University Center for Social Media*, 2007. http://www.centerforsocialmedia.org/sites/default/files/good_bad_confusing.pdf.
2. Aufderheide, P. and Jaszi, P. *Reclaiming Fair Use: How to Put Balance Back Into Copyright.* University of Chicago Press, Chicago, IL, 2011.
3. Bruckman, A. Studying the Amateur Artist: A Perspective on Disguising Data Collected in Human Subjects Research on the Internet. In *Ethics and Information Technology* 4 (2002), 217-231.
4. Busse, K. and Farley, S. Remixing the Remix: Fannish Appropriation and the Limits of Unauthorized Use. *M/C Journal: A Journal of Media and Culture 16*, 4 (2013).
5. Charmaz, K. *Constructing Grounded Theory: A Practical Guide Through Qualitative Analysis.* SAGE Publications, London, UK, 2006.
6. Cheliotis, G., Nan, H., Yew, J., and Jianhui, H. The Antecedents of Remix. *CSCW '14: Proceedings of the 17th ACM Conference on Computer Supported Cooperative Work & Social Computing*, (2014).
7. Cook, E., Teasley, S.D., and Ackerman, M.S. Contribution, Commercialization & Audience: Understanding Participation in an Online Creative Community. *GROUP '09: Proceedings of the ACM 2009 International Conference on Supporting Group Work*, (2009).
8. Coppa, F. A Brief History of Media Fandom. In K. Hellekson and K. Busse, eds., *Fan Fiction and Fan Communities in the Age of the Internet.* McFarland Press, 2006, 41–59.
9. Diakopoulos, N., Luther, K., Medynskiy, Y., and Essa, I. The Evolution of Authorship in a Remix Society. *HT '07: Proceedings of the 18th Conference on Hypertext and Hypermedia*, ACM Press (2007).
10. Ellickson, R.C. Of Coase and Cattle: Dispute Resolution Among Neighbors in Shasta County. *Stanford Law Review 38*, (1986), 623–687.
11. Felten, E.W. A Skeptical View of DRM and Fair Use. *Communications of the ACM 46*, 4 (2003), 56–59.
12. Fiesler, C. and Bruckman, A.S. Copyright Terms in Online Creative Communities. *CHI 2014 Extended Abstracts*, (2014).
13. Fiesler, C. and Bruckman, A.S. Remixers' Understandings of Fair Use Online. *CSCW '14: Proceedings of the 17th ACM Conference on Computer Supported Cooperative Work & Social Computing,* (2014).
14. Fiesler, C. Everything I Need To Know I Learned from Fandom: How Existing Social Norms Can Help Shape the Next Generation of User-Generated Content. *Vanderbilt Journal of Entertainment and Technology Law 10*, 3 (2008), 729–762.
15. Fiesler, C. The Chilling Tale of Copyright in Online Creative Communities. *XRDS: Crossroads, The ACM Magazine for Students 19*, 4 (2013).
16. Goggins, S.P., Mascaro, C., and Mascaro, S. Relief Work after the 2010 Haiti Earthquake: Leadership in an Online Resource Coordination Network. *GROUP '12: Proceedings of the ACM 2012 Conference on Computer Supported Cooperative Work*, (2012), 57–66.
17. Graveline, J. Debunking Common Misconceptions and Myths. *College & Undergraduate Libraries 17*, 1 (2010), 100–105.
18. Hoare, M., Benford, S., Jones, R., and Milic-Frayling, N. Coming in from the Margins: Amateur Musicians in the Online Age. *CHI 2014*, (2014).
19. Humphreys, S. The Challenges of Intellectual Property for Users of Social Networking Sites: A Case Study of Ravelry. *MindTrek '08: Proceedings of the 12th International Conference on Entertainment and Media in the Ubiquitous Era*, (2008).
20. Jackson, S.J., Gillespie, T., and Payette, S. The Policy Knot: Re-integrating Policy , Practice and Design in CSCW Studies of Social Computing. *CSCW '14: Proceedings of the 17th ACM Conference on Computer Supported Cooperative Work & Social Computing*, (2014).
21. Jamison, A. *Fic: Why Fanfiction is Taking Over the World.* Smart Pop, Dallas, TX, 2013.
22. Lampe, C., Arbor, A., Vitak, J., Bldg, H., Wing, S., and Ellison, N. Users and Nonusers: Interactions between Levels of Facebook Adoption and Social Capital. *CSCW '13: Proceedings of the 2013 Conference on Computer Supported Cooperative Work*, (2013).
23. Larsen, L.O. and Nærland, T.U. Documentary in a Culture of Clearance: A Study of Knowledge of and Attitudes Toward Copyright and Fair Use Among

Norwegian Documentary Makers. *Popular Communication 8*, 1 (2010), 46–60.

24. Lawrence, J. and Tar, U. The Use of Grounded Theory Technique as a Practical Tool for Qualitative Data Collection and Analysis. *The Electronic Journal of Business Research Methods 11*, 1 (2013), 29–40.
25. Lessig, L. *Remix: Making Art and Commerce Thrive in the Hybrid Economy*. Penguin Group, New York, 2008.
26. Lombard, M., Snyder-Duch, J., and Bracken, C.C. Content Analysis in Mass Communication: Assessment and Reporting of Intercoder Reliability. *Human Communication Research 28*, 4 (2002), 587–604.
27. Marshall, C.C. and Shipman, F.M. Saving, Reusing, and Remixing Web Video: Using Attitudes and Practices to Reveal Social Norms. *WWW '13: Proceedings of the 22nd International Conference on World Wide Web*, (2013).
28. Monroy-hernández, A., Hill, B.M., Gonzalez-Rivero, J., and Boyd, D. Computers Can't Give Credit: How Automatic Attribution Falls Short in an Online Remixing Community. *CHI '11: Proceedings of the SIGCHI Conference on Human Factors in Computing Systems*, (2011).
29. Roth, J. and Flegel, M. 'I'm not a lawyer but...': Fan disclaimers and claims against copyright law. *Journal of Fandom Studies 1*, 2 (2013), 201–218.
30. Sawyer, M.S. Filters, Fair Use & Feedback: User-Generated Content Principles and the DMCA. *Berkeley Technology Law Journal 24*, (2009), 363–404.
31. Singh, V., Johri, A., and Kathuria, S. Newcomer Integration and Learning in OSS Technical Support Communities. *CSCW '12: Proceedings of the 2012 ACM Conference on Computer Supported Cooperative Work*, (2012).
32. Strauss, A. and Corbin, J. *Basics of Qualitative Research: Techniques and Procedures for Developing Grounded Theory*. SAGE Publications, Thousand Oaks, CA, 1998.
33. Tushnet, R. Legal fictions: Copyright, fan fiction, and a new common law. *Loyola LA Entertainment Law Journal 17*, (1997), 651-686.
34. Tushnet, R. Economies of Desire: Fair Use and Marketplace Assumptions. *William and Mary Law Review 51*, (2009), 513–536.
35. Tushnet, R. Remix nation. *Communications of the ACM 54*, 9 (2011), 22.
36. Tushnet, R. 'I'm a Lawyer, Not an Ethnographer, Jim': Textual Poachers and fair use. *The Journal of Fandom Studies 2*, 1 (2014), 21–30.

Emotion Map: A Location-Based Mobile Social System for Improving Emotion Awareness and Regulation

Yun Huang[1], Ying Tang[2] and Yang Wang[1]
School of Information Studies[1], Department of Psychology [2]
Syracuse University
{yhuang,ytang,ywang}@syr.edu

ABSTRACT
Effective emotion regulation can benefit many aspects of our lives such as mental health and work performance. Informed by emotion regulation theories and in consultation with our university counseling center, we designed a novel location-based mobile social app, Emotion Map, to help improve people's awareness and regulations of their emotions. The app allows users to log their emotions with the associated time, location, and activity information. Users can keep these logged emotions to themselves or share them with others publicly or anonymously. We conducted a 4-week field trial of the app with 14 university students. Combining usage logs and in-person interviews, our analysis shows promising results of the app. Specifically, we found that the app improved some participants' self-knowledge of their emotions, supported their various emotion regulations, and enabled better awareness of the emotion statuses of their friends and communities.

Author Keywords
Mobile Applications; Emotion Regulation; Emotion Sharing; Location Awareness.

ACM Classification Keywords
H.5.m. Information Interfaces and Presentation (e.g. HCI): Miscellaneous

INTRODUCTION
Effective emotion regulation has been linked to advantageous outcomes in the areas of mental health [13], physical health [30], relationship satisfaction [20], and work performance [7]. Psychological research has shown that deficits in emotion regulation skills may be an important antecedent of mental disorders [1]. For example, diagnosable depression may be the result of prolonged periods of distress experienced on a daily basis by individuals who cannot effectively manage their emotions [13].

One of the important prerequisites of effective emotion regulation is accurate self-knowledge of one's emotions [10]. One example of the impact of poor self-awareness of emotions was brought up by the student counseling center staff at our university. They commented that a common issue that they had observed in students with clinical symptoms was their inability to remember the causes and contexts of their emotions. Similarly, prior research has shown that people in general have blind spots in their self-knowledge, and they may not always understand their emotions very accurately [28]. Thus an efficient and effective tool to help individuals track, reflect and regulate their emotions is highly desirable.

Recent work discovered how *visual, locative, temporal and social contexts* as four types of cues can trigger memories of events and associated emotions [9]. In fact, location is also a fundamental contextual trigger for emotions [10] as regular daily activities have been found to occur at particular locations [15]. Therefore, naturally, locations along with other situational elicitors of emotions may be recurring [35]. For example, a weekly meeting in the same room might lead to recurring and anticipatory anxiety. These findings inspired us to design a location-based mobile app, called Emotion Map, which can assist individuals in tracking their emotions at different locations and over time. In particular, the app allows users to log emotions with location, time and activity information and visualize the emotions on a map. Such a tool intends to improve people's emotional memory and their awareness of how daily activities and locations may affect their emotions, enabling people to better regulate their emotions.

Furthermore, emotion sharing could make emotion regulation more effective. From a developmental perspective, emotion regulation is essentially an interpersonal process that involves extensive emotion sharing (e.g., infants cry out to caregivers when experiencing anxiety). In fact, much evidence with the adult population has also shown the prevalence and importance of sharing emotion in adult emotion regulation [27]. Prior literature has also found that social networking sites (SNSs), such as Facebook, could potentially promote social connections [32], and emotions are contagious on social media [6]. Emotion Map was designed to further capitalize on the unique benefits of emotion expression and regulation in the context of social media.

However, emotion sharing may encounter much hindrances, such as social judgment, shame, and guilt, which nevertheless could be mitigated by various privacy or anonymity features on SNSs [17]. SNSs can be a helpful alternative for individuals who may otherwise have difficulty in seeking face-to-face emotional support. They may also afford prompt feedback and elicit rich social support. Therefore, we were mo-

CSCW 2015, March 14–18, 2015, Vancouver, BC, Canada.

http://dx.doi.org/10.1145/2675133.2675173

tivated to enable emotion sharing and social support in Emotion Map. Given the personal and potentially sensitive nature of emotions, we also designed privacy-preserving features such as the option to share emotions anonymously. Self-reported social media content has also been used to explore physical community's well-being [26]. Emotion Map provides unique community-level data, namely aggregations of community emotions that help people better understand their communities.

Given the above rationale, in this paper, we present the design of Emotion Map and investigate the following research questions. Can Emotion Map enhance users' knowledge of their own emotions? Can the app improve users' awareness of the community-level emotion trends? How do people use the app to build these types of knowledge? Will enhanced awareness help users better regulate their emotions? What are users' concerns about logging and sharing emotions in such a social environment?

To answer the above questions, we conducted a 4-week field trial of the app with 14 university students and interviewed most of them about their experiences. It is important to note that our field trial aimed at understanding how users may perceive and use the app in their natural environment rather than statistically validating the effectiveness of the app. Our study yielded rich and promising results regarding the functions and design of the app; in particular, it improved users' self-knowledge of their own and others' emotions, and supported them in applying various emotion regulation strategies.

BACKGROUND AND RELATED WORK

Our work was informed by different lines of literature, including self-knowledge of emotion, emotion sharing and emotion regulation.

Self-knowledge of Emotion

Literature on self-knowledge of emotions has revealed that people often hold biased views or are unsure about the causes or intensities of their emotions [31]. This is likely due to the fact that people's short-term emotion memories are largely guided by episodic knowledge, i.e. experiences that are inextricably bound with details of time and place [28]. Nevertheless, one's ability to retrieve such episodic or experiential information linked to time and location declines quickly over time. Consequently, any later reporting of emotions is likely to result in a loss of certain details of relevant emotion episodes [29]. Emotion Map, which enables users to log emotions in a moment that is close to their occurrences, can be a valuable tool to combat such memory biases, offering a rich repertoire of emotion self-knowledge.

Emotion Sharing

There are many benefits of emotion sharing. For example, researchers have found that people who are able to engage in self-disclosure of intimate emotions tend to be more well-liked [5]. In addition, emotion sharing promotes social integration, social bonding, and propagation of social knowledge, thus suggesting the importance and advantages of emotion disclosure on both personal and collective levels [27].

However, by letting emotions play a central role in our lives, we assent to being exposed to a certain extent; we relinquish some privacy in order to be able to live emotionally [3]. In other words, emotion sharing can be risky because it may invite ridicule or even rejection, thereby placing the discloser in a socially awkward or vulnerable position [23]. For one, society has developed social norms about what one should or should not discuss with others. In addition, emotion sharing is particularly difficult when the discloser experiences shame and guilt [27]. To circumvent these constraints of emotion sharing, research has shown that online communication lends itself to self-disclosure [16]. Because of the relative anonymity that online interactions may offer, the risks of self-disclosure may be greatly reduced, and disclosers should be much less fearful of potential condemnation or rejection. Our Emotion Map incorporates features of anonymity where users could post emotion-related contents without exposing their identities. Such features are likely to reduce inhibition of social sharing and promote more unrestrained self-expression.

Emotion Regulation

While interpersonal emotion sharing is an intrinsically important aspect of emotion regulation [27], there are other important intrapersonal ways in which emotions are regulated. Admittedly, emotion is an intuitive yet theoretically challenging concept. Theorists have debated for centuries the nature and constitution of emotion and how it is regulated. On one end of the spectrum, researchers from the basic emotion camp believe that there are intrinsically concrete and categorical emotion states, such as anger, sadness, and fear, each of which is associated with unique biological, physiological and behavioral outcomes. On the other extreme, emotions are viewed as completely socially constructed, and are socio-cultural performances that are prescribed by specific role contexts [12]. Both of these extreme perspectives fail to highlight the intuitive and important role of individual agency and meaning-making in the process of emotion generation and regulation.

For the purpose of this work, we have largely been informed by two perspectives - appraisal and psychological construction perspectives that lie somewhere in between the two aforementioned extreme perspectives - which approach emotion from an interactive angle, highlighting the exchange between person and situation, and the importance of appraisal and psychological construction in shaping one's emotional experiences [12].

According to the appraisal model, it is assumed that emotions are distinct functional states but they are considered to be emergent products of individuals' active meaning making. The consequence of emotion regulation could be to increase, maintain, and decrease positive or negative emotions [22]. Emotion regulation in this perspective prescribes five major strategies that individuals can employ to intervene with their own emotions, including situation selection, situation modification, attention deployment, cognitive change, and response modulation. In other words, essentially, this perspective entails that one of the most initial ways to regulate an emotion is to be aware of the situations that trigger it, and in turn to avoid or approach certain people, places and objects that may elicit certain types of emotions. Once a situation and its corresponding emotion are unavoidable, one adopts various cognitive strategies to regulate the emotion.

On the other hand, the psychological construction model increasingly views emotion generation and emotion regulation as one continuous process [12]. This view further emphasizes emotion as being the products of various psychological ingredients, such as psychological, cognitive, chemical and even physical interventions. In this view, modifying any of the psychological ingredients could lead to changes in emotions. For example, emotion regulation strategies informed by this perspective could be behavioral interventions (e.g., exercise) or cognitive interventions (e.g., change knowledge about emotions). However, researchers have noted that to the extent that the emergent products of emotions have constituent properties across various psychological ingredients, emotions could be regulated by processes described in the appraisal model.

Taken together, it is established that there are close connections between person and situation in the forces leading to an emotion. The intimate linkage between emotion and situations, which could broadly refer to location, activities, people, events and time, was one of the main motivators for the design of Emotion Map. To serve users' different emotion regulation needs, Emotion Map contains many features informed by emotion regulation mechanisms such as *Situation Selection*, *Attention Deployment*, and *Response Modulation*. *Situation Selection* refers to choosing the situation in which to expose oneself, e.g., choose to leave home at 6am instead of 8am to avoid frustration in traffic. *Attention Deployment* means reallocating or focusing attention to specific features of a situation in order to attune an emotion, e.g. distracting oneself from feeling down by not thinking about a tragedy. *Response Modulation* refers to directly changing and adjusting the physiological, behavioral, and experiential response to an emotion, e.g., going for a jog to alleviate lethargy.

It is worth noting that there are an increasing number of systems designed to facilitate emotion regulation. For instance, McDuff et al. built a desktop application called Affectaura, which continuously logs physiological and contextual data, predicts users' emotional states, and allows users to reflect on their past emotional experiences [19]. Pina et al. designed a mobile app that helps parents better handle their children who have attention deficit hyperactivity disorder (ADHD) [24]. This app detects negative emotions of the parents and then sends them supportive or informative messages to help their parenting [24]. Similar to these systems, our Emotion Map app also supports emotion regulation. Moreover, Emotion Map also supports emotion logging and sharing as well as reflection of emotional states of users themselves, their friends and communities.

EMOTION MAP DESIGN

In this section, we present the design goals and current features of Emotion Map, and explain how and why we designed these features. Overall, the design of Emotion Map was informed by the relevant literature we reviewed previously as well as in consultation with the student counseling center and a clinic-health Psychology professor in our university.

Before designing the app, we visited our university's student counseling center. We expressed our interests in building a mobile app to help students better track and manage their emotions. The counseling center staff shared their counseling experiences and provided us with good input that motivated our system design. Firstly, they commented that college students at their age usually lack self-analytic skills, and often times, they can not explain/remember their emotions or fail to associate what may contribute to those emotions. Secondly, people may experience the same emotions in different ways. For example, people may have different symptoms for nervousness, e.g., some may have a headache while others may tend to sweat. Therefore, the counseling center staff suggested that it would be important to allow people to describe the content of their emotional experience rather than simply labeling the emotion (e.g., happy or sad). Thirdly, due to a limited number of therapists at the counseling center and long time intervals between therapy sessions, it is challenging for the therapists to have a comprehensive perspective of a client's emotional history. Emotion Map has the potential to bridge the gap to meet this need by providing real-time tracking of a client's emotional experience.

We also discussed these ideas with a clinical/health psychology professor in our university and he strongly supported our Emotion Map idea. He suggested that it would be interesting to allow people to associate their emotions with location context, such as home, school, office or gym and their activity, such as family time, study, work, or exercise. He commented that people might not be aware that they have certain negative emotions when doing certain activities at certain locations, e.g. having a headache and being nervous all the time whenever that one needs to meet with someone, therefore an app such as Emotion Map might help people to identify that association. He also supported our idea of presenting emotions on a map. He also suggested that we should study how one perceives others' emotions on the map, as they may be influenced by that information.

Based on our prior literature review and informed by the practical needs voiced by mental health professionals, we defined the following design goals of the Emotion Map app. Emotion Map should enable users to report their emotions, describe the emotions in details, and associate the emotions with contextual information including location, time, and activity; it should provide customizable reports of emotion history to enhance people's knowledge of their emotions; it should allow users to share emotions with others and seek/provide social support; it should create a sense of community of emotions on a map and allow people to interact around one particular emotion of interest.

We now present the current design of the app that attempts to achieve the above goals. Figure 1 shows the homepage of the app, displaying a map view, centered by the user's current location. The map shows the emotions shared by the user herself, her friends, and other users. As shown in Figure 1, we color coded these three types of shared emotions on the map to help the user differentiate them. Overall, this design presents emotion-related representation on a map, encouraging people to build the spatial context of their and others' emotions.

More specifically, on the left side of the homepage, there is a list of buttons. For illustration purposes, we denoted them in Figure 1 as four groups, i.e. L, S, R and C. The L button is for logging an emotion; the three S buttons are for searching emotions shared by the user herself or other users; the two R buttons are for displaying the user's own historical emotions; and the three C buttons are for configuring the user's connections in the app and app settings, and reviewing the user's app usage data. The goal of L and R is to build self-knowledge of users' emotions, and the goal of S is to promote social awareness of community emotion statuses in a spatio-temporal manner. Next, we will focus on the L, R and S features and explain their design rationale.

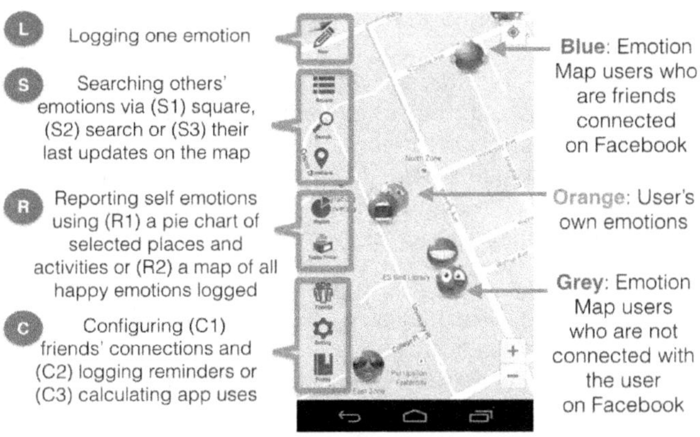

Figure 1. App Menu (4 Groups of Buttons) and Color Coding.

Logging, Sharing and Self-Reflecting Emotions

Emotion Map enables structured emotion logging of rich contextual information such as the corresponding time, location, and activity of the logged emotion [14, 9]. Figure 2 (L1) displays the emotion logging screen. To log an emotion, the user needs to choose one of the emotion icons that we designed. In this app, we chose 16 emotions that fall squarely into the four cells from the valence by arousal orthogonal structure of affect [8]. This structure argues that emotions or affect could be described along two dimensions: valence (i.e., positive vs. negative) and arousal (i.e., highly aroused vs. lowly aroused). These two dimensions in combination could generate the core types of human emotions. While this model has its limitations (e.g., only having two dimensions), it is one of the most widely accepted models for categorizing human emotions. It has also been theoretically validated and empirically tested. In short, this model provides us with a comprehensive yet not overwhelming set of basic human emotions. While our system design is not locked to this model, we consider it a reasonable starting point. We plan to further enrich the list of emotions in the future.

After choosing an emotion, the user need to choose a type of place and an activity that are associated with the current emotion. The user can also optionally enter thoughts, comments or descriptions associated with that emotion in the text box.

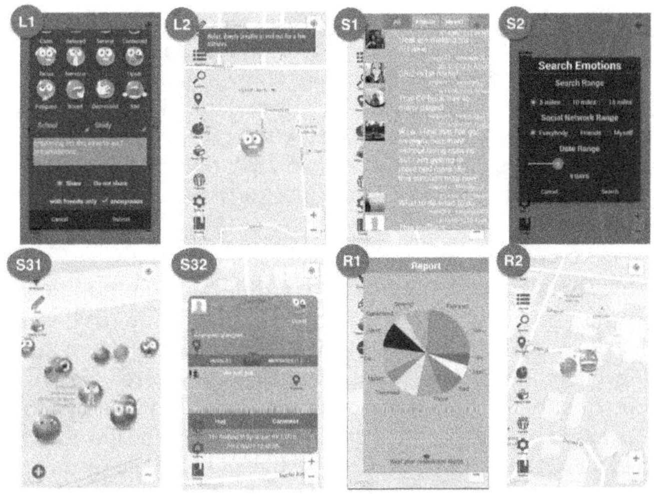

Figure 2. App Screenshots. Group L: (L1) The user interface for logging one emotion, (L2) A message triggered by one negative emotion. Group S: (S1) Square, (S2) Search, (S31) and (S32) Last updated emotions on a map. Group R: (R1) Customized emotion reports based on selected locations and activities, (R2) Positive emotions saved in a Happy folder.

Emotion Map provides a range of privacy settings for emotion status sharing in the same interface as Figure 2 (L1). Since anonymity could increase self-disclosure [25], the system provides an anonymous sharing option. Emotion Map users can choose to share their logged emotions with their friends only or the general public with or without their identities, or simply log the emotion as completely private information. Such privacy sharing settings can be adjusted for each emotion status. For example, as shown in Figure 2 (L1), a "depressed" emotion face was selected, the location was "school," the activity was "study," and it was shared anonymously with everyone in the system.

As discussed in the related work, the emotion regulation theory suggests that people can use a variety of strategies to regulate their emotions [10]. Emotion Map has features that support several of these strategies. For example, Emotion Map allows users to log emotions and their corresponding contextual information, and uses the map and reports to visualize the impact of location, time, and activity on one's emotion patterns. These features enhance the users' awareness of the situations which provoke certain types of emotions, making *Situation Selection* easier and more accurate.

Right right after a user logs an emotion, the system will send a message to the user based on the type of that emotion. We called this feature "triggering message." In general, if a positive emotion is selected, the corresponding message (e.g. "Take a few seconds to remember this moment and how you end up here.") attempts to remind people to remember what makes them feel this way, either by sharing it with friends, reinforcing the emotions, or prolonging the moment. If a negative emotion is logged, the message would attempt to direct the user's attention away, recommending reconsideration of the situation or other behavioral suggestions. An example message is "Go exercise for half an hour." Technically, the system has pre-loaded messages and randomly displays a message that is appropriate according to the type of the emotion. For example, as shown in Figure 2 (L2), a message "Relax, deeply breathe in and out for a few minutes." is displayed after the user entered a "stressed" emotion. The design of the triggering messages corresponds to various emotion regulation strategies such as *attention deployment* (e.g., "Now go do something creative") and *response modification* (e.g., "Go for a jog").

Learning Emotion Statuses of Others or Communities

As shown in Figure 2 (the S screens), the app affords different features to increase users' social awareness of community-level emotions. One way is to click the "Square" button, the first button in the S group in Figure 1, to view others' shared emotions with the most recent one listing on the top. As shown in Figure 2 (S1), there are three tabs on the result page. The "All," "Friends," and "Myself" tabs show, respectively, the emotions shared publicly by all Emotion Map users, emotions shared by the user's friends who are also Emotion Map users, and the user's own emotions (either shared or private).

Another way to view others' shared emotions is to click the "Search" button, the second button in the S group in Figure 1, to explicitly search emotions based on three criteria: physical distance from the user's current location (e.g., 5 miles), type of users (every user, friends only, or the user herself), and day(s) since the emotion was shared (e.g., 5 days). The search results will be displayed on a map similar to what Figure 2 (S31) shows. Users can click on each of the faces, and the owner and contents of that emotion will appear unless the owner chose to share it anonymously. For example, Figure 2 (S32) shows an anonymously shared emotion, where the profile picture of the owner is hidden. Additionally, within this window, other users can provide social feedback or support to that emotion by "hugging" or "messaging" the owner. If this is a publicly shared emotion, then everybody can see the messages and write follow-up comments. However, only the owner can delete any particular message.

Reporting Emotions

As shown in Figure 2 (S1), a user can view her own emotions by clicking the "Myself" tab in the Square feature. To further assist users in improving their awareness of their own emotions, Emotion Map presents an interface to display exclusively a user's own emotions. This feature is shown in Figure 2 (R1). The user clicks the first button in the R group in Figure 1, and the app will generate a pie chart of the amount of different types of emotions logged by this user. The user can also see a report of her emotion distribution for a particular location (e.g., school) or activity (e.g., study). The user can also adjust the range of time for her emotion logs to be shown in the report.

In order to facilitate review of particular types of emotions, we also designed a "Happy Folder" feature which allows one to quickly access the happy moments that one has logged, thereby supporting the *attention deployment* strategy. To use it, the user clicks the second button in the R group in Figure 1, and the app will show all the "positive" emotions that this user logged on a map. This design was in part inspired by the "feel good" email folder idea of Radhika Nagpa when she reflected on how she dealt with the stress of being a university professor [21]. The "feel good" folder keeps all the emails that can point to her happy moments. However, we do acknowledge the potential utilities of both negative and positive emotions especially in terms of their goal-instrumentality (e.g., feeling nervous may help a person perform better on a task and therefore is a functionally useful emotion, albeit negative in a layman's sense) [33]. In the future, we plan to explore emotion folders for other types of emotions.

FIELD TRIAL

To evaluate how people would perceive and use Emotion Map in their natural environment, we released a trial version of the app on Google Play and conducted a 4-week field trial with 14 university students (the same population that the university counseling center serves). To observe how students would use Emotion Map in situations where they may have emotional issues, we decided to conduct our study around the period of final exams since this period is usually stressful for students. In addition, to examine how people's social networks may affect their emotion regulation, we also sought to recruit participants who already knew each other. However, it was very challenging to recruit such student participants during the finals' period since they were busy.

At the beginning of the study, each participant came to our lab, read and signed the study consent form, and installed the app on their Android phones. To help users leverage their existing social network connections, the app asked users to login via their Facebook accounts.

The participants used the app for two weeks, then participated in an in-person mid-term interview. We conducted the mid-term interviews at this time, because many participants were about to leave campus for the summer. Before each interview, we aggregated and printed out the participant's behavioral logs on Emotion Map such as the emotions they shared and the interaction they had with other users. During the interview, we interviewed participants' regarding their general behaviors on social media, and their general perception of and experience with Emotion Map. We also asked the participants to log into Emotion Map and walk us through the emotions they logged or shared as well as the interactions they had with other users. While we intentionally did not explain the purposes of the app features and how to use them during the first 2 weeks, during the interviews, we went through each button to identify any confusion or difficulty they might have had with the app. We also sought their suggestions to improve the app. Each interview took about an hour. These interviews allowed us to gain a deeper understanding of the feature usage. We lost contact with one participant P6 after the first week, and he was the only participant who did not participate in the mid-term interview.

After the mid-term interviews, most participants continued to use the app for about another two weeks. When the participants finished the study, they came to our lab and finished a short exit interview (less than 20 minutes). During the exit interview, we paid participants for participating in the study, and we asked if they had any other questions or comments regarding the system. Only half of the participants were able to make the exit interview because of summer internships in other states or travels.

In terms of participation compensation, each participant received 10 cents for each logged emotion, for up to one dollar each day. The visibility of a logged emotion (i.e., whether it is logged privately or shared publicly) did not affect the compensation. Participants also received five dollars for participating in the mid-term interview. The study was approved by our university IRB office beforehand.

RESULTS

Our results are organized according to our research questions that investigate participants' perceptions and usage of the app, as well as the impact of the app on participants' emotion awareness and regulation.

Demographics and Emotion Loggings

Participants consisted of nine male and five female students from a wide range of majors, as shown in Table 1. Eight were master's students and six were undergraduate students.

ID	Gender	Major	Status	Total	Pos.	Neg.	Days
P1	M	IM	M	5	2	3	21
P2	F	IM	M	52	37	15	28
P3	F	IM	M	17	12	5	28
P4	F	AS	U	102	55	47	28
P5	M	CS	M	19	12	7	14
P6	M	CS	M	11	6	5	7
P7	M	CE	M	17	14	3	14
P8	M	BN	U	23	13	10	28
P9	F	PN	U	49	28	21	28
P10	F	PC	U	8	3	5	14
P11	M	AS	U	14	7	7	14
P12	M	AS	U	47	25	22	28
P13	M	CE	M	69	51	18	28
P14	M	ME	M	4	2	2	20

Table 1. Summary of participants' demographics and emotion sharing. Participants' majors include IM (Information Management), AS (Art & Science), CS (Computer Science), CE (Computer Engineering), BN(Biology & Neuroscience), PN (Psychology &Neuroscience), PC (Psychology & Chemistry), and ME (Mechanical Engineering). Their statuses include M (Master student) and U (Undergraduate student). The "Total" column shows the total number of emotions logged for each participant, while the next column displays the numbers of positive and negative emotions logged, respectively. The "Days" column shows the number of days people participated in the study.

Our system logs show that participants varied in the amount of emotion logging in Emotion Map (the number of emotion logged per participant: mean=31, sd=28). There were also more positive than negative emotions logged (average number of emotions logged per participant: positive=19, negative=12). However, the difference was not statistically significant.

Based on the level of app usage and emotion logging, we categorized the 14 participants into three groups — *active*, *regular*, and *inactive* users. Figure 3 shows which group each participant belongs to. More specifically, four *active* users (P2, P4, P12, P13) logged roughly two to four emotions per day, looked up others' emotions and used app features daily. Six *regular* users (P5, P6, P7, P8, P9, P11) logged about one emotion each day. Four *inactive* users (P1, P3, P10, P14) logged very few emotions during the entire study and three of them (P3, P10, P14) looked up others' emotions on the same day when logging their emotions. P1 looked up others' emotions seven days, but only logged in four days. P1 later reported a bug in the app that blocked him from logging emotions. We also found that there was at least one user in each group who looked up others' emotions more frequently than logging his or her own. This suggests that both emotion logging and consumption are important aspects of the app user experience.

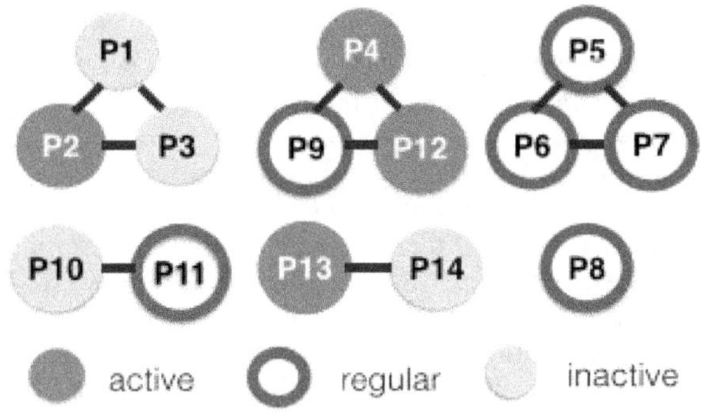

Figure 3. User friendship connections and user groups based on emotion logging behaviors. All participants except P8 knew at least another participant before the study.

Improving Self-Awareness of Emotions

More than half of the participants mentioned that the emotion report feature improved the self-awareness of their emotions. For instance, P4 said *"[the report] made me more aware of my emotions. I didn't realize how tired I was."*. P4 has been involved in a lot of university activities and one part-time job. Similarly, the emotion report also helped P9 realize aspects of her emotions that she would not have known otherwise. She told us, *"I'm always busy with my many part-time jobs, and I was glad to see the report showing I had so many happy moments at work and around campus. I don't think I relax a lot, but looking at this report, surprisingly, "relaxed" is really frequent here, but I never really thought that way. It made me feel better because I am handling myself well."* It is encouraging to see that the emotion report not only improved the self-awareness of one's emotions but also in turn made this participant feel better about herself, highlighting the benefits of this feature. P8 commented *"The report gives me an idea about what happened. [I should] try to do something that is fun."*

P13 also spoke highly of this feature, *"The reporting feature is very useful. I can know better about myself from the reports. Like, why I have been so nervous? Well, now I know it is the finals. This is reasonable, so I don't have to worry about it. But if it is an unusual reason, then I want to pay attention."* This example clearly illustrates the incorporation of *Attention Deployment* as an effective emotion regulation strategy.

There was one participant who saw no value of this report feature. P5 said *" I don't like to think back. I only look at the present. I don't want to carry what has happened previously. Every day is a new day. I don't see the report has value to me."* Although theory informs us that an, accurate understanding of ones past emotion can help individuals be aware of their emotions, which in turns facilitates emotion regulation, in real life, however, some people may refuse to examine their past emotions for different reasons. Thus, we should provide other features to help people understand their own emotions better. In our study, we have found that one effective alternative strategy is to leverage social and community level emotion information, which is discussed in further detail in the following section.

In summary, the report feature was well-received by the majority of our participants as a way to improve self-awareness of their emotions, and we also received valuable suggestions to improve this feature. For example, P1 wanted to see line charts. He explained *"I had experienced a down moment when I was in college, and it took me two years to get over it. Now when I was in difficulty again, I knew something good will happen after this. So I'd like to see a graph showing this up and down over time."* This suggestion will help us strengthen the temporal visualization of emotional history in the next version of the app. In addition, P13 and P7 made a good suggestion that we should provide interactive charts to help users interpret the reports, where options can be clicked and related emotions can be displayed on the map.

Improving Awareness of Community Emotions

The home screen of the Emotion Map app is a map, where by default last updated emotions are displayed on the map centered by user's current location. The color coding indicates friending relationships of emotion owners to the app user. We designed these features to help improve users' awareness of the emotion statuses of their friends and communities, and hoped this could help users reflect on their own emotions and even allow them to adapt certain behaviors so as to avoid negative emotion. Our interview results offered some good evidence.

P1 told us a story about relieving his stress: *"I was really stressed out by the finals. I saw [on Emotion Map] someone that I didn't know was watching a cricket game. I knew about the game but forgot about the time. I then went watching the game. I felt much relaxed afterwords."* In this case, Emotion Map helped the user gain knowledge of other people whom he did not know and yet led to a behavior change (i.e., watch the game) that reduced his stress.

Similarly, P5 said *"I was just watching a movie on April 30, thinking the exam would be easier. Then I saw [on Emotion Map] my friends posting in the library and preparing for the exam. Why am I sitting here? I should study for my exams too."* The new knowledge of the participant's friend in his community also led the participant to a behavior change, namely studying for exams to avoid possible anxiety during the exam. P5 also commented *"If I am feeling bored and other friends are happy, then I want to know why. To make myself happy, I can do the same thing. If they are enjoying it, I can go to the location and do the same thing."* This explains why he felt the location information is important because he can identify and visit locations that may make himself happy.

Other participants (such as P1, P4, P9, P10, P11, P13) also expressed they liked to check emotions on the map. For instance, P11 liked to use the Map to see others' emotions and understand the spatial patterns of emotions. He said *"I like to zoom out as much as possible. I remembered very far away there was one using the app. It is very interesting. There was a cluster of fatigue around the school during finals. It's interesting to see where people are the most upset. Simply reinforce the fact that I don't want to go to DMV. Correlation between places and emotions. "* This underlines the benefit of showing emotions and their locations on a map, helping users aggregate emotions in locations and identify where the community thinks as the "happy" or "upset" locations. A few participants said that during the finals week, there were many sleepy faces on the map, which made them feel a sense of community and belonging.

In addition to the Map (Figure 2 - S31), Square (Figure 2 - S1) allows users to check all the shared emotions with the most recent one on the top. Clicking each news feed on the Square will direct users to the particular emotion displayed on the map, so that users can see the details. Participants like P2, P12 and P8 found the Square easier to use, because they could find more emotions quickly.

All of these anecdotes suggest that Emotion Map helped participants discover activities of people (either friends or strangers) in their communities, improved participants' temporal, spatial, and social awareness of the emotion statuses of others. Participants were found to often adjust or adapt their own behaviors and emotions to conform to the community patterns, suggesting possible powers of peer influence.

Facilitating Social Support

In addition to improving the emotion awareness of users themselves, their friends and the community, our participants also reported providing and receiving social support via Emotion Map. Here, we use social support to denote either "commenting" on others' shared emotions or "hugging" others in the app.

Figure 4 depicts the days in which participants logged emotions, looked up others' emotions (defined as clicking others' emotion faces on the map or opening the square to read the emotion newsfeed in the community) or provided social support to others. 8 participants (including 1 active, 4 regular, and 3 inactive participants) looked up others' emotions on some days when they did not log their own emotions, and all participants except P5 provided social support to others in the app during the study. We only compensate participants for logging an emotion, not sharing it or looking up/commenting/hugging others' emotions, thus this result shows that participants were generally "curious" to know about others' emotions, and the majority of them used the social support features if they felt necessary.

For instance, it took P10 quite some days to get the app to work on her phone (noticing she started her first log on the

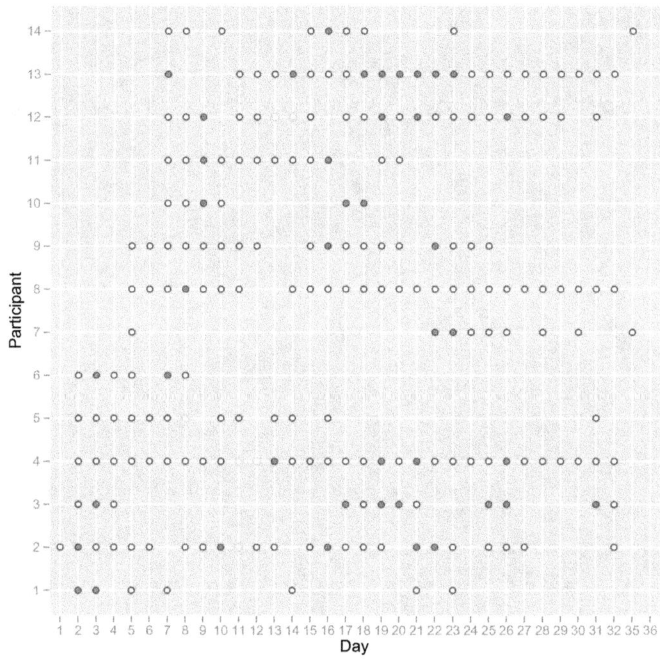

Figure 4. Emotion Logs, Emotion Lookup and Social Support: the days in which each participant made the following actions at lease once on that day, i.e. logged emotions (either shared or private) - green circles, looked up others' emotions - blue circles, and showed social support to other users (e.g., comment or hug one emotion in the app) - red dots.

8th day), after her boy friend fixed some security configuration in her phone. Then she posted a very happy emotion with *" We got the app to work!"*. P8 did not know P10, but hugged that emotion (as a greeting). P10 mentioned in the interview that *"It's cute to hug and I once commented someone's emotion saying 'you can do it'. Hopefully it is helpful to them. It's worthy of trying."* Our system log shows that P10 made the comment "You can do it!" on one of P8's stressful emotions "Very stressed out for orgo and genetics...not gonna be able to sleep tonight." Since P8 did not know any other participants, we explicitly asked if he noticed any interaction between him and others in Emotion Map. He did mention that *"I remembered I was commented by a female participant [looking at the Facebook image], it is good that someone commented".*

Other such encouraging stories also abound. P9 often looked through her friends' emotions. She said, *"It's interesting to see her [P4] posts, so they give me a better understanding of her. That's cool. (Those are) things she wouldn't talk to me in person, but big enough for her to post...It gives me the opportunity to help her."* For example, P9 found P4 shared a fatigue emotion in early morning with *"I don't want to get out of bed yet!"* and P9 sent a hug to P4. P9 nicely summarized her perceptions of Emotion Map: *"it serves two functions: a personal way to express themselves, and a way to understand friends and the community at a different level."* P12 also mentioned he noticed P4 shared a lot of negative emotions with her knee problem, and he sent text messages to her. In addition, P5 mentioned that social support is important for him to log or even share emotions. *"I'd like to have more people using the app. I only have a few friends using it. I don't feel posting many emotions. It's like no one cares for you.... The most important part of one's life is caring."*

These are all excellent examples of how Emotion Map facilitates social support, provided by both friends and strangers, to other community members.

Supporting Emotion Regulation Strategies

Improving knowledge of self and others' emotions, as well as seeking and receiving social support are all part of the design effort to facilitate people better regulating their emotions. But the following features are explicitly informed by the literature on emotion regulations, and we now present how the participants found them effective and their feedbacks in details.

Expression

The Emotion Map app helped people express both negative and positive emotions. Many participants expressed away their negative emotions on Emotion Map. For example, P10 gave us an example in which she relieved her frustration by sharing her emotions on Emotion Map. The emotion had a 78-word long description *"Why can't everyone just let me do what major I want?... "* She explained *"I didn't have anyone to share. Grandma told me she didn't approve my major. It's really frustrating. I felt a little better after posting it. I didn't have any outlet and I want somebody to hear it..."* In this case, the participant purposefully wanted people to hear her complaint. Emotion Map became her outlet to vent her negative emotions. Unlike P10, participants like P9 tended to share her positive emotions in Emotion Map which made her feel good. She said *"posting positive emotions are very helpful. Very good reminder. When I am down, I can look back. Seeing most of the time I am OK."*

While description (as a way to express details that relates to an emotion) is optional when logging an emotion, 90% of the total of 437 logged emotions had descriptions. Two active users (P2, P4), three regular users (P6, P7, P9), and an inactive user P14 logged a total of 43 emotions without descriptions. This indicates that most of the time, participants took the opportunity to describe their feelings while logging their emotions. The window for typing in description currently show two lines of texts, not designed to display a long description. But when participants feel strong emotions, they used the limited space to type long descriptions.

Triggering Messages

The triggering message feature was designed to support people's emotion regulation strategies such as *Attention Deployment* and *Response Modification*. Some triggering messages are famous quotes and some are advice to take a particular action that corresponds to a particular emotion regulation strategy, such as *Attention Deployment* (e.g., "Now go do something creative") or *Response Modification* (e.g., "Go for a jog"). Almost all interviewed participants except P2 liked this feature. For instance, P9 said, *"They are really cute. The quotes are very cool, especially those about happiness."* She told us one time she was really upset and posted an emotion *"Can't put money in my account for printing, don't know what to do"*, and then received a message "Relax, deeply breath in and out for a few minutes." She did that and felt a little better. This is a good example of response modification because she modified her behavioral response to the negative emotion by taking a deep breath which in turn mitigated the negative emotion.

P8 also thought positive of this feature. He said *"I do enjoy the messages. Very engaging, which is a good thing...I posted a stressful emotion and I remembered being a little relieved in a way."* He referred to a post he made at school that read *"Psychology Poster Session tomorrow from noon to 4. This week needs to be over already."*

In terms of other feedback, P12 suggested the messages to be *"something more introspective"* and P13 wanted *"concrete suggestions, for example some coupons for some sport event"*. P5 felt the messages were helpful only when he felt bad: *"I like the triggering messages. The app is counseling me. As long as the message is simple, it hits me. The messages were only helpful when I was having negative emotions. When I am happy, I don't need those messages. "* Additionally, P2 gave a different feedback *"I don't like the trigger function. If I post and exit the app, the message stays on the screen. Sometime it's not relevant. I don't want it at all, and I want to turn it off. If I feel an emotion, I don't think any generic message can fit into my situation."* P2 may or may not like the feature even after we provide more concrete messages. Either way, this indicates that we should enable an on and off setting for this feature.

Overall, the triggering message received strong positive feedback from most of the participants. In the meantime, participants gave suggestions and important feedback to the usability of the feature.

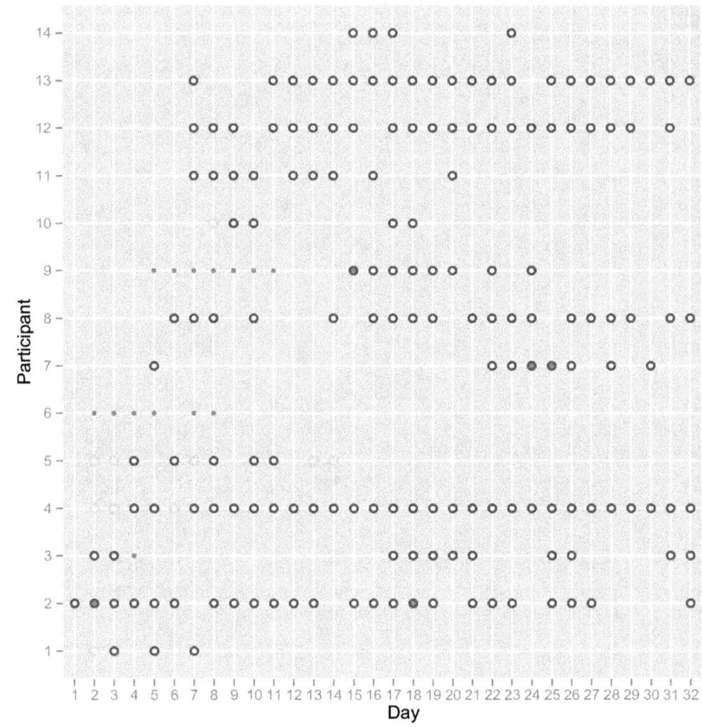

Figure 5. Visibility of logged emotions: the days in which each participant logged/shared emotions publicly, anonymously, or privately. The blue and green circles denote a participant who shared at least one emotion publicly and anonymously (without his/her identity) on that day, respectively. The red dot denotes a participant who logged at least one emotion privately (i.e., only the participant can see it) on that day.

Privacy-Preserving Emotion Sharing

Because emotions are personal and can be sensitive, we designed private and anonymous sharing to mitigate people's potential privacy concerns in logging and sharing their emotions. As shown in Figure 5, our participants usually shared their emotions publicly, but more than half of the participants, including two active (P2 and P4), four regular (P5, P6, P7 and P9), and three inactive (P1, P3, P10) used the private or anonymous features during the study.

In particular, five participants P9, P2, P3, P6 and P7 used private logging. They kept 36, 3, 1, 11, 3 private emotion logs respectively, and shared 13, 49, 16, 0 and 14 emotions publicly with their identities. A total of 29 positive emotions and 25 negative emotions were kept private. P6 showed great interests in participating in the study, unfortunately he never replied to our interview request.

We were very curious about why P9 consistently logged private emotions at the beginning, and then after more than a week of use, she started to share everything publicly. P9 said *"I typically try not to post emotions on [social networks, e.g.] Facebook, because they are too personal and there are a lot of people on Facebook that I actually do not know very well. At first I thought the emotion statuses that I post on Emotion Map would post on Facebook [because Facebook account is used to login the app], so I chose to record the emotions privately, as a way to monitor how my own mood fluctuate personally. Then I realized that the statuses do not show up on Facebook. Even though there are strangers on the app, it is for a community of people who are able to express their emotions freely, not just to draw attention. "* This quote indicates that P9 was concerned about sharing emotions on Facebook but felt comfortable doing that in Emotion Map.

P2 was an active user, but she shared one exciting emotion privately with the description *"received offer letter! Best day ever!"* She said *"I don't want to push on their [my friends] faces, people who don't have internships. I want to remember the day, how I was feeling, so I post it."* The other two private posts are negative ones, *"missing home"* and *"last meet for a loooong looong time"*. She said *"I either share it [the emotion] with everybody [with identity] or keep it private. If it's very personal, I just like it to be my private."* For P2, she used the private logging feature to avoid either social awkward situations or exposing her very personal feelings.

Four participants P1, P4, P5 and P10 used anonymous sharing with the public. They anonymously shared 2, 3, 5, and 1 emotion(s) respectively, a total of 4 negative emotions and 7 positive emotions. The negative emotions are P4's *"I got nothing accomplished today :("* and *"Long day and it's not even 5"*, and P5's *"Exam preparation time. A little confused on how to start where to start and what to read."* and *"Very boring day ... How come waiting eagerly from the semester to begin"*.

We also noticed that all these four participants posted anonymous sharing at the very beginning of using this app. For example, P5 posted *"Feeling excited to be part of a study at the school."* P1 posted positive emotions e.g. *"Waiting for the weekend bash!!!"* anonymously and he posted it twice within one minute. Interestingly, he posted three negative emotions publicly with identity, such as two fatigue ones *"Working on weekends"*, Listening to presentation for the last 5 hours, and one bored *"Last Project paper!!!!"*. P1 said *"I usually posted on social networks for major milestones, like graduation. I think people showing off on social media such as Facebook is spreading ego-centric negative emotion. This app is for emotion, so it makes me comfortable to share very emotional statuses."* Thus, he was using the two positive emotions to test if his posts were shared on Facebook at the very beginning. Once he found the answer, he was willing to share emotions in the app.

Protection of user privacy can better help participants disclose their emotions with comfort. In particular, private logging gives participant a safe place to store their emotional experiences with the great comfort in keeping personal emotions only accessible to themselves. Almost all participants mentioned they like the anonymous sharing feature.

DISCUSSION

Our field trial study gave us insights into how people used the Emotion Map app to improve self-knowledge of their own emotions, and how visualizing emotions on a map helped them build temporal, spatial and social contextual awareness of community emotions. Further, such enhanced awareness and different features of the app (e.g. describing emotions, triggering message, hugging and commenting) enabled participants to adapt their behaviors, subsequently regulating their emotions. The privacy-preserving features were well-received and used by most participants to log their emotions with comfort. We present our reflections on the results in details below.

Self-Knowledge

Prior research has shown that people have blind spots in their self-knowledge, and they may not always understand their emotions very accurately [28]. Due to memory and other cognitive biases, people often overlook important situational and social information that contributes to their emotional lives, and thus compromise their awareness of the causes and contents of their emotions. A few participants such as P4 and P9 were surprised about their emotion history when reviewing their reports, highlighting the aforementioned cognitive biases. User feedback suggests that the reports indeed helped improve people's self-knowledge of their emotions.

The report presents past emotions in a pie chart, which explicitly drew users' attention to their own emotions in an aggregated manner. In addition, allowing users to log an emotion and listing emotion logs in the Square implicitly improved self-awareness of their current or past emotions.

One observation we had during the interviews was that when we pointed at one particular emotion from a participant's Emotion Square, the participant's first reaction was to click it and view the emotion log on the map, identifying where it was logged. Usually they would quickly identify this was around home or campus, and they would associate the description and the time to retrospect what happened at that moment. This suggests visualizing emotion logs on a map helped people recall their emotional states using location as a cue.

Spatial, Contextual, and Social Awareness of Emotions

We gained a better understanding of how people built their knowledge of community emotions. Visualizing emotions on the map emphasizes the location aspects of the emotions, and listing the emotion logs on Square highlights the time aspect of the emotions. Participants varied in their preferences. Even though they accessed community emotions differently, the interview results suggest that participants had a good sense of the community emotion states on Emotion Map. For instance, several participants noticed that the campus was plagued with fatigue on the map around finals' week. When users identified a community whose emotional trends were consistent with their own, they were likely to feel a sense of community and camaraderie.

We also found instances where knowledge of strangers' or friends' emotions led to changes of emotions and behaviors of the users. In both cases, peer pressure and social comparison were at play. During the interviews, participants also mentioned that they needed a way to know if someone commented or hugged their emotions. The app had push notification implemented, but it was not well received by the participants. The notifications were either failed to deliver or cluttered. Thus many times, the participants either noticed a comment some days after the comment was made, or they just did not know they were commented until they revisited some of the previous logs during the interviews. The desire to enhance social interaction in the app and the majority of emotion logs being shared publicly suggest that participants value social interactions in this community.

Emotion Regulation Strategies

Different emotion regulation strategies tend to work differently for different people in varying occasions.

Expression

Our results show that simply writing about what happened and what was related to a particular emotion can be helpful to release one's frustration (e.g., P10 wrote a long description on how her grandma didn't approve her major) or strengthen one's enjoyment (e.g., P2 did not share her job offer with others). Expressive writing was found to be helpful to ease stress and cope with emotional problems [2]. Participants P5, P7 and P13 would also like to post pictures with emotions. We think expression may not be limited to text, and our future work should allow expressions in other modalities, such as audio or video and compare their effectiveness.

Triggering Messages

Overall, the feature of triggering messages was well received by most participants, even though they tended to differ in their preferences of the format and content of these messages. P2 did not like the triggered message at all, and she preferred a way to turn it off. Future design should recognize these individual and situational differences and perhaps allow users to choose their preferred strategies or intelligently pick the appropriate strategy for the user based on the context. In the field trial, each emotion had 5 pre-loaded triggering messages. To avoid users from getting bored of the same messages and to retain a long term use of the app, the triggering messages need to be updated. We plan to build a crowdsourcing mechanism that will allow people to contribute different emotion regulation practices for various types of emotions.

Privacy and Anonymity Concerns

Our findings of privacy-preserving logging is in line with the previous research on the impact of anonymity on computer-mediated communication, and how it may facilitate self-disclosure and self-expression [34]. Participants seemed to have only utilized the privacy/anonymity functions selectively, usually when they were sharing certain emotion statuses that were very sensitive or private. One interesting observation was that none of the participants used both anonymous and private features in the 4-week study. Either they used the anonymous feature (or they kept private logs), otherwise, they will choose to share their logs with the public. In future work, we will further investigate how and why people differentiate and use the two features.

In addition, in our current app, a shared emotion would take the user's current location at the time of logging and the location can not be changed. Even when users log and share their emotions anonymously, such location information may still raise location privacy issues to some users. In the future, we will implement another type of sharing where the emotion owner's location information can be protected from other users, and we will investigate if such a sharing will be adopted by people who have location privacy concerns.

Emotion Map vs. Facebook for Emotion Sharing

Many social networking sites such as Facebook allow people to tag emotion faces. Since our participants used their Facebook accounts to log into our app, we knew they are Facebook users. During the interviews, we asked them how they would compare these two platforms. Compared with Facebook, participants thought that Emotion Map focuses on emotion logging, sharing, and the utilities focus on emotions. They felt more comfortable in sharing details about their emotions in this community, which is different from general social networks such as Facebook.

Sharing emotion on Emotion Map can help people to build social awareness of community emotions, but this is only one of the many purposes that Emotion Map can serve. Emotions logged and kept for users themselves can serve many other objectives such as enhancing self-awareness, and enabling reflection on current and past emotions. Without any emotion sharing, the app can still serve self-counseling purposes to some extent. This is a major difference between our app and tagging emotion faces on other social media apps such as Facebook. Sharing emotions on Emotion Map therefore can serve a different purpose than simply trying to obtain popularity on social networks [4].

Design Implications

After implementing the system, we showed our app to one therapist assigned by the counseling center, seeking their feedback. The therapist was very positive of our work and was impressed by all the features. To improve the app, she suggested adding more emotion choices similar to what the participants requested. She also liked the triggering messages and she suggested to consolidate all suggestions to each emotion in one place, such that without logging emotions, people can still look up all the suggestions on how to regulate their emotions and practice the ones they select. She believed this feature could serve as a handy and self-counseling tool. The other reason why she liked to have such a central place for regulation suggestions is that those who do not want to log or share emotions may still find this system helpful.

We did not explain the app features and how to use the app to the participants when they started the trial. It turned out that the app was largely usable. Participants figured out the majority of the functions by themselves and used them without any problem, except some participants had difficulty with customizing the reports. Because the customized button was located at the bottom of the report page, and it is hard to notice. We will fix this usability issue in the next app version.

All participants thought positively of the private and anonymous sharing features, and they used them in different occasions. We believe these are important features that could improve user experiences and address people's potential privacy concerns. Therefore, they should be considered by social media services. However, anonymous sharing may lead to sensitive, controversial, or even problematic content. In addition, the privacy settings were presented as part of the structured emotion sharing task on Emotion Map, which reduces the transaction cost of thinking about and controlling one's privacy. While usually privacy is at best a secondary task in sharing on SNSs, making the privacy options as part of the sharing task nudges people to think about the privacy implications of the sharing and can potentially avoid sharing emotions that they later regret.

Challenges, Limitations and Future Improvement

We faced several challenges during this study. First, recruiting Android users who are already connected on Facebook and would stay on campus for an extended period of time after the finals was very difficult. Secondly, the list of emotions was not meant to be comprehensive, and indeed many participants complained that the 16 emotions provided were not sufficient for them. The current location and activity options were not sufficient either. Participants reported that they preferred to specify a particular location and activity, e.g. gym, TV instead of choosing "others". Ideally, we would like users to be able to choose self-input locations and activities rather than choosing from a drop-down menu of pre-designed options. Thirdly, according to the exit interview, the Happy Folder feature (as shown in Figure 2 (R2)) did not receive a lot of attention from the participants. Only one or two participants understood the design purpose of this feature and used the folder to recall happy locations and moments. To better enable situation awareness, allowing people to engage in more comprehensive self-reflections about a variety of emotions, in our next release of the app, we plan to add search features which allow users to access summaries of different individual emotions, other than "happiness".

According to the literature [11], older people show greater emotional control than younger people, and 89% of the users of social networking sites are from 18 to 29 years old [18], thus we expect running this study in older people is likely to generate different results. To be successful outside of campus, Emotion Map should not rely on people "sharing" emotions, but more on "logging" emotions regardless of sharing with the public or not. The app should also be useful for anyone, who has ups and downs in their daily lives. In the mean time, we hope the app can help people who have regular emotional issues and plan to deploy a customized version of the app for patients in our university counseling center. For example, we can provide one view for the patients to practice different regulation strategies and another view for therapists to watch the progress of the patients.

CONCLUSIONS

Effective emotion regulation is the gateway to a plethora of positive psychosocial benefits, yet it remains an untenable task for many individuals. Some particular challenges lie in the fact that self-awareness of emotions is frequently amiss, emotion sharing is hindered, and social support is compromised. In this paper, we present our design and study of Emotion Map which tackles some of the issues head-on. The system allows people to log and share emotions in a spatio-temporal and privacy-preserving manner. We conducted a 4-week field trial study with 14 college student participants. Our interview results and data analysis of app logs show that the app improved the participants' self-knowledge of their own emotions; helped them build spatial contextual and social awareness of their community well-being; and facilitated different emotion regulation strategies. Emotion Map is a promising tool in the age of mobile app to help us study how to leverage social network influences to help address people's emotional and mental health needs.

ACKNOWLEDGEMENTS

We thank Yu Sun, Tong Jin and Qianyi Wang for their contribution to the implementation of the Emotion Map app. We also thank Minjung Doh, Laura Kay Thompson and Craig Ewart for their great input to our research.

REFERENCES

1. Aldao, A., Nolen-Hoeksema, S., and Schweizer, S. Emotion-regulation strategies across psychopathology: a meta-analytic review. *Clinical Psychology Review 30* (2010), 217–237.
2. Baikie, K. A., and Wilhelm, K. Emotional and physical health benefits of expressive writing. In *Advances in Psychiatric Treatment* (2005).
3. Ben-Zeev, A. Privacy, emotional closeness, and openness in cyberspace. *Computers in Human Behavior 19* (2003), 451–467.
4. Christofides, E., Muise, A., and Desmarais, S. Privacy and disclosure on facebook: Youth and adults' information disclosure and perceptions of privacy risks. In *The Office of the Privacy Commissioner of Canada* (2010).
5. Collins, N. L., and Miller, L. C. Self-disclosure and liking: A meta- analytic review. *Psychological Bulletin 116* (1994), 457–475.
6. Coviello, L., Sohn, Y., Kramer, A., Marlow, C., Franceschetti, M., Christakis, N., and Fowler, J. Detecting emotional contagion in massive social networks. In *PLoS ONE* (2014).
7. Diefendorff, J. M., Hall, R. J., Lord, R. G., and Strean, M. L. Actionstate orientation: Construct validity of a revised measure and its relationship to work-related variables. *Journal of Applied Psychology 85* (2000), 250–263.
8. Feldman-Barrett, L., and J.A., R. Independence and bipolarity in the structure of current affect. *Journal of Personality and Social Psychology 74*, 4 (1998), 967–984.
9. Gouveia, R., and Karapanos, E. Footprint tracker: Supporting diary studies with lifelogging. In *Proceedings of the SIGCHI Conference on Human Factors in Computing Systems*, CHI '13, ACM (New York, NY, USA, 2013), 2921–2930.
10. Gross, J. The emerging field of emotion regulation: An integrative review. *Review of General Psychology 2*, 3 (1998), 271–299.
11. Gross, J., Carstensen, L., Tsai, J., Skorpen, C., and Hsu, A. Y. Emotion and aging: experience, expression, and control. In *Psychol Aging* (1997).
12. Gross, J. J., and Barrett, L. F. Emotion generation and emotion regulation: One or two depends on your point of view. *Emotion Review 3*, 1 (2011), 8–16.
13. Gross, J. J., and Munoz, R. F. Emotion regulation and mental health. *Clinical Psychology: Science and Practice 2* (1995), 151–164.
14. Han, K., Shih, P. C., Rosson, M. B., and Carroll, J. M. Enhancing community awareness of and participation in local heritage with a mobile application. In *CSCW'14* (2014).
15. Hasan, S., Zhan, X., and Ukkusuri, S. V. Understanding urban human activity and mobility patterns using large-scale location-based data from online social media. In *Proceedings of the 2nd ACM SIGKDD International Workshop on Urban Computing* (2013).
16. Joinson, A. N. Self-disclosure in computer-mediated communication: The role of self-awareness and visual anonymity. *European Journal of Social Psychology 31*, 2 (2001), 177–192.
17. Lin, H., and Qiu, L. Sharing emotion on facebook: network size, density, and individual motivation. In *CHI Extended Abstracts*, J. A. Konstan, E. H. Chi, and K. Höök, Eds., ACM (2012), 2573–2578.

18. MarketingCharts. Social networking adoption trends, by age group, http://www.marketingcharts.com/wp/interactive/social-networking-adoption-trends-by-age-group-35692/attachment/pew-socnet-site-use-by-age-aug2013/.

19. McDuff, D., Karlson, A., Kapoor, A., Roseway, A., and Czerwinski, M. Affectaura: An intelligent system for emotional memory. In *Proceedings of the SIGCHI Conference on Human Factors in Computing Systems*, CHI '12, ACM (New York, NY, USA, 2012), 849–858.

20. Murray, S. L. Regulating the risks of closeness: A relationship-specific sense of felt security. *Current Directions in Psychological Science 14* (2005), 74–78.

21. Nagpal, R. The awesomest 7-year postdoc or: How i learned to stop worrying and love the tenure-track faculty life, http://blogs.scientificamerican.com/guest-blog/2013/07/21/the-awesomest-7-year-postdoc-or-how-i-learned-to-stop-worrying-and-love-the-tenure-track-faculty-life/.

22. Parrott, W. Beyond hedonism: Motives for inhibiting good moods and for maintaining bad moods. In *In D.M. Wegner & J.W. Pennebaker (Eds), Handbook of mental control* (1993).

23. Pennebaker, J. W. Confession, inhibition, and disease. In *In L. Berkowitz (Ed.), Advances in Experimental Social Psychology*, New York: Academic. (1989), 211–244.

24. Pina, L., Roseway, A., Czerwinski, M., and Rowan, K. In situ cues for adhd parenting strategies using mobile technology. In *IEEE Pervasive Health*, IEEE Pervasive Health (May 2014).

25. Qian, H., and Scott, C. Anonymity and self-disclosure on weblogs. *Journal of Computer-Mediated Communication 12*, 4 (2007), 1428–1451.

26. Quercia, D., Ellis, J., Capra, L., and Crowcroft, J. Tracking "gross community happiness" from tweets. In *CSCW'12* (2012).

27. Rime, B. Emotion elicits the social sharing of emotion: Theory and empirical review. *Emotion Review 1*, 1 (2009), 60–85.

28. Robinson, M., and Clore, G. Episodic and semantic knowledge in emotional self-report: evidence for two judgment processes. *Journal of Personality and Social Psychology 83*, 1 (2002), 198–215.

29. Rubin, D., and Wetzel, A. One hundred years of forgetting: A quantitative description of retention. *Psychological Review 103* (1996), 734–760.

30. Sapolsky, R. M. Stress, stress-related disease, and emotional regulation. In *In J. J. Gross (Ed.), Handbook of emotion regulation.*, New York: Guilford Press. (2007).

31. Schwartz, N., and Xu, J. Why don't we learn from poor choices?: The consistency of expectation, choice, and memory clouds the lessons of experience. *Journal of Consumer Psychology 21* (2011), 142–145.

32. Sheldon, K., Abad, N., and Hinsch, C. A two-process view of facebook use and relatedness need-satisfaction: Disconnection drives use, and connection rewards it. *Psychology of Popular Media Culture 1*, S (2011), 2–15.

33. Tamir, M. What do people want to feel and why? pleasure and utility in emotion regulation. *Current Directions in Psychological Science 18*, 2 (2009), 101–105.

34. Valkenburg, P., and Peter, J. Preadolescents' and adolescents' online communication and their closeness to friends. *Developmental Psychology 43* (2007), 267–277.

35. Voelkle, M., Ebner, N., Lindenberger, U., and Riediger, M. Here we go again: Anticipatory and reactive mood responses to recurring unpleasant situations throughout adulthood. *Emotion 13*, 3 (2013), 424–433.

MoodLight: Exploring Personal and Social Implications of Ambient Display of Biosensor Data

Jaime Snyder°, Mark Matthews°, Jacqueline Chien°, Pamara F. Chang*, Emily Sun°, Saeed Abdullah°, Geri Gay°*
Cornell University
°Information Science Department
*Department of Communication
{js2829, mark.matthews, jtc229, pfc46, es765, sma249, gkg1} @cornell.edu

ABSTRACT
MoodLight is an interactive ambient lighting system that responds to biosensor input related to an individual's current level of arousal. Changes in levels of arousal correspond to fluctuations in the color of light provided by the system, altering the immediate environment in ways intimately related to the user's private internal state. We use this intervention to explore personal and social implications of the ambient display of biosensor data. This study provides greater understanding of the ways in which the representations of personal informatics, with a focus on ambient feedback, influence our perceptions of ourselves and those around us.

Author Keywords
Personal informatics; self-discovery; biofeedback; stress management; light; color; ambient display.

ACM Classification Keywords
H.5.m. Information interfaces and presentation (e.g., HCI): Miscellaneous.

INTRODUCTION

> "To *reveal* is to allow to be known what has heretofore been hidden (a passive act)...and to *disclose* is to act, to make known an occurrence that has been under consideration but, for valid reasons, has been kept under wraps" [22, p. 238].

We are now several years into an era of biosensor research in the field of human computer interaction [cf. 19]. The devices for gathering micro-metric data about even the smallest fluctuations in our biological forms are shrinking in size, becoming more reliable and are increasingly and seamlessly integrated into our environments.

Much of the research in this area has been motivated by a desire to reveal more about ourselves and to provide users with tools to cultivate an increased sense of self-awareness. For example, Affective Health [10; 31] is a bio-sensing tool designed to support stress management by helping people to track trends associated with the response the body has to day-to-day activities and environments. Like similar systems [e.g., 5; 26], Affective Health uses a combination of skin conductance, heart rate and accelerometer sensors to collect data that are displayed on a user's mobile phone in real-time. The designers of this system have explained that "by finding patterns in their own behavior, users can start [to figure] out both what stresses them and how to cope" [31, p. 48].

Extending from this and similar work, we created Moodlight, an interactive ambient lighting system that responds to an individual's physiological markers of arousal. We were interested in learning more about the mechanics of self-awareness provided by real-time display of an individual's biosensor data, particularly in social contexts. We wanted to investigate how the representation of self that is offered by these systems interacts with and influences an individual's own sense of wellbeing. Biosensor systems for self-awareness carry the benefits of ubiquitous and automatic data collection but also embody real risks associated with removing control from users [16; 19]. These systems challenge the ways we have traditionally thought about the process of self-discovery [33] and intentionality of self-disclosure [21].

MOTIVATION

The motivation for MoodLight grew out of two focus group sessions and a series of conversations with clinicians who provide mental health counseling to college students, a population particularly susceptible to stress [9; 34]. For these mental health practitioners, working with students to cultivate successful stress management skills typically involves assessing stress levels, encouraging non-judgmental self-awareness through talk therapy, teaching

CSCW '15, March 14-18, 2015, Vancouver, BC, Canada.
Copyright 2015 ACM 978-1-4503-2922-4/15/03...$15.00.
http://dx.doi.org/10.1145/2675133.2675191

traditional relaxation tools such as deep breathing and, in particular, mindfulness meditation, a stress management technique which places an emphasis on developing a detached awareness of momentary cognitive and emotional experience. Research in psychology has shown that cultivating a sense of non-judgmental mindfulness or awareness of present-moment experience can produce substantial improvements in wellbeing, especially for people suffering from pain and distress [1; 4].

The counselors reported that many students find it extremely challenging to practice relaxation techniques, like mindfulness meditation, both at home and in the clinic. One counselor explained: *"Students can self-experiment with some of the therapeutic exercises but I don't feel that they actually reflect on these experiments, It would be nice to have a way to help them reflect, [to] provide convincing evidence [that it works]."*

Another therapist mentioned the benefits of supporting self-discovery in social contexts by making feelings and emotions "more concrete," visually representing them not only to the individual but also to others in a group session, thereby helping session members validate and acknowledge the feelings of others. She anticipated that a visual display might be particularly helpful for students who lacked or were in the process of developing a vocabulary for their emotions. A third clinician commented that the visual representation of an internal state could provide the opportunity for students to reflect on and accept even negative emotions (their own or others) without judgment, shutting down or denying their existence, thereby supporting healthy self-discovery in the future.

With input from these clinicians, a design probe was deployed to observe MoodLight being used by college students singly and in pairs. During the study we spoke with the students about the experience of seeing their internal, affective state represented in an ambient display. The practical goal of the study was to explore the possibility of using MoodLight in clinical and home settings to cultivate mindfulness, provide a novel outlet for self-discovery, and enhance stress management interventions by supporting social engagement. Our more formative goal was to use this domain to look more reflectively at the process of self-represention through the use of biosensor data and the ways in which this influences our perceptions of ourselves and those around us.

RELATED WORK

Technology for mindfulness

A variety of intervention techniques have been used to encourage self-awareness including mindfulness meditation [13], breathing exercises, progressive muscle relaxation [25], and acceptance and commitment therapy [30]. Many people, however, find mindful practices such as meditation difficult to learn and apply in daily life [4]. Also, many traditional approaches to self-awareness are practiced in isolation, making it challenging to support the stress management process through positive social engagement.

One prominent example of technology-based interventions to support self-reflection and relaxation is biofeedback [33]. This technique involves using sensor technologies to measure and represent changes in typically automatic biological signals like heart rate, skin conductance and brain activity in order to learn how to voluntarily control them. Biofeedback research in the domain of human computer interaction typically involves designing systems that combine one or more of these detection techniques in order to provide users with an enhanced ability to track their own behaviors and activities. For example, Microsoft Research's Food and Mood project [5] deploys biofeedback in the service of intervention and behavior change. Users wear sensors embedded in their clothing in order to track behaviors and affective states associated with emotional eating so that they can curb undesirable habits. The Affective Health project mentioned above uses a similar set of biometric collection points with the goal of empowering users with the ability to interpret and find their own meaning in the signals as a reflective practice.

Biofeedback and similar affective systems are often screen-based, providing sensor output via a digital graphical display. Some systems present feedback through traditional data visualizations while others use visual metaphors. For example, AffectAura measures head position, posture, voice activity, electrodermal activity (EDA), and GPS to provide participants with an interactive visualization of the user's predicted affective state [26].The team involved in designing and developing the Affective Health system have explored more lyrical expressions of the temporal aspect of biosensor data through displays based on layers and spirals [36].

As the devices for collecting and displaying biosensor data become more refined, attention is shifting to the position of these systems within social contexts. Although not yet a standard component of collaborative work interfaces, there is great potential for biosensor feedback to be used as a means for cultivating co-presence and awareness, especially in distributed contexts. For example, mood sharing applications like MobiMood [6] and the MoodJam project [27] encourage awareness of the emotion climate or collective mood of a shared space.

Self-revelation and automated disclosure

We chose an ambient output for our system in order to explore both the personal and social impacts of representations of self generated from biosensor data. Based on ubiquitous computing investigations of the mechanics of automated disclosure [21; 32], we anticipated that there would be interesting tensions between the passive and automatic process of *self-revelation* provided by the sensing device and traditional practices of *self-disclosure* that are typically characterized by intentionality. In particular, we found through the process of designing the MoodLight system that our own understanding of the nature of these practices of revelation and disclosure were challenged.

Self-revelation refers to the passive and often inadvertent act of exposing something about yourself in a tacit manner [11; 22]. For example, we reveal clues about personality, preferences and disposition through body language, the arrangement of our personal spaces, and even through the silences in our speech patterns. Levenson [22] describes the process of self-revelation in social situations as inevitable, inadvertent and continuous. The practice of recognizing and interpreting the unconscious self-revelations of others is poetically referred to by Levenson as "exquisite attention" [22, p. 239]. In this sense, biosensor tools offer us a means to cast "exquisite attention" on ourselves, enabling us to notice subtle and unattended details that signal internal states of being.

On the other hand, self disclosure traditionally refers to "an interaction between at least two individuals where one intends to deliberately divulge something personal to another" [12, p. 411]. In spite of cultural and social taboos against sharing personally sensitive information, psychology research indicates that self-disclosure, especially to friends and family members, can play an important role in constructing relationships and coping with stressful or traumatic events [cf. 12]. Greene et al. [12] posit that nondisclosure, especially in stressful situations such as being informed of a serious illness, correlates to psychological inhibition, suppression of cognitive processing and other physical symptoms of anxiety. Not only do mindfulness practices help us to mitigate stress by encouraging non-judgmental self-awareness of negative feelings, but they can also lead to the intentional expression these emotions to others [1; 4].

Recent research looking at computer-mediated interactions has shown that the perceived anonymity offered by online environments can affect our disclosure practices, often encouraging more spontaneous sharing of personal details [17; 35]. While users largely remain in control of self-disclosure decisions on social media sites through the voluntary nature of posts, with sensor-based systems that can passively and continuously track personal information there are risks associated with *automated disclosure* [cf. 21; 32]. Managing disclosure in daily life "is an intuitive, situated social process" [21, p. 2] while managing disclosure in ubiquitous computing is complicated by the seamlessness with which these systems strive to operate. Lederer et al. looked at ways to support intentional disclosure in ubiquitous systems, particularly where the data may be disclosed automatically [20; 21]. They identified a tension between the risk of unintentional revelation of personal information and the burden of having users provide permission for the release of each piece of information about themselves to which the system has access.

Our study was designed to probe representations of self through biosensor data by focusing on the blurred line between inevitably inadvertent self-revelation and the mechanics of automated disclosure. When users make the explicit choice to use sensing technology, this can be seen as intentional acquiescence to automated disclosure (especially when the system is embedded in a social context). However, in many current systems, users quickly lose control of those data points as their personal information is fed into a complex system [16]. What might have begun as an act of intentional disclosure becomes an experience of passive self-revelation [22, p. 240]. Understanding this shift should be of particular concern to researchers in the CSCW community who envision exploiting affective and bio-sensing technologies in the service of establishing and maintaining trust, cohesion and coordination in distributed teams.

Summary

The capacity for bio-sensing tools to support self-awareness has been the subject of previous work. However, as these tools become more seamlessly embedded in our everyday lives, the data and representations of self that they offer are increasingly integrated into our social landscape. We contribute to this work by viewing representations of self that are offered by bio-sensing systems in terms of not just self-awareness and mindfulness practices, but also within the context of more socially grounded practices of self-revelation and evolving notions of automated disclosure.

DESIGN OF MOODLIGHT

Design considerations

The first design consideration we addressed dealt with the recent surge of interest in personal informatics systems driven by low-level biometric and movement sensors [38]. Biofeedback is no longer a specialized therapeutic technique. Readily available sensor-based activity trackers like the Basis wristwatch (http://www.mybasis.com) enable individuals to use high-frequency sampling of low-level outputs in order to see a view of themselves that was previously unavailable. This information provides new opportunities for self-awareness: Do I recognize myself in this micro-level data? We were interested in investigating these representations in the context of self-discovery.

Second, we were sensitive to students' vulnerabilities when it comes to the relationship between avoidance behaviors and technology use [23]. Avoidance behavior, a by-product of stress, refers to any activity a person engages in to avoid facing a source of stress, resulting in a negative impact on everyday life. Examples include gambling, watching television, and playing computer games. According to the American Psychiatric Association's Diagnostic and Statistical Manual of Mental Disorders (DSM-5), newly identified conditions such as Internet addiction could be the result of a strong relationship between technology use and a range of avoidance behaviors. Because of this connection, the design for MoodLight system needed to remove the screen and introduce an element of ambient experience to users.

Third, in order to support social engagement, we designed the system around the notion of playful interaction, with two modes: single play and paired play. It is a passive, ambient display that encodes output as colored light. During single play, the system responds to input from an individual. In the paired play, biometric data from both participants is combined to produce a visible representation of their shared interaction. We did not present a specific goal to participants, but encouraged open-ended exploration of the system.

System description

The MoodLight system consists of EDA sensors, an android device, a series of commercially available programmable light bulbs produced under the HUE brand by Philips, and a set of desk lamps. Using this technology, it is possible to change the color and/or intensity of the light cast by the bulbs in response to changes in arousal.

Measuring arousal

The Personal Input Pod (PiP), a commercially available sensor used in the MoodLight system, is a novel implementation of standard EDA technology (Figure 1, left). The PiP sensors are about 2cm wide by 3cm long, non-invasive and are held lightly between the participant's thumb and forefinger (Figure 1, left). When the participant makes contact with two separate metal plates on either side of the device, a safe and imperceptible electric charge (13 microamps) is passed through the fingers. The level of conductance is then measured. Readings are taken at regular intervals in order to establish trends of increasing or decreasing arousal for an individual.

EDA sensors can detect changes in an individual's arousal levels via the autonomic nervous system by measuring subtle changes in skin conductivity [8]. The amplitude and rise time of EDA pulses vary between individuals making direct comparisons challenging. The algorithm for assessing changes in individual EDA levels takes this into account by applying Least Means Squares (LMS) on successive windows of data to determine the slope of the EDA curve, and also uses a threshold up/down counter to reject spurious peaks/troughs. An accumulator is used to increment the arousal trend in one direction (stressed) or the other (relaxed). While EDA sensors can detect arousal, or a heightening response to stimuli, they cannot disambiguate whether an individual perceives that sensation of arousal as positive or negative. EDA levels between individuals can vary greatly depending on age, skin type and other factors. For initial testing, the system used a generic profile for interpretation of EDA data.

Figure 1. PiP (left) and setup (right)

Interactive lighting

MoodLight uses the Philips HUE interactive lighting system hardware and API [29]. The system includes programmable LED light bulbs and a wireless bridge that enables the lights to communicate. Three types of LED, producing a relatively wide range of colors and intensities, define the color profile of the lights. MoodLight has been initially optimized to work within the range of colors available through this system, mapping to ten discrete hues (Figure 2), with transitions moving from magenta-red to blue-violet (discussed below).

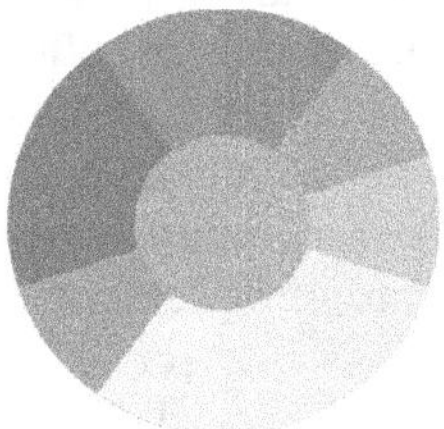

Figure 2. Ten hues representing the MoodLight color range, with red at the top of the circle, moving clockwise to orange, yellow, green, white and blue-violet

EDA readings are sent via bluetooth to an Android device, which in turn sends a signal to the programmable light bulbs. This information is used to control the hue of ambient lighting conditions in a room, essentially controlling the output of the lights with input representing the participant's current level of arousal.

During use, a participant holds the PiPs between their fingers (Figure 1, left). The EDA sensors pick up increasing, decreasing or stable levels of arousal. Depending on the signal, the lights change color, with increasing arousal triggering a transition to warmer (red) end of the spectrum and decreasing arousal signaling the lights to transition to the cooler (blue-violet) end of the spectrum. When either end of the scale is reached, a soft chime sounds.

Light, color and affect

There are multiple theories regarding color, emotion, culture and physiology [cf. 3; 40]. Researchers have shown that exposure to light has both *visual* and *biological* effects [18; 37]; there are non-visual, biological impacts of being exposed to certain colors or levels of light under different circumstances. One example of this type of effect is the influence of light on circadian rhythms. There is also support for a positive association between arousal and color wavelength. Walters et al. [37] showed that subjects who made color preferences throughout the day exhibited a systematic tendency for long-wavelength colors (towards the red end of the spectrum) to induce feelings of high arousal and short-wavelength colors (towards blue) to induce feelings of low arousal.

Supported by this research and a pilot study exploring associations between different colors of light and levels of stress and relaxation, we designed MoodLight with the anticipation that most participants would associate relaxed states with cooler colors like blue and purple and heightened levels of arousal with warm colors such as red and orange.

METHOD

There is limited research that makes an association between face-to-face public display of personal information and social dynamics of self-discovery; therefore, we designed an open-ended protocol that would allow us to observe participants using the system both on their own and in the presence of a friend or acquaintance.

Our study included four stages: 1) a preliminary interview during which we learned about participants' relationship with stress; 2) interaction with the MoodLight system singly providing an opportunity to explore the relationship between the system and self-discovery; 3) interaction with the system in pairs during which we observed a range of behaviors associated with emergent self-awareness in a social context; and 4) an exit interview during which we asked participants to reflect on their experience with MoodLight.

Each recruit for the study was asked to bring a friend or acquaintance when they came to the lab to participate in the study. All individuals completed a preliminary interview and individual session, and those who were able to bring a companion also participated in the second paired session.

Setup

Two empty offices in an academic department close to the center of campus were used to run the study. Decorations, personal items and unneeded furniture were removed from the rooms. A table was set up in each room with a chair on either side, one for the researcher and one for the participant. A plain white cloth was spread over each desktop. There was a laptop computer in each room, as well as two desk lamps, each utilizing a programmable light bulb (Figure 1, right).

Protocol

Preliminary interviews

A preliminary interview gathered information about typical experiences of stress and actions taken to mitigate stress. We asked participants about typical sources of stress, steps taken to mitigate negative feelings and the role that social interaction played in their approach to stress management.

Single and Pair Play

Individual sessions began with a brief introduction to the MoodLight system, including an explanation of the relationship between typical experiences of stress and relaxation in relation to the arousal data used in the system. Individual participants were asked to playfully interact with the MoodLight system by trying to make the lights respond to their EDA input (Figure 3). Most participants engaged with the system for approximately 10 minutes before indicating that they were ready to move on to the next phase of the study. At that point, a partner participant was brought into the room.

For the paired interactions with the MoodLight system (Figure 4), each individual held one of the PiPs. The lights were controlled using the aggregate of EDA input from both participants. We chose to combine the signals in the output in order to emulate the experience of being involved in a face-to-face conversation where it is not always completely clear who contributes what to the overall tone or mien of the discussion. For example, it is not uncommon to find oneself in a tense discussion with a spouse or partner and have competing beliefs about who instigated the conflict.

During paired interactions, the color encoding used was similar to that of the individual version, signaling changes in level of arousal with warmer color for increasing arousal and cooler color for decreasing arousal. For the pairs, we added an additional representation of synchronicity. When both participants were "in sync," meaning both were simultaneously experiencing either increasing or decreasing arousal, the light became brighter. This was intended to function similarly to the many ways we typically signal conversational coordination and involvement, such as mirroring body language, aligning speech patterns and synchronizing vocabulary.

Participants were not asked to complete a specific task, but were encouraged to playfully engage the system with their partner. Many participants began by negotiating a goal; for example, whether they would try to cooperate by simultaneously trying to reach an aroused or un-aroused state or try to compete by trying to reach opposite ends of the spectrum. When the paired participants had exhausted their play, they moved on to individual exit interviews.

Exit interview

At the conclusion of their session, participants were asked a series of questions about their interactions with the MoodLight system. They were asked to reflect on their abilities to control the lights, the appropriateness of colors in reflecting momentary experiences of arousal, and how they might use MoodLight in their day-to-day lives.

Figure 3. Single play, light transitioning from blue (far left) to green (center) to red (right)

Figure 4. Pair play, light transitioning from red (left) to blue-violet (center) to white (right)

Participants

Thirty participants were recruited at a large university in the northeast of the US. During recruitment, participants were asked to bring a friend for the paired observations. Although not all were able to do so, many of the paired participants were friends or acquaintances prior to joining the study. This was a convenience sample, yet participants were reasonably representative of the underlying population. Our sample consisted of 68.8% undergraduate students, 21.8% postgraduates, 3.1% postdoctoral researchers and 9.5% staff members (underlying population: 66% undergrad, 33.5% postgrad). Genders were evenly distributed at 50%, compared to underlying sample of 51.5% male, 48.5% female. Most participants (87.5%) were in the 18 to 25 age range, with the rest being 26-34 years of age. The ethnic background of participants (59.5% American, 28.1% non-American and rest unknown) is similar to the underlying population (64.7% American, 29.6% non-American and rest unknown).

All 30 individuals completed the preliminary interview and were observed interacting with the MoodLight individually; and 22 were observed using the system in groups of two (11 pairs).

Analysis

Qualitative analysis of individual and paired play involved reviewing field notes from all sessions; audio recordings of interviews (30 preliminary interviews and 27 exit interviews due to technical issues with recording equipment); and video recordings when available (26 single play videos, 9 pair play videos).

RESULTS

Our analysis focused on (1) observing verbal and non-verbal practices related to self-revelation during engagement with the MoodLight system singly and in pairs; and (2) specific statements made by participants during play with the system or interviews in response to emergent self-awareness, self-discovery and representations of self.

Engagement with MoodLight

All participants were able to intentionally change the color of the lights either by relaxing or stressing. Participants reported that in order to reach the high-arousal end of the continuum, they tried to think about a stressful situation in their current or recent experiences (62%); made a mental to-do list (15%); performed physical activities such as jumping, running in place or doing push-ups (15%); or think about relationships (12%). When attempting to reach the low-arousal end of the scale, participants indicated that they tried some sort of deep breathing technique (54%), followed in frequency by thinking about something relaxing or enjoyable (42%) like visits with family or trips to the beach. Others talked about trying to clear their minds (19%) or thinking about nothing (12%). Only one person used the term "meditating" to describe these activities.

Interestingly, there were a small number of people who said that they did not need to try to reduce their level of arousal (12%), it just happened naturally. An equal number attempted to relax their neck and shoulders by rolling their head or loosening their posture (12%). A smaller percentage of participants told us that they simply thought about some form of physical activity that they found relaxing (8%).

As participants tried to control the lights, they manifested outward, non-verbal indicators of their internal state. When attempting to become increasingly aroused, they exhibited some common physical characteristics: rapid blinking, sitting forward in their chair, staring intently, short or constricted breathing, clenched jaw, and increased micro-movements or fidgeting. Participants who were attempting to decrease arousal tended to close their eyes, to lean back in their chair, to keep their head/gaze turned downward, or to be very still.

The paradigm of playful engagement with the system enabled us to provide a minimal amount of structure to the paired interactions without drawing attention to a specific goal. In fact, most paired play sessions began with a negotiation between participants regarding whether they would try to get "stressed" or "relaxed," or if they would try to reach opposite ends of the continuum. While social interactions "in the wild" do not always explicitly begin with this sort of alignment work, we know from sociolinguistic research that similar implicit coordination behaviors are highly typical in face-to-face interactions [14; 39]. Regardless of the strategy selected, during the paired play, participants used many of the same techniques they had tried during single play (deep breathing to decrease arousal, fidgeting or other tense physical movements to increase arousal).

During the single play observations, social interactions such as asking participants to describe aloud what they were experiencing or participants asking the researcher a question appeared to increase the arousal level of some participants. In contrast, during paired play, informal chatting appeared to reduce arousal in some people. We observed a distinct pattern in physical proxemics [24] between the pairs. When attempting to become increasingly aroused, participants were more likely to confront each other, look each other in the eye, be facing each other, and mirror each other's movements. When attempting to become less aroused, the pairs were more likely to sit at an angle to each other, to not make direct eye contact and to curtail mimicking or mirroring behaviors.

Risks and rewards of technology-mediated self-discovery

Participant quotes from exit interviews provided some of the richest insights related to user attitudes, assumptions and expectations about the intersection of emergent self-discovery and social engagement provided by the MoodLight system. Therefore, we focus the remainder of the results on reporting these qualitative observations.

Is that me?

Through behaviors such as peeking at the lights after sitting with eyes closed for a period of time, it was clear that participants used the light for feedback about how they were doing, as a tool for achieving the "exquisite attention" described by Levenson as a hallmark of self-revelation [22]. Although the majority of students in the study told us that they know when they are stressed, there was still curiosity about how the lights would represent their momentary arousal level and transitions between states. In this sense, the color of the light revealed to the participant information about his or her own internal affective state. A student explained, *"When I saw the red lights, I was, like, happy and I thought I was achieving what I wanted to do, so then I could relax and just take a deep breath."*

Another participant also expressed a belief that the system would help her to see herself more clearly, imagining using the lights at home: *"I can't fall asleep when I'm stressed and that'd be a good indicator because sometimes I'm not always aware."*

For some of the students, the representation of their internal state was not a welcome discovery. They were susceptible to a negative feedback loop created by the red light not only revealing a state of high arousal, but at times *causing* elevations in stress levels: *"Looking at the light makes me stressed, so I am not going to look at it!"* When asked about using MoodLight at home, a participant articulated the tension between the unconscious experience of self-revelation and the intentional act of self-disclosure by remarking that he did not *"want to wear my emotions on my sleeve."* Another student expressed her hesitation by explaining: *"I already know I'm stressed and I have these...lights that are reflecting how I feel and I already know I'm having a bad day."*

During exit interviews there was a range of responses regarding whether people thought the hue was representative of how they were feeling. While some thought the red and blue extremes accurately depicted their maximum stress and relaxation states, others thought the colors should be different. One participant said she would have preferred a soft green instead of blue-violet at the relaxed end since she considers blue to be sad and dark. Another participant thought the white color was equally as stressful as red.

Although the students talked about customizing the color of the lights, surprisingly, none of them questioned whether the lights were accurately representing their internal state. Based on our observations, participants had different understandings about how the system worked, typically erring on the side of attributing omniscience to MoodLight, even when the output of the lights contrasted or conflicted with the way they were currently feeling. For example, one participant felt that she was highly aroused, "stressed" in her words, although the output of the lights was a steady blue-violet. Rather than questioning the accuracy of the reading, she concluded, *"I guess I've gotten better at not being totally enraged."*

Which one of us is that?

Typically, participants initiated a paired session with a brief conversation about their experience interacting with the system singly and then decided on an approach to the paired session. Conversation generally dropped off after this initial coordination; however, two pairs continued to chat informally about a range of topics not related to the study for the duration of the paired play. These exchanges were characterized by a willingness to share details about their personal experiences and preferences, clear examples of traditional socially driven self-disclosure that stood in contrast to the automated disclosure provided by the lamps. In both cases, the lights indicated a high degree of coordination and steady decrease in level of arousal. The relaxed state achieved by the two chatting pairs supports observations by psychologists that healthy self-disclosure has measurable physiological implications [12].

In the majority of other cases, as talking decreased there was a reduction in standard markers of conversational involvement such as mirroring of gestures and body position, eye contact, leaning towards each other [15; 24]. Particularly when trying to decrease arousal, participants in a pair would often become silent, physically turn away from each other and turn gazes downward indicating internal reflection. During exit interviews, we learned that, in fact, many of these participants were engaged in a form of *indirect coordination*. Although eyes might appear closed, they were often just softened, allowing the participants to use the colored light reflecting off the walls and ceiling to gather information about the state of their joint interaction [7].

During paired interactions, variations in the lights became not only an external representation of the pairs combined arousal level, but also a collaborative platform for the practice of passive self-revelation in a social context. This became evident through statements such as, *"One of us is getting stressed, that's for sure!"* as the room filled with a red-orange glow. Along with this passive self-revelation came a sense of responsibility: *"I don't want to be the one who turns it red."*

We saw evidence of a continuum between self-revelation and automated disclosure through statements such as, *"I don't want to be the person to just make the...light bad— or like stressed out, so I tried to relax myself even more."* Another student felt that the presence of another person inhibited her ability to use the light in a reflective way:

> *"I just felt like everything that we tried to do together we'd get like the opposite. We tried to relax and it was stressful lighting, and tried to get pale lighting and it was a dark purplish. So it was kind of the opposite of what I was trying to achieve. But when I was by myself, I was like, 'I want a pale green,' and I could almost imagine what it would take to get that color."*

The passive nature of the display prompted some participants to think more explicitly about their role in the conversation. While subtle linguistic adjustments to increase rapport or alignment are common during predominantly verbal conversations, the feedback provided by the lights highlighted the fact that a participant was getting information about both themselves and their conversation partner, to which they were not accustomed. One participant explained,

> *"When both of us talk and like the colors suddenly change, it also affects me because I start thinking about why it's changing: is it because of me, or is it because of my partner, what is he thinking, what am I thinking? I also think the color affects me a lot."*

Another student articulated the way in which the lights made him aware of the fact that he and his partner were actually at odds with each other:

> *"Or, I guess with the changing intensity thing...I don't know, I felt like that was harder to— 'cause it was somebody else too, so it was harder to gauge what was...affecting the lights, you know what I mean? I didn't know if—'cause it was dim for a lot of it, which means that [maybe] he was more stressed and I was going the other way trying to relax."*

These findings are closely related to statements from the therapists in our focus group who expressed an interest in visually and externally representing the effects of self-awareness in group settings. In the MoodLight system, the automatic nature of data collection and representation removes the locus of choice from the user and places it in the system, while the representation of self offered by that system still performs some of the social functions of traditional self-disclosure. Statements from participants reflect tensions between the inadvertent act of self-revelation and automated disclosure practices when bio-sensing devices are used for self-awareness in social contexts.

LIMITATIONS

As mentioned above, there are limitations to the current system related to 1) the system-wide representation of the arousal matrix, 2) individual differences in associations between colors and affective states, and 3) the ability of EDA technology to measure nuances in an individual's experience of arousal. However, observing participants engage with MoodLight during this design probe study provided the opportunity to engage with these limitations, as discussed in the next section. Now we move on to implications of this work for the display of personal information through low-level biometric data.

DISCUSSION

One of the most promising aspects of bio-sensing technology lies in the potential for these devices to help us see ourselves more clearly and more completely. This was at the heart of our interest in developing the MoodLight system to assist therapists in their work introducing stress management techniques to college students. However, the representation of self that is offered through biosensors and other affective systems can be problematic: "A central issue faced by affective computing systems is how to balance the personal, subjective nature of experienced human emotions with the external, objective representations of emotions which computers require to function" [19, p. 425].

Further complicating this issue is the likelihood that, as low-level biometric sensors become more deeply embedded in our environments, the resulting data will find its way more quickly into social media channels and ubiquitous displays. This convergence of personal information and increasingly public display will require a more refined understanding of the dynamics of technology-mediated self-revelation and an appreciation of the risks of minimally controlled automated disclosure [21; 32].

Dialectics of technology-mediated revelation and disclosure

Psychologists refer to the process of deciding what personal information to share with whom as the *dialectics of self-disclosure* [28]. Making a conscious decision to reveal information about oneself can be an important part of building lasting relationships. However, not all forms of disclosure are beneficial or healthy. Sharing personal details too soon in a relationship or sharing information that is too private can be inappropriate, especially when not reciprocated. Our study revealed tensions between these dialectics and the passive revelation offered by "always-on" activity trackers and biometric sensors. The process of intentionally deciding what to reveal and to whom is disrupted because the system has the ability to display personal information that users might not be aware of themselves.

By using a very simple game-like paradigm for the design probe, we were able to highlight basic social practices of coordination and alignment that we typically perform throughout our daily interactions, often unconsciously. Some users of MoodLight approached the passive revelation offered by the system as an opportunity for self-reflection and self-discovery. In the context of paired interactions, the momentary display of arousal level through the colored lights provided real time feedback about the current state of their social interaction, enabling users to adjust themselves to try to optimize their shared experience. The aggregated nature of the display also provided an opportunity for participants to reflect on their own complicity in co-constructing the overall tone of their conversation. From a therapeutic perspective, the process of untangling who contributes what to an exchange is an important step to exploring a range of interpersonal dynamics.

Höök et al. talk about this in terms of *affective loop experiences*, described as "experiences where it is not possible to separate the intellectual from sensual experiences, nor to single out what is [an] individual experience from the overall experience arising in a dialogue with a friend or in dialogue with a system" [16, p. 248]. In observing participants interacting with each other through the MoodLight system, we saw these affective loop experiences become increasingly complex when participants were involved in dialogue with a friend *and* in dialogue with the system. The simplicity of our system enabled us to begin to grapple with the ways that the representation of biosensor data played a role in these dynamics.

The use of ambient colored light also allowed us to observe the ways in which the form and format of the representation of personal information could serve as both description and inadvertent intervention. *Negative feedback loops* occurred when some participants experienced high levels of arousal that triggered the lights to transition to the red end of the spectrum. Immersive exposure to the red light heightened arousal further, making it very difficult for these users to break out of what they perceived as an undesirable cycle. Although Höök et al. talk about loop experiences as being a constructive feature of affective systems, our study highlights the potential of interactional loops to be a negative experience for users.

Agency, skepticism and uncertainty

Although students had varying opinions about the hue associated with their level of arousal, surprisingly no one questioned the authority of the system itself. There was a marked lack of skepticism about the omniscience of the system. This may be due, at least in part, to working with students in a research lab setting, lending the experience an overall sense of credibility. However, this observation did prompt us to review interviews and video recordings of interactions with the system with a particular eye to understanding the ways in which the students *assumed* the system worked.

In many ways, the design of the MoodLight system aligns with principles of empowerment through affective tools advocated by Höök et al. [16], Leahu et al. [19], and Boehner et al. [2]. From this perspective, affective systems have the potential "to embody a different kind of interaction, one that positions the user as an expert who makes sense of his or her emotional states with the help of the system, in contrast to a more rigid interaction between a passive user and an expert system" [19, p. 433].

In spite of the relatively open-ended ambient display, the interactive nature of the system, and the co-constructed aggregated signals in the paired interactions, we did not reach a state of pervasive interpretive and interactive empowered across all of our participants. In fact, many of the students in our design probe abdicated the role of self-awareness to the system, seeming to expect (and trust) the lights to tell them how they were feeling. There was a tendency to give more credit to the system than to themselves in terms of knowing how they were feeling in the moment. This was true even in cases when subjective feelings contradicted the information displayed via the lights.

These issues raise questions about the ways in which we present low-level biometric feedback to participants and responsibly explain the uncertainty and complexity that underlies much of this information. When working with biometric data, readings need to be made consistently and analysis depends on identifying patterns in the data. It is rarely a case of definitive black and white declaration, and more typically an instance of identifying a trend in a particular direction. This is due as much to the nature of the signals themselves as to the specifics of the sensing technology.

While it is relatively easy to spot check the accuracy of some types of activity monitors, such as step trackers, it is not as easy for users to check the reliability of biometric sensors such as EDA. Arousal is a complex physical and psychological phenomenon that some users in our study tended to reduce to a binary stress-relaxation axis. Future iterations of the MoodLight system will seek to represent emotion as a balance of subjective and objective interpretation [19] co-constructed through interaction with the system and the revelations provided by it [2], taking into consideration the social influences on this process identified through this design probe.

DESIGN IMPLICATIONS

Ephemerality of Ambient Light

The use of ambient light is a particularly promising medium to cultivate healthy self-awareness in social contexts, including both therapeutic and home settings. Feedback in the form of ambient light places minimal constraints on users: they can maintain a conversation, remain facing each other and sustain eye contact – all common features of therapeutic work. In particular, the use of ambient light supported a rich variety of physical positioning, in ways not possible via screen-based displays. Pairs were able to remain connected even with their eyes almost shut or when facing away from each other. Additionally, there are distinguishing qualities to light that are particularly suited to supporting mindfulness practice. Ambient light provides momentary feedback with an emphasis on the present moment. Unlike a graph, the past is invisible, thereby placing a focus on the present, a key aspect of therapeutic mindful, meditative and reflective practices. Lastly, this technology can be embedded in everyday environments (e.g., a therapeutic clinic, a living room, a bedroom) and serve multiple purposes, enabling individuals to easily pick up the system for brief periods of use without any prior setup, and then to easily return to prior activities.

Understanding the signals

Mindfulness involves being aware of a broad range of mental components and associations that make up everyday perception and experience [4]. Effective design of affective systems that rely on biosensor data means ensuring that users have the information and freedom they need to interpret technology-mediated representations of themselves. It also means enabling users to negotiate inadvertent self-revelation and the risks of automated disclosure. Based on the findings of this design probe study we believe MoodLight will be most effective when used alongside or after a period of training during traditional face-to-face therapeutic sessions. The system is currently being piloted by clinicians in this context as a tool for introducing self-awareness practices to their patients.

Individual Control

To account for individual and cultural differences and variance, monitoring/feedback systems should allow users to choose the display parameters that are meaningful to them. For MoodLight, this entails allowing users to choose the hues that are meaningful to them. Choosing the colors that represent arousal states acts essentially as a private key that only the individual knows, preventing others from interpreting the meaning behind the signal. Enabling color choice is not just about supporting personal preference. Perhaps more importantly, it returns a measure of control to the individual over self-revelation that was taken away by the mediation of technology. Although it is possible with most personal informatics to turn sensors off or opt out of sharing data, for biofeedback systems measuring and representing underlying physiological factors in real-time, this output is less controllable by users. As reflected by Höök et al.'s work on interactional empowerment [16], giving individuals the ability to be involved in the representation of this information ensures the locus of control remains with them.

CONCLUSION

The passive nature of data capture and the ambient display of personal information provided a compelling opportunity for observing the mechanics of technology-mediated self-awareness and the negotiation of automated disclosure in face-to-face social engagement. Data are only meaningful and useful when the user has the ability to understand what is being represented about him or herself. Our design probe showed that the display of momentary arousal levels via ambient light supports self-discovery, enabling students to develop awareness of communication practices related to self-revelation. The study also revealed tensions between control over presentation of self and passive sensing devices that will be increasingly important to address in personal informatics displays designed to be embedded in daily work and living environments.

REFERENCES

[1] Bishop, S.R., Lau, M., Shapiro, S., Carlson, L., Anderson, N.D., Carmody, J., Segal, Z.V., Abbey, S., Speca, M., and Velting, D., 2004. Mindfulness: A proposed operational definition. *Clinical Psych: Sci and Prac, 11*, 3, 230-241.

[2] Boehner, K., Depaula, R., Dourish, P., and Sengers, P., 2007. How emotion is made and measured. *IJHCS, 65*, 4, 275-291.

[3] Butterfield, J., 1996. *The art of light and space*. Abbeville.

[4] Carmody, J., 2009. Evolving conceptions of mindfulness in clinical settings. *J Cogn Psychotherapy, 23*, 3, 270-280.

[5] Carroll, E.A., Czerwinski, M., Roseway, A., Kapoor, A., Johns, P., Rowan, K., and Schraefel, M.C., 2013. Food and Mood: Just-in-Time Support for Emotional Eating. *Humaine Assoc ConfAffective Computing and Intelligent Interaction.*

[6] Church, K., Hoggan, E., and Oliver, N., 2010. A study of mobile mood awareness and communication through MobiMood. *Proc NordiCHI*, 128-137.

[7] Clark, H.H., 1996. *Using Language*. Cambridge University Press, NY.

[8] Cohen, S., Kessler, R.C., and Gordon, L.U., 1995. *Measuring Stress: A Guide for Health and Social Scientists*. Oxford Unive Press, Oxford, UK.

[9] Darling, C.A., Mcwey, L.M., Howard, S.N., and Olmstead, S.B., 2007. College student stress: the influence of interpersonal relationships on sense of coherence. *Stress and health 23*, 4, 215-229.

[10] Ferreira, P., Sanches, P., Höök, K., and Jaensson, T., 2008. License to chill!: how to empower users to cope with stress. *Proc NordiCHI*, 123-132.

[11] Frank, K.A., 1997. The role of the analyst's inadvertent self-revelations. *Psychoanalytic Dialogues 7*, 3, 281-314.

[12] Greene, K., Derlega, V.J., and Mathews, A., 2006. Self-disclosure in personal relationships. In *The Cambridge Hdbk of Personal Relationships*, 409-427.

[13] Grossman, P., Niemann, L., Schmidt, S., and Walach, H., 2004. Mindfulness-based stress reduction and health benefits: A meta-analysis. *J Psychosomatic Res, 57*, 1, 35-43.

[14] Gumperz, J.J., 1982. *Discourse Strategies*. Cambridge Univ Press, Cambridge, UK.

[15] Harrigan, J.A., 2005. Proxemics, Kinesics and Gaze. In *The New Handbook of Methods in Nonverbal Behavior Research*, J.A. Harrigan, R. Rosenthal and K.R. Scherer Eds. Oxford Univ Press, NY, 137-198.

[16] Höök, K., Ståhl, A., Sundström, P., and Laaksolaahti, J., 2008. Interactional Empowerment. *Proc SIGCHI*, 647-656.

[17] Joinson, A.N., 2001. Self-disclosure in computer-mediated communication: The role of self-awareness and visual anonymity. *Euro J Soc Psych, 31*, 2, 177-192.

[18] Knez, I., 2001. Effects of colour of light on nonvisual psychological processes. *J Envir Psych, 21*, 2, 201-208.

[19] Leahu, L., Schwenk, S., and Sengers, P., 2008. Subjective objectivity: negotiating emotional meaning. *Proc DIS*, 425-434.

[20] Lederer, S., Mankoff, J., and Dey, A.K., 2003. Who wants to know what when? privacy preference determinants in ubiquitous computing. *Proc SIGCHI*, 724-725.

[21] Lederer, S., Mankoff, J., Dey, A.K., and Beckmann, C., 2003. *Managing personal information disclosure in ubiquitous computing environments*. Report No. UCB/CSD-3-1257. Computer Science Division (EECS), Univ. of California Berkeley.

[22] Levenson, E.A., 1996. Aspects of self-revelation and self-disclosure. *Contemp Psychoanalysis 32*, 2, 237-248.

[23] Malaney, G.D., 2004. Student use of the internet. *J Educ Tech Sys 33*, 1, 53-66.

[24] Manusov, V. and Patterson, M.L., 2006. *The Sage Handbook of Nonverbal Communication*. Sage Publications, Thousand Oaks, CA.

[25] Matsumoto, M. and Smith, J.C., 2001. Progressive muscle relaxation, breathing exercises, and ABC relaxation theory. *J Clinical Psych, 57*, 12, 1551-1557.

[26] Mcduff, D., Karlson, A., Kapoor, A., Roseway, A., and Czerwinski, M., 2012. AffectAura: an intelligent system for emotional memory. *Proc SIGCHI*, 849-858.

[27] Moodjam.Org, Verified 9/23/2010.

[28] Petronio, S. and Bantz, C., 1991. Controlling the ramifications of disclosure:" Don't tell anybody but...". *J Lang and Soc Psych. 10*, 263.

[29] http://developers.meethue.com/coreconcepts.html.

[30] Powers, M.B., Zum Vörde Sive Vörding, M.B., and Emmelkamp, P.M.G., 2009. Acceptance and commitment therapy: A meta-analytic review. *Psychotherapy and psychosomatics 78*, 2, 73-80.

[31] Sanches, P., Höök, K., Vaara, E., Weymann, C., Bylund, M., Ferreira, P., Peira, N., and Sjölinder, M., 2010. Mind the body!: designing a mobile stress management application encouraging personal reflection. *Proc DIS*, 47-56.

[32] Sapuppo, A. and Seet, B.C., 2012. An Empirical Investigation of Disclosure of Personal Information in Ubiquitous Social Computing. *Intl J Computer Theory & Eng, 4*, 3.

[33] Schwartz, M.S. and Andrasik, F.E., 2003. *Biofeedback: A practitioner's guide*. Guilford Press.

[34] Smith, A., Rainie, L., and Zickuhr, K., 2011. College students and technology. *Pew Internet & American Life Project 19*.

[35] Suler, J., 2004. The online disinhibition effect. *Cyberpsychology & Behav, 7*, 3, 321-326.

[36] Vaara, E., Silvăşan, I., Ståhl, A., and Höök, K., 2010. Temporal Relations in Affective Health. *Proc NordiCHI*, 833-838.

[37] Walters, J., Apter, M.J., and Svebak, S., 1982. Color preference, arousal, and the theory of psychological reversals. *Motivation and Emotion 6*, 3, 193-215.

[38] Waltz, E., 2012. How i quantified myself. *IEEE Spectrum 49*, 9, 42-47.

[39] Wardhaugh, R., 1985. *How Conversation Works*. Blackwell, NY.

[40] Ware, C., 2012. *Information Visualization: Perception for Design*. Elsevier.

Social Sharing of Emotions on Facebook: Channel Differences, Satisfaction, and Replies

Natalya N. Bazarova
Department of Communication
Cornell University
Ithaca, NY 14853
nnb8@cornell.edu

Yoon Hyung Choi
Department of Communication
Cornell University
Ithaca, NY 14853
yc863@cornell.edu

Victoria Schwanda Sosik
Department of Information Science, Cornell University
Ithaca, NY 14853
vls48@cornell.edu

Dan Cosley
Department of Information Science
Cornell University
Ithaca, NY 14853
drc44@cornell.edu

Janis Whitlock
Bronfenbrenner Center for Translational Research, Cornell University
Ithaca, NY 14853
jlw43@cornell.edu

ABSTRACT
People often share emotions with others in order to manage their emotional experiences. We investigate how social media properties such as visibility and directedness affect how people share emotions in Facebook, and their satisfaction after doing so. 141 participants rated 1,628 of their own recent status updates, posts they made on others' timelines, and private messages they sent for intensity, valence, personal relevance, and overall satisfaction felt after sharing each message. For network-visible channels—status updates and posts on others' timelines—they also rated their satisfaction with replies they received. People shared differently between channels, with more intense and negative emotions in private messages. People felt more satisfied after sharing more positive emotions in all channels and after sharing more personally relevant emotions in network-visible channels. Finally, people's overall satisfaction after sharing emotions in network-visible channels is strongly tied to their reply satisfaction. Quality of replies, not just quantity, matters, suggesting the need for designs that help people receive valuable responses to their shared emotions.

Author Keywords
Social sharing of emotions, emotion, Facebook, social media, interpersonal emotional regulation.

ACM Classification Keywords
H.5.2 [Information Interfaces and Presentation]: User Interfaces - Interaction styles.

General Terms
Human Factors

CSCW 2015, March 14–18, 2015, Vancouver, BC, Canada.

http://dx.doi.org/10.1145/2675133.2675297.

INTRODUCTION
Experiencing emotions is a fundamental part of human existence [4]. Although an emotional experience begins as an internal private process, it often leads to the social sharing of emotions with others [41, 42]. Social sharing of emotions refers to the verbal expression of an emotion to others by the person who experienced it [50]. Across age, gender, personality type, and culture, people share emotions with others in over 80% of all emotional episodes (see for review, [41, 42]).

A key reason for social sharing of emotions is that it allows for interpersonal emotion regulation, defined as attempts at managing emotions through social interaction [49]. Emotions often affect people well after the initial emotion-generating episode, leading people to share these emotions with others, particularly those which are stronger and more salient [42]. Such sharing supports both self-oriented (self-soothing, expression of feelings) and other-oriented (receiving support and validation) mechanisms that help people move back into emotional equilibrium [41].

Most research on social sharing of emotions has been limited to offline and dyadic contexts (see for review, [42]) because such sharing has typically involved a single and often relationally close target. However, people are increasingly sharing emotions with large and diverse groups on social networking sites (SNSs), including tweets on Twitter and network-visible Facebook channels such as status updates and posts on others' timelines [8, 26]. Motivations for this form of sharing are diverse [7]; one possible motivation that has so far received limited consideration is that SNSs are good tools for interpersonal emotion regulation, allowing people to reach both broad and targeted audiences depending on their needs around a particular emotional experience.

In this paper we examine how listeners' replies to social sharing of emotions on Facebook affect sharers' overall satisfaction, their sense that the overall goal for this message has been achieved. We investigate overall satisfaction as a function of intensity, personal relevance, and valence of expressed emotions, as well as based on Facebook channel (i.e., status updates, posts on others' timelines, and private messages) in which emotions are shared. As Facebook offers several communication channels with different levels of network visibility and interaction directedness, we also explore whether the intensity, personal relevance, and valence of expressed emotions differ across these channels. In addition to type of channel and characteristics of expressed emotions, overall satisfaction may be affected by listeners' replies to emotional content and whether sharers find these replies to be gratifying and useful. In light of this, we also examine how quantity (number of comments and likes) and perceived quality (as measured by sharers' ratings of gratification and usefulness, henceforth called "reply satisfaction" and "reply usefulness", respectively) of replies affect overall satisfaction with sharing emotional experiences in network-visible channels on Facebook.

RELATED RESEARCH

Characteristics of Expressed Emotions in Different Facebook Channels

Understanding how people share emotions in social media has become an important research topic in CSCW and related venues. One stream of this research has focused on describing and predicting emotions by analyzing the language of social media posts (e.g., [11, 28, 29]) and how factors including individuals' emotional states [18], time of day and location [21], socio-economic events such as elections and holidays [9, 29], and the weather [37] relate to expressed emotions on Twitter and Facebook. These expressions, in turn, can affect others via emotional contagion, the spread of emotional expressions in a social network from one person to another in a sequence of similarly valenced social media posts [16, 30].

Properties of these networks can themselves influence social sharing of emotions. For instance, larger and sparser social networks are associated with increased expression of both positive and negative emotion on Twitter [26], while people with a high ratio of Twitter followers to followees tend to share more positive and fewer negative emotions than people with a lower ratio [17]. Different motivations such as relationship management and self-expression also moderate the relationship between network density and sharing of emotions in Facebook [33].

Social media affordances also affect how people express emotions. Although comparisons between platforms are rare, research has looked at how differences in channels available within the same platform may affect emotional expressions and their functions. For instance, Facebook channels differ in network publicness and interaction directedness, which, in turn, shape potential audiences and communication actions [7]. Status updates are broadcasts, typically visible to a profile owner's entire network. They are not directed at any particular person and are more likely to be "author-centric," [36] that is, contain information pertaining to the author in some way [31]. Posts that people write on others' timelines are typically visible to those others' Facebook friends. They are also targeted at a particular person; this other-directedness leads them to be more concerned with the receiver than status updates are [7, 12]. Finally, private messages are typically sent to an individual in chat, so they are both directed and private, i.e., not visible to a network.

People express fewer negative emotions in network-visible communication (i.e., status updates and posts on others' timelines) than in private messages, while expression of positive emotions in status updates is often strategic, serving to manage a profile owner's self-presentation [8]. People also tend to share more intimate information in private messages than in network-visible Facebook communication, although this result was found in relation to self-disclosure overall, not just sharing of emotions [7]. This tendency may also be linked to Facebook social norms, as people regard intimate expression in network-visible communication as less appropriate than in private messages [5] and as a violation of social norms [35].

Thus, we predict that expressed emotions are less intense and more positive in network-visible channels (status updates and posts on others' timelines) than in private Facebook messages. Further, we predict that directedness affects sharing of emotions. In particular, we expect that people share more personally relevant emotions in author-centered status updates than in posts on others' timelines or in private messages [8, 31]:

H1: People share a) more intense and b) less positive emotions in private messages than in their status updates or posts on others' timelines.

H2: People share more personally relevant emotions in status updates compared to private messages or posts on others' timelines.

Overall Satisfaction After Sharing Emotions on Facebook

Social Sharing of Emotions Framework

We now turn to factors that influence the degree of overall satisfaction people experience after sharing emotions in different channels on Facebook. Social sharing of emotions is often driven by the goal of managing, or regulating, emotional responses [41, 42]. An emotional experience, whether positive or negative, can leave lasting social and cognitive traces. After experiencing an emotional event, it is common for people to cognitively replay and reassess the event in order to make sense of it. Cognitive reassessment of positive emotional episodes reactivates positive emotions, boosting feelings of self-esteem and self-efficacy [41, 50]. Cognitive reassessment of negative emotions can reduce cognitive dissonance and promote understanding of how the emotion-causing event fits in to one's life narrative [42]. Social contact and conversations aid in sense-making through the opportunity to retell the story and make social comparisons; they can also lead to the provision of support and solidarity. Taken as a whole, this process can decrease stress and anxiety associated with negative emotions while enhancing positive affect through reliving positive emotional experiences in conversation.

Although developed in the context of face-to-face communication, the social sharing of emotions theory [42] has been recently applied to emotional communication in different media. A recent study compared affective outcomes of sharing "most important" personal events across multiple media, including Facebook, face-to-face, texting, and phone calls [14]. People reported feeling better after sharing positive emotions and feeling worse after sharing negative emotions in all media, with face-to-face providing the most positive and least negative affect. People were less likely to share significant emotional events in Facebook status updates, using Facebook more for "everyday habitual communication" [14, p. 539].

When emotions are expressed in network-visible Facebook channels, they are overwhelmingly positive [44]. This is likely due to impression management concerns typical for public interactions [8, 44], but there may be additional benefits in sharing positive events in network-visible compared to private Facebook interactions [44]. Interviews with participants who shared their memorable experiences on Facebook suggest that these benefits may be both intrapersonal (e.g., re-experiencing a positive event and enhancing the positive emotions associated with it) and interpersonal (e.g., strengthening relationships with others by entertaining and connecting with them). Further, feedback left on an individual's wall can enhance a positive experience by publicly validating the event [44].

Taken together, especially to the extent that people pursue different goals in different Facebook channels, these studies suggest that characteristics of Facebook channels may affect not just how people share emotions but the outcomes they experience after doing so. In particular, we look at how both the characteristics of shared content and the replies people receive interplay with Facebook channels to affect the overall satisfaction people experience from sharing emotions.

Effects of Emotional Valence, Intensity, and Personal Relevance on Overall Satisfaction in Private vs. Network-Visible Channels

Offline research shows that people share more intense emotions more widely. According to Rimé and colleagues, people experience a greater need to regulate intense emotions, leading to sharing them with more people and more frequently [41, 42, 43]. Network-visible Facebook channels offer an easy way to share with many people compared to private channels, reducing the costs of communicating and the need for repeated interactions [45, 48]. Thus, people may feel more satisfied after sharing personally relevant and intense emotions in network-visible channels compared to a single receiver in Facebook private messaging. Furthermore, people generally feel happier after sharing positive versus negative emotions [14]. Therefore, we predict that positivity and interactions between intensity and personal relevance with Facebook communication channel affect overall satisfaction:

H3: People experience greater overall satisfaction after sharing more positive emotions on Facebook.

H4a: The effect of intensity is moderated by Facebook channel such that people feel more satisfied after expressing more intense emotions in network-visible than in private channels.

H4b: The effect of personal relevance is moderated by Facebook channel such that people feel more satisfied after expressing more personally relevant emotions in network-visible than in private channels.

Effects of Replies on Overall Satisfaction in Network-Visible Facebook Channels

While people can experience benefits from the mere act of sharing emotions socially, listeners' replies to emotional posts (i.e., likes and comments) may play an important role in overall satisfaction. One of the main functions of audience in emotional regulation is to signal that listeners share in a discloser's emotional experience [49]. For a positive emotional episode, listeners help maintain *capitalization*, in which sharing a positive emotional event with others enhances positive affect beyond the satisfaction received from the event itself [32]. For a negative episode, replies serve as a signal that the discloser is not alone [49]. By providing social support, attention, and empathy [42], listeners' replies can also buffer the negative feelings reactivated when sharing a negative experience. The role of replies may be especially important in network-visible channels where people seek social attention and validation [7] and replies can signal attention, co-presence, and partaking in the shared emotional experience [45].

H5: People experience greater overall satisfaction after receiving a) more likes and b) more replies to their Facebook status updates and posts on others' timelines.

However, not all replies are equal. Comments can be perceived as awkward, face-threatening, or challenging to one's desired self-presentation [34], while one reply from a trusted friend may be worth ten from distant acquaintances. Likes, on the other hand, generally carry a positive connotation and are often displayed as an aggregate number in the interface, making them less subject to issues of tone and tie strength. Thus, we predict that overall satisfaction is affected by the quality of replies (reply satisfaction and reply usefulness).

H6: People's overall satisfaction after sharing emotions in status updates and on others' timelines depends on both reply satisfaction and reply usefulness.

METHODS

Participants

Undergraduate and graduate students (*N*=141) from a northeastern United States university were compensated with either a $5 Amazon.com gift certificate or extra credit in communication, psychology, human development, or business courses. The data for this study were collected during May to December of 2013 as part of a larger study, which excluded a small proportion of the population with a history of mental illness (e.g., depression, psychological distress, and self-injury behaviors). The sample was 64.5% female (*N*=91) and 35.5% (*N*=50) male, ranging in age from 18 to 45 (*M*=21.16, *SD*=3.95). On average, participants had a Facebook account for close to six years (*SD*=1.57), spending over 80 minutes (*SD*=88) a day and having over 800 friends (*SD*=448) on Facebook.

Procedure

Our strategy was to ask participants retrospective questions about recent Facebook content in which they shared emotion. To do this, we created a Facebook application that collected relevant data. After giving consent, participants were asked to log on to their Facebook account and to explicitly give the application permission to access their Facebook communication data. The application then accessed the participant's own status updates, posts they wrote on others' timelines, and private messages they sent to another person (both in chat and asynchronously) within the past 60 days. Items less than three words long were eliminated to avoid messages such as "Happy Birthday". To increase the chance of selecting content that included expressed emotions, items were also filtered based on whether they contained any affect words from the LIWC 2007 dictionary (Linguistic Inquiry and Word Count [38]), which has been used in prior Facebook research (e.g., [8, 30]) to determine the presence of emotional content. This procedure did not guarantee all items retained had emotional content and might have excluded some items expressing emotions that failed to contain affect words, but it was a reasonable way to target posts of interest.

From this group of recent status updates, posts on others' timelines, and private messages that contained at least one affect word and were at least three words long, the most recent six items from each channel were displayed. For network-visible items (i.e., posts on others' timelines and status updates), comments and likes were displayed along with the original post. Since some participants use certain channels of Facebook infrequently, the application sometimes showed fewer than six items per channel. The items were displayed in the same order for all the participants: own status updates first, posts they wrote on others' timelines next, and private messages last. For each item, the application presented a set of questions described in the message-level variables below. Overall, we collected data for 754 private messages, 560 posts on others' timelines, and 314 status updates (total *N*=1628).

Message-Level Variables

Participants answered questions pertaining to the intensity and personal relevance of expressed emotions using 7-point scales (e.g., 1="Completely non-intimate", 7="Completely intimate"). Intensity[1] was operationalized by the extent of depth or intimacy of expressed emotions. The scale contained three bipolar items adapted from a prior study [5]: non-intimate/intimate, impersonal/personal, and public/private, α=.70. Personal relevance included three original items: not personally significant to me/personally significant to me, not important to me/important to me, not central to my core self/central to my core self, α=.88. For emotional valence, participants rated each message on a 7-point bipolar scale, with anchors of 1="Very Negative" and 7="Very Positive".

Overall satisfaction was operationalized with two original questions: "After sharing this message, to what extent do you feel satisfied with the outcome?" and "To what extent do you think your goal for this message has been achieved?", α=.84. For posts in network-visible channels (i.e., status updates and posts on others' timelines), participants were also asked about their reply satisfaction: "To what extent did you like the responses (comments and likes) to your post?" and "To what extent were you satisfied with the responses to your post?", α=.94. They also answered questions about reply usefulness: "To what extent did you find the responses to your post useful?" and "To what extent did you find the responses to your post valuable?", α=.92. These questions were all measured on a 5-point scale, with 1="Not at all" and 5="Very much."

To control for frequency, we used post timestamps to calculate the time span in hours of all retained posts within a channel (*M*=383.26, *SD*=361.36) for each participant and the time in hours since the previous message was posted within a channel (*M*=78.85, *SD*=154.29). The values for time variables were divided by a constant to make their variances comparable to other variables to reduce difficulties in achieving model convergence when large differences in variance exist across variables [27].

---

[1] Note that emotional intensity can be measured in different ways, from intensity of impact the event had on individuals and their level of control of an emotional situation (e.g., [43]) to emotional valence (e.g., [14]). To avoid overlap with our measures of emotional valence and personal relevance, we chose to operationalize intensity by the extent of depth or intimacy of expressed emotions, similar to measurements of self-disclosure intensity (e.g., [20]).

Variable	1	2	3	4	5	6	*M*	*SD*
1) Emotional Intensity	-						4.06	1.56
2) Personal Relevance	.49**	-					4.19	1.45
3) Emotional Valence	-.008	.23**	-				5.52	1.55
4) Reply Satisfaction	.09**	.22**	.17**	-			3.44	1.09
5) Reply Usefulness	.21**	.29**	.04	.44**	-		2.45	1.15
6) Overall Satisfaction	.06*	.17**	.39**	.59**	.28**	-	3.92	.95

$p<.05$. ** $p<.01$.

Table 1. Pearson Correlation of Message-Level Variables.

For posts on others' timelines and status updates, information about the number of likes (M=4.26, SD=8.99) and comments (M=1.03, SD=2.37) were recorded. For private messages, the conversation thread for each message was recorded. 73.3% of private messages had other messages from the same thread, and participants had private messages from 1 to 6 different threads (M=2.92, SD=1.05).

RESULTS

Since there were multiple messages for each participant, the analyses were conducted with multi-level modeling to control for potential non-independence of residuals due to repeated observations clustered within each participant. Message-level characteristics were modeled as first-level factors, while participants' characteristics (age, gender, ethnicity) and Facebook use (number of friends, time spent on Facebook per day, number of years having an account) were modeled as second-level factors. We controlled for time effects using the per-channel time span and time since previous post measures described earlier. All of the above variables were included in each model; only those that had a significant effect are reported in the analyses. Independent variables were grand mean-centered. Table 1 reports correlations, means, and standard deviations for the message-level variables across all replies and channels.

Characteristics of Expressed Emotions

First, we ran Model 1 to examine differences in emotional intensity between network-visible and private channels. Based on the null model with no predictors, the intraclass correlation (ICC) was equal to .36, suggesting that 36% of the total variance in emotional intensity of messages was attributed to between-participant differences in how intense their sharing of emotions was on average. Consistent with H1a, there was an overall effect of Facebook channel, $F(2, 230)=73.02$, $p<.001$, effect size $\eta=.46$. Specifically, emotions expressed in private messages were more intense than those expressed in posts on others' timelines, $p<.001$, or status updates, $p<.001$. The difference in intensity between status updates and posts on others' timelines was also significant, $p=.03$ (Table 2).

		Status Updates	*Posts on Others' Walls*	*Private Messages*
Intensity *(Model 1)*	*M*	3.17[a]	3.48[b]	4.73[c]
	SE	(.21)	(.21)	(.20)
Valence *(Model 2)*	*M*	5.44[a]	6.03[b]	4.89[c]
	SE	(.19)	(.19)	(.18)
Personal Relevance *(Model 3)*	*M*	4.30[a]	3.94[b]	4.16[ab]
	SE	(.21)	(.21)	(.20)

Note: Different superscripts indicate significant differences between mean values within rows.

Table 2. LS Means and SE for Emotional Intensity, Valence, and Personal Relevance for Each Facebook Channel.

Model 2 examined differences in emotional valence between the channels, with ICC equal to .16. Similar to H1a, we found a significant difference between channels, $F(2, 243)=50.63$, $p<.001$, effect size $\eta=.27$. Although expressed emotions were overall positive (*Median*=6), private messages expressed fewer positive emotions compared to posts on others' timelines, $p<.001$, or status updates, $p<.001$, consistent with H1b. The difference between posts on others' timelines and status updates was also significant, $p<.001$.

Model 3 tested differences in personal relevance of expressed emotions across the Facebook channels (H2), with ICC equal to .32. The effect of channel was significant, $F(2, 225)=3.46$, $p=.03$, effect size $\eta=.02$, with people sharing more personally relevant emotions in status updates than on posts on others' timelines, $p=.01$. There were no significant differences in personal relevance between the other channels, $p>.05$ (see Table 2). Age also had a significant effect, $F(1, 115)=4.77$, $p=.03$, with older people sharing more personally relevant emotions, $\beta=.05$, $SE=.02$.

The above analyses show that, consistent with H1a and H1b, emotions expressed in private messages are generally more intense and less positive than those expressed in network-visible posts. However, although people share more personally relevant emotions in status updates than in posts on others' timelines, there is no difference in personal relevance of shared emotions between status updates and private messages, so H2 was only partially supported.

Characteristics of Emotions and Overall Satisfaction

To test hypotheses about the effect of characteristics of emotional expression on overall satisfaction (H3, H4a, H4b), we ran a model with the following predictors: Facebook communication channel, characteristics of emotional expression (emotional intensity, personal

Predictor	*DF*	*F*	*p*
Facebook channel	(2, 245)	1.57	.21
Emotional intensity	(1, 1417)	.82	.37
Valence	(1, 1452)	86.04	<.01
Personal Relevance	(1, 1460)	21.72	<.01
FB channel*Personal Relevance	(2, 1255)	4.57	.01
Gender	(1, 126)	4.08	.05

Table 3. Predictors of Overall Satisfaction for Emotions Shared on Facebook (Model 4).

relevance, and valence), and controls for time effects and individual-level characteristics (gender, ethnicity, age, Facebook network size, time spent on Facebook per day, number of years having a Facebook account). Since H4a and H4b predicted interaction effects between message characteristics and Facebook channel, all two-term interactions between message characteristics and communication channel were also included.

After eliminating non-significant interactions and individual-level controls, Model 4 retained Facebook channel, gender, message characteristics (emotional intensity, valence, personal relevance), interaction between personal relevance and Facebook channel, and gender (Table 3). The ICC for this model was .30. Including fixed predictors reduced residual variance by 9% of the variance remaining after partialing out between-individual differences in how satisfied people felt.

As predicted by H3, people experience more overall satisfaction after sharing more positive messages, β=.14, *SE*=.01. Emotional intensity did not have a significant effect on overall satisfaction, β=.02, *SE*=.02, *p*=.37, nor did the interaction between intensity and Facebook channel, *p*>.05. Thus, H4a was not supported.

As predicted by H4b, the effect of personal relevance was moderated by Facebook channel, indicating that people felt more satisfied after sharing more personally relevant content in network-visible status updates, β=.15, *SE*=.03, *p*<.001 and posts on others' timelines, β=.08, *SE*=.03, *p*<.01, but not in private messages, β=.04, *SE*=.03, *p*=.17.

Finally, gender also had a significant effect on overall satisfaction, with females (*M*=4.00, *SE*=.06) being more satisfied than males (*M*=3.80, *SE*=.08) after sharing emotions on Facebook (see Table 3).

Overall Satisfaction and Replies in Network-Visible Communication

Our final two hypotheses examined the role of reply quantity (number of comments and likes) and quality (reply satisfaction and reply usefulness) in predicting overall satisfaction after sharing emotions on Facebook (H5, H6). To test H5 about the effect of the number of comments and number of likes, we first ran a model that included the number of likes and comments received for status updates and posts on others' timelines,[2] characteristics of emotional messages, and individual-level and time controls. After eliminating non-significant individual-level and time controls, Model 5 retained Facebook channel, message characteristics, number of comments, number of likes, and gender (Table 4). The ICC was .27 based on the null model with no fixed predictors.

Predictors	*Model 5* β *(SE)*	*Model 6* β *(SE)*
Facebook channel	-.35*** (.09)	-.33***
Emotional intensity	.04	.01
Valence	.14***	.11***
Personal Relevance	.08**	.03
Comments	.05***	.02†
Likes	.02***	.01**
Reply Satisfaction	-	.35***
Reply Usefulness	-	.05†
Gender	-.21†	-.18†
Deviance	.40	.33

† *p*<.10. * *p*<.05. ** *p*<.01. ****p*<.001.

Table 4. Effects of Replies on Overall Satisfaction in Network-Visible Facebook Channels (Status Updates and Posts on Others' Walls).

As seen from Table 4, the results of Model 5 suggest that overall satisfaction is linked to both the number of comments and the number of likes received for emotional content, as well as personal relevance and valence of this content. To untangle the effect of the number of replies from their quality (reply satisfaction and reply usefulness) and to test H6, we next ran Model 6, which added sharers' reply satisfaction and reply usefulness to the predictors in Model 5. Valence was still positively associated with overall satisfaction, suggesting that people felt more satisfied after sharing more positive emotions regardless of the replies they received and their reply satisfaction.

However, when controlling for reply quality as measured by reply satisfaction and reply usefulness, the number of comments and the effect of personal relevance were no longer significant on overall satisfaction. Reply satisfaction and number of likes were important to overall satisfaction;

[2] Here we focus on network-visible communication to untangle the effect of quantity of responses (since more than one response or like can be received for a network-visible comment) from their perceived quality; comments and likes are not meaningful for private messages.

reply usefulness was not. Finally, people felt generally more satisfied after sharing emotions in posts on other people's walls (M=4.10, SE=.05) than in status updates (M=3.77, SE=.06). The inclusion of the fixed predictors in Model 6 reduced the residual variance by 31% of the variance compared to the null model with no fixed predictors and by 17.5% compared to deviance in Model 5.

One explanation for the number of comments and personal relevance becoming non-significant after controlling for reply quality is that they have an indirect effect on overall satisfaction through the mediator of reply satisfaction. Full mediation is established when four conditions are met [3]: A predicts B, A predicts C, C predicts B, and A's predicting B disappears when C is included. Here, personal relevance and number of comments are A, overall satisfaction is B, and reply satisfaction is C, and Models 4 and 6 have already shown that the conditions are met except for A predicts C. An additional analysis shows that both personal relevance, β=.13, SE=.03, p<.001, and number of comments, β=.08, SE=.01, p<.001, do predict reply satisfaction, showing that they are important for overall satisfaction insofar as they increase reply satisfaction.

DISCUSSION

This study presents an analysis of how people share emotions via Facebook and how the emotional content of communication and listeners' replies are associated with sharers' overall satisfaction. The results show that people share more intense and less positive emotional content in private than in network-visible communication, while non-directed status updates display more personally relevant emotions than directed posts on others' timelines. The emotional content, in turn, is associated with the level of overall satisfaction people experience after sharing it with others: they feel more satisfied after sharing positive content in all channels, as well as after sharing personally relevant content in network-visible status updates and posts on others' timelines. Listeners' replies to network-visible emotional content are very important, with people feeling more satisfied overall when they receive more likes and gratifying comments (i.e., reply satisfaction), while number of comments influences overall satisfaction indirectly by enhancing reply satisfaction. Below we discuss theoretical contributions of these findings and their implications for understanding sharing of emotions in social media, as well as for designing systems that support social sharing of emotions.

Theoretical Contributions and Implications

Our results help understand why people share emotions on Facebook. Prior research has suggested that people who use the Internet and especially Facebook receive more social and emotional support from others [22], but have not detailed the mechanisms through which this phenomenon occurs. Our findings suggest that one such mechanism is that expressing emotions and receiving feedback may serve emotional regulation needs of Facebook users.

Social Media Affordances and Emotional Content

The results about how people share different emotional content in different Facebook channels contributes to the understanding of how people adapt their communication behaviors, including emotional expressions, to media affordances and potential audiences [8]. Consistent with other research (e.g., [7, 10, 31]), our findings show that people express less intense and more positive information in network-visible than private channels. This could be due to higher self-presentational concerns in public exchanges [24], norms for positivity and less intimate information in Facebook public communication [5, 35], or less control over the spread of information [10] when sharing with broad audiences.

People may compensate for the lack of audience control in public Facebook channels by exercising tighter message control, i.e., sharing less intimate and less private information in status updates and on others' timelines compared to Facebook private messages. It is not clear, however, to what extent this process is driven by conscious attempts to shape emotional expression or by a more situated, spontaneous process where social media affordances and the audience representations embedded within them elicit different types of emotional expressions. Future studies that focus on the mechanisms that cause these differences between channels would help clarify the theoretical picture and might give guidance into designing affordances that improve choices and outcomes around social sharing of emotions.

Furthermore, these studies would need to take into account differences between users, including age, gender, and personality factors, as these factors might influence both experiences with social media and people's expectations and outcomes around sharing emotions online. For example, although not the focus of the current study, we found that older people shared more personally relevant information, which is consistent with other research showing that as people get older, they also seek more meaningful social connections on Facebook [6] as part of their adaptive response to changing social motivations [13].

Emotional Content and Overall Satisfaction

People derive intrinsic value from sharing personal information and emotions with others [41, 42, 43, 46], but different types of emotional content are associated with different levels of satisfaction. As our findings show, people derive more value from sharing positive emotional content regardless of communication channel, number of likes or replies they receive, or the quality of responses. This is consistent with the phenomenon of capitalization, in which sharing positive emotions serves to re-experience and enhance positive affect for the sharer. Since emotions that people share on Facebook are predominantly positive, capitalization may explain the self-affirmation value of Facebook communication [47] and the fact that posting on Facebook is associated with a higher level of well-being independent of listeners' feedback [19].

We also found that the personal relevance of emotions is associated with increased satisfaction in network-visible Facebook communication. This is an interesting finding given that communication in network-visible Facebook posts is mostly described as being mundane in nature [14], but is consistent with offline studies of social sharing of emotions showing that people have a greater need to share more personally important and salient emotional events with others [41, 42]. However, personal relevance was only associated with satisfaction in network-visible Facebook channels, not in private messages. This may be because people derive meaning and social value from the private context of communication itself [5, 8]. Meanwhile, in network-visible channels, the influence of personal relevance on overall satisfaction works by increasing sharers' reply satisfaction, that is, sharers find responses to personally relevant content more gratifying.

The Importance of Replies for Overall Satisfaction

Finally, our study contributes to understanding the role of feedback in how people derive satisfaction from sharing emotions in network-visible Facebook communication. We investigate whether others' replies matter or whether people derive satisfaction from the act of sharing emotions itself, regardless of the feedback they receive. In other words, what is the role of "social" in social sharing on Facebook?

Our results indicate that replies do matter both in terms of quantity (number of likes) and quality (reply satisfaction): satisfying replies are more important for overall satisfaction than their number or their perceived usefulness, although the number of replies also increases posters' reply satisfaction. This might be because one of the salient goals for sharing in network-visible Facebook communication is obtaining validation and approval from others [7]; gratifying comments appear to provide such validation to posters' emotional experiences. Even more than useful responses, they may be particularly instrumental for satisfying sharers' socio-affective needs, which, in turn, enhances their overall satisfaction. The number of likes was important even after controlling for reply satisfaction, suggesting that likes, often displayed as an aggregate number in the interface, also serve as a signal of validation and legitimization of a sharer's emotional experience.

This shows the importance of listeners' feedback to social sharing emotions. Most work on sharing personal information, including emotions, focuses on the production side—sharers' characteristics and motivations or properties of the disclosed content. However, both the main effects of reply satisfaction and our mediation analysis of the relationship between content, responses, and outcomes show that accounting for respondents is important for understanding effects of sharing emotions in social media (which in turn will affect future decisions around social sharing of emotions [39]).

The value of responses may also help explain the mismatch between dyadic models of disclosure that predict restricted, intimate sharing of emotions to close ties and observed sharing behavior in SNSs with larger networks. Such broadcasting of personal information is often derided as over-sharing, but sharing emotional episodes with a larger audience likely increases the chances of receiving empathy, social validation, and support from others [42] while reducing costs.

Designing to Improve Social Sharing of Emotions

More generally, the high-level story of Models 5 and 6 is that responses are key drivers of how satisfied people are when sharing emotions. Thus, design features that improve the likelihood, quantity, and value of responses are one path to improving people's outcomes from sharing emotions with others.

Algorithms to Increase the Chance of Receiving Responses

The filtering algorithms services use when distributing activity to network members often have a "rich get richer" effect around attention. Content that receives initial positive responses is promoted both in public lists (as with upvotes in reddit) and by filtering algorithms, while content that doesn't receive early attention may languish. This would lead to worse outcomes from sharing emotions with others, especially to the extent that negatively valenced items receive fewer responses.

Although these filtering algorithms are subject to practical, financial, and ethical constraints, they could be made sensitive to content indicating emotional needs. Work around detecting emotion in social media (e.g., [11, 28, 29]) could be used to identify content that is likely to contain expressed emotions and that would benefit from a response. Then, information about tie strength and responsiveness of people in their networks could be used to route such content to the people who are likely to respond (c.f. intelligent task routing [15]).

Sharing Hints for Algorithms

People could help these algorithms out by suggesting the right audiences for sharing of particular kinds of emotional content. This idea is inspired by Twitter @-mentions, which route public messages to specific individuals, Google+ circles, which route messages to particular audiences, and the tagging of people in Facebook, which leads to notifications for the tagged recipients. Each has flaws for supporting social sharing of emotions: Twitter, although often author-centric, is more about activity than emotion; circles require predefined groups that are often not suited to the social nuances of sharing [1]; publicly directing emotional content at specific individuals through tags may impose awkward obligations to respond.

Instead of explicit instructions for distribution, as in the above channels, it might be useful to allow people to give "hints" to the algorithms. Facebook's mobile client has a new feature that renders privacy settings in the form of a "To:" field similar to that of an email client. A "Feed:" field that lets people specify names they would like to share a particular item with might help people flexibly and precisely target audiences that they believe will support their goals. This would in turn provide algorithms useful information about social relationships they could use for other purposes. Further, unlike @-mentions, circles, and tagging, these are just suggestions; the algorithm could ignore the request (if it deemed other things more important for those recipients), providing plausible deniability for those who do not respond [2].

Lightweight Interfaces for Providing Support

A final idea is to explore lightweight interfaces for providing support. It can be hard to respond to negatively valenced emotional expressions: people may find it awkward or uncomfortable to comment on it, or if it indicates specific needs such as mental health concerns, they may not have the knowledge needed to say something helpful. Meanwhile, it would be odd to "like" the news that someone was fired, became ill, or lost a loved one.

Interface elements that support lightweight emotional connection and support—such as the like button, but with different semantics—is worth exploring. In Kaye et al.'s Virtual Intimate Objects, people can click a button that lights up a partner's button to provide a feeling of connection [25]. The "Yo" app (http://www.justyo.co/), for all its apparent silliness in letting people only send the message "Yo" to each other, performs a similar function. It's unclear what the right abstractions are for lightweight responses to expressed emotions—Hearts? Hugs? I Empathize?—but it is a direction that might have real impact on both social sharing of emotions and its outcomes in SNSs.

Limitations

A key limitation of this study comes from the fact that we have a relatively narrow sample in terms of age and Facebook experience. We also have the standard "WEIRD" (Western, educated, industrialized, rich, and democratic) biases articulated in [23] and skew young because of our subject population. In our sample, older people shared more personally relevant content; factors such as age, experience with Facebook, or cultural background may be important in understanding sharing of emotions and responses to it and should be further studied.

Our study also focused on likes and comments as the measure of replies, meaning we were unable to say much about the effects of replies in private messages. Private messages are also often part of a longer-term exchange between people. Thus, we see the need for further studies with designs that target the role of response and sequence in sharing emotions in private channels.

Our design also collected self-ratings of both content characteristics and outcomes after the fact. We focused on recent posts to minimize the effects of time on people's ratings, but experience sampling-based designs that capture responses closer to the actual sharing of the emotional experience might give more ecologically valid results. Our analysis was also correlational, and though it is hard to picture ethical designs where we could control the responses people saw, this, too, should be kept in mind when interpreting the results.

CONCLUSION

This study adds to the growing body of literature on how people use social media to share and manage emotions in both network-visible and private communication channels. Variations in emotional valence, intensity, personal relevance, and outcomes by channel suggest that individuals selectively use SNS channels to support specific interpersonal emotion regulation goals. Further, the key role of replies and satisfaction with those replies warrants more attention to the role of recipients in understanding social sharing of emotions. Our findings substantiate the value of research on the role SNSs play in the context of larger individual emotion regulation strategies and how design elements of SNSs might better facilitate that role.

ACKNOWLEDGMENTS

This work is supported in part by the National Science Foundation (IIS-1405634), a NSF graduate research fellowship, and the Bronfenbrenner Center for Translational Research at Cornell University. We acknowledge research assistance from Jessie Taft, as well as helpful comments on previous versions of this document from three anonymous reviewers and the Associate Chair.

REFERENCES

1. Ackerman, M. S. The intellectual challenge of CSCW: the gap between social requirements and technical feasibility. *Human-Computer Interaction, 15,* 2–3 (2000), 179–203.
2. Aoki, P. M., and Woodruff, A. Making space for stories: Ambiguity in the design of personal communication systems. In *Proc. CHI 2005,* ACM Press (2005), 181–190.
3. Baron, R. M., and Kenny, D. A. The moderator-mediator variable distinction in social psychological research: Conceptual, strategic, and statistical considerations. *Journal of Personality and Social Psychology, 51* (1986), 1173-1182.
4. Barrett, L. F. Solving the emotion paradox: Categorization and the experience of emotion. *Personality and Social Psychology Review, 10,* 1 (2006), 20–46.

5. Bazarova, N. N. Public intimacy: Disclosure interpretation and social judgments on Facebook. *Journal of Communication, 62* (2012), 815–832.
6. Bazarova, N. N., Chang, P. F., Choi, Y. H., and Loeckenhoff, C. Online social networking across the life span: Extending socioemotional selectivity theory to social network sites. *Presented at 7th ICWSM.*
7. Bazarova, N. N. and Choi, Y. H. Self-disclosure in social media: Extending the functional approach to disclosure motivations and characteristics on social network sites. *Journal of Communication, 64* (2014), 635-657.
8. Bazarova, N. N., Taft, J. G., Choi, Y. H., and Cosley, D. Managing impressions and relationships on Facebook: Self-presentational and relational concerns revealed through an analysis of language style. *Journal of Language and Social Psychology, 32* (2013), 121–141.
9. Bollen, J., Mao, H., and Pepe, A. Modeling public mood and emotion: Twitter sentiment and socio-economic phenomena. In *Proc. 5th ICWSM* (2011), 450–452.
10. Brandimarte, L., Acquisti, A., and Loewenstein, G. Misplaced confidences privacy and the control paradox. *Social Psychological and Personality Science, 4* (2013), 340–347.
11. Brubaker, J. R., Kivran-Swaine, F., Taber, L., and Hayes, G. R. Grief-stricken in a crowd: The language of bereavement and distress in social media. In *Proc. 6th ICWSM* (2012). 42–49.
12. Burke, M., Marlow, C., and Lento, T. Social network activity and social well-being. In *Proc. CHI 2010,* ACM Press (2010), 1909–1912.
13. Carstensen, L. L. The influence of a sense of time on human development. *Science, 312* (2006), 1913–1915.
14. Choi, M., and Toma, C. Social sharing through interpersonal media: Patterns and effects on emotional well-being. *Computers in Human Behavior, 36* (2014), 530-541.
15. Cosley, D., Frankowski, D., Terveen, L., and Riedl, J. SuggestBot: Using intelligent task routing to help people find work in Wikipedia. In *Proc. 12th IUI,* ACM Press (2007), 32–41.
16. Coviello, L., Sohn, Y., Kramer, A. D. I., Marlow, C., Franceschetti, M., Christakis, N. A., and Fowler, J. H. Detecting emotional contagion in massive social networks. *PLoS ONE 9,* 3 (2014).
17. De Choudhury, M., Counts, S., and Gamon, M. Not all moods are created equal! Exploring human emotional states in social media. In *Proc. 6th ICWSM,* (2012), 66–73.
18. De Choudhury, M., Gamon, M., Counts, S., and Horvitz, E. Predicting depression via social media. In *Proc. 7th ICWSM,* (2013), 128–137.
19. Deters, G. F., and Mehl, M. R. Does posting Facebook status updates increase or decrease loneliness? An online social networking experiment. *Social Psychological and Personality Science, 4* (2013), 579–586.
20. Durcharme, J., Doyle, A. B., and Markiewicz, D. Attachment security with mother and father: Associations with adolescents' reports of interpersonal behavior with parents and peers. *Journal of Social and Personal Relationships, 19* (2002), 203–231.
21. Golder, S. A., and Macy, M. W. Diurnal and seasonal mood vary with work, sleep, and daylength across diverse cultures. *Science, 333* (2011), 1878–1881.
22. Hampton, K., Goulet, L. S., Rainie, L., and Purcell, K. Social networking sites and our lives. Report, Pew Internet & American Life Project (2011).
23. Henrich, J., Heine, S. J., and Norenzayan, A. The weirdest people in the world? *Behavioral and Brain Sciences, 33,* 2–3 (2010), 61–83.
24. Goffman, E. (1967). *On face-work: An analysis of ritual elements in social interaction.* Garden City, NY: Anchor Books.
25. Kaye, J. J., Levitt, M. K., Nevins, J., Golden, J., and Schmidt, V. Communicating intimacy one bit at a time. In *CHI Extended Abstracts 2005*, ACM Press (2005), 1529–1532.
26. Kivran-Swaine, F., and Naaman, M. Network properties and social sharing of emotions in social awareness streams. In *Proc. CSCW 2011*, ACM Press (2011), 379–382.
27. Kline, R. B. (2010). Principles and practices of structural equation modeling (3rd ed.).
28. Kouloumpis, E., Wilson, T., and Moore, J. Twitter sentiment analysis: The good the bad and the OMG! In *Proc. 5th ICWSM,* (2011), 538–541.
29. Kramer, A. D. I. An unobtrusive behavioral model of "gross national happiness." In *Proc. CHI 2010,* ACM Press (2010), 287–290.
30. Kramer, A. D. I. The spread of emotion via facebook. In *Proc. CHI 2012,* ACM Press (2014).
31. Kramer, A. D. I., and Chung, K. Dimensions of self-expression in Facebook status updates. In *Proc. 5th ICWSM,* (2011), 169–176.
32. Langston, C. A. Capitalizing on and coping with daily-life events: Expressive responses to positive events. *Journal of Personality and Social Psychology, 67* (1994), 1112–1125.
33. Lin, H., and Qiu, L. Sharing emotions on Facebook: Network size, density, and individual motivation. *Ext.*

Work-in-Progress CHI 2012, ACM Press (2012). 2573–2578.

34. Litt, E., Spottswood, E., Birnholitz, J., Hancock, J., Smith, M. E., and Reynolds, L. Awkward encounters of an "other" kind: Collective self-presentation and face threat on Facebook. In *Proc. CSCW 2014,* ACM Press (2014), 449–460.
35. McLaughlin, C., and Vitak, J. Norm evolution and violation on Facebook. *New Media & Society 14,* 2 (2012), 299–315.
36. Naaman, M., Boase, J., and Lai C. Is it really about me? Message content in social awareness streams. *In Proc. CSCW 2010*, ACM Press (2010), 189–192.
37. Park, K., Lee, S., Kim, E., Park, M., Park, J., and Cha, M. Mood and weather: Feeling the heat? In *Proc. 7th ICWSM,* (2013), 709–712.
38. Pennebaker, J. W., Booth, R. J., and Francis, M. E. (2007). Linguistic Inquiry and Word Count (LIWC 2007). Austin, TX: http://www.liwc.net.
39. Petronio, S. (2002). Boundaries of privacy: Dialectics of disclosure. New York, NY: State University of New York Press.
40. Radovanovic, D., and Ragnedda, M. Small talk in the digital age: Making sense of phatic posts. *In Proc. 2nd #MSM Workshop*, (2012), 10–13.
41. Rimé, B. Interpersonal emotion regulation. *Handbook of Emotion Regulation,* (2007), 466–485.
42. Rimé, B. Emotion elicits the social sharing of emotion: Theory and empirical review. *Emotion Review, 1* (2009), 60–85.
43. Rimé, B., Mesquita, B., Philippot, P., and Boca, S. Beyond the emotional event: Six studies on the social sharing of emotion. *Cognition and Emotion, 5* (1991), 435–466.
44. Sas, C., Dix, A., Hart, J., and Su, R. Dramaturgical capitalization of positive emotions: The answer for Facebook success? In *Proc. 23rd BCS-HCI* (2009), 120–129.
45. Sosik, V. S., and Bazarova, N. N. Relational maintenance on social network sites: How Facebook communication predicts relational escalation. *Computers in Human Behavior, 35* (2014), 124–131.
46. Tamir, D. I., and Mitchell, J. P. Disclosing information about the self is intrinsically rewarding. *Proceedings of the National Academy of Sciences, 109,* 21 (2012), 8038–8043.
47. Toma, C. L., and Hancock, J. T. (2013). Self-affirmation underlies Facebook use. *Personality and Social Psychology Bulletin, 39,* 321–331.
48. Tong, S. T., and Walther, J. B. Relational maintenance and computer-mediated communication. In K. B. Wright & L. M. Webb (Eds), *Computer-mediated communication in personal relationships* (pp. 98–118). New York: Peter Lang Publishing (2011).
49. Zaki, J., and Williams, W. C. Interpersonal emotion regulation, *Emotion, 13* (2013), 803–810.
50. Zech, E., Rimé, B., and Nils, F. Social sharing of emotion, emotional recovery, and interpersonal aspects. *The Regulation of Emotion* (2004), 157–185.

Coordination-Artifacts Suiting: When Plans are in the Midst of Ordering Systems

Ilaria Redaelli
Università della Svizzera italiana
G. Buffi, 9 Lugano, Switzerland
ilaria.redaelli@usi.ch

Antonella Carassa
Università della Svizzera italiana
G. Buffi, 9 Lugano, Switzerland
antonella.carassa@usi.ch

ABSTRACT
This paper addresses the received understanding of the status of plans in cooperative work—that is, artefacts that anticipate future ways of performing activities, to challenge the received understanding of the plan's capacity to anticipate interdependencies as an immutable feature of plans. We propose conceptualizing the plan's capacity to anticipate interdependencies at work as an emergent, distributed and artifact-mediated activity that might be uncovered studying plans, planning and the plans application as work objects and activities occurring within a multiplicity of coordinative artifacts and protocols. This way we can expand our knowledge on how the plans anticipation is maintained in changing environments to support work coordination and we might support designers of computer-supported cooperative work (CSCW)' efforts for the design of CSCW systems.

Author Keywords
Artifacts; Anticipation; Coordination; Ordering Systems; Plans; Planning

ACM Classification Keywords
H.5.3 [Group and organization interfaces]: Computer supported cooperative work; theory and models

INTRODUCTION
The objective of this paper is to contribute to the understanding of the role of plans in supporting coordination at work by proposing an approach that focuses on how the plan's capacity to anticipate interdependencies at work is maintained in face of changes in surroundings to ensure stability in the coordination of different stakeholders.

Several computer-supported-cooperative work (CSCW) scholars [7; 13; 15; 29; 43; 16] have examined how the plans' executors deal with the anticipated courses of events that plans set up in real settings. This stream of research has significantly contributed to our understanding of how plans are used within work settings. Previous researchers have always taken as an object of inquiry plans as "static artifacts" that one person develops and another one has to use or, said in other words, as artifacts whose capacity to define in advance interdependencies at work can never be changed by the plan executors. But what happens when plans change over time? Is it possible to conceptualize the plans capacity to anticipate interdependencies among work activities as an emergent, distributed and artifact-mediated activity that still ensure stability in the coordination of complex work activities? This is the research question that inspired this paper and that we answer focusing on how plans are used in combination with other artifacts, thus approaching the study of plans in a way that still needs to be exploited by CSCW scholars. In particular, we take the concept of "ordering system" developed by Schmidt and Wagner [44] as particularly inspiring in that it promotes the necessity to study specialized coordinative practices as essentially linked with coordinative artifacts and to understand practices and artifacts designed to address very specific coordinative issues as interrelated. This way, the study of work must include the understanding of the complex interconnections actors establish to interrelate specific objects and practices to ensure order at work.

We propose the term "coordination-artifacts suiting" to focus on the set of local practices and coordinative artifacts that permit individuals to keep plans on track—that is, to ensure the usability of plans over time, even if changes in surroundings occur. In order to develop our argument, we first present and comment on coordination-artifacts studies, then we examine coordination dynamics studies in airport and traffic control settings, and finally we focus on research on plans and planning in CSCW. We then present the ethnographic study used as a meaningful case and we conclude by providing insights into the design of CSCW systems.

CSCW '15, March 14 - 18, 2015, Vancouver, BC, Canada.
Copyright 2015 ACM 978-1-4503-2922-4/15/03...$15.00.
http://dx.doi.org/10.1145/2675133.2675136

ARTIFACTS AND WORK COORDINATION
The preoccupation with coordination that is at the basis of CSCW research has fostered the study of how artifacts contribute to the realization of cooperative work.

Exemplar in this sense is Schmidt and Simone's work [42]. Drawing on Strauss' work [49], these scholars defined cooperative work as the kind of work "constituted by multiple actors who are interdependent in their work in that they interact through changing the state of the common field." They further defined articulation work as the means to "curb the distributed nature of complexly interdependent activities." Based on these definitions, they identified coordination mechanisms as the "protocols encompassing a set of explicit conventions and prescribed procedures and supported by distinct artifacts with a standardized format, that stipulate and mediate the articulation of distributed activities so as to reduce the complexity of articulating distributed activities of cooperative ensembles" (pp. 16-21). The role of the artifacts in the coordination mechanism is thus "to provide persistence to the precomputations of the protocol and to make them publicly available" (p.35).

Several CSCW scholars have examined interrelated material artifacts vis-à-vis coordinative practices. Among others [2], Schimidt and Wagner [44] explored the fundamental concept of "coordination mechanisms" and developed the concept of "ordering systems" to address clusters of coordinative protocols and concomitant coordinative artifacts. In their study, they sought to overcome the biases that the study of coordination through the study of coordination mechanisms could engender [45; pp.17-21] as well as outline an approach that "supports the analyst in embracing the motley of coordinative practices required in highly complex cooperative work settings" [25; p. 23]. Other scholars have instead focused on the role of "boundary objects" [11; 48] as material artifacts that mediate the relationship among different cooperating groups. Such studies, focusing on how objects mediate the relationship among different communities of practices, developed the concepts of "prototypes" [51], "intermediary objects" [9], "boundary negotiating artifacts" [30], boundary-object trimming [8] and boundary objects as punctuated crystallizations [31]. These studies have not only highlighted the functions of boundary objects in facilitating the crossing, pushing, and establishing of boundaries [30; p.333] and the role of objects in knowledge dynamics [9]; but they have also—and most relevantly—introduced the study of how boundary objects are created and used within information flows. In other words, they have discussed the processes by which such objects are made progressively intelligible to members of the receiving communities. We draw on such conceptualizations and put ourselves within the stream of research interested in the study of the creation and management of coordination artifacts for the understanding of plans as coordination mechanisms, focusing on the change and crystallization of artifacts in instable environments, instead of the processes involved in the standardization of their informational content. Among the studies quoted above, we find particularly inspiring Bossen et al.'s study [8] on boundary-object trimming in that it highlights the kind of articulation work necessary to "keep-on-course boundary-objects whose structural form and informational content need to be maintained and updated during their use" to ensure the smooth execution of work and stresses "the dynamic and directional aspects of work" (p.101).

ARTIFACTS AND WORK COORDINATION IN FLIGHT AND AIRPORT MANAGEMENT

Several studies investigated how coordination is achieved in the management of airport activities and flight execution since these activities are highly distributed in space and need to be coordinated in time following the trajectories [50] of the flights execution. The Lancaster group' s studies [among others 4.; 26; 27] strongly impacted the CSCW community for their focus on how to link the ethnographic study of the setting with the development of software design while other research provided insights into the functioning of the flight management and particularly how flight strips are used by air traffic controllers. Such studies investigated the coordinative functions of flight strips wondering how to replace the papered versions of flight strips by software [5; 6; 17; 25; 33; 34]. They highlighted different aspects of the flight strip use, such as their being aids to memory [33]; their supporting peripheral awareness among colleagues within the room [34]; their being the means by which flight scheduling is achieved when they are used in conjunction with other equipment, namely the radar and the radio connection with pilots [24]. Information provided by strips, radar and radio with the controllers' knowledge of the kind of reasons that might determine planes not being in the place indicated at the time indicated allow to foresee their position in the next future thus "solving the sequencing problem as a matter of moment-to-moment problem," more than as a matter of following procedurally defined rules [24; p. 142].

Other research projects [5; 17; 22; 23] focused on the use of boundary objects between the air traffic control and the flight control tower and between the airport control tower and other ground services. Halverson, [22] and Halverson and Ackerman [23] showed that artifacts work as intermediary objects when they recontextualize expert knowledge across organizational boundaries and work as memory aids in that they crystallize previous solutions to routine problems. Similarly, Berndtsson and Normark [5] analyzed the coordinative function of a closed-circuit television-system that transmits the view of the flight strip rack between adjacent sectors, such as the apron tower and the air traffic control centers. They noticed that such a system worked as an "awareness mediator" that supported coordination among services reducing the necessity to draw on other form of communication, such as telephone calls.

Last but not least, it is possible to identify studies that focused on the activities necessary to the execution of flights that occur on the ground [21; 54; 55]. Goodwin and Goodwin [21] showed that to see a plane in a manner that is relevant for the task at hand (i.e. to load baggage) it is necessary to situate it within organizational networks and that this is possible only drawing on an heterogeneous collection of technological artifacts and a social organization that allows the transformation of individual expertise into an element of the working culture of the operation room.

Suchman [54] studied the activity of the operators of an operations room who have to participate in the ground traffic control. She noticed that operators coordinate pilots and operators on the ramp by means of "embodied articulation" in that they craft messages and their timing to such stakeholders in different ways to achieve the orderly movement of planes given what video cameras allow them to see as regarding the movements of planes on the ground. Suchman [55] also showed how the interplay between the structure of the workplace, the assigned location of operators within the room and their interactions allow for the continuous transformation of restricted and public areas thus supporting both joint activities and different structure of attention among the operators. Another of Suchman's concerns was the understanding of how "prescriptive devices," such as airline schedules, operate [56; p.23]. She noticed that "any normative prescript requires, for its routine enactment, the management of inevitable contingencies of actual events." Schedules thus are both resources for the actors' organizing of their activities and regimes created elsewhere to which participants' activities are accountable [56; p.28]. We consider Suchman [56] and Harper and Hughes's [24] studies particularly relevant for the analysis of how the stand and gate allocation plan are set up and changed in that they face the problem of how prescriptive devices are enacted. We will refer to these papers in the following sections.

PLANS, PLANNING AND RE-PLANNING

To date, several CSCW scholars have focused on how plans and planning are used in work settings focusing alternately on planning as a process and plans as artifacts.

Highlighting that actions are inevitably situated in that they depend in essential ways upon the material and social circumstances of their occurrence, Suchman [53], recognized that the efficacy of plans inevitably depends on their relationship with the circumstances in which actions occur. Plans, in fact, cannot represent all the changing circumstances of their occurrence; thus, they should be considered "weak resources" for the execution of actions as their usefulness depends only on their bringing "past experience and projected outcome to bear on our present actions" [53; p. 185]. This implies that — in order to get the work done well, it is necessary to deviate from the plan.

Schmidt [43] strongly criticized Suchman's conceptualization of plans by demonstrating that plans might or might not determine our actions. The role of plans, in fact, depends on the extent to which it is possible to identify and model interdependencies in advance. In addition, he asserted that Suchman had underestimated the normative dimension of plans as constructs that provide criteria for whether or not a particular action is correctly executed [46; p. 366].

Bardram [1] suggested that plans could be conceptualized as planning—that is, a situated activity. Bardram's analysis of the daily clinical work showed that hospital patients' assistance draws on a socially constructed planning activity that is enhanced by and simultaneously shapes the work activities. As a result, plan implementation allows for the adjustment of the plan to the conditions of the specific situation. Bardram also identified the "anticipation of future ways of performing activities as the strength of plans" [1; p. 24].

Dourish [16; p. 52] highlighted the role of plans as "organizational accounting devices." Focusing on workflow technologies he examined how such technologies are taken to be effective for the coordination of work despite the fact that their pre-defined formal descriptions of working processes do not match with the improvised accomplishment of work [on this topic see, among others 52; 10]. In Dourish's opinion, workflows are so widespread because they do not act as mere coordination technologies, but instead as "organizational accounting devices"—that is, they render work activities "observable-and-reportable as being the activity they describe" [16; p. 55]. Said in other words: workflow helps explain work. Such a conceptualization of workflow permits them to be designed as systems that support the visualization of work thus overcoming the conceptualization of workflow as technologies that pre-specify work, in favour of their conceptualization as technologies that visualize the order of work.

Rönkkö et al. [41; p. 433] argued the necessity to study "the way plans become an accountable matter in organization activity" to understand how they help co-ordinate the development of work. They draw on Gerson and Star's s definition of "due process" [19], that sustained the necessity to study the articulation and coordination process around planning documentation to understand how inconsistencies that might arise in the accomplishment of work that formal description cannot fully anticipate and provide for, might be resolved.

Other researchers [7; 15] showed that plans do not themselves ensure that work is done in an orderly manner, but that such orderliness depends on everyday work. This means that efforts have to be made to deal with planned deadlines [8], to give significance to formal plans within the situated rationality of social actions [4] or to make sense of work [11].

Redaelli and Carassa [39; 40] instead focused on how a team sets up and modifies plans showing that plans might be set up so as to make the realization of the planned work activities feasible. If, in fact, plans might define deadlines in an inconsistent manner, they might also be designed and changed so as to promote the organizations' capability to deal with disruptions both at the level of work coordination and at the level of the maintenance of the organizational functioning on the whole.

On the other hand, Bardram and Hansen [3] investigated the relationship between plans and situated actions to understand how and why plans are changed. They suggested considering planning in hospitals as a continuous activity adjusted to the conditions of specific situations. Continuous planning is therefore necessary when it is impossible to anticipate every contingency that might arise in carrying out a series of tasks. Consequently, the distinction between the planning phase and the execution phase fades as planning never ends, even if it might be carried out following different priorities over time, such as the optimization for utilization during the planning phase and the optimization for performance during the execution phase. Similarly, Munkvold et al. [35] investigated the process of planning, showing that planning is a collective and ongoing achievement that needs to be supported as such even though this might be in detriment to the standardization of work practice that plans usually support.

In summary, plans have mainly been studied as "static artifacts" whose capacity to define in advance interdependencies at work can never be changed by the plan executors. CSCW studies have thus focused on how such artifacts are used by people who have to apply or realize them. As such, plans like checklists might be useful resources that help execute the planned activities or artifacts that might fail to adequately support courses of action if particular adaptive efforts devoted to match the plan content with the real situation are not made. When the focus of attention is instead on the process of planning rather than on plans as artifacts, planning is conceptualized as the adjustment to the concrete conditions of the context [3] and the relevance of plans as tools that might support the execution of action is minimized or even dismissed. In such cases, in fact, plans are conceptualized as trajectories that are the outcome of continual articulation work [35]. This undermines the possibility to study them as interdependent. Furthermore, the studies discussed thus far have been oriented to the study of such artifacts and processes in a disconnected manner from the other artifacts that inhabit the organizational settings. Only Rönkkö et al. [41] attempted to link the study of plans with other planning documents, showing that the members' reference to the project plan and the company-wide project models make it possible for people not to cease to orient to plans even as they change. Indeed, the combined use of such documents makes the project plan useful even when it does not work out as it contributes to the identification of deviations between the plan and the project's reality. However, a systematic attempt to understand how plans work as coordination mechanisms when used in combination with other artifacts is still missing. All this suggests that our understanding of plans might be incomplete.

RESEARCH SITE

The study was carried out in the ramp control tower (RCT) of an Italian airport where the operators plan the use of parking areas for aircrafts (i.e., the stands) to ensure a proper area will be available when planes arrive for the entire duration of handling activities on the ground. Such operators also plan the use of gates to ensure the availability of gates when boarding has to start and for the duration of passengers' boarding. Their planning activities not only play a key role in ensuring the orderly movements of planes on ground, but also ensures the orderly execution of flights in that they support the timely execution of the planes' assistance on the ground which is crucial for the execution of flights as scheduled. In particular, the stand and allocation plan work as coordination mechanisms in that they permit the convergence of personnel involved in assisting the plane on the ground (bus, fuelling, and towing truck drivers; ramp agents; utility workers for aircraft cleaning and luggage loading and unloading; drivers of follow-me trucks and of belt-loader vehicles) upon the planes' arrivals and the convergence of airport personnel and passengers at the gates.

The airport it is home to both passenger and cargo flights; thus it is active 24 hours a day meaning the RCT operators have to ensure the continuity of planning over time. They do this both by planning in advance twice a day and engaging in re-planning whenever necessary. The operators' advance planning consists of planning before the plan is executed. The operators match stands and gates with flights when the airline companies send them the rotation lists (i.e., documents in which scheduled flights are assigned to planes). This way, the RCT operators know how long each plane will stay on the ground between the execution of subsequent flights and can therefore allocate stands and gates as necessary. The operators' re-planning occurs during the plan's execution and it is devoted to compensating for changes in the execution of flights or in the rotation lists. As a result, the most frequent causes of changes to plans are flight delays or arrivals ahead of time, flight cancellations or the addition of charter flights, changes in the size of aircrafts used to carry out flights, or changes in the match between flights and planes.

The RCT operators match planes with stands by considering the size of the aircrafts and the technical features of stands. Planes have different and varied sizes while stands offer different features. Some of them allow for the self-maneuvering of aircraft while others do not, and sometimes the possibility for using certain stands depends on whether adjacent stands are in use or not as access to some stands overlap with other parking areas. In addition, stands offer different capacities and can be used to park aircrafts of various dimensions, up to their maximum capacity. Similarly, gates have different capacities and might allow for boarding solely by bus, solely on foot, or both. This implies that the RCT operators have to match flights with gates while also respecting the number of passengers to board and the security requirements that might involve boarding by bus for certain flights. In addition, some stands are structurally linked with gates; RCT operators have to take this into consideration when planning. Thus, the way stands and gates might be used depends on choices made when planning.

It is also worth considering that, during the last ten years, the airport has ensured a progressive increase in air transport movements and that low-cost companies provide the majority of flights hosted by the airport. As a result, the operators have to handle aircrafts on the ground while respecting short turnaround times. The stand allocation plan is set up using software available to the RCT that represents the stand plan in the form of a Gantt's chart for the occupation of stands over time. The operators drag and drop flight numbers from a list over to the Gantt's chart, where icons representing the length of planes' stay on ground appear. The software highlights potential conflicts in the stand allocation—namely, the mismatch between the dimension of the stand and those of the plane as well as the overlapping of allocations for each stand during both the plan setup and execution if changes in the execution of flights occur. The gate allocation plan is set up and printed once finished, without the support of any alarm system. As a result, the operators must pay attention to overlaps or mismatch in the use of gates.

The RCT operators work in an environment full of artifacts. As the image below shows, the operators have two workspaces at their disposal for the set up and change of the gate and stand allocation plans and for the coordination of all the ground activities connected with the departure and arrival of planes. The operators sit at their workstations where one of them manages incoming flights, while the other manages departures. Some tools are available to both operators, while others are not. Big windows in front of the operators' workspaces permit the direct view of most of the ramp and taxiway.

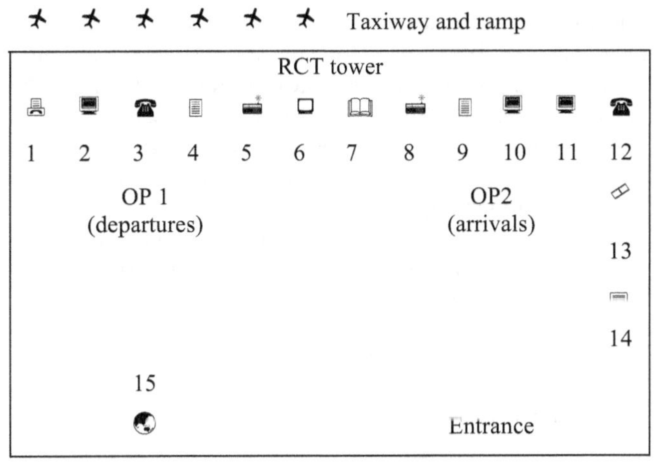

LEGEND

Operator's 1 workspace	**Operator's 2 workspace**
1 Telex	8 Radio
2 Computer	9 Stand allocation plan (paper version)
3 Telephone	10 Gate allocation plan (electronic version)
4 Gate allocation plan (paper version)	11 Computer
5 Radio	12 Telephone 13 Close circuit camera
Shared tools	
6 Strip rack	14 Printer
7 Block-notes	15 Airport map

Figure 1. Layout of the RCT

The RCT uses a closed-circuit system for the surveillance of the parking areas, a monitor showing the electronic strip-rack, and software for the allocation of stands and gates. The electronic strip rack offers various information on flights, such as the estimated block-off time (EOTB) and the calculated take-off time (CTOT) for departing flights, which allows the operator to know at what time the flight is scheduled to depart and at what time the plane will actually depart. The strip rack also provides information about flight status for incoming planes. Such statuses change from inactive to active, radar, and landed, corresponding with the plane's approach to the airport. The strip-rack also provides different evaluations of the estimated time of arrival (ETA) so that the closer the plane is to the airport, the more accurate and reliable the estimations of the arrival time are. Meanwhile, the software for the allocation of gates allows the operator to have an overview of the gate allocations and to monitor the number of passengers boarded for each flight. The data on the scheduled flights included in the system for the gate and stand allocation need to be manually updated when changes in the scheduled time or the numbers of planes occur. The airline companies send such information in the form of telex or e-mail messages to the operation room where the operators update the database information. RCT also uses a block-note that lists the messages that refer to daily occurrences, such as ongoing maintenance procedures at gates, stands and aircrafts; particular messages received by airline companies; to-do lists (i.e. messages to send or to receive) that the RCT operators progressively update. The operators might also consult documents glued on furniture that provide the list of gates and stands whose allocations need to be coupled; security protocols that specify which gates and stands can be used for extra-Schengen flights; a big map of the airport on the wall that provides information on the technical features of stands.

RESEARCH METHODS

The study is an ethno-methodologically oriented ethnography [14; 18; 38]. The objective of the data collection was the study of the operators' planning practices in allocating resources. We followed Llewellyn and Spence's [32] conceiving practices as members' phenomenon. Therefore, data collection was oriented to the identification of patterns of activities that are intersubjectively organized and recognized by operators as embodying (or not) a certain practice. Our main goal was to understand how RCT operators carry out such activities and how they make those activities "accountable" to others in order to understand how such artifacts contribute to the coordination of ground activities. We did this in accordance with the ethnomethodologically inspired studies of work that take as topic the study of work as "lived experience" [38]. Empirical materials were collected within the RCT where 18 people (12 males and 6 females, aged from 30 to 40) work. The majority of them started working in the airport ten years before the beginning of the research, while only two of them started working in the service more recently. Some of the operators are part of teams that define the organization of the ground activities, others in teaching professional courses, but each of them is equally able to manage the routine work in the RCT. The data collection was carried out by means of the direct observation of the operators' planning and re-planning activities. Data collection lasted eight months by spending at least two days a week in the service for a total amount of more than 500 hours. The operators were observed at different times of the day and night according to the operators' shifts to catch their planning and re-planning strategies during the occurrence of hourly, daily and seasonal variations. After one month the direct observation was accompanied by the audio-recordings of naturally occurring conversations. Due to security requirements, we were not allowed to videotape and take pictures of work activities. This, of course, makes the fine-grained analysis of how discourses relate with activities as, for example, Nevile [36] did studying the flight execution, impossible. Detailed notes were taken regarding the activities carried out by the operators and were linked with the discourses that occurred during their execution and we made drawings to fix the layout of tools and documents.

Field notes and the majority of the recorded conversations were transcribed for a total amount of 223 pages of field notes and 197 pages of transcripts. We decided to transcribe all conversations occurring between the operators during planning and re-planning, but not all the ones with pilots, who transmit data regarding the kind of maintenance planes need once on the ground, and the operators on the ramp with whom they talk about the execution of ground activities. We transcribed conversations drawing on a modified orthography (see the table 1) that allowed for us to keep track of the "sounds as uttered" [57] to catch the operators' inferential work that emerges in lexical choices, in the way words and utterances are produced and sequentially organized. But it is worth specifying that we decided to use the standard numeric symbols for the representation of numbers to make the reading and the analysis of transcripts easier. Transcripts of conversations are presented here following Jordan's [28] presentation of the ethnographic study conducted at the San Jose international Airport [12] to show the relationship between discourses and actions. We also carried out 47 unstructured ethnographic interviews [47] while observing the operators' setting up and changing the plans. The questions were devoted to the understanding of how the operators realized the necessity to change the plans, of how they reached a solution to re-allocation problems and to the identification of the strategies they usually adopt for the plans setup. The interviews thus were carried out at the workplace making it possible to discuss the features and functions of artifacts. We interviewed all the operators with the exception of one who refused to be interviewed and audio-recorded. Field notes were verified with participants and the analysis of data was carried out triangulating all collected empirical materials. The empirical materials presented here were selected to highlight the issue of how the plans capacity to anticipate interdependencies is maintained despite contingencies that might arise in carrying out a series of tasks so as to help the coordination and development of work.

PLANNING AND RE-PLANNING IN THE APRON TOWER

As previously explained, both the stand and gate allocation plans are coordination mechanisms. The stand and gate allocation plans are sent to all personnel involved in providing plane assistance on the ground and to the airport's personnel to ensure the convergence of ground personnel at stands and of airport personnel and passengers at gates. This means that changes in such plans might create disruptions in the execution of airport activities. But plans also have to compensate for changes in the execution of flights or in the airlines' efforts to match planes and flights. The RCT operators who work to match the airport with the flight activities are bound to deal with conflicting exigencies; plans are at the interface of such a tension between stability and flexibility. This is why we focused on how the operators set up and modify plans.

Planning Practices and the Anticipation of Events

Planning for the Likely Case Scenario and Preventing Delays

As Suchman noticed [56], the RCT operators are oriented to achieving a normal order of on-time arrivals and departures as prescribed by the flight schedule. They participate in the achievement of such a goal by means of planning the allocation of stands and gates. Using Suchman's words [56; p. 27], like other operators involved in the flight execution [24], they work "to maintain a consistent relationship between an order of events prescribed via the schedule and events at the local site." They do this by means of precise planning and re-planning practices. The RCT operators, in fact, are able to anticipate the occurrence of some events on the basis of their knowledge of "how things usually go." As a consequence, they are able to plan so as to provide resources to compensate for changes in the flight execution and to ensure the execution of the ground activities as planned.

The interviews indicated that RCT operators, unlike what Bardram and Hansen noted [3], do not plan based on the best-case scenario (i.e., all flights will be carried out as scheduled), but rather on the basis of their knowledge of how flights are usually executed. Thus, for example the operators set up the stand allocation plan, ensuring the availability of slack space, i.e. at least one free stand on the ramp, and of slack time between subsequent flights to compensate for changes in the number or timetable of flights. But the RCT operators not only plan to adapt to likely-to-occur changes in the execution of flights. In fact, they, on the basis of their knowledge of how planning the use of stands and gates impact on the timely execution of the ground activities, also plan so as to prevent the occurrence of delays in the execution of flights thus contributing to their execution as planned. They do this planning to ensure the timely execution of the handling activities—that is, by planning to avoid delays in the execution of boarding, favouring the exchanges of crews and allocating planes in order to avoid bottleneck situations. The operators avoid delays in the execution of boarding by maximizing the use of stands that allow the boarding and disembarkation on foot and matching the gate dimensions with the number of passengers to board.

All of us here know that you have to exploit at maximum the stands that allow boarding and disembarkation on foot so we do not need to use busses and such procedures are carried out quicker than by bus. So, for example I assign the flights that depart first in the morning to those stands so that they will be free for subsequent flights. If I put there flights that depart late in the morning, then I block their use (Track 5 10/07/2011).

With the Sxxair we have to start boarding a long time before the flight departure, so you need the space to place the passengers in; otherwise, you board 6 passengers and then you have to stop. This way, you do not gain time. So we have to avoid assigning crowded flights to gates that have a small fingers (Track 36 10/25/2011).

The operators also plan in such a way to shorten the time necessary to exchange crews (i.e., move from one plane to another one).

When looking at the rotation lists and we detect an aircraft change, we try to put the two planes next to each other so the crew will not take a long time to move from one plane to the other one. You know, the low cost companies do not provide vehicles for the crews to move on the ground, so if we do not do this it might take a long time for them to walk from one side of the ramp to the opposite one, increasing the risk of a delay in the flight departure (Track 14 10/07/2011).

Moreover, the operators allocate planes and gates so as to avoid overlaps in the aircrafts' and passengers' movement on ground.

This is another thing you have to keep in mind. If I assign the plane that departs first in the morning to the gate 16 instead of 14, I risk having to stop the boarding for stand 14 if the plane at stand 16 is ready to go. Stand 16, in fact, is a self-manoeuvring and its exit way overlaps the path passengers use to reach stand 14 (Track 14 10/07/2011).

If we cannot avoid using the stand 24, we put there the flight that departs first because this stand has to be free as soon as possible. It is a pushback stand and it is on the exit way of all these other self-manoeuvring stands. So if it is not free, we have to push back all the flights that, as a consequence, cannot leave the stands in self-manoeuvring so we risk causing delays because we have few pushback tractors and we have to push all those planes that, early in the morning, depart almost at the same time (Track 37 10/14/2011).

Such planning practices contribute to the execution of flights as planned in a significant way, even though they are not enough to compensate for changes in the flight execution. The RCT operators are therefore forced to engage in re-planning.

Re-planning Practices and the Anticipation of Events

Planning and re-planning are different activities in that during planning the RCT operators can repeatedly change the allocations until they are satisfied—that is, until they think that the plans allow for the optimization of the use of airport resources and the orderly movement of planes on the ground.

First, I assign stands to be sure that flights fit in them; then I cancel everything and I start assigning the crowded flights with the gates that allow boarding on foot, and I put the international flights on the other side next to the gates dedicated to international flights (Track 37 10/1472011).

In this way, the operators make the plans resistant to changes thus reducing the need to re-plan, which is a costly activity for planners who have to re-plan while executing other activities. Moreover, changes in the allocation of stands and gates might disrupt airport activities because, for example, passengers have to move from one gate to another; and airport operators have to make additional efforts to re-coordinate their activities according to the change. In addition, during re-planning, it is more difficult to change plans while ensuring the optimization of resources in that they do not have the possibility to use whatever stand or gate, but only those not in use at that moment or in the near future. Yet, changes to the plans cannot always be avoided. Thus the operators have to recognize the necessity to change plans and decide how to change them in advance so as to ensure the smooth execution of flights and ground activities. The RCT operators do this according to shared discursive practices and the use of artifacts as emerging from the analysis of the naturally occurring conversations between them. The transcripts analyzed here are translated from Italian. The following fragments represent routine talk within the RCT.

Transcription conventions	
.	Falling intonation
?	Rising intonation
,	Flat or slightly rising intonation, talk which sounds incomplete
(2.0), (0.5)	Silence measured in seconds and tenths of seconds
word_word	Bounded words
(xx)	Incomprehensible talk
[writing]	Description of actions occurring during the talk
Pronunciation of numbers	
1	One
9 8 7 5	Nine eight seven five
12	Twelve
References of numbers	
9 8 7 5	Flight number
12	Stand number
11	Gate number
21	Time (hours and minutes)

Table 1: Transcription conventions

In the following transcript one of the two operators detects the necessity to change the stand and allocation plans and involves the colleague in the solution of the re-allocation problem.

Extract 1 (Track 18 11/25/2011)

1. FRANK It's too narrow for us here with the **4 7 0 6**

[Looking at the stand allocation plan (electronic version)]

2. TINA Even there?

[Inserting data into the database]

3. FRANK It's at 16. **4 8 8 6, 4 7 0 7** is it already there?

[Looking at the stand allocation plan (electronic version)]

4. TINA *18* and *22* but it's inactive

[Looking at the strip rack]

5. FRANK The **4 8 8 6** is already on ground the **4 8 8 5**

[Looking at the stand allocation plan (electronic version)]

6. TINA Yes_yes. The **4 7 0 7** is arriving *10* minutes ahead of time at 16

[Looking at the strip rack]

7. FRANK Okay. Let's see, Tina, let's see

[Looking at the stand allocation plan (electronic version)]

8. TINA Can we switch them with another flight?

[Looking at Frank]

9. FRANK Not here, they're all full. 14 18 it should go at 13. Shall we change the gate immediately and put it at 13? It leaves at *19* and *50*. Can we take it easy? Let's change it

[Looking at the stand allocation plan (electronic version)]

10. TINA We can wait until it goes on radar and then we'll decide

[Looking at Frank]

11. FRANK Okay, let's wait until it goes radar and then we'll decide

[Looking at Tina]

12. TINA Okay

[(any record)]

13. FRANK But the 13 is free. Let's check for another gate. Mh (13.0)

[Looking at the software (opening the manager of gate allocation)]

14. TINA *14, 15*

[Looking at the gate allocation plan]

15. FRANK No there is also the *19*

[Looking at the software (manager of gate allocation)]

16. TINA But if the passengers are already at the gate it'll be a mess moving them

[Looking at Frank]

17. FRANK *16* they're already there, you are right, then *15*

[Looking at the software (manager of gate allocation)]

18. TINA *15* is the closest

[(any record)]

19. FRANK *15* is the closest. So in the end we'll change it

[(any record)]

Does a Contingency Matter?

As explained above, the stand and gate allocation plans are set up to ensure the availability of slack space and time so as to compensate for changes in the flight execution. This means that not all the contingencies require changes to the plans. The RCT operators detect the necessity to change the stand allocation plan in that its representation as a Gannt's chart allows for the detection of the shortening of the slack time between subsequent flights even before the activation of the alarm color code in that such a representation shows time in terms of space (extract 1, turn 1).

Assessing a Viable Solution

Once the operators detect the necessity to change the plans, they have to find a viable solution to the re-allocation problem. They re-allocate stands by both looking at the stand allocation plan and at the representation of the strip rack. This way, in fact, they are able to identify the free stands at disposal (extract 1, turns 5 and 9) and to assess which planes might be moved from their original allocations. Planes that are already on ground might be moved but this is a time consuming activity whose occurrence interferes with the movement of planes on the taxiway. This is the reason why the operators solve re-allocation problems by changing the allocation of flights that are going to arrive. They select the plane to move on the basis of the distance of the aircraft from the airport. Usually the farthest, the better in that it is unlikely that the re-allocation negatively impacts the execution of' ground activities. The operators assess the planes positions looking at the strip rack and in particular focusing on the status of flights (extract 1, turn 4). Inactive flights are the farthest while the radar flights are the closest to the ground.

To Re-plan or not to Re-plan?

Drawing on the information provided by the strip rack the RCT operators can also decide to postpone the change to the plan up to the achievement of more reliable information about the time of arrival of planes (extract 1, turns 9, 10, 11). Usually, in fact, the estimations of the arrival time change with the plane approaching the airport thus making the re-allocation no longer necessary. The operators, in fact, might decide to use the slack time between subsequent flights to compensate for changes in the scheduled flight time. To do this safely they check the strip-rack for the estimations of the arrival time that are more and more accurate with the time passing. In addition they might use the statuses of flights as deadlines along which to organize their re-planning activity (extract 1, turn 11). Changing the flight status from "inactive" to "radar" is a means to balance the RCT operators' concern of preserving the plan as it was set up as much as possible with the necessity to inform the operator on ground in time to avoid disruptions in the execution of ground activities. In particular the RCT operators consider "inactive flights" as sort of mere hypothesis of how thing will go, while they consider the status "radar" as highly reliable and as fixing the optimal deadline for re-planning. The status "radar" occurring 30 minutes before the arrival of the plane permits the change of plans and the re-coordination of ground activities.

Re-allocating Gates

Once the RCT operators have re-allocated stands, they re-allocate gates if necessary. Similarly with the gate re-allocation, they need to know the location of passengers (already at the gate or not) in order to find the less disruptive solution. They can monitor the passengers' position looking at the software at their disposal for the allocation of gates. They, in fact, can check the foreseen time of boarding to assess the presence of passengers at the gate and, on the basis of their knowledge of the airport structure and of the stands available at that moment, decide which is the less disruptive solution in the given circumstances (extract 1, turns 16, 17).

Departing Flight

The use of artifacts not only supports re-allocation when incoming flights change their scheduled times, but also supports the identification of delays in planes leaving the stands. As the extract 2 shows, Freddy asked the colleague to check whether they might have problems at stand 31 since the plane is next to land and the plane previously assigned to that stand is still on ground. It, in fact, is on the strip rack but not ready for departure.

Extract 2 (Track 66 11/04/2011)

1. FREDDY Check the 31, does it fit?

[Looking at strip rack]

2. MARK Maybe let's say maybe

[Looking at the stand allocation plan (electronic version)]

3. FREDDY Maybe? (10.0) let's put this on ice

[Looking at Mark]

4. MARK If it fits ok otherwise I see that there is the yellow air at 9 that we could put at 7 that is beside. The red air (XX) is going to leave first, isn't it? it is still sixty

[Looking at the software (boarding page surveillance)]

The colleague shares with the colleague the developed back-up plan. He thinks that it is possible to use the stand 7 since the plane at that stand is going to leave. That plane, in fact, arrived ahead of time thus permitting the timely beginning of boarding procedure. Mark is saying that the plane is going to leave because, looking at the boarding page surveillance he notices that only 60 passengers have yet to be to boarded.

Tidying the Plans

Extract 3 (Track 37 11/09/2011)

1. ALAN The Stansted is bothering me. In any case there is a stand free

[Looking at the strip rack]

2. TINA A stand free?

[Looking at the stand allocation plan (electronic version)]

3. ALAN My 13 is free

[Looking at the stand allocation plan (paper version)]

4. TINA Because there is 28 to move to 13. That won't do there, we have to use 13 or we should move this one down. Oh no this is 14. This one? No because it is the first one to leave. Can't we put something there? This one? Let's move this Stansted. Oh no we can't. Guess what we can do? Move this one and this down there

[Moving the cursor on the stand allocation plan (electronic version)]

5. ALAN In fact I was moving it to 14, if possible

[Looking at Tina]

6. TINA Yes but what do you care? Oh yes let's have the disembarkation, let's do that. But at what time does that one leave though? *20* and *40*. And this will arrive at? *20* and *45*, no I cannot. No, why is that? Yes it fits. Okay let's put the **4 1 9 7** at 14. Then here at 13 we can put another flight. Let' s see. Otherwise we could have moved this one up and the other one down, you see? We could have put this one down and moved this one

[Moving the cursor on the stand allocation plan (electronic version)]

When re-planning, the RCT operators try to optimize the use of airport resources and to maintain the possibility of changing plans over time as much as possible. This means that very often for the operators the simplest solution—finding a free stand for an unexpected plane—is not the best solution even though this means to change several allocations to solve a single re-allocation problem (extract 3, turns 4, 6). In addition, due to the possibility to change the plans, optimizations in the use of airport resources impossible during its set up might become viable in the course of the day. Again the use of the representations of plans and of the strip rack plays a key role in such processes. In other words, the operators always "tidy up" the plans to maintain them as optimal working tools for themselves and next colleagues.

Extract 4 (Track 1 11/25/2011)

1. FRANK I'm moving the **8 7 8 6** that was at 14 to 13

[Changing the stand allocation plan (electronic version)]

2. LISA But

[Looking at the stand allocation plan (papered version)]

3. FRANK What?

[(any record)]

4. LISA This other one swaps. Cannot we put this one closer to the16? (XX) The crew that has to board on the 12 now is at 15 and then at 22 but now we have space here

[Looking at the stand allocation plan (papered version) and then pointing at the stand allocation plan (electronic version)]

5. FRANK At 12 well done

[Looking at the stand allocation plan (electronic version)]

6. LISA At 13

[(any record)]

7. FRANK Wait isn't it already at 13?

[Looking at the stand allocation plan (electronic version)]

8. LISA No here it is written at 11. It's departing as **4 5 6 1**

[Looking at the stand allocation plan (paper version)]

The papered and electronic version of the stand allocation plan, in fact, representing the changes in the plan at different speed (the electronic version is updated as new data are received and inserted into the system, while the papered version is updated by the operators at any re-allocation) permit both an overview of the decisions made during planning (the papered version) and an image of events in real time (the electronic version) thus allowing the review of the plan and therefore the identification of areas of improvement that re-allocation have made possible (extract 4, turn 4). Different representations of the stand allocation plans allow for the evaluation of whether pre-planned solution are still good enough and to crosscheck whether "first glance sound solutions" are feasible or not thus avoiding mistakes in the re-allocation of stands (extract 4, turn 8).

DISCUSSION

The RCT operators' work, similarly to the work of other operators involved in flight execution, is bound by the requirements of the flight plan. Other researchers [24; 56] have highlighted the kinds of efforts that operators have to accomplish to execute the flight plan despite the occurrence of inevitable contingent events to enact the plan. Our work does the same, focusing on the relationship between the coordination of ground activities and the execution of flight schedules as well as on the role of plans in such a process. It shows that the stand and gate allocation plans not only are supposed to not only compensate for changes in the execution of flights, but also promote the execution of flights as expected. They reach this objective thanks to both to planning and re-planning practices that draw on different principles. Planning is developed based on the implementation of preferred scenarios, such as the movement of aircrafts on ground, while re-planning is implemented based of "what-if scenarios"—that is, the evaluation of possible consequences determined by the change of the plan. Yet despite these differences, both planning and re-planning are oriented to the anticipation of the courses of events. Anticipation in the planning phase draws on the operators' local knowledge [37] of how flight schedules are changed and how ground activities are executed. Anticipation is characterized by two elements: It is oriented to ensuring slack resources with which to deal with contingencies (at least a certain amount of them) and to the prevention of disruptions in the execution of the planned activities. Re-planning, instead, anticipates events successfully because it is carried out based on the basis of the detection of the necessity to re-plan in advance; it is oriented to the identification of successful solutions to emergent problems and it is carried out in a timely manner in terms of the execution of the ground activities it coordinates. Such activities are possible in that RCT operators can use a set of tools to support their execution. It is worth noting is that the majority of such tools are not designed to support re-planning, but to monitor the flight execution. Nevertheless, the RCT operators use the information provided by such tools and transform them into information useful for re-planning purposes. In particular, RCT operators transform data provided by the equipment in terms of changes in the timetable of scheduled flights into data regarding the position of planes. Similarly, they exploit instruments developed to control the ground activities (i.e., the CCC) and the functions provided by the software system for gate allocation to assess the position of passengers. In this way, they determine the availability of stands and gates and identify the elements on which it is possible to act so as to solve contingent problems. In addition, the operators use the information regarding flight status to fix the timing of re-planning, thereby reducing the occurrences of re-planning and avoiding disruptions in the execution of the re-planned activities. Last but not least, the different representations of the same plan support the recursive optimization of the use of airport resources and the maintenance of the possibility to change the plan over time despite the recurring changes to its content that, in turn, ensure the reliability of the plans. This means that the successful use of the stand and gate allocation plans depends on the combined use of artifacts and the deployment of local knowledge coupled with the constant monitoring of the execution of the flight plan.

Anticipation is recognized as one of the features of plans supporting coordination, but researchers still need to understand how anticipation for planning purposes is achieved in changing environments. Anticipation has also been seen as the "Achilles' heel" of plans in that they cannot foresee all contingencies ahead of time. Thus, when several changes occur, plans cannot do anything else but fail to support the execution of course of actions. Our data instead show that anticipation can be an emergent, distributed and artifact-mediated activity that, at the same time, does not undermine the possibility to determine the action of its users—namely, the RCT operators and the ground personnel. Anticipating events in the RCT is a complex set of interrelated planning and re-planning practices supported by the use of a composite set of tools. This means that anticipation emerges as the outcome of complex interconnections established by RCT operators to interrelate specific objects and practices to ensure order at work. RCT operators' combined use of specialized coordinative artifacts is instrumental in maintaining anticipation. As a result, even if plans in the RCT change, they never cease to ensure stability in the coordination of complex work activities and they never cease to be used to pre-compute interdependencies during the allocation of stands and gates. Thus, anticipation even if depending on the use of different tools, essentially draws on the use of the representations of plans.

Our study suggests that the understanding of how plans can maintain their capability to anticipate events in changing environments is possible by taking a precise analytical stance. Indeed, when we extend the analytical focus over the study of the specific purposes, plans serve to encompass the understanding of the relationship they have with all the artifacts that support the orderly accomplishment of work; thus, we can understand how plans are kept on track despite the changes that might occur in the work conditions.

This is the reason why we think that we should conceptualize the study of plans as part of ordering systems [44]—that is, clusters of artifacts and practices necessary to ensure order at work. In our case, this refers to the tools and practices necessary to coordinate the execution of flights with the accomplishment of ground activities. When we adopt such a perspective, we might understand not only how consistency is maintained across distributed and interdependent activities, such as the flight execution and ground activities but also how ordering systems might support the maintenance of one of the artifacts of the cluster. We are mulling over efforts to keep the plans on track by using the term "coordination-artifact suiting."

We know that our definition of the kind of work necessary to prevent the deterioration of plans might be understood as echoing the concept of "boundary-object trimming" developed by Bossen et al. [8], but we contend that these concepts are radically different. Bossen et al.' s study, like ours, involved a group whose core task is the articulation work necessary to keep an artifact on course, and coined the term "boundary-object trimming" to address the kind of articulation work necessary for the maintenance of a boundary object. The term "coordination-artifact suiting" instead refers to both the participants' articulation work and the broader "artifact's landscape" in which single artifacts are included for the dynamic maintenance of artifacts. In addition, the term "coordination-artifacts suiting" refers to the prevention of artifacts going off use, while the concept "boundary-object trimming" refers to the activities necessary to maintain optimal working tools which according to Bossen et al. includes their orderly completion and registration.

We contend that the concept of "coordination-artifact suiting" can be as used a descriptive and a heuristic concept. In fact, the term "coordination-artifact suiting" can be used to describe all the cases in which ensembles of coordinative artifacts and practices are functional to the dynamic maintenance of one or more coordination mechanisms belonging to a cluster. It can also work as a sensitizing concept in that it carries a precise methodological insight—namely, that the understanding of how coordination artifacts are updated when their information content needs to be changed during their use might require expanding the analytical focus beyond the study of a single artifact.

CONCLUSION

Our data suggest that anticipation, which plays a key function in the coordination of work and is often crystallized in plans, needs to be studied by focusing on the set of coordinating artifacts that always inhabit complex work settings. In this way, the utility of plans might be understood even when they need to be changed throughout the day. Contrary to the results of studies by Bardram and Hansen [3] and Munkvold et al. [35], our data indicate that the reference to artifacts remains the basis of the possibility to progressively pre-compute interdependencies during both the planning and re-planning phases when the dynamic anticipation of events is possible. Our findings thus suggest the need to distinguish between cases in which continuous planning is associated with the possibility to anticipate events for all practical purposes from the cases in which this is not possible as it requires approaching software design in different ways. Indeed, our findings, even if not oriented to the development of software, open the question on how to design software to support anticipation as a cooperative and mediated activity. The study of plans as articulation artifacts that have highlighted the need to support users' possibility to skip the prescriptions of the plan and monitor such deviations [1; 3; 42] cannot be applied to support RCT operators' activities as planning in the RCT depends on the use of several tools. Thus software should be designed not to produce a single workflow system, but to make planning and re-planning possible by distributing meta-content over a cluster of technologies to permit the transformation of the information provided for planning purposes. We recognize that "awareness technologies," such as the strip rack, the software for the gate allocation and boarding monitoring and the CCC, thereby affording information regarding work activities carried out in related and distributed settings (on the ground and in the flight control tower), play a key role in the operators' capability to anticipate events. However, they are not enough. All the information about the timing of events and positions of stakeholders is useless if not transformed into information about the possibility to act upon objects and persons to solve allocation problems. Distributing affordances [20] such as alarm systems over several tools based on the recurrent patterns of planning and re-planning, as highlighted in the previous sections, might help operators both compute interdependencies and display aspects of their activities of relevance for colleagues. In this way, operators might be adequately supported in the identification of the need to revise the plans, in developing provisional solutions and identifying them as such, in assessing the timing of re-planning, and in evaluating the appropriateness of solutions to allocation problems as necessary to address slack resources and to prevent delays during both the planning and re-planning phases.

We think that the concept of "coordination-artifact suiting" helps CSCW scholars understand the interplay of work practices and the use of tools for the dynamic change of artifacts' information content, and we hope that other CSCW scholars will try out our insights.

ACKNOWLEDGMENTS

We thank all the reviewers for their valuable comments on earlier versions of this paper and Dave Randall for stimulating discussions and feedback on early thought.

REFERENCES

1. Bardram J. E. Plans as situated action: an activity theory approach to workflow systems. In *Proc. ECSCW 1997,* Kluwer Academic, (1997), 17-34.
2. Bardram, J. E., Bossen, C. A web of coordinative artifacts: collaborative work at a hospital ward. In *Proc. SIGGROUP 2005,* ACM Press (2005), 168-176.
3. Bardram, J. E., Hansen, T. R. Why the plan doesn't hold: a study of situated planning, articulation and coordination work in a surgical ward. In *Proc. CSCW 2010,* ACM Press (2010), 331-340.
4. Bentley, R., Hughes, J. A., Randall, D., Rodden, T., Shapiro, D., Sommerville I. Ethnographically-informed systems design for air traffic control. *Proc. CSCW,* ACM (1992), 123-129.
5. Berndtsson, J., Normark, M. The coordinative functions of flight strips: air traffic control work revisited. In *Proc. SIGGROUP 1999,* ACM Press (1999), 101-110.

6. Berndtsson, J., & Normark, M. *Coordination in Air Traffic Control.* Internal report, Center for Tele-Information, Technical University of Denmark, Lyngby, Denmark (1999).
7. Bossen C, Markussen R. Infrastructuring and ordering devices in health care: medication plans and practices on a hospital ward. *Computer Supported Cooperative Work* 19,6 (2010), 615–637.
8. Bossen, C., Jensen, L. G., Udsen, F. W. Boundary-Object Trimming: On the Invisibility of Medical Secretaries' Care of Records in Healthcare Infrastructures. *Computer Supported Cooperative Work 23,*1 (2014), 75-110.
9. Boujut, J. F., Blanco, E. Intermediary objects as a means to foster co-operation in engineering design. *Computer Supported Cooperative Work 12,* 2 (2003), 205-219.
10. Bowers, J., Button, G., Sharrock, W. Workflow from within and without: technology and cooperative work on the print industry shopfloor. In *Proc. ECSCW'95,* Springer (1995), 51-66.
11. Bowker, G. C., Star, S. L. *Sorting things out: Classification and its consequences.* MIT press (1999).
12. Brun-Cottan, F., Forbes, K., Goodwin, C., Goodwin, M., Jordan, B., Suchman, L., & Trigg, R. H. The workplace project: Designing for diversity and change (Videotape). *Xerox Palo Alto Research Center, 3333* (1991).
13. Button, G., Sharrock, W. The organizational accountability of technological work. *Social Studies of Science 28,*1 (1998), 73-102.
14. Carassa, A. La conoscenza entra in azione. In: Mantovani G. (ed) *Ergonomia.* Il Mulino, Bologna (2000), 123–150.
15. Dant, T., Francis, D. Planning in Organisations: Rational Control or Contingent Activity?' *Sociological Research Online* 3, 2 (1998), http://www.socresonline.org.uk/3/2/4.html.
16. Dourish, P. Process descriptions as organizational accounting devices: the dual use of workflow technologies. In *Proc. SIGGROUP 2001,* ACM Press (2001), 52-60.
17. Fields, B., Amaldi, P., Tassi, A. Representing collaborative work: the airport as common information space. *Cognition, Technology & Work 7,* 2 (2005), 119-133.
18. Garfinkel, H. *Studies in ethnomethodology.* Prentice Hall, Englewood Cliffs (NJ) (1967).
19. Gerson, E. M., Star, S. L. Analyzing due process in the workplace. *Transactions on Information Systems (TOIS), 4,* 3 (1986), 257-270.
20. Gibson, J. J. *The ecological approach to visual perception.* Lawrence Erlbaum Associates, New Jersey (1979).
21. Goodwin, C., Goodwin, M. H. Seeing as situated activity: Formulating planes. In Engeström, Y., Middleton, D. (eds) *Cognition and communication at work.* Cambridge University Press, Cambridge, (1998), 61-95.
22. Halverson, C. A. Traffic management in air control: Collaborative management in real time. *ACM SIGOIS Bulletin, 15,* 2 (1994), 7-11.
23. Halverson, C. A., Ackerman, M. S. Yeah, the Rush ain't here yet-Take a break: Creation and use of an artifact as organizational memory. In *Proc. Annual Hawaii International Conference,* IEEE (2003),10 pp.
24. Harper, R. H., Hughes, J. A. What a F-ing System! Send 'em All to the Same Place and Then Expect Us to Stop 'em Hitting. Making Technology Work in Air Traffic Control. In (ed) Button, G. *Technology in Working Order.* Routledge, London, (1993), 127-144.
25. Harper, R. R., Hughes, J. A., Shapiro D. Z. "Harmonious working and CSCW: Computer Technology and Air Traffic Control." *Studies in Computer Supported Cooperative Work.* North-Holland Publishing Co. (1990).
26. Hughes, J. A., Randall, D., Shapiro, D. Faltering from ethnography to design. *Proc. CSCW,* ACM (1992), 115-122.
27. Hughes, J. A., King, V., Rodden, T., Andersen, H. Moving out from the control room: Ethnography in system design. *Proc. CSCW,* ACM (1994).
28. Jordan, B. Technology and social interaction: Notes on the achievement of authoritative knowledge in complex settings. *Talent Development & Excellence 6,1* (1992), 95-132.
29. Koskinen, I. Plans, Evaluation, and Accountability at the Workplace. *Sociological Research Online* 4, 4 (2000) http://www.socresonline.org.uk/4/4/koskinen.html.
30. Lee, C. P. Boundary negotiating artifacts: Unbinding the routine of boundary objects and embracing chaos in collaborative work. *Computer Supported Cooperative Work 16,* 3(2007), 307-339.
31. Lutters, W. G., Ackerman, M. S. Beyond boundary objects: collaborative reuse in aircraft technical support. *Computer Supported Cooperative Work 16,*3 (2007), 341-372.

32. Llewellyn, N., Spence, L. Practice as a members' phenomenon. *Organization Studies 30*,12 (2009), 1419-1439.

33. Mackay, W. E., Fayard, A. L., Frobert, L., Médini, L. Reinventing the familiar: exploring an augmented reality design space for air traffic control. In *Proc. SIGCHI 1998*, ACM Press (1998), 558-565.

34. MacKay, W. E. Is paper safer? The role of paper flight strips in air traffic control. *ACM Transactions on Computer-Human Interaction (TOCHI)*, *6*, 4 (1999), 311-340.

35. Munkvold, G., Ellingsen, G., Monteiro, E. From plans to planning: the case of nurse care plans. In *Proc. CSCW 2007,* ACM Press (2007), 21-30.

36. Nevile, M. *Beyond the black box: Talk-in-interaction in the airline cockpit.* Ashgate Pub Ltd, (2004).

37. Randall, D., O'Brien, J., Rouncefield, M., Hughes, J.A.Organizational Memory and CSCW: Supporting the 'Mavis' Phenomenon. In Grundy, J., Apperley, M. (eds.) *Proc. HCI (OzCHI '96*), IEEE (1996), 26-35.

38. Randall, D., Harper, R., Rouncefield, M. *Fieldwork for design.* Springer, London (2007).

39. Redaelli, I., Carassa, A. Temporality in planning: the case of the allocation of parking areas for aircrafts. In: *Proc. ECSCW 2013*, Springer (2013), 45–62.

40. Redaelli, I, Carassa, A. Reconsidering the Role of Plans and Planning in the Management of the Unexpected. In: Proc. COOP 2014, Springer (2014).

41. Rönkkö, K., Dittrich, Y., & Randall, D. When plans do not work out: How plans are used in software development projects. *Computer Supported Cooperative Work 14,*5 (2005), 433-468.

42. Schmidt, K., Simone, C. Coordination mechanisms: Towards a conceptual foundation of CSCW systems design. *Computer Supported Cooperative Work 5,*2-3 (1996),155-200.

43. Schmidt, K. Of maps and scripts: The status of formal constructs in cooperative work. *Information and software technology 41,*6 (1999), 319-329.

44. Schmidt, K., Wagner, I. Ordering systems: Coordinative practices and artifacts in architectural design and planning. *Computer Supported Cooperative Work 13,*5-6 (2004), 349-408.

45. Schmidt, K. Cooperative work and coordinative practices. In Schmidt, K. (ed) *Cooperative Work and Coordinative Practices*. Springer, London, (2011) 3–27.

46. Schmidt, K. Frail foundations. In Schmidt, K. (ed) *Cooperative Work and Coordinative Practices.* Springer, London, (2011), 359–389.

47. Sherman, Heyl, B. Ethnographic interviewing. In P. Atkinson, A. Coffey, S. Delamont, J. Lofland, L. Lofland (eds) *Handbook of ethnography*, Sage, London, (2001), 369-383.

48. Star, S. L. This is not a boundary object: Reflections on the origin of a concept. *Science, Technology & Human Values*, *35*,5 (2010), 601-617.

49. Strauss, A. Work and the division of labor. *The Sociological Quarterly*, *26,*1, (1985), 1-19.

50. Strauss, A. L., Fagerhaugh, S. Y. *Social organization of medical work.* Transaction Publisher (1997).

51. Subrahmanian, E., Monarch, I., Konda, S., Granger, H., Milliken, R., & Westerberg, A. Boundary objects and prototypes at the interfaces of engineering design. *Computer Supported Cooperative Work 12,*2 (2003), 185-203.

52. Suchman, L. A. Office procedure as practical action: models of work and system design. *ACM Transactions on Information Systems (TOIS)*, 1, 4 (1983), 320-328.

53. Suchman, L. A. *Plans and situated actions: the problem of human-machine communication.* Cambridge University Press, New York (1987).

54. Suchman, L. Supporting articulation work. In (ed) Kling, R. *Computerization and controversy: Value Conflicts and Social Choices*, *2* Academic Press (1996), 407-423.

55. Suchman, L. (1996). Constituting shared workspaces. In Engeström, Y., Middleton, D. (eds) *Cognition and communication at work.* Cambridge University Press, Cambridge (1998), 35-60.

56. Suchman, L. Practice and its overflows: reflections on order and mess. *TECNOSCIENZA: Italian Journal of Science & Technology Studies*, 2,1 (2011), 21-30.

57. Ten Have, P. *Understanding qualitative research and ethnomethodology*. Sage (2004)

From The Matrix to a Model of Coordinated Action (MoCA): A Conceptual Framework of and for CSCW

Charlotte P. Lee and Drew Paine
Human Centered Design & Engineering
University of Washington, 425 Sieg Hall, Seattle, WA 98195
cplee@uw.edu, pained@uw.edu

ABSTRACT
The CSCW community is reliant upon technology-centric models of groupware and collaboration that frame how we examine and design for cooperative work. This paper both reviews the CSCW literature to examine existing models of collaborative work and proposes a new, expanded conceptual model: the Model of Coordinated Action (MoCA). MoCA is a broader framework for describing complex collaborative situations and environments including, but not limited to, collaborations that have diverse, high-turnover memberships or emerging practices. We introduce MoCA's seven dimensions of coordinative action and illustrate their connection to past and current CSCW research. Finally, we discuss some ramifications of MoCA for our understanding of CSCW as a sociotechnical design space.

Author Keywords
CSCW; Conceptual Frameworks; Theory

ACM Classification Keywords
H.5.3 [Group and Organization Interfaces]: CSCW

General Terms
Theory

INTRODUCTION
What is the phenomenon of study in CSCW? As computerized technologies and the practices they support continue to grow in diversity, ubiquity, complexity, and scale, the number and type of research topics related to the study of collaborative systems have simultaneously continued to proliferate within CSCW and the larger umbrella of HCI. It has become increasingly urgent to find ways to describe the problem space in which CSCW researchers work. Focusing on name changes for our field is to inspect bandages without attending to the wound itself. A conceptual grounding—e.g. theoretical framework—is needed to help us define and describe what it is that the field of CSCW actually studies. In order to further discussions in our field, this article first reviews models of CSCW and then turns to positing a new conceptual model, the Model of Coordinated Action (MoCA).

Technology-centric models of groupware and CSCW have influenced and continue to influence how we think about cooperative work. Existing frameworks continue to be useful, yet we need a larger conceptual model that allows us to be explicit so that when we are modeling work we might hold these models up for inspection, rather than letting our models of work linger in the shadows, designed for but unarticulated. When we design systems to support collaboration, we are modeling sociality. Popular conceptual frameworks for explaining what it means to design for collaboration, or icons like the time-space matrix that models teams, have a bias towards individuals and small groups. These frameworks thus ensure that we have a model for only a very small subset of sociality.

Instead of trying to map an infinite variety of types of work on to a relatively smaller number of technologies that are rapidly changing and proliferating—we instead propose mapping technologies on to a more comprehensive model of work, such as the one proposed here. Doing so is sensible for understanding whole "ecosystems" of technologies that may be used in concert, whether or not they were designed at the outset to be used together. Sociotechnical coordinated actions may require the combined use of mundane technologies such as MS Excel and Access in conjunction with bespoke business process-specific applications [21].

A new conceptual model is needed that can help us to understand CSCW as a *comprehensive and coherent* design field that is neither overly constrained by an allegiance to "work" per se, nor is so open that any description of any computational technology used by two or more people is considered relevant. The theoretical development of our field has struggled to keep up with the rapidly increasing diversity of sociotechnical configurations, therefore landing us in an exciting era of research, but also one in dire need of conceptual grounding.

Below we present an overview of existing models of collaborative work within CSCW that are helpful for

CSCW '15, March 14-18, 2015, Vancouver, BC, Canada.
Copyright 2015 ACM 978-1-4503-2922-4/15/03...$15.00
http://dx.doi.org/10.1145/2675133.2675161

understanding how the field historically frames its design space. These technology-centric models of groupware and CSCW continue to influence how we think about cooperative work. We next present our elaborated model of collaborative work, the Model of Coordinated Action (MoCA). MoCA is our attempt to better map the larger design space that reflects today's CSCW challenges of supporting not only small, homogeneous groups, but also larger, heterogeneous groups coming from different communities of practice [56]. We then apply MoCA to two examples from the CSCW literature to illustrate the potential our model affords the community. Finally, we discuss directions for further development of the theoretical bases for the design space around collaborative work.

BACKGROUND

The call for a broader conceptualization of the design of systems for collaborative work is far from new. In 1992, Schmidt and Bannon [46] had already pointed to the need to expand the scope of research to settings that are unstable, large, open, and diverse. They state:

> *Also, we do not want to restrict the scope of CSCW to those special settings where the responsibility of accomplishing a task has been allocated to or assumed by a relatively closed and stable collective. The concepts of 'group' and 'group work', however, invariably connote special types of cooperative relations characterized by shared responsibilities. This conceptualization of CSCW will tend to ignore or even dismiss the major challenges posed by the design of systems that support cooperative work arrangements that are characterized by a large and maybe indeterminate number of participants, incommensurate conceptualizations, incompatible strategies, conflicting goals and motives, etc. (p.17)*

While European CSCW has, overall, had a more organizational bent, including more investigations of heterogeneous organizations [19,20,45], the field of CSCW in the United States, has emphasized to a greater degree developing technologies to support relatively homogeneous, small groups [19]. The historical bias in the US towards the study of small, homogeneous groups has contributed to a lack of necessary theories of the larger, "woolier" collaborations to which Schmidt and Bannon [46] refer. Despite progress internationally, the theoretical foundation of CSCW has been "patchy and incoherent" [49]. Here we posit a conceptual framework that is by, for, and of CSCW research—a theory native to CSCW and HCI.

The growth of studies of "new" social media and large-scale and long-term infrastructures are putting pressure on extant models of collaborative work in CSCW. Social media is increasingly used for organizing [1,52], bringing US CSCW research back to the table of organizational work. It should be noted here that throughout this work we are referring to models of CSCW that are either used or posited as being comprehensive models of the field. There are myriad fine models on various subtopics of the field that we do not elaborate on here, for example the work of Olson et al. [40] on the five factors that contribute to the success of a collaboratory (computer-mediated science, usually at a distance): the nature of the work, common ground, collaboration, readiness, management, and technical readiness; and the work of Chudoba et al. [8] modeling distance workers, "virtual teams", collaborating through computer-mediated communication and facing the "discontinuities" of team distribution, workplace mobility, and variety of workplaces.

MODELS OF CSCW

In this paper when we discuss "models" of CSCW we refer to conceptual models that posit the elements that compose Computer Supported Cooperative Work. The models we have had of CSCW thus far have been largely descriptive and the model proposed below is not yet different.

Historically groupware-ware centric models, of which there is much work in HCI, are still held up by the larger HCI community as the typical way to model collaborative technologies. The field of CSCW formally began in 1984 and initially focused on developing software to support the work of small groups [19]. The HCI community has long used taxonomies of cooperative systems to better understand how to design for people working together. Grudin posits one such conceptual model, see Figure 1, where each ring shows the link between "*one focus of computer systems development and the principal customer or user of the resulting technology*" [19, p.20]. The outermost ring (Organization) is described as emerging originally as the research province primarily of Information Studies while the innermost ring (Individual) emerged soon after as the focus of HCI research. The diagram notes CSCW's emphasis on the "Small group" level with occasional efforts at the "Project" level noted.

At the same time, Grudin acknowledged that CSCW as a field need not restrict itself to the level of small groups and the associated groupware, but that it draws from more than one ring of his model: "*People study, for example, the use, in group and organizational settings, of applications developed for individual users: the ways in which software, developed to support groups, affects individuals and is adapted to different organizational contexts: and systems developed to support organizational goals as they act through individuals, groups, and projects" [19, p.21].* CSCW was posited as "residing" at the small group level but also venturing to other levels. Our point here is not to dwell on the fact that development and technology have changed over the past 20 years, nor on the fact that CSCW is no longer limited to groupware, rather our point here is to *draw attention to the ways in which we think about collaboration and collaborative technology.*

Our conceptual frameworks for what it means to design collaborative technologies have changed remarkably little since Grudin's discussion in 1994. The HCI community has long used taxonomies of cooperative systems, such as Johansen's [24] matrix, to better understand how to design for people working together.

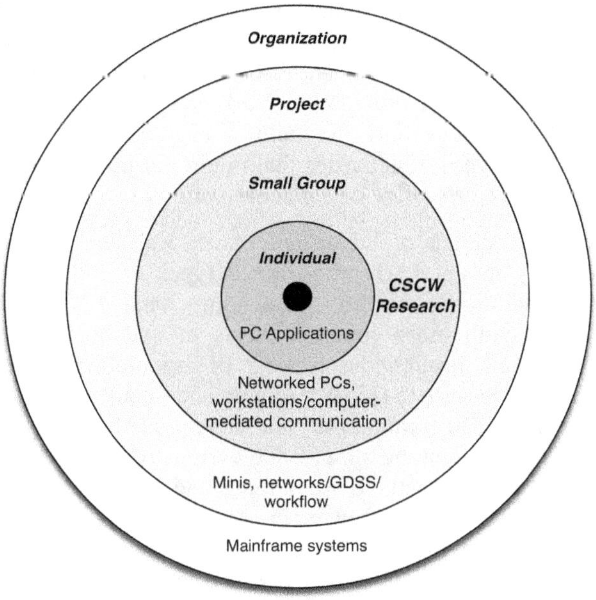

Figure 1. A recreation of Grudin's (1994) model for the design space of CSCW with the technological systems and associated principal customers or users in each ring. For simplicity we do not list the software development and research areas included on the original, although we do note the indication of CSCW research on the Small Group ring.

Johansen's taxonomy of groupware tools [24] is such a storied, long-standing element of HCI research that it is a requisite part of the education of anyone stepping foot into the HCI community attempting to support groups, and certainly for the CSCW community whose historical core has been in the research and design of groupware tools. Johansen's matrix may even be considered an icon within CSCW: "*This matrix has become a common language amongst the CSCW community*" [12, p.692].

Latour [26] makes a distinction between future science where what is known is still being debated (for example in recent publications) and established science which is taught as factual and known in textbooks. In the field of HCI, textbooks continue to discuss Johansen's matrix, itself derived from an earlier typology of group support systems [11], as a known fact. Shneiderman et al. [50] cites Ellis [14] in a brief discussion of Johansen's matrix, describing the matrix as the "*the traditional way to decompose cooperative systems.*" Johansen's matrix is not merely a way to decompose cooperative systems but is "the" way. Dix et al. [12] discusses Johansen's matrix in terms of systems to support groups and states that while groupware can be classified by function (e.g. meeting support or group authoring), the matrix is considered "*a very useful shorthand to refer to the particular circumstances a groupware system aims to address.*"

Below we see the original Matrix from p. 44 of [24], Figure 2. We see the familiar axis of time, which is broken down in to synchronous and asynchronous and also the axis of place (unlabeled but described in the text), which is broken down into co-located and remote meetings). We also see the familiar dichotomy between. However, we also see something quite interesting: the other axis concerning place is labeled face-to-face vs. electronic *meetings*. Closer inspection of the book's chapter reveals that this table is part of an extended discussion focused quite clearly and explicitly on, and only on, supporting team meetings.

	Time	
	Synchronous	*Asynchronous*
Face-to-face meetings	1. Facilitation services 2. Decision support 8. Beyond white board 17. Nonhuman participants	4. Presentation software 5. Project management 14. Memory management 16. Comprehensive support
Electronic meetings	3. Telephone extension 9. Screen sharing 12. Teleconference aid 15. Spontaneous interaction	6. Calendaring 7. Group writing 10. Computer conferencing 11. Text filtering 13. Conversation structuring

Figure 2. Johansen's (1988) time-space matrix.

Furthermore, Johansen presents an adjacent table contrasting small group work versus large group work (Table 3 on p.43 in [24]). While he does not explicitly theorize the small group/large group division, the table is presented as no more or less important than the divisions presented in the time vs. location matrix. The matrix was originally created to understand only electronic meetings and was also originally presented along with another typology that presented small vs. large group work as conceptually and practically distinct. The textbook discussions of CSCW only present the electronic meeting matrix and do not present Johansen's adjacent table contrasting small vs. large group work [12,50]. In other words, *the matrix has been taken out of context and half of Johansen's conceptual model—which includes large group work—has been ignored.*

HCI researchers have extended the electronic meeting portion of Johansen's model in the intervening years since 1988. However, the extensions have largely been focused on issues surrounding the dichotomous division of synchronous vs. asynchronous. Dix et al. [12] critique and extend the matrix by pointing out that the distinction between synchronous and asynchronous work is overly simplistic. For example work can be *concurrent synchronized* (e.g. videoconferences), *serial* (e.g. argumentation tools), *mixed* (able to be synchronized or serial for example through locking), or *unsynchronized* (e.g. email). Grudin's [19] iteration of Johansen's matrix divides place into same place, predictable different place, and unpredictable different place vs. same time, predictable different time, and unpredictable different time (p.25). Despite the many useful iterations of Johansen's matrix [2,3,19,20], this conceptual model does not and was not designed to be able to grapple with the variety and complexity of the systems that we are attempting to design today nor the great variety in the types of work in contemporary societies. Are the elements of place and time really all that are salient in the composition of cooperative work systems? Previous work suggests no [14,24], and yet also continues to only incrementally build on the Matrix [2,19].

The notion of groupware as an organizing concept for collaborative systems is further problematized by Andriessen [2] in his own iteration of the matrix. Andriessen notes that although the matrix suggests a sharp distinction between systems, many advanced systems are "*sets of more or less integrated modules and functionalities, that can be tailored to specific usage,*" or in other words, he highlights that actual work often requires the use of many applications together.

When discussing the Johansen taxonomy, we often consider it to be a taxonomy of tools, but the Johansen taxonomy is also a framework that implicitly describes work itself. In the matrix, the salient elements of work are considered to be whether or not it is asynchronous or synchronous and whether or not it is local vs. distributed (alternately described as same place vs. different place). While it seems specious to suggest that many actual CSCW researchers today consider the matrix to be representative of our understanding of work and of technologies that help people to work together, the model is considered, as noted above, to be not only part of a common lexicon but also as a traditional way to decompose cooperative systems (i.e. break them into their constituent parts).

Finally, while not a model of CSCW per se, in the field of Human Factors and Ergonomics, Patel et al. [41] posit the CoSpaces Collaborative Working Model (CCWM) of collaboration that lists "various factors that make up or influence collaboration at work." This framework is a useful tool for providing guidance to systems developers structuring iterative development, evaluation, and implementation and is therefore relevant to CSCW. However, despite a purported dual focus on both factors that "make up" or influence collaboration, the model focuses on factors that *influence* collaboration and on collaborative engineering in particular. The CCWM model does not take on the task of defining collaboration itself.

For the field of CSCW, which is increasingly grappling with a proliferation of types of collaboration including non-engineering work and even non-work, a nuanced model of collaboration itself is important. In CSCW, we not only lack models to put in our textbooks, but we also lack a contemporary, comprehensive model for decomposing cooperative systems in their great variety.

ARTICULATION WORK AND THE EDGES OF CSCW

The model we introduce later builds on some existing comprehensive models of CSCW and collaborative technologies. However, as we discuss in this section, there are some "edge cases" which are cases of collaboration that are not technically "collaborative" yet are now falling within the purview of current research in our field. Here we discuss notions of articulation work and non-routine work in order to show how the field is changing and is now embracing types of activities that might not traditionally be considered cooperative or collaborative.

While the models of Johansen's matrix and later iterations implicitly model fairly constrained types of collaborative work, additional work in Sociology and CSCW has grappled with more complex forms of collaboration and organization through the concept of articulation work as posited by Strauss [54] in Sociology, and later built upon on by Schmidt and Simone [48] and Gerson [18]. Articulation work is about making sure all the various resources needed to accomplish something are in place and functioning where and when they're needed in the local situation [54]. Key concepts worth interrogating here are the spectra posited by Strauss of collaborative work projects falling on a continuum from simple to complex and also the notion of the "common field of work."

Articulation work is implicitly reliant upon the notion of the *common field of work* that Schmidt and Simone [48] posit. Schmidt and Simone note that the common field of work is the site of action for coordinative work:

> *constituted by the interdependence of multiple actors who, in their individual activities, in changing the state of their individual field of work, also change the state of the field of work of others and who thus interact through changing the state of a common field of work.* [48, p.158]

Interaction *through* a common field of work is considered a fundamental distinction of cooperative work. Articulation work as a result is necessary to help to restrain the distributed nature of the "complexly interdependent activities" that are taking place. Schmidt and Simone also note that cooperative work and articulation work are recursively related, leading to re-arrangements of the work at hand before further articulation work and so on.

Later work by Gerson [18] takes on much more diffuse, networked types of collaborations where he coins the term "metawork" to discuss the subset of Strauss's articulation work conceptualization that consists of aligning tasks and subprojects. The notion of metawork accounts for non-local arrangements of different "kinds of activity" that may be larger and more abstract. Despite these differences, both metawork and local articulation focus on modifying a "common field of work."

Might there be room for less direct interdependence where the relationship between the person and the common field of work is slightly more distant? To take a mundane example: a Person who drops off canned food at a shopping mall that will later be taken to a food bank. The common field of work is the food bank where people in need come to pick up food. But the Person is only interacting directly with the shopping mall. The reader might object here that the common field of work is actually at the shopping mall where the food is exchanged, but then a conceptual gap arises between the shopping mall and the actual, situated, goal-centered work whose state the actors want changed. This is not so different from what Friedman et al. [16] argued when they noted that system stakeholders are not just those who have their hands on a system. And in fact, Schmidt and Simone [48] foreshadow this when they note that one person's work is another person's articulation work.

The point here is not to argue that a common field of work is no longer important for CSCW—to the contrary—rather we are simply arguing for greater recognition that for complex endeavors there may be more distance between relevant participants and the "common field of work" than in simpler endeavors. There may be multiple overlapping common fields of work; people may be working in a concerted and coordinated fashion and yet might have slightly different, but compatible, goals.

Strauss' Work Spectra: The Need for More Detail

In his discussion of articulation work, Strauss introduces spectra from routine to non-routine work and from simple to complex [54]. The contention that projects range from simple to complex and from routine to non-routine still holds, however, as we will discuss below, there are many ways in which a collaboration can be simple or complex, or new or old. For example, a project can be complex because it is has many people, or involves many communities of practice, or has no communities of practice. A project can also be complex because there is a high turnover of participants, or because it is highly physically distributed, or is highly asynchronous, or because of the extremes of being temporary, or of being very long term.

Any of these things could make a collaboration more complex. Similarly for the notion of routine, elements of a collaboration can be routine while other elements may stay the same. For example a team may be stable, but their artifacts (e.g. tools or systems) may be changing rapidly, or the type of problem being solved may be routine, but an organization may have become geographically distributed requiring new collaboration practices. The question then becomes not only whether a project is simple or complex, and not only whether a collaboration is routine or non-routine, but how is it simple or complex? How is it routine or non-routine? In what ways?

It should be noted that even supposedly routine work must confront unexpected change from time to time either from within the collaboration [22,33] (e.g. a key team member gets sick) or without (e.g. organizational restructuring or economic pressures). To some extent, then, all work is developing, progressing, materializing. While this is the case, there is still a range from more established to more emergent, or developing, collaborations.

In order to sufficiently understand collaborative technology, we need a more sophisticated understanding of collaborative work itself and to develop models that are in line with the variety and complexity of the systems that we are designing and using today. However, as the "groups" supported by HCI research grow increasingly large, diverse and distributed, so does our focus. We have expanded our conceptualization of collaborative technologies to not just tools, but whole systems or aggregates of tools and systems, which exist outside of currently employed taxonomies. In the following section we examine well-known dimensions of models of collaborative work in greater detail while also positing additional lesser-known dimensions relevant in today's research, development, and practice landscape.

MODEL OF COORDINATED ACTION (MOCA)

In this section we introduce the Model of Coordinated Action (MoCA). The conceptual models of CSCW discussed above have been largely descriptive, as mentioned earlier, and the model that we propose here is currently descriptive as well. However, with additional investigation, MOCA could be further developed to document even more fully the relationship between the dimensions of the model.

As per the previous section about the need for room for less direct interdependence between the person and the common field of work, we call our new model a model of "coordinated action" rather than one of "collaborative work." We chose the word "action" to emphasize the importance of goal-directedness implied by the word "work" while also being inclusive of goal-directed action that may not traditionally be considered work (e.g. serious leisure [53] or relationship work [55]).

MoCA shows us that there are many ways for coordinated action to be diffuse (well beyond physical distribution and asynchronous work) and this requires us to broaden our notions of interdependence that require individuals to interact through changing a common field of work. Rather we posit that individuals may have a shared goal (even if in name only) and that while interdependence remains key, individuals may actually be working to support others in changing a field of work. Therefore we suggest a slight change to the wording but a marked change in perspective. We suggest that coordinated action is the core of our modern field of CSCW and that it is constituted by the interdependence of two or more actors who, in their individual activities, are *working towards a particular goal through one or more overlapping fields of action.*

What this shift does is make room in how we conceptualize CSCW for action that supports, feeds into, and is necessary for accomplishing goal-directed actions—but may not be taking place through a common field of work itself. In other words, tying ourselves to conservative notions of what "common" means in the notion of a "common field of work" actually prevents us from studying a whole variety of collaborative and organizational forms where interests and tasks might be aligned only partially (e.g., slightly, temporarily, hastily, or even poorly). Rather than this being considered a problem, we might consider this to be a rather normal state for endeavors that are at all complex.

MoCA consists of seven dimensions of coordinated action. While the time-space matrix implies a binary division between local and distributed and synchronous vs. asynchronous, in our model we describe each of these "dimensions" as falling on a continuum. Again, we are describing actual collaborative work arrangements in all their great variety, as opposed to collaborative technologies per se. This new conceptual mapping of types of collaborative work enables a fuller representation of the design space for collaborative systems. By focusing this model on collaboration per se, we open up more room to investigate how multiple technologies can be mapped to a single collaborative action—a sociotechnical aggregation of actors and technologies. The figure below, Figure 3, demonstrates one way of depicting a full range of coordinated action.

We introduce below all seven dimensions and illustrate their connections to CSCW literature. The characteristics of each these seven dimensions have already been described in some way in the CSCW literature, MoCA provides a way to tie together these many "loose threads." More specifically, the model provides conceptual parity to dimensions of coordinated action that are particularly salient for mapping profoundly socially dispersed and frequently changing coordinated actions. As discussed in the previous section, the first two dimensions represent concerns that are well acknowledged within HCI and are captured by Johansen's matrix as well as any number of iterations of that matrix. Therefore we spend less time discussing these two dimensions. Building off of our community's decades of work and elaborating further upon these dimensions as part of our model, we are not suggesting dismissing the traditional model itself, rather we are setting up the traditional model to be incorporated into a larger, more elaborated model.

Dimension One: Synchronicity

The first dimension, taken from Johansen's original matrix about electronic meetings, is one of the two "typical concerns" or considerations [47] within extant CSCW models. Here it is slightly renamed as *synchronicity*. To iterate for the sake of setting up a parallel discussion for the third through seventh dimensions to be introduced later: the first dimension of *synchronicity* concerns a continuum of coordinated action ranging from being conducted synchronously, or at the same time, to asynchronously, or at different times. In deference to earlier work [12], the continuum of this dimension allows for coordinated actions to be a mix of asynchronous and synchronous. We do, however, give up some of the nuance of all the historical discussions [19,20] in that this dimension does not account for predictability of time. However, appreciation for predictability, or lack thereof, is implied in dimensions described later.

Dimension Two: Physical Distribution

The second dimension, also taken from Johansen's original matrix, is *physical distribution*: a continuum which concerns whether coordinated actions are taking place in the same geographic location at one end of the continuum or at completely different geographic locations at the other end. As this dimension is on a continuum, a collaborative undertaking can be more or less synchronous or physically distributed, including being mixed as per Dix et al. [12]. As with synchronicity, this dimension does not account for predictably of place. However, appreciation for predictability, or lack thereof, is implied in dimensions described later. Finally, as Olson and Olson [39] note, "*Collaborative work at a distance will be difficult to do for a long time, if not forever,*" and furthermore distance will continue to matter; the nature of some kinds of work (e.g., tight vs. loose coupling) are affected by distance even despite technological advances.

Dimension Three: Scale

The third dimension is *scale*, or the number of participants involved in the collaboration. The dimension of scale is often an afterthought in the discussions on synchronicity and physical distribution. On the other hand, large scale is often taken as a given for studies of infrastructure or social media. Coordination theory tells us that when "*multiple actors pursue goals together, they have to do things to organize themselves that a single actor pursuing the same goals would not have to do*" [34, p. 5]. Even when technologies are modular and easily extensible, an increase in participants requires more complicated social arrangements and new practices. In large-scale collaborations it has been found that mechanisms for coordination need to scale dramatically to adequately support large-scale distributed work [9]. In other words, scale matters.

Dimension Four: Number of Communities of Practice

The fourth dimension is *Number of Communities of Practice (NCoP)*. The Communities of Practice framework is itself a complex multidimensional theory; for this dimension we focus specifically on the *number* of communities of practice *represented* in the coordinated action.

Wenger's Community of Practice framework, built on the notion of legitimate peripheral participation [27], is a theory of learning whereby newcomers are exposed to experienced members of a community. Over time, newcomers learn and adopt the values, norms, practices, and artifacts (e.g. tools) of an expert community. A community of practice, however, takes time to form. Individuals must have repeated and enduring exposure to each other to form a community and to teach and learn from each other. Notions of teams and groups tend to assume the existence of a community of practice. Recent research in HCI, however, has increasingly explored collaboration where communities of practice are far less developed and where the notion of "community" (already a stretch beyond the idea of a team) becomes increasingly hard to pinpoint. The CoP framework is useful for understanding learning and socialization to a given social world but oftentimes in our field we must investigate coordinated actions where multiple communities of practice are *represented* by individuals, groups, or networks and where a social group may yet need to be created. Having briefly described CoP, we note that the dimension here is not meant to capture the whole, complex theory of socialization but merely the number of CoP.

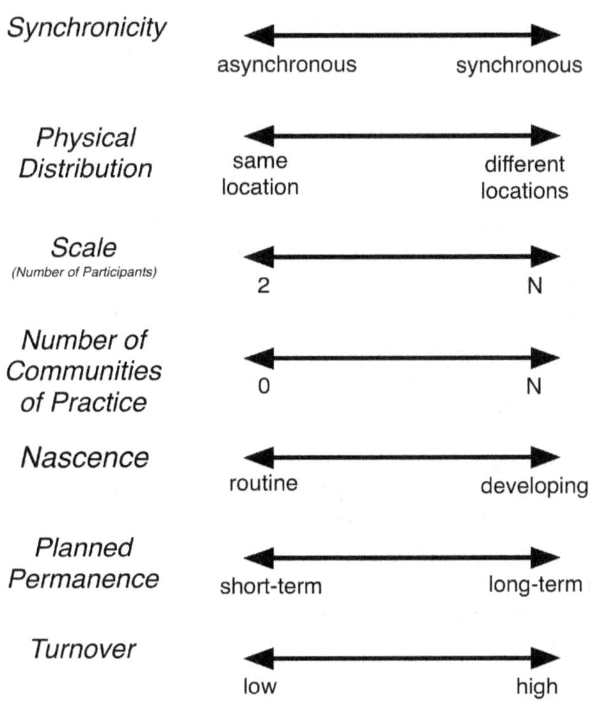

Figure 3. The Model of Coordinated Action (MoCA) and its seven dimensions with the end points of each continuum.

One way to look at the dimension of NCoP is through the lens of interdisciplinarity. When collaborators come together to work from different disciplines—science, design, or another background—there is a lot of thrash. There is confusion about roles, about how and why artifacts and tools have been created and should be used, and there is confusion about terminology [28,57]. In other words, there is not a lot of group cohesion. It is a team or community-in-the forming that is trying to develop practices, artifacts, and nomenclature. This mish mash of background, perspectives, artifacts, and tools is a natural occurrence when trying to foment creativity and innovation by putting together a diversity of skills and perspectives.

The dimension of NCoP then pertains to a type of cultural diversity including diversity in norms, practices, tools, and language. Towards one end of the dimension are small, homogeneous teams comprised of people with similar backgrounds and training. However, there is a more extreme possibility: in theory, it should be possible for people to come together who belong to no relevant community of practice. Examples of this include children with no previous experience trying to form a theater group, or novice adults trying to accomplish something in which none of them have significant relevant experience—e.g. building a deck together when none has such experience, in which case no CoP are involved. We expect that this case of 0 might be relatively rare, however.

A more common scenario would be a very culturally diverse team, and we indeed pass that waypoint as we travel to the endpoint of the continuum, but in fact if we go to the far end of the dimension we find diversity bounded only by the vast mélange of people who have access to computational systems and the Internet. At a very high N, we may see a scenario we have seen in studies of smaller collaborations of design teams [28,57], where there are several people involved, and while the coordinated action itself is still forming its own community of practice, the individuals involved bring the expectations, norms, and practices of their own relevant community of practice very much to bear on the work of the coordinated action.

Also, individual project members may belong to existing communities of practice and have access to those practices. A newly formed, very small team comprising four team members from different disciplines, for example, can be said to have an NCoP of 4. In these two latter cases the coordinated action cannot truly be considered to be 0 on the dimension of communities of practice.

Dimension Five: Nascence

The fifth dimension of MoCA is *nascence*, which discusses un-established (e.g. new) versus established (e.g. old) coordinated actions. Nascence, it should be noted is not merely a simple synonym for "newness" rather it implies a "coming in to being"—a special kind of instability rife with future potentialities. Thus we might see nascence in a reformed and rebooted coordinated action. Rather than posit one end of the spectrum as simply the opposite of routine, we describe it as developing. It is well understood that even routine work has developing characteristics. As previously mentioned, even seemingly routine work may confront unexpected change either from within the collaboration [22,33] (e.g. a key team member take a prolonged leave) or without (e.g. new market demands).

A relevant concept for nascence is the notion of *boundary negotiating artifacts,* which, while not exclusive to this dimension, might be found most commonly in un-established coordinated actions. The term *boundary negotiating artifacts* (BNAs) [28] has been used to describe the creation and use of temporary, unstandardized artifacts to support collaboration. The related notion of boundary objects as originally conceived is reliant on the existence of standardized practices [28]. The notion of BNAs posits that artifacts can be unstandardized yet functionally useful but also suggests that the organization of collaborative work itself can be in flux and yet functionally useful. It is not just nascence that characterizes these collaborations that are highly in flux, however. Some collaborations are not just new, but they are also, by design, temporary.

Dimensions Six: Planned Permanence

The sixth dimension is the *planned permanence* of the collaborative arrangement. *Planned permanence* refers to the intended permanence of a coordinated action. Relatively little research in CSCW has focused explicitly on notions related to this dimension. The dimension of planned permanence refers to planned or intended permanence, because it often cannot be predicted how long a coordinated action will actually last, nor is it straightforward to decide at what point something is actually "permanent." Another way to think about this is whether the collaboration is intended to be short-term or long-term. Works by Lee [28] and Yasuoka [57] studied small teams doing non-routine, nascent, and short-term collaborative work involving people from different communities of practice or "knowledge backgrounds."

Research has studied the special character of collaborations that were not intentionally created to be long term or global by assigning them a name: *local and temporary alignment of practices* (LTAP) [57]. A characteristic of LTAP is the creation of project jargon to create local and temporary alignment of practices during the early design period of short-term projects. While some modes of communication were learned during participants' professional education, others were invented during the project period. Within nascent and short-term teams, where participants belong to different communities, the creation of practices, artifacts, and special shared terms, i.e. jargon, is necessary if not crucial for success.

Whether a coordinated action is temporary or permanent, the participants need to create shared practices, artifacts, and terms; however, with strong *planned permanence*, participants may endeavor to create not just temporary artifacts, but in fact the standardized artifacts and practices that are requisite for stable boundary objects. The coordinated action, then is substantively different—the difference between a family setting up tents and a campsite for a weeklong stay vs. the same family building a home meant to last for decades. Again, we are referring to planned and not actual permanence, because the plan is to what people are orienting their actions.

It should be noted however, that a temporary collaboration is not necessarily "easier" than a more permanent one. While a more permanent one has high overhead in the planning and creation of administrative and coordinative practices and tools required for long-term collaborations, temporary collaborations can struggle due to a lack of common jargon, methods, practices, and understanding.

Dimension Seven: Turnover

The seventh dimension of MoCA is *turnover*. The turnover dimension refers to the stability of the participant makeup of a given collaboration. More specifically, this refers to the rapidity with which participants enter and leave. Implicit within this dimension are collaborations that range from closed, private collaborations where participants leave slowly, if at all, to collaborations that are fully open and public where "the masses" may participate. While nascence and turnover may seem to be overlapping, it is important to note that they can be independent. For example a long-standing coordinated action can suddenly undergo a significant amount of turnover due to internal events (e.g. a favorite manager being fired) or external (e.g. the advent of a favorable job market).

Instances of mass participation serve as examples of collaborations that are high on the dimension of turnover. For example, recent work on mass participation explores not the work of teams or organizations, but of the "crowd". The crowd is a very different animal where anyone can participate or stop participating at any time. We see loose collaborations ranging from individuals writing and editing articles for public wikis [25,35,36], websites that allow collaborative editing, to tweeters sharing information about disasters through microblogging [51,52].

EXAMINING THE LAST THREE DIMENSIONS: NASCENCE, PLANNED PERMANENCE AND TURNOVER

The seven dimensions of MoCA include two dimensions, synchronicity and physical distribution, that have been explicitly recognized in CSCW for quite some time; and two more dimensions, scale and number of communities of practice, that have been explicitly and implicitly recognized. We examine the last three dimensions of MoCA in more depth here using two examples drawn from previous CSCW literature since they are relatively less explored in the field.

The three dimensions of *nascence*, *planned permanence*, and *turnover* are dimensions that are necessary for understanding the more diffuse coordinated actions that are of increasing interest in CSCW. These diffuse coordinated actions are often characterized by emergent ways of organizing and a complex ecosystem of fields of work. We are not suggesting that for emergent collaborations and organizations the other dimensions are not salient; they are. Rather we wish to explicitly draw attention to how these more abstract, dimensions play out in actual practice.

We use these two examples to illustrate how MoCA can help us understand sites of study that are of interest to CSCW researchers. The first example is an emergent disaster relief virtual organization from Starbird and Palen [52]. The second is work to develop and sustain the CAMERA metagenomics cyberinfrastructure from Bietz, Ferro, and Lee [5]. Since these projects were not undertaken to explicitly gather data to address these seven dimensions, interpretation of the data presented in the articles is necessary. *Thus, this analysis is undertaken for demonstration purposes and is not intended to represent an empirical contribution.*

Example One: Humanity Road (HR)

Our first example uses Starbird and Palen's [52] examination of a disaster relief virtual organization, Humanity Road (HR), to explore what the dimensions look like in a coordinated action. Starbird and Palen describe how Humanity Road arose as an emergent organization in the aftermath of the 2010 Haiti earthquake. Humanity Road started as a group of people affiliated through social media and eventually morphed into a non-profit organization. The authors emphasize that since its inception and evolution in 2010, HR is, and always has been, a virtual organization comprised of a global network of volunteers in support of humanitarian relief.

Humanity Road used various social and collaborative media, including Twitter, Skype, and Google Docs. Twitter was the primary mechanism through which active disaster information was collected and disseminated while Skype and Google Docs were used to coordinate volunteers' participation. Work in this realm was episodic and dependent upon volunteers' ability to obtain information, sort through it to ascertain its correctness and utility to emergency management groups, and to disseminate information determined to be correct and useful.

Key to the process of collecting and disseminating information were "episodic" and long-term volunteers. Serving as a volunteer in HR ranged from retweeting tweets to disseminating current information about the disaster, to helping create and coordinate event diaries (later renamed situation reports) that helped track the knowledge being tweeted. Participation was open to people around the globe. "Long-term volunteers" were persons who contributed both during and in-between disasters, and as of 2011 included six "seasoned" participants.

While Starbird and Palen refer to these persons as "long term" or "now seasoned" this by no means indicates that there was a stable core of participants over time. Some of these seasoned participants were with the organization since a year prior to it's 2010 inception as a formal non-profit and some joined afterwards. Episodic volunteers on the other hand contributed during a single disaster event and could be entirely new to the collaboration with no previous experience or understanding of the emerging norms for disseminating disaster information through social media. The collection of members who volunteered over the long-term was not entirely stable and could turn over in less than a year's time. Still others came and went over a longer period of time.

During an unfolding crisis the high turnover in participants from event to event led to a muddled information collection and dissemination process. New long term or episodic volunteers could jump into the middle of ongoing work at any time during a disaster, leading to confusion regarding the state of verified and disseminated information. The high turnover led the long-term volunteers to take charge and develop a structured set of documents for the information collection and dissemination process. This process and associated artifacts enabled new participants to contribute to the disaster relief effort without disseminating incorrect information. The development of such artifacts and processes, however, took time and only emerged over the course of multiple disaster events as long-term volunteers adapted their work to the situations at hand.

The ability of anyone who was invited and willing to undergo a minimal amount of training to participate in Humanity Road's efforts reduced the virtual organization's ability to form a community of practice due to a constantly changing stream of participants. Humanity Road therefore found it necessary to "*bake in mechanisms into their work*" (e.g. the structured set of documents to organize work tasks) to make their larger overall strategy and goals possible. Starbird and Palen point out, however, that the development of these mechanisms did, over time, allow episodic volunteers to more freely enter and exit the collaboration while freeing long term volunteers to focus on other organizational goals.

In applying MoCA to the briefly discussed example above, it enables us to make sense of the coordinated action itself. Rather than looking at "collaboration" or "cooperative work" or even "coordinated action" as unchartable territory, perhaps we can begin to look for patterns and similarity. In the following discussion, we use the ordinal rankings of low, medium, and high, as crude placeholders for potential future empirically derived measures. In essence, we are "kicking the tires" a bit to demonstrate the potentiality of having such a framework such as MoCA. Indeed the only way to be sure about this data would be to have collected this data at the time that the study was undertaken.

Working primarily through Twitter and Skype, we see that volunteers are widely distributed, with participants scattered around the globe. While the potential number of people participating in the coordinated action is quite large, in actuality there is a small group of longer-term volunteers along with a somewhat larger group of episodic volunteers. The example of Humanity Road shows that high *turnover* for collaborations involving the "crowd" confounds the formation of a community of practice since participants may enter or exit at any time. Yet at the same time there are some stable members over time so there is also evidence of medium turnover. Thus, in the MoCA dimensions, we might say that Humanity Road covers a range on the continuum rather than simply being high or medium.

We also see that Humanity Road changes with regards to *planned permanence* over time. It starts out as a group of interested people and then eventually becomes a non-profit organization. However, our data for planned permanence is incomplete based on the above example. We know that once HR became a formal organization, we consider the planned permanence to be much higher than none, but still to be less than some ecological science infrastructures for example that are planned to last several decades if not a century. On the dimension of *nascence*, HR is mixed because during the course of the study it is truly brand new with many new practices needing to be established, whereas after a core group is established, the nascence is less. Thus on the dimension of nascence, HR is both medium and high. Given that coordinated actions change over time, it is sensible that how a coordinated action looks on the dimensions of MoCA changes over time as well.

Example Two: Development of the CAMERA Cyberinfrastructure (CI)

Research in CSCW has also looked at the transforming nature of collaborations for developing scientific cyberinfrastructures (CIs). In the following example, we examine the development of a cyberinfrastructure in more detail to further illustrate an emergent sociotechnical system from the literature. We are using the example of an ethnographic study of a marine metagenomics CI from Bietz, Ferro, and Lee [5]. Cyberinfrastructures are virtual organizations comprised of people and large-scale scientific computational infrastructures. Cyberinfrastructures have been described as being fundamentally emergent [43] and as being iteratively developed over time in response to a climate of constant scientific and technological change [6].

Bietz, Ferro, and Lee studied scientists who are collaborating to create a new database-centric system that will support new scientific methods, specifically metagenomic or environmental genomic methods. This project is the Community Cyberinfrastructure for Advanced Marine Microbial Ecology Research and Analysis (CAMERA). CAMERA is the collaborative endeavor of multiple organizations. The authors studied the project over a three-year period. In CAMERA participants were designing new collaborative practices and organizational structures in order to create new infrastructures to support new ways of doing science. Below we briefly describe findings from that original study, Bietz et al. [5], before launching in to our own analysis of it using MoCA.

In Bietz, Ferro, and Lee [5] the author's examine how "*the developers of CAMERA understand, manage, and respond to change*" in the course of their work to accomplish an infrastructure for marine metagenomics research. The author's especially focus on the strategies the individuals use to sustain the development and maintenance of CAMERA through changing organizational and scientific contexts. Bietz et al. discuss studying the CAMERA project in two phases, with the first phase begun around two years after the first. This enabled them to capture "*two snapshots in the life of the project*" for their analysis.

Between the first and second round of data collection Bietz et al. found that the human infrastructure [31] of the CAMERA project had changed substantially. Originally, CAMERA was a partnership of two US research institutes: the J. Craig Venter Institute (JCVI) and Calit2. JCVI is an independent genomic sciences institute in Maryland, while Calit2 is a research institute of the University of California, San Diego (UCSD). During their first round of data collection Bietz et al. ascertained that JCVI was leaving the CAMERA project. This was significant since JCVI provided both technological and biological expertise to the project. The authors note that CAMERA's leadership therefore quickly sought to partner with another organization to fill this gap and enable them to sustain the project and its stated goals.

At the end of the author's first round of data collection the CAMERA leadership selected a new organizational partner, the Center for Research on Biological Systems (CRBS). The CRBS had previous experience with other similar cyberinfrastructure projects and importantly was also located at UCSD. By the second round of data collection, the organizational leadership had also shifted from Calit2, even though it was still part of the project, to CRBS. CRBS members occupied "key leadership positions" and were leading the development work for the CI.

The author's note that the CAMERA project's transition from the JCVI to the CRBS organization was "easier than it might have been" thanks to CRBS and Calit2 being embedded in many of the same structures at UCSD. Mechanisms for moving money between the organizations and the purchase and use of common computing systems were more easily accomplished thanks to these structures. Bietz et al. note that the shared structures readily enable the CI developers to leverage existing infrastructural relationships to enact productive new relationships. In addition, the transition from JCVI to CRBS was "managed in phases so as to minimize disruption to the infrastructure." Members from each organization were therefore able to enact productive relationships over the course of these phases and key members who stayed on were able to take on larger roles that helped to keep historical information within the project. This relationship work sustained the development of CAMERA through changes in the organizations, technology, and scientific goals as it grew from a nascent to a more established entity.

The CAMERA project's organizational changes led to significant turnover in the project development staff. However, as Bietz et al. note the larger human infrastructure of CI projects is more expansive. This motivated the authors' examination of other stakeholder groups who found that the composition of the executive committee, the program officer, and the 10-person scientific advisory board did not change significantly between their two rounds of data collection. This provided stability to the project since these entities helped keep the project funding stable and its vision and goals aligned in the same direction.

Turning now to briefly apply MoCA to the CAMERA example, we see that as with many infrastructure efforts, CAMERA stays consistently high on the continuum of *planned permanence* as it is meant to be a lasting research infrastructure for many researchers who can, in turn, create their own sets of tools to work with that infrastructure. Across the author's two rounds of data collection one of the key organizations on the project changes, yet the overarching goal of accomplishing an infrastructure is sustained and enacted due to the human infrastructure.

Nascence is ranked on the high end of medium or the low end of high over the course of Bietz, Ferro, and Lee's study as the coordinative action of CAMERA is not entirely brand new during most of the course of the study, and thus cannot be said to be high, yet at the same time the project does reach an identifiably stable and established state. Certainly it does not rank low in nascence where there would be a clear "business as usual" feeling.

Finally, the example discusses *turnover* at great length showing that while there is some stability in the form of continuity in executive and advisory members and a few members of the project staff, overall the project staff had a great deal of turnover. Therefore we can consider the coordinated action of CAMERA on the dimension of *turnover* to be both medium and high.

We take the discussion of these two examples as a neonate thought exercise. Each of the two examples is distinct from early CSCW studies of electronic team meetings, being among the coordinated actions that are less centralized and exhibit a lot of change. We drew on already-published research to show that highly emergent organizations are already being studied within CSCW and furthermore that they, and their emergent qualities, can be at least partially understood and profiled by grappling with their relationships to the dimensions of nascence, planned permanence, and turnover. While the other dimensions of MoCA, too, are necessary to help us chart the realm of coordinated action, these three dimensions in particular are useful for us to be able to identifying and talk about emergent ways of organizing and also complex ecosystems of work.

DISCUSSION

Having discussed how three particular dimensions might help us to index and talk about emergent collaborations, we now take a step back to look at the "big picture": the larger context of MoCA. In particular, we elaborate on the utility of the shift from traditional notions of cooperation to the notion of coordinated action. This shift is helpful for assisting with investigations of more complex forms of multi-person action. We then go on to discuss how emergent coordinated actions have been of enduring interest to our field. Growing interest in emergent types of action such as infrastructural work to support "big data" and social media that support mass participation are exerting pressure on our field to redefine its scope more broadly. In the final subsection of this discussion, we list some of the theoretical and practical implications of MoCA.

Coordinated Action

Coordinated action can still be conceived of as people working together toward a shared goal. But shared goals can be very diffuse and ill-defined and we also see that "working together" may sometimes feel more like a series of fleeting microblog exchanges or people working rather separately on different systems that still need to interoperate with a larger, sprawling infrastructure. Research on information infrastructures has explored the idea that not only are infrastructures virtual organizations [10], but they are also systems of systems [13] comprised of a shifting patchwork of stakeholders who have different but overlapping interests [4,6]. The easiest way to describe this is to note that many organizations and computing systems are partially but not completely interoperable, and have overlapping but non-congruent interests and priorities.

Research has shown that people developing parts of infrastructures are usually spending a lot of their time on other projects as well [4,7,29]. The people involved in these infrastructure efforts, like most people, participate in many communities of practice. And yet these infrastructure efforts often do not feel like communities of practice: when people are working together *and productively* on a funded infrastructure project they may not agree on the target audience and the precise goals of the component of work that they are working on. For example in one study of infrastructure developers, participants had a few different ideas about who the "community" was that they were serving and therefore also different ideas about what their design priorities should be [30].

Collaborations that are low on planned permanence overall and high on the dimensions of turnover and communities of practice (including zero CoP) may also have another interesting quality however, which is that with a lack of routine practices and artifacts, the nature of work is rather special. Wenger's notion of a community of practice requires enduring participation, yet with very little enduring participation, we have coordinated actions bringing together people from many communities of practice. As mentioned earlier, it is possible for people to come together who belong to no community of practice, relevant to the coordinated action in which case none are involved.

Alternatively, there could be a coordinated action where many different people hail from many different communities of practice. In such a situation it is not hard to believe that there may not be a well defined, shared goal. Perhaps we are both interested in helping with disaster relief. You tweet from where the disaster happens and I re-tweet your tweet, exchanges that have been documented in the literature [51]. We may never otherwise interact although we may be following some of the same microblogging feeds. This is a very, very lightweight coordinated action where there is little interdependence. It is arguable whether the Twitter feed itself is "the common field of work" or if it is the disaster area where participants want help to be rendered, but it still represents people working on a shared goal of some kind: helping disaster victims.

The notion of coordinated action frees us from having to decide on only one common field of work and one clear-cut goal. Removing the bias towards smaller, tightly knit cooperation allows room for our field to continue studying not only those cooperations, but also larger, more loosely knit coordinated actions.

Emergence

How can we make sense of the types of coordinated action that are making a new model such as MoCA necessary? We posit here the notion of *emergent coordinated action* as a way of describing some of the edge cases that are pressuring CSCW to reconsider what is indeed the phenomenon of study. The model presented above might provide a tool for discussing how to support and design for collaborations that exhibit emergence, particularly *social emergence* [44] (the processes whereby the actions and interactions of agents result in the global behavior of a system). All social systems, and thus all sociotechnical systems, are emergent to some degree. Innovative types of work, such as design or scientific work, seem to exhibit more emergence. Coordinated actions that have high turnover, are low on planned permanence, are high on nascence (or some combination of those) could be considered highly emergent.

In research on intensional networks from more than a decade ago, Nardi et al. [37] found that actors deliberately formed intensional networks and that furthermore these networks had two properties: history (shared knowledge) and emergence (described by the authors as characterized by rapid formation to accomplish particular tasks). In their more recent work on complex and multiply-determined systems, Edwards et al. [13] describe a challenge of "navigating processes of planned vs. emergent change."

In research also from more than a decade ago, Furnas [17] discusses a framework for the context for designing IT as a mosaic of responsive adaptive systems (MoRAS) in the context of future HCI (denoted by Furnas as ++HCI):

> *The framework views the world relevant to ++HCI design as being composed of a whole set of systems, ranging from parts of the human mind to workgroups, communities, markets, and societies. The dominant considerations that shape the structure and dynamics of this set of systems arise by noting that they individually respond to their environments and adapt to remain viable* over *time. Further, they are coupled with one another in a kind of multiscale mosaic, influencing each other in a variety of ways. [17, p.208]*

In the extended example on cyberinfrastructure development described earlier [5], we see more recent research describing similar ways that collaborations can be emergent: different groups form at different times and different actors are working to reshape their collaborations and technical arrangements depending on their needs of the moment. The collaboration is described as a complex and rapidly shifting kaleidoscope of interactions, technologies, and collaborations from teams to multiple organizations.

Additional research in CSCW has investigated design in emergent sociotechnical systems. In research on complex collaborations around organizational software, Pollock et al. [42] investigate the seeming contradiction in design contexts where there exist standardized software solutions and, simultaneously, a great diversity of organizational settings to which those solutions are to be applied. Looking at "generification work" with organizational software packages, they describe a process of extending and morphing that enable software packages to move from place to place and in to new settings. The extensions of software packages, however, also enable organizations to align themselves with the software. Individuals and larger social structures, such as organizations, exist and coevolve in relation to one another.

Our investigations of coordinated action and how to model it has pushed us far beyond our starting point of looking at synchronous and asynchronous and co-located vs. distributed work. Our journey here has also taken us past another waypoint that looked at routine and non-routine and simple vs. complex coordinated action. We have now gone far beyond simple binaries to looking at a very multi-dimensional design space.

While the notion of emergence is not new to CSCW and related literatures [38,44], coordinated actions that exhibit social emergence are becoming ever more ubiquitous in our research, and increasingly relevant to everyday life given the extended reach of social media and information technologies more generally. Having emergent qualities is a fundamental reality of many contemporary coordinated actions. As we start to consider more types of coordinated action that are "complex," or more extreme, on any number of the seven dimensions of MoCA (i.e., synchronicity, physical distribution, scale, nascence, NCoP, planned permanence, turnover), the challenge of designing to support emergence will become increasingly important. Exploring the design space of emergent collaborations and emergent organizations is timely and deserves more attention.

Conceptual Frameworks for CSCW: A Way Forward

The Model of Coordinated Action represents but one way forward. While it touches upon many years of empirical research in CSCW, it is yet an early step in a larger project to contribute to theory that originates from the CSCW community and that is for the CSCW community—and perhaps beyond. We propose here a particular kind of theoretically driven empirical program. It is our hope, however, given the continued prominence of historical models such as Johansen's matrix, that the community is ready to consider an expanded model. Should MoCA stimulate or contribute to conversations about what the phenomenon of study is within CSCW or should MoCA inspire the development of other conceptual frameworks that put all manner of research and technologies that support coordinated action in dialog with each other, then this model will have served an extremely useful purpose and our time here will already have been well spent. However, we do not wish to stop there.

The future practical implications of MoCA are that it may provide *a shared way* to find and talk about what we study in CSCW despite its electrifying and daunting diversity. We are not recommending that everyone adopt this wholesale and make this the object of their research, rather we suggest that this model could provide a useful common reference similar to GPS coordinates. Further exploration of models like this, whether or not they are MoCA, could assist with finding some of our own common ground for talking about and comparing:

- Change within one coordinated action over time
- Differences and similarities within particular domains (e.g. health, science, education)
- Differences and similarities within particular types of activity (e.g. mass participation, infrastructure development)
- Differences *across* domains and spheres of activity (e.g., Wikipedia scholars in CSCW might find similarities with scientific collaboration scholars in CSCW whereas they might not have before)
- The development of a way to index different coordinated actions *at the time of data collection* so that we may search for similar coordinated actions that may not be in our sub-disciplinary area
- Identification of the equivalent of personas for different types of coordinated action: profiles of coordinated actions
- Identification of technologies that have proven relevant or useful to coordinated action that fits certain profiles
- Identification of constellations of technologies that are relevant to coordinated actions that fit certain profiles

Related to the last point of identification of constellations, we note that research has already usefully taken notice that groups of individuals are combining different types of technologies in different ways [15,21]. However we still need to know more about when, how, or why. We suspect given the examples already in the CSCW literature that the technical needs of more emergent systems are somewhat different from those that are less emergent—for example what constitutes agile and modular ways of working? We already see that people are using ecologies of tools and technologies to collaborate [21,23], therefore we can perhaps start to get a sense of what classes of tools and systems, and what clusters of those same classes, are useful for what sorts of collaborations.

The seven dimensions of MoCA (i.e. synchronicity, distribution, scale, number of communities of practice, nascence, planned permanence, and turnover) provide researchers, developers, and designers with a vocabulary and range of concepts that can be used to tease apart the aspects of a coordinated action that make them easy or hard to design for. If we are sensitized to the notions of planned permanence, turnover, and number of communities of practice, etc. we then have standardized tools (concepts in this case), with which to read, recognize, compare and talk about the unique features of each design space.

MoCA starts to reveal some of its power when a design or research team is provided with this conceptual framework for comparing one design or research project with another. If we become aware that while our previous projects involved few communities of practice, extreme distribution, high planned permanence and low turnover and our new project entails extreme distribution, low planned permanence, and high turnover, we can be proactive about anticipating new challenges for research and design pertaining to those dimensions which are different from our earlier work. Furthermore, we can document and learn from the differences.

MoCA's major implications for design, however, as per the bullet list above, are twofold: 1) to more precisely, yet with appropriate flexibility, describe the CSCW design space and 2) to provide fine-grained ways to understand and locate related work such that we do not forever relegate ourselves to domain silos (e.g. health informatics, Wikipedia, science, ubiquitous computing for the home) or methodological silos. Coordinated actions that are similar in terms of synchronicity, distribution, nascence, turnover, and scale in, for example, health informatics and ubiquitous computing for the home, might have more in common with each other than coordinated actions in the same domain that rate very differently on those same dimensions. To reduce this to a simple example: designing for a small, nascent undistributed coordinated action in medical research informatics (e.g. a tablet app to support wet lab activities) might have more in common with another small, nascent, undistributed coordinated action in, say, ubiquitous computing for the home (e.g. a tablet app to support family chores) than it would with a large, established highly distributed coordinated action (e.g. a legacy system for electronic medical research records). With frameworks like MoCA it could become much easier to locate and explain such "cross-silo" comparisons than it is currently. The implication of this work for design is to help CSCW by mapping our new, larger and more complex design space and by maximizing our use of existing research.

CONCLUSION

Rather than seeing this model as a foray in to turning CSCW into a "pure" social science, to the contrary we see this work as taking seriously the notion that CSCW is, in fact, a design field. If we are designing to support coordinated action we should know more about what coordinated action is, and furthermore, we should have better ways to talk about the variations among them. In this way, we might get closer to understanding what it means to design for sociotechnical systems that can be simultaneously socially and technically complex and are subject to frequent changes from both within and without.

For systems that are very large and complex "design" almost feels like a misnomer. The developers of these systems are somewhat powerless in the schema of very diffuse organizations that do not have central control, but might be seen more accurately as facilitators. While CSCW has sought to investigate the political ramifications and methodological challenges of involving users in processes of change, the field still suffers from the lack of a understanding of how people involve themselves, in larger, more complex sociotechnical systems.

More recent work in HCI, particularly in CSCW, investigates very different types of coordinated actions such as Wikipedia communities, crowd working, and infrastructural development [4,35,36,42,51,52]. Of course smaller, changeable collaborations have been under our nose all along but have received less attention [28,57]. These collaborations, where the cast of characters and the work practices and artifacts are often necessarily changing, and changing frequently, are likely to continue yielding interesting questions, insights, and design opportunities.

For historical reasons we do not actually object to adherence to the use of the words "collaboration" or "cooperation," but we chose to use the words coordinated action in this paper and for this model in order to be consistent and technically correct about what we consider to be the focus of CSCW research and development. What we propose here is a simple and straightforward extension of existing models of CSCW that also represents a bold shift. The shift lies in giving up on narrow idealized notions of goal-directedness, which suggest that goals are clear and well-defined and that people working in concert necessarily have the exact same goals. The shift also lies in opening our conceptual roadmap to include the notion that very loosely knit ways of doing things together (whether it be for work or leisure or enrichment) are now part of the landscape. What we hold on to from our theoretical past is the notion that a keystone of our field of CSCW is not "Computer Supported Cooperative Work" per se, but investigating goal-directed coordinated action to better inform technology design research and practice.

Löwgren and Stolterman [32] note that design theory is "*knowledge focused on creating new conditions for design, different patterns of thinking and acting, new design examples, and a general understanding of the conditions for creative and innovative work.*" If, in the future, we succeed in coming up with values for the dimensions described above, we open up the possibility for CSCW researchers to retrieve research on similar types of collaborations. That would be immensely valuable.

Individual intrepid researchers in HCI have already been venturing into the frontiers of accepting and exploring these ways of coordinating action together—we do not argue otherwise. However, our theory and conceptual frameworks should follow suit. This work represents an effort to stimulate more dialog about what the phenomenon of study of CSCW really is and how we might represent it so that we can understand our work and ourselves better and—at the very least—have a model to put in our HCI textbooks that are more reflective of advances in our field.

ACKNOWLEDGMENTS

We offer our grateful thanks to the anonymous reviewers of this paper and also those of earlier versions for thoughtful and constructive feedback. Thanks also to Kate Starbird, Behzod Sirjani, and Stephanie Steinhardt. While in no way responsible for any of the content of this paper, we also offer our warm gratitude to Matthew Bietz, Paul Dourish, Tom Finholt, and Elihu Gerson for timely encouragement. Any errors are ours. This work has been supported in part by National Science Foundation grants IIS-0954088, ACI-1302272, OCI-1220269, IIS-0712994, and OCI-0838601.

REFERENCES

1. Al-Ani, B., Mark, G., Chung, J., & Jones, J. (2012). The Egyptian blogosphere: a counter-narrative of the revolution, Proceedings of the ACM 2012 conference on Computer Supported Cooperative Work (pp. 17-26). Seattle, Washington, USA: ACM.

2. Andriessen, J. H. E. Working with Groupware: Understanding and Evaluating Collaboration Technology. Springer, London, UK, 2003.

3. Baecker, R. M., Grudin, J., Buxton, W. A. S., & Greenberg, S. Readings in Human-Computer Interaction: Toward the Year 2000 (2nd ed.). Morgan Kaufmann Publishers, 1995.

4. Bietz, M. J., Baumer, E. P. S., & Lee, C. P. Synergizing in Cyberinfrastructure Development. Computer Supported Cooperative Work (CSCW), 19, 3-4 (2010), 245-281. DOI= http://dx.doi.org/10.1007/s10606-010-9114-y.

5. Bietz, M. J., Ferro, T., & Lee, C. P. (2012). Sustaining the development of cyberinfrastructure: an organization adapting to change, Proceedings of the ACM 2012 conference on Computer Supported Cooperative Work (pp. 901-910). Seattle, Washington, USA: ACM.

6. Bietz, M. J., & Lee, C. P. Collaboration in metagenomics: Sequence databases and the organization of scientific work. ECSCW 2009 (2009), 243-262.

7. Bietz, M. J., Paine, D., & Lee, C. P. (2013). The work of developing cyberinfrastructure middleware projects, Proceedings of the 2013 conference on Computer supported cooperative work (pp. 1527-1538). San Antonio, Texas, USA: ACM.

8. Chudoba, K. M., Wynn, E., Lu, M., & Watson-Manheim, M. B. How virtual are we? Measuring virtuality and understanding its impact in a global organization. Information Systems Journal, 15, 4 (2005), 279-306. DOI= http://dx.doi.org/10.1111/j.1365-2575.2005.00200.x.

9. Costa, J. M., Cataldo, M., & Souza, C. R. d. (2011). The scale and evolution of coordination needs in large-scale distributed projects: implications for the future generation of collaborative tools, Proceedings of the SIGCHI Conference on Human Factors in Computing Systems (pp. 3151-3160). Vancouver, BC, Canada: ACM.

10. Cummings, J., Finholt, T., Foster, I., Kesselman, C., & Lawrence, K. A. (2008). Beyond being there: A blueprint for advancing the design, development, and evaluation of virtual organizations.

11. DeSanctis, G., & Gallupe, R. B. A Foundation For The Study Of Group Decision Support Systems. Management Science, 33, 5 (1987), 589-609.

12. Dix, A., Finlay, J., & Abowd, G. D. Human-computer interaction. Prentice hall, 2004.

13. Edwards, P. N., Jackson, S. J., Bowker, G. C., & Knobel, C. P. (2007). Understanding Infrastructure: Dynamics, Tensions, and Design (Workshop Report).

14. Ellis, C. A., Gibbs, S. J., & Rein, G. L. (1991, January 1991). Groupware: Some Issues and Experiences. Communications of the ACM, 34, 38-58.

15. Ferro, T., & Zachry, M. Networked Knowledge Workers on the Web: An Examination of US Trends, 2008-2010. Handbook of Research on Business Social Networking: Organizational, Managerial, and Technological Dimensions (2011).

16. Friedman, B., Kahn Jr, P. H., Hagman, J., Severson, R. L., & Gill, B. The Watcher and the Watched: Social Judgments About Privacy in a Public Place. Human-Computer Interaction, 21, 2 (2006), 235-272. DOI= http://dx.doi.org/10.1207/s15327051hci2102_3.

17. Furnas, G. W. Future design mindful of the MoRAS. Hum.-Comput. Interact., 15, 2 (2000), 205-261. DOI= http://dx.doi.org/10.1207/s15327051hci1523_6.

18. Gerson, E. M. Reach, Bracket, and the Limits of Rationalized Coordination: Some Challenges for CSCW Resources, Co-Evolution and Artifacts. M. S. Ackerman & C. A. Halverson & T. Erickson & W. A. Kellogg, Eds. Springer London, 2008, 193-220. DOI= http://dx.doi.org/10.1007/978-1-84628-901-9_8.

19. Grudin, J. Computer-supported cooperative work: history and focus. Computer, 27, 5 (1994), 19-26. DOI= http://dx.doi.org/10.1109/2.291294

20. Grudin, J., & Poltrock, S. E. Taxonomy and theory in computer supported cooperative work. The Oxford Handbook of Industrial and Organizational Psychology. Oxford University Press, New York (2012).

21. Handel, M. J., & Poltrock, S. (2011). Working around official applications: experiences from a large engineering project, Proceedings of the ACM 2011 conference on Computer supported cooperative work (pp. 309-312). Hangzhou, China: ACM.

22. Heath, C., & Luff, P. Collaboration and Control: Crisis Management and Multimedia Technology in London Underground Line Control Rooms. Computer Supported Cooperative Work (CSCW), 1, 1 (1992), 69-94. DOI= http://dx.doi.org/10.1007/bf00752451.

23. Jirotka, M., Lee, C. P., & Olson, G. M. Supporting Scientific Collaboration: Methods, Tools and Concepts. Computer Supported Cooperative Work (CSCW), 22, 4-6 (2013), 667-715. DOI= http://dx.doi.org/10.1007/s10606-012-9184-0.

24. Johansen, R. Groupware: Computer Support for Business Teams. The Free Press, New York, NY, 1988.

25. Kriplean, T., Beschastnikh, I., & McDonald, D. W. (2008). Articulations of WikiWork: Uncovering Valued Work in Wikipedia Through Barnstars, Proceedings of the 2008 ACM conference on Computer supported cooperative work (pp. 47-56). San Diego, CA, USA: ACM.

26. Latour, B. Science In Action. Harvard University Press, Cambridge, MA, 1987.

27. Lave, J., & Wenger, E. Situated Learning: Legitimate Peripheral Participation. Cambridge University Press, Cambridge, UK, 1991.

28. Lee, C. P. Boundary Negotiating Artifacts: Unbinding the Routine of Boundary Objects and Embracing Chaos in Collaborative Work. Computer Supported Cooperative Work (CSCW), 16 (2007), 307-339.

29. Lee, C. P., Bietz, M. J., Derthick, K., & Paine, D. (2012). A sociotechnical exploration of infrastructural middleware development, Proceedings of the ACM 2012 conference on Computer Supported Cooperative Work (pp. 1347-1350). Seattle, Washington, USA: ACM.

30. Lee, C. P., Bietz, M. J., & Thayer, A. Research-Driven Stakeholders in Cyberinfrastructure Use and Development In Proc. International Symposium on Collaborative Technologies and Systems, IEEE Press (2010), 163-172.

31. Lee, C. P., Dourish, P., & Mark, G. The Human Infrastructure of Cyberinfrastructure. In Proc. CSCW, ACM (2006), 483-492.

32. Löwgren, J., & Stolterman, E. Thoughtful Interaction Design: A Design Perspective on Information Technology. MIT Press, 2004.

33. Lutters, W., & Ackerman, M. Beyond Boundary Objects: Collaborative Reuse in Aircraft Technical Support. Computer Supported Cooperative Work (CSCW), 16, 3 (2007), 341-372. DOI= http://dx.doi.org/10.1007/s10606-006-9036-x.

34. Malone, T. W. (1988). What is coordination theory? Cambridge, MA: Massachusetts Institute of Technology.

35. Morgan, J. T., Bouterse, S., Walls, H., & Stierch, S. (2013). Tea and sympathy: crafting positive new user experiences on wikipedia, Proceedings of the 2013 conference on Computer supported cooperative work (pp. 839-848). San Antonio, Texas, USA: ACM.

36. Morgan, J. T., & Zachry, M. (2010). Negotiating with angry mastodons: the wikipedia policy environment as genre ecology, Proceedings of the 16th ACM international conference on Supporting group work (pp. 165-168). Sanibel Island, Florida, USA: ACM.

37. Nardi, B., Whittaker, S., & Schwarz, H. NetWORKers and their Activity in Intensional Networks. Computer Supported Cooperative Work (CSCW), 11, 1-2 (2002), 205-242. DOI= http://dx.doi.org/10.1023/A:1015241914483.

38. Nelson, H. G., & Stolterman, E. The Design Way: Intentional Change in an Unpredictable World (2nd ed.). MIT Press, Cambridge, MA, 2012.

39. Olson, G. M., & Olson, J. S. Distance matters. Hum.-Comput. Interact., 15, 2 (2000), 139-178. DOI= http://dx.doi.org/10.1207/s15327051hci1523_4.

40. Olson, J. S., Hofer, E., Bos, N., Zimmerman, A., Olson, G. M., et al. A theory of remote scientific collaboration. Scientific Collaboration on the internet (2008), 73-97.

41. Patel, H., Pettitt, M., & Wilson, J. R. Factors of collaborative working: A framework for a collaboration model. Applied Ergonomics, 43, 1 (2012), 1-26. DOI= http://dx.doi.org/http://dx.doi.org/10.1016/j.apergo.2011.04.009.

42. Pollock, N., Williams, R., & D'Adderio, L. Global Software and Its Provenance: Generification Work in the Production of Organizational Software Packages. Social Studies of Science, 37, 2 (2007), 254-280.

43. Ribes, D., & Finholt, T. A. The Long Now of Technology Infrastructure: Articulating Tensions in Development. Journal of the Association for Information Systems, 10, 5 (2009), 375-398.

44. Sawyer, R. K. Social emergence: Societies as complex systems. Cambridge Univ Press, 2005.

45. Schmidt, K. Divided by a common acronym: On the fragmentation of CSCW. ECSCW 2009 (2009), 223-242.

46. Schmidt, K., & Bannon, L. Taking CSCW seriously. Computer Supported Cooperative Work (CSCW), 1, 1 (1992), 7-40. DOI= http://dx.doi.org/10.1007/bf00752449.

47. Schmidt, K., & Bannon, L. Constructing CSCW: The First Quarter Century. Computer Supported Cooperative Work (CSCW), 22, 4-6 (2013), 345-372. DOI= http://dx.doi.org/10.1007/s10606-013-9193-7.

48. Schmidt, K., & Simone, C. Coordination mechanisms: Towards a conceptual foundation of CSCW systems design. Computer Supported Cooperative Work (CSCW), 5, 2 (1996), 155-200. DOI= http://dx.doi.org/10.1007/bf00133655.

49. Schmidt, K., & Wagner, I. Ordering Systems: Coordinative Practices and Artifacts in Architectural Design and Planning. Computer Supported Cooperative Work (CSCW), 13 (2004), 349-408.

50. Shneiderman, B., Plaisant, C., Cohen, M., & Jacobs, S. Designing the user interface: strategies for effective human-computer interaction (5 ed.). Addison-Wesley Computing, 1998.

51. Starbird, K., & Palen, L. (2012). (How) will the revolution be retweeted?: information diffusion and the 2011 Egyptian uprising, Proceedings of the ACM 2012 conference on Computer Supported Cooperative Work (pp. 7-16). Seattle, Washington, USA: ACM.

52. Starbird, K., & Palen, L. (2013). Working and sustaining the virtual "Disaster Desk", Proceedings of the 2013 conference on Computer supported cooperative work (pp. 491-502). San Antonio, Texas, USA: ACM.

53. Stebbins, R. A. Serious Leisure: A Conceptual Statement. The Pacific Sociological Review, 25, 2 (1982), 251-272. DOI= http://dx.doi.org/10.2307/1388726.

54. Strauss, A. The articulation of project work: An organizational process. The Sociological Quarterly, 29, 2 (1988), 163-178.

55. Thayer, A., Bietz, M. J., Derthick, K., & Lee, C. P. (2012). I love you, let's share calendars: calendar sharing as relationship work, Proceedings of the ACM 2012 conference on Computer Supported Cooperative Work (pp. 749-758). Seattle, Washington, USA: ACM.

56. Wenger, E. Communities of practice: Learning, meaning, and identity. Cambridge University Press, Cambridge, UK, 1998.

57. Yasuoka, M. (2009). Bridging and Breakdowns - Using computational artifacts across social worlds. IT University of Copenhagen, Copenhagen, Denmark.

The Effects of View Portals on Performance and Awareness in Co-Located Tabletop Groupware

David Pinelle and Carl Gutwin
Department of Computer Science, University of Saskatchewan
110 Science Place, Saskatoon, Saskatchewan, Canada
david.pinelle@usask.ca, carl.gutwin@usask.ca

ABSTRACT

Tabletop work surfaces have natural advantages for co-located collaboration, but also have physical constraints that can make group work difficult. View portals have been proposed as a way to provide access to other parts of a table surface, and as a way to re-orient content for group members in different locations; however, there is little research on whether portals really do improve group performance, how much they help, and whether they change other aspects of collaboration. We report on two studies that evaluate the effects of portals on group performance and behavior. Our first study showed significant performance advantages for portals: people were able to complete tasks more quickly and with more equal division of labor. Our second study, with a realistic design task, showed that people used portals extensively and saw them as valuable, but that they affected people's ability to maintain awareness, coordinate access to objects, and understand the organization of the workspace. Our work demonstrates benefits and potential drawbacks of portals for tables, and suggests that designers should carefully consider both individual and group needs before implementing these and other tabletop view augmentations.

Author Keywords

Tabletop groupware; portals; performance; awareness

INTRODUCTION

Digital tabletops are now becoming common in research labs and organizational settings. One reason for the interest in these devices is that tables are a natural setting for collaboration, and provide many advantages for co-located group work. For example, tables traditionally allow for easy verbal and visual communication, simple and rich awareness of others' presence, location, and activity, and enough space to support both individual work and shared group areas.

However, there are also limitations presented by physical table settings. For example, the arrangement of the group around the table means that some people must look at work artifacts sideways or upside down (when they are being used by others), that people can interfere with one another when they are working in the same place, and that it can be difficult to see and reach other parts of the surface (either because of distance or occlusion from others' arms and bodies).

Figure 1. Tabletop portals – the left user has a portal that is showing the contents of the right person's work area.

Researchers have proposed augmentations to digital surfaces that are intended to address some of these limitations – for example, long-distance reaching techniques such as tractor beams, wormholes, or cursor extensions allow people to select and manipulate objects anywhere on the table (e.g., [1,20,23,38]); individual views provide additional or private space for people to work (e.g., [11,16,26,27]); and view portals allow people to temporarily duplicate regions of the table for easier access to objects or tools (e.g., [12,19,34,38]).

Augmenting tabletop collaboration with techniques like these poses a question for groupware designers: is it better to preserve the well-understood affordances and supports of a traditional tabletop setting (and live with the limitations), or is it better to add to the capabilities and affordances of a digital table to try and overcome the traditional limitations. The risk in augmenting digital tables is that the new techniques may compromise some of the characteristic benefits of tables (communication, awareness, and flexibility) that are so useful for collaboration.

Some research has shown that changes do occur – that group activity changes based on different factors in the tabletop setting. For example, the type of input device [9], the type of interaction (direct or indirect) [10], the type of embodiments used on the table [6,24], and the use of personal views [16]

CSCW 2015, March 14–18, 2015, Vancouver, BC, Canada.

ACM 978-1-4503-2922-4/15/03...$15.00.
http://dx.doi.org/10.1145/2675133.2675196

have led to a variety of effects on group performance, coordination, conflict, and territoriality at a digital table.

There is little previous research, however, about the effects of view portals on collaboration. Portals can substantially increase the power of a tabletop system – they can provide access to distant parts of the table, can allow reorientation of work objects to each user's perspective, and can allow people to work in the same area of the table without physical collisions – but these new capabilities could also take away from the existing strengths of tabletop settings. For example, the duplicate views that portals create can break the explicit connection between a user's embodiment and the artifacts being manipulated, possibly reducing awareness; similarly, portals create visual discontinuities in the table surface, potentially making it more difficult for users to understand the organization of the workspace and others' locations in it.

To provide initial knowledge about how view portals affect both group performance and group behavior, we carried out two studies. The first study looked at the potential performance benefits of portals in controlled conditions – that is, we examined whether, and by how much, portals can solve problems of reach and orientation on tables. The second study looked at how portals affected collaboration in a realistic and open-ended task, and collected subjective data about group awareness, coordination, and conflict, about people's ability to understand the overall organization of the workspace, and about overall performance and preferences.

The results of our first study show that in terms of performance, view portals do provide the intended benefits – they significantly reduce the time needed to reach distant objects, and they significantly reduce time and errors when working with objects that are oriented away from the user. In a two-person task, portals also led to more equality in the amount of work done by the two people – although participants reported being less aware of the other person's activities when portals were used.

In the second study, which used a realistic and open-ended task, participants all chose to use portals to organize their work activity, all stated that portals provided benefits in terms of reaching and orientation, and eight of twelve people said that portals improved the collaboration. However, participants again reported negative subjective effects of portals on their ability to keep track of what the other person was doing, and on their ability to understand the spatial organization of the workspace. Comments and interview responses from participants showed that portals introduced new barriers to awareness, understanding, and coordination – in particular, portals made it harder to see others' actions, which led to poor awareness and increased conflicts, and portals also led to people becoming overly focused on a single view rather than observing the entire tabletop.

These results indicate that view portals present groupware designers with a tradeoff between the needs of the individual and the needs of the group. Our studies are the first to demonstrate that portals can improve performance and reduce limitations of the table setting – but that there is a cost to issues important to the group. Our work shows that designers must carefully assess the need for awareness, coordination, and workspace understanding before deciding to make use of this (potentially high-performance) technique.

RELATED WORK

Tabletop workspaces and constraints

In tabletop work, people naturally divide the workspace into nearby personal areas and into more centrally located group work areas [29]. However, tabletop work often has a mixed focus in which people move back and forth between individual activities, subgroup interactions, and shared activities with the entire group [8,22]. This means that peoples' work locations can change over the course of an activity, and that they may need to access a variety of locations and artifacts on the tabletop. Three main problems can arise during mixed-focus collaborative work on a tabletop: that items are out of reach, that people can interfere with each other's access to different parts of the table, and that shared artifacts can only be oriented towards one person.

Reaching. When people switch between these work modes, they often change the artifacts and tools that they are working with, but the items they need are sometimes out of their reach [20,23]. People can adopt different strategies to retrieve the items that they need [36]: for example, they can lean across the table, stand up and walk around the table, or ask another person to pass the item. This problem has also been encountered with large wall displays (e.g., [12]).

Interference and access. When people have to work in a limited area (e.g., with a particular artifact or on a set of artifacts), they can have difficulties managing access due to space limitations. For example, several studies describe instances where people blocked another person's view or interfered with their ability to interact with the workspace [19,36]. Similarly, Doucette et al have shown that people avoid crossing over another person's arm on the table, meaning that people need to coordinate access when they need to use objects in different areas of the workspace [6].

Orientation. Orientation plays an important role in collaborative work on tables: collaborators use the orientation of shared resources to comprehend information, to communicate, and to coordinate work [15]. Orientation enables comprehension since repositioning an object enables individuals to read its contents more easily. As Kruger and colleagues found, people turn objects toward others during conversation, and use object orientation to help to partition the tabletop workspace into individual and group spaces [15]. In many tabletop situations, people must often try to interpret and make use of objects that are oriented away from them, and several sources indicate that it is difficult to comprehend information in this setting. Prior work in psychology (e.g. [13]), suggests that people are significantly slower when reading text that is oriented away from them. Wigdor and Balakrishnan [39] show similar results, but argue that the effects are less than the previous studies, since people can often accommodate some degree of rotation by changing the posture and position of their head and body.

Augmenting tables with new view techniques

Several solutions to the limitations of traditional tables have been proposed in prior work. These solutions often take the form of augmented view techniques for digital tables that provide people with new capabilities. Three of the main types of augmentations are techniques for reaching and reorientation, personalizable views, and digital portals.

Techniques to improve reaching and reorientation

Several techniques have been proposed for increasing a person's reach on large surfaces. These techniques use a variety of mechanisms, including pointing, distance reduction, miniatures, and wormholes.

Pointing-based reaching techniques allow people to point to distant objects on the table and drag them into proximity. For example, Tractor Beam [23] and "laser pointing" [20] use this method; simple indirect input with a mouse (e.g., [6]) uses similar principles.

Distance-reduction approaches magnify a person's reaching motions. There are two ways in which this can be done – by extending the user's locus of control (e.g., the Pantograph technique [20] or the I-Grabber tool [1]), or by bringing targets closer after an initial directional movement (e.g., using target proxies in the Drag-and-Pop technique [2]).

Wormholes provide regions on the display that will transport dropped objects to other places. This idea has been used for object transfer in multi-display environments (e.g., using different mouse buttons [6] or a list of displays [4]), and also on tables – the Dynamic Portals system [38] allows people to position the two sides of a wormhole anywhere on the table and move objects through the hole.

Workspace miniatures enhance reaching by creating a new representation where all objects are close (but much smaller). Miniatures give an overview of complex environments (e.g., [4]) but are also fast: for example, Nacenta et al. showed that reaching with a "radar view" miniature was faster than either a pantograph technique or laser pointing [20].

In addition, techniques have been developed to allow easier rotation of artifacts (e.g., RNT [14] or TNT [17]) or the entire table (e.g., DiamondSpin [31]). These simplify the process of reorienting content for a single person, but do not solve the problem of conflicting orientation for the entire group.

Personalized views for tabletop work

Researchers have considered several techniques that provide individuals with different views around a digital table – either to increase the available work area of the table, or to provide private information for each person.

For example, the tabletop workspace can be extended with people's personal devices such as smartphones or tablets (e.g., [29,34]). This approach is common in situations such as a shared card table, where each person's hand of cards is shown on a personal device. Other technologies have also been explored for extending the table – for example, the MisTable system presents 'fog screens' between each user and the table surface that can show individual views [27].

The space of the table itself can also be multiplexed to show different views to different people. A simple approach is to use transparency (e.g., for popup menus) so that people working in the same part of the table can still see their work artifacts [40]. Other technologies can provide completely different views. One approach uses LCD shutter glasses to divide the refresh rate of the table between multiple individualized views. This method, which can show both shared objects and private objects, was used in the early Single Display Privacyware technique [32], as well as the more recent Permulin table system [16]. Another approach uses physical display materials that provide different information depending on the user's position. For example, the Lumisight table [18] gave four users individual views of the workspace using Lumisty film, and the PiVOT system used multiple LCD displays, Lumisty, and an overhead projector to provide flexible and moveable personal views overlaid on top of a shared visual workspace [11].

Personalized view systems are dependent upon specialized hardware, which can limit the number of collaborators. In addition, the approach of providing a different view for each person moves away from one of the original advantages of tabletops – that everyone can see the same shared workspace. This can reduce consequential communication and feedthrough [8] and cause conflicts that do not occur in typical tabletop work (e.g., when people put their personal views into the same physical space on the table [16]). Portal-based systems, in contrast, maintain a single view for all participants, even though the table content is rearranged.

Digital Portals

Multiple views of a large workspace have been known since the first windowed user interfaces; however, the idea of views that are part of the workspace itself is more recent. One of the first common implementations was in the portals of the Pad++ system [3], which were rectangular regions that looked onto other parts of the workspace. Pad++ portals could be scaled arbitrarily, and provided long-distance visibility and long-distance action to other regions of the space. WinCuts is a similar idea [35] that allows users to create new windows that reference regions of existing windows on the desktop, letting them build customized interfaces for particular tasks. Tan and colleagues [35] also propose using WinCuts in co-present collaboration, where users create WinCuts of work areas on their laptops and share them on a large public display.

Several portal and view systems have been developed for large vertical displays. The Frisbee system [12] provides a portal to another region on a wall display, and users can pan and resize the portal area. Actions performed within the Frisbee portal are the equivalent of interacting with the referenced display area. Kahn et al. propose further modifications to the Frisbee system, such as support for multiple portals and the ability to rotate the content of the target area. Bezerianos and Balakrishnan [5] describe a related implementation, called canvas portals, that allows users to reach to distant areas on a large display. The system has several additional enhancements including variable shapes for portals, portal resizing, grouping of portals, and division bands within a portal.

Portals have also been implemented on tabletops – here we separate the specialized technologies that could be used to provide individualized views (discussed above) from the idea of displaying another region of the workspace in a portal (which is possible with any table system). Morris et al. [19] suggest that portals can play an important role in helping to coordinate group work in tabletop systems. Streitz et al. [34] describe the InteracTable, a tabletop system which allows users to create customizable views of other regions of the workspace. The views can be repositioned and reoriented so that they are tailored to each user's perspective. Tang et al. [36] describe a technique called ShadowBoxes that allows users to create views of other areas of the tabletop, with limited control over orientation and size of the view area.

Shen et al. [30] developed CoR2Ds, a portal based widget for providing access to tools that are far away; the widget can be rotated, moved, and resized (but only allows access to controls, not content). Finally, the Dynamic Portals technique (primarily used as an object-transfer technique, as described above) can also provide a view of the table at the other side of the wormhole; and manipulations of the portal can provide effects such as scaled views [38].

The effects of table augmentations on collaboration

Previous work has considered the ways that changes to group and table size, input technique, and embodiment type change the nature of collaborative activity on digital tables. Early work showed that although group size strongly affected collaboration in a shared construction task, table size had little effect [28]. Several projects have compared direct and indirect input in terms of their effects on performance [9], coordination and conflict [10,21,24], and spatial interference [36,37]. Some evidence suggests that indirect input changes natural collaborative behaviours such as territoriality [29], and leads to an increase in coordination problems [22].

Recent work has also looked at tabletop embodiments, which are necessary when a table system uses indirect input (such as mice) for interaction with the table. For example, Pinelle et al. [24] carried out a broad exploratory study that looked at ways that different arm embodiments affected behaviours in a tabletop game; they found differences between physical and digital arms, but that different types of digital embodiments had little effect (although people preferred more realistic representations). Doucette and colleagues have also looked at the effects of different arm embodiments on reaching and arm-crossing behaviour on tables [7]. This work also shows a dramatic difference between physical and digital embodiments, and very little difference between different types of digital representation. These researchers also showed that some of the effects of physical arms (e.g., reduced arm crossing) could be reintroduced by adding tactile feedback or motion changes to digital embodiments.

The effects of personalized views on collaborative coupling was tested in an evaluation of the Permulin system [16]. The study found that the individual views enabled greater parallelization of work, but that when work was loosely coupled, participants stayed almost entirely in their own individual views, reducing awareness of the other person.

These previous study show that augmenting the capabilities of a traditional tabletop can change collaboration in a variety of ways. The specific effects of portals on collaboration has not been considered, however – and portals differ substantially from techniques such as individualized views because portals, and the actions within them, are always visible to all participants around the table. In the following sections, we describe our implementation of a portal system for tabletops, and then report on two studies of how portals affected collaborative performance and behavior.

CUTOUTS: PORTALS FOR DIGITAL TABLES

We developed a representative portal-based interaction technique for tabletop groupware (called *cutouts*) that provides multiple flexible views of the artifacts on a shared tabletop [25]. Our implementation is based on three design goals that capture the main features seen in existing portal techniques (e.g., [12,18,34]): enable users to see and access any area of the table, regardless of distance or others' locations; enable users to work near another person without bumping into them; and enable users to orient digital artifacts to suit their current position at the table.

Cutouts provide portals to other regions of the workspace (Figures 1, 2, 3). Each portal is bound to a region on the table called its 'reference area,' and provides a duplicate virtual view all of the objects that are contained in the reference area. The portal can be moved anywhere on the table, and can be rotated to any angle (Figure 3). Users can interact with the objects shown in the portal, and all operations are applied to the original objects located in the reference area. A cutout is only a view, so destroying it does not affect the original.

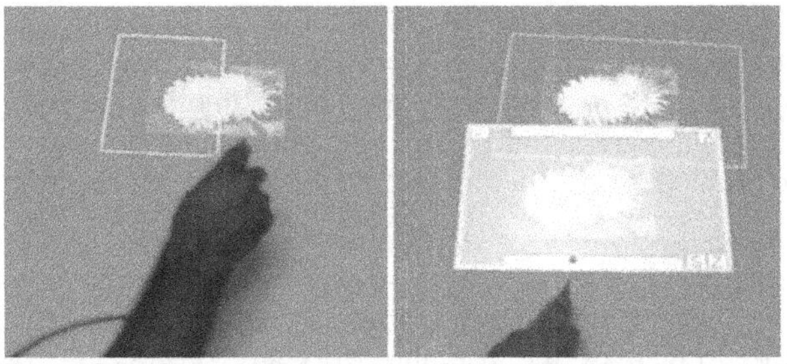

Figure 2. Left: creating a cutout. Right: the new cutout and dashed rectangle indicating reference area.

All instances of an artifact are 'live' and can be manipulated by users. If two users grab the same object, we use a "last-moved" strategy to determine where the object goes, allowing people to use social protocols to resolve the conflict. To aid in maintaining awareness of people's actions in a portal, cutouts display telepointers that show pen movements in both the reference area and the cutout.

Users can also change the coordinates of the reference area that is displayed in the portal using panning controls, and they can change the size of the reference area (which also changes the size of the portal). Finally, they can use zoom controls to shrink and enlarge the objects shown in the portal. These controls allow users to create a variety of customized views that show areas of the table at any size and orientation.

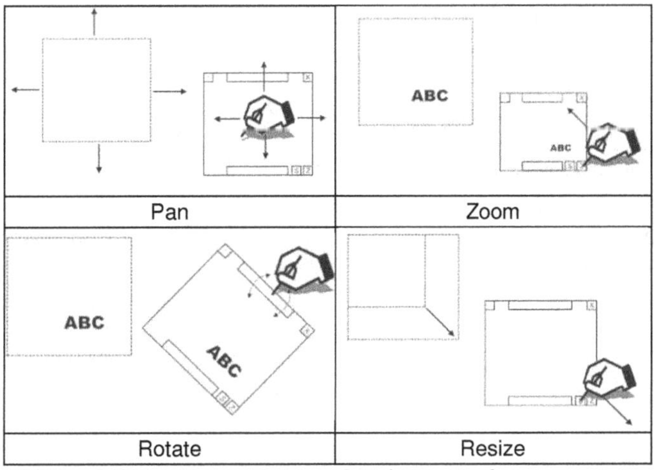

Figure 3. Pan, zoom, rotate, and resize operations on cutout (dashed rectangle indicates change to reference region).

Users can also change the coordinates of the reference area that is displayed in the portal using panning controls, and they can change the size of the reference area (which also changes the size of the portal). Finally, they can use zoom controls to shrink and enlarge the objects shown in the portal. These controls allow users to create a variety of customized views that show areas of the table at any size and orientation.

Users create cutouts by dragging their pen to define the reference area (see Figure 3). Initially, the portal has the same size as the reference area, and has toolbar regions at the top and bottom that provide several controls. A dashed line is drawn around the reference area using a random color, and the same color is used on the cutout border. Users can destroy a cutout by clicking on the "X" button in the portal's toolbar.

We conducted two studies to evaluate the usefulness of portals as a way of managing shared work in tabletop systems. Our overall goal was to assess the quantitative and qualitative effects that cutouts have on the group process. The first study was a controlled experiment where we assessed the effects that cutouts have on group performance and participation. The second was a qualitative study where we evaluated cutouts during a more realistic task, where pairs of people designed a series of webpages.

STUDY 1: PERFORMANCE BENEFITS OF PORTALS

We carried out a controlled study to examine the potential benefits of portals in situations where people need to reach other areas of the table, and where they need to work with artifacts that are oriented away from them. This study established baselines using simple atomic actions that are building blocks in more realistic tasks, and also combined these actions in a simple two-person puzzle game. Our goals were to determine whether portals had a beneficial effect on performance, and what the size of that benefit was.

Methods

We recruited 20 participants (10 men, 10 women, mean age 25.6 years), from a local university. Participants were recruited in same-sex pairs. All were regular computer users (more than 8 hours/week), and 9 had previous experience with using tabletop display systems.

The experiment was conducted on a top-projected table (125x160cm) with 1024x768 resolution. A custom study system was built in Java; all participant input was handled using a Polhemus Liberty tracking system with two pens. Interaction with the table in all conditions involved touching the table with the pen to manipulate objects. There were two within-participants study conditions: the *standard table*, which provided no augmentations, or *portals*, which provided an additional view portal to address distance or orientation limitations for the task, as described below.

Tasks

Baseline tasks: reaching and orientation

The first tasks involved simple reaching and matching activities to determine baseline effects on performance. In the reaching task, participants repeatedly reached for objects and dragged them to a central location (Figure 4, left). For the standard table, objects were positioned 100cm from the central location, and participants had to lean forward to touch the objects with the pen. In the portals condition, a portal of the objects and the central location was created before the trial, scaled to 25%, and positioned in front of the participant. The Fitts's Law index of difficulty for the two tasks are the same (since although the targets are closer, they are also smaller); however, the standard view requires much larger movements of the whole arm.

In the orientation task, participants had to match a given shape to one of four shapes on the table. In the standard setup, we tested two cases: the cue shape was right-side up for the participants, but the reference shapes could be either upside-down or right-side-up; in the portals condition, a portal was used to create a copy of the reference shapes that was oriented towards the participant (Figure 5).

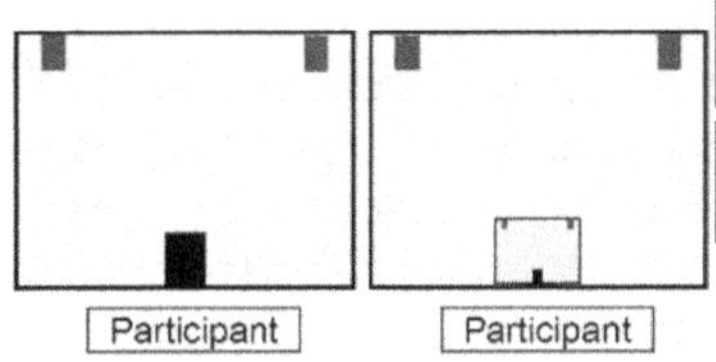

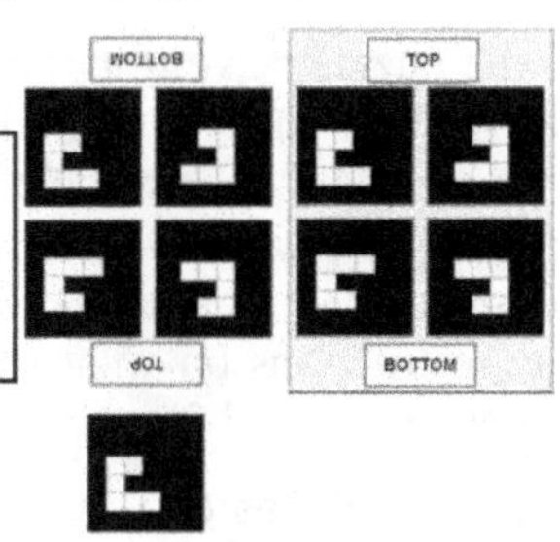

Figure 4. Reaching task (standard left, portal right) **Figure 5. Orientation task (standard left, portal right)**

Group task: puzzle game

Participants sat on opposite sides of the table from each other. During each game, eight targets were displayed on the table (see Figure 6). Each target displayed two white cursive letters on a black background. All targets and all letters faced the same direction (right-side-up for participant A).

Match cards were shown at the corners of the table. When a user tapped on a card, it turned over and rotated to face them. Participants were instructed to select the target card that matched these cards; when a correct match was made, a new match card would appear. Sound feedback indicated correct and incorrect matches. Each game included 16 cards, two for each target. Cards were presented in random order. The game ended when all cards were matched with their targets.

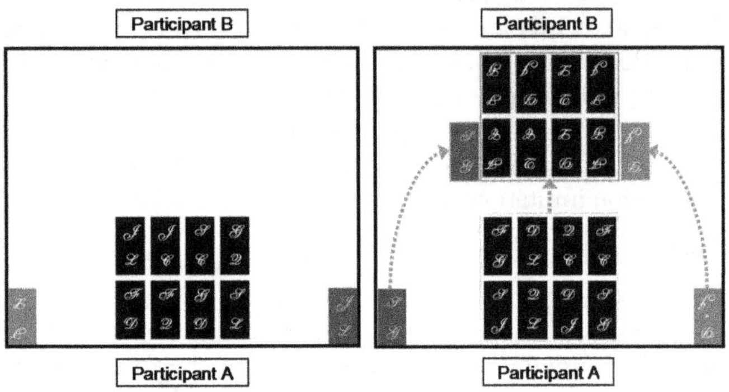

Figure 6. Puzzle game. Standard table shown at left, portals at right. Arrows connect cutouts and their reference areas.

Groups completed two games, one with the standard table (where participant B had to view the targets upside-down, and reach to the other side of the table for the cards), and one with portals, such that participant B saw a rotated view of the targets, and closer versions of the match cards.

Procedure

Participants were given basic training with the table and the input devices, and the experimenter demonstrated the tasks in each condition. Participants carried out the baseline tasks individually, and then completed the puzzle task as a group.

For the reaching baseline task, participants completed one training block and one test block of 24 trials each. For the orientation task, participants completed one training block of four trials and then three test blocks of four trials each. A different set of targets were used in each block.

In the puzzle task, groups carried out short training tasks in each condition, and then eight experimental tasks (four in each of the standard-table and portals conditions). In all cases, participants were instructed to work together and to complete the task as quickly as possible; they were not given any instructions on what strategy to use. A different set of targets were used for each game.

Experiment Design

We analysed performance for each task separately. For the reaching task, we used a single factor design (*table configuration*) with two levels (standard and portals). For the orientation task, we had three levels (standard right-side up, standard upside-down, and portals). For the puzzle game, we used two levels (standard and portals). Condition order was balanced using a Latin square. The study system recorded all dependent measures (e.g., completion times, errors, and the number of cards completed by each user in the puzzle game). Subjective data was collected using a questionnaire. Analyses used ANOVA and Repeated-Measures ANOVA tests, and Tukey Honestly Significant Difference tests for follow-up comparisons.

Results – Baseline tasks

Reaching

Participants took considerably more time (almost one second per trial) to carry out the task on the standard table than in the portal view (Figure 7). A one-way ANOVA showed that the difference was significant ($F_{1,9}$=30.1, p<0.001, η^2_p=0.62).

Orientation (Matching task)

RM-ANOVA showed a significant main effect of table configuration on completion time ($F_{2,38}$=36.35, p<0.001, η^2_p=0.66). A Tukey HSD test showed that the upside-down condition was significantly slower (by about 3 sec per trial) than the right-side-up and portal conditions (p<0.05), but that there was no difference between the latter two (Figure 7).

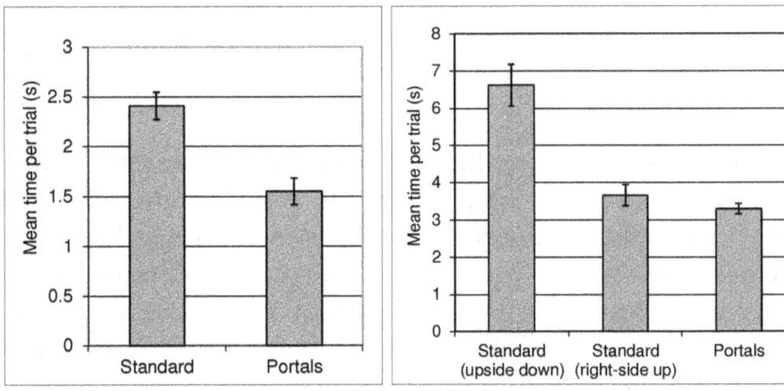

Fig. 7. Performance in reaching (left) and orientation (right).

Results – Group puzzle game

Completion time

Mean completion times are shown in Figure 8. RM-ANOVA showed a significant main effect of configuration ($F_{1,9}$=30.67, p<0.001, η^2_p=0.77). With cutouts (mean 42 sec), the group was faster than with direct touch (52 sec).

Group participation levels

We compared the number of cards that were correctly matched by each player. RM-ANOVA showed a significant main effect of configuration ($F_{3,57}$=54.73, p<0.001, η^2_p=0.74). Figure 8 shows the mean number of cards correctly matched in each condition (each game consisted of 16 cards). On the standard table, the player who saw the targets upside down averaged only 6 of 16 cards; with portals, the portal user averaged 8.4 of 16. A Tukey HSD test showed that this difference was significant (p<0.01).

We also examined error rates for the group puzzle task, but RM-ANOVA showed no significant difference between the configurations ($F_{3,57}$=1.30, p=.284).

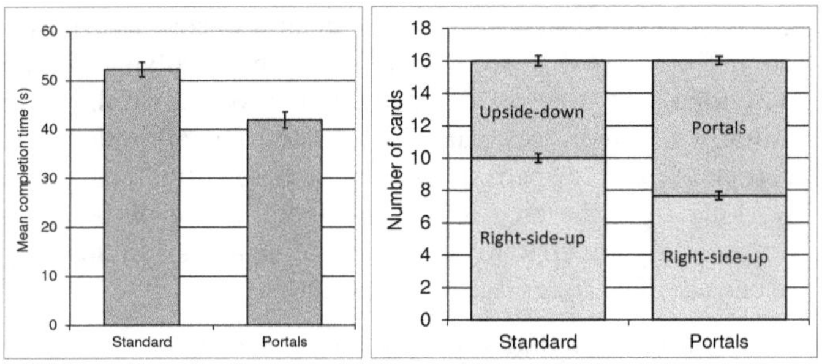

Figure 8. Completion time (left), participation level (right).

Questionnaire responses

Participants answered a series of open ended questions in a questionnaire administered at the end of the study. We summarize the results below.

Working together as a group. Participants were asked which technique allowed them to work together as a group more effectively. Most selected portals (19/20). When asked why, most participants (12/20) indicated that portals allowed them to work together without interfering with each other. Several people indicated that portals minimized physical collisions, for example: "when we had a cutout, we did not have to cross arms." Others indicated that cutouts helped them to avoid occlusion problems: "With no cutouts, either I blocked the other person's view or I was blocked."

Benefits and drawbacks of using portals. People stated that portals provided several benefits: they reduced physical effort, made rotated objects easier to understand, and were faster because they brought items nearer. A few participants also stated some drawbacks. Four people felt that there was less interaction with their partner when using portals. One person stated that that he "didn't really feel like we were collaborating." Another person wrote that she "was unaware of my partner's actions until the cards ran out."

Summary of Study 1

Our results demonstrate that portals can significantly improve performance in situations where the limitations of a physical table setting are apparent – i.e., reaching and re-orientation. Portals allowed people to complete the tasks faster when they were in a disadvantaged setting (far away, or across the table); and in the puzzle game, this led to a more equal distribution of work between the two people.

It is important to note, however, that portals were not essential for success – people were still able to reach to the other side of the table, and were able to interpret upside-down artifacts – it just took them longer to do so. In addition, the performance improvement with portals, although significant, was not enormous – e.g., improvement of a second in a reaching tasks, or three seconds in a matching task, or two extra cards in a 16-card puzzle. This indicates that the limitations of traditional table settings do not (usually) prevent collaborative success, but rather act as a hindrance. This means that the need for portals depends on the performance requirements of the task – and portals will become more important as performance becomes more of an issue. They are likely to become more valuable as the number of reaching actions or the number of reorientation tasks grows, or as tables become larger (thus increasing the performance advantage over standard reaching).

In addition, the study showed early indications that portals can change the way in which collaboration occurs. Although only a few participants commented on these changes, those that did felt that qualities such as group awareness and a shared group focus were reduced by the portals.

STUDY 2: EFFECTS OF PORTALS ON COLLABORATION

Our second study focused on the subjective effects of view portals on group collaboration behaviors – maintaining awareness, coordinating access to shared objects, avoiding conflicts, and working together smoothly. In this study, we used a realistic open-ended task (designing webpages), and we gathered observations, questionnaire results, and interview data, rather than performance measures as seen above, in order to explore the qualitative effects that portals have on collaboration processes.

Methods

We recruited 12 participants from a local university (mean age of 24.6 years; 1 female). All were Computer Science students, and all were frequent computer users (more than 20 hours a week). Ten participants had past experience with using tabletop display systems, but none had used portals.

The experiment setup was similar to that described above, but with a larger table (1536x1024 pixels, display area of 178x118cm). A custom study system was built in Java; participant input was again handled using a Polhemus Liberty tracking system with two pens.

Task

Pairs completed two website design tasks (see Figure 10) that involved manipulation and arrangement of several web-page elements on the table surface (e.g., pictures, headings, text boxes, and icons). The elements existed as separate objects on the table, and could be dragged and rotated using the stylus. This task incorporates basic actions that are part of many real-world activities carried out on tables – such as moving and rotating individual items, accessing tools and resources that are common to all participants, and organizing objects using the space of the table.

Participants were given a design scenario and were asked to create a mockup that shows the visual layout for two web pages from the site, maintaining a consistent overall look. Each group completed two design scenarios (one for an online florist, and one for a travel website), and they were given 15 minutes for each. Participants were told to create the home page and a detail page in both tasks, but they had freedom to choose content and layout, to move around the table, and to use any strategy for carrying out the task.

The application provided tools and catalogs of pictures that could be used to create the pages. The catalogs contained both generic interface items (e.g., buttons and icons) and scenario-specific content (e.g., pictures of flowers and holiday destinations). Participants could create handwritten labels for the text on the page. At the end of the table, two rectangular "paste-up" areas were provided to produce the webpage designs. Portals were implemented as described above, and users had access to all of the controls (move, rotate, zoom, resize, pan).

Figure 10. Web design task. Web pages are at the bottom and both users (top and left) have a cutout of that area.

Procedure

Participants were given basic training with the table and the input devices. The experimenter explained the application, demonstrated each of the web design tools, and explained and demonstrated the portals. Participants then completed a 15 minute training trial, where they were asked to create portals and to experiment with the controls. After the training session, they completed two 15-minute sessions, where they designed pages for two different websites. Participants were asked to switch locations at the end of the first session. At the end of the session, participants completed a questionnaire about the collaboration (Figure 9) and provided additional comments that were discussed in a short follow-up interview.

How did portals affect:
1 ... your ability to work together as a group? 2 ... your ability to track others' actions during the task? 3 ... your ability to understand where objects are located? 4 ... your ability to work with objects that are not near you? 5 ... your ability to work with objects that are not oriented to you? 6 ... the amount of physical effort needed to interact with objects? 7 ... the amount of mental effort needed to interact with objects?

Figure 9. Experience questions given at the end of the session (7-point scales, and space for open-ended comments).

Results

Use of portals during the task

All of the participants stated that they felt comfortable using portals by the end of the training session, and all twelve people used portals during both of the tasks. The portals took some time to set up, but there were no noticeable problems using the controls while carrying out the tasks. Most groups adopted a similar strategy in using portals. Their personal territories were perpendicular to the paste-up regions at the end of the table, so they both created portals that could be scaled and rotated to fit into their own workspaces at the sides of the table (see Figure 10). In addition, most of the groups moved the tools and image catalogs near to the paste-up regions, so that they would also be available in the individual portal views. People had to move around the table initially in order to create the cutouts, but after this was complete, people spent most of their time sitting down and working from the area in front of them. Some participants occasionally got up to look at the paste-up areas, but this only occurred a few times during the session.

People used their individual portals extensively during the trial, and most of their interactions with the table were carried out through a portal. Pan and resize controls were often used when setting up a portal, when the person was trying to get the cutout positioned so that they could view the regions of the table where they were going to design the website. Zoom controls were used when people were trying to fit the cutout into their personal territory.

Four of the groups interacted regularly throughout the task, and jointly worked on the webpages, but not necessarily at the same time. People had ongoing discussions about the designs that they were developing and about the elements that they were adding to the pages. However, two other groups used a divide and conquer approach, where the participants each worked on a separate page, and little direct interaction took place between them.

Questionnaire responses

The questionnaire asked people about how portals affected their collaboration, in terms of awareness, understanding of the table space, managing orientation differences, reaching, and mental and physical effort (see Figure 9). The seven-point scale used semantic anchors ("made it much easier" at one end, "no difference" in the middle, and "made it much more difficult" at the other end).

The results are summarized in Figure 11. Portals were ranked favorably in several areas: working together as a group, working with distant objects, managing orientation differences, and physical effort. People had a more negative opinion of cutouts in three other areas, although most of the responses in these areas are close to the "no difference" value on the scale. These areas are tracking others' actions, understanding object location, and mental effort.

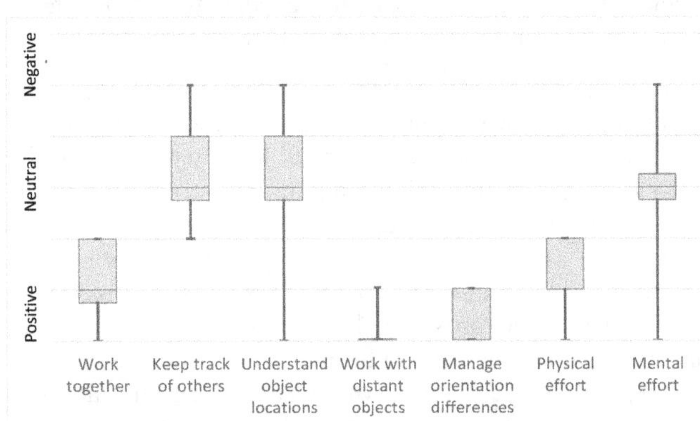

Figure 11. Questionnaire responses (box shows Q1-Q3 and median; whiskers show maximum and minimum)

Participant comments and discussion
Additional information about the topics in the questionnaire were gathered through open-ended areas on the survey form, and through follow-up questions in a short interview. In the following paragraphs we summarize participants' views on each of the topics considered in the questionnaire.

Working with objects and areas that are far away
Participants were uniformly positive about the value of portals both for seeing and reaching different areas of the table. One person stated "I could reach far places and I could see far places easier" (P3); others said "I never had to reach" (P1), "no more reaching!" (P9), and "very awesomely easy" (P8). Two participants mentioned that the portals meant that they did not have to get up as often to move around the table ("I didn't have to get up" (P4), "I didn't have to reposition the chair" (P11)). One participant also mentioned that the zoom function can bring items closer even within the portal (P12), which echoes the results of the reaching task in Study 1. The only negative comments about reaching had to do with the time it took to set up the portals and get them sized and rotated appropriately for the task (P6, P7, P8).

Working with objects that are oriented away from the user
Participants were also very positive about the portals' ability to reorient work artifacts to suit their own position at the table. This was seen as easy to do with the cutouts tools (e.g., "easy to reorient objects to my desired perspective" (P1), "when I needed to I could just re-orient the cutout" (P9)), and it was clear to the participants that this reorientation worked for all of the group members (e.g., "everyone can have the cutout oriented towards them" (P2)). In addition, two participants stated that having the correct orientation was particularly important for a design task – one stated that "alignment and orientation are very important for artistic design" (P3). Finally, one participant said that portals let him make better use of the space of the table ("with cutouts, it was easy to use the other side of the table" (P7)).

Effects on physical effort
Overall, participants felt that the portals reduced the amount of physical effort they had to expend during the task. As discussed above in terms of reaching, the reduced effort was due to a reduction in the distance that people had to reach, and a reduction in the number of times that people had to stand up and move around the table. Participants stated that with portals, there is "no reaching or standing up or moving around the table" (P1) and that "I can do the whole thing just sitting" (P2). This was clearly seen as a benefit, as stated by one participant: "Yay – [it] helped a lot by minimizing reaching and movement distance" (P6).

As we discuss further below, however, reduced movement can also have implications for the group as a whole. Movement around the table is something that is costly to the individual, but that is valuable to the group – in that people standing up and walking to different locations is an obvious signal of their activities and focus.

Effects on mental effort
The questionnaire responses about mental effort were much more divided than those about physical effort (see Figure 11), and people's comments also showed a much wider variance. Participants discussed both positive and negative aspects of portals, relating to three different kinds of mental effort in the task. First, people discussed the reduced mental effort that came from having task objects oriented right side up (e.g., "objects aligned to me are easy to understand" (P3). Second, several participants mentioned that having multiple parts of the table that were copied and reoriented could be confusing, at least at first. For example, one person said "keeping track of what is in where was a bit more difficult" (P9); another stated that "it was confusing [...] between cutouts, table, and other cutouts" (P2). Third, participants mentioned the additional effort needed to learn and manage the portal tools themselves – one person said "there is definitely a learning curve" (P1); another said "[there was] a little effort getting the cutouts set up and positioned" (P2).

Ability to track others' actions during the task
This question on maintaining awareness led to the least positive results in the questionnaire (although still more neutral than negative), and to several comments from participants. The main result from the discussions was that portals appeared to allow people to focus more on their own work, at the expense of maintaining awareness of the other person. There were numerous comments in this area: for example, "I was too busy looking at my own work" (P1), "I did not really notice them at all" (P2), and "I didn't really follow his actions" (P3). It is possible that this reduction in awareness would occur on a standard table as well (e.g., if people became immersed in their local work), but it does seem clear that portals increased the effect. As described above, people moved around the table much less often, and made fewer large reaching gestures – both of which provide obvious awareness cues. Similarly, the ability to have all the necessary artifacts within one's personal work area may have reduced the need for people to look over at the other person's area – as one person stated, "I could look over whenever I wanted to see the other person's work, but when I focused on my task I wasn't very aware of him" (P8).

The second awareness issue that came up in discussions was that of the telepointers that were used to show others' actions in portals (or in reference areas). Several people mentioned that they were not able to see the telepointer adequately – for example, one person stated "embodiment was a problem, as I found it difficult to know from the cutout if he was flipping through pictures or not" (P5); another said "I could not tell clearly what the other user was doing" (P6). These comments suggest that awareness representations in a tabletop's large and visually busy space may need to be made more obvious than what would be needed for other kinds of groupware.

The lack of awareness did on occasion lead to conflicts in the system, in which both people would simultaneously attempt to grab a picture or page through the image catalog. Three participants mentioned these coordination difficulties – for example, one said "sometimes, if I wasn't paying attention, we got in each other's way" (P4).

Ability to understand the organization of the table

This question received neutral rather than positive scores, and there was a mixture of positive and negative comments from participants. Some people felt that they had no difficulties understanding the table surface (e.g., "the cutout didn't change my ability to understand where objects are located" (P5), or "spatial location understanding was not really affected" (P6)). Several others, however, made comments that suggest that there were some problems. For example, one person said "I would get confused between the cutout and the original and try to move one or the other where it could not go" (P1); another said "the different frame of reference between the cutout and the page view made it a little counter intuitive to drag between them" (P2). Part of the problem is caused by the duplicate views, each with different locations and orientations, but the reduced awareness may have also contributed to spatial confusions – as one person stated, "things moved without my seeing someone move them, so it was a bit harder" (P9).

One result of the added complexity of the table surface (with portals) was that some participants focused more on their own areas and portals – which may have reinforced the lack of awareness discussed above. For example, one person stated "I just took my own view and went ahead with it" (P11); another stated that, "I may think of where [an object] is in my setup rather than where it is on the table" (P8).

Overall effect on ability to work together as a group

Participants were overall very positive about the effects of portals on the collaboration – both in their questionnaire responses and their comments. The improved access to the different areas of the table, and the ability to both work with right-side-up artifacts were mentioned by several participants as main benefits – to the group, and not just to the individual. This suggests that group members see the overall efficacy of the group as a critical aspect of the overall task of "working together," and that allowing everyone to contribute equally may outweigh the reduced awareness of others' activity or of the workspace's organization.

Our task was not highly interdependent (people needed to maintain consistency and ensure that their pages were similar, but could still divide the task fairly completely), and it may be that portals made it possible for people to parallelize their activity more than a standard table would allow. This is reflected in participant comments: one person said "[portals] were good for divide and conquer style – we mostly worked individually, but towards a common goal and working off of one another" (P8); another stated that a main benefit of portals was that they allowed "more freedom" in the task (P12). A third participant summed up this effect of portals on the overall collaboration by saying "it was easier to do cooperative work, with each working on their own, but difficult to coordinate on the same page" (P10).

At the end of the interview, we asked people whether they would choose to use portals if they were available in the future. Nine of the twelve participants said that they would use portals, and three did not state a preference.

DISCUSSION

Our studies show that view portals can have substantial effects on group work at digital tables. Both study 1 and study 2 show that portals can overcome some of the limitations presented by the table environment – allowing people to reach distant areas of the table, allowing them to reorient artifacts to their own perspective, and allowing people to work in the same area without physical conflicts. However, there are also effects on collaborative behavior – most notably on group awareness, coordination, and understanding of the organization of the table surface. These effects are to some degree a result of the way that groups organized their portals (i.e., with each person having a view of the page layout space), but represent a common organization of portal views, and therefore a common set of drawbacks that can occur.

View portals therefore present a tradeoff for groupware designers – in which the system can support the needs of either the individual or the group, but not both simultaneously. This general issue has been noted in previous CSCW research [8], but for distributed groupware rather than co-located collaboration at tables. This is an interesting comparison, because in some ways view portals take the co-located setting of a table and make it more like distributed groupware – that is, if each group member creates a portal and focuses only on that window, things become very similar to the distributed setting where each person looks at their own display's view of the workspace [33]. Given that the natural collaborative affordances of tables are one of the main reasons why people gather around them in the first place, it seems to be an odd choice to disable those affordances through the use of portals (or personalized views, which go even further in this direction).

Tabletops provide a strong group focus by enforcing a working style that can disadvantage some people and some types of work organization. Designers can attempt to get some of the best of both worlds, by providing the power of portals but attempting to repair some of the awareness or coordination problems that can result from their use. In our implementation of portals, we attempted to address the need for additional awareness information by using a telepointer. However, our studies suggest that some people did not see the pointer because it was not large enough to stand out from all of the other visual information present in the workspace (including work objects and multiple portals and reference-area markers). It is possible that larger and more obvious telepointers will increase the noticeability of others' actions within a portal – and that other techniques from distributed groupware (such as enlarged actions, or persistent traces [8]) can improve people's ability to maintain awareness.

As mentioned above, however, moving too far down this path could lead to a situation where the natural value of co-located tabletops is lost; more work is needed to determine an appropriate balance between the needs of individuals and groups in tabletop groupware settings. It is clear from our realistic-task study that users see the value of portals, and choose to use them when they have the chance. Participant comments in this study also showed that users see the success of the overall collaboration, to some degree at least, as the sum of the individual contributions from the group members rather than the level of shared group focus that exists during the task. This echoes earlier discussions in CSCW of "mixed-focus" collaboration [8,16,22], in which most of the work is individual, but carried out in a context of others' activity. If mixed-focus collaboration is in fact the norm, then it may be that designers should be focusing as much on features that enhance individual work as they are on features that support the group as a whole.

Generalization to other technologies and settings

Three factors in tabletop collaboration are important in considering the generalization of our results to other settings – group size, input technology, and other types of tabletop augmentations. First, it is likely that increasing group size – and therefore increasing the number of portals on the table – will accentuate both the positive and negative results seen in our studies. For example, more people around the table may lead to increased difficulty in accessing different work areas, which could increase the usefulness of portals in allowing different people to reach distant areas and work in the same region. However, the increased visual clutter from multiple portals is also likely to further reduce understanding of the workspace and group awareness, potentially leading to local conflicts (e.g., trying to manipulate the same object) or problems with higher-level coordination.

Second, our results can also generalize to other types of input technology and other types of display. Changing the type of input (e.g., to multi-touch finger input instead of pens) is not likely to change the way that portals are used – but it does mean that awareness techniques such as telepointers may have to be altered (e.g., to show "video arms" rather than individual pointers). Changes to the table environment may also affect our results – for example, larger tables make reaching more difficult, which can in turn make portals and other reaching techniques more valuable. We also expect our results to apply to vertical displays as well as horizontal tables – although orientation is not an issue in these settings, both the reaching benefits and the potential awareness drawbacks could occur when using portals on wall displays.

Third, we expect that some of our results will also generalize to other types of table augmentations. Reaching techniques such as the pantograph [20] or the I-Grabber [1] may also have negative effects on awareness, since they allow people to manipulate artifacts without the obvious awareness cue of a physical body [7]. However, these techniques do not break the continuity of the table's work surface (the way that a portal does), which may reduce problems of understanding; similarly, reaching techniques are temporary and add less visual clutter to the workspace. Finally, the negative effects of portals on awareness are likely to be exaggerated in situations where the table provides people with separate individualized views. When others cannot see a person's view at all, it becomes very difficult to maintain awareness of their work [16]; the consistent visibility of everyone's views may be a collaborative advantage of portals, despite the increased visual clutter.

CONCLUSION

Portals have been proposed as a way to overcome some of the limitations of co-located tabletops – they can provide access to other parts of a table surface, and can allow re-orientation of content for group members in different locations. We carried out two studies to examine the effects of view portals on collaborative performance and collaborative behavior. Our first study showed significant performance advantages for portals: people were able to complete tasks more quickly and with more equal division of labor. Our second study, with a realistic design task, showed that people used portals extensively and saw them as valuable, but that they affected people's ability to maintain awareness, coordinate access to objects, and understand the overall organization of the workspace. Our work demonstrates both benefits and potential drawbacks of portals, and suggests that designers will need to carefully consider both individual and group needs before implementing portals in tabletop groupware.

REFERENCES

1. Abednego, M., Lee, J., Moon, W., Park, J. I-Grabber: expanding physical reach in a large-display tabletop environment through the use of a virtual grabber. *Proc. ITS 2009*, 61-64.
2. Baudisch, P, et al. Drag-and-pop and drag-and-pick: Techniques for accessing remote screen content on touch- and pen-operated systems. *Proc. INTERACT'03*, 57-64.
3. Bederson, B., and Hollan, J., Pad++: A Zooming Graphical Interface for Exploring Alternate Interface Physics, *Proc. UIST 1994*, 17-26.
4. Biehl, J. and Bailey, B. ARIS: an interface for application relocation in an interactive space. *Proc. Graphics Interface 2004*, 107-116.
5. Bezerianos, A., Balakrishnan, R., View and Space Management on Large Displays. *IEEE CG&A*, 25(4), 2005, 34-43.
6. Booth, K., Fisher, B., Jui, C., Lin, R., and Argue, R. The mighty mouse multi-screen collaboration tool. *Proc. UIST 2002*, 209-212.
7. Doucette, A., Mandryk, R.L., and Gutwin, C., Sometimes When We Touch: how arm embodiments change reaching and collaboration on digital tables, *Proc. CSCW 2013*, 193-202.
8. Gutwin, C., and Greenberg, S., Design for Individuals, Design for Groups: Tradeoffs between Individual Power and Workspace Awareness, *Proc. CSCW 1998*, 207-216.

9. Ha, V., Inkpen, K.M., Mandryk, R.L., Whalen, T. Direct Intentions: The Effects of Input Devices on Collaboration around a Tabletop Display. *Tabletop 2006*. 177-184.
10. Hornecker, E., Marshall, P., Dalton, N.S., Rogers, Y. Collaboration and interference: awareness with mice or touch input. *CSCW 2008*. 167-176.
11. Karnik, A., Plasencia, D., Mayol-Cuevas, W., and Subramanian, S. PiVOT: personalized view-overlays for tabletops. *Proc. UIST 2012*, 271-280.
12. Khan, A., Fitzmaurice, G., Almeida, D., Burtnyk, N, and Kurtenbach, G., A Remote Control Interface for Large Displays, *Proc. UIST 2004*, 127-136.
13. Koriat, A. and Norman, J. Reading rotated words, J. *Experimental Psychology* 11(4), 1985, 490-508.
14. Kruger, R., Carpendale, S., Scott, S., & Tang, A., Fluid integration of rotation and translation. *Proc. CHI 2005*.
15. Kruger, R., Carpendale, S., Scott, S., & Greenberg, S., How people use orientation on tables: Comprehension, coordination and communication. *Proc. Group 2003*.
16. Lissermann, R., Huber, J., Schmitz, M., Steimle, J., and Mühlhäuser, M. Permulin: mixed-focus collaboration on multi-view tabletops. *Proc. CHI 2014*, 3191-3200.
17. Liu, J., Pinelle, D., Sallam, S., Subramanian, S., and Gutwin, C., TNT: Improved Rotation and Translation on Digital Tables, *Proc. Graphics Interface 2006*, 25-32.
18. Matsushita, M., Iida, M., Ohguro, T., Shirai, Y., Kakehi, Y. Lumisight table: a face-to-face collaboration support system that optimizes direction of projected information to each stakeholder. *Proc. CSCW 2004*, 274-283.
19. Morris, M., Ryall, K., Shen, C., Forlines, C., Vernier, F., Beyond 'social protocols': multi-user coordination policies for co-located groupware. *CSCW 2004*, 262-265.
20. Nacenta, M., Aliakseyeu, D., Subramanian, S., and Gutwin, C., A comparison of techniques for multi-display reaching. *Proc. CHI 2005*, 371-380.
21. Nacenta, M.A., Pinelle, D., Stuckel, D., Gutwin, C. The effects of interaction technique on coordination in tabletop groupware. *GI 2007*. 191-198.
22. Nacenta, M.A., Pinelle, D., Gutwin, C., Mandryk, R.L. Individual and Group Support in Tabletop Interaction Techniques. *Tabletop 2010*, 303–333.
23. Parker, J., Mandryk, R., and Inkpen, K., TractorBeam: seamless integration of local and remote pointing for tabletop displays. *Proc. Graphics Interface 2005*, 33-40.
24. Pinelle, D., Nacenta, M., Gutwin, C., Stach, T. The effects of co-present embodiments on awareness and collaboration in tabletop groupware. *Proc. GI 2008,* 1-8.
25. Pinelle, D., Dyck, J., Gutwin, C., and Stach, T. *Cutouts: multiple views for tabletop groupware*. Technical report HCI-2006-01, available at http://hci.usask.ca.
26. Plasencia, D., et al. ReflectoSlates: personal overlays for tabletops combining camera-projector systems and retroreflective materials. *Proc. CHI 2014*, 2071-2076.
27. Plasencia, D., Joyce, E., and Subramanian, S. MisTable: reach-through personal screens for tabletops. *Proc. CHI 2014*, 3493-3502.
28. Ryall, K, Forlines, C., Shen, C., and Ringel Morris, M. Exploring the effects of group size and table size on interactions with tabletop shared-display groupware. *Proc. ACM CSCW 2004*, 284-293.
29. Scott, S., Carpendale, S., Inkpen, K. Territoriality in collaborative tabletop workspaces. *CSCW'04*. 294-303.
30. Shen, C., Hancock, M., Forlines, C., and Vernier, F., CoR2Ds: Context-Rooted Rotatable Draggables for Tabletop Interaction, *Proc. CHI 2005*, 1781-1784.
31. Shen, C., Vernier, F., Forlines, C., and Ringel, M., DiamondSpin: an extensible toolkit for around-the-table interaction, *Proc. CHI 2004*, 67-174.
32. Shoemaker, G., and Inkpen, K. Single display privacyware: augmenting public displays with private information. *Proc. CHI 2001*, 522-529.
33. Stefik, M, Bobrow, Foster, G., Lanning, S., Tatar, D. WYSIWIS revised: Early experiences with multiuser interfaces. *ACM TOIS*, 5(2), 1987, 147-167.
34. Streitz, N., Tandler, P., Muller-Tomfelde, C., Konomi, S. Roomware: Towards the Next Generation of Human-Computer Interaction Based on an Integrated Design of Real and Virtual Worlds. In *Human-Computer Interaction in the New Millennium*, 2001, 553-578.
35. Tan, D., Meyers B., and Czerwinski, M., WinCuts: Manipulating Arbitrary Window Regions for More Effective Use of Screen Space, *Proc. CHI 2004*, 25-28.
36. Tang, A., Tory, M., Po, B., Neumann, P., and Carpendale, S., Collaborative coupling over tabletop displays. *Proc. CHI 2006*, 1181-1190.
37. Tse, E., Histon, J., Scott, S.D., Greenberg, S. Avoiding interference: how people use spatial separation and partitioning in SDG workspaces. *CSCW 2004*. 252-261.
38. Voelker, S., Weiss, M., Wacharamanotham, C., and Borchers, J. Dynamic portals: a lightweight metaphor for fast object transfer on interactive surfaces. *Proc. ITS 2011*, 158-161.
39. Wigdor, D. and Balakrishnan, R. Empirical investigation into the effect of orientation on text readability in tabletop displays. *Proc. ECSCW 2005*, 205-224.
40. Zanella, A., and Greenberg, S. Reducing interference in single display groupware through transparency. *Proc. ECSCW 2001*, 339-358.

The Perverse Effects of Social Transparency on Online Advice Taking

Duyen T. Nguyen, Laura A. Dabbish, Sara Kiesler
Human-Computer Interaction Institute
School of Computer Science
Carnegie Mellon University, Pittsburgh, PA, 15213

ABSTRACT
Increasingly, the advice people receive on the Internet is socially transparent in the sense that it displays contextual information about the advice-givers or their actions. We hypothesize that activity transparency—seeing an advice giver's process while creating his or her recommendations—will increase advice taking. We report three experiments testing the effect of activity transparency on taking mediocre advice. We found that the presence of a web history increased the likelihood of following a financial advisor's advice and reduced participant earnings (Exp. 1), especially when the web history implied greater task focus (Exp. 2, 3). CSCW research usually emphasizes how to increase information sharing; this work suggests when shared information may be inappropriate. We suggest ways to counter activity transparency's potential downsides.

Author Keywords
Social transparency; online advice; decision making; persuasion; credibility; information sharing

ACM Classification Keywords
H.5.3 Group and Organization Interfaces: Computer-supported cooperative work

General Terms
Experimentation, Human Factors

INTRODUCTION
Many people go online to get advice in domains ranging from medical care to financial decision-making [e.g., 23]. Frequently, this advice has unknown or unclear sources [27]. Increasingly, however, advice seekers see more information about potential sources of advice. This information might include ratings of advisors or their profiles, evidence of others' use of the advice, or even source code. We argue here that social transparency about the online activities of an advisor can lead to a sense of familiarity and trust in the advice. If the advice is wrong or misleading, this information will have the perverse effect of increasing the persuasive impact of the advice.

CSCW '15, March 14 - 18, 2015, Vancouver, BC, Canada.

http://dx.doi.org/10.1145/2675133.2675253

In this paper, we test how a form of social transparency called "activity transparency" [55] affects advice taking. Activity transparency means that advice seekers can see some or all of the advisor's online activity [55]. In three experiments, participants were shown mediocre advice before they made financial investment decisions. We varied whether the advisor's web history was visible (Exp 1), the work-related content of the web history (Exp 2), and the presence of non-work web history (Exp 3). We measured whether participants took the advice. This work contributes to the CSCW literature by extending our understanding of the impact of new forms of social transparency. We demonstrate how information about a source's actions can seem informative and cause people to adopt the source's mediocre advice.

BACKGROUND
Erickson & Kellogg [19] introduced the term *social translucence* to describe communication system designs that provide mediated visibility of other participants. Stuart et al. [55] extended the notion of social translucence to include visibility of actions on information artifacts. Examples of this *activity transparency* are found in systems such as the open-source repository of GitHub that displays the number of changes to a shared document, or commits to a software project [37], Wikipedia, which displays the editors' discussion about an article's content [33], and websites that display the date and time of the latest updates to a webpage.

Activity transparency can improve the perceived quality of information when it showcases the source's expertise in a subject matter [33], or it can make information seem less reliable, for example when it suggests flaws and conflicts in the information creation process [60]. For example, Towne et al. [41] found that Wikipedia editing information reduced an article's credibility when it revealed conflict, lack of expertise, and inefficiencies among the editors. In this situation, activity transparency gave strong negative cues about the editing process.

Seeing a source's work activity also can affect perceptions of a source's credibility [27, 22, 21]. Wikipedia changes suggest contributors' expertise [33, 56, 62]. Users of GitHub intuit developers' level of expertise from relevant activity histories of other users [16]. Shoppers rate websites that display photographs of a company's past selling and buying activities as more credible than websites that do not display such photographs [47].

HYPOTHESES

Most previous studies of social translucence and transparency have focused on the transparency of a source's identity [31, 37, 59] or content [e.g., 21, 22]. This prior work is consistent with theoretical research in social psychology on how people use social cues to verify the utility and quality of information [28, 29]. Petty & Cacioppo's Elaboration Likelihood Model [43] suggests that when people lack the ability or expertise to evaluate the quality of information directly, they rely on irrelevant social cues to accept or reject the information.

Extending this prior work to activity transparency, we suggest that incidental information displayed online about the activities of an information source will increase the influence of the source's information. Consistent with this idea, Cramer et al. [14] found that those using an online art recommender tended to follow system recommendations more if they were given information on why the recommender system picked certain works of art to recommend (i.e., the algorithm the system used for making recommendations). We extend this work to show that activity transparency can increase advice taking even when the advice is of poor quality.

We hypothesized:

H1: Activity transparency will increase the influence of mediocre advice.

Prior work also suggests that activity transparency may increase advice taking through its effect on perceived credibility [e.g., 27]. Source credibility has long been known to increase trust [8] and advice taking [11, 58].

H2: Activity transparency will increase the advisor's credibility.

H3: Perceived advisor credibility will increase the influence of mediocre advice.

To test these hypotheses, we conducted three online experiments. In these experiments, participants completed a financial investment task. They received advice from an unfamiliar advisor, either with or without activity transparency--a snapshot of the advisor's web history. We measured whether participants adopted the advice, how they performed on the financial task, and how credible they rated their advisors and the advice they gave.

GENERAL METHOD FOR ALL EXPERIMENTS

The participants were asked to select a hedge fund to invest from a list of funds. The best performance was a choice that took potential profit, risk, and fees into account to obtain the highest net value of the investment.

Task

Participants completed a financial investment decision task adapted from Godek and Murray [24]. Participants chose one fund from a list of hedge funds that promised the largest return. They were given data on each fund about its risk (on a scale from 1 to 10), potential return (1 to 10), flat fee (a percentage, such as 2%), and performance fee (ranging from 20% to 25%) (see Table 1).

Fund	Risk	Return	Flat fee	Performance fee
Mainoways	4	4	2%	22%
Carisies	5	6	2%	22%

Table 1. Two sample funds & the attributes to evaluate them

We chose this financial investment task for several reasons. First, financial investment is a common task among adults, but it is new to virtually all of our participants, and thus is interesting to them. Second, it is easy enough that they could learn (with a practice phase) which objective investment was a good choice, but also hard enough that an advice will be seen as useful. As it is hard for participants to evaluate the correctness of the advice, this task is not demonstrable, and thus it reduces bias towards either accepting or rejecting the advice [10]. Fourth, the task has a measureable outcome, based on the quality of the hedge fund people chose.

Procedure

Experiments 1, 2 and 3 all involved the same procedure as shown in Figure 1. Participants read a page of information about investing in hedge funds, completed a comprehension check, and practiced evaluating 10 hedge funds. They were asked to rate them on a scale of 1 (Bad) to 3 (Good). They then viewed the funds' historical performance in the market so they could compare their ratings with the 'correct' historical ratings. To reinforce learning, we asked participants to report their own number of correct ratings (based on the historical standard) and their opinions of the practice.

After their practice, participants completed an investment decision task three times (center box of figure 1). The first time they completed the task, they viewed a list of funds, rated the funds and selected an investment (steps A and C

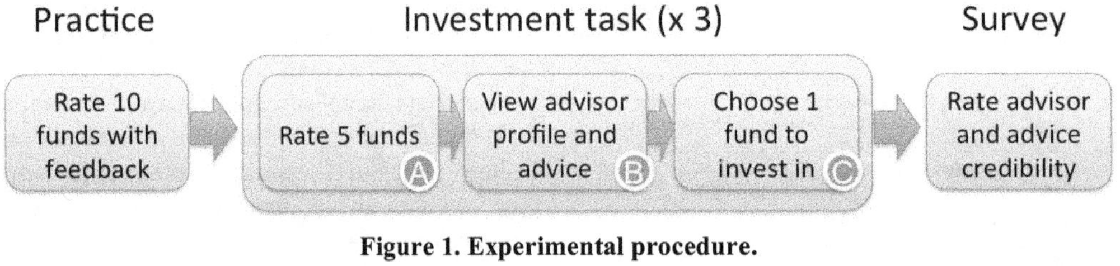

Figure 1. Experimental procedure.

only in Figure 1). This selection served as our baseline condition to assess performance without any advice. The participants then completed the investment task two more times and were shown professional advice (step B in Figure 1). As we are interested in adoption of poor quality advice, the advisor always gave mediocre advice—a fund with a historical rating lower than 3—but not so poor that the advice would be unbelievable.

All participants earned at least $5. We also gave them a bonus of up to $5, based on their performance in the investment tasks. Participants earned a higher bonus if they chose to invest in funds with a historical rating of 3 (Good).

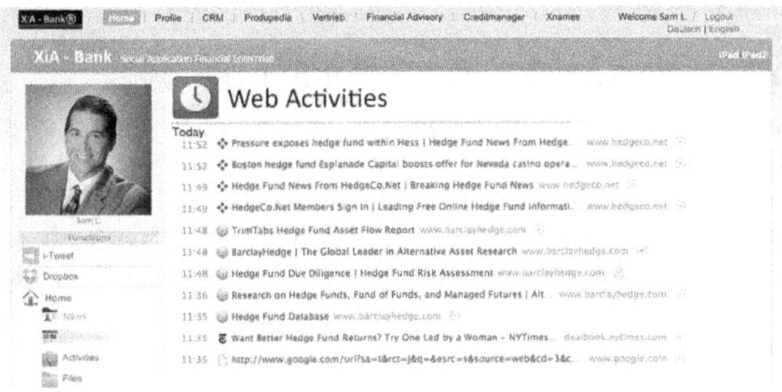

Figure 2. Profile page of the advisor in the activity transparency condition.

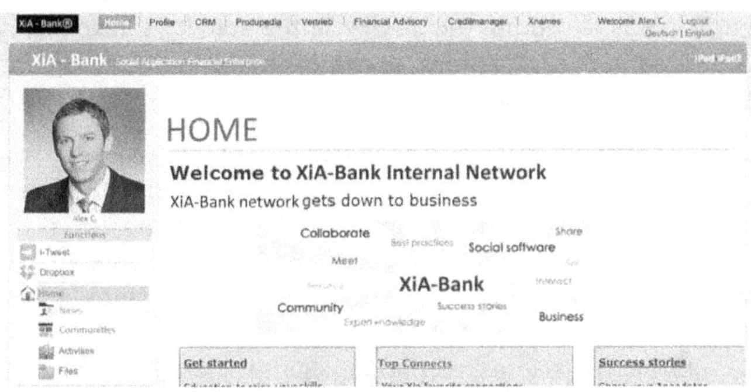

Figure 3. Profile page of the advisor in the no transparency condition.

Activity Transparency Manipulation

Each participant chose three investments. To "help" with two of the choices, the participant got advice from two different advisors. The advisor in the activity transparency condition had a profile page with a snap shot of his web activity on the right (Figure 2). The one in the no transparency condition had a profile page without the web history log (Figure 3). The activity transparency manipulation is thus within-subject.

The advisors shown came from XiA bank, had profile pages of the same design with blue and gray theme and with the photos shown in Figure 2 and 3. Advisor photos were professional images of a white male, aged 25 to 30. The names of the advisors were Alex C. and Sam L. Their names and photos were countered-balanced so that each person appeared equally often across the transparency and no transparency conditions.

We told participants the web history snapshot was taken while the advisor was constructing the advice. The web history reflected the advisor's activities leading to his advice, such as the websites he consulted or information he searched. Browsing histories are common online activity traces that can be found, and are currently used by third parties to improve online services [39, 41].

Dependent Measures

We collected 3 dependent measures: 1) behavioral measurements of advice taking, 2) credibility ratings of the advisor and the advice, and 3) performance measurements of participants' three chosen funds.

Advice taking. For the second and third investment tasks, participants received recommendations from the advisors about which fund to choose and then made their decisions. We recorded the fund that participants picked, and created a binary dependent variable of whether participants chose the same (mediocre) fund recommended by the advisor. We were interested in how transparency would affect adoption of bad advice. Therefore, higher adoption score is equivalent to investing in a poorer hedge fund.

Credibility of advisor. After the 3 investment tasks, participants completed a questionnaire to measure their evaluation of the advisor and advice and to assess their demographic characteristics. To measure the advisor's credibility, we adapted eight Likert items (1 – strongly disagree to 7 – strongly agree; Table 2), from Meyers [40] and Fogg and Tseng [22]. We created a credibility scale by averaging the items (Cronbach's α = .95) (Table 2).

Survey Items
This analyst was competent.
This analyst was experienced with hedge fund investment.
This analyst was an expert about hedge fund investment.
This analyst was trustworthy.
This analyst was reliable.
This analyst was honest.
This analyst was helpful to me during this task.
This analyst was unbiased.

Table 2. Advisor credibility scale.

Earnings. We calculated the amount of money participants earned as a bonus based on their performance in the three investment tasks. Specifically, they earned $1.50 per task if they chose a fund with good historical value, $0.5 if they chose funds with moderate historical value, and $0.10 if they chose funds with a bad historical value. They earned $5 if all three funds they chose had good historical value, and $0 if all three funds had bad historical value.

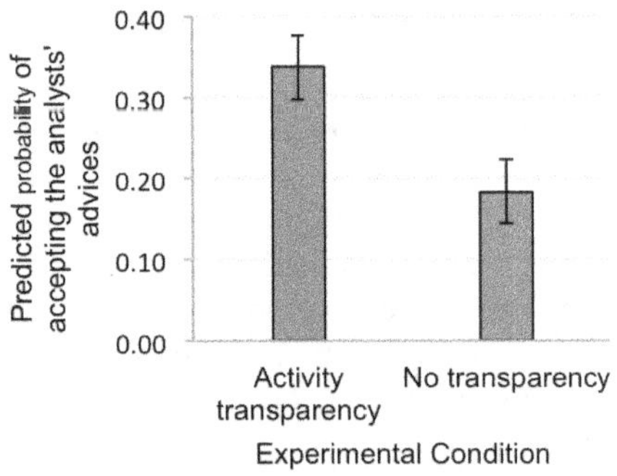

Figure 4a. Predicted probability of accepting mediocre advice, controlling for order of condition.

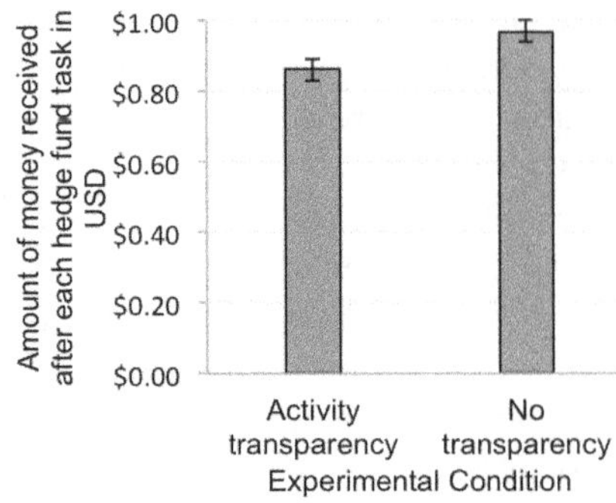

Figure 4b. Participants' earnings in USD after each hedge fund task.

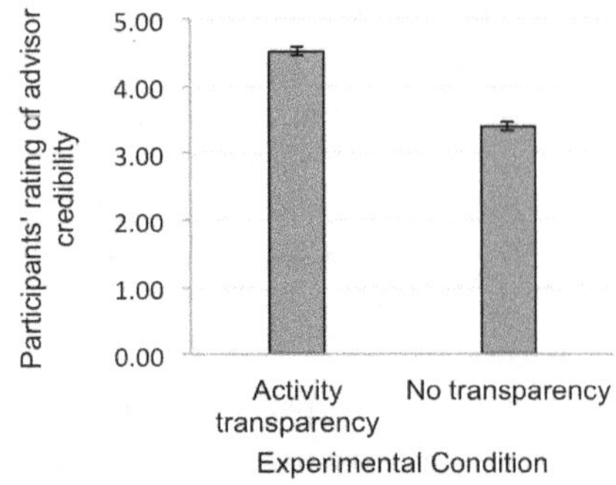

Figure 4c. Participants' rating of advisor credibility.

Figure 4. Experiment 1: Advice taking, earnings, and advisor credibility as a consequence of activity transparency

EXPERIMENT 1: EFFECT OF SHOWING AN ADVISOR'S WEB HISTORY ON TAKING HIS MEDIOCRE ADVICE

The purpose of this experiment was to test the hypothesis that a web history (activity transparency) would increase the influence of an advisor giving mediocre advice. The method of this experiment followed the general method described above.

Participants

We recruited 266 participants aged 18 to 65 (151 undergraduates, 9 graduate students, 75 employees, 9 retirees, 25 unemployed; 59% female) from an online participant pool. Participants were given $5 to $10 Amazon or Starbucks e-gift cards, depending on their investment performance. Only three participants held jobs in finance; none had experience with hedge fund investments. On a scale of 1 (no knowledge at all) to 7 (extremely knowledgeable), their average level of financial investment knowledge prior to the experiment was 2.5 (*SD* = 1.54).

Method

The method followed the general method describe above. In the activity transparency condition, the profile of the advisor contained a web browsing history showing only professional financial investment sites such as bloomberg.com. In the no activity transparency condition, the profile did not show any web history or any other activity information.

Results

Of 266 participants, 229 (86%) reported the analyst in the activity transparency condition did more research than the analyst in the no transparency condition, a probability of 0.86, SD = 95% CI [0.82, 0.90], significantly larger than 0.50 in a two-tailed Chi-square test (χ^2 [1] = 154.19, $p < .001$).

Advice taking

We predicted that participants would be more likely to follow the mediocre advice from an advisor in the activity transparency condition (H1). To test this hypothesis, we conducted a mixed effects logistic regression on whether participants accepted the advice in the two tasks on which they received advice. Mixed effects logistic regression is used to analyze repeated binary response variables [30]. We included as fixed factors the experimental condition (activity transparency or no transparency), the order of the tasks in these conditions (activity transparency first or second), the interaction between experimental conditions and order of the tasks, and performance in the baseline condition with no advice. Because the design was within-subjects, participants were a random effect. We used the glmer function of the lme4 package in R [3].

Only the transparency experimental condition (activity transparency vs. no transparency) had a significant effect on the likelihood of accepting the mediocre advice (β = .95, SE = .31, 95% CI [.34, 1.55], z = 3.089, $p < .01$). The odds of participants accepting the advice in the activity transparency condition was 2.59 times as high as the odds in the no transparency condition, with 95% CI [1.42, 4.76] (fig. 4a).

Did participants recognize the advice they had received was poor quality? After the task was over, we asked participants to rate, from 1 (strongly disagree) to 7 (strongly agree), if the advice given by the advisors was good. The mean response was 3.40, SD = 1.55, 95% CI [3.28, 3.54], significantly smaller than 4 (neutral) in a two-tailed t-test (t [525] = -8.62, $p < .001$). We also asked participants to rate all the funds in the list on a scale of 1 (Bad) to 3 (Good) in terms of their value for investment before they saw the advisor's recommendation (see fig. 1). The mean of this value rating for the hedge fund that the advisor recommended was 1.80, SD = .69, 95% CI [1.74, 1.86], significantly lower than 2 (average) in a two-tailed t-test (t [530] = -6.45, $p < .001$). These data show that, before seeing the advice, participants did not think the funds recommended by the advisors were of high quality. Yet, in the transparency condition, they were likely to follow this advice.

Earnings

We conducted a mixed-effect ANOVA on the payment received for each task, with advice taking and performance in the baseline condition task (no advice) as fixed factors. We found a significant negative effect of advice taking on earnings (β = -0.34, SE = 0.02, 95% CI [-0.37, -0.30], F [1, 518.3] = -16.59, $p < .001$). Thus, following mediocre advice was not simply an intellectual exercise; it reduced participants' monetary pay for the experiment. On each of the two hedge fund tasks where participants received advice, those who accepted the mediocre advice received on average \$.40 (SE = .03). Those who didn't follow the advice received on average \$1.09 (SE = .02), about 69 cents more than those who did (Cohen's D = -1.19) (fig. 4b).

Advisor credibility

H2 and H3 predict that activity transparency increases advice taking through its influence on perceived advisor credibility. Based on Preacher and Hayes [46], to test this mediation effect of advisor credibility, we first tested the effect of activity transparency on advisor credibility using a mixed-effect ANOVA with advisor credibility as the dependent variable, experimental conditions, order of the tasks, and their interaction as fixed effect, and participants as a random effect (R^2 = 0.42). We found that activity transparency had a significantly positive effect on advisor credibility (β = 0.55, SE = 0.04, 95% CI [0.47, 0.63], F [1, 264] = 166.51, p < .001), and no other variable was significant. Participants rated the advisor in the activity transparency condition (M = 4.53, SE = 0.07) more credible (Cohen's D = 1.04) than the advisor in the no transparency condition (M = 3.41, SE = 0.07) (fig. 4c). H2 was supported.

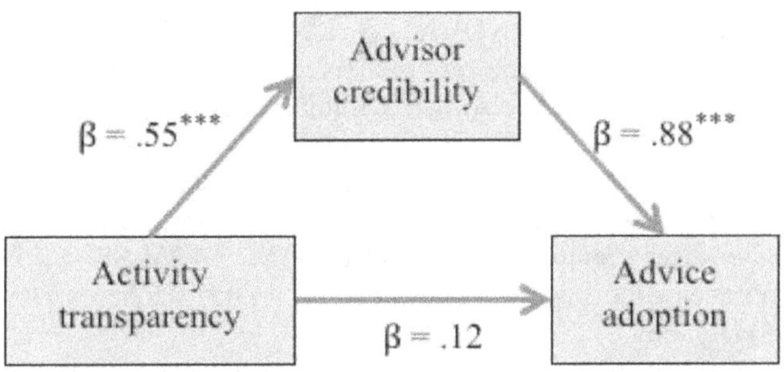

Figure 5. Experiment 1: Mediation effect of advisor credibility. 2-tailed p values: * p <= .05, ** p < .01, *** p < .001.

We then retested the effect of activity transparency on advice adoption using a mixed-effect logistic regression similar to the model we used to test H1, but with the addition of advisor credibility as a fixed factor. We found that the effect of activity transparency on advice adoption became insignificant (z = 0.36, p = 0.71), and the effect of advisor credibility on advice adoption was significant (β = .88, SE = .12, 95% CI [.65, 1.12], z = 7.03, p < .001). H3 was supported. A Sobel test [1, 51] showed the mediated effect of activity transparency on advice adoption was significant (t = 5.25, SE = .17, p < .001). These results show that seeing an advisor's web history affects advice adoption indirectly through its effect on advisor credibility. Figure 5 shows the mediation effect.

Discussion of Experiment 1

The findings of Experiment 1 were that a snapshot of an advisor's web searches increased the likelihood of people following his mediocre advice. Statistically, the effect occurred because the web history information made the advisors look more credible than when there was no web history shown. The positive effect of activity transparency on advice adoption in Experiment 1, however, may be due to the fact that the web history consisted of only URLs related to financial research. What if the web history also includes searches for off-task or non-work information? Some literature suggests that this might not hurt; it could increase perceptions of the advisor as a normal person like us [9, 35, 42]. We therefore decided to test the effect of showing non-work and work-related web history on an advisor's persuasiveness.

EXPERIMENT 2: EFFECT OF SHOWING SOME NON-WORK WEB HISTORY ON TAKING AN ADVISOR'S MEDIOCRE ADVICE

In Experiment 1, because we did not vary what was shown in the advisor's web history, it is unclear whether the effect of that history was due to the presence of any history or the particular content of that history. Many studies [63, 4, 5, 49] show that any information about a person can increase positive responses to that person.

Independent Variable

To explore these explanations, in Experiment 2 we used the same general method but varied the content of the web history shown to participants. Each participant was randomly assigned to one of two types of web history for the advisor with a web history shown: a web history with only work-related URLS (about financial sites), or a web history with both work-related and non-work URLs (e.g., Youtube.com for online videos, Yelp.com for online shopping and service recommendations). We hypothesized that visibility of some non-work URLs in the advisor's history might create an impression of a distracted advisor and thus negatively affect his credibility.

Participants

One hundred and eight participants saw the web history with only work-related URLs (work-related only condition), and 110 participants saw the history with both work-related, and non-work URLs (mixed work and non-work condition). They were 61% female, and aged 18 to 65, with education ranging from high school diplomas to graduate degrees and little financial knowledge. They completed an online survey with the same tasks, procedures, measures, and payment scheme as those used in Experiment 1. No participant had experience with hedge fund investments before the experiment.

Results

Figure 6 shows the effect of activity transparency on the three dependent variables: advice taking, participants' earnings after each hedge fund task, and participants' rating of advisor credibility.

Advice taking

We conducted a mixed-effect logistic regression on advice adoption, with fixed effects of activity transparency vs. no transparency and work-related history vs. half non-work related history nested within these conditions. (The effect of

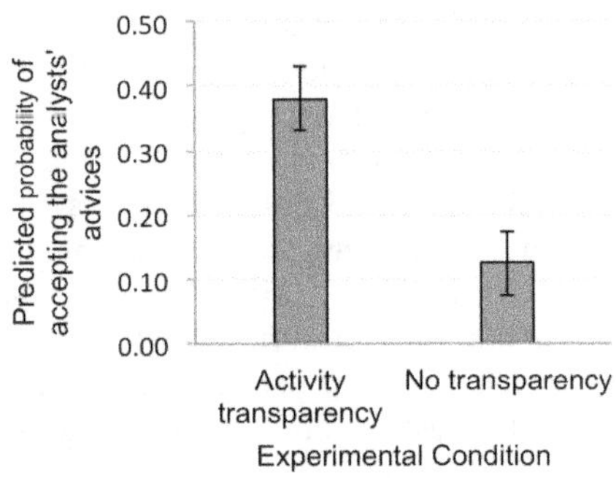

Figure 6a. Predicted probability of accepting mediocre advice from an advisor.

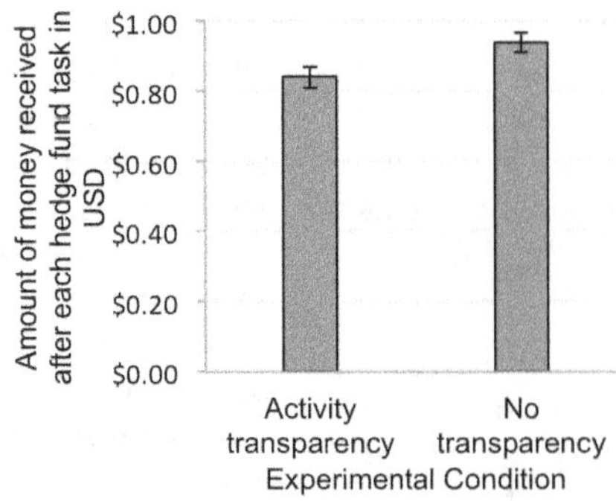

Figure 6b. Participants' earnings in USD after each hedge fund task.

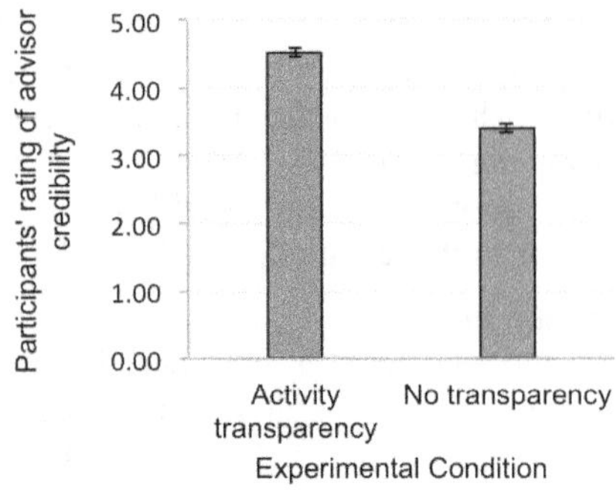

Figure 6c. Participants' rating of advisor credibility.

Figure 6. Experiment 2: Advice taking, earnings, and advisor credibility as a consequence of activity transparency.

web history content is nested within experimental conditions because such effect is not meaningful in the no transparency condition.)

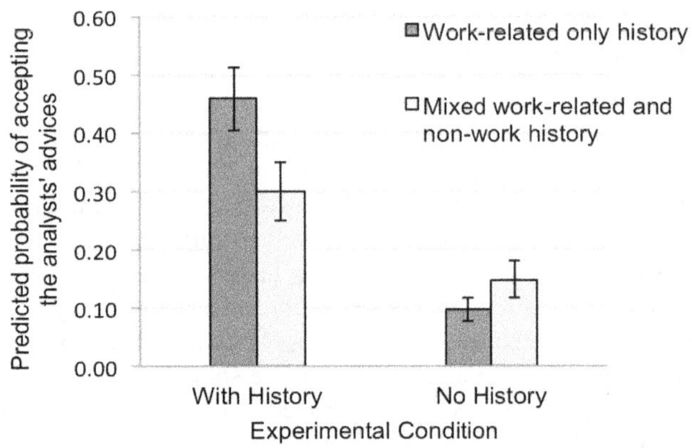

Figure 7. Probability of accepting mediocre advice from an advisor as a consequence of activity transparency (seeing the advisor's web history vs. not seeing) and the content of that activity.

We found a significant effect of experimental condition (β = .91, SE = .33, z = 2.71, p < .01), and a significant effect of the work-related websites when participants saw the web history (β = .68, SE = .29, z = 2.36, p = .01). These effects show that advice adoption was influenced both by seeing the web history and by its content as work-related. The odds that participants would accept mediocre advice after seeing an advisor's web history was 2.48 times higher (95% CI [1.30, 4.74]) than after seeing no history (fig. 6a). The odds that the participant who saw only work-related websites (about hedge fund research) would adopt the advice was 1.97 times higher (95% CI [1.11, 3.48]) than one who saw the mixed work and non-work history.

Figure 7 shows the likelihood of advice adoption when participants saw only work-related websites in the web history and when they saw a mixture of work and non-work websites. The results show that the nature of the web history matters; however, either kind of web history had a stronger impact than no history at all.

Earnings

We found a significant negative effect of activity transparency on earnings (β = -.05, SE = 0.02, 95% CI [-.08, -.01], F [1, 225] = 4.26, p = .04). Participants in the activity transparency condition earned on average $.84 (SE = .04). Those in the no transparency condition earned on average $.94 (SE = .04), 10 cents more than those in the activity transparency condition (Cohen's D = -.16) (fig. 6b).

Advisor credibility

A mixed effects ANOVA on advisor credibility with experimental condition as the fixed factor showed that activity transparency also had a significant effect on advisor credibility (β = .35, SE = .04, 95% CI [.27, .42], F[1, 224] = 55.42, p < .001), controlling for the work-related content of the web history. Participants rated the advisor's credibility higher after seeing either web history (M = 4.35, SE = .07) than seeing no history (M = 3.65, SE = .07) (Cohen's D = .68) (fig. 6c).

We analyzed the effect of activity transparency further by dividing the participants into two groups: participants who saw the work-related only history versus those who saw the mixed work and non-work history. We conducted a mixed-effect ANOVA on the advisor's credibility, with experimental condition as the fixed effect. Participants who saw only work-related activities rated the advisor significantly higher in credibility after seeing the history (M = 4.65, SE = .09) than if they did not see it (M = 3.41, SE = .09) (β = .62, SE = .06, 95% CI [.50, .73], F[1, 112] = 100.36, p < .001). Those who saw the mixed work and non-work history did not increase their credibility ratings as compared to seeing no history at all (β = .07, SE = .07, F[1, 112] = 1.17, p = .28).

A mixed-effect logistic regression on advice adoption with advisor's credibility as the fixed effect showed that, as in Experiment 1, credibility had a significant positive effect (β = .93, SE =.12, z = 7.43, p < .001) on advice adoption.

To evaluate mediation effects, we conducted a mixed-effect linear regression on the analyst credibility with experimental condition, and web history content nested in experimental condition as the fixed effects, and participants as the random effect ($R^2 = .31$). We found that when participants saw a web history, the content of that web history significantly influenced the participants' ratings of the analyst's credibility (β = .30, SE = .07, 95% CI [.16, .43], $F[1, 298] = 16.82$, $p < .001$). Participants who saw the web history with only work-related URLs rated the advisor higher in credibility (M = 4.65, SE = .09) than those who saw the history with mixed work and non-work URLs (M = 4.04, SE = .09) (Cohen's D = .40).

After participants saw all advisors, and finished all investment tasks, we asked them what they noticed about the activities of the two analysts displayed on their profile page. Participant comments provide a window into their thought processes when they saw financial web activity:

"Thoroughly researched list and lots of effort." P25

"It showed a lot of hedge fund websites and general information you would expect an analyst to look up for you when trying to make good choices about what to invest in." P100

On the other hand, participants who saw a web history with mixed work and non-work URLs from the advisor perceived the advisor to be distracted or unfocused.

"(He was) procrastinating." P56

"He wasn't doing his job. he was on sites like amazon, and was listening to music on spotify. also, he had lots of general google searches... not the sort of thing you want from an analyst." P78

Discussion of Experiment 2

Our results show that the likelihood of accepting an advisor's mediocre advice is enhanced significantly by work-related activities that raise the advisor's credibility. However, even when the advisor was shown as searching both non-work and work-related sites, participants were still more likely to adopt his mediocre advice than when there was no web history in his profile at all. In Experiment 3, we examined whether an advisor with only a non-work web history would still have an influence on advice taking.

EXPERIMENT 3: EFFECT OF SHOWING ONLY HIS NON-WORK WEB HISTORY ON TAKING AN ADVISOR'S MEDIOCRE ADVICE

In Experiment 3, the web history of the advisor in the activity transparency condition showed only non-work URLs. We used the same tasks, procedures, dependent measures, and payment scheme as those used in experiments 1 and 2 (fig. 1). The only difference from the first two experiments was the independent variable.

Independent Variable

In Experiment 3 we manipulated the presence of a non-work activity history within subjects. Participants saw one advisor with a profile with a non-work web history consisting of six URLs from Amazon.com, Yelp.com, and Youtube.com. The other advisor had a profile without any web history.

Participants

Sixty one participants (67% female), aged 18 to 65 with highest education ranging from high school diplomas to graduate degrees and little financial knowledge, completed the study with the same tasks, procedures, measures, and payment scheme as those used in Experiment 1.

Results

Figure 8 shows the effect of activity transparency on three dependent variables: advice taking, participants' earnings after each hedge fund task, and participants' rating of advisor credibility.

Advice taking

To test the net effect of activity transparency and content of the history on advice taking, we first conducted a mixed-effect logistic regression on advice taking, with experimental condition as the fixed effect. We found no significant effect of experimental condition on advice taking (β = .62, SE = .45, $z = 1.37$, $p = .17$) (fig. 8a). This result suggests that the negative implications of the non-work activity history cancelled any positive effect of mere transparency. We next included the advisor's credibility in the mixed model regression. (The Pearson's correlation between credibility and experimental condition is $r = -.46$.)

We found that when controlling for the advisor's perceived credibility, the non-work web history increased advice taking significantly compared to the no transparency condition (β = 1.33, SE = .53, 95% CI [.29, 2.36], $z = 2.50$, $p = .01$). Given two advisors rated equally in credibility, the odds that participants would adopt the mediocre advice from the advisor with a non-work activity history was 3.78 times higher (95% CI [1.33, 10.60]) than the odds of accepting the advice from the advisor without any web history. As in our first two experiments, we also found that credibility had a significant positive effect on advice adoption (β = .83, SE = .27, 95% CI [.30, 1.35], $z = 3.07$, $p < .01$).

Earnings

We conducted a mixed-effect ANOVA on the payment participants received after each hedge fund task that they were given an advice, with experimental condition as the fixed factor. We did not find any effect of activity transparency on payment ($F[1, 60] = 2.7$, $p = .10$) (fig. 8b). On each hedge fund task, participants in the activity transparency condition made on average \$.98 (SE = .07). Those in the no transparency condition made on average \$1.01 (SE = .07).

Advisor credibility

We tested whether transparency of non-work activities lowered the advisor's credibility compared to not seeing any history. We conducted a mixed model ANOVA on the ratings of the advisor's credibility with experimental condition (activity transparency vs. no transparency) as the fixed effect, and participants as the random effect.

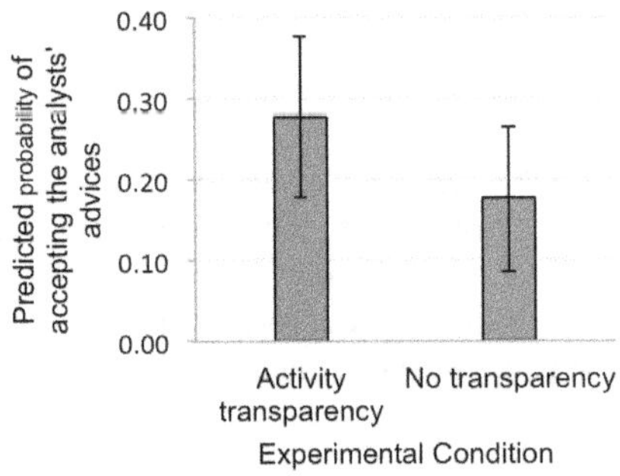

Figure 8a. Predicted probability of accepting mediocre advice from an advisor.

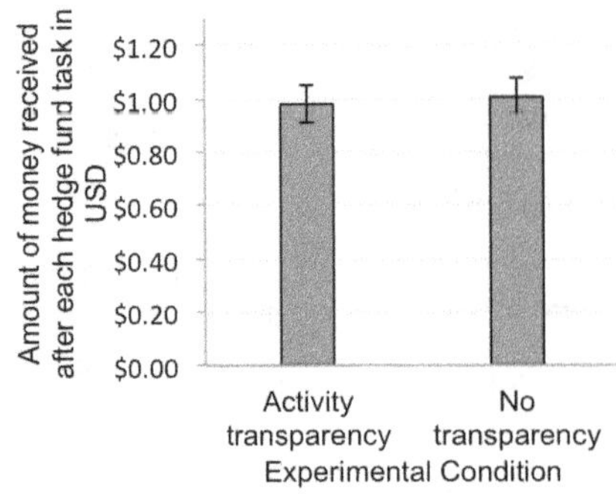

Figure 8b. Participants' earnings in USD after each hedge fund task.

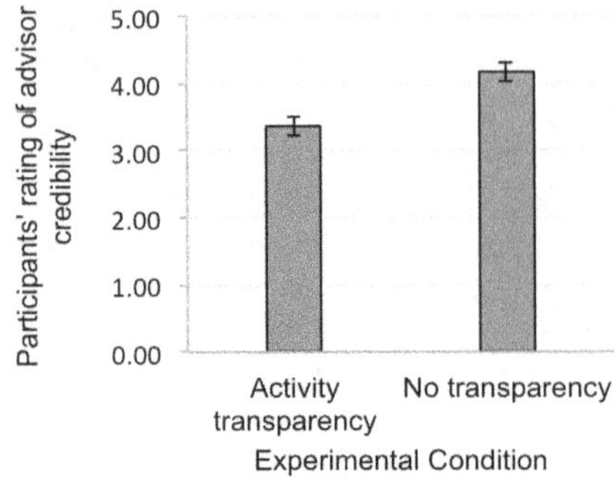

Figure 8c. Participants' rating of advisor credibility.

Figure 8. Experiment 3: Advice taking, earnings, and advisor credibility as a consequence of activity transparency.

As expected, we found a significant negative effect of seeing the non-work web history (β = -.39, SE = .09, 95% CI [.21, .56], F[1, 60] = 19.34, p < .001). Participants rated the advisor with activity transparency (of non-work URLs) lower in credibility (M = 3.36, SE = .14) than the advisor with no activity transparency (M = 4.16, SE = .14) (Cohen's D = .74) (fig. 8c).

Discussion of Experiment 3

In experiment 3 the advisor's credibility was damaged by the non-work web history and participants were no longer inclined to take his advice over the advisor without a web history. However, it should be noted that the non-work web history did not reduce advice taking below that of the advisor without a web history. Moreover, controlling statistically for the effect of credibility, the non-work web history actually increased advice taking. These statistical analyses imply that just showing a web history could cancel the impact of poor credibility. We discuss some of the potential mechanisms below.

GENERAL DISCUSSION

Our results extend the literature about social transparency by explaining how it influences advice taking. Although previous studies [e.g. 16, 47, 8] show the effect of social transparency and information source credibility on trust and other social perceptions, none have investigated how transparency can cause people to adopt poor quality advice. Our study shows that activity transparency increased the persuasive impact of poor quality advice except when the web history showed the advisor to be working completely off task (e.g., on Amazon searches). Our study and the earlier Towne et al.'s study on Wikipedia change histories [60] are not entirely comparable because of the difference in people's tasks and the dependent measures, but both studies suggest activity transparency can reduce people's ability to objectively evaluate an information source.

Why transparency works

Participant comments and the credibility ratings from our experiments suggested that participants used the advisor's web history to evaluate the amount of effort and concentration the advisor gave to the advising task. Non-work searches in the web history suggested a lack of effort or distraction. However, the statistical analyses suggested that the impact of web history might have gone beyond its impact on advisor credibility.

One possibility is that the extra data about the advisor's activity increased people's sense of familiarity with the advisor, and indirectly increased comfort with the advisor's advice. However, the proposition that transparency increases people's sense of familiarity with advice needs to be tested in the future.

Activity transparency also might influence advice taking by increasing the memorability of an advisor. In our experiments, showing the advisors' web activities could have provided additional anchor points for participants' representation of them in memory, increasing their social impact [52, 53, 57]. Studies also suggest that people have a more positive attitude towards a person or organization if they see information that makes that person seem more realistic and lively [1, 36,]. New research could help us understand the effect of activity transparency by varying the vividness of the activity information in an advisor's profile (e.g., still photos of the advisor at work versus a video of the advisor at work).

Finally, activity transparency might influence advice taking by reducing psychological distance from an advisor. Things far removed from our direct experience, such as far-away places and events in the future) can feel psychologically distant [61]. Being able to see an advisor's activity may have given participants the impression that the advisor was real or close by, reducing their psychological distance from him. We could examine whether the effects of transparency on psychological distance vary as the physical or temporal distance of advisor activity changes.

Activity transparency second-order consequences

Participants in our study were more susceptible to bad advice and performed more poorly when they were exposed to a web history log of the advisor. Prior work shows the collaborative benefits of more awareness of another's activities for supporting opportunistic connections among people or avoiding coordination conflicts (e.g., [55, 48]). By contrast, our work suggests that more awareness may have deleterious effects on people's ability to objectively evaluate information from another person. The second-order consequence might be to damage collaborations by injecting bad information into group decisions.

In remote teams, where participants are not well-acquainted and span disciplines, not all team members have the knowledge to assess information in an unfamiliar field of expertise. People may less objectively evaluate information and advice from collaborators in the remote work setting when these collaborators have heightened activity transparency. There might be a difficult tradeoff between enhanced connectivity and coordination among members of a remote team with activity transparency, versus indiscriminate information use and poor decision-making quality. Researchers will need to examine how activity transparency influences information use in a team, and how collaborative technology can counteract the potential negative performance impact of increased transparency while supporting coordination and awareness among members.

Limitations & future directions

We used experiments so that we could control important variables: the advisor's characteristics and expertise, the nature of the advice, and the measures of advice taking. The repeated measures, counterbalanced design allowed us to make comparisons for each person, controlling the impact of the participant's own expertise and motivation. We therefore can draw valid implications of the impact of activity transparency on advice taking in this online setting, but we cannot generalize to everyday advice taking without further research.

Web history reflecting the information gathering process in the making of an advice, while common and easy to access [39], may not be a realistic representation of the types of activity traces that web users normally see online. Future studies can employ a more realistic type of activity transparency such as the changes to a document, or the date and time of the last edits to a document.

Hedge fund investment choices are only one kind of online decision-making on which people want expert advice. To generalize beyond this task would require research using other types of online tasks and other advisors, and varying the expertise of the recipients of the advice.

We also did not vary the quality of the advice; in each case, the advisor gave mediocre advice, not the worst investment but not the best either. Varying the quality of the advice could help us understand if people will accept really bad advice with high activity transparency. The earning scheme that forms our performance measure was designed to reflect the real-life consequences of trusting mediocre advice to a certain extent, but it cannot be generalized beyond the experimental settings. Future work should consider more realistic performance measures.

CONCLUSION

In three experiments, we found that activity transparency increased adoption of a financial advisor's mediocre advice and reduced earnings in an investment task, and that the effect of transparency was greater the more it revealed work-related activity of the advisor. Our study calls attention to the potential negative social effects of activity transparency and contributes to the literature on the direct and second order effects of social transparency. When designing for online platforms for Q&A, recommendations, or advising, in order not to help bad advisors, and to counter inappropriate persuasion [44], we should implement features such as rating systems for advice that would encourage people to use discretion.

ACKNOWLEDGMENTS

This research is supported by NSF grants CNS-1040757, CNS-1040800, CNS-1040801, and ACI-1322278. We thank Tatiana Vlahovic and the anonymous reviewers for their feedback on the previous versions of the paper.

REFERENCES

1. Allen, D. G., Van Scotter, J. R., & Otondo, R. F. (2004). Recruitment communication media: impact on pre-hire outcomes. *Personnel Psychology, 57*, 143–171.
2. Baron, R. M., & Kenny, D. A. (1986). The moderator mediator variable distinction in social psychological research: Conceptual, strategic, and statistical considerations. *Journal of Personality and Social Psychology, 51,* 1173-1182.
3. Bates, D., Maechler, M., Bolker, B., Walker, S. (2014). *Linear mixed-effects models using Eigen and S4*, version 1.0-6[computer software]. Available from: http://cran.r-project.org/web/packages/lme4/index.html.
4. Bornstein, R. F. (1989). Exposure and Affect: Overview and Meta-Analysis of Research, 1986–1987. *Psychological Bulletin, 106,* 265–289.
5. Bornstein, R. F., & D'Agostino, P. R. (1992) Stimulus Recognition and the Mere Exposure Effect. *Journal of Personality and Social Psychology, 63,* 545–552.
6. Bonhard, P., Harries, C., McCarthy, J., & Sasse, M. A. (2006). Accounting for taste: using profile similarity to improve recommender systems. *In Proceedings of CHI '06*, 1057-1066. New York: ACM.
7. Brenoff, A. (2013). What bad advice did this heart attack survivor get? *Huffington Post.* Retrieve from: http://www.huffingtonpost.com/2013/09/24/online-myths_n_3954799.html
8. Briggs, P., Burford, B., De Angeli, A., & Lynch, P. (2002). Trust in online advice. *Social Science & Computing Review 20, 3*, 321-332.
9. Cain, D. M., Loewenstein, G., & Moore, D. A. (2005). The Dirt on Coming Clean: Perverse Effects of Disclosing Conflicts of Interest. *Journal of Legal Studies, 34, 1,* 1–25.

10. Campbell, J. & Stasser, G. (2006). The Influence of Time and Task Demonstrability on Decision-Making in Computer-Mediated and Face-to-Face Groups. *Small Group Research, 37*, 217-294.

11. Casaló, L. V., Flavián, C., & Guinalíu, M. (2011). Understanding the intention to follow the advice obtained in an online travel community. *Computers in Human Behaviors, 27, 2*, 622-633.

12. Chung, M., Oden, R. P., Joyner, B. L., Sims, A., & Moon, R. Y. (2012). Safe Infant Sleep Recommendations on the Internet: Let's Google It. *Journal of Pediatrics, 161(6)*, 1080-1084.

13. Coker, B. (2011). Freedom to surf: the positive effects of workplace Internet leisure browsing. *New Technology, Work and Employment, 26*, 238–247.

14. Cramer, H., Evers, V., Ramlal, S., van Someren, H., Rutledge, L., Stash, N., Aroyo, L., & Wielinga, B. (2008). The effects of transparency on trust in and acceptance of a content-based art recommender. *User Model User-Adap Inter, 18*, 455–496.

15. Crocco A. G., Villasis-Keever M., & Jadad A. R. (2002). Analysis of cases of harm associated with use of health information on the Internet. *Journal of American Medical Association, 287(21)*, 2869–2871.

16. Dabbish, L., Stuart, C., Tsay, J., & Herbsleb, J. (2012). Social coding in GitHub: transparency and collaboration in an open software repository. *Proc. CSCW '12*,1277-1286.

17. De Alfaro, L., Kulshreshtha, A., Pye, I., & Adler. B. T. (2011). Reputation systems for open collaboration. *Commun. ACM 54, 8*, 81-87.

18. Dembroski, T. M., Lasater, T. M. & Ramirez, A. (1978). Communicator Similarity, Fear Arousing Communications, and Compliance with Health Care Recommendations. *Journal of Applied Social Psychology, 8*, 254–269.

19. Erickson, T. & Kellogg, W.A (2000). Social translucence: An approach to designing systems that support social processes. *Proc. CHI'00*, 59-83.

20. Erickson, T., Smith, D. N., Kellogg, W. A., Laff, M., Richards, J. T., & Bradner, E. (1999). Socially translucent systems: social proxies, persistent conversation, and the design of "babble". Proc. CHI '99, 72-79.

21. Fogg, B. J., Marshall, J., Laraki, O., Osipovich, A., Varma, C., Fang, N., Paul, J., Rangnekar, A., Shon, J., Swani, P., & Treinen, M. (2001). What makes Web sites credible?: a report on a large quantitative study. *Proc. CHI '01*, 61-68.

22. Fogg, B. J., Tseng, H. (1999). The elements of computer credibility. *Proc. CHI'99,* 80-87.

23. Fox, S., & Duggan, M. (2013). One in three American adults have gone online to figure out a medical condition. *Pew Internet & American Life Project.* Retrieve from: http://pewinternet.org/Reports/2013/Health-online/Summary-of-Findings.aspx.

24. Gilbert, E. (2012). Designing social translucence over social networks. Proc. CHI '12, 2731-2740.

25. Gino, F. (2008). Do we listen to advice just because we paid for it? The impact of advice cost on its use. *Organizational Behavior and Human Decision Processes, 107,* 234-245.

26. Godek, B., & Murray, K. B. (2008). Willingness to pay for advice: The role of rational and experiential processing. *Organizational Behavior and Human Decision Processes, 106, 1*, 77–87.

27. Golbeck, J. & Fleischmann, K. R. (2010). Trust in social Q&A: the impact of text and photo cues of expertise. In *Proc. ASIS&T '10, 47*, Article 77, 10 pages.

28. Griffin, D., Gonzalez, R., Varey, C. (2001). The heuristics and biases approach to judgment under uncertainty. In *Blackwell Handbook of Social Psychology: Intraindividual Procresses (A. Tesser & N. Schwarz Eds.)*, 207-235.

29. Hancock, J. & Dunham, P (2001). Impression formation in computer-mediated communication revisited: An analysis of the breath and intensity of impressions. *Communication Research, 28*, 3, 325-347.

30. Hu, F. B., Goldberg, J., Hedeker, D., Flay, B. F., & Pentz, M. A. (1998). Comparison of Population-Averaged and Subject-Specific Approaches for Analyzing Repeated Binary Outcomes. *American Journal of Epidemiology, 147, 7*, 694-704.

31. Janiszewski, C., & Meyvis, T. (2001). Effect of brand logo complexity, repetition, and spacing on processing fluency and judgement. *Journal of Consumer Research, 28,* 1, 18-32.

32. Kinnaird, P., Dabbish, L., & Kiesler, S. (2012). Workflow transparency in a microtask marketplace. *Proc. GROUP '12*, 281-284.

33. Kittur, A., Suh, B., & Chi, E. H. (2008). "Can You Ever Trust a Wiki?". *Proc. CSCW'08,* 477.

34. Lee, U., Kang, H., Yi, E., Yi, M., & Kantola, J. (2012). Understanding mobile Q&A usage: an exploratory study. *Proc CHI '12,* 3215-3224.

35. Loewenstein, G., Cain, D. M., Sah, S. (2011). The Limits of Transparency: Pitfalls and Potential of Disclosing Conflicts of Interest. *American Economic Review, 101, 3*, 423-428.

36. Nisbett, R. & Lee, R. (1980). *Human Inference: Strategies and Shortcomings of Social Judgment.* Englewood Cliffs, NJ: Prentice-Hall.

37. Marlow, J., Dabbish, L. & Herbsleb, J. (2013). Impression formation in online peer production: activity traces and personal profiles in github. *Proc. CSCW '13,* 117-128.

38. Mas, A. and Moretti, E. (2009). Peers at work. *American Economic Review, 99, 1*, 112-145.

39. Meyer, J. R. & Mitchell, J. C. (2012). Third-party web tracking: policy and technology. *Proc. SP 2012*, 413-427.

40. Meyer, P. (1988). Defining and measuring credibility of news- papers: Developing an index. *Journalism Quarterly, 65,* 567– 574.

41. O'Reilly, D. (2011, Nov 1st). How to know who is tracking your web activities. *CNET Tech Culture.* Retrieved from: http://www.cnet.com/how-to/how-to-know-who-is-tracking-your-web-activities/

42. Pearson, S. D., Kleinman, K., & Rusinak. D. (2006). A Trial of Disclosing Physicians' Financial Incentives to Patients. *Archives of Internal Medicine, 166,* 623–628.

43. Petty, R. E., & Cacioppo, J. T. (1986). The Elaboration Likelihood Model of Persuasion. In *Communication and Persuasion – Springer Series in Social Psychology*, pp. 1-24. New York, NY: Springer.

44. Petty, R. E., & Cacioppo, J. T. (1977). Forewarning, cognitive responding, and resistance to persuasion. *Journal of Personality and Social Psychology, 35,* 9, 645-655.

45. Pirolli, P., Wollny, E., & Suh. B. (2009). "So You Know You're Getting the Best Possible Information: A Tool that Increases Wikipedia Credibility." *Proc. CHI'09,* 1505.

46. Preacher, K. J., & Hayes, A. F. (2007). Addressing Moderated Mediation Hypotheses: Theory, Methods, and Prescriptions. *Multivariate Behavioral Research, 42, 1,* 185-227.

47. Riegelsberger, J., & Sasse, M. A. (2001). Trustbuilders and trustbusters: The role of trust cues in interfaces to e-commerce applications [WWW page]. *Paper presented at the 1st IFIP Conference on E-commerce, E-business, E-government.* Available: http://www.cs.ucl.ac.uk/staff/J.Riegelsberger/trustbuilders_and_trustbusters.htm

48. Scupelli, P., Kiesler, S., & Fussell, S.R. (2005). Project view IM: A tool for juggling multiple projects and teams. *Proc. CHI'05,* 1773.

49. Shapiro, S. (1999). When an Ad's Influence Is beyond Our Conscious Control: Perceptual and Conceptual Fluency Effects Caused by Incidental Ad Exposure. *Journal of Consumer Research, 26,* 16–36.

50. Sillence, E., Briggs, P., Harris, P., & Fishwick. L. (2006). A framework for understanding trust factors in web-based health advice. *International Journal of Human-Computer Studies 64, 8*, 697-713.

51. Sobel, M. E. (1982). Asymptotic intervals for indirect effects in structural equations models. In S. Leinhart (Ed.), *Sociological methodology* (pp.290-312). San Francisco: Jossey-Bass.

52. Slusher, M. P., & Anderson, C. A. (1996). Using causal persuasive arguments to change beliefs and teach new information: The mediating role of explanation availability and evaluation bias in the acceptance of knowledge. *Journal of Educational Psychology, 88,* 110-122.

53. Srull, T. K., Lichtenstein, M., & Rothbart, M. (1985). Associative storage and retrieval processes in person memory. *Journal of Experimental Psychology: Learning, Memory, and Cognition, 11,* 2, 316-345.

54. Steel, E. and Fowler, G. Facebook in privacy breach. *Wall Street Journal*, 2010.

55. Stuart, H. C., Dabbish, L., Kiesler, S., Kinnaird, P., & Kang, R. (2012). Social transparency in networked information exchange: a theoretical framework. *Proc. of CSCW '12*, 451-460.

56. Suh, B., Chi, E.H., Kittur, A., and Pendleton, B.A. Lifting the veil: Improving accountability and social transparency in Wikipedia with wikidashboard. *Proc. CHI '08,* 1037-1040.

57. Tversky, A. & Kahneman, D. (1973). Availability: A heuristic for judging frequency and probability. *Cognitive psychology, 5*, 2, 207-232.

58. Tausczik, Y. R., & Pennebaker, J. W. (2011). Predicting the perceived quality of online mathematics contributions from users' reputations. *Proc. CHI '11,* 1885-1888.

59. Toma, C. L. (2010). Perceptions of trustworthiness online: the role of visual and textual information. In *Proc. CSCW '10,* 13-22. New York, NY: ACM.

60. Towne, B. W., Kittur, A., Kinnaird, P., & Herbsleb, J. (2013). Your process is showing: controversy management and perceived quality in Wikipedia. *Proc. of CSCW '13,* 1059-1068.

61. Trope, Y., & Liberman, N. (2010). Construal-level theory of psychological distance. *Psychological review, 117,* 2, 440-463.

62. Viégas, F.B., Wattenberg, M., and Dave, K. Studying cooperation and conflict between authors with history flow visualizations. *Proc. CHI '04,* 575-582.

63. Zajonc, R. (1968). Attitudinal effects of mere exposure. *Journal of Personality and Social Psychology, 9,* 2, 1-27.

An Agent for Deception Detection in Discussion Based Environments

Amos Azaria
Dept. of Machine Learning
Carnegie Mellon University,
Pittsburgh, PA

Ariella Richardson
Dept. of Industrial
Engineering
Lev Academic Center, Israel

Sarit Kraus
Dept. of Computer Science
Bar Ilan University, Israel

ABSTRACT
Extensive use of computerized forums and chat-rooms provides a modern venue for deception. We propose introducing an agent to assist in detecting and incriminating a deceptive participant. We designed a game, where deception in a text based discussion environment occurs. In this game several participants attempt to collectively detect a deceptive member. We compose an automated agent which participates in this game as a regular player. The goal of the agent is to detect the deceptive participant and alert other members, without raising suspicion itself. We use machine learning on the data collected from human players to design this agent. Extensive evaluation of our agent shows that it succeeds in raising the players collective success rate in catching the deceptive player.

Author Keywords
Deception Detection; Human Agent Interaction; Suspicion Evasion; Machine Learning

ACM Classification Keywords
I.2.m Computing Methodologies: ARTIFICIAL INTELLIGENCE—*Miscellaneous*

INTRODUCTION
Many activities in our everyday lives involve sharing opinions with peers through computer-mediated communication. People participate in forum discussions on important topics such as: how to raise their children, what medication they should use and how to improve their business. It would be nice to assume that all of the people participating in these discussions have a common, honest goal and that malicious participants are spotted by moderators. However, this is often not true. Pedophiles manage to infiltrate kids' chat rooms, commercial products are pushed in forums by dealers posing as regular users, and business forums are probably full of advice that actually assists their competitors. Computer-mediated communication has provided a modern venue for deception [30], and encouraged research on the extent of deception online [21]. For example, consider a salesperson that participates in a chat discussion on buying a specific car. The salesperson may try to promote the car, and may be confronted by other participants as being dishonest. The salesperson would likely deny being a salesperson, and may accuse other participants of being a salesperson trying to promote another car. It can be difficult to determine which of the participants is presenting an honest opinion, and which is motivated by an ulterior motive. Many chat environments are not monitored by an administrator, or loosely monitored. Sometimes the moderator does not wish to intervene (this could be for various reasons, for example if the administrator is only responsible for the infrastructure and not for the content). Furthermore, even in monitored environments a user (or a group of users) may have personal preferences to the type of moderation they require. We suggest introducing an agent to the chat environment, that participates in the chat as a regular user. We expect this agent to have three capabilities. First, the agent must be able to find the salesman. Second, the agent should convince other users that this participant is a salesman. Third, we expect our agent not to raise suspicion as being a salesman himself. Such an agent could decrease deception in this environment.

CSCW 2015, March 14–18, 2015, Vancouver, BC, Canada.

ACM 978-1-4503-2922-4/15/03$15.00
http://dx.doi.org/10.1145/2675133.2675137

In his book "Telling Lies" [12], Ekman states that "it is not a simple matter to catch lies" (pg. 80). Ekman explains (pg. 82) that when people are dishonest, they choose their words with care, however they tend to give away the lie through body language and tone. This knowledge from Psychology has motivated studies on the automatic detection of lies based on video and audio data [8, 25, 15, 4]. However, in many web-based environments, in which a group forms a discussion, such as chat rooms and forums, there is no audio or visual information. Such environments are based solely on short text messages.

Inspired by this, we investigate scenarios where several participants attempt to collectively detect a deceptive member. We also study how and if they may be assisted by an autonomous agent. As a first step towards reducing deception by human subjects, in discussion based environments, we designed an agent. This agent participates in a discussion based game that involves discussion and deception. The agent joins a group of human players as a regular member, and has no enforcement capabilities on other players. The agent must detect the deceptive participant and alert other members of suspicious behavior while not raising suspicion itself.

We designed a game to deploy and evaluate our agent in a text-based discussion environment. In this game there are several credible participants and one dishonest participant (a pirate). In the first phase of the game the participants con-

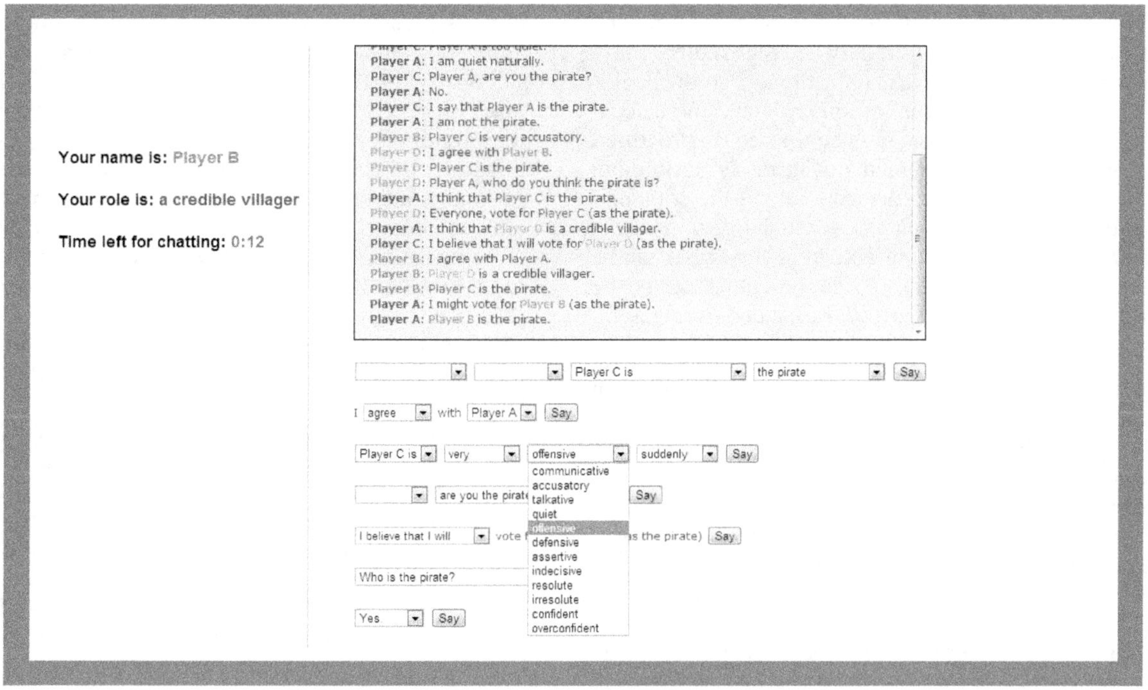

Figure 1. A screen-shot of the pirate game in progress.

duct a textual discussion in an attempt to uncover the liar, and later they cast their votes as to whom they think the liar is. The game is played either with a human set of participants, or with a mixture of human participants and an autonomous agent that plays as a regular participant. We evaluate the contribution of the agent to the credible participants in the following two different game versions: the first version of our game allows the pirate to be as active or inactive as he chooses and the second version encourages the pirate to be more active. The second version is similar to one where a salesman is pushing a commercial product. The credible participants performed no better than chance at spotting the pirate in both versions of the game. However, once one of the credible participants was replaced by the agent that we built, the group had significantly greater success in finding the pirate.

We use machine learning on the data collected from human participants to determine whether a player is honest or not. The agent uses this information to catch the pirate. We also apply machine learning methods in order to learn when players fall under suspicion. This information is also used by our agent in order to minimize the suspicion that it raises. We focus on the discussion dynamics such as tendencies towards accusation, denial or agreement.

In this paper we provide a platform for studying deception detection within a text based game that supports group discussion. In this game we deploy an agent that is required not only to detect deception and lead other participants to recognize the deceiver, but also to refrain from raising suspicion itself. Previous approaches use corpora to perform off-line deception detection, whereas we have perform on-line detection during multi-player interaction. To the best of our knowledge we are the first to deploy an autonomous agent in any such environment. We provide extensive evaluation of our agent in both game settings.

THE PIRATE GAME

In order to simulate the environment which we are interested in studying (deception in chat-rooms and forums), we need a game which will provide us with the following properties:

1. The game is played by a group of people.
2. The game uses text-based communication.
3. The game is based on a discussion, using short messages and in which players refer to one another.
4. The deceiver has some motivation to deceive.
5. The other players have some motivation to catch the deceiver.

To satisfy these properties we introduce the Pirate Game; a game, with four players and two roles. Three players are the honest players, the "credible villagers", and the fourth player plays the deceptive participant, the "pirate". All players are informed of their own role but not of anyone else's. The participants are told that they are a group of villagers who went on a journey to find a treasure. They have found a treasure of coins and can split it. However, one of the participants is a pirate and can steal the coins unless he is detected. In order to detect the pirate a discussion phase is held. After the discussion, all credible villagers cast votes as to whom they think is the pirate (or an empty vote if they wish). In our game we do not allow the pirate to vote, as allowing the pirate to vote would make the game harder and less fun for the players and demotivate them. The votes are concealed until all players cast their votes. If there is a majority of votes for the pirate he is "caught" and the money is split between the credible players. Otherwise the pirate receives all the money. At the beginning of the game each player is told his role and the discussion phase begins. The discussion is composed of structured sentences (examples are presented in Figure 1). Although we do not use free chat, our frame-work allows the composition of approximately $4,000$ sentences (which is, for instance, much richer than the options available in [11] or what can be achieved using icons as in [2]). A video demonstrating the user interface can be found at: http://azariaa.com/pirate.avi.

We use structured sentences rather than free text for several reasons. First of all, structured sentences, as opposed to open text, enable focusing on the dynamics of the discussion, and less on the syntax. Furthermore, the structured sentences encourage participants to use meaningful sentences, and they also encourage players to speak and be active because the player merely selects a sentence rather than phrasing his own. Since the players have limited time, slow typists may not have time to respond. Structured sentences limit the effect of typing speed (since this environment is new to everyone). Finally, the controlled environment also makes it easy to add an agent that plays similarly to other players and keeps the agent inconspicuous. This does not mean that an agent cannot be deployed into an unstructured environment, but adding "social credentials" to the agent were not the focus of this work. An open chat environment requires solving NLP challenges in order to automatically tag sentences. These are difficult challenges, but recent progress in NLP seems promising [28]. Once these challenges are solved it would be straightforward to adapt our agent to incorporate the NLP tagging.

We also implemented a second variation of the game. This variation is different only for the scenario where the pirate manages to escape (does not receive a majority of the votes). In this variation the pirate is told that one of the credible villagers will turn him over to the village ruler, if he escapes with the money. This results in neither the pirate nor the other players receiving any money, unless the pirate manages to convince the other players to cast at least one vote against the villager. In this case the villager will be considered unreliable (to the village ruler) and the pirate will gain all of the coins, that he escaped with. This setting encourages the pirate to be active in the game. We call this version of the game the "informer version" and differentiate it from the "basic version". A description of the formal model for the Pirate game can be found in the Appendix.

RELATED WORK

Of all existing games, the "Pirate Game" we introduce is most similar to the Mafia games (also known as "werewolf"), however pirate game is a simpler game which is closer to actual situations which take place in real life. In the mafia game once a player is accused to be a malicious player (or the werewolf") by a majority of votes, this player is eliminated from the game and the game continues. The mafia game also includes a phase in which the malicious player (or the werewolf") eliminates a credible player. Furthermore, every time a player is eliminated his real role is revealed. This elimination process receives considerable attention in studies which examine this game. However, in real-life situations there is very seldom a situation where some users are eliminated and the discussion continues without them. We therefore introduce the pirate game which we believe resembles real-life situations much better. The mafia game has been used as a platform for studying communication, coordination and functionality in situations where participants have different amounts of information, and have also raised much interest in theoretical analysis [18, 6]. Dias et al. [11] introduce MIXER (Moderating Interactions for Cross-Cultural Empathic Relationships), which is a platform incorporating intelligent and interactive characters and is based on the mafia game. They study the level of human reasoning (e.g. if someone wanted to eliminate a player which turned out to be a credible villager he may be the werewolf), and the level of reasoning which is required for an agent in order to play well. Aylett et al. [2] use the MIXER platform for studying the attitude children adopt towards cultural differences. They had children play the mafia game using two different sets of rules and observed how a child playing in one set of rules reacts when exposed to a group playing the game under a different set of rules. The mafia game has also been used for detecting deceptive participants using audio and video data [8, 25]. Chittaranjan and Hung [8] use non-verbal audio cues such as: the length of speaking intervals, the number of speaking turns, interruptions and pitch. They achieve an F-Measure of 0.62 for deception detection. These cues are used to detect suspicious behavior. They also show that the degree of speaker activity influences the group decision. In a later work, Raiman, Hung and Englebienne [25] combine these audio features with low quality visual data, in which facial expressions cannot be recognized, but gestures can. Combining the audio data with the video results in an improved detection rate with an F-measure of 0.76.

A similar study was performed by [15] who use digital audio tape to detect deceptive speech. They use both prosodic features (which do not use the actual words) such as pitch, loudness, duration, etc. and lexical features such as denials and flags for positive and negative emotion words (a total of 20 features). The best combination resulted with an accuracy of 64.4%. Our experiment is run under the assumption that the conversation is performed over the web where visual and audio data are unavailable.

Zhou et al. [30], use a text-based environment in which deceptive senders have to persuade receivers to make decisions which they know to be incorrect. This experiment tests whether the automatic extraction of linguistic cues contributes to differentiation between deceptive and non-deceptive texts. In their work, though subjects were motivated to play the game, there was no special motivation for the deceptive players to be deceptive. In the game we design we make a point of motivating the deceptive player to act accordingly. The deceptive senders were found to be more expressive than honest senders. This is contrary to previous work that shows that liars tend to be less expressive. This result was explained by the fact that previous studies were conducted in an interview type scenario where a liar had to answer in real time without planning or editing, as opposed to this experiment where liars can think about and edit the message before they send it. This work was later extended [31] to a chat-based environment where the effects of the type of environment on deception detection by human subjects were studied. They observed that humans felt that viewing the messages assisted detection more than viewing video of the actual typing of the liars. However, the accuracy of the human deception detection in all settings was lower than 50%. Although the text-based domain that we use is similar to the domains used by Zhou et al., our research differs substantially from these studies. We use machine learning to differentiate between deceptive and non-deceptive texts as opposed to these studies that either collected statistics on the existence of automatically extracted phrases or used humans for detecting deception.

Newman et al. [20] and Toma and Hancock [29] find that certain words are chosen more often by liars. Zhou et al. use text-based computer mediated environments to study what linguistic-based cues are used more in deceptive texts than in non-deceptive texts [31] and how modality affects human deception detection in chat-based environments [30]. However they do not build a model for deception detection with machine learning.

Another study on deceptive language is performed by [19]. Their data consists of paragraphs written by subjects who were asked to write their opinion on a topic and then write the opposite opinion. Naive Bayes and Support Vector Machines were used to classify words in this data set. Words that are connected to the self such as "I, friends, self" are often used in the honest text. In contrast, detached words such as "you, other, human" appear more often in the deceptive text. When topics were evaluated separately, an average detection rate of 70.8% was found. When testing the portability of the classifiers across topics, accuracy dropped to 59.8% on average.

Toma and Hancock analyze text which is presented in online dating profiles [29]. This is a setting where the subjects have time to revise their descriptions, and make sure they sound honest. Yet again deceptive participants use less self-references, and use more negations. 63% of the profiles were correctly classified using logistic regression. Ott et al. conduct a study [23] in which they try to differentiate honest hotel reviews from fake ones. They asked Mechanical Turk workers to write fake *positive* reviews for a set of hotels and fetched (presumable) truthful *positive* reviews from TripAdvisor. One of their proposed methods reaches a success rate of nearly 90%. Ott et al. also conduct a recent similar study [22] for *negative* reviews. These types of studies are inherently different to the discussion environment that we study, since in a discussion environment people are part of a group and refer to each other, while in writing a review etc. each person merely posts the review, doesn't refer to anyone else and isn't required to later post any additional response. While writing a review, description or opinion is composed of a large bulk of text; in a discussion environment the messages are short and fast. As we chose to focus on the dynamics of the discussion and therefore use structure sentences, most of the features which heavily rely on syntax features are not applicable to our work.

Mancilla-Caceres et al. [17] developed a game in order to identify children who act as bullies within a social network. The game involves a restricted set of resources and two tasks. One is collaborative and the other competitive. The communication between participants is through text messages. Mancilla et al. manually classify the messages exchanged and, using machine learning, are able to detect the bullies with an accuracy of slightly above 60%. This game is reminiscent of our game as it uses text messages and players are given a set of resources. However our game is aimed at assessing dishonest behavior and not aggressive behavior.

Similar work dealing with cyberbullying was performed by Bosse and Stam [5]. They deploy an agent in a game in order to reduce cyberbullying in it. However, their agent is given special capabilities over the ordinary players, such as using rewards and punishments. Additionally, since they do not deal with deception, their agent is not required to appear trustworthy to the other players.

Human-agent interaction has taken a major role in the negotiation environment [27, 14, 3]. Occasionally, in such environments, agreements aren't enforceable and thus an agent must reason about the probability or the likelihood that the opponent might be deceiving and will not keep his promise. However, to the best of our knowledge, in this realm, predictions are based merely on the user's actions and monetary promises and not on verbal or textual context.

Our work should not be confused with the following works on deception and deception detection in agents, [26, 16, 7, 9], where agents must determine whether other agents are lying, or agents use deception themselves. Santos an Li [26] study deception detection in a multi-agent environment. They focused on the agent's reasoning process in a medical inference system. In this system the agents infer medical information in an intensive care unit. Some of these agents are simulated to be deceptive. Correlation between the various agents in the system are used to make predictions on the agent reasoning process and are then used to detect deception. Kaluža, Kaminka and Tambe [16] propose a two step approach for detecting suspicious behavior in agents. In their study they simulate an airport domain, where agents simulate passenger behavior. Some of the agents simulate suspicious behavior. The detection of suspicious agents is based on sequences of events performed by the agents. In the first stage trigger events are detected, and in the second multiple events are combined to determine suspiciousness. An interesting study is performed by Bridewell and Isaac [7]. They developed a framework for socially aware inference, using deception as an example of social behavior. They model the mental states of other agents using beliefs, goals and intentions. Christian and Young [9] use strategic deception in a planner in order to achieve certain goals. The deception is used in order to improve planning. This is an example to the agent being deceptive itself rather than detecting deception in others.

THE DIG AGENT

We present the Deception In Group detector and catcher Agent (DIG). The DIG agent is capable of participating in the pirate game while posing as a regular player. During an ongoing session of the pirate game, DIG uses input from multiple previous games, along with input from the current game, and outputs the next sentence it wants to contribute to the discussion. DIG has four components. The first is used to detect the deceiver and is called the *'Suspector'*. The second component, the *'Output Selector'*, aims to avoid raising suspicion (as being the pirate). The third component is the *'Accuser'*; it directs the other credible players towards DIG's suspect. The fourth component, the *'Responder'*, responds to sentences other players may direct to DIG.

The structure of DIG is presented in Figure 2. All of the sentences from the chat in the current game are provided as input to the *'Suspector'* component which (using machine learning) outputs an ordered list of suspects. This list of suspects is provided as input to the *'Accuser'* and is used to output a time-dependent list of possible sentences for the DIG agent to use. In addition, the last sentence in the current chat is input to the *'Responder'*. In the case this sentence is referred to DIG, the *'Responder'* (Using training data) outputs another optional sentence set. Based on the sentences in the chat and the optional sentence set, the *'Output Selector'* (using machine learning) selects a sentence for DIG to output. We describe the components in detail.

The Suspector Component

The 'Suspector' relies on a machine learning model built offline that classifies various users' texts and whether or not they played the role of a deceiver. We use data from previous games. For each player in each game we build a feature vector. We use the feature set mentioned below and label each player vector as being the pirate or a credible villager. We used an SVM classifier with a linear kernel [10] which is built on these player vectors. The *'Suspector'* is interested in the SVM-score (the signed distance from the separating hyperplane) and not in the actual SVM classification. The online part of the component works as follows: it extracts feature vectors from all of the sentences that appeared in the game. The feature vectors are fed to the model (built offline), and the model outputs the degree of suspiciousness for each of the players. The component then sorts the players according to their degree of suspiciousness. The *'Suspector'* is used mainly by the *'Accuser'* component.

The Output Selector Component

The 'Output Selector' gets a set of sentences from the *'Accuser'* and the *'Responder'* components and using another machine learning model outputs the least suspicious sentence from the perspective of human players (the sentence that would raise the least suspicion if said at the current time). Similarly to the model used in the *'Suspector'* component, the model we build here (offline) uses player feature vectors and uses SVM as described above. However, this model uses different labeling. The player vectors are labeled as being suspicious or not, based on whether they received votes or did not (rather than whether the player was a pirate or not). Note: just as the *'Suspector'* component, this model is built on a group of sentences and not on single sentences. The model is fed with features derived from all of the sentences that appeared in the game, together with each option provided as input by the *'Accuser'* or *'Responder'*. Based on the SVM-score obtained from this model, for each of the options, the *'Output Selector'* chooses the sentence which would raise the least suspicion, towards DIG, if said at the current time. In addition to the above, a random delay was added to each sentence said by DIG, in order to appear human.

The Accuser Component

The 'Accuser' is awoken by a clock at given times[1] and selects possible sentences for DIG to say. The list of sentences output by this component is based on a manual tagging of all sentences. For example, some sentences were tagged as opening sentences, such as "Who is the pirate", "I am not the pirate" and "I am a credible villager". Other sentences were tagged as accusing sentences, as alter justification (standing up for a different player) and as questions to other players. The *'Accuser'* component could also output an empty sentence as part of the set of sentences. Depending on the time left until the end of the game and according to a manually constructed table which determines which sentence tags are appropriate for which time, and based upon the *'Suspector'*s suspects, the *'Accuser'* provided the *'Output Selector'* a set of possible sentences to output. For example, when 100 seconds remain till the end of the game, the *'Accuser'* component provides all sentences which were either tagged as accusing sentences (towards the *'Suspector'*s top suspect) or tagged as alter justification sentences (towards the *'Suspector'*s least suspected player). The sentence tags are determined under the assumption that as time progresses, more confident sentences should be chosen. The exact sentence to say is chosen by the *'Output Selector'*. The *'Accuser'*s main goal is to encourage the other players to vote for DIG's suspect. This component is also in charge of casting a vote (on the *'Suspector'*'s leading suspect) in the voting phase.

The Responder Component

The 'Responder' is activated when someone referrers to DIG in the previous sentence. The *'Responder'* then searches the data set for sentences used by other players when posed with the same question or statement. The *'Responder'* provides these sentences to the *'Output Selector'* which determines which sentence to output. Similarly to the *'Accuser'* component, if any of these sentences require reference to another player (if the sentence is tagged as accusing or alter justification), the player which the *'Responder'* refers to depends on the list of suspects obtained from the *'Suspector'*.

DIG Feature Selection

For the machine learning used in DIG's *'Suspector'* and *'Output Selector'* components we need to define the feature set obtained from the structured chat. We used 41 features, some of which are mentioned in [30] and the rest were dedicated

[1]We used fixed time values, however, these clock values may be learned online and updated according to performance.

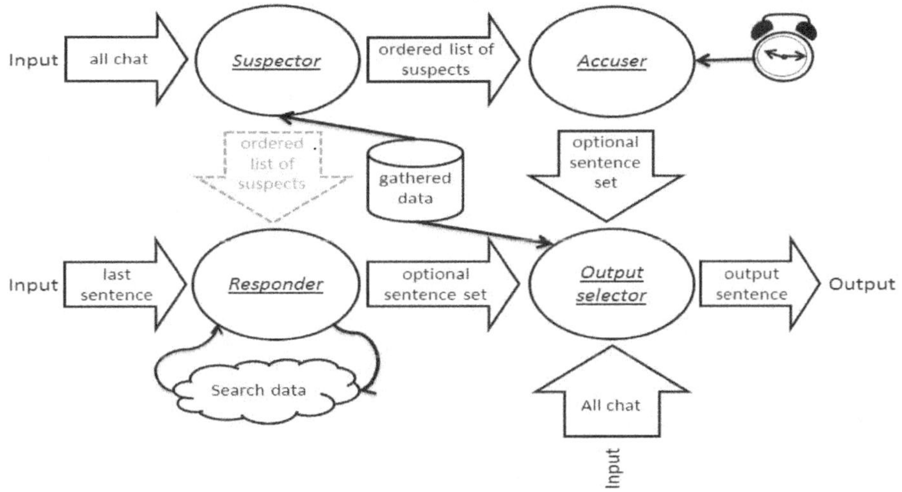

Figure 2. The structure of the DIG agent. Circles represent components, arrows represent input and output.

to our problem. Since we wanted our approach to be scalable and suitable also for a free chat environment, we used more general features such that other sentences (which do not appear in the structured sentences) may be mapped to these features as well. Some of the features also depend on the order of the sentences and not solely on whether a sentence was said (or how many times it was said). For the learning, each player is treated as an instance which must be classified. All of the 41 features that we used had a positive impact. The top 10 features are:

- **Fraction of talking:** the fraction of sentences said by the player out of the total number of sentences said (in current game).
- **Accusations:** the number of accusing sentences used by the player. And the fraction of accusations from all sentences said by that player.
- **Consistency:** indicates the level of accusation consistency towards the other players. A player who always accused the same other player will have a high value, while a player who accused all three other players equally will have a low value. This feature calculates the maximum among the accusations towards each of the other players and divides it by the total number of accusations.
- **Characteristics:** indicates how many times a player referred to a different player's characteristics such as being too quiet, talkative, accusatory etc. This was easily identified since we used structured sentences (see the third form of sentences in Figure 1).
- **First sentence:** indicates whether the player was first, second, third or fourth to say his first sentence.
- **First Accusation:** indicates whether the player was first, second, third or fourth to accuse a different player of being the pirate.
- **Self-justification:** indicates how many times the player stood up for himself (saying he is not a pirate etc.).
- **Alter justification:** indicates how many times the player stood up for a different player (saying that a different player is not a pirate etc.).
- **Agreeing:** indicates whether a player agreed with other players (and how many times).
- **Agree to accusation:** indicates whether a player agreed with another player when that other player accused someone (and how many times).

EXPERIMENTS

All of our experiments were performed using Amazon's Mechanical Turk service (AMT) [1][2]. Participation in all experiments consisted of a total of 320 subjects from the USA, of which 47.8% were females and 52.2% were males. The subjects' ages ranged from 18 to 67, with a mean of 32 and median of 30. All subjects had to pass a short quiz to assure that they understood the rules and had to practice the usage of the structured sentences before they could play. We ran experiments with the two versions of the game ("informer" and "basic"), each with two different setups. We ran the game with only human players and then with an agent playing the role of one of the credible villagers (the agent is never the pirate). The subjects weren't told about the agent and therefore assumed all players were humans. According to comments we collected, no players suspected a nonhuman player.

Participants had to play 5 games each. Each game was played with different participants, so no deductions based on participants' behavior can be made between games. The discussion phase was limited to 240 seconds and the voting phase was limited to 30 seconds. The average number of sentences per

[2]For a comparison between AMT and other recruitment methods see [24].

game was 36.6. The subjects were paid 62 cents for participating in the study. They gained 12 cents for every time they were a credible villager in a group that managed to catch the pirate and 36 cents if they were a pirate who managed to escape with the gold. A stake of 36 cents for a single game is relatively high in AMT (58% of total payoff for 5 games). This is in order to increase the players' incentive to play seriously.

The players enjoyed the game very much. When asked whether they enjoyed the game, on a scale between 1 to 5 they gave it on average a score of 4.01 (standard deviation of: 1.06). The players also provided very positive feedback such as: "It was the best survey or game I have done...", "This was really fun... Thanks for the good time!" and "That was so much fun! ... I could play it all day!". . Interestingly, the subjects found the "informer version" of the game more enjoyable than the "basic version": 4.22 vs. 3.79 ($p < 0.01$). This can be explained by the fact that in the "informer version" both the pirate (needs to incriminate a certain player) and the credible villagers (need to find who is trying to incriminate a different player) have a clearer task. On average the subjects did not seem to believe that they played very well. The subjects were asked how well they believed that they played (on a 1 to 5 scale) and the average response was 2.89 (standard deviation of: 1.05). Interestingly, the subjects seemed to believe that they played slightly better in the "informer version": 2.94 vs. the "basic version": 2.84, however, these differences are not statistically significant and have no support in the actual results (as presented later).

DIG Construction

Recall that two of DIG's components (the 'Suspector' and the 'Output Selector') are based on machine learning. We now describe their construction.

Constructing the 'Suspector' component

The *'Suspector'* component builds a model that identifies whether a player is a pirate or a credible villager. We used the results obtained from the all-human games (with no agent) as our learning data for this component. For the "basic version" we used 204 examples and for the "informer version" we used 272 examples. We obtained an accuracy of 72.1% and an F-Measure of 0.69 for the "basic version" of the game, and similarly an accuracy of 72.8% and an F-Measure of 0.7 for the "informer version". Some interesting insights into the pirate's behavior are: The pirate is an average talker (not too much, not too little), doesn't talk much about himself, avoids direct accusation but hints that someone else is the pirate, is often the third to talk (rarely the first). In the "informer version" the pirate talks mostly about the same player, and in "basic version" the pirate talks about others quite equally.

Constructing the 'Output Selector' Component

We use this component to supply DIG with information regarding which sentences to use and which to avoid. The model of this component was less accurate (using the same feature-set above), with only 56.4% accuracy and an F-Measure of 0.56 in the "basic version". This result implies that we aren't very successful at predicting which players will receive votes and which will not (possibly because the subjects themselves might have voted almost randomly). The accuracy in the "informer version" was slightly higher at 61.0% and an F-Measure of 0.61, implying that in the "informer version" we were more successful at identifying whom the other players suspect. We found that people think that the pirate is quiet, is the first to talk, and that the pirate tends to agree with others, especially when making accusations.

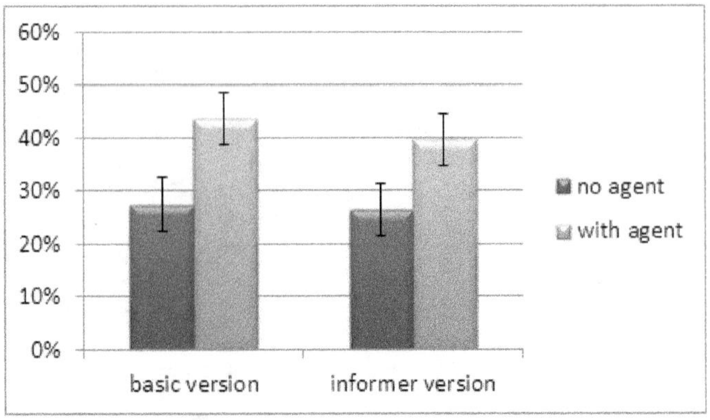

Figure 3. Success rate in catching the pirate. Compares both versions of the game, with and without an agent.

Based on this model, the *'Output Selector'* component chose to say "I am a credible villager" at the beginning of the game, and decided to use "Alter justification" (stood up for other players) with the least suspicious player (when such sentences were optional according to the *'Accuser'* component's output). The *'Output Selector'* component tried to avoid any accusations, and therefore started to accuse a player only towards the end of the game (when the *'Accuser'* component only provided sentences tagged as accusing). It always avoided asking other players whether they were pirates, as this was also shown to raise suspicion. The *'Output Selector'* preferred sentences which clearly said for whom it would vote "I will vote for..." rather than using a phrase such as "I believe that I will vote for..." as, once again, while the first is shown to lower the other players' suspicion, the latter is shown to raise it.

Experimental Results

Figure 3 presents the success rate of the credible villagers at catching the pirate in both versions of the game, with and without the agent. In both versions of the game the groups including the DIG agent (basic: 43.7%, informer: 39.7%) significantly outperform (using chi square test, with $\alpha = 0.05$) the groups that didn't include the DIG agent (basic: 27.5%, informer: 26.5%). The performance of the human players without the agent is very close to the expected utility of random voting which is 0.26 (see random voting analysis in the appendix).

Table 1 summarizes the voting results. These should not be confused with the success rate. The number of correct votes in the setting that includes DIG were higher than those without DIG. This is true both in the "basic version" of the game (41.9% with DIG vs. 35.9% without DIG) and in the "informer version" (42.4% with DIG vs. 33.8% without DIG).

game version	agent participation	correct votes	agent correct votes	human correct votes
basic	no agent	35.1%	-	35.1%
basic	with agent	41.9%	48.3%	38.6%
informer	no agent	33.8%	-	33.8%
informer	with agent	42.4%	46.6%	41.6%

Table 1. Voting Accuracy (random vote = 33.3%)

Even more interesting are the number of correct human votes. Humans cast more correct votes when DIG participated than when humans played alone (see Table 1 for details). This is true both for the "basic version" and for the "informer version". This implies that not only did DIG help the group by casting more accurate votes, but DIG also seems to improve the number of correct votes cast by the humans in its group. We would also like to mention that very rarely did subjects cast an empty vote (only in 4% of the cases).

We end this section by testing the ability of DIG to avoid suspicion (as being the pirate). Recall that one of DIG's properties is to choose sentences that reduce suspicion. We measure suspicion by counting the number of votes cast by the other credible villagers against DIG. Note, that as DIG was never the pirate, a low vote percentage is better than a high one. In the "basic version", 32.2% of the votes were cast against DIG (meaning they falsely thought DIG was the pirate), which is still a little below average (which is 33.3%) and therefore may be reasonable. However, unfortunately, 37.6% of the votes in the "informer version" were cast against DIG (which is higher than the average). We explain this by the fact that DIG tried to encourage the other humans to vote for the player which DIG detected as the pirate, as required by the *'Accuser'* component. This act in the "informer version" probably raised suspicion (as players might have incorrectly assumed that DIG is the pirate and therefore trying to incriminate the informer). Another reason that could have caused suspicion in both versions is that people might have noticed that DIG doesn't play as a completely normal player, as the *'Responder'* component was not the focus of this study. We believe that had we not selected DIG's sentences with care using the *'Output Selector'* component, the suspicion would have been greater. We plan to investigate this in future work. An example of one of the games played by DIG (in the basic version) can be found at: http://azariaa.com/GameExample.htm.

DISCUSSION

One might wonder how the use of open chat rather than structured sentences would affect the relationship between the success rates of human players and the agent. Previous work [31] has shown that people are roughly as good as chance at detecting liars. We believe that since we succeeded while using structured sentences, using free text, and extracting features from it should be even more successful, but requires additional research.

We designed our agent to remain unsuspicious, as we did not want it to be falsely accused as being the pirate, and since we wanted it to be able to influence other players. We believe that if the agent seemed human these goals would be accomplished. However, behaving like a human was not a goal by itself. It is unclear how well the agent would perform, if the context was one not restricted to structured sentences, and the agent could identify it-self as non-human. This would require additional research. On the other hand, it would be easier for DIG to function in such an environment.

In our game people had little experience at deceiving. It is interesting to know how well DIG would perform against experienced deceivers. Note that this problem is not specific to our work, but a known challenge in deception detection in general. People, who would be experienced in deceiving in these types of environments, would be experts at deceiving people, rather than agents. We have shown people use different features for deception detection than DIG. Experienced deceivers would probably avoid the features picked up by humans. However they may still display other features, which DIG would pick up. Therefore, DIG may be able to succeed in detection of experienced deceivers as well. This has not been determined.

If DIG does not have enough data collected yet, it could use data from a similar domain. Alternatively DIG can collect data from Mechanical Turk, or ask humans to tag discussions.

In our game, we have a single deceptive participant. We would expect that in a scenario where there may also be zero or multiple deceptive participants DIG will not perform as well, but will still perform much better than humans (who will also not perform as well). An extension to this work would need to design a new game to account for multiple deceptive participants.

CONCLUSIONS AND FUTURE WORK

In this paper we presented "the pirate game" as a platform that enables the study of deception in a computerized discussion text-based environment. We presented two versions of the game, the "basic version" where the deceiving participant could hide and an "informer version" where the deceptive player was encouraged to be active. In both versions we found that humans' success rate in catching the deceptive player was similar to the success rate of random votes achieved when all players cast a random vote. This result is consistent with previous studies which show that people do not perform much better than chance when asked to detect deception.

We introduced DIG, an agent that uses machine learning to build a successful strategy for deception detection. DIG was successful at detecting the deceptive player in both versions of the game. DIG provided two contributions to the group of players. The first is that as we look at a group task, the ability of DIG to cast a correct vote increases the group ability. The second contribution of DIG is the indication that other players have higher detection rates when the agent participates.

The platform we introduce is a first step towards decreasing deception in textual discussion based environments. The input method relies on the use of structured sentences. Although, this method has many benefits, as we described, many natural discussion based environments use free text. As

NLP continues to develop and improve, it is natural to extend our work to include NLP tagging and integrate it into our agent.

In future work we also intend to pursue a method for the agent to select its sentences so that it increases its probability of detecting the pirate. The agent will need to find a question for each situation that, when answered, may either increase or decrease the probability that the agent's current suspect is the real pirate. This is a very challenging issue since each sentence may change the behavior of the rest of the game.

ACKNOWLEDGMENT

This work was supported in part by ERC grant #267523, and ARO grants W911NF0910206 and W911NF1110344.

REFERENCES

1. Amazon. Mechanical Turk services. http://www.mturk.com/, 2012.
2. Aylett, R., Hall, L., Tazzyman, S., Endrass, B., André, E., Ritter, C., Nazir, A., Paiva, A., Höfstede, G., and Kappas, A. Werewolves, cheats, and cultural sensitivity. In *AAMAS'14* (2014), 1085–1092.
3. Azaria, A., Aumann, Y., and Kraus, S. Automated strategies for determining rewards for humanwork. In *AAAI'12* (2012).
4. Bhaskaran, N., Nwogu, I., Frank, M., and Govindaraju, V. Lie to me: Deceit detection via online behavioral learning. In *FG'11* (march 2011), 24 –29.
5. Bosse, T., and Stam, S. A normative agent system to prevent cyberbullying. In *WI-IAT'11*, vol. 2, IEEE (2011), 425–430.
6. Braverman, M., Etesami, O., and Mossel, E. Mafia: A theoretical study of players and coalitions in a partial information environment. *Annals of Applied Probability 18*, 3 (2008), 825–846.
7. Bridewell, W., and Isaac, A. Recognizing deception: A model of dynamic belief attribution. In *Advances in Cognitive Systems: Papers from the 2011 AAAI Fall Symposium* (2011), 50–57.
8. Chittaranjan, G., and Hung, H. Are you a werewolf? detecting deceptive roles and outcomes in a conversational role-playing game. In *ICASSP* (2010), 5334–5337.
9. Christian, D., and Young, R. M. Strategic deception in agents. In *AAMAS'04*, IEEE Computer Society (2004), 218–226.
10. Cortes, C., and Vapnik, V. Support-vector networks. *Machine learning 20*, 3 (1995), 273–297.
11. Dias, J., Aylett, R., Reis, H., and Paiva, A. The great deceivers: Virtual agents and believable lies. In *CogSci 2013* (2013), 2189–2194.
12. Ekman, P. *Telling Lies: Clues to Deceit in the Marketplace, Politics, and Marriage*. W. W. Norton & Company, 1991.
13. Farrell, J., and Rabin, M. Cheap talk. *The Journal of Economic Perspectives 10*, 3 (1996), 103–118.
14. Gal, Y., Kraus, S., Gelfand, M. J., Khashan, H., and Salmon, E. Negotiating with people across cultures using an adaptive agent. *ACM TIST 3*, 1 (2012).
15. Graciarena, M., Shriberg, E., andFrank Enos, A. S., Hirschberg, J., and Kajarekar, S. Combining prosodic, lexical and cepstral systems for deceptive speech detection. In *Proc. IEEE ICASSP* (2006).
16. Kaluža, B., Kaminka, G. A., and Tambe, M. Detection of suspicious behavior from a sparse set of multiagent interactions. In *AAMAS'12* (2012), 955–964.
17. Mancilla-Caceres, J. F., Pu, W., Amir, E., and Espelage, D. Identifying bullies with a computer game. In *AAAI* (2012).
18. Migdal, P. A mathematical model of the mafia game. *CoRR abs/1009.1031* (2010).
19. Mihalcea, R., and Strapparava, C. The lie detector: Explorations in the automatic recognition of deceptive language. In *ACL/AFNLP (Short Papers)* (2009), 309–312.
20. Newman, M. L., Pennebaker, J. W., Berry, D. S., and Richards, J. M. Lying words: predicting deception from linguistic styles. *Pers Soc Psychol Bull 29(5)* (2003), 665–75.
21. Ott, M., Cardie, C., and Hancock, J. Estimating the prevalence of deception in online review communities. In *WWW '12*, ACM (2012), 201–210.
22. Ott, M., Cardie, C., and Hancock, J. T. Negative deceptive opinion spam. In *HLT-NAACL 2013* (2013).
23. Ott, M., Choi, Y., Cardie, C., and Hancock, J. T. Finding deceptive opinion spam by any stretch of the imagination. In *HLT '11 - Volume 1* (2011), 309–319.
24. Paolacci, G., Chandler, J., and Ipeirotis, P. G. Running experiments on Amazon Mechanical Turk. *Judgment and Decision Making 5*, 5 (2010).
25. Raiman, N., HayleyHung, and Englebienne, G. Move, and i will tell you who you are: detecting deceptive roles in low-quality data. In *ICMI '11*, ACM (2011), 201–204.
26. Santos, E., and Li, D. On deception detection in multiagent systems. *Systems, Man and Cybernetics, Part A: Systems and Humans, IEEE Transactions on 40*, 2 (march 2010), 224 –235.
27. Simari, G. I., Broecheler, M., Subrahmanian, V., and Kraus, S. Promises kept, promises broken: An axiomatic and quantitative treatment of fulfillment. In *KR* (2008), 59–69.
28. Toledo, A., Katrenko, S., Alexandropoulou, S., Klockmann, H., Stern, A., Dagan, I., and Winter, Y. Semantic annotation for textual entailment recognition. In *Advances in Computational Intelligence*. Springer, 2013, 12–25.

29. Toma, C. L., and Hancock, J. T. Reading between the lines: linguistic cues to deception in online dating profiles. In *CSCW '10*, ACM (2010), 5–8.

30. Zhou, L., Burgoon, J. K., Nunamaker, J. F., and Twitchell, D. Automating linguistics-based cues for detecting deception in text-based asynchronous computer-mediated. *Group Decision and Negotiation 13* (2004), 81–106.

31. Zhou, L., and Zhang, D. Typing or messaging? modality effect on deception detection in computer-mediated communication. *Decision Support Systems 44*, 1 (2007), 188 – 201.

APPENDIX

FORMAL MODEL

In the formal model, the Pirate Game consists of k players $P = \{p_1, p_2, ..., p_k\}$, one of which is a pirate. We assume $k \geq 4$. The identity of the pirate player is known only to the pirate himself. The game includes two phases: the first phase consists of a communication phase where all players can discuss their strategy. The communication in this phase bears no cost and is not binding ("cheap talk" [13]). The second phase is a voting phase where all players except the pirate may simultaneously cast their vote $v(p)$, where $v : P \rightarrow \{\{p_1\}, \{p_2\}, ..., \{p_k\}, \phi\}$ and ϕ indicates an empty vote. It is assumed that the pirate always casts an empty vote ϕ. If the majority of the votes are cast against the pirate, all players but the pirate receive a point and the pirate receives zero points. Otherwise the pirate receives a point and the other players receive zero points. More formally, we define a function for a player's role:

$$r(p) = \begin{cases} 0 & \text{if p is the pirate} \\ 1 & \text{else} \end{cases} \tag{1}$$

We will use $\overline{r(p)} = 1 - r(p)$. The reward function for each player $u(p)$ is given by:

$$u(p) = \overline{r(p)} + (\text{-}1)^{\overline{r(p)}} \cdot$$
$$\mathbb{1}\Big\{\Big(\sum_{i=1}^{k} \sum_{p' \in v(p_i)} \overline{r(p')}\Big) \geq \Big\lceil \frac{1 + \sum_{i=1}^{k} |v(p_k)|}{2} \Big\rceil\Big\} \tag{2}$$

where $\mathbb{1}\{\}$ is the indicator function.

Equilibrium Strategies

Assuming all players are perfectly rational, the communication phase doesn't reveal any information regarding the pirate's identity, since the pirate may act as if he were a credible player. We provide the equilibrium strategies analysis in order to compare human performance to that of perfectly rational players.

Pure strategy equilibrium

Given a player p', the strategies $\forall p | r(p) = 1, v(p) = \{p'\}$ are in equilibrium, since any deviation from the equilibrium by a single player will not change the final result[3]. Assuming p' is random, this equilibrium assures an expected utility of $\frac{1}{k}$ for the credible players (and $1 - \frac{1}{k}$ for the pirate). Although it is in equilibrium, agreeing upon the player to vote for (p') requires the communication phase to allow simultaneous messaging. Assuming simultaneous messaging, all players must choose a random number $x(p)$ between 1 and k, simultaneously publish it, and then vote for player p_l where $l = \sum_{p \in P} x(p) \pmod{k}$. Although the pirate may choose a non-random number, since he has no knowledge of the numbers chosen by the other players, the result remains random. This method was also proposed in [6].

Mixed Equilibrium

Following is a mixed equilibrium for the game:
$\forall p | r(p) = 1, \forall p' | p' \neq p, v(p) = \{p'\}$ with probability $\frac{1}{k-1}$. The expected utility for the credible players using this equilibrium is given by the following binomial distribution mass function: $\sum_{j=\lceil \frac{k}{2} \rceil}^{k-1} \binom{j}{k-1} (\frac{1}{k-1})^j \cdot (1 - \frac{1}{k-1})^{k-1-j}$

When $k = 4$, the above mixed equilibrium yields a slightly greater expected utility than the pure equilibrium mentioned before (0.26 vs. 0.25). Being symmetric towards all players, the mixed equilibrium doesn't require any prior communication. However, as k increases, the mixed equilibrium yields a very low expected utility for the credible players. For example, when $k = 7$ the expected utility of the credible players goes down to 0.01.

Alternative Models

Informer version

We also consider a model with a slight modification to the pirate's utility function, where there exists a player $\bar{p}$ whose identity is known only to the pirate. The pirate's utility function is identical to Equation 2, except if $\bar{p}$ doesn't receive even a single vote, in which case the pirate's utility is 0 regardless of the other votes. Formally, if $\sum_{i=1}^{k} \sum_{p' \in v(p_i)} \bar{r}(p') = 0$, then the pirate's utility is 0. This change doesn't affect the equilibria, as they do not depend on the pirate's actions.

Voting pirate

Allowing also the pirate to vote significantly reduces the credible villagers' probability of catching him. In addition to allowing the pirate to vote, one might also consider requiring that the pirate need only receive the plurality of votes (rather than the majority), where in case of a tie, the chosen player is defined by a toss of a coin. This drastically changes the equilibria for all games. As long as all players vote and no player votes for himself, almost any mixed strategy is in equilibrium with an expected utility of $\frac{1}{k}$ for the credible players, since, in every game, one and only one player is chosen. For symmetric reasons, there is a probability of exactly $\frac{1}{k}$ that this player is the pirate.

[3] if the majority of players plus one have a strategy of $v(p) = \{p'\}$, all other players may have any other strategy and still be in equilibrium. Although additional equilibria exist, in this appendix we give only a few examples of equilibria and do not try to list them all.

Characterizing Online Rumoring Behavior Using Multi-Dimensional Signatures

Jim Maddock†*, Kate Starbird†, Haneen Al-Hassani, Daniel E. Sandoval†, Mania Orand†, Robert M. Mason*
HCDE†, iSchool*, DUB
University of Washington, Seattle WA, 98195
{maddock, kstarbi, haneen1, dansand, orand, rmmason}@uw.edu

ABSTRACT

This study offers an in-depth analysis of four rumors that spread through Twitter after the 2013 Boston Marathon Bombings. Through qualitative and visual analysis, we describe each rumor's origins, changes over time, and relationships between different types of rumoring behavior. We identify several quantitative measures—including temporal progression, domain diversity, lexical diversity and geolocation features—that constitute a multi-dimensional *signature* for each rumor, and provide evidence supporting the existence of different rumor types. Ultimately these signatures enhance our understanding of how different kinds of rumors propagate online during crisis events. In constructing these signatures, this research demonstrates and documents an emerging method for deeply and recursively integrating qualitative and quantitative methods for analysis of social media trace data.

Author Keywords

Social computing; misinformation; rumoring; information diffusion; Twitter; crisis informatics;

ACM Classification Keywords

H.5.3 [Information Interfaces & Presentation]: Groups & Organization Interfaces - Collaborative computing, Computer-supported cooperative work; K.4.2 Social Issues

INTRODUCTION

Increasingly, social media platforms are becoming places where people affected by a crisis go to share information, offer support, and collectively make sense of the event [23]. Rumoring and its byproduct, misinformation, present a threat to the utility of these platforms, as noted by media [12] and emergency managers [13,14]. Distinguishing between misinformation and truth in online spaces is difficult, especially during the high-volume, fast-paced action of a crisis event as it unfolds. There is growing interest in technical solutions that could help detect misinformation [5,20,24] or preemptively reduce its ability to spread [4,7], and indeed these solutions would be quite useful in the crisis context. However, to generate the best strategies for identifying and reducing the impact of misinformation, we may first need to better understand how false rumors take shape and spread through online spaces.

Existing research on the spread of rumors online is primarily quantitative, including descriptive studies of trace data [9,15,26], theoretical research on network factors [4,7], and prescriptive studies that experiment with machine learning methods to classify rumors as true or false [5,15,24]. When qualitative methods are employed in this space, they typically consist of manual coding of large numbers of tweets, followed by quantitative methods—i.e. descriptive and statistical analyses—to infer meaning from patterns of codes [3,20,22]

Our research, a descriptive study intended to inform future predictive efforts, takes a different approach by profoundly and recursively integrating qualitative and quantitative methods to gain an in-depth understanding of how rumors develop and spread through social media after disaster events. This approach features the use of multi-dimensional *signatures*—or patterns of information propagation—to help understand, characterize, and communicate the diffusion of specific rumors. In this study, we examine four rumors that spread via Twitter after the 2013 Boston Marathon Bombings, establishing connections between quantitative measures and the qualitative "story" of rumors, and revealing differences among rumor types.

BACKGROUND

Definitions of Rumor and Rumoring

Rumor can be defined in a number of ways. In the social computing literature, Qazvinian et al. define a rumor as "a statement whose truth-value is unverifiable or deliberately false" [24, p. 1589], and Spiro et al. [26] offer a broader definition of rumor that includes any kind of informal information—i.e. not from "official" sources—without specifically considering its veracity.

Researchers of social psychology use a slightly different definition—for example, DiFonzo & Bordia define rumors as unverified statements that arise out of "danger or potential threat, and that function to help people make sense and manage risk" [8, p. 13]. Social psychologists often treat

CSCW '15, March 14-18, 2015, Vancouver, BC, Canada.
Copyright 2015 ACM 978-1-4503-2922-4/15/03...$15.00.
http://dx.doi.org/10.1145/2675133.2675280

rumor as a process—i.e. *rumoring* [3,25]. Rumoring, in this perspective, is a collective activity that arises in conditions of uncertainty and ambiguity as groups attempt to make sense of the information they have [1,25]. Rumoring is also related to anxiety [2], and can be motivated at times by emotional needs—i.e. sharing information with others after an emotionally powerful event can be cathartic [10].

The Problem of Misinformation during Crisis

A byproduct of rumoring behavior is misinformation, which can be a problem in the context of disaster events [12,16]. The perception of online spaces being overrun by misinformation may limit the utility of these platforms during crisis situations, and some emergency responders are reluctant to include social media in their decision-making processes due to fear of misinformation [13,14]. There is a clear need for better understanding how and why misinformation spreads after disaster events.

Approaches for Studying Online Rumoring

Studying the diffusion of an online rumor presents an interesting methodological challenge. Important aspects of that rumor exist on two very different levels of analysis—i.e. both within patterns of information diffusion at the scale of thousands of posts, and within the specific content of individual tweets or links that help to shape, catalyze and propagate the rumor. Existing research has largely focused on the former unit of analysis and typically takes one of three approaches.

Quantitative Analysis

The first approach is purely quantitative and focuses on developing a high level understanding of the diffusion of rumors. This work includes descriptive, empirical studies [e.g. 9,15,26], as well theoretical research [e.g. 4,7]. Several of these studies analyze network features to understand the flow of misinformation [4,7,26]. Kwon et al. [15] include descriptive analysis of temporal characteristics, finding false rumors on Twitter have more spikes than true rumors. Friggeri et al. [9] examine the interaction between rumor corrections (via posted links to Snopes articles in comments) and the spread of rumors on Facebook, finding that large rumors keep propagating despite corrections.

Qualitative Coding with Quantitative Analysis

A second approach, which is largely descriptive, utilizes mixed methods. It first employs qualitative analysis to code large numbers of individual posts and then uses quantitative analysis to interpret patterns across those codes and over time [3,20,22]. The most influential of this research works to connect online rumoring to rumor theory from social psychology [1,25], using this knowledge to inform research questions and qualitative coding schemes. For example, studying rumor behavior in online discussion groups, Bordia & DiFonzo [3] identified five kinds of rumor statements, coded posts accordingly, and presented a model of rumor progression with four stages characterized by different proportions of each statement type. Oh et al. [22] coded tweets related to various rumors for six attributes, statistically analyzed how those codes related to each other, and found evidence that anxiety, personal involvement, and source ambiguity contribute to the spread of rumors online.

In research on Twitter use after the 2010 Chile Earthquake, Mendoza et al. [20] coded tweets related to several rumors as confirming or denying. They confirmed claims that the online crowd questions false rumors, and hypothesized that it might be possible to identify misinformation by automatically detecting those corrections.

Automatic Classification of Rumors as True or False

A third type of research focuses on developing machine learning algorithms for automatically detecting misinformation. In a follow up study to [20], researchers trained a machine classifier to determine the credibility of a news topic related to a set of tweets using corpus-level features that could relate to "questioning" behavior [5]. Qazvinian et al. [24] developed a machine-learning approach for classifying tweets as related to a false rumor, and as confirming, denying, or doubting a rumor. Their technique showed high precision and recall using content-related features in the tweet, and had reasonably high recall and precision for network and Twitter-specific features (i.e. hashtags and URLs). Kwon et al. [15] also explored solutions for automatically classifying rumors as either true or false by building off the Castillo et al. model [5], but introduced three types of additional features: temporal (looking at spikes over time), structural (looking at friend/following relationships) and linguistic (employing sentiment analysis). They found their feature set to be more effective than the features from Castillo et al [5].

Each of these machine learning studies measures the efficacy of their models—typically through accuracy, precision and recall scores—and provides some insight into a feature's relative predictive strength. Yet few studies provide significant insight into *how* and *why* rumors spread, and classification research has been limited to distinguishing between true and false information.

OUR APPROACH: CHARACTERIZING RUMORS THROUGH MULTI-DIMENSIONAL SIGNATURES

This research seeks to advance understanding of how online rumors form and spread, and to identify and distinguish between different types of rumors. We employ a unique methodological approach that relies upon a deep and recursive integration of qualitative and quantitative methods to construct multi-dimensional *signatures*—i.e. patterns of information flow over time and across other features [21]—that can be used to characterize rumors.

Preliminary research [27] describes the temporal signatures of three rumors across two codes (misinformation and correction). This study expands to include a more nuanced coding scheme—including speculation—and several more features that constitute dimensions of each rumor's signature. We use mixed-method analysis to tell the story of four distinct rumors spreading on Twitter after the 2013 Boston Marathon Bombings. Shifting repeatedly between quantitative and qualitative analysis, we describe each rumor's origins, propagation over time, relationships between rumor behavior types (e.g. sharing misinformation vs. correcting), prevailing URLs and domains, and lexical diversity, and work to connect each rumor's qualitative "story" to quantitative measures that reflect that narrative.

Event Background: 2013 Boston Marathon Bombings

On Monday, April 15 at 2:49pm, two bombs were detonated near the finish line of the Boston Marathon, killing three individuals and injuring 260 others. The instigators of the bombing fled the scene and a police investigation began immediately.

The FBI released photographs of two suspects on April 18 at 5:20pm. Three hours later, following an armed robbery near MIT, two men—who were later identified as bombing suspects—shot a police officer, carjacked an SUV, and engaged police in a violent firefight nearby Watertown, MA. One attacker was killed, but the other suspect escaped, setting off a manhunt through the Watertown neighborhood that concluded the next evening.

Between the bombings and the capture of suspects, the FBI requested photos or videos of the scene from the public. This call for information resulted in a massive volume of material, and social and mainstream media coverage of this information "resulted in a lot misinformation and false leads" [17]. During that time, social media users collectively and publicly searched through available photos and videos to find the perpetrators themselves. In some cases, innocent individuals were called out and accused, a behavior characterized as "digital vigilantism" [18].

Several other rumors took shape in social media spaces and began to spread. Like the errant search for suspects, some of these rumors stemmed from the online crowd's attempts to make sense of the situation, while others were simply falsehoods that targeted the emotions of an affected public.

Data Collection

For data collection, we used the Twitter Streaming API, tracking the following search terms: blast, boston, bomb, explosion, and marathon. We initiated this collection at 5:25pm[1] on April 15 and discontinued it at 5:09pm on April 22. Significantly, our collection did not cover the first few hours after the bombing and suffered several periods of data loss later in the event. It was also rate-limited (at ~50 tweets a second), causing data loss during the first six hours. It resulted in 10.6 million tweets contributed by 4.7M different authors. 56% were retweets and 47% contained a URL link, though another limitation of this data is that the data storage technique did not record metadata associated with a retweeted tweet or embedded URL, so these were calculated using textual searches, likely resulting in under-estimations for both measures.

Identifying rumors

In preliminary analysis of this Twitter data, we examined the most popular individual and co-occurring hashtags and noted a large number of viral stories. Further exploration of tweet text revealed certain hashtag groupings to be associated with specific rumors. From these we initially selected a subset of six rumors that were both diverse and highly visible during the event. Later, we eliminated two of these due to limitations in our collection that resulted in significant data loss (found to be >50%) for those which propagated during early periods of diffusion.

For each of the remaining rumors, we then identified a search string that returned from our total collection a comprehensive, low-noise set of tweets. For example, for Rumor #1, we used the following MySQL search string:

```
WHERE (text LIKE '%propos%' OR text LIKE
'%marry%') AND (text LIKE '%girl%' OR text
LIKE '%woman%')"
```

Table 1 lists the four rumors with total volume and number of distinct tweets in each rumor subset.

#	Rumor	Total	Distinct
1	Woman killed before proposal	3,371	1591
2	Girl killed while running	93,353	3275
3	Navy Seals as perpetrators	4,525	1996
4	Falsely accusing Sunil Tripathi	29,416	7445

Table 1. Rumor Subsets: Total Volume and Distinct Tweets

Tweet Coding

We coded each tweet within each rumor subset into one of seven distinct categories related to the rumor behavior type: *misinformation*, *speculation*, *correction*, *question*, *hedge*, *unrelated*, or *neutral/other*. These categories were developed through an iterative process during preliminary coding. We began with misinformation and correction, but as subtleties between rumor behavior types became salient, we added other codes. Table 2 provides examples for each of these codes (as they relate to Rumor #4, below).

Tweets coded as *misinformation* support the rumor without doubt, relaying the rumor as established fact and consequently spreading false information. *Speculation* tweets develop or support a growing rumor, and often introduce new information or commentary. The speculation tweet in Table 2 demonstrates this by inferring that the bomber 'may be' Sunil. In a *Hedge* tweet, an author passes along an existing rumor with some doubt about its veracity. These tweets show hesitancy, illustrating an unwillingness to declare the rumor as accurate, but continue to spread the

[1] All times are in EDT, local time in the affected region.

false information without a clear challenge. By contrast, a *question* tweet actively challenges or questions an existing rumor. Finally, *correction* tweets clearly negate the rumor.

Tweets coded as *neutral/other* are related to the rumor yet do not fit into one of the existing categories because the position is either neutral or unclear to researchers. Tweets that show no association to the rumor but exist within the subset due to search term noise are coded as *unrelated*.

Code	Example Tweet
Misinfo	`The 2 Boston suspects are mike muligeta and Sunil Tripathi. Sunil is still on the loose.`
Speculation	`This may be a shot in the dark but, I think the missing Ivy League student, Sunil Tripathi, is the guy responsible for the Boston bombings`
Hedge	`MIT suspects, per police scanners, are Mike Mulugeta and Sunil Tripathi. Probable, but not confirmed connection, with Boston Marathon Bombs`
Question	`Based simply on height, Boston suspect #2 doesn't look 6'2" Sunil Tripathi is. I just dont buy that its him.`
Correction	`Suspect #2 is NOT Sunil Tripathi! Both NBC and MSNBC confirmed this! #Boston`
Neutral/ Other	`Help us find Sunil Tripathi FB page was taken down within the 15 minutes... weird #Boston`
Unrelated	`Boston bombings, EQ and Sunil Narine!! The harlem shake. 3 disasters strike on the same day.`

Table 2. Coding Categories for Rumor-Related Tweets

Coding Process

Two researchers coded every distinct tweet (after removing retweets and close matches) in each rumor subset. Table 1 shows the number of distinct tweets per rumor. After the first round of coding, a third coder arbitrated disagreements by choosing the most appropriate code. Each rumor provided its own challenges, and initial agreement ranged from 70-90 percent. The most difficult distinctions occurred between *misinformation* and *speculation, speculation* and *hedge,* and for Rumor #3 in particular, *question* and *correction.* Agreement for collapsed categories (where misinformation includes speculation and hedge, and where correction includes question) was consistently much higher.

Analysis

This research utilizes a mixed-method approach, integrating quantitative, qualitative and visual analyses of tweets, to describe and characterize four rumors related to the Boston Marathon Bombings. These methods include the following:

Qualitative and visual analysis to understand the origins and evolution of each rumor: Using its temporal signature as a guide, we explore the progression of each rumor over time. The visual signatures allow us to identify significant moments in the rumor's propagation, and qualitative analysis enables us to understand the nature of the peaks, valleys, and interactions between rumor behavior codes.

Calculation of lexical diversity: To assess differences in the unique rumor behaviors present in tweet content, we calculate the lexical diversity—i.e. the number of different words that tweets in this corpus use. For each rumor behavior category, we create a dictionary containing every unique word mentioned by tweets with that code. Due to large imbalances in tweet volume for the different code categories, we normalize this calculation by selecting 100 random distinct tweets (excluding retweets) from each corpus.

Analysis of URL propagation and domain diversity: We explore the relationship between the rumoring behavior code of a tweet and URL links embedded in its text, as the latter represents a virtual link to content beyond the 140 character limit. Due to over-representation of a few domains across our rumor set, analysis at the domain unit is often more useful than focusing on individual URLs. We describe the domain diversity of each rumor—i.e. the distribution of embedded URLs across different domains—focusing predominantly on the top ten domains for each subset. Our data storage technique only retained the text of the current tweet (not upstream original tweets), which truncated a significant number of URLs.

Geolocation analysis: For the limited subset of tweets that include GPS data, we analyze tweet location to draw parallels between event proximity and rumor propagation.

FINDINGS

Rumor #1: Proposal Rumor

Rumor #1 claimed that a woman whose boyfriend was going to propose after the marathon died while running the race. This rumor may have developed from a small number of tweets sent prior to the bombings that mentioned a proposal taking place at the finish line. Soon after the bombings, the story appears to have morphed into a false rumor asserting that the woman had died. The first tweet in our dataset referencing this rumor is a retweet, which appears 55 times in our data set.

```
(April 15, 6:30pm): RT @TweeterA: a girl who
ran in the marathon was killed due to the
bombing & her boyfriend was gonna propose to
her afterwards
```

In our dataset, Rumor #1 consists of 3371 total tweets. It began to propagate a few hours after the event and had mostly run its course by about 11:00pm April 17, by which time 90% of volume had passed. The rumor reached a peak volume of 63 tweets per 10 minutes at 10:00pm April 15, but also had several subsequent local maximums. Figure 1 shows volume over time by rumor behavior code.

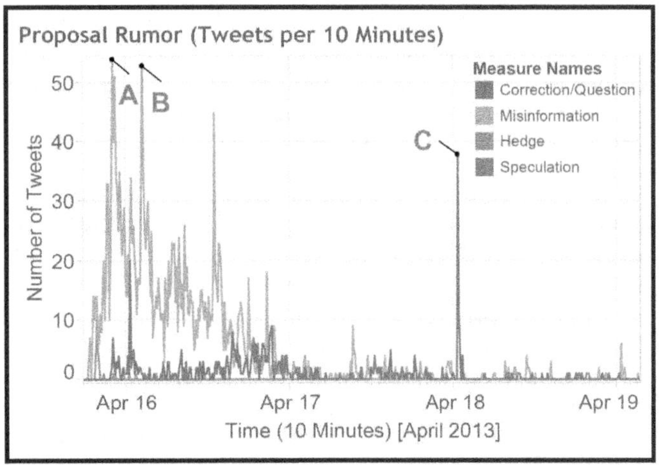

Figure 1. Rumor Codes Over Time for Proposal Rumor

An Added Photograph Sparks a Second Burst

The first peak largely consisted of text-only tweets. New variations of the rumor, where downstream authors restated the existing rumor in slightly different words, often led to subsequent increases in propagation and small spikes visible in Figure 1. The highest peaks (Figure 1, A & B) were generated by multiple variations of the rumor propagating at the same time.

Less than an hour after the rumor appeared, Twitter users began to introduce variations that included links to a photo:

```
(April 15, 7:11pm): this guy found his
girlfriend dead he was devastated he was
going to propose to her after the marathon
http://t.co/ZfIi7r4c3x
```

The above tweet has an embedded image showing a man at the scene of the blasts attending to an injured woman. This photo was originally published by the Boston Globe with a caption describing the scene as a man comforting a victim near the finish line. The URL links to a new copy of the photo posted within the pic.twitter.com domain without attribution. Manual analysis suggests that a large number of distinct tweets—i.e. different forms of the rumor—have this same photo embedded in them, an observation supported by URL and domain analysis. Figure 3 shows that while the first (and highest) peak in misinformation in Rumor #1 stems from mostly textual variations, the second major peak (Point B) is largely constituted by rumor variations that linked to a photo. These findings suggest the introduction of photos catalyzed additional bursts in the overall rumor.

Characterizing the Correction

13% of tweets in Rumor #1 were coded as corrections. Notably, the first correction of the photograph's context occurred hours before the peak volume of tweets containing the photo, indicating that the correction did little to stop the rumor's propagation. A much later burst of corrections, one that occurred days after the apex of misinformation (Figure 1, C), was a highly retweeted reprimand of rumor-spreading behavior more broadly:

```
(April 18, 12:30am) Some of these Boston
stories are so fake, like the one about dude
going to propose to the girl after the race.
That shit was made up
```

Differences and Interactions in Rumor Behavior Codes

Tweets coded misinformation dominated this rumor. Significantly, the rumor began as misinformation—i.e. very few tweets were coded as speculation. The crowd produced some corrections, but the overall ratio of correction to misinformation was small at about 3 to 16. The signal of misinformation for this rumor was therefore stronger than the signal of correction. Furthermore, corrections appear to get less amplification from the crowd; tweets coded as correction were somewhat less likely to be retweets than those coded as misinformation (51% vs. 65%). This difference is significant (Chi Square test, $p<0.01$).

Code	Total # Tweets	% RT	Lexical Diversity
Total	3576	54.9%	370
Misinformation	2586	65.2%	322
Speculation	2	50.0%	--
Hedge	34	70.6%	--
Question	22	27.2%	--
Correction	481	51.1%	379

Table 3. Tweets Per Code for Proposal Rumor

Lexical Diversity

Qualitative and visual analysis suggests that a large percentage of misinformation tweets use similar words. Subsequent quantitative analysis reveals that the combined textual content of misinformation tweets possessed a much lower lexical diversity than that of correction tweets. Taking a random sample of 100 distinct tweets from each coded category and averaging the results over 100 iterations results in a dictionary of 322 unique words for misinformation tweets compared to one of 379 words for correction. These differences in lexical diversity support the observation that corrective tweets tended to contain more original content than those that spread misinformation.

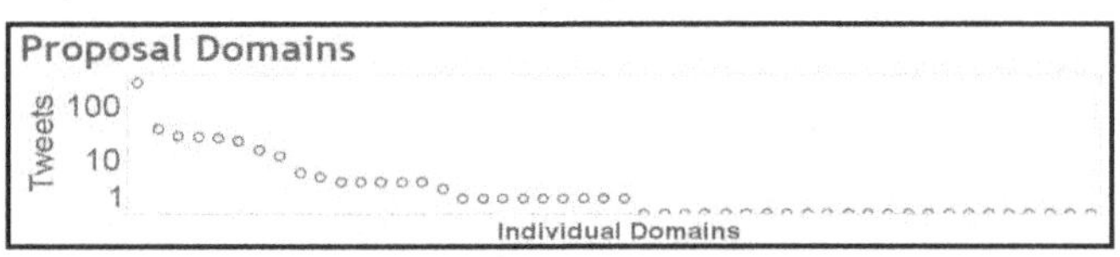

Figure 2. Domain Diversity, Proposal Rumor, Log Scale

Domain Diversity and Propagation Over Time

The distribution of tweets across the domains in the Proposal rumor is long-tailed (Figure 2). Twitter was the top domain (far left), linked to by 275 tweets; CNN.com, the second most sited domain was included only 39 times. Of the top domains, each maps almost exclusively to a single code—misinformation or correction. Though our sample is too small to make a large generalization, here misinformation associated with social media domains—in this case Twitter and Instagram—while correction tweets that included URLs primarily linked to the CNN domain.

Examining the temporal relationships between URLs and rumor codes (Figure 3) indicates that certain domains seem to rise and fall in tandem with peaks of misinformation and correction. Both the Twitter and CNN domain groupings correspond to—and indeed match the shape of—a second peak of misinformation or correction, respectively. Because our URL counts are artificially low, it is likely that these domain signals are even stronger, and therefore fit the overall plots even more closely. Recall that the Twitter domain was associated with the photo that helped catalyze the rumor's spread; though we cannot claim that external content provided by URLs drives social media conversation, it does appear to facilitate both propagation and correction of rumors.

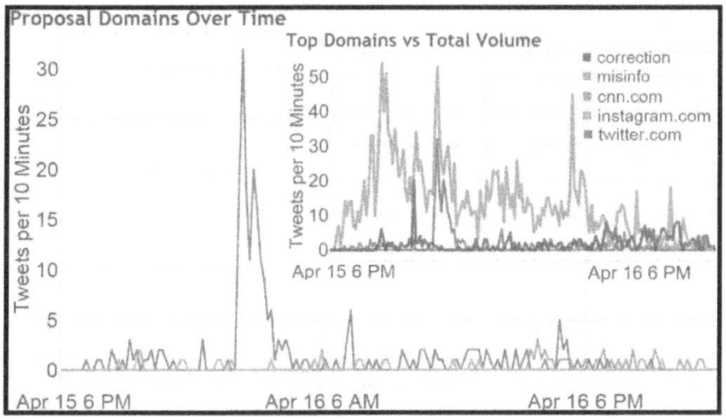

Figure 3. Domains Over Time for Proposal Rumor

Rumor #2: Girl Running Rumor

Rumor #2 stated that an eight-year-old girl died while running the Boston Marathon. This rumor may have originated from sense-making activities of the crowd as it attempted to process official information that an eight-year-old child had been killed at the bombings. An early tweet in our collection lends evidence to this hypothesis:

```
(April 15 6:09pm): What if one of the people
who died's baby girl was running her first
marathon ever today? #PrayForBoston
```

It's unclear whether this tweet is indeed connected to the rumor, but an hour later the rumor transformed into distinct misinformation:

```
@tweeterB (April 15 7:17pm): An eight year
old girl who was doing an amazing thing
running a marathon, was killed. I cant stand
our world anymore
```

This rumor has many similarities to the proposal rumor, and began to propagate only about 45 minutes later. However, Rumor #2 had a much higher tweet volume than Rumor #1, consisting of 93,353 tweets within our dataset. It began to spread rapidly at about 8:15pm on April 15 and reached its peak rate (2,287 tweets in ten minutes) at 9:50pm. It started to fade rapidly by midnight and 90% of its volume completed by 10:45am the next morning. Figure 4 shows volume over time by rumor behavior code.

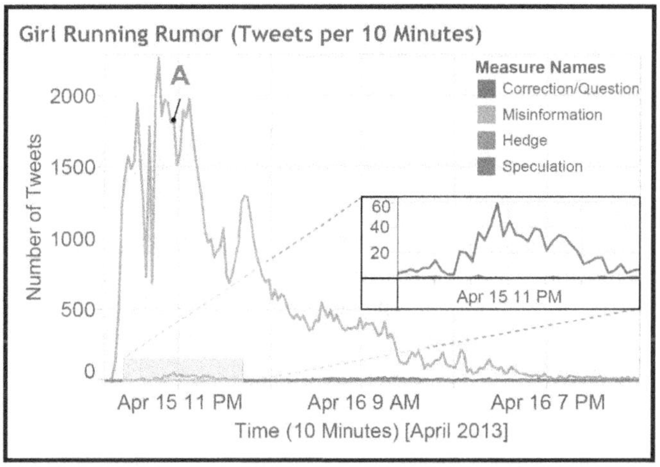

Figure 4. Rumor Codes Over Time for Girl Running Rumor

Similar Signatures: Propagation through an Image

The tweet generated by @tweeterB was the first instance of the Girl Running rumor, but it only received two retweets. The next version, which was retweeted much more widely (555 times), appeared four minutes later. It included a key addition—a link to an image of a young girl running a race.

```
(April 15 7:21pm): The 8 year old girl that
sadly died in the Boston bombings while
running the marathon. Rest in peace
beautiful x <link>
```

This photo was clearly an intentional false addition to the rumor, at least initially. As various other versions of the rumor began to spread in the following hours, most included that photo. Shortly after 11:20pm, the volume of misinformation increased dramatically, and at least 82% of tweets related to the rumor during that period included the image. By 9:50pm misinformation reached a peak volume of 2266 tweets per ten minutes.

Characterizing the Correction

Corrections only constitute about 2% of the total volume of the rumor. Until 9:50pm on April 15—at about the time that misinformation was reaching its highest tweet rate—they remained relatively rare. Corrections peaked less than an hour later at 56 tweets per ten minutes. Figure 4 shows the alignment and stark difference in amplitude between correction and misinformation signals.

The set contained a few different forms of correction. The first simply refuted the rumor outright:

```
(April 15, 11:42pm): Whoever started this
8yo girl dying while running the Boston
marathon for Sandy Hook needs to be dealt
with swiftly. #hoax
```

Another correction contradicted the rumor, offering a logical explanation for why it could not be true:

(April 15 11:46pm): An eight year old girl did not die today in Boston while running the marathon. You have to be 18+ to be in it. Come on, people!

Finally, a third type attacked the rumor, refuting it with a factual explanation:

(April 16, 10:35pm): The 8-year-old victim today was a boy: <link> Please stop RTing nonsense about it being a girl running for a cause.

It is impossible using our methods to establish a causal connection between the rise in corrections and the decline of misinformation, yet the temporal graph might indicate an interaction. Misinformation volume dropped dramatically, though temporarily, at 10:40pm on April 15 (Figure 4, A), while correction volume peaked at 56 tweets per 10 minutes during that same interval. However, by about an hour later misinformation had peaked again, before beginning a steady decline, interrupted by one more burst.

Code	Total # Tweets	% RT	Lexical Diversity
All Codes	93,353	96.0%	362
Misinformation	90,841	97.6%	260
Speculation	4	25.0%	NA
Hedge	8	37.5%	NA
Question	112	27.7%	NA
Correction	1931	48.2%	414

Table 4. Tweets Per Code for Girl Running Rumor

Differences and Interactions in Rumor Behavior Codes

Similar to the Proposal rumor, the Girl Running rumor contained much more misinformation than correction (48:1) and little speculation. In contrast to Rumor #1, here the percentage of retweets within tweets coded as misinformation is high, at 97.6%, demonstrating that the retweet mechanism played a major role in the overall signal of misinformation for the Girl Running rumor.

Domain Diversity and Propagation Over Time

Quantitative analysis of domains reveals similar patterns between the Proposal and Girl Running rumors. Again, the distribution of tweets across domains was long-tailed, with a sharp drop off between the top domain (twitter.com at 17,356) and the next domain (instagram.com at 288). CNN was the fourth most-tweeted domain at 202 mentions. Domains appear to map primarily to a single code—i.e. either misinformation or correction but not both. The Facebook domain is one exception, balancing relatively evenly between misinformation (14 tweets) and correction (11 tweets). Social media constitute much of the top ten domains in this rumor, and all strongly associate with misinformation. Again, CNN is the one domain primarily linked to by correction tweets (201 times).

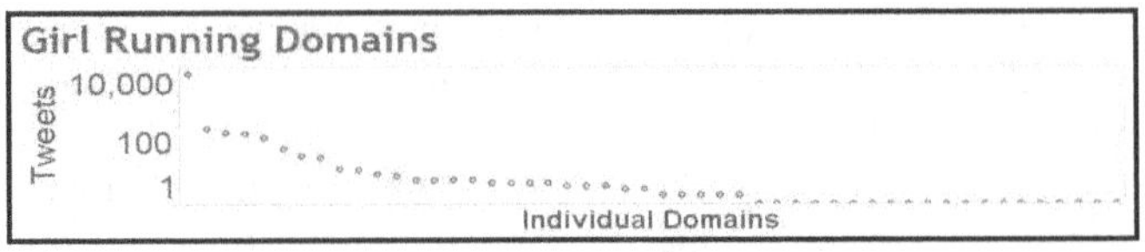

Figure 5. Domain Diversity, Girl Running Rumor, Log Scale

The shape of the temporal signatures of the Twitter domain—in this case photos on pic.twitter.com—again matches the shape of the misinformation signal overall (see Figure 6). For Rumor #2, it appears that the Twitter domain played a role in the propagation of misinformation from a very early stage, which aligns with our qualitative findings. Additionally, the CNN domain peaks at about the same time as corrective tweets, indicating some interaction between external sources and the propagation of correction as well.

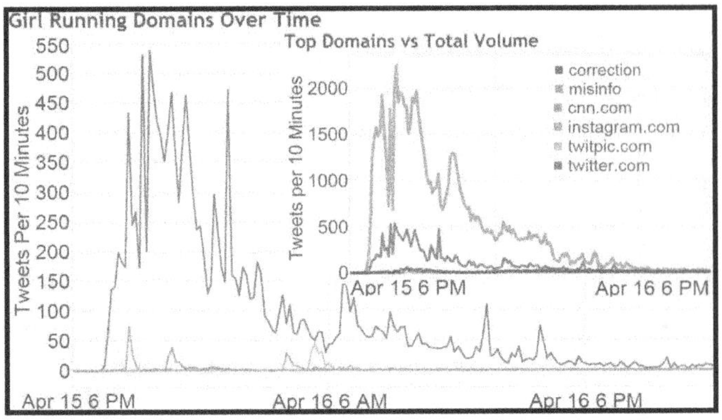

Figure 6. Domains Over Time for Girl Running Rumor

Rumor #3: Navy Seals Rumor

Rumor #3 speculated that either the Navy Seals or Craft Security facilitated the Boston Marathon Bombings. This rumor was associated with a popular #falseflag hashtag in our dataset. A "false flag" is a term used to describe an attack designed to appear as if carried out by someone other than its perpetrators.

At 6:44pm, April 15 the first tweet related to this rumor appeared in our data set:

RT @TweeterD: BOSTON BOMBINGS HAVE CIA BLACK OPS WRITTEN ALL OVER IT! BALL BEARINGS IN BOMBS - PLACEMENT OF BOMBS - PATRIOTS DAY - JUST SAYIN...

Similar tweets appeared sporadically over the subsequent 24 hours. Initially, the rumor propagated at extremely low volumes, never exceeding two tweets an hour.

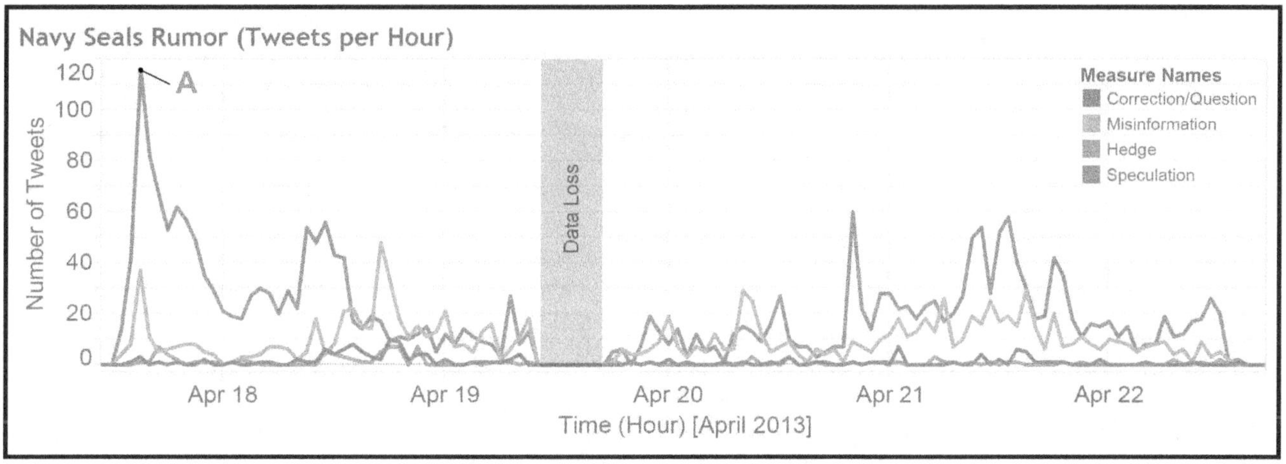

Figure 7. Rumor Codes Over Time for Navy Seals Rumor

That changed at about 1:40pm on April 17 when 35 tweets referencing the rumor were shared within one hour. Almost all included a link to an InfoWars.com article arguing that Navy Seals were behind the bombings:

```
(April 17, 1:38pm) Truth has been revealed:
Boston Bombing culprits found as NAVY SEALS
UNDERCOVER http://t.co/PFahtn28qy
THIS IS UNBELIEVABLE.
```

InfoWars is an independent media outlet run by Alex Jones, who also has a popular radio show. Links to the InfoWars website were the first links to appear in any tweets related to this rumor. Their precipitation to the first peak in misinformation further demonstrates how external content can help Twitter rumors evolve and spread.

Code	Total # Tweets	% RT	Lexical Diversity
All Codes	4151	30.1%	503
Misinformation	1171	35.4%	489/310*
Speculation	2551	28.5%	437/273*
Hedge	102	24.5%	NA/NA
Question	54	20.1%	NA/345*
Correction	87	18.4%	NA/368*

Table 5. Tweets Per Code for Seals/Craft Rumor
*** Due to low volume of distinct tweets for each code, the 2nd number here was calculated using only 50 random tweets.**

The total volume of tweets related to the Seals Rumor is 4525, similar to the Proposal rumor. This rumor, however, demonstrates a very different pattern over time than the first two with a much longer temporal range. Rumor #3 first appeared in significant volumes on April 17 and was still propagating at a consistent rate at the end of our collection period on April 22. The peak volume of 163 tweets per hour occurred between 3pm and 4pm on April 17. Though the volume did drop significantly after the initial peak, it continued to fluctuate between 20 and 70 tweets per hour for the remainder of the collection period.

This rumor notably contained two distinct variations, accusing either the Navy Seals or private agents from Craft Security. These different versions seem to arise from new interpretations of images and explanations from "experts" within the online crowd's sensemaking activities.

Speculative Signatures

In contrast to the first two, the Seals Rumor was largely driven by speculation, which accounted for 61% of the total volume. Additionally, it began with speculative tweets, and speculation largely constituted the first major peak (Figure 7, A)—which occurred from 3pm to 5pm, April 17. Multiple identical versions of the following tweet made up the majority of this initial peak, appearing 125 times in that period (and 699 times overall):

```
(April 17 2:44pm) Navy SEALs Spotted at
Boston Marathon Wearing Suspicious Backpacks
- http://t.co/4iIEKLyZtd
```

These tweets propagated not as retweets, but as original tweets with the same words, though often with different shortened links. All pointed to the same webpage, another article on the InfoWars site, and were likely generated by a tweet button on that page.

A Weak Correction

Correction and question tweets occurred in similar volumes for this rumor and were often hard to differentiate. However, even taken together, both categories make up only 3.4% of the rumor. This rumor therefore spread without much correction. When tweets containing corrections or questions did appear, they were less likely to be retweeted than speculation or misinformation tweets.

Lexical Diversity

Qualitative analysis suggests that tweets containing speculation and misinformation tended to vary more textually than they did in the previous two rumors. Where variations on a small group of initial tweets defined both the Girl Running and Proposal rumors, from the Seals rumor multiple themes emerged over the course of several days.

```
(April 18 5:50pm): RT @TweeterC: 4 #BostonMarathon #Bombing Images show Operatives of Craft Inter, a Blackwater-style private military/security Inc <link>

(April 20 12:12pm): FBI Boston Bombing Video Altered To Hide Fact Bomber Was Black Ops Mercenary? http://t.co/viUcjRs92I via @BeforeItsNews
```

Measures of lexical diversity support these observations, showing the Seals Rumor to be much more diverse overall—503 unique words in 100 random tweets compared to 362 for Rumor #1 and 370 for Rumor #2. Again, corrections show more lexical diversity than misinformation. This pattern is not only consistent across the correction code for all four rumors, but also seems to extend to other similar categories—i.e. correction and question both have higher lexical diversity than misinformation and speculation.

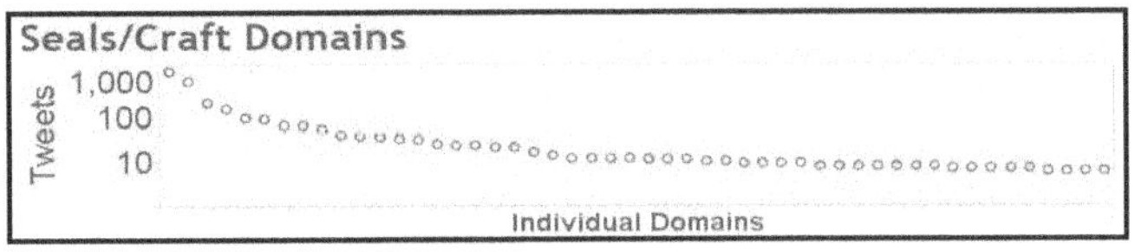

Figure 8. Domain Diversity, Seals Rumor, Log Scale

Domain Diversity and Propagation Over Time

The Seals rumor had a much higher level of domain diversity than Rumors #1 and #2—i.e. tweets in this rumor linked to many different domains. Figure 8 shows the signal of domain diversity, demonstrating a less steep slope than the previous rumors.

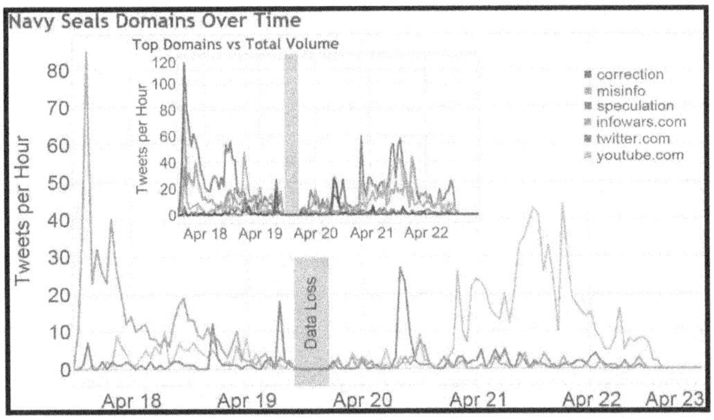

Figure 9. Domains Over Time for Navy Seals Rumor

None of the top domains were primarily associated with tweets coded as correction. Unlike the first two rumors, Twitter was not the predominant domain (219 tweets) and fell significantly below both Youtube.com (1083 tweets) and InfoWars.com (663 tweets), incidating that a different kind of external content shaped this rumor. Other alterative news sites appear in the top ten most tweeted domains, including beforeitsnews.com (160 tweets) and secretsofthefed.com (54 tweets). Conversation was therefore aided by outside media sources, but it was never addressed by traditional, "mainstream" outlets.

The temporal signature created by domains (Figure 9) again tends to align with spikes of misinformation. Similar to the previous rumors, volume increases among the top domains appear to correspond to spikes of misinformation and speculation. The initial maximum correlates to the appearance of the InfoWars domain, while the somewhat consistent spikes later in the window rise in tandem with YouTube.com, almost all linking to a video of a retired U.S. Army officer asserting that the attack was a false flag.

Rumor #4: Falsely Accused Rumor

Rumor #4 asserted that missing Brown University student Sunil Trapathi was a suspect, partially based on photos published by the FBI shortly after 5pm on April 18. After the actual suspects were identified, this rumor became a symbol for the negative impacts of online misinformation during the event.

Our dataset indicates that more than one person seeded this rumor, and that it likely existed elsewhere online prior to appearing on Twitter (e.g. Reddit). The first two tweets in our collection, sent about two hours after the photos were released, appear to be independent observations alleging similarities between Trapathi and images of a Boston Marathon suspect:

```
(April 18 7:38pm) Sunil Tripathi - Some might think he looks like the kid in Boston. But the FBI photos are too grainy to say for sure. http://t.co/9y5CivjlCX

(April 18 7:47pm) Sunil Tripathi. One of the Boston bombers. I'm calling it
```

The total volume of the Falsely Accused rumor was 29,416 tweets. Its lifespan was relatively short, beginning on April 18 at 7:38pm and tapering significantly by April 19 at 10pm. Peak volume was 4675 tweets per ten minutes at 3:00am on April 19.

Building Speculation Becomes Misinformation

The first few hours of the rumor were characterized by persistent, low-level speculation (520 of the first 725 tweets); a large number of these linked to a specific sub-Reddit thread. This trend changed drastically at 2:50am April 19, when the following tweet was shared:

```
(April 19, 2:50am): BPD scanner identified the names: Suspect 1: Mike Mulugeta Suspect 2: Sunil Tripathi. #Boston #MIT
```

Notably the reference to the police scanner added a layer of complexity to the Falsely Accused rumor; however, the scanner never actually claimed that Trapathi was a suspect. Yet after that point, due to a large number of retweets and references to the scanner claim, the signal of misinformation began to dominate.

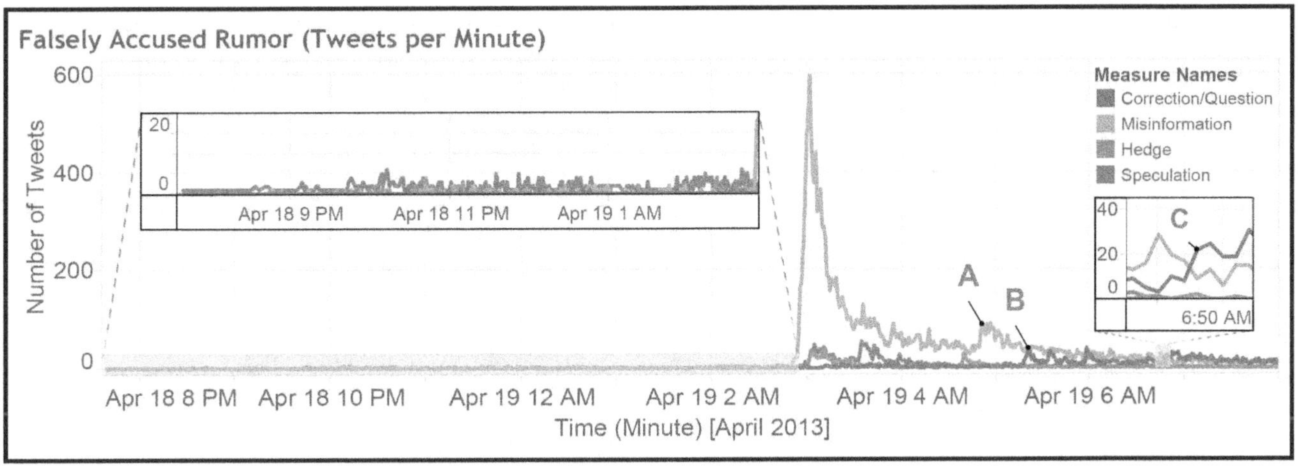

Figure 10. Rumor Codes Over Time for Falsely Accused Rumor

Interactions between Rumor Codes: The Crowd Corrects

Among the four, the Falsely Accused rumor is the only one where correction volume eventually surpassed misinformation. Early on, the combined signal of correction and question flickered at a few tweets per hour, including:

```
(April 19, 2:40am): Come on, you've been
watching way too many thrillers. Sunil
Tripathi doesn't look at all like one of the
Marathon bombing suspects. (Question)
```

```
(April 19, 3:20am): No, the scanner DID NOT
say suspect missing was Sunil Tripathi, they
said repeatedly light skinned, white.
#MITshooting #Boston (Correction)
```

After a second rolling maximum of misinformation before 5am (Figure 10, A), largely driven by a tweet claiming to show Tripathi in the same photo as the young boy who was killed in the blasts, correction volume began to approach misinformation volume, reaching about 40 tweets a minute on several occasions. These pulses never reached the volume of the initial peaks in misinformation, but they did approach (5:21am) and eventually surpass (6:48am) the volume of misinformation at those times. The first of those points (Figure 10, Point B) corresponds to a rise in tweets quoting an NBC statement that Tripathi was not one of the suspects. The second (Figure 10, Point C) occurred as Twitter users begin to widely share similar information from the AP that named Tsarnaev as the actual suspect.

After its peak, correction volume did not rapidly decline as with other rumors, but remained greater than the volume of misinformation for the remainder of the rumor's lifespan. Much of this persistent activity focused on public reprimand of the crowd for falsely accusing Tripathi.

Lexical Diversity

Lexical diversity for tweets related to the Falsely Accused rumor was much higher overall—at 555 unique words per 100 distinct tweets—than the Proposal (370) and Girl Running (362) rumors, and slightly higher than the Seals rumor (503). Consistent with patterns seen in other rumors, speculation and misinformation tweets had less lexical diversity than correction and question tweets.

Code	Total # Tweets	% RT	Lexical Diversity
All Codes	27,522	77.0%	555
Misinformation	19,024	80.0%	486
Speculation	2620	73.2%	442
Hedge	1222	70.9%	463
Question	546	49.8%	575
Correction	4110	70.6%	554

Table 6. Tweets Per Code for Falsely Accused Rumor

Domain Diversity and Propagation Over Time

Domain diversity was high for the Falsely Accused rumor as well. Though the rumor contained roughly a third of the total tweet volume compared to the Girl Running rumor, the number of domains with relatively high representation was significantly larger. Interestingly, many of the domains in the top ten most tweeted were social media sites, including Twitter, Reddit, Imgur, rt.com, YouTube, Twitchy, and the Tumblr account of celebrity Perez Hilton. This domain distribution differs sharply in slope from the first two rumors, and drastically in content from the third.

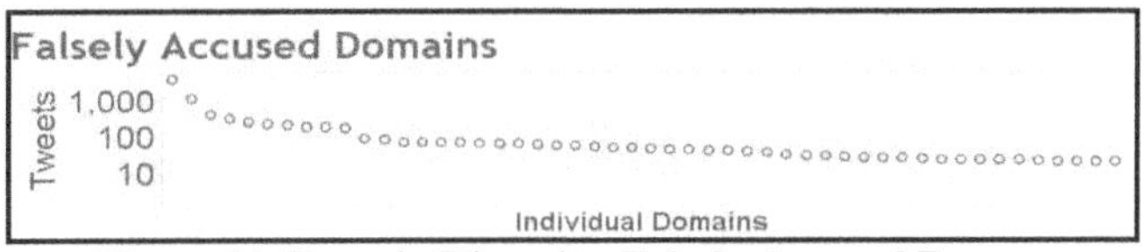

Figure 11. Domain Diversity, Falsely Accused Rumor

Domains were again strongly associated with either misinformation or correction, and Facebook.com was again a notable exception to this with a misinformation to correction ratio of about 2:1. YouTube.com had a somewhat balanced ratio at 5:1. NDTV.com, an Indian news site, represented the only correction-dominated domain in the top 10.

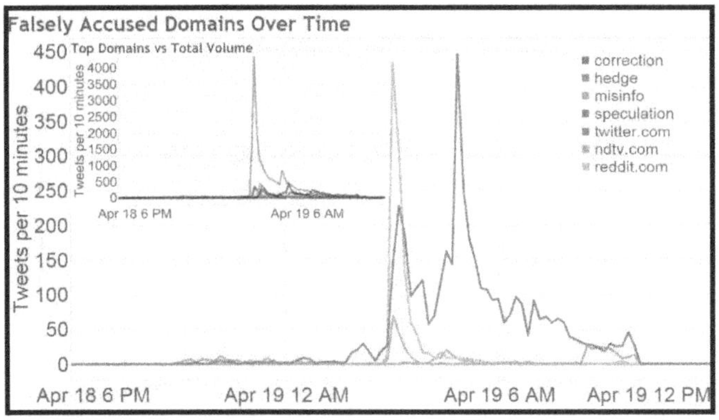

Figure 12. Domains Over Time for False Accused Rumor

Temporal analysis (see Figure 12) shows relatively similar parallels between domains and total tweet volume, though as with top domain analysis, the temporal shape differs to reflect the rumors' dissimilar origins. The Reddit.com domain group increases sharply first and is only later replaced by Twitter as the conversation migrated across platforms. Tweets that fall within the Twitter domain group again rise with misinformation, but notably less intensely after peak total misinformation. Aligned with patterns for correction-heavy domains in two previous rumors, the NDTV domain rises and falls with correction and peaks at nearly the same time as maximum correction.

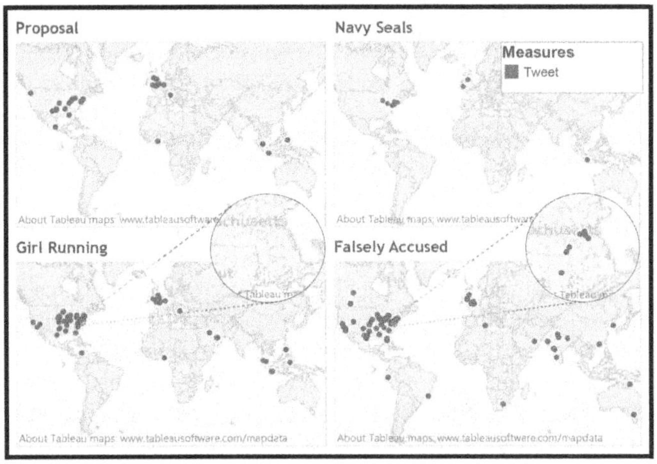

Figure 13. GPS Locations for Geo-located Tweets by Rumor

Geolocation and Rumor Propagation

The Falsely Accused rumor also stands out from the other rumors when we examine the GPS coordinates in geo-located tweets within the set, though the percentages of geo-located tweets are very small (<1% for each rumor). Figure 13 shows the GPS location of each geo-located tweet in each rumor. Interestingly, none of the rumors contain more than a single tweet posted from the Boston area (within 50-mile radius of the city's central point) *except* for the Falsely Accused rumor (8 tweets). The difference between Falsely Accused and Rumors #1 and #2 in the distribution of local vs not-local tweets is statistically significant (Chi Square, $p<0.05$). Though the geo-data is too sparse to draw strong conclusions, this analysis suggests that Rumor #4 was locally relevant in a way that the other rumors were not. Additionally, this rumor is also the only one with tweets geolocated to India, likely due to the fact that Tripathi was of Indian heritage.

DISCUSSION: MULTI-DIMENSIONAL SIGNATURES OF ONLINE RUMORS

This paper presents an in-depth examination of rumoring behavior, providing several empirical insights into how misinformation spreads via social media after disaster events and demonstrating how certain visual and quantitative measures reflect the qualitative "story" of a rumor. This work also documents a novel method for doing mixed-method research on information diffusion through social media, using multi-dimensional *signatures* to characterize large volumes of tweets related to a topic.

The concept of signatures has been introduced briefly in previous work [21,27], but here we explore the concept more deeply and discuss how it can be operationalized.

Signatures are a conceptual metaphor for understanding information diffusion online. A signature is a distinctive *representation* of information diffusion—in this case, a rumor spreading through Twitter—that allows us to quantitatively describe phenomena that are complex, multi-dimensional, and (we argue) largely qualitative.

Identifying Signature Dimensions for Characterizing the Spread of Rumors

Signatures consist of multiple *dimensions* that help to describe and represent salient features of the data. In this work, we explored five dimensions of rumor propagation: temporal progression of rumor spreading behavior (within individual tweets), URL domain diversity, domains over time, lexical diversity, and geolocation information.

Temporal graphs of tweet volumes over time clearly demonstrate (visually) the concept of a *signature*. Kwon et al. [15] connect temporal properties of rumors to rumor veracity, though they claim false rumors contain more repeating spikes over time, a pattern that is not consistent in the crisis-specific rumors analyzed in this paper. Examining temporal interactions across rumor behavior codes in additional to volume, as we do here, allows for additional insight into a rumor's origin and propagation.

Domain volume and diversity are markers of the influence of outside sources on rumor propagation. Like temporal signatures by code, peaks in a domain's temporal signature potentially demonstrate critical moments in rumor development when news, social media, or other external sources alter the content or course of the rumor. The shape of the domain diversity curve indicates interaction between tweets and outside sources.

Lexical diversity in textual communication has been identified as a marker of truthfulness [29]. Our research suggests that lexical diversity is also an important feature of rumor propagation, providing a measure of how much a rumor changed over time, and possibly reflecting the number of unique messages and voices that participated in its spread. Lexical diversity appears to correlate with different kinds of rumor spreading behavior—e.g. speculation has a higher lexical diversity than misinformation. Combining these observations, rumors with a low lexical diversity spread virally without substantial content variation, while rumors with high lexical diversity are more "conversational" and seem to more fully engage the crowd in collaborative sensemaking.

The geographic patterns of tweets may be another important feature in a rumor's signature. Though our geo-location data was sparse, we could see patterns suggesting Rumor #4 was more "locally relevant" than the other rumors. Using other techniques to increase the proportion of geo-located data [e.g. 6] could increase the utility of this feature.

Using Signatures for Comparing Rumors

Like a hand-written signature, a data signature is distinctive and recognizable. Signatures can therefore be used as tools for representing, communicating and identifying something that is fairly complex, such as patterns over large volumes of data. Signatures can also be operationalized as a tool for comparative studies. For example, some rumors may have similar signatures that can belong to specific rumor types. This research shows strong support for at least one rumor type—the *Internet Meme* rumor.

Internet Meme Signatures

The Girl Running and the Proposal rumors developed and propagated in very similar ways, and their signatures have many similarities. Both began as misinformation, and started to diffuse widely with the addition of a photograph. Both had very weak corrections when compared with the overall signal of misinformation. They also had relatively low measures of lexical diversity; they were spread by many authors, but through very similar content. We believe that these two rumors show a possible common "type" of rumor propagating through social media.

A Conspiracy Theory Signature?

The other two rumors were quite distinct from the first two and from each other. The Navy Seals rumor was largely speculative, beginning with and persisting primarily as speculation. Like the "false" rumor pattern in the Kwon et al. study [15], the Navy Seals rumor's signal pulsed repeatedly, often in tandem with links to a specific domain that was promoting this theory of the event. Much of the information related to this rumor came from outside of Twitter. Both domain diversity and lexical diversity were much higher than the Internet meme rumors, as participants in the conversation added their own evidence and explanation. This rumor may be indicative of a conspiracy theory type rumor, but analysis of more rumors will be needed to establish this as a type.

A Collective Sensemaking Signature?

Though similar to the Navy Seals rumor in some ways, the Falsely Accused rumor likely represents another type of rumor signature. This rumor also began with speculation, as members of the crowd attempted to make sense of available information and identify the bombers. Later, the rumor shifted from speculation to misinformation, as downstream individuals passed along early theories as fact. Eventually, for this rumor (and only this rumor), correction caught up and surpassed misinformation, demonstrating the concept of the self-correcting crowd [11,20]. Lexical and domain diversity were both high, indicating wide participation as opposed to simple amplification. Notably this was the only rumor in the set, according to geo-location data in the tweets, that resonated among accounts in the Boston area. This rumor may be part of a larger category of collective sensemaking signatures, though again future research is needed to confirm this type.

Using Multi-Dimensional Signatures as a Method for Analyzing information Diffusion

In this research, we also explore how multi-dimensional signatures can be used as a structuring construct to guide a method of analysis that deeply integrates qualitative and quantitative methods.

Here, we utilize the concept of signatures as a tool for recursive data analysis. These signatures are central components of a repeating process of data representation, observation and reflection, employed to iteratively make sense of the complexity of high-volume information diffusion. For each rumor, we generated a signature (feature by feature), often creating a visualization or some other quantitative representation. These representations were not final results, but opportunities to return to the data with new questions. For example, visualizations of tweets over time revealed peaks and troughs that often aligned with critical moments in rumor development. Subsequent qualitative analysis at those "points of interest" provided insight into how a rumor formed, evolved, and spread.

Throughout this process, qualitative findings provided insight into which features to measure and what representations to create. For example, initial qualitative coding led us to believe that lexical diversity would be an important feature for distinguishing between corrections and misinformation, and possibly for characterizing different types of rumors. This approach aligns with Starbird and Palen's [28] work that used in-depth qualitative analysis to identify important quantitative features of information diffusion.

Each quantitative representation is therefore both an outcome of qualitative research (to identify the dimensions) and an instrument for qualitative research. As the features are identified and the dimensions represented, the signature then becomes a tool for conceptualizing patterns across large amounts of data—for both understanding and communicating how the rumor formed and spread.

Demonstrating and Documenting an Emerging Method

Qualitative analysis of large amounts of Twitter data is hard to perform and perhaps even harder to communicate. The process is largely iterative, moving from data exploration; to sampling; to iterative rounds of qualitative analysis (including open coding of small data samples and mass coding of large swaths of data); to creating quantitative and visual representations of this coding; to reflecting on those representations; and perhaps returning to data exploration with new questions. This paper demonstrates how multi-dimensional data signatures can be tools for structuring and communicating this emerging method of analysis.

FUTURE WORK

This study is part of a larger research effort that aims to improve techniques for automatically identifying and classifying rumors propagating on Twitter. The current study identifies several features that may be useful in distinguishing between true and false rumors. In future work, we intend to leverage this concept of signatures, in combination with our growing understanding of how and why rumors propagate, to develop methods of categorizing different types of rumors. The three rumor types identified here are likely part of a larger set, and future research will expand and refine this list of prototypical signatures as we converge on the most useful set of categorizations.

CONCLUSION

In this paper, we integrate qualitative, quantitative, and visual analysis to examine the spread of four rumors propagating via Twitter after the 2013 Boston Marathon bombings. We identify five quantitative features that reflect salient aspects of the qualitative story of each rumor, including temporal progression of rumor behavior codes, URL domain diversity, domain propagation over time, lexical diversity, and geolocation information. These features constitute multi-dimensional *signatures* that can be used to characterize different types of rumors. In constructing these signatures, this research demonstrates and documents an emerging method for deeply and recursively integrating qualitative and quantitative methods for analysis of social media trace data.

ACKNOWLEDGMENTS

This research is a collaboration between the emCOMP Lab and SoMe Lab at UW and was partially supported by NSF Grants 1342252 and 1243170. The authors thank Shawn Walker for his efforts to transform the original Twitter data into datasets that were more easily accessed and analyzed.

REFERENCES

1. Allport, G. W. & Postman, L. An analysis of rumor. *Public Opinion Quarterly 10*, 4 (1946), 501-517.
2. Berger, J. Arousal increases social transmission of information. *Psychological Science 22*, 7 (2011), 891-893.
3. Bordia, P., & DiFonzo, N. Problem solving in social interactions on the Internet: Rumor as social cognition. *Social Psychology Quarterly*, *67*, 1 (2004), 33-49.
4. Budak, C., Agrawal, D., & El Abbadi, A. Limiting the spread of misinformation in social networks. In *Proc. of WWW 2011*, ACM, 665-674.
5. Castillo, C., Mendoza, M., & Poblete, B. Information credibility on twitter. *WWW 2011*, ACM, 675-684.
6. Cheng, Z., Caverlee, J., & Lee, K. You are where you tweet: A content-based approach to geo-locating twitter users. *Proc. of Conference on Information and Knowledge Management, CIKM 2010*, 759-768. ACM.
7. Chierichetti, F., Lattanzi, S., & Panconesi, A. Rumor spreading in social networks. In 36th *Intl. Colloquium on Automata, Languages and Programming (ICALP)*, pp. 375–386. Springer, 2009.
8. DiFonzo, N, & Bordia, P. *Rumor psychology: Social and organizational approaches*. American Psychological Association, 2007.
9. Friggeri, A., Adamic, L. A., Eckles, D., & Cheng, J. Rumor Cascades. *AAAI, 2014*.
10. Gantz, W., & Trenholm, S. Why people pass on news: Motivations for diffusion. *Journalism & Mass Communication Quarterly 56*, 2 (1979), 365-370.
11. Herrman, J. Twitter is a Truth Machine. Blog in *Buzzfeed*. (October, 2012). Available at: http://gofwd.tumblr.com/post/34623466723/twitter-is-a-truth-machine
12. Hill, K. Hurricane Sandy, @ComfortablySmug, and the Flood of Social Media Misinformation. *Forbes.com*. (October 30, 2012). Available at: http://www.forbes .com/sites/kashmirhill/2012/10/30/hurricane-sandy-and-the-flood-of-social-media-misinformation/
13. Hiltz, S. R., Kushma, J., & Plotnick, L. Use of social media by US public sector emergency managers: Barriers and wish lists. *Proc. of ISCRAM, 2014*.
14. Hughes, A. L., & Palen, L. The evolving role of the public information officer: An examination of social media in emergency management. *J. of Homeland Security & Emergency Management 9*, 1 (2012), 1-20.
15. Kwon, S., Cha, M., Jung, K., Chen, W., & Wang, Y. Prominent Features of Rumor Propagation in Online Social Media. In *IEEE 13th International Conference on Data Mining, ICDM 2013*, 1103-1108.
16. Leberecht, T. Twitter Grows Up in Aftermath of Haiti Earthquake, *CNET News*, (January 19, 2010) http://www.cnet.com/news/twitter-grows-up-in-aftermath-of-haiti-earthquake/

17. Leonard, H. B., Cole, C. M., Howitt, A. M., & Heymann, P. B. Why was Boston strong? Lessons from the Boston Marathon Bombing. Program on Crisis Leadership and Program in Criminal Justice Policy and Management, Harvard Kennedy School, April 3, 2014.

18. Madrigal, A. Hey Reddit, Enough Boston Bombing Vigilantism. The Atlantic. (April 17, 2013). http://www.theatlantic.com/technology/archive/2013/04/hey-reddit-enough-boston-bombing-vigilantism/275062/

19. Madrigal, A. #BostonBombing: The Anatomy of a Misinformation Disaster. *The Atlantic* (2013, April 19) http://www.theatlantic.com/technology/archive/2013/04/-bostonbombing-the-anatomy-of-a-misinformation-disaster/275155/

20. Mendoza, M., Poblete, B., & Castillo, C. Twitter under crisis: can we trust what we RT?. *Proc. of 1st Workshop on Social Media Analytics 2010*, ACM, 71-79.

21. Nahon, K., Hemsley, J., Mason, R. M., Walker, S., & Eckert, J. Information flows in events of political unrest. *Proc. of iConference 2013*, 480-485.

22. Oh, O., Agrawal , M., & Rao , H. (2013). Community Intelligence and Social Media Services: A Rumor Theoretic Analysis of Tweets During Social Crises. *MIS Quarterly, 37*, 2 (2013), 407-426.

23. Palen, L, Anderson, K.M, Mark, G, Martin, J, Sicker, D, Palmer, M., and Grunwald, D. A Vision for Technology-Mediated Support for Public Participation & Assistance in Mass Emergencies & Disasters, in *Proc. of ACM-BCS Visions of Computer Science* (2010), 1-12.

24. Qazvinian, V., Rosengren, E., Radev, D. R., & Mei, Q. Rumor has it: Identifying misinformation in microblogs. In *Proc. of the Conference on Empirical Methods in Natural Language Processing*, (2011), 1589-1599.

25. Shibutani, T. *Improvised news: A sociological study of rumor*. Ardent Media, 1966.

26. Spiro, E. S., Fitzhugh, S., Sutton, J., Pierski, N., Greczek, M., & Butts, C. T. Rumoring during extreme events: A case study of Deepwater Horizon 2010. *Proc. of ACM Web Science Conference 2012*, ACM, 275-283

27. Starbird, K., Maddock, J., Orand, M., Achterman, P., & Mason, RM. Rumors, False Flags, and Digital Vigilantes: Misinformation on Twitter after the 2013 Boston Marathon Bombing. *iConference 2014*, 654-662.

28. Starbird, K. & Palen, L. (How) Will the Revolution be Retweeted? Information Propagation in the 2011 Egyptian Uprising. In *Proc. of CSCW 2012*, 6-17.

29. Zhou, L., Burgoon, J. K., Nunamaker, J. F., & Twitchell, D. Automating linguistics-based cues for detecting deception in text-based asynchronous computer-mediated communications. *Group Decision & Negotiation*, 13(1), (2004), 81-106.

Capture the Moment: "In the Wild" Longitudinal Case Study of Situated Snapshots Captured Through an Urban Screen in a Community Setting

Nemanja Memarovic[1], Ava Fatah gen. Schieck[2], Holger Schnädelbach[3], Efstathia Kostopoulou[2], Steve North[3], Lei Ye[3]

[1]University of Zurich
Zurich, Switzerland
memarovic@ifi.uzh.ch

[2]University College London
London, UK
{ava.fatah, efstathia.kostopoulou.10}@ucl.ac.uk

[3]University of Nottingham
Nottingham, UK
{holger.schnadelbach, steve.north, l.ye}@nottingham.ac.uk

ABSTRACT
Urban screens are becoming a common element of our city landscape. As such they offer new ways of connecting people that occupy public space, e.g., by taking situated snapshots through a display-attached camera. In this paper we present a first longitudinal case study of 12 weeks of such an application – Moment Machine – deployed "in the wild" on an urban screen facing the street. We report findings from 1189 photos taken, 13 interviews, and 3 weeks of observations that show engagement stimulated by situated snapshots within a place-based community where the screen is located. We also analyze interaction log files to describe how often users interacted, what type of interactions they had and how long they lasted, and overall engagement on a weekly basis and throughout the week. Based on our experience, we provide three take-away snippets for designers of similar urban screen experiences.

Author Keywords
Urban screens; situated snapshots; community interaction; urban computing;

ACM Classification Keywords
H.4.3 [Communications Applications]: Bulletin boards; H.5.1 [Multimedia Information Systems]; H.5.3 [Group and Organization Interfaces]

INTRODUCTION
Large public displays are "painting" the urban landscape and are becoming a common element of the urban scenery [10]. As urban screens are part of public spaces where place-based (or geographical, territorial) communities [2] thrive, an interesting research agenda lies in understanding their *social impact*, i.e., how urban screens can stimulate community interaction – interaction between community members within the public space [4, 16]. Within this space researchers and artists have investigated the use of simple video links [3, 6, 7, 25]; text messages uploaded from mobile phones [27]; user-contributed photos from a custom created website/social network [12, 26] or from an existing photo sharing website, e.g., Flickr [23] or Instagram [20]; or *situated snapshots* created through an on-display camera [8, 14, 22]. Situated snapshots via public displays are fundamentally different from any photo sharing application as they require a person to be situated in front of a display in order to take a photo in a "mirror like" fashion, and unlike other photo sharing display applications that support remote access and participation through a website/social network [12, 20, 23, 26]. This difference can also be connected to previous research [13] that explored the design space for limiting content input and access on communal public displays and pointed out the differences between "tethered" interaction that is situated and tied to a display and remote interaction via mobile devices or other means (for example, tethered interactions lead to social congregation around a display).

In this paper we report on the first longitudinal, open, "in the wild" study that investigated the use of such a medium without any constraints. While previous studies has

Figure 1 - Passers-by interacting with the Moment Machine application (a red rectangle) and capturing a moment/ image: In a) we see them interacting capture the image and b) the resulting image, a few seconds allow to pose.

CSCW '15, March 14 - 18 2015, Vancouver, BC, Canada

ACM 978-1-4503-2922-4/15/03...$15.00
http://dx.doi.org/10.1145/2675133.2675165

investigated some aspects of posting situated snapshots it has either been focused on a) stimulating civic engagement within a certain age group – young adults –and allowing them to express their opinions and views about issues in a city through photo-stories created through displays [8]; or b) on soliciting user opinions on the potential use of situated snapshot through short-term user trials [14]. Also all of the above studies were much shorter than the one reported here and did not consider long-term effects of such a medium. The contribution of this work is two-fold:

- We provide first insights into the use of urban screens for taking situated snapshots over a course of 12 weeks within a community setting. By analyzing 1189 photos and interaction log files we provide a detailed description of user engagement, i.e., frequency of user interactions, type of interactions they had and their duration, and overall engagement on a weekly basis and throughout the week. We also provide the first categorization of the photos captured through this medium.
- We show engagement stimulated by viewing and posting photos on a display on a place-based community located around the community center, collected through 13 interviews with community members and 3 weeks of observations. These include reasons for taking the photos, social interaction stimulated by the application, impact on community interaction and awareness, properties that describe situated snapshots taken through an urban screen as a communication medium, and networked aspects and interest in other places.

In the following sections we first describe related work. Next we describe the Moment Machine deployment and the community setting where the application was running. After that we present the analysis of the photos taken through the Moment Machine application and show how frequent people interacted with the application. We also show 10 photo themes from the photos that were taken with the application. We then summarize qualitative insights obtained from the interviews conducted with 13 returning users/groups as well as observations taken over the course of 3 weeks and provide insights into how the application was used over 12 weeks on a multipurpose urban screen. Finally, we discuss our findings and provide concluding remarks and directions of future work.

RELATED WORK

Some of the pioneering research on urban screens has been conducted in the early 80s through the 'Hole in Space' [7] project that connected two urban spaces in New York and Los Angeles through a video link. Similar and more recent projects are Connected Urban Spaces [3], Hole in the Earth [6], and Telectroscope [25]. Recently, research on urban screens has shifted from stimulating interaction through video links into creating more interactive multimedia applications [9, 15]. For example, FunSquare [15] is an application that creates place-relevant information on the fly by connecting information sensed around display vicinity with information coming from elsewhere. This intriguing piece of information stimulates social interaction between passers-by. On the other hand Jose et al. [9] investigated how we can use familiar paradigms, i.e., pins and posters, to allow community members to express themselves on an public screens. More generally, researchers have also investigated how urban screens/public displays can be integrated within existing communication services [17] and identified the multi-faceted challenges in creating engaging experiences for communities [16].

The work reported in this paper falls in the category of applications that allow people in a community setting to express themselves through photos, more precisely using *situated snapshots* taken through a display-attached camera. In the area of situated snapshots the work reported here is closest to UBI-Postcards [22], Ubinion [8], and our prior preliminary study [14]. UBI-Postcards [22] allows passers-by to take photos using a camera attached to a display – once the photos are taken users can send the photo to an email address. However the study of the use and impact of this application was not documented. Similarly, Ubinion [8] used urban screens as an input device: young adults/teenagers could use them to create posters with speech bubbles that would represent their concerns about the city of Oulu. Posters created on displays would be posted on dedicated Facebook and Twitter accounts. In our prior short user trail study [14] we investigated people's expectations towards situated snapshots within urban setting (the study took place in total 7.5 hours). The study reported here complements the above mentioned ones, as the first longitudinal and open-ended study of such a medium in a community setting.

THE MOMENT MACHINE DEPLOYMENT

In order to investigate the uptake and effects of posting and viewing situated snapshots on urban screens, we use the Moment Machine application [14], an urban screen application that allows passers-by to take images through a display-attached camera. Its user interface is shown in Figure 2. The interface shows a live video feed (1) and allows passers-by to take an image by simply pressing a button with a hand icon (3). By selecting a filter before taking a photo (2) users can change the look-and-feel of their snapshot: this is somewhat similar to the popular social media application Instagram[1]. Pictures are taken with a five seconds delay indicated with a countdown timer. After taking a photo users have thirty seconds to decide if they want to leave the snapshot on the display (4) or discard it. Also, passers-by can scroll and browse the snapshot from all 4 locations where the application is installed (5). Each instance of the application is showing the last 100 photos taken from all 4 locations.

[1] http://en.wikipedia.org/wiki/Instagram, accessed on 7.10.2014

Figure 2 – Moment Machine user interface.

We deployed the application "In the wild" on a multipurpose urban screen as part of the "Screens in the Wild" screen network [4, 20]. The project used an iterative methodology to integrate the screen placement, content development, local interactivity and distributed connectivity of four screen nodes connecting Nottingham, UK at Broadway (a media center and cafe) and New Arts Exchange (a culture hub) with London, UK at Leytonstone (a public library) and the Mill (a hub for local communities). The displays were installed in 2012 behind glass allowing touch by people who pass-by from the street side: first installed in Nottingham in February/March followed by London at Leytonstone in May, and finally at the Mill in September, which is the focus of the study presented in this paper. Since then there were a couple of applications installed and the displays have more than a single application running throughout the day, where some are interactive while others are not [20]. However, unlike the multipurpose displays in Oulu [22], there is never more than one application running at a time: if people pass by they will see only one application running and they need to pass during another time period in order to understand that there is more than one application.

As a first step in understanding the impact of the application we have decided to focus on thorough examination of its use and the effects on one location at first. We had better connections with stakeholders in Leytonstone and the Mill, and hence we have decided to conduct the first user trials "in the wild" in both locations [14]. We then focused on the Mill where we have the most contacts with the community; and it is the richest of the two settings; providing different levels of engagement and how the locals relate to the building: this includes people who: 1) visit the community hub often or regularly, 2) live around it, and 3) people who pass regularly in front of the community building as part of their daily routine without/ or with less connection to its activities. In this paper we describe the uses and effects of the application at the Mill. The application was deployed in early March 2013 and it has been running since. We report on the first 12 weeks of use (March – May), and overall research of the Screens in the Wild project. The application had a changing schedule in the system, running most of the time from 12 PM until 8AM and from 2PM until 4PM (88.1% of the deployment period). These periods were identified as the most active through observations of daily interactions i.e., (2-4 pm) when school kids pass in front of the screen and (after 12 pm- i.e., when dark) when the screen is visually noticeable. Also, these time slots fitted in the schedule of other applications running on the screen.

Setting The Scene

In our work we are investigating the impact of the Moment Machine application on a place-based community, typically defined through geographical proximity within a certain area where members spend time (in the area) on a regular basis [2]. The Mill where the urban screen is located is in a residential area linking the local market on the way to the local primary school and a local park. It is a community center established after a passionate community campaign to keep the Mill Street Library open. The local residents won funding to support community-led innovation. At the Mill various groups meet – residents can share information and services in a self-determined way. Currently over 40 different groups gather regularly for different purposes such as poetry, knitting, photography or over 65s' social life improvement [21]. In this context, the community in our work are members of the Mill, neighbors, as well as school kids that attend the local primary school. One of the goals of the Moment Machine came out of our direct collaboration with the community champion who wanted to get more engagement and attention from the neighbors and kids that pass by. In order to understand how the community at the Mill interacted with the Moment Machine application we analyzed images and conducted 13 semi-structured interviews with returning users, i.e., people who came back and used the application more than once, as well as 3 weeks of observations in May 2013. We also analyzed interaction log files in order to better understand how users interacted with the application. We will explain the analysis of each part in the appropriate sections.

FINDINGS

The evaluation of local interactions mediated through the Moment Machine application and its impact on the community draws on both qualitative and quantitative data. The quantitative data is collected through interaction log files and documents how often users interacted with the application during the 12 weeks of deployment on a monthly and weekly basis; how they used the applications and what type of interactions they had. On the other hand, the qualitative data documents impressions from community members – this way of evaluating the impact on the place-based community draws on methods reported by prior research [16] that documented the evaluation of three public display applications and their impact on place-based communities. In addition, the qualitative photo analysis reveals how situated snapshots captured through an urban screen are used and what type of photos passers-by take.

As a first step in analyzing user engagement over 12 weeks, we manually examined all the photos – 1189 – from the Mill - this comprises 35.05% of photos taken across the four locations (overall: 3390, Leytonstone 1146 photos or 33.81%, Broadway 877 photos or 25.87%, and New Arts Exchange 178 photos or 5.25%). The goal was to understand what age groups the application attracted, how people used it as a means of expression and self-expression, and how many people returned to interact (we call them returning users) and how often they interacted. A researcher labeled each photo with: 1) the number of people on it, 2) their estimated age group, 3) labels that describe the photo's theme, e.g., "single portrait" for a single person's portrait or "showing objects" if people are showing objects, 4) identifiers of users who came back to interact with the application on two different days, and 5) sequential number/id of a photo session, where a photo session is defined with same people appearing in the photo (one session can have just one photo). Labeling was done by a single researcher using iPhoto for recognizing returning users. The procedure was repeated several times in order to improve consistency and lasted in total 3 months of 8 hours everyday analysis. Overall it is similar in nature to the data analysis described in [5], which was also conducted by a single researcher.

Overall, in the manual analysis we counted 509 users on the photos out of which 93 (18.27%) were returning users. We show the estimated age group of both returning and non-returning users in Figure 3.

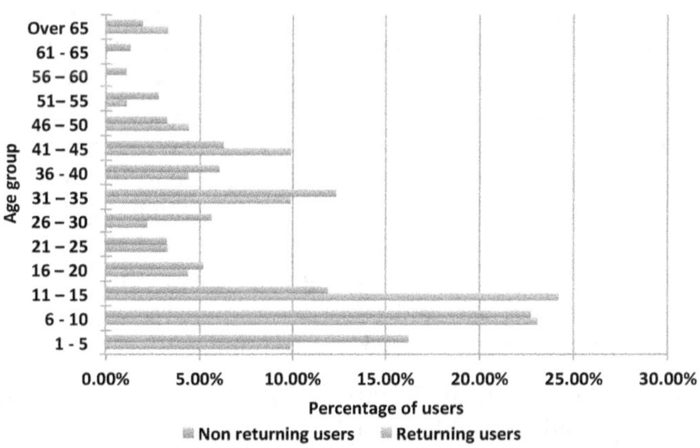

Figure 3 – User age group distribution (estimate)

Most of the people in the photos were recognized as kids, i.e., age groups 1 – 5 (16.23%), 6 – 10 (22.73%), and 11 – 15 (11.90%) followed by people in their early thirties (31 – 35, 12.34%). As shown in Figure 3 the largest portion of returning users are children in the age groups of 11 – 15 (24.18%) and 6 – 10 (23.08%). Most returning users returned once (54.84%), followed by users who returned 2 to 5 times (34.41%), while a smaller portion returned 6 or more times (10.75%). Some returning users (48.39%) returned at a "standard time" when they interacted with the screen, i.e., their returning times did not vary much (for 35.48% of users STD is <=5 minutes and for 50.54% STD is <= 20 minutes). We classify all returning users based on their return frequency in 3 groups (Figure 4):

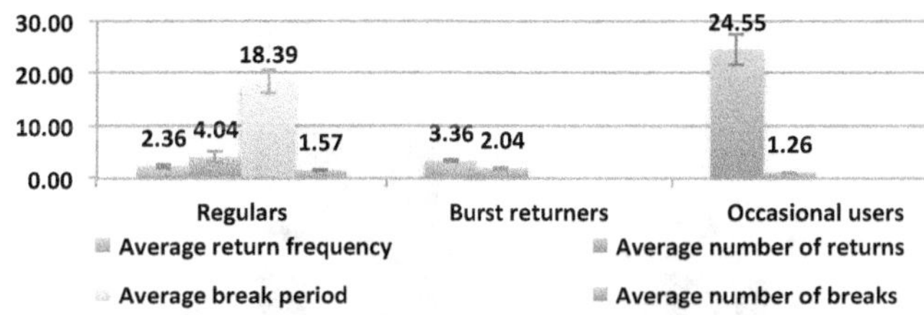

Figure 4 - Three groups of returning users: a) regulars, b) weekly returners, and c) occasional passers-by

- *Occasional users* (24.73% of returning users) are characterized with returns that took more than a week. On average this type of users returned after 24.55 days (SEM 2.87 days) and they returned 1.26 times (SEM 0.15 times).
- *Burst returners* (50.54% of returning users) returned in periods less than a week, on average after 3.36 days (SEM 0.33 days) 2.04 times in a row (SEM 0.33 times).
- *Regulars* (24.73% of returning users) has mixed behavior as the above two groups. They had periods when they returned on a weekly basis returning after 2.36 days (SEM 0.43 days) 4.04 times in a row (SEM 1.03 times). However they also have a "break" in interaction. On average this break lasted 18.39 days (SEM 2.2 days) and occurred 1.57 times (SEM 0.14 times). One of the reasons for such a behavior could be because of holidays (Easter) that happened during the deployment.

In total passers-by took 1189 photos: 51.39% were taken by returning users and 48.61% by non-returning users. Top contributors among returning users were school kids aged 11 – 15 whose interactions accounted for 22% of the photos produced. In order to better understand how the community used this medium a researcher used open-ended coding to label all the photos with different themes that appear in them. Thirty-three labels were identified and then regrouped into 11 themes. In Table 1, 10 themes are shown in descending order from the top left corner (theme "Empty" is not included, i.e., when no one in the photo). A photo had multiple codes that describe it, so the sum of labels is more than 100%. Identified themes are:

- *Action:* a sequence of photos catching people in "action". Most of the photos in this category were taken by a group of school kids that took the photos "jumping" in the air on their way back from school (see also R1, which is mentioned later in Table 2). Another big portion was taken

Action, 24.3%: being caught in action 	**Single portrait, 23.1%** 	**Group portrait, 22.2%** 	**Accidental, 8.6%**: caught on camera by chance 	**Posing, 8.5%**: striking a pose for the photo 
Facial expressions, 7.5%: e.g., funny face, tongue out 	**Signs, 5.3%**: signs with hands 	**Showing objects, 2.3%**: e.g., cards, book, cans 	**Inappropriate, 1.5%**: middle finger 	**Affection, 1.2%**: kissing or hugging 

Table 1 - Photo themes with example image for each, their percentage in the photo corpus, and a short description.

during a community organized event – Star Wars day – where kids played around the screen and "shot" at it.

- *Single portrait*: a person having a portrait photo facing the camera frontally.
- *Group portrait*: a group of people having a portrait photo.
- *Accidental*: people being caught on camera while passing by or people who are not fully in the photo, looking down like they are "checking out" the user interface.
- *Posing*: striking a "pose" for the photo, e.g., acting like "zombies" or "tuff guys". Mainly group photos.
- *Facial expressions*: having a facial expression in the photo, e.g., lolling/showing tongue out, making a "silly" face, or duck mouth. Similarly to signs, these were performed in combination with single or group portrait.
- *Signs:* people performing signs with their hands. Signs ranged from waving at the screen/saying "hi"; showing "peace" or "victory" with fingers; giving "bunny ears" to another person; showing "rock'n'roll" gesture; "thumbs up"; and creating a "heart" with both hands. Mostly they were in combination with a single or group portrait.
- *Showing objects*: showing an object in the photo, e.g., a bottle, soda can, or notebook.
- *Inappropriate*: showing the middle finger or middle and index finger as well as "mooning".
- *Affection:* people showing affection to each other, for example kissing or hugging each other.

Interviews and Observations

In order to understand people's experience around the Moment Machine application, how they view its impact on their community and how they may relate to other people in their immediate vicinity/locality, we conducted 13 semi-structured interviews with returning users, who are members of the local community. All of the interviewees are located within the screen's vicinity at the Mill and are 1) either active members of the Mill's community where screen is placed (R3, R4, R5, B2, B4, O1, U1); or 2) part of its immediate neighborhood – B3 lives just across the location, O2 and U2 rent office spaces on top of location it; or 3) are part of the local neighborhood where screen is situated, such as the local primary school located roughly 480 meters away (R1, R2, B1).

The interview questions revolved around 1) when and how the users encounter the Moment Machine application, 2) how they find the user interface and the experience, 3) how they interact with the application, and 4) its effects on community interaction and awareness (identified through capturing if 1) they browse the photos, 2) recognize someone on them, and 3) recognize other locations). We used a snowball recruitment approach starting with the community champion [26] – our strongest contact person in the community (R4 in Table 2). With her we browsed the photos and found returning users with whom she could put us in contact. We then scheduled an interview with the identified person and also asked her/him at the end of the interview if s/he could recommend someone to go through our interviews. Interviews lasted between 20 and 45 minutes depending on the interviewee's availability. Three interviews were unplanned, i.e., during our observations we noticed three groups of returning users interacting with the application (R1, R2, and B1) so we invited them to short interviews (lasted between 5 and 10 minutes).

We conducted overall 13 interviews with 7 individuals and 6 groups and were able to capture 12 regulars (1 individual, 1 group of 7 users and 2 groups of 2), 5 burst returners (3 individual and 1 group of 2 users), and 2 occasional users. Two groups were unclassified as they were not recognized as returning users through the photos, but they explicitly stated interacting with the application multiple times. We

ID and description
R1: Group of 6 schoolboys age 11 – 15. Took the photos on their way back from school. Their interactions accounted for 15.31% of overall photos (182/1189). Mainly pictures of action, them jumping in the air. Returned 12 times.
R2: Two schoolgirls, age 11 – 15. Take the photos on their way back from school, their interactions accounted for 3.53% of the photos (41/1189). Mainly group portraits. Returned 21 times.
R3: Mother, age 31 – 35 and daughter, age 11 – 15. Take the photos on a weekly basis before entering the Mill, group portraits with facial expressions. Returned twice, took 5 photos.
R4: Community champion, age 31 – 35, in charge of the Mill. Took 6 photos, single or group portraits. Returned 5 times
R5: Schoolgirl, age 11 – 15, takes the photos on her way to the Mill where her mom (O1) works. Mainly single portraits, posing and silly faces. Sometimes group portraits with silly faces with O1. Returned 7 times and took 32 photos.
B1: Two schoolgirls, age 11 – 15. Take the photos on their way back from school. Group portraits, showing objects and posing. Returned 1 time and took 4 photos.
B2: Volunteer at the Mill, age 56 – 60. Takes the photos on his way back from a pub. Single portraits, sometimes with facial expressions. Returned twice and took 12 photos.
B3: Neighbor who lives across the Mill, age 41 – 45. Takes the photos on his way to the Market Square. Single portrait. Returned 4 times and took 7 photos.
B4: Worked for 2 weeks everyday on repairing the heating at the Mill, age 26 – 30. Group and single portraits, posing and facial expressions. Returned 6 times and took 9 photos.
O1: Woman, age 41 – 45, volunteer at the Mill. Takes the photos with her daughter R5. Group portrait and facial expressions. Returned once and took 2 photos.
O2: Man, age 35 – 40, working in the office space above the Mill. Takes the photos with his kid, group portrait with action, on the way up. Returned once and took 6 photos.
U1: Family, woman 31 – 35, boy 11 – 15, girl 6 – 10. Part of the Mill's community, take the photos before/after entering the space. Posing, action, and facial expressions. Took 16 photos.
U2: Family, woman 31 – 35, boys 6 – 10 and 1 - 5, rents the office space on top of the Mill. Kid takes the photos when they application is running, action (fighting), took 16 photos.

Table 2 - Interviewees and their descriptions. 'R' stands for regular, 'B' stands for burst returner, 'O' stands for occasional, and 'U' stands for unclassified.

describe our interviewees in Table 2 and code them with a letter and number for identifying their responses later on.

Additionally, observations were conducted during 3 weeks in May, lasting 1-2 hours depending on the availability of the researcher. We observed information such as coordination, engagement, and social interaction around the application, and paid a particular attention to spotting returning users. We summarize 5 most important findings that came out of the analysis, i.e., 1) general impressions of the application and reasons for taking the photos, 2) social interaction stimulated by the application, 3) impact on community interaction and awareness, 4) properties that describe situated snapshots taken through an urban screen as a communication medium, and 5) networked aspects and connectivity with other places.

General Impressions and Reasons for Taking the Photos

Users found the application very easy and intuitive for use. Some participants thought it added more interactivity to the display (R4, O1, O2) stating "It's definitely made that screen far more interactive than it was before" (O2). As for the reasons for taking the photos we were able to distill 6 different ones. The strongest one is that *the application is integrated in passers-by daily routine*. They liked that whenever s/he passed by the display the Moment Machine application would be running (R1, R2, R3, R4, R5, B1, B2, B3, B4). They would encounter the application when going to/from school/work, or when entering/leaving the community space. Taking photos was seen as *part of a group activity* (R1, R2, R3, B1, O1, O2, U1). As R3 stated "When we come on Tuesday we normally come a little bit early and she likes to take a few photos, pull silly faces, play with the different effects, see what other pictures people have taken." Also R1 is an example of this behavior: whenever they would pass by a display they took photos as a group.

Getting attention is another reason for taking the photos. The statement from R4 about R2 best captures this "Tall girl used to knock on the window and then stared and waved. […] she wasn't trying to hide, she was trying to be annoying. But since the app was installed she stopped that." This was also confirmed by R2 who stated they "want to be seen and [they take photos because] we know others 'on the network' will see it." *Curiosity* is another reason for taking the photos. People were curious about the application or what the photos will look like (B2, O1). When asked about the reasons for taking the photos with his kid O2 replied "To be captured the same size like you really are. Literally like a mirror. Curious, both curios." Similarly B1 stated they "just wanted to see what the photos will turn out like."

Another reason for interaction is *the honey pot effect* [1]. We observed this behavior and also our interviewees reported similar reasons for taking photos. For example O2 notes "I just noticed them [a group of kids] taking the photos, not knowing much about it really. [I took the photos] Not far after them. I picked up my son about half past 3, walked into the studio and on returning the machine for taking the photos was on, so I just indulged to keep my son happy, he saw the children doing it. We both saw the kids". There are two interesting aspects of the honey pot effect that we noticed during observations and interviews. First, as noted in the above quote *it is important to see people from the same age group interacting with the application*. The kid saw other kids interacting with the application and expressed a desire to interact with it. Similar example is illustrated in Figure 5 where we can see a little girl standing in the back next to the mailbox. She observed other kids interacting. Once they were done she approached the display and started interacting. However, *seeing people form other age groups than ones can repel people from interacting*. This is best captured by a quote from B2 who commented on Moment Machine's ability to connect people "there's a fear element, maybe it's a generational thing, you see kids playing around with it, messing around with it". In other words, he hesitated from interacting with the application because he saw children interacting with it.

Figure 5 - Honey pot effect working with the same age group

Social Interaction Around the Moment Machine Application

As mentioned previously taking photos was seen as part of a group activity (R1, R2, R3, B1, O1, O2, U1). In turn this stimulated social interaction between the ones who knew each other. Some of the interactions were quite local, e.g., talking with the people from the community (R4, O1, O2, U1), while some went outside the locality, e.g., talking with other school kids about the application (B1). For example, R4 stated "It's easy to talk to strangers when you're interacting with the application". Similarly U1 said "We have a reason, we have an excuse, to stand out there and take some photos outside. Sometimes the children are quiet/busy and you can linger a bit more. [...] You stop and got a few moments to kind of speak to people". U1 also mentioned that the application created time for adults with children to socialize: while the kids were playing with the application parents had time to talk to other people.

For kids the application *stimulated play and imagination*. Some interviewees explicitly mentioned their children love to "play with it" (O2, U1, U2), while others mentioned seeing children play (R4, B4, O1). Besides R1 who appropriated the application and took the photos jumping in the air, during observations we noticed two games children played. In one game kids pressed the hand button to take the photo and then rapidly pressed the filter button in order to randomize their picture, as the final filter of the photo would be made by chance. In another game kids would stand still in a place waiting for the counter to go down and then they would "duck" in order not be captured in the photo (cf. Figure 6). These examples show how children easily embrace and appropriate the application. However, we also observed other aspects between R1 and R2, i.e., territoriality – defending their time to interact with the application. In one instance R1 were interacting and R2 asked them to use it. The boys said repeatedly "No" and the girls left. This shows there can be conflicts between groups who are at the display at the same time.

Figure 6 – Kids playing the "duck" game

Community Interaction and Awareness

The communal nature of taking situated snapshots is best captured by U1 "[takes the photos] out of community spirit because you're really putting it out there for absolutely anybody to see it." When asked if they recognize someone in the photos interviewees gave different answers. For example, R4, R5, and O2 recognized R1, the most famous group of people on the photos who took 15.31% of the overall photos. Their impact on the display is best captured by a quote from R4 "The most obvious one is the group of young boys who come really every day after school and I mostly, usually hear them, they're quite loud, they're like a hurricane, you can hear them laughing, hitting the app, the window, a lot of that comes across the pictures but it's quite different when you see them. When they're around I know that the app is running". Others had a more general awareness of the application users. R3 stated seeing "children, typically school children who live here or elsewhere" while O1 identified more than a single user group "Regulars stopping there to take their picture every day, you get a lot of kids, a couple of teenagers, you get young adults, people in their 20s, 30s. A mixture, some of them are people that come to the Mill, some of them are from the area, and some of them are on their way to the park". These examples show how situated snapshots can stimulate *different levels of awareness about a community*.

When people talked about the Moment Machine application some of them mentioned *events or photos they remembered* (R3, R4, B1, U1). For example, R4 remembers talking to others about the application in general, but also about "the whole dog sequence, which I showed to everybody" – a sequence of photos where people held their dogs and took a photo with them. Similarly R3 remembered "a man pulling a stand, but that was ages ago". U1 was able to specifically remember when the event happened stating "two weeks ago I was out there with children and a cousin of mine passed and I told her she can take the photos". The strongest memory of a photo or event is connected with an event organized by the community. On Saturday May 4 (week 9) the community organized the Star Wars day where community members and kids dressed up as Star Wars characters. During the event people took the photos inside the Mill, but as they noticed the Moment Machine application running they went out and started playing and interacting outside. As O1 stated "[there was] a lot of action on Star Wars. [...] people came with their costumes and they wanted their photo taken." Similarly B1 notes "We had an event at the Mill based on Star Wars, I was dressed as a storm trooper, so let's let people know what's going at the Mill." The above examples show how situated snapshots help in creating shared memorable events for a specific location and enhance, stimulate, and aid in capturing ongoing ones.

Situated Snapshots as a Communication Medium

We distilled 3 properties of situated snapshots as a communication medium: 1) relevance of the locality for the medium, 2) inclusive and egocentric nature of the use, and 3) communicating through situated snapshots.

This type of medium brings attention to the place where the display is located. As O2 stated "It's great, brings attention to the fun of the shop for children [referring to the Mill], which is also one of the goals. It's a great reactive element to the Mill, it's perfect for the Mill. [...] The novelty wore off once it [the display] was installed, but since the first photography was installed that's much more interactive obviously." R4 had similar comments and saw engagement with the application as engagement with the place. However, this also means the reach of the medium can be quite local. Although there were school kids who talked to their peers about the application (B1) and came back with more friends thus bringing in new users, there were also others (R5) who did not talk about the application "because none of my friends live in the area." In other words, reach of the application with respect to social interaction can be quite local and depends if the users have friends in the area.

During the interviews a strong property of this medium emerged – its *inclusive but also egocentric nature of use.* Regarding the inclusive nature of the medium participants stated, "anyone feels like they can use" (O1), "this is your content" (R4), and simply "It's very democratizing" (U1). Although passers-by could browse the photos of others, some interviewees were more interested in looking at their own photos (R3, B1, B2, B3, O1, O2). We observed that after taking a photo people come back to browse and find their own photo as shown in Figure 7, occasionally bringing in more people to show them the photo(s) they took.

Figure 7 - B1 taking photos (left) and coming back the day after to browse (right).

Communicating through this medium is done through replication, i.e., mimicking behavior of others. As R4 stated "I think one of the good things about the app is that it creates a conversation, people copy the pose, like the dog photos, something links spontaneously and people take photos". This can be connected to her previous statement where she said she likes New Arts Exchange because kids do similar things there. The overall impression about this type of communication is nicely summarized B2 "Not gonna save the world, maybe it could make a world a better place for us who live in it, i.e., by communicating it [the world]". The uniqueness of taking photos through the Moment Machine application is best captured by R4 "Less editorial control, it's the same location you always have the same backdrop you're always concentrated on the expression or the action. I find it difficult, I'm not great in being in photos, but children find it very easy as they are great with telling stories with photos". and O2 "This is a media without me having any sort of like interface, this is a media as in... percentages luck, that I'm passing the screen, percentage is luck that I know that's it taking photographs".

Networked Aspects And Connectivity With Other Places

The Moment Machine application was running in 4 locations in 2 major cities. While some did not know there were photos from other locations (O1) or there was no raised interest in them (B4), for others (R4, R5, B1, O2, U1), for some people seeing images of people from those locations stimulated interest in them. For example, R4 stated "I recognize families from the neighborhood and people from the app, e.g., Leytonstone. I might not know them but I recognize them from the app. I've seen them historically from the other photos". U1 and B1 had similar comments. For example, U1 stated "It's nice to have another place so close by [referring to Leytonstone] because it's easy recognizable. It's so close by it may just happen to see faces of people who used the application, it becomes better known. It's nice that other camera is close by so you may come across someone". Overall, the above quotes show how situated snapshots can stimulate interest in other communities and places.

However, some showed interest in locations from Nottingham (R4) "Yes, I'm interested. I like the 2nd location [New Arts Exchange] in Nottingham, school kids do similar things to ours. They do similar things with application wherever they are." People noticed places that had similar age groups and behavior, but also ones that were different "[R4 continued] But the other Nottingham location, Broadway, had a lot more adults and that's more unusual for us because we have more kids using the app". This shows how the networked aspect of the application may help *enrich local life*. Other interviewees made similar statements as well (B1) "More interest in Nottingham because I don't know about it, Leytonstone is too close". For some people interest was raised because of the activities at that location, e.g., (U1) stated "There are photos from people going ought late at night (referring to Leytonstone)[...] That was kind of new, as we would usually see pictures of school kids, kind of boring; we want to know if something more exciting is happening". Furthermore, R5 was interested only in people and what they do, regardless of their location. Some interviewees wanted *more connections with physical places*. For example R5 wanted more local displays, e.g., in the Market Square, school, and library close to the Mill where she passes-by the most. Others wanted connections with places they visited in the past (B1, O2). When asked if they would like to access the photos through other means, e.g., Facebook, or have more displays R5 and B1 chose more displays: R5 stated "just like it the way it is", while B1 stated that this would give him connection to more people.

Engagement During 12 Weeks From Interaction Logs

With the manual analysis conducted on the photos, described in the introduction of the 'findings' section, we got very crude information regarding when a user starts and ends interacting, as we would only get their interactions when they took a photo (and sometimes it would be just one photo). Also, this excludes any other interaction that did not result with a posted photo, e.g., interactions that included only browsing the photos or exploring the UI without saving a photo. In order to get more detailed insights into users' interactions, we automatically analyzed interaction log files, as we did not have video recordings of interactions (due to legal constraints). We analyzed the "pauses" between touch events – periods of inactivity – in order to find the best time for determining when an interaction session starts/ends. We compared automatically classified sessions with manually labeled photo sessions – ground truth – to see the match between the interaction sessions. We did so by comparing filenames of the photos in the automatic session with filenames of the photos in the manually labeled one: if both sessions had the same photos this was then classified as an exact match. We obtained best match with interaction pauses of 35 seconds having 69.05% of exact matches.

Session types and their properties are shown in Table 3. Besides exact matches we had three other types of sessions: 1) merged, i.e., two or more sessions that were manually labeled as different sessions were merged into one session in the automatic analysis (25.47%); or 2) they were split, i.e., manually labeled sessions were classified as multiple sessions in the automatic analysis (4.21%). A small portion was both 3) split and merged with another session (1.05%). Overall we classified 671 sessions that lasted on average 69 seconds (SEM 4 seconds). Majority of the sessions were photo sessions, i.e., 431 out of 671 (64.23%). Average photo sessions lasted 85 seconds (SEM 6 seconds), and had on average 2.76 photos (SEM 0.21 photos) and 36.67 scrolls (SEM 2.16) – number of times a user pressed the up or down arrow (5 in Figure 2). Out of 671 sessions 99 (14.75%) were "browsing only", i.e., users only scrolled and looked at the photos. These sessions on average lasted 72 seconds (SEM 10 seconds). There are also sessions that did not result with a photo nor were they browsing only (category "other" in Figure 8 and Figure 9).

Type	Property	Min	Max	Avg.	SEM
Photo sessions (overall)	Duration	3s	1216s	85s	6s
	Photos	1	45	2.76	0.21
	Scrolling	0	415	36.67	2.16
Exact match	Duration	3s	677s	63s	5s
	Photos	1	26	1.99	0.13
	Scrolling	1	246	32.82	1.79
Split	Duration	4s	623s	107s	18s
	Photos	1	18	3.25	0.5
	Scrolling	0	200	43.10	6.49
Merged	Duration	21s	1216s	201s	33s
	Photos	1	45	7.32	1.36
	Scrolling	0	415	46.07	9.04
Browse only	Duration	1s	207s	40s	3s
	Scrolling	1	415	35.94	3.14
Other	Duration	1s	161s	40s	3s

Table 3 - Session types and their properties: a) duration of the session is in seconds, b) photos in number of photos and c) scrolling in number of times "scroll" button was pressed

In Figure 8 and Figure 9 we show engagement with the application over 12 weeks and on a weekly basis respectively. The two graphs were obtained in the following way. After examining interaction events we determined there are periods with high and low interactivity that match different times of the day, i.e., morning (6AM – 12PM, low), afternoon (12PM – 6PM, high), evening (6PM – 12AM, high) and night (12AM – 6AM, low). In order to balance engagement between periods of high and low interactivity and have them in accordance, and in order to balance the varying/different amount of time the application was running in them we divided all daily interactions into the 4 above-mentioned periods and normalized the number of interactions in them by dividing the number of sessions for a period with the number of hours application was running in it. As application schedule changed 11 times and the application was not running always in all the periods we calculated the weighted sum of the average normalized number of sessions, in order to show user engagement with the application for a deployment week and for a day of the week. We want to note here that results on engagement are of a descriptive nature.

For Figure 8 the weighted sum of the average normalized number of sessions for a day was calculated in the following way: if the application was running 2 hours in the morning we divide the number of interaction sessions by 2. Then we calculate the average number of sessions for that period for that week. Lastly, we calculate a weighted sum of the averages to produce the one number shown in Figure 8. Here, weighting was done by multiplying the average normalized number of sessions for a period with a fraction representing how many times that period appeared in that week (e.g., if morning period appeared 2 times the average normalized number of sessions would be multiplied by 2/7). For example, this leads to 1.3 photo sessions in week 1 in Figure 8. We calculated similarly the daily engagement with the application in Figure 9. We calculate the average

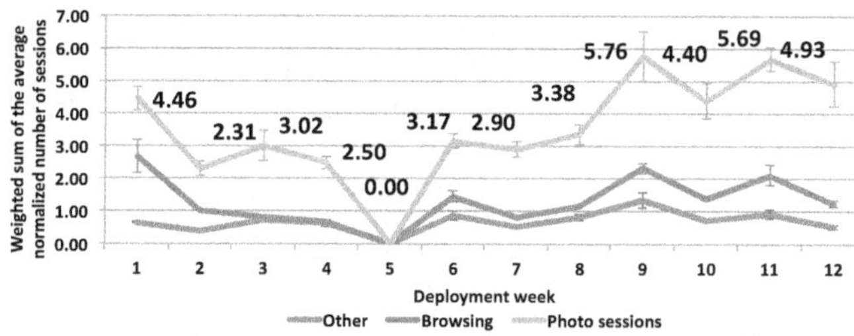

Figure 8 - Daily engagement with the Moment Machine application over 12 weeks. The stacked graph shows weighted average of the normalized number of sessions for a day.

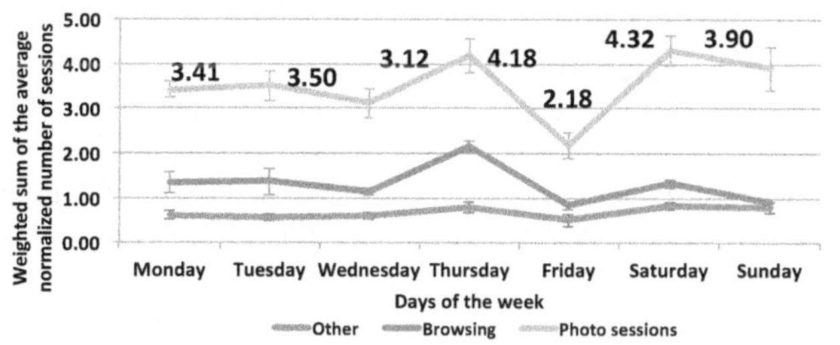

Figure 9 – Daily engagement with the Moment Machine application over a week. The stacked graph shows weighted average of the normalized number of sessions for a day.

normalized number of sessions for a period for a particular day of the week. Weighting is done by multiplying the average with the number of times that period appeared for that day of the week during the deployment.

As shown in Figure 8, user engagement with the application varied from 2.31 (week 2) to 5.76 interaction sessions (week 9). In the last four weeks of the deployment users engaged with the application more, and engagement ranged from 4.4 to 5.76 interaction sessions. In week 5, there were no sessions because the application was not running for 4 days that week, while there was no engagement in the remaining 3 days. One possible reason for no interaction during those 3 days is that it was Easter break during that week, meaning that people were on holidays. In Figure 9, we see that on a weekday the basis application usage ranged from 2.18 sessions on Friday to 4.32 sessions on Saturdays. On average the application was used more in the weekend (4.11 sessions) than in weekdays (3.28 sessions).

DISCUSSION

As we have outlined, the medium allowed very broad participation as "anyone feels like they can use [the application]" (O1) and content was seen as a public property: "this is your content" (R4). Because of the long-term deployment of Moment Machine, we can now reflect on three important aspects of its use, contributing to a growing body of design knowledge in the field. Firstly, we were able to see how user engagement fitted into users' daily routines and the rhythm of a place. Secondly, we can reflect on people's motivations emerging from one particular install location and finally, we discuss the relationship between community awareness and individual motivations for interacting with situated snapshots.

Engagement and Rhythm of Place

Our longitudinal study shows that this type of medium generates consistent usage following a startup period. Over the 12 weeks the number of interaction sessions grew from 2.31 (week 2) to 5.69 (week 11). When people have more time they will use the medium more, with more interaction sessions during the weekend compared to weekdays (4.11 vs. 3.28 sessions). Bucking this trend are school children who took 22% of all snapshots during the weekdays. An important behavior of users engagement is that returning users come back to interact, but you will not see them every day as they have breaks in their interactions (cf. Figure 4). To best of our knowledge behavior of returning users described in Figure 4 is the first description of returning users and the way they behave around interactive urban displays.

For designers, it will be essential to consider the extent to which an application fits into the rhythm of a particular place as interaction session on average are short – the overall average was 85 seconds (cf. Table 3). A consistent schedule brings benefits for this: Moment Machine analysis showed that nearly 50% of returning users returned at the same time, i.e., their return times did not vary much (for 35.48% of users STD is <=5 minutes and for 50.54% STD is <= 20 minutes). In addition, events near an install location can be considered as this generates increased use. The highest use of the application was during the Star Wars day event (5.76 sessions, week 9 in Figure 8) and in the longest session, 20 minutes and 18 seconds (cf. Table 3) 45 photos were taken. More generally, weekends might provide people with more time to 'play', while it is even more important to fit a schedule around the dominant user groups, for example school children in the case of Moment Machine. Deciding on the best schedule is a matter of careful observations at install locations in addition to drawing on local knowledge. For example R4 suggested that the application runs "9-10, 15-16, 17-19, give the chance for different kinds of people to use it, commuters, shoppers – drop their kids and run errands, after school for school kids."

On the other hand, if the application would run for the whole day over a certain period of time it could capture the rhythm of the place and passer-by as the application has a low threshold for interaction and taking situated snapshots is done willingly by the users (e.g., O1, "anyone feels like they can use [the application]"). This would allow capturing user demographics (cf. Figure 3) as well as when and how often users interact with a display, informing the design of other applications that could run on a display.

Motivations at Install Location

We uncovered 11 usage categories because of the unframed and open use of the application. The two most prominent were *action* (24.31%) and *portrait* (single 23.13% and group 22.2%). Photos in the category *action* were predominantly taken by the school kids, while single and group *portraits* can be associated with people wanting to convey positive image of themselves as they are part of the neighborhood and/or community located around the Mill. As U1 noted, she wanted to look the best in the photo, as she is a "perfectionist". The application stimulated play and imagination, especially for children, as shown by themes action (24.31%), facial expression (7.49%), and posing (8.49%). In this sense, the usage categories presented in Table 1 also reflect back at the community at a location.

Overall, designers need to consider the possible motivations for usage at each of the install locations for the main user groups as this can inform the design or suggestions for use of other applications. As highlighted above, motivations might derive from regular contact and play. For some people it became a standard group activity and part of a routine – strongest examples are R1, R2, and B4 who took the photos whenever they passed by the display: this can signal that similar applications that stimulate group play would be welcomed, e.g., [18, 19]. Desire to present one-self (well) to the public would be another motivation, telling us that similar applications that allow expression of one's or group's personality and interests are welcome, e.g., [1, 9, 12]. Or the motivation might be to leave a message, showing that applications like [11, 24] could be suitable.

Community Awareness and Photo Taking

A certain sense of community awareness emerged through the longer exposure of the people to the application. Interviewees reported on different levels of awareness, ranging from recognizing the most prominent group (R1) to having general knowledge of people who use the application. This behavior is also supported though session analysis – 99 sessions (14.75%) were browsing only and photo sessions on average had 36.67 scrolls (cf. Table 3). This shows that people were exposed to seeing pictures of others and posting a lot of photos resulted in greater visibility within the setting, as confirmed by R4, R5, and O2 who recognized R1.

Designers need to consider how to best harness the duality of the medium, where self-expression (taking a snapshot and browsing through one's own snapshots) is intertwined with the desire to see what others have been doing (browsing other people's snapshots). B2 summarized this behavior *"Certainly, if you see photos of other people instinctively you, well, I'm looking at you, well take a look at me and I want to look my best and that's the vanity thing."* This could be supported in a number of different ways. For example, the system might show bigger photos of top contributors, display the images for a longer period, or rank the photos in a certain way (likes or number of photos a person has taken). This form of highlighting the ways that one can leave a 'mark' on the location are then likely to increase awareness of the community, as it is captured through snapshots, while also increasing the motivation for people to take a snapshot of themselves. As mentioned previously, users could be incentivized to interact with the application by seeing photos of their interest and age group of preference, however this could hinder their overall awareness of diverse groups that are interacting with the urban screen, or in an extreme case cold even drive away certain age groups that are not presented enough.

In cases of multipurpose public displays where other applications and content are running they could benefit from this type of duality of the situated snapshots, e.g., while browsing through the photos users could see advertisement or previews of other applications and services that a display offers (e.g., ones that match users motivation as explained in previous subsection).

CONCLUSIONS AND FUTURE WORK

In this paper, we report on the first open longitudinal case study of how urban screens can be used for posting and viewing situated snapshots via a display-attached camera. We investigated the use of this novel medium "in the wild" in a community setting and report on the uptake and interactions over the course of 12 weeks. Our findings show how situated snapshots stimulate engagement within place-based communities and highlight aspects that inform the design of future systems. In future work, we will investigate how the application is used across the four locations.

ACKNOWLEDGMENTS

We thank Screens in the Wild team members and members of the UbiComp group from the University of Lugano. This research is partially funded by the UK DE Programme (grant EP/I031839/1 and EP/I031413/1) and the Future and Emerging Technologies (FET) programme within the 7th Frame-work Programme for Research of the European Commission, un-der FET-Open grant number: 244011.

REFERENCES

1. Brignull, H., and Rogers, Y. 2003. Enticing people to interact with large public displays in public spaces. In *Proceedings of INTERACT*. 17-24.
2. Clark, A. 2007. Understanding community: A review of networks, ties and contacts. NCRM Working Paper.
3. Fatah gen. Schieck, A, Fan. S. 2012. Connected urban spaces. In *Proceedings of Eighth International Space Syntax Symposium.*, Chile.
4. Fatah gen. Schieck, A., Schnädelbach, H., Penn, A. 2012. Research in the Wild: Exploring the potential of Networked Urban Screens for Communities and Culture. *In DIS 12 workshop: Research in the Wild: understanding 'in the wild' approaches to design and development, DIS 12*, Newcastle, UK.
5. Fortin, C., Neustaedter, C., and Hennessy, K. 2014. Posting for Community and Culture: Considerations for the Design of Interactive Digital Bulletin Boards. In *Proceedings of the 32nd annual ACM conference on Human factors in computing systems*. ACM, 1425-1434.
6. Hole in the Earth, http://bit.ly/1exeai0
7. Hole in Space, http://bit.ly/de6vOG

8. Hosio, S., Kostakos, V., Kukka, H., Jurmu, M., Riekki, J., and Ojala, T. 2012. From school food to skate parks in a few clicks: using public displays to bootstrap civic engagement of the young. In *Pervasive Computing*. Springer, 425-442.

9. Jose, R., Pinto, H., Silva, B., and Melro, A. 2013. Pins and posters: Paradigms for content publication on situated displays. *IEEE Computer Graphics and Applications 33*, 2, 64-72.

10. Kostakos, V. and Ojala, T. 2013. Public Displays Invade Urban Spaces. *IEEE Pervasive Computing* 12, 1, 8-13.

11. Lévesque, M., Be´langer, L., and Lewis, J. 2006. p2P: Cityspeak's reconfiguration of public media space. *Wisc. J. Mob. Digi. Comm. Net. 1*, 1.

12. McCarthy, J. F., Farnham, S. D., Patel, Y., Ahuja, S., Norman, D., Hazlewood, W. R., and Lind, J. 2009. Supporting community in third places with situated social software. In *Proceedings of the fourth international conference on Communities and technologies*. ACM, 225-234.

13. Memarovic, N., Cheverst, K., Langheinrich, M., Elhart, I., and Alt, F. 2013. Tethered or free to roam: The design space of limiting content access on community displays. In *Proceedings of the 2nd ACM International Symposium on Pervasive Displays*. ACM, 127-132.

14. Memarovic, N., gen Schieck, A. F., Kostopoulou, E., Behrens, M., and Traunmueller, M. 2013. Moment machine: Opportunities and challenges of posting situated snapshots onto networked public displays. In *Human-Computer Interaction–INTERACT 2013*. Springer, 595-602.

15. Memarovic, N., Langheinrich, M., Alt, F., Elhart, I., Hosio, S., and Rubegni, E. 2012. Using public displays to stimulate passive engagement, active engagement, and discovery in public spaces. In *Proceedings of the 4th Media Architecture Biennale Conference: Participation*. ACM, 55-64.

16. Memarovic, N., Langheinrich, M., Cheverst, K., Taylor, N., and Alt, F. 2013. P-LAYERS--A layered framework addressing the multifaceted issues facing community-supporting public display deployments. *ACM Transactions on Computer-Human Interaction (TOCHI) 20*, 3.

17. Memarovic, N., Langheinrich, M., Rubegni, E., David, A., and Elhart, I. 2012. Designing interacting places for a student community using a communicative ecology approach. In *Proceedings of the 11th International Conference on Mobile and Ubiquitous Multimedia*. ACM.

18. Müller, J., Eberle, D., and Tollmar, K. 2014. Communiplay: a field study of a public display mediaspace. In *Proceedings of the 32nd annual ACM conference on Human factors in computing systems*. ACM, 1415-1424.

19. Müller, J., Walter, R., Bailly, G., Nischt, M., and Alt, F. 2012. Looking glass: a field study on noticing interactivity of a shop window. In *Proceedings of the SIGCHI Conference on Human Factors in Computing Systems*. ACM, 297-306.

20. North, S., Schnädelbach, H., Fatah gen Schieck, A, Motta, W., Ye, L., Behrens, M., and Kostopoulou, E. 2013. Tension space analysis: Exploring community requirements for networked urban screens. In Human-Computer Interaction–INTERACT 2013. Springer, 81-98.

21. Motta, W., Fatah gen Schieck, A., Schnädelbach, H., Kostopoulou, E., Behrens, M., North, S., and Ye, L. 2013. Considering communities, diversity and the production of locality in the Design of Networked Urban Screens. In *Human-Computer Interaction–INTERACT 2013*. Springer, 315-322.

22. Ojala, T., Kukka, H., Lindén, T., Heikkinen, T., Jurmu, M., Hosio, S., and Kruger, F. 2010. UBI-hotspot 1.0: Large-scale long-term deployment of interactive public displays in a city center. In *Proceedings of Internet and Web Applications and Services (ICIW)*. IEEE, 285-294.

23. Peltonen, P., Salovaara, A., Jacucci, G., Ilmonen, T., Ardito, C., Saarikko, P., and Batra, V. 2007. Extending large-scale event participation with user-created mobile media on a public display. In *Proceedings of the 6th international conference on Mobile and ubiquitous multimedia*. ACM, 131-138.

24. Schroeter, R. 2012. Engaging new digital locals with interactive urban screens to collaboratively improve the city. In *Proceedings of the ACM Conference on Computer Supported Cooperative Work*. ACM, 227–236.

25. Telectroscope, http://www.telectroscope.net/

26. Taylor, N., and Cheverst, K. 2009. Social interaction around a rural community photo display. *International Journal of Human-Computer Studies* 67, 12, 1037-1047.

27. Wouters, N., Huyghe, J., and Vande Moere, A. 2013. OpenWindow: citizen-controlled content on public displays. In *Proceedings of the 2nd ACM International Symposium on Pervasive Displays*. ACM, 121-126.

Measuring Urban Deprivation from User Generated Content

Alessandro Venerandi
University College London
Gower Street
London WC1E 6BT, UK
alessandro.venerandi.12@ucl.ac.uk

Giovanni Quattrone
University College London
Gower Street
London WC1E 6BT, UK
g.quattrone@cs.ucl.ac.uk

Licia Capra
University College London
Gower Street
London WC1E 6BT, UK
l.capra@cs.ucl.ac.uk

Daniele Quercia
Yahoo Labs
Barcelona, Spain
dquercia@acm.org

Diego Saez-Trumper
Yahoo Labs
Barcelona, Spain
dsaez-trumper@acm.org

ABSTRACT

Measuring socioeconomic deprivation of cities in an accurate and timely fashion has become a priority for governments around the world, as the massive urbanization process we are witnessing is causing high levels of inequalities which require intervention. Traditionally, deprivation indexes have been derived from census data, which is however very expensive to obtain, and thus acquired only every few years. Alternative computational methods have been proposed in recent years to automatically extract proxies of deprivation at a fine spatio-temporal level of granularity; however, they usually require access to datasets (e.g., call details records) that are not publicly available to governments and agencies. To remedy this, we propose a new method to automatically mine deprivation at a fine level of spatio-temporal granularity that only requires access to freely available user-generated content. More precisely, the method needs access to datasets describing what urban elements are present in the physical environment; examples of such datasets are Foursquare and OpenStreetMap. Using these datasets, we quantitatively describe neighborhoods by means of a metric, called *Offering Advantage*, that reflects which urban elements are distinctive features of each neighborhood. We then use that metric to *(i)* build accurate classifiers of urban deprivation and *(ii)* interpret the outcomes through thematic analysis. We apply the method to three UK urban areas of different scale and elaborate on the results in terms of precision and recall.

Author Keywords

Empirical methods, quantitative analysis, socio-economics, user generated content, Foursquare, OpenStreetMap

CSCW 2015, March 14–18, 2015, Vancouver, BC, Canada.

http://dx.doi.org/10.1145/2675133.2675233

ACM Classification Keywords

H.2.8 Database Management: Database Applications—*Spatial Databases and GIS*; H.1.2 Models and Principles: User/Machine Systems—*Human information processing*

INTRODUCTION

The world is undergoing a process of fast urbanization and it is estimated that by 2050 6.2 billion people will live in cities (68% of the total global population) [9]. Although this process is supported by governments as it is expected to bring important advantages (e.g., better and less expansive public services, better living standards due to the concentration of economic activities) [30], recent research has also shown that inequality is dangerously on the rise, with some areas benefiting substantially more than others from public investments and economic growth [28]. Quantifying urban poverty promptly, and at a fine level of spatial granularity, has thus become a priority for governments worldwide, so to be able to monitor the impact of urbanization, and to make data-driven decisions as to how to allocate limited financial resources for regeneration projects.

Traditionally, socioeconomic deprivation has been measured using data acquired through household surveys; while such data is semantically rich, it is also very expensive to obtain and process. As a result, it is acquired with a rather low frequency that varies from few years for developed countries like the UK, to several years for developing countries like Cote d'Ivoire. To remedy this, computational social scientists have started to develop new methods that aim to automatically derive metrics of deprivation from alternative data sources, that afford finer spatio-temporal granularity than survey data. Data sources used to date span from call detail records (e.g., [10, 25, 40]), to satellite images (e.g., [11, 12, 29]), to transit data (e.g., [41]). A common limitation to all these methods is the reliance on datasets that are very difficult to obtain, thus severely limiting the applicability of the methods themselves.

In this paper, we propose a new method that aims at accurately computing urban deprivation at a fine-grained spatio-temporal granularity, while relying on easily accessible datasets. More precisely, in terms of datasets, our method relies on user-generated content that captures which urban features are present in a neighborhood. Examples of such datasets are Foursquare and OpenStreetMap. We made this choice inspired by qualitative works in the public health domain that have found important relationships between the presence of certain urban elements in a given area, and the socioeconomic well-being of its residents. For example, researchers have found that health-promoting amenities (e.g., golf courses in Australia [14], fitness centers and dance facilities in USA [32]) are more concentrated in well-off areas; on the contrary, potentially health-harmful resources (e.g., fast food outlets in England and Wales [8]) are more concentrated in poorer areas. From these datasets, our method automatically extracts a metric called *Offering Advantage* that intuitively reflects which urban elements are distinctive features of each neighborhood. Using correlation analysis, we prune down these features so to consider only those that are significantly correlated with urban deprivation; we then use those significant features to build classifiers of urban deprivation and finally, by means of thematic analysis, interpret the outcomes. We illustrate how to apply the method in practice in three UK urban areas of different scale (i.e., Greater London, Greater Manchester, West Midlands); finally, for these three case studies, we elaborate on the precision and recall of the results.

In the reminder of the paper, we first provide an overview of related works in this domain. We describe the datasets, and the method developed to leverage them. We then present the results of our evaluation, before concluding the paper with a discussion of implications, limitations and future work.

RELATED WORK

In an attempt to measure socioeconomic deprivation at a fine level of spatio-temporal granularity, researchers have started to develop computational methods that automatically mine a variety of data sources, looking for significant and strong signals of deprivation. To this end, three main sources of data have been used.

Call Detail Records (CDRs). These are records about calls and text messages measured by telecommunication providers for billing purposes. CDRs contain information about time, duration, caller ID, callee ID and location of the antenna tower through which the call or the text message is sent. Features extracted from these datasets have then been used to assess socioeconomic well-being of populations. A pioneering work in this domain has been conducted by Eagle *et al.* [10]; they studied the relationship between CDRs from land lines and mobile phones in England and the Index of Multiple Deprivation (IMD). Their results highlight a strong correlation between call network diversity and deprivation, confirming the hypothesis that having a varied set of contacts is a signal of socioeconomic well-being. A few years later, Mao *et al.* investigated the relationship between features of calls in Cote d'Ivoire and some economic indexes of ten areas of high economic activity [25]. They discovered that the ratio of outgoing calls per area, relative to the total of outgoing plus incoming calls, has high correlation with annual income. Smith *et al.* analyzed the same mobile phone dataset and found that features of network diversity and introversion (i.e., ratio of within-area calls vs. inter-area calls) strongly correlate with deprivation [40]. A common limitation to these studies is the difficulty to gain wide access to CDR data, as telecommunication operators do not tend to make that data publicly available.

Satellite imagery. A completely different approach has looked into analyzing patterns from satellite images, in order to map economic development. In particular, researchers have extracted a feature called Night Time Light (NTL) from images, that is, the total surface lit during night time. Elvidge *et al.* found a correlation between NTL and countries' Gross Domestic Product [11, 12]. Similarly, Noor *et al.* studied the relationship between NTL and a composite index of wealth for several administrative regions of some African countries [29]. The correlations found were initially high; however, more recent research showed far lower correlations. These findings suggest that, as the penetration of electrical lightning reaches saturation, the signal present in these datasets disappears. Satellite images are as hard to get as CDRs; furthermore, the methods seem only applicable in under-developed countries up to the point where electricity becomes a commodity.

Transit data. Another source of information which researchers have been analyzing to get insights into deprivation is urban transit data. Smith *et al.* [41] used Oyster Card data (i.e., electronic ticketing system capturing journeys made within the London public transport network) to derive features of mobility flow between areas, and of transport modality choice. They then used these features to build a classification model to identify highly deprived areas, as measured by the UK Index of Multiple Deprivation. Although the model achieves high prediction accuracy, it can only estimate deprivation for 10% of London (i.e., where a tube station is present). Furthermore, similar to works on CDRs data, this line of work requires access to datasets that are very difficult to get hold of (if available at all).

All lines of research above require access to datasets that are very difficult to get. An alternative approach is to rely on more easily accessible user-generated content (UGC) for the same purpose. User-generated content comes in a wide variety of forms, thanks to the big popularity and uptake of social media applications, especially in developed countries. These data sources have been used by researchers to develop a better understanding of our cities. For example, geo-coded tweets have been analyzed to quantify sentiment/mood, as it varies between neighborhoods of different socioeconomic standing [35]; Twitter has also been analyzed to investigate the relationship between the topic of discussion in a certain area, and the deprivation score of that area [38]; Foursquare check-ins have been used to redefine neighborhood boundaries, by categorizing different areas of a city through a clustering model that leverages similarity of urban functions, rather than using super-imposed administrative boundaries [7].

In line with this last stream of research, we propose to use user-generated content to mine urban deprivation. Inspired by previous qualitative works in the public health domain that found correlations between the presence of certain urban venues and deprivation [14, 32], we propose to automatically extract such urban features directly from easily accessible user-generated content datasets, specifically, Foursquare and OpenStreetMap. In the next section, we describe the datasets, before providing the details of our method.

DATASETS

To conduct this work, we needed access to two types of datasets: on one hand, indicators of socioeconomic deprivation at a fine-grained spatial granularity; on the other hand, detailed records of which physical elements are present in the built environment. We use the Index of Multiple Deprivation for the former, and both Foursquare and OpenStreetMap for the latter.

Index of Multiple Deprivation (IMD)

As measure of deprivation, we use the UK Index of Multiple Deprivation (IMD),[1] computed at the level of small census areas known as Lower-layer Super Output Areas (LSOAs). LSOAs were defined to roughly include always the same number of inhabitants (around 1.500) [27]. IMD is a composite score, calculated as the weighted means of seven distinct domains: income deprivation, employment deprivation, health deprivation, education deprivation, barrier to housing and services, crime, and living environment deprivation. The higher the IMD score, the more deprived the neighborhood, and viceversa; overall, IMD scores follows a normal distribution [27]. For the purpose of our study, we collected IMD scores for three UK urban areas that differ in terms of population size and geographic span, so to test the applicability of our approach to case studies of different scales. Those are: Greater London, Greater Manchester, and West Midlands.

We chose Greater London as an example of large metropolitan city. Greater Manchester and West Midlands are both examples of mid-size cities instead, albeit with a rather different population density. General information about these cities is provided in Table 1.[2]

Urban area	*Population*	*Density*	*Area*
Greater London	8,204,100	5,218 ppl per km^2	1,572 km^2
Greater Manchester	2,685,400	2,105 ppl per km^2	1,276 km^2
West Midlands	2,738,100	3,039 ppl per km^2	902 km^2

Table 1. Population, population density, and area for the three UK urban areas.

Foursquare

Foursquare is a mobile social-networking application launched in 2009 and is also one of the most popular location-based social-networking websites.[3] In Foursquare, when registered users visit a venue, they can 'check-in' on the mobile application to share their location with their friends. In April 2012, Foursquare reported 20 million registered users, with more than 2 billion check-ins [20]. Aside from checking-in at existing venues, Foursquare users can also create new ones. Possible conflicts in the definition of venues are solved in a bottom-up fashion: the more accurate a description, the more likely users will be able to recognize (check-in to) it. Foursquare then attempts to merge multiple descriptions that are likely to refer to the same venue using a Venue Harmonization procedure,[4] which includes the use of developer-contributed geographic databases. At the minimum level, each venue needs to be defined by a pair of latitude/longitude coordinates, a name, and a category (e.g., Church, School, Pub). Janne Lindqvist *et al.* have recently studied why people check-in and found five factors, one of which is particularly relevant to the creation of places [22]: individuals tend to use Foursquare to see where they have been in the past and ultimately curate their own location history. In cities where Foursquare has high penetration, the venues recorded in this service should thus collectively form a well-curated land use dataset. For the purpose of this work, we use the official Foursquare API to crawl all Foursquare venues for the three UK urban areas under consideration.[5] We performed this step between 04/03/2014 and 08/04/2014; a summary of the dataset obtained is reported in Table 2. Given that the three cities show different orders of magnitude in the number of venues, applying our method to them is likely to translate into interesting insights about our method's applicability to different urban contexts.

Urban area	*# Venues*	*# Check-ins*	*# Categories*
Greater London	178.756	26.344.132	503
Greater Manchester	43.874	3.235.174	421
West Midlands	37.370	2.424.546	435

Table 2. Number of Foursquare venues, number of check-ins, and number of Foursquare categories across the three UK urban areas.

OpenStreetMap

OpenStreetMap (OSM) is perhaps one of the most successful examples of geographic crowd-sourcing, with currently over 1.6M users, collectively building a free, openly accessible, editable map of the world.[6] OSM data covers three types of spatial objects: *nodes*, *ways*, and *relations*. Nodes broadly refer to Points of Interests (POIs), ways are representative of roads, and relations are used to group together other objects (e.g., administrative boundaries, bus routes). For the purpose of this study, only nodes are relevant. Similar to Foursquare venues, an OSM node consists of three main attributes: a geographical position (latitude and longitude), a name, and a category (called amenity type in OSM jargon). Differently from Foursquare, OSM categories are not chosen through a given taxonomy, and contributors are free to use whatever words they find most suitable. We downloaded OSM node data for the three cities under consideration on 07/05/2014; summary statistics are provided in Table 3.

Urban area	*# Nodes*	*# Categories*
Greater London	79.343	896
Greater Manchester	24.321	381
West Midlands	27.885	465

Table 3. Number of OSM nodes and number of OSM categories across the three UK urban areas.

Preliminary analysis on Foursquare and OSM datasets for Greater London (Figure 1) shows that categories follow a

[1] `https://www.gov.uk/government/uploads/system/uploads/attachment_data/file/6871/1871208.pdf`

[2] `http://www.ons.gov.uk/ons/dcp171778_270487.pdf`

[3] `https://foursquare.com/about`

[4] `https://developer.foursquare.com/overview/mapping`

[5] `https://api.foursquare.com`

[6] `http://download.geofabrik.de/`

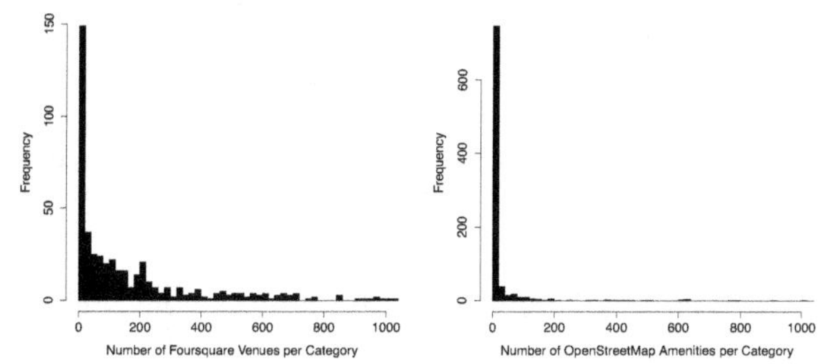

Figure 1. Frequency distribution of Foursquare categories (left) and OSM categories (right).

long-tailed distribution, with few categories having large number of venues/nodes, and many categories with very few venues/nodes instead. Furthermore, we notice that, although Foursquare and OSM conceptually provide the same kind of information (e.g., physical elements present in the urban environment), their users map different things. In fact, while the most frequent Foursquare categories are restaurants, pubs and cafes, the most frequent OSM categories are bus stops, crossings and post boxes. This is not surprising, given the fundamentally different purposes behind these services: Foursquare is mainly used to share locations with which users like to be associated; conversely, OSM is mainly used to capture in full what is present in the world. Our work takes advantage from the complimentary nature of these two UGC datasets, as we hypothesize that more accurate area profilers can be built by combining the peculiarities of the two datasets, rather than using them in isolation, thus potentially unveiling a broader set of features that correlate with urban deprivation.

METHOD

In this section, we describe the method we have developed to estimate urban deprivation from UGC data (Foursquare and OSM in particular). We begin with a description of the adopted spatial unit of analysis, and of the motivation behind this choice. We then define the metric implemented to automatically extract, from UGC data, the urban features characterizing these spatial units. Finally, we provide a step-by-step description of how to apply our method in practice: from correlation analysis to identify urban features related to deprivation, to classifiers to estimate deprivation levels, to thematic analysis to interpret results.

Unit of Analysis

The goal of this work is to measure the socioeconomic deprivation of different areas within a city by capturing the urban elements that are physically present in each neighborhood. To do so, we need to define a spatial unit of analysis that is representative of a city neighborhood. As mentioned in the previous section, IMD is available at a fine-grained spatial granularity, that of LSOAs. However, these units, which have been introduced relatively recently (in 2001), are too small and too arbitrarily defined to be meaningful to urban residents. Indeed, we calculated the average LSOA for Greater London to be no bigger than 33 hectares; furthermore, they are identified through alphanumeric codes (e.g., E01008881) which do not represent neighborhoods as recognized by citizens. We therefore choose a different spatial unit called *ward*. Wards have a much longer history compared to LSOAs (they have existed since the Middle Ages). Wards are defined by the UK Government[7] and represent both electoral subdivisions and ceremonial entities; their geographic extension exceeds that of the LSOAs with an average area size for Greater London of about 250 hectares. Finally, wards are identified through human-understandable toponyms (e.g., Highgate). For all these reasons, we argue that wards, more than LSOAs, are good representations of citizens' neighborhoods. Using official geographic definitions of wards in the UK,[8] we computed 625 wards for Greater London, 215 for Greater Manchester and 163 for West Midlands. For simplicity, in the next sections we will refer to wards as 'neighborhoods'.

Offering Advantage Metric

Having defined our spatial unit of analysis, we now need to profile each ward in terms of the urban features that characterize it. In doing so, we aim to capture not just what urban elements are physically present in a neighborhood, but more importantly what elements make it distinct with respect to other neighborhoods. As shown in the previous section, some categories are much more frequent than others, so that a simple count of what amenities are present is not sufficient to elicit distinctiveness. Rather, we propose to use a metric called *Offering Advantage*, which weights categories by their popularity; intuitively, the presence of one element from an unpopular category is much more significant in profiling a neighborhood than the presence of one element from a very popular category. In practice, this measure relies on a concept used in economics called Revealed Comparative Advantage (RCA) [17]. This is used to measure whether a country exports more of good i (as a share of its total exports), than the average country; if so, then $RCA > 1$.

The RCA of a country c is usually evaluated with this formulation:

$$RCA_{c,i} = \frac{goods_{c,i}}{goods_c} \cdot \frac{world}{world_i}$$

where $goods_{c,i}$ denotes how many goods i are exported by country c; $goods_c$ denotes the total number of goods exported by the country c; $world$ is the total number of goods exported all around the world; finally, $world_i$ indicates how many goods i are exported all around the world.

In our context, this measure reflects to what extent a neighborhood n_k provides more (Foursquare/OSM) POIs of a certain category c_i than the average neighborhood. More specifically:

$$OA(c_i, n_k) = \frac{count(c_i, n_k)}{\sum_{j=1}^{N} count(c_j, n_k)} \cdot \frac{\sum_{j=1}^{N} count(c_j)}{count(c_i)}$$

[7] `http://www.ons.gov.uk/ons/guide-method/geography/beginner-s-guide/administrative/england/electoral-wards-divisions/index.html`

[8] `https://geoportal.statistics.gov.uk/Docs/Boundaries/Wards_(E+W)_2011_Boundaries_(Full_Extent).zip`

where $OA(c_i, n_k)$ denotes the *Offering Advantage* of a (Foursquare/OSM) POI category c_i in the neighborhood n_k; $count(c_i, n_k)$ counts how may POIs of category c_i are present in the neighborhood n_k; N is the total number of (Foursquare/OSM) POI categories; finally, $count(c_i)$ counts how many (Foursquare/OSM) POIs of category c_i are present in the whole urban area. This metric has been recently used in a preliminary study on a Foursquare dataset for Greater London [37] and showed to provide better association with deprivation compared to a raw count of number of POIs for each category in a ward. We thus rely on the same metric to study deprivation and we apply it on two datasets of user generated content and on three cities.

Approach

Having defined our spatial unit of analysis (i.e., UK wards) and the metric we use to quantitatively profile these areas (i.e., *Offering Advantage*), we can now describe our proposed approach.

Correlation Analysis to Identify Significant Urban Features

Each area (ward) is described by a vector that reports the OA metric for each Foursquare/OSM POI category in that area. Although there are several hundred POI categories, not all of them will bear significant signals of deprivation. For example, the very same POI category (e.g., school) may be equally present in well-off and deprived wards. To filter out all those categories that do not consistently signal deprivation within the urban area under consideration, we use correlation analysis between the OA metric automatically derived from user-generated content, and the Index of Multiple Deprivation (IMD) that acts as ground truth in this context. To do so, the following three steps had to be performed: first, we had to reconcile the spatial unit of analysis at which IMD is available (i.e., LSOA), with the spatial unit of analysis used in this work (i.e., ward). We did so by computing the IMD score of a ward as the average of the IMD scores of the LSOAs it spatially contains. One may wonder if, by doing so, we cause significant data loss and inaccuracies. We found this not to be the case, since deprivation scores for LSOAs which belong to the same ward are very consistent (the standard deviation of IMD values related to LSOAs contained within wards is smaller than the corresponding average value, for all wards).

Second, since we are dealing with geographical data, we had to address the problem of spatial auto-correlation in our data. This, in fact, can lead to incorrect conclusions. Spatial auto-correlation is the tendency for measurements located close to each other to be correlated, a property that generally holds for variables observed across geographic spaces [21]. In broader terms, this is the direct quantitative demonstration of Tobler's First Law of Geography, which states that 'everything is related to everything else, but near things are more related than distant things' [43]. When high spatial auto-correlation occurs, traditional metrics of correlation (e.g., Pearson and Spearman) that require independence in the observations cannot be applied. We tested our data for spatial auto-correlation and we found it to be indeed high. To overcome this problem, we used a method familiar to natural scientists [15] and introduced by Clifford *et al.* [6]. This approach addresses the 'redundant, or duplicated, information contained in geo-referenced data' [16] – the effect of spatial auto-correlation – through the calculation of a reduced effective sample size. The significance of the correlation coefficients presented in the next section is obtained through the implementation of Clifford *et al.*'s method, partly accounting for spatial auto-correlations.

Third and lastly, since we are performing simultaneous correlation tests with multiple variables (i.e., our POI categories), the chance of incorrectly rejecting the null hypothesis for some of these variables (and thus of obtaining false positive results), increases. To quantify this threat, we implement a statistical control technique commonly used among researchers dealing with datasets comprising a large number of distinct variables (e.g., in genomics) called False Discovery Rate (FDR) [42]. In practice, the method analyses the distribution of p-values of the tested variables, and produces a list of so-called q-values, each varying between 0 and 1, indicating the expected proportion of false discoveries within the list of findings. In the next section, we will report q-values, computed using the FDR method, over the list of variables found to be significantly correlated when using the Clifford *et al.* correlation method.

Note that there exists a temporal discrepancy between the IMD dataset (2011), and the Foursquare/OSM datasets (2014). We expect this discrepancy to have limited impact on the findings we will report in the next section, as IMD values did not significantly vary in the last two reporting periods (i.e., 2008 and 2011).

Classification Tool of Deprivation

Once we have identified the POI categories that correlate with deprivation in the urban areas, we can then build a classifier of deprivation. One might wonder what the advantage of such a classifier is, if we still need IMD scores to be able to identify what urban features signal deprivation in the first place. We envision two uses of this approach that would make it more affordable than running citywide household surveys every (few) year(s): a first approach would require the completion of household surveys only in a small subset (e.g., 25%) of the city neighborhoods; our method would then apply correlations analysis to derive features upon which to build classifiers for the remaining (e.g., 75%) areas. A second approach would see the completion of citywide household surveys, from which to compute IMD scores manually, only once every several years: at these times, correlation analysis would be conducted. Once this is done, for the several years in between surveys, the classifiers would then be used to estimate deprivation at no extra cost. This second approach is based on the assumption that, although the deprivation score of an area may vary year by year (e.g., as a result of processes of urbanization, migration, and gentrification), the relationship between deprivation scores and urban features is much more stable; that is, certain POI types remain concentrated where wealth – or deprivation – is higher (although we do not know whether that is because people move towards area with certain POI types, or because areas with some POI types attract people of certain economic status, or both).

Thematic Analysis to Derive Significant Themes

The correlation analysis potentially identifies tens of Foursquare/OSM POI categories that are associated with deprivation; some of these might be redundant (e.g., bus, bus stop), and some others might be due to chance. The outcome of the classification tool built atop of these categories might thus be fragmented and difficult to interpret. To avoid this, our proposed method requires the application of inductive thematic analysis [4] to the filtered Foursquare/OSM POI categories, so to group together those categories that are semantically related. The result is a very small set of meta features, or themes, that represent simple and distinctive urban characters.

In the next section, we apply our method to three UK urban areas of different scale (i.e., Greater London, Greater Manchester, West Midlands), and discuss precision and recall of the results.

RESULTS

We first illustrate the results of the correlation analysis that is carried out to identify which POI categories (out of the hundreds present in Foursquare and OSM) are significantly associated with deprivation. Second, we build classification tools based on the identified categories, and assess their accuracy compared to a baseline classifier and to a state-of-the-art approach. Finally we illustrate which meta-features emerged from the thematic analysis.

Finding Signals of Deprivation

We explore to what extent we can exploit land use data extracted from user-generated content to get useful insights about the socioeconomic status of city neighborhoods. To this end, we calculated *Offering Advantage* for all Foursquare and OSM categories for each urban area and, through the Spearman's rank correlation coefficient r_s, we correlated it with IMD. Tables 4 and 5 show the number of Foursquare and OSM categories correlated (positively or negatively) with IMD, grouped by strength of correlation. From the analysis of these two tables, we highlight two important observations: first, there is a higher number of categories significantly correlated with deprivation in Foursquare than in OSM; this suggests that most OSM categories are conceptually less associated with socioeconomic aspects of cities. Second, the number of weak-to-moderately correlated categories ($r_s \in [0.2, 0.4)$ or ($r_s \in [0.4, 0.6)$) is high across all cities (15 categories for Greater London, 24 for Greater Manchester, and 34 for West Midlands), suggesting there is indeed a wealth of urban features we can mine from UGC to study deprivation for cities of different scales (in terms of area size, population, and user-generated content). Tables 6 and 7 show the top three categories most positively and most negatively correlated with IMD, using Foursquare and OSM data respectively. Note that, while Foursquare categories provide detailed information about services and facilities (e.g., Student Center, Caribbean), OSM categories tend to give more information about road system elements (e.g., traffic signals, crossing). The two datasets thus offer complimentary information at times, and they should thus be studied together.

	$\lvert r_s\rvert \in [0.05, 0.2)$	$\lvert r_s\rvert \in [0.2, 0.4)$	$\lvert r_s\rvert \in [0.4, 0.6)$
Greater London	23	15	0
Greater Manchester	30	24	0
West Midlands	17	33	1

Table 4. Number of Foursquare POI categories (positively or negatively) correlated with IMD (all results shown are statistically significant, $p < 0.05$)

	$\lvert r_s\rvert \in [0.05, 0.2)$	$\lvert r_s\rvert \in [0.2, 0.4)$	$\lvert r_s\rvert \in [0.4, 0.6)$
Greater London	4	2	0
Greater Manchester	1	4	0
West Midlands	1	9	0

Table 5. Number of OSM POI categories (positively or negatively) correlated with IMD (all results shown are statistically significant, $p < 0.05$)

To quantify the expected proportion of false discoveries among the previously identified POI categories, we then followed our proposed methodology and applied the FDR control technique. More precisely, we first ranked our variables by their p-values (from the lowest to the highest), and then computed q-values on the ranked list. Table 8 shows summary results: for each dataset (Foursquare and OSM), and for each city under study (Greater London, Greater Manchester and West Midlands), we report the computed q-values for each quartile of the (ranked) variables. Let us consider Foursquare-related results first: the expected proportion of false positive correlations is less than 9% across all POI categories considered significant for Greater Manchester, and at most 20% for West Midlands. For Greater London, the expected proportion is at most 14% for half of the discovered variables (those with lowest p), though it increases to 40% when looking at the whole set. Results for OSM-related variables are less promising instead: with the exception of West Midlands, where the q values are low over the entire set of variables, for Greater London up to 63% of the findings are expected to be false discoveries, and up to 41% for Greater Manchester. For the purpose of the present study, the Foursquare dataset would thus appear more suited; indeed, the majority of significant POI categories, and the themes derived from them (which we are going to present next), come from Foursquare.

Building Classifiers of Deprivation

We now test whether we can exploit land use data extracted from user generated content to build accurate classifiers of urban deprivation. As we pointed out in the Method section, there are two possible ways to carry out this task: conducting household surveys on a small subset of city neighborhoods and estimating deprivation for the remaining ones; or conducting citywide surveys in one year and estimate deprivation for the subsequent ones. We evaluate the former approach next (we cannot test the latter, as we do not have UGC for different time steps). We proceeded as follows: we selected Greater London as case study (similar results were obtained for Greater Manchester and West Midlands), and divided IMD values into ten deciles, adhering to the methodology applied in the official IMD document [27]. We then randomly split our data in 25% train and 75% of test, thus obtaining 156 neighborhoods for the train test and 469 neighborhoods for the test set respectively. We then built a variety of classifiers that take in input the *Offering Advantage* values of the Foursquare/OSM POI categories that show statistically

	Greater London	*Greater Manchester*	*West Midlands*
Top positively correlated	Caribbean (0.37)	Bus Station (0.32)	Car Wash (0.38)
	African (0.32)	Residential (0.27)	Temple (0.34)
	Fried Chicken (0.31)	Student Centre (0.24)	Desserts (0.32)
Top negatively correlated	Indian (-0.27)	Italian (-0.36)	Golf Course (-0.42)
	Italian (-0.26)	Golf Course (-0.28)	Salon Barbershop (-0.35)
	Golf Course (-0.24)	Gastropub (-0.26)	Farm (-0.31)

Table 6. Foursquare categories most (positively and negatively) correlated with IMD. In parentheses, the Spearman correlation values (at statistical significance $p < 0.05$) computed with the Clifford *et al.* method are shown.

	Greater London	*Greater Manchester*	*West Midlands*
Top positively correlated	traffic signals (0.29)	traffic signals (0.25)	tram stop (0.31)
	crossing (0.25)	taxi (0.24)	billboard (0.29)
	community center (0.18)		artwork (0.29)
Top negatively correlated	parking (-0.14)	post box (-0.26)	parking (-0.30)
	garden center (-0.10)	kindergarten (-0.22)	
		restaurant (-0.18)	

Table 7. OSM categories most (positively and negatively) correlated with IMD. In parentheses, the Spearman correlation values (at statistical significance $p < 0.05$) computed with the Clifford *et al.* method are shown.

Dataset	*Urban area (# categories)*	*1st Qu.*	*Median*	*3rd Qu.*	*Max.*
Foursquare	Greater London (35)	0.04	0.14	0.30	0.40
	Greater Manchester (54)	0.02	0.03	0.05	0.09
	West Midlands (50)	0.06	0.10	0.14	0.20
OSM	Greater London (6)	0.32	0.32	0.63	0.63
	Greater Manchester (5)	0.20	0.21	0.31	0.41
	West Midlands (10)	0.07	0.07	0.14	0.14

Table 8. q-values per quartiles of POI categories, computed using the False Discovery Rate technique.

significant (positive or negative) correlations with IMD values in the training set. Next, we present results obtained using a Naive Bayes classifier – the classifier that, among the tested ones (i.e., Decision Tree j48, Logistic Regression), showed the best performance.

Classification accuracy results are shown in Table 9. We note that the highest Precision and Recall values are obtained for classes a and j, which represent the 10% least deprived and the 10% most deprived neighborhoods. This suggests that our method is most suitable to identify and monitor problematic areas, while performing less well for middle cases. Also, at first glance, Precision and Recall are not particularly high in absolute values. However, in almost all cases, the predicted class only differs of a few positions (two or three) from the actual one, as evidenced by the Confusion Matrix reported in Table 10.

Precision	*Recall*	*F-Measure*	*Class*
0.320	0.356	0.337	a: 10% more deprived
0.189	0.227	0.206	b: from 10% to 20% more deprived
0.200	0.137	0.163	c: from 20% to 30% more deprived
0.135	0.102	0.116	d: from 30% to 40% more deprived
0.125	0.067	0.087	e: from 40% to 50% more deprived
0.143	0.080	0.103	f: from 50% to 60% more deprived
0.165	0.357	0.226	g: from 60% to 70% more deprived
0.194	0.255	0.220	h: from 70% to 80% more deprived
0.214	0.115	0.150	i: from 80% to 90% more deprived
0.262	0.364	0.305	j: from 90% to 100% more deprived

Table 9. Classification accuracy of urban deprivation for Greater London. IMD is subdivided in 10 bins.

At this point, one may wonder how our proposed method performs compared to both state-of-the-art approaches (e.g., [10, 25, 40]) and simpler benchmarks derived from UGC datasets.

a	b	c	d	e	f	g	h	i	j	← classified as
16	11	5	3	3	1	2	1	0	3	a: 10% more deprived
10	10	4	4	4	0	7	3	1	1	b: from 10% to 20% more deprived
4	9	7	7	3	4	7	4	3	3	c: from 20% to 30% more deprived
7	4	4	5	3	3	17	2	2	2	d: from 30% to 40% more deprived
2	6	5	2	3	2	11	6	3	5	e: from 40% to 50% more deprived
4	4	6	2	1	4	12	4	4	9	f: from 50% to 60% more deprived
0	5	0	3	2	4	15	6	1	6	g: from 60% to 70% more deprived
2	3	1	5	1	3	11	12	3	6	h: from 70% to 80% more deprived
4	1	3	2	3	5	4	14	6	10	i: from 80% to 90% more deprived
1	0	0	4	1	2	5	10	5	16	j: from 90% to 100% more deprived

Table 10. Confusion Matrix associated with our classification model.

To answer the former, we compare our classification results with those reported in [40], where public transit data was used to estimate deprivation for Greater London, using the same ground truth data (IMD published in 2011) we rely upon. To ease comparison, since the work in [40] divided the IMD distribution in two bins only (i.e., below and above the median value), we re-computed our classification using these two bins separated by the median value as output. To address the latter, we built a simple benchmark that estimates deprivation of a London ward by means of a Naive Bayes classifier that takes in input the number of Foursquare check-ins, the number of Foursquare POIs, and the number of OSM POIs present in that area; the intuition behind this benchmark is that, the higher the number of check-ins and POIs in a ward, the less deprived the ward is.

Table 11 shows results for our model, together with the performance gain over the basic benchmark. Our model reaches a Precision between 0.763 (for above-median deprivation) and 0.713 (for below-median deprivation); the best performing classifier presented in [40] achieved an overall Precision of 0.805; however, note that such result only holds for 10% of the wards in London (where a tube station is present), while our results cover the whole of Greater London. By taking these two observations together, we argue that the performance of our classifier is indeed comparable to state-of-the-art approaches that require access to datasets that are not publicly available. As for the performance of our model compared to the simpler benchmark, we observe significant improvements (shown in parentheses in Table 11) for both Precision and Recall in both classification classes. This result demonstrates the suitability of the *Offering Advantage* metric over simple counts of check-ins and POIs.

Precision	*Recall*	*F-Measure*	*Class*
0.763 (+41%)	0.692 (+17%)	0.726 (+28%)	50% more deprived
0.713 (+37%)	0.780 (+39%)	0.745 (+38%)	50% less deprived

Table 11. Classification accuracy of urban deprivation for Greater London. IMD is subdivided in 2 bins. In parenthesis, the percentage difference w.r.t. the results of a basic benchmark is shown.

Deriving Themes

The previous results show that our method has competitive classification accuracy. To interpret those results, we conduct a thematic analysis [4] of the POI categories identified through correlation analysis, and group them together in coherent themes. The analysis consisted of three iterations, separately conducted by an urban designer and a computer scientist. In the first iteration, the whole set of POI categories was scanned and initial codes were generated; this was followed

Themes	*Category*	*Greater London*	*Greater Manchester*	*West Midlands*
		Foursquare		
Health harmful food	Fried Chicken	0.31	0.15	0.19
	Fast Food		0.22	0.31
	Wings	0.11		
Faith	Mosque	0.27	0.22	
	Church	-0.18	-0.15	
Non-local cuisines	African	0.32		0.25
	Caribbean	0.37		0.21
	Asian			0.23
	Italian	-0.26	-0.36	-0.25
	Indian	-0.27	-0.17	
	Spanish		-0.20	
	Chinese		-0.22	
Beauty & aesthetics	Dentist's Office	-0.22	-0.21	-0.15
	Nail Salon		-0.17	-0.19
	Salon Barbershop	-0.15		-0.35
Sports	Golf Course	-0.24	-0.28	-0.42
	Cricket	-0.13		-0.23
	Tennis Court		-0.23	
Open spaces	Other Outdoors	-0.15	-0.24	-0.25
	Lake	-0.12	-0.13	
	Campground		-0.22	-0.23
	Field	-0.15	-0.23	
	Playground		-0.22	
	Trail		-0.21	
	Outdoors and Recreation		-0.14	
Bus service	Bus	0.15		0.23
	Bus Station	0.28	0.32	
	Bus Stop	0.18		
		OSM		
Road system elements	traffic signals	0.29	0.25	
	crossing	0.25		
	mini roundabout			0.24

Table 12. Spearman correlation values r_s between Foursquare and OSM categories considered by the thematic analysis and IMD (all results shown are statistically significant, $p < 0.05$).

by merging semantically-related codes into broader themes using relevant urban studies as guidance; finally, identified themes were refined and named. In the end, a total of eight common themes were identified: (derived from Foursquare) *health harmful food*, *faith*, *non-local cuisines*, *beauty & aesthetics*, *sports*, *open spaces*, and *bus service*; (derived from OSM) *road system elements*. Table 12 shows the Foursquare and OSM categories related to each theme, along with the Spearman correlation values for each category within these theme, computed through the Clifford *et al.* method [6] between their *Offering Advantage* and IMD. Note that these correlation values are only valid for the three cities under study; as these three cities belong to the same country, it is not surprising that values for the same POI category are similar across them. However, if we were to apply this method to other cities in the world, the same POI category could bear opposite correlation with deprivation. While correlation findings are expected to differ, the same method could still be applied to other urban contexts, as long as UGC is available. We next briefly elaborate on each of the derived themes; in most cases, to gain confidence in their validity, we mention similar results in the literature.

Health harmful food

We created this theme to include all the Foursquare venues that are related with restaurants selling unhealthy food. These are Fried Chicken, Fast Food and Wings. Those venues are positively associated with neighborhoods with IMD scores above the median. This finding is consistent with some studies in preventive medicine: using qualitative investigations, MacDonald *et al.* found that the higher the density of chain fast-food restaurants, the higher the neighborhood deprivation for England and Scotland [8]. Other studies have been carried out in New Zealand [31] and in the USA [2] and found similar results, thus suggesting the same correlation sign for this theme could be found in cities within these other countries too.

Faith

This theme includes two Foursquare venues: Mosque and Church. However, the two bear opposite correlation with deprivation: mosques tend to have higher concentration in areas with IMD above the median, while churches are more concentrated in areas with IMD below the median. Previous research has shown that there is a link between high concentrations of Muslim residents in London wards and below the median IMD values [5]. This seems to be consistent with part of our finding; however it is also true that Muslims might not live where their places of worship are located. To ascertain this missing point, we studied the relationship between the percentage of Muslims living in a certain area (relative to the total number of religious people in that area) and the *Offering Advantage* for the Foursquare category Mosque. We did so by extracting information from the Census Data 2011 for Greater London at the level of ward.[9] We indeed found a positive correlation between the presence of mosques in a neighborhood and percentages of Muslim residents in it ($r_s = 0.40$, $p < 0.01$). This seems to be congruent with the hypothesis that neighborhoods with Muslim predominance, which are generally associated with above-median IMD values in Greater London [5], have a higher-than-normal number of mosques.

Non-local cuisines

We created this theme to include all Foursquare venues that are related to restaurants but exclude those covering local cuisine (i.e., Pub, Fish & Chips Shop, English Restaurant), as the latter did not bear strong correlation with IMD. Within this broad theme, we identified two sub-themes: one comprising cuisines that, in the cities under consideration, had positive correlation with deprivation (e.g., African, Asian and Caribbean), and one comprising cuisines that, once again for the three cities under consideration, had negative correlation with deprivation (e.g., Italian, Chinese, Spanish, Indian).

Beauty & aesthetics

This theme comprises three Foursquare venues: Dentist, Nail Salon and Salon Barbershop. All these categories are negatively correlated with IMD, suggesting that beauty and aesthetics facilities concentrate in neighborhoods with IMD below the median. We found a reference to this finding for the category Dentist's Office. Previous studies have, in fact, demonstrated that high socioeconomic status is significantly associated with good oral health [23]; our results seem to be congruent with those findings. However, this is an example of a finding that may not generalise to other geographic contexts: for example, previous research has found a link between the prevalence of beauty salons in areas of the USA and their socio-economic deprivation [39]. Note that, although

[9] `http://www.nomisweb.co.uk/census/2011/ks209ew`

the finding itself might not generalise, the methodology we propose to discover whether this is indeed the case remains the very same.

Sports
This theme includes all the Foursquare categories related with physical activity facilities. These are Golf Course, Cricket and Tennis Court. These venues are negatively correlated with deprivation, suggesting that sport facilities tend to be concentrated in areas with low IMD scores. Previous qualitative studies are consistent with this finding: researchers found that golf courses in Australia [14], fitness centers and dance facilities in the USA [32] tend to be more commonly available in wealthier areas.

Open spaces
We create this theme to include all the Foursquare facilities related to public open spaces. These are Lake, Outdoors and Recreation, Playground, Campground, Trail, Field and Other Outdoors. All these categories are negatively correlated with deprivation. Previous studies are congruent with these results and found similar outcomes for the Netherlands [24], in Howard County, USA [13] and for Portland, USA [3].

Bus service
This theme includes the Foursquare categories for Bus, Bus Stop and Bus Station. These venues are positively correlated with deprivation; their concentration in an area is thus signal of higher than average deprivation. This finding is consistent with a recent report issued by Transport for London that shows that, for Greater London, the share of bus trips increases with the decrease of household incomes [44].

Road system elements
This theme includes all the OSM amenity types related with the traffic management system. These are traffic signals, crossings (i.e., elements which guarantee safe pedestrian crossing) and mini roundabouts. All of these OSM amenities are positively correlated with deprivation and therefore tend to be concentrated in areas with IMD scores above the median. Higher-than-normal presence of these elements may be associated with road infrastructures (e.g., junctions, highways, main roads), which might make a neighborhood less attractive to live in.

IMPLICATIONS, LIMITATIONS AND FUTURE WORK

In the previous sections, we have proposed and evaluated a new method that mines urban data obtained from easily accessible UGC datasets (namely, Foursquare and OpenStreetMap) to extract features that correlate with metrics of socioeconomic deprivation at the level of cities' neighborhoods. We have shown that we can use these features to build accurate classifiers of deprivation and that the corresponding results are in line with previous findings.

Implications
This work has both practical and theoretical implications. From a practical standpoint, the suggested method affords the ability to build 'neighborhood profiling' tools that different stakeholders can use for different purposes: for example, residents may use them to decide where to buy a property or rent a flat; visitors may consult them to decide in which hotel or rent-house to stay; and city planners and administrators may use them to analyze and compare what makes a well-off *vs.* a deprived neighborhood in their cities. From a theoretical standpoint, our method can be used by urban designers and social science researchers to advance knowledge in their fields: for example, to understand the relationship between the built environment and deprivation, as it varies across different cities and cultures; and to analyze the relationships between the built environment and deprivation as it varies in response to different processes such as urbanization and gentrification. Note that, when analysing different geographic contexts, findings elicited with our methodology may well differ; however, the methodology itself is generally applicable, and indeed can be applied in different geographic settings to discover these variations.

Limitations
When selecting to apply our proposed method, one needs to take into consideration the following limitations. First, both Foursquare and OSM datasets have geographic and social biases. The two datasets, in fact, do not have a uniform coverage of urban features across space; rather, coverage is concentrated in city centers, thus affording us only a partial picture of what elements are present in areas further away [26]. In terms of social bias, both Foursquare and OSM users belong to a rather specific demographic group (i.e., young, educated, wealthy); one may thus question how representative the data they produce is of what indeed exists in the physical space. When applying our methodology, one should first check for geographic and social biases, for example using the method proposed in [33]; for cities where such effects are large, our methodology is more likely to return invalid results.

The second limitation which ought to be acknowledged concerns the multiple comparison problem. Our method requires the simultaneous test of multiple variables, and this might increase the chance of finding false positive correlations. Statistical control techniques like FDR should be applied, before deciding whether risks of invalid findings are low. In the case studies presented in this work, we applied FDR to estimate such risk; results appear robust when using Foursquare data, especially for the cities of Greater Manchester and West Midlands.

The third limitation has to do with the coarse-grained classification granularity. We have demonstrated clear performance advantage of our method over a plausible baseline and over a state-of-the-art method that classifies urban deprivation in a binary fashion. In the future, to perform finer-grained classifications, researchers might use multi-modal machine learning approaches to combine features derived from multiple datasets. For example, they could combine social media data with image data coming from Google Street Views, to obtain information about the aesthetic capital afforded by many neighborhoods around the world [19, 36].

Finally, for moderate levels of urban deprivation, classification accuracy should be improved, since our classifier performs really well only at the two extremes of the distribution. One way of doing so is to explore metrics other than

Offering Advantage. There might be metrics that capture different notions of a neighborhood's potential offering (e.g., what types of POIs are within walking distance) and that express those notions with alternative mathematical formulations (e.g., graph-based ones [18]).

Future work

Our future work spans two main directions: on one hand, we aim to expand the method so to capture other urban features (e.g., walkability) that pertain the physical layout of neighborhoods. OSM data is particularly well-suited to extract such features, as it comprises not just POI data (as is the case for Foursquare), but also road network information. Examples of features we might computationally capture include average block size and road density, that urban studies have previously linked to indicators of neighborhood well-being [45, 1]. On the other hand, we aim to quantify the applicability of our method to measure deprivation in different geographic contexts, especially in developing countries where accurate and up-to-date indexes of deprivation like IMD are very difficult to build. We note that, in these contexts, UGC data as obtained by social media services like Foursquare is probably of very little value (too sparse); however, OSM penetration has been shown to be high also in developing countries [34], thus suggesting our method could be used in these more challenging contexts too, especially once we have expanded our set of features to comprise those that we can extract from the road network.

Acknowledgments

This work has been carried out thanks to the Engineering and Physical Sciences Research Council (EPSRC) and the Centre for Urban Sustainability and Resilience (USAR) at University College London.

REFERENCES

1. Alberti, M. The effects of urban patterns on ecosystem function. *International Regional Science Review 28*, 2 (2005), 168–192.
2. Block, J. P., Scribner, R. A., and DeSalvo, K. B. Fast food, race/ethnicity, and income: a geographic analysis. *American journal of preventive medicine 27*, 3 (2004), 211–217.
3. Bolitzer, B., and Netusil, N. R. The impact of open spaces on property values in Portland, Oregon. *Journal of environmental management 59*, 3 (2000), 185–193.
4. Braun, V., and Clarke, V. Using thematic analysis in psychology. *Qualitative Research in Psychology 3*, 2 (2006), 77–101.
5. Brimicombe, A. J. Ethnicity, religion, and residential segregation in London: evidence from a computational typology of minority communities. *ENVIRONMENT AND PLANNING B PLANNING AND DESIGN 34*, 5 (2007), 884.
6. Clifford, P., Richardson, S., and Hemon, D. Assessing the significance of the correlation between two spatial processes. *Biometrics 45*, 1 (1989), 123–134.
7. Cranshaw, J., Schwartz, R., Hong, J. I., and Sadeh, N. The Livehoods Project: utilizing social media to understand the dynamics of a city. In *Proc. of ICWSM*, AAAI (2012).
8. Cummins, S. C. J., McKay, L., Witten, K., and MacIntyre, S. McDonalds restaurants and neighborhood deprivation in Scotland and England. *American Journal of Preventive Medicine 29*, 4 (2005), 308–310.
9. Department of Economic and Social Affairs. World urbanization prospects, the 2011 revision: highlights. Tech. rep., Population Division United Nations, 2011.
10. Eagle, N., Macy, M., and Claxton, R. Network diversity and economic development. *Science 328* (2010), 1029–1031.
11. Elvidge, C. D., Baugh, K. E., Kihn, E. A., Kroehl, H. W., and Davis, E. R. Mapping city lights with nighttime data from the DMSP Operational Linescan System. *Photogrammetric engineering and Remote Sensing 63*, 6 (1997), 727–734.
12. Elvidge, C. D., Imhoff, M. L., Baugh, K. E., Hobson, V. R., Nelsonc, I., Safran, J., Dietz, J. B., and Tuttle, B. T. Night-time lights of the world: 1994-1995. *Photogrammetry and Remote Sensing 56*, 2 (2001), 81–99.
13. Geoghegan, J. The value of open spaces in residential land use. *Land use policy 19*, 1 (2002), 91–98.
14. Giles-Corti, B., and Donovan, R. Socioeconomic status differences in recreational physical activity levels and real and perceived access to a supportive physical environment. *Preventive Medicine*, 35 (2002), 601–611.
15. Grenyer, R., Orme, C. D. L., Jackson, S. F., Thomas, G. H., Davies, R. G., Davies, T. J., Jones, K. E., Olson, V. A., Ridgely, R. S., Rasmussen, P. C., Ding, T., Bennett, P. M., Blackburn, T. M., Gaston, K. J., Gittleman, J. L., and Owens, I. P. F. Global distribution and conservation of rare and threatened vertebrates. *Nature 444* (2006), 93–96.
16. Griffith, D. A., and Paelinck, J. H. *Non-standard spatial statistics and spatial econometrics*. Springer, 2011.
17. Hidalgo, C. A., Klinger, B., Barabási, A. L., and Hausmann, R. The product space conditions the development of nations. *Science 317*, 5837 (2007), 482–487.
18. Hillier, B., and Hanson, J. *The social logic of space*. Cambridge University Press, 1984.
19. Hwang, J., and Sampson, R. J. Divergent Pathways of Gentrification: Racial Inequality and the Social Order of Renewal in Chicago Neighborhoods. *American Sociological Review* (2014).
20. Lacy, S. Foursquare closes $50M at a $600M valuation. Tech. rep., TechCrunch, 2011.
21. Legendre, P. Spatial autocorrelation: trouble or new paradigm? *Ecology 74*, 6 (1993), 1659–1673.

22. Lindqvist, J., Cranshaw, J., Wiese, J., Hong, J., and Zimmerman, J. I'm the mayor of my house: examining why people use Foursquare - a social-driven location sharing application. In *Proc. of CHI*, ACM (2011), 2409–2418.
23. Locker, D. Deprivation and oral health: a review. *Community dentistry and oral epidemiology 28*, 3 (2000), 161–169.
24. Luttik, J. The value of trees, water and open space as reflected by house prices in the Netherlands. *Landscape and Urban Planning 48*, 3 (2000), 161–167.
25. Mao, H., Shuai, X., Ahn, Y. Y., and Bollen, J. Mobile communications reveal the regional economy in Cote d'Ivoire. In *Proc. of NetMob* (2013).
26. Mashhadi, A., Quattrone, G., and Capra, L. Putting Ubiquitous Crowd-sourcing into Context. In *Proc. of CSCW*, ACM (2013), 611–622.
27. McLennan, D., Barnes, H., Noble, M., Davies, J., Garratt, E., and Dibben, C. The english indices of deprivation 2010. *London: Department for Communities and Local Government* (2011).
28. Moreno, E. L., Bazoglu, N., Mboup, G., and Warah, R. State of the world's cities 2008/2009 - harmonious cities. Tech. rep., UN-HABITAT, 2008.
29. Noor, A. M., Alegana, V. A., Gething, P. W., Tatem, A. J., and Snow, R. W. Using remotely sensed night-time light as a proxy for poverty in Africa. *Population Health Metrics 6*, 5 (2008), 81–99.
30. Overseas Development Institute. Briefing paper 44: Opportunity and exploitation in urban labour markets. Tech. rep., 2008.
31. Pearce, J., Blakely, T., Witten, K., and Bartie, P. Neighborhood deprivation and access to fast-food retailing: a national study. *American journal of preventive medicine 32*, 5 (2007), 375–382.
32. Powell, L., Slater, S., Chaloupka, F., and Harper, D. Availability of physical activity-related facilities and neighborhood demographic and socioeconomic characteristics: a national study. *American Journal of Public Health 96*, 9 (2006), 1676–1680.
33. Quattrone, G., Capra, L., and Meo, P. D. Theres No Such Thing as the Perfect Map: Quantifying Bias in Spatial Crowd-sourcing Datasets. In *Proc. of CSCW*, ACM (2015).
34. Quattrone, G., Mashhadi, A., and Capra, L. Mind the map: the impact of culture and economic affluence on crowd-mapping behaviours. In *Proc. of CSCW*, ACM (2014).
35. Quercia, D., Ellis, J., Capra, L., and Crowcroft, J. Tracking Gross Community Happiness from Tweets. In *Proc. of CSCW*, ACM (2012).
36. Quercia, D., Ohare, N., and Cramer, H. Aesthetic Capital: What Makes London Look Beautiful, Quiet, and Happy? In *Proc. of CSCW*, ACM (2014).
37. Quercia, D., and Saez, D. Mining urban deprivation from Foursquare: implicit crowdsourcing of city land use. *Pervasive Computing, IEEE 13*, 2 (2014), 30–36.
38. Quercia, D., Séaghdha, D. O., and Crowcroft, J. Talk of the city: our tweets, our community happiness. In *Proc. of ICWSM*, AAAI (2012).
39. Small, M. L., and McDermott, M. The presence of organizational resources in poor urban neighborhoods: An analysis of average and contextual effects. *Social Forces 84*, 3 (2006), 1697–1724.
40. Smith, C., Mashhadi, A., and Capra, L. Ubiquitous sensing for mapping poverty in developing countries. In *Paper submitted to the Orange D4D Challenge (2013)* (2013).
41. Smith, C., Quercia, D., and Capra, L. Finger on the pulse: identifying deprivation using transit flow analysis. In *Proc. of CSCW*, ACM (2013), 683–692.
42. Storey, J. D., and Tibshirani, R. Statistical significance for genomewide studies. In *Proc. of NAS* (2003), 9440–9445.
43. Tobler, W. R. A computer movie simulating urban growth in the Detroit region. *Economic Geography 46* (1970), 234–240.
44. Transport for London (TFL). Travel in London, Supplementary Report: London Travel Demand Survey (LTDS). Tech. rep., 2011.
45. Tratalos, J., Fuller, R. A., Warren, P. H., Davies, R. G., and Gaston, K. J. Urban form, biodiversity potential and ecosystem services. *Landscape and Urban Planning 83*, 4 (2007), 308 – 317.

Avoiding the South Side and the Suburbs: The Geography of Mobile Crowdsourcing Markets

Jacob Thebault-Spieker
GroupLens Research
University of Minnesota
thebault@cs.umn.edu

Loren Terveen
GroupLens Research
University of Minnesota
terveen@cs.umn.edu

Brent Hecht
GroupLens Research
University of Minnesota
bhecht@cs.umn.edu

ABSTRACT
Mobile crowdsourcing markets (e.g., Gigwalk and TaskRabbit) offer crowdworkers tasks situated in the physical world (e.g., checking street signs, running household errands). The geographic nature of these tasks distinguishes these markets from online crowdsourcing markets and raises new, fundamental questions. We carried out a controlled study in the Chicago metropolitan area aimed at addressing two key questions: (1) What geographic factors influence whether a crowdworker will be willing to do a task? (2) What geographic factors influence how much compensation a crowdworker will demand in order to do a task? Quantitative modeling shows that travel distance to the location of the task and the socioeconomic status (SES) of the task area are important factors. Qualitative analysis enriches our modeling, with workers mentioning safety and difficulties getting to a location as key considerations. Our results suggest that low-SES areas are currently less able to take advantage of the benefits of mobile crowdsourcing markets. We discuss the implications of our study for these markets, as well as for "sharing economy" phenomena like UberX, which have many properties in common with mobile crowdsourcing markets.

Author Keywords
Mobile crowdsourcing; volunteered geographic information;

ACM Classification Keywords
H.5.3 [Information Interfaces and Presentation]: Group and Organization Interfaces – Computer-supported cooperative work.

INTRODUCTION
Mobile crowdsourcing markets are a recent development in crowdsourcing that has attracted substantial attention from both academia and industry. These markets are similar to purely online (or virtual [35]) markets like Amazon Mechanical Turk, but offer tasks that are situated in the physical world. For instance, the mobile crowdsourcing market Gigwalk has worked with Microsoft Bing to collect 3D panoramas [39]. Another market, TaskRabbit, suggests that people "outsource household errands and skilled tasks" (e.g. minor home repairs, grocery shopping, cleaning one's house, assembling Ikea furniture) [40].

Despite the growing interest in mobile crowdsourcing markets (e.g. [25,35]), no work has focused on understanding these markets from a geographic perspective, a perspective that is fundamental to the physically-situated nature of mobile crowdsourcing tasks. As a result we have little understanding of the geography of mobile crowdsourcing markets. For instance, the relationship between a task's location and the price at which a crowdworker will perform the task is unknown. Even more fundamentally, the same is true for the relationship between a task's location and the likelihood of finding a mobile crowdworker willing to do the task at all.

This paper seeks to address this gap in the literature through a survey deployed on *TaskRabbit,* a popular mobile crowdsourcing market. Through quantitative and qualitative analysis of our survey results, we find that two types of areas are disadvantaged on TaskRabbit: areas with low socioeconomic status (SES) like the "South Side" of Chicago and suburban (and rural) areas. People in both types of areas have access to significantly fewer mobile crowdsourcing workers. Additionally, in many cases, they will have to pay more to get a task completed. With respect to low-SES areas, this result is especially problematic as it suggests that when it comes to mobile crowdsourcing, it is "expensive to be poor" [9] and people who live in low-SES areas are less able to leverage the efficiencies of mobile crowdsourcing (e.g. spending time on longer-term goals that may increase one's SES versus "crowdsourceable" household labor).

Our quantitative and qualitative analyses reveal several mechanisms behind this unequal geography of mobile crowdsourcing markets. Our statistical modeling shows that both distance to a task and the SES of a task area influence whether a worker is willing to accept a task, and that

CSCW 2015, March 14–18, 2015, Vancouver, BC, Canada.

http://dx.doi.org/10.1145/2675133.2675278

distance is the dominant predictor of task price. Qualitative responses to our survey suggest that perceptions of higher crime in lower SES areas reduces workers' willingness to go to these areas to complete a task. Additionally, very few survey respondents reported living in low-SES areas, leading to longer travel times – and increased prices – even when people in these areas are able to find a crowdworker. This is particularly the case where the socioeconomic residential segregation that is endemic to most major metropolitan areas leads to large low-SES districts (e.g. the South Side of Chicago, west Oakland, north Minneapolis).

This work also contributes to our understanding of the role of gender in crowdsourcing markets. In particular, our survey reveals that women are far more likely than men to avoid doing a task, primarily for safety and distance reasons. As such, although women made up the majority of our respondents, the number of available tasks is somewhat smaller for them than it is for male workers. A larger pool of women are likely competing for a smaller pool of tasks, which may have an effect on wages over time.

We next discuss related work, followed by a description of the study we deployed on the mobile crowdsourcing market TaskRabbit. We then present both the quantitative modeling and qualitative analysis results of our study. Finally, we discuss in more detail the implications of our findings.

RELATED WORK

Our work is informed by research on several topics: general properties of crowdsourcing markets, motivations of mobile crowdworkers, and geographic coverage biases in geowikis (e.g. OpenStreetMap) and social media VGI (e.g. geotagged tweets and photos).

Non-mobile crowdsourcing markets

Non-mobile (or "virtual" [35]) crowdsourcing markets like Amazon's Mechanical Turk (AMT) have been the subject of intense study. Work in this area ranges from novel applications like word processors backed by the crowd [3], to complex architectures exploring the best way to organize people [16,19], to understanding and supporting the labor dynamics of crowd workers [15]. One of the more common uses of AMT is data processing, ranging from translation of text [8] to annotation of images [29].

More directly relevant to this work is research on the demographics of workers on AMT (e.g. [14,26,30]). As AMT gained popularity and success, the demographics of workers started to shift, from predominantly US-based workers using AMT as a second income source, towards a very large proportion of workers based in India using AMT as a full-time job [14,30]. This shift in the demographics of AMT, and the role that crowdsourcing plays as an income source for these groups has led some to build technology to try to address the power imbalance between workers and Amazon [15].

In this work, we focus on mobile crowdsourcing markets rather than virtual markets like AMT. The inherently geographic nature of mobile crowdsourcing markets results in substantially changed dynamics – e.g. distance and environmental effects – relative to AMT and other virtual crowdsourcing markets.

Mobile crowdsourcing marketplaces

Mobile crowdsourcing marketplaces are the geographic counterpart to virtual crowdsourcing markets like AMT [35]. A number of companies have sprung up to build mobile crowdsourcing marketplaces (e.g. GigWalk [41], Field Agent [42], and TaskRabbit [40]). While these marketplaces are still relatively new, they have quickly attracted interest from researchers. Initial work has focused on participant behavior. For example, Teodoro et al. [35] conducted a qualitative study to investigate the motivations of workers in TaskRabbit and Gigwalk. They found that monetary compensation and control of working conditions (time of day, rate of pay, the tasks they do) were primary factors for joining these systems.

Rather than studying mobile crowdworkers on existing platforms, Alt et al. [1] independently developed a mobile crowdsourcing system. They asked people to complete tasks using a smartphone and observed their behavior. They found that workers were more willing to do tasks before and after business hours, tasks that were near their home or office, and very simple tasks (e.g., taking photos).

Although neither Teodoro et al. nor Alt et al. focused on the geography of mobile crowdsourcing markets as we do here, both observed that how far people have to travel appears to influence their attitude toward a task, a finding that is a reflection of the important principle of distance decay in geography (or that as the distance between two locations increases, interaction between them tends to decrease, e.g. [10]). Similarly, Musthag and Ganesan [25] studied distance-to-task as a factor in a study of the behavior of "power users" in a mobile crowdsourcing system. They found that power users travel further per day, earn more per mile travelled, and account for 84% of total earnings and 80% of the completed tasks in the system. As detailed below, we enrich our understanding of the role of distance in mobile crowdsourcing markets by including it in a model of decisions related to pricing and willingness to complete a task. We learned additional context (e.g. the relationship of distance to other factors like SES) and new specifics (e.g. quantifying the relationship of distance to price).

Coverage problems in mobile crowdsourcing

Mobile crowdsourcing markets exist in a broader mobile crowdsourcing universe, which also includes phenomena like geowikis (e.g. OpenStreetMap and Cyclopath [27]), and physically-situated citizen science projects (e.g. [31]). Research has shown that these systems can have drastic geographic coverage problems (e.g. [12,21,24,28,37]). For instance, Quattrone et al. [28] show that countries with higher GDP and a lower Power Distance (more egalitarian) have better coverage in OpenStreetMap. Similarly, Haklay et al. [12] find that within Britain, the most deprived areas (according to the Index of Deprivation, an aggregate metric of SES factors) tend to have worse coverage than those areas that are less deprived.

Volunteered geographic information (VGI) [11] is a concept from the geography and geographic information science communities that is closely related to mobile crowdsourcing. According to Goodchild [11], VGI is "the widespread engagement of large numbers of private citizens, often with little in the way of formal qualifications, in the creation of geographic information". However, despite this "widespread engagement", VGI systems [20,23] also have been shown to have socioeconomic biases. Li et al. [18] studied Flickr and Twitter, demonstrating that low SES areas and rural areas both have worse coverage (less data) than higher SES and urban areas. Similarly, Hecht and Stephens [13] found that people from rural areas produce less social media VGI (e.g. Twitter, Flickr, Foursquare) per capita than their urban counterparts.

This research

Prior research has demonstrated coverage biases in mobile crowdsourcing systems that correlate with differences in socioeconomic status and presents qualitative evidence that distance matters to crowdworkers as they consider what tasks to take on. We extend prior research in several ways. (1) We formalize the decision-making of crowdworkers as consisting of two sequential steps: **willingness** to do a task, and how much compensation they require for the task (i.e. the **price** of the task). (2) We do a **controlled study** of crowdworkers from one of the most popular marketplaces for mobile crowdwork, TaskRabbit. (3) We use **formal statistical modeling** to quantify the effect of distance-to-task and SES status of the task area on workers' decisions regarding willingness and compensation. (4) We enrich the results of our formal model through **qualitative analysis** that reveals the reasons behind workers' decisions.

RESEARCH QUESTIONS

As noted above, mobile crowdworkers must ask themselves two questions when confronted with a potential task: "Am I **willing** to do this task?", and second, "Is the **price** acceptable?" (or in the case of some markets, "What price would I ask?"). Our two research questions in this study are targeted at better understanding each step of this process from a geographic perspective. Our first question, aimed at the first step, is thus:

RQ-Willingness: *Where will participants in mobile crowdsourcing markets be willing to go to complete tasks?*

The related work outlined above led us to hypothesize that two geographic factors may influence workers' willingness to complete a task. First, the SES-related coverage biases observed in domains like geowikis and volunteered geographic information suggest that SES may play a role in this step of the process. Second, within geography and related fields, distance is often thought of as a cost function [10]. This leads to concepts like distance decay, which has been observed in mobile crowdsourcing systems. Therefore, we hypothesized that:

H-Willingness: *As distance to a task increases, willingness to complete the task will decrease (H-Willingness-Distance), and as the SES of a task's surroundings increases, willingness to complete a task will increase (H-Willingness-SES).*

Once crowdworkers have decided they are *willing* to complete a task, they must then decide on a *price* for the task. In TaskRabbit, this can either be accepting an offer, or making a bid. To address this second stage in the decision-making process, we ask our second research question:

RQ-Price: *How does geography affect how much participants in mobile crowdsourcing markets request in payment?*

The literature discussed in the previous section led us to hypothesize that SES and distance would also affect the price a worker charges for a task. More specifically, we hypothesized that:

H-Price: *Participants will demand a higher price for tasks farther away from where they work and live (H-Price-Distance) and in lower SES areas (H-Price-SES).*

STUDY DESIGN

To address the above research questions and evaluate the corresponding hypotheses, we developed a survey and deployed it on TaskRabbit. TaskRabbit is a well-known mobile crowdsourcing market used by task requesters for the completion of physically-situated tasks ranging from delivering flowers to helping build IKEA furniture to helping task posters move large items.

We deployed our survey in an organic fashion by posting it as a task to TaskRabbit's Chicago metropolitan area site just as a typical task requester would post a task. Only TaskRabbit workers local to the Chicago area could fill out the survey, for which we paid respondents $5 in 15-minute intervals, capped at an hour (e.g. a person who took more than 15 minutes but less than 30 would receive $10).

To add context to our survey results, we first asked respondents a number of questions about themselves, such as their gender, their preferred mode of transportation, and their activity level on TaskRabbit. We also asked respondents to select their home census tract[1] on a map we provided, and to do the same for census tracts that they visited at least once a month.

[1] Census tracts are geographic areas defined by the U.S. census and "generally have a population size between 1,200 and 8,000 people, with an optimum size of 4,000 people" [36].

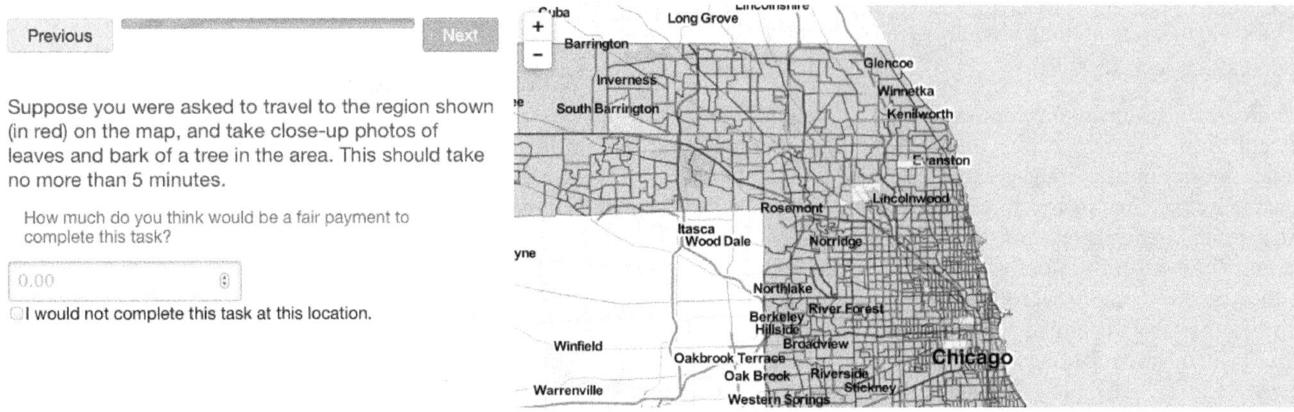

Figure 1: A screen grab from the survey taken by workers on TaskRabbit. The green census tract is the worker's self-reported home tract and the blue tracts are those that the worker reported visiting at least once a month. The red tract is the tract about which the worker is currently being questioned (Note: screen grab is cropped for space and, for privacy reasons, the figure does not depict an actual crowdworker's responses).

After respondents answered questions about themselves, they began the main portion of the survey, which was dedicated to investigating *RQ-Willingness* and *RQ-Price*. This portion of the survey involved prompting respondents with census tracts in Cook County, Illinois, which contains Chicago and many of its suburbs[2]. For each census tract, the respondent had the option to either check a box labeled "I would not do this task at this location" or to name what they felt would be a fair price to complete the task (see Figure 1) were they to be asked to do it by a task requester.

In order to control for task-specific attributes, each tract was randomly assigned one of three hypothetical tasks designed to vary the level of engagement with the local area (Table 1). These tasks ranged from one that could be done without leaving a vehicle to one that required interaction with a person in the area. Tasks were designed so that they would not take more than five minutes.

Task	Engagement Level
Task 0: Suppose you were asked to travel to an intersection in the region shown (in red) on the map, and photograph all of the signs at that intersection. This should take no more than 5 minutes.	Low
Task 1: Suppose you were asked to travel to the region shown (in red) on the map, and take close-up photos of leaves and bark of a tree in the area. This should take no more than 5 minutes	Medium
Task 2: Suppose you were asked to travel to the region shown (in red) on the map, visit someone's home, and ask the owners to respond to a single question about local politics. This should take no more than 5 minutes	High

Table 1. Tasks in our survey and their hypothesized engagement level.

Each participant received 20 census tracts (18 unique). Fourteen of the tracts were randomly selected (without replacement), and these tracts were the tracts that were considered in our quantitative analysis below. In order to enrich our qualitative understanding of the geography of mobile crowdsourcing markets, we also considered four special-case tracts: the highest-income and the lowest-income tracts and the highest-crime[3] and the lowest-crime tracts. The other two tracts were repeated from the randomly chosen set of 14 in order to verify intra-rater reliability. The repeated tract was presented no fewer than 5 tracts after the original.

Upon seeing and responding to all 20 of the tracts with either a price or by stating that they would not complete the task, we asked respondents several open-ended questions whose answers were entered into text boxes. Specifically, we asked respondents about how they made their pricing decisions and why they would not complete certain tasks (if they checked that box at least once).

RESULTS

Forty respondents completed the survey, which we ran during Spring 2014. 57.5% of respondents were women (42.5% men). The median respondent performed a task on TaskRabbit between once a week and once every two weeks. 30% of respondents indicated that they complete multiple tasks per week, while only 20% of respondents indicated that they complete a task once a month or less.

[3] As reported by the Chicago Police Department (Cook County-wide crime data is not available).

RQ-Willingness

Because price is irrelevant if a worker will not complete a task, we first sought to understand the geography of workers' *willingness* to complete tasks. To do so, we built a logistic mixed effects model with three fixed effects:

- Distance to task from the closest census tract visited by the respondent at least once a month (as indicated in the survey)
- Median household income of the task tract, as an indicator of socioeconomic status. Many other socioeconomic variables are well known to be correlated with income (e.g. educational attainment, occupation). To reduce the effect of the long-tailed distribution of wealth, we log-transformed this variable. Median household income data was gathered from the United States Census' American Community Survey 2006-2010 dataset.
- Task ID, to make sure we understand the effect of distance and median income in the context of a given task.

The models' random effects were intercepts for respondent and by-respondent slopes for the effects of income and distance. The model's dependent variable was whether or not the survey respondent had checked the "I would not do this task at this location" box for a given tract. Overall, respondents indicated that they would not do 34% of the tasks. The few census tracts that had a reported median income of zero (e.g. the tract that consists of O'Hare International Airport and a few hotels[4].) were excluded

Fixed Effect	Estimate	*p*-value
Travel time (in hours)	-3.15 (0.99)	0.001
Log_2[Task tract income in $10k]	0.87 (0.36)	0.014
Task ID (baseline = Task 0)	1: 0.37 (0.40) 2: -0.92 (0.40)	0.003
Constant	1.81 (0.82)	0.028

Table 2: The results of our *willingness* model (p-value for Task ID was calculated with an ANOVA).

Fixed Effect	Estimate	*p*-value
Travel time (in hours)	10.10 (2.27)	<0.001
Log_2[Task tract income in $10k]	0.40 (0.52)	*n.s.*
Task ID (baseline = Task 0)	1: -1.73 (0.85) 2: 0.28 (0.87)	0.024
Constant	16.92 (2.90)	<0.001

Table 3: The results of our *price* model (p-value for Task ID was calculated with an ANOVA).

To operationalize distance, we used travel time rather than Euclidean distance to better match the lived experience of mobility in Chicago. We used the Google Distance API to calculate the off-peak travel time between the centroid of the task tract and the centroid of the nearest (to the task tract) tract that the respondent indicated visiting frequently (more than once a month). The API supports multiple transportation modes, and we calculated travel time with respondents' self-reported preferred mode of transportations.

Table 2 shows the results of our model. All fixed effects are significant. Returning to our hypothesis *H-Willingness*, we find that both *H-Willingness-Distance* and *H-Willingness-Price* are supported. Socioeconomic status of the task location and distance to the tract both have an effect on whether or not a worker on TaskRabbit is willing to accept a task, with SES having a significant positive relationship and distance having a negative one. According to the model, for every doubling of task area median income, there is a 2.38x increase in likelihood that a worker will accept a task. In other words, holding the other variables constant, our model suggests that the likelihood of a worker accepting a task will more than double if the task is in a tract with a median income of, for instance, $60K rather than a tract with a median income of $30K. As shown in Figure 2, $60K is a relatively normal median household income in northern Chicago and the Chicago suburbs, with $30K median household incomes common on the South Side.

With respect to travel time, our model indicates that for every hour of travel time there is a substantial decrease in willingness. Specifically, workers are about 4.3% as likely to be willing to do a task an hour away as they are one located in their immediate vicinity. We also saw that respondents were significantly less willing to do the most engaging task relative to the others ($p < .05$). Further investigating this phenomenon, especially with regard to its interaction with SES, is a direction of future work (see below).

Examining our willingness results in more detail, we found an interesting result with regard to gender. While 78% of women said they would not complete at least one task, the equivalent number for men was 53%. In addition, the grand mean willingness (mean of means) for women is 57.1%, for

[4] One respondent indicated living in this tract. While we did not consider samples where the proposed task was in this tract (and other zero-income tracts), we did include this user's responses about tasks in other tracts because there are reasonable residential options in this tract (though temporary ones).

men it is 77.7%. Our qualitative results below suggest that both distance and crime factors play a role in women's explicit willingness decisions, but these are the same factors also indicated by men. Although further research is needed, it is likely that women have a lower threshold for one or both of these factors.

RQ-Price

We next turned our attention to analysis of the price respondents indicated they would charge for a task, assuming they were willing to complete it. We began our analysis of the price data by ensuring that it had sufficiently high intra-rater reliability. We did so by calculating the Pearson's correlation coefficient between the first and second price judgments for repeated tracts. The coefficient was $r = 0.96$ across all respondents, indicating that respondents' pricing decisions were very consistent.

To understand the geography of prices on TaskRabbit and the effects of distance and SES on these prices, we built a linear mixed effects model with identical independent variables as our willingness model but with reported task price as dependent variable.

The results of this price model can be seen in Table 3. The table reveals that travel time was indeed positively related to price, supporting *H-Price-Distance*. Indeed, the model suggests that for every hour of travel time, price goes up at a rate of $9.97/hour.

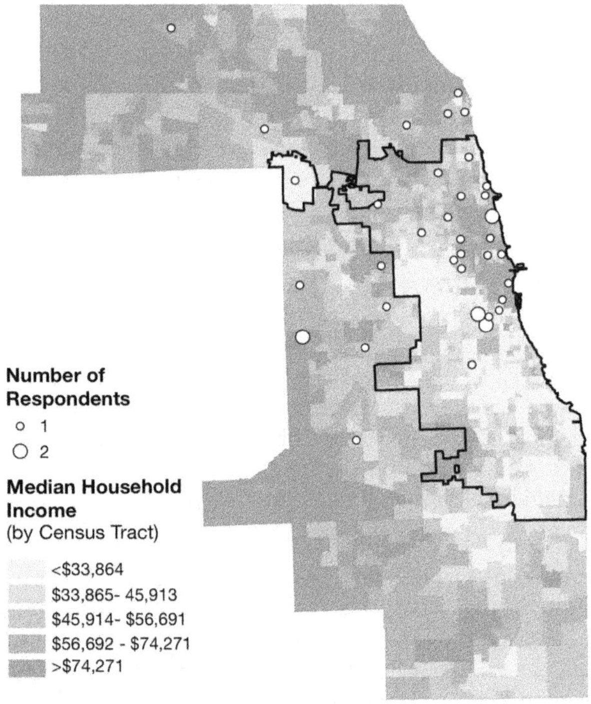

Figure 2. Survey respondents' self-reported home census tracts (centroids) and median income in Cook County, Illinois. Very few respondents live in low-income tracts. Note that the low-SES south side of Chicago (Chicago is outlined with a bold border) has only one respondent, and no respondents live in the poorest parts of south Chicago. Median income color classes are determined via the quantile method, meaning each class represents a quintile of the household income dataset.

Task tract income, on the other hand, was not significant; the median household income of the tract does not have a significant effect on price. In other words, *H-Price-SES* was not supported.

However, examining the geography of where our respondents live provides additional context for the role of distance in TaskRabbit. Figure 2 shows the self-reported home tracts of all 40 respondents on top of a map of income by census tract in Cook County. Immediately visible in Figure 2 is that very few respondents live in the heart of low-income areas. Indeed, most respondents seem to cluster around the very high-income portions of northern Chicago. Only a single respondent lives well within the lower-income South Side of Chicago. As a result, a low-income resident of the South Side would have to pay more for mobile crowdsourcing services (e.g. someone to take care of errands to make time for longer-term goals) than someone in wealthier areas of Chicago, and is likely to have a harder time finding someone willing to accept this request for services in the first place.

This suggests that the character of the socioeconomic residential segregation that is common to many metropolitan areas around the world – i.e. the "Big Sort" [4] – may play an important role in the price of mobile crowdsourcing market tasks. Where this segregation results in large-area low-income districts like the South Side, the people who live in these districts will live far from mobile crowdworkers, resulting in longer travel times, and higher prices for tasks. However, where low-SES pockets are much smaller (e.g. the lower income pockets in the suburbs just north of Chicago), the effect on travel time, and therefore price, will be minimal.

It is also important to note that distance not only disadvantages lower SES areas, but also disadvantages people who live in distant suburbs. Figure 2 shows that workers are concentrated in the dense city of Chicago rather than the suburbs. However, as can also be seen in Figure 2, suburban people have higher incomes than people on the South Side of Chicago, and thus they can potentially afford the increased costs. In addition, in many cases, even people in somewhat remote suburbs are closer to one of our respondents than a person in south Chicago.

Further, while United States suburbs tend to be relatively wealthy, the opposite is true in many cities around the world (e.g. France and Latin America [6,10]). Where this is the case, mobile crowdsourcing will likely be drastically more expensive and less accessible in these areas. As we note below, investigating these phenomena in cities with different socioeconomic segregation patterns is an important direction of future work.

QUALITATIVE RESULTS

Thus far, our quantitative models and our descriptive statistics have revealed a number of properties of the geography of mobile crowdsourcing, e.g. crowdworkers are less willing to do tasks in lower SES areas, and prices are higher in areas far from the areas frequented by crowdworkers. We now turn to our qualitative results to attempt to help understand *why* these dynamics are at play in mobile crowdsourcing markets. To do so, a single investigator looked for themes in the survey responses, focusing on ideas related to the geographic concepts *site* and *situation*. We use this framing to discuss the results of our qualitative data.

Site and *situation* are core concepts from geography used to describe the attributes of an area [10,17,22]. Broadly stated, *site* attributes are properties of an area that are not directly dependent on other areas (e.g. mineral deposits, quality of terrain, local weather). *Situation* attributes describe connectivity of one place to another (e.g. located on a major highway connected to a big city, has a seaport).

In the context of this work, *site* attributes refer to reputation of a census tract, the perception of safety in that tract, poverty in that tract, and so on. *Site* attributes do not change with the crowdworker being asked. *Situation* attributes, on the other hand, are those that vary by relative location with respect to the crowdworker. These include properties like easy access to the location, travel cost with respect to mode of travel, the time of day the task was requested for, distance to the location, etc. We will discuss each of these themes in turn.

Site attributes

Perceptions of high crime in the task's census tract was a site attribute that was very commonly mentioned by our respondents as a reason they ticked the "will not do" box. For instance, respondent 27 (R27) wrote:

I think the high incidence of gang-related crime makes many Chicagoans too nervous to visit some parts of the city. We always refer to Chicago as being a "city of neighborhoods" but the truth is that many Chicagoans feel uncomfortable visiting a huge portion of our city. The nature of the crimes that occur on the South and West Sides (gang-related) makes me particularly nervous because there's nothing you can do to prepare/protect yourself. I realize that I might have some biases but it's less about location for me and more about crime rate. I do wish Chicagoans (and visitors) could feel more comfortable exploring and enjoying more neighborhoods without worrying about crime."(R27)

In the above quote, R27 discusses the unease she perceives among others in Chicago and the (reported) reputation that the South Side and West Side of Chicago have for having large amounts of violent, gang-related crime.

R39 specifically addresses her gender as part of the reason she did not consider certain tasks, saying:

"I wouldn't feel safe in some areas as a female by herself." (R39)

R9 is a member of the TaskRabbit Elite. This is a designation one can earn within TaskRabbit after earning an average rating of 4.9 stars (ratings are given by task posters upon completion), completing a large number of tasks, and not violating any of TaskRabbit's policies. R9 offered similar feedback to R27:

I am an Elite member of TaskRabbit and I do a lot of tasks. I do not do tasks anything below the loop of Chicago [i.e. the South Side] *so it has to be on the north side for me to work. It is purely for safety concerns. (R9)*

R4, a relatively new resident of Chicago, similarly makes decisions about where to participate within the city based on the reputation of certain areas with respect to crime. In this case, she explicitly mentions poverty as well, providing qualitative support for our SES results.

I only moved to Chicago last May (2013) so I don't know much about the city except that there are large pockets of poverty, inequality and high crime. In terms of general areas of the city I understand that large swaths of the south side and west side include these pockets of poverty and high crime. Without specifics about which neighborhoods/blocks/streets are safe I essentially ruled out anything on the south or west side of the city. For the most part, I think the western suburbs are safe but I know nothing about the southern suburbs so I erred on the side of safety and avoided those areas as well. (R4)

Other participants raised this idea of generalizations about, and reputations of, unsafe areas as well:

Whether or not my assumptions of lack of safety were correct, I wouldn't put myself in danger for a few dollars (R16)

Situation attributes

As can be expected from our quantitative models, the respondents' qualitative feedback suggests that proximity or convenience of the task location is a very important factor in their pricing and willingness decisions. Here, R4 explicitly discusses the role of convenience in her pricing decisions.

Mostly how much of a pain it was going to be to get there. If it was a place I could stop by on my way to or from work or the gym= cheap. If it required getting in my car=more. If it required an extensive drive to a far flung suburb=more. (R4)

Others, like R16, discuss the role of transportation mechanisms and time it would take to travel to areas to complete tasks.

Other areas were too far from the Metra [the commuter rail system in Chicago] *to make it worth my while. Others were still close to the Metra but far enough away where the ticket round trip would be a bit pricy. (R16)*

Recognition of diminishing returns was also raised by other participants, like R23, R31, and R39, who discussed the tension between traveling long distances and being able to complete a task at a "fair" price:

"I didn't think any price would be worth the commute and risk while still offering even a marginally fair price." (R23)

"The distance was too far to justify any fair price for completing task. The price would have to be higher/greater than 25 dollars to justify it." (R31)

"getting there would take me longer than actually completing the task" (R39)

More specifically, these crowdworkers discuss needing to ensure they could afford to complete the task, and were balancing a trade-off between distance, the time it would take, and the cost of travel to these locations. The diminishing returns were both internal (e.g. it wouldn't make sense for them to travel), and external (e.g. it would be too expensive for the task poster to hire me to do this).

DISCUSSION

Above, we examined the geography of mobile crowdsourcing markets through quantitative and qualitative lenses, finding that the SES of a task area and distance to a task are key factors in access to the benefits of these markets. Below we discuss additional themes emergent from our findings and highlight our findings' implications for mobile crowdsourcing markets and related platforms like car-sharing services (e.g. UberX).

Relationship between Income and Crime

One important theme that emerges when comparing our quantitative and qualitative results is that perceived danger from crime may be an important mechanism through which low SES areas are disadvantaged in mobile crowdsourcing markets. In our qualitative feedback, crime was far more frequently discussed as a reason for declining a task than SES, but crime and SES are known to be highly correlated (e.g. [2,5,7]). Indeed, we obtained violent crime data from the Chicago Police Department (equivalent data for the entire study area was not available, since it extended outside the Chicago city limits) and found that the Pearson's correlation with median household income was quite high ($r = 0.70$). In other words, it may be fear of crime that is at least partially driving the SES effects we saw in our model.

It is important to note that there is likely some disagreement between perception and reality when it comes to crime. For instance, while the South Side does have some very dangerous areas, it also has significantly safer areas. The safer areas – low SES or otherwise – may be grouped together with the more dangerous by crowdworkers, leading to less access to crowdworkers' services even in these safer South Side areas.

Similarly, it is also important to note that due to the tremendous economic inequalities that occur across racial and ethnic lines in the United States, our results suggest that specific racial and ethnic groups have differential access to mobile crowdsourcing market resources. Specifically, we observed that the percent of the population that self-identifies as *white (non-Latino)* (a designation used by the U.S. census) has a strong correlation with income in our study area ($r = 0.67$). Therefore, *because of these correlations,* many of the patterns we saw for SES factors may be true for race/ethnicity as well. To illustrate this point, we found that in a version of our willingness model that used percent white (non-Latino) as a fixed effect instead of income, white (non-Latino) was marginally significant ($p = 0.06$).

These relationships reflect a set of real and *perceived* correlations in our study area (and in the United States as a whole) between SES factors, neighborhood safety, and race/ethnicity. Our inquiry into the factors that influence mobile crowdworkers' willingness to travel to a particular area to do a task made it inevitable that these relationships and correlations would surface. We think it is intellectually appropriate to acknowledge them, situate them in proper context, and exercise caution in interpreting results based on them. We hope that other researchers looking at similar problems will do the same.

Implications for Ride-Sharing Platforms

Another interesting point of discussion ensues from the rise of car-sharing platforms like UberX, which have strong similarities to mobile crowdsourcing markets. In UberX, drivers (i.e. workers) have agency in terms of which regions they visit to try to find fares, just as TaskRabbit crowdworkers can choose which tasks to accept. As such, UberX may be subject to similar phenomena as we observed for TaskRabbit. Namely, our results suggest that people who live in low SES areas (or high crime areas) may find it significantly more difficult to take advantage of services like UberX, especially in terms of available drivers and, in certain areas, in terms of higher prices. Indeed, there is growing anecdotal evidence that this is the case, with Uber being increasingly accused of ride-sharing "redlining", or providing less service and higher prices in lower SES areas (e.g. [32,33]). Uber is currently the subject of widespread discussions with respect to transportation policy, and we hope this work can provide a related data point in these discussions. Repeating this work with UberX drivers is a valuable direction of future work.

Crowdworker Recruitment and Background Checks

Although we have focused on the benefits of mobile crowdsourcing markets for task requesters, another benefit of these markets comes from the ability to find work as a crowdworker. However, our results also indicate that people in low SES areas again are disadvantaged in this respect. The vast majority of respondents reported living in census tracts whose median household income is well above the United States federal poverty line for a household of four (Figure 2). Indeed, the median of the median household incomes of respondents' census tracts was \$51,216 (over 200% of the poverty line). While it is possible that some respondents are much poorer than their tract's median, it is unlikely that this is true of a substantial number. In addition, only one respondent lives in the very poor western and southern areas of Chicago (and s/he lives in a relatively wealthier tract), meaning that that these populations are not yet leveraging TaskRabbit for work.

One reason for the underrepresentation of low SES crowdworkers is likely TaskRabbit's set of requirements for new crowdworkers. For instance, TaskRabbit mandates that crowdworkers pass a background check and have a smartphone and a bank account, both of which are found less often in low-income households than higher-income households (at least in the United States [34,38]). Interestingly, UberX also has requirements that would restrict lower income people from becoming drivers, e.g. owning a car, having insurance.

Our results suggest that reducing the barriers to entry for potential workers would be an effective way of increasing the accessibility of the benefits of mobile crowdsourcing markets. Not only would this bring in more low-income mobile crowdworkers, but many of these low-income workers would likely live in lower income areas, decreasing the distance to the nearest crowdworker for people in these areas. Our model indicates that this would both increase the number of workers willing to complete tasks and decrease prices for these people. Straightforward means of reducing barriers to entry would include providing mobile crowdworkers with a specialized smartphone (Uber does this) and paying workers through means that do not require a bank account.

It's "Expensive to be Poor" in Mobile Crowdsourcing

One of the major benefits of mobile crowdsourcing markets is that they allow task requesters to use their time more efficiently in an economic sense. For instance, consider a Silicon Valley worker with a high salary and many demands at her job. If she can find a TaskRabbit to do her laundry, pick up her packages, go to the grocery store for her, etc. at say, \$20/hour, she can focus on succeeding at work, which has much higher potential payoffs over the long term. Our results suggest that these efficiencies are harder to obtain through mobile crowdsourcing in low SES areas. This is a classic "expensive to be poor" [9] scenario in a new domain.

Other Directions of Future Work

An important direction of future work for us will involve looking at the implications of this papers' findings for rural areas. The fact that distance was significant both in willingness and in price does not bode well for the success of mobile crowdsourcing markets in rural contexts. Rural areas are some of the least-covered spaces in other types of mobile crowdsourcing (e.g. [13,37]) and it appears it is cost-prohibitive to use existing mobile crowdsourcing markets there as well.

Because of residential segregation, we might anticipate that distance and accessibility discrepancies are bi-directional, but this is an interesting direction for future work. Would locals to low-SES areas travel to higher-SES areas to perform crowdwork? What about equally-distant low-SES areas? Addressing each of these questions would add to our understanding of price and willingness in mobile crowdsourcing markets.

Finally, we also are looking further into the gender dynamics in mobile crowdsourcing markets. We hope to uncover additional details with regard to the differences in willingness between men and women that we saw in our survey, as well as better understand the potential economic implications (e.g. on overall wages).

Limitations

While the above work sheds new light on the role of SES and geography more generally in mobile crowdsourcing markets, our study also has several limitations that are important to discuss.

First and foremost, some participants in their qualitative feedback indicated that the time we allocated for a task had an effect on their decision making. For instance, TR5 wrote:

> *"If it was too far from my home or my job I would not travel to that location to take a picture for 5 minutes." (TR5)*

This dynamic may have affected the participation and price dynamics of some of the locations. Therefore, our future work will involve investigating the role task duration plays (even in the context of flat-rate vs. hourly pricing).

Second, our study was performed on a single county. While we believe our results are generalizable to most cities, it will take additional research to be sure.

CONCLUSION

We presented evidence from a quantitative and qualitative survey of TaskRabbit indicating that mobile crowdsourcing markets advantage the advantaged and disadvantage the disadvantaged. Specifically, we show that the SES of a task area is associated with the willingness of crowdworkers to complete a task, with lower SES leading to fewer willing crowdworkers. We also discuss how distance to the task – which affects both the willingness of a worker to complete a task and the price at which the worker is willing to complete it – can act as an agent of SES in certain contexts due to endemic residential segregation in metropolitan areas. Qualitatively, we find that concerns about safety are a primary mechanism for our SES-related finding. By showing the uneven geography of mobile crowdsourcing markets, it is our hope that this work can help bring the benefits of mobile crowdsourcing (and related concepts like ride-sharing) to a wider audience.

ACKNOWLEDGEMENTS
This work was supported in part by NSF grants IIS-1218826 and IIS-0808692 and a Yahoo! ACE Award. We would like to thank Darren Gergle, Shilad Sen, Aaron Rendahl, and our GroupLens colleagues for providing valuable feedback during the course of this work.

REFERENCES

1. Alt, F., Shirazi, A.S., Schmidt, A., Kramer, U., and Nawaz, Z. Location-based Crowdsourcing: Extending Crowdsourcing to the Real World. *October*, (2010).
2. American Psychological Association (APA). *Violence and Socioeconomic Status*. 2010.
3. Bernstein, M.S., Little, G., Miller, R.C., et al. Soylent: A Word Processor with a Crowd Inside. *Artificial Intelligence*, (2010), 313–322.
4. Bishop, B. *The Big Sort: Why the Clustering of Like-minded America is Tearing Us Apart*. Houghton Mifflin Harcourt, 2008.
5. Browne, A., Salomon, A., and Bassuk, S.S. The Impact of Recent Partner Violence on Poor Women's Capacity to Maintain Work. *Violence Against Women 5*, 4 (1999), 393–426.
6. Brunn, S.D., Williams, J.F., and Zeigler, D.J. *Cities of the World: World Regional Urban Development*. Rowman & Littlefield Publishers, 2003.
7. Buka, S.L., Stichick, T.L., Birdthistle, I., and Earls, F.J. Youth Exposure to Violence: Prevalence, Risks, and Consequences. *American Journal of Orthopsychiatry 71*, 3 (2001), 298–310.
8. Callison-Burch, C. Fast, Cheap, and Creative: Evaluating Translation Quality Using Amazon's Mechanical Turk. *Proceedings of the 2009 Conference on Empirical Methods in Natural Language Processing: Volume 1 - Volume 1*, Association for Computational Linguistics (2009), 286–295.
9. Ehrenreich, B. It Is Expensive to Be Poor. *The Atlantic*, 2014.
10. Fellmann, J.D., Getis, A., and Getis, J. *Human Geography: Landscapes of Human Activity*. McGraw-Hill, 2007.
11. Goodchild, M.F. Citizens as sensors: the world of volunteered geography. *GeoJournal 69*, 4 (2007), 211–221.
12. Haklay, M. How good is volunteered geographical information? A comparative study of OpenStreetMap and Ordnance Survey datasets. *Environment and Planning B: Planning and Design 37*, 4 (2010), 682–703.
13. Hecht, B. and Stephens, M. A Tale of Cities: Urban Biases in Volunteered Geographic Information. (2014).
14. Ipeirotis, P.G. *Demographics of Mechanical Turk*. 2010.
15. Irani, L.C. and Silberman, M.S. Turkopticon: Interrupting Worker Invisibility in Amazon Mechanical Turk. *Proceedings of the SIGCHI Conference on Human Factors in Computing Systems*, ACM (2013), 611–620.
16. Kittur, A., Smus, B., Khamkar, S., and Kraut, R.E. CrowdForge: Crowdsourcing Complex Work. *Proceedings of the 24th Annual ACM Symposium on User Interface Software and Technology*, ACM (2011), 43–52.
17. Lanegran, D.A. and Natoli, S. *Guidelines for Geographic Education in the Elementary and Secondary Schools*. Association of American Geographers, 1984.
18. Li, L., Goodchild, M.F., and Xu, B. Spatial, temporal, and socioeconomic patterns in the use of Twitter and Flickr. *Cartography and Geographic Information Science 40*, 2 (2013), 61–77.
19. Little, G., Chilton, L.B., Goldman, M., and Miller, R.C. TurKit: Tools for Iterative Tasks on Mechanical Turk. *Proceedings of the ACM SIGKDD Workshop on Human Computation*, (2009), 29–30.
20. Mashhadi, A., Quattrone, G., and Capra, L. Putting ubiquitous crowd-sourcing into context. *Proceedings of the 2013 conference on Computer supported cooperative work - CSCW '13*, (2013), 611.
21. Mashhadi, A., Quattrone, G., and Mooney, P. On the Sustainability of Urban Crowd-Sourcing for Maintaining Large-Scale Geospatial Databases Categories and Subject Descriptors. (2012).
22. McKnight, T.L. *Regional Geography of the United States and Canada*. Prentice Hall, 2004.
23. Mislove, A., Lehmann, S., Ahn, Y.-Y., Onnela, J.-P., and Rosenquist, J.N. Understanding the Demographics of Twitter Users. *ICWSM 11*, (2011), 5th.
24. Mooney, P., Corcoran, P., and Winstanley, A.C. Towards quality metrics for OpenStreetMap. *Proceedings of the 18th SIGSPATIAL International Conference on Advances in Geographic Information Systems - GIS '10*, (2010), 514.
25. Musthag, M. and Ganesan, D. Labor dynamics in a mobile micro-task market. *Proceedings of the SIGCHI Conference on Human Factors in Computing Systems - CHI '13*, (2013), 641.

26. Pavlick, E., Post, M., Irvine, A., Kachaev, D., and Callison-Burch, C. The Language Demographics of Amazon Mechanical Turk. *ACL '14*, (2014).

27. Priedhorsky, R., Masli, M., and Terveen, L. Eliciting and Focusing Geographic Volunteer Work. *CSCW '10: 2010 ACM Conference on Computer Supported Cooperative Work*, (2010).

28. Quattrone, G., Mashhadi, A., and Capra, L. Mind the Map: The Impact of Culture and Economic Affluence on Crowd- Mapping Behaviours. *CSCW '14*, (2014).

29. Rashtchian, C., Young, P., Hodosh, M., and Hockenmaier, J. Collecting Image Annotations Using Amazon's Mechanical Turk. *Proceedings of the NAACL HLT 2010 Workshop on Creating Speech and Language Data with Amazon's Mechanical Turk*, Association for Computational Linguistics (2010), 139–147.

30. Ross, J., Irani, L., Silberman, M.S., Zaldivar, A., and Tomlinson, B. Who Are the Crowdworkers?: Shifting Demographics in Mechanical Turk. *CHI '10 Extended Abstracts on Human Factors in Computing Systems*, ACM (2010), 2863–2872.

31. Sheppard, S.A., Wiggins, A., and Terveen, L. Capturing Quality: Retaining Provenance for Curated Volunteer Monitoring Data. *CSCW '14*, ACM (2014), 1234–1245.

32. Silverstein, A. Uber and Lyft Are Being Accused of Redlining Again, But Is That Actually Happening? *Dallas Observer*, 2014.

33. Singer, C. Ridesharing and Redlining: Uber, Lyft, Race and Class. *Daily Kos*, 2014. http://www.dailykos.com/story/2014/05/27/1302417/-Ridesharing-and-Redlining-Uber-Lyft-Race-and-Class#.

34. Smith, A. *Smartphone Ownership 2013*. Pew Internet & American Life Project, 2013.

35. Teodoro, R., Ozturk, P., Naaman, M., Mason, W., and Lindqvist, J. The motivations and experiences of the on-demand mobile workforce. ACM Press (2014), 236–247.

36. United States Census. 2010 Geographic Terms and Concepts - Census Tract. http://www.census.gov/geo/reference/gtc/gtc_ct.html.

37. Zielstra, D. and Zipf, A. A comparative study of proprietary geodata and volunteered geographic information for Germany. *Conference on Geographic Information 1*, (2010), 1–15.

38. *2011 FDIC National Survey of Unbanked and Underbanked Households*. Federal Deposit Insurance Corporation, 2011.

39. Gigwalk Announces $6 Million In Funding, Expands Relationship With Microsoft, And Names New CEO. http://gigwalk.com/press/gigwalk-announces-6-million-in-funding-expands-relationship-with-microsoft-and-names-new-ceo.php.

40. TaskRabbit. https://www.taskrabbit.com.

41. GigWalk. http://gigwalk.com.

42. Field Agent. http://www.fieldagent.net.

Connecting in the Kitchen: An Empirical Study of Physical Interactions while Cooking Together at Home

Jeni Paay, Jesper Kjeldskov and Mikael B. Skov
Department of Computer Science / Centre for Socio+Interactive Design
Aalborg University, Selma Lagerlöfs Vej 300, DK-9220 Aalborg East, Denmark
{jeni, jesper, dubois}@cs.aau.dk

ABSTRACT

Recent research has explored the role technology might play in future kitchens, including virtually dining together, recipe sharing, augmented kitchen furniture, reactive cooking utensils and gestural interaction. When people come together in a kitchen to cook it is about more than just production of sustenance – it is about being together, helping each other, exchanging stories, and contributing to the gradual emergence of a shared meal. In this paper we present a digital ethnography of how people coordinate and cooperate in their kitchens when cooking together for the purpose of inspiring the design of social natural user interactions for technologies in the kitchen. The study is based on 61 YouTube videos of people cooking together analyzed using the frameworks of proxemics and F-formations. Our findings unfold and illustrate relationships between people's spatial organization, their cooking activities and physical kitchen layouts. Based on these we discuss the kitchen as a design space and particularly the opportunities for social natural user interaction design.

Author Keywords

F-formations; proxemics; natural user interaction; cooking together; digital ethnography; digital kitchens; the home

ACM Classification Keywords

H5.3 Computer-supported cooperative work

INTRODUCTION

In the past decade there has been a marked increase in CSCW research centered on the home, rather than the office. This indicates an enormous potential for innovation in domestic information technology [51]. At the same time with the advent of off-the-shelf availability and affordability of motion sensing natural interaction technologies, such as Microsoft's Kinect, perhaps we can look beyond the realms of family participation in gaming and envision new approaches to technologies for the home, exploring new opportunities and applications. In thinking about natural user interactions as inputs to technologies in the home, it follows that we need to understand of the kinds of physical and gestural interactions that happen in co-located domestic shared activities.

Studying and analyzing human behavior in physical space, and the way we use technology and other artifacts around us, are not new ideas. As discussed by Rogers [49], a number of theories from other disciplines, new or relatively unknown to the fields of CSCW and HCI, are currently making their way into our research. Some of these, she argues, represent "the beginnings of a 'turn to space'", including schematic frameworks for modeling people's interactions with each other in physical space, such as *proxemics* and *F-formations.* Developed for analyzing social interactions outside the technology domain, these theories and frameworks have recently proved to be highly valuable in relation to interaction design as this domain broadens itself, embracing the challenges of digital ecologies and pervasive and ubiquitous computing. Our approach is supported by Reitmeier et al. [48] who state: *"Two major conceptual lenses used to describe and analyse co-located situations and interactions are Adam Kendon's F-formations and Edward Hall's proxemics".*

In past work, using proxemics and F-formations, we studied how people physically orient themselves when they are cooking together [44]. We found that the spatial organization of behavior in the context of the shared cooking activity goes beyond the kinds of formations found in purely conversational contexts, and is directly influenced by the architectural design of kitchen spaces, which structures the kinds of interactions and social activities that take place there. Cooking activities and artifacts used in cooking also contribute to the kinds of patterns that occur.

In this paper, we analyze the juxtaposition of the physical formations reported in our earlier papers [43, 44] against the different kinds of cooking activities that people are involved in to better understand the ways multiple people coordinate and cooperate when cooking, including both physical and conversational interactions. We then extend our thinking to general ideas on how our findings might be applied to the design of cooperative natural user interaction technologies to enhance the cooking experience - being assistive, social, and celebratory [13] in approach.

CSCW '15, March 14-18, 2015, Vancouver, BC, Canada.
Copyright 2015 ACM 978-1-4503-2922-4/15/03...$15.00
http://dx.doi.org/10.1145/2675133.2675194

RELATED WORK

There is a small but extant literature in HCI and CSCW regarding the actual practices of cooking, covering a wide range of different perspectives and interests. Cooking and eating are central activities of human experience and as such are relevant to these disciplines [23]. To support the design of technology solutions for kitchens that are usable, useful and facilitate enjoyable experiences, researchers are working to provide grounded understandings of the needs and activities of cooks in different contexts [27].

Ethnographically inspired approaches such as direct observations combined with interviews are the most common techniques to understanding the current practices of people cooking and eating, such as in the work of Bell et al. [2], Chamberlain and Griffiths [7], Crabtree et al. [10] and Kerr et al. [27]. This has been done across different cultures to achieve a new perspective on the activity of cooking [2], and to understand user goals and practices in meal preparation [7, 27]. Sometimes the focus is on how people appropriate new and old kitchen technologies in their cooking [2, 37]. Other studies use indirect methods to gather data, such as the work by Hupfeld and Rodden [23] who use self reporting in the form of photographs of family meals with follow up interviews, or Clear et al. [8] who use fixed cameras mounted in kitchens for automatically recording cooking activities.

The outcomes of these "understanding" studies take a variety of forms, e.g. design strategies [2], cooking personas [27], implications for design [8, 23], all aimed at informing the design of kitchen technologies. Extending this body of work, our own research focuses explicitly on understanding cooking practices as a social activity embedded in a particular physical space. This has encouraged us to explore the 'turn to space' in CSCW and HCI research encouraged by, amongst others, Rogers [49] and Greenberg et al. [12], through the use of frameworks for modeling people's interactions with each other in physical space, such as proxemics and F-formations.

Proxemics covers a topic concerned with peoples' use of their immediate physical space in their interaction and communication with each other. It was originally developed by Edward Hall, a cultural anthropologist, in the early 1960s [16], but has recently gained renewed momentum as a framework for describing and understanding people's interaction with devices and displays around them. In brief, Hall proposed that (in the USA) four interpersonal distances govern social interaction: *intimate* (0-0.46m), *personal* (0.46-1.22m), *social* (1.22-3.66m) and *public* (>3.66m). In the context of CSCW this provides a useful framework for analyzing and designing interactive technology for people working together. Examples of this include Obata and Sasaki' virtual visiting system [38], Heaton's case studies of social interaction in virtual workspaces [20], and more recently in a general interaction design context, the works of Greenberg et al. on Proxemic Interactions [12].

F-formations is part of a conceptual framework about people's interpersonal spacing and orientation developed by Adam Kendon, a leading researcher in the study of gesture, in the late 1970s [25, 26]. The notion of F-formations helps explain how people arrange themselves spatially with respect to others, and to artifacts, in different kinds of social interactions and collaborations. It can also be used to explore the influence of physical environment on the interpersonal interactions taking place there. It was developed by Kendon in response to previous studies in proxemics in order to draw attention to the fact that *"participants in occasions of interactions of all sorts may enter together into a cooperative relationship to sustain, through time, a more or less constant pattern of spatial orientational arrangement"* [Kendon 2012, pers. comm.].

Briefly described, in an F-formation system, individuals have a space called a *transactional segment,* which is the space where they focus attention and manipulate artifacts. This space is defined in relationship to their lower body, and changes in size depending on the kind of activity people are doing. An F-formation is formed when the transactional segments of two or more people overlap and create a shared inner space, where the shared activity of those people occurs. This is called the *o-space* [25] or the *use-space* [26].

Like proxemics, the work on F-formations has recently attracted interest among CSCW and HCI researchers concerned with design and use of technology embedded in the physical environment, for example in the works of [21, 21, 30, 31, 34, 35, 41]. In the study by Marshall et al. [31] the F-formation system is used for analyzing social interactions between visitors and staff in an information center for tourists. They show how the presence or absence of F-formations can explain the relationship between co-located interactions and the physical environment, and how this can inform technology design. Mentis et al. [34] conduct a similar analysis but in the context of work practices in neurosurgery theatres. This leads to insight about the spatial organization of shared work practices in this specific setting, and to understanding design implications for touch-less interaction with medical technology. Other uses of F-formations in HCI include investigating the spatial relationships between humans and service robots during cooperative tasks [21], detecting F-formations from video footage for analyzing social behavior in crowded environments [21], and for supporting cross-device interaction [30].

F-FORMATIONS IN COOKING TOGETHER

Through a study of user-created videos on YouTube we analyzed how people arrange themselves spatially in their kitchens while cooking together. In previous papers [43, 44] we observed four of Kendon's known F-formations, *Side-by-side, L-shaped, Vis-à-vis*, and *Semi-circular*, but also identified four *new formations* not described previously. We named these new formations *wide V-shaped*, *Spooning*,

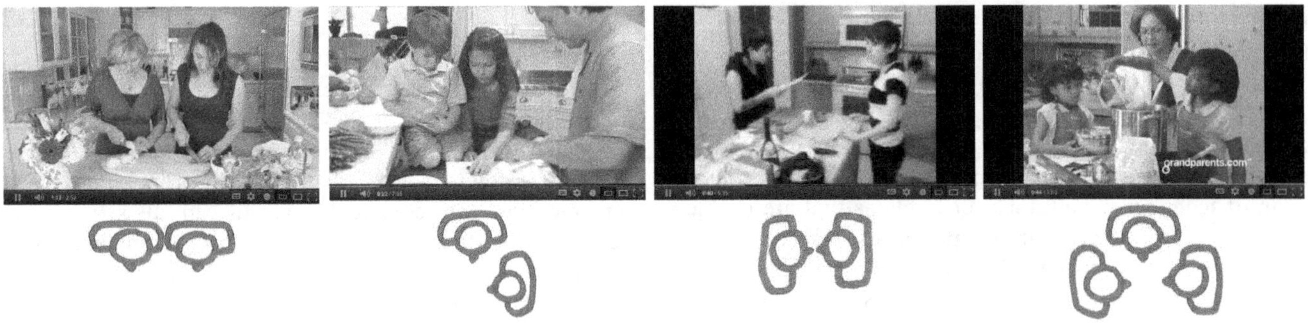

Side-by-side L-shaped Vis-à-vis Semi-circular

Figure 1. Known F-formations observed while cooking together

Z-shaped, and *reverse L-shaped*. As these eight formations all play an important part in our further analysis of interactions while cooking together presented in this paper, we will briefly describe them.

Figure 1 illustrates the four known F-formations observed while cooking together: *Side-by-side, L-shaped, Vis-à-vis, and Semi-circular*. The *Side-by-side* formation occurs when two people are standing next to each other abreast and facing in the same direction. As described by Kendon [26] this is a common formation when people are jointly concerned about something in their immediate environment. While cooking together, this formation was typically observed when people were working at the same kitchen bench. The *L-shaped* formation occurs when people are standing or sitting with their torsos orthogonal to each other and facing towards a shared transactional space in front of them. Kendon relates this formation to conversations between two people where the topic is disembodied. This formation was often observed when working on a shared task at the corner of a bench while cooking together. The *Vis-à-vis* formation occurs when people are standing opposite and facing each other, creating a shared transactional space between them. Unlike the L-shaped formation, Kendon relates this formation to conversations between two people where the topic is related to their relationship. While cooking together this formation was often observed when working on two sides of a freestanding kitchen bench. The *Semi-circular* formation occurs when more than two people are standing in a circular shape with one side of the circle open. This formation is common when more than two people are engaged in a shared conversation while either watching the same thing or being open to other people joining in. This formation was often observed when gathered around a stove or similar shared point of focus.

While it is in itself interesting to observe how known F-formations appear slightly differently from purely conversational situations in the context of human-food interaction, the more remarkable finding was that the activity of shared cooking clearly made way for new formations notably different from those normally found in interpersonal communication, illustrated in Figure 2: *wide V-shaped, Spooning, Z-shaped, and reverse L-shaped*. The *wide V-shaped* formation occurs when two people are standing next to each other, but rather than facing in the same direction are turning their bodies slightly towards each other so that they are facing the same shared space in front of them. While cooking together, this formation occurs frequently when people are working along the same kitchen bench but also engaged in conversation or collaboration. The *Spooning* formation describes a rather intimate interaction occurring when one person approaches another from behind and enters closely into facing the same direction and sharing the same immediate space in front of them both. While cooking together this formation was often observed when the physical layout prevented other ways of

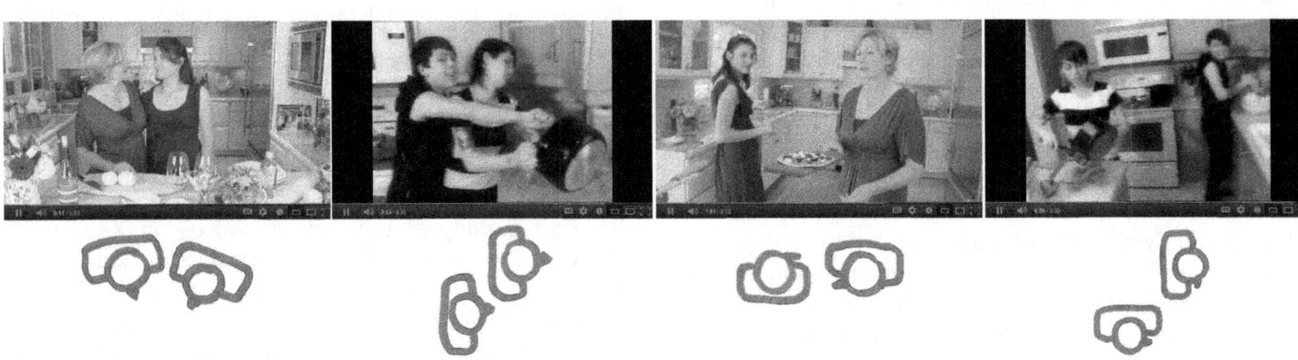

Wide V-shaped Spooning Z-shaped Reverse L-shaped

Figure 2. New formations observed while cooking together

sharing the same transactional space, and where the people cooking together had a close personal relationship (e.g. partners or parents with their children). The *Z-shaped* formation occurs when two interacting people are standing side-by-side but facing in opposite directions. This would seldom happen in a purely conversational context, but appears to be quite a comfortable way of interacting while cooking together. Here it is often observed when people are working at different kitchen benches, or when passing each other, while also engaged in conversation or collaboration. Finally, the *reverse L-shaped* formation occurs when two people are placed orthogonal to each other but with their torsos facing *away* from each other. This would seldom happen during normal conversation, but was observed often when people are working on orthogonal kitchen benches.

COOPERATION IN COOKING TOGETHER

The findings presented above and further below are based on an observational study of people cooking together in their own kitchens. However, in order to gain access to such situations we have had to deal with some methodological challenges. As discussed several times in CSCW and HCI research (e.g. [9, 36]), and charmingly illustrated in Hamer's movie "Kitchen Stories" [18], although the home is relatively easy to access, it is not always possible or desirable to meaningfully do traditional direct observation in people's homes. Not only is it a well-known social phenomenon that people alter their behavior when being watched (The Hawthorne Effect), but researcher presence in people's *private homes* is also likely to disrupt the flow of household activities as they would normally unfold, and raises new challenges of ethics and preservation of privacy. Consequently, conducting research in a home presents its own set of particular challenges, and although anthropologists have been faced with these for decades, and valuable insights on the practical aspects of such research exists (e.g. [1, 28, 39]), these challenges are still considered difficult to overcome with traditional methodological tools.

In response to some of these challenges, research into the domestic domain has explored a range of data collection approaches, including installing video cameras in people's homes [9], and has to a large extent turned to methods of self-reporting for obtaining insight into people's daily lives with minimal interference. This has been done through various techniques and data collection media, such as cultural probes [15], technology probes [24], experience sampling [36], and diaries [45]. Taking a step further, Masten and Plowman [32] suggest that if we really want to understand people and their everyday lives then we need to rethink and reconfigure the principles and techniques of traditional ethnography to include *digital* realms to a much greater extent. As many aspects of our everyday lives today leave an increasing digital footprint, we should use this as a key source of data. Masten and Plowman propose the notion of "digital ethnography" as a form of ethnography where the source of information includes all sorts of digital technology capable of sensing aspects of their surroundings. In using these data sources for digital ethnography, researchers make use of digital data, such as written words, images, audio files, video and online communities, about the phenomenon of interest, which is often publically available in vast amounts.

Using YouTube as a Data Source

Inspired by the notion of digital ethnography, and other studies making use of YouTube as a data source (e.g. [3, 4, 19, 50]), we have explored an alternative approach to obtaining insights into what happens in people's private homes while cooking together by drawing on user-generated video recordings posted on YouTube. Using YouTube videos as a data source in an ethnographic-type study is not a new idea and has previously been used to good effect in other studies. For example, YouTube video postings were used by Blythe and Cairns [4] to study user engagement with a specific digital musical instrument, by Harley and Fitzpatrick [19] to study social contact between older and younger people, and by Rotman and Preece [50] to study the creation of online communities through video sharing. When chosen carefully, Blythe and Cairns [4] argue that YouTube potentially provides several interesting avenues of inquiry as a digital on-line data source. However, working with YouTube data in a digital ethnography also presents a number of challenges and potential limitations that need to be acknowledged.

While YouTube videos potentially give us access to study life and behavior in real world settings that are difficult to study with traditional ethnographic techniques, it is important to notice that the context in which these videos were produced is very different from the context of an observational study by an ethnographer or anthropologist. Firstly, it is important to acknowledge that ethnographic engagements are rarely matters of detached objective observation but rather built upon researcher participation, or membership, where the observer can inquire into the details of a situation, and move beyond their own "local" reasoning into the reasoning of the observed parties. In the case of using YouTube videos, or similar video material detached from the actual situation, this participation is obviously restricted, limiting the extent of possible insight. In relation to this, it is also important to recognize that some contextual cues are bound to be missing from the relatively low-fidelity recordings posted on YouTube (compared to in-person observation), and that context, which might have been recognized as important by a researcher, may not have been attended to by the camera-person due to the different purpose of the recording. This means that important things may well be happening off-screen and go unnoticed by the digital ethnographer. Consequently, YouTube videos cannot be treated as documentation of particular situations to the same degree that researcher video recordings might be. These limitations need to be considered when analyzing YouTube video data.

Another challenge in the use of YouTube video material is their potentially "performative" nature. Here it is important to recognize that YouTube videos are particular media artifacts in their own right, and not necessarily neutral recordings of the world around us. YouTube videos are often filmed and published for a particular purpose, and may carry an implicit view or perspective of the person who created and uploaded it. This means that YouTube videos are not always pure captures of home life, but are sometimes "staged" performances for the camera and for the YouTube medium. This clearly introduces a potential Hawthorne Effect (possibly different from the one introduced by researcher presence), which needs to be taken into consideration when analyzing such videos.

Despite these challenges and limitations, however, we find that there is some merit in exploring the use of YouTube videos as a source of data for digital ethnography in CSCW and HCI research, provided that they are acknowledged for what they are, and what they are not, in relation to the observational power that we assign to them. In fact we feel that the vast amount of video recordings from ordinary people's lives is a potentially rich source of additional data for ethnographic research in CSCW and HCI. But as with any new source of data, of course, we need to learn how to best analyze it, and understand its limitations.

Method

As people voluntarily and enthusiastically share a variety of different cooking situations from their homes on YouTube, we chose this as our data source for investigating the physical interactions of people cooking together at home. Through "purposeful sampling" [47] of YouTube material we were able to rapidly gain access to a breadth of data about a variety of people's social cooking activities across different generations, cultures and situations.

Using the keyword phrase "cooking together", 169 videos were found on YouTube through a search on 15th November 2010. After discarding duplicates and unrelated videos (e.g. a song with the words "cooking together" in the lyrics), a final set of 61 videos of people cooking together remained. Three trained researchers all analyzed these 61 videos from three different conceptual perspectives (using different analytical lenses): *1. Spatial Arrangements*; *2. Social Interactions*; and *3. Cooking Situations*. Early findings from our analysis of spatial arrangements are described in a previous paper [44], while in this paper we are looking across all three perspectives.

As the first step of our analysis, inspired by Blythe an Cairns [3, 4], we conducted a qualitative content analysis of the 61 videos in order to establish their purpose, what they were about, who was in them, etc. This analysis showed that the videos spanned a range of genres, people and social settings. The majority of videos were made by families and friends in their home kitchens. The largest group were home videos showing amateurs cooking together as part of daily life (28 videos) or for sharing cooking advice with others (13 videos). Others were "mini documentaries" with both professional and amateur cooks (10 videos). A small number were educational to teach children how to cook (5), or professional cooking shows and ads for such shows (5).

As the second step, we used Kendon's diagramming practice for recording F-formations at a birthday party [25] to "transcribe" the videos, recording patterns of behavior by creating a series of maps of the physical kitchen layouts (figure 3), showing the arrangements and movements of people and cameras within that space.

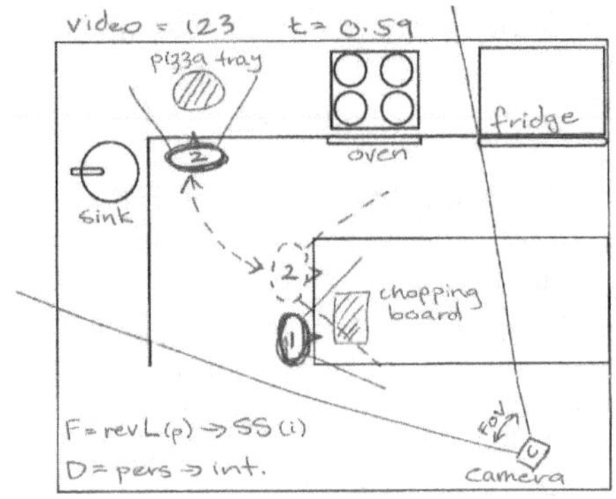

Figure 3. Map transcription from video 123 at t=0:59

Each map is time stamped *(t)* and records a newly established position of individuals. People are shown as numbered ovals with two lines extending to show their transactional segment, and hence where these intersect to create an F-formation. Previous positions and paths of movement through spaces are represented, as are kitchen artifacts currently being used. We also documented the virtual position of the camera and its field of view. Finally, we noted each person's current activity, the topic of conversation (from the audio track), and the focus of the current camera shot.

As the third step, we examined the map transcriptions of the 61 videos through applied thematic analysis [14]. As our guiding themes of analysis we used Kendon's framework of F-formations [25] to identify the interpersonal spacing and orientation between the cooks, and Hall's framework of interpersonal distances [16] to identify their proximity. Subtle differences in F-formations, such as the side-by-side versus the wide-V formation, were established by looking at the overlap between people's transactional space, and the angle between their upper bodies (less than 180°). While the map transcriptions mostly provided enough detail for the applied thematic analysis, such subtleties sometimes required going back to the video recordings.

As the final step, we revisited the identified formations in the 61 videos, using timestamps from the map transcription. Looking at these formations we were able to further identify three distinguishable task-related configurations, and four related collaboration-oriented actions. This gave us an awareness of different interdependencies between

Figure 4. Working on related tasks with: side-by-side (top row) and L-shaped (bottom row)

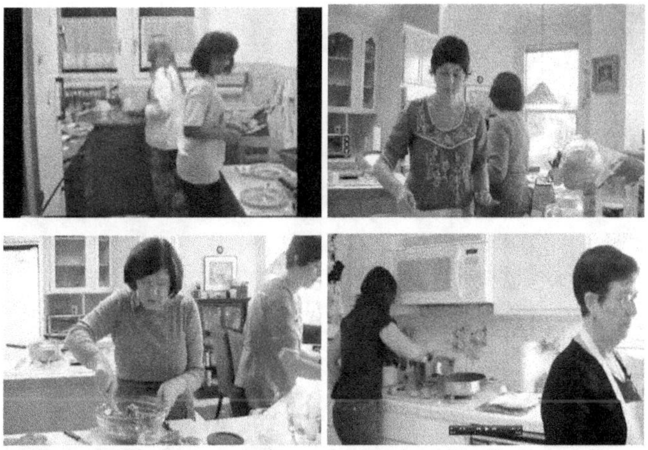

Figure 5. Working on independent tasks with: Z-shaped (top row) and reverse L-shaped (bottom row)

cooking tasks, interpersonal interactions, and spatial patterns of cooks in respect to the kitchen layout.

FINDINGS

In the following sections, we describe and illustrate the different cooking situations identified in our analysis, and the spatial formations that characterize them. These are three distinguishable task-related configurations: working on *related tasks*, working on *independent tasks* and working on *shared tasks*; and four related collaboration-oriented actions: *observing*, *checking*, *helping* and *showing*.

Task-Related Configurations

Working on Related Tasks

When cooking together people often work on related tasks, e.g. chopping up vegetables for a meal. In such situations, people will distribute sub-tasks between them, and they will often be working in parallel on tasks that are related to each other, but can advantageously be done at the same time. This often happens, for example, during the early stages of producing a meal where various food materials and ingredients need to be prepared for later stages, including cleaning and chopping up vegetables, seasoning meats, and mixing ingredients. In these situations, we found that people often work in either Side-by-side or L-shaped formation, depending on the layout of the specific kitchen (see figure 4). In kitchens with long bench tops and bench tops placed along a wall, the Side-by-side formation is prevalent. In kitchens with freestanding benches accessible from several sides, the L-shaped formation is also characteristic of this situation. The reason for these formations happening while working on related tasks is that these tasks often naturally take place in the same area of the kitchen, requiring the collaborating cooks to negotiate this space between them. This can be done by standing abreast or orthogonal to each other, depending on the layout and other affordances of the physical cooking space.

Working on Independent Tasks

The distribution of responsibilities while cooking together also happens in relation to tasks that are not closely related, e.g. one mixing up ingredients while another is washing up dishes. This means that at some point of the joint production of a meal, people start working individually on independent tasks. These independent tasks are typically coordinated, but do not need close collaboration and may be quite different. This often happens at the intermediate and late stages of meal production, and involves working with different food materials, working on different dishes, and using different types of tools. In these situations we found that people tend to spread out more in the shared kitchen space, and enter into formations that are quite different from those found in relation to interpersonal communication. We especially found that while working on independent tasks, people often enter into Z-shaped or reverse L-shaped formations, subject to the layout of the kitchen and location of particular artifacts such as ovens, stoves, sinks, etc. (see figure 5).

In kitchens with two parallel benches, the Z-shaped formation is prevalent. In kitchens with orthogonal benches, formed in a corner, the reverse L-shaped formation is prevalent. In kitchens with freestanding cooking islands, both Z-shaped and reverse L-shaped formations occur. The reason for these two formations happening while working on independent tasks is that they typically involve working in different places in the kitchen, resulting in the collaborating cooks facing away from each other, while still talking to each other.

Working on Shared Tasks

Contrasting distributed work on independent tasks, cooking together also involves situations of closer collaboration where people work together on the same shared task. This happens at all stages of the meal production, from preparation of ingredients, handing over or exchanging food materials at intermediate stages, to putting together and

Figure 6. Working on shared tasks with: wide V-shaped (top row), semi-circular (middle row), and vis-á-vis (bottom row)

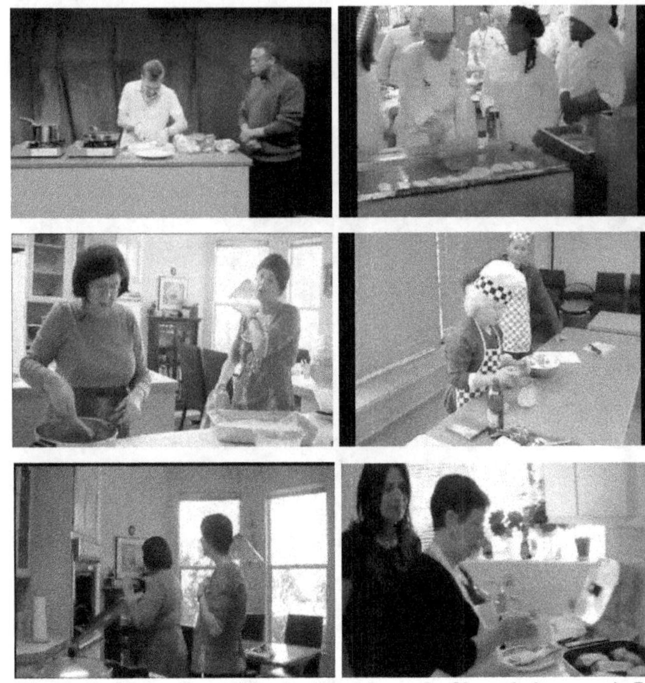

Figure 7. Observing with: L-shaped - end of bench (top row), L-shaped – along bench (middle row), and spooning (bottom row)

arranging the final meal, and typically involves working together on the same food materials or with the same tools. In these situations we found that people often work in wide V-shaped, Semi-circular or Vis-à-vis formations depending on group size and the layout of the kitchen (see figure 6).

In groups of two the wide V-shaped formation is very common, and typically occurs when working along the same kitchen bench. Here it is often observed that two collaborating cooks will shift between working Side-by-side on related tasks to a wide V-shaped formation when exchanging or mixing the materials they were each working on independently. In groups of more than two, the wide V-shaped formation is often extended into a Semi-circular formation with people standing around a common focus point, such as a bowl or tray on the bench, or a pot or pan on the stove. In kitchens with a freestanding bench, working on a shared task is sometimes done across the bench from opposite sides in a Vis-à-vis formation.

Collaboration-oriented actions

Observing

While cooking together is mostly an activity where all people involved are active, we further identified situations where only one person would be working or cooking while others just passively observed this person. This often happens when one person is demonstrating a cooking technique, or explaining something related to a particular cooking task or food product. It also happens when a person has finished what they were doing but the other still has something to do. In these situations people tend to enter into the facing formation typically associated with interpersonal communication about a disembodied topic, namely the L-shaped formation (see figure 7). This means that they place themselves orthogonal to the person cooking and sometimes the cooking bench. Depending on the kitchen layout, this can either be along one side of the bench, or, if the bench sticks out into the room, by standing at the end of it. Alternatively, in some situations, people enter into a Spooning formation observing over the shoulder of the person in front of them.

Checking

Somewhat related to the situations where people observe someone else who is currently engaged with a cooking task, people cooking together often check up on what their co-cooks are doing. Sometimes this would happen only briefly while in between doing other tasks and served the general purpose of creating and maintaining a level of common ground throughout the overall joint activity of creating the meal. In other situations where children were involved in the cooking activity, checking would happen when parents (or other adults) checked up on the task of the children. In both situations, people are able to align what they do with the tasks and doings of others, and they are also able to intervene if deemed necessary. The difference between observing and checking is that observation is typically passive and removed, while checking is active and focused with the person knowing what they are looking for. When checking up on what others are doing, people typically enter into formations looking over the other person's shoulder – sometimes with intimate proximity – in order to

Figure 8. Checking with: spooning-intimate (top row), spooning-personal (middle row), and L-shaped (bottom row)

Figure 9. Showing with spooning-intimate (top row), spooning-personal (middle row), and L-shaped (bottom row)

be able to see up close what the other person is seeing and doing. Depending on their relationship, formations are typically the Spooning or L-shaped type (see figure 8). If the collaborating cooks are intimate others (i.e. partners, parents with young children, close friends, etc.) the Spooning formation is often observed. If they are not, then more distance and personal space is usually maintained, which is possible in L-shaped formations.

Showing

When people cook together they sometimes need to intervene with what the other person is doing and show them how to do it, e.g. adding seasoning to a meal. This means that they will sometimes enter into the other person's transactional space and modify their actions or sometimes even take over completely. This often happens during the middle or final stages of meal production where attention to detail is important, and involves specific actions such as adding herbs or spices, stirring or turning, removing food from a heat source, changing the temperature of the oven or stove, etc. In these situations we found that people very often enter into Spooning configurations with partially or completely overlapping transactional spaces in front of them (see figure 9). The reason for this particular formation, which is not usual during, for example, normal interpersonal communication, is that intervention is often something that needs to happen quickly, and will only last for a very short time before control is handed back. Hence, when entering into a Spooning configuration one does not force the other to withdraw from the task they are working on – in fact by standing behind someone in a Spooning formation at a bench or stove it becomes rather difficult for the other person to withdraw. When showing in a Spooning formation, you are merely providing an extra pair of hands and eyes for a short period of time.

Depending on their level of intimacy, people may show things in a way that is less intrusive of the other person's physical space. Here the L-shaped formation allows for reaching into another person's transactional space from either side without bodies touching or breaching the other person's intimate distance (figure 9, bottom left). The L-shaped formation can also be observed when the intervention is major and will not be brief, for example when taking over a task completely (figure 9, bottom right).

Helping

When producing a meal together, situations sometimes occur that require very close and coordinated collaboration between two or more people acting together as one to help each other. This typically happens when a task simply requires more than one pair of hands, such as operating a particular tool, shifting food between pots or bowls, moving something in or out of the oven, etc. It also happens if a person simply needs help with a particular task because they are inexperienced with it, for example when cooking with children. Situations of helping occur at all stages of meal production, from preparing food materials, cooking different parts of the meal, to putting together and arranging the final meal. Depending on the specific task, the kitchen layout, the number of people, and their relationship, it leads to a variety of different physical configurations of people, most notably Vis-à-vis, L-shaped, Spooning and Semi-circular formations (see figure 10). Depending on the layout

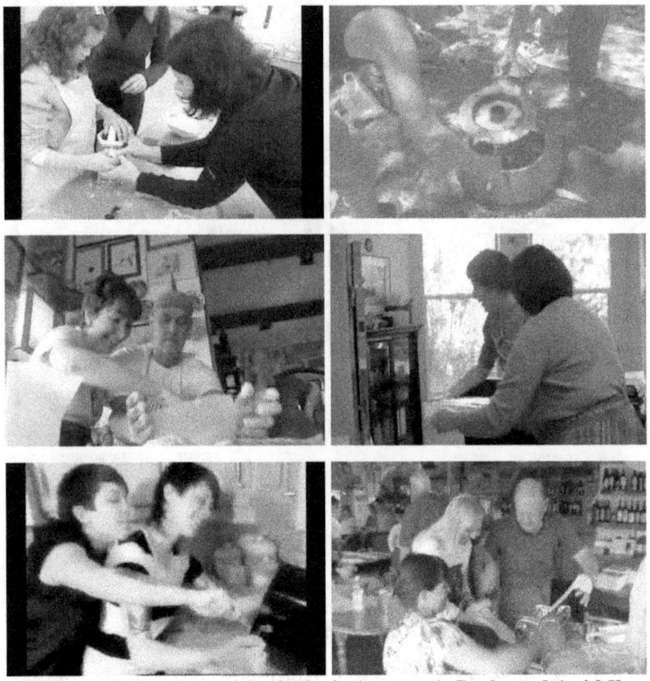

Figure 10. Helping with vis-á-vis (top row), L-shaped (middle row), and spooning and semi-circular (bottom row)

of the kitchen, the Vis-à-vis formation allows two people to help on food and tools in the transactional space between them, such as grating a piece of fruit (figure 10, top left) or shifting something hot or heavy (figure 10, top right). If working along the same side of a kitchen bench, or directly in front of an appliance, helping often takes place by entering into L-shaped or Spooning formations. As described earlier, the L-shaped formation is the less intimate of the two, and allows for the creation of a shared transactional space by standing orthogonal to each other and reaching into the area in front without breaching intimate distance and having bodily contact (figure 10, middle left and right). The Spooning configuration, however, allows two people to completely share a transactional space in front of them both, simply allowing more than one pair of hands to operate in this space, like when scraping food out of a pot (figure 10, bottom left). In Semi-circular formations, people are able to help with food or tools in their shared transactional space, like operating a pasta maker (figure 10, bottom right).

DISCUSSION

The kitchen as a design space

We reviewed CSCW and HCI literature for research on the design of innovative technologies for the home, specifically the kitchen. Of the designs that we found, most aim to provide cooking assistance in the form of digital recipe systems or how-to-cook applications. Notable examples of purpose built kitchens which explore this concept are AR Kitchen [5] which gives real time recipe assistance to cooks by projecting steps, quantities and temperatures onto kitchen surfaces, and Ambient Kitchen [42] which uses a combination of projectors, cameras, RFID tags and readers, object mounted accelerometers, and under-floor pressure sensing to guide people with dementia through a cooking session. Both involve natural interactions with technology. In the AR Kitchen people use a combination of touch and mid-air gestures to control the advance of recipe instructions. In the Ambient Kitchen people interact with the system by physically moving around the kitchen, by working with augmented cooking utensils and by turning pages of a paper based recipe book.

Natural user interactions in the kitchen make good sense when we think about the other roles that hands must play in the activity of cooking. People are handling ingredients and cooking implements while operating kitchen equipment such as stoves and ovens. Their hands go through various stages of business, wetness and messiness making traditional direct manipulations interfaces, and interaction devices such as keyboards and mice problematic. Some systems have tried to work with this problem. The eyeCOOK recipe system progresses a cook through the recipe using the natural input modalities of eye movement and speech [5]. Cooking Navi [17] uses a foot switch to replace the mouse, and a waterproof touch pen for use on a touch screen for operating their daily cooking assistance system. More recently, Panger [46] explored the use of a Microsoft Kinect in the kitchen to implement a recipe navigator, timer and music player using touch-less gestural control during the activity of cooking with messy hands. Although these designs explore natural interactions in the kitchen, they are aimed at supporting a single cook, which in reality is not always the case. Often the kitchen becomes a meeting place for families and friends, where people come together and share their daily experiences, while participating in the activity of preparing a meal.

Of more interest to us within the context of our study were: 'Living Cookbook' [52] and 'Personal Chef' [33]. The 'Living Cookbook' enhances the social aspects of cooking while learning to cook. It includes a touch screen display mounted on a cupboard in front of the cooks, in a vis-à-vis configuration. Videos of friends/instructors cooking, ingredients and recipes are shown on the screen, and sometimes involve multiple cooks at the same location. Multiple cameras were used to video both the cook and the preparation area. Similarly 'Personal Chef' aims to support the social process of cooking using a multi-display, dual-perspective interactive kitchen counter. Their upright display is also in a vis-à-vis configuration, behind the stove with a second display on the counter top. So, when these designs add the presence of a video tutor or video link, they place it in the vis-à-vis configuration with the cook – just like traditional video conferencing - but in the total number of formations (929) that we identified in the videos of people cooking together, only 7% were vis-à-vis. It was not a typical way for people to relate to each other when cooking together, nor was it used for the activities of observing, checking, showing or helping.

In designing for the situation of people cooking together, a deeper understanding of the social and physical nuances of cooking becomes extremely important. The systems we reviewed, rather than being built on empirical findings, were technology driven, deployed as technology probes [24], and then evaluated with users to find design ideas and opportunities for redesign. Our approach in exploring human-food interaction technologies as a potential design space [13] was to study multiple cooks coordinating and cooperating in a home kitchen. From this we have provided an empirically devised catalogue of physical interactions in the kitchen based on the configurations and actions people engage in when cooking together. From this, we can then start to think about different design opportunities for new technologies in the kitchen.

Designing for social natural user interaction

Motion sensing natural interaction technologies, such as Microsoft's Kinect, invite a new approach to the interaction design of technologies for the kitchen. Rather than the kinds of direct manipulation interfaces that predominate most cooking support systems surveyed, we can start to think about proxemics and formations of multiple people as inputs to technology. By understanding concurrent activities and movements, within a variety of kitchen layouts, we can imagine a system that aligns with and augments different aspects of the cooking experience for people sharing the activity of cooking. With multiple cooks it becomes important to consider both the physical aspects of food preparation and the social aspects of cooking together. Our findings give a useful starting point from which to consider the kinds of opportunities available for touch-less gestural control of technology in the kitchen. For example, one could imagine gestural controls designed specifically to be available and functioning from a range of different interpersonal spatial arrangements and distances. Studies that propose informed designs for natural user interfaces for emerging technologies, such as Microsoft's Kinect, Nintendo Wii, and wearable sensing devices in non-gaming areas are starting to appear in CSCW and HCI literature. This is especially pertinent in situations where users are trying to achieve important and timely tasks, and where touch-less interaction and gestural input are necessary for reasons of hygiene (e.g. surgery [40]), messiness (e.g. cooking [46]) or movement (e.g. physical training [11], learning physics theory [29]).

In one of our related studies on collocated intergenerational cooking [37] we watched different combinations of grandchildren, parents and children cooking together in their home kitchens. In our findings, we note that the hands of cooks are often busy or fully engaged, using tools, picking up ingredients, or communicating to each other through gestures and even physical touch. So when considering the usefulness of natural interaction technologies in the home kitchens we need to be mindful that the gross physical movements required by contemporary gestural sensors, such as Microsoft's Kinect, and input from multiple closely positioned users could be problematic in a cluttered cooking space. The amount of movement in the kitchen, comprising body movements, as well as hands moving to communicate and undertake cooking tasks, has implications for technology attempting to capture specific inputs.

It is therefore valuable to be able to assign meaning to different configurations of spatial positioning within the cooking context. Design approaches should not intervene directly in cooking activities to the extent that they distract from the experience of cooking but rather that they complement it [37]. In our user-centered approach to designing technology for the kitchen, it is the knowledge and understandings of current practice generated through studies of people cooking together that should be used to inspire creative interventions that add to the experience.

We suggest that in designing technology to augment the cooking together experience, displays, touch screens and cameras installed at a single location in the kitchen do not cater for the varied physical movements and social interactions that take place around food preparation and make it a meaningful and positive experience. The kinds of designs we envisage use multiple sensing devices, for example, several Kinect camera's taking in people's positions from various angles, not just face-to-face. Or using ceiling mounted Kinect camera's to recognize and relate our task-related configurations to kitchen architecture and cooking artifacts, or to register proxemic distances between cooks. When combining this with gestures as input to the system it should be possible to provide both ambient and instrumental additions to the cooking experience that align with human actions and desires.

Digital Ethnography with YouTube Videos

Our study is based on a data set of YouTube video postings, which we have analyzed by looking at people's spatial arrangements and interpersonal distances. As we have discussed earlier, although YouTube offers an appealing amount of rich video data, and in some sense a window into people's lives, using video postings as part of an ethnographic study is not without challenges and potential limitations. Firstly, we were not able to enquire further into what was happening in the kitchens, and outside the scope of the camera, as one would during participating observation. In our particular study, however, we did not find this to be a significant problem as the spatial arrangements and interpersonal distances could be observed visually, and did not rely on the reasoning of the observed participants. To investigate further *why* people arrange themselves in the way observed, and *what it means* that they arrange themselves in these ways, one would have to include additional techniques, such as cued recall, or direct observation and interviews as we have done in a follow-up study [37]. Secondly, because YouTube videos are not just neutral video recordings, but particular media artifacts produced and posted with a purpose and audience in mind, one has to be sensitive to how this may potentially impact what is seen. In our study, we were particularly conscious and attentive to the fact that some videos might be staged performances, and perhaps take place in studio settings, which could influence the way people arrange themselves spatially. In looking at the videos, however, we were surprised to see that most take place in home kitchens and the camera typically appears to recede into the background, with people clearly focusing on the social cooking activity, with very little performing for the camera (see figures 4-10). Hence, the presence of the camera, and the fact that the video might end up on YouTube, did not appear to influence the way people were cooking together and arranging themselves spatially in the kitchens.

CONCLUSIONS

We have taken an empirical approach to understanding what it is that people do when they are cooking together in their home kitchens. We have analyzed 61 YouTube videos in a digital ethnography and identified formations made while people share the activity of food preparation. We did this to understand the spatial patterns that people form when cooking together and relate this to cooking activities and kitchen architecture.

Our contribution includes 8 identified spatial formations of people cooking together, which are very different from formations characterizing purely conversational situations. We have also identified three distinct task-related configurations: working on *related tasks*, working on *independent tasks* and working on *shared tasks*; and four related collaboration-oriented actions: *observing*, *checking*, *showing* and *helping*. This catalogue of the relationships between formations, cooking situations and kitchen architecture is a way to understand and represent the physical interactions of people cooking together.

Our research has shown that cooking together is a complex activity and based on our findings, we have reflected on possible ideas and implications for technology designed to enhance the cooking experience that accounts for the fact that people coordinating in a kitchen do so by positioning and interweaving their bodies within the available space to connect, converse, coordinate, cooperate and cook.

REFERENCES

1. Arnold, J.E., Graesch, A.P., Ragazzini, E. and Ochs, E. *Life at Home in the Twenty-First Century: 32 Families Open Their Doors.* The Cotsen Institute of Archaeology Press. 2012.
2. Bell, G., Blythe, M. and Sengers, P. Making by Making Strange: Defamiliarization and the Design of Domestic Technologies. *TOCHI, 12,* 2 (2005), 149-173.
3. Blythe M. and Cairns P. Tenori-On Stage: YouTube As Performance Space. In *Proc. NordiCHI 2010,* ACM (2010), 72-81.
4. Blythe, M. and Cairns, P. Critical Methods and User Generated Content: the iPhone on YouTube. In *Proc. CHI 2009,* ACM (2009), 1467-1476.
5. Bonanni, L., Lee, C. and Selker, T. Attention-Based Design of Augmented Reality Interfaces. In *Proc. CHI 2005 EA,* ACM (2005), 1228-1231.
6. Bradbury, J., Shell, J. and Knowles, C. Hands on Cooking: Towards an Attentive Kitchen. In *Proc. CHI 2003 EA,* ACM (2003), 996-997.
7. Chamberlain, A. and Griffiths, C. Wild Food Practices: Understanding the Wilder Implications for Design and HCI. In *Proc. UbiComp 2013,* ACM (2013), 575-584.
8. Clear, A., Hazas, M., Morley, J., Friday, A. and Bates, O. Domestic Food and Sustainable Design: A Study of University Student Cooking and its Impacts. In *Proc. CHI 2013,* ACM (2013), 2447-2456.
9. Crabtree, A. and Rodden, T. Domestic Routines and Design for the Home. *Computer Supported Cooperative Work, 13,* 2 (2004), 191-220.
10. Crabtree, A., Rouncefield, M. and Tolmie, P. Cooking for pleasure. In P. Tolmie and M. Rouncefield (Eds.) *Ethnomethodology at Play.* Ashgate, 2013, pp. 21-52.
11. Fritz, T., Huang, E., Murphy, G. and Zimmerman, T. Persuasive Technology in the Real World: A Study of Long-Term Use of Activity Sensing Devices for Fitness. In *Proc. CHI 2014,* ACM (2014), 487-496.
12. Greenberg, S., Marquardt, N., Ballendat, T., Diaz-Marino, R. and Wang, M. Proxemic interactions: the new ubicomp?. *Interactions, 18,* 1 (2011), 42-50.
13. Grimes, A. and Harper, R. Celebratory Technology: New Directions for Food Research in HCI. In *Proc. CHI 2008,* ACM (2008), 467-476.
14. Guest, S., MacQueen, K. and Namey, E. *Applied Thematic Analysis.* SAGE, 2012.
15. Haines, V., Mitchell, V., Cooper, C. and Maguire, M. Probing user values in the home environment within a technology driven Smart Home project. *Personal and Ubiquitous Computing. 11,* 5 (2007), 349-359.
16. Hall, E.T. *The Hidden Dimension.* Anchor Books, 1966.
17. Hamada, R., Satoh, S., Okabe, J., Sakai, S., Ide, I. and Tanaka, H. Cooking Navi: Assistant for Daily Cooking in Kitchen. In *Proc. MM 2005,* ACM (2005), 371-374.
18. Hamer, B. *Kitchen Stories* (Salmer fra kjøkkenet) [Motion picture]. Norway, IFC Films, 2003.
19. Harley, S. and Fitzpatrick, G. Creating a conversational context through video blogging. *Computers in Human Behaviour,* 25, 3 (2009), 679-689.

20. Heaton, L. Preserving Communication Context: Virtual Workspace And Interpersonal Space In Japanese CSCW. In *Proc. of Cultural Attitudes Towards Com. and Tech. 1998,* U Syd (1998), 207-230.

21. Huettenrauch, H., Eklundh, K., Green, A., Topp, A., 2006. Investigating Spatial Relationships in Human-Robot Interaction. In *Proc. IROS 2006* (2006), 5052-59.

22. Hung, H. and Kröse. Detecting F-formations as Dominant Sets. In *Proc. ICMI 2011* (2011), 231-238.

23. Hupfeld, A. and Rodden, T. Laying the Table for HCI: Uncovering Ecologies of Domestic Food Consumption. In *Proc. CHI 2012,* ACM (2012), 119-128.

24. Hutchinson, H., Mackay, W., Westerlund, B. et al. Technology probes: inspiring design for and with families. In *Proc. CHI 2003,* ACM (2003), 17-24.

25. Kendon, A. *Conducting Interaction: Patterns of Behavior in Focused Encounters.* Cambridge University, 1990.

26. Kendon, A. Spacing and orientation in co-present interaction. In *Proc. COST 2009,* Springer (2010), 1-15.

27. Kerr, S., Tan, O. and Chua, J. Cooking personas: Goal-directed design requirements in the kitchen. *Int. J. Human-Computer Studies, 72* (2014), 255-274.

28. Lareau, A. *Unequal Childhoods: Class, Race, and Family Life.* University of California Press. 2011.

29. Lewis, S., Acholonu, U. and Ju, W. Using Low Cost Game Controllers to Capture Data for 6th Grade Science Labs. In *Proc. CSCW 2012,* ACM (2012), 1115-1124.

30. Marquardt, N., Hinckley, K. and Saul Greenberg, S. Cross-device interaction via micro-mobility and f-formations. In *Proc. UIST 2012,* ACM (2012), 13-22.

31. Marshall, P., Rogers, Y. and Pantidi, N. Using F-formations to analyse spatial patterns of interaction in physical environments. In *Proc. CSCW 2011*, ACM (2011), 445-454.

32. Masten D. and Plowman, T. Digital Ethnography: The next wave in understanding consumer experience. *Design Management Journal. 14,* 2 (2003), 75-81.

33. Mennicken, S., Karrer, T., Russell, P. and Borchers, J. First-Person Cooking: A Dual-Perspective Interactive Kitchen Counter. In *Proc. CHI 2010 EA,* ACM (2010), 3403-3408.

34. Mentis, H., O'Hara, K., Sellen, A. and Trivedi, R. Interaction proxemics and image use in neurosurgery. In *Proc. CHI 2012,* ACM (2012), 927-936.

35. Morrison, C., Jones, M., Blackwell, A. and Vuylsteke, A. Electronic patient record use during ward rounds: a qualitative study of interaction between medical staff. *Critical Care, 12,* 6 (2008), R148.

36. Nagel, K., Hudson, J. and Abowd, G. Predictors of Availability in Home Life Context-Mediated Communication. In *Proc. CSCW 2004,* ACM (2004), 497-506.

37. Nansen, B., Davis, H., Vetere, F., Paay, J., Skov, M. and Kjeldskov J. Kitchen Kinesics: Gestural Communication within Familial Cooking Interactions. In *Proc. OZCHI 2014, ACM and SIGCHI* (2014)

38. Obata, A. and Sasaki, K. Office Walker: a virtual visiting system based on proxemics. In *Proc. CSCW 1998,* ACM (1998), 1-10.

39. Ochs, E. and Kremer-Sadlik, T. (Eds.) *Fast Forward Family.* University of California Press. 2013.

40. O'Hara, K., Harper, R., Mentis, H., Sellen, A. and Taylor, A. On The Naturalness Of Touchless: Putting The "Interaction" Back Into Nui. *TOCHI, 20* (2013).

41. O'Hara, K., Kjeldskov, J. and Paay, J. Blended Interaction Spaces for Distributed Team Collaboration. *TOCHI, 18,* 1 (2011), Article 3.

42. Olivier, P., Xu, G., Monk, A. and Hoey, J. Ambient Kitchen: designing situated services using a high fidelity prototyping environment. In *Proc. PETRA 2009,* ACM (2009), Article 47.

43. Paay, J., Kjeldskov, J., Skov, M. and O'Hara, K. Cooking Together: A Digital Ethnography. In *Proc. CHI 2012 EA,* ACM (2012), 1883-1888.

44. Paay, J., Kjeldskov, J., Skov, M. and O'Hara, K. F-formations in Cooking Together: A Digital Ethnography using YouTube. In *Proc. Interact'13* (2013), 37-54.

45. Palen, L. and Hughes, A. When home base is not a place: parents' use of mobile phones. *Personal and Ubiq. Comp. 11,* 5 (2007), 339-348.

46. Panger, G. Kinect in the Kitchen: Testing Depth Camera Interactions in Practical Home Environments. In *Proc. CHI 2012 EA,* ACM (2012), 1985-1990.

47. Patton, M. *Qualitative Research & Evaluation Methods.* Sage Publications, Thousand Oaks, CA, 2002.

48. Reitmaier, T., Benz, P. and Marsden, G. Designing and theorizing co-located interactions. In *Proc. CHI 2013,* ACM (2013), 381-390.

49. Rogers, Y. *HCI Theory: Classical, Modern, and Contemporary.* Morgan & Claypool, 2012.

50. Rotman, D. and Preece, J. The 'WeTube' in YouTube – creating an online community through video sharing. *International Journal of Web Based Communities, 6,* 3 (2010), 317-333.

51. Sellen, A., Harper, R., Eardley, R., Izadi, S., Regan, T., Taylor, A. and Wood, K. HomeNote: Supporting Situated Messaging in the Home. In *Proc. CSCW 2006,* ACM (2006), 383-392.

52. Terrenghi, L., Hilliges, O. and Butz, A. Kitchen Stories: sharing recipes with the Living Cookbook. *Personal and Ubiq. Comp., 11,* 5 (2007), 409-414..

Taking Our Time: Chronic Illness and Time-Based Objects in Families

Andrea Barbarin[1] andbar@umich.edu
Tiffany C. Veinot[1,2] tveinot@umich.edu
Predrag Klasnja[1,2] klasnja@umich.edu
University of Michigan, School of Information, Ann Arbor, MI 48109, USA[1]
University of Michigan, School of Public Health, Ann Arbor, MI 48104, USA[2]

ABSTRACT
This study examined the use of time-based objects by patients and their families to manage chronic illnesses at home. Calendar systems and medication containers, the main types of time-based objects studied, were used as part of two family-based collaborative work practices: 1) prompting health management activities, and 2) safeguarding these activities. Additionally, these artifacts were part of two social interaction patterns that managed emotional intimacy: 1) expressing support, and 2) hiding and disguising illness. Accordingly, home-based illness management may be more collaborative than previously recognized. Moreover, through their interactive incorporation into family life, time-based objects are laden with psychosocial significance. Breakdowns in temporal support were also evident, and were accompanied by: missed medication events; rationing of medications; medication errors; and difficulties with preparation for medical appointments. We propose novel artifact designs to better support patients and their families in managing the temporal aspects of chronic illness together.

Author Keywords
Health Informatics; Families; Calendars; Pill Boxes; Medication; Patient Portals; Visual Methods; Qualitative.

ACM Classification Keywords
J.3 [Life and Medical Sciences]: Health; J.3 [Life and Medical Sciences]: Medical information systems.

INTRODUCTION
The twentieth century saw a significant shift from acute to chronic illness disease patterns in Western countries [41]. People with chronic illnesses face long-term management of conditions that can be controlled but not cured; this typically entails home-based treatments such as medication administration. Additionally, to slow the rise in healthcare costs, care previously provided in healthcare facilities is increasingly being shifted to the home [23]. Short hospital stays accompanied by community rehabilitation are becoming more common [33]. Increasing proportions of citizens in countries such as Canada, Belgium, Great Britain, the Netherlands, and the United States also now die at home [28, 31, 45, 61]. Self-management supported by governmental health information provision is also a health policy focus in Western countries such as Canada and Great Britain [59]. Given the rising number of people involved in home-based care, and its health information policy emphasis, it is critical that home-based illness management systems are effective and designed to fit the informational demands of the home context. Support for home-based care necessitates attention to personal health information management.

CSCW '15, March 14- 18 2015, Vancouver, BC, Canada.

ACM 978-1-4503-2922-4/15/03$15.00
http://dx.doi.org/10.1145/2675133.2675200

Personal health information management, a complex aspect of life with chronic illness, involves synthesizing information from diverse sources and sharing it in varied environments using a range of technologies [51]. Although important for all patients, personal health information management is critical for chronically ill patients because it affects self-care and illness management practices and must typically be sustained over an extended period of time.

Time-related information has heightened significance for chronically ill patients and their families. Onset of serious illness is typically experienced as disruptive and may shift routines, physical experiences, relationships, and identities [16]. Illness may improve or worsen; time's passage may signify days to live or triumph over disease [12]. Days may be structured partly by treatment regimens, including coordination of inner experience of time, clock time, and temporal demands of medication dosage [44]. Thus, chronic illness may create a complex relationship with time.

Given the centrality of time to the chronic illness experience, we investigate the use of time-based information objects, including medication containers and calendar systems, among patients and their families. As we will show, the use of such objects is profoundly *social*. They are often used by more than one person, and reside in shared spaces. They support *collaborative* activities, which Computer-Supported Cooperative Work (CSCW) researchers define as activities that share "one objective, but [are] distributed onto several actors, each performing one or more actions according to the overall shared objective of the work" [2]. Moreover, in keeping with CSCW's embodied interaction theory [21], family interactions with time-based objects involve creating and sharing *meaning*, specifically regarding relationships. Although time-based objects may effectively support home-based care, we describe circumstances where this support fails and suggest ways that developing technologies could better facilitate collaborative, family-based care.

RELATED WORK

Moen and Brennan [46] identified four health information storage strategies in the home: 1) "just-in-time," which tends to stay in a person's physical proximity because it is potentially needed at any moment; 2) "just-at-hand," which is highly accessible, functioning as a cue for action; 3) "just-in-case," stored for a future need; and 4) "just-because," formerly important information that one holds onto while deciding whether to discard it. In work with breast cancer patients, Klasnja et al. [38] extended this concept of "just-in-time" storage to "unanchored settings" where patients do not have their health information with them. This work highlighted the fragmentation of patients' information, and challenges in bringing the information to healthcare appointments [38]. To address the challenges, they developed a personal health information management system that integrated information from a variety of sources into a smartphone calendar to facilitate easy access during medical appointments [39].

While this previous research laid important groundwork in understanding personal health information management, unanswered questions remain. Moen and Brennan [46] researched healthy people without chronic illness. While Klasnja et al. addressed information management in the illness context, the focus was on unanchored settings; it is unclear whether chronically ill patients use similar information practices at home [38].

Importantly, previous personal health information management studies have tended to focus primarily on individuals, whether patients or "home health information managers" [46, 51]. Yet, 40% of American adults care for an adult or child with significant health issues [49]. Moreover, half of health-related Internet searches are conducted on behalf of someone else [26]. Accordingly, personal health information management related to chronic illness may often be collaborative and its use may be focused, in part, on care and support. We investigate these possibilities by including both patients and their families in this study.

Health-related research in Human-Computer Interaction (HCI) and CSCW has, in contrast, paid attention to families. Grimes, Tan, and Morris [30] identified opportunities for technologies to support families in collaboratively using diet and exercise data. Building on this, Colineau and Paris [14] developed experimental technologies supporting "healthy lifestyle"-related goal-setting and feedback for the family group as a whole. Khan et al. [37] developed a mobile application to facilitate dietary tracking and feedback among low-socioeconomic status (SES) parents and teens. While demonstrating the feasibility of technologies geared towards families, this research has focused on health promotion rather than chronic illness. Attention to the chronic illness context, however, is important because illness impacts family members differentially.

There is also extensive HCI and CSCW literature on the use of calendar systems, a central type of time-based object. While early work in this domain focused on the use of calendars in the enterprise (e.g., [48]) more recent work has examined use of calendars to manage personal lives, showing that they are used for "life scheduling"—the process of coordinating work and personal commitments [29]—and managing friendships and romantic relationships [55]. Calendars also play a key role in managing household activities. Family calendars are used for interpersonal coordination and keeping household members aware of plans [47]. While Neustaedter et al. [47] found that family calendars are usually primarily maintained by one person, they serve as shared representations for negotiation and holding family members to agreed-upon obligations [17]. Along with recent work by Eschler, et al. [24], we extend this research through our focus on a chronic illness context.

Finally, the consumer health market has produced a number of time-based digital applications for everyday use. Stawartz, Cox and Blandford [53] highlight the vast array of mobile applications that provide alarms as reminders to take medications. An alternative approach to adherence is "smart" containers. Lee and Dey [42] used sensor-enabled pill boxes to provide tablet-based feedback to older adults regarding medication-taking. Commercially, AdhereTech [35] uses touchscreen technology to monitor levels in a pill bottle, and GlowCaps [1] use sound and light emanating from the bottle to serve as reminders. Efforts to integrate digital technology into containers are promising, but it is unclear to what extent they meet varied time-related needs in families.

This work extends prior research by examining the following questions: (1) *What kinds of illness-related time-based objects do chronically ill patients and their families use? (2) How and why are these time-based objects used? (3) What are the strengths and weaknesses of current time-based objects and their uses?*

METHODS

This research focuses on 38 families (97 individuals) who participated in a longitudinal, two-year study involving five waves of semi-structured interviews (two individual and three group interviews). Patients defined the parameters of their "family" units and recruited family members into the study. To represent experiential variation based on different treatment regimens (e.g., pills for HIV/AIDS versus pills/injections, diet and exercise for diabetes), we recruited families in which at least one member was living with either HIV/AIDS or type 2 diabetes. These two different diseases were also selected due to their differing social dynamics; previous research has shown that high levels of perceived stigma affect the information behavior of people with HIV/AIDS and their family members [58], whereas such a relationship was not established in a diabetes context. With deliberate sampling for such variance, we sought to understand time-based object use generally, rather than to identify differences between illnesses. Patient participants were recruited through three methods: 1) when attending appointments at a Veteran's Affairs Medical Center in the Midwest; 2) *via* flyers distributed to clients of three disease-specific nonprofit organizations in the Midwest, or 3) *via* a university online research participant recruitment system.

In addition to the interviews all families participated in, a subset of 24 families (59 individuals) consented to an optional home tour photography session [32, 46], during the fourth wave of interviews. Each home tour began with a participants identifying illness management activities (e.g., making medical appointments, reordering prescriptions, etc.) conducted at home. They led the researcher through the home and described the processes and artifacts/devices used to carry out each activity while a second researcher took photos based on a content/sequence protocol that structured the photography of referenced artifacts/devices, and the zone and room in which they were stored and used [15]. Field notes were drafted to capture observations.

Audio recordings of semi-structured interviews (including home photography sessions) were transcribed verbatim. Transcripts for all interviews with 38 families were analyzed with QSR NVivo 10 software through a grounded theory approach [11]. Thus, interview transcripts were analyzed using initial, line-by-line coding [11]. Gerund-based coding highlighted the processes of object use [11].

Personally identifiable information (PII) was removed from photographs and a final set of 794 unique photos was selected. Visual analysis, conducted in four steps, combined established methods from visual anthropology [15, 36, 50]. First, two researchers reviewed contact sheets for all photos, noting overall patterns and areas for further analysis. Second, initial coding [11] was based on material content, spatial arrangements, and use activities. Third, the entire corpus was reviewed and broader findings identified. Finally, the researchers discussed approximately 80 photos in depth in the context of coding field notes and transcripts.

Next, focused coding [11] further developed concepts regarding use of time-based objects (e.g., "prompting activity"). Finally, theoretical coding [11] was conducted. Following Charmaz [11], this coding focused on changes in and consequences of the use of time-based objects. The research was approved by the University of Michigan Health Sciences and Behavioral Sciences Institutional Review Board (HUM00041535).

RESULTS

Characteristics of Participants

As Table 1 shows, 20 families affected by diabetes and 18 by HIV/AIDS participated in the study. The majority of patients had more than one chronic condition. Most families had access to the Internet (84.2%), and to a patient portal from their healthcare provider (89.5%). On average, participants were in their mid-50s. Slightly more than half (57.7%) were female. The majority were White (62.9%) or Black (29.9%). Thirty-five percent were employed, with large proportions unemployed (30.9%) or retired/disabled (26.8%). Close to half had a college degree (45.4%).

Overview of Time-Based Objects

Families used two main types of time-based objects: 1) calendar systems, and 2) medication containers. These objects primarily facilitated attendance at medical appointments and medication taking.

	Total Study Participants	**Home Tour Participants**
Family Groups	**N=38**	**N=24**
Diagnosis of patient		
Diabetes	20 (52.6%)	13 (54.1%)
HIV/AIDS	18 (47.4%)	11 (45.8%)
Comorbidity (patient has >1 condition)	36 (94.7%)	23 (95.8%)
Access to Technology		
Internet access (home/mobile)	32 (84.2%)	22 (91.7%)
Patient portal access	34 (89.5%)	21 (87.5%)
Individuals	**N=97**	**N=59**
Age (in years) (mean (s.d.))	53.31 (13.2)	55.64 (11.9)
Gender		
Female	54 (55.7%)	35 (59.3%)
Male	43 (44.3%)	24 (40.7%)
Race/Ethnicity		
White/European American	61 (62.9%)	38 (64.4%)
Black/African American	29 (29.9%)	17 (28.8%)
Hispanic/Latino	4 (4.1%)	2 (3.4%)
Asian or Native American	3 (3.1%)	2 (3.4%)
Employment		
Employed (full or part time)	36 (37.1%)	21 (35.6%)
Unemployed	30 (30.9%)	18 (30.5%)
Retired/Disability	26 (26.8%)	16 (27.1%)
Student (full or part-time)	5 (5.2%)	4 (6.8%)
Education		
High School or less	21 (21.6%)	12 (20.3%)
Some college	30 (30.9%)	16 (27.1%)
College degree	44 (45.4%)	31 (52.5%)

Table 1. Characteristics of participants

Calendar Systems

Calendars systems included two sub-types: 1) *calendars*, which measured time at the level of days, weeks, and months; and 2) *day planners*, which offered participants finer-grained views of time, typically at the level of weeks, days, and hours. Depending on the family, calendars and day planners were in either paper-based or digital formats.

Calendars offered "overviews" [6] of temporally-structured activities and commitments. While a range of calendars (e.g., online patient portal calendar, dry-erase board calendar, etc.) were utilized, all families had at least one traditional wall calendar (i.e., a grid in which each cell corresponded to a date) on which notes were often written. These were rarely moved; they were often large and nailed or pinned to surfaces, and posted high on walls and doors to maximize visibility. Many families had multiple calendars, with each calendar serving a different role. Some were used by and reflected the activities of individual family members, whereas others were shared. Shared calendars aggregated information from individual calendars (e.g., medical appointments), as well as information relevant to the entire family (e.g., birthdays). Some calendars, used only for certain types of information (e.g., illness management), stayed in private locations such as bedrooms.

Day planners organized daily activities, including medical appointments. They came in various forms, including paper and smartphone applications and were either the sole site of particular information or replicas of wall calendars, but not copies of other daily schedules. More mobile than calendars, they easily fit into purses or bags and were often referred to throughout the day.

Calendar systems functioned as *reminders*, especially for infrequent activities such as appointments, and in a few cases, refilling prescriptions and supplies. However, a few patients with irregular schedules used additional memory triggers for daily medications. On digital devices such as smartphones, they programmed alerts. For paper-based calendar systems, they affixed post-it notes, appointment cards, and post cards to the calendars next to the scheduled activity (see Figure 1). Reminders were typically prominently displayed, or kept with a person.

Figure 1. Medical appointment card and postcard reminder clipped to a diabetic's day planner.

Medication Containers

Containers such as pill boxes, pill bottles, and injection kits temporally structured medication taking by aligning supply with consumption time. We observed no use of "smart" pill boxes. At home, medication containers were fixed objects, occupying established locations. Most patients taking more than one medication used pill boxes subdivided into compartments and labeled by product designers with time units for particular days and/or hour spans. Other patients, usually those with fewer medications, kept their medication in the original prescription pill bottles. In some cases, patients filled and otherwise monitored the medication containers themselves; in others, a family member managed them. Several patients modified medication containers: one diabetic who took health supplements stored them in old prescription bottles with self-written instructions in permanent marker on the outside; two families attached medication lists with dosage instructions to pill boxes.

Many participants used features of pill containers as *reminders*. In particular, they used the status of a day/time compartment as empty or full, or open or closed container tops, to determine whether medications had been taken.

How and Why Time-Based Objects are Used

Patients and their families used calendar systems and medication containers to support instrumental, time-bound illness management activities that were often collaborative. Instrumental uses included 1) prompting illness management activities and 2) safeguarding these activities. Time-based objects were also used to construct and share meaning regarding intimacy and care in family relationships. These uses included: 1) expressing support, and 2) hiding and disguising illness.

Prompting Illness Management Activities

Time-based objects prompted patients and families to engage in time-dependent illness management activities, such as taking medications. Depending on the family, these activities were either individual or collaborative. In the latter cases, family members shared in the objective of managing their loved one's illness, and undertook actions—often on a repeated basis—that contributed to illness management activities as a whole.

Taking medications was typically repetitive and took place in a stable environment, as part of a recurring activity set such as waking up and getting ready for the day. As one patient said, *"You wake up, it's one of the first things you do...you go to the bathroom, brush your teeth, do that...so it's easy to remember."* Medication routines included objects such as pill boxes, which patients noted reduced their mental effort: *"[T]hat keeps me [sic] track of the days...I just look to see what day it is...and then just take the [meds]"*. Medication-taking activities also depended upon spatial arrangements within rooms, such as prominently placing medication containers within a recurring line of activity. As this patient related, *"the containers that are out...when I come back home and walk into my room, I see the bottles and then I'll take them...because I'm getting ready to bed down."* Such routines could be collaborative as well. As this HIV-positive person said, his partner *"used to lay the pill bottle on my side of the bed when I would go to bed."*

The stable and recurring nature of these activities meant they became habits triggered by the patient's context and no longer needed additional reminders. As one patient said, *"I don't need an alarm... I know I've got to take them twice a day."* However, patients noted that adherence became challenging when routines were disrupted, or if their travel and work schedules made the establishment of a routine especially challenging. In such cases, patients more frequently spoke of using alarms to remember medications.

For more infrequent activities such as medical appointments, objects such as calendars were more likely to be used to prompt activity. However, this only worked if they were regularly consulted. To address this problem, several participants developed routines for consulting their calendars. For instance, one person with HIV/AIDS noted, *"I glance at this [the calendar] every day... I won't forget to do that."* The husband of another person with HIV/AIDS looked at a calendar each morning after he woke up: *"I get up and it's [the calendar] hard to miss because I'm on this side of the bed...and so I check it out."* Another patient with a complex health status consulted her patient portal daily to see whether appointments had been added without her knowledge.

For infrequent events, time needed to be dedicated to record keeping. This involved recording appointments on a calendar system, often transferring them from cards obtained at visits or letters from healthcare providers. Contributing to the often-collaborative objective of appointment attendance, appointments were recorded on by both patients and family members. As one diabetic patient said of his spouse, *"[S]he puts all the appointments on the calendar... so then we know."* Several patients with smartphones or other digital devices said they programmed alarms as reminders. As one person with HIV/AIDS said, *"I'll put [appointments] on the phone... I use two day as my reminder for it. So this thing in my phone keeps popping up for the last two days..."* When possible, patients with unpredictable schedules developed recurring appointment times to aid in memory. As this diabetes patient said, *"I'm accustomed to the second Friday of every month, I know that I have appointments."*

Furthermore, wall calendars were valued as coordination tools for illness management activities, *"so everyone can see it,"* as one person with HIV/AIDS said. This was particularly valuable when multiple family members were involved in appointment attendance, or shared resources such as cars. We also found that family members acted as "human reminders" for infrequent activities such as appointments or medication refills, often with the aid of time-related objects. For example, a diabetic's wife saw an upcoming medical appointment written in her day planner and was prompted to start verbally reminding her husband. As the patient related, his wife started reminding him a week in advance: "'*You've got an appointment on the day,' walk in the house, 'Hey, you know you've got an appointment on this day?' she won't leave it alone!"* To which his wife responded, *"If I don't, he doesn't remember*." Similarly, another person with HIV/AIDS said of the family member with whom he lived, *"[S]he'll always know and she says, 'Well you've got an appointment coming up.'* Family members also reminded patients about medication refills. As a diabetic's wife explained, *"I do his pills...I'll put them in this [pill box] there for two weeks at a time. When I know he's getting low, I'll say, "[Husband], you've got to order this...And a couple of days later I'll remind him and ask him if he did refill it."*

Safeguarding Illness Management Activities

Patients and their families also pursued instrumental, collaborative activities to ensure that illness management activities took place correctly, and when needed. Such activities included creating activities with feedback loops, often with the aid of medication containers. For instance, one diabetic's wife examined his pill bottles to be sure he had used all the pills before discarding the container. He appreciated his wife's assistance with this: *"It... keeps you in check, that way you're double checking to make sure that you didn't mess up and miss it."*

Another approach to safeguarding activities involved completing an illness management task collaboratively. After a medication dosage error (to be discussed later), one couple attempted to prevent future errors by setting up the pill box together, using a verified list. As the spouse said, *"So we go through [the pill boxes] about every month. And I've got a list at home and we read the list, what goes where, and how much and everything. So it's all set up and it's all right, at that point...the last thing I need is another overdose of stuff."*

Patients and their family members also maintained multiple time-based objects, accessible to everyone, to ensure attendance at medical appointments. As this participant said, *"[I]t's marked on both calendars, so if they get...misplaced, if one gets moved, then the other one's here, but I usually keep both of them right here together."* Patients also kept back-up, personal copies of time-based objects to ensure that an appointment was remembered, *"I have a pocket calendar that I carry in my purse...but I make sure that what's on that is on here [shared calendar] and visa-versa* [sic]." Another patient noted that although his spouse maintained the shared calendar, he held onto appointment cards: *"I keep them on my desk, some place wherever I can find room, and I know that's when my appointment's in there."* Patient portal-based calendars were occasionally used as "authoritative" sources to ensure that other calendars were accurate.

Additionally, some families used time-based objects to verify that the patient was engaging in adequate illness management. One partner of a person with HIV/AIDS described how she inspected a pill box for evidence that the patient was adhering to his medication schedule: "*[H]e'll get busy and I just know...[he'll] be out all day and...the pill is still in the 'A.M.' or 'P.M.' tray...I just ask him, 'Have you taken [the medicine],' and he'll tell me the truth.*" Rather than feel irritated by this, the patient appreciated her concern: "*I'm glad she does it....*" Similarly, a diabetes patient said that his wife "*makes sure I take them too because there's a couple of times I've forgot.*" This patient was grateful for her support and care, noting after a recent health crisis, "*if it wasn't for her, I'd probably been dead.*"

Expressing Family Support

Interactions mediated by time-based objects also expressed emotional support and care within the family, largely due to their integration into other aspects of caregiving. Because patients and families tended to use multiple time-based objects, they often needed to integrate information across systems by copying information between them. This integration of information was incorporated into a broader role that often included responsibility for activities such as cooking, medications, etc. Thus, the family member who assisted the patient the most with illness management generally took on coordinating responsibilities as well. The wife of one person with HIV/AIDS jokingly likened her family management role to a job and the home to a work environment: "*I'm the bookkeeper and all of that...I run the 'office.'*"

Information integration across time-based objects served an instrumental function, but it also met relational and emotional needs of patients and their families. One person with HIV/AIDS said he "trusts" his wife to accurately record duplicate entries for his medical appointments in all of their calendars. Thus, these activities provided an opportunity for her husband to rely on her; integrating calendars became a tangible expression of the couple's interdependence.

Knowing the patient's schedule also allowed family members to be aware of and attend health activities. While this facilitated logistical planning (e.g., what time to leave home for an appointment), it also allowed family members to sustain emotional connections. For instance, the partner of a diabetes patient stated, "*Anything... that happens with her, I put in mine [calendar] so I know, so I don't schedule something...she generally wants me to go with her.*" Thus, coordinating information between the patient's calendar and her own became an expression of attunement to the other person's emotional needs surrounding illness management.

Hiding and Disguising

Patients and family members also used time-based objects to shroud themselves from others' scrutiny. While focused on self-protection and privacy, these activities were nevertheless interactive because they took place in reference to other people. Thus, although patients and families placed many time-based objects in visible locations, some were deliberately obscured. They remained accessible but were strategically hidden or disguised to keep them private and out of the hands of certain individuals. Obscuring health artifacts often reflected a desire to not disclose the existence of an illness and prevent perceptions of lack of control over the home environment.

In particular, people with HIV/AIDS were concerned that extended family members or other guests visiting their homes might see more than they were willing to share. For instance, one HIV-positive couple, who had not publicly disclosed their HIV statuses, stated that all HIV/AIDS information in the family home was "*under lock and key.*" Additionally, the family had the following strategy for dealing with guests at their home: "*If we do have guests...if they have to use the restroom we just direct them to [our son's] bathroom because there's nothing in there... that we have to hide.*"

Despite these efforts, one member of this couple also kept HIV medication stored in his bathroom in a pain reliever bottle to disguise the pills. He also password protected access to his digital calendar *via* desktop computer, and on the slight possibility that anyone would see it, used notation not easily discernable by others. This couple was concerned that discovering their HIV status this would needlessly worry their extended family members. They also feared potential rejection by members of their community.

Additionally, one diabetic woman who took medication throughout the day chose containers based on her desire to downplay medication-taking in public. As she described it, "*[I]t holds...a week to 10 days...of medication, and it's also a little more discreet...I don't want I have this big dramatization of me taking medicine ...I think I'm slightly embarrassed that I'm so young taking medicine.*"

Some families, all of whom were of lower SES, believed they did not have full control over their home environment. This led to additional efforts to hide time-related objects. As a diabetic's wife stated, "*[P]eople look through the window and they see the [diabetes] drugs on the table..., they see them sitting there...and we go away, they might break in so we just put them right up in there [the bedroom closet].*" To which the patient responded, "*Out of sight, safety.*" Another diabetic who lives in public housing was concerned that the property managers had access to her home. She kept her medical records, including previously used day planners, protected in a safe and in her bedroom with a self-installed lock. As she explained, "*[M]y landlords walk in here when they want to...not explaining why... anything of major importance has to either go in there [the locked bedroom] or go in my safe.*"

Strengths and Weaknesses in Time-based Object Use

Many participants were satisfied with their use of time-based objects to prompt and safeguard illness management activities. When describing reasons for liking current systems, participants made statements such as *"It works for me," "It's easy,"* or *"We don't have any problem that way."* Some also viewed their systems as simply good enough: *"[I]t is what it is...I'm neutral on it."* Indeed, families created their illness management systems and believed they could easily change them if unsatisfied. Nevertheless, as discussed below, specific issues arose for families in the use of the main types of time-based objects.

Calendar Systems

Calendars excelled at providing an overview of upcoming time commitments, and calendar reminders effectively captured participants' attention. From a safeguarding point of view, many participants noted that the accuracy of their calendars was improved by having multiple versions, and by the timely telephone or mail appointment reminders sent to them by their healthcare providers. The ability of calendar systems to effectively prompt appointment attendance was supported by the fact that only one participant, a non-calendar user, reported missing a medical appointment during the two years of the study.

Despite the strengths of calendar systems, certain weaknesses were apparent. Both paper and digital calendars are useful for recording the timing of events, with many digital calendars now also permitting the scheduling of recurring events. However, existing calendar systems do not well support "contingent timing," or "tasks for which their ideal time is dependent upon some other activity in the timescape" [4, p. 107]. In line with this concept, per health insurance guidelines and controlled substance policies, medication refills can typically only proceed when a certain amount of previous medications have been taken. Refill timing was also complicated by the multiple medications taken by most participants. Given the difficulty of determining this contingent timing with paper calendars, it is perhaps unsurprising that only a few participants used them for medication/supply refills. Nevertheless, one family member, worried by his relative with HIV/AIDS's medication lapses, said he wanted them to use the family wall calendar to write *"when they need to get refills or when they ran out of something... put more medication-wise stuff on there."* Such refill problems persisted despite the fact that a majority (see Table 1) of patients had access to a patient portal calendar with the capability of placing medication refill requests, although such systems did not typically provide refill alerting capabilities.

Calendar systems also provided incomplete support for prompting the multiple, interrelated activities involved in preparing to attend medical appointments. Weeks in advance of an appointment, for example, people with HIV/AIDS were required to have a laboratory-based blood draw for their regular CD4 and viral load tests. Weeks or days in advance, many participants needed to arrange travel to an appointment, particularly if they used a transportation service or relied upon another person for a ride. Several participants regularly brought lists of questions for their providers, with varied time horizons accompanying their advance preparation. For instance, one couple always kept a notepad accessible at home, collaboratively building the list of questions to bring to provider appointments every few months. Provider-driven medication reconciliations also took place at many appointments, especially for participants with multiple healthcare providers. To prepare for this, several patients attempted to compile medication lists in advance. However, prompts could be helpful since this step was not always remembered; this diabetic female participant noted problems *"when I'm at the doctor's office and they want to know what medications I'm on, and I haven't thought to print out a list."* Further support could be embedded in prompts for this preparation, as evidenced by the excess work performed by this participant with three physicians: *"[T[hey always want a copy of it, so that's the pain, they copy it because it's three pages long...I just write it all out ahead of time and take it in and give it to them."*

A further limitation of calendar systems concerns the extent to which they accommodate the shifting involvement of (geographically dispersed) family members in patient care. Over a two-year period, many participants noted changes in family relationships. From drifting apart to fractious conflicts, from a new job to the birth of a child, and from moving across the country to worsening health, the involvement of some network members reduced over time. Family members were also newly engaged in care as patients expanded the circle of people who knew about their health status. As this partner of a diabetic patient said, she could ask her husband's friends for transportation to medical appointments, *"Now that they know how bad his sugar is."* Short-term health challenges such as broken bones also engaged previously-uninvolved family members in tasks like providing transportation. Participants also formed new relationships with partners and friends, some of whom quickly became involved in their care. Thus, static, place-bound calendars were ill-suited to engaging everyone involved in appointment preparation, and to maintaining accurate representations of the changing family care network. Of those participants using digital calendars, only one couple shared calendars digitally. Furthermore, no participants reported using currently-available online care coordination applications.

Figure 2. Pill boxes of a person with HIV/AIDS, as well as comorbidities.

Medication Containers
As described above, participants generally praised the ways pill boxes prompted medication taking by making the task more automatic. Yet pill boxes were insufficient to support the complex medication regimens managed by some participants. It was possible to exceed the capacity of existing boxes because *"there's just too many pills to go in there,"* as one diabetic patient said. (See Figure 2 for one family's solution to this problem: multiple pill boxes used for a single day.) Commonly taken medications (e.g., insulin) were also not in pill form, which meant they required additional effort and supplies (e.g., needles) to administer. Some patients collected additional supplies in makeshift "kits" or bags. Insulin and other medications required refrigeration and were kept separate from other parts of the medication regimen. In these cases, medication containers had to be proactively incorporated into larger and more complex routines, reducing some of the simplicity benefits of pill boxes alone.

In addition, as mentioned earlier, medication containers were less effective as prompts when patients and family deviated from routines. Such deviations were not rare; throughout the two years of the study, many patients reported missed dosages for this reason. Patients reported missing doses on weekends, when traveling, and when at social engagements. Family responsibilities could also spark missed medications. As one diabetic said, *"I did not take my medication yesterday... I do have...stress in my life...I have a set of twins at my house... it was... a lot of running yesterday."* For another family, missing could be prompted by small routine changes: *"We usually take it when we eat dinner... I put it on the table, we know we got to take it...it's right there. And that's the way I had a problem...'Cause if it's in the room, we forget...he goes into his office... I go and watch my shows..."*

With regard to prompting, pill containers also only partially addressed the most common temporal medication-related problem: lapses in medication and medical supply refills. As described, participants used the visual indication of a pill bottle getting "low" as a prompt to reorder medications. However, refills were completed late at least some of the time for the majority of families. For some, this was due to difficulties managing the delay between ordering and receiving medication, especially with mailed prescriptions. This could result in missed dosages due to a lack of medication on hand; one participant said her spouse ran out of HIV medications *"about five times a year,"* which he confirmed: *"Yeah, yeah about."* A diabetic patient said at one of her interviews, *"I was asleep at the switch a few weeks ago and I didn't notice that I was almost out of [medication]....It's winging its way to me... but it isn't here yet and I'm going to run out on Tuesday."* Four patients also had supply problems due to interruptions in health insurance coverage during this study. To deal with this, three "stretched medications" to make them last longer. For example, risking possible medication resistance over time, one person with HIV/AIDS who had lost insurance said, *"[T]o kind of make it last, I've been doing it every other day for my pills, just to keep it stretched. But not go without taking them."* Similarly, a diabetic who lost insurance explained his recent poor blood glucose results as follows: *"Instead of every day... I might only take [insulin] only every three days...so it's not going to be as effective..."* Frequent regimen changes and insurance limits rarely allowed patients to "stockpile" medications to safeguard against supply lapses.

Despite their safeguarding efforts, medication errors emerged in two pill box-using families during the study; both events required hospital visits. In one case, the problem emerged from the pill box design, which made it difficult to identify whose medications were whose. As described by this participant, *"[M]y sister is [diabetic] and her husband's also [diabetic], but he takes different medicines and she took his by accident and it threw her in the hospital."* In another case, mentioned earlier, a dosage error arose from inaccuracy. As this family member explained, *"[S]he was in the hospital... because she was over-medicating herself and not realizing it. She's putting too many [pills] in the [pill box]...she's only supposed to go to 800 [mg], she was putting 1200 [mg]."*

DISCUSSION
This study describes two main types of time-based objects, 1) calendar systems, used most often for infrequent events such as medical appointments, and 2) medication containers, which were used daily. Such objects were used instrumentally and collaboratively to prompt and safeguard illness management activities. Additionally, they were used to produce and share relational meaning, particularly regarding intimacy. We also identified instrumental strengths and weaknesses of these systems.

Illness Management as a Collaborative Activity
Our research shows that family members are often critical sources of patient support in illness management. Family members engaged in actions mediated by time-based objects, such as prompting and checking, to accomplish the shared objective of illness management. We extend previous family-based CSCW research by examining a situation in which family members share a common work objective [18]. We found that family members can and do

adopt the shared objective of maintaining the well-being of their loved ones. They also contribute to larger illness management activities such as pill taking. Researchers, however, have typically approached personal health information management as an individual effort. Moreover, technologies focused on illness management rarely aim to support collaboration. For example, medication reminder applications largely focus on the patient alone (e.g., [53]). This suggests a need to broaden understanding of the uses of consumer-facing informatics applications, particularly those of a temporal nature. We discuss this issue further below.

In keeping with the collaborative nature of illness management, we note that family members used time-based objects such as calendars in ways that have been observed by other CSCW researchers in both workplace and family contexts. For example, in line with workplace-based research, our participants gathered information about others' activities by assessing changes in time-based objects, a process that has been called "feedthrough" [20]. As in other research on families [24, 47], we observed that they often have multiple calendars which may be maintained by one person on behalf of others, and that the calendar maintainer may remind others of shared activities. In our study, like others [6], calendars provided an "overview" function. Similar to our findings, previous home-focused research has also documented the practice of placing objects in the pathways of routine activity to communicate messages, such as reminders [22]. Recent research by Eschler, et al. [24] also documented the practice of keeping multiple calendars to prevent missed healthcare appointments. Despite these similarities, we extend this prior work with our focus on illness management in the context of the complete family unit.

More than Instrumental: Interactive Time-Based Objects' Use and Relational Meaning

Generally, previous research has not directly addressed personal health information management outside of instrumental considerations such as storage strategies related to information needs [46]. We found that instrumental uses of time-based objects did not capture the full range of interactions by which personal health information management is incorporated into the lives of patients and their families.

This study revealed that time-based objects were used to express family support and care. Previous CSCW research has highlighted ways in which digital calendar sharing may be used to maintain and develop relationships [55]. Similarly, social psychologists note that the synchronization of calendars becomes an expression of intimacy [25]. We extend this prior work by showing that, like sharing of health-related documents in general [60], time-based objects may serve as vehicles for expressions of emotional support when managing illness. Additionally, time-based objects supported families in maintaining awareness of a patient's health happenings (e.g., medical appointments), facilitating offers of assistance. These interactions allowed family members care for patients and express concern for their health, which patients recognized and appreciated. From a clinical perspective, this family involvement is important because patients who perceive emotional support from family members experience better health outcomes [56].

Interactive time-based objects' use also reflected relational meanings that were more negative, but nonetheless took other people into account. Navigating the world as a person with HIV/AIDS or type 2 diabetes can be stigmatizing [43]. Diabetics tend to think others will blame them for their illness and judge them for it [10]. Hence, diabetics may believe it is in their interest to not disclose that they have the disease. Additionally, people with HIV/AIDS often want to conceal their illness to avoid reactions that can range from viewing them as sickly, weak individuals to a highly contagious viral "contaminant" [13]. Such perceptions of people with HIV/AIDS are not only personally hurtful, but in extreme cases could lead to outright discrimination. By considering the broader social context in which patients and their families live and operate, we found that practices of illness concealment extended to time-based object use as well. While Klasnja, Hartzler, et al. [39] found that privacy was important in the design of personal health information management systems for cancer patients, our research offers new insights into the need to develop time-based objects that permit obfuscation as well as more straightforward modes of access control.

Challenges in the Transition to Home-Based Care

As described at the outset of this paper, healthcare in Western countries has been increasingly transitioning from institutions to the home. At a policy level, this has often been accompanied by a focus on cost containment. For example, under the US Affordable Care Act (2010), "readmission penalties" are applied to Medicare (government-funded health insurance for the elderly) fee-for-service payments. Accordingly, payments are reduced for hospitals that experience higher-than-expected rates of readmission after patient discharge. This incentivizes healthcare providers to ensure that care upon discharge, often to the home, is coordinated and implemented well to avoid readmission [9]. Patient- and family-facing technologies are often lauded as core enablers of re-admission prevention and other efforts to ensure the effectiveness of home-based care [3]. However, our findings suggest inadequacies in the time-based objects currently used by patients and their families. For example, our research identified breakdowns in temporal support accompanied by missed medication events, rationing of medications to deal with delayed refills, episodes of erroneous medication administration, and difficulties with collaborative activities leading up to important medical appointments. To realize effective home-based care, time-based illness management systems must be improved.

Improving Support Provided by Time-Based Objects

Two technological trends currently underway in healthcare could help solve the temporal challenges we identified: 1) smart pills and medication containers; and 2) patient portals. Extending these technologies could provide support while adding minimal complexity to the care process and preserving the relational significance of time-based objects.

Smart Pills and Medication Containers

A key trend relevant to time-based objects is the increasing use of ingestible and other miniature sensors for tracking medication and food intake [19]. While the current generation of "smart pill" technologies are activated when a pill is swallowed, medication containers should soon be able to sense which pills have been removed. This functionality would help solve many problems patients face without requiring them to change their current practices.

Smart pills could help in three ways. First, as described above, medication containers could simplify medication-taking and provide contextual cues amendable to daily routine; however, disruptions in routine may lead to missed medication. This finding is consistent with the literature on habits, which demonstrates that even small changes in context cues can disrupt triggering of the habitual activity [62, 63]. As is now possible in commercial applications, containers that can sense that a pill has not been taken within a certain window could send a reminder (e.g., a text message) if medication is missed, while minimizing burden by not using reminders at other times. Furthermore, while systems such as GlowCap [1] permit notices to be sent to caregivers, our findings provide empirical support for the value of the involvement of "human reminders." In some families, reminding is an integral part of the expression of care and support, with both patients and family members cherishing the opportunity to interact as well as ensure medication adherence. Thus, families should have a range of options for sending alerts, such as patient only; simultaneous notification of patient and family member(s); patient first with a delayed reminder to the family member(s); and family member(s) only. Given the dynamic nature of family networks, systems should also make it easy to add or remove family member(s) and change notification settings depending on circumstances, such as a bout of the flu that impedes a patient's independence for a short time.

Second, medication containers that are aware of what pills, liquid, or ointment remain in them could fully or partially automate refill requests. This would reduce how often patients find themselves without their medications. Given the possibility of frequent changes in insurance coverage in the US, in such an environment smart pill bottles could just alert the patient and/or family members about the need to a refill without ordering it on their behalf. In more stable healthcare contexts, however, a refill request could be automatically made in the patient portal, reducing fallibility in one of the most crucial aspects of long-term medication adherence.

Third, smart pills could reduce the risk of overdosing, since medication containers could be programmed with exact medication regimens, enabling them to know if the correct dose has been prepared for each pill-taking event. The frequent medication regimen changes in our sample highlight the need for a straightforward mechanism for updating regimens that would be programmed into a container.

Using our study results and healthcare-based patient safety initiatives as a guide [7, 52], we contend that it is also important to support patients and their families in safeguarding medication taking. The design of smart pill containers we described here presupposes an electronic version of a medication list that can be used to program containers and alert schedules. This assumption is grounded in patients' current practices since they already maintain lists of medications they are asked for at every appointment. If such lists were available electronically, it would be possible to provide safety checks on medication regimens by cross-checking them against publically available databases such as RxNorm [57] and flagging potential duplicates and interactions. This could be helpful given that patients often receive prescriptions from multiple clinicians, and take over-the-counter medications. A system that checked medication lists could flag concerns and enable patients to involve providers in medication reconciliation.

Our findings further indicate that while some chronically ill patients benefit from easily visible containers, some desire to hide their medication from others. To support both processes, containers could take non-traditional shapes. For instance, pill boxes could be incorporated into decorative objects such as vases or art pieces, enhancing the aesthetics of an environment rather than emphasizing the presence of illness. Such containers could be out in the open, serve as visual reminders to patients, and be enjoyed by visitors while preserving patients' privacy. The reminding function of smart pill boxes could be handled in a similar way. The object could softly glow or provide another kind of subtle cue that the patient would recognize as a reminder while others present perceived as part of the aesthetic object.

Calendars and Patient Portals

Calendars do not easily support many of the more sophisticated operations related to medical appointments, such as managing preparatory information or sharing events with family members who provide logistical support.

Patient portal access was common in our study population. Portals are web-based, patient-facing applications connected to electronic health records (EHRs) that coordinate between patients and providers *via* features such as patient access to lab reports and appointment scheduling. They have recently been introduced by numerous healthcare organizations in the US due to federal policy that provides incentives for "meaningful use" of health IT [5]. While the value of portals to patients and families largely remains to be demonstrated [27], extended capabilities could address the identified limitations of calendars using two main approaches.

First, by providing patient-facing data storage that is not part of an official medical record, portals could extend the kinds of temporal information they support; this could include information patients need that is not strictly clinical. Patients could use portals to connect to upcoming appointments and upload medication lists, questions, notes, and other types of information, giving them access to all information needed for that appointment. Prior work has shown the promise of this approach [40], but embedding personal health information management functionality in a portal could be more effective than in previous designs, allowing patients to work smoothly with both clinical information (e.g., test results), and ad-hoc information (e.g., question lists) to manage their illness.

Second, patient portals could enable patients to selectively give—and revoke—access to their data, enabling them to keep the right people abreast of their condition and, potentially, to receive more offers of assistance based on the social network's clearer understanding of their health needs. Additionally, the coordination of assistance could be facilitated by linkages with existing care applications such as *LotsaHelpingHands* [34] or *CaringBridge* [54]. If necessary, and similar to Bossen et al. [8], care coordination features could involve both family members and paid caregivers. The ability to use care coordination applications to allocate shared resources such as vehicles or request assistance from a routine provider (e.g., an insurance company) could also smooth appointment planning processes.

Additionally, to facilitate emotional support, an extended portal could allow users to offer feedback to one another. For instance, the system could allow them to express a "like" or "thanks!" to others when health milestones are reached or family members confirm that they will attend an appointment with a patient, providing a public way to encourage and acknowledge support. While the system would need to avoid encouraging public shaming, good things could be acknowledged in a public way.

Lastly, for patients who use electronic calendars, it would be relatively straightforward to incorporate monitoring of events such as travel that might interfere with medication taking. The system could alert patients of potential conflicts, enabling them to plan for routine disruptions.

While further development of smart pills, medication containers and patient portals may be costly and time consuming, it would align with healthcare institutions' and governments' financial incentives to keep patients out of emergency rooms and reduce re-hospitalizations. Such incentives could drive development, increasing the likelihood of patients and families ultimately gaining access to these technologies through their healthcare providers.

Study Limitations

As our study comprises ethnographic interviews with 38 families and 97 individuals, the generalizability of its findings is limited. Nevertheless, the sample was large and diverse for a qualitative cohort, and provided in-depth insight into the research questions. Only 24 of 38 families agreed to participate in a home tour, which may reflect the personal nature of one's home environment. However, there were no notable demographic differences between the 24 families that participated in home tours and the full sample.

CONCLUSION

This paper describes how chronically ill patients and their families use the illness-related time-based objects of calendars and medication containers as support for the temporal aspects of illness management in the home. These objects were used as part of two family-based collaborative work practices: 1) prompting health management activities, and 2) safeguarding these activities. Additionally, they were part of two social interaction patterns that managed emotional intimacy: 1) expressing support, and 2) hiding and disguising illness. We also describe the strengths and weaknesses of existing systems. Of concern were the ways in which existing objects could not address the complexity of medical appointment attendance nor prevent several cases of medication errors and lapses. Based on these findings, we note three key contributions of our research.

First, the current research demonstrates that use of time-based objects by patients and their families is not only shaped by instrumental considerations, but also reflects the collaborative and interactive nature of illness management. Thus our work suggests the value of developing or extending *collaborative* technologies to support the temporal aspects of illness management. Such technologies should be informed by consideration of their relational meanings as well as the tasks that they support.

Second, while calendars and medication containers can effectively prompt and safeguard illness management activities, they have certain limitations. Calendars are limited in supporting tasks characterized by contingent timing (e.g., medication refills), in prompting cascading activities leading up to events (e.g., preparing current medication lists), and in accommodating the shifting involvement of family members in care. Medication containers are limited in supporting complex medication regimens and in providing prompts in instances of routine deviation. This suggests a need for technologies that better accommodate the temporal and social complexity of both appointment attendance and medication taking.

Third, to address the identified limitations of current objects, we identify potential extensions to two widely-available consumer health technologies: patient portals and smart pill containers. Our recommended design options remain sensitive to the instrumental and social uses identified in our research. For example, decorative medication containers would allow users to "hide and disguise" their illness as desired.

As time-based objects for home health management continue to be developed, we hope that the findings and recommendations reported here will inspire the creation of technologies that support a wider range of temporal illness management activities, and allow patients and family members to generate relational meaning in ways that meet their social and emotional needs.

ACKNOWLEDGMENTS

This research was made possible by funding from the Institute of Museum and Library Services (grant #: RE-04-10-0038-10), which we gratefully acknowledge. All views, findings, and conclusions expressed in this article are ours and do not necessarily represent those of the funder. We also thank our participants for generously sharing their experiences with us.

REFERENCES

1. About GlowCap. *Vitality*. http://www.vitality.net/glowcaps.html.
2. Bardram, J. Designing for the dynamics of cooperative work activities. In *Proc. CSCW 1998*, ACM Press (1998), 89-98.
3. Bauer, A. M., Thielke, S. M., Katon, W., Unützer, J. and Areán, P. Aligning health information technologies with effective service delivery models to improve chronic disease care. *Preventive Medicine 66*, (2014), 167-172.
4. Birth, K. *Objects of time: How things shape temporality*. Palgrave Macmillan, New York (2012).
5. Blumenthal, D. and Tavenner, M. The "meaningful use" regulation for electronic health records. *New England Journal of Medicine 363*, 6 (2010), 501-504.
6. Bødker, S. and Grönvall, E. Calendars: Time coordination and overview in families and beyond. In *Proc. ECSCW 2013*, Springer (2013), 63-81.
7. Borchard, A., Schwappach, D. L., Barbir, A. and Bezzola, P. A systematic review of the effectiveness, compliance, and critical factors for implementation of safety checklists in surgery. *Annals of Surgery 256*, 6 (2012), 925-933.
8. Bossen, C., Christensen, L. R., Grönvall, E. and Vestergaard, L. S. CareCoor: Augmenting the coordination of cooperative home care work. *International Journal of Medical Informatics 82*, 5 (2013), e189-e199.
9. Boutwell, A., Silber, S., Nguyen, D., Ryan, L. and Melville, L. Post-Acute care: What does it have to do with me? *Current Emergency and Hospital Medicine Reports 2*, 1 (2014), 9-15.
10. Browne, J. L., Ventura, A., Mosely, K. and Speight, J. 'I call it the blame and shame disease': A qualitative study about perceptions of social stigma surrounding type 2 diabetes. *BMJ Open 3*, 11 (2013).
11. Charmaz, K. *Constructing grounded theory: 2nd Edition*. SAGE, Los Angeles (2014).
12. Charmaz, K. *Good days, bad days: The self in chronic illness and time*. Rutgers University Press, New Brunswick (1991).
13. Chenard, C. The impact of stigma on the self-care behaviors of HIV-positive gay men striving for normalcy. *Journal of the Association of Nurses in AIDS Care 18*, 3 (2007), 23-32.
14. Colineau, N. and Paris, C. Motivating reflection about health within the family: The use of goal setting and tailored feedback. *User Modeling and User-Adapted Interaction 21*, 4-5 (2011), 341-376.
15. Collier, J. and Collier, M. *Visual anthropology: Photography as a research method*. University of New Mexico Press, Albuquerque (1986).
16. Corbin, J. and Strauss, A. Managing chronic illness at home: Three lines of work. *Qualitative Sociology 8*, 3 (1985), 224-247.
17. Crabtree, A., Hemmings, T., Rodden, T. and Mariani, J. Informing the development of calendar systems for domestic use. In *Proc. ECSCW 2003*, Springer (2003), 119-138.
18. Crabtree, A. and Rodden, T. Domestic routines and design for the home. *Computer Supported Cooperative Work 13*, 2 (2004), 191-220.
19. Digital Health Feedback System. *Proteus Digital Health*. http://www.proteus.com/technology/digital-health-feedback-system.
20. Dix, A. Computer supported cooperative work: A framework. In D. Rosenberg and C. Hutchison (eds.) *Design issues in CSCW*, Springer, New York (1994), 9-26.
21. Dourish, P. *Where the action is: The foundations of embodied interaction*. MIT Press, Cambridge, Mass. (2004).
22. Elliot, K., Neustaedter, C. and Greenberg, S. Time, ownership and awareness: The value of contextual locations in the home. *UbiComp 2005: Ubiquitous Computing Lecture Notes in Computer Science 3660*, (2005), 251-268.
23. England, K. Home, work and the shifting geographies of care. *Ethics, Place & Environment 13*, 2 (2010), 131-150.
24. Eschler, J., Kendall, L., O'Leary, K., Vizer, L., Lozano, P., McClure, J., Pratt, W. and Ralston, J. Shared calendars for home health management. In *Proc. CSCW 2015*, ACM Press (2015).
25. Flaherty, M. G. *The textures of time: Agency and temporal experience*. Temple University Press, Philadelphia (2011).
26. Fox, S. and Jones, S. *The social life of health information, 2011*. Pew Research Center & California HealthCare Foundation, Washington, DC (2011).
27. Goldzweig, C. L., Orshansky, G., Paige, N. M., Towfigh, A. A., Haggstrom, D. A., Miake-Lye, I., Beroes, J. M. and Shekelle, P. G. Electronic patient

portals: Evidence on health outcomes, satisfaction, efficiency, and attitudes: A systematic review. *Annals of Internal Medicine 159*, 10 (2013), 677-687.
28. Gomes, B., Calanzani, N. and Higginson, I. J. Reversal of the British trends in place of death: Time series analysis 2004-2010. *Palliative Medicine 26*, 2 (2012), 102-107.
29. Grimes, A. and Brush, A. Life scheduling to support multiple social roles. In *Proc. CHI 2008*, ACM Press (2008), 821-824.
30. Grimes, A., Tan, D. and Morris, D. Toward technologies that support family reflections on health. In *Proc. GROUP 2009*, ACM Press (2009), 311-320.
31. Hansen, S. M., Tolle, S. W. and Martin, D. P. Factors associated with lower rates of in-hospital death. *Journal of Palliative Medicine 5*, 5 (2002), 677-685.
32. Hartel, J. and Thomson, L. Visual approaches and photography for the study of immediate information space. *Journal of the American Society for Information Science and Technology 62*, 11 (2011), 2214-2224.
33. Haycock-Stuart, E. and Kean, S. Shifting the balance of care? A qualitative study of policy implementation in community nursing. *Journal of Nursing Management 21*, 6 (2013), 867-877.
34. How to Help the Community and Provide Caregiver Support. *Lotsa Helping Hands*. http://www.lotsahelpinghands.com/how-it-works/.
35. Jeffries, A. Smart pill bottle measures meds using touchscreen technology. *The Verge*. http://www.theverge.com/2012/10/8/3473218/smart-pill-bottle-adheretech-capacitance.
36. Jewitt, C. and Van Leeuwen, T. *The handbook of visual analysis*. SAGE, London (2001).
37. Khan, D. U., Ananthanarayan, S., Le, A. T., Schaefbauer, C. L. and Siek, K. A. Designing mobile snack application for low socioeconomic status families. In *Proc. PervasiveHealth 2012*, IEEE (2012), 57-64.
38. Klasnja, P., Civan Hartzler, A., Unruh, K. T. and Pratt, W. Blowing in the wind: Unanchored patient information work during cancer care. In *Proc. CHI 2010*, ACM Press (2010), 193-202.
39. Klasnja, P., Hartzler, A., Powell, C., Phan, G. and Pratt, W. Health weaver mobile: Designing a mobile tool for managing personal health information during cancer care. In *Proc. AMIA Symposium 2010*, AMIA (2010), 392-396.
40. Klasnja, P., Hartzler, A., Powell, C. and Pratt, W. Supporting cancer patients' unanchored health information management with mobile technology. In *Proc. AMIA Symposium 2011*, AMIA (2011), 732-741.
41. Kramarow, E., Lentzner, H., Rooks, R., Weeks, J. and Saydah, S. *Health, United States, 1999 with health and aging chartbook*. National Center for Health Statistics, Hyattsville, MD, United States (1999).
42. Lee, M. L. and Dey, A. K. Real-time feedback for improving medication taking. In *Proc. CHI 2014*, ACM Press (2014), 2259-2268.
43. Lee, R., Kochman, A. and Sikkema, K. Internalized stigma among people living with HIV-AIDS. *AIDS and Behavior 6*, 4 (2002), 309-319.
44. McCoy, L. Time, self and the medication day: A closer look at the everyday work of 'adherence'. *Sociology of Health & Illness 31*, 1 (2009), 128-146.
45. Meeussen, K., Van Den Block, L., Echteld, M. A., Boffin, N., Bilsen, J., Van Casteren, V., Abarshi, E., Donker, G., Onwuteaka-Philipsen, B. and Deliens, L. End-of-Life care and circumstances of death in patients dying as a result of cancer in Belgium and The Netherlands: A retrospective comparative study. *Journal of Clinical Oncology 29*, 32 (2011), 4327-4334.
46. Moen, A. and Brennan, P. F. Health@ Home: the work of health information management in the household (HIMH): implications for consumer health informatics (CHI) innovations. *Journal of the American Medical Informatics Association 12*, 6 (2005), 648-656.
47. Neustaedter, C., Brush, A. and Greenberg, S. The calendar is crucial: Coordination and awareness through the family calendar. *ACM Transactions on Computer-Human Interaction 16*, 1 (2009), Article No. 6.
48. Palen, L. Social, individual and technological issues for groupware calendar systems. In *Proc. CHI 1999*, ACM Press (1999), 17-24.
49. Parker, K. and Patten, E. *The sandwich generation: Rising financial burdens for middle-aged Americans*. Pew Research Center, Washington, DC (2013).
50. Pink, S. *Doing visual ethnography: Images, media, and representation in research*. SAGE, London (2007).
51. Pratt, W., Unruh, K., Civan, A. and Skeels, M. M. Personal health information management. *Communications of the ACM 49*, 1 (2006), 51-55.
52. Shekelle, P., Wachter, R., Pronovost, P., Schoelles, K., McDonald, K., Dy, S., Shojania, K., Reston, J., Berger, Z. and Johnsen, B. *Evidence report/technology assessment - No. 211: Making health care safer II: An updated critical analysis of the evidence for patient safety practices*. Agency for Healthcare Research and Quality, Rockville, MD, United States (2013).
53. Stawarz, K., Cox, A. and Blandford, A. Don't forget your pill!: Designing effective medication reminder apps that support users' daily routines. In *Proc. CHI 2014*, ACM Press (2014), 2269-2278.
54. Support for Your Health Journey. *Caring Bridge*. http://www.caringbridge.org.
55. Thayer, A., Bietz, M. J., Derthick, K. and Lee, C. P. I love you, let's share calendars: Calendar sharing as relationship work. In *Proc. CSCW 2012*, ACM Press (2012), 749-758.
56. Thoits, P. A. Stress, coping, and social support processes: Where are we? What next? *Journal of Health and Social Behavior 35*, (1995), 53-79.

57. UMLS: RxNorm. *U.S. National Library of Medicine*. http://www.nlm.nih.gov/research/umls/rxnorm.
58. Veinot, T. "A lot of people didn't have a chance to support us because we never told them" Stigma management, information poverty and HIV/AIDS information/help networks. In *Proc. American Society for Information Science and Technology 2009*, Wiley (2009), 1-20.
59. Veinot, T. Power to the patient? A critical examination of patient empowerment discourses. In R. M. Harris, C. N. Wathen and S. Wyatt (eds.) *Configuring health consumers: Health work and the imperative of personal responsibility*, Palgrave Macmillan, New York (2010), 30-41.
60. Veinot, T. C. E., Kim, Y.-M. and Meadowbrooke, C. C. Health information behavior in families: Supportive or irritating? In *Proc. American Society for Information Science and Technology 2011*, Wiley (2011), 1-10.
61. Wilson, D. M., Truman, C. D., Thomas, R., Fainsinger, R., Kovacs-Burns, K., Froggatt, K. and Justice, C. The rapidly changing location of death in Canada, 1994-2004. *Social Science and Medicine 68*, 10 (2009), 1752-1758.
62. Wood, W. and Neal, D. T. A new look at habits and the habit-goal interface. *Psychological Review 114*, 4 (2007), 843-863.
63. Wood, W., Tam, L. and Witt, M. G. Changing circumstances, disrupting habits. *Journal of Personality and Social Psychology 88*, 6 (2005), 918-933.

"Preventative" vs. "Reactive": How Parental Mediation Influences Teens' Social Media Privacy Behaviors

Pamela Wisniewski
The Pennsylvania State University
University Park, PA
pam@pamspam.com

Haiyan Jia
The Pennsylvania State University
University Park, PA
hjia@psu.edu

Heng Xu
The Pennsylvania State University
University Park, PA
hxu@ist.psu.edu

Mary Beth Rosson
The Pennsylvania State University
University Park, PA
mrosson@ist.psu.edu

John M. Carroll
The Pennsylvania State University
University Park, PA
jcarroll@ist.psu.edu

ABSTRACT
Through an empirical, secondary analysis of 588 teens (ages 12 – 17) and one of their parents living in the United States, we present useful insights into how parental privacy concerns for their teens and different parental mediation strategies (direct intervention versus active mediation) influence teen privacy concerns and privacy risk-taking and risk-coping privacy behaviors in social media. Our results suggest that the use of direct intervention by itself may have a suppressive effect on teens, reducing their exposure to online risks but also their ability to engage with others online and to learn how to effectively cope with online risks. Therefore, it may be beneficial for parents to combine active mediation with direct intervention so that they can protect their teens from severe online risks while empowering teens to engage with others online and learn to make good online privacy choices.

Author Keywords
Adolescent online behavior; parental involvement; privacy

ACM Classification Keywords
K.4.1 [Public Policy Issues]: Ethics, Human safety, Privacy

General Terms
Human Factors; Theory; Design.

INTRODUCTION
According to Pew Research, 95% of American teens between the ages of 12 and 17 are online [34], and 81% of online teens use some kind of social media, such as Facebook or Twitter. These teens are sharing more personal information about themselves through social media sites than ever before, yet report relatively low levels of privacy concern [33]. In contrast, 81% of their parents are "somewhat" to "very" concerned about their teens' online privacy [31]. In this paper, we explore the co-influences of parental privacy concerns and mediation strategies on teens' privacy concerns and social media privacy behaviors, including both risk-taking and risk-coping behaviors. We do this through a secondary analysis of the 2012 Pew Research Center's Internet and American Life Project's ***Teens and Privacy Management Survey*** of 588 teen (ages 12 – 17) and one of their parents living in the United States. The nationally representative data were collected from July 26 to September 30, 2012 [31-34].

Through an empirical analysis of this large-scale survey data, we developed useful insights into how parental privacy concerns for their teens and different parental mediation strategies may influence teen privacy concerns and social media privacy behaviors on Facebook. We identify and examine two types of parental mediation strategies from the 2012 Pew survey: 1) ***direct parental intervention*** through the use of parental controls and/or reading and setting up a teen's social media privacy settings for him or her; and 2) ***active parental mediation*** which includes talking with the teen about what he or she posts, reviewing information the teen posts, and/or commenting on or responding to posts made by the teen on Facebook. We found that parental privacy concerns are significantly and positively associated with teen privacy concerns, as well as both types of parental mediation strategies.

We also examine two types of teen social media privacy behaviors: 1) ***privacy risk-taking behaviors***, which include teens' sharing of *basic information* (e.g. photos, real name, birth date, and relationship status), sharing of more *sensitive information* (e.g. videos of him or herself, cell phone number, email address, etc.), and partaking in *risky interactions* (e.g. online communication with strangers, regrettable information disclosures, and automatic location

CSCW 2015, March 14–18, 2015, Vancouver, BC, Canada.

http://dx.doi.org/10.1145/2675133.2675293

sharing); and 2) ***privacy risk-coping behaviors***, which include *seeking advice* from others and taking *remedy/corrective measures*, such as posting fake information, deleting posted content, blocking or deleting individuals, and/or deactivating one's account.

We found that direct parental intervention is significantly and negatively associated with teens' basic information disclosures and remedy/corrective behaviors, but positively associated with advice-seeking. This suggests that when parents are directly involved in teens' social media disclosure decisions, teens tend to be more risk-adverse in disclosing basic information online and seek more advice on how to manage their online privacy, thereby preventing the need to take remedy or corrective actions. In contrast, we found parental active mediation to be positively associated with teens' disclosure of sensitive information and remedy/corrective behaviors. This suggests that active parental mediation may afford teens a higher level of autonomy to make more risky disclosure decisions but also encourages teens to learn from their mistakes and take corrective actions to protect their online privacy in a more reactive fashion. We further compare and contrast the apparent "preventative" versus "reactive" motivations behind these two parental mediation strategies and investigate how they influence teen outcomes. Our results suggest that the use of direct intervention alone may have a suppressive effect on teens, reducing their exposure to online risks but also their ability to engage with others online and to learn how to effectively cope with online risks. Therefore, it may be beneficial for parents to combine active mediation with direct intervention so that they can protect their teens from severe online risks while empowering them to benefit from online engagement and make good online privacy choices.

BACKGROUND

Technology use and the coordination of use within the context of families and between parents and teens have become important areas of interest within the CSCW community [1]. For instance, CSCW researchers have examined how teens use instant messaging for interpersonal communication [18], how teens interact with social media [25], how and why teens use video chat [7], what teens ask their online social networks [16], and how parenting influences teen moral judgments regarding various online behaviors [46]. A common theme that emerges across all of these studies is that teens benefit from technology use and online engagement; however, doing so also exposes them to privacy-related risks. In terms of privacy, the CSCW community has also established that a fundamental social-technical gap exists between how individuals manage the dissemination of personal information in everyday social situations versus how this is done explicitly through the use of technology [2]. Systems do not provide the flexibility, nuance, or ambiguity inherent in normal social situations and instead often require users to make intentional and complex disclosure decisions [2].

This gap only widens when socially developing adolescents are the ones making difficult information disclosure decisions when they engage with others through social media. Researchers have confirmed a disconnect or "privacy paradox" between teens' stated privacy concerns, level of awareness, and the vast amounts of information they continue to share through social media [4, 25]. Yet, relatively few CSCW studies have solely focused on understanding the extent of this privacy gap and finding ways to address it. The majority of studies in this space [7, 16, 18] employ qualitative approaches with small samples of teens to understand more generally how teens use various communication technologies and report privacy implications as one of their many nuanced findings. Thus, we extend the extant literature by conducting an in-depth analysis specifically to examine teens' privacy concerns and social media privacy behaviors in relation to parental privacy concerns and mediation strategies.

Even outside of the CSCW community, relatively few U.S.-based, large-scale, nationally representative surveys have been conducted to understand adolescent online privacy risks and online disclosure behaviors and experiences. One of the most recent and notable surveys was the ***Teens and Privacy Management Survey*** conducted by Pew Research Center's Internet and American Life Project in 2012 [31-34] that focused on teens' social media privacy management behaviors. Data were originally obtained through Random Digit Dial (RDD) telephone interviews with a sample of 802 teens aged 12 - 17 years, and their parents living in the United States. To ensure a nationally representative sample, the data were collected to match national parameters for both parent and teen demographics [31].

This survey collected dyadic-level data from both parents and teens regarding social media use, privacy concerns, parental mediation strategies, and teen social media privacy behaviors [31-34]. Pew Research's initial reports mainly focused on descriptive characteristics of the teen data and the parental data separately; however, they did uncover some initial trends between parent and teen factors. For instance, parents of younger teens were more concerned about their teens' online privacy than parents of older teens and were also more likely to employ the use of parental controls [31]. Meanwhile, younger teens were more likely to seek advice from their parents on how to manage their online privacy than older teens [32]. However, to date, Pew Research has not published an in-depth report on how parental privacy concern and mediation strategies relate directly to teen privacy concerns and social media privacy behaviors. Fortunately, given the dyadic-level data published publically by Pew Research, we were able to further analyze this data set to understand how parental factors are related to teen social media privacy concerns and behaviors.

CONCEPTUAL FRAMEWORK

To group items from the Pew survey conceptually and build an empirically testable framework, we drew from relevant constructs previously explored in adolescent online safety and developmental psychology literature. Building from that understanding, we performed data reduction techniques on the survey responses to build statistically stable factors [44] that were consistent with past theoretical constructs. Factors that were statistically robust were added as constructs to our research framework below and kept for further analysis; items that did not load sufficiently with the emergent factors or that lacked clear theoretical basis were removed from our analysis. In this section, we present the conceptual foundations of our framework. Later, in the methodology section, we will provide further details on how statistically robust constructs were developed to empirically test the salient relationships between constructs in our conceptual framework.

Privacy Concern

Privacy concern has often been measured in privacy research as a proxy measure for information privacy and shown to be one of the strongest predictors of privacy-related behavior [12, 35, 41, 47]. However, very few studies have examined how parental and/or teen privacy concerns about technology use relate to teens' subsequent online behaviors. While past literature consistently suggests that parental concerns over teen online safety are high [19, 31, 42] and teen privacy concerns are low relative to those of their parents [33], very little research helps explain how privacy concerns relate to parental mediation strategies or teen online privacy behaviors. For example, Crossler et al. found no evidence of a relationship between parental concerns for information privacy and their awareness of privacy regulations or perceived privacy risks for their teens [8]. Thus, in our model, we wanted to explore the relationship between parental and teen privacy concerns, different parental mediation strategies, and teen social media privacy behaviors in more depth.

Parental Mediation Strategies

Most of the ***parental mediation strategies*** examined in past research were originally derived from Valkenburg et al.'s parental mediation strategies for regulating children's television viewing. These included instructive (active) mediation, restrictive mediation, and social co-viewing (monitoring) [45]. With respect to online interactions, *active mediation* has been adapted to mean interaction and discussions between parents and teens regarding online activities; *restrictive mediation* occurs through rules and limits placed on a teen's online activities; and *monitoring* is non-interactive surveillance of a teen's online activities, such as checking text messages or web browser history [28]. Some studies have also included *technical mediation* as a mediation strategy, for example the use of parental monitoring software applications [14, 28].

In our model, we examine two types of parental mediation strategies. The first strategy is ***direct parental intervention*** through the use of parental controls and/or reading and setting up a teen's social media privacy settings for him or her. Direct parental intervention strategies reflect more *restrictive* parenting and the use of *technical mediation* in order to proactively and directly intervene in teens' social media privacy decisions.

The second type of parental mediation strategy we examine is ***active mediation***, which includes parents talking with their teens about what they post, reviewing information teens post, and/or commenting or responding to posts made by their teens on Facebook. These strategies tend to reflect *more instructive (active)* and *monitoring*-based strategies used by parents as a way to guide their teens' online behaviors as these behaviors occur. Parental active mediation allows teens to be more experiential and reflective because their parents are not attempting to directly control their social media privacy behaviors.

We expect that direct parental intervention and active mediation will function to influence teen privacy behaviors in different ways. For instance, past research has found that active mediation is more effective than restrictive mediation because it allows teens to better interpret their media experience [11], and it better educates teens as media consumers, especially in highly interactive environments such as the Internet [23]. We also note that parents may choose to employ none, one, or both of these parental mediation strategies when attempting to mediate their teens' online privacy behavior. Therefore, we later explore the potential interaction effects for when these two strategies are used in isolation or combined.

Teen Privacy Risk-Taking Behaviors

Teens are by nature sensation-seeking and more likely to take greater risks than children and adults [26]. Therefore, a number of studies have focused on ways parents can mitigate teen risk-taking behaviors and experiences, thus viewing adolescent online safety through a lens of risk-adversity, or shielding teens from online risks. As such, the two most prominently studied dependent variables in this stream of research include attempting to reduce teens' propensity to disclose personal information online and limiting their exposure to online risks. Many past studies have been interested in understanding how parental mediation can reduce teen exposure to online risks; teen risk experiences examined in past research include but are not limited to exposure to unwanted sexual materials or pornographic imagery, harmful user-generated content, sexual solicitations, and online harassment or cyberbullying [13, 30, 36-38, 40].

However, the Pew survey focused specifically on teens' privacy-related risks in social media. Therefore, in our framework, we specifically examine three types of teen privacy risk-taking privacy behaviors in social media: ***Basic***

information disclosures include basic information sharing, such as sharing one's real name or relationship status through social media. ***Sensitive information disclosures*** involve more intimate disclosures, such as personal videos and direct forms of contact information, such as cell phone number and email address. We also examine ***risky interactions*** that teens report experiencing through social media, such as communicating online with strangers, viewing inappropriate ads, automatic location sharing, and other regrettable interactions.

Some past studies have discovered interesting associations between parental mediation strategies and teens' information disclosure decisions. For instance, explicit parental restrictions against giving out personal information online have actually been associated with a higher likelihood that teens disclose such personal information [29]. Shin et al. [40] confirmed from a sample of parents and teens in Korea that parental mediation was not significantly related to tweens' (ages 9 – 12) willingness to disclose personal information online, although the larger the discrepancy between parental and tween perceptions of online restrictive mediation, the more willing tweens were to make online disclosures.

The relationship between parental mediation strategies and the risky interactions teens engage in through social media have also been examined, but often in conjunction with other types of risk exposure. Livingstone and Helsper [29] found that parental mediation strategies were ineffective or non-significant in terms of reducing teen online risk exposure, including exposure to pornography, violence, privacy, and contact-related risks. Later, Dürager and Livingstone [13] actually found a positive correlation between parents talking to their teens about their online safety and various types of teen risk exposure, including pornography, cyberbullying, contact with unknown others; they suggest that these discussions may have occurred as a consequence of risk exposure, not as a causal agent. Also, active mediation of Internet use and restrictive mediation were found to be negatively associated with teen risk exposure; however, restrictive mediation reduced risk exposure by limiting the overall time a teen spent online, thereby also reducing potential opportunities that teens may garner from online engagement [13]. Technical monitoring was found to have either a non-significant [13] or relatively weak negative association with online risk exposure, reducing risk exposure but also potentially reducing teen Internet proficiency [30].

These past studies tend to frame teen online risk experiences using a broader conceptualization of risks as exposure, which implies a sense of teen victimization or lack of agency. However, our research focuses specifically on teens' social media privacy-related risk-taking behaviors, which include their self-reported basic information disclosures, sensitive information disclosures, and risky interactions. Given the conceptually varied and often counter-intuitive results found in past research regarding teen online risk experiences, we believe that further examination of how parental mediation strategies are related to these specific teen social media risk-taking privacy behaviors is warranted.

Teen Privacy Risk-Coping Behaviors

In literature, very few studies have attempted to better understand teen online protective or risk-coping behaviors that occur in response to risk exposure, as opposed to attempting to prevent teens' exposure to online risks. D'Haenens et al. [10] was one of the first studies to point out that teens' exposure to online risks did not necessarily equate to harm. In fact, the ways in which teens responded to or chose to cope with negative online experiences ultimately influenced whether or not they were bothered by online risk exposure. They found that teens who took ***risk-coping behaviors***, such as talking to someone or taking proactive, problem-solving approaches when confronted with a problem tended to be less upset about a negative online experience than teens who took a more fatalistic or passive approach [10]. This finding is consistent with developmental psychology theory, which explains that resilience is the process of overcoming negative effects of risk exposure and successfully adapting, despite challenging or threatening circumstances. Importantly, resilience cannot be expressed without risk [43]. From this perspective, restricting teens' risk experiences too drastically might actually be detrimental, stunting their developmental growth [5-6].

Similarly, parents cannot shield their teens from all negative online experiences without also limiting the potential for positive online experiences that promote their teens' developmental growth. Therefore, instead of focusing on teen risk-taking behaviors as our dependent variable of interest, we focus on factors that may contribute to teen risk-coping behaviors when confronted with online risks. The Pew survey focused specifically on teens' privacy-related risks in social media. Therefore, we examine two types of privacy risk-coping behaviors: The first is ***advice-seeking***, which is a communicative process wherein teens solicit advice from others on how to manage their online privacy; the second is ***remedy/corrective behaviors***, which are problem-solving actions teens take to protect their online privacy.

Figure 1 depicts a summary of the constructs represented in our conceptual framework. From extant literature, we know very little about the salient relationships among parental privacy concerns, parental mediation strategies, teen privacy concerns, and teen privacy risk-taking versus risk-coping behaviors. Because past research has provided very few consistent insights regarding the potential significant relationships between our constructs and because our goal was to develop a conceptual framework through an exploratory analysis of the data, we did not hypothesize specific relationships between our constructs prior to our analysis. However, we do expect to see some general trends based on past research findings. For instance, consistent with more traditional risk avoidance approaches to adolescent online safety, we expect direct parental intervention to be associated with fewer teen risk-taking behaviors. Conversely, we expect active mediation to function more reactively, being triggered by teens' risk behaviors and encouraging teens to take more risk-coping measures in order to mitigate these risks. We test these general propositions in our empirical analyses.

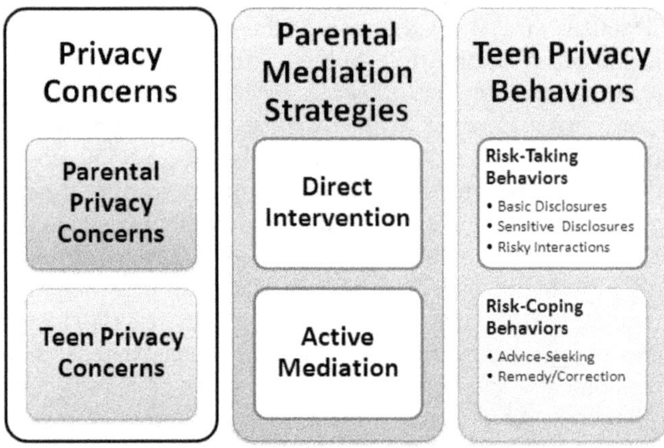

Figure 1: Conceptual Framework

METHODOLOGY

Pew Data Set

We conducted a secondary analysis of an existing, open-source data set[1] collected from July 26 to September 30, 2012, prepared by the Princeton Survey Research Associates International, and provided publicly by the Pew Research Center's Internet and American Life Project [31]. The Pew data set included paired responses from parents and teens regarding general Internet usage, social media usage, privacy concerns, parental mediation strategies, teen online privacy management behaviors, demographic variables, and more. Many of the questions were specific to various privacy management strategies teens employed for different social media platforms, such as Facebook, Twitter, and Instagram. Ninety-four percent of teens reported having an active Facebook account, followed by 26% with a Twitter account, 11% with an Instagram account, and so forth [31]. Given the high prevalence of teens with active Facebook accounts, our analysis eliminated responses from teens who did not report having a Facebook account and focused on privacy behaviors associated with their Facebook usage.

Operationalizing Constructs

A latent factor of parental privacy concern was constructed based on relevant ordinal-level items, and the Cronbach's alpha was reported as an indication of internal consistency [27, 44]. To construct factors of the other dichotomous items ("yes" or "no" questions) measuring parental mediation strategies, teen privacy risk-tasking behaviors, and teen privacy risk-coping behaviors, we utilized categorical principal component analyses (CATPCA). Similar to classic principal component analysis, CATPCA is used specifically for assessing the dimensionality of dichotomous or categorical variables [20]. To assess the reliability of these factors, Eigenvalues were reported and compared to the standard CATPCA criterion of being greater than one [22, 27]. After confirming that the resulting CATPCA factors were robust and aligned with past theoretical conceptualizations, we created additive indices for each factor and used these indices in our structural analysis.

Privacy Concerns

Parental privacy concern was measured with four questions asking parents how much they were concerned (on a 4-point scale from "not at all concerned" to "very concerned") about their teens' technology usage when it came to how their teens managed their reputation online, how much information third parties could learn about their teens, how their teens interacted with strangers, and how their teens' online behaviors might affect their academic or employment future. A reliability test indicated acceptable internal consistency among the four-item measurement, with *Cronbach's* $\alpha = 0.77$. As such, a scale of parental privacy concern (ranging from 1 to 4) was created and used for further analyses. ***Teen privacy concern*** was measured in the survey by asking one question to teens regarding the degree (on a 4-point scale from "not at all concerned" to "very concerned") of personal concern over the information that they share on the social media that might be accessed by third parties without their knowledge.

Parental Mediation Strategies

The Pew data set included six questions regarding parental mediation strategies for teen technology use, including whether or not the parent had previously read at least one privacy policy of a website that the teen was using; searched the teen's information online; used parental controls to block, filter or monitor the teen's online activities; helped the teen set up privacy settings; talked with the teen about concerns with their online postings; or commented or responded directly to the teen's online postings. Using parental strategies delineated in past research as our theoretical justification, we reduced these six items using CATPCA [20] into two distinct factors: ***Direct Intervention*** (including items of reading privacy policy; using parental controls; and setting up privacy settings), which resulted in an Eigenvalue of 2.04, and ***Active Mediation*** (talking with teens; searching teens' information; and responding directly to teens' online posts), with an Eigenvalue of 1.21. For both direct parental intervention and active parental mediation factors, we

[1] http://www.pewinternet.org/datasets/september-2012-teens-and-online-privacy/

created additive indices based on the number of different strategies parents reported having used ("yes") in the past (each ranging from 0 to 3).

Teen Privacy Risk-Taking Behaviors

Teens' risk-taking behaviors were measured with a variety of questions in the Pew survey, and three major dimensions were revealed: The dimension of ***basic information disclosures*** (Eigenvalue = 2.24) consisted of six items including posting real name, birth date, school name, relationship status and photos online; the dimension of ***sensitive information disclosure*** (Eigenvalue = 1.47) consisted of eight items, such as posting sensitive information including cell phone number and email address, personal interests, something which "later caused a problem" or "got [the teen] in trouble at school," or other types of "sensitive" information; and the dimension of ***risky interactions*** (Eigenvalue = 1.55) consisted of five items, including online postings/sharing that the teen later regretted; automatically sharing location; viewing inappropriate content; being contacted by strangers; and meeting someone they first met online, offline. Again, we created additive indices for these three factors based on the number of behaviors teens reported having taken in the past (ranging from 0 to 6, 0 to 8, and 0 to 5, respectively).

Teen Privacy Risk-Coping Behaviors

Teen's risk-coping behaviors emerged as two dimensions; the first dimension labeled as ***advice-seeking*** (Eigenvalue = 2.66) was measured by asking whether the teen had ever sought advice about managing their online privacy from a friend or peer, a sibling, a parent, a teacher, or online resources. The second dimension of teen risk-coping behaviors was labeled ***remedy and corrective behaviors*** (Eigenvalue = 1.64) and were measured with eight items asking whether the teen had blocked someone, deleted someone from their friends' list, removed tagging of themselves, deleted comments from others, deleted or edited their own posts, posted fake information in order to protect their privacy, shared inside jokes or coded messages between friends, and deleted or deactivated their account. We created additive indices for these two risk-coping behaviors (advice-seeking and remedy/corrective behaviors) based on the number of strategies teens reported having taken in the past (ranging from 0 to 5 and 0 to 8, respectively).

Data Analysis Approach

After the constructs for our model were established, covariance-based structural-equation modeling (CB-SEM) tests were conducted using Amos 22.0 [3] to explore the relationships between parental privacy concern, parental mediation strategies, teens' privacy concern, and teens' risk-taking and risk-coping behaviors. We began our analysis by testing a semi-saturated model, which included all possible paths between the parental constructs and teen constructs in our model (**Table 1**) [17]. Next, similar to a backward stepwise regression [44], but also taking into account relevant theory [24], we fitted the model by iteratively trimming insignificant paths between our constructs and adjusting the model based on suggested modification indices until all paths that remained were significant. Therefore, our final model (**Figure 2**) represents all significant paths between the constructs and implies that all paths not drawn in our final model were found to be insignificant.

Descriptive Statistics

Missing data were removed and data were also filtered to only retain parent-teen dyads with teens who specified having an active Facebook account. Thus, the final dataset that was used for analyses consisted of 588 teens (292 males and 296 females) and one of their parents. A majority (77.6%) of the respondents were Caucasian, with teens on average aged 15 and parents on average aged 47. Approximately 37% (N = 217) of the parents who responded to the telephone interview were male, while approximately 50% (N = 292) of the teens were male. About 70% of the parents indicated having some college education, including an associate's degree or higher. Also, 55% of parents reported having a household income equal to or higher than the U.S. average household income for the year 2011 ($50,000 and above). They were also adequately technology-savvy, as 69% reported having experience using social networking sites.

RESULTS

Structural Model Results

In order to examine the relationships between the constructs in our model, a series of analyses were conducted. First, a semi-saturated model was tested in order to examine the influences between parental and teen factors. The semi-saturated model indicated a good fit of the model to the data, $\chi^2 = 3.86$, $DF = 8$, $p = 0.87$; $CMIN/DF = 0.48$, $CFI = 1.000$, $RMSEA = 0.000$ (Note: A "good" model fit is characterized by a χ^2 that is not statistically significant, or $p\text{-}value > 0.05$; $CMIN/DF <$ or approaching 1; $CFI > 0.90$; and $RMSEA < 0.05$ [39]). **Table 1** reports the standardized estimates of the path coefficients for the semi-saturated model.

Path Analyses	*Standardized β*	*p-value*
Parental Privacy Concern → Parental Direct Intervention	0.226***	0.000
Parental Privacy Concern → Parental Active Mediation	0.208***	0.000
Parental Privacy Concern → Teen Privacy Concern	0.134**	0.001
Parental Direct Intervention → Teen Basic Information Disclosures	-0.101*	0.014
Parental Direct Intervention → Teen Sensitive Information Disclosures	-0.013	0.737
Parental Direct Intervention → Teen Risky Interactions	-0.010	0.797
Parental Direct Intervention → Teen Privacy Concern	-0.062	0.137
Parental Direct Intervention → Teen Advice-Seeking	0.135**	0.002
Parental Direct Intervention → Teen Remedy/Correction	-0.091*	0.014
Teen Basic Information Disclosures → Parental Active Mediation	0.058	0.142
Teen Sensitive Information Disclosures → Parental Active Mediation	0.106**	0.010
Teen Risky Interactions → Parental Active Mediation	0.042	0.288
Parental Active Mediation → Teen Privacy Concern	0.019	0.616
Parental Active Mediation → Teen Advice-Seeking	-0.037	0.397
Parental Active Mediation → Teen Remedy/Correction	0.100**	0.007
Teen Basic Information Disclosures → Teen Sensitive Information Disclosures	0.289***	0.000
Teen Sensitive Information Disclosures → Teen Risky Interactions	0.308***	0.000
Teen Risky Interactions → Teen Privacy Concern	0.097*	0.017
Teen Basic Information Disclosures → Teen Advice-Seeking	0.003	0.941
Teen Sensitive Information Disclosures → Teen Advice-Seeking	-0.031	0.478
Teen Risky Interactions → Teen Advice-Seeking	0.069	0.104
Teen Privacy Concern → Teen Advice-Seeking	0.188***	0.000
Teen Basic Information Disclosures → Teen Remedy/Correction	0.034	0.339
Teen Sensitive Information Disclosures → Teen Remedy/Correction	0.110**	0.003
Teen Risky Interactions → Teen Remedy/Correction	0.457***	0.000
Teen Privacy Concern → Teen Remedy/Correction	0.103**	0.003
Teen Advice-Seeking → Teen Remedy/Correction	0.117***	0.000

Table 1. Parameter Estimates of the Semi-Saturated Structural Model.

As noted in **Table 1**, a number of paths in this model were non-significant; therefore, a parsimonious model was created by omitting all paths that were found non-significant in the semi-saturated model, which also yielded a good model fit, $\chi^2 = 22.21$, $DF = 19$, $p = 0.27$, $CMIN/DF = 1.69$, $CFI = 0.994$, $RMSEA = 0.017$. Therefore, the results from this more parsimonious model are illustrated in **Figure 2** and discussed in the sections that follow. Due to the non-significant paths that were removed, there may be slight differences between the path coefficients shown in Table 1 and Figure 2; however, the overall results remain the same. Our final model explained 5% of the variance in teens' advice-seeking behaviors and 32% of the variance in teens' remedy/corrective behaviors. The recommended threshold of 10% is considered an indication of substantive explanatory power in social sciences [15].

Effects of Teens' Privacy Concern and Risk Behaviors

Although we are most interested in how parental factors contributed to teens' risk-coping privacy behaviors, we also controlled for differential effects of teens' own privacy concern and risk-taking behaviors on their risk-coping strategies. Such effects became useful in understanding the effects of the parental factors that followed. *Teen privacy concern* was positively associated with both types of risk-coping behaviors: *advice-seeking* ($\beta = 0.19$, $p < 0.001$) and *remedy/corrective actions* ($\beta = 0.10$, $p < 0.01$). The more concerned teens were about their online privacy, the more likely they were to seek advice from others and take remedy/corrective actions to protect their online privacy.

In terms of teen risk-taking behaviors, we found that less "risky" teen disclosure behaviors were likely to contribute to more "risky" teen behaviors. For instance, teens' online *basic information disclosures* were positively associated with their disclosure of *sensitive information*, ($\beta = 0.29$, $p < 0.001$); in turn, disclosure of *sensitive information* was positively associated with *online risky interactions*, ($\beta = 0.31$, $p < 0.001$). Consequently, *teens' privacy concern* increased as a result of such *risky interactions* ($\beta = 0.10$, $p = 0.017$). The more "risky" privacy behaviors also tended to be the ones that were significantly and positively associated with teens' remedy/corrective behaviors. Specifically, teens who disclosed more *sensitive information* about themselves through social media ($\beta = 0.12$, $p < 0.001$) and engaged in more *risky interactions* ($\beta = 0.46$, $p < 0.001$) online tended to also take more *remedy/corrective measures* to protect their online privacy. However, none of the teen risk-taking behaviors were significantly related to teen advice-seeking. Though, when teens *sought advice* from others, they were more likely to take *corrective/remedy actions* ($\beta = 0.12$, $p < 0.001$).

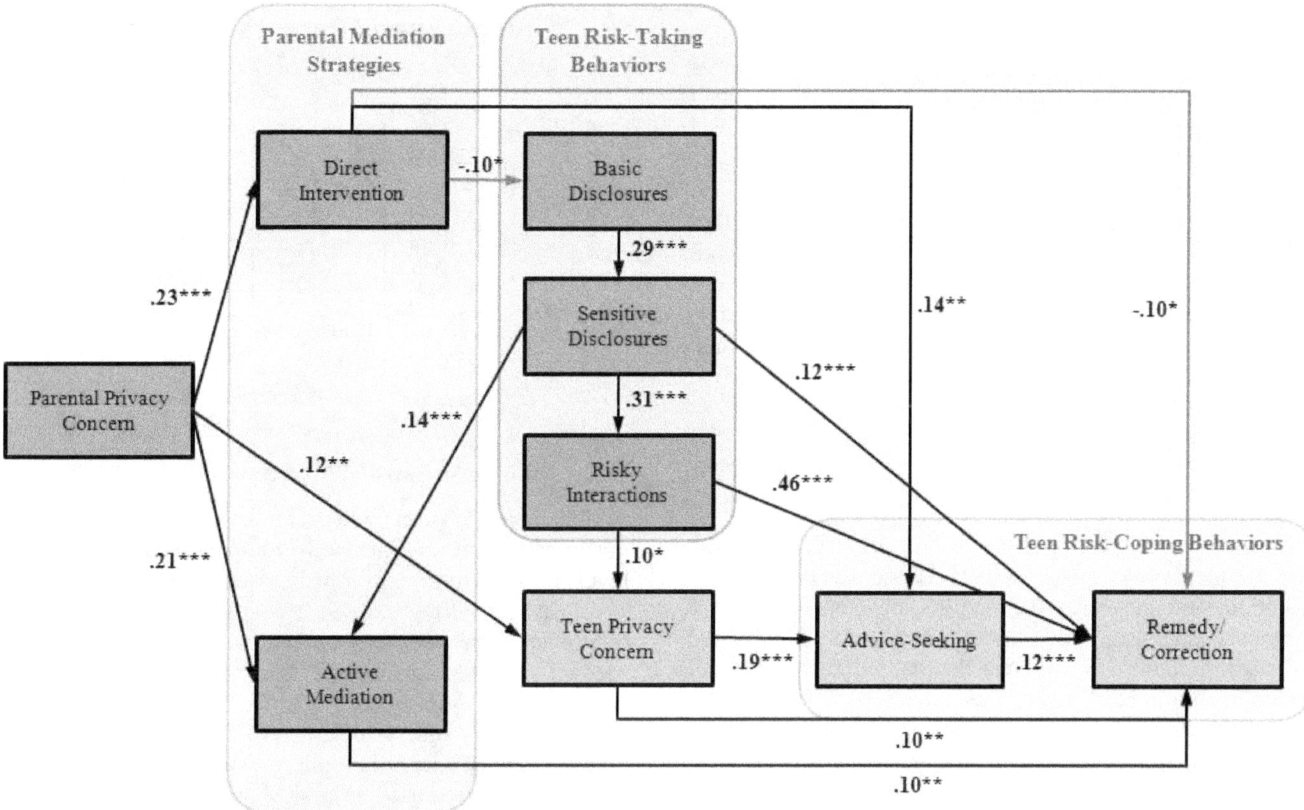

Figure 2: Structural Model. Statistically significant paths are shown with standardized coefficients and *p-values* indicated (* <= *0.05, ** <= 0.01, * <= 0.001*).**

Effects of Parental Privacy Concern

The extent to which parents were concerned about their teens' online privacy showed significant effects on both parental mediation strategies as well as teens' concern about privacy. Specifically, *parental privacy concern* was positively associated with *direct intervention* ($\beta = 0.23, p < 0.001$) and *active mediation* ($\beta = 0.21, p < 0.001$). *Parental privacy concern* also was positive related with *teens' privacy concern* ($\beta = 0.12, p < 0.01$). Parental mediation strategies and teens' privacy concern, in turn, influenced teens' online privacy behaviors, as discussed below.

Effects of Direct Parental Intervention

Direct Parental intervention appeared to influence teens' risk-coping privacy behaviors both directly and indirectly. For the direct effects, *direct parental intervention* was positively associated with *teens' advice-seeking behaviors* ($\beta = 0.14, p < 0.01$) and negatively associated with *teens' remedy/correction behaviors* ($\beta = -0.10, p < 0.05$). Direct parental intervention also affected teens' risk-coping behaviors through its effect on teens' risk behaviors; in particular, the structural model showed that *direct intervention* was negatively associated with *teen's basic information disclosures* ($\beta = -0.10, p < 0.05$). The less basic information teens disclosed online, the less likely they would engage in higher-risk, online privacy behaviors, reducing their need to take remedy/corrective actions. However, direct parental intervention showed no significant direct effects on other types of teens' risk behaviors, such as *sensitive information disclosures* ($\beta = -0.01, p = 0.74$) and *risky interactions* ($\beta = -0.01, p = 0.80$); nor did it affected *teens' privacy concern* directly ($\beta = -0.06, p = 0.14$).

Effects of Active Parental Mediation

Active mediation was found not only positively associated with parental privacy concern, but was also positively associated with teens' sensitive information disclosures. The more *sensitive information* teens disclosed online, the more likely parents were to engage in *active mediation* ($\beta = 0.14, p < 0.001$). There were no statistically significant relationships between teens' *basic information disclosures* ($\beta = 0.06, p = 0.14$), or *teens' risky interactions* ($\beta = 0.04, p = 0.29$), and *active mediation*. The structural model further showed that parental active mediation's influence on teens' risk-coping strategies was only through its direct effect on teens' remedy/correction behaviors. Increased *parental active mediation* appeared to enhance *teens' remedy/correction behaviors* ($\beta = 0.10, p < 0.01$). However, no effect of *active mediation* was found on *teens' advice-seeking* ($\beta = -0.04$ $p = 0.40$); or *teens' privacy concern* ($\beta = 0.02, p = 0.14$).

Parental Mediation Strategies Post Hoc Analysis

Because direct intervention and active mediation had such divergent influences in our model, we wanted to further understand the potential benefits and drawbacks associated with each parental mediation strategy, as well as the potential interaction effects when they the strategies were used individually or combined. Therefore, prior to discussing the implications of our results, we further explored the relationship between the two parental mediation strategies represented in our model with some of the contextual teen variables that were captured in the data set. To do this, we first dichotomized the two parental mediation strategies (direct intervention and active mediation) into "High" and "Low" categorical variables using median split (Direct Intervention: *Mean* = 1.35, *Median* = 1.00; Active Mediation: *Mean* = 1.34, *Median* = 1.00).

As illustrated in **Figure 3,** of the 588 parent respondents the most frequent categorization for the combined parental mediation strategies was "Low/Low" (blue bar) with 38% of parents exhibiting few direct intervention and active mediation behaviors. However, the second most frequent parental mediation strategy across parents was "High/High" (green bar) direct intervention and active mediation with 27% of parents falling into this category. This suggests that most parents (65%) are consistently low or consistently high on both parental mediation scales.

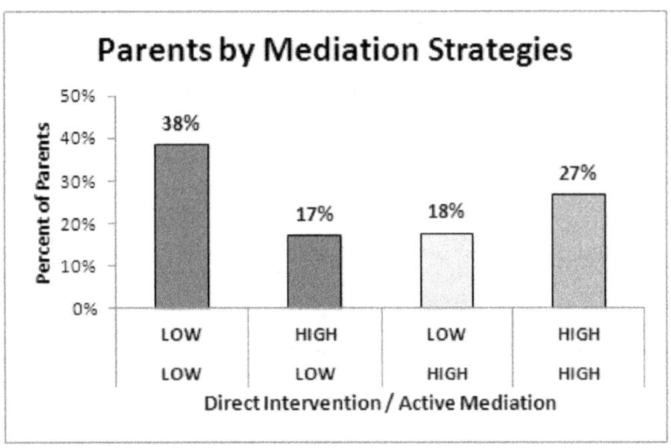

Figure 3: Distribution of Parents by Mediation Strategies

Next, we examined the relationship between parental mediation strategies and teen age. Teen age was categorized in to three levels using a tertiary split: younger teens (12-14-years-old, N = 214), mid-teens (15-years-old, N = 120), and older teens (16-17-years old, N = 254), and chi-square tests were conducted to examine the relationship between teen age and parental mediation strategies. As shown in **Figure 4**, the relationship between direct parental intervention and teen age was relatively linear while the relationship between teen age and active mediation was more nuanced.

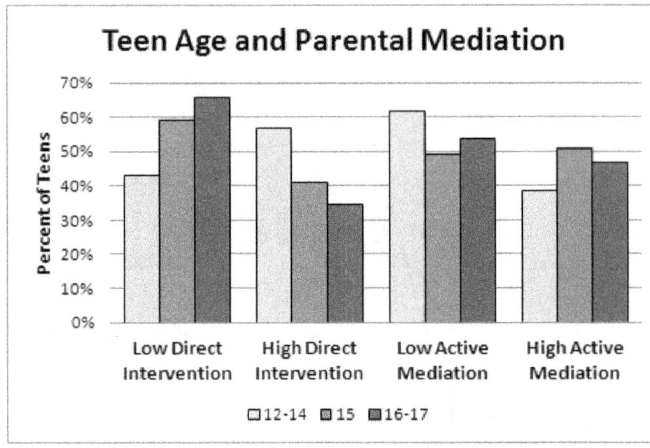

Figure 4: Parental Mediation and Teen Age

A high level of direct intervention was more likely to be observed among parents with younger teens, while a low level of direct intervention was associated with older teens, χ^2 (2, N = 588) = 24.99, p < 0.001. Conversely, the relationship between active parental mediation and age seemed almost curvilinear, resulting in only a near-significant chi-square test χ^2 (2, N = 588) = 5.654, p = 0.06, which suggests that a high level of active mediation was more generally adopted among parents of older teens. With further examination of **Figure 4**, parents seem to exhibit even higher levels of active mediation for mid-teens (15-year-olds) than for older teens (16-17-year-olds). This suggests that 15 may a pivotal age where teens are becoming more autonomous, parents are beginning to reduce direct intervention, but do so by more actively mediating their mid-teens' online behaviors. Once teens get older, direct intervention may no longer be an option so parents continue to actively mediate their older teens but to a lesser extent.

We also conducted Analysis of Variance (ANOVA) tests to explore how the combined parental mediation strategies influenced teens' frequency of SNS use and the complexity of teens' SNS networks. For teens' frequency of SNS use, we saw a main effect of both direct intervention and active mediation. Low levels of direct intervention were associated with significantly higher levels of SNS use (*Mean* = 4.88, *SE* = .09) than high levels of direct intervention (*Mean* = 4.61, *SE* = .09), F (1, 582) = 4.71, p < .05. In contrast, high levels of active mediation (*Mean* = 4.94, *SE* = .09) were associated with increased SNS frequency for teens compared to a low level of active mediation (*Mean* = 4.54, *SE* = .09), F (1, 582) = 19.69, p < .01. The interaction effect on teens' SNS frequency was not statistically significant, F (1, 582) = 1.00, p = .32 (see **Figure 5**, Note: asterisks denote significant differences between levels, such that A > B and C > D; bar colors are consistent with parental mediation strategies depicted in **Figure 3**).

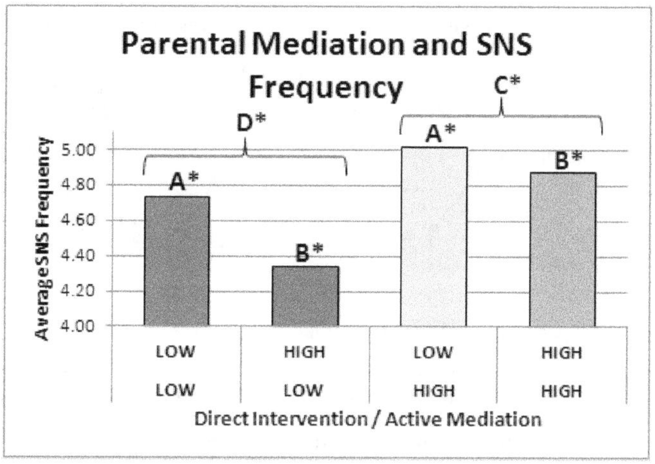

Figure 5: Parental Mediation and Teens' SNS Frequency

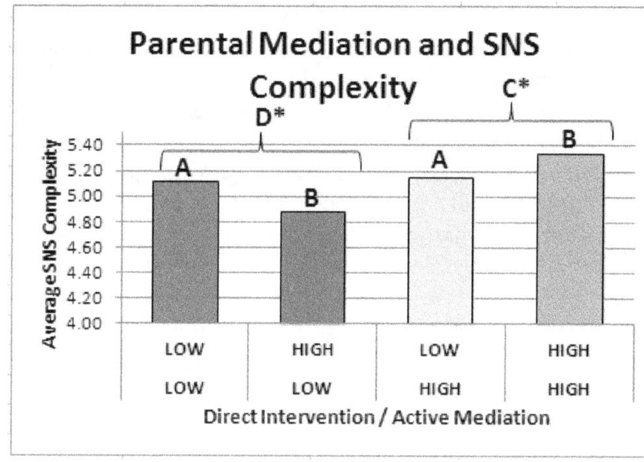

Figure 6: Parental Mediation and Teens' SNS Complexity

Therefore, teens who used SNSs the least frequently (red bar) tended to be those who experienced high levels of direct intervention and low levels of active mediation; teens who used SNSs most frequently (light blue bar) tended to be those under low levels of direct intervention and high levels of active mediation. Therefore, our findings suggest a potential *suppressive* effect where high levels of direct parental intervention (red bar) may reduce teens' SNS frequency of use.

Teens' SNS complexity was measured based on the self-reported network composition of teens' Facebook friends, ranging from closer networks of family and real friends to more open networks, which included acquaintances and strangers. High active mediation ($Mean$ = 5.24, SE = .08) was associated with a greater complexity of teens' online social networks than low active mediation ($Mean$ = 5.00, SE = .08), F (1, 584) = 4.70, p < .05. Direct intervention showed no effect on teens' SNS complexity, F (1, 582) = .05, p = .82; however, the interaction effect was approaching statistical significance, F (1, 582) = 3.20, p = .07 (see **Figure 6** Note: asterisks denote significant differences between levels, such that C > D; bar colors are consistent with parental mediation strategies depicted in **Figure 3**). The near significant interaction effect suggests that, in cases of high direct intervention (B), active mediation had a greater influence on teens' SNS complexity (Given B, C > D), but for low levels of direct intervention (A), active mediation showed little influence on teens' SNS complexity. As such, teens with the least complex SNS networks (red bar) tended to be those who experienced high levels of direct intervention and low levels of active mediation, and teens with the most complex SNS networks (green bar) tended to experience both high levels of direct intervention and active mediation. Thus, similar to SNS frequency, we observed a possible *suppressive* effect of high levels of direct intervention coupled with low levels of active mediation (red bar), which may restrict teens' from having a variety of different SNS connections.

However, we also saw a potential *empowering* effect from combining high levels of active mediation with high levels of direct intervention (green bar), which seemed to encourage teens to have a broader range of SNS social connections, despite the increased parental oversight.

DISCUSSION

By focusing on dyadic-level data of both parents and teens, conceptually grouping individual survey questions from the Pew telephone interviews using construct development and statistical factor reduction, and by performing various path analyses, our work provides unique, empirical insights into the salient relationships among parental and teen privacy concerns, parental mediation strategies, and teens' risk-taking and risk-coping behaviors when teens engage with others through social media. We will highlight some of the key insights provided by our findings, discuss implications for design, summarize the limitations of our findings, and discuss potential opportunities to extend our research in the future.

Key Insights

Parental and Teen Behaviors are Multi-Dimensional

Our factor analyses of the Pew data revealed two dimensions of parental mediation strategies (direct intervention and active mediation), three types of teen risk-taking behaviors (basic information disclosures, sensitive information disclosures, and risky interactions), and two distinct teen risk-coping strategies (advice-seeking and remedy/corrective actions). The underlying dimensionality of these various parental and teen behaviors, combined with the differential relationships between each of these factors, highlights the importance of examining parental and teen behavior at more granular levels in order to detect nuanced relationships.

For example, our model found that direct intervention is positively associated with teen advice-seeking but negatively associated with teen remedy/corrective behaviors, even though both were framed as teen risk-coping behaviors in past literature. If these two dimensions of risk-coping behaviors had been grouped as one latent construct in our model, we would not have uncovered these unique relationships. This finding suggests an important distinction between teen advice-seeking and remedy/corrective behaviors. Advice-seeking appears to be a less autonomous, more dependent teen behavior that is associated with higher levels of direct supervision from parents. In contrast, remedy/corrective behaviors appears to be a more direct risk-coping behavior that teens employ to reactively problem-solve once they encounter online risks. The low explanatory value of our model for teen advice-seeking (5%) compared to the high explanatory value for remedy/corrective behaviors (32%) also suggests that advice-seeking behaviors may not be equivalent to remedy/corrective risk-coping strategies. Neither parental nor teen factors contribute much explanation to whether or not teens seek advice regarding their online privacy, and even though advice-seeking is associated with remedy/corrective actions, seeking advice does not necessarily always translate into actionable privacy behaviors. Therefore, future research may consider treating advice-seeking as a mediating factor of risk-coping instead of as an endogenous dimension of risk-coping.

If we had not performed factor analyses prior to our structural analysis, we may not have uncovered this and other interesting and important differences between the various parental mediation and teen privacy behaviors in our model. Yet, a limitation is that our analysis only focused on the parental mediation strategies, teen risk-taking behaviors, and teen risk-coping behaviors that emerged from our data. Therefore, future studies may want to examine the unique relationships between other parental mediation strategies and teen risk-coping behaviors in more depth.

"Preventative" vs. "Reactive" Parental Mediation Strategies

As previous literature on adolescent online privacy indicated, adults may adopt various mediation strategies in order to protect their teens' online privacy. Our analyses has revealed a dynamic process through which parents make decisions as to which strategies to implement; the positive relationship between parents' concern about the teens' online privacy and both types of mediation strategies provides empirical evidence that parental concern is one of the fundamental reasons parents become involved in their teens' online privacy management. Our analyses also confirmed that both direct intervention and active mediation influence teen risk-taking and risk-coping behaviors, but they do so in very different ways. **Figure 7** illustrates the different motivations and influences of the two parental mediation strategies.

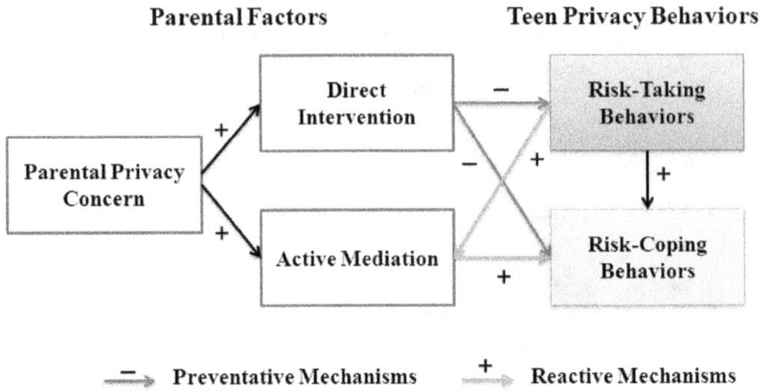

Figure 7: Preventive versus Reactive Parental Mediation

Based on our findings, we characterize direct intervention as a "*preventive*" parental mediation strategy, where parents use measures such as reading website privacy policy, helping set up privacy settings and using parental monitoring software to filter or block content to prevent their teens from experiencing online risks. Unlike teens who tend to generally be more risk-seeking, parents who mediate their teens through direct intervention tend to be more restrictive and risk-adverse, and this approach is reflected in the privacy behaviors of their teens. Teens who experience higher levels of direct parental intervention tend to be younger, disclose less basic information online, rely on external resources (parent, peer, professionals, or websites) for privacy management advice more heavily, have less extensive SNS networks, and use SNSs less frequently overall. On the other hand, they also have less of a need to take remedy and corrective behaviors because of their limited information revelation and risk experiences.

Alternatively, we characterize active parental mediation as a more "*reactive*" approach to teen online safety. Parents who actively mediate their teens' online behaviors may monitor the information their teens post online, talk with their teens, and comment on their teens' online posts, but they do not necessarily directly intervene in their teens' online privacy behaviors. Teens who experience higher levels of active mediation tend to be older, have more complex SNS networks, use SNSs more frequently, and disclose more sensitive information online. The positive relationship found between teens' online disclosure of sensitive information and parents' adoption of active mediation strategies suggests that this kind of parental involvement may be triggered reactively when parents perceive that their teens' online behavior has made them particularly vulnerable to privacy risks. Therefore, parents of these teens may be compelled to initiate discussions with their teens when they observe that their teens are disclosing too much sensitive information through social media, and in turn, these discussions may prompt teens to take subsequent corrective measures to mitigate potential risks. This reactive type of parental involvement appears to afford teens more autonomy to take risks but also to take corrective actions to mitigate the risks that they take.

Our findings confirm and extend the results from a smaller, qualitative study of parents and teens that recently found a potential relationship between parents who are actively engaged in what their teens to online, but do not heavily restrict their online activities, and teens who exhibit higher levels of moral judgment in their online behaviors. Similarly, teens who exhibited lower levels of moral judgment online tended to have parents who were either highly restrictive or overly indulgent of their teens' online behaviors [46]. For instance, our post-hoc analysis can be used to categorize these particular parental mediation strategies into four distinct parenting profiles, based on low/high levels of direct intervention and active mediation, respectively. We label these profiles as follows: 1) "*Unengaged Parents,*" who exhibit low direct intervention and low active mediation; 2) "*Controlling Parents*," who exhibit high direct intervention and low active mediation; 3) "*Counseling Parents*," who exhibit low direct intervention and high active mediation; and 4) "*Highly Engaged Parents*," who exhibit both high direct intervention and high active mediation.

Overall, "*controlling parenting*" tended to have the most suppressive effect of teens' online behaviors, both limiting online privacy risks through fewer basic disclosures and reducing the need for protective adaptations, but also restricting teens' general online experiences, such as their SNS frequency and network complexity. In contrast, active mediation appeared to have more of an empowering effect, allowing teens to actively engage with others online, experience some level of risk, and form coping strategies for protecting themselves from harm. This effect is particularly evident for teens of *"highly engaged parents"* who still maintained frequent use of SNSs and a relatively complex online social network, despite the restriction from direct parental intervention.

Risk Perception Triggers Concern and Behavior

We found a quite interesting pattern of risk escalation between the three teen risk-taking behaviors, from basic information disclosures, to sensitive information disclosures, to risky online interactions. This highlights an experiential learning process through which teens mitigate online privacy risks by taking protective actions when they feel their privacy boundaries may have been compromised (for a more in-depth discussion on the effects of teens' privacy risk behaviors, privacy concern, and risk-coping behaviors, see [21]). Our combined findings suggest an inherent level of perceived risk that both parents and teens associate with each of these risk-taking behaviors, which seem to trigger subsequent responses.

Our findings further validate and provide additional insights into the apparent "privacy paradox" [4, 25] between teens' privacy concerns and their information disclosure behaviors. For teens, only risky interactions were significantly associated with heightened levels of teen privacy concern, which in turn, was positively associated with advice-seeking and remedy/corrective risk-coping behaviors. Sensitive information disclosures and risky interactions were associated with more frequent remedy/corrective behaviors, but basic information disclosures were not. A possible explanation is that teens simply do not appraise basic information disclosures online as particularly risky. It is only once these disclosures escalate into regrettable social interactions that teens become concerned about their online privacy and take measures to protect themselves. Thus, teens' privacy behaviors may be less paradoxical than they appear; instead their privacy behaviors may be simply more post hoc or retroactive in nature. This may be, in part, due to how teens choose to cope with the social-technical privacy gap [2] between how they socialize offline and social media privacy affordances online.

While teens' self-reported, risky online interactions, such as connecting to strangers or being contacted in a way that make them feel uncomfortable, was the most alarming type of privacy risk perceived by teens, this risk-taking behavior was not associated with either type of parental mediation. Only sensitive disclosures made by teens were associated with higher levels of active parental mediation. We believe the reason this association is not present in our model is because risky interactions may be less transparent to parents than sensitive information disclosures that can be more readily discovered by actively searching the teens' social media profile. Therefore, parents may be less aware of when their teens are engaged in risky online interactions. Be it that these risky interactions take place beyond parents' monitoring, or that the teens are unable or unwilling to communicate the unease that they have experienced online, this raises a major concern because neither preventative nor reactive parenting approaches appear to be effective in terms of addressing the most "risky" privacy behaviors that teens may engage in online. This is an issue with growing significance, as emerging SNSs and mobile applications (e.g., Snapchat, Secret, Yik Yak, etc.) support more discreet ways of teen communication. Parents will need better ways to understand and/or monitor teens' online activities and gauge teen risk exposure.

Implications for Design

Findings from this study have yielded practical implications for designing measures to improve teens' online privacy safety. For example, the preventive and reactive mechanisms of parental mediation (**Figure 6**) identified in this study provide a conceptual foundation for building more effective parental monitoring software. Currently, parental monitoring software primarily facilitates direct parental intervention strategies of blocking and restricting teen online behavior. However, this approach tends to limit the shelf life of parental monitoring software, as past studies show that such restrictive monitoring is not really a viable option for older (15-16-year old) teens who demand more trust from their parents [46]. Furthermore, our study suggests that highly engaged parenting, which involves both high levels of active mediation and direct intervention, may be the best approach for mitigating teen online risk exposure while allowing them to engage in meaningful interactions online. Therefore, one potential design implication is a call for parental monitoring software that helps parents engage in conversations with their teens about their online risk-taking and risk-coping behaviors instead of primarily functioning to block any exposure to online risks. In this way, parental monitoring software could be transformed into a tool to teach teens about appropriate online behaviors and to raise parental awareness regarding high-risk teen behaviors.

The effect of teens' sensitive information disclosures on parental mediation, as well as the lack of effect for teens' risky online interactions, highlights the need for more sophisticated mechanisms to detect teens' privacy risks that are less visible to parents. For example, new parental monitoring software features may integrate with the Facebook application platform (or the currently most popular SNS for teens) in order to provide parents with a summary how often and with whom their teens engage online. This becomes a particularly urgent need as many websites and mobile applications increasingly support a higher level of anonymity and ephemerality in teen online communication. Parents need to be educated of emerging technologies and of the risks that are associated with such communication methods. In addition, online safety software could also cater to the needs of teens as end users by making hidden privacy risks more apparent to teens themselves, in order to enhance their privacy awareness and encourage voluntary risk-coping behaviors.

Limitations and Future Research

Even though the Pew data set afforded numerous strengths, such as a large, nationally representative and dyadically paired sample of parents and teens, many of the limitations of our study also come with the secondary data set that we used for analyses. First, the level of measurement used in the Pew telephone interviews was often dichotomous; therefore, limiting, to some extent, the explanatory power of our structural model. Secondly, we were limited to item wording as it was presented to respondents during the Pew telephone interviews. Some of the questions were double-barreled, such as one item that asked parents whether they had ever, "used parental controls or other means of blocking, filtering or monitoring [their] child's online activities." In this case, we had to rely on the data-driven results of the CATPCA, which determined that this item loaded best with Direct Parental Intervention, even though it included an aspect of Active Mediation (i.e., monitoring). Third, teens' privacy concern was measured using a single-item question, which may not fully capture the full extent of teens' privacy concerns.

Given the inherent strengths and weaknesses of analyzing a large, secondary data set, our work both informs future research directions and motivates the need for follow up studies. For instance, future work can improve measurement accuracy and reliability by adopting established scales from the privacy literature and further examining the empirically validated relationships in our model. Otherwise, subsequent studies may benefit from operationalizing new measures based on existing theoretical conceptualizations, as opposed to deriving factors from existing survey items, as we did from the Pew data. In our future work, we plan to confirm and extend our current findings regarding privacy concerns, parental mediation strategies, teen social media privacy behaviors, and other relevant parent-teen factors by combining both of these approaches.

Finally, the cross-sectional survey methodology used by Pew constrains our capability to confirm causal effects between the various constructs in our model. We have observed a number of correlation relationships between different parental mediation strategies and various teen privacy behaviors, as well as privacy concerns. Therefore, we had to make some analytical decisions based on the given wording of the survey questions and the positive or negative path coefficients produced by our structural model in order to specify the direction of some of the paths in our model. For example, if we had specified in our model that parental active mediation led to more sensitive disclosures made by teens, this interpretation would imply that teens react rebelliously against parental attempt to protect their online privacy. Instead, we chose to acknowledge that parents and teens can influence one another bi-directionally [9], and, in this case, a more plausible explanation is that active parental mediation is a reaction to teens' sensitive information disclosures online. However, future studies should involve either a longitudinal approach or an experimental design to confirm the causal relationships between the various factors in our model. For example, we are currently in the process of conducting a two month diary study of parents and teens in order to understand teens' online experiences and the role of parental involvement.

CONCLUSION

This paper highlights the bi-directional influences between parents and teens when it comes to privacy concern, parental mediation strategies, and adolescent social media privacy behaviors. Parents can employ preventative strategies that protect their teens from initial online risk exposure and reduce teens' need for corrective privacy measures, and/or parents can employ more reactive strategies as a result of their teens' risk-taking behaviors, which encourage teens to take subsequent protective measures. However, parents who implement preventative, restrictive measures without being actively engaged in what their teens are doing online may risk limiting the potential benefits their teens may garner from online engagement. Thus, balancing preventative parental strategies with reactive strategies may be the best option for protecting teens online while allowing them to learn and benefit from their online experiences. As such, our findings present a unique opportunity for the CSCW community: Helping parents and teens *collaboratively* manage teens' social media privacy behaviors may be one way to narrow the social-technical privacy gap [2] for adolescents, allowing them to safely engage with others online.

ACKNOWLEDGMENTS

First, we would like to thank Mary Madden, Senior Researcher at Pew Research Center, who enabled our access to the Pew data set. Also, this research was supported by the U.S. National Science Foundation under grant CNS-1018302. Part of the work of Heng Xu was done while working at the U.S. National Science Foundation. Any opinion, findings, and conclusions or recommendations expressed in this material are those of the authors and do not necessarily reflect the views of the U.S. National Science Foundation.

REFERENCES

[1] *The 17th ACM Conference on Computer-Supported Cooperative Work & Social Computing Conference Program*. 2014, http://cscw.acm.org/2014/cscw2014_program.pdf.

[2] Ackerman, M. S. The intellectual challenge of CSCW: the gap between social requirements and technical feasibility. *Human-Computer Interaction*, *15*, 2 (2000), 179-203.

[3] Arbuckle, J. L. *Amos* SPSS, City, 2006.

[4] Barnes, S. B. *A privacy paradox: Social networking in the United States*, 2006.

[5] Baumrind, D. A developmental perspective on adolescent risk taking in contemporary America. *New directions for child development*, 37 (1987), 93-125.

[6] Baumrind, D. Patterns of parental authority and adolescent autonomy. *New Directions for Child and Adolescent Development*, *2005*, 108 (2005), 61-69.

[7] Buhler, T., Neustaedter, C. and Hillman, S. How and Why Teenagers Use Video Chat. In *Proc. CSCW 2013* (2013).

[8] Crossler, R. E., Bélanger, F., Hiller, J. S., Park, J.-M., Hsiao, M., Channakeshava, K., Bian, K. and Korbich, E. Determinants of Protection Behaviors for Online Privacy of Children. In *Proc. 39th Annual Meeting of The Decision Sciences Institute* (2008).

[9] Cummings, E. M., Bergman, K. N. and Kuznicki, K. A. Emerging Methods for Studying Families as Systems. In *Proc. PSU 20th Annual Symposium on Family Issues* (2012).

[10] D'Haenens, L., Vandonink, S. and Donoso, V. *How to cope and build resilience*. EU Kids Online, 2013, http://eprints.lse.ac.uk/48115/1/How%20to%20cope%20and%20build%20online%20resilience%20%28lsero%29.pdf.

[11] Desmond, R. J., Singer, J. L. and Singer, D. G. Family Mediation: Parental Communication Patterns and the Influences of Television on Children. In J. Bryant (ed.) *Television and the American Family*, (1990), 293–309.

[12] Dinev, T., Xu, H. and Smith, H. J. Information Privacy Values, Beliefs and Attitudes: An Empirical Analysis of Web 2.0 Privacy. In *Proc. Proceedings of 42th Hawaii International Conference on System Sciences (HICSS 42)* (2009).

[13] Dürager, A. and Livingstone, S. *How can parents support children's internet safety?* , 2012, http://www.lse.ac.uk/media@lse/research/EUKidsOnline/EU%20Kids%20III/Reports/ParentalMediation.pdf.

[14] Eastin, M. S., Greenberg, B. S. and Hofschire, L. Parenting the Internet. *Journal of Communication*, *56*, 3 (2006), 486-504.

[15] Falk, R. F. and Miller, N. B. *A primer for soft modeling*. University of Akron Press, Akron, OH, 1992.

[16] Forte, A., Dickard, M., Magee, R. and Agosto, D. E. What do teens ask their online social networks?: social search practices among high school students. In *Proc. Proceedings of the 17th ACM conference on Computer supported cooperative work & social computing*, ACM (2014), 28-37.

[17] Gefen, D., Rigdon, E. and Straub, W. D. An Update and Extension to SEM Guidelines for Administrative and Social Science Research. *MIS Quarterly*, *35*, 2 (2011).

[18] Grinter, E. R. and Palen, L. Instant Messaging in Teen Life. In *Proc. Proceedings of the 2002 ACM conference on Computer supported cooperative work* (2002), 21-30.

[19] Hasebrink, U., Görzig, A., Haddon, L., Kalmus, V. and Livingstone, S. *Patterns of risk and safety online: indepth analyses*. The London School of Economics and Political Science, London, UK., 2011,

[20] IBM. *Categorical principal components analysis (CATPCA)*. 2014, http://pic.dhe.ibm.com/infocenter/spssstat/v20r0m0/index.jsp?topic=%2Fcom.ibm.spss.statistics.help%2Fidh_cpca.htm.

[21] Jia, H., Wisniewski, P., Xu, H., Rosson, M. B. and Carroll, J. M. Risk-taking as a Learning Process for Shaping Teen's Online Information Privacy Behaviors. In *Proc. Computer-Supported Cooperative Work and Social Computing* (2015).

[22] Kaiser, H. F. The application of electronic computers to factor analysis. *Educational and psychological Measurement*, *20* (1960), 141-151.

[23] Klein, P. S., Nir-Gal, O. and Darom, E. The Use of Computers in Kindergarten, With or Without Adult Mediation; Effects on Children's Cognitive Performance and Behavior. *Computers in Human Behavior*, *16*, 6 (2000), 591–608.

[24] Kline, R. B. *Principles and Practice of Structural Equation Modeling*. The Guilford Press, New York, 2011.

[25] Lampe, C., Gurzick, D., Stutzman, F., Yardi, S. and Bruckman, A. Get Off My e-Lawn: Mulching Youth and Technology. In *Proc. CSCW 2010* (2010).

[26] Lerner, R. M. *Adolescence: Development, diversity, context, and application*. Prentice-Hall, Upper Saddle River, NJ, 2002.

[27] Linting, M., Meulman, J. J., Groenen, P. J. F. and van der Koojj, A. J. Nonlinear principal components analysis: Introduction and application. *Psychological Methods*, *12*, 3 (2007), 336-358.

[28] Livingstone, S., Haddon, L., Görzig, A. and Ólafsson, K. *Risks and safety on the internet: The perspective of European children*. EU Kids Online, 2011, http://eprints.lse.ac.uk/33731/.

[29] Livingstone, S. and Helsper, E. J. Parental Mediation of Children's Internet Use. *Journal of Broadcasting & Electronic Media*, *52*, 4 (2008), 581-599.

[30] Livingstone, S., Ólafsson, K., O'Neill, B. and Donoso, V. *Towards a better internet for children: findings and recommendations from EU Kids Online to inform the CEO coalition.*, The London School of Economics and Political Science, London, UK., 2012,

[31] Madden, M., Cortesi, S., Gasser, U., Lenhart, A. and Duggan, M. *Parents, Teens, and Online Privacy*. Pew Research Center's Internet & American Life Project, 2012, http://pewinternet.org/Reports/2012/Teens-and-Privacy.aspx.

[32] Madden, M., Cortesi, S., Gasser, U., Lenhart, A. and Duggan, M. *Where Teens Seek Online Privacy Advice*. Pew Research Center's Internet & American Life Project, 2013, http://www.pewinternet.org/2013/08/15/where-teens-seek-online-privacy-advice/.

[33] Madden, M., Lenhart, A., Cortesi, S., Gasser, U., Duggan, M., Smith, A. and Beaton, M. *Teens, Social Media, and Privacy* 2013, http://www.pewinternet.org/Reports/2013/Teens-Social-Media-And-Privacy.aspx.

[34] Madden, M., Lenhart, A., Duggan, M., Cortesi, S. and Gasser, U. *Teens and Technology 2013* Pew Internet, 2013, http://www.pewinternet.org/Reports/2013/Teens-and-Tech/Summary-of-Findings.aspx.

[35] Malhotra, N. K., Kim, S. S. and Agarwal, J. Internet Users' Information Privacy Concerns (IUIPC): The Construct, the Scale, and a Causal Model. *Information Systems Research*, *15*, 4 (December 2004), 336-355.

[36] Mesch, G. S. Parental Mediation, Online Activities, and Cyberbullying *CyberPsychology & Behavior*, *12*, 4 (2009), 387-393.

[37] Mitchell, K. J., Finkelhor, D. and Wolak, J. Youth Internet Users at Risk for the Most Serious Online Sexual Solicitations. *American Journal of Preventive Medicine*, *32*, 6 (2007), 532-537.

[38] Rosen, L. D., Cheever, N. A. and Carrier, L. M. The association of parenting style and child age with parental limit setting and adolescent MySpace behavior. *Journal of Applied Developmental Psychology*, *29*, 6 (2008), 459-471.

[39] Schermelleh-Engel, K., Moosbrugger, H. and Müller, H. Evaluating the fit of structural equation models: Tests of significance and descriptive goodness-of-fit measures. *Methods of psychological research online*, *8*, 2 (2003), 23-74.

[40] Shin, W., Huh, J. and Faber, R. J. Tweens' Online Privacy Risks and the Role of Parental Mediation. *Journal of Broadcasting & Electronic Media*, *56*, 4 (2012), 632-649.

[41] Smith, H. J., Dinev, T. and Xu, H. Information Privacy Research: An Interdisciplinary Review. *MIS Quarterly*, *35*, 4 (2011), 989-1015.

[42] Sorbring, E. and Lundin, L. Mothers' and fathers' insights into teenagers' use of the internet. *New Media & Society*, *14*, 7 (2012), 1181-1197.

[43] Stevenson, F. and Zimmerman, M. A. Adolescent Resilience: A Framework for Understanding Healthy Development in the Face of Risk. *Annual Review of Public Health*, *26* (2005), 399-419.

[44] Tabachnick, B. G. and Fidell, L. S. *Using Multivariate Statistics*. Pearson Education, Inc., Boston, 1996.

[45] Valkenburg, P. M., Krcmar, M., Peeters, A. L. and Marseille, N. M. Developing A Scale to Assess Three Styles of Television Mediation: "Instructive Mediation," "Restrictive Mediation," and "Social Coviewing". *Journal of Broadcasting & Electronic Media*, *43*, 1 (1999), 52-66.

[46] Wisniewski, P., Xu, H., Rosson, M. B. and Carroll, J. M. Adolescent Online Safety: The "Moral" of the Story. In *Proc. CSCW 2014* (2014).

[47] Xu, H., Dinev, T., Smith, H. J. and Hart, P. Examining the Formation of Individual's Privacy Concerns: Toward an Integrative View. In *Proc. Twenty Ninth International Conference on Information Systems* (2008).

"This is a Throwaway Account": Temporary Technical Identities and Perceptions of Anonymity in a Massive Online Community

Alex Leavitt
Annenberg School for
Communication & Journalism,
University of Southern California
aleavitt@usc.edu

ABSTRACT
This paper explores temporary identities on social media platforms and individuals' uses of these identities with respect to their perceptions of anonymity. Given the research on multiple profile maintenance, little research has examined the role that some social media platforms play in affording users with temporary identities. Further, most of the research on anonymity stops short of the concept of varying perceptions of anonymity. This paper builds on these research areas by describing the phenomenon of temporary "throwaway accounts" and their uses on reddit.com, a popular social news site. In addition to ethnographic trace analysis to examine the contexts in which throwaway accounts are adopted, this paper presents a predictive model that suggests that perceptions of anonymity significantly shape the potential uses of throwaway accounts and that women are much more likely to adopt temporary identities than men.

Author Keywords
Anonymity; multiple profile maintenance; reddit; throwaway account; selective self-presentation; social news sites

ACM Classification Keywords
H.5.3. Group and Organization Interfaces–Web-based Interaction

INTRODUCTION
Even though anonymity plays such a crucial role in the history of computer-mediated communication (CMC), online identity management remains a significant issue in the technology industry [19]. For example, Google's initial decision to forbid anonymous accounts on the young Google+ social networking service led to a dramatic disturbance among its members, many of whom felt that anonymous profiles should be allowed [44].

However, some social media platforms have implemented features that afford a variety of boundary management techniques for information disclosure or identity performance. These affordances play a key role in how some users negotiate identity boundaries through the creation of multiple accounts, such as in moments when someone does not want particular information linked to the primary representation of him- or herself. I call these types of accounts "temporary technical identities," where the particular sociotechnical system affords an individual to create a provisional pseudonymous username. This paper explores one online platform, reddit.com, which permits users to create numerous accounts (under any pseudonym) easily, leading to the emergent phenomenon of "throwaway accounts."

CSCW '15, March 14-18 2015, Vancouver, BC, Canada.

ACM 978-1-4503-2922-4/15/03 $15.00
http://dx.doi.org/10.1145/2675133.2675175

This paper explores the typology and uses of temporary technical identities within the sociotechnical and cultural context of reddit guided by two research questions:

RQ1: *How and in what contexts do social media users navigate boundary management around identity with particular affordances of some sociotechnical platforms?*

RQ2: *How do CMC factors, especially perceptions of anonymity, play into an individual's potential use of a temporary technical identity?*

To investigate these questions, this paper draws from a dataset of self-identified throwaway accounts as well as a survey of reddit users to see how perceptions of anonymity, willingness to self-disclose, and the size of the imagined audience play into the potential adoption of temporary technical identities. The paper concludes with a discussion of multiple profile maintenance with respect to reddit's peculiar community subculture and the implications of affordances for temporary identity creation toward the design of online communication platforms.

RELATED WORKS
This paper investigates the use of temporary technical identities at the intersection of a number of research areas: multiple profile maintenance; selective self-presentation and imagined audiences; and affordances for anonymity.

Multiple Profile Maintenance

Multiple profile maintenance (MPM) focuses on the practices and motivations of sustaining multiple alternate identity profiles within a communication service, platform, or technology. Some researchers have identified the use of multiple accounts as an emergent practice, particularly around boundary regulation and privacy management [40, 26, 50], though few look at platforms that purposefully afford multiple technical identities.

Other research has provided empirical insights into the use of multiple profiles. For example, Gross [17] examined the use of multiple email addresses and instant messenger screen names. Individuals described reasons for use from wanting multiple identifiers to regulating access to personal information based on work, family, and acquaintance boundaries. Stutzman & Hartzog [45] conducted a similar study of social network site users who maintained more than one profile on the same social media platform. They similarly found that privacy is the primary motivation for MPM, with identity, utility, and propriety in the range of secondary motivations. From interviews, they also constructed a spectrum of boundary regulation processes, fluctuating from pseudonymity (separate incognito and unlinked identities) to practical obscurity (separate visible identities) to transparent separation (separate public identities purposefully linked).

Selective Self-Presentation & Imagined Audiences

MPM involves boundary regulation within the context of particular user-audience relations. Selective self-presentation is an affordance of CMC where individuals can decide what information to share about themselves without the context of face-to-face interaction [48]. The prior literature [17, 45, 31] shows that people take into account each platform's varying audience dynamics when dealing with particular profile performances. Imagined audiences do impact real decisions to disclose, which are then displayed to the actual audience (though underestimating the size of this actual audience can be common [3]). For example, email communication is directed and more confidential, while communication on Twitter is sometimes more broadcast and accessible, so individuals employing MPM take into account the potential of the unknown, imagined, and unintended audiences to access information. Marwick & boyd [33] note that issues like context collapse (see also [8]) emerge from networked communication technology because expectations around information access are unexpectedly broken down by others accessing particular bits of communication meant for certain audiences, and some people will create multiple accounts to deal with the management of these fluctuating boundaries.

Some social media platforms differ from social network sites [11] in that they rely more on broad information sharing practices rather than the curation of personal information distributed to a select number of viewers (friends, followers, etc.). Online forums and newsgroups, image boards, microblogs, video-game social hubs, and social news sites [30] provide systematic ways for users to communicate with other individuals without adhering to the "profile and friend list" format of social network sites.

Research on disclosure and selective self-presentation has rarely focused on social news sites, particularly within the "broadcast-to-all" context that this genre of website affords. Strategic self-presentation literature (e.g., [24]) has detailed the motivations that go into communication choices, but more recent scholarship has identified aspects of CMC situations specifically like non-identifiability (anonymity) and invisibility (from audiences) that create effects – for instance, the disinhibition effect – which lead to greater disclosure [46]. Joinson [21] especially identifies that disclosure increases with the combination of anonymity and private self-awareness, so people that use CMC are more likely to disclosure when the risk is lower. Therefore, one may expect that individuals who are uncomfortable disclosing personal information would use multiple profiles, especially temporary ones.

H1: *People who are less willing to disclose personal information are more likely to use a temporary identity.*

Scholarship on the impact and influence of audiences on self-disclosure vary. Butler [5] posits that membership size and communication activity are opposing forces that unbalance resources and benefits for members within online social structures. Valacich et al. [48] asserts the opposite, saying that an increase in the group's size in anonymous CMC leads to increased productivity within the group. And from traditional psychology, research has shown that group size can determine the intensity of audience effects [28, 25, 27].

Voelpel et al. [51] found that the bystander effect in virtual communities – while theoretically predicted to negatively affect participation in these communities as group size increased – actually had a parallel, positive effect as group size approached large or very large. In other words, participation overall was high in very large groups (though they find that quality of content diminished). In a direct study of perceived audience on anonymous communication, Okdie [36] found the opposite: there was no relationship between bloggers' willingness to disclose personal information and their anonymity in the face of unknown audiences. In the context of social network sites, Vitak [49] found that audience size does impact disclosures (and other uses of affordances like privacy settings), though in a positive direction (opposite of what was expected).

Yun [55] studied perceptions of anonymity in relation to the perception of the size of the online community, and he found support for group size's effect on disclosure. Thus, perception of the imagined audience may impact people's information sharing behaviors. This paper takes the stance that if an individual perceives a large, unknown audience for their disclosure – especially if that audience could include an acquaintance – then personal risk increases, and the individual would prefer to use a temporary identity to disclose information.

H2: *People are more likely to use a temporary identity in the face of larger perceived audiences.*

Affordances & Anonymity

While Stutzman & Hartzog [45] touch on temporary identities in MPM, their prior research does not explore in detail the affordance of some sociotechnical platforms allowing users to create temporary technical usernames in addition to their primary crafted identities. In relation to the MPM literature, then, it is not necessarily that these accounts are maintained as much as generated and cast away through convenience of the platform's affordances, making these accounts relatively anonymous.

Anonymity and pseudonymity play a key role in the technical production of identity in CMC, as anonymous communication usually is implemented through pseudonymous usernames. Some platforms even institute absolute anonymity, forcing individuals to adopt particular identity strategies and signals to make themselves memorable [5]. The affordance of creating *temporary* usernames can have adverse effects toward creating reliable reputation systems; as Resnick & Friedman [42] argue, "cheap pseudonyms" create distrust within a community, particularly around new participants. Conversely, the social identity model of deindividuation (SIDE) has shown that anonymity can increase the salience and success of collective identity [41]. This paper, though, takes an ambivalent position regarding the effect of anonymity on community dynamics, instead opting to show how different types of anonymity might affect individual information sharing behaviors.

While many scholars have focused on the impact of anonymity or pseudonymity on communication and – both positive and negative – behavior [20, 1, 6, 54, 47, 22, 35, 7], usually the research literature has used a dichotomized concept of anonymity (it is either "on" or "off," or people "have it" or don't). Few have taken the next step to examine how levels in the perception of anonymity change these behaviors. Some, such as Hayne & Rice [18] built on the dichotomy with assumptions like "partial anonymity." Notably, Joinson [21] and Qian & Scott [39] approached the issue with a basic perception-driven, scaled concept. Yun [55] also examined various aspects of perceived anonymity and concluded that "self anonymity" contributed the most to a total perception of anonymity (alongside "other anonymity" and "discursive anonymity"). In addition, all three scholars point to some increase in disclosure with the increase in anonymity.

Finally, regarding anonymous and pseudonymous profiles within the framework of MPM, Stutzman and Hartzog [45] note that users created multiple profiles under the guise of feeling anonymous because "[p]seudonymity both conceals information and encourages disclosure… As a result of the disassociation with the primary identity, individuals can disclose with less reservation, knowing that the pseudonymous profile is 'invisible' to search engine queries on the individual's name, for example" (774). Therefore, I expect that temporary identities are more likely to be used when individuals feel less anonymous in the particular setting of their potential disclosure.

H3. *People are more likely to use a temporary identity in cases of lower perceived anonymity.*

METHOD & DATA

This paper employs a mixed methods approach to understanding the details and dynamics behind temporary technical identity practices. A temporary technical identity is defined as a username or other technical implementation of an individual's presence within a sociotechnical platform that the individual creates and then uses for a short time or only once to produce a strategic self-presentation. These accounts are not maintained and are kept distinct and separate from the individual's primary representation.

The paper first uses public data from self-identified throwaway accounts on reddit to describe the nature of reddit's non-persistent identity affordance and contextualize what I found with ethnographic observations from general site use and user conversations. Then, the paper examines the results of a survey of reddit users to examine the impact of perceptions of anonymity and selective self-presentation on the likelihood of a reddit user to use a temporary identity on the social news site.

The motivation to explore reddit stems from its current popularity and massive userbase; the ease of creating alternate identities; and the small amount of research about social news sites. Social news sites allow users to contribute links and posts that can be made visible by the community through the technical mechanisms of voting these posts up or down [15, 34, 29, 43]. The highest voted posts then reach the most visibility, usually the top of an aggregated page. Reddit's architecture is especially consequential for how people use the platform: because subreddits (specific topical communities) are created by anyone, they range in size, purpose, social norms, and levels of activity. The site curates "default" subreddits that all new contributors (and viewers without accounts) are subscribed to, so these particular subcommunities gain the most visibility within the platform. The potential audience for content shared in these default subreddits then exponentially increases compared to newer, smaller subreddits.

The primary alternate identity practice on reddit involves what are colloquially known as "throwaway accounts." Social media companies will sometimes embed a logic of multiple identities directly into their system (e.g., the ability to directly switch between multiple accounts); however, many platforms do not, and while they can afford broadcasting particular content to specific audiences [23], they frequently discourage the use of multiple accounts (ie., Facebook and Google+). Reddit, though, allows one-time-use accounts that are easily created by signing up only with a new username, password, and CAPTCHA (even an email address is not required). The site also explicitly encourages the use of throwaway accounts in their site FAQ[1]. Because the "throwaway account" has become so well known within this community of practice, the ecosystem (including third-party, community-developed add-ons like the Reddit Enhancement Suite[2]) essentially warrants the frequent use of these multiple, temporary identities.

Study 1 uses a qualitative grounded theory approach [16] in participant observation to understand how users talk about the contexts for adopting temporary technical identities. These observations are also situated within 3 years of ethnographic participation across reddit's various communities, where I spent time participating in a wide range of topical communities; talking casually on- and offline with ordinary users, moderators, and admins; and recording notes and screenshots. The conclusions are drawn from a trace ethnographic technique [14] in which self-identified throwaway accounts were curated and crawled for their contribution histories. These conversations and notes were reviewed, coded, and summarized, and they were synthesized with observations taken from the database of accounts and messages. Self-identified throwaway accounts were used for this study because of the difficulty of distinguishing throwaway accounts when nearly every username is pseudonymous and the ethical considerations of linking individuals' primary accounts with any throwaway accounts they might possess.

To collect self-identified throwaway accounts, Python and MySQL were used to crawl reddit.com's public API to search for mentions of the word "throwaway" in either post titles, post text, or usernames across the top 500 most-subscribed subreddit communities[3] in the past year. In total, 15,469 messages were collected from 372 of the subreddits from 13,681 unique user accounts. There are many approaches that could be taken to identify throwaway accounts from the collected messages. Noted from an exploratory stage looking at 241 messages that explicitly mentioned, "This is a throwaway account," 78.8% of the accounts – based on their contribution history – had posted only once, while 96.3% had posted 3 or fewer times. Therefore, to look further at the contexts of using throwaway accounts, all of the 13,681 accounts' contribution histories were crawled, and a subsample of accounts was selected that had posted only once and whose comments were restricted to the same subreddit, resulting in 5,102 distinct accounts. While usernames that have posted only once do not account for all types of throwaway accounts, they represent a notable sample of temporary technical identities on reddit.

Study 2 uses the results of a general survey of 113 reddit users conducted in April 2012. The survey participants were recruited on reddit.com's /r/AskReddit subreddit (a default community to which all new accounts are subscribed) and self-selected into the study. All respondents had created at least one account on reddit and had at least one week of experience using the platform (months as a user, mean = 13.76, s.d. = 12.63). The participants ranged in age from 13 to 61 (mean = 21.81, s.d. = 6.65), with 46.0% of them identifying as female and 62.8% located within the United States.

The survey instrument was constructed using established scales from previous research, adapted for the current study. The survey was pilot tested (n = 39) to clarify question wording. Responses to all reddit-related questions referred to participation on reddit.com specifically and ranged on a 7-point Likert scale from Strongly Disagree (1) to Strongly Agree (7).

Perception of size of imagined audience. To measure the perception of the size of the imagined audience, the survey used a modified version of Yun's [55] community size question to assess the size of the perceived community in an online forum (also readjusted on an exponential scale; "*When a post on reddit reaches the top of a large subreddit (like r/AskReddit), how many users do you think will read the post?*") and converted to a log-transformed measure before analysis (mean = 5.363, s.d. = 1.053).

Perception of anonymity. The perception of anonymity was measured using Yun's [55; p. 63] scale of perception of self-anonymity in an online forum. Eight items measured individuals' perceptions of what other members of the community might know about some aspect of the individual's personal identity or personality ("*I feel that some members can… 1) recognize my username, 2) recognize my name, 3) tell my profession,*" etc.). The scale was modified to include 6 of the items ($\alpha = .734$): each item was measured on the 7-point Likert scale, and they were summed into an aggregated score representing perception of anonymity (on a scale of 0 to 36, representing low to high anonymity; mean = 8.559, s.d. = 7.051).

Selective self-presentation. The estimate of selective self-presentation was measured using one scale, adapted from Yun's [55] online public disclosure scale: 8 items measuring an individual's willingness to contribute certain information to an online community and concern about the information's reception ("*I am willing to talk about my shameful experiences in this online community,*" "*I am willing to talk about my hurt feelings in this online community,*" etc.). This scale ($\alpha = .918$) was measured on the 7-point Likert scale and was summed into an aggregated score representing willing to disclosure private information

[1] http://us.reddit.com/wiki/faq

[2] http://redditenhancementsuite.com/

[3] For a list, see http://www.redditlist.com/

(on a scale of 0 to 48, representing low to high willingness to disclose; mean = 25.5, s.d. = 11.061).

Use of a throwaway account was measured with a Yes/No question asking if the individual had ever created and used a throwaway account.

Control variables. Four additional variables that are likely to influence perception of anonymity and willingness to disclose were considered as controls: gender, age, location, and time as a reddit.com user. Gender was considered as a control variable given gender differences on self-disclosure and privacy [13] and was assessed through one demographic question. Age and Location were also included; both were assessed through individual demographic questions. Months as a Reddit User was included given that users acclimate to certain social norms given ample time [52, 12, 55]. Time spent was assessed through one introductory survey question.

RESULTS

Study 1

Study 1 was conducted to establish an understanding of practices and contexts for throwaway account adoption on reddit.com. This section examines 5,102 curated accounts that mentioned "throwaway" and had only posted once in their entire contribution history (from 203 of the top 500 subreddits). Below, the paper presents three themes from observations of contexts and stated reasons for use of temporary technical identities.

Disclosure of personal information

Though each of the top 500 subreddits was queried for mentions of "throwaway" accounts, a particular subset of communities returned hundreds of messages each, while two-fifths did not return any results. The vast majority of the five thousands accounts posted to subreddits related to relationships, sex, gender, confessions, or general question-asking in order to tell personal stories, ask for advice, and receive feedback on particular questions or issues. Use in these subreddits illustrates that temporary usernames have become commonplace in discussion communities where the individuals frequently share personal information. For example, in a health and exercise community, a user writes, "I just wanted to know if this sort of thing is normal and what the causes may be. I hope this will be taken seriously. Obvious throwaway." In a confession and complaint subreddit, another user explains about a depressed friend, "What I'm looking for is a wake me up call, please someone just tell me the harsh wake up call I need so I can be a better person and be there for her without feeling like it's a chore."

When a throwaway account posted to a subreddit where throwaways were uncommon, they still tended to be sharing personal information around a particular issue in which feedback was solicited from the specific community. Sometimes people use these accounts to post information that individuals find controversial and therefore don't want connected to their main accounts on the site. For instance, in a niche financial subreddit, one user explains, "These companies have very strict policies about sharing earnings, so I've made a throwaway and censored all personal details." In another small, location-based community, a second individual asks for advice, writing, "(throwaway, of course, for fear of looking like a stupid idiot)."

Widespread adoption & "obviousness"

Whether individuals make their uses explicit or not, throwaway accounts pervade reddit. Still, it was surprising to find that at least 1 in 10 of the throwaway accounts in our sample mentioned that using a temporary account was "obvious." There are many instances of this, such as, "Using a throwaway for this post for obvious reasons," "Sorry for the obvious throwaway, but I'll try to keep it short. I hope to get some advice from y'all," or "I'm a 15 year old guy, and this is obviously a throwaway." After disclosing the "obvious" use of the throwaway account, each individual usually then wrote a lengthy explanation of a personal or controversial situation that they posed to the respective community for feedback.

Given their widespread use, throwaway accounts also manifest across different types of adoptive practices. As mentioned above, reddit's FAQ emphasizes the use of throwaway accounts, but the actual practice of their implementation can vary. Of the accounts I discovered that self-identified, 2,084 (40.8%) of the accounts included the word "throwaway" within the username, marking them as temporary identities even if the contributed message does mention the nature of the account. And as stated in the methods section, it can be difficult to categorize a throwaway as a temporary technical identity, given that "temporary" could mean only once or a short but still bounded period of time. For example, in our observation of throwaway account uses, some accounts labeled with "throwaway" in the username were merely used as additional – but sustained – pseudonymous accounts, such as for pornographic subreddits, which suggests that some members of the community have adopted the term "throwaway" as a marker for some degree of further anonymity. The ubiquitous character of throwaway accounts within reddit's ecosystem means that the everyday meanings of participants shape throwaway account use in different ways, though – as explained in the next section – throwaways appear to be adopted primarily to further distinguish accounts that the individual would rather remain anonymous to some larger degree.

Privacy & boundary management

As the literature reviewed above illustrates, individuals that engage in MPM do so in large part to maintain strict boundaries between social circles in order to share information to any particular one but not others. In the case of the throwaway accounts in this sample, a similar dynamic emerges, but instead of boundaries between particular groups of acquaintances, the line is drawn

	Exp(β)	SE	Z	P
Intercept	*1.674*	*1.878*	*0.274*	
Gender (0: Male, 1: Female)	2.634	0.470	2.061	*
Age	1.028	0.047	0.589	
Country (0: USA, 1: not-USA)	2.433	0.476	1.866	.
Months as a Reddit User	1.040	0.022	1.780	.
Willingness to Publicly Disclose *(H1)*	1.008	0.020	0.429	
Perception of Audience Size *(H2)*	0.925	0.228	-0.343	
Perception of Anonymity *(H3)*	0.901	0.036	-2.860	**

Significance: . $p < 0.1$, * $p < 0.05$, ** $p < 0.01$, *** $p < 0.001$

N: 113 McFadden Pseudo-R^2: 0.278

AIC: 139.67 ROC Area Under Curve: 0.785

Table 1. Results of a logistic regression model predicting the likelihood of a reddit user using a throwaway account.

between the individual and one or more specific contacts, whom the information should never reach. In particular, a distinct separation in made between the contributing individual's primary reddit account and the throwaway account, removing any trace of the contributed information from the primary account (and thus resisting the permanence and searchability of this data).

Some people explicitly state the groups they are distancing themselves from in the use of a throwaway account. For example, one individual names fellow students and writes, "Using a throwaway, because I'm deep within the Bible Belt and some of my more narrow-minded classmates use this site." A second person mentions a parent: "[T]hrowaway because I want no karma and just some advice from the wisest people I know, also because my mother knows I reddit and I don't want her finding this out." Another explains, generally, "This is a throwaway account because there's some personal stuff in here that I wouldn't want traced back to me."

In particular, participants mention the use of a sustained reddit account that they do not want the information they are contributing linked to their primary technical identity. One person clarifies, "I would like to build a PC for my girlfriend and give it to her for Christmas. ... I'm using a throwaway since she knows my primary account name." Other individuals refer to a "real" account that embodies their day-to-day activities, such as, "Want to start by saying this is a throwaway account, created only to tell this. I have a real account, but I do not wish to use that one here. Sorry," or "Throwaway because my crazy ex knows my real account."

For some members, it is not an issue with particular information but with the type of communication, like complaining: "I don't want this sort of relationship drama on my primary account." One person even explains that she does not want to be reminded of the information she is asking advice about: "i apologize for the wall of text and the throwaway, but i can't deal with having this on my main account. after being in very intensive therapy for a while, i've learned how to cope and get over a lot of things, but this doesn't seem to be one of them. [sic]"

All of these reactions fall in line with Stutzman and Hartzog [45] who found that individuals maintained multiple, sustained profiles to separate distinct spheres of their lives. However, temporary identities like throwaways allow the user to avoid issues like context collapse and unexpected audiences that might still occur if an unintended individual were to come across one of the maintained profiles (eg., employer gaining access to a personal account), even if effort was made to separate these spheres.

Study 2

Study 1 provided insight into the contexts that necessitate the use of throwaway accounts on reddit, especially within situations where others can identify you and what you are willing to disclose. In Study 2, I use a predictive model to look at factors that might affect adoption of throwaway accounts on reddit. To test the hypotheses outlined above, I ran a logistic regression to predict the likelihood of an individual to create a throwaway account, using three independent variables (willingness to disclose, perception of audience size, and perception of anonymity) and four control variables (gender, age, country, and months as a user). The results are summarized in Table 1 above.

Hypothesis 1 stated that people who are less willing to disclose personal information (ie., select self-presentation increases) are more likely to use a temporary identity. The relationship was not significant, and therefore H1 was not supported.

Hypothesis 2 stated that people would be more likely to use a temporary identity in the face of larger perceived audiences. The relationship was not significant, and H2 was not supported.

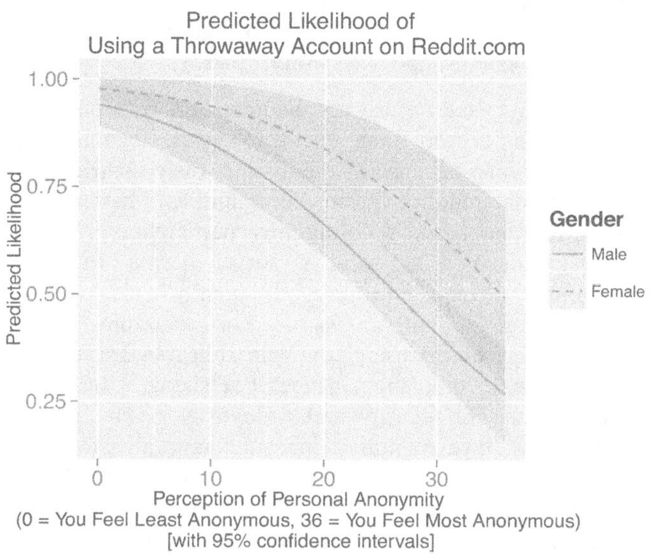

Figure 1. Summary of the significant results (perception of anonymity and gender) from the logistic regression model predicting throwaway account use on reddit (holding all other variables at their means).

Finally, Hypothesis 3 stated that in cases of lower perceived anonymity people are more likely to use a temporary identity. The relationship was significant, so this hypothesis was supported: a one-unit increase in the anonymity perception scale (ie., feeling more anonymous) results in a 9.9% decrease in likelihood of using a throwaway account (controlling for all other variables).

According to the model, the control variable of gender produced an additional significant effect. Compared to men, women are 154% more likely to use a throwaway account (controlling for all other variables). I discuss this additional finding below. Both of the significant findings are illustrated in Figure 1.

DISCUSSION

This paper provides an overview of temporary technical identities, an exploration of their use on reddit.com, and a predictive model that highlights the importance of perceptions of anonymity and gender in the creation of multiple profiles in sociotechnical systems. The first study shows how throwaway accounts on reddit enable people to disclose personal or controversial information in a quick and convenient manner without consequences tied back to their primary identity on the site. It also demonstrates generally how throwaways are used for momentary disclosure rather than act as sustained profiles for multiple purposes, as well as how pervasive throwaway accounts have become on reddit to the point of "obvious"-ness. The second study illustrates how perceptions of anonymity significantly frame the use of throwaway accounts, in addition to the impact that the gender of the person has on creating temporary identities.

Affordances for Profile Maintenance

Because reddit in its most basic form is a text-based forum, participants must navigate a significant lack of communication cues. As the literature points out, sometimes pseudonyms can complicate community dynamics like reputation and trust. Yet throwaway accounts afford individuals to smoothly disclose information separate from their main accounts, and the community has adapted to their widespread use.

Reddit's various communities still occasionally encounter issues with throwaways. For example, Bergstrom [2] illustrates the emergent norm of contacting a community's moderator to verify particular accounts' contributions, when throwaway accounts were initially embraced within the reddit community. While moderators police much of the low-level information that makes it through to the larger audience of reddit.com readers, ordinary members must still rely on posters' cues and trust in their personal statements and stories, so verifications of identities do help reduce uncertainty and increase trust in these communities (such as the /r/IAmA question-asking subcommunity). Still, throwaways afford benefits to many people, particularly in the separation of particular information from their main identity representation, providing them opportunities still to post personal information without repercussions from being identified.

As far as being an affordance for identity management, throwaway accounts also come with some difficulties. For instance, ethnographic observations produced some instances where the posters stated they were not going to use a throwaway. For example, "I usually break out my throwaway for this sub, but I really don't care this time." Sometimes the decision seems arbitrary, while in other circumstances, the use exhibits more-critical situations like safety and personal risk: "I am very nervous writing this, I was considering using a throwaway account since I live in the middle east but I decided against it." The perception of the audience particularly plays into the decision making process. For example, one user actually expressed the hope that eventually some acquaintance would come across the posted message: "I'm not using a throwaway because I kinda want people to know this happened, but I'm nervous about telling them explicitly... [I]f you read this and you know me, or think you might know me, I would really love it if you came to me and addressed this." Others merely feel comfortable expressing personal information or confessions, such as one person who wrote, "This is not a throwaway. I'm accepting of my shame." These personal debates tend to point to a willingness to disclose personal information whether or not the disclosed information can be tied back to the individual's primary identity. Future research could examine how catharsis plays into the motivation to use (or not use) temporary technical identities. For instance, one study has shown that the use of throwaway accounts in the context of mental health disclosures can result in individuals' "decreased feelings of vulnerability and increased self-disclosure" (p. 8) as well as responses from other users that were more emotional [9].

Anonymity and Temporary Technical Identities

Study 2 also highlights the importance of the role of perceptions of anonymity within the context of identity performance and self-disclosure. The model suggests a strong relationship between individuals that have both created throwaway accounts and reported lower perceptions of anonymity. Based on individuals' self-reports, willingness to disclose and awareness of imagined audience size seem unlikely to explain adoption of throwaway accounts. In total, the results suggest that being identifiable has more impact on using a temporary technical identity than what you say or to how many people you say it. These findings seem to complement the ethnographic observations from Study 1, in that users expressed more concern with particular individuals discovering their disclosed information than a larger audience of unidentified others reading the information that was disclosed or any hesitancy to share it in the first place.

With respect to the literature of MPM, the issue of privacy from very particular audiences again seems to be core to the use of multiple profiles. Individuals may be willing to share any particular type of information, but one specific piece shared with one specific person may compel them to selectively self-present with afforded identity mechanisms. Temporary account adoption linked to perceptions of anonymity also has implications for theories of context collapse [33, 8], which currently does not preempt interactions with specific individuals around contentious information (instead depending primarily on post-hoc anecdotes). These results have particular design consequences for online communities, especially those that deal in the exchange of controversial or personal information. Designers might consider affordances that allow moments of anonymity for public-facing comments that still allow the individual to control the traces they make public (rather than consistently switching between multiple technical identities).

The impact of gender particularly stands out in the results, given its large effect size. The community that drives reddit heavily skews male [37], and the dominant culture that thrives within the platform reflects that population [56]. Prior research in online anonymity and gender point to a lack of equality amongst genders (e.g., [38]), and even Stutzman and Hartzog [45] suggest that some women use multiple profile maintenance to counteract gender stereotypes. As one of their interview participants stated, "I guess as a woman you kind of want to be gender neutral because it used to be that you had to be careful going online, because if you were a woman you would be the subject of all kinds of either stalking or spamming or, just, you know, its just not pleasant" (773). In particular, Flanagin et al. [11] found that, in CMC group contexts, women are more likely than men to use strategies to keep cues reduced in anonymous online contexts (while men "introduce those cues into CMC to regain an interactional advantage lost through anonymity," p. 82).

In addition to safety, privacy, and comfort with disclosure, female reddit users may use throwaway accounts more often than men because of the distinct male-centric culture that pervades reddit's various communities. Massanari [35] identifies that reddit's community participants engage in complex debates to solidify social norms within the community, but discourse frequently clashes with participation of other users. For example, in my ethnographic observations, the subreddit /r/ABraThatFits – for women to talk about proper bra sizing – has had to debate issues of identity and anonymity given that some male users have exploited the subcommunity for sexual purposes. Earlier in 2013, one moderator posted, "[I]f you do not want creepers to stalk your account, please, USE A THROWAWAY. We cannot stop them from sending you PMs. Some women do not mind the creepy PMs, they can just ignore them, but if you think that kind of thing will get under your skin do not use your main account when posting here."[4] The emphasis on using temporary accounts to evade privacy issues and avoid sexual stalkers points to the adoption of throwaways not for identity performance but specifically to reduce interaction with repulsive and detrimental participants in the larger community. While this example represents an acute instance of consequential boundary regulation, it still falls in line with our observations of the convenient nature of temporary identities to continue participating on the platform.

Limitations

Three limitations to this study of temporary technical identities could be noted. First, as noted before, the identification of throwaway accounts is difficult when the user does not make it explicit, and ethical concerns remain regarding linking these accounts to individuals' primary identities. Interviews, in addition to the ethnographic observations presented here, could help illuminate the motivations and other factors that go into the adoption of throwaway accounts. Future research could employ better sampling techniques to map out the full range of temporary technical identity practices.

Second, as with most surveys, self-reported data and respondents' recollection of past behaviors may affect the generated data. In a post-hoc simulation of statistical power, while H3 was strong, H1 and H2 showed lack of power to detect their small effects given the sample size. Still, the survey measures used might require more specific items rather than general questions about throwaway account use that encompass every situation. Some survey measures, such as willingness to disclose information,

---

4 http://www.reddit.com/r/ABraThatFits/comments/1bg186/mod_post_not_an_aprils_fool_joke_i_just_have_bad/

measured a scale based on recollection, and future research could improve on this study by examining motivations in the moment before the creation of a temporary identity. Other factors like perception of anonymity or audience size could be affected by similar temporal and perceptual dynamics. For the purpose of this study, though, these initial measures allow us to view their impact at a general, high level given individuals' participation on reddit as a whole.

And third, the results found in this study may not necessarily be generalizable to other platforms. The findings found in Study 1 about the contexts when individuals adopt temporary throwaway accounts of course can occur in many different online environments (though these platforms might not on a technical level let participants create additional accounts). Also, I found similar results related to anonymity and gender as other research papers have reported. Still, the social norms and community dynamics of reddit may inflect how well particular results in this study could translate to other online environments and user practices.

CONCLUSION

While the technology industry has pushed in recent years toward identifiable technical representations of individuals, throwaway accounts – and temporary technical identities broadly – afford people who use online communication to disclose particular information without repercussions of being limited to only a single account. By examining throwaway account usage and describing factors that impact their adoption, this paper shows how the use of multiple profiles goes beyond maintenance of sustained technical identities when particular social media platforms afford such opportunities. Given the beneficial nature of these accounts, especially for those individuals who tend to feel less anonymous in particular situations, designers should consider alternatives to permit these identity performances within their own systems.

ACKNOWLEDGMENTS

The author would like to thank Josh Clark, Dennis Wixon, Peter Monge, Brian Keegan, Nick Jackson, Dmitri Williams, and Peggy McLaughlin for their feedback on early drafts of this paper, as well as the anonymous reviewers who provided amazingly detailed feedback and questions during the review process. This research was supported by a USC Annenberg Graduate Fellowship.

REFERENCES

1. Anonymous. 1998. "To Reveal or Not to Reveal: A Theoretical Model of Anonymous Communication." Communication Theory 8 (4): 381 – 407.
2. Bergstrom, Kelly. 2011. "'Don't feed the troll': Shutting down debate about community expectations on Reddit.com." First Monday 16: 8.
3. Bernstein, Michael, Eytan Bakshy, Moira Burke, and Brian Karrer. 2013. "Quantifying the Invisible Audience in Social Networks." Proceedings of the 2013 ACM Conference on Human Factors in Computing Systems. CHI '13. Paris, France: ACM.
4. Bernstein, Michael, Andres Monroy-Hernande, Drew Harry, Paul Andre, Katrina Panovich, and Greg Vargas. 2011. "4chan and /b/: An Analysis of Anonymity and Ephemerality in a Large Online Community." Proceedings of the 2011 AAAI Conference on Weblogs and Social Media. ICWSM '11. Barcelona, Spain: ACM.
5. Butler, Brian. 2001. "Membership Size, Communication Activity, and Sustainability: A Resource-Based Model of Online Social Structures." Information Systems Research 12 (4): 346 – 362.
6. Chester, Andrea, and Gillian Gwynne. 1998. "Online Teaching: Encouraging Collaboration Through Anonymity." Journal of Computer-Mediated Communication 4 (2).
7. Christopherson, Kimberly. 2007. "The Positive and Negative Implications of Anonymity in Internet Social Interactions: 'On the Internet, Nobody Knows You're a Dog.'" Computers in Human Behavior 23: 3038 – 3056.
8. Davis, Jenny, and Nathan Jurgenson. 2014. "Context Collapse: Theorizing context collusions and collisions." Information, Communication, & Society 17 (4): 476 – 485.
9. De Choundry, Munmun, and Sushovan De. 2014. "Mental Health Disclosure on reddit: Self-disclosure, Social Support, and Anonymity." Proceedings of the 2014 AAAI Conference on Weblogs and Social Media. ICWSM '14. Ann Arbor, MI: ACM.
10. Ellison, Nicole, and danah boyd. 2013. Sociality through Social Network Sites." In Dutton, W. H. (Ed.), The Oxford Handbook of Internet Studies (151 – 172). Oxford, England: Oxford University Press.
11. Flanagin, Andrew, Vanessa Tiyaamornwong, Joan O'Connor, and David Seibold. 2002. "Computer-Mediated Group Work: The Interaction of Member Sex and Anonymity." Communication Research 29 (1): 66 – 93.
12. Gibbs, Jeremy, Nicole Ellison, and Rebecca Heino. 2006. Self-presentation in online personals: The role of anticipated future interaction, self-disclosure, and perceived success in Internet dating. Communication Research 33 (2): 1 – 26.
13. Gibbs, Jeremy, Nicole Ellison, and Chih-hui Lai. 2010. "First Comes Love, Then Comes Google: An Investigation of Uncertainty Reduction Strategies and Self-Disclosure in Online Dating." Communication Research 38 (70).

14. Gieger, Stuart, and David Ribes. 2011. "Trace Ethnography: Following Coordination through Documentary Practices." Proceedings of the 2011 Hawaii International Conference on System Sciences, 1 – 10. HICSS '11. Kauai, HI, USA: IEEE.

15. Gilbert, Eric. 2013."Widespread Underprovision on Reddit." In Proceedings of the 2013 ACM Conference on Computer Supported Cooperative Work, 803–808. CSCW '10. San Antonio, TX, USA: ACM.

16. Glaser, Barney, & Anselm Strauss. 1967. The Discovery of Grounded Theory: Strategies for Qualitative Research. Chicago, IL: Aldine.

17. Gross, Ben. 2009. "Names of Our Lives." In Proceedings of the 2009 IEEE International Conference on Computational Science and Engineering (4): 747-752. CSE '09. Vancouver, Canada: IEEE.

18. Hayne, Stephen, and Ronald Rice. 1997. "Attribution Accuracy When Using Anonymity in Group Support Systems." International Journal of Human-Computer Studies 47: 429 – 452.

19. Hogan, Bernie. 2012. "Pseudonyms and the Rise of the Real-Name Web." In J. Hartley, J. Burgess, & A. Bruns (Eds.), A Companion to New Media Dynamics (290 – 308). Chichester, UK: Blackwell Publishing Ltd.

20. Jaffe, Michael, Young-Eum Lee, Lining Huang, and Hayg Oshagan. 1995. "Gender, Pseydonyms, and CMC: Masking Identities and Baring Souls." Paper presented at the 1995 Conference of the International Communication Association. Albuquerque, NM, USA.

21. Joinson, Adam. 2001. "Self-disclosure in computer-mediated communication: The role of self-awareness and visual anonymity." European Journal of Social Psychology 31: 177 – 192.

22. Kang, Hye-Seung, and Hee-Dong Yang. 2004. "The Effect of Anonymity on the Usage of Avatar: Comparison of Internet Relay Chat and Instant Messenger." Proceedings of the 2004 Americas Conference on Information Systems. AMCIS '04. New York, NY, USA: AIS.

23. Kairam, Sanjay, Michael Brzozowski, David Huffaker, and Ed Chi. 2012. "Talking in Circles: Selective Sharing in Google+." Proceedings of the 2012 ACM Conference on Human Factors in Computing Systems. CHI '12. New York, NY: ACM.

24. Kellermann, Kathy. 1992. "Communication: Inherently Strategic and Primarily Automatic." Communication Monographs 59.

25. Knight, Martha L., and Richard J. Borden. 1979. "Autonomic and affective reactions of high and low socially-anxious individuals awaiting public performance." Psychophysiology 16: 209 – 213.

26. Lampinen, Airi, Vilma Lehtinen, Asko Lehmuskallio, and Sakari Tamminen. 2011. "We're in It Together: Interpersonal Management of Disclosure in Social Network Services." Proceedings of the 2011 ACM Conference on Human Factors in Computing Systems. CHI '11. Vancouver, BC, Canada: ACM.

27. Latané, Bibb. 1981. "The psychology of social impact." American Psychologist 36: 343 – 356.

28. Latané, Bibb, and Stephen Harkins. 1976. "Cross-modality matches suggest anticipated stage fright as multiplicative function of audience size and status." Perception and Psychophysics 20: 482 – 488.

29. Leavitt, Alex, and Joshua Clark. 2014. "Upvoting Hurricane Sandy: Event-Based News Production Processes on a Social News Site." Proceedings of the 2014 ACM Conference on Human Factors in Computing Systems. CHI '14. Toronto, Canada: ACM.

30. Lerman, Kristina. 2006. "Social Networks and Social Information Filtering on Digg.." Proceedings of AAAI 2007 International Conference on Weblogs and Social Media. ICWSM '07. Boulder, CO, USA.

31. Litt, Eden. 2012. "Knock, Knock. Who's There? The Imagined Audience." Journal of Broadcasting & Electronic Media 56 (3): 330 – 345.

32. Massanari, Adrienne. 2013. "'Reddit hates EVERYTHING, including Reddit': Identity, Community, Participatory Culture, and Engagement on Reddit.com." Paper presented at the 2013 Association of Internet Researchers Conference: Denver, CO, USA.

33. Marwick, Alice, and danah boyd. 2010. "I tweet honestly, I tweet passionately: Twitter users, context collapse, and the imagined audience." New Media & Society 13 (1): 114 – 133.

34. Muchnik, Lev, Sinan Aral, and Sean J. Taylor. 2013. "Social Influence Bias: A Randomized Experiment." Science 341 (6146): 647 – 651.

35. Nissenbaum, Helen. 2006. "The Meaning of Anonymity in an Information Age." The Information Society: An International Journal 15 (2): 141 – 144.

36. Okdie, Bradley. 2011. "Blogging and Self-Disclosure: The Role of Anonymity, Self-Awareness, and Perceived Audience." PhD Dissertation (University of Alabama).

37. Pew Internet & American Life Project. 2013. "Six percent of online adults are reddit users." Retrieved from http://www.pewinternet.org/2013/07/03/6-of-online-adults-are-reddit-users/

38. Postmes, Tom, and Russell Spears. 2002. "Behavior Online: Does Anonymous Computer Communication Reduce Gender Inequality?" Personality and Social Psychology Bulletin 28 (8): 1073 – 1083.

39. Qian, Hua, and Craig R. Scott. 2007. "Anonymity and Self-Disclosure on Weblogs." Journal of Computer-Mediated Communication 12 (4): 1428 – 1451.

40. Raynes-Goldie, Kate. 2010. "Aliases, creeping, and wall cleaning: Understanding privacy in the age of Facebook." First Monday 15 (1).

41. Reicher, S.D., Russell Spears, and Tom Postmes. 1995. "A Social Identity Model of Deindividuation Phenomena." European Review of Social Psychology 6.

42. Resnick, Paul, and Eric Friedman. 1999. "The Social Cost of Cheap Pseudonyms." Journal of Economics and Management Strategy 10 (2): 173 – 199.

43. Singer, Philipp, Fabian Flöck, Clemens Meinhart, Elias Zeitfogel and Markus Strohmaier. "Evolution of Reddit: From the Front Page of the Internet to a Self-referential Community?" Proceedings of the 23rd World Wide Web Conference. WWW '14. Seoul, South Korea.

44. Skud. 2011. "Preliminary results of my survey of suspended Google+ accounts." Retrieved from http://infotrope.net/2011/07/25/preliminary-results-of-my-survey-of-suspended-google-accounts/

45. Stutzman, Fred, and Woodrow Hartzog. 2012. "Boundary Regulation in Social Media." Proceedings of the ACM 2012 Conference on Computer Supported Cooperative Work. CSCW '12. Seattle, WA: ACM.

46. Suler, John. 2004. "The Online Disinhibition Effect." CyberPsychology & Behavior 7 (3): 321 – 326.

47. Tanis, Martin, and Tom Postmes. 2003. "Social Cues and Impression Formation in CMC." Journal of Communication 53: 676 – 693.

48. Valacich, Joseph, Alan Dennis, and J. F. Nunamaker. 1992. "Group Size and Anonymity Effects on Computer-Mediated Idea Generation." Small Group Research 23 (1): 49 – 73.

49. Vitak, Jessica. 2012. "The Impact of Context Collapse and Privacy on Social Network Site Disclosures." Journal of Broadcasting & Electronic Media 56 (4): 451 – 470.

50. Vitak, Jessica, and Jinyoung Kim. 2014. "'You Can't Block People Offline': Examining How Facebook's Affordances Shape the Disclosure Process." Proceedings of the ACM 2014 Conference on Computer Supported Cooperative Work and Social Computing. CSCW '14. Baltimore, MD: ACM.

51. Voelpel, Sven, Robert Eckhoff, and Jens Forster. 2008. "David Against Goliath? Group Size and Bystander Effects in Virtual Knowledge Sharing." Human Relations 61 (2): 271 – 295.

52. Walther, Joe. 1993. "Impression Development in Computer-Mediated Interaction." Western Journal of Communication 57: 381 – 398.

53. Walther, Joe. 2007. "Selective self-presentation in computer-mediated communication: Hyperpersonal dimensions of technology, language, and cognition." Computers in Human Behavior 23 (5): 2538 – 2557.

54. Wayner, Peter. 1999. "Technology for Anonymity: Names by Other Nyms." The Information Society: An International Journal 15 (2): 91 – 97.

55. Yun, Haejin. 2006. "The creation and validation of a perceived anonymity scale based on the social information processing model and its nomological network test in an online social support community." PhD Dissertation (Michigan State University).

56. Zuckerman, Esther. 2012. "'Why Is Reddit So Anti-Women?': An Epic Reddit Thread Counts the Ways." The Atlantic. Retrieved from http://theatlanticwire.com/entertainment/2012/07/why-reddit-so-anti-women-epic-reddit-thread-counts-ways/55080/

Models and Patterns of Trust

Bran Knowles[1], **Mark Rouncefield**[1], **Mike Harding**[1], **Nigel Davies**[1], **Lynne Blair**[1], **James Hannon**[2], **John Walden**[2], **Ding Wang**[1]
[1] Lancaster University, Lancaster, UK, and [2] InTouch Ltd, Morecambe, UK
b.h.knowles@lancaster.ac.uk, m.rouncefield@lancaster.ac.uk, hardingm@comp.lancs.ac.uk, nigel@comp.lancs.ac.uk, lb@comp.lancs.ac.uk, james@intouch-ltd.com, john@intouch-ltd.com, d.wang4@lancaster.ac.uk

ABSTRACT
As in all collaborative work, trust is a vital ingredient of successful computer supported cooperative work, yet there is little in the way of design principles to help practitioners develop systems that foster trust. To address this gap, we present a set of design patterns, based on our experience designing systems with the explicit intention of increasing trust between stakeholders. We contextualize these patterns by describing our own learning process, from the development, testing and refinement of a trust model, to our realization that the insights we gained along the way were most usefully expressed through design patterns. In addition to a set of patterns for trust, this paper seeks to demonstrate of the value of patterns as a means of communicating the nuances revealed through ethnographic investigation.

Author Keywords
Trust; pattern language; cooperative work; mobile work; highways maintenance; ethnography

ACM Classification Keywords
H.5.m. Information Interfaces and Presentation (e.g. HCI): Miscellaneous

INTRODUCTION
In the context of real world social interactions, people have an implicit understanding of the trust that solidifies relationships or the lack of trust that fails to. In the latter case, it is fairly easy to identify lack of trust as a contributor to a range of problems — be it the poor quality of work resulting from collaboration, a failure to complete tasks at all, or the stress and frustration generated when having to interact with people who are untrustworthy (or who think you are untrustworthy). Interpersonal and inter-organizational trust dynamics are no less important within technologically mediated cooperative work, but our language for understanding and describing these dynamics with respect to technology is comparatively under-developed. For example, the success or failure of a system to accommodate and support trust is rarely identified as a contributor to the quality of the resulting system or its uptake. To design successful cooperative work systems, greater understanding is required about a) the role that technology plays (or not) in the breakdown of trust, b) how technology can be successfully deployed in fostering greater trust, and c) what effects greater trust has as it relates to both the outcomes of cooperative work and the culture in which that work is produced.

CSCW'15, March 14–18, 2015, Vancouver, BC, Canada.

http://dx.doi.org/10.1145/2675133.2675154

In previous work [18], we identify trust as a catalyst for enabling new, more efficient organizational processes. This goes beyond the facile understanding of trust as a necessary ingredient of successful collaborative work, and suggests instead that trust — or rather the *degree* and *quality* of trust existing between collaborating parties — circumscribes the possibilities for how parties undertake and complete work. Although we cannot test this hypothesis in all scenarios, we feel it is safe to generalize that greater trust not only enables different processes, but also enables smoother, more efficient, and more successful processes. For this reason, it is worth trying to gain a better understanding of how systems can be developed to foster trust as an intentional outcome of its use.

For the past three years, as part of a project called FAITH, we have been developing systems with the explicit aim of fostering trust between stakeholders. Our chosen domain was highways maintenance, where the lack of trust between local councils, highways contractors and subcontractors, field-workers and the public is especially prevalent and contributes (tangibly) to significant inefficiencies and their associated costs. As noted in greater detail in our previous work [18], fear of litigation has driven efforts to verify the accuracy of maintenance data collected in the field, costing the UK public some tens of millions of pounds per year. What seems especially noteworthy is that these efforts have done little to produce *trust* in that data, a symptom of a failure to sufficiently attend to the various social factors that enable trust to thrive. And in the absence of trust in the people who generate such data, these organizations are unable to break free of their dependence on inefficient and high-cost re-inspection routines.

In contrast to our previous publication [18] which focused on design decisions for one system in particular, here we aim to communicate the insights we gained regarding trust that span across our experiences of developing multiple systems in this domain. To this end, we develop a set of design *patterns*, which isolate dynamics of trust that we encountered repeatedly in the context of developing our systems for highways maintenance and are likely to occur in other contexts when developing collaborative systems. In addition to providing useful insight for successfully navigating these dynamics, we use patterns to provide some much needed clarity about what trust *is* and what trust *does* in this context, to demystify its relevance to systems development.

To provide adequate background for these patterns, we begin by summarizing the evolution of our thinking about trust, which began with the creation, testing and refinement of a trust model. We critique the value of this model as both a tool for informing the development of our systems and as a means of capturing and expressing the wisdom gained along the way, which serves to justify the use of patterns as a more appropriate (and ultimately valuable) output of the FAITH project. Then we present five patterns inspired by the challenges we encountered throughout the project, and use examples of the systems we developed to help illustrate the solutions they encapsulate.

DEVELOPING A TRUST MODEL

Collaboration within and between organizations presupposes trust. In complex forms of organizational and individual collaboration, it is not only persons that must be trusted, but also, and inevitably, different electronic information sources and data that mediate these relationships and can (if done well) enable trust. But 'trust' is evidently a difficult topic, and has been the subject of numerous sophisticated, sometimes conflicting, philosophical and social scientific speculations and theories. A range of theories have identified the basic grounds for the foundation of trust — in such things as individuals' reputation, performance and appearance — and indicate a range of different relational, psychological and cultural dimensions [1, 11, 12, 14, 16, 19, 20, 28, 30, 31, 32].

As an initial entry point into our exploration of trust, we began by outlining some of these understandings of the concept to produce a holistic trust model. This model, which we refer to as the Trust Wheel (Figure 1), integrates three separate but interrelated dimensions of trust: trust in systems, trust in people, and trust in processes. Our thinking behind these dimensions was as follows. As people engage with a system, when the system performs well, it may be deemed more trustworthy; but the result of distrust can be anything from user stress, to efficiency impairment, to rejection and abandonment of the system. Therefore, ensuring that a system performs well enough to be trusted is a key component of any trust model. Trust in processes is highly interrelated with trust in both systems and people. For example, when people do not trust the technical component of the process of doing their work, they may circumvent it, thereby disrupting the processes and making it less trustworthy to others. Alternatively, if people can trust the process, they are more likely to follow it and ensure that work is completed as planned.

The Trust Wheel is a simplified representation of the complex map we constructed to integrate a number of existing but thus far distinct models of trust (see Figure 2). In addition to providing insight into some of the dependencies between constituent features of trust (i.e. some needing to be in place as a prerequisite of others), the map helped us identify potential points of intervention (orange circles) that could contribute to the growth of trust by impacting on one or more of these components.

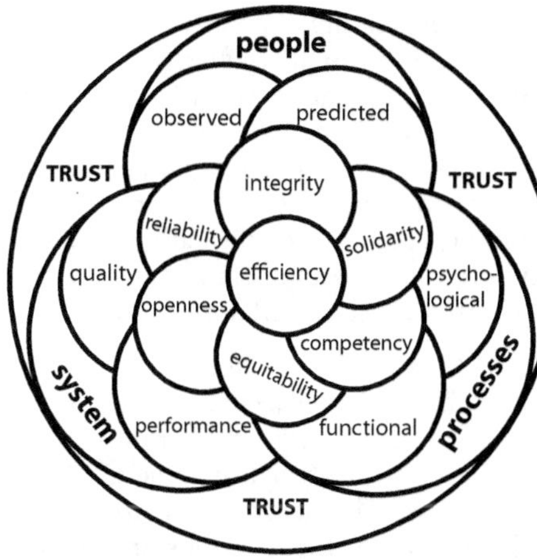

Figure 1. FAITH Trust Wheel, identifying three broad dimensions of trust — trust in systems, including both quality and performance dimensions, trust in people, both their observed and predicted behavior, and trust in processes, both functional concerns (to do with whether the process works for the desired end) and psychological concerns (related to the feelings that a process evokes) — and six related concepts (reliability, openness, equitability, competence, solidarity and integrity) that overlap with these dimensions and influence the development of trust.

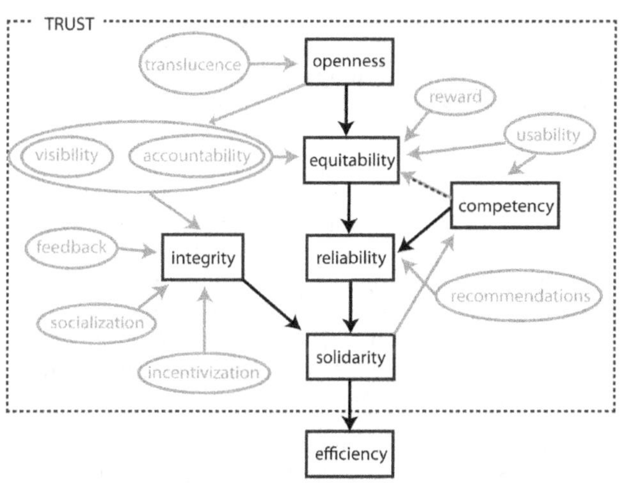

Figure 2. Trust Map, showing relations between core concepts. Rectangles contain key ingredients in creating trust; circles represent potential benefits that can be delivered through digital systems to foster the production of these ingredients.

Testing the trust model

One of the problems with such neat conceptual models is that they rarely survive any encounter with 'real life'; so we were interested in the extent to which the model might be validated or modified by our empirical research — both by the general processes of everyday work in highways maintenance and specifically by the experiences of using the technology as a part of that work. What we anticipated might emerge was an improved understanding of precisely what relationship this model of trust has to explicit organizational goals, such as increasing efficiency, and the extent to which we can perceive, and perhaps measure, some of the more nebulous benefits of increased trust, such as a general 'good feeling' associated with trusting relationships. In the process we also hoped to develop an improved, more empirically grounded model that might feed into design recommendations for developing trust producing or 'trustworthy' [18] applications.

We tested our trust model through fieldwork on various aspects of highway maintenance and repair in several locations around the UK, identifying where trust manifested and considering the extent to which our model deals effectively with such instances. The fieldwork involved informal, semi-structured interviewing, focus groups and periods of simple ethnographic observation, and was undertaken by two ethnographers (with further input on these fieldnotes from a third ethnographer). In addition to informing broad requirements for the development of systems that would be deployed in these contexts, the purpose of the fieldwork was to determine whether the model adequately identifies the various stakeholders and the forces that influence the trust relationships between them; whether the threefold division — people, process and system — was the only or best way of understanding the different interests involved (of stakeholders, beneficiaries, actors); and whether the individual components of the trust model — integrity, solidarity, competence, equability, etc. — could be easily discerned in the everyday work documented in the fieldwork.

When we looked for trust in the fieldwork we found it manifested in various ways, some of which might be more consequential for our trust model and ultimately for design than others (to be discussed in detail in the latter half of this paper). Overall we believe that the conceptual trust model held up satisfactorily when evaluated against all the empirical data on highways maintenance; and as a conceptual model of how trust works and what factors appear important in the development of trusted relationships, the model operates rather well. There were however some aspects, some ideas, that emerged quite strongly from the empirical data and which were either absent or relatively marginal to the trust model — and accordingly we suggest the model could be redesigned to incorporate some of the following ideas:

- 'Trusted data' as a separate and important factor in fostering trust between various stakeholders, which computing systems can be particularly adept at delivering (cf. [18]);

- The 'political' dimension of trust — i.e. the role of existing power relationships, which are tacitly negotiated as part of the social reality of collaborative work and delineate the parameters of trust formation;

- The issue of temporality, reflecting the fact that understandings of trust, who can be trusted, and what constitutes a 'trustable' procedure or 'trustable' data, change over time, which is especially relevant in the continued maintenance of trust.

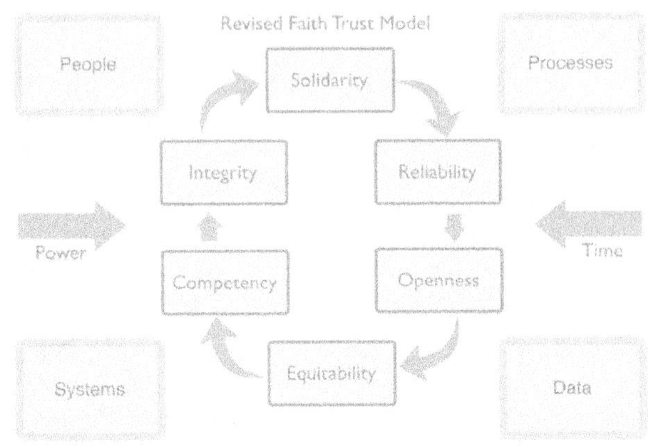

Figure 3. Revised trust model.

A revision of the trust model incorporating these ideas is reproduced in Figure 3.

Benefits and limitations of a model

There is a powerful temptation at this point to go into greater depth about how this revised trust model integrates existing theories on trust, to validate it with the ethnographic data we think demonstrates these different components and their interrelations, and to explain how this model might be usefully applied by other practitioners. While claiming ownership of a comprehensive trust model might seem like the holy grail in academic circles, we have doubts about the value that any such model can offer for practitioners who simply need to know how to design systems that work.

This is not to say that the process of creating and refining such a model is wasted effort. Our model was integral to the evolution of our group's thinking about trust, which ultimately made it possible for us to design several successful systems. In the early stages, creating a theoretically robust model forced us to familiarize ourselves with other existing models and understandings of trust. Tidying up the connections we found between the literature and representing it in a simple, elegant way forced us to refine our research questions so that what remained represented the areas that we were most interested in pursuing further. Having a manageable list of concepts and understanding the theory underpinning each gave us initial targets for technological interventions that might yield greater trust. As we began to develop technical solutions, we came to understand the greater complexity and the 'moving parts' that were affected by technology, and at that point our model provided a useful benchmark for how our thinking about trust was evolving over time. Throughout, it gave us a shared language with which to make sense of our fieldwork and to communicate the rationale behind design decisions that were being made.

But a model cannot do justice to the most important lessons we learned about trust that we will carry forward into the development of future systems. Models are not appropriate tools for expressing nuance; and as it happens, designing to support trust requires understanding of some subtle yet important concepts. We have therefore arrived at patterns as a more appropriate legacy for the FAITH project. Patterns are useful for 'establishing a relationship between a context, a system of forces which arises in that context, and a configuration which allows these forces to resolve themselves in that context' [3]. The advantage of articulating our new insights as patterns is that they allow us to communicate our detailed knowledge of the dynamics of trust *in situ* (i.e. in our experience with highways maintenance systems deployed in the field) as part of the explication of more broadly applicable insights about trust in the design of systems, while doing so in a way that is implementable by other practitioners. Indeed, there may be a natural affinity between ethnography and patterns [23], as both attempt to provide insight that can be used to ensure that systems are developed in a way that suits the context of their deployment. We hope to demonstrate that patterns are an appropriate tool for analyzing the successes (or failings) of specific systems while extracting knowledge from ethnographic fieldwork that is useful for other practitioners in a range of other contexts.

METHODS

Patterns have been developed in a range of disciplines for a variety of domains. Within computing, patterns were first developed to solve recurring problems in object oriented programming [13], but have since been developed to address a number of problem areas within HCI (e.g. [4, 6, 8, 10, 15, 23, 26]). Despite their popularity — or perhaps because of it — there is no consensus within HCI about how to develop patterns, or to what purpose. For this paper, we defer to the original (Alexandrian [3]) spirit of patterns, which identify the core of a solution to a repeating problem, stated in such a way that it can be creatively adapted by others to the specific 'local conditions' where the fostering of trust is needed, 'without ever doing it the same way twice' [3]. Developing patterns that are generative in this way requires more than translating into patterns the successful characteristics of a single system (as described in [18]). Instead, we attempt to look across the several systems we created in the past three years as part of the FAITH project, to understand why there tends to be a lack of trust between collaborating parties, how technology can be used to remedy that lack of trust, and what the effect of increased trust is on the culture in which the technology is deployed.

Earlier work [22] focused on some grossly observable features of a range of settings as the genesis of the patterns, and in order to provide a focus on the issues of importance to designers the authors attempted to develop a set of generative principles for patterns. These principles broadly divided into two main sets.

- ***Spatially oriented features*** that focus on the physical nature of the work and the observable arrangements within the workplace;
- ***Work oriented features*** that focus on the principles of social organization used to structure and manage the cooperative work.

Some of the patterns generated, such as 'artefact as audit trail' or 'multiple representations of information' [22] are easily visible in our current work, but here we had a rather different and perhaps more complex purpose — the generation of what might be regarded as 'normative' patterns — specifically patterns associated with the idea of 'trust' — and so we developed a third set of generative principles.

- ***Trust oriented features*** that focus on the role of trust in facilitating the everyday social organization of cooperative work.

This approach is consistent with Alexander's notion of 'quality' ('The Quality Without A Name') [2], which consists of answering questions such as 'what makes a good café?' Here 'quality' refers not to some mystical characteristic but to features that ensure that buildings, organizations, activities 'really work', that they fit with the social circumstances of use. For us the question is 'what makes a trusted organizational relationship?' — and our approach is to break down this question into more manageable, more digestible segments of organizational work, and to document the patterns that comprise this 'work' in a number of empirical examples.

As such, the patterns we describe here are rooted in the empirical data captured and analyzed by a team of ethnographers throughout the development and deployment of these systems. This is to say, the development of the FAITH systems was informed by our trust models and by reacting to our observations in the field, and the patterns we describe in the next section were identified after the fact as a way of drawing out lessons about designing for trust that we had tacitly absorbed along the way.

The patterns below adhere to following template:

- Name: encapsulates a characteristic of successful design;
- Problem: describes a challenge in fostering trust that consistently surfaces in a range of contexts;
- Discussion: presents the ethnographic data that was used to reveal the solution;
- Pattern: describes the core of a solution for addressing the problem successfully;
- Example(s): shows this solution in action in one or more of the FAITH systems — The Works Orders Management System (WOMS), Inspections, StreetSmart, and the FAITH Window.

PATTERNS OF TRUST

The following patterns describe the dynamics of trust that presented design challenges in our attempts to develop systems for successful cooperative work. CSCW has always struggled to make the leap from ethnography to design [9], so part of what we hope to demonstrate through these patterns is how ethnographic fieldwork can generate key insights that can inform the design of real world systems that work.

1–Chances to fail

Problem

Trust can be defined as a subjective assessment of the reliability that a person will perform a given action [12]. This assessment is often informed by that person's track record of past performance in approximately equivalent situations [27]. Without evidence of a person's reliability, there will be no evidence from which others can form trust in him/her.

Discussion

One strategy for ensuring that work is completed satisfactorily is to remove any opportunities for individuals to make mistakes. For example, in highways maintenance, supervisors will give their maintenance crews job sheets which they must complete in order without deviation, because the workers are not trusted to take care of works in an appropriate order and are assumed, instead, to try to cherry-pick easy or nearby jobs.

There are two problems with the removal of opportunities to fail, however, as it relates to trust:

1. Successful completion of work in this scenario does not contribute evidence of a person's trustworthiness, because there is no way of knowing whether work was completed satisfactorily as a result of the person's trustworthiness or as a result of having been micro-managed well (i.e. can they be trusted to deliver the same results without such micro-management?).
2. Often the minimization of mistakes is achieved by eliminating workers' opportunities to make decisions, which can create festering resentment when workers perceive a better route to take that they are unable to pursue. This can lead, in some cases, to deliberate sabotage or insubordination; or in other instances, it may lead to a perceptible diminishment of worker motivation; both of which provide management even less reason to trust the worker.

Furthermore, for external observers (management, the public), objective performance of a worker is not necessarily the only criterion that is considered in the evaluation of trustworthiness. Factors such as expectations and perception also play an important role. Hence, attempting to synthesize worker performance through tight system controls does not provide any guarantees that workers will be perceived trustworthy through their actions. Parker et al. [25] refer to this as the 'performance paradox', where performance may be rated highly but satisfaction remains low.

Pattern

More important than not making mistakes is the ability for an individual to exceed expectations. Whereas successful completion of a task one was expected to complete successfully (because of tight controls) may not contribute to increased trust, successful completion of a task that one could have failed to complete will generate evidence of their trustworthiness. So design opportunities for people to fail... and then *make sure they don't fail.* Rather than automating all decision making wherever technically possible, systems should instead defer decision making to the user particularly when that user has the expertise or competency to be able to make as good a decision as the system or better. When the system can offer sufficient support to ensure that a user completes a task satisfactorily — i.e. when the system can add some assurances that they will not fail and end up producing evidence that might indicate that they should not have been trusted in the first place — it may also be beneficial to defer decision making to the user.

Example(s)

The FAITH Inspections system succeeds in fostering trust because it empowers the people who are highly capable of succeeding in making decisions (see [18] for more details). Rather than having to follow an inefficient cleaning regimen designed by their supervisors, Inspections allows fieldworkers to make decisions about which assets do or do not need maintenance, based on a) their vast local knowledge, and b) the data accumulated by their peers, which is visible to them as they make decisions. Instead of feeling like robots whose intelligence (and, indeed, humanity) is undervalued, workers report feeling competent and engaged, and find job satisfaction in being able to contribute to the success of their company's maintenance activities. The result has been more efficient maintenance, and greater public safety, with less required supervision — all of which demonstrates that the workers can be trusted to do a good job.

2–Empowering for real

Problem

Empowerment typically results in a greater ability for an individual to influence the organization or larger system of which they are a part (cf. [21]). Empowerment, therefore, necessarily disrupts existing power relationships. When empowerment is ostensibly enabled by technologies, it can be undermined by participant stakeholders who for whatever reason do not wish to defer power. In these cases, designing for empowerment does not contribute to increased trust.

Discussion

Various factors — including a) the increased viability of public reporting due to the prevalence of smart phones, b) the need to cut costs associated with in-house inspections, and c) the UK government's Big Society initiative — have led to a turn toward citizen sensing and citizen reporting. Instead of relying on trained inspectors to systematically locate and classify highways defects, the public is asked to inspect their local areas and report any faults. As a cost-saving measure, this makes sense; but it has its downsides (cf. [17]), as one frustrated scheduler explained to one of our ethnographers in the following extract:

> *"So [the public have] got influence over what can happen — or what [the council] can or can't do, so... I think in effect, say for a road, or scheme as they call it, 'scheme A', they've got 40 thousand pound to spend on say five roads in that area. They tried to get a consensus of opinion in the neighbourhood. So you're then empowering people that don't really know a lot about the job. And then everyone wants everything done outside their own house. [Interviewer: Right, and then everything's done in the most inefficient way ever.] Exactly ...But that's the modern way, of empowering people; but you're empowering people that don't know anything about it, or what it costs. [Interviewer: So you're empowering people to make the worst decision.] Probably,*

yeah... And I find that more and more in life: ... [the] people that are actually paid to make decisions don't make decisions."

As noted in [18], empowerment literature frequently points to the following: 1) people have natural strengths that they can use and build upon [29]; and 2) people understand their own needs better than anyone else does, and should have the power to act on them [7] (cf. [21]). As a corollary to the previous pattern, this suggests that where people do not have natural strengths in the area and where they do not understand their needs better than the traditional forces in power, empowering them through technology is an empty gesture. Firstly, they will show themselves to be untrustworthy when they are unable to make intelligent decisions. Secondly, those formerly entrusted with these responsibilities may resent the input of less qualified individuals and distrust their contributions out of hand. And thirdly, when individuals have been led to believe they can contribute and then expend the effort to do so to the best of their abilities only to have their data ignored, they will feel betrayed, entrenching feelings of distrust toward those in power.

Pattern

Systems cannot effectively empower without ensuring that a) those to be empowered are adequately prepared for their new responsibilities, and b) those who are losing power are willing to entertain the possibility of trusting those gaining power. As part of the former, it is important to empower the right people, by identifying their unique strengths and abilities and matching those to the tasks the technology enables them to perform. But also, where there are potential deficiencies, the technology must include some educational component that enables them to do the job well. As for the latter, it is important to try to resolve any resistance to this empowerment before the system is introduced. Simply launching the technology and hoping the stakeholders will resolve their distrust over time is unlikely to work.

Example(s)

The StreetSmart system enables members of the public to perform localized, collective decision-making over the priority local councils give to street infrastructure defects when scheduling work. Specifically, the application empowered citizens to a) collaborate with other citizens and emphasize reported issues (e.g. through indicating that they had also encountered the same problem reported in the system) that the public felt were priorities for the council, and b) directly exchange information about issues they would like to see resolved, with a feedback mechanism for managing authorities to share information about the actions performed to resolve the issue.

What we found in practice was that the empowerment we had designed for these individuals was not real, in the sense that councils struggled in practice to defer such decision making to the public. In part, this stemmed from unresolved trust issues related to the history of litigiousness that the council feared would be exacerbated by sharing further information with the public — e.g. there was a pervasive concern that the public could use data about street defects to purposely seek out damage that they could sue the council for. In short, the council was not keen to engage in the two-way dialogue the system afforded. But further, there was no reason for the council to assume the public was capable of doing a good job, or that they were motivated by the best interests of all. In the end, StreetSmart users were frustrated by their inability to influence the council's decision making, with negative impacts on that trust relationship.

3–Baggage Handling

Problem

Within a collaborating group, people will a) manifest different levels of dispositional trust, i.e. one's baseline inclination to be trusting [24], and b) may have different histories of trustworthy or untrustworthy relationships to draw on, either in the context of that work environment or from other experiences in their past. This suggests that individuals will bring 'baggage' to any new trust context, that must be managed effectively as part of the development of a successful system.

Discussion

People who work together do not always know precisely what others are doing at any given time. In groups that have built up a healthy level of trust, each tends to assume that others can be trusted to be taking care of their responsibilities. But when people are predisposed to distrust others for whatever reason (fairly or unfairly), not being able to see what others are doing, or not understanding why they are doing what they are doing, leaves room for people to fill in these blanks with negative assumptions about others' untrustworthiness.

Public perception of civic authorities is traditionally one of incompetence and an incapability to deliver adequate civic services (e.g. social welfare, highways maintenance). Key factors that contribute to this perception include a) restrictive public awareness of on-going activities performed, and b) limited feedback on the status of reports provided by managing authorities after public members have raised issues of concern, affording citizens the opportunity to make assumptions regarding their council's trustworthiness.

As a case in point, when asked to comment on how the highways were maintained in his local area, one citizen answered:

> *"Yes, basically [the problem is] potholes around the village where I live. There are hundreds of them but they [the civic authority] don't seem to bother to repair them. I've contacted the council and neighbors have on several occasions. They took the details but did nothing."*

Having conducted extensive observation of identification and scheduling of maintenance jobs, we understand how decisions are made regarding which potholes to repair; but it is also clear that this decision making is opaque to citizens. In practice, citizens may witness civic authorities repair a subset of potholes in a given road. To the average citizen the obvious strategy would be to fix all of the potholes in a street before moving on to the next location. However, all pothole defects are categorized according to their severity and have strict targets in terms of repair time. In order to meet these targets the civic authority may well be prioritizing critical repairs, hence making multiple visits to a single location to subsequently attend to lower priority repairs. But in this case, without visibility of the contractor's efforts to meet stringent safety requirements, the public will tend to assume them to be untrustworthy.

Additionally, we commonly found in our fieldwork that different stakeholders assumed that each other *"just sits around doing nothing all day."* In part, this may have been fed by experiences of untrustworthy individuals who did not do what they were expected to do. But the larger problem was that neither party was entirely sure what the other's job entailed.

Notably, however, when someone had firsthand knowledge of the day-to-day requirements of another's job, they were less likely to assume the other to be lazy or unproductive. For example, in instances when a scheduler had previously been a member of a maintenance crew, he was more trusting that crew members were working hard and taking breaks only when necessary.

Pattern
Negative assumptions can be difficult to shake once they take hold, so it is best to avoid giving people the opportunity to fill gaps with their own assumptions in the first place. When introducing any new system, assume low levels of dispositional trust in users. Systems should be designed to be reassuring, by providing information along the way that shows how work is progressing; and if there are delays, to provide room for workers to explain these delays, rather than leaving it to the user to draw their own conclusions. As part of this, where 'black boxes' are contributing to speculation about what people may or may not be doing in the completion of work, revealing the inner complexity of interdependent processes can reduce detrimental speculation about what these workers' jobs entail and how decisions are ultimately made.

Example(s)
The StreetSmart system aimed to minimize public uncertainty about council maintenance activities by supporting a context-sensitive two-way dialogue stream. The system enables citizens to communicate freeform text information regarding reported issues, and allow local highways maintenance operatives to provide real-time updates and feedback on the progress of work (such as the acknowledgment of receiving reports), estimate completion times of work, and provide potential reasons for delay. Users of the system highlighted the importance of supporting a two-way dialogue in the system to make a more informed judgement as to whether they trusted the council were meeting their expectations and dealing with the problem accordingly.

Another example of 'Baggage Handling' is demonstrated by WOMS, the FAITH Works Orders Management System. WOMS provides a means of creating jobs that need to be done, scheduling them to fieldworkers, and then enabling fieldworks to either complete these jobs or send them back for rescheduling, along with an explanation of why the work could not be completed. At any given point in this process, individuals with access to the WOMS system can view the real-time status of jobs, along with other jobs that are ahead of it in the queue; so if someone is waiting for a specific job to be done, they can see that work is being done toward getting it completed. Additionally, this gives collaborating parties (e.g. the council, or other departments within the contractor company) a greater understanding of the decision making that goes into completing these works, which we have found cuts down on any tension that had tended to build up when collaborators were left to make assumptions about each others' trustworthiness.

4–Team spirit

Problem
Assessments of a person's trustworthiness is informed, in part, by an understanding of that person's motivations and goals [1, 32]. When these motivations and goals are understood to be in conflict with the desired behavior, trust is reduced — i.e. one might assume someone to be less likely to perform the desired behavior. Within collaboration, when individuals understand others to have motivations and goals that differ from their own, this can create a lack of trust between stakeholders.

Discussion
There is a general trend within highways maintenance (as in other sectors) to move from paper records to digital. This required getting maintenance workers, sometimes lifelong ones (typically committed technophobes), to adopt new technology. Initially, this was met with some resistance, and crews would revert to paper based systems, complaining that using the device took too much time and that it was slowing them down. They would say that if the contractor is going to force them to use these devices, then they are going to have to recognize that it means they will not be able to complete as much work. Meanwhile, the schedulers assumed that the crews were making excuses and exaggerating how much of a burden this really was. In particular, they thought that crews were *"pulling the wool over your eyes"* when they said they couldn't input information in the device while they are driving because they have to look at the map; the schedulers claim that these guys never look at the map because they know the area and have been working there for years. Furthermore, the crews are not being paid per job — they are being paid per day — so the schedulers assumed they were upset less about not being able to get as many jobs done and more because they like something to complain about.

Symptomatic of the same problem, once they had finally welcomed the mobile technology in principle, getting fieldworkers to *accurately* record their activities was another matter. In order to successfully perform their own duties, it was necessary for the supervisors that this field data was accurate; but whether this data was accurate did not tangibly help the fieldworkers succeed in meeting their goals. Fieldworkers were motivated largely by the desire to get their work done quickly, and spending time to record the data accurately was, again, an impediment to them achieving this goal. Although mobile data capture solutions that were introduced (preceding the FAITH project) attempted to enable the capturing of accurate data, accurate or not, this data was not *trusted* to be accurate. In part, this was because management was aware of fieldworkers' main motivations, which did not include data accuracy.

Pattern

Systems should be designed to align collaborators motivations so that there is an understanding of a shared goal that unites them as a team. The key is to make the achievement of Person A's objective otherwise beneficial to Person B. For example, if users cannot be trusted to use a device, then make using that device otherwise beneficial for them (so that it aligns with their goals). More specifically, where accuracy of data is a key concern for certain stakeholders, but not necessarily that of the people entrusted to gather that data, design the system so that accurate data is *useful* to the individual capturing it.

Exmaple(s)

The importance of team spirit in enabling more effective work processes is revealed by the FAITH Window (see Figure 4). This system was developed to provide managing civic authorities with a real-time, shared visualization of highways maintenance activities performed by remote contractors. In use, it has demonstrated capabilities to re-align contractor and client (civic authority) objectives while collaborating remotely. Specifically, providing a shared awareness of contractor activities has helped foster a sense of 'working together' on a shared activity, and as a result has enabled managing authorities to transition from a) a reliance on a costly inspections to confirm that work has been carried out in the field to b) a more trusted partnership where organization motivations are focused on the primary (shared) goal of delivering reliable maintenance services to the public.

In other instances, the systems we have designed have succeeded in fostering team spirit through realignment of users' motivations. For example, the introduction of WOMS succeeded where other similar devices had failed because the maintenance crews benefitted from being able to send their completed jobs to the office from the field. Primarily, this meant that if they had finished their jobs for the day — especially in instances when they were unable to do several jobs on their list for whatever reason — the scheduler could then send them different jobs to do. While this may seem a disincentive, the workers understood that it was better to do a steady number of jobs per day than to have to run around like headless chickens if these jobs started to back up. And as another example, the Inspections system enables the fieldworkers themselves to view the data that they and their peers capture, to use it to do their jobs faster and more effectively. In this case, their motivation for collecting accurate data is that it helps them achieve their primary goal: to finish work quicker.

Figure 4. Above, FAITH Window prototype, indicating information displayed in each panel; below, gesture operated FAITH Window system in use, allowing collaborating parties to share a real-time view of works that are being completed.

5–Weighting the Trust Dial

Problem

Trust builds slowly as evidence of trustworthiness is accumulated. It can take a long time and significant effort to forge trust between collaborating parties, or between individuals and the systems they use. Meanwhile, as a continual threat to this trajectory, trust is very easily lost. Whereas one positive incident rarely produces trust, one negative incident can entirely erode hard-won trust.

Discussion

One of the reasons that trust is so valuable to collaborating groups is because it represents the achievement of numerous hard-won individual and collective achievements. If trust were as easy to gain as it is easy to lose, individuals would be thought trustworthy for one-off successes, for meeting expectations on a single assignment, or for a casual remark that reveals their trustworthiness in a particular context.

But no — trust is gained through consistency; and the fact that a single mistake can eliminate trust means that it is always easier to lose trust than it is to gain. An early workshop with various highways maintenance stakeholders captured this dynamic with the image of a 'trust dial' that is spring-loaded so that one is always pushing against the force of this spring when trying to increase trust, and one slip-up snaps the dial swiftly back to the start.

Pattern

Systems are unlikely to foster significant, lasting trust unless they simultaneously and continuously prevent against the loss of trust. Various mechanisms are likely to be required as dampeners for the loss of trust; and anticipating where potential losses of trust may occur is a key ingredient of system success. Likewise, certain organizational processes can make it particularly hard to gain trust while making it that much easier to lose trust. In these cases, it is especially beneficial to introduce a technological disruption to this process, to give people a greater likelihood of earning trust.

Example(s)

This spring-loading action was observed in initial deployments of the FAITH Window (a shared visualisation component that shows WOMS information in real-time). During one trial, the window system failed, causing council workers to assume the whole WOMS system had failed, quickly leading to complete loss of trust in the FAITH project suite. The loss of trust in the system is not easily recovered in this case, which highlights as one necessary (if obvious) mitigation against the loss of trust the need to thoroughly bug-test systems before deployment in an organization.

There were, however, several more positive examples in FAITH of having appropriately mitigated against the loss of trust. For example, both WOMS and Inspections include wizarding functionality to prevent users from failing to enter all necessary data — a significant improvement on paper records, which were frequently missing information required for the contractors' legal record keeping. Further, WOMS pre-empts the loss of trust that may occur from a failure to deliver expectations, by showing the progression of jobs, and allowing users to send alerts via appropriate channels to warn collaborators of any potential delays, so that when they did occur, they were less detrimental to that trust relationship.

And as explained in more detail in [18], Inspections was particularly successful in fostering trust in remote fieldworkers because it specifically disrupted a dynamic that was disproportionately weighted toward them being seen as untrustworthy. In the past, it was far easier for fieldworkers to lose the trust of their managers than gain it, because their only route to gaining trust was to clean a set number of gullies per day, and in practice this was often not possible due to a range of factors external to the fieldworkers' ability or desire to complete the work (e.g. gullies being blocked by parked cars, problematic weather conditions, traffic delays). But because Inspections disrupts this dynamic by allowing workers to make intelligent decisions about how to keep the roads safe, the system offered them new routes to gaining trust, namely to design for themselves a more efficient schedule. And indeed, they were unlikely to craft *less efficient* schedules than those where they previously had to clean every single gully, so the trust dial in this case was effectively spring-loaded in the reverse direction, toward inevitable increased trust.

DISCUSSION

Bannon argues that 'a critical issue for research lies in determining ways of transforming the ethnographic material in such a way that remains sensitive to the practices of designers themselves and thus can readily be used by them in the design process' [5, p. 250]. Like others, we were drawn to patterns as a way of communicating knowledge about a workplace to a multidisciplinary design team [23] — or as Diggins and Tolmie [9] put it, we are concerned with 'how to make ethnographic findings tractable to the exercise of design.' In our approach, patterns complement our ethnographic fieldwork. They are a resource 'to be used after the fieldwork stage and as part of the process of analysis and design' [23]. Consequently this work is intended to explore 'the efficacy any such representations have for the conduct of situatedly relevant collaborative work,' given 'the need to provide some kind of formulation for design purposes' [9]. We believe our attempt to focus on 'trust' patterns brings attention to an often neglected aspect of everyday work and the design of systems to support cooperative work — that 'success' and 'failure' in collaborative work is often not simply a matter of spatial location or process and sequence but of human relationships characterized by trust and mistrust.

We began this paper by discussing our process of developing a trust model. As useful as this process was, the real insights that helped us develop systems, and understand why they were or were not working — i.e. the patterns described in the previous section — were not derived from our models; nor do we feel are they adequately captured by them. The patterns come directly out of our ethnographic work and our experience working with the development team to address the dynamics of trust that we had identified on numerous occasions. And yet we cannot make decisive claims about the superiority of patterns over models in all cases involving ethnographic analysis and systems design, or indeed in this one, without further study comparing the use of both. It is not our intention, however, to incite conflict between those who do or do not find value in models as a way of communicating insights gained from research projects — and clearly, we found them useful at certain stages of our system development. Rather, we wish to encourage other researchers who conduct 'messy' ethnographic studies to attempt to structure their findings in the form of patterns as a possible means of increasing the applicability of their insights to practitioners developing systems in other contexts.

Even having decided on patterns as the most suitable means of articulating our insights, there are many other levels we may have pitched our patterns. For example, we might have written patterns that pertain to the various constituent features of trust identified in our modelling stage — e.g. concepts such as openness, equitability, reliability, integrity, and solidarity; or we might have written patterns about the various technological characteristics that may foster or otherwise affect each of these constituent features — e.g. usability, accountability, translucence (from our Trust Map, Figure 2) or principles such as performance, provenance, and so forth which we have described elsewhere in non-pattern form [18]. Instead, we thought we could make a greater contribution to the CSCW community by going 'higher up', reflecting more broadly on *what happens* to create trust or lack of trust. From this perspective, the patterns are intended to identify strategic goals (rather than technical solutions) that might serve as guidance for developers, while still leaving plenty of room for them to experiment with technical mechanisms for achieving those goals.

We recognize that for any given pattern, it can be difficult to determine the extent to which it represents a repeating, generalizable problem and solution, as opposed to an instance that worked for a specific context. While we cannot know for sure how well these patterns apply to other domains beyond highways maintenance until researchers attempt to apply them elsewhere, we have attempted to circumvent this issue as much as possible by being selective in the patterns we chose for inclusion. While there were other insights that may have made interesting patterns that touched on specifics of the contexts we found ourselves investigating, we opted for generalizability over comprehensiveness and included only those that isolated a readily recognizable, if not universal, human characteristic or dynamic that influences the formation of trust. Having said that, we welcome the continued evolution of these five patterns as others apply them in developing systems in other domains and determine where they work and where they fall down. And we similarly encourage the addition of further patterns as part of a growing pattern language for trust, which may include many patterns of varying granularity, such as those we chose not to detail here, and of varying contextual applicability, to help the community better understand when to use one pattern over another.

CONCLUSION

We have covered a lot of ground in this paper. We have discussed four systems developed for the FAITH project, and explored why we think they have succeeded (or failed) with respect to fostering trust between stakeholders. We have isolated cross-cutting trust dynamics found in the ethnographic research conducted in preparation for and during development of these systems; and having articulated them in the form of patterns, we have attempted to offer other developers strategic insight into designing successful systems, without having to design future systems as clones of our FAITH systems. In doing so, we have tried to show the benefits of patterns as a means of communicating wisdom for future systems design compared to the more typical reliance of models (which nonetheless serve an important function in the process) — these patterns serving as reminders of what to consider when developing systems to support effective collaboration, whether or not the ultimate intention is, specifically, to increase trust between collaborators. Finally we offer the FAITH project as an example of how CSCW may use ethnographic research to inform the design of cooperative work systems, how important trust is to consider in their design, and how important it is to more deeply investigate the many facets of trust.

ACKNOWLEDGMENTS

The research leading to these results has been conducted as part of the FAITH: Building Trust Between Citizens, Local Authorities and Contractors project funded by the EPSRC/TSB under grant TS/I002537/1.

REFERENCES

1. Ajzen, I. The theory of planned behavior. *Organizational behavior and human decision processes 50*, 2 (1991), 179–211.
2. Alexander, C. *The Timeless Way of Building*, vol. 1. Oxford University Press, 1979.
3. Alexander, C., Ishikawa, S., Silverstein, M., Jacobson, M., Fiksdahl-King, I., and Angel, S. *A Pattern Language: Towns, Buildings, Construction*. Oxford University Press, New York, 1977.
4. Arvola, M. Interaction design patterns for computers in sociable use. *Int. J. Comput. Appl. Technol. 25*, 2/3 (Feb. 2006), 128–139.
5. Bannon, L. *Workplace Studies: Recovering Work Practice and Informing System Design*. Cambridge University Press, 2000, ch. Situating workplace studies within the human-computer interaction field.
6. Borchers, J. O. A pattern approach to interaction design. In *Proc. DIS '00*, ACM (2000), 369–378.
7. Cochran, M. The parental empowerment process: Building on family strengths. In *Child psychology in action: Linking research and practice*, J. Harris, Ed. Croon Helm Publishers, Brookline, MA, 1986, 12–33.
8. Crabtree, A., Hemmings, T., and Rodden, T. Pattern-based support for interactive design in domestic settings. In *Proc. DIS '02*, ACM (2002), 265–276.
9. Diggins, T., and Tolmie, P. The 'adequate' design of ethnographic outputs for practice: some explorations of the characteristics of design resources. *Personal and Ubiquitous Computing 7*, 3-4 (2003), 147–158.
10. Erickson, T. Lingua francas for design: sacred places and pattern languages. In *Proc. DIS '00*, ACM (2000), 357–368.
11. Erickson, T., and Kellogg, W. A. Social translucence: An approach to designing systems that support social processes. *ACM Trans. Comput.-Hum. Interact. 7*, 1 (Mar. 2000), 59–83.
12. Gambetta, D. *Trust: Making and breaking cooperative relations*. 2000, ch. Can we trust trust?, 213–237.
13. Gamma, E., Helm, R., Johnson, R., and Vlissides, J. *Design patterns: elements of reusable object-oriented software*. Addison-Wesley Longman Publishing Co., Inc., Boston, 1995.
14. Hechter, M., and Kanazawa, S. Group solidarity and social order in japan. *Journal of Theoretical Politics 5*, 4 (1993), 455–493.
15. Herrmann, T., Hoffmann, M., Jahnke, I., Kienle, A., Kunau, G., Loser, K.-U., and Menold, N. Concepts for usable patterns of groupware applications. In *Proc. GROUP '03*, ACM (2003), 349–358.
16. Hoffman, L. J., Lawson-Jenkins, K., and Blum, J. Trust beyond security: an expanded trust model. *Communications of the ACM 49*, 7 (2006), 94–101.
17. King, S. F., and Brown, P. Fix my street or else: Using the internet to voice local public service concerns. In *Proc. ICEGOV '07*, ACM (2007), 72–80.

18. Knowles, B., Harding, M., Blair, L., Davies, N., Hannon, J., Rouncefield, M., and Walden, J. Trustworthy by design. In *Proc. CSCW '14*, ACM (2014), 1060–1071.

19. Lee, M. K., and Turban, E. A trust model for consumer internet shopping. *International Journal of electronic commerce 6* (2001), 75–92.

20. Liang, Z., and Shi, W. PET: A personalized trust model with reputation and risk evaluation for P2P resource sharing. In *Proc. HICSS '05*, IEEE (2005), 201b–201b.

21. Lord, J., and Hutchison, P. The Process of Empowerment: Implications for Theory and Practice. *Canadian Journal of Community Mental Health 12*, 1 (1993), 5–22.

22. Martin, D., Rodden, T., Rouncefield, M., Sommerville, I., and Viller, S. Finding patterns in the fieldwork. In *Proc. ECSCW '01*, Kluwer Academic Publishers (2001), 39–58.

23. Martin, D., Rouncefield, M., and Sommerville, I. Applying patterns of cooperative interaction to work (re)design: e-government and planning. In *Proc. CHI '02*, ACM (2002), 235–242.

24. McKnight, D. H., Cummings, L. L., and Chervany, N. L. Initial trust formation in new organizational relationships. *Academy of Management Review 23*, 3 (1998), 473–490.

25. Parker, S. C. *State of trust: How to build better relationships between councils and the public*. Demos, 2008.

26. Remy, C., Weiss, M., Ziefle, M., and Borchers, J. A pattern language for interactive tabletops in collaborative workspaces. In *Proc. EuroPLoP '10*, ACM (2010), 9:1–9:48.

27. Waguih, H. A proposed trust model for the semantic web. *Enformatika 11* (2006).

28. Wang, Y., and Vassileva, J. Bayesian network-based trust model. In *Proc. IEEE/WIC '03*, IEEE (2003), 372–378.

29. Whitmore, E. Participation, empowerment and welfare. *Canadian Review of Social Policy 22* (1988), 51–60.

30. Xiong, L., and Liu, L. PeerTrust: Supporting reputation-based trust for peer-to-peer electronic communities. *IEEE Transactions on Knowledge and Data Engineering 16*, 7 (2004), 843–857.

31. Yu, B., and Singh, M. P. A social mechanism of reputation management in electronic communities. In *Cooperative Information Agents IV – The Future of Information Agents in Cyberspace*. Springer, 2000, 154–165.

32. Zhang, X., and Zhang, Q. Online trust forming mechanism: approaches and an integrated model. In *Proc. Electronic Commerce*, ACM (2005), 201–209.

Privacy as Articulation Work in HIV Health Services

Chrysanthi Papoutsi
Department of Medicine
Imperial College London
369 Fulham Road, SW10 9NH,
London, UK
c.papoutsi@imperial.ac.uk

Ian Brown
Oxford Internet Institute
University of Oxford
1 St. Giles, OX1 3JS,
Oxford, UK
ian.brown@oii.ox.ac.uk

ABSTRACT
Normative accounts on health information privacy often highlight the importance of regulating data sharing. Yet, little attention has been paid to how health professionals perform and negotiate privacy practices in highly multidisciplinary, technologically-mediated medical work. This paper examines information privacy practices in two HIV outpatient clinics based in two NHS hospitals in London (UK). Methods include 46 semi-structured interviews, primarily with health professionals and technology developers, ethnographic observation and document analysis. Drawing on an empirically informed understanding of privacy as 'articulation work', we focus on the indeterminate nature of information privacy practices and examine the work required to translate privacy, from a normative professional duty to an enacted medical practice. This analysis also highlights the invisibility of privacy practices and their coordinating role in delivering technologically-supported medical care. The paper ends with a discussion of implications for practice and technology design.

Author Keywords
Information privacy; medical confidentiality; articulation work; HIV; design.

ACM Classification Keywords
J.3 [Life and Medical Sciences]: Health. K.4.1 [Public Policy Issues]: Ethics – Privacy. K.4.3 [Organizational Impacts]: Computer-supported collaborative work. K.7.4 [Professional Ethics]: Ethical dilemmas.

INTRODUCTION
The importance of health information sharing and interoperability among healthcare providers has been underlined in a number of policy initiatives in different countries [12, 25]. Yet, striking a balance between information accessibility and patient confidentiality in technologically mediated healthcare work remains a challenge. Privacy considerations have long accompanied plans for the implementation of electronic records and integrated systems in healthcare [28]. In the UK, 186 serious data breaches were reported to the Department of Health between 2011-2012 [13] and efforts to alter the technological landscape in the English National Health Service (NHS) raised privacy and confidentiality concerns in recent years [2, 10, 31].

Against this background, patient confidentiality remains a highly valued professional duty and a cornerstone of medical practice [20]. Legal provisions and codes of ethics outline standards for protecting patient information, provide a framework for appropriate professional conduct and specify repercussions from a confidentiality breach. Although useful as templates for professional practice, these normative accounts do not fully capture the lived experiences of clinicians who manage patient confidentiality within health settings. Healthcare provision often involves unexpected events and information needs that are not always predictable. In addition, medical work is becoming increasingly multidisciplinary, including not just a wider range of health professionals, but also social care and other occupations.

To better support service delivery and technology use, it is important to gain an empirical understanding of how information privacy and confidentiality are enacted in practice to manage the collaborative and distributed nature of medical work. Recent literature reviews in the area emphasise the importance of empirical research that transcends the individual level of analysis, to use case studies and ethnographic methods looking at collaborative, rather than individual, privacy practices from the perspective of data users [4, 5, 11, 23, 27, 34, 35, 38].

This paper focuses specifically on collaborative information privacy practices from the perspective of health professionals working in outpatient clinics for people living with the Human Immunodeficiency Virus (HIV) in two NHS hospitals in London (UK). HIV health services provide a unique context to study privacy and confidentiality practices because of the sensitivity of HIV patient information and the potential for stigmatisation. To

CSCW '15, March 14 - 18, 2015, Vancouver, BC, Canada.
Copyright 2015 ACM 978-1-4503-2922-4/15/03…$15.00.
http://dx.doi.org/10.1145/2675133.2675204

account for confidentiality concerns, HIV health services in the UK were historically organised in isolation to mainstream care, using segregated practices for service delivery and patient management. With current treatments extending life expectancy, however, HIV is increasingly managed in ways similar to other chronic conditions that require strong collaboration and information exchange between different medical specialties [1]. As medical care extends beyond a single discipline or health setting, HIV patient information is also often necessary beyond the boundaries of HIV clinics to support appropriate medical decisions and safe care. This paper examines how health professionals manage patient confidentiality using a number of different systems at the interface between HIV and mainstream care. The analysis informs the debate on shifting privacy practices for HIV care and contributes to the discussion on how these would be best technologically supported.

The rest of this paper is structured as follows. The next section provides the background literature review, followed by the theoretical framework underpinning this work. The research methods are then presented, together with a section on HIV health settings explaining how HIV patient care is organised in the UK. Key findings on privacy as articulation work and as an invisible practice are contained within the next two sections. The discussion follows, including implications for design and practice, and the paper ends by highlighting the main conclusions from this work.

LITERATURE REVIEW

A large body of literature has been devoted to examining privacy as a set of elements, states or categories. Westin [43] observes that there are four basic privacy states between an individual and society: solitude, intimacy, anonymity and reserve. Similarly, Gavison [15] argues that secrecy, anonymity and solitude constitute the three elements of privacy, importantly highlighting, however, that these are: 'distinct and independent, but interrelated, and the complex concept of privacy is richer than any definition centred around only one of them'. The richness and complexity this conveys permeates many contemporary views.

Instead of looking for a common denominator to what constitutes privacy, Solove [36] focuses on conceptualising privacy problems and proposes a taxonomy of information harms. More recent work discusses the relevance of context relevant informational norms in framing an understanding of privacy as contextual integrity [24]. Following a similar approach, Palen and Dourish [26] conceptualise interpersonal privacy as dynamically and dialectically managed in response to competing tensions and circumstances in sociotechnical environments.

In this work, we adopt a view of information privacy as a set of contextual and situated practices, drawing on recent work that seeks to overcome the rigidity of previous privacy conceptualisations and to problematise the fluidity of public/private distinctions [17, 21, 22, 24, 32, 36]. We are interested in privacy not as an abstract trade-off, a technical property or a set of preferences, but as an inherent part of interrelated and performative social and cultural practice [14]. This approach transcends the idea of privacy as fixed and stable, to draw attention to its ongoing collaborative accomplishment.

Although significant work has been done on collaborative practices in health settings from a CSCW perspective, privacy has more often been examined as an individual value or preference, or as a consequence, rather than as a collaborative practice in its own right [5, 35]. Only recently have researchers focused more explicitly on how privacy is managed and enacted at the group-level [11, 23].

One of the studies within this strand of research specifically examined the different mechanisms and workarounds emergency care staff used to enact privacy while carrying out medical work [23]. Drawing on the theory of contextual integrity, another ethnographic study in three different settings outlined three types of group dynamics and discussed the implications for appropriate privacy management [11]. Both studies point to the challenges of aligning privacy policies and technological design within highly distributed, collaborative work practices in dynamic environments.

The work presented here focuses on a different context, that of HIV health services, to expand the body of literature looking at privacy as a highly situated collaborative practice. In doing that, we employ concepts of articulation and invisible work to examine how privacy practices are accomplished in practice, as explained in the following section. This introduces a novel theoretical conceptualisation for studying privacy, which holds potential for illuminating aspects more difficult to clearly articulate as technical requirements or specifications, or to stipulate in organisational policies.

THEORETICAL FRAMEWORK

According to Gerson and Star [16], articulation work is defined as a series of coordination tasks carried out to support work practices and respond to local contingencies within highly complex collaborative settings. This is achieved 'by packaging a compromise that 'gets the job done', that is closes the system locally and temporarily so that work can go on' [16]. In this respect, articulation work refers not only to the activities and tools employed to cope with the distributed nature of cooperative work, but also denotes mechanisms of interaction and communication, which require continuous articulation work in themselves to successfully fulfill their role [29].

As a theoretical concept, articulation work sensitises towards the 'continuous efforts required in order to bring together discontinuous elements [...] into working configurations' [40]. This brings to the fore elements of background practices that are often not clearly included in formal representations of work, but remain crucial for the accomplishment of collaborative tasks [3, 16, 29, 39]. The idea of 'invisible work' also relates closely to articulation as it seeks to highlight informal tasks performed in the background with discretion [37].

A number of CSCW studies have encompassed articulation work as a crucial aspect in making sense of and addressing the implications of distributed, collaborative work across different settings [3, 19, 39, 42]. This has been particularly highlighted in studies looking at the management and use of patient records in health settings [6-8]. Yet, this theoretical lens has not been explicitly considered in understanding how privacy and confidentiality practices are produced and configured. This paper argues that privacy work contains significant elements of articulation in the process of translating a normative professional duty to an enacted medical practice, work that often happens silently in the background. An emphasis on articulation allows invisible practices that are 'relegated to a background of expectation' [37] to come to the fore and become explicitly recognised [40]. This has implications on who gets to define what counts as privacy work, how it should be done and how it should be effectively designed in record keeping systems.

The case studies presented here highlight how privacy practices are embedded in managing the distributed nature of medical work within HIV centres and across hospital departments. In this, we look not just at how privacy practices are part of the articulation work necessary to carry out clinical tasks, but also at how privacy practices themselves require articulation work to be accomplished. This highlights how privacy becomes socially and collaboratively produced, in ways that are not always formally acknowledged in organisational policies and codes of conduct, or supported by technological systems.

METHODS

This paper draws on two case studies on privacy and confidentiality practices in HIV clinics. Fieldwork began in October 2009 with a pilot project in the HIV unit of a teaching hospital in the South East of England. Following that, the main part of the research was carried out in two HIV outpatient specialist centres in east London between April and October 2010. These sites were in the process of negotiating changes to the way they managed HIV patient information, from using stand-alone systems to integrating their HIV records with the rest of the hospital. These negotiations opened a productive space for engaging in privacy discussions with staff members and brought to the fore different experiences with providing integrated HIV care while protecting patient information.

A total of 46 semi-structured interviews were conducted, primarily with health professionals, including HIV medical consultants and other specialties, junior doctors and registrars, nurses and nursing assistants, health advisors, administrative employees, IT developers, a pharmacist and a patient representative. The majority of staff looking after HIV patients in the clinics and most of the IT staff involved in the integration negotiations were interviewed, following purposive and snowballing sampling methods. Relevant 'experts' from academia, government agencies and community organisations who had an insight on the integration project were also involved in interviews to provide some background and contextualise privacy practices for HIV care. Table 1 presents a breakdown of participants based on their roles. Each interview lasted one hour on average. Interview questions evolved throughout the study and were adapted for different professional groups, but high-level topics included perceptions around privacy and confidentiality practices in HIV care, experiences with using paper and electronic records, challenges emerging from the use of segregated technological systems and practices adopted to overcome communication and collaboration barriers.

Roles	#
Consultants	10
Registrars and junior doctors	3
Nurses & nursing assistants	10
Health advisors	5
Pharmacist	1
IT developers	7
Administrative staff	4
General management	2
'Experts'	3
Patient representative	1

Table 1. Roles of participants.

Interviews were supplemented by ethnographically informed observation in the two HIV outpatient centres for an average of 2-3 days a week over a period of six months. Areas observed included outpatient waiting rooms, reception areas and different staff offices (HIV nurses, doctors and health advisors). The researcher also observed a number of meetings looking at HIV clinical care, multidisciplinary meetings discussing patient cases, service provision, training as well as executive and management meetings, among others.

Document analysis was also used to inform the interpretation of findings. Minutes of meetings between 2005-2010, hospital policies, risk registers, risk assessment forms, confidentiality policies, clinic guidelines, incident reports, codes of conduct, HIV process flow diagrams, discussion papers and other documents related to the integration negotiations were reviewed and analysed where relevant to guide fieldwork and contribute to the findings.

The data from the interviews, observation and documentation were analysed using thematic analysis with emerging codes iteratively added to a pre-defined coding framework [44]. Ethical approval for the project was granted by University College London Hospital (UCLH) Research Ethics Committee Alpha (ref. 09/H0715/78).

SETTING: HIV HEALTH SERVICES

According to the most recent prevalence statistics produced by the Health Protection Agency (HPA), an estimated 100,000 people live with HIV in the UK, out of whom one fifth have not been diagnosed [18]. By the end of 2012, the number of patients accessing HIV care had doubled since 2003, with the total number reaching 77,610 individuals. The majority of cases and new diagnoses are reported in London, with a higher prevalence in the most deprived boroughs of the east where this research was focused.

In the UK most HIV specialist outpatient centres operate models of anonymous testing and treatment, due to the increased level of confidentiality restrictions applicable to sexual health information, as set out in legislation and professional codes of practices. Although medical confidentiality remains important in all medical settings, HIV clinics have historically adopted particular privacy practices: they use their own unique identifiers and are not obliged to link patients' identities to their NHS numbers as routinely done in other settings; they also use separate paper and electronic records which cannot be shared with health professionals even when co-located in the same hospital.

The two HIV centres studied here had adopted these practices, with record-keeping systems and information flows historically designed to retain the segregation of patient information. The HIV units were thus using their own stand-alone clinical support systems, which did not communicate with the hospital Electronic Patient Record (EPR). This entailed separate confidentiality practices and distinct privacy regimes between the HIV clinics and mainstream hospitals, which raised interesting questions as to how privacy practices would be managed in collaborative medical work at the intersection of HIV and general patient care.

This way of organising HIV services, however, is being questioned as HIV has shifted from being a terminal condition to one where chronic treatment is available [1, 30, 33, 41]. The long-term nature of the disease and the changing demographics of patient populations create new challenges as to how heterogeneous and distributed practices of HIV care will be best technologically supported. This led the British HIV Association (BHIVA) to recommend integrated clinical records for the management of HIV patients, therefore encouraging a shift from HIV-specific to generic confidentiality practices as relevant for any other patient in a hospital setting [9]. Adoption of this recommendation had been slow but provided interesting opportunities for examining privacy practices as the two HIV outpatient centres were still operating at the interface of mainstream care and HIV models at the time this research was carried out.

HIV PATIENT TRAJECTORIES

In the two clinics, HIV patients were seen either for follow-up routine appointments every 3-4 months or on a walk-in basis. Two weeks before their scheduled appointment they visited the clinic to have blood taken, usually by a nurse. They then attended on the day to receive the results, discuss with the doctor and, if necessary, receive drug prescriptions.

Drop-in clinics served HIV patients with semi-acute problems between regular appointments. Apart from face-to-face patient clinics, HIV professionals frequently held what they called virtual clinics, where they used paper and electronic records to discuss patients with their team.

To account for the medical and social implications of an HIV diagnosis, care was multidisciplinary and team-based within the HIV units. Psychologists and social workers were often involved to support patients. Also, occupational therapists offered treatment and rehabilitation services to people living with HIV who encountered problems with everyday tasks as a result of their condition or who needed help after being discharged from the hospital. Other services were also involved on a needs basis, ranging from dieticians to mental health specialists. To protect from stigma and accidental disclosure within the clinics and become embedded with the larger patient body, people living with HIV were not referred to as HIV patients but as 'medical' patients in the HIV clinics.

The care of pregnant women living with HIV was transferred to the hospitals' antenatal departments, where a team of HIV specialists and obstetricians followed them until delivery. By adhering to therapy, receiving specialist obstetric care and avoiding breastfeeding, they could significantly reduce the chances of vertical (mother-to-child) transmission. After the pregnancy, care continued normally in the HIV clinics.

When the HIV specialist unit was closed, patients presented to the Accident & Emergency (A&E) Department or other NHS walk-in clinics. One of the hospitals had no dedicated inpatient ward for patients whose problems were primarily HIV-related so they were transferred to a different site. There were still patients living with HIV, however, who were hospitalised for problems not directly associated to their positive status. These patients were under the care of different specialties acting on a liaison basis with HIV doctors on matters of drug interactions and other complications. Apart from such ad hoc communication, few connections existed between HIV and other medical teams. In the second hospital, the HIV team coordinated care in an inpatient ward where most people living with the condition were admitted, although this was not a formally dedicated HIV ward.

ARTICULATION WORK & PRIVACY PRACTICES

The segregation of record-keeping systems between HIV clinics and mainstream hospital departments entailed increased articulation work (in the sense of background practices) to manage collaboration needs in multidisciplinary teams inadequately supported by existing information infrastructures. Due to the condition often considered stigmatising, articulation work was done to fill in the gaps created by the privacy practices adopted in the two hospitals and to sustain absolute confidentiality for HIV patients.

Creating HIV patient trajectories

When a patient was admitted to hospital, they were either triaged in emergency admissions or sent to the acute care unit directly through a referral from their General Practitioner (GP), before being admitted to other hospital wards if necessary. Patients living with HIV often required the attention of an HIV clinician as part of their multidisciplinary team. With little information sharing between the HIV centres and mainstream hospital departments, articulation of HIV patient trajectories often took place in ad-hoc and contingent ways, as the junior doctor below explains:

How we get informed [...] varies. It doesn't always work completely. Most patients who are admitted to the hospital come through the Acute Care Unit and the HIV Liaison Nurse was going to their ward round every morning. [...] And also the hospital teams, there's information that basically if they have any patient with HIV they should inform us. And sometimes it comes through the Pharmacy if they are written up for ARVs [HIV medication] and we get informed. So [...] any patients who have HIV tests in the hospital, any positive results get phoned through to either our Health Advisors or [the HIV Liaison Nurse] again. (Junior Doctor)

The role of the liaison nurse was to provide the link between acute admissions and HIV clinics, carrying out the background work that allowed the initiation of HIV patient trajectories. This was necessary in order to be able to draw on HIV-specific expertise, but also to gain access to the information contained in the separate set of patient notes held at the HIV centre for patients already treated there (as the notes were not allowed to leave the HIV centre). Articulation work was done to attach the appropriate medical team and draw a relevant care plan, thereby overcoming the implications of distributed work and retaining HIV-specific confidentiality.

Working with HIV patient records

For HIV patients who attended scheduled appointments in the hospital, another layer of articulation work had to be performed. In one of the hospitals studied, the antenatal clinic for pregnant women living with HIV took place in the obstetrics department rather than in the HIV centre. This meant that attending HIV Consultants had to bring a number of resources together to support clinical interactions: paper notes had to be transferred from the HIV centre, access to one of the HIV-specific systems needed to be set-up in the obstetrics department, while also drawing on the mainstream hospital system. Often in collaboration with a midwife and an obstetrician, HIV Consultants coordinated across these resources, to acquire the relevant background to the consultation and document medical encounters in a way that would support further multidisciplinary care, both in obstetrics and crucially also in the subsequent trajectory of the patient back in the HIV centre after labour:

Now there, I'm in the antenatal clinic and there I manage all the patients on EPR. [...] When I'm in [the HIV centre] I use [System 1] and [System 2] as my prime sources and then if I have to look up EPR it will be a subsidiary thing. There [antenatal clinic] they are on EPR. Their blood results are done on EPR, everything is on EPR and I use [System 1] as a subsidiary thing. But I have [System 2] in both places and I put the data in from both into that. Of course you've got to bear in mind at all times I will have the paper record as well. And in the Antenatal Clinic I will have the paper record from the hospital, I will have the paper record from [the HIV centre], I will have the woman's handheld notes and in terms of previous pregnancies I'll have all her previous handheld notes and if I want to find out about the baby I will have another set of paper notes as well. So, and that's as well as the computer. (HIV Consultant)

Articulation work for the care of pregnant women living with HIV was necessary because the infrastructure developed to support the obstetrics department did not take in account HIV specificities neither did it allow communication and information exchange with the HIV centre. Since the main hospital system provided few options in supporting the HIV privacy culture, this meant clinicians had to use a number of different practices to address this difference, engaging in articulation work to accomplish privacy in practice: articulating what medical confidentiality meant for people living with HIV, while also supporting the tasks necessary to retain this sense of confidentiality in collaborative practices within HIV centres and across boundaries.

Crossing the boundaries of different privacy regimes also involved physical movement to a different space when HIV technologies and patients were not co-located:

[...] then you maybe have to see the patient in one room and then go back to another room to write their prescription and check their results. (Junior Doctor)

Similar information seeking, translation and coordination work to support collaborative practice was carried out in many departments within the same hospital, since HIV patients could have different types, versions and combinations of electronic records and paper notes. Often health professionals had to use resources additional to their electronic and paper records to obtain a more complete picture of a patient's health and social situation, by phoning colleagues, establishing contact with other departments, holding meetings or following-up with liaison or community nurses. Of interest here is the articulation work performed to allow people to work well together across privacy regimes, while still keeping their record-keeping practices separate, driven by the need to respond to privacy concerns about perceptions of stigmatisation around HIV.

Engaging in discovery and translation

In the clinics, an investigation and discovery process similar to the one followed in cross-boundary collaboration with other settings, was also performed. To produce a view of the patient that informed and guided locally and temporally relevant clinical decisions, HIV professionals drew on a number of sources within the centres: one system containing patient demographic information, another system containing prescriptions and two more systems primarily including blood results, as well as HIV paper notes - each with different or overlapping parts of patient health information. Multiple systems were used to provide the required functionality in the clinics, but also to allow for privacy options in terms of different access levels between staff. Depending on their role, some would only have access to the system containing demographic information, while others would have access to all systems, having to coordinate the information to be able to provide appropriate care while still protecting patient confidentiality.

The HIV nurse quoted below, provides an example of how she would read the information fragments included within each of the different systems, comparing and contrasting between them to support HIV care:

You look through [System 2] to check the trend of their viral loads, CD4 and if they are for blood tests, which blood tests they need to have and whether they need any other bloods, whether they are immune to hepatitis B or they need a vaccination. Then you check [System 3] as well, to check on a result like their glucose, their NEPs and their full blood count and their liver and kidney to see if they were abnormal last time. And then you check [System 4] for their previous appointment, whether they've been attending and whether they have future appointments because that will determine whether they need more medications or not. Yeah. Whereas [System 2] would have told you when that day was, it's keeping their prescriptions, you know, that you can ask them why did you run out of medications. (HIV Nurse)

Another consultant discussed this as a type of translation process between the interfaces available through the different systems, where each supported the clinical interaction differently, while sometimes information was incongruent and remained at the discretion of the clinician to make sense of the discrepancies:

The interfaces are different and the data I can get about the patient in each place are different and the way you get the data in each system is completely different. There are a few bits with common data in them but on the whole all three are holding different things about patients. The demographics ought to match on a good day but then sometimes the name might be spelt slightly differently or there will be something that isn't quite the same. (HIV Consultant)

Often this process of information discovery and translation of records was not formalised or planned, but depended on the clinicians deciding which aspects of existing record-keeping practices were deemed relevant and important:

It's just very, kind of dependent on a particular clinician knowing and utilising selective bits of each system to find out the whole thing. (HIV Consultant)

Accessing technological systems

Being able to use the different record-keeping systems in the first place required further background work as each system had to be accessed separately using different log-in details. Although designed as security mechanisms, the large number of passwords and the rate with which they changed, meant that in practice they could compromise confidentiality, as they had to be easily remembered or shared to fulfil clinical work, or could compromise medical care, if they posed obstacles even to legitimate access to patient records. As the following clinician notes in relation to the work required for retrieving her details and gaining access to patient information:

[...] I try to impose some human values on it. So I will make sure I've got one password for them but they change their rhythm of passwords at different times, so I've always got three passwords, and I lock myself out regularly because I've put the wrong one in to the wrong system [...] 30% of the time I have to get help to actually log on because I've put in the wrong thing to start me off. (HIV Consultant)

This section discussed how privacy-driven background work was embedded into producing HIV patient trajectories, records and clinical interactions, especially when it came to more intricate and complicated tasks. This work was made necessary in the first place because of the increasingly collaborative nature of HIV care in the context of information sharing restrictions in the two hospitals studied. In essence, articulation work was done to manage the privacy implications of providing multidisciplinary care to patients living with HIV, both within outpatient centres and across the boundaries with other hospital departments.

In turn, this articulation work was also an integral component of sustaining privacy practices specific to HIV care.

INVISIBILITY OF PRIVACY PRACTICES

During fieldwork, health professionals explained how translating the professional ideal of confidentiality in practice was not always straightforward, but was done in silent and invisible ways. Many privacy practices were successful exactly because they were part of background articulation work; they remained largely invisible to patients and often to health professionals outside HIV clinics, yet done in way that communicated the information relevant to accomplish clinical tasks.

Record-keeping

Staff members in the HIV clinics had developed their specific codes to fulfil HIV confidentiality requirements in their record-keeping practices. For example, to be able to easily distinguish paper notes belonging to HIV patients against general sexual health service users, clinics used coloured stickers attached to the front of the notes. Marked HIV paper records where unintelligible to outsiders but still easy to identify by staff members, therefore avoiding confusion between notes when retrieving and classifying folders, while also providing the potential to protect information with higher levels of sensitivity more efficiently by locking them in separate cabinets. Staff members also commented on how they tried to reverse paper records so that the front page containing the patient's name would not be visible, although this seemed much more difficult to achieve in practice.

Clinical consultations

Privacy practices were also invariably performed in clinical interactions with individual patients in ways subject to the discretion of HIV professionals. When clinicians were in the consultation rooms, they communicated with the reception of the HIV centre through an electronic patient list on their computer screen. As soon as a patient attended for their appointment, their name would change colour to inform the clinician that they were waiting to be called in the room. The appointment list, however, included the names of all patients who would be seeing the same clinician on the day. This meant that staff members had to make sure the list was not visible on the screen when the patient entered the room or that it did not appear as they were switching between the different systems to look at patient information:

Then you bring [the patient] in and you sit them down, but they can see all these names [pointing to the patient list on the computer screen]. So it's very important to click on their name only. (Nursing Assistant)

Interacting with other departments

HIV care had to be done even more invisibly in the main hospitals to protect patient confidentiality. This did not only entail bringing together segregated records and aligning medical practices, but also involved how clinicians physically moved and behaved to manage the privacy implications of their recognisability. Many doctors discussed how they turned their identity badges over so that HIV patients on the hospital wards would not feel that they were being stigmatised or to avoid accidental disclosure to relatives or healthcare staff who would be able to see their specialty. One of the consultants described HIV doctors as '*a walking breach of confidentiality*' and explained how they have to be '*alert to what [they] are embodying in what [they] do*'.

Interviewees also referred to the invisibility of privacy practices when discussing how electronic records were discreetly attributed the role of informing health professionals about a patient's HIV status. Due to the fragmented and distributed nature of patient records, patients did not always fully understand what parts of their information were shared and how between clinicians. As one A&E Consultant suggested, many HIV patients presenting to A&E expected the system to inform healthcare staff about their status automatically, especially when it came to treating open wounds and potential transmission risk. In such an open-plan, busy environment patients could find but few opportunities for disclosing sensitive information such as their status. Therefore, technology was attributed the role of discreetly, invisibly articulating sensitive information and essentially protecting patient dignity and confidentiality:

You know the system should have made sure that the staff knew so that they as a patient don't have to worry about always having. They don't like having to announce their status in a, 'I'm a leper kind of way'. They would much rather that the system discreetly informs the staff and that their consultation appeared to be unaffected by this bug. [...] To have to sit there going, 'You need to be careful because I'm infectious', is not a pleasant place. It reinforces a stigma that they would prefer was handled more discreetly. (A&E Consultant)

Another example of privacy practices where information protection was done invisibly relates to blood tests and drug prescriptions. Instead of printing patient names and other identifiable information on the label attached to the blood vials, as was the norm for other hospital departments, HIV clinics used their own unique identifiers. This meant that test results would then return to the HIV clinic through a separate path, rather than be entered on the main hospital system. Drug prescriptions were also printed on paper and delivered to the pharmacy by the patients themselves, instead of being sent electronically as for the rest of hospital patients.

Although this was intended to protect patient confidentiality, it also meant that HIV medical work was less recognised in the rest of the hospital. HIV professionals often narrated cases where paper referrals to other departments were rejected because they had not been sent electronically from the main hospital system. This meant that HIV professionals had to explain their practices and justify the invisibility of their privacy work to other clinicians:

Having the X-ray department sort of ringing us up and saying: 'Oh we can't take pieces of paper, only GPs send us bits of paper.' We said: 'No, no we do as well.' (HIV Consultant)

'Doing' privacy meant that HIV medical work became less visible and subsequently less legitimised when other hospital practices had been streamlined electronically and homogenised through the integration of records on the hospital system. For privacy practices to reinforce HIV-specific confidentiality, however, they needed to be invisible, in the sense of being performed in the background with the agreement of all parties involved. When this agreement broke down, the legitimacy of these practices was questioned. This difference required articulation work to sustain the privacy afforded to HIV patients and to enforce recognition of the circumstances of HIV care.

DISCUSSION

This paper looks at how health professionals working in a collaborative and technologically-mediated context describe the accomplishment of privacy practices. To understand the nuances in their narratives we have employed articulation work as a novel theoretical approach to study privacy. Although articulation work has often been examined in studies of medical work [8, 39, 42], little attention has been paid to how it can elucidate aspects of collaborative privacy practices in healthcare. Privacy studies have not often engaged in empirically driven analysis, while previous work has also tended to view privacy as a consequence or implication, rather than a social and collaborative practice.

This work focuses on HIV health services where multiple confidentiality practices are employed in patient care. With HIV management changing as a result of the long-term nature of the condition, HIV professionals are called to manage the ongoing tensions between treatment and side-effects, co-morbidities and an ageing patient population, medication adherence, drug interactions and resistance, the potential for transmission in HIV pregnancies and late diagnoses. As a result information needs extend beyond the boundaries of HIV clinics, with health professionals in other specialties increasingly required to provide care for HIV patients.

In the interest of 'reconciling incommensurate assumptions and procedures' [16] embedded in historically segregated information practices, health professionals engage in background work to accomplish medical encounters, both within HIV centres and across hospital departments. The articulation work depicted in their narratives does not just relate to the achievement of clinical tasks, but also constitutes privacy work in its own right, as it is done to facilitate collaboration across privacy regimes with the aim to sustain patient confidentiality.

Confidentiality in healthcare settings happened invisibly and silently, as for example when HIV professionals discussed how they made sure their appointment list was not on the computer screen when they saw a patient or how they covered their name badges to avoid disclosure by inference. To paraphrase Suchman [40]: 'the better [privacy] work is done, the less visible it is to those who benefit from it'. Attention to articulation work further points to the difficulties HIV professionals faced when they tried to 'construct an arena of voice' [37] that would make their privacy work recognisable across settings (e.g. getting pharmacy prescriptions or radiology referrals accepted in the main hospital) and to maintain a common information space.

By looking at privacy practices as articulation work, one can begin to understand the nuanced and detailed mechanisms health professionals employ in managing multiple and conflicting confidentiality requirements. This expands our understanding of privacy by taking in account the local contingencies [16] entailed in doing privacy in different contexts and generates further insight into how compromise becomes relevant to make things work from a confidentiality perspective. It also supports the view that privacy practices are not episodic and fragmented, but continuous and interrelated. While often presented as clear-cut ethical requirements, translation in practice requires multiple processes of articulation that require careful disentanglement.

Design implications

Looking at confidentiality practices as articulation work draws attention to the complex ways confidentiality is produced and maintained within record-keeping practices. When composing models of work, it is important to capture the detailed ways through which health professionals translate normative imperatives of confidentiality in practice. Privacy practices done invisibly and silently might be easier to neglect when designing systems to support collaborative work.

In the hospitals studied, existing systems were not able to manage multiple co-existing confidentiality practices as required by HIV specificities (and potentially other conditions). The large number of passwords required and the difficulties logging on to the relevant systems when necessary also created frustrations. As HIV care practices were not adequately supported, health professionals had to engage in increased articulation work to carry out medical tasks while keeping confidentiality in check. This created an ongoing tension between requirements for HIV-specific and general patient confidentiality, which led to negotiations for the integration between the systems used in the HIV clinics and the EPR in the main hospital.

Issues with role-based access control systems and 'all-or-nothing' security controls have also been identified in previous work [e.g. 11]. Although useful in certain situations, these security mechanisms have not yet been developed to the extent that they are able to manage privacy dynamically in response to competing requirements and changing circumstances. A conceptual understanding of privacy as articulation work would allow an in-depth understanding of the mechanisms that facilitate articulation work for confidentiality management while medical tasks are being accomplished.

Instead of introducing rigid mechanisms and homogenising privacy regimes, an alternative would be to work towards understanding and developing information infrastructures with the potential for ambidexterity. This would mean incorporating the capability to handle different degrees of confidentiality (e.g. in the context of HIV health services this would entail HIV-specific and general medical confidentiality). This would accommodate, rather than eradicate, difference for people living with HIV and other conditions, stigmatising or not. Design methodologies should engage with the multiple degrees of confidentiality relevant in medical work for the same patient under different circumstances and acknowledge the articulation work performed as part of and for privacy practices. Privacy enhancing technologies and alternative authentication solutions that embrace the flexibility required in dynamic and collaborative healthcare settings might further support medical work, although their implementation remains slow.

CONCLUSION

This paper examined how confidentiality practices are performed within the information seeking, translation and coordination work conducted to support HIV health services. As a result of historically segregated practices between HIV centres and main hospital departments, clinicians had to engage in articulation work to coordinate privacy practices across different contexts. Even within clinics, background articulation work was necessary to combine information from multiple systems, which were used to provide the required functionality, but also to allow for privacy options. The analysis highlighted how privacy practices are often done invisibly and in the background of clinical tasks. Many of these privacy practices remained largely invisible to patients and often to health professionals outside HIV clinics, yet were done in way that communicated the information relevant to accomplish clinical tasks.

Differences in record-keeping practices, however, meant that HIV medical work was less visible by other specialties in the main hospital, thus becoming less legitimised. We suggest that design methodologies taking better account of privacy as articulation work could allow the development of patient record systems that concurrently support differing privacy needs in different contexts.

ACKNOWLEDGMENTS

The authors would like to thank the AC and the three anonymous reviewers for their constructive comments. We are grateful to those who participated in this research and to the field sites that hosted the project. Unfortunately, they have to remain anonymous for confidentiality reasons. Special thanks to Dr Fadhila Mazanderani for her comments on an early draft of this work. The research was supported by a grant from the UK Engineering and Physical Sciences Research Council as part of the Privacy Value Networks project (EP/G002606/1).

REFERENCES

1. Anderson, J. Ethical issues in relation to HIV care in the UK. *Medicine*, 37, 7 (2009), 330-332.
2. Anderson, R., Brown, I., Dowty, T., Inglesant, P., Heath, W. and Sasse, A. *Database State*. Joseph Rowntree Reform Trust, York, 2009.
3. Bardram, J. E. and Bossen, C. Mobility Work: The Spatial Dimension of Collaboration at a Hospital. *Computer Supported Cooperative Work (CSCW)*, 14, 2 (2005), 131-160.
4. Barkhuus, L. The mismeasurement of privacy: using contextual integrity to reconsider privacy in HCI. *Proc. SIGCHI Human Factors in Computing Systems 2012*, ACM Press (2012), 367-376.
5. Belanger, F. and Crossler, R. E. Privacy in the Digital Age: A Review of Information Privacy Research in Information Systems. *MIS Quarterly*, 35, 4 (2011), 1017-1041.
6. Berg, M. and Bowker, G. The Multiple Bodies of the Medical Record: Toward a Sociology of an Artifact. *The Sociological Quarterly*, 38, 3 (1997), 513-537.
7. Berg, M. The politics of technology: On bringing social theory into technological design. *Science, Technology, & Human Values*, 23, 4 (1998), 456-490.
8. Berg, M. Accumulating and Coordinating: Occasions for Information Technologies in Medical Work. *Computer Supported Cooperative Work (CSCW)*, 8, 4 (1999), 373-401.
9. BHIVA. *Standards of care for people living with HIV 2013*. British HIV Association, London, 2012.
10. Brown, I., Brown, L. and Korff, D. Using NHS Patient Data for Research Without Consent. *Law, Innovation and Technology*, 2, 2 (2010), 219-258.
11. Chen, Y. and Heng, X. Privacy management in dynamic groups: understanding information privacy in medical practices. *Proc. CSCW 2013,* ACM Press (2013), 541-552.
12. Department of Health. *The power of information: Putting all of us in control of the health and care information we need*, London, UK, 2012.

13. Department of Health. *Information: to share or not to share? The Information Governance Review*. London, UK, 2013.
14. Dourish, P. and Anderson, K. Collective Information Practice: Exploring Privacy and Security as Social and Cultural Phenomena. *Human-Computer Interaction*, 21, 3 (2006), 319-342.
15. Gavison, R. Privacy and the Limits of Law. In F.D. Schoeman (Ed.), *Philosophical Dimensions of Privacy*, Cambridge University Press (1984), Cambridge, 364-404.
16. Gerson, E. M. and Star, S. L. Analyzing due process in the workplace. *ACM Transactions on Information Systems (TOIS)*, 4, 3 (1986), 257-270.
17. Gutwirth, S. *Privacy and the Information Age*. Rowman & Littlefield Publishers, Oxford, 2002.
18. Health Protection Agency. *HIV in the United Kingdom: 2013 Report*. Health Protection Services, London, 2013.
19. Heath, C. and Luff, P. Collaboration and control - Crisis management and multimedia technology in London Underground Line Control Rooms. *Computer Supported Cooperative Work (CSCW)*, 1, 1-2 (1992), 69-94.
20. Hope, R. A., Hope, T., Savulescu, J. and Hendrick, J. *Medical ethics and law: the core curriculum*. Churchill Livingstone/Elsevier, London, 2008.
21. Marx, G. T. Murky conceptual waters: The public and the private. *Ethics and Information Technology*, 3, 3 (2001), 157-169.
22. Mazanderani, F. and Brown, I. *Privacy as a Practice: Exploring the Relational and Spatial Dynamics of HIV-Related Information Seeking*. Springer, City, 2011.
23. Murphy, A. R., Madhu, C. R. and Heng, X. Privacy practices in collaborative environments: a study of emergency department staff. *Proc CSCW and Social Computing 2014,* ACM Press (2014), 269-282.
24. Nissenbaum, H. *Privacy in Context: Technology, Policy and the Integrity of Social Life*. Stanford University Press, Stanford, California, 2010.
25. ONC. *Connecting Health and Care for the Nation: A Ten Year Vision to Achieve Interoperable Health IT Infrastructure*. The Office of the National Coordinator for Health Information Technology, 2014.
26. Palen, L. and Dourish, P. Unpacking 'privacy' for a networked world. *Proc. SIGCHI Human factors in computing systems,* ACM Press (2003), 129-136.
27. Pavlou, P. A. State of the Information Privacy Literature: Where Are We Now and Where Should We Go? *MIS Quarterly*, 35, 4 (2011), 977-988.
28. Rindfleisch, T. C. Privacy, Information Technology, and Health Care. *Communications of the ACM*, 40, 8 (1997), 93-100.
29. Schmidt, K. and Bannon, L. Taking CSCW Seriously: Supporting Articulation Work. *Computer Supported Cooperative Work*, 1(1992), 7–40.
30. Selwyn, P. A. and Forstein, M. Overcoming the False Dichotomy of Curative vs Palliative Care for Late-Stage HIV/AIDS. *JAMA: The Journal of the American Medical Association*, 290, 6 (2003), 806-814.
31. Sheather, J. and Brannan, S. Patient confidentiality in a time of care.data. *BMJ*, 347(2013).
32. Sheller, M. and Urry, J. Mobile Transformations of 'Public' and 'Private' Life. *Theory, Culture & Society*, 20, 3 (2003), 107-125.
33. Siegel, K. and Lekas, H.-M. AIDS as a chronic illness: psychosocial implications. *AIDS*, 16 (2002), S69-S76.
34. Smith, H. J., Milberg, S. J. and Burke, S. J. Information Privacy: Measuring Individuals' Concerns about Organizational Practices. *MIS Quarterly*, 20, 2 (1996), 167-196.
35. Smith, H. J., Dinev, T. and Xu, H. Information Privacy Research: An Interdisciplinary Review. *MIS Quarterly*, 35, 4 (2011), 989-1015.
36. Solove, D. J. *Understanding Privacy*. Harvard University Press, Cambridge, 2008.
37. Star, S. L. and Strauss, A. Layers of silence, arenas of voice: The ecology of visible and invisible work. *Computer Supported Cooperative Work*, 8, 1-2 (1999), 9-30.
38. Stewart, K. A. and Segars, A. H. An Empirical Examination of the Concern for Information Privacy Instrument. *Information Systems Research*, 13, 1 (2002), 36-49.
39. Strauss, A. L., Fagerhaugh, S., Suczek, B. and Wiener, C. *Social Organization of Medical Work*. Transaction Publishers, New Brunswick, 1997.
40. Suchman, L. A. Supporting articulation work. In R. Kling (Ed.), *Computerization and Controversy: Value Conflicts and Social Choices*. Academic Press (1996), London, 407-423.
41. The Antiretroviral Therapy Cohort Collaboration Life expectancy of individuals on combination antiretroviral therapy in high-income countries: a collaborative analysis of 14 cohort studies. *The Lancet*, 372, 9635 (2008), 293-299.
42. Vikkelsø, S. Subtle redistribution of work, attention and risks: Electronic patient records and organisational consequences. *Scandinavian Journal of Information Systems*, 17, 1 (2005), 3-30.
43. Westin, A. *Privacy and freedom*. Atheneum, New York, 1967.
44. Ziebland, S. and McPherson, A. Making sense of qualitative data analysis: an introduction with illustrations from DIPEx (personal experiences of health and illness). *Medical Education*, 40, 5 (2006), 405-414.

Designing for Discomfort: Supporting Critical Reflection through Interactive Tools

Helen Halbert
The iSchool @ UBC
University of British Columbia
Vancouver, CA V6T 1Z1
helenhalbert@gmail.com

Lisa P. Nathan
The iSchool @ UBC
University of British Columbia
Vancouver, CA V6T 1Z1
lisa.nathan@ubc.ca

ABSTRACT
A focus of human-computer interaction work and a central principle of user experience is that design should avoid discomfort and aim to craft positive experiences for individuals. However, for contexts in which an uncomfortable reaction is intended, instrumental, or indeed inevitable, we recognize that it is inappropriate to design for a positive or "feel good" experience. Herein we describe an investigation into the use of interactive technologies to support transformative learning, a process through which individuals engage with feelings of discomfort. The project is grounded by work with graduate students enrolled in a course that employed decolonizing pedagogies. Throughout the course students responded to uncomfortable, problematic scenarios through interactive tools. We present our analysis of students' learning experiences, their interactions with technologies and their reflections on the effectiveness of these engagements in terms of supporting opportunities for critical reflection, a crucial stage of the transformative learning process.

Author Keywords
design; negative affect; critical reflection; decolonization

ACM Classification Keywords
K.4.2 [Computing Milieux]: Computers and Society---Social Issues; H.5.2 [Information Interfaces and Presentation]: User Interfaces---theory and methods

INTRODUCTION
A focus of the human-computer interaction (HCI) work and a central principle of user experience (UX) is that design should avoid discomfort and aim to craft positive experiences for individuals [21]. As stated by Hassenzahl and Tractinsky in their framing of UX research within HCI,

CSCW 2015, March 14–18, 2015, Vancouver, BC, Canada.

ACM 978-1-4503-2922-4/15/03…$15.00.
http://dx.doi.org/10.1145/2675133.2675162

"To prevent frustration and dissatisfaction had always been a core objective even of the most cognitively driven perspective on HCI. What is new in UX research is a focus on positive emotional outcomes such as joy, fun and pride" ([21], p.93). However, for contexts in which a negative reaction is intended, instrumental, or indeed inevitable, we recognize that it is inappropriate to engineer a positive or "feel good" experience for the user. HCI scholars are beginning to conduct empirical work within such contexts (e.g., the de-gamification of military technologies [23], post-genocide reconciliation [36,49]. In addition, a generative body of work is exposing the assumptions behind dominant HCI research paradigms, advocating for a decentering of the field and engaging critically with the diversity of human experience (e.g., [3,5,6,16,24]). Drawing inspiration from these scholars, we set out to explore the context of discomfort that arises when people engage with societal tensions that are systematic and intergenerational (e.g., colonization) rather than contained and confined by an interaction.

In this paper we describe a blended graduate level seminar course that employed decolonizing pedagogies—philosophies, teaching practices and tools with an aim to "create a sense of the complexity of colonial oppression and how it is systematically exercised" ([25], p.124). We introduce the theory of transformative learning and describe how we applied this lens to our project. We present our analysis of students' learning experiences, their interactions with select educational technologies and their reflections on the effectiveness of these engagements in terms of supporting opportunities for critical reflection.

The goal of the research was to investigate the potential and pitfalls of incorporating interactive technologies into the transformative learning process, through which individuals engage with feelings of discomfort, stress, and uncertainty leading to significant change in perspective. The work is informed by scholarship that explores the reciprocal, intertwined nature of technological engagements (e.g. [30,48]). Our work does not provide a decontextualized functional analysis of tool features. Rather we engage the socio-cultural contexts and histories that mediate and are mediated through technological practice. In summary, our major contributions include:

- Articulating the need for ethically grounded studies of discomfort and negative affect;
- An example of investigating difficult-to-quantify dimensions of human experience and ongoing processes (e.g. decolonization);
- The theoretical grounding and pragmatic examples of extending interactive system design to include negative affect;
- An initial set of criteria for system affordances that encourage the process of transformative learning, including shared practices of critical reflection; ideologically- and emotionally-contextualized information discovery; slowing down; liminal space; and communication backchannels
- Scholarship that acknowledges human diversity and the risks of generalizing (neutralizing) the term *user experience*.

LEARNING, NEGATIVE EMOTION AND DESIGN

The concept of transformative learning, first developed by sociologist Jack Mezirow, is often understood and referred to as perspective transformation: "the process of becoming critically aware of how and why our presuppositions have come to constrain the way we perceive, understand, and feel about our world; of reformulating these assumptions to permit a more inclusive, discriminating, permeable, and integrative perspective; and of making decisions or otherwise acting on these new perspectives" ([33], p.14).

According to Mezirow's theory, the multi-step process is first triggered by a disorienting dilemma resulting from a disconnect between one's understanding of the world and one's own concept of self. Yet, at this point instead of minimizing mental discomfort as predicted by theories from information science, psychology, and communication studies (e.g., information avoidance, cognitive dissonance, and selective exposure [10,51]), individuals engaged in transformative learning are willing to prolong a state of internal inconsistency.

Scholars across the social sciences have extended Mezirow's work, interrogating the experiences of transformative learning (also termed *pedagogies of discomfort*) [50] through anti-oppressive frameworks (including anti-racist, anti-classist, anti-sexist/feminist, and others critical of expressions of oppression). Upsetting emotions such as denial, contempt, and guilt are commonly experienced, but there is also potential for the negative to foster constructive dialogue, encourage action and allyship, and improve individual self-esteem through increased awareness and mindfulness [41,43].

The theory is not without critiques. The body of research tends to center on the educational benefits for individuals newly encountering dissonance between their understanding of the world and their concept of self. We note that for marginalized people who regularly experience systemic oppressive forces there are different concerns:

- The experience of 'uncomfortable content' (e.g., racist, classist, sexist, transphobic, heterosexist systems or attitudes) is likely daily and ongoing;
- It is never a question of 'willingness' to be subjected to or to prolong mental or emotional discomfort;
- Further exposing oneself to disturbing perspectives does not have the same 'transformative' potential. It can be harmful if threatening to the process of healing and taxing to the human psyche [18];
- Educating others of their "difference" [31] is another burden along with having to find information and perspectives that agree with their own (e.g. seeking a virtual community to experience "a 'presence' that is denied elsewhere ([34], p. 492).

In short, we agree with de jesus: a theory that posits exposing individuals to uncomfortable perspectives as categorically *good* suggests that we are (once again) taking on the perspective of people with privilege [12]. The balance of harms and benefits is complex and nuanced. Yet, for the context in which we situated this work (discussed below), the benefits appear well worth pursuing, albeit cautiously. Ongoing initiatives suggest that developing compassion and understanding often leads to some level of healing and perhaps reconciliation, even for survivors of past harm and those experiencing ongoing oppression (e.g., the work of Canada's Aboriginal Healing Foundation and the Indian Residential School Survivors Association).

Although researchers and designers have started to engage the role of discomfort in UX through work in serious games [32], adversarial interactions [4,13], and in developing the overall concept of engagement [38] the dominant approach is to engineer experiences which are intended to be engrossing and entertaining for the user (e.g., an impossibly difficult video game). It remains a challenge for those who endeavour to "confront participants with difficult decisions involving culturally challenging issues" ([4],p. 2009) to avoid approaches that frame the experiential as episodic, contained and confined by the interaction. It is common for scholars to articulate interaction as a contained experience to be manipulated, with rising action (building suspense); climax (the moment of discomfort); falling action (release of tension); and dénouement (post-experience reminiscence and retelling) [4]. This is problematic when addressing societal tensions that are often systematic, intergenerational and ongoing [18], often unaddressed in the final design.

In this project we are studying design for mediation (a *process* of listening and reflection) rather than agitation (a *state* of provocation). We take into consideration scholarship that explores the role of systems and settings—including discussion boards, content recommendation platforms, user anonymity, and collaborative editing software (e.g., [7,15,28,37,38,44])—in fostering dialogue or listening, encouraging reflection or empathy, supporting learning and engagement in situations of discomfort (i.e., unfamiliar and intimidating environments), and enabling perspective transformation. However, we view tool engagement as an evolving practice that is influenced by the diversity of experiences, levels of awareness, group identities, and backgrounds of our participants along with the broad socio-technical context [16,24].

Most broadly, our research investigates how technological practice can support engagement in contexts, circumstances, or interactions that are likely to provoke uncomfortable or distressing responses. Our inquiry frames a series of generative research questions: What socio-technical practices show promise for facilitating the experience of negative emotion and scaffolding the transformative learning process? What interaction challenges face those who wish to support engagement in contexts of negative affect? In what ways can interaction design support the process of critical reflection?

ETHICAL PRACTICE: QUESTIONS OF ACTION

A significant challenge for this project was determining an appropriate context to conduct the work. We wanted to ensure that individuals were informed about the potential for discomfort before participation. We conducted the study with graduate students at the University of British Columbia enrolled in an elective class entitled "Information Practice and Protocol in Support of Indigenous Initiatives". We argue that through the description of the course (see Box 1), students who enrolled were aware that course material, assignments, and discussions might prove uncomfortable. Through this approach we hoped to alert anyone who had experience negotiating oppressive frameworks so she or he could avoid additional harms exposure to views expressed in this course might inflict. Students were told about the study and provided with copies of the consent form during the first class meeting by a third party. The instructor was not present. Students were asked to sign consent forms after the course was over. At that time they were better positioned to provide informed consent concerning the use of their data.

A second concern for the project was that the co-leads for the project are non-Indigenous scholars. Neither of us claim to hold or represent Indigenous perspectives. However, as settlers in Canada working with Indigenous colleagues on Indigenous initiatives, we have direct experience with discomfort, negative affect, critical reflection and the transformative learning process. Marginalized peoples do not bear the sole responsibility for inquiries that address bias, oppression and racism.

METHODOLOGY

Mezirow's theory begins with the *experience of discomfort*. It is the first stage in the transformative learning process [8]. Many studies have indicated that the second major stage labeled *critical reflection*—more so than any other—is essential to the transformative learning process [8,33,44]. Though many experience negative emotions when confronted with materials that question their assumptions and worldviews, only those who critically engage with the feelings and question the premises that underlie these assumptions and worldviews (i.e., critical reflection [44] p. 186), develop the foundations necessary for perspective transformation.

Researchers of transformative learning acknowledge the difficulty of quantifying and measuring the process; there is, however, consensus that perspective transformation is a long-term and gradual, incremental process [7,8,15,44], with some work suggesting that the incidence of and capacity for transformation increases with time [8].

Course Goals:

This course prepares students to work effectively with Indigenous peoples, communities and organizations in support of ongoing developments in Indigenous culture and languages, self-government, treaty negotiation and litigation. Processes of information creation, sharing, storage, access and use within the information professions can support and/or negate these initiatives. Students will engage with the knowledge traditions, histories, government policies, and litigation that influence contemporary practice and protocols that shape interactions between Indigenous peoples and information systems. Students will develop an appreciation for the range of Indigenous and settler perspectives on information-related topics including: intellectual property; repatriation; knowledge; knowledge organization; orality; and the digitization of cultural heritage. At the end of the course, students will be positioned to undertake experiential learning opportunities within Indigenous-oriented information organizations, including but not limited to libraries, archives and cultural centres.

Please note: Students are welcomed from widely varied backgrounds. Some students are of Indigenous heritage, well aware of contemporary Indigenous issues and interests and the ongoing influence of colonization. Other students are unfamiliar with Indigenous perspectives and alternate histories of colonization...Students are expected to reflect on these differences while engaging with course materials and interacting with their colleagues.

Box 1

In this study, we sought to avoid getting caught up in decisions of who among our participants had already been 'decolonized'. Instead of seeking to verify individual students' transformative learning process or corroborate their judgments of whether they were undergoing transformative learning, our interest was on investigating the ways in which practices, mediated through interactive tools, can contribute to critical reflection.

Students were assigned six problematic scenarios to read and respond to at six different points in the term. Each scenario highlighted discriminatory, yet standard, information and/or archival situations. Box 2 provides one example, a session description from a regional library conference. It is a real world example of information professionals framing oral culture as a "lesser than" (and detrimental, backward) way of being. Members of a regional Indigenous information professional interest group shared the examples that we used as the scenarios. Reading, discussing and responding to the scenarios provided opportunities for discomfort for our participants, students in the process of adopting identities as information professionals.

PROBLEMATIC SITUATION #4

You are an active member of your regional professional librarian association; you've served on the conference committee in the past and still contribute your time to the peer-review process to review and recommend papers and submissions. You eagerly look forward to the program every year and while flipping through your pre-conference information package you notice the following session description:

"Can We Talk? Bridging the Gap between Oral Culture and Print Culture"

Oral culture orientation is a main determinant of poverty. This session will focus on how to assist oral culture individuals in gaining the print culture skills necessary to be successful in their own and their family's education. When family members have the skills and the confidence to master print culture skills they can be their child's first and best teacher. Find out how libraries can help to bridge that gap between oral and print culture.

How do you react?

Box 2.

For each scenario they were asked to respond using the private journal (student/instructor only), discussion board (full class), or group wiki (small group access). Journal entries were private, only the student posting to her/his journal and the instructor could view these entries. Discussion board entries were posted by and viewable to all students. Group wikis were editable and viewable by groups of 3 or 4 students. The tools were all part of the Blackboard 9.0 learning management system (LMS). This LMS is provided, endorsed and supported by our university. Ethical and legal concerns related to student privacy, data security and access were (partly) addressed by this choice.

Each tool was assigned twice. The tools offered students a different range of functionality through which to develop a response when viewed from private-public, individualistic-collective, and rhetorical-discursive continuums. We did not seek to contrast the use of the three tools with each other; rather we focused upon how students used the different tools to support a particular type of pedagogical tool (the scenarios) in a specific context.

Engagements with and through the LMS were designed to complement other course activities (readings, short films, lectures, trips to Indigenous-oriented libraries, museums and resource centres) and in-class discussions. In the last three weeks of the class, students contributed to a series of participatory-design-inspired workshops during which they were encouraged to reflect on, critique, imagine, and "mock up" interactions that support critical reflection leading to transformative learning. The workshops were envisioned as an inclusive and collaborative design space with students as learning technology stakeholders [14, 35]. The workshops provided opportunities for students to further contribute to the research by considering other interactive systems outside of our initial selection. Through the application of participatory design methodologies, we sought to minimize the potential for information avoidance, disengagement, and self-censorship within the specific context of transformative learning, engaging uncomfortable content in the classroom. Our intention was that by taking on the role of designers, students would be prompted to imagine and consider a plurality of perspectives, be provided more distance for reflection on the transformative learning process than they would as just "users", and would feel empowered to speak authoritatively, informed by their direct experiences engaging with course content.

ANALYSIS

Once grades were submitted for the course the authors gained access to student consent forms and learned that all 11 students agreed to let us include their course submissions and engagements in the project. For this paper our data set consists of students' responses to the 6 problematic situations (22 individual journal posts, 8 collaborative wiki posts, 2 discussion threads with submissions from all 11 students, 11 written reflections of the design workshop reflections). The workshop reflections included discussions of students' experiences with the course, its content, and activities. We took into account quantitative measurements available through contemporary LMS (e.g. number of posts, page view count, time on page), but do not explore these substantively.

We used grounded theory methods as developed by Charmaz [11] to conduct qualitative content analysis of our data via the online analysis tool Dedoose. Charmaz articulates well the controversy over drawing upon existing theory in grounded theory research ([11], pp.305-310). Our iterative analysis benefitted greatly from multiple passes through transformative learning scholarship. Specifically, we draw the reader's attention to Table 1, which is linked to our review of relevant literature. We used the table to first hypothesize whether we would find evidence of tool use supporting aspects of critical reflection in responses to the scenarios [20]. We returned to the table throughout our analysis to help articulate disconnects between what we expected and what emerged from the interactions. These discussions were generative in developing our themes.

Critical Reflection Activity	Evidenced in Literature		
	Board	Journal	Wiki
Writing as externalization of thought [15, 44]	●	●	●
Socio-communicative exchange (vs. an individual activity) [7, 15, 28, 44]	●		●
Space for collaborative sense-making (i.e. with opportunities for debate, dialogue, agreement, confrontation, negotiation) [7, 15, 28, 44]	●		●
Consensus-oriented [28]			●
Access to information subjective norms (i.e. implicit primers and/or framing for response provided by others) [7, 8, 15, 28, 44]	●		●
Full or partial anonymity possible with response [37]	●		❍
Non-public channels for participation and contribution (e.g. from lurking to liking) [28, 37]	●		❍
Group identification process [7, 44]	❍		●
Asynchronous communication [15]	●		❍
Accountability, autonomy and individual ownership of ideas and actions [7, 15, 28, 44]	❍	●	

Table 1: Critical Reflection Activities in Context

● Evidence that tool use in context strongly afforded the critical reflection activity

❍ Evidence that tool use in context partially affords the critical reflection activity

FINDINGS

Based on the analysis introduced above, we are positioned to discuss themes drawn from: 1) participants' reported reasoning in response to the problematic scenarios (i.e. their statements regarding the modeling of and strategies for engagement, and awareness of social and professional norms); 2) participants' reflections on technology use (including opinions and evaluations of the different tools); and 3) participants' technological use (i.e. their behaviour as evidenced through their technology interactions).

In the following subsections we introduce and expand upon themes that emerged from students' engagements with and through the different tools and their reflections on these engagements: negotiating a professional response; mediating information; the role of time; and qualities of space. We use italics to indicate direct quotations from students' responses.

Negotiating A Professional Response

Frequently students responded to uncomfortable comments, insensitive requests, or offensive viewpoints, by first suggesting that these were a result of an unfortunate but accidental choice of wording or an outdated policy that had no real bearing on standard, contemporary organizational practice. Lack of information was also cited as leading to the situations described in the problematic scenarios. GG noted that oppression and paternalism emerge "*most often from very well intentioned people armed with a great deal of misinformation.*"

Given that our participants were aspiring information professionals, articulations of tolerance are not surprising. Often participants referred to professional norms or quoted directly from the American Library Association's core competencies of librarianship. CC's contribution underscored the professional stance of not lecturing patrons on "*the appropriateness of their views*" and HH described the job of a librarian as someone who helped "*patrons find information in a friendly and non-judgmental way…no matter how culturally insensitive*" [the request].

These statements advocating tolerance and expressing a willingness to presume good intentions on behalf of others persisted even when participants reported negative affect (e.g., hurt, dismay, or offense) in reaction to a scenario, such as when PG viewed part of a scenario description as deliberately racist yet still did not "*want to assume that in an initial assessment*". For MW, this was related to perspective taking; while a scenario could be interpreted offensively—a patron or colleague showing a callous attitude—"*a more positive outlook is that* [the patron or colleague] *is simply not aware.*" Similarly, EE thought one should strive "*to see such encounters more as opportunities for polite, good-humoured, 'information-added' education.*"

Some participants noted that the ability to exercise tolerance was often related to an individual's emotional awareness, particularly in contexts of negative affect when potential triggers and strong emotions could overpower or interfere with the ability to approach situations tolerantly. For example, to PG, it was important to be "*aware of my initial reaction in order to respond … in a respectful and appropriate manner*" and mindful of the need to "*take more time to consider the situation and to look at where it comes from.*" The limits of emotional awareness for sustaining perspective taking and open-mindedness in the context of negative affect are worth noting. As previously mentioned with respect to de jesus' writings, in these contexts an extra burden is placed on those who frequently experience oppressive forces and there is little to entice such individuals to engage. In fact, there are many discouraging factors, for example, past experiences that have eroded one's ability to give others the benefit of the doubt.

Mediating Information: Objectivity, criticality and plurality

Drawing upon previous encounters to interpret events and determine the validity of new information is just one of multiple strategies used for making sense of our world [33]

as well as a key teaching of information literacy instruction [1]. Participants in our study often proposed several courses of action in response to scenarios dependent upon what they knew about the precise characteristics of the individuals (e.g. their level of expertise with a topic, their cultural identity, any invested interests or biases, etc.) involved and the broader context of the situation.

Information—understood here as documents and resources regarded as authoritative, but also 'facts' considered common knowledge and conventional wisdom—was also used as a tool for thinking through and formulating responses to scenarios. Given the emotionally charged and at times polarizing nature of the scenarios, some participants viewed information as a mediator and aspired to "let the facts speak for themselves" when possible.

For example, in reaction to a scenario on the use of the word genocide to describe the government of Canada's treatment of Aboriginal peoples, many participants cited, and relied on, the UN's definition in drafting their responses. Here information was deployed as an intermediary, neutral platform of expression and voicing disagreement with others by making it clear that the source of disagreement was not personal grounds, but factual ones; BB stated "*the best, and most diplomatic way to stand up to the Federal Government [was] to cite the UN.*"

While this may seem a reasonable approach to responding to the scenario, and, according to communication theory such as non-violent communication, can be a powerful strategy for fostering constructive dialogue [40], in certain contexts, information could become viewed as objective and indisputable—by the same information professionals who were acutely aware of the biases and prejudices that seep into the construction of knowledge.

As previously mentioned, many participants' comments suggested that it was lack of accurate information which stood in the way of perspective transformation or more inclusive and less discriminatory opinions among others. In our study, information was readily invoked by participants in times of uncertainty and while discussing contentious and complicated issues. For example, to return to the political use of the term genocide in Canada, AE's comment on the matter was that the "*United Nations Office of the Special Adviser on the Prevention of Genocide lays out a pretty black and white definition*"—suggesting that the issue described in the scenario was also clear-cut.

While information can serve as a necessary scaffold for thought and frame of reference for those experiencing uncertainty and discomfort, it can also yield to reductionist thinking. Exercising plurality in opinion was a challenge for participants, as was the ability to hold, and honour, different perspectives at one time.

The Roles of Time

While EE wondered if the challenge of pluralism was caused by a pervasive "*sense of there being one right answer*" which could "*inhibit full exploration of the complexities of some issues*," our data suggests that there were other factors at play too, including time.

We believe such an effect would be especially pronounced in a context of classroom behaviour and graded assignments, and, in particular, would manifest in the wiki assignments, which were designed as collaborative activities for participants who had to develop one scenario response per small group rather than an individual response (as was the case for the journal and discussion board).

We anticipated that the wiki assignments would provide interesting insights into the process and practices of consensus building, and would prove more of a challenge for our participants in comparison to the activity of responding as just an individual to problematic scenarios. However, we learned that many participants viewed the wiki as a tool that privileged consensus, or the appearance thereof, over acknowledging diverse perspectives among participants. EE was of the opinion that an orientation towards collective agreement and collaboration from the onset could result in consensus being "*too easily achieved.*" Despite our expectations that the wiki would encourage the debate and negotiation of ideas, for participants "*there did not seem strong enough motivation to put forward what might seem a weird, negative, or even contrarian perspective.*"

Consensus building practices were related to the time constraints of coursework and the pressures to produce work within a short timeframe. Some participants reported a practice of agreeing with the group's direction in order to get an assignment finished and submitted. Even DD— who enjoyed the wiki format, preferred it over the other tools used during the study, and thought it allowed students to "*collaborate to form one answer that is greater than the sum of its parts*"—was aware that the "*process forced some ... opinions and thoughts to be discarded in the final response.*" Not all agreed there was not enough time, however; AE thought the two weeks was "*too long to have the wiki 'open'*" as no one even bothered to participate until the second week. AE acknowledged this was likely because "*everyone works on different schedules*" depending on their other commitments (shifts at work, assignment deadlines for other classes, etc.).

For EE, the time constraints made it difficult to have "*organic*" sharing and sense-making processes or create circumstances under which all members of a group could contribute "*in a relaxed, confiding way.*" When contributions from all members were incorporated in a final group response, the process was not always done in a considerate or consultatory manner, and participants saw their words misused or ideas misrepresented. There was neither enough time for all group members to state their opinions or for the group to come up with an approach that was inclusive, if not fully representative, of all ideas.

Time can also have an important effect on an individual's critical reflection processes, including their formulation of ideas, and development or evolution of perspectives. As previously mentioned, taking the necessary time to emotionally and mentally refuel and recharge can be critical for those processing disturbing and upsetting content and mediating the experience of negative emotion.

In contrast to the wiki, the journal and discussion tools provided better support for these needs and the practice of taking time for reflection. DD appreciated the asynchronous nature of these technologies and found it helpful for engaging more deeply with class content, especially sensitive material; compared to face-to-face interactions and in-class discussions, "*the opportunity to think about one's response and conduct some quick background research before hitting 'submit' [was] certainly an advantage*." EE also noted the benefits of having access to other people's comments on the discussion board over the course of a week, as well as the value of reading and reflecting on "*what other people were thinking*" before crafting and posting a response of your own.

This relationship between time and the process of critical reflection is also found in the literature on transformative learning. Specifically, it reinforces Taylor's finding of the "significance of having time to reflect" for transformative learning during asynchronous, online interactions ([44], p. 182). Similarly comments by participants in Boyer's study of transformative learning in online settings reflect on the value of having "time away" ([7], p. 348) from an onslaught of negative emotions be it panic, sadness, or self-doubt.

Space: Safe, Marginalized, Liminal, Shared, Delineated

The idea of having time away from a system and its content also echoes sentiments from participants on the importance of creating space.

For the participatory design activities, students worked in small groups to develop strategies for both physical facilities and virtual systems. One group planned an online portal for teachers to access the resources of the National Research Centre (NRC) for the Truth and Reconciliation Commission of Canada and discover materials for teaching and learning about the residential school system. CC described how their group strived to keep the "*emotional well being (of teachers, students, parents) at the forefront of our discussions*" and emphasized on "*laying the groundwork for establishing a safe and respectful environment in which to discuss [the] difficult subjects*" related to this recent chapter of Canadian history. This was envisioned through featuring information on available health services to support any trauma experienced by engaging with the content. Design considerations also included deliberate liminal spaces intended "*for preparatory interactions with students, parents, and colleagues*" that would provide an emotional buffer and precede users' access to the NRC's resources.

Another group, that deliberated on the physical gallery/exhibit space that would house digital access points to the NRC's online systems, had a similar approach. FF also described how the priority of supporting the well being of visitors led to the design of exits stationed throughout that would "*allow [visitors] to remove themselves into another space where they can reflect and recover from the potentially hurtful information being displayed*." As well as having multiple exits, the group also designed different entry points in order to accommodate visitors of different backgrounds, knowledge, interest, and levels of engagement with the NRC.

In addition to space away, i.e. necessary mind space for emotional processing and reflection, safe space [43] that is "free of manipulation, coercion, and so on" has been identified as an important precursor for constructive dialogue and the transformative learning process ([17], p. 269) which is often characterized by moments of uncertainty and vulnerability. "Safe space" can mean different things to different people (e.g. in the context of our university, it refers to respectful and supportive environments for lesbian, gay, bisexual, queer, transgender, two-spirited and intersex persons); in this paper, we use "safe space" to refer to learning environments that foster trust (e.g. the feeling that others acknowledge and listen to your ideas) as well as support (e.g. the feeling that you can voice your ideas and that others will/can recognize you are in a place of learning and there is room for making mistakes). We do not mean a place where everyone (i.e. everyone who has privilege) is entitled to *not* having to feel discomfort so that voices of dissent (i.e. voices of those without privilege) are either silenced "under the pretence that it makes [others] feel 'unsafe'" ([46], p. 160) or else gentrified to become more palatable forms of discourse [41].

With regards to our participants' experiences throughout the class, it is unclear whether "safe space" was adequately conveyed or provided by the design of the course.

EE believed "*the combination of different modes [of communication] was especially effective*," adding that having to reply to problematic scenarios through discussion board "*postings would have been inhibitory ... had they not been combined with the smaller group experience*." However, MW noted that overall "*it was a bizarrely untalkative class all semester*," even noting that during brainstorming activities – which were part of the participatory workshops and designed to encourage collaboration – "*few people seemed comfortable discussing anyone else's suggestions*." This was also reflected in the class' use of the discussion board tool, which for the most part was used by individuals to post one-off comments, rather than replies to other threads or to engage in back-and-forth conversations.

While it is tempting to conclude this was entirely due to the uncomfortable or challenging nature of the course material, we think the classroom environment also played a large role in shaping participants' expectations and understandings of how to use the different tools in the learning management system. Students mentioned how engagements with course tools were influenced by the motivation to do well in the course and earn a satisfactory grade or participation credits. AE pointed out that *if* the instructor had explicitly indicated that posts in response to someone else's post would still 'count' as a submitted assignment, more students would have been encouraged to "*create more of a discussion instead of just writing their response and putting it up in the discussion board*."

Similarly, there is evidence that use of the wiki was influenced by participants' desire to demonstrate their contributions to this collaborative space. Unlike the popular MediaWiki platform used by Wikipedia, the Blackboard wiki did not provide participants a detailed breakdown of revisions for shared workspaces beyond who had last edited a page. They took significant steps to accomplish this, either by using horizontal lines and different coloured fonts to indicate authorship or through meta-commenting—explicitly stating what they had changed (some even elected to use discussion boards for collaboration and then migrate finished content over to the wiki).

Interactions with other students in the class proved influential in participants' learning experiences. Final reflections from participants suggested that for some, the actions of other students in the class at times detracted from their experiences with course content, as well as the creation of a safe space. Interestingly, this was not restricted to a difference in opinions or problematic comments voiced in class or online, but extended to attitudes, efforts, and the perceived commitments of other students to their learning. For example, a student expressed disappointment with facilitating a discussion on a topic for which many had not done the assigned reading. The final reflections from some of the participants suggested there was a lack of trust among students; more than one participant reflected how the use of online tools seemed to undermine accountability for group work, and expressed scepticism of other students' claims of technical difficulties, seeing it instead as an easy excuse for avoiding work. Additional communication, even to the point of redundancy, would have been welcome in instances such as when AE was left waiting more than a week for group members to reply or when PG's wiki response was never commented on or edited.

RECOMMENDATIONS: SCAFFOLDING EXPLORATION AND DEVELOPMENT

The recommendations section is structured in the form of a narrative rather than compartmentalized, quickly scannable bullet points or a requirements checklist. We use italics to emphasize short form recommendations within the broader framing. Our choice of structure is integral to our content and will be expanded upon at the end of the section. For now, we encourage readers to go through the text slowly, deeply and reflectively and to avoid surface scanning.

We begin by addressing the influence of identity processes and politics on our participants' capacity for exercising tolerance, open-mindedness, and emotional awareness, qualities underpinning sustained engagement in contexts of negative affect and contributing to critical reflection.

In our study, the most relevant identity politics were those related to the information profession. In framing their responses to problematic scenarios, our participants drew from their knowledge of professional norms; their actions were shaped by their understandings of their roles as professionals. We acknowledge this to be a factor of our research design; however, we believe it is applicable to the general design of virtual systems, which are shaped by the existing practices of a community of users.

Technologies mediate practices—this is a foundational tenet of HCI research—but can also challenge or enhance facets of identity [29] and contribute to the development or expression of new ones [34]. A specialist system for disrupting, de-biasing, and decolonizing standard information professional practice would vary considerably from a system designed for a different profession; however, design approaches that *seek to create a shared identity of critical reflection and respectful dialogue among all users of a system* are not only platform-agnostic but can be of equal value to diverse communities. In addition to the positive effect a shared identity can have on cooperation, interpersonal relations, and conflict resolution [22], previous research on online communities recognizes the *opportunity for platform rules, policies, and user agreements to contribute to the development of a shared identity intertwined with shared practices* [9]. While we appreciate the critiques that approaches such as Adversarial Design [13] apply to consensus-based, community-oriented processes, we argue that it is critical to *do more than give voice to dissent. Contentious voices and actions need to be heard.* We saw evidence of frustration followed by disengagement when participants felt ignored or dismissed by their colleagues (concerns articulated but unheard). We believe influencing practice through design has the potential to minimize these types of frustrations.

In particular, we view the application of community code of conducts and anti-harassment policies—such as those adopted by conferences and open source projects like Code4Lib and Django—as strong examples of how to *convey the values and communicate the expectations of using a system and participating on a platform while also creating a culture of critical reflection.* According to the Ada Initiative, an organization that supports women in open technology and culture, an effective code of conduct will: List specific common behaviours that are not okay; Include detailed directions for reporting violations; Have a defined and documented complaint handling process [2].

Effective code of conducts outline what is considered inappropriate and state that there is no tolerance for abusive and discriminatory comments—although, *in order to be successful, system affordances must provide ways to enforce and react to violations of the code of conduct as well as dispute and iterate on the codes themselves.*

Participants' ability and willingness to exercise open-mindedness and engage in perspective taking, such as when encountering an institution's problematic policy, often depended on what they knew about the organization (or individual) with which they were engaging. A code of conduct provides the necessary framing: all individuals are subject to the conditions of the code and presumably in agreement with them as users of a system, making it easier to presume good intentions (e.g., when an outdated term is posted). Organizations that author or adopt a code of conduct provide more transparency to users by explicitly stating its values and commitments to upholding them.

With regards to identity, we also note *the difference in experiences and interactions between those with privilege and those without in a given context (privilege being relative and situational)*. In thinking about information practices and tools, we return to the challenge faced by marginalized peoples who may be asked or feel the need to educate others and explain the oppression they experience. We envision information systems that *privilege the voices, perspectives, and experiences of these individuals (e.g.,* Aboriginals in discussions of self-determination and colonization, the working class in discussions of social stratification, cis and trans women in discussions of sexism). *Yet these systems must take care to avoid placing unfair demands or expectations upon these individuals, nor assume that there is homogeneity, complete agreement, or one defining experience within these diverse communities.*

We appreciate the complexity and challenges of designing for this context, but there are approaches and affordances in development that may provide support for engagement and the process of critical reflection. We look to Kriplean's et al's ConsiderIt platform [27] and other work in the area of de-biasing interfaces for promising designs.

Users of ConsiderIt are encouraged to create pro/con lists that are representative of their stances yet demonstrate contemplation of both sides of a political issue; there is also a distinctly social dimension to the platform whereby users can include their lists on a site-wide "continuum of conviction" (which acts as an ideological barometer for user activity), as well as consult lists made by others to incorporate new arguments into their own lists with an easy click. The continuum further serves to aggregate and visualize the prevailing positions on issues, both pro and con, allowing users to explore these positions broken down by different attributes or characteristics of users.

By requiring users to include both the pros and cons of an issue, Kriplean's platform *affords and supports pluralism*, especially in comparison to other systems, such as our study's wiki, which privilege consensus and contribute to a perception of total agreement. In addition to the value in *viewing the nuances and variation in opinions among people with different levels of investment in an issue* or who are disproportionally affected by the social and community processes related to an issue, we also see potential in *aggregating user-contributed content in order to crowdsource ideologically contextualized information, and indicate where there are gaps in understanding.*

Designs that serve to *'situate' users* are also of interest to our inquiry. They can *help newcomers—whether to a platform or a way of thinking—identify users who either may be willing to provide mentorship and point to helpful resources or are in a similar place in their learning and welcoming of peer-to-peer support and learning opportunities.* Such an affordance is one that creates a liminal space outside of direct engagement with system content. Wikipedia's Teahouse—"A friendly place to help new editors become accustomed to Wikipedia culture, ask questions, and develop community relationships" [47]—is a good example of liminal space that acknowledges through its design that there are differences among users that need to be respected in order to sustain and increase engagement.

Similar to use of space, designs should also *be responsive to time and its relationship to critical reflection and individuals' capacity to engage with uncomfortable content and negative emotions.* Research on slow technology—and its effects on reflection [39] and information processing [45]—suggests there may be value in further exploring the experience of time when designing for transformative learning. Specifically, slow design theorists argue that slow technologies have the potential to *reveal experiences that are often overlooked by a user and induce deeper reflection and contemplation* [19].

While there are technical ways to slow down the pace of user interactions (for example, periods of disabled access, delayed message relaying, etc.), it's also possible to *design a system such that the time constraints are a product of users' engagements with content and other users.* For example, another platform developed by Kriplean, the Reflect interface [28] add-on, provides a "backchannel" for communication which encourages users to demonstrate they have understood the comments of another, and to seek confirmation of their interpretation, before responding in turn. Users are also able to indicate they have 'heard' another's ideas—but not rate or express agreement or evaluations of the ideas.

While originally envisioned as a design for saving time for users (by allowing succinct and scannable summaries of long online discussions), Reflect slows the discussion board exchange and concentrates users' energies on finding common ground and negotiating understanding in asynchronous interactions. In addition to providing more time for reflection, we see this as a particularly useful functionality *for supporting collaborative work processes in platforms such as wiki that may not preserve the integrity of ideas and perspectives from multiple users.*

This affordance also *provides participation pathways for users* who may not necessarily want to post to the discussion board but are still able to demonstrate that they have read, listened, or understood another's ideas—which can prove key for users *who may be reluctant to publicly engage* because of difficulty articulating their own opinion due to uncertainty, powerful emotional reactions or else fear of getting it wrong. We think a *backchannel for conveying information related to collaboratio*n—availabilities to work on a project, indication of changes, gratitude for others' efforts, emotional states, degree of certainty or comfort one feels about their contribution—may also provide increased support for individuals working with uncomfortable content.

Through the content of the recommendation discussion we highlight tensions that arise when designing for negative affect. Through the structure of the discussion we attempt a (Kriplean-esque) meta reflection encouraging readers to read slowly, deeply and reflectively. We hope that highlighting real-world examples of innovative *and* functional system designs that could be used to support critical reflection and transformative learning will motivate others to consider this area of design scholarship.

CONTRIBUTIONS

Specific contributions of our work include:

Demonstrating a theoretical grounding (transformative learning) for extending interactive system design and the potential for interaction design to contribute to transformative learning processes;

An example of investigating difficult-to-quantify dimensions of human experience and ongoing processes (e.g. decolonization);

Offering an initial set of criteria for system affordances that encourage the process of transformative learning, including shared practices of critical reflection; ideologically- and emotionally-contextualized information discovery; slowing down; liminal space; and communication backchannels;

Providing examples of how to build on these criteria to extend our understanding of interactive system design;

Aware of harms that result from efforts to generalize, normalize and homogenize people and their activities, particularly through research practices (discussed in [5,6,26,42]), we cautiously put forward that aspects of the work *may* have applications for other environments, particularly those with opportunities for actors to undergo paradigm shifts and to engage 'pedagogies of discomfort'. These understandings can be critiqued, expanded upon and developed through future work designing and implementing systems that support the process of transformative learning.

Most broadly, through this project we join others working to add depth and nuance to the way the field of HCI conceptualizes 'user experience' (e.g., [3,5,6,16,24]). In a world fraught with inequities and conflict there remains much to learn concerning the use of interactive tools in support of understanding, healing and reconciliation.

ACKNOWLEDGMENTS

Students: We thank the individuals enrolled in LIBR 569a fall, 2013, for their participation in the study, including Alexandria Everitt, Michele Adams, and Patricia Geddes who expressed interest in being acknowledged in our write-up. Participants Alexandria Everitt (AE), Patricia Geddes (PG), and Michael Wynne (MW) also indicated that they wanted their quotations to be attributed to them by name, rather than to an anonymized participant label (AA-HH).

Problematic scenarios: We gratefully acknowledge the contributions from the members of the of the Advisory Group for the iSchool @ UBC's First Nations Curriculum Concentration for sharing the problematic scenarios that were used throughout the course to create experiences of negative affect. These scenarios were drawn from their experiences as Indigenous and non-Indigenous information professionals contributing to Indigenous initiatives.

Consent: Dr. Richard Arias Hernandez for assistance with the consent protocols

Editorial assistance: Graduate student Maggie Castor for helping with final formatting and proofreading references.

REFERENCES

1. Association of College & Research Libraries, Information Literacy Competency Standards. http://www.ala.org/acrl/standards/informationliteracycompetency.
2. Aurora, V. How to design a code of conduct for your community. http://adainitiative.org//02/howto-design-a-code-of-conduct-for-your-community/.
3. Bardzell, S. Feminist HCI: Taking stock and outlining an agenda for design. *Proc. CHI '10*, ACM, (2010), 1301-1310.
4. Benford, S., Greenhalgh, C., Giannachi, G., Walker, B., Marshall, J. and Rodden, T. Uncomfortable interactions. *Proc. CHI'12*, ACM, (2012), 2005-2014.
5. Bidwell, N.J., Siya, M., Marsden, G., Tucker, W.D., Tshemese, M., Gaven, N., Ntlangano, S., Eglinton, K.A. And Robinson, S. Walking and the social life of solar charging in rural Africa. *ACM TOCHI 20*,6 (2013), 1-33.
6. Bidwell, N.J. And Winschiers-Theophilus, H. Audio pacemaker: Walking, talking Indigenous knowledge. In *Proc. SAICSIT '12*, ACM (2012), 149-158.
7. Boyer, N.R., Maher, P.A. and Kirkman, S. Transformative learning in online settings: The use of self-direction, metacognition, and collaborative learning. *Journal of Transformative Ed. 4*, 4 (2006), 335-361.
8. Brock, S.E. Measuring the importance of precursor steps to transformative learning. *Adult Education Quarterly 60*, 2 (2010), 122-142.
9. Butler, B., Joyce, E., and Pike, J. Don't look now, but we've created a bureaucracy: The nature and roles of policies and rules in Wikipedia. *Proc. CHI '08*, ACM, (2008), 1101-1110.
10. Case, D.O., Andrews, J.E., Johnson, J.D. and Allard, S.L. Avoiding versus seeking: the relationship of information seeking to avoidance, blunting, coping, dissonance, and related concepts. *Journal of the Medical Library Assoc. 93*,3 (2005), 353-362.
11. Charmaz, K. *Constructing grounded theory: A practical guide through qualitative analysis*. Sage, 2006.
12. de jesus, nina. The filter bubble is a misguided, privileged notion http://satifice.com/octofice/2014/02/21/the-filter-bubble-is-a-misguided/.
13. DiSalvo, C. *Adversarial Design*. MIT Press, 2012.

14. DiSalvo, C., Nourbakhsh, I., Holstius, D., Akin A., & Louw, M. The Neighborhood Networks project: a case study of critical engagement and creative expression through participatory design. *Proc. PDC'08*, ACM (2008), 41-50.
15. Donnelly, R. The nexus of problem-based learning and learning technology: Does it enable transformative practice? *European Journal of Open, Distance and E-Learning 2*, 2009.
16. Dourish, P. & Mainwaring, S. Ubicomp's colonial impulse. *Proc. UbiComp '12,* ACM (2012), 133-142.
17. Fetherston, B. & Kelly, R. Conflict resolution and transformative pedagogy: A grounded theory research project on learning in higher education. *Journal of Transformative Education 5,*3 (2007), 262-285.
18. Friedman, B. & Nathan, L.P. Multi-lifespan information system design: A research initiative for the HCI community. *Proc. CHI'10*, ACM (2010), 2243-2246.
19. Grosse-Hering, B., Mason, J., Aliakseyeu, D., Bakker, C., & Desmet, P. Slow design for meaningful interactions. *Proc. CHI'13*, ACM (2013), 3431-3440.
20. Halbert, H., & Nathan, L.P. Designing for negative affect and critical reflection. Poster presented at CHI'14. *Proc. CHI'14*, ACM (2014), 2569-2574.
21. Hassenzahl, M. & Tractinsky, N. User experience – A research agenda. *Behaviour & Information Technology*, *25*, 2 (2006), 91-97.
22. Hinds, P.J, & Mortensen, M. Understanding conflict in geographically distributed teams: The moderating effects of shared identity, shared context, and spontaneous communication. *Org. Science 16,*3(2005), 290-307.
23. Hourcade, J.P. & Bullock-Rest, N.E. HCI for peace: A call for constructive action. *Proc. CHI'11*, ACM (2011), 443-452.
24. Irani, L., Dourish, P. And Hall, D.B. Postcolonial interculturality. *Proc. IWIC '09,* ACM (2009), 249-252.
25. Iseke-Barnes, J. Pedagogies for decolonizing. *Canadian Journal of Native Education 31*,1 (2008), 123-148.
26. Kovach, M.E. *Indigenous Methodologies: characteristics, conversations, and contexts*. University of Toronto Press, 2010.
27. Kriplean, T., Morgan, J.T., Freelon, D.G., Borning, A., and Bennett, L. Supporting reflective public thought with ConsiderIt. *Proc. CSCW '12*, ACM (2012), 265-274.
28. Kriplean, T., Toomim, M., Morgan, J., Borning, A. and Ko, A. Is this what you meant? Promoting listening on the web with Reflect. *Proc. CHI'12*, ACM(2012), 1559-1568.
29. Lamb, R. & Davidson, E. Information and Communication Technology challenges to scientific professional identity. *The Information Society: An International Journal, 21*,1 (2005), 1-24.
30. Latour, B. On technical mediation: Philosophy, sociology, genealogy. *Common Knowledge 3*, 2 (1994) 29-64.
31. Lorde, A. Age, Race, Class and sex*:* Women redefining difference. In *Out There: Marginalization and Contemporary Culture*. MIT *(1992),* 281-287.
32. Marsh, T. & Costello, B. Experience in serious games: between positive and serious experience. *Proc. SGDA '12*, Springer (2012), 255-267.
33. Mezirow, J. *Fostering critical reflection in adulthood: A guide to transformative and emancipatory learning*. Jossey-Bass Publishers, 1990.
34. Mitra, A. Voices of the marginalized on the internet: examples from a website for women of South Asia. *Journal of Communication 54*, 3 (2004), 492-510.
35. Muller, M.J. & Druin, A. Participatory design: The third space in HCI. In J.A. Jacko and A. Sears, eds., *Human Computer Interaction Handbook*. Lawrence Erlbaum Associates, 2003, 1051–1068.
36. Nathan, L.P., Lake, M., Grey, N.C., Nilson, T.T., Utter, R.F., Ring, M., Kahn, Z. & Friedman, B. Multi-lifespan information system design: Investigating a new design approach in Rwanda. *Proc. iConference '11,* ACM, (2009), 591-597.
37. Nonnecke, B., Andrews, D. and Preece, J. Non-public and public online community participation: Needs, attitudes and behavior. *Elec. Comm. Research*, *6*, 1 (2006), 7-20.
38. O'Brien, H.L. Exploring engagement in online news interaction. *Proc. ASIS&T '11,* (2011), 1-10.
39. Odom, W.T., Sellen, A.B., Banks, R., Kirk, D.S., Regan, T., Selby, M., Forlizzi, J.L., and Zimmerman, J. Designing for slowness, anticipation and re-visitation: A long term field study of the Photobox. *Proc. CHI '14*, ACM (2014), 1961-1970.
40. Rosenberg, M.B. *Nonviolent Communication: A language of life*. PuddleDancer Press, 2003.
41. Schulman, S. *The gentrification of the mind: Witness to a lost imagination.* University of California Press, 2012.
42. Smith, L.T. *Decolonizing methodologies: Research and Indigenous peoples*. Zed, 2012.
43. Tatum, B.D. Talking about race, learning about racism: The application of racial identity development theory in the classroom. *Harvard Ed. Review 62*, 1 (1992), 1-25.
44. Taylor, E.W. An update of transformative learning theory: A critical review of the empirical research (1999–2005). *Inter. Jour. of Lifelong Ed.26*, 2 (2007), 173-191.
45. Teevan, J., Collins-Thompson, K., White, R.W., Dumais, S.T., and Kim, Y. Slow search: information Retrieval without Time Constraints. *Proc.HCIR'13*, ACM (2013).

46. Wang, J. Against innocence: Race, gender, and the politics of safety. *LIES: A journal of materialist feminism 1*, 2012, 145-171.

47. Wikipedia Teahouse http://en.wikipedia.org/wiki/Wikipedia:Teahouse.

48. Verbeek, P. Acting Artifacts: The technological mediation of action. In *User behavior and technology development: Shaping sustainable relations between consumers and technologies,* P.P. Verbeek & A. Slob Eds. Springer, 2006, 53-60.

49. Yoo, D., Lake, M., Nilsen, T., Utter, M.E., Alsdorf, R., Bizimana, T., Nathan, L.P., Ring, M., Utter, E.J., Utter, R.F. & Friedman, B. Envisioning across generations : A multi-lifespan information system for international justice in Rwanda. *Proc. CHI '13*, ACM (2013), 2527–2536.

50. Zembylas, M. & McGlynn, C. Discomforting pedagogies: Emotional tensions, ethical dilemmas and transformative possibilities. *British Ed. Research Journal 38*, 1 (2012), 41-59.

51. Zillmann, D. & Bryant, J (eds). Selective exposure to communication. Lawrence Erlbaum, 1985.

Collective Smile: Measuring Societal Happiness from Geolocated Images

Saeed Abdullah
Information Science
Cornell University
sma249@cornell.edu

Elizabeth L. Murnane
Information Science
Cornell University
elm236@cornell.edu

Jean M. R. Costa
Information Science
Cornell University
jmd487@cornell.edu

Tanzeem Choudhury
Information Science
Cornell University
tanzeem.choudhury@cornell.edu

ABSTRACT

The increasing adoption of social media provides unprecedented opportunities to gain insight into human nature at vastly broader scales. Regarding the study of population-wide sentiment, prior research commonly focuses on text-based analyses and ignores a treasure trove of sentiment-laden content: *images*. In this paper, we make methodological and computational contributions by introducing the *Smile Index* as a formalized measure of societal happiness. Detecting smiles in 9 million geo-located tweets over 16 months, we validate our Smile Index against both text-based techniques and self-reported happiness. We further make observational contributions by applying our metric to explore temporal trends in sentiment, relate public mood to societal events, and predict economic indicators. Reflecting upon the innate, language-independent aspects of facial expressions, we recommend future improvements and applications to enable robust, global-level analyses. We conclude with implications for researchers studying and facilitating the expression of collective emotion through socio-technical systems.

Author Keywords

Sentiment Analysis; Image Processing; Twitter

ACM Classification Keywords

H.5.m Information Interfaces and Presentation: Misc.

INTRODUCTION

The science of observing and interpreting human behaviors, thoughts, and feelings has been fundamentally changed by computer-mediated communication technologies and specifically social media platforms. Of particular interest to a wide array of researchers from psychology, sociology, HCI, economics, healthcare, and politics is the socially embedded affective and cognitive experience of how people perceive the quality of their lives. In the mid 1980s, Diener formalized this notion comprising positive affect, negative affect, and life satisfaction as *subjective well-being* (SBL) [15]. The corresponding Satisfaction with Life (SWL) score has since been developed to quantify happiness and compare societies of people in terms of fulfillment with life on the whole [16].

CSCW 2015, March 14 - 18 2015, Vancouver, BC, Canada

ACM 978-1-4503-2922-4/15/03...$15.00
http://dx.doi.org/10.1145/2675133.2675186

In recent years, continued efforts have been made by scholars and policymakers to measure and promote subjective perceptions of well-being for individuals and groups at community, regional, national, and global levels. The term Gross National Happiness (GNH) originated as a holistic measure of well-being [68, 72], and GNH principles have inspired initiatives to measure national happiness from governments and organizations across multiple continents [80, 85, 74, 73, 83]. In 2012, the United Nations General Assembly resolved to design well-being indicators, launching the annual World Happiness Report [86] to rank countries by happiness. Similar agendas to calculate happiness for countries around the globe continue to grow each year [84, 79]. Measurement typically relies on polls, surveys, and other forms of self-report from individuals and households. However, this approach is costly in terms of time, money, and manpower and therefore is typically administered with limited samples of the population and only annually or less frequently [26, 54, 53].

Opportunely, a growing body of research demonstrates that an unobtrusive, inexpensive, and scalable solution to such challenges is implicit sentiment analysis using public social media data such as blog posts [9, 49], Facebook status updates [41, 53], and tweets [2, 18, 54]. This computational form of well-being monitoring aligns well with the aforementioned indices for both individuals and entire communities. However, approaches focus on text analysis, which has its own limitations, especially when input has complex semantics (e.g., sarcasm or humor) or syntax (e.g., unrecognized characters, non-English words, or typographical errors).

At the same time, the use of internet- and camera-capable smart devices is becoming increasingly prevalent. 1.8 billion new smartphones were sold in 2013 alone [71], and there are an estimated 7 million mobile subscriptions worldwide as of May 2014 [76]. Furthermore, numerous tools and sites have appeared that revolve around photo sharing and image curation, activities in which 62% of internet users take part [81]. This has produced a shift in online user-generated content from predominantly text-based data to richer forms of image-based media. 300 million images are uploaded daily on Facebook alone (7 petabytes worth of data per month) [69]; and between Facebook, Instagram, Flickr, Snapchat, and WhatsApp, 1.8 billion images are uploaded every day [82].

Recognizing this opportunity and necessity to design next-generation methodologies, we explore images on social media as a resource for sensing societal characteristics, focusing in this study on collective happiness. We apply our approach to 9 million geo-located images on Twitter and analyze aggregated emotional trends across multiple timescales. Interpreting uncovered mood patterns in light of culturally and politically significant events that took place during the captured window, we relate our findings to research from quantitative psychology and discuss important considerations such as the variety of cultural contexts in which users may be embedded and the implications of predicting happiness on a mass scale.

Our contributions are thus *methodological*, *computational*, and *observational*:

- We provide a novel technique for large-scale sentiment assessment based on smiles detected in images shared on social media.
- We present our analyses, which demonstrate our approach's ability to: i) track how societal happiness changes over time and in response to emotionally significant events; ii) characterize communities from a socio-economic perspective; and iii) predict consumer confidence.
- Lastly, we discuss theoretical and practical implications of our work, including the potential that images hold as a far-reaching, fast, and low cost alternative to existing methods for capturing collective characteristics and social behavior.

RELATED WORK

Facial Expression, Emotion, and Photography

The relationship between facial expressions and emotions has been extensively studied, leading to central theories from various fields that together suggest these brief non-verbal cues reveal a great deal about individuals' emotional states [60, 42]. Facial expressions can be annotated according to a number of core emotions [19], including 6 initially identified by Darwin: anger, disgust, fear, happiness, sadness, and surprise. Ekman's Facial Action Coding System (FACS) has been used to characterize facial expressions such as smiles according to more fine-grained features [20]. Multiple studies have used FACS to code smile intensity [28, 57].

When it comes to *conveying* emotions and opinions, visual imagery proves a highly effective medium. Recent studies show that expression of positive affect in photographs can be indicative of an individual's long term well-being and happiness as well as provide insight into underlying personality traits that shape social, cognitive, and behavioral tendencies and responses [36]. Notably, two longitudinal studies by Seder et al. [57] show that smile intensity in Facebook profile pictures is positively associated with social relationships and is a robust predictor of self-reported life satisfaction after 3.5 years for both male and female participants.

That being said, a complete and overarching theoretical framework explaining the causal relationship between happiness and smiling in photographs has yet to be developed. Specifically, it is important to consider individual differences in the expression of emotion in photographs as well as the authenticity of emotion displayed. Prior research on posing and smiling in photos suggests that high-status and dominant individuals tend to smile less in photos than submissive types and that men smile less than women [27]. Smiling in spontaneous, candid photos is regarded as an indicator of authentic happiness [40], and though some photographed smiles may not reflect true happiness or may even mask negative emotions, the proportion of such smiles is generally small compared to the ones displaying genuine emotion, for people from both Eastern and Western cultures [30]. Regarding this last point, the role of culture is another factor requiring further attention when measuring emotion from photos. We address the feasibility of our framework for cross-cultural sentiment analysis in the latter portion of our Discussion section.

Assessing Sentiment with Social Media

Today's unprecedented access to records of self-expression and social interaction archived on social media has empowered the CSCW community to explore data-driven social science questions. Significant research has leveraged this resource both to extend our understanding of human behaviors and contexts as well as to contemplate practical implications such insights can have on sociotechnical research happening across diverse fields.

Considerable recent attention has been given in particular to leveraging online social networks and content-sharing platforms to assess the affective states of individuals and groups, for example to study mood sharing and emotional expression [38, 63]; population-wide assessment and diagnosis of mood and mental health [11, 12]; and public emotional responses to political events such as debates [45] and armed conflicts [13].

Prior work has also shown social influence to be a major factor impacting subjective well-being [24], further motivating our use of data contributed within the social setting of a platform like Twitter. With respect to societal happiness in particular, a growing body of work related to large-scale sentiment analysis has recognized the opportunity social media affords to study trends of collective mood. This research typically applies natural language processing (NLP) techniques and uses tools such as the Linguistic Inquiry Word Count [52] to quantify sentiment. Kim et al. [37] use Affective Norms for English Words (ANEW) [4], a list of terms with emotional ratings, to track mood on Twitter. Bollen et al. [2] infer sentiment from tweets by extending the psychometric measurement Profile of Mood States (POMS) [47], which consists of mood adjectives. Dodds et al. [18] compile and apply an emotion-annotated corpus of words to measure the happiness expressed in tweets.

Computational Emotion Recognition

In parallel to the psychological and sociological studies on emotion, systems-focused researchers have also undertaken work to detect as well as foster emotional expression.

Much work from Computer Vision and Processing has pursued the development of hardware and algorithms for facial expression recognition, including for smile detection [64]. There has also been increased interest in the development of computational frameworks capable of automatically inferring about the emotion associated with digital images [35].

Considering the beneficial influence smiling can have on overall affective state, a number of systems developed by the HCI community focus on encouraging smiles. Tsujita et al.

[61] use household cameras to detect smiles and provide feedback to users in order to increase self-awareness about smiling behavior and mood. Hernandez et al. [29] station cameras on a college campus to detect smiles in real time and reflect upon the community's emotional reactions. Visualizing patterns in collective sentiment over time and in relation to campus events, their experiment finds that trends in smiling strongly reflect events such as exam periods and graduation.

Thus to summarize, by building on findings from psychology, leveraging large-scale emotionally-rich image data from social media, and applying facial recognition techniques from computer vision, we pursue a novel methodology for detecting smiles in online user-contributed content that allows for the assessment of collective emotion on a global scale and over fine-grained time intervals. In the sections that follow we describe our technique, the results of our validation experiments, and the insights we derive from these applications.

METHODOLOGY

Data

In this study, we use a dataset of nine million geo-tagged tweets with images that were posted between January 1, 2012 and April 30, 2013, a time window that gives us access to content posted during emotionally significant political and cultural events in the United States such as the presidential inauguration of Barack Obama and the Boston Marathon bombings. We obtain the tweets via Twitter's "garden hose" — the service's official sample of approximately 10% of all tweets. Our dataset is thus the subset of garden hose tweets containing images that were posted during our collection period.

We determine the geographic locations of tweets from the latitude and longitude coordinates provided in the *geo* metadata field. Figure 1 illustrates the distribution of the tweets' counties of origin across the United States normalized by population. To handle timezone differences across geographical regions, we use the same *geo* metadata to convert a tweet's Coordinated Universal Time (UTC) formatted creation-time to local timezone for fine-grained temporal analysis.

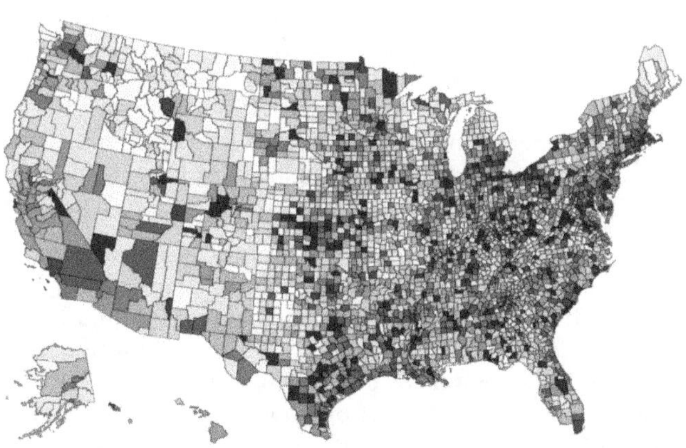

Figure 1. Distribution of tweets per-capita across counties in our dataset

It is worth noting here that Twitter (along with other popular social media sites including Facebook) remove metadata (e.g., Exif data) from images. As a result, it is impossible to differentiate when and where an image is captured vs. when and where it is posted, based on information available in Twitter's datastream. Researchers whose work depends on the assumption that posting happens at the same time and location as capture should thus be aware to either seek data from sources that do not strip this metadata or take steps such as survey follow-ups to ensure geography and recency of content. Photos posted by tourists vs. locals may be the main source of discrepancy [25, 77]. That being said, prior work has shown that in general, users do share information on social media in real-time and post geotagged tweets from their current locations (e.g., [67]). Particularly relevant is the CityBeat project [66], which uses geotagged social media photos to classify diverse events such as car accidents, fires, and music concerts. The high accuracy they achieve in detecting these events demonstrates the geographical and temporal reliability of such image data at the hyper-local level. Relatedly, the transient nature of the Twitter medium encourages users to focus on current as opposed to past events, and this in-situ nature of tweets has been confirmed by a number of projects with focuses ranging from real-time news detection to emergency support during events such as earthquakes [56]. Given the large-scale nature of our data, we therefore expect that any potential noise-to-signal ratio resulting from individual sharing habits would be small.

The images in our tweets were uploaded using the official photo-sharing service provided by Twitter. Around 12% of these images were inaccessible at the time of crawling, presumably due to user deletion. Of all the accessible images, around 40% contain a human face according to our smile detection framework, which we describe next.

Smile Index Framework

Figure 2 shows the phases of our happiness assessment. One of our key aims is building a system that is both fast and reliable given the large size of current and future data sources.

Extracting images

The first step is processing our Twitter dataset to extract images. To determine whether a tweet contains any image, we use the post's associated metadata. Specifically, we check the *media* field in the *Entity* metadata[1] and retain a tweet for further processing if the media element has a type *photo* associated with it. An exploratory look into a random sample from the API shows that more than 72% of all images uploaded in Twitter use the site's official photo-uploading service; all images in our dataset have been uploaded using this service. After identifying image-containing tweets, we parse the metadata to build a database of links for crawling the images directly from Twitter. Since the images from Twitter can have different encoding formats, we perform image conversion to ensure all the images are in a standard JPEG format. We also convert RGB images to grayscale since subsequent phases in our framework do not use color information.

[1] `https://dev.twitter.com/docs/platform-objects/entities`

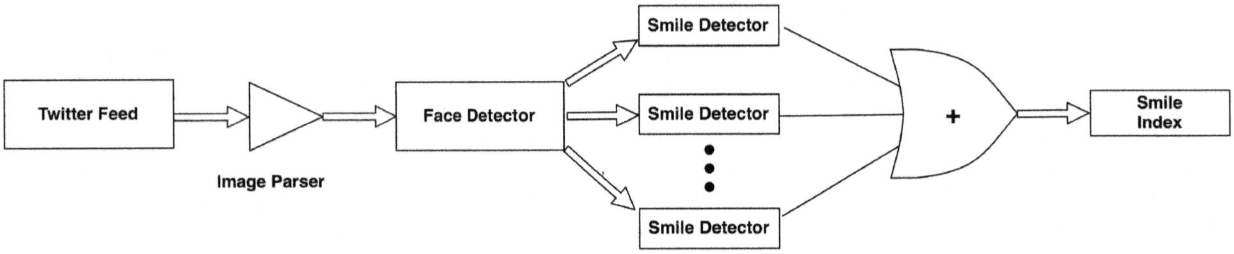

Figure 2. Framework for assessing happiness through Smile Index

Face and smile detection

To detect faces within images, we use a cascade of boosted classifiers with Haar-like features [62]. The classifier uses the change in contrast between adjacent rectangular regions instead of intensity of individual pixels to determine relative dark and light areas. These features can be easily scaled, which allows efficient detection of objects of various sizes. The final classifier is a cascade of several stages, where each individual stage consists of boosted classifiers. We use a trained cascade consisting of twenty stages from Lienhart et al. [43]. The processing in these stages allows for the efficient elimination of false positives. Ultimately, we achieve 100% accuracy in detecting faces in our test dataset. Such high accuracy is expected since we are leveraging well-established and well-tested facial detection techniques [62]. After this phase, we retain only images containing human faces.

Next, we detect smiles in these images by using a Haar feature based classifier trained by Hormada et al. [31], who manually labeled images from multiple sources including the photo sharing site Flickr. The classifier achieves an AUC (area under the ROC curve) score of 0.9, a strong prediction rate. If an image contains multiple human faces, we run the smile detection algorithm for each detected face and combine the results by performing a logical OR since individuals are likely to show similar sentiment in a photo. This means that if any face detected in an image is smiling, we consider that a positive instance of smiling.

To test our system, we use the public GENKI [64] database, which consists of images of people from publicly accessible personal web pages. The people in the images are diverse in gender, ethnicity, age, geographical location, facial features (e.g., eyeglasses, facial hair), and photo setting (e.g., indoor and outdoor). Our system achieves 0.85 accuracy and F-Score of 0.71 on GENKI-4K[2], a subset of 4000 images manually labeled for smile presence.

Quantifying happiness

Our final step is building our Smile Index of happiness. A possibility for computing this measure over a time period t for a given geographical area is using the total count of images in which smiles are detected:

$$S_t = \sum_{i \in I_t} f_{smile}(i)$$

I_t is the total number of images in time period t from that geographical area, and f_{smile} represents our smile-detection output (1 if the image i contains any smiling human face and 0 otherwise). However, Twitter's growth in popularity and contributed content over time means that the volume of tweets in our dataset increases significantly over the collection period. Simply using a raw smile count as seen in Figure 3 would therefore lead to a systematic bias where the Smile Index would merely reflect the increasing contribution levels in Twitter rather than the happiness levels of those contributors.

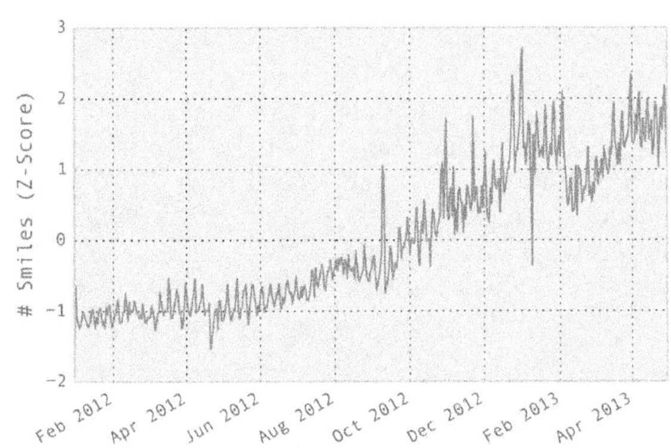

Figure 3. Smile count (normalized using z-scores) in tweets over time

For this reason we use another metric — the ratio of smile-containing images to the total number of images posted during a given time period:

$$R_t = \frac{S_t}{I_t}$$

Our Smile Index is thus a normalized smile frequency — that is, the number of images containing smiles normalized by the total number of images posted in the same time period. Figure 4 shows the resulting distribution of this ratio for U.S. tweets.

Not only does this ratio prevent the bias just described, but it also allows for the comparison of Smile Index measurements arising from datasets of different sizes. It should be noted that we do not use the ratio of smiling faces to the number of faces because images that do not contain faces might still convey important information about external events. This is particularly true because given the nature of social media, if an image contains a face it is more likely to be a smiling one, causing the ratio of smiling faces to total face count to be relatively constant over time. Instead, setting the total count

[2]MPLab GENKI-4K database `http://mplab.ucsd.edu`

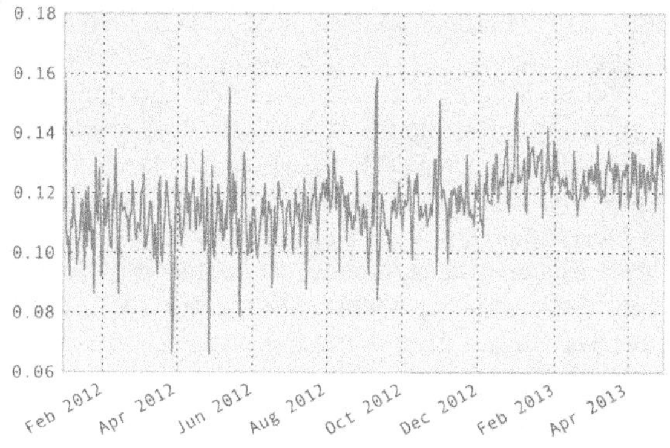

Figure 4. Ratio of images that contain smile(s)

of images as the denominator lets us quantify the appearance of smiles within a given time-period in a broader context. For example, during Hurricane Sandy, we see a discernible rise in the number of images that do not contain faces but that do capture the surroundings and communicate about the event in that way. This lower ratio of smiles to the total number of images allows us to correctly detect the negative sentiment associated with this event.

A key question is whether the image-based methodology we propose is reliable and enables the robust study of emotional and sociological phenomena. To address this, we now compare our approach with a state-of-the-art text-based analysis as well as with ground-truth self-reported happiness data.

Dodds et al. [18] publish a daily happiness score[3] computed over 100 million words per day from Twitter. Given that our and Dodds et al.'s indices use different scales, we normalize the time series to a $[0, 1]$ scale using the following equation:

$$h_{\text{norm}} = \frac{h - h_{\text{min}}}{h_{\text{max}} - h_{\text{min}}}$$

To compare the happiness scores computed from smiles and from text, we perform statistical equivalence testing. Using two one-sided tests (TOST) with interval margin $\delta = 0.3$, the null hypothesis that the difference between the samples' means is larger than the specified margin threshold can be rejected with p-value < 0.001. In other words, we find statistical equivalence between happiness computed via traditional text-based and our image-based analyses. It should be noted though that our paper's focus is not to compare and contrast our alternative methodology with existing text-based techniques or to argue that our approach is superior. Rather, our intention is more primarily about mining, analyzing, and exploring a previously unplumbed datastream. In fact, it would be desirable to combine both textual and image based sentiment analyses together to play on the strengths of each. For instance, text-based analysis is computationally simpler; but in many cases text is malformed, not in a processable language, or simply non-existent, which motivates the use of an alternate, text-independent approach such as ours.

[3] `http://hedonometer.org/`

We also compare our Smile Index with the Gallup-Healthways Well-Being Index [70], which tracks the ratio of Americans experiencing "lots of happiness and enjoyment" and "lots of stress" using daily telephone surveys. While Gallup's index is limited in the sense that it tracks the extreme ends rather than the full happiness spectrum, we still find expected correlations with our Smile Index, as seen in Table 1. Day-to-day changes in happiness and stress are also strongly correlated with detected smiles: 0.5*** and −0.43***, respectively. To further compare the Gallup happiness index and our Smile Index, we again perform statistical equivalence testing. Since our Smile Index is a ratio (of images with smiles to all images), we normalize the Gallup happiness score to the same $[0, 1]$ scale as we did when making the comparison with text-analysis. The result shows that the happiness time series of Gallup and of our Smile Index are statistically equivalent with an interval margin of $\delta = 0.3$ and $p < 0.001$.

	Happiness/Enjoyment	Stress/Worry
Smile Index	0.26^{***}	-0.22^{***}

Table 1. Smile Index compared with Gallup Well-Being Index. (Throughout the paper, we use $^{*} = p < 0.05$, $^{**} = p < 0.01$, $^{***} = p < 0.001$ to mark level of statistical significance)

EXPERIMENT AND RESULTS

Temporal Smile Distribution

Here we examine temporal trends in the Smile Index across different timescales (hours, days, and weeks).

Daily patterns of happiness

As the term "Blue Monday" indicates, there is a commonly held cultural belief about the relationship between affective state and the day of the week. To see if we observe such an effect, we compute the distribution of smile-containing images across days of the week, aggregated over the United States. The result is shown in Figure 5.

There is a clear peak during the weekend, which makes sense intuitively and also conforms with prior research that observes the expression of increased positive sentiment and lower negative sentiment on weekends [44]. A sharp decay occurs after the weekend, but we see the minimum reached mid-week on Wednesday. A number of previous studies [59, 48, 18] have similarly reported the absence of a Blue Monday

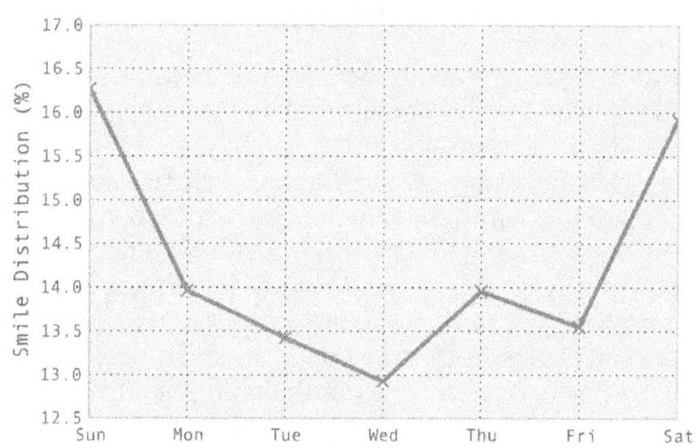

Figure 5. Distribution of smiles in U.S. tweets over days of the week

phenomenon in their findings, and the mid-week dip in happiness has also been observed in prior work based on blog-post data [48] and tweets [17]. We conjecture that relatively higher Monday happiness is a result of inertia from the preceding weekend and note the analogy of the Wednesday mid-week mood dip with the known mid-day dip [50].

Hourly patterns of happiness

Examining the hourly pattern in the appearance of smiles, we find a diurnal rhythm as shown in Figure 6. Our data shows a gradual increase in happiness during the morning, which then levels off and reveals the mid-afternoon dip. The patterns we observe are consistent across workdays and weekends as shown in Figure 7.

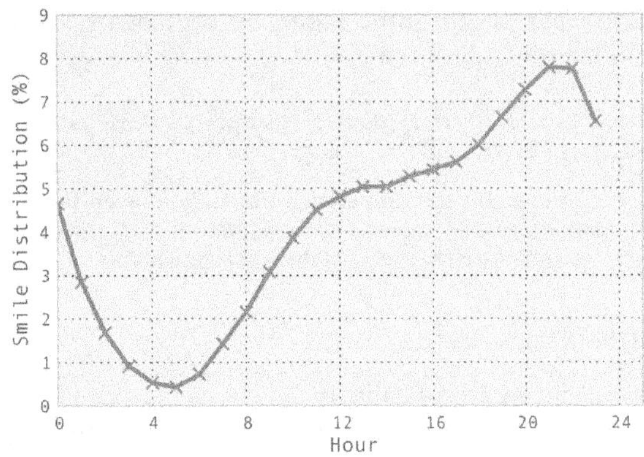

Figure 6. Distribution of smiles detected in U.S. tweets over hours

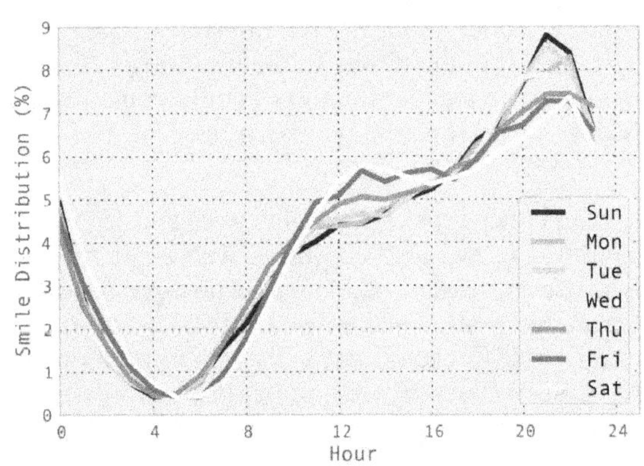

Figure 7. Daily breakdown of hourly smile distribution

Clark et al. [8] in a study on undergraduate students note a similar plateau effect in the middle of the day, albeit their reported dip lasts from noon to 9 pm. In the evening, we see smiles again increasing steadily with a peak around 9-10 pm, then dropping to a minimum in the middle of the night, which is when research shows depressed individuals tend to be more active on Twitter [11]. A recent study by Golder et al. [26] uses text-based content from Twitter to analyze patterns in positive and negative affect and finds trends similar to ours — a peak in Positive Affect (PA) in the morning and another at midnight as well as a minimum in PA around 5 am. However, the peaks from Golder et al. have similar PA values to each other, while we see much higher levels in the evening.

Public mood surrounding emotionally significant events

To investigate whether public mood is reflected by smiles in uploaded images, we look closely at a variety of societal events. While Twitter is a global service, the majority of its users are from the United States, so for reasons of scope in this study we consider only U.S. events: the Boston Marathon bombings, the inauguration of President Obama, the period during Hurricane Sandy and its aftermath, and New Year's Eve. To keep the dataset diverse, we focus on particular geographical regions of the country during our analyses. Figure 8 summarizes our findings from these case studies.

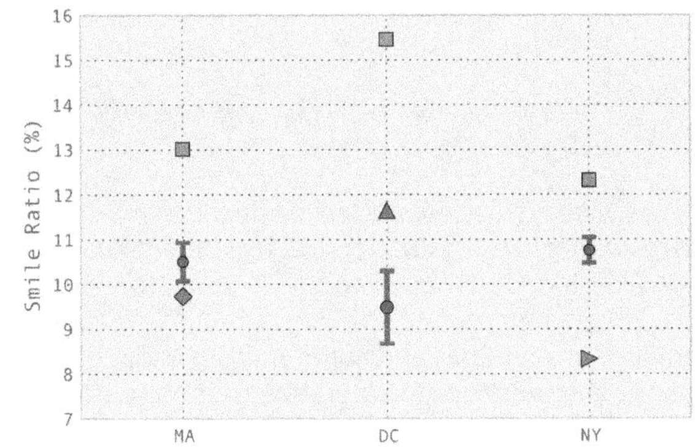

Figure 8. Smile Index (SI) of indicated events. • shows the mean for each of the three geographical regions, and 99% confidence interval is included. ♦ indicates SI in Massachusetts during Boston Marathon Bombings and subsequent manhunt period; ▲ marks SI during Presidential Inauguration in DC; ► indicates SI during Hurricane Sandy in NY; ■ represents SI in the corresponding areas during New Year's Eve

First, we analyze images posted April 15-19, 2013 from Massachusetts during the tragic Boston Marathon bombings and subsequent manhunt. The mean of daily smiles detected during this period falls with a margin of more than 7% compared to the total time period in our dataset. In other words, even though the number of images increased during this time period, the Smile Index was significantly lower.

Second, we measure smiles detected in images from Washington D.C. during the second inauguration of Barack Obama as President of the United States. The event included concerts, a swearing-in ceremony, a parade, and other activities spread over January 19-21, 2013; so we use images posted during these dates. For this time frame, we see a 22% increase in the Smile Index compared to the overall mean. Figure 9 shows an example of a smile-containing image posted during this period and relevant to the event.

Figure 9. Example of a smile-containing image contributing positively to the Smile Index for the 2013 U.S. Presidential Inauguration

Third, we study images from NY posted during and after Hurricane Sandy, a Category-3 storm that caused severe devastation, including 147 deaths and a damage estimation exceeding \$50 billion [75]. Its storm-force winds at one point had a diameter of 1000 miles. Hurricane Sandy made landfall in NY on October 20, 2012, so we use images posted from this date until November 1, 2012. Comparing to the overall mean, the Smile Index during this period drops 22.5%.

Finally, we also analyze images posted from each of these geographical areas on New Year's Eve (on December 31, 2012 and Jan 1, 2013 to be specific). As shown in Figure 8, there is a substantial increase in the Smile Index during this holiday.

Hence for all four events, there is a noticeable increase or decrease in our Smile Index. The ratio of images containing smiling faces increases during positively affective celebrations and decreases during negatively affective calamities, and the difference in each case is significant with $p < 0.01$. In these case studies, our simple smile metric thus proves an effective barometer of public mood during societal events.

Happiness and Economy

Understanding the potential link between well-being and various economic phenomena is arguably one of the most mainstream topics in Economics. This is evidenced by Clark's [6] recent comparison of article titles between 1960 and 2000 in the electronic bibliography of The American Economic Association — the publishing rate of articles on well-being and happiness increased more than 8 times after 2000. Researchers from the discipline commonly assume that happiness is a representation of true internal utility with some noise. Rafael et al. [14] note that if this signal-to-noise ratio in the available data is large enough, a measurement of happiness can enable study of numerous topics ranging from determinants of political economy to the effects public policies have on social welfare. In the following sections, we draw on this expanding literature to look into the relation between economic phenomena and our Smile Index of happiness.

Median household income

The connection between income and happiness has been well-studied. Generally, the relationship is suggested to be positive but with diminishing returns [7], and a number of studies argue in favor of relative rather than absolute income as a determinant of well-being measurement [23].

Using the U.S Census Bureau's 2007-2011 American Community Survey 5-year estimate data[4], we compare the distribution of median household income with per-capita smile count across New York City zip areas. We use per-capita smile count since this analysis focuses on community characteristics rather than temporal trends. We see a high degree of variation in median household income — the maximum is \$232,031 in Manhattan and the minimum is \$19,840 in the Bronx.

Table 2 shows the correlation between per capita smile count and median household income. Income does positively correlate with the smile metric, though perhaps more interesting

	Correlation
Overall	0.173074^{*}
Black Majority Area (> 50%)	-0.586325^{**}
Black Majority Area (> 75%)	-0.726471^{**}
White Majority Area (> 50%)	0.312572^{*}
White Majority Area (> 75%)	0.536020^{**}

Table 2. Spearman correlation between median household income and smile count per-capita across NYC areas

is the clear pattern that emerges when we take racial demographics into consideration. Specifically, the correlation goes from positive to negative in black majority areas (i.e., higher income is associated with lower positive sentiment and vice versa), while the correlation is more positive in white majority areas. The correlations for other races are not statistically significant in our dataset. Note that we follow the 2010 Census in treating Hispanic as an ethnicity but not a race. To better isolate the relationship between racial distribution, income, and smile data, we use the following regression model:

$$L1 : C_z = \alpha + \beta_i I_z + \beta_b B_z + \beta_w W_z + \beta_o O_z + \epsilon_z$$

where C_z is the number of smile-images per capita, I_z is the median income, B_z is the fraction of the population identifying as black in zipcode z, and W_z is the fraction identifying as white. O_z represents the other racial proportions in that region. Table 3 presents the result estimated by Ordinary Least Squares regression. As the summary statistics show, there is no serious auto-correlation problem with the model. The strong positive coefficient for W_z indicates that an increased white population proportion in a given zip code corresponds to an increase in the number of images with detected smiles.

	Coeff	Std. Err.	t
I_z	-0.001	0.00	-0.731
W_z	0.774	0.2	3.8^{***}
B_z	-0.224	0.4	-0.5
O_z	0.186	0.17	1.06
Summary	DW	Adj-R	F-Stat
	1.4	0.059	4.101^{**}

Table 3. Summary and coefficient statistics of $L1$. DW stands for Durbin-Watson statistic, a measure of residual auto-correlation

Given the relatively small coefficient associated with income in $L1$, we also look into the correlation between racial distribution and images with smiles across the NYC area. The results are shown in Table 4. For this analysis, we use the percentage of black populations and white populations in every zip code and compare against the number of per capita images with smiles. We find a strong positive correlation for the white populations, while the correlation for black populations is negative.

Race	Correlation
White	0.464114^{***}
Black	-0.371355^{***}

Table 4. Statistically significant correlation between race and number of images with smiles per-capita across zip codes in NYC

[4] http://www.census.gov/acs/www/

This intriguing finding is consistent with extant research on happiness and well-being. For instance, using surveys between 1957 and 1972, Campbell et al. [5] found 32% of whites to be "very happy" compared to only 18% of blacks. More recent studies [33, 10] report that although declining, there still remains a discernible black-white gap in terms of well-being and happiness.

Public Opinion Polls

Following the observed correlations between our Smile Index and economic factors, we investigate to what extent our metric may also capture trends in public opinion polls. In particular, we are interested in the consumer confidence index, which captures the collective degree of optimism that people express about the overall status of the economy and their personal financial situations. Such measurements are of substantial value to both governments and business entities since high consumer confidence indicates higher spending and often results in economic growth.

A methodology based on surveys and polling has been extensively utilized to understand such attitudes of population samples, and data collected with these methods are often considered a gold standard when it comes to public opinion. Thus, comparing against these indicators provides an additional validation of the reliability of our approach. A number of surveys attempt to measure consumer confidence in the U.S. For instance, Reuters/University of Michigan Surveys of Consumers maintains the monthly-published Index of Consumer Sentiment (ICS)[5]. However, since we have temporally fine-grained data from Twitter, we prefer a consumer dataset with more frequent observations and use the daily-administered economic confidence index from Gallup[6], which is calculated from a 3-day rolling average where each data point is based on interviews with 1,500 Americans aged 18 and older. The aggregated Gallup economic index is known to correlate well with ICS, and both indices do correlate strongly for the duration of our study ($r = 0.59, p = 0.01$).

We also find that the consumer confidence index from Gallup correlates strongly with the normalized frequency of smile-containing images ($r = 0.608$, $p < 0.0001$). However, we are more interested in whether variations in detected smiling is a reflection of consumer confidence. To formally test the relationship between these two time-series, we use the well-known econometric technique of Granger causality analysis.

Granger causality analysis

Granger causality tests for the ability of one series to predict another one — in our case, whether our Smile Index provides information to forecast the economic index. More formally, the analysis uses two linear models G_1 and G_2 to predict E_t as shown in equations (1) and (2). The first model, G_1, uses endogenous information — only the lagged value of E_t. G_2 incorporates another variable, H_t, combining the lagged value of both E_t and H_t. If the variance of the regression model G_2 decreases by including G_t, then H_t is said to Granger-cause E_t. The assumption here is that if H_t causes E_t, then the lagged value of H_t will strongly correlate with E_t. We note that this analysis is not asserting true causation but rather the presence of useful predictive information.

$$\mathbf{G_1}: \; E_t = \alpha + \sum_{i=1}^{k} \beta_i E_{t-i} + \epsilon_t \tag{1}$$

$$\mathbf{G_2}: \; E_t = \alpha + \sum_{i=1}^{k} \beta_i E_{t-i} + \sum_{i=1}^{k} \gamma_i H_{t-i} + \epsilon_t \tag{2}$$

In the equations, ϵ_t represents noise and k is the lag parameter, which is free in Granger causality analysis. In our case, we are interested in the trend of daily change, and so we use the difference in values across subsequent days:

$$E_t = EI_t - EI_{t-1}$$
$$H_t = S_t - S_{t-1},$$

EI_t and S_t are respectively the values of Gallup's economic index and the frequency of images with smiles, on day t. The Granger causality analysis assumes that the data is stationary, which the differencing measurement ensures.

Lag	F-statistic	p-value
1 day	4.74	0.03*
2 days	4.64	0.01*
3 days	2.5047	0.058

Table 5. Summary of bivariate Granger causality analysis between Gallup Economic Confidence Index and frequency of images with smiles

We estimate equations (1) and (2) using an Ordinary Least Squares regression model. Table 5 shows the result of the causality analysis. In this case, the model G_2 performs significantly better than G_1. The F-statistic here is proportional to the relative change in the residual sum of squares between models. In other words, we can reject the null hypothesis that our Smile Index does not predict consumer confidence with a high level of confidence.

Forecasting analysis

The result of our preceding Granger analysis indicates that our image based Smile Index captures predicative information about consumer economic confidence. To further validate, we train and evaluate our model in a rolling forecast setting. Similar to Brendan et al. [51], we use a one variable least-square model:

$$EI_t = \alpha + \beta \sum_{i=0}^{k-1} S_{t-i} + \epsilon_t \tag{3}$$

For a given hyperparameter k, the model uses a k-day window for training. In other words, to predict the forecast on day t, the slope and bias parameter of the model β and α are fitted using data from $t - k$ to $t - 1$ days. The fitted model is then used for prediction. For evaluating in a rolling forecasting setup, we introduce another hyperparameter L:

$$EI_{t+L} = \alpha + \beta \sum_{i=0}^{k-1} S_{t-i} + \epsilon_t \tag{4}$$

[5] `http://www.sca.isr.umich.edu/`

[6] `http://www.gallup.com/poll/122840/Gallup-Daily-Economic-Indexes.aspx`

The parameter L determines how many days in the future we are forecasting. In other words, for a target forecast date $t+L$, we train the model through $t-k$ to $t-1$ days and predict using the value from the last day of the window, day t.

To evaluate performance, we use Mean Absolute Error (MAE). We find that the best model for forecasting 7 days ahead uses 13 days of historical data. That is, we use the data from days $t-13$ to $t-1$ to learn the parameters of the model, and we then ask the model to use the value from day t to predict day $t+7$. We then measure the error in this predicted value compared to the actual eventual outcome. Figure 10 illustrates the alignment between this forecast and the actual Gallup economic confidence index.

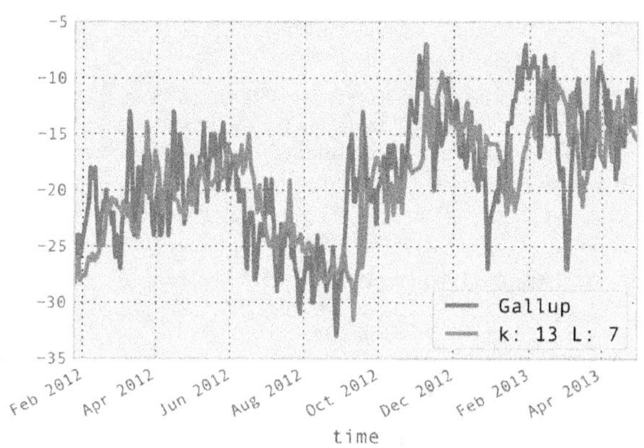

Figure 10. Rolling forecast of Gallup economic confidence index using Smile Index

Performance for alternative lag parameters is shown in Table 6. For $k = 13$, the 7 days ahead forecast has a mean absolute error of 3.53. We compare that result with a baseline model that uses endogenous values for prediction. In other words, the baseline model uses the lagged self-value for prediction ($EI_{t+L} = \alpha + \beta \sum_{i=0}^{k-1} EI_{t-i} + \epsilon_t$). We find that this baseline performs slightly worse with a mean absolute error of 3.55.

	$L = 7$	$L = 10$	$L = 14$
$k = 7$	3.70	3.95	4.19
$k = 13$	3.53	3.68	4.10
$k = 10$	3.61	3.75	4.05

Table 6. Mean Absolute Error (MAE) for rolling forecast of economic confidence (L = # of days in the future we forecast, k = # of days of historical data used to train model)

Overall, the performance of this simple model thus validates our finding from the Granger analysis: smile-containing images hold predictive information about the economic confidence index. The performance of the model is also encouraging since the rich content of social media could be used as a faster and lower-cost supplement for expensive traditional polling. Given the deep reach and broader scope of social media, being able to combine such signals in this way would not only allow us to measure well-being but also to analyze factors that may contribute to it.

DISCUSSION

Methodological Implications

In this study, we set out to explore the potential of using pictures shared on social media to assess collective well-being. By applying computer vision techniques and calculating the proportion of photos in which we detect smiling faces, we proffer our methodological contribution: the *Smile Index* — a quantifiable proxy for happiness that capitalizes on the ever-expanding supply of social media hosted images, which are shared by users frequently, naturally, and globally.

Examining temporal trends, our Smile Index reveals patterns of happiness that are highest during mornings, evenings, and weekends and that drop during late night, mid-day, and mid-week. In our case studies on four emotionally significant U.S. events, we verify that the Smile Index considerably increases in response to celebratory events and holidays, while it substantially sinks during tragedies and disasters. In connecting emotional health with demographic and economic indicators, we find positive correlations between income and positive sentiment in white-majority geographical areas yet the reverse relationship in black-majority areas. In testing the predictive power of the Smile Index, we demonstrate the metric's ability to forecast consumer confidence 7 days ahead using just 13 days of historical data. Altogether, these results showcase our approach's potential for monitoring population-level emotion.

Further, our methodology can benefit stakeholders from multiple domains including CSCW disciplines, government, and business. For example, a primary intended outcome of our work was unlocking a rich data source and offering a new lens through which future research can extend existing understandings of human behavior, emotion, and communities of practice. In particular, our work helps advance computational social science's aim to leverage social media as part of data-driven social science research, which continues to gain interest within CSCW. Along the same lines, our work further provides novel image-based computational techniques that scholars can apply to develop psychological and sociological theory.

Our findings, especially those regarding the relationship between events and public mood, highlight the insight our method provides about one such notable behavioral dynamic: how people's offline activities and emotional states impact their online behaviors. In this way, social media's ability to reflect the well-being of real world communities has important implications for the role such online communication platforms can play in connecting leaders and constituents in order to help improve people's quality of life and welfare, for example through better public health intervention, allocation of public services, or regional planning.

Looking for evidence of the reverse phenomenon would be desirable as well — that is, to what extent being exposed online to emotionally-charged content influences emotions and behaviors in the physical world. Prior work on mimicry and emotional contagion find that viewing pictures containing smiles can influence a person's own happiness [39, 65], and it would therefore be worthwhile to explore whether pictures containing smiles not only signal current levels of collective sentiment but also are responsible for stimulating similar emotions in other users or even fueling emotional cascades. Researchers may similarly investigate whether content containing pictures has more influence over other users' behavior than purely text-based content does, for instance in posts that encourage users to join protests, charity events, or other forms of collective action. This sort of study could also make space for new generations of personalized early warning systems that inform people about major events that will personally impact them, based on local patterns of emotional arousal trending in their social media streams.

Practical Implications

From a practical perspective, our proposed system additionally offers ways to overcome a number of limitations faced by current methods for assessing sentiment. First, in contrast to survey-based methodologies — which may struggle with low response rates, are typically administered infrequently and retrospectively, and can be difficult to scale — our approach is unobtrusive, enables live and continuous affective monitoring, and provides access to ever-wider global populations as social media adoption continues to grow. Such real-time monitoring, which our prediction and forecasting analyses demonstrate is feasible, can have particularly important implications during times of crisis, for instance when communities require prompt and accurately targeted aid. Second, current NLP techniques for text-based sentiment analysis are language-dependent, and most available corpora and dictionaries only exist for the English language. This impedes not only international-level studies but even research within the United States. For instance, an estimated 200 languages are spoken in New York City alone [78], and studies using sentiment analyses restricted to text in English may be biasing results and missing opportunities to investigate the full emotional characteristics of such highly diverse regions. Again in contrast, our text (and hence language) independent method facilitates an analysis of emotions expressed by individuals spanning multiple languages and cultures.

Cultural Differences in Emotion and Photography

To further push on this idea of using photographed smiles to assess sentiment cross-culturally, we investigate viability by comparing our Smile Index across countries. For the 15 countries with more than 100,000 tweets in our dataset, we find it to be relatively consistent, as shown in Figure 11. Additionally, the standard deviation of the Smile Index across these countries is 0.02, and this low value further suggests that our proposed sentiment assessment framework would be applicable for use with countries beyond the US. These results provide some evidence that the universal nature of smiling would permit the use of our system cross-culturally, though researchers should be aware of cultural variations.

While the universality of emotion across cultures has been long debated by psychologists [21, 55], an extensive survey of the related literature by Elfenbein et al. [22] concludes that the core six emotions are universally recognized. Key to our research is that even researchers critical of universality

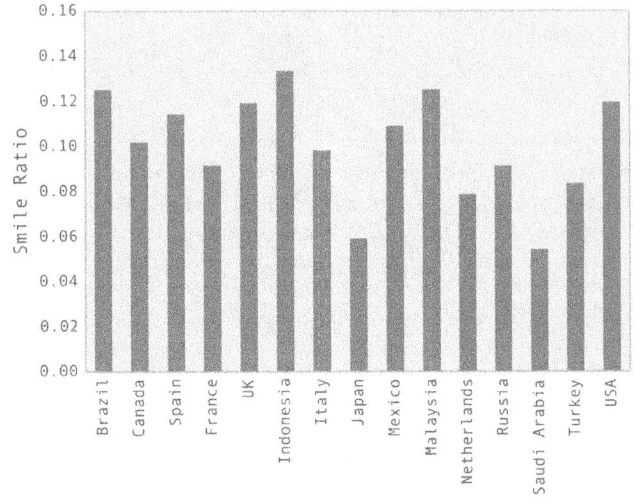

Figure 11. Smile ratio across countries with more than 100,000 tweets in our dataset. Low standard deviation (0.02) indicates that Smile Index is consistent, highlighting the potential of using our framework in cross-cultural setups

models find that facial expression for *happiness* is consistent across cultures [34].

Regarding the influence of culture on photography, East Asians' facial expressions in particular tend to display lower intensity in photographs, and images from East Asia also focus more on contextual details. This phenomenon is observed on social media as well — for instance, East Asian users often de-emphasize faces in Facebook profile pictures, resulting in a smaller face-to-background size ratio compared to users from the United States [46]. Nonetheless, vital to our research is the determination that the *ratio of smiling and non-smiling images is the same across cultures* [32] — though as seen in Figure 11, photos from Japan do exhibit lower smile ratios as expected.

Overall, such prior work as well as our own preliminary inspection are a sign that using smile features to build an index of happiness could improve cross-cultural sentiment analysis, especially compared to word-based approaches, which are tightly coupled with specific languages and obligate complicated feature engineering such as cross-language dictionaries [3] or multilingual annotations [1] to study the sentiment of speakers with different languages.

Future Work

This paper illustrates the merits of our current study, but as a nascent step towards using pictures as a measurement tool for societal happiness, further attention is required to address some limitations.

The first is a question of population bias. While the wide adoption of social media platforms like Twitter increasingly offers the potential to access broad groups of people, at this point concerns can be raised about the issue of representativeness for these sorts of datasets. Around 15% of online adults in the U.S. use Twitter, resulting in a user base in which younger generations and minorities are overrepresented compared to the overall population [58]. Combining this with the fact that we have access to only 10% of all posts, we acknowledge that our dataset is a non-uniform subsample from a non-representative population and that our happiness metric is based on the sentiments of some people more than others. Especially since a core motivation of our work is the creation of techniques with which to perform global and cross-cultural assessments of sentiment, a key next step is therefore extending our study to ensure more representative coverage and to utilize additional datasets, including from countries around the world of diverse languages and cultures.

Second, it is also necessary to more fully investigate the quality of image-based data streams for sentiment analysis. Though extant research and our own comparison studies suggest our data is reliable in terms of the authenticity of positive affect that detected smiles express, there are some complex questions herein that require deeper investigation. One is whether the social convention of smiling while being photographed might artificially inflate our smile based happiness index. That is, smiling might not always indicate good mood but rather be the result of nuanced posing etiquette and customs, which can vary with culture, gender, and age as discussed in earlier portions of the paper. On the reverse hand, pictures suggestive of happiness may not always contain smiles or even faces or people, necessitating strategies to detect alternate signals of sentiment in photos, such as sustainable crowdsourcing techniques for labeling emotions in photos. Another issue is the extent to which the images people share on social media are pictures of themselves and friends as opposed to popular memes that may contain smiles but not be truly reflective of the contributing user's own emotional state. In our earlier description of our dataset, we also noted potential complications due to discrepancies between when and where images are captured vs. posted, though we explained why this concern should likely be minimal.

Alongside these issues regarding the reliability of image data, it is worth pointing out that the *existing* approaches to happiness measurement suffer from their own analogous challenges. For instance, text-based sentiment analysis techniques typically struggle with syntactic errors and properly handling linguistic mechanisms like sarcasm, and survey-based approaches must deal with response veracity and can suffer from reflective self-report biases. Going forward, it would be worthwhile to make further comparisons between various image, text, and survey-based methods for happiness assessment to determine the key advantages and limitations of each approach, with a focus on combining the methods in ways most appropriate for the phenomenon being studied.

Finally, in this study our focus was on developing a new technique for *measuring* happiness, so it is desirable to next look more deeply into what factors may actually *generate* that happiness. While our findings demonstrate a number of clear correlations between smiling and sentiment, we cannot yet claim causation without such further inquiry. Similarly, careful examination of potential confounding factors, such as the effect of education on income and happiness, will help to strengthen interpretations regarding the reasons underlying observed emotional characteristics.

Given these concerns, we therefore emphasize the need to further unravel our findings by undertaking additional qualitative work. Such research could involve more rigorous analyses of the images themselves to identify subtleties in the expression of emotion in photographs. Interview studies could also be conducted with individuals who contribute image content in order to better understand the motivations behind their sharing practices and the authenticity of emotion displayed in their pictures, as well as the extent of geographical and temporal differences between when they capture vs. post images, and finally their reactions to having their content used as part of automatic sentiment tracking.

CONCLUSION

In this paper, we presented a novel methodology for utilizing user-contributed pictures on social media to infer public happiness. We provided evidence of the potential to assess population-wide sentiment from such large-scale, geographically diverse, and temporally dispersed image-based content.

In the first attempt to use images for large-scale sentiment analysis, we leveraged established computer vision techniques to detect smiling faces from photos posted on Twitter in order to track societal patterns of happiness, sense underlying political and cultural events, and uncover community characteristics. We verified that this data source aligns well with established survey-based methods for assessing public mood and yet is less costly to obtain in terms of time, financing, and human resources. In addition to this comparison with ground-truth data, we also compared our technique to traditional text-based approaches for analyzing sentiment, laid out strengths and weaknesses of each, and considered how they might be combined.

Through multiple analytic experiments and case studies, we explored how publicly posted pictures can reveal temporal trends in happiness, serve as an indicator of mood during societal events, and be used to study relations between socioeconomic factors. Finally, we discussed the theoretical and practical implications of our research along with directions for future work, giving particular attention to the issues of overcoming population bias, achieving cross-cultural generalizability, and remaining cognizant of the social contexts in which individuals who share photos are embedded.

Acknowledgements

The authors would like to thank Chris Danforth and Peter Dodds from UVM's Computational Story Lab for providing valuable comments and making the research data available.

Development of these methods for non-US data was originally supported by the Intelligence Advanced Research Projects Activity (IARPA) via DoI/NBC contract number D12PC000337. The US Government is authorized to reproduce and distribute reprints of this work for Governmental purposes notwithstanding any copyright annotation thereon. Application of these methods to US data was undertaken by the authors on their own.

REFERENCES

1. Boiy, E., and Moens, M.-F. A machine learning approach to sentiment analysis in multilingual web texts. *Information retrieval 12*, 5 (2009), 526–558.
2. Bollen, J., Mao, H., and Pepe, A. Modeling public mood and emotion: Twitter sentiment and socio-economic phenomena. In *ICWSM* (2011).
3. Boyd-Graber, J., and Resnik, P. Holistic sentiment analysis across languages: multilingual supervised latent Dirichlet allocation. In *EMNLP'10*, ACL (2010), 45–55.
4. Bradley, M. M., and Lang, P. J. Affective norms for english words (anew): Instruction manual and affective ratings (1999).
5. Campbell, A., Converse, P. E., and Rodgers, W. L. *The quality of American life: Perceptions, evaluations, and satisfactions*, vol. 3508. Russell Sage Foundation, 1976.
6. Clark, A. Happiness, habits and high rank: Comparisons in economic and social life.
7. Clark, A. E., Frijters, P., and Shields, M. A. Relative income, happiness, and utility: An explanation for the Easterlin paradox and other puzzles. *Journal of Economic Literature* (2008), 95–144.
8. Clark, L. A., Watson, D., and Leeka, J. Diurnal variation in the positive affects. *Motivation and Emotion 13*, 3 (1989), 205–234.
9. Cohn, M. A., Mehl, M. R., and Pennebaker, J. W. Linguistic markers of psychological change surrounding September 11, 2001. *Psychological Science 15*, 10 (2004), 687–693.
10. Coverdill, J. E., López, C. A., and Petrie, M. A. Race, ethnicity and the quality of life in america, 1972–2008. *Social Forces 89*, 3 (2011), 783–805.
11. De Choudhury, M., Counts, S., and Horvitz, E. Major life changes and behavioral markers in social media: Case of childbirth. CSCW (2013), 1431–1442.
12. De Choudhury, M., Counts, S., Horvitz, E. J., and Hoff, A. Characterizing and predicting postpartum depression from shared facebook data. CSCW (2014), 626–638.
13. De Choudhury, M., Monroy-Hernández, A., and Mark, G. "Narco" emotions: Affect and desensitization in social media during the mexican drug war. CHI, ACM (2014), 3563–3572.
14. Di Tella, R., and MacCulloch, R. Some uses of happiness data in economics. *The Journal of Economic Perspectives 20*, 1 (2006), 25–46.
15. Diener, E. Subjective well-being. *Psychological Bulletin 95* (1984), 542–575.
16. Diener, E., Emmons, R. A., Larsen, R. J., and Griffin, S. The satisfaction with life scale. *Journal of personality assessment 49*, 1 (1985), 71–75.
17. Dodds, P. S., and Danforth, C. M. Measuring the happiness of large-scale written expression: Songs, blogs, and presidents. *Journal of Happiness Studies 11*, 4 (2010), 441–456.
18. Dodds, P. S., Harris, K. D., Kloumann, I. M., Bliss, C. A., and Danforth, C. M. Temporal patterns of happiness and information in a global social network: Hedonometrics and twitter. *PloS one 6*, 12 (2011).
19. Ekman, P. An argument for basic emotions. *Cognition & Emotion 6*, 3-4 (1992), 169–200.
20. Ekman, P., and Friesen, W. V. Facial action coding system: A technique for the measurement of facial movement. *Consulting Psych. Press* (1978), 271–302.
21. Ekman, P., Friesen, W. V., O'Sullivan, M., Chan, A., Diacoyanni-Tarlatzis, I., Heider, K., Krause, R., LeCompte, W. A., Pitcairn, T., and Ricci-Bitti, P. E. Universals and cultural differences in the judgments of facial expressions of emotion. *Journal of personality and social psychology 53*, 4 (1987), 712.
22. Elfenbein, H. A., and Ambady, N. On the universality and cultural specificity of emotion recognition: a meta-analysis. *Psychological bulletin 128*, 2 (2002).
23. Ferrer-i Carbonell, A. Income and well-being: an empirical analysis of the comparison income effect. *Journal of Public Economics 89*, 5 (2005), 997–1019.
24. Fowler, J. H., Christakis, N. A., Steptoe, and Roux, D. Dynamic spread of happiness in a large social network: longitudinal analysis of the framingham heart study social network. *British medical journal* (2009), 23–27.
25. Girardin, F., Calabrese, F., Fiore, F. D., Ratti, C., and Blat, J. Digital footprinting: Uncovering tourists with user-generated content. *Pervasive 7*, 4 (2008), 36–43.
26. Golder, S. A., and Macy, M. W. Diurnal and seasonal mood vary with work, sleep, and daylength across diverse cultures. *Science 333*, 6051 (2011), 1878–1881.
27. Hall, J. A., LeBeau, L. S., Reinoso, J. G., and Thayer, F. Status, gender, and nonverbal behavior in candid and posed photographs: A study of conversations between university employees. *Sex Roles 44* (2001), 677–692.
28. Harker, L., and Keltner, D. Expressions of positive emotion in women's college yearbook pictures and their relationship to personality and life outcomes across adulthood. *Personality and social psych. 80*, 1 (2001), 112.
29. Hernandez, J., Hoque, M. E., Drevo, W., and Picard, R. W. Mood meter: counting smiles in the wild. In *UbiComp*, ACM (2012), 301–310.
30. Hess, U., Beaupré, M. G., Cheung, N., et al. Who to whom and why: cultural differences and similarities in the function of smiles. 187.
31. Hromada, D. D., Tijus, C., Poitrenaud, S., and Nadel, J. Zygomatic smile detection: The semi-supervised Haar training of a fast and frugal system: A gift to opencv community. IEEE (2010), 1–5.

32. Huang, C.-M., and Park, D. Cultural influences on facebook photographs. *International Journal of Psychology 48*, 3 (2013), 334–343.

33. Hughes, M., and Thomas, M. E. The continuing significance of race revisited: A study of race, class, and quality of life in america, 1972 to 1996. *American Sociological Review* (1998), 785–795.

34. Jack, R. E., Garrod, O. G., Yu, H., Caldara, R., and Schyns, P. G. Facial expressions of emotion are not culturally universal. *Proceedings of the National Academy of Sciences 109*, 19 (2012), 7241–7244.

35. Joshi, D., Datta, R., Fedorovskaya, E., Luong, Q.-T., Wang, J. Z., Li, J., and Luo, J. Aesthetics and emotions in images. *Signal Processing Mag. 28*, 5 (2011), 94–115.

36. Keltner, D. Ekman, emotional expression, and the art of empirical epiphany. *Journal of Research in Personality 38*, 1 (2004), 37–44.

37. Kim, E., Gilbert, S., Edwards, M. J., and Graeff, E. Detecting sadness in 140 characters: Sentiment analysis and mourning Michael Jackson on twitter. *Web Ecology 3* (2009).

38. Kivran-Swaine, F., and Naaman, M. Network properties and social sharing of emotions in social awareness streams. CSCW, ACM (2011), 379–382.

39. Kleinke, C. L., Peterson, T. R., and Rutledge, T. R. Effects of self-generated facial expressions on mood. *Jour. Personality & Social Psych. 74*, 1 (1998), 272.

40. Kotchemidova, C. Why we say "cheese": Producing the smile in snapshot photography. *Critical Studies in Media Communication 22*, 1 (2005), 2–25.

41. Kramer, A. D. An unobtrusive behavioral model of gross national happiness. In *CHI*, ACM (2010), 287–290.

42. Levenson, R. W., Ekman, P., and Friesen, W. V. Voluntary facial action generates emotion-specific autonomic nervous system activity. *Psychophysiology 27*, 4 (1990), 363–384.

43. Lienhart, R., Kuranov, A., and Pisarevsky, V. Empirical analysis of detection cascades of boosted classifiers for rapid object detection. *Pattern Rec.* (2003), 297–304.

44. Logunov, A., and Panchenko, V. Characteristics and predictability of twitter sentiment series. In *Internat. Congress on Modelling and Simulation* (2011).

45. Maruyama, M. T., Robertson, S. P., Douglas, S. K., Semaan, B. C., and Faucett, H. A. Hybrid media consumption: How tweeting during a televised political debate influences the vote decision. CSCW, ACM (2014), 1422–1432.

46. Masuda, T., Gonzalez, R., Kwan, L., and Nisbett, R. E. Culture and aesthetic preference: Comparing the attention to context of east asians and americans. *Personality & Social Psych. Bull. 34*, 9 (2008), 1260–75.

47. McNair, D., Lorr, M., and Droppleman, L. Profile of mood states. *San Diego, California 53* (1992), 6.

48. Mihalcea, R., and Liu, H. A corpus-based approach to finding happiness. In *AAAI, Computational Approaches to Analyzing Weblogs* (2006), 139–144.

49. Mishne, G., and de Rijke, M. Capturing global mood levels using blog posts. In *AAAI, Computational Approaches to Analyzing Weblogs* (2006), 145–152.

50. Monk, T., Buysse, D., Reynolds, C., Berga, S., Jarrett, D., Begley, A., and Kupfer, D. Circadian rhythms in human performance and mood under constant conditions. *Journal of sleep research 6*, 1 (1997), 9–18.

51. O'Connor, B., Balasubramanyan, R., Routledge, B. R., and Smith, N. A. From tweets to polls: Linking text sentiment to public opinion time series. *ICWSM'10*, 122–9.

52. Pennebaker, J. W., Chung, C. K., Ireland, M., Gonzales, A., and Booth, R. J. The development and psychometric properties of liwc2007. *liwc.net* (2007).

53. Quercia, D. Don't worry, be happy: The geography of happiness on facebook. In *Proceedings of the 5th Annual ACM Web Science Conference*, ACM (2013), 316–325.

54. Quercia, D., Ellis, J., Capra, L., and Crowcroft, J. Tracking gross community happiness from tweets. In *Proc. CSCW'12*, ACM (2012), 965–968.

55. Russell, J. A. Is there universal recognition of emotion from facial expressions? a review of the cross-cultural studies. *Psychological bulletin 115*, 1 (1994), 102.

56. Sakaki, T., Okazaki, M., and Matsuo, Y. Earthquake shakes twitter users: real-time event detection by social sensors. In *WWW*, ACM (2010), 851–860.

57. Seder, J. P., and Oishi, S. Intensity of smiling in facebook photos predicts future life satisfaction. *Social Psychological & Personality Sci. 3*, 4 (2012), 407–413.

58. Smith, A., and Brenner, J. Twitter use 2012. pew.

59. Stone, A. A., Hedges, S. M., Neale, J. M., and Satin, M. S. Prospective and cross-sectional mood reports offer no evidence of a "blue monday" phenomenon. *Journal of Personality and Social Psychology 49*, 1 (1985), 129.

60. Tomkins, S. S. Affect, imagery, consciousness.

61. Tsujita, H., and Rekimoto, J. Smiling makes us happier: enhancing positive mood and communication with smile-encouraging digital appliances. In *Proceedings of the 13th international conference on Ubiquitous computing*, ACM (2011), 1–10.

62. Viola, P., and Jones, M. Rapid object detection using a boosted cascade of simple features. In *Computer Vision and Pattern Recognition*, vol. 1, IEEE (2001), I–511.

63. Wang, W., Chen, L., Thirunarayan, K., and Sheth, A. P. Cursing in english on twitter. CSCW (2014), 415–25.

64. Whitehill, J., Littlewort, G., Fasel, I., Bartlett, M., and Movellan, J. Toward practical smile detection. *Pattern Analysis and Machine Intelligence* (2009), 2106–2111.

65. Wild, B., Erb, M., and Bartels, M. Are emotions contagious? evoked emotions while viewing emotionally expressive faces: quality, quantity, time course and gender differences. *Psychiatry research 102*, 2 (2001), 109–124.

66. Xia, C., Schwartz, R., Xie, K., Krebs, A., Langdon, A., Ting, J., and Naaman, M. Citybeat: real-time social media visualization of hyper-local city data. In *WWW* (2014), 167–170.

67. Xie, K., Xia, C., Grinberg, N., Schwartz, R., and Naaman, M. Robust detection of hyper-local events from geotagged social media data. In *13th Internat. Workshop on Multimedia Data Mining*, ACM (2013), 2.

68. Bhutanese gross national happiness commission. `http://www.gnhc.gov.bt/`.

69. Facebook has 220 billion of your photos to put on ice. `http://gigaom.com/2012/10/17/facebook-has-220-billion-of-your-photos-to-put-on-ice`.

70. Gallup Healthways Well-Being Index. `http://www.gallup.com/poll/106915/gallup-daily-us-mood.aspx`.

71. Global mobile statistics 2014 part A. `http://mobithinking.com/mobile-marketing-tools/latest-mobile-stats/a`.

72. Gross national happiness. `http://www.grossnationalhappiness.com/`.

73. Gross national happiness USA. `http://www.gnhusa.org/`.

74. Guangdong to use index to gauge happiness. `http://china.org.cn/china/2011-10/12/content_23601655.htm`.

75. Hurricane/post-tropical cyclone sandy service assessment. `http://www.nws.noaa.gov/os/assessments/pdfs/Sandy13.pdf`.

76. Ict facts and figures. `http://www.itu.int/en/ITU-D/Statistics/Documents/facts/ICTFactsFigures2014-e.pdf`.

77. Locals and tourists. `https://www.flickr.com/photos/walkingsf/sets/72157624209158632/`.

78. NYC planning - population facts. `http://www.nyc.gov/html/dcp/html/census/pop_facts.shtml`.

79. Oecd guidelines on measuring subjective well-being. `http://www.oecd.org/statistics/guidelines-on-measuring-subjective-well-being.htm`.

80. Office for national statistics - measuring national well-being. `http://www.ons.gov.uk/ons/guide-method/user-guidance/well-being/index.html`.

81. Photo and video sharing grow online. *PEW 2013.*

82. Planet selfie. `http://www.businessinsider.com/were-now-posting-a-staggering-18-billion-photos-to-social-media-every-day-2014-5`.

83. State of American Well-Being. `http://info.healthways.com/wbi2013`.

84. The lottery of life. `http://www.economist.com/news/21566430-where-be-born-2013-lottery-life`.

85. The role for well-being in creating the big society. `http://cles.org.uk/wp-content/uploads/2011/01/LW-105-Well-Being-and-Big-Society1.pdf`.

86. World happiness report 2013. `http://unsdsn.org/resources/publications/world-happiness-report-2013/`.

Engagement and Well-being on Social Network Sites

A.K.M. Najmul Islam[†‡] **Sameer Patil**[†§ϕ]
[†]Helsinki Institute for Information Technology HIIT / Aalto University
P O Box 15600, 00076 Aalto, Finland
[‡]Information Systems Science, University of Turku, 20500 Turku, Finland
[§]Department of Information Systems and New Media, University of Siegen, 57068 Siegen, Germany
[ϕ]Yahoo Labs, 701 First Avenue, Sunnyvale, CA 94089, USA
najmul.islam@utu.fi, sameerpatil@yahoo-inc.com

ABSTRACT
Prior research has reported contradictory findings on the relationship between the use of Social Network Sites (SNS) and psychological well-being. We addressed this shortcoming by incorporating a finer measure of SNS user engagement and hypothesizing a U-shaped rather than purely linear relationship between the two. We tested our hypotheses via a Web based questionnaire administered to 289 Facebook users. Ordinary least squares approach confirmed the hypothesized U-shaped relationship. Our results further show that User Engagement, and in turn well-being, is associated with the number of SNS friends. These findings indicate that well-being derived from SNS usage could be optimized by avoiding underuse as well as overuse.

Author Keywords
Content production; Facebook; Facebook vitality; Social Network Sites; SNS; user engagement; well-being.

ACM Classification Keywords
H.5.m. Information Interfaces and Presentation (e.g. HCI): Miscellaneous

INTRODUCTION
In recent years, Social Network Sites (SNS) have become an integral form of social and professional online interactions. Therefore, it is important to examine how interactional capabilities of SNSs are connected with the well-being of their users. Such understanding could then be translated into improvements that promote greater well-being and mitigate issues that could have an adverse impact on users.

In the physical world, engagement with everyday social activities has been shown to be positively associated with subjective well-being [22, 25]. In fact, such impact was also observed in the early days of the Internet when it was a *substitute* rather than a *medium* for social interactions [16]. In this paper, we introduce user *engagement* [13] as a lens for characterizing SNS usage. Further, we utilize the concept of *vitality* [26] to measure psychological well-being and examine how it is associated with SNS engagement.

CSCW 2015, March 14–18, 2015, Vancouver, BC, Canada.
Copyright © 2015 ACM 978-1-4503-2922-4/15/03 ...$15.00.
http://dx.doi.org/10.1145/2675133.2675299

We operationalized these constructs in the form of a questionnaire administered via the Web to users of Facebook, the most widely adopted SNS. Based on responses from 289 Finnish participants, we found that psychological well-being follows a U-shaped relationship with the level of SNS engagement.

We begin by positioning our contribution in relation to prior research. We then explain the theoretical background informing our hypothesized relationships between SNS engagement and psychological well-being. Next, we describe questionnaire formulation and administration followed by the details of the analyses employed to validate our constructs and test our hypotheses. We conclude with implications of our findings for theory and design.

RELATED WORK
Several past studies have investigated the relationship between SNS usage and well-being using self-reported questionnaires as well as usage logs. For instance, Ellison et al. [10] found that SNS use was associated with increased self esteem and life satisfaction. Similarly, Burke et al. [6] discovered that SNS participation measured using log data showed a positive relationship with self-reported psychological well-being. In contrast, more recent research suggests that young SNS users experience low levels of subjective well-being [17]. We aimed to reconcile these somewhat contradictory findings by further unpacking the relationship between SNS usage and well-being.

We tackled this objective by addressing two gaps in prior research. First, in most prior research, SNS use has been measured in terms of the *frequency* and/or the *duration* of use [10, 17] and the level of *participation* in different activities such as commenting, liking, sharing, following, etc. [6]. We believe that frequency, duration, and participation do not sufficiently capture the extent to which the user is *attentive* and *aware* when participating in SNS interactions. As a result, we focused on *active user engagement.*

Second, prior research treated the association between SNS use and psychological well-being [6, 17] as a linear relationship. Given the opposing findings of Burke et al. [6] and

Kross et al. [17], we questioned this assumption of a linear relationship. Instead, we hypothesized a U-shaped relationship between SNS use and well-being.

THEORETICAL BACKGROUND AND HYPOTHESES

In this section, we describe the theoretical background that informed our hypotheses. We conceptualized psychological well-being using the concept of 'vitality' [26] from the psychology literature. Hwang and Throng [13] refer to user engagement as observable user behavior or psychological state of users toward a system. Therefore, we characterized SNS user engagement in terms of 'mindfulness' (i.e., *attentiveness*) and 'content production' (i.e., *active participation*). Mindfulness is connected to the psychological state while content production captures observable user behavior. We further examined whether user engagement is related to the Number of Friends one is connected to via SNS.

Vitality

The concept of vitality is used to describe one's psychological well-being [26]. Vitality is defined as the subjective experience of being energetic and alive [1]. An individual who possesses vitality experiences a sense of enthusiasm, liveliness, and energy available to the self [26]. Vitality is considered an aspect of well-being and has often been linked to various positive and energetic psychological states, such as vigor [1]. Vitality has been characterized as a complex and dynamic outcome influenced by factors such as social and psychological satisfaction or demands [27]. It has been argued that social events may lead a person to feel excited and energized, or, alternatively, stressed and drained [26]. Consequently, participating in social activities via SNSs (e.g., updating status, sharing and 'liking' content, writing comments, etc.) may influence vitality. As SNSs have become an integral part of people's social lives, it is particularly meaningful to investigate how participation in SNSs influences vitality.

The literature has conceptualized vitality at two levels – individual [26] and state [23]. At the individual level, vitality is considered an on-going and enduring characteristic of a person. In contrast, the state level conceptualization deals with the state of vitality only during a specific activity. Since we are interested in the specific activity of SNS usage, we adopted the state level conceptualization and adapted it to the context of Facebook. This adaptation led us to define 'Facebook Vitality' as the subjective experience of feeling energetic and lively during Facebook use.

Mindfulness

We examined the attentiveness facet of user engagement via the concept of mindfulness (or, conversely, mindlessness). Mindfulness traces its roots to Buddhist philosophy where conscious attention and awareness are actively cultivated [5]. In psychology, mindfulness has been conceptualized in three ways – state, trait, or cognitive ability. As a state, it facilitates positive psychological flow or well-being [5]. As a trait, it is employed to develop personality scales and examine differences among individuals [18]. As a cognitive ability, it describes an individual's typical mode of thinking, remembering, or problem solving [29].

Regardless of which conceptualization is considered, mindfulness reflects one's attentiveness to, and awareness of, events taking place in the present. A core characteristic of mindfulness has been described as open or receptive awareness and attention, which may be reflected in sustained consciousness of ongoing events and experiences [5]. In contrast, mindlessness is the absence or reduction of mindfulness and can be placed at the other end of a continuum [18]. An individual in a state of mindlessness fails to acknowledge or attend to a thought, emotion, motive, or object of perception [5]; the individual behaves automatically or habitually, without awareness of, or attention to, his or her behavior [18].

Since we utilized the state level treatment of vitality, for the sake of consistency, we chose to adopt the state level characterization of mindfulness. Consequently, we conceptualized 'Mindful Facebook Use' as the state of user engagement reflecting Facebook interactions toward which the user pays active and focused attention. In contrast, 'Mindless Facebook Use' is the state of user engagement corresponding to automatic and habitual Facebook activities, without conscious awareness or attention.

Content Production

In addition to conscious attention and awareness, a second aspect of user engagement is *active* behavior such as production of content on SNS. Content production takes place when SNS users update their status, upload photos, comment on posts, tag friends in their photos, etc. Content production is also referred to in other ways, such as 'directed communication' [6] or 'active participation' [15].

Relationship between Psychological Well-being and User Engagement

To formulate our hypotheses, we reviewed the literature on the relationship between psychological well-being (vitality) and user engagement (mindfulness and content production).

The literature suggests two opposite views on the relationship between vitality and mindfulness. First, automatic and habitual nature of mindless behavior relegates it to the subconscious, thus saving time and freeing up cognitive resources for other (presumably more important) tasks [19]. The higher availability of cognitive resources can translate into greater feeling of vitality. In the context of Facebook, this view suggests that routine and/or mundane SNS activities that could be performed without mindful attention keep cognitive resources free to experience vitality, thus indicating a positive association between Facebook Vitality and Mindless Facebook Use. From the second point of view, mindfulness enhances one's vitality because it involves conscious attention and raised awareness of the ongoing situation [5]. In the context of Facebook, this implies that mindful engagement would be associated with increased vitality and vice versa, leading to a negative association between Facebook Vitality and Mindless Facebook Use. We suspected that initially the former effect might dominate but will eventually diminish as mindless usage gradually accumulates to capture higher amounts of cognitive resources owing to cumulative volume and cognitive burden. This reasoning implies an inverted U-shaped relationship between Facebook Vitality and Mindless Facebook Use. Consequently, we hypothesized the following:

H_1: *Facebook Vitality follows an inverted U-shaped curve as the level of Mindless Facebook Use increases.*

SNSs are interactive systems where users produce content not just on their own but also in response to the content produced by others. Receiving (positive) responses to the content one produces has been shown to increase one's self-esteem and well-being [10, 30]. These findings largely align with the psychology literature showing that social relationships and interaction have a positive influence on psychological well-being [9]. Typically, there is a positive correlation between the production of content and responses received from others. In other words, greater content production on Facebook can be expected to drive larger volume of responses from others, resulting in enjoyable experiences that reduce anxiety and stress and enhance well-being. Consequently, we formulated the following hypothesis:

H_2: *Facebook Vitality is positively and linearly associated with the level of Content Production.*

Relationship between User Engagement and Number of Friends

Individuals possess limited cognitive resources [11]. An increase in the number of SNS friends creates a corresponding increase in incoming communication and information, such as messages, news feed posts, etc. As a result, it becomes increasingly difficult for an individual to process incoming information and keep track of SNS interactions. Such information overload likely leads to increased mindlessness as one finds it challenging to maintain attentive engagement with the large volume of incoming content. This led us to the following hypothesis:

H_3: *Mindless Facebook Use is positively and linearly associated with the Number of Friends on SNS.*

Burke et al. [6] reported that time spent on SNS was highly correlated with friend count and content produced. Since both friend count and content produced were highly correlated with time spent on the site, we hypothesized a correlation between content produced and friend count. Arguably, as one gathers more friends on SNS, one tends to produce more SNS content, suggesting a positive association between Content Production and Number of Friends. However, as the number of friends increases beyond a threshold, 'context collapse' could set in. Consequently, concerns related to privacy and impression management may result in greater self censorship and reduced content production. Such a relationship suggests an initial increase in Content Production as the Number of Friends increases, followed by a gradual decrease once the Number of Friends passes a threshold. We captured this in the following hypothesis:

H_4: *Content Production follows an inverted U-shaped curve as the Number of Friends increases.*

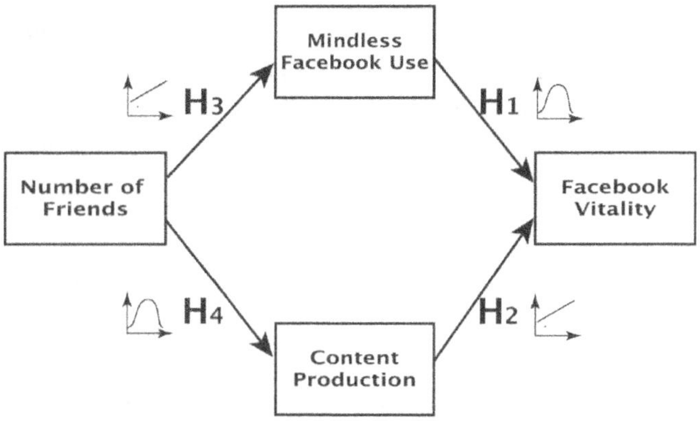

Figure 1. Hypothesized relationships between SNS User Engagement, Well-being, and Number of Friends.

	Items	Loadings
FV_1	When I use Facebook, I feel alive and vital.	0·82
FV_2	When I use Facebook, sometimes I feel so alive I just want to burst.	0·84
FV_3	When I use Facebook, I have energy and spirit.	0·88
FV_4	When I use Facebook, I feel I am fully living.	0·84

Table 1. Facebook Vitality items.

How often do you engage in the following Facebook activities? (Choices: *Never, Seldom, Sometimes, Often, and Very often)*

	Items	Loadings
CP_1	Update my status	0·76
CP_2	Add photos to my galleries	0·72
CP_3	Comment on other users' postings	0·78
CP_4	'Like' other users' postings	0·77
CP_5	Tag my friends to the photos I have added to my galleries	0·72

Table 2. Content Production items.

Figure 1 combines the above four hypotheses into a single model that depicts the hypothesized relationships between SNS user engagement, well-being, and number of friends.

METHOD

We operationalized the constructs outlined in the previous section in the form of a questionnaire administered via the Web. The items for measuring Facebook Vitality, Mindless Facebook Use, and Content Production were derived from the literature and adapted with appropriate wording changes to fit the Facebook context. The measures for Facebook Vitality were adapted from Bostic et al. [3] (see Table 1) while the measures for Mindless Facebook Use (see Table 3) were

	Items	Loadings
MFU_1	I could be experiencing some emotion when using Facebook and not to be conscious of it until some time later.	0·73
MFU_2	I share overly sensitive information on Facebook because of carelessness or not paying attention.	0·71
MFU_3	I find it difficult to stay focused on what is happening in my circle of friends on Facebook in the present.	0·39
MFU_4	I tend to try out different things quickly without paying attention to what I experience after trying.	0·71
MFU_5	I tend not to notice postings of friends until they really grab my attention.	0·35
MFU_6	I forget a person's name almost as soon as I've become friend with him/her on Facebook.	0·33
MFU_7	It seems I am 'running on automatic' when using Facebook, without much awareness of what I am doing.	0·77
MFU_8	I visit pages on Facebook on 'automatic pilot' and then wonder why I visited those pages.	0·80
MFU_9	I do things (e.g., launching apps, playing games) on Facebook automatically without being aware of what I am doing.	0·71
MFU_{10}	I rush through activities (e.g., posting status updates, commenting, launching apps, joining groups) on Facebook without being really attentive to them.	0·72
MFU_{11}	I get so focused on the goal I want to achieve that I lose touch with what I do on Facebook to get there.	0·73
MFU_{12}	I find myself using Facebook and listening to someone talking to me at the same time.	0·74
MFU_{13}	I find myself preoccupied with the future or the past when I use Facebook.	0·73
MFU_{14}	I find myself doing things on Facebook without paying attention to them.	0·80
MFU_{15}	I quickly check updates from Facebook without being aware that I am using it.	0·72

Table 3. Mindless Facebook Use items.

adapted from Brown and Ryan [5]. The measures for Content Production were adapted from Mäntymäki & Islam [20] (see Table 2).

An initial draft of the English questionnaire was reviewed by two senior scholars. After incorporating their edits, the questionnaire was reviewed by 10 Ph.D. students, resulting in further refinement. The refined questionnaire was translated into Finnish by a native Finnish speaker, with the translation verified by another native Finnish speaker. Disagreements were resolved by discussion among the two Finnish speakers.

In order to ensure construct validity, we employed card sorting [21]. We recruited four native Finnish speaking Ph.D. students to serve as judges. Each judge was provided with definitions of the constructs (viz., Facebook Vitality, Mindless Facebook Use, and Content Production) and a randomly sorted list of questionnaire items in Finnish. The judges were then told to assign each item to one of the constructs or mark it as 'ambiguous' if they were unsure about the categorization. The average hit ratio (i.e., the proportion of items correctly placed in the target category [21]) was 95% across all dimensions. The Cohen's Kappa was 0.85, well above than acceptable level of 0.70 [4].

The English version of the questionnaire items is shown in Tables 1, 2, and 3 along with corresponding loadings from a confirmatory factor analysis. Each item for Facebook Vitality and Mindless Facebook Use was measured using a five point Likert-type scale, with answer choices ranging from 'Strongly disagree (1)' to 'Strongly agree (5).' The items measuring content production were on a five point frequency scale, using adjectives deemed to indicate approximately equal intervals: never, seldom, sometimes, often, and very often. In addition, the questionnaires gathered other relevant information, such as gender, age, and number of Facebook friends. The questionnaire was advertised in October 2013 to a randomly selected sample of 1,500 students from the University of Turku in Turku, Finland. Participants were offered a movie ticket worth € 10 as a reward for completing the questionnaire. We received 289 valid responses, yielding a response rate of 19.27%. About two thirds (68%) of the respondents were female; 10% were less than 20 years old. Slightly more than half (55%) of the respondents were between 20 to 30 years old.

FINDINGS

We first verified the validity of our constructs and then tested each of the hypotheses outlined in the previous section.

Construct Validity and Reliability Assessment

We evaluated construct validity by carrying out a confirmatory factor analysis and examining convergent validity, discriminant validity, and internal consistency of our measures [8]. Prior research has recommended item loadings greater than 0.7 as acceptable [12]. All loadings for the items for Facebook Vitality were within 0.82–0.88 range (see Table 1). The item loadings for Mindless Facebook Use were within 0.71–0.80 for all items, except three (MFU_3, MFU_5, and MFU_6: see Table 3). Therefore, we deleted these items from the Mindless Facebook Use scale. Finally, item loadings for Content Production ranged from 0.72–0.78 (see Table 2), thus meeting the criterion for convergent validity for all items.

Cronbach's αs for Facebook Vitality, Mindless Facebook Use, and Content Production were 0.86, 0.81, and 0.84, respectively. These values are well above the recommended threshold of 0.7 [24]. The values of Average Variance Extracted (AVE) for Facebook Vitality, Mindless Facebook Use, and Content Production were 0.70, 0.55, and 0.58, respectively, exceeding the recommended cutoff of 0.5 [24]. These Cronbach's α and AVE values further confirmed sufficient convergent validity of our constructs. To verify discriminant validity, we verified that the square root of the AVE for each construct was higher than the correlation between the construct and any other construct [7].

We tested the hypotheses using the Ordinary Least Squares (OLS) approach. Although more powerful methods exist, OLS has been deemed acceptable when sample size is reasonably high [14]. Composite scores for Mindless Facebook Use, Content Production, and Facebook Vitality were calculated by summing the scores for corresponding individual items. The skewness of the composite scores ranged from -1.28–1.78, indicating that the scales were not highly skewed.

Relationship between Psychological Well-being and User Engagement

In order to test H_1 and H_2, we compared four regression models, viz., Model 1–4. $Model_1$ assumed that Mindless Facebook Use and Content Production are both linearly related to Facebook Vitality. $Model_2$ assumed that Mindless Facebook Use exhibits a quadratic relationship but Content Production holds a linear relationship with Facebook Vitality. $Model_3$ assumed that Mindless Facebook Use is linearly related, but Content Production is quadratically related to Facebook Vitality. Finally, the assumption of $Model_4$ was that both Mindless Facebook Use and Content Production exhibit a quadratic relationship with Facebook Vitality. The models are captured in the following four equations, respectively:

Model$_1$: $Facebook\ Vitality = \beta_0 + \beta_1 * (Mindless\ Facebook\ Use) + \beta_2 * (Content\ Production) + \epsilon$

Model$_2$: $Facebook\ Vitality = \beta_0 + \beta_1 * (Mindless\ Facebook\ Use) + \beta_2 * (Content\ Production) + \beta_3 * (Mindless\ Facebook\ Use)^2 + \epsilon$

Model$_3$: $Facebook\ Vitality = \beta_0 + \beta_1 * (Mindless\ Facebook\ Use) + \beta_2 * (Content\ Production) + \beta_3 * (Content\ Production)^2 + \epsilon$

Model$_4$: $Facebook\ Vitality = \beta_0 + \beta_1 * (Mindless\ Facebook\ Use) + \beta_2 * (Mindless\ Facebook\ Use)^2 + \beta_3 * (Content\ Production) + \beta_4 * (Mindless\ Facebook\ Use) * (Content\ Production) + \beta_5 * (Content\ Production)^2 + \epsilon$

The results of testing the four regression models are provided in Table 4. The results show that the R^2 of $Model_1$ was 0.13. Adding the quadratic term for Mindless Facebook Use increased R^2 to 0.17 for $Model_2$. The F-change statistic showed that the increase was statistically significant. However, the R^2 change for $Model_3$, resulting from adding the quadratic term of Content Production to $Model_1$, was not statistically significant. Finally, when we added the quadratic terms of both Content Production and Mindless Facebook Use to generate $Model_4$ and compared the R^2 change with respect to $Model_2$, we observed that the change was not statistically significant. Taken together, the analyses indicated that $Model_2$ was the most appropriate among the four models.

The regression results for $Model_2$ suggest that Mindless Facebook Use ($\beta_1 = 1.45, p < 0.001$) is positively associated with Facebook Vitality and its squared term ($\beta_3 = -1.25, p < 0.001$) is negatively associated Facebook Vitality. These results confirm an inverted U-shaped relationship between Facebook Vitality and Mindless Facebook Use, thus supporting H_1. The results also indicate a positive association between Facebook Vitality and Content Production ($\beta_2 = 0.23, p < 0.001$), supporting the linear relationship hypothesized by H_2.

Relationship between Number of Friends and User Engagement

To test H_3, we compared two alternate regression models, viz., Model 5 and 6. The assumption of $Model_5$ was that Mindless Facebook Use is linearly related to Number of Friends, while $Model_6$ was based on the assumption of a quadratic relationship between Mindless Facebook Use and Number of Friends. These models are described by the following two equations respectively:

Model$_5$: $Mindless\ Facebook\ Use = \beta_0 + \beta_1 * (Number\ of\ Friends) + \epsilon$

Model$_6$: $Mindless\ Facebook\ Use = \beta_0 + \beta_1 * (Number\ of\ Friends) + \beta_2 * (Number\ of\ Friends)^2 + \epsilon$

The results of testing the regression models 5 and 6 are shown in Table 5. From the table, we observe that the change in R^2 between $Model_5$ and $Model_6$ was not statistically significant. Therefore, $Model_5$ is more appropriate; Mindless Facebook Use is positively and linearly associated with Number of Friends ($\beta_1 = 0.17, p < 0.01$), as hypothesized in H_3.

Finally, we tested H_4 by comparing two further regression models, viz., Model 7 and 8. The assumptions of $Model_7$ and $Model_8$ were that the relationship between Content Production and Number of Friends is linear and quadratic, respectively. The corresponding equations are:

Model$_7$: $Content\ Production = \beta_0 + \beta_1 * (Number\ of\ Friends) + \epsilon$

Independent Variables	$Model_1$	$Model_2$	$Model_3$	$Model_4$
Mindless Facebook Use	$0{\cdot}21^{***}$	$1{\cdot}45^{***}$	$0{\cdot}21^{***}$	$1{\cdot}61^{***}$
Content Production	$0{\cdot}27^{***}$	$0{\cdot}23^{***}$	$0{\cdot}17^{ns}$	$0{\cdot}10$
(Mindless Facebook Use)^2	–	$-1{\cdot}25^{***}$	–	$-1{\cdot}25^{***}$
(Content Production)^2	–	–	$0{\cdot}10^{ns}$	$0{\cdot}25^{ns}$
(Content Production) $*$ (Mindless Facebook Use)	–	–	–	$-0{\cdot}21^{ns}$
	$R^2 = 0.13$	$R^2 = 0.17$	$R^2 = 0.13$	$R^2 = 0.17$
		F-change $14{\cdot}58^{***}$	$F - change$ $0{\cdot}9^{ns}$	F-change $0{\cdot}34^{ns}$

***: $p < 0.001$; **: $p < 0.01$; *: $p < 0.05$; ns: non-significant

Table 4. Relationship between Psychological Well-being and User Engagement.

Independent Variables	$Model_5$	$Model_6$
Number of Friends	$0{\cdot}17^{**}$	$0{\cdot}36^{*}$
(Number of Friends)^2	–	$-0{\cdot}20^{ns}$
	$R^2 = 0.03$	$R^2 = 0.03$
		$F - change$ $1{\cdot}38^{ns}$

***: $p < 0.001$; **: $p < 0.01$; *: $p < 0.05$; ns: non-significant

Table 5. Relationship between Number of Friends and Mindless Facebook Use.

Independent Variables	$Model_7$	$Model_8$
Number of Friends	$0{\cdot}41^{***}$	$0{\cdot}78^{*}$
(Number of Friends)^2	–	$-0{\cdot}40^{**}$
	$R^2 = 0.16$	$R^2 = 0.18$
		$F - change$ $6{\cdot}8^{**}$

***: $p < 0.001$; **: $p < 0.01$; *: $p < 0.05$; ns: non-significant

Table 6. Relationship between Number of Friends and Content Production.

$Model_8$: $Content\ Production = \beta_0 + \beta_1 * (Number\ of\ Friends) + \beta_2 * (Number\ of\ Friends)^2 + \epsilon$

The results of testing regression models 7 and 8 are shown in Table 6. As the table shows, the R^2 of $Model_8$ was statistically significantly higher than that of $Model_7$, indicating $Model_8$ as more appropriate. The regression results of $Model_8$ show that Content Production exhibits a positive association with Number of Friends ($\beta_1 = 0.78, p < 0.05$) and a negative association with the squared term of Number of Friends ($\beta_2 = -0.40, p < 0.01$). Therefore these results support H_4; Content Production follows an inverted U-shaped curve with increase in Number of Friends.

IMPLICATIONS AND CONCLUSION

From a theoretical point of view, our results establish sufficient validity and reliability for the construct of *mindfulness* when examining SNS use. Therefore, our findings promote mindfulness as a useful and deeper measure of SNS usage, capturing attentiveness and awareness in interactive practices.

Our results show that the relationship between SNS user engagement and psychological well-being is neither wholly positive nor negative as suggested in prior literature [6, 17]. We found that subconscious and habitual Facebook use is positively associated with psychological well-being. Such use arguably requires little mental processing [5], leaving cognitive resources free to experience vitality. This suggests that frequent and routine Facebook activities (such as liking, commenting, updating status, tagging photos, etc.) may serve to freshen one's mind. After a certain point, however, we found that routine usage is negatively associated with well-being. At high levels of routine use, individuals might lose interest and experience low vitality. Thus, an initial positive association between engagement and well-being is later reversed, suggesting that underuse as well as overuse of SNS is associated with diminished well-being.

Such a U-shaped relationship, however, holds only for the attentiveness and awareness component of user engagement. Engagement via production of SNS content exhibits a linear positive association with well-being, supporting the findings of Burke et al. [6]. However, the linear relationship between content production and well-being is impacted by an increase in the number of friends. After a certain threshold, an increase in the number of friends shows a negative association with the amount of content one produces.

Indeed, it has been found that users do worry about and experience negative effects of social media overuse, leading them to take breaks [28], limit usage, or leave the platform altogether [2]. Our findings suggest that concerns regarding overuse could potentially be addressed by user experience improvements that distinguish between mindful and mindless usage. For instance, SNSs could enhance their algorithms to populate users' news feeds with content that fosters greater engagement. Further, machine learning and automation techniques could be employed to detect when a user approaches a threshold at which well-being may start being adversely affected. At such points, the user could be encouraged to take a break from SNS use or be guided toward SNS activities or content requiring mindful attention.

LIMITATIONS

Several limitations must be taken into account when considering the generalizability of our findings. First, the study covered a specific SNS (Facebook) and the respondents were drawn from a university community in Finland. Replicating the study with other SNSs and cultural contexts is necessary to verify broader applicability of these findings. Second, we utilized self-reported measures using Likert-type scales. Such measures may suffer from various biases and errors. Third, we described *associative* relationships between SNS engagement and well-being. We plan to repeat the study and use further analyses to identify potential causal relationships.

ACKNOWLEDGMENTS

We thank the participants of the study. We acknowledge anonymous reviewers for insightful comments that helped us revise and refine the paper. This research was supported in part by the Helsinki Institute for Information Technology (HIIT) project on Future Networks, Society and Modeling (FuNeSoMo) funded by Tekes - the Finnish Funding Agency for Innovation.

REFERENCES

1. Akin, A. The relationship between Internet addiction, subjective vitality, and subjective happiness. *CyberPsychology, Behavior, and Social Networking 15*, 8 (2012), 404–4010.
2. Baumer, E. P., Adams, P., Khovanskaya, V. D., Liao, T. C., Smith, M. E., Schwanda Sosik, V., and Williams, K. Limiting, leaving, and (re)lapsing: An exploration of Facebook non-use practices and experiences. In *Proceedings of the SIGCHI Conference on Human Factors in Computing Systems*, CHI '13, ACM (New York, NY, USA, 2013), 3257–3266.
3. Bostic, T. J., Rubio, D. M., and Hood, M. A validation of the subjective vitality scale using structural equation modeling. *Social Indicators Research 52*, 3 (2000), 313–324.
4. Boudreau, M.C. Gefen, D., and Straub, D. W. Validation in Information Systems research. *MIS Quarterly 25*, 1 (March 2001), 1–16.
5. Brown, K. W., and Ryan, R. M. The benefits of being present: Mindfulness and its role in psychological well-being. *Journal of personality and social psychology 84*, 4 (2003), 822–848.
6. Burke, M., Marlow, C., and Lento, T. Social network activity and social well-being. In *Proceedings of the SIGCHI Conference on Human Factors in Computing Systems*, CHI '10, ACM (New York, NY, USA, 2010), 1909–1912.
7. Campbell, D. T., and Fiske, D. W. Convergent and discriminant validation by the multitrait-multimethod matrix. *Psychological bulletin 56*, 2 (1959), 81.
8. Cook, T. D., Campbell, D. T., and Day, A. *Quasi-experimentation: Design & analysis issues for field settings*. Houghton Mifflin, Boston, MA, USA., 1979.
9. Diener, E., Suh, E. M., Lucas, R. E., and Smith, H. L. Subjective weil-being: Three decades of progress. *Psychological Bulletin 125*, 2 (1999), 276–302.
10. Ellison, N. B., Steinfield, C., and Lampe, C. The benefits of Facebook "friends:" Social capital and college students' use of online social network sites. *Journal of Computer-Mediated Communication 12*, 4 (2007), 1143–1168.
11. Eppler, M. J., and Mengis, J. The concept of information overload: A review of literature from Organization Science, Accounting, Marketing, MIS, and related disciplines. *The Information Society 20*, 5 (2004), 325–344.
12. Fornell, C., and Larcker, D. F. Evaluating structural equation models with unobservable variables and measurement error. *Journal of Marketing Research 18*, 1 (1981), 39–50.
13. Hwang, M. I., T. R. G. The effect of user engagement on system success: A meta-anlaytical integration of research findings. *Information & Management 35* (1999), 229–236.
14. Kaptein, M. C., Nass, C., and Markopoulos, P. Powerful and consistent analysis of Likert-type rating scales. In *Proceedings of the SIGCHI Conference on Human Factors in Computing Systems*, CHI '10, ACM (New York, NY, USA, 2010), 2391–2394.
15. Koroleva, K., Krasnova, H., Veltri, N., and Günther, O. It's all about networking! Empirical investigation of social capital formation on social network sites. In *International Conference on Information Systems*, ICIS 2011 (2011).
16. Kraut, R., Patterson, M., Lundmark, V., Kiesler, S., Mukophadhyay, T., and Scherlis, W. Internet paradox: A social technology that reduces social involvement and psychological well-being? *American psychologist 53*, 9 (1998), 1017.
17. Kross, E., Verduyn, P., Demiralp, E., Park, J., Lee, D. S., Lin, N., Shablack, H., Jonides, J., and Ybarra, O. Facebook use predicts declines in subjective well-being in young adults. *PLOS ONE 8*, 8 (2013), 1–6.

18. Langer, E. J. *Mindfulness*. Addison-Wesley/Addison Wesley Longman, Reading, MA, USA, 1989.
19. Maddux, J. E. Habit, health, and happiness. *Journal of Sport and Exercise Psychology 19*, 4 (December 1997), 331–346.
20. Mäntymäki, M., and Islam, A. Voyeurism and exhibitionism as gratifications from presuming Facebook. In *European Conference on Information Systems*, ECIS '14 (2014).
21. Moore, G., and Benbasat, I. Development of an instrument to measure perceptions of adopting an information technology innovation. *Information Systems Research 2*, 3 (September 1991), 192–222.
22. Mosley Jr, T. H., Perrin, S. G., Neral, S. M., Dubbert, P. M., Grothues, C. A., and Pinto, B. M. Stress, coping, and well-being among third-year medical students. *Academic Medicine 69*, 9 (1994), 765–7.
23. Nix, G. A., Ryan, R. M., Manly, J. B., and Deci, E. L. Revitalization through self-regulation: The effects of autonomous and controlled motivation on happiness and vitality. *Journal of Experimental Social Psychology 35*, 3 (1999), 266–284.
24. Nunnally, J. C. *Psychometric Theory*, 2nd ed. McGraw-Hill, New York, NY, USA, 1978.
25. Rowe, J. W., and Kahn, R. L. Human aging: Usual and successful. *Science 237*, 4811 (1987), 143–149.
26. Ryan, R. M., and Deci, E. L. From ego depletion to vitality: Theory and findings concerning the facilitation of energy available to the self. *Social and Personality Psychology Compass 2*, 2 (2008), 702–717.
27. Ryan, R. M., and Frederick, C. On energy, personality, and health: Subjective vitality as a dynamic reflection of well-being. *Journal of personality 65*, 3 (1997), 529–565.
28. Schoenebeck, S. Y. Giving up Twitter for lent: How and why we take breaks from social media. In *Proceedings of the SIGCHI Conference on Human Factors in Computing Systems*, CHI '14, ACM (New York, NY, USA, 2014), 773–782.
29. Sternberg, R. J. Images of mindfulness. *Journal of Social Issues 56*, 1 (2000), 11–26.
30. Valkenburg, P. M., Peter, J., and Schouten, A. P. Friend networking sites and their relationship to adolescents' well-being and social self-esteem. *CyberPsychology & Behavior 9*, 5 (2006), 584–590.

PaperChains: Dynamic Sketch+Voice Annotations

Jennifer Pearson, Simon Robinson, Matt Jones
Future Interaction Technology Lab, Swansea University, SA2 8PP, UK
{ s.n.w.robinson, j.pearson, matt.jones } @swansea.ac.uk

ABSTRACT
In this paper we present a novel interface for collaborative creation of evolving audio-visual documents. *PaperChains* allows users to sketch on paper and then augment with digital audio, allowing both the physical and digital objects to evolve simultaneously over time. The technique we have developed focuses on affordability and accessibility in its design, using standard cameraphones and telephone connections, which allow it to be used in regions where literacy, technological experience and data connections cannot necessarily be taken for granted. The main use-case that we focus on in this paper is for collaborative storytelling, an area which has been well studied and previously proven to be of value in resource constrained environments. To investigate the relevance of the approach in these contexts, we undertook two usability evaluations in India and South Africa. Results from these investigations indicate users' ability to both create and interpret stories using the software, as well as demonstrating high overall usability and enjoyment. We end with a discussion of the implications of our design and opportunities for use in other contexts.

Author Keywords
Sketching; audio; photographs; cameraphones; resource-constrained environments.

ACM Classification Keywords
H.5.3 Group and Organization Interfaces: Collaborative computing; H.5.2 User Interfaces: Interaction styles; H.5.1 Multimedia Information Systems: Audio input/output.

INTRODUCTION
In this paper we present PaperChains – a novel method of connecting paper-based material with digital audio using low-tech, easily accessible equipment. We make use of standard cameraphone handsets to photograph physical content, and then allow the photographed item to be augmented with digital audio in multiple locations via interaction with the image. Unlike previous approaches, the design supports evolving physical-digital narratives, allowing sketches, memorabilia, photos and other physical objects to be built up with audio content over time. The technique is unique in that it also allows modification of the underlying physical content, without compromising on recognition – something that similar approaches (e.g., [6, 12, 29] or augmented reality apps such as Blippar or Aurasma) do not support. The core contribution of the paper, then, is the provision of a lightweight technical platform for evolving audio-physical documents, with a wide range of uses.

CSCW '15, March 14 – 18 2015, Vancouver, BC, Canada.
Copyright 2015 ACM 978-1-4503-2922-4/15/03...$15.00.
http://dx.doi.org/10.1145/2675133.2675138

Our approach uses two precisely placed QR (quick response) codes printed on paper, allowing the PaperChains system to detect the item, its orientation, and its dimensions, with any camera-enabled mobile handset. The system then corrects the photograph for skew and rotation, and lets users add audio snippets anywhere on the image. This method ensures the approach requires no additional specialist hardware (such as a dock or camera-pen) – users interact directly with the photograph using the phone as a proxy. Further, our technique has the additional advantage of being able to utilise an Interactive Voice Response (IVR) system over a standard telephone line as the audio content store, in contrast to the internet connectivity or local private database used by other approaches.

The PaperChains technique has promise in many different scenarios, as we discuss in more depth later. However, we feel it has a particularly strong use case in resource constrained environments. Its appropriateness can be seen in both the interactions it affords and in its low technical requirements, making it an attractive tool for regions where literacy, technological familiarity, power and data connectivity can be low. In particular, using a standard telephone connection to connect with a remote voice server ensures that PaperChains can be used with existing devices and infrastructure. Previous work in this area (e.g., [13, 21]) has shown that IVR systems are a valuable resource, as they are easy to adopt and compatible with any handset. Our technique aims to follow this same strategy by requiring a minimum of technology and experience from the user. PaperChains runs on standard mobile handsets – we studied the design using an Android smartphone, and have also developed a feature-phone version. During a recent ethnographic study in India, we investigated the costs of low-end smartphones in a slum in Mumbai, finding a wide range of so-called "China phones" that support the system, available for as little as \$15–35 USD (see Fig. 1 for a sample).

We see one particular application—collaborative storytelling—as an especially attractive and appropriate use for the technique. Previous work has investigated the use of storytelling in resource constrained contexts, focusing in particular on mobile story capture (e.g., [8, 23, 26]). A common theme that emerges from this research has been a desire for collaborative authoring, with a particular focus on the importance of audio. Our approach enables these types of interactions, and makes it possible to build up digital-physical narratives over time. Consider the following scenario, which illustrates the approach:

Twelve year-old Chitra lives in a remote part of rural Gujarat with her parents and younger siblings, but her older brother, Nirav, has recently moved to New Delhi—a 20-hour journey away—to work. Chitra misses him badly, and wants to share some of the recent family experiences with him in a personal way; but neither of them can afford to visit each other often, and she does not have an internet connection. She begins drawing a story, then takes a photograph of the page with her phone, using the on-screen tool to add audio hotspots over each section of her drawing. After recording voiceovers for her pictures she passes the paper on to her sister, Aditi, who draws several sketches. Aditi then takes her own photograph of the page and begins adding audio. Finally, their brother Ram adds his own content. Once the story is complete, Chitra puts it in an envelope and posts it to her brother.

A few days later, Nirav receives the letter. After taking his own photograph of the document, he can hear audio recordings of their voices by touching on each section of the image on-screen, thus preserving both the paper and spoken records of the family story. He can also add his own content and send the letter back to his family.

This scenario reflects the desire of many migrant workers for a sense of connectedness, as reported in [14]. In the context of resource constrained environments such as this example, then, we argue that PaperChains is a novel and compelling way of collaborating to combine the story emerging on paper with the story emerging in the audio.

The rest of this paper is organised as follows. We first describe previous research related to our approach, then detail the technical implementation of our design. To explore the system in resource-constrained environments, we carried out two usability-focused evaluations in India and South Africa. These studies illustrated the value of the approach by demonstrating users' ability to both create and interpret stories (such as the one described in the scenario), as well as showing an appreciation of the system and overall enjoyment of the experience. We end with a discussion of the work, future directions and other applications for the system.

BACKGROUND

The key previous research area related to PaperChains involves augmenting images with sound, animations and all sorts of multimedia. These approaches, now seen in commercial apps, work by taking a picture of an object or a document, processing it to find key elements that allow it to be recognised quickly, and uploading these discriminants to a server. When another picture of the same object is taken, the system can search its database and identify the object and the annotation. However, unlike our design, changes to the original item can mean subsequent attempts to recognise it will fail. These approaches, then, are unable to support PaperChains' core functionality.

Figure 1. A set of low-end touch-screen smart phones that are capable of running PaperChains. These phones were purchased for $15-35 USD each from a shop in Dharavi, a slum in Mumbai.

Augmenting paper with digital content

Many research systems have been developed that attempt to close the gap between the affordances of paper and the benefits of digital content. Early work, such as the DigitalDesk [31], allowed the properties of paper to be preserved while supporting digital annotation and manipulation. More recent work in this area has lowered hardware requirements, adopting technology such as Anoto[1], which uses dot-marked paper and a camera below a digital pen's nib to recognise document areas while writing. Other work has investigated how traditional methods of interaction could be replicated digitally (e.g., [17]), or, how augmentation of physical objects could provide additional information—see, for example, the audiophotography work of Frohlich [7], or the many commercial mobile apps that are focused around adding digital content to physical items.

Since the DigitalDesk, which used a projector and camera above a desk, more portable designs (such XLibris [27]) have allowed users to scan in paper documents and mark them digitally with freeform annotations on a tablet-like device. Later approaches, such as that of Guimbretière [10], lowered the hardware requirements for digital-physical annotation systems, making use of Anoto-marked paper to support notes that could be replicated digitally. Guimbretière aimed to allow cycles between digital and physical documents, arguing for cohabitation of the two forms of media, rather than replacement of one with the other. We had similar motivations in the design of PaperChains, aiming to allow cohabitation of (and collaboration around) digital annotations and physical media. Our approach was to use two QR code markers in opposing corners of the document area that identify and align it in a photograph taken of the item. Previous work has used photographs of paper documents in similar ways to extend document interactivity. For example, Parikh et al. [20] added QR codes next to form fields to improve data entry in rural India; Seifert et al. [28] turned photographs of interface designs into interactive prototypes; and, Erol et al. [6] used image recognition of a document and comparison to a ground truth version to detect the regions of a page in a photograph.

These methods are similar to those taken by the many augmented reality applications that add interactive overlays to physical objects, such as Aurasma[2], Blippar[3] and Daqri.[4] These apps overlay a realtime camera preview with digital content associated with the object in the frame. Other designs for this form of interaction have aimed to add more interactivity to the process – for example, Mistry et al.'s pico projector-based

[1]See: anoto.com; [2]aurasma.com; [3]blippar.com; [4]daqri.com

design [19] allowed users to frame objects with their fingers while wearing coloured tags to request associated interactive digital content. However, none of these types of approaches allow the underlying document to change or evolve while at the same time preserving the annotations that have been added – a key difference between these methods and our design.

Annotating with audio

In this work we focus on linking paper documents with audio annotations. Previous work in this space ranges from immersive audio story books (e.g., [1]) to the audio greetings cards and interactive picture books that have been commercially available for many years. These designs commonly use buttons or simple sensors to start sound playback. Various research approaches have been taken to synchronising audio recordings with physical documents automatically. Audio d-touch [3], for example, used fiducial markers to create a simple tangible audio interface, where the positions of markers under a camera were reflected in the sounds that were played. The Audio Notebook [30] was a custom hardware tablet that allowed users to take paper notes and record audio simultaneously, then skim-review later, referencing the correct recording position from the notes. Erol et al. [5] took a similar approach to synchronising a slideshow presentation with notes made on a handout – barcodes on the printout automatically linked notes with the correct positions in a later video of the talk.

Our approach uses photos of paper items to link them with digital annotations. PaperChains is clearly related to audiophotography (explored in depth by Frohlich [7]), which is the general area of associating audio with photos. Implementations of audiophotography have ranged from adding short audio transcripts to digital photos on-camera (cf. [7]), to using overhead image recognition for selecting and browsing audio associated with printed photos (e.g., [9]). Audiophotographs traditionally associate only one annotation with each photograph, however; and, more importantly, the audio track is associated with the photograph taken, rather than the object pictured in the photo.

More similar to our approach, then, are systems that link audio annotations with specific places on physical documents. Klemmer et al. [12] created Books with Voices, using barcodes printed in the margins of paper history books to retrieve video interviews with historians talking about the material. West et al. [32] used Anoto-marked paper in a scrapbook, supporting various user-drawn symbols to associate audio and other content with scrapbook items. Liu et al. [16] had similar goals, but removed the need for Anoto paper, instead using photos of the page, and recognising preprinted marks that signified media the author had associated with the document. In a more resource constrained context, Smith and Marsden [29] created a client-free mobile platform for media retrieval based on taking a picture of an image representation that was then recognised and returned to the requester via Bluetooth. Our approach is adapted from that taken in [25], which used digital markers to indicate the edges of the content area. However, our design does not focus on retrieving audio content from products and posters; instead, we support document annotation and audio narration in a flexible, dynamic manner that allows both the document and annotations to be changed over time.

	Affordable, accessible	Modifiable documents	Modifiable audio	Collaborative authoring	Flexible item sizes	No data connection	Proximate sharing	Remote sharing
PaperChains	✔	✔	✔	✔	✔	✔	✔	✔
Img. recog.	✔	✘	✔	✘	✔	✘	✔	✔
Pen-based	✘	✔	✔	✘	✔	✔	✘	✘
Tablet-based	✘	✔	✔	✘	✘	✔	✔	✘
Table-based	✘	✔	✔	✔	✘	✔	✔	✘

Table 1. A comparison of features between PaperChains and several general classes of previous work. Each broad category is illustrated by, for example: Image recognition (Aurasma[2]); Pen-based [32]; Tablet-based [22]; Table-based [2].

Annotation as storytelling

We believe the PaperChains design shows strong potential for interactive, evolving physical-digital storytelling. Previous work in this area includes systems such as KidPad [4], which extended existing sketching software to create a storytelling environment, or PicoTales [24], which supported group-based collaborative sketching via gestures and pico projectors. Unlike traditional digital storytelling (which has focused around creating short self-narrated digital films), or these previous approaches, PaperChains lets physical sketches or other objects and digital elements coexist as part of the narrative.

Cao et al.'s TellTable [2] supported sketch-based storytelling on an interactive table, aiming to encourage incorporating physical objects into stories via 'capture tools' that inserted photos directly on to the story surface. Other approaches have included those of Jacoby and Buechley [11], who used conductive ink to allow sketches to be augmented with digital content; de Lima et al. [15], who used pen and paper sketches to insert characters into a virtual world; or, Wood et al. [33], whose barcode scanning approach linked digital tales to physical books. Yeh et al.'s approach [34] aimed to produce a merged digital version of both Anoto-marked paper notebooks and related photos. More similar to our design is the approach of Raffle et al. [22], who used a drawing tablet and 'stamp,' to associate audio recordings with sketches on the page. However, their design required both a custom hardware package, and supported only local playback of the content.

A comparison of PaperChains to previous work

PaperChains is a lightweight platform for evolving, collaborative, audio-physical documents, and thus differs from previous work in several ways. Table 1 compares the PaperChains approach with general examples of previous work. The approach is *affordable* and *accessible*, which we define as being compatible with existing or low-cost devices and suitable for users with low technology experience. PaperChains supports *collaborative authoring* – audio is created by users of the system (rather than content producers); and, interaction with the audio uses a photograph of the page that is content-agnostic. Because of this, both the *documents* and the *audio* are modifiable, unlike most other systems. The few other approaches that do allow modification require specialised hardware (e.g., Anoto pen or overhead camera), which prevents easy sharing of the content, and makes group-based creation

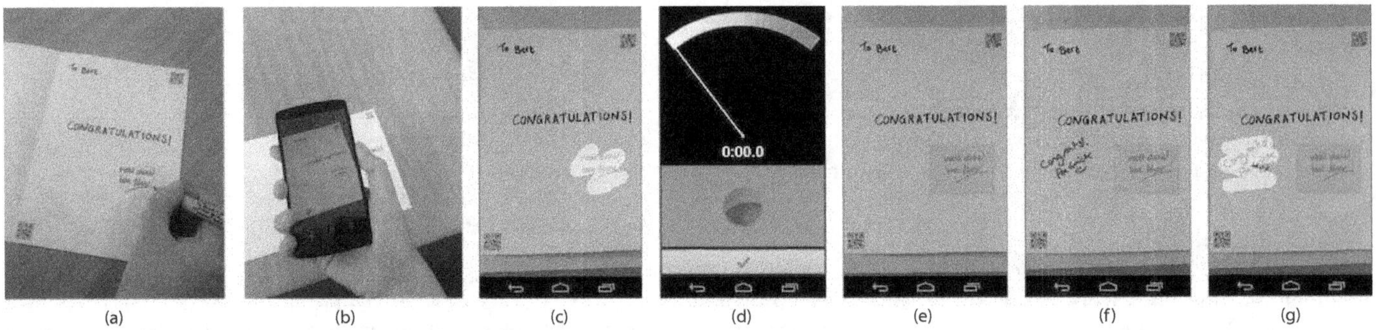

Figure 2. The PaperChains system, illustrating the process of scribbling and recording audio hotspots. From left to right: (a) annotating on paper; (b) taking a photograph of the document; (c–e) adding audio; (f–g) other users adding additional audio.

and collaboration more difficult. PaperChains supports *flexible item sizes* and multiple annotations on the same item, whereas many other methods (e.g., most augmented reality apps) are limited to a single position for an annotation on any one physical object. It also needs *no data-connection*, because the system is able to utilise IVR systems for content storage. Finally, the technique supports both *proximate* and *remote sharing* of audio-augmented documents, which, as Table 1 shows, is offered by only one of the alternative methods.

TECHNICAL FEATURES AND IMPLEMENTATION

PaperChains provides a simple way to merge paper and audio annotations, by using a photograph of the annotated document as a proxy for adding and browsing audio hotspots. The approach affords rich interactive experiences with physical items, allowing any marked-up object to be augmented with audio. PaperChains documents can be created or edited by any user, allowing collaborative and shareable audio annotations.

Creating PaperChains documents

The process of creating a PaperChains document begins with a user adding a physical annotation—anything from sketching to writing to pasting items—on a QR code-augmented object (Fig. 2a). Then, using a standard smartphone, they take a photograph of the entire object, making sure to include both QR codes in the frame (Fig. 2b). The picture is captured automatically once both QR codes are detected. This photograph can now be used as a collage to add audio to the physical annotations. Audio is added by 'scribbling' over the part of the object that the user wishes to narrate (Fig. 2c and 2d), creating a bounding-box audio 'hotspot'. Once audio recording has finished, the new audio area is visible on the photo (Fig. 2e).

Further hotspots can be added, or other users can add their own physical and digital annotations at any time, by repeating this procedure. The process is identical for every user – when a photo is taken, the system recognises the same document as before, and allows access to previous users' annotations (Fig. 2f). Others can add their own audio messages to the canvas via the same scribbling technique (Fig. 2g). This process can be repeated as often as required.

Browsing PaperChains documents

To listen to the audio associated with PaperChains documents, the same process is used – first a photo is taken of the document. Touching anywhere on the photograph plays the audio for that location. When listening to the audio there are no visual cues as to where the hotspots are located, to avoid interfering with the natural browsing and exploration of the document. Users wishing to interpret someone else's PaperChain document do so in an exploratory manner, discovering audio areas by touching different regions of the photograph.

Technical implementation

PaperChains consists of two main components: a client application and a remote telephone service. The client application is used to take the initial photograph and provide tools such as pan, zoom, selection and editing of the audio content. The remote telephone service is an IVR system that stores the audio recordings and all information associated with the underlying physical object. One particularly attractive aspect of this setup is that the client application is completely independent of the information with which it is interacting – all data, including the audio recordings, are stored on the telephone server and retrieved via DTMF requests over the phone line (see below). This ensures that no internet connection is required for listening, editing or retrieving updated audio recordings.

The main technical aspect of the system, which allows the flexibility of photographing and augmenting items without any additional hardware, is the placement of the two QR codes on the physical item. These QR codes, which are placed in the corners of PaperChains-augmented objects, identify the item and allow boundary detection and image correction, in the same way as [25]. When a user holds the camera over an item, the system takes a photo automatically as soon as it detects the two QR codes. The image is corrected for skew and rotation, and the object's dimensions are inferred according to a simple grid coordinate system. The grid system is based on the size and positions of the QR codes in the image, as in the example shown in Fig. 3. This grid system is then used to determine the exact position of a user's touch on the photo. This method makes recognition quick and accurate, and—more importantly—allows the underlying document to be modified while still being recognisable.

Once a photograph has been taken and the dimensions calculated, the client application decodes the QR codes' information to retrieve an IVR telephone number and identifier unique to the item. It then calls this number to connect to the remote

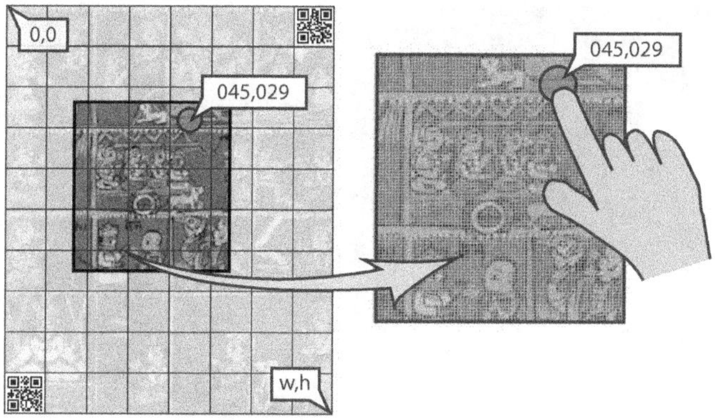

Figure 3. The grid system used by the PaperChains technique. The QR codes detected on the item are used to calculate a coordinate grid from the upper left [0, 0] to the lower right [width, height] of an object, as shown in the overlay (the grid is not visible during usage). Touch point positions are calculated based on this grid. When the image is touched, a six-digit DTMF-encoded request is sent to the server over the phone line, and the requested audio is played in response. As shown in the inset image, the resolution is high enough to allow very precise touch positions.

service. This live telephone call is now "listening" to any touches made on the photograph. Touching a position on the photograph triggers the application to determine the exact coordinate of the touch, convert this into a DTMF tone, and play it down the live telephone call, much like a touch tone keypad. The listening server then interprets this information and performs the correct action. For example, if the application is in creation mode, it will ask the user to narrate an audio snippet for that location, and associate this with the location selected. Similarly, in browsing mode it will check to see if there are any audio recordings in that location, then play them in real time down the phone line.

Viability in resource constrained environments

Table 1, discussed earlier, compared the benefits of the PaperChains approach with general examples of previous approaches in this area. Clearly, there are further considerations we must be aware of when designing for resource constrained environments, such as the cost and availability of the hardware and consumables required to make use of the design.

Although affordable smartphones are becoming widely available (see Fig. 1), we are well aware that many people in these areas own lower-end phones that do not include a touchscreen. With this in mind, we have implemented a Java ME version of PaperChains, compatible with lower-end, camera-enabled feature phones. This version works in the same way as the original application, but uses the phone's joystick or directional pad to navigate the image – a slightly clumsy but viable approach to facilitate use on lower-end devices.

Turning now to consumables, PaperChains requires items to be augmented with two QR codes to function. These QR codes can be created with our simple browser-based tool,[5] and printed onto standard paper using a low-end desktop printer. Several previous systems in this area have demonstrated how partnership with local organisations, community computer centres or NGOs can support systems requiring consumables (e.g., [8, 18]). Another possible use case, which does not require new QR sheets each time, is the notion of a reusable PaperChains surface. Consider, for example, a community noticeboard made of a wipe-clean material—such as a typical school whiteboard—augmented with PaperChains QR codes in each corner. Users could mark-up the board, augment it with audio, and then erase the marks when necessary to make way for a new mark-up session.

[5]Available for use and download at http://enterise.info

USABILITY EVALUATIONS

In order to test how well users from resource constrained contexts can make use of PaperChains, we undertook two group-based user evaluations of the system. The purpose of these studies was to explore the usability of the system, and find out how PaperChains could support storytelling from a functional point of view.

The first study took place in Mumbai, India; the second in Langa, a township in Cape Town, South Africa. Both studies followed the same procedure. Eighteen people took part in each location, with six taking part in each session (i.e., three groups per site). Each of the people in the groups of six were friends or relatives, to ensure they had shared experiences with one another. Video and audio equipment was used throughout all stages of the studies to record usage of the system, with consent obtained from all participants prior to commencement. Local facilitators ran both the Indian and South African studies and helped with communication with participants.

Procedure

After a short introduction and obtaining informed consent, the six people in each group were given an overview of the study procedure and a demonstration of the PaperChains system. Once each participant had been given the opportunity to try using the system, they split into two groups of three to undertake storytelling tasks separately. Each group sat separately to the other so they could not hear the other group.

Each group was provided with a blank A3 PaperChains sheet (i.e., a blank sheet of paper with QR codes in two corners), a pack of 12 fibre-tipped coloured pens and a PaperChains phone. The groups were then asked to sketch and discuss a shared experience, documenting it using the PaperChains system. This step involved taking turns drawing parts of the story and augmenting them with audio using the phone provided. A member of our research team observed each group and was available to answer any questions they might have throughout the study.

Once each group was happy with their creations, the groups swapped their story sheets with each other. Each group then attempted to interpret the other's story, first taking a new photograph, then using it to listen to the audio hotspots. Following this, the groups came back together and we conducted a semi-structured focus group interview, asking participants to rate the system on several subjective Likert-like scales (1–10, 10 high). These questions probed difficulty (*"To what extent was the system easy or difficult to use?"*), enjoyment, (*"To what extent was the system enjoyable to use?"*), and also ability to, first, tell their own stories (*"To what extent did the system support*

Figure 4. A group of users collaboratively authoring a PaperChains document in the Indian evaluation.

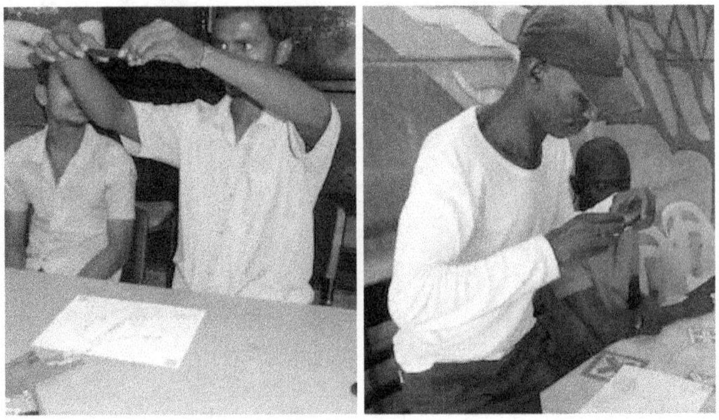

Figure 5. Users in the Indian evaluation (left) and in the South African evaluation (right) experimenting with methods for framing the image for the photograph early on in the study session.

telling a story?"), and second, interpret others' stories (*"To what extent could you understand other people's stories?"*). The groups were then thanked and each person was given an incentive of 200 Rupees (India) / 120 Rand (South Africa).

We chose to use slightly higher-end, touch-screen smart phones in both studies rather than the lower-end ones we found on sale in the Mumbai slum. Our decision to use these more expensive handsets rather than the $15 versions, or even lower-end camera-enabled feature phones, was two-fold. Firstly, we wanted to ensure the system was as robust as possible for the usability evaluations – something we could not currently guarantee on the sometimes counterfeit devices sold in these areas. Secondly, there is strong evidence to suggest that the trajectory of smart phone use in these areas over the next 5–10 years is heading towards the type of handset we were testing on. It was our desire, therefore, to explore how well participants would cope with not only the PaperChains system, but the increasingly sophisticated hardware they are likely to have access to in the near to mid-term future.

Study 1: Mumbai, India

Our first study involved 12 male and 6 female participants aged 20 45 from Mumbai, India. Education levels of the group varied from none at all (i.e., no literacy), to education to a 7th grade level (11–12 years; i.e., a basic level of literacy in the local Marathi language). Access to affordable data connections was very low for this set of users, as was higher-end technology exposure. Basic feature phones or lower-end 'dumb' handsets were the dominant device within the cohort (17 of 18 people). One participant owned a touch-screen phone, and only 6 of the remaining 17 had tried using one before.

Results

All participants were able to collaboratively create stories on paper, and augment them with audio recordings (see Figs. 4 and 6). Participants were also able to use the system to interpret the other group's stories effectively, and provided useful feedback on general use of the system.

Ratings and observations: The results of the Likert-like ratings across both studies are summarised in Table 2. Due to the low technological familiarity of the groups, we anticipated

Question	India (s.d.)	SA (s.d.)	Avg
Ease of use	7.0 (2.3)	8.9 (1.0)	8.0
Enjoyment	9.7 (0.6)	9.6 (1.1)	9.7
Telling stories	7.3 (2.0)	9.4 (0.9)	8.4
Understanding stories	8.8 (1.8)	8.0 (1.9)	8.4

Table 2. Summary of PaperChains ratings across the two studies (range 1–10, 10 high; standard deviations in parentheses).

encountering problems with using smartphones. At the start of the study, each participant was given the opportunity to use the system until they felt comfortable using it. Although a minority had problems in framing the photograph initially (see Fig. 5), participants quickly learned how to use the system effectively, rating it 7.0 on average for ease of use.

It was also clear from the observations made during the study sessions, and the post-study interviews, that users enjoyed the experience. Participants rated the system 9.7 on average for how fun the system was to use, with comments such as: *"it was amazing because if I had to tell one of my friends I would never be able to attach audio to the picture before"*, *"I found it really fun"* and *"we like that we can draw our own pictures."* Conversely, there were some complaints about the volume of the audio playback; one participant stated she felt uncomfortable sketching as she did not see herself as a capable artist; and, another had reservations about the possibility of the system being used for unfavourable purposes: *"it is 99 percent good but 1 percent problem because it shouldn't be misused."*

When asked how well they were able to convey their stories to others, participants gave an average score of 7.3. In terms of how participants created stories collaboratively, we observed several different behaviours within the six groups. The majority of the time, group members took it in turns to draw on the paper then add their own voice to that section. This action would then repeat with the next person sketching and adding their own voiceover. At times, we did observe participants making additions to other participants' drawings (drawing over or around existing illustrations) as well as attempting to add additional audio on top of existing hotspots. It was also clear from the studies that participants liked to listen back to their own voices after recording. Other behaviours

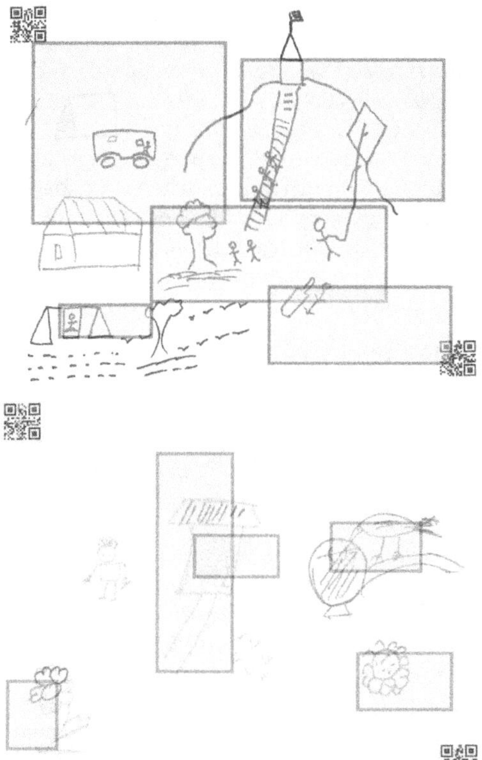

Figure 6. Two example stories from the Indian evaluation. The upper story is a group narration about childhood, while the lower scene consists of individual anecdotes about each of the items pictured. Grey shaded areas indicate where participants added audio to their sketches.

included all participants talking on the same recording, as well as a single person taking charge of all sketching for the group. However, all participants appeared to be collaboratively working together in order to help create a single, unified story.

The average score given for the ease of understanding other people's stories was 8.8. Groups were engaged while attempting to interpret stories, with multiple members touching to select drawings to listen to, and huddling together to be closer to the microphone on the phone. It was evident during the sessions that locating the actual audio hotspots within the image was sometimes challenging – several groups missed some of the hotspots from the other group's story. This did not seem to distract from the overall storytelling experience, however. In fact, many participants commented that they enjoyed the exploratory nature of the process, discovering the hotspots for themselves. Despite this, further development of the design of the interface could include some form of visual cue as to where hotspots exist to aid with this process.

Comparison to other methods: When comparing the PaperChains approach to current methods of storytelling that they used, participants appreciated the PaperChains approach, with several stating that they preferred the system to simply reciting a story over a telephone (something they regularly did). This was illustrated well by one participant, who said: *"it is better than using the telephone – it's better to show the picture than just explaining what I saw."* Participants were also excited about how they could make use of the technology in their day-to-day lives. For example, activities such as documenting accidents, sharing with children, and using PaperChains for directions to inform others on how to get to a particular place were all mentioned as possible uses for the system.

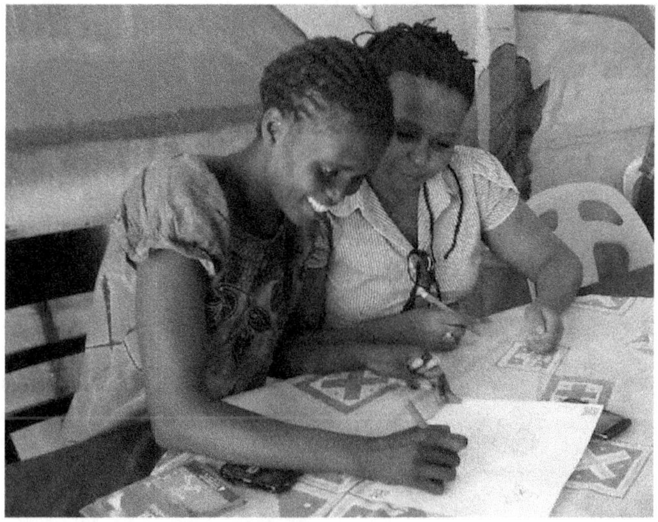

Figure 7. A group of users collaboratively creating a story in the South African evaluation. (The third participant is off-camera to the right.)

Study 2: Langa, South Africa

Our second study involved 9 male and 9 female participants aged 18–37 from Langa, a township near Cape Town in South Africa. Users from this cohort were moderately educated with mixed levels of literacy in both English and the local isiXhosa language. Access to affordable data connections was slightly higher in Langa than in Mumbai, but still beyond the reach of many. For example, data connections are relatively cheap on Blackberry phones (R60 for 30 days) but far more expensive on other devices. Technological exposure was also higher in Langa than Mumbai – although the majority of participants owned only feature phones, most had experience with using touch screens and all have access to a local internet cafe.

Results

As with the Indian evaluation, all groups managed to create and view each others' stories successfully (see Figs. 7 and 8). It was also clear, based on the ratings, that the groups enjoyed using the system to tell stories – the groups gave an average score of 9.6 regarding enjoyment. Participants' comments regarding the experience strengthened the findings here: *"the whole in general was iyoba! [fantastic]"*, *"it was an interesting fun activity"*, and *"it's really dramatic and exciting."* That said, however, some negative points were also raised, with one participant stating: *"it's a little childish – imagine a business man doing this."* As in the Indian evaluation, there were some participants who felt uncomfortable drawing and, this time, two who suggested less-educated people might find the system harder to use. There were similar initial issues with framing the photograph as in the previous study, but these were overcome quickly, leading to an average ease of use score of 8.9.

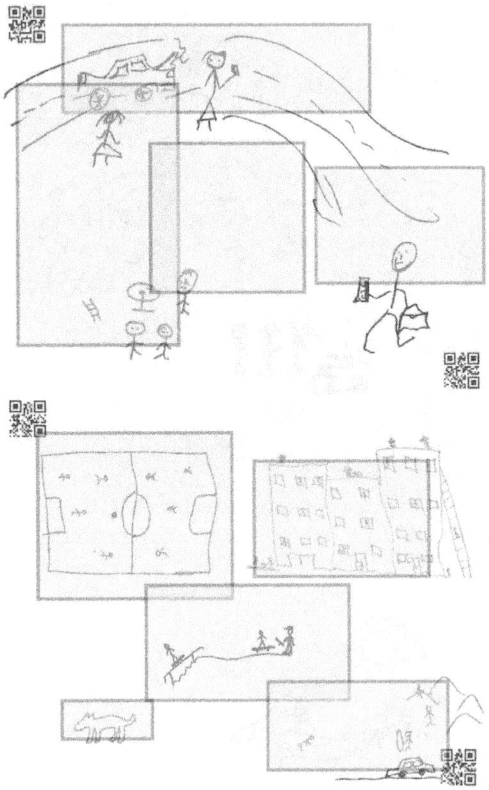

Figure 8. Two example stories from the South African evaluation. As in the first study, groups varied in the methods and layouts chosen. The upper story here is a collective effort about road issues and a car breakdown; the lower image is a collection of individual stories about the sketched items. Shaded areas indicate audio hotspots.

The average ratings for ease of telling and understanding stories were 9.4 and 8.0, respectively, and the methods of creating and interpreting stories were broadly similar to those in the first evaluation. Participants tended toward taking turns to draw and speak, with individuals occasionally adding to or modifying others' images, and often multiple people speaking on the same recording. Similar issues with finding audio hot spots when interpreting others' stories were observed in this study, indicating that a visual cue solution would be beneficial.

After participants had used PaperChains, we asked what they thought the role of the audio was in the storytelling experience. Comments such as: *"it's more descriptive with audio; you get a sense of who is talking – it works nicely together"*, *"[the audio] is very helpful because you can always refer back to the recoding; it's great"* and *"[the audio] makes it easier for those who can't read and write"* strongly indicate that the audio annotations complement the paper sketches well. Some even felt that the audio was an essential part of the experience, and without it the drawing would have been very difficult to interpret: *"with the help of the audio it was easy to understand, but without it it would have been very hard to understand"*.

Comparison to other methods: After some discussion about how the PaperChains approach differed from participants' usual methods of telling stories, it became apparent that most participants felt that they were able to go into more depth with PaperChains than usual: *"this is more detailed than face-to-face – more practical," "[PaperChains] lets you elaborate more and be more creative,"* and *"for me the drawing approach is a way of exercising my mind more, and I'm able to express myself more this way."* One individual went further, commenting that the system enabled him to share his thoughts and feelings when he usually could not: *"[PaperChains] takes my mind off things because as an introvert I think too much, so it was good fun. I can share my emotions and my feelings to people now,"* suggesting that PaperChains could be a powerful tool to support sharing emotional content.

Participants also offered suggestions about how they would make use of the system. Common examples included using the system for people who are not as literate, or for older people to help them communicate. One participant commented that he would use the technique to draw a map and describe directions for someone, while another suggested it could be useful to mark up school assignments. Another common scenario was to use the system for people who are not physically in the same location. For example: *"I would use it a lot to communicate with my child who does not live with me," "Valentine's day for a long distance relationship – an original way to create for lover," "I will be able to send to my mum if I'm away and I can share my experience with her"*, and *"[PaperChains] makes a person who is not around feel like they are around"*.

CONCLUSIONS AND FUTURE WORK

We began this paper with a strong motivation from existing research, highlighting the lack of techniques that allow both the audio and the visual component of a story to evolve simultaneously. This incentive to create sketch+voice narratives that emerge and grow over time led to the development of PaperChains – an audio annotation system specifically designed with high affordability and accessibility in mind. We now discuss the system's benefits, the limitations of this work, and areas for future research.

PaperChains' novel technique makes use of an interactive voice response (IVR) backend, using standard, widely-recognised DTMF codes to communicate with client handsets over a normal phone line, removing the need for a potentially costly data connection. In addition, the approach works with even the lowest-end of the smartphone market (or camera-enabled feature phones), making it particularly appropriate for users in resource constrained environments.

Our usability evaluations of PaperChains have demonstrated its ability to support the creation and interpretation of dynamic audio-annotated documents. All groups in both Mumbai and Langa were able to use the system to sketch and annotate their own stories, and to understand other groups' stories. During the studies, participants mentioned other scenarios that they imagined the system being useful for, including specific aspects of the expressivity that the system enables that made it particularly useful. There were also strong statements about its usability, and the majority of participants stated that they enjoyed using the system.

Clearly, there are opportunities for further work to refine the system's operation. When sketching and annotating, users

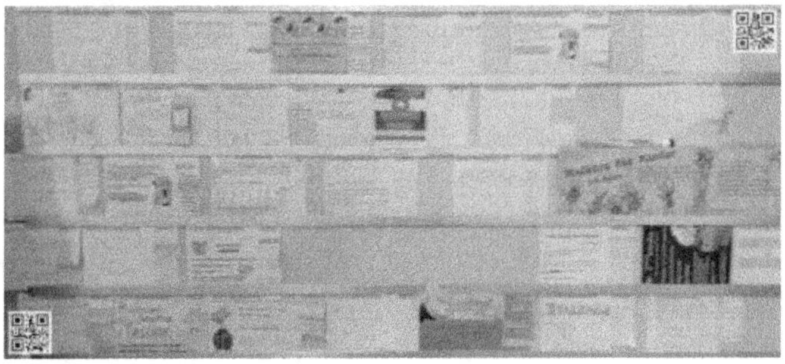

Figure 9. Noticeboards—such as this local advert board—could easily be augmented with PaperChains content after adding two small QR codes.

tended to sketch in more areas than they eventually annotated, or annotated only a small section of the sketch rather than the entire object. It was apparent in both evaluations that the exploratory nature of the audio discovery process that this annotation behaviour led to was enjoyable. However, further development of the design could investigate ways to draw users toward audio areas in an unobtrusive manner.

While the results from our studies have been highly encouraging, the experiments we have conducted to date have been in a lab-like environment. As a result, usage of the system so far has not been contextualised in the type of storytelling scenario we imagine the system being used. Our next task is to deploy the PaperChains system in a more naturalistic environment in order to gather feedback on real-world experiences from users. One possible way to achieve this could be to distribute PaperChains-augmented paper via a local NGO or community group within the regions we have been working in. Monitoring uptake and the types of documents created would provide useful information about long-term usage of the system.

A further alternative for a more longitudinal and in-the-wild investigation in this area would be to explore the use of annotated community notice boards (see Fig. 9). If we consider the nature of group notice boards, it is clear that they are built-up and modified by multiple users over time, making them an ideal use-case for the PaperChains technique. An additional benefit of such an application, as mentioned earlier, is that a notice board is static and can therefore be reused, reducing the consumable materials required to use the system.

Stepping back from resource constrained environments, we also believe that our approach has benefits for more developed contexts. For instance, in areas where data-costs are higher than usual (such as when data roaming abroad), an IVR-based rather than internet-based method could significantly lower costs for this type of interaction. Alternatively, modifying the system to use an internet-based backend would better suit areas where data connectivity is cheap. In this context, we imagine using the technology for the archive of personal media. For example, this could include building up scrap- or baby-books over time, including various physical keepsakes such as photographs or memorabilia augmented with personal anecdotes from family and friends. A specific instance of this idea, then, could be to use the PaperChains technology as a method of creating interactive greetings cards, which could be particularly useful when there are multiple well-wishers who would like to leave a message, as explored in the following scenario:

Liam is leaving the office for several months to take up a summer internship. To wish him well, his friends buy a PaperChains greetings card, and over the next few days the card is passed around the lab for everyone to sign. At their turn, each person writes in the card, then uses their phone to take a photo, scribbling on-screen over their handwritten message to leave an audio greeting. The space fills up over time, and soon the card is crowded with penned notes and paired audio messages.

Liam takes the card with him while away. At any time during the trip, he can take a photo of it and touch the handwritten notes to hear the accompanying voice messages. When Liam gets back he writes his own note on the card and adds audio comments about the experience, then pins the card to the lab noticeboard. Anyone in the office can take a photo of the card and hear about his summer visit – the card is now an interactive memento of the experience.

As illustrated in the scenario, we see benefits of the PaperChains approach in wider situations than that demonstrated in this work. The aim of this paper has been to explore the notion of evolving collaborative digital-physical artefacts in resource-constrained contexts. We hope that this work stimulates discussion on ways to provide advanced services with low technological requirements, and motivates further work of this type in these contexts

ACKNOWLEDGMENTS
This work was funded by EPSRC grant EP/J000604/2. We thank Minah Radebe (South Africa), and our colleagues at IIT Bombay (India), for their help running usability evaluations.

REFERENCES

1. Back, M., Cohen, J., Gold, R., Harrison, S. and Minneman, S. Listen reader: an electronically augmented paper-based book. In *Proc. CHI '01*, ACM (2001), 23–29.
2. Cao, X., Lindley, S. E., Helmes, J. and Sellen, A. Telling the whole story: anticipation, inspiration and reputation in a field deployment of TellTable. In *Proc. CSCW '10*, ACM (2010), 251–260.
3. Costanza, E., Giaccone, M., Kueng, O., Shelley, S. and Huang, J. Ubicomp to the masses: a large-scale study of two tangible interfaces for download. In *Proc. UbiComp '10*, ACM (2010), 173–182.
4. Druin, A., Stewart, J., Proft, D., Bederson, B. and Hollan, J. KidPad: a design collaboration between children, technologists, and educators. In *Proc. CHI '97*, ACM (1997), 463–470.

5. Erol, B., Hull, J., Graham, J. and Lee, D.-S. Prescient paper: multimedia document creation with document image matching. In *Proc. ICPR '04*, vol. 2. 2004, 675–678.
6. Erol, B., Antúnez, E. and Hull, J. J. HOTPAPER: multimedia interaction with paper using mobile phones. In *Proc. MM '08*, ACM (2008), 399–408.
7. Frohlich, D. Audiophotography. Springer (2004).
8. Frohlich, D. M., Rachovides, D., Riga, K., Bhat, R., Frank, M., Edirisinghe, E., Wickramanayaka, D., Jones, M. and Harwood, W. StoryBank: mobile digital storytelling in a development context. In *Proc. CHI '09*, ACM (2009), 1761–1770.
9. Frohlich, D., Clancy, T., Robinson, J. and Costanza, E. The audiophoto desk. In *Proc. 2AD Demos*, 2004.
10. Guimbretière, F. Paper augmented digital documents. In *Proc. UIST '03*, ACM (2003), 51–60.
11. Jacoby, S. and Buechley, L. Drawing the electric: storytelling with conductive ink. In *Proc. IDC '13*, ACM (2013), 265–268.
12. Klemmer, S., Graham, J., Wolff, G. and Landay, J. Books with voices: paper transcripts as a physical interface to oral histories. In *Proc. CHI '03*, ACM (2003), 89–96.
13. Kumar, A., Rajput, N., Chakraborty, D., Agarwal, S. and Nanavati, A. WWTW: the world wide telecom web. In *Proc. NSDR workshop at SIGCOMM '07*, ACM (2007).
14. Lang, X., Oreglia, E. and Thomas, S. Social practices and mobile phone use of young migrant workers. In *Proc. MobileHCI '10*, ACM (2010), 59–62.
15. Lima, E. S. de, Feijó, B., Barbosa, S. D., Furtado, A. L., Ciarlini, A. E. and Pozzer, C. T. Draw your own story: paper and pencil interactive storytelling. *Entertainment Computing* 5.1 (2014), 33–41.
16. Liu, Q., Liao, C., Wilcox, L., Dunnigan, A. and Liew, B. Embedded media markers: marks on paper that signify associated media. In *Proc. IUI '10*, ACM (2010), 149–158.
17. Lucero, A., Holopainen, J. and Jokela, T. Pass-them-around: collaborative use of mobile phones for photo sharing. In *Proc. CHI '11*, ACM (2011), 1787–1796.
18. Maunder, A., Marsden, G. and Harper, R. Making the link—providing mobile media for novice communities in the developing world. *International Journal of Human-Computer Studies* 69.10 (2011), 647–657.
19. Mistry, P., Maes, P. and Chang, L. WUW – wear ur world: a wearable gestural interface. In *Proc. CHI EA '09*, ACM (2009), 4111–4116.
20. Parikh, T., Javid, P., K, S., Ghosh, K. and Toyama, K. Mobile phones and paper documents: evaluating a new approach for capturing microfinance data in rural India. In *Proc. CHI '06*, ACM (2006), 551–560.
21. Patel, N., Chittamuru, D., Jain, A., Dave, P. and Parikh, T. S. Avaaj Otalo: a field study of an interactive voice forum for small farmers in rural India. In *Proc. CHI '10*, ACM (2010), 733–742.
22. Raffle, H., Vaucelle, C., Wang, R. and Ishii, H. Jabberstamp: embedding sound and voice in traditional drawings. In *Proc. IDC '07*, ACM (2007), 137–144.
23. Reitmaier, T., Bidwell, N. J. and Marsden, G. Field testing mobile digital storytelling software in rural Kenya. In *Proc. MobileHCI '10*, ACM (2010), 283–286.
24. Robinson, S., Jones, M., Vartiainen, E. and Marsden, G. PicoTales: collaborative authoring of animated stories using handheld projectors. In *Proc. CSCW '12*, ACM (2012), 671–680.
25. Robinson, S., Pearson, J. S. and Jones, M. AudioCanvas: internet-free interactive audio photos. In *Proc. CHI '14*, ACM (2014), 3735–3738.
26. Sawhney, N. Voices beyond walls: the role of digital storytelling for empowering marginalized youth in refugee camps. In *Proc. IDC '09*, ACM (2009), 302–305.
27. Schilit, B. N., Golovchinsky, G. and Price, M. N. Beyond paper: supporting active reading with free form digital ink annotations. In *Proc. CHI '98*, ACM Press/Addison-Wesley Publishing Co. (1998), 249–256.
28. Seifert, J., Pfleging, B., Hermes, M., Rukzio, E. and Schmidt, A. Mobidev: a tool for creating apps on mobile phones. In *Proc. MobileHCI '11*, ACM (2011), 109–112.
29. Smith, G. and Marsden, G. Providing media download services in African taxis. In *Proc. SAICSIT '11*, ACM (2011), 215–223.
30. Stifelman, L., Arons, B. and Schmandt, C. The audio notebook: paper and pen interaction with structured speech. In *Proc. CHI '01*, ACM (2001), 182–189.
31. Wellner, P. Interacting with paper on the DigitalDesk. *Communications of the ACM* 36.7 (1993), 87–96.
32. West, D., Quigley, A. and Kay, J. MEMENTO: a digital-physical scrapbook for memory sharing. *Personal and Ubiquitous Computing* 11.4 (2007), 313–328.
33. Wood, G., Vines, J., Balaam, M., Taylor, N., Smith, T., Crivellaro, C., Mensah, J., Limon, H., Challis, J., Anderson, L., Clarke, A. and Wright, P. C. The dept. of hidden stories: playful digital storytelling for children in a public library. In *Proc. CHI '14*, ACM (2014), 1885–1894.
34. Yeh, R., Liao, C., Klemmer, S., Guimbretière, F., Lee, B., Kakaradov, B., Stamberger, J. and Paepcke, A. ButterflyNet: a mobile capture and access system for field biology research. In *Proc. CHI '06*, ACM (2006), 571–580.

Piloting TrACE: Exploring Spatiotemporal Anchored Collaboration in Asynchronous Learning

Brian Dorn
Univ. of Nebraska at Omaha
Omaha, NE, 68182
bdorn@unomaha.edu

Larissa B. Schroeder
University of Hartford
West Hartford, CT 06117
schroeder@hartford.edu

Adam Stankiewicz
University of Hartford
West Hartford, CT 06117
astankiew@hartford.edu

ABSTRACT
The use of multimedia content such as video is becoming more prevalent in educational environments. However, current platforms for hosting these media provide few collaborative tools to foster social learning between students or request help from instructors. In this paper, we explore the potential of *spatiotemporal anchored collaboration*, and we present a prototype media-playback environment called TrACE that exemplifies the approach. We examine a first design-based research (DBR) pilot deployment of TrACE in two post-secondary courses. Results indicate that students do take advantage of the system's affordances to interact in meaningful ways, though overall student annotation authoring was limited. Using the pilot data, we propose socio-technical modifications for the next iteration in the DBR cycle. Specifically we focus on tools to support instructors' use of the system and for promoting collaboration between students.

ACM Classification Keywords
H.5.3. Information Interfaces and Presentation (e.g. HCI): Group and Organization Interfaces—*asynchronous interaction, collaborative computing, computer-supported cooperative work*

Author Keywords
anchored collaboration; computer-supported collaborative learning; flipped courses; video annotation

INTRODUCTION
Digital media is playing an increasing role in educational environments, particularly at the post-secondary level [39, 43, 17]. Many simultaneous changes have accelerated the adoption of streaming video content in education. A 2010 Sloan Consortium study showed online higher education enrollments that were growing at ten times the rate of face-to-face offerings and projected continued robust growth in online education for the foreseeable future [2], and massive open online courses (MOOCs) have garnered considerable public attention in recent years [31]. In both MOOCs and other online courses, video lectures and tutorials are the most common form of primary instruction. At the same time, educational institutions are experimenting with blended or hybrid learning environments in which some instruction occurs online, while other aspects take place in face-to-face settings. "Flipped classrooms" [29, 7], in which students independently watch video lectures online prior to class and devote in-class time to collaborative problem-based and discussion-oriented tasks, have become a major discussion point among STEM educators in recent years (see, e.g., [16, 8]). While the educational merits of both MOOCs and flipped classes are still a subject of debate and ongoing research [18, 8], the importance of online video in education is undeniable.

A significant challenge in fully and hybrid on-line educational environments is the inability to tailor instruction to the immediate needs of the students when they first engage with content. In these contexts video consumption is conceptualized as an individualistic activity and implicitly couched in the behaviorist view of instruction centered around direct knowledge transmission. Within some MOOC platforms (e.g., Coursera) learners may be presented with individual formative assessment quizzes to check their developing understanding, but such tools are not broadly available. Thus, it is no surprise that instructors of flipped courses report that students express frustration about a lack of help while watching videos, and they observe students consuming media passively rather than actively engaging with the content [37]. Further, lack of timely instructor feedback in blended courses may lead students adopt the view that they must "learn it all on their own" and perceive that the course requires more work [38]. Paradoxically, recommended practices in flipped classes, like giving graded entrance quizzes to ensure videos are viewed [30], may exacerbate these perceptions among weaker students who struggle with content of course videos.

In typical video playback tools available to instructors and students, the only means of interacting with the video and other learners is with comments that are often occluded below the visible content. Not only do disconnects between educational media and collaborative spaces inhibit interaction [23], but they make it difficult for learners to engage in more student-centered learning activities like debate, critique, and analysis that are commonly the goals of knowledge building [35] and constructivist learning environments [33, 14].

We see an opportunity to explore the potential of socio-technical systems that explicitly recognize learning from videos as a different process than simply viewing videos. In this paper, we present the initial design and pilot deployment

CSCW'15, March 14–18, 2015, Vancouver, BC, Canada
Copyright 2014 ACM 978-1-4503-2922-4/15/03...$15.00
http://dx.doi.org/10.1145/2675133.2675178

of a novel media-playback environment called TrACE, the Transformative Anchored Collaboration Environment. It is intended to enable collaborative annotation and discussion of video content as a first-order learning activity, facilitating more student-centered activities in the online space. In particular, we examine the role of *spatiotemporal anchored collaboration* affordances (ie., the ability for learners to embed discussions at particular locations and times within videos). Thus we use the initial TrACE prototype as a form of technological probe [27], allowing us to explore the adoption and impact of these features for both instructors and learners.

In the remainder of this paper, we first discuss related work in computer-supported collaborative learning (CSCL). Next we introduce the initial prototype of TrACE and discuss its design. We then outline a pilot deployment using TrACE in two post-secondary courses and present the study results. Lastly, we reflect on the implications of these findings for the future design asynchronous video playback environments.

BACKGROUND AND RELATED WORK

We are employing an iterative, design-based research (DBR) approach [4] in the design and evaluation of TrACE. DBR recognizes the significant influence that instructional context has on the ultimate success of new educational technologies and learning environments. DBR espouses a process of progressive refinement, placing early versions of an educational artifact in real learning contexts, with the goal of deriving lessons learned to guide the next phase of design within the socio-technical learning environment [15]. At the same time, DBR recognizes the pragmatic issues of instruction that might limit an instructor's ability or willingness to adopt the newly designed artifact. In this section we synthesize the relevant literature informing the design of the initial system prototype used for the first round of DBR evaluation.

Collaboration and Knowledge Building

Scardamalia and Bereiter pioneered the development of collaborative knowledge building tools [35, 34], namely CSILE (later, Knowledge Forum). Central in knowledge building environments is the ability for learners to engage in discourse—positing ideas to the group along with supporting evidence. Importantly, these tools also allow learners to collaboratively evaluate, discuss, and augment each others' work to advance the whole class understanding of phenomena being learned [34]. Knowledge Forum and other modern systems (e.g., Science Online [19]) explicitly promote the salient forms of discourse in the target educational context. In this work, we aim to stimulate class-level discourse about instructional media so that learners actively engage and help each other to a deeper understanding. Thus, we adopt and adapt features from other knowledge building environments like procedural facilitation and categorization of contribution types to guide students toward productive forms of discourse.

Guzdial and Turns define *anchored collaboration* in CSCL environments as embedding, or anchoring, collaboration tools near the media to which they refer [20]. Early anchored collaboration environments demonstrated that placing links to threaded discussion areas within static Web pages of instructional content increased the likelihood that students would engage in collaborative discourse and increased the quality of that discourse [23]. In this paper, we extend this approach for time-based instructional media (e.g., videos) and anchor collaborative discussion spaces in both "place" and "time" within the media itself to preserve the original context in which discussions begin. Thus, we refer to this approach as *spatiotemporal anchored collaboration*.

Annotation Systems

The HCI and CSCL communities have a long history of exploring the use of multimedia and annotation platforms as vehicles to provide instruction. In the mid-nineties and early 2000s researchers developed a wide variety of computational tools to support students in using multimedia for learning course content (e.g., MediaText [25], Classroom 2000 [1], and Goal-Based Scenarios [36]). Classroom 2000 was designed to capture course content through ubiquitous computing techniques to be made available for students to later access asynchronously over the web [1]. It employed instructor-specified annotations within the media as bookmarks, and allowed learners to contribute additional annotations on separate course wikis [22]. While evaluation studies of Classroom 2000 showed promising results, the level of learner interaction within the environment was limited by the web-based development techniques available at the time.

In the intervening decade, there has been an explosion of Web 2.0 interfaces, social and crowd-sourced platforms, and a generation of learners who have grown up interacting with the web as co-creators of content [6, 32]. Accordingly, there has been a renewed interest in collaborative annotation environments for various documents and media (e.g., [47, 44]). Zyto et al. argue that this is due in part to the fact that "the socio-technical environment of the classroom has evolved to the point where the barriers that were encountered by earlier annotation tools have lowered enough to be overcome by motivated teachers and students" [47]. Zyto's text document system employs a spatial annotation technique, and their evaluation efforts show significant increases in the amount of student-to-student discourse occurring online [47].

Recent work by several different research teams has also revisited annotation of course videos. Wong's system, EVA, provides a collaborative temporal annotation system allowing learners to associate comments with specific time-segments in a video [45]. The Choreographer's notebook, developed by Carroll et al., allows users to asynchronously attach critique feedback to relevant regions of videos recorded during dance rehearsals [40]. While both dancers and choreographers can contribute annotations, researchers found that the vast majority of annotations were unidirectional from the choreographers to the dancers [12]. Kim's Toolscape [28] provides an interface for navigating workflow annotations within online tutorial videos. Toolscape's playback system leverages annotations as bookmarks that allow for quick indexing to important parts of the tutorial, but the annotations themselves are not intended as points of discussion between users. Lastly Zaption [46], a commercial start-up venture, allows instructors to place a variety of interactive widgets like discussion boards and quiz questions at specific points in instructional videos. Zaption's discussion widget (when enabled by the

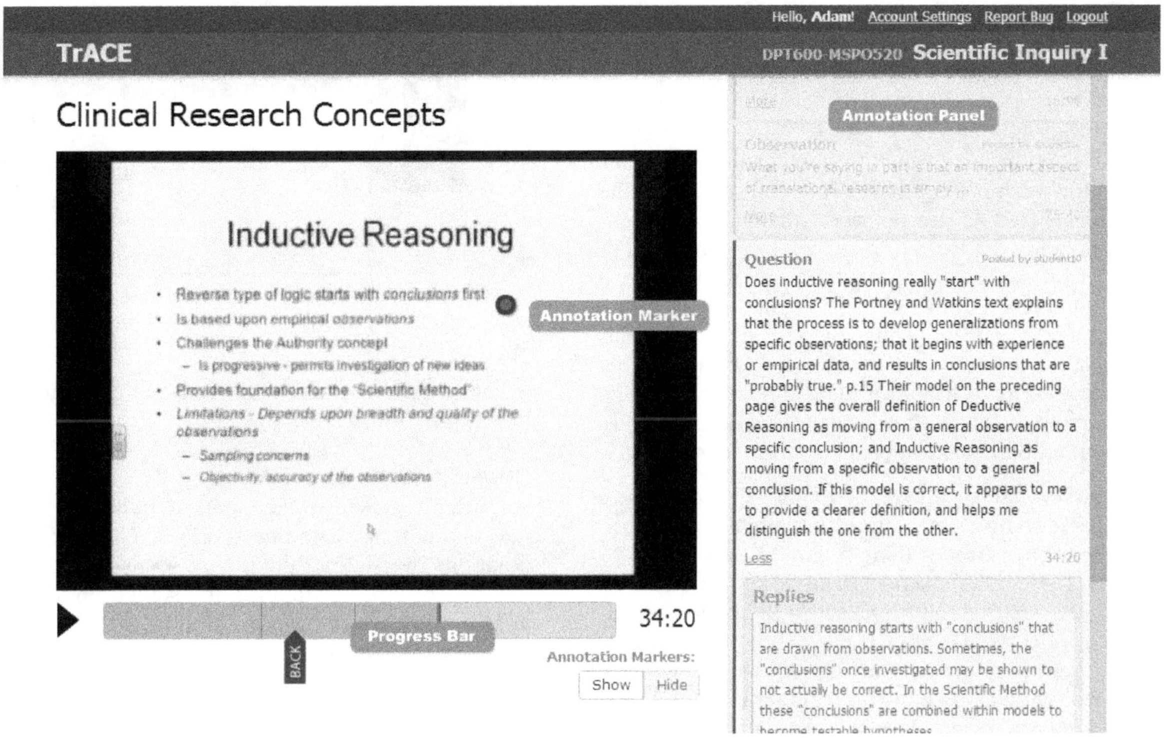

Figure 1. A student view of watching a video in TrACE

instructor) associates student posts with the video's current timestamp, but comments and replies are free-form and do not explicitly aid learners in the task of authorship.

Our design of the TrACE system synthesizes ideas from each of these systems and differs from prior work in one or more of the following ways:

- TrACE provides robust referential comments, associating annotations with both a timestamp in the video *and* a specific location inside the 2D media frame at that timestamp.
- Contributed annotations serve as bookmarks in the media and allow quick navigation and non-linear access.
- TrACE supports both asynchronous and synchronous collaboration between users.
- Top-level annotations in TrACE are treated as starting points for group discussion, allowing others to reply directly and collaboratively make sense of the media.
- Annotation authoring in TrACE supports categorization and directed reflective prompts to enhance the quality of the resulting discourse between users.

In the next section, we illustrate each of these design features as they appear in the current TrACE prototype.

OUR DESIGN PROTOTYPE

TrACE is implemented as a web application using HTML5, JavaScript, PHP, and AJAX. This implementation choice allows for write-once-run-everywhere functionality in modern web browsers, including those on mobile devices. This ensures a wide degree of flexibility for how students view the media associated with a course, and it provides a seamless interaction experience as students and instructors move between their various computing devices.

Upon logging into TrACE, learners are presented with a list of courses in which they are enrolled. Students can then navigate to a specific course and view its associated videos. Once they select a video from this list, they are presented with the media playback interface illustrated in Figure 1. This screenshot illustrates many of TrACE's core features.

Annotation Panel

The annotation panel at the right of Figure 1 displays all annotations in the system for the displayed video. Rather than hiding annotations below the video, annotations are placed alongside the media to maximize the learner's ability to refer back and forth between the media and annotations.

Each annotation carries a timestamp indicating where its author placed it within the video. During playback, timestamps are used to automatically position the panel's scroll bar such that the annotations of temporal relevance to the video's playback position are always visible. Annotations that are not currently relevant are also faded to reduce visual clutter, and replies are only shown when the user explicitly views the top-level annotation. These techniques leverage progressive disclosure to minimize cognitive workload [24] and focus the viewer's attention on the annotations of immediate importance. It also enables learners to quickly evaluate whether another person has asked a similar question at this point in the video.

Further, annotations are categorized and color-coded in the annotation panel and playback interface (e.g., "Questions" are blue, and "Links" are red). This simplifies recognition of the type of contribution within the system.

Annotation Markers

In addition to providing information about an annotation's temporal location within the media (i.e., timestamps in the annotation panel), TrACE also provides referential capabilities for learners, allowing them to place a visual marker at or near an item of interest in the video frame. For example, a student might annotate a confusing term or definition, or the introduction to a new concept. Thus, not only are annotations tagged with respect to *when* in the video they are made, but they are also tagged as to *where* in the 2-dimensional video frame the poster left the annotation using a circular marker. In Figure 1 an annotation marker appears near the word "first".

Annotation markers are displayed as though floating above the media and are visible for a short, but predictable, window of time on either side of their original timestamp. As the video plays, these markers appear and disappear based on which annotations are currently relevant to the point the student is at in the video. This unobtrusive technique allows for annotations to appear as though they belong within the content of the video while also giving an indication of the social interactions which are taking place at a given position.

The expository and/or demonstrative nature of most educational videos motivates the need for our spatiotemporal approach. It enables students to refer to and ask about steps, items, and concepts in the moment, which is a critical element in developing both conceptual and procedural understanding [10]. Further, anchoring comments in space and time allows users to visually indicate specific, relevant details of their questions. Preserving this referential context about the initial annotation increases the likelihood that subsequent viewers will be able to understand the original point made and engage meaningfully in authoring a reply.

Progress Bar

TrACE employs a context-aware progress bar beneath the media that not only indicates the learner's current playback position within the video, but also the relative position of all annotations placed by others in this video (seen as the colored vertical bars in the progress bar in Figure 1). This can serve as an advance organizer [3], giving students an indication of which annotations are present and cuing their attention to sections of the video where significant activity has taken place. Further, this visualization provides instructors with an immediate formative assessment tool [11], allowing them to evaluate which parts of the media may need additional discussion.

The video player and annotation markers, the progress bar, and the annotation panel are designed such that interactions in one area affect all others. For example, advancing the progress bar will move both the video and the annotation panel to that position. Further, clicking on an annotation will cause the video and progress bar to jump to the location where that contribution was made. Thus, each annotation serves as a bookmark; learners are able to index into the media to points

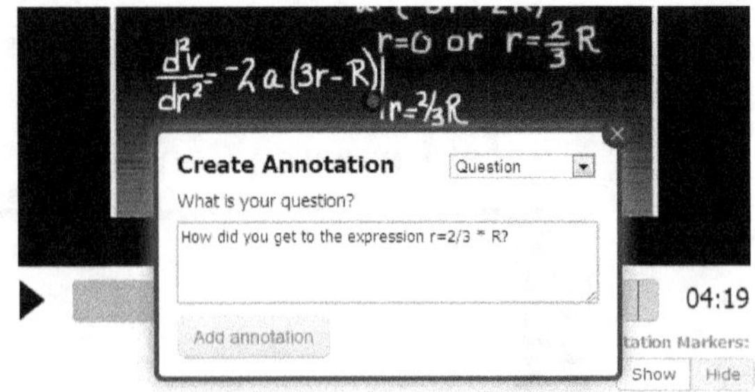

Figure 2. Creating a new annotation

of interest rather than being restricted to viewing the content in a strictly linear fashion [13].

Creating a New Annotation

As a user is viewing media in TrACE, he or she can contribute new annotations as the need arises. Users construct new annotations by clicking the mouse at a specific position within the video frame (or tapping the screen on a mobile device). This mimics the pointing gesture a student might make in a classroom while saying, "I don't understand where this value came from in the equation." The location in which the student clicked or tapped provides the new annotation's anchor point for both where and when it occurred.

When a user initiates an annotation, a new marker appears on the video and the user is presented with a multi-step wizard to scaffold the creation of an annotation (a simplified view of the process is shown in Figure 2). Each of the different annotation types features a customized dialog that assists students in the process of contributing a productive question, comment, link, etc. These question types and prompts are determined based on instructor input prior to the term. The goal is that, rather than posting generic comments, learners are guided to think through specific aspects of their contributions. Similar guided approaches to reflection have been shown to produce more educationally effective discourse in other collaborative learning environments [35, 20, 5].

Viewing an Annotation and Replying

Once submitted, the new annotation automatically appears and becomes the starting point for a new anchored discussion in the annotation panel to which other students and the instructor can post replies (see Figure 1). Figure 3 illustrates how learners and instructors can then view existing replies for any given annotation as well as contribute a new reply. When an annotation is clicked (either by the marker within the video frame or by the annotation in the panel), the video is advanced to the point in which the annotation was added and then paused. The annotation then expands within the panel to show all replies (which are also categorized) along with a text area that can be used to post a new reply. The reply wizard follows the same conventions as creating a new annotation in order to create constructive and meaningful replies.

SPRING 2013 PILOT STUDY

During Spring 2013 we deployed TrACE in our first DBR iteration. The early TrACE prototype was piloted in two courses, Scientific Inquiry and Calculus I, both of which used

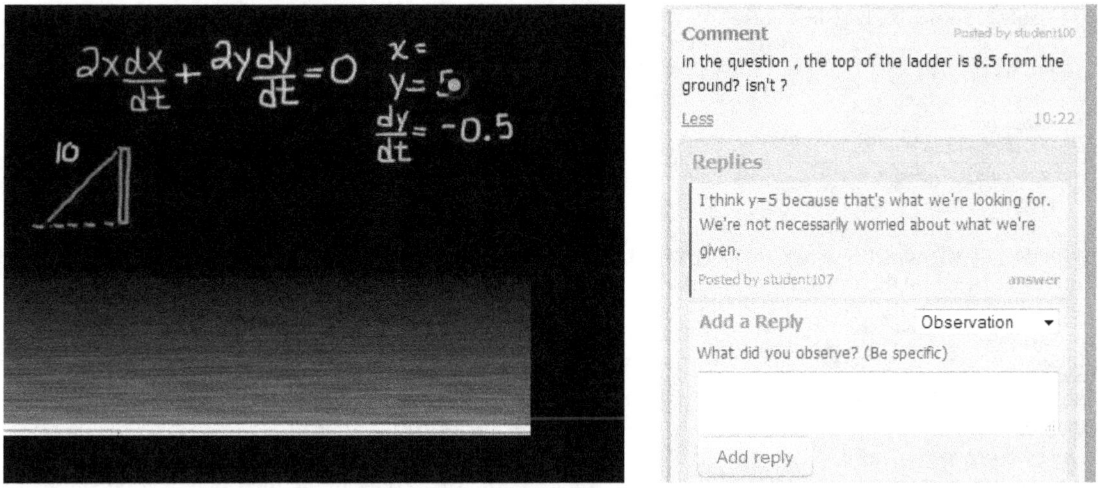

Figure 3. Adding a reply to an existing annotation

videos as an integral component of instruction. Scientific Inquiry (SciInq), a graduate level course taken by masters and doctoral students in the rehabilitation sciences, provides an introduction to research methods used in physical therapy. This course was taught in a hybrid format, with the class meeting face-to-face every two to three weeks; in the intervening weeks, students were expected to watch video lectures recorded by the course instructor. SciInq videos were predominately recorded in a lecture-capture format showing static slides interleaved with full motion video of the instructor at a podium. Of the 63 students enrolled in this course, 41 agreed to participate in the study data collection, and 35 were active[1] within TrACE. Videos were simultaneously available in both the course LMS (ie., Blackboard) and TrACE during 14 weeks of instruction, and students were allowed to view videos using one or both systems.

Undergraduate students from two sections of an inverted/flipped Calculus I (Calc) course also participated in the pilot study for a 5-week period at the end of the semester. Videos in Calc took on an interactive format, where slide-based presentations with minimal pre-existing content were written upon by the speaker with a stylus while explaining mathematical ideas. Other videos made use of interactive simulation software to demonstrate the relevant concepts. Of the 45 students enrolled in these sections, 30 consented to participate in the study, and 28 of them were active in TrACE. Throughout the entire semester, students in the inverted Calc classes were expected to view one or two 10–15 minute long videos before each class meeting period. During pilot study data collection at the end of term, videos were only available through TrACE and were no longer available through the LMS as had been the case earlier in the semester.

Beyond obvious differences between the level and content of these courses, the instructors adopted different approaches to the integration of videos. Table 1 outlines a number of these differences. While students in Calc were expected to watch more videos per week, the videos were much shorter

Table 1. Video Properties by Course

	Sci Inq	Calc
weeks of instruction with TrACE	14	5
# videos available	22	14
average # videos per week	1.57	2.8
minimum video length (mm:ss)	17:52	5:25
maximum video length	56:46	17:59
average video length	36:50	11:38
mean expected viewing time per week	54:01	32:34

in length. Notably, the shortest video in SciInq was roughly equal in length to the longest Calc video. All told, the average expected viewing time per week[2] for Calc students was about half that of SciInq students.

Differences in course expectations seem natural given that SciInq students watched videos in lieu of attending class, whereas Calc students viewed videos on their own time to enable hands-on activities during normal class sessions. Other pedagogical variations that arose due to differing course content, teaching strategies, and the needs of students served as variables with which to study usage and adoption of TrACE. In this pilot deployment, we also needed to balance pragmatic concerns instructors had about the new technology with our research goals. Nonetheless, the SciInq and Calc courses provided interesting (and somewhat typical) use cases for asynchronous educational videos and thus were good environments in which to pilot the system.

We posed the following exploratory questions:

Q1 How and to what extent do students make use of the collaboration tools within TrACE?

Q2 How and to what extent did the collaboration tools support interactions between users?

Q3 What socio-technical limitations can be identified in the pilot deployment to inform future iterations?

[1]We define *active users* as those who consented for the study and viewed at least one video in TrACE.

[2]Calculated as the total running time of all videos in a course divided by the number of weeks of instruction using TrACE.

Table 2. Session Activity by Course

	SciInq	Calc
Total number of sessions	393	363
Avg # sessions per student	11.2	13.0
Avg # sessions per student per week	0.8	2.6
Avg session length (mm:ss)	32:04	15:42
Avg player events per session	17.2	15.6

The first two questions explore the ways in which users collaborate within TrACE, while the third focuses broadly on the interaction between instructional context and the system.

Data Collection

In both courses, students were allowed to use TrACE regardless of whether or not they participated in the study. Data presented here is from only the consenting, active participants and is masked to preserve anonymity. User interaction in TrACE was recorded automatically for both server-side events (logging in, viewing a course, opening a video) and client-side events (playing/pausing a video, seeking within a video, viewing and authoring annotations). 13 action types were logged along with relevant details about each like timestamps, user ids, etc. In total, we recorded 16,347 such actions. We also aggregated the actions for each student into viewing sessions. A *session* in this context is defined as when a student begins viewing a video and continues until an action that takes the user off the video page (e.g., returning to the course media page, logging out of TrACE).

Logfile data provided quantitative interaction data, but we also examined student and instruction contributions in the system to develop a qualitative understanding of participants' use. Lastly, we administered an online survey to student users at the end of the term to gather additional feedback on TrACE.

Results

Students in the two courses exhibited distinct viewing patterns. In total, SciInq students viewed videos 425 times, while Calc students generated 418 video viewing events. However, given that Calc students used the system only for the last third of the term, they generated significantly more views per week per student on average (2.99) than their SciInq counterparts (0.87) ($t(38.1) = -4.92, p < 0.001$). On the whole, Calc students also demonstrated more consistent viewing patterns week-to-week up until final exams where viewership dropped off. SciInq students, on the other hand, showed more erratic viewership patterns in TrACE.

Session-Level Interactions

Aggregating log events at the session level provides another perspective from which to view the use of TrACE. Table 2 presents additional details about students' activity levels in viewing sessions. Calc students generated significantly more viewing sessions per week on average than SciInq students ($t(39.2) = -4.52; p < 0.001$). Further, SciInq students generated markedly fewer viewing sessions per week than would be expected given the number of weekly assigned videos (see Table 1). The average SciInq session was shorter than the average video length in the course, implying that most sessions ended before the entire video was played. On the other hand, Calc students' typical sessions lasted about 35% longer than the average course video's length, suggesting the potential of activity in the interface beyond simple playback. These trends held when we examined students' total session length per week, with Calc students viewing videos in TrACE for considerably more time per week than those in SciInq (40:44 vs 22:46, respectively). While the average number of playback interface events in a typical session was similar in the two courses, Calc students were significantly more active in their interactions with the media when controlling for session duration ($t(636.4) = -2.78; p < 0.001$).

Table 3. Annotation Related Statistics by Course

	SciInq	Calc
Total number of annotations	29	46
% of annotations contributed by students	62%	43%
% of videos with annotations	36%	64%
By Conversation Threads		
Total number of conversation threads	14	30
Avg # threads per video	0.64	2.14
Avg thread length	2.07	1.53
% of threads initiated by students	92.9%	40.0%
Student Authorship/Viewing Behaviors		
% who authored an annotation or reply	8.6%	21.4%
% who viewed annotations, but didn't author	62.9%	39.3%
% who watched videos, but didn't view annotations	26.6%	39.3%

Use of the Annotation System

Beyond basic interaction data, we examined how participants made use of the TrACE annotation system. Table 3 presents quantitative data about annotation authoring. The remainder of this subsection explores example annotation threads within the system to highlight its use in the two courses.

Pointing and Asking: In both courses, students and instructors took advantage of TrACE's spatiotemporal features by leaving annotation markers near content within the video, where in at least some cases the position of the annotation markers resolved ambiguities for the reader. Calculus students left annotation markers near diagrams being discussed or near variables of interest in equations. For example, the interaction depicted earlier in Figure 3 shows student100 expressing confusion about a portion of a video where the professor is solving a related rate problem about a ladder sliding down a wall. From the student's comment alone, it is not clear to which part of the currently visible content within the video frame he is referring. The associated annotation marker, however, removes all doubt as it is placed directly on top of the $y = 5$ in the visible content. This enables student107 to recognize that student100 is wondering why y is not 8.5 instead, and allows her to respond based on her understanding of the situation.

Additionally, we noted instances where the physical position of the annotation markers was not essential to the posted content; however, the temporal dimension played an important role. In particular, SciInq students often asked more general questions about the current topic of discussion. In these cases the particular visible content in the video frame was not of direct relevance. In Calculus, one instructor would often place annotation markers in the margins of the video at particular times when challenging students to try working a problem:

[Instr4] Comment: *You should try this on your own - pause the video and then check your work.*

Deliberate Seeding: One of the Calculus instructors made a regular and deliberate effort to seed the environment with potential points of discussion for the students. As a result, videos from Calc were more likely than those from SciInq to contain at least one annotation. For example:

[Instr4] Question: *Is a left rectangular approximation always an under-approximation and is a right rectangular approximation always an over-approximation?*

Unfortunately, many of these instructor contributed annotations received no student replies, limiting the instructional impact of these meta-cognitive reflection points. We posit that students may have considered these annotations merely rhetorical questions from the instructor, rather than questions to which a response was needed.

Student-to-Teacher: A large proportion of the student contributed annotations garnered only a single reply from the course instructor, with no other students taking part in the conversation whether or not the instructors' intention was to facilitate or terminate the interchange. For example, in the exchange below from Calc, the student directly addresses the question to the instructor using the pronoun "you." The instructor's response is an invitation for further discussion among the class, but goes nowhere.

[Stu110] Question: *how did you get* $Pi \cdot r^2 h$ *?*

[Instr4] Answer: *What is the volume of a right circular cylinder?*

This type of interaction was most frequent in SciInq where a majority of the top-level annotations were contributed by student users, and nearly all these threads began with a question or comment from a student followed by an answer from the course instructor. One interaction like this is shown below, where a student provided feedback to the instructor, asking for a specific example.

[Stu10] Comment: *An example might be useful right about now ... this is hitting the limit of my capacity to relate the various pieces in the abstract ...*

[Instr1] Answer: *Operational Definition Example - Assessment of Pain: Pain will be assessed using a VAS (Visual Analog Scale) The patient will be given a paper copy of the 10 point scale that ranges from 1 (no pain) to 10 (unbearable pain). The patient will place a mark on the pain scale to indicate his/her choice. The closest numerical value to the mark will be recorded as the pain indicator for that sample.*

In fact, on several occasions SciInq students explicitly began their posts with "Dr. XXX, . . . " Unfortunately doing so may signal to other students that they need not reply, potentially preempting meaningful collaborative discourse. Students appear to be naturally transferring the face-to-face practice of directing their individual questions to the teacher, rather than posing the question to the whole class for discussion. It may be necessary to help students adopt a broader notion of their audience when authoring posts.

Student-to-Student Collaboration: While there were some instances of student-driven discussions within TrACE, they were a small minority and far less frequent than we had anticipated. In almost all cases such threads did not exceed a single reply. All told, only about 20% of Calc students authored an annotation, including both top-level contributions and replies. The remaining 80% of students were evenly split between lurking behaviors (viewing, but never posting annotations) and seemingly ignoring the annotations all together. Less than 10% of SciInq students authored any annotations, but the majority viewed at least some of the existing annotations as they watched the videos. Only about a quarter of SciInq students viewed all videos without examining annotations. Encouraging more student interaction is a clear obstacle to overcome if the goal is to sustain discourse between students about course material in the future. We return to this and other implications in the discussion section.

Student Feedback

In addition to data collected through TrACE, sixteen students (n = 4, Calc; n = 12 SciInq) responded to our end of semester survey. Their responses to the survey questions provide limited opinions about TrACE, but when asked to describe what they liked responses could be grouped into two categories: one applying directly to TrACE and one related to video-based instruction in general.

Students liked the interactivity of TrACE (n = 5) (i.e., the ability to ask questions, to receive feedback, and to read comments), its ease of use (n = 6), and the general ability to view/re-view material (n = 3). When asked to compare experience with TrACE to watching course videos posted on YouTube, a Calc student reflected:

Advantages for both video platforms: the ability to pause and replay videos if something was not fully understood.I personally enjoyed the ability to full screen on youtube. However, I liked the TrACE platform more b/c I was able to ask questions.

Respondents indicated a high degree of comfort with TrACE, without significant instruction on its functions. 12 of the 16 (75%) were confident that they knew how to create new annotations and 11 of them were confident that they knew how to reply to existing annotations in TrACE. However all but 4 students indicated that they had never authored one. When asked why they had not contributed, common responses were:

I didn't have any questions during the viewing of the videos.

I have contributed one time but I feel that the power points are really self explanatory.

Students' criticisms of TrACE centered on the lack of some common video UI tools in the protoype used for the study (e.g., lack of a zoom feature and volume control widgets). Other suggestions for improvement included thread notifications and the ability to "follow" posts, embedded quizzes, and integration with the university LMS. Some survey respondents also felt that instructors should require students to post comments or questions in TrACE or somehow otherwise encourage more participation.

Student responses on open-ended questions also discussed logistical issues with the course content that influenced their behaviors. For example, a SciInq student brought up issues related to the video length and its presentation style:

The videos on trace work much better than blackboard echo. I do not use the tool properly, though, because the video lectures are just the professor reading the PowerPoint slides posted to download. It is quicker to read the slides than watch the video. I only use the video for the lab assignments.

DISCUSSION AND IMPLICATIONS

Classrooms are complex sociotechnical environments that make it difficult to isolate the multiple variables influencing collaborative student behavior [41]. Nonetheless, these results highlight pedagogical and technological issues to be considered in order to improve opportunities for spatiotemporal anchored collaboration, to support learning, and to provide a direction for the next iteration of TrACE.

Pedagogical Issues

The limited degree of collaboration between users during this pilot study raises a number of questions about general absence of collaboration observed in both courses. One possible explanation could be the students' academic background in the sciences. Guzdial et. al. [21] attributed the lack of collaboration between students enrolled in math, science, and engineering courses to competition inherent to these programs, the reluctance to seek help, and the perception of single correct answers as the discipline standard. The students enrolled in this study fit a similar profile. SciInq students, studying rehabilitation sciences, have extensive studies in the sciences. Similarly, students enrolled in Calc I are predominantly science, math or engineering majors.

Anecdotal reflections from the instructors suggest that the limited student collaboration in TrACE may not be due to lack of questions about content. For example, at the beginning of each class one of the Calc instructors regularly asked students to respond to the prompt, "state three questions that you still have about the video." In this formative assessment, students raised considerably more questions than were in TrACE for the same video. Thus, the limited interactions may be due to students' unwillingness to expose their lack of understanding to the class as a whole in the semi-public TrACE environment. While prior CSCL environments have demonstrated that online media can reduce classroom conversation inhibitions (see, e.g., [26]), design features of TrACE—namely, usernames derived from student first and last names—may have unintentionally amplified traditional classroom anxiety about asking questions given today's concerns about the longevity of social media posts.

Both of these possible explanations speak to classroom culture that may best be addressed through explicit discussion of classroom norms and social expectations.

Instructor Intentionality

Instructors play a key role in students' adoption of technologies. The sparse collaboration within TrACE during this pilot study suggests a need for more intentional integration between online activities in TrACE, instructors adoption practices, and face-to-face classroom activities. Stahl et. al. [42] highlight the importance of considering CSCL technologies as part of the "larger motivational and interactive context." As first time users of the system, our instructors were experimenting with both online content delivery and the TrACE platform during the pilot study. As a result, clearly articulated plans for integrating TrACE into the course structure and modifying their own teaching practice was absent from this pilot study. Instead, both instructors viewed TrACE as a means of addressing a perceived shortcoming of using videos for instruction—the inability of students to ask questions as they are viewing the content for the first time.

To enhance the opportunities for spatiotemporal anchored collaboration to positively impact student learning, we see a need for instructors using TrACE to set clearer expectations for student interactions on-line and to integrate asynchronous discussions with in-class instruction. Instructors need to be aware of how their own behavior in the system can impact the quality of student interactions and send tacit signals about the locus of authority and knowledge in the online environment. For example, the phrasing of an instructor's replies may either encourage extension or termination of a discussion.

Ultimately, we believe that instructors using TrACE need to explicitly establish and communicate a rationale for why the online interactions are valuable to students both individually and as a group—something that was largely absent in both courses during this pilot test.

Technical Issues

In addition to social issues that arose here, we also identified some technical limitations in the prototype that can be resolved prior to future deployments.

Tools to Promote Collaboration

One of the difficulties within any asynchronous collaboration environment is recognizing what happened since the user last logged in. In course settings like those here, many students watched videos once and then never returned, regardless of whether or not important questions or conversations had taken place since the original viewing. TrACE did not provide any visual clues as to which videos had recent annotation activity for student viewers, making it difficult to entice students to revisit videos. In fact, students mentioned social media inspired features as a potential improvement to TrACE on the end of term survey; for example:

> *Like on Facebook, when someone comments on a post your made you are notifies that a response has been made to your post. And an option to [c]hoose whether you want thread notifications or not.*

Features like thread following and activity notification emails would provide more activity awareness for students and may propel them back into the system. Not only might this encourage them to revisit media, but ultimately this may increase collaboration activities like viewing annotations and extending existing threads with new replies.

To address students' reluctance to expose their lack of understanding to peers, future prototypes should give authors the ability to anonymize annotations on a post-by-post basis. This may alleviate concerns about posting questions or comments about which students are not completely confident.

Instructional Supports

The results of this pilot also suggest some areas where TrACE did not fully support the instructors' needs. First, we saw that instructors contributed annotations for unique reasons, like attempting to seed student discussion, but the version of TrACE in this study provided a uniform set of annotation tools to all users in all courses, regardless of the user's role. Instructors need greater flexibility to adapt the set of available annotation types to fit the kinds of discourse best suited to their discipline. Further, annotation types that help users distinguish posts from students versus the instructor may help direct students' attention when necessary. Providing an expanded set of annotation types tailored to individual courses may help instructors integrate TrACE more easily. For example, bookmarks in the video could provide the instructor with a way of creating an advance organizer for the video, or allowing instructors to insert a pause point in the video with a specific prompt for student response may be one way to eliminate uncertainty as to whether or not a question is rhetorical.

Limitations and Future Work

The nature of this pilot study naturally serves as a limit to what can be said about TrACE and spatiotemporal anchored collaboration in general. Because neither course exclusively used the system for the entire instructional term, students and instructors may not have had time to establish norms around its use that would increase interaction. Further limited data about instructor intentions and student motivations was available, partially due to low survey response rate. However, broad generalizability is not the primary goal at this early stage. Instead, the results of this study have identified numerous revisions to both the TrACE system and pedagogy to be explored more formally in the following DBR evaluation.

We have already incorporated many of the interface modifications mentioned in the previous sections (e.g., customized annotation types, anonymous posting) and are collecting new data about system use in a wider variety of course settings. In particular, we are deploying the system as the sole video content source with multiple courses and different instructors of the same course for the full academic term. This will provide a broader understanding of variations in course integration and the impact of those variations on student activity in TrACE. We have three primary questions going forward: (1) What aspects of system usage correspond to higher student performance? (2) What types of collaborative discourse take place in TrACE? (3) To what extent do instructors intentionally integrate TrACE into their practices, and how does this shape student participation and collaboration in the system?

The first two questions focus on students and their interactions. First, we intend to correlate measures of user engagement derived from system logfile data to study how students' viewing and annotating patterns in TrACE relate to various course performance metrics (e.g., exam grades, final course grades). These metrics will help us quantify both viewing behaviors and collaboration activities, and this analysis will help us uncover which behaviors align with greater student performance. Beyond the quantity of posts, we also will assess the quality and types of annotation content using a qualitative framework derived from that of Borge and Goggins [9]. This tiered framework allows for evaluative distinctions to be made between posts—for example, those that share unsubstantiated facts, attempt to revoice content of others, synthesize multiple concepts, or represent metacognitive reflection. In addition to uncovering a great deal about student's observed behaviors, these data will also be used to purposefully sample student users for follow-up interviews to examine their perceptions of the overall instructional environment.

The last question specifically addresses the role of instructors within a socio-technical system and the impact of their instructional decisions on students' interactions. To this end, instructors will participate in a weekly journaling activity to reflect on the trajectory of instruction during the past week, the impact of TrACE on teaching and learning, and any instructional changes planned for the upcoming week. In addition, instructors will be interviewed at the end of the term about their experiences, using their own journal entries as an artifact on which to elaborate. Coupling a qualitative thematic analysis of these data with the quality of annotation content and student performance data may help us understand how to encourage the types of classroom integration practices and student participation in TrACE that enhances learning.

CONCLUSION

As educational innovations continue to grow the use of web-based media, technical advancements in collaborative learning tools must also be made for both small scale environments like flipped classes and large scale environments like MOOCs. In this paper we have outlined the initial design of TrACE, the Transformative Anchored Collaboration Environment, and presented results of a pilot study involving two different post-secondary courses. We have extended prior work in CSCL to include *spatiotemporal anchored collaboration*, and TrACE exemplifies a set of interaction techniques for enacting it. Results of our pilot study suggest a variety of factors that may influence students' usage patterns in the system and highlight the need for additional pedagogical and technical supports to foster interaction and collaboration over course media delivered asynchronously online.

ACKNOWLEDGMENTS

We sincerely thank the instructors of the two courses and students that piloted TrACE during the academic term. We also thank the anonymous reviewers for their generous feedback on earlier versions of this paper.

This work is funded in part by the National Science Foundation under grants IIS-1318345 and DUE-1245059. Any opinions, findings, and conclusions or recommendations expressed in this material are those of the authors and do not necessarily reflect the views of the NSF.

REFERENCES

1. Abowd, G., da Graça Pimentel, M., Kerimbaev, B., Ishiguro, Y., and Guzdial, M. Anchoring discussions in lecture: an approach to collaboratively extending classroom digital media. In *Proc. CSCL'99* (1999).

2. Allen, I. E., and Seaman, J. *Class Diferences: Online Education in the United States, 2010.* Babson Survey Research Group, 2010.

3. Ausubel, D. In defense of advance organizers: A reply to the critics. *Review of Educational Research* (1978), 251–257.

4. Barab, S., and Squire, K. Design-based research: Putting a stake in the ground. *The Journal of the learning sciences 13*, 1 (2004), 1–14.
5. Bell, P., and Linn, M. C. Scientific arguments as learning artifacts: Designing for learning from the web with KIE. *Intl. J. of Science Education 22*, 8 (2000), 797–817.
6. Bennett, S., and Maton, K. Beyond the 'digital natives' debate: Towards a more nuanced understanding of students' technology experiences. *J. of Computer Assisted Learning 26*, 5 (2010), 321–331.
7. Bergmann, J., and Sams, A. *Flip Your Classroom: Reach Every Student in Every Class Every Day*. Intl. Society for Technology in Education, 2012.
8. Bishop, J. L., and Verleger, M. The flipped classroom: A survey of the research. In *ASEE National Conference Proceedings, Atlanta, GA* (2013).
9. Borge, M., and Goggins, S. Towards the facilitation of an online community of learners: Assessing the quality of interactions in Yammer. In *Proc of ICLS'14* (2014), 753–761.
10. Bransford, J. D., Brown, A. L., and Cocking, R. R. *How People Learn: Brain, Mind, Experience, and School*, expanded ed. National Academy Press, Washington, D.C., 2000.
11. Buchanan, T. The efficacy of a world-wide web mediated formative assessment. *J. of Computer Assisted Learning 16*, 3 (2000), 193–200.
12. Carroll, E. A., Lottridge, D., Latulipe, C., Singh, V., and Word, M. Bodies in critique: a technological intervention in the dance production process. In *Proc. CSCW'12* (2012), 705–714.
13. Chen, S. A cognitive model for non–linear learning in hypermedia programmes. *British journal of educational technology 33*, 4 (2002), 449–460.
14. Collins, A., Brown, J. S., and Newman, S. E. Cognitive apprenticeship: Teaching the crafts of reading, writing, and mathematics. In *Knowing, learning, and instruction: Essays in honor of Robert Glaser*. LEA, Hillsdale, N.J., 1989, 453–494.
15. Collins, A., Joseph, D., and Bielaczyc, K. Design research: Theoretical and methodological issues. *Journal of the Learning Sciences 13*, 1 (2004), 15–42.
16. Deslauriers, L., Schelew, E., and Wieman, C. Improved learning in a large-enrollment physics class. *Science 332*, 6031 (2011), 862–864.
17. d'Oliveira, C., Carson, S., James, K., and Lazarus, J. MIT opencourseware: Unlocking knowledge, empowering minds. *Science 329*, 5991 (2010), 525–526.
18. Fischer, G. Beyond hype and underestimation: identifying research challenges for the future of moocs. *Distance Education 35*, 2 (2014), 149–158.
19. Forte, A., and Bruckman, A. Writing, citing, and participatory media: Wikis as learning environments in the high school classroom. *Intl. J. of Learning and Media 1*, 4 (2009), 23–44.
20. Guzdial, M., Hmelo, C., Hübscher, R., Nagel, K., Newstetter, W., Puntambekar, S., Shabo, A., Turns, J., and Kolodner, J. L. Integrating and guiding collaboration: lessons learned in computer-supported collaborative learning research at Georgia Tech. In *Proc. CSCL'97* (1997), 95–105.
21. Guzdial, M., Ludovice, P., Realff, M., Morley, T., and Carroll, K. When collaboration doesn't work. In *Proc. ICLS'02* (2002), 125–130.
22. Guzdial, M., Rick, J., and Kehoe, C. Beyond adoption to invention: Teacher-created collaborative activities in higher education. *J. of the Learning Sciences 10*, 3 (2001), 265–279.
23. Guzdial, M., and Turns, J. Effective discussion through a computer-mediated anchored forum. *J. of the Learning Sciences 9*, 4 (2000), 437–469.
24. Harper, S., Michailidou, E., and Stevens, R. Toward a definition of visual complexity as an implicit measure of cognitive load. *ACM Trans. on Applied Perception (TAP) 6*, 2 (2009), 10.
25. Hay, K. E., Guzdial, M., Jackson, S., Boyle, R. A., and Soloway, E. Students as multimedia composers. *Computers and Education 23*, 4 (1994), 301–317.
26. Hudson, J. M., and Bruckman, A. Disinhibition in a cscl environment. In *Proc. CSCL'02*, International Society of the Learning Sciences (2002), 629–630.
27. Hutchinson, H., Mackay, W., Westerlund, B., Bederson, B. B., Druin, A., Plaisant, C., Beaudouin-Lafon, M., Conversy, S., Evans, H., Hansen, H., et al. Technology probes: inspiring design for and with families. In *Proc. CHI'03*, ACM (2003), 17–24.
28. Kim, J. Toolscape: enhancing the learning experience of how to videos. In *CHI EA '13* (2013), 2707–2712.
29. Lage, M. J., Platt, G. J., and Treglia, M. Inverting the classroom: A gateway to creating an inclusive learning environment. *J. of Economic Education 31*, 1 (2000), 30–43.
30. Onchwari, G., Oigara, J., and Keengwe, J., Eds. *Promoting Active Learning Through the Flipped Classroom Model*. IGI Global, 2014.
31. Pappano, L. Year of the MOOC. *The New York Times* (Nov 2 2012), ED26.
32. Prensky, M. *Teaching digital natives: Partnering for real learning*. Corwin Press, 2010.
33. Roschelle, J. Learning by collaborating: Convergent conceptual change. In *CSCL: Theory and Practice of an Emerging Paradigm*, T. Koschman, Ed. Lawrence Erlbaum Associates, Mahwah, NJ, 1996, 209–248.

34. Scardamalia, M. Collective cognitive responsibility for the advancement of knowledge. In *Liberal education in a knowledge society*, B. Smith, Ed. Open Court, Chicago, IL, 2002, 67–98.

35. Scardamalia, M., and Bereiter, C. Computer support for knowledge-building communities. *J. of the Learning Sciences 3*, 3 (1994), 265–283.

36. Schank, R. C., Fano, A., Bell, B., and Jona, M. The design of goal-based scenarios. *J. of the Learning Sciences 3*, 4 (1994), 305–346.

37. Schroeder, L., Xue, F., and McGivney, R. Flipping three different mathematics courses: Common conclusions and plans for the future. *MathAMATYC Educator 4*, 2 (2013), 63–67.

38. Senn, G. Comparison of face-to-face and hybrid delivery of a course that requires technology skills development. *J. of Information Technology Education: Research 7* (2008), 267–283.

39. Severance, C. Teaching the world: Daphne koller and coursera. *Computer 45*, 8 (august 2012), 8–9.

40. Singh, V., Latulipe, C., Carroll, E., and Lottridge, D. The choreographer's notebook: a video annotation system for dancers and choreographers. In *Proc. of C&C'11* (2011), 197–206.

41. Stahl, G. A model of collaborative knowledge-building. In *Proc. ICLS'00* (2000), 70–77.

42. Stahl, G., Koschmann, T., and Suthers, D. Computer-supported collaborative learning. In *Cambridge Handbook of the Learning Sciences*. Cambridge University Press, New York, 2006, 409–426.

43. Thompson, C. How khan academy is changing the rules of education. *Wired Magazine* (2011), 1–5.

44. van der Pol, J. *Facilitating Online Learning Conversations*. PhD thesis, Universiteit Utrecht, 2007.

45. Wong, W. Y., and Howie, P. Teaching developmental psychology using an interactive online video platform. In *Proc ASCILITE'10* (2010).

46. Zaption. `http://www.zaption.com/` Last accessed October 9, 2014.

47. Zyto, S., Karger, D., Ackerman, M., and Mahajan, S. Successful classroom deployment of a social document annotation system. In *Proc. CHI'12* (2012), 1883–1892.

Learnersourcing Subgoal Labels for How-to Videos

Sarah Weir[1] Juho Kim[1] Krzysztof Z. Gajos[2] Robert C. Miller[1]

[1]MIT CSAIL
Cambridge, MA USA
{sweir, juhokim, rcm}@csail.mit.edu

[2]Harvard SEAS
Cambridge, MA USA
kgajos@eecs.harvard.edu

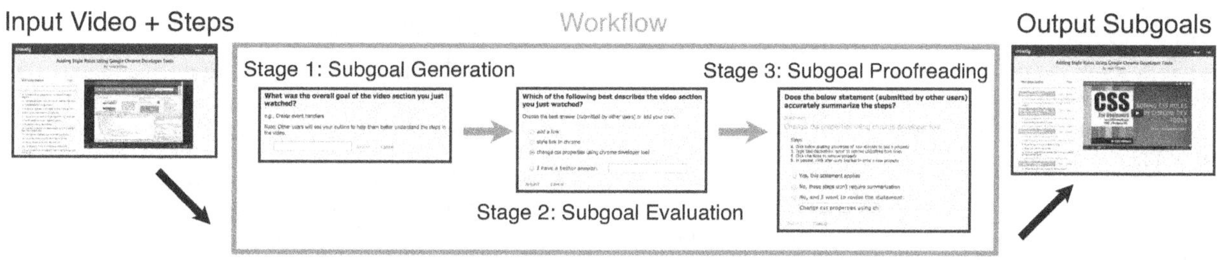

Figure 1. We present a three-stage workflow to generate labels for groups of steps (subgoal labels) for how-to videos. This workflow is designed to engage people actively trying to learn from the video to contribute the information.

ABSTRACT
Websites like YouTube host millions of how-to videos, but their interfaces are not optimized for learning. Previous research suggests that people learn more from how-to videos when the videos are accompanied by outlines showing individual steps and labels for groups of steps (subgoals). We envision an alternative video player where the steps and subgoals are displayed alongside the video. To generate this information for existing videos, we introduce *learnersourcing*, an approach in which intrinsically motivated learners contribute to a human computation workflow as they naturally go about learning from the videos. To demonstrate this method, we deployed a live website with a workflow for constructing subgoal labels implemented on a set of introductory web programming videos. For the four videos with the highest participation, we found that a majority of learner-generated subgoals were comparable in quality to expert-generated ones. Learners commented that the system helped them grasp the material, suggesting that our workflow did not detract from the learning experience.

Author Keywords
Video learning; subgoal labels; learnersourcing.

ACM Classification Keywords
H.5.1. Information Interfaces and Presentation (e.g., HCI): Multimedia Information Systems: Video.

ACM 978-1-4503-2922-4/15/03...$15.00.
http://dx.doi.org/10.1145/2675133.2675219

INTRODUCTION
More and more people are turning to the web to learn. While massive open online course (MOOC) platforms such as edX and Coursera have become popular for academic material, platforms like YouTube and Vimeo host millions of how-to videos that teach short procedural tasks ranging from putting on makeup to using Photoshop, to creating a two column layout using CSS.

Our long-term goal is to leverage research findings on how people learn and to find scalable approaches for improving the learning experience for viewers of existing how-to videos. In this work we specifically focus on the benefits conferred by augmenting instructional videos with textual outlines. Previous research [20] has shown that people learn better from videos if they are simultaneously presented with the *subgoals*, which capture meaningful conceptual pieces of the procedure covered in the video (Figure 2). Presenting subgoals improves learning by reducing learners' cognitive load by abstracting away low-level details, and by encouraging learners to self-explain why a set of steps have been grouped [4]. Ideally, to help people learn better from how-to videos, a video interface could display a list of subgoals as learners watch a video. Traditionally, labeling subgoals requires domain experts and knowledge extraction experts [5], but this process will not scale to the millions of existing how-to videos on the web. While makers of how-to videos may eventually be convinced to add subgoal labels for each video they create, we seek a scalable mechanism for improving the learning experience for viewers of existing videos.

In this paper, we turn to learners for help in generating subgoal labels at scale for how-to videos on the web (Figure 1). We introduce *learnersourcing*, a method for human computation for gathering information from people trying to actively learn from a video. Learnersourcing is a conceptual model in which learners collectively generate useful content for future learners while engaging in a meaningful learning experience themselves. Unlike a paid crowd, learners are incentivized to watch these videos based on their own desire to learn, and not because they will receive payment. Learners may provide higher quality answers than a paid crowd because they are motivated by their interest in the instructional material. Like other crowd-powered systems, our system relies on a large number of micro-contributions and a computational mechanism to aggregate them. Unlike paid crowd workers, however, learners are unlikely to engage with tasks that appear tedious or irrelevant to their learning. A challenge in learnersourcing task design, therefore, is motivating learners to engage in the tasks while providing positive impact on learning experience or outcome. In other words, in learnersourcing we attempt to design meaningful human computation tasks while leveraging learners' natural activities.

While the idea of learnersourcing could have many applications, this paper presents a specific application for human computation in the educational video domain: subgoal labeling for how-to videos. Our solution is a three-stage workflow with microtasks for learners to complete as they watch the videos. We hypothesize that learners will be able to generate expert-quality subgoals with our workflow.

In the learnersourcing workflow we developed for constructing subgoal labels, as learners watch a video, the video stops periodically and the system asks one of three questions. The choice of question depends on how much information has already been gathered for that section in the video, and the questions are designed to engage learners to reflect on the content. In the first stage of the workflow, learners are asked to summarize the preceding short video section, which generates candidate subgoal labels for the section. After enough candidate subgoals have been generated for a video section, learners are routed to the second stage where they answer an automatically generated multiple choice question. The question asks them to pick the best subgoal from candidates contributed by previous learners. Learners' answers are then used by the system to evaluate the learner-generated subgoals. In the third stage, learners make improvements to the most popular subgoal by considering its scope and language. Once learners stop making changes to a subgoal, we can consider it final and future learners can be presented a final list of subgoals when watching the video.

To test our learnersourcing approach, we built Crowdy, a prototype system powered by the learnersourcing workflow. It features how-to videos on introductory web programming that demonstrate how to accomplish procedural tasks in HTML, CSS, and jQuery. We conducted a two-part deployment of Crowdy. The first was an in-class deployment at a university course on user interface design. We used results from that deployment to refine the interface and the workflow. We then conducted an in-the-wild study over a period of 25 days, where we made Crowdy publicly available. We found that in both deployments, learners were able to generate subgoals close to expert quality. In the live deployment, 14 out of 17 subgoals evaluated had at least one out of four evaluators rate the learner subgoal as matching or better than the subgoal generated by experts. We interviewed three learners who emailed us to ask questions or express interest while using the site. We recognize that this sample is biased toward learners who used the site and is not representative of the entire population, especially those who dropped out. These learners felt the learnersourcing workflow helped them pay attention to the video and increased their understanding of the material. Based on these findings, we believe that learnersourcing is a viable solution for generating subgoal labels for how-to videos.

The contributions of this paper are as follows:

- An introduction of learnersourcing, a context-specific form of crowdsourcing in which learners engage in human computation tasks while trying to learn a new skill.
- An implementation of a three-stage learnersourcing workflow to generate high-quality subgoal labels from how-to videos in a scalable way.
- Results from an in-the-wild study demonstrating the workflow's effectiveness in generating high-quality subgoals. 14 out of 17 subgoals had at least one out of four evaluators rate the learner-generated subgoal label as equal to or better than the expert-generated label.
- Results from interviews with learners who participated in the in-the-wild study suggesting that the system helped them pay attention to videos and grasp the material better.

RELATED WORK

Previous work suggests that presenting learners with subgoals for procedural tasks improves learning. Eiriksdottir and Catrambone [8] explored the effects of presenting learners with different forms of instructional material. They discovered that including specific instructions helped learners complete the initial task but those learners did not retain the information. Conversely, learners presented with more holistic instructions had greater learning and transfer. Margulieux et al. showed that instructions including both specific steps and subgoals [20] resulted in improved learning and transfer, compared to those with the specific steps alone. Buykx and Petrie [3] included subgoals in recipe instructions and showed that displaying steps and subgoal information improves understanding in domains other than software applications. The TAPS method [5] proposes a systematic workflow for extracting subgoals for existing lecture videos with a domain expert and a knowledge extraction expert working together. This work suggests that knowledge extraction experts, who are novices in their domains, are a viable source for providing information to help other domain novices.

A rich body of previous research has looked into tutorial interfaces for learning software applications. Some of these interfaces focus on ways to visualize and discover the most suitable tutorials [17, 23], while other systems enhance tutorial content by building on the metadata available in software applications [6, 9, 16, 24]. The success of these systems in helping people learn to use software suggests that using existing information (such as the transcript to a tutorial video)

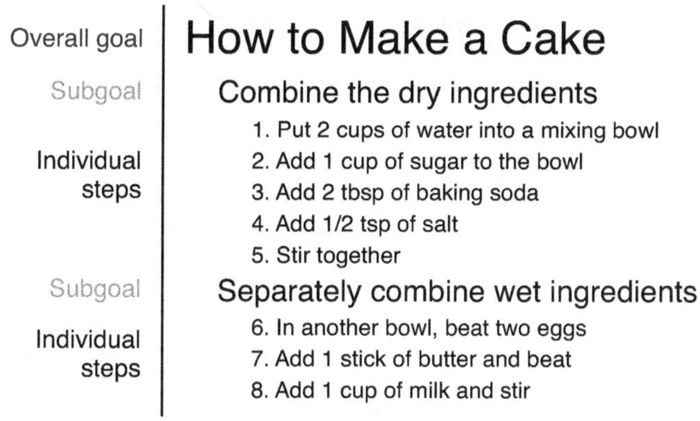

Figure 2. An example of the breakdown between goal, subgoals, and individual steps for a procedural task. Creating subgoals from individual steps requires self-explanation and summarization.

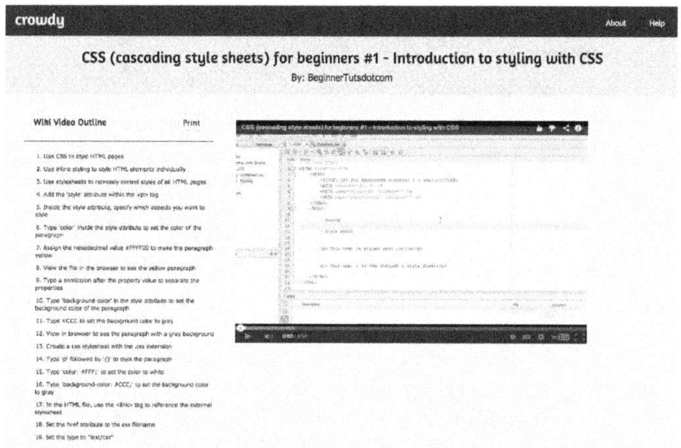

Figure 3. For each video on Crowdy, we show the video player as well as a side panel with the individual steps. After learners answer a question, the subgoal they added or picked appears in the outline. Learners can click on steps or subgoals to jump to various parts in the video. The question block (Figure 4, 5, 6) temporarily replaces the video player when it appears.

is an effective way to improve learning. However, many of these systems rely on the underlying structure of software applications to generate content [9, 17, 23, 24] and cannot easily be generalized to domains other than software.

Systems have also been built to leverage the power of the crowd to generate information on educational videos. For example, VidWiki [7] is a platform to crowdsource incremental improvements to educational videos with annotations. Additionally, ToolScape [16] used a Mechanical Turk crowd to generate step-by-step annotations for how-to videos. The fact that these systems were successful suggests that crowdsourcing is an effective way to create additional content for educational videos.

A number of prior crowd-powered systems [1, 16, 19, 22] use multi-stage workflows to generate expert-quality material in a variety of domains. Our three-stage workflow is inspired by previous research, but is designed explicitly for a crowd of learners who are naturally watching the video with their own desire to learn. Designing human computation tasks for voluntary learners presents a unique set of challenges, which we address with our workflow.

LEARNERSOURCING SUBGOAL LABELS

In order to generate subgoal labels for how-to videos, we use a learnersourcing approach. Our design goals are:

- To create a method for generating subgoal labels that does not require experts,
- To enable learners to generate expert-quality subgoals collaboratively,
- To design human computation tasks that are engaging and do not detract from the learning experience.

Due to the variety in video domain and presentation style on the web, an automatic approach to generating subgoals does not seem feasible. For example, some videos include text, some are silent and only show a person completing certain actions, and others rely on video and sound for demonstration. Automatically adapting to the various presentation and instructional styles is difficult, and we are looking for a solution that can generalize to any how-to video on the web. Additionally, subgoals are often at a higher conceptual level than what the video explicitly mentions, so automatically generating subgoals would require interpreting and understanding the material.

Learnersourcing is a context-specific form of crowdsourcing, in which people who are already trying to learn from a video are asked to complete microtasks while watching the video. Because learners are self-selected based on their interest in the video material, this approach is scalable and generalizable to any video domain. As long as there are learners interested in a video, there is the possibility for input into the system. Learnersourcing complements 'expertsourcing' (domain experts generating subgoal labels) and 'authorsourcing' (video authors generating subgoal labels) because it is designed to add subgoals to videos that already exist. Although not covered in this paper, well-designed learnersourcing prompts may offer a pedagogical benefit to learners.

We built a website, Crowdy, to implement our workflow for learnersourcing subgoal labels. It is an alternative site to watch videos that were originally hosted on YouTube. The front page features all videos for the current deployment. When a user selects a video, Crowdy shows a separate page with an embedded video player and interactive outline (Figure 3). Our learnersourcing workflow asks specific questions as learners watch the videos, and in turn generates high-quality subgoals for them. Crowdy was created using standard web technologies (HTML, CSS, jQuery), with a Django backend and the YouTube API (`https://developers.google.com/youtube/`) for the video player.

WORKFLOW DESIGN

In order to enable learners to generate subgoal labels from how-to videos, we designed a three-stage workflow that engages learners to create and refine each others' subgoal labels.

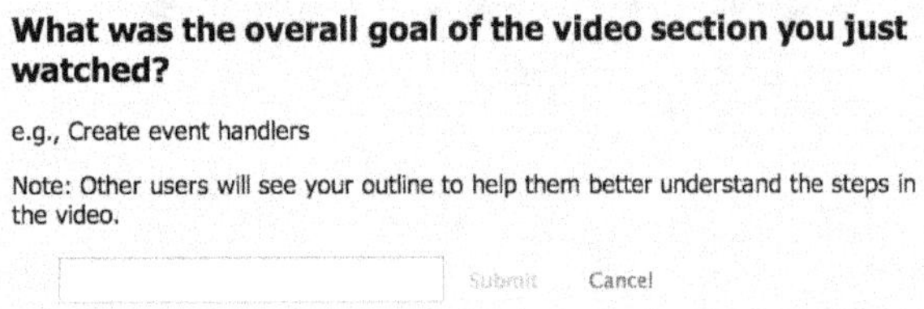

Figure 4. In Stage 1, learners are asked to generate a new subgoal label after watching a video segment.

Initially, learners are presented with a video player and an interactive outline panel seeded with the low level steps that the video goes through (Figure 3). By aggregating the micro-contributions from learners, Crowdy adds subgoal labels to this outline. The steps are presented as a vertical timeline, such that clicking on a step moves the playhead to that time in the video. This research assumes that the low-level steps have already been generated for a video, and focuses only on generating subgoal labels. Although we manually added the steps for this research, individual steps could be obtained by crowdsourcing [16] or automatically in part, possibly by processing a transcript or notes from the video creators.

As learners watch a video, they are stopped periodically and asked a question about the preceding video section. Although we experimented with having a Wiki-like interface where learners were asked to contribute subgoal labels but were not forced to, we found that this direct question approach resulted in more frequent and higher quality participation.

We chose a multi-stage workflow because we wanted to make each task small enough so that learners could complete it without getting too distracted from the video. To ensure a high quality of final subgoal labels, we use three mechanisms used in prior crowd-powered systems: we solicit multiple candidate solutions, we use voting to identify the best candidates, and we allow for iterative refinement.

We automatically route each subgoal to the necessary stage, so a learner might experience different stage prompts even while watching a single video. By removing the need for human intervention and judgment to move to the next stage, we aim to standardize and improve the efficiency of the workflow.

STAGE 1: Generation

The goal of the first stage (Figure 4) is to have learners generate candidate subgoal labels from scratch. After a certain interval, learners are asked to summarize what they have just watched. While the learner is answering the question, the individual steps that were covered in the most recent video segment are bolded in the outline panel. Learners are given the option to cancel out of the question and are not forced to submit an answer.

In order to minimize spam answers, we made sure learners could easily cancel out of the prompt. We also designed the question such that it does not require prior familiarity with the concept of subgoals, but such that the answer to the question can serve as a subgoal label. From our preliminary user tests,

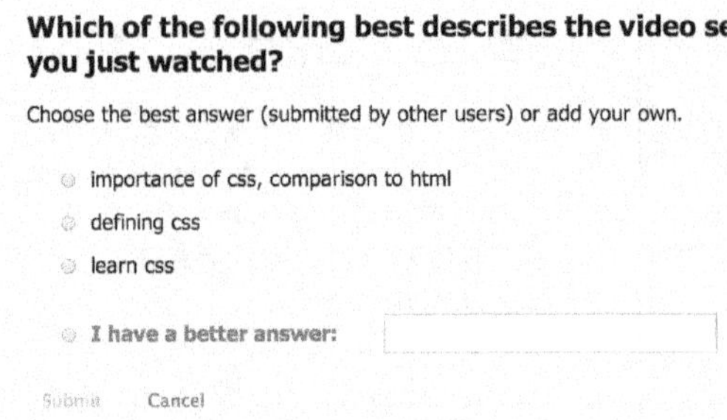

Figure 5. In Stage 2, learners vote on a subgoal they find most accurate.

we found that learners preferred jargon-free questions (i.e., using 'goal' instead of 'subgoal').

When there have been three candidate subgoal labels generated from the first stage, the next set of learners are asked the stage 2 question.

STAGE 2: Evaluation

The subgoal labels that learners generate in stage 1 are not always of the highest quality. Learners may interpret the question in different ways or have different levels of familiarity with the video's topic, which cause their subgoal labels to be different from each other. In stage 2 (Figure 5), learners are presented with the previously generated subgoals and asked to choose which they feel best captures the preceding section.

The goal of the second stage is to choose the most relevant answer for the video section, as well as weed out potential spam answers. The input to the question in this stage are the subgoal labels previously generated by learners. The learners who are presented with the stage 2 question have the option to choose one of the subgoals, add their own, or abstain. We do not give learners any indication as to which subgoal is most popular during this stage. The subgoal that the learner chooses gets an upvote, and the ones that were not chosen receive a downvote. We use the upvote and downvote measures to determine when to move on to the third stage. This helps interpret user actions by weeding out answers that are consistently not chosen and considering newly generated subgoals. When the number of upvotes or the difference in upvotes between the top two subgoals reaches a certain threshold, we accept that subgoal as the winner of stage 2 and route the question to stage 3 for future learners.

STAGE 3: Proofreading

Learners in stage 2 evaluate the previously generated subgoal labels, but the most popular subgoal label from stage 2 is not necessarily a high-quality label by our standards. We define high-quality subgoal labels as having the correct scope (the subgoal label accurately reflects the underlying steps) and being concrete and descriptive. For example, for a section in a CSS video about changing the color of a div, a label like "CSS video" would be too broad, whereas a label such as "Use CSS to change div color" would be more appropriate.

The goal of this stage (Figure 6) is for learners to evaluate the most popular subgoal label from stage 2 for quality and eventually agree on a final label for that subgoal. The input to this

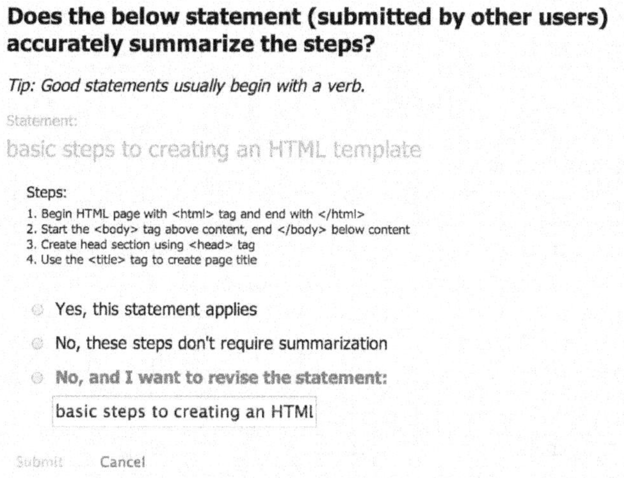

Figure 6. In Stage 3, learners proofread the most popular subgoal for language and scope.

stage is the most popular subgoal from stage 2, determined by the relative numbers of upvotes and downvotes. Learners are presented with this subgoal label and the steps that it covers, and have the option to refine the label or keep it as is. Ideally, when N learners accept the label without making a change we can assume that the label is final and future learners would be shown this subgoal without being asked a question.

We expect alterations at this stage to be minimal because the necessary changes are often subtle and require a certain understanding of the material. By specifically asking learners to iterate on the subgoal label, we envisioned that some would accept the challenge and improve the quality of the subgoal.

Learner Prompts and the Learning Experience

A major concern in designing Crowdy was to design the workflow such that participation in the process of subgoal label creation would not detract from the learning experience. Our core design decision to use short prompts interspersed throughout the video as the way to collect input from learners was informed by prior research in education and learning technologies, which we review here.

The subgoal learning model suggests that the process of grouping a set of solution steps involves self-explanation [5]. Previous research on self-explanation [2, 10, 26] suggests that when learners are asked to explain examples to themselves, they learn the material better and have greater awareness of their own understanding. Self-explanation encourages learners to engage in deep cognitive processing, which results in more robust learning. Our learner prompts also aim to encourage active learning [25], as opposed to passively watching a video, which is shown to engage learners in the learning process and improve retention of the material.

Research on designing learner prompts shows that learners self-correct misconceptions by answering the prompts [27]. Existing online learning platforms such as Coursera add frequent micro-quizzes inside videos to help people learn better from video lectures, and research on retrieval practice might provide support for in-video quizzes [12, 13]. In multimedia learning, different learner prompts are shown to provide different pedagogical benefits [21]. The learning gain was higher when learners picked the best explanation than when they were asked to type in a possible explanation [11], possibly because the higher cognitive load in generating an explanation might break the flow in multimedia learning.

These findings suggest that our tasks may actually offer a pedagogical benefit to learners. In future research we intend to evaluate the impact that participation in Crowdy has on learning and — if the impact is positive — to compare it to the benefit conferred by being presented with subgoal labels while watching a how-to video.

PILOT STUDY

To iterate on the workflow design and get a general sense of the quality of learner-generated subgoals, we conducted a pilot study in a user interface design class at a university. The class covers the theory behind designing usable interfaces, and students are responsible for creating and testing a web interface. Therefore, we felt it was a suitable deployment for a series of introductory web programming how-to videos. While students are expected to complete programming assignments and a project involving web interfaces, these topics are not explicitly covered during class time.

There were approximately 280 students in the class, and most were computer science majors. By the end of the class we had brought together 21 videos on HTML, CSS, jQuery/JavaScript, and Meteor (`https://www.meteor.com/`), a JavaScript platform for building web apps) into one place. These videos had an average duration of 6:18 minutes (stdev=2:49). The videos were all existing videos on YouTube. For each video we generated the individual steps and learners went through the three-stage workflow to generate subgoals. There was an average of 76 students participating in each video (stdev=39), 20 subgoals generated per video (stdev=16), and 193 actions (stdev=395), which are logged when learners answer a question or manipulate subgoals in any way. We deployed the videos periodically based on the topics for the upcoming problem sets/projects. The video links were embedded into assignment handouts as a resource. Although students had to be responsible for the material in the videos in order to succeed in the class, watching the videos was optional. We used a group of college students to iterate on our design, but in the future we will consider how using different groups of learners may affect the success of our workflow, especially if there is no constraint on who can participate.

We did not conduct a rigorous evaluation of the results from this deployment, and instead used the periodic deployments as an opportunity to iterate on our design. We found that participation was consistent throughout the semester, although participation varied greatly per video, likely based on video quality and difficulty of the material. In the beginning of the deployment we received a lot of spam answers, which we attribute to unclear instructions on the website that did not emphasize the option to cancel out of a question. Additionally, it was not obvious that a user's answers would be seen by others. The instructions in our final workflow state that the answers will be seen by other learners, and we added a 'Cancel' button to reduce spam.

Design Dimensions Refined through Pilot Study

Through our pilot deployment, we refined important design dimensions for the workflow such as the correct interval to ask questions, whether it is important to show steps, and whether it is important that learners are asked every question. During the deployment, we analyzed the submitted subgoals and talked with users to determine the pain points of our system. For example, we added an interactive tutorial to Crowdy because first-time users commented that they were caught off-guard and confused by the questions. We then iterated on our design and continued our analysis to arrive at our final system.

Question Interval

For the pilot iteration we asked questions at predetermined, fixed intervals because we wanted to focus on the overall design of the questions. We started using a 30-second interval based on our analysis of short (<5 minutes) videos. We arrived at this interval by manually annotating the subgoals for the short videos we used and averaging the time at which the subgoals occurred. However, the web programming videos we used in our pilot deployment were often longer than five minutes. We ended up with a one minute interval for our live deployment, based on users' feedback that frequent stops can be annoying to them. In the future, we would like to make the question intervals adapt to the domain, context, or video length.

Steps vs. No Steps

We also tested whether the workflow would be successful if the individual steps were not shown, in case step generation becomes a future bottleneck. We found no significant difference between subgoals generated when steps were present and not present. However, users liked the extra information provided and the ability to navigate to different points in the video by clicking on the steps. The presence of steps allowed users who may have lost attention during the video to generate a high-quality subgoal by examining the steps that were covered instead of submitting spam. Therefore we decided to show the steps for the live deployment.

Random vs. Not Random

We also tested whether learners would generate high quality subgoals if they were not asked a question at every interval boundary. Half of the users were asked a question randomly at each interval, and we found that the random interval led to subgoals that varied in scope. One learner who had the random condition and was only asked two questions, both at the very end of the video. Both of the subgoals she generated were summaries of the entire video, instead of being related to the preceding short section. Asking questions at regular intervals tended to lead to greater regularity in subgoals.

LIVE DEPLOYMENT

After improving the workflow based on the pilot study, we publicly launched a website, Crowdy, a wrapper interface to embed videos and implement our three-stage workflow. The goal of live deployment was to test our claim that learners can collaboratively generate subgoals of similar caliber to those generated by domain experts.

Study Structure

Our study targeted anyone interested in learning introductory web programming. Crowdy was presented as a way to learn web programming through collaborative video watching. In order for the site to stand alone, we included 15 videos (average duration=6:15, stdev=2:08) covering the basics of HTML, CSS, and JavaScript/jQuery. We refined the original selection of videos from the pilot study to remove less popular ones and added some to increase coverage. A summary of the videos included is presented in Table 1. We manually annotated each of the videos to generate a list of individual steps to be shown alongside the video. All of the videos started with zero subgoals, and all contributions were from people visiting the site voluntarily.

Deployment Strategy and Participation

We used various strategies to promote the website. We emailed to lists at universities, posted on social media (Twitter, Facebook, Reddit, Hacker News), reached out to local hacker schools, and bought keywords on Google Ads. Furthermore, we added our link to YouTube comments on the original videos we used to attract learners watching the videos on YouTube to visit Crowdy. In our analysis, we included data from May 5 to May 29, 2014 (25 days).

During the 25-day deployment, 1,268 users visited 2,838 pages, with an average session duration of 1.3 minutes. The top 4 traffic sources were direct access (41.31%, including mailing list clicks and typing in the URL), Twitter (23.81%), Google organic search (12.39%, which are clicks on search results, not advertisements), and Facebook (8.84%). All traffic data was collected with Google Analytics.

Evaluation Method

We chose the four most popular videos on Crowdy (boldface in Table 1) HTML Intro, Intro to CSS, Making divs side by side, and Intro to selectors) to evaluate the quality of learnersourced subgoal labels. These videos resulted in 17 final subgoal labels.

To judge the quality of the learner-generated subgoals, we compared them to expert-quality subgoals. We recruited two faculty and staff members in computer science at a university, who have extensive experience in web programming, to be our domain experts. After explaining what subgoals are and providing examples, the domain experts watched the four videos that we are evaluating and generated subgoals using our system. Because we only allowed learners to generate subgoals at predetermined intervals, we asked the domain experts to generate labels using the same intervals for direct comparison. In the future, we plan to evaluate subgoals at the entire video level without the set interval. Table 2 compares all the subgoal labels from both the experts and learners. For learner-generated subgoals, we took the subgoals that were in stage 3 or most popular in stage 2 for the four videos we

Video Title	Domain	YouTube Views	Length
Learn HTML- Basic Structure and How to Link Pages	HTML	8,745	4:48
Div and Span	HTML	12,934	6:09
HTML Website Tables & Layouts Tutorial	HTML	210,777	4:19
How to create forms in HTML5	HTML	9,983	9:23
Introduction to styling with CSS	CSS	3,150	6:55
Adding Style Rules Using Google Chrome Developer Tools	CSS	205	4:47
CSS Absolute and Relative Positioning Tutorial	CSS	34,113	6:56
Making Divs Side by Side using CSS	CSS	17,644	4:24
Z-Index CSS Tutorial	CSS	8,158	7:33
Introduction to Selectors	jQuery/JavaScript	40,825	2:06
ID selector	jQuery/JavaScript	36,795	5:53
addClass	jQuery/JavaScript	13,871	4:46
Click Event Handler	jQuery/JavaScript	11,234	6:56
Working on the Drag and Drop Program	jQuery/JavaScript	41,615	9:28
Finishing the Drag and Drop Program	jQuery/JavaScript	38,145	9:16

Table 1. How-to videos used in our live deployment. We evaluated the quality of learnersourced subgoal labels for the four bolded videos because they were the most popular videos on Crowdy.

Subgoals + Steps	Your Evaluation	Subgoals + Steps
Create divs in HTML file	L ✔ R	**What HTML code is used to create side-by-side <div>**
1. Create a new html file	Please explain:	1. Create a new html file
2. In the body section of the html file, create a div with a id="wrap"		2. In the body section of the html file, create a div with a id="wrap"
3. Create another div inside the wrapper with class="left"		3. Create another div inside the wrapper with class="left"
4. Underneath the left div, create another div with class="right"		4. Underneath the left div, create another div with class="right"

Figure 7. An excerpt from the worksheet given to domain experts to evaluate learner-generated subgoals. The subgoals were randomly placed on the left and right so experts had no notion of which was which. Evaluators were asked to choose whether the subgoals matched, or which was better, and provide an explanation.

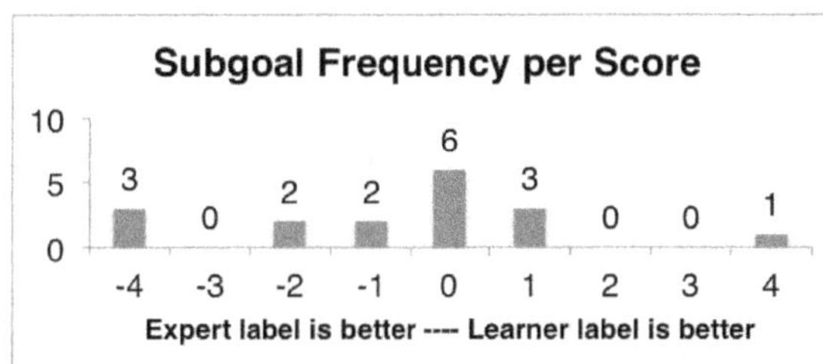

Figure 8. The distribution of subgoal label scores. The scoring scheme assigned -1 if an expert label is better, 1 if a learner label is better, and 0 if they match. While a majority of the subgoals were within the -2 and 2 range, three subgoals had unanimous votes for the expert label, and one subgoal had unanimous votes for the learner label.

selected. At the end of our deployment, five of the subgoals were in stage 3, but most had a clear majority.

To measure how the learner-generated subgoals compare to the expert-generated subgoals, we created a worksheet (Figure 7) to have another group of domain experts rate whether the subgoals matched or which one was better, and why. We randomized which side of the worksheet each of the subgoals was on, so evaluators did not know which were generated by learners and which were by experts. They were instructed to rate based on how well the subgoals covered the given steps, and whether they were concrete and descriptive. We recruited four domain experts who were graduate students in computer science with substantial web programming experience to rate 17 subgoals in the four videos.

We used a scoring scheme to better compare the subgoal labels. Each evaluator's rating is assigned either -1 (expert label is better), 0 (expert and learner label match), or 1 (learner label is better), which match the three options the evaluators were given for each subgoal. The score of -4 means all raters thought the expert label was better, while 4 means all raters thought the learner label was better.

Results

During the 25 day deployment, learners generated 109 subgoals in stage 1, added 14 new subgoals in stage 2, and edited 3 subgoals in stage 3. There were 109 upvotes in stage 2, and 13 upvotes in stage 3. Based on our logging, we found that 119 users (unique sessions) participated in a single video, 17 participated in two, and 14 participated in three or more.

Table 2 shows all 17 labels generated by experts and learners. For 14 out of 17 labels, the learner label was voted as matching or better than the expert label from at least one of the four raters. When we used majority voting to determine a winner in the comparative evaluation, eight labels were considered

Expert Subgoal	Evaluation	Learner Subgoal
Learn HTML- Basic Structure and How to Link Pages		
Create top-level structure of an HTML file	Expert better	The video stopped right as it was starting to talk about the head section
View HTML page in a Web browser	Expert better	Save and open a HTML document in the browser
Add a hyperlink	Learner better	Create link to another page
Create target page of the hyperlink	Match	Create another page to link to and from
View and navigate between both pages	Expert better	Create HTML pages and links
Introduction to styling with CSS		
Understand what CSS is	No majority	Introducing CSS, comparison to HTML
Two kinds of CSS styling	Match	Inline styling, and difference between this and stylesheets
Set text color of a paragraph	Match	Using the style and color attributes of inline styling
Set background color of a paragraph	Expert better	Problems with inline styling, solutions
Create an external stylesheet	Match	Create a stylesheet to set paragraph colors
Linking stylesheet to HTML file	Match	Linking CSS documents to HTML
Making Divs Side by Side using CSS		
Create divs in HTML file	Match	What HTML code is used to create side-by-side <div>
Create CSS for wrapper and left div	Match	Define div appearance with style blocks
Create CSS for right div	Expert better	Style the left and right div, color, height, width
Position divs side by side	Match	Put the two divs side by side and adjust spacing between them
Introduction to Selectors		
Create HTML and JavaScript files	Learner better	Selector introduction
See example of a jQuery ID selector	No majority	Using selectors and jQuery to create event handlers for page objects

Table 2. Expert labels compared to Learner subgoals for the four videos selected for evaluation. For each pair, we identify whether a majority of evaluators felt the subgoals matched or that one was better than the other. In some cases there was no clear majority between evaluators, which we have also noted.

matching between the learner label and the expert label, five were voted in favor of the expert label, two were voted in favor of the learner label, one was a tie between matching and in favor of the expert label, and one was a tie between favoring the expert and learner labels. Figure 8 shows the distribution of scores using the scoring scheme. Due to the highly subjective nature of the matching task, inter-rater reliability (Fleiss' $\kappa = 0.19$) showed a slight level of agreement [18].

We now discuss interesting cases in detail: labels for which the expert label was unanimously voted as better, labels for which the learner label got worse in stage 3, and labels that were voted to be matching.

Example of subgoals where expert's is better

Scoping of a subgoal label matters. Most evaluators judged the subgoals on whether they were accurate representations of the given steps. A common complaint was over subgoals that were too specific, or ones that did not seem to capture the steps at all. Evaluators tended to prefer subgoals that were informative instead of those that captured only generic statements. For example, evaluators preferred the expert subgoal "View and navigate between both pages" over the learner subgoal "Create HTML pages and links" for a subgoal in the introduction to HTML video because the learner subgoal was too broad.

Expert subgoal: View HTML page in a web browser

Learner subgoal: Save and open a HTML document in the browser

Steps:

1. Save file with .html extension
2. Open file in web browser to view

Evaluators felt the expert subgoal was more holistic, whereas the learner subgoal simply enumerated the steps that were covered. This subgoal was added in stage 1, and was chosen over other answers such as "Save and open HTML", "HTML format", "describe page tags", and "Implementation of an HTML page". Out of these choices, "Save and open a HTML document in the browser" is the most accurate and the most specific. However, as a subgoal it is not ideal because it exactly replicates the steps. This subgoal correctly summarizes the steps, as asked in stages 1 and 2, but could have been altered to be less specific in stage 3.

This suggests a lack of instruction on our part in stage 3 where learners are asked to make sure the subgoals cover the provided steps, but are not instructed to make subgoals neither too broad nor too specific. This sort of instruction could be added to stage 3, or we could implement multiple versions of stage 3, where we ask learners about different aspects of the subgoal.

Example where final subgoal got worse in stage 3

Expert subgoal: Create top-level structure of an HTML file

Learner subgoal (most popular subgoal after stage 2): Basic structure of HTML template

Learner subgoal (subgoal altered in stage 3): The video stopped right as it was starting to talk about the head section

In this example, a learner who saw a stage 3 question for this subgoal changed the subgoal to something of much lower quality. The final subgoal in this case does not summarize the video section. Although learners only rarely made a drastic replacement to a subgoal in stage 3, we need to consider mediation methods to prevent this from happening in the future. One possibility is to accumulate votes throughout the stages and only allow minor changes to subgoals that already have a lot of votes.

Example of subgoals that match
Expert subgoal: Set text color of a paragraph

Learner subgoal: Using the style and color attributes of inline styling

Steps:

1. Type 'color' inside the style attribute to set the color of the paragraph
2. Assign the hexadecimal value #FFFF00 to make the paragraph yellow
3. View the file in the browser to see the yellow paragraph
4. Type a semicolon after the property value to separate the properties

These subgoals are slightly different, yet the majority of evaluators felt they accurately covered the steps. This suggests that there can be variability in subgoals. Learners and experts (or people in general) can have different interpretations on what the 'correct' subgoal is. Further study will need to see if learner-generated subgoals, even if imperfect, still lead to improved learning gains as observed in literature.

Interviews with Users

To better understand learners' experiences, we conducted semi-structured interviews with three learners who have used Crowdy. Learners identified themselves to us via email after using our system to ask a question or express their interest in the site. They had various programming experiences, but all were web programming novices. We conducted 30-minute video interviews where we asked them about their experience on the site and tried to learn about their thought process while they answered the questions.

Learners in general felt that being asked questions helped them pay attention, and one specifically noted that answering the questions helped him remember the concepts. This suggests that the learnersourcing prompts may have had a positive effect on learning. Learners also liked being able to reference the video's steps as they watched. According to one learner, *"having the steps there and knowing that I was going to have to fill out goals made me pay attention to the video slightly differently."* In contrast, he felt that if he had watched the video with no steps or questions, he would have mindlessly followed along without learning anything. Another learner commented, *"When I first watched the first video I didn't really know what to expect, but in the second and third videos I was more... attentive to watching, to trying to understand what exactly am I watching instead of blindly watching."* Learners also recognized that the quality of the underlying video affected how well they learned the material, even if the prompts helped them engage with the material.

Learners had different critical approaches to the multiple choice questions in stage 2. One learner never contributed additional subgoals in stage 2 because he felt *"the ones that were there were pretty descriptive already."* Another added his own answers instead of choosing an existing subgoal about 50 percent of the time. He said, *"I would choose one if it was close to what I would have written... I think I was pretty critical, actually."* Learners liked seeing labels added by other learners. One learner said the choices *"...made me feel as though I was on the same wavelength still."*

The set interval for the learnersourcing prompts was hit or miss. For some videos it seemed okay, but for others it felt too short and others too long. Some learners felt the questions were asked at suboptimal times, especially for the shorter videos. One mentioned *"on a really short video, it was a little harder to see the goals,"* and another said, *"The introduction videos didn't cover very much content, so they could use a longer span, while something that covers more information would need to stop more frequently."*

Interview with Video Creator

We also interviewed a creator of one of the videos to get the author's perspective on the value of having subgoal labels added to the video. We contacted some of the authors through YouTube messaging, and one author volunteered to share his thoughts. We showed him the learner-generated subgoals from his video and asked questions over email. For his video, he felt that most of the subgoals were correct except for the last one, which was too broad in his opinion.

He was happy that the outline and the questions might make learners stay and watch the entire video, or be able to easily find the sections that they want to watch. He commented, *"Having pop up questions means the viewer has to be paying attention."* This means that our system can be beneficial to both video learners and video creators because it has the opportunity to enhance what the author has created with the help of learners watching the video.

DISCUSSION

We discuss the value of having each stage and ways to further improve the workflow, as well as the limitations of our current methodology presented in the paper.

Improving the Workflow for Better Subgoal Labels

Stage 1 is necessary for the system to obtain initial subgoals from scratch. The quality of these initial subgoals largely determines the overall quality of the final subgoal label because future steps mostly focus on refining existing steps, not generating completely new ones. In Figure 9, raw subgoals in stage 1 vary in quality. In our deployment, there were power users who submitted a set of high quality subgoals in stage 1, which usually ended up being the most popular all the

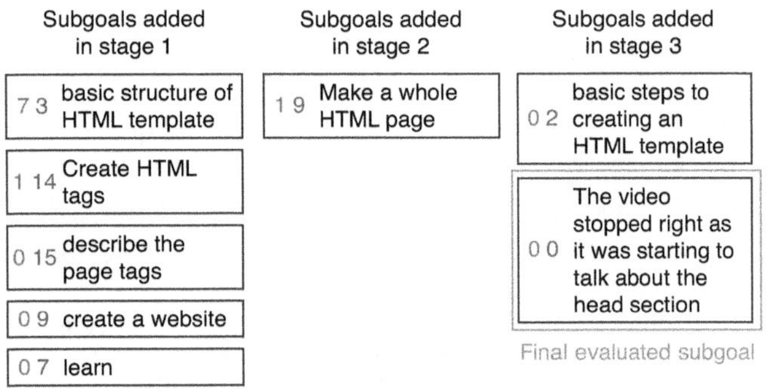

Figure 9. The subgoals that were added in each of the stages for the introduction to HTML video. The green numbers refer to upvotes, and the red numbers refer to downvotes. In stage 3, we expected small iterations, but found that one learner drastically changed the tone of the original subgoal.

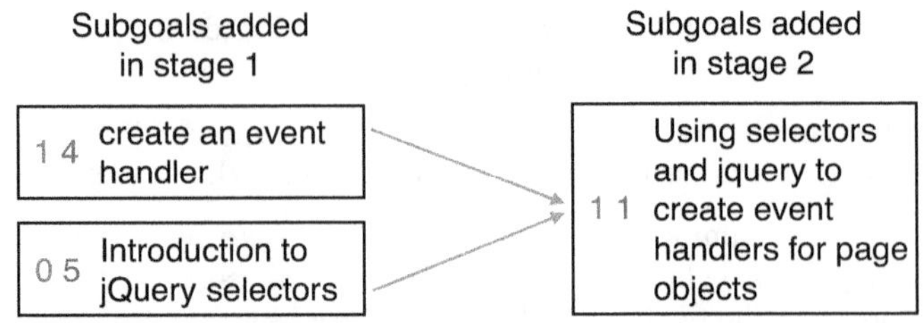

Figure 10. The subgoals that were added in each of the stages for one portion of the introduction to jQuery selectors video. The green numbers refer to upvotes, and the red numbers refer to downvotes. The subgoal added in stage 2 is a combination of the subgoals added in stage 1, which suggests that the learner who created this subgoal may have used the stage 1 subgoals as a baseline.

way through. How can we better guide learners to come up with quality subgoals? The current learner prompt provides an example, but more contextual, domain-specific examples and counterexamples that highlight the desired properties in a subgoal label might help.

Stage 2 is necessary to remove spam and to pick the best label from candidates, but results suggest that more guidance on which one to pick would improve the voting process. Our current design assumes that one label is going to be significantly better than others, but there is the possibility that they will be close. In such cases, the learner prompt can suggest more specific guidelines by encouraging them to consider scope and language and presenting contrasting good and bad examples. Another potential problem we noticed is that learners are reluctant to submit their own labels in this stage and resort to the best one from the candidates, even when they find the existing ones unsatisfactory. We plan to study the voting process in more depth, and design ways to lower the cost of label revision in stage 2.

Stage 3 is necessary to adjust the scope and language for finalization, but it still triggers learner prompts at a pre-defined subgoal label boundary, preventing learners from looking for video-wide consistency and scoping improvements. Also, in stage 3 we expect learners to only make incremental changes, but a learner who totally missed the point could change a previously 'good' subgoal. This is what happened in Figure 9. We are considering mediation methods to prevent later stage input from completely overwriting the earlier stage input and are looking to automatic methods for evaluating subgoals before they are considered final.

In many cases, we found an improvement in subgoals added as learners progressed through the stages. For example, in the "Introduction to Selectors" video, a stage 2 user combined the subgoals "create an event handler" and "Introduction to jQuery selectors" to create the final subgoal "Using selectors and jquery to create event handlers for page objects" (Figure 10). This suggests that even if incomplete, the subgoals in stage 1 are a good baseline for the final selected subgoal.

In general, we found that our learnersourcing workflow succeeded because it allowed many learners to contribute at a micro level, and learners were generally successful at identifying the 'best' subgoal in each set. For learnersourcing systems in general, we believe it is important to consider the amount of information given to learners at each task so they are equipped to contribute without being distracted from learning. The type of prompt is also important so learners are contributing as much information as possible and still benefiting from the original educational material.

In the future, we would like to make the question interval more context-specific. Some ideas for informed segmentation are to analyze the audio track for speech breaks, run topic modeling on the transcript to detect topic transitions, or leverage signals from previous learners' in-video interaction [15, 14]. Allowing learners to move subgoals to the correct spot and making sure questions aren't asked in the middle of words could be a preliminary step. Another approach would be to add additional steps to the learnersourcing workflow to allow learners to contribute the subgoal boundaries.

Only 26% of users participated in multiple videos, so we want to look for ways to encourage learners to stay on the site, perhaps by recommending videos or visualizing the learners' collective progress.

Limitations

More domains: Our live deployment only looked at web programming videos. The videos we chose were how-to videos that had hands-on, concrete, demonstrated tasks through which instructors walked the learners. Although there is nothing in the workflow that is specific to web programming, we don't have any quantitative data about learner-generated subgoals from other domains to show that the workflow is domain-independent. We plan to include videos from other how-to domains such as cooking or home improvement.

Learning benefits: While our task design was based on literature in learning sciences, our current evaluation did not directly measure learning improvements from using our workflow. A careful study is needed to explore the tradeoff between learning benefits and distraction or interruption caused by our learnersourcing prompts.

Longer term, larger deployment: Our 25-day deployment with over 1,000 users was helpful for us to get the initial idea of how our workflow works, but we believe a longer and larger deployment will be helpful. While many people visited the website out of curiosity, not many learners were seriously willing to learn web programming. As a result, not many videos received enough learner input to advance to stage 3. We plan to host more videos and continue the live deployment, which will provide us with more data for a deeper analysis on how learners in the wild use our workflow.

CONCLUSION AND FUTURE WORK

This paper introduces the concept of learnersourcing, a form of crowdsourcing that engages learners in human computation tasks as they interact with educational videos. We built Crowdy, a learnersourcing application for generating subgoal labels from a how-to video, through a multi-stage workflow where learners collaboratively contribute useful information about the video while answering reflective summary questions. Our deployment study shows that a majority of learner-generated subgoals were comparable in quality to expert-generated subgoals, and that learners reported they were paying more attention to the material and felt they understood the material better after going through the workflow.

We envision more advanced learnersourcing applications that enable more constructive and interactive video learning experience at scale. We plan to extend our current workflow to lecture videos on MOOCs that are much less structured than how-to videos. Collaborative summarization on lecture videos might be a useful exercise for learners that deeply engage them in the learning process. Further, we plan to design synchronous learnersourcing workflows for more direct interaction between learners, which can result in more complex and creative outcomes.

ACKNOWLEDGMENTS

The authors thank Philip Guo, Max Goldman, Lauren Margulieux, Mark Guzdial, and the UID Group at MIT CSAIL for suggestions and feedback. This work was supported in part by the MIT EECS SuperUROP Program and Cisco Systems, Inc., by Quanta Computer through the Qmulus project, by NSF award SOCS-1111124, and by a Sloan Research Fellowship. Juho Kim is partly supported by the Samsung Fellowship.

REFERENCES

1. Bernstein, M. S., Little, G., Miller, R. C., Hartmann, B., Ackerman, M. S., Karger, D. R., Crowell, D., and Panovich, K. Soylent: A word processor with a crowd inside. In *Proceedings of the 23rd Annual ACM Symposium on User Interface Software and Technology*, UIST '10, ACM (New York, NY, USA, 2010), 313–322.

2. Bielaczyc, K., Pirolli, P. L., and Brown, A. L. Training in self-explanation and self-regulation strategies: Investigating the effects of knowledge acquisition activities on problem solving. *Cognition and instruction 13*, 2 (1995), 221–252.

3. Buykx, L., and Petrie, H. Recipe sub-goals and graphs: An evaluation by cooks. In *Proceedings of the ACM Multimedia 2012 Workshop on Multimedia for Cooking and Eating Activities*, CEA '12, ACM (New York, NY, USA, 2012), 59–64.

4. Catrambone, R. The subgoal learning model: Creating better examples so that students can solve novel problems. *Journal of Experimental Psychology: General 127*, 4 (1998), 355.

5. Catrambone, R. Task analysis by problem solving (taps): uncovering expert knowledge to develop highquality instructional materials and training. In *2011 Learning and Technology Symposium* (2011).

6. Chi, P.-Y., Ahn, S., Ren, A., Dontcheva, M., Li, W., and Hartmann, B. Mixt: Automatic generation of step-by-step mixed media tutorials. In *Proceedings of the 25th Annual ACM Symposium on User Interface Software and Technology*, UIST '12, ACM (New York, NY, USA, 2012), 93–102.

7. Cross, A., Bayyapunedi, M., Ravindran, D., Cutrell, E., and Thies, W. Vidwiki: Enabling the crowd to improve the legibility of online educational videos. In *Proceedings of the 17th ACM Conference on Computer Supported Cooperative Work & Social Computing*, CSCW '14, ACM (New York, NY, USA, 2014), 1167–1175.

8. Eiriksdottir, E., and Catrambone, R. Procedural instructions, principles, and examples how to structure instructions for procedural tasks to enhance performance, learning, and transfer. *Human Factors: The Journal of the Human Factors and Ergonomics Society 53*, 6 (2011), 749–770.

9. Grossman, T., Matejka, J., and Fitzmaurice, G. Chronicle: Capture, exploration, and playback of document workflow histories. In *Proceedings of the 23rd Annual ACM Symposium on User Interface Software and Technology*, UIST '10, ACM (New York, NY, USA, 2010), 143–152.

10. Hausmann, R. G., Nokes, T. J., VanLehn, K., and Gershman, S. The design of self-explanation prompts: The fit hypothesis. In *Proceedings of the 31st Annual Conference of the Cognitive Science Society* (2009), 2626–2631.

11. Johnson, C. I., and Mayer, R. E. Applying the self-explanation principle to multimedia learning in a computer-based game-like environment. *Comput. Hum. Behav. 26*, 6 (Nov. 2010), 1246–1252.

12. Karpicke, J. D., and Blunt, J. R. Retrieval practice produces more learning than elaborative studying with concept mapping. *Science 331*, 6018 (2011), 772–775.

13. Karpicke, J. D., and Roediger, H. L. The critical importance of retrieval for learning. *science 319*, 5865 (2008), 966–968.

14. Kim, J., Guo, P. J., Cai, C. J., Li, S.-W. D., Gajos, K. Z., and Miller, R. C. Data-driven interaction techniques for improving navigation of educational videos. In *Proceedings of the 27th Annual ACM Symposium on User Interface Software and Technology*, UIST '14, ACM (New York, NY, USA, 2014), 563–572.

15. Kim, J., Guo, P. J., Seaton, D. T., Mitros, P., Gajos, K. Z., and Miller, R. C. Understanding in-video dropouts and interaction peaks inonline lecture videos. In *Proceedings of the First ACM Conference on Learning @ Scale Conference*, L@S '14, ACM (New York, NY, USA, 2014), 31–40.

16. Kim, J., Nguyen, P. T., Weir, S., Guo, P. J., Miller, R. C., and Gajos, K. Z. Crowdsourcing step-by-step information extraction to enhance existing how-to videos. In *Proceedings of the 32nd Annual ACM Conference on Human Factors in Computing Systems*, CHI '14, ACM (New York, NY, USA, 2014), 4017–4026.

17. Kong, N., Grossman, T., Hartmann, B., Agrawala, M., and Fitzmaurice, G. Delta: A tool for representing and comparing workflows. In *Proceedings of the SIGCHI Conference on Human Factors in Computing Systems*, CHI '12, ACM (New York, NY, USA, 2012), 1027–1036.

18. Landis, J. R., Koch, G. G., et al. The measurement of observer agreement for categorical data. *biometrics 33*, 1 (1977), 159–174.

19. Lasecki, W. S., Song, Y. C., Kautz, H., and Bigham, J. P. Real-time crowd labeling for deployable activity recognition. In *Proceedings of the 2013 Conference on Computer Supported Cooperative Work*, CSCW '13, ACM (New York, NY, USA, 2013), 1203–1212.

20. Margulieux, L. E., Guzdial, M., and Catrambone, R. Subgoal-labeled instructional material improves performance and transfer in learning to develop mobile applications. In *Proceedings of the Ninth Annual International Conference on International Computing Education Research*, ICER '12, ACM (New York, NY, USA, 2012), 71–78.

21. Mayer, R. E., and Moreno, R. Nine ways to reduce cognitive load in multimedia learning. *Educational psychologist 38*, 1 (2003), 43–52.

22. Noronha, J., Hysen, E., Zhang, H., and Gajos, K. Z. Platemate: Crowdsourcing nutritional analysis from food photographs. In *Proceedings of the 24th Annual ACM Symposium on User Interface Software and Technology*, UIST '11, ACM (New York, NY, USA, 2011), 1–12.

23. Pavel, A., Berthouzoz, F., Hartmann, B., and Agrawala, M. Browsing and analyzing the command-level structure of large collections of image manipulation tutorials. Tech. Rep. UCB/EECS-2013-167, EECS Department, University of California, Berkeley, Oct 2013.

24. Pongnumkul, S., Dontcheva, M., Li, W., Wang, J., Bourdev, L., Avidan, S., and Cohen, M. F. Pause-and-play: Automatically linking screencast video tutorials with applications. In *Proceedings of the 24th Annual ACM Symposium on User Interface Software and Technology*, UIST '11, ACM (New York, NY, USA, 2011), 135–144.

25. Prince, M. Does active learning work? a review of the research. *Journal of engineering education 93*, 3 (2004), 223–231.

26. VanLehn, K., Jones, R. M., and Chi, M. T. A model of the self-explanation effect. *The journal of the learning sciences 2*, 1 (1992), 1–59.

27. Williams, J. J., Kovacs, G., Walker, C., Maldonado, S., and Lombrozo, T. Learning online via prompts to explain. In *CHI '14 Extended Abstracts on Human Factors in Computing Systems*, CHI EA '14, ACM (New York, NY, USA, 2014), 2269–2274.

From Personal Tool to Community Resource: What's the Extra Work and Who Will Do It?

Erik H. Trainer, Chalalai Chaihirunkarn, Arun Kalyanasundaram, James D. Herbsleb
Institute for Software Research
Carnegie Mellon University
5000 Forbes Ave., Pittsburgh, PA 15213
{etrainer, cchaihir, arunkaly, jdh}@cs.cmu.edu

ABSTRACT
Sharing scientific data, software, and instruments is becoming increasingly common as science moves toward large-scale, distributed collaborations. Sharing these resources requires extra work to make them generally useful. Although we know much about the extra work associated with sharing *data*, we know little about the work associated with sharing contributions to *software*, even though software is of vital importance to nearly every scientific result. This paper presents a qualitative, interview-based study of the extra work that developers and end users of scientific software undertake. Our findings indicate that they conduct a rich set of extra work around community management, code maintenance, education and training, developer-user interaction, and foreseeing user needs. We identify several conditions under which they are likely to do this work, as well as design principles that can facilitate it. Our results have important implications for future empirical studies as well as funding policy.

Author Keywords
Software sharing; scientific software; extra work; scientific communities; qualitative methods.

ACM Classification Keywords
H.5.3 [Information Interfaces and Presentation (e.g., HCI)]: Group and Organization Interfaces – Computer supported cooperative work.

INTRODUCTION
We are in an era of distributed, large-scale science that depends not only on new technological advances, but also on "human infrastructure," complex arrangements of people, organizations and communities [22]. Studies of cyberinfrastructure and e-Science have pointed out that creating this infrastructure is an ongoing task, involving continuous collaboration, alignment, and adjustment among many stakeholders [3]. Sharing scientific resources, a central dimension of this collaboration, has been a topic of great interest to the CSCW community as of late [4,10,29].

Sharing scientific resources requires *extra work*, voluntary or involuntary unpaid labor, to make them generally useful. A significant portion of recent research on sharing in science has documented extra work from the perspective of the recipient: locating data [39], interpreting data [5,29], and assessing their reliability [10,15]. There is also extra work from the perspective of the sharer. Standardizing data, for instance, requires reaching agreement on key terms, creating protocols for data collection, providing tutorials and training on implementing the standards, and translating the standards to forms, spreadsheet templates, and interfaces [2,26].

The above studies have focused primarily on the work scientists do to share *data*. Other than work showing that scientists share software based on social ties [18], we know little about the extra work to make contributions to *software* generally useful, even though software is a major output of the scientific process. More than other assets produced by scientific work, such as published results and archived data, software requires continuous maintenance effort or it soon loses its value, as it becomes incompatible with new releases of operating systems, middleware, and complementary software.

Extra work provides powerful leverage for other scientists who can use the software to produce new knowledge. If a scientist spends 10 hours writing a piece of software, plus an additional hour to make it generally useful, other scientists who use it get the benefit of that 10 hours of work. Even if only 1 other scientist uses it, the benefit from the perspective of the community is 10 hours. If 2 scientists use it, 20 hours, and so on. If we can understand what this extra work is, and under what conditions it is likely to happen, we can find ways to facilitate it.

We therefore address the following research questions:

(1) *What are the kinds of extra work that scientists do to make contributions to software generally useful?*

(2) *Under what conditions are scientists likely to perform (or not perform) extra work?*

(3) *What are the design principles that can facilitate extra work?*

CSCW '15, March 14 - 18 2015, Vancouver, BC, Canada
Copyright 2014 ACM 978-1-4503-2922-4/15/03…$15.00
http://dx.doi.org/10.1145/2675133.2675172

To answer these questions, we conducted a multiple case study of four scientific software communities. We interviewed developers and end users, having them describe contributions to and use of the software, and activities within their communities. We found that our participants conducted a rich set of extra work, and several considerations influenced their decisions to do so. We also identified several principles that can facilitate extra work. In the following sections we review related research, describe our study, present the results of our interviews, and discuss the implications of our findings.

BACKGROUND

The Human Work of Large-Scale Science

The research challenges of today demand large-scale collaborations involving multiple research institutions and scientific domains, often as a condition of funding. Creating the necessary infrastructure for such projects is an ongoing task requiring the establishment and maintenance of people, groups, and technologies. For instance, Bietz et al. [3,4] talk about "aligning," which is the work that developers do to enact a relationship in a way that enables it to produce within a cyberinfrastructure. Developers of middleware, for example, must balance building systems that can be used across multiple projects, while also ensuring that their software meets the needs of funding sources. In order to find potential collaborators, developers attend seminars, watch funding calls from various agencies, and follow trends in multiple scientific domains [4].

Another kind of work, "leveraging," emphasizes how an existing relationship with a person, artifact, or organization can build or strengthen another relationship [3]. To get access to a novel technology, a project may create a partnership with a research project located at the same university that is developing the technology.

Extra Work of Sharing Scientific Resources

In the context of large-scale scientific collaboration, recent research has examined the work of sharing scientific data, not scientific software. A notable exception is work by Huang et al. [18] that identified social practices around the sharing of and control over commercial and open-source software in a bioinformatics research team. For instance, in order to use software that another team developed, scientists leveraged existing relationships with members of the other team and negotiated co-authorship on publications. Our work is distinct by looking at the work to make features of the software generally useful to a community of users, beyond a particular laboratory, and on open-source software in particular.

Much of the research on data has documented work required by the recipient. Zimmerman [39], for example, documented how ecologists locate data for reuse. She found that ecologists devised systematic sampling methods and used research journals to bound their data searches by timeframe and geography.

Other research has focused on the work of data interpretation [5,29]. For instance, Rolland & Lee [29] found that postdoctoral researchers reusing cancer epidemiology datasets spent significant amounts of time consulting manuscripts to see how the data were written about, reading study protocols and documentation to understand how key variables were constructed, and even tracking down former study members in their new jobs.

Recipients of scientific data also assess the data's relevance and trustworthiness. Faniel & Jacobsen [10] observed that earthquake engineering researchers assess relevance by generating criteria related to their research questions and comparing those criteria to colleagues' experimental test setups and parameters, which they find in journal articles describing the experiments or through direct contact with the researchers. To assess trustworthiness, they consult experiment documentation first and speak with colleagues who produce the data to get basic facts or clarify inconsistencies in the data.

Sharing scientific resources also requires extra effort on the part of the sharer. For example, standardizing data for sharing can involve creating laboratory protocols, reaching agreement on definitions of key terms, translating standards to forms, templates, smartphone apps, and web sites, and developing material transfer agreements [2]. In a study of a standardization process in an ecological research community, Millerand et al. [26] documented how developers of the standards created training sessions for information managers at distant sites to teach them how to implement the standard.

There are likely some kinds of extra work that the sharer is in a better position to do, and some kinds of extra work that the recipient is in a better position to do. On the one hand, when deciding to offer up a piece of software for the community, the sharer understands what its functions do, and will be able to modify it more easily than the recipient. It will therefore be appropriate for that scientist to create documentation for the software and fix bugs that surface after it goes into operation. On the other hand, the recipient may know more about intended use cases for the software, or other data and tools with which the software must interoperate. The recipient can also provide the sharer with valuable feedback. The role of the recipient is an important one. In fact, product innovations often come from users, who know more about what the product should do, and what it means to do it better [13,14].

It is clear why recipients do extra work; they are the ones who need and will use what sharers provide. The motivations of sharers, however, are not as easily explained. Undertaking extra work without tangible reward is a very real concern, shown in early CSCW research to be a reason why groupware systems fail [12,27]. Sharers of data may nevertheless get fuller use out of their data, or the ability to negotiate co-authorship on publications produced using the data. To understand why someone would do extra work on software, we turn to the literature on open-source software.

Open-Source Software: Extra Work for Others (for free)

There are three primary individual motivations for contributing to open-source software [8]. *Intrinsic* motivations include fun and enjoyment [21] and learning opportunities [28,31,38]. *Internalized extrinsic motivations* include fulfilling personal needs [20,23].

Extrinsic motivations such as reputation and opportunities for career development have been the focus of increased study in recent years [9,25,28]. Studies of transparent software development environments such as GitHub (http://github.com/) have found that developers actively manage their profiles to gain greater attention and visibility for their work [24]. The number of followers a developer has, for example, signals their status. The transparency into development activities that GitHub provides allows others to gauge developers' expertise [9]. Employers have even started using GitHub to find and recruit potential employees [25].

The trouble is that whereas reputation is an effective motivator in the world of open-source, it is significantly less of a motivator—perhaps even irrelevant—in the world of scientific software. The reason is that scientists receive reputation for the results they publish, not the software they develop. Scientists receive credit for software only indirectly. In a study of BLAST [1], a key bioinformatics tool, Howison & Herbsleb [16,17] concluded that improvements to the software motivated by academic credit were less likely to be integrated. They argued that this is because integration makes it harder to see who did what, undermining the ability of reputation to function as a reward.

METHOD

To address our research questions, we conducted a multiple case study of four scientific software communities characterized by the availability of rich data and community activity. Three considerations influenced our selection of cases. First, we wanted clearly infrastructural projects and end user projects, both in the same domain, in order to understand how the presence of close ties to users influences the kinds of extra work conducted. We found very active bioinformatics projects meeting this criterion in Biopython and Bioclipse. Biopython is a set of Python software libraries designed for use by other scientists who develop software [6]. The project began in 1999, and as of this writing has 69 contributors to the source-code, and 487 "stargazers," people who subscribe to updates made to the repository, on GitHub. The source-code has been "forked," cloned by someone to use it as a starting point for their own contributions, 283 times. Bioclipse, in contrast, is a biological workbench application providing a range of functionality for end user biologists [33,34]. The first release of Bioclipse was in 2007. In 2009, Bioclipse was re-written to allow end users to automate functionality using the Bioclipse Scripting Language, and to share reproducible scripts. The project has 8 contributors, 13 stargazers, and 11 forks on GitHub.

Second, we wanted to look at a project that has paid developers. The existence of a paid core might influence the extra work that volunteers are willing to do, in that volunteers may be less willing to do work that they perceive to be the responsibility of paid developers. Throughout this paper we also use the term "core" to refer to developers who are listed as such on their community's website, who self identify as core, or who others identify as core. All paid developers are core, but not all core are paid.

We found a project with paid developers in Bioconductor, which comprises components, often R packages, for analysis of genomic data generated by biological wet lab experiments [11]. First released in 2001 with 15 packages, Bioconductor now contains 824 packages. Bioconductor's source-code is hosted in a Subversion repository instead of GitHub, so we were unable to collect information about contributors, stargazers, and forks. The Bioconductor website, however, tracks download statistics for all packages. From August 2013 to July 2014, there were 9,354,646 downloads from 2,35,401 IP addresses (http://www.bioconductor.org/packages/stats/). In addition, the Bioconductor mailing list has 3,500 subscribers, suggesting a large community of users. Each package has one or more volunteers who maintain it (although paid developers may also maintain packages). The team of paid programmers is located at the Fred Hutchinson Cancer Research Center in Seattle, Washington, USA. Their job is to review user-submitted components, manage official releases, provide user support, and develop experimental packages.

Third, we wanted another project to contrast with the others on many dimensions, with the intention to see large differences and to see if our findings generalized across these many dimensions. We therefore selected NetLogo, a project used for simulation, instead of analysis [37]. Developed in 1999, NetLogo was closed source until it was moved to GitHub in 2011, where it has 13 contributors, 165 stargazers, and 46 forks. NetLogo is in use by educators as well as researchers in the physical and social sciences. NetLogo end users are also active contributors, adding another dimension to sharing in this particular community. Although they do not make direct source-code contributions to NetLogo, end users do write models using the NetLogo language that simulate various natural and social phenomena, and can share these models with others on the Modeling Commons (http://modelingcommons.org/), a community model sharing site. The Modeling Commons currently lists 1,272 models. End users can also write and share extensions, which are separate plug-ins that add capabilities to the modeling environment. For instance, the R extension (http://netlogo-r-ext.berlios.de/) adds the capability to send data between NetLogo and R and to call

R functions from within NetLogo. The NetLogo extensions page lists 37 user submitted extensions. Like Bioconductor, NetLogo has paid developers.

Among the three biology-related projects in our sample, Bioconductor and Biopython appear to be more popular and actively developed compared with Bioclipse. Using a tool's Google Scholar search results as a rough indicator of its usage in scientific work, we found that 24,800 publications mention Bioconductor, 1,420 mention Biopython, and 263 mention Bioclipse. NetLogo appears to be popular across multiple domains, and the simulation environment, models, and extensions are all actively developed. We found that 8,970 publications mention NetLogo.

Data Collection

We conducted semi-structured interviews with 39 participants (see Table 1). We identified our participants by inspecting a combination of community web pages and wikis, mailing lists, and commit access listings from the source code repositories. For Bioconductor and NetLogo, we targeted participants who were paid developers and participants who contributed in their spare time in order to understand differences in motivations and types of extra work these two groups conducted. For NetLogo, we targeted equally model and extension developers in order to understand differences between extra work associated with each of these end user-submitted tools and the main NetLogo source-code. We solicited participants by e-mail and interviewed them using either Skype or Google Hangouts. In the interviews we first asked participants to talk about their role and activity in the project in general, and then we asked about their recent contributions in greater detail. Interviews lasted 45 minutes on average. A transcription service firm transcribed all interviews.

Analysis

We used techniques from grounded theory [7] to analyze the interview transcripts. We first imported all transcripts into the Dedoose qualitative data analysis software package [32]. We then identified and conducted open coding on statements about work that participants carried out to make the software of general use, and their reasons for doing so. When possible, we triangulated participants' statements with work artifacts hosted in project source-code repositories as well as descriptions of, and discussions about, those artifacts posted in mailing lists and web pages.

In the next phase of analysis we wrote, shared, and discussed descriptive memos about emerging themes in the dataset. We met weekly to unify, refine and collapse codes where there was commonality, using themes from our memos as support. We applied the resulting set of codes to the remaining interviews, sometimes revealing additional behaviors not captured by our existing set. In such cases we extended our codes as appropriate. We continued this process until our data no longer revealed new phenomena captured by our categories.

	Volunteer	Paid
Biopython	P1, P2, P3, P4, P5, P6, P7, P8, P21, P24, P30, P33, P40	
Bioclipse	P17, P18, P22, P26, P29	
Bioconductor	P31, P35, P37, P38, P44	P23, P27, P41, P42
NetLogo	P11, P12, P13, P14, P15, P16, P20, P25, P36	P9, P10, P34

Table 1. Summary of interview participants.

RESULTS

RQ 1: What are the kinds of extra work that scientists do to make contributions to software generally useful?

We found that participants conducted a rich set of extra work. Our analysis revealed five categories of extra work: *community management, code maintenance, education and training, developer/user interaction, and foreseeing user needs.*

Community Management

Participants described doing work that supported community management activities. This work included following community norms and guidelines, attending core team meetings, evaluating potential contributions, promoting the project in the broader community, soliciting contributions from community members, announcing work in progress, and staying aware of community members' activities.

Abiding by Community Norms and Guidelines

Community norms and guidelines provided participants guidance about what extra work to conduct. Participants from Biopython and Bioconductor (P37, P31, P40, P7, P2) described following guidelines, such as thoroughly testing the code, collating examples and documentation, reusing common data structures, following naming conventions, and breaking the code apart into logical pieces. For instance, upon failing the tests required to check his code into the Biopython repository, one respondent described that a core developer told him to change the syntax of his code to make it compatible with all the versions of Python that Biopython supports (P40).

The Bioconductor community has additional expectations about the work that follows code contribution. Members of the paid core (P23, P27, P41, P42) explained that each Bioconductor package has one or more maintainers who address support requests and bug reports.

NetLogo and Bioclipse, in contrast, do not have clear guidelines with respect to contribution. Yet NetLogo end users who shared their models, for instance, learned how to structure those models based on reviewing existing models bundled with the NetLogo software and models shared on the Modeling Commons (P11, P13, P16). From these reviews, participants sensed that models should be simple and generalizable:

> *"What people tend to like are models that are relatively simple, and if you want something else, you put them in a separate model. [My model] on the [Modeling Commons] isn't exactly like that, but the one that's on my hard drive is not at all like that. It's just a bunch of different tools thrown into the same NetLogo model...no one wants to look at that unless they're doing stuff with it." (P11, NetLogo)*

P11 described spending a few hours over a week's time to clean out the extraneous functionality in his model before sharing it on the Modeling Commons. Another participant described that he believed his model was simple enough to be generally applicable, but that he still needed to document it, as suggested by the NetLogo model template, before he felt it was ready to share with others (P13).

Attending Core Team Meetings

Attending face-to-face meetings played an important role for core developers. Members of the Bioconductor paid core team, for example, described meeting every three weeks to discuss challenges related to the development of experimental packages, policies around package reviews, how to make resources on the website more usable, and developing courses on the use of particular Bioconductor packages (P23, P27). NetLogo core developers met face to face every six months to discuss design changes, demonstrate prototype functionality to one another, and discuss future directions for the project with their grant partners (P20, P10).

Evaluating Submitted Contributions

Participants also talked about the work of assessing potential contributions, often doing their best to help the submitter get the contribution into an acceptable state. This typically involved back and forth discussions in a GitHub "pull request," a workflow method where a contributor submits proposed code changes to a project, which are integrated into the main branch only with the repository owners' approval. Pull requests are public; anyone can comment on them. Respondents from projects hosted on GitHub (i.e., Biopython, Bioclipse, and NetLogo) recalled that pull requests generated discussion from repository owners and other developers, who pointed out possible incompatibilities with the code and other tools within their workflows, and suggested possible fixes and improvements (P10, P9, P6, P1, P7, P20, P42).

Paid developers of Bioconductor are responsible for reviewing user-submitted packages. As such, we did not consider their reviews extra work. However, we found that some individuals not paid to work on Bioconductor (e.g., P38) volunteered to review packages, which entailed reading through people's code, checking for adequate unit tests, checking for reuse of common data structures, and looking for thorough documentation. A paid Bioconductor developer explained that the review process usually took a whole afternoon to complete (P42).

Advertising Project, Demonstrating Impact

To promote their software and generate enthusiasm for it among the broader community, participants shared updates to the software on Twitter and Facebook (P10, P34, P44), wrote papers describing the software (P23), and organized workshops (P29, P23, P27).

Often underlying project promotion was motivation to increase the software's perceived scientific impact. Participants talked about the importance of demonstrating to funding agencies their software's value to the community, employing usage indicators to do so (P27, P22, P29, P34). For instance, in annual reports to funders, participants included the Bioconductor download statistics for their packages and citations to key publications (P22, P27). In fact, all projects in our sample provide specific citation guidelines for scientists who publish results obtained using the software.

Soliciting Contributions

Several participants talked about the work of finding project contributors (P7, P38, P34, P42). Upon noticing activities in end users' project "forks," participants e-mailed them asking when the code would be ready to integrate (P7, P8, P38). Some core developers (e.g., P34) also encouraged end users to implement ideas for features discussed on the mailing list.

Several core developers from Biopython and Bioconductor described having ideas for functionality, but prioritized other responsibilities over implementing those ideas (P7, P4, P41, P42). In response, they applied to the Google Summer of Code (GSoC) (https://developers.google.com/open-source/soc/) program to find a student to produce the code. GSoC is an annual program sponsored by Google that pays students to develop features for an open-source project during the summer. In some cases, students continued to contribute after the summer (P4, P5, P8, P44).

Announcing Work in Progress

Participants sometimes made announcements on the mailing list to notify others what they were working on. Participants described that they did this to gather suggestions for improvements (P36, P8, P5) as well as feedback on the usefulness of the functionality (P5). One participant from Biopython described that he preferred to announce proposed changes over the mailing list before making a pull request because the mailing list can potentially reach a broader audience—not just developers but end users as well (P5).

In the Biopython project in particular, GSoC students posted weekly blogs containing descriptions of their ongoing work (P8, P7, P30).

Monitoring other People's Activities

Participants also described trying to get a general sense of what others in the community were doing. To this end they browsed the project mailing lists, GitHub project activity visualization and feeds, and question and answer forums. For example, participants reported periodically checking active forks of their projects to get a general sense of what people were doing with their code (P9, P7, P34, P36). As the de facto leader of Biopython told us: *"I find that useful to know what other people have been up to just in case there's something I need to be aware of" (P7, Biopython).*

Code Maintenance

We found that participants made efforts to ensure that their software worked correctly before and after making it publically available. These efforts included fixing bugs, managing dependencies in the code, monitoring code usage, and testing.

Fixing Bugs

One of the most common types of extra work during maintenance was fixing bugs. Respondents described receiving bug reports through issue tracking systems and through e-mail, over the mailing list, and in pull requests themselves (P12, P37, P20, P24, P1, P35). In many cases, participants were willing to fix reported bugs. In other cases, decisions to fix bugs depended on the importance of the bug, the existence of workarounds, and developers' spare time (P10, P12).

Social capital and reciprocity seemed to play important roles in fixing bugs (P20, P29, P5, P14). For example, one participant recalled a NetLogo extension that he wrote years earlier but no longer used. He described fixing bugs that a former professor of his continued to report even though it was *"kind of a pain to work on it" (P20, NetLogo).* Members of the Bioclipse project contributed to another project on which Bioclipse has a dependency. One respondent explained that this *"giving and taking"* ensured that bugs in the other project were fixed quickly (P29, Bioclipse).

Managing Dependencies

We found that participants spent time resolving dependencies in their code. The most common occurrence was where a participant noticed that their software was failing. The participant would very quickly contact the developer of the depended upon code through e-mail or the mailing list to resolve the error (P37, P31).

Work associated with dependency management seemed to be linked to the architecture of the project. The Bioconductor package system, for example, allows contributors to reuse certain data structures and existing algorithms, enabling reproducible research and interoperability among packages (P27). It is exactly this reuse that creates dependencies. The Bioclipse and NetLogo architectures allow contributors to write extensions, which are like plug-ins, (and models in the case of NetLogo) without needing to know how to modify the core components. This allows extensions to evolve independently (P10), but puts the maintenance burden on extension developers (P10, P15). For example, one NetLogo extension developer maintained two different versions of his extension so that it worked with the older and newer versions of NetLogo (P15). Because Biopython is a set of libraries, it comprises many wrappers for other tools. Participants explained that they were accustomed to new changes in file formats and new switches arising from new functionality included in new releases of BLAST [1] (e.g., P7). Fortunately, very often the fix involved only changing a few lines of code.

Monitoring Code Usage

We found that participants actively kept track of how others used their code. Some participants occasionally checked the number of downloads of their software (e.g., P15, P2). Others, in addition, instrumented their software to collect usage data (P22). Participants described these statistics as important to include in grant reports and funding applications (P22, P27, P10).

Usage information also supported developers in addressing user problems. The core developers of NetLogo described setting up RSS feeds to watch for questions about NetLogo on Stack Overflow (http://www.stackoverflow.com/), a popular question and answer website for programmers (P10, P34). Maintainers of Bioconductor packages watched the mailing list for questions about their components (P31, P44). Actively monitoring how others were using code was relatively rare in Biopython. One respondent mentioned setting up a RSS feed to monitor questions about his contributions. He also set up a special time several days a week to look at questions and answer them. He felt a particular satisfaction in helping people and felt that it was a good learning opportunity to do so (P8).

Testing

The majority of participants from Biopython, Bioclipse, and Bioconductor described regularly testing their software, often as a prerequisite for contribution.

In NetLogo, we noticed more variance. Most end users who wrote NetLogo models at least relied on syntax checkers available in the NetLogo runtime environment (P14, P13, P15, P16, P11). Of that group, some performed additional testing using agent based simulation model validation techniques (P14, P13), especially when they submitted their models for publication. Participants who wrote NetLogo extensions described doing minimal testing, such as spot checking output by hand and having friends try it out to see if it worked on their computer (P11, P12). One participant explained that more extensive testing was unnecessary because it was not big enough to be worth the effort (P12).

Education and Training

Other extra work supported learning about the software. Participants described running tutorials on how to use the software to perform common analyses, mentoring other community members, and using the mailing list to learn about technologies relevant to them.

Running Tutorials

We found that participants in all four communities attended workshops, often collocated with community conferences, aimed to teach people how to use the software. Participants described running tutorials, one or two hour long training sessions where workshop participants learned how to use package APIs to work through a typical analysis on a sample dataset (P41, P38, P7, P1, P11, P27).

Mentoring Others

Several participants described mentoring new, potential members of the community (P1, P42, P7, P4, P41, P40). The most common occurrence of mentoring was GSoC, where active members of the community volunteered to mentor a student while the student proposed and developed features for the project.

The work of mentoring GSoC students typically involved corresponding with students weekly via videoconference or e-mail, over a period of three months, to discuss progress and any difficulties related to proposed goals. Mentors taught students about how to contribute to the project, as well as software engineering practices more generally. Sometimes mentoring was far-ranging, involving career choices and sample applications for jobs (P7, P1).

Studying the Mailing List

A few participants mentioned that they actively read the project mailing list to find new technical knowledge. Questions and answers about modules related to their own work served as resources that could potentially be relevant in the future (P31, P37).

Developer/User Interaction

Much extra work evolved from interactions between developers and end users. These activities included answering end users' questions, adding requested features, and suggesting fixes for others' code.

Answering Questions

Many participants described responding to users' questions related to the software. Their answers clarified how to interpret errors encountered when executing the code (P31, P37, P7), how to extend the software to provide additional functionality (P36, P44, P38, P10), or where to find a particular component that addressed the asker's particular need (P12). Participants described that they had discussions with a lot of back and forth communication, where somebody would ask for more detail, and the conversation would *"keep going like that for a while" (P36, NetLogo)*.

For paid developers of NetLogo and Bioconductor, answering user questions consumed a significant portion of their free time (P10, P42). They therefore selectively answered questions for which they were particularly knowledgeable (P27, P42, P15, P9). This strategy seemed to be a natural fit for Bioconductor package maintainers, who typically only answered questions related to their packages (P31, P37, P35) but we observed that participants from Biopython (e.g., P8, P5) used it as well. Some participants from Bioclipse made themselves available to users in real-time on Internet Relay Chat (IRC) (P29, P18).

Adding Requested Features

Participants often described receiving feature requests from end users through e-mail and over the mailing list (P5, P15, P12, P10). Requests deemed to take more time and effort needed to pass a certain threshold of priority. A request was considered low priority, for example, if there was an existing workaround to achieve the desired result (P42, P12). For instance, a participant described that he had a user request to pass matrices to his NetLogo MATLAB extension, but he didn't implement the feature because the same result could be achieved by writing a loop in NetLogo to pass multiple arrays to his extension (P12).

For projects with funding (i.e., Bioclipse, Bioconductor, NetLogo), the paid core generally considered feature requests as high priority if they aligned with objectives outlined in grants (P34, P10), or if there was a clear community need for them (P34, P10, P27, P42).

Suggesting, Making Possible Fixes to Others' Code

In some instances, participants not only reported bugs but also provided solutions. Often, participants' needs for the corrected functionality motivated their suggestions (P6, P20, P40, P3, P35, P37). Sometimes suggestions turned into pull requests:

> *"When I report issues I usually like to give as much information as possible and even point to possible fixes, and often as I go through that process I just happen to stumble-- I'm like 'Oh, this is how I would fix that' or something like that, so then a report turns into a pull request." (P20, NetLogo)*

Foreseeing User Needs

We found that participants often thought about the needs of end users. Participants modified their code so that others could reuse it, created documentation, and provided detailed snippets of source-code illustrating how to use it.

Creating Flexible Code

Participants often considered the community who would want to use their features, and the range of uses for which they might want to use it (P42, P40, P24, P2). One respondent, who described himself as *"generically selfish,"* said:

> *"...I won't code up something that I would not use. I would not code up something that only I would use and only idiosyncrasies...so I coded up things that I would use and hopefully a lot of other people would." (P24, Biopython)*

To create flexible code, participants made code syntax compatible with multiple versions of the code interpreter (P40), reused common data structures and annotation resources from other developers (P23, P4), broke the code apart into more logical pieces (P37, P11, P4), and provided access to objects via interfaces, which aren't limited to a specific implementation (P31). One participant estimated that making *"something that's maintainable and accessible"* took at least 30% more of his effort (P9, NetLogo).

Participants noted, however, that there were limitations to how much they could predict. Sometimes, making code more flexible was in response to user requests or feedback from source-code submission process (P31, P40).

Creating Documentation

Participants often documented their software contributions (P23, P15, P12). Participants from the Bioconductor and Biopython projects, which uphold certain levels of documentation quality, described creating especially extensive documentation (P35, P37, P31). Participants from Bioclipse expressed creating documentation as well, especially for setting up the Eclipse environment (P18).

We found more variability in the amount and quality of documentation in NetLogo models and extensions. Some of our NetLogo participants expressed that they kept more documentation for themselves than for others (P15, P13, P36), while others provided extensive documentation (P12, P11) and kept *readme* files up to date (P9). One reason for this variability may have been confusion about the documentation requirements (P16), as the core NetLogo team did not review contributions before accepting them, as in Biopython and Bioconductor.

Creating Examples

We found that in some cases, participants described writing additional code that demonstrated how to use their software. In Bioconductor, these examples are required for package acceptance. Contributors must write "vignettes," documents that provide a task-oriented description of the package functionality, and include executable examples.

Some NetLogo extension and model developers described creating examples as well. Extension developers provided one-line code snippets how to call functions in their code (e.g., P12). NetLogo core team members (e.g., P10) wrote whole models to illustrate to end users how to build their own. Indeed, NetLogo end users described incrementally building on these examples in order to create their own (P11, P25, P14, P16).

RQ 2: Under what conditions are scientists likely to perform (or not perform) extra work?

We found that several considerations influenced whether participants were willing to take on extra work. Participants thought about their own interests, others' interests, the relevance of the work to their jobs, their obligations, their current priorities, and their own expertise.

Does the work serve my interests?

Participants often considered whether doing extra work would benefit their own interests. They were willing to do certain kinds of extra work to publish papers describing their software. For example, maintainers of Bioconductor packages felt that *abiding by community norms* during the submission process helped produce something that was a mark of quality in the bioinformatics community (P38, P31, P22), and could be recognized as such through publication. Even though participants sensed that these so-called "software papers" would not be as well regarded as traditional publications, they felt that having a Bioconductor package imparted to them *"extra credit" (P38, Bioconductor)*. Participants who created NetLogo models described that they were willing to provide more thorough *documentation* and conduct extensive *testing* on their models submitted in conjunction with conference and journal papers if they knew that the models would also be subject to peer review (P13, P14).

Similarly, in order for current and future funders to assess their work positively, participants were willing to advertise and *promote their projects*, and *monitor code usage* (P22, P10, P34).

Participants tended to do the extra work of *suggesting fixes* when they needed working features for their own research (P20, P40, P35, P7, P3, P37). They especially escalated their efforts if a feature was high priority for them. As one participant put it:

> *"The more I need a fix, the more time and energy I'm willing to put into it." (P20, NetLogo)*

Participants seemed less likely to report or suggest fixes for issues if they were not relevant to their own research. P16, for instance, described not reporting broken models that were unrelated to his graduate thesis.

Does the work serve others' interests?

In addition to their own needs, doing extra work for free seemed to depend on whether others would benefit from it. When, for instance, developers were developing new features for themselves they often thought about whether others would need similar functionality. For example, one participant, a Bioconductor contributor, talked about an example where he asked his mentor for advice on adding a feature to his GSoC project:

> *"I sent [P42], the other author on the package, just sort of an update, 'Here, this is what I added. Do you think this is useful to the community? Would people actually use this in their workflow?'" (P44, Bioconductor)*

Other participants relied on their intuition (P41, P42, P27) or received information about others' needs in comments of their pull requests (e.g., P20, P40) and in bug reports (e.g., P20). Others *announced their work in progress* over the project mailing list in order to get feedback on whether the work would be useful to others (P5). After getting a sense how useful their contributions could be, participants *suggested fixes*, *created flexible code*, *examples* and *documentation*.

If participants considered their potential contributions too domain specific (e.g., P40, P15) or if their contribution was a personal customization (P20), they would generally not try to create a more generic solution for others.

Does the work align with my job description?
Participants who were funded to work on projects, or whose employers supported their work, tended to engage in certain kinds of extra work, such as *soliciting contributions*, *attending core team meetings*, *fixing bugs*, *mentoring others*, and *advertising and promoting the project*. From their institutes' point of view, their work on the projects served their immediate professional goals and made them look good. As the de facto leader of Biopython explained:

> *"So my employers have been quite flexible and they recognize that [Biopython] is something that is good for my career, it's something the institute is associated with in a positive way...So the practical hands-on work that's done has been related to things that we needed to do here for the research anyway." (P7, Biopython)*

If extra work instead aligned poorly with participants' jobs or career, they tended to ignore extra work such as *adding requested features* or *fixing bugs*. For example, a graduate student we spoke to mentioned that he didn't add a feature that someone else requested because he *"wasn't being paid for it." (P12, NetLogo)*

Am I under obligation?
In some cases, even when extra work was not part of participants' job descriptions, they felt an obligation to do it anyway. For example, becoming a Bioconductor package maintainer created obligations to create *examples*, conduct *testing*, *manage dependencies*, *create documentation*, and *answer questions*. Some participants found that even if they did not find extra work personally useful, peer review panels required the work as part of their criterion for publication (P13, P14). As one NetLogo modeler described:

> *"Many of the journals require if you use models in your—in the research, then they want you to submit your models, and they want them to be documented...I've never [been] a big fan of formally specifying all the units in my models. I just think it's an awful lot of work, and I hadn't found it to be all that useful, but because I have to, I do it." (P13, NetLogo)*

As we mentioned previously, social capital and reciprocity seemed to play a role in the extra work of *fixing bugs* (P29, P20). Participants seemed to feel socially obligated to conduct this extra work.

Is this extra work high enough priority?
Participants prioritized certain kinds of extra work, such as *fixing bugs*, *answering questions*, *mentoring others*, *suggesting possible fixes*, *monitoring code usage*, and *adding requested features*. Even if the work aligned well with participants' job descriptions, they had to prioritize it with respect to other tasks. P10, a core developer of NetLogo, described that critical bugs took priority over bugs with existing workarounds. NetLogo developers also described balancing user submitted bugs against requirements directly from the PI of the grant that supports NetLogo (P10, P34). Requirements originating from the PI often took priority.

Educators teaching NetLogo in the classroom (e.g., P13, P16) prioritized teaching responsibilities over extra work like *monitoring code usage* and *monitoring other people's activities*. Biopython GSoC mentors described that, in recent years, mentor time had become a limiting factor for the number of students they could accept (P7, P1). One former mentor explained that changes in his career, along with having to support his family, made mentoring GSoC students a lower priority than programming:

> *"It's a lot of time to devote; and I think people have a hard time allocating their time sometimes. You know? That's one of the reasons why I can't do as much with [mentoring] now. I have a family and I don't have the time to do that. And it's like you have a certain amount of hours for open-source stuff; and you're like 'why?' And I prefer to code I guess." (P1, Biopython)*

Do I have the expertise?
Participants explained that *suggesting possible fixes* and *answering questions* depended on whether they had the necessary expertise to do so. When participants had the expertise to contribute a fix to a project, for example, they would typically do it (P20, P40, P3). However, if participants did not have the required knowledge, they would not. A member of the NetLogo core team explained how he decided not to contribute a fix to the git project:

> *"For example, I found a bug in git once. I narrowed the bug down to a single line, fixed it for myself, and reported it, but did not contribute my fix. I'm glad I didn't too; when the bug was fixed, it required more extensive knowledge of the coding standards of git, and more extensive knowledge of the programming language (bash in this case), than I had." (P20, NetLogo)*

RQ 3: What are the design principles that can facilitate extra work?

We observed a number of common obstacles and difficulties in performing extra work. For many of them, a subset of participants had worked out effective solutions that we think can be applied more broadly. For others, existing solutions in other domains (e.g., mobile applications) seem to be a good fit to the problem. In this section, we describe a number of these problems and obstacles, design principles we think could be helpful, and the basis for this recommendation.

Use Checklists to Facilitate Learning About Community Norms and Guidelines

Common problem. In addition to learning the technical details of the scientific software under development, scientists also have to learn about the guidelines and norms of the communities. In the first section of the results we discussed that abiding by these norms and guidelines requires extra work from contributors. These guidelines varied significantly across different communities and participants often learned about these through interacting with other members or reading them on the community's websites.

We also found that there is ambiguity in interpreting these guidelines, as one NetLogo participant described:

> *"I'm not exactly sure what the standards are for [the Modeling Commons] I noticed a pretty big range of quality in the models. I definitely have downloaded a few that were literally broken and just didn't run. So I'm not sure what to make of the criteria for what makes an appropriate model to submit there." (P16, NetLogo)*

Sometimes contributors only learn about these guidelines *after* making a contribution. For example, in Biopython, contributors often learn about expected coding standards after they submit a pull request on Biopython's GitHub repository (e.g., P40). This is time consuming and only compounds the extra work that already comes with following guidelines.

Design principle. We believe many communities could benefit by borrowing an idea from Bioconductor, which maintains a short checklist of things to do before submitting a contribution. This checklist helped contributors learn and gauge the extra work required; all of our Bioconductor participants understood the expectations associated with package submission. Therefore, the extra work involved in *abiding by community norms and guidelines* may be considerably reduced by investing in checklists that help to ensure consistency and completeness in submitting contributions.

Provide Automated Support for Asking Questions

Common problem. We observed that a majority of scientists were involved in answering questions on mailing lists, which we found was another form of extra work. However, mailing lists are known to have obvious drawbacks. For instance, due to the large volume of emails, users may sometimes fail to notice certain queries of relevance to them. We found that scientists overcome some of these limitations by adopting strategies such as checking emails frequently (P42), using email filters (P31), and prioritizing questions (P34).

Design principle. Other communities may benefit from the NetLogo core team's (e.g., P34, P10) practice of using Stack Overflow, instead of mailing lists, for asking questions:

> *"People that go and ask a question on a mailing list don't usually search for the archives of the list before asking their question. Stack Overflow kind of gives you that for free because it analyzes the text of the question, automatically suggests similar questions that could have an answer that's relevant for you." (P10, NetLogo)*

Social Q&A sites such as Stack Overflow allow users to efficiently manage and answer questions. One of the biggest advantages that such Q&A sites offer is the ability to view questions that are similar and relevant to the one that is being raised. In addition, users can mention similar questions by simply specifying their URLs. Although migrating from traditional mailing lists to sites such as Stack Overflow might be one possible solution [35], it may not be entirely feasible, since scientists may not readily adopt new tools that do not directly benefit their domain task [30]. Therefore, providing this extended functionality in a way that allows users to continue using mailing lists can significantly reduce the extra work associated with *answering questions*.

Allow Contributors to Choose Between Private and Public Modes of Evaluating Submitted Contributions

Common problem. Code contributions in open-source software are often reviewed and discussed by other members before the code is accepted. The use of pull requests on GitHub to submit code contributions makes this process transparent and easier for community members to review and improve the code. However, we found that scientists are not always comfortable with making the review process public. For example, in Bioconductor, the discussions between the reviewer and the contributor happen through private emails and only the revised code is uploaded to the public repository. While this form of review takes more time than using pull requests, it allows new contributors to learn in a friendlier environment and prevents any embarrassment that they might often face (P42). However, a few Bioconductor contributors we interviewed did not mind if their code reviews were accessible to all (P31). On the other hand, a transparent review process in a community like Biopython might deter potential contributors.

Design principle. Drawing from projects with very different levels of transparency in the evaluation process, we believe that other communities may find it helpful to allow contributors to choose between these forms of evaluating code contributions rather than enforcing a protocol. In some cases, this may help facilitate *evaluating submitted contributions*.

Allow Users to Provide Feedback Within the Software, in as Few Steps Possible

Common problem. After contributions have been made, we found that feedback allows developers to evaluate how well they serve the needs of others and inform about what they should do to serve those needs. For example, P12, who developed an extension for NetLogo, mentioned that he had updated the documentation a few times after he received emails from the users. However, some participants (e.g. P9, P36) said that they rarely received feedback from users, although they were aware that their software was being used due to the number of downloads.

Design principle. We think that communities could benefit from techniques applied in the mobile applications domain, which allow users to rate and provide comments directly within the software. Examples include one-time rating popups and easy to remove banners at the top of the screen. By allowing users to effortlessly provide feedback on how they are using the software and, if possible, who they are, these designs would not only facilitate extra work around *monitoring code usage*, but also give developers more information that could help *foreseeing user needs* for other contributions. These techniques could therefore reduce the effort of users to find a channel for giving feedback to developers.

Separate Requested Features from Reported Issues

Common problem. There was a sense among our participants (e.g., P34, P35) that GitHub is a place for developers whereas the mailing list is a place for end users. In typical software development practices, bugs and requested features are reported to a central issue tracking database. In many cases, the interfaces to these databases reside on GitHub. Whereas developers may expect to find user needs in these systems, we found a portion of developers' extra work involved finding user requests on the mailing list. An additional complication with the mailing list is that developers were already conducting extra work to filter and prioritize postings of interest. If the right person does not see the message at the right time, it may never be addressed.

Design principle. It seems useful to separate requested features from reported issues in order to direct developers to requests with high user demand. As our participants pointed out, *foreseeing user needs* was an important aspect of their work, but there was a limit to what they could predict. A central dashboard dedicated to requested features may decrease the likelihood that important needs become buried under reported bugs, giving developers insight into what is needed and how many people need it. An interface, possibly a variation of the reddit (http://www.reddit.com/) format, where developers and end users can view and sort requested features by popularity, and vote on them with a simple "thumbs up" and "thumbs down" button, might prove helpful.

DISCUSSION

Based on our findings, we discuss three themes in the extra work that scientists do. The first theme is that of sharing as a continuing commitment. The second theme is that of grasping the needs of scientists and conveying developer intent. The third theme is that of efficiently distributing extra work among sharers and recipients.

Sharing as a Continuing Commitment

Some modes of sharing are an event, e.g., I give my data to a data manager, thus I have shared it and my effort is complete. Our findings illustrate that much extra work for scientific software occurs throughout the lifecycle, not only as a specific sharing event. We found that, as part of their regular work practices, when developing a new feature, participants often first considered the possible range of uses for their contributions. Consider P40, the developer who determined his code would be too domain specific to share with Biopython, P22 who wrote documentation and provided examples of his NetLogo extension in action, and P44 who sent an e-mail to the maintainer of a Bioconductor package asking if certain functionality would be useful. In many cases, the work did not stop there, particularly for Bioconductor package maintainers. Extra work actually reflected an ongoing commitment, in which participants continued to fix bugs, manage dependencies, answer questions on the mailing list, implement new features, and monitor the code usage after the software was in operation.

Some kinds of extra work seem to come at predictable intervals, whereas others do not. In Bioconductor, for instance, when preparing initial contributions, would-be contributors follow specific guidelines outlining submission requirements. *Promoting the software*, and *demonstrating its impact* are especially important when calls for funding appear. Other kinds of extra work are more dynamic, occurring in response to new uses of the software (e.g., *evaluating new submissions*, *monitoring code usage*) and changes to other tools on which the software interoperates (e.g., *managing dependencies*). We note, however, that the choices scientists make about the extra work they perform early on can affect what happens later. For example, once a scientist writing software understands a need well enough (e.g., by *announcing work in progress*), it is likely efficient at that time to *create examples*, *write documentation*, and *make the code flexible*. Otherwise, the scientist will have to spend more time later on *fixing bugs*, *adding badly needed features*, and *answering questions* that could have likely been foreseen earlier.

Grasping User Needs, Conveying Developer Intent

Knowledge about broader uses of scientific software must somehow make its way into the development process if community needs are to be well served. The participants that we interviewed considered possible future uses of their software, often relying on their own intuitions and experience (e.g., P40, P42). End users often users nudged developers by suggesting ways to make software contributions more general, reporting bugs, requesting more complete documentation, and asking for new features.

We found, however, relatively fewer instances of developers conveying the intent of their development trajectories. In many cases, developers announced new features and major releases of the software, or held workshops on analyses possible with new analysis packages—but after the software went into operation. Although developers could track activities of other developers using activity cues available in GitHub, we found that, in general, end users did not use these features. Without ways for developers to convey the intent of their development activities, potential users may simply be unaware or, or even have any way to discover, that the functionality they need exists. Broad exposure would also help increase the probability that errors are corrected before they have the opportunity to break commonly used workflows or creep into publications.

Efficiently Distributing Extra Work

It seems useful to think about efficient divisions of labor for extra work. As we mentioned in the background section, sharers are in a better position to do some extra work whereas recipients are better suited to do other extra work. Interestingly, the incentives to do the work do not necessarily line up to create an efficient division of labor, because the recipient, who, as a potential user, has a pressing current need, generally has a more obvious incentive.

Future Work

Future studies might investigate variables that influence who should do extra work. The predictability of the need for the extra work, for instance, may be of interest. If the sharer understands what is actually needed, the sharer will be in a better position to implement it, since the sharer understands the code. Another variable of interest might be how many people actually need what the extra work accomplishes. If many people will benefit, the sharer may be more inclined to do the extra work, especially if the use of the software matters to them for funding purposes (e.g., P27, P22, P29, P34). In sum, we hypothesize that if a need is predictable, and many users need it, it is more efficient for the sharer to do the work. Otherwise, the recipient should do the work because the sharer does not sufficiently understand what is actually needed, and only the recipient will benefit.

In addition, future studies might explore architectural principles for scientific software that lower the barriers to contribution and allow end user customization, thereby relaxing dependencies on the original developers. Usable APIs for instance, may make it easier for end users to contribute functionality. NetLogo end users, for example, can contribute small Java extensions without understanding the core functionality of NetLogo, which is written in Scala, another programming language. These extensions serve the contributor's needs, and potentially many others', without imposing extra work on the core developers. Toolkits [13] that allow end users to make customizations to the software but maintain the same look and feel of the core software (e.g., same user interface elements), may be valuable in instances, for example, where few users need the features.

Finally, future work might include broadening studies of extra work on software to other scientific disciplines where software sharing behaviors may be less prevalent. For instance, Velden [36] found that the field of synthetic chemistry emphasizes individual skill and personal reputation over team efforts and collective achievements. Chemical databases that specify molecular structures play a particularly crucial role in the routine work of synthesis, and discussions of important synthesis details are often kept private in order to hold competition at bay. Field specific characteristics may therefore influence questions around the conditions in which scientists are likely to perform extra work. In particular, *serving others' interests* may in fact be a disincentive, rather than an incentive, to share.

Implications for Funding Agencies

As others have argued, studies of scientific collaborative work can have important implications for funding policy [19]. This paper provides a comprehensive list of the extra work associated with developing open-source scientific software, as opposed to developing such software for oneself. The results suggest important considerations for funding scientific work of which software development is a component. The potential payoffs of extra work are substantial, provided that there exists a sizable community to use the software, because other scientists can use the software to discover new knowledge. Understanding the rich variety of extra work that scientists conduct can better inform funding policy makers of how to design practices and formulate objectives that align with these efforts. Such an understanding may also support proposal reviewers in evaluating software maintenance strategies, which are currently part of data management plans. Recognizing the value of this extra work, funders may be more willing to provide more substantial financial support to address scientific software maintenance efforts. There may also be a role for industrial funders in motivating scientists to perform extra work. Scientists interested in commercializing their software, for example, may align with industry partners who recognize its commercial potential and are willing to fund its development or pay a portion of their own developers directly to work on it. With adequate support, the software can continue effectively, building new functionality, and supporting users over time.

CONCLUSION

Our work is part of a growing body of research on the sharing and circulation of scientific resources. It is one of the few studies to examine extra effort associated with sharing software, even though software is of vital importance to nearly every scientific result. We found that both paid and unpaid contributors conducted a rich set of extra work, and that several considerations led them to do it. We also identified design principles that can facilitate extra work among sharers and recipients. In contrast to previous work showing that *reputation* for contributions to software does not matter to scientists [16,17], we found that software *use* matters to them for funding purposes. Moreover, developers might do more to convey their intent to end users if extra work is to be efficiently distributed.

Our results open up opportunities for tool design, policy, and future empirical studies of scientific software development in CSCW.

ACKNOWLEDGMENTS
We wish to thank all of our participants for their time, and our anonymous reviewers for their valuable feedback on an earlier version of this paper. We also gratefully acknowledge support of the Alfred P. Sloan Foundation, the National Science Foundation awards 1064209, 1111750, and 0943168, and the Google Open Source Programs Office.

REFERENCES
1. Altschul, S.F., Gish, W., Miller, W., Myers, E.W., and Lipman, D.J. Basic local alignment search tool. *Journal of Molecular Biology 215*, (1990), 403–410.
2. Bietz, M. Standardization in Large-Scale Collaborative Science: The Ocean Sampling Day. *Workshop on Sharing, re-use and circulation of resources in cooperative scientific work at CSCSW 2014*, (2014), 1–2.
3. Bietz, M.J., Baumer, E.P.S., and Lee, C.P. Synergizing in Cyberinfrastructure Development. *Computer Supported Cooperative Work (CSCW) 19*, 3-4 (2010), 245–281.
4. Bietz, M.J., Paine, D., and Lee, C.P. The work of developing cyberinfrastructure middleware projects. *Proceedings of the ACM 2013 conference on Computer supported cooperative work*, ACM Press (2013), 1527–1538.
5. Birnholtz, J. and Bietz, M. Data at Work: Supporting Sharing in Science and Engineering. *Proceedings of the 2003 international ACM SIGGROUP conference on Supporting group work*, (2003), 339–348.
6. Cock, P.J. a, Antao, T., Chang, J.T., et al. Biopython: freely available Python tools for computational molecular biology and bioinformatics. *Bioinformatics (Oxford, England) 25*, 11 (2009), 1422–3.
7. Corbin, J. and Strauss, J. *Basics of Qualitative Research: Techniques and Procedures for Developing Grounded Theory*. Sage, 2008.
8. Crowston, K., Wei, K., Howison, J., and Wiggins, A. Free/Libre open-source software development: what we know and what we do not know. *ACM Computing Surveys 44*, 2 (2012), 1–35.
9. Dabbish, L., Stuart, C., Tsay, J., and Herbsleb, J. Social Coding in GitHub: Transparency and Collaboration in an Open Software Repository. *Proceedings of the ACM 2012 conference on Computer Supported Cooperative Work*, (2012), 1277–1286.
10. Faniel, I.M. and Jacobsen, T.E. Reusing Scientific Data: How Earthquake Engineering Researchers Assess the Reusability of Colleagues' Data. *Computer Supported Cooperative Work (CSCW) 19*, 3-4 (2010), 355–375.
11. Gentleman, R.C., Carey, V.J., Bates, D.M., et al. Bioconductor: open software development for computational biology and bioinformatics. *Genome biology 5*, 10 (2004), R80.
12. Grudin, J. Why CSCSW Applications Fail: Problems in the Design and Evaluation of Organizational Interfaces. *Proceedings of the 1988 ACM conference on Computer-supported cooperative work*, (1988), 85–93.
13. Von Hippel, E. and Katz, R. Shifting Innovation to Users via Toolkits. *Management science 48*, 7 (2002), 821–833.
14. Von Hippel, E. *The Sources of Innovation*. Oxford University Press, New York, New York, USA, 1988.
15. House, N. Van, Butler, M., and Schiff, L. Cooperative Knowledge Work and Practices of Trust: Sharing Environmental Planning Data Sets. *Proceedings of the 1998 ACM conference on Computer supported cooperative work*, (1998), 335–343.
16. Howison, J. and Herbsleb, J.D. Scientific software production: incentives and collaboration. *Proceedings of the ACM 2011 conference on Computer supported cooperative work*, (2011), 513–522.
17. Howison, J. and Herbsleb, J.D. Incentives and integration in scientific software production. *Proceedings of the ACM 2013 Conference on Computer-Supported Cooperative Work*, ACM Press (2013), 459–470.
18. Huang, X., Ding, X., Lee, C.P., Lu, T., Gu, N., and Hall, S. Meanings and Boundaries of Scientific Software Sharing. *Proceedings of the ACM 2013 conference on Computer supported cooperative work*, (2013), 423–434.
19. Jackson, S.J., Steinhardt, S.B., and Buyuktur, A. Why CSCW needs science policy (and vice versa). *Proceedings of the ACM 2013 Conference on Computer-Supported Cooperative Work*, ACM Press (2013), 1113–1124.
20. Lakhani, K. and Hippel, E. Von. How open source software works: "free" user-to-user assistance. *Research policy 32*, July 2002 (2003), 923–943.
21. Lakhani, K. and Wolf, R. Why Hackers Do What They Do: Understanding Motivation and Effort in Free / Open Source Software Projects. *Perspectives on free and open source software*, (2005), 1–27.
22. Lee, C.P., Dourish, P., and Mark, G. The human infrastructure of cyberinfrastructure. *Proceedings of the 2006 20th anniversary conference on Computer supported cooperative work*, ACM Press (2006), 483–492.

23. Lerner, J. and Tirole, J. Some Simple Economics of Open Source. *The journal of industrial economics 50*, 2 (2002), 197–234.

24. Marlow, J., Dabbish, L., and Herbsleb, J. Impression Formation in Online Peer Production: Activity Traces and Personal Profiles in GitHub. *Proceedings of the ACM 2013 Conference on Computer-Supported Cooperative Work*, ACM Press (2013), 117–128.

25. Marlow, J. and Dabbish, L. Activity traces and signals in software developer recruitment and hiring. *Proceedings of the ACM 2013 conference on Computer supported cooperative work*, ACM Press (2013), 145–156.

26. Millerand, F., Ribes, D., Baker, K.S., and Bowker, G.C. Making an Issue out of a Standard: Storytelling Practices in a Scientific Community. *Science, Technology & Human Values 38*, 1 (2012), 7–43.

27. Orlikowski, W. Learning from notes: Organizational issues in groupware implementation. *Proceedings of the 1992 ACM conference on Computer-supported cooperative work*, (1992), 362–369.

28. Roberts, J.A., Hann, I., Slaughter, S.A., and Donahue, J.F. Understanding the motivations, participation, and performance of open source software developers: A longitudinal study of the Apache projects. *Management science 52*, 7 (2006), 984–999.

29. Rolland, B. and Lee, C. Beyond trust and reliability: reusing data in collaborative cancer epidemiology research. *Proceedings of the ACM 2013 conference on Computer supported cooperative work*, (2013), 435–444.

30. Segal, J. Some Problems of Professional End User Developers. *IEEE Symposium on Visual Languages and Human-Centric Computing (VL/HCC 2007)*, Ieee (2007), 111–118.

31. Shah, S. Motivation, Governance, and the Viability of Hybrid Forms in Open Source Software Development. *Management Science 52*, 7 (2006), 1000–1014.

32. SocioCultural Research Consultants, L. Dedoose, web application for managing, analyzing, and presenting qualitative and mixed method research data. 2013.

33. Spjuth, O., Alvarsson, J., Berg, A., et al. Bioclipse 2: a scriptable integration platform for the life sciences. *BMC bioinformatics 10*, (2009), 397.

34. Spjuth, O., Helmus, T., Willighagen, E.L., et al. Bioclipse: an open source workbench for chemo- and bioinformatics. *BMC bioinformatics 8*, (2007), 59.

35. Vasilescu, B., Serebrenik, A., Devanbu, P., and Filkov, V. How social Q&A sites are changing knowledge sharing in open source software communities. *Proceedings of the 17th ACM conference on Computer supported cooperative work & social computing*, ACM Press (2014), 342–354.

36. Velden, T. Explaining field differences in openness and sharing in scientific communities. *Proceedings of the ACM 2013 Conference on Computer-Supported Cooperative Work*, ACM Press (2013), 445–458.

37. Wilensky, U. NetLogo. 1999. http://ccl.northwestern.edu/netlogo/.

38. Ye, Y. and Kishida, K. Toward an Understanding of the Motivation of Open Source Software Developers. *Proceedings of the 2003 International Conference on Software Engineering*, (2003), 419–429.

39. Zimmerman, A. Not by metadata alone: the use of diverse forms of knowledge to locate data for reuse. *International Journal on Digital Libraries 7*, 1-2 (2007), 5–16.

(Re)defining Land Change Science through Synthetic Research Practices

Alyson L. Young, Wayne G. Lutters
Department of Information Systems
UMBC, Baltimore, MD, USA
alyson1@umbc.edu, lutters@umbc.edu

ABSTRACT
This paper investigates the co-evolution of scientific practice and supporting technologies for the interdisciplinary research community of Land Change Science. Through three and a half years of iterative fieldwork and system design, we have developed a deep understanding of their synthetic research practices, specifically regarding meta-studies. Here we detail the challenges researchers face conducting meta-studies and how this collective effort advances the entire scholarly community. We illustrate how our understanding of this synthetic research practice informs the design and refinement of cyberinfrastructure to better support their work.

Author Keywords
Cyberinfrastructure, e-Science, Land Change Science, Research Synthesis, Sociotechnical Systems

ACM Classification Keywords
H.5.3 [Group and Organization Interfaces]: Computer-supported cooperative work.

INTRODUCTION
Computational innovation is rapidly transforming our processes of scientific inquiry. New tools allow us to ask new questions about the world around us. While this has long been the case, the past decade has seen the pace quicken and the impact deepen as entire new scientific subfields have emerged. For example, in genomics, advances in DNA amplification techniques and new sequencing technologies have made it possible for researchers to study entire communities of microorganisms, giving rise to the field of metagenomics [3].

Simultaneously, transformation in the sciences drives innovation in information and communication technology. This has resulted in a number of cyberinfrastructure projects designed to support novel practices and the communities that form around them [2,18,26,27].

Increasingly, researchers are confronted with intellectual and scientific challenges at such scales and complexity that single disciplinary perspectives are no longer adequate, thus demanding the expertise of multi-disciplinary teams [22]. Climate change is a classic example of this. Scientific cyberinfrastructure seeks to support interdisciplinary research by providing tools for data and resource sharing, knowledge transfer, and collaboration across geographical, institutional, and organizational boundaries [2,28]. Understanding this situated interplay in sociotechnical systems has long been central to the CSCW research agenda.

Examining extreme cases of scientific transformation can be quite instructive. Young communities, still in the active process of institutionalization, often foreground phenomena that can be lost in more mature disciplines, such as negotiations around community identity, scientific methods, and knowledge production. We are studying an emergent scientific interdiscipline enabled by computational advances. While our story is not unlike that of bioinformatics [21,22], with advances in remote sensing, modeling, and synthesis enabling new questions and new types of analyses, our community is still in a state of flux, working to define itself, and solidify the processes that give it meaning. Although it has established itself enough to have the norms and structures of a maturing transdiscipline (i.e., an organizing scientific body, core conferences, and journals), they continue to debate their identity. These tensions are brought to the fore and made visible, affording us a unique opportunity to observe their self-reflection and self-definition.

Land Change Science
Understanding the full complexity of Earth systems is one of the most challenging contemporary scientific problems. Historically, this has been examined in many different ways by many different disciplines, such as earth sciences (e.g., hydrology, geophysics, and remote sensing), biological sciences (e.g., plant science, soil science, and agricultural science), social sciences (e.g., geography, sociology, and anthropology), environmental sciences (e.g., ecology, environmental engineering, and environmental conservation) and economics (e.g., public policy, econometrics, and cultural economics) [23,34].

In the 1990s a group of natural and remote sensing scientists aligned with the International Geosphere Biosphere Programme (IGBP) came to the conclusion that in order to understand land-cover dynamics, a comprehensive understanding of land-use change was needed. This required engaging with social sciences to understand how people

CSCW 2015, March 14–18, 2015, Vancouver, BC, Canada.

ACM 978-1-4503-2922-4/15/03...$15.00.
http://dx.doi.org/10.1145/2675133.2675183

make land use decisions. The IGBP subsequently approached the International Social Science Council (ISSC) to explore the possibility of creating a joint core research program. In 1996, this IGBP-ISSC working group established the Land Use Cover Change (LUCC) project. In the United States, NASA responded by developing the LCLUC research program, taking elements from LUCC for use in its science plan [24].

These programs helped form the foundation for what would become Land Change Science (LCS). The LCS community was forged by a shared worldview that the changing interactions among human systems, the terrestrial biosphere, atmosphere, and other Earth systems are best understood as mediated by human use of land [33]. Institutionally, much of the LCS community is respondent to the Global Land Project (GLP). This multi-year coordination project was the result of a series of scoping meetings that began in 2001, culminated with a Science Plan in 2005, and the establishment of the GLP International Project Office in 2006 [38]. The GLP is commissioned by the ISSC and the International Council for Science (ICSU) and supported by both the IGBP and the International Human Dimensions Programme on Global Environmental Change (IHDP) [34]. In 2016, the GLP will transition to Future Earth, a new 10-year international research initiative aimed at transforming Earth systems science and human dimensions research.

Traditionally, the referent disciplines generated knowledge through local case studies based on detailed field observations of land use change or regional studies that combine remote sensing observations with socio-economic and biogeophysical data. However, the influence of LUCC and the GLP drew attention to the need for more integrative assessments of the drivers and impacts of land change as part of global environmental change [34]. This led to the adoption of synthetic practices such as integrative remote sensing products (e.g., anthromes [10]) and agent-based models. It is argued that only through these synthetic practices of comparative research and theory development can the LCS knowledge base become more systematic.

Based on our field research we have identified these processes of research synthesis to be one of the most informative examples of the interplay of technology and scientific process for the LCS community.

RESEARCH SYNTHESIS

Across the entire scientific enterprise, the need for more systematic methods of data analysis and integration to answer larger, more complex questions has led to an increased interest in the use of research synthesis [13,14]. In most disciplines, this refers to the process of integrating research questions, methods, theories, and data across dissimilar scales of analysis, study systems, and levels of expertise in an effort to uncover consistencies and account for differences in similar-appearing studies [9,12]. The objective is to increase the generality and applicability of the findings [16]. While research synthesis methods have been around since the 1970's, with Glass's 1976 article in education believed to be the first publication to introduce meta-analysis to a wider audience, their use stayed fairly consistent until 1990 [32]. At that time the use of synthesis methods across disciplines saw an exponential increase from 0.02 to approximately 1.4 percent in 2010 [32].

Research synthesis is used extensively in a number of scientific fields, including health sciences [5,6,7,32] and ecological sciences [12,14,15]. Within the health sciences meta-analysis in particular has had a significant impact on the transformation of research practices [32]. For example, in epidemiology synthesis is used as a way to make timely decisions about risk assessment and public health concerns [7], and in pharmacology it has led to the discovery of new uses for existing compounds. In the ecological sciences, synthesis methods have been adopted in an effort to consolidate current knowledge into general patterns and principles that can be used to advance the field and inform policy decisions [15].

Data Sharing and Data Reuse

Research synthesis relies on data being shared in a reusable format that is both accessible and understandable. Within CSCW the challenges of data reuse are well known. Lack of contextual information on how and where data are produced [11] leads to difficulties in data interpretation [4] and concerns about data quality [37]. Understanding how variables are constructed is a highly collaborative and time-consuming effort [29]. Often engagement with original study staff is the only way to obtain the contextual information needed to assess data relevance for reuse [20].

Standardization

One of the ways heterogeneity, both in terms of disciplinary differences and data formats, is being addressed is through standardization. It is argued that in order to talk about data in the aggregate, we one must first classify it [8]. Standardization through classification thus facilitates interoperability [20,28] and comparability [8]. Standards have been proposed, designed, and deployed to better facilitate data sharing [18] and data reuse [11] among and across many scientific disciplines. For example, in ecology, the Long-Term Ecological Research (LTER) Network introduced the Ecological Metadata Language (EML) to standardize data collection and reporting across the network [18]. Although intended to preserve datasets for the long-term, the process of ascribing standardized metadata paradoxically resulted in a loss of contextual information that was needed for data reuse [17].

The move towards standardization is one of the reasons why synthesis has been successful in highly structured, mature fields such as biology. Standardized study procedures, data reporting, and metadata practices across subdisciplines makes data reuse and integration more tractable [5]. Disciplinary databases, such as the sequencing database

GenBank, further simplify synthesis by providing standardized data in one centralized location. The same cannot be said for LCS. Logistical and technical challenges in locating and integrating large sets of cases from its vastly differing disciplines, and variations in research questions, scales of analysis, and theoretical models make research synthesis a particular challenge for LCS.

METHODS AND APPROACH

The data we present here are based on an ongoing multi-year ethnographically informed field study of synthetic processes in Land Change Science. This study informs a larger NSF-funded research project, GLOBE, which seeks to design cyberinfrastructure to support LCS meta-study practices [36]. The authors have been core team members from the project inception as designers, UX evaluators, and participant observers.

At the time of this writing, we have been observing this research community for 42 months. We have facilitated a community-driven survey; we have undertaken observations at international workshops and scientific meetings; and we have conducted lab visits and semi-structured interviews. We have also completed a systematic document review of 21 LCS meta-studies.

The survey was a community driven examination of the state and trajectory of LCS research. All questions were designed by community representatives to reflect their own collective interests and concerns. It was administered to the 650 attendees of the premier conference venue for LCS – the triennial Global Land Project Open Science Meeting (OSM) in Berlin Germany, in 2014. This afforded us the rare opportunity to survey the majority of the international LCS population at a point of communal self-reflection. Through the survey we were able to obtain a baseline understanding of the community, including their common practices, tools, and perspectives. This helped us to situate our field findings within the larger population. The final survey sample consisted of 205 respondents, representing a 32% response rate. The majority of web-based survey questions were open-ended.

Our attendance at the OSM also afforded us the opportunity to meet and interact with conference participants, observe sessions, and test the beta-release of the GLOBE system with prospective users via tutorial sessions and a staffed help-desk.

In contrast, our participation in the workshops was strictly observational. This provided unimpeded access to unprompted community reflection and discussion on the strengths, challenges, and opportunities of research synthesis in LCS. Four international workshops have been observed to date: 1) Australia (November 2011), which focused on improving scientific tools to support an integrated understanding of human dimensions of global change; 2) The Netherlands (May 2012), which focused on synthesis methods in LCS; 3) the United States (June 2013), which focused on the content of LCS meta-studies; and 4) Germany (March 2014), which focused on the use of synthesis in land change modelling.

The semi-structured interviews and lab visits have allowed us to further understand the reasons why LCS researchers have adopted research synthesis methods, and the techniques and processes they use for producing their meta-studies. Twelve in-depth interviews have been completed with individuals who have either finished a meta-study or who are in the process of conducting a meta-study. Interviewees were all academics and held the following positions: Associate Professor (2), Assistant Professor (5), Postdoctoral Researcher (4), and recent PhD graduate (1).

The authors transcribed all data for iterative open-coding in Nvivo, generated and reviewed analytic memos of core themes, and visualized emergent categories in a flow diagram. We actively cross-compared survey findings with the field data.

FINDINGS

Research Synthesis in Land Change Science

In the survey, we asked respondents if they had ever conducted a research synthesis of land use change: 51% indicated that they had; 40% indicated they had not; and, 8% were unsure. We then asked them to indicate which types of research synthesis they had conducted, with categories adopted from [23], prompting them to select all types that applied to their experience (see Figure 1). The most highly reported form of research synthesis was the literature review (74%), followed by cross-site comparisons (49%) and remote sensing analyses (49%). Case-oriented meta-analyses, variable-oriented meta-analyses, and cross-site data analyses were each reported by 25% of respondents, and cross-site meta-data analyses were reported by 22%. Sixteen percent indicated that they had conducted a meta-analysis of effect sizes.

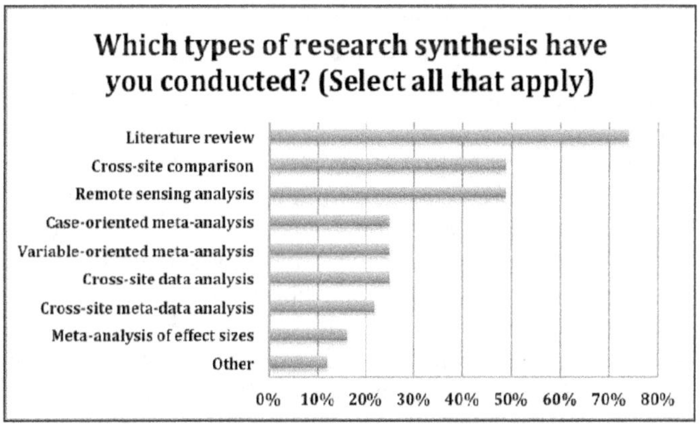

Figure 1: Percentage of respondents who had conducted each type of LCS research synthesis

(Re)defining Land Change Science Through Research Synthesis

In the survey and interviews we asked participants to reflect on what they considered to be the foremost strengths and weaknesses of research synthesis in LCS. A common theme emerged: Research synthesis was seen as a way to move the community forward, from an interdisciplinary group of researchers towards a unique transdiscipline with its own holistic approach. As we continued our analysis, we came to see that this view was prevalent throughout the many workshops, scientific meetings, and conferences we had observed. There was a general sense that synthesis is what "*makes [LCS] a discipline, as opposed to a set of individual fields with shared agendas*" (survey respondent 114).

Integrating Disparate Knowledge

At its core, research synthesis is about integrating disparate knowledge and information to elicit novel findings or insights [16]. Our participants viewed knowledge integration as a strength of synthesis in LCS as it affords the consolidation of knowledge produced in multiple individual case studies. Research synthesis enables the "*bringing together of data and lessons from multiple cases to assess the variety of drivers and outcomes of land-change*" (SR76). It also facilitates the integration of knowledge from the diverse disciplines that study LCS, thereby "*making links between research areas explicit and allowing the field to build on existing findings and experience*" (SR113).

Through this integration our participants believed that new patterns and trends would emerge from the data. This new information would then facilitate a greater understanding of the underlying reasons for differences and commonalities. It would uncover common characteristics of land change processes, drivers, and their consequences, and it would elicit information on how many locations were experiencing the same phenomena. This in turn would afford a "*systematic overview of what knowledge already exists*" (SR196), guiding future research directions and supporting greater generalization of findings.

Our participants also believed that through knowledge integration they would be able to uncover trends in the LCS knowledge base. This includes both trends in what types of research have been conducted and understanding what areas of the world have been over- or underrepresented in studies. An associate professor in our interview sample described how his study of swidden (i.e., slash and burn agriculture) in the tropics allowed him to uncover an unequal distribution of studies. He found that while studies in Central America were numerous, there were very few studies of swidden in Africa. Similarly, a postdoctoral researcher described how she used a meta-analytic approach to understand the distribution of research on the Sahel[1]. In this process, she identified gaps in coverage that she then used to drive her future research projects. Knowledge integration therefore enables LCS researchers to point to "*the next research agenda*" (SR118).

Finally, our participants expressed a belief that knowledge integration would drive standardization. Through synthesis, the LCS community would be able to establish a "*common understanding of terms, research priorities, and concepts*" that would make LCS "*appear less diffuse*" (SR26). It could thus enable a transformation from an interdiscipline with divergent methods and goals to a formalized transdiscipline with a common language, research vision, and methodology.

Geographic Information Systems (GIS) provide a central means of standardization in LCS. As a community focused on studying specific Earth systems, rather than abstract processes such as in chemistry, spatial context is paramount. Spatiality is a fundamental component of all LCS research and is one of the ways that the community is defining what it means to be a LCS researcher: All data and findings must be reported relative to specific locations on the planet. For researchers from other disciplines interested in doing LCS research, they must therefore learn to situate their data in space and care about more than just reified processes.

Generating New Knowledge

Through research synthesis, LCS researchers generate new insights. Our participants identified three main ways this new knowledge advances the field. First, they described how synthesis enables theory building. This finding is consistent with a recent study of 181 LCS meta-studies that found that one-third of those studies were aimed at theory generation (comment at US workshop; see also [23]). One survey respondent described this desire to theorize as:

> I think trying to come up with generalizable outcomes across these various case studies is a lofty and necessary goal, because of a need for generalized theory making about how land change occurs and the many interactions across spatial and temporal aspects of those things affecting those changes (SR61).

As a research community whose goal is often to inform practice, coherent theories about how land use changes are important for decision-making and to direct the future of land use policy. These theories can also be used to inform the development of tools to help guide future research directions: "*[global theory is] important in the area where research informs practice because we can use this theory in places where case studies [are] not yet done to help build models, scenarios, predictions*" (SR164). Understanding

[1] The Sahel represents the semidesert area of the Sahara that stretches from Mauritania to Chad.

the global context of local knowledge allows for this knowledge to be transferred to areas of the world that have not yet been examined and for LCS researchers to make informed predictions about these places.

While theory building is a prime motivator of research synthesis in LCS, an epistemic tension exists between those researchers who believe that the integration of disparate knowledge can lead to generalized theories of land use change and those who contend that due to the biases inherent in case study and interdisciplinary research, synthesis can only provide a general overview of interesting patterns and trends. Context is the crux of this tension. An interviewed associate professor identified three biases of case study research that impact the usefulness of research synthesis for theory building: 1) disciplinary biases, which refer to choices of concepts and indicators used in a case study; 2) sampling biases, which deal with when, where, and at what scale a case study was conducted; and, 3) doctoral dissertation biases, which refer to the fact that dissertations, which make up the bulk of the case study literature, seek to prove that a specific problem exists to demonstrate their novel contribution. This individual further argued that LCS researchers cannot avoid these in their research synthesis because there is an overrepresentation of case studies in the literature that fall victim to these biases.

In light of these biases, some of our participants stressed the importance of not overgeneralizing the findings of research synthesis. They cautioned against "*trying to extract too globally applicable lessons, whilst most decisions driving land-change are taken locally under the influence of locally specific contexts*" (SR76). They urged researchers to pay attention to the different contexts in which land change science is conducted (SR112) and they encouraged others to account for the limitations in the synthetic approaches used and to not overstate findings (SR113). Whether or not LCS researchers believe synthesis can enable generalized theories of land use change depends largely on their worldview. Those researchers who hold a more positivist perspective are more likely to agree that generalization is possible through synthesis, whereas more interpretivist and critical researchers downplay this possibility. A main challenge of LCS research therefore is the ability to "*transgress current biases imposed by differences in paradigm between researchers*" (SR114).

Our participants also described how synthesizing data benefits policy. In the survey and workshops, synthesis was expressed as a way to concisely explain trends, patterns, drivers, and impacts of land use change to non-scientists. Indeed, one workshop participant argued that if nothing else "*meta-analyses should make the findings from the literature more accessible to policymakers*" (Amsterdam workshop, presenter slides). While academics generally appreciate nuance, policy makers typically want simple guidance on what to do (comment at US workshop). Synthesis makes access to scientific results relevant for these policy makers through the reduction of extraneous data. This finding is also consistent with the previously mentioned study, which found that one-fifth of meta-studies were focused on informing policy (comment at US workshop; see also [23]).

Additionally, the respondents noted that research synthesis methods could be used to support and enhance model building. In a workshop at the GLP-OSM, they described how synthesis, and more specifically meta-studies, could be used to determine the types of behaviour that are likely to be important for the model. It could also be used to identify missing parameters that should be included in the model, as well as to parameterize the model, using the literature to ensure that variables were reporting in the correct range. Throughout the workshop, synthesis was viewed as a means to enhance models, whereas models were never discussed as a way to enhanced synthesis research. This finding is also consistent with [23], which found that 7% of meta-studies were focused on informing model building.

Comparing the Incomparable

Our participants identified a number of impediments to useful synthesis. Issues of data comparability, in terms of different methods, scales of analysis, and context, greatly impact researchers' ability to adequately synthesize data:

> For a good synthesis, you need research that is comparable to a certain degree. As research characteristics are sometimes very specific or local, it is difficult to know whether cases are comparable with each other (SR40).

The lack of comparable data means that LCS researchers are confronted with the reality that to do research synthesis means having to find ways to "*compare the incomparable*", such as when trying to integrate qualitative interview results with statistical spatial analyses (SR188). Research synthesis is further complicated by the fact that case studies frequently differ on how they report and weight variables; important factors in one study are often absent in another study. This results in a "*small universe of usable cases*" for synthesis (US workshop, presenter slides).

While these challenges are generally well known in CSCW, LCS differs in meaningful ways that make data integration particularly difficult for this community. One notable complication is "*dealing with [the] complexity of the coupled human-natural system*" (SR120). LCS research does not focus systems, human and natural, in isolation, but rather examines the interplay of the two. Mixing bio-physical data with socio-economic data is a much more complex form of cross-disciplinary knowledge integration than dealing with each system independently.

Another difficulty is dealing with the many different scales at which land use changes are studied. Effectively linking land change science processes with "*material cycles and other biogeochemical dynamics in different spatial and temporal scales*" (SR118) is a particular concern. Our participants called for the need to find ways to harmonize the data in order to resolve these mismatches in scale.

Conducting Research Synthesis: Tools, Techniques, and Processes

Like all scientific endeavours, research synthesis relies on the use of specific tools, techniques, and processes. In this section we describe how these are used by LCS researchers, with a focus on how they both enable and constrain synthesis activities.

Searching for Data

All research syntheses start with a search to identify published results from projects investigating issues relevant to the purpose of the meta-study. We found that in LCS this consists of two approaches: the use of multidisciplinary citation databases, such as Web of Knowledge, which allow for searching across many disciplines simultaneously, and social searching, tapping into one's social network to obtain difficult to locate data. Each of these is described in turn.

The survey suggests that locating cases almost always begins with a keyword search in Web of Knowledge or Google Scholar, similar to the following:

> keywords: (swidden or shifting cultivation or (slash and burn)) and (change or driver* or impact) for studies published in 2000-2010) (Amsterdam workshop, presenter slides).

A postdoctoral researcher in our interview sample explained how he used keyword searches to locate cases for his synthesis study on agricultural change in Europe. As these types of land changes have been studied by different disciplines, he chose Web of Knowledge in order to systematically search across publications from multiple disciplines simultaneously. In the process, he uncovered a core challenge of LCS research: determining the correct keywords or keyword combinations. His searches either yielded too many or too few results. He finally settled on a 'good enough' sample of 3,000 cases, which he narrowed down to 200 that he reviewed individually for relevancy. This resulted in a sample of 60 cases, which he further expanded to 140 cases following a cross-referencing exercise in Google Scholar.

Not all synthesis studies in LCS lend themselves to the use of citation databases. In some cases, the data researchers' rely on is not found in peer-reviewed journals or conference proceedings, but rather in the grey literature of government reports and project websites. For these types of studies, Google is most often used for basic searches to get a sense of the general landscape. Most REDD+ projects[2], for example, have not been published in academic venues and therefore citation databases are not effective search tools:

> Peer-reviewed journals don't help with REDD+ projects because the information I'm after is not published in peer-reviewed journals. So I have to access project ports, which is more the type of grey literature but which is more inclusive in the way they report things... only very few REDD+ projects have also peer-reviewed publications out on their project. Actually it's quite rare. That's the thing about doing land use science... the real information you need is often not available in peer-reviewed publications but you need to get it through stakeholders or grey literature or other sources (interview, postdoctoral researcher).

To overcome some of the logistical challenges imposed by the limitations of citation databases, LCS researchers are turning to their social networks and original case study authors to obtain this difficult to find information. In the survey, respondents proclaimed that, *"Colleagues and social networks have been more important for finding difficult to obtain datasets"* (SR71) and the *"best "technology" [is to] contact the authors behind the data!"* (SR149)

This social search approach not only helps address issues in locating data across disciplinary boundaries, but also with obtaining full case details. If results are published at all, they are often incomplete as this scholar notes:

> I mean without their input this analysis would not be possible because it's often data that is not published yet or is data that is even if it would be published ... it's information that is not provided in one publication (interview, postdoctoral researcher).

Enlisting the help of colleagues and original authors then is often the only way to obtain the provenance information required for successful synthesis. However, this may also unnecessarily complicate the search process and delay the meta-study. One of our associate professors described how his invitation to experts to submit additional papers for his meta-study meant that the dataset was constantly evolving. Each time a new paper was submitted, he had to update the Excel spreadsheet and the analysis had to be redone. He eventually stopped this process because he needed to reach a point where the dataset was complete so the final analysis could be done.

Transforming Data

A challenge of all interdisciplinary research is that data comes in multiple formats and these formats are usually not readily comparable. Researchers must then first transform the data to a standardized format before it can be

[2] REDD+ stands for Reducing Emissions from Deforestation and Forest Degradation. Its main objectives are to mitigate climate change by reducing and removing greenhouse gases through enhanced forest management in developing countries

synthesized: "*Each paper talks differently about the same topic. They don't use the same words. But in the end if you want to summarize you need to put them in an overarching category*" (interview, assistant professor).

In LCS, data transformation is a do-it-yourself project achieved with the help of different end user programming tools [25]. The two most commonly identified in the survey were R and Microsoft Excel. The use of these reflects differences in how the community understands and deals with the amount and types of data that need to be transformed. While all data is quantified for research synthesis in LCS, the degree to which data is separated from its context during this process differs.

The use of the statistical language R was a favourite among LCS researchers working with large datasets:

> I like program languages, in general, because data comes in different formats and have to be organized before being used for modeling and research (SR72).

While this community also uses native quantitative data, our participants expressed far fewer concerns about the need to transform this type of data. In the interviews, they consistently mentioned the processes they used to transform qualitative data to allow for quantitative comparison. A post-doctoral researcher, for instance, showed how he had transformed qualitative descriptions of significant drivers of land use change from a narrative account to a numeric representation that would allow him to run statistical analyses on the data (see Figure 2). If the case study authors had reported that a driver had a significant relation to land use change, he coded this as a "1" if present and "0" if not.

In the process of transforming qualitative data, contextual information about the data is lost. In an effort to preserve some context, some LCS researchers have adopted coding practices that not only quantify qualitative data but that also provide qualifiers for why the data was transformed in a particular way. In describing his data transformation practices, another post-doctoral researcher indicated that he tries to retain contextual information by attaching qualifiers to his codes: "*If I put a 1, I note or give a quote from the report qualifying why there is a 1*" (interview, postdoctoral researcher).

The desire to balance the need for large-scale data transformation on the one hand with the preservation of context on the other hand, has led some LCS researchers to adopt programs such as Excel that afford data transparency:

> I was thinking of using a database manager like Access or others and developing a form to put in a structured way the data, but I found that is sometimes too restrictive and that it's more easy if you have one [Excel] spreadsheet where you can easily add a column or skip through columns and compare and so on. Of course… it can get a lot of columns, but somehow this makes it more transparent. And you are better able to understand your data (interview, postdoctoral researcher)

While this participant identifies the potential benefits of using a database manager to create forms to transform, organize, and search across his data, he also realizes the limitations it would impose, in particular the loss of data transparency.

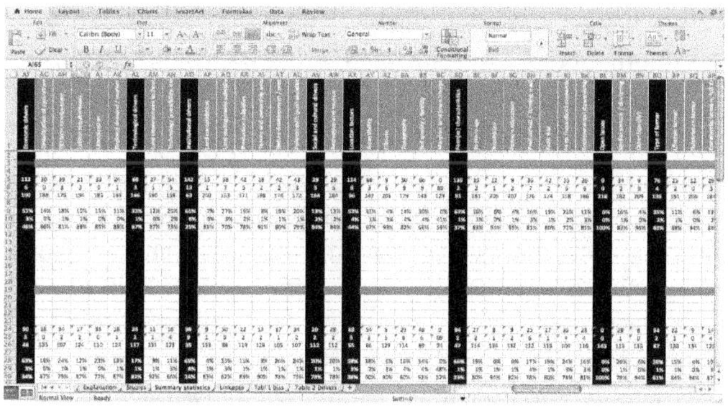

Figure 2: Interview participant's Excel spreadsheet providing an example of how data is transformed to enable synthesis

Interpreting Data

Like others who have studied data reuse in CSCW, we observed challenges with data interpretation and concerns about data quality. Participants likened data interpretation in LCS to "*comparing apples to oranges*" since land use change has been studied from so many different disciplinary perspectives (SR65). To overcome this they have adopted a number of specific techniques.

The use of global datasets of variables that geographically cover the extent of the Earth's terrestrial surface is one way to deal this complexity. While we continue to investigate the different ways in which these datasets are used in LCS, our initial findings point to two ways they help fill gaps in understanding. This is reported in one LCS meta-study as:

> A common problem in the meta-analysis of qualitative and narrative case studies is the comparability of the driving factors mentioned, and the limitations on extrapolating the results due to their qualitative character. We have, therefore, used georeferenced datasets, in addition to the commonly-used qualitative meta-analysis, to describe in a comparative manner, the location conditions of the case-studies [1:2].

As discussed previously, data transformation is a necessary process of data synthesis. Instead of inferring what the case study authors meant by certain variables and then organizing similar variables into an overarching category, these researchers chose to use global datasets to help interpret and describe the locational conditions of the case studies used in their meta-analysis. This takes an alternative, top-down approach to research synthesis, focusing more on which cases can be used to represent certain parts of the world and using global datasets to provide ground support to explain the global results.

In a second example, global datasets are used to help explain and identify predictors of REDD+ project design:

> It would be kind of socioeconomic indicators for different countries or regions that the projects are in for the REDD+ projects. So kind of see if there are indicators on economy, on governance, on biodiversity, that can kind of explain why certain projects are designed the way they are (interview, postdoctoral researcher).

In contrast to the previous example, here global datasets were not used to transform qualitative data to a comparable format, but rather to identify global and regional socioeconomic patterns or indicators that can help explain differences and similarities in REDD+ project design for the regions in which the projects are based.

Another way that LCS researchers deal with data complexity and interpretation is by enlisting the help of original case study authors. Across the workshops participants highlighted the importance of recruiting pertinent case study authors to participate in the meta-study process. Echoing general concerns of data reuse, our participants stressed the importance of author involvement particularly in correctly interpreting data context across disciplines. Through this *participatory meta-analysis* approach, meta-study researchers are better able to ensure the validity in their codes and resulting models.

Our participants described two participatory meta-study styles [35]. The first approach was a *partnered* meta-study, which involved asking case study authors' questions about their study site and having them code their cases based on a standardized classification scheme. In the interviews, an associate professor described how case study authors or experts helped the first author of their meta-study with any uncertainties she had with the cases. These authors provided cases that they themselves had worked on.

The second approach was an *interpretative* meta-study, which involved asking case study authors to confirm whether their cases were interpreted correctly and coded accurately. The original authors were then able to amend codes where necessary.

Despite this expressed need for greater cross-disciplinary integration, engaging case study authors from different disciplines is not an easy task. Our participants described difficulties in networking across disciplinary boundaries because they did not know anyone from the other disciplines that they wished to engage. Even in instances where they are able to identify these individuals, there is no guarantee they will be willing to help. To entice case study authors to work with them, participants reported offering co-authorship in exchange for assistance, thus providing an incentive for participation in a project for which they may otherwise not be invested.

Contextualizing Scientific Inquiry through Geographic Information Systems

In the survey, our participants reported the use of Geographic Information Systems to support nearly all stages of the research synthesis process. For instance, GIS is used for "*organizing spatial data*" (SR71) and to find "*GIS layers*" (SR132). This use of GIS by our participants points to the previously discussed inherently spatial nature of LCS research: To do LCS means understanding the spatial situatedness of your data and findings. Another interviewed associate professor described how he used GIS tools to understand the spatial distribution of the case studies used in his meta-analysis. By placing his cases on a map, he was better able to understand where his cases were situated thus identifying underrepresented areas of the world (see Figure 3).

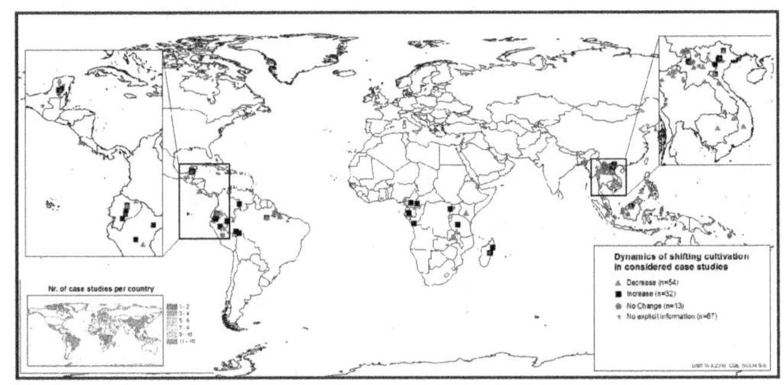

Figure 3: Spatial map of case studies as presented at the Amsterdam Workshop (presenter Slides).

BUILDING CYBERINFRASTRUCTURE TO SUPPORT RESEARCH SYNTHESIS

The LCS research community is working to establish new standards and to define itself as an independent scientific field. Similar to other e-science projects, LCS is an emergent interdiscipline trying to figure out how best to work together given their referent disciplinary differences. Remember that in a related CSCW study, the LTER community adopted an Ecological Metadata Language to standardize data reporting and curation across their network. In general, this was successful, but there were several serious problems translating local practices to global standards [17]. The LCS community is wrestling with a similar problem: Coming up with its own standards to better facilitate interdisciplinary collaboration and to define LCS-style research. Our field study points to four ways they are trying to standardize their discipline: 1) adoption of synthetic research practices; 2) preferences for particular analytic methods; 3) specific processes of data transformation; and 4) an emphasis on the spatial situatedness of data and findings.

It is in this context that we are working to build cyberinfrastructure to better support research synthesis in

LCS. The objective of the GLOBE project is to develop and deploy a suite of tools that will support and advance this scientific practice without necessitating systemic change. We do not want to duplicate efforts that are already working, but rather to identify and address current gaps or deficiencies in the practice that can be better supported. We also seek to amplify meta-study researchers' abilities to manage an order of magnitude more data than they are currently able. In an ideal world, GLOBE-enabled analyses will become one of the new standards for LCS; similar to how EML became foundational for the LTER network. We will now illustrate a few examples of how these findings have come to inform the design and refinement of GLOBE.

Supporting Geographic Search

The value of search lies in its ability to return results relevant for the user's query. Our research reveals that for certain types of information traditional keyword searches may not be adequate. We observed in the interviews, for example, that disciplinary differences in language and representation made it challenging for our participants to correctly determine the appropriate keywords or keyword combinations necessary to find relevant information for synthesis. As a community grounded in geography, traditional citation databases do not effectively support geographically based search. While place name keyword searches can pull cases that reference a specific geographic location, such as "Brazil", they cannot confirm if the case is actually located in the specified area. Representing data on a map assists both with general search but also with sense-making across the results: LCS researchers can better assess data relevance when they understand where in the world the data is located. Visualizing case searches in space is therefore quite powerful for them.

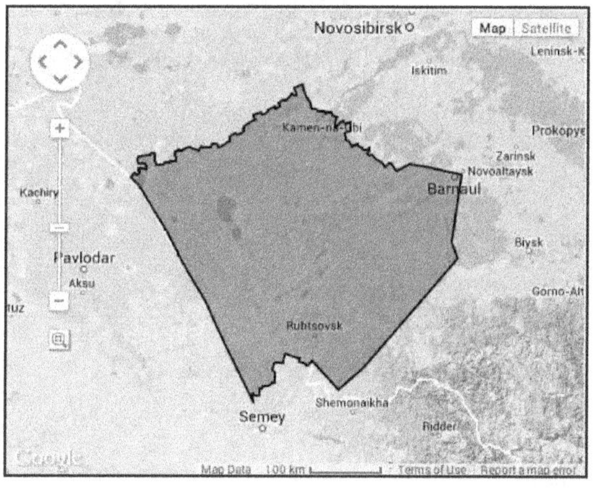

Figure 4: Geographic representation of a case study in GLOBE

We designed GLOBE as a geographic search engine specifically for this purpose. We wanted to make it easier for LCS researchers to understand and interpret their data in a way that makes sense to them: Grounded on a map. While other location-based search engines exist (e.g., JournalMap[3]) they are based solely on points (i.e, latitude by longitude coordinates), providing very little detail about the actual study site. GLOBE goes deeper by providing full geometries that represent the actual case study area (see Figure 4).

However, GLOBE does not just provide simple geographic search; it also allows users to search for similar cases based on a wide array of global variables. This similarity search assesses the degree to which a particular case study site (or geographic location) is similar to other areas of the Earth's surface based on user-defined variables and filters. Similar cases are then represented on a map and can be saved to a collection for use in a meta-study (see Figure 5).

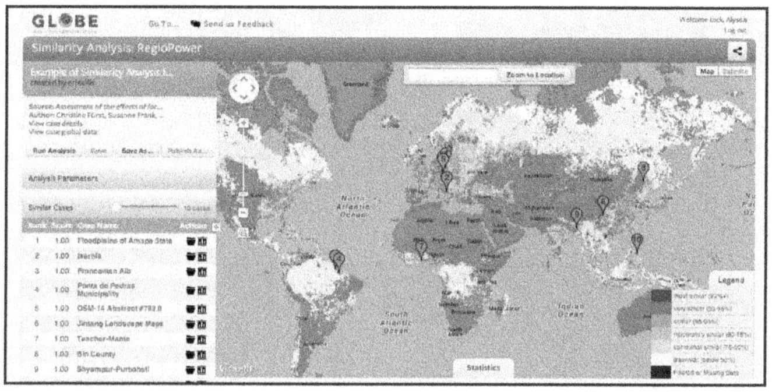

Figure 5: GLOBE similarity analysis

Linking Cases to Authors

As discussed earlier, often the data needed for research synthesis is not available in peer-reviewed journals, but commonly found in the grey literature of reports and project websites. Even when data is accessible, it may not always be understandable. In the process of moving from study site to publication, important details about study procedures are often lost through the deletion of process [19]. Recall that in line with what [29,37] have suggested, we found that meta-study practice is not a sole author activity, but often involves enlisting the help of original study authors to both access difficult to obtain data and to learn about how the data were constructed. While author engagement has been found in other studies of data reuse, few studies have suggested ways of designing cyberinfrastructure to support this relationship. One noticeable exception is the C-IKnow Project [31] which provides a way for researchers to find the original authors for the project data they are using in their study.

GLOBE makes case study author identification and participation a central focus of the system. Where we differ from the C-IKnow project is in facilitating direct contact by providing links to the author's verified email and personal website (see Figure 6). Each case entered into GLOBE is attached to an originating author with clear provenance

---

[3] JournalMap is a scientific literature search engine that offers location-based and variable search.

metadata. System-generated quality metrics help identify cases with weak links that will likely be difficult to interpret and integrate. In these cases authors are invited by the system to work collaboratively with case contributors to verify, correct, or reenter case details and geographic information. Cases vetted in collaboration with case study authors earn higher quality scores.

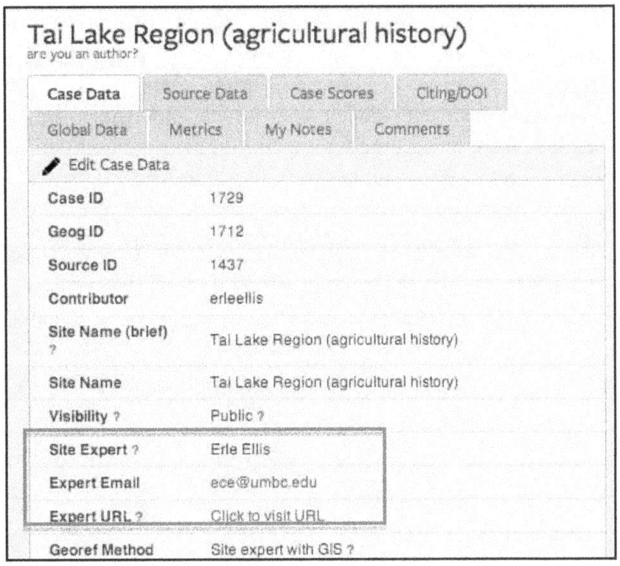

Figure 6: Case study author contact information

Linking cases to authors also allows meta-study researchers to more easily identify and build a network of individuals conducting research in a particular area of the world, on a specific topic, or variable. This information can be used to not only develop a network of potential future collaborators, but also to help identify underrepresented areas to study and potentially mobilize research resources to address this deficiency.

Designing for Transparency

Recall that research synthesis requires that diverse data be transformed to enable comparability. In LCS, this need for data transformation is often weighed against the need to preserve context. Understanding under what local conditions the data was produced is important to fully comprehend the data. This is particularly true of qualitative data. Data transformation risks loss of context by reducing complex narrative explanations to mere binary reporting of "absence" or "presence" for statistical analysis. In an effort to simultaneously preserve context and transform data, we found that our participants adopted tools that would support both tasks.

The LCS community's value of transparency for data transformation has changed (and continues to change) our design of GLOBE from an opaque system, obscuring the mechanics of data transformation, to a more transparent system that provides visualizations and metrics about data transformation. Initially all analyses in GLOBE were black boxed by design. Similarity and representativeness are nuanced mathematical concepts and required fairly intricate manipulations in the core Global Collaboration Engine [30]. Given this complexity, we had decided that it would be best to hide the algorithmic processing from the user. However, in the process of beta testing, we learned that this lack of transparency made it difficult for users to understand and trust the output. They were used to the iterative control they had in R or visual representations they had in Excel.

An instructive example of this tension is in the process of binning for representativeness. A representativeness analysis assess the degree to which a given collection of study sites represents an unbiased sample of a specified global extent based on a set of global variables, answering the question: how much of the variance across the planet is explained, or represented, by my case collection? Binning is used to understand how the universe of all cases is parsed against a collection of cases based on a set of global land variables. The resulting output informs the user to the degree and nature of the biases in their collection (see Figure 7). In testing the system with users we learned that in order to be understandable, the processes involved in binning required more transparency than we initially provided. This led us to include contextual information about each bin, including how many cases were needed to make the collection less biased. We also added interactive features that allow users to toggle between different scales (e.g., log and ordinal). The latest system update includes an interface for users to easily find cases to add to their collection to make it more representative.

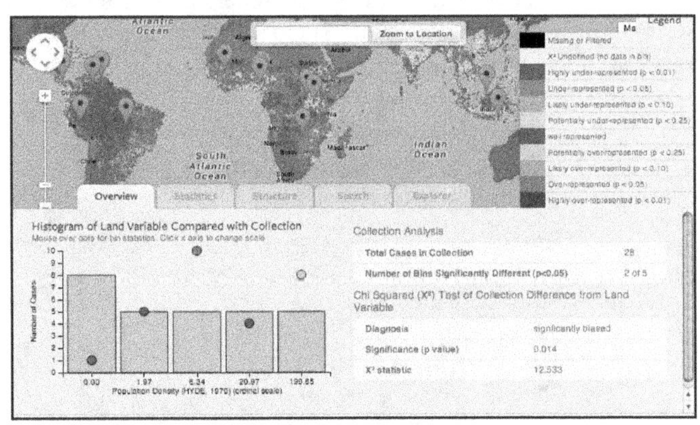

Figure 7: Binning visualization in GLOBE

CONCLUSIONS

In this paper, we have examined research synthesis in the emergent interdiscipline of Land Change Science. Through our investigation, we have uncovered new insights into the sociotechnical interplay between scientific practice and the tools used and designed to support this practice. Our study shows how technology not only enables research synthesis by providing the tools needed to find and integrate large datasets, but also constrains the process due to mismatches in what current tools support and what the community actually needs.

By exposing the geographic situatedness of LCS research and the strategies for involving authors, we have furthered our understanding of synthetic processes. The identification of geography as a core component of the LCS identity helps us to rethink the ways we approach the design for data search. Traditional keyword searches afforded by citation databases may not be the most practical or useful way to search for multi-disciplinary data or for data that does not lend itself well to textual descriptions. For research communities with a common characteristic that is core to their identity (as geography is to LCS) and which is computationally tractable, the design of interactive search visualizations that support the way the community understands their data will help improve and simplify research activities.

This study also extends the data reuse literature by providing a better understanding of the strategies used for engaging original authors in the research synthesis process. Through *participatory meta-analysis*, case study authors are enlisted to either code their cases based on a pre-defined classification scheme or to confirm whether or not their cases have been coded properly. As incentive for their participation, they are offered co-authorship on the resulting meta-analysis.

By identifying the role of research synthesis for LCS and how this community has adopted tools to support this scientific practice, we have been able to develop cyberinfrastructure that will ideally address deficiencies in current approaches and enhance researchers' ability to do research synthesis in the future. This understanding of the role of sociotechnical systems in actual collaborative work practices has long been a central focus of CSCW.

ACKNOWLEDGMENTS

We would like to thank the LCS community and the Global Land Project for their support of this research. We would also like to thank our fellow GLOBE team members, in particular Erle Ellis and Jared Margulies. This research has been supported by NSF award #115210 'GLOBE: Evolving New Global Workflows for Land Change Science'.

REFERENCES

1. Asselen, S. van, Verburg, P.H., Vermaat, J.E., and Janse, J.H. Drivers of Wetland Conversion: a Global Meta-Analysis. *PLoS ONE 8*, 11 (2013), e81292.
2. Bietz, M.J., Ferro, T., and Lee, C.P. Sustaining the development of cyberinfrastructure: an organization adapting to change. *Proceedings of the ACM 2012 conference on Computer Supported Cooperative Work*, ACM (2012), 901–910.
3. Bietz, M.J. and Lee, C.P. Collaboration in Metagenomics: Sequence Databases and the Organization of Scientific Work. In I. Wagner, H. Tellioğlu, E. Balka, C. Simone and L. Ciolfi, eds., *ECSCW 2009*. Springer London, 2009, 243–262.
4. Birnholtz, J.P. and Bietz, M.J. Data at work: supporting sharing in science and engineering. *Proceedings of the 2003 international ACM SIGGROUP conference on Supporting group work*, ACM (2003), 339–348.
5. Blake, C. and Pratt, W. Collaborative information synthesis I: A model of information behaviors of scientists in medicine and public health. *Journal of the American Society for Information Science and Technology 57*, 13 (2006), 1740–1749.
6. Blake, C. and Pratt, W. Collaborative information synthesis II: Recommendations for information systems to support synthesis activities. *Journal of the American Society for Information Science and Technology 57*, 14 (2006), 1888–1895.
7. Blettner, M. and Schlattmann, P. Meta-Analysis in Epidemiology. In W. Ahrens and I. Pigeot, eds., *Handbook of Epidemiology*. Springer Berlin Heidelberg, 2005, 829–857.
8. Bowker, G.C. and Star, S.L. *Sorting things out: classification and its consequences.* MIT Press, 1999.
9. Cooper, H. and Hedges, L.V. *The Handbook of Research Synthesis.* Russell Sage Foundation, New York, 1994.
10. Ellis, E.C. and Ramankutty, N. Putting people in the map: anthropogenic biomes of the world. *Frontiers in Ecology and the Environment 6*, 8 (2007), 439–447.
11. Faniel, I.M. and Jacobsen, T.E. Reusing Scientific Data: How Earthquake Engineering Researchers Assess the Reusability of Colleagues' Data. *Computer Supported Cooperative Work (CSCW) 19*, 3-4 (2010), 355–375.
12. Hackett, E.J. and Parker, J.N. Research Groups. In W. Bainbridge, ed., *Leadership in Science and Technology: A Reference Handbook*. SAGE Publications, 2011, 165–174.
13. Hackett, E.J. and Parker, J.N. Ideas, Emotions, and Coherent Group Development. 2013.
14. Hackett, E.J. and Parker, J.N. Ecology reconfigured: Organizational innovation, group dynamics and scientific change. In M. Merz and P. Sormani, eds., *The Local Configuration of New Research Fields*. Springer, 2014.
15. Hackett, E.J. and Parker, J.N. From Solomon's house to synthesis centers. In T. Heinze and R. Muench, eds., *Institutional and Organizational Innovation in Science*. Palgrave Macmillan, 2014.
16. Hampton, S.E. and Parker, J.N. Collaboration and Productivity in Scientific Synthesis. *BioScience 61*, 11 (2011), 900–910.

17. Karasti, H., Baker, K.S., and Halkola, E. Enriching the Notion of Data Curation in E-Science: Data Managing and Information Infrastructuring in the Long Term Ecological Research (LTER) Network. *Computer Supported Cooperative Work 15*, 4 (2006), 321–358.
18. Karasti, H., Baker, K.S., and Millerand, F. Infrastructure Time: Long-term Matters in Collaborative Development. *Computer Supported Cooperative Work (CSCW) 19*, 3-4 (2010), 377–415.
19. Latour, B. and Woolgar, S. *Laboratory Life: The Construction of Scientific Facts.* Princeton University Press, 1979.
20. Lee, J., Zhang, J., Zimmerman, A., and Lucia, A. DataNet: An emerging cyberinfrastructure for sharing, reusing and preserving digital data for scientific discovery and learning. *AIChE Journal 55*, 11 (2009), 2757–2764.
21. Lenoir, T. Shaping Biomedicine as an Information Science. *Proceedings of the 1998 Conference on the History and Heritage of Science Information Systems*, Information Today, Inc (1998), 27–45.
22. Lutters, W.G. and Winter, S. Virtual Organizations. In W. Bainbridge, ed., *Leadership in science and technology: A reference handbook.* SAGE Publications, Thousand Oaks, Calif., 2012, 334–343.
23. Magliocca, N.R., Rudel, T.K., Verburg, P.H., et al. Synthesis in land change science: methodological patterns, challenges, and guidelines. *Regional Environmental Change*, (2014), 1–16.
24. Moran, E.F., Skole, D.L., and Ii, B.L.T. The Development of the International Land-Use and Land-Cover Change (LUCC) Research Program and Its Links to NASA's Land-Cover and Land-Use Change (LCLUC) Initiative. In D.G. Gutman, A.C. Janetos, C.O. Justice, et al., eds., *Land Change Science.* Springer Netherlands, 2004, 1–15.
25. Nardi, B.A. *A Small Matter of Programming: Perspectives on End User Computing.* The MIT Press, Cambridge, MA, 1993.
26. Ribes, D. and Bowker, G.C. Organizing for Multidisciplinary Collaboration: The Case of the Geosciences Network. In G.M. Olson, A. Zimmerman and N. Bos, eds. *Scientific Collaboration on the Internet.* The MIT Press, 2008, 310–330.
27. Ribes, D. and Finholt, T.A. Representing Community: Knowing Users in the Face of Changing Constituencies. *Proceedings of the 2008 ACM Conference on Computer Supported Cooperative Work*, ACM (2008), 107–116.
28. Ribes, D. and Lee, C.P. Sociotechnical Studies of Cyberinfrastructure and e-Research: Current Themes and Future Trajectories. *Computer Supported Cooperative Work (CSCW) 19*, 3-4 (2010), 231–244.
29. Rolland, B. and Lee, C.P. Beyond trust and reliability: reusing data in collaborative cancer epidemiology research. *Proceedings of the 2013 conference on Computer supported cooperative work*, ACM (2013), 435–444.
30. Schmill, M.D., Gordon, L.M., Magliocca, N.R., Ellis, E.C., and Oates, T. GLOBE: Analytics for Assessing Global Representativeness. *International Conference on Computing for Geospatial Research and Application (GEOCOM)* (2014) 25–32.
31. Science of Networks in Communities Laboratory. 2011.
32. Sheble, L. Research synthesis: Overview of an intersection with ILS. *Proceedings of the 2012 ASIS&T Annual Meeting*, (2012).
33. Turner, B.L., Lambin, E.F., and Reenberg, A. The emergence of land change science for global environmental change and sustainability. *Proceedings of the National Academy of Sciences 104*, 52 (2007), 20666–20671.
34. Verburg, P.H., Erb, K.-H., Mertz, O., and Espindola, G. Land System Science: between global challenges and local realities. *Current Opinion in Environmental Sustainability 5*, 5 (2013), 433–437.
35. Young, A. and Lutters, W. Collaborative Interpretation in Land Change Science Meta-studies. *Proceedings of the Companion Publication of the 17th ACM Conference on Computer Supported Cooperative Work & Social Computing*, ACM (2014), 269–272.
36. Young, A., Lutters, W.G., Magliocca, N.R., and Ellis, E.C. Designing a System for Land Change Science Meta-study. *CHI '13 Extended Abstracts on Human Factors in Computing Systems*, ACM (2013), 1473–1478.
37. Zimmerman, A. Not by metadata alone: the use of diverse forms of knowledge to locate data for reuse. *Int. J. Digit. Libr. 7*, 1 (2007), 5–16.
38. The Global Land Project. *Global Land Project: Background.* hwww.globallandproject.org/home/background.php.

Anticipation Work: Cultivating Vision in Collective Practice

Stephanie B. Steinhardt
Cornell University
Department of Communication
sbg94@cornell.edu

Steven J. Jackson
Cornell University
Department of Information Science
sjj54@cornell.edu

ABSTRACT
Problems of temporality in distributed cooperative work have emerged as an important theme of CSCW and HCI work. This paper draws on ethnographic fieldwork into large-scale infrastructure development in ecology and ocean science and analyses of futurism in science and technology studies to call attention to "anticipation work": the practices that cultivate and channel expectations of the future, design pathways into those imaginations, and maintain those visions in the face of a dynamic world. We advance three basic claims: first, that long term technological development and sustainability in science is guided by complex and distributed forms of futurism; second, that *all* actors (both individual and collective) orient towards the future (at both temporally close and distant scales); and third, that actors engage in complex and skilled forms of anticipation work – individual and collective, formal and informal – that guide and shape the present character and experience of collaborative life.

Author Keywords
Anticipation; time; temporality; futures; collaboration; infrastructure; ecology; oceanography; futurism.

ACM Classification Keywords
K.4.3 Computer supported collaborative work.

General Terms
Human Factors.

INTRODUCTION

> *"Imaginations of the future, like imaginations of the past, are devices for living in the present."*
>
> Sanz-Menéndez & Cabello [41]

Big data and big science have captured the attention and imagination of scientists and policymakers alike with glossy visions of innovation reaping benefits on a societal scale. Many of our deepest hopes and fears for the future manifest in new trends for data science like "quantified self," "algorithmic living" and "the internet of things" and in the generation of terabytes of data about our communication, bodies, behaviors and Earth. Previously unseen amounts of capital are invested into developing infrastructures which will support the storage and acquisition of these large data sets, whether it be billion-dollar initiatives in social media like Facebook or Twitter, in cybersecurity like those of the NSA, open government such as data.gov, or biotechnology such as 23andMe. And, as climate change, urbanization, and ocean acidification permeate both our public and scientific dialogues about the Earth, researchers and policymakers have been faced with the pressures of planning, constructing and maintaining new scientific systems that produce unprecedented stores of data to answer grand challenge questions, expanding not only the functional ability but also the imagination of science. These innovations are pointed towards the long term, at scales from years to decades to centuries. Answers to the grand challenge questions facing science today depend on whether the future lies in our understanding of a passing present quickly accumulating into one highly auditable trace of big data that represents the world around us.

At the heart of this dialog is a complex bridging between past and future, a fundamental turn to futurism and an increased need for understanding the complex work practices that support and maintain visions of technological advancement. This is a call to more squarely integrate futures – and the work we do to imagine, contest, and produce them – into our studies of sociotechnical systems.

We offer the theory of "anticipation work" as a forward-looking frame to capture practices in the present that cultivate our expectations of the future, design pathways into those imaginations, and maintain those visions in the face of a dynamic world. Anticipation work is the realized, pragmatic and attainable ways actors move toward some imagined future (ex. designing protocols for handling specimens, formalizing data standards, establishing support groups). It is a persistent and permanent feature of everyday life (much like our core theories of articulation and cooperative work), illuminating that which we wish to represent and embody. Anticipation work sensitizes the analyst toward the temporal factors at play in collaborative life and links to spheres broader than the immediate project of study.

Through these actions we can more clearly and critically see futurism in our studies of collaboration, technology development, and big data. Different groups mobilize

CSCW '15, March 14 – 18, 2015, Vancouver, BC, Canada.

http://dx.doi.org/10.1145/2675133.2675298

resources in order to inscribe their visions into the design of systems, including social and organizational structures. While futurism often is wrapped in pledges to build, promises for tomorrow, and vaporware, anticipation work traces the real-time work and adjustments that underwrite any master narrative about the future. Anticipation work helps to us to ask questions of these efforts like: what and who are we building for? Whose voices are found in the design and what are their visions? Who is left out? What will be valued and devalued by design?

We begin by exploring the forms of future work necessarily involved in core CSCW theories of coordination and articulation work, then follow with literatures concerning temporality, futures and anticipatory governance external to CSCW scholarship. Second, we highlight three cases from field work around large-scale collaborative projects in ecology and oceanography that locate anticipation work within arenas of common CSCW concern: standardization, planning and project evolution. Lastly, we assert the ubiquity of anticipation work and discuss its relationship to broader design and policy concerns, both within and beyond the worlds of large-scale collaborative science addressed here.

LITERATURE REVIEW

Concerns and assumptions of a temporal kind are present but muted within even the earliest generations of collaboration scholarship. In fact, the very introduction that conceives CSCW's core theory of articulation work builds from a future-oriented frame:

> "Each project, as defined by its initiator(s), must begin with a vision-an image, an idea, a notion---of what can, might, or should be done. Because the vision does not yet constitute reality, or even necessarily a sense of how to make the vision into reality, the initiator (whether more like a dreamer or a planner) must consider ways and means of implementing the vision; otherwise disruptive problems will haunt the entire project. What is required to attain the goal? What modes of action, what types of work or sequences of tasks, what resources?" [47, p. 166]

Articulation work is motivated and defined by both a futuristic sensibility and by the temporal orderings of work between ad hoc practices and more permanent, institutionalized policies or procedures. Likewise, the theories of cooperative work and coordination mechanisms are contextualized by their temporal boundaries (short-term, long-term, perpetual), where performance and practice are impacted by the time for task and the time limitations of proceduralized work [41]. Each form of work is faced with concerns of a distinctly temporal and forward-thinking manner, yet often in our analyses of cooperative work futurism becomes thinkable only within the confines of project goals and schedules.

In recent years, this recognition has led to a growing chorus of CSCW work arguing that many of the pressing questions around collaborative life turn centrally on problems of *time*. Karasti et. al. [31] call out CSCW's strength in addressing short-term distributed collective practice, yet assert the need for analytic modes that will tackle the growing temporal scales of infrastructure built for the long term. Work concerning "the long now" [36] and "the long term" [18] emphasizes the temporal orientations of infrastructure, bringing to light the complex alignment of goals and social organization across individual, institutional and broader policy arenas that sustain development, maintenance and use. Jackson et. al. [26] argue that all distributed collective action is subject to the ebbs, flows and evolution of rhythms across organizational, infrastructural, biographical and phenomenal dimensions of work and life. Tensions with these temporal forms often highlight the entwined nature of career, life and technological systems and practices which reorient these forms with the long term goals of an infrastructure [12].

Many of these insights have emerged from a body of CSCW work around the challenges and complexities of large-scale collaboration and infrastructure development in the sciences [29], long central to CSCW research. Formative collaboration theory has arisen from the scientific spaces of the WORM genetics community (infrastructure [44]), the Department of Energy's CORE prototype (the collaboratory [51]), and the Stanford Research Institute (groupware [20]). These foundational works provide us understanding of social phenomena that we now take as given: illuminating how collaborative technologies loosen or break bounds between close and distant [35], disciplinary and interdisciplinary [45], and human and nonhuman [33].

In recent years this coupling of CSCW scholarship and sites of scientific inquiry has been legitimized and amplified by the increased funding of research efforts through the National Science Foundation and more direct integration of social science analysis into the scientific research process more broadly (e.g. Charlotte Linde, ethnographer at NASA). This in turn has produced new waves of CSCW scholarship and insight into the dynamics of large-scale collaborative work and practice: the political and economic implications of open or closed data sharing, production and curation [5, 49]; the connection of new infrastructural development to changes in the basic values, experiences and identities of scientific work [28]; the dynamics of scientific software development [25]; the role of materiality in collaborative practice [4, 39]; and opportune strategies for connecting ethnographic analysis with design and policy implications [17, 27].

Over the same period, a largely separate body of work in the fields of science and technology studies and the broader social sciences has called out the remarkable extent to which collaborative practice is influenced by the futures embedded in scientific systems. The future and how people anticipate it (on a continuum of abstract speculation to concrete prediction) is integral to understanding action.

This is an idea tracing back to early works by Max Weber concerning "dual futurity," in which all humans are oriented toward the future and guided by this orientation for action in the present [51]. Expectation is a pathway toward which actors calibrate both private and public behaviors, and provides grounds for negotiation between actors [7]. From the personal, possible and close (ex: "I will get fired for this.") to the collective, abstract and distant (ex: "Humans will need to relocate to another planet."), the continua of anticipation structures and drives human behavior in striking ways.

The anticipatory behaviors that comprise the design, use and maintenance of systemic structures are integral to our understanding of collaborative life across scales. In their conception of the "sociotechnical imaginary," Jasanoff & Kim [30] provide a compelling empirical case in which actors at the national level derive strikingly different expectations of their (nuclear) futures, drawing distinctive demarcations between scientific interest, safety regulation and national innovation [33]. The analysis is rooted in understanding the practices of activism, licensing and litigation which, in aggregate, represent the broader (and quite different) positions of the U.S. and South Korea on nuclear containment - what was regulated and considered hazardous, whose voice was heard in litigation and policymaking, what was imported and trusted, etc. Futures and visions are not merely reflections of the world but are mindfully curated and impact how actors perceive themselves in relation others in the world [10].

While futures in Jasanoff & Kim's piece are defined and pursued, futures can just as easily be broken and lost. For example, despite being touted as the greatest achievement of applied biology, with the potential for bringing adequate food and protein to poor populations and developing nations, Collingridge's illustration in "The Social Control of Technology" [13] shows that the Green Revolution's food production did not lead to a healthier diet for those it intended to impact. The adoption and dissemination of the new infrastructure instead fell to the social realities of poor credit, high costs of produce, inadequate accumulation of land, and widespread discrimination.

Concerns of this kind address the social and political nature that accompanies sites of CSCW scholarlship and the affective character of temporal work. Adams et. al [1] draw the abstract notion of time down to the individual experiences of it. Actors tack between futures, presents and pasts in order to characterize their status, optimize and secure their 'best possible futures' and inhabit a feeling of hopefulness despite uncertainty [1]. The everyday interactions and behaviors of individuals are guided by the positive or negative valence of futures, closely tied to the distance and speed at which those futures are approaching [36]. Adherence to or belief in a particular future can dictate an individual's likelihood to adopt or reject new sociotechnical structures [3, 38, 43]. Technological intervention does not ensure a future and the lived future will differ from the past representations of it [8].

From science and technology studies, the worlds of anticipatory governance and knowledge both emphasize the ways in which the expected consequences of an action, construction or policy may encourage a vision's proliferation or disaster – the continua of anticipation structures and drives human behavior at the individual and collective levels. "Anticipation, then, takes on a Heisenbergian dimension as a form of knowledge that not only guesses about events in the world but directs them in unintended but unavoidable ways" [24, p. 558]. Rather than anticipation being a path dependent form in which the future is inevitably a continuation of the past, anticipatory governance looks at prediction as one among a host of possibilities that shape everyday action and policymaking.

In this paper, we borrow the adjective of "anticipation" and the "work" of Strauss and Schmidt to illuminate how practices in the present define, orient and accommodate to expectations of the future that are often sidelined in our current understandings of collaborative life. This paper tackles the problem of anticipation work: the complex behaviors and practices that define, enact and maintain vision across individual and collective, and temporally close and distant scales. In the context of collaborative life, anticipation work does important things. It illuminates that all actors orient towards the future and places futurism at the center of design and long term sustainability of technological development. And, it sensitizes the analyst toward the temporal factors, emergence and change in the formal and informal performance of everyday action.

The sections that follow explore these propositions in the context of large-scale infrastructural development in ocean science and ecology. We offer three vignettes that trace how actors gather and align futures, and in doing so form regularities which support those futures (and just as often break them). We conclude with three basic arguments: first, that long term technological development and sustainability in science is guided by complex and distributed forms of futurism; second, that all actors (both individual and collective) orient towards the future (at both temporally close and distant scales); and third, that actors engage in complex and skilled forms of anticipation work – individual and collective, formal and informal – that guide and shape the present character and experience of collaborative life.

METHODS

The accounts that follow draw on more than three years of ethnographic fieldwork into patterns of computational change and large-scale infrastructure development in the American earth science research communities, with special attention to two projects – the National Ecological Observatory Network (NEON) and the Ocean Observatories Initiative (OOI) – central to current changes in their respective fields. This included more than 200 interviews with actors in both fields ranging from scientists, engineers, project managers, staff, postdocs, and policymakers. Our observational work took place across a wide variety of sites: actual fields, ecological towers, ships, docks, construction facilities, laboratories, and formal meeting places. This included time spent with boots in mud, at meetings, collecting bugs and small fish, deploying instruments and learning the knots that fasten them.

Transcribed interviews, field notes, photos and related documents (scientific or news media articles, etc.) were collected and qualitatively coded following a grounded theory approach [14, 22]. Each investigator performed fieldwork within a single domain, then together exchanged thoughts, memos, stories and field notes. The emergent themes were then further developed into subsequent memos that guided later round field work and provided the basis for the analysis presented here.

ANTICIPATION WORK & E-INFRASTRUCTURE DEVELOPMENT

The cases that follow build on two leading examples of contemporary collaborative infrastructure development in the sciences. Our first case follows a suite of changes unfolding in American ecology in recent years, driven in part by the development of the U.S.-based National Ecological Observatory Network, or NEON. With a construction budget of $434 million and a thirty-year operation plan, NEON plans to build and distribute consistent and long-term data across more than 100 carefully selected sites that would, taken collectively, provide crucial new input to pressing scientific and public questions around the ecological impacts of climate change, land use change, and invasive species. Building on core data from satellite observation, tower and remote sensing units, and a standardized field sampling program, and a suite of computational and post-processing tools that will package network data into a series of higher level data products, NEON aims to provide the first continental scale portrait of ecological change as it unfolds at the organism, biome, and regional levels. Having successfully navigated its design and planning phases, NEON is now in the midst of a five-year construction process scheduled to culminate in full operational status by 2017 (though parts of the observatory are already collecting live data).

In comparable ways to NEON in ecology, our second site, the Ocean Observatories Initiative (OOI), is breaking down traditional configurations of oceanography that are deeply repositioning the way scientists are relating to their work, their colleagues, their field and their lives outside of science. OOI is an unprecedented undertaking in the field of oceanography worldwide. It is the first observatory of its kind, touted as “the instrumented ocean:” a form of data-centric infrastructure predicated around distributed sensors and sample collection wired continuously to the ocean basin, sea-floor-walking robots, buoys, and gliders - each transmitting data to two dedicated satellites above for open and real-time access to big ocean data for at least 25 years. Scaling upward in both size and in longevity, the OOI is an evolving portrait of the ocean, relaxing many of the constraints of temporality built into more monolithic systems and introducing both immediate access and long-term archives. Not only is OOI operating at multiple temporal scales, but it also mutates as it progresses: adding new connections, instrumentation, geographies and data types as new questions are asked of it. At once long term and malleable, the observatory is not static, nor bounded by a concrete set of potential operations and uses. This is not just a day-by-day change in the form and function of the data network, but also decade-by-decade.

These developments are of deep CSCW interest in their own right: NEON and the OOI each attempt to build, in part through computational means, a form and scale of collaboration that would change the nature of ecological and oceanographic work and organization, with deep implications for practice, training, and policy, but also the core vocational identities that shape and define research as a way of life [27, 28]. But they are also of interest for the significant changes they spell for the basic temporal practice and orientations of their fields. As the following examples make clear, such reorientations initiate and rely on new cascades of anticipation work through which individual and collective futures are imagined, produced, and negotiated.

Case #1: Standards as Anticipation Work

Our first case involves the work of standards and protocol development that dominates current NEON development efforts. As stressed to us repeatedly by informants, standards are central to everything NEON seeks to accomplish. Standards are needed to ensure the comparability of data across space and time, ensuring that measures taken by sensors or field technicians in one time and place can be meaningfully correlated with those emerging from parallel activities in other times, groups, and places. Standards operate as a hedge against human and infrastructural variability, producing consistencies in method and practice across the vast human, natural and temporal scales that NEON is called upon to span. Taken in the abstract, standards are needed to separate the often subtle and complex signals of ecological change from the noise of field variability. More concretely, they establish the line between random collections of bugs in jars (or numbers in spreadsheets) and an integrated and comparable body of data and evidence from which complex scientific work and public decision can proceed.

In practice this proves challenging to achieve, for a wide variety of reasons. Some stem from the range and heterogeneity of field conditions that NEON protocols are required to address (rivers that freeze in the winter or dry up in the summer; soil conditions ranging from rich to non-existent; land cover conditions that lend themselves well to satellite and remote sensing analysis vs. those ill-suited to such methods; etc.). Others connect to the highly distributed nature of NEON field operations, and the need to ensure consistency across a large and dispersed staff of varying backgrounds and research experiences. Others connect to the embedded histories of work by specific sites and investigators, and the widespread hope that NEON will build continuities, not ruptures, with this past. At the most profound level, NEON faces the challenge of standardizing a radically *un*standardized field (or more precisely: a field that has struggled to converge on method and technique above the level of the individual site or PI research program). As one staff scientist explained to us,

> "Because of the breadth of those sampling activities, plants, insects, mammals, aquatic environments and so on, you're sourcing information from a variety of different communities. And even within each of those communities, there are no standard methods of practice. One PI and another PI will differ quite strenuously about the right way to do it, and so there is no standard within the community of practice."

To map and constrain this variability, staff scientists charged with developing the NEON instruments and field protocols engage in elaborate practices of consultation, codification, and field-testing. Coordinators of the various NEON science areas (microbial, plant and insect ecology; soil science; remote sensing; etc.) work closely with area specialists and advisory boards to arrive at standards workable and defensible across the range of disciplines and field conditions connected to NEON operations. As the network moves closer to operations, staff scientists also work increasingly closely with the growing field operations staff to ensure that protocol descriptions are clear, unambiguously described, and implementable across the range of regional sites that constitute the network. This includes processes of 'cold-testing' in which protocol descriptions are handed to field technicians 'raw' to see if the rules and procedures described can be accurately and consistently deciphered from description. It also includes elaborate training exercises in which regional managers and field staff – most with generalist science training, but none with disciplinary expertise across the comparatively vast range of procedures NEON field teams will be called on to perform – are trained in the methods and underlying science questions guiding NEON data collection efforts. These exercises are meant to build consistencies across organizational and geographic variance: ensuring that teams operating in the x and y regions, for example, are sampling air, soil, water and organisms in ways that preserve the integrity and comparability of data across teams and sites. But they are also meant to build consistencies *across time*, guarding against differential interpretation, the accretion of unstructured workarounds, and other forms of protocol 'drift' in ways that ensure that data points produced in 2017 hold the same general meaning as those produced under the potentially radically different conditions of 2047. This work is rendered additionally complicated by the fact that the scientific, natural, and technological worlds NEON is meant to respond to are themselves in flux, in ways that must *also* be accommodated moving forward. In this way, NEON (like other longterm research projects, c.f. [9]) must fix without freezing a complex landscape of change, managing the boundary between constancy and change in ways that protect the 'liveness' and relevance of the project without sacrificing the integrity of its core data products as they shift and evolve through time [9]. The sum total of these efforts, performed through a multiplicity of mundane actions that characterize the ordinary work of NEON in its day-to-day operations, constitutes anticipation work of a particularly skilled and complex sort.

The example above indicates a core form of anticipation work, as played out under the distinctive conditions of new collaborative network formation in the sciences. Standards work represents a powerful bid to anticipate, shape and gather future action across a wide variety of actors and contexts, building new regularities of action that will sustain (if successful) the core integrative interests of NEON. To do so, it must also manage and curtail deviations from the standard, the subtle forms of customization, drift and workarounds that may constitute perfectly reasonable responses to local conditions, but undermine the integrity of the whole. But the same strategies are required to respond artfully to the futures that *can't* be fully anticipated and controlled: changes in biomes and landscapes that bring new phenomena to the center of scientific attention, changes in the technological landscape, and changes in the core questions and interests that science and the public may call on ecological research to answer. NEON must bend and answer to these futures too.

Case #2: Moving from Construction to Operations

During the period of our fieldwork (2010 to the present) NEON passed or approached two central milestones. The first was the successful completion of its pre-construction planning phase, a process running in various forms for more than a decade and completed with approval of the final NEON science and operations plans, its incorporation into the FY 2012-2013 presidential budget request, and the subsequent Congressional appropriation of the first round of NEON construction funding. The second concerns the transition from construction to full-scale operations – a milestone that will formally conclude with the completion of facilities construction scheduled for 2017, but which NEON as an organization (and individual groups and actors within NEON) has been increasingly orienting towards as the project moves forward.

The move from planning to construction marked major changes, both to NEON as a project and NEON Inc., the legally constituted entity formed to plan and build the proposed network. During the period of our fieldwork NEON staff grew from a team of 12 operating out of temporary space near the Boulder airport to a group of more than 120 occupying a sizable office building in central Boulder. This growth has included the introduction or significant expansion of new disciplinary types and roles, including project management, systems engineering, environmental permitting, civil engineering, human resources, and other functions tied to the growing scale and construction orientation of NEON. The same period has seen a related shift in organizational structure and culture: from a relatively flat and fluid model (which some informants likened to a 'start-up' culture) to a more complex, hierarchical, and internally differentiated model marked by the complex division of labor within and between groups, systems of managerial accountability, and a more professional culture of project management imposed in part by the requirements of Congressional accountability and borrowed in part from project management and systems engineering methodologies developed in the worlds of large-scale physics, astronomy, space contracting, and the defense industries. For some (especially those coming from past histories in engineering and industry) this was perceived as a natural and welcome change. For others (especially those coming from ecology's own organizational roots in small-scale lab and field traditions) these changes were received more ambivalently.

The move to operations spells a further set of changes, which NEON as a whole and individual actors within NEON are now working to anticipate, unpack, and respond to. As alluded to above, an important element of this is the rise of a large and distributed field operations staff. Rendered obscure under earlier descriptions of the project (which cast field operations under the oblique but impressive sounding title of 'Fundamental Sentinel Units'), field operations will eventually come to constitute the bulk of NEON staff and the largest single budget item for the network going forward. Conversely, as the network enters operation, the role and size of the science and engineering teams is likely to shift, from active design of the protocols, instrument suites, computational tools and data products that will define NEON science, towards more of a trouble-shooting and maintenance role, dealing with problems and breakdowns as they occur. NEON itself as an organization is likely to become more stable, predictable, and in the words of more than one informant, "boring."

Through the period of our fieldwork, many of our informants were actively thinking towards a life in post-construction NEON. Some spoke with regret about the sense of growth, excitement and collective endeavor that has accompanied NEON in its ramp-up phase, and expressed concern that NEON in its steady state would become a less dynamic (albeit less chaotic and demanding) work environment. Others viewed the shift to operations more positively, and saw in it an opportunity to rebalance a series of commitments – family, outside interests, the development of one's own research program – that had been challenged or compromised under the intensity of the NEON development phase. Several of the NEON staff we spoke with were actively contemplating a life post-NEON altogether, and were taking steps (or tying to) to ensure their relevance and legibility to post-NEON job markets. This included efforts to maintain or restore individual research and publishing programs in ways that might support post-NEON transitions back into academic job markets. This connected in turn to a larger and sometimes contentious discussion within NEON around how the autonomous research programs of its PhD scientists (perhaps especially early career scientists) should be credited and supported. Several of our informants spoke of the 'google' or '80/20' model that had been floated within the organization, in which 80% of staff scientist time was to be devoted to NEON business, with the other 20% spent on individual research projects or simply "keeping a hand in" the science. (In practice, as at Google, this model has proved hard to achieve; several of our respondents noted that the sheer volume of required NEON work meant that 'their' 20% amounted to a voluntary add-on from personal time on top of an already 60-80 hour work week). Periodic discussions broke out around the nature of the NEON 'career ladder', including questions around how and whether things like external academic publication ought to be figured within the review and promotional policies of the organization. Still others sought to establish and valorize a new kind of scientific role within ecology, emphasizing the managerial skills, training, and experiences that former NEON employees might bring to other research operations.

In all these ways, actors within NEON have begun to orient to an operational future. For some, this means an accommodation (sometimes a happy one) to an adjusted role in science, as the organization as a whole and their role within it changes shape, texture and function once again. For others, this means leaving NEON altogether – and setting in motion the plans, steps, and processes needed to make that transition effective.

Case #3: Diversity, Inclusion, and Biographical Adjustment

If anticipation work shows up in more formal guise in planning and procedural activities like those associated with standards and protocol development at NEON, it is also found in the mundane and everyday interactions that drive and define what are sometimes personal or alternative sets of values, hopes and ambitions associated with collective projects. To emphasize this point we turn to a set of oceanographers pursuing a vision (which echoes that of early internet manifestos [2]) in which the new infrastructure of the OOI and big data will level the playing field for the doing of science across the currently unequal distribution of race, gender, class and geography in the field. These participants each described how data-intensive science could open new worlds of research that might not differentiate between male and female bodies in the way that traditional forms of ship-based work have in the past. While women were confronted with many barriers to entry on ships and particularly submarines even into the last decade [11], participants noted the shifting tides of gender awareness and the potential for open data and infrastructure to support discovery without the physical and social barriers of sexuality, strength, or more subtle forms of sexism that once deterred engagement. Much like that of Donna Haraway's cyborg fiction [25], these participants are building their vision where all genders have the capacity to assert power through the ocean's coming big data resources.

This appears at first glance an unlikely future, as data-intensive ocean science sits at the corner of two particularly gendered STEM disciplines - oceanography and computer science. One participant stressed direct mentoring and caring for young women in this path to help them navigate and engage the science in meaningful and sustainable ways, while acknowledging the often subtle forms of discouragement that may arise. Another participant engaged the communication director of her institution to ensure that public-facing OOI documents and websites include imagery that references a more diverse array of genders, ages and ethnicities. She detailed her arguments over the cover photo of a recent expedition press release: under the headline was a photo of the two established, older white male founders. The participant strongly asserted that this photo reifies the diversity concerns for engagement that permeate the field, and suggested instead that the header include a mosaic of the people and roles who were invested in the project. Still another participant detailed her efforts to connect with women, both advanced and early career, through regular lunch outings, coffee breaks and trips to the bar. She detailed the ways in which this everyday social organizational work is critical to feelings of inclusion and may garner open communication for women as they traverse this space, setting an example for generations of mentors to come.

Much of this work was done with the recognition that these scientists will not see equality during their tenures, and was rather driven by a need to shepherd in and open opportunities for the next generation. One participant noted that while the number of women within her institution dramatically increased with the introduction of the OOI on campus, the number of men increased at a similar rate, leaving the statistical balance of gender untouched. But, the mere presence of additional female scientists – and the anticipation of more to come – inspired the participant to mobilize a collective initiative for female inclusion, support and sustainability in the ocean sciences. These efforts were then paralleled across institutions within the OOI and linked to similar efforts in the broader oceanographic community, forming a network of allies, generating awareness and initiating actionable items to build toward more equal futures. This resulted in formalized diversity initiatives by members of the OOI, a number of papers published about their efforts and visions, and work with the universities to address concerns and change institutional supports.

The OOI example above calls attention to forms of local, mundane, and value-based anticipation work that may feed into collective action in unique and powerful ways. These practices advocate and reflect the open, communal and democratic virtues desired to build into the future of a more inclusive ocean science community. Actors within the OOI are working to identify and pursue a distinctly cultural vision of the future that may stem (but not without work) from the possibilities raised by new infrastructures and the forms of work and organization they support. Through this example, we see that actors define their own positions and then strategize with regard to their expectations of the future [15]. Anticipation work flows outside of the bounds of the OOI and has legs in the universities, the governing bodies and the field more broadly. Actors reorient their personal plans and trajectories in light of the evolving shape and expectation of the project. The example sheds light on the core frames of anticipation work in building an envisioned future through mobilizing resources, aligning political and scientific interests, and evangelizing imagined worlds.

DISCUSSION

As the above accounts have shown, collaborative life is constituted in ways that are temporally driven, framing what our futures might in time inhabit. Our empirical examples show how much of the present work of our participants is oriented to a sense of building and maintaining futures, from establishing social support networks within data-intensive oceanography to the adherence to formalized protocols that dictate engagement in the operations of the ecological observatories.

A substrate of this work materializes from "ordinary futurisms'; the mundane, local, and sometimes highly personal accommodations to the future that always accompany the more formalized and/or speculative dimensions that are often called out in the planning and futurism literatures. The temporal orientation of these vignettes enmeshes actors (individuals and collectives) into a broader narrative connecting local and immediate action with larger spheres of influence in important and remarkable ways.

We have shown how standardization is employed to hedge against human and infrastructural vulnerability (including protocols, rules, procedures) and build consistencies across time. We have mapped NEON's impending transition from construction to operations and the forms of work underway to prepare for, absorb, or depart from that future. Lastly, our example of the OOI presents a spectrum of formal and informal working orders that reorient biographical trajectories for diversity and equality across the field.

But such examples only scratch the surface of the multiple forms of anticipation work at play in the ongoing development of the OOI and NEON: writing grants which make use of the infrastructures, learning a programming language on the side of construction activities to prepare for the data-intensive science that is to come, or even gaining public momentum for a research venture through a photography exhibition at the Smithsonian around a particularly beautiful deep sea creature; in all these ways, OOI, NEON, and the diverse array of individual actors that constitute both, are engaged in futurism of a very specific and consequential sort.

Beyond its grounding in the specific cases at hand, we believe the notion of anticipation work complements our understanding of collaborative life and practice in at least five important ways.

First, anticipation work builds common futures around which distributed actions can be coordinated and calibrated. Actors are actively engaged in the production and maintenance of social (sociotechnical) imaginaries. Our participants coalesce through formalized grant proposals or new protocols for operations and development, in what de Laat & Laredo [16] describe as "from predictive to procedural." The formalized practices that reconcile the complexities of NEON guide collective action through what others have theorized more deeply within customization, categorization, standardization, and regulation frames [e.g. 6, 21]. Though standardization work is often viewed merely as a bureaucratic device, it often finds its footing in the everyday anticipations of individual graduate students, administrators and researchers.

Anticipation work (and the futures that work is building toward) can become procedural, but unification can also materialize through purposeful, yet casual interactions with colleagues and in interactions via mentorship and group support. This symbiosis may converge or conflict with the formalized plans and goals of a project, like those of the NEON affiliates prepared for the re-balance of work and life post-operations. Much like plans themselves, anticipations are not determinate and can contradict or complement across actors within a sociotechnical system. As with our example of establishing research activities amidst construction obligations in NEON, anticipation work is an important mechanism by which individual futures get (re)calibrated to the formal and evolving shape of collective plans. The mindful practices of anticipation work not only develop order but are ordered themselves, ranging from the first order issues that ensure the following day will follow smoothly to a broad ideal type less easily attained.

Second, anticipation work asserts normative claims: the nature of a proper life in science, the values of a community, the forms of knowledge and infrastructure that are of greatest importance, or the kinds of technical resources that will persist into future generations. In many ways, the frame of anticipation work illuminates not only the styles of work and practice that are currently in fashion (e.g. high postmodernist construction) but may provide insight into the long term trends that will persist into future generations (e.g. big and open data, a distributed collaborative culture). The form of work that builds our infrastructures carries into the ways expected and appropriate behavior is defined, how values are enforced, and how dependencies are drawn. Taken together with the first point, we see that sometimes mundane anticipations shape not only the ways in which actors align themselves to, work towards, or rationalize their own stakes in the planned future of a project but also how such working, aligning, or rationalizing shapes the planned future itself.

Third, anticipation work is crucial to temporal alignment at scales from the individual and close to collective and distant. Anticipation work gives us the ability to place the practices of standardization and planning against a broader backdrop of historically-embedded and future-oriented narratives across biographical, organizational, infrastructure and phenomenal temporal scales: rhythms and events called out by Jackson et. al. [26] and Steinhardt & Jackson [46]. Actors organize their behavior in the present in real-time to reconcile the multiplicity of temporalities, some of which are currently in motion and others that are being newly engendered. Through the lens of anticipation work we draw out the active temporal work and strategic practices that align and reconcile the predictable and unpredictable nature of collaborative life.

Fourth, anticipation work is key in scaling between local and institutional forms, addressing a longstanding tension of performing CSCW work most recently called out by Ribes [37]. "We should travel across the scales mirroring the footsteps of our informants', and when we do so we will discover that scaling is the sometimes mundane, but often esoteric, work of actors." [37, p. 169]. Anticipation work follows this bridge from local practice to institutions. Expectations and their ends are often met by factors external to the individual, forcing our attention outside of the practice of one and into the larger ecology within which that individual is embedded. Anticipation work calls out an under-theorized set of practices that cross over the boundaries of a single project and align individuals at local level with institutions, planning and policies at a larger scale. Anticipation work makes visible the actors within our empirical cases as actively engaged in practices for managing the size of the project, both in the number of human and nonhuman resources as well as in their long term temporal scales.

Fifth, anticipation work breaks from risk and uncertainty in important ways. Local circumstances often break the expected trajectory of a formality or imaginary, forcing a recalibration of work practice to reclaim order [48]. It may be paradoxical to say, but the future is not fact: the one inevitability in social systems is error. Broken or irreconcilable visions can unfold as a scandal (e.g. natural disaster derails the construction of ecological sensing unit) or fall silently and passively into the background (e.g. the debilitated morale of an individual scientist takes the attention of a colleague away from their formalized goals).

Often this thinking leads us directly to limits and contingency: a series of questions subsumed under "risk" and "uncertainty." However, this framing diminishes the purposive actions and temporal forms that direct and give meaning to practices. Our empirical example sheds light on more than what some participants noted as "Squirrel Away Funds" or "Extraordinary Maintenance" risk measures. Anticipation work captures both the formalized and the ordinary adjustments that hedge investment into a role, a project or a lifestyle. To paraphrase sociologist, Howie Becker, "in any interaction everyone always has a side bet." But what other names can we give to this futures work that is not fully predictive, that makes claims on a future it can't easily control, and is prone to producing effects even (perhaps especially!) when it's wrong?

Finally, while we may plan and hedge, the realities of the collaborative world span further than its formalized project plans and into a world full of improvisation, opportunistic change, and adaptation. We are reminded of the beautiful synthesis of John Dewey and Thelonious Monk by Nathanial Klemp et. al. [32]:

> "From Dewey's earliest work on perception (1896) and even logic (1893), he always insisted that activities are organized in time, at a particular time often at just the right time, and always with a simultaneous concern for both the future and the past." [32, p. 4-5]

For our three cases, we see that improvisation and adaptation are an integral part of anticipation work where a harmony at the collective level can result in new standards and routines that carry forward through the collaboration. As in the quotation, a sense of the past (e.g. the absence of standardization in ecology or the limitations of gender expression in oceanography) is important to any respective imagination of the future and to the jointly planned and improvised trajectory that constructs them as reality.

CONCLUSION

The paper above has argued that long term technological development and sustainability in science are guided by complex and distributed forms of futurism. All actors (both individual and collective) orient towards the future (at both temporally close and distant scales) and engage in complex and skilled forms of anticipation work – individual and collective, formal and informal – that guide and shape the present character and experience of collaborative life. These insights have important application in the world of large-scale collaboration and infrastructure development in the sciences but, they also speak to the dynamics of collaborative life and experience more generally, including in spheres well outside of the worlds of science studied here.

CSCW has long and strong traditions for analyzing and understanding collaborative practice in the present and has more recently begun building a body of work concerning time, rhythm and temporality in collaborative systems. This is a call to extend these trends and more squarely integrate futurism into our studies of sociotechnical systems. We offer "anticipation work" to bring to the fore the often invisible and forward-thinking practices of preparation and positioning that drive, unite and calibrate individual and collective action. Anticipation work illuminates the immediate actions that are building the near future, and centers these practices within dynamic spheres of collaborative life. It is a critical frame which forces the analyst to acknowledge the voices that are built into infrastructures and those voices that protest or hedge, and to be mindful of whose future is being built.

ACKNOWLEDGMENTS

We wish to thank our participants for their time and feedback, as well as Steve Hilgartner, Poppy McLeod and Kate Achille for their contributions to early drafts of this work. This research was funded under NSF CAREER #0847175 and EAGER #1258927.

REFERENCES

[1] Adams, V., Murphy, M. Clarke, A. Anticipation: Technoscience, life, affect, temporality. *Subjectivity* 28, (2009), 246-265.

[2] Barlow, J.P. A Declaration of the Independence of Cyberspace. https://projects.eff.org/~barlow/Declaration-Final.html.

[3] Bazerman, M.H. The study of "real" decision making. *Journal of Behavioral Decision Making* 14, (2001), 353-355.

[4] Borgman, C.L. The conundrum of sharing research data. *Journal of the American Society for Information Science and Technology* 63, 6 (2012), 1059-1078.

[5] Blanchette, J-F. A Material History of Bits. *Journal of the American Society for Information Science* 62, 6 (2011), 1042–1057.

[6] Bowker, G. and Star, S.L. *Sorting Things Out.* MIT Press, Cambridge, 1999.

[7] Borup, M., Brown, N., Konrad, K. and Van Lente, H. The sociology of expectations in science and technology. *Technology Analysis & Strategic Management* 18, (2006), 285–298.

[8] Brown, N., Rappert, B. and Webster, A. Introducing contested futures: From looking into the future to looking at the future. In Brown, N., Rappert, B. and Webster, A. (eds.) *Contested Futures*, Ashgate Publishing, Aldershot, 2000, 3-20.

[9] Burton, M. and Jackson, S.J. Constancy and change in scientific collaboration: coherence and integrity in long-term ecological data production. In *Proc. HICSS '12*, IEEE (2012), 353-362.

[10] Castree, N. Differential geographies: place, indigenous rights and 'local' resources. *Political Geography* 23,

(2004), 133-167.

[11] Clark, L. Women in oceanography: 20 years of progress, change and challenges. *Oceanography* 21, 3 (2008), 38-43.

[12] Cohn, M. Lifetimes and legacies: Temporalities of sociotechnical change in a long-lived system. PhD dissertation, Information and Computer Science, University of California, Irvine, 2013.

[13] Collingridge, D. *The Social Control of Technology*. Palgrave Macmillan, New York, 1981.

[14] Corbin, J.M. and Strauss, A. *Basics of Qualitative Research: Techniques and Procedures for Developing Grounded Theory*. Sage Publications, Thousand Oaks, CA, 2007.

[15] De Laat, B. Scripts for the future: technology foresight, strategic evaluation and socio-technical networks: the confrontation of script-based scenarios. PhD thesis, University of Amsterdam, 1996.

[16] De Laat, B. and Laredo, P. Foresight for research and technology policies: From innovation studies to scenario confrontation. In Coombs, R., Green, K., Richards, A. and Walsh, V. (eds.) *Technological Change and Organization*. Edward Elgar Publishing, Cheltenham/Northampton, 1998, 150-179.

[17] Dourish, P. Implications for design. In *Proc. CHI 2006*, ACM Press (2006), 541-550.

[18] Edwards, P. Infrastructure and modernity: Force, time, and social organization in the history of sociotechnical systems. *Modernity and technology*, 2003, 185-225.

[19] Edwards, P.N., Mayernik, M. S., Batcheller, A.L., Bowker, G.C., and Borgman, C.L. Science friction: Data, metadata and collaboration. *Social Studies of Science* 41, 5 (2011), 667–690.

[20] Engelbart, D. Augmenting human intellect: A conceptual framework. Summary Report AFOSR-3233, Standford Research Institute, 1962.

[21] Gerson, E.M. Reach, bracket, and the limits of rationalized coordination: Some challenges for CSCW. *Computer Supported Cooperative Work*, 2008, 193-220.

[22] Glaser, B. and Strauss, A. *The Discovery of Grounded Theory: Strategies for Qualitative Research*. Aldine Transaction, Chicago, 1967.

[23] Gusterson, H. Nuclear futures: Anticipatory knowledge, expert judgment, and the lack that cannot be filled, *Science and Public Policy* 35, 8 (2008), 551–560.

[24] Haraway, D.A. Cyborg Manifesto: Science, Technology, and Socialist-Feminism in the Late Twentieth Century. *Simians, Cyborgs and Women: The Reinvention of Nature*. Routledge, New York, 1991, 149-181.

[25] Howison, J. and Herbsleb, J.D. Scientific software production: Incentives and collaboration. In *Proc. CSCW 2011*, ACM Press (2011), 513–522.

[26] Jackson, S.J., Ribes, D., Buyuktur, A., and Bowker, G.C. Collaborative rhythm: Temporal dissonance and alignment in collaborative scientific work. In *Proc. CSCW 2011*, ACM Press (2011), 245–254.

[27] Jackson, S.J., Steinhardt, S.B., and Buyuktur, A. Why CSCW needs science policy (and vice versa). In *Proc. CSCW 2013*, ACM Press (2013), 1113-1124.

[28] Jackson, S.J., Barbrow, S. Infrastructure and vocation: Field, calling and computation in ecology. In *Proc. CHI 2013*, ACM Press (2013), 2873-2882.

[29] Jackson, S.J., and Buyuktur, A. Who killed WATERS? Mess, method, and forensic explanation in the making and unmaking of large-scale science networks. *Science Technology and Human Values* 39, 2 (2014), 285-308.

[30] Jasanoff, S. and Kim, S.H. Containing the atom: Sociotechnical imaginaries and nuclear power in the United States and South Korea. *Minerva* 47, (2009), 119-146.

[31] Karasti, H., Baker, K.S., Millerand, F. Infrastructure time: Long-term matters in collaborative development. *Computer Supported Cooperative Work* 19, 3-4 (2010), 377–415.

[32] Klemp, N. Plans, takes and mis-takes. *Critical Social Studies* 1, (2008), 4-21.

[33] Lee, C.P., Dourish, P., Mark, G. The human infrastructure of cyberinfrastructure. In *Proc. CSCW 2006*, ACM Press (2006), 483-492.

[34] Michael, M. Futures of the present: From performativity to prehension. In Brown, N., Rappert, B., and Webster, A. (eds.) *Contested Futures: A Sociology of Prospective Technoscience.* Ashgate, Aldershot, 2000, 21-39.

[35] Olson, G., and Olson, J. Distance Matters. *Human-Computer Interaction 15*, 2 (2000), 139–178.

[36] Ribes, D. and Finholt, T.A. The long now of technology infrastructure: Articulating tensions in development. *Journal of the Association for Information Systems* 10, 5 (2009), 375–398.

[37] Ribes, D. Ethnography of scaling, or, how to fit a national research infrastructure in the room. In *Proc. CSCW 2014*, ACM Press (2014), 158-170.

[38] Rosenberg, N. On technological expectations. *Economic Journal* 86, (1976), 523-535.

[39] Rosner, D.K. The material practices of collaboration. In Proc. CSCW 2012, ACM Press (2012), 1155-1164.

[40] Sanz-Menéndez, L.S. and Cabello, C. Expectations and

learning as principles of shaping the future. Brown, N. Rappert, B. and Webster, A. (eds.) *Contested Futures: A Sociology of Prospective Science and Technology*. Ashgate Press, Aldershot, 2000, 229-249.

[41] Schmidt, K.J. Cooperative work: A conceptual framework. Rasmussen, B. and Leplat, J. (eds.), *Distributed Decision Making: Cognitive Models for Cooperative Work.* Wiley & Sons, Chinchester, 1991, 75-109.

[42] Scott, J.C. *Seeing Like a State: How Certain Schemes to Improve the Human Condition Have Failed*. Yale University Press, New Haven, 1999.

[43] Shapin, S. *The Scientific Life: A Moral History of a Late Modern Vocation.* Chicago University Press, Chicago, 2008.

[44] Star, S.L. and Ruhleder, K. Steps toward an ecology of infrastructure: Design and access for large information spaces. *Information Systems Research* 7, 1 (1996), 111– 134.

[45] Star, S.L., and Griesemer, J.R. Institutional ecology, `translations' and boundary objects: Amateurs and professionals in Berkeley's Museum of Vertebrate Zoology, 1907-39. *Social Studies of Science* 19, 3 (1989), 387–420.

[46] Steinhardt, S.B. and Jackson, S.J. Reconciling rhythms: Plans and temporal alignment in collaborative scientific work. In *Proc. CSCW 2014,* ACM Press (2014), 134-145.

[47] Strauss, A. The articulation of project work: An organizational process. *The Sociological Quarterly* 29, 2 (1988), 163–178.

[48] Suchman, L. *Human-Machine Reconfigurations: Plans and Situated Actions.* Cambridge University Press, Cambridge, 2007.

[49] Vertesi, J. and Dourish, P. The Value of Data: Considering the Context of Production in Data Economies. In *Proc. CSCW 2011*, ACM Press (2011), 533–542.

[50] Weber, M. From Max Weber: Essays in Sociology. Oxford University Press, New York, 1946.

[51] Wulf, W.A. The collaboratory opportunity. *Science* 261, 5123(1993), 854–855.

Social Eye Tracking: Gaze Recall with Online Crowds

Shiwei Cheng[a,b], Zhiqiang Sun
[a]Zhejiang University of Technology
swc@zjut.edu.cn,
sunzhiqiang89@163.com

Xiaojuan Ma
Noah's Ark Lab
xiaojuan.ma@gmail.com

Jodi Forlizzi, Scott Hudson, Anind Dey
[b]Carnegie Mellon University
{forlizzi, scott.hudson, anind}@ cs.cmu.edu

ABSTRACT
Eye tracking is a compelling tool for revealing people's spatial-temporal distribution of visual attention. But quality eye tracking hardware is expensive and can only be used with one person at a time. Further, webcam eye tracking systems have significant limitations on head movement and lighting conditions that result in significant data loss and inaccuracies. To address these drawbacks, we introduce a new approach that harnesses the crowd to understand allocation of visual attention. In our approach, crowdsourcing participants use mouse clicks to self-report the positions and trajectory for the following valuable eye tracking measures: first gaze, last gaze and all gazes. We validate our crowdsourcing approach with a user study, which demonstrated good accuracy when compared to a real eye tracker. We then deployed our prototype, *GazeCrowd*, in a crowdsourcing setting, and showed that it accurately generated gaze heatmaps and trajectory maps. Such an approach will allow designers to evaluate and refine their visual design without requiring the use of limited/expensive eye trackers.

Author Keywords
visual attention; fixation; crowdsourcing.

ACM Classification Keywords
H.5.m. Information interfaces and presentation (e.g., HCI): Miscellaneous.

INTRODUCTION
Eye tracking can measure and record gaze positions and movements of an individual. More researchers are using this technology to obtain insights into users' behavioral and cognitive processes used in problem solving [1], such as to explore usability problems in user interfaces, and improve a user's efficiency in searching, navigating and manipulating. However, traditional eye tracking hardware is not suitable for use in all contexts. It has three main shortcomings [28]: 1) most commercial eye trackers are too expensive for anyone other than researchers and practitioners to own; 2) a limited number of users from narrow demographic groups can participate in eye tracking experiments, as they must be co-located with the eye tracker, and only one user can use it at a time; 3) cheaper web-camera based eye trackers greatly constrain the location and motion of a user's head, are not robust to different lighting, have low sample rates, leading to significant data loss and inaccuracies [6].

We propose a device-independent and easily accessible method to complement or even replace current eye trackers for some measurements. In particular, our method leverages crowdsourcing in which multiple users self-report the regions (or gaze points) of stimuli that they focus on visually. These results can be aggregated to generate an overall understanding of how people allocate their visual attention on these stimuli. This approach can be executed cheaply, as it requires no expensive equipment beyond a computer and an Internet connection, and can be used by many users in parallel, with varying demographics.

Our approach collects a range of eye tracking data: location of *first gaze*, location of *last gaze* and *location and order of all gazes*. These eye movement measures are important for understanding the spatial-temporal distribution of visual attention. For example, first gaze usually reveals the most salient part of a visual stimulus, and can be used to select between multiple graphical user interface (GUI) design solutions, *e.g.*, to determine whether an important menu can be easily found. Last gaze can indicate objects that have low visual saliency, *e.g.*, an icon located in the bottom-left corner of an interface may be the last item seen by a user. The sequence of all gazes can help understand how visual attention is allocated over time. By having users recall (*i.e.*, self-report) their gaze trajectory in the presence or absence of a given task, we can also identify the use of different kinds of visual attention mechanisms, such as bottom-up and top-down [7], and identify problems with UI designs.

Our approach displays a visual stimulus and asks users to recall which parts of it they looked at. To validate the accuracy of these self-reports, we conducted a laboratory experiment (user study 1) where we compared the recall results of first gaze, last gaze, and all gazes to those obtained from an eye tracker, and found high consistency between each individual's self-reports and actual gaze data. User study 1 validated that an individual's recall data for a user was similar to his/her own eye-tracking data. We conducted a second experiment in a crowdsourcing setting (user study 2), to then validate that aggregated crowd data is similar to the aggregated eye-tracking data from study 1. We obtained gaze recall data and aggregated crowdsourced results to generate gaze heatmaps and trajectory maps comparable to eye trackers and models of visual attention.

CSCW '15, March 14 - 18, 2015, Vancouver, BC, Canada.
Copyright 2015 ACM 978-1-4503-2922-4/15/03...$15.00.
http://dx.doi.org/10.1145/2675133.2675249

User study 2 validated that the recall approach also had good performance on a crowdsouricng platform. Finally we discuss how to reduce the limitations of our approach and apply it to guide visual design or design evaluation tasks.

Our contributions of this paper include:

- Validated the use of structured participant recall for recording gaze data (first gaze, last gaze, all gazes) with accuracy comparable to *infra-red* web camera-based eye trackers. This gaze recall data can be captured in task-oriented and browsing situations, leveraging both bottom-up and top-down visual cognition mechanisms.
- Developed a prototype crowdsourcing system for collecting aggregate measures of visual attention. Our approach is efficient, inexpensive, and induces low workload in collecting eye motion data in a real crowdsourcing environment. Most importantly, it produces heatmaps and trajectory maps, comparable to eye tracking systems and models of visual attention.

RELATED WORK

Traditional commercial eye trackers are expensive (usually US $10,000 to $30,000 each) and allow only a single user at a time. These issues make it difficult to acquire gaze data from a large number of users with high efficiency. Hence, different methods were proposed to address these issues.

Webcam-based eye tracking. Compared to high quality, commercial eye trackers, webcam-based eye tracking systems use much cheaper and simpler cameras built into computers to detect users' gaze locations. For example, the ITU *Gaze Tracker* (gazegroup.org/downloads) performs remote eye tracking using a web camera with a modified camera lens and two infrared lights (total cost is US$100). It has a sampling rate of 30 Hz and a mean error of 59 pixels, approximately twice the error of the Tobii *T60* binocular eye tracker (sampling rate of 60 Hz, mean error of 31 pixels) [20]. There are also a number of open source eye trackers that use unmodified webcams, such as Opengazer (inference.phy.cam.ac.uk/opengazer/), but they tend to have even worse errors.

Developers have improved these open source eye trackers and deployed them as services for conducting remote user study service, such as *GazeHawk* (gazehawk.com) and *EyeTrackShop* (eyetrackshop.com), for evaluating advertisements, website designs, *etc*. Using these systems, gaze data can be recorded on participants' computers and then uploaded to a study server, for the generation of analytic reports and visualizations. However, these systems still have some limitations: 1) low data sampling frequency and accuracy. A typical commercial eye tracker has accuracy of less than one degree of visual angle and 60 Hz sampling frequency at least; in contrast, due to imperfect lighting conditions, poor quality webcams, on-screen distractions, an infrared webcam produces results with accuracies of 1.5 to 2 degrees of visual angle at best, but usually with less accuracy, such as 2 to 5 degrees of visual angle and use at most a sampling frequency of 30 Hz [20]; 2) low tracking robustness. In addition, participant head movement and a lack of robustness to imperfect lighting conditions, leads to a greater proportion of participants whose data will be lost [6]; 3) device dependent. For example, the ITU *Gaze Tracker* requires a special camera lens and infrared illuminations; 4) hard to use. For example, the technical sophistication required to compile a package like Opengazer with a number of external dependencies and then configure the system, is quite high; 5) users' limitations. Ordinary web-cam based eye trackers do not perform well if users wear glasses.

Visual attention model-based eye tracking. Visual attention is a process that enables humans to quickly select the most relevant regions of a scene. Visual attention models usually take into account a bottom-up cognition mechanism that highlights regions that are different from their surroundings. They are used to predict eye movement data (*e.g.*, fixations), and to generate salience maps. Although these models can accurately predict fixations when compared to real eye tracking data and can be executed very quickly [8], most of them do not focus on the top-down cognitive process that is driven by task. This results in saliency maps that are quite different from actual eye movement when people observe images or videos with interactive, complex, and dynamic tasks [7].

Mouse movement-based eye tracking. There is some coordination between eye movements and mouse movements. Chen *et al.* [9] asked users to browse web pages, and used an eye tracker to record their gaze and mouse movement data at the same time. They found that of the regions that a mouse cursor visited, 84% of them were also visited by gaze, and for the regions that the eye gaze did not visit, 88% of them were also not visited by the mouse cursor. However, just five participants were involved in this study, and they were given no specific tasks when browsing the web pages. Most users moved their mouse according to their eye gaze, only when they had specific tasks, such as clicking highly relevant target results on web search result pages [27].

Another similar method, restricted focus viewer (RFV) [5], blurred a test image, but allowed users to see a small region of the image in focus, with the region being dynamic based on the position of the mouse. By assuming that users only focus on the unblurred region of the stimulus the tracked mouse movement can be considered as equivalent to gaze movement. Although the RFV was introduced as a complementary tool for eye tracking, it could not track users' visual attention well when solving complex problems like identifying as many bugs in a program as possible [4]. In these situations, the visual attention data recorded using the RFV and eye tracker differed significantly. Moreover, the blurring of the stimuli changed users' natural visual attention strategies and increased mental and physical workload. Jones and Mewhort [21] suggested that the size and characteristics of the view in focus affected the information search strategies, and the users who relied on peripheral data would have to exert more effort to search for information using the mouse.

Social computing -based eye tracking. As mentioned above, these methods aim to be a complementary or even alternative tool for real eye trackers, but they have not yet achieved high accuracy, efficiency and convenience. Recently, a social computing-based eye tracking method has been proposed. It applies a human computation mechanism to involve crowds in completing specific and simple tasks, and aggregates the crowd's interaction data to indicate eye movement. For example, researchers developed an online game system where users are shown a small part of an image, and are asked to click where it belongs in the original full image [2]. The system considered the most well mapped image regions to be the most salient parts, and generated a saliency map. An evaluation revealed that the saliency map contained the most essential visual elements and features of the image. However, elements that people pay attention to such as human faces or traffic signs, are not always chosen in saliency maps based on traditional visual attention models. In addition, unlike with real eye trackers, this method cannot capture gaze trajectories (gaze sequences over time).

Rudoy *et al.* [28] proposed a different crowdsourcing method, which acquires gaze data using self-reports of what users were looking at in video clips. Users viewed an input video for a few seconds, and immediately after the video ended, were shown a labeled grid where the video was displayed. The grid was displayed for a short period of time and disappeared afterwards, at which point, users were asked to enter the grid label corresponding to the region of the video they had seen most clearly. These self-reports were shown to be comparable to eye-tracking data. However, this kind of approach still has three limitations:

(1) This method only asked each participant to recall the last gaze on the screen and did not track the first gaze, and all the gazes and their trajectories over the whole period of time when the stimuli was displayed. The first gaze is more important than last gaze, as it typically reveals the most salient region, and the remaining gazes are chosen to maximize information gain, given the first gaze [13] [18]. In addition, the information about all gazes, such as how many there are, their positions, and the overall trajectory (sequences of gaze points over time) is also important for us to understand spatial-temporal distributions of visual attention. For example, gaze trajectories (also called scan paths) may indicate higher cognitive strategies (*e.g.*, visual search strategies for UIs) and states [24] [16].

(2) Participants were just asked to recall gaze positions based on the bottom-up visual mechanism, but use of top-down mechanisms were not considered. Bottom-up is mainly based on characteristics of visual scene (stimulus-driven) [25], and is involuntary [7]. Areas of interest that attract our visual attention in a bottom-up manner must be sufficiently distinctive with respect to surrounding features. In contrast, top-down (goal-driven or task-driven) is voluntary, determined by cognitive phenomena like knowledge, expectations, tasks and goals [7] [17]. So eye movements will differ considerably for the same scene if users were or were not assigned a task, or if assigned different tasks [29]. The bottom-up mechanism can only explain a small fraction of eye movements since the majority of them are driven by the top-down mechanisms [14]. Hence, supporting the collection of gaze information based on the bottom-up mechanisms alone is not sufficient.

(3) The mechanism for specifying recalled gaze can be made more efficient. Participants were asked to enter a label consisting of several characters for reporting their gaze locations, and this can increase both physical and mental workload and reduce efficiency, unnecessarily.

We propose a method to facilitate gaze recall with online crowds that builds on this past work of Rudoy *et al.* [28]. We address the shortcomings discussed above: 1) Besides recording the last gaze, we also record the first gaze, all gazes and their trajectories; 2) In addition to simply browsing images (bottom-up), our approach also applies to task-driven recall (top-down); 3) Instead of having to recall multi-character labels, participants are asked to only click on regions of interest when recalling gaze. The scope of our method is broader, making the results more applicable across different application domains and scenarios. Furthermore, we performed a detailed analysis of the accuracy of our approach, comparing it to eye tracking data. Finally we validated our method with a prototype system deployed on Amazon Mechanical Turk. We now describe our approach in detail and the evaluation of our approach.

USER STUDY 1: GAZE RECALL EVALUATION

To determine if recall of what a participant views in an image can approximate gaze data, we used an eye tracker to collect users' gaze data as ground truth, and recorded users' recalled gaze points (mouse clicks) simultaneously. Then we evaluated users' recall performance for their first gaze, last gaze, all gazes, and trajectory of gazes compared with the ground truth.

Participants & Apparatus

We recruited 20 participants (8 female and 12 male) from a local participant pool. They were aged between 18 and 61 years (M=28.6, SD=10.7), and none of them were color-blind or had any visual impairments. We used the SMI^{TM} iViewX RED remote eye tracker to record gaze data. The eye tracker has two infrared cameras and the gaze sampling rate was configured to 250Hz. Its operating distance is 50cm to 70cm, and it supports free head movement (40cm × 20cm at 70cm distance to screen). In this context, the gaze data sampling accuracy is 0.5 degrees of visual angle. It works with most glasses and contact lenses. Study stimuli were shown to participants on a 21-inch LCD screen with a resolution of 1680×1050.

Procedure

We first gave the participants a brief introduction to our experiment, and then asked them to sit in front of the monitor about 50cm (30° of visual angle) away from their eyes. We performed an 8-point calibration for each participant with the eye tracker. Our study had 4 different sessions: training session (5 images), first gaze recall session (16 images), last gaze recall session (8 images), all gazes recall session (with specific tasks (3 images) and without specific tasks (14 images)). Without specific tasks, a bottom-up, stimulus-driven approach is used. In contrast, to explore task-driven (top-down) gaze recall, we gave participants two kinds of tasks that have high complexity: detection tasks and problem-solving tasks [12]. For *detection tasks*, we asked participants to locate predefined objects embedded in the stimuli; for *problem-solving tasks*, we ask participants to answer one cognitive-ability question, such as reporting the number of people in an image. The study lasted between 30 to 50 minutes for each participant.

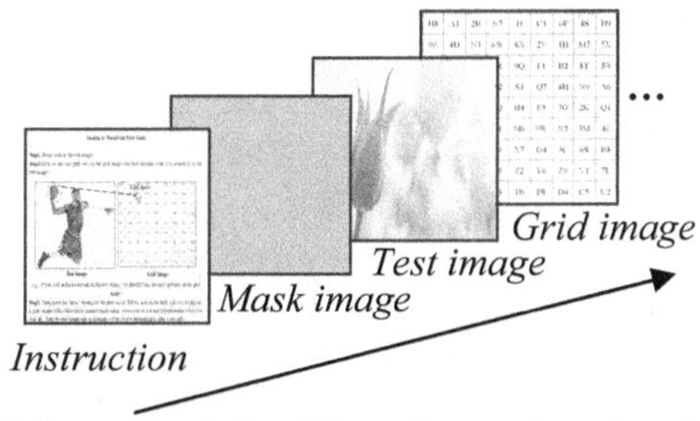

Figure 1. Sequence of stimuli in each experiment session.

A recall session is shown in Figure 1. During each session, there are four different types of frames displayed on the screen: instruction, mask image, test image and grid image.

- Instruction: describes the task and how to recall the gaze and click the grids. For example, for first gaze, the instruction provided was "Please look at the test image; then click on the one grid cell (in the grid image) that best matches what you first looked at in the test image".
- Mask image: a blank gray image displayed for 1 second. It acts as a visual mask, allowing any high contrast stimuli from the previous screen to fade, reducing the persistence of vision [15]. In addition, it can also reduce visual fatigue.
- Test image: image resolution was 1152×864, and displayed for a given duration (*e.g.*, 250 milliseconds). We used a total of 20 different test images collected from Internet, including abstract salient scenes (*e.g.*, one yellow dot among green dots), human faces, sports activities, flowers, posters and advertisements, *etc.*
- Grid image: a blank white image with a 9×9 grid placed over it. Each grid cell was marked with characters, which had no specific meaning but could help participants to discriminate different cells easily. We provide the grid as a visual aid, to help participants locate their gaze positions, but record the actual pixel location of their clicks. Participants recalled their gaze(s) from the previous displayed test image and clicked one (or more) grid cells to indicate their gaze based on the instructions. The size of the grid image was equivalent to the test image, which ensured the grid covered the test image.

All experimental sessions followed a similar sequence, and we only varied the duration for displaying the test image. For the first gaze recall session, the test image duration was set to 250ms, 500ms and 1000ms. After a stimulus is attended to for a short while (*e.g.*, 100-1000ms), inhibition of return (IOR) [22] promotes exploration of new, previously unattended regions in the scene by preventing attention from returning to already-attended regions. So if we display the test image for a long period of time, the participant will shift her gaze to other regions of the stimulus. Thus, we displayed the test image no longer than 1000ms to capture first gaze. For the last gaze recall session, the test image duration time was 1000 and 2000ms. Here, we leveraged the inhibition of return phenomenon in our favor. By showing the test image for longer periods, users will shift their gaze beyond their initial gaze point. For the all gaze recall sessions without a task, the test image duration time was also 1000 and 2000ms, so participants had enough time to browse more of the test image and recall multiple gazes. For the all gaze recall session with a task, the duration was unlimited, so a participant could close the image manually when she finished the task (but the completion time was M=7.3 seconds, SD=7.6).

Additionally, before each experimental session, we displayed 2 or 3 images (not repeated in the experimental sessions themselves) to train participants how to perform different kinds of gaze recall. We provided additional instructions to the participants who did not understand how to recall gazes or made mistakes during recall (*e.g.*, clicking two grid cells when recalling only the first).

The nature of our recall-based experiments allowed users to explicitly recall their gazes. To ensure that the recall did not impact how they allocated visual attention, we incorporated an additional data collection during the first training session. We displayed test images that would later be seen during the experimental settings. Participants were provided with no instructions other than to browse the images (*i.e.*, no recall). The gaze data (*e.g.*, fixation count) was treated as ground truth and compared to the later browsing of these images with explicit recall. We found that there was no significant difference in the fixation count for the "no recall" and "recall" conditions, for example, for one test image with natural browsing and the first gaze recall, a paired samples t-test showed no significant differences ($t(19)=-.665$, $p=0.257$). These results suggest that our explicit recall method did not impact participants' visual attention.

Results

Results of first gaze recall

We measured the geometrical distances between each participant's first gaze points (eye tracking fixations) and her recalled gaze points (mouse clicks) to evaluate the accuracy of gaze point recall. The smaller the distance, the more accurate the recall. Across all test images, the distance ranged from 6 pixels to 393 pixels (*M*=116, *SD*=83). A 100-pixel distance equates to a visual angle error of ~3 degrees.

The distribution of distances revealed that distances shorter than 20 pixels (1.2% of the screen's width) accounted for only 3.4% of the distances, corresponding to 0.5 degrees (equivalent to the accuracy of most commercial eye trackers, *e.g.*, SMI™ iViewX RED) of visual angle (with the viewing distance between participant's eyes and screen set to 50cm). Distances corresponding to 1, 2, 3, 4, and 5 degrees accounted for 15.9%, 32.5%, 54.1%, 62.8% and 73.4%, respectively. The most effective webcam eye trackers have accuracies of 1.5 to 2 degrees (but often 3 to 5). However, these suffer from requiring modification to the camera to be infrared-based, and data loss due to imperfect lighting, webcam quality, and head motion. While our accuracy for first gaze recall is comparable to the infra-red webcam systems, it does not have these data loss issues.

For each test image, a one-way within subjects (or repeated measures) ANOVA was conducted to compare the effect of test image display duration on distance for the 250ms, 500ms and 1000ms conditions. There were significant effects of display duration for all the test images. For example, in one test image that had an abstract scene, there was a significant effect of display duration, F (2, 18) = 10.68, p =.001. Three paired samples t-tests were used to make *post-hoc* comparisons between conditions. The first paired samples t-test found a significant difference in the distances for the 250ms (*M*=156.59, *SD*=101.93) and 500ms (*M*=64.13, *SD*=56.81) conditions; $t(19)$=4.74, p<0.001. A second paired samples t-test indicated that there was a significant difference in the distances for the 250ms (*M*=156.59, *SD*=101.93) and 1000ms (*M*=77.5, *SD*=71.37) conditions; $t(4)$=2.97, p = .008. But a third paired samples t-test indicated that there was no significant difference for the 500ms and 1000ms conditions; $t(19)$=-.599, p=.556.

These results suggest that when a test image was displayed to participants for 250ms, their recall was significantly less accurate (higher distances) than when the test image was displayed for 500ms and 1000ms. These results were consistent across our set of test images. One reason for these results is that when a test image is only displayed for 250ms, it is too short for a participant to be conscious of her first gaze, so she cannot recall its position with high accuracy. When the test image is displayed longer, such as 500/1000ms, the participant has time to be aware of the first gaze made, and can better recall its position.

However, the first gaze recall still has some errors when compared to the first fixation data from an eye tracker. We found that if there were some highly salient objects around the first fixation, people tended to remember them rather than the actual first fixation. This is because people are sensitive to salient objects around their fovea centralis, the part of the eye responsible for sharp central vision.

We did observe some interesting differences across our images and participants. Across all conditions of test image display duration, on average, participants were more accurate with some images compared to others. The average visual angle distance on each image from participant recall to the eye tracker data was 3.7 degrees (*SD*=1.2), but ranged from 2.1 to 5.7 degrees. Similarly, there was variance among our participants. The average visual angle distance was 3.7 degrees across the participants (*SD*=1.2), but some participants averaged as low as 1.8 degrees across all the images, while others were as high as 5.5 degrees.

Results of last gaze recall

The metric for the last gaze recall is the same as for the first gaze recall. We calculated the distance between the last gaze point and the recalled gaze point. For all test images, the distances ranged from 5 pixels to 689 pixels (*M*=102, *SD*=105). The distribution of distances revealed that distances shorter than 20 pixels represented 5.6% of all distances, corresponding to a visual angle of 0.5 degrees. Distances corresponding to 1, 2, 3, 4, and 5 degrees accounted for 20.0%, 53.1%, 68.8%, 73.1% and 81.9%, respectively. Our last gaze recall accuracy results are again comparable to web camera eye trackers.

For each test image, a paired samples t-test was conducted to compare the effect of test image display duration on the values of distance for the 1000ms and 2000ms conditions. There were no significant effects of display duration on recall accuracy for any of the test images. The reason is that participants rarely depend on the test image duration to streamline the recall, because: 1) there is a very short interval (less than 100ms) between the last gaze and when participants start to recall, so participants can accurately remember the position of their last gaze; 2) the test image and grid image are temporally adjacent, so when the grid image displays, the effects of persistence of vision can facilitate participants in still "seeing" the area where their last gaze was located.

Results of all gazes recall

All recalled gazes generate a multiple-point sequence that is similar to "scanpath" (sequence of fixations). Hence, we are inspired by scanpath comparison methods for comparing the scanpaths as measured by the eye tracker and the corresponding recalled points. Jarodzka *et al* [19] proposed five dimensions to measure scanpath similarity: shape, fixation position, length, direction and fixation duration. However, our participants' recalled point sequence is not a true scanpath, as it contains no information about duration. Also, this method for calculating the similarity of two scanpaths, does not discriminate between different fixation points in the same area of interest (AOI). Hence, we refine this method, by replacing the AOI-oriented calculation with a pixel-oriented calculation, and then propose three new measures more appropriate for our study: *point count ratio* (*CR*), *trajectory comparison distance* (*D*) and *recall order ratio* (*RR*), with descriptions as follows:

Point count ratio (*CR*): the fixation count and recalled point count are denoted as *n* (n>0, as we displayed the image long enough, so as to record one fixation at least) and *m* (m>0, as we asked the participants to click one point at least), respectively. The *point count ratio CR=m/n*, and the closer *CR* is to 1, the more accurate the recall.

Trajectory comparison distance [3] (*D*): we consider a trajectory as a sequence of positions over time, and define the fixation trajectory $F=\{(x_1, y_1),(x_2, y_2),\ldots,(x_n, y_n)\}$, x_i and y_i are the coordinates of fixation i (i=1,2,...n); and the recalled point trajectory $R=\{(a_1, b_1),(a_2, b_2),\ldots,(a_m, b_m)\}$, a_j and b_j are the coordinates of recalled point j (j=1,2,...m). For each time step t (t=1, 2... k and k= minimum (n, m)), the distance between fixation and its recalled point positions is given by $d_t=\sqrt{(x_t-a_t)^2+(y_t-b_t)^2}$. We do not know which fixation point a recalled point represents, so we assume it is the nearest one. Then we can use the mean of these distances $D=\frac{1}{k}\sum_{t=1}^{k} d_t$ to indicate the similarity of trajectory *F* and trajectory *R*.

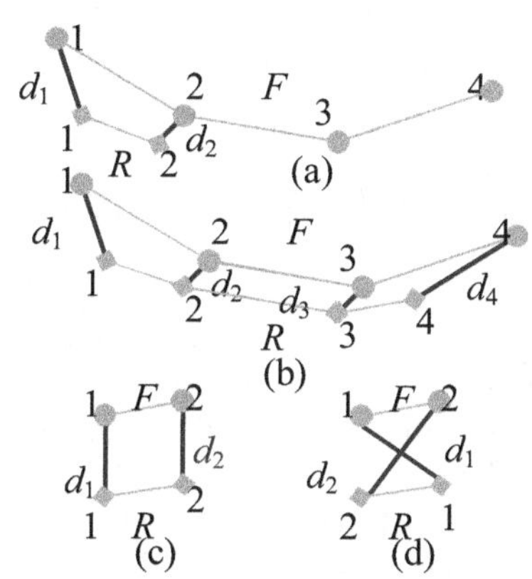

Figure 2. Examples of trajectory comparisons (D).

For example, as shown in Figure 2(a), *F* has four fixations, *R* has two recalled points (local similarity); in contrast, *F* and *R* in Figure 2(b) are more similar (both have four fixations and recalled points) with some offset. However, *D* in Figure 2(a) may be smaller than in 2(b). So we cannot make a conclusion about distance only based on *D*: *R* in Figure 2(a) is more accurate than in Figure 2(b), leading us to consider the point count ratio *CR* as well. *CR*=2/4 in Figure 2(a), but 4/4 in 2(b). Based on *CR*, we can say that the recall performance in Figure 2(b) is better than in 2(a).

Recall order ratio (*RR*): an additional factor to consider is the order of recalled points in the trajectory. To illustrate, the result of *D* and *CR* in Figures 2(c) and 2(d) are quite similar. However, the point order of *R* in Figure 2(c) (*e.g.*, 1, 2) is the same as *F* (*e.g.*, 1, 2), but the point order of *R* in Figure 2(d) (*e.g.*, 2, 1) is reversed with *F* (*e.g.*, 1, 2). So we denote the number of recalled points, which are in the correct order according to the real fixations, as *r*, and then the *recall order ratio* $RR=r/m$ (as $0\leq r\leq m$, $0\leq RR\leq 1$).

D and *CR* indicate recall performance with regard to spatial distribution: *CR* indicates local/global similarity, and *D* detects scale and spatial-offset similarity. *RR* indicates recall performance with regard to temporal distribution, such as detecting offsets and reversed similarity. Ideally, we want recall results with low *D*, and both *CR* and *RR* close to 1, indicating a high similarity between trajectories *F* and *R*.

For all gaze recall trials without tasks: 1) *RR* ranged from 0% to 100% (*M*=64%, *SD*=30%), and with 57% of the instances being higher than 60%. 2) *CR* ranged from 11% to 400% (*M*=90%, *SD*=69%), and 68% of the instances being higher than 60%. 35% of the instances were higher than 100% (*i.e.*, there were more recalled points than actual fixation points), and this was mainly because some participants recalled the visual objects in the test images using many clicks along the objects' boundaries, instead of clicking one or two points representing the objects. 3) *D* ranged from 11 pixels to 433 pixels (*M*=119, *SD*=68), and 44% of instances were shorter than 100 pixels. Moreover, there was no significant difference of *RR*, *CR*, *D*, in display duration (1000ms and 2000ms conditions) for most of the test images. For two complex test images (*e.g.*, advertisement poster with human face), *CR* was significantly smaller in the 2000ms condition than the 1000ms condition. In the 2000ms condition, the eye tracker recorded more fixations than in the 1000ms condition for these complex visual scenes, but most participants were unable to recall the increased number of fixation points.

For all gaze recall trials with detection and problem solving tasks: 1) *RR* ranged from 0% to 100% (*M*= 66%, *SD*=27%), and 60% of the instances being higher than 60%. 2) *CR* ranged from 1% to 171% (*M*=44%, *SD*=42%), and 30% of instances being higher than 60%, and 13.3% of them being higher than 100%. 3) *D* ranged from 23 to 202 pixels (*M*= 98, *SD*=46), and 60% of instances being shorter than 100 pixels. There were no significant differences in these metrics between the two conditions: with and without tasks, except for *CR*. *CR* was smaller in the with tasks condition, as most participants spent more time executing tasks (with tasks had no time limit), resulting in more fixations being recorded and less accuracy in point count recall.

From these results, we can conclude that, in general, participants can recall their gaze trajectories well, when compared against the gaze data from the eye tracker. *RR* (recall order ratio) was ~66% in both with task and without task conditions, *CR* (count ratio) was quite high (90%) without tasks, but much lower (44%) with tasks, due to the increased number of fixation points, and *D* (distance) was ~100 pixels for both conditions. The gaze trajectories typically contained between 3 and 8 recalled points, each corresponding to an AOI in the image. The recalled count (*CR*) was low for the with-tasks condition, as participants recalled AOIs, and not fixation points that were in the transitions between AOIs. While the recall order ratio (*RR*) was lower than we would like to see, the distance (*D*) had about a 3 degree error in visual angle. Additionally the count ratio (*CR*) was quite good for the without-tasks case, and for the with-tasks case, the viewed AOIs were recalled, even if every fixation within each AOI was not recalled. Furthermore, we found that the more complex the test image, the harder it was for participants to recall all fixations. For example, for the without-tasks case, one image only showing some rectangles has higher *RR* (*M*=78%, *SD*=25%) than another involving many flowers and leaves (*M*=49%, *SD*=35%).

Comparison with webcam based eye tracker

As mentioned earlier, a webcam based eye tracker is an alternative option if a commercial eye tracker is unavailable, and commonly available to crowdsourcing workers as many are now built into laptops. Hence we compared our recall approach (just for first gaze) with a webcam based eye tracker to better understand the differences in accuracy. In practice, most users do not have infrared webcams or infrared lamps, which the great majority of the public eyegaze tracking software assume, such as ITU Gaze Tracker. Instead we used a regular webcam (Logitech Webcam Pro 9000 with Carl Zeiss glass lens and autofocus, resolution of 640×480) along with a combination of open source eye tracking systems: Webcam Gaze-Tracking (www.luiwenhao.com/project/gazetrack/), with a refined algorithm from Opengazer.

We conducted a pilot study with 6 participants (3 female, 3 male), with ages from 19 to 25 (*M*=22, *SD*=2.6). Each participant was shown 9 predefined points, one at a time, on the same screen described earlier. We used both the SMI eye tracker and our webcam based eye tracker to record participants' gaze data when they view the points, and also asked participants recall these points. Our lab settings had good illumination conditions, and we asked participants to keep their heads stable. However, despite this, the results showed that webcam based eye tracker had much lower accuracy (*M*=18.1°, *SD*=8.8°) and higher data loss rate (29%) than both our recall approach (*M*=2.8°, *SD*=2.1°, 0% data loss) and SMI eye tracker (*M*=0.7°, *SD*=0.3°, 0% data loss). Subjective feedback from a post-test questionnaire showed that participants also believed that our approach was more accurate (*M*=4.2, *SD*=0.8) than the webcam eye tracker (*M*=3.2, *SD*=1.5) on a 5-point scale.

Discussion of Validation Results

Based on the evaluation of the first and last gaze recall results, we found that our gaze recall approach had reasonable accuracy: 3.4%-5.6% of the trials were equivalent to using real commercial eye trackers whose minimal visual angles are 0.5 degrees; and between 73.4-81.9% of the trials were equivalent to webcam based eye trackers for which the maximum visual angle error is 5 degrees. Our results also validated the feasibility of, and reasonable accuracy for, recalling all gazes and trajectory.

In terms of the duration of displaying test images, we found that participants had higher recall accuracy for the first gaze in the 500ms and 1000ms conditions than in the 250ms condition. For last gaze recall, we found no significant difference in accuracy for durations of 1000ms and 2000ms. The same was true for all gaze recall, except for visually complex images, where the 1000ms duration led to higher accuracy than the 2000ms duration. Based on these results, and to reduce the fatigue of using our system in an online setting (by having the minimal possible duration), we chose to display images for 500ms for the first gaze recall, and 1000ms for the last gaze and all gazes recall.

USER STUDY 2: GAZE RECALL OF ONLINE CROWDS

Based on User Study 1, we know that our gaze recall method has reasonable accuracy and is feasible when applied in lab settings to individuals. We now apply this approach in a crowdsourcing setting where we look to see if an *aggregate* of a large number of participants' data is comparable to that of eye trackers and visual attention models. We conducted a followup online study without an eye tracker to validate our approach in a real crowdsourcing environment, and demonstrate its efficiency for collect gaze data to generate heat maps and trajectory maps.

Participants and Procedure

We recruited 227 participants (85 female and 142 male) from Amazon Mechanical Turk (AMT), which is the most widely used environment for crowdsourcing as it is easy to recruit worldwide participants, manage tasks and data, and make payments. They were aged between 18 and 67 years (*M*=30.0, *SD*=9.1), and none reported being color-blind or having visual impairments. We designed and developed a website called *GazeCrowd* to conduct an online study, and integrated it with AMT. When participants opened *GazeCrowd*, they were presented with a consent form, and upon giving consent, were shown the study page. The test images and sequences were the same as in study 1. Subjects were told that the test session would take 15 minutes (actual duration was *M*=621.6 seconds, *SD*=428.1), and each participant received $0.20 USD.

As opposed to traditional eye-tracking experiments, it was not possible to observe participants and detect any fake results. Hence, to filter out cheating (fake data) or noisy data from participants, we designed three mechanisms to insure the quality of test data: 1) each participant went through a training session similar to our previous study; 2) each participant received a code from *GazeCrowd* after finishing all test sessions, and had to provide this code to receive payment; 3) if the test session completion time was very short (*e.g.*, much shorter than the minimum duration in our lab test), we did not use this participant's data. In our study, we removed 13 of 227 (5.7%) participants who submitted invalid codes or had short test durations.

We also designed mechanisms to reduce noisy data generated by our system. For example, to limit the impacts of network delay, test images were pre-loaded to a participant's local drive while she read the instructions at the start of a session. To avoid issues with different screen resolutions, we dynamically generated the grid images to cover the test images, regardless of screen or browser used.

Results

For each image in the first and last gaze recall tasks, we visualized all the participants' mouse clicks as heatmaps [11], which provides a clean depiction of aggregate gaze by combining gaze points from multiple viewers. Then we compared the heatmaps generated with our approach with 2 other approaches: eye tracker data and a salience-based visual model. Figure 3 shows 3 example images, on which the 3 approaches were applied. From left to right, the first column has the original images, the second column has heatmaps generated with the *iLab Neuromorphic Vision C++ Toolkit* (http://ilab.usc.edu/toolkit/home.shtml) based on a bottom-up saliency-based visual attention model (denoted as VHM) [17], and the third column has heatmaps generated from eye tracker fixation data from the first study (denoted as FHM), using the SMI BeGaze™ software. In the fourth column, heatmaps were generated from mouse clicks from the online crowdsourcing study (CHM).

The first row shows the results of the *first gaze* recall (with test image display duration of 500ms). All the heatmaps are similar, but the VHM has a greater number of hot spots than both the FHM and CHM. The second and third rows show results for the *last gaze* recall (image display durations are both 1000ms); although all the heatmaps are similar, VHM is not very sensitive to people in the images, especially faces (*e.g.*, second column, third row). These results indicate that compared to FHM and VHM, CHM appears to be robust and accurate, in identifying salient aspects of these images.

We also found that our gaze recall approach can capture both bottom-up and top-down visual mechanisms. We compared the heatmaps from the all gaze recall without and with specific tasks. VHM was not applied in this analysis because it only applies to the bottom-up mechanism. Figure 4(a) (CHM) and 4(c) (FHM) had no tasks assigned. Driven by the bottom-up visual cognitive mechanism, most participants only focused on the high intensity human face in the middle of the image. Figure 4(b) (CHM) and 4(d) (FHM) show the results given the task of counting how many people were in the image. Driven by the top-down visual cognitive mechanism, participants had more gazes on each person in the image. Similarly, as shown in Figure 4(e) to 4(h), when participants were given the task to find the Nike logo in the image (4f, 4h corresponding to CHM and FHM), they narrowed down the area for visual search, and allocated greater visual attention where the logo was located, compared to the without task case (4e and 4g). All figures indicate a high consistency between the CHM and FHM. This indicates that our gaze recall approach can identify both bottom-up and top-down visual mechanisms.

Participants were fairly consistent in what regions they looked at but not in what order they viewed them [26]. However, heatmaps do not depict gaze order. Instead we used a transition map [23] to illustrate the gaze trajectories from all participants. We divided each test image into a number of AOIs on the basis of the gestalt laws (*e.g.*, "law of closure", "law of similarity"). Then we recorded the count of fixations or mouse clicks located in each AOI, and the frequency of gazes (or clicks) that transitioned from one AOI to another. Note that we removed the fixations from the eye tracking data that did not correspond to any AOI (most were image backgrounds), as users rarely report these and they were not salient in our images.

Taking one test image as an example (Figure 5), we identified 3 AOIs in the test image (corresponding to the 3 objects), and recorded the count of fixations or mouse clicks located in each AOI, and the frequency of gazes (or clicks) that transitioned from one AOI to another.

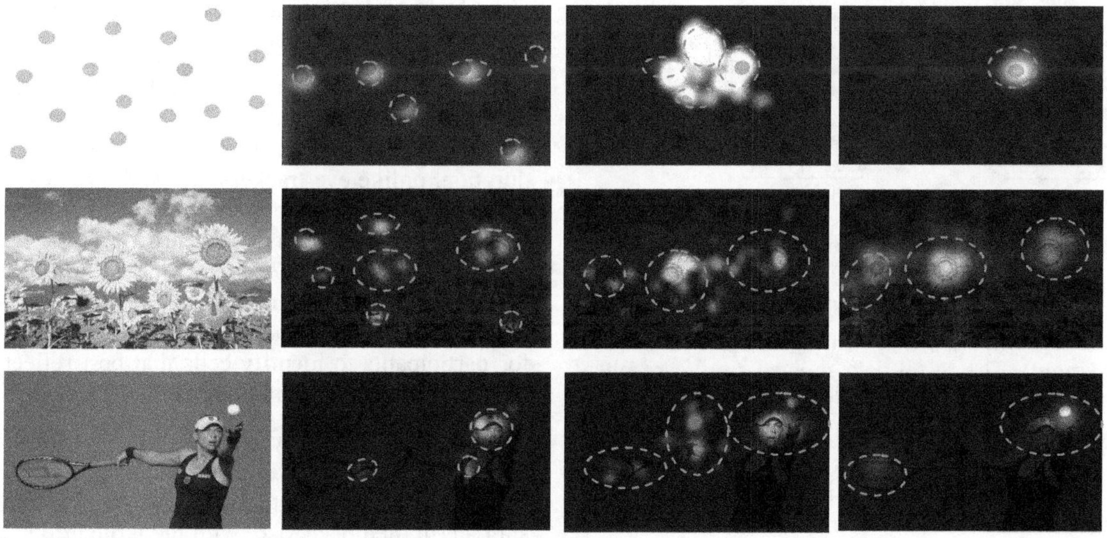

Figure 3. Examples of heatmap comparison without tasks for the first (row 1) and last gaze recall (rows 2 & 3). Ovals indicate the parts of the image that were the most visually salient (from a visual attention model, from eye gaze data, and from our recall data).

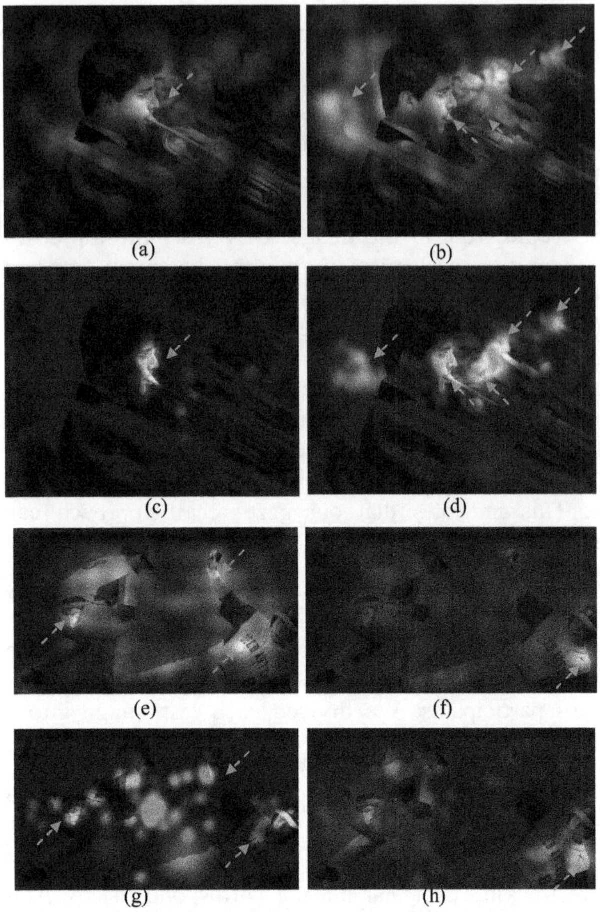

Figure 4. Examples of heatmap (generated from crowdsourced mouse click data (a, b, e, f) and eye tracker data (c, d, g, h) comparison for the all gaze recall, without (first column) and with specific tasks (second column). Arrows indicate the areas that received the most visual attention.

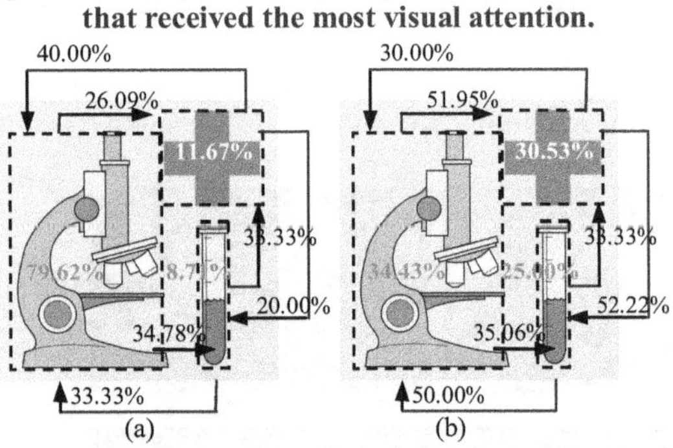

Figure 5. Transition map of gaze trajectory aggregated by a) eye tracking data b) crowdsourced click data.

As shown in Figure 5(a), from the eye tracking data, for the AOI on the left (microscope), 26% of gaze transitions moved to the red cross (top right), and 35% to the red test tube (bottom right). The recall data showed similar results: 52% to the red cross, and 35% to the test tube. The recall data was very accurate for half of the transitions: microscope to test tube, test tube to red cross, and red cross to microscope. However the transitions in the opposite direction were not as accurate. Future work is necessary to understand the uni-directional nature of our approach.

GENERAL DISCUSSION

Our crowdsourced approach for gathering fixation data has comparable accuracy to the more standard device-based eye tracking methods, particularly for point-count ratio, trajectory distance and first and last gaze heatmaps. While participant recall of gaze cannot capture real eye movement data, and relies on short-term memory to achieve fast and accurate performance, it trades off this potential inaccuracy against the cost and convenience of being able to conduct a study online efficiently with no special equipment. In our crowdsourced study, we collected data from 227 participants from all over the world in 5 days, at a total cost of US$45.4. In contrast, a commercial eye tracker, while much more accurate (0.5° of visual angle error), costs tens of thousands of dollars, and can only be used with a single participant at a time. Our initial lab study also took 5 days, but for only 20 participants, at a cost of $200.

Our approach does not require new hardware, and does not have the limitations of webcam based eye trackers. It was interesting that some participants had much lower visual angle errors than others. The mean error was 3.7°, (range: 1.8 to 5.5°). Similarly, some images resulted in lower error than others. In the future, we will explore why some users and images performed better, to identify opportunities for refining our approach to improve recall accuracy overall. We will show participants the same image multiple times (interleaved with other images), and use an aggregate of their recall data, to reduce noise.

Our approach is appropriate for those who want to collect a lot of gaze data cheaply and quickly. It can be applied to identify visual distractors of interfaces or images. Visual distractors will likely be found using the first gaze recall approach. A second example is refining visual layout. Using the last gaze and all gaze results, both a heatmap and a scan path can be generated, respectively. Together, these can reveal the distribution of visual attention on the stimuli, and a designer can use these to refine the layout, *e.g.*, by grouping relevant interactors to create a more logical layout.

Our approach also has some limitations: 1) with short term memory, participants cannot recall more than a few gaze points and have difficulty recalling gaze order, especially for complex scenes or tasks; 2) it does not obtain gaze duration, unlike eye trackers; 3) we did not explore the size of the grid cells which may influence recall performance. We used 9×9 grids in our current research, with the size of each grid cell being 77 pixels wide and high (1.5 to 2° of visual angle). A larger number of smaller cells would allow for finer-grained selection, but may also make it difficult for participants to identify cells that best reflect their gaze; 4) we did not test dynamic images, *e.g.*, videos.

Our approach currently works well for static images (*e.g.*, poster and webpage design), which do not include many independent AOIs, so that they can be recalled easily with short-term memory. Also, with the large grid size, we could not test very tiny AOIs, such as text. To reduce these limitations, we could: 1) divide dynamic images (*e.g.*, video) into a number of static frames to be used in a recall task, and aggregate the recall data later to produce a scan path; 2) explore whether the grid size influences recall performances and the impact on users' mental workload; 3) for complex images, ask users to review either their own or others' recall results and allow them to correct or refine them.

CONCLUSION

We measured eye movement using crowdsourcing instead of a real eye tracker, by having online crowds recall their gazes. We validated this approach through a lab-based user study, and found that participants could recall their gazes with reasonable accuracy when compared to commercial and webcam eye trackers. We then developed a prototype system, *GazeCrowd*, which leverages the crowd to collect a large amount of eye gaze data. The aggregated data produced heatmaps and transition maps similar to those from eye trackers and visual attention models. Our approach is a good complement to traditional eye- tracking, and it is cheap and efficient in collecting gaze data and trades these features for accuracy when compared to more expensive commercial eye tracking systems, and is robust to head movement and imperfect lighting conditions, and data loss typical of web cameras. Next we will apply it to remote usability tests for assessing and refining visual designs, or social recommendation systems that share gaze visualization to improve decision- making [10].

ACKNOWLEDGMENTS

We thank our study volunteers, and reviewers who provided helpful comments. This work was supported by NSF grant SES-0968566 and NSFC grant 61272308.

REFERENCES

1. Andrienko, G., *et al.* Visual analytics methodology for eye movement studies. *IEEE Trans. on Visualization and Computer Graphics 12*, 18 (2012), 2889-2898.
2. Aznar, F., Pujol, M., Rizo, R. Generating saliency maps using human based computation agents. *Current Topics in Artificial Intelligence* (2010), 252-260.
3. Baud, O., *et al.* Trajectory comparison for civil aircraft. *Aerospace Conference* (2007), 1-9.
4. Bednarik, R., Tukiainen, M. Validating the restricted focus viewer: a study using eye-movement tracking. *Behavior Research Methods 39*, 2 (2007), 274-282.
5. Blackwell, A.F., Jansen, A.R., Marriott, K. Restricted focus viewer: a tool for tracking visual attention. *Theory and application of diagrams* (2000), 162-177.
6. Bojko, A. Eye tracking the user experience: a practical guide to research. New York: Rosenfeld (2013), 8-9.
7. Borji, A., Itti, L. State-of-the-art in visual attention modeling. *IEEE Trans. on Pattern Analysis and Machine Intelligence 35*, 1 (2013), 185- 207.
8. Borji, A., Sihite, D. N., Itti, L. Quantitative analysis of human-model agreement in visual saliency modeling: a comparative study. *IEEE Trans. on Image Processing 22*, 1 (2012), 55-69.
9. Chen, M.C., Anderson, J.R., Sohn, M.H.What can a mouse cursor tell us more?: correlation of eye/mouse movements on web browsing. *CHI 2001*, 281-282.
10. Cheng, S. Third eye: designing eye gaze visualizations for online shopping social recommendations. *Extended Abstracts CSCW 2013*, 125-128.
11. Duchowski, A. T., Price, M. M., Meyer, M., Orero, P. Aggregate gaze visualization with real-time heatmaps. *ETRA 2012*, 13-20.
12. Gegenfurtner, A., Lehtinen, E., Säljö, R. Expertise differences in the comprehension of visualizations. *Educational Psych. Review 23*, 4 (2011), 523-552.
13. Henderson, J.M. Human gaze control during real-world scene perception. *TRENDS in Cognitive Sciences 7*, 11, (2003), 498-504.
14. Henderson, J.M., Hollingworth, A. High level scene perception. *Ann. Rev. Psychology 50*, (1999), 243-271.
15. Holmes, T., Zanker, J. Eye on the prize: using overt visual attention to drive fitness for interactive evolutionary computation. *GECCO 2008*, 1531-1538.
16. Hornof, A.J., Halverson, T. Cognitive strategies and eye movements for searching hierarchical computer displays. *CHI 2003*, 249-256.
17. Itti, L., Koch, C. Computational modeling of visual attention. *Nature Reviews Neuroscience 2*, 3 (2001), 194-203.
18. Itti, L. Models of bottom-up attention and saliency. In *Tsotsos (Eds.), Neurobiology of Attention*, Elsevier (2005), 576-582.
19. Jarodzka, H., Holmqvist, K., and Nyström, M. A vector-based, multidimensional scanpath similarity measure. *ETRA 2010*, 211-218.
20. Johansen, S. A., San Agustin, J., Skovsgaard, H., Hansen, J. P., Tall, M. Low cost vs. high-end eye tracking for usability testing. *CHI 2011*, 1177-1182.
21. Jones, M. N., & Mewhort, D. J. K. Tracking attention with the focus-window technique: The information filter must be calibrated. Behavior Research Methods, Instruments, & Computers, 36 (2004), 270-276.
22. Klein, R.M. Inhibition of return. *Trends in Cognitive Sciences 4*, 4 (2000), 138-147.
23. Lessing, S., Linge, L. IICap: A new environment for eye tracking data analysis. Master's thesis. University of Lund (2002), Sweden.
24. Marshall, S.P. Identifying cognitive state from eye metrics. *Aviation, Space, and Environmental Medicine 78*, 5(2007), 165-185.
25. Nothdurft, H.C. Salience of feature contrast. Neurobiology of attention. Academic Press, (2005).
26. Privitera, C. M. The scanpath theory: its definitions and later developments. *SPIE 2006*, 87-91.
27. Rodden, K., Fu, X., Aula, A., Spiro, I. Eye-mouse coordination patterns on web search results pages. *Extended Abstracts CHI 2008*, 2997-3002.
28. Rudoy, D., *et al.* Crowdsourcing gaze data collection. *CI 2012*, 1-8.
29. Yarbus, A.L. Eye-movements and vision. Plenum, 1967.

Strategic Voting Behavior in Doodle Polls

James Zou
Microsoft Research
Cambridge, MA
jazo@microsoft.com

Reshef Meir
Harvard University
Cambridge, MA
rmeir@seas.harvard.edu

David C. Parkes
Harvard University
Cambridge, MA
parkes@eecs.harvard.edu

ABSTRACT
Finding a common time slot for a group event is a daily conundrum and illustrates key features of group decision-making. It is a complex interplay of individual incentives and group dynamics. A participant would like the final time to be convenient for her, but she is also expected to be cooperative towards other people's preferences. We combine large-scale data analysis with theoretical models from the voting literature to investigate strategic behaviors in event scheduling. We analyze all Doodle polls created in the US from July-September 2011 (over 340,000 polls), consisting of both hidden polls (a user cannot see other responses) and open polls (a user can see all previous responses). By analyzing the differences in behavior in hidden and open polls, we gain unique insights into strategies that people apply in a natural decision-making setting. Responders in open polls are more likely to approve slots that are very popular or very unpopular, but not intermediate slots. We show that this behavior is inconsistent with models that have been proposed in the voting literature, and propose a new model based on combining personal and social utilities to explain the data.

Author Keywords
Event scheduling; strategic voting; Doodle; group dynamics.

ACM Classification Keywords
H.5.m. Information Interfaces and Presentation (e.g. HCI): Miscellaneous

INTRODUCTION
Online platforms for scheduling events are used more than ever. A recent survey has found that over 30% of Internet users use specialized online tools to schedule their meetings.[1] Among those tools, perhaps the most popular is the online calendar and scheduling website *Doodle* (`www.doodle.com`). In a typical Doodle poll, a *poll initiator* defines the possible dates and time slots (say, for an upcoming event), and sends a link to the poll to other participants, by e-mail or other means.

[1] `http://en.blog.doodle.com/2011/07/13/`

CSCW 2015, March 14–18, 2015, Vancouver, BC, Canada.

http://dx.doi.org/10.1145/2675133.2675273

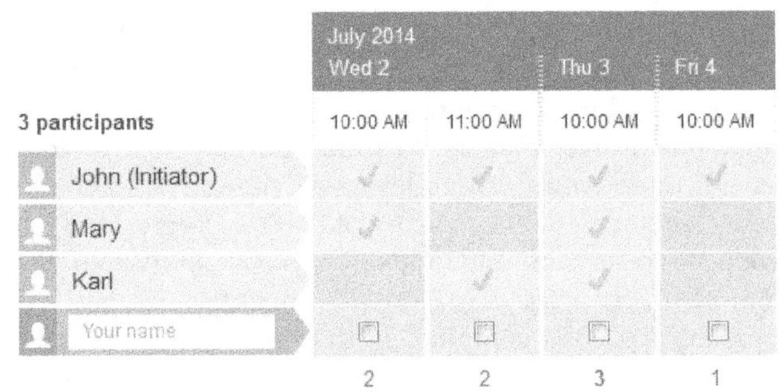

Figure 1: An open Doodle poll, as seen by the fourth voter.

Upon receiving the link, each participant can mark any number of time slots as available, see Figure 1. The poll initiator then uses the reported availability to determine the event time.

Much research has been dedicated to the adoption of scheduling tools, the conditions under which people are willing to use them, and how scheduling activities fit within the larger context of a workflow or a relationship [22, 25, 28]. We focus on the complementary question of user behavior during the scheduling process. Given that a group of people already decided to use a scheduling tool and have preferences over time slots, how do they report their availability? For example, we are interested in whether people apply strategic considerations, for example choosing to report as non-available some slots in which they could actually attend (but prefer not to).

One way to think about Doodle polls is as a *voting mechanism*. That is, after the possible slots have been announced, each participant is a voter, with preferences over event times. These preferences may be derived from constraints and considerations such as convenience of commuting, other events on the same day, and so forth. Each participant may approve a subset of the slots by marking these as available. By doing so, a participant discloses partial information about her preferences, which is then aggregated with the votes of others. If we assume that the option approved by most participants gets selected, then this voting mechanism is known in the social choice literature as *Approval voting* [14] (where a voter can vote for as many alternatives as she likes). Strategic voting has been widely studied and discussed within the social choice literature, and so by rephrasing the group scheduling problem as a voting problem, we hope to gain important insights on the strategies that participants may apply.

In the simplest case, a participant may vote for exactly the time slots for which she is available. But in reality there is a range of differing time slots, some of which may be feasible but inconvenient. How would she vote in this case? She may take into account various strategic and social considerations when casting her vote. For example, she may hide some of her available slots in hope that another, more convenient slot will be selected. Alternatively, she may mark a less convenient slot if she believes that this would enable more participants to attend the meeting. Perhaps this is done in order to be cooperative, or because she personally benefits from a time that allows as many to attend as possible. Such sophisticated behavior can depend on how earlier participants have voted. Models from the voting literature offer predictions on how individuals would behave under these settings.

Doodle polls provide a unique opportunity to study the range of strategies that people apply in group scheduling situations. Consider the following three reasons. First, there is a huge database of polls that can be used for analysis. In this paper we use more than 14 million votes from 2 million responders in over 340,000 polls.

Second, the data consists of both *hidden polls*, where participants do not see the other votes, and *open polls*, where participants can see the votes of previous participants. By using the hidden-poll data as a baseline, we can study how voting behavior is affected by the group information available to the participant and avoid other confounds (for example, changes in responses that occur due to whether a response is placed early or late, and thus closer to the associated event). This also allows us to explore the implications of design decisions made by the initiator, in terms of setting a poll to be open versus closed.

Third, Approval voting has been extensively studied in the economics, political science and AI literature, and there are many models of both truthful and strategic voting. The Doodle data can be used to test the assumptions underlying these models in a particular real scenario, as well as their predictions on voting outcomes.

Summary of Key Findings and Contributions

1. The average reported availability is higher in open polls compared to hidden polls.

2. In both open and hidden polls, there is a decline in reported availability over time. The relative rate of decline is similar between open and hidden polls.

3. Responses in open polls have higher positive correlation with previous responses compared to hidden polls.

4. Open polls have higher response rates for very popular *and* very unpopular time slots compared to hidden polls. Intermediate time slots have similar response rates between open and hidden polls.

We show that some of these empirical observations are inconsistent with standard models of Approval voting. We propose a new theoretical model, whereby a responder in an open poll votes for her preferred time slots, while also voting for highly popular slots that she does not disprefer, while also trying to appear cooperative, to explain the data.

Related work

Reinecke et al. [27] study how cultural differences between countries are reflected in scheduling patterns on Doodle. In particular they show that participants in collectivist countries tend to coordinate more with one another in open polls. Recognizing this, we use data from a single country (US) to avoid confounding due to such cultural differences.

The phenomenon of vote coordination in open online polls is related to a theoretical model of *herding* [5, 30, 17, 1], where information revealed in early votes influences voting dynamics and leads to a failure of information aggregation. Herding typically refers to situations where a voter faces a binary choice (e.g., to recommend a product or not, or choosing between two alternatives), and is learning about the best option from the responses of others rather than bringing her own preferences to bear.

The implications of sequential voting in more complex scenarios have also been studied [2, 9]. However these models deal with equilibrium analysis, thereby assuming very sophisticated participants. Moreover, these models do not consider Approval voting.

The role of incentives in scheduling has also received attention in the AI literature. However these papers focus mainly on the design of novel scheduling systems with various guarantees [10, 8]; or on optimizing the behavior of automated agents who operate on behalf of users [11, 7]. We are interested how human participants behave in an existing scheduling system.

Approval voting

Brams and Fishburn [3] offered the first systematic model of strategic behavior under Approval voting. They assume that voters have a weak transitive preference order over alternatives, and define a vote as *sincere* if the voter prefers all alternatives on which she votes over all other alternatives. Crucially, a voter may have more than one sincere way to vote. Brams and Fishburn prove that a voter who has at most three levels of preference[2] is always better off by voting sincerely. However, a voter may prefer to vote insincerely if she has four or more levels of preference.

A key issue in strategic voting models is the assumption about what information a voter has when deciding on her vote. Brams and Fishburn assume that voters have no knowledge whatsoever about the preferences or actions of others. A more elaborate model for Approval voting was studied by Weber [29], based on a general voting theory [23]. Here voters have a common prior distribution over the total number of votes obtained by each alternative, and they each try to maximize their expected utility w.r.t. this distribution. Weber shows that the optimal vote (i.e., the rational best response of a voter to any distribution) is sincere.

While the Weber model assumes that voters are highly sophisticated, capable of probabilistic calculations, a heuristic strategy called the *leader rule* has been suggested by Laslier [13].

[2]That is, alternatives can be partitioned to three sets, such the voter prefers all alternative in a set to all alternatives in the next set, but is indifferent between the alternatives in each set.

This is a simple and sincere strategy (see details in the next sections), and Laslier was able to show that it is optimal for a rational voter in a special case of the Weber model in which there is a common prior on the *rank order* of alternatives.

Other researchers have studied social factors affecting voting behavior, albeit not under the Approval system [6, 18]. In particular, the MBD model, named after Manski [19], Brock and Durlauf [4], assumes that a voter tries to meet the expectations of her peers (see [18]). The MBD model completely ignores any self-interested aspect of voting: the alternative that actually gets selected does not factor into the utility of the voter (assuming that the number of voters is high and thus every single vote is negligible). The simple model that we propose and support with the Doodle poll data combines both social and self-interest considerations.

EMPIRICAL RESULTS

Data collection

The dataset consists of all the polls created by US users on Doodle over the three month period July-September, 2011. It was collected and anonymized by Doodle and shared with the authors under a research agreement. We focus our analysis on polls with at least three participants, at least four time slots and only yes/no options. In Doodle, it is also possible to set up a poll where the participants can choose from one of three options (yes/no/maybe) for each time slot. However, there are very few three-option polls and we exclude them from our analysis. There are two types of yes/no polls: *open* and *hidden*. In open polls, responders can see all the previous responses. In hidden polls, a responder does not see any previous responses. We have 345,297 open polls and 7,390 hidden polls that pass this filtering. While there are fewer hidden polls, there are sufficiently many hidden polls to perform meaningful statistical analysis.

Key assumption. In our analysis, we compare certain statistical properties of the open polls with that of the hidden polls. We do this to isolate the effect of observations of previous responses and to avoid confounds. In order for this comparison to be reasonable, we need open and hidden polls to be generated from similar distributions of activities or events, so that the main difference in response patterns are driven by the fact that responders see previous responses in open polls. Our collection of polls has a median of 5 responders and 12 time slots. The patterns we discuss below are robust if we stratify and compare open and hidden polls with the same number of responders and time slots, where there is sufficient sample size for analysis.

Hypotheses

Our goal is to investigate how responders' behavior changes when all previous responses are public. We state several hypotheses, and later test whether they are corroborated by the data. Our first hypothesis is bidirectional, as it is not *a priori* clear whether seeing previous responses would make the next responder approve more slots:

[H 1.1]. The fraction of time slots approved by voters differs between hidden and open polls.

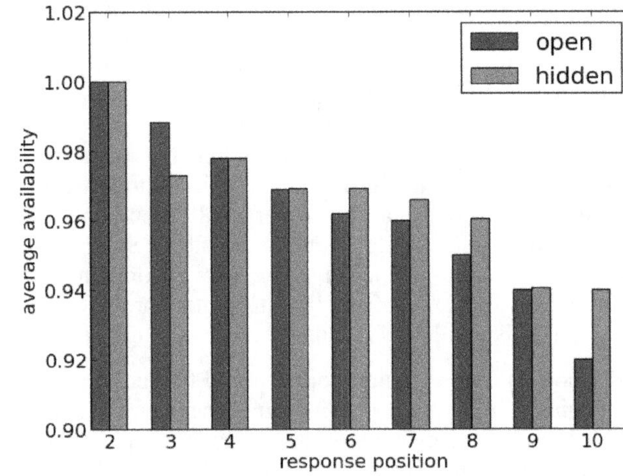

Figure 2: Normalized average availability as a function of responder position in hidden and open polls.

We hypothesize that Doodle responders, on average, will select time slots that work for other people, and will do this to a greater extent in open polls:

[H 1.2]. The correlation of the votes of a participant and the aggregated votes from previous participants is positive and is higher in open polls than in hidden polls.

We also conjecture that participants in open polls will tend to vote more for popular alternatives (i.e. time slots that have received relatively large number of votes from previous participants), and will be more reluctant to approve unpopular alternatives:

[H 1.3]. The probability that a voter will approve a popular alternative is higher in open polls than in hidden polls.

[H 1.4]. The probability that a voter will approve an unpopular alternative is lower in open polls than in hidden polls.

Average availability

We define the *aggregate availability* of a poll to be the average proportion of 'yes' votes from all responders. Open polls have average availability of 0.53, which is significantly higher than the 0.39 average availability of hidden polls ($p < 10^{-5}$).

After controlling for the number of time slots and participants in polls as covariates in a linear regression, we still obtain significantly higher availability in open polls. In addition, we compute the average availability for each time slot, aggregated over all polls. We observe uniform availability across the time slots in both open and hidden polls, showing no bias in approvals for 'leftmost slots' (early times) or 'rightmost slots' (late times) in. Moreover, for each time slot, open polls have higher availability than hidden polls. We conclude that Hypothesis 1.1 is supported, in the positive direction.

We can also measure the availability for the first responder, second responder, and so forth. The availability of an individual is the fraction of time slots she approves. In both open and hidden polls, we observe that the average availability declines monotonically for later responders. This decline could be due to responders of the poll becoming more constrained the more they wait to answer the poll. It is also possible that busier people tend to respond later to polls and are also more constrained in the number of time slots they approve.

Both open and hidden polls have similar rate of decline. We see this in Figure 2. This plots the normalized average availability for responders 2 through 10, in each of open and hidden polls. We ignore responder 1 since this person is likely to be the poll creator and an outlier,[3] and normalize availability by dividing the availability by responder 2's availability.

Correlation with previous responders

For each responder we compute the Pearson correlation between her availability and the aggregated availability of all previous responses. This measures how likely she is to agree with earlier participants.

In both open and hidden polls, the correlation increases monotonically in response position (see Figure 3). Open polls have significantly higher correlation than hidden polls, supporting Hypothesis 1.2 ($p < 0.01$). This suggests that later participants actively try to match the previous responses that they observe. This finding is also consistent with Reinecke et al. [27], who found that participants in open polls tend to reach a consensus more often.

As a control, we randomize the open and hidden polls by permuting each row of a poll. The randomized polls, as expected, have zero correlation for all the response positions. The small positive correlation observed in hidden polls could be because a subset of slots are intrinsically more popular among all responders, and they are also more likely to be selected by later responders who have additional constraints.

Thus the Doodle data supports Hypothesis 1.3, and rejects Hypothesis 1.4. In fact, H1.4 is *inverted*, as we observe significantly higher response rates ($p < 10^{-5}$) for the least popular time slots in open polls than in hidden polls.

Which time slots get the extra availability?

To understand why there is higher availability in open polls, we investigate the distribution of votes for different types of time slots in open and hidden polls. We compute the *response curves* for the responder in position $n = 11$, focusing on polls with ≥ 11 responders (32,527 open polls and 2434 hidden polls). The response curve is computed by looking at the response of the 11th responder, averaged across all polls. See Figure 4. The dots show the probability that the 11th responder inputs 'available' (y-axis) conditioned on i out of the first 10 votes 'available' for $i = 0, 1, ..., 10$ (x-axis). Both curves are S-shaped due to mean-reversion.

Open polls show higher response rate relative to hidden polls for time slots with both low availability and high availability

[3]Indeed, responder 1 shows 12% and 20% higher availability than the poll average in hidden and open polls, respectively.

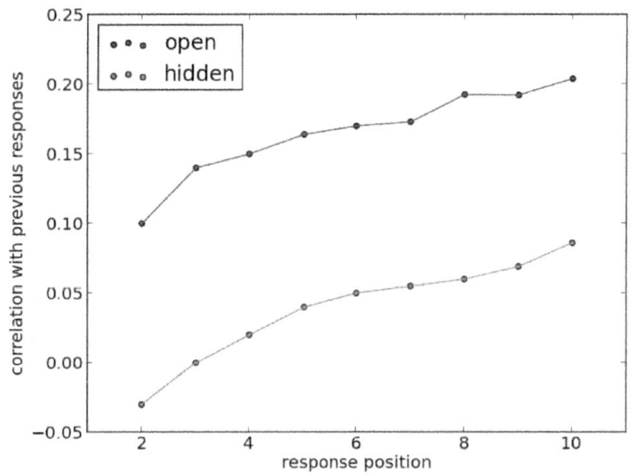

Figure 3: Correlation with previous responses in hidden and open polls.

($p < 0.01$). Both kinds of polls show similar response rates for time slots with intermediate popularity (4/10 and 5/10). To additionally verify this result, we also compute the response curves at $n = 6$ (see Figure 5). There are 160,574 open polls and 5105 hidden polls with at least 6 participants. Again, open polls exhibit consistently higher response rate compared to hidden polls, with the smallest gap for the intermediate time slot with 2/5 popularity. The difference in response rates for the intermediate time slots between hidden and open polls is not statistically significant.

Conditional response rate

The response curves in Figures 4 and 5 are aggregated over all voters. Two possible explanations for the observed patterns are: (a) responders choose to mark both highly popular and highly unpopular slots; or (b) there are two types of voters, where some tend to mark the popular slots, and others tend to mark the unpopular ones (possibly a minority group whose preferences differ from the rest). We compute conditional response rates and show that this supports the first explanation.

Conditioned on the $n = 11$ individual having approved a 10/10 time slot (i.e., a very popular one), we compute her response rate for other time slots. In particular, we are interested in her conditional response rate for other popular (9/10, 8/10), intermediate (5/10, 4/10) and unpopular (1/10, 0/10) time slots. See Table 1. Comparing the conditional response rates between open and hidden polls reveals several surprises:

1. In open polls, people who have voted for a 10/10 slot are significantly more likely to approve unpopular slots (0/10 and 1/10) than in hidden polls ($p < 0.01$).

2. In open polls, people who have voted for a 10/10 slot are significantly less likely to approve an intermediate (5/10) slot than in hidden polls ($p < 0.01$).

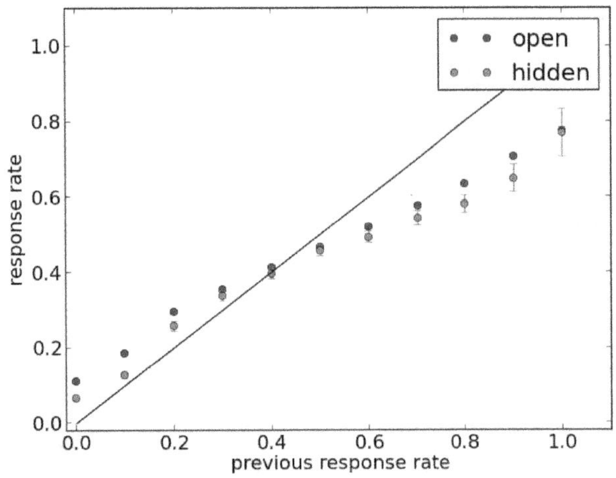

Figure 4: **Response curve for the 11th responder.** Each dot represents the probability that the 11th responder approves a slot (y-axis) if the slot has been approved by i out of the first 10 responders (x-axis), for $i = 0, ..., 10$. Error bars shows the 95% confidence interval. The open poll error bars are small.

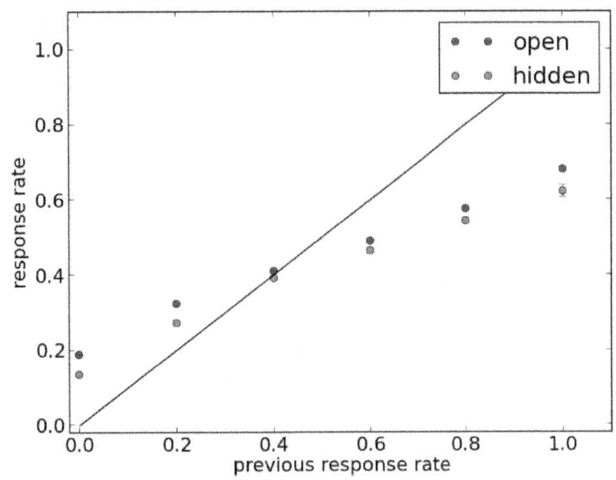

Figure 5: **Response curve for the 6th responder.** Each dot represents the probability that the 6th responder approves a slot (y-axis) if the slot has been approved by i out of the first 5 responders (x-axis), for $i = 0, ..., 5$. In both Figures 4 and 5, open polls show statistically higher response rates for popular and unpopular time slots compared to hidden polls. For intermediate time slots, the difference between open and hidden polls is not statistically significant.

3. In contrast, the conditional response rates for other popular time slots are similar between open and hidden polls.

To further validate these results, we also compute the conditional response rates for the $n = 11$ individual who has approved a 9/10 time slot, and observe similar patterns (Table 2). This means that the same responders who approve popular slots are in effect shifting some of their votes from medium to unpopular slots.

Table 1: Conditional response rates for individuals who have approved a 10/10 slot.

	0/10	1/10	4/10	5/10	8/10	9/10
open	**0.08**	**0.20**	0.44	0.51	0.70	0.76
hidden	0.05	0.09	**0.55**	**0.66**	0.69	0.76

Table 2: Conditional response rates for individuals who have approved a 9/10 slot.

	0/10	1/10	4/10	5/10	8/10	10/10
open	**0.14**	**0.24**	0.46	0.51	0.69	0.81
hidden	0.03	0.23	**0.50**	**0.56**	0.68	0.83

ANALYSIS

The patterns observed in the previous section suggest that in open polls responders may resort to *strategic* behavior, whereby they do not simply mark all feasible time slots. In order to analyze possible incentives for such behavior, we introduce a preference model and concepts commonly used in the theory of Approval voting. This formal notation is required for a precise presentation and analysis, however we also explain each component in words.

Let $A = \{a_1, a_2, ..., a_M\}$ denote the time slots designated by the initiator of the poll. We denote the responders (or *voters*) by $V = v_1, v_2, ..., v_N$, where voters are in temporal order so that v_n is the n'th responder to the poll. The *response* (or *vote*) of v_n, denoted as r_n, is the set of slots that she approves. We also think of r_n as a binary vector, with $r_n(a) = 1$ if she approves slot a and $r_n(a) = 0$ otherwise.

For a set of votes R, we denote by $s(a, R) = \sum_{r \in R} r(a)$ the *score* of alternative a, aggregating all votes in R. We denote by $\mathbf{s}(R) = (s(a, R))_{a \in A}$ the score vector over R. Let $R_{\leq n} = (r_i)_{i \leq n}$ denote the collection of all votes by voters up to and including v_n. We adopt $s_{\leq n}(a)$ and $\mathbf{s}_{\leq n}$ as a shorthand for $s(a, R_n)$ and $\mathbf{s}(R_n)$, respectively. Given the first n voters, we divide the time slots with the highest, middle, and lowest number of votes into three sets $\{\text{Popular}_{\leq n}, \text{Intermediate}_{\leq n}, \text{Unpopular}_{\leq n}\}$.

The preference of voter v_n is a partition of $\{a_1, ..., a_M\}$ into sets $\{A^n_1, ..., A^n_K\}$ such that voter v_n is indifferent about slots in the same set A^n_k, and strictly prefers any slot in A^n_k to any slot in $A^n_{k'}$ if k is less than k'. We allow the possibility that a set is empty.

The K levels can be thought of as *preference levels*. A responder with $K = 2$ is called *dichotomous*, and is simply "available" at some times and "unavailable" at others. A responder with $K = 3$ may distinguish between times that are convenient, available but inconvenient, and not available. W.l.o.g., since levels can be empty, we assume that all the responders have the same number of levels K.

A vote r_n is *sincere* if for all $a \in r_n, a' \notin r_n$, it holds that she prefers a to a'. In words: if all of the approved slots are preferred by the voter to all of the slots that are not approved.

A vote r'_n *dominates* vote r_n if for all actions of other voters, voter v_n prefers the outcome had she voted r'_n to the outcome had she voted r_n.

A vote r_n is *admissible* if there is no vote r'_n that dominates r_n. Intuitively, if a voter has fixed preference levels and is only interested in the outcome of the vote (that is, in which slot is selected), then she will always submit admissible votes.

PROPOSITION 1 (BRAMS AND FISHBURN [3]). *A vote r_n in an Approval voting system is admissible if and only if $A^n_1 \subseteq r_n$ and $A^n_K \cap r_n = \emptyset$.*

In words, a vote is admissible if and only if a voter approves all top-level choices and no bottom-level choices. Given this viewpoint, the behavior of responder v_n can be described by a *response function* f. This function takes as input the preferences P_n and the available information on previous responses $\mathbf{s}_{\leq n-1}$. The output of response function f is a subset of time slots r_n, taken to be the vote, and the function f may or may not be deterministic. We say that a response function f is sincere if it always generates a sincere vote. Different voters may apply different response functions, but ideally we would like to be able to explain voting behavior using a small number of simple response functions, or even a single response function.

Testing response functions

We describe some response functions that have been suggested in the literature.

In order to test some of the models (i.e., response functions), we run *social simulations* of open polls, albeit very simple ones. We assume that in hidden polls, responders submit admissible votes consistent with Prop. 1. Recall that by our other key assumption, the actual availability/preferences of participants in hidden and in open polls follow the same underlying distribution. This means we can use the open polls to derive some information on the preferences of participants in the hidden polls. In particular, to test a particular response function, we generate synthetic preference profiles using data from the hidden polls, and then run simulations of open polls where voters vote sequentially according to a particular response function and for each of the generated preference profiles. Then, we compare the patterns observed in the simulation with those described in the previous sections.

Random cutoff.

The simplest response function is to mark the most preferred $q \geq 0$ candidates, where q is fixed or is sampled from some distribution. We call such a response function *q-cutoff*. In the *random cutoff*, q is sampled uniformly from $\{0, 1, 2, \ldots, M\}$. Some variations of the random cutoff function have been studied in [26]. They also describe a more general class of response functions which they call *size independent*. Crucially, all size independent functions only use the preferences P_n as input, and all are sincere. Another variation is to choose an availability level $q > 0$, and approve all slots in A^n_k, $k < q$, plus a random subset in level A^n_q. We refer to this variation as the q-level cutoff function.

Irrespective of the particular variation, the responder does not use any information based on votes from previous responders. Hence it cannot explain the difference that we observe between open and hidden polls.

Lazy responses.

Determining one's own availability for a certain time slot may require some effort. Recognizing this, we consider a simple variation of the cutoff model, where responders refrain from even checking their own availability for time slots that do not seem like they are going to be selected. Thus a *lazy q-level cutoff* function only considers responding to plausible time slots (each responder might have her own threshold for what level of support makes a slot plausible). A lazy response function requires access to $\mathbf{s}_{\leq n-1}$, i.e. the votes placed so far. Lazy responses may not be sincere, and may not even be admissible if the voter refrains from assessing implausible slots in A^n_1.

In the lazy model, conditioning on voting for a Popular time slot, we would expect the responder to be less likely to vote for an Unpopular slot in open polls than in hidden polls. Empirically we observe the opposite, and thus reject this model.

The Leader rule.

Let x and y be the *leader* and the *challenger* after the first $n-1$ votes. That is, $x = \text{argmax}_{a \in A}\, s_{\leq n-1}(a)$, $y = \text{argmax}_{a \neq x}\, s_{\leq n-1}(a)$. In case of tie, a leader and a challenger is randomly selected from the set of candidates with the most votes. The Leader Rule [13] stipulates that voter v_n will approve all candidates that she strictly prefers to x, and will approve x if and only if x is strictly preferred to y. It is easy to see that the Leader rule is sincere.

To test the Leader Rule, we generate synthetic preference profiles as follows. For each hidden poll responder, we assume all of her m approved slots are in level 1 (most preferred); this is consistent with Prop. 1. Then we assign a random preference ordering (starting from $m+1$ onward) to the other slots. Thus for each responder, we obtain a preference ordering over all time slots. Then we simulate an open poll with the same number of voters and slots by adopting the Leader Rule. Figure 7 (left) shows the $n = 11$ response curve for these synthetic open polls. It exhibits uniformly higher response rates in open polls across all slots. In particular, simulated open polls show significantly higher ($p < 0.01$) response rates for Intermediate slots.

We conclude that the Leader Rule does not replicate the pattern in Figure 4, where only Popular and Unpopular slots get additional votes and Intermediate slots show statistically similar response rate between open and hidden polls. Therefore we reject this model.

A SOCIAL VOTING MODEL

In many scenarios there are factors that affect the utility of the voter other than just the outcome. For example, voters may prefer an outcome that is also convenient for others [15], or vote in accordance to the expectations of their peers, as in the MBD model [19, 4]. Other considerations may bias voters towards a strategy that is truthful or sincere, that is, in accordance with the voter's own preferences [21, 24].

Social utility is one possible explanation for approving popular slots in a meeting context, as participants may prefer a time that is convenient to more people or allows more people to attend. But why would a responder mark an unpopular slot? Other than being able to see the responses of the previous participants, responders in open Doodle polls can also see their peer names, including after the poll is over. Social theories suggest when workers in a group monitor one another, they incentivize members of the group to hold up to the group norms [12].

We conjecture that there is an implicit social expectation that every responder will mark as many slots as possible. Therefore a responder in open polls may be motivated to mark more slots. In other words, bearing in mind that other participants can see her name and vote, a participant may want to approve more time slots to *appear more cooperative* and even if they are less convenient for herself. While any additional slot that is approved increases the social utility, voting on inconvenient slots is also risky for a participant, since these slots may come out as winners in the end. The risk is lower if the additional inconvenient slots are very unpopular, as these would be unlikely to win.

Motivated by this consideration, we propose the following **Social voting** response function for a voter v_n. For simplicity, we consider three level preferences, $K = 3$, in defining Social voting:

- Approve A_1^n.
- Approve $A_2^n \cap$ Popular.
- Approve $A_2^n \cap$ Unpopular.

In words, a voter approves all of her most preferred slots, irrespective of their popularity. In addition, among the slots at her second preference level, the voter approves those slots that are either very popular or very unpopular. No slot of the third preference level is approved.

By this theory, the Unpopular slots are marked to appear cooperative with the social norm, and since they have a low chance of getting selected anyways.[4]

PROPOSITION 2. *Social voting is admissible and (for $K = 3$) sincere.*

The proof follows immediately from Proposition 1 of Brams and Fishburn [3]. The proposition shows that by following this Social voting response function, a voter can gain additional social utility without a substantial loss of "strategic" utility, and still remain sincere.

[4]A variation of the Social voting model is for the responder to also approve $A_3^n \cap$ Unpopular (note that this variation is neither admissible nor sincere). In our simulation framework (below), this leads to much higher response rates for Unpopular slots than observed in real open polls, hence we reject this alternative.

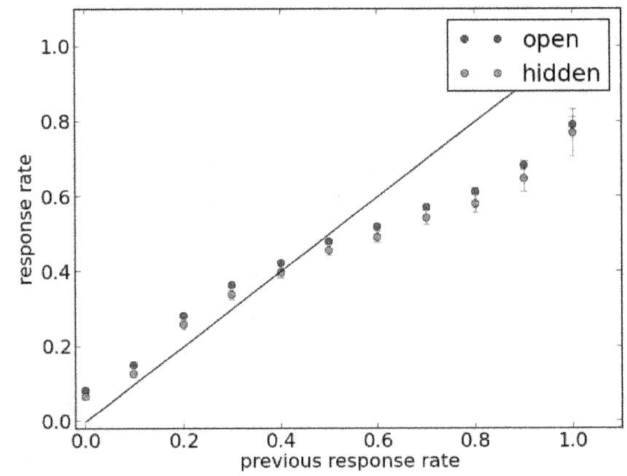

Figure 6: Response curve for synthetic open polls generated by the Leader rule. Hidden polls are from the real data.

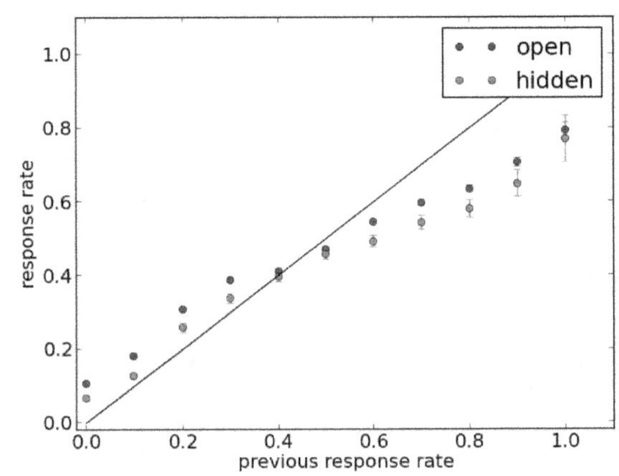

Figure 7: Response curve for synthetic open polls generated by the Social voting rule (compare with the Leader rule in Figure 6). The Leader rule does not generate data matching the observed response rates, while the Social voting rule does reproduce the observed pattern.

Simulation Results

We show that our proposed behavioral model produces response curves patterns qualitatively similar to that observed in the real data. As in testing the Leader Rule, we take the real hidden polls and generate synthetic open polls based on this behavioral model. For each hidden poll, we assume that a responder v_n approves A_1^n (all most preferred slots). To generate a responder $\hat{v}^n$ for the corresponding synthetic open poll, we set: $\hat{A}_1^n = A_1^n$; $\hat{A}_2^n$ to be a random subset among the time slots *not* approved by v_n; and $\hat{A}_3^n$ to be the remaining slots. We choose the size of the random subsets $\hat{A}_2^n$ so that the availability averaged over all the synthetic open polls when participants adopt the Social voting rule matches the average availability of the real open polls. Given these assumed preference levels, each voter v_n in a synthetic open poll partitions the time slots into Popular$_{\leq n-1}$, Intermediate$_{\leq n-1}$ and

$\text{Unpopular}_{\leq n-1}$ and approves $\hat{A}_1^n \cup (\hat{A}_2^n \cap (\text{Popular}_{\leq n-1} \cup \text{Unpopular}_{\leq n-1}))$, as specified by the Social voting response function.

Figures 6 and 7 show the $n = 11$ response curve for these synthetic open polls under this behavior model, combined with the curve for real hidden polls. The synthetic open polls have significantly higher ($p < 10^{-5}$) response rates for popular and unpopular slots, and there is no statistically significant difference with hidden polls for intermediate slots. The pattern we see in the social simulations matches the pattern observed in the real data (see Figure 4).

DISCUSSION

Standard models of user behavior in voting were mostly developed in the context of strategic voters who are trying to affect the identity of the selected candidate or alternative. However social factors beyond those that relate to the choice of the winning candidate can play some role in voters' decisions. Our analysis demonstrates that in social settings, such as scheduling a group meeting, voters may have other incentives that are also important.

We show that responders are more likely to approve highly popular and unpopular time slots in open polls than in hidden polls. When a popular slot emerges, a responder might feel the need to approve it, in order to be cooperative or because she personally benefits from a time that allows as many to attend as possible. Moreover, because votes are public in open polls, there might be social pressure for responders to mark as many slots as possible to appear flexible. In this case, the 'safe' strategy is to vote for unpopular slots that are unlikely to win in addition to her preferred slots. We propose a social voting model that captures this phenomenon and qualitatively reproduces the same patterns as in the Doodle data. All of our analysis are based on data from the Doodle platform. It would be interesting to see if similar patterns can be found in other online and offline scheduling systems.

In future work we intend to further explore and model social utility. In particular, we would like to have a distinction between the social utility gained from *being* more cooperative to that gained from *appearing* as such. A complete behavioral model should take into account both the utility structure and the epistemic state of the voter [23, 20]. In that respect, it is important to mention that strategic voting in itself is not *a priori* harmful, and may often increase the overall social welfare of the group [16]. Further research is required to determine the welfare implications of various strategic behavior patters in Doodle.

Another interesting direction is to understand more fine-grained social dynamics in online scheduling. For example, if one has observations of the same group of individuals over multiple polls, then it should be possible to infer the influence of each member in terms of the effects of her votes on other members' votes. It would then be interesting to investigate whether influential members tends to vote early or late, as well as how members try to maximize their influence.

Finally, further understanding these social incentives and voter behavior, through empirical or theoretical analysis, also has important implications for the design of group interaction mechanisms. For example, Doodle currently offers a binary choice between hidden polls (where voters' responses are hidden both throughout the poll and after it) and open polls. Our results suggest that while open polls provide opportunity for coordination, they also provide incentives for strategic behavior that does not benefit the group and could lead to miscoordination (marking unpopular slots). A clear separation between these features and their effects may allow the design of better mechanisms for preference aggregation in everyday group decision making.

Acknowledgement We would like to David Gubler at Doodle for extracting the data and Doodle and Katharina Reinecke for sharing the data. We have also benefited from insightful discussions with Katharina Reinecke, Krzysztof Gajos and Myke Näf.

Parkes was supported in part by NSF grant CCF #1301976 and the SEAS TomKat fund.

REFERENCES

1. Ali, S. N., and Kartik, N. Herding with collective preferences. *Economic Theory 51*, 3 (2012), 601–626.
2. Battaglini, M. Sequential voting with abstention. *Games and Economic Behavior 51*, 2 (2005), 445–463.
3. Brams, S. J., and Fishburn, P. C. Approval voting. *The American Political Science Review* (1978), 831–847.
4. Brock, W. A., and Durlauf, S. N. Discrete choice with social interactions. *The Review of Economic Studies 68*, 2 (2001), 235–260.
5. Callander, S. Bandwagons and momentum in sequential voting. *The Review of Economic Studies 74*, 3 (2007), 653–684.
6. Coleman, S. The effect of social conformity on collective voting behavior. *Political analysis 12*, 1 (2004), 76–96.
7. Crawford, E., and Veloso, M. Opportunities for learning in multi-agent meeting scheduling. In *Proceedings of the AAAI 2004 Symposium on Artificial Multiagent Learning, Washington, DC* (2004).
8. Crawford, E., and Veloso, M. Mechanism design for multi-agent meeting scheduling. *Web Intelligence and Agent Systems 4*, 2 (2006), 209–220.
9. Desmedt, Y., and Elkind, E. Equilibria of plurality voting with abstentions. In *Proceedings of the 11th ACM conference on Electronic commerce*, ACM (2010), 347–356.
10. Ephrati, E., Zlotkin, G., and Rosenschein, J. S. A non-manipulable meeting scheduling system. In *Proceedings of the 13th international workshop on distributed artificial intelligence* (1994), 105–125.
11. Garrido, L., and Sycara, K. Multi-agent meeting scheduling: Preliminary experimental results. In

Proceedings of the Second International Conference on Multiagent Systems (1996), 95–102.

12. Kandel, E., and Lazear, E. P. Peer pressure and partnerships. *Journal of political Economy 100*, 4 (1992), 801.
13. Laslier, J.-F. The leader rule: A model of strategic approval voting in a large electorate. *Journal of Theoretical Politics 21*, 1 (2009), 113–136.
14. Laslier, J.-F., and Sanver, M. R. *Handbook on approval voting*. Springer, 2010.
15. Lee, H. Algorithmic and game-theoretic approaches to group scheduling. In *Proceedings of the 2014 international conference on Autonomous agents and multi-agent systems*, International Foundation for Autonomous Agents and Multiagent Systems (2014), 1709–1710.
16. Lehtinen, A. The welfare consequences of strategic behaviour under approval and plurality voting. *European Journal of Political Economy 24*, 3 (2008), 688–704.
17. Leskovec, J., Huttenlocher, D. P., and Kleinberg, J. M. Governance in social media: A case study of the wikipedia promotion process. In *Proceedings of International Conference on Weblogs and Social Media* (2010).
18. Li, J., and Lee, L.-f. Binary choice under social interactions: an empirical study with and without subjective data on expectations. *Journal of Applied Econometrics 24*, 2 (2009), 257–281.
19. Manski, C. F. Identification of endogenous social effects: The reflection problem. *The review of economic studies 60*, 3 (1993), 531–542.
20. Meir, R., Lev, O., and Rosenschein, J. S. A local-dominance theory of voting equilibria. In *Proceedings of the fifteenth ACM conference on Economics and computation*, ACM (2014), 313–330.
21. Meir, R., Polukarov, M., Rosenschein, J. S., and Jennings, N. R. Convergence to equilibria in plurality voting. In *AAAI'10* (2010).
22. Mosier, J. N., and Tammaro, S. G. When are group scheduling tools useful? *Computer Supported Cooperative Work (CSCW) 6*, 1 (1997), 53–70.
23. Myerson, R. B., and Weber, R. J. A theory of voting equilibria. *The American Political Science Review 87*, 1 (1993), 102–114.
24. Obraztsova, S., Markakis, E., and Thompson, D. R. Plurality voting with truth-biased agents. In *SAGT'13*. 2013, 26–37.
25. Palen, L. Social, individual and technological issues for groupware calendar systems. In *Proceedings of the SIGCHI conference on Human Factors in Computing Systems*, ACM (1999), 17–24.
26. Regenwetter, M., and Tsetlin, I. Approval voting and positional voting methods: Inference, relationship, examples. *Social Choice and Welfare 22*, 3 (2004), 539–566.
27. Reinecke, K., Nguyen, M. K., Bernstein, A., Näf, M., and Gajos, K. Z. Doodle around the world: Online scheduling behavior reflects cultural differences in time perception and group decision-making. In *Proceedings of the 2013 conference on Computer supported cooperative work*, ACM (2013), 45–54.
28. Thayer, A., Bietz, M. J., Derthick, K., and Lee, C. P. I love you, let's share calendars: calendar sharing as relationship work. In *Proceedings of the ACM 2012 conference on Computer Supported Cooperative Work*, ACM (2012), 749–758.
29. Weber, R. J. Approval voting. *The Journal of Economic Perspectives 9*, 1 (1995), 39–49.
30. Wu, F., and Huberman, B. A. How public opinion forms. In *Internet and Network Economics*. Springer, 2008, 334–341.

Structuring, Aggregating, and Evaluating Crowdsourced Design Critique

Kurt Luther[1], Jari-Lee Tolentino[2], Wei Wu[3], Amy Pavel[3], Brian P. Bailey[4], Maneesh Agrawala[3], Björn Hartmann[3], Steven P. Dow[1]

[1]Carnegie Mellon University {kluther,spdow} @cs.cmu.edu

[2]University of California, Irvine jltolent@gmail.com

[3]University of California, Berkeley {amypavel,maneesh,bjoern} @eecs.berkeley.edu

[4]University of Illinois at Urbana–Champaign bpbailey@illinois.edu

ABSTRACT

Feedback is an important component of the design process, but gaining access to high-quality critique outside a classroom or firm is challenging. We present CrowdCrit, a web-based system that allows designers to receive design critiques from non-expert crowd workers. We evaluated CrowdCrit in three studies focusing on the designer's experience and benefits of the critiques. In the first study, we compared crowd and expert critiques and found evidence that aggregated crowd critique approaches expert critique. In a second study, we found that designers who got crowd feedback perceived that it improved their design process. The third study showed that designers were enthusiastic about crowd critiques and used them to change their designs. We conclude with implications for the design of crowd feedback services.

Author Keywords

Design; critique; feedback; social computing; crowdsourcing

ACM Classification Keywords

H.5.3 Group and Organizational Interfaces: Computer supported cooperative work, web-based interaction

INTRODUCTION

For centuries, critique has provided a foundational exercise for art and design, and also more recently, for project-based education in computing and engineering [23]. The traditional studio critique is a co-located communication activity where someone presents preliminary work and then critics—often teachers and peers—provide feedback to improve the design [5, 2]. Critiques can help novices to understand key principles in a domain [12], to compare alternatives [7, 27], to articulate the goals and assumptions behind their work, and to recognize how others perceive their work [15]. The critique providers also learn by developing domain-specific vocabulary [4] and rehearsing the mechanics of the crit process.

CSCW 2015, March 14–18, 2015, Vancouver, BC, Canada.

ACM 978-1-4503-2922-4/15/03 ...$15.00
http://dx.doi.org/10.1145/2675133.2675283

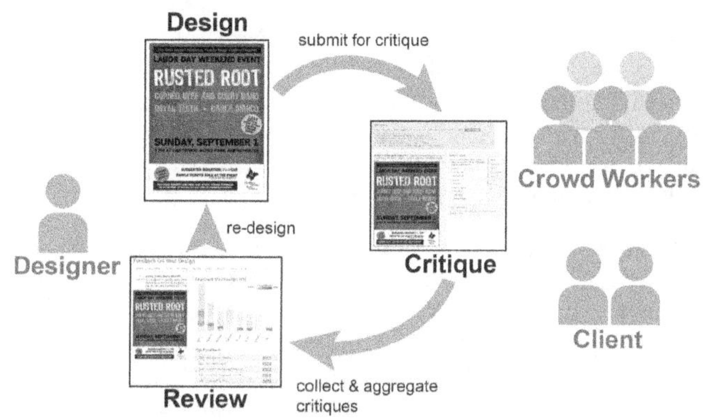

Figure 1. CrowdCrit allows designers to submit preliminary designs to be critiqued by crowds and clients. The system then aggregates and visualizes the critiques for designers.

Critique leads to knowledge sharing and helps inculcate important values and aesthetics.

Feedback can be valuable to a wide audience, from professional designers to design students to everyday designers working on slide decks and flyers. Unfortunately, high-quality critique can be difficult to obtain outside of a design firm or classroom. There are numerous online design communities where people seek feedback (e.g. Forrst [14], Photosig [32]), but these often yield sparse, superficial comments [32]. Some (e.g. Dribbble [18]) are invitation only, and most require members to build a reputation and feel comfortable sharing preliminary work. Novice designers in particular may experience evaluation apprehension and avoid sharing their works-in-progress alongside experts [18].

Recently, a number of academic and commercial efforts have explored how to leverage paid crowdsourcing platforms like Amazon Mechanical Turk (MTurk) within a design process. These platforms are attractive because they provide fast, scalable access to human intelligence at a reasonable cost, but most crowd workers lack design knowledge and cannot provide useful critiques. Most of these efforts, therefore, focus on using crowds to provide high-level impressions [11, 13] or learn more about a target audience [8]. Others (e.g. Voyant [33]) decompose the feedback process into microtasks but do not focus on the process and language of design critique.

In this paper, we propose and evaluate a different approach. We built a web-based system called CrowdCrit (Figure 1) that allows designers to submit preliminary designs, receive critiques from many crowd workers, and explore the aggregated results using an interactive visualization. Rather than searching a large crowd for design experts, CrowdCrit provides a structured interface, inspired by scaffolding theory, to help non-expert crowds submit critiques. CrowdCrit integrates with MTurk to leverage the speed, scale, and cost benefits of paid crowds, but is designed to work with any type of crowd (classmates, coworkers, user communities, etc.).

We evaluated CrowdCrit with three studies, focusing on the experience of designers and the characteristics of crowd critiques. The first study compared the characteristics of crowd critiques (N=14) to expert critiques (N=3) of the same set of poster designs. Crowd and expert critiques had comparable internal consistency, though it was low. The results also show that aggregating crowd critiques trends towards approximating expert critiques, with 10–14 crowd workers finding 40–60% of design issues identified by experts.

The second study (N=14) used interviews to explore designers' reactions to crowd critiques and examples and patterns of use in the context of a poster design contest. We found that designers of varying experience levels considered crowd critiques valuable and used them to make changes to their designs. We describe how designers explored and interpret crowd critiques, weighing attributes like crowd expertise and critique frequency against their own intuitions.

The third study (N=18) is, to our knowledge, the first controlled experiment to examine the specific impact of crowd-generated design feedback against a baseline. In a second contest, half of designers received crowd critiques and half received generic feedback. The study found that with crowd critiques, designers reported noticing more issues, making more changes, and producing an overall better design. However, third-party ratings of designs found few conditional differences, suggesting that CrowdCrit may lead designers to focus on refinement, rather than broader changes.

In the following sections, we review related work on crowdsourcing and feedback and describe the CrowdCrit system and our evaluations. We conclude with design implications for crowd feedback services.

RELATED WORK

Theories of learning and assessment

To inform our interface design, we draw on learning theory literature that explores how best to teach new concepts to students. *Scaffolding* refers to a teaching technique where learners are given significant support — by teachers or computer-based tutors, for example — to help them learn new material [25, 3]. Our system, inspired by scaffolding theory, structures the visual design critique process for the crowd by suggesting design issues and concepts as a set of pre-authored critique statements.

Sadler reviewed different feedback approaches and argued that good feedback must help a student grasp the concept of a standard (*conceptual*), compare the actual level of performance with this standard (*specific*), and engage in action that closes this gap (*actionable*) [22]. Our system structures crowd workers to include all three components in the context of visual design critique.

Peer critique vs. external feedback

Recently, researchers have explored the viability of online critique within an educational context. Tinapple et al. [26] developed CritViz, a system which enables peer critiques of designs. Kulkarni and Klemmer [16] also developed a peer critique system for use in a Massive Open Online Course (MOOC), and Easterday et al. [10] developed a mixed face-to-face and online critique system for design students in a classroom environment. These systems were shown to be effective in a formal educational setting, with students of fairly uniform levels of knowledge and motivation. Alternatively, Dow et al. [8] explored the utility of external crowds to contribute outside perspectives to add authenticity to a design course. CrowdCrit seeks to leverage the diverse capabilities of crowd workers and focuses their efforts on producing visual design critique.

Reputation vs. anonymity

Many commercial sites like Dribbble [18] and Forrst [14] allow members to upload their own creative projects and provide feedback on each other's work. However, novices are likely to experience evaluation apprehension and feel intimidated sharing their work alongside professionals [18]. CrowdCrit operates in a double-blind fashion, so that designers do not feel reluctant to share and critique providers are not influenced by the designer's reputation.

Payment vs. reciprocity

Systems that follow the reciprocity model do not require a financial transaction, but they often fail to produce enough useful feedback in a timely manner. Xu and Bailey [32] studied critique behaviors in the online photography community PhotoSIG, where members voluntarily critique each other's photos and hope for reciprocity. They found that 80% of photos received less than four critiques, which most users found insufficient. The paid crowdsourcing paradigm used by CrowdCrit provides a novel opportunity to deliver large quantities of feedback quickly and at a reasonable cost.

Impressions vs. structured feedback

Sites like Five Second Test [13] and Feedback Army [11] allow users to pay crowds to provide feedback on their designs or websites, typically in the form of overall impressions or general reactions. This kind of feedback is valuable for getting an audience's perspective on a design, but it does not illuminate why a design works well, or suggest what to change. Even in online communities for professional designers, shallow reactions, rather than detailed critique, are the norm [32].

Xu et al. [33] created the Voyant system to obtain crowd feedback on visual designs by creating structured micro-tasks. Most of the feedback types supported by Voyant centered around audience reactions (e.g. which elements are noticed first, general impressions of the design). The system also paid the crowd to rate, on a Likert scale, how well the design meets the guidelines of alignment, contrast, proximity, and repetition. CrowdCrit builds on these ideas by structuring not only the crowd's ability to *recognize* a wide range of design issues, but also the *process* and *language* of constructing a critique.

Aggregating crowd feedback

Most commercial and academic critique software is not designed to scale to large quantities of critique. CritViz [26] supported peer critique in a college course of 75 students, but each assignment received only five critiques. Voyant [33] supports large quantities of crowd feedback, using visualizations such as word clouds and histograms. Our research builds on this idea by using a stacked bar chart visualization to aggregate rich critique data, including valence (positive/negative), text comments and graphical annotations, and expertise across seven design principles.

General solutions for aggregating crowd-generated content are also germane. For example, CommentSpace [30] provided interactive visualizations and structure to help crowds perform social data analysis. We implemented several of these papers' recommendations, such as linked discussions and structured comments to support deeper analysis. Our system differs in that it focuses on the unique requirements of design critique and operates as a service for designers, providing distinct interfaces for critique collection (from crowds) and critique aggregation (for designers).

PRELIMINARY STUDIES

To better understand the challenges of crowd-generated critique and the appropriate type of structure, we conducted a series of preliminary studies on MTurk (Figure 2) to see what type of feedback crowds provided, given minimal training or structure. In our first pilot, we paid three crowd workers to write open-ended feedback on a set of eight designs. A quick analysis showed that only five of 65 responses fulfilled Sadler's [22] requirements for high-quality feedback. Next, we added some structure to the task, asking three different workers to provide feedback on four designs using two text boxes: one for describing the problem and one for explaining why it was a problem. However, these workers still failed to identify and justify significant issues with the designs. In our third pilot, we embedded design knowledge into the structure, asking three new workers to critique nine designs by considering a list of pre-authored critique statements and checking the box next to ones that applied to the given design. This approach showed promise; the three workers agreed on 65% and 52% of the issues in the two checklists we provided.

Overall, these pilots suggested that eliciting open-ended critique without appropriate task structuring led to predominantly low-quality responses that lacked conceptual grounding and action-oriented advice. Introducing structured checklists was more successful and suggested that given this type of domain-specific structure, crowd workers might identify legitimate design problems and generate reasonably useful feedback. These early findings, along with the prior work reviewed above, informed the design of our CrowdCrit system, described in the next section.

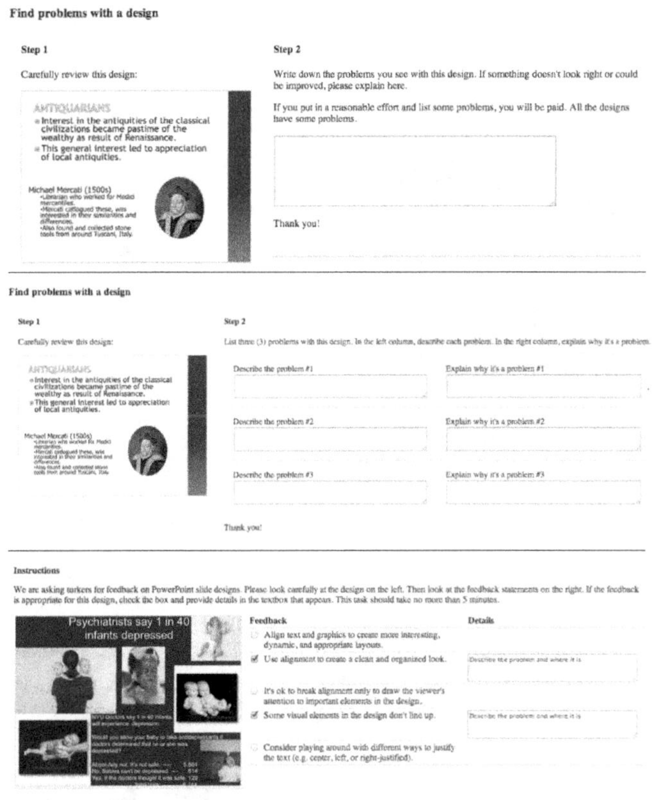

Figure 2. Crowdsourcing interfaces used for the first three pilot studies that indicated some drawbacks of open-ended designs feedback and benefits of additional structure.

THE CROWDCRIT SYSTEM

CrowdCrit is a web-based system built in Python and JavaScript that allows a user to request, receive, and review design critiques generated by an online crowd. To use the system, a designer uploads an image and provide some contextual information, such as a title, brief description, and intended audience. Next, crowd workers provide feedback on the design using a scaffolded critique interface. Finally, the designer can explore the crowd critiques using an aggregation interface which includes an interactive visualization. This process can be repeated whenever the designer seeks a new round of feedback.

Eliciting critique

CrowdCrit is designed to elicit valuable critiques from any online crowd, even those with limited design experience. Our preliminary studies and prior work suggested a structured interface could help novice crowds adopt the process and language of visual design critique. This required solving two problems: first, generating structured design knowledge based on best practices; and second, embedding this material in an interface suitable for non-expert crowd workers.

Critique statements

There is no universally agreed-upon reference for visual design critique, but our survey of widely cited design textbooks and other resources revealed significant overlap in terminology, concepts, and best practices. Therefore, two authors

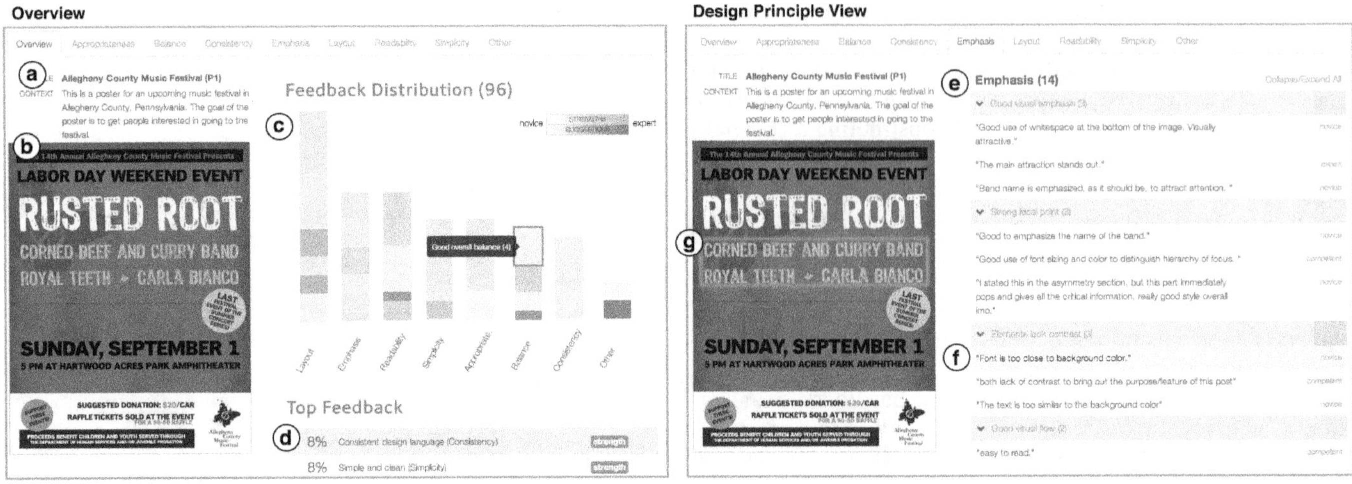

Figure 4. The Overview (left) and Design Principle view (right) for the CrowdCrit aggregation interface.

Figure 3. The CrowdCrit critique interface.

with design experience performed a bottom-up analysis of key sources [21, 31, 17, 6] to generate material for structuring our critique interface. They began by reviewing each text for lists of best practices or principles and extracting these along with definitions and examples. Next, they grouped related concepts together based on overlapping terminology, similar examples, their own knowledge and experience, and direct references in the text. After several iterations, they produced a list of seven key design principles: *Readability, Layout, Balance, Simplicity, Emphasis, Consistency,* and *Appropriateness*. The principles are distinct, but not mutually exclusive, as there are often multiple effective ways to identify issues with a design. This general approach is inspired by similar efforts in the HCI community to produce other types of design principles (e.g. [20, 28, 29]).

Each principle is composed of a set of pre-authored "critique statements" about more specific issues. CrowdCrit follows from traditional critique [12] and provides both positive and negative critique statements. For example, critique providers can praise the appropriateness of the design ("Reaches intended audience") or raise concerns about it ("Wrong audience"). A total of 70 critique statements are available across the seven principles.

Finally, each critique statement has a short name and a longer, more detailed description. The description identifies the specific issue, connects it to a broader design principle, and (in most cases) offers a generic solution. This format is meant to embody Sadler's [22] criteria for good feedback and provide a basic level of utility. For example, within the *Simplicity* principle, there is a critique statement with the name "Too much text" and the description: "The abundance of text makes this difficult for viewers to comprehend. Consider condensing this text by focusing on the essential message."

Critique interface

Crowd workers begin by completing a survey of self-reported design experience and a design knowledge quiz, used to categorize their expertise as low, moderate, or high. Next, workers are presented with the critique interface (Figure 3). The design's contextual information (a), including intended audience, along with the design itself (b), appears on 1 side, and the critique tools are shown on the other. The interface uses progressive disclosure [24] to avoid overwhelming novice critique providers with information about design. There are tabs for each of the seven design principles, plus an "Other" tab for critiques that our list may overlook (c). Crowd workers click a tab to reveal the critique statements for that principle and hide the others (d). Workers can mouseover the short statement names to display the longer description as a tooltip. After selecting a statement, the worker can use annotation tools, such as markers or polygons, to indicate the relevant area of the design (e). Workers can also elaborate on the critique using a text box (f). Finally, the worker saves the critique, and it appears on the comment list (g). The worker can repeat this process for as many critiques as they desire.

Aggregating and presenting critique

Once workers have critiqued the design, the designer needs to be able to review the feedback in a meaningful way. This poses interesting challenges compared to a traditional studio critique, which unfolds linearly, in real time, from a small number of co-located participants. In contrast, CrowdCrit generates potentially large quantities (50+) of individual critiques from online, distributed providers in a nonlinear, asynchronous format. We needed to design an interface that would handle these requirements and allow the user to identify the most significant issues with a design.

Aggregation interface

The CrowdCrit aggregation is shown in Figure 4. Like the critique interface, it leverages progressive disclosure to avoid overwhelming the user with details. The design and contextual information appear on one side (a, b), and an interactive visualization providing an overview of all critiques as a stacked bar chart (c) appears on the right (Figure 4, left). Each bar represents a design principle, and each bar segment indicates a critique statement chosen by workers. Bars are ordered by decreasing critique count so that the principle with the most critiques appears first. Color encodes critique valence; positive critiques are green and negative critiques are purple. We use lightness values to encode crowd expertise; darker shades indicate critiques from workers with higher expertise. Below the visualization, a "Top Feedback" section lists the most frequently used critique statements (d).

The designer can click a bar or segment to drill down on the detailed critiques for that principle (e), ordered by decreasing frequency (Figure 4, right). The interface displays each critiquer's text comment and expertise (f); we label workers in the bottom quartile of design expertise as novices, workers in the middle quartiles as competent, and workers in the top quartile as experienced. Hovering over a critique causes any corresponding annotations to appear on the design itself (g).

STUDY 1: COMPARING CROWD VS. EXPERT CRITIQUE

Our first study focuses on how crowd critiques compare to expert critiques. We consider the following research questions:

- How internally consistent are crowd vs. expert critiques?
- How similar are individual and aggregated crowd critiques to expert critiques?

Methods

We designed a controlled experiment using three event poster designs gathered online (Figure 5). Each poster received critiques from a group of 14 crowd workers and a group of three expert designers. The crowd workers came from MTurk and were recruited with the same criteria described above. The expert designers all had degrees in design and had worked full-time as professional designers. Both crowd workers and experts provided critiques independently, using the CrowdCrit interface.

The crowd produced between 38 and 58 critiques for each of the three designs (approximately four crits per design), using between 25 and 33 unique critique statements. Experts generated between 21 and 24 critiques for the designs, using 18–20 different statements. Finally, we generated a set of random critiques as another baseline. We generated 14 groups of four random critiques per design, to approximate the quantity of crowd-generated critiques.

Figure 5. Poster designs for Study 1, used to advertise real events (collected from the web).

To measure consistency among more than two raters, we used Fleiss's κ. For each of the 70 possible critique statements offered by CrowdCrit, we calculated how many critiquers used that statement, and how many didn't.

To compare crowd and random critiques to experts, we use an approach inspired by Nielsen and Molich [20] to validate usability heuristics. For each design, we produce a "gold standard" list of expert critiques which is the union of the statements chosen by each expert independently. We chose the union rather than intersection due to the low levels of agreement observed among experts, described below. This yielded 18, 19, and 20 "correct" statements for designs 1, 2, and 3, respectively. If crowd or random critiques include the same statements as experts, we can think of this as a "match" or as both groups identifying the same issues and problems.

Finally, to understand the impact of false positive, we calculate precision, recall, and f-measure (combined precision and recall) for crowd and random critiques vs. expert critiques.

Results and discussion

Internal consistency of crowd vs. expert critiques

The crowd's κ scores ranged from 0.04 to 0.09, while experts ranged from -0.05 to 0.20. Random critique κ scores ranged from -0.01 to 0.01. All of these scores are considered poor or slight agreement. Yet, across all designs, crowd workers converged on a subset of statements ($\leq$33 of the available 70), and on average each statement that was used received two different crits. The highest crowd agreement occurred in design 1, where six of 14 workers (43%) chose the statement, "Lacks background contrast."

Individual crowd workers vs. experts

We found the average worker identified 6–8% of expert critiques, though workers provided only about four crits per design. The best workers produced crits that matched 17–25% of the expert list. Random critiques fare worse, with average matches ranging between 3–6%, and a maximum of 11%, even with equal or higher numbers of critiques vs. the crowd condition.

Aggregate crowd workers vs. experts

While individual crowd workers provide relatively few matching critiques, one of the benefits of crowdsourcing platforms is that we can easily recruit more workers and generate

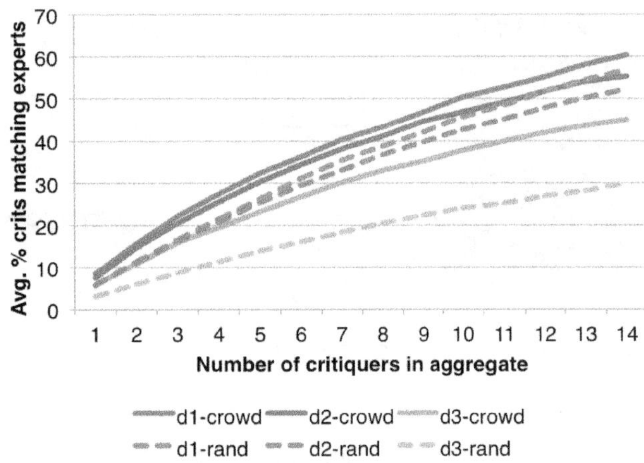

Figure 6. Proportion of expert critiques matched by aggregated crowd vs. random critiques.

more critiques. However, we first need to understand the relationship between more workers and better expert matches.

For design 1, the crowd identified 60.3% of the experts' selections, compared to 56.9% of random crits. For design 2, the crowd found 55.3% of the expert issues, compared to 52.2% for random crits. For design 3, the crowd found 45% of the issues, compared to 30% for random crits. These results suggest that more workers produce better results (8x to 10x more matches). Data on >14 workers is needed to determine if higher matches are possible.

Figure 6 shows how match percentage changes with aggregation. For each design, we ran 500 trials randomizing the order in which the crowd critiques were aggregated. Overall, the trend suggests a linear relationship between number of crowd critiquers and proportion of expert issues identified. An aggregate of 10 workers yields 40-50% of the issues, while 14 workers find 45–60% of the problems.

Precision/recall scores for crowd critiques

The above analyses consider how well crowds match the results produced by experts, but they don't address crowd critiques that don't match the experts, i.e., false positives. Figure 7 graphs the precision, recall, and f-measure scores for crowd and random crits across all designs. The crowd achieves better scores across the board, on average 0.12 points higher (out of 1.0) for precision and recall. This supports the above evidence that crowd critiques match experts better than random, and also suggests that crowds miss fewer expert crits and offer fewer false positives.

However, not all false positives are bad critiques. Nielsen and Molich [20] observed few false positives, and in fact revised their expert list post-hoc to include new issues identified by novices. Similarly, our informal analysis finds many crowd critiques that point out legitimate, if minor, issues.

Overall, compared to random critiques, crowd critiques show higher internal consistency, individual workers identify a greater percentage of expert issues, and aggregate percentages are also higher. Additionally, crowd critiques may provide richer feedback, in the form of optional annotations and text comments, that random critiques lack. The first study suggests that crowd critiques could benefit designers, but we know little about how designers might respond to crowd critiques or incorporate them into their actual design process. We address these issues in the following two studies.

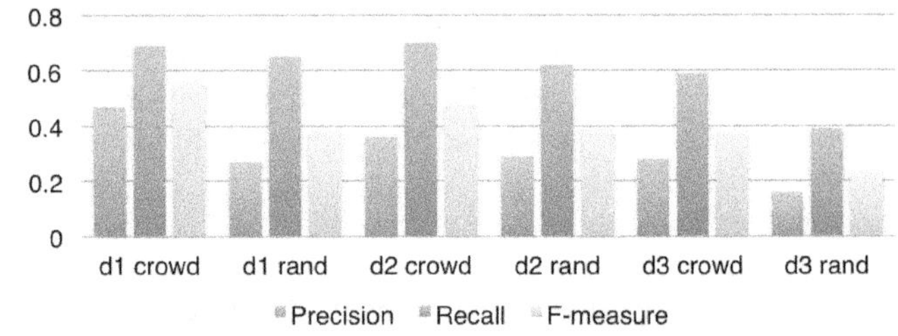

Figure 7. Precision, recall, and f-measures for crowd and random critiques vs. expert critiques.

STUDY 2: DESIGNER REACTIONS TO CROWD CRITIQUE

This exploratory study examines how designers leverage CrowdCrit in the context of a visual design contest. It seeks to answer three key research questions:

- How do participants react to the critiques and the aggregation interface?
- How do participants react to the source of crowd critiques?
- How do participants use crowd critiques?

To facilitate rich data collection and comparison across participants, we organized a poster design contest with real clients (organizers of a local music festival) and real prize money ($250 for the best poster). Participants used their own laptops and software and were provided with crowd feedback from CrowdCrit.

Method

We recruited 14 participants (six female) ranging in age from 20 to 33 ($\mu = 25$) by posting flyers at a university campus and advertising on neighborhood email lists, Craigslist, and Reddit. We sought to recruit participants with a wide range of experience, which we later categorized into three groups: *novice* designers, who had little or no design experience; *competent* designers who had taken a design course or had done some freelance design work; and *experienced* designers who had earned a degree in design or had worked full-time as a designer. To motivate participants while acknowledging their primary role as research participants, we compensated each participant $10/hour ($30 total), the standard rate for research participation at our institution, and awarded the $250 contest prize to the winning participant. The study consisted of two design sessions separated by a week to provide time to generate feedback from both the crowd and client.

Design session 1

In the first design session, each participant came to our lab and completed a pre-survey about their design experience. We then explained the goals of the contest and presented a design brief, written in collaboration with the clients, which included information about the event and other requirements, such as using the festival logo. Participants then had one hour to design a draft of their posters.

Crowd and client critique
After all participants had completed the first design session, we used CrowdCrit to gather crowd and client critiques for each design.

To gather crowd critiques, we recruited 50 crowd workers on MTurk and paid each the US minimum wage ($7.25/hour, or $3.50 for this 25-minute task). All workers were US-based to reduce the impact of cultural differences on perceptions of design. After completing a pre-survey and a tutorial video, each worker critiqued three randomly selected posters from the group, completed a brief post-survey about their opinions of the system, and received payment.

To gather client critiques, we arranged an hour-long, face-to-face meeting with two of the festival organizers. They discussed each of the 14 initial designs and provided feedback using the same critique interface as the crowd. We also asked them to share their impressions of the critique and aggregation interfaces.

Design session 2
After one week, each participant returned to the lab for a second design session. We demonstrated the aggregation interface and asked participants to explore the crowd and client critiques using a think-aloud protocol. Participants then had another hour to iterate on their original version and submit a final design, using the aggregation interface and critiques as much or as little as they wanted. We then conducted a semi-structured interview covering design process, thoughts on the crowd and client critiques, and experience with the interface. The combination of think-aloud and interview lasted, on average, 27 minutes per participant. Pre- and post-critique versions of all 14 designs can be viewed in Figure 8.

Client judging
We set up a second face-to-face meeting with the clients where we showed them each participant's first draft, the client and crowd critiques, and the final design. We asked clients to comment on how the designs had changed and how well the participants had responded to their feedback. The clients also voted on a winning poster (P6).

All client and participant interview data was audio-recorded, fully transcribed, and analyzed using a bottom-up approach. In our first pass, we annotated quotes which addressed one of our research questions above, and in several subsequent passes, we grouped related quotes together to elicit broader themes, presented in the next section.

Results and discussion

How do participants react to the critiques and the aggregation interface?
Quality: On the whole, participants found the majority of critiques to be helpful, especially given the crowd's minimal qualifications and the lack of moderation. They mentioned specific reasons such as causing them to notice issues they hadn't considered (P5), appreciating the concreteness and rich detail (P6), and feeling like the critiques were carefully considered (P8). Some participants particularly appreciated positive critiques; P6 noted, "I tend to always second guess my work, so hearing affirmation, hearing people say 'This is a strength,' it helps a lot."

Quantity: Overall, each poster received an average of 69 ($\sigma = 12$) critiques, where 26 ($\sigma = 17$) critiques were positive and 43 ($\sigma = 20$) critiques were negative. Clients contributed 4% of all critiques. The majority of participants were satisfied by the number of critiques they received, with some expressing pleasant surprise at receiving more than they expected. P7 characterized the general attitude towards quantity, saying, "The more feedback, in my opinion, the better, because there's a chance that you'll be able to see a larger trend." P1 agreed, "It feels like if it's only two people [critiquing], that's just their taste. [With CrowdCrit] you get a sense of, 'Overall, people like the alignment,' [or] 'Overall, people like this.'"

Speed: We asked participants how quickly they'd prefer to receive crowd critiques, and most responses ranged between one day and several days for each round of feedback, depending on the project. For this study, the CrowdCrit system generated critiques for all 14 posters in less than two hours, or on average, less than 10 minutes per design. We shared this with participants, and most found the turnaround time to be surprisingly fast. In P1's words, "If you can do it in an hour, it's perfect—I think that will really justify the price."

Cost: The total cost to collect critiques for all 14 designs was $175, or $12.50 per design on average; workers were paid an hourly rate equivalent to minimum wage in our location. We asked participants how much they'd be willing to pay for the critiques of their poster drafts. For novices, who typically designed for themselves, the most common response was a flat rate of around $5–10 per round of feedback. Given the abundance of feedback provided in this study, we speculate that a service like CrowdCrit can provide value at the $5–10 price point.

Interface Participants generally found the aggregation interface easy to use. They described it using phrases such as "easy to understand" (P1), "simple and clean" (P5), "clear-cut" (P6), and "intuitive" (P7). P12 praised the "straightforward" design, saying, "the brilliance of this interface is the fact that it's really simple."

One of the most popular features was the ability to hover over individual critique text to reveal the corresponding graphical annotations (e.g. markers or selected regions) on the design itself. P6 liked that annotations added specificity to ambiguous comments; without them, critique statements like "Lacks balance" would seem, in her words, "fake."

How do participants react to the source of crowd critiques?
Crowd expertise: When exposed to critiques from a variety of sources, participants usually considered client critiques first and crowd critiques second, often commenting that client satisfaction trumped everything else. Among crowd critiques, participants paid closer attention to expert critiques because they perceived them to be higher quality. Responses to novice feedback were more varied. Some experienced designers

Figure 8. All drafts (left) and final designs (right) from the Study 2. P6 won the contest.

tended to disregard novice feedback because the experienced designers felt more knowledgeable. P6 said, "Not to sound pompous or anything, but I feel like I do know a little bit more than general people who don't really know much about design." Other participants felt that novice critiques were valuable in their own distinct way. P3 felt that novices provided "good emotional feedback" while experts offered "a higher-level technical critique." P1 saw novices as representative of the target audience of her design: "[Novices] are the customer, too—they are the ones that are going to the show."

Crowd vs. client critiques: Participants found both client and crowd feedback to be valuable, albeit in different ways. The crowd, as mentioned above, provided both designerly critique and audience reactions. The clients, on the other hand, were sources of domain-specific knowledge, providing input on the music festival and the goals for the poster. For our design contest, participants needed to consider both types of feedback to succeed. P5 noted that clients provided feedback specific to the festival (e.g. add a photo of the band Royal Teeth), while the crowd provided "more generic" feedback about effective design (e.g. "the font size should change"). The clients also saw their role as complementary to the crowd's. Their "general feedback" supplemented the crowd's "high-end visual feedback" (Client).

Some participants viewed the clients' lack of design expertise as problematic, and crowd critique as an exciting possible solution. They imagined "hav[ing] a crowd behind you, backing you up" (P1), i.e., using the crowd's feedback as empirical evidence to persuade clients to abandon a poor idea (P1) or embrace one favored by the designer (P3).

Crowd vs. other critique sources: Participants also compared the crowd critiques they received to other feedback sources. Participants who worked as freelancers (P1) or as the lone designer within an organization, such as a university department (P6, P8), struggled to find reliable sources of meaningful feedback beyond their clients, and these clients frequently lacked design backgrounds. Some isolated participants turned to online feedback sources, like Dribbble [18] and design forums, but were generally unsatisfied with the results. P6 praised the crowd critique for being "more specific, like it addressed very, very specific issues better than just vague 'I like it' or 'I don't like it'" comments typical of design websites. She added that the "guiding points" and "categories" of the crowd critique system seemed effective for preventing the misunderstandings and mean-spirited remarks which deterred her from these other sites.

Privacy and identity: Participants generally expressed little concern over sharing their works-in-progress with the crowd for the purposes of critique. Several mentioned that any apprehensions they might have were eased because the system was double-blind; designers were anonymous to critiquers and vice-versa. P1 said, "I like anonymous... They don't see my name, I don't see theirs. That's good." She added that she was grateful that the system did not support direct interaction between designers and crowds, fearing that direct communication could lead to arguments and defensiveness.

How do participants use crowd critiques?

Most participants used the feedback to make changes to their design. For example, P1 increased the legibility of the top of the design and removed a distracting image; P5 changed the placement of a photo and made the background less "flashy"; and P9 changed an inappropriate typeface and added color to create visual interest.

Participants also used the feedback to decide what *not* to change. For example, P6 saw that the clients "liked how clean and simple it was so instead of changing my design to make it more flowery or whatever, I just decided to mostly keep it the way it was." Participants also mentioned situations where they agreed with feedback, but chose not to act on it. For example, P13 agreed with a crowd worker's suggestion that creating an illustration would help tie together two images, but he felt he lacked the drawing skill to execute it. The clients gave P8 negative feedback on the "stars" motif he had chosen, but he kept it because he felt he was too far along with the original concept.

Summary

This study offered evidence that crowd feedback provides value to designers across a range of backgrounds and skill levels. It demonstrated how a crowdsourcing platform could be leveraged to provide design critique for a contest scenario. Participants were generally enthusiastic about the quality, quantity, cost, and speed of crowd critiques, and found the aggregation tool straightforward and helpful. Participants also described their reactions to this novel source of critique. They compared crowds favorably to more familiar feedback sources and identified unique benefits of crowds, such as providing a broader range of perspectives, preserving limited social capital, and protecting privacy and anonymity. Finally, the study revealed how participants used crowd critiques in their design processes, weighed expertise against their own intuitions, and even used crowds to justify design decisions.

STUDY 3: IMPACT OF CROWD CRITIQUE ON DESIGN PROCESS AND RESULTS

The second study provides qualitative evidence for the efficacy of gathering crowd critique for a realistic design scenario. However, it did not directly compare crowd critique to the feedback typically available on a design contest platform. Therefore, we conducted a controlled between-subjects experiment to isolate these effects. Specifically, we investigated the following research questions:

- How do designers perceive crowd critique in comparison to the generic feedback typical on contest platforms?
- How does crowd critique affect designers' final products in comparison to generic feedback?

Method

Site

We ran our experiment on 99designs [1], a popular host of online design contests. The site has hosted nearly 300,000 contests since it was founded in 2008.

Participants

Eighteen designers (five female, ages 19–55) participated in the experiment. All but three reported their occupations as designers. They had won, on average, 5.6 contests on 99designs (min: 0; max: 33). All 18 designers were paid $10 for participating, and the winner (D18) received an additional $599 in prize money.

Experimental conditions

We randomly assigned half (nine) of the designers to the experimental condition, where they received crowd critiques via URL. The remaining nine designers, assigned to the control condition, received the following "generic" feedback: *"We checked out your design and wanted to tell you that you're on the right track. Keep up the good work!"* This type of feedback is typical of contest sites like 99designs, where many hosts provide little or no feedback to designers.

Procedure

We initiated a 99designs contest to design a poster advertising an upcoming lecture series hosted by a U.S. university. We worked with the lecture series coordinator to develop a design brief, which contained information about the lecture series and target audience, as well as more specific requirements like size and sponsor logos.

The contest lasted one week from start to finish. Participants (hereafter "designers" for sake of clarity) completed a demographics pre-survey and submitted a draft of their poster design by the end of Day 3 of the contest. On Day 4, we generated crowd critiques for all 18 designs from a total of 30 crowd workers on MTurk, and distributed these crowd critiques to designers in the experimental condition. Designers in the control condition were sent generic feedback. All designers were asked to consider their feedback, iterate, and submit a final poster design on Day 7. Pre- and post-critique versions of all 18 posters, totalling 36 unique designs, are shown in Figure 9.

Following the contest deadline, all designers completed a post-survey about their impressions of the contest and feedback. Designers who had received only the generic feedback were given the URL for the crowd critiques, which we generated on Day 4 but did not reveal until this time (Day 8). These designers completed a second post-survey about their reactions to the crowd critiques.

The final posters were evaluated by both the client (the lecture series coordinator) and crowd workers from MTurk. We sought evaluations from people with design knowledge, so we required crowd workers to score 80% or higher on a true/false design knowledge quiz that was previously validated [9]. Thirty-seven crowd workers passed the quiz and participated in the evaluation.

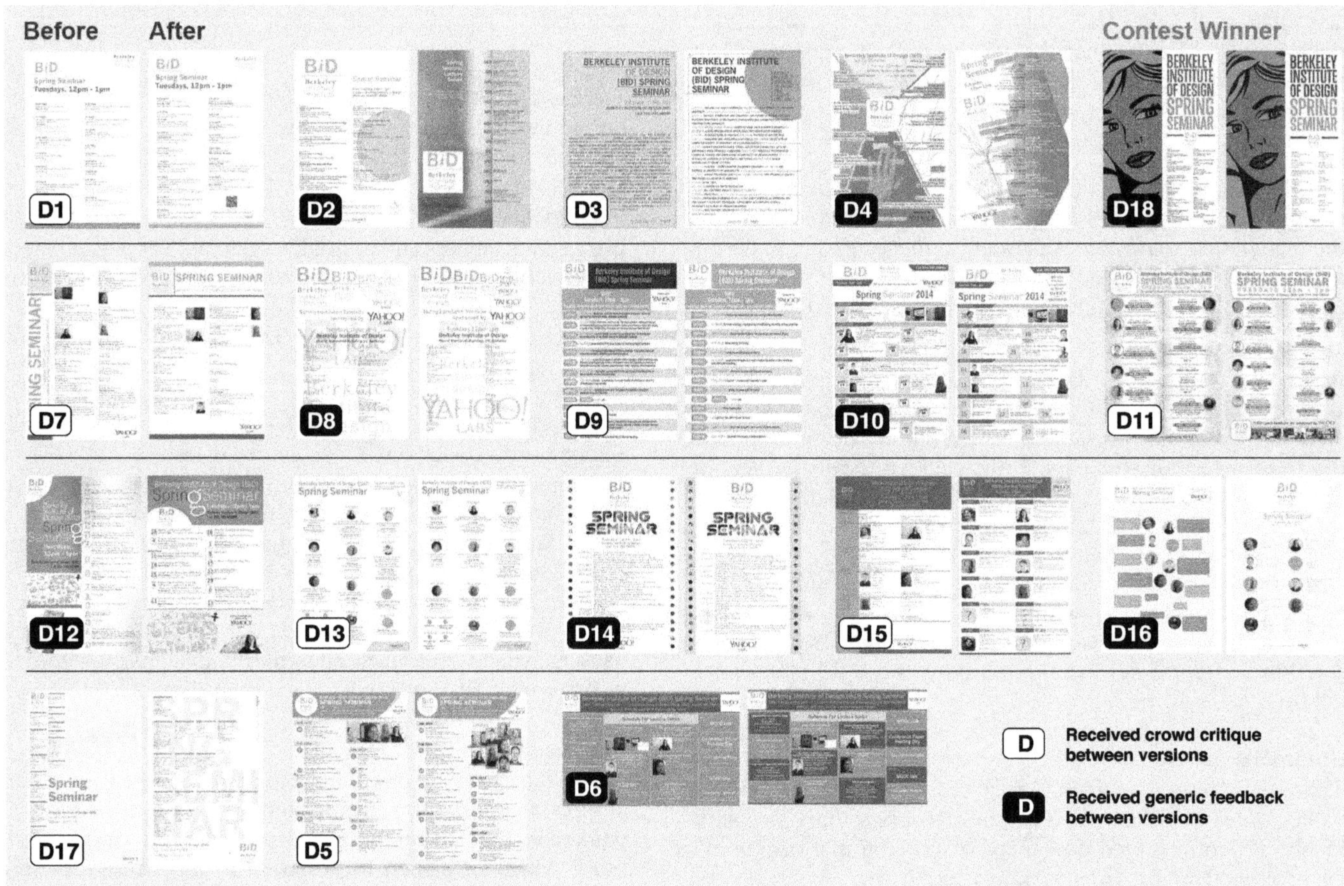

Figure 9. All drafts (left) and final designs (right) from Study 3. D18 won the contest.

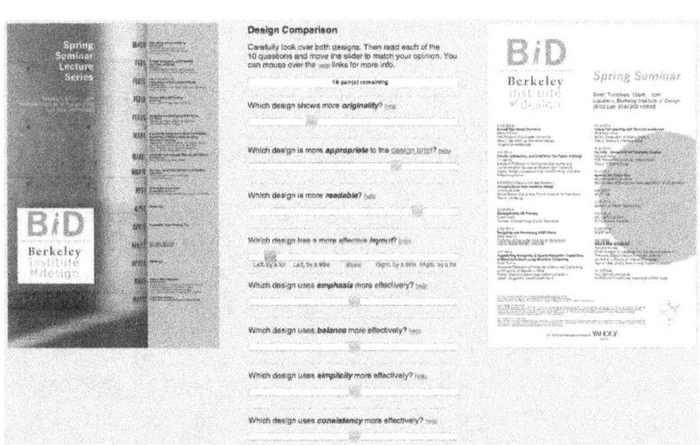

Figure 10. The rating interface used by crowd workers and the client to evaluate the 18 poster designs along 10 dimensions.

Raters viewed both poster versions from all 18 participants (36 designs total), unlabeled and in random order. They compared two versions across 10 dimensions: adherence to the seven design principles, originality, similarity, and overall quality (see Figure 10). Raters moved a slider left or right, more towards one design or the other, to indicate which design embodied each dimension more effectively.

Analysis

To analyze the non-parametric survey data, we ran independent samples Mann-Whitney U-tests. We also analyzed designers' responses to open-ended questions about the feedback and share illustrative quotes below.

To analyze the posters, we first calculated intraclass correlation (ICC) scores to establish the reliability of the crowd's ratings (see Table 1. Eight of the 10 dimensions scored 0.75 or higher (considered "excellent" on a scale of 0–1), and the remaining two dimensions, Balance and Appropriateness, scored 0.60 or higher (considered "good"). Thus, there was high agreement among crowd raters.

For each designer, we computed the average change in score between his or her initial and final designs (delta), as rated by the crowd workers on a 0–10 Likert scale. The maximum delta was ±5 points, except for Similarity, which was a 0–10 scale. Positive deltas indicate the post-feedback design improved along that dimension.

We ran independent samples t-tests comparing the crowd feedback deltas across all 10 dimensions to the generic feedback deltas. these deltas across conditions. We also examine poster ratings by design experience. For the latter analysis, we divided the participant pool into thirds according to the number of 99designs contests they had won.

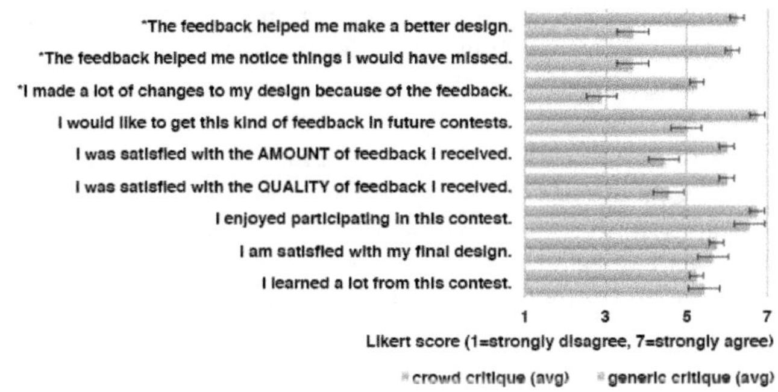

Figure 11. Post-survey results. Only the first three questions (marked with *) have statistically significant different responses between conditions (p<0.05).

Dimension	ICC score	Crowd avg. Δ	Generic avg. Δ
*Simplicity	0.94‡	+0.09	+0.63
Balance	0.71†	+0.44	+0.67
Consistency	0.84‡	+0.25	+0.40
Appropriateness	0.64†	+0.20	+0.26
Readability	0.88‡	+0.74	+0.81
Layout	0.86‡	+0.65	+0.69
Emphasis	0.88‡	+0.54	+0.52
Originality	0.95‡	+0.20	+0.12
Similarity	0.99‡	6.51	6.19
Quality	0.84‡	+0.69	+1.00

Table 1. Average change (Δ) between pre-critique and post-critique designs for the 10 dimensions evaluated. Only Simplicity (marked with *) was significantly different between conditions (p<0.05). ICC scores with ‡ have "excellent" agreement; scores with † have "good" agreement.

Results and discussion

Survey responses are shown in Figure 11, and poster evaluation results are shown in Table 1. In general, designers rated the feedback from CrowdCrit higher than the generic feedback. Designs improved along most dimensions between the initial and final iterations, but there was no significant difference between conditions.

Designers receiving crowd crits felt they noticed more issues

Designers who got crowd critiques reported noticing significantly more issues they would have ordinarily missed (6.13 vs. 3.67, $p<0.05$). Some attributed this to the higher quantity and variety of critiques available on CrowdCrit. D10 wrote, "I didn't realise that in a design there are so many points to look for... now I know what to look for in my future designs." D2 wrote, "The feedback about lacking contrast, imagery and the bottom text being too small were right on. (I can't believe I didn't see it myself)."

Designers receiving crowd crits felt they made made better designs, but third-party ratings show little difference

Compared to generic feedback, designers felt that crowd critiques helped them make a significantly better overall design (6.25 vs. 3.67, $p<0.05$). Many provided specific examples of crowd feedback that led them to make improvements. D11 described how, after reviewing critiques in the Balance tab, he "noticed that the bottom part of my entry lacks something to balance the whole thing... so I added edited photos of the university to fill in the gap." D15 described "changing the layout of the dates to make it less confusing", and D13 "[c]hanged a lot of things that weren't making sense at all like using dark colour fonts under the dark background."

However, despite designers' greater sense of improvement in the crowd feedback condition, the third-party ratings show no significant differences between conditions for nine of the 10 dimensions. Only final designs receiving generic feedback scored significantly higher on Simplicity than designs getting crowd feedback (+0.63 vs. +0.09, $p<0.05$). Designs tended to improve modestly (≤ 1 point) across all dimensions following either type of feedback.

Designers receiving crowd crits felt they made bigger changes, but ratings show only inexperienced designers did

The third significant survey result helps to explain the discrepancy between designers' perceptions and the poster ratings. Compared to generic feedback, designers reported making significantly more changes to their designs as a result of crowd critiques (5.25 vs. 2.89, $p<0.05$). Some mentioned that the higher specificity and concreteness of crowd critiques made it easier to recognize problems and make changes. D1 appreciated that crowd feedback "showed where the change was needed...in a graphical manner." D4 wrote, "[Crowd] feedback was precise, detailed and to the point. Even though it didn't favor my design it was better than someone saying they like it, or nice and not giving any more details."

The poster ratings partially support these claims. As mentioned above, there was no significant difference in Similarity when designers of all experience levels are analyzed together. Separating the analysis by designers' contest experience, however, tells a different story. High-experience designers who received crowd critique produced more similar final designs (8.47 vs. 8.01, $p<0.05$), while low-experience designers getting crowd critique produced less similar final designs (4.81 vs. 5.44, $p<0.05$). As these means suggest, inexperienced designers made bigger changes between iterations, regardless of feedback type. Generic feedback was correlated with higher Simplicity scores, regardless of experience ($p<0.05$). There were no other significant differences across dimensions.

IMPLICATIONS

Evidence from the first study suggested that aggregated crowd critiques can address many of the issues raised by expert critique providers. Designers from the 99designs contest site expressed enthusiasm for crowd critiques and offered concrete examples of how they influenced their design process, echoing the findings of our second study. Compared to the generic feedback condition, designers who got crowd critiques reported significantly better recognition of issues, more changes, and better overall designs. By mitigating "good subject" effects [19] through our controlled experiment, these results show that CrowdCrit provides value over the generic feedback typical in design contests.

Yet, when we examine independent ratings of their designs, we see no significant difference in quality or most other dimensions. One interpretation of these results is that crowd critique leads designers to think they are making significant improvements, when in fact, they tend to make minor revisions. The opportunity to respond to specific issues, provided by CrowdCrit, may fixate designers on addressing minor, easily-addressed problems rather than contemplating broader, more substantive changes. The aggregation interface provides a "Top Feedback" section aimed to mitigate this problem, but this orientation towards simple frequency may have oriented designers towards issues that were popular or easily identified (e.g. a typo) rather than important. Further, presenting critiques in list form may have led to changes that were idiosyncratic, rather than contributing to a more synergistic improvement. This could have resulted in designs that were "busier" but not necessarily better, possibly explaining why crowd critique led to more complex designs. Our first study, which found that many designers approached their revisions by working their way through the list of critiques, also supports this interpretation.

Another partial explanation may come from the nature of our study site, a host of online design contests. Typically only the winner is paid, so designers may find that submitting multiple revisions to fewer contests is a less effective strategy than submitting a single reasonable version to many contests. The culture of 99designs may have discouraged designers from making significant changes, even if the crowd critiques were considered valuable. Our finding that designers with more contest experience made fewer changes, regardless of critique type, also supports this interpretation. Crowd critique led inexperienced designers to make bigger changes, possibly because they had not yet embraced this "shotgun approach" as more productive.

Systems like CrowdCrit may be most appropriate for domains in which quality is somewhat subjective, experts frequently disagree, and a rich diversity of feedback is valued. Although usability heuristics have now been widely adopted as a foundation of HCI practice, Nielsen and Molich found little correlation between evaluators, experts adjusted their rubrics in response to novice feedback, and the average novice found only 20–50% of issues identified by experts. They acknowledge that usability evaluation is challenging, yet argue convincingly that it is still worthwhile because "even finding some problems is of course better than finding no problems" [20]. We propose that a similar argument may apply to crowdsourced design critique and possibly other domains of crowdsourced feedback.

FUTURE WORK

Enhance scaffolding

Scaffolding allows novices to quickly become productive within an unfamiliar domain to gradually learn to do new things without support. As such, scaffolding can come in many forms. Our critique statements provided a first approximation at scaffolding visual design critique, but we did not measure the effect on crowd worker learning, or implement techniques such as progressively "fading" scaffolds, requiring the learner to draw on memory to fill new gaps [25]. Crowd feedback systems could be modified to monitor critique providers and, as they gain experience, remove supports for structured feedback. For example, CrowdCrit could adapt the pre-authored critique statements to match a worker's skill level, perhaps starting with surface-level elements (like fonts, text, and images), moving to more abstract principles (like balance and emphasis), eventually dropping all of these in favor of more open-ended critique.

Support new principles

For crowd feedback services to generalize across domains, they should offer flexibility in *how* they structure novice behavior. For CrowdCrit, this could mean allowing designers to author their own set of visual design principles or to modify the ones provided in our system. This feature could also make CrowdCrit useful in other domains, such as interface design or architectural design, and to other types of crowds, such as user communities or concerned citizens.

Explore new power dynamics

This paper focused on the practical scenario of introducing feedback in design contests. As a result, we had the opportunity to observe interactions between designers, crowds, and clients (or contest hosts). The introduction of crowd critique created the potential to challenge the traditional relationship between the designer and client. Instead of merely responding to the clients' whims, designers saw an opportunity to use crowd feedback as empirical support for certain design decisions. The crowd, in a sense, represents both the target audience and a body of knowledgeable designers. Future work on crowd feedback systems can explore new interaction models where clients also view and interpret crowd feedback.

CONCLUSION

We presented CrowdCrit, a system which uses crowdsourcing to provide designers with a fast, scalable, and reasonably priced source of feedback. We built a working prototype of CrowdCrit and deployed it in three studies. This paper makes the following contributions. First, we present the CrowdCrit system itself, demonstrating how to structure the complex task of design critique for crowd workers, and how to aggregate and present large, diverse quantities of crowd feedback for review. Second, we compared crowd and expert critiques, showing how aggregated crowd critiques converges towards expert feedback, and demonstrating that agreement trends low among both novice and expert critiquers. Our second study used interviews to provide rich descriptions of a diverse group of designers' attitudes, concerns, and enthusiasm towards crowd feedback and patterns of use in a real-world design context. Our third study showed that crowd feedback led designers to report noticing more issues, enacting more changes, and producing better designs that the generic feedback more typical of online contest hosts. It also identified a gap between designers' perceptions and independent ratings of changes to their final designs. These evaluations are among the first to attempt to describe and quantify the value of crowd feedback. Finally, we discuss design implications for building crowd feedback systems that provide valuable and equitable services to both designers and crowd workers.

ACKNOWLEDGMENTS

The authors wish to thank our designer participants, crowd-workers, Allegheny County (PA) Parks Department, 99designs.com staff, and our anonymous reviewers. Financial support provided by the National Science Foundation under IIS grants 1210836, 1208382, and 1217096.

REFERENCES

1. 99designs. `http://www.99designs.com/`.
2. Barrett, T. A comparison of the goals of studio professors conducting critiques and art education goals for teaching criticism. *Studies in art education* (1988), 22–27.
3. Bransford, J. D., Brown, A. L., and Cocking, R. R., Eds. *How people learn: brain, mind, experience, and school.* National Academy Press, Washington, D.C., 2000.
4. Dannels, D., Gaffney, A., and Martin, K. Beyond content, deeper than delivery: What critique feedback reveals about communication expectations in design education. *Int. J. Schol. Teach. & Learn. 2*, 2 (2008).
5. Dannels, D. P., and Martin, K. N. Critiquing critiques a genre analysis of feedback across novice to expert design studios. *Jo. Bus. & Tech. Comm. 22*, 2 (2008), 135–159.
6. Dondis, D. A. *A primer of visual literacy*. MIT Press, Cambridge, Mass., 1973.
7. Dow, S., Fortuna, J., Schwartz, D., Altringer, B., Schwartz, D., and Klemmer, S. Prototyping dynamics: sharing multiple designs improves exploration, group rapport, and results. In *Proc. CHI 2011* (2011), 2807–2816.
8. Dow, S., Gerber, E., and Wong, A. A pilot study of using crowds in the classroom. In *Proc. CHI 2013*, CHI '13 (New York, NY, USA, 2013), 227–236.
9. Dow, S. P., Glassco, A., Kass, J., Schwarz, M., Schwartz, D. L., and Klemmer, S. R. Parallel prototyping leads to better design results, more divergence, and increased self-efficacy. *ACM Trans. Comput.-Hum. Interact. 17*, 4 (Dec. 2010), 18:1–18:24.
10. Easterday, M. W., Rees Lewis, D., Fitzpatrick, C., and Gerber, E. M. Computer supported novice group critique. In *Proc. of DIS '14* (2014).
11. Feedback army. `http://www.feedbackarmy.com/`.
12. Feldman, E. *Practical Art criticism*. Prentice Hall, Englewood Cliffs, NJ, 1994.
13. Five second test. `http://www.fivesecondtest.com/`.
14. Forrst. `http://www.forrst.com/`.
15. Klemmer, S. R., Hartmann, B., and Takayama, L. How bodies matter: five themes for interaction design. In *Proceedings of DIS*, ACM (2006), 140–149.
16. Kulkarni, C., and Klemmer, S. R. Learning design wisdom by augmenting physical studio critique with online self-assessment. Tech. rep., Stanford U., 2012.
17. Lidwell, W., Holden, K., and Butler, J. *Universal principles of design*. Rockport Pub, 2010.
18. Marlow, J., and Dabbish, L. From rookie to all-star: Professional development in a graphic design community of practice. In *Proc. CSCW 2014* (2014).
19. Nichols, A. L., and Maner, J. K. The good-subject effect: investigating participant demand characteristics. *The Journal of general psychology 135*, 2 (Apr. 2008), 151–165. PMID: 18507315.
20. Nielsen, J., and Molich, R. Heuristic evaluation of user interfaces. In *Proceedings of the SIGCHI Conference on Human Factors in Computing Systems*, CHI '90, ACM (New York, NY, USA, 1990), 249–256.
21. Reynolds, G. *Presentation Zen: Simple ideas on presentation design and delivery*. New Riders, 2011.
22. Sadler, D. R. Formative assessment and the design of instructional systems. *Instr. Sci. 18*, 2 (1989), 119–144.
23. Schön, D. *Educating the Reflective Practitioner*. Jossey–Bass Publishers, San Francisco, 1990.
24. Shneiderman, B. The eyes have it: a task by data type taxonomy for information visualizations. In *Proc. VL/HCC 1996* (1996), 336–343.
25. Soloway, E., Guzdial, M., and Hay, K. E. Learner-centered design: the challenge for HCI in the 21st century. *interactions 1* (April 1994), 36–48.
26. Tinapple, D., Olson, L., and Sadauskas, J. Critviz: Web-based software supporting peer critique in large creative classrooms. *Bulletin of the IEEE Technical Committee on Learning Technology 15*, 1 (2013), 29.
27. Tohidi, M., Buxton, W., Baecker, R., and Sellen, A. Getting the right design and the design right. In *Proceedings of CHI*, ACM (2006), 1243–1252.
28. Wattenberg, M., and Kriss, J. Designing for social data analysis. *IEEE Transactions on Visualization and Computer Graphics 12*, 4 (2006), 549–557.
29. Willett, W., Heer, J., and Agrawala, M. Strategies for crowdsourcing social data analysis. In *Proceedings of the SIGCHI Conference on Human Factors in Computing Systems*, CHI '12, ACM (New York, NY, USA, 2012), 227–236.
30. Willett, W., Heer, J., Hellerstein, J., and Agrawala, M. Commentspace: structured support for collaborative visual analysis. In *Proc. CHI 2011* (2011), 3131–3140.
31. Williams, R. *The Non-Designer's design book*. Peachpit Press, 2008.
32. Xu, A., and Bailey, B. What do you think?: a case study of benefit, expectation, and interaction in a large online critique community. In *Proc. CSCW 2012* (2012), 295–304.
33. Xu, A., Bailey, B. P., and Huang, S.-W. Voyant: Generating structured feedback on visual designs using a crowd of non-experts. In *Proc. CSCW 2014* (2014).

Back in Sight, Back in Mind: Picture-Centric Support for Mobile Counseling Sessions

Tobias Giesbrecht
University of Zurich
Binzmuehlestrasse 14, Zurich
giesbrecht@ifi.uzh.ch

Tino Comes
University of Zurich
Binzmuehlestrasse 14, Zurich
comes@ifi.uzh.ch

Gerhard Schwabe
University of Zurich
Binzmuehlestrasse 14, Zurich
schwabe@ifi.uzh.ch

ABSTRACT
This paper explores unique challenges of mobile consultancy and offers a picture-centric solution. We study the example of a policeman counseling a homeowner on how to prevent burglary. As in a stationary set-up, consultants and clients collaborate to co-create solutions to match the clients' problems. Concurrently, in a mobile set-up, problem and solution information are bound to the physical environment of the house. Moving through the house, both clients and consultants forget crucial location-bound information, severely impairing their collaboration. We propose supporting such collaboration with a tablet-based application that is centered on pictures of the physical environment, called *SmartProtector*. In an evaluation, we show that both clients and consultants remember substantially more information when using the *SmartProtector*. With this study, we contribute to the ongoing research discussion on collaborative memory, memory aid systems and mobile collaboration, highlighting the roles of pictures and their large potential to enhance collaborative work practices.

Author Keywords
mobile collaboration; collaborative memory; memory aid; counseling service; working with pictures; design science

ACM Classification Keywords
H.5.2 [Information Interfaces and Presentation]: User Interfaces – Screen design

INTRODUCTION
Mobile counseling sessions between a consultant and a client, e.g., crime prevention counseling or energy counseling sessions at a client's home, are knowledge-intensive and require high cognitive capabilities from both actors. A mobile counseling session is a collaboration between a consultant and a client, where first, the physical environment is an essential part of the collaboration, containing crucial information. Second, the actors are moving around during their collaboration collecting information from the surrounding environment. In such mobile collaborations, actors not only have to exchange information with one another but also need to process information from the surrounding environment. In our investigation of mobile crime prevention counseling, we observed that while consultants and clients move through the client's house, they frequently forget crucial location-bound information: in their on-site discussions, consultants and clients refer to physical objects in their immediate surroundings to explain specific issues, e.g., the front door with a specific lock. Once they move on, they struggle to remember detailed information related to this object, e.g., the particular type of door lock. As a result, they have to interrupt their collaboration to bring the respective information "back into mind", by, e.g., physically revisiting the front door. We refer to this generally well-known phenomenon as the "out of sight, out of mind" (OOS-OOM) phenomenon. This forgetting, as well as the individuals' strategies of dealing with it, shapes - to an amazing degree - the process of mobile counseling sessions and how actors behave and interact with one another.

CSCW '15, March 14-18, 2015, Vancouver, BC, Canada.

ACM 978-1-4503-2922-4/15/03...$15.00
http://dx.doi.org/10.1145/2675133.2675169

These cognitive challenges have been addressed by current research. In the psychology research literature, the cognitive capabilities of individuals and the role of the physical environment thereupon are discussed extensively [cf. 27,28,31]. Research on memory aid systems highlights suitable technical support to recall information [cf. [11,15,16,21]. However these current research discussions address mostly the individual level or single-user scenarios, and insights on the cognitive aspects in mobile collaborations and how the individuals' cognitive capabilities influence their collaborative behavior are scarce. To provide appropriate support, it is important to understand the role of the OOS-OOM phenomenon in mobile collaborations. This brings us to our first research question: **RQ1**: *How does forgetting influence mobile counseling sessions*?

The cognitive aspects in collaborations are broadly discussed in research on computer supported collaborative work (CSCW). Researchers provide high-level insights on the concept of *collaborative memory* [2,24] and extensively discuss how to support collaboration partners to create and use a collaborative memory [1,2,19]. However, current research focuses mostly on stationary scenarios, and insights on the novel challenges and their influence on group members' cognitive capabilities and the creation of a collaborative memory are lacking. Current research on mobile memory aid systems addresses the individual's cognitive capability, and presents diverse solutions to facilitate memory cue creation [15,16,21]. However, research insights on suitable support accounting for multiple users are scarce. Both the collaborative situation of the client-consultant relationship and the mobile setting give rise to new challenges for developing suitable support systems. We thus asked ourselves how an appropriately designed "memory aid" could support actors to create and use a collaborative memory in their mobile collaboration. After reviewing related literature on psychology research, CSCW-research and memory aid systems, as well as discussing different design options, it was "working with pictures" that turned out to be a surprisingly useful concept for responding to the characteristics of mobile collaborations and to bring information back into the minds of the actors. Thus, in this study we further pursue the second research question **RQ2**: *How can pictures improve the memories of consultants and clients in their mobile collaboration?*

We follow a design science research approach [7,23] for providing an in-depth problem specification and designing a concept for picture-centric mobile counseling support. We instantiate the concept in the *SmartProtector* prototype, that supports consultants and clients in their mobile crime prevention counseling sessions and evaluated it in a user test with real consultants and clients. By means of our exemplary instantiation of the picture-centric support, we highlight the powerful roles of pictures in mobile collaborations supporting all participants to overcome the cognitive challenges from the OOS-OOM phenomenon and establish a fruitful collaboration. Finally, we discuss the meaning and effects of our insights: on current CSCW research on collaborative memory, on memory aid systems research and on counseling support systems research. This research output is relevant beyond the emerging research stream of mobile counseling services. It can be generalized to other face-to-face collaborations between actors where the physical environment contains crucial information, e.g., an architect discussing structural changes with workers at a construction site.

RELATED WORK

The mobile counseling encounter between consultants and clients represents a knowledge-intensive collaboration. The main objective of this consultant-client-collaboration is to enable clients to resolve their problems on their own [33]. To reach this objective, they develop solutions (the consultant's area of expertise) that suit the client's problems (the client's area of expertise). To explore clients' problems in the mobile counseling session, the consultants and clients move from one physical problem object (e.g., the kitchen window) to another, thereby continuously integrating new information originating from the changing physical environment. These interactions require high cognitive capabilities from participants, as they constantly need to remember, exchange and process information.

The actors' cognitive processes not only comprise the individual's internal mental processes, but also their interactions with others as well as with the physical artifacts in the surrounding environment. In this context, the changing environmental context can influence individual's cognitive capabilities considerably. In psychology research literature, researchers discuss extensively the individual's cognitive processes and the role and effects of the environmental context on an individual's cognitive capabilities [cf. 3,8,10,27,28,31]. Studies report on different effects (e.g., environmental reinstatement [28], where changing the physical environment causes individuals to remember fewer memories) and propose measures to reduce the resulting context-dependent forgetting (e.g., multiple-learning-context-technique [27], where individuals learn information in different environmental contexts rather than one). Whereas these studies provide useful insights on how to enhance a human's cognitive capabilities, they mainly discuss them on the individual level, when reporting on several actors and how they influence each other's memories, discussions remain mostly conceptual. These interactions between actors can enhance individual's cognitive capability, e.g., by either cross-cueing [9], where information from others trigger memories of an individual that s/he would not have remembered alone, or impair it, e.g., by the "outshining"-effect [28], where an individual's memories are "outshone" by easier-to-access information. However, current research studies barely provide insights how corresponding effects influence actors' behaviors in collaborations.

Current research on counseling support systems investigates consultants' and clients' collaborative work practices from different perspectives. Novak [17] describes the hampering effects of *information overload* in shared problem solving, where actors' ability to make decisions deteriorates due to the presence of too much information. Novak and Schwabe [18] highlight the impact of *sticky* information that is bound to a specific location (physically, mentally) aggravating the exchange of information. Nussbaumer et al. [20] discuss the information asymmetry between consultants (as experts) and clients (as laypersons), and report on the negative effects, thwarting collaborative interactions. Schmidt-Rauch and Nussbaumer [25] give insights into actors' collaborative task of co-creating the value of counseling and show how to design appropriate support to help them becoming more equal co-creators. In their solutions, these researchers give insights into collaborative work practices in counseling collaborations, showing how technical support systems should be designed to support users appropriately. However, they rarely consider the individuals' cognitive aspects in storing and recalling information, and do not discuss how they influence the individual's collaborative behavior. Furthermore, they focus mostly on stationary scenarios, disregarding the actors' physical environment and its role and effects within the consultant-client collaboration.

Current research on memory aid systems attempts to increase individuals' cognitive capabilities. Lin et al. [15], for instance, describe how micro-notes support individuals in recalling memories. They claim that for ideal support: corresponding technical devices need to be continuously present and the phase of recording should be simple and fast. In a health-related context, Palen and Aalokke [21] analyze how elderly manage remembering to take their medicine, and derive principles for the design of assistive health technology, e.g., technology by invitation or support of personalized medication management. Similarly, McGee-Lennon et al. [16] formulate technology guidelines for assisted living, addressing design aspects like personalization, autonomy, or shared spaces. While these studies provide useful insights into designing IT-based memory support, they focus mostly on single user scenarios, neglecting the influence of human-human interactions on individuals' cognitive capabilities. These interactions between actors can affect the individual's cognitive capability (e.g., by cross-cueing [9]) or impairing it (e.g., by the "outshining"-effect [28]).

Since the 1980s, researchers in CSCW-research discuss extensively the support of synchronous collaborations [cf. 1,2,12,13,14,19]. One of the core discussion topics is how actors can create and use a shared *collaborative memory* [2,24], for larger groups it is also called group memory. Collaborative memory describes a common repository containing the issues and minutes of a group discussion so that it is available for future review by the collaboration partners [2,24]. It is required to get a tangible product at the end of collaboration [14] as well as to have partial results of single collaborative tasks to be reused during ongoing collaboration [2,19]. Collaborative memory is created during the actors' information sharing activities. Specifically, actors have to share information in a "memory-able" form, meaning that it could be reused for later recall of information, e.g., writing on a flipchart to explain an idea and refer to the writings in a later discussion. The lack of an effective collaborative memory has been found to negatively affect group member's task performance and decision making [1].

In the current research discourse, researchers extensively discuss how to create collaborative memory during group work. Kane et al. [14], for instance, discuss the creation and validation of collaborative memory. They describe the fundamental preconditions, that collaborative memory should be created without diverting from the face-to-face collaboration, it should require only little (if any) processing, and provide for a multitude of potential uses. Kalnikaite et al. [12] address the specific note-taking activities of individual actors during collaboration. Their solution based on automatic speech recognition and annotation possibilities, should reduce the individuals' cognitive workload in order to maintain their verbal contribution to the collaboration while taking notes. With their "Livenotes"-system, Kam et al. [13] present a solution for cooperative note-taking between students, emphasizing the value of co-created notes to facilitating more efficient reuse of collaborative memory.

Current research studies in CSCW provide useful insights on the creation and use of collaborative memory, describing how corresponding support can be designed and applied. However, researchers focus mostly on stationary collaborations and rarely discuss mobile collaboration scenarios and the novel challenges that occur. It is important to understand these challenges and their implications on the design of suitable support systems: The integration of the changing physical environment in the mobile collaboration can increase the cognitive workload for the actors substantially, causing them to struggle more with information overload and ultimately hampering their collaborative work severely.

RESEARCH APPROACH

To answer the research questions, we followed a design research approach proposed by Peffers et al. [23], consisting of six activities to be followed when conducting a design science research project: 1) defining and justifying the research problem, 2) defining the objectives for a solution, 3) designing and developing the artifact, 4) demonstrating the use of the artifact, 5) evaluating the artifact and 6) communicating the results. We address these activities in the following four sections:

Problem specification: To answer the first research question (RQ1), we engaged in the first activity of justifying the core problems that consultants and clients experience due to the OOS-OOM phenomenon. We conducted an exploratory field study in the context of mobile crime prevention counseling services. In November 2012, two researchers conducted semi-structured interviews with four clients and two consultants from the crime prevention department of the police of a major Swiss city. The clients for the semi-structured interviews were randomly selected from the usual clients of the police's counseling service. Furthermore, the researchers observed the same two consultants in three counseling sessions (one consultant twice) with three additional clients, and interviewed the consultants and clients afterwards to uncover their collaborative behavior. These three clients were also randomly selected from the police department's usual clients. The observed counseling sessions lasted 45 minutes, on average. The observation guidelines and the interview questions were based on: Wilson's model of human information behavior [35], the *needs-driven approach* [26], and the *servqual* measuring tool [22].

Design: To address the second research question (RQ2), we engaged in further activities proposed by Peffers et al. [23]. We first derived specific goals that an artifact resolving the OOS-OOM-related problems should accomplish (activity no. 2). Second, we described the key design ideas for picture-centric mobile counseling support and comprehensively illustrated our design rationale, based on current research literature. Third, we implemented a prototypical system to support consultants and clients in their mobile crime prevention counseling sessions (activities no. 3 and no. 4).

Evaluation: We applied experimental techniques to evaluate the extent to which the developed artifact helped accomplishing the goals. We conducted a within-subject user test, where the same two consultants from the police gave advice to 12 clients (activity no. 5). Detailed set-up of the experiment is described in the evaluation section.

Discussion: We discussed the findings of our research, highlighting the powerful roles of pictures in mobile collaborations. We discussed the meaning and effects of current research on CSCW research, memory aid systems and counseling support systems (activities no. 6).

PROBLEM SPECIFICATION: COGNITIVE CHALLENGES IN MOBILE CONSULTANT-CLIENT COLLABORATIONS

The mobile counseling session is characterized by intensive information exchange: between consultants and clients, and between the actors and their physical environment. All information has to be memorized, processed and integrated into the problem-solving activities to advance the collaboration, working toward the counseling objective to develop solutions matching the client's problems. These solutions may not be accomplished without input from both actors. The client provides information about her needs and preferences (her area of expertise) and the consultant provides information about possible solutions (his area of expertise). Thus, solutions developed in the counseling session must be co-created. The consultant and the client get involved in expert-layperson collaboration, where their respective roles can influence their respective behavior substantially.

Current work practices in crime prevention counseling

A normal citizen not only has little knowledge on crime prevention but also has difficulties in explaining her problem situation. Therefore, a consultant from the police visits the client "on site." In a briefcase, the consultant carries paper-based standardized information on home security or fact sheets on security products, i.e., security locks or safes.

In the counseling session's first phase, the consultant and client move around the house exploring the physical problem objects, where burglars could break in, "on site" (e.g., the front door). They collectively examine structural weaknesses while exchanging information to establish a shared problem understanding. The client provides information about her needs; the consultant asks detailed questions to refine the problem understanding. He also addresses simple solution possibilities, e.g., "always turn the key in the lock twice." During their tour around the house the consultant carries his briefcase with him, but usually does not make use of it. We call this phase the *"mobile exploration" phase*.

In the second phase, the consultant and client sit together at a central location, e.g., the client's kitchen table. They readdress the problems verbally and discuss possible solutions. In their discussions, the consultant takes some brochures and flyers from his briefcase to show the client standard product information, e.g. a security lock information sheet. Meanwhile, the client provides the consultant with information about her criteria for suitable solutions, e.g., price range. Together, they evaluate the different solution possibilities in order to choose the most suitable one. We refer to this second phase as the *"discussion" phase.*

Finally, the consultant creates the final product of the counseling session, the "security plan." This consists of a few handwritten notes, e.g., on buying a new door lock or an alarm system. Together with some product brochures, the consultant hands over to the client the notes that document the collectively developed security recommendations.

The OOS-OOM phenomenon in crime prevention counseling sessions

In their mobile crime prevention counseling sessions, consultants and clients face a number of cognitive challenges. In the following paragraphs, we report from an explorative field study (cf. research design section for details) where we identify the most influential collaboration problems caused by the OOS-OOM phenomenon.

The client forgets: the problem of information incoherence

The clients in all observed counseling sessions reported that although they could remember the developed solutions, they could not remember all discussed details regarding the corresponding problems. As a result, they were later unable to sufficiently explain the solutions, e.g., to their partner or a security firm's employee. One client stated: "As I told my husband about the lock bars, I remembered the consultant saying something about the bathroom window, but I couldn't recall it [...]. We had to call the consultant, who told us that our wall was too thin." (All quotes were translated into English by the authors). The consultants also mentioned this issue: "Quite often, clients come back after some months, to ask again how a solution fits their problem [...] extremely time consuming." Furthermore, there were negative effects during the actual counseling encounter: all three clients repeatedly had difficulties in understanding the explanations of the consultant and interrupted the counseling process with clarifying questions, e.g., "This safety lock should be applied where? The front or the terrace door?" A major reason for the clients' shortcoming was the lack of environmental context in the "discussion" phase of the counseling session. Differing environmental contexts negatively affect an individual's capability to remember information significantly [27,28]: The client cannot sufficiently link the solutions to the corresponding problems. We refer to this as the *problem of information incoherence (**P1**).*

Why traditional pen-and-paper is insufficient: The paper-based documents that consultants mostly use consist of standardized information. These technical drawings or standard product fact sheets often do not match the actual problem object. As a result, the consultant's solution explanations detach even further from the original environmental context of the problem and increasingly impede the client's efforts of recalling the corresponding context.

The consultant forgets: the problem of outshone information

In their discussion on-site of a physical problem object, consultants provided solution information constituting an important part of the final solutions. However, our observation revealed that none of the consultants re-addressed these solutions and thus did not include them in the final security plan. As a result, the clients missed important information for later implementation of the solutions. We explain this forgetting via *the outshining effect* [27,28], which describes the effect when memory cues bound to a specific environment are later "outshone" by stronger, non-contextual memory cues, e.g., verbal cues [28]. The consultants also referred to this *problem of outshone solution information (**P2**)*. One consultant stated: "I would mention this information in the final discussion, if I remembered it [...] I rely on my documents to explain the security measures and hardly remember other measures I proposed."

Why traditional pen-and-paper is insufficient: The standardized documents provide consultants with context-independent memory cues. These cues help them to recall information about the specific product, e.g., the price of a security lock. But they do not help them to recall previously discussed solution information, as these memory cues do not contain information about the physical problem objects. In the end, the context-independent memory cues in the documents "outshine" the more-difficult-to-access mental cues on the solution information discussed on-site.

Consultant and client fail to synchronize: the problem of asynchronous information levels

The counseling encounter is also a collaboration between an expert and a layperson [25]. Consultants take on the role of experts, applying their expertise to establish a shared problem understanding with the client, enabling them to co-create suitable solutions. However, the knowledge and experience asymmetry causes the consultant and client to show different cognitive behaviors, affecting their collaboration negatively: In the "discussion" phase of the observed sessions, the client (as layperson) at some point faces more difficulties than the consultant in recalling the "out of sight" problems. Clients needed clearer and/or more memory cues to remember the location-bound problems and start lagging behind in their mental processing. Our observations revealed that the lack of a clear understanding of a problem hindered the client from participating as active co-creator in the development of solutions. Two clients specifically mentioned this aspect of "can't contribute to developing the solution" in the interviews. Additionally, the clients' delayed mental processing also resulted in delayed comprehension questions, disrupting the counseling process. As a result, consultants repeatedly had to help the clients to re-establish a sufficient understanding of the problem before proceeding with co-creating solutions. In two cases of the observed counseling sessions, this even forced actors to interrupt their discussions since they needed to revisit the physical problem object to renew their problem understanding. The measures of re-synchronizing the information levels increase the cognitive workload for both actors and complicate developing a coherent security plan. We refer to this as the *problem of asynchronous information levels (**P3**)*.

Why traditional pen-and-paper is insufficient: The paper-based documents (e.g., product fact sheets) do not provide any information about the client's actual physical problem objects. In consequence, consultants and clients have to depend on their cognitive capabilities to recall the problems in their mind and link them to the solution information presented in the standardized brochures, thus increasing the actors' cognitive workload substantially.

In answering RQ1, we identified three problems representing the negative influences of the OOS-OOM phenomenon on the mobile consultant-client collaboration. To show how an IT-artifact can be designed to support consultants and clients to overcome the identified problems (P1 to P3), we derive three specific design goals.

First goal (addressing P1): The clients' difficulties in linking received solution information to the individual location-bound problems (P1) affect them severely, not only during their collaboration with the consultants (inability to actively collaborate), but also after the counseling session (restricted ability to implement the solutions). Thus, we formulate a corresponding first design goal *to improve linking of location-bound problem and solution information.*

Second goal (addressing P2): Both actors frequently fail to recall essential information during their collaboration: 1) the consultant forgets essential parts of the solution when they get "outshone" and 2) the client struggles to link the problems with the developed solutions, as the missing local context hampers their recall. To help the consultant access the "outshone" solution information and the client to recall "out of sight" information, we state a second design goal: *to improve the recall of problem and solution information.*

Third goal (addressing P3): The missing synchronicity of the actors' cognitive processing strongly influences the mobile collaboration between consultants and clients, and thus hampers their joint problem-solving activities. Therefore, a supportive artifact should *increase information synchronicity between consultants and clients.*

SOLUTION: PICTURE-CENTRIC MOBILE COUNSELING

The OOS-OOM-phenomenon can strongly affect consultants and clients in recalling information. To respond to the identified challenges, we designed the concept of a picture-centric mobile counseling service addressing the developed goals and instantiated this concept in the *SmartProtector* (an 11.6' tablet computer with the corresponding software).

Key design ideas

To show how a corresponding artifact should be designed to address the occurring challenges in mobile collaborations (RQ2), we developed a set of key design ideas. These design ideas can be seen as technological guidelines that should be considered when developing IT-artifacts supporting mobile collaborations between consultants and clients.

***"Taking pictures"** for fast and simple externalization of information:* To facilitate linking location-bound problems with solutions (first goal), consultants and clients need a profound problem understanding. When they manipulate shared external representations, they explicate their meanings and beliefs, thus facilitate establishing a shared problem understanding [30]. Thus, external representations may encourage the client to become an active co-creator, helping her to internalize the problems. In the mobile counseling session, the actors need to capture the physical environment, containing the problem, and create external representations. In doing so, the pictures become external memory cues reminding actors of previously discussed ideas [30]. They can facilitate actors' cognitive process by serving as substitute reference for the actual problem object [3]. Externalization of information should not disturb the evolving consultant-client-relationship. Thus, the switching cost between problem exploration and memory cue creation should be low, as Lin et al. called for in their work [15]. Hence, we argue that supportive artifacts should *enable users to take pictures* (design idea 1) for capturing the physical environment and easily document discussed problem information.

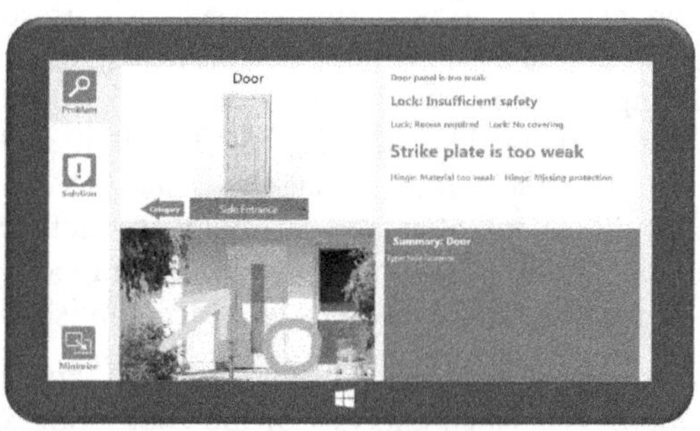

Figure 1. Picture-centric notecard in the *SmartProtector*

***"Drawing on pictures"** to create memory cues:* We argue that "taking pictures" alone does not suffice. For better recall of information (second goal), the information that matters on the picture needs to be highlighted to differentiate surrounding context from kernel memory cues. Customizing the representation can support reasoning and problem solving [10]. Additional explanatory information on the problem object needs also to be added to the corresponding picture to link them together (third goal). Similar to "taking pictures," actors need to make these refinements without disturbing their work relationship. Drawing on the pictures constitutes a suitable means to add additional information, not only because it is an intuitive and self-evident action on pictures, but drawing and the actors' concurrent verbal discourse occupy different mental resources (visual and verbal) and thus can prevent increasing the cognitive workload of the actors [cf. 34]. Furthermore, memory cue creation activities need to be quick and easy [15]. Therefore, we argue that supportive artifacts should *enable drawing on pictures* (design idea 2) to allow users to create additional memory cues. Therewith, actors should be able to better integrate the memory cue creation activities into their ongoing verbal discussion. Figure 1 shows the picture that the consultant and the client took from the front door and on which they draw additional information about structural weaknesses.

***"Creating picture-centric notecards"** to promote cross-linking location-bound problem and solution information:* In the mobile counseling session, the problems are mostly discussed on-site of the physical problem object (cf. Figure 2), whereas the discussions of solutions take place location-independent, e.g., at the kitchen table. Thus, it is useful to cross-link the pictures of the individual problems, e.g., a door lock, with corresponding solution information, e.g., a product information sheet. We argue that creating these links by adding solution information to a picture of an individual problem should preserve this connection (first goal). Therefore, we propose that supportive artifacts should enable actors to *create picture-centric notecards* (design idea 3). These notecards contain the problem information organized around the physical problem objects' picture and provides additional means to externalize information on solutions. The picture-centric notecard can function as boundary objects that both actors can use to explain their thoughts and ideas on discussed problems. Boundary objects are objects that are shareable across different problem solving contexts [5], thus can help to establish a shared context [29]. The picture-centric notecards can facilitate establishing a shared understanding as starting point for collaborative problem-solving (third goal). Integrating picture-centric notecards as integral part of the collaboration allowing them to physically refer to the problem objects (or their representations), which can facilitate their cognitive processes [3].

Figure 2. The *SmartProtector* in use during mobile exploration

Working with pictures as a simple, but surprisingly powerful concept

"Working with pictures" is a simple, but powerful core concept. Pictures serve as shared artifacts and boundary objects. Both consultants and clients can create their shared understanding based on a jointly viewed picture and process it with their individual cognitive capabilities. Pictures can also serve as collaborative memory aid, allowing both actors to recall information concurrently, to synchronize their knowledge levels and help them to collaborate more effectively. Furthermore, pictures are useful information carriers:

drawing on pictures enables the actors to refine the information content and create a more in-depth problem description. The actors can distribute the multitasking workload of documenting information and discuss it on different mental resources, thus facilitating their collaborative work [34]. "Taking pictures" captures a lot of information in a very short time. Writing down the information allows users to create more personal memory cues, but creating them takes too much time. Recording on video would be a fast and easy way to store information, but reviewing continuous video data during collaborative work is simply impractical [11]. Thus, we argue that taking pictures, drawing on them and referring to them in later discussions will overcome the deficiencies of current approaches and allow users to establish a balanced effort-benefit ratio to store and recall information. Figure 3 summarizes the roles of pictures in our picture-centric support concept for mobile collaborations.

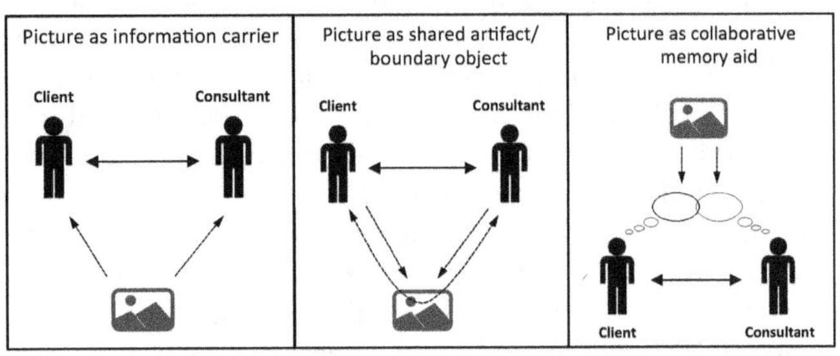

Figure 3. The roles of pictures to support mobile collaborations between consultants and clients

EVALUATION

Following the methodology of Peffers et al. [23], we assessed the extent to which the IT-artifact helped to accomplish the formulated goals (cf. problem specification section). We evaluated the *SmartProtector* in a within-subject test (in April 2013), collecting data about the differences between conventional and artifact-supported counseling sessions. The two consultants from the police gave advice to 12 clients (12 conventional and 12 artifact-supported sessions). Each client received one conventional and one artifact-supported session (experiencing both consultants). Afterwards they reported on the differences between the two sessions. Each consultant conducted six conventional and six artifact-supported counseling sessions in alternating order. Afterwards, they reported on the differences between the two kinds of counseling sessions. The clients were recruited among the crime prevention department's usual clients. Seven clients were male and five female; average age was 44. A counseling session lasted about 45 minutes; the duration did not vary, on average, between conventional and artifact-supported sessions.

We recorded all 24 counseling sessions on video and encoded them manually. We collected all discussed problems and solutions (including who addressed them, content and start/end time of discussion). We could thus see how much and which information was externalized or recalled. We collected all questions asked by the clients to provide us with observable characteristics of the clients' cognitive processing. Furthermore, we complemented our analysis with participants' direct feedback in a questionnaire and semi-structured interview. The questionnaire was used to assess the IT-artifact's fit within the consultant-client collaboration. It included items for technology acceptance [32], e.g., intention to use: "I plan to use the IT-tool in the next few month.", and user satisfaction [4], e.g., "I'm satisfied with using the IT-tool in the counseling session.". The semi-structured interviews were based on the same topics as the questionnaire, helping us to understand the reasons behind the actors' behavior during the counseling sessions.

Results

In general, the *SmartProtector* was well accepted and successfully integrated into the mobile counseling sessions. Participants valued their perceived satisfaction with the tool well (on average 6.5 for clients and 6.7 for consultants on a Likert scale; 7 = pos. max.). In addition, five of twelve clients especially highlighted the improved personal relationship with the consultant experienced during the artifact-supported session (despite their inverse expectations).

During the artifact-supported sessions, consultants and clients recalled and re-addressed during the final "discussion" phase, on average, 91% of the initially discussed information. In contrast, they only re-addressed, on average, 68% during the conventional sessions. The difference is significant (two-sided t-test, $T(22)=3.53$, $p=0.002$). This result gives the first evidence that the *SmartProtector* supports consultants and clients in recalling substantially more information. In the following paragraphs, we report the extent to which the individual goals were accomplished.

Externalize and link location-bound problem with solution information: The video analysis of the counseling sessions showed that the consultants externalized substantially more of the discussed information while using the *SmartProtector*. They externalized, on average, six problems and six solutions in the artifact-supported sessions, whereas in the conventional sessions, they externalized only three problems and four solutions. In this context, the clients accentuated the feature of taking a picture and attaching it to a notecard. They confirmed that this was both a fast way to capture the visited problems and also beneficial, as the picture facilitated the subsequent recalling and discussion of the problems. In addition, the *SmartProtector* encouraged the clients to participate more actively in the counseling sessions, helping them to internalize the new information: in the artifact-supported sessions, the clients asked more questions about the implementation of specific solutions than they did in the conventional ones (on average four questions in the artifact-support session, but only one in the conventional sessions). One client stated afterwards: "I knew directly when the consultant opened a [memo] card that the information would be linked with it [...] I could concentrate on understanding the solution."

Recall problem and solution information: In the conventional counseling sessions, the consultants only re-addressed 68% of the problem information during the final "discussion" phase, i.e., they forgot 32%. This happened due to the consultant prematurely closing some issues (by providing both problem and solution information on-site of the problem) without documenting them. Whereas most of this information got lost in the conventional sessions, consultants and clients recalled them in the artifact-supported sessions. Concretely, the picture-centric notecards encouraged consultants to provide more detailed information: our video analysis revealed that whenever they saw the picture of a discussed problem or the remarks drawn upon, they repeated the problem information. The consultants explained their behavior and one stated: "I wanted to explain to the client what we already documented [...] to check if we forgot something." Another consultant stated: "I really like the photographs with the remarks. They remind me of the conversation [...] I was able to repeat all the details."

Establish information synchronicity: Lacking information synchronicity (P3) between consultants and clients manifested most strongly in the form of "delayed" questions. That is, while the consultants moved from discussing one problem and its solution to the next one, the clients stayed behind mentally, asking questions about the "old" discussion. The results indicate that in the artifact-supported sessions, consultants and clients could establish information synchronicity better. In the artifact-supported setting, the average number of delayed questions was less than one, whereas in the conventional setting, they asked three delayed questions, on average. Furthermore, the video analysis revealed that pictures were the main triggers, activating the clients to ask their questions: 70% of all questions asked by clients during the "discussion" phase coincided with them looking at one of the pictures. The picture is always one of the first things appearing on a notecard, thus clients were encouraged to take on the role of the active co-creator early in the problem-solving process, allowing them to comprehend and memorize the solution better [25].

When not working with pictures...: In the artifact-supported sessions, whenever consultants needed to make written notes in addition to taking pictures, they had to interrupt the verbal conversations. In twelve sessions 18 corresponding situations occurred. These interruptions negatively influenced the evolving consultant-client relationship. The consultants pointed out these negative effects. One consultant stated: "When I wrote information in the tool, I had to interrupt the conversation."

DISCUSSION

The evaluation revealed that the picture-centric support concept implemented in the *SmartProtector* helped consultants and clients to externalize and recall substantially more information, overcoming the cognitive challenges of the OOS-OOM phenomenon (cf. P1 to P3). As a consequence, consultants and clients could establish and reuse a collaborative memory more effectively. In their picture-centric mobile collaboration, the actors could become more equal and more active co-creators of the counseling's value.

Whereas previous CSCW research discuss group members' activities for creating a collaborative memory in stationary collaborations [cf. 1,2,12,13,14,19], mobile collaborations create novel challenges. We could show, that the OOS-OOM-caused problems that consultants and clients face in mobile collaboration (cf. P1 to P3) do severely influence them in creating and using a collaborative memory. In answering our research questions, we contribute to the ongoing scientific discussion on collaborative memory in CSCW. In greater detail, we continue and extend the work of, e.g., Kalnikaite et al. [12], Berlin et al. [2] or Kane et al. [14] by highlighting, first, the influences of mobility on the creation and use of collaborative memory, and, second, how they can be diminished:

Actors create collaborative memory while sharing information in "memory-able" form. In doing so, the effort to create corresponding information represent an influential determinant of the actors' collaborative behavior in mobile collaborations. In the mobile collaboration, the physical environment becomes an essential part of these information sharing activities, increasing the actors' cognitive workload and affecting them to create an adequate collaborative memory. Current CSCW-research focus on facilitating the actors' writing activities and complementing them with voice entry possibilities to enable more efficient creation of collaborative memory [cf. 12,13,14].

Based on our research insights, we argue that when supporting mobile collaborations, another improvement is necessary: from writing or speaking to *working with pictures*. Using pictures is an appropriate and necessary extension to (re-)establish an adequate ratio between the efforts of creating and the benefits of using collaborative memory: First, "taking pictures" allow actors to collect comprehensive information on location-bound problems in short time and with barely disrupting their verbal discussions, as also Lin et al. [15] called for. Writing or voice entry possibilities do hardly fit the task as resulting records do restrict on the (presumably) essential information and missing necessary environmental context information. Second, whereas for written and spoken documentation support, actors have to explicitly create "memory-able" information, taking pictures do not require such processing and thus do not additionally burden the actors' cognitive workload and allow them to focus on their collaboration. In addition, creating sharable information using pictures do not require actors to search for and explain technical terms, but to simplify documentation and to focus entirely on their collaboration, while still creating a comprehensive collaborative memory. Researchers can profit from our insights and learn about actors' collaborative behaviors in mobile collaborations, its triggers, and how working with pictures can represent a suitable next step for support systems for mobile collaborations. Developers of future IT-artifacts can benefit and use our key design ideas to improve system design, creating mobile collaboration support that allows for a more balanced effort-benefit-ratio to increase the effective creation and use of collaborative memory.

In mobile collaborations, the actors' cognitive capabilities to memorize and recall location-bound information come to the fore. Thus, preventing cognitive "overload" should guide the design of future IT-systems supporting mobile collaborations. Using pictures in mobile collaborations, help actors to distribute their cognitive workload on different mental resources (visual and verbal) and thus diminishing the risk of cognitive "overload". Furthermore, using pictures can facilitate the creation of a information space for distributed cognition [8], where the changing physical environment is integrated as cognitive resource. With our research, we contribute to the ongoing scientific discussion on the design of IT-system supporting mobile collaborations by highlighting the benefits of a picture-centric support concept. In detail, we continue the work of, e.g., Kalnikate et al. [12], Kam et al. [13] or Lin et al. [15], showing how to design IT-systems that not only facilitate creating collaborative memory in mobile collaborations but concurrently help preventing cognitive "overload" and maintain the actors as active contributors to the collaboration.

In contrast to the related work on memory aid systems focusing on single users [e.g., 15,16], the situation of the mobile consultant-client collaboration can substantially differ. Collaboratively used memory aid systems require addressing the users' different cognitive styles to memorize and recall information. Researchers and developers of memory aid systems can benefit from our insights on the powerful and diverse roles of pictures with the capability of supporting multiple users in their collaboration in creating and using a collaborative memory. Therewith, we contribute to the current scientific discussion on memory aid systems, deepening the understanding of the novel application area of expert-layperson collaborations. Allowing users to take pictures, to draw on them for refinements and to integrate them (cf. key design ideas) into the collaborative work combines both memory aid and collaboration support capabilities, and thus should be considered by developers when designing future collaboratively used memory aid systems.

With our research insights on mobile consultant-client collaborations, we also contribute directly to the current research discourse on IT-enabled collaborative work practices in consultant-client collaborations. The cognitive perspective on the actors' collaborative behaviors provides corresponding researchers with a deeper understanding of the underlying reason for collaborative behavior. We continue and extend the work from, e.g., Heinrich et al. [6] or Schmidt-Rauch and Nussbaumer [25], by adding the neglected perspective of memory support. Extending their solution artifacts with our research findings on how to integrate pictures into consultant-client collaborations adds to their developed solutions, bringing us closer to providing comprehensive counseling support, comprising all collaboration-relevant characteristics.

We argue that the picture-centric design concept instantiated in the *SmartProtector* can be generalized to similar face-to-face collaborations. Counseling collaborations with the same role allocation (expert/layperson) and setting, e.g., energy counseling at one's home, are very similar. Potentially, other mobile collaborative settings, such as mobile learning with an equivalent role allocation (teacher/pupil, etc.) could also profit from our insights, as the identified OOS-OOM caused problems are not domain specific.

Whereas "working with pictures" provides suitable support for quick and simple creation of a collaborative memory in mobile collaboration, the study also revealed that consultants repeatedly had to interrupt the verbal conversation with the clients when adding written notes. In the design of suitable systems supporting mobile collaborations, these issues could be addressed through implementing, e.g., speech-recognition functions, location-aware notification functions or using more ubiquitous technology (e.g., google glass) to facilitate note-taking.

CONCLUSION AND LIMITATIONS

In this paper, we identified the novel (cognitive) challenges occurring in mobile collaborations between consultants and clients. We, first, highlight how these challenges influence actors' collaborative behavior to create and use a collaborative memory and, second, developed a picture-centric design concept for IT-systems supporting mobile collaborations addressing these challenges.

While working with real consultants allowed us deep insights, the setup also comes with limitations. Our study is based only on two consultants, as the city (500,000 citizens) does not have more consultants. Thus, the results could be biased and need to be validated in other settings before we can develop a more rigid design theory. At the time of this writing, the *SmartProtector* has moved on from the experimental stage to the pilot stage in which two consultants use *SmartProtector* as part of their everyday work. Furthermore, additional tests with six consultants from other Swiss cities are currently running. This offers the opportunity to deepen our research and validate our research findings.

REFERENCES

1. Alavi, M. GROUP DECISION SUPPORT SYSTEMS A Key to Business Team Productivity. *Journal of Information Systems Management 8*, 3 (1991), 36–41.
2. Berlin, L.M., Jeffries, R., O'Day, V.L., Paepcke, A., and Wharton, C. Where did you put it? Issues in the design and use of a group memory. *Proc. INTERACT'93 and CHI'93*, ACM (1993), 23–30.
3. Blandford, A. and Furniss, D. DiCoT: a methodology for applying distributed cognition to the design of

teamworking systems. In *Interactive systems. Design, specification, and verification*. Springer, 2006, 26–38.
4. Briggs, R.O., Reinig, B.A., and Vreede, G.J. The yield shift theory of satisfaction and its application to the IS/IT domain. *Information Systems Theory*, (2012), 185–217.
5. Carlile, P.R. A pragmatic view of knowledge and boundaries: Boundary objects in new product development. *Organization science 13*, 4 (2002), 442–455.
6. Heinrich, P., Kilic, M., Aschoff, F.-R., and Schwabe, G. Enabling Relationship Building in Tabletop-supported Advisory Settings. *Proc. CSCW'14*, (2014).
7. Hevner, A.R., March, S.T., Park, J., and Ram, S. Design science in information systems research. *Mis Quarterly*, (2004), 75–105.
8. Hollan, J., Hutchins, E., and Kirsh, D. Distributed cognition: toward a new foundation for human-computer interaction research. *Transactions on Computer-Human Interaction (TOCHI) 7*, 2 (2000), 174–196.
9. Horton, G., Chelvier, R., Knoll, S.W., and Gors, J. Idea Engineering: A Case Study of a Practically Oriented University Course in Innovation. *System Sciences (HICSS), Proc. HICSS*, (2011), 1–7.
10. Hutchins, E. *Cognition in the Wild.* MIT Press, 1995.
11. Ju, W., Ionescu, A., Neeley, L., and Winograd, T. Where the wild things work: capturing shared physical design workspaces. *Proc. CSCW'04*, ACM (2004), 533–541.
12. Kalnikaitė, V., Ehlen, P., and Whittaker, S. Markup as you talk: establishing effective memory cues while still contributing to a meeting. *Proc. CSCW'12*, ACM (2012), 349–358.
13. Kam, M., Wang, J., Iles, A., et al. Livenotes: a system for cooperative and augmented note-taking in lectures. *Proc. CHI'05*, (2005), 531–540.
14. Kane, B.T., Toussaint, P.J., and Luz, S. Shared decision making needs a communication record. *Proc. CSCW'13*, ACM (2013), 79–90.
15. Lin, M., Lutters, W.G., and Kim, T.S. Understanding the micronote lifecycle: improving mobile support for informal note taking. *Proc. CHI'04*, (2004), 687–694.
16. McGee-Lennon, M.R., Wolters, M.K., and Brewster, S. User-centred multimodal reminders for assistive living. *Proc. CHI'11*, (2011), 2105–2114.
17. Novak, J. MINE, YOURS… OURS? Designing for Principal Agent Collaboration in Interactive Value Creation. Proc. *Wirtschaftinformatik*, (2009).
18. Novak, J. and Schwabe, G. Designing for reintermediation in the brick-and-mortar world: Towards the travel agency of the future. *Electronic Markets 19*, 1 (2009), 15–29.
19. Nunamaker, J.F., Dennis, A.R., Valacich, J.S., Vogel, D.R., and George, J.F. Electronic Meeting Systems to Support Group Work. *Communications of the ACM 34*, 7 (1991), 39–61.
20. Nussbaumer, P., Matter, I., and Schwabe, G. "Enforced" vs."Casual" Transparency–Findings from IT-Supported Financial Advisory Encounters. *Transactions on Management Information Systems (TMIS) 3*, 2 (2012), 11.
21. Palen, L. and Aaløkke, S. Of pill boxes and piano benches: home-made methods for managing medication. *Proc. CSCW'06*, (2006), 79–88.
22. Parasuraman, A., Zeithaml, V.A., and Berry, L.L. Servqual. *Journal of retailing 64*, 1 (1988), 12–40.
23. Peffers, K., Tuunanen, T., Rothenberger, M.A., and Chatterjee, S. A Design Science Research Methodology for Information Systems Research. *Journal of Management Information Systems 24*, 3 (2007), 45–77.
24. Rajaram, S. and Pereira-Pasarin, L.P. Collaborative Memory: Cognitive Research and Theory. *Perspectives on Psychological Science 5*, 6 (2010), 649–663.
25. Schmidt-Rauch, S. and Nussbaumer, P. Putting Value Co-Creation into Practice: A Case for Advisory Support. Proc. *ECIS'11*, (2011).
26. Schwabe, G. and Krcmar, H. Der Needs Driven Approach-Eine Methode zur bedarfsgerechten Gestaltung von Telekooperation. *Herausforderung Telekooperation Einsatzerfahrungen und Lösungsansätze*, (1996), 69–88.
27. Smith, S.M. A comparison of two techniques for reducing context-dependent forgetting. *Memory & Cognition 12*, 5 (1984), 477–482.
28. Smith, S.M. and Vela, E. Environmental context-dependent memory: A review and meta-analysis. *Psychonomic bulletin & review 8*, 2 (2001), 203–220.
29. Starr, S.L. The structure of ill-structured solutions: Boundary objects and heterogeneous distributed problem solving. *Readings in Distributed Artificial Intelligence*, (1989).
30. Suthers, D.D. and Hundhausen, C.D. The effects of representation on students' elaborations in collaborative inquiry. *Proc. CSCL'02*, (2002), 472–480.
31. Tulving, E. Cue-Dependent Forgetting: When we forget something we once knew, it does not necessarily mean that the memory trace has been lost; it may only be inaccessible. *American Scientist 62*, 1 (1974), 74–82.
32. Venkatesh, V., Morris, M.G., Davis, G.B., and Davis, F.D. User Acceptance of Information Technology: Toward a Unified View. *MIS Quarterly 27*, 3 (2003), 425–478.
33. Warschburger, P. *Beratungspsychologie.* Medizin Springer Verlag, Heidelberg, 2009.
34. Wickens, C.D. Multiple Resources and Mental Workload. *Human Factors: The Journal of the Human Factors and Ergonomics Society 50*, 3 (2008), 449–455.
35. Wilson, T.D. Human information behavior. *Informing science 3*, 2 (2000), 49–56.

Designing Mobile Experiences for Collocated Interaction

Sus Lundgren[1], Joel E. Fischer[2], Stuart Reeves[2] and Olof Torgersson[1]

[1]Interaction Design, Dept of Applied IT
Chalmers University of Technology/
University of Gothenburg
{sus.lundgren, olof.torgersson}@chalmers.se

[2]The Mixed Reality Laboratory
School of Computer Science
University of Nottingham
{jef, str}@cs.nott.ac.uk

ABSTRACT

Many of our everyday social interactions involve mobile devices. Yet, these tend to only provide good support for *distributed* social interactions. Although much HCI and CSCW research has explored how we might support *collocated*, face-to-face situations using mobile devices, much of this work exists as isolated exemplars of technical systems or interaction designs. This paper draws on a range of such exemplars to develop a practical design framework intended for guiding the design of new mobile experiences for collocated interaction as well as analysing existing ones. Our framework provides four relational perspectives for designing the complex interplay between: the social situation in which it takes place; the technology used and the mechanics inscribed; the physical environment; and the temporal elements of design. Moreover, each perspective features some core properties, which are highly relevant when designing these systems. As part of presenting the framework we also explain the process of its construction along with practical advice on how to read and apply it.

Author Keywords

Collocated interaction; face-to-face; design framework; interaction design.

ACM Classification Keywords

H.5.2 [Information Interfaces and Presentation]: User Interfaces.

General Terms

Design

INTRODUCTION

Physical collocation and 'face-to-face' forms of interaction are now a pervasive and mundane feature of much technology use. We might navigate through streets with others [12], share photos [36], listen to music together or jointly edit a document using mobile devices. Yet, many portable technologies—particularly consumer electronics like smartphones and tablets—tend to be strongly oriented towards supporting *distributed* interactions, and have only limited built-in support for *collocated* use where face-to-face interactions play a key role [39]. For example, taking and sharing group photos with your co-present friends and family can be an awkward endeavour. 'Support' for collocated action is provided by the possibility of 'showing' another person the screen of a phone or tablet or simply handing the device over. Sharing copies, however, often ends up being done by email, despite being collocated.

Technological support of collocated collaborative work is a central feature of CSCW. This research has often revolved around describing topics such as collocated awareness and coordination practices [8,23,25]. A classic exploration of this domain may also be found in single display groupware systems [27]. Recently, there has been significant research exploring more inherently *mobile* settings, examining novel collaborative ways of supporting physically collocated mobile device users beyond simple screen sharing practices described above [1,16,36]. While this strong line of work offers a large corpus of knowledge for CSCW, little coherent design synthesis of it has taken place.

In this paper we present a design framework to help analyse and design for collocated interaction. The framework is the outcome of a process *focussed on helping designers shape mobile experiences which support collocated interaction.* Our process of exploration has included a conference workshop with researchers, design activities with students, reflection on our own design experiences, and reviewing the literature on collocated mobile experiences, all of which aimed to cover and describe various perspectives and properties that are relevant for design within this domain.

The resulting framework has two *representational forms*: a *diagrammatic form* and a *list form*. Respectively these provide both a relational map and a set of design properties. The framework is intended for two main forms of use:

- As a **design tool** for ideating and (re)-designing through selection and adaptation of the framework's properties;
- As an **analytic tool** for systematically describing interactive systems for collocated mobile experiences.

The core contribution of this work is to help understand how we can practically design interactive systems that support, enable, or augment face-to-face group interactions that occur in collocated settings.

We firstly review a range of literature that informed the framework's construction. The paper then offers a presentation of the framework itself. Finally we provide

CSCW '15, March 14 - 18, 2015, Vancouver, BC, Canada.

http://dx.doi.org/10.1145/2675133.2675171

guidelines for its practical application, using design examples, discuss a set of reflections on the process of developing the framework and lastly consider it as describing a 'genre' of experiences.

RELATED WORK

Research on the design of digital tools and experiences for collocated settings and situations spans from classic CSCW research on technology support of collocated office environments [24,52] to diverse domains such as visiting cities [11], galleries and museums [19], theme parks [14], sports events [30], learning [4], playing [5], therapeutic situations [29], or sharing photos [36].

A range of systems have been designed to support collocated group identification, often employing multiple modalities including physical proximity, orientation, audible talk or other aural fingerprinting means, similarity of visual view and so on (e.g. see [2,31]). Various interaction techniques for collocated settings also allow users to leverage a range of novel modalities to manually indicate group situations, from touch and collocated display couplings [37,3], through to audio-based proximity groupings of mobile devices [22,49].

Beyond this, a related body of work has drawn attention to the empirical study of collocated social interactions surrounding system use [38,39] and their various design implications. This work points out the need to consider how technology fits or rubs up with the interactional resources people employ in face-to-face interaction, such as gaze, gestures, and bodily co-orientation. Examples include how environments may foster F-formations [42], how insights from studies of visual conduct may be used to design more sociable robots [32], how mutual observability of action may be a key resource for tabletop collaboration [27], or how collocated groups employ embodied resources to manage mobile notifications [16]. Whilst the focus of *this* paper is on practical design matters, we suggest this kind of collocated interaction analysis [26] is useful in future evaluations of experiences designed with our framework.

In order to ground our framework in design examples, we first review experiences from the literature. Although many examples involve off-the-shelf hardware like phones and tablets, we designed our framework to be agnostic to hardware details. Further, while mobile devices are often used in these experiences, *bodily mobility* is not always a necessary feature [cf. 38]; and vice versa, whilst the experience may entail physically moving through space, the technology may be stationary. Moreover, our framework is not bound to certain kinds of modalities, e.g. different forms of input and output such as 'natural' interaction techniques. In our framework these are options for design, rather than requirements. Instead our framework attempts to emphasise relevant design properties that are specific to and characteristic of collocation.

Mobile collocated experiences

Our framework was developed from a wide range of examples of experiences designed for settings that feature collocated interaction. Due to the broad range of domains we intend to cover with our framework, we limit the review to illustrate the breadth of this work. When constructing our framework we used four distinct domains: cultural visiting experiences, leisure-related systems, pervasive and urban games, and mobile apps.

Cultural visiting experiences aim at enhancing shared visitor experiences, for example through audioguides for galleries [21], sculpture parks [20], or city tour guides [10].

Leisure-related work often has a playful and collaborative component related to *photographs, sharing and co-creation*: Automics [14] is an experience in which groups create photo-memories together; InstaCampus [16] instead features groups collaborating in photographing a campus; MobiPhos [36] is a photo-sharing application where users need to be collocated to share and explore each other's photo collection; MobiComics [37] instead revolves around co-creating photo comics on phones and public displays.

Pervasive and urban games often have elements of collocated interaction and collaboration. Research around these experiences often reports on issues relevant to the CSCW community, such as 'live' orchestration from a control room [13], collaboration between people on the ground and online [18], and giving and following instructions in teams [50,44]. Some of these experiences may also have an educational character [51], or they may be classified as a 'serious' game, for example to study team coordination in a disaster response scenario [17].

Mobile apps are now a routine part of mobile device use. Apps we particularly drew on for our framework's development were games, simply because there are several digital versions of board games that require gamers to be collocated, either as game interaction is not technologically mediated or requires a central shared device such as a board (e.g. Scrabble for phones and a tablet). There are also a few games where the core gameplay is collocated collaboration; one example is SpaceTeam, in which players instruct each other what to do on their respective phones. However there are also some work-related collaborative apps within our chosen design space, e.g. iBrainstorm, which will be described further below.

While the framework was constructed in view of the broad literature we reviewed, we describe three very different design examples from different domains in more detail. We will later refer to them when describing and grounding the various design properties in the following sections.

Rufford audioguide is an interactive audio-based mobile visiting app by Fosh et al. [20]. It has been designed specifically for couples visiting a particular sculpture garden, with carefully selected content for each sculpture. Exploring together, the visitors can choose their own path through the garden, triggering a sequence of sculpture-specific audio, audio instructions (e.g. inviting the visitors to observe the sculpture from a particular angle), and interpretive information provided after these. The design drives visitors to have both isolated (via headphones) moments, as well as and shared moments of talk around the sculptures.

Atomic Orchid [17] is a location-based mobile disaster response game, i.e. a 'serious game'. Participants either play the role of first responders on the ground, or in an HQ. First responders are assigned a specific role: medic, soldier, transporter or fire-fighter, all which have different abilities. Their task is to rescue distributed virtual targets (representing human casualties and resources) by 'carrying' them to a drop off zone, something that often requires cooperation between roles—all whilst staying alive, and before the area is covered by a radioactive cloud. Responders are equipped with a 'Geiger counter'-app, messaging, and a real-time map to locate targets and teammates. HQ players instead have a dashboard showing field responders' location, health levels, targets, and the cloud, and run the operation.

iBrainstorm[1] is a commercially available productivity app that supports creativity work in groups. It features a Bluetooth connection between an iPad and up to four iPhones. The phone app provides the ability to write virtual Post-Its and send them to the tablet with a 'flick' gesture. The tablet app allows for adding, colouring, editing and arranging the Post-Its as well as scribbling on the background. Sessions can be saved and shared.

Design frameworks

While our framework's main focus is on supporting design of experiences for face-to-face group interactions that occur in a range of settings, there exist a number of relevant interaction design frameworks beyond CSCW. Firstly, some frameworks are intended to capture the qualities that may be used to describe the *subjective user experience*, e.g. Löwgren's and Stolterman's [35] use qualities, or Wright et al's. [53] four types of experiences (sensual, emotional, and spatio-temporal). In contrast, other frameworks focus on the *building blocks of interactive experiences*, such as attributes of designing for location in pervasive games[2] or the design languages for interaction gestalts of Lim et al. [33,34]. Drawing on the above, Lundgren [40] created a framework of interaction-related properties describing categories of interaction, expression, behaviour, complexity, change and time, and users. Most specifically relevant to our work, Schuster et al. have developed a taxonomy related to collocated interaction that frames a pervasive social context [46], using the four dimensions Space, Time, People, and Information. However, Schuster et al. suggest limiting the taxonomy to categorise artefacts. Although our framework is similar in some respects, it is useful not only for analysis and categorisation, but particularly, we argue, for design.

A further influence has been Benford et al.'s trajectories framework, which captures the spatio-temporal journey through the user experience that extends over space and time, traversing multiple roles and interfaces [6]. It represents a similar kind of framework to ours, in that it is not just about the building blocks of interactive experiences, but also how they may be used to create specific user experiences.

[1] http://www.ibrainstormapp.com

[2] http://designforlocation.org

FRAMEWORK OVERVIEW

The process of the framework's construction is explored in more depth in a later section, but in brief it was constructed using a combination of two sources: firstly, a literature review; secondly, practical experience applying the framework with design students.

In short, the framework consists of four different perspectives, which are complemented with relevant design properties which in turn can have different states. It has two complementary *representational forms*; the diagrammatic form (Figures 1 and 2) and the list form (Table 1). Before we unpack the framework in full, we here provide a brief overview to prime the reader and to inform subsequent discussion.

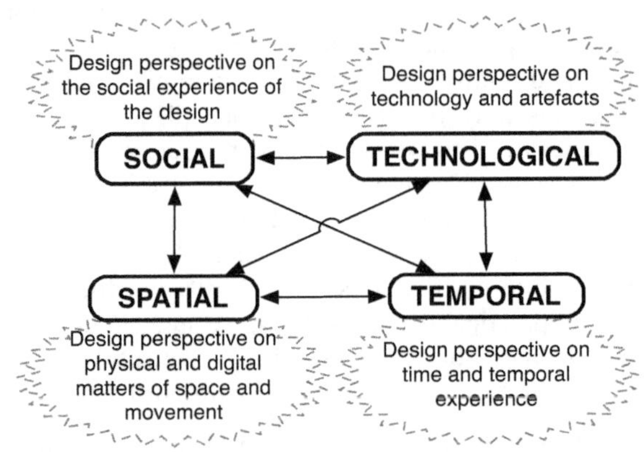

Figure 1: Framework overview (diagrammatic form)

Four perspectives

The framework's four broad overarching *design perspectives* help the designer to systematically address the design of collocated interactive systems: Social, Technological, Spatial and Temporal.

The *Social Perspective* describes design properties related to the social features of collocated situations, e.g. the design of the face-to-face setting, the actors and their relationships within that setting.

The *Technological Perspective* describes design properties related to software and how it utilises existing hardware. It encompasses information flow, interaction abilities and actions that trigger progress.

The *Spatial Perspective* describes design properties related to all aspects of space, location and the physical environment.

The *Temporal Perspective* describes design properties related to the temporal experience of system users, involving the synchronisation and pacing of user activity.

Properties and states

Each of the four *perspectives* has associated *properties* that we have found to be the most relevant. In turn, properties also have various associated (suggested) *states*. We have found through our process that states can be used for pinpointing differences between designs. For example, while all designs have the FOCUS-property, their respective state (e.g. collaborative vs. competitive) instantiates these as distinct experiences. In addition, states support the use of the framework as a design tool, as will be shown in a later section (Using the Framework).

For clarity the properties and their states formatted in the following way: 'PROPERTY [*state* | *state* | ...]'. They are listed in order of importance.

Relations

A key feature of understanding this framework is that it is *relational*. Firstly, the perspectives both shape and are shaped by the other perspectives in the framework (see Figure 2). Hence, a methodical approach to using the framework takes each perspective in turn and uses it as a particular 'standpoint' from which to examine impacts on other design elements. Secondly, many properties are closely intertwined or dependent on each other, e.g. giving users different possibilities to interact with the system (*asymmetric* INTERACTION ABILITIES) supports the state *combining actions* in the property COORDINATION OF ACTIONS.

We detail example implications of the relational approach in subsequent sections describing the framework in detail.

THE FRAMEWORK

In the rest of this section we now describe each perspective and their associated properties, providing examples of how they interrelate. We also ground descriptions of the properties and states through reference to the example experiences introduced earlier in this paper: Atomic Orchid, iBrainstorm and the Rufford audioguide.

The Social Perspective

The Social Perspective is the most complex and the least directly controllable by design. It describes the social 'design' of the experience. It encompasses considerations regarding the intricacies of the social situation that arise during the interactive experience: for instance users may take on different roles (e.g. as user or spectator, leader or sub-ordinate, adult and child). Moreover, users already have some sort of relationship to each other, which may be unknown to the designer, and they may either have or lack specific capabilities (e.g. driving skills or good eyesight). This perspective has three properties: FOCUS, COORDINATION OF ACTIONS and FRAMING.

FOCUS [*collaboration* | *communication* | *competition* | *combined*]. This design property sets the major interaction goal for the whole design, shaping the overall social focus of the activities engaged in by users. It describes the focus of users' social actions, for example as collaborative, communicative and / or competitive.

For example, iBrainstorm's design creates a strong focus on *communication* of ideas between users and ways to support *collaboration* around these. For Atomic Orchid the focus is also on *collaboration*, and *communication* is a requirement to accomplish the task. As for many other experiences, there may be a combination of states, so a competitive team-based game would incorporate all three, i.e. *collaboration* and *communication* within teams, and *competition* between teams. However, one of these must always be the main focus of design, steering the others.

COORDINATION OF ACTION *[timing actions* | *combining actions* | *combined]*. This property is concerned with how users perform actions together, thus shaping the interplay of interactions between users. They can either aim to carry out actions simultaneously, or combine their efforts (e.g. by complementing each other's skills), or both.

Atomic Orchid combines both in that rescue of targets requires teams of responders with complementary roles to be at the same place at the same time, e.g. *timing actions* and *combining actions*. In contrast, iBrainstorm only expects users to *combine actions*, i.e. write Post-Its, move and sort Post-Its, scribble notes etc.

FRAMING [*public* | *private* | *combined*]. This is the main social 'situation' where the activities are carried out and it thus affects design decisions related to how that situation is defined; one can demand very different things from users depending on whether they are in public or in private.

Atomic Orchid, like many pervasive games, to a great extent takes place in *public* and participants must conduct their activities in light of all that being in public implies (e.g. acting professionally, taking into account those who are not part of the simulation, etc.).

Relations

These various properties associated with the Social Perspective can implicate and be implicated by each of the other perspectives. Here we outline some of these for illustrative purposes.

- FOCUS is closely tied to the Technological Perspective since design decision regarding INFORMATION SYMMETRY, INFORMATION DISTRIBUTION and INTERACTION ABILITIES help regulate it.
- COORDINATION OF ACTION between users or between users and the system is perhaps most frequently related to properties from the other perspectives. It is tied to the

Spatial Perspective since it affects or is affected by properties like PROXIMITY and LOCATION(S). Its state *Timing actions* is clearly linked to SYNCHRONISATION (Temporal Perspective). Lastly, several properties within the Technological Perspective shape how, or when actions can be carried out, e.g., EVENT TRIGGERS and INTERACTION ABILITIES. Atomic Orchid exemplifies this very well.

- FRAMING is tied to the Spatial Perspective since it affects LOCATION(S) and MOVEMENT. These are more likely to affect the design when FRAMING is public.

The Technological Perspective

In contrast to the Social Perspective, the Technological Perspective is perhaps the most controllable by design. Underlying concerns within this perspective relate to choosing the hardware based on capabilities and limitations. For example, this includes the combination of devices (e.g. whether users should have tablets or phones) and their connectivity. Broadly speaking, the ratio of devices per user may also matter; if users share a device, they are bound to get the same information, for instance, and they are more likely to stay together. Lastly, the information within the system must be considered—e.g. is it system-generated (e.g. tracking positions), or user-generated?

This perspective has four properties: INFORMATION SYMMETRY, INTERACTION ABILITIES, INFORMATION DISTRIBUTION, and EVENT TRIGGERS.

INFORMATION SYMMETRY [***symmetrical*** | ***asymmetrical***]. This property is powerful in shaping user communication and behaviour, and is linked to INFORMATION DISTRIBUTION. It regulates whether all users have access to *the same type* of information or not. For instance, each user might know their own position on a map, i.e. it is *symmetrical* across users. In case information is *asymmetrical*, different users have access to different kinds of information. For example, one participant might have access to information on locations to go to, while another might have information on which locations are interesting.

INFORMATION SYMMETRY has previously been identified as an important feature of team working (e.g. [48]) and has been used to create simulations of fire emergency responder training practices [51]. Differential access to resources for awareness activities in CSCW (e.g., [25]) is also relevant for this property.

Atomic Orchid features *asymmetrical* information in that the headquarters has an 'omniscient' point of view including 'seeing' the radioactive cloud, whereas the field responders only have a Geiger counter reading for their current location. iBrainstorm on the other hand is *symmetrical*, in that all users can see both the contents on the shared tablet and on their own phone (e.g., the Post-Its currently being written).

INTERACTION ABILITIES [***symmetrical*** | ***asymmetrical***]. This property shapes how users can act and interact within the experience, taking into account any special abilities the system can provide to different types of users. It can appear in many different ways, e.g. in rights to add / edit / delete content, rights to manage other users, rights to perform certain actions, and so on.

Atomic Orchid features asymmetry in many ways, e.g. field responders have *asymmetrical* different abilities in relation to each other (being medics, fire fighters etc.), but in addition field responders as a group have very *asymmetrical* INTERACTION ABILITIES in relation to HQ: the former can actually rescue targets whereas the latter can only assess and inform. iBrainstorm can be seen as *symmetrical* since all participants have a phone, from which they may add Post-Its, and share access to the tablet.

INFORMATION DISTRIBUTION [***free*** | ***unfolding*** | ***limited*** | ***shared*** | ***combined***]. How to distribute information to users and spectators strongly affects how users act and interact. This issue of how information is physically and virtually distributed has long been a concern in CSCW (e.g. in the situated physical representations of distributed cognition [28]). For this property, *free* implies that all information is accessible for anyone anytime. *Unfolding* implies that more information is becoming available over time, either as a result of actions, or just time passing. *Limited* implies that there is some information that a certain user will never get (e.g. certain information about other users). Lastly one may, or may not, allow users to *share* information via the system.

As an example, information is *free* in the Rufford audioguide; all the content is available at the touch of a button. In iBrainstorm, users share information and ideas as they ideate along, i.e. it combines *unfolding* and *shared* information. In Atomic Orchid, field responders have *limited* information but they also get *shared* information communicated by the HQ.

EVENT TRIGGERS [***information-based*** | ***time-based*** | ***proximity-based*** | ***combined***]. This property describes what users or the system need to do in order to trigger an event that changes or causes progress in the system in some way. Triggers may be arriving at the right location or person (*proximity-based*), entering content in the system (*information-based*), or the passing of a deadline (*time-based*). The resulting events may be notifications, points, state changes, or another form of system output. *Proximity-based* EVENT TRIGGERS are often employed to support collocation (e.g. [9, 43]) but are not as central as other properties in this perspective.

When the tablet and phones of iBrainstorm 'detect' each other, it is a *proximity-based* EVENT TRIGGER that causes the application to start running. This in turn enables *information-based* TRIGGERS uploading written Post-Its. The Rufford audioguide also features *proximity-based* EVENT TRIGGERS for sculptures: when close enough users may evoke the relevant information for the particular sculpture they are at (i.e. the event). In contrast, the expansion of the radioactive cloud in Atomic Orchid is a *time-based* TRIGGER, putting field respondents in danger and thus regulating their movement.

Relations

The Technological Perspective has many relations to other perspectives; overall, it is perhaps the most controllable by design.

- INFORMATION SYMMETRY and INTERACTION ABILITIES are closely tied to COORDINATION OF ACTION in the Social Perspective, since users may have different means to carry out certain actions; similarly they are tied to SYNCHRONISATION in the Temporal Perspective.
- INFORMATION DISTRIBUTION is related to FOCUS from the Social Perspective, since the means of distributing information help shape whether and how users *communicate* (*shared*) or *collaborate* (*shared, unfolding*); similarly asymmetrical INFORMATION SYMMETRY opens up for more communication.
- EVENT TRIGGERS are closely related to Spatial and Temporal Perspectives. Do users need to be within PROXIMITY with each other, be at a certain LOCATIONS, carry out an action with SYNCHRONISATION? Equally, in what ways do EVENT TRIGGERS impact the COORDINATION OF ACTION among social actors?

The Spatial Perspective

The Spatial Perspective involves the consideration of the physical and virtual space(s) in which the experience takes place. In this, it encompasses any aspect from designing for 'anyplace anywhere', a specific area anywhere or a specified location (e.g. a certain museum). It has three properties: PROXIMITY, LOCATION(S) and MOVEMENT.

PROXIMITY ***[people | devices | objects | locations | combined]*****.** This property regulates which things need to be close in order for an activity, or event to play out. PROXIMITY may involve *people, devices, objects* (e.g., a statue), or *locations* in any combinations (e.g. *people* with *people*, *devices* with *locations*, *objects* with *locations* etc.) Although devices are almost always equal to people this must not be taken for granted.

For example, iBrainstorm relies on PROXIMITY between *devices* (phones and tablet are connected via Bluetooth), which implies proximity between *people*, and between *people and devices*. Atomic Orchid features virtual objects (placed on LOCATIONS defined by GPS-coordinates) that are to be rescued by players, requiring proximity between *people and locations*.

LOCATION(S) ***[one or more | none]*****.** This property is important when designing for a larger space. It defines whether there are any specific locations or places within the spatial boundaries that matter for the experience. For example, these could be different exhibits in a museum, or the place where the treasure is hidden in a game.

For the Rufford audioguide the sculptures serve as locations. In Atomic Orchid, locations that matter are

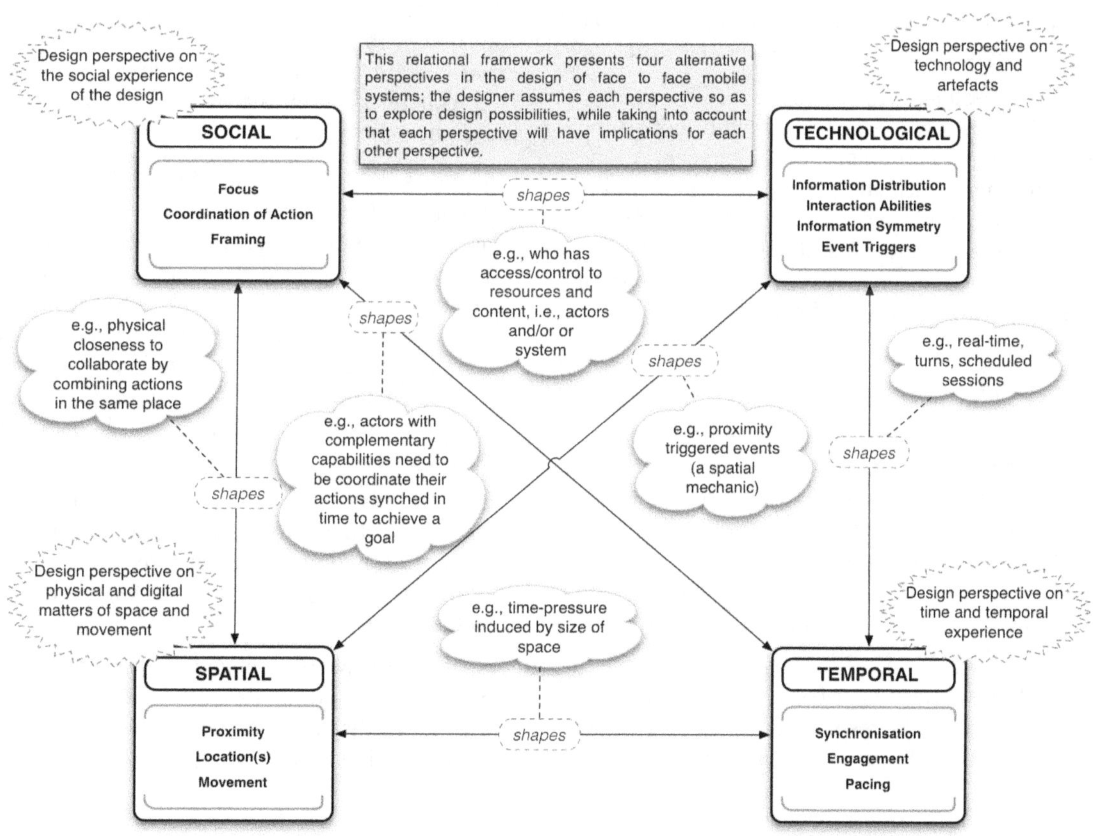

Figure 2. Framework for designing mobile experiences for collocated interaction (diagrammatic representation).

defined by the geo-locations of virtual objects and drop-off zones. iBrainstorm in contrast has *none*.

MOVEMENT [*on the go* | *sedentary* | *combined*]. This property describes design decisions about user movement through the space as part of the experience. Is movement through space an inherent feature of the experience (e.g. visiting support for museums or cities)? And which kind of movement is desired (e.g. running, walking, cycling, or driving)?

iBrainstorm is designed to be used whilst *sedentary* (e.g., sitting). Atomic Orchid combines *sedentary* players in the HQ with field responders being *on the go* in their efforts to carry virtual objects to drop-off zones).

Relations
This is the one perspective with most interrelated dependencies: MOVEMENT and LOCATION(S) are closely tied, and so are PROXIMITY and LOCATION(S). They also have links to other perspectives.

- PROXIMITY is very closely linked to EVENT TRIGGERS (Technological Perspective) which are *proximity-based*. It can also be related to the Social and Temporal perspectives respectively since it may be required for either COORDINATING ACTIONS or SYNCHRONISATION.
- LOCATIONS are related to the Social Perspective in that they are affected by or affecting the FRAMING of a situation.
- MOVEMENT in space relates to the Temporal Perspective particularly for ENGAGEMENT and PACING. For example, a movement design that switches from *sedentary* activities to running creates strong contrasts in PACING.

The Temporal Perspective
The Temporal Perspective is concerned with how time plays a role both as a particular design concept to be employed explicitly by the designer, as well as an inevitable feature of experience. Thus it encompasses the course and possible order of actions and events, the pace and possibly rhythm of the experience. It integrates some concepts from the trajectories framework by Benford et al. [4].

Properties of this perspective are SYNCHRONISATION, ENGAGEMENT and PACING.

SYNCHRONISATION [*user-driven* | *system-driven* | *combined*]. This property describes the synchronisation of actions within a temporal frame—if any—and as such is most central for collocation-oriented designs. Possibilities for this property revolve around whether users control this themselves, or if the system enforces synchronisation in some way (including perhaps prompting or rewarding *timing actions* as a means of COORDINATION OF ACTION).

In Atomic Orchid, SYNCHRONISATION is *system-driven* in that the system requires field responders to be physically close to each other and an object at the same time in order to rescue it. Examples of *user-driven* SYNCHRONISATION would be users agreeing to meet somewhere to carry out an action together, as in the Rufford audioguide.

ENGAGEMENT [*continuous* | *intermittent* | *sporadic*]. This refers to users' broad temporal patterns of action within the experience, such as how intensely and how often they will engage with it and each other. This is highly dependent on the length of a session. Designers of a long-term pervasive game will for example more or less inherently assume and design for an *intermittent* or *sporadic* engagement [15].

For example, iBrainstorm allows intermitting ENGAGEMENT, however one can assume *continuous* ENGAGEMENT during a focused collocated brainstorming session. Atomic Orchid, on the other hand, requires *continuous* ENGAGEMENT during its relatively short sessions (~30mins).

PACING [*high-paced* | *slow* | *user-paced* | *combined*]. Pacing describes the way in which actions are distributed over time: is it stressful, relaxing or just right, and how does this affect social interaction between users?

Atomic Orchid is *high-paced* as it provides many actions (many targets to rescue, spread out on a relatively large area) in combination with the time-pressure provided by the spreading radioactive cloud (a *time-based* EVENT TRIGGER), resulting in an intense experience with much communication between users. For the Rufford audioguide the PACING is instead *user-paced*.

Relations
While elements of the Temporal Perspective are controllable by design, those more closely related to the *experience* of time are arguably less so. Nevertheless there is a general relationship to other perspectives, here we highlight some of these.

- There is a relation to the Social Perspective in that the manner of COORDINATION OF ACTION between collocated users will shape and be shaped by the minutiae of ENGAGEMENT, SYNCHRONISATION and PACING. For instance *timing actions* is tied to SYNCHRONISATION; and if that is user-driven it requires or creates ENGAGEMENT. Similarly, if there are many actions to be carried out this may lead to either a *high-paced* PACING, or a lot of communication between users in choosing which actions to carry out.
- Additionally, ENGAGEMENT, SYNCHRONISATION and PACING will be affected by some design decisions made in the Technological Perspective, e.g. choice of *time-based* EVENT TRIGGERS, or *unfolding* INFORMATION DISTRIBUTION.
- Spatial Perspective-related design decisions regarding MOVEMENT and LOCATION(S) affect temporal aspects, e.g. large distances between locations that participants have to visit will affect both ENGAGEMENT and PACING.

	PROPERTY	STATES	DESCRIPTION
SOCIAL	FOCUS	*collaboration | communication | competition | combined*	What it is that users do together, i.e., what is the focus of their social actions intended to be.
	COORDINATION OF ACTION	*timing actions | combining actions | combined*	Whether, and if so, how actors perform coordinate actions together.
	FRAMING	*public | private | combined*	The main social situation in which the activities are carried out.
TECHNOLOGICAL	INFORMATION SYMMETRY	*symmetrical | asymmetrical*	Whether all users have access to *the same* information or not.
	INTERACTION ABILITIES	*symmetrical | asymmetrical*	Whether different users have different abilities/possibilities to interact with or in the system.
	INFORMATION DISTRIBUTION	*free | unfolding | limited | shared | combined*	The ways in which information is being distributed to users and spectators.
	EVENT TRIGGERS	*information-based | time-based | proximity-based | combined*	What users or the system need to do in order to trigger an event that may change or cause progress in the system.
SPATIAL	PROXIMITY	*people | devices | objects | locations | combined*	The ways in which proximity is used as a mechanic, including the entities and relations for which proximity matters.
	LOCATION(S)	*One or more | none*	One or more specific location(s) or place(s) that matter for the experience.
	MOVEMENT	*on the go | sedentary | combined*	Whether users move through space as part of the experience.
TEMPORA	SYNCHRONISATION	*user-driven | system-driven | combined*	The ways in which actions within a temporal frame are synchronised.
	ENGAGEMENT	*continuous | intermittent | sporadic*	Users' temporal patterns of action within the experience.
	PACING	*high-paced | slow | user-paced | combined*	How the intensity of action is distributed across the experience, e.g. number of actions per time-frame.

Table 1. Framework for designing mobile experiences for collocated interaction (list form).

USING THE FRAMEWORK

The framework we have presented offers a way of codifying knowledge about the design of mobile systems supporting collocated interaction. It has been argued [7,45] that such frameworks offer a variety of applications in practice, providing sensitising concepts, shared design languages, or performing as 'boundary objects', in the sense of providing loose, flexible artefacts that can withstand multiple interpretations and conflicting perspectives [47] between interdisciplinary co-creators. In this section we offer practical advice on how it may be used, and broader implications on how it may be 'read'.

Using the framework: for redesign

Building on photo-sharing as a familiar collaborative activity, we now show how key collocated design aspects of a photo-sharing system we created—Automics [14]—were changed to create InstaCampus [16]. Automics is a system that allow visitors of a theme park to co-create photo story souvenirs of their day out together [14]. Each visitor has a mobile phone; they take photos that they annotate with speech bubbles, and select for photo story templates. All photos are automatically shared across the group, i.e. INFORMATION SYMMETRY is *symmetrical*. PROXIMITY to key *locations* across the theme park serve as *proximity-based* EVENT TRIGGERS, prompting notifications to invite photo taking and annotating (i.e. events). Newly available photos also serve as *information-based* EVENT TRIGGERS in that a notification is sent to each group member.

After a trial, group members remarked that they did not need notification of other member's actions that they could see themselves (being collocated), and moreover our observations showed that group members were simultaneously engrossed in using the mobile app, instead of interleaving device use with face-to-face interaction; they were 'alone together'.

Consequently, we changed the mechanics relating to collocation to investigate the issues we observed further, resulting in the InstaCampus app. Based on the same code base as Automics, InstaCampus was trialed to support a collaborative photo-taking exercise undertaken between multiple groups of participants. Their task was to collectively create a campus guide for new students and staff. Photos for the guide were mainly created by participants as they explored the campus, but this was supplemented by georeferenced images that were 'seeded' by us as designers before the trial. While similar to Automics, InstaCampus offered key differences in that photo-sharing between one group and another became selective and not broadcast to all group members.

In the terms of the framework, InstaCampus' INFORMATION SYMMETRY was made *asymmetrical* in that one collocated team member received photo notifications (i.e. *asymmetrical* INFORMATION SYMMETRY) as the result of PROXIMITY to locations (i.e. *proximity-based* EVENT TRIGGERS): these indicated that they had 'found' images taken nearby (i.e. the georeferenced, seeded photos). In contrast with Automics' *symmetric* distribution of notifications of newly taken photos, for InstaCampus, only a single local group member gets *information-based* EVENT-TRIGGERS (notifications) when the remote group has taken new photos. Moreover, the 'seeded' photos could only be added to the shared pool by one member of a given group, hereby introducing *asymmetrical* INTERACTION ABILITIES.

Note how PROXIMITY was not only used to trigger notifications in terms of *proximity to locations* but also in terms of *proximity between people,* so as to limit alerts of action to that of remote group members that could not have been observed.

As a result of the added asymmetry introduced to InstaCampus, the content of notifications were frequently brought up in conversations and shared between collocated group members [16]. While designers may have different goals for their collocated experiences, we felt that the frequent observations of how members made device use part of the face-to-face interaction was a compelling case of a successful design for collocated interaction.

In the terms of the framework, the design evolution from Automics to InstaCampus further demonstrates how certain properties can be harnessed to support collocated interaction. In this case, INTERACTION ABILITIES, INFORMATION SYMMETRY, and PROXIMITY have been instantiated to specifically support collocated interaction. The use of concepts akin to our INFORMATION SYMMETRY in related work focusing on face-to-face collaboration [48,51,25] further stresses their essential character.

Using the framework: for ideation

Speaking more generally, a framework such as this (featuring properties and states) can also be used to ideate initial designs: we have tried this with students on several occasions. This activity is more open than the redesign example above, thus we recommend as a guideline that designers decide on 4-6 properties and a state for each, and take it from there. The properties can be chosen at random or one can ensure that there is at least one from each perspective. For redesign we suggest using the 'skewing method' [41]: an artefact is analysed in terms of properties and states, and some of the states are then changed, hence asking *"What if...?"* in a structured way. For instance a group of students were given the following combinations: *user driven* SYNCHRONISATION, PROXIMITY between *people*, *high-paced* PACING and *unfolding* and *shared* INFORMATION DISTRIBUTION. Students designed a simple game where pairs of players get the same image on their phone; they then need to find each a match as fast as possible and register each other's names. The last pair to find each other in each round is eliminated from the game.

Guidelines for reading the framework

Understanding how to *read* the framework is important. We also argue that these guidelines may have relevance for reading frameworks in general.

Control versus outcomes. Some properties of the framework are inherently more controllable, while others are less so. For example, (Spatial) PROXIMITY between people may be very controllable through technological means, such as enforcing a group of users to meet up at a specific LOCATION in order to proceed with their COORDINATION OF ACTION, whereas specifying how system use is (Socially) FRAMED can be extremely difficult to pull off successfully. On the other hand, we may pursue a policy, as designers, of deliberately ceding control because we desire a wide variability of outcomes.

The situation. This is about what actually happens when the design is put to work. All designs must face 'the world as it is discovered'. Technology, people, physical places, infrastructures and social practices are all things that will necessarily be encountered in the course of some design being used, yet preceded the design. Outcomes thus depend on a mixture of what is 'discovered' through the engagement with the design, and the ability of the designer to successfully construct controls for the particular situation they have intervened in. For instance, if we are designing a mobile app a museum, it will be used in what is a primarily public space, there will be restrictions on what is 'reasonable' conduct in that space, and there will likely be some sort of set of pre-existing roles assumed like an 'audience' in the form of other visitors, staff, guards, etc.

DISCUSSION

We close with reflections on the participatory process we engaged in to help generate the framework itself, and the ways in which the framework may help define the genre of experiences for collocated interaction.

Developing the framework

Often when frameworks are presented, little is said about the process of creating frameworks. We provide a reflection on this process so as to inform others wishing to use this particular framework and / or to develop other frameworks. In constructing the framework we have made various assumptions and glosses in order to arrive at a practically usable tool for designers. This section also exposes these matters of limitation and compromise to the reader.

Inception

The genesis of the framework was a workshop conducted at ECSCW '13 that explored various instances of mobile systems that were deliberately designed to support collocated interactions in some way. Some basic properties of the framework list form emerged during this meeting. Thus the idea of a synthesis was born.

Initial framework construction and evaluation

Now a team of co-authors had been formed. We conducted a more formal review of the mobile collocated experiences highlighted at the workshop, enriched by further examples from research and commercial products. From this we derived a list representation of the framework containing many of the properties outlined in this paper. The next phase consisted of attempting more participatory practical classroom-based engagement with students training on an Interaction Design programme at the University of Gothenburg. The activity was part of the concept generation phase in the 'Mobile Computing' course and thus fit very well with the students' work as they were at the stage of developing ideas for their projects. The initial framework list form (an expanded version of Table 1) was presented as a one hour lecture to the students who subsequently had a further two hours to use the framework in a mobile app design activity.

Refining the framework

Our interaction with the students formed an initial evaluation to iterate the framework. At the same time we began seeking out a diagrammatic way to present the framework, which in turn exposed its relational aspects, thus offering refinements that were emergent due to the combinations of other properties.

Further, from the student exercise we uncovered a number of reflections that fed into our iterative process. Firstly, we noted that frameworks have 'fingerprints' of their sources. By this we mean that our initial literature review that fed the framework tended to subtly colour the focus of the designs that the students ideated from it. We rectified this by analysing broader examples and improving the framework accordingly. Secondly, the framework design itself necessarily has to exclude a range of design possibilities. This was reflected in student feedback that certain properties were 'missing'.

Thirdly, we noted that frameworks are worked with as 'prescriptions'. Students found that the framework could be used for any kind mobile system, not just design for collocated interactions. At the same time they attempted to 'stay true' to the framework's perceived intentions for the genre of designs that it was seen to prescribe. This became evident in the students' designs. In addition, reviewer feedback provided on the initial version of this paper encouraged us to cut down the number of properties, focusing them on aspects that we felt are 'critical' to the genre of collocated interaction design.

The genre of experiences for collocated interaction

As a final part of this discussion we would like to offer our rationale for how the properties define the 'genre' of experiences for mobile collocated interaction. We had a long list of properties initially, but we distilled it to its essence by asking: *is this property characteristic for the design of mobile experiences which support collocated interaction?* We excluded properties that were too general, the results of other design decisions, or described phenomena related to 'the world as it is discovered' and thus out of the designers' control.

Returning to the properties of our framework, there are strong arguments for all of them. FOCUS, COORDINATION OF ACTION, INTERACTION ABILITIES, EVENT TRIGGERS, PROXIMITY, and SYNCHRONISATION are all closely tied to making users meeting up and joining efforts, this covering the collocation-aspect. INFORMATION SYMMETRY and INFORMATION DISTRIBUTION and to some extent ENGAGEMENT support this further by regulating communication (and *need* for communication) between users. FRAMING, LOCATION(S) and MOVEMENT adhere to the mobile / mobility aspect, and although it is possible to provide INTERACTION ABILITIES, INFORMATION SYMMETRY, INFORMATION DISTRIBUTION, EVENT TRIGGERS and PACING with analogue techniques, using digital interactive systems enables a larger design space. Thus, the chosen properties help outline the design space for this particular genre: systems or experiences that aim to support or even enforce social, collocated activities as supported by mobile technology.

CONCLUSION

We have presented a framework for the design and analysis of mobile systems that support, enable or augment social, collocated interactive experiences, supported by mobile technology. The framework presents four interrelated design perspectives that shape and are shaped by each other. We have offered both a diagrammatic and a textual list form of the framework to support this process, specifically for: 1. focussed hands-on design *ideation* activities; 2. and *analytic* dissection of existing designs into their elements and relationships.

In order to show how the framework can be used, we have discussed a case-specific redesign process in detail. We also provided guidelines on *how to read* the framework, which had implications for reading other frameworks as well. We particularly drew attention to the tensions inherent in any design framework where the designer's desire for control over its aspects (and the variation of this control-ability) rub up against the fact that the design must exist in the world and in some sense be shaped by the world 'as we find it'.

Finally, our work offered an account of the (limited) ways we attempted *operationalisation* and *practical application* during the framework's construction through simple design activities with students, and periods of repeated refinement. We have tried to show how the process of *constructing design frameworks itself* can be an iterative, participatory process that involves evaluation, reflection and redesign. As such we see potential for researchers developing future CSCW-related design frameworks to adopt this approach.

ACKNOWLEDGMENTS

Thanks to the students taking 'Mobile Computing' in 2013 at the Chalmers University of Technology; their feedback helped us to develop the framework. This work is supported by EPSRC grants EP/I011587/1 and EP/K025848/1.

REFERENCES

1. Aoki, P.M., R.E. Grinter, A. Hurst, M.H. Szymanski, J.D. Thornton, and A. Woodruff. Sotto voce: exploring the interplay of conversation and mobile audio spaces. *Proc. CHI '02*, ACM Press (2002), 431-438.
2. Bao, X. and Choudhury, R. R. 2010. MoVi: mobile phone based video highlights via collaborative sensing. In *Proc. MobiSys '10*. ACM, New York, NY, USA, 357-370.
3. Bedwell, B. *A Framework to Guide the Design of Environments Coupling Mobile and Situated Technologies*. PhD Thesis, University of Nottingham, UK, 2010.
4. Benford, S., D. Rowland, M. Flintham, A. Drozd, R. Hull, J. Reid, J. Morrison, and K. Facer Life on the edge: supporting collaboration in location-based experiences. *Proc. CHI* '05, ACM Press (2005), 721–730.
5. Benford, S., Crabtree, A., Reeves, S., Sheridan, J., Dix, A., Flintham, M., Drozd, A. The frame of the game: blurring the boundary between fiction and reality in mobile experiences. *Proc. CHI '06,* ACM Press (2006), 427-436.
6. Benford, S., Giannachi, G., Koleva, B., Rodden, T. From interaction to trajectories: designing coherent journeys through user experiences'. *Proc. CHI '09,* ACM Press (2009), 709–718.
7. Benford, S. & Giannachi, G. *Performing Mixed Reality*. MIT Press, September 2011.
8. Bentley, R.M., Hughes, J.A., Randall, D., Rodden, T., Sawyer, P., Shapiro, D. and Sommerville, I. Ethnographically informed systems design for air traffic control, *Proc. CSCW '92,* ACM Press (1992), 123–129.
9. Bjork, S., Falk, J., Hansson, R., and Ljungstrand, P. Pirates! using thc physical world as a gamc board. In *Proc. of INTERACT '01*, IFIP, pp. 423–430, 2001.
10. Brown, B., and Chalmers M. Tourism and mobile technology. *Proc. ECSCW '03,* Klewer Academic Press (2003), 335-355.
11. Brown, B., M. Chalmers, M. Bell, M. Hall, I. MacColl, and P. Rudman Sharing the square: collaborative leisure in the city streets. *Proc. ECSCW '05,* Springer (2005), 427–447.
12. Brown, B., McGregor, M., Laurier, E. iPhone in vivo: video analysis of mobile device use. *Proc. CHI '13,* ACM Press (2013), 1031-1040.
13. Crabtree, A., S. Benford, Rodden, T., Greenhalgh, C., Flintham, M., Anastasi, R., Drozd, A., Row-Farr, J., Tandavanitj, N. and Steed, A. Orchestrating a mixed reality game 'on the ground'. *Proc. CHI '04*. ACM Press (2004), 391-398.
14. Durrant, A., Rowland, D., Kirk, D.S., Benford, S., Fischer, J.E, and McAuley, D. Automics: Souvenir generating photoware for theme parks. *Proc. CHI '11,* ACM Press (2011), 1767–1776.
15. Fischer, J.E., Benford, S. Inferring player engagement in a pervasive experience. *Proc. CHI '09.* ACM Press (2009), 1903-1906.
16. Fischer, J.E., Reeves, S., Moran, S., Greenhalgh, C., Benford, S. and Rennick-Egglestone, S. Understanding mobile notification management in collocated groups. *Proc. ECSCW'13*. Springer (2013), 21-44.
17. Fischer, J.E., Jiang, W., Kerne, A., Greenhalgh, C., Ramchurn, S.D., Reece, S., Pantidi, N. and Rodden, T. Supporting team coordination on the ground: requirements from a mixed reality game. *Proc. COOP '14*, Springer (2014), 46-67.
18. Flintham, M., Benford, S., Anastasi, R., Hemmings, T., Crabtree, A., Greenhalgh, C., Tandavanitj, N., Adams, M., and Row-Farr, J. Where on-line meets on the streets: experiences with mobile mixed reality games. *Proc. CHI '03,* ACM Press (2003), 569-576.
19. Flintham, M., Reeves, S., P. Brundell, Glover, A.T., Benford, S., Rowland, D., Koleva, B., Greenhalgh, C. Adams, M. Tandavanitj, N. and Row-Farr, J. Flypad: designing trajectories in a Large-Scale Permanent Augmented Reality Installation. *Proc. ECSCW '11*, Springer (2011) 233–252.
20. Fosh, L., Benford, S., Reeves, S., Koleva, B., Brundell, P. See me, feel me, touch me, hear me: trajectories and interpretation in a sculpture garden. *Proc. CHI '13*, ACM Press (2013), 149-158.
21. Fosh, L., Benford, S., Reeves, S., Koleva, B. Gifting personal interpretations in galleries. *Proc. CHI '14.* ACM Press (2014), 625-634.
22. Goel, M., Lee, B., Aumi, M.T.I., Patel, S., Borriello, G., Hibino, S. and Begole, B. SurfaceLink: using inertial and acoustic sensing to enable multi-device interaction on a surface. *Proc. CHI '14*. ACM Press (2014), 1387-1396.
23. Gross, T., Stary, C. and Totter, A. User-centered awareness in computer-supported cooperative work-systems: structured embedding of findings from social sciences. *Int. Journ. of Hum.-Comp. Interact. 18*, 3 (June 2005), 323-360.
24. Grudin, J. Computer-supported cooperative work: history and focus. *Computer 27*, 5, (1994), 19-26.
25. Heath, C. and Luff, P. (1992) Collaboration and control: Crisis Management and Multimedia Technology in London Underground Line Control Rooms. *Journ. of CSCW 1,* 1 (1992), 24-48.
26. Heath, C., J. Hindmarsh, and P. Luff (2010): *Video in qualitative research*. Sage.

27. Hornecker, E., P. Marshall, N. S. Dalton, and Y. Rogers Collaboration and interference: awareness with mice or touch input. In: *Proc. CSCW '08,* ACM Press (2008), 167–176.

28. Hutchins, E. *Cognition in the Wild.* MIT Press, Cambridge, MA, USA, 1995.

29. Hwang, I., Yoo, C., Hwang, C., Yim, D., Lee, Y.., Min, C., Kim, J. and Song, J. TalkBetter: family-driven mobile intervention care for children with language delay. *Proc. CSCW '14.* ACM Press (2014), 1283-1296.

30. Jacucci, G., Oulasvirta, A. and Salovaara, A. Active construction of experience through mobile media: a field study with implications for recording and sharing. *Pers. Ubi. Comp. 11*, 4 (2007), 215–234.

31. Kim, T., Chang, A., Holland, L., and Pentland, A. 2008. Meeting mediator: enhancing group collaboration using sociometric feedback. *Proc. CSCW '08.* ACM Press (2008), 457-466.

32. Kuzuoka, H., K. Pitsch, Y. Suzuki, I. Kawaguchi, K. Yamazaki, A. Yamazaki, Y. Kuno, P. Luff, and C. Heath. Effect of restarts and pauses on achieving a state of mutual orientation between a human and a robot. *Proc. CSCW '08*, ACM Press (2008), 201–204.

33. Lim, Y., Stolterman, E., Jung, H. and Donaldson, J. Interaction gestalt and the design of aesthetic interactions. *Proc. DIS '07*, ACM Press (2007), 239-254.

34. Lim, Y., Lee, S. and Lee, K.: Interactivity attributes: a new way of thinking and describing interactivity. In: *Proc. CHI '09*, ACM Press (2009),105-108.

35. Löwgren, J. and Stolterman, E.: *Thoughtful interaction design.* MIT Press (2004).

36. Lucero, A., Holopainen, J. and Jokela, T. Pass-Them-Around: Collaborative Use of Mobile Phones for Photo Sharing. *Proc. of CHI '11*, ACM Press (2011), 1787-1796.

37. Lucero, A., Holopainen, J. and Jokela, T. MobiComics: collaborative use of mobile phones and large displays for public expression. *Proc. MobileHCI '12*, ACM Press (2012), 383-392.

38. Luff, P. and Heath, C. Mobility in collaboration. In: Proc. CSCW '98, ACM Press (1998), 305–314.

39. Luff, P. and Jirotka, M. Interactional resources for the support of collaborative activities: common problems in the design of technologies to support groups and communities'. *In: Community Computing and Support Systems, Social Interaction in Networked Communities*, Springer-Verlag (1998), 249–266.

40. Lundgren, S. Interaction-Related Properties of Interactive Artifacts. *Proc. Ambience '11,* CTF (2011), 112-121.

41. Lundgren, S. and Gkouskos, D. Escaping the obvious: skewing properties of interaction. *Proc. NORDES '13*, Nordes (2013), 32-39.

42. Marshall, P., Rogers, Y. and Pantidi, N. Using F-formations to analyse spatial patterns of interaction in physical environments. *Proc. CSCW '11,* ACM Press (2011), 445–454.

43. Mitchell, K., McCaffery, D., Metaxas, G., Finney, J., Schmid, S., and Scott, A. Six in the city: Introducing Real Tournament - a mobile IPv6 based context-aware multiplayer game. *Proc. of NETGAMES '03*, ACM Press (2003), 91–100.

44. Moran, S., Pantidi, N., Bachour, K., Fischer, J.E., Flintham, M., Rodden, T., Evans, S. and Johnson, S. Team Reactions to Voiced Agent Instructions in a Pervasive Game. *Proc. IUI '13.* ACM Press (2013), 371-382.

45. Reeves, S. *Designing interfaces in public settings: Understanding the role of the spectator in Human-Computer Interaction.* Springer, January 2011.

46. Schuster, D., Rosi, A., Mamei, M., Springer, T., Endler, M., Zambonelly, F. Pervasive social context: taxonomy and survey, *ACM Trans. on Intelli. Sys. and Tech. 4,* 3, (June 2013).

47. Star, S. and Griesemer, J. Institutional ecology, 'translations' and boundary objects: amateurs and professionals in Berkeley's museum of vertebrate zoology, 1907-39. *Social Studies of Science* 19, 3 (1989), 387–420.

48. Stasser, G., and Titus, W. Pooling of unshared information in group decision making: biased information sampling during group discussion. *Journ. of Personality and Soc. Psych.* 48, 6 (1985), 1467-1478.

49. Sun, Z., Purohit, A., Bose, R., and Zhang, P. Spartacus: spatially-aware interaction for mobile devices through energy-efficient audio sensing. *Proc. MobiSys '13.* ACM Press (2013), 263-276.

50. Tolmie, P., Benford, S., Flintham, M., Brundell, P., Adams, M., Tandavantij, N., Row Far, J. and Giannachi, G. "Act natural": instructions, compliance and accountability in ambulatory experiences. *Proc. CHI '12.* ACM Press (2012), 1519-1528.

51. Toups, Z. O. and Kerne, A. 2007. Implicit coordination in firefighting practice: design implications for teaching fire emergency responders. *Proc. CHI '07.* ACM Press (2007), 707-716.

52. Weiser, M. The computer for the 21st century. *SIGMOBILE Mob. Comput. Commun. Rev. 3*, 3, (1999), 3–11.

53. Wright, P., Wallace, J., McCarthy, J.: Aesthetics and Experience-Centered Design, *ACM Trans. on Comp.-Hum. Interact. 15*, 4 (November 2008).

Searchable Objects: Search in Everyday Conversation

Barry Brown, Moira McGregor, Donald McMillan
Mobile Life @ Stockholm University
SE-164, Kista, Sweden
{Barry, Moira, Don}@mobilelifecentre.org

ABSTRACT
This paper examines mobile internet search, presenting search not as a process of information retrieval, but as part of conversation and talk. Through video extracts of mobile search we explore how mobile phones are interwoven into talk, and how searchers manage the participation of other conversationalists alongside the search itself. We introduce the notion of a 'searchable object' – an object that arises in conversation that can be searched for online – and document how such an object occasions a search. In turn we discuss the differing roles of the device 'driver' and 'passenger', and how participation is managed through questions and narration. Rather than search being solely about getting correct information, conversations around search may be just as important. We conclude by critiquing some of the pessimistic views of interaction around mobile phones and their use in ordinary life and talk.

Author Keywords
Collaborative search; mobile; phone interaction; video analysis

ACM Classification Keywords
H.5.2. User Interface

INTRODUCTION
In this paper we examine how search is used in conversation, in particular collaborative search [15]. We follow the example of how *forgetting* is used in talk put forward in Chuck Goodwin's paper "Forgetfulness as an interactional resource" [7]. Here, Goodwin presents the argument that forgetfulness can be something more than just a cognitive impairment. The paper starts with an extract of a conversation in which, while telling a story, a speaker forgets the name of a guest who had appeared the previous evening on a television talk show. This prompts the other parties to the conversation to give suggestions for the guest's name. In his analysis of this clip, Goodwin shows how forgetting is used by the main speaker to change the participation of the listeners to his story: "a display of uncertainty provides resources for [...] rearranging the structure of the current interaction" [7, p128]. Forgetting – in interaction with others – lets the speaker talk in ways sensitive to the presence of parties who might already know the story being told, who can be included in the telling by giving them the opportunity to aid the speaker's memory.

CSCW '15, March 14 - 18, 2015, Vancouver, BC, Canada.
Copyright 2015 ACM 978-1-4503-2922-4/15/03...$15.00.
http://dx.doi.org/10.1145/2675133.2675206

The prominence of mobile phones, and the ability to quickly conduct searches in the presence of others – 'collaborative search' – appears to be a frequent occurrence, with some reports that collaborative search accounts for as much as 63% of mobile search [21]. Internet searches that arise in conversation are now a grossly observable feature of everyday interaction. Yet while this searching is commonplace, we have little data on how this searching is arranged, how it influences conversation, and how we might design search to take into account its conversational role. Indeed, current narratives around mobile device use have followed a somewhat predictable path of critiquing the potential for distraction, cognitive impairment, and damage to our social lives with others – e.g. [13, 22].

Yet Google is changing our everyday conversations. Through close examination of videos of collaborative search we document how search is connected with and used in interaction with others. We discuss how mobile collaborative searches are 'occasioned' by the surrounding talk or environment. Searching at a particular point in a conversation is not random but dependent upon having something that can be searched for – a *searchable object*. We go on to document how narration and questioning are used to manage participation, how search results format and influence conversational sequence, and talk is structured into candidates and evaluation slots. As with Goodwin's example of forgetting, during search the participation of those present is managed through narration, questioning and following the given structure of search results.

This close examination of search leads us to engage with a crucially important question: are mobile devices – and activities like search when conducted in the presence of others – actively changing or even damaging our conversation and interaction? We attempt to understand this relationship and feed this back into the design of search, to understand how search applications could be aligned not just for the efficiency of information retrieval but to support their role in interaction with others. More broadly we document the implications of interactional research for understanding the role of mobile devices in our daily lives and interactions with others – distracting or engaging, detrimental or advantageous.

RELATED WORK

Search has been extensively investigated as both an individual, and more recently, collective activity [1, 2, 17]. One early concept was 'information foraging' [17], clearly encapsulating the notion of an individual searching for and evaluating different results to a search. Information foraging explains how search is organised so as to satisfy the need for information, with a tradeoff between conducting further searches for information, and the declining returns of further search. 'Collective search' more broadly is search involving others, including cases where searchers are co-present with each other. Teevan et al's [21] survey of mobile search users reported that 63% of incidents of mobile search took place in a 'social context' and were discussed with someone co-present. Collective search has come to the fore in part because of the growth of mobile search and the increasing support that mobile device interfaces offer for such search. Morris conducted a survey based inquiry into collaborative search, identifying high amounts of co-located web searching, with as much as 93% of smartphone owners reportedly engaging in co-located collaborative searches [17]. In terms of design, Amershi's [19] paper introduces some useful concepts around co-present search, while Amini focuses specifically on mobile search [1]. Church and her colleagues [5, 6] have discussed the different types and uses of mobile and social search, using diary and interview methods.

Much of this work has reviewed search behaviour broadly, however we have little detailed understanding of the moment by moment involvement of talk and search. In particular, how does conversation and interaction interface with search? We began to investigate this in [4] where we used video data to examine co-present mobile device use, including search. Giving pairs of users a single, instrumented phone around which to interact and recording a day of data as the participants explored a city (figure 1) we noted that projected location was an important factor in the initiation and content of social search.

We situated this in the controversy around co-present device use. A series of debates have developed around the argument that this use of devices in the presence of others (such as in conversation, while driving [11], or during university lectures [22]) is distracting or even alienating users [13] – mobile devices portrayed here as machines which are increasingly drawing us away from our valuable presence with others [20]. As a contrasting view Whittaker *et al* discuss 'Information Curation' [25] that can be seen as a social use of mobile computing where familiar information is used as a personal resource to be kept, managed, and exploited in every day life, supporting claims that mobile phones can bring us closer to our families [24] and friends [12]. While these debates are perhaps recognisable to any witness of the growing use of mobile devices, there is something of a paucity of data. How is our interaction with others influenced by mobile device use? While this paper focuses on search we can also use our data to inform these debates.

Figure 1: Participant is wearing camera in map bag around her neck. The left picture is taken from one wearable camera, with the image from the iPhone recording and the second camera on the right.

METHODS

One inspiration was Moore et al [16] and their use of video analysis to look at search, drawing on the notion of 'third position repair' to explain how search enquiries follow a sequence of specification of search terms, followed by results, followed by a further re-specification of search terms. Could mobile search be examined using video recordings of *in situ* search? Close attention to relatively small number of recordings of search would lack the easy generalisability of the quantitative data usually deployed to inform search design. Classically, bucket tests provide strong evidence for the superiority of particular search approaches over others, and have been fundamental to the refinement of search among major search engine designers.

Yet we felt that video data provides the opportunity to generate more fundamental understandings of what is going on in the search process – not just improvements in queries but how and why particular search results might be conducted. This is particularly the case in mobile situations where both the search situation is less well understood, and where there is the potential for the context to be more varied and to play more of a role in the search itself. Video recordings have been one longstanding method used for a range of different analytic purposes, but particularly to document interaction with and around technical artifacts [9, 23]. This research has extensively studied interaction around screens, capturing on-screen interactions as part of ongoing complexes of work practice (e.g. [10]). Video has proven valuable in illuminating aspects of activities neglected by previous methods, particularly drawing on conversation analysis to understand technology in use. In some senses video forces attention on the moment-by-moment production of technologically mediated action.

Accordingly we used a relatively lightweight video method that made use of wearable cameras, combined with iPhone screen recording software. This method allows us to gain something of a new perspective on mobile device use and, importantly, lets us study in detail how the environment and device are connected during search. Our participants wore multiple portable wearable cameras that recorded their actions relatively unobtrusively (figure 1). These videos were combined with phone screen recording software to allow us to unobtrusively capture the onscreen use of mobile phones. We combined this with experimenting with studying multiple participants together, each wearing portable cameras from which to capture multiple viewpoints of device use, resulting in video recordings of the device user (from their companion) alongside video recorded by the device user, a recording of screen use and an audio recording of everything said around the phone.

We collected a corpus of video recordings of phone use involving participants asked to spend a couple of hours enjoying a 'city daytrip'; in total 20 participants (14 female, 6 male) took part across 13 sessions in Stockholm and London, including 9 locals and 11 visitors. All were iPhone users recruited via advertisements in local cafes, visitor websites and social media. All participants were fluent in English and we asked them to interact in English - though some switched to other languages at points during their daytrips. With one exception, all sessions involved two people, both wearing small cameras and one person leading the iPhone use. A researcher accompanied a single participant in five of the sessions. Otherwise, remaining participants were set up in pairs, with equipment and sent off without the researcher.

In earlier work we have reported more generally on the use of mobile devices in interaction during city visits from this data, documenting map use, and co-present interaction around the device [4]. Our goal in this work was not to provide a statistical breakdown of the uses of the mobile device. In many ways this is already well catered for in the existing log-based literature. Rather our goal was to better understand the details of particular situations of use. One researcher watched all 24 hours of video data and flagged clips that included search. This resulted in 205 one to two minute clips which were then used for focused analysis in group data sessions. These clips were used to generate analytic concepts which we then looked for in the other search relevant clips. We focus on cases of mobile collaborative search – naturalistic examples of search which took place on users' iPhones while they were participating in our trial. Our analysis involved in-depth examination of the clips looking to understand the different resources individuals brought to bear on the interaction and use of technology. As is often the case with data of this kind, the presence of groups in the data let us examine how their analysis of the situation echoed our own interpretation of the data. Here we focus on three incidents which most succinctly illustrate our broader analytic themes; each clip features different aspects of how search is done in conversation, but also some of the variety in how search is interlaced with conversation. In the first clip we see how search can be occasioned by a topic that comes out of conversation. In the second clip we look more closely at how the participation of others in the search is managed by the searcher. Lastly, we look at how decisions are jointly made around searches. Each clip also illustrates a different type of search – using Google in the first clip, the iPhone "Yelp" app in the second, and lastly through navigation and discussion around a website's contents.

RESULTS

In our first clip two participants are walking around a museum exhibition together. This clip lets us introduce three important aspects: how conversation works to occasion a search, the introduction of what we call a "searchable object", and how 'drivers' and 'passengers' work together to manage the search. Note how the search terms come from both participants:

The first transcript (Figure 2) begins with a preamble before the search where discussion is sparked by an observation about one of the displays.

Transcript Notation: Participant A takes the role of 'driver', i.e., they hold the device. Participation is highlighted by [dark grey] when only A is looking at the device, [light grey] when only B, and [medium grey] when both. ↑ = rising pitch, (.1) = a timed silence or . short break, colon = exte:e:nded syllables, [*] = image included.

```
A: He's (.) he does like to stand behind.
   He's gonna get pooped on if he's not
   careful
   ((Participant points to exhibition signage
   which illustrates the relative size of the
   prehistoric animals in the museum by using
   diagrams of them standing beside a human
   form. It looks as if the human is standing
   directly behind the animal.))
B: Have you se:e:en that footage of the guy
   in the zoo and he's cleaning out the
   elephant pen (.) and he's sweeping and the
   elephant reverses and his head goes up the
   elephant's ass↑ [*]
A: Heh heh ha ha
A: Is that online?
B: It's on YouTube.
A: That we have to find.
A: Right eh. Search (.) What do-what do we
   search for?
A: Elephant arse man.
B: Uh yeh. Elephant head (.) elephant ass
   head [Hhh heh heh]
A:      [Hhh heh heh] (9s)
A: elephant man head arse
   ((A taps in 4 worded
   search to YouTube))
A: Hey hey there you=is
   that the one?
   ((B points to item in
   results listing)) [*]
B: Yep that'll be it.
```

Figure 2: Searching for elephant video

The search starts with a "`have you seen`" sequence. This is arranged in the form of two 'stories'– first a very short "`he's going to get pooped on`" remark about a sign in the museum that the two friends are visiting. This is followed by the description of a video of a reversing elephant. Clearly this elephant story doesn't come out of nowhere, but is linked to the illustration on the sign and the first friend's remark. As Sacks [18, vol ii p764] points out, these 'second stories' often get proceeded by questions like: "`have you seen`", that act to introduce the second story in a topically connected way, and also to set up a possible next action (go and see this video).

Occasioning Search: Searchable Objects

With a smartphone it is possible to pull it out and do a search at just about anytime. Why then is the search done here? One of our key questions was what *occasions* a search– what is it that makes an internet search a reasonable thing to be done at *this* point in time? This can be broadly described in terms of how a conversation 'occasions' the search. That is, the way in which a conversation proceeds that sets up the situation where the all elements required for a search are present – although whether a search is actually conducted at that point is a matter of circumstances and decisions of those involved. The usage is not triggered by the conversation, but becomes a relevant thing to do.

```
B: Have you se:e:en that footage of the guy
   in the zoo and he's cleaning out the
   elephant pen (.) and he's sweeping and the
   elephant reverses and his head goes up the
   elephant's ass↑
A: Heh heh ha ha
A: Is that online?
B: It's on YouTube.
A: That we have to find.
```

Figure 3: Have you seen

One of the first things that seems to 'occasion' a search here is the question and answer sequence: "`Have you se:e:en`" / "`That we have to find`". The first line is a recommendation of an unusual video, and with the YouTube app on the iPhone the video is available there and then. We might then suppose that questions could occasion a search. Yet questions and answers are an exceedingly common part of conversation and many of them seem to do little to encourage or occasion an internet search. More specifically in this clip the question actually produces something that is essential for a search – what we call a 'searchable object'. We can start to define such an object as something that can be found via a search – a video, the the case above, or an answer to a query, such as to the question "Is Joni Mitchel sami?" (as in one of our other clips). For a conversation to occasion a search of some sort it needs to provide such an object, however the presence of a searchable object is just one ingredient in occasioning a search.

It is possible to propose further constraints on what a searchable object might be, in that it needs to be something that could be searched for and found *at that point and time.* If, for example, the conversation mentioned a television show then perhaps it would not be appropriate to do a search there and then and start watching the show. However, a clip from that show could be found, or details of that show (such as actors, episode names etc).

Here the video is an amusing clip that is short and can be watched there and then. One class of 'searchable objects' then might be those that can be searched for, found and quickly consumed; a fact, an answer to a question, a short video – these are 'searchable objects' in that they can be searched for and consumed there and then. The searchable object may be something stored on the internet (such as a video or song), or it may be something (like the answer to a question) which can be produced using materials found on the internet (such as a wikipedia page). We emphasise that the occurrence of a searchable object in conversation does not force or trigger the search. Rather the introduction of a 'searchable object' into the conversation provides a slot where a search can be performed relatively naturally (what we called 'occasioning' a search). Those involved might choose to search or not to search, of course, but that action is a 'relevant next action'.

The decision to do a search there and then has some possible dangers in an interaction, in that it might reasonably be a little frustrating for the person who does not have the phone to have their companion searching on the phone and then watching a video. They might, for example, wander off, choose to pay attention to something else or simply dis-attend to the search. This leads us to the second aspect of search: managing participation.

Managing Participation: Driver & Passenger

As in our introductory example, Goodwin [7] discusses the practice of managing participation by those telling stories where forgetting – and specifically the use of questions by the speaker – provides an opportunity to manage the participation of others in an activity – in that they reliably require an answer from the recipient, and 'involve' them in the story telling – or in our case, the search [8].

One of the challenges in using a phone when others are co-present is managing their participation so that they are not excluded from the activity on the phone. That is, when using a device how do you manage the participation of those who are present with respect to the device usage? At times this could mean excluding those co-present, but in the cases we look at here device users actively attempt to engage those who are co-present in the search itself.

A first point about the interaction is that there is something of an asymmetry in that one individual holds the phone and has direct interactional access to the device, whereas the other has only visual access (mostly), which is mediated by the individual holding the device. Drawing an analogy with studies of driver-passenger interaction we will differentiate between 'driver' and 'passenger' (as in [19]). Of course, the device can be passed from one individual to another, swapping the driver and passenger, but here these roles remain static.

```
A: Right eh. Search (.) What do-what do we
   search for?
A: Elephant arse man.
B: Uh yeh. Elephant head (.) elephant ass
   head [Hhh heh heh]
A:      [Hhh heh heh]
```

Figure 4: What do we search for

So in figure 4 the phone-using participant (the 'driver' - A) uses the YouTube app to search for the video, and what follows is a short discussion of the search terms. The question, "What do we search for?" is followed by a self answer of "elephant arse man", and then a list of terms produced by the co-participant without the phone ('the passenger'): "elephant ass head". The search query is a list of terms that are to be typed into the YouTube app. The choice of these three terms is interesting in that they are both minimally adequate for the search.

The search terms, 'elephant arse', 'elephant man', 'arse man' – could be ambiguous in that one can at easily conceive of videos that might be found instead. The listing of the three nouns (by both participants) summarises the supposedly amusing event caught on video: man (or head), elephant and the noun 'arse' (or 'ass') acting as the crux of 'the action' (see also [15]).

The 'driver' could have chosen to plug in the search query themselves, but the question and the short discussion act to bring the co-present passenger in as a minimal participant in the search. If the search fails, they might be called upon to supplement future searches. What is actually typed in by the driver is a mix of the search terms given by both participants: "elephant man head arse" – this mix displays 'listening to', and also the participation of, the non-phone holding participant. When the search results load the searcher then asks, "is that the one".

After the selection of search terms, the participants move to stand side by side, with one participant on a ledge and the second slightly closer arranging their participation around the phone, both with visual access to the screen but also the ability to interact with the screen and gesture above it. As the results are returned, and before the driver asks "is that the one", the passenger points at an item on the list of returned search results (image bottom right in figure 2).

One feature of a small device like a phone then is that it provides for the easy reconfiguration of a limited number of multiple participants around a screen, even while the small size does place some limits on visibility and joint interaction. In this case though the two participants quickly engage in 'joint interaction' and just as quickly disengage. It is worth noting that this configuration does not rely upon any furniture or special arrangements in the environment, just the movement of bodies, hands and eyes. After the video is found and loaded, both the participants face the screen and watch the video. After a minute or so of narration the video gets to 'the action' and we finally get to see the participants watching the video together (figure 5).

```
B: this is it
   ((YouTube video runs with continued
   narration for 40secs till video shows a
   keeper's head accidentally going up an
   elephant's rear))
A: oh:h:h:h ma:ate heh heh heh heh that is
   s:o:o wrong [heh heh heh heh]
B:             [sheh heh heh heh]
```

Figure 5: So wrong

As soon as the clip has played, the passenger moves away from the phone but both of them continue laughing together about the clip.

This first clip sets up some of the key things that go on when searching as part of a conversation. We talked about how a search is 'occasioned' – what makes an opportunity for a search to happen in the first place. Important here are 'searchable objects'– things that come up in conversation or interaction that can be searched for. During the search the driver 'manages the participation' of the passenger, involving the other participant in the search, through questions and the like.

Clip 2: Questions and narration

Now lets move onto our second clip (figure 6, next page). This time we get to see how search results themselves are used. In this clip, the 'driving' participant uses their phone to look through a set of results on the Yelp application (a local information site) searching for the term 'shopping'. The couple are looking for a new bag, although as we will see this leads to a search for shopping establishments. Here we can see how the participation of the 'non driver' is managed by the participant who is holding the phone. Unlike our first example, there is no conversation or interaction around the search term which is entered into the 'Yelp' app. Yelp is a website that lists local establishments and services, and it has a companion application that is used by the participant to see if they can find a suitable store. It is not until the search results are returned that conversation engages with the search.

What this clip does show quite nicely, however, is how the results of a search can be engaged with jointly in discussion with a co-present other. Here the two participants are facing each other over a restaurant table, so cannot jointly interact with the device. The phone can, however, can be passed over the table so that they can share the search results and information on the display.

As with the first example *managing participation* is one key aspect of talk around the device. Again we can see how questions are used, (what's a hobby shop) as well as narration, (there's mood shopping centre). Secondly, we will discuss how the timing of the interaction with Yelp is arranged in the conversation. Distinguishing this search from the earlier transcript, the two searchers here are also jointly deciding what they will do on that day. The inspection of different items is consequential, in that they will visit one of these places to look for the bag (I'm trying to find like where I might buy a bag). The 'searchable object', then, is a shop or set of shops where bags could potentially be purchased. Yet alongside

((A starts a search holding the phone under the table as she dines with her partner))

A: I'm trying to find like where I might buy a bag (.2) or where there like are vintage shops or-
A: There's mood shopping centre stockholm. (.) There's the olens.
A: There's one (.2)
A: what's↑a hobby shop
B: trains↑
A: huh
B: trains
A: I don't think so.
A: The things it has are (.2) ((participant
1 waits for page to download))
A: it's whole bunch of stuff ((A scrolls through pages and describes images))
A: like for biking (.) for backpacking (.) for making your deck, for your pool. Interesting↓ It's kinda like a homegoods store.
B: Okay.
A: There was one (.4) used vintage constignment-consignment place
B: yeh (.1) okay
A: But I think it could be more of a book store
((A selects Rönnells Antivariat again and waits for the page to load))
A: yeh, like used books.
2 B: Why do you say that?
A: It's not (.) It's like the third or fourth thing in its list of what it is, but I feel like it could be the
B: The first thing it says is books↑
A: No it's like the fourth thing↑
A: But I just. Yeh it's mostly books (.2)
A: I mean, look it's a bookstore ((A turns the screen towards B opposite then back to herself again))
B: alright, well (8s)
A: yeh i think this area is mostly (4s)
B: What did'y, did you get Martha's email↑
B: She wants to visit august 15th to 19th
((A conversation about Martha's email follows…))
A: There's supposedly shopping in Kungsholmen
B: Yeah sure. You wanna go there↑

Figure 6: Searching for a shop

this search for shops, there is also a decision that must be made collectively as to where to actually go. This is somewhat similar to the situation discussed in [3], in which a group of tourists is working around a map to find things on the map and also trying to collectively decide what to do on the day. So the search here is also a process in joint decision making.

The heart of the exchange, however, takes place over two question and answer sequences (marked 1 and 2). In the first exchange, the question "what's a hobby shop" starts a discussion of what a hobby shop might be, and the answer "trains" is compared with the results from the store's website (which seems to offer a range of goods that are not fitting with the description 'hobby shop'). In this exchange the website for the store is used to correct Yelp's misleading categorisation (from hobby shop to home-goods store).

The second exchange takes place in a similar way ("there was one used constignment-consignment place"), although with an evaluation followed by a query and then an answer. In this case it is also the store website that allows for a correction of the description given in Yelp – (from "consignment store" to bookshop). The source of the conversation in each piece is the category that Yelp puts each store into, with the searchers trying to 'decode' the description into something more understandable to them. In particular, since they are searching for a store that sells bags, the relevant question is whether each store will sell bags – and the sort of bags they are looking for too. In each case, it seems like the categories that Yelp use do not quite fit with the local Swedish stores being described. Indeed, Clas Ohlson, the 'hobby shop', is in some ways an almost 'uncategorisable' store as covers more than home-goods.

Since the couple are deciding where to go together, the participation of both parties is of some relevance. For similar reasons to do with 'managing participation' found in the first clip (figure 2), we see questions being asked about the search results – although here the passenger also queries the description 'used books'. While these may certainly be genuine questions to clarify what Yelp has returned, they also have the result of bringing the passenger into the phone interaction, as does the second exchange. Yet, even in the second case of the 'used vintage consignment' shop there is a puzzle set up in terms of this shop being "more of a book shop" – which prompts the question "Why do you say that?" and finally the turn to share the phone screen.

Alongside *questions*, the driver here also *narrates* aspects of the search as it is conducted. Again this narration of the search acts to include the passenger in the search even though they have no visual access to the screen. The narration allows the driver to ask questions without having to explain again the context of their activity. Narration here thus works as a kind of ongoing commentary to the activity that covers for the lack of visual availability of the screen that we saw in the first extract.

Timing and insertion sequences

Much of the above discussion has focused on how the talk is organised around the search itself, but we might now move on to consider how it is that search itself is organised to take into account its role in conversation. Now much of the arrangement of the search is dictated by the tool or website being used – indeed, there is an almost fixed pattern of input of search terms followed by output of search results which can then be sequentially inspected. Yet the system also has situations where it waits for input by the user, and where the system can be 'paused'. There are also situations where the system itself pauses as it has to fetch the given results or website.

As Licoppe [14] discusses, the delays of the interface can be used to help manage aspects of the conversation. For example, "`but I think it could be more of a book store`", is said as the webpage for the book store is selected, an operation which takes much longer than moving around the interface of the Yelp application. This following conversation is thus 'timed' to happen in a lull in interacting with the phone, where the attention of the driver is freed up. We can see aspects of the interaction which take into account the attention of the driver – leading to pauses where the driver visibly reads, and there is no talk filling the gaps.

The organisation of narration also indicates to co-present others when there may exist a opportunity to introduce a different conversation topic; in transcript 2 participant B around the end waits for a pause in the spoken summary of the search results, to raise the subject of a mutual friend's email, (`What did'y, did you get Martha's email?)` which is discussed for several minutes, before A returns to the task in hand of researching a shopping area. This sequence can be seen as a form of 'insertion sequence'– interludes of talk and interaction inserted within the main task of conducting an online search. This also displays something of the temporal organisation of mobile device use, in that the search can be 'paused' and another matter attended to with no concern about the task lapsing on the phone. Devices wait until the next action so long as there is no realtime action (such as game playing) unfolding.

Clip 3: Result and conversational mirroring

Each of our clips so far has dug into how the searchers manage the search results in their conversation with each other. What we are seeing is the ways in which a search is conducted, not only with regard to the interface of the website or search engine, but how talk and the search itself is interlaced by those talking. In these clips the search is as much about the talk as it is about the search technology.

Yet how the results are displayed and parsed can also have a substantive role on conversation – to the point of ordering and shaping what is talked about. Figure 7 contains our final clip, and we return to our two participants from our first clip. In this instance we are at the start of their day out where they are deciding what they might do for the daytrip.

((A runs a search in Google for things to do in London when it's raining and sits down while waiting for search results to fill in. Participant B looks over to the handset from the left))

B: Is there actually a thing that says when it's raining↑
A: It's rainy day activities=things to do when it's ra:ining ((A turns handset screen round more towards B))
B: aw right I see
B: yes ((B checking pockets for something))
A: eat ((A turns the phone and zooms in to read detail on the page))
A: Rainy days (.) find out what's on in (.) London's top museums (.) finds out… what's, °secret galleries°

A: what's a, what's a secret gallery?
B: that's a good question
A: we could go and walk around the Barbican
B: oh yeh (.) is there (.2) anything fun in there?
A: if not=yes there's all sorts of things on in there. Don't know what's on there at the moment
((A scrolls down a page of 'secret gallery' listings))

B: °read them out°
A: we've got Auto Italia [*] on the Old Kent Road
A: [*] uh (.) yeah no, that's just some
A: Banner repeater [*] in Hackney >i told you we should go to hackney<
B: heh heh heh
A: uh (.) The Cabinet gallery in Old Street (.3) uh
[Cabinet gallery discussion deleted]
A: Where w:was the Barbi-Barbican?
((short discussion of camera position, user goes back to rainy days page and then selected the Barbican page))
A: RAIN ROOM
B: ah
A: they've got something called the rain room
B: oh [let's go there]
A: [okay let's go there then]

Figure 7: Searching for a destination

In this extract we see again a prolonged search, again taking place around 'what to do' – although unlike our earlier example which was based around which shop to visit, this search seems more open ended, constrained not by the search for a particular purchase but initially by the weather; 'things to do in London when its raining'.

The first hit for the google search 'things to do in London in the rain' leads to a page from 'Time Out', the website for the popular listings and guide magazine. This page is selected and loads at the beginning of our extract and after some complaining about the speed of the page loading, the non-phone using participant asks a question about the results, leading the 'driver' to turn the phone to the other participant at the start of the clip. The rest of the extract then takes place on the Time Out website as different activities suggested for a 'rainy day' are inspected, before the decision is made to go to the 'rain room.'

As in our previous two clips 'the driver' takes on the role of narrating features of the search, and in particular describing the different options from the website. Again, we can see the use of questions about the items to manage the participation of the non-driving user – such as "`what's a secret gallery`" and "`where was the barbican`". As the website is scrolled through we have a narration by the driver which in turn leaves slots for conversation by the second participant, and at times is explicitly prompted by the driver. While the driver talks more the second participant clearly has an involvement in their final choice of visiting the barbican – commenting "`oh yeh (.) is there (.2) anything fun in there?`" when it is first mentioned, and "`oh let's go there`" when the rain room in the Barbican is mentioned. Clearly both participants are orientated towards the joint nature of their activity and the need for an agreement about what to do, informed by the details of their search. In the extract in

```
A: [*] RAIN ROOM
B: ah
A: they've got something called the rain
   room
B: oh [let's go there]
A:    [okay let's go there then]
```

Figure 8: Deciding on the rain room

figure 8 we can see how the conversation follows the format of the search results from the Time Out website.

The website is organised in three 'levels' of a hierarchy, and the conversation takes place within 'Galleries'. The Barbican centre is mentioned quite early on, but rather than accept this as their destination the driver proceeds with the search and conversation through three of the 'secret gallery' entries. This is perhaps an attempt at a 'reasonable' search, where alternatives are considered without taking the first (or the second) suitable destination, leaving some time to consider alternatives. At some point the list of alternatives seems not to be raising preferable candidates, and so the 'secret gallery' line is abandoned and the search then jumps to see what exactly they might go and see at the Barbican, since it is a large arts centre with multiple exhibits.

One point to make about this traversal is that the order is 'seen in common' by both participants seated around the phone. While most of the items are narrated by the driver, the Barbican is actually first mentioned by the passenger. The sequence of the conversation then follows in a fairly straightforward way. After visiting the Cabinet Gallery website the 'secret galleries' list is abandoned (it has four entries) and they return to the original 'Rainy days' page.

Candidate-evaluation slots

Even more than our previous clip, this extract takes the form of sequences of 'candidate-evaluation'. Or perhaps a more fitting description is 'candidate-evaluation *slot*', since many of the comments that are given about each establishment are not clearly positive or negative. Rather perhaps it is that the narration brings up candidates which can be evaluated (or not), with the search for a 'positive evaluation', which will help the joint choice. In fact the two participants come quite quickly to an agreement at the end, both picking the Rain Room simultaneously.

The organisation of the talk in terms of 'candidate-evaluation slot' works well with the overall task of the day: to decide together on a place to go. This relies upon a sensitivity between the conversationalists to not force an option that they might find desirable yet to express their own evaluations (which may be very vague), yet do this within the bounds of a mutual accommodation of each other that necessitates an amortisation of one's own desire.

Or, as Brown and Laurier put it, in discussing some similar data: "By bringing up each place tentatively they allow others to express a desire or interest in each of these activities, to gradually come to an agreement on what would be fun for all of them. The ambiguity of their conversation is not a problem for the friends, rather it is a feature of the geography of the route they are producing, one which weds the plan to their activity" [3].

Through *not* commenting on the possibilities raised by the search, the participants then allow each other to express their view, but also to take into account uncertainty over what to do that day. Simply put, as planning a day out is a step into the unknown whatever they choose to do will be something of a guess and the conversational organisation here affords this uncertainty in some ways.

DISCUSSION

We have presented here results to open up some aspects of how devices and conversations are integrated with each other. Each of these cases present different aspects of how searches get started, and how participation comes to be managed drawing on the nature of search results and using it to structure and manage the conversation.

Rethinking search results

While previous search research has documented how information seeking goals shape search, here we show how the search activity is one that is conducted in concert with conversation and the interaction with others. Broadly then, we would argue that search should integrate with the conversational context as much as it does with the goals of a single searcher. Search is interwoven with conversation.

Take, for example, the initial points about occasioning search; it should be possible to produce devices that would apply speech recognition to all talk occurring around the device. Interaction in the background has been pioneered commercially recently with "Google Now". This could be taken further, and lead the device to look for 'occasions' for search thus pre-empting search, placing results on the home page. Two ways of doing this might be to identify searchable objects that occur in talk and offer results, or find nouns or questions and offer these as search terms.

A second set of implications might be found in how the hierarchy of results and how their role in conversation plays out. The simultaneously of talk and search here does present some challenges to spoken word and audio search solutions, since these potentially might not support the different modalities as well as an existing text and screen based search might. Some applications take a more hybrid approach than a conversational one – with spoken words leading to a more traditional list of search results, and in fact this might fit better with the nature of search in interaction.

A third strand could be the ways in which the user can manage the expansion of the one-user-one-device interaction paradigm to allow for this socially inclusive use of a primarily personal device. Detecting when more than one person is focused on the screen and delaying incoming message alerts or other such personal information while increasing the size of fonts, volume, or brightness may be a first step towards more integrated designs where, if such a situation is detected, the participants devices and others in the location could collaborate to provide a larger input and output space.

Devices and interaction

Alongside these design issues, however, we are also deeply concerned with questions on the roles of devices in interaction and talk. There has been growing popular concern and attention on the role of mobile devices as forms of 'distraction', for example in education and driving [11, 22]. More recently, there has been growing discussion of the detrimental role of devices in our interaction with others [13]. Are mobile devices destructive to that important realm of human sociability – the conversation?

A full account of these questions is outside the scope of this paper. What we can say, however, is that we see considerable attention, effort and thought given to co-conversationalists while using a mobile device. Rather than shutting off conversationalists from each other, the devices become a site of investigation and discussion. As with any object or device that is predominantly designed for single person use we might question how limited these resources and adoptions might be, but it is apparent that the devices do not kill or negate conversation, but rather that they are skilfully deployed in conversation with others. This is not to say this is always, or even frequently, the case but rather that these facilities are grossly present in multipart interaction.

Moreover, we have a natural scepticism as this debate seems to arise with nearly every new technology encouraging both dystopian and utopian discourses. Mobile phones have been through this before, with questions and debates around the initial use of voice and text-messaging. Within much of the literature around device use, the concept of distraction has been a common motif. Yet this might simply be an inadequate concept for understanding device use, as it implies an agent with a central singular focus who is then distracted by a device, or by a conversation, and so whom then must maintain multiple separate interactions. Rather in the videos that we examine here both conversation and device use are co-produced, with both the conversation influencing device use and device use influencing the conversation. This is not to say that devices do not distract, or that one cannot find cases where devices cause problems for focused proximate interaction. Rather our point is that for these cases of ordinary interaction – collected during cases of everyday usage – we find this threading much more prevalent than problematic incidences of distraction. We suggest then that work seeking to understand the nexus of talk interaction and device use, rather than seeing them as necessarily separate or in conflict, is likely to be more promising.

CONCLUSION

This paper has examined in detail how social search is part of conversation with co-present others. Firstly, we documented how talk occasions search, providing the example of a "searchable object" – something referenced in conversation that can be found with an online search. Secondly, we described how multi-party interaction around a small mobile device naturally falls into a division between driver and passengers, in that one is holding, interacting with, and orienting the display of the device and the others are observing. However, both the driver and the passengers are involved in the search – through the talk around the search we have shown that those in both roles are active even if only one directly controls the interface. Specifically, we discussed how questions and narration are used to involve and manage the participation of those co-present. We then discussed the role of timing and the search interface, and how the hierarchical organisation of search results in a list form can be mirrored in conversation. Finally, we talked about situations where one result must be collaboratively chosen (such as a shared destination) and how in such situations, the conversation tends to be arranged as an example of candidate and evaluation slots.

Through these extracts and the broader corpus we have uncovered complexity in how search comes to be threaded with conversation. Clearly devices do not simply take us away from interaction with others. The notion of distraction is much too simplistic to explain the situations here. Rather our results point once again to the diversity of device use in everyday life. Our interactions display a robustness and richness that escapes the attention of those who wish for simplistic narratives of technological disruption.

ACKNOWLEDGEMENTS

The research was made possible by a grant from the Swedish Governmental Agency for Innovation Systems to the Mobile Life VinnExcellence Centre, in partnership with Ericsson, Microsoft, Nokia, IKEA and the City of Stockholm.

REFERENCES

1. Amini, S., Brush, A. J., et al. Trajectory-aware mobile search. In Proceedings of the 2012 ACM annual conference on Human Factors in Computing Systems (2012),2561-2564 ACM.
2. Bouidghaghen, O., Tamine, L., et al. Personalizing Mobile Web Search for Location Sensitive Queries. In 2011 12th IEEE International Conference on Mobile Data Management (MDM),110-118 IEEE.
3. Brown, B. and Laurier, E. Maps and Journeys: An Ethno-methodological Investigation. Cartographica, 40, 3 (2005), 17-33.
4. Brown, B., McGregor, M., et al. iPhone in vivo: video analysis of mobile device use. In Proceedings of CHI '13, Paris, France., ACM Press (2013).
5. Church, K., Cousin, A., et al. I wanted to settle a bet!: understanding why and how people use mobile search in social settings. In MobileHCI 2012 (2012),393-402 ACM.
6. Church, K. and Oliver, N. Understanding mobile web and mobile search use in today's dynamic mobile landscape. In Mobile HCI 2011 (2011),67-76 ACM.
7. Goodwin, C. Forgetfulness as an interactive resource. Social Psychology Quarterly, 50, 2 (1987), 115-130.
8. Goodwin, C. Participation, stance and affect in the organizations of activities. Discourse and Society, 18, 1 (2007), 15-73.
9. Heath, C. and Luff, P. Technology in action. Cambridge university press, Cambridge, 2000.
10. Heath, C., Svensson, M. S., et al. Configuring awareness. Computer Supported Cooperative Work (CSCW), 11, 3 (2002), 317-347.
11. Hosking, S. G., Young, K. L., et al. The Effects of Text Messaging on Young Drivers. Human Factors: The Journal of the Human Factors and Ergonomics Society, 51, 4 (2009), 582-592.
12. IJsselsteijn, W., van Baren, J., et al. Staying in touch: Social presence and connectedness through synchronous and asynchronous communication media. Human-Computer Interaction: Theory and Practice (Part II), 2(2003), 924-928.
13. Kuss, D. J., van Rooij, A. J., et al. Internet addiction in adolescents: Prevalence and risk factors. Computers in Human Behavior, 29, 5 (2013), 1987-1996.
14. Licoppe, C. and Figeac, J. Patterns of Gaze Switching in the "Naturally-Occurring" Uses of Smartphones in Urban Mobile Settings. Department of Economics and Social Sciences TELECOM ParisTech, 2013.
15. Meredith Ringel, M. Collaborative search revisited. In Proceedings of the 2013 conference on Computer supported cooperative work (2013) ACM.
16. Moore, R. J., Churchill, E. F., et al. Three sequential positions of query repair in interactions with internet search engines. In Proceedings of the ACM 2011 conference on Computer supported cooperative work (2011),415-424 ACM Press.
17. Pirolli, P. Information Foraging Theory: Adaptive Interaction with Information. Oxford University Press, USA, 2007.
18. Sacks, H. Lectures on conversation: vol 1 & 2. Basil Blackwell, Oxford, 1995.
19. Saleema, A. and Meredith Ringel, M. CoSearch: a system for co-located collaborative web search. In Proceedings of the SIGCHI Conference on Human Factors in Computing Systems (2008) ACM.
20. Srivastava, L. Mobile phones and the evolution of social behaviour. Behaviour & Information Technology, 24, 2 (2005), 111-129.
21. Teevan, J., Karlson, A., et al. Understanding the importance of location, time, and people in mobile local search behavior. In Proceedings of the 13th International Conference on Human Computer Interaction with Mobile Devices and Services (2011), 77-80 ACM.
22. Tindell, D. R. and Bohlander, R. W. The Use and Abuse of Cell Phones and Text Messaging in the Classroom: A Survey of College Students. College Teaching, 60, 1 (2012), 1-9.
23. vom Lehn, D., Heath, C., et al. Exhibiting Interaction: Conduct and Collaboration in Museums and Galleries. Symbolic Interaction, 24, 2 (2001), 189-216.
24. Wajcman, J., Bittman, M., et al. Families without Borders: Mobile Phones, Connectedness and Work-Home Divisions. Sociology, 42, 4 (2008), 635-652.
25. Whittaker, S. Personal information management: from information consumption to curation. Annual review of information science and technology, 45, 1 (2011), 1-62.

Supporting Developers' Coordination in The IDE

Anja Guzzi*, **Alberto Bacchelli**
Delft University of Technology
Delft, The Netherlands
{a.guzzi, a.bacchelli}@tudelft.nl

Yann Riche
Microsoft
Redmond, WA, USA
yannr@microsoft.com

Arie van Deursen
Delft University of Technology
Delft, The Netherlands
{arie.vanDeursen}@tudelft.nl

ABSTRACT
Teamwork in software engineering is time-consuming and problematic. In this paper, we explore how to better support developers' collaboration in teamwork, focusing on the software implementation phase happening in the integrated development environment (IDE). Conducting a qualitative investigation, we learn that developers' teamwork needs mostly regard coordination, rather than concurrent work on the same (sub)task, and that developers successfully deal with scenarios considered problematic in literature, but they have problems dealing with breaking changes made by peers on the same project. We derive implications and recommendations. Based on one of the latter, we analyze the current IDE support for receiving code changes, finding that historical information is neither visible nor easily accessible. Consequently, we devise and qualitatively evaluate BELLEVUE, the design of an IDE extension to make received changes always visible and code history accessible in the editor.

Author Keywords
Developers' coordination; IDE extension; qualitative study.

ACM Classification Keywords
D.2.6 Software Engineering: Programming Environments

INTRODUCTION
Software engineering is often a team effort. It is not unusual for hundreds of professionals collaborate to design, build, evaluate, and maintain software systems [71]. However, teamwork remains one of the most difficult and pervasive problems of software engineering, and developers face a plethora of teamwork problems at different levels [18].

Key to this teamwork are tools and processes that revolve around it, source code management, and development. Most of developers' time is spent within the Integrated Development Environments (IDE) [48], thus researchers are trying to leverage them by augmenting their collaborative capabilities (*e.g.,* [17, 27, 32, 33]). Nevertheless, the IDE remains a tool that primarily helps individual programmers to be more effective in the classical edit-compile-run cycle [73].

*Anja Guzzi was an intern with the User Experience Team, Microsoft Developer Division, Microsoft, Redmond, USA in the summer of 2012 when this work was carried out.

CSCW 2015, March 14–18, 2015, Vancouver, BC, Canada.

ACM 978-1-4503-2922-4/15/03 ...$15.00.
http://dx.doi.org/10.1145/2675133.2675177

In this paper, we explore how to better support collaboration in teamwork within the IDE. Our research is set up in two phases: An exploratory investigation, followed by the design and evaluation of a medium fidelity click-through prototype.

In our investigation, we explored how developers in large development teams experience collaboration and identify problems they face when working in team. To this end, we (1) conducted a brainstorming session with 8 industry experts working on the development of IDE solutions at Microsoft; (2) identified three core opportunities for the design of improved collaborative solutions, which we refined through semi-structured interviews with developers; and (3) interviewed 11 professional developers with various degrees of experience and seniority, from 9 different companies to contextualize those opportunities.

In our investigation, we report how, while our participants reported collaborating with others on code, they spend a limited amount of time actively engaged in collaboration. As a consequence, one of the core issue emerging revolves around managing dependencies between activities, rather than working together contemporarily on the same (sub)task. Our interviews with developers also confirm that issues arise due to the lack of information (*i.e.,* imperfect information) when working on shared code, and uncover existing strategies to prevent or resolve them. Dependencies are often mediated through code, in the form of code changes. Yet, our investigation illustrates how dealing with code changes remains a common source of issues despite existing tools and strategies when working on the same project. This emerges as one of the main causes of frustration in interviewees' experience of teamwork. From our findings we derive implications and recommendations for improving coordination in modern IDEs.

In the second phase of this study, we focus on an investigation of how to improve handling teams code changes from within the IDE. Using common usability heuristics [56], we describe opportunities to better support teamwork in the IDE by supporting information needs about change history. Consequently, we leverage this analysis to: (1) derive requirements for an IDE extension, (2) describe the design of BELLEVUE, a prototype fulfilling these requirements, and (3) iteratively evaluate a design called BELLEVUE with 10 senior developers from different companies and backgrounds.

BELLEVUE makes incoming code changes always visible during development, eases the use of that history in the context of the developer's tasks and flows. It shows historical information within the active code editor to let users modify the code without context switch. To achieve this, BELLEVUE takes already available historical change data and offers an interactive view that shows detailed historical information for files and code chunks with respect to a previous version.

EXPLORATORY INVESTIGATION: METHODOLOGY

In this section, we define the scope of our research, and our research methodologies (illustrated in Figure 1), divided into the following main steps: brainstorming, semi-structured interviews, and data analysis with card sorting.

Scoping

We scoped our initial focus by tapping in the collective knowledge of eight industry experts engaged in the design and implementation of development tools (including one of the co-authors, and the first author as researcher intern). To do so, we organized a brainstorming on the challenges and opportunities revolving around team development. The brainstorming led to the identification of the following areas for further investigation: *awareness* (*i.e.,* knowing other people's work to anticipate issues and to proactively seek out information when needed), *work dependencies* (*i.e.,* anticipating and understanding who I depend on and who depends on me), and *breaking changes* (*i.e.,* anticipating what and whom will be impacted by the breaking change I am about to release). As we will explore in more depth later, those areas describe times where lack of information can lead to resource- and time-consuming situations. Such situations are common not only in development situations, but in teamwork in general where situation of *imperfect information* is the norm [38].

Consistently, literature reported that developers often have difficulties facing questions such as: "*What have my coworkers been doing?*" "*How have resources I depend on changed?*" "*What information was relevant to my task?*" "*What code caused this program state?*" [7, 26, 45, 68] In our work, we iterate on this by providing a more in-depth view of some of those specific problems, and by illustrating and validating ways of addressing them within the flow of activities developers engage in.

Semi-structured Interviews

To gather more details about the context in which those issues emerge, and current strategies for addressing them, we conducted *semi-structured* interviews [50] with professional developers. In total, we interviewed 11 developers from a varying in experience, team sizes, and companies. Table 1 summarizes interviewees' characteristics.

We conducted each 90-min interview on the phone, and transcribed the interviews for latter analysis. After each interview, we analyzed the transcript and split it into smaller *coherent units* (*i.e.,* blocks expressing a single concept), which we summarized by using an interview quotation or an abstractive sentence. In addition, the interviewer kept notes (*i.e., memos*) of relevant and recurring observations in a document iteratively refined and updated. Out of the interviews, 56 memos emerged.

ID	Overall experience	In current team Time	Role	Team Size
D1	7.5 years	4.5 months	dev	4
D2	10 years	6 years	dev lead	7
D3	2 months	2 months	junior dev	4
D4	1.5 years	1.5 years	sql dev	5
D5	20 years	10 years	senior dev	4
D6	25+ years	7 years	senior dev	15
D7	21 years	2 weeks	senior dev	10
D8	25+ years	10 years	senior dev	16
D9	1 years	1 years	dev	5
D10	15 years	5 years	dev lead	5
D11	20 years	6 years	senior dev	11

Table 1. Interviewed developers

To analyze our data, we created the 562 cards from the transcribed coherent units and the memos. Each card included: the source (transcript/memo), the interviewee's name (if from the transcript), the unit/memo content, and an ID for later reference. We used *card sorting* [69] to extract salient themes, leveraging a combination of open and closed card sorts. After macro categories were discovered, we re-analyzed their cards to obtain a finer-grained categorization. Finally, we organized the categories using *affinity diagramming* [52].

EXPLORATORY INVESTIGATION: DATA

In this section, we present the results of our exploratory investigation. When quoting raw data, we refer to the individual cards using a [D*X*.*Y*] notation, where *X* represents the developer, and *Y* (optional) the card (*e.g.,* [D2.03] refers to card 03 from the interview with D2).

Teamwork from the developers' perspectives

According to the interviewees, collaboration in teamwork is defined by a wide spectrum of activities:

Communication - Collaboration is communication: As D8 said: "*It is all about communication. If you have good communication, you have good collaboration.*" Communication can be both one-to-one and one-to-many, can be formal or informal, and goes through different channels. Channels are "conventional," such as email and instant messaging (IM), but also more domain specific ones, such as interactions via project management tools (*e.g.,* source code management systems and requirement tracking systems) and source code; as D4 explains: "[to communicate] *typically we use* [IM]*, but we also have an internal wiki that we use*". [D4.02, D7.09, D8.(01,02)]

Helping each other by sharing information - As D9 said: "*Collaboration is just sharing information and ideas.*" In particular, according to interviewees, collaboration means being proactive and sharing useful information to make it easier for others to complete their work (*e.g.,* "*make* [the acquisition of information] *as easy as possible on the other co-workers, so that they don't have to struggle*" [D7]). This aspect of collaboration involves voluntarily sending notifications (*e.g.,* "*FYI–for your information*" messages) and starting discussions (*e.g.,* "*let's coordinate on this change*

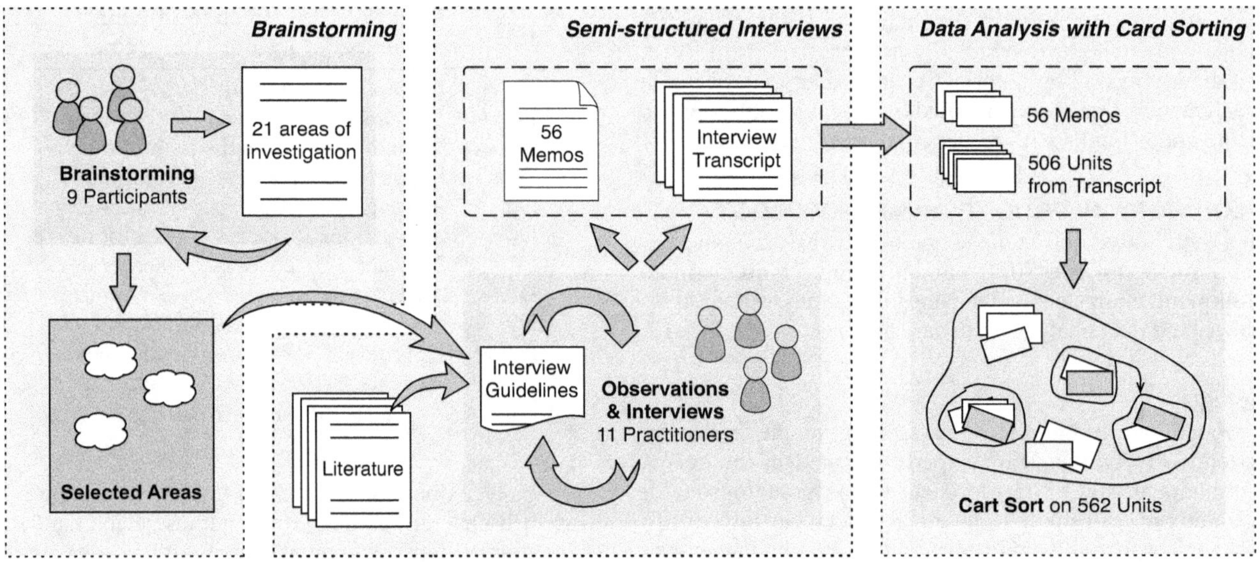

Figure 1. The research method applied in the first phase

I need to make") [D7]. Resource sharing involves not only knowledge on the actual source code of the project, but also information from external resources, for example about new technologies or coding style; as D9 stated: "*We also like send each other things, like, style tips and like interesting articles about how other companies do things*". [D2.02, D7.(02,03,06), D9.(01,04,05)]

Knowing what others know - Collaboration, from the interviewees' perspective, also means to stay aware of the experts on the different parts of the system (*i.e.,* "*the domain experts*") and to understand artifacts and code changes done by colleagues. D11 explains: "[collaboration] *is keeping track of what everybody is working on and being able to know how the different pieces are in place*". According to interviewees, knowing what the others know has the aim both of preventing problems and of reacting faster when they occur. [D2.01, D4.03, D7.04–07, D11.47]

Working on the same goal, doing different things - Overall, developers see collaboration as working toward the same goal (*e.g.,* product releases), by acting in parallel on different parts of the same project (*e.g.,* working separately on different code artifacts): "*Collaboration is we are all working towards the common goal, but maybe working on different parts of it, but these components do interact*" [D7]; "[Collaborating meant] *we divided up the work* [...], *we went off these directions, and as things started to merge together, we go on* [merging] *on a case by case base.*" [D3]. [D1.2, D3.01, D4.01, D7.01, D9.(02,06)]

Dealing with imperfect information in teamwork

To investigate how developers deal with imperfect information, we outlined three concrete teamwork scenarios in which the existence of imperfect information can generate problems. The scenarios were derived from teamwork situations commonly described as problematic in literature.

Inefficient Task Assignment

Scenario. One developer is assigned to a task, while another is already working on a similar or related task. This introduces inefficiencies in the team (and potential collisions).

Related literature. Software engineering researchers have recognized task partition and allocation as important endeavors in the context of teamwork [44, 46]. If dependencies and common traits among tasks are not correctly handled, developers can reduce their efficiency and generate unexpected conflicts [37]. Literature suggests different techniques, with varying results, for efficient task assignment (*e.g.,* [16, 24]). In particular, the assignment of bug fixes (or new features to implement), from a repository of issues or requests to the most appropriate developers, is one of the main instances of task assignment investigated by researchers [1]. Researchers reported that bug triaging is a time consuming task, which requires non-trivial information about the system, and that often leads to erroneous choices [2]. A number of techniques has been devised to tackle the triaging problem, *e.g.,* [53, 41].

Interviews' outcome. Although considered realistic, our participants did not see this scenario as a core issue. In fact, the task assignment processes of teams are in general considered effective to prevent the problematic scenario to take place. In some teams supervising figures (*e.g.,* managers) do the task assignment (*e.g.,* "[a new task] *goes to a manager, who decides whom to assign*" [D8], and "*the boss will tell you about a task* [to do]" [D9]); in the other teams, tasks are divided during team meetings, with various degrees of developers' interaction (*e.g.,* "*we are using daily SCRUM meetings*" [D1], and "*we break up the code, and if the* [task] *is in your code, it's yours*" [D5]).

Simultaneous Conflicting Changes

Scenario. Developers find themselves in a situation where there is a merge conflict (*i.e.,* when different people are touching the code at the same time).

Related literature. A recent significant effort in the software engineering research community is devoted to detect concurrent modifications to software artifacts (*e.g.,* [35, 36, 59, 65]). In fact, developers making inconsistent changes to the same part of the code can cause merge conflicts when changes are committed to the code repository, which leads to wasted developers' efforts and project delays [13, 42, 66]. Grinter conducted one of the first field studies that investigated developers' coordination strategies [29]. She observed that it is sometimes difficult for developers (even for expert ones) to merge conflicting code without communicating with the other person who worked on a module. Later, de Souza *et al.*, in an observation of the coordination practices of a NASA software team, observed that developers in some cases think individually trying to avoid merging, while in others think collectively by holding check-ins and explaining their changes to their team members [21].

Interviews' outcome. Our participants reported only rarely encountering a situation where more than one person was working on the same file at the same time ("*we don't run into those situations a lot*" [D2]). Most of our participants' teams were organized to make developers work on different parts of the system, with a key person in charge of coordinating development to prevent those issues, typically a lead developer or an architect. Some participants also used technical solutions to avoid concurrent edits (*e.g.,* "*We put a lock on* [the file]*, so it does not get edited* [by others]" [D1]). When a merge conflict happens, our participants reported resolving it quickly and easily (*e.g.,* "*The best and quickest solution you have is to undo, we roll back and* [fix it]." [D1]; "*typically, it is solved really quick*" [D2]), and often using merging tools (*e.g.,* "*we don't have to do much manually*" [D8]). Although automatic merging was used, our participants also explained that they manually checked each conflict, revealing that it is not entirely trusted.

Breaking changes

Scenario. A developer/team changed some parts of the code, rendering the work of another developer or team unusable or obsolete.

Related literature. Researchers consider breaking changes problematic, not only for developers who receive the change and have to understand and adapt their code, but also for developers who are making a change that might break the functionalities of many clients [3]. Literature shows investigations (*e.g.,* [22]) on the effect of dependencies that break other people's work, and proposed methods to address subsequent problems, at the scale of both single system (*e.g.,* [10, 72]) and ecosystems (*e.g.,* [32, 61]).

Interviews' outcome. The reaction of our participants was different according to the *origin* of the breaking changes. When the origin was considered to be *external* to the team or company or when participants felt they had opportunity for neither intervening nor displaying their disappointment to 'the breaker', they accept the breaking changes with no strong negative emotions but rather as inevitable. This happened even when resolving the issue might take long time (*e.g.,* "*more than year*" [D2]) or when it resulted in large operational or maintenance costs (*e.g.,* "*this* [break] *was costing the company many thousands of dollars per minute.*" [D7]).

However, when the origin was *internal* to the company/team, participants reported strong negative emotions (*e.g.,* frustration). This seemed in part due to the mismatch between the expected communication that is made possible by being in the same company/team, and the "waste" of time spent finding the cause of the issue, which might in turn be resolved relatively quickly (*e.g.,* "*I spend a couple of hours to find out the error* [...] *fixed in 5 minutes.*" [D3] and "*I spent a day fixing the problem I spent three days finding.*" [D8]). Generally, breaking changes leading to syntactical errors were not considered an issue, because they could easily be spotted with static analysis tools (e.g. pre-compilers) and fixed. In effect, those particular breaks were considered as a direct consequence of the lack of coordination effort from the person introducing the breaking code [D1]. Some of our participants insisted that breaking changes when the origin of the break is internal to the team or company should be handled more smoothly and proactively. For example, some would prefer stricter rules to avoid internal breaking changes: "*people breaking other's people code* [...]*, I'd like to see management being more rigorous about it*" [D8].

Receiving a code change

Managing internal breaking changes is the most problematic scenario that emerged from our analysis, in this section, we analyze how developers deal with changes made by peer developers working on the same project.

Our participants reported that they investigated changes in the code-base when they were notified of them (*e.g.,* via automatic emails from versioning systems). However, they mostly did so to discover whether they had an impact on their own code. While they are not interested in building a holistic view of the whole code base, they use this approach to discover whether the changes will impact their own work. In doing so, they first need to assess how relevant the change is to their current or upcoming work to decide whether or not to investigate further. In some rare occasions, developers use this opportunity to explore other's work not as it impacts theirs, but from a style/aesthetics perspective, looking at coding styles, norms, approaches, and solutions, especially is changes are emitted by a respected colleague (for learning/inspiration) or a novice (for peer reviewing).

When our participants reported discovering an error caused by a change made by someone else, their most prominent complain regarded the lack of coordination that they felt should have accompanied the change (*e.g.,* they would have expected an "heads up" email). However, in the case of clear syntactic errors (*e.g.,* compilation errors, or runtime errors generating a stack trace), participants did not feel the kind of frustration they expressed in the case of semantic errors (*e.g.,* caused by a library that changes some sorting order, therefore impacting the dependent code) or unclear alteration in the behavior. In fact, semantic errors required participants to perform a deeper and more time-consuming analysis to understand their cause [D3.(47,49), D8.(28,29,36)].

Once they found the cause, they explained they proceeded to measure the impact on their code by, for example, measuring how many files or lines of code needs to be changed (as D8 explained: *"I measure the impact of a change* [looking at] *how many files/lines it affects. A few? Hundreds?"*). Usually, the developers receiving the breaking change were those automatically responsible of adapting and fixing their own code. However, when a change had a deep impact on the code-base, and required more information about the change (*e.g.,* the rationale of the change) and the code-base, developers usually wanted to contact the author.

Participants also reported that, when the change introduced a defect, those receiving were responsible for deciding to file an issue report against the change to the change author (*e.g.,* D5 explained: *"if the bug is in your code, it's your bug to fix.* [...] *I send a bug request."*) [D3.(06,09,31), D5.06], or, occasionally, if the fix took little time, they would directly change the code to fix it (D3 said: *"If it's small I just fix it and notify the author"*) [D3.59, D5.107, D8.38, D9.60]. The time spent fixing the problem in the code does not seem to bring frustration *per se* (*e.g., "Diagnosing is almost always harder than to fix it. With the majority of bugs, once you know where the problem is, it's easy to fix"* [D8.29]). The rationale to fix it directly is that the developer already has the necessary information, which would require time to share with the author of the faulty code.

Some participants mentioned that the lack of testing contributes to faulty changes being committed to the repository (*e.g., "we are really bad at testing* [...], *you pull and you get a file you try to run and it fails"* [D9], *"If I'd tested it better, I wouldn't have put [this code] in the build"* [D5]). Nevertheless they also warned that running all the tests for each change would be too expensive (*"all tests, to run them all, it would take 3 weeks. Unfeasible to take 3 weeks for each check in"* [D6]). They also warned that testing performed on a setup might unreliable on a different one (*"we test and it's all good, but then they test on their end and it might break* [...]. *It's something to do with customizing."* [D2]), and that many semantic changes could not be detected by tests (*"even if there are tests that check* [most] *things, you'd still end up with edge cases.* [...] *You still need to see that you break, and then react, and then fix it"* [D6]).

EXPLORATORY INVESTIGATION: INTERPRETATION

Teamwork Collaboration Is Coordination

The terminology used in many disciplines [51] defines coordination as *"managing dependencies between activities,"* and collaboration as *"peers working together."* In this light, what participants consider as collaboration in teamwork is mostly *coordination*, needed to organize the individual work toward achieving a shared goal.

By analyzing the data from the interviews, coordination emerged—after individual work—as the dominant interaction level when working in team, rather than collaboration. In particular, our participants described that:

1. They spend most the time doing individual work;
2. Most of their interaction is to coordinate (*e.g.,* through daily stand-ups);
3. In their work, collaboration happens infrequently and on a need basis (*e.g.,* with (bi-)weekly sprint meetings).
4. Most of the time, their intention for collaboration is coordination leading to individual work.

By abstracting the explanations of interviewees, we model developers' interaction in three levels (from lowest to highest degree of interaction): individual work, coordination, and collaboration. Individual work corresponds to no interaction (*e.g.,* a developer working on her own), while collaboration means developers working together at the same time on the same (sub)task (*e.g.,* pair programming). Coordination is an intermediate level of interaction, where developers interact but are not working together on the same (sub)task (*e.g.,* during task assignment).

An activity is a working state that can be placed as a point on the corresponding level of interaction. In a set of activities done to accomplish a certain subtask (*i.e.,* 'working situation'), particular events often serve as a transition between levels of interaction, for example, steps from individual work to coordination (*e.g.,* "[when a file is locked] *we just* [ask]*: 'hey what are you working on? And then when you think I can do it?' to the author."* [D2.10]), and from coordination to collaboration (*e.g., "sometimes we* [...] *get together and talk about* [similar things], *then realize how we can do these things together and do them together"* [D11.45]). Figure 2 depicts our model of developers' interactions.

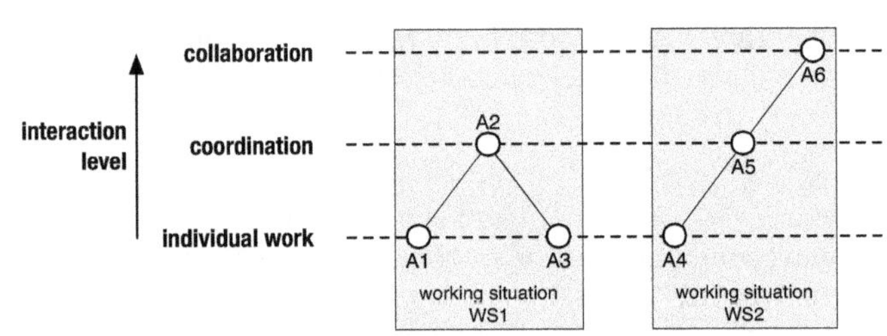

Figure 2. Model of developers' interactions in working situations

Figure 2 shows two working situations: In the first (WS1), a developer doing individual work asks another developer to make a change in their code (*e.g., "I asked one of the guys: '*[...] *I need a method that would return* [a special object], *can you write* [it] *for me?' He was able to write* [it] *and knew exactly where to go"* [D3.(09,15)]). This requires going from individual work (A1) to coordination (A2) when asking to make a change to the other, and back to individual work (A3) when they reach an agreement, without reaching a state of collaboration. In the second situation (WS2), two developers decide to work together on a subtask. This requires moving from individual work (A4) to coordination (A5) when they decide, then to collaboration (A6) for the actual work.

The steps between the different levels of interaction in the model are not necessarily discrete: Intermediate interaction levels can be reached. For example, while the activity of task assignment can generally be placed on the coordination level, when the task assignment is *discussed together in a meeting* it can be put on a level between coordination and collaboration.

Implications

Our participants report that most of their time is spent in doing individual work, while, unexpectedly, they report to spend very little time *collaborating* on the same subtask. A direct consequence is that interactions revolving around coordination are a more actionable area, with better research opportunities and with greater potential impact, than areas considering purely the collaboration aspects. For example, better support to communication would have more relevance than tools for concurrent real-time coding.

In addition, techniques for supporting information sharing among developers should take into account that developers spend most of their time doing individual work. Considering that most of this individual work is spent in the development environment (the IDE) [48], tools that support coordination within the IDE have potential to lead to greater impact.

The role of information.

In our study, we uncovered how available information was pivotal in transitioning between levels of interaction (Figure 3). This happened when our participants acted on information they had already acquired earlier, reacted to incoming information, or sought out to gather new information, for example, through communication or by understanding code changes done by colleagues.

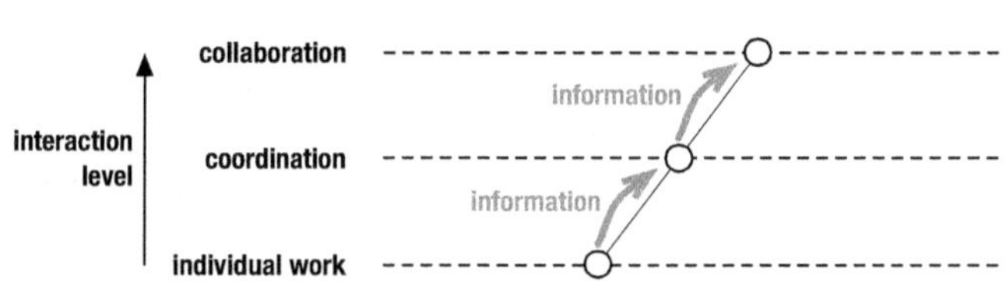

Figure 3. The role of information in developers' interaction

Researchers have been studying the importance of information sharing for teamwork over the years from different angles. For example, Cataldo *et al.* introduced the notion of *socio-technical congruence*, and provided evidence that developers who share information when making changes in dependent software components complete tasks in less time [15]. Other researchers similarly showed that missing information correlates with coordination problems and project failures [14, 63, 47]. Ko *et al.* analyzed the information needs of developers in collocated teams and found they have difficulties in answering questions related to information about colleagues' work and software component dependencies [45].

From our interviews, developers reported to know how to deal with the investigated scenarios involving imperfect information, except when they received an internal breaking change. We suggest that this is connected to how easy it is to access the information they need to address the problem. Analyzing the ways developers/teams successfully deal with a condition of imperfect information, we see that the solutions to the problematic scenarios require information to be shared in two ways: (1) via direct communication (*e.g.,* during a meeting), and (2) by making it visible (*e.g.,* in a tool).

Scenario	Needed Information	
	Communicated	Visible
Task assignment	✓	✓
Simultaneous changes	✗	✓
Breaking changes	✗	✗

Table 2. Information in investigated scenarios

Table 2 shows that for non-problematic scenarios, the needed information is communicated or visible. In the case of task assignment, the inefficiencies are avoided by centralizing the task assignment to the team leader, who has all the information "visible" in mind, or by conducting group meetings in which the information is communicated. Other researchers report evidence of this behavior: Begel *et al.* described that industrial program managers and developers have regular team meetings to effectively prioritize bugs and to coordinate component completion schedules [8]; and Guzzi *et al.* reported that when open source software developers meet in person, they manage to advance the coordination of their projects better [31]. In the case of simultaneous changes that were not avoided with the team policies (*i.e.,* through modularization and technical locks), the information necessary to solve the merge conflict is immediately visible through the merge tool. In their analysis of parallel development practices, de Souza and Redmiles similarly reported that issues were averted through the mediation of configuration management tools [22]. In the case of breaking changes, we suggest that the needed information is neither communicated in time nor easily accessible/visible. As a result, developers can spend a long time finding the information they need to coordinate. This is in agreement with other studies that report how breaking changes are due to missing information and lead to significant loss of time (*e.g.,* [61]).

Implications

Our analysis showed that the efforts spent in gaining the information developers are missing can be a source of negative emotions. This underlines the importance of information sharing practices, both active (*e.g.,* communicated) and passive (*e.g.,* visible via a tool).

Researchers proposed a number of tools (*e.g.,* Palantìr [65] and FASTDash [9]) to detect merge conflicts and tested them in laboratory settings with seeded conflicts. These tools helped developers to spend less time to resolve conflicts and encouraged communication. An interesting venue for future research is to verify the overall impact of these tools on teams whose structure maps the software architecture, as our participants reported not encountering this issue.

In addition, in most of our investigated scenarios, we observed that—unexpectedly—developers already had means to deal with missing information, or did not considered these scenarios as issues. In contrast, the results of the study by deSouza and Redmiles put in evidence the significant differences that two unrelated companies have when they deal with the management of dependencies and the underlying information sharing [22]. This suggests that what is considered a critical issue for a company/project could not important for another. As a consequence, it is important, when investigating potential problems generated by lack of information, to first study whether and how the target developers already employ any method to supply this missing information.

Changes and dependencies

As de Souza and Redmiles explained: "it is not possible to study changes in software systems without studying dependencies" [22]. In this light, our analysis of coordination and receiving changes is related to the work by Begel *et al.* [8] and by de Souza and Redmiles [22].

Begel *et al.* conducted a survey of Microsoft developers, testers, and program managers to see how these coordinate on dependencies (*e.g.,* tasks) within the same team and among different teams. The study reported that most Microsoft developers (63%) minimize code dependencies to mitigate problems. This is similar to our interviewees who use software modularity to avoid inefficient task assignment or merge conflicts. Similarly to our findings, Begel *et al.* also reported that lack of communication often led to coordination problems, and that email is the common means by which developers kept track dependencies. In contrast, our study outlines the difference between internal and external dependencies and changes. Begel *et al.* found that internal dependencies are managed by "send[ing] an email and pay[ing] a personal visit to the person blocking their work," [8], and surveyed developers do not report any negative emotion. Our findings underlined that, in the case of internal breaking changes, the process preceding the communication with the person blocking the work (*i.e.,* finding the source of the problem) is cause of dissatisfaction and frustration in cases where the expected communication did not take place. Moreover, the two studies present different definitions of *external* dependencies and breaking changes: (1) According to Begel *et al.*, dependencies are 'external' if in different teams within the same company, with which it is possible to communicate personally; (2) according to our findings, dependencies are 'external' if in different companies, with which it is extremely difficult to communicate. In the former case, Begel *et al.* reported that developers have to maintain personal communication with external teams to remain updated of changes, and the existence of unexpected changes from external teams generates anxiety. In the latter case, our interviewed developers did not report anxiety (even though unexpected changes happen and lead to loss of time), rather acceptance of the situation as part of the natural business model of the industry.

In their work, de Souza and Redmiles investigated the strategies software developers use to handle the effect of software dependencies and changes in two industrial software development teams [22]. The two teams deal with *internal* dependencies according to our definition. One team (MVP) allows parallel development and the modularity of the system is low, the other team (MCW) focuses on modularity by using a reference architecture. Our interviewed developers have complains similar to those in the MCW team, which also has strikingly similar practices: In both studies these teams avoid inefficient task assignment with modularity, their developers have problems identifying their impact network (they do not know who is consuming their code or whether changes can modify the component they depend on) and are only interested in changes in particular parts of the architecture that impact them. Moreover, developers in both MCW and our study have expectation that major changes are accompanied by notifications about their implications, yet are worried about information overload resulting from too frequent notifications. Conversely, the MVP practices seems to align with our participants' description of an ideal scenario where emails are sent to update about changes, everybody reads notification emails, management urges developers to notify about breaking changes, and such email even suggest courses of action to be taken to minimize the impact. As a result, despite the parallel development, coordination in MVP seems smoother than in our participants' experiences. One important characteristic of MVP, mentioned by de Souza and Redmiles, is that most developers have worked on the project for at least two years, and their experience could also be the cause of the difference with MWC, which is a newer project. Our results, though, do not seem to corroborate this hypothesis, since interviewed developers reported similar issues regardless of project maturity and personal experience. Our additional analysis of code changes looks at coordination from a low level perspective; we found that most information developers need to coordinate is typically available, but not necessarily accessible.

Implications

Our study confirms that lack of coordination leads to late discovery of unexpected errors or behaviors in the code, followed by a time-consuming analysis to find the code changes that are the source of the issue. This calls for better support for coordination when developers make and receive changes, and for when they need to investigate a change to determine its impact. As the existing body of research suggests, impact analysis and support for change understanding in software development scenario remains problematic. Research prototypes have not yet reached widespread usage in the IDE, and our findings underlines the substantial practical relevance of further research in these areas.

The differences between coordination practices between our interviewees' teams and the MVP team described by de Souza and Redmill [22] are an interesting venue for future research. In fact, compelling is the hypothesis that the modularity adopted by our interviewees' teams and MWC could create asymmetries in engineers' perceptions of dependencies [30], thus being at the basis of the differences and generating the reported coordination issues.

By investigating how developers currently handle received code changes in the IDE, we realized that they do many tasks manually, and spend a lot of effort to collect and remember change information. The data that would help developers in their tasks is available (*e.g.,* data recorded by the versioning systems), but not easily accessible. This implies that better support for integrating change information in the IDE is needed and it would impact development and coordination.

DESIGNING AND EVALUATING BELLEVUE

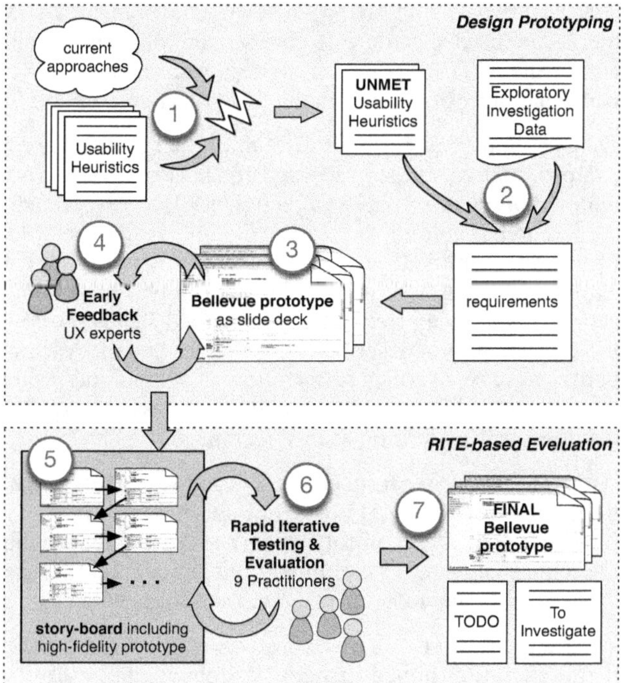

Figure 4. The research method applied in the second phase

Building upon our findings from our interviews, we aimed to design a tool to help developers anticipate, investigate, and react to breaking changes in a collaborative development environment. Figure 4 outlines the process.

Design requirements

We first analyzed the current approaches for receiving changes in the IDE under the light of widespread usability heuristics [56] (Point 1 in Figure 4). We found several unmet heuristics that, together with the data collected in the exploratory investigation, we used as a basis to derive requirements for our IDE extension to improve receiving changes and support teamwork (Point 2).

Recognition over recall

"Memory for recognizing things is better than memory for recalling things" [49].

Once a developer decides to merge a received change with the local version, the information about the integrated change disappears. For this reason, when developers encounter a bug, they must recall which change occured and whether any of them could have generated the problem. One participant explained that the frustration when he encounters a bug comes from *"figuring out where the problem is: Trying to figure out what really has changed"* [D5]. We suggest that when looking for the cause of a bug, developers' memory can be aided by tools to navigate change history, but existing tools require to switch from the current development context, and typically give the information outside of the development context.

Visibility of system status

"The system should always keep users informed about what is going on" [56].

Once changes are integrated, development tools provide no distinction between code already present before merge, and the newly integrated one. Therefore, there is no clear visibility of the system status with respect to its history. *"It's kind of impossible to know every single line of code that everybody else on your team changed"* [D3]. While historical information is available, it typically resides in dedicated tools or views, out of the current development context, thus the status is neither self-evident nor easily accessible: *"there isn't really an easy method [...] that let you see [that] these ten files are different from what you had in your current time"* [D5].

Clearly Marked Exits

"A system should never capture users in situations that have no visible escape" [55].

In software engineering, code repositories typically provide change history which gives developers an escape: If they find something not working after they merged some changes into their local working copy, they can roll back to the status prior to the merging. Problems with this approach are: (1) The exits are not evident, and (2) the exit strategy is binary.

The first issues means developers sometimes do not realize that their problems could be addressed by undoing the merge, instead of trying to find an error in their own code. The second issue means that developers can only undo *all* the merged changes at once, although the error can be caused by a mistake in a small fraction of the changed code. Once the code is rolled back, developers have to reconsider all the undone changes and realize which ones could have caused the error, without having the full IDE context at disposal, but only the change information, and integrate all the unrelated changes back again. D1 explained: *"It's a loss of time, we have to roll back, figure out* [what the problem was]*, and roll again. It's a loss of time, definitely."*

Help and Documentation

"*[Documentation should]* be easy to search, focused on the user's task, list concrete steps to be carried out, and not be too large" [56].

In development processes, documentation also consists in the explanations software developers write as they commit their changes to the shared repository. It also includes other sources of information, such as descriptions of work items or bugs, stored in bug management or work item management tools. These pieces of information are accessible to the developer, and the commit messages are available to inspect upon receiving code changes, but once the changes are integrated they disappear, unless the user performs a number of steps navigating the history of the code in specialized windows or applications. Additionally, comments in the code commit and the work management tools are often disjointed. For example D5 complained: *"When you get the latest* [changed files] *you get tons of files"*; he found it very difficult to search the necessary help or information due to information overload. Finally, when developers integrate more than one commit into their local copy, often they see only the last commit message, even though a line of code could have been changed several times between their local copy and the current status.

Help users recognize, diagnose, and recover from errors

Current code change management in IDEs make it difficult to recognize and diagnose errors generated by integrated code changes, because they are not visible and the history has to be analyzed outside of the current development context. One interviewed developer explained that, despite the availability of external history tools, *"one of the problems is trying to figure out what really has changed [and] what's the impact on your code"* [D5]. In fact, as D3 explained, external tools are not helpful because *"version control gives you a list of files that changed and not the specific lines"*: Seeing exactly which part changed and how takes many steps. Moreover, the only possibility to recover from errors is to do a complete undo of the merged changes, while it might be be enough to modify a small part of code to fix the error.

System design requirements

To address our current concerns with imperfect or missing information in development tasks, we suggest the following requirements for development tools:

(1) Received code changes should always be visible, (2) Information should be provided in context, both semantic (code) and procedural (history, project) without undue actions by the user, both at the project and file level (3) History of code chunks should be easily accessible, possibly using progressive disclosure to prevent information fatigue (4) Error identification ad diagnostics should be supported through a fluid integration of code history, (5) Code changes should be reversible at the sub-file level, and (6) Requiring context switches to acquire the necessary knowledge to solve a task should be avoided.

Prototype and evaluation

Consequently, we devised an IDE extension, named BELLEVUE, to fulfill the requirement outlined above and to serve as a tool to explore our preliminary design ideas (Point 3 in Figure 4). The prototype allowed us to communicate our ideas to various experienced designers and practitioners at Microsoft, and to get their feedback, reveal early problems, and improve the initial concept (Point 4 in Figure 4).

We devised a detailed storyboard including a high-fidelity prototype of BELLEVUE (Point 5). This was implemented as a PowerPoint presentation with a sequence of believable action steps of interaction with the prototype. Each step was devised to let the participants of the evaluation phase observe what was happening, explain what they would do, and describe the effects they would expect as a consequence of their actions. We used this prototype to evaluate BELLEVUE with professional software developers, using the RITE (Rapid Iterative Testing & Evaluation) method [54], to evaluate and identify problems in the prototype, quickly fix them, and then empirically verify the efficacy of the fixes (Point 6).

Participants in the RITE study were selected among a population with the following characteristics: More than three years as a professional developer, more than one year in the current company, and more than three months in the current team. Moreover, interviewees had to spend at least 20 hours per week on writing and editing code, their team had to use a source control management system, and they had to have at least browsed the change history, encountered a change merge, or used the file diff comparison view in the month before the RITE. Evaluation invitees were thanked for their participation by a gratuity in the form of Microsoft software.

Each session occured in a full usability lab on the Microsoft campus, and was video recorded for later analysis. To mitigate the *moderator acceptance bias* [28], we explained that the researcher guiding the session did *not* created the product. Moreover, to mitigate any *social desirability bias* [28], and to encourage discussion, the storyboard plot was describing the actions taken by a proxy developer named James. Following the storyboard plot described by the slides and the researcher, participants were solicited to follow a think-aloud protocol, and indicate what they saw, would do, and would expect as a result of their actions on each screen page.

After 9 iterations we reached a stable and validated design. At the end of the process (Point 7 in Figure 4), we had: (1) the finalized BELLEVUE prototype, (2) a set of changes to implement but that were not eventually integrated, and (3) a set of candidate aspects to be investigated as future work.

We designed BELLEVUE as a prototype code editing and navigation solution aimed at being a lightweight, ready to be used, without requiring developers to change their working style. It takes the historical change information that is already available, but currently neither visible nor easily accessible, and displays it in a non-obtrusive way. BELLEVUE offers an interactive view that shows detailed historical information for files and specific chucks with respect to a previous version. We detail the features of BELLEVUE, as they were at the end of the RITE phase, and the feedback from participants (mentioned as R1–9). The final version of the slide-deck used in the RITE is available as a file accompanying this paper.[1]

Recognizable changed files and blocks

BELLEVUE decorates changed files with an arrow (Figure 5, Point 1), and denotes changed lines with a blue[2] colored sign, both at a fine-grained granularity (Point 2), to see them in the context of the current text window, and a more coarse-grained one (Point 3), to see them in the context of the entire file. One can decide (Point 4) to see only the files that were just merged into the current local version. This design supports recognition over recall: Once new changes are merged into the local version, their traces remain visible. It also enhances the visibility of the system status, with respect to changes.

RITE participants' feedback—All the participants appreciated this feature. In particular, they liked that it helps filtering out irrelevant information when looking for the reason of an error that could have been introduced by a received change: *"Knowing what I can ignore is huge, the larger the project, the more beneficial it comes"* [R1]. Concerning the way in which changes are made recognizable, some users did not find it intuitive, or appropriate: *"I'd prefer a bar or something*

[1] Also available at: `http://www.st.ewi.tudelft.nl/~guzzi/`

[2] This color has been chosen because it is currently considered a neutral color in the IDE. As opposed to green or red, which are often associated to versioning systems or debuggers.

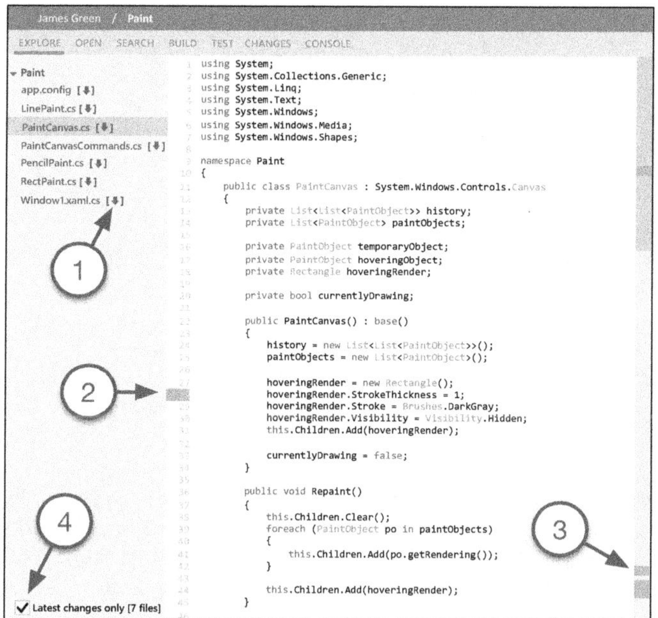

Figure 5. Recognizable changed files and blocks, and filtering

much more visibile [than a blue-colored sign] *to see that it's different*" [R2]. Nevertheless, after they continued in the scenario and experienced the following features of BELLEVUE, they withdrew their concerns. Some participants suggested to let the users personalize the color to denote changes; other participants suggested to use different colors to clearly distinguish added, removed, or modified lines, as it currently happens in tools that display code differences.

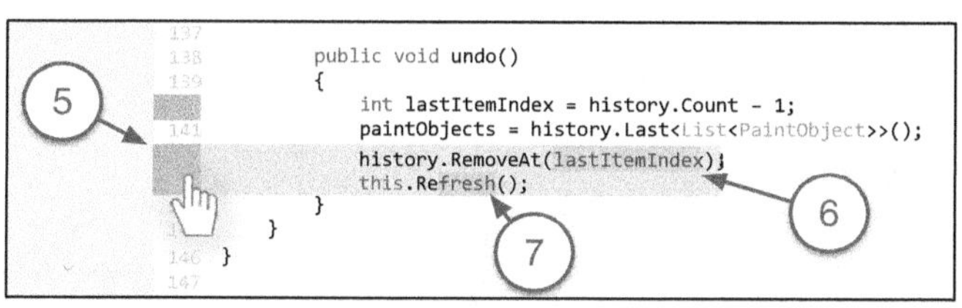

Figure 6. Visibility of changes' effect by mouse hovering

Visible changes' effect

To show the effect of the change in the code, the user can hover on any colored block to see the latest changes. For example, in Figure 6, the user decided to look at the changed block that was not visible in Figure 5. Then, by hovering on the colored sign on the left (Point 5), (s)he can see the effect of that change: The argument of the `RemoveAt` method call has changed (Point 6), and the `Refresh` method call has replaced a call present before on the same object (Point 7).

RITE participants' feedback—This feature was introduced in the third iteration of the tool, after considering the feedback received by the first participants. As an example, one participant had some expectations when hovering the lines indicating a change: "*toggle to highlight what's different from the last version, to quickly diagnose, I don't need a true side by side*" [R3]. Once introduced, this feature was well received by all the remaining participants (*e.g.*, "*ok, good! I can see here how* [this part] *changed!*" [R6]), because it also helps with the progressive disclosure of the information about the changes: Users can quickly verify whether the changes seem relevant and, only if necessary, investigate more.

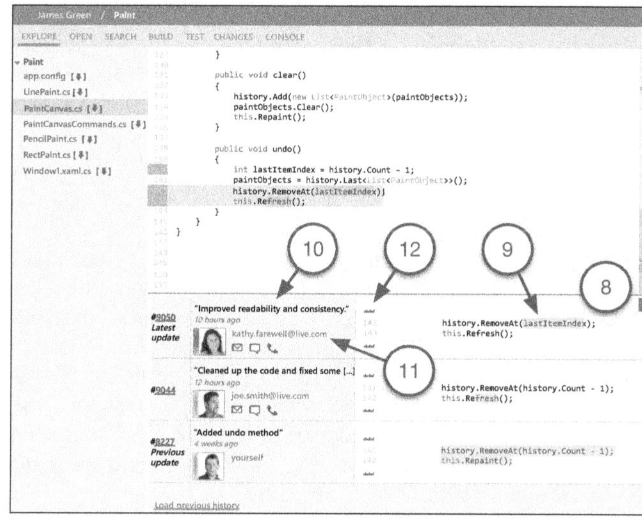

Figure 7. Accessible historical details

Accessible historical details

In BELLEVUE the user can see the code history of any block that was changed with respect to the previous local version. This is achieved with one click on the colored sign on the left of the interesting block. For example, in Figure 7, the user decided to further inspect the history of lines 142–143 because they led to an unexpected behavior. Once the block is clicked, a pane appears from the bottom (Point 8): It contains the historical details of the changes happened to that block since the last update of the user. Each item represents a change and shows the changed code with respect to the previous commit (Point 9), the commit message to document it (Point 10), and the contact information of the change author (Point 11). The changed code only regards the chosen block, but it is possible to extend it by clicking on the '...' before and after. It is also possible to inspect also previous history (Point 12).

RITE participants' feedback—As for the other steps, before showing what would happen next, the interviewer asked the participants how they would interact with the design and what their expectations would be. In particular, for this feature, the interviewer asked what participants expected it would happen by clicking on the colored sign on the left (Point 5). In this way, we learned that the participants wanted to have something similar to a diff with the previous version (*e.g.*, "*I'd do a compare versus the previous version, and just look at those particular changes*" [R3]). The BELLEVUE solution was, thus, very much appreciated and it often exceeded their expectations: "*All the details! This is exactly what I was looking for: It tells me who* [...] *and it tells me what did each one, and how long ago!*" [R1]; "*oh I see, so this is exactly what I was looking for. It's even better!*" [R8]. Seeing the version that could have introduced the error (*i.e.*, #9044) was a clearly marked exit: Some participants considered to recover the error by reverting that particular change, because that would not imply reverting entirely to a more complex change set.

Through the iterations, we added the clickable revision number (to open a panel to see all the changes in a revision), and the hovering function to show the full commit comment.

Participants' suggestions that we did not eventually include in the iterative evaluation, due to time reasons, mostly regarded the possibility of selecting specific parts to see the history, instead of the contiguous block (*e.g., "I want to see the whole function* [history, by] *right clicking on a function*" [R2]).

Editable code

BELLEVUE allows editing code while reviewing the history (Figure 8), because it integrates history within the active editing context. It also highlights the new code differently (Point 13 in Figure 9) and automatically adds a new item to the list (Point 14) to put it in its historical context. This differs from current approaches for visualizing history, which involve opening a distinct context or application, and do not make it possible to edit code (*e.g.,* to fix a bug) and see history in the same context, at the same time.

RITE participants' feedback—This feature was very well received by all the participants. In particular, many were positively surprised and realized the possibilities of having code changes better integrated in the IDE: "*I have a diff view, but I am not trapped in that* [...] *I got my editor and my diff view, so the split view is very very helpful* [...]. *Let me do what I want to do, while looking at the information I needed to make my change*" [R1]; "*Now that I see, I know what is happening* [...]. *That is intuitive to me: Just clicking, edit, and go*" [R7]. They also appreciated the immediate feedback of the change in the local history (Figure 9): "*Oh, I like it shows it's local*" [R4].

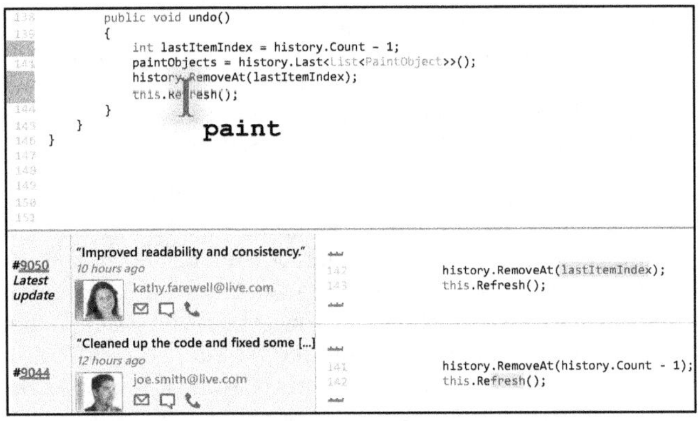

Figure 8. Editable code while accessing historical details

Contacting change's author

The author's photo and contact pane is inspired by CARES [32], a tool to help developers discover and choose relevant colleagues to speak with when seeking information or coordinating action. In BELLEVUE, the communication icons are for contacting the author of a given commit. Figure 10 shows the email template automatically generated by clicking on the email icon for commit #9044; it includes the diff with the previous commit, for easier reference.

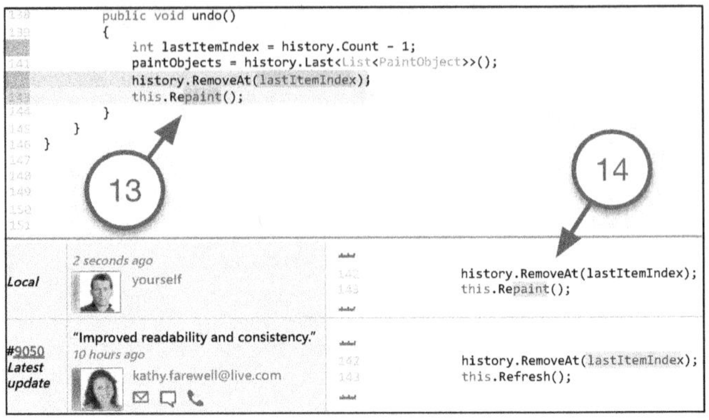

Figure 9. New local change added to history

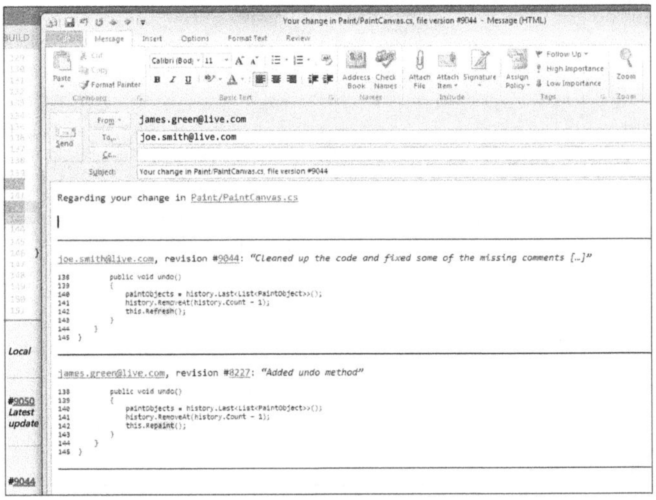

Figure 10. Contacting the author of a change from the IDE

RITE participants' feedback—The social interaction within the view was extremely well received by all the participants. They especially appreciated the possibility of quickly using email and IM: "*I really like that. I'd click on chat*" [R6]. When discussing the email they would write to the author of the buggy change, they all specify the things they would like to ideally see in the email, and when they see it, they like how it includes everything they wanted: "*That is perfect.* [It is] *exactly what I would have sent*" [R1]. However, some would have liked to obtain the diff view as BELLEVUE shows it in the IDE, while "*now it's like standard diff*" [R6].

Participants' suggestions not integrated for time reasons are: Adding an *email all* feature, change the email title to give information about method and class in which the new change is taking place, support for copy and paste from history to email, and add communication clients (*e.g.,* IRC or Skype).

Evaluation Debriefing

After each RITE session, participants filled two short questionnaires about their experience with the tool: A System Usability Scale (SUS) questionnaire [11] and a proprietary 7-point Likert scale questionnaire standardly used at Microsoft. The SUS answers were overall positive: The mean SUS score is 85.1 (answers had $\sigma = 0.66$, on average), which is considered a high value across different domains [5, 6, 67]; as an example, the statement "*I think that I would like to use this product frequently*" scored 4.7/5.0 ($\sigma = 0.50$). The proprietary survey was equally positive: Mean score was 5.4/7.0 (the higher the better: items only included positive wordings [40]), with $\sigma = 1$ on average. For example participants gave 5.4/7.0 ($\sigma = 1.13$) to the statement "*This product has powerful functionality and excels at what it was designed for*" and "*This product is something I am likely to share information about*" scored 5.9/7.0 ($\sigma = 0.78$).

COLLABORATIVE SOFTWARE DEVELOPMENT TOOLS

Coordination in software development has been studied in the fields of Software Engineering and Computer Supported Cooperative Work since the 1980s, and researchers have produced a wide range of analyses and tools [62].

BELLEVUE uses historical change information to support developers' coordination. Sarma *et al.* present a comprehensive review of coordination tools and defines a framework that classifies those technologies according to multiple coordination paradigms [66]. In this framework, tools such as versioning systems and issue tracking systems support the development process and are at the basis of the more sophisticated tools that provide meaningful and automatically aggregated information: These are research prototypes and industrial applications conceived to better support developers coordination in the IDE. Such tools includes full-fledged platforms, specific workspace awareness solutions, information discovery approaches, and code information visualization tools.

Full-fledged platforms, such as Jazz [39] and Mylyn [25], are at the far end of the spectrum in terms of complexity [66], and aim at transforming the IDE experience. Jazz, or Rational Team Concert, is an IDE platform, built on top of Eclipse and Visual Studio, that integrates several aspects of the software development process, including integrated planning, tracking of developer effort, project dashboards, reports, and process support. Relations between artifacts can be defined and leveraged to gather project information. Jazz also offer support for communication within the IDE (*e.g.,* instant messaging), more advanced than BELLEVUE. Mylyn and its successor, Tasktop Dev [70], are based on Eclipse and Visual Studio and use task context to improve the productivity of developers and teams [43]; for example, they reduce information overload by providing developers with just the artifacts and information necessary for their current code modification task, and offer a comprehensive task repository to support teamwork by sharing information on tasks and their context. Both platforms support the creation of novel information (*e.g.,* tasks and work items, and relations among artifacts) to support developers productivity, and encourage a task or work item based approach to evolution. BELLEVUE aims at using already available data and visualizing it in a non-obtrusive way. Another example of improved communication in the IDE is REmail [4], which integrates developers' email communication in the IDE to support program comprehension; REmail can be used in conjunction with BELLEVUE to extend the communication feature of the latter.

Workspace awareness solutions, such as Palantìr [64], Lighthouse [19], CollabVS [23], Syde [34], and Crystal [12] are concerned with changes before they are committed to the source code repository, to address the conflict detection or real-time development information. For example, Syde tracks fine-grained real-time changes and alerts developers on the code editor and on a view when potential conflicts are emerging. Given the goal of these tools, differently from BELLEVUE, they do not show change history related information.

Interestingly, BELLEVUE design could be included in environments such as Mylyn and Jazz, and could be used concurrently with workspace awareness tools, in order to offer coordination support from a complementary perspective.

Information discovery approaches, such as Ariadne [20] and Tesseract [63], seek and assemble information to perform tasks such as expert finding and socio-technical network analysis. Recommender systems, such as Seahawk [57, 58], exploit change information and externally generated data to support software development and comprehension. Similarly to BELLEVUE some of these approaches also use historical code information to inform their users. Given their goal, they offer different, complementary views on data and integration with the development environment.

Code information visualization tools include the "blame" functionality offered, for example, by git or svn.This feature allows to see who did the last change on each line of code of a file, and when. Another tool is the concept presented by Rastkar and Murphy, in which the developer is able to see for a summary of commit messages connected to a line of code in the IDE [60]. In contrast, BELLEVUE offers an interactive view that shows detailed historical information for specific chucks with respect to a previous version. BELLEVUE always displays which files and lines changed, so it does not require the developer to actively ask for the commit message of the line, because the developer may not be already aware of the relevance of the file and the line. In our exploratory investigation narrowing down a breaking change to the file and line causing the issue emerged as one of the most problematic and time-consuming efforts for developers.

FINAL REMARKS

In our study we explored how to support developers' collaboration in teamwork. We focused on teamwork in the software implementation phase, which takes place in the IDE, and we conducted a qualitative investigation to uncover actionable areas for improvement. We identified internal breaking changes as one of the most important areas for improvement, because current IDE support for receiving changes is not optimal. Consequently, we designed BELLEVUE to enable developers better coordinate, by making historical information visible and more accessible in the IDE.

Overall, this paper makes the following main contributions:

1. A qualitative analysis indicating that teamwork needs mostly regard coordination, that developers are able to face scenarios considered problematic in literature, and that dealing with breaking changes is hard, but it only generates frustration if the breaker is internal to the project.

2. Recommendations on how to improve collaboration in teamwork in the software implementation phase, such as to focus on interactions revolving around coordination rather than on collaboration on the same (sub)task.

3. Requirements for a tool to support teamwork based on currently unmet usability heuristics and the results of our qualitative analysis. For example, to favor recognition of code changes over recall, and to increase the visibility of the codebase status with respect to received changes.

4. The design and evaluation of BELLEVUE, an IDE extension to support teamwork by improving the integration of code changes in the IDE. BELLEVUE makes received changes visible inside the editor, and makes the history of code chunks easily accessible using progressive disclosure.

ACKNOWLEDGMENTS

We want to express our gratitude to the anonymous reviewers, whose valuable comments significantly helped to improve the paper. We warmly thank Andrew Begel for his first-class feedback on the revision of this paper, and Monty Hammontree for his support during Anja's internship.

REFERENCES

1. Anvik, J., Hiew, L., and Murphy, G. C. Who should fix this bug? In *Proceedings of ICSE 2006 (28th International Conference on Software Engineering)*, ACM Press (2006), 361–370.
2. Anvik, J., and Murphy, G. C. Reducing the effort of bug report triage: Recommenders for development-oriented decisions. *ACM Transactions on Software Engineering and Methodology 20*, 3 (Aug. 2011), 10:1–10:35.
3. Arnold, R., and Bohner, S. *Software Change Impact Analysis*. Wiley-IEEE Computer Society Press, 1996.
4. Bacchelli, A., Lanza, M., and Humpa, V. RTFM (Read The Factual Mails) –augmenting program comprehension with REmail. In *Proceedings of CSMR 2011 (15th IEEE European Conference on Software Maintenance and Reengineering)* (2011), 15–24.
5. Bangor, A., Kortum, P., and Miller, J. An empirical evaluation of the system usability scale. *International Journal of Human-Computer Interaction 24*, 6 (July 2008), 574–594.
6. Bangor, A., Kortum, P., and Miller, J. Determining what individual SUS scores mean: Adding an adjective rating scale. *Journal of Usability Studies 4*, 3 (May 2009), 114–123.
7. Begel, A., Khoo, Y. P., and Zimmermann, T. Codebook: Discovering and exploiting relationships in software repositories. In *Proceedings of ICSE 2010 (32nd ACM/IEEE International Conference on Software Engineering)*, ACM (2010), 125–134.
8. Begel, A., Nagappan, N., Poile, C., and Layman, L. Coordination in large-scale software teams. In *Proceedings of the CHASE 2009 (2nd International Workshop on Cooperative and Human Aspects of Software Engineering)*, IEEE Computer Society (2009), 1–7.
9. Biehl, J. T., Czerwinski, M., Smith, G., and Robertson, G. G. FASTDash: a visual dashboard for fostering awareness in software teams. In *Proceedings of CHI 2007 (25th SIGCHI Conference on Human Factors in Computing Systems*, ACM (2007), 1313–1322.
10. Black, S. Computing ripple effect for software maintenance. *Journal of Software Maintenance 13*, 4 (Sept. 2001), 263–.
11. Brooke, J. SUS: A 'quick and dirty' usability scale. In *Usability Evaluation in Industry*, P. W. Jordan, B. Thomas, I. L. McClelland, and B. Weerdmeester, Eds. CRC Press, 1996, ch. 21, 189–194.
12. Brun, Y., Holmes, R., Ernst, M. D., and Notkin, D. Proactive detection of collaboration conflicts. In *Proceedings of ESEC/FSE 2011 (8th Joint Meeting on Foundations of Software Engineering)*, ACM (2011), 168–178.
13. Brun, Y., Holmes, R., Ernst, M. D., and Notkin, D. Early detection of collaboration conflicts and risks. *IEEE Transactions on Software Engineering 39*, 10 (2013), 1358–1375.
14. Cataldo, M., Mockus, A., Roberts, J. A., and Herbsleb, J. D. Software dependencies, work dependencies, and their impact on failures. *IEEE Transactions on Software Engineering 35*, 6 (Nov. 2009), 864–878.
15. Cataldo, M., Wagstrom, P. A., Herbsleb, J. D., and Carley, K. M. Identification of coordination requirements: Implications for the design of collaboration and awareness tools. In *Proceedings of CSCW 2006 (20th Anniversary Conference on Computer Supported Cooperative Work)*, ACM (2006), 353–362.
16. Chen, W.-N., and Zhang, J. Ant colony optimization for software project scheduling and staffing with an event-based scheduler. *IEEE Transactions on Software Engineering 39*, 1 (Jan. 2013), 1–17.
17. Cheng, L.-T., de Souza, C. R., Hupfer, S., Patterson, J., and Ross, S. Building collaboration into IDEs. *ACM Queue 1*, 9 (2003), 40–50.
18. Curtis, B., Krasner, H., and Iscoe, N. A field study of the software design process for large systems. *Communications of the ACM 31*, 11 (Nov. 1988), 1268–1287.
19. da Silva, I., Chen, P., der Westhuizen, C. V., Ripley, R., and van der Hoek, A. Lighthouse: Coordination through emerging design. In *Proceedings of ETX 2006 (OOPSLA Workshop on Eclipse Technology eXchange*, ACM Press (2006), 11–15.
20. de Souza, C. R. B., Quirk, S., Trainer, E., and Redmiles, D. F. Supporting collaborative software development through the visualization of socio-technical dependencies. In *Proceedings of GROUP 2007 (International ACM SIGGROUP Conference on Supporting Group Work)*, ACM (2007), 147–156.
21. de Souza, C. R. B., Redmiles, D., and Dourish, P. Breaking the code, moving between private and public work in collaborative software development. In *Proceedings of GROUP 2003 (International ACM SIGGROUP Conference on Supporting Group Work)*, ACM Press (2003), 105–114.
22. de Souza, C. R. B., and Redmiles, D. F. An empirical study of software developers' management of dependencies and changes. In *Proceedings of ICSE 2008 (30th ACM/IEEE International Conference on Software Engineering)*, ACM (2008), 241–250.
23. Dewan, P., and Hegde, R. Semi-synchronous conflict detection and resolution in asynchronous software development. In *Proceedings of ECSCW 2007 (10th European Conference on Computer Supported Cooperative Work)*, Springer (2007), 24–28.
24. Duggan, J., Byrne, J., and Lyons, G. J. A task allocation optimizer for software construction. *IEEE Software 21*, 3 (May 2004), 76–82.
25. Eclipse Foundation. Mylyn. [Software]. Available: https://www.eclipse.org/mylyn/ [Accessed: Jun 4, 2014], 2014.
26. Fritz, T., and Murphy, G. C. Using information fragments to answer the questions developers ask. In *Proceedings of ICSE 2010 (32nd ACM/IEEE International Conference on Software Engineering)*, ACM (2010), 175–184.
27. Frost, R. Jazz and the eclipse way of collaboration. *IEEE Software 24*, 6 (2007), 114–117.
28. Furnham, A. Response bias, social desirability and dissimulation. *Personality and Individual Differences 7*, 3 (1986), 385 – 400.
29. Grinter, R. Supporting articulation work using software configuration management systems. *Computer Supported Cooperative Work 5*, 4 (1996), 447–465.

30. Grubb, A. M., and Begel, A. On the perceived interdependence and information sharing inhibitions of enterprise software engineers. In *Proceedings of CSCW 2012 (ACM Conference on Computer Supported Cooperative Work)*, ACM (2012), 1337–1346.

31. Guzzi, A., Bacchelli, A., Lanza, M., Pinzger, M., and van Deursen, A. Communication in open source software development mailing lists. In *Proceedings of MSR 2013 (10th IEEE Working Conference on Mining Software Repositories)* (2013), 277–286.

32. Guzzi, A., Begel, A., Miller, J. K., and Nareddy, K. Facilitating enterprise software developer communication with CARES. In *Proceedings of ICSM 2012 (28th IEEE International Conference on Software Maintenance)* (2012), 527–536.

33. Hattori, L. *Change-centric Improvement of Team Collaboration*. PhD thesis, Università della Svizzera Italiana, February 2012.

34. Hattori, L., and Lanza, M. Syde: A tool for collaborative software development. In *Proceedings of ICSE 2010 (32nd ACM/IEEE International Conference on Software Engineering)* (2010), 235–238.

35. Hattori, L., Lanza, M., and D'Ambros, M. A qualitative analysis of preemptive conflict detection. Tech. Rep. 2011/05, University of Lugano, Sept. 2011.

36. Hegde, R., and Dewan, P. Connecting programming environments to support ad-hoc collaboration. In *Proceedings of ASE 2008 (23rd IEEE/ACM International Conference on Automated Software Engineering*, IEEE CS Press (2008), 178–187.

37. Henderson, R. M., and Clark, K. B. Architectural innovation: The reconfiguration of existing product technologies and the failure of established firms. *Administrative Science Quarterly 35*, 1 (Mar. 1990), 9–30.

38. Herbsleb, J. D., Mockus, A., and Roberts, J. A. Collaboration in software engineering projects: A theory of coordination. In *Proceedings ICIS 2006 (International Conference on Information Systems)* (2006).

39. IBM. Rational Team Concert. [Software]. Available: http://jazz.net/projects/rational-team-concert/ [Accessed: Jun 4, 2014], 2014.

40. Jeff, and Lewis, J. R. When designing usability questionnaires, does it hurt to be positive? In *Proceedings of CHI 2011 (29th Conference on Human Factors in Computing Systems)*, CHI '11, ACM (2011), 2215–2224.

41. Jeong, G., Kim, S., and Zimmermann, T. Improving bug triage with bug tossing graphs. In *Proceedings of ESEC/FSE 2009 (7th Joint Meeting on Foundations of Software Engineering)*, ACM (2009), 111–120.

42. Kasi, B. K., and Sarma, A. Cassandra: Proactive conflict minimization through optimized task scheduling. In *Proceedings of ICSE 2013 (35th International Conference on Software Engineering)*, IEEE Press (2013), 732–741.

43. Kersten, M., and Murphy, G. C. Using task context to improve programmer productivity. In *Proceedings of FSE 2006 (14th ACM SIGSOFT International Symposium on Foundations of Software Engineering)*, ACM (2006), 1–11.

44. Kirsch, L. J. The Management of Complex Tasks in Organizations: Controlling the Systems Development Process. *Organization Science 7*, 1 (Jan. 1996), 1–21.

45. Ko, A. J., DeLine, R., and Venolia, G. Information needs in collocated software development teams. In *Proceedings of ICSE 2007 (29th ACM/IEEE International Conference on Software Engineering)*, IEEE Computer Society (2007), 344–353.

46. Kraut, R. E., and Streeter, L. A. Coordination in software development. *Communications of the ACM 38*, 3 (Mar. 1995), 69–81.

47. Kwan, I., Schroter, A., and Damian, D. Does socio-technical congruence have an effect on software build success? a study of coordination in a software project. *IEEE Transactions on Software Engineering 37*, 3 (May 2011), 307–324.

48. LaToza, T. D., Venolia, G., and DeLine, R. Maintaining mental models: a study of developer work habits. In *Proceedings of ICSE 2006 (28th ACM International Conference on Software Engineering)*, ACM (2006), 492–501.

49. Lidwell, W., Holden, K., and Butler, J. *Universal Principles of Design, Revised and Updated: 125 Ways to Enhance Usability, Influence Perception, Increase Appeal, Make Better Design Decisions, and Teach through Design*, 2nd ed. Rockport Publishers, January 2010.

50. Lindlof, T. R., and Taylor, B. C. *Qualitative Communication Research Methods*. SAGE Publications, Inc., 2010.

51. Malone, T. W., and Crowston, K. The interdisciplinary study of coordination. *ACM Computing Surveys 26*, 1 (Mar. 1994), 87–119.

52. Martin, B., and Hanington, B. *Universal Methods of Design: 100 Ways to Research Complex Problems, Develop Innovative Ideas, and Design Effective Solutions*. Rockport Publishers, 2012.

53. Matter, D., Kuhn, A., and Nierstrasz, O. Assigning bug reports using a vocabulary-based expertise model of developers. In *Proceedings of MSR 2009 (6th International Working Conference on Mining Software Repositories)*, IEEE Computer Society (2009), 131–140.

54. Medlock, M. C., Wixon, D., Terrano, M., Romero, R. L., and Fulton, B. Using the RITE method to improve products: A definition and a case study. In *Proceedings of UPA 2002 (Usability Professionals Association)* (2002).

55. Molich, R., and Nielsen, J. Improving a human-computer dialogue. *Communications of the ACM 33*, 3 (Mar. 1990), 338–348.

56. Nielsen, J. 10 usability heuristics for user interface design. http://www.nngroup.com/articles/ten-usability-heuristics/, January 1995.

57. Ponzanelli, L., Bacchelli, A., and Lanza, M. Leveraging crowd knowledge for software comprehension and development. In *Proceedings of CSMR 2013 (17th European Conference on Software Maintenance and Reengineering)*, IEEE CS Press (2013), 57–66.

58. Ponzanelli, L., Bacchelli, A., and Lanza, M. Seahawk: Stack overflow in the ide. In *Proceedings of ICSE 2013 (35th International Conference on Software Engineering)*, IEEE CS Press (2013), 1295–1298.

59. Proenca, T., Moura, N., and van der Hoek, A. On the use of emerging design as a basis for knowledge collaboration. *New Frontiers in Artificial Intelligence 6284* (2010), 124–134.

60. Rastkar, S., and Murphy, G. C. Why did this code change? In *Proceedings of ICSE 2013 (35th ACM/IEEE International Conference on Software Engineering)*, IEEE Press (2013), 1193–1196.

61. Robbes, R., Lungu, M., and Röthlisberger, D. How do developers react to api deprecation?: The case of a smalltalk ecosystem. In *Proceedings of FSE 2012 (20th ACM SIGSOFT International Symposium on the Foundations of Software Engineering)*, ACM (2012), 56:1–56:11.

62. Sarma, A. A survey of collaborative tools in software development, isr. Tech. rep., Institute for Software Research, University of California, Irvine, 2005.

63. Sarma, A., Maccherone, L., Wagstrom, P., and Herbsleb, J. Tesseract: Interactive visual exploration of socio-technical relationships in software development. In *Proceedings of ICSE 2009 (31st International Conference on Software Engineering)*, IEEE Computer Society (Washington, DC, USA, 2009), 23–33.

64. Sarma, A., Noroozi, Z., and van der Hoekvan der Hoek. Palantìr: Raising awareness among configuration management workspaces. In *Proceedings of ICSE 2002 (23rd International Conference on Software Engineering)*, IEEE CS Press (2003), 444–454.

65. Sarma, A., Redmiles, D., and van der Hoek, A. Empirical evidence of the benefits of workspace awareness in software configuration management. In *Proceedings of FSE 2008 (16th ACM SIGSOFT International Symposium on Foundations of Software Engineering*, ACM Press (2008), 113–123.

66. Sarma, A., Redmiles, D., and van der Hoek, A. Categorizing the spectrum of coordination technology. *IEEE Computer 43*, 6 (June 2010), 61–67.

67. Sauro, J. *A Practical Guide to the System Usability Scale: Background, Benchmarks and Best Practices*. CreateSpace, 2011.

68. Sillito, J., Murphy, G. C., and Volder, K. D. Questions programmers ask during software evolution tasks. In *Proceedings of FSE 2006 (14th ACM SIGSOFT International Symposium on Foundations of Software Engineering)*, ACM (2006), 23–34.

69. Spencer, D. Card sorting: a definitive guide. http://boxesandarrows.com/card-sorting-a-definitive-guide/, April 2004.

70. Tasktop. Tasktop Dev. [Software]. Available: http://www.tasktop.com/dev [Accessed: Aug 1, 2014], 2014.

71. Whitehead, J. Collaboration in software engineering: A roadmap. In *Proceedings of FOSE 2007 (Future of Software Engineering)*, IEEE Computer Society (2007), 214–225.

72. Yau, S. S., Colofello, J. S., and MacGregor, T. Ripple effect analysis of software maintenance. In *Proceedings of COMPSAC*, IEEE Computer Society Press (1978), 60–65.

73. Zeller, A. The future of programming environments: Integration, synergy, and assistance. In *Proceedings of FOSE 2007 (Future of Software Engineering)*, IEEE Computer Society (2007), 316–325.

'Is' to 'Was': Coordination and Commemoration on Posthumous Wikipedia Biographies

Brian C. Keegan
College of Social Sciences and Humanities
Northeastern University
Boston, Massachusetts, USA
bkeegan@acm.org

Jed R. Brubaker
School of Information and Computer Sciences
University of California, Irvine
Irvine, California, USA
jed.brubaker@uci.edu

ABSTRACT
Following the deaths of notable people, Wikipedians incorporate this new knowledge by updating or creating biographical articles. Drawing on literature from death studies and peer production, we demonstrate how the creation of these "wikibituaries" requires complex coordination work and highlight processes of commemoration and memorialization within socio-technical systems. Using the corpus of 6,132 articles about people who died in 2012, we examine the network relationships and contribution dynamics of users who perform this work and identify behavioral and content dynamics on the biographical articles about the deceased. The collaborations that emerge from posthumous editing of these biographies are sites of significant activity that coalesce into complex but temporary collaborations. Based on these findings, we argue that Wikipedia has re-imagined the obituary into a genre for creating memory spaces in which the death of a subject prompts a form of "death work" involving the collective re-evaluation of article content and a transition into a new mode of data stewardship.

Author Keywords
Wikipedia; death; obituary; cybermemorial; collective memory; network analysis; peer production; death work

ACM Classification Keywords
H.5.3 Information Interfaces and Presentation: Group and Organization Interfaces (collaborative computing, computer supported cooperative work); K.4.2 Computers and Society: Social Issues

INTRODUCTION
Even in death, the famous and powerful do not want for attention. Their passing—like anyone's—is an occasion for family and friends to commemorate and reflect. But what do we remember about the deceased? Wikipedia biographies are a unique kind of artifact that users collectively create to document the lives of notable people. These encyclopedia articles are intended to be historical accounts, but their mutability reveals that what is remembered about important people changes after death. Just as importantly, Wikipedia data can provide a window into *how* this memorialization is done and *who* makes these changes.

CSCW'15, March 14–18 2015, Vancouver, BC, Canada.

ACM 978-1-4503-2922-4/15/03...$15.00.
http://dx.doi.org/10.1145/2675133.2675238

Wikipedia's open collaboration model has proven remarkably adept at covering current and breaking news events [24, 25]. The death of political leaders, artists, and other notable people are examples of news events that lead strangers to create and modify their biographical articles. Wikipedia users' responses to the death of living people exhibit surprising similarities as well as differences to posthumous activity on other socio-technical systems such as Facebook and other social network sites [4, 5]. Articles become gathering places for large numbers of people, but the types of content and activity that are permitted are governed by strong social and stylistic norms emphasizing notability, a neutral point of voice, and reliable sourcing that would seem to pre-empt practices of memorialization.

However, the Wikipedia community has demonstrated substantial capacity to re-interpret non-encyclopedic norms and practices such as journalistic writing [25]. We find evidence that Wikipedia has re-imagined the obituary into a genre for creating memory spaces in which the death of a subject prompts collective re-evaluation as well as a transition into a new mode of stewardship [3]. Rather than simple revisions of verb tenses ("*is* an actor" to "*was* an actor") and vital statistics, the death of notable people prompts bursts of focused activity among contributors with diverse backgrounds.

Who authors these "wiki-bituaries"? Do previous contributors participate in the posthumous collaboration or are there users who specialize in this genre of writing? What content changes after the death of a subject? Are there systematic biases in the posthumous attention some biographies receive over others? How is the structure of collaborations different before death versus the days and weeks following the death? These questions highlight how socio-technical scholarship overlooks the importance of death for creating communicative spaces for participants to encode collective memories into more durable knowledge artifacts.

Drawing upon a mixture of quantitative and qualitative methods, we examine the changes in the features of posthumous biographical articles as well as changes in the composition of their contributors. Shifting between these levels of analysis reveals significant differences in attention, the development of specialized skills, and the emergence of complex structures that distinguish posthumous collaborations from other types of peer production on Wikipedia. We identify editors who cluster their edits on particular days and use this strategy to qualitatively examine their history of revisions as well as their practices on these articles. We find the articulation of a posthumous biography draws on practices in journalistic obituary writing, but embeds the deceased in a web of connections to their contributions [32].

BACKGROUND

Wikipedia is a peer-produced online encyclopedia that has become one of the largest reference works and most-trafficked websites in the world. While Wikipedia has adopted rules that emulate centuries-old norms of encyclopedic production [28], the technological affordances of a wiki platform has also expanded the possibilities of the genre. In particular, the potential to rapidly update encyclopedic content in reaction to new information has led the Wikipedia community to develop structures to support "newswork" that journalists traditionally engage in around evaluating source credibility, synthesizing information, and sharing timely content [25].

Prior research has examined Wikipedia's coverage of current and breaking news events. Large-scale collaborations emerge following major natural disasters such as the 2011 Japanese earthquake and tsunami and generate real-time accounts of events as they unfold. The coordination of this work involves user communities specializing in newswork, users with relevant domain and process expertise, as well as technological tools to prevent vandalism and standardize content [22]. Compared to other Wikipedia collaborations, the structures of these breaking news collaborations are marked by the rapid emergence of a connected core of users [24] and dense patterns of user interactions and content modifications [23]. The encyclopedia has also adopted policies that expand its mission into quasi-journalistic coverage of news events [25].

In this study, we focus on a more subtle form of newswork—the journalistic practice of writing obituaries—as a genre of high-tempo knowledge collaboration involving large-scale self-organization, time-sensitive coordination, and conflicting norms. Obituaries of notable people allow us to look at another journalistic practice that has been re-interpreted by Wikipedians for encyclopedic functions of documenting social memory and history. Obituaries report the news, but they also serve as an authoritative account of an individual's life. Given the variety of stakeholders, Wikipedia's articles for "notable people" may potentially be sites of tension. If obituaries are a cultural practice in which a life narrative is concretized and the deceased is symbolically put to rest, there are open questions about who stewards this narrative and what types of engagement that requires over time.

To provide some background for the "death work" performed on Wikipedia, we start with a brief history of the obituary as a genre of journalistic writing. Next, we talk about the cultural functions that obituaries serve—namely, they reflect and encapsulate a culture's shared, but evolving, values and ideals. While obituaries outside of Wikipedia are static, we turn to related literature around online memorialization over the last twenty years as a way of understanding how individuals' practices and online user-generated content are shifting memorials from static content to communal sites of interaction around evolving content. We then bridge research on obituaries and Wikipedia by considering the role both play in the material construction of memory. Finally, we outline the relevant policies and guidelines on Wikipedia that inform the practices we describe.

Obituaries as Journalistic Practice

Obituaries are news articles that report the death of an individual and provide a summary of their life. They are conventionally authored by a journalist and published in newspapers and other news media [38].[1] While newspapers are dedicating increasing amounts of space for the publication of obituaries [37], historically they have been reserved for celebrities and the famous whose deaths qualified as "news" [1].

Obituary writing presents significant ethical challenges. Editorial staff must make decisions about who to cover, what content to include, and the overall style [38, 39]. Scholarship has noted journalistic bias that privileges men [31], cultures that are proximate to the newspaper [17], as well as stylistic differences across different countries [37].

Posthumously reviewing a subject's life is "a formidable exercise of authority" [38]. More comprehensive than a death notice, contemporary obituaries must balance elements of opinion with historical fact. It is through this balance that obituaries serve as a record of our cultural history as well. Examined across time, obituaries reflect a culture's shared, but evolving values and ideals. As Hume writes: "An obituary distills the essence of a citizen's life, and because it is a commemoration as well as a life chronicle, it reflects what society values and wants to remember about that person's history" [19]. Post-war obituaries, for example, are notable for references to valor and patriotism [19], while the contemporary obituaries in the United States increasingly celebrate ordinary, "every American" qualities [20].

Today the obituary genre has been popularized in use and is more populous in its content. Many follow its format when posting a notice of a loved one's death in classified advertisements or when creating a written memorial. This democratization of the obituary genre, however, raises questions about a genre that is based on "distinction" [11]. It is this distillation that we examine in the context of Wikipedia. We consider how existing encyclopedia articles are reframed to not only include a person's death as part of their overall history, but how content is commemorated as well.

In the context of Wikipedia, questions rise about who is engaging in obituary-styled journalistic practices. Are there editors who specialize in obituary-styled writing? How many

[1] Even though the announcement family or loved ones place in a newspaper is commonly called an "obituary", the technical term for this is a "death notice"

and what kinds of users become involved in posthumous editing? Do "wiki-bituaries" reproduce the biases found in journalistic obituaries that privilege some types of individuals over others? In what ways does a dynamic wiki-platform challenge the authority of the static journalistic obituary?

User-Generated Content and Online Memorials

In order to understand how individual practices and online user-generated content (UGC) might impact obituary work, we turn to research on online memorials to understand how individuals' practices and UGC online are shifting memorials from static spaces or content to communal sites of interaction around evolving content. "Virtual memorial" sites can be traced back to the early days of the Internet [35]. Most memorials were written in the style of an obituary or eulogy, and a few of the larger memorial sites included rudimentary "guest books" that allowed visitors to author a message that would be displayed with the memorial [36]. Likewise, as newspapers have migrated online, some have included spaces for visitors to leave comments.

Greater scholarly attention, however, has focused on the use of social media sites for memorialization. User profiles on social network sites over the last fifteen years have provided natural spaces for interactive memorials. As Brubaker and Hayes note, the continued presence of profiles on these sites post-mortem have enabled the development of post-mortem social networking practices [4].

Three features of practices on social networking sites (SNS) are relevant when considering practices on Wikipedia. First, memorials on social media allow large groups of individuals to visit and participate in content creation. Many academics have noted the potential benefits of support these communal spaces provide [7]. Studying celebrity death, Radford & Bloch have argued that by sharing information fans validate their view of the deceased and incorporate the reality of their death [33]. However, the public visibility of these spaces creates potential privacy concerns about who is allowed to participate [30]. Second, like Wikipedia articles, social media profiles exist prior to the owner's death. Unlike a traditional obituary that reviews an individual's life, posthumous activity on social network sites and Wikipedia may be better conceptualized as a "reappraisal" of existing content. Finally, open and evolving memorial spaces can create tensions between existing and new content [3, 4], as well as the disparate depictions of the deceased [5].

Recent work has begun to consider what claims survivors might appropriately have over deceased's accounts or data, and the roles that stewarding each entails [3]. Similar tensions might exist with Wikipedia between providing a factual historical account of an individual's life and the types of ongoing engagements that might occur as people connect to, edit, augment, and shape the content. In the context of Wikipedia, the quality of the user-generated content relies on implicit and explicit coordination among contributors [26].

UGC shifts obituaries from a codified accounting of the deceased's life to a site of ongoing engagement and contestation. A similar tension manifests in Wikipedia between providing a factual historical account of an individual's life and the types of ongoing engagements that might occur as people connect to, edit, augment, and shape the content. Our contention here is that systems that support UGC are shifting their memorial, obituary, and encyclopedic content from static entries to communal spaces in which content can be reappraised and revised. This raises the question of who are the users generating this content? How do their temporal and structural patterns of contributions change in the aftermath of the subject's death? Do these revisions co-occur simultaneously with other attempts at re-appraisal and for how long does this behavior persist?

Collective Memory

Finally, we bridge death studies and Wikipedia by considering the role both memorials and Wikipedia play in the material construction of memory. Based on the sociological work of Halbawach [15], memory is understood as a collective function that is constructed in the individual through interactions with others. Sites of collective memory, then, are places where what is considered worthy of remembering is negotiated. Arguments have been made for both obituaries and Wikipedia as sites of collective memory. An obituary provides "a rare instance when an average person can become part of collective thought, part of what Americans might believe in common about the worth of a life" [20]. Examined as a whole, obituaries serve as a repository for our collective memory [11, 19]. Pentzold applies the same theoretical lens when studying Wikipedia as a site of collective memory. He argues that the web presents both a vast archive and endless potential for communicative interactions. As such, when considering the role of online content in relationship to collective memory, is not simply the transition from communicative to cultural modes, but "also interactions between the canon and the archive" [32].

Given the role that Wikipedia plays in collective memory of events and individuals, we expect to see significant changes in biographical articles' content, contributors, and contexts. What types of content are introduced or removed from the deceased's Wikipedia article? Is the death of a subject an occasion for adding new content and links to contextual information about legacies? Is there anything that marks the "hand-off" between editor communities dedicated to policing biographies of living people to those coordinating biographies of the recently deceased and finally those stewarding historical biographies?

Wikipedia Guidelines

Not everyone who dies has an article on Wikipedia. Wikipedia is governed by an extensive body of explicit rules as well as implicit norms [2, 10], and specific rules have evolved to determine who is worthy of a biographical article. Wikipedia includes a "Notability" policy that explains that only individuals who are "worthy of notice" by virtue of being "significant, interesting, or unusual enough to deserve attention" are eligible for a "written account of that person's life." While these criteria are subjective, Wikipedia operationalizes "attention" as "significant coverage in multiple published secondary sources."[2] Wikipedia explicitly acknowledges that biographical articles are intended to be historical records, but despite its participatory ethos, it enforces distinctions about who and what is included in this cultural memory through formal rules and institutional routines.

The notability policy is further reinforced by Wikipedia's policy enumerating all the things "Wikipedia is not."[3] Part of this policy states that "Wikipedia is not the place to memorialize deceased friends, relatives, acquaintances, or others who do not meet [the notability requirements]." This rule stems from early debates about the boundaries of Wikipedia's identity during the aftermath of the September 11, 2001 terrorist attacks when some users attempted to create articles for every single victim [25]. Although the rule is intended to provide a bulwark against appropriating Wikipedia as a site for "virtual memorials," commemoration nevertheless plays a significant role in editing behaviors [9]. Thus we expect that the recently deceased who had no Wikipedia articles in life may yet still "earn" an article in death. This may be a function of new information coming to light that passes the notability criterion, enumeration practices in which users create articles in response to lists of the recently deceased, as well as memorialization and commemoration practices among users.

Articles about living people also have to abide by an additional set of guidelines called the "Biographies of Living Persons" (BLP).[4] This policy emphasizes that biographical articles about living people must be held to a higher standard of verifiability and neutrality to ensure they do not run afoul of libel, defamation laws, respect for privacy of non-public figures, and maintained norms around the presumption of innocence. This, in turn, motivates a very active policing and maintenance of biographical articles through dedicated taskforces and communities. These communities have also developed tools for monitoring changes and automating reversion, as well as specialized administrative processes for alerting administrators and removing content. However, this policy states that it generally does not apply to "material concerning people who are confirmed dead by reliable sources" unless the individual recently died or the death is particularly notable. Thus, biographical articles for deceased people are not held to the same set of governing policy and do not receive the same level of monitoring and oversight. This heightens questions about how articles change posthumously and what stewardship practices are involved.

METHODS

We conducted a mixed-methods empirical study of revisions to English Wikipedia articles about people who died in 2012. We used 2012 data to ensure that data for analyses that look at the year following the death were not censored, but analysis of data for deaths in 2013 show similar patterns. Like many open collaboration platforms, the MediaWiki software running Wikipedia includes a complete revision history of every change to an article. These revisions document the changes in content as well as metadata such as the contributor and timestamp. We collected the complete revision histories for 6,132 biographical articles in the "2012 deaths" category[5] using a Python script to retrieve data from the English Wikipedia's MediaWiki API.[6] This generated an original corpus of revisions containing 528,980 revisions from 117,829 unique users from between July 2001 and May 2014. The data returned by the API may omit revisions deleted by administrators that are blatant copyright violations or contain offensive/disruptive material.[7]

We then extracted attributes about the subjects of the biographies from WikiData, which provides an extensive corpus of labels for articles covering attributes such as gender,[8] birth and death places,[9] and birth and death dates,[10] among others. However, these data are not extensive across all articles in the parent "2012 deaths" corpus. WikiData contains information on death dates for 3,734 articles, gender for 3,918 articles, and birthplaces for 2,016 articles.

Despite the importance of bots in the ecology of work on Wikipedia, especially in anti-vandalism and stylistic standardization [14], we removed contributions associated with bot users from our dataset so as to focus on people who directly engage in posthumous journalistic and memorializing practices. Automated editing is so deeply embedded within Wikipedia's editing practices that it requires several iterative steps to identify and filter out most of these revisions with any confidence. We began with the set of automated users formally flagged as bots in the "All Wikipedia bots" category.[11] Removing contributions associated with bot users, there were 491,826 revisions from 117,412 unique users remaining.

In addition to the bots, we also found that the users who contributed to the most articles in each of the pre- and postmortem coauthorship networks were ranked among the top 10 users with the most edits.[12] Many of these users employ semiautomated tools such as "AutoWikiBrowser"[13] and "Twinkle"[14] to generate hundred of revisions for repetitive or minor tasks. Because these semi-automated generalists would appear as prominent users in nearly any corpus of articles or revisions, we also exclude them to focus on contributions more specific to biography or "wiki-bituary" writing.

[2] https://en.wikipedia.org/wiki/Wikipedia:Notability_(people)

[3] https://en.wikipedia.org/wiki/Wikipedia:What_Wikipedia_is_not

[4] https://en.wikipedia.org/wiki/Wikipedia:Biographies_of_living_persons

[5] https://en.wikipedia.org/wiki/Category:2012_deaths

[6] http://en.wikipedia.org/w/api.php

[7] http://en.wikipedia.org/wiki/Wikipedia:Revision_deletion

[8] https://www.wikidata.org/wiki/Property:P21

[9] https://www.wikidata.org/wiki/Property:P19

[10] https://www.wikidata.org/wiki/Property:P569

[11] http://en.wikipedia.org/wiki/Category:All_Wikipedia_bots

[12] http://en.wikipedia.org/wiki/Wikipedia:List_of_Wikipedians_by_number_of_edits

[13] http://en.wikipedia.org/wiki/Wikipedia:AWB

[14] http://en.wikipedia.org/wiki/Wikipedia:Twinkle

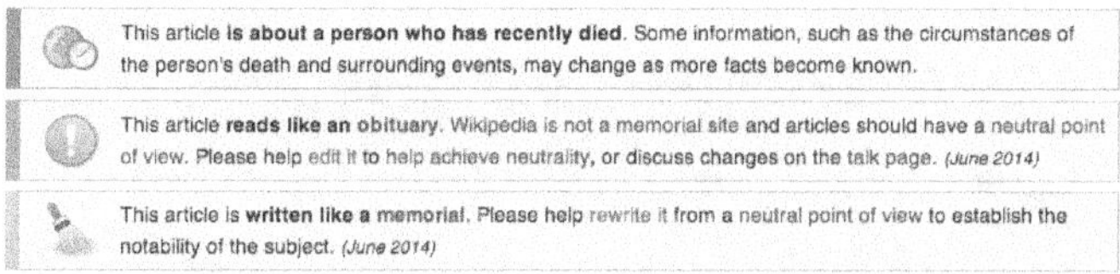

Figure 1. Examples of template messages used as disclaimers or warnings about biographical articles for the recently deceased.

Previous work has employed a number of methods to identify and filter out these "cyborg" users based on their implausible productivity of making continuous contributions without taking a break for six hours [13, 16]. Because we sampled on articles rather than on users, their contributions to articles outside the corpus are censored, which limits our ability to filter users based on the continuity of their activity. Instead, we use the flags many of these semi-automated tools include within revision comments to filter "cyborg revisions" rather than "cyborg users." We adopted a method to filter revisions containing these tags by adapting queries suggested by the Wikimedia Foundation [12].[15] Removing these semi-automated revision, there were 458,818 revisions from 116,010 unique users remaining in the final revision corpus.

In the set of 3,738 articles about deaths in 2012 for which a specific death date was coded on WikiData, 2,865 of these articles existed before the day of the death ("pre-mortem") and 873 (23%) have their first revision occurring on or after the day of the death ("post-mortem"). There are a total of 235,875 pre-mortem revisions from 68,994 unique users and 226,248 post-mortem revisions from 48,941 unique users. Note that we will employ the term "users" throughout the paper to refer to individuals who author changes to an article, rather than consumers of article content.

To evaluate whether there are significant differences in post-mortem attention, we specify a multiple regression model to evaluate the simultaneous effects of gender, age, birthplace, and revisions in the preceding year on the number of revisions in the subsequent year as an outcome. We also compare the state of the content in the article the day before the death as well as a week after the death. We specifically measure the number of categories, external links to other websites, and internal links to other Wikipedia articles. Because the distributions of these variables are not normal, we use a non-parametric version of an ANOVA called the Wilxocon signed-rank test is used to test the null hypothesis that the medians of these two related groups are the same [8].

We explore the results in two separate sections. The first focuses on articles as the unit of analysis. We examine the practices and changes that occur on biographical articles after the subject's death, how changes to the article differ in the year following the death compared to the years preceding death, and finally whether there are biases in the response of Wikipedians to subjects based on gender, age, or birthplace. The second set of results focuses on users as the unit of analysis. We examine how the network of users contributing to articles evolves over time to incorporate different types of users and changes in the structural patterns. We also examine the most active contributing users on different days reveals distinct social roles and orientation to maintaining these articles.

Pre-mortem		Post-mortem	
Title	*Users*	*Title*	*Users*
Whitney Houston	3239	Whitney Houston	488
Neil Armstrong	2800	Donna Summer	441
Rodney King	2243	Jenni Rivera	436
Ray Bradbury	1822	Ray Bradbury	420
Arlen Specter	1122	Rodney King	376
Joe Paterno	1116	Davy Jones	356
Donna Summer	1016	Joe Paterno	338
Gore Vidal	975	Rajesh Khanna	327
Sun Myung Moon	917	Andy Griffith	325
Sally Ride	907	Robin Gibb	322

Table 1. List of articles with the most unique users in the pre- and post-mortem coauthorship networks, after filtering out bots and "cyborg" users.

ARTICLE-LEVEL RESULTS

As a way of exploring practices of re-evaluation, this section explores changes in the properties of biographical articles following the death of the subject. To provide some context for the results in this section, Table 1 enumerates the top ten articles with the most unique users in the pre- and post-mortem eras. Both lists are predominantly composed of major figures from the spheres of politics and entertainment, however there are substantial differences in the rank of individuals between lists. The subjects of the most widely-edited post-mortem articles are generally marked as "unexpected" deaths and many involve actors or musicians rather than political figures, business people, or scientists.

Death Work on Wikipedia

The work of administering content about the recently deceased occurs in several places and involves three notable practices. First, biographical articles are labeled with categories that include the year of the subject's birth, and after they die, the year of their death. In addition to adding the death year category, contributing users also remove the "Living People" category that marks the article as warranting Biographies of Living Persons (BLP) protections.

Second, the article is added to a list such as "Deaths in 2014" that enumerates all of the individuals who died by day alongside a short biographical summary.[16] Some of these articles are "red linked" which reflects the fact there is no corresponding article for the person, and thus invites other users to create a new article.

In a rare third step, when individuals of particular importance and notability die, their biographical article can be added to a section on the homepage of Wikipedia. Inclusion criteria for this section emphasize the need for an individual to have occupied a "high-ranking office," have made a "significant

[15] `https://wiki.toolserver.org/view/MySQL_queries#Automated_tool_and_bot_edits`

[16] `https://en.wikipedia.org/wiki/Deaths_in_2014`

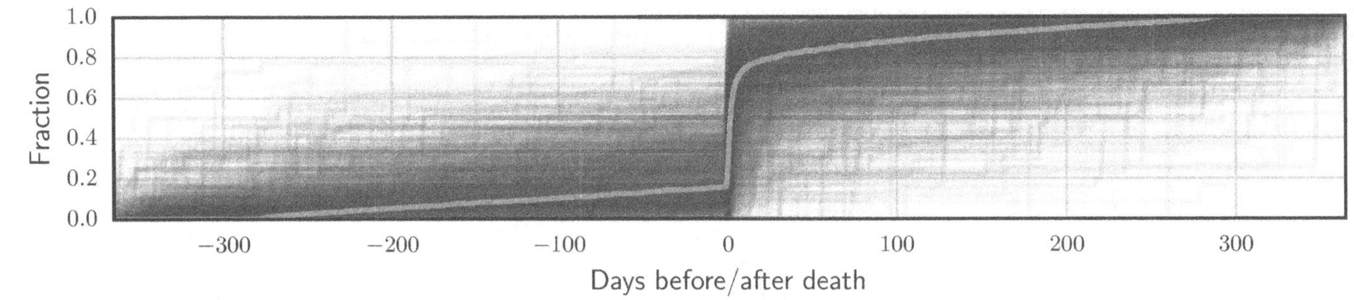

Figure 2. Cumulative number of normalized revisions made to biographical articles in year before and after subject's death ($x = 0$). Each line corresponds to a single article's cumulative revision history. Median trajectory in red.

contribution or impact," or made a "major impact" on current events.[17] Users can nominate biographical articles for inclusion, after which other users can discuss and come to a consensus about whether this "recent death" warrants inclusion on this homepage for a few days. In addition to being a more prominent acknowledgment of an individual's notability, links from the homepage generate substantially more traffic and editorial attention from the community.

A variety of social communities as well as technological and administrative tools have also been implemented to support the process of updating biographical articles to reflect the subject's death. These include templates about current events,[18] which include a template explicitly for recent deaths.[19] As seen in Figure 1, these templates are intended to be disclaimers applied to biographies to warn readers about the fast-changing state of the article. But these templates can also be used by editors to label articles so they might attract the attention of other users, who in this case are interested in contributing to posthumous articles. Still other templates exist to warn readers that the biographical article is in violation of style guidelines and reads like a memorial or obituary.[20] These warnings invite users to rewrite the article to establish a neutral point of view or sufficiently demonstrate the notability of the subject. These findings all point to how "death work" on Wikipedia has highly been structured into highly specialized and routinized processes.

Temporal Dynamics

How does editing an article after the subject's death differ from pre-mortem edits? An initial way to examine this question is to compare how much editing occurs on the days leading up to a subject's death to the editing that occurs in the days following their death. Figure 2 plots the normalized cumulative time series of revision activity for each Wikipedia articles in the year before and the year after the date of the subject's death ($x = 0$). The data is normalized in two ways to make it comparable across articles with very different scales of response. First, all articles start the period with 0 revisions 365 days before the subject's death to provide a baseline to measure changes over the subsequent two years. Second, the number of revisions 365 days after the death of the subject are normalized again to 1 to create a fractional index of number of revisions as a total of the final revisions.

There is an obvious "jump" in editing activity on the day of the subject's death. Little editing activity precedes the subject's death relative to the final amount of edits, reflecting death as a newsworthy event that Wikipedians document, as well as a moment in which Wikipedians begin to integrate and re-evaluate biographical content as a whole. The days immediately following the subject's death see very large changes in the number of normalized revisions relative to the editing activity over the year beforehand. This reflects the need to incorporate new information, but the scale of activity in such a short time period suggests complex coordination work involving multiple users working in parallel.

The data in Figure 2 examined only the year before the death, which eliminates possible changes occurring in earlier years. Looking at the four years before the death of the subject, we also find that editing patterns in general are consistent during pre-mortem years. Figure 3 plots the changes in the revisions, users, and bytes changed in the articles in the four years preceding the death and the year following the death. In addition to significantly more revisions ($\widetilde{r_{pre}} = 1, \widetilde{r_{post}} = 15, p < 0.001$), there are significantly more unique users ($\widetilde{u_{pre}} = 1, \widetilde{u_{post}} = 8, p < 0.001$) as well as significantly larger changes in the article content (bytes added) in the year following the death ($\widetilde{b_{pre}} = 0, \widetilde{b_{post}} = 2073, p < 0.001$) than in any of the preceding four years.

These findings suggests that the death of the subject is potentially an occasion for "finishing" a biography. They provide evidence that death on Wikipedia, rather than prompting existing users to make minor changes such as changing verb tenses or adding information about the death, actually prompts substantial collaborative activity involving many users making large changes over many revisions, relative to articles' previous four years of history.

[17] `https://en.wikipedia.org/wiki/Wikipedia:In_the_news#Deaths`

[18] `https://en.wikipedia.org/wiki/Wikipedia:Current_event_templates`

[19] `https://en.wikipedia.org/wiki/Template:Recent_death`

[20] `https://en.wikipedia.org/wiki/Template:Obituary`,`https://en.wikipedia.org/wiki/Template:Memorial`

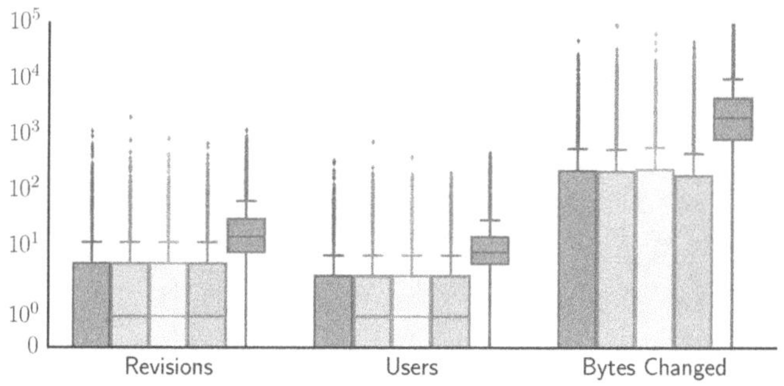

Figure 3. The number of revisions, users, and bytes changed in the year following the death (red) are significantly higher than in any of the four years (other four bars) preceding the death.

	β	S.E.	p
Male	−0.107	0.043	*
Death age	−0.192	0.016	**
Asia	0.208	0.100	*
Caribbean	0.067	0.236	
Eurasia	−0.090	0.123	
Europe	0.057	0.092	
North America	0.217	0.093	*
Oceania	0.087	0.142	
South America	−0.019	0.123	
Article age	0.175	0.017	**
Revisions before	0.586	0.016	**
Constant	−0.036	0.097	

Table 2. Multiple regression model. Standardized coefficients (β) are reported. $N = 2,139$, $R^2 = 0.478$; $^*p < 0.05$; $^{**}p < 0.01$

Biases in Attention

In the previous section we observed large changes in the behavior of a biographical article following the death of the subject. However, prior research has suggested that English Wikipedia articles have systematic biases against women, historic figures, and people from the Global South [6, 18, 34], a tendency that emulates biases observed in the selection of subjects for obituaries [17, 31, 37]. If this is true, we expect that posthumous editing activity will show significant differences based on the gender, and birthplace of individuals. Likewise, prior research indicates that online memorials skew towards younger deaths [4, 7]. If this is a byproduct of online memorializing practices generally and not just the social networks on social media, we would expect to see a difference on Wikipedia based on age as well. Using WikiData to code articles by their subject's gender, birth year, and birth location, we compare editing behavior in the year preceding and following their death.

To assess the direction, strength, and statistical significance of these demographic features on editing behavior, we specified a multiple regression model. Using the age of the article (days since first edit) and the number of revisions in the year preceding the death as control variables, we estimated the effects that the age at death, gender (female as base category), and birthplace (Africa as base category) had on the number of revisions in the year following the subject's death. This model is estimated on the 2,139 articles for which we had complete information, but Figures 4 through 6 plot the univariate relationships between pre-mortem (light green) and post-mortem (dark green) revision activity across these variables. We extended the analyses of revisions to the number of unique users and cumulative bytes changed in article content and found similar patterns to those we report below. Because we employed standardized coefficients to compare effect sizes, the estimates should be changes in standard deviations rather than count of revisions.

The model estimates several significant effects. The strongest effect ($\beta_{Before} = 0.586, p < 0.01$) on the number of post-mortem revisions is the number of pre-mortem revisions: individuals who are popular in life are also popular in death. Similarly, the age of the article also has a significant and moderate ($\beta_{ArticleAge} = 0.175, p < 0.01$) effect on post-mortem activity: the longer a biographical article has existed the more revisions it attracts after the subject has died. These variables on popularity and history are important controls to test subsequent effects of biases owing to demographic differences.

We find mixed evidence of biases in post-mortem attention based on demographic features. First, articles about men attract significantly less post-mortem revisions than articles about women, but this effect is moderate ($\beta_{Male} = -0.107, p < 0.05$). This inverts our expectation that Wikipedia should award greater post-mortem attention to men, but it may also be an artifact of gender-biased censoring. Wikipedians write more articles about men (4,285) than women (693) and thus the women present in the sample may be more important than the semi-notable men.

Second, the biographies of older people attract less post-mortem activity than articles about younger people. The direction of this moderate effect ($\beta_{DeathAge} = -0.192, p < 0.01$) replicates other findings around online memorialization in which attention skews towards younger people. This reflects the confounding of several potential processes: younger people having articles are rarer and as notability requires the accumulation of many accomplishments, they are also demographically less likely to die, and their deaths are more prominently covered in the news media and popular culture as unexpected and tragic.

Third, we find mixed evidence of biases in post-mortem activity across birthplaces. Biographies of people born in Asia ($\beta_{Asia} = 0.208, p < 0.05$) and North America ($\beta_{N.America} = 0.217, p < 0.05$) both have significantly and substantially larger post-mortem attention than biographies of African-born people. While North America shows a strong and significant effect, we observe no similar effect for Europe or Oceania which also are typically classified into the Global North. Thus, we have mixed evidence that biographies of people from the Global South are significantly underrepresented in post-mortem activity.

Changes in Hyperlinked Content

In this section, we examine how the content of biographical articles changes over time. We expect that postmortem revisions should lead to an integration with a larger cultural

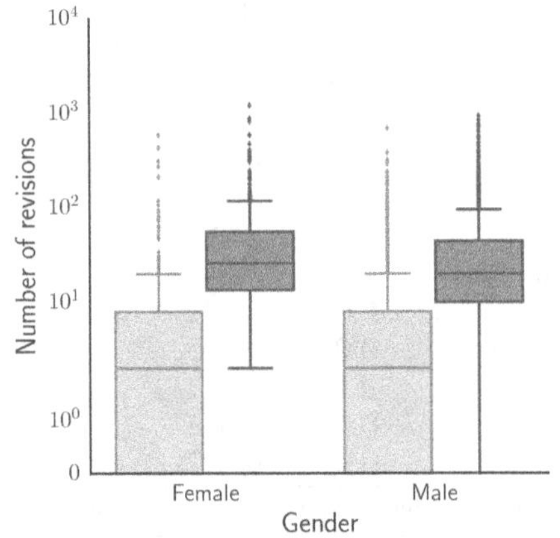

Figure 4. Revisions in the year before (light green) and the year after (dark green) death by gender of the biographical subject.

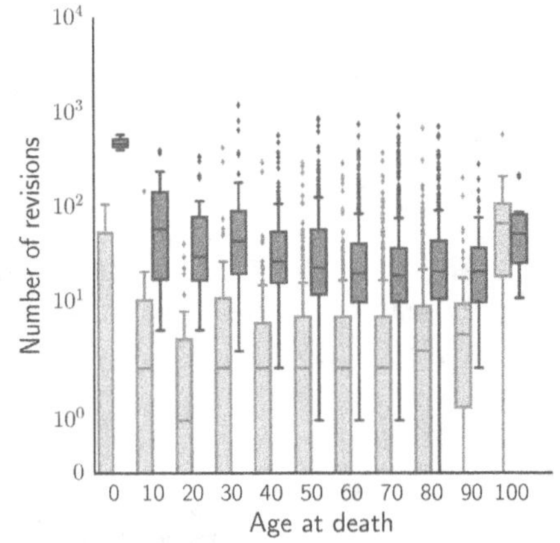

Figure 5. Revisions in the year before (light green) and year after (dark green) death by age of the biographical subject.

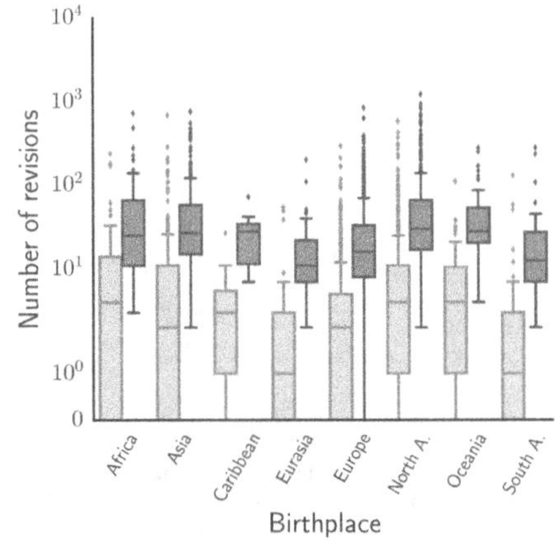

Figure 6. Revisions in the year before (light green) and year after (dark green) death by birthplace of the biographical subject.

account of the subject's contributions. Practices of commemoration emphasize that people will try to make claims on the subject's legacy and one part of grieving is placing the subject's contributions into a larger context, which we capture through the addition of links to other content and inclusion of new categories for classifying the subject. Furthermore, we also expect the external links used in the articles' citations and references will become more diverse as more information comes to light through published obituaries about the individual's contributions.

Figure 7 plots the differences in the number categories, number of links to external website, and the number of links to other Wikipedia articles for 1 day before death (left bar) and 7 days after (right bar) the death of the subject. We used the Wilcoxon signed-rank test to test the differences between the medians of these distributions. There were the same number of media categories pre-mortem ($\widetilde{c_{pre}} = 9, \widetilde{c_{post}} = 9, p = 0.108$), more post-mortem external links ($\widetilde{e_{pre}} = 3, \widetilde{e_{post}} = 4, p < 0.001$), and fewer post-mortem internal links ($\widetilde{i_{pre}} = 25, \widetilde{i_{post}} = 23, p < 0.001$). This implies the significant uptick in post-mortem revisions we observed in Figure 3 did not translate into the creation of new categories, but did result in the removal of internal links and the addition of external links. These differences are very slight and suggests that much of the changes could reflect stylistic (copy editing) or procedural (anti-vandalism) changes than adding new relationships.

While Figure 7 suggests the median change in links between the day before the death and 7 days after the death is close to zero, it also hides within-article changes. Plotting the distribution of within-article changes in Figure 8 reveals there is substantial variance in behavior across articles. First, we observe articles see both positive and negative changes in new internal links, external links, and category memberships. This means that there are hundreds of articles that have a net *loss* of links, rather than gain, following the death of the subject. Second, we observe this distribution is peaked around 0 but there are "long tails" of both positive and negative changes in linked content. Thus while the median biographical article has small changes in content in the week following the death of the subject when most editing activity occurs, there are hundreds of articles that see the addition of dozens of new links, references, and categories.

For example, when closely examining deaths from 2013, we see the article for activist Aaron Swartz grew in size and connectivity following his death, going from 14 categories, 17 external links, and 34 internal links the day before his death to 30 categories, 82 external links, and 151 internal links just 7 days after his death. Conversely, the article for the Taliban commander Hakimullah Mehsud lost 10 external links as citations for speculation about his whereabouts was replaced with information about the circumstances of his death. Other articles that saw major losses of external links such as politician Frank Lautenberg are attributable to the removal of tangentially-related navigation templates that often contain dozens of links. Articles like those of author Doris Lessing saw the removal of 10 categories in response to redundant or over-zealous categorizing; for example, simultaneously including "English women writers," "21st-century women writers," and "Women novelists."

This distribution and these linking examples point to at least two interwoven post-mortem practices. First, linking is a form of contextualization that creates semantic adjacencies. The death of a subject is an occasion for other media outlets to publish obituaries and information. This new information may reflect topics that previous contributors overlooked or were unable to reliably reference, but now become inputs to the article. The addition of these new links move the article from the periphery and make it more embedded within the project as a whole.

Second, the death of a subject also provides an occasion that prompts other members of the community to police the content and style of articles and make them conform to norms and standards when information is most available about the subject. The death of a subject also causes the knowledge artifact to undergo a transition as it is prepared and made ready to

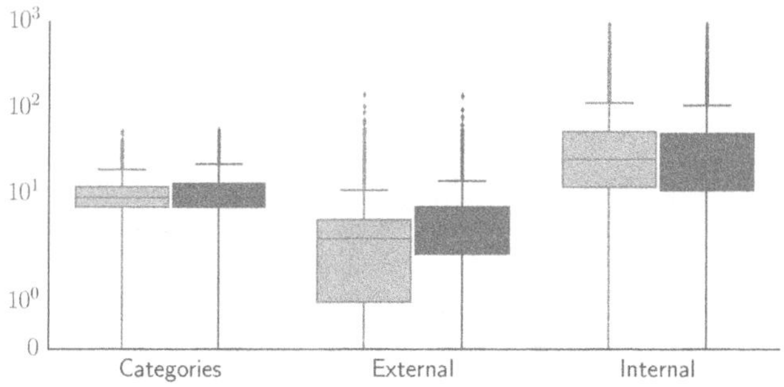

Figure 7. The number of categories, external links, and internal links on the day before (left, in light red) and 7 days following the death (right, in dark red).

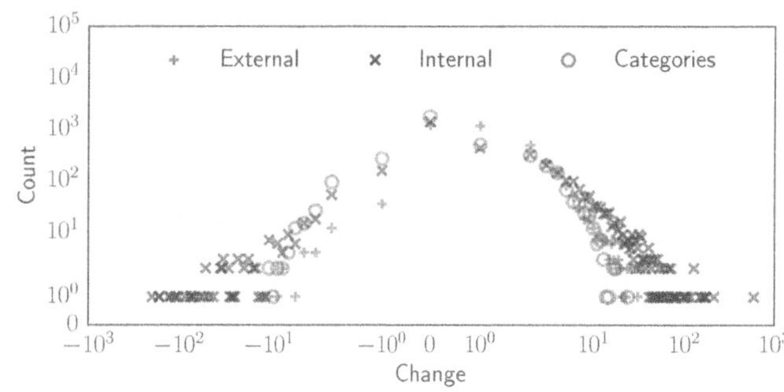

Figure 8. The distribution of changes to categories (green), external links (red), and internal links(blue) between the day before and 7 days following the death

join the set of articles about other historical figures. Articles about other historical figures can be used as templates and can lead to reframing as an entity of historical importance, rather than contemporary interest. Furthermore, because the subject is no longer living, Wikipedia's BLP policies are no longer in force. As a result, the article will receive less close scrutiny from users who specialize in anti-vandalism or regular cleanup of BLP articles. There may be "handing off" practices from users who specialize in editing living people to users who edit the recent dead or historical figures.

USER-LEVEL RESULTS

In this section, we shift the unit of analysis from the article to the users who are making contributions to these articles. Who edits biographical articles after the death of the subject? We differentiate between the population of users who edited the article before death as "pre-mortem" users and the set of users who made their first edit after the death of the article's subject as "post-mortem" users. In the first subsection, we examine how the composition of users shifts from pre-mortem to post-mortem users. We also analyze how the networks of users contributing to articles change over time. Finally, we identify and compare the contributions made by some of the most active users on two different days.

Coauthorship Network Evolution

The users most involved in shaping a biographical article while the person was alive may potentially have their contributions drowned out by new contributors arriving to edit the recently-deceased's article. This disparity is not necessarily bad as it may be the case that users who specialize in obituary writing or editing current news events have more relevant expertise during these most acute phases of article editing. To get at whether pre-mortem users are being crowded out by new users in the post-mortem era, Figure 9 plots how many pre-mortem editors return to edit the article on each post-mortem day. This distribution is the fraction of revisions from pre-mortem users divided by revisions from all users on each post-mortem day, averaged across all articles. Plotting time on a log-scale on the x-axis highlights the differences in the earlier post-mortem days while compressing the differences in later days.

We observe that pre-mortem users make up approximately 20% of the revisions and contributors on the day of the death. This falls to approximately 10% of the revisions and contributors on average for the remainder of the week, and then never rises above 20 until several months later. While pre-mortem users' activity never makes up a majority of the post-mortem activity, these users are most active on the day of the subject's death and then their contributions are subsequently outweighed by new users.

The analyses of structure in the previous section demonstrates substantial similarities in the structure of pre- and post-mortem collaborations. However, we know that the post-mortem activity on articles is intensely concentrated in the days immediately following the death and then recedes to more typical levels. In this section, we examine the properties of the networks that emerge on the day of a subject's death and how these daily networks change over time relative to the subjects' deaths.

We borrow from the methods we used above to place all articles on a relative timescale. Like Figure 2, we center the activity for each article to 0, which represents the day of the subject's death and then look at the activity over the preceding and following 365 days. We then construct daily networks based on this relative time scale. For example, user U_1 may edit article A_1 on the day of that subject's death in March and U_1 may also edit article A_2 on the day of that subject's death in October. Using this relative timescale approach with daily collaboration networks, user U_1 is connected to both article A_1 and article A_2 in the network for relative time 0, even though these contributions actually occurred at very different absolute times. This approach thus focuses on the collaborations that emerge in response to the death. Substantively, a dynamic network analysis like this also captures macroscopic patterns that emerge from users' microscopic decisions to autonomously self-select into contributing to specific articles at particular points in their history relative to the lives of their subjects. Changes in the structure of the network reflect changes in editors' behavior as they choose to adopt practices to contribute broadly or narrowly.

How does the structure of these collaborations change? Figure 10 plots three other network statistics over the daily relative time collaboration networks. These network statistics

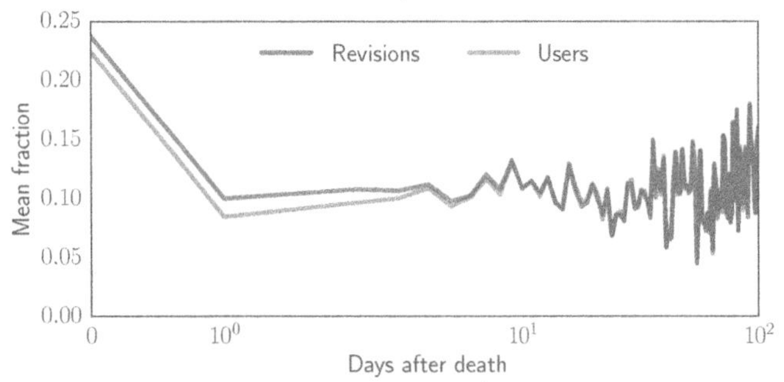

Figure 9. Average fraction of pre-mortem users (red) and their revisions (blue) each post-mortem day (log-scaled) peaks on day of death and then does not recover for weeks.

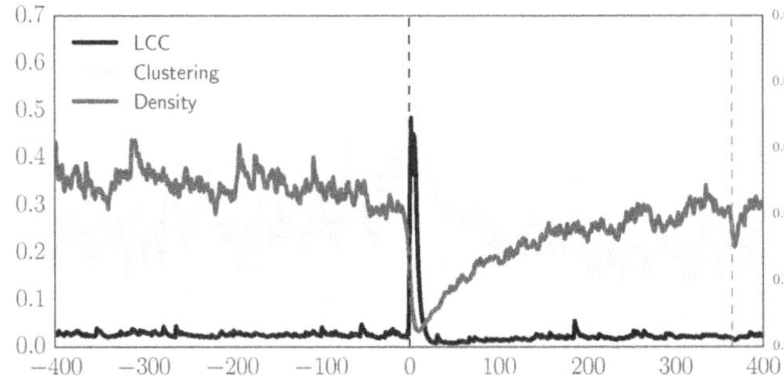

Figure 10. Changes in the daily co-authorship network structure relative to the day of death. The fraction of nodes in the largest connected component (LCC), the average bipartite clustering coefficient, and the bipartite network density The 1-year anniversary is marked by a red dotted line.

are defined specifically for bipartite coauthorship networks in the `NetworkX` analysis package and defined in prior scholarship [27].[21] The *density* is the ratio between the number of edges in the observed network and the number of edges in a completely-connected network of the same size. The *average clustering* captures whether users tend to share articles in common and whether articles tend to share users in common. The *LCC fraction* captures how many user and article nodes are in the largest connected component (LCC). Each of these measures captures distinct structural signatures of how users and articles are interrelating and then tracks how they change over time.

Again, we observe significant changes in the daily structure of the collaboration networks on the relative date of death. First, the density (red, right y-axis) falls and does not recover to pre-mortem levels until approximately 200 post-mortem days later. This loss of density implies sparser collaborations where users edit only a few articles among the many possible articles on each relative day. In the pre-mortem era, users contribute to several articles that are being edited on any given relative day but in the post-mortem aftermath, it becomes unfeasible for all users to contribute to all articles that are being edited by all other users on the same day. Thus, collaborations on the day of subjects' deaths appear to be generally characterized by users' focused editing on a few articles rather than users' contributing across many articles.

Second, the average clustering (yellow) exhibits substantial day-to-day variation but nevertheless spikes on the day of death. This effect decays rapidly and returns to pre-mortem ranges within approximately a month. High levels of clustering imply that editors who work together on one article also work together on other articles. This finding presents a potential paradox as it suggests the post-mortem collaboration is both less dense and yet more clustered than the pre-mortem collaborative. However, density is a metric for the entire network while the average clustering is a local metric for each article and user: the network is clustered by virtue of editors working together on some articles but the network is also sparse by virtue of most editors working on only a few articles rather than all articles on each day.

Third, the fraction of nodes in the LCC (black) also spikes on the day of death before falling rapidly back to baseline levels within several days. The LCC finding in Figure 10 suggests pre-mortem collaborations involve users typically operate in relative autonomy from other users' contributions. This manifests as few users being in the largest component. However on the day of the death, this "autonomy" evaporates and a giant component emerges in which up to 60% of users and articles are indirectly connected to one another rather than operating in isolation. The emergence of a "giant component" on the day of a subject's death reflects contributions from users who specialize in "death work" by making revisions across multiple articles in the hours and days following the death.

Active Contributing Users

The pre- and post-mortem levels of aggregation presented in Tables 1 obscure the dynamics and distributions of users' contributions. Previous findings suggest there were "hand offs" between old pre-mortem and new post-mortem user groups. To explore *who* these users are, we examined how users' contributions clustered by daily relative time. Figures 11 and 12 show the users who cluster their contributions a year, a month, a week, a day before and after the day of death. Each cell in a row is the percentage of revisions (within in the 2012 revision corpus, not across all contributions) from that user on that relative day. For example, user "Makecat" made no revisions on any day in the pre-mortem period, made 42% of his revisions within the corpus on the day of the subject's death, 26% of revisions the day after, and then 0% thereafter. To prevent users who made a single contribution or edited a single article from saturating these results, we have subsetted the data to those users who contributed to 10 or more articles in the corpus. This biases our inferences, but it tries to capture users engaged in biographical work broadly and examines whether editing activity is differentiated across (relative) days.

Figure 11 plots the top 10 user contributions, sorted for highest percentage for day 0. Although sickness or injury may foreshadow the death, it is obviously difficult to consistently predict the date of death. As such, we see little evidence of the active users contributing to biographies in advance of the

[21] **http://networkx.lanl.gov/reference/algorithms.bipartite.html**

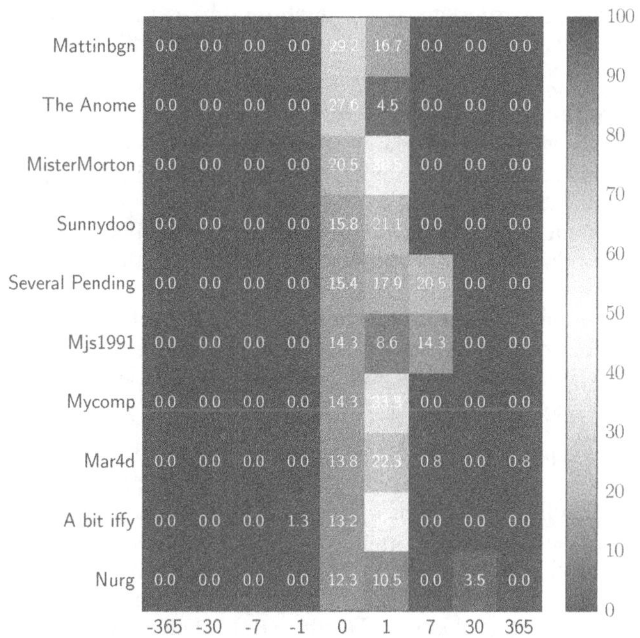

Figure 11. Among users making post-mortem contributions to 10 or more articles, the top 10 users' percentage of contributions by post-mortem day, sorted on highest percentage for day 0. Colors are percentage of edits.

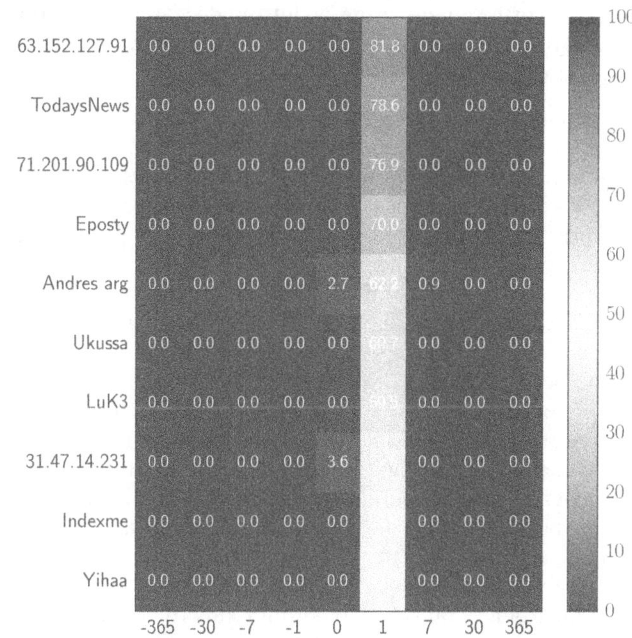

Figure 12. Among users making post-mortem contributions to 10 or more articles, the top 10 users' percentage of contributions by post-mortem day, sorted on highest percentage for day 1. Colors are percentage of edits.

subject's death. Instead, these users who cluster their contributions across articles on day 0 are the "first responders". This cohort of top day 0 users nevertheless makes less than 50% of their contributions on the day of the death, suggesting their revisions are spread out over longer periods of time in our data. This suggests a group of users who are motivated to make the earliest updates to the article but also remain active in editing biographical articles the day following the death. These first responders make no contributions a week later, suggesting they move on to other topics after a few days.

Some of the users who appear in Figure 11, such as "Makecat" and "Callanecc," are actively engaged in anti-vandalism efforts that are not specific to obituary work. Rather, their contributions are reverting vandalism made by other users who were presumably attracted by the timeliness of the article. Other users such as "MisterMorton" are focused more on topics such as actors or "Droodkin" on Middle Eastern politicians and athletes, that leads them to contribute based on the intersection of these topics and their mortality.

Figure 12 plots the top 10 user contributions, sorted for the highest percentage for day 1. A very different cohort of users and contribution behavior emerges from this sorting and none of the top users from Figure 11 are found here. These users are wholly distinct behaviorally as well as few of them edit on day 0 and more than 60% of their contributions in the corpus are focused on this single day. Like the other users above, this engagement is very short-lived and these users no longer make contributions after a week or more. Users such as "Martyn Smith" and "Andres arg" specialize in "death work" by contributing extensively to articles such as the "2012 deaths" over long periods of time. The unregistered user 63.152.127.91 edited several posthumous biographies almost exclusively over a week in May, but did not contribute again. User "Eposty" edits "date" articles (i.e., "December 31") which list major historical events as well as deaths, which was the focus of his contributions.

The sampling strategy we adopted overlooks users who may engage heavily in editing a single article as a form of commemoration and focuses instead on users who engage more broadly. This includes users whose contributions are in response to the attention and activity of vandals who are motivated by the temporary attention afforded recent deaths, users who specialize in death work of updating and enumerating information to articles such as "2012 deaths" as a part of an ongoing routine, users whose contributions abut obituary work by virtue of their topical interests in actors or athletes, and users who contribute in a short burst and then leave the community. Like other forms of breaking news coverage [23], posthumous biography writing thus involve users with varied motivations, backgrounds, and social roles temporarily coming together to manage the transition of living biographies to posthumous biographies.

DISCUSSION

Wikipedia's biographies are intensively updated following the death of their subject. We used quantitative methods to demonstrate the significant differences in posthumous behavior across a large sample of articles. We used qualitative methods to explore the death work on Wikipedia and the practices of prominent users in the corpus. Our results highlight how death work on Wikipedia is not only a reappraisal of what is worth remembering about the deceased, but a reappraisal of the kinds of collaborative work practices enacted and adapted within socio-technical systems.

Our analyses were conducted at the level of articles and users as both are irreducibly entangled in these posthumous and self-organized collaborations. At the level of the article, Wikipedia employs a number of highly specialized tools and practices that served to routinize and even privilege the death work that migrates biographies away from the policies and content only appropriate for a "living person." The need for these resources is apparent when examining the extreme concentration of editing activity in the immediate aftermath of the death as well as the significant increases in the number of revisions, users, and content changes in the year following the death. Wikipedia reproduces some but not all of the systematic biases and inequalities found in its biographical coverage and in journalistic obituary practices more generally, but differences in posthumous activity as a result of gender, age, or birth place were moderate and mixed. Finally, while the differences in the overall connectivity of post-mortem articles compared to pre-mortem articles were minor, we did find extremely skewed distributions in these content-level changes. Post-mortem re-appraisals involve not only the addition of new content about the circumstances of the death of the subject and their legacy, but also the removal of hyperlinked and referenced content suggesting death is an occasion to re-evaluate the article as a whole.

At the level of the user, Wikipedia's posthumous collaborations exhibit remarkable dynamism in their composition. Over the course of the post-mortem collaboration, pre-mortem users did more work on the day of the subject's death than at any subsequent post-mortem point in time. The reduction in these users' contributions suggests they accede to the contributions made by the new post-mortem users that appear in subsequent days. This dynamic suggests pre-mortem users are highly motivated to be among the first to makes the initial changes to the article, but users specializing in obituary writing appear over subsequent days to revise the article to more general standards. This is emblematic of the "hand-off" between communities: users who edited articles about living subjects make a concerted effort on the day of the death to update the article, but users who specialize in death work take over stewarding articles about the recently deceased.

The networks of users contributing to articles after death show major, but temporary, disruptions in scale and structure when compared to the pre-mortem collaborations. Post-mortem collaborations involve users working closely with a few other users (high clustering) on select articles (low density) connected indirectly to many other users and articles (high LCC fraction). Rather than relying on a few highly central specialist users, post-mortem contributions are coordinated through a distributed network of tight clusters connected by weak ties. The post-mortem collaborations are evolving networks of users who edit a single article as well as brokers who stitch this collaboration together and may be able to ensure consistency of death work across articles. Finally, there is variation in top users' contribution patterns across post-mortem days, which reinforces the need for different social roles throughout the stages of death work.

Limitations and Future Work

While we report on a large-scale dataset using a variety of descriptive, temporal, and network methods to identify prominent users and articles, our methods do not provide a rich account of the purpose or meaning of the rapid succession of edits that happen post-mortem. Specifically, literature from memory studies and death studies about the "contested distribution" of collective remembrances [29, 40] suggest that a deeper qualitative analysis of edits might reveal the tensions between consensus and contestation on Wikipedia generally that play out in obituary news work [32].

Many questions also open remain for quantitative researchers. The deaths of subjects can serve as a valuable instrument for conducting naturalistic experiments to evaluate complex phenomena like peer or spillover effects. Death may prompt increased pageview and editing attention not only on the biographical article but also for the articles linked from it as forms of re-evaluation. Death may also change the psychological states of editors, which could manifest in changes in the types of articles edited or differences in language used in subsequent revisions. Memorialization on biographies may also provide opportunities to evaluate how to recruit and socialize new users into the community.

Given that changes can continue indefinitely, how are post-mortem articles edited over the span of decades? Are obituaries "revised" to stay in sync with the shifting cultural norms? Are "wiki-bituaries" involving different users, norms, and times even comparable? If so, what might this say for our sense of cultural memory, the cultural memories of past generations, and our ability to surface these disparities from long-term archives? This problem, of course, is inherent to larger encyclopedic practices where the demand for an authoritative account asks temporal questions around how authority is maintained in a network.

Our examination of posthumous collaborations likewise focused solely on the English language Wikipedia. Death practices vary immensely across cultures [21]. We do not expect that Anglophone practices of memorialization generalize to these contexts, but rather that there will be significant variation across other language editions that may reflect local cultural practices. This underscores the need for more multilingual work to illuminate the social construction of cultural practices by their selective implementation and appropriation by socio-technical systems.

CONCLUSION

"Death work" on Wikipedia highlights the tensions between encyclopedic documentation of social memory and cultural history versus journalistic practices of commemoration and democratization. While its policies warn against memorialization of biographies, Wikipedia's flexibility enables a form of participation that emulates post-mortem social networking practices of participation, stewardship, and shares similar tensions around content and contributions. Wikipedia, like journalism, relies upon specialists who can be best characterized as "obituarists" to update biographies of the recently deceased rather than relying upon either previous contributors or newcomers to make these changes. This work does not merely encompass minor grammatical changes ("is" to "was") but a larger re-appraisal of both the article and its subject. The constitution of posthumous biographical collaborations reflects a series of "hand offs" between communities of users who edit the biography of the living person, manage the transition to death, and then steward biographies about deceased subjects.

Our study of the death work on Wikipedia opens up our understanding of the ways existing social and technical structures in a community like Wikipedia come to be differently enacted due to contexts that extend beyond the boundaries of the community—in this case, mortality. The mutability of articles afforded by Wikipedia, not only in content but also in contributors, raises important questions for both practices of stewarding collective memories and how collaborative networks shift that can be overlooked in human-computer interaction and computer-supported cooperative work: whose stories do we end up telling? How does what we say in them change over time?

Socio-technical systems that rely upon user-generated content are fundamentally shifting who gets to participate and what types of content are privileged in memorials, obituaries, and other forms of cultural memory [32]. These systems have the potential to be communal spaces that can support on-going re-appraisal of what is worth remembering through interaction, but institutionalized routines and norms can also undermine this potential. However this problem is not unique to Wikipedia, but rather reflects how Wikipedia's posthumous collaborations emulate journalistic obituaries that portray the deceased relative to contemporary values [19], which can naturally shift over time. What remains an open question is when and how Wikipedia and other socio-technical systems that serve as cultural repository archive will evolve in relationship to these values.

ACKNOWLEDGMENTS

We would like to thank Navid Dianati, Darren Gergle, Ryan Patrick Kennedy for input on statistical analyses; Scott Hale, Stuart Geiger, Aaron Halfaker, and other members of `wiki-research-l` for feedback on data cleanup; and Deborah Keegan for copy-editing.

REFERENCES

1. Barry, E. From epitaph to obituary: Death and celebrity in eighteenth-century British culture. *International Journal of Cultural Studies 11*, 3 (2008), 259–275.
2. Beschastnikh, I., Kriplean, T., and McDonald, D. W. Wikipedian self-governance in action: Motivating the policy lens. In *Proc. ICWSM 2008*, AAAI (2008), 27–35.
3. Brubaker, J. R., Dombrowski, L. S., Gilbert, A. M., Kusumakaulika, N., and Hayes, G. R. Stewarding a legacy: Responsibilities and relationships in the management of post-mortem data. In *Proc. CHI 2014*, ACM (2014), 4157–4166.
4. Brubaker, J. R., and Hayes, G. R. "We will never forget you [online]": An empirical investigation of post-mortem myspace comments. In *Proc. CSCW 2011*, ACM (2011), 123–132.
5. Brubaker, J. R., Hayes, G. R., and Dourish, P. Beyond the grave: Facebook as a site for the expansion of death and mourning. *The Information Society 29*, 3 (2013), 152–163.
6. Callahan, E. S., and Herring, S. C. Cultural bias in Wikipedia content on famous persons. *Journal of the American Society for Information Science and Technology 62*, 10 (2011), 1899–1915.
7. Carroll, B., and Landry, K. Logging on and letting out: Using online social networks to grieve and to mourn. *Bulletin of Science, Technology & Society 30*, 5 (2010), 341–349.
8. Corder, G. W., and Foreman, D. I. Comparing two related samples: The Wilcoxon signed ranks test. In *Nonparametric Statistics for Non-Statisticians*. John Wiley & Sons, Inc, 2009, 38–56.
9. Ferron, M., and Massa, P. Psychological processes underlying Wikipedia representations of natural and manmade disasters. In *Proc. WikiSym 2012*, ACM (2012), 1–10.
10. Forte, A., Larco, V., and Bruckman, A. Decentralization in Wikipedia governance. *Journal of Management Information Systems 26*, 1 (2009), 49–72.
11. Fowler, B. Mapping the obituary: Notes towards a Bourdieusian interpretation. *The Sociological Review 52* (2004), 148–171.
12. Geiger, R., and Ribes, D. Trace ethnography: Following coordination through documentary practices. In *Proc. HICSS 2011*, IEEE (2011), 1–10.
13. Geiger, R. S., and Halfaker, A. Using edit sessions to measure participation in Wikipedia. In *Proc. CSCW 2013*, ACM (2013), 861–870.
14. Geiger, R. S., and Ribes, D. The work of sustaining order in Wikipedia: The banning of a vandal. In *Proc. CSCW 2010*, ACM (2010), 117–126.
15. Halbwachs, M. *On collective memory*. University of Chicago Press, 1992.
16. Hale, S. A. Multilinguals and Wikipedia editing. In *Proc. WebSci 2014*, ACM (2014), 99–108.
17. Hanusch, F. Valuing those close to us. *Journalism Studies 9*, 3 (2008), 341–356.
18. Hecht, B., and Gergle, D. Measuring self-focus bias in community-maintained knowledge repositories. In *Proc. C&T 2009*, ACM (2009), 11–20.
19. Hume, J. *Obituaries in American Culture*. University Press of Mississippi, 2000.

20. Hume, J. "Portraits of Grief," reflectors of values: The New York Times remembers victims of September 11. *Journalism & Mass Communication Quarterly 80*, 1 (2003), 166–182.

21. Kastenbaum, R. *The psychology of death*. Springer Publishing Company, 2000.

22. Keegan, B., Gergle, D., and Contractor, N. Hot off the wiki: Dynamics, practices, and structures in Wikipedia's coverage of the Tōhoku catastrophes. In *Proc. WikiSym 2011*, ACM (2011), 105–113.

23. Keegan, B., Gergle, D., and Contractor, N. Staying in the loop: Structure and dynamics of Wikipedia's breaking news collaborations. In *Proc. WikiSym 2012*, ACM (2012), 1–10.

24. Keegan, B., Gergle, D., and Contractor, N. Hot off the wiki structures and dynamics of Wikipedia's coverage of breaking news events. *American Behavioral Scientist 57*, 5 (2013), 595–622.

25. Keegan, B. C. A history of newswork on Wikipedia. In *Proc. WikiSym 2013*, ACM (2013), 1–10.

26. Kittur, A., Lee, B., and Kraut, R. E. Coordination in collective intelligence: The role of team structure and task interdependence. In *Proc. CHI 2009*, ACM (2009), 1495–1504.

27. Latapy, M., Magnien, C., and Vecchio, N. D. Basic notions for the analysis of large two-mode networks. *Social Networks 30*, 1 (2008), 31–48.

28. Loveland, J., and Reagle, J. Wikipedia and encyclopedic production. *New Media & Society 15*, 8 (2013), 1294–1311.

29. Martin, D. D. Identity management of the dead: Contests in the construction of murdered children. *Symbolic Interaction 33*, 1 (2010), 18–40.

30. Marwick, A., and Ellison, N. B. "There isn't wifi in heaven!" negotiating visibility on Facebook memorial pages. *Journal of Broadcasting & Electronic Media 56*, 3 (2012), 378–400.

31. Moremen, R. D., and Cradduck, C. 'How will you be remembered after you die?' gender discrimination after death twenty years later. *Omega: Journal of Death & Dying* (1998), 241–254.

32. Pentzold, C. Fixing the floating gap: The online encyclopaedia Wikipedia as a global memory place. *Memory Studies 2*, 2 (2009), 255–272.

33. Radford, S. K., and Bloch, P. H. Grief, commiseration, and consumption following the death of a celebrity. *Journal of Consumer Culture 12*, 2 (2012), 137–155.

34. Reagle, J., and Rhue, L. Gender bias in Wikipedia and Britannica. *International Journal of Communication 5*, 0 (2011), 1138–1158.

35. Roberts, and Lourdes A. Vidal, P. Perpetual care in cyberspace: A portrait of memorials on the web. *OMEGA: The Journal of Death and Dying 40*, 4 (2000), 521–545.

36. Roberts, P. The living and the dead: Community in the virtual cemetary. *OMEGA: The Journal of Death and Dying 49*, 1 (2004), 57–76.

37. Starck, N. Posthumous parallel and parallax: the obituary revival on three continents. *Journalism Studies 6*, 3 (2005), 267–283.

38. Starck, N. Revelation, intrusion, and questions of taste: The ethical challenge for obituary editors. *Journalism Practice 1*, 3 (2007), 372–382.

39. Starck, N. Death can make a difference: A comparative study of "quality quartet" obituary practice. *Journalism Studies 9*, 6 (2008), 911–924.

40. Unruh, D. R. Death and personal history: Strategies of identity preservation. *Social Problems 30*, 3 (1983), 340–351.

Don't Wait! How Timing Affects Coordination of Crowdfunding Donations

Jacob Solomon
Michigan State University
solomo93@msu.edu

Wenjuan Ma
Michigan State University
mawenjua@msu.edu

Rick Wash
Michigan State University
wash@msu.edu

ABSTRACT
Crowdfunding sites often impose deadlines for projects to receive their requested funds. This deadline structure creates a difficult decision for potential donors. Donors can donate early to a project to help it reach its goal and to signal to other donors that the project is worthwhile. But donors may also want to wait for a similar signal from others.

We conduct an experimental simulation of a crowdfunding website to explore how potential donors to projects make this decision. We find evidence for both strategies in our experiment; some donate early while others wait till the last second. However, we also find that making an early donation is usually a better strategy for donors because the amount of donations made early in a project's campaign is often the only difference between that project being funded or not. This finding suggests that crowdfunding sites need to develop designs, policies and incentives that encourage people to make immediate donations so that the site can most efficiently fund projects.

Author Keywords
Crowdfunding

ACM Classification Keywords
H.5.m. Information Interfaces and Presentation (e.g. HCI): Miscellaneous

General Terms
Human Factors; Design

INTRODUCTION
Crowdfunding sites are a type of online community where large groups of people come together in order to realize a new idea or project that requires financing. Crowdfunding is a form of collective action that requires the participation of people in varying user roles, such as project creators, donors, or site administrators. Success in crowdfunding is achieved when the individual actions of users are well coordinated so that everyone's effort is put to use, not duplicated by other users, or not withheld from the group. Crowdfunding sites have many features that enable this coordination, either by affording direct communication between users, by providing information about users and their collective behavior, or by providing rules and structure that assist users in their decision making.

CSCW 2015, March 14–18, 2015, Vancouver, BC, Canada.

ACM 978-1-4503-2922-4/15/03 ...$15.00.
http://dx.doi.org/10.1145/2675133.2675296

One feature in many sites that assists in coordination is the setting of a deadline for projects to collect the required funds. This deadline typically accompanies an "All-or-nothing" style of crowdfunding where refunds are given to donors if a project does not meet a specified goal before the deadline [20]. Often in this style of crowdfunding, the site is designed to provide real-time status information about the progress of a project towards its goal. Kickstarter, for example, displays for each project the up-to-date total for how much the project has received, how many people have donated, and how long until the deadline (see Figure 1).

This combination of design features presents an interesting choice for anyone who might consider contributing to a crowdfunding project. *When* should one make a donation? Should donors immediately donate, or wait some period of time before donating? There are good reasons for either choice. It may make sense to wait to see whether other people donate, because the donations of others may be sufficient and a donor could free-ride and reap the benefits of the project without contributing. It might also make sense to donate immediately, because a donation may be used as a signal to others that the project has quality and encourage them to donate.

Both choices are relevant to coordination. Signals sent to other users of a site through donation (or lack of) will influence the way groups coordinate to fund projects, and likely the degree to which they are successful at this collective effort.

We explore this decision from the perspective of crowdfunding donors by conducting an experimental simulation of a crowdfunding site. This study seeks to understand how the decision of when to donate affects coordination on crowdfunding sites. We primarily explore how the degree of interest or preference that donors have for projects (both as individuals and collectively as a cohort of potential contributors) affects their decisions, and how this subsequently affects coordination and crowdfunding outcomes. We show that making an immediate donation is generally a better strategy for potential donors, particularly if they are strongly motivated to see a project completed. We do find however, that waiting till the end can be a successful strategy in some circumstances.

Figure 1. An example Kickstarter project

Later, we will discuss the implications of this finding for the design of crowdfunding sites.

CROWDFUNDING, COORDINATION AND TIMING

Recent years have seen the rise of a wide variety of crowdfunding websites [8], including Kickstarter (which funds creative projects), IndieGoGo (which funds a wide variety of ideas and new businesses), Spot.Us (which funds investigative journalism), and Donors Choose (which funds K–12 classroom projects). These websites have enabled people with ideas to raise large amounts of money to support their projects. Kickstarter has raised over $1 billion in funding for a variety of projects from over 6 million people[1]. Donors Choose has raised over $240 million for over 450,000 projects in K-12 classrooms[2].

Projects on crowdfunding websites offer two forms of value to donors. Many projects offer a *public good* – a valuable good that everyone can benefit from, even if they don't back the project. For example, recently Kickstarter was used to raise money to create a new Veronica Mars movie that we all can now watch. Additionally, many crowdfunded projects offer specific value to individual donors, usually in the form of project-related rewards, product pre-orders, or equity in what is produced. Crowdfunding is rarely used solely as a sales mechanism; almost all crowdfunded projects include some public goods component. Belleflamme et al.[6] argue that in the absence of any public good aspect, crowdfunding theoretically "yields exactly the same outcome as seeking money from a bank or equity investor."

Crowdfunding is an effective method of raising funds for projects. Many crowdfunding websites have funding rates higher than 40%: 43%–49% of projects on Kickstarter are fully funded [15, 12]; 43.5% of projects on Spotus are fully funded [11], and almost 70% of projects on Donors Choose are fully funded [19]. Mollick [15] observes that projects that ask for less money have higher funding rates than larger projects.

Crowdfunding Needs Coordination

Crowdfunding enables a large number of people to collaborate through the creation of and donations to projects to produce a public good. Crowdfunding works because people donate to crowdfunding projects irrespective of geography [1]. However, this creates a coordination problem for the people involved: with scarce resources, how can donors and creators decide which projects to put their effort and money behind?

Crowdfunding requires several forms of coordination. Much of the CSCW research on crowdfunding has looked at coordination between project creators and donors or potential donors. Gerber and Hui [7] found that establishing long-term connections with backers and building awareness are important motivations for project creators to use crowdfunding. In other work [10] they show that building a community around one's project and engaging with that community is important for the success of crowdfunded projects. Likewise, Xu et al. [21] showed that effective project updates during the course of a Kickstarter campaign keep backers engaged and positively influence the chance of success for a project. Mitra and Gilbert [14] describe how the language used in project descriptions signals the quality of projects to potential donors.

Another form of coordination on crowdfunding sites is coordination and collaboration between project creators. Hui et al. [10] found that a number of communities have formed around crowdfunding, where creators discuss and critique ideas. Project creators may learn not only from other creators, but also from their own repeated experiences as project creators [9, 16].

Wash and Solomon [20] demonstrated that the discrete nature of many crowdfunding projects creates complementarities in donors' preferences, which means that coordination is required in order for all donors to get what they desire out of crowdfunding. They showed that in some cases, such as when a crowdfunding site uses an "all-or-nothing" mechanism and refunds donations to incomplete projects, getting more in donations may not lead to more projects being funded if the donations are not well coordinated.

Crowdfunding donors face a coordination challenge in that, while donors typically know how much they value a project, they don't necessarily know how others value it. This may be inferred from the amount of backing a project has received previously, but if people are free-riding, this inference could be incorrect and a project may not receive some donations simply because it does not appear to donors that others will also contribute.

Theory of Donation Timing in Charitable Giving

Crowdfunding projects collect donations over an extended period of time. The choices donors make about when to donate may have significant effects on the outcomes of crowdfunding projects. Agrawal et al. [2] argue that crowdfunding prompts "rational herding" where people are more likely to donate to projects when they have already received some donations from others, and that as a project nears its deadline the rate of donations accelerates. This finding has similarly been shown in a micro lending sites [22], which resemble crowdfuding. Kuppaswamy and Bayus [13] found that projects on Kickstarter tend to experience a "bathtub" pattern of donations over time: projects typically get many donations immediately after being posted, go through a period where few donations are made, and then as the deadline approached, re-

[1] `https://www.kickstarter.com/help/stats`, retrieved on June 4, 2014

[2] `http://www.donorschoose.org/about/impact.html`, retrieved on June 4, 2014

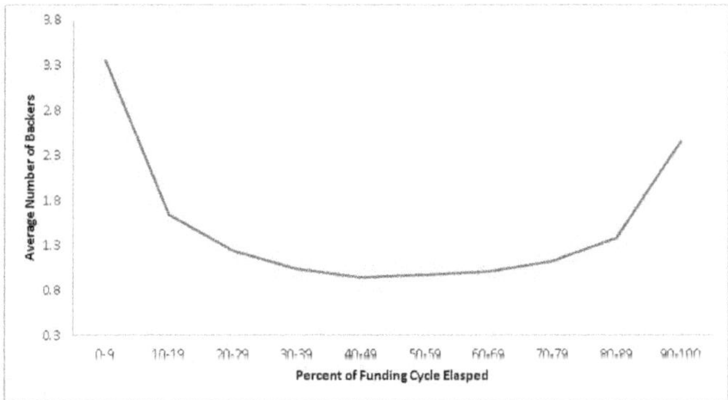

Figure 2. The timing of donations made to Kickstarter.com, as reported by [13]

ceive a last-minute surge of donations. Figure 2 illustrates their finding.

Public goods are often funded through philanthropy: charitable giving by wealthy (and sometimes not-so-wealthy) donors. Economists have identified a number of rational strategies for choosing when to give to a public good. First, many people choose to free-ride. That is, they choose to not donate to the public good, allow others to fund the good, and then reap the benefits once it is funded. This is a very common and rational strategy. However, if everyone chooses this strategy, then no public good would ever be funded.

A second strategy is to wait until asked to donate, and then contributing to whichever charity asked. Dubbed "the Power of the Ask", this strategy is a minimal-effort strategy that allows people to make charitable donations without the effort of deciding where to donate [4]. Together, these first two strategies represent a *lack of coordination*. Anyone using these donation strategies is explicitly forgoing coordinating with other donors about which projects or charities to fund.

Many donors often intentionally choose a wait-and-see approach to charitable donation. Because there is risk associated with donating, it is rational for a potential donor to wait and see how many other people are donating. This allows the potential donor to assess the likelihood that the project will be completely funded, or to assess the quality of a project based on the assessment of the crowd [3]. By waiting, donors may also benefit if the project is able to be completed without their donation at all.

Because many potential donors take a wait-and-see approach, another strategy is to make a large donation early during a fundraising campaign. Charities often solicit a "leadership donation" – a large donation from a well-known donor for 25%-50% of the total funds needed. Andreoni argues that leadership donations provide a credible signal that a charity or project is high quality and also that the project is likely to receive the funds it needs [5]. It also reduces the remaining funds needed, making the fundraising goal easier to achieve. Thus, by giving early, leadership donors can influence which projects are funded both directly through their donation and indirectly by inducing others to donate.

Timing Donations on Crowdfunding Websites

These donation timing strategies present an interesting coordination dilemma for donors on a crowdfunding site. Typically, no single donor can fund a crowdfunding project, so it is important that donors coordinate their donations to ensure that the project of their choice receives the funds it needs. However, each person might prefer a different project be funded, and therefore must coordinate with others to decide which projects will be funded with the scarce resources available in the crowd.

Wash [19] found evidence of a "completion bias" in crowdfunding projects on Donors Choose: the last person to make a donation to a completed project typically donates far more than an average amount. This could be a selection-and-timing effect, where people who want to make large donations intentionally wait until they are certain that their donation will go to a successful project – the wait-and-see approach identified for charitable giving. Or it could be that donors who hear about a project later experience very little risk, and thus are willing to make an increased donation.

Shin and Jian [17] found evidence of leadership giving in crowdfunding. They observed that most early donations to projects come from friends or family of the project creator (who may be most motivated for the project to succeed). However, leadership giving is risky; if the project never reaches its goal and receives the funds it needs, then the money that was donated is tied up for a period of time, unable to be used more productively.

It is difficult to determine from existing research and data on crowdfunding which of these strategies are being used. Perhaps those who wait till the end of a campaign are waiting because they are trying to free-ride off the donations of others. Or they may be herding and only see value in a project because enough other people have expressed value through their donations. We do not know with enough precision the motivation or value that a donor has for making the donation. We also can't know whether people who donate early are the ones who really like the project most and want to encourage others, or if they are simply expressing support for the creator because of the personal connection and not as much for the project itself. Similarly, those who wait may be the ones who like the project most, and the completion bias found by Wash [19] offers some evidence for this. Without having more specific information about individual donors' motivations and valuations of projects, our understanding of the timing dynamics is incomplete. In this paper, we report on a lab-based study where we control people's preferences and thus are able to better understand the strategies being used.

METHODS

In order to understand timing choices in crowdfunding, we created an experiment that provided people an opportunity to make decisions about when to donate to crowdfunding projects. This experimental approach allows us to completely control the environment: we controlled exactly which projects could receive donations, each person's budget for donating to crowdfunding projects, and the number of other potential donors.

Also, critically, we were able to assign *preferences* to subjects. For each available project, every subject was assigned a payoff – a number of credits that they would receive if that project is fully funded (regardless of whether that subject donated to the project). At the end of the experiment, subjects exchanged the credits that they earned for real money (100 credits = $1 USD). Vernon Smith showed that by assigning preferences and paying based on credits earned, this structure effectively induces the subjects to value the projects as they are assigned to [18]. Once subjects value the projects, they are likely to make decisions about these projects in similar ways as they do about real-world projects that they value. This Induced Value Theory [18] has been the basis of much of experimental economics in the last 30 years.

Assigning preferences to subjects also allows us to control the difficulty of the coordination problem. If we assign high preferences to many people for a given project, then that project is easy to fund. Likewise, if few people value a project, then that project will be more difficult to fund. Thus, we can effectively create a variety of different types of projects simply by varying the distribution of preferences for a given project across subjects.

Simulated Crowdfunding Website

Our experiment followed a similar setup to the crowdfunding game used by Wash and Solomon [20]. A group of six subjects formed a crowd of visitors to a simulated crowdfunding site. In this setup, subjects were allotted credits that they could donate to the three projects on our simulated crowdfunding site. Projects were available for donations for 60 seconds, and subjects could make donations at any point during the period. The three projects had no descriptions and were labeled only as "Red", "Yellow", or "Blue" projects. Each project had a goal of 100 credits. Figure 3 shows the site as subjects saw it.

Subjects were instructed that if the project was funded by the end of 60 seconds, they would receive their pre-specified payout as a bonus payment in credits. Each subject was given a budget of 30 credits per project that could be donated, and this budget could not be transferred to other projects. This feature of the design ensures that projects on the site are not actually in direct competition with each other for donations. Donating to the Red project, for example, does not in any way diminish one's ability to donate to the Blue project. Although they appear on the site simultaneously, there was no economic incentive to withhold donations or make a strategic choice about timing donations from one project because of the status of any other project. This reflects the common view that people make independent donation decisions about crowdfunding projects, rather than comparing projects and deciding which to donate to. This also allows us to treat the projects as independent in our analysis.

Subjects were free to donate any amount within their budget at any time during the 60 seconds. Subjects were also free to donate as many times to a project as they wished. For this reason, the number of donations that could be made to a project was limited only by the time available. The total amount in credits of donations was only limited by the budget.

Project:	Difficult		Easy		Medium	
Condition:	1	2	1	2	1	2
Subj. 1	0	15	30	30	45	25
Subj. 2	0	15	30	30	45	25
Subj. 3	0	15	30	30	45	25
Subj. 4	15	15	30	30	15	25
Subj. 5	15	15	30	30	15	25
Subj. 6	15	15	30	30	15	25
Total	45	90	180	180	180	150

Table 1. Payoff a subject receives, in credits, when a given project is funded. In condition 1, the medium project has the same total payout as the easy project but unevenly distributed payouts. In condition 2, the medium project has a lower total payout but everyone has identical payouts.

A strategy that we expected to see was for subjects to wait until the last possible moment to submit a final donation. Because we wanted to be sure that we captured all such attempts to make a "last-second donation" and not have the results depend on subjects' ability to time their clicks of the mouse button precisely, we configured the interface to treat the final ten seconds of the round as being effectively the final second. For this reason, in the final ten seconds of each round, project totals stopped being updated on subjects' screens and subjects could only submit one tim in this period. Subjects were instructed to treat this period as the "final second."

Groups played three practice rounds followed by fifteen live rounds where earnings were recorded. After each round, groups were re-formed to avoid problems that can arise from repeated games [3].

We recruited 120 undergraduate students (54% female, average age of 20 years) by email from our university to play this crowdfunding simulation. Only 33% of subjects indicated that they had ever visited a crowdfunding website previously. Subject earned an average of about $20 for participating in this hour-long study.

Creating Projects and Preferences

Projects varied only in the preferences assigned to the potential donors, as induced by the payouts offered for completion. Table 1 lists the payout structure of the experiment. This payout structure created three classes of projects that relate to how much total interest there was in a project (i.e. the sum of all donors' payouts) and the distribution of those payouts (i.e. evenly spread out so all donors receive the same payout, or uneven payouts where some donors receive larger payouts than others).

We have labeled these projects in this description according to their relative difficulty in funding, as determined by the results of the study. Easy projects were funded most frequently, medium projects were funded somewhat rarely, and difficult projects were almost never funded (because funding this project required irrational donating). We anticipated how difficult each type of project would be to fund through pilot testing, and structured the experiment into two conditions that represent two different versions of a crowdfunding site. Each

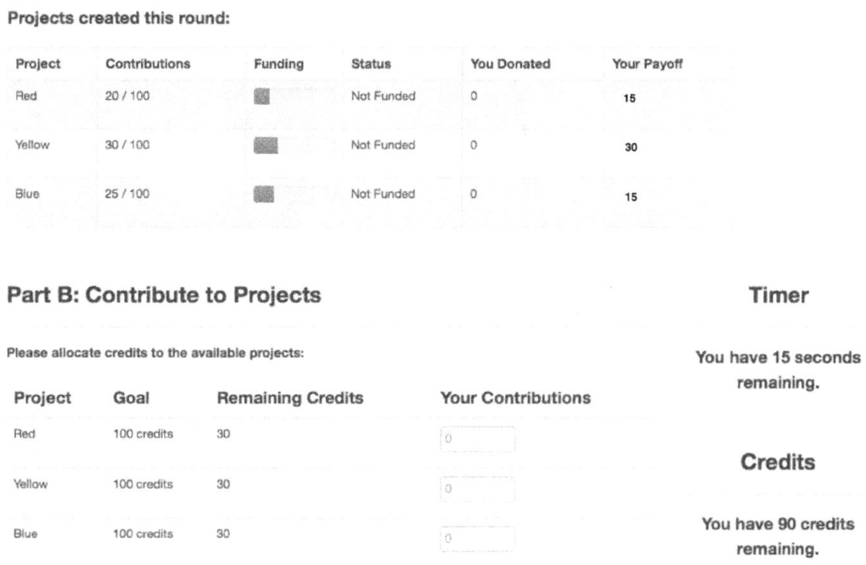

Figure 3. Crowfunding interface used in the experiment

site had three projects, one that was easy, one medium, and one difficult. The primary difference between the two sites was the nature of the medium project. In condition 1, the medium project had a high degree of overall interest, based on the sum of all payouts, but the payouts were unevenly distributed so that some people valued it more than they had budget to donate, and others had only a small preference. This created difficulty because if any one person with a high value decided to free-ride or take a wait and see approach, it became difficult for the rest of the group to rationally fund the project. Likewise in condition 2, the medium project had evenly spread out preferences but they were smaller overall. This similarly reduces the margin of error that users have for coordinating their donations successfully and still earning a payout from the project.

Subjects knew their own payouts for each project, but were not explicitly given any information of others' payouts. Any information they gained about other donors had to be inferred by observing donations to projects over the course of the 60 seconds.

RESULTS

Descriptive analysis

How much did people donate?

Of the 30 credit allotment given for each project, subjects donated an average of 10.39 (SD = 10.23) credits to each project on the site. Figure 4 shows the distribution of donations made to a project broken down according to the subject's payout if the project was completed. Subjects on average made 1.3 donations to a given project over the 60 seconds in the round. Figure 5 describes this distribution. Repeated donations from the same donor occurred in less than half of all observations. It was more common to either free-ride or to only make a single donation.

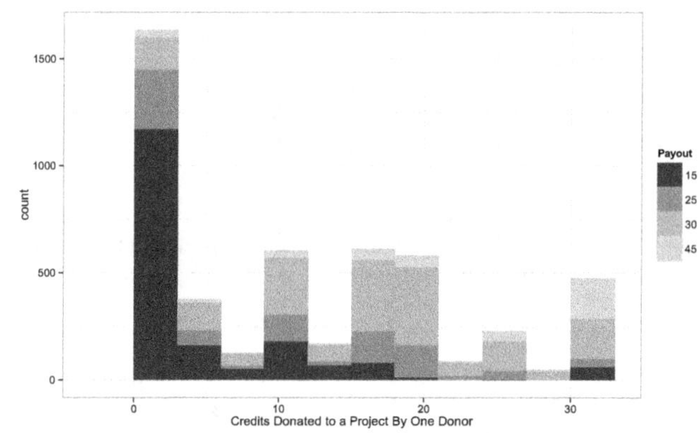

Figure 4. Distribution of donation amounts

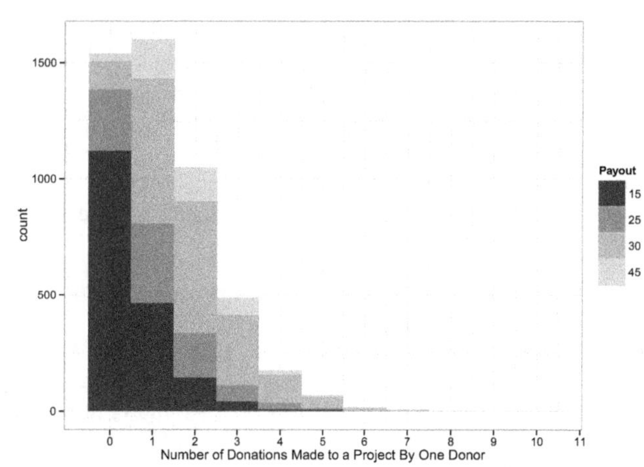

Figure 5. How many times each person donated

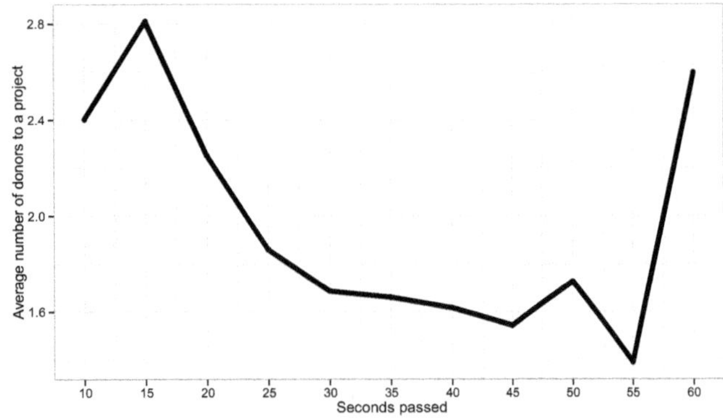

Figure 6. Average number of donations to a project over time

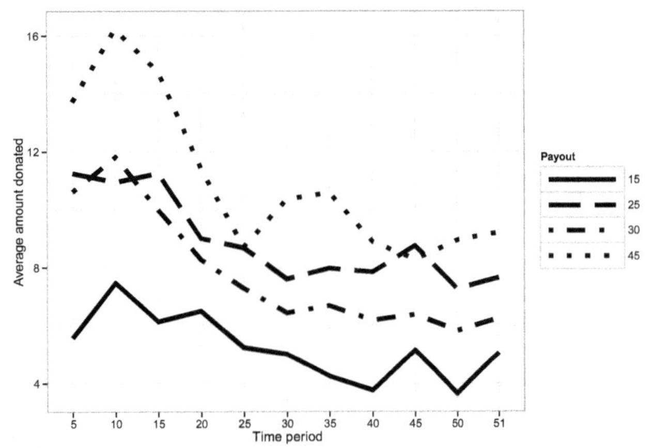

Figure 7. Average donation amount at each time period. These averages exclude non-donations in the period

Together, these results illustrate that free-riding – donating zero or a very small amount and letting others contribute most of the needed funds – was a popular strategy among donors. Free-riding was particularly common when subjects had a payoff of 15 credits, which was a low payout amount.

When did people donate?

Figure 6 describes how many donations were made to projects over the course of the 60 second campaign. Donations quickly hit a peak between about 10 and 15 seconds into the 60-second fundraising campaign and then slowly decreased in frequency until another peak right before the end. This pattern is highly similar to what has been observed by other research on live crowdfunding sites (compare Figure 6 to the Kickstarter data shown in Figure 2 above).

When subjects did make donations, there was a general tendency to make larger donations towards the beginning of the round, and smaller donations later on. Figure 7 shows the average size of donations made at each 5-second block within the round (not including donations of 0). This is in contrast to the finding of Wash [19], who found that the last donation of a project was usually much larger than other donations.

How successful were the crowds at funding projects?

	Project:	Difficult	Easy	Medium
Cond. 1	Success Rate	0%	54%	35%
	Credits Received	13.7	96.0	85.9
	# of Donations	1.3	11.8	9.5
	Payouts	Uneven	Even	Uneven
Cond. 2	Success Rate	1%	52%	18%
	Credits Received	19.2	94.0	65.3
	# of Donations	1.8	11.5	7.2
	Payouts	Even	Even	Even

Table 2. Donation statistics for each project type, averaged across all projects of that type

The projects varied widely in their likelihood of being funded. The easy project was, unsurprisingly, the most frequently funded project, and the difficult project was only funded once. The medium projects, however, showed an interesting pattern. The medium project with a high total payout but preferences unevenly spread through the crowd was funded 35% of the time. The other medium project, with a lower total payout but an even distribution of preferences, was funded 18% of the time. This difference is statistically significant according to a Chi-square test ($p < .001$). This suggests that it is better to have more total interest in the community than to have everyone like it somewhat. Table 2 describes the outcomes for all types of projects.

Identifying Strategies

One of our goals was to identify different strategies that subjects use when making donations. To do this, we used k-mean clustering analysis. The unit of analysis is the amount of donation from an individual at a time period. We cut the entire 60 second session into 3 periods: The first 15 seconds, 16 to 50 second and 51 to 60 seconds. This was based on our initial analysis (Figure 6) where we noted that these three periods had different donation patterns overall. In this analysis, we only examine first-time donations to a project. The first-time donation is the best representation of a donor's strategy, and first time donations are more fairly comparable to each other than subsequent donations. This is because donor's have the choice to make a first-time donation at any point in the round, and they always have an equal amount of budget when making the donation. Subsequent donations are biased towards the end of the round, which makes it difficult to assess the degree to which they act as leadership donations. Additionally, the vast majority of users make only 0 or 1 donation to a project (see Figure 5).

The goal of the cluster analysis was to find donations that were similar in terms of the timing and amount of the donation, the donor's payout, and the amount the project had already received. This is done by finding groups that maximize the distance between clusters and minimize the distance within. Through exploration, we found that seeking four clusters provided only marginal improvement in overall fit compared to three, so we settled on three clusters.

Figure 8 illustrates the clusters, broken down by the timing and amount of donation made by the observations. Each

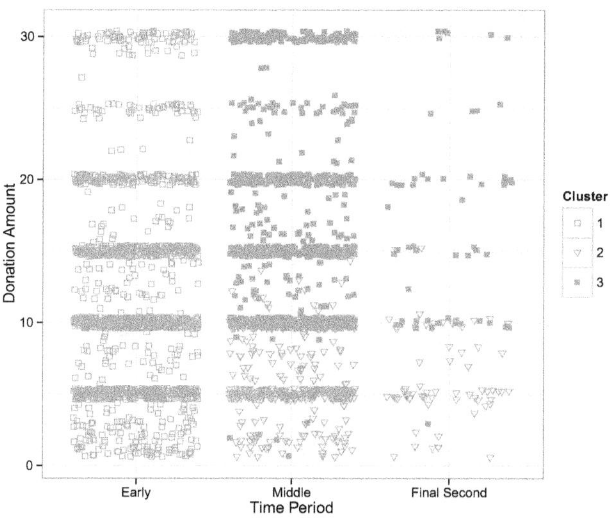

Figure 8. Strategy clusters

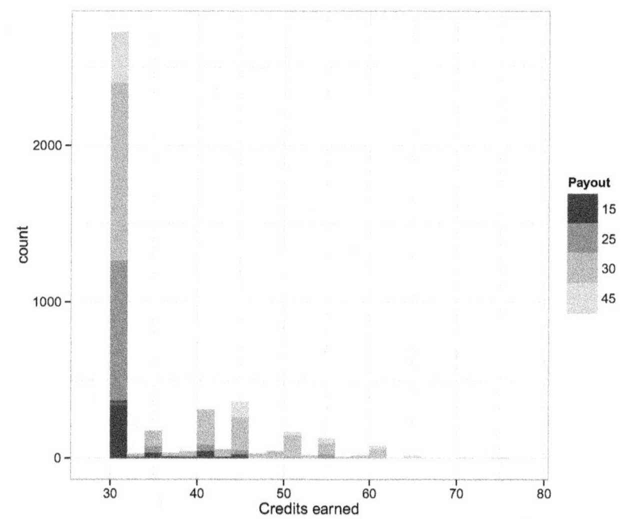

Figure 9. Distribution of the number of credits earned from a project

of the three clusters represents a separate strategy taken by donors. One strategy involved making a donation of any size in the initial 15 second period of the round (cluster 1). Another strategy was to make a larger donation (approximately 10 credits or greater) in either the middle period or the "Last chance" period (cluster 2). The third strategy was to make only a small donation in the middle or final stages of the round (cluster 3).

These clusters only include instances where a subject made any donation in the round. There is a fourth strategy which can clearly be seen in Figure 4 which was to completely free-ride and never make a donation.

We speculated that the size of one's payout would be related to which strategy a donor chose to take. However, removing payouts as one of the factors led to almost no changes in the clusters. We also noted in a visual analysis of donations that the proportion of donations made by each payout level remained constant over the course of the round on average. This means that the size of one's payout did not influence donors' strategies.

These clusters roughly correspond to the strategies identified in the literature review above. Donations in cluster 1 are leadership donations – early donations that signal to others which projects are likely to succeed. Cluster 4 (non-donations) are free-riding. Clusters 2 and 3 appear to be variations on the wait-and-see strategy, though it isn't clear how that strategy is playing out.

Having an Impact

To examine which strategy worked best for donors, we plotted the growth patterns for the three types of fundable projects in Figure 10. Projects that were ultimately funded differ from the unsuccessful projects. A separation in growth appears within the first 15 to 20 seconds for each type of project. For the High Interest projects – the easy project and the medium project with a large payout and uneven spread – this separation does not grow much, if at all, over the rest of the round. For these types of projects, the difference between being funded or not is a direct effect of the donations made early on. In the middle period of the round, the growth rates are equivalent. But the extra donations made early make it more likely that when the final second comes, that someone will donate to complete the project.

For the Medium difficulty project with lower, evenly spread payouts, the early donations are even more important. Unlike the High Interest projects, donations slow down considerably for this kind of project when it does not receive many early donations. When this project was funded, it received a slightly higher rate of initial donations which then was sustained somewhat constantly over the round until it was funded. When these early donations did not happen, donors ignored this project and it received few further donations.

This suggests that as a strategy for personal gain in our crowdfunding simulation, it is generally better for a donor to make an early donation than to wait. To examine this idea in more detail, we ran a set of regression models that estimate the profitability of different donation strategies.

When a project is not funded, the all-or-nothing structure of the site meant that the subject would still earn 30 credits. Since less than 40% of projects were funded, the distribution of earnings was somewhat unusual and heavily inflated with earnings of 30 (see Figure 9). Therefore, we built two models to analyze whether donating early led to better outcomes for donors. The first model estimates the probability that a subject earned any "profit" at all (payout greater than 30) using logistic regression.

When removing projects that were not funded, the remaining distribution is approximately a poisson distribution. Therefore in our second model we estimated the number of credits earned from a funded project based on the timing of the first donation grouped into 15 second intervals. For this model we used a poisson regression – a generalized linear model where

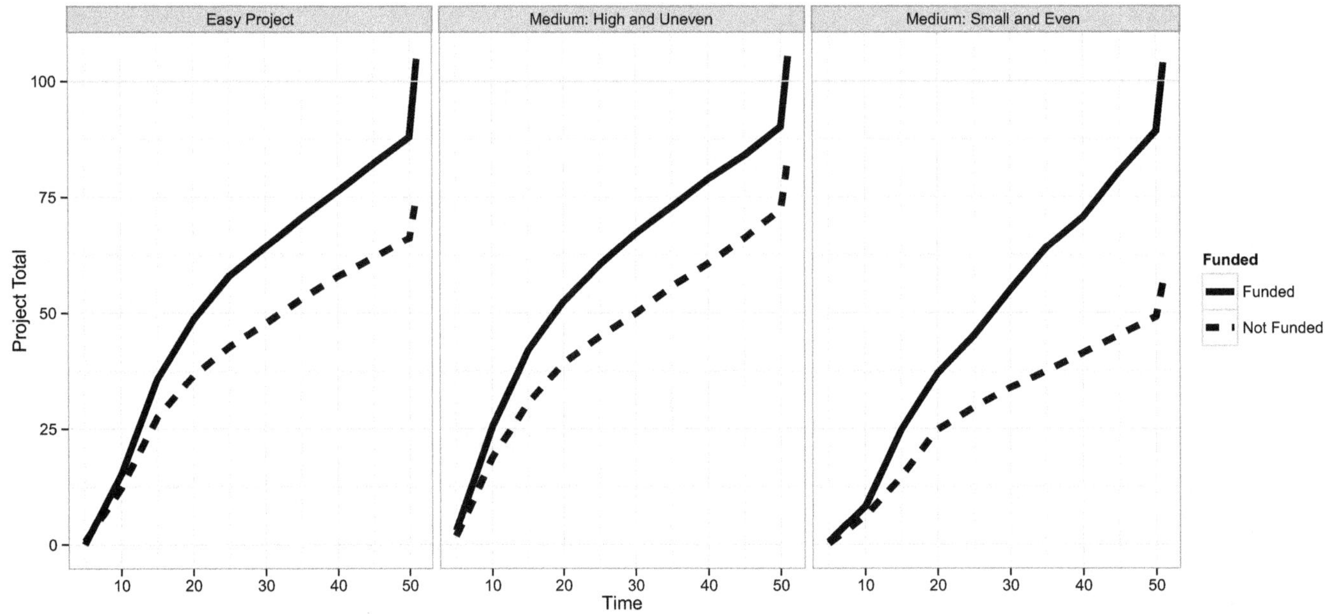

Figure 10. Comparison of growth of funded and un-funded projects

the errors are distributed according to a poisson distribution and the natural logarithm as a link function. These models are represented in Table 3. Both models include the subject's payout for the given project and a random effect of the subject (due to the repeated nature of the game). The Intercept in these models represents those who donated in the first 15 seconds. The estimates represent the changes in log odds of earning a profit (Model 1) and the natural logarithm of credits earned above 30 (Model 2) that can be expected from a one unit change in the independent variable.

Model 1 suggests that it is a poor strategy to wait longer than the initial 15 second period to make a donation, though waiting until the last moment is almost as good. Subjects who donated between 15 and 45 seconds were less likely to earn additional credits from the project. Additionally, subjects who never made a donation were very unlikely to earn additional credits. This model describes the probability of earning a profit, but in our study, this is nearly completely synonymous with the probability of a project being funded (since subjects almost always donated less than their payout). Therefore, model 1 can also be interpreted as the effect of the timing of one's donation on the probability of that project being funded.

However, model 2 suggests that if a project was funded, the subjects who waited till the end or did not donate did in fact earn more credits. To get a better overall picture for the value of being an early contributor, we conducted a Wilcoxon Rank Sum test on the total credits earned from a project that compared those who donated early (within the first 15 seconds) and those who did not. The test indicated that those who donate early did earn more credits ($p < .001$), although the difference in means between the two groups was less than 1 credit.

	Dependent variable:	
	Profited?	Earnings
	(1)	(2)
Intercept	−0.102	1.462***
	(0.073)	(0.047)
15-30 Seconds	−0.239***	0.033*
	(0.083)	(0.019)
30-45	−0.282**	0.186***
	(0.113)	(0.025)
After 45	−0.091	0.295***
	(0.130)	(0.027)
Never	−1.626***	0.569***
	(0.134)	(0.030)
Amount Donated	−0.019***	−0.022***
	(0.005)	(0.001)
Payout		0.041***
		(0.001)
Note:	*p<0.1; **p<0.05; ***p<0.01	

Table 3. Effect of donation timing on earnings from projects

It is worthwhile to note that free-riding was a very poor strategy in this study. Free-riding on average led to much lower earnings than when even small donations were made. This likely speaks to the value of a donation both as an act of funding a creator's idea but also as a coordination signal sent to other potential donors.

DISCUSSION

Donors in the experiment, like real users of crowdfunding sites, face a difficult decision around when to make a donation. Donating early sends a behavioral signal to others that encourages them to donate as well, and improve the chances of the project being successful. However, the project may be successful without one's donation, and by waiting, donors may be able to reap the benefits of a completed project without donating or may only need to make a smaller donation towards the end. This is a potential cost of sending coordination signals to other users.

In our study however, donating early was overall a better strategy for donors. This was particularly true for donors with the most to gain from a project being funded; donating early leads to a higher likelihood of profit. Though, once you know the project will be funded, it is better to donate late because that allows you to partially free-ride using a smaller donation. Conversely, those with only small payouts, equating to those with relatively low preference, may do better by waiting till the end and making a small donation if the project is close to being funded.

This result has some important implications for crowdfunding sites. First of all, it suggests that the rigid all-or-nothing deadline structure of many crowdfunding sites may create some inefficiencies with the way people coordinate to fund projects. Deadlines may create an incentive for people to wait, and if too many people wait then projects that otherwise have enough interest to be completed may not be funded. In our simulation, the collective payouts of most projects was over 100, meaning that it was profitable for the crowd of donors as a whole to fund the project. Since this happened less than 40% of the time for these projects, we argue that there was inefficient coordination among the donors on a site.

A noteworthy result is that the medium project with uneven preferences was funded less frequently than the easy project. Although this was expected, it is noteworthy because the sum total of all payouts to donors was actually the same for both projects. The only difference between them was the difference in how those payouts were distributed. In some subsequent exploration of this result, we noted that the medium project almost always failed if one of the three donors with high preference (45 credit payout) decided to wait or to free-ride altogether. When projects have an uneven distribution of preference across the population of potential donors, it is critical that those with with high preference donate early because if they do not, there is not likely to be anyone else who will. When preferences are evenly distributed, there is a greater chance of early donation because if one person free-rides or waits, there is a larger pool of potential replacements for that donation.

Deadlines do have an important role in crowdfunding. Deadlines are necessary for the all-or-nothing style or crowdfunding to be functional. All-or-nothing crowdfunding minimizes the risk for a donor associated with donating [20]. Therefore, it seems logical that this approach would encourage more early donations. Our data do show many early donations, as do real crowdfunding data collected from Kickstarter [13]. But in our study, one or two "missing" donations in the early period was frequently the only difference between funded and un-funded projects. Therefore, it is critical for projects to absolutely maximize their early donations. Even though all-or-nothing may minimize the incentive to wait, it does not eliminate it. People can still estimate for themselves that they may be able to free-ride and still reap the benefits of the project, or at least minimize the size of contribution they need to make. It is also very important to consider that waiting to donate towards the end was a good strategy if the project was funded. That is to say, if a project only needed a small donation at the deadline, the person who waits till the end then makes that small donation ends up with a large profit.

Design Implications

What can crowdfunding sites do get people to donate at the start of a project's campaign? One existing structure likely has a positive influence. Many projects offer potential donors some form of personalized reward or perk in exchange for a donation. Often, projects set limits on how many of these rewards are given out to donors, which gives an incentive to donate immediately. It is a limitation of our study design that we have treated crowdfunding projects as pure public goods, when in fact the rewards offered by projects add some additional complexity.

One potential design for crowdfunding sites that could maintain the all-or-nothing structure, but possibly lead to more early donations, would be to set a mandated pace for donations. Projects might have multiple check-in points during the time period of the campaign, and failure to maintain a pre-specified funding pace at any of these points would result in the project being closed and donations being immediately refunded. This design may relieve the coordination dilemma that can occur because it encourages people to send signals of interest in a project (by way of donating) immediately, which then gives other potential donors a more accurate estimate of the true interest the crowd has in a project.

Another design might keep the current status or the total funding goal hidden from donors when the project gets close to reaching its goal. In this design, when a project meets its goal, it remains open for some period of time and can collect additional donations, since the status is not communicated. As a project grows beyond its goal, donations would not go to the project but rather to early donors. In our experiment, project status was not updated to donors in the final period and as a result, most projects that were funded received some excess donations. Returning these donations to early donors would offer a new incentive to donate early and express one's preference for a project rather than waiting or free-riding.

Limitations

This study has several limitations that should be considered. In our experiment, we created a simplified replication of a crowdfunding site that is has some clear differences from most real crowdfunding sites, such as the extremely limited amount of time of a campaign and the limited amount of information available about projects. In particular, our experiment was designed such that the only information donors had with which to coordinate was a project's funding total at a given moment in the campaign, whereas much richer information is available to donors making real crowdfunding decisions. Future work should examine how other type of information or communication afforded by crowdfunding platforms might influence timing decisions, or how our results may be moderated in more authentic crowdfunding scenario.

Our study also simulates the decisions of a large number of distinct people by having a smaller number of people make multiple decisions, such as how many times to donate and how many projects to donate to. This is demanded by the complexity of recruiting and coordinating participation in an experiment. Although the study successfully replicated the results of real crowdfunding sites by condensing the "crowd" in this way, it should be noted as a limitation because our simulation may have achieved similar results but for different reasons.

CONCLUSION

Overall, we can conclude that all-or-nothing crowdfunding with a deadline creates an inefficiency because it encourages people to withhold their donation. By withholding donations, people not only withhold funds from a project but also a signal to others about the crowd's interest in a project. Without these signals, donors do not efficiently coordinate and fund projects even when there is sufficient interest. Crowdfunding sites should explore ways to increase early donations so that crowd interest in projects is effectively communicated and donations are coordinated.

ACKNOWLEDGEMENTS

This work was supported by the National Science Foundation, award number CCF-1101266.

REFERENCES

1. Agrawal, A., Catalini, C., and Goldfarb, A. The geography of crowdfunding. NBER Working Paper #16820, February 2011.
2. Agrawal, A. K., Catalini, C., and Goldfarb, A. Some simple economics of crowdfunding. Tech. rep., National Bureau of Economic Research, 2013.
3. Andreoni, J. Why free ride?: Strategies and learning in public goods experiments. *Journal of Public Economics 37*, 3 (1988), 291 – 304.
4. Andreoni, J. Philanthropy. In *Handbook of Giving, Reciprocity, and Altruism*. Elsivier / North Holland, 2005.
5. Andreoni, J. Leadership giving in charitable fundraising. *Journal of Public Economics 8*, 1 (2006), 1–22.
6. Belleflamme, P., Lambert, T., and Schwienbacher, A. Crowdfunding: Tapping the right crowd. Tech. Rep. 1578175, Social Science Research Network (SSRN), April 2012.
7. Gerber, E. M., and Hui, J. Crowdfunding: Motivations and deterrents for participation. *ACM Transactions on Computer-Human Interaction (TOCHI) 20*, 6 (2013), 34.
8. Greenberg, M., and Gerber, E. Crowdfunding: A survey and taxonomy. Tech. Rep. 12-03, Northwestern University Segal Design Institute, 2012.
9. Greenberg, M. D., and Gerber, E. M. Learning to fail: experiencing public failure online through crowdfunding. In *Proceedings of the 32nd annual ACM conference on Human factors in computing systems*, ACM (2014), 581–590.
10. Hui, J. S., Greenberg, M. D., and Gerber, E. M. Understanding the role of community in crowdfunding work. In *Proceedings of the 17th ACM Conference on Computer Supported Cooperative Work and Social Computing*, CSCW '14, ACM (New York, NY, USA, 2014), 62–74.
11. Jian, L., and Usher, N. Crowd-funded journalism. *Journal of Computer Mediated Communication 19*, 2 (January 2014).
12. Kickstarter. Statistics. `http://www.kickstarter.com/help/stats`, June 2014.
13. Kuppuswamy, V., and Bayus, B. L. Crowdfunding creative ideas: the dynamics of projects backers in kickstarter. *SSRN Electronic Journal* (2013).
14. Mitra, T., and Gilbert, E. The language that gets people to give: Phrases that predict success on kickstarter. In *Proceedings of the 17th ACM Conference on Computer Supported Cooperative Work and Social Computing*, CSCW '14, ACM (New York, NY, USA, 2014), 49–61.
15. Mollick, E. The dynamics of crowdfunding: An exploratory study. *Journal of Business Venturing 29*, 1 (2014), 1–16.
16. Pak, C., and Wash, R. Importance of recent experience and initial overconfidence:factors of crowdfundiners' limited learning. Working Paper, June 2014.
17. Shin, J., and Jian, L. Driving forces behind readers' donation to crowd-funded journalism: The case of spot.us. Working paper, University of Southern California, 2012.
18. Smith, V. L. Experimental economics: Induced value theory. *American Economic Review 66*, 2 (May 1976), 274–279.
19. Wash, R. The value of completing crowdfunding projects. In *International Conference on Weblogs and Social Media (ICWSM)*, AAAI Press (July 2013).
20. Wash, R., and Solomon, J. Coordinating donors on crowdfunding websites. In *Proceedings of the 17th ACM Conference on Computer Supported Cooperative Work and Social Computing*, CSCW '14, ACM (New York, NY, USA, 2014), 38–48.
21. Xu, A., Yang, X., Rao, H., Fu, W.-T., Huang, S.-W., and Bailey, B. P. Show me the money!: An analysis of project updates during crowdfunding campaigns. In *Proceedings of the SIGCHI Conference on Human Factors in Computing Systems*, CHI '14, ACM (New York, NY, USA, 2014), 591–600.
22. Zhang, J., and Liu, P. Rational herding in microloan markets. *Management science 58*, 5 (2012), 892–912.

Manifestation of Depression and Loneliness on Social Networks: A Case Study of Young Adults on Facebook

Sungkyu Park[1] **Inyeop Kim**[2*] **Sang Won Lee**[3] **Jaehyun Yoo**[3] **Bumseok Jeong**[3] **Meeyoung Cha**[1]

[1] Graduate School of Culture Technology, KAIST
[2] Division of Web Science and Technology, KAIST
[3] Graduate School of Medical Science and Engineering, KAIST
{shaun.park, kiyeob4416, leesangwon, jaehyun.yoo, bs.jeong, meeyoungcha}@kaist.ac.kr

ABSTRACT

As people around the world are spending increasing amounts of time online, the question of how online experiences are linked to health and well-being is essential. This paper presents how activities on Facebook are associated with the depressive states of users. Based on online logs of 212 young adults, we show not only the sheer size of the network but also the frequency and diversity of interactions on social networks have close associations with depression. Depressed individuals reported smaller involved networks regarding comments and likes, the two popular forms of interactions. In contrast to the decreased level of interactions, depressed individuals showed an increase in the wall post rates and were active online during midday, which can be interpreted as an endemic behavior linked to the perceived degree of loneliness among young adults who are avid users of social media. We discuss these findings from theoretical, empirical, and subjective perspectives.

Author Keywords

Social media; online activities; depression; mental health; Facebook; Web application

ACM Classification Keywords

H.3.4 Systems and Software: User profiles and alert services; J.3 Life and Medical Sciences: Health

INTRODUCTION

Online social networks have become a common part of everyday life. The frequent intermingling of online life and offline life means that social networks can be an appealing platform to study human behaviors and moods. In response, researchers have studied how online experiences affect the daily interactions and well-being of users. A number of studies found online social links help maintain one's offline relationships better [2] and increase social capital, for individuals with low self-esteem [47] or among those who live across far geographical distance [51]. However, some have found a detrimental impact: frequent accesses to online social networks was shown to incur addiction and decreased the subjective well-being for young adults [32].

Moving beyond the debate of whether constant use of social networks is a benefit or a harm, recent studies have utilized data from online social networks to predict individual's well-being. For instance, population happiness [14], reactions to pandemics [17], unemployment or suicide rate [26, 54] can be predicted from sentiments in social media. These studies investigate whether online activities and sentiments indicate the presence of a particular social trend and collective mood of individuals. These efforts help attain a better understanding of individual's and societal needs and a design of right policies to further promote health and well-being through online experiences.

Continuing on the efforts, this paper seeks to understand how depressive moods and loneliness of young people in their 20s are manifested as online activities on Facebook, one of the most popular Internet destinations. We chose depression because it is the most common mental disorder, affecting more than 350 million people worldwide of all ages [11]. Depression is also the leading cause of death in many developed countries, especially among young adults [54]. Despite the severity of the problem, existing diagnostic tools often face challenges in reaching vulnerable individuals due in part to the perceived stigma of acknowledging depressive symptoms and visiting psychiatrists [46, 57]. Remarkable efforts have been paid to raising awareness to depression, including a social media-based research that guessed the possible depressive state of online friends based on wall posts, network structure, and interactions on Facebook and visualized the prevalence of depression [20].

As a joint effort between psychiatrists and data scientists, we designed a study framework that investigates the relationship between various activity metadata and one's depressive state. The ultimate goal of this project was to raise awareness to depression at the university where the study was conducted, which had seen an increase in the suicide rate of its students. Because all activities are digitally logged, online social networks can be used to analyze psychological attributes such as mood states [10, 38] as well as any pathological social net-

*This author contributed equally to the work with the first author.

CSCW '15, March 14 - 18 2015, Vancouver, BC, Canada.
Copyright 2015 ACM 978-1-4503-2922-4/15/03...$15.00.
http://dx.doi.org/10.1145/2675133.2675139

work use such as Internet addiction [33]. Our project is in line with on-going efforts of online health communities that try to reach and detect a large number of depressed individuals at low cost [24, 37, 39].

Our methodology is based on a Web application implemented within Facebook. The application provides easy access to the Center for Epidemiological Studies-Depression (CES-D) scale, a well-proven self-report test for measuring depressive symptomatology in the general population [41]. The application also contained tips and games that would appeal to young people and gave feedback on the depression test. The users could invite their peers and share test results if they wished. Having the study targeted for one school, we could further conduct face-to-face interviews, through which a psychiatrist supported validity of the online evaluation system.

The application-based methodology is novel in three perspectives. First, compared to offline depression diagnosis, we may correlate one's online and offline behaviors. Second, compared to the recent papers that infer users' moods based on snapshot data, our approach considers moods as a dynamic entity. The depression test is designed to measure the past week's mood and so we examine activities from the corresponding time period, which allows us to separate out the effect of mere topology (i.e., listed as friends) from the involved network (i.e., active interactions). Third, by logging how users answer each depression questionnaire, our approach can gain deeper insight into the precise depression aspects (e.g., somatic and interpersonal affects) and test which online behaviors are prominent. For instance, we can check if users who experienced restless sleep were more active during late hours than usual.

Described below are the key observations and findings from this research.

1. The depressed young adults owned fewer friends and posted fewer logs of physical activity (e.g., geotags) on Facebook. In addition, they constructed smaller 'involved networks'—the network of friends a user actually interacts with during a given period of time on Facebook (as opposed to the mere number of friends)—than the non-depressed participants.

2. In contrast to the decreased level of interactions, communication intensity was not different between the two groups. Inside the small involved networks, depressed young adults sent a similar number of comments to each interacting friend compared to the non-depressed participants. Yet, in comparing the ratio of inbound and outbound comments, there was a tendency in the more depressed ones to be more passive in communicating with others.

3. The depressed young adults showed an increase in the wall post rates compared to the past months and were active online during the midday. Analysis of each depression statement and face-to-face interviews suggested that these behaviors are linked to compensating for loneliness in the offline world through activities in the online world.

These observations help us to better understand how users interact with features such as 'likes' and 'comments' on Facebook. Our findings also contribute to understanding users' needs and psychological states in general within social media platforms—a natural collaborative system for sharing emotional support, which are important lines of research within the computer-supported cooperative work community. For instance, here is some related research: recent research investigated how moods are affected by interactions [34], depression is portrayed within social networks [13, 24], personality traits are discovered from sharing preferences [18], and how people manage vast amount of their digital traces over time [55].

BACKGROUND

Our study was built upon a large body of relevant research.

Conventional Studies on Depression

The following socio-demographic factors have been found to be associated with depression: female gender, young adulthood, old age, single parenthood, social isolation, financial difficulties, and stressful environments [12, 25, 29]. Researchers have also confirmed that psychological factors such as perfectionism, self-criticism, and sensitivity to loss and rejection are important correlates of depression [5].

Wall Posts & Outbound Interactions Volume, and Active Time

Loss of interest, lack of energy, and fatigue are the main symptoms that can be detected by the fifth edition of the diagnostic and statistical manual of mental disorders (DSM-5), a popular test widely used for diagnosing mental disorders, including depression, in the psychiatric field [1]. In regard to somatic features, one study proposed that dyssomnia is a major manifestation of depression, mood disorders, and anxiety disorders [49]. Furthermore, another study that assessed 38,000 subjects from ten countries concluded that insomnia and lack of energy are the most common symptoms related to depression [52].

Networks Size

Considering the interactions via offline social networks, it has been revealed that depressed people engage in smaller and less supported social networks than non-depressed people. A social psychology research synthesized existing findings on depression to find that depressed people feel uncomfortable interacting and they have fewer meaningful contacts with others compared to non-depressed people [4].

Personal Traits and Depression Seen from Online Data

Recent research has utilized the Internet and social network data to find correlates of personal traits and various disorders. One study investigated online surveys such as the Big 5 test to collect personal traits and then suggested the feasibility of predicting participants' personal traits based on social media posts in Twitter [18]. The study found a relationship between participants' personal traits and their preferences in sharing the prediction results via social media. Another study observed a strong geographical correlation between the ratio of suicidal tweets (e.g., bullying) and the actual suicide rates at the state level in the United States [26]. Research on the national suicidal rate of South Korea has also revealed one word

Himdeulda, which means tired or exhausted in Korean, to be the most powerful predictor as more people used this word in social media, the national suicide rate has risen [54].

Inbound Interactions Volume

A recent study concentrated on the relationship between the textual expression of loneliness indicating how people perceive loneliness and the number of sent tweets on Twitter [28]. They found that people who wrote about loneliness with transient remarks (e.g., *"OMG, I'm so lonely right now."*) and sent more tweets than those who wrote with prolonged remarks (e.g., *"I Hate feeling like this, I'm so lonely and depressed all the time."*). Moreover, people who wrote about loneliness with prolonged remarks were much less likely to get responses from others. These findings are in line with conventional studies concluding that language use is closely associated with psychological states.

Not only the raw text, but also Internet metadata or application logs can be used for the same purpose. A study of college students revealed those who exhibited signs of depression were more likely to use file-sharing services, send emails, and chat online than non-depressed students [31]. Depressed students had a tendency to use high-bandwidth applications (such as online videos and games) and showed random behaviors, for instance erratically switching between applications. Another intervention study asked college students to increase their rate of social network usage and found this to decrease the subjective well-being of subjects [32].

Among research that utilizes online social network data, one study examined a list of content that people 'liked' on Facebook and found that this information can be used to accurately predict various private traits, such as personality and sexual preference, as well as other demographic variables [30]. Another study found that people who feel lonely tend to disclose themselves more negatively and to establish fewer friends and also have less communication activity on Facebook [27]. This self-disclosure appears to be a common behavior on social media, as Major Depressive Episodes (MDE) could be detected in the wall posts of Facebook [37] as well as on the micro-blog platform Twitter [38].

Wall Posts & Outbound Interactions Volume

Other studies revealed whether people facing psychological anxiety over social interactions tend to cling on to online social media. Unlike the conventional notion that depression is connected to lethargy or loss of interests [1, 52], one study by surveying 568 users of Usenet newsgroups via e-mails found that people who feel lonely or psychological anxiety on social interactions are more likely to express themselves and to form intimate relationships over the Internet in order to dispel loneliness [35]. Another study measured the state of depression and loneliness of 368 undergraduate students by surveying the participants offline [7] and found that depressed individuals tend to prefer interacting online to face-to-face. This finding implies that depressed individuals try to find a safer alternative to the face-to-face interactions, in which they experience the difficulties in overcoming or compensating for social incompetence in their personal lives.

Finally, a recent work discussed the behavioral changes of new mothers who gave birth and had signs of postpartum depression [13], which based on an extensive set of activities within Facebook found clear distinguishing signs of postpartum depression, such as increased use of first person pronoun and reduced activity in general. We extend upon these studies and try to understand which activities within Facebook correlate with depressive moods.

Research Hypotheses

Based on the related literature, we test the following hypotheses to reveal whether depressed peoples' ways of expressing themselves and interacting with others in social media would be different from those discovered by the previous works in the real world:

H1 (Networks Size): Depressed users have smaller social networks compared to non-depressed users [4].

H2 (Wall Posts Volume): Depressed users write fewer wall posts compared to non-depressed users [28, 35, 52].

H3 (Inbound Interactions Volume): Depressed users receive fewer comments and likes compared to non-depressed users [28].

H4 (Outbound Interactions Volume): Depressed users send out fewer comments and likes compared to non-depressed users [4, 7, 35, 52].

H5 (Active Time): Depressed users are more active during night compared to non-depressed users [49, 52].

METHODS

Application Design

We developed a Facebook web application for this study. The main purpose of the application was to measure depressive states of users by an authorized psychological questionnaire and to cull user data. Upon accessing the application for the first time, users were shown a consent form asking permission to access personal data. When users agreed, the application provided depression questionnaires, gathered data from Facebook, and stored it on the application server. For those users who did not give consent, the application terminated. Participants were recruited from a large university through online and offline advertisements, where the application could be accessed from both mobile devices and desktop computers.

The application is designed for both desktop computer and mobile environments, and it therefore has two different versions, one for the desktop computer and one for the mobile device. The two versions share the same database; thus, if a user completed the depression test on a mobile device, he or she cannot do this on a desktop computer later, and vice versa. We designed the application to be compatible with both environments to guarantee that users can access the application anywhere and at any time. There were no differences in the user interfaces of the desktop computer and mobile versions.

Once users took the depression test, the application provided three types of feedback according to the depression scale: non-depressed, mild depression, and severe depression. The feedback was carefully designed by psychiatrists to inform users of the depression test results and suggest guidelines that promote healthier psychological state. The screen snapshots in Figure 1 illustrate the process for asking user consent, the front page of the application, the flyer used to gather participants, and the test results.

The application provided another function, learning general knowledge about depression (100 facts and tips). We embedded this function not only to raise the awareness of users but also indirectly to measure the interest level of users toward depression. The main menu of the front page contains buttons to bring up the depression test and tips and facts page simultaneously so that users can freely access both pages without any given directions. However, once users access the depression survey, the corresponding button disappear from the main menu. Thereby, users can complete the depression test only one time whereas they can repeatedly access other functions. The application offered a points system to motivate users, where users could accumulate points every time they clicked on any function within the application.

Once getting permission from the participants we acquired users' access tokens on Facebook and stored them into the database of our application. With the access tokens, we could directly access additional information stored on Facebook by utilizing FQL (Facebook query language). Also, some additional information such as the texts of wall-posts, was collected through the application and stored in the database of the application server. Therefore, additional information was collected through both Facebook and the application.

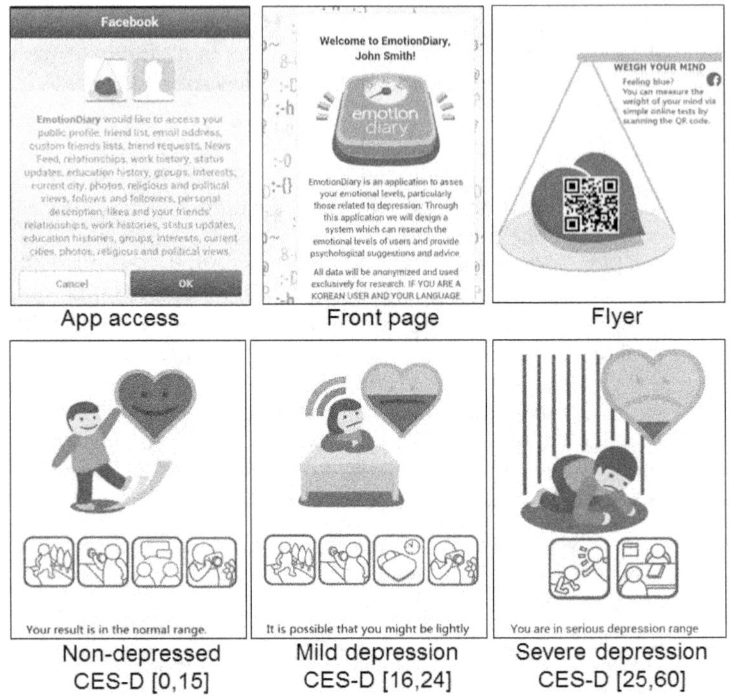

Figure 1. Screen snapshots of the developed application, illustrating the process for asking user consent, front page, flyer to recruit participants, and the three types of feedback given to users.

Depression Survey

The application provided the Center for Epidemiological Studies-Depression (CES-D) scale [41], a test widely used in epidemiological studies. It is a self-report scale and contains 20 simple statements, each designed to identify markers of somatic, positive, and interpersonal affects related to depression. The test questions are shown in Table 1, which is re-organized to highlight three major subscales of depression. Participants were asked to judge each statement based on experience from the previous week. The items of the CES-D test were presented in a regular sequence from question #1 to #20 to follow the general surveying method used in the psychiatric field.

The degree of depressive symptom for each statement is rated from 0 (weak) to 3 (strong) scores, except for the positive affect subscale, whose severity is in reverse order from 3 to 0. The total score range of the CES-D is between 0 and 60 and cutoffs of 16 and 25 have been suggested in various literature to detect depression [22]: a score up to 15 indicates low probability of depression, a score between 16 and 24 indicates mild depression, and a score of 25 or above indicates a major depressive disorder. We followed this guideline to provide feedback to users. For presenting findings, however, we used different cut-off values and categorized participants into two groups: depressed and non-depressed. We chose the cutoff value 21 because it is a commonly used threshold with adequate sensitivity and specificity in community or school settings [3, 8].

In this study one explicit consideration went to preventing potential bias in data. Crowdsourced surveys often suffer from inaccurate data [15], because users participate for monetary rewards and could fill in answers inaccurately. Our survey was hence designed as voluntary-based and offered no explicit reward. To further ensure reliability of the depression test, a subset of users (115 participants) were asked to additionally take an alternative depression test (Beck Depression Inventory, BDI) and their scores were checked for consistency [56]. We did not find any abnormal trends between the CES-D and BDI results. Another subset of users were invited to perform the depression test in a laboratory setting (e.g., a desktop computer was provided) and data from these users were later used to check bias.

Participant Recruitment

A total of 234 participants were recruited from a large university among users who had Facebook accounts for at least a year. Participants were gathered over two periods of time, April and December in 2013, during which they did not overlap with major exams. Three distinct methods were utilized: (1) flyers distributed across the campus, (2) online advertisements at the school's bulletin board system, and (3) a survey booth installed at the largest cafeteria. Recruited participants showed a high response rate and a large majority of 212 (90%) completed the depression test; 161 (76%) were males aged between 19 and 38 (Mean=25.61, SD=3.72) and

Subscale affect & item	Depressed	Non-depressed
Somatic & Depresssed		
1. I was bothered by things that usually don't bother me.	1.58	0.54
2. I did not feel like eating; my appetite was poor.	1.04	0.27
3. I felt that I could not shake off the blues even with the help from family or friends.	1.75	0.42
5. I had trouble keeping my mind on what I was doing.	1.46	0.77
6. I felt depressed.	1.58	0.28
7. I felt that everything I did was an effort.	1.67	0.58
11. My sleep was restless.	1.17	0.57
17. I had crying spells.	0.83	0.15
20. I could not get "going".	1.46	0.35
Positive		
4. I felt that I was just as good as other people.	1.25	0.79
8. I felt hopeful about the future.	1.83	0.71
12. I was happy.	1.54	0.68
16. I enjoyed life.	1.75	0.68
Interpersonal & Depressed		
9. I thought my life had been a failure.	0.96	0.12
10. I felt fearful.	1.50	0.32
13. I talked less than usual.	1.58	0.51
14. I felt lonely.	1.67	0.44
15. People were unfriendly.	1.17	0.45
18. I felt sad.	1.67	0.42
19. I felt that people dislike me.	0.83	0.26
Total CES-D Score (Mean, SD)	28.29, 6.13	9.31, 4.76

Table 1. The CES-D questionnaires and the average scores from the study. Participants were asked to answer based on the previous week's experience and to give scores from 0 (Rarely or less than 1 day), 1 (Some or 1-2 days), 2 (Occasionally or 3-4 days), to 3 (Most or 5-7 days). The scores for the positive affect subscale are reversed: 3 (Rarely) to 0 (Most). The depressed group indicates users who received a total of at least 21 scores and the non-depressed group is up to 20 scores.

the remaining 51 (24%) were females aged between 19 and 33 (Mean=24.06, SD=2.69).

We explained the purpose of study and the list of personal data fields that we planned to analyze. The application explicitly cited the name of the hospital in charge of the study, should participants have any question about how the data would be used. Informed written consent was obtained prior to participation and the school's Institutional Review Board approved this study.

For 212 participants, we had access to all activities over the recent two weeks that appeared on their walls. For 129 of them, we further asked for agreement to access more detailed information on their Facebook usage, including the complete set of likes, comments, and wall posts through which they interacted with others during the past six months. Then we set up a range for the number of Facebook friends from five to 1,000—the threshold 1,000 was chosen based on the value of +3SD while five was chosen based on the observation that the participants whose friends numbered less than five did absolutely no activity on Facebook—to filter out outliers who would show extraordinary behavioral patterns on Facebook compared to common users [39]. As a consequence, three participants with fewer than five friends and two participants

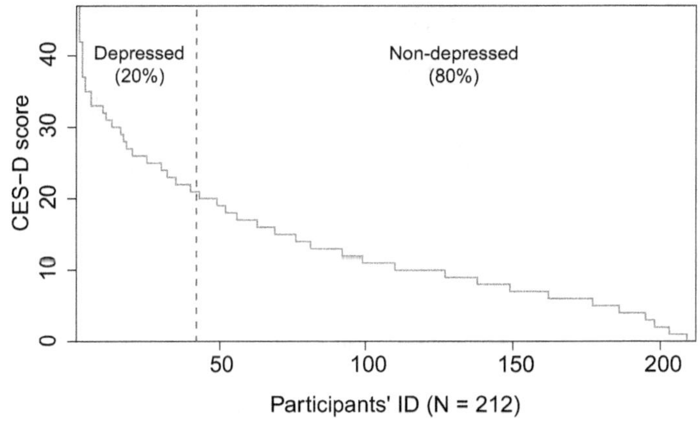

Figure 2. Distribution of the depression test results.

with more than 1,000 friends were excluded. The eventual data of 124 participants (i.e., 53% of the 212 participants) accounted for a total of 17,157 activities. We used everyone's data (i.e., 212 participants) for most of the analyses and we limited the focus to the 124 participant subset when detailed information was necessary.

We particularly paid attention to 'likes' and 'comments' as a proxy of lightweight and effort-taking interactions respectively. These two functions are the two most popular forms of interactions on Facebook, and hence have received much attention. For instance, a recent study demonstrated that the two functions serve different purposes: relationships grew closer from composed content (e.g., writing on the timeline or leaving comments) than from simple on-click features (e.g., likes) [6].

RESULTS

Out of the 212 participants, 170 (80%) of them obtained a CES-D score of between 0 and 20 indicating a low probability of depression. The remaining 42 obtained a CES-D score of between 21 and 60, which means a high probability of depression. For convenience, we simply refer to these two groups as *non-depressed* and *depressed*, respectively. The overall CES-D distribution is shown in Figure 2.

We checked the efficacy of online depression screening through both quantitative and qualitative approaches. The quantitative approach involved comparing the CES-D score with an alternate test, BDI [56], and the qualitative approach involved face-to-face interviews. The application sent a personal invitation message to all participants who obtained a high CES-D score (i.e., 21–60) and offered free counseling at the university's hospital. The turnout rate was low. Only six participants out of 42 corresponding individuals agreed to meet, for whom a psychiatrist assessed their depressive symptoms through the Hamilton Depression Rating Scale (HAM-D), a widely practiced structured interview for determining one's depression level [21].

Three participants reported chronic depressive symptoms that

Feature	Individual level(N=212) Pearson's r	p-value	Group level(N=124) Depressed(N=90) Mean	SD	Non-depressed(N=34) Mean	SD	Ratio	p-value
Profile & App Activity								
Friends	-0.25**	<.01	190.57	141.59	336.26	183.71	0.57***	<.001
Tips checked	0.39***	<.001	3.65	4.07	1.02	2.37	3.58**	<.01
Geotags	-0.16	.48	1.5	0.58	4	3.89	0.38*	.01
Area of gyration	-0.20	.16	560.26	1942.74	5385.28	23534.49	0.10	.24
Wall posts	0.16	.17	1.85	3.16	1.74	3.58	1.06	.92
Wall post rate	0.26*	.02	0.21	0.28	0.10	0.17	2.13	.18
Fan pages	0.14	.11	73.96	256.51	44.55	69.12	1.66	.59
Inbound Likes								
Total	-0.11	.34	18.80	26.25	44.60	69.18	0.42*	.03
Avg per wall post	-0.24	.05	6.56	6.60	10.34	11.19	0.63	.10
Distinct friends	-0.23	.05	13.60	15.52	29.25	29.30	0.46*	.01
Avg per friend	.07	.60	1.23	0.41	1.31	0.50	0.94	.56
Inbound Comments								
Total	-0.08	.52	8.60	10.68	22.49	38.55	0.38*	.02
Avg per wall post	-0.17	.15	3.79	5.75	4.86	4.60	0.78	.51
Distinct friends	-0.13	.28	6.20	5.75	12.42	4.60	0.50*	.01
Avg per friend	-0.13	.34	1.25	0.30	1.52	0.61	0.82*	.04
Outbound Comments								
Total	-0.24*	.01	5.04	5.08	8.24	5.78	0.61*	.01
Distinct friends	-0.27***	<.001	3.83	3.65	7.14	5.18	0.54***	<.001
Avg per friend	0.17	.09	1.28	0.36	1.19	0.31	1.07	.34
In-Out ratio	0.16	.08	0.87	1.62	0.42	0.82	2.07	.21

Table 2. The depressed and non-depressed participants are compared (1) at the individual level through the Pearson's test and (2) at the group level through the two sample t-test. Significance of the results are marked (*$p<.05$, **$p<.01$, ***$p<.001$).

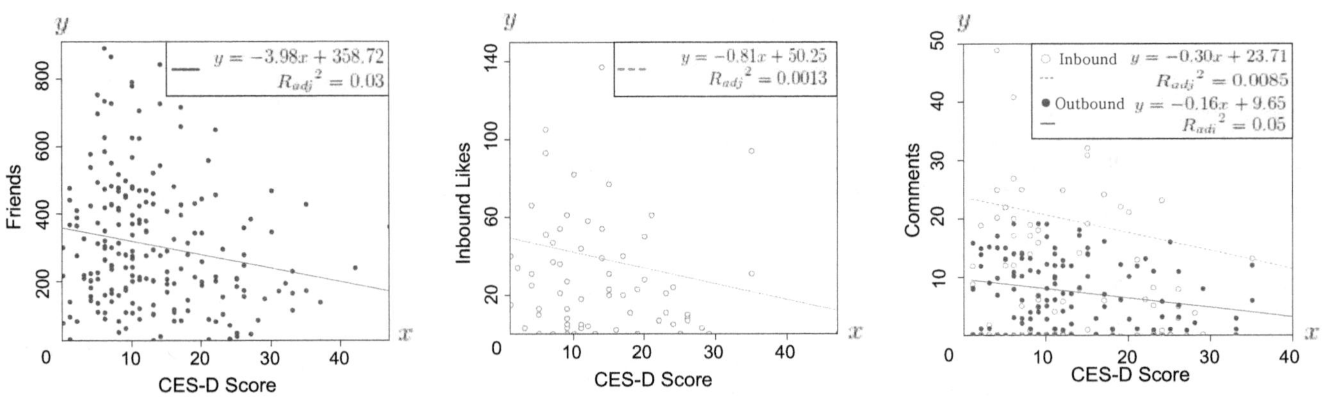

(a) Number of friends (b) Number of inbound likes (c) Number of in & outbound comments

Figure 3. Scatter plot of the depression test result (CES-D) along with major features on Facebook.

involved depressive mood and loss of interest: they rated moderate scores in HAM-D (mean=16). The other three no longer showed signs of distress during the interview, yet they had experienced depressive episodes at the time of online screening. One participant even had experienced a major depressive episode during the online screening period, and the face-to-face interviews conducted by a psychiatrist supported the validity of the online screening system. Among the six interviewees, two of them had prior experience visiting a psychiatrist. However, the other four—including a student with chronic depression—had no prior experience and hence our application could effectively raise awareness to depression to these students. We discuss implications of the qualitative analysis in the later section together with findings from quantitative analysis.

Profile and Application Activities

Among various relationships that our research allows us to explore, we focused on user-level metadata related to interpersonal activities such as likes and comments. The relationship between online social activities and the CES-D scores was measured by the Pearson's correlation coefficient as well as simple linear regression analysis. The difference between the depressed and non-depressed groups was measured by independent two-sample t-test as well as the calculated mean, standard deviation, and ratio of the means.

As a first step, we examined the mere counts as a function of the participant's depressive state. Table 2 indicates that depressed participants (1) owned fewer friends, (2) shared fewer geolocation tags, and (3) covered a smaller area of movement based on geotags compared to non-depressed participants; on the other hand, they (4) viewed more tips about depression through the application, (5) liked more pages on Facebook, (6) updated as many wall posts in total, and (7) even showed an increase in wall post rates compared to the past months. We note that the described correlations are specific to the participants and the choice of statistical test.[1]

As these results can be influenced by samples, we do not bring into focus on the specific values in the regression analysis but rather focus on the overall trend of the features. For instance, geotags may be a proxy that represents a user's activity scope in the real world. On average the area of gyration of the non-depressed individuals was wider than that of the depressed participants, where the area of gyration was calculated by utilizing the geolocation tags posted by users over the past six months and then finding a radius that covers all geotagged locations from the mean location of that user. While it is debatable whether depressed participants traveled shorter distances or simply they did not post updates frequently enough than the non-depressed participants, a lower rate of physical activity is related to the common signs of depressive symptoms (e.g., lethargy, fatigue, weariness) [1, 52].

Wall Posts Activities

Updating posts on the wall page is one of the basic functions on social networks. A post, which can be of various forms (e.g., texts, photos, web links), serves as the medium through which other social interactions begin (e.g., comments, likes). We examined how many wall posts participants shared during the two-week period and how much interaction they evoked. Some participants did not update any wall posts: 34.7% and 41.5% of participants in the depressed and non-depressed groups, respectively, posted none. Among the rest of the users who posted at least once, on average depressed participants wrote as much wall posts as the non-depressed participants.

Since the mere number of postings gives limited information, we normalized the posting rate for participants for whom we had longitudinal trace and defined a metric termed 'wall post rate', which compares the posting rate from the recent two weeks against that of the previous six months. This measure is useful for tracking behavioral changes of individuals with acute depression (as opposed to those with chronic depression), which typically takes up the majority of depressive symptoms among young adults. Because acute depression develops suddenly, it could leave a visible activity marker over time. We may now examine whether acute depression increases or decreases one's wall post rate.

The data showed that wall posting activity became more prevalent for depressed participants. For increment of 1 unit in the depression test result (i.e., higher likelihood of depression), the wall posting rate increased 0.26 times over a six month period (p=.02). At the aggregate level, on average the depressed group increased the wall post rate more quickly than the non-depressed group. These observations rejects the second hypothesis, which assumes that depressed users write fewer wall posts compared to non-depressed users.

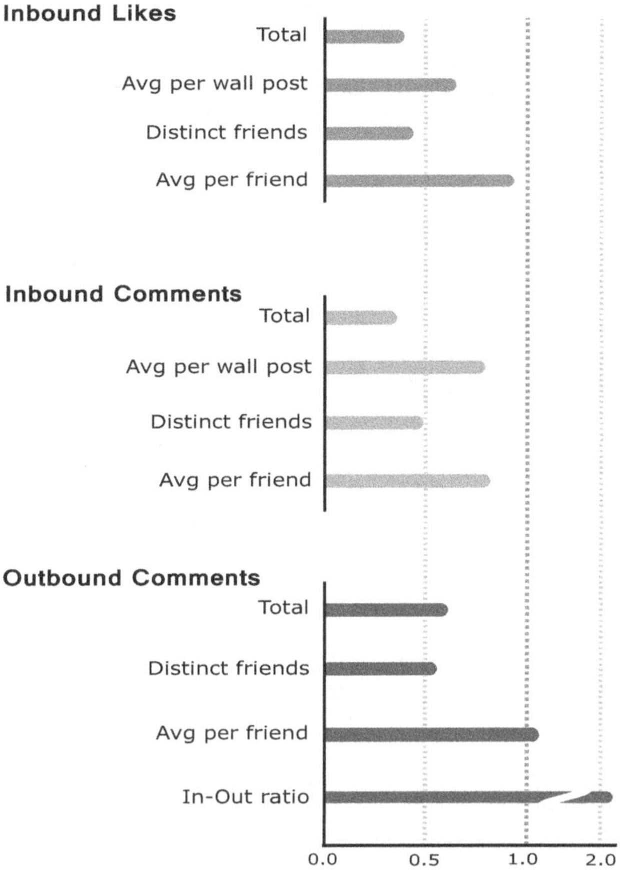

Figure 4. The relative amount of likes and comments activities on Facebook by participants in the depressed group compared to those in the non-depressed group for the observed two-week period: x-axis is the value of the ratio where 1.0 indicates an equal quantity and y-axis is the title of each activity feature. For visual clarity, we grouped activity features into similar categories and added space between them: Inbound Likes, Inbound Comments, and Outbound Comments.

Likes Interactions

The likes activity is a popular way to express a relatively positive reaction to a story that one has just read on Facebook. Likes are lightweight because they are an alternative to taking time to deploy mental energy in giving a written response [19]. The likes activity showed several meaningful relationships with depression.

Depressed participants received 4.2 likes for every 10 likes that non-depressed participants received during the observed two-week period (see the row termed Total in the Inbound Likes category of Table 2). Normalizing the number of inbound likes per wall post gives a similar picture: on average the depressed participants received fewer likes for every wall post they wrote (see Avg per wall post). Moreover, the depressed participants owned 0.46 times fewer distinct friends

[1]When we use the Mann-Whitney U test, which has greater efficiency than the t-test on non-normal distributions, the following five features can be interpreted as significant: Friends and Tips checked from the Profile & App Activity category as well as Total, Distinct friends, and In-Out ratio from the Outbound Comments category.

from whom they received likes (see Distinct friends). However, on average the number of likes received from each interacting friend was similar between the two groups (see Avg per friend).

Comments Interactions

Users can interact with one another through writing or replying to comments on a wall post. As one might imagine, the correlation between inbound likes and inbound comments was prominent (Pearson ρ=0.91): those who received many comments received many likes. In addition, the number of inbound comments was predictive of owning depression (see the Inbound Comments category). Perhaps because writing each comment takes more thought and energy than pressing the like button, its relative quantity was more pronounced between the depressed and non-depressed groups. Depressed participants received 3.8 comments for every 10 comments that non-depressed participants received and had a 50% smaller involved network that sent comments during the two-week period.

We next looked into the effect of giving a comment as opposed to receiving one (see the Outbound Comments category). Giving was as rewarding as receiving: the number of outbound comments was a meaningful indicator of depression. For the two weeks depressed participants sent 6.1 comments for every 10 comments that non-depressed participants sent and had a 54% smaller involved network that received comments. In contrast, the correlation between the inbound and outbound comments was relatively low (ρ=.02), indicating that those who write many comments on wall post of others do not necessarily receive back many comments on their wall posts. The conversation intensity, measured as the average number of comments sent for each interacting friend, was not meaningfully different between the depressed and non-depressed participants.

There was no obvious trend related to depression in (1) the time difference between inbound and outbound comments (i.e., how quickly one comments back) or (2) the time interval between two consecutive outbound comments (i.e., how frequently one leaves comments) at both individual and group level tests. This means diversity and intensity of interaction with the involved network are key predictors of depressive moods, rather than immediacy of interactions.

To further investigate what happens to the depressed participants' involved networks, we examined the ratio of inbound and outbound comments for the depressed and non-depressed groups (see the In-Out ratio row). In calculating this ratio, we divided the number of inbound comments by the square of the outbound comments, as the latter quantity was usually far smaller than the former. The in-out ratio would be 1.0 should one receive and send the same number of comments. The ratio showed a marginally significant positive correlation to the depression score, whereas its average ratio for the depressed participants was greater than that of the non-depressed ones. We discuss implications of these findings in the later section.

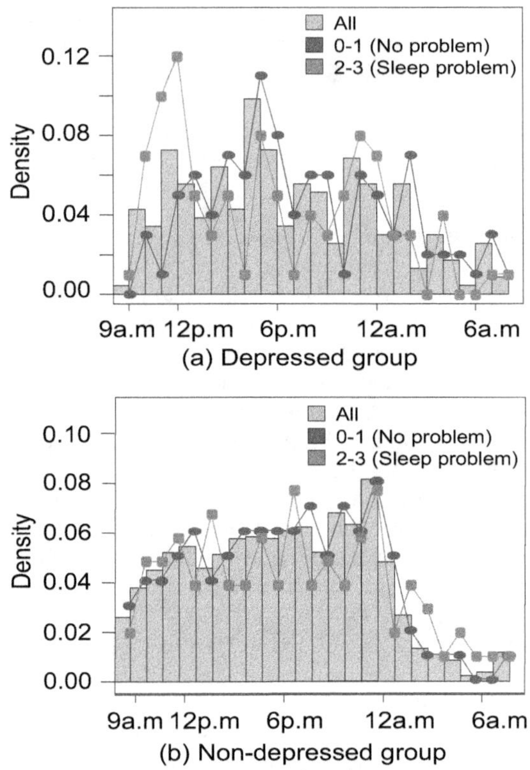

Figure 5. Correlation between metadata of active hours and the 12th CES-D statement, "My sleep was restless".

Manifestation of Perceived Mood

Depression is a complex disorder that involves various somatic and emotional affects. Having analyzed the user metadata, we now attempt to understand how the self-perceived mood states are manifested as online activities on Facebook. This analysis is possible because the application stored information about how participants judged each statement in the depression test. We demonstrate the idea with three cases: the 12th, 14th, and 19th statements in Table 1.

The first statement we consider is, "*My sleep was restless*", which reveals physical symptoms such as insomnia. We grouped participants: the first group answered 'rarely' or 'some' to the statement (i.e., score of 0–1) and the second group answered 'occasionally' or 'most' to the statement (i.e., score of 2–3). We then counted the frequency of all activities each cohort showed throughout the day. Figure 5 shows the diurnal trend. Frequent activities are shown during the day time compared to after midnight for both depressed and non-depressed groups. The pattern for the non-depressed group is smoother due to a larger sample size. Among the depressed participants, those who experienced restless sleep (i.e., score of 2–3) had higher chance of being active online in the early morning. The non-depressed participants did not show any visible trend related to whether they experienced restless sleep.

The next statement we investigated is "*I talked less than usual*". While giving a high score (2–3) generally increases the probability of depression, the depressed participants had

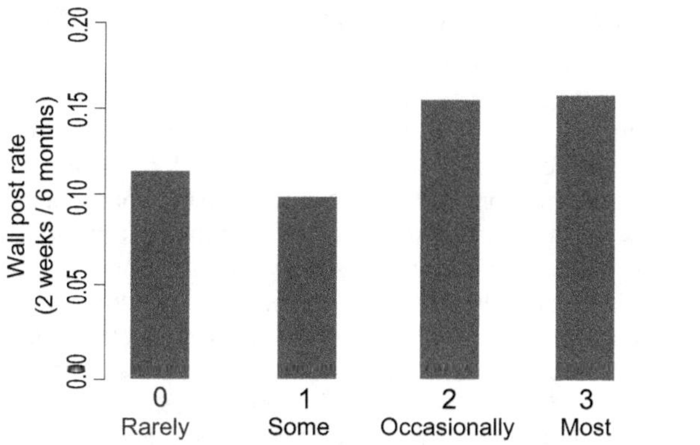

Figure 6. The relationship between the speed of wall posting and the 14th CES-D statement, "I talked less than usual".

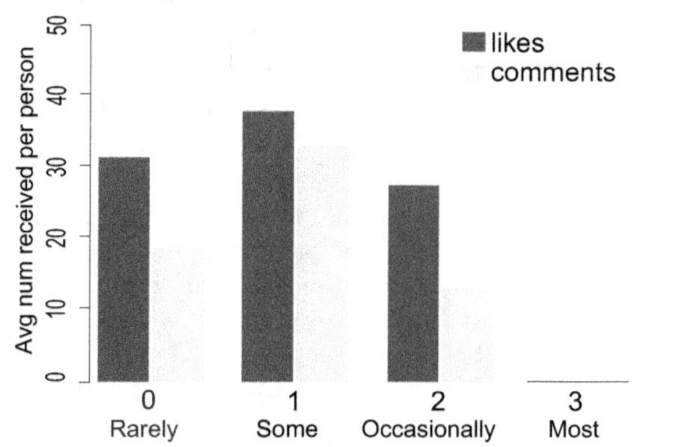

Figure 7. The relationship between metadata of inbound interactions and the 19th CES-D statement, "I felt that people dislike me".

posted almost the same number of text-based wall posts as listed in Table 2. Then, to investigate the trend in detail, we checked whether participants who identified themselves as "having talked less" showed slower wall post rates. After grouping participants based on their scores (by two groups: 0–1 and 2–3), an opposite trend emerged as indicated in Figure 6: participants who answered 2–3 (i.e., talked less than usual) currently posted more text-based wall posts than usual when compared to those participants who answered 0–1 (i.e., did not talk less).

The final statement we examined is *"I felt that people dislike me"*, which we associated with the aggregate number of comments and likes that participants received from friends over a two-week period. We classified users into two groups based on their answers: the first group who answered 0–1 (rarely or some) and the next group with answer of 2–3 (occasionally or most). While none of the non-depressed students gave a score of 3 (i.e., most of the time), none of the depressed students gave a score of 0 (i.e., rarely). Figure 7 shows the trend between the aggregate number of likes and comments students received for their text-based wall posts as a function of their perceived feeling toward others. Those who perceived that others disliked them (i.e., 2–3) in fact received fewer comments and likes than those who did not indicate so (i.e, 0–1).

DISCUSSION

Principal Findings

While we do not attempt to claim a causality between online activities and depression, we discuss how shrinking of interpersonal relationships and loss of interests, which are common factors linked to depression in the real world, correlate with depression through the medium of social media. One of our research achievements is to quantify the interpersonal relationships by utilizing social media data because it has been a difficult task with conventional offline studies. We found certain traits of online interactions (e.g., a small involved network and a large value of the in-out ratio of comments on Facebook) are highly associated with a person's depressive moods. We revisit the five main hypotheses that we discussed earlier and provide possible explanations.

H1: Depressed users have smaller networks — Supported

The size of a person's network had a strong correlation with depressive moods. Even the mere number of friends had an association with depression, which was similarly shown in related studies on depressive symptoms, dysthymia, and loneliness [27, 42]. While these studies considered a single snapshot of the network (i.e., the total number of friends), our work considered a temporal aspect and focused on how many peer users interacted over a short period of time. We found that the depressed participants reported qualitatively and quantitatively smaller involved networks through which they interchanged thoughts and emotions with peers via likes and comments.

There are two possible ways of explaining why the size of network is related to depression: one is that participants with a larger involved network may find more opportunities for support from friends and hence are less inclined to be depressed [50]. For instance, receiving positive feedback (i.e., likes) on one's social network profile may enhance self-esteem and the sense of well-being, as a study of older adolescents demonstrated [47]. On the other hand, another explanation is that participants who are suffering from depression may experience difficulties in engaging and maintaining a social network. However, providing the causality will require qualitative interviews over a long period of time and is beyond the scope of this study.

H2: Depressed users write fewer wall posts — Rejected

Depressed participants showed an increased rate of wall posts compared to the past months, not in line with our expectation. Face-to-face interviews and surveys provided possible reasons for this behavior. A more frequent posting pattern is a specific feature of young adults who are avid users of social media, and this trait may be linked with loneliness—a signal shown in those who fail to express themselves; the depressed users may be eager to compensate for loneliness in the offline world by activity posting updates in the online world [53].

Unfortunately, the one way communication did not reciprocally trigger sufficient positive feedback to the depressed participants from friends, and hence could not ameliorate depressive moods. In the real world, the depressed individuals did not converse actively with their friends due to loss of energy and interest. However, they found it easy to be active in online platforms like Facebook, because of the high accessibility and ease of interactions such platforms provide. Thus, our finding is an endemic trait of the depressed young adults on social networks, which designers of the future social networks and health care policy makers may be interested in.

H3: Depressed users have smaller inbound interactions such as receiving likes and comments from peers — Supported

H4: Depressed users engage less in outbound interactions such as sending likes and comments to peers — Rejected

We examined social activities in the form of comments and likes. Although the depressed group had fewer friends who sent likes, their average number of likes received for each interacting friend was close to that of the non-depressed group. However, the depressed users had fewer aggregate friends who sent comments and further received a smaller number of inbound comments per friend than the non-depressed users. These observations together indicate that friends of the depressed users tend not to send comments to the depressed friends, while they do not hesitate to send likes. The reason for this behavior may be either that it is difficult to make comments on content the depressed users typically share or simply they do not wish to expend more energy than that involved in merely sending likes, which is a kind of threshold. From the result, we may state that, for receiving traits, the depressed participants' friends might have the perception that 'likes' is a lightweight interaction while 'comments' is a more energy-driven interaction.

Meanwhile, outbound activities demonstrate the opposite trend from receiving activities. The depressed users sent almost the same volume of comments (1.07) for each interacting friend. Unfortunately, due to the limitation of the Facebook API (application programming interface) we cannot cull the correct data of outbound likes. The result may mean that depressed participants interact through comments at a level of effort similar to the non-depressed participants.

Indeed, if we only looked at the number of comments and likes it would be difficult to find any differences. However, since we deeply investigated the interaction that occurs inside the involved network, we could find endemic traits of the likes and comments features and surmise that users perceive the likes and comments functions on Facebook differently based on their depressive states.

Moreover, the proportion of inbound comments to outbound comments grew as a person had a higher likelihood of depression, meaning that a depressed user sends fewer comments than he or she receives. At first glance, the depressed participants' intention to actively communicate with focused friends—although they are fewer—is not profoundly different from non-depressed participants. Yet, analysis of the interaction intensity implies that the communication tendency of depressed participants is still passive. This may be linked to a previous study that found that spending money (i.e., an outbound activity) on others as a method of social support makes the spender more happy and improves his or her social well-being [16].

H5: Depressed users are more active on late at night than non-depressed users — Rejected

The depressed group showed a peak at the working hour of around 5 p.m., in contrast to the non-depressed group who showed the highest activity at around 11 p.m. We have two explanations for why the depressed participants used Facebook during working hours, which in the real world are commonly used for studies or social interactions. One explanation is that the depressed participants do not have enough energy to engage in real social interactions. Loss of interest and energy are main symptoms of depression, and thus the depressed participants might give more attention to easy interactions that can occur on social networks. They might replace the real world activities with social network activities, which could also be confirmed through qualitative analysis. This pattern was more prominent for those who indicated restless sleep, suggesting that a sleep problem can aggravate their lack of energy and the day time activities.

An alternative explanation is related to a deficit in real social relationships that could mitigate depressive symptoms [36]. Lack of social support is a main risk factor of depression [40], and depression can reduce the breadth of a social network [48]. Depressed participants in our study may not have received enough support from their real world network, and hence they might have tried to interact with friends through online social networks to compensate for their deficits in social support. This may also explain why participants who answered "having talked less than usual" in the CES-D scale had in fact posted more (text-based) wall posts online.

Interestingly, the depressed individuals without sleep problems had more activities in the middle of the night than the depressed individuals with sleep problems. Subjective satisfaction of sleep quality and duration did not always align with the objective findings; this can be influenced by the individuals' differences in the composition of sleep [43]. Thus, the subjective sleep problem cannot reflect their behavior directly, but the problem can be influenced by individuals' physical and cognitive states.

Some of our observations are unexpected and would not have been found if we had not checked the individual CES-D statements. Moreover, for those observations showing unexpected outcomes we could provide reasonable explanations and novel insights with the presented methodologies for investigating profiling frequencies and interacting patterns on Facebook as well as with qualitative analysis.

Feedback on User Experience

The application we developed raised awareness of depression among students, most of whom had no experience of visiting a psychiatrist. The application identified other unexpected findings, for example, depressed participants were eager to view tips provided about depression. In discussing implications, it is important to consider how participants perceived the application.

We conducted a survey a week after the test, asked the participants to complete four questionnaires: the first two were objective and the other two were descriptive. The objective questionnaires asked for a general assessment of the application and whether a participant intended to seek a psychiatrists' support if they had emotional difficulties in the future. The descriptive questionnaires asked participants to write about whether the application was helpful and how it could be improved. We asked participants to give the feedback in detail. Regarding the scales used in the survey, participants were asked to estimate general assessment of the application by rating it on a scale of 0 to 10 and to provide information on the preference of psychiatrists' support with a Likert-like scale of one to five: *never; don't want; don't know; want; actively want.*

In the overall result, 63% of the participants responded to the survey. On the objective questions, 48% from the responding participants evaluated the application as good (7–10), 11% of respondents evaluated it as bad (0–3), while the rest of respondents evaluated it as average (4–6). In addition, 67% from the responding participants indicated that they did not want psychiatrists' support, whereas 18% of the respondents intended to ask psychiatrists for help if they suffered from emotional problems. Therefore, it is a crucial future task to design a user experience so that users feel comfortable in contacting and getting aid from psychiatrists through the application when they are in need.

Considering positive feedback from the descriptive questionnaires, while most participants answered that they found the application to be useful in learning about their depressive moods, others found it useful in ways that we did not expect. For instance, several participants mentioned that the experience of self-awareness was rewarding in a manner similar to meditation. Below are some sample quotes from the positive responses.

> *"The app made me think about my emotions, which I liked. Perhaps periodically using this app will help me know about myself better."*

> *"The feedback shown after the test was useful. It showed an emotional state that I was not well aware of in daily life. Easy-to-try recommendations were given, which I found practical."*

> *"I took this app as an opportunity to sit quiet and look back on myself. As I took the test, I thought deeply about which elements affect my emotion."*

> *"I became more aware of the current feeling than feelings from the past week [which the app asked]. Maybe the application can provide more directions to help users focus on feelings from the past week."*

We also received non-positive comments, which we plan to utilize to improve the system. One participant said it was difficult to focus on the past week's experience (which the depression test is based on), as he became constantly aware of the instantaneous feelings. Another user found the user interface could be designed better.

Limitations

This study is limited and can be extended in several ways. First, the findings are dependent on the participants' demographics, and hence they cannot be generalized. Most online surveys are known to suffer from potential bias [15] in that respondents are found to be in a more educated and affluent group and also disproportionately in male. However, our data showed a different bias: the proportion of females (26%) was marginally higher than the rate of overall female students (21%). One approach to alleviate this bias is to increase the number of participants of the online survey, for instance, by including it on a voluntary basis in a school's yearly physical check-up service for students. We hope to address the sampling bias and investigate how cultural specifications come into play in the future.

Second, our findings are limited to the particular platform used in this study and any change in the platform may make some correlations weaker or stronger. The way Facebook activities are designed and the level of social interactions promoted will affect how users perceive and behave. For instance, social networks such as Tumblr or Snapchat, where social interactions are more focused on smaller groups, could incur different user behaviors. In order to address this concern, we hope to replicate the study in a number of different platforms. The methodology and high-level implications, however, will remain consistent. For instance, certain interactions require heavier or weaker attention to users (e.g., comments versus likes), for which we found different level of correlations. Although we examined a single platform, its activities, such as wall posting and photo tagging, are easily found in most social networks.

Third, we are not sure whether depression is a unique trait associated with online behaviors and interactions. Other personal categories such as personalities, interests, and other mental as well as physical diseases may be linked to users' online behaviors and interactions as well. Hence, we need to investigate the relationships of other categories and carefully compare them to the trait of depression.

Fourth, we have not checked the users' amount of time spent on Facebook. Since time spent on Facebook may influence various actions that can be taken, the amount of time spent can be a confounding variable to consider. However, we were focusing on not just passively consuming the content on Facebook but actively uploading content and sending out likes and comments to interact with others; these active behaviors may or may not be correlated with the time spent on Facebook. We also considered receiving feedback from a user's friends, and it is also unclear whether these features are related to the user's time spent on Facebook. Therefore, more research needs to be conducted to reveal the relationship between the amount of time spent and the volume of online inbound and outbound activities to contemplate the confounding variable.

In regard to the confounding variable, there are other factors, such as various demographics and offline user activities, that should be looked at as well. Considering other demographic and offline user activity variables like age, occupation, social status, and specific time events, we think we have relatively homogeneous participants because we recruited young adults at a single university. Furthermore, we could not find any significant correlations between the CES-D scores and the listed variables in our participants. Consequently, we believe we have removed some major confounding variables.

Lastly we did not examine any linguistic features or content shared by users, an area that future studies can look into. In particular, sentiment and topic analysis may reveal clues as to why the depressed users receive fewer comments and likes than the non-depressed [44]. Such an investigation may help us understand the potential factors that could play a role in making friends hesitate to respond in online interactions.

CONCLUDING REMARKS

Recent studies have proposed the potential for utilizing data from social network sites to identify references for well-being of people. This paper investigated what kinds of interaction metadata of Facebook is related to depressive moods and identified several strong associations between the social network usage patterns and depression symptoms. The research was conducted by an interdisciplinary group and took a mixed methodology and conducted both qualitative and quantitative analyses. Some of our findings are new in the sense that they have not yet been shown in previous studies, for which we provided explanations.

The 212 study participants, recruited from a single university through fliers, covered various levels of depression from mild and moderate to severe. Overall, 20% of the participants were judged to be depressed based on the CES-D screening and the remaining 80% were judged as non-depressed. The overall depression level in our sample was 1.18 times higher than the nation-wide average of people in their 20s and 30s (which was based on offline diagnostic studies [9]). Whereas our analysis was limited to the dataset of a single university, a similar level of prevalence between the studied demographics and the nation-wide sample suggests that online screening is a viable approach to reaching vulnerable individuals, especially young adults.

While this research is observational, the presented research methodology and findings have implications for future intervention designs that can improve the well-being of users. Among various possible directions, one can envision designing a cost-effective online campaign that increases awareness to depression by providing a diagnostic tool that alleviates the stigma associated with offline detection methods [57]. Online social media-based diagnostic tools may be particularly useful in countries, where open discussion of depression is suppressed. One can also envision an application that regularly monitors users and their online behaviors such as wall-posting over time to summarize users' mood states, which can then be provided to health professionals during hospital visits to help diagnose symptoms more thoroughly. By this method, the application may be an effective communication channel between users and psychiatrists.

Young adults make up the largest population on Facebook: those aged between 18 and 34 are the largest proportion (47.7%) among all age groups [45]. Moreover, 48% of them report reading Facebook streams is the first activity to do in the morning as soon as they wake up [23]. Hence, young adults might find a Facebook application-style screening less intrusive (compared to visiting and taking written screening tests), who are as well the group that could potentially benefit the most from online depression screening. We hope observations from our research contribute toward building mental capital of cognitive and emotional resources that influence well-being of young adults in the future [11].

ACKNOWLEDGMENTS

We appreciate the anonymous reviewers for their incisive and detailed comments to improve the quality of this work. We also thank Young Bok Lee for sharing his thoughtful opinions in discussing the implications and Sangyoon Lee for cooperating in developing the web application. This paper was supported by the BK21 Plus Postgraduate Organization for Content Science (or BK21 Plus Program) in Korea, by grant for KAIST Future Systems Healthcare Project from the Ministry of Education, Science and Technology (N10140010, N01140087, G04110085) and in part by grants (NRF-2012R1A1A2001 and NRF-2006-2005372 to B. Jeong) from National Research Foundation, and by the ICT R&D Program of MSIP [I0114-14-1016, Youth crisis forecasting and real-time response technology development by big data analysis] and the Creative Vitamin Project in Korea.

REFERENCES

1. American Psychiatric Association. *The Diagnostic and Statistical Manual of Mental Disorders: DSM-5*. bookpointUS, (2013).
2. Arnaboldi, V., Conti, M., Passarella, A., and Dunbar, R. Dynamics of personal social relationships in online social networks: A study on twitter. In *Proc. COSN 2013*, ACM Press (2013).
3. Bailly, D., Beuscart, R., Collinet, C., Alexandre, J., and Parquet, P. J. Sex differences in the manifestations of depression in young people. *European Child & Adolescent Psychiatry* (1992).
4. Barnett, P. A., and Gotlib, I. H. Psychosocial functioning and depression: distinguishing among antecedents, concomitants, and consequences. *Psychological bulletin 104*, 1 (1988), 97.
5. Blatt, S. J. The destructiveness of perfectionism: Implications for the treatment of depression. *American Psychologist* (1995).
6. Burke, M., and Kraut, R. E. Growing closer on facebook: changes in tie strength through social network site use. In *Proc. CHI 2014*, ACM Press (2014).
7. Caplan, S. E. Preference for online social interaction a theory of problematic internet use and psychosocial well-being. *Communication Research 30*, 6 (2003), 625–648.
8. Cho, M. J., and Kim, K. H. Use of the center for epidemiologic studies depression (CES-D) scale in Korea. *The Journal of Nervous and Mental Disease* (1998).

9. Cho, M. J., Nam, J. J., and Suh, G. H. Prevalence of symptoms of depression in a nationwide sample of korean adults. *Psychiatry research* (1998).

10. Choudhury, M. D., Counts, S., and Horvitz, E. Predicting postpartum changes in emotion and behavior via social media. In *Proc. CSCW 2013*, ACM Press (2013).

11. Collins, P. Y., Patel, V., Joestl, S. S., March, D., Insel, T. R., and Daar, A. S. Grand challenges in global mental health. *Nature* (2011).

12. Cyranowski, J., Frank, E., Young, E., and Shear, M. Adolescent onset of the gender difference in lifetime rates of major depression: a theoretical model. *Archives of General Psychiatry* (2000).

13. De Choudhury, M., Counts, S., Horvitz, E. J., and Hoff, A. Characterizing and predicting postpartum depression from shared facebook data. In *Proc. CSCW 2014*, ACM Press (2014).

14. Dodds, P. S., and Danforth, C. M. Measuring the happiness of large-scale written expression: songs, blogs, and presidents. *Journal of Happiness Studies* (2009).

15. Dudaa, M. D., and Nobilea, J. L. The fallacy of online surveys: No data are better than bad data. *Human Dimensions of Wildlife* (2010).

16. Dunn, E. W., Aknin, L. B., and Norton, M. I. Spending money on others promotes happiness. *Science* (2008).

17. Eysenbach, G. Infodemiology and infoveillance: framework for an emerging set of public health informatics methods to analyze search, communication and publication behavior on the internet. *Journal of Medical Internet Research* (2009).

18. Gou, L., Zhou, M. X., and Yang, H. Knowme and shareme: Understanding automatically discovered personality traits from social media and user sharing preferences. In *Proc. CHI 2014*, ACM Press (2014).

19. Hackett, P. M. W. Facebook and Uncritical Contemporary Culture *SocialScienceSpace*. http://tinyurl.com/lhl3oly, (2014).

20. Haimson, O. L., Ringland, K., Simpson, S., and Wolf, C. T. Using depression analytics to reduce stigma via social media: Bluefriends. In *iConference* (2014).

21. Hamilton, M. Rating depressive patients. *Journal of Clinical Psychiatry* (1980).

22. Haringsma, R., Engels, G., Beekman, A., and Spinhoven, P. The criterion validity of the Center for Epidemiological Studies Depression Scale (CES-D) in a sample of self-referred elders with depressive symptomatology. *International Journal of Geriatric Psychiatry* (2004).

23. Hepburn, A. Facebook Statistics, Stats and Facts For 2011 *digitalBuzz. http://goo.gl/EUKhRE*, (2011).

24. Homan, C. M., Lu, N., Tu, X., Lytle, M. C., and Silenzio, V. Social structure and depression in trevorspace. In *ACM CSCW* (2014).

25. Jacobs, D. Analysis of effects of sex and age in response to items on the CES-D scale. *Psychiatry Research* (1981).

26. Jashinsky, J., Burton, S. H., Hanson, C. L., West, J., Giraud-Carrier, C., Barnes, M. D., and Argyle, T. Tracking Suicide Risk Factors Through Twitter in the US. *Journal of Crisis Intervention and Suicide Prevention* (2013).

27. Jin, B. How lonely people use and perceive facebook. *Computers in Human Behavior* (2013).

28. Kivran-Swaine, F., Ting, J., Brubaker, J. R., Teodoro, R., and Naaman, M. Understanding Loneliness in Social Awareness Streams: Expressions and Responses. In *Proc. ICWSM 2014*, AAAI Press (2014).

29. Klerman, G. The current age of youthful melancholia: Evidence for increase in depression among adolescents and young adults. *British Journal of Psychiatry* (1988).

30. Kosinskia, M., Stillwella, D., and Graepel, T. Private traits and attributes are predictable from digital records of human behavior. *PNAS* (2013).

31. Kotikalapudi, R., Chellappan, S., Montgomery, F., Wunsch, D., and Lutzen, K. Associating depressive symptoms in college students with internet usage using real Internet data. *IEEE Technology and Society Magazine* (2012).

32. Kross, E., Verduyn, P., Demiralp, E., Park, J., Lee, D. S., Lin, N., Shablack, H., Jonides, J., and Ybarra, O. Facebook use predicts declines in subjective well-being in young adults. *PLoS One* (2013).

33. Kuss, D., Griffiths, M., Karila, L., and Billieux, J. Internet Addiction: A Systematic Review of Epidemiological Research for the Last Decade. *Current Pharmaceutical Design* (2013).

34. Mark, G., Iqbal, S., Czerwinski, M., and Johns, P. Capturing the mood: facebook and face-to-face encounters in the workplace. In *Proc. CSCW 2014*, ACM Press (2014).

35. McKenna, K. Y., Green, A. S., and Gleason, M. E. Relationship formation on the internet: Whats the big attraction? *Journal of social issues 58*, 1 (2002), 9–31.

36. Miller, P. M., and Ingham, J. G. Friends, confidants and symptoms. *Social Psychiatry* (1976).

37. Moreno, M. A., Jelenchick, L. A., Egan, K. G., Cox, E., Young, H., Gannon, K. E., and Becker, T. Feeling bad on facebook: Depression disclosures by college students on a social networking site. *Depression and Anxiety* (2011).

38. Park, M., McDonald, D. W., and Cha, M. Perception Differences between the Depressed and Non-depressed Users in Twitter. In *Proc. ICWSM 2013*, AAAI Press (2013).

39. Park, S., Lee, S., Kwak, J., Cha, M., and Jeong, B. Activities on Facebook reveal depressive state of users. *Journal of Medical Internet Research* (2013).

40. Paykel, E. Life events, social support and depression. *Acta Psychiatrica Scandinavica* (1994).

41. Radloff, L. S. The ces-d scale a self-report depression scale for research in the general population. *Applied Psychological Measurement* (1977).

42. Rosen, L. D., Whaling, K., Rab, S., Carrier, L. M., and Cheever, N. A. Is facebook creating idisorders? the link between clinical symptoms of psychiatric disorders and technology use, attitudes and anxiety. *Computers in Human Behavior* (2013).

43. Rotenberg, V., Indursky, P., Kayumov, L., Sirota, P., and Melamed, Y. The relationship between subjective sleep estimation and objective sleep variables in depressed patients. *International Journal of Psychophysiology* (2000).

44. Rude, S., Gortner, E., and Pennebaker, J. Language use of depressed and depression-vulnerable college students. *Cognition and Emotion* (2004).

45. Saul, D. The 2014 Facebook Demographic Report *iStrategyLabs*. http://goo.gl/E3ADUS, (2014).

46. Sirey, J. A., Bruce, M. L., Alexopoulos, G. S., Perlick, D. A., Raue, P., Friedman, S. J., and Meyers, B. S. Perceived stigma as a predictor of treatment discontinuation in young and older outpatients with depression. *American Journal of Psychiatry* (2001).

47. Steinfield, C., Ellison, N., and Lampe, C. Social capital, self-esteem, and use of online social network sites: A longitudinal analysis. *Journal of Applied Developmental Psychology* (2008).

48. Stice, E., Ragan, J., and Randall, P. Prospective Relations Between Social Support and Depression: Differential Direction of Effects for Parent and Peer Support? *Journal of Abnormal Psychology* (2004).

49. Taylor, D. J., Lichstein, K. L., and Durrence, H. H. Insomnia as a health risk factor. *Behavioral Sleep Medicine 1*, 4 (2003), 227–247.

50. Valkenburg, P., Peter, J., and Schouten, A. Friend networking sites and their relationship to adolescents' well-being and social self-esteem. *Cyberpsychology & Behavior* (2006).

51. Vitak, J. Facebook makes the heart grow fonder: relationship maintenance strategies among geographically dispersed and communication-restricted connections. In *Proc. CSCW 2014*, ACM Press (2014).

52. Weissman, M. M., Bland, R. C., Canino, G. J., Faravelli, C., Greenwald, S., Hwu, H.-G., Joyce, P. R., Karam, E. G., Lee, C.-K., Lellouch, J., et al. Cross-national epidemiology of major depression and bipolar disorder. *The Journal of the American Medical Association 276*, 4 (1996), 293–299.

53. Wohn, D. Y., and LaRose, R. Effects of loneliness and differential usage of facebook on college adjustment of first-year students. *Computers & Education* (2014).

54. Won, H.-H., Myung, W., Song, G.-Y., Lee, W.-H., Kim, J.-W., Carroll, B. J., and Kim, D. K. Predicting national suicide numbers with social media data. *PLoS One* (2013).

55. Zhao, X., Salehi, N., Naranjit, S., Alwaalan, S., Voida, S., and Cosley, D. The many faces of Facebook: Experiencing social media as performance, exhibition, and personal archive. In *Proc. CHI 2013*, ACM Press (2013).

56. Zich, J. M., Attkisson, C. C., and Greenfield, T. Screening for Depression in Primary Care Clinics: The CES-D and the BDI. *International Journal of Psychiatry in Medicine* (1990).

57. Zivina, K., Eisenberg, D., Gollust, S. E., and Golberstein, E. Persistence of mental health problems and needs in a college student population. *Journal of Affective Disorders* (2009).

Coming of Age (Digitally): An Ecological View of Social Media Use among College Students

Yiran Wang[1], Melissa Niiya[2], Gloria Mark[1], Stephanie Reich[2], Mark Warschauer[2]

[1]Department of Informatics
University of California, Irvine
{yiranw2,gmark@uci.edu}

[2]School of Education
University of California, Irvine
{mniiya,smreich,markw@uci.edu}

ABSTRACT

We take an ecological approach to studying social media use and its relation to mood among college students. We conducted a mixed-methods study of computer and phone logging with daily surveys and interviews to track college students' use of social media during all waking hours over seven days. Continual and infrequent checkers show different preferences of social media sites. Age differences also were found. Lower classmen tend to be heavier users and to primarily use Facebook, while upper classmen use social media less frequently and utilize sites other than Facebook more often. Factor analysis reveals that social media use clusters into patterns of content-sharing, text-based entertainment/discussion, relationships, and video consumption. The more constantly one checks social media daily, the less positive is one's mood. Our results suggest that students construct their own patterns of social media usage to meet their changing needs in their environment. The findings can inform further investigation into social media use as a benefit and/or distraction for students.

Author Keywords

Social media; Facebook; computer logging; *in situ* study; college students

ACM Classification Keywords

H.5.3 [Information Interfaces and Presentation]: Group and Organization Interfaces; K.4.m [Computers and Society]: Miscellaneous.

General Terms

Human Factors

INTRODUCTION

The rapid adoption of social media has shaped contemporary culture. In widespread use for less than ten years, social media has become broadly adopted with over two billion users worldwide [40] and with Facebook alone claiming 1.3 billion active users in a given month [41].

The largest cohort of social media users is the Millennial generation. The Millennial generation, the largest in history (with over 80 million in the U.S. aged 19-33 years), is rapidly entering the workforce, and it is already reshaping cultural institutions with new communication and coordination habits. Specifically, the current generation of college-aged students (i.e., those approximately age 18-22) is the first college cohort to grow up with social media, and as a group is one of the heaviest users of social media [32].

This group's heavy use of social media raises many questions about how students incorporate social media into their lives and whether doing so supports or hinders students' broader social and academic development, as reflected by the ability to read deeply, think critically, and form authentic friendships. The influences of social media will likely permeate the workforce as college students graduate. For example, Gartner [10] predicts that social media will transform information work into activity that is less routine, hyper-connected, and with higher reliance on weak social links.

Considering the scale of social media adoption, the size of the Millennial cohort, and the potential for both users and media to transform social life and work, we feel that examining social media usage patterns could yield valuable insights into the utility and impacts of social media use on the workplace, in relationships, in social life, and on health and well-being. As a first step to begin to understand the phenomena brought about by social media, we focus on its use among college students.

To date, CSCW has examined a variety of aspects related to social media use such as social relationships [20], tie strength [11], credibility [27], enterprise use [24], and in signaling affect [1]. However, studies of social media use in CSCW have largely focused on the use of individual applications such as Facebook, Twitter, or Pinterest. Some exceptions include studying broad social media usage in the enterprise [13, 24]. Although Facebook continues to be the most widely used form of social media [29], social media use on the whole can by no means be characterized as commensurate with Facebook use. A range of social media sites such as YouTube, Twitter, Instagram, and Reddit, created primarily for social and/or leisure purposes, are also widely used by Millennials, and by college students in particular [29]. We therefore seek to widen the lens of investigation beyond any single social media site and

CSCW '15, March 14 - 18, 2015, Vancouver, BC, Canada.
Copyright 2015 ACM 978-1-4503-2922-4/15/03…$15.00.
http://dx.doi.org/10.1145/2675133.2675271

consider the *entire ecology* of social media use, examining how young people use an assemblage of social media sites in their daily lives. Though the Millennial generation roughly includes those born after 1980, we focus on a particular sub-group, college students, because 1) compared to all Millennials this is a more homogeneous group, and 2) this enables us to compare our results with other studies of social media by college students [e.g., 1, 9, 15, 21].

We seek to provide an accurate and grounded understanding of both the extent and ways college students embed social media in their lives. Specifically, the goal of this study is to examine patterns of social media use in the aggregate and how these might be associated with students' characteristics and attitudes toward social media as a type of digital activity. We use a mixed methods approach of precision tracking with sensors and daily surveys to capture the data. This paper is part of a larger study investigating IT use and its impact on education among college students.

RELATED WORK: SOCIAL MEDIA USE AMONG COLLEGE-AGED MILLENNIALS

Although social media is a recent phenomenon, its use among the Millennial generation has been the subject of increasing study. The majority (90%) of those 18-29 year olds have a social media profile, and nearly all (97%) use the Internet [31, 32]. Of those in college, 96% use the Internet and 86% have created a social media profile [45]. Whereas Facebook use is predominant [29], other social networking sites (SNSs) and social networking apps also play a role; for example, Facebook, Instagram, and Twitter are among the top ten most used mobile apps by young people [29].

Social Media in College Life

Social media usage among college students is not only highly prevalent but also socially important as it can improve social fluency [4], increase college students' bridging and bonding social capital, and compensate for low self-esteem [9], anxiety, and shyness [7, 48]. Certain behaviors, such as one-to-one communication rather than broadcasting behaviors and simple actions such as "likes," are particularly important for developing social ties [3], as are profile enhancements [47] and the strategic displays of online relationships [46]. Social media use can also help maintain geographically distant friendships [43, 49], which may be particularly important among college students as they transition from high school to college and from college to careers. Participation in social media may help satisfy psychosocial needs during these times of change. For example, maintaining contact with high school friends through Facebook is associated with higher life satisfaction and perceived social support [23, 43].

Daily Social Media Use and Distractions

A recent survey of college students found that they spend more time online than studying [43]. Research on Facebook alone has found that college students spend an average range of 10-60 minutes daily, checking about 6 times a day [12, 14, 15]. Unfortunately, time estimates of use based on self-reports can be unreliable. For example, studies show that self-reports of computer and Facebook usage overestimate time dramatically [6, 16].

Examining the frequency of usage may help identify how social media may be distracting or whether its use is associated with deficits in other areas. Survey studies of a range of users suggest that heavy and light users may be distinct groups. Heavy and chronic media multitaskers are significantly more susceptible to distractions from the environment [30] and social media app use can develop into problematic behaviors including overuse and interference with schoolwork [22]. Some users, however, are aware of social media as a distraction and alter their behaviors as a result. Baumer et al. [2] found that approximately 31% of the Facebook users they sampled had currently or previously deactivated or deleted their accounts, noting productivity issues and problematic behaviors. In a study on quitting Twitter for lent, Schoenebeck [36] found that concern for spending too much time on social media is one of the primary reasons why users took breaks from it. In addition to restricting site visits, some students chose not to use their device(s), forming a sort of *techno-resistance* [1]. Thus, for some students, social media, especially when used in combination with schoolwork, may pose a cognitive burden [30].

Social Media Use and Mood

Although social networks can be used to cope during stressful times, they can also increase stress [3]. For example, college students may feel pressured to quickly respond to social media notifications and to maintain a "constant connection" with peers [1]. For those who mainly consume SNSs content rather than use it to connect directly with friends and family, there may be negative effects on wellbeing and social capital [5].

Social media interactions may affect wellbeing and mood in other ways. A study of emotional "contagion" on Facebook suggests that status updates with emotional content can flow to other users [19]. As a population with high rates of SNSs adoption and use, college students may be especially affected. A study in the workplace found that higher duration of Facebook use was associated with more positive affect [24]; SNSs use might also have an impact on positive affect for college students.

Although a growing number of studies such as these have investigated social media use among college students, they have been based solely on self-reports, proven to be unreliable [6, 16], focused on a single social media application such as Facebook, or examined only smartphone usage. In contrast, we take an *ecological perspective* (i.e., across social media sites and devices) exploring the duration and frequency of checking social media, contrasting differences among heavy and light users, and assessing how patterns of use connect to mood. We use a mixed-methods approach of precision tracking on both computers and smartphones along with daily surveys.

Our study thus makes the following contributions:

- To overcome the problems of unreliability with self-reports, we use precision tracking to determine exact measures of social media use.
- As most studies have focused on usage of a single social media site, we provide an ecological perspective of social media usage across sites and devices.
- Most studies generally treat college students as a single cohort in their social media usage. We examine patterns in heavy and light users and those that are younger and older.
- As results are unclear how social media may affect mood, we examine how social media usage is associated with mood.

RESEARCH QUESTIONS

Building on the research discussed, we are interested in identifying social media use patterns and their effect on mood. We address the following research questions

RQ1. *What are the habits of checking behavior of social media among college students?* Studies have reported that social media is a distraction from schoolwork [cf 25]. Recent research also reports that some college students have reduced or halted their time on social media due to it hindering their productivity [1, 2]. However, studies that measured amount of social media use have generally focused solely on Facebook use [12, 14, 15] or all online activity [43]. Given that people self-report that they use social media often [31, 45], it is an open question as to exactly how often and how frequently students check social media sites throughout the day. Checking behavior is important to study as it can be associated with frequent distractions from schoolwork. We investigate here the differences in people who check social media continually versus infrequently, including their perceptions of their use, and potential reasons for the checking habits.

RQ2. *Can we identify patterns and clusters of social media usage?* While Facebook is the dominant social media platform among college students [29], there are a myriad of other sites available. Again, studies that have examined college students' use of online media have generally focused on either Facebook or more broadly, the Internet. To our knowledge, no study has objectively tracked a range of actual social media usage. Examining social media use is important because social media as a whole (and not just Facebook) can provide information, social support, and entertainment as well as be a "break" from work. In this research question we examine whether we can find patterns of preferences for social media use. For example, those people who prefer Youtube may also prefer other content sharing sites such as Reddit. Others may prefer to use sites with more direct communication features. We may find that people show clear preferences for visiting social media sites that offer particular affordances. Our goal in this research question is to see if we can identify an underlying structure of usage among social media sites, given the wide choices available to produce and consume user-generated content. If such a structure exists, this could potentially illuminate some of the information and social needs of college students, which would be useful for the design of social media sites.

RQ3. *Are differences in social media use associated with mood?* Because of the prevalent use of social media among college students, and because college life is a critical developmental experience [23, 43], we feel that it is important to examine whether social media use has an effect on mood. Prior research has found mixed results, with some results showing that social media increases negative affect and stress [5] and others finding increased positive affect [19] and lower stress with use [25]. These studies, however, relied on self-reports to gauge amount of social media use and have only looked at Facebook use. Again, social media use encompasses far more than Facebook. We will examine the relationship between mood and aggregate social media use.

METHODOLOGY

We conducted an *in situ* observational study at a large public university on the U.S. West Coast in the spring of 2013. Since our interest was in capturing fine-grained social media activity, we used a mixed-methods approach with automatic computer and phone logging as the primary method of data collection. In order to capture the context of students' life at school, their mood, and their perceptions and attitudes towards social media, we also used daily surveys and a one-time general survey on attitudes and demographic information. Data collection occurred over seven days, with logging done during all waking hours.

Participants and Procedure

Participants were recruited from various undergraduate classes, resident communities, and snowball sampling. In total, we collected data from 48 undergraduates, 27 males and 21 females. Due to the availability of monitoring software and its limitations, the study was restricted to students who used both Windows computers and Android phones. Students' ages ranged from 18 to 26 years (mean=19.6); and the median college year was sophomore. The average age when participants started using a computer was 9.4 years and using the Internet, 10.8 years. We divided their declared majors into STEM and non-STEM majors for further analysis according to NSF STEM classification [28]. Their self-reported GPAs ranged from 1.6 to 3.8.

On Day 1 of the study, participants visited a campus laboratory where the computer and phone logging software were installed on their devices. Students who also had desktop computers were given software installation instructions. Participants were instructed to continue to use their devices as usual. They were also sent a link to an online general survey on Day 1 and instructed to complete it before the end of the study (by Day 7). An online daily survey was sent to the participants at 9PM for each day of the study and they were asked to complete it before going to bed. Semi-structured interviews were conducted on Day 7. Participants were asked about their general experiences during the study, their technology and social media habits, their various projects and responsibilities, and beliefs about how technology could affect stress, productivity, and mood. The interviews were on average 15 minutes long. In addition to quantitative analyses of logs and surveys, open coding, including descriptive and process codes, were used to identify key themes that emerged from these interviews [35]. Participants were paid $100 for their participation.

Measures

Data were collected from 48 students from social media usage logs from their computers and phones and seven days of self-reported measures. We also monitored heart rate variability and used experience sampling to measure stress levels both objectively and subjectively. Since stress is not the focus of this paper, these measures are not presented. The following measures were used:

Social media logs. Participants' technology use was collected by an automatic logging program: Kidlogger (kidlogger.net). The software has Windows and Android versions, which were installed on participants' computer and phone, respectively. Kidlogger generated one log record each time a user opened a new window or switched between already open windows on a computer or phone. A window can be an application or a web browser tab. Each log record included the starting time and duration of the active window, the name of the application and a URL if the window was a web browser tab (including incognito or private browsing tabs), and idle time. Timestamps are accurate to the second. Only time spent in the window that was currently in use was measured. In other words, if a Word program was open in the background while the user was actively browsing Facebook in the foreground, our software only counted the time spent in Facebook.

Two coders independently categorized the computer logs of the top 421 most frequently visited URLs (each having at least 20 visits), based on the domain name of the website. The coders iteratively developed 10 website categories, with social media as one of the 10 categories, which were loosely defined as Internet-based applications that allow the creation and exchange of User Generated Content [18]. Out of the 421 URLs, there were disagreements in 34 of these URLs. After discussion, the coders reached consensus for all 421 URLs. For this paper, we only focus on the subset of computer logs that are marked as social media, which includes websites such as Facebook, Twitter, Tumblr, YouTube, and Livejournal. Wikipedia was excluded from the list as we believe that college students generally use it for non-leisure purposes, though the content of the site is collaboratively generated. Phone logs were annotated using the same coding scheme. Note that social media use on the phone includes both URLs (i.e., a user browsed a social media site from a phone browser) and individual applications such as a Facebook or Twitter app. Our measures of social media usage were based on the combination of both computer and phone logs that were categorized as social media, described above.

Survey measures. We obtained demographic information along with students' study and technology use habits in the general survey. Table 1 summarizes the measures and the questions asked in surveys. In addition to demographics, we asked about GPA, students' course load, class standing. Using a Likert scale of 1-5, we asked a cluster of questions regarding feeling lack of control online and expectations for using social media. These questions on subjective attitudes were pilot tested among the research team and analyzed individually, thus we did not include validity test. An established workplace empowerment scale [26, 39] was adapted for college students. In order to measure overall mood, we deployed the PANAS scale [50], a well-validated mood measure that is comprised of two dimensions – positive and negative affect, each measured on a scale of 10 to 50. In an end-of-day survey, participants reported their daily mood using the PANAS, which was modified for a daily measure. Each day they also noted the classes they attended; on a Likert scale of 1-5, their perceived productivity, and how influenced they were by deadlines and work/study pressure.

RESULTS

Of 48 participants, two (one female, one male) were excluded from the analysis. For one participant, our logging software was blocked by anti-virus software on their computer. Another participant was noncompliant, using another personal computer without Kidlogger installed.

We collected a total of more than 1350 hours of computer logs from 46 participants, excluding computer idle time; and 412 hours of phone logs from 45 participants – due to technical difficulties, we could not download the logs from one participant's phone. Combining both computer and phone logs, we captured 471 hours of social media use and a total of 33,566 visits to social media. Of these, 393 hours and 78 hours of social media use are from computers and phones, respectively.

An Overview of Social Media Use

We first present an overview of daily social media usage by our sample. Table 2 shows average daily duration, average number of visits per day (frequency), and average duration per visit averaged over all users, averaged over all full days of logging. Participants in our sample on average spent over 1 1/2 hours daily on social media sites (median=1 hour 33 minutes). Participants also visited social media sites on average about 118 times daily (median = 90.5). Each visit was counted if there was a unique record of a social media site URL recorded in the logging program. When a user browsed a social media page (e.g., a Facebook news feeds) and was involved in relevant activities that did not cause a URL change (e.g., scrolling down the page, liking a status,

Measure	Explanation
General measures (self-reported from general survey)	
Demographics	Age, gender, class standing, major, GPA, year of adoption of SNSs, smartphone, and Internet
Course load	*How many credit hours (units) are you taking this term?*
Lack of control online	(1 = Strongly, 5 = Strongly agree) **Distracted** - *I feel that on the whole social media distracts me from what I need to do.*
	Behind_schoolwork - *I feel that because I use social media so much I am falling behind my schoolwork.*
	Use_SM_less - *I would like to use social media less time during the day.*
	Addicted_to_Internet - *I feel that I am addicted to the Internet.*
Feeling of empowerment at school (**Empowerment**)	The overall Empowerment score is aggregated from these 12 questions, adapted from [26, 39]: *1) The work I do at school is very important to me. 2) I am confident about my ability to perform well as a student. 3) What I do as a student has a large effect on the school where I am enrolled. 4) My school activities are personally meaningful to me. 5) I have a great deal of control over what happens at the school where I am enrolled. 6) I have significant autonomy in determining what work I do as a student. 7) I am self-assured about my capabilities to perform well in school. 8) I have considerable opportunity for independence and freedom in performing school work. 9) I have mastered the skills necessary to be a good student. 10) I have significant influence over what happens at the school where I am enrolled. 11) I can decide on my own how to go about doing my student work. 12) The school work I do is meaningful to me.*
PANAS	Measures positive (**PANASPOS**) and negative (**PANASNEG**) affect dimensions [50]. Scale of 10-50.
Expectations of using social media	(1 = Strongly, 5 = Strongly agree) **Connect_close_friends** - *I feel that I should maintain connections with close friends using social media*
	Connect_acquaintances - *I feel that I should maintain connections with acquaintances using social media.*
	Maintain_presence - *I feel that I need to maintain a presence on social media, i.e. that others are aware that I am active on social media sites.*
	Keep_informed - *I feel that I need to keep current with the information posted on social media sites.*
Daily Measures (from end of the day survey)	
Daily PANAS	Measures positive (**PANASPOS**) and negative (**PANASNEG**) affect dimensions [50]. Scale of 10-50.
Productivity	How productive do you feel you were today? (1 = Not at all, 5 = Extremely)
Deadline	I feel that deadlines influenced me today. (1 = Strongly, 5 = Strongly agree)
Under pressure	I feel that I was under work/study pressure today. (1 = Strongly, 5 = Strongly agree)

Table 1. Summary of general and daily survey measures.

commenting on a status update), there was one record of Facebook in the log. But if the user clicked on a video or picture that took her to another site, then there was another Facebook record generated when she returned to Facebook. We considered the latter case as two Facebook visits. Switching from one Facebook page to another was also counted in our log as two visits since there was a URL change. Therefore, our estimate of frequency is likely an overestimate. The duration per each visit to social media was short, averaging slightly over one minute (median = 1 minute and 4 seconds).

For the 45 participants we obtained both computer and phone logs, 44 used social media sites on both devices, one used only their computer for social media. Based on a paired t-test, students spent more time on social media per visit on phones (median=71.32 sec.) than computers (median=56.03 sec.), t(43)=2.78, p<.01). We did not find significant differences in social media use based on daily duration for full days, between genders, STEM and non-STEM majors, class standing, or weekday/weekend use.

		Duration/ day	Visits/ day	Duration/ visit
Total SM	Mean	1:41:01	117.92	0:01:06
	Median	1:33:40	90.5	0:01:04
	(sd)	(1:06:21)	(101.21)	(0:00:35)
Facebook	Mean	0:49:34	52.32	0:01:06
	Median	0:39:48	31.5	0:01:05
	(sd)	(0:43:48)	(57.49)	(0:00:31)
Other SM	Mean	0:51:27	65.60	0:01:08
	Median	0:40:02	45.20	0:01:05
	(sd)	(0:45:53)	(71.38)	(0:00:41)

Table 2. Average daily duration, visits, and duration per visit averaged over all participants. Duration in h:mm:ss. N=46.

General patterns of site usage

We present an overview of general patterns of different site usage. The top 10 social media sites in our sample, based on total hours of use observed, are shown in the left half of Table 3. Facebook and YouTube were the most popular social media sites; almost all of the participants in our sample used these two sites. However, Facebook is not the only site used; students tended to use multiple social media sites. Of the 10 most-used sites, participants used an average of at least 5 of them (M=5.3, sd=2.12, min=1, max =9) over the week of the study. Facebook was the primary social media site for 32 participants (in terms of time duration). Users who predominately use Facebook (M_{Age}=19.34) were significantly younger than other users (M_{Age}=21), t(44)=-3.04,p<.005) and were comprised of more freshmen and sophomores compared to other users who were mainly juniors and seniors ($X^2_{(1)}$=4.44, p<0.05). In general, the mean age of lower classmen (i.e. freshmen and sophomores, N=30) was M_{Age}=18.8, sd=0.71; the mean age of upper classmen (juniors and seniors, N=16) was M_{Age}=21.81, sd=1.72.

Social media	# users	Avg. daily use* (h:mm)	Primary site usage			
			Cont-inual	Infre-quent	Hea-vy	Lig-ht
Facebook	45	0:49	9	4	7	6
YouTube	45	0:21		4		3
Reddit	20	0:20		2	1	1
Tumblr	32	0:07			1	
Instagram	24	0:09				
Twitter	22	0:09	1		1	
Weibo	1	3:00	1		1	
Imgur	27	0:02		1		1
Livejournal	3	0:12				
Google+	12	0:02				

Table 3. Average daily social media use. N=46. *Average daily use is calculated based only on users of the site.

RQ1. Habits of Checking Social Media

As table 2 shows, college students in our sample visited social media sites often, averaging an hour and 40 minutes per day. However, a measure of duration does not indicate how frequently students might be checking social media, which could potentially be interrupting other activities. To analyze frequency of checking over time, we first divided our total logged computer and phone time into 5-minute windows. We then computed a ratio between observed social media use and total computer and phone use in each 5-minute window (**SM ratio**). The ratio was computed by first flagging whether social media was used or not in the 5-minute window. Then, we examined overall the percentage of 5-minute windows of time where social media was used. This ratio gave us a measure of the spread of SM checking throughout the period of computer and phone use. A large value of the ratio indicates that someone's day was filled with frequent visits to social media sites. A small ratio value indicates that someone visited social media sites very infrequently relative to their total computer and phone usage. Note that the ratio does not take into account the *extent* to which one uses social media within the 5-minute window; rather it gives us a measure of how temporally distributed one's social media use is compared to her overall computer and phone use. This measure thus provides us with an estimate of spread of social media use throughout the day.

For the 46 participants, the values of the SM ratios were normally distributed (M=38.38%, sd=18.38%, min=2%, max=77%). We then divided our sample into *continual checkers*: the top 25th percentile (N=11, mean= 62.9%, sd= 8.1%), and *infrequent checkers*: the bottom 25th percentile (N=11, mean= 15.9%, sd=7.5%) of SMRatios. Even though the absolute number of times visiting social media sites per day is likely to be an overestimate as discussed earlier, continual checkers (M=237, sd=101) visited social media pages daily more than six times as often as infrequent checkers (M= 39, sd=34).

Next we explored the patterns of use, comparing whether continual and infrequent checkers visited the same sites. We found differences in primary social media sites used (see the right half of Table 3): continual checkers predominantly used Facebook (9 of 11 users) compared to infrequent checkers (4 of 11 users). The primary sites that infrequent checkers visited were content-focused sites of Youtube and Reddit.

Table 4 shows the results from the questionnaires, with the means and standard deviations of the entire sample shown in the far right column. We found age differences with continual checkers being mostly lower classmen whereas infrequent checkers were predominately upper classmen. Continual checkers revealed a lack of control of social media use: they agreed significantly more that it distracts them, that they were falling behind on schoolwork, they would like to use social media less, and feel addicted to use the Internet. Continual checkers also had significantly heavier course loads. Yet we found no difference in reasons for using social media. Continual and infrequent checkers

Variables	Heavy vs. Light social media use				Continual vs. Infrequent social media use				Total N=46 Mean (sd)
	Heavy	Light	t (df)	Sig.	Continual	Infrequent	t (df)	Sig.	
Class Standing	More freshmen and sophomores	More juniors and seniors	NA	*	More freshmen and sophomores	More juniors and seniors	NA	*	
Course load	14.8	13.6	1.264 (20)	N.S.	14.96	12.73	2.320 (20)	*	14.56 (2.98)
Distracted	3.82	3.18	1.328 (20)	N.S.	4.18	2.91	2.945 (20)	**	3.57 (0.98)
Behind_schoolwork	3.27	2	2.609 (20)	*	3.36	1.91	3.150 (20)	**	2.78 (1.23)
Use_SM_less	3.73	2.91	1.649 (20)	N.S.	3.91	2.73	2.298 (20)	*	3.26 (1.22)
Addicted_to_Internet	3.91	2.82	2.524 (20)	*	3.91	2.82	2.524 (20)	*	3.17 (1.32)
Maintain_presence	3.09	2.18	2.344 (20)	*	2.73	2	1.698 (20)	N.S.	2.50 (1.11)
Keep_informed	3.55	2.55	2.079 (20)	*	3.18	2.55	1.078 (20)	N.S.	2.83 (1.31)

Table 4. Demographics and questionnaire results for Heavy vs. Light social media users and Continual vs. Infrequent social media users. * = p<0.05, ** = p<0.01, *** = p<0.001

did not differ in their reported need to use social media for maintaining social relationships, maintaining a presence, or keeping current with information on social media. We found no differences in gender, major, GPA, overall mood, year of adoption of SNSs or a smartphone, or overall feeling of empowerment at school.

Thus, continual checkers are younger, favor Facebook more, and report having more of a lack of control with social media compared to infrequent checkers.

Heavy and light usage: duration of use
The SM ratio provided us with a measure of how often one checks social media; we compared the results with duration of use. We divided our sample into the top 25th percentile of duration spent on social media daily (heavy users: N=11, M=3 hours, 16 minutes) and the bottom 25th percentile (light users: N=11, M=25 minutes). The continual checkers and heavy users overlap with 5 people in common; infrequent checkers and light users overlap with 9 people in common.

We found the characteristics of heavy and light duration users to be similar to continual and infrequent checkers, see Table 4 (note there is substantial overlap in groups). The majority of both heavy and light users used Facebook as their primary social media site. Heavy users were more likely to be lower classmen while light users were more likely to be upper classmen ($X^2_{(2)} = 6.108$, $p<.05$). Similar to continual checkers, heavy users agreed significantly more that they were falling behind on schoolwork and that they were addicted to the Internet (see Table 1 for the questions). In contrast to continual checkers, heavy users agreed significantly more that they need to maintain a presence on social media and to keep informed with current information. No other differences were found.

Qualitative analysis: amount of usage and habits
The open-ended interviews also help shed light on students' habits of social media use. Consistent with our findings above, was a reoccurring theme during interviews that social media use was a practice with which people felt guilty or stressed about—particularly in relation to the amount of time spent on academic work. Some students felt that their use of social media interfered with their academic achievement: "*I wake up and it's the first thing I check and the last thing I look at before I go to sleep. I'm always on it even when I'm supposed to be studying*" (P15).

Interviews among upper classmen, reported growing away from intense social media use, which supports our age difference finding for heavy to light use and continual to infrequent checking of social media. Of these upper classmen, 8 mentioned that they had at least tried to curb their social media use, e.g., "*I'm not big on Facebook. Not anymore. I don't use it as much as other people, it's a distraction*" (P25); "*I tried to quit it before, but it's almost like a necessity because all my friends and my co-workers are on there*" (P19); "*I don't usually go on SM. I used to like a year ago. Not anymore. Too much of a hassle. I just found it more work than it's worth I suppose*" (P41). Another student also mentioned that his impending graduation played a role in his moving from Facebook to other social media such as LinkedIn: "*it's kinda right there on my doorstep right now. I would say that it did change how much I use one social media over another*" (P27).

Also consistent with the quantitative results, continual checkers revealed concerns with their practice of social media use. As an illustration, one student reported: "*I spend most of my days overdosed. I spend most of my day on Reddit, YouTube, and Facebook*" (P35). Seven of the 11 continual checkers spoke about wanting an app that would prevent them from using the Internet or social media. However, one frequent checker also mentioned that there were benefits from switching between social media and academic work: "*It increases productivity, and it also increases distraction time. So it's a trade-off I feel*" (P18).

Continual checking: uncovering reasons
Participants described many reasons for why they used social media frequently throughout the day ranging from killing time to routine behavior. Many noted the desire to relieve boredom and pass the time: "*I usually just go on Facebook, Instagram, and Twitter. And then Foursquare too...If I'm bored, I'll just go on Twitter or something like that. Just to see if there's anything new*" (P33).

Continual checking was also noted as a way to avoid doing academic work: "*I do my studying and I have a monitor next to this one so I'll have a document on my large monitor. Then I have Facebook open on my other one. I would just multitask on it...Try to not think about doing homework*" (P7). One participant noted that he "*already hated doing homework*" (P36) and that social media was just one way to avoid it. Other students described social media use as normative and routine. For example, one female (P24) described her use of Facebook: "*It's like my job.*"

RQ2. Patterns of Social Media Site Use
Our second research question addressed whether we could uncover a structure of preferences of social media site use. We conducted a factor analysis of daily duration of site use across users. Factor analysis is used to uncover an underlying structure among correlated variables. Our goal was to identify how social media sites cluster according to usage (e.g., do those who spend more time on Facebook also spend more time on Twitter?). Based on average daily duration per participant for the top 10 social media sites, we performed a factor analysis using a Varimax rotation. A scree plot revealed four factors, accounting for 61.9% of the variance. Table 5 shows the four factors and the social media sites that comprise them.

Factor 1 is comprised of Tumblr, Instagram, Twitter, and Livejournal. We interpret this factor as sites where users "follow" or subscribe to accounts that are of interest to them to receive or post (micro)blog-like content. Because of the interest-based and content-focused nature of these communities, we infer that students use these types of social media to primarily stay informed and perhaps have an audience. *Factor 2* is comprised of one site: Google+. Google+ is different from other content-focused social media in that it focuses on customized content sharing to different social circles and integration with other Google services such as Hangouts (text and video chat) and email. *Factor 3* consists of only YouTube. In contrast with the other factor loadings, YouTube users consume video instead of text or images and socialize less with other users. *Factor 4* consists of Reddit and Imgur. Imgur began as an image hosting service inside of Reddit and later gained popularity as a stand-alone site. Content shared in Reddit and Imgur is often through memes or topic-based discussion. There is less relationship-driven communication in this factor compared with factors 1 and 2.

Facebook did not load onto these factors. However, Facebook had moderate weights in 3 factors, indicating that Facebook use occurs in conjunction with the other social media sites identified in these factors (shown in parentheses in table 5). The factor loading of Facebook in factor 4 was moderately negative, suggesting that students who spend more time on Reddit and Imgur are less likely to use Facebook. Reddit and Imgur use represents content-focused anonymous communication while Facebook use represents relationship-based communication that requires a real identity. The contrast suggests that different students might have different preferences for anonymity online.

Infrequent checkers are mostly associated with Factor 3 (Youtube and Facebook, seven participants) and Factor 4 (Reddit and Imgur, three participants); whereas continual checkers were more distributed over the factors: two continuous checkers did not belong to any factor group, indicating that they did not have site preferences, four chose Factor 1 (Tumblr, Instagram, Twitter, LiveJournal, and Facebook), and five chose Factor 3.

Thus, we uncovered a structure of preferences in social media use. While Facebook is used along with other sites, students tend to exhibit patterns of preferences for sites. For example, people who prefer one type of content-focused site such as Twitter, also prefer to use Tumbler, Instagram and. These results support the notion that people develop

Factors	Social media sites
1. Content-focused social sharing	Tumblr, Instagram, Twitter, LiveJournal, *(Facebook)*
2. Social networking for customized friend circles	GooglePlus, *(Facebook)*
3. Video streaming	YouTube, *(Facebook)*
4. Text and image-based entertainment and discussion	Reddit, Imgur

Table 5. Factor analysis results of social media usage

habits of social media use to some extent, i.e. habits of clustering usage of certain types of sites, which might indicate interest and utility of social media for college students.

RQ3. Social media use and mood

Our third research question examined the connection between mood and social media use. The PANAS scale measures mood in terms of two dimensions: positive and negative affect [50]. Independent t-tests showed no differences between continual and infrequent checkers in overall positive and negative affect.

Using a Linear Mixed Model (LMM) to model both fixed and random effects due to non-independence, we included each participant's daily end-of-day PANAS positive affect score and daily PANAS negative affect score as the dependent variable for the two models, respectively. Given the exploratory nature of our study, we used relevant daily measures as independent variables, entered them by hand into the LMM, and chose the best fitting model based on the smallest BIC measure[1]. The daily measures used included daily social media ratio (SM ratio, i.e. checking behavior), whether it was a weekday or weekend, how productive one felt, how much one was under the influence of a deadline, and work pressure. We controlled for gender, age, class standing, course load, and GPA, as these variables could affect mood.

The best fitting model for daily positive affect (Table 6) shows that, overall, daily SM ratio was *negatively* correlated with their daily positive affect. The more constant SM checking was, the lower the positive mood. There was a significant interaction between the SM ratio and how productive one felt that day. Specifically, the less productive a student felt that day, the more that continuous checking decreased the positive affect. With daily duration included in the model instead of daily SM ratio, the model produced a consistent result with similar BIC measure. Daily negative affect showed no association with social media use.

Qualitative analysis: Explaining social media use and mood

From the interview data, we identified two main themes: how social media use helps one de-stress, and how unintentional overuse could lead to bad time management

	β	F	df	P
Daily SM ratio	-0.141	17.98	(1,216)	<.001
Feeling productive x daily SM ratio	0.037	14.73	(1,199)	<.001

Table 6. Model for daily positive affect

[1] Schwarz's Bayesian Criterian (BIC) is commonly used as the criterion to find the best fitting linear mixed model [37]. Models are chosen based on having the lowest score.

and low productivity, which in turn could negatively affect a student's mood.

Some students discussed using social media to improve their mood by taking their minds off work, as one freshman reported: *"If I get frustrated, I go on Facebook to relax and forget about the work"* (P43). Social media breaks offer stress relief because *"If I'm just looking at stuff casually I'll be more happy than if I'm studying for a midterm."* (P34) However, quite a few participants indicated that the effect of social media use on mood is, as P39 put it, *"for a short period of time"*. There seems to be a tension between temporary happiness and productivity in the long term, as P13's discussion pointed out: *"I think there's a difference between being happy and being distracted. I find that sometimes when I'm happy I'm not in a work mode."*

Since the daily PANAS measure was taken once at the end of the day, rather than immediately after each social media use, we think that the negative association between continual checking throughout the day and positive mood could be due to the accumulated effect of social media use on productivity. For example, one freshman commented: *"Sometimes I feel like I'll be on those SNSs or playing games, because I spent so much time on it, I'll have to work at night, and that increases my stress."* (P3) Another freshmen claimed that Facebook relieved stress yet was a distraction that negatively affected mood: *"Although Facebook de-stresses me, I feel like it's a waste of time for me to go on Facebook. When I see myself going like half an hour or more, I think that's just a distraction and it's not productive"* (P39). The quantitative and qualitative results together suggest the potential different temporal effects of social media use on mood.

DISCUSSION

Social media has been in widespread use for just over a decade, yet for college students, there is still little understanding of their patterns of use across sites. Our study provides several contributions that distinguish it from other studies of social media. First, rather than relying on self-reports of use, which tend to be unreliable [6, 16], we captured a fairly comprehensive picture of social media use with precision tracking methods of computer and phone usage over a seven day period, coupled with daily surveys and interviews. Second, while studies of online behavior generally focus on single social media sites, this methodology enabled us to examine *the array* of daily social media practices among college students. This is important since a focus on Facebook or any single social media site does not fully capture students' daily social media usage routine.

Social Media Use as A Habit

Our results revealed that students who constantly check social media did not report higher need or motivation to use social media, such as to maintain social relationships, maintain a presence, or keep current with information, compared to infrequent users. Rather, continual checkers often reported feeling a lack of control. These findings point to a possible explanation of constant checking: the establishment of social media routines might not be driven by different social needs, but rather by a lack of self-discipline. Avoiding studying, passing time, and procrastinating were mentioned often in the interviews and point to a potential lack of self-control. This finding could partially explain why some people, despite their desire to change, find it difficult to break the pattern of continual checking. Habits can become ingrained and hard to break [51], an idea supported by the participants who mentioned that they wanted an app to prevent them from using social media when studying. As more research begins to address how to develop healthy social media use habits [36], understanding ways to discipline one's behavior might be a future research direction, in addition to identifying various social and information needs.

Our findings also found differences in the types of social media sites used by continual and infrequent social media checkers. Continual checkers primarily used Facebook whereas infrequent checkers primarily used content-focused sites such as Youtube and Reddit. Perhaps a need for social connection or the pressure to be available online [e.g., 1] was another motivation for the students who felt compelled to constantly check, even though continual checkers did not report so in surveys. On the other hand, information from content-focused social media sites does not require constant attention (as Facebook might), but rather, can be "batch processed."

We found that although most students used sites such as YouTube and Facebook, college students showed patterns of preferences across sites with some students favoring content-focused social sharing sites and others preferring information/video consumption or customized friends' circles for social networking. These results examining preference patterns support the notion that people cluster their usage of certain types of sites based on key features or affordances. This clustering might also indicate that college students are selective in their consumption of social media, targeting sites that fit their developmental needs for such things as intimacy and connection or independence and autonomy [42]. While we have labeled the factors based on the sites' affordances, it is possible that other underlying factors may lead people to cluster usage. For example, sites that are popular or trendy may be used in a cluster.

Our results reveal that the more constantly one checks social media daily, the less positive is one's mood. We have several explanations for this result. One explanation from the interviews is that social media could be perceived as a distraction in the context of a schoolwork environment, lessening students' opportunities to feel productive and successful in school. It is also possible that the content and interactions on social media could lessen positive moods, increasing social comparison and contributing to feelings of isolation. Also, as discussed earlier, lack of self-regulation appears to be associated with constant use, and this awareness of social media as a distraction could negatively impact one's mood. Given that college students spend significant amounts of their waking hours using social media, it is important to identify the possible mechanisms connecting social media use with lower positive affect.

From the questionnaires and interviews, students report being aware of many of the benefits and deficits of the frequency and duration of their social media use. This awareness is key in the cultivation of self-regulatory skills for managing social media use. The data from our interviews suggests that some students, particularly upperclassmen, have engaged in purposeful activities to curb their social media use and suggests that some young Millennials are aware of the benefits and hindrances of social media use. Future studies could examine in more depth how students can develop self-regulatory strategies to use social media in a balanced way.

Shifting Needs in College

We found differences of social media use with age. Specifically, lower classmen were more likely to be continual and heavy users of social media, whereas upper classmen were more likely to be light and occasional users of social media. These findings expand on the results of Pempek et al. [33] who found that upper classmen used Facebook less.

There are several possible explanations for this pattern. Lower classmen are, for the most part, more recent arrivals to a new university community and thus have a greater need to develop social capital and to maintain connections with old friends. As such, they may spend a lot of time on social media to maintain these connections. Others have found maintenance of connections with family and friends from high school a main reason for using social networking sites [43]. Upper classmen, on the other hand, may feel a greater need to concentrate on their studies and for preparation for graduate school or careers. Thus they may cut down on their use of social media and shift toward informational (e.g., Reddit) or career network sites (e.g., LinkedIn) and away from Facebook. Interviews with upper classmen support this possible explanation. Research has found that attitudes, beliefs, critical thinking skills, and self-regulated strategies differ for younger and older college students (e.g., [17]). The shift in social media use might just be one that such differences are manifest. A cohort effect could also be a possible explanation for these findings. It is possible that these cohorts are simply different, and when these particular freshman and sophomores reach junior and senior status, they will continue to use social media, and Facebook, as much as they do now.

Social Media Use as A Situated Practice

Since we took a weeklong snapshot of students' social media use, we cannot interpret how social media use might change over time. For this reason, we now draw from the notion of situated action [cf 44] to help contextualize our results of social media use. Situated action considers a person's actions in a real world setting, as a flow of ongoing activity. As opposed to a laboratory setting, we observed and tracked social media use of people in their real world environment of college life. This ecological approach enabled us to observe our participants' full range of social media activity as it unfolded over time and among other digital activities. Situated action gears its lens to how people react to the contingencies of their environment. Our data show that college students' daily lives are filled with brief and frequent social media visits. Students may thus gravitate to particular social media as a response to contingencies of the environment, such as checking social media updates while standing in line or waiting for a class to start, or internal needs that arise in the course of their day, such as needing a study break or seeking relief from stress. Coupled with their preferences for sites, checking behavior may have become a routine response to contingencies. For example, Facebook may offer social support or simple access to friends who are online, whereas YouTube may offer light humor or step-by-step instructions for study.

In general, people construct their own patterns of social media usage, revealed by our factor analysis of clusters of site preferences. We propose that people select those tools in response to situational needs that stem from social, academic, and environmental factors as they arise over the course of the day. Some people may have developed habits and even reliance on particular sites. Social media in all its forms is a flexible media, adaptable, with a range of affordances, and thus a good fit to meet contingencies that arise in young students' lives. To this end, as a situated practice, social media use may not accomplish long-term goals directly but may instead help young people to navigate through their current changing environments and experiences. Future research could address a more detailed examination of the relation of social media use to the real world environment.

Limitations

Although a first step toward a better understanding the ecology of social media use, our study was limited. First, our sample was small and drawn from one university. Therefore, it is possible that students at this university have unique traits that differentiate them from other students. Our sample was not particularly diverse in terms of race or income, and due to our logging software, we could only use participants who had PCs and Android phones. Given that race and income are related to device operating system [38], these underlying factors may contribute to individual differences. For example, some social apps may be used as an alternative to texting in order to save money, such as free texting and instant messaging apps like WhatsApp, Vine, or even Facebook instant messaging function. All of these issues contribute to our limited ability to determine what socioeconomic, cultural, and device-based factors might contribute to the types of social media sites that college students choose. A longitudinal study over years might better be able to examine how this process of social media adoption occurs, what individual factors influence this process, and whether and to what effect social media use might change as students transition into the workforce.

CONCLUSION

The ecology of social media use includes more than just Facebook and entails numerous other sites, varying patterns of use, and different levels of integration into daily life, from continual checking to selective use and with contrasting perceptions on costs and benefits. Understanding the differences in how college students use and adapt social media to fit their socioemotional and academic needs is the first step toward determining how best to provide social computing systems that better fit these needs. Future research can build on our initial findings into how these young Millennials might engage with social media from a range of perspectives: from communication and distraction to site preference and regulating use.

ACKNOWLEDGMENTS

This material is based upon work supported by the National Science Foundation under grant #1218705.

REFERENCES

1. Ames, M. G. Managing mobile multitasking: the culture of iPhones on Stanford campus. In *Proc. CSCW'13,* ACM Press (2013), 1487-1498.
2. Baumer, E. P., Adams, P., Khovanskaya, V. D., Liao, T. C., Smith, M. E., Schwanda Sosik, V. and Williams, K. Limiting, leaving, and (re) lapsing: an exploration of Facebook non-use practices and experiences. In *Proc. CHI'13,* ACM Press (2013), 3257-3266.
3. Burke, M. and Kraut, R. E. Growing closer on Facebook: changes in tie strength through social network site use. In *Proc. of CHI'14,* ACM Press (2014), 4187-4196.
4. Burke, M., Kraut, R. and Marlow, C. Social capital on Facebook: Differentiating uses and users. In *Proc. of CHI'11*, ACM Press (2011), 571-580.
5. Burke, M., Marlow, C. and Lento, T. Social network activity and social well-being. In *Proc. of CHI'10*, ACM Press (2010), 1909-1912.
6. Collopy, F. Biases in retrospective self-reports of time use: An empirical study of computer users. *Management Science*. 42 (1996), 758-767.
7. Desjarlais, M. and Willoughby, T. A longitudinal study of the relation between adolescent boys and girls' computer use with friends and friendship quality: Support for the social compensation or the rich-get-richer hypothesis? *Computers in Human Behavior, 26* (2010), 896-905.
8. Duggan and Smith, 6% of Online Adults are reddit Users. Pew Research Center. (2013). http://www.pewinternet.org/files/old-media//Files/Reports/2013/PIP_reddit_usage_2013.pdf
9. Ellison, N. B., Steinfield, C. and Lampe, C. The benefits of Facebook "friends:" Social capital and college students' use of online social network sites. *JCMC 12*, 4 (2007), 1143-1168.
10. Gartner says the world of work will witness 10 changes during the next 10 years, Gartner, 8.4.2010. http://www.gartner.com/newsroom/id/1416513
11. Gilbert, E. and Karahalios, K. Predicting tie strength with social media. In *Proc. of CHI'09,* ACM Press (2009).
12. Hew, K. F. Students' and teachers' use of Facebook. *Computers in Human Behavior* 27, 2 (2011), 662-676.
13. Jacovi, M., Guy, I., Kremer-Davidson, S., Porat, S. and Aizenbud-Reshef, N. The perception of others: inferring reputation from social media in the enterprise. In *Proc. CSCW'14*, ACM Press (2014).
14. Junco, R. The relationship between frequency of Facebook use, participation in Facebook activities, and student engagement. *Computers & Education 58*, 1 (2012), 162-171.
15. Junco, R. Too much face and not enough books: The relationship between multiple indices of Facebook use and academic performance. *Computers in Human Behavior 28*, 1 (2012), 187-198.
16. Junco, R. Comparing actual and self-reported measures of Facebook use. *Computers in Human Behavior 29*, (2013), 626–631.
17. Justice, E. and Dornan, T. Metacognitive differences between traditional-age and nontraditional-age college students. *Adult Education Quarterly* 51, 3 (2001), 236-249.
18. Kaplan, A. M. and Haenlein, M. Users of the world, unite! The challenges and opportunities of Social Media. *Business horizons 53*, 1 (2010), 59-68.
19. Kramer, A. D. The spread of emotion via Facebook. In *Proc. CHI'12*, ACM Press (2012), 767-770.
20. Lampe, C., Ellison, N. and Steinfeld, C. A Face (book) in the crowd: Social searching vs. social browsing. In *Proc. of CSCW'06*, ACM Press (2006).
21. Lampe, C., Ellison, N. B. and Steinfield, C. Changes in use and perception of Facebook. In *Proc. of CSCW'08,* ACM Press (2008), 721-730.
22. Lee, U., Lee, J., Ko, M., Lee, C., Kim, Y., Yang, S.,Yatani, K., Gweon, G., Chung, K. and Song, J. Hooked on Smartphones: An Exploratory Study on Smartphone Overuse Among College Students. In *Proc. CHI'14*, ACM Press (2014).
23. Manago, A. M., Taylor, T. and Greenfield, P. M. Me and my 400 friends: the anatomy of college students' Facebook networks, their communication patterns, and well-being. *Developmental psychology 48*, 2 (2012) 9.
24. Mark, G., Guy, I., Kremer-Davidson, S. and Jacovi, M. Most Liked, Fewest Friends: Patterns of Enterprise Social Media Use. In *Proc. of CSCW'14*, Baltimore, MD, ACM Press (2014).

25. Mark, G., Wang, Y. and Niiya, M. Stress and multitasking in everyday college life: an empirical study of online activity. In *Proc. of CHI'14*, ACM Press (2014), 41-50.
26. McGraw-Hill Higher Education. Student empowerment scale. (2006). http://highered.mheducation.com/sites/0070876940/student_view0/chapter6/activity_6_5.html
27. Morris, M., Counts, S., Roseway, A., Hoff, A. and Schwarz, J. Tweeting is believing?: understanding microblog credibility perceptions. In *Proc. of CSCW'12*, ACM Press (2012), 441-450.
28. National Science Foundation. NSF STEM classification of instructional programs crosswalk. (2010). https://www.lsamp.org/help/help_stem_cip_2010.cfm
29. Nielsen Company. *Millennials: Breaking the myths.* (2014). http://www.nielsen.com/us/en/reports/2014/millennials-breaking-the-myths.html
30. Ophir, E., Nass, C. and Wagner, A. Cognitive control in media multitaskers. *Proc. of the National Academy of Sciences 106*, 37 (2009), 15583–15587.
31. Pew Research Center. Internet User Demographics. (2014). http://www.pewinternet.org/data-trend/internet-use/latest-stats/
32. Pew Research Center. Social Media User Demographics. (2014). http://www.pewinternet.org/data-trend/social-media/social-media-user-demographics/
33. Pempek, T. A., Yermolayeva, Y. A. and Calvert, S. L. College students' social networking experiences on Facebook. *Journal of Applied Developmental Psychology 30*, 3 (2009), 227-238.
34. Roblyer, M. D., McDaniel, M., Webb, M., Herman, J. and Witty, J. V. Findings on Facebook in higher education: A comparison of college faculty and student uses and perceptions of social networking sites. *The Internet and Higher Education 13*, 3 (2010), 134-140.
35. Saldaña, J. *The coding manual for qualitative researchers* Sage, (2012).
36. Schoenebeck, S. Y., Giving up Twitter for Lent: How and Why We Take Breaks from Social Media. In *Proc. of CHI'14,* ACM Press (2014), 773-782.
37. Schwartz, G. Estimating the dimension of a model. *Annals of Statistics 6*, 2 (1978), 461-464.
38. Smith, A. Smartphone owners: 2013. (2013). http://www.pewinternet.org/2013/06/05/smartphone-ownership-2013/
39. Spreitzer, G. M. Psychological empowerment in the workplace: Dimensions, measurement, and validation. *Academy of Management Journal, 38* (1995), 1442-1465.
40. Statista. Number of social network users worldwide from 2010 to 2017. (2014). http://www.statista.com/statistics/278414/number-of-worldwide-social-network-users/
41. Statista. Number of monthly active Facebook users worldwide. (2014). http://www.statista.com/statistics/264810/number-of-monthly-active-facebook-users-worldwide/
42. Steinberg, L. and Morris, A. Adolescent Development. *Annu. Rev. Psychol.* 52 (2001), 83–110.
43. Subrahmanyam, K., Reich, S. M., Waechter, N. and Espinoza, G. Online and offline social networks: Use of social networking sites by emerging adults. *Journal of Applied Developmental Psychology 29*, 6 (2008), 420-433.
44. Suchman, L. *Plans and Situated Actions: The Problem of Human-Machine Communication.* (1987). Cambridge: Cambridge University Press.
45. Taylor, P. and Keeter, S. Millennals: A portrait of generation next. Confident. Connected. Open to change. Pew Research Center, (2012).
46. Utz, S. Show me your friends and I will tell you what type of person you are: How one's profile, number of friends, and type of friends influence impression formation on social network sites. *JCMC,* 15 (2010), 314–335.
47. Utz, S., Tanis, M. and Vermeulen, I. It is all about being popular: The effects of need for popularity on social network site use. *CyberPsychology, Behavior & Social Networking 15*, 1 (2012), 37-42.
48. Valkenburg, P. and Peter, J. Preadolescents' and adolescents' online communication and their closeness to friends. *Developmental Psychology 43*, 2 (2007), 267-277.
49. Vitak, J. Facebook makes the heart grow fonder: relationship maintenance strategies among geographically dispersed and communication-restricted connections. In *Proc. of CSCW'14,* ACM Press (2014), 842-853.
50. Watson, D., Clark, L.A. and Tellegen, A. Development and validation of brief measures of positive and negative affect: the PANAS scales. *Journal of personality and social psychology 54*, 6 (1988), 1063.
51. Wood, W. and Neal, D. T. A new look at habits and the habit-goal interface. *Psychological review 114*, 4 (2007), 843.

Risk-taking as a Learning Process for Shaping Teen's Online Information Privacy Behaviors

Haiyan Jia
The Pennsylvania State University
University Park, PA
hjia@psu.edu

Pamela Wisniewski
The Pennsylvania State University
University Park, PA
pam@pamspam.com

Heng Xu
The Pennsylvania State University
University Park, PA
hxu@ist.psu.edu

Mary Beth Rosson
The Pennsylvania State University
University Park, PA
mrosson@ist.psu.edu

John M. Carroll
The Pennsylvania State University
University Park, PA
jcarroll@ist.psu.edu

ABSTRACT

Through a secondary data analysis of a nationally representative Pew survey [35-36], we empirically test the validity of two contrasting theoretical models of adolescent information privacy behaviors. Our results suggest that in seeking to understand the underlying processes of teens' privacy risk-taking and risk-coping behaviors within social media, a "risk-centric" framework may be more useful than a traditional "concern-centric" framework that emphasizes privacy antecedents and outcomes. Our newly proposed and validated "risk-centric" framework implies a possible risk escalation process wherein teens make online disclosures and render themselves more susceptible to experiences of risky online interactions; in turn, these risky experiences are associated with higher levels of teen privacy concern. Higher levels of teen privacy concern predict both advice-seeking and remedy/corrective risk-coping behaviors. Drawing on theories of information privacy and developmental psychology, we discuss these findings from the perspective of allowing teens to experience some level of online risk so that they can learn how to navigate the dangers and reap the benefits of online engagement.

Author Keywords

Adolescent online behavior; privacy; risk; coping

ACM Classification Keywords

K.4.1 [Public Policy Issues]: Ethics, Human safety, Privacy

General Terms

Human Factors; Theory; Design.

INTRODUCTION

Compared to adults, teenagers tend to underestimate their self-efficacy to avoid risk, but they still engage in more risk activities as they also underestimate risk [15]. In online environments, this general pattern may help to explain why teens are observed to engage in more risk-taking behaviors than adults [32, 53]. Within the context of online risk-taking, self-management of information privacy has been the target of considerable attention, controversy [16] and research [4], because the online world creates a wide variety of options for collecting, processing and distributing users' personal information. Yet, no existing law protects the online information privacy of teens who are 13 or older, making this population more vulnerable to dangerous online encounters and safety hazards [34][56]. Particularly, the rapid emergence of Social Network Sites (SNSs), such as Facebook, MySpace, and Pinterest, as well as emerging social networking applications such as Instagram, Vine, and Snapchat, are rife with opportunities for teens to reveal personal information and/or form risky online relationships [29, 31]. Therefore, we examine teens' privacy behaviors in the context of Facebook in order to empirically test two competing theoretical models of teens' online information privacy behaviors.

Specifically, we examine and contrast two theoretically different perspectives of teen online information privacy behaviors: (1) An established "***concern-centric***" model, which accentuates privacy concern in determining risk-related behavioral outcomes; and (2) a novel "***risk-centric***" model, which theorizes a direct effect of teen's risk-taking behaviors on psychological factors such as privacy concern, thus shaping teens' risk-coping behaviors. Further, we focus on two types of teen information privacy behaviors: ***risk-taking behaviors*** (such as information disclosures and choice of social connections) and ***risk-coping behaviors*** (such as seeking advice and/or help and taking protective measures to reduce risk); both types of privacy behaviors might be enacted by teens online to engage with others and/or protect themselves from online threats.

http://dx.doi.org/10.1145/2675133.2675287

From a developmental standpoint, teens and adults are clearly in different cognitive stages, so the concern-centric model of information privacy antecedents and outcomes created and validated for adults [51] may not be adequate to explain teens' online privacy management. Our newly proposed risk-centric model, in contrast, embodies an experiential learning process, highlighting the role that teens' own risk-taking behaviors may take in developing their risk-coping mechanisms. Specifically, we propose that teens' online privacy risk-taking behaviors serve as learning opportunities, through which teens practice and develop risk-coping strategies to manage distinctive types of privacy risks. We focus specifically on teens' privacy risks in the context of SNSs, as privacy threats to this age group and in this context are especially abundant, and may quickly become complicated due to highly interactional situations [24, 29]. Teens' SNS privacy risks appear not only inherent to the social nature of online social networks, which motivates teenage users to maintain relationships with different levels of intimacy [45], but also multidimensional in terms of their nature and severity, with some aspects or dimensions of privacy risks being particularly unique and relevant to teens [41].

This paper reports the empirical results of testing the "concern-centric" versus the "risk-centric" theoretical models using a nationally representative dataset provided by Pew Research Center's *2012 Teens and Privacy Management Survey*. In the course of our model building and evaluation activities, we examine teens' online privacy behaviors and identified three unique dimensions of risk-taking behaviors, which vary based on increasing levels of privacy risk: 1) ***Basic Information Disclosures***; 2) ***Sensitive Information Disclosure;*** and 3) ***Risky Interactions***. We also identified two distinct dimensions of risk-coping behaviors, which include: 1) ***Advice Seeking*** and 2) ***Remedy/Corrective Behaviors***. We use these empirically constructed components of teens' online privacy risk-taking and risk-coping behaviors to explore the relationships between various demographic, individual-difference and psychological factors and these two behavioral variables. In doing so, we provide confirmatory evidence that our "risk-centric" framework of teens' online information privacy behaviors represents a better fit to the data than the previously established "concern-centric" model. Our results suggest that teens have uniquely different cognitive processes than adults that drive their information privacy decisions online.

We present our research using the following structure: First, we establish our research motivation and articulate how our work contributes to the extant literature on teens' online information privacy behaviors. Second, we present two competing theoretical models for understanding teens' online information privacy behaviors. Third, we describe our methodology for empirically testing these competing models and present our results. Finally, we discuss the theoretical and practical implications of our findings and suggest design opportunities for promoting adolescent online safety through leveraging risk-taking as a learning process that can help teens' make more prudent information privacy decisions online.

RESEARCH MOTIVATION AND CONTRIBUTIONS

Social scientists have argued that teens are still developing self-regulatory competence; their risk perceptions and risk appraisals may not yet be effective at guiding their online privacy behaviors [52]. Working from these assumptions, previous studies have focused primarily on intervention strategies that prevent teens from online risk exposure or that mitigate potential harm. For example, researchers have identified external factors that might protect teens online, such as governmental legislation, industry self-regulation, website warnings, and parental mediation strategies [60, 62-63]. However, fewer studies have focused on the internal belief structures and decision strategies of teens themselves in order to understand the processes through which teens are exposed to, and cope with, online privacy risks.

Furthermore, scholars who have investigated teen-related factors have largely focused on perceptual variables, such as privacy risk perceptions [63], information privacy self-efficacy [11], and social and self-expressive needs [31]; these factors influence teens' online privacy disclosures and management. However, underlying these perceptual variables is a view of privacy risk as a cognitive and psychological *state*, rather than as *behaviors* that teens actually engage in and experience. The cognitive approach aids in identifying psychological mechanisms but limits our understanding of the role that privacy behaviors may play in psychological processes. Our research attempts to fill the gaps in the current research by understanding the underlying cognitive mechanisms that drive teens' online information privacy behaviors. Specifically, our unique research contributions include:

- Establishing and contrasting two theoretical frameworks (i.e. "concern-centric" vs. "risk-centric") of teens' online information privacy behaviors
- Identifying multi-dimensional aspects of teens' information privacy risk-taking and risk-coping behaviors
- Empirically testing the theoretical models to conclude that the "risk-centric" framework may be a more appropriate framework for understanding the underlying psychological mechanism through which teens process, evaluate and respond to risks
- Providing theoretical and practical implications for improving teens' online safety through an autonomy-promoting and developmental framework of online information privacy

THEORETICAL FRAMEWORKS

APCO Macro Model

A cohesive model of privacy-related factors is essential for building an understanding of the social and psychological mechanisms of privacy and for predicting cognitive, affective, and especially behavioral responses. Scholars have approached information privacy from many angles, with theories and frameworks proposed from a range of backgrounds, as discussed in more detail below. However, due to the relative lack of such efforts in the privacy literature dealing with adolescents, we began with a general, empirically validated framework that provides a comprehensive view of predictors, processes, and outcomes of information privacy. This interdisciplinary, overarching model of information privacy is called the "Antecedents→ Privacy Concerns→ Outcome" or "APCO" Macro Model [51]. While this theoretical model was built based on a meta-review of 320 privacy articles and 128 books across multiple disciplines, we believe that we are the first to apply it to the unique context of teens' privacy behaviors for online information privacy management.

The APCO model [51] shows versatility as it includes information privacy-related factors ranging in different levels from individual and group to organizational and societal. More importantly, it incorporates numerous empirical privacy studies and identifies commonly studied relationships among these factors. At the center of the APCO model, ***privacy concern*** functions as a "proxy" for information privacy, representing the beliefs, attitudes, and perceptions of privacy at the individual level of analysis. APCO then abstracts various antecedents and outcomes of privacy concern across various disciplines of literature. ***Antecedents*** of privacy concern have included negative privacy experiences, privacy awareness, personal differences, demographic differences, and culture/climate [51]. ***Outcomes*** that have been characterized as resulting from privacy concern include behavioral reactions, such as willingness or intent to disclose personal information at the individual level, or regulatory actions that occur at a group or societal level [51]. **Figure 1** provides a high-level, simplified overview of the APCO Macro Model.

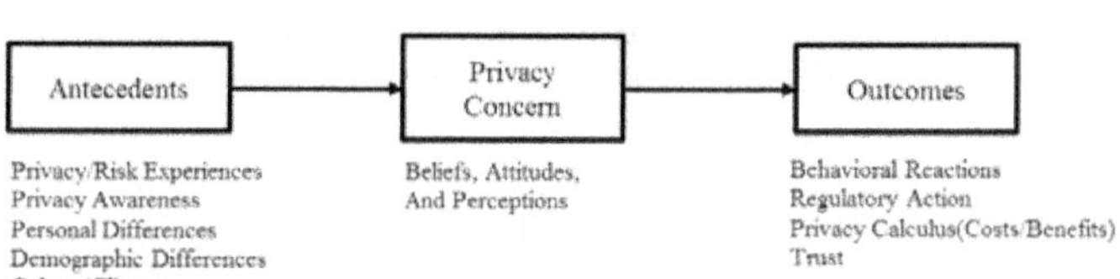

Figure 1: High-Level Overview of APCO Macro Model

The generalizability of the APCO framework provides ample flexibility for us to test relevant factors that are specific and unique to teens' online privacy risk management. Following the APCO framework, and based on an extensive literature review of other relevant privacy theories and studies, this paper will discuss the theoretical relationships between several key factors related to teen online privacy, in particular, their risk-taking versus risk-coping behaviors, privacy concern, and demographic and contextual factors, such as gender and SNS frequency, to propose a modified model of online information privacy for teens. Further, the proposed model is tested with empirical data to verify its validity and predictive power, and contrasted with an alternative model that is discussed below.

"Concern-Centric" versus "Risk-Centric" Frameworks

Two contrasting theoretical models of teens' online information privacy are proposed to theorize relationships between predictors such as demographics, other contextually relevant factors, privacy concern, teen risk-taking and risk-coping behaviors (see **Figures 2 & 3**). First, we examine the hypothesized relationships from the original APCO framework as mapped to our teen factors above; we call this baseline model our ***concern-centric*** approach to teen online privacy management (**Figure 2**).

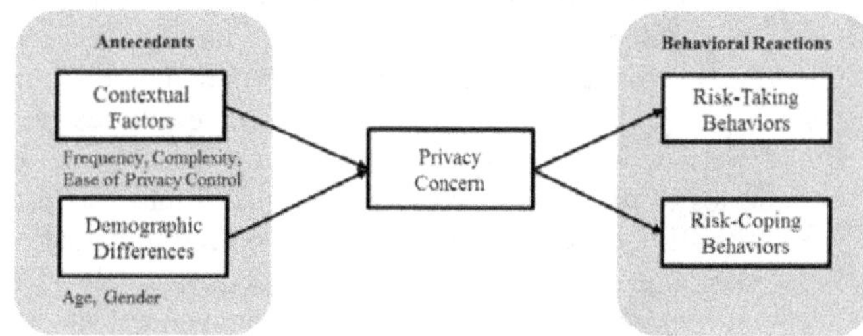

Figure 2: Concern-Centric APCO Framework

This concern-centric model hypothesizes that teens make rational privacy choices based on their concern for information privacy. Therefore, higher levels of concern would translate into more risk-adverse privacy strategies, resulting in lower levels of risk-taking and higher frequency of risk-coping behaviors. However, acknowledging that teens may operate under bounded rationality and have a limited capacity to properly assess risk, we also propose an exploratory ***risk-centric*** model (**Figure 3**) where teens' higher propensity to take risks contributes to new risk experiences, influencing privacy concern, and triggering risk-coping behaviors.

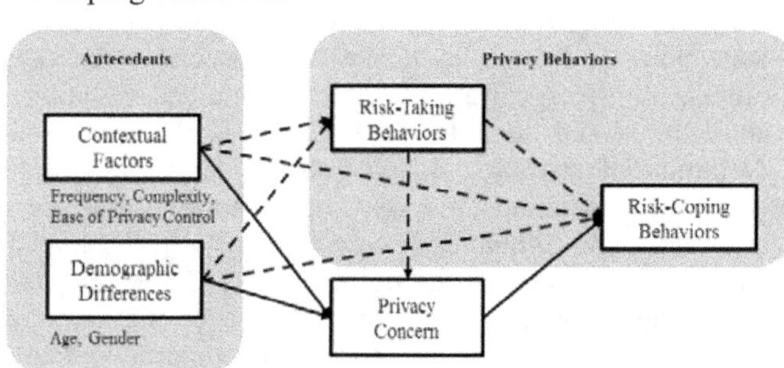

Figure 3: Risk-Centric Risk-Coping Framework

Figure 3 illustrates the new, exploratory hypotheses using dashed lines, while the original APCO hypotheses are shown with solid lines. We empirically test the concern-centric vs. risk-centric theoretical frameworks using the Pew dataset. Toward this end, we first conduct categorical principal component analyses to identify three different types of risk-taking behaviors (basic information disclosures, sensitive information disclosures, and risky interactions) and two risk-coping behaviors (advice-seeking and remedy/corrective behaviors), followed by examining their respective interrelationships between the various behaviors and other factors in our model to identify how the multidimensionality of the various behaviors uniquely effect the teen factors in our models. We further discuss the teen specific factors in the sections below.

Teen Privacy Behaviors

We specifically focus our research outcomes on teens' privacy behaviors in the context of online privacy management, not on external interventions imposed on teens by parents or regulators. Therefore, we focus on teens' risk-taking and risk-coping behaviors in the two theoretical models. From an experiential learning perspective, individuals' conception of privacy varies with life experiences [28] and is an ongoing negotiation of boundaries of disclosure, where an individual must balance the trade-offs between sharing and withholding information in a way that meets one's privacy needs [2, 44]. The decision-making process of privacy management is not fixed but often reactive to social and situational factors. This may be especially true for teens, as they may lack an effective model of self-regulation, especially when exposed to novel risk situations. Teens' experiences and negotiations through various levels of privacy threats and invasions may directly trigger their risk-coping behaviors; or it may indirectly guide the development of risk-coping strategies through increased concern. Therefore, we characterize teen privacy behaviors as an integral part of this negotiation and experiential learning process by representing teens' online privacy management behaviors as both ***risk-taking*** and ***risk-coping*** behaviors.

Risk-Taking Behaviors: A range of privacy risks have been identified with regard to teens' SNS use, such as inability to control information access, distribution, collection, or misuse by other users (social threats) or organizations (organizational threats), inability to maintain anonymity, and identity theft [26, 50]. However, the definition of privacy risk-taking behaviors varies greatly based on communicative or social norms: the social affordances of communication technologies have "forced" teens to alter conceptions of privacy [37]; as a result, contact and conduct viewed risky for an adult may serve as a self-representative or self-expressive opportunity that a teen seeks [32]. Also, relatively safe online information privacy behaviors (e.g., disclosure of age, gender and relationship status) are correlated with riskier behaviors (e.g., disclosure of personal identity information, sensitive personal information, and stigmatizing information) [40], further blurring the line between the two. In recognition of such adult-teen discrepancy in defining risk and risk escalation pattern, we define information privacy risk-taking behaviors as a spectrum of behaviors related to information disclosure and social interactions, varying from sharing basic personal information (e.g., gender and age) to disclosing highly sensitive and personal information, and further to engaging in risky social interactions.

Previous studies of teenage Facebook users have shown that basic information disclosure is positively related with disclosure of sensitive information, which in turn links with risky interactions with unknown others [43]. The social motivation for information sharing makes information privacy "intricately" related to interactional privacy—the type of privacy that relates to the control and management of social encounters and relationships [10]—especially in intimate and connected settings [13]. Further, different aspects and dimensions of a teens' risk-taking behavior may demonstrate different effects as well. For instance, a recent empirical study [26] showed that only social risk experiences (e.g., uncontrollable actions, bullying, stalking, etc.) is an influential predictor of users' intentional risk-coping; other privacy risk experiences, such as accessibility, organizational threats, and identity theft showed little to no effect. In our empirical models, we differentiate among three distinct types of risk-taking behaviors that emerged from the survey data: basic information disclosures, sensitive information disclosures, and risky interactions.

Risk-Coping Behaviors: Risk-coping behaviors refer to users' self-defensive measures to protect privacy rights as a response to their perceptions of privacy risks [48]. Teens do engage in risk-coping behaviors online, which help shield them from information privacy breaches, but very little attention has been focused on these more positive, yet often more reactive behaviors. Research in adolescents' risk-coping strategies [18, 48] suggests two main coping dimensions: approach and avoidance/withdrawal. For teens, the approach dimension refers to functional strategies such as problem-solving, information- or advice-seeking, and accepting social support, whereas the avoidance dimension includes dysfunctional strategies to withdraw from the situation without trying to change or improve it. Following this categorization, Youn [63] suggested two coping styles for dealing with privacy risks, one being approach strategies such as providing false or incomplete personal information, seeking alternative services that do not ask for personal information [63], and seeking help, information or social support; the other style includes avoidance strategies such as refusal to use the websites or services.

Help or information seeking as a risk-coping strategy is of great importance because it implies external influence such as parental guidance. Importantly however, proactive seeking of advice functions very differently for adolescent development compared to imposed intervention. In Baumrind's [6] developmental framework of adolescents' risk-taking, the importance of respecting adolescents' growing need for autonomy and self-regulation, while maintaining a certain level of parental authority and control, is paramount. Pathological observations showed that lack of authoritative parenting tended to result in lower self-esteem, rebellious activities and psychological issues. In an attempt to understand why and how teens seek for help, Boldero and Fallon [7] found that help-seeking behaviors were predicted in part by gender and problem type (social problems as a significant predictor). Alternative help-seeking resources, such as the Internet, were found to be under-used by teens in a 2002 survey study [22]. Among the online help-seeking teens, only 14% found the Internet helpful, and the majority used it as a supplemental, rather than substituting, source for help.

Privacy Concern

In APCO, privacy concern has been accentuated as an important mediating factor between information privacy antecedents and outcomes, such as behavioral reactions, trust, and regulatory actions [51]. It is as a determinant of information disclosure behavior [3], protective behaviors [39], and online activity, or rather, the avoidance of it [40]. Although scholars have proposed positive consequences of privacy concern (e.g., motivating risk-coping behaviors) among adolescents [38][60], the moderating effect of privacy concern on online privacy behaviors is quite limited, especially among adolescents who lack the digital skills (e.g., [33]). SNS use, in particular, is found to weaken teens' online privacy concern [20], with only a weak impact on subsequent behaviors such as Facebook profile visibility and information disclosure [1, 55]. Many studies have reported that privacy concern has a limited to null effect, especially for information disclosure behaviors (e.g., [14]); this phenomenon is described by Barnes [5] as a "privacy paradox." What is paradoxical is that, on one hand, Internet users complain about their privacy being violated, while on the other hand, it appears that users provide personal information freely [42]. For example, information disclosure was not significantly related to online privacy concern in a survey of college students [56]. Instead, students preferred to manage their concerns by adjusting profile visibility or using fake names, not by restricting information. Deliberate restriction of personal information revelation was only influenced by direct social threats [26].

Theories of privacy, bounded rationality and trust have been used to explain the paradox of privacy concerns and behavior. For example, a factor like trust in social ties, a variable that is particularly salient within SNSs, may undermine the effects of concern [61]. Following Altman's [2] conceptualization of privacy as an optimization between disclosure and withdrawal, scholars (i.e., [8, 57, 59]) have pointed to a possible role for self-disclosure dynamics including impression management/self-presentation [21], identity expression [46], and social connections [19]. APCO suggests that measuring behavioral intent as a proxy for actual behavior may also be a contributing factor to this apparent paradox [51].

Demographic and Contextual Antecedents

Previous studies of online information privacy of teens and young adults have identified demographic differences and contextual factors seem to be antecdents of privacy-related factors. For instance, age is negatively associated with teen self-disclosure on Facebook [43]. An analysis of college students' Facebook privacy settings showed that restricting accessibility of personal profile as a risk-coping strategy was positively associated with a higher level of online activity (e.g., higher frequencies of log-ins, profile updates, browses of other profiles, etc.); presumably more active users have "more to hide" [30]. Other determinants of risk-coping strategies include frequency of Internet use, parenting, and observed peers' risk experiences [41]. In our empirical model, we examine age and gender as key demographic differences, and use SNS usage frequency, complexity, and ease of privacy control as contextual SNS factors that may influence teens' privacy concern, risk-taking, and risk-coping behaviors on Facebook.

"Concern-Centric" vs. "Risk-Centric" Perspectives

Given the contradictory and confounding relationships present in past literature, we decided to compare two contrasting models of how teens might regulate their online privacy through risk-taking and risk-coping behaviors. We argue that the concern-centric model may not be predictive of teens' privacy behaviors given that teens are not fully capable of privacy appraisals due to the difference between their cognitive developmental stage and that of an adult. Instead, a risk-centric model may better describe the privacy risk management strategies of the high risk-taking, high risk-coping teens. The bounded rationality hypothesis is especially critical for understanding teens' online privacy risk-coping behaviors, as their informational and cognitive limitations might render their abstract concern that they have in mind ineffective in fully determining their behavioral reactions. Rather, teens' risk-taking behaviors and subsequent experiences may inform privacy concern, and the two may function dynamically on forming risk-coping behaviors. Yet, researchers (e.g., [41]) tend to examine the relationship between antecedents and privacy concern, and that between privacy concern and outcomes, respectively, without attempts to examine the direct effect of risk-taking behaviors on risk-coping behaviors. Meanwhile, the mediating effect of privacy concern is unclear for younger generations according to the existing literature.

Privacy literature has found that privacy concern does not directly affect the amount of information disclosure; instead users tend to engage in remedy or corrective behaviors such as restricting information visibility to chosen groups or providing unidentifiable information [21]. For example, one survey study [49] revealed that young adults are pragmatic, rather than highly concerned, about their online privacy. The researchers argued that the pragmatic users assumed a "contextual approach toward privacy" by constantly learning and forming behavioral strategies to deal with privacy concerns as they faced new situations to assess and respond accordingly. This supports what we have offered as the "risk-as-a-learning-process" paradigm, which may explain why younger generations may take a more risk-centric approach to online privacy than a concern-centric approach.

Furthermore, recent research has shown that exposure to a certain level of risk may be more effective in shaping privacy attitudes and behavior than general awareness. For instance, Debatin et al. [17] found through an online survey that users' personal experiences of privacy invasion, rather than claims of understanding privacy issues, are likely to lead to risk-coping behaviors (e.g., changing privacy settings). Similarly, a study of young adults' privacy beliefs and behaviors [23] showed that female users who were more likely to be exposed to negative online experiences were more concerned and more likely to engage in proactive privacy protection behaviors (regularly review privacy settings, monitoring profiles, careful about pictures posted onto profiles, un-tag pictures, careful about who to friend, set viewing access to friends only, set Facebook activities not to show on newsfeed).

Theoretical frameworks from developmental psychology that are specific to adolescent population also emphasize the importance of teens' risk experiences. Baumrind argues that restricting teens' experiences and limiting their overall ability to take any risks may actually be detrimental to their developmental growth [6]. According to Stevenson & Zimmerman's [54] challenge and inoculation models of adolescent resilience, exposing teens to low levels of risk may be beneficial as they provide the teens with "a chance to practice skills or employ resources." From a developmental view, repetition of such mild challenges will demonstrate an inoculation effect and prepare teens to overcome more severe risks in the future. Such a risk-as-a-learning-process approach provides a framework that examines teens' internal management of online privacy risks out of the traditional frameworks with a significant emphasis and reliance on external factors such as parental mediation or school intervention.

These prior works have encouraged us to build an understanding of the dimensions of privacy risks centered on the teens' own conceptions, and serves as a rationale for modeling the direct and indirect effects of risk experiences on teens' concern for privacy and risk-coping strategies. With the "risk-as-a-learning-process" paradigm, our new "risk-centric" model proposes alternative and more dynamic relationships than proposed in APCO to include this new experiential learning hypothesis. Specifically, theoretical emphasis is put on teens' risk-taking behaviors as an influential factor with direct effects on both privacy concern and risk-coping strategies. Meanwhile, privacy risk-taking behaviors, as well as risk-coping strategies, are hypothesized as potentially having direct associations with the various antecedents, not mediated by privacy concern.

METHODOLOGY

We tested the concern-centric and risk-centric theoretical frameworks of teens' risk-taking and risk-coping behaviors for online privacy management using a nationally representative sample of teens provided by Pew Research. In the paragraphs below, we describe how the Pew data set was collected, followed by explaining how our measures were operationalized and our method of analysis for testing our two competing models.

Pew Data Set

We analyzed a data set from the *2012 Teens and Privacy Management Survey*, conducted from July 26 to September 30, 2012 as a telephone survey using random digit dial (RDD) to gather a nationally representative sample of 802 teens aged 12 to 17 years living in the United States. The survey was conducted by Princeton Survey Research Associates International for the Pew Research Center's Internet and American Life Project [35-36]. Many of the questions were specific to teens' use of social networking sites such as Facebook, and a vast majority (94%) of respondents reported having an active Facebook account. Given the high prevalence of teen respondents who reported having active Facebook accounts, those who did not have a Facebook account were excluded from our analysis.

The final dataset consisted of 588 valid responses. 49.7% of the responses were from males (N = 292); a majority (77.6%) were Caucasian with 15.3% being African-American; and the average age was 15 years old. Almost all respondents had access to the Internet; 80.4% reported access with mobile devices. Facebook is the most frequently used social networking site; 68.4% use this SNS at least daily. 67.9% were connected with their parent(s) through Facebook and 32.3% were connected with their teachers or coaches. 32.8% reported said that on Facebook they were connected to people they had never met. 89.2% considered it not too difficult or not difficult at all, to manage privacy controls on Facebook. Only 7% and 34.5% reported as very concerned and somewhat concerned about their online privacy, respectively.

Operationalization of Measures

The Pew telephone interviews asked teens about their general trust, device ownership, Internet use, mobile use, social media use (Facebook and Twitter in particular), privacy concern, perceived ease to manage online privacy, information disclosure behaviors, privacy management behaviors, and demographic items. Prior to our analysis, the

Pew survey items had no theoretical groupings except by these various topics of interest. Thus to process the dataset, we first identified theoretically robust constructs that exhibited both face and construct validity based on the individual survey items. We then manually reviewed the survey items and responses for items that could be meaningfully mapped to the APCO theoretical framework. Working from past literature, we identified age and gender as two important demographic differences, and grouped SNS frequency, SNS complexity, and ease of SNS privacy control as salient contextual factors. We also identified items that measured teen privacy concern, risk-taking, and risk-coping behaviors. Other demographic, contextual, and privacy-related factors were identified and analyzed but dropped from the final models because of either insufficient factor loadings or insignificant influence in our models. **Appendix A** and **B** summarize all items that remained in our final models and their psychometric properties.

Data Analysis Approach

We first used categorical principal components analyses (CATPCA) [38] to construct various dimensions of teens' privacy risk-taking and risk-coping behaviors using the 21 items identified as risk-taking behaviors and the 13 items identified as risk-coping behaviors. As in the classic PCA, CATPCA produces eigenvalues associated to each of the dimensions. Each eigenvalue is a measure of the importance of the corresponding dimension in capturing the variability of the observed variable. In this study, we follow the Kaiser criterion [25] to retain dimensions with eigenvalues higher than 1. We did this to both understand the multi-dimensionality of different risk-taking and risk-coping behaviors as well as to ensure construct validity. In this survey, the original behavior items were measured as dichotomous, categorical values (e.g. "Yes" or "No"). Thus, once we identified found items loaded on a given factor, we converted each set of dichotomous data into continuous variables by creating additive indices. Using these additive indices as our risk-taking and risk-coping constructs, we then used path analyses to assess the validity of the concern-centric and risk-centric models.

RESULTS

Principal Components Analyses

Teen Risk-Taking Behaviors

The CATPCA analysis produced three constructs related to teen risk-taking: ***Basic Information Disclosures*** (items such as posting name, birthday, school, relationship status, etc., on personal profile); ***Sensitive Information Disclosures*** (items such as posting email address, cell phone number, sensitive information that he or she later regret, etc., online); and ***Risky Interactions*** (items such as receiving unwanted communication, being contacted by or connecting with strangers, automatically sharing geo-locations, etc.). After standardization, all constructs ranged from 0 to 1, with skewness statistics between -1/+1. Specifically, for basic information disclosure, *Mean* = 0.68, *SD* = 0.22; for sensitive information disclosure, *Mean* = .25, *SD* = 0.23; and for risky interaction, *Mean* = .32, *SD* = 0.17.

Teen Risk-Coping Behaviors

Two constructs of risk-coping behaviors were revealed in the analysis. We labeled these as ***Remedy/Correction*** (consisting of items such as deleting comments, a post, a friend or an account, untagging from a photo, falsifying personal information, etc.) and ***Advice Seeking*** (consisting of items such as seeking advice of online privacy management from a friend, a parent, a sibling, a teacher, or a website). After standardization, the constructs ranged from 0 to 1, with skewness statistics between -1/+1. Specifically, remedy/correction has a *Mean* = 0.46, with *SD* = 0.22; and advice-seeking with *Mean* = .28, *SD* = 0.24.

Concern-Centric (APCO) Structural Model Results

Figure 4 summarizes the path analysis results from our test of the baseline "concern-centric" (APCO) model (Model 1). It suggests that the risk-adverse, teen privacy management perspective may not be the best fit given our data. The path analysis results (see **Table 1** and **Appendix C**) indicated poor model fit (Schermelleh-Engel et al.'s goodness-of-fit criteria were adopted, including a non-significant χ^2 value or the *p*-value associated with the χ^2 larger than 0.05; the ratio χ^2/df lower than 2; the Comparative Fit Index, or *CFI*, of 0.97 or higher; the Normed Fit Index, or *NFI*, of 0.95 or higher; and the Root Mean Square Error of Approximation, or *RMSEA*, of less than 0.06 [47]), with a number of insignificant paths, and overall low explanatory values.

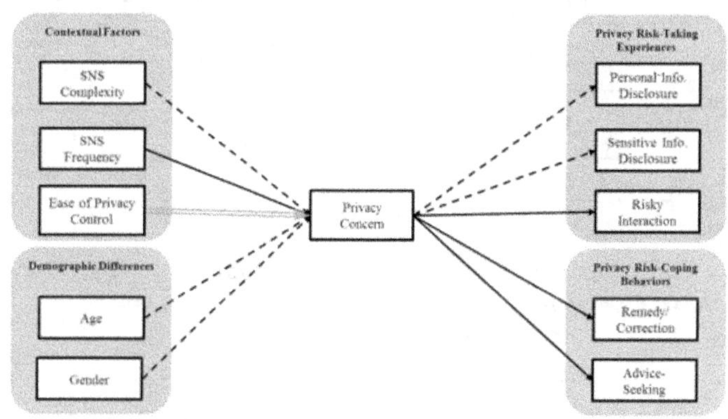

Figure 4: Concern-Centric Model (Model 1) Results.
Note. *Solid lines show paths significant at .05 level; double lines indicate negative path coefficients.*

More specifically, the Model 1 analysis indicated that SNS frequency and ease of privacy control are the only significant antecedents of teen privacy concern. Being a more frequent SNS user is associated with higher levels of concern (β = 0.13, p < 0.001) while higher levels of perceived ease of use for SNS privacy controls are negatively correlated with privacy concern (β = -0.19, p < 0.001). Privacy concern predicts risk-coping behaviors as expected, with increased levels positively associated with both advice seeking (β = 0.19, p < 0.001) and remedy/corrective behaviors (β = 0.18, p < 0.001). However, privacy concern does not have the expected inverse relationship with respect to any of the risk-taking behaviors. The paths from privacy concern to basic information disclosure and sensitive information disclosure behaviors are both non-significant, while the *positive* relationship between privacy concern to risky interactions (β = 0.10, p < 0.05) is contrary to the hypothesized model.

Risk-Centric Structural Model Results

A nearly saturated risk-centric model (Model 2) was tested, yielding some indicators of good model fit, yet included a number of insignificant paths (**Appendix D**). Further path analyses were guided by the modification indices and yielded a more parsimonious model containing only statistically significant paths (Model 3). Model 3 (**Figure 5**) was also seen to have good model fit. **Table 1** summarizes the fit statistics across all three models. Model 3 offers the most parsimonious results with acceptable fit indicators. Therefore, the final model results reported in **Figure 5** and discussed below are based on Model 3.

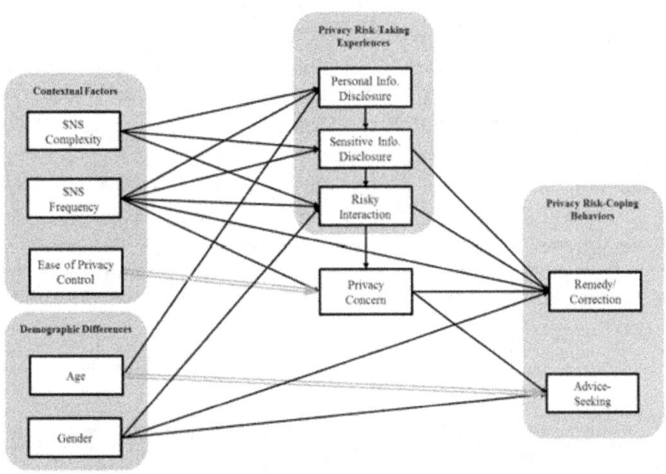

Figure 5: Risk-Centric Model (Model 3) Results.
Note: *All paths shown are significant at .05 level; double lines indicate negative path coefficients*

	χ^2 (*DF*)	NFI	CFI	RMSEA	R^2 (Remedy/ Correction)
Model 1	448.736 (31)	0.378	0.374	0.152	0.036
Model 2	1.519 (1)	0.998	0.999	0.030	0.341
Model 3	18.882 (23)	0.974	1.000	0.000	0.330

Table 1. Summary of model estimates.

The relationships in Model 3 imply an escalation trajectory for risk-taking. Specifically, basic information disclosure is positively associated with sensitive information disclosure (β = 0.22, p < 0.001), which in turn is positively associated with risky interaction (β = 0.23, p < 0.001). All three types of risk-taking behaviors are positively predicted by SNS complexity (basic information disclosure: β = 0.20, p < 0.001; sensitive information disclosure: β = 0.23, p < 0.001; and risky interaction: β = 0.36, p < 0.001) and SNS frequency (basic information disclosure: β = 0.21, p < 0.001; sensitive information disclosure: β = 0.17, p < 0.001; and risky interaction: β = 0.11, p < 0.01). Furthermore, basic information disclosure is positively associated with age (β = 0.16, p < 0.01), whereas risky interaction is significantly associated with gender (β = 0.11, p < 0.01). The level of privacy concern is positively associated with frequency of teens' SNS use (β = 0.14, p < 0.01) as well as their online risky interaction (β = 0.10, p < 0.05), and is reduced by perceived ease of privacy control (β = -0.18, p < 0.001). Finally, similar to the concern-centric model, privacy concern appears to be a significant and positive predictor of both types of risk-coping behaviors. More interestingly, risk-taking behaviors such as sensitive information disclosure (β = 0.14, p < 0.001) and risky interaction (β = 0.44, p < 0.001) also are directly associated with remedy/corrective behaviors. Some demographic factors also have demonstrated significant relationships: a gender effect is found such that girls engage more frequently in both types of risk-coping behaviors; and age is negatively associated with advice-seeking.

DISCUSSION

In this section, we summarize our results, discuss their theoretical implications, and consider opportunities for design. We conclude by pointing to some limitations of our study and areas for future research.

Summary of Results

We used categorical principal components analyses to identify distinctive dimensions or aspects of teen privacy risk-taking (resulting in three dimensions) and risk-coping behaviors (resulting in two dimensions). We then used structural equation modeling to test the validity of a concern-centric versus a risk-centric theoretical model of teens' online information privacy management. We found that the risk-centric model was a much better fit to our empirical data and that the final model revealed complex relationships between the privacy-related factors.

More specifically, SNS-related contextual factors were significant predictors for all three types of privacy risk-taking behaviors; age predicted only basic information disclosure. Both SNS frequency and risky interactions were positively associated with privacy concern, while perceived ease of privacy control appeared as a negative predictor of concern. With respect to privacy risk-coping behaviors, remedy/correction behaviors were positively associated with SNS frequency, sensitive information disclosures, risky interactions, and privacy concern. Privacy concern was also a positive predictor of advice seeking, whereas age was negatively associated with advice seeking behaviors.

Theoretical Implications

Privacy Behaviors are Multi-dimensional and Inter-related

Teen risk-taking behaviors emerged as three separate statistical factors, and teen risk-coping behaviors emerged as two additional factors. Furthermore, these different risk-taking and risk-coping behaviors functioned very differently than one another in our model. This suggests that different privacy behaviors should be tested in future models, instead of assuming that risk-taking and risk-coping behaviors are one-dimensional.

Our findings also suggest that not all risk-taking behaviors are equally as risky and that there may be a pattern of risk escalation between the three risk-taking factors. We saw accumulative effects of risk-taking behaviors, where lower levels of risk-taking are predictive of higher levels risk (basic information disclosures → sensitive information disclosures → risky interactions). At face value, we would automatically assume that risky interactions are more dangerous than disclosing sensitive information online, which in turn would be more risky than disclosing basic personal information online. Again, logically this makes sense. If a teen shares sensitive information, such as his or her phone number through social media, this would put him or her at higher risk of engaging in potentially dangerous offline interactions with strangers. However, this may not necessarily be true if a teen just shared basic information, such as his or her real name and relationship status.

Our risk-centric model offers statistical evidence of risk escalation, showing that basic information disclosures are positively associated with sensitive information disclosures but not risky interactions, yet showing that sensitive information disclosures are positively associated with risky interactions. Also, only risky interactions are positively associated with heightened teen privacy concerns. It is also noteworthy that basic information disclosures are not significantly related to teen risk-coping behaviors, suggesting that disclosing basic information about oneself online may not be perceived by teens as risky at all.

Teen Privacy Management as Experiential Learning

Both empirically tested theoretical models suggest that in the case of teens, privacy concern has a direct influence on risk-coping behaviors but not on teens' propensity to take risks. The risk-centric model provides empirical evidence of teens' propensity to first seek risks, and then take corrective actions to protect their online privacy. It makes sense that teens taking more risks also take more remedy/corrective actions to protect their online privacy after-the-fact. Yet, teen privacy concerns are not significantly related to their personal or sensitive information disclosure behaviors. Teens share personal and sensitive information through social media regardless of their concern for privacy. However, when teens report engaging in risky online interactions that they view as regrettable, that behavior is positively associated with their privacy concern. The most logical explanation for this relationship would be that risky interactions heighten teens' concerns about privacy, not that teens who already experience who already experience higher levels of concern seek more frequent risky interactions online. Furthermore, teens' privacy concern, once elevated, is positively associated with both risk-coping (advice-seeking and remedy/corrective) behaviors. Therefore, when all of these significant relationships are combined, they suggest that teens do care about their online privacy; nonetheless, they are willing to take privacy risks. And, through a process of experiential learning, where risk-taking behaviors contribute to risk-learning experiences, teens mitigate these risks later by taking protective actions when they feel their privacy boundaries may have been compromised. This reasoning, in combination with our empirical results, we propose **Figure 6** as a theoretical model for understanding the process of privacy regulation for teens' online privacy management in future research.

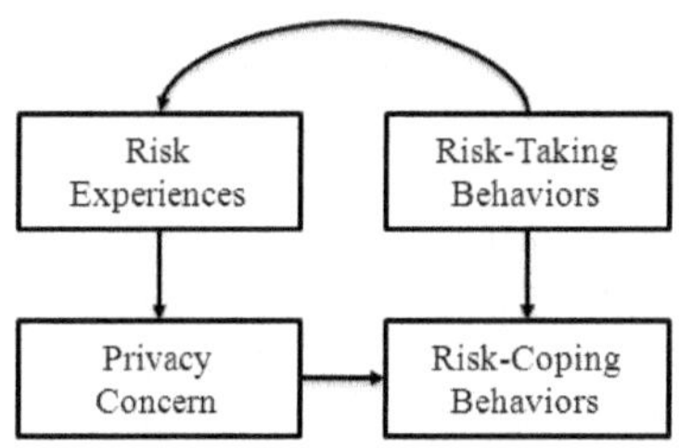

Figure 6: Theoretical Framework of Teen Online Privacy Management

Developing Privacy Awareness and Coping Strategies

Even though information disclosure does not appear to enhance teens' privacy concern, the risk-centric model reveals that disclosing sensitive information is associated with higher likelihood of remedy and corrective behaviors. This relationship indicates that teens perceive risks related to sensitive information disclosures and are more likely to take protective measures to reduce privacy breaches and threats. Risky interactions, on the other hand, appear to exceed teens' comfort level of managing the potential threats by themselves and are, thus, associated with higher levels of privacy concern. Increased privacy concern may, in turn, encourage teens to turn to external resources for guidance and help.

This dynamic relationship between the different types of privacy risks and teens' risk-coping responses lends insight into how teens negotiate their information boundaries. It suggests a developmental process through which teens' awareness and coping mechanisms of information privacy risks are shaped in response to their accumulative risk experiences. If the privacy risks experienced by teens are moderate and manageable, as the inoculation model suggests, they will develop resilience to future privacy risk events. This "risk-as-learning-process" model highlights how today's younger generations who are digital natives form their own risk perceptions and protective strategies from personal experiences with social technologies [37].

It also suggests that teens are, to some extent, capable of identifying the manageable level of risk and adopting different coping strategies accordingly; they will cope with low-level risks by themselves, but they cope with high-level risks using external help systems. This process may be beneficial as it supports proximal development of the teens to allow them to experience and learn and at the same time to protect them from significant harms. In order to assist the identification process, effort should be put to helping teens understand potential and hidden risks, enhancing their awareness of risk invasion and threats, and thereby encouraging them to seek for information and aid when they face privacy risks.

In this sense, the so-called "privacy paradox" [5] may be misleading, at least when it is used to describe the privacy behaviors of this age group. In other words, it is not that their privacy concern fails to moderate their disclosure behaviors; rather, there is a mismatch between their conceptions of risk and the traditional conceptions tied to information disclosure. Therefore, privacy concern is not the effective motivator of risk-coping, but a potential mediating factor underlying the restrictive effect of highly risky behaviors on privacy risk-coping. For this younger generation, risk management should not be equated with *insulation* from risk; instead, we should see exposure to privacy risk and subsequent coping behaviors as an opportunity to influence today's adolescents. With their privacy perceptions and behaviors shaped by the emerging affordances of communication technologies, teens may develop novel ways of evaluating risks in general, and this new outlook and psychology of risk may have significant implications at both personal and societal levels [9].

Implications for Design

Contrasting the concern-centric and risk-centric models, we might infer that, for the generally technology-savvy younger generation, we should explore ways to *enhance risk awareness* in their frequently-used cyberspaces rather than implementing restrictive interventions, so that they can better learn from online privacy risk experiences. For example, design effort and policy-making could focus on mitigation of potential harms in social networking sites, especially those related to social threats, instead of trying to limit teens' SNS use or basic information disclosures. The risk-centric model has implications for designing more effective online security and safety mechanisms for teens. It highlights the importance of educating teenage users about possible privacy risks as they are encountered, and providing opportunities for them to seek help when risks become more dangerous than they can handle on their own. This "learning at the moment of experiencing" is in line with previous literature (e.g., [27]), which suggests embedded training as a more effective practice compared to, for instance, sending separate security emails and notices that are not specifically attached to a contextualized "learning moment," to educate users about phishing and protect them from such attacks.

The accumulative nature of information privacy risks, and especially the fact that only high-level risks such as risky interactions can lead to heightened privacy concern, indicate the importance of educating teens about the correlative relationship between low-level and high-level risks, including instruction on how disclosing basic information can potentially lead to more severe privacy invasion and harm. Education concerning privacy risk, digital literacy and cybersecurity offered through schools, workshops or online courses (e.g., MOOCs) can effectively increase teens' awareness of less apparent privacy risks and encourage them to seek help from external resources.

Beyond educating teens, SNS service providers might also be proactive in helping teens to autonomously engage with others online, while simultaneously implementing interface features that discourage them from exposing themselves to extreme, imminent risks. For example, natural language processing has been explored as a way to identify cyberbullying on Twitter [12]. Using similar and other (e.g., identifying messages sent from outside of one's network) approaches, SNSs may be able to identify common patterns leading to risky behaviors and alert teen users of these risks before they occur. Doing so may heighten teens' awareness of their own sensitive information disclosures or potentially risky interactions so that they can adjust accordingly.

Limitations and Future Research

We would like to address some of the limitations of our findings that can be leveraged as opportunities for informing future research. First, we used cross-sectional survey data to test the theoretical models of teen online privacy management, and this leads to some ambiguity between antecedents and outcomes. Therefore, future longitudinal and/or interview studies should be conducted to confirm the process-level relationships that we theorize in **Figure 6**. Second, important factors such as trust (in other users and/or in service providers), perceived security, self-efficacy, etc. were not measured in the Pew dataset; therefore, these relationships could not be examined in our models. On one hand, the Pew data set is a strength of our research because it provided a large, nationally representative sample of teens, which is a challenging population to study. On the other hand, our empirical test was constrained by the sample data because we had to construct factors from the items already measured in the survey. While we were able to leverage CATPCA to develop more theoretically and statistically robust factors, we recognize that some of the factors used in our empirical models could have been operationalized with more precision. Future studies would benefit from crafting their own survey instruments in order to pre-validate measures and test additional salient factors.

Our study suggests that a moderate level of risk experience may serve as a learning opportunity in teens' developing awareness of information privacy risks and the adoption of risk-coping strategies. However, we also note that risks beyond a certain threshold can cause significant harm. Future research is needed to identify the amount and types of risk experiences that teens can be exposed to achieve an optimal amount of learning without privacy harms, or a "zone of proximal development" [58] conceptualized in cognitive development literature, in order to understand the design space and the policy space for what a teen can learn from certain types or levels of risk experiences and when a teen may need external help or guidance.

CONCLUSION

This paper theoretically constructed and empirically compared two theoretical models of teens' online information privacy risks. Using nationally representative data, the study provides a taxonomy of teens' privacy risk-taking behaviors and risk-coping behaviors. It further revealed that a concern-centric approach that emphasizes the cognitive reasoning in conceptualizing and managing information privacy risks is less applicable to teenagers than other populations studied; rather, teens develop their risk-coping strategies as direct and indirect responses to their personal experiences of privacy risks. This risk-centric approach offers a "risk-as-learning-opportunity" framework and highlights the importance of rethinking teens' conceptions of risks and strategies to reduce and prevent privacy harms for teens from a developmental perspective.

ACKNOWLEDGMENTS

First, we would like to thank Mary Madden, Senior Researcher at Pew Research Center, who enabled our access to the Pew data set. Also, this research was supported by the U.S. National Science Foundation under grant CNS-1018302. Part of the work of Heng Xu was done while working at the U.S. National Science Foundation. Any opinion, findings, and conclusions or recommendations expressed in this material are those of the authors and do not necessarily reflect the views of the U.S. National Science Foundation.

REFERENCES

1. Acquisti, A., & Gross, R. Imagined communities: Awareness, information sharing, and privacy on the Facebook. In *Privacy enhancing technologies*, (2006), 36-58.

2. Altman, I. *The Environment and Social Behavior: Privacy, Personal Space, Territory, and Crowding.* Brooks/Cole Publishing, Monterey, CA, 1975.

3. Bansal, G., Zahedi, F. and Gefen, D. The impact of personal dispositions on information sensitivity, privacy concern and trust in disclosing health information online. *Decision Support Systems*, *49*, 2 (2010), 138-150.

4. Barkhuus, L. and Dey, A. K. Location-Based Services for Mobile Telephony: a Study of Users' Privacy Concerns. *INTERACT 3*(2003), 702-712.

5. Barnes, S. B. *A privacy paradox: Social networking in the United States*, 2006.

6. Baumrind, D. A developmental perspective on adolescent risk taking in contemporary America. *New directions for child development*, 37 (1987), 93-125.

7. Boldero, J., & Fallon, B. Adolescent help-seeking: What do they get help for and from whom? *Journal of Adolescence*, *18*, 2 (1995), 193-209.

8. boyd, d. Why Youth (Heart) Social Network Sites: The Role of Networked Publics in Teenage Social Life In D. Buckingham (ed.) *YOUTH, IDENTITY, AND DIGITAL MEDIA*, *Berkman Center Research Publication No. 2007-16*, (2007).

9. Breakwell, G. M. *The psychology of risk* Cambridge University Press, Cambridge, 2007.

10. Burgoon, J. K., Parrott, R., Le Poire, B. A., Kelley, D. L., Walther, J. B. and Perry, D. Maintaining and restoring privacy through communication in different types of relationships. *Journal of Social and Personal Relationships*, *6*, 2 (1989), 131-158.

11. Chai, S., Bagchi-Sen, S., Morrell, C., Rao, H. R., & Upadhyaya, S. J. Internet and online information privacy: An exploratory study of preteens and early teens. *IEEE Transactions*, *52*, 2 (2009), 167-182.

12. Chen, Y., Zhang, L., Michelony, A. and Zhang, Y. 4Is of social bully filtering: identity, inference, influence, and intervention. In *Proc. Proceedings of the 21st ACM international conference on Information and knowledge management*, ACM (2012), 2677-2679.

13. Cho, H., & LaRose, R. Privacy issues in Internet surveys. *Social Science Computer Review*, *17*, 4 (1999), 421-434.

14. Christofides, E., Muise, A., & Desmarais, S. Information disclosure and control on Facebook: are they two sides of the same coin or two different processes? *CyberPsychology & Behavior*, *12*, 3 (2009), 341-345.

15. Cohn, L. D., Macfarlane, S., Yanez, C., & Imai, W. K. Risk-perception: differences between adolescents and adults. *Health Psychology*, *14*, 3 (1995), 217.

16. Consumers-Union. *Consumer Reports Poll: Americans Extremely Concerned About Internet Privacy*. 2008, http://www.consumersunion.org/pub/core_telecom_and_utilities/006189.html.

17. Debatin, B., Lovejoy, J. P., Horn, A. K., & Hughes, B. N. Facebook and online privacy: Attitudes, behaviors, and unintended consequences. *Journal of Computer Mediated Communication*, *15*, 1 (2009), 83-108.

18. Dumont, M., & Provost, M. A. Resilience in adolescents: Protective role of social support, coping strategies, self-esteem, and social activities on experience of stress and depression. *Journal of youth and adolescence*, *28*, 3 (1999), 343-363.
19. Ellison, N. B., Steinfield, C. and Lampe, C. The benefits of Facebook "friends:" Social capital and college students' use of online social network sites. *Journal of Computer-Mediated Communication*, *12*, 4 (2007), 1143-1168.
20. Feng, Y. and Xie, W. Teens' concern for privacy when using social networking sites: An analysis of socialization agents and relationships with privacy-protecting behaviors. *Comput. Hum. Behav.*, *33* (2014), 153-162.
21. Goffman, E. *The presentation of self in everyday life*. Anchor, New York, USA, 1959.
22. Gould, M. S., Munfakh, J. L. H., Lubell, K., Kleinman, M., & Parker, S. Seeking help from the internet during adolescence. *Journal of the American Academy of Child & Adolescent Psychiatry*, *41*, 10 (2002), 1182-1189.
23. Hoy, M. G., & Milne, G. Gender differences in privacy-related measures for young adult Facebook users. *Journal of Interactive Advertising*, *10*, 2 (2010), 28-45.
24. ISTTF. *Enhancing Child Safety and Online Technologies*. Harvard University's Berkman Center for Internet and Society, Internet Safety Technical Task Force, 2008,
25. Kaiser, H. F. The Application of Electronic Computers to Factor Analysis. *Educational and Psychological Measurement*, *20*, 1 (April 1, 1960 1960), 141-151.
26. Krasnova, H., Günther, O., Spiekermann, S., & Koroleva, K. Privacy concerns and identity in online social networks. *Identity in the Information Society*, *2*, 1 (2009), 39-63.
27. Kumaragruru, P., Rhee, Y., Acquisti, A., Cranor, L. F., Hong, J. and Nunge, E. Protecting people from phishing: The design and evaluation of an embedded training email system. In *Proc. SIGCHI Conference on Human Factors in Computing Systems*, ACM (2007), 905-914.
28. Laufer, R. S. and Wolfe, M. Privacy as a Concept and a Social Issue: A Multidimensional Developmental Theory. *Journal of Social Issues*, *33*, 3 (1977), 22-42.
29. Lenhart, A. and Madden, M. *Teens, Privacy & Online Social Networks, PEW Internet & American Life Project*. 2007, http://www.pewinternet.org/ppf/r/211/report_display.asp .
30. Lewis, K., Kaufman, J., & Christakis, N. The taste for privacy: An analysis of college student privacy settings in an online social network. *Journal of Computer Mediated Communication*, *14*, 1 (2008), 79-100.
31. Livingstone, S. Taking risky opportunities in youthful content creation: Teenagers' use of social networking sites for intimacy, privacy, and self-expression. *New Media & Society*, *10* (2008), 393-411.
32. Livingstone, S., i Helsper, E. Gradations in digital inclusion: children, young people and the digital divide. *New Media & Society*, *9*, 4 (2007), 671.
33. Livingstone, S., Ólafsson, K. and Staksrud, E. Risky Social Networking Practices Among "Underage" Users: Lessons for Evidence-Based Policy. *Journal of Computer-Mediated Communication*, *18*, 3 (2013), 303-320.
34. Lwin, M. O., Stanaland, A. and Miyazaki, A. Protecting children's privacy online: How parental mediation strategies affect website safeguard effectiveness. *Journal of Retailing*, *4*, 2 (2008), 205–217.
35. Madden, M., Cortesi, S., Gasser, U., Lenhart, A. and Duggan, M. *Where Teens Seek Online Privacy Advice*. Pew Research Center's Internet & American Life Project, 2013, http://www.pewinternet.org/2013/08/15/where-teens-seek-online-privacy-advice/.
36. Madden, M., Lenhart, A., Cortesi, S., Gasser, U., Duggan, M., Smith, A. and Beaton, M. *Teens, Social Media, and Privacy* 2013, http://www.pewinternet.org/Reports/2013/Teens-Social-Media-And-Privacy.aspx.
37. Marwick, A. E. and boyd, d. Networked privacy: How teenagers negotiate context in social media. *New Media & Society* (July 21, 2014).
38. Meulman, J. J. and Heiser, W. J. *SPSS-Categories*. 2004, http://www.helsinki.fi/~komulain/Tilastokirjat/IBM-SPSS-Categories.pdf.
39. Milne, G. R. and Culnan, M. J. Strategies for reducing online privacy risks: Why consumers read (or don't read) online privacy notices. *Journal of Interactive Marketing*, *18*, 3 (2004), 15-29.
40. Miyazaki, A. D., & Fernandez, A. Consumer perceptions of privacy and security risks for online shopping. *Journal of Consumer Affairs*, *35*, 1 (2001), 27-44.
41. Moscardelli, D. M., & Divine, R. Adolescents' Concern for Privacy When Using the Internet: An Empirical Analysis of Predictors and Relationships With Privacy Protecting Behaviors. *Family and Consumer Sciences Research Journal*, *35*, 3 (2007), 232-252.
42. Norberg, P. A., Horne, D. R., & Horne, D. A. The privacy paradox: Personal information disclosure intentions versus behaviors. *Journal of Consumer Affairs*, *41*, 1 (2007), 100-126.
43. Nosko, A., Wood, E. and Molema, S. All about me: Disclosure in online social networking profiles: The

case of FACEBOOK. *Computers in Human Behavior*, *26*, 3 (2010), 406-418.

44. Palen, L. and Dourish, P. Unpacking "privacy" for a networked world. In *Proc. Proceedings of the SIGCHI conference on Human factors in computing systems*, ACM (2003), 129-136.

45. Rachels, J. Why privacy is important. In D. G. J. J. W. Snapper (ed.) *Ethical issues in the use of computers*, (1985), 194-200.

46. Schau, H. J. and Gilly, M. C. We are what we post? Self-presentation in personal web space. *Journal of Consumer Research*, *30*, 3 (2003), 385–404.

47. Schermelleh-Engel, K., Moosbrugger, H. and Müller, H. Evaluating the fit of structural equation models: Tests of significance and descriptive goodness-of-fit measures. *Methods of psychological research online*, *8*, 2 (2003), 23-74.

48. Seiffge-Krenke, I. *Stress, coping, and relationships in adolescence*. Lawrence Erlbaum, Mahwah, NJ, 1995.

49. Sheehan, K. B. Toward a typology of Internet users and online privacy concerns. *The Information Society*, *18*, 1 (2002), 21-32.

50. Shin, D. H. The effects of trust, security and privacy in social networking: A security-based approach to understand the pattern of adoption. *Interacting with Computers*, *22*, 5 (2010), 428-438.

51. Smith, H. J., Dinev, T. and Xu, H. Information Privacy Research: An Interdisciplinary Review. *MIS Quarterly*, *35*, 4 (2011), 989-1015.

52. Steinberg, L. Risk taking in adolescence: what changes, and why? *Annals of the New York Academy of Sciences*, *1021*, 1 (2004), 51-58.

53. Steinberg, L. A social neuroscience perspective on adolescent risk-taking. *Developmental review*, *28*, 1 (2008), 78-106.

54. Stevenson, F. and Zimmerman, M. A. ADOLESCENT RESILIENCE: A Framework for Understanding Healthy Development in the Face of Risk. *Annual Review of Public Health*, *26* (2005), 399-419.

55. Tan, X., Qin, L., Kim, Y., & Hsu, J. Impact of privacy concern in social networking web sites. *Internet Research*, *22*, 2 (2012), 211-233.

56. Tufekci, Z. Can You See Me Now? Audience and Disclosure Regulation in Online Social Network Sites. *Bulletin of Science, Technology & Society*, *28*, 1 (February 1, 2008 2008), 20-36.

57. Utz, S., & Kramer, N. The privacy paradox on social network sites revisited: The role of individual characteristics and group norms. *Cyberpsychology: Journal of Psychosocial Research on Cyberspace*, *3*, 2 (2009).

58. Vygostky, L. S. *Mind in Society: The Development of Higher Psychological Processes*. Harvard University Press, Cambridge, Mass, 1978.

59. Walther, J. B. Computer-mediated communication: Impersonal, interpersonal, and hyperpersonal interaction. *Communication Research*, *23* (1996), 3-44.

60. Wisniewski, P., Xu, H., Rosson, M. B. and Carroll, J. M. Adolescent Online Safety: The "Moral" of the Story. In *Proc. CSCW 2014* (2014).

61. Xu, H., Parks, R., Chu, C. H., & Zhang, X. L. Information disclosure and online social networks: From the case of Facebook news feed controversy to a theoretical understanding. In *Proc. AMCIS 2010* (2010).

62. Youn, S. Parental influence and teens' attitude toward online privacy protection. *Journal of Consumer Affairs*, *42*, 3 (2008), 362-388.

63. Youn, S. Teenagers' perceptions of online privacy and coping behaviors: a risk–benefit appraisal approach. *Journal of Broadcasting & Electronic Media*, *49*, 1 (2005), 86-110.

Appendix A. Categorical Principal Components Analysis Results.

Measures of Constructs	Eigenvalue
Information Privacy Risk-Taking Behaviors	
Basic Information Disclosure	**2.24**
Is your birthdate posted to your profile or account?	
Is your real name posted to your profile or account?	
Is your school name posted to your profile or account?	
Is a photo of yourself posted to your profile or account?	
Do you ever share photos of yourself online?	
Is your relationship status posted to your profile or account?	
Risky Interaction	**1.55**
Have you ever received online advertising that was clearly inappropriate for your age?	
Are you friends with or otherwise connected to other people you have never met in person?	
Have you ever been contacted online by someone you did not know in a way that made you feel scared or uncomfortable?	
Do you ever post updates, comments, photos or videos that you later regret sharing?	
Do you ever set up your profile or account so that it automatically includes your location on your posts?	
Sensitive Information Disclosure	**1.47**
Is your email address posted to your profile or account?	
Are your interests, such as movies, music, or books you like, posted to your profile or account?	
Have you ever shared sensitive information online that later caused a problem for you or others in your family?	
Is your cell phone number posted to your profile or account?	
Do you ever share videos of yourself online?	
Are videos of you posted to your profile or account?	
Have you ever said you were older than you are so you could get onto a website or sign up for an online account?	
Have you ever posted something online that got you in trouble at school?	
Information Privacy Risk-Coping Behaviors	
Remedy/Correction	**2.66**
Do you ever delete people from your network or friends' list?	
Do you ever remove your name from photos that have been tagged to identify you?	
Do you ever delete comments that others have made on your profile or account?	
Do you ever delete or edit something that you posted in the past?	
Do you ever post fake information like a fake name, age or location to help protect your privacy?	
Do you ever share inside jokes or coded messages that only some of your friends would understand?	
Do you ever block people?	
Do you ever delete or deactivate a profile or account?	
Advice-Seeking	**1.64**
Have you ever turned to a friend or peer for advice about how to manage your privacy online?	
Have you ever turned to your brother, sister or cousin for advice about how to manage your privacy online?	
Have you ever turned to your parent for advice about how to manage your privacy online?	
Have you ever turned to a teacher for advice about how to manage your privacy online?	
Have you ever turned to a website for advice about how to manage your privacy online?	

Appendix B. Measurement of Key Variables in the Models.

SNS Complexity

Are you friends with or otherwise connected to…?

1. Your parents
2. Your brothers or sisters
3. Extended family
4. Friends at school
5. Other friends that don't go to your school
6. Teachers or coaches
7. Celebrities, musicians or athletes
8. Other people you have never met in person

Frequency of SNS Use

About how often do you visit social networking sites? (Reverse-coded)

1. Several times a day
2. About once a day
3. 3 to 5 days a week
4. 1 to 2 days a week
5. Every few weeks
6. Less often

Ease of Privacy Control

Overall, how difficult is it to manage the privacy controls on your Facebook profile?

1. Very difficult
2. Somewhat difficult
3. Not too difficult
4. Not difficult at all

Privacy Concern

Thinking again about the social network site that you use most often, how concerned are you, if at all, that some of the information you share on the site might be accessed by third parties without your knowledge? (Reverse-coded)

1. Very concerned
2. Somewhat concerned
3. Not too concerned
4. Not at all concerned

Appendix C. Parameter Estimates of Model 1.

Parameter Estimate	*Standardized*	*p*
SNS Complexity → Concern	0.059	0.151
SNS Frequency → Concern	0.134	0.001
Ease of Control → Concern	-0.187	0.000
Age → Concern	-0.004	0.922
Gender → Concern	0.043	0.281
Concern → Basic Disclosure	0.022	0.594
Concern → Sensitive Disclosure	0.016	0.696
Concern → Risky Interaction	0.101	0.014
Concern → Remedy/Correction	0.189	0.000
Concern → Advice-seeking	0.180	0.000

Appendix D. Parameter Estimates of Model 2.

Parameter Estimate	*Standardized*	*p*
SNS Complexity (SC) → Basic Disclosure (BD)	0.198	0.000
SC → Sensitive Disclosure (SD)	0.225	0.000
SC → Risky Interaction (RI)	0.361	0.000
SC → Concern	0.045	0.314
SC → Remedy/Correction (RC)	-0.002	0.967
SC → Advice-seeking (AS)	0.030	0.502
SNS Frequency (SF) → BD	0.205	0.000
SF → SD	0.169	0.000
SF → RI	0.112	0.004
SF → Concern	0.135	0.001
SF → RC	0.078	0.029
SF → AS	0.044	0.304
Ease of SNS Privacy Control (EC) → BD	-0.030	0.441
EC → SD	0.028	0.490
EC → RI	-0.072	0.062
EC → Concern	-0.183	0.000
EC → RC	-0.027	0.443
EC → AS	-0.070	0.090
Age → BD	0.164	0.000
Age → SD	0.007	0.856
Age → RI	0.054	0.172
Age → Concern	-0.004	0.931
Age → RC	0.005	0.885
Age → AS	-0.111	0.009
Gender → BD	-0.007	0.850
Gender → SD	-0.120	0.002
Gender → RI	0.058	0.124
Gender → Concern	0.037	0.361
Gender → RC	0.163	0.000
Gender → AS	0.097	0.017
BD → SD	0.221	0.000
SD → RI	0.226	0.000
BD → Concern	-0.022	0.615
SD → Concern	-0.020	0.647
RI → Concern	0.096	0.016
BD → RC	0.019	0.604
BD → AS	-0.004	0.924
SD → RC	0.135	0.000
SD → AS	0.198	0.000
RI → RC	0.442	0.000
RI → AS	0.051	0.257
Concern → RC	0.225	0.000
Concern → AS	0.361	0.000

Flock: Hybrid Crowd-Machine Learning Classifiers

Justin Cheng and Michael S. Bernstein
Stanford University
{jcccf, msb}@cs.stanford.edu

ABSTRACT

We present hybrid crowd-machine learning classifiers: classification models that start with a written description of a learning goal, use the crowd to suggest predictive features and label data, and then weigh these features using machine learning to produce models that are accurate and use human-understandable features. These hybrid classifiers enable fast prototyping of machine learning models that can improve on both algorithm performance and human judgment, and accomplish tasks where automated feature extraction is not yet feasible. *Flock*, an interactive machine learning platform, instantiates this approach. To generate informative features, Flock asks the crowd to compare paired examples, an approach inspired by analogical encoding. The crowd's efforts can be focused on specific subsets of the input space where machine-extracted features are not predictive, or instead used to partition the input space and improve algorithm performance in subregions of the space. An evaluation on six prediction tasks, ranging from detecting deception to differentiating impressionist artists, demonstrated that aggregating crowd features improves upon both asking the crowd for a direct prediction and off-the-shelf machine learning features by over 10%. Further, hybrid systems that use both crowd-nominated and machine-extracted features can outperform those that use either in isolation.

Author Keywords

Crowdsourcing, interactive machine learning

ACM Classification Keywords

H.5.m. Information Interfaces and Presentation (e.g. HCI): Miscellaneous

INTRODUCTION

Identifying predictive features is key to creating effective machine learning classifiers. Whether the task is link prediction or sentiment analysis, and no matter the underlying model, the "black art" of feature engineering plays a critical role in success [10]. Feature engineering is largely domain-specific, and users of machine learning systems spend untold hours experimenting. Often, the most predictive features only emerge after many iterations [36]. And though feature engineers may have deep domain expertise, they are only able to incorporate features that are extractable via code.

CSCW 2015, March 14–18, 2015, Vancouver, BC, Canada.

ACM 978-1-4503-2922-4/15/03 ...$15.00.
http://dx.doi.org/10.1145/2675133.2675214

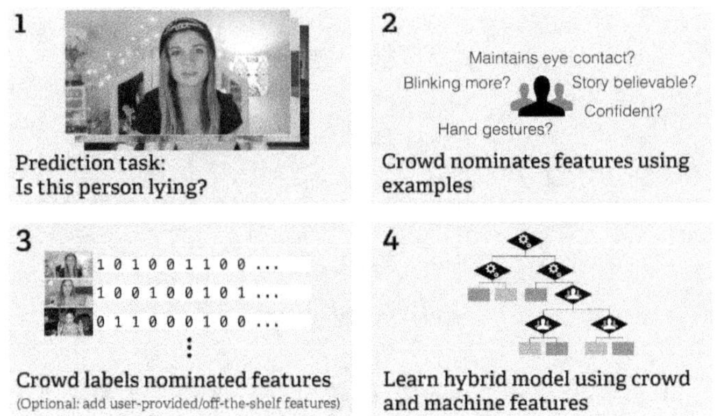

Figure 1. Flock is a hybrid crowd-machine learning platform that capitalizes on analogical encoding to guide crowds to nominate effective features, then uses machine learning techniques to aggregate their labels.

However, *embedding crowds inside of machine learning architectures* opens the door to hybrid learners that can explore feature spaces that are largely unreachable by automatic extraction, then train models that use human-understandable features (Figure 1). Doing so enables fast prototyping of classifiers that can exceed both machine and expert performance. In this paper, we demonstrate classifiers that identify people who are lying, perform quality assessment of Wikipedia articles, and differentiate impressionist artists who use similar styles. Previous work that bridges crowdsourcing and machine learning has focused on optimizing the crowd's efforts (e.g., [8, 21, 39]): we suggest that inverting the relationship and embedding crowd insight inside live classifiers enables machine learning to be deployed for new kinds of tasks.

We present *Flock*, an end-user machine learning platform that uses paid crowdsourcing to speed up the prototyping loop and augment the performance of machine learning systems. Flock contributes a model for creating hybrid classifiers that intelligently embed both crowd and machine features. The system allows users to rapidly author hybrid crowd-machine learners by structuring a feature nomination process using the crowd, aggregating the suggested features, then collecting labels on these new features. It loops and gathers more crowd features to improve performance on subsets of the space where the model is misclassifying many examples. For instance, given a decision tree that uses machine-readable features, Flock can dynamically grow subtrees from nodes that have high classification error, or even replace whole branches. In addition to improving performance, these constraints can help focus the crowd's brainstorming on a subset of the example space to generate more informative features.

Flock's success relies on crowds generating informative features. While crowds of people can excel at generating ideas [49, 22] and labeling subtle behavioral signals, they are generally poor at introspecting on the signals they use to make decisions [13], and even poorer at weighing evidence properly to make a decision [18]. In fact, there are many tasks where the crowd's predictions are significantly worse than even naïve algorithms — for instance, in identifying deceptive online reviews [31], or in categorizing businesses [46]. Nevertheless, crowds can identify useful attributes to classify images [25], suggesting that proper scaffolding of the process might lead to success. Comparing and contrasting examples highlights similarities and differences, and encourages deeper thinking [15]. To this end, we introduce an approach inspired by analogical encoding [14]: Flock asks crowd members to guess which of two examples is from a positive class and which is from the negative class, then write a reason why. These reasons become features: Flock automatically clusters the reasons, then recruits crowds to normalize each cluster and produce features. These features are then used by the crowd to annotate each example.

Rather than help people weigh evidence correctly, we recognize that this is a straightforward task for most learning algorithms. Thus, systems can harness the crowd's collective insight through repeated comparisons to identify potentially predictive features, including ones that require subtle human judgment, and then use statistical machinery to identify those that actually matter.

We demonstrate Flock's effectiveness through an evaluation of six broadly different prediction tasks, including discerning videos of people telling the truth or lying and differentiating between paintings by impressionist artists. We find that aggregating crowd features is more accurate than asking for a direct prediction from the crowd, and produce strong evidence that hybrid crowd-machine systems such as Flock can outperform systems that only use either. On these prediction tasks, these hybrid systems improve on both direct predictions and off-the-shelf classifiers by an average of over 10%.

Though crowdsourcing has generally either been portrayed as a stopgap solution for machine learning systems [43] or a goal for artificial intelligence to optimize [8], our work reinforces the benefits of a productive synthesis. Using crowds, classifiers can begin working minutes after a request, and gradually transition from a crowd-based to machine-based classifier. In this paper, we present a model for such a synthesis.

RELATED WORK

We start by reviewing systems that support the development of machine learning models. These include end-user systems designed to streamline the development process, as well as interactive machine learning systems. We then examine research at the intersection of crowdsourcing and machine learning. Prior work here has mainly focused on optimizing the monetary cost of crowdsourcing and on using crowds as part of the learning process, either through labeling or feature suggestion. This line of work suggests a trajectory toward integrating the entire machine learning pipeline with crowds, from feature generation to prediction.

Flock builds on these approaches by leveraging the strengths of both crowds and machines to learn hybrid models that can be iteratively improved. Extending the literature on integrating crowds and machines, Flock provides a generalized framework for augmenting machine learning models with crowd-nominated features. In particular, the crowd generates (and labels) features, doing so in ways that can integrate with machine learning algorithms to support weak areas of a machine-only classifier.

Supporting Machine Learning

Interactive machine learning systems can speed up model evaluation and helping users quickly discover classifier deficiencies. Some systems help users choose between multiple machine learning models (e.g., [17]) and tune model parameters, for instance through visualizing confusion matrices [44]. Others enable rapid iteration by making model re-training instantaneous (e.g., [40]), or allowing for fast switching between programming and evaluating example attributes [35].

In interactive machine learning systems, end-users train classifiers by providing focused input. These systems may focus on example generation (e.g., [19]), labeling (e.g., [11]), re-ranking (e.g., [12]), or even feature selection (e.g., [40]). Nevertheless, the available features are often built into the system, and the user's goal is to efficiently explore that feature space and label examples. By identifying and training new features to extend the feature space using systems such as Flock, these tools could be made even more effective.

Crowdsourcing and Machine Learning

Artificial intelligence techniques have largely been applied to optimize crowdsourcing efforts. Algorithms such as expectation maximization enable better estimates of worker quality and improved aggregation of responses (e.g., [8], [21], [47]). Other approaches construct behavioral models to predict future performance [39] or estimate task appropriateness [38].

For instance, crowds can be directly integrated into the learning process by focusing on specific questions or features posed by an algorithm (i.e. active learning). Even if the crowd lacks the expertise to answer the high level prediction task, they can effectively label features, or answer questions that help algorithms answer it (e.g., [32, 34]). In computer vision, supervised learning approaches have been applied to object classification by asking crowd workers questions to reduce label uncertainty [6], or by highlighting portions of an image corresponding to a given annotation [45]. Where these active learning systems seek to optimize algorithm performance within a pre-specified feature space, Flock tries to actively learn the feature space itself, by exploring and generating new features that can help when it is performing poorly.

Alternatively, crowdsourcing can augment AI by performing tasks that are difficult for machines to handle alone. Large numbers of labeled examples can be generated on-demand (e.g., [9, 24]); the crowd can even be asked to find difficult examples that tend to be misclassified (e.g., [4]). Apart from labeling examples, crowds can group sets of examples (with categories later automatically inferred [16]). They can even directly identify and label potential features [25]. In both cases, these approaches have been shown to be more effective than directly asking the crowd for the desired categories. Flock demonstrates how to integrate both human features and machine features intelligently into a joint classifier.

Drawing on research in machine learning and crowdsourcing, Flock is an attempt at designing an end-to-end system that generates models consisting of both human-generated, as well as machine-generated features. It utilizes the crowd to define and populate the feature space, then generates a hybrid human-machine model. By identifying weak areas and then learning new features, these models can then iteratively improve themselves.

FLOCK

By leveraging the complementary strengths of the crowd in exploring features and machine learning algorithms in aggregating these features, we can prototype and develop hybrid human-machine learning models that improve on existing methods. Flock, a platform that allows users to develop these hybrid models starting from a written description of the problem, instantiates this approach.

The user workflow has three main components (Figure 2):

- uploading training and test data, along with class labels and any pre-computed machine features
- launching crowdsourcing tasks to nominate features through paired example comparison and suggestion aggregation, then collecting crowd labels for the new features
- training a hybrid crowd-machine classifier, looping to focus new crowd features on areas where performance is poor

Creating a hybrid classifier

Flock is aimed at end users who have a basic understanding of machine learning. Users begin a new project by defining their prediction task in words (Figure 2a). For example: "Is this Wikipedia article a good article (GA-grade), or bad article (C-grade)?" The user then uploads a file containing training and test examples, as well as their classification labels. Users can add their own machine-generated features (e.g., the number of editors) as columns in this file. Flock can automatically generate some additional features, including n-grams for text or those of a randomized PCA in RGB space for images.

The user triggers the learning procedure by choosing the classifier type: Flock currently supports decision trees, logistic regression and random forests. If the feature vector is high-dimensional, as with automatically-generated n-gram features, Flock recommends a linear model such as logistic regression. When the user is ready, Flock asks the crowd on the CrowdFlower microtasking market [1] to generate and aggregate features that can help classify their dataset. For example, suggestions such as "broken down into organized sections" and "thorough and well-organized" are aggregated into a feature that asks, "Is this article well-organized or structured?" Simultaneously, Flock collects gold standard (ground truth) feature labels for each of these possible features. Once the crowd has completed this task, Flock shares the nominated features with the user (Figure 2b). The user chooses which features they want to keep, and can add ideas of their own. Flock then launches crowdsourced feature labeling tasks where workers assign a value to each training and test example across the new features.

Flock now trains the hybrid classifier using available machine features and crowd features on the training data (Figure 2c), using cross-validation to prevent overfitting. If the model is a decision tree, internal nodes may be either machine features or crowd features. Flock shows the tree to the user and suggests improvements by highlighting any leaf nodes that are impure and misclassify more than a threshold (2.5%) of all training examples. If a random forest model is used, Flock trains many hybrid decision trees on random subsets of the input data, then produces the averaged "forest" classifier and highlights commonly impure nodes in the trees inside the forest. If a logistic regression model is used, Flock first trains a decision tree on crowd features only to partition the input data into more coherent subsets, then trains parallel logistic regression classifiers for each leaf nodes at the bottom of the tree using machine features and that partition of training data. Flock highlights any leaf classifiers that perform poorly as possible candidates for additional features in the partition. While Flock currently only supports binary classification, this approach can also be extended to support multi-class or regression problems.

The user can then improve the initial learned models by adding targeted crowd features to weak parts of the classifier. The user can choose any node, including the ones that Flock highlighted earlier as impure, and expand that part of the classifier with new crowd features. When this happens, Flock's process loops and the system launches a new set of crowd tasks to nominate new features on the subset of the data that belongs to the selected node.

At each step, Flock trains multiple models with different feature subsets. It does so to show the user the performance of multiple prediction methods on the test set. These models include *Crowd prediction* (a baseline asking workers directly to guess the correct label for the example), *ML with off-the-shelf* (the chosen machine learning model using only out-of-the-box features such as n-grams), *ML with crowd* (the chosen machine learning model using only crowd features), or *Hybrid* (the full Flock model using both machine and crowd features). This also allows end-users to decide whether the performance improvement of a hybrid model is worth the additional time and cost associated with crowdsourcing.

To enable this workflow in Flock, we must (1) generate high-quality features, (2) gather feature labels for those features, and (3) train hybrid machine-crowd models. Next, we expand upon Flock's approach to solving each problem.

Nominating features with analogical encoding

Crowdsourcing can help discover and test a large number of potential features: more eyes on the prediction task can min-

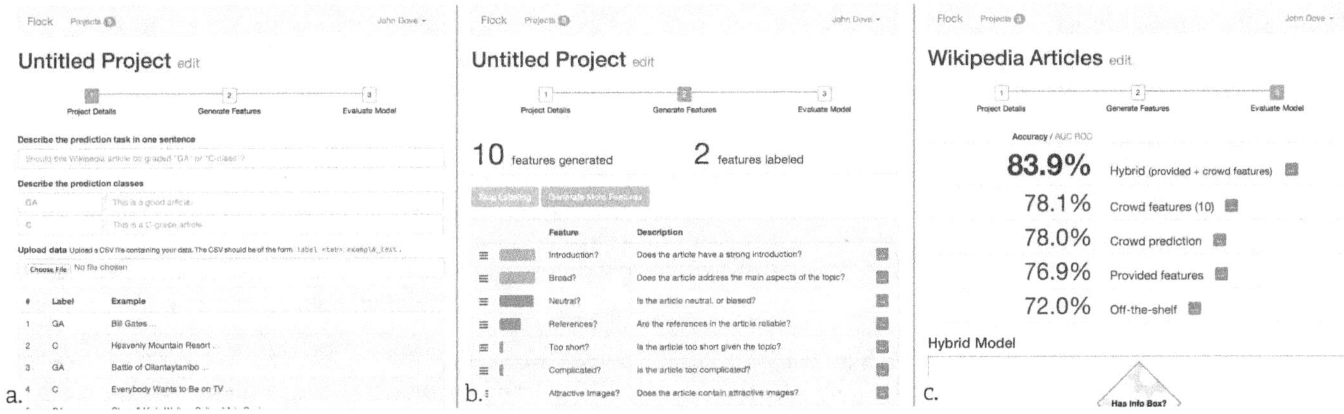

Figure 2. Workflow: (a) Users define the prediction task and provide example data. (b) Flock then automatically gathers features, combining them with machine-provided features if the user provided them. (c) Flock then allows users to visualize the features and results and compare the performance of the different models (e.g., human guessing, human features, machine features, a hybrid model).

Figure 3. Crowd workers generate feature nominations in Flock by comparing two examples, predicting which example is in each class, and explaining how it is possible to tell them apart.

imize functional fixedness and surface counterintuitive features. Prior work suggests that the crowd may be able to generate features that can differentiate classes of input: previously, crowds have labeled training data for learning algorithms [24, 43], discovered classes of input that a classifier has never seen and tends to misclassify [4], brainstormed in creative settings (e.g., designing chairs [49]), extracted high-level concepts from unstructured data [3, 7, 23], and suggested features to classify images [25]. Querying the crowd also has the added benefit of nominated features being easily interpretable (e.g., "Does this painting tend to hide peoples' faces in shadow?"), in contrast to automatic but opaque features by computer vision algorithms such as SIFT [30].

In principle, any task that asks the crowd for predictive features could suffice here. Unfortunately, asking the crowd to generate features directly from examples often elicits poor responses — crowds are likely to be unfamiliar with the problem domain and generate surface-level features. For example, when presented with the task of deciding whether a joke will have popular appeal, the crowd gravitated towards responses such as "it makes me laugh" or "it depends on the person".

Previous research on analogical encoding has found that when considering single examples, people tend to focus on surface-level details, but when they compare examples, they focus on deeper structural characteristics [14]. So, instead of asking the crowd to *deduce* relevant features from a task description, Flock asks them to *induce* features from contrasting examples. Crowds can extract schemas from examples [48], and these suggestions (e.g., factors to consider when buying a camera) tend to exhibit long-tail distributions — while there is high overlap for a few dimensions, individual workers also suggest a large number of alternatives [23]. We hypothesize that eliciting features through contrasting examples will allow crowds to produce predictive features even when they have minimal domain expertise.

Flock first gathers feature suggestions from the crowd by generating crowdsourcing tasks on CrowdFlower. These tasks, which are automatically generated based the example type (text, image, or web page), show workers a random input from the set of positive training examples, and another random input from the set of negative training examples (Figure 3). However, the class labels are hidden from the worker. Workers are first asked to guess which of the two examples belongs to each class (e.g. matching paintings to Impressionist artists with similar styles). They are then asked to describe in free text how these examples differ. Typically, each explanation focuses on a single dimension along which the two examples differ. In early iterations, we showed the label to the workers and asked them for a reason directly, but hiding the label led them to engage in deeper reasoning about the differences between the examples [20]. Flock launches 100 comparison tasks with three workers each per dataset, resulting in 300 nominated features for about six cents per label ($20 total).

Next, Flock must aggregate this large number of free-text suggestions into a small set of potential features to show the user. The features have considerable overlap, and manual categorization suggested that the 300 nominations typically clustered into roughly 50 features. So, Flock clusters the suggestions and asks the crowd to generate an exemplar feature for each cluster (Table 3). First, the system splits each response into multiple suggestions (e.g. by sentence, newlines, and conjunctions such as "and"). The system then performs k-means clustering ($k = 50$) using tf-idf weighted bigram text features. With these clusters in hand, Flock launches another task to CrowdFlower showing workers one cluster at a time and asking them to summarize each into a single representative question (or feature) that has a yes or no answer (e.g., "Is this person shifting their eyes a lot?"). Three candidate features are generated for each cluster.

A subsequent task then asks crowd workers to vote on the best of these three features, and label five examples using that feature in order to bootstrap the gold standard questions [28] for Flock's subsequent feature-labeling tasks. Question rewriting costs 5 cents per question, and each vote and five example labels costs 4 cents, for a total of about $15 to generate 50 features. CrowdFlower's adaptive majority voting algorithm (similar to Get Another Label [41]) aggregates the votes to decide on the correct feature label.

Gathering feature labels

After the crowd-generated features are returned, a user can edit them, filter them to remove ones they don't like or reduce cost, and add any new features that occur to them. They then launch the feature labeling process, which crowdsources labels for each of these user-validated features.

Flock spawns a CrowdFlower task for each feature to gather labels for that feature on the training and test examples. Each task shows workers one example input and asks them to pick a label for each feature (e.g., does this painting contain flowers?). Three workers vote on each feature label, for one cent each, and CrowdFlower's majority voting decides on the correct label.

Hybrid machine-crowd learners

When the feature labels are complete, Flock is ready to train a hybrid classifier (in addition to training other models such as *ML with off-the-shelf* so that they can be compared using the Flock user interface). The initial hybrid model begins by training using k-fold cross-validation on any pre-engineered machine features as well as any crowd-generated features. The exact form of hybridization depends on the user's choice of machine learning algorithm. Decision trees have access to both crowd and machine features, so nodes on the tree may be either a crowd feature or a machine feature. Random forests work similarly, aggregating many decision trees built on samples from the training data. A simple approach to hybridization with logistic regression would be to extend the crowd's features with the feature vector of machine features. However, we may be able to do better by using crowd features to partition the space so that previously ineffective machine features are now effective in one or more subregions of the space. So, the hybridized logistic regression first trains a decision tree at the top level using crowd features, then trains separate logistic regression classifiers as leaf nodes using only machine features. This approach tends to perform at least as well as simple logistic regression. Other linear classifiers (e.g., SVMs) could be added to Flock similarly.

Flock also enables the crowd to selectively supplement weak regions of the classifier. For example, crowds can be used to dynamically extend decision trees at nodes with high impurity, where the decision tree fails to correctly classify its examples. Flock can then ask the crowd to generate new features for examples at that node, providing a constrained space for brainstorming as these examples are already similar in some aspects. These features can then be used to grow a new subtree at that node, improving overall classification accuracy.

To do this, the model-building loops automatically as long as there exist impure nodes that misclassify large numbers of training examples. By default, one decision tree leaf node misclassifying 2.5% of all training examples triggers another round of targeted crowd feature generation. With random forests, we average the number of misclassified examples for each leaf node across all trees in the forest and use a similar filter. With logistic regression, Flock again triggers on leaf-node logistic regression models within the tree that are performing poorly. This process loops until either there exist no more impure nodes, or adding additional features does not improve the previous impure node.

This process can also be iterative and driven by user input. With automatic improvement turned off, Flock's interface highlights impure nodes that the user might consider extending with additional crowd features (Figure 4). When the user chooses a part of the model to improve, the crowd loops again through the process to perform a more targeted brainstorm on just training examples in the poorly-performing region.

Flock then allows any decision tree to add the new features as children of the selected subtree or node. (In the case of hybridized logistic regression, the new crowd features further partition the space and Flock trains new classifiers within the selected region.) Doing so ensures that the extra cost of generating these labels is constrained to inputs that need the help. For example, a user may start by identifying a few extractable features to differentiate good Wikipedia articles from mediocre ones (e.g. the page has missing citations, short sections, or no section headers). While a decision tree built on this algorithm classifies many of the examples well, it performs poorly on examples where none of the visual or structural red flags are triggered. Flock then provides only these difficult examples to the crowd, focusing the crowd's feature generation on a subset of pages where the heading structure is fine and the pages are of reasonable length to generate features like whether the article's introduction is strong.

EVALUATION

Flock's main thesis is that crowds can rapidly produce high-quality classifiers in tandem with machine learning techniques. In this section, we test this thesis by comparing Flock's predictions to those of machines across prediction tasks that require domain expertise, predict popularity and detect deceit. In particular, how effective are crowds at feature nomination? Does using crowd-nominated features perform better than other approaches such as direct prediction by the crowd? And finally, can crowd and machine features be combined to create effective hybrid crowd-machine learners?

Method

To understand the effectiveness of human-generated features and features generated by hybrid human-machine systems,

Dataset	# Examples	Purpose	Accuracy (ROC AUC)				
			Crowd Prediction	ML w/ off-the-shelf	ML w/ engineered	ML w/ crowd	Hybrid
Paintings	200	Predict expertise	0.64 (0.64)	0.69 (0.78)	-	0.74 (0.74)	**0.77 (0.83)**
Fake Reviews	200	Identify deception	0.65 (0.65)	0.87 (0.93)	-	0.72 (0.73)	**0.92 (0.96)**
Wikipedia	400	Evaluate quality	0.78 (0.78)	0.72 (0.72)	0.77 (0.77)	0.78 (0.78)	**0.84 (0.84)**
Jokes	200	Estimate popularity	0.58 (0.58)	0.56 (0.59)	-	0.63 (0.64)	**0.65 (0.64)**
StackExchange	200	Predict behavior	0.60 (0.60)	0.57 (0.57)	0.62 (0.62)	0.65 (0.65)	**0.71 (0.71)**
Lying	200	Identify deception	0.53 (0.53)	-	-	**0.61 (0.61)**	-

Table 1. A performance comparison of human and machine-learning-based approaches to different prediction tasks. Aggregating crowd-nominated features using machine learning consistently outperforms the crowd's direct predictions, and hybrid crowd-machine systems perform better than either crowd-only or machine-only models (unless either model was poor to begin with).

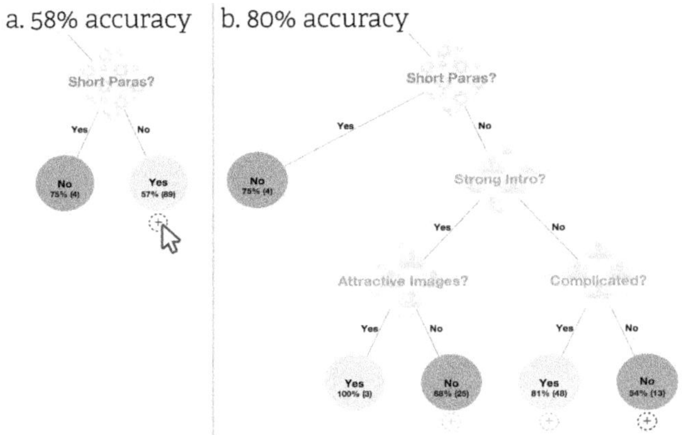

Figure 4. Users can augment weaker parts of the tree by requesting additional human features at specific nodes (a, highlighted). Flock will then automatically generate a new subtree based on these new features (b, highlighted).

we evaluated Flock's crowd feature generation against direct crowd classifications, off-the-shelf machine learning features, engineered features and a hybrid model that includes both crowd features and machine features (for a total of five conditions). For breadth, similar to related work (e.g. [7]), we used six different problem domains.

The problem domains encompass a large range of possible prediction tasks:

- PAINTINGS — differentiating between impressionist paintings by Claude Monet and Alfred Sisley. These painters are often confused due to similar styles. This task represents a learning goal that typically requires domain expertise.
- REVIEWS — telling honest from deceptive hotel reviews [31]. The goal is to identify subtle textual signals of honesty or deception.
- WIKIPEDIA — telling "good" and "C-grade" Wikipedia articles apart. This task requires domain expertise tantamount to that of an experienced Wikipedia editor.
- JOKES — identifying jokes that will have popular appeal. This task was chosen for its similarity to information cascade and popularity tasks in networks.
- STACKEXCHANGE — guessing which answer a question asker would pick as "best".
- LYING — discerning videos of people telling the truth or lying. Here, we try to identify subtle behavioral cues.

In each instance, we generated balanced datasets of at least 200 examples (e.g. for paintings, half were by Monet, and half by Sisley). In other words, random guessing would result in 50% accuracy. For PAINTINGS, images of Monet's and Sisley's paintings were obtained from claudemonet-gallery.org and alfredsisley.org respectively. REVIEWS consisted of a publicly available dataset of truthful and deceptive hotel reviews [31]. For WIKIPEDIA, articles were randomly sampled from a list of all Good Articles and all C-grade articles. JOKES were sampled from Reddit's /r/AskReddit joke threads — jokes with popular appeal were defined as those where the proportion of up-votes was in the upper quartile of the distribution, and those without had a proportion of up-votes in the lower quartile. All jokes received at least ten votes. Questions and answers for STACKEXCHANGE were randomly sampled from the set of all questions with at least two answers and a selected "best" answer on StackExchange's English Language & Usage community. Finally, for LYING, we sampled claims from YouTube videos of people playing "two truths and one lie tag", a game in which they tell truths and lies about themselves and the viewer must guess which is which.

In one baseline condition, *Crowd Prediction*, the crowd is directly asked the prediction question. Three independent workers were directly asked the prediction problem for each example, with CrowdFlower's adaptive majority voting algorithm deciding on the eventual class label. These direct crowd predictions appear to be robust; for example, prediction performance for REVIEWS is slightly better than that described in previous work [31]. One machine learning condition, *ML with Off-the-shelf*, used features that did not require any programming. These consisted of logistic regression on text bigrams for the problems with text content (REVIEWS, WIKIPEDIA, JOKES, and STACKEXCHANGE), and using a randomized PCA model on RGB space for the image prediction task (PAINTINGS). A third condition, *ML with Engineered*, focused on features that a domain expert might extract. For WIKIPEDIA and STACKEXCHANGE, nine features were extracted by the authors, and random forests used for the prediction. For WIKIPEDIA, these features include the structural features extracted in previous work (e.g., infoboxes) [5]. For STACKEXCHANGE, these features are similar to those that were most predictive in a study of a question's long-lasting value (e.g., number of comments, user reputation) [2].

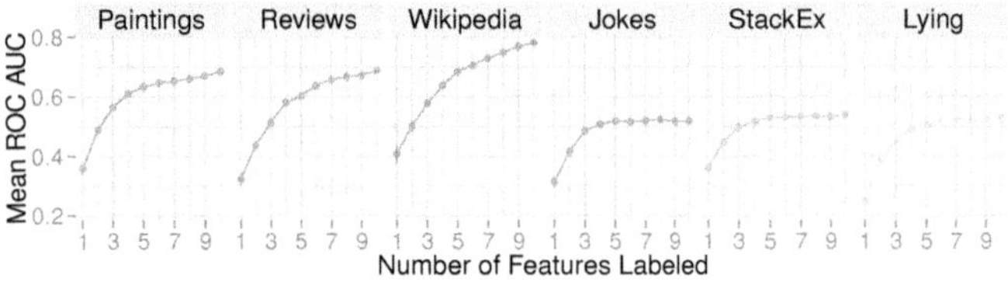

Figure 5. Mean classifier performance with random subsets of features gathered for each prediction task. As more features are collected, the overall performance of the classifier generally improves. Nevertheless, noisy features can impact performance.

In the *ML with Crowd* condition, Flock gathered and aggregated suggestions to generate crowd-nominated features. A final prediction was made by using machine learning to learn the best combination of these features. From the set of nominated features, ten features were chosen at random for labeling. Three different workers labeled each feature for each example, with CrowdFlower's adaptive majority voting algorithm determining the final feature value. Random forests ($n = 100$) were used to aggregate these nominated features, and backward feature selection performed afterward.

A final condition, *Hybrid*, combines crowd-nominated features (the same features as in the *ML with Crowd* condition) and machine features (user-engineered or off-the-shelf such as n-grams). By default, a decision tree model was used, but when the total number of features was large ($\geq$40), we tested both simple logistic regression, which combines both crowd-nominated and machine features into a single feature vector, and hybridized logistic regression, which trains a decision tree at the top level using crowd features, then trains separate logistic regression classifiers as leaf nodes using only machine features.

In all conditions, performance was evaluated using leave-one-out cross-validation.

Results

For each domain on average, 51 workers generated 334 feature nominations ($35 for nomination and aggregation in total), and 263 workers generated 1200 labels for each of 10 features during feature labeling ($12 per feature). Similar to prior work, we find that these feature nominations followed a long-tail distribution. A summary of results can be found in Table 1. While people performed essentially at chance in trying to detect lies on YouTube, *ML with Crowd* was able to detect lying 61% of the time. For other tasks, results were even stronger: for example, *Hybrid* was 92% accurate at detecting fake reviews, 84% accurate and judging Wikipedia page quality, and 77% accurate at differentiating Monet paintings from Sisley.

Aggregating crowd-nominated features outperforms direct predictions from the crowd, off-the-shelf features, and engineered features. In all datasets, aggregating crowd-nominated features (*ML with Crowd*) consistently outperforms directly asking the prediction task (*Crowd Prediction*), with an average improvement of 6% on an absolute scale. People effectively had access to the same features in both cases, but a machine learning architecture was more effective at combining the evidence to make a decision. Further,

Dataset	Top Correlated Features
Paintings	A Monet (i) contains flowers (0.31), (ii) lilies (0.24), (iii) is abstract (0.24), (iv) does not contain people (0.23), and (v) uses broad brushstrokes (0.22).
Reviews	An honest review mentions (i) negative aspects of the stay (0.43), (ii) the prices (0.29), (iii) local activities (0.24), (iv) things only a guest would know about (0.20), and (v) getting something for free (0.17).
Wikipedia	A Good Article (GA) has (i) a strong introduction (0.52), (ii) attractive images (0.39), (iii) is well-structured (0.36), (iv) discusses the topic in detail (0.34), and (v) is not too short to sufficiently cover the topic (0.32).
Jokes	A popular joke (i) uses repetition (0.21), (ii) is long (0.15), (iii) is a "classic" joke (0.12), (iv) does not use toilet humor (0.10), and (v) is not offensive (0.09).
StackExchange	A selected answer (i) is well-written (0.20), (ii) has references (0.19), (iii) uses examples (0.18), (iv) makes logical sense (0.18), and (v) is detailed (0.16).
Lying	When lying, people (i) shift their eyes (0.14), (ii) keep sentences short (0.13), (iii) look confident (0.12), (iv) do not mention details (0.10), (v) and do not use gestures (0.09).

Table 2. For each dataset, the crowd-nominated features that were most correlated with the classification labels for each dataset (correlations in parentheses).

we find that this approach can exceed the performance of off-the-shelf classifiers, or even models with engineered features.

These nominated features were fairly informative and diverse: the mean correlation (Pearson's r) of nominated features with the actual labels was 0.15 (σ=0.09), suggesting that individual features are not strongly predictive but still carry some signal; a mean pairwise correlation between features of 0.19 (σ=0.12) suggests that most nominated features were not restatements of similar concepts. The median maximum correlation of any feature with the crowd predictions was 0.23, suggesting that crowds were not basing their decisions on any single feature. The only exception was WIKIPEDIA, where having a strong introduction was highly correlated (0.49).

Table 2 shows the most correlated features extracted by the crowd for each task. While some features appear subjective (e.g. abstractness for PAINTINGS or a strong introduction for WIKIPEDIA), they nonetheless carry important information. We coded these features to identify how many might be extractable through automated techniques, meaning that off-the-shelf classifiers exist (e.g., sentiment detection) or a simple algorithm can be written to do so (e.g., if an XPath selector could extract the number of headings in a web page). We find that a mean of 25% are easily extracted with machines, suggesting a straightforward approach to automating the collection of some of these features. Future work could study the effectiveness of using only machine-extractable features.

To get a sense of the number of features a user should gather, we plotted mean classifier performance on random subsets of features of different sizes. As Figure 5 shows, performance generally increases with the number of features, although substantial improvements tend to only be seen with four or more features gathered. Nevertheless, feature selec-

Suggestion cluster	Crowd-generated features
looks away from the camera several times · looks away from the camera · look away from the camera or use her hands · glances away from the camera slightly (+4 additional)	**Does she look away from the camera too much?** · Is there too much breaking of eye contact? · Why does she look away like shes trying to get someone elses opinion?
her eyes are shifty in the second video · Her eyes were too shifty in the second video · is shifty in the second video (+3 additional)	Do the eyes shift round causing suspicion of lying? · **Is this person shifting their eyes a lot?** · Is it unnatural?

Table 3. Crowds are able to generate features by summarizing clusters of suggestions into representative features (worded as yes/no questions), and then voting on them (feature with the most votes bolded).

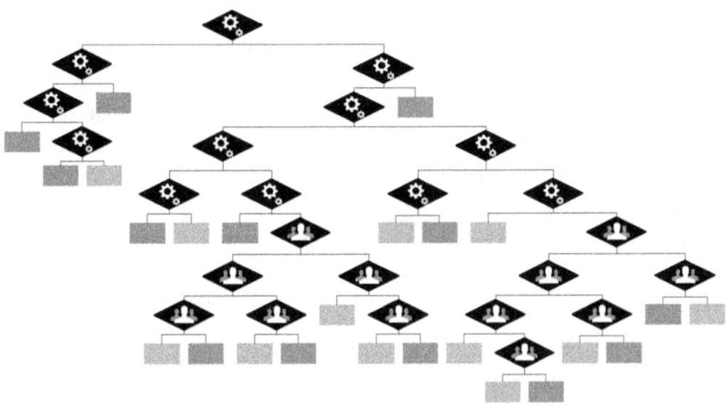

Figure 6. The decision tree used to differentiate "good" (green) and "C-grade" articles (red) on Wikipedia, where machine-extractable features (nodes with gears) were augmented with crowd-nominated features (nodes with people).

tion is important, especially for datasets where features may be noisier or uninformative, and using all nominated features can result in diminished performance (e.g., JOKES).

When comparing classifiers that use crowd-nominated features with those that use engineered features, we note that more time and effort could always have been spent to increase the number of available crowd-nominated, or engineered features. Nevertheless, prior work suggests that the engineered features we use are among the most predictive [5, 2], suggesting that these engineered features produce a classifier in the same performance neighborhood as one that would be more carefully optimized. Figure 5 also suggests that a relatively small number of crowd features is required to achieve reasonable performance as well.

In other words, Flock can help build classification systems that perform roughly as well or better than systems with engineered features with significantly less developer effort, and no programming involved. For example, Flock could be used to prototype and rapidly deploy classification systems that initially are entirely powered by the crowd, with machine-extracted features gradually replacing the crowd over time.

Crowds were able to generate predictive features, but were poor at estimating their features' predictiveness. The feature nomination pipeline generated an average of about 42 potential features (out of 334 unique suggestions) across the 100 examples. k-means clustering identified consistent clusters of suggestions, and crowds were able to extract representative features from these (see Table 3 for examples). Comparing the extracted features with a manually annotated set on the LYING dataset, we found that 80% of features suggested at least five times were identified by k-means and generated by the crowd. Accurately extracting rarer, but more informative features remains future work. Surprisingly, the crowd was also able to identify features that suggested specialized knowledge — for instance, correctly pointing out that the presence of flowers (or lilies) in a painting are indicative of a painting by Monet.

These crowd-nominated features can be gathered reasonably quickly — nomination tasks that asked for 3 independent feature suggestions on 100 examples were 90% complete in roughly nine hours, and finished entirely in 12.5 hours on average. Labeling these features is significantly quicker: the mean time to 90% completion was 1.5 hours, and labels for all 200 examples were complete in 2.8 hours on average (σ=1.6).

Our results showing that *ML with Crowd* outperforms *Crowd Prediction* suggests that crowds do not estimate the importance of the features they generate very well, underlining the importance of machine weighting. To better understand this, for each task, we asked ten workers to independently rank the importance of the ten crowd-nominated features, and compared this ranking with that generated by the absolute correlation of each feature with the provided labels. A Kendall's tau test reveals a coefficient of between -0.184 and 0.156 (a value of 1 corresponds to perfect agreement, 0 to independence in the rankings, and -1 to a completely reversed ranking). These results suggest that people's rankings of features are almost entirely uncorrelated with the true importance of these features with respect to the task. In fact, this coefficient was exactly zero in the case of STACKEXCHANGE. These ranking differences can be striking: for instance, repetitive structure was the strongest feature in JOKES but ranked on average as the least important feature. This experience reinforces the idea that Flock should balance popular suggestions with outlier but potentially very informative suggestions: a classic exploration vs. exploitation tradeoff.

Not only are workers individually poor at predicting feature importance, but the number of workers that suggest each feature is a weak indicator of relative importance. Here, τ ranges between -0.244 and 0.556. When τ is larger, semi-random exploration of the feature space weighted by the number of suggestions for each feature would reasonably discover important features; when τ is small, it would be a poor approach. These results demonstrate the strength of machine learning algorithms in revealing "surprising" features — features that people would not expect to be important.

Combining crowds and machines is better than using either in isolation. On average, hybrid systems that use both crowd-nominated and machine-extracted features improved upon the crowd-only approach by 7%, and on machine-only approaches by 8% (on an absolute scale). While crowd-nominated features are useful and potentially provide more information than machine-generated features, crowds are not always consistent in how they label features [6], and are thus less reliable than completely automatic approaches. By combining these two types of features, we can then take advantage of the strengths of both. For example, a decision-tree approach improves overall accuracy in WIKIPEDIA and STACKEXCHANGE by 7% and 9%, respectively, in comparison to using engineered features, and 6% in comparison to using crowd-nominated features. Figure 6 shows the tree generated by this approach.

The crowd helped most when a Wikipedia page does not have obvious visual or structural indications of needing additional work (e.g. missing citations or very short sections). In these cases, the decision tree often predicts incorrectly, but the crowd focusing on these examples nominates features related to the content of the article (e.g. level of detail) to help differentiate. If we examine the individual nodes where subtrees were added, we find the performance increases here are substantial — 12% in the case of WIKIPEDIA. For different parts of the tree, crowds nominated different features, and again, different features turn out to be important for each subtree. For example, covering a topic broadly and in detail was important when an article contained broken links, but article complexity and text relevance were important when it did not.

In cases when the total number of features is large (e.g., when using n-gram features), performance using either logistic regression or hybridized logistic regression was comparable: for REVIEWS, accuracy using the first approach is 0.92 (AUC=0.96) and 0.90 (AUC=0.90) using the second; for JOKES, the resulting accuracies were 0.65 (AUC=0.64) and 0.63 (AUC=0.64) respectively. Overall, improvements are substantial: 5% over crowd-nominated features for PAINTINGS and 5% over off-the-shelf features for REVIEWS, the next-best performing method for each.

Scale

It may not be realistic to pay workers to label several features for each item to be classified, especially as the number of inputs grows. We thus wanted to see whether we could learn individual classifiers for features that the crowd had nominated, using off-the-shelf features. Such an approach would enable Flock to scale to inputs of arbitrary size with no additional crowd input required, after gathering training data (or feature labels) for a small subset of examples. We expanded the WIKIPEDIA dataset to 1000 examples, instead of 400 previously. For each feature, we trained a bigram classifier on random subsets of 200 labeled examples, and predicted the feature value for the other 800 examples. Across all ten human-nominated features, we obtained a mean accuracy of 0.84 (mean AUC=0.61).

Using these predicted feature values, we again attempted the original prediction task. A model using only these predicted features had an accuracy of 0.74 (AUC=0.74), and a hybrid model that combined these predicted features with off-the-shelf features had an accuracy of 0.79 (AUC=0.79). Only the original *Hybrid* condition with crowd-provided feature values attained better performance. Future work could look at more expressive off-the-shelf classifiers to further improve performance; for some features (e.g., if an article contained reputable references), the bi-gram classifier performed at chance.

Limitations

While our results suggest that our approach generally improves on existing methods, there are several limitations to the system. Like machine-only classifiers, performance suffers when class membership is potentially inconsistent (i.e. in cases where extrinsic factors strongly influence class membership, e.g., JOKES, where a joke may only become popular because it was the first to be posted).

And in some cases such as REVIEWS, a straightforward application of machine learning approaches already performs reasonably well. Although crowds can improve on the performance of these systems (e.g. 92% accuracy using a hybrid system vs. 87% using only off-the-shelf features), the tradeoff between improved performance and cost of crowdsourcing additional features should be considered. In the opposite case, where the machine-only model is poor to begin with (e.g. JOKES), using just crowd features alone can lead to performance comparable to a hybrid model, underlining the importance of comparing these different approaches. In this case, text models were unable to extract useful signals of popular appeal, possibly because such models work best with longer documents and a large number of examples.

Specific to Flock is its dependence on whether features can be easily perceived and identified by a crowd worker. Even if the crowd is poor at guessing, Flock can still perform reasonably well if the crowd can identify differentiating characteristics (e.g. "Does the joke use repetition?"). But while the crowd can generate useful features, both objective and subjective, they sometimes make suggestions that are restatements of the problem ("This seemed more genuine" for REVIEWS), or are too subjective ("It made me laugh" for JOKES) to be similarly interpreted by different workers. The phrasing of the prediction task is important in avoiding these degenerate features. Also, if features are hard to come up with, the features that do matter may not end up being captured in the first place.

We note that gathering more features does not always result in improved performance (i.e. the curse of dimensionality). In all cases, feature selection methods are useful in identifying the features that truly matter.

Finally, while Flock is designed as a tool with significant automation behind it, a laboratory user study which compares Flock with other workflows would provide insight into how it is used in practice.

DISCUSSION

Through Flock, we can build classifiers that are both effective and interpretable. As opposed to off-the-shelf models that use thousands of features and require significant effort to understand, models generated by Flock use explainable crowd-nominated features. We see several promising future directions: in improving the feature nomination process, in considering monetary, developer and computation costs in combination, and in devising methods to better automate such crowd-machine systems. Further, as Flock's design is fairly modular, each component (e.g., feature nomination, feature aggregation, or learning algorithms) can be easily replaced as more effective approaches are found.

Improving feature nomination

To start, we consider possible improvements to Flock's feature nomination process. Currently, examples are paired at random, and the crowd has little guidance as to the type of features to produce. By instead providing similar examples to users, alignable differences between these examples can become more salient (e.g., if one wanted users to focus on article layout when judging Wikipedia article quality by presenting two articles with similar content) [15]. Further, curriculum learning suggests that providing progressively more difficult-to-categorize training examples for training may further improve the crowd's ability to identify subtler features [42].

Different interfaces may also lead to beneficial outcomes: an input-agreement game, where users are incentivized to describe examples using keywords to each other to see if they were presented the same example, may uncover other features [27]. In cases where a larger number of examples can be presented simultaneously (e.g., images), complementary agreement games would allow users to rapidly identify and categorize examples with common characteristics [26]. For highly specialized prediction tasks, automatically targeting groups of workers, possibly by demographic [29], may also improve the quality of nominated features (e.g., identifying art lovers to build a classifier for Monet paintings).

Alternatively, exploring other approaches to feature aggregation such as tagged hierarchies [7] may lead to higher quality features, but at higher cost. More sophisticated algorithms could automatically identify high-level candidate features by clustering on subsets of confused examples when it is possible to automatically generate a large number of low-level features [33]. Pairing examples near the classifier's decision boundary, where the examples are currently most confused, is also a potential approach to improving performance at subnodes of a tree.

One downside to hybridized crowd-machine learning systems is monetary cost, especially with larger datasets. In some cases it may not be financially feasible to permanently wire crowd feature labeling into a system. We see several ways forward: to use Flock to prototype machine feature-driven systems, to more intelligently utilize crowd features, or to learn and then replace these features altogether.

In its current form, Flock could be used as a prototyping tool. While features that the crowd nominates may not be easy to code, our goal is to instead provide inspiration for related machine-extractable features. This approach allows the user to prototype features and understand their effectiveness before sinking hours into writing code to extract them.

We may also consider a system that directly integrates direct crowd guesses and machine features, as collecting a single prediction for each example is significantly cheaper than gathering multiple features. Our initial experiments are promising: on average, the resulting classifier performs better than either guessing or a machine-only classifier, but worse than the complete hybrid model. On ARTISTS, a hybrid system combining the crowd's direct predictions and off-the-shelf features had an accuracy of 0.72 (AUC=0.77). Future hybrid systems could weigh a crowd's direct predictions more heavily amongst other nominated features.

Alternatively, decision-theoretic models could step in to optimize the balance between crowd and machine features [8, 21]. Decision trees could then be optimized for cost-effectiveness and performance by using crowd-nominated features deeper in the hierarchy. Multi-armed bandit strategies could help balance the tradeoff between exploration (gathering more features and labels for these features) and exploitation (improving the quality of specific features or optimizing the existing set of features). Using an active learning approach, one could model the informativeness of each crowd feature, and selectively query the crowd for specific features on specific examples when needed, but also have the flexibility to simply generate more features on-demand.

And while crowd-nominated features improve the performance of machine learning systems, a natural goal would be to eventually replace each crowd feature with its own machine learning classifier. Our analysis of the WIKIPEDIA dataset shows promise in trying to learn classifiers that predicts crowd responses [37], assuming that crowd behavior can be effectively encoded in the classifier's feature space. Another approach could be to have the crowd recursively break down features into simpler sub-features (e.g. "whether a painting uses warm colors" could potentially be broken down into multiple instances of "whether a painting contains a particular color"), until each is simple enough to be automatically extracted. Alternatively, the crowd might be able to author that classifier themselves with appropriate end-user machine learning tools (e.g., [11]).

CONCLUSION

In this paper, we integrate crowdsourcing into machine learning to develop hybrid learners with crowd-nominated features, machine-driven aggregation of these features, and targeted hybrids that use both crowd and machine features. We present Flock, a machine learning platform that allows end users to inspect existing models, launch targeted, crowd-driven feature generation tasks, and guide the feature aggregation and selection process. In an evaluation across domains such as quality evaluation and deception detection, these hybrid systems offer significantly improved performance. Hybrid crowd-machine learning systems may offer a route to rapid prototyping and exploration of the feature space, even in traditionally difficult domains. Flock suggests a future where an end user could create a machine learning system just by explaining the prediction goal into a free-form textbox. A combination of crowds and algorithms could take over from there to collect examples, extract features, then tune and monitor a classifier that becomes useful to the end user within hours.

ACKNOWLEDGMENTS

We would like to thank Noah Goodman, Walter Lasecki, and our reviewers for their invaluable input, as well as CrowdFlower for their support. This work was supported by NSF Grant 1351131 and a Stanford Graduate Fellowship.

REFERENCES

1. Crowdflower. `http://www.crowdflower.com`.
2. Anderson, A., Huttenlocher, D., Kleinberg, J., and Leskovec, J. Discovering value from community activity on focused question answering sites: a case study of stack overflow. In *Proc. KDD* (2012).
3. André, P., Kittur, A., and Dow, S. P. Crowd synthesis: Extracting categories and clusters from complex data. In *Proc. CSCW* (2014).
4. Attenberg, J., Ipeirotis, P. G., and Provost, F. J. Beat the machine: Challenging workers to find the unknown unknowns. In *Proc. AAAIW* (2011).
5. Blumenstock, J. E. Automatically assessing the quality of wikipedia articles. *UCB School of Information* (2008).
6. Branson, S., Wah, C., Schroff, F., Babenko, B., Welinder, P., Perona, P., and Belongie, S. Visual recognition with humans in the loop. In *Proc. ECCV*. 2010.
7. Chilton, L. B., Little, G., Edge, D., Weld, D. S., and Landay, J. A. Cascade: Crowdsourcing taxonomy creation. In *Proc. CHI* (2013).
8. Dai, P., Weld, D. S., et al. Decision-theoretic control of crowd-sourced workflows. In *Proc. AAAI* (2010).
9. Deng, J., Krause, J., and Fei-Fei, L. Fine-grained crowdsourcing for fine-grained recognition. In *Proc. CVPR* (2013).
10. Domingos, P. A few useful things to know about machine learning. *Communications of the ACM* (2012).
11. Fails, J. A., and Olsen Jr, D. R. Interactive machine learning. In *Proc. IUI* (2003).
12. Fogarty, J., Tan, D., Kapoor, A., and Winder, S. Cueflik: interactive concept learning in image search. In *Proc. CHI* (2008).
13. Gazzaniga, M. S., LeDoux, J. E., Gazzaniga, M., and LeDoux, J. *The integrated mind*. 1978.
14. Gentner, D., Loewenstein, J., and Thompson, L. Learning and transfer: A general role for analogical encoding. *Journal of Educational Psychology* (2003).
15. Gentner, D., and Markman, A. B. Structure mapping in analogy and similarity. *American Psychologist* (1997).
16. Gomes, R. G., Welinder, P., Krause, A., and Perona, P. Crowdclustering. In *Advances in Neural Information Processing Systems* (2011), 558–566.
17. Hall, M., Frank, E., Holmes, G., Pfahringer, B., Reutemann, P., and Witten, I. H. The weka data mining software: an update. *ACM SIGKDD Explorations* (2009).
18. Hammond, K. R., Hursch, C. J., and Todd, F. J. Analyzing the components of clinical inference. *Psychological review* (1964).
19. Hartmann, B., Abdulla, L., Mittal, M., and Klemmer, S. R. Authoring sensor-based interactions by demonstration with direct manipulation and pattern recognition. In *Proc. CHI* (2007).
20. Kahneman, D. A perspective on judgment and choice: mapping bounded rationality. *American psychologist* (2003).
21. Kamar, E., Kapoor, A., and Horvitz, E. Lifelong learning for acquiring the wisdom of the crowd. In *Proc. JCAI* (2013).
22. Kim, J., Cheng, J., and Bernstein, M. S. Ensemble: Exploring complementary strengths of leaders and crowds in creative collaboration. In *Proc. CSCW* (2014).
23. Kittur, A., Peters, A. M., Diriye, A., and Bove, M. Standing on the schemas of giants: socially augmented information foraging. In *Proc. CSCW* (2014).
24. Lasecki, W. S., Song, Y. C., Kautz, H., and Bigham, J. P. Real-time crowd labeling for deployable activity recognition. In *Proc. CSCW* (2013).
25. Law, E. *Attribute Learning using Joint Human and Machine Computation*. PhD thesis, 2012.
26. Law, E., Settles, B., Snook, A., Surana, H., Von Ahn, L., and Mitchell, T. Human computation for attribute and attribute value acquisition. In *FPGV* (2011).
27. Law, E., and Von Ahn, L. Input-agreement: a new mechanism for collecting data using human computation games. In *Proc. CHI*, ACM (2009).
28. Le, J., Edmonds, A., Hester, V., and Biewald, L. Ensuring quality in crowdsourced search relevance evaluation: The effects of training question distribution. In *Proc. SIGIR* (2010).
29. Li, H., Zhao, B., and Fuxman, A. The wisdom of minority: Discovering and targeting the right group of workers for crowdsourcing. In *Proc. WWW* (2014).
30. Lowe, D. G. Object recognition from local scale-invariant features. In *ICCV* (1999).
31. Ott, M., Choi, Y., Cardie, C., and Hancock, J. T. Finding deceptive opinion spam by any stretch of the imagination. In *Proc. ACL* (2011).
32. Parameswaran, A., Sarma, A. D., Garcia-Molina, H., Polyzotis, N., and Widom, J. Human-assisted graph search: it's okay to ask questions. *Proc. VLDB* (2011).
33. Parikh, D., and Grauman, K. Interactively building a discriminative vocabulary of nameable attributes. In *CVPR* (2011).
34. Parkash, A., and Parikh, D. Attributes for classifier feedback. In *Proc. ECCV*. 2012.
35. Patel, K., Bancroft, N., Drucker, S. M., Fogarty, J., Ko, A. J., and Landay, J. Gestalt: integrated support for implementation and analysis in machine learning. In *Proc. UIST* (2010).

36. Patel, K., Fogarty, J., Landay, J. A., and Harrison, B. Investigating statistical machine learning as a tool for software development. In *Proc. CHI* (2008).

37. Raykar, V. C., Yu, S., Zhao, L. H., Valadez, G. H., Florin, C., Bogoni, L., and Moy, L. Learning from crowds. *JMLR* (2010).

38. Rzeszotarski, J., and Kittur, A. Crowdscape: interactively visualizing user behavior and output. In *Proc. UIST* (2012).

39. Rzeszotarski, J. M., and Kittur, A. Instrumenting the crowd: using implicit behavioral measures to predict task performance. In *Proc. UIST* (2011).

40. Settles, B. Closing the loop: Fast, interactive semi-supervised annotation with queries on features and instances. In *Proc. EMNLP* (2011).

41. Sheng, V. S., Provost, F., and Ipeirotis, P. G. Get another label? improving data quality and data mining using multiple, noisy labelers. In *Proc. KDD* (2008).

42. Skinner, B. F. Reinforcement today. *American Psychologist* (1958).

43. Snow, R., O'Connor, B., Jurafsky, D., and Ng, A. Y. Cheap and fast—but is it good?: evaluating non-expert annotations for natural language tasks. In *Proc. EMNLP* (2008).

44. Talbot, J., Lee, B., Kapoor, A., and Tan, D. S. Ensemblematrix: interactive visualization to support machine learning with multiple classifiers. In *Proc. CHI* (2009).

45. Vijayanarasimhan, S., and Grauman, K. Large-scale live active learning: Training object detectors with crawled data and crowds. In *CVPR* (2011).

46. Wais, P., Lingamneni, S., Cook, D., Fennell, J., Goldenberg, B., Lubarov, D., Marin, D., and Simons, H. Towards building a high-quality workforce with mechanical turk. In *Proc. NIPSCSS* (2010).

47. Whitehill, J., Ruvolo, P., Wu, T., Bergsma, J., and Movellan, J. R. Whose vote should count more: Optimal integration of labels from labelers of unknown expertise. In *Proc. NIPS* (2009).

48. Yu, L., Kittur, A., and Kraut, R. E. Distributed analogical idea generation: Inventing with crowds. In *Proc. CHI* (2014).

49. Yu, L., and Nickerson, J. V. Cooks or cobblers?: crowd creativity through combination. In *Proc. CHI* (2011).

Bridge the Gap! What Can Work Design in Crowdwork Learn from Work Design Theories?

Obinna Anya
IBM Research – Almaden
650 Harry Road, San Jose CA 95120
obanya@us.ibm.com

ABSTRACT

Integrating crowd-based systems to organizations is highly complex. A major of source of this complexity stems from the nature of organizational work design. Work design and configurations of work performance, in the traditional organizational model, are tightly woven into the structure and functions of organizations, whereas crowdwork leverages an undefined network of people without an organized managerial or hierarchical model. This paper examines work design theories in organizational studies with a view to exploring their potential for addressing the fundamental challenges of work design in organizational crowdwork. Drawing on review of extant literature on crowdwork and analysis of perspectives in work design theories, the paper outlines ways in which crowdsourcing research, on one hand, can interpret and utilize work design theories, and on the other, contribute to redesigning work design theories to keep pace with the important and rapid transformation of work from the traditional staffing paradigm to crowd and open models.

Author Keywords

Crowdsourcing; Work Design Theory; Organizational Work.

ACM Classification Keywords

H.5.3 [Computer-Supported Cooperative Work]:

General Terms

Human Factors; Design

INTRODUCTION

Social computing technologies have made possible new techniques and tools for harnessing the skills and expertise of the crowd – "an undefined (and generally large) network of people" [36] – for problem solving. Organizations have begun to embrace this trend as a way of scaling and enhancing work execution, with businesses accomplishing work via crowdsourcing sites such as InnoCentive and Mechanical Turk, for example. However, taking work outside the realm of formal, clearly defined, organizational structures, either as a form of outsourcing to the crowd or a new way of distributing work beyond the traditional employee base, is inherently disruptive. Often, the processes required to implement crowdwork in organizations appear to stand in diametric dissonance with the closed and structured models of work performance in those organizations.

Organizational crowdwork thus poses interesting challenges for both academic and industrial research along multiple perspectives, including the social, human factors, organizational, and technological dimensions. Despite the remarkable promises of the crowdwork model, the development of effective structures that will establish crowdwork as an organizational process remains poorly understood. For example, there have been reports of significant difficulties in managing work and coordinating engagements with the crowd within the framework of existing organizational structures [46]. Current crowdsourcing systems appear to focus predominantly on micro-tasks [39], and hardly take account of the rich and complex nature of organizational work [20, 1]. To date, researchers report that poorly designed work requests remain a major cause of low work quality in organizational crowdwork [20, 1, 16, 47].

Arguably, a major barrier to effective integration of the crowd work model in organizations stems from the nature of organizational work design. Work design[1] refers to *the study, creation, and modification of the composition, content, structure, and environment within which jobs and roles are enacted* [56]. For more than forty years, research in work design has contributed to a better understanding of "the processes and outcomes of how work is structured, organized, experienced, and enacted" [29]. Work design theories remain a pivotal factor in the design of effective structures for managing the relationships between organizations and those that perform the labor for them. At the core of work design research is the idea of the central role of work design as an actionable feature of the context

CSCW 2015, March 14–18, 2015, Vancouver, BC, Canada.

http://dx.doi.org/10.1145/2675133.2675227

[1] In the work design literature, the terms "work design" and "job design" are often used interchangeably (e.g. [30, 61, 57]). As such, "work" and "job" are treated as the same unit of analysis by most work design researchers. Campion et al. [7] observe that choosing an appropriate unit of analysis in any work design initiative is "a pragmatic issue".

of work [45], and a core component of the execution of work and the experience of workers in any work arrangement. As a result, work design offers a basis for how work – at any level and for whatever purpose, e.g. crowdwork – should be conceived and composed.

Historically, organizations have enjoyed an implicit capability to prefigure, organize, and enact the organization and management of work performance [53, 65], including the composition and management of skills and resources needed to perform work [83]. Crowdwork follows the open world assumption [74, p. 1, 35], and leverages a horizontally distributed and undefined network of workers that lacks the very structure that has enabled organizations to manage work performance so efficiently. As a result, the capacity of organizations to structure the work environment and manage work performance appears to be lost, or adversely weakened, in crowdwork. This gives rise to a range of open questions for researchers in crowdsourcing. For example, how can research enable organizations to manage their role as the ordering structures for work in crowdwork? How can the design of work be understood and delineated for enhanced work quality and worker satisfaction in organizational crowdwork?

This paper describes the challenges that researchers and practitioners face when designing work and managing work performance in organizational crowdsourcing. The analytic framework is organized around a systematic review of the literature in crowdsourcing, as well as an exploration of theories of work design with a view to ascertaining what could be learned from them for the benefit of research and practice in organizational crowdwork. Given the long-standing tradition in CSCW [32, 14, 33] to ground the design of computer support for work on established theories and methodologies that often come from other fields, CSCW has a crucial role to play in guiding thoughts toward effective appropriation of work design theories for crowdwork design. It is the hope that this synthesis will contribute to defining more effective approaches for organizational uses of the crowd by sensitizing the crowdsourcing research community to build bridges with scholars in other disciplines who have addressed similar challenges that militate against the development of effective computer support for organizational crowdwork[2].

Organizational Crowdwork

A wide range of terminology, e.g. crowdsourcing, citizen science, human computation, open innovation, collective intelligence, and participatory sensing, is used to describe the phenomenon of leveraging crowds to accomplish work of different forms and shapes [46, 37, 35, 20, 8]. This paper focuses on *organizational crowdwork*. By organization crowdwork, I mean *work that is organized by an organization, and performed for the organization by paid distributed crowd workers, and for which the organization stands to make business profit.* In this sense, organizational crowdwork mirrors fundamentally the nature of work in organizational studies and CSCW. As such, how it is designed and constituted through a set of relationships that connects organizations, people, technologies, and work activities, becomes very critical.

The definition relates nicely with the notion of enterprise crowdsourcing in [89], and has a lot of resemblance in meaning with Kittur et al.'s concept of "paid, online crowd work" [46]. Organizational crowdwork offers remarkable opportunities for on-demand and scalable work performance, social mobility, and improved productivity, but has tremendous implications on such things as incentives, intellectual property rights, and information security. For the remainder of this paper, we will highlight the challenges of work design in organizational crowdwork, and discuss perspectives in work design theories with a focus on the implications for crowdwork design.

THE CHALLENGE OF WORK DESIGN IN ORGANIZATIONAL CROWDWORK

To bring to light the challenge of work design in organizational crowdwork, existing literature on crowdsourcing and related research areas, such as human computation, CSCW, CHI, and future work design [89, 20, 74, 77, 1, 22, 46], was reviewed. It was found that very few papers particularly in crowdsourcing have focused directly on the problem of work design. However, the challenge of work design on organizational crowdsourcing has been well highlighted in several studies across the fields searched. I describe a meta-analysis to underscore the challenges.

Study Approach

The approach adopted in this work was a structured literature review. The proceedings of CHI, CSCW, HCOMP, Information Systems and related conferences/workshops from 2010 to February 2014 were searched for papers that have directly or indirectly highlighted the challenge and implication of work design in crowdsourcing. The following keywords, which have correlations with crowdwork design and are deemed relevant in understanding the problem of work design, were used in the search: *work coordination, quality of work, worker satisfaction, motivation, collaboration, knowledge sharing, value capture, crowdsourcing design, crowdwork environment, and task design*. A number of other related terms were used, for example, *incentivization and microtask* were used as related terms for motivation and task design respectively. After removing duplicates, editorial introductions, posters,

[2] At a panel discussion at the First International Conference on Human Computation and Crowdsourcing (HCOMP) in Palm Spring, California in November 2013, it was noted that most of the problems we face in crowdsourcing today relate nicely to challenges that have been (partly) addressed in other disciplines, e.g. social science, humanities, and organizational studies. As such, research in crowdwork could potentially benefit from works in these disciplines if we "mind the gap" between crowdsourcing and the disciplines.

tutorials, and publications that contain the search keywords but focus on other issues, the total of 76 papers were left. They were reviewed to identify the challenges of work design to organizational crowdwork. Other studies in crowdsourcing that have adopted the same analytical tool of systematic literature review appear in [93, 34, 67, 82].

Analysis and Findings

Review followed a meta-analysis of extant literature on crowdwork. Data collection and analysis were carried out simultaneously. Initial search included a small set of search terms; as the retrieved publications were analyzed, new relevant terms were found, and used to build a bigger set of search terms for subsequent searches. Attributes and categories related to *the challenge of crowdwork design* were identified. Related attributes and categories were collected and abstracted into themes. For example, through identification, iterative comparison, and grouping of the characteristics commonly associated with the search terms, four broad themes that relate to the challenges of work design in organizational crowdsourcing were identified. These include: a) *Organizational motivation, concerns, and challenges (C1)*, b) *Worker desires and fears (C2),* c) *Work representation in crowdwork (C3)*, and d) *Configuring and managing organizational crowdwork environment (C4).* See Table 1 for more details.

Organizational Motivation, Concerns and Challenges: The papers reviewed indicate that organizations turn to the crowd for a variety of reasons, including access to a scalable workforce, enhancing competitive advantage, advancing understanding, and creating new knowledge resources (see also [20, 89, 35]).

Emergent Themes	Descriptors
Organizational Motivation, Concerns, and Challenges (C1)	• Increased productivity, value capture, and competitive advantage [89, 20] • Reduction in cost of labor [22] • Poor work quality, fraudulent tasks, untimely delivery of results [46, 1, 8, 16, 59, 76] • Security and confidentiality concerns, intellectual property (IP) leakage and loss of 'tribal' knowledge [20, 49, 42, 58, 59] • Workers' dysfunctional behaviors, gaming, and the difficulty in holding workers accountable [16, 59, 25, 90, 49, 48] • Task often misunderstood by workers [16] • Task decomposition, work coordination, and direction-setting or supervision [46, 1] • Safeguarding organizational knowledge capital [90, 22, 71] • Access to scalable knowledge and creativity, advancing understanding [90, 71, 20] • Involves hidden overhead [20, 1, 90, 19, 8]
Worker Desires and Fears (C2)	• Poor articulation of tasks [1, 34, 25] • Low pay, uncertainty about pay, exploitation, and dehumanization [46, 21, 58, 76] • Crowdwork as human-as-a-service leads to microlabor alienation [75, 74, 41, 39, 85] • Belonging and self-protective motives [46] • Job security, and prospects for career growth and skill development [46, 70] • Feedback, participative decision making, nuanced support, perspective-taking are hardly supported, uncommunicative requesters [1, 46, 76] • Seemingly arbitrary work rejections, lean job role and worker invisibility leading to alienation and unethical work practices [40, 75, 76, 54] • Both extrinsic and intrinsic motivations matter [44, 38, 70, 81, 73]
Work Representation (C3)	• Poor work decomposition, workflow, and result aggregation mechanisms lead to low work quality [16, 50, 46, 2, 8, 25, 79, 59] • Work design for the anonymous worker [40] • Task descriptions focus on microwork and lack contexts of work [39, 41, 37] • Task significance [46, 68] • Obscures the complexity of organizational work, workflows, task dependencies, and requester-worker relationship [1, 77, 75] • Tension in determining appropriate levels of work visibility leading to inefficiency [77, 46] • Prohibitive time limits, and short-lived work processes [76, 73, 34]
Configuring and Managing the Crowdwork Environment (C4)	• Incentives focus narrowly on motivation and other simple mechanisms [73, 68] • Access to the crowd exist in two categories – internal and external crowds [20, 1] • Uncertainty in crowdwork environment and work management; varying non-standardized approaches to work design, process management, task assignment, and result aggregation [46, 25, 1, 20, 46, 34, 76, 89] • Poor alignment between the interests of workers and organizations [73, 46, 8] • Trust mechanisms [12, 73, 59] • Minimal support for large-scale organizational tasks [37, 1, 20] • Crowd knowledge management [1, 20, 71] • Governance and compliance issues, payment, taxation, labor laws, and control mechanism [67, 73, 46, 22, 25, 90]

Table 1. Challenges of organizational crowdwork design (the categories are not mutually exclusive; papers reviewed fit into more than one category).

Analysis shows that a much deeper concern and challenge for organizations was how to harness the crowd workforce within the context of an economy that equally "brings new social classes to the fore and creates a different world for business" [3]. The problems in organizational crowdwork embody technical, social, economic, organizational, sociological, and even philosophical issues. However, organizations and crowdwork designers, as indicated in most papers reviewed, are yet to devise adequate work design techniques for managing the interdependencies among these dimensions of work design problems. For example, getting quality work done through a crowdsourcing system and accounting for overhead remain a significant challenge [1, 8].

Worker Desires and Fears: From this perspective, this study indicates that a fundamental challenge of organizational crowdwork is that designers, in framing crowdwork as professional work [46], fail to adequately conceptualize the role of workers and the relationship they have with organizations that request work from them. As noted by Silberman et al. [75], all too often crowdworkers are treated just like an API call. The crowdsourcing literature is heavy with references to the term "human-as-a-service" – a technology and business model that views the crowdwork labor market as large distributed systems in which a worker is analogous to a processing node that can solve a task requiring human intelligence [46, 74, 41]. While "as-a-service" is laudable as a technical concept allowing programmers to manage complexity and improve efficiency in large-scale systems development, it strikes a different note when used with humans, and suggests "a hierarchy of value and division of labor" [41, p.13] in which the server (worker) is to prone to manipulation, by duty or by reward, to the will of the served (organization).

Experience, however, has highlighted the potential inefficacy of the "as-a-service" model. In a study on redesigning the assembly lines at IBM in the 1950-60s, Vough and Asbell [87], cited by [88], point out that although a (factory) worker can be manipulated to enrich his company at his own expense, the truth is that "a man on the job can outfox the company almost every time". Crowdwork design models need to allay the legitimate fears of workers, and meet their desires, for example, by going beyond low-level tasks and deskilled labor prevalent today to designing enriched work models, for example, with support for trajectories to learning and career growth [46].

Work Representation: Analysis shows that crowd and open systems enable, and even demand, fundamentally different approaches to designing and representing work. In much of the work reviewed, a good number of which focused on Amazon's Mechanical Turk as the system of study, work is represented as a set of small, independent, and homogenous tasks, known as microtasks [46, 41]. Microtask offers designers a viable approach to design work for unknown workers, where the organization is concerned, and rightly so, by such issues as intellectual property leakage. However, in practice, microtasking involves a lot of hidden overhead that are often not accounted for in crowdwork design [1]. There are indications that microtask impoverishes job content, and curtails the creativity of workers, who hardly see the larger context, i.e. the significance [68], of the work they do. For example, there are some indications that workers are able to introduce creative ways of doing work that requesting organizations wouldn't have known to ask for [50]. Representing work as microtasks hardly supports such universally crucial work design goals as designing for task significance, autonomy, creativity, and worker satisfaction.

Some papers reviewed also indicate that most crowdwork design approaches lead to poor specification often because of lack of "direction-setting" [46, p.1304], and the fact that the requester and the worker occupy separate worlds demarcated by the organization-crowd boundary [46, 1]. Indeed, analysis suggests that existing models of work representation in crowdwork do not reflect not only the complexity of organizational work, but also the complexity of organizational crowdsourcing.

Configuring and Managing the Crowdwork Environment: The papers reviewed reveal that organizations face an enormous challenge in dealing with a complex work environment that lacks a physical job site, often includes anonymous participants [22], and is characterized by an economy that is "vast, automatic, and invisible" [3]. As noted by Emery and Trist [18, p.21] nearly half a century ago, a major challenge in organizational change is that "the environmental contexts in which organizations exist are themselves changing, at an increasing rate, and towards increasing complexity". Literature review shows that designers are yet to devise effective techniques of computer support for work performance in the crowd work environment.

Many forms of open and crowd work environments lack adequate support for control, management and authority. Analysis indicates that crowdwork environments represent particular sites in which dueling tensions play out between organizations and workers. Opening up access to the work introduces potential for shifts in how it is controlled and managed – taxation, recruitment, knowledge management, work supervision, etc. As indicated by references to poor quality in most papers reviewed, workers often exert dominant control over the process of work performance, often leading to gaming of the work process. This resonates with a finding by Emery and Trist [18] namely; an organization can design a task in a way that will meet its business goals. However, it can hardly describe in the same concepts the specific course that the performance of the task will take. This is because the process is mostly affected by numerous factors that play out differently and even unpredictably in *open and crowd work environments* – where the traditional hierarchical and managerial methods of organizing and assigning work do not exist, and where work could be assigned outside functional roles or an organization's employee base, primarily on short-lived and loose-contractual bases.

Discussion

The four emergent themes described above lay the foundation for understanding the critical role of work design "as a strategy for attempting to improve simultaneously the productivity and the quality of the work experience of employees" [31, p.250] in crowdwork. The results illuminate the central fact of the disruptions or what Weisbord [92, p.196] calls "the turbulent environment" that organizations face in using the crowd. Organizations are oriented pre-theoretically, at least within orthodox social science – in general, and work design theory – in particular, as an objective structure that shapes the conduct out of which work emerges [53]. As noted earlier, organizational influence on the conduct of work becomes weakened in crowdwork as outside events, characterized by increasing complexity and new forms of participation that leverage technology-enabled sociality, interacted to produce conditions organizations can hardly control nor afford to ignore [18, 92].

The findings equally illustrate the interplay between the characteristics of work (representation, configuration and management) and the characteristics of people (organizations and crowdworkers), which, according to Hackman et al. [31], is essential to determine when a particular work design will lead to beneficial outcome, and when it will not. The interplay between characteristics of work and characteristics of people dovetails nicely with three "critical psychological states", which underlie most perspectives in work design research [31], and which describe the factors necessary for individuals in contemporary organizations to perform effectively on their jobs. These include *1) experienced meaningfulness of the work, 2) experienced responsibility of the work, and 3) knowledge of work results.* The three psychological states postulate that individuals have positive experience about their work to the extent that they *learn of their performance through feedback* (knowledge of work results), *feel personally accountable and responsible for the work results* (experienced responsibility), and have *participated on a task that they care about and consider valuable* (experienced meaningfulness).

Work can be designed to evoke a sense of meaningfulness when it is designed to address such issues as (see also Table 1): a) high degree of task significance, b) a clear cycle of perceived closure of a work process, c) high visibility of process transformation and of final work outcome, c) built-in opportunities for learning and career growth, and d) increased trust and proper alignment between the interests of organizations and workers. Designing work for experienced responsibility entails including support for a) increased sense of belonging and self-protective motives, b) greater participative decision making, and c) higher worker visibility. Knowledge of results calls for a work design approach that, among other things, a) provides support for feedback, and b) addresses issues of security, confidentiality, and knowledge management in crowdwork within a manageable work environment. Taken together, the three psychological states emphasize that quality improvement in crowdwork highly depends on a work design approach that recognizes both organizations and crowdworkers as integral to the innovation process of the organization.

The issues denoted by the four emergent themes resonate equally well with the politics of making work visible as demonstrated in the works of Suchman [78] and Bannon [4], and the concept of value co-creation in service science [86]. The questions of work, how work is represented, and what the various entities involved in the doing of work (should) afford to each other, have been of interest to CSCW. Arguably, they take a more intimate tone in crowdwork. Their understanding will potentially enable a better delineation of what resources and accounts of work practices organizations should provide, and which crowdworkers themselves should create and use for improved productivity and maximum worker satisfaction.

Next, I discuss perspectives in work design theories with a view to exploring their potentials and shortcomings in addressing the challenges of work design in organizational crowdwork.

PERSPECTIVES IN WORK DESIGN THEORIES

Work design research in organizational studies has led to a wide range of theories, models, and perspectives for dealing with the challenges of work performance [6, 62, 65, 30, 29, 88, 61, 60, 27, 30]. These theories have provided frameworks and tools for qualifying and gauging the experiences and behaviors of workers [30] and for evaluating and improving job outcomes and organizational productivity [65]. A number of major work design perspectives are discussed below. The list is not exhaustive; more comprehensive accounts of work design theories are available [13, 64, 83, 62, 60, 5, 6, 91, 57, 29, 63]. The goal here is to review relevant developments in work design theories that have influenced the design of work and employer-worker relationship in the doing of work, and highlight their implications for crowdwork research.

Job Simplification and Scientific Management: The founding principle of work design theories in this perspective, which took center stage during the Industrial Revolution, is that division of labor or the idea of breaking down complex jobs into simpler ones, could serve as a way of enhancing performance, improving worker dexterity, and reducing cost [64, 62]. By focusing on job simplification, the theories gave rise to empirical research that led to amelioration of the psychological consequences of repetitive tasks [64]. For example, the concepts of job rotation, horizontal job enlargement, and the recognition of the importance of employees' attitudes in shaping work behavior and productivity. The notion of job simplification is at the core of Taylor's idea of 'Scientific Management' [80], and is profoundly a part of almost all work design efforts of the industrial era and even beyond [64]. A central tenet of 'Scientific Management' is the application of science to the engineering of work processes in order to ensure maximum efficiency and benefit for both the employer and the employee.

Work Characterization: Interest in work characterization emerged in response to the Job Characteristic Model (JCM) introduced by [30]. JCM is perhaps one the most well-known and complete theories for characterizing work [83, 57], and seeks to explain job design for the important purpose of increasing worker motivation and improving job performance. According to JCM, any job can be described in terms of five 'core job characteristics', namely *skill variety, task identity, task significance, autonomy, and feedback*. JCM has catalyzed an impressive array of related research that has studied, for example, the impact of work redesign and worker attitude, absence and turnover, and the effects of work context on work satisfaction and performance [62, 83].

Process Improvement: Process improvement is a major tenet of quality improvement theory and a key concern in 'Scientific Management'. Work design theories for process improvement derive from the notion that understanding how work is accomplished in principle during various stages of the work process is key to successfully improve or redesign work [83, 29].Within and across organizational units, work is accomplished through processes involving "specific ordering of work activities across time and space" [11] during which value is added [86]. For process improvement to occur, all work activities in a work process must be known and formally specified.

Team Working: The sociotechnical systems theory (STS), conceptualized by Eric Trist was the first to take a broader organizational perspective on work design by focusing on teams rather than an individual worker [64]. The overarching goal of the STS theory is the joint optimization of the social and technical aspects of work design [83, 84]. It enhances job satisfaction and improves productivity through a design process that emphasizes the interdependencies among people, technology and the work environment [84]. Applications of STS theory gave rise to work design that reflects the actual engagement between employees and their work environment, serves as the basis for conceptualizing autonomous work groups, and underlies the formation of team-based structures now prevalent in organizations [64, 83].

Job Enrichment: Job enrichment includes approaches concerned with designing worker satisfiability into work. The goal is to overcome the problem of repetition and tedium that occur as a consequence of designing work to maximize efficiency [57]. An example of work design theory focusing on job enrichment is the Two-Factor Theory [62]. The perspective aims to build into people's jobs specific motivations and greater scope for personal achievement, recognition, and more challenging and responsible work [66]. The idea of job enrichment is central to contemporary notions such as learning on the job, worker independence, and empowerment [62].

Technology Support: Theories in this perspective aim primarily to account for work changes that occur as a result of the introduction of new technologies for work support. Two theories – technostructural change models (TCMs) and the adaptive structuration theory (AST) – are particularly prominent. TCMs explain organizational structure largely as a function of contextual factors such as size of organization, environment of work, technology, or scale operation [24]. They effect change in work design by altering the organization's technology and structure [83]. In practice, such change is achieved through such interventions as functional design, work reengineering, and structural designs including self-contained work units, matrix organizations, and network-based structures [83]. AST offers a framework for studying the variations in organizational change that occur as technologies are introduced and implemented. According to AST, technology use in organizations involves a great deal of appropriation that could be examined from two vantage points: the types of structures provided by technologies, and the structures that actually emerge as people work with these technologies. As such, AST offers new insights into the relationship between work design as intended by designers and the actual work practices that emerge over time.

Social Information Processing Perspective: This perspective argues that workers' job perceptions and attitudes do not primarily derive from objective work characteristics, nor from new technologies and tools used to support work, but rather from how the work is socially constructed by cues from such sources as co-workers, managers, clients, family members, as well as the worker's past behaviors and experiences [29, 72]. There is, to date, in work design research debate as to whether objective job characteristics, rather than social cues, determine how workers perceive and react to job [29, 62]. Many studies nevertheless show that it is important to consider both when designing work.

Interdisciplinary Perspective: Interdisciplinary perspective, introduced by Campion and colleagues [6], was aimed to broaden the work design literature beyond an almost exclusive focus on motivationally-oriented approaches by integrating views from other scientific fields. To achieve this, the perspective comprises four different models: 1) the mechanistic model, 2) the motivational model, 3) the perceptual model, and 4) the biological model [57, 62, 29]. Taking the models into account when designing work has been shown to result in increased efficiency, as well as reduced training costs and physical stress [57].

Shortcomings of Work Design Theories

Despite their long-standing status and enormous success in managing the person-job relationship [56, 88], work design theories have many shortcomings that may not be obvious to the crowdsourcing research community. Firstly, most approaches to work design were driven by narrow concerns posed by prevailing changes in work. For example, the scientific management was largely adopted as an off-shoot of the industrial revolution; TCMs and AST focused almost exclusively on understanding how technology use unfolds in the performance of work. As a result, the most general criticism of work design theories in organizational studies is that they are narrowly conceived [62]. An interesting trade-off to this, however, is that they focus on tangible organizational problems. For example, Grant et al. [29] note that work design theory and research has enabled practitioners to "describe, diagnose, and resolve important practical problems in organizations" [p.418], e.g. during the industrial revolution and the information age. While not ignoring the associated shortcoming, can crowdsourcing research take advantage of the ability of work deign theories to resolve the practical challenges in organizational crowdwork design?

Secondly, although work design theories aim to understand work characteristics for the purpose of improving individual and organizational outcomes, they focus on a limited set of characteristics and outcomes. They often fail to consider the overhead, antecedents, and contextual factors that influence or constraint the choice of work design [9, 62]. Work design antecedents can include internal organizational factors, such as managerial or supervisory style, nature of task, and organizational strategy; external factors, such as nature of environment, political or labor institutions, nature of labor markets, and social and economic customs; and crowdsourcing-related factors, such as trust, security, and IP leakage. In particular, JCM has been criticized for failing to recognize that the five job characteristics are not always separable aspects of jobs [10], and for encompassing a narrow range of characteristics that ignore such crucial factors as social and knowledge characteristics of work [62, 63]. Process improvement has been criticized because more often than not relevant implicit entities such as contextual variables and work practice activities that are crucial to work performance are poorly accounted for, and TCMs, for leading to downsizing and for lack of flexibility in task assignment. Arguably, crowdwork is affected by a much wider range of work characteristics. It thus becomes crucial for crowdsourcing research to identify those characteristics preferably by extending those in work design theories.

Thirdly, work design theories assume motivation to be the main or even sole mechanism that underlie the relationship between work features and outcomes, and, as such, do not fully identify individual and organizational factors that might influence the effectiveness or appropriateness of particular work configurations. For example, STS has been criticized for insufficient attention to organizational culture and individual differences [62]. Unfortunately, this is one area where crowdsourcing research, knowingly or unknowingly, appeared to echo work design research – with the increasing number of research in crowdwork that focus on motivation. Motivations and incentives play a crucial role in effecting how workers carry out their jobs in both traditional and crowdwork models, and help align the interests of employees and organizations [29, 73]. However, research [63, 55] has shown that there are other factors far and above motivations why people seek to work.

Finally, despite the critical role of work design theories [29], they have been criticized for their inability to explain adequately the design of work in new work environments [83], or how "the broader occupational and organizational context might impact work design" [56, p. 351]. In addition, there is remarkably little research-based guidance for the process of work design [62, 57], particularly in relation to crowd and open work models. Typically, work design is disruptive, and usually involves "a redistribution of responsibility and power" [62] that is often not evenly received by all stakeholders. This raises critical questions for organizational crowdsourcing, for example, to what extent should both organization and crowdworkers participate in work design and how should this process be managed? Work design is usually a dynamic and evolving intervention, rather than a straightforward or short-term one, that requires learning and adjustment. As such, consideration of all stakeholders (organization, crowdworkers, etc.), and alignment between the work design system and other organizational systems [60] – all of which require research-based guidance – become crucial.

THE INTEGRATIVE MODEL OF WORK DESIGN

Given the implications of the shortcomings of existing work design theories, a wide range of research efforts have focused on infusing new perspectives into work design research [27, 63, 57]. However, most efforts have focused largely on the shift toward knowledge work [17], the service-based economy [86], telecommuting [23], workplace virtuality [26], contract and temporary employment status [64], and corporate volunteering [28]. Little research has focused on redesigning work design theories for crowd and open work models.

One of the biggest attempts in work design research to redesign and elaborate work design theories to keep pace with changes in work is represented by the integrative model of work design [62, 57, 55, 28, 64, 29, 63]. Primarily, the model offers a basis for understanding how dimensions of a task, social, and the broader physical and organizational work environment as well as worker needs interrelate for improved outcome and satisfiability [55]. It acts a framework for adding new work features to work design, and gauging their impact on work outcome. It has led to an expansion of the view of work design from a narrow set of motivational work features to one that incorporates broader social, knowledge, and contextual elements [64, 27, 55]. The model emphasizes the inherent values of the "critical psychological states" [31] of work design, often underlined by the concept of Growth Need Strength, which is the preference or need workers have for stimulating and challenging work [57, 31].

The integrative model of work design is the result of research attempts to broaden work design theories to include task, physical, contextual, knowledge, and social characteristics of work, as well as to account for uncertainty, dynamism, proactivity, and creativity in the work performance [29, 62]. As a result, the model is basically an integration of both the classic and contemporary perspectives in work design [29]. Overall, scholars in work design make it clear that classic perspectives such as long-standing concerns with job simplification remain salient. But at the same time, they give added weight to calls to broaden the work design approach to account for changes brought about by advanced technologies, as well as the increasing interconnectedness, openness, and social mobility that have become the hallmark of today's workplace and workforce [62, 27, 64].

Efforts to elaborate work design through the integrative model have benefited from two emerging perspectives in work design, namely the relational and proactive perspectives [27]. Relational perspectives are concerned with how jobs, roles and tasks are more socially embedded in a networked world, while proactive perspectives are concerned with the notion of independent workers – the growing tendency of employees to initiative and create changes in how their work is performed. Both perspectives are critically important to efforts at elaborating work design theories for open and crowd work. Social embeddedness and worker empowerment orchestrated by notions of work marketplace and DIY represent key descriptors of crowd-enabled work transformations. Others are aimed at expanding the operational space of work design theories within the organizational work environment. As noted by Torraco [83], work design can occur at any point along the continuum between the design of individual tasks and organization-wide work structures. This corresponds to a focus of work design on individual-level and team-level work [88]. A crucial question in relation to crowdwork becomes how to extrapolate this continuum to account for the doing of organizational work at the crowd-level.

POTENTIAL CONTRIBUTIONS OF WORK DESIGN THEORIES TO CROWDWORK

I will situate the discussion of potential benefits of work design theories to crowdwork within the broader context of the use of theory in CSCW research [32, 33]. Three broad categories of such benefits are identified: *1) to provide orienting concepts and perspectives needed to make sense of the world and understand specific settings of system use, 2) to inform the design of technical systems, and 3) to guide evaluation strategies.*

Providing orienting concepts and perspectives needed to make sense of the world and understand system use

One of the uses of theories in CSCW research is to provide designers with concepts to orient how they make sense of the world and understand specific settings of use being designed for. This is particularly crucial in situations where there has been a significant change in design paradigm, for example, the transition from the traditional employee-based work paradigm to the crowd model. As a result, work design theories could lead to more insightful explication of the problems of work design in crowdwork through a framework for broadening the scope of discourse in crowdsourcing. They could help crowdsourcing researchers better understand the varied contexts for the application of organizational crowdwork. For example, they could help in defining appropriate configurations of crowdworkers and crowdsourcing technologies for a given organizational work, and in delineating which organizational task is (or perhaps more importantly, is not) appropriate for crowdwork. Using work design theories to understand the details of organizational work could potentially lead to the design and adoption of more effective crowd-based systems for organizational work.

Informing design

Theories can be used to make design decisions about a technical system, and to determine which functionality to support and how to implement such functionality [33]. As evidenced by much of the publications reviewed in the study described earlier in this paper, a predominant means for understanding system use in crowdwork is through observational and user-centered studies [46, 93, 34, 67]. In such studies, it often becomes problematic to turn social observation into technical design [15]. In this respect, theories as "the language of generalization" [14] can be used inform design through design guidelines by enabling the development of generalizable knowledge for translating empirical findings into better designs. For example, work design theories could provide a means for how to componentize work into assignable tasks, or microtasks, in a way that addresses the concerns and challenges of both organizations and workers, and leads to better work quality. In addition, work design theories can be applied during analysis as a thinking frame for the development of new theories for work design in organizational crowdwork.

Guiding evaluation strategies

Lastly, theories can be used to guide evaluations of crowdwork technologies, and to interpret findings from crowdwork interventions. Theoretically-informed evaluation strategies that can offer researchers new ways to assess the technologies they are developing [14, 33]. Usually, theories are based on experience or observation [14], and can potentially offer a framework to guide evaluation. For example, most work design theories are the result of studies of practical organizational problems in the history of work. They can, as such, be used to explain or predict future observations, conceptualize future roles and relationships in organizational engagement with the crowd, and guide the evaluation of crowdwork systems to address the needs of both organizations and workers.

POSSIBLE WORK DESIGN MODELS FOR ORGANIZATIONAL CROWDWORK

As noted earlier, a general criticism of work design theories is that they are not elaborate enough to account for all factors, including informational, structural, contextual, and knowledge issues, people's concepts, task characteristics, and social relations that influence and constraint the choice of work design in organization [64]. The range broadens even wider in crowdwork where the use of the crowd brings in further challenges. However, it is not unusual that often theories are insufficient to guide research. In such cases, Hekler et al. [33] note that additional empirical work can be used to generate knowledge, and yield concrete and context-specific findings necessary to support design. Over the last couple of years, empirical research in crowdsourcing has uncovered a wide range of challenges facing crowdwork design. Earlier, I discussed these challenges under four categories: *C1, C2, C3, and C4.* In this section, I will revisit the challenges and underscore their implications for organizational crowdwork design. In particular, we explore how they could be used to enrich the integrative model of work design discussed earlier. For example, can the model support the addition and evaluation of crowd-related work features for more effective work design in open and crowd work?

Table 2 outlines a number of considerations to guide the elaboration of the integrative model of work design to address many of the challenges of crowdwork design as depicted in Table 1. The work characteristics are as defined by the integrative model in work design research. Additional and expanded work characteristics are as used by various work design researchers, and denote extra characteristics aimed to elaborate the model. I outline five possible work design models for organizational crowdwork. The aim is to enable the development of a work design model that is sufficiently elaborate to address the many challenges of crowdwork design, and yet grounded in established principles of work design theories.

Designing for task significance and greater autonomy

Since the JCM model [30], task significance and autonomy have remained two of the most important characteristics of work in work design research. By focusing on microwork (C3), existing crowdwork systems have, however, led to a conceptualization of work as "atomized" routine tasks [52] that obscure a view of the real context of work, weaken knowledge of results, and undermine worker independence. This approach to work design has adversely reduced autonomy as a motivational factor, and made the critical work characteristics of task significance an insignificant aspect of crowdwork design [68].

As noted earlier, work design research has long addressed problems of autonomy and task significance, but within the context of the traditional work model. However, by leveraging work design theories, organizational crowdwork can possibly extend traditional approaches to enabling autonomy and task significance toward the design of a crowdwork system that can allow workers not only "to complete a whole and identifiable piece of work in a way that is satisfying and measurable" [46], but also encourage self-assessment and feedback, and enable participative decision in both the design and doing of the work (C2), (C3), as well as learning (C2) and self-control [92]. Such a system will equally allow the determination of appropriate levels of visibility in a manner that addresses organizational concerns of privacy, security, and IP leakage (C1). Recent efforts at elaborating the integrative work design model to support more antecedents and contingencies will most probably be a good resource in achieving task significance and greater autonomy in crowdwork design.

Designing for mutual affordance and value co-creation

As noted during the review of challenges of organizational crowdwork design, there is a lack of alignment between the interests of workers (C2) and organizations (C1). Although a number of studies have focused on understanding requester-provider engagement in crowdsourcing, problems of trust remain (C4) – often leading to poor work quality (C1), and worker dissatisfaction (C2). There is, in current crowdwork systems, an absence of appropriate consideration of the mutual values that both workers and organizations afford each other. As designers of work support systems, CSCW researchers have a critical role to play in enabling the creation of "contexts in which people will treat each other as human beings in a social relation" [75, p. 43], rather than "systems" and just API calls to be invoked.

What is needed is increased dignity and meaning in crowdwork [92], which calls for notions of value co-creation [86] in crowdwork design. In crowdwork, the requester-worker engagement, no matter how short-lived, is fundamentally an economic exchange, where co-creation of values becomes a core purpose and a central concern [86]. By focusing on productivity improvement and worker satisfiability, work design theories will play a crucial role in the creation of a crowdwork environment in which both workers and organizations are constantly seeking to afford mutual benefits to each other. Aspects of the task and social characteristics in work design theories will be particularly useful in this regard, and could enable participatory crowdwork design that involves both organizations and crowdworkers.

Designing for appropriate level of work visibility

As noted earlier, the four themes – C1, C2, C3, and C4 – resonate pretty well with the question of work visibility. The debate over work visibility is one to which the CSCW research community is always keen to contribute [78, 4, 69]. In organizational crowdwork, the question of work visibility creates a dilemma for designers. On the one hand, workers desire greater feedback and participative decision making that engender, for them, increased sense of experienced responsibility of work outcome, as well as belonging and empowerment (C2). On the other hand, organizations are concerned about issues of security, confidentiality, and intellectual property management in dealing with "unknown" workers (C1). Historically, issues of work representation are entangled in the politics of organizations [78, 4]. However, as argued by Suchman [78], varying levels of work visibility and invisibility are both valuable and inevitable to create an effective and "more intimate view of the workplace landscape". Understanding the perspectives underlying particular methods and techniques of making work visible is relevant in designing computer-based support for work [4].

<table>
<tr><th colspan="2">Categories and Dimensions of Variables of a Model of Work Design</th><th>Definition</th><th>Recommendations for Crowdwork Design</th></tr>
<tr><td rowspan="5">Work Characteristics [57, 33, 28, 64, 27, 55]</td><td>Task Characteristics
Autonomy, Task Variety, Task Significance, Task Identity, Feedback</td><td>Characteristics that arise from the task environment or the work itself [55, 57]</td><td>Consider how to achieve task enrichment without introducing complexity in task specification (C2), (C3) and inefficiency in work performance. Consider the implications of the notion of enriched microtask for crowdwork redesign.</td></tr>
<tr><td>Knowledge Characteristics
Job Complexity, Information Processing, Problem Solving, Skill Variety, Specialization</td><td>Definitions of the knowledge dimensions appear in [57].</td><td>Consider novel approaches for enabling crowd knowledge management. For example, consider work design support for collaborative knowledge building that combines crowd intelligence and tribal knowledge based on mutual trust (C4).</td></tr>
<tr><td>Social Characteristics
Social Support, Interdependence, Interaction outside Organization, Feedback from Others</td><td>Characteristics that arise from the social environment or when working with others [55, 57]</td><td>Consider an extension of work design to support relevant social features such as participative decision making (C2), collaboration and knowledge sharing between organization and crowdworkers based on value co-creation – as a way of managing social complexity in crowdwork [62]. Consider the implications for crowdwork design, particularly in relation to social computing</td></tr>
<tr><td>Contextual Characteristics
Ergonomics, Physical Demands, Work Conditions, Equipment Use, Workload Activity Levels</td><td>Characteristics that arise from the physical and organizational environment [55, 57]</td><td>Given that crowdwork typically occurs outside of the physical and conceptual boundaries of the organizational space (C4), consider the implications of a new space – crowd workspace – for managing the contextual information needed to enable quality work without compromising organizational intellectual capital.</td></tr>
<tr><td>Additional Characteristics
Workday Cycles, Time Pressure, Temporal Horizon, Virtual Work, Skills and Ability Requirements</td><td>Definitions of dimensions of additional characteristics appear in [57, 29]</td><td>Consider a new set of characteristics – crowd characteristics – for handling issues in (C1), (C2), and issues of crowd knowledge management and uncertainties in the crowdwork environment (C4). Erickson et al. [19] identify three such characteristics, namely crowd knowledge, crowd value, and crowd location.</td></tr>
<tr><td colspan="2">Expanded Work Characteristics [64]
Individual-level and team-level characteristics</td><td>See [64, p. 420]</td><td>Consider reducing the uncertainties and complexities that occur when work happens at the crowd-level, and the implications for work redesign. Develop techniques for crowd-level collaboration – akin to team-level collaboration in [64]</td></tr>
<tr><td colspan="2">Antecedents [64]
Organizational culture/history, HR practices, nature of tasks, nature of labor market, technology, uncertainties, politics</td><td>Internal and external organizational factors that can influence or constraint the choice of work design [64]</td><td>Consider crowdwork systems as sites of organizational workplace cultural re-imagining. Re-think current organizational work structures to align with, or speak to, the open and crowd paradigm (C4), for example, open ownership of IP between organization and the public. Consider policies to back "crowd employment" [22]</td></tr>
<tr><td colspan="2">Contingencies [64, 55]</td><td>Factors that moderate the performance of work redesign within particular contexts [64]</td><td>Consider how the need for nuanced support to workers or classes of workers (C2) may facilitate or inhibit crowdwork redesign. Consider new approaches for managing contingencies and uncertainties (C4), and their implications to crowdwork design</td></tr>
<tr><td colspan="2">Work Outcomes [55, 64]</td><td>The product of "worker-work characteristics" or "person-job" [60, 55]</td><td>Consider how challenges related to crowdwork outcome, e.g. trajectories for career growth, perspective-taking, quality assessment, proactive performance, could enhance crowdwork design (C4), (C2)</td></tr>
</table>

Table 2: Considerations for applying work design theories to crowdwork design.

However, in crowdwork, the organizational workplace landscape has remarkably changed both physically and conceptually, and has brought to the fore the need for CSCW to rethink visibility in the era of crowdwork. Work characterizations in work design theories, and perspectives such as the relational perspective [27] will potentially provide a good starting point in this endeavor. Appropriate choice of levels of visibility could streamline work, and lead to greater efficiency for worker and organizations (C3), as well as improved trust and quality of work outcome (C4).

Designing work as a service (WaaS)

As noted earlier, the idea of "as-a-service" gives crowdwork off as an unethical work performance strategy [75]. However, incorporating principles of work design theories into it will potentially change this perspective by enriching "the service" with notions of worker satisfiability, task characteristics, knowledge characteristics, work management, work outcome, and feedback. Designing WaaS will lead to a crowdwork system where work engagements, and not just tasks, are modeled as compositions of interconnected service requests in a manner that separates the work to be performed from the work required to facilitate the performance – the meta-work [1]. This approach will potentially address issues of overhead (C1), and reduce concerns of poor task specification and articulation (C2), (C3). Given that the service-oriented architecture paradigm in computer science comes with a lot of industry standards, the approach will also enable standardization and improved crowd knowledge management (C4). The approach can leverage different variables of a model of work design including work characteristics, expanded work characteristics, antecedents, and outcomes (see Table 2) in defining the varied dimensions of a work engagement.

The notion of WaaS is not entirely new in crowdsourcing. Schall [74] describes the Human-Provided Services framework, which applies the principles of service-oriented architecture to the discovery, composition, and selection of scalable human workforce. Vaculin et al [85] propose a WaaS protocol and meta-model aimed to enable decomposition, delegation, adjustable management, control, and visibility of how the work is coordinated and performed. However, as noted by [75, 41], there is a potential danger in treating workers as an "API call". As such, crowdwork design efforts need to go beyond a narrow technical focus on enabling information technology support for work, and consider profoundly human issues such as work design characteristics, motivation, satisfaction, requester-worker relationship, and value co-creation that are at the core of the doing of work.

Designing support for an encompassing crowdwork ecosystem with a better "person-job" fit

Despite the obvious advantages of organizational uses of the crowd, crowdwork in practice involves tremendous overhead (C1). Integration of crowdwork systems into the organizational work environment is often risky and cumbersome (C4). However, many researchers adopt a narrow focus on motivation as the only inventive for engaging in crowdwork, while microtask seems to have become a "standard" work design technique in most crowdwork systems [46]. This trend portends a huge problem, which, as noted earlier, is not only that crowdwork fails to take account of the inherent complexity of organizational work, but, more importantly, that crowdwork research does not sufficiently take account of the complexity of crowdwork itself (C3).

As noted earlier, the challenges of organizational crowdwork are not just technical problems, but involve profoundly human, social, organizational and philosophical issues. There is a need for a more coherent and broader framework to enable a better fitting of crowdwork into organization. A framework that would employ social computing techniques in managing the relationship between workers and organizations, and extend work design theories beyond a focus on statically defined roles and jobs. Such efforts can benefit from recent research works that aim to elaborate the work design model [64, 27]. Work design research has demonstrated that, under appropriate circumstances, work redesign can result in optimum "person-job" fit, and, consequently, enhance both organizational productivity and worker satisfaction [60]. For example, the interdisciplinary perspective in work design theories will potentially lend support to building a crowdwork ecosystem that takes account of the technical, as well as social and organizational issues of crowdwork design [8, 46, 16]. For CSCW research, the idea of an encompassing crowdwork ecosystem will amount to renewed investigation of crowdwork as a site for rethinking work organization and culture, and not just a socio-technical force for the distribution of work.

APPLYING A WORK DESIGN THEORETICAL PERSPECTIVE

The goal of this paper in undertaking a review of the literature in crowdsourcing and work design has been to explore the implications of applying work design theories to organizational crowdwork design. As shown in Table 1, one of the major challenges of work design in organizational crowdwork hinges on how to reconcile what organizations want out of crowdwork with the desires and fears of workers who perform the work. As argued in the review of perspectives in work design theories, a key potential of the theories lies in their ability to ensure that both the organization and the worker benefit from a work design.

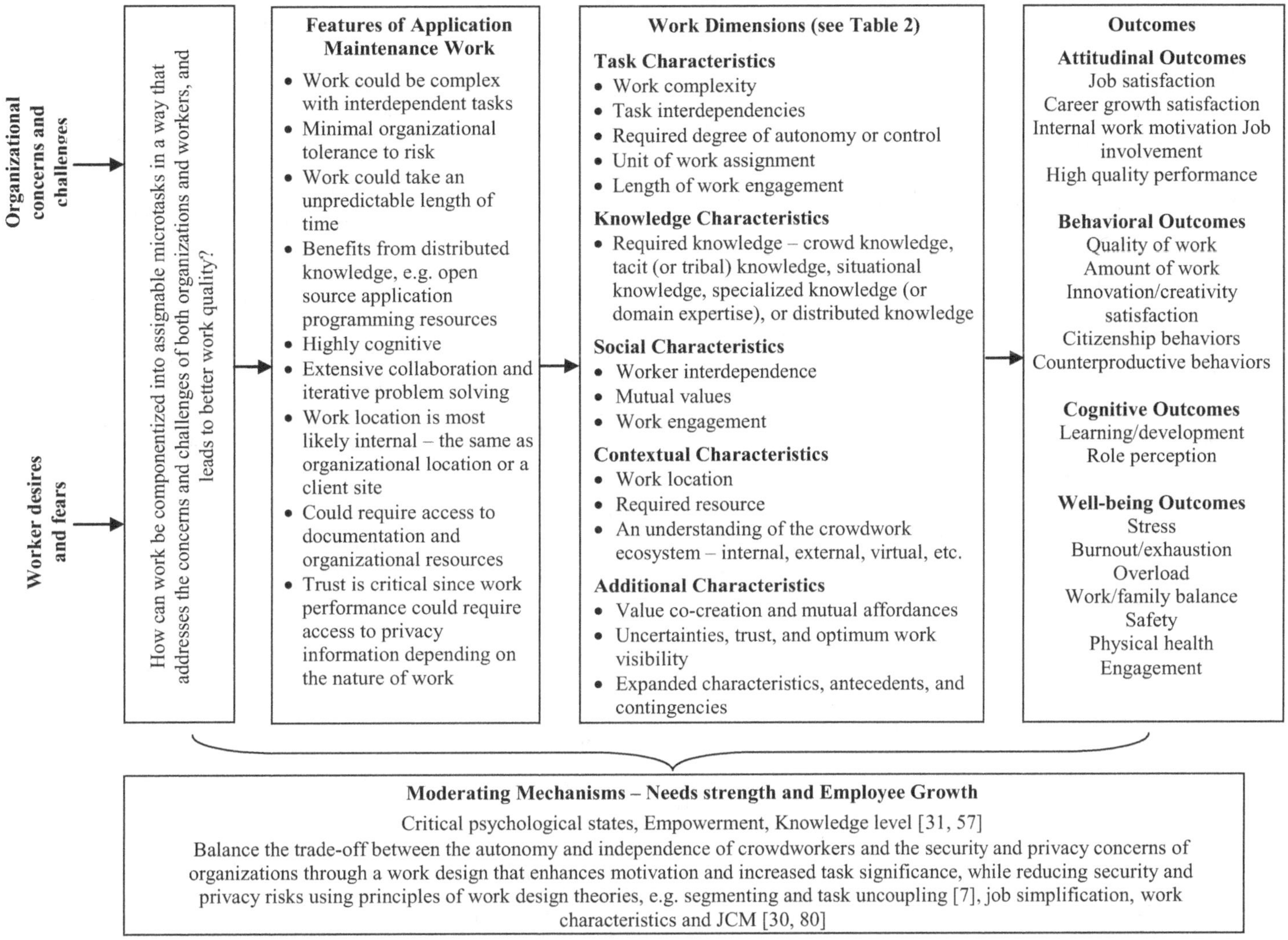

Figure 1: Using work design theories to map crowdwork design challenges (design variables) to outcomes.

While recognizing that principles of the theories cannot transfer naively to the crowdwork platform, this section illustrates how a work design theoretical perspective could be applied to address the problem of crowdwork design using application maintenance work as an example.

Unlike highly prescriptive jobs like call center work [62] that has seen a booming employment of crowdworkers, the use of crowdworkers for application maintenance poses huge challenges [1]. This is largely as a result of the nature of application maintenance as a technical profession [43]. It involves extensive collaboration and shared responsibility. System diagnosis, for example, often requires access to diverse knowledge, and proprietary resources (Figure 1).

In applying work design theories, a key question becomes how to map the design challenges in crowdwork (e.g. in form of design variables), using a work design perspective, such as job simplification, into expected work outcomes. Work design theories allow us to manage the tensions between the needs and challenges of organizations and crowdworkers. Rather than the current method of assigning tasks as "hyperspecialized" microtasks [52], incorporating work design theories would enable a new approach where microtasks are taken from different (but related) stacks of job – A, B, and C (Figure 2) in order to create a new stack of tasks, e.g. using segmenting [7], JCM [30], etc. The resulting stack of tasks provides better task significance to a crowdworker without any risk of exposing organizational knowledge capital. Because each task is taken from a different stack at a microtask level, concerns such as privacy, security, and protection of IPs are lower, and because the crowdworker has a new challenging "macrotask" to perform with such opportunities for self-study learning, on-the-job training, experimentation and/or collaboration with peers and mentors, worker motivation and satisfiability are greatly enhanced.

The example illustrates how a key postulation of work design theories could be applied to enable effective work design in a way that addresses the concerns and challenges of both organization (C1) and crowdworkers (C2), and leads to better work quality. As shown in Figure 2, work that has the potential for cost savings, but poses huge privacy and security risks to the organization if performed through crowdsourcing is redesigned from a work design theoretical perspective in a way that minimizes those concerns. Aspects of task dependencies, workflows, and coordination [51] are not considered in this example. Several aspects of work design theories, such as the mechanistic and motivational approaches introduced by Campion and Thayer [5], offer a set of probing questions that could be used to address such issues, including task clarity, work repetition, and specialization of tools and procedures.

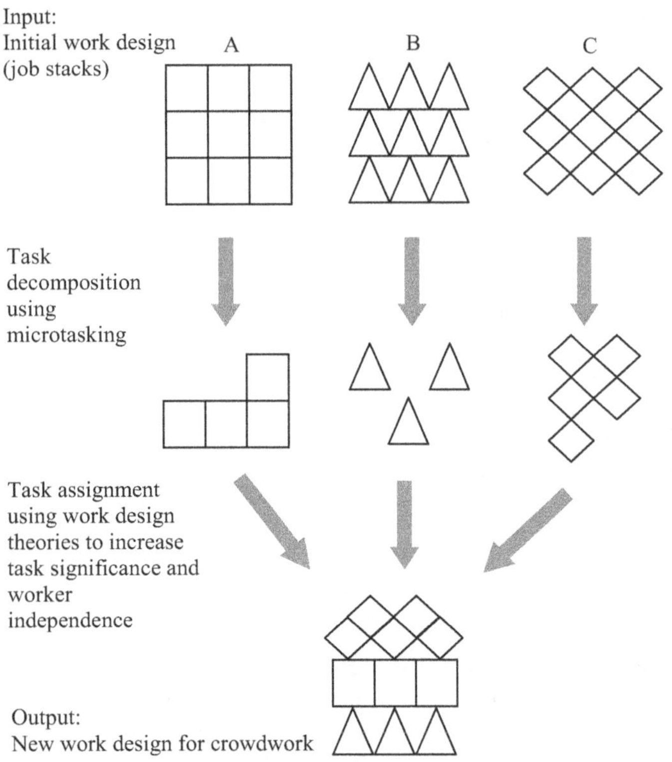

Figure 2. A crowdwork design approach combining microtasking and work design theories.

CONCLUSION

Research in crowdwork has uncovered a wide range of obstacles – most of which derive from empirical data – that stand in the way of effective organizational adoption of crowdsourcing. The goal in this paper was to offer researchers and practitioners in crowdsourcing a moment of deeper reflection on these challenges, and a potential roadmap toward tackling them by leveraging long-standing theories and efforts in work design research in organizational studies.

Bridging the theoretical gap between the crowdsourcing and work design research communities will potentially lead to a better fitting of crowdwork into organizations in a manner that not only leverages advances in CSCW and social computing, but also extends traditional principles in work design. Long-standing theories in work design can provide orienting concepts and perspectives to enable theory-driven analyses of the wide range of observational and empirical studies that have emerged out of crowdsourcing research in the last couple of years. Crowdwork is likely not going to be an all-or-nothing proposition for organizations. As the technology and methods evolve, crowdwork will be applied to different types of organizational work where most appropriate, but will still be integrated with work done by traditional employees. As such, a scientific engagement between the crowdsourcing and work design research communities will most likely, not only result in the mutual strengthening of both communities and an expansion of their horizons, but also lead to effective, efficient, and ethical work design models for open and crowd work.

REFERENCES

1. Anya, O., Cefkin, M., Dill, S., Moore, R., Stucky, S. U. and Omokaro, O. Making Crowdwork Work: Issues in Crowdsourcing for Organizations. *In Proc. HCOMP* (2013).
2. Archak, N. Money, glory and cheap talk: analyzing strategic behavior of contestants in simultaneous crowdsourcing contests on topcoder.com. *Proc. of WWW* (2010).
3. Arthur, B. The Second Economy. *McKinsey Quarterly*, October (2011).
4. Bannon, L. The Politics of Design: Representing Work, *Communications of the ACM*, 38, 9 (1995), 66-68.
5. Campion, M. and Thayer, P. Job design: Approaches, outcomes, and trade-offs. *Organizational Dynamics*, 15, (1987) 66-79.
6. Campion, M. A. Interdisciplinary approaches to job design: A constructive replication with extensions. *Journal of Applied Psychology*, 67 (1988), 467-481.
7. Campion, M. A., Mumford, T. V., Morgeson, F. P. and Nahrgang, J. D. Work Redesign: Eight obstacles and Opportunities, *Human Resource Management*, 44, 4 (2005) 367-390.
8. Cefkin, M., Anya, O., Dill, S., Moore, R., Stucky, S. U. and Omokaro, O. Back to the future of organizational work: crowdsourcing and digital work marketplaces. CSCW Workshop (2014), 313-316.
9. Clegg, C. W. The derivation of job designs. *Journal of Occupational Behaviour*. 5 (1984), 131-146.
10. Cordery, J.L. and Sevastos, P. P. Responses to the original and revised Job Diagnostic Survey: Is education a factor in responses to negatively worded items? *Journal of Applied Psychology*, 78, 1 (1993), 141-143.

11. Davenport, T. H. Process innovation: reengineering work through information technology. (1993), Harvard Business School Press.
12. Davis, J. and Lin, H. Web 3.0 and Crodwsourcing. *In Proc. of AMCIS* (2011).
13. Davis, L. E. and Taylor, J. C. Design of Jobs. (1972), Penguin.
14. Dix, A. Theoretical analysis and theory creation. *In Research Methods for Human-Computer Interaction* (2008), Cambridge University Press.
15. Dourish, P. What we talk about when we talk about context. *Pers Ubiquit Comput*, 8 (2004), 19–30.
16. Dow, S. P., Kulkarni, A., Klemmer, S. R. and Hartmann, B. Shepherding the Crowd Yields Better Work. *In Proc. CSCW* (2012).
17. Drucker, P. F. Managing in the Next Society (2002), St. Martin's Griffin.
18. Emery, F. E. and Trist, E. L. The Causal Texture of Organizational Environments. *Human Relations*, 18 (1965), 21-32.
19. Erickson, L. B., Petrick, I. and Trauth, E. M. Hanging with the right crowd: Matching crowdsouring need to crowd characteristics. *In Proc. of ACIS* (2012).
20. Erickson, L. B., Petrick, I. and Trauth, E. M. Organizational uses of the crowd: developing a framework for the study of crowdsourcing. *In Proc. of Computers and People Research*. (2012), 155-158.
21. Faridani, S. Hartmann, B. and Ipeirotis, P. G. What's the right price? Pricing tasks for finishing on time. *In Proc. of Human Computation* (2011).
22. Felstiner, A. L. Working the Crowd: Employment and Labor Law in the Crowdsourcing Industry. *Berkeley J. of Employment & Labor Law* 32, 1, (2011) 143-204.
23. Gajendran, R. S. and Harrison, D. A. The good, the bad, and the unknown about telecommuting: meta-analysis of psychological mediators and individual consequences. *Journal of Applied Psychology*, 92, 6 (2007), 1524-41.
24. Galbraith, J. R. Environmental and technological determinants of organizational design. *In Studies in organizational design*. (1970), Irwin.
25. Ghosh, A., Kale, S. and McAfee, P. Who moderates the moderators? crowdsourcing abuse detection in user-generated content. *In Proc. of Elect. Commerce* (2011).
26. Gibson, C. B., Gibbs, J. L., Stanko, T. L., Tesluk, P. and Cohen, S. G. Including the "I" in Virtuality and Modern Job Design: Extending the Job Characteristics Model to Include the Moderating Effect of Individual Experiences of Electronic Dependence and Copresence. *Journal Organization Science*, 22, 6 (2011), 1481-99.
27. Grant, A. M. and Parker, S. K. Redesigning Work Design Theories: The Rise of Relational and Proactive Perspectives, *The Academy of Management Annals*, 3, 1 (2009), 317-375.
28. Grant, A. M. Giving time, time after time: Work design and sustained employee participation in corporate volunteering. *Academy of Management Review*, 37, 4 (2012), 589-615.
29. Grant, A., Fried, Y. and Juillerat, T. Work matters: Job design in classic and contemporary perspectives. *In APA handbook of industrial and organizational psychology, S. Zedeck, Ed.,* I (2010), 417-453.
30. Hackman J. R. and Oldham, G. R. Work Redesign. (1980), Addison-Wesley.
31. Hackman, J. R. and Oldham, G. R. Motivation through the design of work: Test of a theory. *Organizational Behavior and Human Performance* 16, 2 (1976).
32. Halverson, C. A. Activity Theory and Distributed Cognition: Or What Does CSCW Need to DO with Theories? *Journal of CSCW II* (2002), 243-267.
33. Hekler, E.B., Klasnja, P. Froehlich, J. Buman, M. Mind the theoretical gap: Interpreting, using, and developing behavioral theory in HCI research. *In Proc of SIGCHI* (2013), 3307-3316.
34. Hetmank, L. Components and Functions of Crowdsourcing Systems – A Systematic Literature Review. *Conf. on Wirtschaftsinformatik* (2013).
35. Howe, J. Crowdsourcing: How the Power of the Crowd is Driving the Future of Business, (2008) Business Books.
36. Howe, J. The Rise of Crowdsourcing, in Wired. 2006.
37. Ipeirotis, P. Analyzing the amazon mechanical turk marketplace. *XRDS*, 17 (2010), 16–21.
38. Ipeirotis, P.G., Provost, F., and Wang, J. Quality management on Amazon Mechanical Turk. *In Proc. HCOMP* (2010).
39. Irani, L. "Microworking the Crowds". *In Limn: Clouds and Crowds,* Seattle: Createspace and on web (2012) http://limn.it/microworking-the-crowd/.
40. Irani, L. and Silberman, M. S. Turkopticon: Interrupting Worker Invisibility in Amazon Mechanical Turk. *In Proc. CHI* (2013), 611-620.
41. Irani, L. The cultural work of microwork. New Media and Society (2013), 1-20.
42. Kanich, C., Checkoway, S. and Mowery, K. Putting out a hit: Crowdsourcing malware installs. *In Proc. of WOOT* (2011).
43. Katz, R. Motivating Technical Professionals Today, *Research-Technology Management*, 48, 6 (2005).
44. Kaufmann, N., Schulze, T., and Veit, D. More than fun and money. Worker motivation in crowdsourcing – A study on Mechanical Turk. *In Proc. AMCIS* (2011).

45. Kirsh, D. The Context of Work, Human computer Interaction 16, 2-4, (2001) 305-322.

46. Kittur, A., Nickerson, J. V., Bernstein, M., Gerber, E., Shaw, A., Zimmerman, J., Lease, M. and Horton, J. The Future of Crowd Work. *In Proc. CSCW* (2013), 1301-18.

47. Kittur, A., Smus, B., Khamkar, S., and Kraut, R.E. Crowdforge: Crowdsourcing complex work. *In Proc. of ACM symposium on User interface software and technology* (2011), 43–52.

48. Kochhar, S., Mazzocchi, S. and Paritosh, P. The anatomy of a large-scale human computation engine. *In Proc. of HCOMP* (2010), 10-17.

49. Lasecki, W. S., Teevan, J. and Kamar, E. Information Extraction and Manipulation Threats in Crowd-Powered Systems. *In Proc. of CSCW* (2014).

50. Lease, M. On quality control and machine learning in crowdsourcing. *In Proc. of Human Computation* (2011).

51. Malone, T. and Crowston, K. The interdisciplinary study of coordination. ACM Computing Surveys, 26 (1994), 87-119.

52. Malone, T. W., Laubacher, R. J. and Johns, T. 2011. The Big Idea: The Age of Hyperspecialization, *Harvard Business Rev* (2011), 4-11.

53. Manning, P. K. Organizational Work: Structuration of Environments, *The British Journal of Sociology* 33, 1, (1982) 118-134.

54. Martin, D. B., Hanrahan, B. V., O'Neil, J. and Gupta, N. Performing Crowdwork. *In Proc. of CSCW* (2014).

55. Morgeson, F. P. and Humphrey, S. E. Job and Team Design: Toward a More Integrative Conceptualization of Work Design. *In Research in Personnel and Human Resource Management*, 27 (2008).

56. Morgeson, F. P., Dierdorff, E. C. and Hmurovic, J. L. Work design in situ: Understanding the role of occupational and organizational context. *Journal of Organizational Behavior*, 31 (2010), 351–360.

57. Morgeson, F. P., Garza, A. S. and Campion, M. A. 2012. Work design. *In Handbook of psychology: Industrial and organizational psychology, 12, Second Edition* (2012), 525-559 John Wiley and Sons.

58. Motoyama, M., McCoy, D., Levchenko, K., Savage, S. and Voelker, G. M. Dirty jobs: The role of freelance labor in web service abuse. *In Proc. of USENIX Security* (2011).

59. Muntés-Mulero, V., Paladini, P., Manzoor, J., Gritti, A., Larriba-Pey, J and Mijnhardt, F. Crowdsourcing for industrial problems. *In Proc. of Citizen in Sensor Networks* (2013), 6-18.

60. Oldham, G. R. and Hackman, J. R. Work Design in the Organizational Context. *In Research in Organizational Behaviour*, 2 (1980), 247-278.

61. Parker, S. K. and Wall T. D. Job and Work Design: Organizing Work to Promote Well-Being and Effectiveness. (1998), Thousand Oaks, CA: Sage.

62. Parker, S. K. and Wall, T. D. Work Design: Learning from the Past and Mapping a New Terrain. *In Anderson, N., Ones, D. S., Sinangil, H. K., Viswesvaran, C. (Ed.), Handbook of Industrial, Work and Organizational Psychology*, 1 (2001), 90-110, Sage.

63. Parker, S. K. Beyond Motivation: Job and Work Design for Development, Health, Ambidexterity, and More. *Annual Review of Psychology*, 65 (2014), 661-691.

64. Parker, S. K., Wall, T. D. and Cordery, J. L. Future work design research and practice: Towards an elaborated model of work design. *Journal of Occupational and Organizational Psychology*, 74 (2001), 413-440.

65. Parks, S. Improving workplace performance: historical and theoretical contexts, *Monthly Labor Review* (1995), 18-23.

66. Paul, W. P. and Robertson, K. B. Job enrichment and employee motivation (1970), London: Gower.

67. Pedersen, J., Kocsis, D., Tripathi, A., Tarrell, A., Weerakoon, A., Tahmasbi, N., Xiong, J., Deng, W., Oh, O. and deVreede, G. Conceptual Foundations of Crowdsourcing: A Review of IS Research. *In Proc. of HICSS* (2013), 579-588.

68. Ren, Y. and Wang, L. S. The Significance of Task Significance in Online Marketplaces for Work. *In CSCW Workshop,* (2014).

69. Robinson, M. and Bannon, L. Questioning Representations. *In Proc. of ECSCW* (199), 219-233.

70. Ross, J., Irani, I., Silberman, M. Six, Zaldivar, A., and Tomlinson, B. Who are the crowdworkers?: Shifting demographics in amazon mechanical turk. *In Proc. of CHI* (2010).

71. Sabou, M., Scharl, A. and Fols, M. Crowdsourced Knowledge Acquisition: Towards Hybrid-Genre Workflows. *Int'l Journal of Semantic Web and Information Systems*, 9, 3 (2013), 14-41.

72. Salancik, G. R. and Pfeffer, J. A social information processing approach to job attitudes and task design. *Administrative Science Quarterly* 23 (1978), 224-253.

73. Scekic, O., Troung, H., and Dustdar, S. Incentives and Rewarding in Social Computing. *Communications of the ACM* 56, 6 (2013), 72-82.

74. Schall, D. Service-Oriented Crowdsourcing: Architecture, Protocols and Algorithms. (2011) Springer.

75. Silberman, M. S., Irani, L. and Ross, J. Ethics and Tactics of Professional Crowdwork. *XRDS*, 17, 2 (2010), 39-43.

76. Silberman, M. S., Ross, J., Irani, L., Tomilinson, B. Sellers' problems in human computation markets, *In Proc. of HCOMP* (2010), 18-21.

77. Starbrid, K. What "Crowdsourcing" Obscures: Exposing the Dynamics of Connected Crowd Work during Disaster. *In Proc. of CI* (2012).

78. Suchman, L. Making Work Visible, *Communications of the ACM*, 38, 9 (1995), 56-64.

79. Sun, Y., Roy, S. and Little, G. Beyond independent agreement: A tournament selection approach for quality assurance of human computation tasks. *Proc. of Human Computation* (2011).

80. Taylor, F. W. The principles of scientific management. (1911) New York: Harper.

81. Teodoro, R., Ozturk, P., Naaman, M., Mason, W. and Lindqvist, J. The motivations and experiences of the on-demand mobile workforce. *In Proc. of CSCW* (2014).

82. Thuan, N. H., Antunes, P. and Johnstone, D. Factors Influencing the Decision to Crowdsource. *In Proc. of CRIWG* (2013).

83. Torraco, R. J. Work design theory: A review and critique with implications for human resource development. *Human Resource Development Quarterly* 16, 1 (2005), 85-109.

84. Trist, E. L. and Bamforth, K. W. Some social and psychological consequences of the long-wall method of coal-getting. *Human Relations*, 4 (1951), 3–38.

85. Vaculín, R., Chee, Y., Oppenheim, D. V. and Varshney, L. R. Work as a Service Meta-model and Protocol for Adjustable Visibility, Coordination, and Control. *In Proc. of SRII Global Conference* (2012), 90-99.

86. Vargo, S. L. Maglio, P. P. and Akaka, M. A. On value and value co-creation: A service systems and service logic perspective. *European Management Journal*, 26, (2008) 145-152.

87. Vough, C. and Asbell, B. Productivity: A practical program for improving efficiency (1975) Productivity Research International.

88. Vough, H. and Parker, S. K. Work Design Research: Still Going Strong. *In Handbook of Organizational Behavior*, 1 (2008) Sage Publications.

89. Vukovic, M. and Bartolini, C. Towards a Research Agenda for Enterprise Crowdsourcing. In *Leveraging Applications of Formal Methods, Verification, and Validation, LNCS*, 6415 (2010) 425-434.

90. Vukovic, M., Laredo, J. and Rajagopal, S. Challenges and experiences in deploying enterprise crowdsourcing service. *Proc. of ICWE* (2010).

91. Wall, T. D. and Martin, R. 1987. Job and work design. *In International review of industrial and organisational psychology*, (1987), 61–91, Wiley.

92. Weisbord, M. R. Productive Workplaces: Dignity, Meaning, and Community in the 21st Century. (2012) Jossey-Bass.

93. Zhao, Y. and Zhu, Q. Evaluation on crowdsourcing research: Current status and future direction. *Information Systems Frontiers* (2012), 1-18.

And Now for Something Completely Different: Improving Crowdsourcing Workflows with Micro-Diversions

Peng Dai [1], **Jeffrey M. Rzeszotarski**[2], **Praveen Paritosh**[1], **Ed H. Chi**[1]
[1]Google, Inc., 1600 Amphitheater Pkwy, Mountain View, CA 94043, USA
[2]Human-Computer Interaction Institute, Carnegie Mellon University, Pittsburgh, PA, USA
daipeng@cs.washington.com, jeffrz@cs.cmu.edu, pkp@google.com, chi@acm.org

ABSTRACT

Crowdsourcing has become a popular and indispensable component of many problem-solving pipelines in the research literature, with crowd workers often treated as computational resources that can reliably solve problems that computers have trouble with, such as image labeling/classification, natural language processing, or document writing. Yet, obviously crowd workers are human, and long sequences of the same monotonous tasks might intuitively reduce the amount of good quality work done by the workers. Here we propose an investigation into how we can use diversions containing small amounts of entertainment to improve crowd workers' experiences. We call these small period of entertainment "micro-diversions", which we hypothesize to provide timely relief to workers during long sequences of micro-tasks. We hope to improve productivity by retaining workers to work on our tasks longer and to either improve or retain the quality of work. We experimentally test micro-diversions on Amazon's Mechanical Turk, a large paid-crowdsourcing platform. We find that micro-diversions can significantly improve worker retention rate while retaining the same work quality.

INTRODUCTION

In crowdsourcing task markets such as Amazon's Mechanical Turk (MTurk), hundreds of thousands of workers take on tasks that are challenging for a computer program to solve automatically. For example, workers create corpora of translation data [5], identify interesting visual features in astronomy data [32], and help curate structured data in semantic entity databases [29]. Workers may even do creative or complex work such as writing news articles or generating novel artifacts with design constraints [27,43].

In paid-crowdsourcing platforms, workers can often perform a large amount of tasks in a single, prolonged setting. Large batches of tasks done in sequence are efficient for workers due to their improving familiarity with the work, and besides, it can be very time-consuming for workers to search for new, interesting work. For work requesters, batched work might be beneficial as well, since workers might develop expertise that can be incorporated into judgments [15,41]. Moreover, long-term, diligent workers have been shown to support more complex workflows and tasks [14,26,27].

However, human workers are quite different from computer programs in their performance characteristics—intuitively, they are not nearly as tireless or reliable. We know from research in other domains that fatigue, both physical and cognitive, can affect workers doing large batches of tasks, not only risking reduced well-being, but also creating lower quality, unreliable data as a result [31]. Imagine, for example, a task asking workers to tag one image. A worker can easily tag the image, and probably have no problem tagging a few more. Now imagine someone who has been working on the same type of tagging tasks during the past hour. Seeking variety and to reduce monotonous work, she might choose to look for another type of task.

In an opt-in setting such as MTurk, workers may choose to stop working, or to find other tasks that pose different, refreshing challenges. Indeed, past MTurk studies show that workers tend to switch tasks once a certain goal has been accomplished [20]. Other research also has demonstrated situations where worker engagement in volunteer crowdsourcing fades over time [33]. Clearly, to obtain good quality and stable results, work requesters want to retain experienced workers.

We are not aware of existing crowdsourcing research on interventions that would help retain good-quality workers. There are, however, great research on how to mitigate quality control issues in crowdsourcing systems using external checks such as CAPTCHA questions, gold standards, majority voting, and behavioral logging [3, 5, 28, 38]. Moreover, crowdsourcing quality control techniques generally assume a consistent model per worker over time [16,41]. Interestingly, some research on temporal probabilistic models of multiple annotators exists [17].

CSCW 2015, March 14–18, 2015, Vancouver, BC, Canada.
ACM 978-1-4503-2922-4/15/03.
http://dx.doi.org/10.1145/2675133.2675260

Here we propose a method to help retain good workers through diversions [1] in the form of small entertaining interruptions. Imagine the previous worker who has been tagging images for 10 minutes. Suddenly she might receive an entertaining diversion. Perhaps she is instead asked to watch a short, funny video if she wants, or is told that she has done a good job so far, together with a leaderboard of how well she is doing compared to other workers. Such small interruptions do indeed incur a cost in context switching as the worker must return to their task afterwards [34,42]. Yet, the act of interrupting also functions as an entertaining time-off from the tasks, potentially refreshing the worker.

We suggest that these refreshing *micro-diversions* might offer benefits that outweigh the tradeoff of context switching, providing a net benefit to crowdsourcing owners. It is important to note that these micro-diversions are different than merely adding fun content to a workflow. They are intended to purposely break the flow of the worker, possibly reducing fatigue, improving alertness, and refreshing workers' cognitive resources.

RELATED WORK

There exists a growing body of research studying human factors and behavior in crowdsourcing markets.

First, improvements in basic task design leverages human behavior to produce better answers. For instance, tasks can be structured so that they resist cheating by requiring more effort, or require explanations to reinforce consideration [25]. Optimizations on design parameters such as the number of questions to ask and payment structure help produce better results with the same budget and time constraints [21]. Even the framing of a task can have a big impact: Chandler and Kapelner [8] demonstrated that workers' perceptions influence their performance, finding that workers who believe that they are working for a charity do a better job. Providing feedback during the tasks, such as strategy advice or good example work by other workers, also result in better quality work [19]. All of these studies take advantage of human aspect of human computation using a Human-Computer Interaction research approach. However, no research that we are aware of thus far has directly tried to improve worker experience through entertaining diversions in crowdsourcing systems.

Second, intuitively, long sequences of monotonous crowdsourcing tasks incite boredom. Unsurprisingly, the psychological and human factors communities have explored boredom and its impact on work. One source for this research is the military, which found itself concerned with fighter pilots sitting in cockpits for long hours and radar operators staring at screens for entire evenings. These vigilance tasks require operators to conduct actions and devote attention over a long period of time. As the task progresses, researchers have found physiological and cognitive effects that reduce performance [36]. Krueger reinforces these findings, demonstrating a linear decay in performance over work time given sustained, possibly sleepless work [31]. Somewhat surprisingly, some tasks cause poor performance not because they are overly taxing, but because they underutilize mental resources, leading to boredom. Pattyn et al. [35] find that underutilization is related to misdirection of attention resources or withdrawal. Carriere et al. [6] relate an underutilization of attention or mistaken redirection to boredom. Later research has identified boredom as a unique condition distinct from underarousal or apathy [7]. However, in crowdsourcing, workers are already free to take breaks anytime they want, and they are also free to switch to other tasks if they choose so, therefore it is possible that micro-diversions are not needed to improve the overall worker experience. Instead, viewed from the work requesters' perspective, our research goal is to retain productive workers and help them stay on the requesters' tasks.

Over long working periods, the opposite of underarousal experiences are flow experiences [10], but these are hard to predict and likely require matching task difficulty to each worker's expertise. Flow experiences, despite being beneficial, might also upset quality control measures when workers unexpectedly increase the quality of their responses. Though relevant, this is outside of the scope of our research goals currently.

Third, while past research shows that diversions can ameliorate boredom, however, their effect also greatly depends on context. Good diversions should be different from the normal, tiring tasks and do not demand an excess of attentional resources [11]. Good diversions may have more impact if they have physical and cognitive conditions that are congruent to the task [18]. For instance, a diversion for a computer operator might involve using computer for something different or stretching the muscles an operator uses for sitting and typing. The length of a diversion interruption is delicate; not too long to require a high context-switch cost, but long enough to refresh the worker. Generally, even small 3- to 30-second breaks can have a measurable impact on workers [18]. This is encouraging for crowdsourcing markets, as micro-diversions might be slipstreamed into workflows automatically.

Fourth, interrupting a workflow has associated costs. Generally speaking, workers might perform poorly after an interruption to their work [30,34]. Interruptions during more complex tasks take longer time to resume [22]. Interruptions also may increase stress [34]. HCI literature suggest that workers often underestimate the costs of interruptions [23]. The costs of interruptions are not consistent either. For participants working on a search task, interrupting them while they were evaluating multiple results was much more costly than interrupting

[1] We use the term 'diversion' because work breaks might be both full rest breaks as well as free-time breaks, in which workers can choose an entertaining activity of their own. Instead we are proposing to prescribe specific entertaining diversions without worker choice.

them while they performed the search query [12, 13]. This has lead to the introduction of numerous intelligent systems and models for locating more optimal moments for interruptions. These systems work to find natural breakpoints in the task or support better task/group awareness [1, 2, 37].

These findings suggest that in a crowdsourcing micro-diversion system, the timing of the interruptions is critical so as to minimize their workflow disruption. Luckily, crowdsourcing workflows have natural breakpoints at the end of task units in a batch. Even better, outside of the crowdsourcing literature, interruptions have been found to improve the performance of workers completing simple tasks by increasing vigilance [39]. We hope to demonstrate that we can retain more of the productive workers in a crowdsourcing system, even though they are free to leave any time.

In summary, based on prior research, here we investigate the potential benefits of micro-diversions, hypothesizing that they outweigh the costs of interruptions at natural breakpoints in human computation tasks. As the literature suggests, on the one hand, micro-diversions might refresh workers and alleviate their boredom. On the other hand, micro-diversions might interrupt the workflow and disrupt working mental states and their flow experiences.

RESEARCH QUESTIONS

We aim to perform experimental studies to find out if micro-diversions have any impact on worker retention and performance in crowdsourcing. Here are the research questions we aim to investigate:

RQ1: Retention Whether and how much does having micro-diversions improve worker retention?

If workers are refreshed by the micro-diversions, then they are likely to stay and do more of the instances of the same task. If they feel that diversions are a distraction, they might actually leave earlier than a no-diversion control condition.

Typical tasks that exist within crowdsourcing platforms might not benefit from micro-diversions, since they typically have short duration, and workers are free to move on to other tasks quickly. However, there is always a switching cost to another task type, since workers would have to search and select a new task, read the instructions, and cognitively prepare for another task structure.

RQ2: Worker Performance In terms of time-on-task and accuracy, do micro-diversions distract workers and bring their performance down, or instead refresh them and either maintain or even boost their performance?

Performance might be measured by both total task-duration per unit work (including the time cost of the diversions) as well as the task accuracy. For our purposes, an increase in time and/or a decrease in accuracy would be considered lower worker performance. If workers do not experience boredom or fatigue, then diversions simply causes increase in total task time. On the other hand, if the workers are refreshed by the micro-diversions, then they might either work faster or maintain/improve their accuracy despite doing more work.

RQ3: Contextual Effects Are different task types affected by the micro-diversions differently? What types of micro-diversions are the most effective in promoting worker engagement?

We aim to study different task types across several domains as well as different micro-diversion types to see if only certain task-diversion combinations work to refresh workers.

RESEARCH METHOD

We conducted our experiments on the Amazon's Mechanical Turk (MTurk) platform, which is a popular platform for crowdsourcing. Tasks on MTurk are grouped into *batches*, which is a set of tasks owned by the same requester that share the same user interface. Workers are paid by a fixed per task rate defined by task requesters. Workers retain full control over which task batch to work on. If a worker likes one batch, she can do as many tasks from the same batch. Therefore, beyond worker task accuracy and speed, the number of tasks completed per worker per batch is a good signal of worker engagements.

Experimental Design

The study used a 3 tasks $\times$ 3 micro-diversions between-subjects design. The three different types of tasks are Image Identification (II), Wikipedia article Quality rating (WQ), and Freebase Entity merging (FE). There were three types of micro-diversions: No Diversions (ND), Game (GD), and Serialized Story (SD). The three task types are crossed with the three micro-diversion types in a between-subjects study design, preventing participants from completing tasks in multiple task and diversion combinations.

In each condition, we provided at least an hour of work for workers to complete in each batch. We also introduced gold standard data so that we could measure work accuracy.

Subjects

We solicited 30 unique workers per condition to stay and do as much as 1-2 hours of work as they could in their assigned task and diversion type combination.

Therefore, the experimental design gives us 3 task types $\times 3$ diversion types $\times 30$ workers $= 270$ unique worker submissions.

Payment

After some deliberations, we decided not to pay workers for time spent in the diversion, since this would have been somewhat awkward for the Game Diversion. However, a worker can quickly skip over a diversion by clicking to proceed to the next question as soon as the diversion UI loads (typically just a few seconds).

This means, for each task type, as long as two workers answer the same number of questions, regardless of how many diversions encountered, they will receive the same amount of monetary reward.

Dependent Variables: Metrics

To measure whether micro-diversions had an effect on workers, we evaluated workers' engagement through retention as well as their average answer time and accuracy.

For RQ1 on retention, we measured the amount of task work units completed by a worker. Retention can be thought of as survival over the multiple instances of a task. The reason we use retention as the main metric here stems from behavioral economics. We regard Mechanical Turk workers as somewhat rational decision makers who decide whether they want to do more work or not each time they see a new task [9]. Since workers opt-in to MTurk tasks, a worker can choose to keep doing tasks in series until her rate of compensation outweighs her calculation of the costs of doing work. We assert that worker boredom and fatigue are part of this cost/benefit calculation that workers make. For example, while a worker may be willing to do many iterations of a task that tags different images, after some time the generous pay may no longer outweigh her boredom, and so she leaves. Thus, if workers in one condition are more engaged than the others, they will stay longer. If more workers stayed to do more tasks in a certain condition, we suggest that that condition was more engaging.

For RQ2 on work performance, we measured the response time and answer accuracy as follows:

Answer response time is measured from the moment a task work unit is served to the worker to the time that the server received the answer for that work unit from the worker. To be fair to the baseline condition containing no diversions, the time a worker spends on a diversion is aggregated with the time she answers the previous question. For example, the answer time a worker spends on one question contains the time she spends both on the question and the coming diversion, if there is one.

Worker accuracy is measured by comparing the workers' answers to the gold standards. A single worker's accuracy is calculated as the percentage of accurate answers in all of her work units. We then aggregated and computed the average of the worker accuracies per task-diversion condition combination.

Independent Variables: 3 Task Designs

As depicted in Figure 1, we introduce three types of tasks here. Obviously, there are many type of tasks we could have studied, so we chose tasks that are somewhat representative of the types used in the research literature.

Wikipedia article Quality rating (WQ)

This task type is a cognitive-intensive task on reading a Wikipedia article and rating the quality of the article, similar to the task used in Kittur et al. [25]. Intended

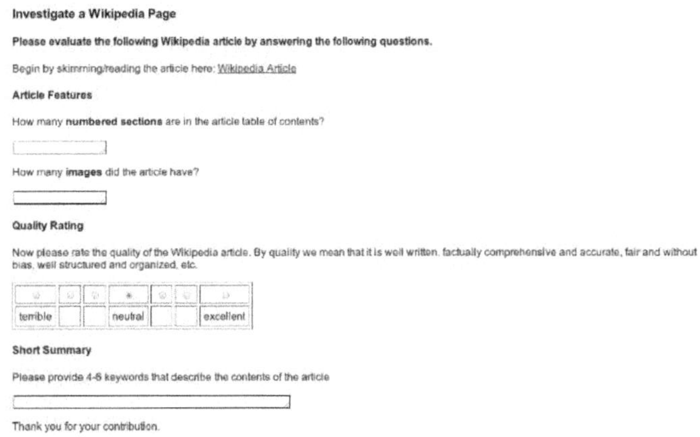

(a) Wikipedia article Quality rating (WQ)

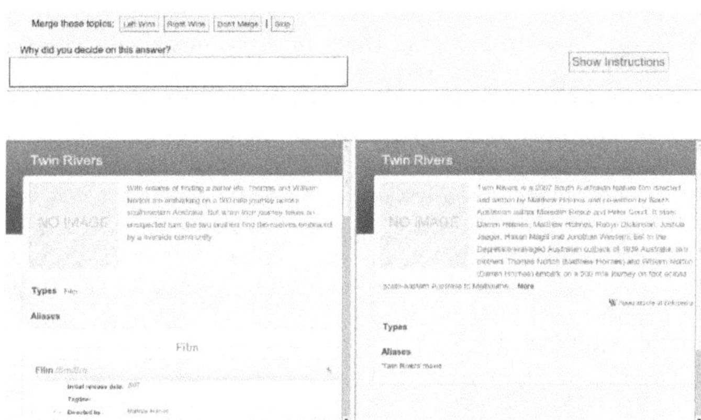

(b) Freebase Entity merging (FE)

(c) Image Identification (II)

Figure 1. Example task types from 3 task domains.

to represent a typical quality judgment task, we incorporated 50 articles from the Wikipedia featured articles list and 50 from the 'needs-cleanup' list that contains lower quality articles. This gave us a mix of good and bad articles that we could use as gold standard. On a Likert scale for article quality, we can measure worker accuracy by comparing whether a worker rated the featured articles better than the cleanup articles on average. As done in Kittur et al. [25], we also asked workers to provide a short summary of the page contents as a proof that they read the article as well as two questions concerning how many images and sections are in the article to deter cheaters. Workers could complete up to 100 tasks for 6 cents each.

Freebase Entity merging (FE)
This task type is also cognitive, making identity judgments for entity resolution of Freebase entities [4] (e.g. one entity might be a tennis player and another a movie star, both with the same first and last names.) In this task, we asked if two different entities were in fact the same entity, and if so, which node's content should get precedence in merging them (e.g. two celebrity entities, one being a nickname for the other.) Typical of a side-by-side judgment task, this task is highly cognitive, as the comparator has to examine both articles looking for consistencies and inconsistencies before making a decision on whether they are in fact referring to the same entity. To deter cheating we asked workers to cite evidence that supports their decision. We extracted 81 different 4-cent merge tasks using the Freebase logs of past entity resolution tasks, with the Freebase adjudicated decision as a gold standard.

Image Identification (II)
This task type is primarily perceptual, asking workers to determine whether each of 12 images contained scenic places or buildings (i.e. 12 images is one task unit.) Image classification and labeling tasks are often used in machine learning research. Compared to other cognitive tasks, perceptual tasks like this are short and relatively easy, so workers could do up to a batch of 100 different, 12-image tasks for 1 cent each. We sampled 600 of the images from panoramio that are of landscapes and landmarks. The other 600 images were sourced from public Google Picasa images, and human judges certified that they did not contain landscapes or landmarks.

Independent Variables: 3 Micro-Diversion Designs
Having outlined the task types above, we now discuss the design of the micro-diversions, which we debated amongst ourselves extensively. In particular, we debated whether (a) micro-diversions should simply be different from the real tasks, so that workers are refreshed just from doing something different? Or (b) diversions should be a real forced-timed rest break/interruption, even though that might risk having workers leave our task completely? Or (c) micro-diversions that are fun and engaging so that we might maximize worker retention and performance? Since there are many possible micro-diversions that we could examine, we decided to opt for (c), leaving the complexity of the issue for future work. Since we were not confident that micro-diversion actually improves retention and performance in crowdsourcing environments, we thought (c) is the most likely to produce an positive effect.

Here we introduce the three diversion types as shown in Figure 2:

Control / No Diversions (ND)
No Diversion is the baseline control condition.

Game Diversion (GD)
We used a simple dice game. Workers were presented with a dialog window that allows them to wager a proportion of the rewards they have accrued so far for more. For instance, the worker could spend 4 cents to have a 50/50 shot at 8 cents, or a 25% chance of getting 16 cents. After picking their wager or choosing not to wager anything, flashing graphics are shown about a rolling dice and finally the amount of payoff. This diversion employs the gambler's fallacy as a gamification mechanic. The gambler's fallacy relies around poor human odds estimation.

In our game, the odds were set completely *n*eutrally—that is, workers should get the same pay over the long run, whether they gambled or not. However, thanks to the gambler's fallacy, a few losses might encourage the worker to try again because they "feel a win coming".

Because the gaming process was easy and encouraged speed, this diversion type is somewhat perceptual, and might relate more easily to the perceptual image tagging (II) task rather than the highly cognitive entity merging (FE) task. Or alternatively, one might surmise that a perceptual diversion would be welcome after a long cognitive load period.

Story Diversion (SD)
Workers received one page of a Hugo-Award-winning narrative webcomic, Digger, by Ursula Vernon [40] (used with permission). This comic features compelling general-interest stories and rich visual designs that continue from page to page. For each diversion, a worker received one page of the comic in the sequence. Worker had to scroll to the end of the page to start their next task. By continuing to work one could see more of the comic and therefore learn more of the story. This introduces a motivation mechanic to continue, though utilizes some cognitive resources. The worker must think and read in order to appreciate the comic.

Because of its narrative and cognitive nature, this diversion might relate more closely to the Wikipedia (WQ) and entity (FE) tasks rather than the Image labeling (II) tasks. Alternatively, one might surmise that a cognitive reading task would be a welcome break to a long perceptual task.

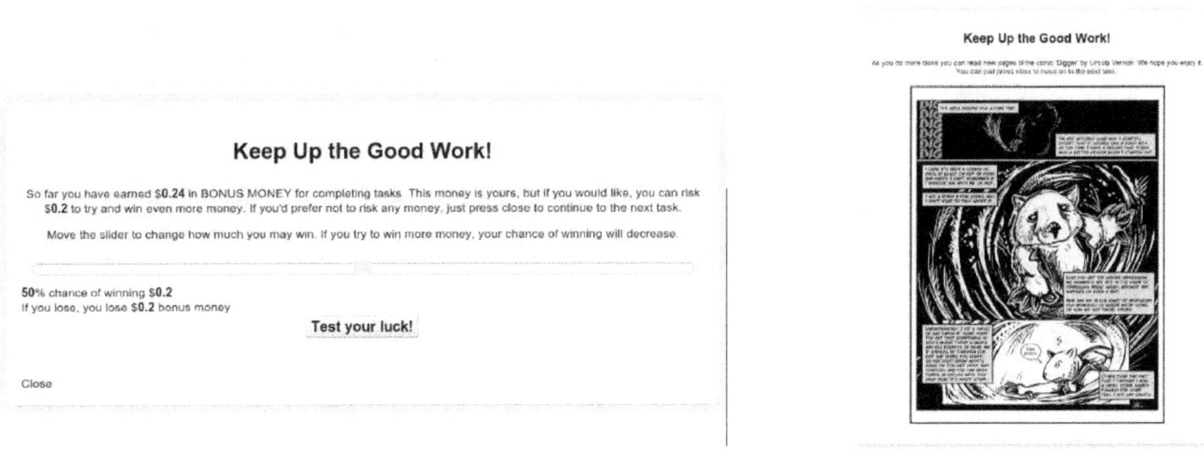

Figure 2. Example micro-diversions. The Control (No Diversions, ND) baseline is not shown here. Left: rolling the dice (Game Diversion, GD). Right: serialized comic (Story Diversion, SD).

Diversion delivery and experiment schedule

We wanted to interrupt the workers with a diversions approximately once every 10 minutes. Therefore, to determine the diversion schedule, we divided 10 minutes by the average answer time per question/work unit (called Human Intelligence Task / HIT on MTurk) and rounded the result to its nearest integer number f. To determine the average answer time per HIT, we ran a calibration pilot over approximately 30 workers for each task type. The values of f for the Wikipedia Quality (WQ), Freebase Entities (FE) and Image Identification (II) tasks were 4, 8, and 6 respectively. We adopted a static diversion schedule of every f HITs, so, on average, we expect a diversion to happen approximately every 10 minutes. We chose to deliver diversions after a set number of tasks rather than exactly 10 minutes to avoid interrupting workers mid-task.

As mentioned previously, a worker can quickly skip over a diversion by clicking to proceed to the next question as soon as the diversion UI loads (typically just a few seconds).

Experiment time: To ensure a similar participant pool, we posted tasks at the same time (4-5PM PST) each day and let them run until all tasks are completed or 48 hours have elapsed.

Subject Experimental Procedure

Server Software: We developed a web server on Google AppEngine that allowed us to deliver controlled batches of tasks to workers through Mechanical Turk. The server maintains state information on each worker.

The experimental procedure for a single worker is as follows:

When a worker asks for a task, her browser queries our server through the external question interface on MTurk. URL parameters encode metadata such as which conditions (task and diversion types) the worker is under. Upon receiving the request, the server examines its database for an entry for that worker's assigned condition combination.

If the worker is in the middle of the batch, it determines whether the worker is due for a diversion. If the worker is not due for a diversion, it randomly chooses a new, uncompleted task in the batch.

The worker is free to leave any time they wished. When they first start, workers are informed they are free to leave at any time and collect payment for the tasks completed so far. In the interface workers saw a large "Finish & Collect Payment" button at the bottom of the screen, which they could press to finish early, or by using standard MTurk UI. We designed our tasks so that Amazon recorded each work unit (HIT) that the workers completed. Later, we paid workers by referring to HIT counts.

The system closes out an experimental condition after a maximum of 30 workers have participated.

RESULTS AND ANALYSIS

In this section, we present the results from our micro-diversion experiment. First, we perform detailed analysis on worker retention. Next, we focus on worker accuracy under various conditions, then we analyze the time on task.

RQ1: Worker Retention

We present worker survival analysis using retention as our dependent measure. For each of the task types, we will first show retention curves and statistics, and then report on ANOVA analysis results on the log transformed *task counts* (the total number of work units completed per worker.) Finally, we show the corresponding results of a negative binomial regression, which is typically used to model repeated binary survival events.

Retention Curves

Figure 3 shows the relative change compared to the Control (No Diversions, ND) baseline for each diversion type.

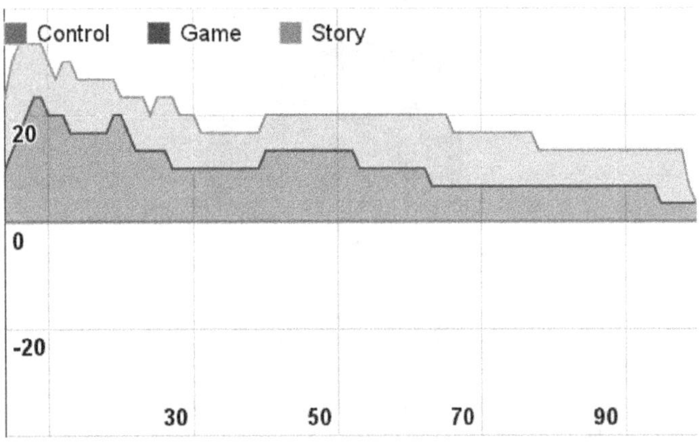

(a) Retention Curve for Wikipedia Quality (WQ) task

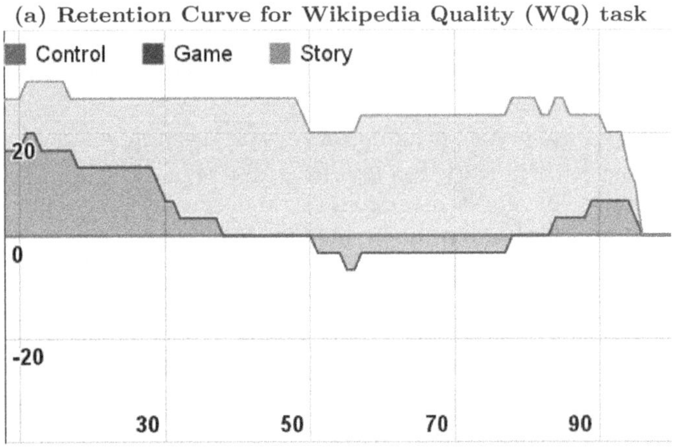

(b) Retention Curve for Freebase Entity (FE) task

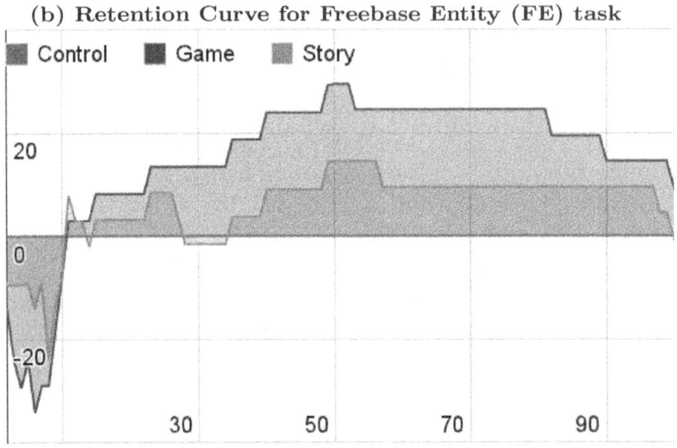

(c) Retention Curve for Image Identification (II) task

Figure 3. Retention (survival) comparison for three different task types under three different diversion types. X-axis is the number of tasks finished by the workers in a task-diversion condition (longer is better). The Control is the baseline and normalized to be flat on the x-axis. Y-axis is the percentage of delta workers retained as compared to the Control baseline (purple) for at least x tasks under the Game (red) and Story (blue) diversion types (higher is better).

The x-axis depicts the total number of tasks completed, and the y-axis shows the percentage difference of the amount of workers who *survived*, or chose to work on more tasks, after finishing a certain number of tasks (x), as compared to the Control baseline. So higher on the y-axis and further to the right on the x-axis are both better. For the three different diversion types, the Control ND is the purple baseline and normalized to be flat on the X-axis, while Game Diversion (GD) type is red, and Story Diversion (SD) is blue.

Wikipedia article Quality rating (WQ) tasks: As shown in Figure 3(a), we find that both the Game and the Story micro-diversion types influenced workers to perform more work when compared to the Control Baseline. More than 20% of workers stayed compared to the Control after finishing half of the tasks. Since workers are essentially paid the same across these different diversion conditions, this is an impressive difference.

Freebase Entity merging (FE) tasks: As shown in Figure 3(b), we see something slightly different from the WQ tasks above. While the Story micro-diversion continues to have a significant, positive impact on worker engagement, the Game condition converges to the Control baseline asymptotically. We surmise that this is due to the cognitive nature of the FE task being too different from our Game diversion, introducing switching costs by distracting workers.

Image Identification (II) tasks: As shown in Figure 3(c), in the beginning, we retained less workers in both the Game and Story diversions, suggesting micro-diversions did not help. Due to the rapid, perceptual nature of the task, it can be completed in a short amount of time with low effort. These tasks are the most profitable when someone completes them in large volume, so workers prefer to do them quickly and without interruption. Even Game condition can be a distraction, since it requires a bit of thinking and planning. Interestingly, after iterating through some instances of the tasks, micro-diversions start to keep more workers around, with Game retaining workers quite well.

Retention Statistics

We computed the means and standard deviations of the number of tasks completed. Results in Table 1 are consistent with our retention curve analysis above, and show that using diversions can improve workers' average survival rate, by a factor of 5 in the best scenario (Story Diversion with the Wikipedia Quality task).

	Wikipedia	Freebase	Image
Control	5.4 (8.6)	12.7 (26.2)	26.3 (30.3)
Game	16.7 (29.3)	16.9 (26.4)	**41.1** (44.8)
Story	**25.3** (37.0)	**35.8** (42.2)	31.85 (38.0)

Table 1. Average number of work units each worker completed for each diversion-task combination. The standard deviations are reported inside parentheses. The best results for each task type are in bold font.

ANOVA Analysis on Retention

We performed a two-way ANOVA analysis on the log transformation of the task count[2]. The results show a main effect on Task Type, $F(2,230) = 8.400, p = .0003$, as well as a main effect on Diversion Type, but instead at the $p < .05$ level, $F(2,230) = 4.203, p = .016$. There were no interaction effects, $F(4,230) = 0.889$, n.s.

Post-hoc Pairwise t-test with Holm-Bonferroni correction at the $p = .01$ level of significance showed that the Image (II) task retained workers longer when compared with Wikipedia (WQ) and Freebase (FE) tasks, but WQ and FE were not significantly different from each other.

Another post-hoc Pairwise t-test with Holm-Bonferroni correction at the $p = .01$ level showed that the Story diversion type retained workers longer than Control and Game types, with Control and Game not significantly different from each other.

In short, the results here suggest that the Image (II) task generally retains workers better than Wikipedia (WQ) and Freebase (FE) tasks. Moreover, the Story type seems to be more engaging to workers than the other diversions.

Negative Binomial Regression Analysis on Retention

Using negative binomial regression, we modeled the influence of the diversions on the number of completed work units using Control with no diversions as the baseline. Results are shown in Table 2.

For the Wikipedia task (Regression 1), the results suggest that both Game and Story diversions improved retention compared to the baseline.

For the Freebase task (Regression 2), the Story diversion has retention effect with a significant coefficient, while the Game diversion does not.

For the Image task type (Regression 3), for both Game and Story conditions, while the coefficient estimates are positive, these results have not reached significance. However, the results here are still consistent with what we have observed with the Wikipedia and Freebase tasks in Regressions 1 and 2.

In general, the results suggest that micro-diversions are more effective in complex, cognitive tasks in retaining workers. Intuitively, there may be a continuum of task domains, where some tasks are so easy that the diversions are not desirable. However, as the tasks become harder, the diversions start to have an effect. Moreover, this is consistent with past literature on interruptions suggesting that context determine whether interruptions might have impact [22, 30, 34].

[2]The task count distribution can be modeled with negative binomial, therefore we applied log transformation to the task count. An alternative statistical test here is to use the non-parametric equivalent of Kruskal-Wallis test, which also resulted in similar conclusions here, with significance on Task Type, $\chi^2(2) = 16.72, p < .001$, as well as Diversion Type, $\chi^2(2) = 6.628, p = 0.036$.

	Regression 1 Wikipedia	Regression 2 Freebase	Regression 3 Image
(Intercept)	**1.6802**	**2.5416**	**3.2682**
Game	**1.0924**	0.2837	0.4478
Story	**1.5185**	**1.0354**	0.1929

Table 2. Negative binomial regression coefficient estimates using Control as the baseline and introducing either a Game or Story diversions. Significant results ($p < 0.01$) are in bold font. A positive coefficient means the condition improves worker retention.

RQ2: Worker Performance

Answer Response Time

	Wikipedia	Freebase	Image
Control	190.2 (112.5)	115.4 (111.5)	52.9 (32.5)
Game	**134.9** (98.9)	80.6 (64.1)	53.6 (43.1)
Story	145.3 (119.9)	**62.3** (86.6)	**50.0** (51.4)

Table 3. Average median time in seconds per worker. The standard deviations are reported in parentheses. The best time values per task type are in bold font.

A two-way ANOVA analysis on the log transformation of the task time yielded a main effect for Task Type at the $p < .01$ level, $F(2,230) = 35.004, p < .001$, as well as a main effect for Diversion Type, $F(2,230) = 6.575, p = .0017$. There were no interaction effects, $F(4,230) = 1.292, n.s.$

Post-hoc Pairwise t-test with Holm-Bonferroni correction at the $p = .01$ level of significance showed that the Wikipedia task type took significantly more time than Freebase and Image task types, but Freebase and Image task types were not significantly different from each other.

Another post-hoc Pairwise t-test with Holm-Bonferroni correction at the $p = .01$ level showed that the Story diversion was significantly faster than the Control, with other comparisons being non-significant.

Based on these results, it seems that task contexts as well as the type of micro-diversions affect answer response time. Indeed, inspecting Table 3, the results suggest that Game and Story both improved answer response time quite a bit for the Wikipedia and Freebase task types.

Worker Accuracy

	Wikipedia	Freebase	Image
Control	66.7 (38.3)	67.8 (32.1)	79.3 (20.1)
Game	**84.2** (23.9)	**69.9** (30.2)	**81.4** (15.7)
Story	68.8 (31.0)	66.9 (33.2)	78.3 (15.3)

Table 4. Worker Accuracy in percentage (%) for each task-diversion combination. The standard deviations are reported in parentheses. The best accuracy values per task type are in bold font.

A two-way ANOVA analysis on accuracy yielded a main effect for Task Type at the $p < .01$ level, $F(2,231) =$

64.62, $p < .001$. However, Diversion Type was not significant, $F(2, 193) = 0.550$, n.s. The interaction effect was also not significant, $F(4, 193) = 0.854$, n.s.

Post-hoc Pairwise t-test with Holm-Bonferroni correction at the .01 level of significance showed that Wikipedia and Image task types were significantly more accurate than Freebase task type, but Wikipedia and Image task types were not significantly different from each other.

The results here suggest that, while micro-diversions did not improve worker accuracy, they did not decrease worker accuracy either. Task type is mainly what determines the accuracy of the workers.

Overall, the results suggest that, with micro-diversions served at fixed frequencies, workers seems faster in completing their tasks (with the exception of the Image task) while retaining the same level of accuracy.

DISCUSSIONS

Here we return to the research questions to see what conclusions we might draw from the results of the experiment.

First, for RQ1 on retention, we saw in the experiment that micro-diversions can significantly retain workers for more work, compared to no diversions. Moreover, certain diversion types appear to retain worker better in some task domains. This is interesting, because the results suggest that we can improve worker experience by introducing micro-diversions into long, monotonous crowdsourcing tasks.

Second, for RQ2 on work performance, we saw in the experiment that workers retained their accuracy, suggesting that micro-diversions are not a significant disruptive interruption to their workflow. It is reassuring that, while micro-diversions did not actually improve worker accuracy (perhaps because workers were already as accurate as they could be), diversions were not a detriment to worker accuracy either.

More interestingly, there are evidences that workers are faster if they receive micro-diversions. In particular, the Story diversion seems to encourage workers to perform faster compared to other diversion types. If workers can maintain their accuracy while working faster, this would have implications for how we should design long, monotonous tasks on crowdsourcing platforms.

Combined with the results from RQ1, we are starting to get a picture that micro-diversions not only can retain workers for longer, but help them work faster, while retaining the same level of work quality! While we did not measure boredom directly, the results are suggestive that workers do experience boredom and that entertaining diversions might enable them to combat these effects.

Finally, for RQ3 on contextual effects, we seek to understand whether specific combinations of task and diversion type might work better than other combinations. While the ANOVA results suggest there is no interaction effects, the negative binomial regression suggests that certain combinations seem to work better than others. Theoretically, since task count is a negative binomial distribution, the negative binomial regression should yield a better model than ANOVA. From this perspective, the results of the regression analysis are worthy of further investigation.

Intuitively, we believe it makes sense that particular diversion types work better with certain task domains. The psychology of tasks suggest that humans are able to deal with fast, instinctive, perceptual tasks separately from the more deliberative, logical, cognitive tasks [24]. The Image identification tasks correspond to the faster, perceptive tasks discussed in Kahneman's work, while the Wikipedia tasks correspond to the more slower, cognitive tasks. Based on our results, more research is necessary to fully understand how these two task types interact, when either type can be the main task or the micro-diversion.

Interestingly, we did not investigate the case where the micro-diversions could also result in useful work. MTurk workers currently curate their own mix of tasks by searching over the available tasks, such that the mix remains interesting to them. Our research suggest some automation might be possible to maximize worker productivity and engagement.

CONCLUSIONS

In this paper, we proposed introducing micro-diversions to crowdsourcing workflows to improve worker experience, so as to retain good quality workers for longer. We implemented an experimental system for delivering micro-diversions interleaved with tasks to crowdsourced workers in a controlled fashion.

We explored different types of micro-diversions, including a wager-based game and a serialized webcomic story. We also examined several different task types, including a Wikipedia quality rating task, an Image identification annotation task, and a Freebase entity resolution task.

We demonstrated that introducing micro-diversions into a workflow can significantly improve worker retention as well as their answer speed, while retaining the same level of work quality. The improved worker retention and performance varied depending on the type of task and micro-diversion they received. Interestingly, in our experiment, tasks and diversions that are more closely aligned in context seemed to perform better. Moreover, the results also suggest that complex cognitive tasks might benefit from micro-diversions more than fast perceptual tasks.

As far as we know, this is the first attempt to improve crowdsourced worker engagement through timely micro-diversions. In the future, we plan to study different reward amount as well as the nature and complexity of the task versus the effectiveness of micro-diversions. We surmise that micro-diversions are more useful when they employ different thinking systems than the main task. We also plan to apply machine learning and decision-theoretic models [15, 33] to dynamically recognize workers' need for a refresh break and schedule them automatically.

REFERENCES

1. Piotr D. Adamczyk and Brian P. Bailey. If not now, when?: The effects of interruption at different moments within task execution. In *Proceedings of the SIGCHI conference on Human factors in computing systems*, pages 271–278, 2004.
2. James Bo Begole and John C. Tang. Incorporating human and machine interpretation of unavailability and rhythm awareness into the design of collaborative applications. *Human-Computer Interaction*, 22(1-2):7–45, 2007.
3. Michael S. Bernstein, Greg Little, Robert C. Miller, Björn Hartmann, Mark S. Ackerman, David R. Karger, David Crowell, and Katrina Panovich. Soylent: A word processor with a crowd inside. In *Proceedings of the 23Nd Annual ACM Symposium on User Interface Software and Technology*, UIST, 2010.
4. Kurk Bollacker, Colin Evans, Praveen Paritosh, Time Sturge Tim, and Jamie Taylor. Freebase: A collaboratively created graph database for structuring human knowledge. In *Proceedings of the 2008 ACM SIGMOD International Conference on Management of Data*, pages 1247–1250, 2008.
5. Chris Callison-Burch. Fast, cheap, and creative: Evaluating translation quality using amazon's mechanical turk. In *Proceedings of the 2009 Conference on Empirical Methods in Natural Language Processing*, pages 286–295, 2009.
6. Jonathan S. A. Carriere, J. Allan Cheyne, and Daniel Smilek. Everyday attention lapses and memory failures: The affective consequences of mindlessness. *Consciousness and Cognition*, 17:835–847, 2008.
7. Jonathan S. A. Carriere, J. Allan Cheyne, and Daniel Smilek. Boredom: An emotional experience distinct from apathy, anhedonia, or depression. *Social and Clinical Psychology*, 30(6):647–666, 2011.
8. Dana Chandler and Adam Kapelner. Breaking monotony with meaning: Motivation in crowdsourcing markets. *CoRR*, abs/1210.0962, 2012.
9. Lydia B. Chilton, John J. Horton, Robert C. Miller, and Shiri SAzenkot. Task search in a human computation market. In *Proceedings of the ACM SIGKDD Workshop on Human Computation*, HCOMP '10, pages 1–9, 2010.
10. Mihaly Csikszentmihalyi. *Creativity: Flow and the Psychology of Discovery and Invention.* HarperCollins, 1997.
11. Mihaly Csikszentmihalyi. *Beyond Boredom and Anxiety: Experiencing Flow in Work and Play.* Jossey-Bass, 2000.
12. Edward Cutrell, Mary Czerwinski, and Eric Horvitz. Notification, disruption, and memory: Effects of messaging interruptions on memory and performance. In *INTERACT*, pages 263–269, 2001.
13. Mary Czerwinski, Edward Cutrell, and Eric Horvitz. Instant messaging and interruption: Influence of task type on performance, 2000.
14. Peng Dai, Christopher H. Lin, Mausam, and Daniel S. Weld. POMDP-based control of workflows for crowdsourcing. *Artificial Intelligence*, 202:52–85, 2013.
15. Peng Dai, Mausam, and Daniel S. Weld. Decision-theoretic control of crowd-sourced workflows. In *AAAI*, 2010.
16. Peng Dai, Mausam, and Daniel S. Weld. Artificial intelligence for artificial artificial intelligence. In *AAAI*, 2011.
17. Pinar Donmez, Jaime G. Carbonell, and Jeff G. Schneider. A probabilistic framework to learn from multiple annotators with time-varying accuracy. In *SDM*, pages 826–837, 2010.
18. Robert A. Henning, Steven L Sauter, Gavriel Salvendy, and Edward F. Krieg. Microbreak length, performance, and stress in a data entry task. *Ergonomics*, 32(7):855–864, 1989.
19. John Joseph Horton. Employer expectations, peer effects and productivity: Evidence from a series of field experiments. *CoRR*, abs/1008.2437, 2010.
20. John Joseph Horton and Lydia B. Chilton. The labor economics of paid crowdsourcing. *CoRR*, 2010.
21. Eric Huang, Haoqi Zhang, David C. Parkes, Krzysztof Z. Gajos, and Yiling Chen. Toward automatic task design: A progress report. In *Proceedings of the ACM SIGKDD Workshop on Human Computation*, pages 77–85, 2010.
22. Shamsi T. Iqbal and Brian P. Bailey. Effects of intelligent notification management on users and their tasks. In *Proceedings of the SIGCHI Conference on Human Factors in Computing Systems*, CHI '08, pages 93–102, 2008.
23. Shamsi T. Iqbal and Eric Horvitz. Disruption and recovery of computing tasks: Field study, analysis, and directions. In *CHI*, pages 677–686, 2007.
24. Daniel Kahneman. *Thinking, Fast and Slow.* Macmillan, 2011.

25. Aniket Kittur, Ed H. Chi, and Bongwon Suh. Crowdsourcing user studies with mechanical turk. In *Proceedings of the SIGCHI Conference on Human Factors in Computing Systems*, pages 453–456, 2008.

26. Aniket Kittur, Susheel Khamkar, Paul André, and Robert Kraut. Crowdweaver: Visually managing complex crowd work. In *Proceedings of the ACM 2012 Conference on Computer Supported Cooperative Work*, CSCW, pages 1033–1036, 2012.

27. Aniket Kittur, Boris Smus, Susheel Khamkar, and Robert E. Kraut. Crowdforge: Crowdsourcing complex work. In *Proceedings of the 24th Annual ACM Symposium on User Interface Software and Technology*, pages 43–52, 2011.

28. Aniket Kittur, Bongwon Suh, Bryan A. Pendleton, and Ed H. Chi. He says, she says: Conflict and coordination in wikipedia. In *Proceedings of the SIGCHI Conference on Human Factors in Computing Systems*, CHI, pages 453–462, 2007.

29. Shailesh Kochhar, Stefano Mazzocchi, and Praveen Paritosh. The anatomy of a large-scale human computation engine. In *Proceedings of the ACM SIGKDD Workshop on Human Computation*, pages 10–17, 2010.

30. John G. Kreifeldt and M. E. Mccarthy. Interruption as a test of the user-computer interface. In *Proceedings of the 17th Annual Conference on Manual Control*, pages 655–667, 1981.

31. Gerald P. Krueger. Sustained work, fatigue, sleep loss and performance: A review of the issues. *Work & Stress*, 3:129–141, 1989.

32. Chris J. Lintott, Kevin Schawinski, Kate L, Daniel Thomas, M. Jordan Raddick, Robert C. Nichol, Dan Andreescu, Phil Murray, and Jan Van Den Berg. Galaxy zoo: morphologies derived from visual inspection of galaxies from the sloan digital sky survey," monthly notices of the royal. *Astronomical Society*, 2008.

33. Andrew Mao, Ece Kamar, and Eric Horvitz. Why stop now? predicting worker engagement in online crowdsourcing. In *HCOMP*, 2013.

34. Gloria Mark, Daniela Gudith, and Ulrich Klocke. The cost of interrupted work: More speed and stress. In *Proceedings of the SIGCHI Conference on Human Factors in Computing Systems*, CHI '08, pages 107–110, 2008.

35. Nathalie Pattyn, Xavier Neyt, David Henderickx, and Eric Soetens. Psychophysiological investigation of vigilance decrement: Boredom or cognitive fatigue? *Physiology & Behavior*, 93:369–378, 2008.

36. Layne P. Perelli. *Fatigue Stressors in Simulated Long-duration Flight: Effects on Performance, Information Processing, Subjective Fatigue, and Physiological Cost.* USAF School of Aerospace Medicine, Aerospace Medical Division (AFSC), 1980.

37. George Robertson, Eric Horvitz, Mary Czerwinski, Patrick Baudisch, Dugald R. Hutchings, Brain Meyers, Daniel Robbins, and Greg Smith. Scalable fabric: Flexible task management. In *Proceedings of the Working Conference on Advanced Visual Interfaces*, pages 85–89, 2004.

38. Jeffrey M. Rzeszotarski and Aniket Kittur. Instrumenting the crowd: Using implicit behavioral measures to predict task performance. In *Proceedings of the 24th Annual ACM Symposium on User Interface Software and Technology*, UIST, pages 13–22, 2011.

39. Cheri Speier, Joseph S. Valacich, and Iris Vessey. The effects of task interruption and information presentation on individual decision making. In *ICIS*, pages 21–36, 1997.

40. Digger U. Verson, 2012. www.diggercomic.com.

41. Jacob Whitehill, Paul Ruvolo, Tingfan Wu, Jacob Bergsma, and Javier R. Movellan. Whose vote should count more: Optimal integration of labels from labelers of unknown expertise. In *NIPS*, pages 2035–2043, 2009.

42. Glenn Wylie and Alan Allport. Task switching and the measurement of "switch costs". *Psychological Research*, 63:212–233, 2000.

43. Lixiu Yu and Jeffrey V. Nickerson. Cooks or cobblers?: Crowd creativity through combination. In *Proceedings of the SIGCHI Conference on Human Factors in Computing Systems*, pages 1393–1402, 2011.

CURIOS: Connecting Community Heritage through Linked Data

Gemma Webster Hai H. Nguyen David E. Beel Chris Mellish Claire D. Wallace Jeff Pan
dot.rural RCUK Digital Economy Research Hub
University of Aberdeen
Aberdeen, UK
[gwebster, hai.nguyen, d.e.beel, c.mellish, c.wallace, jeff.z.pan]@abdn.ac.uk

ABSTRACT
The CURIOS project explores how digital archives for rural community heritage groups can be made more sustainable so that volunteer members can maintain a lasting digital presence. It is developing software tools to help remote rural communities to collaboratively maintain and present information about their cultural heritage. The objective is to investigate the use of semantic web/linked data technology to build a general, flexible and "future proof" software platform that could help such projects to develop digital archives and to be sustainable over time. As an interdisciplinary project we aim to synthesise a narrative that draws from both social science and computer science perspectives by critically reflecting upon the novel approach taken and the on-going results that are being produced.

Author Keywords
Cultural Heritage; Digital Archives; Community heritage; Open Linked Data.

ACM Classification Keywords
E.2 [Data]: Data Storage Representations – Linked representations, J.4 [Computer Applications]: Social and Behavioral Science – Sociology, K.4.0 [Computers and Society]: General.

General Terms
Human Factors

MOVING TOWARDS COMMUNITY DIGITAL HERITAGE
Rural areas are characterised by a strong identity of people with place. These identities draw on a repertoire of cultural norms, knowledge, histories, customs and practices which, taken together, construct unique place identities. This cultural distinctiveness is dynamic given traditional cultural practices are reproduced and others introduced as cultural systems evolve and adapt. Forms of cultural expression, such as story-telling, music and song, poetry and literature, dance and drama, together with material objects, artifacts, sites and cultural spaces, are resources for interacting with the past and for experiencing the present. In the collection and transmission of these collections there has been a growing sense that the traditional methods for doing this are failing [13].

In order to address this problem, digital solutions have been sought but this has been a problematic process due to a number of variances. These include the constant changing of file types, software and codes of best practice, as well problems to do with cost and the sheer amounts of 'analogue' data to convert. National institutions have been leading the way in this process, but with the production of such local cultural repertoires, which as Flynn [6] suggests 'are the grassroots activities' where 'control and ownership of the project is essential', there has been a failure to consider the needs of community heritage groups in these processes [7]. Additionally, such groups do not want to be subsumed into national archives, which they do not control, are not sensitive to their needs and are juxtaposed ideologically to the production of their own 'place history'. Following Creswell's [5] claim that such archives represent 'spaces of marginalized memory' CURIOS is therefore seeking a solution, using open linked data, in which a system can be developed that is attuned to the specificity of a local heritage but can also take advantage of already collected materials from elsewhere.

LINKED OPEN DATA: TOWARDS AN ARCHIVE FOR THE FUTURE?
Digital archives can have several limitations, particularly when collected and maintained by different community groups. Firstly, due to community heritage often being gathered by volunteers there is a wide range of computer literacy across individuals as well as organisations. Secondly the data formats between collections and tools for digitising heritage data are not consistent. For example, some groups may choose to use common multipurpose tools such as spreadsheets to maintain their archives. Others may use pre-existing genealogy software or a traditional relational database. Larger organisations such as national institutions may choose other formats to meet their specific requirements such as Key-Value data-stores for

CSCW 2015, March 14–18, 2015, Vancouver, BC, Canada.
Copyright 2015 © ACM 978-1-4503-2922-4/15/03...$15.00.
http://dx.doi.org/10.1145/2675133.2675247

performance or Resource Description Framework (RDF) triplestores for integration and reusability.

Due to the wide ranging and different types of data formats, it is not trivial for digitalised cultural heritage to be reused and integrated with each other. Most digital archives, therefore, can only be exploited separately, meaning connecting local cultural heritage with national archives cannot be done easily. The integration of knowledge from different digital archives where possible, has been done manually by humans. To automate this process, i.e., to integrate/contextualise contents from different archives, it is important to keep data in an open and reusable format [4].

A solution to an open and reusable data format is the Linked Open Data format. The emergence of the Semantic Web [14] has led to several standard formats for representing and interchanging data [2,8]. In 2009, Tim Berners-Lee proposed linked data as a set of best practices using standard web technologies to publish and link data on the web [11]. These practices involved publishing data using Uniform Resource Identifiers (URIs) such as web addresses and relating those using defined relationships (links). The description of data is then stored as RDF triples in the form:

<subject link object>

where *subject* is a URI, *link* specifies the type of relationship between the *subject* and *object*, and object can be either a literal (i.e., raw data such as numbers, text) or a URI. Using this format, information regarding a subject (e.g., a URI) will be stored as a set of triples in an RDF-supported database, usually referred to as a triplestore.

For example "Angus Macloed lives at 8 Calbost" would be represented in RDF triples as:

<hc:23160 dc:title "Angus Macleod">

<hc:23160 hc:liveat hc:1914>

<hc:1914 dc:title "8 Calbost">

The above example describes two subjects in the Hebridean Connections archive: Angus Macleod (hc:23160) and 8 Calbost (hc:1914) by their titles and the relationship between them, e.g., *hc:liveat* (hc: and dc: are prefixes to identify namespaces for the vocabulary being used). Data holding in the RDF triples can be retrieved and updated by users via SPARQL, a query language for retrieving and maintaining data stored in RDF format.

So far, there has been a vast increase in the number of linked data datasets becoming available on the web [3]. By making use of linked data, cultural repositories would have the potential for reuse and integration with further related data sources. Using Linked Open Data formats, multiple datasets can be integrated and jointly exploited by SPARQL. There have been several attempts to bring cultural heritage data into the Linked Open Data formats such as in the CultureSampo project [10] and the OpenART project [9].

The CultureSampo project aims to create a cultural heritage archive for the whole nation by providing an infrastructures and a set of tools to publish and annotate contents collectively. The case study used in this project is the Finnish cultural heritage archives. On a smaller scale, the OpenART project brings an important arts research dataset, "The London Art World 1660-1735", to the Linked Open Data format so that contents about the art world during that period can be contextualised and linked to the Tate collection and referred to the relevant contemporary art works.

The CURIOS project also aims to overcome the data heterogeneity problem by keeping cultural heritage data in the Linked Open Data format. Yet unlike above projects, which focus on a specific dataset/case-study, CURIOS aims to not only exploit existing linked datasets but also allow the creation of new ones. To do so, CURIOS provides a set of software and tools to assist users with limited Semantic Technology knowledge in producing and consuming their cultural heritage in the form of linked data.

CASE STUDY – HEBRIDEAN CONNECTIONS

In the past 40 years around 20 'Comainn Eachdraidh' have been established in the Outer Hebrides, a group of islands off the West coast of mainland Scotland. Comainn Eachdraidh is a Gaelic phrase meaning 'Historical Societies' and they are community run groups that began in the 1970's with a very specific political and cultural purpose – to preserve the culture, history and language of the primarily Gaelic regions of Scotland. Comainn Eachdraidh across the Outer Hebrides are often very geographically based, both physically within their community space and with a specific focus on their local community history, meaning each can have very different aims and objectives. Such community heritage practices have been described as a 'messy' endeavour with a wide variety of different formal and informal practices [12,17]. The archives embrace different registers of social memory from tangible to intangible heritage, which have been collected and ordered in a variety of different ways: from the highly 'professional' to the more bespoke and sporadic. As the Comainn Eachdraidh groups are voluntary community archives, they are rooted in local historical values, hence there is often little consistency between groups regarding cataloguing, archiving and content management.

Hebridean Connections (HC), which is a community-managed, online historical resource, was formed due to the driving force of a single member of a Comainn Eachdraidh with a background in IT who saw the benefit of digitising and connecting the different historical catalogues [15]. The idea was proposed to the different Comainn Eachdraidh, with four groups (Bernara, Uig, Pairc and Kinloch) actively involved in securing a Heritage Lottery Fund (HLF) bid that funded the creation of the HC website (www.hebrideanconnections.com/). This initial phase fell into abeyance due to a number of reasons (to be discussed in the following section) but has been resurrected through a second funding phase (which is collaborating with the CURIOS Project) and currently has two paid director/administrative staff funded by the Scottish Government's People's Community Fund (PCF) and has expanded from the original four Comainn Eachdraidh to ten historical societies.

HC is one example of a community-built digital cultural heritage repository where their long-term future is unclear. The project website, which was launched in 2006, holds some 100,000 records relating to the genealogy, history, archaeology, and cultural traditions of the Outer Hebrides. The collections are currently expanding as the additional six Comainn Eachdraidh are contributing their collections, and the vision is to expand the collections to incorporate all materials held by the remaining Comainn Eachdraidh. The project is enabling local heritage archives to become accessible to international diasporic communities, especially those with genealogical connections back to the islands. The collections fall outside the national and even local (government) institutional frameworks, hence local people are the 'gatekeepers' of their own heritage and are selecting what to commemorate based on their own customs of remembering. Additionally, the website encourages contributions from its users and therefore has the potential to foster reciprocal knowledge exchange across geographical boundaries. This kind of digital archive can have significant social impacts for the communities involved both at a local and global level. The initiative is heavily dependent upon the volunteer efforts of the Comainn Eachdraidh members and their on-going desire to convert their analogue collections into a digital form.

Sustainability and the Problem Case

The long-term future of Hebridean Connections is unclear, with many issues surrounding the current system arising since the initial grant (as mentioned). In particular, there are concerns around how small communities like this maintain such collections when funding periods have finished. This is something the CURIOS project has been trying to address, with its approach picking up from the failings of the HLF phase of HC. The following section will now detail the problem case for CURIOS before moving to detail the solutions proposed.

The initial website was developed by a private development company using proprietary software funded by the initial grant. The proprietary software restricted the use of the system via licenses and only four licenses were able to be purchased. These licenses were applied to four computers each physically located in Comainn Eachdraidh centres. This restriction on data entry made inputting records difficult and four staff were employed (one at each society) on short-term contracts to actually carry out the data entry to the system. The use of paid staff to digitise the physical records added a barrier to the Comainn Eachdraidh in that it stopped volunteers from being able to contribute to the project and restricted the progress of data entry to one person at a time.

Additionally, two new Comainn Eachdraidh groups decided to join the project but there was no additional funding to purchase licences, meaning a member from each of these groups had to physically travel to another Comainn Eachdraidh to use their computer to enter records. Records were also automatically assigned ownership based on licenses, meaning the two new groups records were automatically assigned to the Comainn Eachdraidh computer they were using, but there was no way for this to be changed without purchasing more licenses.

As the project developed, this situation raised the problem that any changes to the system required more financial investment in the software. For community led cultural heritage groups, funds are always scarce yet as the digital collection grew, the Comainn Eachdraidh became more aware of what was possible through digitisation and wanted to expand. The feasibility of this growth taking place within the constraints of the proprietary was not possible; hence when the HLF funding ended so did this phase of the project. The process of digitisation thus created a number of issues for Hebridean Connections:

- How to expand the project remit without additional funding for developers?
- Scalability issues, such as how can more Comainn Eachdraidh collections be integrated in a closed system?
- How can more volunteers be given access to the system?
- How can appropriate training be given to volunteers?
- How can we maintain our cultural archives independently?

The End of the Proprietary Software

After the HLF ran out there was no funding available to employ paid staff to continue the data entry. This caused a significant pause in the digitisation of the Comainn Eachdraidh collections for a number of reasons: the volunteers had not been responsible for the data entry previously; the software being used was no longer suitable as the project had continued to grow with multiple groups wanting to join but with no way for them to enter data; and finally, the new groups had different types of data within their collections that could not be added to the closed database design.

It was at this point that the CURIOS project began to investigate a suitable solution to the problem of how digital archives for rural community heritage groups can be made more sustainable, so that volunteer members can maintain a lasting digital presence. It was during the initial stages of the CURIOS project that more issues with the existing software became apparent. As all the data had been entered into an external database, in order to access and recover the original digitised data Hebridean Connections had to pay the external software company for access to their own data.

The format of the original data within the database was very restrictive and did not lend itself to being expanded. Some of the data within the database was out of date as it had been given to Hebridean Connections from the Royal Commission on Ancient and Historical Monuments of Scotland (RCAHMS) to enhance the information about important local features of the Outer Hebrides. This data from RCAHMS had been directly copied from their data source but had not been updated since it was copied. Consequently, the database would need to be completely re-designed.

Many of the Comainn Eachdraidh groups that had newly joined the HC project already had some digitized data, but it was within common genealogy software packages such as Brothers Keeper, which use a GEDCOM file format. A GEDCOM file contains genealogical information about individuals and is usually plain text and metadata showing the links between records. GEDCOM has many different proprietary extensions with most genealogy packages allowing the export/import of GEDCOM format but not necessarily the new extensions. This file format in itself caused problems as there was no apparent way to export a GEDCOM file and insert this into the pre-existing database. This meant many Comainn Eachdraidh groups thought they would have to start the digitisation process again.

It was also found that Hebridean Connections now had the only digital versions of some photographs and files. As the Comainn Eachdraidh groups had evolved over time original digital files (not the hard copies) had gone astray with members changing or the physical archives moving locations.

The issues outlined above all helped lead CURIOS to investigate the use of semantic web/linked data technology to build a general, flexible and "future proof" software platform that could help such projects as Hebridean Connections to develop digital archives and to be sustainable over time.

CURIOS

The CURIOS project's aim is to produce a sustainable system that allows a community of users to manage a digital archive of cultural heritage data, or 'cultural repository', releasing them from any specific proprietary software platform. As highlighted in the CrowdMemo project, using 'off the shelf' technologies in new ways can allow for long-term sustainability[1] to achieve this goal, CURIOS has made use of existing open source content management system (CMS) software and Semantic Web standards.

The CURIOS Content Management System

In recent years content management systems have gained popularity on the web by allowing users to build and publish web pages without requiring in-depth knowledge of the underlying web technologies. The CURIOS project has extended the web CMS approach to allow users to manage repositories of linked data. This linked data CMS approach makes use of existing CMS software to retain the usability and scalability of existing tools that are familiar to users, whilst allowing the users to exploit the benefits of linked data.

The Linked Data CMS approach has been implemented as a module for the popular open source web content management system Drupal (http://drupal.org), which we call the CURIOS system. There are three main reasons why Drupal was chosen over other open source CMS systems:

1. Drupal has a strong developer community and a large collection of high-quality and free contributed modules. This makes the system more sustainable and extensible. For example, the users can add new features to their system such as galleries, automatic logout and social media integration easily by installing appropriate modules.
2. The Drupal community has developed an interest in linked data technologies recently, introducing many useful modules to help integrate linked data into Drupal. By using pre-developed modules, the CURIOS project can focus on developing more generic and systematic solutions.
3. Most relevant to the CSCW community is that Drupal has a permissions and roles system that allows simple and effective implementation of collaborative user groups. For each operation, such as creating or updating existing content, there is a corresponding permission whose precondition only allows a special group of users to be able to perform that operation. For instance, if a record is maintained by a historical society, then only users within that historical society can edit or validate the record.

The CURIOS system stores its data in an RDF triplestore and performs SPARQL queries to create, maintain and retrieve the data. However, the complexities of Linked Open Data technologies are hidden away from end-users via a normal CMS user interface. Therefore, CURIOS allows users to consume and, more importantly, produce linked data without users' knowledge of the underneath technology. SPARQL is used as the query language in CURIOS as it is the predominant query language for RDF database format and allows the system to query data from multiple sources and present them as a unified result.

Unlike other approaches combining linked data and CMS, where linked datasets are imported into the CMS internal structures, CURIOS does not maintain the data in the CMS database and all queries and updates are performed directly against the RDF triplestore. As CURIOS does not store the data in Drupal's database, the module is loosely coupled to the dataset. This has the following advantages:

1. The dataset can be exported from the triplestore into different formats (e.g., XML, CSV, JSON…) at anytime without concerning Drupal's operations.
2. The same triplestore and dataset can be reused in other applications. For example, the CURIOS Mobile project also uses the same dataset and triplestore to provide an API so that mobile clients can reuse Hebridean Connections data within a tourist application.

Building the next generation of Hebridean Connections on open source software and web standards has distinct advantages for future development and the use of the system. The Drupal-based system can be maintained by its community of users and can be extended via additional functionality developed by the Drupal open source community, e.g., to support blogging or e-commerce features. This community led maintenance allows for further future development of the cultural repositories as the archives develop.

Validation and User Permissions

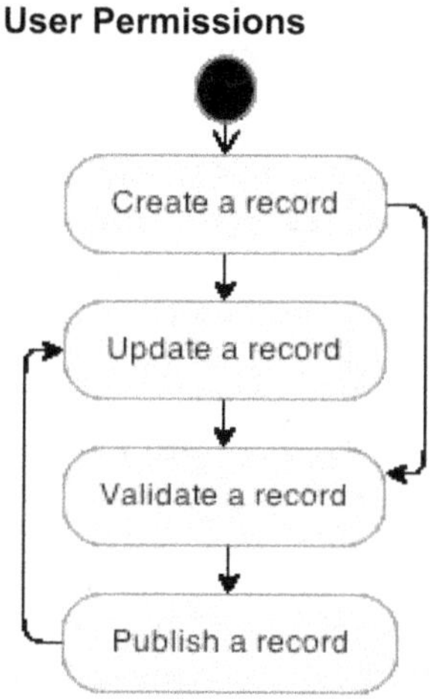

Figure 1: CURIOS record lifecycle

Currently, the record's metadata such as data owner, data maintainer, editing notes and publication status are stored together with the dataset in the RDF triplestore. This approach allows the datasets to be easily reusable in other applications and software without exporting data from Drupal's database. However, as different organisations have different group organisation, as well as policies regarding content creation, maintenance and validation process, CURIOS allows such groups/policies to be implemented in a flexible way by using Drupal permissions and roles system. For example, an "Editor" role allows users to create and update a record maintained by their group, e.g., a Comainn Eachdraidh group. However after being edited, the record will not be available to the public anymore as it needs to be validated by a "Validator", which is also a member of the same group. The lifecycle of a record within the CURIOS system is illustrated in Figure 1.

After a user creates a record, the record's metadata are automatically created by CURIOS: the owner and maintainer of the record is the user's group while the publication status is set to "pending". A user with editing permission can edit the pending record or already published records, given that the maintaining group of that record is also the user's group. However, note that an editor cannot edit the record's metadata and alls record after being edited will become "pending" automatically and hence needs validation. A user with validating permission from the same group can change the publication status of a pending record to "published". Note that in the Hebridean Connection case study, an editor and a validator, although come from the same group, have mutually exclusive permissions. In other words, an editor can only edit the record's content but not the metadata while a validator can only editor the metadata but not the content.

As a group in CURIOS is just a taxonomy-term field in the user's profile, it could be either shared among many users within a group, or made unique for each user. As the Hebridean Connections case study is a multiple group scenarios, we allowed users to shared a group name. In cases where the data is only maintained by group of individuals, we can easily turn the group name into the username, and hence allow a record to be owned and maintained by an individual instead of a group.

Building a CURIOS cultural heritage resource

CURIOS uses a Web Ontology Language (OWL) to describe its dataset classes and properties. Once the ontology is described, it is necessary to provide a separate description of which parts of the data (and the level of detail) are to be managed by the website. This description takes the form of an application-dependent configuration file which is loaded as part of the Drupal module. This file describes the classes, fields, and relationships to be shown in the website and how these relate to the constructs of the ontology [16]. Although the configuration file could be generated automatically, it is a declarative description and can easily be edited by hand.

The configuration file centralises the maintenance of the structure of the CMS with respect to the ontology, e.g., if a new type of page is required, the user can update the configuration and then run the Linked Data CMS mapping. When the CURIOS Drupal module is initialised, it automatically creates a set of Drupal resources and Views based on the configuration file, along with an additional set of pages allowing the linked data to be maintained. Drupal site administrators can then maintain the website generated by the configuration in the same way as a regular Drupal website.

Browsing and Update Functionalities

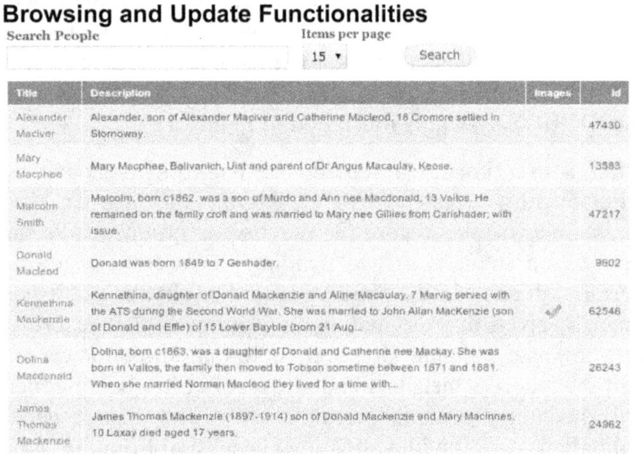

Figure 2: A list of people records

CURIOS allows users to create, update, or delete a record via a user-friendly GUI. For browsing, depending on the parameters such as the URI of a record or the resource types, CURIOS presents data in different ways. For instance, a list of records or details of a record will be displayed depending on whether the record URI is provided (see Figure 2). To support easy navigation between linked individuals, object properties of an RDF individual are presented as hyperlinks to other records as illustrated in Figure 3, instead of the normal text used for data type properties. CURIOS assists users entering data by providing different widgets depending on the data type the user wants to edit (Figure 4).

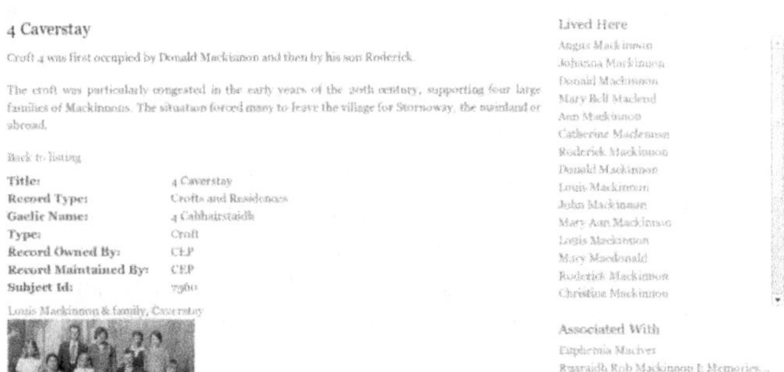

Figure 3: Details of a croft (A Croft is a small rented farm)

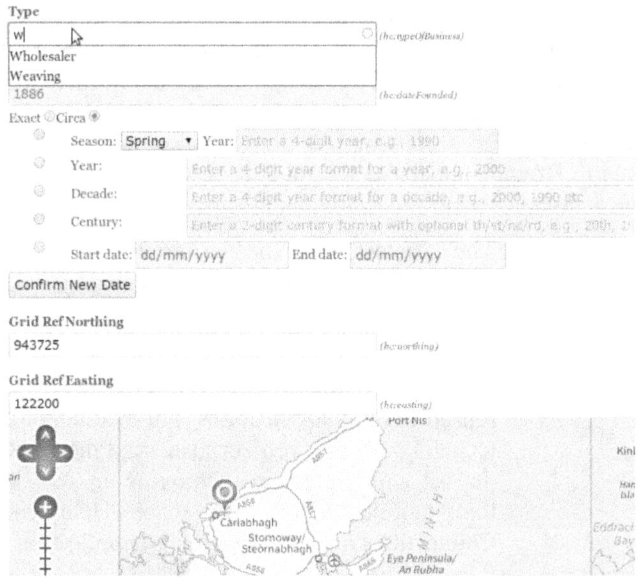

Figure 4: Updating special data types such as dates, geographical coordinates, etc.

For instance,

- Geographical coordinates, a map is displayed to allow users to choose a location rather than to type in the coordinates as text.
- To prevent users from entering incorrect values for some special properties such as an occupation or a type of place, an auto-complete widget is provided.
- It is typical that in the cultural heritage domain, temporal data such as dates are rather vague and not recorded in a consistent format. To facilitate users during data entry process, CURIOS provides a simple treatment to vague dates by introducing the hc:DateRange class which consists of two datetime datatype propertes: hc:dateFrom and hc:dateTo. A user can enter an exact date or a vague date such as a year, a season in a year, a decade, a century, etc, and CURIOS can convert the vague date into an appropriate instance of hc:DateRange. This mechanism separates the presentation of dates in the application-dependent interface from the actual data level.
- To manage object properties (i.e., links) between individuals, CURIOS allows property add and remove operations as presented in Figure 4, which are then mapped onto corresponding SPARQL update queries, e.g., INSERT and DELETE, to insert and remove appropriate triples.

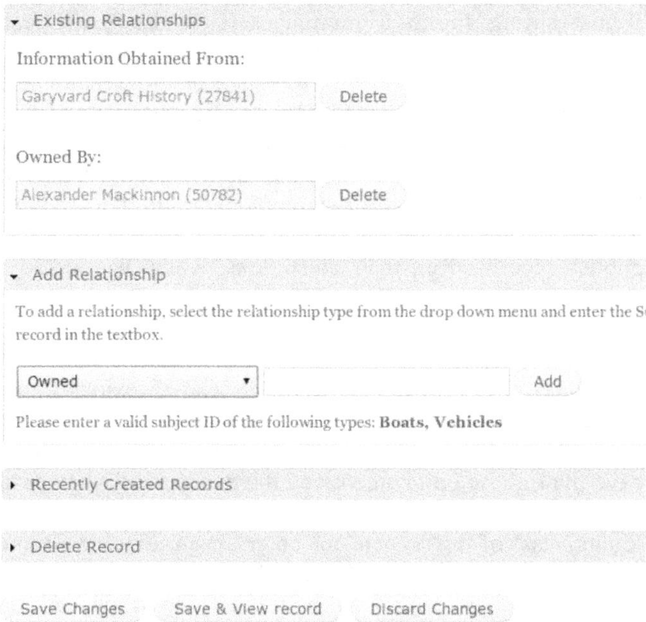

Figure 5: Adding/removing object properties

The CURIOS software has produced a linked data resource for Hebridean Connections documenting different types of information such as people, places, events, boats and businesses. The current instance of the Hebridean Connection data consists of over 700,000 RDF triples, incorporated within a relatively simple OWL ontology. The Drupal website, which was automatically built with the CURIOS tool, is already being used by Hebridean Connections to maintain their data; it is expected that the website will be opened to browsing by the general public shortly.

COLLABORATION

The CURIOS project is currently investigating the changing relationship the Comainn Eachdraidh groups are having with both each other and their collections as they continue the process of digitisation. We are conducting both individual semi-structured interviews with key members of different Comainn Eachdraidh and Hebridean Connections, focus groups/workshops with the different Comainn Eachdraidh groups and ethnographic research.

Through these interviews and focus groups the Comainn Eachdraidh members have repeatedly highlighted why community lead cultural heritage is important to them and how the activities are conducted for the community. Three examples of such points are highlighted in the following quotes:

> *"Something about the community, in the community, and created by the community itself." (1)*

> *"It's the view of the world as seen from Pairc" (3)*

> *"It's about preserving communities history and culture and Gaelic and pictures and all that, for the community itself" (9)*

Data Entry

The new CURIOS system has allowed a shift away from employing staff members specifically for data entry to allowing volunteers to manage and complete the data entry themselves. A Comann Eachdraidh has already inputted upwards of 300 new records into the system completely independently. This move towards empowering the volunteers to manage the process of digitising their repositories is essential in order to embed skills, which, in the long term, makes the process more sustainable:

> *"...because I'm now living in the area and saw an advert for volunteers and time has become available that I wanted to start to take part. So I've found that I'm now able to link an interest with being able to learn more and hopefully learn new skills as well" (13)*

Hebridean Connections Expansion

The new system has also encouraged more Comainn Eachdraidh groups to join the Hebridean Connections project, as the use of open linked data allowed their previous data sources to be cleaned and imported into the new system automatically. This is of key importance within cultural heritage as the sporadic nature of community lead cultural heritage repositories means there is likely to be many different digital archives in different data formats. Without importing the data into a consistent format they will never be able to be easily connected to the wider historical resources.

> *"And slowly but surely it came round to the first phase of Hebridean Connections where four of the Comunn Eachdraidh's were invited to take part. We were quite interested in being one of these but they could only take four on the programme at that time. So the latest, this latest (endeavour), it allows everyone to come in who wants to come in and we're quite pleased about that otherwise we might be another four years before we could have joined" (10)*

Ownership and Collaboration

Through initial evaluations it is becoming apparent that the collaborative nature of the CURIOS tool is allowing Comainn Eachdraidh groups to re-evaluate how they work together and share their collections. In the original proprietary software there was a very restrictive ownership applied to records. Only one group could own a record even if multiple groups had information for that record. This was particularly problematic for records about locations or significant events such as the First World War. This restrictive setting meant if a group wanted to edit a record owned by another Comainn Eachdraidh they had to contact the group and agree transfer of the ownership to the new group. This was not always done as some Comainn Eachdraidh that had put more information into a record felt they should keep their ownership of their data. An example of this ownership issue was highlighted by a Comann Eachdraidh member that was present during the original digitisation:

> *"Well it's interesting seeing the different styles of writing from different Comunn Eachdraidh but when I was putting in to the old system it was clear we were going to have different styles, that's ok – just conform on certain things and that's all right....It happens quite a lot where people have moved from one location to another, now, I think if a child is born on Berneray and then they move away to get married elsewhere, it's often when the married life happens there's more information and my feeling would be that the place where the people were married and had their married life should own the record, although they'd have to be fed in other information. But then you've got ministers and people who move around to various parishes..." (7)*

This issue was one that became very apparent again in the development of the CURIOS system and had no clear solution. In the new CURIOS system originally the data was designed so that ownership could be assigned to a Comann Eachdraidh but multiple groups could be assigned as maintainers by the owners. However it became apparent when the Comainn Eachdraidh groups met together that they were happy to have a much more collaborative approach with ownership no longer used and maintained by all groups that have added anything to a record. This change was observed during a visit to a training activity being conducted by Hebridean Connection with multiple Commainn Eachdraidh around data entry procedures. The change is discussed in detail in Ethnographic Observation 1.

The discussion outlined in Ethnographic Observation 1 lead to a complicated five step validation/user permission process being removed in favour of a simpler, more open process, where a user can edit a record then a second user can approve the changes. These changes in the Comainn Eachdraidh groups opinions to ownership and sharing of their records poses interesting questions around collaboration between groups through digital archives that need further investigation.

> Whilst sitting in on a training session that Hebridean Connections were running to train volunteers to input data, a really interesting discussion opened up around the ownership of digital records. This has been something that has been of constant discussion in the delivery of the new system between CURIOS and HC due to the structure of HC and the autonomy of Comainn Eachdraidh (CE) groups. As independent groups, each have the desire to digitise and publish records from their collections, which has led to a need to collaborate. The discussions therefore centred around the publication of records; who owns them and who has the 'right' to edit such records, especially when an individual may appear in multiple CE. Previously the default choice had been to give the ownership of each record to the CE that first inputs the data and therefore they have the right to edit content and the decision of whether or not to open it up to others. However, the potential 'clunkiness' of this system for others, who may have more and equally valid information for that record becomes very difficult. If they don't have editorial rights, they have to seek permission from the owning CE to add their relevant data and as one pointed question asked 'how do you own a dead person?' especially one that lived in multiple CE areas.
>
> The discussion therefore flowed between the want to retain localised repositories of knowledge and the realisation that in digital form this was not as possible as it used to be. The group wrestled with these issues for some time, representing how issues surrounding value, trust, and 'truth' were being changed through the need to collaborate in a digital archive. Different CEs appeared to have different senses of value towards their records and the digital forms they take. Some saw them as their 'property' directly linked to the people, land and the physical archive of that CE. Therefore, do you trust another group/volunteer to edit a representation of your 'physical' archive in the digital form and to do it in a manner that is accurate or 'truthful' to the record you are representing? Difficult questions but through this discussion, consensus began to develop that, for practicality reasons, a more open system would be better whereby CE would have to trust each other equally (though with some validation still) to edit and maintain each other's records.

Ethnographic Observation 1

FUTURE WORK

The next main developments within the CURIOS project will be the up-coming launch of the Hebridean Connections website to the general public. While investigating the use of the linked data cultural repositories by the public we will also focus on the on-going technical developments of CURIOS and also in-depth investigation of the Comainn Eachdraidh use of the tool. Focusing on:

- Investigation of long-term use by groups and evaluation of whether they change their working practices?

- How do the groups use their data once it's digitised?
- Who does the data entry / is it integrated into part of the collection process?
- Ownership of the records (not in terms of data protection / copyright) – does putting records into a collaborative, open, digital system change how the groups view their ownership or records?

There are also a number of on-going challenges in developing a sustainable user driven cultural repository. Firstly, as new cultural heritage vocabularies and datasets emerge, how can users be encouraged to integrate the Hebridean Connections cultural repository with these datasets and vocabularies? Secondly, the Drupal-based system is currently tailored to the cultural heritage domain. How should the approach be generalised so that it can be released to the open source community and applied to a wider variety of domains on the web? Finally, to investigate how semantic web reasoning technologies can be applied in a scalable way to automatically extract the implicit information from these cultural repositories?

The future technical developments of the system are going to focus on how to automate semantic linking to other data sources such as external cultural heritage repositories or dbpedia. Allow greater data visualisation within CURIOS - how do you visualise linked data in a meaningful way that clearly shows the different sources to the user? Allow users to greater query their data without requiring any specialised knowledge of linked data.

CONCLUSION

Open linked data can help make local cultural repositories sustainable and collective. Linked data allows for collaboration, mutual authoring, distributed responsibilities through community projects and the utilisation of other community or national resources [12]. The CURIOS project is enabling local cultural heritage repositories to become a meaningful identity resource for an international community, who previously had no access to them. By falling outside of national institutional frameworks, local people are the 'gatekeepers' of their own heritage and are selecting what to commemorate based on their own customs of remembering. This kind of digital archive can have, therefore, potentially significant social impacts which need to be better understood. The vision of Hebridean Connections is to expand the collections to incorporate those held by other Comainn Eachdraidh. Additionally, by making use of linked data, there is now the possibility to integrate further sources of data into HC from other historical societies or even national organisations.

ACKNOWLEDGMENTS

We would like to thank Hebridean Connections and the Comainn Eachdraidh for their ongoing commitment to this research. Many thanks to Kim Ross for her assistance in proof-reading however any mistakes held in the report are solely the responsibility of the authors. This work is supported by the Rural Digital Economy Research Hub (EPSRC EP/G066051/1).

REFERENCES

1. Balestrini, M., Bird, J., Marshall, P., Zaro, A., and Rogers, Y. Understanding sustained community engagement. *Proceedings of the 32nd annual ACM conference on Human factors in computing systems - CHI '14*, ACM Press (2014), 2675–2684.
2. Berners-Lee, T., Hendler, J., and Lassila, O. The Semantic Web. *Scientific American May*, (2001), 29–37.
3. Bizer, C., Heath, T., and Berners-Lee, T. Linked Data - the story so far. *International Journal on Semantic Web and Information Systems*, 2009. http://eprints.soton.ac.uk/271285/1/bizer-heath-berners-lee-ijswis-linked-data.pdf.
4. De Boer, V., Wielemaker, J., van Gent, J., et al. Supporting linked data production for cultural heritage institutes: the amsterdam museum case study. *ESWC'12 Proceedings of the 9th international conference on The Semantic Web: research and applications*, Springer Berlin Heidelberg (2012), 733–747.
5. Cresswell, T. Value, gleaning and the archive at Maxwell Street, Chicago. *Transactions of the Institute of British Geographers 37*, 1 (2012), 164–176.
6. Flinn, A. Community Histories, Community Archives: Some Opportunities and Challenges1. *Journal of the Society of Archivists 28*, 2 (2007), 151–176.
7. Han, K., Shih, P.C., Rosson, M.B., and Carroll, J.M. Enhancing community awareness of and participation in local heritage with a mobile application. *Proceedings of the 17th ACM conference on Computer supported cooperative work & social computing - CSCW '14*, ACM Press (2014), 1144–1155.
8. Hitzler, P., Krotzsch, M., Parsia, B., Patel-Schneider, P., and Rudolph, S. *OWL 2 Web Ontology Language Primer (Second Edition)*. 2012.
9. Van Hooland, S., Verborgh, R., De Wilde, M., Hercher, J., Mannens, E., and Van de Walle, R. Evaluating the success of vocabulary reconciliation for cultural heritage collections. *Journal of the American Society for Information Science and Technology 64*, 3 (2013), 464–479.
10. Mäkelä, E., Hyvönen, E., and Ruotsalo, T. How to deal with massively heterogeneous cultural heritage data–lessons learned in culturesampo. *Semantic Web 3*, (2012), 85–109.
11. Manola, F. and Miller, E. RDF Primer. *W3C Recommendation*, 2004. http://www.w3.org/TR/rdf-primer/.

12. Mellish, C., Wallace, C., Tait, E., Hunter, C., and MacLeod, M. Can Digital Technologies increase Engagement with Community History? *Digital Engagement 2011*.

13. Nora, P. *Realms of memory: rethinking the French past. Volume 1: Conflicts and Divisions.* Columbia University Press, 1996.

14. Spector, A.Z. Achieving application requirements. (1990), 19–33.

15. Tait, E., Macleod, M., Beel, D., Wallace, C., Mellish, C., and Taylor, S. Linking to the past: an analysis of community digital heritage initiatives. *Aslib proceedings : New information perspectives 65*, 6, 564–580.

16. Taylor, S., Jekjantuk, N., Mellish, C., and Pan, J.Z. Reasoning Driven Configuration of Linked Data Content Management Systems. *JIST, Seoul, Korea, November 28-30*, (2013).

17. Wallace, C., Tait, E., Macleod, M., Mellish, C., and Hunter, C. Supporting Digital Humanities Creating Sustainable Digital Community Heritage Resources Using Linked Data. *Supporting Digital Humanities: Answering theunaskable Conference*, (2011), 17–18.

Restructuring Human Infrastructure: The Impact of EHR Deployment in a Volunteer-Dependent Clinic

Charlotte Tang[1], Yunan Chen[2,3], Bryan Semaan[4], Jahmeilah Roberson[2]

[1]Department of Computer Science
University of Michigan Flint
Flint, MI, 48502
tcharlot@umflint.edu

[2]Department of Informatics
[3]Institute of Clinical and Translational Sciences
University of California, Irvine
Irvine, CA, 92697
yunanc@ics.uci.edu

[4]School of Information Studies
Syracuse University
Syracuse, NY, 13244
bsemaan@syr.edu

ABSTRACT
Non-profit organizations (NPOs) are often resource-restricted and rely on volunteers to function. As such, their human infrastructure—the social system supporting work—is different from conventional organizations, and technologies that function in a traditional organization with a stable workforce may not work in NPOs. Through an investigation of the deployment of an Electronic Health Record (EHR) system in a safety-net free clinic serving underprivileged populations, we report how the EHR system disrupted the human infrastructure—namely, the work typically enacted by volunteers. Specifically, there was a mismatch between the technological and human infrastructures leading to diminished volunteer roles, an increased workload for paid employees, and a negative impact on the quality of patient care. In turn, employees acted to reconcile the disrupted human infrastructure by creating new work roles for volunteers, re-establishing the quality of patient care, and developing workarounds for volunteers to resume their volunteer work. Finally we discuss how the commercial EHR system failed to support the fluid volunteer-based human infrastructure of the free clinic.

Author Keywords
Free Clinic; Volunteer-Dependent Work Practices; Electronic Health Record; Human Infrastructure; Volunteer Coordination; Technology Deployment

ACM Classification Keywords
H.0 [information systems], K.4.3 [organizational impacts] J3.Life and Medical Sciences: Health, Medical Information Systems

INTRODUCTION
Uncovering the technological and organizational impacts of information systems has long been an interest of the CSCW community. Past studies have identified many critical issues regarding how technologies are implemented, adopted, and adapted, as well as how such systems influence the communication, collaboration, and coordination behaviors within organizational settings [14, 15, 16, 25, 26, 30, 31]. Through a socio-technical lens, these studies point out the important role of the human infrastructure—"the arrangement of organizations and actors that must be brought into alignment in order for work to be accomplished" [21]—in sustaining technological infrastructure in organizations. In particular, Giddens [12] argued that human agency and social structures have a recursive relationship, and Orlikowski [24] showed how a similar relationship exists between technology and human action. On one hand, technology mediates human action; on the other hand, it is also adapted by human action.

Whereas prior work has led to deep empirical and theoretical understandings of how to design, develop, and deploy technologies in organizations, these insights are mostly drawn from conventional organizational environments where the human infrastructure consisted largely of employees[1], and where work performance was typically evaluated through standard business metrics such as productivity and revenue [14, 15, 16, 25, 26, 30, 31]. However, technology adoption and use is not limited to organizations with a stable workforce, but can also be examined within the context of resource-restricted organizations, such as many non-profit organizations (NPOs), where the operations rely on not only paid employees, but also those who volunteer to provide assistance. The challenges of designing and deploying technologies in these settings are considerably different since the human infrastructure underlying work practices are distinctly different [7].

Given the pervasiveness and rapid development of technology, even resource-restricted NPOs have been pressured to adopt new technologies for managing work-related information and enhancing efficiency [20]. Yet, little

CSCW '15, March 14-18, 2015, Vancouver, BC, Canada.
Copyright 2014 ACM 978-1-4503-2922-4/15/03...$15.00.
http://dx.doi.org/10.1145/2675133.2675277

[1] In this paper we use the term employees when referring to the paid staff to distinguish them from volunteers.

is known about the work practices of NPOs and their technology use, including the impacts and challenges of deploying technologies designed for conventional organizations, as resource-restricted NPOs often have to perform work in non-conventional ways due to a lack of financial and human resources [10, 34]. For example, a recent study has found that NPOs had to repurpose database systems designed for conventional organizations in different ways to manage their large pool of volunteers [33].

In healthcare settings, implementing large-scale information systems, particularly Electronic Health Record (EHR) systems, have been found to cause significant disruptions to the routine work practices of healthcare providers [19, 32]. Many unintended consequences have been found after introducing new information systems in clinical settings, such as decreased work efficiency, increased threats to patient safety [1, 8, 13] and end-user resistance and even failure in adoption [3, 5]. These studies highlighted important challenges in designing and deploying new information systems in healthcare organizations, and proposed potential solutions that could alleviate and avoid these problems.

Given government mandates requiring all healthcare organizations to implement an EHR system in the near future, and the goal to achieve improved efficiency and quality of patient care, healthcare organizations are increasingly adopting large-scale EHR systems. As a result, even resource-restricted healthcare organizations, which are typically underfunded, have to purchase and implement EHR systems. Nevertheless, few studies have examined the impacts of EHR system implementation on the work practices and infrastructures, especially the human infrastructure, of these resource-limited healthcare organizations. In particular, non-profit *safety-net* clinics are often limited in resources and volunteers are instrumental to their sustainability. These clinics provide a broad range of healthcare services to medically underserved and uninsured populations, regardless of a patient's ability to pay. Therefore they play an indispensible role in the US healthcare systems. The unique attributes of non-profit safety-net clinic settings make their technology adoption and use an interesting and important research topic to explore.

In this paper, we explore technology deployment and use in a safety-net clinic serving a homeless and poverty-stricken population, paying close attention to the impacts of a new technology on the organization's human infrastructure. Specifically, we observed the rollout of a comprehensive EHR system at the clinic and interviewed key personnel, including those leading and those affected by the transition from paper-based records to the EHR system.

Building on previous work investigating EHR deployment in healthcare settings, we make several important contributions to CSCW scholarship. First, we contribute a better understanding of how the human infrastructure was disrupted when the EHR system, which was not intended for resourced-restricted volunteer-based organizations, was deployed in the non-profit safety-net clinic. The disruption prohibited volunteers from carrying out tasks that they had been trained and were responsible for prior to EHR adoption. Thus, the disruption caused to the human infrastructure greatly mitigated the potential benefits of the EHR system as it disrupted the practices surrounding volunteerism that the operation of the free clinic had heavily relied upon, even though the rollout was generally regarded as being successful. Second, we contribute new insights into how the EHR system caused a change in the social system—in this case, the human infrastructure—where the human infrastructure and work practices were re-structured around the new technological infrastructure. In particular, the way in which work was organized by volunteers and around volunteer services shifted dramatically, as volunteer roles both diminished and changed around the adoption of the new technology. Third, we identified a tension between the goal of achieving interoperability across organizations and the constraint of limited technology options imposed upon resource-restricted organizations. Lastly, we contribute a novel solution, time-sharing licenses, as a financially-viable and HIPAA-compliant remedy for providing EHR access for the volunteer workforce in resource-restricted organizations.

RELATED WORK

Re-thinking infrastructure

Whereas infrastructure is generally regarded as being physical or technical, recent work has investigated infrastructure from a more human-centered perspective [21, 28]. In this view, infrastructure is composed of various social, organizational, and technical components [28], including shared social practices, information and material flows, and the associated processes involved in building and maintaining these practices and flows [27]. Here we are concerned with the social component, or, the human infrastructure.

The human infrastructure is the underlying foundation of a system, in this case social, constituted by the pattern of relationships of people, through various networks and social arrangements [21]. It plays a crucial role in the success of work coordination and collaboration [21], and thus serves as an underlying foundation of social systems like workplaces, and even societies [22]. Importantly, human infrastructure does not exist in a vacuum—it is intertwined with other infrastructures, particularly physical and technological infrastructures [28].

When changes to a social system occur, e.g. from some external force, in what Barley [2] terms "slippages", such events can then trigger new ways to act. Thus, the integration of a new EHR system into a clinical environment can cause the human infrastructure to restructure around the new technological infrastructure. For example, Mark et al. [22], in examining the effects of war on the human infrastructure, described how the physical and/or technological infrastructures would need to be switched so that people could maintain their routines for work and social life when the human infrastructure was disrupted by external environmental factors such as natural disaster or war. In other words, when physical or technological infrastructures are disrupted or changed, the human infrastructure will likely adapt to changes in other infrastructures. This is especially true in clinical settings: when a new technological infrastructure, such as an EHR system, is introduced, this can trigger changes to the human infrastructure, as people often have to reconfigure or adapt their work practices around the new technology. For example, in a hospital environment where people are accustomed to working face-to-face, the introduction of computing technology has since enabled certain types of doctors, such as radiologists, to work remotely, thus at times never interacting with patients on a personal level. Conversely, the human infrastructure may also actively reconfigure the technical infrastructure in order to support former work practices. For example, groups who once relied on certain routine work practices may have to change their practices and develop workarounds that enable them to maintain former practices as a result of the introduction of a new technology.

The infrastructures supporting clinical work in non-volunteer-based healthcare organizations

As information systems become pervasive across organizational domains and contexts, scholars have investigated the social and organizational impacts of information systems, especially EHR systems, in conventional healthcare organizations [14, 16, 25, 26, 31]. Research examining EHR systems in clinical settings has largely focused on identifying the benefits of deploying EHR systems, resulting in new technical infrastructures or uncovering challenges and barriers.

EHR systems have been widely implemented to replace paper medical records in clinical settings. The benefits of EHR systems include improvements in accessibility, patient safety, accountability, and cost-savings [3, 4]. However, the design of these systems has largely focused on EHR systems as information storage and retrieval tools for administrative, research, and legal usage [25], with little attention to how EHR systems can support the human infrastructure via communication, coordination, and collaboration [1, 5]. In fact, properly designed and implemented health IT solutions have the potential to support collaboration among a variety of stakeholders, from patients to clinicians, individuals to institutions, and policymakers at all levels.

Other studies have suggested that EHRs fall short in supporting the work practices of its primary users [e.g. 9, 26]. In particular, Heath and Luff [16] argue that despite the great benefits that the system intends to offer, "the practices through which the document is written, read and used within consultation have been largely ignored." In this regard, many studies have reported cases in which poorly designed IT infrastructures led to unintended consequences after deployment, including dissatisfaction, adoption failures, inefficiencies, and even increased medical errors [6, 8].

Although the impacts of EHR systems are well documented in the non-volunteer-based organizational space, what remains unclear is the extent to which EHR deployment would affect the operations of volunteer-based clinics. The increased adoption of EHR systems in non-profit settings in recent years makes it critically important and timely to address the complex interplay among human, organizational, and technological infrastructures in healthcare settings.

Technology deployment in NPOs

Whereas previous work has mostly been conducted in conventional healthcare organizations—especially in large hospitals [14, 16, 25, 26, 31]—few studies have illuminated the challenges of technology deployment in NPOs [10, 20, 23, 33]. Merkel et al. [23] found that ICTs have been beneficial for volunteer recruitment, public relations, fund raising events, and information management. Moreover, Voida et al. [34] reported how the tensions between standard database systems and the diverse ways of managing data in NPOs forced users to develop and reconfigure their own databases at NPOs. Similarly, Dombrowski et al. [10] described how e-government intermediaries, who assisted low-income households in using welfare systems, often experienced issues of access and trust when working with the technologies available to them. These studies imply that not all members of the human infrastructure are accounted for when technologies are integrated into NPO work practices.

Our study builds on recent work that examines technology use and adoption by NPOs, only our investigation is within the context of a non-profit healthcare organization with limited resources. We identified how the lack of EHR access by volunteers resulted in an unexpected debilitating effect on the clinic's day-to-day operation. We contend that the deployment of an EHR system, without taking into account the way the human and technological infrastructures are intertwined during implementation, can adversely affect the ways work is accomplished. We describe this in the context of an EHR rollout in a nonprofit volunteer-based healthcare clinic.

RESEARCH SITE AND METHODS

To investigate the impacts of EHR deployment on resource-restricted health organizations, we conducted an ethnographic study consisting of field observations and interviews at a free outpatient safety-net medical clinic located in Southern California. We chose to study this free clinic due to a longstanding partnership with the university one of the authors was affiliated with.

Research Setting

The study reported in this paper was conducted in the outpatient medical unit of a safety-net NPO. Founded in 1970, the NPO has been providing high quality service to low-income and homeless individuals and families in the county. It consists of three health units: medical, dental, and mental health counseling services, and two social services units that provide "necessity resources", such as food, clothing, and financial support for housing and transportation. The organization houses about 55 full-time employees offering services supported by over 400 volunteers with various backgrounds. Most paid employees are at supervisory level and they oversee volunteers who carry out their work. The annual budget of the NPO was $7.5 million for the year of 2012-2013, including in-kind donations.

The field site under investigation, which was the medical unit of the NPO, is a free outpatient clinic that serves patients who are uninsured, unemployed and/or do not have a primary care provider. The clinic conducts over 18,000 clinical service encounters annually and about 75 percent of the patients at the clinic require chronic care. Seventy-five to 80 percent of the patients are Spanish speakers, and all of the providers are conversant in medical Spanish to varying degrees. As such, a translator is needed about 10 percent of the time. The medical assistants and front desk staff are fluent in both English and Spanish. Since this is also the only free clinic in the county that serves walk-in patients, on average, the clinic receives 40 new walk-in patients each day. New patients are required to arrive at the clinic between 7:30 AM to 8:00 AM in order to be guaranteed assessment by a provider, and as a result, there is always a long line of patients waiting outside the clinic before 7:30 each morning.

Beyond basic medical services, the clinic also operates under the umbrella of a large non-profit regional healthcare delivery network with hospitals providing comprehensive healthcare services to patients who need further medical assistance, e.g. hospitalization or surgeries. There are four paid providers at the free clinic: two physicians, a physician assistant, and a nurse practitioner. Each of them sees patients 8 out of 10 half days every week. Volunteers at the clinic are mostly college students majoring in the health sciences through the university's community engagement programs. There are also approximately 10 volunteer clinicians who are clinical retirees and they see patients at the free clinic from one half-day a month to a day a week.

Data Collection

The ethnographic study consisted of two phases. First we conducted 40 hours of observations before and after the EHR system implementation to understand the organizational structure, work practices, as well as the changes that occurred during and following the rollout of the system. Two members of the research team conducted field observations, and they were stationed around the main work locations of the clinic to uncover the work practices occurring at these locations. For instance, the observations conducted at the front desk enabled us to understand how patients were registered and how medical records were used at the beginning of medical visits, whereas the observations of the physician assistants while stationed at their workspaces allowed us to observe how work practices differed before, and after the EHR rollout. Other critical locations we studied included hallways, the medical records storage room, and physicians' offices. Each observational session ranged from 2-4 hours in length, during which field notes were taken with pen and paper, and were transcribed soon after observations were completed. We also asked participants brief questions to clarify issues we did not fully understand during observations. Field observations provided us with a comprehensive view of the free clinic's day-to-day operations, enabling us to identify major roles in the clinic and access the people who held those roles. It also allowed us to sample key interviewees for the second phase of the study, and develop an interview protocol. Given the clinic's size, the EHR implementation was undertaken via a big-bang approach, where all functions of the system went live at the same time. As such, observations were split before and after the system rollout and each phase consisted approximately 20 hours.

Second, we conducted 15 semi-structured interviews with 14 participants to obtain a deeper understanding of their experiences with, and perceptions of, the EHR deployment and its subsequent use. The participants[2] had diverse backgrounds, held various roles, and had been with the clinic for different lengths of time from less than one year to over twenty years. Their roles in the clinic included: a medical assistant, a patient advocate, a physician assistant, a nurse practitioner, a medical biller, a health educator, a volunteer coordination manager, a patient service representative, a medical record coordinator, a operations director (previously a volunteer at the free clinic), a pharmacy director, a medical director, and two volunteers. We interviewed the medical director a week prior to and a week after the EHR rollout. The remaining interviews were all conducted over four months after the system rollout. The timing of the study ensured that all participants had sufficient time to interact with the system.

Participants were recruited and sampled during and through our field observations, and we were able to interview the majority of the paid employees. Although more than 400 volunteers worked at the clinic at any given time, it was important to understand the perspectives of paid personnel, considering volunteers mostly carried out routine clerical tasks that were only supportive to the clinical activities at the clinic, e.g. pulling medical charts from storage and calling patients for follow-up information. As such, we sampled volunteers who represented the different volunteer categories at the clinic, e.g. student volunteers who served the clinic only for a few months and senior volunteers who have been with the clinic for years. Since most volunteers took on the same clerical tasks and their involvement in the clinic's operation and system rollout were similar, we felt the two interviews we conducted with volunteers were sufficient to understand their behaviors and perceptions.

[2] Throughout our analysis, we do not include participant roles for several quotes so as to maintain the anonymity of our participants.

The main findings of this paper are based on semi-structured interviews. During interviews, we inquired into how participants carried out their work, volunteer roles, and people's interpersonal interactions before and after deploying the EHR. The interviews were organized into four question blocks covering different issues and were tailored for each interviewee based on insights obtained during observations:

- General questions: What is your position? How long have you been working here? What were your expectations of the EHR system before rollout?
- Questions on pre-EHR work practices: How did you work before the EHR system? What was a typical day like? How did you work with other staff members and volunteers? What kind of support did you receive?
- Questions on the transition experience: What was the transition like? How and for how long was training conducted? Do you feel like you are still in transition or do you feel like you have settled into a routine?
- Questions on post-EHR work practices: How do you work with the EHR system? What is a typical day like? How do you work with other staff and volunteers? What kind of support do you receive?

Interviews lasted between 30-45 minutes and were audio-recorded. Each interviewee was compensated $15.00 for participating in the study. The recorded interviews were transcribed to provide accurate records for data analysis.

Data Analysis

Data analysis was performed using an approach from grounded theory's inductive analytic method through open coding for identifying, naming, categorizing and describing phenomena found in the transcripts in order to establish categories and properties [29]. The transcripts were iteratively read and re-read, and incidents identified were grouped into concepts based on similarity of patterns. For example, incidents related to system procurement, training, and changes in volunteers' work practices were identified and grouped into respective categories. The goal was to understand and make sense of the subjective experience (phenomenology) of the research participants and allow themes to emerge naturally.

We next describe the operations of the clinic, and emphasize the characteristic patient population and the work conducted by volunteers prior to the integration of the EHR system into its daily clinical practices. This sets the context through which we describe how the human infrastructure was affected after the EHR system was deployed.

CLINIC OPERATION PRIOR TO THE EHR DEPLOYMENT

Before the EHR deployment, the clinic primarily relied on paper charts. There was a computerized practice management application for patient scheduling and storing patient demographic information. All other patient care documentation, such as consultation notes, lab and diagnostic test results, and referral requests, were all paper-based and had to be filed in patient charts upon receipt and after use. However, participants described how paper charts were often mishandled—where they were misfiled either in the wrong sections of a chart, or in a wrong chart altogether. These errors often resulted in a lack of access to patient information during medical visits, forcing clinicians to treat patients without knowledge of their medical history. As such, most employees at the clinic were eager to embrace the new EHR system, as it was believed to not only solve the issues associated with the misfiling of patient charts, but also improve work efficiency and reduce workload at the clinic.

Transient patient population

Since the free clinic provides healthcare services to underserved populations, there is typically a high patient turnover rate, requiring a large amount of manpower to address the needs of a constant flux of patients in and out of the clinic. In particular, since this is the only free clinic in the county that serves walk-in patients, the clinic sees an average of 40 new patients each day, in addition to those who return to the clinic (patients who had previously visited the clinic). The new patients often presented varying and complex sets of medical problems; some had also been treated in other medical facilities or hospitalized. The constant turnover of patients created a chaotic atmosphere where patient health history and other information were often lacking. Much effort and time were required to manage patient information and the clinic desperately needed a system that would allow providers to obtain information from other institutions quickly, and to be able to locate its own patient records accurately.

To remedy these issues, the clinic chose to implement an EHR system that was interoperable with the systems used by the hospitals within their affiliated healthcare network so that patient information could be shared across organizations. Other criteria that took into account the non-profit nature of the clinic's operation were also used when choosing the EHR system, such as a limited budget, user-friendly interfaces, and good technical support. Moreover, since patients at the free clinic were often uninsured, it was crucial for providers at the clinic to make requests and send reports to external organizations for free products and services, such as complimentary drugs and *pro-bono* specialty referrals to meet the needs of their underserved patient population. These case-by-case referrals and requests, and the subsequent follow-ups, were labor and time intensive.

Volunteer work before EHR deployment

In order for the clinic to operate efficiently, a large number of volunteers were needed to support and carry out a variety of mundane, yet important tasks. To do so, the free clinic utilized the services of more than 400 volunteers, mostly students, at the same time. Since every volunteer worked at the clinic for only a few hours per week, eight volunteers were needed every morning and every afternoon to handle the clerical work described above. Student volunteers at the clinic were cross-trained so that they could perform a variety of tasks, as needed. More specifically, they were indispensible members of the human infrastructure as they assisted staff in filing charts, obtaining information from charts, and transporting charts intra-organizationally or inter-organizationally, either physically or by using technology, e.g. fax machines, scanners and e-mail. In essence, volunteer work was primarily performed behind the scenes to support the front-end patient care activities conducted by paid employees. As described by a clinical employee, P6:

"Most of our documentation was through just traditional paper charts, so we would see a patient, and have a piece of paper, and read up on the chart, and document our visit on the sheet... All the documentation, and copies of consultant notes, radiology, labs, are all faxes, and so we had papers that we filed in the chart...we were able to obtain help from volunteers to help us look up that information, or to be able to refer patients to alternative providers."

Importantly, the most frequently performed and most challenging task for student volunteers was to locate charts. When a medical chart was not available for a consultation, doctors would have to perform medical evaluations without having any prior medical history to guide them. Nevertheless, this seemingly easy yet critical task was quite challenging for volunteers, as described by our participants:

"45 minute training module on medical records individually as each person comes in here because it was so important that they'd filed appropriately and that, you know, I mean a lost chart is a nightmare and this is a patient's life." (P8)

"Tracking down charts... was one of the big things that we always had was lost medical records." (P9)

"Our biggest issue was finding charts." (P11)

In addition to student volunteers, the free clinic also relied on volunteer clinicians to offer medical care to patients. About 10 retired clinicians volunteered at the clinic and provided medical services sporadically, from one half-day per month to one day a week. These volunteer clinicians were instrumental in providing needed medical care at the clinic. Yet, they all had used only paper charts before their retirement and were generally not tech-savvy. They were comfortable with paper charts and able to perform their medical work without difficulty prior to the EHR rollout.

Volunteers served a central role prior to the deployment of the EHR system at the clinic. Volunteer clinicians provided pro-bono medical care needed at the free clinic and student volunteers ensured timely and accurate performance of clinical work. Together, the volunteers ensured that the clinic operated smoothly, and that patients received proper medical care and treatment.

The deployment of the EHR system ultimately replaced most paper charts circulated at the clinic, and dramatically altered the practices involved with handling patient charts. In the next section, we introduce the EHR system and the implementation process.

IMPLEMENTING EHR AT THE FREE CLINIC

When choosing the EHR system for the free clinic, a leadership team consisting of the IT director, medical director, associate medical director, and the operations director, consulted all the employees for their opinions and ultimately decided to purchase a system that was interoperable with other systems used within the clinic's healthcare network. Considering other members of the healthcare network providing many comprehensive services, such as surgeries and inpatient treatment, for the free clinic, interoperability would allow patient information to be accessible and shared across the entire network.

The EHR system procured for the free clinic offered comprehensive features commonly found in most EHR systems equipped with both practice management and clinical modules. The practice management module was used for storing patient demographic information, scheduling, and billing information, and the clinical module was primarily used to support clinical work and documentation. The latter was also used for ordering lab and diagnostic tests, and receiving reports. It is also capable of administering eReferrals to organizations in the same healthcare network. However, due to the free clinic's reliance on pro-bono services offered by external specialists and health organizations, some capabilities of the EHR system such as eReferrals could not be utilized, which will be described in detail later. Below, we describe how the EHR was implemented, from setting up different levels of access, the pre-rollout training, and the actual rollout process.

Different levels of information access

Before the EHR rollout, all paid employees were consulted to inquire about the information they would need to perform their job. In accordance with the Health Insurance Portability and Accountability Act (HIPAA) Privacy Rule, which was developed with the intention of protecting the privacy of personal health information in the United States [18], the EHR system was set up to provide different levels of user access. The technical implementation was developed so that employees could only access information they needed to carry out their work activities, since it is illegal to access a patient's information if one is not involved in a patient's care. Therefore, the EHR system was customized based on employee roles prior to the rollout. Specifically, the medical director and the associate director had full access to the EHR system. Other employees had access to only specific data that they needed for their job, although every employee was given access to basic patient information, e.g. name and demographic information. All EHR access was password protected and each employee had a unique user name and password, corresponding to the number of licenses billed to the clinic by the service provider.

Sufficient pre-deployment user training

The same leadership team worked together to ensure all users of the EHR system received adequate training prior to the system rollout. Specifically, the operations director worked closely with an implementation specialist from the vendor on the practice management module to make sure the scheduling functions and the billing codes were set up correctly. Afterwards, both the operations director and the implementation specialist started training the staff on practice management for 4 hours in a training room at the clinic.

Next, the implementation specialist trained the operations director intensively for a total of two weeks to show her how to customize the system. All the full-time providers were trained for 12 hours. Other employees received 4 to 8 hours of training depending on their job responsibilities and the extent to which they would be utilizing the EHR.

A well-prepared system rollout

The system rollout occurred in a big-bang approach where the entire EHR went live all at once. In anticipation of possible chaos during the rollout, patient load was intentionally reduced—no walk-in patients were accepted during this period and patient load was cut to 30% of the regular load in the first week, 50% in the second week, 80% in the third week and, finally, 100% from the fourth onwards. Yet, even with the reduced workload, there were challenges embracing the new system and new work practices. As one participant mentioned:

"The day that we switched to [the EHR system], everyone was like running around with their head cut off" (P3).

In the first two months after the rollout, the employees had to work an additional 20 hours per week to cope with the additional tasks during the transition from paper to electronic-based work, since they had to review the paper charts for patients with appointments the next day, and to mark the pages before scanning them into the system. During the fourth month after the rollout, the clinic was operating at 80-90% of its regular patient load. It was expected that patient load would reach 90-100% by the sixth month.

Despite the chaotic atmosphere and emerging issues, we found that, overall, our participants were positive towards the transition from paper to the EHR system, including the training and the support they received, and considered the rollout to be successful. Employees exhibited high morale and considerable understanding of the potential issues that could emerge during the rollout period.

"We helped and asked each other. It was like a working team, unbelievable! Everybody was shoulder to shoulder. Everybody was together when we start to learn everything. It was incredible. This period was like, for me, a very, very, very nice experience. And I am very proud of me, and [giggle] everybody" (P8).

Although we did not observe any major unintended impacts like inefficiencies and system adoption failures that have been reported in prior EHR implementation literature [3, 5], one main issue uncovered in the study was the impact of the new system on volunteer work. In the following sections, we describe how the EHR system led to a breakdown in the human infrastructure, and ways in which members of the clinic attempted to reconcile the newly emerging disruptions to the day-to-day operations of the clinic.

RESTRUCTURING THE HUMAN INFRASTRUCTURE

Although the rollout was considered a success, various problems emerged when the EHR system was deployed into the clinic, as volunteers were not given access to the EHR system. The lack of access to patient information led to a major disruption to the human infrastructure and a restructuring of work around the new technological infrastructure. Volunteers, and employees who relied on volunteers, were no longer able to perform routine tasks as they used to before the system was deployed. As a result of volunteers being excluded from the implementation of the EHR system, a variety of sociotechnical issues emerged within the clinic.

Disruptions to the Human Infrastructure

Prior to the EHR deployment, volunteers were indispensible in a variety of behind-the-scene tasks supporting front-end patient care activities. However, only paid employees of the clinic could access the newly deployed EHR system, substantially affecting the clinic's workflow, mainly because the clinic could no longer utilize its large number of volunteers effectively, as before. This caused a disruption to the human infrastructure, as not only were volunteers affected on an individual level, but there also existed greater consequences across the clinic as other employees who relied on volunteer work were also impacted, as described by a participant:

"We had paper charts so we were able to obtain help from volunteers... now with the new system, we have to do it all ourselves" (P2).

In the following, we describe how volunteer roles diminished, how the diminished role of volunteers impacted employees who relied on volunteers to assist with their work, and finally, how patients and the quality of patient care were impacted.

Diminished role of volunteers

As we have already described, the operation of the free clinic relied heavily on volunteer services. At the same time, volunteer satisfaction, which has been found to contribute to the success of volunteer programs [7], hinges upon whether a clinic can provide their volunteers with a rewarding experience. Thus, a clinic's operation and volunteer program are interdependent. That is, disruption to one can adversely impact the other.

In our field site, the clinic's operation was disrupted as volunteers lacked access to the EHR system. This prohibited them from performing the tasks that they once routinely conducted before the EHR system deployment. Volunteers, many of whom found their roles within the clinic had diminished, also began to feel unsatisfied at the clinic and, understandably, a considerable number of them began to consider alternative places to volunteer. For example, a volunteer (P3) was unhappy as she felt that she could no longer contribute to the clinic. She described how she considered looking for another place where she could contribute her time in a volunteer capacity:

"Now each week my tasks keep getting smaller and smaller... But I've got to find something that I can do every single time so I feel like I'm making a contribution... If I feel like I'm no longer contributing, then, like, I need to find someplace else to be. Some place else that really really wants me to be there. I feel like a lot of volunteers are going to leave or they're just going to cut back on their hours, just because they feel like [the clinic] doesn't need them anymore."

This had a significant impact on the operation of the clinic and the quality of patient care, as the sustainability of volunteer programs is integral to most NPOs, and our study site is no exception.

Increased workload for employees

While volunteers became dissatisfied with their experience volunteering, the employees of the clinic also faced challenges, as they had to assume additional tasks and responsibilities that were previously performed by volunteers. The majority of our participants described how the diminished role of volunteers impacted their day-to-day work practices after the EHR system was deployed. For example, a medical record coordinator described how they could no longer rely on volunteers to help with their work:

"Before, [volunteers] used to help me out, you know, and I was doing different things. Right now I'm doing everything by myself with my friend, [the EHR system]... because it's [an EHR] and we cannot give permission to nobody to, you know, work in our system, I have to do all by myself" (P8).

Also, as discussed by a medical assistant (P15):

"Before, if a volunteer was trained on how to do vitals, then we had the chart, the volunteer used to help us ask the questions for the superbill, have the patient sign, do all the inside questions like allergies, LNP, recent surgeries, any medications, the vitals, everything... Now there is a big impact because... I mean, they're not able to do that."

The increased workload of employees reduced the clinic's capacity to meet the needs of its patients as the employees had to perform additional tasks themselves without the support of volunteers. This had a negative impact on the quality of patient care, due to the sheer number of patients that were visiting the clinic on a daily basis:

"If you come here before 7:45 there's a line from the front door here to the warehouse and those are just mainly new patients coming in... if you saw what was happening in the morning, and then you can see the waiting room how it looks at eight o'clock. And most of those are new people and that's the turnover everyday."

Unintended consequences on patient care quality

The fact that volunteers were unable to access the EHR system also impacted the quality of patient care as some tasks were delayed due to the limited personnel who could access the system. For example, substantial volunteer efforts were required to help with medication dispensing before the EHR system was deployed, and this process was much delayed as it was now conducted entirely by pharmacists with EHR access. As described by the director of pharmacy (P11),

"We did not get medication for our patients for a week. So that was – it could have been really impactful."

Moreover, in order to enable the underserved patients to receive the proper medical care and treatment that they need, the clinic is involved in a number of essential tasks, e.g. requesting complementary drugs from drug companies and requesting pro-bono specialty care for patients with specialized medical needs, that require substantial human effort. For example, these tasks are generally very labor-intensive and time-consuming as they are heavy on paper work and phone calls. Before the EHR deployment, volunteers undertook these tasks, typically in the background. However, without EHR access, volunteers were no longer able to perform these tasks, which impacted the quality of patient care. As described by P11:

"We have a program... where... we use volunteers... they [volunteers] fill out applications for each patient to a specific drug company for a specific drug. And so it's hundreds of applications a day, and thousands a week – a month, thousands a month. And so they need access to the charts to find out phone numbers of these patients, their addresses, what medication they're actually on, if it's changed, the dose has changed, that sort of thing.... Well now they don't have access into that [EHR] and it's very frustrating."

This directly impacted the quality of patient care offered at the clinic as when certain tasks were delayed, patients' health and well-being was also impacted.

Reconciling Disrupted Human Infrastructure

Thus far we have illustrated how the clinic's human infrastructure was disrupted as a result of the EHR system deployment. Volunteers found that they had little left to do as they could not access the system. This led to a shift in the workload from volunteers to paid employees, which negatively impacted the quality of patient care.

In order to ameliorate the negative impact of the EHR system on the human infrastructure, especially with respect to volunteer services, employees of the clinic looked to reconcile the human infrastructure by: *creating new work roles for volunteers*, *re-establishing quality patient care,* and *developing workarounds*. This was important, as volunteers are important resources to NPOs including this free clinic, and, developing and maintaining a volunteer program requires substantial effort and time.

Creating new work roles for volunteers

Employees were concerned with the possible negative ramifications associated with the lack of volunteer work. As such, to reconcile the disrupted human infrastructure, employees were actively seeking new roles for their volunteers. As described by the volunteer coordination manager (P9):

"A lot of volunteers with a whole lot of nothing to do…It's been kind of interesting because I've had to do a lot of nosing around to a lot of different people in a lot of different departments saying, 'I've got some man hours available. Do you have any projects for my kids?'"

The free clinic was being served by a considerable number of volunteer clinicians (who are typically retired clinicians). These older clinicians were not comfortable using a computer. Therefore, a new role emerged where chosen employees began serving as scribes to assist novice technology users in accessing and using the EHR system. As described by the director of pharmacy (P11):

"Those older pharmacists [volunteers], we always told them, 'Don't even worry. You will have a scribe with you at all times. You won't even have to go on the computer, really.'"

In other cases, departments that typically did not rely on volunteers were now assigning volunteers new roles and integrating them into their daily work practices. For example, a patient service representative whose primary responsibility was to link patients with various county health programs, was able to use more volunteers with her work as many volunteers were unable to access the system and accomplish work as they were accustomed to pre-EHR deployment:

"We use the volunteers to mail letters, to call the patients to schedule appointments, or they help us putting the MSI applications together… In the past the volunteers, they were more busier, you know, filing charts, looking for charts. But now there is – they have been helping us a lot" (P10).

Re-establishing Quality Patient Care

The new roles being assumed by volunteers served to empower them. Whereas prior to the EHR system deployment, volunteers only occasionally interacted with patients face-to-face, our participants described how following deployment, patient-volunteer interactions increased and volunteers were given more critical responsibilities within the clinic. Volunteer roles have since become more visible to patients as they now interact with them face-to-face, whereas pre-EHR deployment, volunteers were mostly engaged in clerical work, such as filing charts, behind the scenes. As described by P5:

"We're switching them [volunteers] to be assistants to the medical assistants, so they're helping ask questions, and, you know, they can help do finger sticks, they can help, you know, just prepare the rooms, they can talk to the patients, escort them back to the rooms, so they're doing… more patient care than just being in the file room…"

Volunteers also became more visible in the triage area. They were often asked to escort patients to exam rooms, and were also trained to perform basic medical assessments. As described by P14:

"I'm just starting to figure out, like, how the volunteers are helping out by doing vitals for you… we can have a volunteer at least get it started and have their vitals done so when the MA grabs them, all she has to do is input, she doesn't have to [actually do the vitals]… And it definitely always helps with triage because for most people they need a set of vitals."

Challenges in Reconciling Work Around the EHR

Apart from looking for existing work that volunteers could perform, some employees developed workarounds so that volunteers could assist them with their work. To illustrate, a participant was able to work around the EHR system so that she could continue to utilize the services of some volunteers. As previously described, most patients at the free clinic require referrals for specialty care and it was necessary to contact individual specialty physicians by phone to find out if they would be willing to provide pro-bono services to their patients. The free clinic maintains a list of physicians who could potentially tender the pro-bono referrals. In practice, referral requests are largely conducted through trial-and-error. Therefore, this task is very time-consuming and labor-intensive and had been previously fulfilled by volunteers.

After the deployment of the EHR system, however, our participant switched to first retrieve the EHRs of all the patients requiring a referral and then printed the needed information for volunteers to make the necessary phone calls. The volunteers also faxed patient medical information to specialty physicians for assessment. Finally, the participant documented the referral information in the EHR system with reference to the notes made by volunteers, which were included on printed copies. Through this workaround, the participant was able to perform her job near the level of efficiency before the EHR rollout.

Yet workarounds were not common; in fact, they were severely limited and in many cases not always practical. As described by our participants:

"We have a workaround, but that's pathetically slow and pathetically limited."

"If we didn't have a workaround we wouldn't even use them [volunteers]. And frankly, if we hadn't developed the workaround, we couldn't use them and it would shut down our department. We really rely heavily on volunteers."

Although these two participants revealed the use of workarounds, no further details of how the workarounds were accomplished were provided during our interviews. This is likely because workarounds were generally perceived to be negative, like cutting corners, employees at the clinic were thus cautious of accidental disclosure even though they did express their concern for legal compliance when developing workarounds. As described by our participants:

"Now that we have stricter HIPAA regulations and we have a different system with the electronic health records, some of their [volunteers'] work's been taken away. So we're sort of in transition now figuring out how to use that extra mass of volunteers that we don't have a job for at the moment."

"I'm trying to find the best solution, you know, to implement our volunteers to work with the system, but it's taking time. You have to find the legal solution, because you cannot let everybody to access [the EHR system], and we still, you know, trying to find the best solution for them because we cannot let nobody to get in the system."

It is important to repair a disrupted human infrastructure in a timely manner for an operation to run efficiently. In our study, participants developed several mechanisms to reconcile the disruption caused by the lack of volunteer access to the EHR system. First, new work roles were created to counter disrupted work practices, such as the use of scribes to meet the needs of the older volunteer clinicians so that they could continue to offer services at the clinic. Second, volunteers were brought to the front of the operation increasing their interaction with patients as a means to enhance the quality of patient care. Last, although it was challenging, workarounds were developed to fill in the gaps in work practices, where volunteers could then continue to contribute to the clinic's operations.

DISCUSSION

Based on the findings presented in our study, in this section we first discuss the implications for resource-restricted free clinics adopting new technologies, and then unpack why a commercially designed technological infrastructure was unable to support a volunteer-based human infrastructure at the free clinic under investigation. These discussion points provide an in-depth exploration of the findings we uncovered in the study, and lead to possible implications and approaches for redesigning the human-technological infrastructure to better accommodate volunteer work—especially considering that technology adoption is becoming more and more inevitable even in resource-restricted organizations.

Mismatch between license-based access and volunteer-dependent human infrastructure

Despite a relatively smooth rollout of the EHR system, our study revealed a major disruption to volunteer work stemming from a mismatch between the license-per-user service model and the fluidity of volunteer work practices that were integral to the clinic's operation. As a result, volunteers were unable to access the EHR system and contribute positively to the overall operation of the clinic, since most of their tasks required access to patient information stored in the system. The work previously conducted by volunteers had to be reassigned to, or assisted by, other employees who had access to and could use the system. The loss of valuable manpower that was key to the clinic's operation—in this case, volunteers—created additional work for other employees who were already burdened by the new system.

On the surface, this mismatch appeared to be a system implementation oversight where the designers and management team simply neglected to include volunteers as end-users during system customization. But in reality, the problem was rooted in the EHR system's lack of support for the fluidity and composition of the human infrastructure at the free clinic. Current EHR systems are mostly designed for a steady workforce that is prevalent in conventional healthcare organizations, where a relatively fixed number of access licenses are needed under the license-per-user service model typically adopted for EHR systems. Our study provides a counterpoint; one where the variability in the volunteer workforce at the free clinic revealed the need for a large number of access licenses, e.g., hundreds of licenses, in order to provide each volunteer access to the EHR system despite the fact that volunteers may only work for a few hours each week and in short bursts of time. Given the shortage of financial resources the clinic was facing, it was simply impractical to purchase sufficient licenses for the entirety of the human infrastructure, especially for volunteers, as they were large in number.

Implementing an EHR system is already a substantial financial investment. For example, it was estimated that the cost per physician for a 5-physician practice during the first 60 days following EHR implementation is $32,000 [11]. This is because investments in EHR system implementation include not only the technology—software and hardware—but also a variety of additional costs associated with implementation, such as training, lost productivity during training (and throughout and following the system implementation), as well as various consulting and technical costs. Some of these costs, such as training fees, would increase profoundly if volunteers required training as well.

Moreover, the license-per-user service model is tightly coupled with the HIPAA Privacy Rule, which dictates that only authorized personnel can access and use patient personal health information. The license-per-user model embedded within the current EHR design largely reinforces the HIPAA Privacy Rule since only those who have access to validated user accounts can access protected patient information in the system. Importantly, all information access is logged and can be audited later to decide who have accessed which patient information at what time. In fact, protecting patient privacy is one of the intended benefits of EHR and a motivation behind such large-scale system implementations.

Due to severe financial constraints and the strict HIPAA Privacy Rule, under the current license-per-user model, the free clinic could not purchase enough licenses for every volunteer, nor were they able to create a unified shared-access volunteer account (i.e. an account with the same user name/password for multiple users to use) since they would be unable to identify who actually accessed and documented information in the EHR. Thus, it is critical to think about a more sustainable way to support temporary workers without violating the HIPAA Privacy Rule.

We propose a special license for health organizations housed with a large number of transient workers with variable schedules—a time-sharing license, as opposed to user-based license. Each time-sharing license would allow multiple users to access the EHR system at different times, somewhat similar to the time-sharing of resources in computing or well-known timesharing vacation club programs. In this vein, organizations with large numbers of transient workers would be able to obtain time-sharing accounts, where any one account could allow access by several users who are charged for the amount of time they use the system as opposed to per-user basis. Each time-sharing user would log on the system with his or her own user name and password so that their individual activities are logged as well. Since essentially only one user could log into a time-sharing account at a given time, this account can be billed in a much more affordable way, and the associated individual login information can still identify the user's identity and thus protect patient's privacy and safety in this manner. In this way, the volunteers who work only a few hours at a time will have access to the system, allowing the special license to be best utilized.

Mutual reconfiguration of human infrastructure with technological infrastructure

As we found in our study, without the capacity to access the EHR system, volunteer roles have greatly diminished, to the point where they had little, and in some cases, nothing to do. The tasks that they used to perform had to be shifted to the employees after the system rollout. The diminished volunteer roles, however, had been gradually restructured around the performance of new types of tasks that were not assigned to volunteers previously. For example, student volunteers rarely had the opportunity to interact with patients before the EHR rollout but they became more visible to patients after the EHR system was deployed, such as when they engaged in the new practice around escorting patients to exam rooms.

This finding suggests a co-evolving nature of technology deployment where not only did technologies impact the work practices of the clinic, but the work practices, in particular, the human infrastructure, shifted to better support the system being deployed. The process of reconfiguring human infrastructure was ongoing, particularly when new problems emerged. For instance, although a workaround was developed so that volunteers could help with arranging referrals (as eReferrals were not possible due to the need for pro-bono services), the leadership team continued to work with the vendor to find a long term solution so that the features of the EHR system could be more fully utilized.

Meanwhile, we found that the nature of volunteer work had gradually shifted from being a behind-the-scenes support role, to more visible, collaborative work with employees. The employees, in turn, had to find a way to make volunteer-work work. As such, they served as a mediator between the new technological infrastructure and the volunteer workforce, taking on additional responsibilities as facilitators for volunteer work. Thus, resource-restricted organizations that rely on volunteer work should plan for additional mediation work when adopting new technologies.

Our findings echo what has been reported in prior literature [12, 24], we found a duality existed between the technological and human infrastructures supporting work in the free clinic. The disruption caused by the new technology triggered a process of human infrastructure reconfiguration. The human infrastructure also began to reconfigure practices around the new technological infrastructure, such as by adopting and changing roles. The new roles people assumed even empowered volunteers in some cases, as they assumed roles with greater responsibilities and patient interaction that was not previously part of their workplace identity.

Thus, our results imply that it is a co-evolving process for technologies and human infrastructure to fit together in organizations. Actually defining and reconfiguring the work of volunteers are necessary when more similar organizations are moving into digital-based practices. It is possible that through carefully redesigning the sociotechnical system, volunteers may not always engage in labor and time intensive tasks, but may take on more intelligent and complicated tasks that are complementary to the existing skill sets of the employees. This is important considering that there were more technology related tasks after the system rollout, and the current employees and volunteer clinicians may not always have sufficient skills to perform some of these tasks, whereas the college students who had sufficient computer skills could thus enrich the task force of the free clinic.

The tension in achieving interoperable practices and restricted options for technologies

Our study clinic offers only basic medical care to underprivileged patients who, however, often require further medical attention such as inpatient care, and surgeries. Therefore, the clinic has to rely on a variety of services provided by other healthcare organizations within their affiliated delivery network, such as a nearby comprehensive hospital. In addition to the pervasive pressure from other healthcare organizations in going digital, the free clinic was urged to implement an EHR system so that it could interoperate with the EHR systems used within the healthcare network. The benefits of having an interoperable EHR system have been well recognized as it enhances workflow and data sharing among EHR systems and health care stakeholders [17]. It can also help reduce the number of duplicate lab and diagnostic tests, which is particularly important to the resource-restricted clinic under investigation, so that their limited resources would be best utilized by other patients who were also in need of those services.

However, moving towards digitization so that the free clinic could enjoy the benefits afforded by interoperability was not without its share of challenges. Importantly, the clinic did not have an opportunity to choose a system based on its own needs, or design a system from the ground up. Rather, the choices of EHR systems for the clinic were limited by the requirement of compatibility with other systems in the network. Only three commercially designed systems, all of which were designed for conventional healthcare organizations, were available. The limitation in choices also mitigated the clinic's potential to obtain a more customizable system to meet the specific needs of the free clinic, such as the capability to more flexibly accommodate user licenses for its large number of volunteers.

As demonstrated in our study, the benefits of interoperability clearly limited the possible opportunities for the free clinic to choose the most appropriate technological solution. This observation indicates that there may exist a tension between the technical requirements for interoperable practices and the type of work practices supported by the underlying human infrastructure of resource-restricted organizations. With the rapid digitalization across work domains societally, it is likely the same challenges also exist in other networked systems where intra-organizational collaboration is essential.

Given that the network of organizations may consist of both large companies that are financially stable, and small resource-restricted NPOs that have limited funding, it is critical to ensure that resource-limited organizations are also able to appropriate technologies that suit their own needs. The use of proprietary systems designed for conventional organizations, as we found in our study, cannot always be adapted and effectively used by resource-limited organizations—to use an old adage, technologies are not "one-size fits all".

To that end, we suggest that careful coordination of technology solutions within any given organizational network is crucial. Rather than being forced to use what others have adopted in their network, under-resourced organizations that are most likely to adopt technologies at a later stage should be given the opportunity to voice their needs and concerns earlier in the process. Moreover, we argue that interoperability should be maintained while allowing for any given organization to support its own set of practices so that disruptions to local practices would be minimized. This means that while achieving interoperability, the organization must also take its human infrastructure into consideration, in addition to its technological infrastructure.

CONCLUSION

The study reported in this paper uncovered a major disruption to the human infrastructure in a volunteer-based safety-net free clinic after the implementation of an EHR system, which led to a restructuring of work around the new technological infrastructure. Given the lack of access to patient information by volunteers, members of the clinic were unable to perform routine tasks as they used to before the system was deployed. Thus, employee workloads increased substantially, which brought about unintended consequences that impacted the quality of patient care as some tasks were delayed due to the limited personnel who could access the system.

In order to repair the disrupted human infrastructure, especially with respect to volunteer services, employees of the clinic attempted to reconcile the human infrastructure by creating new work roles for volunteers, re-establishing quality patient care, and developing workarounds. We then discussed implications for resource-restricted free clinics adopting new technologies and why a commercially designed technological infrastructure failed to support a volunteer-based human infrastructure. We also proposed a new type of EHR user license, time-sharing licence, to meet the specific, fluid needs of the volunteer-based clinic. Finally we illuminated the challenges of small resource-restricted healthcare settings in achieving interoperable practices within major healthcare networks. Above all, our work suggests that volunteers should not be overlooked as critical members of the human infrastructure, and offers new knowledge and useful insights for advancing the healthcare system implementation—especially considering that technology adoption is becoming more and more inevitable even in resource-restricted organizations.

ACKNOWLEDGEMENT

We are grateful to the Faculty Mentor Program at the University of California, Irvine awarded to Jahmeilah Roberson that supported the data collection of this work.

REFERENCES

1. Ackerman, M.S., Halverson, C.A., Erickson, T., Kellogg, W.A., Reddy, M., and Dourish, P. Representation, Coordination, and Information Artifacts in Medical Work. In Resources, Co-Evolution and Artifacts. Springer London, 2008, 167–190.
2. Barley, S.R. Technology as an occasion for structuring: Evidence from observations of CT scanners and the social order of radiology departments. *Administrative Science Quarterly* 1986, 31:78-108.
3. Bates, D.W., Ebell, M., Gotlieb, E., Zapp, J., and Mullins, H.C. A Proposal for Electronic Medical Records in U.S. Primary Care. Journal of the American Medical Informatics Association 2003, 10(1):1–10.
4. Bates W, D., Cohen, M., Leape L, L., Marc Overhage, J., Michael Shabot, M., and Sheridan, T. Reducing the Frequency of Errors in Medicine Using Information Technology. Journal of the American Medical Informatics Association 2001, 8(4):299–308.
5. Berg, M., Pirnejad, H., and Stoop, A.P. Bridging information gaps between primary and secondary healthcare. Student Health Technology Information 2006, 124:1003–1008.

6. Boonstra, A. and Broekhuis, M. Barriers to the Acceptance of Electronic Medical Records by Physicians from Systematic Review to Taxonomy and Interventions. BMC Health Services Research 2010, 10:231.
7. Brudney, J.L. Designing and managing volunteer programs. In R.D. Herman (Ed.), The Jossey-Bass Handbook of Nonprofit Leadership and Management. Jossey-Bass, San Francisco 1994, Chapter 13.
8. Campbell, E.M., Sittig, D.F., Ash, J.S., Guappone, K.P., and Dykstra, R.H. Types of Unintended Consequences Related to Computerized Provider Order Entry. Journal of the American Medical Informatics Association 2006, 13(5):547–556.
9. Chen, Y. Documenting transitional information in EMR. Proceedings of CHI 2010, 1787–1796.
10. Dombrowski, L., Hayes, G.R., Mazmanian, M. and Voida, A. E-Government Intermediaries and the Challenges of Access and Trust. ACM Transaction in Computer-Human Interaction 2004, 21(2):Article 13.
11. Fleming, N. S., Culler, S. D., McCorkle, R., Becker, E. R. and Ballard, D.J. "The Financial and Nonfinancial Costs of Implementing Electronic Health Records in Primary Care Practices". Health Affairs 2011, 30(3): 481–9.
12. Giddens, A. The Constitutions of Society: outline of the theory structuration. Berkeley: University of California Press 1984.
13. Han, Y., Carcillo, J., Venkataraman, S., Clark, R., Watson, R., Nguyen, T., Bayir, H. and Orr, R. Unexpected Increased Mortality after Implementation of a Commercially Sold Computerized Physician Order Entry System. Pediatrics 2005, 116:1506-1512.
14. Hartswood, M., Procter, R., Rouncefield, M. and Slack, R. Making a Case in Medical Work: implications for the electronic medical record. JCSCW 2003, 12(3):241-266.
15. Heath, C. and Luff, P. Collaborative Activity and Technological Design: task coordination in London underground control rooms. In Proceedings of ECSCW 1991, 65–80.
16. Heath, C. and Luff, P. Documents and Professional Practice: 'bad' organisational and reasons for 'good' clinical records. Proceedings of CSCW 1996, 354–363.
17. Hillestad, R., Bigelow, J., Bower, A.,Girosi, F., et al. Can Electronic Medical Record Systems Transform Health Care? Potential Health Benefits, Savings, and Costs. Health Affairs 2005, 24(5):1103-7.
18. HIPAA. http://privacyruleandresearch.nih.gov/ accessed on July 30, 2014.
19. Hughes, J.A., Randall, D. and Shapiro, D. Faltering from Ethnography to Design. Proceedings of CSCW 1992, 115–122.
20. Le Dantec, C.A. and Edwards, W.K. The View from the Trenches: organization, power, and technology at two nonprofit homeless outreach centers. Proceedings of CSCW 2008, 589–598.
21. Lee, C.P., Dourish, P., and Mark, G. The Human Infrastructure of Cyberinfrastructure. Proceedings of CSCW 2006, 483–492.
22. Mark, G., Al-Ani, N. and Semaan, B. Repairing Human Infrastructure in a War Zone. Proceedings of the 6th International ISCRAM Conference, 2009.
23. Merkel, C., Farooq, U., Xiao, L., Ganoe, C., Rosson, M.B. and Carroll, J. Managing Technology Use and Learning in Nonprofit Community Organizations: methodological challenges and opportunities. Proceedings of CHIMIT 2007, Article 7.
24. Orlikowski, W. Learning from Notes: organizational Issues in Groupware Implementation. Proceedings of CSCW 1992: 362–369.
25. Paul, S., Das, A., and Patel, V. Specifying Design Criteria for Electronic Medical Record Interface Using Cognitive Framework. AMIA Annual Symposium Proceedings 2003, 594–598.
26. Reddy, M. and Bradner, E. Multiple Perspectives: Evaluating Healthcare Information Systems in Collaborative Environments. In J. Anderson and C. Aydin, eds., Evaluating the Organizational Impact of Healthcare Information Systems. Springer, 2005, 56–74.
27. Sambasivan, N. and Smyth, T. The Human Infrastructure of ICTD. Proceedings of ICTD 2010.
28. Scott, J. T., Rundall, T. G., Vogt, T. M., & Hsu, J. Kaiser Permanente's experience of implementing an electronic medical record: a qualitative study. BMJ 2005, 331(7528):1313-1316.
29. Strauss, A. L. and Corbin, J. M. Basics of Qualitative Research: techniques and procedures for developing grounded theory. Sage, CA, 1998.
30. Suchman, L. Human Values and the Design of Computer Technology, Chapter Do Categories have Politics? The language/action perspective reconsidered, 91–106. Center for the Study of Language and Information, Stanford, CA, USA, 1997.
31. Symon, G., Long, K. and Ellis, J. The Coordination of Work Activities: cooperation and conflict in a hospital context. JCSCW 1996, 5(1):1–31.
32. Tang, C. and Carpendale, S. Evaluating the Deployment of a Mobile Technology in a Hospital Ward. Proceedings of CSCW 2008, 205-214.
33. Voida, A., Harmon, E. & Al-Ani, B. Homebrew Databases: complexities of everyday information management in nonprofit organizations. In Proceedings of CHI 2011, 915–924.
34. Voida, A., Harmon, E. and Al-Ani, B. Bridging between Organizations and the Public: volunteer coordinators' uneasy relationship with social computing. Proceedings of CHI 2012, 1967-76.

Expertise in the Wired Wild West

Joanne I. White & Leysia Palen
ATLAS Institute & Department of Computer Science
University of Colorado Boulder
joanne.white, palen@colorado.edu

ABSTRACT
This ethnographic study reveals how expertise was sought, articulated and actuated across online and offline worlds to enable the evacuation of 38 horses from an isolated ranch in the mountainous region of Northern Colorado following a series of devastating flash floods in September 2013. The shared expertise within a loosely connected community of practice bridged spatial-temporal limitations and afforded opportunities for practical assistance and response, both virtually and on the ground. Interaction via social media articulated the parameters of the emergent problem to be solved, and "cast a net" to find the expertise necessary to address different aspects of the perceived problem. Eventually, more than 60 people with equine expertise converged onto the ranch, bringing their materials to execute a single-day evacuation and relocation of the herd.

Author Keywords
Animals; expertise; crisis informatics; disaster; emergency; equine; livestock; social cognition; social computing.

ACM Classification Keywords
H.5.3. Groups & Organization Interfaces—collaborative computing, computer-supported cooperative work; K.4.2. Social Issues

INTRODUCTION
Disasters create myriad problems. Official responders are often so taxed that they cannot attend to every need in a community. Indeed, the very nature of disaster compels residents of an affected region to take charge in their recovery because the circumstances are dire and the resources are few. People self-organize to "get things done." Many consider community members as the "true first responders" for activities that include rescue, evacuation assistance and medical care [20, 45].

Social Media in Crisis Response
Such arguments have been extended to the study of a new arena of social interaction, that of social media during disaster response. By understanding that the online convergent crowd exhibits similar behaviors as the offline crowd, this body of research looks beyond the noisy online communications to see how subgroups of "digital volunteers" accomplish—or try to accomplish—work through that medium [31,33,36,42,43,47]. Though that research acknowledges that the work of the online effort must connect in some way to activities on the ground to fully assess its import, to date there has been little work that considers how online and offline work in the aftermath of disaster intersects (with exceptions including [41] and [49]). Additionally, we have little understanding about how spontaneous digital volunteers choose the tasks they could attack, and how the medium of social media might influence the topics around which groups organize, though we do see groups working across problem areas, such as crisis mapping [39], medical support [36,41], location information provision [43], situational awareness [33], and notably for this paper, animal welfare [47].

Animals in Disaster
This paper reports on a volunteer activity that responded to livestock concerns during a flooding disaster in Colorado. The matter of animal welfare in disaster is a major problem that community members often must tackle without official support. Over the last decade, the plight of animals in crisis events—both pets and livestock—and how that affects human decision-making about evacuation has been made increasingly clear [9,11,13,17,50]. Many people will not evacuate without their animals, or they may delay their decision to do so. Following Hurricanes Katrina and Rita where approximately 70,000 pets were separated from their families, with less than 3% of these reunited [16,47], the US passed the PETS Act (2006) for the inclusion of companion and service animals in evacuations and sheltering. However, the Act does not address the needs of those who own livestock, including equines and other large animals, even though their owners are often affected in the same way as small animal owners. Furthermore, large animal owners often depend on those animals for their livelihood; disasters can be devastating for these owners in both psychological and financial ways [9]. Naturally, it is difficult or even impossible to logistically evacuate large animals, and the lack of legislative support means that owners of livestock must take the lead on decision-making.

Growing interest among the online pet advocacy community in disaster response was described by White, Palen and Anderson [47], who studied the large-scale self-

ACM 978-1-4503-2922-4/15/03…$15.00.
http://dx.doi.org/10.1145/2675133.2675167

organizing activities of animal welfare advocates to suggest matches between lost and found pets over the months following the 2012 Hurricane Sandy. There was some connection between what was happening online and on the ground, but the extent of this was unclear, even to study participants [47].

Disconnection Between Offline & Online Response

Indeed, a major criticism of much current crisis social media research is that it does not consider the relationship between online work and offline or on-the-ground activities (Wulf, et al. [49] is a notable published location, and it is a discussion often brought up at conferences and in paper reviews). It is an important concern. Does the research fail because the online-to-offline connection is not happening, and therefore all the attention put to social media activity magnifies the role social media are playing (or could play) in disaster? Or is the behavior such that the research cannot tackle it because it is hindered by the logistical difficulties of deploying to a sometimes diffuse and hard-to-access disaster site at the right time to observe and study such activity? Probably some of each is occurring. The majority of online-offline connections that do exist are very subtle and difficult to capture empirically (especially under conditions of disaster).

This paper examines a case where the online work of information gathering was brought to bear on an offline or on-the-ground problem, the sensemaking of which demanded particular kinds of expertise. Where prior research failed because it could not place researchers on the ground in a far away site while simultaneously examining online behavior, we were able to study an event that was an outcome of devastating floods in our own geographical area. We still report on a single event, and the paper aims not to suggest without evidence that this happens frequently: It is rather aiming to learn from a situation that graduated from the online reporting of a problem (which was not a solicitation for help) to the mobilization of interested volunteers who devised and implemented an offline solution over an extended period for a time- and safety-critical situation. That it happened close to our home town where we could access all aspects of it over a protracted time period suggests that these kinds of ensembles of online and offline work in disaster settings are not rare, but that "being there" during the disaster creates the opportunity to witness them.

Research Objectives

This paper examines the case of a "self-assisted evacuation" of 38 marooned horses that were left isolated by extensive road damage on a high mountain ranch in the "wild west" of Colorado, by the devastating floods that occurred there. The account considers how online and offline work came together under conditions of specialized expertise sharing that drew upon people near and far, digitally and physically. In this paper, we examine how a problem with an uncertain solution under time-critical circumstances is solved across people, time, place and materials. In addition to emotionally and financially supporting the ranch owners, the online activity served to "cast a net" to find expertise around the subject of horse-care and ranching. These experts then articulated the problem of the marooned horses and the geography of the mountains they were located in to develop a plan that would allow volunteer "horsepeople" who were connected primarily through social media to converge onto the ranch and evacuate the horses "down mountain" in the uncertain conditions of a post-flood environment without harm to the horses, themselves, or their equipment. Furthermore, the execution on the ground of their expertise was realized and shaped by the layout of the roads, the locations and temperaments of the horses, and the constraints and possibilities yielded by their materials and equipment.

In this online-meets-offline account of cooperative work, we see connections to the classic literature in CSCW around matters of mutual awareness in safety-critical systems [12] that is partially achieved online and only "satisficingly" [38] achieved offline. We see how performances around paperwork intended to connect the online to the offline are once again superficial [44], and that the offline work is refigured at the very end primarily to communicate its successful completion back to a waiting, online crowd. We see how problem definition, work articulation [37], and the materiality of work [27,35] come together to make the work happen in a socially-, spatially-, and temporally- distributed matter [14]. Finally, a main contribution of this research lies in the examination of the solicitation of expertise in a digitally-connected world, where widely distributed and diverse expertise must nevertheless be realized under highly localized conditions.

METHODOLOGICAL APPROACH

Sites of Study

The fieldwork of this ethnographic study first began with online observation of Facebook activity in a group set up specifically during the Colorado Flood event, named *Colorado Equine Evacuation and Disaster Response Network/Fleet of Angels* from September 11 to October 25, 2013. On October 2, a member crossposted a link to the Back Country Horsemen's website calling for volunteers to assist with the needs of a ranch in a mountainous remote area of Northern Colorado at 8500 feet (2600m) above sea level. The ranch, set on 600 acres and the physical site of study, operates as a breeding facility for competitive show horses, each valued in the tens of thousands of dollars.

The ranch owners were evacuated during the 2013 Colorado floods that began on September 11, following days of heavy rain. The region experienced a year's worth of rainfall over a four-day period. The ranchers had to leave what were originally 39 horses behind. Parts of county road access to the ranch eventually washed away and became impassable during the storms and the resulting flash floods. Because of the road status, the horses were "marooned"—

this was the official status of people who were isolated in the mountains for the same reason and had to be airlifted in what the National Guard called the largest air rescue since Katrina [32]. Though domesticated animals were airlifted out with their owners, operating on the directives of the PETS Act, livestock were not.

The threat of the conditions at the ranch was serious: rain and flood waters could mold existing feed and damage or limit access to the little remaining seasonal pasture grass. Horses could be standing in sodden pasture, which could then lead to hoof damage. With the owners so far away with limited access to their property as well as a lack of assurance from officials, it was hard to know how dire the flooding and food situations were, or how quickly they might get worse. What is more, the winter season strikes hard and early at that elevation in Colorado, and, as time passed during the month of September, it was unclear whether the horses could survive for long without proper care. Eventually, a group of volunteer "horsepeople"—experienced owners and caretakers who were loosely connected online but describe themselves as "united by a … common bond and passion" for horses—came to the ranch to move the horses "down mountain" to a temporary ranch location. The "self-assisted evacuation" happened on Sunday, October 6 over the course of 13 hours with more than 60 people—some using their own horses—and approximately 20 trailers participating.

As an important point of clarification early in this story, the number of horses to be evacuated decreased from 39 to 38, which is why both numbers appear in this account. Between the flooding and the evacuation, one of two stallions was killed by the other after they were turned out from their pens into a paddock by a would-be helper long before the expert horsepeople arrived. The stallion's death was a catalyst for a concentrated mobilization of response from horsepeople, both online and offline.

Ethnographic Investigation

Prior to the October evacuation, the first author had been collecting data on other livestock welfare issues in Colorado in the wake of the floods. She had been conducting interviews with ranchers, feed providers, the emergency hay bank and emergency responders. On October 2 she learned of this ranch's situation through a Facebook group she was monitoring. From that point on she collected all prior and current Facebook data related to the ranch. She responded to the call for volunteers for the evacuation as a researcher, and became a participant observer who was in direct contact with those coordinating the evacuation.

She assisted with the evacuation of the horses on October 6, shadowing the ranch owner, Trudy, throughout the day as she traversed her large ranch and engaged with horses and helpers. The morning after the evacuation she drove to the temporary, rented ranch where the horses and owners would spend the winter season. There she spent four hours following up with the ranch owner, employees and two volunteers who had come from Texas to assist. The first author was the only person present at the ranch during the evacuation day who was unfamiliar with horses, a point that delighted Trudy because she knew that the research would not be tainted by the "strong views" that horsepeople often held. We see this research as a multi-sited ethnography [24], with such an approach providing the necessary mobile lens to this particular research environment [2].

We audio-recorded many conversations with Trudy and took nearly 200 photographs of the evacuation. The week following the evacuation, we interviewed seven participants who had volunteered that day plus two officials, a ranch employee, and the owners once again. These interviews were conducted in person and by phone as circumstances allowed. We used photographs taken on the evacuation day in the interviews as probes [1]. In addition we collected personal email correspondence between the evacuation organizers, neighbors and officials. Follow-up questions and interviews by email and telephone clarified points over an even longer duration of time. The interviews were transcribed and then analytically combined with other documents, field notes, and visual data to produce a complete picture of the evacuation's coordination activities. (We note that all names of people and the ranch used in this account are pseudonyms.)

ANALYTICAL DESCRIPTION

This ethnographic reporting focuses on how loosely-connected members of a community of practice with equine specialization mobilized online and offline, and worked with the ranch owners to organize and implement an evacuation. They recruited help from this community to move the horses down-mountain to a temporary ranch over three hours' drive away. We document how a larger distributed group of interested observers articulated the full extent of the problem that Trudy faced through remote, mostly online interaction on Facebook, by email, and telephone, which eventually led a subset of them—who did not otherwise know each other, and with some coming from outside the State—to converge on the mountainous ranch location and evacuate 38 horses on a single day.

We identify times of conflict and challenges that were overcome through the flexibility of experts in circumstances that were unusual and emergent. It reviews matters of coordination between stakeholders who had not worked together before over multiple media before and after, and across physical places; and with respect to the "living" inventory of livestock, which imposes a level of urgency and degree of expertise necessary for such an evacuation.

The next section relays an overview of the features of the evacuation planning and implementation. Some portions of the evacuation are highlighted to convey the "telling" examples [5] of the nature of the coordination.

Flooding & Human Evacuation of the Ranch

The owners of Palisades Ranch were subject to a mandatory human evacuation order on September 12, the second and heaviest day of rainfall during the Colorado floods. Trudy, one of two ranch owners and the prominent figure here, made their situation public by posting on her personal Facebook Timeline. They were able to evacuate with their dogs, but left their 39 equines behind. In the flurry of activity in the hours following the human evacuation, a neighbor of the ranch, Alexander, who owned a small plane and so could evacuate but still fly back and forth when the weather cleared, offered to watch Trudy's herd and fly in grain. Due to the weight of the grain, however, Alexander found he was only able to transport three bags per trip—not enough to feed 39 horses. It became clear this was not a viable long-term plan.

Unfortunately, nearly a week after the human evacuation, an unidentified person entered the property and let loose the two stallions who had been penned. It is likely that the person thought the stallions did not have access to food, not realizing that they must be penned for their own and the other horses' safety. When checking the horses on September 18, six days after the mandatory human evacuation, Alexander found that one stallion had killed the other. He suspected a National Guardsman had been responsible for their release, as they were in the area to check on conditions. When she was told of the death, Trudy was deeply saddened but decided against reporting it to officials, saying, "I would not take someone's joy. He doesn't know horses. He thought he was protecting them."

Online Connection

As Trudy relayed information about her situation to her Facebook friends—many of whom were also horsepeople—they started making suggestions and asking questions to grasp the situation. For example, some did not understand how expansive and rugged the Rocky Mountains are, and that the horses could not be "ponied" or led down to the plains. The online followers of her story became more knowledgeable about the situation as their questions and her answers unfolded. The death of the stallion was a particularly important moment in communicating the gravity of the situation. As in any protracted disaster situation and certainly during the recovery phase, uncertainty rules the day while people wait for changing situational assessments and directions about permissible returns to homes. By the time Trudy realized that a "self-assisted evacuation" was the only practical possibility, in large part due to the information gathering conducted by her growing set of online contacts, 13 days had passed from her own evacuation. It then took only another five days to lease a temporary ranch and evacuate the animals.

Trudy's initial Facebook post provoked an unintended but positive response. Thinking that she was sharing only her frustration and distress, she said that she had "50 mares stuck on the mountain" (Figure 1). Having no expectation that people would come to her aid, what was meant to be an approximate number was transformed into the target that others organized around, and it propagated for the entire time up through the evacuation—and even after the evacuation when there was still uncertainty about the scope of the on-the-ground work that was ultimately conducted.

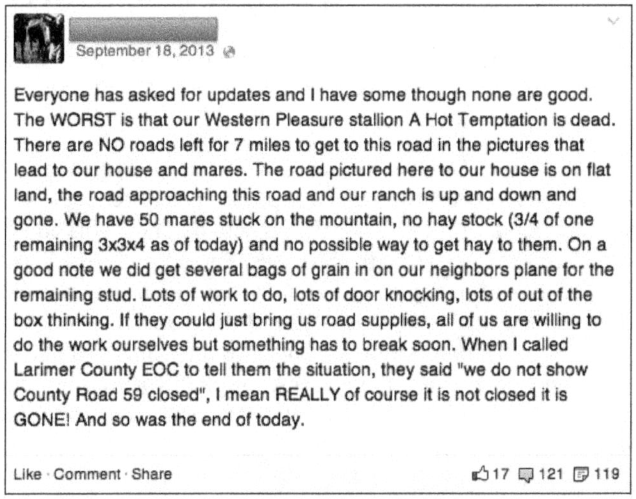
September 18, 2013

Everyone has asked for updates and I have some though none are good. The WORST is that our Western Pleasure stallion A Hot Temptation is dead. There are NO roads left for 7 miles to get to this road in the pictures that lead to our house and mares. The road pictured here to our house is on flat land, the road approaching this road and our ranch is up and down and gone. We have 50 mares stuck on the mountain, no hay stock (3/4 of one remaining 3x3x4 as of today) and no possible way to get hay to them. On a good note we did get several bags of grain in on our neighbors plane for the remaining stud. Lots of work to do, lots of door knocking, lots of out of the box thinking. If they could just bring us road supplies, all of us are willing to do the work ourselves but something has to break soon. When I called Larimer County EOC to tell them the situation, they said "we do not show County Road 59 closed", I mean REALLY of course it is not closed it is GONE! And so was the end of today.

Like · Comment · Share 17 121 119

Figure 1. Trudy's Facebook update.

On the same day that Trudy posted news about the death of the stallion, a horseperson in Missouri saw the post and sent a Facebook message to Jane, a ranch owner she knew in Pueblo, Colorado to solicit in-State help. Jane in turn contacted Frank of the Back Country Horsemen of Northern Colorado (BCHA) by email. Though Jane was located in Colorado and could better leverage the equine social networks there, we note that Pueblo is still over two hours' driving time away from Boulder, Colorado (the nearest city to the ranch, which itself was still a distance away). Jane and Frank together began collecting information about the ranch, including its accessibility. Frank contacted Trudy and over the next few days, the three of them pooled information from their conversations with officials. Together, they brainstormed solutions that could help the horses of Palisades Ranch.

Trudy was initially reluctant to accept help. In a follow-up interview she said,

> *It made me squirm a little bit. I was embarrassed at first ... I'm not used to getting. I'm used to giving. I don't like attention on me.*

This confirms our observation that the mobilization was a ground-swelling, and that though Trudy was involved in supplying information about the situation, significant action was being staged by others on her behalf in preparation for the massive undertaking of a 38-horse evacuation. Trudy had never met Jane or Frank, but understood the motivation of the volunteer response was altruistic, and decided to accept and encourage their help.

Conflicting Official Information

As they conducted their planning for a possible herd evacuation, the volunteers did not act independently of officials. Since the horses were not in immediate danger, officials understandably considered the situation low in priority as they were still locating people on the missing persons register. When Frank shared the initial thoughts for an evacuation of the Palisades horses with the Boulder County Sheriff's Office, he was summarily told there was a roadblock along the planned route, and that those who breached it would be arrested.

Frank, whose career had included 25 years' experience in law enforcement, did not give up. He had better luck with Larimer County Sheriff's Office, where he once worked as a mounted officer with the Sheriff's Posse. A "Posse" is a legal entity of non-paid workers who respond to a sheriff's request, and has its origins in the 1800's American West. In response, deputies from Larimer County Sheriff's Office went up to the ranch themselves, checked road conditions, and relayed that there was in fact no roadblock. The disparity of information between the two agencies reveals the kind of information gaps that frequently occur during mass emergencies and are a source of motivation for people taking problems "into their own hands."

In addition, on September 24, Trudy's husband was told that no hay would be slung in by officials, and that they would need to source and fund the feed and its transport themselves. On September 25, the prohibitively high cost of helicopter rental compounded with imminent winter weather brought Trudy into agreement with Frank and Jane, who had been making evacuation contingency plans the entire time. Trudy began to search for a temporary location for her horses.

Online Support: Raising Money through an Auction

While the remotely distributed volunteers and ranch owners made contingency plans for the evacuation, other online helpers sought complementary ways to support the effort. One person created a Facebook group for support, where people began to donate money along with goods or services to be auctioned, with proceeds going towards the needs of the ranch. The donated items were mostly horse-related (clothing, equipment and even stud fees). Participants used the comment threads to bid. Good-natured bidding and conversations ensued across the auction threads. The group celebrated updates by Trudy. Because the first auction attracted a great deal of support, they held a second.

The auctions were set up unbeknownst to the grief-stricken Trudy who was mourning the loss of the stallion and distressed about the rest of the herd. The two auctions raised an astonishing US$22,000. Trudy discovered the auction's existence after a few days through a reporter who had called her for comment about her "really good friends." Ultimately, the proceeds helped Trudy pay the lease on a temporary ranch and buy hay, which had become expensive due to the water damage of Colorado's hay supply.

Trudy's work led to securing a temporary ranch and the lease was signed on October 1. Trudy, Frank and Jane agreed to set the evacuation to happen five days later—24 days after the rainstorms and flooding began. On October 4, Trudy began to prepare the ranch. Mary, a friend from Texas, came to help, and in turn brought one of *her* Facebook friends, Audrey. Frank continued to make the logistical arrangements for the evacuation, updating Trudy and Jane as he went. Note that this core trio had yet to meet in person.

Information Sharing Built Network of Online Experts

Trudy continued to post online. The posts were shared across the network of horsepeople and organizations, and received many likes and comments, all with messages of support and occasional suggestions of evacuation locations for the horses. The attention of the online community of equine-specialists had clearly been engaged.

When Trudy was securing and preparing a new ranch, she did not have time to post updates on evacuation plans. Instead, Jane and Audrey tagged Trudy in their Facebook posts about the evacuation plans, effectively posting on her behalf since the posts then appeared on Trudy's Timeline.

Date	Event
Sept 12	Ranch owners evacuated.
Sept 18	One of 2 stallions discovered dead.
Sept 19	Jane contacts Frank. Both contact Trudy. Planning begins.
Sept 24	News that there will be no hay drops by FEMA or the State.
Sept 25	Focus turns entirely to a herd evacuation. Trudy begins looking for a ranch to lease.
Oct 1	Temporary ranch lease signed. Evacuation day set. Frank sends email and posts web announcement searching for volunteers, which propagates across social media.
Oct 3	Snow conditions predicted for evacuation day, but team proceeds, with contingency plans.
Oct 4	Trudy moves into temporary ranch. Local reconnaissance on ranch and road network performed.
Oct 6	Evacuation day (with clear weather).

Table 1. Timeline of events.

Expanding the Reach for Help

With the full impact of the planning to move the horses upon them and with time-critical decisions to be made, Frank took on the lead role of soliciting the help of experienced horsepeople through his online networks. Frank asked his partner, Louise, also a horseperson, to take on the role of managing the paper-based administration of the evacuation day, while Frank focused on organizing the volunteers and physical logistics.

On October 1, Frank used his standing and connections as president of the Boulder County Horsemen's Association to attract appropriate volunteers for the evacuation. Addressed to his "fellow equestrians," Frank sent an email outlining his plan, stating that he was looking for:

```
Ten to 12 riders (wranglers), up to 25
4WD three- or four-horse slant load or
stock trailers for transport.
```

To lend authority, Frank explained his recent history with Palisades Ranch and that he was supervising the effort, but that the owners and their employees would have the final say on how the day went. Frank made it clear that "complete cooperation is necessary by all who sign up." The email was shared throughout the equine community by email, websites and Facebook pages.

Between October 1 and October 6 (evacuation day), Frank received about 100 email messages expressing interest. Not all interested people were appropriate for the task. Frank sometimes needed to correct assumptions and use his experience as a horseperson and former Posse lead to select qualified candidates. As Frank explains:

> *I had people telling me ... I don't know how to rope or anything, but I'll come with my horse – and I said, rope? What? What are you going to rope? ... I said no, we don't want a rodeo, we want everything calm and quiet.*

The selected volunteers were emailed an information sheet that included directions to the property, contingencies in case of poor weather, and cell phone numbers of eight people from the Northern Colorado Back Country Horsemen organization whom Frank trusted. He booked more volunteers to come than he thought were required for what he thought were 50 horses. As he anticipated what faced him, including the uncertainty about the numbers of volunteers who would show as well as the psychological state of the horses, he remained flexible. Frank says:

> *Working with volunteers is different to when I worked with the Sheriff's Department and we had an operation. You were deputized and by golly, you were coming. We asked you to come, we're going to order you to come and you come. When you have volunteers you can't hardly hold them to that.*

After seeing a Facebook post, the Weld County Posse also decided to assist with some of their members in an *official* call-out, even though, remarkably, the originating and the destination ranches were not a part of Weld County. On the evacuation day, the Posse members came in uniform, adding visible authority and underscoring their expertise. However, they did not seek to take control. Instead, they saw themselves as supporting the efforts of Frank and his team. As an existing volunteer group, the Posse was able to mobilize more easily than new, episodic volunteers (something we see in other volunteer situations, eg., [46]). Barb, the Weld Posse coordinator explained that she was not flummoxed that Weld participated when the Larimer and Boulder County Posses did not:

> *One of the advantages that Weld County has is that we don't have to carry a weapon or be post-certified, so our numbers are much bigger. They only have seven or eight on the Larimer County Posse, so they don't have a big group to draw from.*

Note again that Frank and Louise were not local to the area, and were working remotely until the evacuation day. Weather remained poor and work demands meant Frank and Louise could not travel to the ranch to check access. Instead of personally surveying the location to establish best routes, they had a friend who lived locally travel the planned route and identify on a map any unrepaired road damage, and suitable places for parking and loading of horse trailers. This happened on Friday October 4, two days prior to the Sunday evacuation.

We also note that, somehow, the actual number of horses—38 after the stallion died—was never accurately figured or communicated by Trudy. Frank was basing his evacuation logistical preparations on the original 50 that Trudy rather casually communicated in her very first post, which had propagated online. It was even reported over time to be as many as 60 horses, and as few as 45 in the digital tracings we reviewed. This was one piece of information that never got corrected, even on the day of the evacuation, though Frank was not worried about this disparity. This suggests that the tracking of the horses was done based on their "presence" in the pasture rather than matched against an inventory. We will return to this issue.

Evacuation Day

Psychologically Readying the Horses

Evacuation day was the first time the ranch owner had seen her horses since she evacuated 24 days before. The reunions were emotional and took some time, as Trudy welcomed each. Some horses approached her directly while others remained dispersed across the ranch pasture, which was now very low on edible grass.

This time spent was critical to successfully herding the horses. Trudy needed to gain the cooperation of the lead mare, which would indicate to the other horses that the activities and new people were acceptable. Most of these horses were not used to being "ponied," (that is, being led with a lead rope by a rider on another horse) and as herding animals, equines prefer to stay with those they know. Frank relied on Trudy's personal knowledge of the horses to determine how best to gather and load them in trailers, but when the *in situ* practicalities of timely decision-making and next-in-line trailer capacities presented themselves, he also used those constraints as his guides. Here we see the applied expert management of the inventory as a skillful interplay between a real-life, time-critical "packing problem" [eg. 22] and the psychological needs of sentient creatures.

Figure 2. Riders pony horses out of the pasture.

Summoning of Expertise Trumps Pro Forma Paperwork

On the day of the evacuation, 44 volunteers signed in on a form prepared by Louise, the volunteer in charge of evacuation-day administration. When Louise and Frank reviewed the sign-in forms after the evacuation, they found that because volunteers filled in the form themselves, only a third were legible and many were incomplete. As researchers, we had thought the form was to be part of a security or tracking effort, but interestingly, in follow-up interviews, the organizers said they were more concerned about thanking volunteers afterwards. In addition, Louise brought waivers for volunteers to sign, but with the focus on the practical aspects of the evacuation, they found it too difficult to manage, so none were completed.

Rather, as the hauling trailers left, a volunteer recorded the license plate and number of horses in the trailers. That was on yet another separate piece of paper—which, once again, was never used. The paper and the data it held were not shared with the destination ranch probably in part due to the lack of phone or data connectivity in the mountainous terrain, though the unworried neglect of all of the paperwork brings into question the very value that this particular system of coordinated work attributed to the paperwork in the first place. Furthermore, even though participants afterward stated intention to connect what had been online relationship development to offline interaction, paper tracking turned out to be largely pro forma for both that purpose as well as for inventory management. It suggests instead that management of the inventory was based on the mere presence of that inventory (the shared understanding that if there's a horse, and Trudy says it is hers, we will move it until there are no more horses). The imagined work during the planning processes involved paperwork, and therefore was once again the rationalized version of work as Suchman's contributions continue to remind us [44].

Furthermore, the *expertise* of the horsepeople was what was being summoned—along with patient cooperation—and the demonstration of their craft to mobilize a heavy and sometimes opinionated inventory was sufficient for granting what resulted in almost unconditional trust. The destination ranch counted the horses as they arrived, but that was primarily to post the information to a waiting audience on Facebook. As Frank said:

> *We didn't know who was going to be there and what their phone number was. I knew somebody was there, but I didn't know who.*

Communication Via Passing By on Set Route

Despite their extensive preparation, new information about the road was discovered on the day of the evacuation. As the first volunteers drove along the seven miles of dirt road towards Palisades Ranch from the highway, they found that in many sections it would be impossible to have two trailers pass each other. The organizers had planned to have trailers coming in and out from the loading area, but they realized that would not work. Instead they staged the trailers further away along the highway at its junction with the dirt road. Two volunteers stayed on the highway with the drivers/trailers and directed them to the "Trailer Loading" area sequentially as it became available. Communication between the two people giving directions and those working in the "Parking & Admin" and "Trailer Loading" areas happened via verbal messages that were passed along between the drivers coming in and out. This worked well, as the two helpers had to only come down twice over the 13 hours to clarify issues.

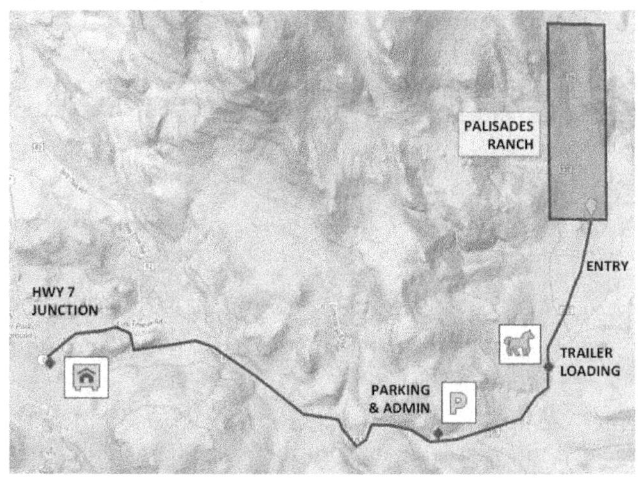

Figure 3. Map of the ranch and the approach.

Indeed, Frank had intended to use radios to communicate across the four staging areas, but their radios relied on line-of-sight and did not work in the woodland terrain. Like the trailer train, riders verbally passed on information at the Trailer Loading Point when horses were loaded and before they headed back into the ranch.

A Distributed Work Environment Enabled by Expertise

The expertise of the volunteers was important to supporting the distributed work arrangements, such that a micro task—for example, ponying a horse—could be performed within the confines of a person's expertise, equipment and tools, while still working as part of the larger coordinated activity of many horses, people and trailers. Their shared familiarity with equines, tools for managing the animals, and a common equine-specific terminology used smoothed the work which was especially important because they did not know each other. Trudy recognized the importance and value of this expertise:

These people have given more than money. They have given time and talent. That's worth so much more...

Figure 4. Posse members in uniform talking with ranch owner.

Conflict with Officials and Neighbors

The property line at the entrance of Palisades Ranch runs directly along the junction of Boulder and Larimer Counties. Frank had different experiences working with the two counties. One county knew of the evacuation plans and provided information to aid in the planning stages, but communications with the other county stopped with the inaccurate instruction about a non-existent roadblock.

On the afternoon before the evacuation, Jason, a second neighbor whose ranch is located directly adjacent to Palisades Ranch on the Boulder County side, heard second-hand about the planned operation and complained to the county. Jason had concerns about the plan to herd the horses through his property, which was necessary because the county road was washed out through both Palisades Ranch and his own. Not knowing the people involved and having only a civil relationship with Trudy, he was worried that the evacuation would be dangerous, and that some of his horses may be collected along the way. There had been no direct communication between Jason and the organizers until late on the day prior to the evacuation, when Jason emailed Frank, questioning the plans. Frank replied that Jason should speak directly with Trudy, and that if Jason also needed ranch assistance, they would be happy to help. At 2:30am on the day of the evacuation, the Boulder County deputy sent an email to Frank, strongly suggesting rescheduling the evacuation, and at minimum recommending the engagement of Animal Control to:

...assess the condition of the horses... and if there is a legitimate need to immediately 'rescue' some or all of them, then maybe we can make something happen.

Up until this point, the effort had internally been called a "rescue," perhaps in part to mobilize interest. Frank had not thought of the external and legal implications of using this term. In addition, the sudden re-engagement of the sheriff at this late stage of planning exposed a critical failure to coordinate with neighbors. Frank assumed Trudy had shared the plan with her neighbors—indeed, Trudy had written on Facebook about her supportive neighbors—but the relationship between her and this particular neighbor had been tense. In fact, Trudy felt direct communication with Jason was unneeded as there was no intention to involve his animals. On the morning of the evacuation, Frank arrived and reached a just-in-time compromise—the plan to herd the horses out got changed to ponying and leading them out—but not before heated words were exchanged between Trudy and Jason. Frank then renamed the effort to be a "self-assisted evacuation," to clarify intent and plans to those outside the effort.

Keeping Track of Horses & Trailers

The ranch owner, her spouse, and their two staff were the only people who knew the horses' names. They were distributed across the ranch and Trailer Loading area, attending to different needs through the day. They did not have consistent contact with the volunteers at the three key sites—Trailer Loading area, Parking & Admin, and the Highway—and therefore could not name and count all the horses as they were loaded.

Figure 5. Loading horses into trailers.

The highway-based volunteers rotated trailers between the two staging areas in batches of five. When each of the loaded trailers reached the highway, the drivers spoke with the volunteers who confirmed directions to the destination ranch 51 miles away at a 4400ft drop in elevation. The drive was three hours long because of road impasses. The remaining roads were in compromised condition in numerous areas, and required a high level of skill to navigate with a fully loaded horse trailer. The drivers discussed the best way to make the trip with the aid of printed maps, but they did not have the benefit of feedback from those who had already made the trip. Happily, as the afternoon progressed, a Boulder County Sheriff's deputy (who came to see the progress) relayed that a major canyon road closed since the floods would reopen late that day. This reduced the trip by one hour, allowing the last few trailers to travel the steepest part during daylight.

Errors that Disrupted the System

Late in the afternoon, coordination around the horse trailers, which had been going well, went awry. A series of miscommunications about the number of horses awaiting evacuation had propagated through the system. A local rider, Angela, who had been ponying horses and was leaving the site on her own horse, passed through each of the staging areas—the Trailer Loading area, and Parking & Admin—and finally she saw five trailers moving toward the Parking & Admin area from the highway. Angela performed a personal calculation of horses that still needed to be evacuated, the trailers she had observed in the parking area as she left, and then those waiting on the highway, and thought some would not be needed. What she did not realize, however, was that Frank had planned that the riders would not do the additional, tiring task of transporting the evacuated horses, given that there were less than the planned 50 horses. In other words, Angela did not have a view of the distribution of labor, and though she had performed a calculation on the material evidence (marooned horses and trailers) and presumed that to be evidence enough (and indeed, that had been how they had been working), the immaterial aspects of work were beyond her ken, and meant that she could not assign proper meaning to the material evidence. With this (observed but incomplete) information as her rationale, she told the five drivers they would not be needed.

Upon hearing this erroneous news, the trailer drivers turned around and returned to the highway where one of the highway volunteers assured them that they *were* needed, emphatically asking Angela where she had gotten her information. Angela was confused but apologetic. In a follow-up email, one of the affected trailer drivers said,

> *I felt confident that [highway volunteer] had been down where the loading was and had the updated information. The person on the horse was riding out so I questioned (in my mind) how she could know how many were left.*

Another problem came up later in the afternoon when a man named Harry who knew the ranch owner personally arrived to help. Trudy and Harry had agreed privately that he would take the single remaining stallion and another equine to the new ranch, but neither had shared this plan with the organizers. When Harry arrived at Palisades in the early afternoon, for some reason he thought the evacuation process was not a good one, and simply informed the volunteers at the Parking & Admin area he would "go down and check it out." The volunteers deferred because he said he was affiliated with the owner—they thought he was an employee. Harry loaded five horses at the Trailer Loading area and brought them up to Parking & Admin where trailers were waiting to go down to the Loading area. Instead he unloaded the horses from his trailer, and reloaded them on the trailers at this higher point in the loading sequence. This reordering of the process disrupted what had been a smooth system. It upset the horses, and disrupted the pattern of coordinated work the volunteers had become accustomed to. After Louise complained, Harry acknowledged her authority and that his adjustments were not helping. They reverted to the original process, and Harry moved only the two animals to the temporary ranch, as originally planned.

We see these disruptions as insights about how much the group grew to depend on repeatable, clear actions taken by others, which was the basis for quick development of intersubjective knowledge between people and horses they did not know, and for a task that they had never done before, but which had to be completed before dark. First, we see how Angela became so dependent on the direct mapping of available-horse-to-available-trailer method that she did not realize that other plans, which were invisible to her, were in place for managing the apparent excess of trailers. Second, we can see how the distributed group used stations in the landscape to mark the stages of work that were repeated for every horse. The breaking of the coordinated patterns of work as they were mapped to the landscape disrupted a system that worked without a great deal of immediate communication between people at the different stations.

Home on the Range: Arrival at the Destination Ranch

There were three volunteers at the destination ranch to receive the trailers as they arrived: Jane, Mary and Audrey, introduced earlier in this narrative. Nobody at the new ranch knew how many trailers to expect, nor when they were likely to arrive because of the spotty cell phone reception. As the trailers began to arrive, it was clear some organization was going to be needed to prevent bottlenecks on the driveway. A fourth volunteer was found in Jodie, an employee from the telephone company who had earlier set up the phone service and wanted to help despite a lack of horse experience. She stationed herself at the driveway entrance, and as trailers arrived, she held them back until Jane and the others were ready to receive a new trailer.

In contrast to the loading at the evacuation site, where attention was paid to putting horses that got along in trailers together, these volunteers had no personal knowledge of how best to paddock the horses together. Rather, Jane, Mary and Audrey, as experienced horsepeople, observed the horses' behavior. Audrey said:

> *I knew to watch them. If there was a problem in the paddock I was ready to go in and remove a mare and put her in the other one.*

Happily, apart from a few scratches and rubs from the side of the trailers, the horses were not injured, and were successfully penned in the new paddock. By 8pm the evacuation was complete. Trudy arrived at the new ranch just after the last trailer had left. Trudy was told the horses were all well, and the evacuation was deemed a success.

DISCUSSION

There are many lessons from this account. We will discuss: first, the *improvisational nature of emergency response*; second, *expertise in safety-critical work*; and third, how these matters play out in *ensembles of online and offline work* where the expanse of digital connection as well as the situated, co-located and collaborative expression of expertise intersect.

Threaded throughout these arguments is the idea of distributed cognition particularly as it materializes in the on-the-ground work, but also through prior online preparation. Through this lens, we see how ideation of solutions sprung from uncertain expressions of problem statements which were quickly forwarded to the local (or local enough) domain experts—horsepeople in Colorado. We see how expertise interacted with the material conditions of work in a way that suspended the need for having prior working relationships with one's colleagues-of-the-day. Much like other specializations—air traffic control [10,23], subway control centers [12], and snow sweeping [18]—the actors do not necessarily know each other, but they trust their own expertise, others' expertise, and common features of the material environment to allow coordinated work. The interesting matter here is that such a large-scale evacuation in an environment impacted by flooding was something that no one had prior experience with; this is where a number of psycho-social phenomena came into play, such as the human tendency to "make do" and improvise with tools at hand, as well as the idea of reciprocal trust springing from mutual liability. From a distributed cognition perspective, we see how Frank as the "expertise concierge" (in the words of McDonald and Ackerman [25]) reduced the macro goal of herd evacuation into a horse-by-horse evacuation, leveraging the constraints of trailers and making use of the road network as a structure to enforce ordering through queuing and sequenced communication. We discuss these aspects in greater detail.

Improvisation

In this account, from the perspective of emergency management we learn how intentional a self-organized response can be. Mass emergencies call for on-the-fly flexibility to adapt to changing circumstances and available resources over large numbers of people. Mendonça, et al. [26] and Kendra and Wachtendorf [20] have characterized this as *improvisation*, which has strong parallels to the conversations in CSCW about the nature of situated cognition or situated work [14,44], as well as the relationship between informal as well as formal aspects of work [30,44]. The difference in the discussions around improvisation is that it is often attached to large-scale endeavors of work. As such, in discussions around mass emergency, a focus is on how members of the public converge onto disaster sites to help physically [7,21,45]—and now digitally as well [42,47].

They interact with formal aspects of the response to use whatever resources they can access to perform even critical tasks like rescue, transportation to hospitals, and debris removal [20,26,45]. Notable is the stunning waterborne evacuation of a reported 500,000 people off Lower Manhattan in the wake of the 9/11 attacks as insightfully told by Kendra and Wachtendorf [19] where a "motley" array of personal and commercial vessels converged onto Battery Park in an orderly though clearly unplanned affair. Though this is a point that social scientists of disasters have been making for years [21,40], it is one that somehow fails to significantly permeate federal policies and even simple everyday conceptualizations about the nature of mass emergency work [30].

As accounts of similar phenomena in the online space are reaching the research world, other doubts ensue about exactly how the online work "matters"—about how it connects to the "real work" on-the-ground. We presented this debate at the opening of this paper, and why it might be justified, but also why it is a problematic question. It is probably being asked too soon and of a world in which it is difficult to have both a watchful eye on the online response and be staged to be in-place to observe the connected activity on the ground, assuming it happens at all.

Here we see that it does happen, though how much is not something we can answer. But a rare disaster put us in the right place at the right time for such behavior to become apparent. This horse evacuation case teaches how the improvisational work of domain experts produces sustained commitments to work (over a month long) with the open-ended parts of the problem being staged online until it could culminate in the execution of offline work, also requiring domain expertise.

Expertise in Time- and Safety-Critical Work

Expertise is a type of embedded knowledge developed within a cultural, social and cognitive environment [6]. Expertise is the ability to apply knowledge in different contexts [6], including in emergent situations that require experts to improvise, as Normark and Randall note [29].

In the horse evacuation, we see how relevant domain expertise made this event come to life, with all the initial ideation arising out of a demonstrable online interplay between statements of distress, problem articulation through public questioning and suggestions, and the alerting of a community of practice around horse care. Indeed, effectively all of the evacuation planning—except for the securing of a temporary ranch—was done by people who were unaffiliated with Palisades Ranch or the owner, Trudy. The volunteers connected through their expertise and mutually witnessed the gradual scaffolding of the problem articulation and solution for a situation that, as fellow horsepeople, alarmed them. We note that as horse lovers, they may have been acting to benefit the horses even moreso than their owner Trudy, as we have seen demonstrated in other studies of pet advocacy mobilization [47]. Some who did not assist with evacuation planning instead participated in auctions online that raised significant funds, but notably around items all related to equestrian matters—reinforcement of this being a community of practice at work.

At the site of the evacuation, participants arrived mostly knowing what roles they would play—riders, drivers, and administrative roles, with those assignments reinforced by the type of equipment and helper-horses they were asked to bring. However, uncertainty was still of course present. This uncertainty was mitigated by intersubjective knowledge that specialized experts share, in this case about the business of equines. Work in flight deck operations [15] articulates how intersubjectivity enables overlays of even incomplete gesture or speech upon artifacts to constitute meaning between only the people who have interacted with such socio-material environments before, even when they have never worked with each other, and we see similar behavior here in the loading and transporting of livestock.

Further, calling upon Fitzpatrick's ideas, this was an environment where expertise was deferred to and leveraged rather than seen as a commodity to be managed in such a way that it strangles innovation [6]. In fact, the pride of specialization enabled professionalism and mutual respect of people because of their craft. In addition, their expertise is *about living creatures* and the uncertainty that comes with horses as social individuals further highlights the respect for equine expertise across a very large and distributed community of practice—the horses were also actors in this ensemble.

We have noted how trustful Trudy had to be of people she did not know—indeed, they are people she cannot even personally thank because the paperwork system "failed." In this event, she knew she would need to relinquish control (which might have been a reason she delayed her decision). But in turn we must also recognize that the volunteers were voluntarily assuming liability in driving in terrain and roads that had been damaged in recent floods, where the connection to the official response was unclear (though earnestly pursued), and in carrying horses on their equipment after a taxing day. We see this as "reciprocity of liability" but critically, it was based *on the implied consent that only experts can give,* and this is what made the arrangements work.

Ensembles of Online and Offline Work

We therefore see features of expertise being leveraged to different advantage in online and offline settings, and that had corresponding temporal qualities.

Digitally Casting a Wide Net to Help with Rare Problems

In the initial weeks, long before Trudy had even imagined a herd evacuation, her distress unintentionally brought experts to the fold who asked her questions and made suggestions that more precisely identified and articulated the problem. They sought details about her ranch, the horses, the terrain, and the post-flood conditions. The digital world allows the casting of a wide net to gather expertise, which can be very useful when the problem is rare or uncertain, as it was in this case.

Expertise In Situ to Execute Solutions

Studies of work practice in co-located safety-critical environments, many of which we named earlier, examine how people employ not only intersubjectivity, but also mutual awareness of action that arises from being co-located [3,12]. This was certainly at play on the ranch in both macro and micro ways. The evacuation of the horses depended on the presence of the horses being in the pasture rather than any kind of starting or even exiting inventory. In micro ways, the riders, loaders, and unloaders "read" the horses' temperaments and relationships to other horses to best lead and load them. They took their cues from where they were in the chain of four staging areas to know what to do next, and from their spatial relationship to each other and the horses. Notably, while these smaller tasks included long stretches of waiting, therefore requiring a great deal of patience over a long and tiring day, these workers remained dedicated and were sustained by a persistent commitment to the larger, shared goal of evacuation. The calm that blanketed the group was a result of their shared expertise, even in an untested situation. Certainly, in the aftermath of disaster, calm operatives are a highly valuable commodity.

The Magnifiers of Uncertainty and Social Media

However, the awareness of the work in the large was imperfect, and based on sometimes hastily written posts by Trudy that said, for example, that her many neighbors were supportive—but no one directly consulted the *adjacent* neighbor whose land they had to traverse to get around road damage. This became a problem during the evacuation and indeed someone affiliated with the recalcitrant neighbor referred online to the event as a "manufactured crisis" and "fiasco." It is not the goal of this paper to judge whether the evacuation was ultimately necessary, but we do highlight the tensions around this issue, which shed light on the function of expertise, the uncertainty of disaster, and social media as a mechanism for participation in disaster response.

We note that there are many indications that suggest that the evacuation was important to the ongoing welfare of the animals and ranchers: One horse had already died, and our direct on-site observations witnessed the surprising and extensive damage of mountain roads. In addition, Trudy remains in her temporary ranch because county road repairs are incomplete at the time of this writing, 10 months after the flooding.

Some participants called the experience "life changing" in that it offered a new view of what they themselves could do and what could be done in community-based disaster response. In an interview a week after the evacuation, Frank, the lead organizer noted how remarkable the effort was, though he also said that once he got up to the ranch he observed that "in my mind, [the situation] was worse than it was." Jason (the recalcitrant neighbor) and some emergency managers also questioned the action. We may believe that in their general unwillingness to support the effort, officials were simply unaware of the needs of livestock in this event. However, Jason, who felt the effort was extreme, is also an expert horseperson who resides directly next to the ranch.

Some may conclude with the benefit especially of Frank's hindsight that the situation was exaggerated, but this is a dangerous place to land, because by doing so we miss many finer points about the nature of collaboration and emergent problems. Note that Frank does not regret the actions he took, only that the actions might not have had as drastic a benefit as perceived a priori. Such is the situation with disaster. We easily dismiss how *uncertain* situations of disaster are or can become, and how a goal in safety-critical work is to avert situations *before* they become problems. Much of the work in safety- and time-critical matters in CSCW appreciates the implications of this goal on vigilance, mutual awareness, and, of course, error, especially propagated error. It is all too easy to blame "pilot error" when a sequence of preceding systemic conditions took place to set a pilot up for perceiving the problem as he or she did [34,48], including one that warns of hazard. Indeed, disaster can *magnify* problems, not necessarily out of proportion, though that can happen, but rather too so that we focus on specific details when many things are happening. Both meanings of magnification are at play in emergent disaster situations that require rapid action as problems are gradually articulated.

We note that neither the officials nor Jason were engaged in the social media attention on the ranch as the evacuation was being planned. Calling upon media theory, which considers how mass media frames and focuses the kind of attention an event receives, e.g., [4,8], social media can do the same. Recall that the event was initially called a "rescue" suggesting immediacy and danger. The death of the stallion was dramatic and unusual. The public display of questions and answers about the situation not only scaffolded understanding of the parameters of the problem, they engaged and compelled a watchful audience. Finally, the Colorado floods achieved international press: it was a significant disaster event. We might see the plight of Palisades Ranch as a "way in" to grapple with the largess of the event that engaged the hearts and minds of a community of practice. The focusing comes from the razor-sharp understanding of the possible problems that can occur in ranching, if not in disaster.

So, notable in this case was that the starting conditions were not known to anyone involved in the earliest planning. Coordination happened "in the dark," that is, without environmental feedback of what they were facing. Even Trudy could not access her ranch—the weather on the Colorado Front Range had been terrible for days, even weeks. Exposed "burn areas" from prior years' wildfires in the mountains created unsafe conditions for traversal by cars at risk from mudslides. Indeed, emergency personnel discouraged passage so that they could continue with missing person recovery and airlifting, which happened for days after the rains stopped. Ranchers were immediately worried about the viability and pricing of the Colorado hay supply. They had concerns about getting supplies up before winter snow storms set in, which weather forecasters said were imminent. The surprising turn of what amounted to glorious weather on the day of the evacuation was seen not as evidence for miscalculation about the severity of the situation, but rather as a stroke of luck by the volunteers who had brought snow chains and cold-weather clothing.

So disaster—that is, uncertainty and threat—combined with the delivery by social media to a very particular audience attenuated the need for action—highly crafted action.

Materiality of On-Site Expertise

Finally, work in CSCW and distributed cognition has long considered how artifacts mediate and enable work, As we have described in this account, physical presence and properties of equipment—specifically trailers in our telling here—played a role in supporting coordination, or even in the failing of it (citing the mistaken rider who told drivers to leave).

The visual traversal of trailers across a shared route, even though there were four different staging areas some miles apart where trailers waited and horses were loaded, meant that over time the coordinated work was made visible as each trailer passed on their way in and out. Riders and drivers also passed on information to the volunteers staged at each site, which ensured a mostly common sense of the state of the work. The presence of breakdowns show that the system was otherwise going smoothly, and the team worked quickly to revert back to a functional state.

Furthermore, to link this back to the matter of expertise, we see that expertise was displayed through material objects: people wore clothing that was consistent with their identification as equine experts (such as boots and cowboy hats), and the Posse members wore their uniforms. At the ranch, one job was to hand out halters and lead ropes to riders. If riders' preferred materials were not available, their expertise allowed them to adapt to what was at hand. As Rosner [35] explains, this goes beyond the "affordances" of objects [28] and instead goes to what the tools represent to their craft and their expert execution of work. Recalling an earlier quote, even the misuse of ropes as a tool when stated only as an *idea—"I don't know how to rope or anything"—* is a sign of a novice.

Conclusion

In this study we describe how the problems incurred by the 2013 Colorado Floods on Palisades Ranch saw the convergence and blending of online and offline expertise. Social media enabled the problem that the Palisades Ranch faced—the marooning of 38 horses—to be made visible, which had the consequence of casting a wide net to locate, engage and mobilize appropriately skilled people throughout a community of practice. These volunteer responders brought their expertise to this unusual context, and improvised throughout the planning and execution of a livestock evacuation. The ever-present information gaps and challenges inherent in disaster response were overcome through the pursuit of coordinated work, which came about through the blending of grassroots and managerial activity; intersubjective knowledge that comes from expertise; and in the physical display of the movements of the horses and equipment across the geographical landscape. Activities conducted on- and offline frequently though discontinuously connected the two spaces across the long span of the event. However, we must recognize that there were also marked breaks of connection between the offline sites too (the two ranches and roads in between), and that those disconnections arose due to the terrain, conditions and distance. In other words, the imagining of work that can be conducted online and offline should not be reduced to simply to a matter of nominality (that is, "online work" versus "offline work"), but rather understood with respect to the disaster conditions that temporally- and spatially distributed collaborative work must accommodate.

ACKNOWLEDGMENTS

We thank the ranch owners and volunteer responders for their participation in this research. This research is funded through the US National Science Foundation grant IIS-0910586. We thank our Project EPIC colleagues for support and critique.

REFERENCES

1. Boehner, K., Vertesi, J., Sengers, P., & Dourish, P. (2007, April). How HCI Interprets the Probes. In *Proc. of CHI*, 1077-1086.
2. Büscher, M., & Urry, J. (2009). Mobile Methods and the Empirical. *European Journal of Social Theory*, *12*(1), 99-116.
3. Dourish, P., & Bellotti, V. (1992). Awareness and Coordination in Shared Workspaces. In *Proc. of CSCW*, 107-114.
4. Downs, A. (1972). Up and Down with Ecology: The Issue Attention Cycle. *Public Interest*, *28*(1), 38-50.
5. Erickson, T. (2008). Knowing the Particulars. In T. Erickson and D. McDonald, (Eds.) *HCI Remixed: Reflections on Works that have Influenced the HCI Community*, 87-91.
6. Fitzpatrick, G. (2003). Emergent Expertise Sharing in a New Community. In (M. Ackerman, V. Pipek, and V. Wulf (Eds.) *Sharing Expertise: Beyond Knowledge Management*, 81-110.
7. Fritz, C. and Mathewson, J. (1957). Convergence Behavior in Disasters: A Problem in Social Control, *Committee on Disaster Studies, National Academy of Sciences, National Research Council*, Washington DC.
8. Gamson, W. A., Croteau, D., Hoynes, W., & Sasson, T. (1992). Media Images and the Social Construction of Reality. *Annual Review of Sociology*, 373-393.
9. Hagar, C., & Haythornthwaite, C. (2005). Crisis, Farming & Community. *The Journal of Community Informatics*, *1*(3), 41-52.
10. Halverson, C (1995). Inside the Cognitive Workplace: New Technology and Air Traffic Control, *UCSD Cognitive Science Department* Dissertation.
11. Heath, S.E., Kass, P.H., Beck, A.M., & Glickman, L.T. (2001). Human and Pet-Related Risk Factors for Household Evacuation Failure During a Natural Disaster. *American Journal of Epidemiology*. (153), 659-665.
12. Heath, C., & Luff, P. (1992). Collaboration and Control: Crisis Management and Multimedia Technology in London Underground Line Control Rooms. *Computer Supported Cooperative Work Journal*, 1(1-2), 69-94.
13. Hunt, M., Al-Awadi, H., & Johnson, M. (2008). Psychological Sequelae of Pet Loss Following Hurricane Katrina. *Anthrozoos*, 21(2), 109-121.
14. Hutchins, E. (1995). *Cognition in the Wild.* MIT Press.
15. Hutchins, E., & Palen, L. (1997). Constructing Meaning from Space, Gesture, and Speech. In *Discourse, Tools and Reasoning*, 23-40.
16. Irvine, L. (2007). Ready or Not: Evacuating an Animal Shelter during Mock Emergency. *Anthrozoos*, 20(4), 355-364.
17. Irvine, L. (2009). *Filling the Ark: Animal Welfare in Disasters.* Philadelphia, PA: Temple University Press.
18. Juhlin, O., & Weilenmann, A. (2002, January). Decentralizing the Control Room: Mobile Work and Institutional Order. In *Proc. of ECSCW*, 379-397.
19. Kendra, J., & Wachtendorf, T. (2006). The Waterborne Evacuation of Lower Manhattan on September 11: A Case of Distributed Sensemaking. Preliminary paper #355, Disaster Research Center, University of Delaware. USA.
20. Kendra, J. M., & Wachtendorf, T. (2007). Community Innovation and Disasters. *Handbook of Disaster Research* Springer New York, 316-334.

21. Kreps, G. A. & Bosworth, S.L. *Organizing, Role Enactment, and Disaster: A Structural Theory*. Cranbury, NJ: Associated University Presses, 1994.
22. Lodi, A., Martello, S., & Monaci, M. (2002). Two-Dimensional Packing Problems: A Survey. *European Journal of Operational Research*, *141*(2), 241-252.
23. MacKay, W. E. (1999). Is Paper Safer? The Role of Paper Flight Strips in Air Traffic Control. *ACM Transactions on Computer-Human Interaction* (TOCHI), 6(4), 311-340.
24. Marcus, G. (1995). Ethnography in/of the World System: The Emergence of Multi-Sited Ethnography. *Annual Review of Anthropology*, *24*(1), 95-117.
25. McDonald, D. W., & Ackerman, M. S. (1998). Just Talk to Me: A Field Study of Expertise Location. In *Proc. of CSCW*, 315-324.
26. Mendonca, D., Beroggi, G., and Wallace, W.A. (2001). Decision Support for Improvisation during Emergency Response Operations. *International Journal of Emergency Management 1*, (2001), 30-38.
27. Nomura, S., Hutchins, E., & Holder, B. E. (2006, November). The Uses of Paper in Commercial Airline Flight Operations. In *Proc. of CSCW*, 249-258.
28. Norman, D. A. (1999). Affordance, Conventions, and Design. *interactions*, *6*(3), 38-43.
29. Normark, M., & Randall, D. (2005). Local Expertise at an Emergency Call Centre. In *Proc. of ECSCW* 347-366.
30. Palen, L., & Liu, S. B. (2007). Citizen Communications in Crisis: Anticipating a Future of ICT-supported Public Participation. In *Proc. of CHI*, 727-736.
31. Palen, L., S. Vieweg, S. Liu, & Hughes, A. (2009). Crisis in a Networked World: Features of Computer-Mediated Communication in the April 16, 2007 Virginia Tech Event. *Social Science Computing Review*, Sage, 467-480.
32. Pearson, M and Howell, G. (September 17, 2013). Hundreds Await Rescue from Colorado Flooding as Helicopter Flights Resume. *CNN*. Available at www.cnn.com/2013/09/16/us/colorado-flooding-monday.
33. Perng, S-Y., Buscher, M., Wood, L., Halvorsrud, R., Stiso, M., Ramirez, L., & Al-Akkad, A. (2013). Peripheral Response: Microblogging During the 22/7/2011 Norway Attacks, *International Journal of Information Systems for Crisis Response and Management*, 5, 1, 41-57.
34. Perrow, C. (1984). *Normal Accidents*. Basic Books.
35. Rosner, D. K. (2012). The Material Practices of Collaboration. In *Proc. of CSCW*, 1155-1164.
36. Sarcevic, A., Palen, L., White, J., Starbird, K., Bagdouri, M. & Anderson, K. (2010). Beacons of Hope in Decentralized Coordination: Learning from On-the-Ground Medical Twitterers During the 2010 Haiti Earthquake." In *Proc. of CSCW*, 47-56.
37. Schmidt, K. & L. Bannon. Taking CSCW Seriously: Supporting Articulation Work. *Computer Supported Cooperative Work Journal*, 1, 1 (1992), 7-40.
38. Simon, H. (1996). *The Sciences of the Artificial* (Third Edition). MIT Press.
39. Soden, R., & L. Palen. (2014). From Crowdsourced Mapping to Community Mapping: The Post-Earthquake Work of OpenStreetMap Haiti. In *Proc. of COOP*.
40. Solnit, R. (2010). *A Paradise Built in Hell: The Extraordinary Communities that Arise in Disaster*. Penguin.
41. Starbird, K. (2013, April). Delivering Patients to Sacré Coeur: Collective Intelligence in Digital Volunteer Communities. In *Proc. of CHI*, 801-810.
42. Starbird, K., & Palen, L. (2011). "Voluntweeters:" Self-Organizing by Digital Volunteers in Times of Crisis. *Proc. of CHI*, 1071-1080.
43. Starbird, K., & L. Palen. Working and Sustaining the Virtual Disaster Desk. In *Proc. of CSCW*, 491-502.
44. Suchman, L. A. (1987). *Plans and Situated Actions: The Problem of Human-Machine Communication*. Cambridge University Press.
45. Tierney, K. & Quarantelli, EL. (1989). Needed Innovation in the Delivery of Emergency Medical Services in Disasters: Present and Future. *Disaster Management*, 2(2), 70-76.
46. Voida, A. Harmon, E. & Al-Ani, B. Bridging Between Organizations and the Public: Volunteer Coordinators' Uneasy Relationship with Social Computing. In *Proc. of CHI*, 1967-1976.
47. White, J.I., Palen, L., & Anderson, K. (2014). Digital Mobilization in Disaster Response: The Work & Self-Organization of On-Line Pet Advocates in Response to Hurricane Sandy. In *Proc. of CSCW*, 866-876.
48. Wiener, E., & Nagal, D. (1988). *Human Factors in Aviation* (Eds.), Academic Press.
49. Wulf, V., Misaki, K., Atam, M., Randall, D., & Rohde, M. (2013). 'On the Ground' in Sidi Bouzid: Investigating Social Media use During the Tunisian Revolution. In *Proc. of CSCW*, 1409-1418.
50. Zotarelli, L.K. (2010) Broken Bond: An Exploration of Human Factors Associated with Companion Animal Loss During Hurricane Katrina. *Sociological Forum*. (25), 110-122.

Exiting the Design Studio: Leveraging Online Participants for Early-Stage Design Feedback

Xiaojuan Ma[1], Yu Li[2], Jodi Forlizzi[3], Steven Dow[3]
[1]Huawei Noah's Ark Lab, Hong Kong; [2]Cornell University, USA;
[3]Human-Computer Interaction Institute, Carnegie Mellon University, USA;
[1]xiaojuan.c.ma@gmail.com; [2]ly257@cornell.edu; [3]{forlizzi, spdow}@cs.cmu.edu

ABSTRACT
Online collaboration tools enable developers of interactive systems to quickly reach potential users for usability testing. Can these technologies serve designers who seek feedback on user needs during the earliest stages of design? *Online needfinding* may help designers create products and services that can target a more diverse user population. To explore this, we conducted a feasibility study to compare face-to-face methods with online needfinding sessions. We found that video can sufficiently capture nuanced reactions to preliminary concept storyboards, but that feedback providers need guidance and structure. We then introduce a tool for collecting early-stage design feedback from online participants and conduct a case study with a professional design team. The team conducted needfinding activities with local participants, as well as a cost-equivalent number of online participants The case study demonstrates that combining online crowdsourcing with a video survey tool provides a simple and cost-efficient way to collect early-stage feedback.

Author Keywords
Design feedback; needfinding; collaboration; crowdsourcing; storyboard scenarios; online video communication.

ACM Classification Keywords
H.5.m. Information interfaces and presentation (e.g., HCI): Miscellaneous.

INTRODUCTION
Designers interact with potential users through a variety of activities, from concept exploration to usability testing, throughout the design process [22]. Tools for online communication and crowdsourcing have made it possible to conduct some of these interactions online. By making participant recruitment easier, faster, and more diverse, the CSCW research community has started to explore how to leverage online participants to shape the design of interactive systems [14, 18, 3, 19, 32]. For example, Martin et al. show that remote asynchronous usability evaluation reveals similar numbers of problems, faster and cheaper than in-person usability testing [23]. This is important as it helps designers discover usability issues before over-investing in development efforts. Further, designers may reach a more diverse sample of potential users online, which is particularly relevant for practitioners designing software intended for millions of people around the world [9].

CSCW '15, March 14 – 18, 2015, Vancouver, BC, Canada.

http://dx.doi.org/10.1145/2675133.2675174

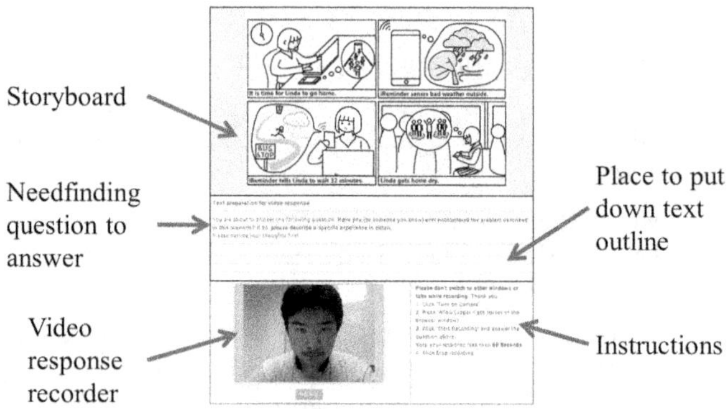

Figure 1. Interface for collecting early-stage design feedback

While online approaches provide a nice option for formative software testing, it remains an open research question whether this translates to the earliest stages of design where the goal is to identify the right problem to solve [16, 28, 33]. Traditional needfinding activities such as "speed dating" with concept storyboards [12] help designers discover the tacit needs and opportunities that ultimately shape a design. At first blush, online strategies seem amenable to helping designers uncover a more diverse set of considerations. However, with in-person needfinding, designers must carefully interpret users' subtle, often non-verbal, reactions to novel interaction scenarios [12]. This issue may make it difficult to conduct needfinding online.

Research by Bietz et al. shows the importance of communication medium when exchanging feedback online; without audio-visual information, creators interpret feedback to be more negative and less credible, and they are less likely to incorporate feedback [7]. The choice of medium can also affect how users formulate their opinions [26, 28].

In this paper, we explore whether online video adequately supports the nuanced communication and interpretation that typically happens during traditional needfinding. Our intention is not to eliminate face-to-face needfinding, but to explore the potential complementary benefits of online methods. First, we conducted a between-subjects feasibility study with 18 participants to contrast in-person needfinding with online video and text-based approaches. We learned that users generally preferred recording their feedback with video rather than typing, as it took less time and effort to verbalize their thoughts and preserved some of the richness of face-to-face interaction. We also identified several factors—such as users feeling timid and providing rambling responses—that could affect online feedback systems.

Second, these findings informed the design and development of an online system for early-stage needfinding through asynchronous video. The system utilizes Amazon's Mechanical Turk (mTurk) [1] to recruit a diverse population of users. It allows designers to tailor and launch their needfinding tasks and to analyze the responses.

Third, we conducted a case study with a professional design team who was creating a mobile reminder app. We compared the speed, sample size and outcomes of needfinding activities performed on our system versus via conventional face-to-face interviews under an equivalent budget constraint. Results show that while each individual online participant generated fewer unique considerations (40% less), collectively, the online approach revealed just as many if not slightly more unique design considerations. Further, the design team discussed the benefits of a more diverse population and how this affected their prioritization of features for a new mobile service. We conclude by discussing future research directions for online needfinding.

RELATED WORK

In this section, we review current practices of early-stage needfinding, and discuss how different media can affect the exchange of design feedback.

Practices for Early-Stage Needfinding

It is essential for designers who target a broad audience to identify the needs common to a global set of users, as well as the preferences of local markets, before settling on a final product or service [13]. Exploring alternatives during the early stages of a design project can help designers solve the right problems [16, 28] and to avoid overinvesting in a particular design direction [13, 16].

Early-stage needfinding can encompass a broad set of methods, including focus groups, field observations, surveys, or interviews [22]. For example, "speed dating" is a rapid-fire technique for exploring early-stage design alternatives where users react to a series of concept storyboard [12]. Designers conventionally conduct these activities with local, co-located participants. This allows designers to instigate a dialogue with users to understand their underlying dreams, values, and needs, [12, 33]. Face-to-face interaction allows designers to pick up on a variety of subtle emotional cues [11] and to interpret possible design opportunities in situ. For example, Tohidi et al. learned that participants worry about offending designers during face-to-face feedback sessions [28]. Designers need to be able to interpret if users favor a design alternative just because they want to appease the designer [28].

This work considers the tradeoffs of conducting early-stage needfinding online. Many of the subtleties of face-to-face communication will be lost, especially when using asynchronous communication [11, 8]. However, designers might be able to more quickly and inexpensively discover user needs by taking advantage of online participants. Online video may provide a means to increase the communication richness while still tapping into a large diverse set of users.

Indeed, video-based crowdsourcing services that collect consumer inputs via webcam such as MindSwarms [24] have gained in popularity. However, designers lack evidence that such an approach provides value for conducting early-stage needfinding activities. This paper aims to fill the gap by exploring whether online collaboration could adequately reveal users' needs, in terms of both quantity and quality, under budget similar to usability testing [25].

How Online Media can Affect Feedback Exchange

Communication medium likely influences how and what feedback providers are willing to share with designers. Hebert and Vorauer showed that critics tended to be more positive when giving specific feedback in person rather than over email [17]. Similarly, Bietz found that writers prefer to hear and see critics (vs. using instant messaging) [7]; writers interpreted text-based feedback as more negative and less credible. Literature on computer-mediated communication indicates the audio-video channel can help create a greater sense of social presence [4], and in turn, establish the trust necessary for an honest exchange of feedback [8].

While video seems valuable for online communication related to design, it may introduce challenges related to anonymity [26] and evaluation apprehension [7]. Feedback providers may be nervous about recording video [4], or prefer to remain anonymous so they have license to be more critical with their feedback.

Our research explores how online video compares with face-to-face and text-based approaches to needfinding. Specifically, we investigate whether online video adequately supports the nuanced interpretation of user reactions to early-stage concepts.

FEASIBILITY STUDY: ONLINE FEEDBACK COLLECTION

To generate insights for an online system for early-stage needfinding, we conducted a feasibility study with three research questions:

1) Do online feedback providers prefer to provide insights via text or video?
2) Will online video adequately capture the nuanced communication that typically happens during in-person needfinding?
3) What considerations affect the design of an online system dedicated to early-stage needfinding?

	Pros (# of participants)	Cons (# of participants)
Face-to-Face	Fast interaction (12) Easy to get points across (8) Easy to clarify ambiguous information (7) Non-verbal cues available (6) Personable, stronger social presence (6)	Reluctant to say more about personal experiences (5) Reluctant to say negative things about the design (5)
Video	Non-verbal cues available (6) Fast interaction (5) Personable, strong social presence (5)	Technical issues e.g. lag or poor sound quality (7) Awkward / weird to talk to a camera (4) Can only see upper torso; incomplete non-verbal cues (2) Intimidated / distracted by the self-view (3)
Text	Not intimidated by seeing each other (8) More time to think (6) Anonymous (3)	Slow interaction (7) ; Takes effort to type (5); spelling issues (3) Non-verbal cues not available (4); it's as not personable (4) Broken flow of communication (3); may forget points (3) Uncomfortable with a permanent record of their feedback (3)

Table 1. Pros and cons of the three communication methods summarized from the post-simulation interviews.

Feasibility Study: Procedure

Simulation of Needfinding Activities

To simulate a speed dating session [33], we generated storyboards using Autodesk SketchBook [2] to depict three scenarios around domestic health: home monitoring, medical records, and diet and exercise (see Figure 2 for an example). Participants reflected on their experiences, perceived needs, and knowledge of existing solutions regarding each of the design scenarios.

Using a within-subject study design, each participant experienced three ways of providing feedback on the storyboard scenarios: 1) talking to a person sitting across from them; 2) talking into a webcam and having their responses recorded; and 3) typing down the answers on Etherpad Lite, an online documentation tool [15]. We counterbalanced the assignment of scenarios and the communication methods.

Post-Simulation Interview

Upon the completion, we interviewed all participants in person and gathered their general reflections, preferences, and thoughts on comfort and ease of use, as well as pros and cons on the three different feedback methods.

Participants

We recruited 18 participants (7 female, ranging from 18-65 years old, from a diverse ethnic background) using a local participant pool and word of mouth. We also pre-screened participants to ensure that they were somewhat familiar with the three health-related scenarios, spoke English as a primary language, and had average (or better) typing skills.

Feasibility Study: Findings

Although all participants picked face-to-face as their favorite communication modality, two thirds of them preferred video over text when having to respond online. Similar to Barksdale et al.'s findings with temporally distributed teams [4], participants noted that, with video, they could present their thoughts faster, and convey complex or subtle messages via gestures and facial expressions (Table 1).

Figure 2. An example four-panel storyboard in Study 1. This story depicts the idea of monitoring health at home.

Interestingly, about 56% of the participants felt that they would more boldly talk about negative experiences or feelings if they did *not* see the immediate reaction of the other party, similar to results presented by Sheer and Chen [26]. According to one participant:

> [I would not] say something negative, probably not face-to-face. Because you want to have the courage to say something bad, you don't want to hurt the person's feelings…

This suggests that even though participants were generally more familiar with face-to-face interactions, online communication may afford a degree of "distance" between designers and users. The reduced social presence of online media compared to face-to-face interviews [8] may encourage critical feedback on designers' ideas. Among those who were not reluctant to share negative information online, participants were (1.5 times) more likely to favor video than text.

Four participants mentioned that they were nervous in front of a camera (Table 1), "*I was kind of conscious of how my hair looks in the video all the time.*" This notion of social awkwardness did not bear out when participants provided text feedback. Three people appreciated its affordance of a greater degree of anonymity and better privacy protection:

> It (text) is definitely the most anonymous. You cannot put a name to a face regarding what they say, so they're probably freer to give their feedback, because they can't be judged since the person isn't actually there.

While text does offer anonymity, designers might suspect the legitimacy of a response if the associated personal identity were less visible, as suggested by Bietz [7].

Beyond social factors, there were several usability issues that might affect an online system for collecting early-stage design feedback. First, across the different techniques, we noticed that many feedback providers needed guidance to provide responses. Over half of participants asked for further clarification or elaboration about the storyboards during the face-to-face interviews. The quality of online feedback may degrade if participants cannot receive prompt assistance from designers [5]. Second, text-based feedback providers would often wrap up their answers in a couple of sentences, or simply put down bullet points. Third, video recordings tended to be verbose and yet relatively content-free. Participants generated almost three times more words per minute in video (75.3) than in text (26.3), but there was no significant difference between the numbers of unique points conveyed using the two media. Some participants suggested that, compared to video, the rehearsability and reprocessability of text allow them to better organize their thoughts and reduce incoherent responses, as observed in previous research [4].

In summary, early-stage feedback activities involve not only exchange of information, but also an interpretation of nuanced user reactions. Our preliminary study confirms prior research on computer-mediated communication and provides evidence that Video-based communication can potentially serve as a means to collect early-stage feedback from online users. Video technology allows designers to collect rich feedback online and to understand subtle reactions to their ideas. This approach also seems to support a degree of separation between the designers and respondents, perhaps enabling feedback providers to be more candid with their input. However, for such an approach to succeed, especially asynchronously, we need an online system that carefully structures the feedback process.

A SYSTEM FOR ONLINE NEEDFINDING WITH VIDEO

To enable large-scale participation, we designed the system to collect online video *asynchronously*, rather than through live video chat. This helps minimize the time commitment and allows data to be collected in parallel, but it provides additional constraints that may affect the quality of such an approach. Given the usability issues discovered in the feasibility study and our decision to support asynchronous data collection, we present several design considerations for online needfinding via asynchronous video.

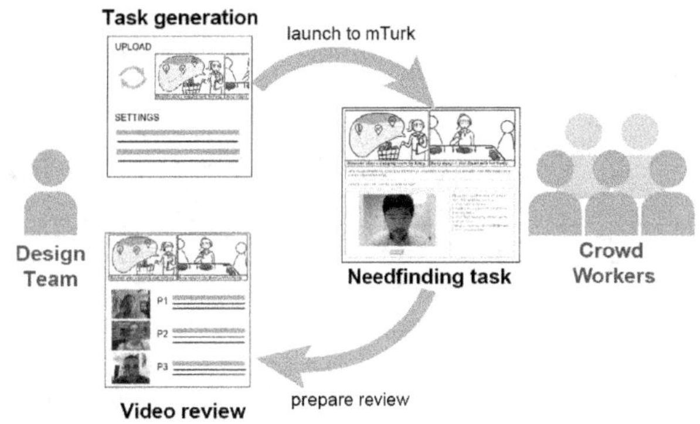

Figure 3. Overview of our online video-based system for collecting early-design feedback.

Design Considerations

Provide Examples to Model Effective Feedback
To set feedback providers' expectations, our system provides positive and negative examples of responses. These examples serve several purposes. First, they show participants the level of detail preferred. Second, examples demonstrate how participants should position themselves in front of the camera with proper lighting in the background. Third, the examples convey the impression that ordinary individuals can talk about their perception, hopefully making participants more confident about the task.

Constrain Data Collection to Yield Concise Responses
To avoid both very short and long, rambling responses we got in the feasibility study, constraints on the length of video responses should be provided. Each response should be no shorter than approximately 20 seconds and no longer than 60 seconds. The examples model the appropriate tone and length for responses. While recording a video, the system gives feedback and visual cues when providers reach the lower and upper time limits.

Allow Rehearsal to Reduce Incoherent Responses
To help respondents provide more coherent feedback, we include a simple re-record function. Likewise, the system allows feedback providers to write a short text outline before recording a video. By rehearsing their response, people do not have to organize their thoughts on the fly. It also reduces the chance of having to redo the whole video if they are not satisfied with a certain part of the response.

System Overview

The system has three parts (see Figure 3): a task generation tool for designers, a crowdsourcing component that automatically posts tasks to Amazon Mechanical Turk (mTurk) through its API [1], and a video review page for designers to view and reflect on the results. The system runs in the Google Chrome browser and was developed using HTML5, Django, and MySQL.

Task Generation Interface
Designers can set up a needfinding activity by filling out a web form (see Figure 3, upper left). Designers can upload and then describe concept sketches or storyboards and list

Figure 4. Sample storyboard panels for Study 2. The team explored four reminder scenarios: bus stops, coupons, weather, and shopping routes. The panels in the top row represent the problem; the bottom row depicts the potential solution.

the questions for the crowd workers. They can also specify various crowd task settings, such as the minimum and maximum length of video responses, the number of feedback providers, the amount of payment per response, the study duration, and screening questions for recruitment.

Crowd Needfinding Task Interface

After the designer configures the task, our system automatically generates the human intelligence task (HIT) for mTurk, and allows designers to monitor the progress and throughput. The system currently uses a dedicated mTurk account to post jobs, but future versions will allow designers to provide their own mTurk account details or to use other participant recruitment methods. Once the task has been accepted, workers watch a short tutorial on recording effective videos, including good and bad example of providing feedback. Workers then view the storyboard and a list of questions specified by the designer. They are prompted to briefly outline each response and then to record a short video (see Figure 3, right). The worker can preview and re-record their video if they wish.

Video Review Interface

Our system provides a video review interface for designers to analyze all user responses for each given scenario (see Figure 3, lower left). The page shows the storyboard presented to the feedback providers followed by one or multiple rows of crowd responses. Each row contains the worker's demographic information as well as the video (or text) responses to the designer's questions. Within this interface, the designer can rate the quality of each response.

CASE STUDY: ONLINE VS IN-PERSON NEEDFINDING

To evaluate our system for collecting early-stage design feedback and to understand its efficacy in comparison with conventional face-to-face methods, we conducted a case study with a professional design team working on a mobile app. We addressed the following research questions:

1) How does feedback obtained through asynchronous online videos compare to in-person interviews under a similarly constrained budget?
2) How would professional designers assess and interpret feedback from online participants, and use it to shape their design decisions?

Case Study: Method

We partnered with an industrial research institution and recruited a four-person design team in the process of conceptualizing and prototyping a new mobile application called *iReminder*. The team had been exploring ideas for a situation-aware intelligent reminder app that could leverage personal data on the phone, context information obtained by embedded sensors, and third-party mobile services.

The team wrote and illustrated four different storyboards to depict scenarios where people might get value from an intelligent reminder app (see Figure 4). The team wanted to know whether these scenarios represented typical needs and what other scenarios people may envision for iReminder.

To draw a comparison between needfinding via our online system and in-person interviews, the design team allocated $72 for each method. With this budget, designers recruited seven local users for the interviews, as advised by Nielson's rule of thumb for discount user testing [25]. This budget supports an equivalent of 10 hours of work at an hourly wage of $7.20 (the current US minimum wage). Therefore, we were able to recruit 20 mTurk workers for a half-hour session each. The case study's goal was to investigate the quality and coverage of responses each method could generate under the same budget.

Procedure for In-Person Participants

The design team sent out recruitment emails to mailing lists of local communities five days prior to the study. The team exchanged on average four emails with each local participant to schedule the time and location for the face-to-face sessions. They also spent about an hour each day to prepare

		In-person	Online crowd
Participant info	# of people	7	20
	Age range	22-29	18-41
	Ethnic groups	2	4
	Distance from design team	12 miles (avg.)	17 cities / towns in US
Ideas Collected	Total valid	36	56
	Ideas/Person	5.14	2.95
Time (avg.)	Task time	27 min	25 min
	Recruitment	5 days, 4 emails/person	10 min to post on mTurk
	Preparation	1 hour	N/A
	Transport time	103 min (round trip)	N/A
Payment (avg.)	Study/Person	$6.45 (1 hr)	$3.60 (30 min)
	Trip/Person	$3.84	N/A
	Total budget	$72.00	$72.00

Table 2. Tradeoffs in time and participant demographics for in-person versus online crowd participants.

the design studio, documents, and video recording equipment in the morning, and transfer data at the end of the day.

When participants arrived, a member of the design team greeted them and interacted with them throughout the study. Participants viewed the four storyboards one by one on an iPad, and had conversations with the designers regarding the needs and solutions related to each usage scenario for iReminder. The questions followed the same script as the online procedure, except that designers could ask for clarification or elaboration on specific points. After commenting on all storyboard scenarios, participants filled out a demographics survey and provided information on their daily practices related to the depicted scenes.

Procedure for Online Crowd Participants

The design team uploaded the same four storyboards to our system and then worked with our research team to configure the crowd task settings. The design team recruited US-only mTurk workers which allowed them to diversely sample their target population, i.e. Americans who are likely to be smartphone users. Once finalized, the system automatically posted HITs on mTurk. When mTurk participants accepted the task, they first reviewed a consent form that explains the study's purpose and asks them to explicitly consent to being video recorded and to allow their video recordings and images be used for research and academic publications. Next, participants checked their audio and video settings by recording a short clip. If the recording feature worked properly, participants went through a video tutorial with examples of good and bad design feedback.

Participants then read a short description about the concept and technology behind the intelligent reminder application, and viewed the design team's storyboard scenarios. For each scenario, participants were instructed to provide responses to two questions: "Have you (or someone you know) ever encountered the problem described in this scenario? If so, please describe a specific experience in detail." and "How effectively do you think the technology in this scenario solves the problem? Elaborate on the features of this technology that could help the situation." The system bounded the video responses so they could be no shorter than 20 seconds and at most 60 seconds.

After providing input on all four storyboards, participants filled out the same questionnaire that was used in the in-person interviews. Our system automatically logged all the data and constructed a review interface for the design team.

Procedure for the Design Team to Review Feedback

After collecting data from both in-person and online participants, our research team met individually with all four members of the design team to examine all 80 online responses (20 participants responding to all four storyboards) and 28 in-person responses (7 participants x four storyboards). For each response, we instructed the designer to extract and tally any valuable insights and to state why they liked or disliked about each response. We then asked each designer to reflect on the pros and cons of online vs. in-person design feedback collection and to discuss their overall perceptions of online needfinding and their expectations for future use regarding the number of participants, response duration, time to yield feedback, and overall costs. Each review session took between 2 and 2.5 hours. We audio recorded each review session, and later transcribed and extracted themes from these sessions.

Case Study: Results

To compare the cost effectiveness between in-person and online needfinding, we first review tradeoffs in time, location, and participant demographics. To analyze the value of each approach, we asked the design team to review p. Finally, we gathered the design team's qualitative reactions to participant responses and to the online feedback collection tool.

Tradeoffs in Recruiting Local vs. Online Participants

Table 2 lists the detailed differences in time, location, monetary costs and participant demographics between in-person participants and online crowds. The face-to-face interviews took 22 to 30 minutes (μ=27 min). Interviewees travelled 20 to 80 minutes (μ=51 minutes one way by public transportation) to the meeting location. Each interviewee received a cash payment (in local currency) equivalent to $6.45. They were also compensated for their round-trip public transportation ($2.60 ~ $6.41, μ=$3.84). Within a pre-set budget of $72, the design team recruited seven local participants. These participants ranged in age between 22 and 29 (μ=25.4) years and all had at least a college degree. Six of seven were from the same Ethnic group; only two were female.

In contrast, each mTurk worker spent 25 minutes on the task page. Approximately 15 minutes were spent on the consent form, examples, the actual feedback task, and final questionnaire. Participants spent the remaining ten minutes learning and testing the video recording feature. Each online worker received $3.60 for his or her participation, comparable to the minimum half-hour wage in the US. Under the same $72 budget, our system recruited 20 participants (14 female) from mTurk. Ages ranged between 18 and 41 (μ=26.9) years. Among the participants, thirteen were Caucasian, three were Hispanic or Latino, two were Asian, and two were African American. They all had received at least some college education.

Design Team's Reactions to In-Person vs. Online Feedback

Members of the design team individually analyzed and compared responses from the online and local participants to extract insights for their design. As shown in Table 2, on average, the design team drew out about 2.95 points of feedback per online participant (SD=1.12) via our system and 5.14 points per person from the in-person interviews (SD = 2.20), and these coalesced as thirteen unique and valuable insights (see summary in Table 3). While in-person interviews yielded more points per participant (likely due to their ability to converse with the design team without constraints [5]), these data show that online communication can provide a viable way to understand users' needs and practices. With only 20 online users, designers were already able to discover all issues identified by the lab-based study of a minimum size, i.e. full coverage. Online participants even raised several points that neither the design team or in-person interviewees had considered (Table 3). The team found online feedback to be as candid and insightful as from the interviews. The following quotes from online participants exemplify two points that were equally valued by both online and local participants:

> **Provide reliable and easy-to-understand information** - "I'd like this to be effective and work properly, but I'm a little skeptical about the app's ability to predict weather circumstances in such a small area." (P3, M, 23 yrs)

> **Be situation-aware and personalized** - "The system could suggest that I can pop into the nearest 7-11 and pick up a disposable poncho or umbrella, which could cost less than five pounds. Or think about alternative transportation, like go into an Underground or an indoor bus stop." (P11, M, 41 yrs)

Design Team's Interpretation and Use of Feedback

The design team considered feedback from both online and in-person participants to be trustworthy, even when they received conflicting opinions. The team found that feedback from both methods covered all aspects that they were particularly interested in: 1) Affirming the problematic scenario. All participants shared personal anecdotes about their life or situations similar to the given scenarios. 2) Envisioning alternative uses for the technology. Online participants proposed five possible use cases for other populations or situations, while the local users only mentioned two. 3) Suggesting how the app should behave. 4) Commenting on specific details of the technology, e.g. privacy protection and battery management. 5) Expressing skepticism or concerns, e.g. on accuracy and adaptability of the app.

Valuable points raised by respondents	O	L
Provide suggestions to users in addition to facts*+	8	3
Minimize the user input by linking to existing apps*+	8	5
Provide accurate, reliable, and interpretable info*+	7	6
Leave sufficient time for users to get prepared+	6	3
Be able to handle big, diverse data	6	3
Be situation-aware and personalized+	5	5
Allow for manual management +	4	0
Be especially informative at unfamiliar locations	4	6
Address privacy issues and reduce interference+	3	1
Be easy to learn and not to complicated	2	2
Be able to correct the user's mistakes*+	1	0
Have good power/battery management*+	1	0
Benefit & challenge for 3rd-party service providers*	1	2

Table 3. Frequency of 13 valuable points (as counted by the design team) generated from online crowd participants (O) vs. local in-person participants (L); those marked with * were initially overlooked by the design team; those marked with + were incorporated into iReminder.

These insights in turn affected how the design team interpreted and shaped the iReminder application, especially the ones that had previously been overlooked in their initial conceptualization of iReminder (marked with * in Table 3). For example, one designer commented:

> I didn't expect that information reliability would have such a big impact on people's adoption of iReminder. I guess we should inform people, maybe explicitly, our source of third-party information and confidence level. When the confidence is low, iReminder should use a softer tone and provide users with more options. We could even ask the users to provide information on the actual situation (Design team member 1).

After reviewing the feedback, the design team continued to develop a working prototype of iReminder, which evolved to account for several valuable points, especially those mentioned by disparate users (marked with + in Table 3).

Design Team's Appreciation of the Online Crowd's Diversity

Overall, the design team found online needfinding to be a viable way to broadly understand users' needs and practices. In particular, the team noted that online needfinding provided a diverse pool of participants from different cities, and neighborhoods, lifestyle choices, and ethnic backgrounds. Despite the diversity of participants, the feedback was dense and useful, likely due to the structure provided in the tool (i.e., examples, time limits, rehearsals, etc.).

When evaluating ideas through in-person interviews, the design team inevitably taps into local participants, people likely to share similar experiences, lifestyle, and culture. As a result, local participant populations may only provide a glimpse of the range of possible reactions to an idea. For example, the design team's office is located in a densely populated metropolis with a public transportation system that effectively shelters travelers from chaotic weather. It is common for the residents to travel by bus and subway, shop at specific stores/malls/supermarkets within walking distance from their home, and dine out regularly near work place or home instead of cooking. Therefore, most local participants felt strongly that iReminder would be mostly useful for emergencies or when traveling to unfamiliar places. Five out of the seven in-person interviewees commented that they would use iReminder to avoid long queues in bus/subway stations and restaurants, rather than as a tool to escape the rain. By also recruiting *online* participants, the design team gained novel perspectives:

> We realized how different the transportation needs are for people in a metropolitan area versus people living in a rural area where driving is the primary means of getting around.

Our system enabled the design team to collect opinions from people with different transportation systems, public facilities, and social norms. Although the design team tried to encourage diversity in the local interviews by recruiting people from different cultural or professional backgrounds, the monetary costs and logistical issues made this difficult.

Design Team's Comments about the System

The design team felt that video gave access to the feedback providers' emotional reactions and engagement in their ideas. Video allowed the design team to pick up on subtle contextual information about the participants—information that could never be captured using text alone. Designers felt that they could make better personal connection to the feedback provider and thus value their responses as more truthful. For example, the team commented on participants' clothing and background décor. They noticed that one participant had many American flags and speculated about her nationalism. They observed one participant owned a cat, because they could see its tail.

Designers picked up on nonverbal cues as an indication of whether people resonate with a given scenario; these cues also lend credibility to the feedback [7]:

> (With video) you get to see their, like, reaction on their face, and also you can hear their voices, and you can see and hear their hesitation or any change of emotions.

While these are minor details, the video data provided a viable and cost-effective way to gain a deeper understanding of their potential audience.

The design team agreed they would use our system on future projects to collect early-stage design insights. However, they also had a number of observations about how to improve the system and crowd needfinding in general. The design team actually wanted more responses than provided by the 20 online participants recruited for this study. They agreed it would be ideal to get feedback from 50 to 100 people and to be able to produce this feedback within two weeks. Our system can handle this demand and may be able to gather feedback in a fraction of this time using a retainer model or other real-time crowd recruitment methods [6].

The design team also felt the video responses should be longer, as one team member stated:

> One-minute videos seem fine from what we just saw. But I feel that we should not set an upper limit. Participants should be able to talk as long as they want.

Although current system limits the recording time to avoid rambling responses based on our results from the feasibility study, we could remove this upper limit (or allow the designer to set it) to accommodate more information. Further, the design team expressed desire for follow-up conversations with particularly insightful respondents:

> I'd love to hear more about the elderly story" or off topic "It is a pity that this person didn't say much as he didn't realize that we have an intelligent engine in the backend.

The designers wanted more interaction with participants, which is something we hope to address in future work. In terms of willingness to pay for such a service, team members said they may pay between \$1 and \$3 per response, "*the price of a cup of coffee.*" But, they would be willing to pay a bonus up to \$10 for exceedingly valuable feedback. "*I am willing to pay more... and I can wait for a longer time as long as there are more interesting responses rolling in.*"

Case Study: Discussion

This research demonstrates how online communication can work *in parallel* with in-person interaction for designers to quickly cast a wide net to capture new insights and discover previously overlooked issues in early-stage design [10]. While designers sometimes felt less sense of presence from online users compared to talking face-to-face and online users generally yielded fewer ideas per person, the crowd as a whole generated more diverse insights. We found that twenty online participants can sufficiently identify issues discovered by seven local interviewees. This approach is also time-and-cost-effective because professional design teams do not need to pay for transportation costs, spend days recruiting participants, or setup a space for interviews.

The study shows that crowd-sourced asynchronous video communication is a viable method for designers to iterate both on their designs and their target audience who are not cultivated for design research. This work provides evidence that workers on mTurk can and will record useful self-reflections on video. For the most part, workers followed our examples to effectively position themselves in front of the camera and to outline their thoughts before capturing the video. Workers re-recorded their videos a total of 28 times out of 100 showing the utility of the rehearsal feature. With properly designed mechanisms, asynchronous online video can successfully support the rich interactions required for early-stage needfinding.

Overall, the design team was impressed by the personal nature of mTurk workers' stories and wanted to learn more. Future versions of our system would allow designers to contact selected workers for follow-up interviews. We also plan to make the system more robust by allowing workers to save their progress and providing features like crowd-enabled speech-to-text transcription to give designers a way to preview the content of videos by reading text.

FUTURE RESEARCH ON ONLINE DESIGN PRACTICES

Our online feedback system can be used in any type of design: product, service, interaction, etc. In future work, storyboards can be replaced by other digital design artifacts such as videos and slideshows, further strengthening the generalizability of this approach. Based on the results and comments received from the two studies, we present some future directions for conducting general design research activities with remote users [10]:

Create effective design artifacts and prompts. This can help feedback providers understand the task, whether it is about a concept, a scenario, or an interaction, and reduce the noise in the feedback. We observed and learned from the post-study interviews in both studies that feedback providers might misinterpret the scenario or miss some of the key messages when they had trouble following the storyboard. This could happen in usability testing and other design activities as well. Therefore, it is critical for the design artifact and prompts that participants interact with to stand-alone, to be easy to understand, and to follow known guidelines (e.g. [29, 30]). Designers can pilot their artifacts and prompts with several participants to test their readability and interpretability before presenting to a larger crowd.

Support more recruitment channels and demographic filters for pre-screening and post-analysis. Designers should identify their target audience and choose platforms or services — crowdsourcing sites, online forums, social networking sites, etc. — that are most likely to provide access to these users. Once people sign up, pre-screening could help ensure quality feedback. Through simple survey methods, designers could capture participants' demographic information, cultural background, and familiarity with the scenarios or design. In addition, when choosing the communication modality, designers should take into consideration target users' literacy and language skills, accessibility to technology (e.g. webcam and decent Internet speed for video chat), and technology fluency (e.g. typing speed). These data could allow designers to pre-screen participants to fit certain criteria or they can be used during data analysis to examine the differences between disparate user populations (e.g., urban vs. rural). As the design activity proceeds, such an approach would help designers flexibly target specific or new participant pools.

Enable information exchange through follow-up strategies. As the case study revealed, designers often want to dig deeper and interact with participants. This is a clear benefit of face-to-face interviews. Our system may support better feedback communication by allowing designers to send follow-up questions to particular users. Going further, online design communication can incorporate both synchronous and asynchronous channels. To take advantage of the scale and relative ease of crowdsourcing, we envision this as a two-stage process. First, the system recruits participants to leave short video responses about designers' concepts (this is currently implemented in the system). Second, if the designer wants to follow up with particular users, the system would help schedule a live video chat between the two parties (future work), much like an in-person interview.

Increase designer presence to promote participant engagement. Designers' degree of social presence, defined as their salience in the mediated environment, may in return affect participants' perception, engagement, trust, and level of satisfaction around the design activity [27]. Online communication systems could further emulate face-to-face interactions by increasing designers' social presence, such as displaying a personable identity or provide voice feedback/appreciation when participants finish the task.

Protect participants' privacy and designers' intellectual property. Privacy features would make both parties more comfortable exchanging ideas online. In the feasibility study, many participants worried that their chat history or video footage would be part of a permanent record. The system should take measures to protect anonymity—for example, by obfuscating the video data and hiding personally identifying information—especially when performing design activities on sensitive topics. Informed consent should be obtained from crowd participants if video data will be used in communication with other stakeholders (our studies followed proper human-subjects protocols). Likewise, the design team in the case study raised the point that presenting novel ideas to a potentially anonymous online crowd raises the risk of leaking intellectual property. The design team proposed that in certain circumstances, participants would need to sign a Non-Disclosure Agreement.

CONCLUSION

This paper showed that, under a similar budget constraint, online crowds can provide early-stage design feedback through asynchronous video with a quality and coverage comparable to face-to-face methods. Through a feasibility study, we first explored the effect of media on feedback providers' experience, comparing face-to-face interviews, online video communication, and text-based chat. Lessons from this feasibility study guided our development of a system for designers to collect asynchronous video feedback from online crowds. We studied its potential impact through a case study with a professional design team and compared the efficacy of online needfinding versus conventional in-person interviews. While the in-person interviews produced more insights per participant, online video responses were cheaper and easier to collect and allowed designers to yield more overall insights from a more diverse pool of people. The design team reacted positively to online video communication, and indicated their desire to use the system for future design projects; they also provided suggestions on improving online feedback collection.

ACKNOWLEDGMENTS

Funded by National Science Foundation grants #1217096 and #1208382, CI Fellows grant #1019343, and REU award #1340291. We thank the design team and all participants.

REFERENCES

1. Amazon's Mechanical Turk. (2014). https://mturk.com/.

2. Autodesk SketchBook. (2012). http://m.autodesk.com/sketchbook/.
3. Andreasen, M.S., Nielsen, H.V., Schrøder, S.O., and Stage, J. 2007. What happened to remote usability testing? An empirical study of three methods. In *Proc. of CHI'07*. ACM (2007), 1405-1414.
4. Barksdale, J., Inkpen, K., Czerwinski, M., Hoff, A., Johns, P., Roseway, A., and Venolia, G. Video threads: asynchronous video sharing for temporally distributed teams. In *Proc. CSCW'12*. (2012) 1101-1104.
5. Bastien, C. Usability testing: a review of some methodological and technical aspects of the method. *International Journal of Medical Informatics*, (2010). 79(4):18-23.
6. Bernstein, M.S., Karger, D.R., Miller, R.C., and Brandt, J. Analytic methods for optimizing realtime crowdsourcing. In *Proc. Collective Intelligence*. (2012).
7. Bietz, M.J. Effects of communication media on the interpretation of critical feedback. In *Proc. CSCW'08*, ACM Press, (2008). 467-476.
8. Bos, N., Olson, J., Gergle, D., Olson, G., and Wright, Z Effects of four computer-mediated communications channels on trust development. In *Proc. CHI'02*. ACM Press, (2002). 135-140.
9. Buxton, B. *Sketching User Experiences*. Morgan Kaufmann Publishers, (2007).
10. Cross, N. Design cognition: results from protocol and other empirical studies of design activity. In: Eastman, C.; Newstatter, W. and McCracken, M. eds. *Design knowing and learning: cognition in design education*. Oxford, UK: Elsevier, (2001). 79–103.
11. Daft, R. L. and Lengel, R.H. Organizational information requirements, media richness and structural design. *Management Science*, (1986). 32 (5):554-571.
12. Davidoff, S., Lee, M.K., Dey, A.K. & Zimmerman, J. Rapidly Exploring Application Design Through Speed Dating. In *Proc. UbiComp2007*, (2007). 429-446.
13. Dow, S., Fortuna, J., Schwartz, D., Altringer, B., Schwartz, D.L., Klemmer, S.R. Prototyping Dynamics: Sharing Multiple Designs Improves Exploration, Group Rapport, and Results. In *Proc. CHI'11*. (2011).
14. Dow, S., Gerber, E., and Wong, A. A pilot study of using crowds in the classroom. In *Proc. CHI'13*. ACM Press. (2013). 227-237.
15. Etherpad Lite (2014). http://etherpad.org.
16. Gaver, B. and Martin, H. Alternatives: Exploring Information Appliances through Conceptual Design Proposals. In *Proc. CHI'00*. ACM Press. (2000).
17. Hebert, B. G., and Vorauer, J. D. Seeing through the screen: Is evaluative feedback communicated more effectively in face-to-face or computer-mediated exchanges? *Comp.in Human Behavior*, 19(2003): 25-38.
18. Hui, J., Gerber, E., Dow, S. Crowd-Based Design Activities: Helping Students Connect with Users Online. In *Proc. DIS'14*. (2014).
19. Kittur, A., Chi, E., and Suh, B., Crowdsourcing for usability: Using micro-task markets for rapid, remote, and low-cost user measurements. In *Proc. CHI'08*. ACM Press, (2008).
20. Kohavi, R., Henne, R. and Sommerfield, D. Practical guide to controlled experiments on the web: listen to your customers not to the hippo. In *Proc. SIGKDD'07*, (2007).
21. Liikkanen L., Kuikkaniemi K., Lievonen P. and Ojala P. (2011) Next Step in Electronic Brainstorming: Collaborative Creativity with the Web. In *Proc. CHI2011*. ACM Press. (2011).
22. Martin, B., Hanington, B. *Universal Methods of Design: 100 Ways to Research Complex Problems, Develop Innovative Ideas, and Design Effective Solutions*. Rockport (2012).
23. Martin, R., Shamari, M.A., Seliaman, M.E., and Mayhew, P. Remote Asynchronous Testing: A Cost-Effective Alternative for Website Usability Evaluation. *International Journal of Computer and Information Technology*. (2014). 3(1): 99-104.
24. MindSwarms. (2014). https://www.mindswarms.com/.
25. Nielsen, Jakob, and Landauer, Thomas K. A mathematical model of the finding of usability problems. In *Proc. INTERCHI'93*. ACM Press. (1993). 206-213.
26. Sheer, V. and Chen, L. Improving Media Richness Theory : A Study of Interaction Goals, Message Valence, and Task Complexity in Manager-Subordinate Communication. *Management Communication Quarterly*. (2004). 18 (76): 76–93.
27. Short,J.,Williams,E.&Christie, B. *The social psychology of telecommunications*. London: Wiley. (1976).
28. Tohidi, M., Buxton, W., Baecker, R., and Sellen, A. Getting the right design and the design right. In *Proc. CHI2006*. ACM Press. (2006). 1243–1252.
29. Truong, K. N., Hayes, G. R. and Abowd, G. D. Storyboarding: An Empirical Determination of Best Practices and Effective Guidelines. In Proc. *Proceedings of the 6th conference on Designing Interactive systems*. (2006), 12-21.
30. van der Lelie, C. The Value of Storyboards in the Product Design Process. *Personal and Ubiquitous Computing*. 10 (2). (2006). 159-162.
31. Xu, A. and Bailey, B. A crowdsourcing model for receiving design critique. In *Proc. CHI'11*. (2011).
32. Yu, L. and Nickerson, J.V. Cooks or Cobblers? Crowd Creativity through Combination.In *Proc.CHI'11*.(2011).
33. Zimmerman, J. Designing for the self: making products that help people become the person they desire to be. In *Proc. CHI'09*. ACM Press, (2009). 395-404.

Procid: Bridging Consensus Building Theory with the Practice of Distributed Design Discussions

Roshanak Zilouchian Moghaddam, Zane Nicholson, and Brian P. Bailey
Department of Computer Science
University of Illinois
Urbana, IL 61801
{rzilouc2, znichol2, bpbailey}@illinois.edu

ABSTRACT
Consensus is a desired but elusive goal in many distributed discussions. A critical problem is that discussion platforms lack mechanisms for realizing consensus strategies and realizing these strategies without tool support can be hard. This paper introduces *Procid*, a novel browser plugin that provides interaction and visualization features for bringing consensus strategies to distributed design discussions. Key features include the ability to organize discussions around ideas, to register and visualize support for or against ideas, and to define criteria for evaluating ideas. It also applies interaction constraints fostering best practices of consensus building. Procid extends the discussion platform of one open source software community. Two evaluations were conducted. The first collected perceptions of the tool from members of the community for their own discussions. The second compared how Procid affects a distributed design discussion relative to the current discussion platform in the community. Results of both studies showed that users found the features of our tool beneficial and perceived it as more effective for consensus building than the existing platform.

Author Keywords
Consensus building; design; open source

ACM Classification Keywords
H.5.2 [Information Interfaces and Presentation]: User Interfaces - Interaction styles.

INTRODUCTION
User interface (UI) design is a complex, communication-driven process where stakeholders with different interests generate and debate design proposals to solve usability problems and integrate new features. Due to the rise in distributed teams (e.g. open source software), many design discussions now unfold through interactive platforms such as Web forums. Building consensus is desirable in these discussions because it improves participants' experience and increases commitment to the outcome [31]. However, existing discussion platforms only offer basic commenting and sometimes voting whereas consensus theory argues for a broader set of strategies [5, 31], e.g., to track alternatives, define evaluation criteria, and promote a positive tone. Such strategies are not directly supported in existing platforms.

Research has shown the need for consensus building in distributed discussions. For example, a study of one large open source software community reported that 42% of the UI design discussions do not reach consensus [35]. This can cause loss of community effort, missed opportunities for enhancing the product, and attrition of community members [35]. In fact, an outflow of Wikipedia volunteers has been attributed to the lack of consensus building mechanisms [3].

In this paper we describe *Procid*, a novel browser extension that enables consensus building strategies to be realized in un-moderated distributed design discussions. Key features of the tool include (i) the ability to visually organize the discussion around idea proposals; (ii) the ability to define persistent criteria and rate the ideas against the criteria; (iii) the ability to register and visualize strong support for or against ideas, empowering individuals with a stronger voice in the discussion; (iv) interaction constraints that promote best practices of consensus efforts, e.g., encouraging the first comment on an idea to be supportive of it; and (v) the ability to identify candidates to invite to active discussions using attributes important for consensus in the domain.

Consensus building involves a broad set of procedural, rhetorical, and social strategies [5, 20, 21, 30, 31, 35]. Procid prioritizes a subset of these strategies that is feasible to implement and would be difficult to realize without tool support or a moderator (e.g. organizing a lengthy discussion around the ideas). Additional strategies can be implemented as experience is gained or integrated into an onboarding process for new members [11]. Procid represents a system design pattern that can be mimicked to bring the benefits of consensus building to online deliberation platforms.

Procid extends the Web-based discussion platform used for distributed design discussions in one mature open source software community (Drupal.org). This approach allows the features of our tool to be experienced and tested in context

ACM 978-1-4503-2922-4/15/03…$15.00
http://dx.doi.org/10.1145/2675133.2675272

of authentic discussions in the community. It also enables novel features (e.g. participant invitations) by utilizing the social structure and interaction history of the community.

Two evaluations of Procid were conducted. For the first, we rendered five active discussions in the community in Procid and invited participants from those discussions to use and provide feedback on the features of the tool and the overall approach. The second evaluation compared how the use of Procid affects a distributed design discussion relative to the existing platform used in the community. Results of both studies showed that users found the features of our tool beneficial for consensus and perceived the tool as more effective for consensus building than the existing platform.

RELATED WORK

We describe the benefits and prior studies of consensus building and how our work differs from prior tools and visualizations used for collaborative problem solving.

Consensus Building

In group decision making, consensus is reached when all participants commit to a proposal despite the fact that objections may remain [10]. The process of building consensus is a distinct form of face-to-face decision making because decisions are reached through mutual consent, each participant is given the power of veto, all stakeholders are invited to participate, and the process is based on openness and trust [30]. Following a consensus approach can increase understanding of the issues, ensure all solution proposals are considered, and encourage commitment to the outcome [30]. Above all, participants should feel good about the social process through which the outcome was achieved. Due to its benefits, consensus building is being increasingly utilized for face-to-face decision making, especially in complex domains such as design where no one person has all the required expertise to solve a given problem [31].

Researchers have recognized the need for and studied consensus building in many distributed communities. For example, Kriplean et al. examined how Wikipedia policies are employed through the consensus building process in talk pages [21]. The authors recommended building tools that summarize behavior to help identify different aspects of a conflict over time and annotating prior instances of consensus and the participants involved. In open source communities, prior work showed that who is involved in the discussion affects consensus and recommended building interface features that allow users to identify other members who could best contribute to the discussion [35]. Research in open source has also shown that the types of arguments and rationale applied in distributed discussions need to be better oriented toward consensus [20]. However, none of these recommendations have been implemented or tested. Without an implementation it is difficult to acquire knowledge about the effectiveness of the recommendations, how users would perceive such a system, or how it would affect consensus. Our research extends prior work on consensus building by developing a system that implements many of the prior recommendations and by evaluating the utility of the system for distributed design discussions.

Tools for Group Decision Making

The CSCW community has a rich history of building tools that support group decision making. The design of these tools typically varies based on the proximity of group members, group size, and the task [13]. For instance, in co-located settings, prior work has studied how collaborative use of large or multiple displays affect negotiation [9], software development [8], and design [4, 27]. In distributed settings, researchers have developed Web-based systems to support tasks such as information security planning [14].

Other research supports decision making by enabling the decision process to be tracked, archived, and reviewed. For example, gIBIS and Compendium support design decision making by tracking issues, positions, and arguments [12, 29]. Pathfinder provides an explicit argumentation model and visualization of that model for engaging citizens in distributed discussions of research questions [25]. Polestar aids intelligence analysts by supporting structured argumentation and fact collection from documents [28] while CommentSpace integrates a small set of tags and link structure with comments to aid evidence gathering and data exploration during collaborative sense-making [33].

Our system is original relative to this prior work because it promotes the social process of decision making in addition to visualizing and tracking the discussion. This is achieved by leveraging consensus theory in its design. Our work also contributes results from a study empirically comparing how the use of our tool affects distributed discussions relative to the use of an existing Web platform.

Visualization for Collaborative Problem Solving

Research has shown that visualization and interaction can foster collaborative problem solving [2, 7, 23, 32]. For instance, Balakrishnan et al. showed that providing a graph visualization of relevant information and shared interaction promotes topical focus and higher solution rates [7]. Alonso et al. proposed a similar graph visualization that represents the closeness of opinions to support consensus building in small groups [2]. Our work is inspired by the success of these types of visualizations for consensus building in lab settings, but our tool provides broader support for the consensus method (e.g. user-defined criteria for rating ideas) and addresses the challenge of aiding real design discussions in an existing open source software community.

Another thread of research has created visualizations to support large-scale deliberation. For instance, ConsiderIt is a visualization tool that promotes public deliberation by guiding people to reflect on the perspectives of others on topics of civic interest (e.g. ballot initiatives) [22]. Opinion Space is a Web interface for collecting and visualizing users' opinions on topics such as politics, parenting, and art

[15]. While these tools focus on visualizing the deliberation process, our work focuses on implementing and evaluating strategies for consensus building in distributed discussions.

STRATEGIES FOR CONSENSUS BUILDING

Developing a system that embodies consensus building in distributed design discussions is a big challenge. To address it, we enumerated many consensus building strategies recommended for moderated face-to-face discussions [5, 20, 21, 30, 31, 35]. See Table 1. The strategies were categorized as social, rhetorical, or procedural. Social strategies relate to who participates in a discussion and their relationships and perceptions. Rhetorical strategies relate to the content of a discussion while procedural strategies relate to how a discussion is organized. As shown in Table 1, we prioritized strategies that would be feasible to implement, be hard to realize without tool support, and form a coherent user experience. This led us to focus on six strategies:

S1: Promote perception of valued contribution and sense of empowerment. All participants should feel welcome to contribute to a discussion, that their comments are valued, and that they have the power to affect the decision outcome. Enhancing these perceptions promotes understanding of the decision and increased commitment to its implementation [5]. Existing discussion interfaces cannot directly support this strategy because they process and represent all comments the same, regardless of who wrote them or if the content conveys strong support for or objection to an idea.

S2: Express concerns in a constructive manner. A discussion needs to be constructive, even when there are strong disagreements [31]. Similarly, when ideas are proposed, the strengths of the ideas should be discussed first and then the weaknesses. In absence of a facilitator, however, distributed discussions can be plagued by destructive comments and flame wars, causing participants to leave the discussion, or discouraging participation.

S3: Build on prior relationships and seek expert advice. Some participants can promote consensus more than others. For instance, experienced and/or trusted participants can promote consensus by helping opposing parties develop options or by identifying barriers to effective negotiation [31, 35]. However, existing discussion platforms do not provide mechanisms for including potential participants based on their ability to promote consensus in a discussion.

S4: Evaluate and decide according to established criteria. Solution alternatives need to be evaluated to find one that best satisfies all stakeholders' interests [31]. The criteria help participants weigh trade-offs and identify the solution that best matches the majority's interest. But in existing discussion forums, criteria must be proposed as part of the text in a comment, thereby becoming fragmented across the discussion. Also, there is no explicit means for evaluating the idea proposals against the set of criteria defined.

Social Strategies
Promote perception of valued contribution (S1).
Build on prior relationships and seek expert opinions (S3).
Promote community ownership of ideas.
Help new members become part of the group.
Rhetorical Strategies
Express concerns in a constructive manner (S2).
Value feelings and show empathy towards strong emotions.
Avoid answering to all the objections to your viewpoint.
Provide descriptive, specific, and tentative feedback.
Disagree with ideas, not people.
Keep the discussion on topic.
Listen for the aspects of an idea that you find attractive and acknowledge the positive when responding.
Procedural Strategies
Evaluate and decide according to established criteria (S4).
Maintain a visual summary of key points of agreement and disagreement (S5).
Mark and revisit influential points of the discussion (S6).
Respond to disruptive behavior.
Generate a wide variety of proposals.
Try to equalize power and balance participation.
Blend ideas together and try to maximize joint gains.
Don't quit after the first good idea.
When all viewpoints have been expressed, state the conclusion toward which the group appears to be moving.
Test for the agreement.
Before proposing solutions, understand the problem.

Table 1. Consensus building strategies derived from prior studies of moderated face-to-face discussions. The strategies were grouped into three categories, but are not intended to be exclusive. The grouping did not affect our design and was done for the purpose of presentation. Highlighted strategies are the focus of our design.

S5: Maintain a visual summary of key points of agreement and disagreement. In moderated face-to-face discussions, a recorder tracks the proposed options and organizes the key points of agreement and disagreement [31], which can be shared during the meeting. This helps the group see the direction of the discussion and maintain task focus [5]. In distributed discussions, the participants carry the burden of tracking ideas and related arguments, making it easy to lose them in the discussion.

S6: Mark and revisit influential points of the discussion. Distributed discussions often contain many comments posted over a wide window of time. It is therefore easy for important discussion points to become lost or forgotten. This is especially problematic for participants who join late, or who enter and leave throughout and only read subsets of comments as time allows. In current discussion platforms, there is no easy way to mark and revisit important discussion points and share these with others.

As shown in Table 1, we selected a subset of the known strategies for our design. Three of the six are procedural (S4-6), which are generally amenable to tool support. Our tool supports these strategies through visualization design. From the remaining strategies, one is rhetorical (S2) while

Figure 1. Procid is a browser script that extends the existing discussion interface in Drupal with a navigation panel on the top and a lens panel on the left. (a) The three icons on the top panel enable navigation between the main discussion page, the idea-centric view, and the invite page. (b) Five filters are available at the top of the lens panel that toggle the highlighting of comments with the corresponding property, e.g., the *must read* (leftmost) lens highlights the comments endorsed as *must read* by participants.

the other two (S1, S3) are social. These are typically more difficult to implement, but are approached in our tool by leveraging content analysis methods, interaction constraints, and the interaction history of the community.

These strategies provide a minimal but reasonable starting point for exploring how to design a system that brings consensus theory to the practice of un-moderated online design discussions. As experience is gained, additional strategies could be implemented or made accessible to community members via onboarding or other newcomer socialization techniques [11].

PROCID

Procid is a browser extension that supports consensus building strategies for distributed design discussions. See Figure 1. We built Procid as an add-on to an existing discussion platform, rather than as a stand-alone system. The benefits are that we can deploy and test our interface in an existing community, recruit participants who care about the discussion topic, and integrate an existing workflow. It also allows us to leverage the community's social structure to build novel features (e.g. participant invitations).

To provide a testbed, we built Procid to augment design discussions in Drupal, an open source content management system initiated in 2001. Drupal is a mature open source community with an established workflow and organization. Drupal's issue management system includes thousands of discussions requesting usability fixes, improved designs or new features for the Drupal product. Members participate in the discussions by proposing design alternatives, critiquing the alternatives, implementing an alternative (writing a patch), reviewing a patch, or offering other insights.

As the Drupal product expands and grows a large user base, adding features or fixing usability issues is getting harder. For example, proposed changes must now often consider customer preferences, product roadmaps, and consistency issues; along with the (strong) opinions of current members. By interacting with the Drupal community for the past four years, the first author has become aware of the need for employing consensus building strategies in the community. This interaction has included participating in and analyzing online discussions in the community, discussing consensus building with members through interviews and existing threads, and presenting at a regional Drupal conference.

Procid organizes its features into three groups: an *idea-centric view* that organizes the proposed ideas, criteria, and comments; an *invite* page that lists potential members to invite to a discussion, and a *lens panel* that wraps the existing discussion and enables filtering of the comments.

Idea-Centric View: Organize Discussions around Ideas

Proposed ideas are the focal point of any design discussion. Keeping track of the ideas enables participants to evaluate or build upon each other's ideas and revisit ideas not yet discussed. For tracking ideas and visualizing agreement and tension, Procid offers an *idea-centric view* of a discussion. This type of view prevents ideas from becoming lost in a discussion [36]. The view summarizes the proposed ideas, their status (Dropped, Ongoing, or Implemented), and the criteria for evaluating the ideas. It also spatially organizes the comments for each idea into supportive, neutral, or constructive categories (Figure 2). Before detailing the features of this view, we will explain how the system knows which comments contain ideas or refer to ideas.

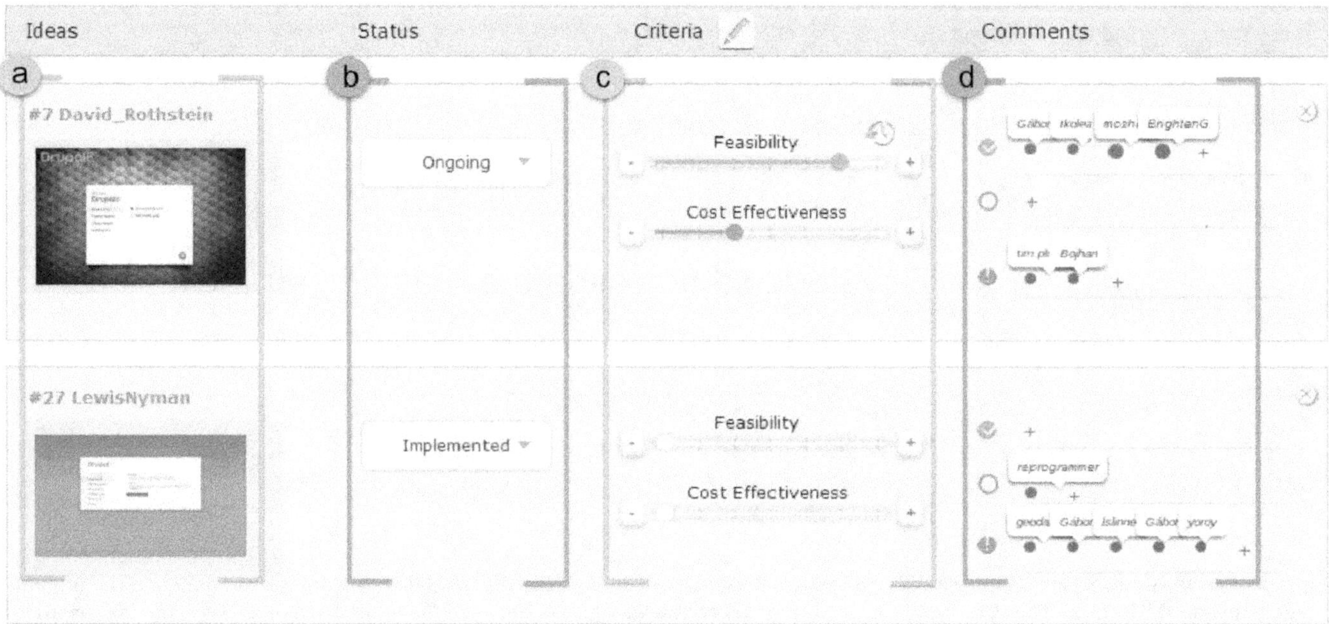

Figure 2. Selecting the light bulb icon from the navigation panel opens the idea-centric view (shown) which contains four columns of information. (a) In this view ideas are represented with the image that was attached to the corresponding comment or the initial text if no image was attached. (b) A menu for setting the status of the idea and (c) a list of user-defined criteria. Each criterion has a shared slider for rating the idea which any user in the discussion can manipulate. (d) The comments referring to an idea are spatially organized into three rows: supportive (top row), neutral (middle) or constructive (bottom). Comments registered as strong support or objections are rendered with larger circles, which are intended to attract more attention than the other comments.

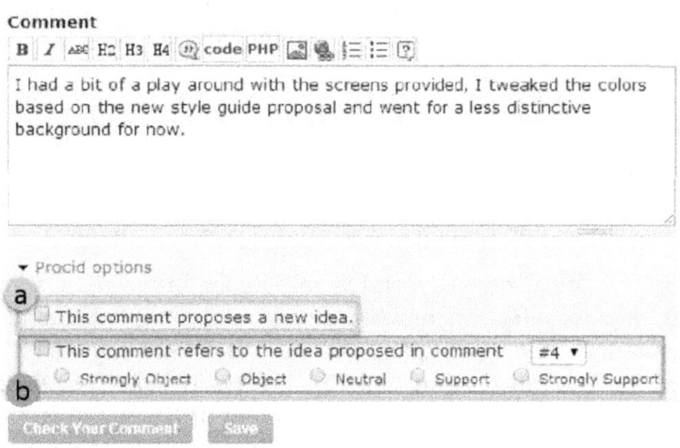

Figure 3. When authoring a comment, Procid allows the user to mark if the comment (a) proposes an idea or (b) refers to an existing idea and, if so, to indicate their disposition toward it.

Identifying Ideas and participants' opinions about ideas

Procid inserts an interaction panel within the existing dialog for authoring a comment. In this panel, a participant can toggle if the comment proposes an idea or if it refers to an existing idea. For the latter, the participant can also indicate her disposition toward the idea (Figure 3). Whether a comment contains an 'idea' can be later changed by selecting the icon inserted by our tool in the bottom right of the rendered view of the comment.

Asking for user input to render alternative views of a discussion follows a long thread of CSCW research (e.g. [12, 25, 28]). A unique aspect of our approach, however, is that we are injecting the request into an existing community interface. This imposes a constraint on how much input we can realistically request for fear of community backlash. It also prevents us from expanding the input to the point of making the system undesirable to use (an important lesson learned from the class of design rationale systems).

Our design therefore only requires this minimal input, but in return can render the view shown in Figure 2. From this view, users can quickly determine which ideas are favored or opposed, which need more attention, patterns in the comments, and how the ideas compare based on the criteria.

Establishing concrete criteria to evaluate ideas

In design discussions, the solution alternatives need to be evaluated to find the one that best satisfies all participants' interests. In the idea-centric view, participants can define the criteria for evaluating ideas. For example, if a solution must have low implementation cost, a participant can add *cost effectiveness* as a criterion. This is achieved using the criteria editor, accessed via the pencil icon (Figure 4).

For each new criterion, a slider is generated and replicated in the row of each idea (Figure 2c). Using the shared slider, participants can specify how much each idea satisfies the criterion on a 7-point scale (unsatisfactory to satisfactory). Upon changing the rating, the participant is prompted to justify the change which will be posted in the discussion (Figure 5). The prompt for rationale is meant to reduce superficial back-and-forth with the ratings. The scales allow

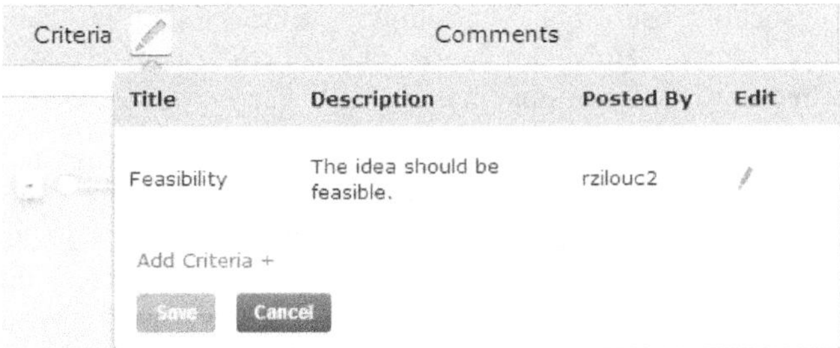

Figure 4. Users can establish new criteria for evaluating the ideas (*Add Criteria +*) and edit the existing criteria.

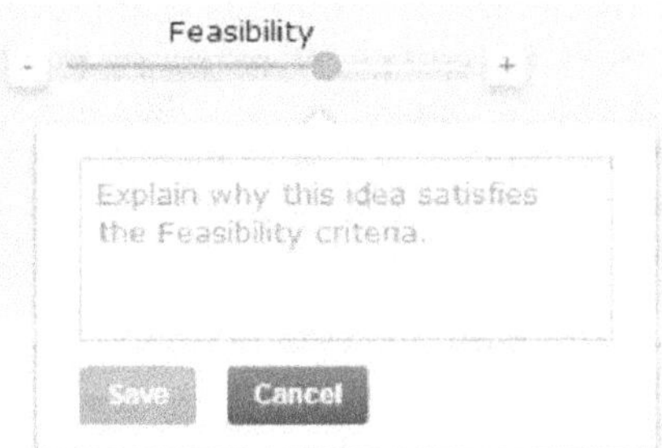

Figure 5. Users can use the generated scale to specify how much each idea satisfies each user-defined criterion.

participants to visualize and discuss trade-offs of ideas and eventually determine the one that best satisfies the criteria.

The criteria scale shows only the most recent rating, but the tool maintains the prior ratings and associated comments. This history can be accessed by selecting the button next to each scale and is intended to prevent prior users from feeling their opinions have been supplanted.

Spatially organizing comments around ideas

The idea-centric view organizes the comments referring to an idea into supportive, neutral, or constructive categories. The category of a comment is determined by the disposition rating provided when it was authored (Figure 3b). A participant can also add a comment from this view by selecting the "+" button corresponding to the desired disposition and idea. The advantage is that this opens the comment authoring dialog with the input parameters already set. When an idea is first posted, the "+" button for constructive (critical) comments is disabled until a neutral or supportive comment is added. The purpose of this constraint is to encourage discussing the strengths of an idea before discussing its weaknesses [19].

When a user is adding a supportive comment for an idea, s/he can register it as *strong support* for the idea (Figure 3b). Alternatively, when users are adding a constructive comment, they can register it as a strong *objection* to the idea. Comments registered as objections or strong support are rendered with larger circles to indicate unusually strong opinions about an idea (Figure 2d). The purpose is to provide participants with a stronger sense of empowerment over the proposed ideas and decision process and make these opinions easily noticeable in the visualization.

Figure 6. The invite page generates a list of users to potentially invite to the discussion. It considers criteria important for consensus such as the number of patches contributed and prior interaction history with participants in the discussion.

If an idea receives several objections, the person who proposed the idea can set its status to "Dropped". This status informs others that the idea need no longer be considered and the ability to add comments is disabled.

Invite Page: Seeking potential contributors

A discussion can become stalled due to controversy over implementation or strong disagreements between parties. Seeking additional expert advice or inviting trusted colleagues can help move the discussion forward. However, there is no useful mechanism for finding people to invite to the discussion who could contribute to the consensus effort.

To explore such a mechanism, the *Invite* page in our tool dynamically creates a list of community members sortable by attributes important for consensus in the domain (Figure 6). The attributes include the duration of membership, number of patches submitted, recent participation, prior interaction with participants in the current discussion, and number of prior discussions involved in that reached consensus (i.e. the discussions were closed). For example, experienced members may bring historical perspectives on the product and past decisions that can influence the direction of the discussion and those with connections to participants in the current discussion may be more likely to accept an invitation to participate. The set of attributes could be expanded in future work, such as including a topic-based relevance score and the number of active discussions to gauge workloads prior to invitation.

Discussion participants can sort the list to seek potential members to invite, and not have to guess, rely on memory, or blindly search for possible contributors. The list can be especially helpful in situations where the user is less familiar with the topic or current participants. To compute these attributes, our tool analyzes the social graph [18], interaction history, and profiles of community members as an offline process and repeats it periodically.

Lens Panel: Gaining a Rapid Overview of Discussion

Procid extracts significant discussion bits from multiple perspectives including community endorsement, the content, and the conversation behavior of the posters. These perspectives are captured in five lenses available in the *lens panel* wrapped around the main discussion page: *must read*, *idea*, *conversation*, *experienced*, and *patch* (Figure 1).

Through these lenses, Procid allows newcomers to quickly gain awareness and existing participants to mark and revisit key points of the discussion (Figure 7). For example the *must read* lens highlights comments that are critical for understanding the discussion's trajectory. Examples include comments that summarize the discussion to date, plot the direction of the discussion, or report conclusions from synchronized discussions. Any participant can endorse a comment as *must read* by toggling an icon that our tool inserts with the comment. It can be toggled off if a participant later feels the comment was incorrectly marked or is no longer deserving of this property.

Figure 7. The idea lens (in blue) highlights all of the comments marked as containing an idea.

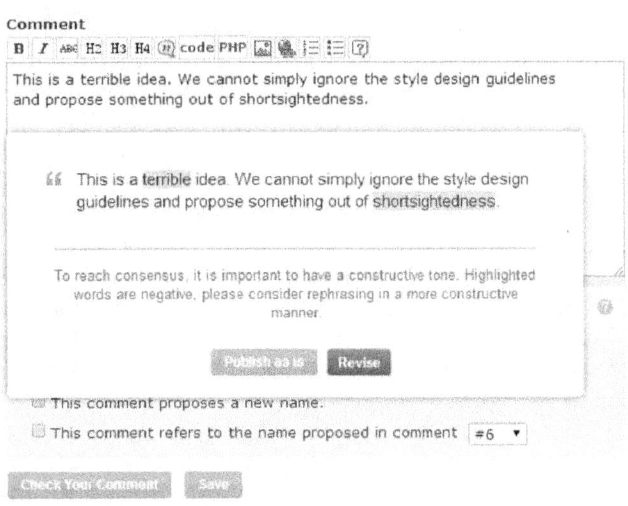

Figure 8. Procid analyzes the sentiment of the comment just before it is posted and, if an overly negative tone is detected, highlights the negative words and encourages revision.

Promoting a Positive Tone

Strong disagreements may result in destructive comments, hindering consensus. Our system promotes a positive tone by detecting when a comment has an overly negative tone relative to prior comments in the community and alerts the author just prior to posting it (Figure 8). The goal is not to censor the user, but to prompt a revision that is more constructive. However, once alerted, the user chooses whether to revise or post it as is.

To determine if a comment is overly negative, we computed the sentiment of 9000 randomly chosen comments from Drupal using AlchemyAPI [1]. We sorted the comments based on their negative sentiment and defined the threshold as the average of the top 1% of the comments. Just before a new comment is posted, Procid compares the sentiment of the comment to the threshold. If exceeded, the negative words in the comment are highlighted and the user is encouraged (but not forced) to revise it [16]. The threshold can be easily tuned or more advanced sentiment analysis techniques can be applied in future iterations. Alternatively, the user can choose to have the system check the tone of the comment and highlight the negative words, regardless of how it compares to prior comments.

Rendering Ongoing Discussions

It is very likely that community members would use Procid to participate in *ongoing* discussions with existing content. For its features to be effective, the tool needs to know which comments propose ideas, which comments refer to ideas, the comment dispositions, etc. One approach is to prompt users to provide this information at first use, but this upfront cost could be large. Instead, we apply heuristics to determine the ideas, comments referring to the ideas, and dispositions of comments toward the ideas and offer interactions for revising the assigned values. For example, Procid detects if a comment contains an idea by calculating a score based on whether the comment contains an image or patch, the number of references to the comment, and the sentiment of the references. If the score exceeds a certain threshold, it marks the comment as an idea.

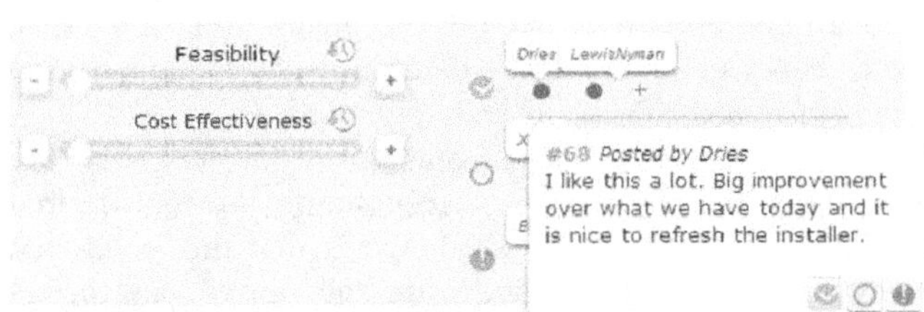

Figure 9. Users can change the classification of comments by selecting the relevant icon at the bottom of the comment box.

For each marked idea, Procid parses the discussion to find the comments referring to it. The tool then uses an internal sentiment analysis tool to categorize the comments. Similar to other tools (e.g. SentiWordnet [6] and LIWC [24]), Procid uses a lexicon that consists of two categories of negative (e.g. disappointment, criticism) and positive (e.g. gratitude, pride) words derived from a commonly used online dictionary. A comment is categorized as *supportive* if it has more positive words, *constructive* if it has more negative words, and *neutral* if it has none or nearly equal negative and positive words. This classification provides a default value, but users can override these values using toggles at the bottom of the comment box (Figure 9).

REVISITING STRATEGIES

We summarize how our tool realizes the six strategies. To promote perception of valued contribution (S1), Procid prominently displays the proposed ideas to ensure that discussion participants do not ignore those contributions and organizes the comments referring to those ideas. This helps participants track the ideas and their status and notice patterns of comments for and against the ideas. Also, to help users consider opposing views, Procid refrains from using colors commonly associated with negative affect (e.g. red) [34]. To cultivate a sense of empowerment (S1), the tool enables registering strong support or objection for ideas and visually emphasizes these dispositions in the idea-centric view (Figure 2d).

To promote constructive tone (S2), Procid analyzes each comment just before it is posted and, if an overly negative tone is detected, cautions the user about posting it and reminds him or her why this is important. For building on prior relationships (S3), Procid generates a list of potential participants for including in a discussion by analyzing their prior contributions, social graphs, and public profiles.

Procid's idea-centric view visually summarizes key points of agreement and disagreement (S5). It lists the ideas along with their supportive and constructive comments (Figure 2). It also allows participants to create concrete criteria and rate the ideas against the criteria (S4). Procid offers five lenses on the main page for marking and revisiting influential points of a discussion based on community endorsement, reply behavior, and content of the comments (S6).

IMPLEMENTATION

Procid was built using a client / server architecture. The client is a user script (JavaScript and jQuery code) that executes on a browser and customizes the appearance and functionality of the existing discussion platform. To track user data and perform data analysis the script connects to the server we built with Ruby on rails and MySQL. Both client side and server side are open source software under Apache license 2.0 and freely available on Github.

As a workaround to Javascript same-origin-policy, the client uses CORS (Cross-Origin Resource Sharing) to communicate with the server and exchange data using JSON. When the user installs the client and opens a discussion, it sends the discussion identifier along with the comments to the server. The server checks whether any records for the discussion exist in the database. It then processes the comments. For each comment, if there is a record in the database, the stored tags (e.g. idea, patch, conversation, etc.) are assigned to the comment. Otherwise the server computes values for as many tags as possible for the comment and stores them in the database. The server then sends the comments, tags, criteria, etc. to the client.

The implementation of the client is customized to work with the Drupal issue management system. It parses Drupal's HTML code and attaches its components to the HTML elements. However, the client uses a modular architecture. Therefore, by updating the parser module (around 15 lines of code) and the HTML elements that the client will attach to (around 10 lines of code), it can work with other issue management systems. The server has its own independent API which is accessible by any client.

EVALUATION

We conducted two studies of Procid. The first study gauged initial reactions to the tool and collected feedback from the community. The second study was a controlled experiment aimed at empirically comparing the use of our tool to the existing community interface for design discussions.

Study 1: Initial Reactions from the Community

We randomly chose five UI design discussions from Drupal. The discussions were active and had recent activity and many comments (μ=124 comments). We then tailored an interface walkthrough for each of these discussions and invited the participants in the discussions to complete the walkthrough. The key point is that a participant could see the discussion s/he was actively participating in rendered in our tool. Participants were informed that their interactions with Procid would not affect the actual discussion because the content had been mirrored on our server.

Nine community members involved in the five selected discussions responded to our invitation to participate. The participants were active members of Drupal. Three (male) were designers with an average of 5.6 years of experience, one (male) was a site builder with four years of experience building websites with Drupal, and one was both a designer and developer (female) with two years of experience in the community. The four remaining participants (male) were developers with an average of 5.25 years of experience.

The walkthrough began by having a participant install Procid in her Web browser. The participant then navigated to a page that mirrored his or her own Drupal discussion along with Procid. The participant then performed specific tasks relating to each main feature of the tool and freely explored that feature of the tool. After each task and exploration, participants rated their perception of the feature and commented on its strengths and weaknesses. Finally, participants rated and commented on the overall utility of the tool and the discussion interface currently used in the community. Participants received \$15 for remuneration.

We collected survey responses and logged interactions. In the survey, participants rated the perceived usefulness of different features of the tool, the tool overall, and the discussion interface currently used. All ratings were made on a 7-point Likert scale ranging from strongly disagree (1) to strongly agree (7).

Results

Participants rated Procid to be more useful for consensus building (μ=4.5, σ=1.2) than the discussion interface currently used (μ=3.4, σ=1.6; (t(8)=4.2, *p*=0.003 using paired samples t-test). Two representative statements are:

> "*I think this could help people see the current status of an issue in a way that our current 'tool' for this (manually-written issue summaries) can't, and in a more in-depth and balanced way than that tool allows.*" [P9]

> "*This tool could help focusing on ideas and not so much on people. Furthermore this tool could help to invite feedback even for long running issues with a lot of comments. Such issues normally are very hard to get into but would profit most from additional input.*" [P5]

The feature that participants found most useful in Procid was the ability to establish criteria (μ=5.9, σ=0.6). As illustrated by P7: "*[Criteria related features are] useful for reviewing: you know what to pay attention to. Useful for establishing what should be in scope of this current issue and what could be a follow-up issue.*"

Participants also agreed that the ability to read the rationale behind idea ratings is useful (μ=5.7, σ=0.7). For example, P9 said: "*I don't think the ranking itself is as important as being able to actually read the rationale behind it (e.g., who gave it the ranking and whether they had something useful and constructive to say about the particular criterion when they did so).*"

Participants found the invitation list and summary of attributes useful for identifying who to invite to the discussion (μ=5.6, σ=0.7). P1 stated: "*This is a good idea, if one wants to get someone involved. Else there is hardly a way to do this if you do not want to use their contact form on d.o. [drupal.org]*". The majority of participants stated that in the proposed list they actually found a member they would like to invite to the discussion (78%). P4 said: "*Yes, I immediately saw people that I should invite to the discussion. The algorithm used for this is interesting.*"

Participants also suggested improvements to the algorithm. For example, one participant stated that selecting people based on experience could miss people who are currently active in the usability discussions. Another participant recommended that the algorithm include topic similarity. P8: "*Facts that person has X patches, or participated in an issue which is now successfully closed, or was recently on the site, can't guarantee that person will be interested in this specific issue. [...] What is useful is relevance, e.g. if person participated in similar issues on the same topic.*" A third participant recommended that we add the invite feature on the comment level as well as the issue level. This would enable the participants to invite members to respond to a particular comment, rather than the whole issue.

Participants found the idea page useful for tracking the ideas (μ=5.1, σ=1.3). P9 said: "*It reminded me of some of the earlier ideas proposed in the drupal.org issue (I'm already a follower of this particular drupal.org issue so I'm somewhat familiar with it, but I'd forgotten about some of the earlier discussion and this helped me remember it).*"

Participants found the five lenses useful for navigating to different parts of the discussion (μ=5.3, σ=0.9) and for identifying important comments (μ=5, σ=0.9). For example, P5 said "*The panel absolutely helped to dive into a bigger, already evolved issue. Usually those issues are very hard to get into and it gets cumbersome to read similar comments over and over again especially if the issue goes on for a longer time period. I especially like the comment highlighting. This feature helps massively to find the comments that bring the meat to the issue so to speak.*"

To make Procid more useful for consensus building, participants suggested ranking the ideas in descending order or adding a status field to communicate the status of the whole discussion. P7: "*Maybe the ideas page can be sorted in reverse, with the latest most current idea on top. Might help focus the discussion on the latest and greatest idea. [..]. Another thing that could be useful is to have some kind of status indication for the issue as a whole: are we still exploring options or are we looking for detailed reviews on an almost done solution.*"

Study 2: Comparative Evaluation

The purpose of the second study was to compare how Procid affects the content, interactions, and user perceptions for distributed design discussions relative to the existing discussion platform used in Drupal. The latter platform is representative of most interactive Web forums used today. Given the limited interaction participants would have with either interface, our focus was on user perceptions of and experiences with the platforms rather than decision quality.

Design Tasks and Participants

The design task was to propose and debate names for a startup and was selected for three reasons. First, the task of naming a startup is a hard design problem. The task is ill-structured, many creative solutions are possible, there are no defined evaluation criteria, and the outcomes matter. Second, many design discussions in the community target selecting effective labels for various interface elements. Finally, proposing and naming a startup does not require user interface design and development expertise, therefore making the task accessible to a wider range of participants.

To make the discussion authentic, we interacted with two technology startups that were seeking effective names. One company is commercializing technology to verify network data flow security and correctness in real time (startup A). The other one is developing a content creation and camera hardware solution that enables users to create immersive experiences for advertising and entertainment (startup B).

We recruited 37 (15 female) participants with diverse disciplinary backgrounds from a large university. None had knowledge of this project. Ages ranged from 18-34. Based on self-reports, about half (18) of the participants frequently participated in Web forums, while the other half did not. Participants received $15 for participating in the study.

Discussion Interfaces and Experimental Design

We created eight issues in the Drupal issue management system for the design tasks and participants created Drupal accounts. Permission to do this was requested and granted from the administrators of Drupal. Our approach allowed participants to use the discussion interface in Drupal and to use Procid as described earlier. To disguise which interface was ours, we always referred to the existing discussion interface as Interface A and our tool as Interface B. Also, participants installed a script for each interface, though the script for Interface A performed no function.

The study was a within-subject design with Interface (our tool vs. existing discussion interface) as the one factor.

	Status quo		Procid	
	Week 1	*Week 2*	*Week 1*	*Week 2*
Startup A	G1	G4	G3	G2
Startup B	G2	G3	G4	G1

Table 2. The naming tasks and interfaces were assigned to the groups using a Latin-square design.

Procedure

Participants went through an informed consent process and were given an overview of the study. Participants were then randomly assigned to one of four groups (G1, G2, G3, G4), each with 10-12 participants. The order of the naming tasks and interfaces used were balanced using a Latin-square design (see Table 2).

The study was conducted over two weeks. During the first week, two groups (G1 and G2) used the status quo interface to name startups A and B, respectively. The other groups (G3 and G4) used Procid to name startups A and B respectively. At the beginning of the week, participants received the installation instructions for the assigned Interface, a video demonstrating its main features, and details of the task in an email. Participants were requested to generate and debate as many names as possible, and to identify their favorite name by the end of the week. Also, participants completed a survey on their experience using the assigned Interface. During the second week, each group switched to use the other Interface for the other design task. The procedure was then the same as the first week.

Each participant was asked to post at least ten helpful comments to a discussion. To motivate participation, we framed the naming tasks as a competition for each week. Groups earned points using a simple point system (Table 3) intended to reward effort and quality. The group with the most points at the end of the week won the competition for that week and each participant received an additional $15.

Contribution	Points
Propose a meaningful startup name.	2
Evaluate a proposed name.	3
Determine criteria to evaluate the names.	3
Post other meaningful comment.	1
Build consensus on a name that company founders chose as their favorite.	15

Table 3. A simple point system was used to motivate participation and determine the winning group.

To make the discussions engaging and realistic, the startup founders gave feedback on the direction of the discussion twice during each week. After the study, we conducted interviews with eleven of the participants asking about their perceptions of and experiences with each interface.

Measures

We collected data from the discussion content, interaction logs, surveys, and interviews. For the content, we measured the number of comments, names proposed, criteria defined, and evaluative statements. The interaction logs recorded each participant's interactions with the features of Procid. For the surveys, participants rated the perceived usefulness of the assigned interface for the consensus-related tasks and its overall usefulness. Ratings were made on a 7-point Likert scale ranging from strongly disagree (1) to strongly agree (7). At the end of the second survey, participants identified what they felt were the important differences between the two interfaces, selected which interface they would use in the future and why, and explained which interface helped the most with consensus building and how. We will refer to survey participants as S#. At the end of the study, we conducted semi-structured interviews with 11 participants (referred to as I#). We asked about their overall perceptions of Procid and the usefulness of its main features. Each interview lasted 15-20 minutes.

		G1	G2	G3	G4
Status quo	**Comments**	36	62	66	40
	Criteria	3	1	2	3
	Ideas	41	36	41	21
	Evaluations	17	34	30	15
Procid	**Comments**	55	59	83	79
	Criteria	3	5	5	4
	Ideas	46	19	18	32
	Evaluations	31	27	53	39

Table 4. Number of comments, proposed ideas, user-defined criteria, and evaluation statements in the discussions.

Results

Participants posted a total of 480 comments during the study. Of those, 254 contained proposed names (ideas) and

26 had criteria for evaluating the names. This shows that the participants were engaged in the study. Examples of some of the proposed ideas were VeriPut, DataRail, Raptor, GreenWall, and SecuraNet for startup A and Phantomizer, Mirage Maker, ProMagix, Luminocity, and Morphology for startup B. The winning name for startup A was *NetGator* and the winning name for startup B was *Astral*, both of which the startup founders thought were creative and had not been considered beforehand. The sets of proposed names were shaped and filtered based on user-defined criteria that emerged during the discussions. Examples of criteria were "*Reflective: The name should reflect the company's idea*", "*Trademark available: Whether trademark is available*", "*Catchiness: How catchy the name is*", and "*Uniqueness: The name should be different from the existing companies.*" For example, the name GreenWall was decided against because it wasn't reflective as S25 pointed out in the discussion: "*The name GreenWall suggests something related to the environment. But the company is focused on security in a network*".

Table 4 summarizes the comments, ideas, criteria, and evaluative statements for both interfaces. Though the trends favored Procid, there were no statistical differences due to the relatively small number of groups.

Overall Preference

From the survey, a large majority of participants (31 out of the 37) experienced Procid to be more helpful for consensus building than the status quo interface and preferred to use Procid for future design discussions. From the open-ended responses, the strong preference for Procid was due to its organization of comments (n=5), the ability to create and evaluate names based on the criteria (n=7), the ability to view the summary of agreements and disagreements with each name (n=7), and the ability to track the proposed names (n=5). Three representative statements were:

> "*Interface B's second screen; a lot more information is presented in a shorter amount of time. Even though I like to read the paragraphs for a poster's entire meaning/explanation behind his or her proposal, I think most forum users/readers do not have the patience to go through an entire thread. Interface B seems to solve that problem by sifting out the important bits and showing the highlights. Though scoring each post at the time may take longer, in the long run and for others on the forum it makes things a lot easier.*" [S4]

> "*It was easier to reach a group consensus on Interface B, because you could make a Positive, Neutral, or Critical vote/comment on someone's proposed name. This made it way easy to see the front-runners in public opinion of the board, rather than trying to keep track of which people agreed, which results in the last discussed names to be the main ones being considered.*" [S19]

> "*B because you can easily view suggested names, provide feedback and rate them in a separate view. In A you have to scan through posts and keep track of the thread.*" [S5]

Questions	Status Quo		Procid		*p*
	μ	σ	μ	σ	
Q1. I felt my comments were considered by others in the discussion.	5.73	1.18	5.62	1.07	0.34
Q2. I felt that I could express strong support for or against a name.	5.24	1.44	5.95	1.11	0.00**
Q3. The proposed names received critical comments after posting.	5.11	1.16	4.95	1.01	0.24
Q4. It is important to have objective criteria for evaluating the names.	5.70	1.21	6.14	0.96	0.00**
Q5. It was easy to establish objective criteria to evaluate the names.	5.08	1.17	5.89	0.95	0.00**
Q6. Participants evaluated the names based on the criteria.	5.00	1.19	5.81	1.01	0.00**
Q7. It was easy to track the discussion and the status of the names.	3.78	1.71	4.97	1.65	0.00**
Q8. It was easy to find other participants' opinions about a name.	4.03	1.75	4.81	1.61	0.03**
Q9. It was easy to find the important comments in the discussion.	3.65	1.76	4.81	1.56	0.00**
Q10. I felt that I was encouraged to add positive comments.	5.14	1.32	5.41	1.17	0.06*
Q11. In our group, we had a collaborative discussion.	5.46	1.20	5.65	0.85	0.23
Q12. This interface supports the consensus building process.	4.76	1.38	5.24	1.12	0.06*

Table 5. Summary of the survey results. From left to right, the table contains the questions, mean and standard deviation for the interfaces tested, and results of a paired-sample t-test. Responses used a 7-point Likert scale ranging from strongly disagree (1) to strongly agree (7).
**** = p < 0.05; *= p < 0.10.**

Conversely, the majority of participants noted the lack of organization of comments and difficulty in tracking names as weaknesses of the status quo interface (Interface A). For instance, S6 wrote: "*It was really hard to keep track of all the posts. Some of them had proposed new criteria, some new names, and some where just supporting, or disagreeing with the suggested names. The main con was that all these posts were in one thread and there was no organization. For example, if you just wanted to know a list of all suggested names you had to read all the posts.*"

Experienced Differences

From the survey, participants reported experiencing three key advantages of Procid relative to the status quo interface. One advantage was the ability to evaluate ideas based on user-defined criteria (n=13). Three representative responses from the surveys and interviews were:

> "*Interface B allowed you to rate names based on criteria and it made it easy to move forward from there. Whereas Interface A was simply a forum discussion.*" [S3]

> "*Interface A was quite plain and not very interactive but got the job done. Interface B on the other hand was very useful and allowed posters to really evaluate other posts and facilitated a meaningful discussion*" [S5].

> "*I feel it's pretty much one of the only ways you can do that sort of thing. It's like you cannot really have an abstract goodness or badness you have to say why it's good why it's bad. I feel like the criteria, really do help you determine why it's good or why it's bad.*" [I5]

As shown in Table 5, the survey responses also showed significantly higher ratings for Procid than the status quo interface on the three questions relating to criteria use (Q4, Q5, Q6). From the content analysis, groups created 14 criteria when using Procid, but created only 9 criteria when using the status quo interface. Participants also wrote 150 evaluative statements based on criteria when using Procid but only 96 statements when using the status quo interface.

A second key advantage was the ability to track the proposed names when using Procid (n=10):

> "*The option for viewing the already proposed names is super convenient because then you don't have to read the whole discussion to see them.*" [S26]

> "*Interface B was easy to follow different names and you can just focus on the specific parts. However, Interface A was simple and much easier to work with. You had to read most of the comments to be aware of discussion.*" [S35]

Procid was also rated as being significantly better for tracking ideas (Q7, Q8) than the status quo interface.

The third major difference was the better organization of comments provided by Procid (n=8):

> "*...[Interface B] seems much more organized. Interface A is simpler, but it can be hard to determine what the key points in the conversation are. This would be particularly true if the discussion is very long.*" [S25]

> "*Interface A was just a discussion that kind of just blended down so like people would just keep going and going which is good but then they forget the stuff that happened before and then we would have to bring that up again and so Interface A was just kind of like a flow of stuff where you could forget the past discussion whereas Interface B you could advance your discussion a lot more better because things in the past are more apparent*". [I9]

In contrast, the main relative strengths of the status quo interface were openness (n=8) and ease of use (n=9).

Feature Use

From the interaction data, we found that the groups used most of the key features of Procid (see Table 6) with Groups 3 and 4 making the most extensive use of them. The most common interactions were with defining criteria, evaluating ideas based on the criteria, checking the tone of the comment, and applying lenses to filter comments. The interaction data also shows that all but one group spent at least 36 percent of their time using the idea-centric view. This usage was balanced toward the latter stages of the discussion when there was more content.

	G1	G2	G3	G4
Rate ideas based on criteria	24	1	18	26
Add a new criteria	3	3	4	4
Check a comment's tone	5	5	26	18
Register strong opinion	0	0	1	4
Drop an idea	0	0	2	4
Tag comment as mustread	3	0	3	7
Click on the mustread lens	10	5	25	24
Tag comment as idea	16	16	11	10
Click on the idea lens	11	10	41	32
Percentage of the time spent on the idea-centric view	36	27	36	36

Table 6. Frequency of actions performed using Procid.

One interesting pattern from Table 6 is that G1 and G2 used the features with the same relative proportions as G3 and G4, but less overall. One explanation is because G1 and G2 used the status quo interface first and, once assigned to use Procid the next week, did not discover its features as quickly as those who used it first.

Opportunities for Improvement

To improve Procid, participants identified wanting better support for comments that contain multiple names or criteria (n=5), better awareness and centrality of the provided features (n=3), and the ability to define an aggregate score for the proposed names. Future work should also address unexpected behaviors observed in the study. For example, one behavior identified by the interviewees was participants positively rating their own ideas, which obviously did not carry much weight. For example, I10 said: "*...I saw there was like three pluses for somebody and I was like oh somebody really likes this idea, and I looked and it was their idea. So, if you are doing such a thing, like three pluses is really good when we were doing* *it, that might confuse people ... that plus feature kinds of need some sifting, you need something to be able to turn that off so you can see what other people think of other people's ideas.*"

DISCUSSION

From both studies, we found support for the six consensus strategies implemented in Procid. There was strong support for S4 (evaluate and decide according to criteria) and S5 (maintain visual summary of agreement and disagreement). The relevant features in Procid were frequently used (e.g. the idea-centric view and criteria interactions) and reported as a distinct advantage of the tool, and the ratings of Procid for the associated tasks were higher than the status quo interface. There was support for S1 (promote perception of valued contribution) as participants rated Procid higher for tracking each other's contributions (ideas, criteria, comments). From Study 1, we found support for S3 (build on relationships and seek expert advice), as community members were able to use the invitation feature of our tool to locate at least one member to include in a discussion who may not have been otherwise considered. S6 (mark and revisit influential points) was supported as the lenses were frequently applied and Procid was rated higher for filtering key comments. Finally, little support was found for S2 (express concerns in a constructive manner). The 'tone' dialog in the tool was accessed, but the comments did not contain an overly negative tone to begin with and therefore the comments were not revised. Despite promising results, our studies focused on perceptions of and experiences with the consensus-based features in Procid. Additional studies are needed to assess how these features are used to shape discussions and how their patterns of use may change over time, with larger groups or with different design problems.

The two studies conducted reported on measures that could be immediately collected (e.g. survey and interaction data). Future field studies should also measure the longer-term impact of a tool such as Procid on a community. For example, measures could include changes in membership duration and turnover, changes in patterns of community discourse, and other health metrics [26]. One challenge of conducting such a study is gaining a critical mass of users [17]. One possible way to approach this challenge is to plant seeds of use that grow over time. For example, the creator of an issue could be given the option of requiring that Procid (or a similar tool) be used for the discussion. Alternatively, the community could identify a subset of threads (e.g. on a particular topic) that would use the tool by default for a period of time. In either case, involving the community in the design of the tool and considering their feedback would help create 'buy-in' and reduce resistance to its adoption. For example, participants in our first evaluation suggested adding a discussion about Procid on drupal.org. This would allow the community members an opportunity to suggest, comment on, and understand the features of our tool.

The implementation of Procid requires knowledge of the structure of the HTML code in a discussion in order to track and manipulate it. We extracted the information necessary to support the discussions in one community, Drupal. This step would have to be repeated to support discussions in other communities. It is also possible with minor extensions to support stand-alone discussions (those not linked to any existing community) in the tool.

Procid was inspired by and targets discussions about design issues, particularly in the UI domain. However, the design of the system should generalize to any situation in which distributed participants need to propose and debate concrete proposals for solving problems, e.g. to name a startup. The system is not tied to the type or content of the discussion.

Procid encourages recommended practices of consensus building, e.g., the first comment on a proposed idea should be positive and even critical points should be written in a constructive tone. We believe, in time, some behaviors encouraged by the constraints introduced in our tool would become integrated into the practice of the community. In addition, for practices that cannot be easily integrated into the tool, communities could include training for consensus building as part of the onboarding process [11].

Our system provides features useful for consensus building, but it is up to the participants to decide how to use these features during the discussion. Even if fully utilized, there is no guarantee that consensus will be reached or that users are satisfied with the experience of the discussion. Finally, there may be situations in which the consensus building approach is not desirable, e.g., participants may be reluctant to concede individual influence to the collective good. In such cases, the use of a tool such as Procid may still aid participants by better organizing the discussion.

CONCLUSION

Reaching consensus is important for distributed design discussions, yet the discussion platforms commonly used do not provide mechanisms for building consensus. Our work has made three contributions to close this gap. First, we built a novel system (Procid) that demonstrates interaction and visualization features for bringing consensus building strategies into distributed discussions. It provides a system design pattern that existing discussion platforms can mimic to better promote consensus building. Second, we extracted and shared consensus building strategies from the literature that can shape the design of systems like Procid. Finally, we reported results from two evaluations showing that users found the main features of the tool useful for consensus building and perceived the tool to be more effective for consensus relative to a status quo discussion platform.

One immediate direction for future work is to conduct a longer study probing how the use of our system affects consensus building in authentic design discussions and how different user categories such as designers and developers utilize the system to meet their needs. Another direction is to integrate more consensus building strategies into the tool and compare how the addition of those strategies affects the discussion experience and outcomes. A third direction is to refine and extend Procid's interface to better support consensus building based on the user feedback collected.

REFERENCES

1. AlchemyAPI *Sentiment Analysis http://www.alchemyapi.com.*
2. Alonso, S., et al. Using Visualization Tools to Guide Consensus in Group Decision Making. *WILF*, 2007, 77 - 85.
3. Angwin, J. and Fowler, G. A. Volunteers Log Off As Wikipedia Ages. *The Wall Street Journal* (Nov. 23, 2009), pages A.1.
4. Applegate, L. M., et al. A group decision support system for idea generation and issue analysis in organization planning. *CSCW*, 1986, 16-34.
5. Avery, M., et al. *Building united judgment: a handbook for consensus decision making*. The Center for Conflict Resolution, Madision, Wis., 1981.
6. Baccianella, S., et al. SentiWordNet 3.0: An enhanced lexical resource for sentiment analysis and opinion mining. *LREC*, 2010, 2200-2204.
7. Balakrishnan, A. D., et al. Do Visualizations Improve Synchronous Remote Collaboration? *CHI*, 2008, 1227-1236.
8. Biehl, J. T., et al. Impromptu: a new interaction framework for supporting collaboration in multiple display environments and its field evaluation for co-located software development. *CHI*, 2008, 939-948.
9. Birnholtz, J. P., et al. An exploratory study of input configuration and group process in a negotiation task using a large display. *CHI*, 2007, 91-100.
10. Briggs, R. O., et al. Toward a Theoretical Model of Consensus Building. *Americas Conference on Information Systems*, 2005.
11. Choi, B., et al. Socialization tactics in wikipedia and their effects. *CSCW*, 2010.
12. Conklin, J. and Begeman, M. L. gIBIS : A Hypertext Tool for Exploratory Policy Discussion. *ACM Transactions of Office Information Systems*, 6, 4 (1988), 303-331.
13. DeSanctis, G. and Gallupe, R. B. A Foundation for the Study of Group Decision Support Systems. *Management Science*, 33, 5 (1987), 589 - 609.
14. El-Gayar, O. F. and Fritz., B. D. A web-based multi-perspective decision support system for information security planning. *Decis. Support Syst.* , 50, 1 (2010), 43-54.
15. Faridani, S., et al. Opinion space: a scalable tool for browsing online comments. *CHI*, 2010, 1175-1184
16. Friedman, R., et al. The Positive and Negative Effects of Anger on Dispute Resolution: Evidence From Electronically Mediated Disputes. *Applied Psychology*, 89, 2 (2004), 369-376.
17. Grudin, J. Groupware and social dynamics: Eight challenges for developers. *Communications of the ACM*, 37, 1 (1994), 92-105.
18. Horowitz, D. and Kamvar, S. D. The anatomy of a large-scale social search engine. *WWW*, 2010, 431-440.
19. Kelley, T. and Littman, J. *The Art of Innovation: Lessons in creativity From IDEO, America's Leading Design Firm.* Doubleday, New York, NY, 2001.
20. Ko, A. J. and Chilana, P. K. Design, Discussion, and Dissent in Open Bug Reports. *iConference*, 2011, 106-113.
21. Kriplean, T., et al. Community, consensus, coercion, control: cs*w or how policy mediates mass participation. *GROUP*, 2007, 167-176.
22. Kriplean, T., et al. Supporting reflective public thought with considerit. *CSCW*, 2012, 265-274.
23. Kriplean, T., et al. Is this what you meant?: promoting listening on the web with reflect. . *CHI*, 2012, 1559-1568.
24. LLWC *Linguistic Inquiry and Word Count. http://www.liwc.net.*
25. Luther, K., et al. Pathfinder: an online collaboration environment for citizen scientists. *CHI*, 2009, 239-248.
26. Matthews, T., et al. *Community insights: helping community leaders enhance the value of enterprise online communities*. 2013.
27. Oehlberg, L., et al. Showing is sharing: building shared understanding in human-centered design teams with Dazzle. *DIS*, 2012, 669-678.
28. Pioch, N. J. and Everett., J. O. Polestar: collaborative knowledge management and sensemaking tools for intelligence analysts. *CIKM*, 2006, 513-521.
29. Shum, S. J. B., et al. *Hypermedia Support for Argumentation-Based Rationale*. 2006.
30. Sidaway, R. *Consensus Building*. Scottish National Rural Partnership, Edinburgh, 1998.
31. Susskind, L., et al. *The Consensus Building Handbook*. Sage Publications, Thousand Oaks, CA, 1999.
32. Tegarden, D. P. Business information visualization. *Communications of the AIS*, 1, 4 (1999).
33. Willett, W., et al. CommentSpace: Structured Support for Collaborative Visual Analysis. *CHI*, 2011, 3131-3140.
34. Yasuda, M., et al. Color and facial expressions. *Journal of Vision*, 7, 9 (2007), 946.
35. Zilouchian Moghaddam, R., et al. Consensus building in open source user interface design discussions. *CHI*, 2012, 1491-1500.
36. Zilouchian Moghaddam, R., et al. Ideatracker: an interactive visualization supporting collaboration and consensus building in online interface design discussions. *INTERACT*, 2011, 259-276.

Content and Network Dynamics Behind Egyptian Political Polarization on Twitter

Javier Borge-Holthoefer **Walid Magdy** **Kareem Darwish** **Ingmar Weber**
Qatar Computing Research Institute
Doha, Qatar
{jborge, wmagdy, kdarwish, iweber}@qf.org.qa

ABSTRACT

There is little doubt about whether social networks play a role in modern protests. This agreement has triggered an entire research avenue, in which social structure and content analysis have been central –but are typically exploited separately.

Here, we combine these two approaches to shed light on the opinion evolution dynamics in Egypt during the summer of 2013 along two axes (Islamist/Secularist, pro/anti-military intervention). We intend to find traces of opinion changes in Egypt's population, paralleling those in the international community –which oscillated from sympathetic to condemnatory as civil clashes grew. We find little evidence of people "switching" sides but observe clear changes in volume with both pro- and anti-military camps becoming more active at different stages.

Our work contributes new insights into the dynamics of large protest movements, specially in the aftermath of the main events –rather unattended previously. It questions the standard narrative concerning a simplistic mapping between Secularist/pro-military and Islamist/anti-military. Finally, our conclusions provide empirical validation to sociological models regarding the behavior of individuals in conflictive contexts.

Author Keywords

Egypt; Twitter; mobilization; polarization; opinion switch

ACM Classification Keywords

J.4 Social and Behavioral Sciences: Sociology

INTRODUCTION

When Time magazine nominated the anonymous protester as the Person of the Year in 2011, it was already clear that online technologies occupied (and occupy) a central spot as the backbone of modern civil protests. Beyond that cycle of turmoil, subsequent events have only reinforced such impression. Public availability and down-to-the-second temporally resolved data have given Twitter an incomparable advantage in addressing important questions, for instance how social networks actually facilitate the emergence and diffusion of protests [18], or how their contents change in time.

This is of particular importance in the Middle-East and North Africa (MENA) region, where chronic political unrest is combined with a speeded adoption of online technologies. Furthermore, the rapid growth of social networking sites since 2011 shifts away from typical social and entertainment uses of online media, towards those that are more political and civic [21]. Indeed, recent turmoil in MENA countries has provided good case studies for online interaction: Iran (2009), Tunisia, Lybia, Egypt and Bahrain (2011), Palestine and Israel (ongoing Gaza conflict) and Syria (2011-present), have witnessed social revolts, violence and even some government changes. And in all of those, online social networks have been claimed to have a key role.

Since 2011, Egypt's society is known to be highly polarized with the two dominant poles typically labeled as "Islamist" and "Secularist". On top of this, the country has experienced much political upheaval during the past year. In such heavily polarized atmosphere, the movement named "*Tamarod*" (meaning *Rebellion* in Arabic) was incepted in Egypt aiming to overthrow president Morsi a few months into his presidency. The efforts of the movement culminated in mass demonstrations and counter-demonstrations on June 30, 2013 and resulted in military intervention (coup or revolution[1]) to displace Morsi on July 3, 2013. The military takeover and ensuing opposition to it has led to significant tension and much violence. As a result, a new pro- *vs.* anti-military intervention dimension has emerged. This latter axis has been widely considered in mass media to be aligned with the previous polarization, in the sense that Islamist/Secularist coincide with anti-military/pro-military, respectively. However, during the violent aftermath of the army's ascent to power, some observers speculated that some of the supporters of the military intervention might have changed their opinion, due to what is mostly viewed –including international observers– as excessive use of force against protesters, with at least several hundred killed.

In this paper, we examine how these events have transpired on Twitter and some of the underlying phenomena. One angle that we are particularly interested in is one of changes in volume or "loudness" of different political camps over time

[1]Different political camps use different terminology to refer to the events surrounding the military intervention on July 3, 2013.

CSCW'15, March 14–18, 2015, Vancouver, BC, Canada.

http://dx.doi.org/10.1145/2675133.2675163

and if these were driven by opinion changes. This question is partly motivated by the fact that "the winds turned" several times for the Muslim Brotherhood, and foreign governments were also struggling to decide which side to support [1].

In particular, we attempt to address some inter-related research questions which –we hypothesize– can be tackled using large amounts of Twitter data. First, we examine whether "opinion switching" between both camps can be detected and estimated. If so, we can move on and question further whether perceived opinion changes are due to (i) people actually switching sides, or (ii) the relevant camps becoming increasingly louder or more muted.

In quantifying the answer to these questions, we learn about the underlying psychological and sociological mechanisms which are at play in conflictive contexts. For instance, it might be more benefitial –or less costly– for an individual to withdraw from an ongoing conflict than to actually switch sides: with a similarly minded social neighborhood, an actor is faced with the "volunteer's dilemma" (in this case, who switches side first); from which the rational outcome is to become mute [10].

Beyond partial accounts, we approach these questions both from the structural (network) side and the semantic (content) side. Concerning content, we used a set of manually labeled hashtags to build a pro- or anti-military-intervention classifier, which is used to classify tweets based on its textual content. On the network side, we used retweets of hand-labeled seed users to derive a Secular *vs.* Islamist leaning for users. We apply our methodology on a set of nearly 6 million Arabic tweets crawled between June 21 and September 30, 2013. From these, we reconstructed the network of Twitter users who authored tweets in the collection, and we crawled all meta information for 120,000 users along with their latest 3,200 tweets prior to December 2013. All the tweets and Twitter user IDs in our collection are publicly available[2], so that researchers can replicate the exact dataset we used for possible future studies.

We are well aware that studies conducted solely on Twitter data have certain limitations and drawbacks. From a general point of view, Twitter can not be regarded as *the* voice of civil society. As a matter of fact, Twitter (and online social networks in general) have been adopted by a minority in these societies. Furthermore, the adoption of these new technologies are not uniformly spread, which implies that the data are, most probably, biased. And yet, we are confident that our study stands on a reliable ground. Though limited, Twitter is a valuable monitor of social dynamics and it is doubtless an influencing actor in modern societies, partially shaping the flow of information among individuals and, in many occasions, performing as an agenda-setting actor. Methodologically, our longitudinal approach tracks not absolute values (raw signal), but rather relative changes (first derivative of the signal) which diminish the impact of inherent biases. Whereas biases are expected to strongly impact the absolute level of, say, Morsi support on Twitter, trends and the direction of *changes* in this level are expected to be more robust.

We find that despite –or because of– the dramatic and violent events there is very little evidence of users changing sides or "switching". We look at switching between Secularist and Islamist camps and between pro-military and anti-military camps. Our network and content analyses indicate that less than 5% of users switched sides. Instead, the main narrative seems to be one of pro-military intervention and Secular users being dominant in terms of volume leading up to July 3, and anti-military intervention and Islamist users gaining in volume afterwards. Furthermore, in contradiction to the dominating narrative in mass media, the correlation between being a secular and a supporter of military intervention is far from perfect. However, some correlation was noticed between being an Islamist and against the military intervention.

EGYPT'S *COUP D'ETAT*: TIMELINE

In this section, we summarize the major events that unfolded in Egypt during the summer of 2013. In general, we can distinguish three major periods: the lead up to the June 30 protests; the military intervention on July 3; and the aftermath of the intervention, including the violent crackdown against the Rabia sit-in. The chronology should help in understanding the conflict in the time period that we cover. We also invite the reader to have a look at a Wikipedia article on the topic[3] and an Al-Jazeera interactive timeline tool for the Egyptian turmoil[4] for more information.

The major events were as follows:

- **Late April, 2013:** A movement named *Tamarod* started in an effort to force the Egyptian president Mohamed Morsi out of office. The movement, which called for mass protests on June 30, 2013, claimed to have collected 22 million signatures by June 29. It was aided by strong media support and major power and gas crises [5]. Tamarod is often branded as a Secularist or pro-military movement.

- **June 28 and 30:** Large anti-Morsi protests take place in Cairo and across the country. Counter-demonstrations in support of Morsi also begin with major sit-ins in Rabia and Nahda squares. The sit-ins continue non-stop until they are disbanded on August 14. Morsi supporters are often branded as Islamists.

- **July 1:** The military issues a two-day ultimatum to the Egyptian president to accept the demands of Tamarod and to call for early presidential elections.

[2] `http://alt.qcri.org/~wmagdy/EgyMI.htm` Only IDs are provided in order not to violate Twitter's terms and conditions.

[3] `http://en.wikipedia.org/wiki/2013_Egyptian_coup_d%27%C3%A9tat`

[4] `http://www.aljazeera.com/indepth/interactive/2013/08/201381712263798l237.html`

[5] `http://www.spiegel.de/international/world/egyptian-army-gives-morsi-of-muslim-brotherhood-a-48-hour-ul html`

- **July 2:** The president, in an address to the nation, concedes to some demands from Tamarod. However, he refuses to step down or to call for early elections [6].
- **July 3:** General Sisi, the head of the military, orchestrates a coup to overthrow the president, suspend the constitution, disband the elected legislature, arrest Morsi's most prominent supporters, and shutdown pro-Islamist television stations. A new interim president is appointed. Protests in support of Morsi continue and grow.
- **July 8:** Clashes between security forces and anti-coup protestors erupt in front of a National Guard compound leading to many deaths.
- **July 24:** General Sisi asks his supporters to demonstrate, so as to obtain a "mandate" to fight "possible terrorism".
- **July 26:** Pro-military protests take place in Tahrir square in response to General Sisi's demands.
- **July 27:** Clashes between security forces and anti-coup protestors erupt near Rabia square, leading to the death of dozens (mostly demonstrators).
- **August 14:** Security forces crack-down on the sit-ins, leading to the death of hundreds of anti-coup protesters. Demonstrators attempt to establish new sit-ins, but these are as well violently disbanded.
- **August 16:** Major anti-coup protests take place, leading again to the death and arrest of many protesters.

Besides the previous specific dates, protests and clashes are intensified on Fridays (prayer day for Muslims) with continuing sit-ins in Rabia and Nahda squares up until August 14.

RELATED WORK

For a helpful contextualization of our work, we focus on three research avenues. First, a general framework is that of temporally resolved social dynamics, i.e. works in which scholars attempt to track the evolution of social phenomena (as opposed to a static snapshot). Within this area, we highlight the studies that zoom in on political events: the growth of grassroots movements, recruitment processes and (bi)polarization of opinions. A second major area –indeed with much work devoted to it– is that of the Arab world, digital media and/or the political/civic use of it. Third, we briefly discuss sociological accounts of opinion dynamics –"switches" and silencing.

In the first line of research, it is possible to identify some works which provide longitudinal accounts of political (protest) events. Some examples are the work by Borge and collaborators [9] (devoted to the growth of the "Indignados" movement in Spain) or González-Bailón *et al.* [19] (recruitment processes again in the 2011 protests in Spain). But closer to the current approach, we pay attention to Weber *et al.*'s work [36, 37], who explore the bipolar political scenario in Egypt (Secular *vs.* Islamist). To do so, they track the retweeting behavior from certain seed users as a signal to deduce a user's political orientation. Furthermore, they transfer the polarity from users to hashtags based on usage patterns – such that a hashtag is tagged as Islamist, Secular or "neutral". In doing so, the authors provide a means to assess real-time online polarization. They provide anecdotal evidence that the increases in this polarity score anticipate periods of political violence.

Needless to say, polarization has been a focus of interest before. Starting with the NOMINATE score [32], to quantify the statement that U.S. politics follows a 1-dimensional left-to-right schema, much research has followed. Focusing on digital media and U.S.-centered politics (i.e. left-*vs.*-right polarization), Adamic *et al.* [4] and Conover *et al.* [12] capitalized on data from the blogosphere and Twitter respectively. The time-resolved retweet graphs constructed from our data set present some similarities to Adamic's work; and yet, the temporal dimension is missing in these articles.

Second, there is a large body of work on the so-called Arab Spring, some of which zoom in on the Egyptian Revolution in particular. These depart from the present work insofar they typically include some discussion on the role of social media during the protests and the revolution, but do not use data from social networks (nor Twitter in particular) to approach polarization or major events. A notable exception is work by Mostak [29], who tests the political hypotheses that "Islamism in an ideology of the poor" with online data. To approach the question, he looks for geographical correlations between census information for income and house value/size, and estimates for how much Islamist activity on Twitter there is originating from a particular region. Down to conflictive situations, we find a plethora of works devoted to the Arab Spring –as the expression "Twitter Revolution" was coined and settled in mass media: some examples can be found in [24, 34, 6, 31, 23, 7], often from a qualitative point of view or relying on surveys. With the use of data from blogs, Al-Ani *et al.* [5] explore alternative news sources –beyond the government-supplied versions of events. However, none of them quantifies online polarization, or provide a longitudinal point of view. Other countries and conflicts have of course caught the attention of researchers, such as Tunisia [39] and Palestine [38]. Closer to this work, Choudhary *et al.* [11] performed time-resolved sentiment and response analysis to Twitter activity during the events in 2011, that eventually led to the displacement of Mubarak and the onset of a transitional period. Apparently, they used English tweets coming from Egypt and relevant news sources. In our work, we focus on Arabic tweets –clearly underrepresented in scholarly articles– to better model people in the region.

Finally, we find literature that focuses on the monitoring of opinion changes and the existence of online "silent crowds". Far from the political debate, some researchers have tried to tackle the fundamental differences between the "vocal minority" and the "silent majority" [30]. In this work, a *caveat* is placed to consider the significant differences between those highly active online media users –who dominate the ongoing discussions over social networks– and the vast majority of

[6] `http://english.ahram.org.eg/NewsContent/1/64/75538/Egypt/Politics-/Egypts-Morsi-defies-calls-to-step-down,-offers-opp.aspx`

people who participate much less frequently. The same line of argumentation is found in Venkataraman *et al.* [35]. A step closer to our politically motivated work, Lin *et al.* [25] exploit sentiment analysis to track political opinions in U.S. – although their method is intended for general purposes. Common to our framework, a real-time, evolving opinion-shift account is offered. Finally, on a more theoretical ground, the work by Chenoweth *et al.* [10] suggests that there are indications that, in a conflictive environment, members of opposing groups do not necessarily switch sides to tip the balance in favor of one of the groups, but they may merely withdraw their support.

DATA COLLECTION

Collecting Relevant Egyptian Tweets

We collected Arabic tweets in the period between June 21, 2013 and September 30, 2013. This period covers the major events in the aforementioned chronology. We used Twitter4J APIs[7] to collect the tweets matching the query "*lang:ar*", (so as to retrieve Arabic tweets). On average, the number of collected tweets per day was 3 million. The Arabic text of the collected tweets was pre-processed using state-of-the-art normalization technique for social Arabic text [15] to facilitate later filtering. The normalization includes letter normalization, diacritics removal, decorative text replacement and word elongation compression.

To extract the tweets that are relevant to Egypt, we constructed a rich set of Boolean queries that cover different facets of Egyptian politics. The set contained 112 requests that represent key players in the Egyptian political sphere: government representatives, political parties, opposition leaders, media anchors and the Twitter accounts of some relevant players. Each Boolean request is prepared to handle different spellings of names, acronyms, and nick-names used by different political groups. As such, an enriched set of queries underlies every request in order to retrieve relevant tweets from the Arabic news platform TweetMogaz[8] [26, 16]. TweetMogaz automatically generates news about Egypt, taking Twitter as the source. By default, the platform uses 84 queries and applies an adaptive tracking algorithm to enrich them, relying on ongoing news [27]. For this work, we manually revised the automatically enriched keywords to ensure a high precision and recall. On top of that, we also considered context keywords, i.e. relevant to that particular period: "revolution", "June 30", "coup", "Rabia" and "massacre". This extra set was picked by two native Egyptian, who regarded these words as most meaningful to the studied turmoil episode.

The number of extracted tweets matching those queries during the mentioned time window was 5.9 million. To ascertain the accuracy of the matching items, we manually judged a set of 500 random tweets, from which only 5 were assessed as not relevant, rendering a 99% estimated accuracy. Figure 1 shows the volume of tweets collected on the filtered set over time. As expected, major events led to peaks in the number of tweets on the days they occurred. There is clear mapping between the peaks in Figure 1 and the events listed in the timeline section (see above), which hints at the fact that Twitter is –among others– a faithful and sensitive monitor of real-world (offline) life.

Collecting Users' Network Data

We identified Twitter accounts that authored/retweeted more than 10 tweets in our collection, to find out their network information for network analysis. In doing so, we guarantee that the monitored users did engage, at some time or another, the ongoing crisis in Egypt. This led to the identification of nearly 120,000 Twitter accounts, out of roughly 1 million in our collection of Egyptian tweets. For each user, we extracted their network information, which comprehends the number of followers, friends and, most importantly, the last 3,200 tweets they authored or retweeted. These latest tweets allowed us to measure the network dynamics of each user through their activities including retweets, mentions, or replies to other accounts. The resulting information exceeded 750GB of user data and more than 300 million tweets for these users. Table 1 summarizes the obtained tweets data collection.

CONTENT-BASED ANALYSIS OF TWEETS

In this section, we describe the analysis we conducted on tweets, based on their textual content. To this end, we built a supervised classifier that groups tweets according to their content, i.e. whether they express support (pro-MI: pro-military intervention) or opposition (anti-MI) to the military intervention, plus a "neutral" category as well. We use this classifier to measure the response to the events in the time window of interest. Later, we deepen our analysis to track for possible opinion changes at the individual level.

Classifying Tweets as Pro/Anti-Military Intervention

The design of the classifier comprehends three main steps. First, we constructed lists of seed hashtags that are either exclusively or predominantly used by either of the two groups. Then, we expanded those lists to identify more tweets that could potentially belong to either group. Finally, we employed a supervised method to classify the tweets.

For the first step (seed lists), we extracted the most frequent hashtags in our collection, which were then tagged as either most likely pro-MI or anti-MI group. The rest of hashtags were neglected. Briefly, we assumed pro-MI hashtags to express support for the army, calls for a regime change or a *revolution* (as opposed to *coup*), opposition to Morsi or his regime or attacks against the Muslim brotherhood. Conversely, the group of hashtags categorized as anti-MI expressed maligning the members of the Supreme Council of Armed Forces (SCAF), the usage of *military coup* (as opposed to *revolution*), expression of support for Morsi or his regime, or rejection to the crackdown against the sit-ins. The lists contained the highest frequent 150 hashtags for each polarity, see Table 2 for some examples.

With the seed lists at hand, we heuristically classified tweets in our collection as belonging to the pro-MI or anti-MI groups if they exclusively contained hashtags belonging to the corresponding lists, for either of the groups. If a tweet contained no

[7] `https://code.google.com/p/tweet4j/`

[8] `http://www.tweetmogaz.com`

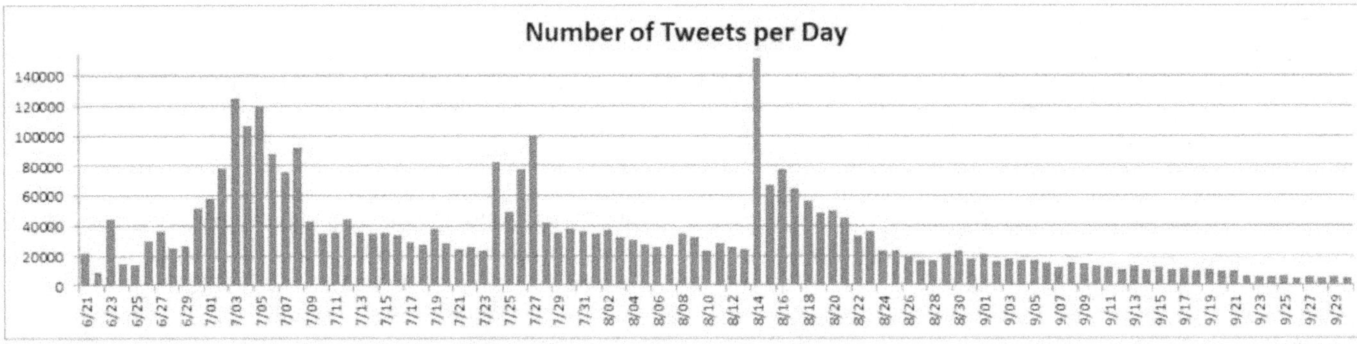

Figure 1. Distribution of the collected tweets about Egypt over time

Data	Description	Included Information	Size
Egyptian tweets	Egyptian tweets between June 21 and October 1, 2013	Tweet ID, text, Twitter user, and Timestamp	5,902,086 tweets
User Data	Profiles of Twitter users with more than 10 tweets in the Egyptian tweets set.	Username, screen name, ID, number of followers and followees. List of last 3,200 posted tweets by the account (prior to the mid of December 2013)	121,003 profiles. Recent 3,200 tweets per profile

Table 1. Tweets data collection used in our study

hashtags indicating polarity or contained hashtags from both lists, it was discarded. Using the filtered tweets, we identified new words and hashtags that exclusively appeared in either group, but not in both. We recursively added these words and hashtags to their respective lists. We repeated this expansion step four times. The resultant lists for the pro-MI or anti-MI group lists contained 1,105 and 1,487 words and hashtags respectively. Exploiting these final filtering lists, we constructed a subset of the tweet collection containing 12% of the tweets in the whole dataset.

Finally, from the filtered tweets subset we randomly selected 500 tweets containing hashtags from each list. These 1,000 tweets were manually verified and judged as exclusively belonging to pro-MI, anti-MI or neutral. Judgments were performed by two Egyptian Arabic speakers, who are keenly aware of the situation in Egypt. The inter-annotator agreement between them was above 93%. In case of disagreement, the annotators discussed over the tweets until consensus was reached. After this process, the agreement exceeded 96%. For the remaining tweets (33), one of the judgments was selected at random. Table 3 shows the distribution of the 1,000 tweets over the three groups. We used a multi-class Support Vector Machine (SVM) classifier to classify tweets as pro-MI, anti-MI, or neutral. We employed the SVMLight Multiclass implementation [13] for classification. We used the following features: word unigrams, word bigrams, and hashtags. We performed 20 fold cross validation over our 1,000 labeled tweets where each fold (containing 5% of the examples) was used for testing and the 19 other folds (containing 95% of the examples) were used for training. The average accuracy for the folds was 87.0% with a standard deviation of 3.4%. Table 4 shows the classifier confusion between the guessed and actual tags.

Pro-MI		Anti-MI	
Hashtag	Translation	Hashtag	Translation
#ارحل_يا_مرسي	Step down Morsi	#noscaf	No SCAF (army)
#السيسي_البطل	Sisi the hero	#السيسي_خائن	Sisi traitor
#ثوره_٣٠_يونيو	30 June revolution	#ضد_الانقلاب	Against coup
#الاخوان_الكاذبين	Muslim brotherhood liars	#مذبحة_رابعة	Rabia massacre

Table 2. Examples of seeding hashtags used for Pro/Anti-military classifier

Pro-MI	Neutral	Anti-MI
35%	9%	56%

Table 3. Distribution of tags in training/test set

Though the undetermined tweets may contain pro-MI or anti-MI tweets, our interest focuses on finding the distribution of tweets belonging to both groups over time. Thus we favored precision. Figure 2 plots the proportion of tweets that were classified as opposing (anti-MI: blue) or supporting (pro-MI: orange) the military intervention over time. As illustrated in Figure 2, before the military intervention on July 3 the proportion of tweets belonging to the pro-MI group was dominant (55% to 75%). After July 3, pro-MI tweets witnessed a significant drop, while anti-MI tweets rose substantially. This can be attributed to many different reasons that we attempt to analyze in the next section.

Given the content of our filtered collection, we analyze the top used hashtags by each group over time. We do so in order to understand the topics of interest for each of the groups and how they evolved in response to major events. We identified the 30 hashtags that achieved the highest per-day volumes for any of the days in the full period, for both groups. We eliminated hashtags, such as *#Egypt*, that were mentioned everyday, achieving the highest aggregate volume over all the

	guess		
Truth	Pro-MI	Neutral	Anti-MI
Pro-MI	**0.817**	0.064	0.119
Neutral	0.125	**0.736**	0.139
Anti-MI	0.054	0.022	**0.924**

Table 4. Confusion between truth and guessed labels for classes

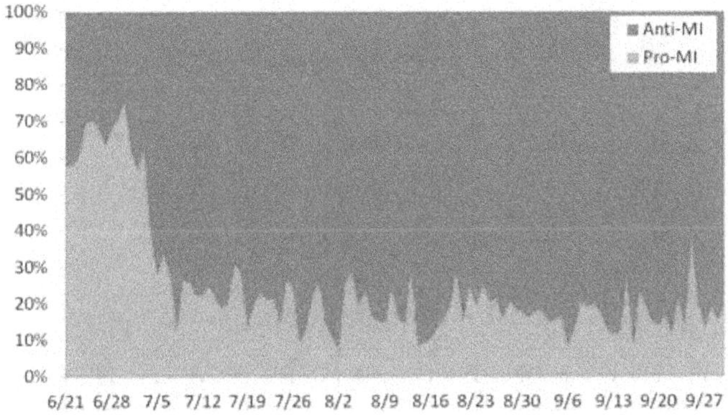

Figure 2. Proportion of tweets per day according to polarity of supporting/opposing military intervention

days –but never exhibited a burst in volume for any given day. Using this scheme, a hashtag that is mentioned 10,000 times in one day is more important than another that is mentioned 1,000 times daily over a span of 100 days. A hashtag showing a spike in volume would likely indicate changes in topics or interest for groups. Figure 3 shows the number of occurrences of the identified 30 hashtags in the period of study. The upper panel shows the most frequent hashtags on the pro-MI group, while the lower panel is devoted to the most frequent ones on the anti-MI group. Surprisingly, the overlap between hashtags representing the topics discussed by each group is almost nonexistent. Only four (out of 30) hashtags are in common in the two groups (*#Morsi*, *#Sisi*, *#Rabia*, and *#Beltagy*). However, the use of these hashtags were different in scale, time periods, and sentiment.

Upon inspection of the tweets and hashtags of the pro-MI group, they are focused more on individuals and organizations. The top hashtag is *#Morsi*. The use of the tag peaked around his ousting on July 3, and the relative volume of the hashtag for the rest of the period continued to be high. Similarly, tweets critically mentioning *#Ikhwan* (Muslim Brotherhood) persisted with relatively high volume for the whole period. *#Tamarod* peaked around Moris's deposition, but dwindled quickly afterwards. Other pro-MI tweets belonging to persons or organizations included support for *#Sisi* (the head of the military), attacks directed at *#Tawakkol_Karman* (Yemeni Nobel prize laureate who was critical of the military takeover) or joy at the arrest of *#Beltagy* (former parliamentarian and a prominent anti-MI figure). Other prominent hashtags can be found related to criticism towards the sit-ins in *#Rabia*, with a peak on August 14, and of the *#subway_sit-in*, with a peak on September 15.

Anti-MI tweets and hashtags instead focused mostly on events, particularly those involving violence and loss of life (*#National_Guard_Massacre*, July 8), *#Rabia_Massacre*, *#Rabia*, *#Rabia_Adawia_Massacre*, *#Rabia_Crackdown_Massacre* (July 27 and August 14) and *#Dilga* (September 16). They also include hashtags for announced protests on specific days or weeks, with activities against the military (*#Defeating_the_Coup* on July 8; *#Egypt_against_Coup*, August 2; *#Last_Friday*, August 8; or *#People_Protecting_their_Revolution*, September 6). The most mentioned individuals in tweets where *#Morsi*, mostly around the time of his ouster, general *#Sisi*, distributed over the entire period, and *#Beltagy*, around the time of his arrest.

Detecting Users Polarity Switching

With a reliable classifier at hand, which provides content-based polarity classification, we can observe the changes in polarity at the Twitter user-level over time. A user polarity switch means that a user who was tweeting pro-MI tweets at t_0 moved to authoring anti-MI tweets at $t_1 > t_0$, or viceversa. We apply this analysis to understand whether this was the reason behind the large decline in the number of pro-MI tweets after the military intervention on July 3 as shown in Figure 2 and the increase in anti-MI tweets.

Two hypotheses are compatible with the observed pattern changes, namely: people switched camps in response to events; or, simpler, one camp became quieter while the other becoming louder. We envisage that the latter is the mechanism behind the phenomenon –in accordance with previous literature [10]. And yet empirical evidence is lacking in a violent context, thus the relevance of the present work.

Detecting switch in user's political leaning requires a minimum number of tweets of that user over the studied period to monitor his leaning over time. The confidence of detecting a switch in leaning increases the larger the number of pro/anti-MI tweets are examined for a given user: more tweets supply more evidence of the user's leaning. Unfortunately, most of the users in our collection did not have large number of tweets classified as pro/anti-MI. Therefore, we relied on a small portion of users who had at least n classified tweets, $n \in \{5, 10, 15, 20\}$. Examining leaning switch of users based on only 5 tweets might be inaccurate, however this leads to the examination of more users in our test set; whereas examining users with at least 20 tweets in our collection leads to a smaller test set, though yielding a higher confidence.

To consider a user polarity switch, we examined the first and last third of tweets for the user. If the average polarity changed from the first third compared to the last third, we assume that the user swapped her leaning. Otherwise, we consider that the user held a coherent (stable) opinion over time. Figure 4 reports the percentage of used switched from anti-MI to pro-MI, or vice versa, and presents the number of users examined in the analysis for different values of n. As shown, for all n values, which reflects different confidence levels, the number of user switching sides are minimal, where it did not exceed 5% of the total number of users examined. For example, the largest percentage when $n = 5$, out of 21,312 users examined, only 970 switched from pro-MI to anti-MI, and 280 switched from anti-MI to pro-MI. The percentage of switching is even less for larger n values, indicating that the higher percentages for smaller n might causes by random

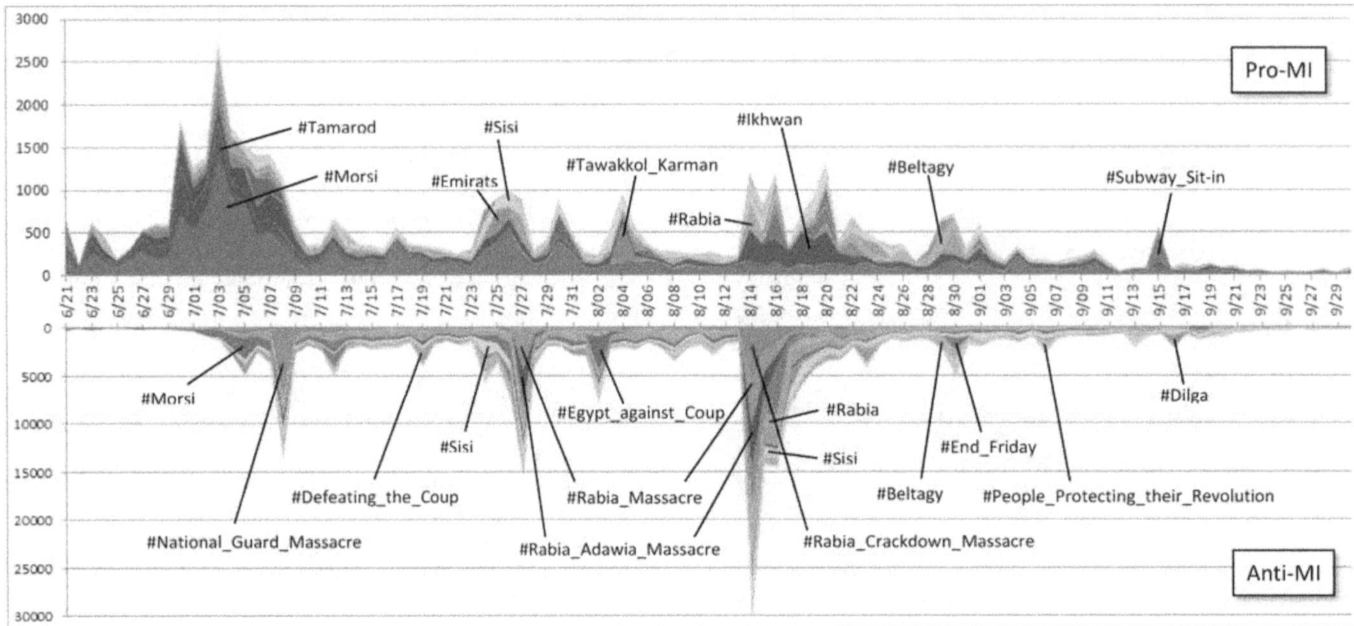

Figure 3. Number of occurrences of the most outstanding 30 hashtags appeared in the pro-MI (upper) and anti-MI (lower) tweets between 21 June and 30 Sep. 2013. Note the scale for the anti-MI plot, which is 10 times the scale of the pro-MI graph. Presented hashtags are translations of the original Arabic ones.

noise in the classifier. In all the switches, the number of users switched against the military intervention are at least triple the number of users switched to support the military intervention.

Our "first third, last third" schema is admittedly an arbitrary one. There are, however, at least two good reasons to proceed in this way. First, an opinion change might not occur in a sudden way, but rather progressively (as events unfold). Thus, it is necessary to focus the attention on the initial opinion state and the final one, with some unobserved time in between. In doing so, we avoid the presence of noise that might "contaminate" our output. For this reason, a $\frac{1}{2}$ – $\frac{1}{2}$ schema would not yield a reliable result (despite its providing larger statistics). In the opposite extreme, a more refined method would be to consider a small initial and final tweeting period (first $\frac{1}{10}$th, last $\frac{1}{10}$th, for instance). We would have obtained a more robust result, at the expense of poor statistics.

Table 5 presents some example tweets (translated from Arabic) for users who switched their polarity. Example 1 in the table is for a Twitter user who was calling for protests against Morsi on June 21, and then he was calling for participation in a march against what he called the military coup on July 19. Similarly, the second example is from pro-MI to anti-MI. On July 4, he expressed approval for the overthrow of Morsi, but then on July 24, he attacked General Sisi[9] for his request for a "mandate". The final example is for a user who switched from anti-MI to pro-MI, where the user showed some solidarity for protestors against military intervention, then after two and half months he showed support for Sisi and opposition to Morsi.

[9]"Sisi" also means pony in Arabic.

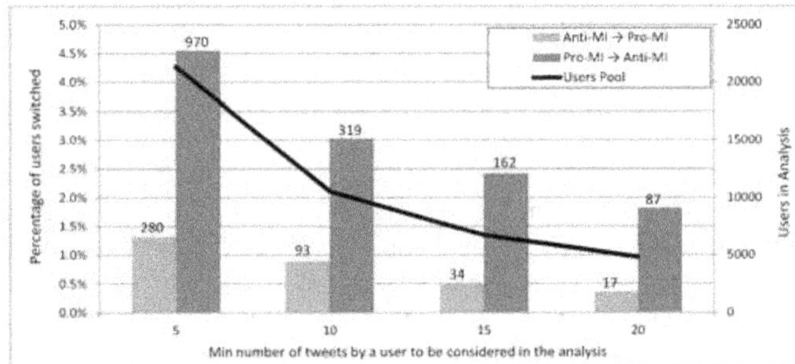

Figure 4. Percentage of users switched from one polarity to the other, and the number of users used for the analysis of switching for different values of n

Although the detected user switches are interesting, they can overall be considered anecdotic: the majority of users tend to express stable opinions. Thus, it can be concluded that the significant changes in polarity proportions in Figure 2 are due to supporters of military intervention becoming quieter and the opponents becoming louder.

NETWORK-BASED ANALYSIS OF TWEETS

From the data collected we built a sequence of temporally-evolving networks (one per day). In these networks, a weighted directed link (i, j, w) is laid between two nodes if user i retweeted a previous tweet by j a number of times w. We used a 3-days overlapping sliding window scheme, where the network on day t is obtained by aggregating 3 days of activity, i.e. retweets from $t-1$ to $t+1$; and the network on day $t+1$ spans from t to $t+2$, and so on. This has some advantages, namely: a 3-day wide aggregation guarantees that retweeting patterns will reflect a certain stability –away from

Switch	Date	Tweets (*English translation*)
Pro-MI → *Anti-MI*	June-21	We will continue to revolt till we reach freedom. Gathering revolution from Alexandria to Cairo to oust Morsi, the sheep.
	July-19	The Mohandseen march is closing the main streets till the police station #No_to_military_coup
Pro-MI → *Anti-MI*	July-04	Everybody, Morsi is displaced. Damn brotherhood who pretend to be Muslims. Long live Egypt
	July-24	I thought you were a Sisi (meaning: pony), but it turned out that you were a fox #Sisi_is_calling_for_civil_war
Anti-MI → *Pro-MI*	July-15	#Egypt_coup gas bombs are thrown inside the Fath mosque and people are trapped inside #Egypt_coup
	Sep-28	Please share the photo of Saied Qotb when he was arrested in a box like the one general Sisi put Morsi, the sheep, inside

Table 5. Sample tweets of Twitter users who switched polarity

the noisy immediacy of events; also, the overlapping scheme allows for a finer tracking of ongoing events.

In general, the sequence of retweet-reconstructed networks exhibit some fairly constant global topological properties. As preliminary steps, "silent" nodes were removed and the (weakly) giant connected component was extracted (typically containing over 95% of the original nodes). Density ($\sim 10^{-4}$), average degree ($2 \leq \langle k \rangle_t \leq 5, \forall t$) or clustering ($\sim 10^{-3}$) display small differences across time. The networks are thus very sparse and highly disassortative, in the sense that a few Twitter users get most of the retweeting activity, with hardly any presence of triadic closure.

Community Sizes

In this work, one of the main motivations was to adopt a network approach to track polarity evolution over time. In this direction, we disregard global (like the ones above) or microscopical (node-level) properties, to focus on changes at the meso-scale or group level. To do so, we applied a well-known community detection technique, namely label propagation [33], as implemented in the C-coded *igraph* network analysis package [14]. This algorithm has some highly desirable features. Apart from obtaining significant values in the modularity optimization process (the higher the modularity Q, the better the quality of the resulting partition), label propagation delivers excellent performance in terms of memory and time.

The algorithm runs with some predefined constraints. First, we use a list of seed users for whom the partisan leaning is out of any doubt, both in the Secularist and the Islamist side [37]. Part of the list was taken from Mostak [29] with additional entries compiled in 2013 by an Egyptian expert[10]. Second, we limit the number of possible communities to two –since we track for a bipolar political scenario in Egypt. Admittedly, it is possible that the network structures (over time) allow for better, higher-Q partitions with more than two communities, but that is beyond the scope of this work. Also, though Secularists and pro-MI group members do not necessarily align, Islamists were more likely to be in the anti-MI group than Secularists, as we show later. To provide an even more efficient running time, we fed the network at time t with the labels obtained in the previous snapshot $t-1$, when possible (thousands of users enter and leave the network at each time step, in the latter case nodes are unassigned initially, and the algorithm eventually imposes the corresponding tag on it).

[10]Due to largely differing degrees in popularity, the list of seed users boils down to Mohamed ElBaradei (@ElBaradei; Secularist camp) and Muhammad Morsi (@MuhammadMorsi; Islamist camp); the rest of the list has secondary effects on the output of the algorithm.

Under these considerations, the label propagation algorithm yields in general high modularity Q values: the average Q-value per snapshot is $Q = 0.4340$ with very few variation, $\sigma_Q = 0.0150$. This implies that in terms of partition quality, communities remain fairly constant over time. To have a solid standpoint regarding the quality of this result, we have generated (and Q-optimized) 100 surrogate versions of the first snapshot. That particular snapshot has an actual $Q = 0.4431$, whereas its random counterparts achieve an average $Q = 0.0468$ with $\sigma_Q = 0.091$. This means the actual Q corresponds to a z-score of 4.3151, i.e. it indeed represents a significant, far-from-random partition.

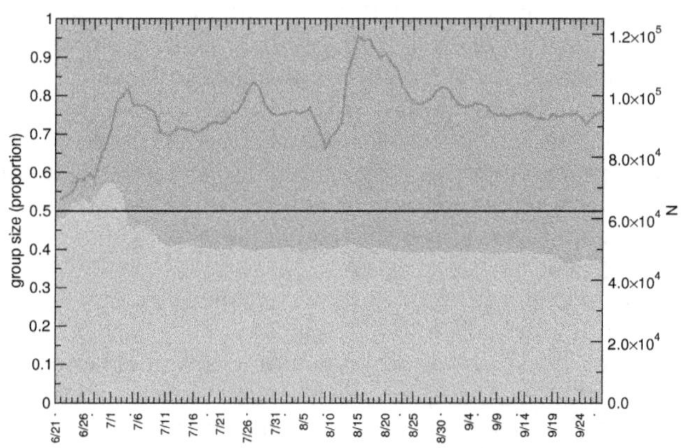

Figure 5. Community sizes corresponding to Islamic (blue) and secular (orange) leanings. The red line tracks the size of the network each day. Dots on the x-axis represent Fridays.

Figure 5 offers a time-resolved view of community size evolution. During the first days of the time window –and up to the military intervention date– Secularists outnumbered Islamists in the retweet network. On July 3, there was a crossover, and the number of Islamists remained larger until the end of the period under study. Even in bursty periods, where the network slices underwent severe changes (note for instance network sizes –red line in Figure 5– around mid-August), Secularists did not (proportionally) recruit newcomers, whereas the Islamist camp did. Unsurprisingly, the network size fluctuated over time, specially as critical events unfold.

Note that it would be overly simplistic to assume "one Twitter user, one vote" and that Twitter user counts perfectly match the proportion in society [28, 22, 17]. This holds both for network-based measures as for content-based measures. Still, the trends in relative sizes of the two camps might be more robust against selection bias and other skews.

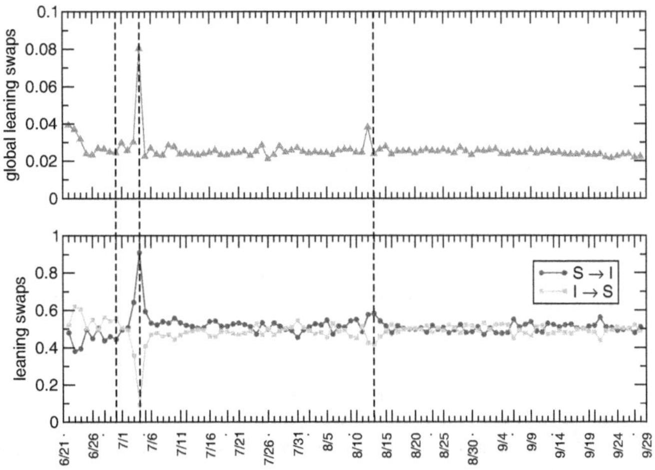

Figure 6. Leaning switches occur at a very low rate (top panel; hardly 3% of switching over time, with a few exceptions on key dates). Also, whenever swapping behavior exists, the direction of these swaps are evenly shared between parties (again, with some exceptions on key dates). Dots on the x-axis represent Fridays.

Global Switching (Islamist vs. Secular)

As stated above, the Islamist dominance of the retweeting scene beyond the 3rd of July is clear. The question remains whether secular sympathizers switched to Islamist positions (as they overwhelmingly belong to the Anti-MI group), thus feeding the growth of the Islamist group as observed in Figure 5. To check this, we measured the global switch ratio (Figure 6, top panel) as the number of observed label switches (from $t-1$ to t), over the total amount of common nodes in the networks corresponding to $t-1$ and t. Notably, switching remained at a very low level with a single exception (July 3) when it climbed up to 8%. In the lower panel of the same Figure, we show the proportion of swaps in either direction, across time. Again, most of the time there is an evenly distributed amount of switching in both directions (from Secular to Islamist, and vice versa) with a noteworthy exception on July 3, when 90% of the switches occurred from a secular to an Islamist position. Though this could be due to actual ideological turnover, it might also just point out that the focus of attention –as expressed through retweeting behavior– is temporarily shifted towards the Islamists –whose president is ousted on that day.

Leaning histogram vs. Tweeting Activity

Besides a longitudinal (across time) view of the leaning evolution, we aggregated all this information to provide soft labels per user. This was easily done either for the whole episode (June 21 – September 30) or for some limited period of interest $[t_0, t_f]$. For each user, we calculated his soft label by adding up every time he was assigned an Islamist leaning and normalizing this value by the total number of times he had been present in the network over time. Thus, an $l_i = 1$ label means that user i was tagged as an Islamist for the whole period under consideration. Labels can take values in the interval $0 \leq l \leq 1$. In Figure 7 we placed these soft labels in a histogram (0.05 bin width; note log scale in the histogram counts axis), to get a global view of the leaning landscape during the unfolding of events. Top panel corresponds to soft labels in the pre-coup period (June 21 – July 3). During this first period, seculars (leaning = 0) and moderate actors ($0 < l < 0.5$) outnumber Islamist ($l = 1$) and pro-Islamic moderates ($0.5 < l < 1$); also, average activity in each of these classes is significantly higher for the former. This scenario drastically changes for the second period (bottom, July 4 – September 30), in which Islamists recruit many new users for their side, as well as the average activity increases. On the secular side, activity drops as the size of the party decreases in relative terms.

In coherence with Figure 5, the number of secular sympathizers is larger (top panel) during the pre-coup period (those with $l < 0.5$), but the opposite is observed for the post-coup period (lower panel). Furthermore, we computed the average strength (number of retweets) per user and per day within each bin (red line in each panel). Clearly, those with a secular leaning are (comparatively) much more active than Islamists during the initial period, but the activity level flattens afterwards –with a slight advantage for the Islamist side.

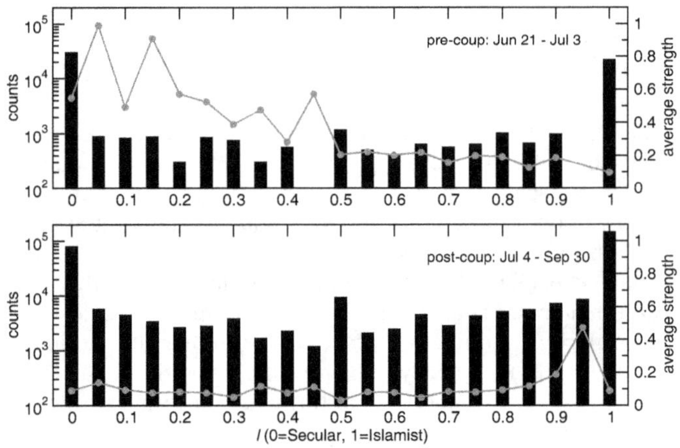

Figure 7. Polarization histograms and average per-day activity (red) for two different periods (pre- and post-intervention, top and bottom panels respectively). Note logarithmic scale for histogram counts (left).

DISCUSSION

At this point, we can attain a global picture of the temporal evolution of the events in Egypt during the time window of interest. On one hand, content-based analysis showed that some group *pro-MI* leaning tweets were flowing in Twitter, and they were especially dominant during the brewing days before the military intervention in early July. Group *anti-MI* activity became dominant soon after July 3, with increasing bursts as violent events unfold. On the other hand, political leaning in the retweet networks underwent a similar transition, i.e. Secularists constitute a larger and more active group up to the coup d'etat, but progressively decrease in number and activity thereafter. These two bipolar schemes (pro/anti-MI, Secular/Islamist) with similar trajectories may lead to the conclusion that Secularists have predominantly a pro-coup standpoint, while Islamist map onto an anti-coup opinion. Such was the general interpretation being projected in classic mass media during the summer of 2013 [2].

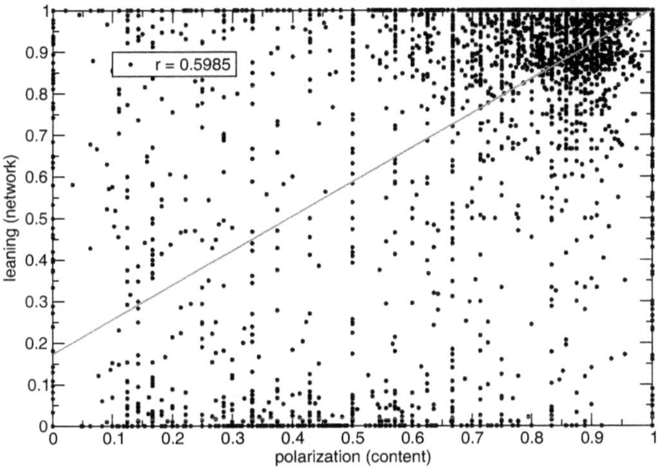

Figure 8. Network-based leaning versus content-based polarity. In the x-axis, lower polarization implies a pro-MI stance, while anti-MI contents are closer to 1. In the y-axis, low leaning values correspond to the Secular camp, whereas Islamists are mapped onto higher ones.

On closer inspection, the scenario turns out to be considerably more complex. If we confront (content-based) group pro/anti-MI polarization scores and (network-based) Secularist/Islamic leaning soft labels for each Twitter users, a relatively strong correlation is found ($r \sim 0.6$, see Figure 8). This means that the leading trend in our analyses (which, noteworthy, have been obtained exploiting different facets of the data) exhibits a significant alignment pro-MI-to-Secularists and anti-MI-to-Islamists; and yet such alignment is far from perfect: ideally, leaning and polarity should meet around the diagonal in the scatter plot. On closer inspection, most of the disagreement occurs on the Secularist side, whereas there seems to be a rather univocal coherence in the Islamist side. Secularists exhibit rather heterogeneous positions regarding the military intervention in the country's politics.

A possible conclusion is that anti-Morsi protests were in fact quite diverse. In this direction, what we labeled here as Secularists might actually be conformed by a heterogeneous collective, including seculars indeed, as well as people without political affiliations and even small groups of Islamists –not necessarily with a pro-MI leaning. On the whole, Islamists exhibited a solid anti-MI stance as the diverse contrarians progressively withdraw. As facts have evolved during this past year, our conclusions seem to grow stronger: indeed, the provisional government led by General Sisi has prosecuted Islamist figures, but also groups or individuals from other ideological stances [3].

Another observation that can be gleaned from our content- and network-based analyses is that switching between pro- and anti-MI groups, and between Secularists and Islamists, is rather limited. Most of the change in volume in observed polarized tweets seems to be mostly due to each group becoming louder or quieter as time progresses. This is consistent with the work of Chenoweth and Stephan [10] where they observed that members of opposing groups in conflict do not necessarily switch sides to tip the balance in favor of one of the groups, but they may merely withdraw their support.

CONCLUSIONS

In this paper we have analyzed how recent turmoil in Egypt in the period between June 21 and September 30, 2013 has transpired in Twitter. We examine the tweets from the perspective of Secularists vs. Islamists and from the perspective of pro- and anti-military intervention. The main lesson from our observations is that the military takeover on July 3 caused major quantitative (volume of polarized tweets), but not ideological (polarity swaps) shifts among Twitter users. Secularist and pro-military intervention Twitter users were very loud before the take-over, but became increasingly silent afterwards. Conversely, Islamists and anti-military intervention Twitter users become significantly louder after the takeover. Furthermore, a close inspection of our results indicate that the axis Secular/Islamist can not be trivially mapped onto a pro/anti-coup opinion –which was the dominant assumption in traditional media at the time of the military intervention. This is specially true for the Secularist-to-pro-MI projection, which is not as aligned as it was generally presumed. The development of the political situation in Egypt during the past year have confirmed our insights.

To reach such conclusions we have exploited two methods, which rely on different (and non-overlapping) aspects of our dataset: the semantic and the structural dimensions. Noteworthy, the trends observed from these varied methodologies converge, on a qualitative basis.

We are aware of the limitations of the present study. Besides the inherent biases in Twitter data [20], other arguments can be put forth. For instance, it is unlikely that an individual publishes a radical change of opinion through a single medium, i.e. such attitude has an associated social cost. Therefore, the availability of other sources (Facebook, blogs, etc.) would be highly desirable. We stress, however, the precise nature of the events we analyze here. We do not expect, in such bipolar scenario, that a Secularist might turn Islamist (or vice versa). But it is possible –and even *probable*, given the turn of the events– that Seculars who held high expectations for a government change, were afterwards deceived as violence and repression grew. Expressing such discontent is not as costly –if it is at all.

For possible future directions, one could analyze the motivation of users who switched polarity to understand reasons for people to change leaning. We could see some examples of users who withdraw support for the military intervention just after it occurred, others after the violent crackdown of the Rabia sit-in, and others who supported the military-intervention after opposing it in the beginning. This non-trivial switching temporal pattern resembles that of "complex contagion", for which a rich theoretical literature is available [8], in which early adopters (early switchers, in this case) pave the way for adoption (switching) cascades. Another essential work direction is to add an additional polarization layer to the Islamist/Secular classification. From the results we have obtained, there might be a missing polarity, which could match old regime supporters (Mubarak's regime). It is known that these were heavily involved in the June 30 protests, and are the strongest supporters of the army. Accounting for them would be interesting, and can give a more complete image of the situation.

On a general framework, the work contributes to an understanding of bipolarized societies –and these are not limited to Egypt: the underlying questions and methods are more widely applicable. The turmoil in Crimea and Eastern Ukraine, the ongoing conflict in Palestine or the Catholic/Anglican dichotomy in Northern Ireland might be other promising case studies.

REFERENCES

1. These are some news stories that illustrate how, as an example, the US administration has re-evaluated its position towards Mohamed Morsi and the Egyptian army over time: http://www.washingtontimes.com/news/2012/jun/24/obama-calls-to-congratulate-morsi-an-islamist-on-w/ http://www.theguardian.com/world/2013/jul/03/egypt-obama-us-mohamed-morsi-crisis http://www.theblaze.com/stories/2013/07/02/obama-calls-egypts-morsi-and-says-u-s-does-not-support-either-side http://www.aljazeera.com/indepth/features/2013/07/201371011352248980l.html http://www.forbes.com/sites/dougbandow/2014/01/20/pharaoh-al-sisi-takes-control-in-egypt-obama-administration-sacrifices-security-human-rights-and-democracy
2. See for instance http://www.project-syndicate.org/commentary/how-egypt-can-avoid-the-fate-of-algeria-in-1992-by–lvaro-d–vasconcelos
3. Prosecution in Egypt beyond the Muslim Brotherhood. Media and secular activists: http://www.aljazeera.com/indepth/interactive/2014/07/freeajstaff-days-jailed-journalism-greste-fahmy-mohamed-b-20147166544671591.html http://www.theguardian.com/world/2013/nov/27/egypt-secular-activists-arrested-protest-law http://www.bbc.com/news/world-middle-east-25484064
4. Adamic, L. A., and Glance, N. The political blogosphere and the 2004 u.s. election: divided they blog. In *LinkKDD@KDD* (2005), 36–43.
5. Al-Ani, B., Mark, G., Chung, J., and Jones, J. The egyptian blogosphere: a counter-narrative of the revolution. In *CSCW* (2012), 17–26.
6. Attia, A. M., Aziz, N., Friedman, B., and Elhusseiny, M. F. Commentary: The impact of social networking tools on political change in egypt's "revolution 2.0". *ECRA 10* (2011), 369–374.
7. Azab, N. A. The role of the internet in shaping the political process in egypt. *IJEP 3* (2012), 31–51.
8. Borge-Holthoefer, J., Baños, R. A., González-Bailón, S., and Moreno, Y. Cascading behaviour in complex socio-technical networks. *Journal of Complex Networks 1*, 1 (2013), 3–24.
9. Borge-Holthoefer, J., Rivero, A., García, I., Cauhé, E., Ferrer, A., Ferrer, D., Francos, D., Iñiguez, D., Pérez, M., Ruiz, G., et al. Structural and dynamical patterns on online social networks: the spanish may 15th movement as a case study. *PLoS One 6*, 8 (2011), e23883.
10. Chenoweth, E., and Stephan, M. J. *Why civil resistance works: The strategic logic of nonviolent conflict.* Columbia University Press, 2011.
11. Choudhary, A., Hendrix, W., Lee, K., Palsetia, D., and Liao, W.-K. Social media evolution of the egyptian revolution. *CACM 55*, 5 (2012), 74–80.
12. Conover, M., Ratkiewicz, J., Francisco, M., Goncalves, B., Flammini, A., and Menczer, F. Political polarization on twitter. In *ICWSM* (2011).
13. Crammer, K., and Singer, Y. On the algorithmic implementation of multiclass kernel-based vector machines. *The Journal of Machine Learning Research 2* (2002), 265–292.
14. Csárdi, G., and Nepusz, T. The igraph software package for complex network research. *International Journal Complex Systems* (2006), 1695.
15. Darwish, K., Magdy, W., and Mourad, A. Language processing for arabic microblog retrieval. In *Proceedings of the 21st ACM International Conference on Information and Knowledge management*, ACM (2012), 2427–2430.
16. Elsawy, E., Mokhtar, M., and Magdy, W. Tweetmogaz v2: Identifying news stories in social media. In *CIKM* (2014).
17. Gayo-Avello, D., Metaxas, P. T., and Mustafaraj, E. Limits of electoral predictions using twitter. In *ICWSM* (2011).
18. González-Bailón, S., Borge-Holthoefer, J., and Moreno, Y. Broadcasters and hidden influentials in online protest diffusion. *American Behavioral Scientist 57*, 7 (2013), 943–965.
19. González-Bailón, S., Borge-Holthoefer, J., Rivero, A., and Moreno, Y. The dynamics of protest recruitment through an online network. *Scientific Reports 1* (2011), 197.
20. González-Bailón, S., Wang, N., Rivero, A., Borge-Holthoefer, J., and Moreno, Y. Assessing the bias in communication networks sampled from twitter. *Social Networks 38* (2014), 16–27.
21. Governance, and Innovation Program, D. S. o. G. Arab social media report, vol. 1, issue 2. `www.ArabSocialMediaReport.com`, 2011.
22. Jungherr, A., Jürgens, P., and Schoen, H. Why the pirate party won the german election of 2009 or the trouble with predictions: A response to tumasjan, a., sprenger, to, sander, pg, & welpe, im "predicting elections with twitter: What 140 characters reveal about political sentiment". *Social Science Computer Review 30*, 2 (2012), 229–234.

23. Khamis, S. The transformative egyptian media landscape: Changes, challenges and comparative perspectives. *IJOC 5* (2011), 1159–1177.
24. Lim, M. Clicks, cabs, and coffee houses: Social media and oppositional movements in egypt, 2004–2011. *JC 62* (2012), 231–248.
25. Lin, Y.-R., Margolin, D., Keegan, B., and Lazer, D. Voices of victory: A computational focus group framework for tracking opinion shift in real time. In *WWW* (2013), 737–748.
26. Magdy, W. Tweetmogaz: a news portal of tweets. In *SIGIR* (2013).
27. Magdy, W., and Elsayed, T. Adaptive method for following dynamic topics on twitter. In *ICWSM* (2014).
28. Metaxas, P. T., Mustafaraj, E., and Gayo-Avello, D. How (not) to predict elections. In *SocialCom-PASSAT*, IEEE (2011).
29. Mostak, T. Social media as passive polling: Using twitter and online forums to map islamism in egypt. Master's thesis, Center for Middle Eastern Studies Harvard University, 2012.
30. Mustafaraj, E., Finn, S., Whitlock, C., and Metaxas, P. T. Vocal minority versus silent majority: Discovering the opionions of the long tail. In *Privacy, security, risk and trust (passat), IEEE 3rd International Conference on Social Computing (SocialCom)*, IEEE (2011), 103–110.
31. Oh, O., Eom, C., and Rao, H. Collective sense-making through the twitter service during the 2011 egypt revolution. In *ICIS* (2012).
32. Poole, K. T., and Rosenthal, H. A spatial model for legislative roll call analysis. *AJPS* (May 1985), 357–384.
33. Raghavan, U. N., Albert, R., and Kumara, S. Near linear time algorithm to detect community structures in large-scale networks. *Physical Review E 76*, 3 (2007), 036106.
34. Starbird, K., and Palen, L. (how) Will the revolution be retweeted?: information diffusion and the 2011 Egyptian uprising. In *CSCW* (2012), 7–16.
35. Venkataraman, M., Subbalakshmi, K., and Chandramouli, R. Measuring and quantifying the silent majority on the internet. In *Sarnoff Symposium (SARNOFF), 2012 35th IEEE*, IEEE (2012), 1–5.
36. Weber, I., and Garimella, K. R. K. #egypt: visualizing islamist vs. secular tension on twitter. In *ASONAM* (2013), 1100–1101.
37. Weber, I., Garimella, V. R. K., and Batayneh, A. Secular vs. Islamist polarization in Egypt on Twitter. In *ASONAM* (2013), 290–297.
38. Wulf, V., Aal, K., Abu Kteish, I., Atam, M., Schubert, K., Rohde, M., Yerousis, G. P., and Randall, D. Fighting against the wall: Social media use by political activists in a Palestinian village. In *Proceedings of the SIGCHI Conference on Human Factors in Computing Systems*, ACM (2013), 1979–1988.
39. Wulf, V., Misaki, K., Atam, M., Randall, D., and Rohde, M. 'On the ground' in Sidi Bouzid: investigating social media use during the Tunisian revolution. In *CSCW* (2013), 1409–1418.

Exploring the Ownership and Persistent Value of Facebook Content

Catherine C. Marshall and Frank M. Shipman
Center for the Study of Digital Libraries and Department of Computer Science
Texas A&M University
{ccmarshall,shipman}@cse.tamu.edu

ABSTRACT
In this paper, we present the results of a study examining 244 participants' attitudes about the value, ownership, and control of social network data. We use Facebook-based scenarios to elicit reactions to hypothetical statements about saving social network content that belongs to others, reusing, repurposing, and monetizing social network data, and removing social network content that is not specifically one's own. Participants also report on their own practices in each of these areas. Findings not only address issues related to ownership, but also explore the use of social networks as documentary records, and the discrepancies between participants' perceptions of how they would like their social network content to be used, and how it is actually used.

Author Keywords
Social networks; social media; saving; reusing; removing; monetizing; digital identity; documentation; records.

INTRODUCTION
Facebook has become a fixture in many people's online lives. Its social networking capabilities have made it a widely accepted and broadly used multi-purpose communication and content-sharing utility [38,43]. It may be a means of keeping a relationship alive [36], a way of seeking information from trusted sources [15], or a place to share emotionally resonant content [44]. Even when it is not foregrounded, many people see Facebook as an implicit constant in their online life and an important means of communication and contact maintenance [11].

As Zhang et al. point out, the online world is still highly volatile [43]. Even well-established services may suffer reversals of fortune. In the face of this volatility, we test participants' attitudes toward the data they have published or shared on Facebook and document users' attitude-shaping practices. We focus on Facebook users and Facebook data, because the service is well-known and fairly stable: participants are likely to have incorporated it into their everyday online lives and to have some investment in content they have shared, social ties they have represented, and profiles they have developed.

CSCW '15, March 14–18, 2015, Vancouver, BC, Canada.
Copyright 2015 ACM 978-1-4503-2922-4/15/03...$15.00
http://dx.doi.org/10.1145/2675133.2675203

In spite of Facebook's ubiquity and entrenchment as a social networking utility, in a recent study, Lindley et al. found that Facebook content was perceived to be of dubious long-term value [19], and, consonant with Zhao et al., that people deliberately curate an ahistorical digital presence in an effort to keep their self-representation current [45]. Follow-on work by Zhao and Lindley revealed that reuse of Facebook content in crafting exercises can change the perception of the material's value [44]. Thus we find ourselves asking, what are the sources of value in social networks, beyond their immediate communicative function? What do people feel they own and control in a co-constructed medium?

In this study, we investigate intertwined notions of value, ownership, and control of social network content. Specifically, we use scenarios and hypotheticals, a technique borrowed from legal education and case-based reasoning [28,32], to identify social norms associated with saving, removing, and reusing social network material in which they have a stake. We test concepts such as the effect of social distance, the difference between individual profiles and shared content, and whether personal data should be used for monetary gain (and by whom). We also ask participants to report on their recent use and curation of social network accounts.

Specifically, we are interested in discovering what people feel they can do with social network content they do not explicitly own, whether social network data can act in the role of archival records (in other words, the reciprocal question of how corporations and public institutions can use individuals' social network content), and the degree to which user-perceived rights deviate from legal reality.

We begin this paper by reviewing several areas of related work. We then describe the method we used to construct the study, recruit participants, and collect data; we also discuss some limitations on our results. Reports of current practice are woven together with quantitative responses to the hypotheticals, organized by the questions they answer. Finally we discuss the answers to our going in questions about ownership and control, as well as exploring the use of social networks as data.

RELATED WORK

Our research is primarily motivated by two confluent strains of related work. One stems from social media archiving, and is directed at answering the question, is there persistent value to the material that is created through and stored in Facebook? To answer this question, it is essential to understand the multiple ways in which Facebook is used, and what contributes to content volatility. The second has to do with ownership, and addresses the question of what people believe they can and should be able to do with co-created social media content. Tied in with these themes are three curation-focused areas: digital identity, privacy, and self-censorship, including questions arising from the deletion or removal of online content.

Social networks and value

Much of our digital identity is formulated and performed online in social media services such as Facebook [45]; in the name of keeping digital media current and digital identity closely curated, personal history is continually renewed and paradoxically destroyed [19]. But Lindley and her colleagues also discovered that users harbored skepticism about the long-term value of the content they have stored in Facebook [19]. To reinvigorate a sense of the content's worth, Zhao and Lindley found that if people crafted something from the content, they became more aware of its value [44]. Gulotta et al. are similarly investigating how value might be explicitly introduced by means of technologies designed to communicate this aspect of their digital possessions [9]. We are exploring value from several standpoints, both archival (value to others and value as historical records [8]) and pragmatic (what people would take with them if they moved to a new service, and whether they are comfortable with the content being monetized by corporate interests or by themselves).

Ownership of co-created social media

The flip side of content value is content ownership. If the content and the social network on services like Facebook has personal or professional value, then we can look at how this content and the social network can be used and reused by others. Previously, we have performed a series of studies looking at the social norms for online content reuse [22, 23, 25, 34, 35]. Generally, we have found a lax attitude toward saving online material, but a much more varied reaction to its reuse, attitudes which may diverge dramatically from law and policy, and which vary by media type and reuse context. Here, we are specifically investigating the reuse of the social graph in other settings.

Curating digital identity

Of course, much of the tension between what is current on services like Facebook, and what is of archival value, stems from a desire to create a robust digital identity. The need for self-representation drives many current identity practices, including a need to manage one's reputation (often seen as frustrating) [42, 40] and to use social media to potentially manipulate search engine results [21]. Farnham and Churchill have shown that people integrate or separate different facets of their online identities to varying degrees [7]; furthermore, sharing and deletion are guided by a sense of audience and social distance [37, 14]. Rainie et al. have established that people that people come and go from Facebook, in part due to curatorial fatigue [31]. These are practices that we used to guide our survey design.

Deletion (and the concomitant act of forgetting) is a valuable part of curation [27]. This may be situation-specific (e.g. after a breakup [33]), or it may be a general part of indicating what's current and what's not of one's online presence [19]. We ask about specific instances of removal to investigate the balance of fixity and fluidity of different portions of one's social network presence, and as a countervailing measure of value.

Finally, privacy is an important influence on many of the behaviors we examine here, especially when it comes to corporate monetization of personal data. Although there are efforts to help users understand their potential exposure [41], some Facebook users rely extensively on hiding in plain sight to achieve privacy through obscurity [13, 38], and attempts to monetize their data may make them feel more exposed (even if distinctions between private and public data follow user privacy settings).

METHOD

This study is implemented as a three-part questionnaire: first, participants responded to 12 demographic questions to characterize themselves. Next, a series of scenarios and 25 associated hypothetical actions were rated along a 7-point Likert scale (from *disagree strongly* to *agree strongly*) to help find the limits of what participants perceive as current social norms. Finally seven multiple choice and open-ended questions elicited participants' reports of their current social networking practices. Two comprehension questions were interspersed among the hypotheticals to help ensure that participants read carefully [15]. A final question asked participants if they would take another survey like this one. The 47 question survey was designed to be completed fairly quickly and to hold participants' interest.

The questionnaire was fielded as an Amazon Mechanical Turk (AMT) HIT. We have refined this technique over the course of four years through experience [24] and the careful application of best practices from the literature [10, 15]. We recruited workers who have at least a 95% acceptance rate for their past work, and pay them as long as they complete the questionnaire regardless of whether we use their data or not. We are conservative about the data we keep. A demerit system means that we discard a participant's data if two or more checks are violated, including: a wrong answer on a comprehension question; no answer or a nonsense answer to an open-ended question; overly brief work time (less than 50% of the average); or suspicious patterns in the Likert scale data (e.g. all responses are the same). In spite of these stringent criteria, we only had to discard data from 6 participants out of the 250 questionnaires administered, leaving us with data from 244 credible participants.

Participants

Current and recent US-based English-fluent Facebook users were recruited to participate in the study; we want participants to be able to understand the scenarios, and respond by reflecting on what they would do, given the situations posed in the hypotheticals. Triangulation among the initial participation requirements, a question in the demographic section of the survey, and another question in the practice section allowed us to verify that all 244 participants were indeed regular Facebook users (2 had recently deleted their accounts; the other 242 had one or more active accounts). Often participants used other social networking services too, including LinkedIn, Google+, Twitter, Instagram, Tumblr, Myspace, and Reddit.

Participants were active online, reporting a median of between 5 and 6 activities. Almost all used email and shopped online; nearly 70% shared videos. Most respondents (68%) had used the Internet for a decade or more.

In keeping with a trend of increased male participation on AMT, 52% of participants reported to be male. Consonant with prior surveys, almost half (48%) were born in the 1980s (although 13% were born in the 1960s or before and 24% were born in 1990 or later) and the group is predominately college educated (only 8% hadn't been to college). At 60/244 (25%), student participation is lower than usual, close to the lowest we have seen in our past AMT surveys. Thus participants in this study represent a population that is fairly young, well-educated, and Internet-literate, but not necessarily technical, nor invested in any particular technological outcome.

Scenarios and hypotheticals

Hypotheticals are a technique borrowed from legal education [28] and case-based reasoning [32]. We describe a basic situation with concrete details that we hope will be engaging for survey participants and will ground their reasoning in similar assumptions. Then a series of hypotheticals is proposed in which specific aspects of actions are varied to test which responses 'fall off a cliff'. For example, we might describe a scenario in which a character saves her profile to her local disk (say, because she intends to delete her account). Then we might propose that instead of just saving her own profile, she saves *some friends' profiles* locally. From there, we might propose that she saves *her friends' friends' profiles* locally, and finally that she saves a stranger's public profile to her local disk. In these hypotheticals, we vary the details in such a way that they are not predictable, thus circumventing the use of any heuristics or shortcuts in reasoning that participants might employ if they notice that the hypotheticals vary too regularly.

We develop the scenarios using situations we have encountered in previous qualitative studies, in published accounts, or in informally observed everyday practice. From there, we consider the features we want to test (for example, in H1-H4[1] shown in Figure 1a, the feature of interest is the effect of social distance on perceived ownership). We then construct a series of statements, changing aspects of the feature. We iterate over the design and language of the scenarios and hypotheticals, since it is important that they are relatable and understandable. Outside reviewers help us identify possible ambiguities in the language or word usages that might lead to misunderstanding. Monitoring early results (especially via the comprehension questions) is a final fail-safe to ensure participants are reading and understanding the scenarios as we intended.

Naturally, because they seek edges, the order in which the hypotheticals are presented can be important; the idea is to start with a banal premise and vary a feature until the statements become controversial. Even if we misjudge the order (for example, it might be more controversial to save one's friends' friends' private profile than a stranger's public profile), it is apparent in the data where we have violated social norms. Out of order statements are not necessarily harmful; they simply highlight "edges" where we did not expect them. Occasionally, to maintain participant interest, we ordered the statements from most controversial to the least. This has the effect of gradually backing off from controversial ideas until changes render them acceptable.

Analysis

The resulting data requires several types of qualitative and quantitative analysis. The Likert-scale data from parallel hypotheticals is compared using the Wilcoxon signed-rank test (a non-parametric test for comparing related samples) to handle the non-normal distributions. Responses in each category are graphed together to visualize trends. Hypothetical grouping generally reflects themes in the study: saving, removing, and reusing social network content either by moving it to a new service or monetizing it. Responses to open-ended questions about social network use have been open-coded using conventional qualitative methods to reveal primary and secondary themes; where possible, we have triangulated among answers to ensure consistency [38].

[1] In this paper, we use the notations H1 through H16 to refer to specific hypotheticals we tested in the study.

Limitations

Any recruiting technique and study population will bring with them inherent limitations on the reach of the results. We note several such limitations on our results. First, we are recruiting participants who may do surveys regularly and who have an interest in the fate of social media. Thus, they may have strong, well-developed opinions about the topic. Second, although the participants are not necessarily of a single socio-economic type [24], they are younger, better educated, and more technology-conversant than a random sample of the US population would be. Yet we were interested in reaching a diverse group of people who had familiarity with and investment in Facebook; we found the limitations introduced by using the Mechanical Turk platform to offer a reasonable trade-off for access to these users. Similarly, we consciously chose to limit our population to current Facebook users; it might be interesting in a future study to reach non-users, since policy questions necessarily affect them too.

We also recognize limitations with this method; we see it as validating and extending the results of earlier interview studies such as [45] and applying the methods used in [25,35] to extend those results to different content types. Accessing real social network data can further validate some of our claims (e.g. identifying unusual uses or which content types are most frequently removed). Although the scenarios are modeled on real-world behavior and have been carefully debugged, we recognize that some participants may not reach the expected interpretation of the situations that are the basis for the hypotheticals.

RESULTS

In this section, we bring together qualitative and quantitative results to explore four primary questions about ownership and value in social networks that we addressed via open-ended questions and hypotheticals.

The first question is connected with saving content. Past studies have shown that saving most types of content locally is primarily sensitive to limits imposed on the action. In other words, participants mostly react when they are told that someone hypothetically *can't* save something, rather than that they can. However, we suspect that some social network content—profiles, for example—may be different because they are so closely associated with identity. How much effect does social distance have on what a person can save? Does content type matter?

The second question stems from removal. Again, because social network curation is so closely associated with digital identity, will effects identified by past research be more pronounced? For example, do people feel they should be able to remove Facebook posts *about* them? Is permission necessary? Prior research has shown that it is important to allow people to untag Facebook posts about themselves [20]. They are concerned about the content's veracity and timeliness. We explore this idea by asking participants what they have removed from Facebook recently and what they would have liked to remove (but couldn't).

The third question pertains to reuse: many people are aware that they consent to a license agreement when they sign up for services like Facebook. They may even be aware that this license grants the service some ownership rights to their data. How do participants feel that this license—combined with the fact that the service is free—influences the service provider's (and their own) rights to reuse the data in a different service?

Ownership can also be seen through the lens of monetization. If Facebook owns your data, can they sell it to another company? Can users sell their data to another company? Should service providers be able to invade the more private reaches of users' personal data (e.g., private messages to other users) to help profile their interests for advertisers? We did not expose which of these data practices are currently in force; instead we asked participants what *should* be done.

Saving social networks and social network content

Saving is invariably the least controversial user action; many people feel they can download material from Internet services such as Flickr and save it with impunity, especially if they have no plans to share it further. But are all of the components of social networks perceived the same way, even those that are more tightly connected with digital identity? Not only do social networking services like Facebook support media sharing, they also encourage users to create rich profiles of themselves and represent their social networks. In turn, people see their profiles as something they have published just as surely as they have published more conventional content such as blog posts and photos [24]. The hypotheticals tested whether participants felt the same way about saving other people's profile content as they did other people's photos, and whether they felt that their social distance from the person mattered.

Susie has been using Facebook since 2005, when she was a college freshman. She has accumulated hundreds of friends, photos, 'likes', posts, and mail. She would like to delete her account, but keep her connections and the content she has posted. Before she deletes her account:

- **H1:** Susie should be able to save her Facebook profile, including who's connected to whom in her network of friends. **(H1: User can save profile and friend list)**
- **H2:** Susie should be able to save contact information for her friends' friends. **(H2: User can save friends' friends)**
- **H3:** Susie should be able to save the content associated with her account, including the pictures in her galleries and her message box (including email to/from her). **(H3: User can save account content)**
- **H4:** Susie should be able to save anything that she can ordinarily reach on Facebook, including pictures from her friends' and friends' friends' galleries. **(H4: User can save all encounterable)**
- **H5:** Susie should only be able to save photos from her friends' Facebook accounts if the photos are public. **(H5: User can save only public photos)**

Figure 1a. Scenario and hypotheticals to test features of saving

In the initial demographic section of the questionnaire, we asked participants the extent to which they had fleshed out their profiles. 71% felt they had normal profiles and 19% reported profiles with more details than normal. Only 10% had minimal profiles. Furthermore, 70% reported their profiles were either stable or growing. Although 30% reported reduced use of the service over time, by these results and others [31], participants seemed to leave their profiles intact. Thus participants were likely to be able to relate to the user described in the scenarios who has had a Facebook account since she went to college, and has a large social network with plenty of accumulated content. In the first set of hypotheticals, our user is now seeking a grown-up job and plans to delete her Facebook account for fear a prospective employer will scrutinize it closely. What can she save locally from her Facebook account? Figure 1a shows an abbreviated version of the scenario and hypotheticals (the labels used in Figure 1b are shown in bold), and Figure 1b shows the results of testing 1a's five hypotheticals.

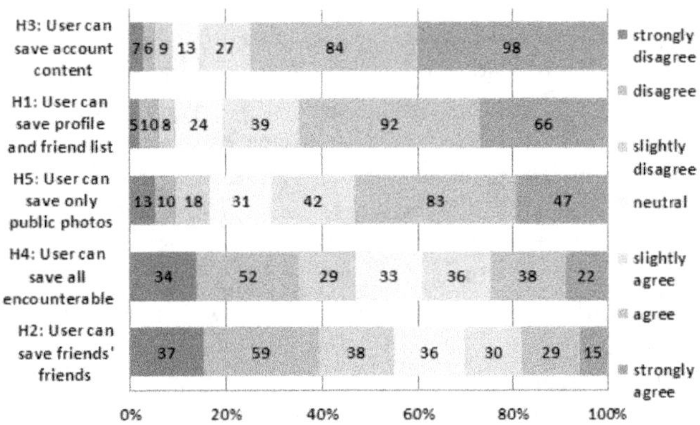

Figure 1b. The results of testing the saving hypotheticals

In this scenario, we are exploring three factors: the effects of social distance, the influence of privacy settings (since saving does not immediately compromise the owner's intent), and whether a profile is similar to (or distinct from) other types of content. Figure 1b shows the results. The strong agreement with statement H3 shows that participants see ownership extending to all of a user's personal content, including their profile. That H1 is less positive (but still positive overall) shows that users distinguish between the ownership of their own profile, and the interconnections among their friends: yes, they can save them, but there is reduced expectation of ownership (Wilcoxon $p=0.005$).

H2 increases social distance (friends of friends), and demonstrates that social distance strongly influences the acceptability of saving. H5 tests the idea that public content is more loosely owned than private. Indeed, participants generally felt it is okay to save public content, far more so than the comparable private content: being able to *reach* content in compliance with a privacy setting does not mean you can *keep* it (but if it is public anyway, you can). H5 is strongly significantly different from H1 (Wilcoxon $p=2.26E\text{-}08$) and H4 (Wilcoxon $p=3.77E\text{-}15$).

Removing social media content

Social network content is fairly fluid relative to other material published on the Internet [18,12]. Users add and remove content regularly. Removal is a significant manifestation of how ownership plays out through identity curation: it may be just as important to manage one's identity by taking things down as it is by adding new content and self-description. But is all removal equivalent? Is removing a photo from Facebook similar to removing a photo from elsewhere on the web? Or are there other concerns when the content is only visible to friends or acquaintances? Is removal of a photo similar to removal of a profile detail like a birthdate? As Das and Kramer found through their large-scale analysis of self-censorship on Facebook, removal is common: 71% of Facebook users in their sample had removed content [6]. We found self-reports of removal to be similarly common: 191/244 (or 78%) reported removing some portion of an account, including the whole thing. Table 1 shows responses to an open-ended question about what participants have recently removed from Facebook.

Content type removed	#	%
Photos	89	36.5%
N/A or nothing	53	21.7%
Posts/comments	53	21.7%
Profile elements	21	8.6%
Unspecified or 1-off	20	8.2%
Entire account	11	4.5%
Friends	8	3.3%
Links	6	2.5%
Game- or app-related auto posts	6	2.5%

Table 1. Recent episodes of content removal by type

There are four primary reasons participants offered for having removed Facebook content: (1) to curate material and keep accounts tidy (*I hard-deleted my old Facebook profile in August and created a new one in its place. I had too many photos and too many friends, and I wanted a 'fresh' profile/account.* [SN193]); (2) to maintain one's online reputation, either directly (*I removed several alcohol related pictures when I started to look for teaching jobs.* [SN024]) or indirectly, for fear an unpopular item will reflect poorly on the participant (*I removed one of my songs that I posted because I didn't have many likes on it...* [SN169]); (3) to reflect a revised understanding of privacy (*[I] removed [my] birthday as it is often a question on a multifaceted security question and answer* [SN011]); and (4) to respond to evolving knowledge about Facebook itself (*After it came out that my content was being monetized with no reimbursement to me, I deleted my entire account.* [SN061]).

Participants were fairly sophisticated about ways to remove unwanted content: not only did they delete items, they also modified privacy settings, untagged posts and photos, and sometimes replaced entire accounts to start over. Participants also managed "likes" and comments, especially since they can appear unexpectedly in search results [21].

We also asked participants what they wish they could've removed; this answer may reflect the character of items that they would ask to be withdrawn from an institutional Facebook archive [26]. Responses indicated that participants mostly felt in control of their social network content; 56% (137/244) said they have no need to remove anything beyond what they are capable of removing already. Thus it's not so much that participants always posted the right thing, it's simply that they feel capable of removing Facebook content they don't want to keep.

A few exceptions are worth noting. The most common is photos; almost one quarter (58/244) say they would have liked to have removed one or more photos, usually because a photo was unflattering; a few represented perceived privacy breaches (*I don't like being mentioned in others photos or having people with lower security than me able to post photos of my kids without having to ask my permission.* [SN166]). In most reported incidents with posts (26/244), removing the post wouldn't have done any good: *I was working for GNC and posted some things on twitter and didn't have my account locked. Needless to say, I was fired for the comments.* [SN227] Profile elements are less frequently a concern, because participants are fairly conscientious about their own privacy settings, although they reminded us that privacy settings may be circumvented via social coercion. SN088 reported, *For a background interview I thought an investigator was only going to search for my profile from a public computer but he actually forced me to login on his own computer....*

Hypotheticals tested four aspects of removal: removal of different constituent media types (e.g. photos versus posts), removing solo pictures versus group pictures, removing photos one has taken versus removing photos of oneself, and whether permission mitigates the other hypothetical conditions. Figure 2a summarizes these hypotheticals.

When Susie searches for her own name, she discovers that her Facebook friend Greg has mentioned her name in conjunction with a political protest:

H6: As part of her clean-up effort, Susie should be able to remove (not just untag) her friend Greg's post about her role in the political protest. **(H6: Susie can remove Greg's post)**

H7: Susie should be able to remove Greg's photo of her at the political protest, especially since there's no-one besides her in the photo. **(H7: Susie can remove Greg's photo of her alone)**

H8: Susie should be able to remove Greg's photo of her at the political protest regardless of who else is in the photo. **(H8: Susie can remove Greg's photo with others)**

H9: Susie should only be able to remove Greg's wall post about her role in the political protest if he gives her his permission. **(H9: Susie can remove post with Greg's permission)**

Figure 2a. Scenario and hypotheticals to test removal features

Because text elements (e.g., posts and profiles) seem so consequential—unlike photos, they remain vulnerable to search engines—we wondered if participants would be more sympathetic to our hypothetical job-seeker's desire to remove a post that might impede her job search. Figure 2b shows the outcome. A substantial proportion (65%) saw permission as a way to resolve uncertain ownership: H9 is viewed less disapprovingly than H6 (the same action without permission), Wilcoxon p=.007. The two photo hypotheticals, H7 and H8, test whether the outcome is influenced by reducing potential ownership conflicts—should Susie be able to remove a photo if she's the only one in it (and sees it as harming her reputation)? It does seem to matter whether she's the photo's only subject: the difference between the two hypotheticals is significant Wilcoxon p=3.24E-18.

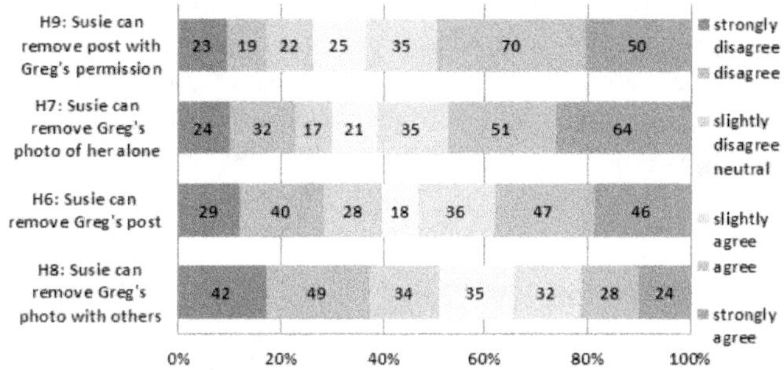

Figure 2b. The results of testing the removal hypotheticals

Reusing social networks

It is fairly easy to come up with realistic scenarios for saving or removing social network data. As our practice results demonstrate, participants readily identify examples of things they have saved or removed. It is more difficult to come up with reuse scenarios that are both specific to the social network setting and align with practice. So we have developed two types of reuse scenarios. The first type involves reuse of an entire account (by moving it to a new service), and the second type couches reuse of complex social network content as data, a form of social network reuse that is apt to be familiar to participants under the guise of 'big data' [1].

Reusing social network content in a different service

Re-entering one's social network data in another Facebook-like service may be seen as needlessly arduous and time-consuming, or it may be an opportunity for a fresh start. We asked an open-ended practice question about this type of reuse: "*If you were to move your social network (say from Facebook to Google+), what would you expect to take with you?*" Participants interpreted this question in several ways: Some thought we were asking what they wanted to take with them (i.e. what was valuable to them); others thought we were asking what they would be allowed to take with them (i.e. who owns the content). Still others speculated on the logistics of taking social network data with them: How would they be able to move this stuff? Would their friends be on the new social networking service too? It is likely that most participants thought of the question as a mix of all three, since they are difficult to usefully separate: you wouldn't care about moving something you don't value or something that is meaningless in the context of the destination service, such as a friends list if your friends aren't on the service.

The responses were coded to reflect how participants framed their answers. If participants enumerated content types, each was tabulated. Categories that subsumed others (e.g. "everything") did not contribute to counts of individual items; rather we tried to capture the general intent and emphasis of the answers.

The elements that the participants specified seem to depend on Facebook's overall role and value. If the service was used primarily as a communication tool, participants might view the accumulated content as transient and not worth moving (except possibly contacts). On the other hand, if Facebook acted a repository for heterogeneous personal information, participants might focus on moving the valuable portion of the content, e.g., photos and messages.

With those constraints in mind, Table 2 shows that over half of the participants (131/244) specifically wanted to take their photos with them (the count would be 155/244, over 63%, if "I want to move everything" answers are included). Some participants had considerable investment in visual media: *I have over 500 videos and thousands of photos on Facebook if I were to move I would expect to take those with me.* [SN217] They felt ownership of photos they'd taken or were featured in: *[I'd expect to take]... tagged posts and photos containing my name.* [SN191] A few anticipated a fight: *Any content I create and I purposely only upload photos with watermarks on them so even if facebook steals a photo everyone knows it.* [SN061]

Content type	# of responses	%
Photos	131	53.7%
Contacts/friends	85	34.8%
Nothing	50	20.5%
Profile information	39	16.0%
Everything	24	9.8%
Statuses	14	5.7%
profile photos	9	3.7%
Messages	9	3.7%

Table 2. What participants expect to take with them from Facebook, given the ability to select multiple options

Facebook's social network is also important to participants. Eighty-five participants specifically referred to wanting to take their contacts or friends with them (again, folding in the "everything" answers brings the count to 109/244, or 45%). A substantial portion of those who thought of Facebook as a communication tool explained that it wasn't important to move their contacts; they would be able to rebuild what they had on Facebook, especially since only a portion of their friends are current: *...A good bit of my contacts on Facebook I am no longer in contact with are not necessary.* [SN182]

Given the results of other explorations of sources of value in social networks [5,9,19,45], it is unsurprising that participants were less interested in moving content such as wall posts and messages. Profile information seems more valuable, if simply because it's time-consuming to rebuild it (and 'likes' may represent significant curatorial effort); still, only 39/244 (16%) singled out their profile as something they wanted to move, and 9 others (less than 4%) were specifically interested in retaining their profile photos. Similarly, only 9 participants (<4%) specifically said they wanted to move their messages; we might expect more participants to call these out if they were an important part of their Facebook assets.

Finally, we can look at the extremes, participants who said they expected to take everything with them and participants who said they expected to leave it all behind. Although only 24 participants (10%) said they expected to be able to take everything, many of those responses were the most passionate: *Everything, All of my photos and photos that I have been tagged in. All of my mail and messages. All of the comments on my pictures and things that I have shared. All of my links that I have shared on my wall since joining. Anything else on my wall others have shared, pictures. links ect... And all of my game activity and causes information.* [SN188] Several respondents had thought about things like their game activity and curatorial work (again, 'likes'). For some, this aspect of Facebook can represent a significant investment of effort: there is evidence that you are what you like [16]. A few even thought that the weight of the content was enough to keep them from moving: [*I would want to take*] *everything or I would not make the move...* [SN011] Of those who wanted to take everything, several explicitly referred to the content's archival value to them.

Twice as many participants were at the other extreme: 50 thought a move would offer a fresh start (*I would hope to start from a clean slate* [SN068]). Others thought it wouldn't be hard to rebuild their social network and that Facebook owned their content anyway (*...it's not their job to work with competitors* [SN205]). SN203 returned to the communication tool theme, saying that he would expect to take *Nothing if I can't remeber [sic] your name your [sic] not that important to keep.*

After she has a new job, Susie thinks it is safe to have a social network presence again. Following her closest friends, Susie decides to move to a new social networking service, Circles.

H11: Because Circles can automatically rebuild a person's social network from their profile on a different network, Susie can use her old Facebook profile (including links to her friends) to move to Circles. **(H11: User can move profile to new service)**

H12: Because Facebook technically owns the information she stored there, Susie cannot use her old Facebook profile to automatically build a new profile on Circles. **(H12: User cannot move profile to new service)**

Figure 3a. Testing the limits of what a user can remove with and without permission

Given this range of responses to the open-ended question, we might expect this varying perception of value to temper participants' responses to the two hypotheticals shown in Figure 3a, testing different justifications for being able to move (or not being able to move) social network data from one service to another. The first offers a pragmatic justification for reusing Facebook data, and the second reminds participants that the license agreement they signed might forbid this type of reuse.

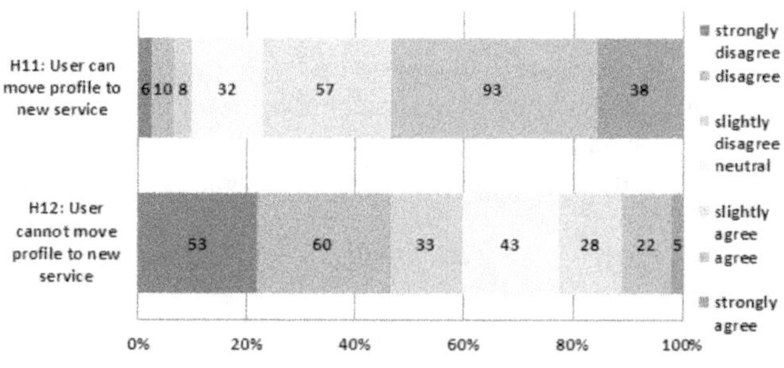

Figure 3b. The results of testing the two social network reuse hypotheticals

Of course, people who agree with the first hypothetical of the set don't necessarily have to disagree with the second. But many of them did. The majority of participants thought they should be able to move their social network data to a new service, and that the license agreement shouldn't prevent this type of reuse: their friends are their friends, not Facebook's (Wilcoxon p= 2.04E-22). This result makes sense when we refer to the practice data: only about 20% were willing to start fresh on a new social network.

Reusing social network content as data.

A second reuse scenario and set of hypotheticals explore the monetization of Facebook data by Facebook and by the user. Because many participants described themselves as having extensive Facebook profiles and user-contributed media collections, it is interesting to pose them as assets that might be valuable to another corporation. Figure 4a shows an abbreviated version of the data reuse scenario and hypotheticals.

Facebook's business model begins to falter. The company needs to develop additional ways to make money. Greg has been using Facebook for many years and has accumulated lots of data.

H13: Facebook should be able to sell the information in Greg's user profile to Amazon so Amazon can create a better profile of Greg's interests. **(H13: FB can sell info to Amazon)**

H14: Facebook should need Greg's permission to sell his profile. **(H14: FB needs permission to sell info)**

H15: Greg should be able to sell the information in his Facebook profile to Amazon to get a cash rebate on his Amazon purchases. **(H15: User can sell FB profile info to Amazon)**

H16: Facebook should be able to analyze the content of Greg's Facebook-internal communication so it can create a better profile of Greg's interests for its own use in selling targeted advertising. **(H16: FB can use internal messaging to improve ads)**

Figure 4a. Testing ownership and monetization

Figure 4b shows participants' reactions to the hypotheticals. Notice that requiring full permission before transferring the data (H14) is the only hypothetical that elicits a strongly positive reaction. But we know from other researchers' practical experience that permission is no panacea: a games archiving project made this assumption (that permission would be granted if requestors offered a polite explanation of their motivation); instead of granting permission, players often denied the request [30]. Given that Facebook data is likely to be personal too, it may be difficult for users to relinquish control of the data without reviewing it in detail.

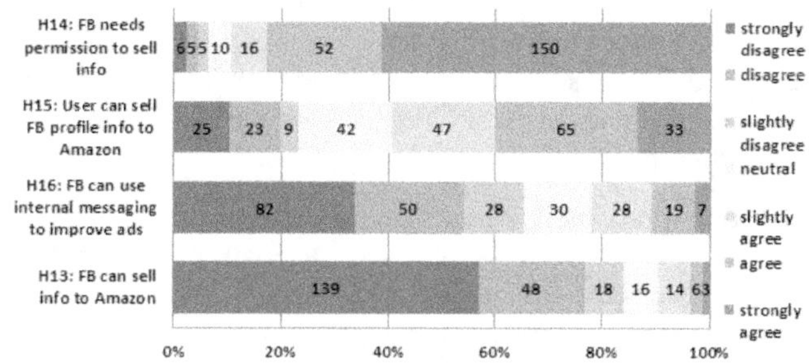

Figure 4b. Results of ownership and monetization hypotheticals

H15 suggests that Greg has sufficient control over his own data that he can sell it to another company (Amazon). This hypothetical is greeted with less enthusiasm than the first (Wilcoxon p= 1.97E-22). But taken together, the responses to both H14 and H15 suggest that users feel they should be able to exert a fair degree of control over what they have put into Facebook regardless of what they agreed to in the service's license agreement.

H16 mimics many modern social media services' personalization strategy: textual message content is analyzed to improve the match of advertising with users' interests. Nearly 75% of participants found this analysis objectionable, in spite of the fact that the participants probably use services that have already adopted this practice (H16 is strongly significantly different than H15, Wilcoxon p= 1.27E-19).

H13, which is based on the premise that Facebook would sell its data assets to Amazon, was the most objectionable hypothetical in our participants' eyes. Over 80% saw this hypothetical as negative, and over 55% thought it was very negative, again strongly significantly different from H16, in which Facebook reused the data internally for commercial purposes (Wilcoxon p= 2.72E-10). In the scenario, Facebook was foundering. Their only asset is the user data they have collected over the last decade. Yet participants were unhappy with the idea that the company might try to monetize this data. This result, taken together with the last set of hypotheticals, suggests that participants might be unhappy if Facebook decided to donate its data to an archive: it does not seem to be solely the monetization of personal data that participants are reacting to. Instead they may be objecting to the idea that if Facebook can use their data as a corporate asset, they are no longer in control of their personal data, and by implication, their own digital footprints [26].

DISCUSSION

What can we learn from participants' attitudes toward heterogeneous social network content? Certainly activities in services like Facebook shed valuable light on design. For example, Wang et al. have discussed the design implications of Facebook practices for privacy protection features [41] and Sas and Whittaker for removing content in the specific circumstances of a breakup [33]. But we believe that the social norms that are expressed through attitudes and practices should have important bearing on law and policy too.

Although practically speaking, ownership provisions are specified by a service's terms of use, users are seldom cognizant of what they consent to: at the outset, when they create an account, they are not able to foresee how they will use it, whether they are going to share five photos or 5,000 photos. They don't know who will look for their account or how it will be interpreted. Nor can they predict how and whether the service will sustain itself over the years: a company may discover alternate uses for user-contributed content or the service may be acquired. Spammers may find convenient ways to repurpose the data too. Users sign license agreements to gain access to a service; they often neither read the terms of use, nor consider their implications for content they have yet to post.

Thus in this study we have focused on social norms and accepted behavior—what participants think is okay in the face of specific circumstances—rather than on licenses and legal interpretations. Furthermore, we are able to compare attitudes and practices distinctive to Facebook data with attitudes toward other media types and user-contributed content in different services, including multiplayer online games and video-sharing sites. We will focus on three such distinctions: (1) the content users encounter on Facebook may be owned by someone they have an explicit relationship with; (2) Facebook accounts are more closely associated with digital identity and self-presentation, and their use as information often leads to conclusions about people (rather than about, say, the potential earnings of a movie); and (3) the personal nature of Facebook content may lead to an especially keen discrepancy between perceived rights and reality.

Who owns our social networks?

Social networking services represent relationships more explicitly than people were previously accustomed to doing (albeit as many have pointed out, in a flattened, less nuanced way than one might like). Thus when Facebook users reuse the content they encounter there, they know whether it belongs to a friend, a friend-of-a-friend, or someone who is socially more remote. Most people are aware of the degree to which it is private insofar as they are able to encounter it.

So what do people feel they can do with the stuff they don't own? Our past studies have shown that saving public online material is uncontroversial (c.f. [22,23]). In other words, if you encounter content on the Web, people feel you should be able to save it to your computer. This effect only holds as long as the content remains under local control of the person who saved it; even storing the content on the cloud compromises one's ability to save it [25]. Social distance imposes a strong effect on whether a person can save something that is posted on Facebook. Even a friend-of-a-friend's powers are limited. This suggests that posting something in a social networking service is very different than publishing it on the public web, *regardless of whether you can reach it or not.* Ownership effects are stronger inside social networking services than they are outside, on the open web. Once individuals are in an explicitly social setting, normal social forces are once again in effect.

Social media as records

Although other types of online content may represent important portions of an individual's digital footprint, our results suggest that people's Facebook accounts are closely aligned with their digital identity and self-presentation. Furthermore, for better or worse, Facebook profiles have become a primary source of data about individuals and their social networks. Hence we may usefully think of Facebook content in personal accounts as records.

In an archival sense, a record is documentation that might be used as evidence; it may have a regular, cohesive structure; and it may suggest a certain rhythm of fixity and fluidity (for example, records may be updated annually or once in a decade) [18]. In this study, we saw a surprising concern for veracity, offset by a desire to permit self-reinvention or to create false identities (for reasons as diverse as convenience or entertainment). At least a certain portion of social network profiles are seen as an accurate reflection of individuals' characteristics—for example, a Facebook profile might be fairly complete documentation of where someone lives, their marital status, their age, where and how much they've been educated, what they like or dislike, and how to contact them.

It is not unusual for this type of informal material to act as a surrogate for more formal records: often historical research turns to ephemera that have serendipitously survived as a way of confirming hypotheses that cannot be validated by intentional sources of documentation such as censuses, tax records, medical records, or military records. Consider mid-century US city directories: they often contained not only telephone numbers, but also addresses, professions, marital status, spouse's names, neighbor relationships (who lived next-door to whom), household size, and where one worked. Yet city directories were transient, something that would be discarded or replaced annually.

When social media profiles are used this way, they reveal at least three sources of tension: (1) What is their rhythm of fixity and fluidity? (2) Can they be trusted as accurate? Who enforces their accuracy? (3) Finally, does a concern for privacy overwhelm their utility? Our hypotheticals posed preliminary tests to resolve these tensions and shed some light on the emerging norms.

Fixity. Our removal results illustrate the tension between fixity and fluidity: can we trust aspects of a social network to remain intact, or are they intrinsically fluid, changing as frequently as each of us wants to change them? Can a resource like Facebook be archived in such a way as to preserve a social network at a given time? Reported practice tells us that people mostly remove content (as opposed to profile elements), e.g. posts that didn't garner responses or seem ill-advised given subsequent scrutiny. It is less common for people to alter their profiles than it is for them to curate the content. The hypotheticals underscore this interpretation: as long as removal doesn't harm someone else's digital footprint, it is generally accepted and expected. If Facebook is seen as a repository of personal documentation, archival policy must work around this level of fluidity.

Veracity. We looked at veracity through several different lenses. First we must acknowledge that in a service like Facebook, people maintain multiple profiles; the majority of our participants did so, sometimes just to separate a professional and a personal identity, but other times for more mischievous purposes. E.g. SN165 admitted, *Like many users, I use multiple, fake profiles on Facebook for trolling purposes (messing with friends, anonymously commenting on sites, or being annoying in general when bored).* This approach to identity is tempered by the thought that it's easy to see through this sort of behavior: *I have multiple profiles... But since both profiles can be found by anyone searching, I don't put anything inflammatory on that one either.* [SN194]. But in general, participants seemed to rely on and appreciate the veracity of certain social network data, even if we interpret our results through a filter of social desirability bias [2].

Privacy and control. Although it is unsurprising that participants are concerned with their own privacy, it is important to understand the degree to which they want to remain in control of their content, as demonstrated by their attitudes toward moving and monetizing their own accounts. A vast majority thought that Susie should be able to take her data, and bring it with her to a new service. Not only that, but when they were contemplating their own social media content, if participants thought the content was worth moving, they were less apt to let it go without objection. That almost 60% thought that users could sell their own Facebook content was a far stronger assertion of ownership than we expected (in spite of the precedent of supermarket affinity cards).

And this brings us to the way that perceived rights can—and do—fly in the face of reality.

Perceived rights and reality

The relatively personal nature of Facebook content may lead to an especially keen discrepancy between perceived rights and the real terms offered users when they sign up for the service. Because there is so much emphasis on data privacy and there is so much communication-centric use, we might expect to see a more profound sense of data ownership, and less thought given to its role as a primary corporate asset.

Although there is a certain level of awareness of governmental use and abuse of social network data, as well as countervailing initiatives to keep governments out of individuals' private data, there is a certain willful ignorance about the equivalent practices in the private sector. Not only is this data acknowledged as a valuable asset, it may also be the basis for an ongoing commercial revenue stream. Government agencies may also surreptitiously use the data (in ways other than the NSA's notorious surveillance program). A 2012 *New York Times* article revealed that, "*LexisNexis has a product called Accurint for Law Enforcement, which gives government agents information about what people do on social networks. The Internal Revenue Service searches Facebook and MySpace for evidence of tax evaders' income and whereabouts, and United States Citizenship and Immigration Services has been known to scrutinize photos and posts to confirm family relationships or weed out sham marriages*." [1] Researchers are aware of the intrinsic risks of bringing together 'big data' resources tied to identity, but there is considerable evidence that users are not [4].

CONCLUSION

In this study, we have explored comingled notions of value and ownership in social networks. Importantly, ownership within a social network is perceived differently than it is on the open web, where many people take strong cues from content type and reuse context; instead, even friends-of-friends are thought to have limited rights to the material that they can reach inside the service. Social strictures seem to play a greater role. Following from this principle, the right to remove content is mediated by the counterbalanced concerns of privacy and damage (would removal for reasons of privacy impinge someone else's desire to curate content?).

Because social network accounts are more closely tied to digital identity than other types of online content, we were interested in testing the limits of reuse, particularly reuse of social networks as data (or records). While participants were comfortable with reusing their own social network content in similar circumstances (e.g. in a similar service), controversy entered the picture when monetization or alternate uses were introduced. A significant number of participants felt they should be able to monetize their own social network data, but the corporate service provider should not be able to traffic in this sort of personal data.

In spite of the unpredictability of social networking services—their use and the nature of their content shifts over time—we feel that it is important to understand the content's larger social role: will it be the basis of a large scale archive? How can corporations and governments use it? What effects will it have on other aspects of life (such as personal legacies)? Although these questions are being resolved in *de facto* ways (for example, by economic forces), we feel that understanding social norms may be crucial to informing more carefully designed policies.

ACKNOWLEDGMENTS

This work was supported in part by National Science Foundation grant DUE–0938074. Cathy Marshall was at Microsoft Research Silicon Valley when this research was performed.

REFERENCES

1. Andrews, Lori. Facebook Is Using You. *New York Times*, February 4, 2012.
2. Antin J. & Shaw, A. Social desirability bias and self-reports of motivation: a study of Amazon Mechanical Turk in the US and India. *Proc. CHI'12*, 2925-2934.
3. Backstrom, L., Boldi, P., Rosa, M., Ugander, J., & Vigna, S. Four Degrees of Separation. (Version 5 Jan 2012) http://arxiv.org/abs/1111.4570.
4. boyd, d. & Crawford, K. Six Provocations for Big Data. Oxford Internet Institute, September 21, 2011.
5. Burke, M., Kraut, R., Marlow, C. Social capital on facebook: differentiating uses and users. *Proc CHI'11*, 671-680.
6. Das, S. & Kramer, A. 2013. Self-censorship on Facebook. *Proc. ICWSM 2013*, 120-127.
7. Farnham S. & Churchill, E. Faceted identity, faceted lives: social and technical issues with being yourself online. *Proc CSCW '11*, 359-368.
8. Good, K. D. From scrapbook to Facebook: A history of personal media assemblage and archives. *New Media & Society 15*, 4 (2013), 557-573.
9. Gulotta, R., Odom, W., Forlizzi, J., Faste, H. Digital artifacts as legacy: exploring the lifespan and value of digital data. *Proc. CHI'13*, 1813-1822.
10. Jakobsson, M. 2009. Experimenting on Mechanical Turk: 5 How Tos. *ITWorld*, September 3, 2009.
11. Joinson, A.N. Looking at, looking up or keeping up with people? Motives and use of facebook. *Proc. CHI'08.*
12. Harper, R., Whitworth, E. & Page, R. Fixity: Identity, time and durée on Facebook. In *Proc. IR 13.0* (2012).
13. Herzog, W. & Stutzman, F. The Case for Online Obscurity, *California Law Review, 101.*
14. Kairam, S., Brzozowski, M., Huffaker, D. & Chi, E. 2012. Talking in circles: Selective sharing in Google+. *Proc. CHI 2012*, ACM Press, 1065-1074.
15. Kittur, A., Chi, E., Suh, B. Crowdsourcing user studies with Mechanical Turk. *Proc. CHI'08*, 453-456.
16. Kosinski, M., Stillwell D.J., Graepel T. Private traits and attributes are predictable from digital records of human behavior. *Proceedings of the National Academy of Sciences 2013.*
17. Lampe, C., Vitak, J., Gray, R. & Ellison, N.B. Perceptions of Facebook's value as an information source. *Proc. CHI 2012*, 3195-3204.
18. Levy, D.M. *Scrolling Forward: Making Sense of Documents in the Digital Age*. Arcade, 2001.
19. Lindley, S., Marshall, C.C., Banks, R., Sellen, A. & Regan, T. Rethinking the web as a personal archive. In *Proc. WWW 2013*, 749-760.
20. Litt, E., Spottswood, E., Birnholtz, J., Hancock, J., Smith, M.E. & Reynolds, L. Awkward encounters of an "other" kind: collective self-presentation and face threat on facebook. *Proc. CSCW '14*, 449-460.
21. Marshall, C.C. & Lindley, S. Motivations and Strategies for Self-Search. *Proc. CHI'14*, 3675-3684.
22. Marshall, C.C. & Shipman, F.M. Social media ownership: Using Twitter as a window onto current attitudes and beliefs, *Proc. CHI'11*, 1081-1090.
23. Marshall, C.C. & Shipman, F.M. The ownership and reuse of visual media, *Proc. JCDL'11*, 157-166
24. Marshall, C.C. & Shipman, F.M. Experiences Surveying the Crowd: Reflections on Methods, Participation, and Reliability, *Proc. WebSci'13*, 234-243.
25. Marshall, C.C. & Shipman, F.M. Saving, reusing, and remixing web video: using attitudes and practices to reveal social norms, *Proc. WWW'13*, 885-896.
26. Marshall, C.C. & Shipman, F.M. An argument for archiving Facebook as a heterogeneous personal store, *Proc. DL'14.*
27. Mayer-Schonberger V. *Delete: The Virtue of Forgetting in the Digital Age*. Princeton University Press, 2009.
28. MacCormick & Summers, (eds.) *Interpreting Precedents*, Ashgate/Dartmouth, 1997, 528-529.
29. Manjoo, F. & Yoffe, E. Resume Robbed: What to do when a colleague steals your job title and description for her LinkedIn profile. *Slate Manners for the Digital Age*, January 10, 2012.
30. McDonough, J., Olendorf, R., Kirschenbaum, M., Kraus, K., Reside, D., Donahue, R., Phelps, A., Egert, C., Lowood, H., and Rojo, S., 2010. Preserving virtual worlds final report, http://hdl.handle.net/2142/17097

31. Rainie, L., Smith, A. and Duggan, M. Coming and going on Facebook. *Pew Research Center's Internet and American Life Project*, 2013.
32. Rissland, E. & Ashley, K. 1986. Hypotheticals as heuristic device. *Proc. Strategic Computing Natural Language*, 165-178.
33. Sas, C. & Whittaker, S. Design for forgetting: disposing of digital possessions after a breakup. *Proc CHI'13*.
34. Shipman, F.M. & Marshall, C.C. Are user-contributed reviews community property? Exploring the beliefs and practices of reviewers. *Proc. WebSci 2013*, 386-395.
35. Shipman, F.M. & Marshall, C.C. Creating and sharing records of multiplayer online game play: practices and attitudes. *Proc. ICWSM'14,* 456-465.
36. Skeels, M. & Grudin, J. When Social Networks Cross Boundaries: A Case Study of Workplace Use of Facebook and LinkedIn. *Proc. Group'09*, 95-103.
37. Sleeper, M., Balebako, R., Das, S., McConahy, A.L., Wiese, J. & Cranor, L.F. 2013. The post that wasn't: exploring self-censorship on Facebook. *Proc. CSCW'13*, 793-802.
38. Strauss, A. and Corbin, J. *Basics of Qualitative Research*, Sage Publications, 1998.
39. Stutzman F. & Kramer-Duffield, J. Friends only: examining a privacy-enhancing behavior in facebook. *Proc. CHI '10*, 1553-1562.
40. Vitak, J. & Kim, J. You can't block people offline": examining how facebook's affordances shape the disclosure process. *Proc. CSCW '14*, 461-474.
41. Wang, Y., Leon, P. G., Acquisti, A., Cranor, L.F., Forget, A., & Sadeh, N. A field trial of privacy nudges for facebook. *Proc. CHI '14*, 2367-2376.
42. Woodruff, A. Necessary, Unpleasant, and Disempowering: Reputation Management in the Internet Age. *Proc. CHI '14*, 149-158.
43. Zhang, H., De Choudhury, M., and Grudin, J. Creepy but Inevitable? The Evolution of Social Networking, *Proc. CSCW 2014*, 368-378.
44. Zhao, X. & Lindley, S. Curation through use: understanding the personal value of social media. In *Proc. CHI '14*, 2431-2440.
45. Zhao, X., Salehi, N., Naranjit, S., Alwaalan, S., Voida, S. & Cosley, D. 2013. The many faces of Facebook: Experiencing social media as performance, exhibition, and personal archive. *Proc. CHI'13*, 1-10.

Participatory Militias: An Analysis of an Armed Movement's Online Audience

Saiph Savage
Universidad Nacional Autónoma de México &
UC Santa Barbara
saiph@cs.ucsb.edu

Andrés Monroy-Hernández
Microsoft Research
amh@microsoft.com

ABSTRACT
Armed groups of civilians known as "self-defense forces" have ousted the powerful Knights Templar drug cartel from several towns in Michoacán. This militia uprising has unfolded on social media, particularly in the "VXM" ("Valor por Michoacán," Spanish for "Courage for Michoacán") Facebook page, gathering more than 170,000 fans. Previous work on the Drug War has documented the use of social media for real-time reports of violent clashes. However, VXM goes one step further by taking on a pro-militia propagandist role, engaging in two-way communication with its audience. This paper presents a descriptive analysis of VXM and its audience. We examined nine months of posts, from VXM's inception until May 2014, totaling 6,000 posts by VXM administrators and more than 108,000 comments from its audience. We describe the main conversation themes, post frequency and relationships with offline events and public figures. We also characterize the behavior of VXM's most active audience members. Our work illustrates VXM's online mobilization strategies, and how its audience takes part in defining the narrative of this armed conflict. We conclude by discussing possible applications of our findings for the design of future communication technologies.

Author Keywords
Social Media; Online Audience; Crisis Informatics.

ACM Classification Keywords
H.5.3. Group and Organization Interfaces; Asynchronous interaction: Web-based interaction.

INTRODUCTION
Militias have historically been defined as a group of three or more citizens that gather together in defense of their community, its territory, property or laws [38]. As social media adoption spreads, militias have started to make use of these networked platforms for organizational purposes [7, 39, 40]. From militia groups in Somalia to right-wing militias in the US, social media has become part of militias' communication strategy [15, 39, 7, 40]. For example, previous work has found that militias in the US use internet technologies because they are user-friendly, reliable, and free [39].

CSCW 2015, March 14–18, 2015, Vancouver, BC, Canada.

ACM 978-1-4503-2922-4/15/03 ...$15.00.

In this paper, we focus on the relationship between militia-related groups on social media and their audiences. Previous work on militia communication practices has identified that some of the goals of these groups when engaging in public channels are to popularize their ideas, distribute propaganda, recruit new militants, and even raise funds [15, 39]. With that in mind, we examine which ideas are most "popular," and which posts "recruit" participants by engaging them in conversation. We guide our exploration of militia groups on social media with the following research questions:

1. What content do these groups share online, and how do their audiences react to such content?
2. What content attracts new participants?
3. What are common attributes of the most active people in these online spaces?
4. What are the characteristics of the most popular content?

We explore these research questions using nine months of data from a Facebook page titled *"Valor por Michoacán SDR*[1] "(VXM), which translates as "Courage for Michoacán." This page was created to inform people of "unsafe situations" or "situaciones de riesgo" (SDR) in the state of Michoacán. This type of activity has been reported in previous work that examined how residents of communities afflicted by violence used Twitter to form alert networks and help one another identify potential danger on the streets [29]. However, shortly after its creation, VXM began to focus more on reporting about the activities of an armed group in the region, the self-defense forces [12].

The movement of the self-defense forces began in 2011 when a group of vigilantes from the town of Cherán in Michoacán expelled a band of illegal loggers backed by the drug cartel of "La Familia" [42]. This uprising became one of the first cases of ordinary citizens joining forces to challenge the powerful drug cartels. Two years later, new armed groups known as the *autodefensas* (self-defense forces) emerged in the same state but much stronger and better organized —and, some argued, with backing from wealthy ranchers [13]. The self-defense forces gained national and international attention after successfully taking over a number of bigger towns previously controlled by the Knights Templar cartel, a spin-off of the

[1] `https://www.facebook.com/ValorPorMichoacan`

La Familia cartel [13, 42]. Although the self-defense forces are a decentralized movement composed of multiple smaller groups, each with their own idiosyncrasics, they share the belief that the government is unable to stop the cartels and bring safety to their towns. Thus, they decided to take action and fight the drug cartels themselves [42]. Notice that we refer to these self-defense forces as a militia following Sumner's definition of a militia being a group of concerned citizens who: (1) are non-professional fighters; and (2) have entered a combat situation to defend their land [38] .

It is important to mention that although the VXM Facebook page documents the activities of the Michoacán self-defense forces, often with access to seemingly privileged information [32], the connection between the page and the militias has not been made official. Furthermore, the administrators of the page remain anonymous. News media, however, often refer to the VXM page as the militias' social media presence [12, 31]. The page is also usually one of the first to provide on-site reports about the militias' battles [32].

We characterize the content that VXM shares and its audience's participation using analytical techniques similar to those for examining discourse between politicians and their audiences [9, 33]. Our aim is to explore the context under which militia-related content gains attention and to investigate the behavioral patterns of VXM's active audience. In particular, we focus on the topics, locations, public figures, and organizations to which the posts or comments refer. We explored topics, organizations, and public figures because they provide a window into people's interests and issues they may want to make more prominent or de-emphasize [33]. For instance, perhaps the most active audience members emphasized certain social aspects of the situation in Michoacán.

We discuss our findings by exploring the factors that have been used previously to interpret the online activity of militias and other social movements [39]. For instance, we examined the role that information and communication technologies play in mobilizing individuals and in helping people narrate or frame their reality [14].

Through our study, we reveal how VXM and its audience appear to construct a participatory space where they collectively define what are important events and who are public figures. Together VXM and its audience propose solutions to the problems they recognize, and specify what each person can do to transform the situation in Michoacán. We also identify the techniques VXM seems to be using to mobilize its audience for offline collective efforts. Our case study highlights how technology is transforming who can frame the narrative of a region and facilitate the mobilization of individuals for collective efforts.

RELATED WORK: SOCIAL MOVEMENTS FRAMEWORK

We position our work within the area of social computing and collective action, particularly focusing on social movements. Social movements are defined as organized collective activities which take place outside political structures, but that attempt to transform existing political, economic, or societal structures [14]. Militias are considered a type of social movement [7].

Posts	6,901
VXM Fans	158,000
Participants (active audience size)	127,374
Comments	108,967
Post Likes	1,481,008
Reshares	364,660

Table 1. VXM Data.

The literature [14, 26] has identified three universal themes recurring across all social movements: mobilizing structures, opportunity structures, and framing processes. We use these themes to interpret our results and further understand what is occurring with VXM.

Mobilizing Structures: mechanisms through which information communication technologies (ICTs) facilitate mobilizing people to promote an ideology or political cause [14]. For instance, in the "Arab Spring" and "Occupy" movements, people used social media to mobilize crowds for street rallies or protests. Similarly, Facebook facilitated the mobilization of political activists in Palestine by letting people connect their private life with their political activities [41]. Lastly, platforms such as Turkopticon allow crowdworkers to mobilize and hold virtual employers accountable for their actions [17].

Opportunity Structures: characteristics of a social system that facilitate or hinder the activity of a social movement [14]. For instance, online donation campaigns take advantage of the immediate emotions after a disaster or of friendships to harvest higher levels of participation and donations [28].

Framing Processes: ways to interpret reality by labeling one's individual experiences within the experiences of society [10, 14]. In social movements, frames represent a set of beliefs and meanings that help to legitimate and motivate the actions of the group. Frames usually emerge by negotiating shared meaning. Diamond et al. [10] found that people used social media to crowd-source framing processes, and collectively create an interpretation of street harassment.

DATA COLLECTION AND ANALYSIS

Using the public Facebook API, we collected nine months of posts, comments, likes, and shares from the VXM page. The data collection took a snapshot of all activity starting from August 14, 2013 to the date of data collection, May 7, 2014. The details of the dataset are shown in Table 1.

Content Analysis

In order to obtain a descriptive assessment of the VXM page content, we extracted common topics, organizations, and public figures referenced in the posts. First, we familiarized ourselves with the VXM page by frequently reading its posts and exchanging notes and observations among the researchers. It is important to note that the researchers are native Spanish speakers originally from México.

Topics. We used a grounded theory approach [37] to identify the main topics in VXM's posts (Table 2). One researcher started by independently extracting topics from a set of 200 randomly selected posts. Then, the other researcher analyzed the emerging topics and adjusted the list accordingly. Finally, we looked at a set of 500 randomly selected posts and produced a final list of mutually exclusive topics.

We used oDesk[2] to hire three Spanish-speaking, college-educated people to categorize the VXM posts independently. First, we asked two coders to categorize each of the 6,901 posts using the topics listed in Table 2. We asked the coders to pick the "most relevant" topic for each post. The two coders agreed on 6,080 posts (Cohen's kappa: 0.54). We then asked the third coder to label the 821 posts upon which the first two coders had disagreed. We then used a "majority rule" approach to determine the topic for those posts.

Public Figures and Organizations. We identified posts that referred to each of the organizations and public figures involved in the conflict, from public officials to cartel members to militia leaders. We manually created a list of full, common, and nicknames and then identified posts that mentioned any of the names. We collected the names from Wikipedia and from *Proceso*[3] magazine. We used the Wikipedia articles, *"Caballeros Templarios Knights Templar cartel"* and *"Grupos de Autodefensa Comunitaria Self-Defense Forces,"* written both in English and Spanish, to manually identify all relevant proper names. We did the same with *Proceso* articles. We used *Proceso's* online search to find articles related to the militias using the keywords *autodefensas* and *caballeros templarios.* We went through each of the articles that appeared in the first page of the search results. We then added or merged the alternate names for each person, both shorter and nicknames. For example, *"Estanislao Beltran"* was also known as *"Papa Smurf,"* and *"Jose Manuel Mireles Valverde"* was usually referred to as just *"Mireles."*

Audience Participation Patterns

Motivated by Van Dijk's work [9], we categorize VXM's most active members by looking the messages they post on the page. We focus in particular on the number of messages they post, and their length, and public figures and locations they mention. We used a clustering method using all of these features, except for locations which are used simply to contextualize the results. We identified VXM's *highly active participants* by finding those individuals whose number of comments was higher than three times the standard deviation (normal procedure to find outliers).

We then profiled the behavior of these active participants by analyzing their total number of comments and the type of public figures and organizations they mentioned. For this purpose, we first grouped all of the public figures and organizations in our list based on their affiliation (i.e., type). For instance, *"Mireles"* and *"Papa Smurf"* were grouped together because both are members of self-defense forces. We obtained the affiliations using data from the *Proceso* and Wikipedia articles mentioned earlier. We assumed that a public figure could have only one affiliation. Through this process, we identified four main types of public figures and organizations: government, militia, drug cartel, and journalist (news reporters), and classified each of the public figures in our list into one of these types.

Next, we measured how often each highly active participant mentioned each public figure in their comments. We then used a probabilistic model to implicitly calculate the degree to which they mentioned a certain type of public figure:

$$P(o,T) = \sum_{f \in \mathcal{F}} P(o)P(f|o)P(T|f), \tag{1}$$

where $P(o,T)$ is the probability an active participant o mentions a certain type of public figures T given her comments; $P(o) = n^{-1}$ is the probability of selecting an active participant o; n is the total number of participants; $P(f|o) = m^{-1}$ is the probability of public figure f appearing in the comments of an active participant o; m is the total number of words that active participant o has used in her comments; $P(T|f) = 1$, when the public figure f is of type T or zero otherwise.

For each highly active participant, we calculated their $P(o,T)$ for all types of public figures and formed a vector representing how often the participant mentioned each type. The size of each vector will correspond to the number of types—in this study, the size is four.

We used the vectors to cluster highly active participants and uncover their behavioral patterns. For instance, people who mentioned governmental public figures more than they mentioned militias might be clustered together. We use mean shift algorithm [4] to group together similar vectors and discover clusters of people. We opted to use mean shift algorithm because it is based on a nonparametric density estimation, and therefore we would not need to know the number of clusters beforehand (unlike K-means). Instead, we let mean shift algorithm discover the clusters from our data. The clusters represent the different behavioral patterns that the most-active audience members exhibited.

We then looked at the characteristics of people in each cluster, particularly (1) the number of comments and words used; (2) the percentage of comments that mention certain types of public figures; and (3) the percentage of comments that reference locations. For the last, we identified comments when each person mentioned a city or town in Michoacán. We used a list[4] from the National Institute of Statistics and Geography to identify comments that referenced such locations.

[2]oDesk is a platform to contract independent professionals from around the world to perform tasks online.
Available at: `http://www.odesk.com/`

[3]*Proceso*, is a well-established magazine covering politics and social issues since 1976. Available at:
`http://www.proceso.com.mx/`

[4]`http://cuentame.inegi.org.mx/monografias/informacion/mich/territorio/div_municipal.aspx?tema=me`

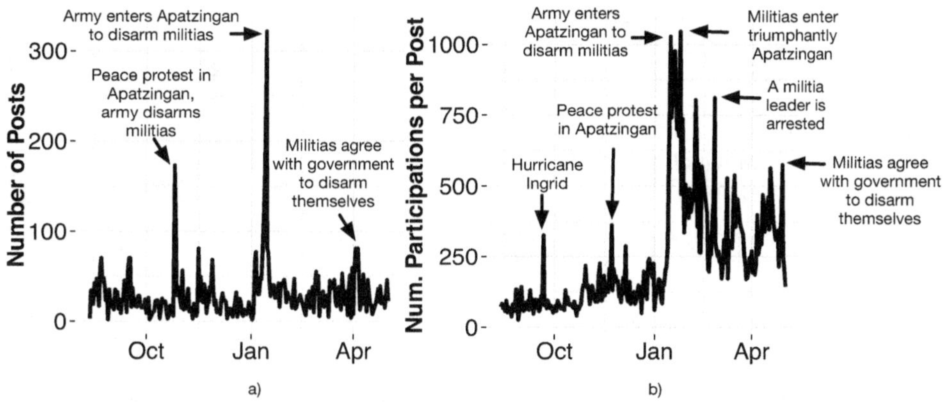

Figure 1. Overview of VXM's posting behavior and audience's activity. In Figure 1a, spikes indicate an increase in the daily number of posts; in Figure 1b, they show an increase in the daily number of audience likes, comments, and shares per post. Together, VXM and its audience appear to signal when there are major events in Michoacán.

RESULTS

RQ1: The VXM Content and Audience Participation

Our first research question explores the type of content that militia-related groups share online, and how unaffiliated civilians respond to and participate in, or interact with such content. For this purpose, we examined (1) the daily activity of VXM and its audience; (2) the public figures that VXM covered; and (3) the topics VXM discussed with its audience.

1. Daily Activity. We plotted the daily number of VXM posts (Figure 1a) and audience participation (likes, comments, and shares) per post (1b). We used this first analysis as an overview of how active the page and audience are.

Figure 1 shows that audience activity per post increased over time, especially in 2014, whereas the the administrators' posting behavior stayed relatively constant. However, both audience and VXM administrators spiked in daily activity. For both, most of the peaks corresponded to times when major offline events occurred in Michoacán, especially events concerning the militias. For instance, on January 14, 2014, the day the Army entered the town of Apatzingán to disarm the self-defense forces, both the number of posts on the page and the number of times the audience participated per post increased.

What is particularly fascinating is that the audience participation also exhibited spikes not related to the administrator's posting behavior. For instance, on February 8, 2014 when the militia took over the Knights Templar headquarters, the audience had one of its largest activity spikes, whereas the administrators did not increase their number of posts during that time. Hence, the audience might help to provide a more complete picture of when important events are transpiring in Michoacán.

2. Public Figures. To further inspect the type of content VXM shares and how its audience reacts, we analyzed the top 10% of names VXM mentioned and studied how the audience responded to these references.

Figure 2 illustrates the total number of posts VXM created about each public figure or organization and compares it with

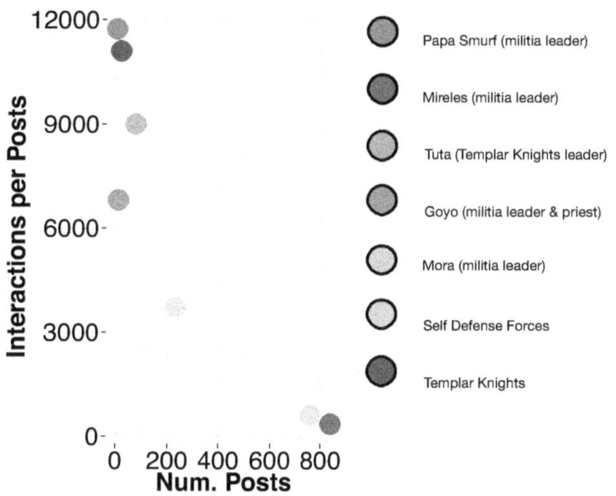

Figure 2. Overview of how much VXM mentions certain public figures and the public figures' popularity. The most popular public figures were not necessarily the ones most mentioned by VXM.

the subject's popularity, measured in terms of the total number of likes, comments, and shares the content received. Each color-coded point represents a public figure or organization. The X axis represents the number of posts about the public figure or organization; and the Y axis, the public figures' popularity. A larger X value represents more mentions by VXM page administrators; a larger Y value represents more popularity with the audience.

Figure 2 shows that public figures and organizations that VXM mentioned most often were not actually the most popular with VXM's audience. We also observed that the audience appeared to be more participatory with posts that referenced individuals, rather than organizations. For instance, posts mentioning Knights Templar' leader *"La Tuta"* and posts mentioning *"Papa Smurf"* were much more popular than posts referencing *"Knights Templar"* or *"Self-Defense Forces."*

What is surprising about Figure 2 is that although *Mora* was the militia leader to whom VXM gave the most coverage, *Mora* was not the most popular. The most popular was actually the other militia leader, *Papa Smurf*, whom VXM hardly covered. *Papa Smurf's* popularity might be due to the deal he negotiated with the government in which the self-defense forces officially became a rural police force [13].

It appears again that the audience is helping to provide a more thorough picture of who and what matters in Michoacán. Together, VXM administrators and its audience might be framing what important events are taking place in Michoacán.

3. Topics: We next examined the type of topics the VXM page presented (Table 2,) and how much coverage the page gave to each (Figure 3).

The dominate topic VXM covered was objective news reports. A distinctive trait of these reports was that they usually made requests to the public for some sort of action. For instance, the following VXM post reported a robbery in the town of Los Reyes and asked the public to help identify the criminals:

> *"#LosReyes there was a burglary in the jewelry shop in downtown Los Reyes today at 7 pm. Please check out the YouTube video. If anyone can identify the criminals, please report them via private message."*

These posts occasionally also included advice for keeping safe:

> *"#Apatzingan in the dance club Layon the organized crime [Knights Templar] is having an event. WE RECOMMEND NOT ATTENDING. IT IS FOR YOUR OWN SAFETY. The club is full of dangerous people."*

VXM's news reporting appears to be factual and caring at the same time. This type of reporting might help the page have a much deeper connection with its audience and facilitate working together towards a common goal [18].

Providing news reports aligned with the page's description in its "About" section:

> *"Here [at VXM] we provide and follow reports about dangerous situations occurring in Michoacán. ...We give coverage to events which take place in the state of Michoacán and are of social interest."*

What is interesting is that VXM also conducted activities not reported in its description, such as sharing propaganda or providing subjective critiques. Of note, VXM incorporated the latter type of content in a subtler way. Only around 10% of all VXM posts were actually propaganda or critiques.

Communication research has shown that it is hard for a message to reach people who are not already in favor of the views the message presents [5]. Thus, for speakers who want to plant their own ideas into an audience, the most effective way is to do it subtly, so that the audience is unaware that a report or commentary is actually indoctrination [20]. Similarly, if VXM only shared propaganda or critiques, the number of people interested in their content could decrease. Subtly sharing indoctrination types of messages might be an effective technique VXM administrators use to maintain their large audience while still promoting their own ideas or opinions.

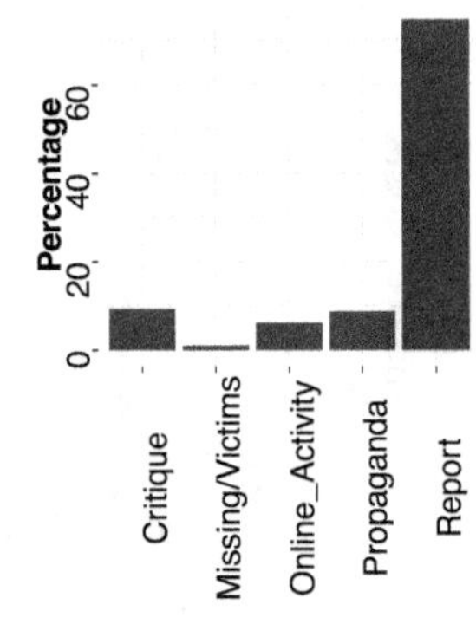

Figure 3. Overview of the percentage of posts VXM creates about each topic. VXM primarily provides News Reports. However, occasionally it shares Critiques and Propaganda. It also provides space for its audience by sharing their missing-persons reports, obituaries, and explaining how to keep safe online.

Another interesting topic the VXM page covered was online activity. These posts tried to explain the online dynamics of the page, such as what type of online content audiences should expect from the page (e.g., news reports), social media sources the page trusted, and how audiences should conduct themselves on the page. The last item focused primarily on giving tips on how people should present themselves online if they decide to participate in VXM.

This topic resembles a theme seen recently in social media content from terrorist groups [40]. Because of the potential danger of being caught, terrorists advise their audiences how to connect to their YouTube videos and present themselves online (e.g., with fake accounts), and which other internet pages are trustworthy allies. Clearly, VXM is not at all related to terrorism. However, there can be value in studying their online activity under the lens of terrorism, especially given the high risks also associated with participating in VXM. The public figures that VXM covered were notoriously dangerous (e.g., drug cartel members). Thus, VXM, just like the terrorists, needed to advise its audience on how to interact in such potentially dangerous online space. Note that the page is an adverse space not necessarily because of its heated discussions, but because drug cartel members could easily eavesdrop on the page's content and violently target audience members whose comments they do not like. It is compelling that VXM makes an effort to explain the page dynamics to its audience and tries to keep them safe.

One topic that was hardly covered by the page (2% of all posts) but was nonetheless very fascinating was the topic of missing people and obituaries. The page not only provided reports about major events occurring in Michoacán, but also provided a space where people could report loved ones that had gone missing, run away, or recently passed away. The VXM page administrators created a space that let people mourn their losses and help each other when they suffered

Topic	Sample Post
Online activity: information on the nature of the VXM page, pointers to other reliable social media sources, and tips.	"If you want to make any complaints about things occurring in your town, try not to publish it on the Facebook wall, send us a private message instead. It is for your own SAFETY. You can also create a fake profile and send to us the complaint, although we will never share your identity."
Critiques: criticism of people or organizations, clearly targeted to attack.	"What do you guys think of this shameless governor, who is a nobody, who wants to report the brave people that told him his truths? Fausto Vallejo [governor of Michoacán] you don't serve as a governor, you are a NOBODY!"
Propaganda: Patriotic or nationalistic messages used to promote or publicize a political cause or point of view.	No more impunity! we see a Michoacán that wants justice that has a hunger for true justice. Only the people can save the people!
News reports: factual reports, and alerts. Occasionally, the messages include commentary of how the report could impact the reader, or actions the reader could take in relation to the report.	"#SDRLosReyes there is a confrontation, the Knights Templar are attacking in Los Reyes through different entrances. Please alert others who pass those zones. If you have a gun please come help the militias."
Missing people and obituaries: Reports regarding runaways, possible kidnappings, and deaths.	"#MissingPerson #Morelia, Michoacán His name is Jose Manuel Molinero Ruiz."

Table 2. Description and sample post of the topics covered by VXM.

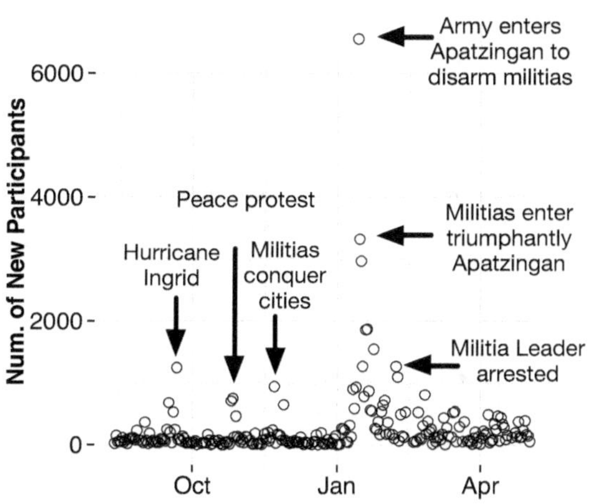

Figure 4. Number of daily new participants. In general, the page saw an increased number of new participants whenever there were major offline events.

personal family tragedies or emergencies. Thus, VXM appeared socially engaged with its community.

RQ2: The VXM Newcomers

Our second research question explored the context under which people started participating in an online space linked to militias. We examined the per-day number of people who participated for the first time with VXM.

Figure 4 shows number of new participants (newcomers) who either liked or commented on VXM page content. Most of the peaks in the number of daily newcomers correspond to major offline events that occurred in Michoacán, especially militia-related events.

For instance, around the time the militias took over the Knights Templar's headquarters on February 8, 2014, the number of newcomers increased. This increase during major offline events might explain the increase in audience participation during the same periods. New, external people suddenly participating in the page could be helping to provide a more complete picture of when there are important offline events in Michoacán.

RQ3: Behavioral Patterns of the Most Active Audience

This research question aimed to investigate the behavioral patterns exhibited by VXM's most active audience members. Using a procedure described in "Audiences Participation Patterns," we found that VXM's most active participants (282 individuals) exhibited three distinct behaviors (i.e., we discovered three clusters).

Cluster A *(Drug Cartel Savvy)*: All individuals in this cluster (33% of the most active) referenced primarily public figures related to drug cartels. On average, each of these individual's comments referenced drug cartels (67%), government (12%), and militias (8%), with no comments mentioning journalists. This apparent knowledge about drug cartels led us to name people in this cluster the *"Drug Cartel Savvy."* Drug Cartel Savvy contributed a median of 112 comments; each comment had an average of 36 words (compared with 2 comments, 10 words from average participants, who never mentioned any public figures). Drug Cartel Savvy contributed the largest number and the longest comments of all the behavioral clusters. Sample comments include:

> *"Yeah right, as if the Templar [Knights Templar] were so innocent. He [the Knights Templar leader] claims they're not stealing or blackmailing us. I think we need to tell la Tuta [Knights Templar leader] what his boys are up [to]. My mom would say that skunks don't realize how much they stink!"*

Forty percent of each of these individual's comments referenced towns in Michoacán (average users never mentioned locations). They also referenced the most locations of all the cluster types. A sample comment with locations:

> *"Right now it is confirmed that Tepalcatepec and Buenavista have those signs [signs that say a town was freed from the Knights Templar]. They look beautiful! I feel pride whenever I see them. God bless the brave people of my neighborhood Loma Blanca! [neighborhood in Tepalcatepec, Michoacán]."*

Cluster B *(Government Gossipers)*: All of these audience members (66% of the most active) mentioned primarily gov-

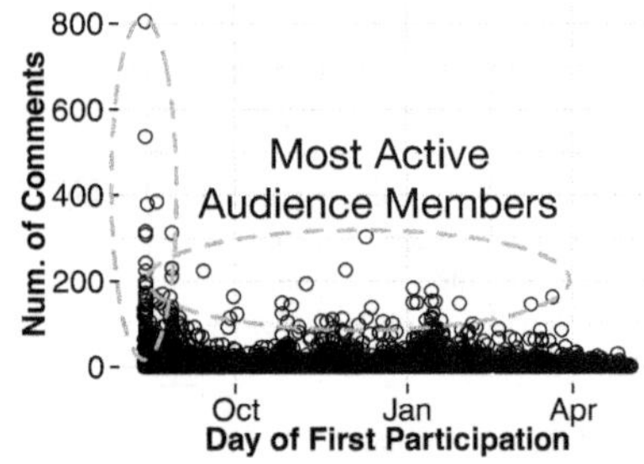

Figure 5. Overview of people's start date and the number of comments they generated. The most active audience members started participating either from the start or when the militias had an offline event.

ernment figures and related organizations in their comments. On average, each of these individuals' comments referenced the government (28%), militias (23%), drug cartels (5%), journalists (1%), and towns or cities (4%). This apparent interest in discussing the government led us to name people in this cluster the *"Government Gossipers."* Government Gossipers contributed a median of 64 comments; each comment averaged 12 words. Government Gossipers contributed the least content of the three clusters. However, the majority of the most active audience belonged to this cluster. Sample comments include:

> *"Oh yeah, but fucking Karam [Attorney General] claims he already rescued Michoacán. Dirty old liar! He and EPN [President] are a disgrace!"*

> *"Come on brothers, don't give up! EPN [President] will just have to learn what the people can do together!"*

We also found that a few (1%) of the Government Gossiper accounts tended to share the exact same comment many times. For instance:

> *"We need to be united as a country, and help the people in Michoacán. The government has committed many injustices against the militias, like throwing them in jail. God isnt with the corrupt. God will not help them."*

> *"Even the drug cartels confirm that they are funded by the US. Do you guys think they'll share this on TV?! It is our responsibility to distribute and share this!"*

This behavior resembles how people use Twitter in war environments where there is a tendency for redundancy [21].

Cluster C *(Geographers Michoacanos)*: These audience members (1% of the most active) did not reference any of the public figures we had on our list. However, they did mention locations. Each person, on average, had some mention or reference to towns and cities in Michoacán in 20% of their comments. We thus decided to name people in this cluster *"Geographers Michoacanos."* Although they did not mention the most locations (Drug Cartel Savvy referenced more), they were the only ones who mentioned locations without apparently involving drug cartels, militias, or the government. The Geographers Michoacanos contributed a median of 74 comments; each comment averaged 17 words.

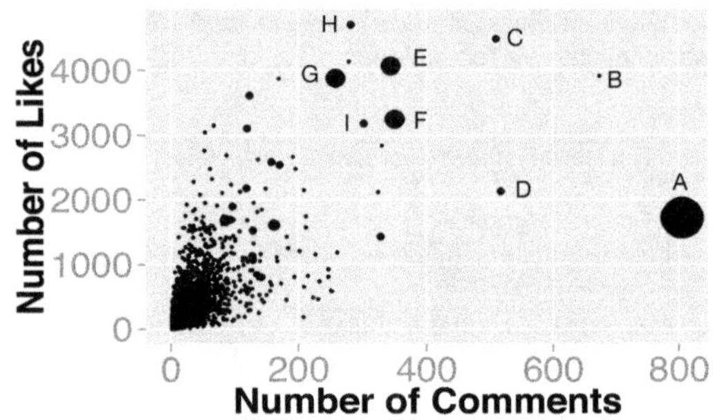

Figure 6. Number of likes and comments for all posts, size of a point is directly correlated with the number of shares of a post. The most popular content was published during major offline events of the militias.

A sample comment:

> *"Michoacán is home to brave, patriotic, and hard working people. In Nueva Valladolid [former town in Michoacán] the first university of all of Latin America was built. The priest Miguel Hidalgo [historical figure] also studied in Nueva Valladolid, today Morelia, [capital of Michoacán]."*

All of the clusters had audience members with varied start dates. Even the Geographers Michoacanos had accounts that started when the page was founded through the middle of 2014. Figure 5 illustrates how much each audience members commented, given their start dates. The X axis shows the date of first comment on VXM; the Y axis shows the number of comments contributed. We highlighted the audience members we considered for this analysis. Note that the majority of the most active participants appear to have started contributing either when the page was first founded or during a major offline event.

Label	Post Description
A	Video of a solider killing an unarmed civilian who supported the militias. (Jan 15)
B	Post announcing that the militias took over the Knights Templar headquarters. (Feb 8)
C	Post describing the type of hardships the militias and people in Michoacán have endured against the Knights Templar. (Jan 15)
D	Video of a corrupt police officer. (Feb 8)
E	Video explaining the militias' motives for fighting. (Jan 19)
F	Video of Father Goyo (priest and militia member) justifying the militias' actions. (Jan 14)
G	Video of Michoacán's youth explaining they are tired of living in the violence generated by the Knights Templar. (Feb 6)
H	Photo of Father Goyo asking civilians to take action against the drug cartels. (Feb 8)
I	Photo of Father Goyo crying because the government wants to disarm the militias. (Jan 18)

Table 3. Characteristics of the most popular content. The most popular content was published during major offline events of the militias.

RQ4: Content Popularity

This research question examined some traits of the content that became the most popular in militia-affiliated online spaces; that is, content that received the most number of likes, comments, and shares. Figure 6 illustrates the number of likes, comments, and shares of each VXM post. The X axis shows the number of comments the post received; the Y axis, the number of likes. The size of the circle relates to the number of shares; the larger the circle, the more the post was reshared. We defined VXM's most popular content as the posts whose total number of likes, comments, and shares deviated by three times the standard deviation. We labeled the most popular posts alphabetically and examined a few of their characteristics (Table 3).

In general, VXM's most popular content emerged during the militias' most important offline events. For instance, over half of the most popular content was created around January 15, 2014, the day the self-defense militias had their biggest confrontation with the government, who wanted to disarm them. The other half of the most popular content was created around February 8, 2014, the day the militias triumphantly entered Apatzingán, a town that had been considered to be the Knights Templar headquarters.

The high number of likes, comments, and shares exhibited during these periods might be due to the increase in newcomers (see Figure 4). Content published during major offline events is likely seen by a larger audience and can become popular more easily.

DISCUSSION

We discuss our results using the previously described themes that tend to appear across all social movements: framing processes, mobilizing structures, and opportunity structures [14, 26].

Framing Processes. Through our case study, we observed that VXM page administrators appeared to: (1) structure and narrate meaning for particular events, public figures, and social life; (2) diagnose what things might need alteration in Michoacán; and (3) propose solutions to the diagnosed problems and, in the process, specify what people can do.

The VXM page administrators are likely framing a shared understanding of the situation in Michoacán with their audience. Such narrative has also been found in the online activity of US militias [2]. However, what is particularly fascinating is that the audience appears to be helping to construct the narrative as well. For instance, we saw how the audience eventually took hold of the space that VXM had set up and participated copiously whenever there were major offline events. The audience helped to provide a more complete picture of what was happening in Michoacán. It was not necessary for VXM to give wide coverage to a certain event or public figure; instead, on its own, the audience adopted the space and participated extensively. The audience appeared to dictate, by itself, what was important.

This behavior has also surfaced in other online spaces. For instance, in "Hollaback!" [10], it was the online audience who defined the meaning behind street harassment. In a Facebook group set up to discuss the Coffee Party in the US, certain audience members assumed advocacy roles and extensively supported certain issues [24]. Group administrators, in fact, usually provide no input. Traditionally, it had been up to the organization's leaders (e.g., page administrators) or people in power to structure and define what matters. Technology, however, is empowering audiences to establish for themselves what is noteworthy.

Mobilizing Structures. We witnessed that VXM was fostering solidarity with its audience by providing safety advice and even assisting them during personal family troubles (e.g., when a loved one passed away). Research on social movements has found that in order to mobilize people and produce action, it is necessary to establish a certain degree of solidarity [39]. It is likely that the time and space that the VXM administrators are dedicating to their audience is helping them create a highly participatory environment. Note that some of these solidarity conducts resemble online strategies that politicians have adopted to encourage participation from citizens [33].

Through our study, we also saw that offline events appeared to be important for mobilizing new participants and popularizing VXM's content. This behavior resembles what has been observed on Twitter [16], where people who joined that service during an emergency event or mass convergence usually became long-term adopters of the technology. Offline events, and the numerous controversies that surround them, might help audiences concentrate on what truly matters to them. This, in turn, is likely helping to increase people's participation in the page. We believe that, in the end, the skillful use of offline events could play a major role in pumping new life into an online group or movement.

Opportunity Structures. Our study revealed that some of VXM's most active participants used the page to actively discuss the drug cartels and the government. There are likely several explanations for this behavior. Smelser [36] identified that social strains (i.e., impairments in the relationship between two actors) usually prompt collective action, and the type of strain generally defines the type of collective action that will emerge. In this study, it is likely that these audience members have a strain with the drug cartels or the government that led them to participate extensively and even exhibit distinct behavioral patterns in VXM. The strains might actually be an opportunity for VXM to recruit highly active participants.

It could also be worth thinking about the role these highly participatory citizens might play in Michoacán or in the country in the long run. Maruyama et al. [23] found that the people who participated on Twitter during a debate were more likely to change their vote in a political election. Their work argued that to take part in an online discussion, people need to process the related information more elaborately; and this could lead to changes in their offline actions. Currently, the offline consequences of citizen participation in militia-affiliated online spaces are unclear. Future work could explore the offline effects that are surfacing from online spaces such as the VXM page.

DESIGN IMPLICATIONS

Our results raise the question of whether showing the framings constructed by an audience could benefit social media.

Summaries of an audience's constructs could certainly help historians make better sense of a social movement or politically charged event. Audience participation coupled with news reports could provide historians with a more complete picture of when important offline events transpired in a region; and also whether organizations or groups tried to frame reality in a certain way, as their reporting could be compared with the audience's.

Interfaces highlighting the narrative of an audience could come in different flavors, such as: visualizations of an audience's size and number of participations through time; or visualizations of the audience's interpretations on various matters. Some social media sites, e.g., Facebook or Twitter, already provide tools to visualize the participation of an audience, mainly to improve people's online communications [3]. Similarly, current research [35, 11] has explored visualizing the interests and social contexts of audiences to facilitate collaborations. Following these ideas, we believe that interfaces which structure and visualize audiences' framings could facilitate collective action. People could better identify collective thinking about a problem, and could work together towards possible solutions.

Many audience members appeared to have specialized knowledge about organized crime, government, and certain geographical regions. There is likely value in designing platforms that can advantageously use audiences' comprehension of the world [43]. Perhaps it is about combining citizens' knowledge with the resources from organizations to create smarter cities [30]. For example, we could design platforms that integrate the audiences' understanding of the crime in their towns or passion for their neighborhoods [6, 25, 34] with government resources to create safer and more lively cities.

On this last point, note however, that currently individuals and organizations have to be savvy and learn on their own the best online strategies to spark collaborations or participation from audiences. As designers, it could also be worth thinking about the type of teamwork we want to facilitate. It is unclear whether it is about just building mechanisms through which organizations can donate resources for citizens to use [22], or if we need to create a more complex platform that intrinsically helps these two players build solidarity with each other.

Finally, our results found that some of the most active audience members appeared to have social strains against certain organizations. When we design collaborative tools, it could be beneficial to consider these strains (e.g., citizens might not trust the government). We likely need to think about how to create platforms that empower citizens and organizations to collaborate towards improving their cities, while taking into account possible fallouts.

LIMITATIONS AND FUTURE WORK

The insights this work provides are limited by the methodology and population we studied. For example, the Facebook page we examined focuses on a particular set of militia groups, hence the results might not generalize to all other armed groups. Future work focusing on militia groups in other latitudes could create a body of literature to better understand this phenomenon.

Also, the methods we used focused on breath rather than depth, as such we do not know much about the identities and motivations of the people behind the Facebook page. Future work could engage in in-depth interviews with the administrators and some of the participants of the page.

Our results also showed that not all major offline events translated into VXM Facebook posts. Previous work has begun an exploration between an individual's online posts and real-world activities [19, 27]. However, the relationship between online posts and real world events in more adverse scenarios has yet to be explored. An understanding of this relationship could impact research areas that range from prediction of a population's activity to crowd-sourced news [1, 8].

We found that VXM page administrators conducted different mechanisms to apparently foster solidarity with their audience. Creating solidarity seems to implicitly help VXM to create a highly participatory online space. Finally, this result suggests that the correlation between the levels of participation of an audience and the solidarity created by page admins warrants deeper investigation.

ACKNOWLEDGEMENTS

This work was partially supported by a UC MEXUS-CONACYT fellowship, and by NSF grant IIS-0747520. Special thanks to Tobias Hollerer, Sergio Rodríguez, Diego Carmona, and the anonymous CSCW reviewers who helped us improve the paper.

REFERENCES

1. Agapie, E., and Monroy-Hernandez, A. Eventful: Crowdsourcing local news reporting.
2. Benford, R., and Snow, D. Framing processes and social movements: An overview and assessment. *Annual review of sociology* (2000), 611–639.
3. Bernstein, M. S., Bakshy, E., Burke, M., and Karrer, B. Quantifying the invisible audience in social networks. In *Proceedings of the SIGCHI Conference on Human Factors in Computing Systems*, ACM (2013), 21–30.
4. Cheng, Y. Mean shift, mode seeking, and clustering. *IEEE Trans. Pattern Anal. Mach. Intell. 17*, 8 (Aug. 1995), 790–799.
5. Cooper, E., and Jahoda, M. The evasion of propaganda: How prejudiced people respond to anti-prejudice propaganda. *The Journal of psychology 23*, 1 (1947), 15–25.
6. Cranshaw, J., Schwartz, R., Hong, J. I., and Sadeh, N. M. The livehoods project: Utilizing social media to understand the dynamics of a city. In *ICWSM* (2012).
7. Crothers, L. *Rage on the right: The American militia movement from Ruby Ridge to homeland security*. Rowman & Littlefield Publishers, 2004.
8. Dailey, D., and Starbird, K. Journalists as crowdsourcerers: Responding to crisis by reporting with a crowd. *Computer Supported Cooperative Work (CSCW) 23*, 4-6 (2014), 445–481.
9. Dijk, V. *Discourse as social interaction*, vol. 2. Sage, 1997.
10. Dimond, J., Dye, M., Larose, D., and Bruckman, A. Hollaback!: the role of storytelling online in a social movement organization. In *Proceedings of the 2013 conference on Computer supported cooperative work*, ACM (2013), 477–490.

11. Forbes, A. G., Savage, S., and Höllerer, T. Visualizing and verifying directed social queries. In *IEEE Workshop on Interactive Visual Text Analytics. Seattle, WA*, Citeseer (2012).
12. García, I. *Redes sociales, el otro campo de accin de las autodefensas.* ADN Politico, 2014. http://www.adnpolitico.com/gobierno/2014/01/14/redessocialeseł-otro-campodebatalladelasautodefensas.
13. Garcia-Ponce, O., and Lajous, A. *How does a drug cartel become a lime cartel?* Washington Post, 2014. http://www.washingtonpost.com/blogs/monkey-cage/wp/2014/05/20/how-doesadrugcartelbecomealimecartel/.
14. Garrett, K. Protest in an information society: A review of literature on social movements and new icts. *Information, communication & society 9*, 02 (2006), 202–224.
15. Gerwehr, S., and Daly, S. *Al-Qaida: Terrorist Selection and Recruitment.* McGraw-Hill, 2005, research report 5, 73–89.
16. Hughes, A., and Palen, L. Twitter adoption and use in mass convergence and emergency events. *International Journal of Emergency Management 6*, 3 (2009), 248–260.
17. Irani, L. C., and Silberman, M. S. Turkopticon: Interrupting Worker Invisibility in Amazon Mechanical Turk. In *Proceedings of the SIGCHI Conference on Human Factors in Computing Systems*, CHI '13, ACM (New York, NY, USA, 2013), 611–620.
18. Jones, E. Ingratiation. *The Journal of Social Psychology* (1964).
19. Kıcıman, E. OMG, I Have to Tweet that! A Study of Factors that Influence Tweet Rates. In *Proceedings of the Sixth International AAAI Conference on Weblogs and Social Media* (2012).
20. King, E. Exposing the age of lies: The propaganda menace as portrayed in american magazines in the aftermath of world war i. *Journal of American Culture 12*, 1 (1989), 35–40.
21. Mark, G., Al-Ani, B., and Semaan, B. Resilience through technology adoption: Merging the old and the new in iraq. In *Proceedings of the SIGCHI Conference on Human Factors in Computing Systems*, CHI '09, ACM (New York, NY, USA, 2009), 689–698.
22. Maruyama, M., Douglas, S., and Robertson, S. Design teams as change agents: Diplomatic design in the open data movement. In *System Sciences (HICSS), 2013 46th Hawaii International Conference on*, IEEE (2013), 1860–1869.
23. Maruyama, M. T., Robertson, S. P., Douglas, S. K., Semaan, B. C., and Faucett, H. A. Hybrid media consumption: How tweeting during a televised political debate influences the vote decision. In *Proceedings of the 17th ACM Conference on Computer Supported Cooperative Work & Social Computing*, CSCW '14, ACM (New York, NY, USA, 2014), 1422–1432.
24. Mascaro, C., and Goggins, S. Brewing up citizen engagement: the Coffee Party on Facebook. In *Proceedings of the 5th International Conference on Communities and Technologies*, ACM (2011), 11–20.
25. Matias, J. N., and Monroy-Hernandez, A. Newspad: designing for collaborative storytelling in neighborhoods. In *CHI'14 Extended Abstracts on Human Factors in Computing Systems*, ACM (2014), 1987–1992.
26. McAdam, D., McCarthy, J. D., and Zald, M. N. *Comparative perspectives on social movements: Political opportunities, mobilizing structures, and cultural framings.* Cambridge University Press, 1996.
27. McKenzie, G., Deutsch, K., Raubal, M., Mooney, P., and Rehrl, K. What, when and where: The real-world activities that contribute to online social networking posts. In *International Workshop on Action and Interaction in Volunteered Geographic Information (ACTIVITY), Leuven, Belgium, edited by Peter Mooney, and Karl Rehrl* (2013), 25–30.
28. Mejova, Y., Garimella, V. R. K., Weber, I., and Dougal, M. C. Giving is caring: understanding donation behavior through email. In *Proceedings of the 17th ACM conference on Computer supported cooperative work & social computing*, ACM (2014), 1297–1307.
29. Monroy-Hernández, A., boyd, d., Kiciman, E., Choudhury, D., and Counts, S. The new war correspondents: The rise of civic media curation in urban warfare. In *Proceedings of the 2013 Conference on Computer Supported Cooperative Work*, CSCW '13, ACM (New York, NY, USA, 2013), 1443–1452.
30. Monroy-Hernández, A., Farnham, S., Kiciman, E., Counts, S., and Choudhury, D. Smart societies: from citizens as sensors to collective action. *interactions 20*, 4 (2013), 16–19.
31. Noticias, R. A. *Autodefensas en Facebook relegan al gobierno a la hora de difundir informacion.* Aristegui Noticias, 2014. http://aristeguinoticias.com/2603/mexico/autodefensasenfacebook-releganalgobiernoalahoradedifundirinformacion/.
32. Processo. *Se enfrentan militares y autodefensas en Michoacan; reportan muerte de civiles.* 2014. http://www.proceso.com.mx/?p=362352.
33. Robertson, S., Vatrapu, R., and Medina, R. Off the wall political discourse: Facebook use in the 2008 u.s. presidential election. *Info. Pol. 15*, 1,2 (Apr. 2010), 11–31.
34. Savage, S., Baranski, M., Chavez, N. E., and Hollerer, T. I'm feeling loco: A location based context aware recommendation system. In *Advances in Location-Based Services: 8th International Symposium on Location-Based Services, Vienna 2011*, Lecture Notes in Geoinformation and Cartography. Springer, 2011.
35. Savage, S., Forbes, A., Toxtli, C., McKenzie, G., Desai, S., and Höllerer, T. Visualizing Targeted Audiences. *COOP 2014-Proceedings of the 11th International Conference on the Design of Cooperative Systems, 27-30 May 2014, Nice (France)* (2014), 17–34.
36. Smelser, N. Theory of collective behavior. *Cambridge New York, Cambridge University Press, Coll.* (1962).
37. Strauss, A., and Juliet, C. *Basics of Qualitative Research : Techniques and Procedures for Developing Grounded Theory.* SAGE Publications, Sept. 1998.
38. Sumner, W. H. *An Inquiry Into the Importance of the Militia to a Free Commonwealth: In a Letter from William H. Sumner... to John Adams, Late President of the United States; with His Answer*, vol. 40. Cummings and Hilliard, 1823.
39. Weeber, S., and Rodeheaver, D. Militias at the millennium. *The Sociological Quarterly 44*, 2 (2003), 181–204.
40. Weimann, G. *New Terrorism and New Media.* Wilson Center Common Labs, 2014.
41. Wulf, V., Aal, K., Abu Kteish, I., Atam, M., Schubert, K., Rohde, M., Yerousis, G. P., and Randall, D. Fighting against the wall: Social media use by political activists in a palestinian village. In *Proceedings of the SIGCHI Conference on Human Factors in Computing Systems*, CHI '13, ACM (New York, NY, USA, 2013), 1979–1988.
42. Zabludovsky, K. *Reclaiming the Forests and the Right to Feel Safe.* New York Times, 2012. http://www.nytimes.com/2012/08/03/world/americas/inmexico-reclaimingtheforestsandtherighttofeelsafe.html.
43. Zambrano, R. New technologies and democratic governance: Towards a more inclusive participation? *IN THE CONSTRUCTION OF DEMOCRACY*, 139.

MoodBar: Increasing New User Retention in Wikipedia through Lightweight Socialization

Giovanni Luca Ciampaglia
School of Informatics and Computing,
Indiana University
919 E 10th St., Bloomington, IN 47409, USA
gciampag@indiana.edu

Dario Taraborelli
Wikimedia Foundation, Inc.
149 New Montgomery St. Floor 6,
San Francisco, CA 94105, USA
dtaraborelli@wikimedia.org

ABSTRACT
Socialization in online communities allows existing members to welcome and recruit newcomers, introduce them to community norms and practices, and sustain their early participation. However, socializing newcomers does not come for free: in large communities, socialization can result in a significant workload for mentors and is hard to scale. In this study we present results from an experiment that measured the effect of a lightweight socialization tool on the activity and retention of newly registered users attempting to edit for the first time Wikipedia. Wikipedia is struggling with the retention of newcomers and our results indicate that a mechanism to elicit lightweight feedback and to provide early mentoring to newcomers improves their chances of becoming long-term contributors.

Author Keywords
Wikipedia; online community; socialization; user retention; experiment.

ACM Classification Keywords
H.5.3 [Information Interfaces]: Group and Organization Interfaces – Collaborative computing, Computer-supported cooperative work, Web-based interaction

INTRODUCTION
Improving the experience and retention of newcomers is one of the main challenges that Wikipedia is facing these days. The base of contributors to the "free encyclopedia that anyone can edit" has been suffering from a gradual deterioration since reaching a tipping point at the end of a rapid growth phase. The number of active editors on the English Wikipedia, defined as all registered users who performed at least five edits in a given month, peaked around 2007 and has been steadily decreasing ever since [32, 34]. This stagnation in the contributor base primarily affects larger and more mature projects like the flagship, English-language edition and less so smaller Wikipedia editions in other languages. However, the trend remains a concern that the Wikimedia Foundation – the nonprofit organization that runs Wikipedia – is currently tackling with dedicated programs and interventions.

CSCW'15, March 14-18 2015, Vancouver, BC, Canada
Copyright is held by the owner/author(s). Publication rights licensed to ACM. ACM 978-1-4503-2922-4/15/03...$15.00
http://dx.doi.org/10.1145/2675133.2675181

Long-term trends in new user retention have caused similar concerns. Longitudinal analysis of cohorts of 'new' editors – editors who reach ten or more lifetime contributions – shows that one year after the 10-edit milestone the fraction of those who performed one or more edits has gone down from about 40%, for 2004 cohorts, to about 10% for those of 2009 [34]. The phenomenon has been acknowledged by the Wikipedia community and covered by popular press outlets, which refer to it as the "decline" of Wikipedia [31, 33].

Wikipedia is a complex socio-technical system, so various factors may contribute to the decline in newcomer retention. In particular, the leading hypothesis suggests that as a result of the desire to maintain high quality standards and to fight vandalism [27] over the years the Wikipedia editor community has become impervious to new contributors [16], who nowadays have to cope with a daunting body of norms and policies [5] and sometimes unpleasant social exchanges, despite producing the same rate of good faith contributions as users who joined the project in earlier years [17]. Such an unintended consequence is not unlikely, since formal and informal norms about contributions [10], socialization [9], and even language use [11] often calcify in online communities. Without adequate support, newly recruited community members may have trouble conforming to these tacit or explicit norms.

One possible solution to deal with a shrinking contributor base is to increase the influx of new users, but competition for attention among different social media platforms [2, 30] implies that this process is largely out of control of any single community – Wikipedia included. A complementary approach consists in increasing the participation and retention of existing contributors once they join the project.

The effect of socialization – the period during which a new member learns the social norms and conventions of a group – on retention has received much attention in the social psychological literature on online communities [6, 9, 14, 24]. Typical socialization tactics include welcoming messages and the creation of safe sandboxing spaces where newcomers have

Happy
i loved it it was omg fun
I am a robot
Everything I have edited is correct.
I love editing but why do u delete my pages ?
I feel powerful, muahahaha.
Sad
I can't edit protected articles
Wikipedia is a proganda. (*sic.*)
I couldn't edit the intro. This needs a lot of work!
wikipedia doesnt let me troll :(
Site is slow again.
Confused
i cant start a new page
too much code :[
The letters are hard to read
Can't change my user name
Editing in Arabic is somehow awkward because of RTL/LTR usual layout problems ...

Table 1: Examples of feedback posted via MoodBar.

an opportunity to learn. These efforts are usually tailored to small groups within a broader community, and are often time-consuming for those who run them. Simpler approaches may have the benefit of reaching a larger audience, but at the same time their effect on retention and engagement may be limited.

The goal of this study is to present results from an experiment on a simple, lightweight socialization process and to understand its impact on the long-term retention of newcomers in an open collaboration community. MoodBar is an experimental feature introduced in Wikipedia between 2011 and 2013 with the goal of eliciting feedback from newly registered users. It allows new users to send feedback (or share their 'mood') about their first editing experience on Wikipedia (Figure 1). Feedback is posted on a public dashboard and replied to by a team of experienced volunteers. As the name suggests, each piece of feedback is characterized by a mood indicator ('sad', 'happy' or 'confused') that gives a simple qualitative clue about the nature of the message. Users experiencing issues with editing can report their problems, typically via "sad" or 'confused' moods, and receive assistance to overcome them. Users can also express gratitude towards the project as a whole or happiness for completing a milestone, such as successfully saving a first edit. Table 1 gives a few examples of feedback posted via MoodBar.

Our hypothesis is that, despite its extreme simplicity, lightweight socialization of the kind provided by MoodBar can be effective at improving the chances that a newly registered user survives as a long-term contributor. By using a combination of observational and experimental methods, we aim to address the following research questions:

RQ 1. *Do users post feedback about their* early *editing experience, or is feedback posted at a later stage?*

RQ 2. *Is reporting feedback associated with a higher productivity by newcomers in the short term?*

RQ 3. *Does posting feedback and receiving a response improve long-term retention of newcomers?*

In the first part of the study we characterize how MoodBar is used and by whom. We analyze how the tool is utilized with respect to the designers' intentions, that is, to report feedback about early editing experience on Wikipedia. We then focus on the productivity of those who used MoodBar to report feedback, and compare them to the larger population of newly registered users. We find that in the early stage of activity MoodBar users are in general more productive than users who do not share their mood and that productivity increases for those users who received a response to their feedback. Usage of MoodBar appears to be strongly associated with higher levels of contribution.

A potential explanation of this result is a self-selection bias. Sending feedback requires locating a small link at top of a page and writing a short (140 characters) message. Having the intention and the ability to send feedback may itself be a strong indicator of the presence of cognitive and social skills required to succeed in a complex socio-technical environment such as Wikipedia [13]. A purely observational method can only reveal whether usage of MoodBar is associated with higher rates of activity and retention, not that the association is a form of causation.

In the second part of this study, we analyze the long-term retention of a large sample of newly registered Wikipedia users. We analyzed the behavior of a group of users who were not able to see or post messages via MoodBar, because the link to post a mood message was suppressed. This group of users served as our control group. We compared their long-term retention to that of a group of users who had regular access to MoodBar (the treatment group), registered shortly before users in the control group.

We found that after 180 days since registration users in the treatment group had a small but significant increase in retention compared to users in the control group. Significant differences in retention between the two groups emerge as early as 120 days after registration. Since the only known difference between the two groups is the availability of MoodBar, this rules out the presence of selection bias and suggests that MoodBar has a positive effect on long-term retention of these users. It should be noted that only a small fraction of newly registered users has the chance of interacting with MoodBar, thus while at the group level the overall effect of MoodBar is very small ($d = 0.22\%$), we estimate that the relative increase must be higher.

The rest of the paper is organized as follows: in the next section we review related work on early socialization in online communities. We then present the methodology used in the study: we describe how MoodBar works, how the data used in this study was collected, and present the methodology used in the remainder of this work. We conclude by discussing design implications of our findings in the final section of the paper.

Figure 1: The MoodBar interface. Left: as soon the user clicks on the "Edit" button of a page for the first time, a yellow tooltip appears inviting the user to send feedback about the editing experience. Right: as the user clicks on the MoodBar link, a larger window appears with a feedback form.

RELATED WORK

A large literature has studied incentives and drivers of participation in online communities, with a focus on early socialization. Early research on Wikipedia and open source software projects suggests that a mix of intrinsic motivation and extrinsic rewards drives participation [18, 20, 36]. Top contributors may have strong intrinsic motives to participate [26]. Non-monetary rewards such as acknowledgements [4, 21, 28, 8], badges [29, 1], and gamified feedback [12] have been shown to increase engagement of users. Certain forms of reward can exert fine-grained control, even though instilling long-term behavior still proves to be difficult [1].

Besides individual incentives, previous studies also stressed the importance of the initial period of socialization in online groups. A successful early socialization experience is associated with, and sometimes even predicts, increased engagement in mailing lists [3], newsgroups [19], social networks [6], and Wikipedia [9, 24], to cite a few. However, the causal structure between socialization, motivation, and participation is still not entirely clear. Strong motivational factors, perhaps in conjunction with individual-level skills [13], may be the cause for both a successful early socialization stage and a later long-term participation. To further establish a causal connection, controlled and field experiments on groups of limited size have been performed, with encouraging results: sharing in a digital information good is increased by social incentives [7], personal messages improve the retention of newcomers to Wikipedia who had their edits rejected [15], and top contributors in a Q&A community contributed more on the long term if they had received a personalized socialization experience [14].

METHODS

MoodBar is an experimental Mediawiki extension, loosely inspired by the Mozilla Firefox Input system [25]. It allows newly registered users to send their feedback (or share their 'mood') about their first edit experience on Wikipedia (Figure 1). Because it is meant to elicit feedback from newly registered users at their first edit, MoodBar activates itself only after the user attempts to edit a page for the first time. Upon

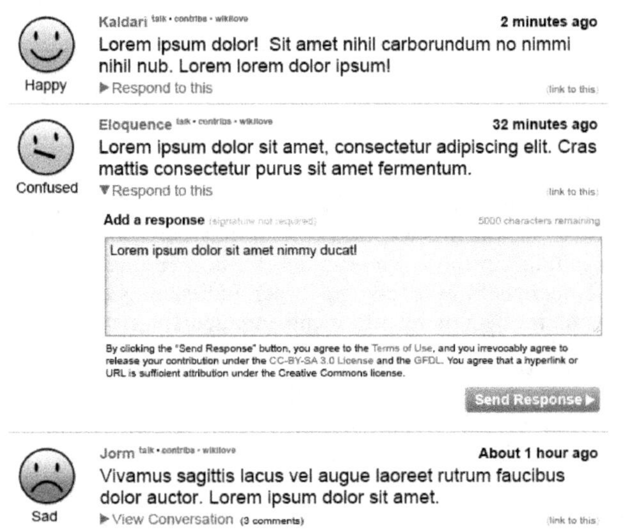

Figure 2: A mockup of the Feedback Dashboard displaying mood messages posted by newcomers that volunteers can respond to.

clicking on the 'Edit' button, a link appears in the upper left area of the screen together with a brief notification in the form of a tooltip, (Figure 1, left).

Clicking on the MoodBar link a non-modal window appears (Figure 1, right), allowing the user to select one out of three moods and post a short feedback message. Feeback posted by the user is displayed on a public Feedback Dashboard (Figure 2), where it can be processed by a team of experienced volunteers. When MoodBar feedback is replied to by a volunteer, a message is automatically published on the talk page of the original poster, and if the user has a verified email address on file an email notification is sent. The original poster can then read the response and, if they find it useful, publicly mark it as such on the Feedback Dashboard.

Group	Start	End	N
Historical	2011-12-14	2012-05-22	528,891
Hist. (Reference)	2011-12-14	2012-05-22	515,438
Hist. (Feedback)	2011-12-14	2012-05-22	8,599
Hist. (Feed.+Resp.)	2011-12-14	2012-05-22	4,164
Hist. (Feed.+Useful)	2011-12-14	2012-05-22	690
Treatment	2012-05-23	2012-06-14	64,652
Control	2012-06-15	2012-06-29	40,389

Table 2: The samples of users of this study. Users who registered an accounts on the English Wikipedia and clicked on the 'Edit' button at least once are assigned to a group based on the registration date.

Datasets

The data we used in this study was extracted from the database of the English Wikipedia, where MoodBar was deployed between July 2011 and February 2013. An earlier version of MoodBar allowed users to report a mood without inserting any message and did not not show any tooltip notification upon activation. In a second iteration, finally deployed in December 2011, the text message was made mandatory and a prominent tooltip was introduced. In this study we only consider data collected from this second version of MoodBar. The samples of users we considered for our analysis are summarized in Table 2.

Observational study

We use the 'Historical' sample (Table 2, top) to perform the observational part of the study. This sample spans about 5 months of new account registrations. Automated accounts (bots) were filtered out using a list of such accounts. We compute two metrics for users in this sample. The first metric is the time lag between the activation of MoodBar (i.e. the first time the 'Edit' button is clicked) and the first feedback posted by a user, if any. If a user did not send any feedback, we include a censored observation, indicating that she could still potentially send one in the future. To estimate the survival rate and filter inactive accounts, we considered only users who performed at least one edit to compute this metric. This reduced the sample size to $N = 95,586$ users, of which only $19,219$ sent feedback (i.e. actual, uncensored observations). The time stamp of the first 'Edit' click was tracked by the 'EditPageTracking' extension [22], an ancillary extension of MoodBar.

The second metric, which we use to quantify short-term productivity, is the cumulative number of contributions measured at 1, 2, 5, 10, and 30 days of days since registration. We counted contributions to any type of page on Wikipedia, including project pages and user talk pages. Contribution data was collected via the 'UserDailyContribs' extension [23]. We computed these metrics for the full 'Historical' sample, but we further distinguish users based on their type of interaction with MoodBar (Table 2, middle). We consider four mutually exclusive groups: all users who attempted to edit and saw the tooltip but did not send any feedback ('Reference'), those who did posted feedback but received no response ('Feedback'), those who posted feedback and got a response but did not mark it as helpful ('Feed.+Resp.'), and those who did mark the response as helpful ('Feed.+Useful'). In the rare case that a user sent multiple feedback messages, we use only the first feedback to determine which of the three sub-groups she belongs to.

Natural experiment

In the second part of the study, we test the socialization effects of MoodBar on long-term retention by identifying a treatment and control group (Table 2, bottom).

The metric we use to quantify long-term user retention is the survival probability at $t = 180$ days since registration, which is defined as the fraction of users who made at least one contribution at any time $t' > t$. To compute it, we collected user contribution data from both cohorts up to a year after the end of the registration window of the latest of the two cohorts. This amounts to an observation window for t' of at least 27 weeks.

To identify the control group we suppressed the link to MoodBar for all users registered during a specific time window. Other approaches, for example showing the link to only a subset of users during the same period could have been possible too, but since we needed to run the experiment on Wikipedia's production servers, we opted for the simplest to implement and deploy.

Power analysis

Users who sent a feedback with MoodBar are a tiny fraction of the overall population of users who saw the MoodBar link. A conservative upper bound from the 'Historical' sample taking into account only users who clicked at least once on the 'Edit' button is equal to 2.5%.

This means that when diluted within the broader population of registered users the difference in retention between the treatment and the control group, if any, is going to be very small. We performed *a priori* power analysis to determine the minimum sample size before collecting data for the treatment and control group cohorts and used the 'Historical' sample to do so, as the most recent available sample of users (see Appendix).

The power of a statistical test is the probability of correctly rejecting the null hypothesis. The minimum sample size required to detect a difference in retention equal to Δ with a test of power $1 - \beta = 80\%$ and significance $\alpha = 5\%$ is given by:

$$N^* = \frac{16\sigma^2}{\Delta^2} \qquad (1)$$

In our case, using the first estimate of π_m (see Appendix), we obtain $N^* = 130,763$ users. Assuming that an underestimate to the average daily of new registered users who activate MoodBar is about $1,600$, this would require us to keep MoodBar disabled for at least 82 days in order to gather enough users for the control group cohort.

UI manipulation

Instead of opting for such a long window, we decided to (1) elicit more feedback by increasing the saliency of MoodBar, and (2) increase the rate of replies on the Feedback Dashboard. Receiving a reply to the feedback is associated to an even higher value of π_m, and thus of Δ. Since we expect the impact of MoodBar on retention to be caused by socialization, i.e. by feedback responses, we calculated that a conservative boosting factor of $b = 1.5$ in the fraction of users who received a reply to their feedback would result in $N^* = 15,329$ and in a registration window of at least 10 days. Based on these considerations, we chose a registration window for the control group of two weeks.

In order to improve the saliency of MoodBar we manipulated the user interface and increased the size of the MoodBar link, and allowed the notification tooltip to stay on screen for a few more seconds before disappearing (see Figure 1). To increase the rate of replies we issued a call to actions to the team of volunteers by asking them to provide replies to incoming posts via the Feedback Dashboard.

RESULTS

Observational study

Our first question is whether MoodBar is effectively being used to post feedback about *early* editing experience. To answer this question we look at the hazard rate, the probability of sending a feedback at a specific time lag given that the user has not sent any feedback before. Figure 3 shows the hazard rate curve estimated on the 'Historical' sample. The time lag on the x-axis is computed since the activation of MoodBar, i.e. since the time the user clicks on the 'Edit' button for the first time. The hazard drops after the first few days: on the tenth day the hazard rate is about 14 times lower than on the first day. This confirms our hypothesis (RQ 1) that MoodBar is indeed used to report on early editing experiences. Looking at the actual mood reported, we find that the median time to report 'confused' and 'happy' moods is roughly 30 minutes, while 'sad' moods take longer, about 2 hours.

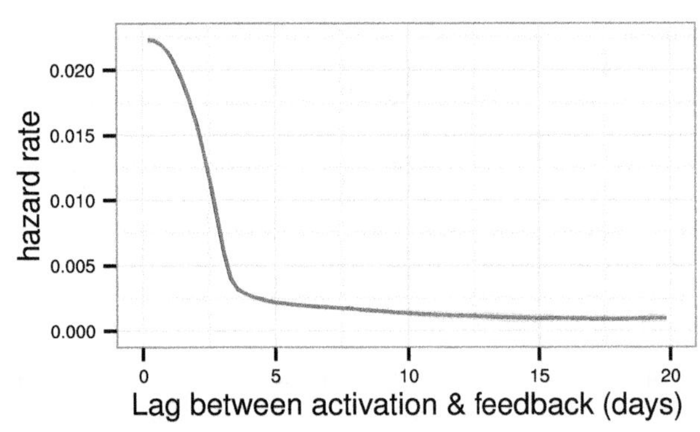

Figure 3: Smoothed hazard rate (see text for definition) of the first MoodBar feedback in the 20 days since the earliest click on the 'edit' button. Resampled 95% confidence bounds are smaller than the width of the line.

Our second question concerns the productivity of MoodBar users against the broader population of registered Wikipedia users who attempted to edit ('Reference'). Table 3 shows the average cumulative number of contribution of users in the 'Historical' sample at various days since registration. MoodBar users are more productive than users in the 'Reference' group. At 30 days since registration those who received a useful feedback ('Feed.+Useful') where about 9 times more productive than those who never sent a feedback.

We confirmed the increased productivity of MoodBar users by performing a regression analysis in which we control for the month of registration, to account for seasonality, and the lag between account registration and activation of MoodBar. Regarding the choice of the regression model, it should be noted that the data is overdispersed, with a variance-to-mean ratio $\sigma^2/\mu > 1$ in all cases. To address this issue we used a negative binomial generalized linear model. The ratio of residual deviance to degrees of freedom in the fitted model is very close to 1 ($D/d.f. = 0.9478$), which indicates a good fit.

We also checked the plausibility of a self-selection bias via a simple observation. By definition, since their feedback did not receive any reply, users in the 'Feedback' group missed the opportunity for socialization offered by MoodBar, so these users should not be different than the reference group. However, according to the regression model, these users are significantly more productive than the reference group by a factor of 2.36 times ($p < 0.001$). We take this as strong evidence for the existence of self-selection bias among MoodBar users (RQ 2).

Natural experiment

We assessed the impact of the increased saliency of the MoodBar link by measuring the weekly volume of feedback messages posted and the weekly ratio of replies to feedback posted during the first seven months of 2012 (Figure 4). Feedback volume spiked during the registration window of the treatment group, and dropped on the third week of June as a consequence of the suppression of the MoodBar link. The volume did not go to zero during this blackout, as MoodBar was still available to users registered before the experiment. For the same reason, the spike in feedback volume reflects feedback posted both by newly and previously registered users.

We can estimate the actual boost factor by comparing the volume of feedback before the UI tweak to that after the end of the control group window. This method yields a boosting factor of $b = 1.54$. The weekly ratio of replies to feedback increased as well, reaching a peak two weeks after the beginning of the registration window of the control group. On that week, the replies ratio was slightly above 100%, since volunteers replied to older feedback too.

To answer the last research question – whether or not MoodBar has a positive effect on long-term retention (RQ 3) – we seek to reject the null hypothesis that the proportion of retained users at 180 days in the control and treatment groups is the same, that is, $H_0 : \pi_m = \pi_{\not m}$. The two samples are

Days since registration	Reference		Feedback		Feed.+Resp.		Feed.+Useful	
1	1.83	(4.95)	3.90	(9.34)	3.70	(8.47)	6.82	(16.96)
2	1.95	(5.63)	4.52	(12.45)	4.18	(10.32)	8.09	(19.09)
5	2.20	(7.56)	5.83	(19.41)	5.22	(15.44)	11.38	(26.65)
10	2.51	(11.10)	7.54	(27.10)	6.37	(22.50)	16.27	(46.10)
30	3.16	(24.20)	11.72	(53.50)	9.55	(58.20)	27.75	(90.70)

Table 3: Mean and standard deviation (in parentheses) of the number of contributions at 1, 2, 5, 10, and 30 days since registration for the different sub-samples of the 'Historical' group.

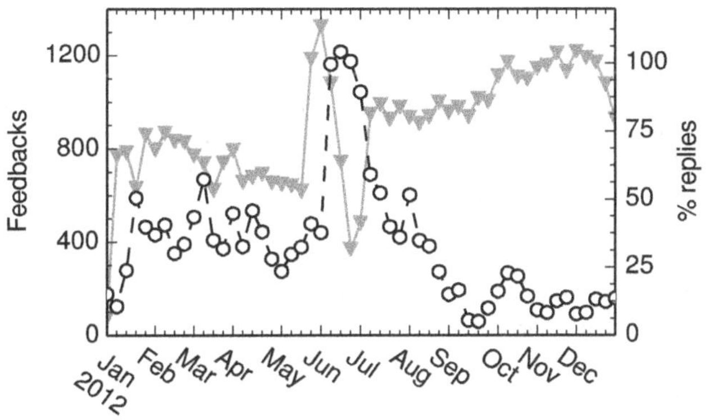

Figure 4: Weekly volume of MoodBar feedback messages posted (gray triangles) and weekly ratio of replies to feedback messages (white circles).

independent, so we use a two-tailed test based on the normal approximation and a pooled estimate of the variance. Using this test, we were able to reject H_0 ($z = -2.56, p = 0.01$). Figure 5 (left) plots the estimates computed from the data, showing a small but clear difference. *Post hoc* power analysis yields a statistical power of $1 - \hat{\beta} = 73.88\%$, consistent to our original expectations.

We also looked at the evolution of differences in retention during the whole 6 month period. Figure 5 (right) shows the full retention curves in the interval $[0, 180]$ days. Differences in retention between the two groups, as evidenced by the overlap between the respective 95% confidence intervals, emerge for a brief period around 50 days. From 120 days onward the two intervals no longer overlap.

DISCUSSION

The two groups we considered in the experiment were cohorts of users registered in two consecutive windows lasting about a month in total. Because we could not control who registered during both periods, our methodology is closer to the category of natural experiments than to that of controlled randomized designs. To the best of our knowledge, no other treatment was administered to users in these cohorts during that period and given the short time frame considered we make the assumption that the composition of the two groups in terms of individual-level skills is homogeneous. Therefore, we can reasonably assume that only difference between the group that is driving the effect is access to MoodBar for users in the treatment group.

One counterintuitive aspect of our experiment is that despite its robustness, the group-level effect of MoodBar on retention, being diluted on the whole sample of registered users, is small in absolute terms. This is a consequence of the limited saliency of MoodBar within the UI of Wikipedia, which results in a very small value of p, the probability that an editor sends a feedback. This means that very few people used MoodBar, and thus their impact on the overall group retention is limited.

Things change dramatically at the individual level, where we see some evidence that MoodBar has marked effects on retention and engagement. The relative increase of the retention of users with successful socialization experience ('Feed.+Useful') over the baseline of those who did not send any feedback ('Reference') is 707%. To at least partially account for the self-selection bias we can use as baseline those who posted feedback but did not receive any reply ('Feedback'). These users never enjoyed the benefits of socialization, so their higher retention rates must be only due to their individual skills/motivation. The relative increase in this case is a more conservative 143%. This line of reasoning, however, does not completely rule out self-selection bias, so these figures should be taken at face value and not as estimates of the individual-level retention increase due to MoodBar.

Finally, the engagement increase of different sub-groups of MoodBar users in the 'Historical' sample (see Table 3) suggests that most benefits of using MoodBar come from receiving a useful reply, which confirms the idea that newcomers benefit the most from active socialization exchanges with existing users, and not just from simply posting a feedback.

CONCLUSION AND FUTURE DIRECTIONS

Our findings provide evidence that early mentoring of newcomers in an open collaboration system through lightweight socialization tools such as MoodBar improves their engagement and retention.

We found that eliciting feedback via simple UI manipulations is an effective way to reach users who are at the earliest stages of their editing experience and might otherwise be unable to receive mentoring and support (RQ 1). We also found that these feedback mechanisms tend to self-select users who have a higher natural propensity to become active contributors (RQ 2). Finally, we found evidence that early interaction with

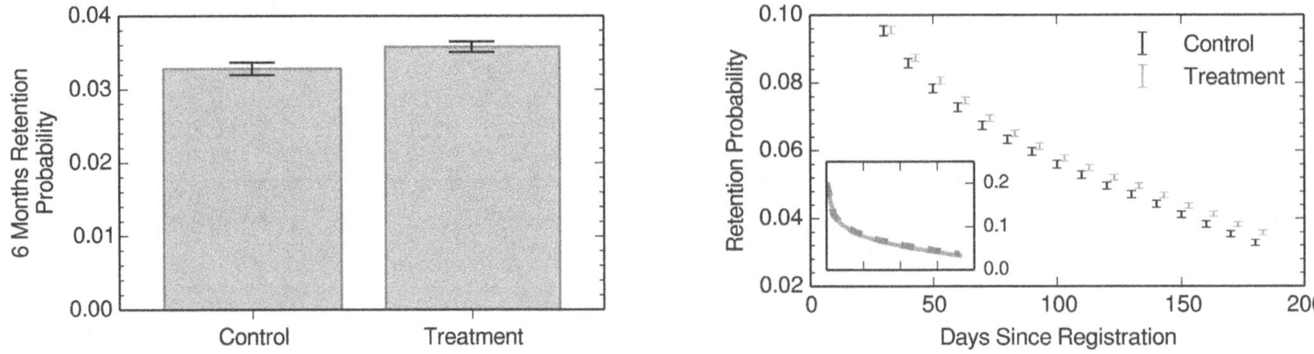

Figure 5: *Left*: Retention probability at 180 days after registration for the two experimental groups. Error bars are 95% confidence intervals. *Right*: A zoomed detail of the full retention curves of the two groups. For ease of comparison, the treatment curve is shifted on the right of 3 days. Error bars are 95% confidence intervals. The inset shows the full curve with no shifting. The red dashed line is the treatment group.

these feedback mechanisms has a significant, long-lasting effect on the retention of these users (RQ 3).

Considering that experienced contributors perform a large amount of work on Wikipedia, we submit that designing interfaces like MoodBar could help mitigate the stagnation and newcomer retention problem Wikipedia is currently facing.

There are a number of limitations and possible research directions that this study did not explore and future research should address.

Despite the fact that a relative small number of experienced users in the "response team" successfully managed to work through a backlog of feedback messages to respond to, our results do not indicate how scalable this approach would be and at what point the ability to socialize a substantially larger number of newcomers would start to break down. We provided evidence that lightweight interaction, based on very short messages and responses, can go a long way in socializing new users but also indicated that the workload was manageable at the current scale. Research indicating that canned, depersonalized messages can negatively impact newcomer retention suggests that any attempt to run the MoodBar model at a larger scale would need to assess the risk of depersonalized communication [15].

We did not perform any kind of qualitative analysis on the type of messages elicited by newcomers to try and understand how self-reported mood and the specific issues being discussed may be associated with engagement and retention. As a result, we do not know what socialization strategy is the most effective, and what aspect in the socialization process afforded by MoodBar drives editor retention. Qualitative analysis of messages exchanged in the context of this lightweight process should be compared with findings from previous studies where more in-depth socialization strategies were considered [24].

Finally, in this study we only considered newcomers on the English Wikipedia. Data from other Wikipedia language editions indicates that other communities have different retention rates for newcomers. As a result, our findings may not immediately generalize to other Wikipedia communities governed by different norms or practices, or composed by a substantially different user demographics. At a broader level, however, our finding applies to any online community where users contribute content, such as ratings, reviews, or photos; wikis are just an example of open collaboration communities and any of these has its own set of norms about contribution. In fact, the problem of socializing a suddenly growing number of newcomers, or "eternal September", dates back to the early period of USENET groups. Our results thus provide evidence that lightweight socialization tools could make newcomer socialization sustainable in other online communities too.

While MoodBar was retired as an experiment from the English Wikipedia in 2013, it is still in use in other Wikimedia projects, so the methodology used in this study could be replicated to other projects to provide an additional validation.

ACKNOWLEDGMENTS

The authors would like to thank all Wikipedia contributors who volunteered at the Feedback Dashboard during the course of the experiment, Jonathan Morgan for useful comments, Howie Fung, Benny Situ, and the Editor Engagement Team at the Wikimedia Foundation for their assistance with setting up the experiment, and the Wikimedia Foundation for supporting the work. Giovanni Luca Ciampaglia was partially supported by the Swiss National Science Foundation under fellowship no. 142353 and by the Center for Complex Networks and Systems Research at Indiana University.

APPENDIX

POWER ANALYSIS

Since we had a sample where any user could potentially access MoodBar, we estimated the expected difference in retention between treatment and control from that of the whole sample by subtracting from it the contribution due to MoodBar users. Let us denote with p the probability that a user posts feedback using MoodBar, with π the probability of retention of a user, with π_m the probability of retention of a MoodBar user, and with $\pi_{\not m}$ the probability of retention of a non-MoodBar user (i.e. a user who does not send any feedback). We are interested in estimating the difference $\Delta = \pi_m - \pi_{\not m}$. It is the case that:

$$\pi = p\pi_m + (1-p)\,\pi_{\not m} \tag{2}$$

And so, substituting for $\pi_{\not m}$ in Δ we have:

$$\Delta = \frac{p}{1-p}\left(\pi - \pi_m\right) \tag{3}$$

which we can easily estimate from the 'Historical' sample. We quantify the effect size using the standardized difference, or Cohen's $d = \Delta/\sigma$ [35], where σ is the pooled standard deviation of the two groups:

$$\sigma = \sqrt{\frac{(N_m - 1)\,\sigma_m^2 + (N_{\not m} - 1)\,\sigma_{\not m}^2}{N_m + N_{\not m} - 2}} \tag{4}$$

where N_m and $N_{\not m}$ are the number of users who sent at least a feedback and of those who did not send any feedback, respectively, and σ_m and $\sigma_{\not m}$ the standard deviations. On the 'Historical' sample, $d = 0.22\%$ for the retention at $t = 30$ days since registration. If we compute π_m and p on the subset of MoodBar users who received a reply to their feedback, $d = 0.09\%$.

REFERENCES

1. Anderson, A., Huttenlocher, D., Kleinberg, J., and Leskovec, J. Steering user behavior with badges. In *Proceedings of the 22nd International Conference on World Wide Web*, WWW '13, International World Wide Web Conferences Steering Committee (Republic and Canton of Geneva, Switzerland, 2013), 95–106.
2. Backstrom, L., Huttenlocher, D., Kleinberg, J., and Xiangyang, L. Group formation in large social networks: Membership, growth, and evolution. In *Proc. of the 12th ACM SIGKDD international conference on Knowledge discovery and data mining* (Philadelphia, PA, USA, 2006).
3. Backstrom, L., Kumar, R., Marlow, C., Novak, J., and Tomkins, A. Preferential behavior in online groups. In *Proc. of WSDM'08* (Dec 2007), 1–11.
4. Beenen, G., Ling, K., Wang, X., Chang, K., Frankowski, D., Resnick, P., and Kraut, R. E. Using social psychology to motivate contributions to online communities. In *Proceedings of the 2004 ACM conference on Computer supported cooperative work*, CSCW '04, ACM (New York, NY, USA, 2004), 212–221.
5. Beschastnikh, I., Kriplean, T., and McDonald, D. W. Wikipedian self-governance in action: Motivating the policy lens. In *Proceedings of the 2nd International Conference on Weblogs and Social Media* (2008).
6. Burke, M., Marlow, C., and Lento, T. Feed me: Motivating newcomer contribution in social network sites. In *Proceedings of the SIGCHI Conference on Human Factors in Computing Systems*, CHI '09, ACM (New York, NY, USA, 2009), 945–954.
7. Cheshire, C. Selective incentives and generalized information exchange. *Social Psychology Quarterly 70*, 1 (2007), 82–100.
8. Cheshire, C., and Antin, J. The social psychological effects of feedback on the production of internet information pools. *Journal of Computer-Mediated Communication 13*, 3 (2008), 705–727.
9. Choi, B., Alexander, K., Kraut, R. E., and Levine, J. M. Socialization tactics in Wikipedia and their effects. In *Proceedings of the 2010 ACM Conference on Computer Supported Cooperative Work*, CSCW '10, ACM (New York, NY, USA, 2010), 107–116.
10. Ciampaglia, G. L. A bounded confidence approach to understand user participation in peer production systems. In *Third International Conference on Social Informatics (SocInfo'11)*, LNCS, Springer Verlang (Singapore, 6 - 8 October 2011).
11. Danescu-Niculescu-Mizil, C., West, R., Jurafsky, D., Leskovec, J., and Potts, C. No country for old members: User lifecycle and linguistic change in online communities. In *Proceedings of the 22nd International Conference on World Wide Web*, WWW '13, International World Wide Web Conferences Steering Committee (Republic and Canton of Geneva, Switzerland, 2013), 307–318.
12. Deterding, S., Sicart, M., Nacke, L., O'Hara, K., and Dixon, D. Gamification. using game-design elements in non-gaming contexts. In *CHI '11 Extended Abstracts on Human Factors in Computing Systems*, CHI EA '11, ACM (New York, NY, USA, 2011), 2425–2428.
13. Egan, D. E. *Handbook of human-computer interaction*. Elsevier Science, New York, 1988, ch. Individual differences in human-computer interaction, 543–568.
14. Farzan, R., Kraut, R., Pal, A., and Konstan, J. Socializing volunteers in an online community: A field experiment. In *Proceedings of the ACM 2012 Conference on Computer Supported Cooperative Work*, CSCW '12, ACM (New York, NY, USA, 2012), 325–334.
15. Geiger, R. S., Halfaker, A., Pinchuk, M., and Walling, S. Defense mechanism or socialization tactic? improving Wikipedia's notifications to rejected contributors. In *Proceedings of the Sixth International AAAI Conference on Weblogs and Social Media*, AAAI (2012), 122–129.
16. Goldman, E. Wikipedia's labor squeeze and its consequences. *J. on Telecomm. & High Tech. L. 8* (2010), 157.

17. Halfaker, A., Geiger, R. S., Morgan, J., and Riedl, J. The rise and decline of an open collaboration system: How Wikipedia's reaction to sudden popularity is causing its decline. *American Behavioral Scientist 57*, 5 (May 2013), 664–688.

18. Hars, A., and Ou, S. Working for free? - motivations of participating in open source projects. *Hawaii International Conference on System Sciences 7* (2001), 7014.

19. Joyce, E., and Kraut, R. E. Predicting continued participation in newsgroups. *Journal of Computer-Mediated Communication 11*, 3 (2006), 723–747.

20. Lerner, J., and Tirole, J. Some simple economics of Open Source. *The Journal of Industrial Economics 50*, 2 (2002), 197–234.

21. Ling, K., Beenen, G., Ludford, P., Wang, X., Chang, K., Li, X., Cosley, D., Frankowski, D., Terveen, L., Rashid, A. M., Resnick, P., and Kraut, R. Using social psychology to motivate contributions to online communities. *Journal of Computer-Mediated Communication 10*, 4 (2005), 00–00.

22. MediaWiki contributors. Extension:EditPageTracking. MediaWiki, The Free Wiki Engine, 2014. [Online at `http://www.mediawiki.org/wiki/Extension:EditPageTracking`, accessed 11-May-2014].

23. MediaWiki contributors. Extension:UserDailyContribs. MediaWiki, The Free Wiki Engine, 2014. [Online at `http://www.mediawiki.org/wiki/Extension:UserDailyContribs`, accessed 11-May-2014].

24. Morgan, J. T., Bouterse, S., Walls, H., and Stierch, S. Tea and sympathy: Crafting positive new user experiences on Wikipedia. In *Proceedings of the 2013 Conference on Computer Supported Cooperative Work*, CSCW '13, ACM (New York, NY, USA, 2013), 839–848.

25. Mozilla, Inc. About Firefox Input :: Firefox Input. [Online at `https://input.mozilla.org/en-US/about`, accessed 11-May-2014].

26. Panciera, K., Halfaker, A., and Terveen, L. Wikipedians are born, not made: A study of power editors on Wikipedia. In *Proceedings of the ACM 2009 International Conference on Supporting Group Work*, GROUP '09, ACM (New York, NY, USA, 2009), 51–60.

27. Priedhorsky, R., Chen, J., Lam, S. T. K., Panciera, K., Terveen, L., and Riedl, J. Creating, destroying and restoring value in Wikipedia. In *Proceedings of the 2007 international ACM SIGGROUP conference on Supporting group work* (Sanibel Island, Florida, USA., November 4–7 2007).

28. Rashid, A. M., Ling, K., Tassone, R. D., Resnick, P., Kraut, R., and Riedl, J. Motivating participation by displaying the value of contribution. In *Proceedings of the SIGCHI Conference on Human Factors in Computing Systems*, CHI '06, ACM (New York, NY, USA, 2006), 955–958.

29. Restivo, M., and van de Rijt, A. Experimental study of informal rewards in peer production. *PLoS ONE 7*, 3 (03 2012), e34358.

30. Ribeiro, B. Modeling and predicting the growth and death of membership-based websites. In *Proceedings of the 23rd international conference on World Wide Web* (2014).

31. Simonite, T. The decline of Wikipedia, 2013. [Online at `http://www.technologyreview.com/featuredstory/520446/the-decline-of-wikipedia/`, accessed 11-May-2014].

32. Suh, B., Convertino, G., Chi, E. H., and Pirolli, P. The singularity is not near: Slowing growth of Wikipedia. In *Proceedings of the 5th International Symposium on Wikis and Open Collaboration*, WikiSym '09, ACM (New York, NY, USA, 2009), 8:1–8:10.

33. The Economist. The future of Wikipedia – WikiPeaks?, 2014. [Online at `http://www.economist.com/node/21597959/print`, accessed 11-May-2014].

34. Wikimedia Strategic Planning contributors. Editor trends study. Strategic Planning, 2011. [Online at `http://strategy.wikimedia.org/w/index.php?title=Editor_Trends_Study`, accessed 11-May-2014].

35. Wilkinson, L., and the Task Force on Statistical Inference. Statistical methods in psychology journals: Guidelines and explanations. *American psychologist 54*, 8 (1999), 594–604.

36. Zhang, X. M., and Zhu, F. Intrinsic motivation of open content contributions: The case of Wikipedia. In *Workshop on Information Systems and Economics (WISE)* (2006).

The Success and Failure of Quality Improvement Projects in Peer Production Communities

Morten Warncke-Wang, Vladislav R. Ayukaev, Brent Hecht, and Loren Terveen

GroupLens Research
University of Minnesota
Minneapolis, MN 55455, USA
{morten,ayukaev,bhecht,terveen}@cs.umn.edu

ABSTRACT

Peer production communities have been proven to be successful at creating valuable artefacts, with Wikipedia as a prime example. However, a number of studies have shown that work in these communities tends to be of uneven quality and certain content areas receive more attention than others. In this paper, we examine the efficacy of a range of targeted strategies to increase the quality of under-attended content areas in peer production communities. Mining data from five quality improvement projects in the English Wikipedia, the largest peer production community in the world, we show that certain types of strategies (e.g. creating artefacts from scratch) have better quality outcomes than others (e.g. improving existing artefacts), even if both are done by a similar cohort of participants. We discuss the implications of our findings for Wikipedia as well as other peer production communities.

Author Keywords

peer production; user-generated content; quality modelling; Wikipedia

ACM Classification Keywords

H.5.3. Information Interfaces: Group and Organization Interfaces – Computer-supported cooperative work

INTRODUCTION

Peer production communities like Wikipedia and OpenStreetMap have been successful at generating large quantities of artefacts, but coverage and content quality of certain subjects can be poor. Popular media reported on Wikipedia's gender bias[1] and argued that it leads to less content about topics with a female audience, a hypothesis that Lam et al. confirmed for articles about movies [23]. Research on biographies comparing Wikipedia to Encyclopædia Britannica found that the former had better coverage and longer articles but was also more likely to be missing articles about women [33], and Wikipedia's related problems with categorisation of novelists has attracted media attention[2]. This type of problem is not limited to Wikipedia: studies of contributions to OpenStreetMap found a much larger variety of tags available to describe places related to prostitution than those related to child care [37], and lower-income areas have considerably lower coverage and content quality [14].

Solutions to these problems have been proposed both from within the communities themselves, as in groups of Wikipedia editors self-organising to improve content (called "WikiProjects") about women scientists[3] and artists[4], and also through formally organised efforts. The Wikimedia Foundation manages the Wikipedia Education Program[5], a project where educators and students across the globe work on improving Wikipedia articles as class assignments.

But the question is: do these "solutions" actually work? Some of these projects have been studied in isolation, for instance the Association for Psychological Science's (APS) Wikipedia Initiative[6], a part of the Education Program, was studied by Farzan and Kraut [10], and WikiProjects were studied by Zhu, Kittur, and Kraut [45]. However, each study took a different approach and used different measurements: Zhu et al. measured amount of effort by counting number of edits made to articles, while Farzan and Kraut measured quality by counting words added and quantifying word survival. Similarly, the Wikimedia Foundation measured quality of work done in the Education Program using human assessments of random selections of articles [34, 43].

Our research begins the process of developing a coherent framework to describe, analyse, and evaluate quality improvement projects for peer production communities. We study five different projects in the English Wikipedia, the largest peer production community in the world, to identify the factors and mechanisms associated with successful projects, resulting in the following three major findings:

[1] http://www.nytimes.com/2011/01/31/business/media/31link.html?_r=0

[2] http://www.nytimes.com/2013/04/28/opinion/sunday/wikipedias-sexism-toward-female-novelists.html

[3] https://en.wikipedia.org/wiki/Wikipedia:WikiProject_Women_scientists

[4] https://en.wikipedia.org/wiki/Wikipedia:WikiProject_Women_artists

[5] http://outreach.wikimedia.org/wiki/Education

[6] http://www.psychologicalscience.org/index.php/members/aps-wikipedia-initiative

CSCW '15, March 14–18, 2015, Vancouver, BC, Canada

ACM 978-1-4503-2922-4/15/03... $15.00
http://dx.doi.org/10.1145/2675133.2675241

1. Projects where participants work individually or in small groups tend to be more effective; an increased number of participants working on each artefact is connected with lower rates of quality increase.

2. Creating new artefacts appears to result in higher quality content than improving existing artefacts.

3. Simply drawing attention to a community's need for quality improvement is not associated with quality improvements; incentives or task structuring also are likely needed.

This work binds several threads of research together to advance how we describe and measure quality improvement projects, as well as our understanding of what factors lead to project success. Our results have implications for both volunteer and professional peer production communities. We begin by looking at related research to show how this paper builds on and extends the current state of knowledge.

RELATED WORK

The motivation for this work arises from two areas of peer production community research: increasing contributions, and quality improvement projects in Wikipedia.

Increasing contributions

In the human resource development literature, peer production communities are commonly referred to as "communities of practice" (CoP), a term from Lave and Wenger's [25] studies of professional training. Research on CoPs has studied participation barriers [12] and motivation [3], finding for example that many participants view their knowledge as a public good, so they have a moral obligation to share it.

Soliciting contributions from consumers of peer produced content is another way to increase activity. Halfaker et al. [15] nudged Wikipedia readers into submitting article feedback, which adds value as long as the system design makes it easy to weed out low quality contributions. A study of the Cyclopath bike-mapping community found that naturally occurring feedback on user behaviour could be used to improve suggested bike routes or add annotations to the map [28].

Intelligent task routing (ITR) uses a recommender system to match contributors with tasks related to their interest. It was first used to request contributions from users in a movie recommender system [7], finding that some personalised strategies were successful, but one was outperformed by the random baseline. ITR has also been implemented in an article recommender for Wikipedia called SuggestBot [8]; in this case, three personalised strategies were about four times more successful than a random baseline at eliciting article edits.

The social psychology literature has provided candidate interventions and appeals. Ling et al. [26] found that appealing to users' unique capabilities and giving them specific and challenging goals resulted in more contributions. In a followup study [32], Rashid et al. discovered that displaying the estimated value of a contribution had a positive impact. Further, identifying with the member group and the way a person viewed the member group also had a positive effect.

Other peer production communities focus on geographic information, known as Volunteered Geographic Information [13] (VGI). Increasing contributions to VGI communities has been studied in the context of Cyclopath [31]. Researchers found that users did considerably more work than explicitly requested, and that user familiarity with a given area strongly affected the type of work done.

Quality Improvement Projects in Wikipedia

Some of the improvement projects we examine in this paper have been studied previously in isolation. The Wikipedia Education Program (WEP) started in 2010 as the Public Policy Initiative (PPI)[7]. Lampe et al. [24] surveyed PPI participants, asking whether the project motivated them to continue contributing to Wikipedia after course completion. Students that reported actively participating and who were aware of Wikipedia's global reach were also more likely to say they would continue contributing. The APS Wikipedia Initiative is another project connected to the WEP. Farzan and Kraut [10] compared project participants with a cohort of similar Wikipedia contributors, finding that project participants added considerably more content, and that their content survived on par with that contributed by subject matter experts with PhDs. Lastly, the Wikimedia Foundation has published two reports on the quality of content added by students in the PPI and WEP projects [34, 43]. They used human assessment of a random selection of articles edited by project participants. The study of PPI found that the average article improved to an intermediate amount of quality, while the WEP study found a smaller increase in quality.

WikiProjects are self-organised groups of Wikipedia contributors interested in a specific topic area (e.g. WikiProject Military History) or type of work (e.g. WikiProject Wikify, which focuses on improving the layout and formatting of articles). These projects have been the focus of several research papers, studying for instance how they coordinate [20, 21], how they support collaboration [11], and how the diversity of group membership affects survival [6]. Some of the WikiProjects run a specific type of improvement project known as "Collaboration of the Week", a project that usually lasts a week or two and aims to improve a specific article or set of articles. These week-long collaborations were studied by Zhu, Kittur, and Kraut [45], who found that these article improvement goals strongly motivated project members to increase the amount of editing they did and that the effect also spilled over to other articles within the WikiProject's topic area.

Opportunity to integrate and expand

Research projects have used different methods and measures, making it difficult not only to compare one improvement project with another, but also to make comparisons within the same project. Take the Wikipedia Education Program, for example, which was studied by Farzan and Kraut [10] as well as the Wikimedia Foundation [34, 43]. Words added and word survival were the measures used in the former, while the latter used human assessment of the quality of a random

[7] `http://outreach.wikimedia.org/wiki/Public_Policy_Initiative`

selection of articles. Like this prior work, we also study the Education Program, but we apply a single form of assessment across this and several other improvement projects to enable cross-project comparisons.

We further extend the existing body of research by studying three improvement projects that have not been studied before:

- The WikiCup[8] is a competition for Wikipedia contributors started in 2007, whose purpose is to "encourage content improvement" and to be "just a bit of fun".
- Todays Article for Improvement[9] (TAFI) is a WikiProject started in mid-2012 that promotes an article per day, seeking to improve its quality.
- Wikipedia's Community Portal[10] is a page on Wikipedia that was created in early 2004 and has since featured an regularly updated list of articles in need of improvement.

In the next section, we present our descriptive framework before using it to describe the quality improvement projects we study. We then go through the datasets we gathered and our technique for measuring content quality in Wikipedia. This technique is then applied to our datasets, we report our findings, and discuss their impact. Lastly we consider some known limitations before final conclusions.

UNIFIED DESCRIPTIVE FRAMEWORK

In order to make comparisons across a diverse set of quality improvement projects, it is first necessary to identify a unified descriptive framework in which to understand these projects. We considered several candidates from the research literature, before settling on Preece's "Online Communities: Designing Usability and Supporting Sociability" [30]. Preece divides the social side of online communities into three components: **People**, **Purpose**, and **Policies**. We use each component as a major theme in our analysis and further explore the components as follows:

People: What *recruitment* method is used to find project participants, and is the work done by *individuals* or *groups*? Recruitment can either be *internal* – participants are already members of the community; *external* – participants are recruited from outside the community; or the project is open to anyone at all.

Purpose: The primary purpose for all the projects we examined was to improve the quality of Wikipedia. We are more interested in dimensions on which projects *differ* and therefore our specific analyses will focus on a project's secondary purpose, e.g. that students in the Education Program achieve academic course credit.

Policies: These comprise the governing structure for a project. Since Wikipedia itself has many policies and guidelines that influence all the projects we study, to avoid confusion, we use the term **structure** to describe the governing rules for individual projects.

[8] `https://en.wikipedia.org/wiki/Wikipedia:WikiCup`

[9] `https://en.wikipedia.org/wiki/Wikipedia:TAFI`

[10] `https://en.wikipedia.org/wiki/Wikipedia:Community_portal`

THE QUALITY IMPROVEMENT PROJECTS STUDIED

We sought a diverse set of improvement projects for our study. The five projects we study, and how they fit into our descriptive framework, are listed in Table 1. Below, we provide additional details:

- **Collaboration of the Week (CotW).** Some of the WikiProjects organise what is known as a **Collaboration of the Week**, where they focus on improving a specific article or a set of articles.

  As we see in Table 1 the **people** in CotW are *internal* as nearly all of them are already Wikipedia contributors and members of a specific WikiProject, and the work is done as a *group*. The collaboration's **purpose** is to achieve the group goal of improving a specific article or set of articles. Similarly the **structure** is a *group collaboration*. The vast majority of the collaborations last *a week or two*, on par with the name, but some last as long as a month.

- The **WikiCup** is a competition for Wikipedia contributors. Since 2009, the cup's organisation has been fairly stable, with four initial rounds followed by a final round, each round lasting approximately two months. There are comprehensive rules, and three judges award points. In each round contestants score points for achieving specific tasks. For example, contributing significantly to an article that successfully passes peer review for Featured Article status (the highest-quality Wikipedia article status) is awarded 100 points. In addition to the competitive aspects, it also is emphasised that the most important rule of the cup is "*just a bit of fun*" (emphasis theirs).

  As with CotW, WikiCup **people** are *internal* to Wikipedia, with contestants most likely already experienced members of the Wikipedia community. Work is done through (and assessed in terms of) *individual* effort. The **purpose** of the WikiCup is described on the cup pages. Of course, its primary purpose is to improve the encyclopedia, but as noted *scoring points* and *having fun* also are called out. Given the point scoring system, the cup **structure** involves *gamification* [9], and the duration is *months*.

- The **Wikipedia Education Program (WEP)** started as an organised effort connecting U.S. and Canadian university instructors and students with ambassadors from the Wikipedia community. The original intent of the program was for students to improve the content of public policy articles as part of class assignments. It has since expanded to other subject areas, countries, and languages. The Wikimedia Foundation says that there have been over 6,500 participants who have added "the equivalent of 45,000 printed pages of quality content"[11].

  The **people** in WEP are *external* to Wikipedia, specifically students at colleges and universities. In some courses, the students work individually on articles while in others they do group work, so we consider the project as having both. Since the work is done as part of college courses, we define the **purpose** of WEP to be *course credit*. Given the

[11] `https://outreach.wikimedia.org/w/index.php?title=Education/About&oldid=66258`

		CotW	WikiCup	WEP	Community Portal	TAFI
People	*Recruitment:*	Internal	Internal	External	Anyone	Anyone
	Individual or group work:	Group	Individual	Both	Individual	Group
Purpose	*Purpose:*	Group achievement	Scoring points, having fun	Course credit	Improve articles	Improve articles
Structure	*Structure:*	Group collaboration	Gamification	Academic coursework	None	None
	Duration:	Weeks	Months	Months	Hours	Day
	Study period:	2006–2009	2009–2013	2010–2013	Dec 2012	2012–2013
	Project size:	852	4,858	2,914	8,246	249

Table 1. The studied quality improvement projects. Abbreviations as follows: CotW: WikiProjects' Collaboration of the Week, WEP: Wikipedia Education Program, TAFI: Today's Article for Improvement. Project size is measured in number of articles.

shared context of post-secondary education and Wikipedia, the **structure** is *academic coursework*. Like the WikiCup, the duration of WEP courses is on the order of *months*, typically a U.S. semester of three to four months.

- The English Wikipedia's **Community Portal** (**CP**) serves several purposes, such as helping visitors learn what Wikipedia is about and how to do various Wikipedia tasks. However, what is relevant to our purposes is that it also features a list of articles that need improvement. The CP is easily accessed through a link in the menu on the left-hand side of any page on the English Wikipedia and is typically viewed about 10,000 times per day.

  While the **people** who visit the Community Portal are already on the Wikipedia site, they might not be members of the Wikipedia community (i.e., editors). Most Wikipedia articles do not require a registered account to be edited, and the Community Portal is a general call to action, which leads us to define the recruitment target as *anyone*. The CP does not feature any group collaboration or awareness mechanisms, so we regard it as *individual* work. The **purpose** of the list of articles that need improvement is simply article improvement. The CP provides no **structure**, and articles typically are promoted for one hour.

- **Today's Article for Improvement** (**TAFI**) is a WikiProject started in July 2012 with the goal of identifying "an undeveloped or underdeveloped article", which would then be promoted through various channels in Wikipedia. As of late May 2014 the project had 109 listed members.

  The **people** who participate in TAFI are recruited on Wikipedia through posts on project members' talk pages[12] and on the Community Portal, but also externally. For instance, some TAFI articles have been promoted on the official Wikipedia Twitter account. Thus, we define this project's recruitment target as *anyone*. Due to TAFI being organised by a WikiProject we see it as primary *group work*, but there likely also are individual efforts being made. There is no obvious secondary **purpose**, as the project is so clearly organised on improving a given article. No **structure** is provided, and the duration of TAFI is a single day.

[12]Every Wikipedia user has a talk page where they can be contacted.

Year	Our Data	Official Count	Our prop. (%)
2009	25	81	30.9
2010	53	135	39.3
2011	61	117	52.1
2012	51	111	45.9
2013	66	127	52.0
Total	256	571	46.4

Table 2. Overview of number of WikiCup participants per year in our dataset compared to the official number reported in the cup statistics.

DATASETS

Collaboration of the Week

We began with the collection of WikiProjects and articles studied by Zhu et al. We removed deleted articles, collaborations that targeted categories, and collaborations where it was unclear which article(s) they worked on. The result is a dataset of 852 articles spanning from 2006 to 2009.

WikiCup

Each WikiCup contestant has a page where they submit the work they have done for scoring review. We mined these pages for contestants in the cups from 2009 through 2013, as those cups have had the same format and a fairly stable scoring system. The result is a dataset with 256 contestants and 4,858 articles. This number of contestants is lower than the "official number" listed on the relevant WikiCup pages, Table 2 gives a yearly overview. We suspect this difference is because some users sign up but withdraw from the competition during a round or get disqualified. Therefore, we do not suspect this results in a distorted sample for our analysis.

Wikipedia Education Program

We mined three sources to gather a dataset covering 258 courses, 2,914 articles, and 2,870 students:

1. The U.S. and Canadian Education Program list of courses[13], which includes the Public Policy Initiative.

2. The Education Program extension's database, which covers the more recent courses in the program.

[13]`https://en.wikipedia.org/wiki/Wikipedia:Education_program/Courses`

3. The APS Wikipedia Initiative's Wikipedia page[14]. The APS Wikipedia Initiative is to some extent a separate project, but it still fits with the Education Program since some of the APS Wikipedia Initiative courses are included in the Education Program lists of courses.

We included data only from courses where individual students selected specific articles to work on, thus yielding an explicit record of the work done.

There also is an Indian Education Program that has worked on articles in the English Wikipedia. We did not include this project in our dataset for two reasons. First, the Wikimedia Foundation published a report[15] that described early contributions as "poor quality and/or ridden with copyright violations", and second, the remaining WEP courses form a fairly coherent group. There are now education programs in several countries and we plan to study these in future work.

The Community Portal

The list of articles that need improvement on the CP is updated automatically by a bot[16] roughly every hour. We mined the edit history of the Community Portal to gather a dataset of articles listed from December 4, 2012 to January 4, 2013. The bot updates 40 articles every time, and during the given time span 741 updates were made. Some articles were featured multiple times, resulting in a total of 8,246 unique articles.

Today's Article for Improvement

Our dataset of TAFI articles was collected from the project's archived schedule[17] as well as any article having the template "Former TAFI" applied to it. This resulted in a dataset containing 249 articles from July 2012 through December 2013.

Common properties of all datasets

For each article in each of the datasets, we gather the source (text and wiki markup) of the article at the start and end of every project. For the WikiCup and WEP, the end of the project is defined as the last edit by any project participant during the project. This is to ensure that we do not also capture additional work done by other editors. The remaining improvement projects are time-bound, e.g. the end of TAFI is the end of the day an article was selected.

We also gather data on the number of contributors working on each article between the start and end of each project. In the Education Program students assign themselves to specific articles, which provides an explicit mapping for us to use. For TAFI, CotW, and the WikiCup, we search the edit history of each article. We remove three categories of contributors: bots, because those are automated tools; those who were reverted by a bot or through common anti-vandal tools since they were likely vandalistic edits; and those who made reverts using common anti-vandal tools as that is maintenance work. The remaining set of contributors should be those who tried to make productive edits to an article.

[14]`https://en.wikipedia.org/wiki/Wikipedia:WikiProject_Psychology/APS-Wikipedia_Initiative`

[15]`https://en.wikipedia.org/wiki/Wikipedia:India_Education_Program/Analysis/Quantitative_Analysis`

[16]Software robot, ref `https://en.wikipedia.org/wiki/Wikipedia:Bots`

[17]`https://en.wikipedia.org/wiki/Wikipedia:Today%27s_articles_for_improvement/Archives/Schedule`

Class:	Stub	Start	C	B	GA	A	FA
Quality:	*Low*						*High*

Table 3. English Wikipedia's seven assessment classes in order from lowest quality (left) to highest quality (right). Abbreviations: GA=Good Article, FA=Featured Article.

MEASURING PROJECT PERFORMANCE

The most important thing to measure about quality improvement projects is how much they improve the quality of the articles within their scope. This means we need a way to assess the quality of the articles in the datasets. There are several possible approaches to doing so, with the majority having appeared in the literature:

1. Using Wikipedia's own article quality assessments.
2. Gathering expert human assessment of randomly sampled articles (e.g. [34, 43]).
3. Crowdsourcing human assessment of a random sample of articles (e.g. [20]).
4. Using proxy measures for quality, e.g. words added and word survival (e.g. [10, 16]).
5. Leveraging machine learning techniques for predicting article quality (e.g. [42]).

Each one of these approaches comes with benefits and drawbacks. Wikipedia's own assessments are done by Wikipedia contributors using the seven-class scale shown in Table 3. This notion of article quality in Wikipedia has been shown to correspond well with existing notions of encyclopaedic quality [39]. However, because these assessments are done by people, there is a potential time lag between substantial changes to an article and its subsequent (re)assessment. As we are interested in measuring the immediate effect of article improvement work, the lag makes us unable to use the reassessments without further analysis.

The drawback of using experts to assess random samples is that it limits the number of samples, which can reduce statistical power. We come across a similar problem in one of our validation datasets, where 257 articles are not enough to tease out the effects we seek to understand (see Appendix A). While crowdsourcing assessments has been shown to be significantly correlated with Wikipedia's own assessments [20], the correlation ($r_s = 0.54$) also suggested disagreements. As we will show, we are able to produce higher correlations using a machine learning approach. Using proxy measures for quality would mean we would end up not capturing many features associated with article quality (e.g. the presence of references to sources or illustrative images). A machine learning approach enables measuring the entirety of the datasets, but will make prediction errors, requiring analysis of where prediction errors occur and how they affect overall results.

In this paper, we take a two-fold approach to quality estimation. Our primary focus is on a machine learning model,

	Est.	Std. Err.	P-val.
Intercept: $Stub\|Start$	-2.57	0.25	***
Intercept: $Start\|C$	-0.12	0.15	
Intercept: $C\|B$	1.30	0.16	***
Intercept: $B\|GA$	3.07	0.19	***
Intercept: $GA\|FA$	4.36	0.23	***
$log_2(n\_contributors)$	-0.51	0.06	***

Table 4. Ordinal Logistic Regression model coefficients for Collaboration of the Week. P-values: * < 0.001**

	Est.	Std. Err.	P-val.
Intercept: $Stub\|Start$	-2.94	0.10	***
Intercept: $Start\|C$	-1.26	0.07	***
Intercept: $C\|B$	0.44	0.07	***
Intercept: $B\|GA$	2.18	0.08	***
Intercept: $GA\|FA$	3.25	0.11	***
$from\_scratchTRUE$	0.47	0.08	***
$n\_contributors$	-0.10	0.03	**

Table 5. Ordinal Logistic Regression model coefficients for Wikipedia Education Program. P-values: ** < 0.01, * < 0.001**

	Est.	Std. Err.	P-val.
Intercept: $Stub\|Start$	-5.35	0.26	***
Intercept: $Start\|C$	-1.23	0.09	***
Intercept: $C\|B$	0.27	0.09	**
Intercept: $B\|GA$	0.43	0.09	***
Intercept: $GA\|FA$	3.15	0.11	***
$from\_scratchTRUE$	1.89	0.08	***
$log_2(n\_contributors)$	-0.63	0.04	***

Table 6. Ordinal Logistic Regression model coefficients for the WikiCup. P-values: ** < 0.01 * < 0.001**

which we demonstrate can outperform published crowdsourcing approaches while at the same time providing assessments of a sufficient number of articles for our analyses. However, our model does have some error, and in order to validate our high-level results, we also repeat our experiments using a set of manual assessments from Wikipedia that we ensured were temporally valid. That is, the only assessments we considered in this second analysis were those that were applied to articles soon after a quality improvement project finished (so that the quality was not affected by subsequent edits). As we will show, we found substantial agreement between the model and the manual assessments. That is, our high-level model results hold across both means of assessing article quality.

The following section of the paper describes our results using the machine learning model to predict quality. In Appendix A, we describe the technical details of how the machine learning model is trained and evaluated, as well as demonstrate its strong performance relative to existing approaches. Appendix A also describes our validation of the results in the section that follows using manual assessments rather than the model's predictions and provides additional details about how we gathered these manual assessments.

RESULTS

This section focuses on three main findings. One relates to the **people** component of our framework, and a second to the **policies/structure** component. The third finding can be seen as relating either to **purpose** or **policies** depending on the improvement project's design. To complete our framework, we discuss this finding under the **purpose** component.

People

Result: More People, Less Quality

A fundamental question facing the designer of any effort to improve quality is: does it pay off to have contributors working individually on each artefact in the effort, or should they work in groups? Three of the studied projects have varying number of contributors per artefact, allowing us to investigate this question. Our results suggest that an *increased number of contributors per artefact* is associated with a *lower rate of increase in artefact quality*.

We examine the relationship between number of contributors and quality in the Collaboration of the Week (CotW), the Wikipedia Education Program (WEP), and the WikiCup. In all of these datasets, we have predicted the quality of each article at the start and end of the project using our quality machine learning model. We also calculated the number of contributors to each article during the project. The distribution of number of contributors is highly skewed in the CotW and WikiCup datasets. This is not uncommon for contributions to online communities. We therefore choose to log-transform these variables. The WEP dataset does not have the skewness issue. Group size in college classes is limited, so the most common size for WEP efforts is 2-5, and only a few outliers have more than 6 people.

To model the relationship between number of contributors and predicted quality we use an Ordinal Logistic Regression [27, 44] (OLR) with the assessment classes in the order shown in Table 3. We have a variable $n\_contributors$ for the number of contributors per artefact and add a binary variable $from\_scratch$ in the WEP and WikiCup dataset to control for articles that did not exist prior to the start of the project (thus having an unknown prior quality).

During our model building we also want to control for two additional issues: the *proportional odds assumption* and whether there is an *interaction effect* between our independent variables. The former is a fundamental assumption upon which OLRs are commonly built. In our case, it means the coefficients explaining the relationship between Stub-class ($P(Stub)$) and higher than Stub-class ($P(\geq Stub)$) also explain all other classes (e.g. $P(C)$ and $P(\geq C)$). We have verified that this assumption holds in all our OLR models. Second, we also verified that there is no interaction effect between our independent variables, which would have indicated that the strength of the effect of starting an article from scratch would be altered by the number of contributors to the article.

The results of our OLR models, one for each effort, are listed in Tables 4, 5, and 6. All predictors are statistically significant in all models. In the CotW model, the intercept (cutpoint) between Start and C-class is not significant. Because this cutpoint is only an estimate of the borderline between the two classes and the predictor's P-value < 0.001, this issue does not invalidate the model.

Across all three efforts the number of contributors has a negative sign indicating that larger numbers of contributors per artefact is associated with slower increase in quality. We also built additional models where we controlled for the quality at the start of the effort, to make sure that our model was not influenced by (for example) a larger proportion of articles starting from a certain quality level. Pre-effort quality was generally also a significant predictor in those models, but did not cancel out the effect of number of contributors. This means that consistently across these projects, an *increase in number of contributors per artefact* is connected with a *negative impact on the rate of quality increase*.

Discussion

We find it particularly interesting that the negative effect of additional contributors per artefact is consistent across all three projects, even though the nature of the "group" is different: in the WEP, participants are explicitly connected to an article, while in the other two projects we count all likely productive editors as participants. Wikipedia articles are of course open to anyone to edit, but WEP students are directed to work in a "sandbox", a personal space where they can draft an article before publishing it, as described in the template syllabi[18]. This usage of personal work spaces likely isolates many of the WEP articles from contributions from non-WEP contributors until they are published.

As we will see in the next section, WEP students seldom take articles above B-class quality, supporting the findings of the Wikimedia Foundation's studies on WEP quality [34, 43]. This could be due to a lack of experience with writing Wikipedia articles, but it could also be due to satisficing [35], they are doing just enough for a reasonable grade but nothing more. Groups of students might also be experiencing social loafing [18], e.g. that some of the group members are trying to free ride their way through the course while other members do the work. Future research on the WEP could try to tease these effects apart.

The groups of contributors in the WikiCup and CotW datasets are more implicit, and the extent to which participants in these efforts use sandboxes to edit articles before publication is unknown. It may be that additional contributors to those two efforts are not aware that they are taking part in an improvement project, which could alter their edit behaviour. These contributors may also differ in experience levels and engagement with the Wikipedia community, previous research has shown that power users in Wikipedia produce higher quality edits from early on [29]. Additional contributors could also be positive as long as only a few contributors are doing the majority of the work, as found by Kittur and Kraut [20], otherwise they just cause more maintenance overhead, similar to how adding people to late software development projects make them even later [4].

These results also beg the question of whether it is better for groups creating artefacts to work individually and sequentially. André et al. [2] found simultaneous work to be less effective than a sequential structure, but the effect was mitigated by assigning specific roles to participants. In Wikipedia there are few formal roles. Some users are promoted to become administrators, a role that is supposed to be janitorial and "not a big deal" [19] (yet research indicates it is an increasingly bigger deal [5]). Instead, users assume informal roles, which they may seek to use to their advantage in conflicts, for instance by questioning other contributors' expertise [22].

	Stub	Start	C	B	GA	FA
NA	3.93	14.88	46.79	18.81	12.50	3.10
Stub	21.43	20.44	37.68	9.61	9.61	1.23
Start	0.95	25.79	44.94	17.25	8.07	3.01
C	0.00	1.49	54.29	25.00	12.87	6.34
B	0.00	1.21	16.92	65.86	6.95	9.06
GA	0.00	0.00	10.58	11.54	61.54	16.35
FA	0.00	0.00	3.08	6.15	7.69	83.08

Table 7. Prior (rows) and post (columns) predicted quality for the Wikipedia Education Program. Proportions are relative to prior quality (rows). NA=Article did not exist prior to start of a course.

	Stub	Start	C	B	GA	FA
NA	0.90	34.11	37.95	3.60	21.46	1.98
Stub	1.18	28.10	40.26	2.09	26.67	1.70
Start	0.00	24.25	17.55	2.08	51.96	4.16
C	0.00	1.18	47.14	3.16	39.05	9.47
B	0.00	0.00	5.74	36.89	47.54	9.84
GA	0.00	0.19	1.23	0.85	89.26	8.48
FA	0.00	0.33	0.33	0.66	7.95	90.73

Table 8. Prior (rows) and post (columns) predicted quality for the WikiCup. Proportions are relative to prior quality (rows). NA=Article did not exist prior to start of a cup round.

In order for a peer production community to be successful, there needs to be collaboration. These results suggests some degree of conflict between individual and group work, when does one approach benefit the community more than the other? We see investigations into how contributor roles, work organisation, conflict, coordination, and concentration of contributor effort affect artefact quality in improvement projects as a promising venue for future research.

Purpose

Result: New Artefacts, Higher Quality

Is it more effective to have participants in a quality improvement project create new artefacts or work on improving existing ones? Two of our efforts, the WikiCup and the Wikipedia Education Program include both types of work. Across both of these, our results indicate that artefacts created from scratch end with a higher final quality.

To investigate this effect, we first look at what level of quality articles reach at the end of a project. Table 7 (WEP) and Table 8 (WikiCup) show the relationship between predicted quality at the start of an improvement project (rows) and at the end (columns), where Good Article is abbreviated "GA" and Featured Article "FA". For the WikiCup, the end of the project

[18] `http://outreach.wikimedia.org/w/index.php?title=Education/Syllabi&oldid=70162`

[19] `https://en.wikipedia.org/wiki/Wikipedia:DEAL#History`

	Stub	Start	C	B	GA	FA
Stub	29.46	40.31	17.83	6.20	4.65	1.55
Start	1.74	46.52	27.39	18.26	6.09	0.00
C	0.00	0.65	69.48	17.53	10.39	1.95
B	0.00	1.45	14.49	72.83	6.52	4.71
GA	0.00	0.00	4.88	2.44	80.49	12.20
FA	0.00	0.00	0.00	9.09	9.09	81.82

Table 9. Prior (rows) and post (columns) predicted quality for Collaboration of the Week. Proportions are relative to prior quality (rows).

is the last edit done by a specific participant on the article that participant submits for scoring, and for the WEP the end is the last edit done by any student assigned to a specific article. For convenience, we have also included the same type of table for the Collaboration of the Week (Table 9) but note that in that project no articles were created from scratch.

In the WEP (Table 7), 65.6% of the articles started from scratch (the "NA" row) reach an intermediate level of quality (C- or B-class). This is not the case for the WikiCup (Table 8), where instead more than one fifth of every new article is predicted as Good Article (GA) or Featured Article (FA) status. We can also see that to a certain degree in the WikiCup, and to a much larger degree in the WEP, many articles do not improve enough to change their predicted quality class.

More generally, our OLR models in Tables 5 and 6 show that the $from\_scratch$ variable is a significant predictor with a positive relationship to end quality. This suggests that in both the WikiCup and WEP projects, *new artefacts have higher end quality* compared to existing artefacts.

Discussion

Here again we have found an effect that is consistent across vastly different improvement projects. As previously noted, many WEP articles are likely isolated from contributions from non-WEP editors due to the extensive use of sandboxes. In contrast, the WikiCup has an "In the news" category for articles that are featured in that section on the English Wikipedia's front page, with the contestant scoring 10 points for each article featured. This will likely lead to the cup containing some breaking news articles [19], newly created articles where the particularly high interest and resulting traffic could lead to quicker improvements in quality.

The result also is interesting because both projects have a long duration, namely months. With that amount of time available, one would not expect there to be a significant difference in quality improvement between new and existing articles, particularly one in favour of new articles. Producing high-quality Wikipedia articles requires access to resources, for instance sources for claims and illustrative images. For some types of content these might be more difficult to find, particularly using online resources, and in the case of existing artefacts resources might already have been exhausted. The lack of online sources could to some extent explain the WikiCup result where participants might strongly prefer them, but it seems unlikely to explain the WEP result, since students should have access to good library resources.

Existing artefacts are also more likely to have some contributors monitoring them. Research on Wikipedia has shown that editors assume ownership of content [16, 41] although Wikipedia's own policy states noone owns an article[20]. This type of territoriality also occurs outside of Wikipedia, expert contributors to a museum tagging system were found to more strongly express ownership of content than novices [40]. When participants in a quality improvement project try to make changes, territoriality by existing contributors is likely a barrier to entry, resulting in reduced quality gain through coordination overhead.

It is also not obvious that peer production communities should always focus on creating new artefacts. If the community already has good coverage (e.g. a large number of articles), it would perhaps instead benefit the most if work was concentrated on improving existing artefacts. Community managers could combine the understanding of this trade-off between coverage and quality with information on audience attention to guide contributions to the areas where they are most needed in order to ensure the community's resources are utilised most efficiently.

Perhaps people work differently if they start with a blank slate than if they have to modify an existing piece of work. In their study on the effect of seeding wikis with content, Solomon and Wash [36] found that not seeding led to significantly more content added, while those who started with seeded content would instead use that as a model. We do not know to what extent this finding also is present in the work WikiCup and WEP participants do on existing articles. There is an opportunity here for both qualitative analysis of live data as well as lab studies to understand the effects that are in play and how to most efficiently produce high quality artefacts.

We also found interesting differences between improvement projects in the patterns of change in predicted quality. The WikiCup results (Table 8) show that few articles move into the B-class. Instead, the cup participants push articles upwards to GA/FA status, a behaviour we interpret to be clearly in line with the cup's incentive mechanism. Successful Good Article nominations score 30 points and Featured Articles 100 points, while getting an article only to B-class scores zero. This is similar to how badges steer user behaviour in Q&A systems [1]: when users have nearly reached a badge threshold, they will modify their behaviour to achieve the badge as quickly as possible.

The results for WEP (Table 7) and the Collaboration of the Week (Table 9) show that for many articles quality does not appear to improve. The CotW's short duration, usually a week or two can explain the effect in that project. Most improvements in CotW occur in low quality articles, confirming Zhu et al.'s description of those articles being the typical collaboration targets [45]. That the Education Program also to a large extent leads to improvements that appear to not substantially change the article quality is more concerning. Students in the program have more time available to affect change, thus we wonder if they are struggling with learning how to write

[20] `http://en.wikipedia.org/wiki/Wikipedia:Ownership_of_articles`

articles in the context of Wikipedia, for instance how to correctly source content with footnotes and citation templates.

Policies/Structure

Result: Structure is Required

Two of the improvement projects we study, Today's Article for Improvement (TAFI) and Wikipedia's Community Portal, do not have a well-defined structure. For example, they are open to anyone, have a very general purpose, and lack a clear incentive mechanism. Our results indicate that unlike the other projects, neither TAFI nor the Community Portal is particularly successful at improving artefact quality.

First, let us investigate the TAFI project. We predicted the quality of each article at the beginning and end of the effort, in this case the day the article was promoted for improvement. Only 9 out of 249 articles (3.6%) saw an improvement in predicted class, and of those all but one moved up a single class, the exception being a Start-class article improving to B-class.

Is the problem lack of participation? TAFI started in mid-2012 and at the end of 2013 the project's member list contained 103 usernames. Still, of the 249 articles in the TAFI dataset 56.2% had no contributors during the day of the effort. We investigated whether the degree of participation changed over the course of the project and found that in the first three months, 1 out of 16 articles saw no contributors, while in the last three months it was 33 out of 47. This is a statistically significant difference (Fisher exact count test $p < 0.001$); the project has seen a significant decline in participation as its membership has increased.

We found a similar problem with participation in the Community Portal. Our dataset covers Dec 4, 2012 to Jan 4, 2013 during which time the portal, according to data from the Wikimedia Foundation[21], saw 314,534 views, for a daily average of 10,146 views. One would hypothesise that these views would directly affect listed articles as visitors to the portal follow links to edit them. To investigate this, we calculated average views/day prior to being listed for the portal articles and removed those that were listed twice on the same day due to our view data having a granularity of one day. We sorted the articles into buckets based on average views/day, using exponential buckets since article popularity follows a power-law distribution. Lastly we calculated views on the day of listing, as well as average views/day up to 14 days after.

Articles are typically listed for only one hour, so one would expect the portal to affect article views less as popularity increases. This is also seen in Table 10, which shows an excerpt of the view results. The remaining part of the table (up to x $\geq$ 16,384 views/day) is left out for brevity as the trend of a decrease in views on the listed day as well as in the period after continues. Based on the results in Table 10 it seems clear that few views appear to come from the Community Portal.

Not surprisingly, since including an article on the Community Portal did not increase how much it was viewed, it also didn't increase participation. We selected portal articles which had no edits in the two weeks prior to being listed, because those articles are most likely getting contributions from the portal. Out of 4,410 articles only eight of them were edited during the time they were listed. This extends data from the Wikimedia Foundation during a redesign of the portal in late 2012, where 220,000 portal views led to 46 saved edits [22]. Since the portal does not lead to participation, there obviously can be no improvements in quality. Therefore it is not an example of a successful improvement project.

Discussion

Both of the unstructured projects studied were largely unsuccessful. The short duration of these projects, an hour in the case of the Community Portal and a day for the TAFI project, might be posited as the explanation for the lack of success. However, the Community Portal is easily accessible from the left-hand menu of any Wikipedia page, and as we saw exposes a lot of readers to its call to action. In our related work we referenced several successful projects with a much similar approach: Cosley et al. [7] suggested edits of movie data on a movie recommender site; a general call to action solicited contributions in the Cyclopath geo-wiki [31]; Halfaker et al. [15] asked Wikipedia readers to submit article feedback. In all three cases more structure and guidance was supplied when necessary, for instance Cosley et al. had a form for inputting data, and the Cyclopath experiment provided volunteers with clear instructions for the work needed.

Comparing TAFI and the Community Portal to the other projects, we also see that these two unsuccessful projects lack a clear purpose, perhaps it is unclear to potential participants what the benefit is to both them and the encyclopaedia. In contrast, many of the WEP courses aim to extend Wikipedia's content in areas where it is lacking (e.g. public policy or psychology), and the WikiCup's scoring system appears to steer participant behaviour, as seen in their movement of articles to the higher quality classes to score points. Neither TAFI nor the Community Portal implements similar incentive mechanisms. Where our initial investigation has pointed to a lack of participation, future work could look at how much structure and what kind of incentive mechanisms are needed to trigger increased participation to cross the border into a successful improvement project.

LIMITATIONS AND NEXT STEPS

This research has several known limitations. First, while the English Wikipedia is the largest peer production community in existence, results from this community might not generalise. For example, a Q&A system like Stack Overflow is also a peer production community with some wiki-like features. Research to determine to what extent our findings also are present there (or in other peer production communities) would be valuable.

Second, our analysis uses Wikipedia's own assessment classes. Wikipedia's notion of article quality has been shown to correspond well with existing notions of encyclopaedic quality [39]. In our analysis of prediction errors, we discovered that in some cases Wikipedia contributors failed to apply

[21] `http://dumps.wikimedia.org/other/pagecounts-raw/`

[22] `https://meta.wikimedia.org/wiki/Research:Community_portal_redesign/Opentask`

Views/Day Bucket	Prior mean views	Listed day gain/loss (%)	Post gain/loss (%)
$0 \leq x < 2$	1.6	126.08	80.34
$2 \leq x < 4$	3.1	33.12	12.10
$4 \leq x < 8$	5.6	6.74	-4.36
$8 \leq x < 16$	11.2	-3.68	-8.50

Table 10. Excerpt of view statistics for articles listed on Wikipedia's Community Portal. Articles are placed in buckets based on prior mean views.

the assessment criteria correctly, leading to articles being assessed into a lower class. This suggests that there is room for improvement in the understanding of how Wikipedia contributors apply the assessment criteria, as well as how these correspond to assessment of quality by non-Wikipedians, and we plan future work in this area.

This paper brings together a diverse set of improvement projects, which means we must also consider limitations imposed by them. There is likely a clear difference in skill levels between some of the efforts. Contestants in the WikiCup and WikiProject members participating in the Collaboration of the Week are probably skilled members of the Wikipedia community, while students in the Education Program have little prior experience with writing for Wikipedia. One way to control for this would be to introduce measures of tenure, for instance the number of edits a contributor has or the amount of time since account registration.

We are also limited by how we define a contributor to a specific article. In the Education Program we use the course pages' explicit definition of which students worked on a specific article, and in the WikiCup we use contestants' submission pages to track which articles they worked on as part of the cup. In the other efforts, we instead use an implicit method of defining participants. This method could potentially be improved by algorithmic content analysis, for instance to account for different categories of contributors (e.g. newly registered users, users without an account, etc).

CONCLUSION

We have studied five diverse quality improvement projects in the English Wikipedia. Our findings suggest three important implications for design:

1. **People:** Increasing number of contributors per artefact is associated with slower increase in quality. Consideration should be given to when working individually can be more effective than group work.
2. **Purpose:** Artefacts created during the improvement project are connected to a higher quality level than existing artefacts worked on during the project. There may even be cases where deleting an old artefact to start over is preferred, although more research is needed.
3. **Policies/Structure:** Unstructured efforts are less likely to succeed. Our results suggest that new efforts should provide a carefully designed socio-technical structure, for instance through incentive mechanisms appropriate for the desired work and the knowledge level of the participants.

To analyse a diverse set of quality improvement projects, we used Preece's three components of online communities (outlined in bold above) as building blocks for an analytic framework. We developed a classifier for assessing Wikipedia article quality and verified its performance, enabling us to bring several existing threads of research together, while at the same time extending the variety of improvement projects studied. This research provides researchers and designers with the knowledge to design and evaluate more effective quality improvement projects in the future.

ACKNOWLEDGEMENTS

We would like to thank Haiyi Zhu and colleagues for access to their Collaboration of the Week dataset, our GroupLens colleagues for their support, the reviewers for their helpful assistance in improving the quality of this paper, the Wikimedia Foundation for facilitating access to Wikipedia data, and all Wikipedia contributors for creating a great encyclopaedia for us to study. This work has been funded in part by the National Science Foundation (grants IIS-0808692, IIS-0968483, and IIS-1111201) and a Yahoo! ACE Award.

APPENDIX A: CLASSIFIER TRAINING AND EVALUATION

To create a classifier that can assess the quality of Wikipedia articles, we built upon our previous work [42] where a Random Forest (RF) classifier was used to predict which of Wikipedia's seven assessment classes (shown in Table 3) to which an article belongs. In that study we found that the RF classifier had the best overall performance, and we therefore chose to use an RF classifier as our starting point. We improve the classifier's performance through four steps:

1. A much larger dataset (N=29,828), which requires us to address the class imbalance problem imposed by Wikipedia's low number of A-class articles.
2. A larger set of quality features extracted from each article.
3. Each feature is tested six times using 10-fold cross-validation to determine how each feature most strongly relates to article quality (raw metric, log-transformed, and four variants of proportions relative to article length).
4. Classifier parameter tuning (again using 10-fold cross validation) to determine forest size, the number of features to use in each tree split, and terminating node size.

There is no gold-standard dataset on which to train a classifier for this task. To gather a suitable set of candidate articles we copied the behaviour of WP 1.0 Bot[23], the software robot that gathers statistics on Wikipedia article assessments. Using Wikipedia's category system to find articles in a specific assessment class we collected 29,828 article assessments, 5,000 from each class with two exceptions: the Featured Article (FA) class had 4,062 articles at that time, and we only found

[23]`https://en.wikipedia.org/wiki/User:WP_1.0_bot`

766 A-class articles. Official statistics listed 1,279 A-class articles and the discrepancy is likely due to duplicates.

The low number of A-class articles creates what is known as a *class imbalance problem* [17]. Random Forest classifiers require reasonably balanced classes, so without remedial action, this would result in poor classifier performance on A-class articles. Typical approaches are oversampling the smaller class, or undersampling the larger classes. We tested both of these approaches and found that they led to lower classifier performance. The 766 articles accounted for only 0.018% of the total number of articles in the English Wikipedia at that time, so, statistically speaking, this article class simply is not used in the encyclopedia. Given the low usage of this class, the probability of an article in our datasets belonging to it is very low, which means that removing it does not significantly impact our study. Therefore, we decided to ignore A-class articles altogether, and we confirmed this significantly increased classifier performance.

WikiProjects "claim" – and thus assess – articles, and multiple projects can claim the same article (e.g., the Barack Obama article is claimed by 14 projects). How do we select an assessment class for an article if different projects disagree on its assessment? We looked at two methods – (1) choose the **highest** class, (2) choose the **majority** class – and found that these two methods disagreed on only 150 out of 29,828 articles (Cohen's Kappa = 0.967 with two raters, p-value $\ll 0.001$). Therefore, we chose to use the highest assessment class as an article's correct class.

For each article in our training dataset, we went through the article's assessment history to find the point in time where it first belonged to a given class. If that revision is not available, for instance revisions sometimes get deleted due to copyright issues, we used the first available more recent revision. We then retrieved the revision content (text and wiki markup) and extracted the following 11 features:

1. article length in bytes (log-transformed)
2. number of references (log-transformed)
3. number of links to other articles (log-transformed)
4. number of citation templates
5. number of non-citation templates (log-transformed)
6. number of categories linked in the article text
7. number of images / article length
8. information noise score (as defined by Stvilia et al. [38])
9. has an infobox template (binary variable)
10. number of level 2 section headings
11. number of level 3+ section headings

In order to verify classifier performance on this dataset, we chose to split the dataset using random selection to get a training dataset (80%) and a test dataset (20%). Using 10-fold cross-validation on the training set we validated our features and identified optimal classifier parameters. A forest with 501 trees and terminating node size 8 showed the best performance. Training a classifier on the entire training dataset and validating its performance on the test set results in the confusion matrix shown in Table 11.

	FA	**GA**	**B**	**C**	**Start**	**Stub**	**N**
FA	546	167	47	9	1	0	770
GA	252	655	54	83	5	0	1049
B	81	151	374	261	129	11	1007
C	25	128	201	471	189	18	1032
Start	1	12	71	201	600	138	1024
Stub	0	0	0	14	166	818	998

Table 11. Confusion matrix for the Random Forest classifier predicting articles in the test set. Rows (italic) are true (assessed) class, columns (bold) are predicted class. Last column (N) is the total number of articles in each class.

	CotW		**WEP**		**WikiCup**	
Distance	**N**	**%**	**N**	**%**	**N**	**%**
5					1	0.1
4			2	0.8		
3	2	3.5	7	2.7	26	2.4
2	8	14.0	38	14.8	40	3.7
1	12	21.1	104	40.5	223	20.8
0	27	47.4	96	37.4	699	65.1
-1	7	12.3	7	2.7	49	4.6
-2	1	1.8	3	1.2	31	2.9
-3					4	0.4
Total	57	100.0	257	100.0	1,073	100.0

Table 12. Prediction errors by distance between reassessed and predicted class for the Collaboration of the Week (CotW), Wikipedia Education Program (WEP), and Wikicup. Positive error means the prediction was a higher quality class.

The difference in number of articles per class in Table 11 is due to fewer Featured Articles (FA) and the random selection. We see that the overall error rate is 41.08%. Similarly as in our previous work, the classifier is often off by one class. If we allow one class leeway the error rate drops to 10.5%. The classifier also often errs on the high side, for instance more Start-class articles are predicted as C than Stub.

While the performance of the classifier on the test dataset is promising, we also wanted to verify its performance on articles after completion of a quality improvement project so as to understand its performance on data more specifically associated with the goals of this research project. Three datasets of articles that were reassessed after a project's completion were gathered, one each from the Collaboration of the Week (518 articles), the Wikipedia Education Program (987 articles), and the WikiCup (1,617 articles).

Many of these reassessments suffer from the time lag described in the section "Measuring Project Performance". For instance in the CotW dataset the median time to reassessment is 157.6 days. In the intervening time the article may have gone through substantial changes. We therefore restricted these datasets to reassessments that occurred within 10 edits, and where the article has changed by less than 100 bytes. When checking some of our prediction errors described below, we also confirmed that this edit/size limitation led to articles only going through minor changes, e.g. copy edits. After applying this limitation we were left with 57 CotW articles, 257 WEP articles, and 1,073 WikiCup articles.

Dataset	Reassessments	Predictions
CotW	N collaborators negatively associated with quality. Significant ($p < 0.01$).	N collaborators negatively associated with quality. Significant ($p < 0.01$).
WEP	Not statistically significant.	Not statistically significant.
WikiCup	N collaborators negatively associated with quality. New articles positively associated with quality. Significant ($p < 0.001$).	N collaborators negatively associated with quality. New articles positively associated with quality. Significant ($p < 0.001$)

Table 13. Comparison between Ordinal Logistic Regression models built on article reassessments and predictions for each reassessment dataset.

For each article, we then predicted their quality class as described earlier in order to enable the comparison of predictions against human assessments post quality improvement. As we were interested in learning specifically to what extent the classifier makes prediction errors, and when it does, how severe these errors are, we chose to measure the error as the distance between predicted and assessed class along the ordinal scale listed in Table 3 (e.g. a B-class article predicted to be Start has an error of -2). We then summed these errors across all classes. The distribution of prediction errors for each reassessment dataset is shown in Table 12.

For the WikiCup, the classifier shows stronger performance than on our test set, while the performance is less for the other two. The large proportion of one-class errors in the WEP dataset led us to investigate further, finding that the majority of the errors come from articles reassessed as C-class (23 articles) and Start-class (64 articles). A random sample of 23 Start-class articles and all 23 B-class articles were selected and verified that they had all gone through only minor changes (e.g. link fixes or minor copy-editing). The English Wikipedia's criteria for Start-class assessment states in part that the article "most notably, lacks adequate reliable sources." Inspection of the Start-class articles by an expert Wikipedia contributor indicated that the vast majority (20 articles) appeared to have several, if not many, reliable sources, suggesting that this subset of articles were not correctly reassessed, an issue that is also discussed in our "Limitations" section and that opens to future work.

The classifier's predictions are strongly correlated with Wikipedia's own article assessments, more so than using a crowdsourcing approach. This is the case across all four evaluation datasets: the test set ($r_s = 0.86$), CotW ($r_s = 0.57$), WEP ($r_s = 0.58$), and the WikiCup ($r_s = 0.82$). In all these cases we have a higher correlation than what was reported when crowdsourcing was used ($r_s = 0.54$) [20].

Using the post-improvement reassessments to perform the same analysis that forms the basis for this paper gives the same results. To determine this we built two Ordinal Logistic Regressions for each of the three reassessment datasets, one each using the reassessment and the prediction as the dependent variable. This set of models can then be checked for agreement and the results are listed in Table 13.

Aside from the lack of statistical significance for WEP, we see in Table 13 that in all cases the pair of models agree with each other. When significant, number of contributors is negatively associated with post-improvement quality, and creating a new artefact is positively associated with quality. Based on the classifier's performance as established by this appendix and its agreement with post-improvement manual assessments, we therefore conclude that our classifier-based results hold when we are analysing the entire datasets, which also allows us to gain statistical significance for WEP.

REFERENCES

1. Anderson, A., Huttenlocher, D., Kleinberg, J., and Leskovec, J. Steering user behavior with badges. In *Proc. of WWW* (2013), 95–106.
2. André, P., Kraut, R. E., and Kittur, A. Effects of Simultaneous and Sequential Work Structures on Distributed Collaborative Interdependent Tasks. In *Proc. of CHI* (2014), 139–148.
3. Ardichvili, A. Learning and Knowledge Sharing in Virtual Communities of Practice: Motivators, Barriers, and Enablers. *Advances in Developing Human Resources 10*, 4 (2008), 541–554.
4. Brooks, F. P. *The Mythical Man-Month*, vol. 1995. Addison-Wesley Reading, 1975.
5. Burke, M., and Kraut, R. Mopping Up: Modeling Wikipedia Promotion Decisions. In *Proc. of CSCW* (2008), 27–36.
6. Chen, J., Ren, Y., and Riedl, J. The Effects of Diversity on Group Productivity and Member Withdrawal in Online Volunteer Groups. In *Proc. of CHI* (2010), 821–830.
7. Cosley, D., Frankowski, D., Terveen, L., and Riedl, J. Using Intelligent Task Routing and Contribution Review to Help Communities Build Artifacts of Lasting Value. In *Proc. of CHI*, CHI '06 (2006), 1037–1046.
8. Cosley, D., Frankowski, D., Terveen, L., and Riedl, J. SuggestBot: Using Intelligent Task Routing to Help People Find Work in Wikipedia. In *Proc. IUI* (2007), 32–41.
9. Deterding, S., Dixon, D., Khaled, R., and Nacke, L. From game design elements to gamefulness: Defining "gamification". In *Proc. of Mindtrek* (2011), 9–15.
10. Farzan, R., and Kraut, R. E. Wikipedia classroom experiment: Bidirectional benefits of students' engagement in online production communities. In *Proc. of CHI* (2013).
11. Forte, A., Kittur, N., Larco, V., Zhu, H., Bruckman, A., and Kraut, R. E. Coordination and Beyond: Social Functions of Groups in Open Content Production. In *Proc. of CSCW* (2012), 417–426.

12. Garfield, S. 10 reasons why people don't share their knowledge. *KM Review 9*, 2 (2006), 10–11.
13. Goodchild, M. Citizens as sensors: the world of volunteered geography. *GeoJournal 69*, 4 (2007), 211–221.
14. Haklay, M. How good is volunteered geographical information? A comparative study of OpenStreetMap and Ordnance Survey datasets. *Environment and planning. B, Planning & design 37*, 4 (2010), 682.
15. Halfaker, A., Keyes, O., and Taraborelli, D. Making Peripheral Participation Legitimate: Reader engagement experiments in Wikipedia. In *Proc. of CSCW* (2013), 849–860.
16. Halfaker, A., Kittur, A., Kraut, R., and Riedl, J. A jury of your peers: quality, experience and ownership in Wikipedia. In *Proc. WikiSym* (2009), 15:1–15:10.
17. Japkowicz, N., and Stephen, S. The class imbalance problem: A systematic study. *Intelligent data analysis 6*, 5 (2002), 429–449.
18. Karau, S. J., and Williams, K. D. Social loafing: A meta-analytic review and theoretical integration. *Journal of personality and social psychology 65*, 4 (1993), 681.
19. Keegan, B., Gergle, D., and Contractor, N. Hot off the wiki: Structures and dynamics of wikipedias coverage of breaking news events. *American Behavioral Scientist 57*, 5 (2013), 595–622.
20. Kittur, A., and Kraut, R. E. Harnessing the wisdom of crowds in Wikipedia: quality through coordination. In *Proc. CSCW* (2008).
21. Kittur, A., Pendleton, B., and Kraut, R. E. Herding the Cats: The Influence of Groups in Coordinating Peer Production. In *Proc. of WikiSym* (2009), 7:1–7:9.
22. Kriplean, T., Beschastnikh, I., McDonald, D. W., and Golder, S. A. Community, Consensus, Coercion, Control: Cs*W or How Policy Mediates Mass Participation. In *Proc. of GROUP* (2007), 167–176.
23. Lam, S. T. K., Uduwage, A., Dong, Z., Sen, S., Musicant, D. R., Terveen, L., and Riedl, J. WP:Clubhouse?: An Exploration of Wikipedia's Gender Imbalance. In *Proc. of WikiSym* (2011), 1–10.
24. Lampe, C., Obar, J., Ozkaya, E., Zube, P., and Velasquez, A. Classroom wikipedia participation effects on future intentions to contribute. In *Proc. of CSCW* (2012), 403–406.
25. Lave, J., and Wenger, E. *Situated learning: Legitimate peripheral participation*. Cambridge university press, 1991.
26. Ling, K., Beenen, G., Ludford, P., Wang, X., Chang, K., Li, X., Cosley, D., Frankowski, D., Terveen, L., Rashid, A. M., et al. Using social psychology to motivate contributions to online communities. *Journal of Computer-Mediated Communication 10*, 4 (2005), 00–00.
27. Liu, I., and Agresti, A. The analysis of ordered categorical data: An overview and a survey of recent developments. *Test 14*, 1 (2005), 1–73.
28. Masli, M., and Terveen, L. G. Leveraging the Contributory Potential of User Feedback. In *Proc. of CSCW*, CSCW '14, ACM (New York, NY, USA, 2014), 956–966.
29. Panciera, K., Halfaker, A., and Terveen, L. Wikipedians Are Born, Not Made: A Study of Power Editors on Wikipedia. In *Proc. GROUP* (2009), 51–60.
30. Preece, J. *Online communities: Designing Usability and Supporting Socialbilty*. John Wiley & Sons, Inc., 2000.
31. Priedhorsky, R., Masli, M., and Terveen, L. Eliciting and Focusing Geographic Volunteer Work. In *Proc. of CSCW* (2010), 61–70.
32. Rashid, A. M., Ling, K., Tassone, R. D., Resnick, P., Kraut, R., and Riedl, J. Motivating Participation by Displaying the Value of Contribution. In *Proc. of CHI*, CHI '06 (2006), 955–958.
33. Reagle, J., and Rhue, L. Gender Bias in Wikipedia and Britannica. *International Journal of Communication 5*, 0 (2011).
34. Roth, A. Student Contributions to Wikipedia. `https://outreach.wikimedia.org/wiki/Student_Contributions_to_Wikipedia`. Retrieved June 2, 2014.
35. Simon, H. A. Rational choice and the structure of the environment. *Psychological review 63*, 2 (1956), 129.
36. Solomon, J., and Wash, R. Bootstrapping wikis: developing critical mass in a fledgling community by seeding content. In *Proc. CSCW* (2012), 261–264.
37. Stephens, M. Gender and the GeoWeb: divisions in the production of user-generated cartographic information. *GeoJournal* (2013), 1–16. 00001.
38. Stvilia, B., Twidale, M. B., Smith, L. C., and Gasser, L. Assessing information quality of a community-based encyclopedia. In *Proc. ICIQ* (2005), 442–454.
39. Stvilia, B., Twidale, M. B., Smith, L. C., and Gasser, L. Information quality work organization in Wikipedia. *J. Am. Soc. Inf. Sci. Technol. 59* (April 2008), 983–1001.
40. Thom-Santelli, J., Cosley, D., and Gay, G. What Do You Know?: Experts, Novices and Territoriality in Collaborative Systems. In *Proc. of CHI* (2010), 1685–1694.
41. Thom-Santelli, J., Cosley, D. R., and Gay, G. What's Mine is Mine: Territoriality in Collaborative Authoring. In *Proc. of CHI* (2009), 1481–1484.
42. Warncke-Wang, M., Cosley, D., and Riedl, J. Tell me more: An actionable quality model for wikipedia. In *Proc. of WikiSym* (2013), 8:1–8:10.

43. WMF. Spring 2012 United States and Canada student article quality research results. https://en.wikipedia.org/wiki/Wikipedia:Ambassadors/Research/Article_quality/Results. Retrieved June 2, 2014.

44. Yee, T. W. The vgam package for categorical data analysis. *Journal of Statistical Software 32*, 10 (2010), 1–34.

45. Zhu, H., Kraut, R., and Kittur, A. Organizing without formal organization: Group identification, goal setting and social modeling in directing online production. In *Proc. of CSCW* (2012), 935–944.

The Effects of Visualizing Activity History on Attitudes and Behaviors in a Peer Production Context

Jennifer Marlow
Human-Computer Interaction Institute
Carnegie Mellon University
5000 Forbes Avenue, Pittsburgh, PA
jmarlow@cs.cmu.edu

Laura Dabbish
Human-Computer Interaction Institute and
Center for the Future of Work, Heinz College
Carnegie Mellon University
dabbish@cmu.edu

ABSTRACT
In a variety of peer production settings, from Wikipedia to open source software development to crowdsourcing, individuals may encounter, edit, or review the work of unknown others. Typically this is done without much context to the person's past behavior or performance. To understand how exposure to an unknown individual's activity history influences attitudes and behaviors, we conducted an online experiment on Mechanical Turk varying the content, quality, and presentation of information about another Turker's work history. Surprisingly, negative work history did not lead to negative outcomes, but in contrast, a positive work history led to positive initial impressions that persisted in the face of contrary information. This work provides insight into the impact of activity history design factors on psychological and behavioral outcomes that can be of use in other related settings.

Author Keywords
Crowdsourcing; Peer production; Activity traces; Transparency; Bias

ACM Classification Keywords
H.5.2 [Information Interfaces and Presentation]: User Interfaces - Interaction styles.

General Terms
Human Factors; Design; Measurement.

INTRODUCTION
As social media functionalities become more integrated into online work environments, details about individuals' work and interaction histories become increasingly visible. For example, sites like GitHub visibly showcase software developers' work history traces in a variety of formats that give insight into their past behavior and can be a source of learning [4]. External observers have access to these traces to learn about individuals' past work, which can help them to form an initial impression of this person's areas of expertise [13]. For example, in an enterprise social media setting, public online activity traces can also be used to infer connections between individuals relating to various aspects of expertise and reputation [7].

Other sites like Wikipedia and Stack Overflow make different design choices in terms of how they present information about users' activity history in varying degrees of accessibility and granularity. There are tradeoffs between aggregating information about activity, such that focusing only on quantitative properties of user behavior (e.g. reputation score, number of answers) can cause people to misclassify active users for knowledgeable ones, or be subject to manipulation [23].

However, the effects of exposure to past traces of activity history in evaluating work done by an unknown individual are not well understood, particularly in a peer review setting where individuals review and correct each other's work. On one hand, making activity history visible can provide useful insight into details of behaviors that previously were inaccessible and encourage more careful review of difficult cases [5].

On the other hand, large amounts of detailed information could be overwhelming and lead to cognitive overload. The way in which the details are presented may be able to mitigate problems of information overload if they are presented in a summary. However, summaries may obscure some of the useful details.

To investigate these competing potential outcomes, we conducted an online experiment looking at the effects of activity history presentation on evaluation of an unknown individual's work in an online peer review/peer production context. Our research questions were as follows:

RQ1. How does exposure to information about an individual's work history influence initial attitudes and behaviors towards that person?

RQ2. How does subsequent experience with the individual's work artifacts influence final impressions of that person and editing behaviors on their work?

CSCW '15, March 14–18, 2015, Vancouver, BC, Canada

ACM 978-1-4503-2922-4/15/03…$15.00
http://dx.doi.org/10.1145/2675133.2675250

RQ3. How does the design and presentation of work history information influence final impressions of that person and editing behaviors on their work?

This work builds upon previous research in the areas of online impression formation and peer production by examining how interpersonal impressions can change over time and how they relate to work-related decision-making and evaluation.

RELATED WORK

Typically, information available about others in peer production contexts like Wikipedia or social Q&A sites is limited. The impact of providing detailed information about a stranger's work history on attitudes and behaviors towards that person is not well known. As Tausczik & Pennebaker [18] point out, minimizing information about a person's activity (e.g. what they have done in the past) can give individuals with little or no reputation the opportunity to produce high quality content. However, the reverse is also true: seeing a user's reputation could be a useful heuristic for assessing the quality of their work and making it easier to identify high quality content. We therefore hypothesize that if work history is seen as indicative of an individual's past performance, then

H1: The valence of work history should inform initial impressions of the person (e.g. a good work history should lead to more positive first impressions than a bad history.)

Advantages of seeing work history and process

One advantage of access to an individual's work process is the fact that aggregated history of behavior should, overall, provide a good basis for reputation even if an individual might behave differently across specific interactions [1]. Work looking at the effects of exposure to different types of discussion histories for Wikipedia articles suggests that access to more information about how an article was written (specifically, how much conflict there was between editors) can shape readers' attitudes towards the quality of an article [19]. In this case, evidence of negative conflicts decreased readers' perceptions of the actual work quality. However, we do not know how exposure to conflict also affected perceptions of the articles' authors.

Qualitative research has provided some insights in this regard. In creative collaborations, Luther et al. [12] found that access to an individual's past work influenced how project leaders evaluated candidates. They equated a high "batting average" (reputation) and evidence of a long activity history with competence and expected them to be able to contribute to a project's success. Similar patterns have been observed in open source software development [13], but these findings have not been experimentally tested.

Bias

As Walther [21] asserts, lack of rich cues in a text-based digital environment can often make information seeking and interpretation cognitively demanding and subject to errors. Despite this, research on impression formation online suggests that first impressions are often unexpectedly robust, although they can be both confirmed and disconfirmed [22].

The potential disadvantage of access to work history is that people may be subject to bias based on whatever they see. When viewers are not motivated or unable to systematically evaluate information, they may be subject to using heuristic shortcuts or cues instead [14]. For example, the confirmation bias can cause individuals to form an initial impression and interpret subsequent information in light of this impression. This can be a problem when making social judgments in cases where the initial impression is inaccurate [6].

In general, the valence of information may also affect the nature of biases formed. While positive stimuli may elicit positive inferences (a positivity bias), and negative stimuli may elicit a negativity bias [16], negative information is often stronger and more influential than positive information [2]. Past work suggests that negative first impressions are often more resistant to change, and negative information is more likely than positive information to have an enduring effect [8].

Prior research on interactions around contributions in peer production provides some evidence of the negativity bias occurring, particularly towards contributors who are perceived to be novices [13, 24]. Based on this, we might expect that a negative first impression of a person will be less likely to change than a positive first impression, even in the face of disconfirming information.

H2a: Initial impressions will persist even in the face of contrary evidence.

H2b: Individuals will change their opinions after new evidence is revealed.

Visualizations of behavior

Past work in a variety of online domains have explored the effects of using simple interface interventions to help people make sense of detailed and potentially overwhelming information about the past behavior of individuals and the artifacts that they create. For example, Liao & Fu have used various indicators of unknown online forum commenters' attitudes and expertise to help increase accuracy of perceptions of these commenters' positions and knowledge [10, 11]. Other research in the realm of peer production has focused on different ways of presenting and displaying information about work history. For example, work in Wikipedia explored ways of visualizing an article's edit history to indicate quality [3].

Psychological principles underlying visualization design may affect the way people interpret the information displayed. Large volumes of information can be presented in great detail or aggregated into a more visual format. This has implications for the amount of processing effort it takes to make sense of the information. For example, work that is harder to perceive (such as text written in a font that is hard to read) requires more mental effort to process, and this has been found to lead to more negative impressions of the text's author [15]. This work suggests the easier a display is to process, the more positive feelings it may engender, thus we hypothesize:

H3a: Reducing the amount of detail in the work history will increase impression positivity.

Reducing detail by summarizing the information could be beneficial, by reducing information overload (which can impose a ceiling on accuracy [20] and make people more subject to bias). At the same time, even uninformative details may increase the clarity of the judge's mental picture of the target [20], which has been associated with increased positive attitudes towards others [17].

H3b: Increasing the amount of detailed information about another worker will increase impression positivity.

In the present research we were therefore interested in exploring the tradeoffs between useful detail and potential information overload by examining when and how presenting information about a worker's past history influences attitudes and subsequent behaviors towards that person and their work.

THE EFFECTS OF WORK HISTORY AND PRESENTATION ON ATTITUDES AND BEHAVIORS

In this study we were interested in understanding the relative effects of work history valence (positive or negative) on subsequent evaluations of that person's work. We also examined the role of information presentation (i.e. the level of detail provided) on impressions and behaviors. To do so, we conducted an online experiment on Mechanical Turk where participants first viewed a worker's past history and then went on to rate and edit new examples of their work.

METHOD

Procedure

Participants were recruited from Amazon's Mechanical Turk to complete what was advertised as a "transcription evaluation" task. The task was posted on January 6, 2014 and we provided a payment of 25 cents for successful completion. Participants were told that the requesters were having people on Mechanical Turk type in the text from images of signs to help compile a database of transcriptions, and that we needed help from other Turkers to check them for quality.

Participants were then told they would first see some information about the past performance of the person whose work they were about to evaluate, including how other "editors" had evaluated their work. After this, participants were then told that they would be shown six new pieces of work that had not been evaluated yet. They were asked to rate the quality of the work and had the option to edit it if needed. After rating the six pieces of new work, participants completed a short questionnaire in which they evaluated the overall quality of the worker, gave a recommendation for using this person for future tasks, and provided demographic information such as age and gender.

Figure 1 summarizes the overall experimental flow:

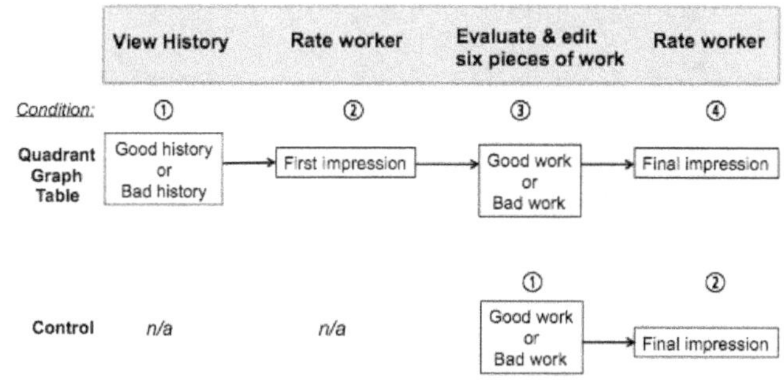

Figure 1. Overall experimental flow and manipulations

Independent variables

We manipulated three independent variables: Work history visualization (3 types: *table*, *graph*, or *quadrant*), work history quality (2 types: good history or bad history), and quality of work to be evaluated (2 types: good work or bad work), for a total of twelve different experimental conditions. We also had two *control* conditions, where participants did not see any history information and evaluated either good or bad work. There were therefore a total of fourteen potential conditions and each participant was randomly assigned to one of these.

Work history visualization

Participants in the work history conditions saw information about how the worker they were evaluating had previously performed on transcribing six images, along with how their work was evaluated by another editor. The visualizations differed in terms of the amount of detail they presented and the degree to which this was listed in textual format or displayed in a more abstract, visual way.

The *table* condition involved a grid filled with the text the participant had typed, the correct answer, the rating by the editor, and the percent of the work that had been completed. The *graph* condition contained this same information, except the percent of the work completed and the rating by the editor were displayed in a visual format (through colored bar graphs.) Finally, the *quadrant* condition was the most abstract and plotted the participant on a grid showing the average completeness of their work and the average evaluation of their work.

Because we were interested in varying the amount of detail and in varying the difficulty of processing the information, the table was designed to be the most detailed but also the hardest to process. The graph was designed to present activity information in a visual summary, using color and visual cues to help make it easier to process. The quadrant was designed as an alternative, easy to process visualization to make sure the particular design of the graph itself was

VISUAL SUMMARIES	DETAILED DISPLAY

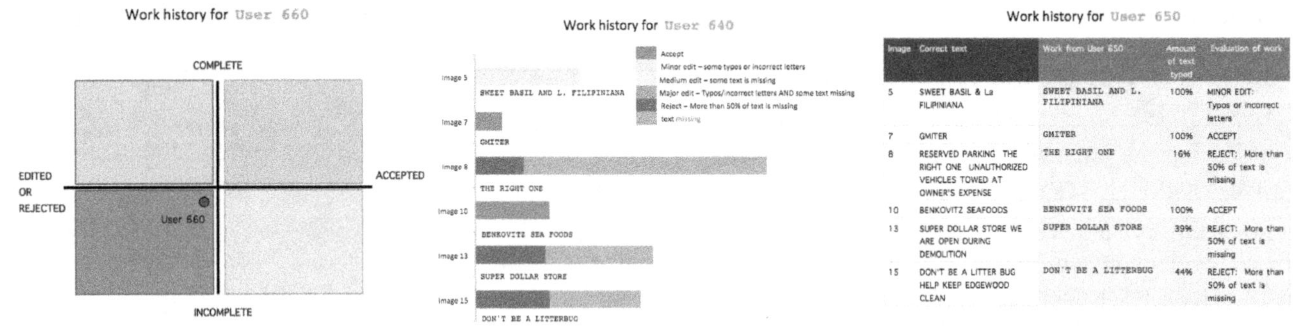

Figure 2. Examples of bad work shown, from left to right: summary (quadrant, graph) and detail (table) formats

not responsible for any observed effects. We used two different visual summaries to ensure that any differences between the table and the visual summaries was due to the difference in abstraction rather than the particular representation chosen (see Figure 2).

Work history quality

We were also interested in how the quality of past work influenced attitudes towards subsequent work (H1). Therefore, we manipulated the quality of the work shown in the past history and in the six examples. The work shown was taken from actual activity history taken from Turkers who had performed the image transcription task previously.

Figure 2 shows an example of the three visualization formats we used (in this case, showcasing "bad" work history). Participants in the control condition were not exposed to any of these work history visualizations. They viewed a neutral image (to ensure that they were still looking at something prior to beginning the work) but this was unrelated to the person whose work they were about to evaluate.

Stimuli used for work quality evaluation

For the work task, participants were shown six new images along with the worker's performance transcribing the image. The instructions for evaluating the work were as follows: *We would like the text transcribed to be as complete a representation of everything in the image as possible. The capitalization of letters does not matter.*

Figure 3. Sample image for transcription

Figure 3 shows one of the sample images used; below are examples of "good" and "bad" work.

Example of correctly transcribed text: `STAGNO'S BAKERY INC. STAGNOS BAKERY`

Example of "good" work: `STAGNO'S BAKERY INC. STANGNOS` [missing 6 characters]

Example of "bad" work: `STAGNO'S BAKERY` [missing 18 characters]

Dependent variables

There were four dependent measures: 1) *First work impression:* The initial impression of the quality of the Turker's past work, measured on a scale from 1-100, after viewing the history; 2) *Work evaluation:* The mean of the six quality ratings given for the pieces of work seen, on a five point Likert scale; 3) *Amount of work fixed:* A measure of relative amount of work edited, calculated as the average increase in number of characters from the original work to the participants' answer, and 4) *Final impression:* The aggregate sum of four five-point Likert scale items assessing overall impressions of the quality of the Turker's work.

RESULTS

Overall, 284 participants completed the task (which had an overall completion rate of 82%). 55% were female, and 45% were male. 59% were located in the USA, 35% in India, and 6% in other countries.

RQ1: Attitudinal and behavioral effects of work history

We initially predicted that the valence of work history would influence initial impressions of the person. We conducted a one-way ANOVA to assess the effects of work history on first impression (on a 100-point scale, with 100 being the highest quality.) This was supported; participants exposed to the "good" work history gave a significantly higher rating of the quality of the Turker's past work (75.94 out of 100) than participants exposed to the "bad" history (33.39 out of 100) ($F(1,217)=329.72$, $p<.001$).

This suggests that participants were able to fairly accurately assess work quality and correctly interpreted the history visualizations.

RQ2: Relationship between initial impression and direct experience with work

RQ2 focused on the degree to which an initial impression was subject to influence or change after direct experience viewing and editing the Turker's work artifacts.

There was a significant main effect of work quality, which is to say that participants exposed to "bad" work rated it, on average, significantly lower (mean rating for six pieces of work=3.97) than "good" work (4.29) (F(1,282)=322.22, p<.001).

Hypotheses 2a and 2b focused on the persistence of initial first impressions after direct exposure to work. In order to test these, we conducted a series of paired t-tests comparing final impressions within each set of history conditions.

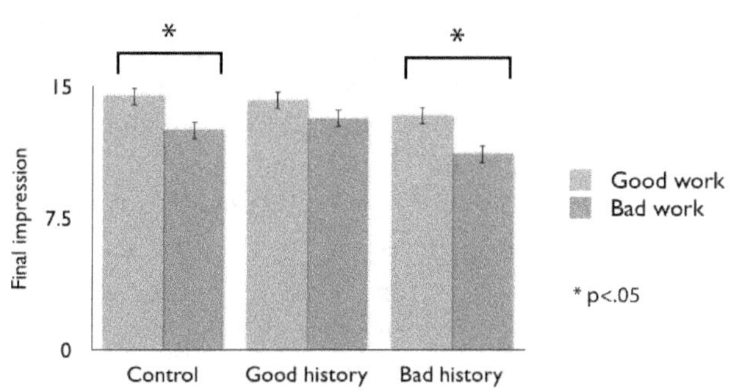

Figure 4. Effects of history and work on final impression

As indicated in Figure 4, participants in the control and bad history conditions had differing impressions of the worker based on the quality of the work they evaluated themselves. When participants had no history to go on (in the control condition), they formed impressions of people in accordance with the work that they saw; final impressions of good work were significantly higher than final impressions of bad work (t[63]=2.49, p=.01). Similarly, when the work history was bad, then participants' final impressions of the worker were, like in the control condition, more based upon the work that they saw, with "good" workers viewed as better than "bad" workers (t[108]=3.01, p<.005).

However, when the work history was good, then subsequent work quality had no effect on the final impressions of the person (t[107]=2.69, p=.10). This suggests the presence of a "positivity effect" and confirmation bias when the history was good, but no such effects when the history was bad.

When comparing the effects of work quality on editing behaviors within history quality types, there was a significant difference in editing behaviors (number of characters edited) in the bad history condition (see Figure 5). Individuals in the bad history condition edited more bad work than good work (t[108]=-3.09, p<.0025). This pattern was not observed for the control condition (t[63]=-.74, p=.46) or the good history condition (t[107]=-1.25, p=.21).

Therefore, we found partial support for both Hypothesis 2a and 2b, depending on the valence of the history information. People who viewed a good history formed impressions that were resistant to change, while people who viewed a bad history were able to change their opinions in the face of new evidence. The bad history also seems to have made people more sensitive to fixing work when it was needed.

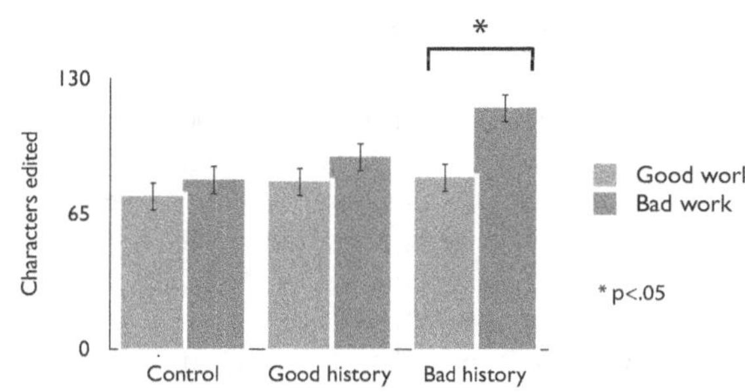

Figure 5. Effects of history and work on amount edited

RQ3: Influence of visualization type

To compare among the three visualization types on first impressions of work quality (testing H3a and H3b), we conducted a one-way ANOVA comparing the three visualizations on first impressions of worker quality. There was no significant main effect of visualization type on first impressions of worker quality (F(2,216)=1.53, p=.21). However, planned contrasts between the table and the two visual summary types of visualizations (graph + quadrant) revealed that the table (aka detailed format) led to more positive first impressions of worker quality than the two summary conditions (F(1,213)=10.93, p<.001). This lent support to H3b, which predicted that more detail would lead to more positive attitudes.

In order to see how the visualization of history affected final impressions and editing behaviors, we once again conducted paired t-tests for each visualization type on final impressions and editing behaviors after exposure to either good or bad work. For the analyses conducted, the graph and quadrant conditions were combined and we refer to them collectively as the "summary" conditions.

The positive first impressions induced by the detailed format (table) seemed to persist and remained immune to further experience with work quality. As shown in Figure 6, participants in the table (detail) condition had equally high final impressions of the worker's quality, regardless of whether they saw examples of good or bad work (t[71]=1.17, p=.24). This did not occur in the control condition (t[63]=2.49, p=.01) or the summary conditions (t[144]=3.38, p<.001).

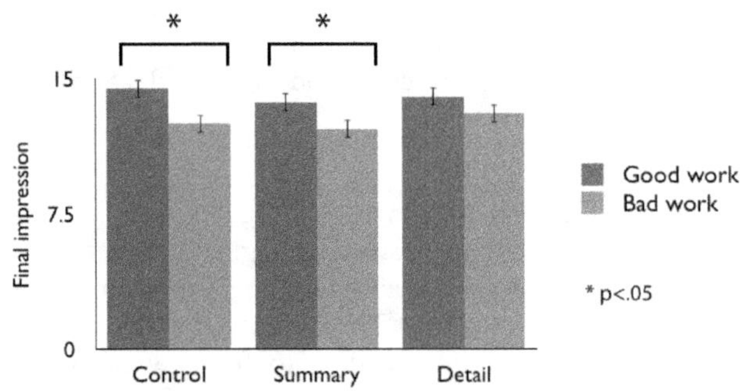

Figure 6. Effects of history visualization and work quality on final impressions of worker

The visualization types also had different effects depending on whether they showed good or bad activity history. As Figure 7 indicates, only participants who had viewed work history in a summary format exhibited a significant difference in editing behaviors (t[144]=-4.26, p<.001). Compared to the control (t[63]=.46, p=.46) or table (t[71]=.45, p=.65) conditions, they fixed significantly more bad work than good work, thus suggesting that they were more sensitive to fixing work in accordance with its actual quality.

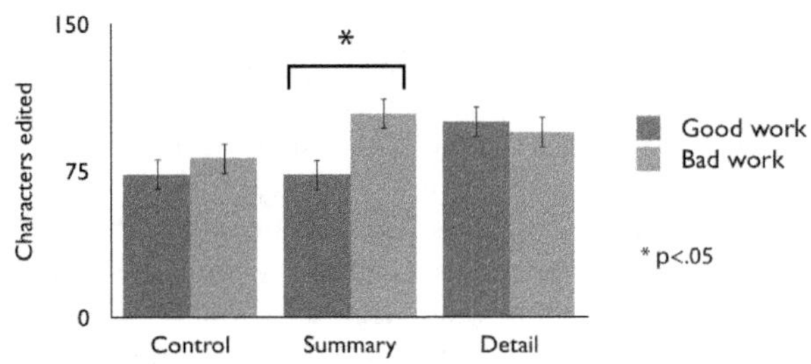

Figure 7. Effects of history visualization and work quality on editing behaviors

DISCUSSION

Implications for theory

In conclusion, we found that positive first impressions based on a "good" work history engendered a positivity effect among participants in that condition. This made them more positively rate the quality of the worker, but at the same time made them neglect to fix more of the work, especially when it was needed. In contrast, a negative first impression seemed to make participants more sensitive to fixing bad work (but did not make them unduly critical towards good work.)

This result is somewhat surprising, since prior research on impression formation has suggested that negative information is typically more enduring than positive information [16]. If this was the case, we would not have seen a significant difference in editing behaviors between the two "bad history" conditions. However, our results are in line with related recent work by Carr & Walther [2], which also saw lack of support for the negativity effect in the context of social media information in a hiring context.

While most evidence of the negativity bias comes from direct interpersonal evaluations online or in the real world, it could be that negative information generated by others (in our case, by a previous editor's assessment) does not carry the same weight in informing impressions. For example, when users know little about the expertise or qualification of a previous rater, they may be less likely to trust past assessments [14].

There may be various explanations for the lack of negativity effect that we observed that are related to the online peer review task and setting. One potential mechanism driving the persistence of negative information is that it is more novel and memorable and also as seen as more non-normative [8]. The negativity bias is expected to be reversed in situations where there is an expectation of negative behavior as the norm. This may have been the case in our task, where participants were primed to look out for work to correct. Additionally, the positivity bias is most clearly observed in neutral situations where the target of evaluation is relatively novel and does not directly influence the observer during the process of evaluation [9].

Implications for design

Differences in behaviors and attitudes between different visualizations of activity history suggest that design choices about how much information to provide and how difficult it may be to fully process have the potential to influence work outcomes. One reason why the summary conditions may have led to differential editing behaviors based on the work could be that their designs featured color coding (using a green for good and red for bad) paradigm that made it easier to visually assess the overall work quality in a way that was not present in the table. Adding color to the table in a similar way could potentially encourage more editing of the work.

There could be other ways of enhancing a detailed work history to encourage more editing behaviors as well. For example, the system could insert artificial and fictitious bad history in cases where a worker might have little to no prior work history in order to induce more sensitivity and attention to fixing their work.

However, one caveat and tradeoff with doing this is that improved editing performance could come at the expense of more negative attitudes towards the worker. This could pose a problem in more collaborative situations with greater interactions between workers (e.g. in Wikipedia or software development). The role of task factors may also play a role in terms of the most desirable information to highlight about individuals.

In our task, which was decoupled and anonymized, participants had little expectation of interacting with the person whose work they were fixing. As a result, in this type of situation it may be fine to highlight problems with their work in order to ensure more accurate editing. On the other hand, in a context where future interaction is expected, interpersonal attitudes and impressions of quality may play a bigger role in terms of outcomes to promote. Future work can address alternative design decisions and further explore their attitudinal and behavioral effects in a variety of collaborative task settings.

CONCLUSION

Overall, our work provides some initial indications that observers are able to form fairly accurate impressions of an individual's past work history, but that both detail and valence play a role in the degree to which these impressions persist in the face of disconfirming evidence.

This work provides initial insights for designers of peer production systems about how various design parameters might influence both interpersonal attitudes and work evaluation behaviors (sometimes in different ways).

Given the increase in transparency of individuals' actions in online work contexts, there is great potential for leveraging this information to jump-start work relationships or to help recommend people for various tasks. However, our results suggest that not only *what* is presented but *how* it is shown can produce differing effects.

ACKNOWLEDGMENTS

This work was supported by NSF grants IIS-1111750, SMA-1064209, OCI-0943168, ACI-1322278, and the Center for the Future of Work, Heinz College, Carnegie Mellon University.

REFERENCES

1. Anderson, C. and Shirako, A. Are individuals' reputations related to their history of behavior? Journal of Personality and Social Psychology 94, 2 (2008), 320.

2. Carr, C.T. and Walther, J.B. Increasing Attributional Certainty via Social Media: Learning About Others One Bit at a Time. Journal of Computer-Mediated Communication, (2014), 922-937.

3. Chevalier, F., Huot, S., and Fekete, J.-D. WikipediaViz: Conveying article quality for casual Wikipedia readers. Pacific Visualization Symposium (PacificVis), 2010 IEEE, IEEE (2010), 49–56.

4. Dabbish, L., Stuart, C., Tsay, J., and Herbsleb, J. Social coding in GitHub: transparency and collaboration in an open software repository. Proceedings of CSCW, (2012), 1277–1286.

5. Hansen, D.L., Schone, P.J., Corey, D., Reid, M., and Gehring, J. Quality control mechanisms for crowdsourcing: peer review, arbitration, & expertise at familysearch indexing. Proceedings of CSCW, (2013), 649–660.

6. Hullman, J., Adar, E., & Shah, P. The impact of social information on visual judgments. Proceedings of CHI, (2011), 1461–1470.

7. Jacovi, M., Guy, I., Kremer-Davidson, S., Porat, S., and Aizenbud-Reshef, N. The perception of others: inferring reputation from social media in the enterprise. Proceedings of CSCW, (2014), 756–766.

8. Kanouse, D.E. Explaining negativity biases in evaluation and choice behavior: Theory and research. Advances in consumer research 11, 1 (1984).

9. Lewicka, M., Czapinski, J., and Peeters, G. Positive-negative asymmetry or 'When the heart needs a reason.' European Journal of Social Psychology 22, 5 (1992), 425–434.

10. Liao, Q. V. and Fu, W-T. Can you hear me now? Mitigating the echo chamber effect by source position indicators. Proceedings of CSCW, (2014), 184-196.

11. Liao, Q.V. & Fu, W-T. Expert voices in echo chambers: effects of source expertise indicators on exposure to diverse opinions. Proceedings of CHI, (2014), 2745-2754.

12. Luther, K., Caine, K., Ziegler, K., and Bruckman, A. Why it works (when it works): success factors in online creative collaboration. Proceedings of GROUP, ACM (2010), 1–10.

13. Marlow, J., Dabbish, L., and Herbsleb, J. Impression formation in online peer production: activity traces and personal profiles in Github. Proceedings of CSCW, (2013), 117–128.

14. Metzger, M.J., Flanagin, A.J., and Medders, R.B. Social and heuristic approaches to credibility evaluation online. Journal of Communication 60, 3 (2010), 413–439.

15. Oppenheimer, D.M. Consequences of erudite vernacular utilized irrespective of necessity: Problems with using long words needlessly. Applied Cognitive Psychology 20, 2 (2006), 139–156.

16. Peeters, G. and Czapinski, J. Positive-negative asymmetry in evaluations: The distinction between affective and informational negativity effects. European review of social psychology, 1, (1990), 33–60.

17. Tanis, M., & Postmes, T. Social cues and impression formation in CMC. Journal of Communication, 53(4), (2003), 676-693.

18. Tausczik, Y.R. and Pennebaker, J.W. Predicting the perceived quality of online mathematics contributions from users' reputations. Proceedings of CHI, (2011), 1885–1888.

19. Towne, W.B., Kittur, A., Kinnaird, P., and Herbsleb, J. Your process is showing: Controversy management and perceived quality in Wikipedia. Proceedings of CSCW, (2013), 1059–1068.

20. Tsai, C. I., Klayman, J., & Hastie, R. Effects of amount of information on judgment accuracy and confidence.

Organizational Behavior and Human Decision Processes, 107(2), (2008), 97–105.

21. Walther, J. Computer-mediated communication impersonal, interpersonal, and hyperpersonal interaction. Communication research 23.1 (1996), 3-43.

22. Walther, J. B., & Tong, S. T. Inventing Partners in Computer-Mediated Communication: How CMC Sustains Self-fulfilling Prophecies and Relational Attributions. In Social Computing and Social Media, (2014), 517-527.

23. Yang, J., Tao, K., Bozzon, A., and Houben, G.-J. Sparrows and Owls: Characterisation of Expert Behaviour in StackOverflow. In *User Modeling, Adaptation, and Personalization*. Springer, 2014, 266–277.

24. Zhu, H., Zhang, A., He, J., Kraut, R.E., and Kittur, A. Effects of peer feedback on contribution: a field experiment in Wikipedia. Proceedings of CHI, (2013), 2253–2262.

"You Never Call, You Never Write": Call and SMS Logs Do Not Always Indicate Tie Strength

Jason Wiese, Jun-Ki Min, Jason I. Hong, John Zimmerman
Human-Computer Interaction Institute, Carnegie Mellon University
{jwwiese, loomlike, jasonh, johnz}@cs.cmu.edu

ABSTRACT

How effective are call and SMS logs in modeling tie strength? Frequency and duration of communication has long been cited as a major aspect of tie strength. Intuitively, this makes sense: people communicate with those that they feel close to. Highly cited research papers have pushed this idea further, using communication as a direct proxy for tie strength. However, this operationalization has not been validated. Our work evaluates this assumption. We collected call and SMS logs and ground truth relationship data from 36 participants. Consistent with theory, we found that frequent or long-duration communication likely indicates a strong tie. However, the use of call and SMS logs produced many errors in separating strong and weak ties, suggesting this approach is incomplete. Follow-up interviews indicate fundamental challenges for inferring tie strength from communication logs.

Author Keywords

Tie strength, smartphone, social graph

ACM Classification Keywords

H.5.m. Information interfaces and presentation (e.g., HCI): Miscellaneous.

INTRODUCTION

Logged communication data collected by smartphones offer a potentially rich way for computer systems to gain more social sophistication and to better understand the changing interpersonal relationships that people have with each other. Recent work points to benefits from more social sophistication, including digital photo frames that adapt based on the relationships of the people in a place [20]; online identity authentication [21]; virtual possession collections that automatically surface based on the social context [30]; and even services that automate the management of privacy settings based on the influence of relationship in people's willingness to share [39].

A wealth of work in social psychology has found that relationship strength between two people influences their pattern of communication. When a relationship has stronger tie strength, there is generally more communication and when a relationship has weaker tie strength there is generally less communication [16,23]. Subsequent research has operationalized this theory by using call frequency and duration as a proxy for tie strength [7,27,31,37].

The theory relating communication frequency to tie strength is based on communication across long periods of time and across all possible channels, including face-to-face. Many recent and highly cited papers, however, have operationalized tie strength using data from one or two communication channels and using small time windows when compared to a person's lifetime [7,27,31,37]. The idea that you can model tie strength with relatively sparse data is tantalizing but dangerous. If it works, it is a discount approach that can easily be adopted by many applications where call logs are readily accessible. However, linking together communications from more data sources is challenging and error-prone. Furthermore, if sparser communication data does not accurately infer tie strength, then our community's ongoing adoption of this untested assumption may lead to many kinds of errors.

To investigate if tie strength can be inferred from sparser communication data sets, we conducted a study based on the call and SMS logs stored on smartphones that had been in use for at least six months. We gathered data from 36 participants, including contact lists, call and SMS logs, and a list of friends from Facebook. We also collected ground truth: participants labeled the type of relationship and rated the tie strength of seventy of their contacts and friends.

The data confirms that high-frequency or long-duration communication is a useful signal for identifying strong ties. However, communication frequency and duration are a noisy signal, producing many errors. In an attempt to reach beyond the simple proxies of frequency and duration, we employed a set of 153 features and developed 9 machine learning models to identify any complex signals in the call logs that might indicate tie strength. In line with previous findings conducted using Facebook data, our binary classifier achieved 91.6% accuracy for inferring tie strength. We confirmed that frequent communication is a useful signal for identifying strong ties. However, this high accuracy can be misleading, because the number of strong ties is much lower than the number of weak ties. Despite the high accuracy of the model, over half of strong ties are incorrectly labeled as weak ties, and only half of the classified strong ties are actually strong ties.

http://dx.doi.org/10.1145/2675133.2675143

To understand the cause of these errors, we interviewed a subset of our participants. We found three explanations: 1) people use many different communication channels, and phone and SMS logs are not representative of their overall communication patterns; 2) face-to-face communication is important, but is not easily observed; and 3) people feel a lingering sense of closeness to friends from a previous stage in their life, though communication has decreased.

In hindsight, these results may seem obvious; interestingly, they are not well represented in the literature. Furthermore, several highly cited papers operationalize tie strength only using call frequency and duration, without acknowledging these limitations, leading to an incomplete construct that may affect their results. While in many cases a more accurate approximation of tie strength may not be feasible, work using call logs to operationalize tie strength should consider these systematic biases and directly address how these limitations affect their claims.

RELATED WORK

Social Science Research in Social Networks

A large amount of social science research has focused on understanding aspects of human relationships. We highlight some related areas and describe how we operationalize these theories in a machine learning system.

Numerous studies have examined how many close ties a person has. A study of 3,000 Americans showed that people average four strong ties, with most having between two and six [6]. Another study of 1,000 adults found that most people had 10 friends they meet or speak with weekly [6]. Our work is focused less on counting ties and instead looks to characterize these ties. A great deal of literature has looked at factors influencing tie strength. Roberts and Dunbar examined how closeness and kinship influence the size of social networks and communication patterns [34,35]. Some studies have used proximity as a proxy for quantity of social interaction between pairs [13,29], showing that communication frequency drops exponentially as members of a pair move farther apart [2,42].

Granovetter identified four dimensions of tie strength: duration, intimacy, intensity, and reciprocity [17]. Gilbert and Karahalios expanded on these dimensions for online communications on Facebook, and built models that could achieve 85% accuracy on binary classification of a person's contacts as strong or weak ties [14]. Using survey data and Facebook data (including passive consumption) from 11,000 participants, Burke developed a linear model for estimating tie strength of contacts on Facebook, which was able to distinguish the closest relationships from others with an accuracy of 71.2% [4]. Our work is similar to the above, and our binary classification accuracy of 91.6% is in line with their results; however, we use a different data source, looking at smartphone usage and not Facebook usage.

Beyond using different data sources, we use a different method for eliciting a participant's contacts to be examined in this study, including: 1) Explicitly asking the participant for their close contacts regardless of whether they are in the participant's contact list; and 2) Selecting contacts with whom the participant has frequent communication. By employing this approach, we can better understand the aggregate of the participant's social relationships. This also enables us to understand the limits of elicitation methods that use only Facebook, or only the mobile contact list.

Backstrom and Kleinberg used Facebook data to analyze network properties of users to identify a specific kind of strong tie: a romantic partner [3]. They identified a new measure of tie strength that they call 'dispersion;' the lack of connectedness between two people's mutual friends. Employing machine learning techniques focused on structural and interaction measures, they correctly identified an individual's romantic partner 70% of the time. The call and SMS log data we used lacked these structural features. The logs contain egocentric network information for each participant, not for each of the participant's contacts. However, we take a similar process of examining several specific features individually before combining them in a machine learning model to infer strong ties.

Using Sensors to Model High Level Context

An emerging thread in UbiComp research has been the use of sensors to model real-world behavior and context [32], including inferring information about people and their social networks. Eagle, *et al.* studied and modeled human social structure using mobility data from mobile phones [11,12]. They were able to infer 95% of friendships based on call records and Bluetooth proximity within their participant pool of two interconnected groups at a university. In that study, inferences were made in a very particular setting: the only potential relationships considered were of classmates who were also participants in the study. Our work differs from this project by making inferences about a much larger pool of relationships.

Cranshaw, *et al.* [8] looked at how to use location data alone to infer friendships on Facebook. Using features extracted from the location data, they created a machine learning classifier that achieved 92% accuracy in making a binary classification for someone appearing in a person's list of Facebook friends. Similar to the reality mining work, this work also focused primarily on a campus population, and the analysis could only include relationships where both people in the dyad were participants using the study system. Both of these projects demonstrate the importance, and also the challenge, of using collocation to infer the presence of a social relationship. In our work we focused on trying to be as complete as possible with identifying a user's strong relationships, rather than identifying a subset of the participant's strong relationships. Our error analysis interviews highlight the necessity of collocation for being able to infer some of a person's strong relationships.

Researchers have used communication data to model social graphs. Past work developed techniques for inferring different groups from email or online social network usage [5,10,28]. Other work looked at inferring tie strength based on communication patterns [4,14,40]. For example, Xiang et al. [40] developed models that would infer the strength of ties between individuals on LinkedIn. Other work looked at using large quantities of mobile phone call logs to model social structure and persistence of ties over time [18].

Other work has created models to infer the life facet (family, work, or social) of contacts using smartphone logs [26], achieving 90% accuracy for contacts that had at least one communication. Our work uses similar machine learning features. Our core contribution is our investigation into inferring tie strength, our analyses of which techniques did and did not work well, and interviews to understand the errors made by the models.

METHOD

We wanted to assess how well tie strength can be inferred from data found on nearly every smartphone: contacts, call logs, and SMS logs. We chose these data sources because we wanted to validate the assumption being used in the research community that communication frequency and duration from these channels can work as an effective proxy for the strength of a relationship. We collected data from participants' Android smartphones and asked them to manually categorize and rate their relationships with individual contacts as our ground truth.

Participants

We recruited 40 participants (13 male and 27 female) living throughout the United States by posting ads in several places: on Craigslist in 6 major US cities, on a nationwide site for recruiting study participants, on a website for posting social relationship research studies, and on a participant pool within our university. We had three selection criteria. First, to avoid privacy concerns with minors, participants had to be at least 18. Second, to focus on people who could benefit from a more computationally sophisticated representation of relationships, participants had to use Facebook and have at least 50 friends through the service. Third, to ensure a sufficient amount of log data, participants had to have used the same Android phone for at least six months prior to the study. 55% of our participants were students (graduate or undergraduate), 35% were employed in a variety of professions, and 10% were unemployed. Participant ages ranged from 19 to 50 years ($mean$ = 28.0 years, $\sigma = 8.9$). Participants were instructed to complete the ground truthing within two weeks, and were compensated $80 USD. Of the 40 participants, we excluded four participants from our analysis: each had fewer than two weeks of data and fewer than 100 phone calls. Findings are based on the remaining 36 participants.

Procedure

Participants downloaded our Android app, which copied their contact list, call log, and SMS log to a database file. Participants then uploaded this file, in addition to their Facebook friends list, to our server through a custom website that was designed for this study. The entire study was conducted through this website. Participants could stop and resume whenever they wanted, and were given two weeks to complete the entire process. By default, Android phones limit the call log to the last 500 calls and typically have a default limit of 200 SMS messages per contact. This resulted in broad differences in how many days the logs represented (range: 21-369; median: 80; mean: 108).

Participants' contact and Facebook lists were much too long for participants to completely ground truth. Through pilot testing, we found 70 contacts to be a reasonable number for participants to rate before becoming overly burdensome: we wanted to maximize participant retention.

The vast majority of any individual's contacts will be weak ties. However, in this work, we wanted to maximize the likelihood of collecting information on strong ties. To accomplish this, we asked participants to generate a list of contacts that fit specific social categories, regardless of their appearance in the phone contact list or Facebook list. Participants listed five people in each of the following categories: *immediate family*, *extended family*, *people they live with*, *coworkers*, *people they feel close to*, and *people they do hobbies with*. We selected these groups based on past qualitative work that suggests these categories will contain an individuals' strong ties [24,36,39]. This resulted in approximately 25 unique names per participant (some names were repeated across the categories). In addition, we selected the 15 contacts with the highest communication frequency for calls, SMS, and Facebook. These characteristics allow us to examine the assumptions that communication is a direct proxy for tie strength: we now have ground truth data for all of the high-communication contacts, and we have identified many of the participant's strong ties by asking for them directly. If call and SMS communication is a perfect proxy for tie strength, these two groups should be the same.

To fill out the list of 70 contacts, we combined category list and the frequency list, removing all duplicates. To get the list of 70 contacts, we added randomly selected individuals from their phone's contact list and Facebook friend list, with participants manually identifying duplicates due to the challenges of automatic merging using names [38]. This process continued until we had a list of 70 distinct names for each participant (hereafter called the *70-person* list).

Participants provided demographics for each contact in the 70-person list, such as sex, age, and relationship duration. Participants also answered four questions about their relationship with each contact, adapted from [22]:

1. How close do you feel to this person?
2. How strongly do you agree with the statement "I talk with this person about important matters"?
3. How strongly do you agree with the statement "I would be willing to ask this person for a loan of $100 or more"?

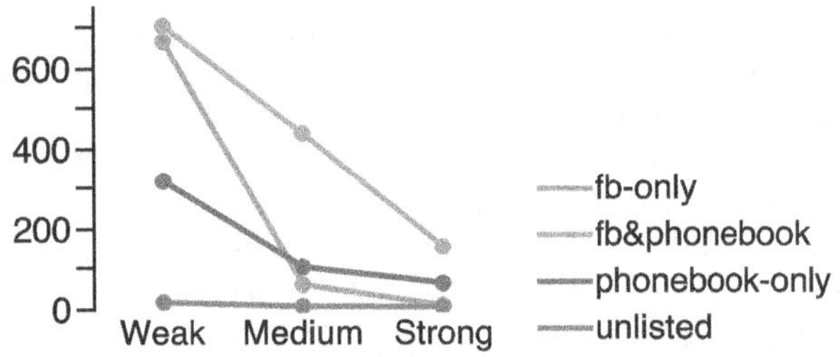

Figure 1. Total number of friends within each tie strength level across all participants, separated by the number of contacts who only appeared in the contact list, only in the Facebook friends list, appeared in both, or neither.

4. How strongly do you agree with the statement "I enjoy interacting with this person socially"?

Participants answered questions using a discrete 5-point scale, following previous work on tie strength [1,4,9,35]. We used a discrete rather than continuous scale to reduce cognitive load and fatigue. Participants provided a large amount of data for many contacts, and we were concerned that the freedom of a continuous slider would be an additional burden. To protect privacy, we did not collect the content of SMS messages. However, we did collect descriptive information such as email domain name, first six digits of phone numbers, and city/state/zip code.

DATA ANALYSIS

We gathered logs for 24,370 phone contacts, 16,940 calls, 63,893 SMS messages, and 1,853 MMS messages. Note: Android phones can be set to automatically sync the phonebook with online contact lists (e.g. Gmail and Facebook). As a first step to explore the validity of using information available on a smart phone (contact list, call logs, and SMS logs) to infer tie strength, we analyzed the answers for the four tie strength questions our participants answered. The questions were highly reliable ($\alpha = 0.91$). This allows us to add together the answers from the four questions to form a scale. This is a standard practice that increases the reliability of a measure [15]. Based on this combined score we generated a ranked list of each participant's contacts based on relationship strength.

Next we partitioned each participant's contacts into three levels. We explored several approaches for identifying these levels. An assessment of the distribution of Z-scores from the combined tie strength metric both across all participants and per-participant revealed no obvious gaps in ratings on which we could split strong and weak ties. Instead, we based these levels on previous work by Zhou *et al*, which finds that "rather than a single or a continuous spectrum of group sizes, humans spontaneously form groups of preferred sizes organized in a geometrical series approximating 3–5, 9–15, 30–45, etc." [41]. They found that the top group represents a person's closest relationships (support group), and the second group represents the next closest set of relationships (sympathy group). The larger sized groups of 50 and 150 people are considered to be less stable, and are referred to as clans or regional groupings.

In constructing each participant's 70-person list, we took multiple steps to increase the likelihood of capturing many of a participant's closest contacts. Because of this, we assigned the contacts into their respective groups based on the numbers from Zhou *et al.* By handling the data in this way, we are able to normalize out individual differences between participants (e.g. a tendency for some participants to use 3 as the baseline and others to use 1, or a participant's negative reaction to a particular question).

We partitioned each contact list accordingly:

- ***strong tie*** - the top group (rank 1-4)
- ***medium tie*** - the middle group (rank 5 – 19)
- ***weak tie*** - the remaining contacts

In cases where multiple contacts tied for a rank, all of those contacts were assigned to the same tie strength level, resulting in a slight variation in group sizes per participant.

With these tie strength groupings, we began to investigate communication patterns as a proxy for tie strength. First, we discuss simple features and their relationship to the tie strength groupings. Next, we describe machine learning models for inferring these tie strength levels.

SIMPLE FEATURES AND TIE STRENGTH

Contact Source and Tie Strength

The properties of the *70-person* list allow us to estimate an upper bound for the percentage of a user's close contacts who could be detected from our two contact sources: only Facebook, only the contact list, or both. As Figure 1 shows, overall 99% of people on the *70-person* list showed up in either a phonebook or Facebook list (range: 95-100%, med: 100%). Overall, 19% of contacts existed only in the phonebook (range: 4-57%, med: 18%); 29% were only in Facebook (range: 0-56%, med: 31%); and 51% were in both (range: 20-90%, med: 52%). Looking across the tie strength categories reveals distinctive trends. We used Spearman's rho (ρ) to measure the non-parametric correlations between tie strength group and presence in the phonebook and Facebook friend list. Being a Facebook-only contact was negatively correlated with tie strength (ρ=-0.32, $p < 0.001$). Being a phonebook-only contact was not correlated with tie strength (ρ=0.03, n.s.), although percentage-wise, more of the closer contacts were only in the phonebook. Being a phonebook-and-Facebook contact was positively correlated with tie strength (ρ=0.27, $p < 0.001$).

The red points in Figure 1 represent the 21 people that were neither in the phonebook nor Facebook list, including people whom participants identified as immediate and extended family members; people participants currently live with; work with; feel close to; and do hobbies with. The orange points in Figure 1 represent Facebook-only contacts and the blue points represent the phonebook-only contacts. 29% of contacts would be missed if using a phonebook-only list to classify tie strength and 19% would be missed if using a Facebook-only list. Both a Facebook-only and a contact-list-only approach would miss some strong ties;

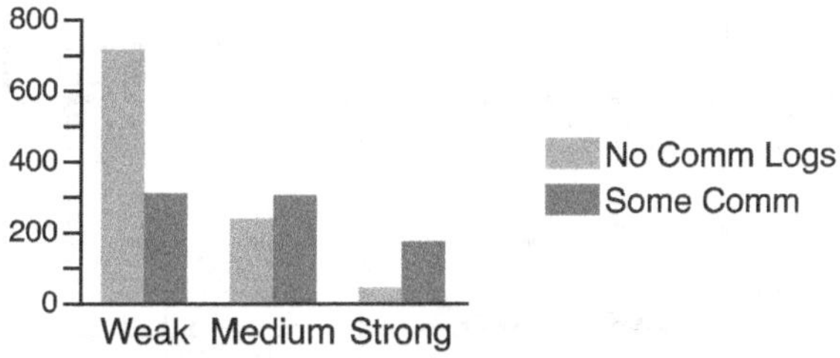

Figure 2. Number of friends in the mobile contact list who exchanged zero or at least one SMS or call with our participants (determined from call log data).

however, the Facebook-only approach would miss a notably larger number of strong ties (29% vs. 4%).

Tie Strength and Phone/SMS Communication

To establish an upper bound for the accuracy of inferring tie strength from phone and SMS communication, we divided the phonebook contacts into two groups by communication history (none vs. some). A reasonable baseline expectation would be that contacts with no communication history would have weak tie strength. Figure 2 shows that most contacts with at least one communication in the dataset tend to have higher levels of tie strength. Additionally, as the tie strength level increases, the percentage of contacts with some communication with the participant also increases (ρ=0.35, $p < 0.0001$). Still, several contacts with strong tie strength have no communication history in the dataset. Thus, attempts to classify tie strength using only call and SMS data could not correctly classify these contacts.

Having at least one communication in the call and SMS logs increases the likelihood of a contact having higher tie strength. However, this is not an absolute rule: there are counter-examples in both directions - strong ties without communication history and weak tie contacts with it.

Next we explored the relationship between communication frequency and duration with respect to tie strength. Figure 3 shows six plots in a grid. The top row shows aggregate call duration (y-axis) against the total number of calls (x-axis) for each contact. The bottom row shows the total number of SMS messages (y-axis) against the total number of calls (x-axis) for each contact. Each column indicates the contact's ground truth tie strength level. Both aggregate duration and frequency are represented as a percentage relative to the total call duration or number of calls per participant. We expected some close contacts to stand out with long call durations, and others to stand out with high frequency. For example, a person might call an old friend infrequently, but chat for a while each time. Conversely, one might regularly make short calls to a roommate to coordinate.

As expected, contacts with more frequent or longer duration communications were more often in the higher tie strength levels. Number of calls, duration of calls, and number of SMS are all positively correlated with tie strength (ρ = 0.42, 0.43, and 0.20, all $p < 0.0001$). Surprisingly, many people in all tie strength levels had very little communication. Weak ties generally had few calls and short durations. For

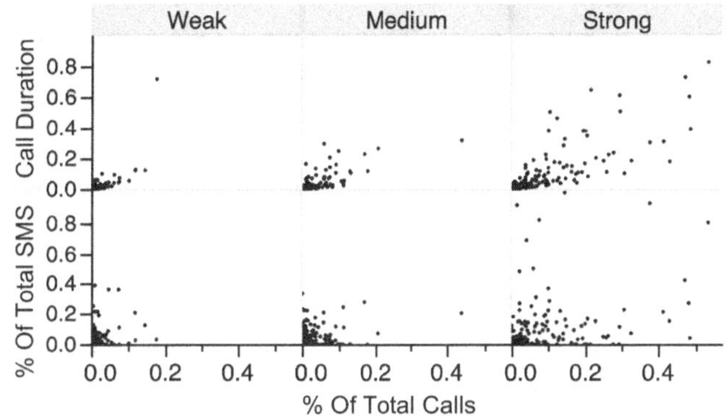

Figure 3. A grid of six plots showing communication frequency and total talk time. The top 3 graphs plot each contact's aggregate call duration (y-axis) against number of calls (x-axis). The bottom 3 graphs plot each contact's number of SMS messages (y-axis) against number of calls (x-axis). For both top and bottom, the columns separate the contacts by tie strength group. The graphs include data for contacts with at least one call or SMS. All numbers are represented as the percentage of a participant's total communication frequency/duration.

strong ties, the ranges increase for number and duration of calls, but a clump of few-and-short contacts persist.

Summary

In this section, we established a basic upper bound of accuracy for inferring tie strength with smartphone communication logs. The data shows that using Facebook as the only data source would miss 29% of strong ties, either because they are not Facebook friends, or because these contacts do not use Facebook at all. Next, there are some strong ties without any record of communication within the phone logs. Finally, while communication frequency and duration of calls can help indicate strong tie strength, low frequency and duration are not clear indications of weak tie strength.

These trends are consistent with tie strength theory: more communication on more channels indicates a strong tie. However, our dataset has a number of counterexamples, pointing to critical challenges for automatically inferring tie strength from communication behavior.

CLASSIFYING TIE STRENGTH

While the above findings already indicate significant issues for using call and SMS logs to indicate tie strength, we wanted to explore the possibility that a combination of more subtle features than frequency and duration might indicate tie strength. To explore this prospect, we developed several machine learning models to classify tie strength based on call and SMS log data.

Features Used for Characterizing the Data

We defined a total of 153 machine learning features: 17 from the contact list, 66 from call logs, 36 from SMS logs, and 34 from combined calls and SMS. These features are based on Min *et al.* [26], and more details on the specific features can be found in that paper. These features include:

- *Intensity and regularity:* The number of and duration of communications has been used to infer tie strength in past

				Strong ties		Medium strong ties		Weak ties	
Class Condition	Dataset	Accuracy	Kappa	Precision	Recall	Precision	Recall	Precision	Recall
3-class	all	69.60%	0.279	0.503	0.399	0.399	0.209	0.759	0.907
3-class	contactlist	61.11%	0.251	0.491	0.423	0.414	0.242	0.677	0.845
3-class	somecomm	46.28%	0.179	0.449	0.473	0.440	0.425	0.496	0.498
2-verystrong	all	91.55%	0.361	0.537	0.323	→		0.937	0.973
2-verystrong	contactlist	88.64%	0.361	0.545	0.343	→		0.914	0.961
2-verystrong	somecomm	75.46%	0.297	0.480	0.432	→		0.829	0.855
2-mediumstrong	all	75.00%	0.367	0.693	0.420	←		0.764	0.920
2-mediumstrong	contactlist	68.06%	0.317	0.683	0.460	←		0.680	0.843
2-mediumstrong	somecomm	63.11%	0.192	0.707	0.724	←		0.488	0.467

Table 1. The results of 9 classifiers constructed using SMO. The prediction classes are tie-strength categories. For 2-verystrong, the middle and low tie strength classes are combined and for 2-mediumstrong the middle and high classes are combined.

work [19,35]. We modeled this factor using features like total number and total duration of calls.

- *Temporal tendency*: In their friends-acquaintances work, Eagle and Pentland observed the temporal tendency in contacting people [11]. For example, calling particular contacts at different times of day and days of the week.
- *Channel selection and avoidance*: People favor a certain communication medium based on the person they are communicating with [25]. We modeled this using features like the ratio between SMS and phone calls.
- *Maintenance cost*: Roberts and Dunbar [35] find that people apply different amounts of effort in maintaining different kinds of relationships, based on the time to last contact. To model maintenance cost, we used the number of communications in the past two weeks (short-term view) and in the past three months (longer-term view).

Inferring Tie Strength Using Communication Logs

Using all of the features described above, we tested how well a model could infer tie strength. The nature of tie strength poses a challenge for building this model. Tie strength could be treated as a numeric class value based on the answers to the tie strength questions. However, the difference between a rating of 1 and 2 is not necessarily equal to the difference between a rating of 2 and 3. Additionally, our early iterations treating this as a continuous value tended to push scores closer to the middle, with very few people classified as being weak ties. Therefore, we used the tie strength levels of *very strong tie, medium strong tie,* and *weak tie* as nominal class values in these models (explanation of these categories on page 4).

We evaluated our models using the Weka Toolkit's [43] implementation of a support vector machine (SMO). We conducted a leave-one-participant-out cross-validation (each fold contained data from one participant). This prevents any anomalies within a particular participant's data from causing a performance overestimate. We trained 9 models, varying two aspects of input data. First we varied what the model was classifying (First column of Table 1):

- ***3-class***: classifies as strong, medium-strong, or weak
- ***2-verystrong***: binary classifier that combines medium-strong and weak ties into one class
- ***2-mediumstrong***: binary classifier that combines strong and medium-strong ties into one class

We also varied the input data for the classifier (Second column of Table 1):

- ***all*** includes all contacts on the *70-person* list
- ***contactlist*** includes only contacts from the *70-person* list who appear in the user's phonebook (see Figure 2)
- ***somecomm*** includes only contacts from the *70-person* list with at least one logged SMS or call (see Figure 3)

Classification results vary considerably (Table 1), ranging from 46.28% (κ=0.179), to 91.55% (κ=0.361). The Kappa statistic measures the agreement between predicted and observed categorizations, correcting for agreement that occurs by chance. Table 1 reveals clear trends. First, within each of the class conditions, classifiers perform best for *all*, second best for *contactlist* and worst for *somecomm*. Figures 2, 3, and 4 provide some insight into these results. Most of the contacts who are not in the contact list (thus excluded from *contactlist* models) or who have no communication history (thus excluded from the *somecomm* models) are not strong ties, and thus are easier to classify. As a result, the models that include them perform better.

The most successful class condition is *2-verystrong*, followed by *2-mediumstrong*. *3-class* performs the worst. This is typical of multi-class models, which usually take a performance hit compared to binary classifiers.

The models incorrectly classified more strong ties as weak than were correctly classified as strong (in Table 1, the recall values for the strong tie class are the percentage of strong ties correctly classified). Also, about half of ties that were classified as strong were actually not strong (in Table 1, the precision values for strong ties is the percentage of contacts that were classified as strong ties who were actually strong ties). The plots from Figure 3 offer insight into these errors. These misclassifications emphasize the weakness of using call and SMS logs to infer tie strength, and thus the problem with using those logs as direct proxies for tie strength. This result is even more pronounced in recall values for the strong tie class of the *2-verystrong* models in Table 1. The *2-verystrong-all* model, the model with the best performance, only detects 1/3 of strong ties.

ERROR ANALYSIS PARTICIPANT INTERVIEWS

Motivated by the particularly low recall of the *strong* tie class in these models, we conducted semi-structured interviews with 7 of our participants. For each participant, we selected 5 to 10 contacts they had labeled as strong ties that we misclassified as weak ties, (58 contacts total). An error analysis of the data led us to focus on strong ties that were classified as weak. In the error analysis, we referenced tie strength theory to consider communication expectations for medium and weak ties. It is not that we expect people to *only* communicate with strong ties, so the presence of some communication with weak ties is reasonable. However, if participants had more communication with more of their strong ties, the model would have been better able to distinguish between strong and weak ties. This led us to focus on strong ties with little or no communication, rather than weak ties with some communication.

Interviews took place over the phone, lasted about a half an hour, and were recorded to facilitate note taking. We asked participants open-ended questions about the nature of their relationship and communication with each selected contact:

- When and how did you meet this person?
- What led to this being a close relationship?
- Has anything changed between the time that you became close and now?
- Was there anything different about the channels that you used to communicate with this person or the frequency of communication that you used with this person between then and now?

Interview Results

We iteratively coded participants' responses about each contact for themes to provide insight into the misclassifications. Several themes surfaced that help explain the discrepancy between communication frequency and tie strength. We present them in two categories: *Communication Channel* and *Relationship Evolution.*

Communication Channel

We used to talk on the phone more when we first became close (7 of 58 contacts). In these cases, participants indicated that they spoke on the phone more frequently before, but that they speak on the phone less frequently now, mostly just to catch up. In some cases, this seemed to be a result of a change in life stage (either for the user or for their contact) and/or a change in their geographic location, replicating findings from prior work [36]. For example, one participant complained that he used to keep up with a friend much more regularly before that friend got married, and now they hardly speak at all. Change in life stage and change in geography are discussed more in the *Relationship Evolution* section below.

Other contacts in this category appear to be in relationships in decline, yet the feeling of closeness lingers. One participant spoke about reaching out to a friend multiple times without reciprocity: "I'd like to be friends, but it doesn't work unless we both put in the effort."

In-person communication (11 of 58 contacts). Participants also identified people whom they mostly interacted with in person. A contact's close proximity to the home seems to play an important role. One participant described talking to her neighbor opportunistically, when they see each other. Another detailed how she spoke with her 11-year-old son regularly, just not over the phone. Three participants described friends from classes and their dorm with whom they spoke when they saw each other.

Extended family often fell into this category. Many participants reported primarily speaking with parents, siblings, and other family members in person. In one case, a participant reported going to her parents' house a couple times per month, but mostly not calling her dad on the phone. In these cases, lack of communication logs did not mean lack of effort in maintaining the relationships. In discussing these contacts, some participants specifically mentioned making an effort to travel once a year to see each other, or making a special effort to get together when they do happen to be in the same place.

Other communication channels (25 of 58 contacts). For some strong ties, participants noted that they communicate regularly, but not via phone calls or SMS. For several participants, communication with a contact happened almost exclusively using Facebook. Other participants used instant messenger, email, Skype, or SMS replacements such as WhatsApp to stay in touch with close contacts.

Relationship Evolution

Different location or different life stage (27 of 58 contacts). When asked what was different about their relationship between when they became close and now, many participants responded immediately that either they or their contact had moved. As in the literature [36], participants said that with the change in geography, the communication frequency had changed, but not the perception of closeness. The move was often triggered by a change in life stage (e.g., going to college, graduating, getting a new job). However, even without moves, a significant life stage change could trigger a communication change on its own (e.g. getting married or having a child).

Family is close regardless of communication (17 of 58 contacts). Many misclassified participants were family members. Several participants described specific familial relationships from the perspective of obligation, which hinted at a greater underlying complexity. For example, one participant said that she refused to take her grandmother's phone calls, stating that she calls too frequently and repeats herself. Yet, the participant still reported feeling very close to her grandmother. Another participant, the mother of an 11 year old, said "of course I am close to him," but that it is not necessary for them to talk on the phone. Another participant said her uncle was "definitely close, but he's different from the other close people. He's that really strict uncle that wants to tell me how to live my life, so I don't talk to him too much, maybe every couple months."

Interview Summary

These interviews highlight the limited effectiveness of the tie strength models. A major issue is the temporality of a relationship. In particular the circumstances under which two people became close are not necessarily the same as the current circumstances of the relationship, even if the two people remain close. The communication logs only capture relatively recent behavior. Therefore, they do not contain the data that indicates a strong long-term relationship. The other main component is that there remains a large amount of interpersonal interaction that happens outside of phone calls and text messages, including communication in other media, as well as face-to-face communication. Call and SMS-based models do not account for this.

DISCUSSION

Our work investigates the growing practice of using communication frequency and duration as a proxy for social tie strength. While the social psychology theory identifies that frequency and long durations across all communication channels indicate strong ties, our community has used behavior across a few communication channels and over relatively short time windows as a tie strength proxy. We wanted to know if the call and SMS logs stored on a smartphone held enough information to infer tie strength.

Communication Is an Indicator of Tie Strength, But...

Our results support the tie strength theory literature, showing a strong relationship between tie strength and communication patterns [14,35]. Higher levels of communication frequency, call duration, and, in particular, communication initiated by the phone's owner are all indicators of a strong tie. However, we found that when operationalizing this theory with call and SMS logs, the signal is very noisy. Low levels of communication do not accurately identify weak ties: our participants had many strong ties who they rarely called or SMSed. Our interviews probing strong ties with little communication revealed several explanations for this pattern that we believe pose fundamental challenges for inferring tie strength.

First, a person's communication via phone and SMS does not capture all of their communications. Interactions happen through many other channels (e.g., Skype, instant messenger, landline phones), in some cases replacing communication via phone or SMS. Second, face-to-face communication remains a primary form of communication for some very close contacts, but capturing this kind of communication today is difficult. Third, strong ties may form in an earlier life stage and persist across stages even as communication frequency diminishes. Even if we could capture data across multiple channels and do so for longer periods of time, it is not clear that this would be sufficient to improve the models of tie strength.

A breadth of recent and highly-cited research has assumed that call and SMS behavior is a good proxy for tie strength [7,27,31,37]. These contributions do not attempt to identify all strong ties exhaustively. Rather, they only identify strong ties who use a specific communication channel. Our *contactlist* and *somecomm* datasets best match this task. The models for these datasets produce similar errors; they also indicate that communication frequency and duration are an incomplete signal for determining tie strength. While theory supports the relationship between communication frequency and duration and tie strength [19], these communications should not be operationalized only through the call and SMS logs stored on a person's phone.

Alternatives for Identifying Tie Strength

Researchers looking for a way to separate strong ties and weak ties need to consider alternatives to using short term communication logs from one or two channels, such as those available of today's smartphones.

One alternative is to collect data from more communication channels. This approach has several challenges. First, beyond a couple of obvious additional sources (i.e. email, Facebook), researchers are likely to face diminishing returns when adding additional data sources. For example, some people use Skype, while others use Google Hangouts. Similarly, there are many text message replacement apps (e.g., WhatsApp, GroupMe, Kik). The number of communication channels continues to grow, people have different preferences for which channels they use and for what purposes, and people switch between services based on fads, or on what services friends are using. Second, many of these services offer no API for accessing this data. Third, correctly linking contact identities across multiple communication sources is non-trivial and error-prone.

Another way of augmenting this process while still using communication data to separate strong and weak ties is to use *a lot more data*; data that extends back to when close relationships first began, which could be on the order of years or even decades. Since this data does not currently exist, the only way to evaluate this is to start collecting the data now and see if it helps several years from now. Current data collection and retention practices are not helping to solve this challenge for researchers. For example, Android devices by default only store the last 500 calls and 200 SMS messages. Furthermore, there are no standard APIs to access one's data, and no unified structures for storing user data and maintaining history as users change devices and services. If this kind of work is ever going to be possible, these practices will have to change.

Investigating message content might also help to improve the separation of strong and weak ties. It is possible that in cases where there is some communication, the content of the communication with strong ties is different from weak ties in a systematic way. A drawback to this approach, and the reason that we did not explore this avenue, is that many people are uncomfortable with the privacy implications of granting content level access to calls and SMS.

Another approach is to try and differentiate relationship maintenance communications with strong ties (which can be less frequent but very important to maintaining the strong tie) from other communication. There are many possible opportunities. One example might be to see whom a person calls or visits when traveling (factoring in time of day to differentiate between a likely work contact versus a social contact). Another example might be to use age or the inferred life stage of individuals and incorporate that into tie strength models. For instance, college students, 40-year-old parents, and senior citizens likely have different kinds of people in their strong ties. This idea would require much deeper investigation into how people's friendships change over time and how life stage affects these relationships.

The most reliable (and the most obvious) option for distinguishing strong and weak ties is to include users in the process through interviews [36], or a survey as we did. Some research has also looked at computer supported tools for collecting this kind of data [33]. The primary challenge here is that, even in the case that labeling is efficient, this approach still requires the time and effort of the user.

The primary drawback to all of these approaches is that in general, researchers who use communication frequency as a tie strength proxy do so because it is easily available. Many of the datasets that are being analyzed were collected and anonymized for a different purpose, often by a third party such as a telecommunications company. These researchers do not have the possibility of collecting more data, or have any access at all to the actual participant. Furthermore, many of these datasets contain the data of far too many users for a non-automated approach to be possible.

Using Communication Frequency as Tie Strength

We expect researchers to continue to use communication frequency as a tie strength proxy because it is now available due to the increasing use of smartphones. Here, we offer some implications for those that make this choice.

Researchers should carefully consider how the imperfect proxy of communication frequency as tie strength limits the strength of their claims. Does the fact that a strong tie might have some in-channel communication (which means that they would be included in an experiment), but has less communication than some weak ties hurt the strength of a claim being made on that data? It will depend on the claims being made, and to what extent those claims rely on a clear separation between strong and weak ties.

One solution for researchers in these situations is to modify the claims in their papers so that instead of relating their claims to *tie strength*, they relate the claims directly to *communication frequency*. For example, the existing work [7,27,31,37] that equates tie strength and communication frequency are valuable contributions. The issue with these works is that explaining their findings in the context of "tie strength", while convenient, gives the false impression that the work is based on a reliable measure of tie strength. This can negatively impact the reader's ability to correctly interpret their findings. If tie strength is important to an argument, researchers should also explain how they believe tie strength and communication frequency are related to each other within their dataset, and should explicitly identify that communication frequency is a limited proxy.

In this initial work, we have not yet explored the possibility of systematic per-user differences based on demographics, behavioral characteristics, or life stage, that affect our ability to separate strong ties from weak ties. If any such effects exist, they may well have an impact on the claims that can be drawn from using communication frequency to classify tie strength. Similarly, it is conceivable that there are other dimensions of interpersonal relationships that communication frequency is capable of detecting. Perhaps through this process, we can further our definition and understanding of the nuances of tie strength as a concept.

CONCLUSION

Having a computational model of tie strength could be useful for a number of domains. Past work has used call log data as a proxy for tie strength. However, our analysis of 36 participants' data suggests that this operationalization of tie strength is incomplete, missing more strong ties than it correctly identifies. Interviews with our participants revealed several explanations for low frequency, short duration communication with close contacts – these explanations indicate fundamental limitations when using communication logs to infer close relationships.

ACKNOWLEGEMENTS

This work was supported by the Yahoo InMind project, The Stu Card Fellowship, A Google Faculty Research Award, NSF Grant No. DGE-0903659 and ONR N66001-12-C-4196. The authors thank Eliane Wiese for helping strengthen the message of this paper.

REFERENCES

1. Ackerman, J.M., Kenrick, D.T., and Schaller, M. Is friendship akin to kinship? *Evolution and Human Behavior 28*, 5 (2007).
2. Allen, T. Managing the flow of scientific and technological information. 1966.
3. Backstrom, L. and Kleinberg, J. Romantic partnerships and the dispersion of social ties. *In Proc. CSCW '14.*
4. Burke, M. Reading, Writing, Relationships: The Impact of Social Network Sites on Relationships and Well-Being. 2011.
5. De Choudhury, M., Mason, W.A., Hofman, J.M., and Watts, D.J. Inferring relevant social networks from interpersonal communication. *In Proc. WWW '10.*
6. Christakis, N.A. and Fowler, J.H. *Connected: The Surprising Power of Our Social Networks and How They Shape Our Lives*. 2009.
7. Conti, M., Passarella, A., and Pezzoni, F. A model for the generation of social network graphs. *In Proc. WWMMN '11.*

8. Cranshaw, J., Toch, E., and Hong, J. Bridging the Gap Between Physical Location and Online Social Networks. *In Proc. Ubicomp '10*, .
9. Cummings, J.N., Lee, J.B., and Kraut, R. Communication technology and friends during the transition from high school to college. In *Computers, phones, and the Internet: Domesticating information technology*. 2006.
10. Danezis, G. Inferring Privacy Policies for Social Networking Services. *AISec*, (2009).
11. Eagle, N., Pentland, A., and Lazer, D. Inferring Social Network Structure using Mobile Phone Data. *PNAS 106*, 36 (2009).
12. Eagle, N. and Pentland, A. Social serendipity: Mobilizing social software. *IEEE Pervasive Computing 4*, 2 (2005), 28–34.
13. Festinger, L. Informal social communication. *PsychRev 57*, 5 (1950), 271–282.
14. Gilbert, E. and Karahalios, K. Predicting tie strength with social media. (2009), 211–220.
15. Gliem, J.A. and Gliem, R.R. Calculating, Interpreting, And Reporting Cronbach's Alpha Reliability Coefficient For Likert-Type Scales. (2003).
16. Granovetter, M. The strength of weak ties. *The American Journal of Sociology*,, (1973).
17. Granovetter, M. The Strength of Weak Ties: A Network Theory Revisited. *Sociological Theory*, (1983).
18. Hidalgo, C.A. and Rodriguez-Sickert, C. The dynamics of a mobile phone network. *Physica A: Statistical Mechanics and its Applications 387*, 2008, 3017–3024.
19. Hill, R.A. and Dunbar, R.I.M. Social network size in humans. *Human Nature 14*, (2003), 53–72.
20. Kim, J. and Zimmerman, J. Cherish. *In Proc. CHI EA '06*, (2006), 953.
21. Kim, T.H.-J., Yamada, A., Gligor, V., Hong, J., and Perrig, A. RelationGram: Tie-Strength Visualization for User-Controlled Online Identity Authentication. *Financial Cryptography and Data Security*, (2013).
22. Marin, A. and Hampton, K.N. Simplifying the Personal Network Name Generator. *Field Methods 19*, 2007.
23. Marsden, P. V and Campbell, K.E. Measuring tie strength. *Social Forces 63*, 1984, 482–501.
24. McCarty, C. Structure in personal networks. *Journal of Social Structure 3*, 1 (2005).
25. Mesch, G.S. Social context and communication channels choice among adolescents. Computers. *Human Behavior 25*, (2009), 244–251.
26. Min, J.-K., Wiese, J., Hong, J.I., and Zimmerman, J. Mining smartphone data to classify life-facets of social relationships. *In Proc. CSCW '13*.
27. Miritello, G., Moro, E., Lara, R., et al. Time as a limited resource: Communication strategy in mobile phone networks. *Social Networks*, (2013).
28. Neustaedter, C., Brush, A.J.B., Smith, M.A., and Fisher, D. The Social Network and Relationship Finder: Social Sorting for Email Triage. *In Proc. CEAS '05*.
29. Newcomb, T. *The acquaintance process*. New York: Holt, Rinehart, & Winston, 1961.
30. Odom, W., Zimmerman, J., and Forlizzi, J. Teenagers and Their Virtual Possessions: Design Opportunities and Issues. *Proc. of CHI '11*, .
31. Onnela, J.-P., Saramäki, J., Hyvönen, J., et al. Structure and tie strengths in mobile communication networks. *PNAS*, (2007).
32. Pentland, A. *Honest Signals: How They Shape Our World (Bradford Books)*. The MIT Press, 2008.
33. Ricken, S.T., Schuler, R.P., Grandhi, S.A., and Jones, Q. TellUsWho: Guided Social Network Data Collection. *HICSS '10*.
34. Roberts, S.G.B., Dunbar, R.I.M., Pollet, T. V., and Kuppens, and T. Exploring variation in active network size: Constraints and ego characteristics. *Social Networks*, (2009).
35. Roberts, S.G.B. and Dunbar, R.I.M. Communication in social networks: Effects of kinship, network size, and emotional closeness. *Personal Relationships*, (2011).
36. Spencer, L. and Pahl, R. Rethinking Friendship: Hidden Solidarities Today. 2006.
37. Wang, D., Pedreschi, D., Song, C., Giannotti, F., and Barabasi, A.-L. Human mobility, social ties, and link prediction. *In Proc. KDD '11*.
38. Wiese, J., Hong, J.I., and Zimmerman, J. Challenges and opportunities in data mining contact lists for inferring relationships. *In Proc. Ubicomp '14*.
39. Wiese, J., Kelley, P., Cranor, L.F., Dabbish, L., Hong, J.I., and Zimmerman, J. Are you close with me? Are you nearby? Investigating social groups, closeness, and willingness to share. *In Proc. UbiComp '11*.
40. Xiang, R., Neville, J., and Rogati, M. Modeling relationship strength in online social networks. *In Proc. WWW '10*, .
41. Zhou, W.X., Sornette, D., Hill, R.A., and Dunbar, R.I.M. Discrete hierarchical organization of social group sizes. *In Proc RSBS '10*.
42. Zipf, G. *Human behavior and the principle of least effort*. 1949.
43. Weka 3: Data Mining Software in Java.

Dwelling Places in KakaoTalk: Understanding the Roles and Meanings of Chatrooms in Mobile Instant Messengers

Da-jung Kim, Youn-kyung Lim
Department of Industrial Design, KAIST
291 Daehak-ro, Yuseong-gu, Daejeon 305-701, Republic of Korea
{dajungkim, younlim}@kaist.ac.kr

ABSTRACT
Recently, a great amount of conversation is taking place through mobile instant messaging (MIM) applications. The emergence of mobile messengers has enabled people to spend significant time in MIM, *dwelling* with close people. To investigate how this persistent use of MIM shaped the roles and meanings of MIM chatrooms, we conducted semi-structured interviews with ten users of KakaoTalk, one of the most popular MIM applications in South Korea. By understanding how participants determine the notion of centrality in MIM, we discovered three functional regions, namely, *primary, secondary,* and *tertiary regions*, which respectively support different functions not only in communication, but also in social interaction with various types of relationships: *performing everyday life, connecting to the maintained social capital,* and *connecting to the expired relationship*. Based on the valued meanings and user behaviors in those regions, we highlight two approaches that would trigger a new perspective in the design of messaging applications.

Author Keywords
Mobile Instant Messaging Application; Human Territoriality; Virtual Possessions; Personal Boundary; Design

ACM Classification Keywords
H.5.m. [Information interfaces and presentation (e.g., HCI)]: Miscellaneous.

General Terms
Human Factors; Design.

INTRODUCTION
Recently, a great amount of conversation has taken place through mobile instant messaging (MIM) applications such as KakaoTalk [11], WhatsApp, WeChat, LINE, and Facebook Messenger. As people spend a significant amount of time in MIM applications, O'Hara et al. [14], from a reflection on Ingold's notion of dwelling [10], proposed that people are *dwelling* in MIM. According to O'Hara et al., in MIM, intimacy is enacted through sharing small and continuous tidbits and moments of life, thereby developing the knowledge of others and a sense of being together with those whom they care about. Given that people can dwell in a *place*, this work enabled us to rethink the differences of *virtual places* where we communicate, such as chatrooms in MIM and traditional CMC applications. A chatroom, in PC-based IM and Internet Relay Chat (IRC), has been regarded as a *temporal place* that is repeatedly created and extinguished whenever users want to talk to other users in the systems. As those chatrooms are demonstrated in mobile systems through MIM, however, they become a more *persistent place* that is carried by people everywhere. Thus, MIM provides a sustained spatial anchor in which the previous conversation threads are kept and people keep staying and continuing the conversation whenever they want. In this sense, O'Hara et al. claims that MIM provides "a particular way of being together, knowing, and dwelling, that is casual and never-ending [14]."

Since such shift in the nature of chatroom experience makes MIM more pervasive in everyday life, we thought that it has become very important to understand the roles and meanings of MIM chatrooms in people's social life in order to better support their digital dwelling. In this sense, we aim to investigate how people perceive and value chatrooms in the context of MIM. To do so, we draw a concept of *centrality* from the theory of human territoriality [20, 23], which refers *how critical a place is* in the life of a person or group. We thought that investigating how the concept of centrality can be defined in the MIM context would provide a new perspective in the design of MIM as well as other forms of social media. It is because the territories, which can be classified by the level of centrality, are closely related to personal boundary regulation, privacy experiences, and the practices around virtual possessions, which are all emerging issues in the design of social media.

As a result of this motivation, we conducted semi-structured interviews with ten regular users of KakaoTalk, the most popular MIM application in South Korea (i.e., where we conducted this study). Through the analysis, we classified three types of dwelling places in KakaoTalk by the level of centrality in MIM, namely, the *primary, secondary, and tertiary region.* By explaining the characteristics of each region and the regional behaviors, we will discuss how the concept of centrality can be

CSCW 2014, March 14–18, 2015, Vancouver, BC, Canada.

ACM 978-1-4503-2922-4/15/03…$15.00.
http://dx.doi.org/10.1145/2675133.2675198

interpreted in the MIM context and how this perspective can inform the design of messaging applications.

BACKGROUND

In this section, we provide an introduction of themes that are closely related to this work: human territoriality in the physical and virtual world and the characteristics of MIM.

Human Territory & Centrality

Human territory refers to fixed spaces that, in some way, belongs to a person or a group. Altman distinguished three types of territories, namely, primary, secondary, and public territory, according to the amount of control an individual or a group expects to have on an area [1]. Individuals or groups exclusively own, use, and control *primary territory* on a relatively permanent basis, and it plays a central role in the daily lives of the occupants. It is often marked or personalized by the owners to identify ownership, and outsiders need permission to enter this area, otherwise the owners may generate defensive responses. *Secondary territory* is less central, pervasive, and exclusive area where an individual or a group has some control and ownership, but not to the same degree as they have over a primary territory. Secondary territories are a bridge between primary territory and the *public territory* that is accessed and temporarily used by almost every individual.

This typology came from Altman's privacy regulation model, which regards *territorial behaviors* as one of the mechanisms that people use to achieve the desired level of privacy [1]. Taylor, however, argues that territorial experience cannot be treated merely as a subset of privacy experience, because territorial behaviors, such as the personalization of a place and the practices around possessions, do not always intend for privacy to be achieved. Rather, he classifies human territory by the *centrality,* which refers to how important a space as a supportive context for individual's or group's daily functioning [23].

Our approach to understand human territoriality in this study is to start from exploring how Taylor's centrality concept works in an MIM context, because Taylor's approach suggests a primary criterion that defines human territory. Then, we will determine whether or not Altman's typology can be extended in the MIM environment. By doing so, we aim to discuss not only the privacy experience, but also more diverse behaviors within the MIM environment, such as personalization and possessions.

Territory in Social Media

In the online environment, where the boundary between "my space" and "your space" become unclear, territoriality has been studied in the perspective of personal boundary regulation and privacy [17, 24, 27]. This body of work has discussed the coping strategies for privacy concerns in SNSs (e.g., filtering, blocking, and withdrawal) and the self-disclosure practices in Facebook. While this body of work has built the understanding of how people regulate personal boundary in SNSs, little work has been done in the MIM context. Also, the results of those works were primarily focused on information disclosure management, rather than the role of virtual space as a person's dwelling place. Among few works, we could find several initial attempts that regard online as a personally meaningful space. For instance, Lindley et al. proposed that the web becomes a personal storage area [12]. Also, Zhao et al. elaborated that people experience Facebook Timeline as a space for performing and exhibiting self-presentation and keeping personal archives [28]. To extend such initial works and to overcome the lack of research, we will explore how people's notion of territory is shaped in MIM.

Mobile Instant Messaging Applications

For this research, we decided to recruit the users of KakaoTalk because it is a representative application that realizes the digital dwelling of people in South Korea. KakaoTalk is a dominant MIM application, which holds 88% of the domestic market share. Also, it is deeply pervasive in Korean's everyday lives, as they often say, *"Kakao me,"* or *"Let's Ka-talk."* While KakoTalk is not very dominant in the Western market, it still has common features with popular MIM applications such as WhatsApp and WeChat that enable the digital dwelling in MIM.

More specifically, like many other instant messaging applications, KakaoTalk is an over the top application, which is independent from network providers. Since it does not charge for sending and receiving messages, people see MIM as more fluid and never-ending compared to SMS, which limits the way people create messages within a single packet due to the cost [5]. Users can send and receive texts, photos, videos, digital gifts, and GPS information about certain locations to individuals or a group of people. Also, the application provides delivery notification and a timestamp of incoming messages. The number of people who did not read yet will be displayed beside each message, and it will be removed if (all) receiver(s) read the message. Users can control the delivery notification of chatrooms both selectively and as a whole.

STUDY METHOD

The approach we adopted for the study was to enable us to deeply understand individuals and their diverse types of relationships in KakaoTalk. To do so, 18 applicants were screened through the pre-interviews about their occupations, family types, domestic environments, and daily or weekly activities, to ensure that we recruited people with different lifestyles. As a result, we recruited 10 participants (6 female and 4 male) who are in their 20s or 30s and are regular users of KakaoTalk. Although our participants were a part of main user groups that do not encompass teens and people over the age of 40, we expected that the range of their relationships in KakaoTalk would be sufficient to be firstly explored because they were the people who, as young adults, actively build, interact, and thereby, dwell with various relationships. The ages of the participants varied from the early 20s to mid-30s. Their occupations varied from university and graduate students to researchers and office workers. Most of them were away from family and living alone or with housemates. Also, they were involved in the various types of relationships with their partners (i.e., a pre-marriage couple, distant/campus couple, recently broken-up couple, and a married couple with a child) and social groups (e.g., work, study, hobbies, and religion).

Semi-structured interviews with each participant were conducted for 60 to 120 minutes. Interviews aimed to probe what kinds of chatrooms were persistently used and how their behaviors (e.g., managing relationships, privacy, and possessions) were related to the roles and meanings of those chatrooms. For a deep understanding of each participant, we deployed two drawing activities: a network map and a centrality map. We began by asking participants to draw a *network map* that describes the KakaoTalk chatrooms in which they were involved. We encouraged the participants to review the list of their previous chatrooms and to draw a range of chatrooms as diverse as possible (Figure 1(a)). We also asked them to either explain or draw the chatrooms that were formerly used, but had been removed from the list. We then asked the participants to describe each chatroom by explaining what kinds of people they interact with, what they talk about, and how they behave in each chatroom. They were also asked to color the chatrooms to indicate which are similar or different according to their own criteria.

Since participants naturally introduced themselves while drawing and explaining chatrooms and their behaviors in those chatrooms, this drawing activity was not only helpful for participants to be easily engaged in the activity, but also useful for researchers to comprehensively learn and build knowledge about each participant's use of chatrooms. Also, although we did not intentionally guide them to use specific visual elements, the participants spontaneously exploited those elements, which were meaningful in seeking to understand their perceptions toward, and the relations among chatrooms. For instance, P4 differentiated the thickness and the length of lines connected to the circles, which indicates individual or group chatrooms, to represent the frequency of conversation. Also, the colors represent how private the conversation is in each room and the dashed lines define how chatrooms are related to the kinds of his social life. In this sense, the network map (Figure 1(a)) enabled us to walk through the "tour" of participants' vivid perceptions and experiences of their chatrooms.

The second activity we requested for the participants was to draw a *centrality map*, which visualizes the chatrooms that appeared on the network map in the order from high centrality to low centrality. For instance, as shown in Figure 1(b), P6 arranged her chatrooms from high centrality (left) to low centrality (right) and divided them with several segments. Since the purpose of this activity was to investigate how and why people think of a chatroom as a "central" space in KakaoTalk, we did not provide a specific

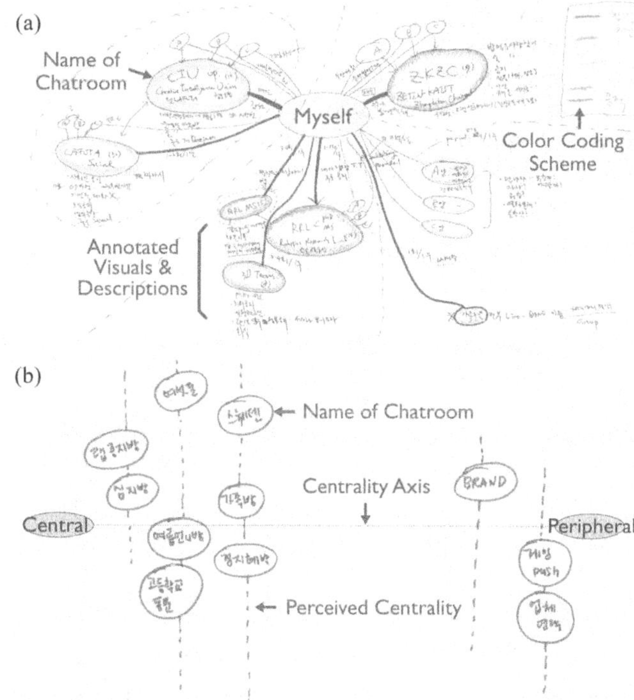

Figure 1. (a) P4's network map and (b) P6's centrality map

definition of centrality. Rather, we had more focus on how they describe the rationales of their centrality maps. Based on these centrality maps, we also triggered further discussion on the reasons for their territorial behaviors in each chatroom (e.g., control over interpersonal interaction, information access and preservation, and personalization).

All interviews were audio-recorded and nearly 15 hours of recordings were transcribed. The transcripts were segmented by each entity of chatroom, which produced 161 chatrooms and verbal descriptions about each chatroom. Although we had only ten participants, the study with them produced 161 chatrooms that are the sample data for our study. In addition, since we thoroughly inquired about each chatroom during the interview, the rich verbal and visual expressions regarding each chatroom created a significant amount of data to confirm the analysis results. Indeed, the data was saturated when we got to the analysis of the chatrooms from six participants, and the rest of data from the other four participants further confirmed our analysis.

THREE FUNCTIONAL REGIONS IN ONE PLATFORM

We first analyzed how participants explained the rationales when they decided upon the position of each chatroom on their own centrality maps. Although the rationales varied according to the participants (e.g., intimacy, frequency of use, amount of conversation, the level of attention), there were two overlapping dimensions that determined "central" places in MIM: *i) the relevance of a conversation to a user's current life (from high to low relevance)* and *ii) the degree of actual participation in the conversation (from active to no participation)*. These were quite well matched with the original concept of centrality by Taylor [23], since it refers how critical a space is as a supportive context for performing daily life. For example, while we first thought that a chatroom for an intimate chitchatting group would be placed as more central space than a chatroom for a work-related group, all of the participants clearly explained that both of them are central in terms of their personal and professional life respectively.

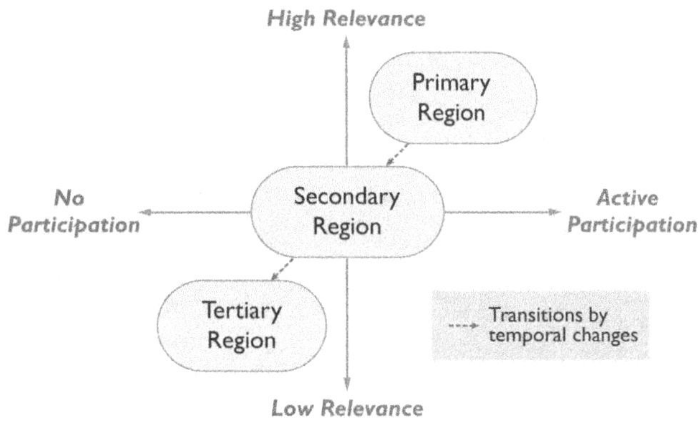

Figure 2. Three regions in KakaoTalk

Based on these dimensions, we arranged the 161 chatrooms and came up with three groups of chatrooms by centrality, namely, the *primary*, *secondary*, and *tertiary region* (Figure 2). The numbers of chatrooms in each region were 79, 64, and 18, respectively. In each region, we also identified chatrooms that are in a transitional stage from one region to another region as time goes on. Also, we could find that participants attempted to visually express the boundary of different centralities by remarkably distancing one group of chatrooms from others or by drawing a clear division line (see Figure 1(b)), which further supported our classification.

We adopted Altman's typology of human territoriality, as the characteristics of the three regions we found from the analysis were quite overlapping with those of the three territories he proposed. However, the concept of publicity and privacy did not fully resonate with the characteristics shown in KakaoTalk; given that a user can enter a chatroom only by the invitation of a member of the chatroom, there was no specific public space that everybody can access in MIM. Therefore, we selected the term *tertiary region* to refer chatrooms with the least centrality, instead of using the term *public territory* in Altman's typology.

In what follows, we describe the definitions and general characteristics of conversation in each region. Also, we present representative relationships that were often discovered in each region, although these were a bit different, in some cases, depending on the individual differences in the level of intimacy with each type of relationship. We refer to each participant and their chatroom by participant number and the relationship with chat partners (e.g., P1, family group). In addition, we connect the related visual expressions in both the network map and centrality map with each region's characteristics.

Primary Region: Performing Everyday Life

Consistent with the characteristics of a *primary territory*, the chatrooms in the *primary region* was the most central spaces where people were actively engaged in ongoing conversation as they performed daily life at home, work, and in social places. In this region, participants usually communicated with family members, romantic partners, colleagues, close friends, and groups of those individuals. Most of them were geographically close and interacted with the participants on a daily or regular basis, both in KakaoTalk and in other offline places. Although some family members and couples were geographically distant, their chatrooms were also included in the primary region, because their conversation was as highly relevant to their lives as other chatrooms in this region and the participants were actively using them. As the word "primary" suggests, the circles of chatrooms in this region in the network map were often centered, highlighted, color-marked, contoured, and connected through thick lines by participants to denote the frequency of use and significant relevance to their lives.

Conversation in this region was usually never-ending and did not have typical starting and ending talk, as illustrated in [5, 14]: *"(P5, lab mate) We talk about just everything." "(P7, boyfriend) We talk from morning till night."* With intimate relationships, they were engaged in chitchatting and sharing gossip and every single moment of life second by second. The use of chatrooms was similar, even with colleagues. Chatrooms with co-workers were pervasively used for efficient communication during the work hours. Thus, their conversations were also continuous and somewhat mixed with casual conversations. By doing so, they had a high level of understanding about others' lives.

Secondary Region: Connecting to the Maintained Social Capital

A *secondary region* is not directly related to everyday performance, but is essential in order to keep regular or irregular offline social interactions. Although most people in this region were geographically distant and had a lower frequency of offline gathering than the primary region, the participants still cherished the relationships with those people, which called *maintained social capital* [6]. It usually encompasses school reunions, social groups to which the participants have belonged for enjoying hobbies and religious activities, and family or relatives who live far away. The role of the secondary region was closely aligned with the arguments that the persistent and pervasive nature of ICTs (such as SNSs) contributes to maintain relationships that would have otherwise faded [3, 8, 25].

In general, conversation in this region was sporadically activated and used to keep updated on others' lives and to plan and comment on important events for group. Unlike the primary region, however, the degree of participation varied in this region. In the chatrooms where participants were actively engaged in the conversation, the members were intimate and the size of the groups was usually small (i.e., encompassing less than ten members). On the contrary, in the chatrooms where participants do not talk much, the size of the groups was often very large (e.g., sometimes including more than 100 members). Thus, it seemed hard to find a common identity or topic of interest. For this reason, the size of a group sometimes, but not always, forced a group that is supposed to be used as the chatroom in the primary region to move to the secondary region. As a result, individuals' or small group's chatrooms in this region, once activated, were usually perceived and used just as a primary region, while even sometimes providing serendipitous experiences: *"(P10, friends from school days) Although we talk once every six months, it's still fun. If I receive a message from this group, it gives me serendipity."*

However, in a bigger group's chatroom, conversation could be continued only when there were regular offline gatherings or a significant amount of life sharing through KakaoTalk. Otherwise, conversations were easily deactivated or loosely continued only by a few people, who kept chitchatting anyway, or by the people who announced important social events in the group: *"(P5, elementary school union) When this [chatroom] was opened, I got 400 incoming messages in only a few minutes. In the beginning, we were all busy to catch up on each other's lives... There was a spark in the conversation due to the delight that we felt because we had all gathered and connected. However, since we are a bit far from each other's daily lives, this chatroom becomes inactive afterward. We only talk and gather when we have very important affairs to announce, such as one's wedding or a parent's funeral."*

As P5 illustrated, this *falling conversation* seems natural as the relationships change over time and conversations with those people become less related to everyday life. These chatrooms with falling conversation were often placed at the outer circle of the network map and at the right part of the centrality map, which indicates the chatroom's low priority and the participant's limited participation in these chatrooms: *"(P10, past group) These rooms are almost all over the 'milky way,' out of my attention. I barely respond and read."*

One interesting relationship that belongs to the secondary region was a relationship with a brand account, which is called "Plus Friend" in KakaoTalk. Two of the participants had several Plus Friends on their chatroom list for the purpose of receiving useful information, such as ongoing events of a brand or news from a daily food recipe magazine. Another interesting relationship was the friends who only send and receive the Kakao Game push. While participants were not engaged in the normal forms of conversation, they tried to maintain these relationships because they saw them as a kind of social capital which broadens the examples related to the concept of maintained social capital: *"(P7, Plus Friend) I often look through the news from McDonald to check the discount information." "(P6, game friend) We are not intimate and we haven't talked for years. Game push is annoying for everybody, but we are a kind of a partner in Kakao game, who understand each other."*

Tertiary Region: Connecting to the Expired Relationship

The *tertiary region* refers to the chatrooms in which social relationships have expired and the conversation is no longer active. Although some relationships were explicitly expired, such as dating situations, some relationships implicitly expired as one's status changed over time (e.g., by graduating) or as they gathered for event-specific purposes (e.g., to plan a social event or to do a group assignment). Except for the past romantic partners (e.g., an ex-boyfriend and ex-girlfriend), participants could not easily come up with the specific relationships in this region. One reason is that chatrooms in the tertiary region were subsets of those in the primary group, as P1 illustrated, *"(P1, birthday party group currently deleted) On his (a lab member's) birthday, I and my lab members created a secret chatroom that excluded him. We talked through the chatroom to prepare a party, and when it ended, all of us went back to our original chatroom, where every member is, and we no longer talk here."*

Another reason of unawareness of the chatrooms seems to have a relation with the way KakaoTalk displays the chatroom history. It shows the chatrooms that were recently used by the members at the top in the list of all of the past and the current chatrooms. Unless users explicitly leave the rooms, those chatrooms will remain on the list. They will be automatically moved from the top to the bottom of the list. Therefore, participants often predicted that a chatroom they had been using every day would soon "*disappear*," which implies that those chatrooms would be out of their sight and mind, unless they intentionally searched for it: *"(P8, temporary study group) We gathered temporarily to carry out a group assignment. This chatroom will disappear in the next week when we finish the presentation."*

This example clearly shows why a chatroom for an event-specific purpose might be easily moved from the primary region to the tertiary region. Thus, reflecting on such volatility, the circle of chatrooms in the tertiary region was often drawn with a dashed line or signified with black color to express the temporal nature.

REGIONAL BEHAVIORS

Regarding the aforementioned regions, we also analyzed how their characteristics were related to the behaviors within each region. To highlight the differences between the regions and the tensions that people experience in the transitional region, we drew four regional behaviors that seem to trigger a worthwhile discussion in the CSCW community: i) personal boundary regulation and self-disclosure, ii) maintaining group boundaries, iii) keeping and sharing virtual possessions, and v) personalization.

Personal Boundary Regulation & Self-Disclosure

Since the use of KakaoTalk is very pervasive and sometimes disturbs people, each participant had their own strategies to manage their social interactions within it. One way to do so was to selectively control the delivery notifications of each chatroom. For example, participants usually did not turn off the delivery notifications from the primary and tertiary regions, since the former is important and sometimes requires their prompt action, and the conversation in the latter is usually deactivated at that moment and, thus, there is little possibility to be disturbed by this region. However, they often turned off the notifications from chitchatting groups in both the primary and secondary regions. In this case, participants turned off the notifications in the primary region in order to read and respond to the messages by freely pausing and resuming the conversation whenever they are available. In contrast, in the secondary region, participants turned off the notifications in order not to be involved the unnecessary interactions with the people with whom they do not keep the normative behaviors. Following examples show some *avoidance behaviors* [2, 4] in social media within the context of MIM: *"(P6, past club members who are still close, primary region) Since I receive 300 messages every 30 minutes from this group, I can't do anything if I don't turn off the notification. I check it all at once. It is like receiving a news feed in Facebook."*

"(P8, department batch, secondary region) There are 120 people in this group, but only five close people keep talking to each other. I can't understand why they are chitchatting in this room. However, I should scan through their conversation just to make sure that I didn't miss something important to me."

While aforementioned practices were a kind of static setting that were controlled in advance, as Altman claimed [1], the participants also dynamically regulated their personal boundaries to achieve the desired level of privacy from over-loading messages. The privacy was achieved through intentionally pending or selectively replying to the messages, as P9 contrasted his behaviors in response to messages from his girlfriend and other chitchatting groups: *"(P2, girlfriend vs. housemates) Even if I am too busy, I reply [to her] something like, 'Sorry, I am busy now,' because she is an important person to me and she worries if I don't reply. But I just delay the response to my housemates."*

Another way of regulating a personal boundary was to differentiate self-disclosure practices depending on the audience of each chatroom, which resonates with Goffman's notion of self-presentation [7]. For example, participants behaved differently, as P6 clearly contrasted her behaviors when she talks with her friends and clients: *"(P6, best friend vs. clients) In this chatroom with my best friend, I often use shortened words or dynamic emoticons without any hesitation. I even use this chatroom for leaving my personal notes or for uploading personal files so that I can check it later without using cloud storages. In contrast, when talking to clients, I use very formal and professional words."*

As a final strategy to manage personal boundaries, we observed the attempts to manage *context collapse* [13, 24, 26], the way that social media group individuals' various relationships into a single context, which is often termed like "KakaoTalk friends." For example, one participant turned off the auto sync function that automatically adds user's contacts to the KakaoTalk friend list in order to avoid potential interaction with her professional network in KakaoTalk. In extreme cases, P2 and P6 decided to use another MIM to exclusively communicate with their strong ties, instead of fighting for their space in already-buzzing KakaoTalk. This also resonates with the example of creating another Facebook account to divide one's professional and personal networks, which was noticed in the recent study [26]: *"(P6, KakaoTalk vs. LINE) Since there are so many group chatrooms and incoming messages, I couldn't distinguish the messages I should really care about. Therefore, I migrated to LINE and now I am exclusively using LINE with people who are most important and intimate."*

Maintaining Group Boundary

While managing an individual's boundary was a troublesome practice for the users, maintaining group boundaries was another practice into which people put a tremendous effort. Given that outsiders cannot come into the chatroom or even know about its existence without an insider's invitation, unlike the physical world, the attempts to maintain the group boundaries were focused on the people who intentionally or accidently leave the room.

Whereas the tertiary region is no longer active and the primary region has a relatively stable boundary, the struggles to keep the social boundary were mostly observed in the secondary region. This was also well described in the analogies that P1 used to describe her sense of boundary in two different chatrooms: *"(P1, family group) This [room for my family and fiancé] is like a building that was firmly established, but when it comes to these rooms [in the secondary region], it's like a temporary frame tent where everybody comes and goes."*

As a region that is not directly connected to daily lives, some people left the room without any explanation. Then, the other members who care about their departure, usually a representative or creator of the group, re-invited those who had left. However, we could speculate *the tensions between the departees and inviters* from P3's description: *"(P3, past social group) I really want to leave, but they (inviters) don't let me, because they have to re-invite me when they have things to say to me. I don't have any option. I give up."*

In addition, most people were worried about the mark that notifies who had left the room, which is automatically shown in the application. It is because others could misunderstand it as a sign of withdrawal from a relationship: *"(P1, past project group) I am worried what the others [in this chatroom] would think about me if I left with the mark that I have left."*

Nevertheless, those chatrooms were likely to enter the tertiary region at the end, as people no longer care about other's departures and get into the stage of estrangement: *"(P4, past social group) We (all the members) don't talk here and ten people already left, but nobody re-invited them. There's no reason that I have to be here."*

On the other hand, in the primary region, another concern arose when one of the members became *an accidental outsider* as the member's status changed. We observed *an emotional tension between the accidental outsider and the remaining occupants* when they disclosed secured information or noticed the absence of previous members: *"(P6, colleague group) She finished her summer internship at our company, but didn't leave the chatroom for a while. At that time, another member asked for the password of our FTP server. It was a bit embarrassing to provide the information because the password shouldn't be shared with the outsider. It was also awkward to ask her to leave the room by herself. We finally created another room for the current members."*

"(P1, lab mates group) When she (a junior student) graduated and left this chatroom, I was sad. It was like the end of our conversation and relationship."

Keeping and Sharing Virtual Possessions

Although KakaoTalk is a communication platform, we observed the practices of keeping and sharing virtual possessions [15] that were created across the three regions. In the primary region, we observed compelling evidence that the ritual exchange of trivial messages in KakaoTalk often embodied the meaning as a *virtual gift-giving* [22] and enhanced the sense of connectedness. All of the participants exhibited their attachments to the ritual exchange of meaningful digital things, which varied from trivial text messages, to the web links of which the contents would be interesting to their conversation partners, and to photos of a distant romantic partner or a distant family member including pets: *"(P3, a group of three friends who decided to exercise together) In the morning, we check whether or not everybody woke up. Even after we exercise, we take care of each other's condition in the afternoon by exchanging small talks and photos of what each member had for lunch. At night, we plan when we are going to exercise tomorrow. Although the content is not very special, I want to keep this conversation since it enables me to feel that somebody is taking care of me every day."*

However, these gifts-like digital things were usually kept in the conversation stream in KakaoTalk and an actual attempt to locally store them happened less frequently than we expected based on the participants explanations of what they mean to them. This behavior seemed to be attributed from the belief that they will be persistently stored in the KakaoTalk server, as P3 add to the aforementioned morning exercise group, *"but I didn't try to save this conversation in a special way because I can always access to this chatroom on the application, unless I leave the room."*

Motivations of locally storing those digital things were often emerged around special events. For example, the cherished parts of conversation streams were saved in the form of digital photos by downloading the shared photos or by capturing screenshots: *"(P1, fiancé, while showing a series of screenshots of the chatroom with her fiancé) It was the day we announced our wedding on Facebook. I screen captured all of the conversation we had at that moment into five different pictures. It was quite an impressive and unforgettable moment, so I thought this [part of the conversation] was very special."*

Although they extracted those cherished digital items, it did not seem to be easy to create, retrieve, and reminisce over a meaningful collection of them. It is because once people download photos or capture the screen, then the extracted photos are automatically saved in a default photo application in a smartphone and mixed with other photo archives. Thus, such archiving mechanisms often interfered with the flow of revisiting experiences, as P9 illustrated: *"(P9, a group of his two sisters) It is inconvenient to launch the gallery app to see the photos that have been saved from KakaoTalk. The photos of my nephew are all mixed with work-related photos."*

Thus, some of the participants preferred to use the application's function that displays all of the photos in a chatroom at once, even after they downloaded the copy of those photos in the local storage of their mobile phone. This reflects the fragmentation of archiving and revisiting experience, which would imply a concern of designing a personal archive in online services. Otherwise, participants collectively found a more systematic way of managing their co-owned digital items, especially with the people in the primary region. P1 created a Facebook group with close friends to create a collection of wedding items that had been shared through KakaoTalk. Also, P2 and his housemates created a Google spreadsheet to record and calculate their living expenses. In this way, those in the primary region, i.e., strong ties, were using multiple means of communication and it seemed to enhance their relationship as well, following the concept of *media multiplexity* [9].

While participants screen-captured the conversation stream to keep for a longer term in the primary region, they exhibited the same behavior in the secondary region for a temporary reason, such as to remember the notices of offline gatherings. Thus, the participants did not have much emotional attachment to the record. Rather, they cherished the presence of the chatroom that connects with distant people. Following examples clearly show how persistent and pervasive KakaoTalk maintain the relationships that would have otherwise faded:

"(P6, friends met during travel) Since I don't have the phone number of some friends [in this group], this room is the only way to be connected with those people."

"(P3, high school reunion) Nowadays, increasing number of my friends [in this group] plans to get married. I should keep this chatroom to maintain these relationship so that I can ask somebody [in this group] for a favor to deliver my money gift in the case I can't attend their weddings."

Also, some people cherished the symbolic meaning associated with those chatrooms:

"(P10, all members of her father's family and her cousins) I wonder how many families have this kind of Kakao room where we take care of each other. I am very proud of being in this family and in this Kakao room we share."

"(P5, high school reunion) We don't make a phone call to each other, but if this room is closed, I would feel like I was disconnected from these people. I feel [that] I am connected with these friends through this room."

"(P4, my high school teacher) He sends me lines of the Bible from time to time. Since I already get the Bible text everyday through a different application, the text itself does not mean much to me. Rather, I would say that this is the place where I can reminisce about my childhood with the teacher I respect."

Whereas aforementioned examples in the primary and the secondary region illustrate the attachments to the records of conversation and the chatroom themselves, the participants generally showed a lower attachment to the tertiary region. This may be attributed to the event-specific use of a chatroom. Regarding the management of virtual possessions in the tertiary region, there were three types of people: deleter, holder, and keeper.

Deleters think that they do not have to keep the finished conversation and they regularly leave the rooms, which automatically deletes all of the conversation data in those chatrooms: *"(P1, finished project group) I can leave without any hesitation, because it's finished and all of the important information was shared through email or cloud storage."*

Holders keep the expired conversation without any specific intention, just in case. Although they did not intentionally save those conversations, the records sometimes provided a clue to restart the conversation with people who do not regularly talk as illustrated by P4: *"(P4, friends who rarely talk) I don't remove all of the chatrooms from the list, just in case I need a record of the conversation. When I start talking with people I contact every six months, I was curious about what we have talked about before. By referring to the previous threads, I can naturally restart the conversation. If it has been deleted from the list, it is as same as deleting it from my memory."*

Very occasionally, there were explicit *keepers* who strongly cherished the conversation as a personal record. Most of these chatrooms had been used in the primary region for a while. However, contrary to the typical practices in the primary region, the participants wanted to keep the whole range of conversation stream from the beginning to the end: *"(P4, ex-girlfriend who broke up a month ago) I exported all of the conversation we had as a text file. She was the most important person in my life. I am still keeping her Kakao room. I will leave when I can be convinced that the relationship has expired."*

This example may imply that a sudden transition from the primary to tertiary region creates strong emotional attachment even to a single history of conversation, which has been taken for granted when a chatroom was still in the primary region, and motivate people to locally store the whole conversation stream as a kind of digital memento [19]. However, if so, there seemed to be a lack in maintaining the authenticity of data. For instance, P1 still remained in the chatroom, even after exporting the text files of whole conversation as well: *"(P1, a group of friends who helped her and her fiancé to take self-wedding photos) I downloaded all of the photos and texts, but I can't leave. It was a special event and this conversation stream shows the happy moment. However, when I review the exported text files, I cannot feel such vivid happiness. So, I won't leave here, even if all the others leave."*

Personalization

As participants expressed their attachment to the data that had accumulated in the primary region, they also cherished the place itself. Therefore, they tended to personalize the virtual space, just as we do in our primary territory in the physical world, for example, as in our own homes. Participants often changed the title and the background of the individual's and group's chatroom in a way that reflects the relationship or group's identity: *"(P1, fiancé) I changed the title of the chatroom of my fiancé from his name, to his nick name, and to 'my husband.'"*

Occasionally, some participants treated a number of group chatrooms in special ways (e.g., making a logo of the group or assigning special title). Although the participants said that they personalized the chatrooms for a practical purpose (e.g., to quickly find them on the chatroom list), we could speculate that the participants were expressing their ownership and attachments to the relationship and the chatroom through the personalization that needed extra effort, as illustrated in the following excerpts: *"(P3, a group of three friends who decided to exercise together) It is my own group that I initiated and created. I didn't just name it something like 'close friends.' Rather, I thought for a while to come up with a special name."*

As these examples indicate, many components of a chatroom could be exploited not only for decorating its appearance, but also for expressing and enhancing the shared identity among the members. In addition, the ways to deploy those elements in the secondary and tertiary region would be another area to be researched.

DISCUSSIONS

Before starting a discussion about this research, we must comment on the limitation of our data because the participants were recruited from only one part of Asia. Given that there is a well-known distinction between Western individualistic, low-context cultures and Eastern collectivistic, high-context cultures, there could be cultural differences in the use of MIM in terms of group interaction, possessions, and personalization. For instance, the attachment to the social groups and the efforts to maintain the social boundary and identity might have been more emphasized in this work. However, as studies in Europe have shown [5, 14], we can expect that users around the world may commonly use the MIM platform not only as a communication tool, but also as a place where they spend time and create memories while dwelling with people they care about. To better support such behaviors, we came up with two approaches in the design of MIM, based on the conceptual framework of three regions in MIM.

Improving the Workaround in Each Region

The first approach is to improve the workarounds in each room to reduce the tensions that people often experience in MIM applications. In the primary region, we have seen many workarounds when keeping and revisiting cherished virtual possessions. For this reason, *supporting the curation of digital artefacts*, such as a digital photo album that is connected to each chatroom, seems to have potential. Since people actively participate in the primary region, we can also think about the *collective creation or curation of digital collections* with a chat partner and group members. This may involve different kinds of co-creation, such as an example of a couple's co-evaluation of photos discovered in [15]. Thus, the reminiscing and revisiting experiences will also be enhanced, not only because those collections are not mixed with other archives, but also because they create an opportunity to collectively reminisce about memories.

In the secondary region, the most challenging issue was the tension between departees and inviters. We could find two layers of information that create this tension; one was for important notices or opinion-gathering discussions that everybody has to check and the other was for continuous chitchatting. In this context, dividing two layers of information and controlling them respectively could reduce the tension. This kind of function, which is called "announce," already exists in KakaoTalk, which displays important messages over the conversation in chatroom. However, it needs to be more enhanced because users cannot control the notification of the announcement layer individually, and they cannot review the previous announcements, which are sometimes also important. Also, while pursuing this notion, the ways to enable users to fluidly move between the two layers should be further researched so that the advantages of a current streaming interface are not degraded.

Also, we can think of applying the characteristics of *third place* [16], which refers to the social surroundings that afford and foster the informal social interaction of a community, provides welcoming by the "regulars" and a playful mood through conversation and thus, giving sense of home away from home. If this kind of characteristics is affordable in the secondary region through, for example, a designation of regulars to a member, light-weight welcoming interactions, such as with an emoticon or the poke button in Facebook, then it might be able to smooth the interaction between small talkers and passive readers.

The tertiary region will be discussed in the following section because the value of chatrooms in this region can be better described in the second approach.

Supporting Functional Transitions over Time

Although the first approach highlighted the enhancement of the functional characteristics of each region, there has already been a similar effort in the MIM industries. For instance, KakaoTalk became a part of the Kakao platform and connected with many applications in the platform, such as Kakao Group and Kakao Story. Although those vertical SNSs are designed to support more diverse types of communications and activities, for example, through a shared calendar, a group photo album, and post-based news feed, we think that there will still be a unique value if these activities can be supported within MIM applications.

For this reason, we suggest the second approach: *supporting functional transitions over time*. To design and develop a MIM of which functions evolve along with the changes of a user's social relationships, the collaborations among many professions, such as sociology, computer science, and design, will be essentially required. With that in mind, we will highlight three of many possible transitions among the regions, as those transitions inspire the new design implications.

Transitions from Primary Region to Secondary Region

One of driving factors of the transitions from the primary region to the secondary region is a geographical movement of users as the users' status changes, such as moving to another city as a person graduates from school. Since these chatrooms become more cherished by their existence and symbolic meaning, *enhancing the sense of place* may orient these chatrooms as a place where people far away can visit and be connected with the maintained social capital. The personalization of a chatroom can be a mechanism that enhances the sense of place and the sense of ownership to the place. We can think of many spatial metaphors (e.g., a front entrance, wall, or signpost) that can be used for the personalization of individual or group chatrooms. By doing so, it can be a place which allows a user to feel a sense of belonging and connection to other people, thereby curing friendsickness [18] and homesickness.

Transitions from Primary Region to Tertiary Region

When a chatroom falls directly from the primary region to the tertiary region, we can assume that there have been dynamic changes in a relationship, such as the breakup of a couple. If this usage pattern can be identified by the system, then functions can be activated to support the practices around virtual possessions from the expired relationship. For instance, to overcome the authenticity problem of the exported data (as shown in P1 and P4's experiences), the temporal metaphor, such as "time freeze," could be used to support the maintenance of the digital collections as they appeared in the chatroom. Otherwise, a system could be designed to support forgetting the sore memory, as proposed in [21].

Transitions from Tertiary Region to More Central Regions

Instead of maintaining or enhancing the connections with the chatrooms that lost their centrality, we can also think of the chatrooms that suddenly gain centrality. In this context, the reasons for gaining centrality and the types of social relationships would inspire new approaches to design social interaction in MIM applications. For example, the first messages from the friends who were contacted long time ago could be delivered in a special way by maximizing serendipitous and gladsome experiences.

Although we described two approaches that focus on the mobile phone context, taking other platforms into account in the design of MIM application would create a richer user experience (e.g., collective reminiscence or management of family photos on TV at the dispersed family's homes) because the findings of our study were also closely integrated with the parallel use of KakaoTalk in PCs or tablets.

CONCLUSION

From the study of KakaoTalk with ten participants, we suggested three types of regions that function differently in users' lives. Such a group includes a primary region for performing various functions associated with daily life, a secondary region for connecting to maintained social capital, and a tertiary region for connecting to the expired relationship. We discussed regional behaviors and tensions regarding the maintenance of social boundaries, the act of keeping virtual possessions, and the personalization of places. Although the proposed divisions of the regions should be examined in different cultures, as groundwork, this study provides a new perspective on the current discussion on the design of MIM and social media.

ACKNOWLEDGMENTS

We appreciate all the participants of our study for their time and the reviewers for their valuable comments on this work.

REFERENCES

1. Altman, I. 1975. *The environment and social behavior.* Brooks/Cole Monterey, CA.
2. Bryant, E.M., & Marmo, J. 2012. The rules of Facebook friendship: a two-stage examination of interaction rules in close, casual, and acquaintance friendships. *Journal of Social and Personal Relationships 29*, 8, 1013-1035.
3. Burke, M., & Kraut, R. 2014. Growing closer on Facebook: changes in tie strength through social network site use. *Proc. of CHI'14*, 4187-4196.
4. Canary, D.J., Stafford, L., Hause, K.S., & Wallace, L.A. 1993. An inductive analysis of relational maintenance strategies: comparisons among lovers, relatives, friends, and others. *Communication Research Reports 10*, 1, 5-14.
5. Church, K., & Oliveira, R. 2013. What's up with Whats-App? comparing mobile instant messaging behaviors with traditional SMS. *Proc. of MobileHCI'13*, 352-361.
6. Ellison, N.B., Steinfield, C., & Lampe, C. 2007. The benefits of Facebook "Friends:" social capital and college students' use of online social network sites. *Journal of Computer-Mediated Communication. 12*, 4, 1143-1168.
7. Goffman, E. 1959. *The Presentation of Self in Everyday Life.* Doubleday Anchor, New York.
8. Hampton, K.N., Lee, C., & Her, E.J. 2011. How new media affords network diversity: Direct and mediated access to social capital through participation in local social settings. *New Media & Society 13*, 7, 1031-1049.
9. Haythornthwaite, C. 2005. Social networks and Internet connectivity effects. *Information, Communication & Society 8*, 2, 125-147.
10. Ingold, T. 2011. *Being alive: Essays on movement, knowledge and description.* Abingdon, UK: Routledge.
11. KakaoTalk, http://www.kakao.com/services/8
12. Lindley, S., Marshall, C.C., Banks, R., Sellen, A., & Regan, T. 2013. Rethinking the web as a personal archive. *Proc. of WWW'13*, 749-759.
13. Marwick, A., & boyd, d. 2010. I tweet honestly, I tweet passionately: twitter users, context collapse, and the imagined audience. *New Media & Society 13*, 1, 114-133.
14. O'Hara, K.P., Massimi, M., Harper, R., Rubens, S., & Morris, J. 2014. Everyday dwelling with WhatsApp. *Proc. of CSCW'14*, 1131-1143.
15. Odom, W., Zimmerman, J., et al. 2013. Fragmentation and Transition: Understanding perceptions of virtual possessions among young adults in Spain, South Korea and the United States. *Proc. of CHI'13*, 1833-1842.
16. Oldenburg, R. 1999. *The Great Good Place: cafe's, coffee shops, community centers, beauty parlors, general stores, bars, hangouts, and how they get you through the day.* New York: Marlowe & Company.
17. Palen, L., & Dourish, P. 2013. Unpacking "Privacy" for a networked world. *Proc. of CHI'03*, 129-136.
18. Paul, E., & Brier, S. 2001. Friendsickness in the transition to college: Precollege predictors and college adjustment correlates. *Journal of Counseling and Development 79*, 1, 77-89.
19. Petrelli, D., & Whittaker, S. 2010. Family memories in the home: contrasting physical and digital mementos. *Personal and Ubiquitous Computing*, 14, 153-169.
20. Sack, R.D. 1986. *Human Territoriality: Its Theory and History.* Cambridge University Press.
21. Sas, C., & Whittaker, S. 2013. Design for Forgetting: Disposing of digital possessions after a breakup. *Proc. of CHI'13.* 1823-1832.
22. Taylor, A.S., & Harper, R. 2002. Age-old Practices in the 'New World': a study of gift-giving between teenage mobile phone users. *Proc. of CHI'02*, 439-446.
23. Taylor, R.B. 1988. *Human Territorial Functioning: An empirical, evolutionary perspective on individual and small group territorial cognitions, behaviors, and consequences.* Cambridge University Press.
24. Vitak, J., & Kim, J. 2014. "You can't block people offline": examining how Facebook's affordances shape the disclosure process. *Proc. of CSCW'14*, 461-474.
25. Vitak, J. 2014. Facebook makes the heart grow fonder: relationship maintenance strategies among geographically dispersed and communication-restricted connections. *Proc. of CSCW'14,* 842-853.
26. Vitak, J., Lampe, C., Gray, R., & Ellison, N.B. 2012. "Why won't you be my Facebook friend?": Strategies for managing context collapse in the workplace. *Proc. of iConference'12*, 555-557.
27. Wisniewski, P.J., Lipford, H.R., & Wilson, D.C. 2012. Fighting for my space: coping mechanisms for SNS boundary regulation, *Proc. of CHI'12*, 609-618.
28. Zhao, X., Salehi, N., Naranjit, S., Alwaalan, S., Voida, S., & Cosley, D. 2013. The many faces of Facebook: Experiencing social media as performance, exhibition, and personal archive. *Proc. of CHI'13*, 1-10.

Collaborative Affordances of Hybrid Patient Record Technologies in Medical Work

Steven Houben, Mads Frost, Jakob E. Bardram
The Pervasive Interaction Technology Laboratory
IT University of Copenhagen, Rued Langgaardsvej 7, DK-2300 Copenhagen, DK
{shou,madsf,bardram}@itu.dk

ABSTRACT
The medical record is a central artifact used to organize, communicate and coordinate information related to patient care. Despite recent deployments of electronic health records (EHR), paper medical records are still widely used because of the affordances of paper. Although a number of approaches explored the integration of paper and digital technology, there are still a wide range of open issues in the design of technologies that integrate digital and paper-based medical records. This paper studies the use of one such novel technology, called the Hybrid Patient Record (HyPR), that is designed to digitally augment a paper medical record. We report on two studies: a field study in which we describe the benefits and challenges of using a combination of electronic and paper-based medical records in a large university hospital and a deployment study in which we analyze how 8 clinicians used the HyPR in a medical simulation. Based on these empirical studies, this paper introduces and discusses the concept of *collaborative affordances*, which describes a set of properties of the medical record that foster collaborative collocated work.

Author Keywords
Hybrid Patient Record; Collaborative Affordance; Hospitals; Electronic Health Record; EHR; Mixed Reality Interaction

ACM Classification Keywords
H.5.2 [**Information Interfaces and Presentation**]: User Interfaces; J.3 [**Computer Applications**]: Life and Medical Science.

INTRODUCTION
Information management in medical work in hospitals is centered around medical records: a legal document containing detailed information about the patient's treatment. Medical records are organizational and coordinative artifacts that are used to share, communicate and manage complex treatment procedures [7]. To improve efficiency and quality in care, the Western world is investing significant resources in digitizing healthcare with a special focus on creating an integrated Electronic Health Record (EHR) [16]. The EHR offers a number of fundamental advantages over the Paper Medical Record (PMR) related to quality of health care, efficiency in use and a higher level of patient safety [11].

Despite this ongoing trend, hospitals still use PMRs as part of the daily workflow [5, 12, 37]. The significance and affordances of paper have been drawn together in Sellen and Harper's book — *The Myth of the Paperless Office* [36] — and are also highlighted in reflections on PMRs in clinical work [16]. Studies show that paper makes clinicians more efficient at their work [34] and that the use of paper forms increases significantly after the introduction of an EHR [35]. In fact, there is little to no evidence about the actual effectiveness of some of the new digitized workflows [8, 43] or EHRs [19]. Moreover, the EHR often operates as a passive information repository and is therefore often supplemented with a PMR which holds more informal documentation, such as ad hoc notes, as part of a *working record* [15]. Furthermore, PMRs frequently function as *transitional artifacts* [12] that mediate the information flow between day to day work in the hospital and the EHR, while also providing redundancy of information [10, 14]. As a consequence, clinicians *"... continue to maintain a hybrid documentation environment"* [13][p. 160] and a typical setup in many hospitals is that the EHR system does not replace the PMR, but a *double record* consisting of both a paper and electronic part is maintained. This double medical record, however, introduces a number of configuration and coordination problems related to finding, using, updating, communicating and managing both records.

To address the ubiquity of paper in workplaces like hospitals, a number of technologies that integrate paper and digital technology have been proposed. Paperlink [2], or the commercial solution Anoto, provides a digital pen as a synchronization mechanism between written documents and digital storage of that data. Building on this idea, other examples such as the Paper Augmented Digital Documents (PADDs) [20], Paperproof [39] and PapierCraft [27] provide support for digital annotation of paper documents using pen input. Other approaches focus on the medical record. Penbook [40] supports capturing handwritten prescriptions by providing a hybrid setup using a touch screen and projector equipped with a digital pen. NOSTOS [3] supports data capture in emergency

CSCW 2015, March 14–18, 2015, Vancouver, BC, Canada.

ACM 978-1-4503-2922-4/15/03 ...$15.00.
http://dx.doi.org/10.1145/2675133.2675164

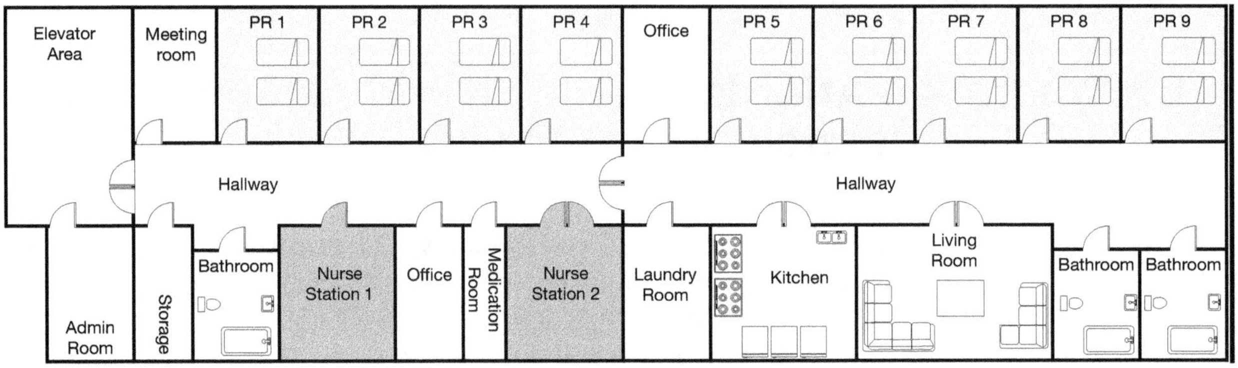

Figure 1. The physical layout of one of the wards from our field study. A typical ward consists of an administration desk, a number of patient rooms (PR), stations for the nurses, offices for the doctors, storage and medication rooms for medical equipment and finally bath- and living rooms for patients.

rooms and combines digital pens, wall displays and a digital desk to augment and enhance the PMR and form with digital patient information. Finally, the Augmented Paper Chart [41] provides seamless integration of paper notes with digital storage by using the Anoto pen.

This paper investigates one specific approach, called the Hybrid Patient Record (HyPR) (Figure 7) [23], for integrating the paper-based and electronic medical record. The HyPR device is attached to the PMR (like a notepad clip) and augments it with a notification system (color and sound), location tracking and ad hoc integration to a tablet that provides access to contextual relevant electronic patient data. By supporting various mechanisms to integrate the PMR and the EHR, the HyPR is designed to be a transitional artifact [12] that helps clinicians to gradually introduce digital tools in their use of medical records.

In this paper we make three contributions. First, we provide results from a detailed field study on the collaborative alignment and integration of PMR and EHR in different medical departments of a university hospital. This study verifies prior findings on collaboration in hospitals, but also contributes to the body of knowledge on the relationship between paper-based and electronic medical records. Second, we describe a study of the HyPR in a clinical simulation environment where 8 clinicians used the HyPR devices over two days performing scenarios originating from the field study. This study provides detailed insights into the use of hybrid or mixed reality technologies in collocated clinical work. Finally, we introduce and discuss the concept of '*collaborative affordances*', which is used to understand what features of a tool (be it paper-based or electronic) foster and support collocated collaboration. We analyze the collaborative affordances of the existing paper-based medical records and describe how they translate to the hybrid technology. Collaborative affordances thus extend the set of paper affordances identified by Sellen & Harper [36].

STUDY OF DOUBLE RECORD KEEPING

To thoroughly understand the nature of double record keeping, we conducted a field study on the use of the PMR and EHR in a large university hospital. The objective of the study was twofold; first, to obtain insights into the mechanisms clinicians adopt to collaboratively align and configure the two medical records in daily work and second, to prepare for the clinical simulation study of the HyPR technology.

Setting

The study took place in a university teaching hospital with about 3,000 employees providing care for a municipality of about 400,000 people in greater Copenhagen, Denmark. The study involved five connected medical departments, covering two patient bed wards, two surgical departments and the emergency department. All five departments are located in the same building and work in close collaboration with each other. Patients treated in the surgical or emergency departments are sent to the bed wards for recovery and post-op care. Each of the bed wards admit 20 to 30 patients and employ about 15 staff members including doctors, nurses and administrative personnel. The bed wards share the same architecture and consist of a set of patient-related rooms, including patient rooms, living area, bathrooms and a set of rooms used by doctors, nurses and secretaries including the meeting room, nurses stations, medication room, ward offices and the administrative room (Figure 1).

Method

The field study applied participant observations, contextual inquiries and interviews. Observations included task-centric, artifact-centric, place-centric and person-centric observations of work in all the wards and departments. Task-centric observations provided an understanding of the tasks and activities performed in the different wards and departments. Artifact-centric observations studied the use of paper-based artifacts including the PMRs; the different medical information systems used including the EHR; other computing devices, such as digital whiteboards, mobile PDA devices, traditional desktop computers; specialized medical equipment and monitors; and other physical artifacts like whiteboards, carts and medical equipment. Place-centric observations studied the flow of work in and between departments, wards, meeting rooms and patient rooms. Person-centric observation comprised of contextual inquiries of nurses and doctors for one day followed by a post-hoc interview to get a more detailed understanding of the work in each department. In total there were 7 shadowing sessions, 5 follow-up interviews and 10 days of observation material (images and notes). The data were collected and recorded using photographs, audio tapes and extensive note taking, and were analyzed into reports, diagrams and workflow charts. To conclude the study, we conducted a follow-up workshop after the observations in which our findings were presented and verified.

The Medical Record Workflow

At the hospital, the medical record consists of a unique PMR. It is a legal requirement that this record is at all times present at the ward that is currently treating the patient. Although the content of the PMR varies between different departments, the record itself is standardized within the entire hospital. The record consists of a plastic cover that is marked with color-coded sections for different types of documentation (Figure 2). Documentation includes basic patient data, the narrative treatment record (called the 'continuation'), nursing documentation, various schemes and forms, observations, test results (e.g., radiology examinations) and messages from other medical professionals. Each record carries a label that uniquely identifies the patient by stating name and social security number both in text and encoded in a barcode. This label is attached to the front of the record. Normally, the PMR is between 2 and 3 cm thick, but the size of a record can take extreme proportions. In one case, the record of a cancer patient had to be distributed over several physical folders because of the large amount of documents accumulated over a long treatment period. At a patient ward, there are typically up to 25 active PMRs in use.

Figure 2. The standard PMR consists of a plastic folder that is labeled with the name and ID of the patient. The record holds all patient documentation and provides separate color-coded sections, e.g., for nurse notes, treatment history or other forms and observations.

Next to the PMR, the hospital provides a set of Health Information Systems (HISs), such as a Radiology Information System (RIS), an Electronic Medication System (EMS), a Patient Administration System (PAS), a Blood Bank System (BBS) and many others. Clinicians can access these applications through a system portal, which collates all applications into one interface, that is referred to as the EHR. Both the paper and digital information are often used simultaneously and are of equal importance. But in order to have electronically stored information 'ready-at-hand', information like lab results and radiology examinations are printed and added to the physical PMR.

Figure 3 shows the four main processes involving the medical record. The color code indicates whether only the PMR (blue), only the EHR (green) or both records (red) are used for that part of the process. The patient is referred to the hospital (e.g., for surgery) by the general practitioner (GP), who fills in an online form. This form is printed by the administration of the hospital when setting up an appointment for the patient. The form is stamped and approved by a doctor and sent

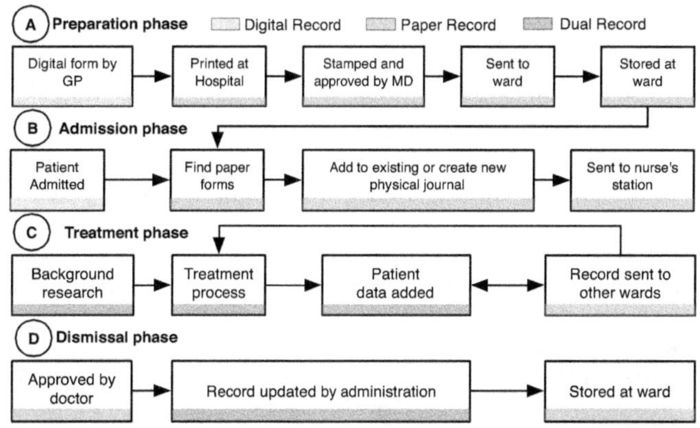

Figure 3. The life cycle of the PMR consists of a (A) preparation phase, (B) admission phase, (C) treatment phase and (D) dismissal phase (GP: general practitioner; MD: medical doctor).

to the ward responsible for the patient (Figure 3A – *preparation phase*). In the hospital, the general workflow surrounding the PMR is primarily managed by the ward secretaries and the nurses. When a patient is admitted to the hospital, the ward secretary locates the PMR. Most patients are readmitted to the same department and this 'home' department hence physically stores the PMR in the storage room. However, if a patient was previously treated at another department, locating the PMR can be a rather cumbersome process. Once located, the referral letter (e.g., from the GP) is added to the PMR. If a new patient with no PMR is admitted to the ward, one is created. The record is then sent to the nursing station the day before (or on the morning) the patient arrives. During the morning conference between the doctors and nurses, the record is used to prepare the arrival of the patient and to plan the treatment (Figure 3B – *admission phase*). Once the daily treatment and care of the patient has ended (Figure 3C – *treatment phase*), the medical continuation is updated by a ward secretary while nurses update the nursing record, the medicine scheme and add relevant examination results to the record (Figure 3D – *dismissal phase*). Once the patient is discharged from the department, the PMR is finalized and stored at the ward. This implies that hundreds of archived records are at the department.

FINDINGS

The field study on the use of (double) medical records provided three main findings related to: (i) establishing workflows, awareness and coordination; (ii) micro- and macro-mobility of medical records; and (iii) how medical record sub-artifacts are collated and aligned. These findings relate well to those from other studies of the use of (electronic) medical records in hospital environments, but also add a detailed insight into how medical professionals handle such double record keeping.

Workflow, Awareness and Coordination

Several studies (e.g., [12, 33, 37]) have shown that the PMR serves as a key coordination mechanism between clinicians, which is confirmed in our study. The PMR is used as a coordination mechanism between nurses and doctors inside the patient ward where the doctor can give orders concerning the patient via the PMR and in turn, the nurses note information in the record that helps the physician decide what to do next for the patient. In our study, we found that the PMR is actively used during coordination of patient treatment and care during the morning conference. The content of the record including the latest examination results is key in deciding on treatment and care as well as the allocation of doctors and nurses to the patient. As such, the record is essential in coordinating treatment within and between departments, which is reflected in the fact that the record is always required by law to follow the patient to other departments.

Figure 4. The placement of a PMR (e.g., spatial orientation or opening the record) is used to signal information to other clinicians.

The PMR is also key in a more subtle coordination inside the ward as its physical form helps to achieve local coordination and awareness. The physical placement of records often reveals status information and can be used for signaling and for drawing attention to important matters. For example, the PMRs shown in figure 4 are deliberately placed on the desk by a nurse to signal to the doctor that the paper forms in the record should be inspected and validated. Similarly, the PMR would often be placed in the bed of the patient inside a patient room, visible from the hallway. This is a signal to the porter that this patient is ready for pick-up and can be moved, e.g., to surgery. This phenomenon of signaling through document placement was also observed by Bång et al. [3] who noted that if, e.g., a physician wanted a laboratory test, the request was attached to the folder that was then placed at a designated spot on the desk. Hence, our study confirms that the processes of signaling and monitoring are used in medical work to constitute mutual workplace awareness [6]. However, an interesting addition to prior research is that in this case, not only humans but also computational devices work as active signaling actors. For example, printing lab results directly on the ward's printer is a signal from the lab to the ward. In general, the spatial arrangement of documents bestows local importance on the workplace and provides an overview and deposition of information that facilitates memory recall and the tracking of work processes. The placement of a record inside the ward, the nurses station, the filing cabinet or storage room convey information about their role in the overall workflow.

Micro- and Macro-mobility

Medical work in hospitals is inherently nomadic [4], which implies that clinicians and the tools they use move around inside wards, departments and the entire hospital. This mobility includes the PMR, which moves between different departments, wards and locations within the ward [32]. As such, the mobility affordance of PMRs fits medical work well, as they are easy to move around inside a hospital. Our study showed that the PMR is primarily moved around inside the patient ward and is mostly used in the ward offices, nursing stations, doctor's offices and at the bedside of the patient. However, since it is a legal requirement that the record is present during medical treatment, the record always 'travels with the patient'. For example, when patients are sent to other departments (e.g., for x-ray or surgery), the record is mounted in a special container on the side of the patient's bed and travels with the patient to the receiving department. This flexible mobility affordance of the PMR, however, also introduced significant challenges since it often was lost or misplaced both inside the ward and in other departments. Significant time was spent looking for records, especially by the ward secretaries. Hence, a core challenge to a paper-based workflow is that sometimes the physical record is misplaced or not available. As one of the nurses explained:

> *"Doing background research on a patient can be difficult when the patient does not belong to our ward. Then the PMR is elsewhere and the digital data might not be up to date. All we can do is wait for the patient and improvise."*

But also finding records inside the ward offers its own set of challenges. Finding the right PMR is difficult because there is no visual differentiation between different records; they are all stacked upon each other and scattered all over the ward in the nurses station, the secretary offices and in the storage room.

In addition to mobility on a macro level, micro-mobility of a PMR plays a central role in medical work [28]. Micro-mobility is *the way in which an artifact can by mobilized and manipulated for various purposes around a relatively circumscribed, or 'at hand', domain.* For example, during the ward round a physician and nurse jointly worked on a PMR by standing next to each other reading the record. They handed over parts of the record to each other, pointing out specific results. Furthermore, the record was often broken open and the individual records, results, forms and graphs were spread out on, e.g., a desk for better overview. This micro-mobility affordance of a PMR hence supports clinicians in achieving an overview of the medical situation at hand [9].

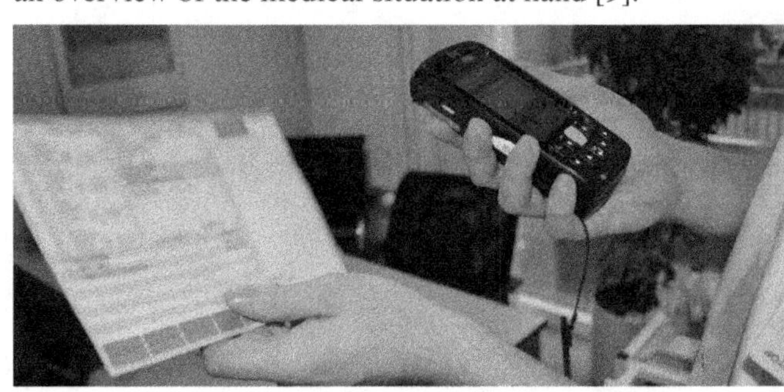

Figure 5. A nurse completing a form while using a PDA to scan the vacutainer after taking a blood sample.

Moreover, as seen in figure 5, nurses often 'break open' the record by only taking parts of the record with them, while interacting with patients. In this specific case, a nurse has brought the record and placed it on the table before taking a blood test from the patient, scanning the tube with the PDA and adding the form to the PMR. In current work practices, this kind of micro-mobility alignment between paper and digital information is often cumbersome. Additionally, since the

PDA only provides limited access to the patient data (in this case only the blood work), the clinician will have to return to the nurses station to manually add any data to the electronic record. The mobile device as such is only used to ensure the blood test was taken from the correct patient.

Artifact Collation and Alignment

Core to medical overview and decision making is the collation and alignment of information from many sources. This includes both the many different paper forms and records in the PMR, as well as the information located in the EHR. Hence, significant effort was put into collation and alignment of medical information for several sources to get a comprehensive overview of a patient's medical state. As seen in figure 6, both the paper and digital information are of equal importance and are thus often used simultaneous. This implies that while some information is duplicated in both records, other information only exists in one of both.

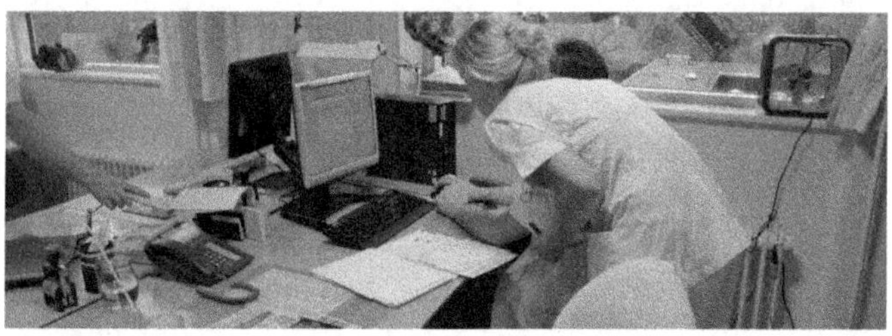

Figure 6. Clinicians are using both the PMR and EHR to coordinate information.

Managing the dual record introduces a number of configuration challenges related to managing, synchronizing, communicating and cross-referencing both versions of the record. Current work practices still include printing a significant amount of information, which is then stored in the PMR. Furthermore, most of the digital applications can only be used to request or add new medical data (such as blood test or MRI). The results of these requested tests are often still sent by paper trough internal mail or by sending the results to the printer located at the requesting ward. This places a large and important coordinative role on the printer, which essentially operates as a communication and awareness mechanism. It also implies that although a lot of time and effort is invested in printing, often these printouts are quickly outdated compared to the digital record, or even get lost throughout the printing process. There was a general recognition that aiming for a completely 'paperless hospital' would be naive. Moreover, information on large whiteboards were also constantly updated to align information across several records and other coordinative artifacts. The need for collation and alignment of information across such a 'web of coordinative artifacts' is known to be essential for the general flow and coordination of medical work [5].

HYBRID MEDICAL RECORD TECHNOLOGY

As argued above, there is a significant set of configuration challenges related to managing, synchronizing, communicating and cross-referencing both versions of the medical record.

Figure 7. The HyPR device augments the PMR with a notification system (color and sound), location tracking and near-field communication that uniquely identify the medical record, which allows clinicians to pair a tablet with the HyPR to display the digital information associated with the present PMR.

In order to provide a technical design to mitigate these problems, we have previously proposed an augmented hybrid patient record or HyPR device (Figure 7) [23]. The HyPR device is a small sensing and computing platform that supports notification through colored light and sound, location tracking and unique identification using near-field communication (NFC). The HyPR device is designed to be 'clipped on' to the paper-based record as an augmentation of the plastic folder used now. Hence, one HyPR device should be deployed for each PMR in use in a hospital department.

As shown in Figure 7, the HyPR device is attached to the PMR and, by placing a mobile device like a tablet computer or a smart phone on top of the record, relevant electronic information from the EHR is loaded and displayed. The HyPR embeds a unique id, which is communicated to the mobile device using NFC and Wifi and is used to retrieve relevant patient information in the EHR. On the side of the HyPR device, an array of LED lights can be used for signaling purposes and the device also has a small buzzer for sound notifications. These notification features can be used to convey status information about a patient, such as when the patient is ready for the ward round or should be prepared for surgery. The HyPR also embeds a location tracking tag that allows for tracking the location of the physical paper record. This allows clinicians to retrieve the location of a record when missing. Additionally, they can turn on the buzzer or set the colored lights to blink, to visually or auditory locate the HyPR.

The overall design goal of the HyPR approach is to create a transitional artifact allowing clinicians to easily move between paper-based and digital records. Clinicians thus benefit from both the portability and flexibility of paper-based records as well as the easy access and information processing capabilities of electronic medical records. As such, the goal is to reduce the amount of configuration work required to use and setup this dual record. Specifically, the HyPR approach supports: easy and fast *configuration* of the dual record by allowing clinicians to connect the paper and digital information, *coordination* by providing a notification system equipped with dynamic colored lights and sound and *mobility* by including location tracking capabilities to the portable device. The HyPR approach supports flexible and dynamic configuration of paper and digital information, which allow for a gradual transition between paper and digital. For example, paper-based forms can be digitized and stored in the EHR or digital material can be printed and stored in the PMR, all of which can be handled by the HyPR approach.

HYBRID MEDICAL RECORD STUDY

Previous studies of the HyPR device have only provided preliminary insights into its overall usability and usefulness [23]. Therefore, there is a need to understand the details of how this technology supports collaborative work in hospital departments, in particular, how it helps alleviating configuration challenges related to managing, synchronizing, communicating and cross-referencing both versions of the medical record. The study investigated to what degree the HyPR supports and potentially enhances existing clinical practices.

Since doing a field deployment of this type of technology is technically, legally and organizationally unfeasible, we conducted a clinical simulation in a separate 1:1 simulation environment. In the medical domain, a clinical simulation is a methodology frequently applied to train and educate clinicians in critical clinical scenarios, such as surgery, medicine prescription and administration and emergency cases. It has proved very efficient and reliable for the initial phase of training and assessment of clinical staff [1]. However, since the clinical simulation approach attempts to bring the dimension of clinical context into stronger focus, the method has lately been used also as a method for testing clinical systems with representative users doing representative tasks, in an ecologically valid setting [24]. The main source for this medical simulation was the data and insights obtained from the original hospital field study, which provided input for the physical setup, the scenarios and the configuration of the technology.

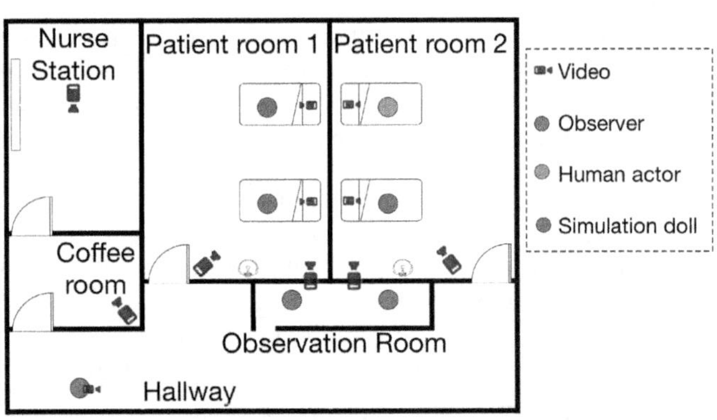

Figure 8. The simulation setup was comprised of a medical ward with five zones including two patient rooms, a nurse station, a coffee room and a hallway. The simulation facility is equipped with hidden cameras and an observation room behind a one-way mirror. The simulation included three simulation dolls (patients) and one human acting as a real patient.

Setting and Participants

The study was conducted at a 1:1 clinical simulation and training facility in a large hospital. This simulation facility supports the simulation of different hospital departments ranging from patient wards to surgical department and emergency ones. For our study, we set up the facility to be identical to a fully equipped patient ward with two patient bed rooms. Figure 8 shows the layout of the setup consisting of five zones: two patient rooms, a nurse station, a coffee room and the hallway. One human actor performed as a patient in a bed in room 2 (Figure 7, green dot). The other patient beds were equipped with simulation dolls, each connected to a monitor displaying the vital signs of the 'patient' (such as heart rate, saturation, blood pressure, temperature, etc). The setup included artifacts such as a traditional whiteboard with patients' data, desks in the nursing station with a stationary computer and nursing carts with medical equipment.

During the two-day simulation, 8 senior clinicians with different specialties (such as surgery, psychiatry and intensive care) participated in the experiment. Participants included 5 doctors, 2 nurses and a psychologist. The entire simulation was recorded using video and audio as well as extensive note taking and observations from inside the observation room through a one-way mirror.

Method

The study applied a scenario-based evaluation of the HyPR approach. The scenarios were drawn directly from the initial field study and revolved around interacting with the patients (both the actor and simulation dolls) to assess the patient case, update the status in the EHR and add or remove all necessary documents to the PMR. Scenarios included:

S1 *Ward Round* – Clinicians were asked to perform a ward round to assess the situation of four patients. By examining the patients and monitoring vitals signs on the monitor, they had to calculate an Early Warning Score (EWS) to describe their current status.

S2 *Blood Result* – Clinicians were asked to order a blood test result while working on the case of patient P1. After receiving the results they had to visit the patient, re-calculate the EWS and discuss the situation with the patient.

S3 *Lost Record* – Clinicians were asked to find a number of PMR, which, after a shift change, were not at their usual place. For this scenario, they could employ information on the patient's location, the last treating doctor, the current treatment procedure and the location of the HyPR.

After welcoming the participants, a brief introduction was delivered on the concept, the system and the physical layout of the ward. Participants were then asked to perform the three scenarios above. We did not provide any detailed instructions on how to perform the scenarios, which patients to look at first or how to use the system. Because we were interested in how clinicians would leverage their existing practices while using the HyPR setup, the scenarios were deliberately open ended: no explicit instructions or training on the system was given to them and the facilitator only intervened to solve technical issues. Because the initial field study showed that most medical work is highly collaborative, involving both doctors and nurses, the scenarios were conducted in pairs of two clinicians from the same department.

Artifact and Technology Setup

A list of patient cases with realistic names, backgrounds, social security number and medical background was compiled for the study. The PMRs used in the simulation contained real blood tests, EWS forms, admission forms, doctor and nurse notes and other medical information. The whiteboard placed in the nurse station listed all the patients with room number, treatment plan, responsible doctor and nurse and admission date. Four HyPR devices and three Nexus 7 tablet computers were used. We equiped the simulation facility with the Sonitor[1] ultrasound location tracking system in all rooms, excluding the hallway.

Since there was no open access to the medical information system in the hospital, we implemented a simple Activity-Centric EHR application to be used in the simulation. This application contained all patient cases with a set of medical entries such as blood test results, continuation records and nursing notes. The adaptable web application runs on phones, tablets and desktop computer and supports two views: (i) an overview screen and (ii) a patient details screen. The overview screen lists all patients currently active on the ward and provides basic information, such as name, assigned color, room number and ongoing medical procedures on each patient (Figure 9A). Using the 'Blink' button causes the colored lights of the HyPR to start blinking (Figure 7), asking for attention until a tablet is paired. The 'Buzz' button can be used to turn on a buzzing sound to quickly find a record. The buzzing sound is automatically stopped after 15 seconds.

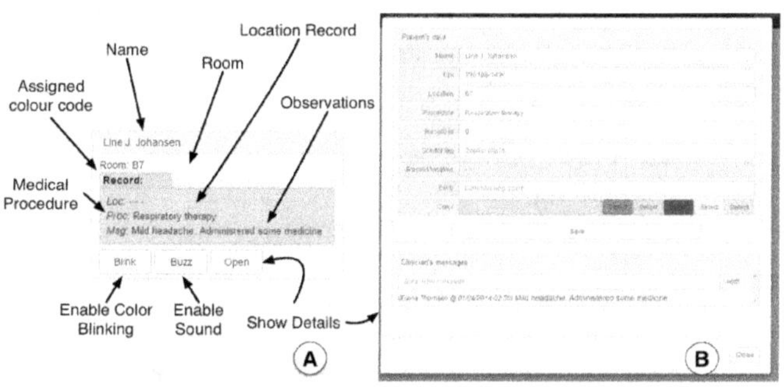

Figure 9. The details of the patient record.

By placing the tablet on the HyPR device, the patient information (Figure 9B) is displayed. This screen allows clinicians to inspect prior observations and update medical information (e.g., EWS), add a message, or change the status color of the patient. Changing this color in the EHR will cause the color of the HyPR device to change accordingly (see Figure 7). The EHR on the tablet computer can also be used while not paired with an HyPR device. In this case, if new data (medical observations or a message) for a patient is entered into the EHR application, the patient's HyPR device (attached to the patient's PMR) will start to blink. In this way, the physical record signals changes in the digital record. Once a tablet is paired with the HyPR record, the patient information is displayed and the device stops blinking. All patient information is thus organized in 'patient activities' which are visualized in the overview screen and can be quickly and easily accessed through physical or remote interaction.

FINDINGS

The objective of the simulation was to study how work practices observed in the field study would translate to the HyPR. As such, we were interested in relating the observations of the HyPR approach to current work practices at a medical ward. The discussion of the simulation findings are therefore framed in the three main findings from the field study on the use of medical records in the hospital; (i) establishing workflows, awareness and coordination; (ii) micro- and macro-mobility of medical records; and, (iii) how medical record sub-artifacts are collated and aligned.

Workflow, Awareness and Coordination

Since the HyPR encloses the PMR, it was used as a coordination mechanism in exactly the same way as seen during the field studies. Clinicians would use the record for information sharing, during clinical conferences and as the key coordination mechanisms between doctors and nurses during, e.g., the ward round. It was, however, interesting to observe how the features and functionality of the HyPR sparked new workflows, awareness and coordination practices.

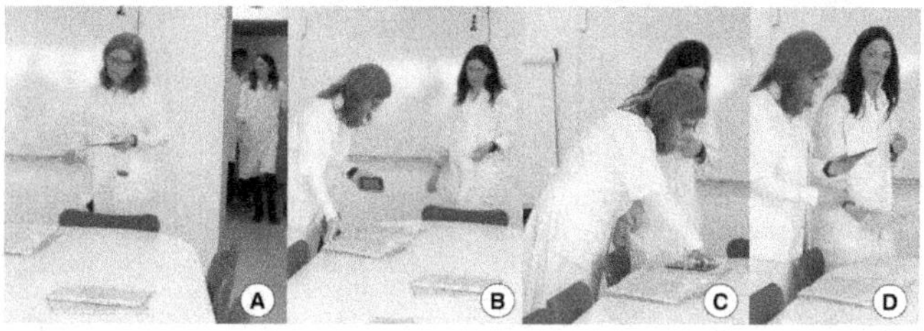

Figure 10. Clinicians glance at the PMRs (A) and notice that a colored light is blinking, indicating a new message (B). They pair a tablet computer with the record to read the message on the tablet (C) and finally consult the paper forms for more details (D).

First, the colored lights of the HyPR triggered a number of novel workflow coordination mechanisms. The color was quickly appropriated as part of the externalization of the EWS. This meant that clinicians would use the color to organize and structure their ward round. One doctor, for example, mentioned that the colors helped him prioritize his patients during the ward round by using blue, green and red colors to indicate low, normal and acute patient cases. Colors were also used to reveal workflow status information. For example, during one of the ward round scenarios, a nurse had already appropriated the use of colored light as a method to keep track of the workflow:

> *"This [patient record] is green and it is not blinking, so he is fine." – P7*

Colors were also used for revealing if new content was added to the PMR. Figure 10 shows a video fragment of two nurses picking up a new message via the HyPR. First, the two nurses pass by the nurse station and glance at a number of PMRs in active use (Figure 10A). One nurse notices a blinking colored light indicating that new content has been added to the record (such as a new observation, message, or lab test result) (Figure 10B). The clinicians approach the record and, by placing the tablet on top of the record, they are able to read the updates (Figure 10C). They realize that they need more detailed information and align it with the paper documentation (Figure 10D) to construct a shared overview of all patient data.

Second, placement of the HyPR combined with the color light was also used for deliberately signaling status information.

[1] http://www.sonitor.com

Placing PMRs in the patient's bed was a signaling mechanism often observed during the field study. The simulation study showed that this work practice was continued and enhanced using the HyPR. We observed that clinicians carefully considered location and orientation when placing the HyPR. In the patient rooms, for example, clinicians would often position the records in such a way that the lights were visible from the hallway. This mechanism was adopted so that clinicians could easily glance inside the room and check if the colored light was changed or if a new message was received. They considered the colored lights to be an important collaborative affordance that helped them share and externalize the status of the patient in a fast and efficient way.

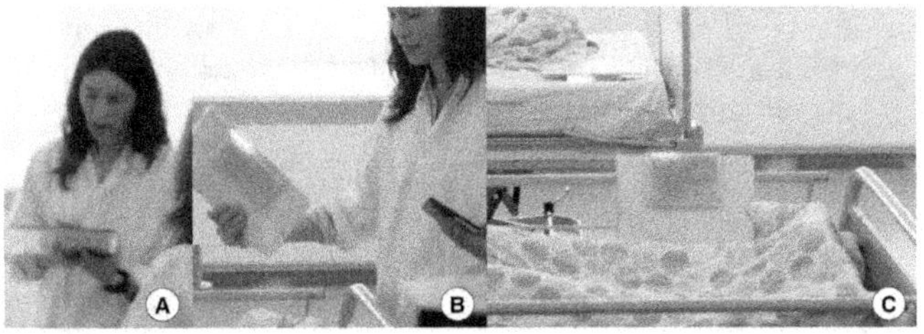

Figure 11. The clinician uses the record (A), checks if the colored light matches her assessment (B) and places both records in such a way that they are visible from the hallway (C).

Figure 11 shows a video fragment of a nurse using the HyPR for signaling. After finishing assessing the patient case (Figure 11A), the clinician double checks the color to see if it matches her assessment color (Figure 11B) and then positions the record to allow for visibility from the hallway (Figure 11C). Interestingly, this positioning was done differently depending on the location of the bed in the patient room:

> *"Then I should place it so one can see the light.. now it lies across his legs, then I should probably move it.. there!" – P8*

As seen in Figure 11C, the record on the second bed in the background is positioned differently than the one on the bed in the foreground. This was done because the bed in the foreground was close to the wall, implying it would not be visible from the hallway if it were flat on the bed. With the current positioning both records where visible from the hallway.

Micro- and Macro-mobility

The HyPR device is designed to maintain the macro-mobility affordance of regular PMRs. The medical simulation study clearly showed that a HyPR was carried around in the simulation facility just like regular PMRs are carried around. This can be seen in the video fragments in Figures 11, 14 and 16. However, as observed during the field studies, there are a number of problems related to mobility in clinical work, including the problem of lost PMRs and the lack of support for accessing the EHR while roaming the ward or hospital. The HyPR was designed to mitigate these problems by supporting location tracking of the HyPR and by allowing access to the EHR via a tablet that is paired with the PMR.

During the simulation, clinicians very quickly appropriated these features and we observed a number of recurring patterns in the mobile use of the HyPR. Figure 12 shows a video

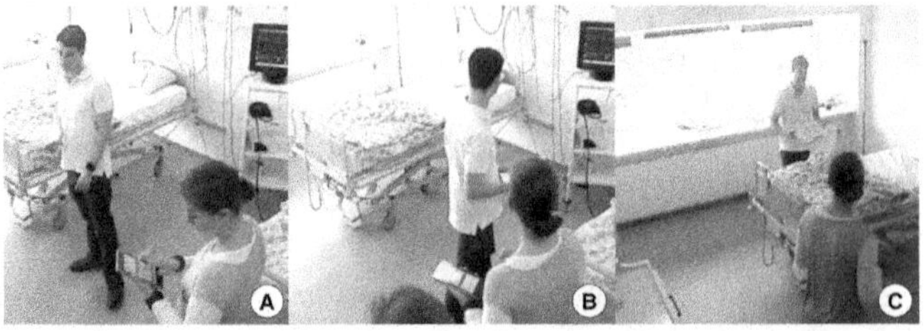

Figure 12. Clinicians use the color blinking (A) and buzzing feature (B) to identity the location of the record (C).

fragment of two clinicians searching for a lost PMR. The search strategy was very similar for most clinicians. First, they use the tablet computer to look up the location of the HyPR PMR. Since location tracking is room-based, they enter the room and look for the record. If it is not immediately visible, they use the tablet to turn on a blinking pattern on the record (Figure 12A). This approach only works if the PMR is in plain sight, e.g., on a desk or on a stack of other records, but not if the record is in a cupboard or drawer. Clinicians therefore turn on the buzzing sound and divide the mobility work between both of them. One clinician holds the tablet and repeatedly presses the buzz button while the other clinician tries to identify the location of the record with the instructions of the clinician that is holding the tablet and who has a better idea on where the sound is coming from (Figure 12B). After finding the tablet, it is still blinking from the initial search attempt, thus helping them verify that they have found the correct PMR (Figure 12C).

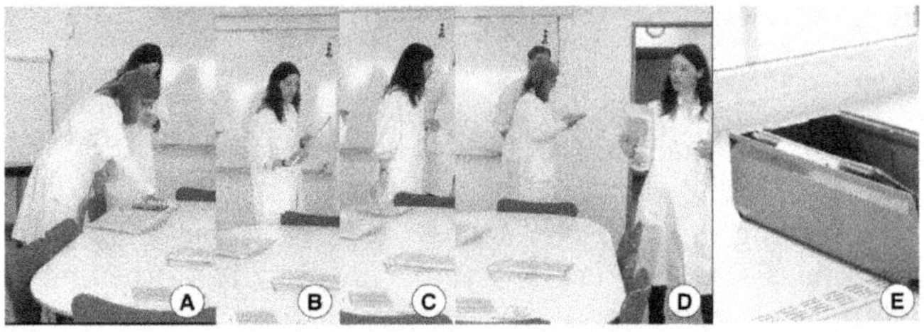

Figure 13. Clinicians inspect a pile of PMRs (A), select the one that they need (B) and position it strategically on the table while discussing it (C). Afterwards the doctor takes it (D) and places it in the out-tray with the colored lights clearly visible (E)

The field study also revealed extensive micro-mobility of PMRs; the spatial orientation and positioning of the record often carry a meaning as it symbolizes and reflects work processes. During the simulation, we observed similar micro-mobility use patterns with the HyPR as depicted in the video fragment in Figure 13. Clinicians inspect a pile of records and spatially categorize them based on their importance (Figure 13A). After selecting and inspecting a particular PMR (Figure 13B), the doctor places the record on the corner of the table (Figure 13C) to indicate that this is the record they are currently using. After discussing the patient case, they realize that this patient is no longer at the ward and the record is therefore no longer needed at the ward, but has to be sent to another ward (Figure 13D). The doctor then places the record in the out-tray with the colored lights facing upwards and clearly visible (Figure 13E).

Artifact Collation and Alignment

The original field study revealed significant work associated with aligning and collating PMR with EHR. A first observation from the simulation study reveals that record alignment and collation no longer takes place at the desk in the nurses station (as seen in Figure 6), but can be done by clinicians while roaming around inside the entire ward. All clinicians followed a very similar strategy in aligning the PMR and EHR. Figure 14 shows a video fragment showcasing the new approach available through the HyPR, performed by the patient's bedside. The clinicians first pair the paper and digital record to get an overview on the patient case (Figure 14A). They then jointly inspect both the paper and digital information and explicitly check if any new observations were added to the digital or PMR (Figure 14B). After discussing the case with the patient, they add a new observation to the digital record and place the paper forms back in the record (Figure 14C).

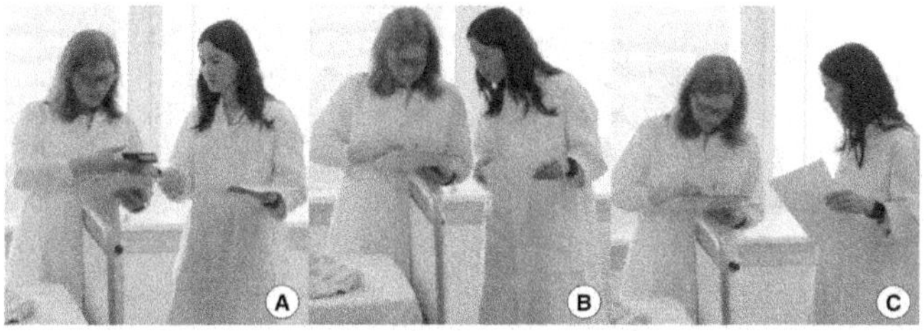

Figure 14. Clinicians first align the paper and digital record (A), then inspect both types of documentation (B) and finally update the documentation in both records (C).

While interacting with a patient, clinicians would divide the PMR between both of them. One clinicians would thus hold the PMR and inspect all the printed blood tests and paper forms, while the other clinicians would consult the paired tablet for the EHR. However, while moving to another patient or room, one clinician would carry both the HyPR and tablet, while the other clinician would focus on the patient. One clinician is thus often "left behind". Busy adding information to the electronic record using the tablet, the other clinician moves to the next patient. Interestingly, we also observed that although clinicians had easier access to both records, they sometimes were reluctant to use all its features. At one time a nurse, for example, whispered to the doctor:

> *"I am very much against that we should be writing it in here. We should do this at the nurses station." – P4*

She essentially disliked using the system in front of patients, as she argued that it detached the contact between the clinician and the patient.

During the EWS assessments of patients, we often observed that clinicians would spatially organize information that was needed to better understand the case. The video fragment in Figure 15 shows two clinicians doing a ward round while using the patient bed to organize and collate all the paper forms stored in the PMR and in the tablet computer. They first collate the prior blood results paper, EWS forms and digital messages (Figure 15A). Based on this information, they discuss

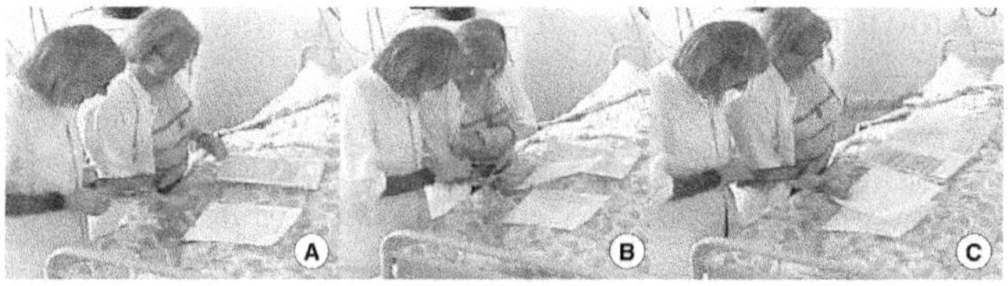

Figure 15. Two clinicians are using the patient bed to spatially organize both the paper and digital record of the patient (A-B), before adding content to the digital record (C).

the patient case and compare the previous data to the live information on the monitor (Figure 15B). Finally, they complete a new EWS form and add the form to the PMR while at the same time recording the EWS score to the digital record (Figure 15C).

When a physical surface was not available for spatial organization, clinicians would perform the collation in a much more mobile setting. The video fragment in Figure 16 depicts two clinicians that are collating medical forms, blood tests and digital record entries. While talking to the patient, the doctor (Figure 16A — on the right) is studying previous data. Based on the vital signs on the monitor, he requests the other clinician (Figure 16B — on the left) to update the electronic record with his assessment. He also asks the other clinician to update the color of the record to match his assessment (Figure 16C). Before leaving the patient room, the doctor checks the HyPR to see if the color has been updated based on his assessment of the patient (Figure 16D).

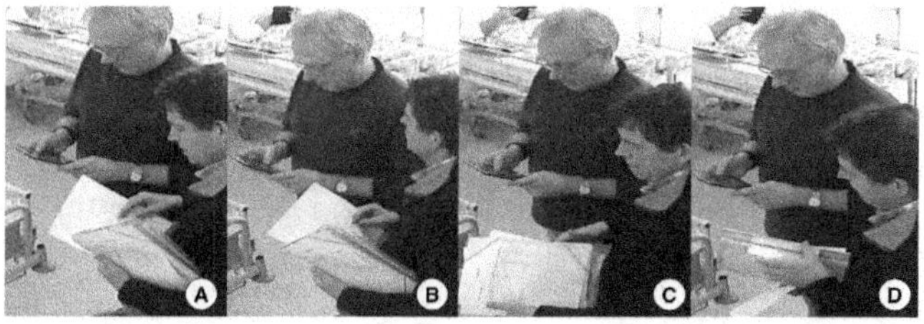

Figure 16. During the ward round, two clinicians are collating the paper and digital record (A-B) of the patient while standing at the bed assessing the patient case (C-D).

DISCUSSION

Prior studies [5, 12, 37] as well as this paper show that paper documentation remains to play an important central role as it is persistently and pervasively used during medical work in hospitals. This intensive use of paper documentation seems to be independent from the degree to which EHRs are integrated as paper simply makes clinicians more efficient in parts of their work [34]. Based on Gibson's theory of affordances [18], Sellen and Harper have argued that paper in general possesses a set of affordances, that makes it especially efficient in use [36]. These affordances include the ability to quickly navigate through documents, read across multiple documents at once, mark up a document while reading and interweave reading and writing. Looking more specifically to the medical domain, Harper et al. [21] point to the affordances of *flexibility*, *markability*, *portability* and *accessibility* of the anesthesia record that makes it easy to fill out, share and use during surgery.

Collaborative Affordance - *Affords the ability to*
Mobility and Portability
Physically carry, share and use the record in different places
Collocated Access
Simultaneous and collocated read and update the record
Shared Overview
Collectively create an overview of the content on the record
Mutual Awareness
Signal and monitor information between users

Table 1. The Collaborative Affordances of PMR and HyPR.

Based on the two studies reported in this paper, we argue that the core benefit of a paper-based medical record does not solely lie in its core basic affordances, but that a set of *collaborative affordances* exist that support clinicians in coordinating work. Rather than applying the original definition of affordance provided by Gibson [18], we rely on Norman's interpretation for human-computer interaction[2], in which affordance refers to those action possibilities that are *readily perceivable* by an actor [29]. In this definition, affordances depend not only on the physical capabilities of an actor, but also on the actor's goals, plans, values, beliefs and past experiences. Gaver describes that the perception of affordances is "*embedded in the observer's culture, social setting, experience and intentions*" [17]. Although affordances exist as a configuration of physical properties, its perceptible meaning is often dependent on the social strata and can thus change or differ between environments or social setting. Within the framework of distributed cognition, Zhang and Patel [42] refer to this dependency to culture as *cognitive affordance*. Using Activity Theory, Kaptelinin and Nardi reconceptualize affordances in a social-culture background describing them as *mediating actions* [25]. Similarely, Vyas et al. [38] describe that *affordances in interaction* exist between the user and environment, emerges from activities and practices and are therefore socially and culturally constructed. Finally, Kreijns and Kirschner [26] introduced *social affordances* as properties of collaborative environments "*which act as social-contextual facilitators relevant for the learners social interactions.*"

Based on these prior interpretations of the social role of affordances, we describe *collaborative affordances* as 'physical' properties that afford — make possible different actions for a person perceiving the object — collaborative perceptions and actions within a specific social context. Collaborative affordances do not replace the normal affordances of paper, but rather contextualize them in a social structure. Table 1 lists four basic collaborative affordances of the medical record which were observed in both studies. As technology comes closer to paper (as in the HyPR approach), questions arise on how these collaborative affordances translate to technology. Using the field study and the clinical simulation as case studies, we describe below how the four collaborative affordances described in Table 1 were observed in the initial study and how they translate into the HyPR approach.

[2]Although Norman nowadays prefers the terms perceived affordance [30] or signifier [31] over affordance.

Mobility & Portability

Portability, the ability to carry, maneuver and navigate, is an important affordance of paper [36], hence, also of the PMR [21]. From a collaborative stance, the portability and mobility of PMRs is a central reason for its success in mediating cooperative medical work. As argued by Østerlund [32], a PMR serves as a *portable place* in the sense that it can move across space and time but retain the indexical structure which points out relevant participants, places and times. This collaborative affordance allows several clinicians to use the record on the move as they continuously perform care activities for many patients across multiple locations. Such macro-mobility inside and across patient wards was also found in both of the presented studies: PMR as well as HyPR were carried around and used during care activities (e.g., ward rounds) and this portability of the record helped clinicians to jointly accomplish their work. Although the HyPR in its current state is relatively heavy and bulky due to the sensor platform, the technology essentially incorporates support for mobility as there was less mobility work [4] required to configure the work setup. The mobility and portability affordance of the HyPR is much closer to that of a PMR, specially if compared to other approaches that attempt to include mobility use for the EHR (e.g., Computers on Wheels (COW) [37]). By using the PMR as a contextual surface that auto-configures the paired tablet, HyPR mitigates the high cost of information access [37] and physical [21] challenges of handling digitized medical information at the bedside.

Collocated Access

Paper has a high degree of configurability as it affords simultaneous access through reading and writing [36]. These affordances are key to PMRs, since *working records* [15] and *transitional artifacts* [12] are used by clinicians as a coordinative reflective tool to bridge the gap between day to day work in the hospital and managing the EHR. In the course of the working shift, clinicians keep these documents to continuously gather information on the move and gradually transfer them back to the official record [32]. Our studies of the use of PMRs and the HyPR approach emphasize the collaborative nature of such simultaneous access to medical records. Records were often used in a collocated setting in which typically a pair of a nurse and a doctor would break open the record and simultaneously inspect and access the documents and forms. Examples of situations in which collocated access of the medical record is evident include the ward conference situation and the use of the record at the patient's bedside during a ward round (Figure 14). Such situations are examples of *standard operation configurations* [4] in a hospital, which are spatial setups fostering easy cooperation because of a common knowledge and agreement as to how to use and navigate the artifacts involved. A core requirement for medical records is that they embed this collaborative affordance of collocated access, which enables them to be part of such standard operation configurations. Using HyPR provides clinicians with a high degree of plasticity to import a digital device into standard operation configurations. Furthermore, by using a tablet computer with a size that fits into the clinicians' white coat pockets, the tablet can easily be brought in and out of the configuration. Although the sensors of the HyPR device are clearly visible to the clinicians, the technology was considered to be transparent as clinicians did not mention the mediating hardware at all, but rather talked about the HyPR as a 'smart paper-based medical record'.

Shared Overview

One of the most prominent affordance of paper is that it supports quick and flexible navigation and simultaneous access of multiple documents [36]. This is extensively used in a clinical setting, in which the PMR is key in obtaining an overview of the treatment and care of a patient [9]. Our studies of both the PMR and HyPR showed that this creation of an overview is primarily a collaborative effort, as the records afforded the creation of a shared overview by aligning documents. In the case of the PMR, we observed that clinicians would collate and align medical information from several sources (both PMR and digitally, as shown in Figure 6) to get a comprehensive overview of a patient's medical state. Moreover, during the study of the HyPR record, we often observed that clinicians would spatially organize information that was needed to better understand the case. For example, the video fragment in Figure 15 shows two clinicians doing a ward round while using the patient bed to organize and collate all the paper forms stored in the PMR and in the tablet computer. The micro-mobility associated with this specific operation configuration, thus includes digital devices that can essentially be handled similar to another paper artifact while providing a portal into the EHR. As concluded by Bossen and Jensen:

> *"Collaborative overview requires a display that can be shared by two or more people in the many ad hoc conversations that take place, for example a display that can be carried and handed around like paper (like the printed lists), providing essential overview, but also making it possible to go into specifics"* [9][p. 11].

How the device contextualizes, integrates and visualizes large, complex and specialized EHRs to achieve *seamless integration* remains an important open question [14]. Nevertheless, HyPR can be used as a long term *stable concept* for a gradual movement towards a higher degree of integration and a less paper-centric hospital.

Mutual Awareness

Paper is not only easy to annotate and manipulate, but also provides an intrinsic historical account on these actions or changes [36]. Physical records are extensively used in achieving workplace awareness [6] in a hospital setting, as also evident in our studies of the PMR and HyPR. For example, the PMRs shown in figure 4 are deliberately placed on this desk to signal the hand-over from the nurse to the doctor. And, while using the HyPR record, clinicians positioned the HyPR in various ways (e.g., in the patient bed) to signal a status change, as seen in the video fragment in Figure 11. Similarly, clinicians were able to monitor places to pick up awareness information on status changes. For example, monitoring the printer in the ward office for lab results, as well as the HyPR records in the out-tray for status changes (Figure 13). Mutual awareness is a collaborative affordance as the medical record should allow the creation and perception of awareness information through the physical artifact. The physical properties of a PMR allow for placement in different places and positions — something that the EHR does not. HyPR did not remove any of the original collaborative affordances of the PMR, but rather supports and amplifies existing ones. The colored lights, for example, were used as *signifiers* [31] that allowed clinicians to externalize work practices into signals that helped them to optimize and prioritize interaction with patients. As such, medical records — PMR, EHR or HyPR — should be designed with the affordance of mutual awareness in mind, thus, providing clinicians with tools to *configure awareness* [22].

CONCLUSION

Medical records are key in coordinating treatment and care of patients in modern hospitals. Historically, they were paper-based, but due to the increased digitizing of medical information, more and more patient information is stored in different medical information systems. This creates a situation in which clinicians need to maintain and use a double record consisting of both a paper-based and electronic part. A detailed field study of the use of such a double record in a large university hospital revealed that a paper-based medical record is key in the subtle coordination inside the ward as its physical form helps to both achieve local coordination and awareness, as well as facilitates micro- and macro-mobility. These results echo previous findings, but our study highlighted that these paper-based affordances are not transferred to the electronic medical record used in the hospital. Specifically, our study showed that managing the dual record introduces a number of configuration challenges related to managing, synchronizing, communicating and cross-referencing both versions of the record. Different technologies for bridging the gab between paper-based and digital records have been proposed and we did a detailed study of one particular technology called the HyPR device. The study was conducted in a simulated medical ward environment with 8 clinicians performing a set of scenarios. Although the study was limited to 8 clinicians, it already showed that the HyPR approach has the potential to function as a transitional artifact that helps integrate and synchronize paper-based and digital information while maintaining some of the benefits from both the paper-based and digital records. Based on these two studies we introduced the concept of collaborative affordances, which denotes a set of properties of physical devices and artifacts that supports collaboration. These collaborative affordance include: mobility and portability, collocated access, shared overview and mutual awareness. The concept of collaborative affordances can be used in the analysis and design of collaborative technologies.

ACKNOWLEDGMENTS

This work was supported by the EU Marie Curie Network iCareNet grant number 264738. Special thanks to Sanne Jensen for facilitating the medical simulation study. Mathias Schmidt, Thomas Snaidero and Vaidas Sirtautas helped implement and test the HyPR technology. We thank our anonymous reviewers, Evi Vlassaks and Paolo Tell for their feedback and helpful suggestions for the improvement of the manuscript.

REFERENCES

1. Ahmed, K., Jawad, M., Abboudi, M., Gavazzi, A., Darzi, A., Athanasiou, T., Vale, J., Khan, M. S., and Dasgupta, P. Effectiveness of procedural simulation in urology: a systematic review. *The Journal of urology 186*, 1 (2011), 26–34.
2. Arai, T., Aust, D., and Hudson, S. E. Paperlink: a technique for hyperlinking from real paper to electronic content. In *Proceedings of the ACM SIGCHI Conference on Human factors in computing systems*, ACM (1997), 327–334.
3. Bång, M., Larsson, A., and Eriksson, H. Nostos: A paper–based ubiquitous computing healthcare environment to support data capture and collaboration. In *AMIA Annual Symposium Proceedings*, vol. 2003, American Medical Informatics Association (2003), 46.
4. Bardram, J. E., and Bossen, C. Mobility work: The spatial dimension of collaboration at a hospital. *Computer Supported Cooperative Work (CSCW) 14*, 2 (2005), 131–160.
5. Bardram, J. E., and Bossen, C. A web of coordinative artifacts: collaborative work at a hospital ward. In *Proceedings of the 2005 international ACM SIGGROUP conference on Supporting group work*, ACM (2005), 168–176.
6. Bardram, J. E., and Hansen, T. R. Context-based workplace awareness. *Computer Supported Cooperative Work (CSCW) 19*, 2 (2010), 105–138.
7. Berg, M. Accumulating and coordinating: occasions for information technologies in medical work. *Computer Supported Cooperative Work (CSCW) 8*, 4 (1999), 373–401.
8. Berger, R. G., and Kichak, J. Computerized physician order entry: helpful or harmful? *Journal of the American Medical Informatics Association 11*, 2 (2004), 100–103.
9. Bossen, C., and Jensen, L. G. How physicians' achieve overview': a case-based study in a hospital ward. In *Proceedings of the 17th ACM conference on Computer supported cooperative work & social computing*, ACM (2014), 257–268.
10. Cabitza, F., Sarini, M., Simone, C., and Telaro, M. When once is not enough: the role of redundancy in a hospital ward setting. In *Proceedings of the 2005 international ACM SIGGROUP conference on Supporting group work*, ACM (2005), 158–167.
11. Chantler, C., Clarke, T., and Granger, R. Information technology in the english national health service. *JAMA 296*, 18 (2006), 2255–2258.
12. Chen, Y. Documenting transitional information in emr. In *Proceedings of the SIGCHI Conference on Human Factors in Computing Systems*, ACM (2010), 1787–1796.
13. Dykstra, R. H., Ash, J. S., Campbell, E., Sittig, D. F., Guappone, K., Carpenter, J., Richardson, J., Wright, A., and McMullen, C. Persistent paper: the myth of "going paperless". In *AMIA Annual Symposium Proceedings*, vol. 2009, American Medical Informatics Association (2009), 158.
14. Ellingsen, G., and Monteiro, E. A patchwork planet integration and cooperation in hospitals. *Computer Supported Cooperative Work (CSCW) 12*, 1 (2003), 71–95.
15. Fitzpatrick, G. Integrated care and the working record. *Health Informatics Journal 10*, 4 (2004), 291–302.
16. Fitzpatrick, G., and Ellingsen, G. A review of 25 years of cscw research in healthcare: contributions, challenges and future agendas. *Computer Supported Cooperative Work (CSCW) 22*, 4-6 (2013), 609–665.
17. Gaver, W. W. Technology affordances. In *Proceedings of the SIGCHI conference on Human factors in computing systems*, ACM (1991), 79–84.
18. Gibson, J. J. The theory of affordances. *Hilldale, USA* (1977).
19. Greenhalgh, T., Potts, H. W., Wong, G., Bark, P., and Swinglehurst, D. Tensions and paradoxes in electronic patient record research: A systematic literature review using the meta-narrative method. *Milbank Quarterly 87*, 4 (2009), 729–788.
20. Guimbretière, F. Paper augmented digital documents. In *Proceedings of the 16th annual ACM symposium on User interface software and technology*, ACM (2003), 51–60.
21. Harper, R., O'Hara, K., Sellen, A., and Duthie, D. Toward the paperless hospital? *British journal of anaesthesia 78*, 6 (1997), 762–767.
22. Heath, C., Svensson, M. S., Hindmarsh, J., Luff, P., and Vom Lehn, D. Configuring awareness. *Computer Supported Cooperative Work (CSCW) 11*, 3-4 (2002), 317–347.
23. Houben, S., Frost, M., and Bardram, J. Hypr device: Mobile support for hybrid patient records. In *Proceedings of the 2014 ACM international conference on Interactive tabletops and surfaces*, ACM (2014).
24. Jaspers, M. W. A comparison of usability methods for testing interactive health technologies: methodological aspects and empirical evidence. *International journal of medical informatics 78*, 5 (2009), 340–353.
25. Kaptelinin, V., and Nardi, B. Affordances in hci: toward a mediated action perspective. In *Proceedings of the SIGCHI Conference on Human Factors in Computing Systems*, ACM (2012), 967–976.
26. Kreijns, K., and Kirschner, P. A. The social affordances of computer-supported collaborative learning environments. In *Frontiers in Education Conference, 2001. 31st Annual*, vol. 1, IEEE (2001), T1F–12.

27. Liao, C., Guimbretière, F., and Hinckley, K. Papiercraft: a command system for interactive paper. In *Proceedings of the 18th annual ACM symposium on User interface software and technology*, ACM (2005), 241–244.

28. Luff, P., and Heath, C. Mobility in collaboration. In *Proceedings of the 1998 ACM conference on Computer supported cooperative work*, ACM (1998), 305–314.

29. Norman, D. A. *The psychology of everyday things*. Basic books, 1988.

30. Norman, D. A. Affordance, conventions, and design. *interactions 6*, 3 (1999), 38–43.

31. Norman, D. A. The way i see it signifiers, not affordances. *interactions 15*, 6 (2008), 18–19.

32. Østerlund, C. S. Documents in place: demarcating places for collaboration in healthcare settings. *Computer Supported Cooperative Work (CSCW) 17*, 2-3 (2008), 195–225.

33. Park, S. Y., and Chen, Y. Adaptation as design: Learning from an emr deployment study. In *Proceedings of the SIGCHI Conference on Human Factors in Computing Systems*, ACM (2012), 2097–2106.

34. Saleem, J. J., Russ, A. L., Justice, C. F., Hagg, H., Ebright, P. R., Woodbridge, P. A., and Doebbeling, B. N. Exploring the persistence of paper with the electronic health record. *International journal of medical informatics 78*, 9 (2009), 618–628.

35. Sands, D. Z., Rind, D. M., Vieira, C., and Safran, C. Can a large institution go paperless? *Studies in health technology and informatics 52* (1997), 60–63.

36. Sellen, A. J., and Harper, R. H. *The myth of the paperless office*. MIT press, 2002.

37. Tang, C., and Carpendale, S. Evaluating the deployment of a mobile technology in a hospital ward. In *Proceedings of the 2008 ACM conference on Computer supported cooperative work*, ACM (2008), 205–214.

38. Vyas, D., Chisalita, C. M., and Van Der Veer, G. C. Affordance in interaction. In *Proceedings of the 13th Eurpoean conference on Cognitive ergonomics: trust and control in complex socio-technical systems*, ACM (2006), 92–99.

39. Weibel, N., Ispas, A., Signer, B., and Norrie, M. C. Paperproof: a paper-digital proof-editing system. In *CHI'08 Extended Abstracts on Human Factors in Computing Systems*, ACM (2008), 2349–2354.

40. Winkler, C., Seifert, J., Reinartz, C., Krahmer, P., and Rukzio, E. Penbook: Bringing pen+ paper interaction to a tablet device to facilitate paper-based workflows in the hospital domain. In *Proceedings of the 2013 ACM international conference on Interactive tabletops and surfaces*, ACM (2013), 283–286.

41. Zamarripa, M. S., Gonzalez, V. M., and Favela, J. The augmented patient chart: Seamless integration of physical and digital artifacts for hospital work. In *Universal Access in Human-Computer Interaction. Applications and Services*. Springer, 2007, 1006–1015.

42. Zhang, J., and Patel, V. L. Distributed cognition, representation, and affordance. *Pragmatics & Cognition 14*, 2 (2006), 333–341.

43. Zhou, X., Ackerman, M. S., and Zheng, K. I just don't know why it's gone: maintaining informal information use in inpatient care. In *Proceedings of the SIGCHI Conference on Human Factors in Computing Systems*, ACM (2009), 2061–2070.

Visible but Unseen? A Workplace Study of Blood-Test Icons on Electronic Emergency-Department Whiteboards

Arnvør á Torkilsheyggi
Computer Science and Informatics
Roskilde University
Universitetsvej 1, 4000 Roskilde, Denmark
arnvoer@ruc.dk

Morten Hertzum
Royal School of Library and Information Science
University of Copenhagen
Birketinget 6, 2300 Copenhagen, Denmark
hertzum@acm.org

ABSTRACT
Studies have shown that whiteboards support much cooperative work by for example strengthening awareness, improving communication, and reducing mental workload. In line with these predominantly positive findings, an emergency department (ED) turned to its whiteboard to improve the coordination of its work with blood tests. We investigate this use of the whiteboard through observations and informal interviews in the ED and analyze the ability of the whiteboard to support coordination and awareness in the work with blood tests. Our findings show limitations in the ability of the whiteboard to support awareness in a setting where the users are (locally) mobile, specifically in regard to information that requires continuous monitoring. We do however also find that the whiteboard safeguarded the work with blood tests against some risks by making blood-test information socially visible.

Author Keywords
Electronic whiteboards; Healthcare; Blood tests.

ACM Classification Keywords
H.5.3 [Information Interfaces and Presentation]: Group and Organization Interfaces – Computer-supported cooperative work.

General Terms
Human Factors.

INTRODUCTION
Whiteboards support the coordination of much cooperative work by making information visible to collaborating actors and thereby facilitating awareness, communication, and joint scheduling [8, 27, 31, 34]. In emergency departments (EDs), electronic whiteboards are replacing dry-erase whiteboards, and studies show that the electronic whiteboards may strengthen the clinicians' overview of their work [17], improve their communication [33], and reduce their mental workload [12]. In line with these predominantly positive findings, an ED at a medium-sized hospital in Region Zealand, Denmark, turned to the vendor of their electronic whiteboards with the request to have icons showing the status of the blood tests added to the whiteboard. With this integration of the whiteboard and the laboratory system, the whiteboard was expected to improve awareness of the status of blood tests, shorten the response time to available blood-test results, and ensure that ED clinicians acknowledged having seen the results. Our study, conducted when the icons had been in use for about six months, shows however that the whiteboard icons did not have the intended effect.

On the basis of observations and informal interviews, we find that except during a few work procedures the blood-test information visualized on the whiteboard remained largely unseen by the ED clinicians. We consider this finding interesting because it speaks against the majority of whiteboard studies, which conclude that whiteboards serve an important coordinative function in much cooperative work [1, 2, 5, 8, 15, 22, 31, 33, 34]. By studying the coordination of blood-test results, our intention is therefore to contribute to a better understanding of the ability of the whiteboard to support coordination and thus to derive at some implications for the design and use of electronic whiteboards for supporting awareness and coordination. To understand the coordination of blood-test results in the ED, we focus on how clinicians attend to blood-test results and the technologies they use for this purpose. The focus on blood-test results is important, since studies show that between 1% and 75% of test results lack follow-up, with impacts ranging from no negative effect to patient death [11].

The work in the ED is conducted in cooperation with other departments in the hospital. For example, physicians from the medical department (MD) work some of their shifts in the ED and are responsible for the clinical part of the treatment of patients with medical problems. The MD physicians constitute the majority of physicians working in the ED and are highly dependent upon blood-test results in diagnosing and treating patients. In our observations in the ED, we focused on these physicians.

In the ED, electronic whiteboards were introduced in May 2011. The whiteboards are mounted on the wall in central locations in the ED. The basic layout of the whiteboards is a row for each patient, with columns displaying selected information about the patient, such as triage level, room, chief complaint, responsible nurse, responsible physician, and

CSCW '15, March 14–18 2015, Vancouver, BC, Canada
Copyright 2015 ACM 978-1-4503-2922-4/15/03...$15.00
http://dx.doi.org/10.1145/2675133.2675228

Figure 1: The electronic whiteboard.

current treatment activity (see Figure 1). The clinicians can interact with the system by tapping the wall-mounted touchscreens and by mouse and keyboard. A study conducted before the whiteboard was extended with blood-test icons showed that it was an important coordinative artifact in the ED [16].

The functionality of showing icons that visualize the blood-test process was added to the whiteboard in April 2012. The icons show the status of each patient's blood tests by means of color-coding. A blood test goes through four steps: ordered (blue), taken (yellow), results available (green, red, or red and flashing), and acknowledged (grey). The icon is green when results are within the normal range and red when results are abnormal. If a result is critically abnormal, the red icon flashes. Prior to the introduction of the blood-test icons, the clinicians in the ED used the laboratory system to look up information about blood tests. Information about blood tests can still be accessed in this way. The whiteboard icons aim to increase the clinicians' awareness of the status of blood tests by making information that the clinicians otherwise have to look up in the laboratory system readily available by means of visual cues. The ED is the only department with a whiteboard that shows blood-test icons. In the rest of the hospital, the laboratory system is the only way to access information about blood tests.

RELATED WORK

In the following, we account for related work on the role of whiteboards in supporting the coordination of cooperative work and highlight challenges in the work with blood tests.

The Role of Whiteboards in Supporting Coordination

Multiple studies have found that whiteboards support coordination and have emphasized different ways in which whiteboards provide this support [5, 8, 33, 34]. Some studies focus on the role of whiteboards when users meet to coordinate their activities. These studies, for example, find that large whiteboards promote collective reading and interpretation during clinical activities such as nursing handovers because they provide shared access to relevant information [8, 23]. Similarly, Whittaker and Schwarz [31] argue that the public visibility of the whiteboard they studied promoted individual and collaborative behaviors that improved the participants' joint scheduling and negotiation of how to balance the workload in their projects. Scupelli et al. [22] extend these findings by emphasizing the importance of the physical setting to the success of whiteboards in supporting ad hoc meetings. Whiteboards appear especially successful when they provide for at-a-glance reading in passing the whiteboard or provide a space in front of the whiteboard for users to confer with their colleagues [34].

Whiteboards also support asynchronous coordination, for example by bringing together information that was previously distributed across multiple people and places [12, 33]. Bjørn and Hertzum [8] argue that this bringing together of information on the whiteboard integrates information relevant to different staff groups. One of the characteristics of work in, for example, EDs is that it is difficult to plan activities according to a schedule. Therefore, ED clinicians have to synchronize their activities in an ongoing, ad hoc manner. Without a preset schedule to tell them what to do next, the clinicians rely on continually working out how to mesh their interdependent activities. To succeed in this articulation work [20], the clinicians need to maintain an overview of the current state of affairs in the ED. The transition from dry-erase to electronic whiteboards in EDs appears to improve the clinicians' overview of their work because information can be made available on distributed electronic whiteboards without the need for repeated manual entry [1], because electronic whiteboards can be interfaced with other clinical systems and automatically show information about, for example, laboratory tests [2], and because electronic whiteboards may, as a result, be accompanied by more patient-focused work practices [23]. In a systematic review of electronic ED whiteboards, Rasmussen [19] found that whiteboards had affected the work in EDs at multiple levels, but that the results were of a mixed and somewhat inconclusive nature. He therefore called for more research targeting the effects of implementing electronic whiteboards, for example studies of interface design and integration with other clinical systems. This call is similar to that of Hertzum and Simonsen [15] who contend that valuable lessons about the design and use of whiteboards can be acquired by extending the functionality of whiteboards and then studying the impact of their implementation on clinical work. Our study can contribute in such a manner.

The concept of overview is often linked with that of awareness [4, 18]. Though awareness has been studied extensively within the field of CSCW [13, 21], it still appears to be a challenge to describe the process of *arriving* at the state of overview. For example, Bossen and Jensen [9] found that although the studied physicians had an opinion about what information they needed to have confidence in their overview of their work, it was difficult for them to explain how they got, maintained, and interrelated this information. Bossen and Jensen [9] conclude that the process of achieving an overview should be viewed as an "actively pursued, reflective understanding of one or more patients' situation." Whiteboards may support clinicians in pursuing this understanding by making readily available information that otherwise has to be searched [5]. It is, however, a limitation of wall-mounted whiteboards that they "may go unnoticed if they are located off the beaten track" [22: 1778]. That is, whiteboards must be attended in order for the whiteboard information to support users in their work. While this statement is self-evident, it is not self-evident that whiteboards will be attended with sufficient consistency in a dynamic ED environment in which clinicians are locally mobile and may be away from the coordination centers of the ED for extended periods of time. This could suggest limitations in the types of information a whiteboard can be used to broadcast. Such limitations have however not been a focal point in existing studies, which instead have tended to document positive effects of whiteboards on cooperative work. The exceptions from this tendency are mainly studies finding that the shift from dry-erase to electronic whiteboards comes at a cost [7, 29].

Working with Blood Tests

Hawkins [14] reports evidence suggesting that the most error-prone parts of the blood-test process are before and after the blood test is in the laboratory for analysis. This evidence indicates that improvement efforts should target the patient departments that order the tests and receive the test results. According to Callen et al. [11] failure to follow up on test results is a critical issue. In an ED setting the reasons for such failures include the multiple people involved in the blood-test process and the complexity of aligning this process with patient trajectories [28]. The ED is a particularly challenging setting due to its high patient throughput, team-based care, unpredictable numbers of acute patients with urgent problems, and lack of continuous relationships between patients and clinicians [11, 32].

Physicians value to be alerted when new test results are available [6]. In continuation of this finding, systems that rely on clinicians to 'pull' information from the system are not sufficient [11], partly because critical results are overlooked and partly because clinicians waste time accessing the system in vain before the results are available. The alternative approach of 'pushing' information to physicians by means of alerts does, however, not ensure consistent follow-up on test results [25]. Physicians who receive a large number of alerts may, for example, experience alert fatigue and stop reacting promptly to alerts [24]. The diligence required of clinicians in order for them to attend quickly and consistently to new test results is also strained by the finding that the number of tests ordered differs considerably across clinicians, suggesting that much diagnostic testing may be unnecessary and warrant neither alerts nor the attention of clinicians [32].

METHOD

The present study was approved by the management of the ED and MD. The observed and interviewed clinicians were individually informed about the study and orally consented to take part.

Departments

The ED received 40-45,000 patients a year and consisted of a total of 21 patient rooms divided onto a fast-track area for walk-in patients, two acute areas for patients arriving by ambulance, and a long-term area. The ED employed 120 nurses and 13 full-time physicians. In addition to the full-time physicians, a number of physicians from other departments, in particular the MD, worked part of their shifts in the ED. Physicians from the MD were responsible for the clinical treatment of ED patients with medical problems but the ED retained responsibility for the overall organization of work in the ED.

The MD consisted of four wards and a number of outpatient clinics. We focused on the ward for respiratory medicine, the ward for cardiac medicine, and the ward for gastroenterological medicine.

Procedure

We conducted an ethnographic study in which the blood-test processes in the ED and MD were investigated by means of observation and informal interviews. The observations consisted of shadowing mainly medical physicians in the ED and in the MD for periods of a couple of hours at a time as they went about their work. Shadowing the medical physicians in different contexts allowed for the observer to get an overall understanding of the physicians' evolving tasks and a more specific understanding of how the work with blood tests was integrated into their clinical work and to what extent the whiteboard and, specifically, the icons supported these activities. The shadowed physicians also consented to answering questions about the work they were performing, thereby explaining individual activities, clarifying relations among activities, and offering informed opinions. To increase our understanding of the work with blood tests in the ED, we similarly shadowed a number of other clinicians. The observations in the ED consisted of shadowing three junior physicians (i.e., residents) working full-time in the ED and two nurses. In addition, we also observed three instances of a practice the clinicians referred to as timeouts. During a timeout, which lasts 10-15 minutes, the clinicians gather around the whiteboard to discuss the admitted patients. In total, the observations of medical physicians and the other clinicians in the ED amounted to 19 hours, spread across the day shift. In addition, informal interviews were conducted with one chief physician, two surgical physicians working their shift in the ED, two nurses, two laboratory technicians, a coordinating nurse, a triage nurse, and a secretary. These informal interviews mainly served the purpose of elaborating upon the observations and verifying our findings.

To increase our understanding of the medical physicians' work, we performed supplementary observations in the MD. These observations amounted to 9 hours in total and took place during the ward rounds and during a practice we will refer to as the end-of-shift check, where senior physicians before ending their shifts checked for blood tests lacking follow-up. We chose these observation periods in the MD because most follow-up on blood tests took place during these periods.

All observations and interviews were conducted by the first author and documented in real time in detailed notes. In our analysis, we first read through our data from the observations and interviews and divided them into initial categories. These categories included issues to do with maintaining an overview, the frequent interruptions, and understanding when and for what purposes the whiteboard icons were used. The overall theme that emerged from the analysis concerned the activities for which clinicians needed to be aware of blood-test information and the extent to which the whiteboard icons supported this awareness. In the following section, we therefore structure our results according to the identified activities and describe to what extent the whiteboard and the icons in particular supported the clinicians' coordination and awareness of the information of blood tests.

RESULTS

Using the Whiteboard to Gain an Overview

When the physicians from the MD worked in the ED, they were working together with clinicians from other departments in the aim to treat and care for acute patients. Some of these clinicians were permanent ED staff (nurses and physicians), while others, like the physicians from the MD, represented the specialty of their base department. The physicians from the MD thus had to collaborate with a multitude of other clinicians, who were responsible for various tasks in the patients' trajectory through the hospital. This entailed considerable coordination in order for them to gain an overview of who was responsible for which patients, at what time, and to know when to perform the tasks for which they were responsible. The two examples that follow show how they used the electronic whiteboard as their main artifact in gaining this overview.

When patients arrived to the ED, they were assessed by a triage nurse in order to determine the priority of their treatment based on the acuteness of their condition. In addition to this assessment, the triage nurse also assessed which resources to call upon, typically, whether the patient should be examined by a medical or a surgical physician. After completing her/his assessment, the triage nurse updated the patient's information on the whiteboard with a label indicating, whether the patient was 'surgical' or 'medical'. From this point the whiteboard displayed the patient as the responsibility of either the physicians from the MD or the physicians from the surgical department. Whereas the organization of work in the ED thus aimed at distinguishing between a medical and a surgical track for the patients, it was however clear that in practice these tracks were interwoven in several ways. Physicians from different hospital entities were dependent upon the same resources (nurses, equipment, specialists, beds etc.) and even though they were present in the ED as representatives for a specific specialty, they shared responsibilities for several activities in the ED.

One of these activities was the supervision of junior physicians. Before choosing their medical specialty, junior physicians take their basic clinical training (in Danish: KBU) at different departments. In the ED, the junior physicians can get medical experience while working under the supervision of senior physicians. The junior physicians received this training by performing an initial examination of the less acute patients and documenting this examination in the patient record. When the junior physician finished this task, s/he updated the patient's information on the whiteboard to indicate that the patient was ready to be examined by a senior physician. While the junior physicians typically performed this initial examination on their own, we did however observe several cases, where the junior physicians sought senior physicians to ask for their advice on how to interpret results and observations. When the physicians from the MD worked in the ED, they also participated in this activity of supervising the junior physicians. In one of our observations, a medical physician was going back and forth between four or five patients, and then suddenly went looking for a junior physician, because he had noticed that another patient's pulse was critically high and he wanted to make sure that the responsible junior physician was taking care of it. Our field notes read: *"He goes searching for the responsible junior physician and finds her as she is leaving the conference room. They sit down and start talking about the patient, what symptoms to look for and how to treat them."*

The ED is thus a setting, where many activities take place simultaneously. The medical physicians used the whiteboard as their main artifact for navigating among these activities and maintaining an overview of which patients to examine next. When they approached the whiteboard, they stated that they were mainly looking for two things: which patients were medical, and whether the junior physician had completed the initial examination.

Approaching the Whiteboard in Between Patients

The medical physicians' primary activity in the ED is to treat and stabilize medical patients and in this process their main goal is to arrive at a conclusion about whether the patients are well enough to be discharged or they need to be transferred to other departments for further treatment. When the physicians in our observations approached the whiteboard, it was primarily when they had reached such a decision and therefore needed an overview of which patient to examine next. Like in the following example, where a physician approached the whiteboard after having devised a plan for a patient: *"The physician explains that he uses the whiteboard to see which patients have been labeled as medical patients. For two of these patients he can see that they are still being examined by the junior physicians. He will not see to them until the junior physicians have finished their examination."* He then changed the status for another patient on the whiteboard to indicate that he was taking responsibility for this patient, wrote the patient's social security number in a little notebook, and sat down by a computer to prepare for the examination. He then accessed the patient's record in the electronic patient record (EPR) system and read previous notes about the patient's condition and medical history. In this process he also accessed the laboratory system through a menu in the EPR system to check for new blood-test results.

This observation was verified by similar observations of other medical physicians. The physicians approached the whiteboard in between patients to gain an overview of what to do next, but we never saw them approach the whiteboard with the sole purpose of attending the blood-test icons. Rather, they chose to sit down to prepare for the examination and in this process they accessed the laboratory system to check for and evaluate blood-test results. One of the medical physicians in our observation stated that because a great deal of her time was used on coordination with nurses, medical students, junior physicians, other departments, transferals and so forth, she felt that she was struggling to complete the treatment of her patients and reach a decision about whether to discharge or transfer them. Her struggle to maintain a focus on the treatment of individual patients also affected how she managed the blood-test results and what technology she chose to use for this purpose. She explained that to her it would seem like just another interruption, if she had to regularly approach the whiteboard to keep an eye on the icons: *"When I sit down, I check for test results"*. Constantly monitoring the icons on the whiteboard was seen as an interruption to her primary activity of finishing the treatment of patients. She therefore integrated the evaluation of blood-test results with the treatment of the individual patients, that is by attending to blood-test results while she prepared for her examination of the patient.

Activities that Require Immediate Attention

Though the medical physicians in most cases strived to align their evaluation of blood-test results with their preparation for the examination of individual patients, there were two activities that required them to perform an immediate evaluation of blood-test results: to follow-up on critical results and to secure free beds for arriving patients.

In the case of critical results, the icon on the whiteboard flashes to indicate that the results require immediate attention. However, it was clear that the clinicians did not monitor the whiteboard closely for flashing icons. In one of our observations, we asked a clinician about who was responsible for attending to an icon that had been flashing for a while. One of the nurses replied that it was primarily the nurses, who noticed the flashing icons, but they would then try to find the responsible physician. In an interview, a nurse however stated that a flashing icon did not always require immediate attention: *"A flashing icon is not necessarily life threatening. Sometimes it is just one of the values in the test that is slightly off. So we do not always react promptly. We know that the laboratory will call us on the phone, if the results are critical."* They therefore relied more on the procedure that the laboratory in these cases is required to phone the ED to inform them about the results. It is primarily nurses in the ED, who receive these calls, whereafter they forward the information to the right physician.

Whereas the medical physicians were highly engaged in the treatment of medical patients, they also had to engage in the activity of securing the flow of patients through the ED. This activity was about managing the flow of patients through the ED and securing free beds for the unpredictable numbers of patients that would be arriving. Because the physicians prioritized the treatment of the most acute patients, less acute patients would sometimes be waiting and thereby occupying a bed, until the physician had time to complete the examination and reach a decision about the patient. In one of our observations, one of the admitting nurses even stated: *"That is the problem with less acute patients. If the patient had been more critical, the physicians would have more focus on the patient."* In several of our observations, we observed how the medical physician would inform the nurses that a patient could be discharged, if the results of a laboratory test came back normal. Because the nurses were aware that the physicians often awaited the results of blood tests before reaching a decision about what should happen to the patient, they saw the arrival of new test results as an opportunity to notify the physicians and thereby get the physician to attend to these patients. When the nurses approached the whiteboards to update information about patients, we observed how they also used these opportunities to attend to the blood-test icons and then inform the physicians about available blood-test results.

Thus, in the case of critical results or if the flow in the ED was under pressure, the medical physician had to be interrupted to perform an immediate evaluation of blood-test results. It was however clear that the whiteboard was not sufficient in calling the physicians' attention to critical results. Even though there were clinicians in the proximity of the whiteboard, who could see the flashing icons, they would rather rely on having the laboratory calling the nurses, when the results were of such a nature that they warranted the physicians' prompt attention. When the patient flow was under pressure, the physicians relied on having the nurses inform them of the availability of results about less-critical patients, who in most cases could be discharged from the ED. Notably, in both of these cases, the clinicians reported that it was most likely the nurses, who would notice the changing colors of the icons.

Using the Whiteboard at Timeouts

Whereas most of the coordination in the ED happened continually and in an ad hoc manner, we did observe one scheduled practice (the timeouts), where the clinicians met to discuss the overall status of the department. Timeouts were held up to four times a day and lasted 10-15 minutes. During a timeout the clinicians met by the whiteboard (see Figure 2) and walked through the patients in the ED. If at all possible, medical and surgical physicians had to suspend their treatment of their patients to participate in the timeout. The ED nurses and the junior physicians also participated. As the following excerpt from our observations illustrates the clinicians, in walking through the patients, repeatedly made reference to the whiteboard information. *"Two physicians are standing in front of the whiteboard. One of them, the chief physician, asks, if everyone is ready. He then starts to talk about the first patient on the whiteboard (the top row); they are waiting for blood-test results. If they come back normal, the patient can be discharged. He then points to the second row and mentions the name of the next patient. Another physician takes over and informs the others of his treatment of the patient. The chief physician offers advice about what can be done."* During another timeout, the chief physician on two occasions tapped on the blood-test icons on the whiteboard. This action prompted the opening of a pop-up window displaying the values of the blood-test results, thereby opening up to a collective evaluation of the results. This activity also provided an opportunity for junior physicians to seek advice on how to interpret test results and for senior physicians to provide advice on additional possibilities to consider. We also observed how the chief physician delegated relevant tasks to the junior physicians, and the more experienced physicians offered them advice on how to perform these tasks.

Figure 2: Timeout in front of the whiteboard.

The timeout was the only incident, where we observed physicians actually tapping on icons to view blood-test results. A junior physician explained that apart from during timeouts she would not use the whiteboard to evaluate tests, because she did not want to disturb others that wanted to look at the whiteboard and because she saw her individual evaluation of the results as a task that should be performed on a personal computer. Outside of the timeouts the physicians only made changes to the whiteboard, when they updated the whiteboard with information about their own activities. They never used the whiteboard to look up additional information about blood-test results but, instead, used a personal computer to look up such information in the laboratory system.

Negotiating the Clinical Relevance of Acknowledgement

In the studied hospital, it was a formal requirement that all tests should be acknowledged. This requirement had been introduced to prevent that blood-test results were missed or neglected. One of the aims of introducing icons on the ED whiteboard was to increase the physicians' awareness of

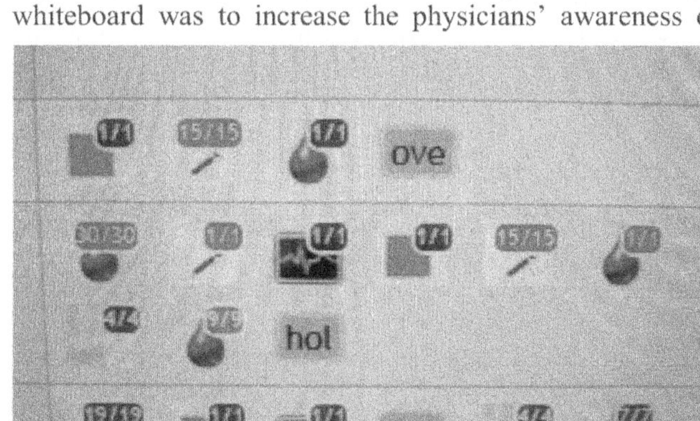

Figure 3: Whiteboard icons with colors indicating their status.

blood-test results that needed to be acknowledged. A red or green icon indicated that the blood-test results had not yet been acknowledged, a grey icon that the results had been acknowledged (see Figure 3). During our observations it was however apparent that the physicians were confronted with several challenges in regard to integrating the requirement to acknowledge blood-test results with the clinical activity of evaluating the test results.

Though test results were evaluated during timeouts, they were never acknowledged during this practice. There were at least two reasons for this. First, while the whiteboard provided for evaluating blood-test results, it was not possible to acknowledge test results on the whiteboard. Second, a chief physician in the ED stated that timeouts were primarily a collaborative activity, and the acknowledgement of test results should be performed by individual physicians in the course of treating individual patients. We observed several instances of medical physicians acknowledging results in the laboratory system while they were sitting by the computer and preparing for examining their patients, but they clearly did not acknowledge all test results. The observed physicians provided several explanations for omitting to acknowledge test results. In one of our observations, a physician stated that she would not acknowledge the results, because some of the multiple values in the test were still missing. In another, a lesser-experienced physician stated that he would not acknowledge a test result, because he was concerned that if he did then a more experienced physician would not examine the results. In both of these cases, the physicians appeared unwilling to comply with the requirement to acknowledge test results, because it clashed with their primary activity of ensuring competent treatment of the patients.

In the Medical Department, the management had implemented a practice (the end-of-shift check), where the senior physicians, before ending their shifts, took turns to acknowledge the blood-test results that had not been acknowledged during the ward rounds. However, several medical physicians in our study stated that they felt that the acknowledgement of blood-test results mostly served managerial purposes. This was also recognized by the head of the Medical Department, who during an initial meeting with us stated: *"It is not the acknowledgement that is important to the clinicians. Rather, their concern is to perform a proper evaluation, which can then lead to a better treatment of the patients."*

When a patient leaves the ED, the information about the patient disappears from the whiteboard and there is, consequently, no visual reminder to help the physicians remember to acknowledge blood-test results. At the time of our study, the ED had not implemented any practice to ensure any form of follow-up on blood-test results for patients that had left the ED. If the ED physicians do not follow up on these test results, the requirement to follow up on and acknowledge them is propagated to the physicians in the receiving department. In one of our observations at the Medical Department, we observed how the blood-test results that had been ordered by the ED had not been acknowledged: *"The medical physician accesses the patient's blood tests. Some of the tests have not been acknowledged – including some from the ED. 'This happens frequently!' the physician says."* This finding points to challenges in managing the blood-test results of patients that are transferred to other departments, and emphasizes that these challenges have not been managed simply by providing the physicians with access to the blood-test results of transferred patients.

DISCUSSION

The aim of the ED in introducing the blood-test icons on the whiteboard was to improve the ED clinicians' awareness of the status of blood tests, shorten their response time to available blood-test results, and ensure that they acknowledged having seen the results. While related work generally finds that whiteboards succeed in supporting awareness and coordination, the present study has shown that the blood-test icons on the studied whiteboard were rarely attended by the physicians.

The Whiteboard Is Not Continuously Monitored

To improve the ED physicians' awareness of the status of blood tests and shorten their response time to available results, the physicians must continuously monitor the whiteboard. Continuous monitoring is, however, at odds with ED work.

First, ED physicians are locally mobile and, thus, away from the centrally located whiteboard for considerable periods of time to attend their patients. In accordance with previous studies [22, 34] we find that the whiteboard supports the clinicians in gaining an at-a-glance overview when they pass by the whiteboard, but such ad hoc scanning of the whiteboard is very different from continuous monitoring. Without continuous monitoring the changed status of a blood test will not be noticed until a clinician passes by and attends the whiteboard, not even if the icon is flashing.

Second, ED clinicians face many interruptions and, consequently, work to receive interruptions when they disrupt the least. Previous work shows that ED clinicians are interrupted as much as an average of 15 times an hour [26], often with the result that they fail to return to the interrupted task or hasten to complete it to compensate for the time 'lost' in interruption [30]. We find that the physicians seek to attend to one patient at a time; that is, to complete their current examination of a patient before they turn to the next patient. To do so they do not attend to blood-test icons for their other patients until they have completed their current patient and need to decide whom to attend next. Attending to the blood-test icons in between patients is consistent with studies suggesting that the cost of being interrupted is lower at the boundary between tasks than in the middle of a task [3]. However, this strategy means deliberately avoiding a continuous monitoring of the whiteboard and, thereby, postponing the response to available blood-test results.

Third, in an ED setting many blood tests have become irrelevant before their results arrive because the patient's condition has changed or the physicians' understanding of it has evolved. For example, Torkilsheyggi et al. [28] report that predefined sets of blood tests are ordered by the admitting ED nurse. While that practice aims to avoid delays waiting for test results, it also means that the tests are ordered before a physician has assessed which tests are needed to diagnose the patient, thereby risking that many of the tests are irrelevant. When general experience, or concrete knowledge about a specific patient, shows that blood-test results have often been superseded by other developments when they arrive, physicians become less preoccupied with remaining minutely aware of the status of blood tests. This reinforces the strategy of attending to the blood-test icons in between patients rather than doing it continuously.

Fourth, to see the actual blood-test results the physicians need to tap on the icons to open a pop-up window. The physicians are however reluctant to perform such interactions at the whiteboard because they perceive it as occupying, though only briefly, an artifact intended for shared use with information relevant only to their individual needs. Therefore, the physicians normally look up the actual blood-test results by accessing the laboratory system from a desktop computer rather than via the icons on the wall-mounted whiteboard. This practice contributes further to making the whiteboard less important to how the physicians attend to blood tests.

The Status of Blood Tests Becomes Socially Visible

While the physicians do not continuously monitor the whiteboard for changes in the status of blood tests, the icons have made the status of blood tests socially visible. In the laboratory system, information about blood tests is only visible to the physician looking it up for a specified patient. On the whiteboard, the status of all blood tests is visible to all clinicians. We emphasize three implications of this social visibility.

First, the arrival of test results has become visible to the nurses. This visibility has affected the interactions between the activities of treating the patients and of maintaining the flow of patients through the ED. When the nurses need to free beds in the ED to make room for new patients, they keep an eye on the arrival of blood-test results. Upon their arrival a nurse alerts the physician responsible for the patient to the possibility – and need – of completing the treatment of the patient and freeing the bed. This use of the blood-test icons illustrates that the whiteboard serves and meshes a multiplicity of practices [8]. In addition to supporting the nurses in maintaining the flow of patients through the ED, the nurses' alertness to the blood-test icons in these situations also supports the physicians in their strategy of restricting their own attention to the blood-test icons to the periods in between patients. When this strategy conflicts with the activity of maintaining the flow, the nurses will alert the physicians of new blood-test results.

Second, the blood-test information is routinely attended at the timeouts during which the physicians suspend patient treatment to walk through the currently admitted patients. The timeouts is one of very few standard procedures that involve the ED physicians as a group, and it evolves around the content of the whiteboard. The introduction of the blood-test icons has made blood tests more prominent during the timeouts, and in this collaborative context the physicians make frequent use of the possibility to tap on an icon to see details about the results of the test. This way, the blood-test icons have changed the timeouts from a discussion based on one physician's reading (ahead of the timeout) of the blood tests toward one of collective reading and interpretation by the physicians at the timeout. Simonsen and Hertzum [23] have previously reported a similar effect of a large, shared display on nursing shift handovers.

Third, while it might be expected that the social visibility of unacknowledged blood tests would increase the physicians' impetus to acknowledge having seen test results, this has not happened. One explanation for the absence of such an effect is that it is, at present, not possible to acknowledge test results on the whiteboard. Other explanations include that the physicians may act on test results without acknowledging having seen the results, thereby reducing the acknowledgement to a formal requirement of importance to quality management but not to the physicians' primary activity of patient treatment. This explanation is reinforced by the procedure that the laboratory must phone the ED whenever a blood test yields critically abnormal results. Receiving this information consistently on the phone makes it even safer for the physicians not to monitor the whiteboard continuously and not to worry a lot about unacknowledged blood tests. A supplementary explanation for the many blood tests that remain unacknowledged may be that patients disappear from the whiteboard when they leave the ED. Because most patients are only in the ED for a few hours, unacknowledged blood tests tend to disappear from view quite quickly. In the MD, where patients stay longer and their condition evolves more slowly, the end-of-shift check provides a procedure for avoiding unacknowledged blood-test results. Notably, the medical physicians' care in attending to the acknowledgement of test results in the MD did not transfer to their shifts in the ED.

Implications for the Design and Use of Whiteboards

Our study has five implications that extend previous work on the design and use of whiteboards for supporting awareness and coordination. First, whiteboards do not seem to be effective at supporting continual awareness of time-critical information in settings where participants are locally mobile. Rather, whiteboards appear useful for supporting information needs that are periodic, such as between patients (for physicians) and when beds need to be cleared (for nurses). This distinguishes settings like EDs from settings with the characteristics of a control room, in which people can be expected to monitor whiteboards near continuously.

Second, whiteboards are perceived as shared artifacts and should build on this perception by aiming to enhance cooperative practices such as timeouts. In contrast, users should not be expected to perform individual tasks at the whiteboard, unless they are trivial and very brief. The primary type of individual use appears to be at-a-glance reading.

Third, by making information socially visible, whiteboards can serve to create safeguards against individual persons' oversights as well as opportunities for coordination of seemingly conflicting activities. While it may be tempting in the planning of future design initiatives to consider sending blood-test information directly to the physician responsible for the specific patient (e.g., by text messages on a smartphone), it must be considered that such an approach does not make information socially visible and necessitates replacements of the practices that rely on this visibility.

Fourth, by making information socially visible whiteboards support ad hoc coordination well but the social visibility is likely insufficient to foster consistent compliance with formal requirements, especially if the visibility is transient. The MD illustrates that the consistent acknowledgement of having seen blood-test results is dependent on enforced procedures and does not require a whiteboard.

Fifth, it might seem banal to point out that even if a whiteboard makes information visible, it cannot be taken for granted that clinicians will see the information. It appears, however, that the effect expected from the blood-test icons presupposes that the clinicians continuously monitor the whiteboard. This misunderstanding could, probably, have been avoided if the design of the icons had been informed by an ethnographic study of the work in the ED. Although it is an often-made point in CSCW studies that technologies are designed without taking work practices into account [10], our study suggests that it is a point still worth making.

CONCLUSION

In the studied ED, blood-test icons were introduced on the whiteboard to improve awareness of the evolving status of blood tests, shorten response time to available results, and ensure that clinicians acknowledged having seen the results. However, the physicians did not attend appreciably to the icons, except at timeouts and in between patients. The main reasons were that continuously monitoring the whiteboard for changes in the status of blood tests was incompatible with the physicians' local mobility and the high number of interruptions they already experienced. As a result, the icons had little effect on the work activities performed by the physicians individually. Instead, the social visibility of the blood-test information on the whiteboard facilitated coordination between clinicians who were otherwise engaged in seemingly separate activities. It, for example, improved the timeouts by providing for collective reading of test results, thereby incorporating the supervision of junior physicians better in the activity of patient treatment. It also facilitated the coordination between patient treatment and the activity of maintaining the flow of patients through the ED. In spite of the social visibility of the icons many blood tests remained unacknowledged.

ACKNOWLEDGEMENTS

This study was co-funded by Region Zealand as part of the Clinical Communication project. Thor Brygge approved the observations and interviews at the Medical Department. We want to thank Gustav From, who participated in the planning of the study and facilitated access to the ED and the MD. Special thanks are due to the observed and interviewed clinicians.

REFERENCES

1. Abujudeh, H.H., Kaewlai, R., Kodsi, S.E., and Hamill, M.E. Improving quality of communications in emergency radiology with a computerized whiteboard system. *Clinical Radiology 65*, 1 (2010), 56–62.
2. Aronsky, D., Jones, I., Lanaghan, K., and Slovis, C.M. Supporting patient care in the emergency department with a computerized whiteboard system. *Journal of the American Medical Informatics Association 15*, 2 (2008), 184–194.
3. Bailey, B.P. and Iqbal, S.T. Understanding changes in mental workload during execution of goal-directed tasks and its application for interruption management. *ACM Transactions on Computer-Human Interaction 14*, 4 (2008), 21:1–21:28.
4. Bardram, J.E. and Bossen, C. Mobility work: The spatial dimension of collaboration at a hospital. *Computer Supported Cooperative Work 14*, 2 (2005), 131–160.
5. Bardram, J.E., Hansen, T.R., and Soegaard, M. AwareMedia - A shared interactive display supporting social, temporal, and spatial awareness in surgery. *Proc. CSCW'06*, ACM Press (2006), 109–118.
6. Batley, N.J., Osman, H.O., Kazzi, A.A., and Musallam, K.M. Implementation of an emergency department computer system: Design features that users value. *The Journal of Emergency Medicine 41*, 6 (2011), 693–700.
7. Bisantz, A., Pennathur, P., Guarrera, T.K., Fairbanks, R.J., Perry, S.J., Zwemer, F., and Wears, R.L. Emergency department status boards: A case study in information systems transition. *Journal of Cognitive Engineering and Decision Making 4*, 1 (2010), 39–68.
8. Bjørn, P. and Hertzum, M. Artefactual multiplicity: A study of emergency-department whiteboards. *Computer Supported Cooperative Work 20,* 1&2 (2011), 93–121.
9. Bossen, C. and Jensen, L.G. How physicians 'achieve overview': A case-based study in a hospital ward. *Proc. CSCW'14*, ACM Press (2014), 257–268.

10. Bowers, J., Button, G., and Sharrock, W. Workflow from within and without: Technology and cooperative work on the print industry shopfloor. *Proc. ECSCW'95*, Kluwer (1995), 51–66.

11. Callen, J., Georgiou, A., Li, J., and Westbrook, J.I. The safety implications of missed test results for hospitalised patients: A systematic review. *Quality & Safety in Health Care 20*, 2 (2011), 194–209.

12. France, D.J., Levin, S., Hemphill, R., Chen, K., Rickard, D., Makowski, R., Jones, I., and Aronsky, D. Emergency physicians' behaviors and workload in the presence of an electronic whiteboard. *International Journal of Medical Informatics 74*, 10 (2005), 827–837.

13. Gross, T. Supporting effortless coordination: 25 years of awareness research. *Computer Supported Cooperative Work 22*, 4-6 (2013), 425–474.

14. Hawkins, R. Managing the pre- and post-analytical phases of the total testing process. *Annals of Laboratory Medicine 32*, 1 (2012), 5–16.

15. Hertzum, M. and Simonsen, J. Work-practice changes associated with an electronic emergency department whiteboard. *Health Informatics Journal 19*, 1 (2013), 46–60.

16. Hertzum, M. and Simonsen, J. Effects of electronic emergency-department whiteboards on clinicians' time distribution and mental workload. *Health Informatics Journal*, (in press).

17. Hertzum, M. Electronic emergency-department whiteboards: A study of clinicians' expectations and experiences. *International Journal of Medical Informatics 80*, 9 (2011), 618–630.

18. Hornbæk, K. and Hertzum, M. The notion of overview in information visualization. *International Journal of Human-Computer Studies 69*, 7-8 (2011), 509–525.

19. Rasmussen, R. Electronic whiteboards in emergency medicine: A systematic review. *Proc. IHI'12*, ACM Press (2012), 483–492.

20. Schmidt, K. and Bannon, L. Taking CSCW seriously: Supporting articulation work. *Computer Supported Cooperative Work 1*, 1-2 (1992), 7–40.

21. Schmidt, K. The problem with 'awareness.' *Computer Supported Cooperative Work 11*, 3 (2002), 285–298.

22. Scupelli, P.G., Xiao, Y., Fussell, S.R., Kiesler, S., and Gross, M.D. Supporting coordination in surgical suites: Physical aspects of common information spaces. *Proc. CHI'10*, ACM Press (2010), 1777–1786.

23. Simonsen, J. and Hertzum, M. Iterative participatory design. In J. Simonsen, J.. Bærenholdt, M. Büscher and J.. Scheuer, eds., *Design Research: Synergies from Interdisciplinary Perspectives*. Routledge, 2010, 16–32.

24. Singh, H., Wilson, L., Reis, B., Sawhney, M.K., Espadas, D., and Sittig, D.F. Ten strategies to improve management of abnormal test result alerts in the electronic health record. *Journal of Patient Safety 6*, 2 (2010), 121–123.

25. Sittig, D.F. and Singh, H. Improving test result follow-up through electronic health records requires more than just an alert. *Journal of General Internal Medicine 27*, 10 (2012), 1235–1237.

26. Spencer, R., Coiera, E., and Logan, P. Variation in communication loads on clinical staff in the emergency department. *Annals of Emergency Medicine 44*, 3 (2004), 268–273.

27. Tang, A., Lanir, J., Greenberg, S., and Fels, S. Supporting transitions in work: Informing large display application design by understanding whiteboard use. *Proc. GROUP'09*, ACM Press (2009), 149–158.

28. Torkilsheyggi, A. á, Hertzum, M., and From, G. Whiteboard icons to support the blood-test process in an emergency department: An observational study of temporal patterns. *Studies in Health Technology and Informatics 192* (2013), 303–307.

29. Wears, R.L., Perry, S.J., Shapiro, M., Beach, C., Croskerry, P., and Behara, R. A comparison of manual and electronic status boards in the emergency department: What's gained and what's lost? *Proc. HFES Annual Meeting*, HFES (2003), 1415–1419.

30. Westbrook, J., Coiera, E., Dunsmuir, W.T.M., Brown, B.M., Kelk, N., Paoloni, R., and Tran, C. The impact of interruptions on clinical task completion. *Quality & Safety in Health Care 19*, 4 (2010), 284–289.

31. Whittaker, S. and Schwarz, H. Meetings of the board: The impact of scheduling medium on long term group coordination in software development. *Computer Supported Cooperative Work 8*, 3 (1999), 175–205.

32. Wilson, G.A., McDonald, C.J., and McCabe, G.P. The effect of immediate access to a computerized medical record on physician test ordering: A controlled clinical trial in the emergency room. *American Journal of Public Health 72*, 7 (1982), 698–702.

33. Wong, H.J., Caesar, M., Bandali, S., Agnew, J., and Abrams, H. Electronic inpatient whiteboards: Improving multidisciplinary communication and coordination of care. *International Journal of Medical Informatics 78*, 4 (2009), 239–247.

34. Xiao, Y., Lasome, C., Moss, J., Mackenzie, C.F., and Faraj, S. Cognitive properties of a whiteboard: A case study in a trauma centre. *Proc. ECSCW'01*, Kluwer (2001), 259–278.

Comparing Health Information Sharing Preferences of Cancer Patients, Doctors, and Navigators

Maia Jacobs, James Clawson, Elizabeth D. Mynatt
College of Computing
Georgia Institute of Technology
Atlanta, GA 30332, USA
mjacobs30@gatech.edu, {jamer, mynatt}@cc.gatech.edu

ABSTRACT

As technologies such as personal health records and symptom trackers become more common, we are seeing an increase in patients actively engaging in health tracking behaviors. Patient collected data can provide valuable insight for healthcare providers, particularly in the area of breast cancer. Thus far, little work has examined whether the health information that patients are willing to track and share aligns with the information needs of healthcare providers. Our work provides a comparison between the health information sharing preferences of breast cancer patients, doctors and navigators. We identify discrepancies between stakeholders' preferences, such as patients' hesitation to share feelings of loneliness, signifying where technology can play an important role in helping patients prioritize the health information shared with providers. We present design implications from this work to guide the development of future health information sharing tools that consider the differing needs of healthcare stakeholders.

Author Keywords

Health Tracking; Physician-Patient Communication; Cancer Care; Cancer Navigation

ACM Classification Keywords

H.5.3 Group and Organization Interfaces: Collaborative computing, Organizational design; J.3 Life and Medical Sciences: Health, Medical Information Systems

INTRODUCTION

Personal health tracking is changing the landscape of healthcare. Patient-centered tools such as personal health records (PHRs), and symptom trackers are allowing people to actively engage in their personal healthcare. With these changing practices, health systems have the opportunity to utilize patient collected data to tailor and improve the care provided to their patients.

CSCW '15, March 14 – 18, 2015, Vancouver, BC, Canada.

ACM 978-1-4503-2922-4/15/03...$15.00.
http://dx.doi.org/10.1145/2675133.2675252

Breast cancer care provides one area of healthcare that could greatly benefit from patients tracking and sharing health information. Cancer care is often modified for individual patients and one's symptoms and side effects can heavily influence the treatment plan [7]. Cancer treatment can often encompass a complex trajectory, distributed across multiple healthcare organizations. Thus, patients become responsible for communicating vital health data to help the medical teams monitor treatment impacts.

While patient self-monitoring and sharing of health information has the potential to benefit patient care, little work has identified whether the health information patients are willing to track and share aligns with the health information needs of the providers. By considering the relative needs of these distinct stakeholders, future tools could encourage patients to prioritize reporting health information that is of particular importance to their healthcare providers. Further, these patient centered tools may expand to provide greater collaboration between patients and providers.

In order to enhance our ability to develop tools that consider the needs of these multiple user groups, we compare the health information sharing preferences of breast cancer patients, doctors, and cancer navigators (professionals who help cancer patients navigate the complex healthcare system by providing individualized support and resources). We aim to call attention to the need for future health information sharing tools to promote greater collaboration between patients and their healthcare network, an area where CSCW researchers can have a significant influence on improving patient experiences. Our work provides the following contributions:

- We examine the health information sharing preferences of patients, doctors, and cancer navigators across 23 distinct health factors relevant to the breast cancer journey. Our results highlight the willingness of those involved in the cancer care process to utilize tools that encompass a robust set of health factors.
- We reveal discrepancies between patients, doctors, and cancer navigators' health information sharing preferences. Misalignment was particularly evident in regards to sharing emotional health factors. The finding points to an opportunity for technologies to bridge the

gap so that patient tracking behaviors align with the informational needs of their healthcare network.

- We identify four design implications to guide the development of future health sharing tools that will consider the needs of patients and providers.

RELATED WORK

Benefits and Challenges of Health Tracking

Patient Perspective

Patient engagement is becoming increasingly recognized as a significant aspect of healthcare, particularly in the cancer care process. Personal health tracking can allow patients to receive the necessary help in stressful situations, directly influence treatment decisions, and improve health outcomes [13,19,22]. Health tracking practices can help mitigate limitations in the existing health system, in which a patient must recall as much information as possible during time-constrained meetings with their providers [2].

Continuous patient engagement brings new challenges alongside the benefits. Patients often must share basic medical information with concerned family members and friends. In parallel, patients may also track side effects to share with their oncologist to help in determining future steps and influence health outcomes [22]. Overall as the network of care enlarges, the burden falls on the patient to share the appropriate information with each person within their formal and informal healthcare networks [17].

Provider Perspective

For healthcare providers, including doctors and cancer navigators, the increase in patients tracking their own health provides a wealth of information. Such information can help doctors and cancer navigators to more efficiently focus their time [6]. While doctors and navigators will often work to assess patients' health status during appointments, a more accurate understanding of a patient's health situation can be gained by the patient providing his or her own assessments [21]. Receiving this health information prior to appointments can also allow a more direct focus on areas that require a doctor's or a navigator's attention during in-person patient meetings.

The challenge with utilizing this information is that these valuable data are not yet regularly incorporated into healthcare treatment [2]. Providers have discussed viewing the information that patients track and add to PHRs as medically useful, especially when patients' medical records are not available [24]. However, these same providers did not have access to electronic records that could interoperate with the patients' own records. By providing more detailed insight into which specific health factors could benefit cancer providers, we hope to encourage the development of tools that support both patient health information sharing as well as the incorporation of the patient collected health information into cancer care.

Perceptions Toward Sharing

Social computing research has identified many scenarios in which a person may wish to share different pieces of information, or provide different levels of access, to others [5,10,18]. In the health field, we see a desire from patients to share subsets of health information with selected groups. For instance, one study found that users of mobile health tools opted to share more information with strangers than with friends or family [16]. The Digital Family Portrait provides another example in which a subset of personal information was shared with family members [12]. These studies demonstrate the importance of understanding the social context that can influence sharing behaviors. In addition, a study examining diabetes patients found that these preferences and attitudes towards health information privacy can change over time [14].

Such studies help us gain an understanding of the personal beliefs and desires that underpin health information privacy. We aim to expand on this work by investigating the social and medical implications of health monitoring for the cancer care system, as the severity and complexity of the disease can bring additional challenges.

Personal Health Tracking Tools

Emerging technologies are encouraging patients to actively engage in tracking their own health. PHRs provide one such technology. PHRs provide a single location for patients to collect information about their medical history, treatments, and medications [23]. The challenge with many existing online medical records, as discussed in a recent study, is that these records utilize an all or nothing access model that does not consider the various levels of sensitivity intrinsic in certain health information [3]. Thus, while patients may engage more directly with their health records, they do not necessarily have tools that support their preferred health information sharing practices, nor the preferences of those receiving the information.

Symptom trackers provide another tool that allows patients to actively manage their healthcare. Patel et al. found that utilizing real-time tracking tools helped cancer patients keep more accurate symptom data and enhanced communication between patients and their doctors [15]. Patel's work also called for future health trackers to provide patients with greater ownership of their data, and the freedom to specify which data to share with different individuals.

Mobile technologies are also emerging as useful tools for patients' health management. The HealthWeaver mobile project used a mobile phone application to allow cancer patients to capture ad hoc symptoms and questions for their doctors [11]. Similarly, the My Journey Compass project used tablets to provide cancer patients with a symptom tracker and provider contact information within a broader suite of cancer related applications [8].

While technologies such as these help patients track important health information, they have yet to provide features that allow providers to incorporate health information sharing preferences as a way to focus patient behaviors. We aim to provide a comparative study examining patient, doctor, and cancer navigator preferences, ensuring that future tools are beneficial to all those involved in cancer care.

METHODS

We designed this study to better understand health-sharing preferences of breast cancer patients, doctors, and navigators. We utilized surveys, interviews, focus groups, and a card sorting activity to elicit information from our participants. All of our participants were a part of the cancer care system in a residential town in the southern United States. The town consists of a community that spreads across the full socio-economic spectrum. The health system serves a geographic area of over 500 square miles with a population around 100K. In 2013, the health system treated 260 breast cancer patients. To date, the local cancer care system utilizes a process in which patients decide if they want to track and share their personal health information with their providers. Our study provides foundational information to improve this process, alleviate some of the responsibility from the patients, and make available more relevant information to providers.

Patient Surveys

To understand patients' willingness to share health information with various groups in the cancer care network, we developed a survey that asked patients to identify whether or not they would feel comfortable sharing 23 different health information factors with 7 different groups of people. The health information factors include basic biometric information, physical side effects, and emotional issues pertinent in a cancer journey. Through discussions with cancer navigators, doctors and patients, we selected the health information factors that were relevant for breast cancer patients. To further ensure the appropriateness of the list, we asked participants of this study whether any important factors were missing. Participants commented that the list was comprehensive.

The final list of health factors included two biometric factors, fourteen physical health factors and nine emotional factors. Biometric factors included height and weight. Physical health factors included pain, nausea, constipation/diarrhea, fatigue, hot flashes, sleeplessness, hair loss images, medication adherence, surgery details, cancer stage, survival statistics, scar images, breast images, and diet. Emotional factors included stress, anxiety, loneliness, fear, seeking support, 'I am having a good day' and 'I am having a bad day'. Height was used as an initial factor that possessed few emotional implications as a way for patients to get acclimated with the survey questions.

In the survey, patients were asked to indicate for each factor whether or not they would feel comfortable sharing the information with the following groups: Me, Caregiver, Navigator, Oncologist, Social Media, and Society.

'Me', as explained to participants, was a way for a person to indicate whether each health factor would be something they were interested in monitoring themselves throughout their cancer journey. 'Caregiver' was used to represent any person in the patient's health network who helps look after the patient (usually a close relative or friend).

'Navigator' was used for asking whether or not patients would share health factors with their cancer navigator. Cancer navigators provide patients with individualized support to mitigate barriers to care, including emotional, financial, and logistical issues that typically arise during the cancer journey [9]. Barriers can vary based on a number of factors, including diagnosis, treatment plan, and socioeconomic status. Thus, navigators offer a range of services, including answering health related questions, providing emotional support and therapy, and accessing vital resources such as gas cards (for those who can't afford the increase cost of driving to daily treatments) or health insurance. In Rome, GA, cancer navigators play a central role in the breast cancer care process. The navigation organization exists outside of the network hospitals and cancer clinics but works with these health institutions to provide personalized support for cancer patients. Navigators will typically meet with patients at their first meeting with the general surgeon and continue to meet with them throughout their treatment.

'Social Media' represented any social networking sites used by participants. Many of our participants engaged to a various degree with Facebook and other social media. For participants who did not, we asked them whether or not they thought they would feel comfortable sharing the information online. 'Society' was used as a means to ask patients if they would feel comfortable sharing certain health information in public settings, such as a public forum or open cancer awareness event.

We asked about these distinct groups in order to gain a more holistic view of patients' health information sharing preferences as they relate to their entire healthcare network. For the purpose of this study we focus on their preferences for sharing health information with their doctors and navigators.

Patient Interviews

To compliment the survey, we wished to gain a deeper understanding of the thought process used to decide what information patients were willing to share with the various groups. We developed a card sorting activity that mirrored the information collected in the survey. In the activity, the health information factors and groups were written on cards. The groups were placed along the top of a table to create individual columns. Patients would then receive the health factor cards. For each group, the patient would place the health factor card in one of two piles below the group heading to indicate whether they would or would not be willing to share that health factor with that group. During the activity patients were encouraged to think aloud and the interviewers would occasionally ask probing questions to better understand the thought process. Table 1 shows a sample of data collected after a patient went through the first four health factors. Figure 1 shows a photograph of the activity after all of the health factors had been laid out.

All interviews took place in the cancer navigation office and lasted 1-2 hours. We found that responses from the interviews were comparable to the survey responses, while providing some additional information about the thought process behind the results.

Patient Participants

The survey was sent out to 67 breast cancer patients in the Rome, GA community. We also ran interviews with four additional patients (represented in this paper as P1-P4). All patients were female and had been diagnosed with breast cancer within the past year. Patients' average age was 60 years old. Patients had varying stages of breast cancer and treatment plans, but all received treatment in Rome, GA.

We received 20 survey responses (a response rate of 29.9%). Three of the survey responses were removed from the analysis because the participants marked the same answer for each question. When combined with the responses from the four patients who participated in the interviews, we analyzed a total of 21 patient responses.

Participants who were interviewed had participated in previous interviews with the researchers for a separate study. We hoped that this on-going relationship would result in open, honest conversation, which could otherwise prove challenging due to the personal and sensitive nature of the information discussed.

Doctor Focus Group

In addition to understanding how patients felt about sharing health information, we wished to get a sense of the types of patient information doctors would be interested in monitoring. We ran a focus group with three doctors: a medical oncologist, a radiation oncologist, and a general surgeon. All three doctors work with the breast cancer

Figure 1: Image of a completed card activity

patient population described above. We conducted a focus group as opposed to individual interviews due to the preferences and availability of the doctors.

With these doctors we ran an activity similar to the card activity used with patients. For every health factor, each doctor stated their interest in receiving and monitoring information about that factor collected by their patients, and whether or not they currently collect that information. Upon completion, we asked the doctors to rank the health factors they were most interested in monitoring. This ranking allowed us to gain an understanding as to which features would be necessary on future health monitoring tools to encourage provider use.

Cancer Navigator Interviews

We ran the same card activity with two of the cancer navigators (represented in this paper as N1 and N2). Both navigators were nurse navigators. Nurse navigators' work straddles the medical and emotional aspects of the cancer journey and they deal directly with many of the health factors included in the patient survey. Interviews were conducted with each of the navigators individually due to their differing availability.

Data Analysis

Two researchers reviewed the survey and interview data. The researchers used an iterative analysis to cluster segments from the survey responses and transcripts and develop thematic concepts. Researchers focused on preference reasoning, discrepancies between sharing

Willing to Share?	Me	Caregiver	Oncologist	Navigators	Social Media	Society
Yes	Height, Weight, Pain, Nausea	Height, Weight, Pain, Nausea	Height, Weight, Pain, Nausea	Height, Weight, Pain, Nausea	Height	Height
No					Weight, Pain, Nausea	Weight, Pain, Nausea

Table 1: Sample of data collected after a patient completed the first four health factors

preferences, and technology design implications. The two researchers reviewed each other's analysis and came to a consensus on the themes.

FINDINGS

In this section we provide an overview of the doctor, navigator, and patient responses, summarized in table 2. We then examine some interesting factors that influenced patient preferences, including patient assumptions, cancer identity, and concerns about imposing on others. Finally, we examine the misalignment between patient and doctor responses.

Doctor Responses

The focus group activity with the medical oncologist, radiation oncologist and general surgeon revealed that eleven of the health factors would be important to all three doctors for continuous monitoring. These factors included both biometric factors (height and weight), four physical factors (nausea, constipation/diarrhea, hot flashes, and medication adherence), and five emotional factors (stress, anxiety, loneliness, fear, and seeking support). The medical and radiation oncologists were interested in an additional four physical factors: pain, fatigue, sleeplessness, and diet. While this list includes many distinct factors to track, all three of the doctors emphasized that the combination of information across many factors would be important in allowing them to better understand the context when issues do occur.

When asked to rank the factors in terms of their importance, each doctor agreed that pain, nausea, and constipation/diarrhea are typically the most important as they can greatly influence a patient's daily life. However, the doctors also stated that these can change depending on the patient, and anything that could negatively impact quality of life will be important for the doctor to monitor. As the general surgeon noted:

"The quality of life issues [are most important]. Most patients, if you ask them, their goal is to have some semblance of a good quality of life. Well, you can't have a good quality of life if you're in pain all the time, if you're sick, if you're having diarrhea... These are things that really impact their day to day." - surgeon

Thus, based on the doctors' feedback, health tools that monitor a range of quality of life factors, including both physical and emotional factors, will be most beneficial to them, despite the large amount of information.

Navigator Responses

Both navigators stated that they currently talk to patients about eleven of the health factors. These include six physical factors (pain, constipation/diarrhea, fatigue, medication adherence, surgery details, and cancer stage) and five emotional factors (anxiety, stress, loneliness, fear, and 'I am having a bad day'). In the future, the navigators discussed a desire for health tracking tools to include these factors. Both navigators were also interested in including nausea and sleeplessness to their practice through future tools. N1 expressed interest in monitoring additional health factors, including height and weight (due to their impact on BMI), diet, seeking of support, hair loss images and scar images. N2 stated an interest in monitoring hot flashes.

The main similarity between the two rankings is that loneliness is viewed as critical to both of the navigators, ranked first and second in their individual orderings. However, when looking at their top ten ranked health factors we can see differences emerge. N1's top ranked health factors included (in order) loneliness, surgery details, pain, medication adherence, constipation/diarrhea, nausea, fatigue, stress, sleeplessness, and weight. N2's top ranked health factors included cancer stage, loneliness, anxiety, fear, stress, surgery details, fatigue, diet, pain, and constipation/diarrhea.

Looking at these rankings side by side, N1 focused more on medical issues while N2 ranked the emotional issues higher. These differences were primarily due to the fact that the navigators work with different groups of patients. N1 works with a wider range of cancers than N2, who works exclusively with breast cancer patients. A broader array of health challenges result from the additional cancer diagnoses. Ultimately, such variations demonstrate the need for health tracking tools designed for cancer navigators to include both physical and emotional health factors. Further, tools must be agile so that they may be tuned to best serve the individual journey of the patient.

Patient Responses and Motivations

Table 2 shows the percentage of respondents who indicated a willingness to share each health information factor with their oncologist and navigator. The table shows that overall patients are willing to share their health information with doctors and cancer navigators. The interviews provided some additional context around these responses, particularly into how patients make health information sharing decisions. Here we discuss three influential factors that arose during our conversations with patients.

Assumptions

Two assumptions made by the patients seemed to drive information sharing preferences. The first assumption dealt with the perceived interest of the receiver, while the second assumption focused on the receiver's ability to help the patient. When looking at these assumptions alongside our conversations with the doctors and navigators we begin to see that these patient assumptions do not always align with the beliefs of doctors and navigators.

1. Perceived Interest

The first assumption that influenced information sharing was whether or not the patient thought the receiver cared about the information. For example, P2 specifically stated that she would not share feelings of nausea on social media because her friends on social media "don't really care." Perceptions of interest also motivated the sharing of information. P2 stated that she was willing to share her fear with her family and cancer navigators:

"Caregivers, they really want to know that because they're afraid, they're very afraid for you. Navigators, they want to be there [for you]." - P2

2. Ability to Help the Patient

The second assumption patients mentioned involved the ability for the receiver to help the patient with her issue. In general, this was discussed in interviews as a reason for not sharing health information. For example, P3 discussed a previous experience in which she chose not to tell the doctors about the side effects of her treatment:

"I never usually have swelling but the first time I took Tamoxifen, I took it on a Friday night. The next morning I woke up and my hands were like the Pillsbury Doughboy's. My fingers were swelled together. I've never seen anything like it. And doctors said 'you should have come to the emergency room.' And I said 'Well, and what would you have done? Nothing.' So I just kind of watched it." – P3

In this situation, an assumption led a patient to not share health details with her doctor. Such an example demonstrates the need to make the ways in which doctors can help with managing certain symptoms and side effects clear to patients. These perceptions help explain why patients and doctors did not always concur on what information ought to be shared with one another. In the next section, we explore this finding in greater detail, describing how this misalignment can hinder a patient's cancer care and how future technologies may help ameliorate this gap in care.

Health Factor	Percent of patients willing to share		General Surgeon	Medical Oncologist	Radiation Oncologist	N1	N2
	(Doctors)	(Navigators)					
Height	100	100	X	X	X	X	
Weight	95	81	X	X	X	X	
Pain	100	95		**X**	**X**	**X**	X
Nausea	100	90	**X**	**X**	**X**	X	X
Constipation/diarrhea	100	90	**X**	**X**	**X**	X	X
Fatigue	100	95		X	X	X	X
Sleeplessness	100	95		X	X	X	X
Heat Flashes	95	90	X	X	X		X
Hair Loss Images	90	76				X	
Medication Adherence	100	90	X	X	X	X	X
Surgery Details	100	95				**X**	X
Cancer Stage	100	100				X	**X**
Survival Statistics	90	90					
Scar Images	90	86				X	
Breast Images	90	71					
Diet	86	90		X	X	X	
Stress	71	86	X	X	X	X	X
Anxiety	76	81	X	X	X	X	**X**
Fear	71	76	X	X	X	X	X
Loneliness	76	71	X	X	X	**X**	**X**
Seeking Support	86	86	X	X	X	X	
Good Day	90	86					
Bad Day	86	81				X	X
Totals:			2 biometric 4 physical 5 emotional	2 biometric 8 physical 5 emotional	2 biometric 8 physical 5 emotional	2 biometric 11 physical 6 emotional	9 physical 5emotional
Top Ranked:			Nausea, constipation/ diarrhea	Pain, nausea, constipation/ diarrhea	Pain, nausea, constipation/ diarrhea	Loneliness, surgery details, pain	Cancer stage, loneliness, anxiety

Table 2. The percentage of patients who indicated a willingness to share the health factor with their doctor and navigator, and the health information sharing preferences of each of the providers.

Cancer Identity

A surprising result that emerged from discussions with cancer patients was the association between a patient's assumed cancer identity and the willingness to share health information. N1 described to us how she has witnessed patients adopt varying cancer identities:

"Sometimes cancer is a small part of their lives, and they'll say 'cancer is a small part of my life and I'm not going to let it dictate my future, it's not my whole life.' And then sometimes cancer becomes... they get stuck in that. That's their whole life." – N1

Our conversations with patients helped to reveal the way in which they perceive their cancers differently. For example, P2 described her cancer as a small hurdle:

"I feel like this is a bump in the road, you get over it, and you move on down." – P2

When examining P2's sharing preferences, she spoke of being open and willing to share symptoms such as nausea, fatigue, and pain with her doctors, caregivers, and navigators. She was also comfortable sharing some information on social media, such as feelings of stress, anxiety and her diet. For society at large, P2 said she would be willing to share her experiences with hair loss, stress, anxiety, diet, and seeking support. The dialogue centered on sharing in an effort to overcome the disease and to help others. In contrast, P3 seemed to disassociate herself from the cancer:

"I just didn't want any one to know. Except my own children know, and my brother and sister in law know... I try to act like I don't have it I guess. I don't want to be my cancer." – P3

This perspective also seemed to affect her willingness to share health information. In general, P3 was less comfortable sharing health information. She was less willing to share information with the cancer navigators and said she would not discuss some personal health details, such as weight or constipation/diarrhea side effects with her caregiver. Further, she would not share any health information on social media or society at large. P3 also said that throughout treatment other people in her life, such as her boss, did not know about her diagnosis because she didn't want to be seen as a cancer patient. When discussing her sharing preferences for health information generally, P3 focused mainly on protecting her privacy.

These contrasting viewpoints help to provide a glimpse into the types of personal traits that can influence a patient's willingness to share health information. Future research could delve deeper into the influence of a patient's cancer identity on daily behavior and relationships with others.

Imposing on Others

The desire to not impose one's problems on other people seemed to cause some patients to share less personal health information. P1 specifically stated that she tries to keep her pain to herself because she doesn't want to bother other people. P4 also stated that her desire to not "whine and complain" caused her not to share information on social media or to society at large. Further, P4 stated:

"I tend to even with [my husband and children], not want to complain, put a pretty good face on it... And you know, not wanting to trouble them or worry them, so a lot of times I just won't share things that I think will hurt them or upset them." – P4

Other studies have noted similar results in which patients wished to "maintain positive impressions" around the people close to them [1]. Interestingly, a patient taking on this burden to deal with issues and side effects by herself was apparent to the cancer navigators. N1 described a conversation she has with numerous patients. When she asks patients "why have you been hurting for two weeks and you didn't tell me?" A common response from the patient is "I didn't want to bother you."

Patient/Provider Discrepancies

Through our results described above, and summarized in table 2, we can see that some misalignments between patient, doctor, and navigator preferences exist. For instance, we can see that some health factors were only of interest to the cancer navigators, and yet fewer patients were willing to share this information with their navigators than with their doctors. This misalignment can be seen in the responses to health factors such as hair loss images and 'I am having a bad day'. Also apparent in table 2 is the willingness and interest patients possessed to share health factors that were not of interest to any of the providers. This can specifically be seen in the breast images factor, in which 90% of patients said they would be interested and willing to share these with their doctors. These misalignments begin to show the need for technologies that help focus patients' health tracking and sharing behaviors, so that they may better support the needs of their healthcare network.

The health information sharing preferences surrounding the emotional factors lead to some interesting discrepancies as well. As we discuss below, we have found inconsistencies dealing with loneliness and patient satisfaction.

Loneliness Gap

Our findings revealed that 24% and 29% of patient participants stated they would not share feelings of loneliness with their oncologist or navigator, respectively. P2 stated she would not share loneliness because "doctors really don't care if you're lonely." Other patients discussed not sharing emotional factors, such as loneliness, because they did not feel that doctors could help in coping with these emotions. However, the medical oncologist gave an example of a recent patient to describe why communicating feelings of loneliness can be so important:

"If any one of these [factors] is off the charts it could be bad. It could be loneliness. I had a woman today. I was like 'how are we going get her home?' She won't reach out to her best friend. And because of that she's scared to death, and because of that she's scared about coming in to treatment and doesn't know if she wants to do it. And it all stems from loneliness." – medical oncologist

The navigators also brought up loneliness as an issue. Both navigators ranked loneliness high on their list of important health factors to monitor, but recognized that patients do not always share this information outright. Sometimes it falls on the navigator to identify hints that loneliness may be an issue for a patient. As N1 described:

"Loneliness is something that is very shameful and embarrassing to them. So if I sense that this person is alone I need to be there a lot more then." – N1

This "loneliness gap" begins to show that some misalignment exists between what patients, doctors, and navigators each feel are important health factors to share. The navigators noted that emotional issues are generally the most challenging for patients to share, specifically referencing loneliness, fear, and anxiety.

Addressing this gap carries two main challenges. First, in order to track loneliness or other emotional issues, a useful measurement must be utilized. As the general surgeon noted: "I don't know how you would define loneliness." The second challenge involves increasing patients' willingness to share loneliness issues with their doctors and navigators. This may be possible if health-tracking tools highlight doctors' interest in emotional issues and how they may be able to help the patient.

Tracking Patient Satisfaction

Although we did not specifically ask about patient satisfaction, stories concerning their satisfaction with the health system came up frequently in our conversations with patients. For instance, P2 shared one memorable moment with us:

"I remember one time I was going through a depression. I remember going to [my doctor], and he was busy writing, he had his back turned to me and I was on the exam table. And I said things are pretty rough, I feel pretty sad. And he never even looked at me." – P2

Following this situation, P2 told her doctor directly that their interaction had upset her and received positive results in return. She stated that following that incident and subsequent discussion her doctor makes a more concerted effort to shake her hand and focus on her during appointments. However, not all patients are as willing to confront their doctors. For example, P3 shared that she once felt extremely upset with her care when she felt that she could not reschedule one of her radiation treatments:

"I don't like being treated like that. I like having a choice. And it was never made clear to me why I didn't have a choice. [My doctor] would want me to tell him, but I just, I just can't. Because, number one, they're not going to change." – P3

Clearly, experiences like these can leave lasting impressions on patients. P3 finished treatment several months prior to the interview, but got visibly upset when sharing this story, showing the long-term emotional impact of patient satisfaction during the cancer journey.

Interestingly, patient satisfaction also leaves lasting impressions on the doctors. In the focus group, the doctors also brought up patient satisfaction and their desire to have patients share their feelings and negative experiences with them earlier. The general surgeon discussed his desire to improve the cancer care experience for his patients:

"You find out sometimes after you've gone through the entire process that somebody early in the course of care was unhappy about something... It would be nice if somewhere they were keeping a log that we had access to that says how happy are they with the way things are going. It gives us a chance early on in the care to realize [we have a problem]. But we can solve it. What happens is the problem has already occurred and three months later comes to my office. Well, I could have fixed that. Give me real-time data. Let me affect the patient's experience by knowing their not having a good experience. I can do something about that. Give me an opportunity." - surgeon

Similar to the issue of loneliness, some patients revealed feeling hesitant to share dissatisfactions about their healthcare to their doctors. Notifying doctors of satisfaction issues through technology may help alleviate the challenge of confronting the doctors directly. Ultimately, a more defined process for tracking and sharing emotional issues and enhanced communication between doctors and patients may help to address these contrasting preferences.

Summary

Table 2 provides an overview of the health information sharing preferences across patients, doctors, and navigators. To our surprise, all of the providers indicated a need to receive a set of both physical and emotional health factors. Further, they all preferred receiving a wide range of health factors, which provide greater context but take more time to monitor and understand. We also found several factors that can influence patients' willingness to share, including assumptions about others' interest and ability to help, patients' cancer identity, and concerns about imposing on others. Through a comparative analysis, we identified discrepancies between patient, doctor, and navigator health information sharing preferences. Such misalignments point to the need for future tools to help bridge the needs of healthcare providers with the behaviors of patients engaging in personal health tracking.

DISCUSSION

Cancer care is becoming an increasingly collaborative process between patients and providers. While existing tools such as PHRs and symptom trackers help patients collect health information, research has yet to examine whether this information aligns with the health information needs of healthcare providers, such as doctors and cancer navigators. We examined the health information sharing preferences of cancer patients, doctors, and navigators in order to explore how future tools can incorporate the needs of these stakeholders and enhance the utility of patient collected information in their healthcare.

In reflection, our findings highlight four specific design implications. These implications aim to reduce discrepancies between patients, doctors, and navigators' sharing preferences. For these design opportunities we also discuss challenges that ought to be considered in the development of future health information sharing tools.

Allow Recipients to Select Important Health Factors

Undoubtedly, patients need control of their health tracking tools. Providing control not only to the patient but also allowing those in a patient's healthcare network to select which factors they want to receive may help increase the utility of health trackers. The main motivation for this feature is that we saw discrepancies between each of the doctors and navigators regarding which features they were interested in monitoring. Today, health information tracking and sharing tools place the responsibility on patients to decide with whom to share [3]. Providing this feature to a patient's healthcare network may also help to reduce the concern patients felt about sharing health information with people who did not care about that particular information. Allowing recipients to select the information they wish to monitor may help alleviate the burden placed on patients of trying to guess who in their healthcare network should receive select health information.

Challenge: Determining Frequency of Sharing

Allowing both the sharer and recipients of health information to influence the sharing process does bring additional questions that ought to be considered in future designs. Determining how often patients should share health information with their doctors and navigators remains an open question for health tracking processes. Capturing and sharing health information more frequently requires a greater time commitment from patients. However, less frequent sharing hinders the potential benefit of health tracking tools to provide early warning signs that health problems are hurting a patient's quality of life.

When asked about current sharing processes, each of the doctors and navigators stated that patients brought up health factors "when there is an issue." While all of the participants agreed that more frequent sharing would benefit the cancer care process, the appropriate pace of health information sharing was not identified. Examining how different sharing frequencies influence health-tracking practices could greatly help the design of future health tracking tools.

Support Sharing of Past Experiences

An important feature for future health information sharing tools and processes is the ability for patients to learn from the past experiences of providers and other patients. This need falls under broader requirement to educate patients about how providers can use the information they share. We found that some patients hesitate to share information if they don't think the person receiving the information can help. Demonstrating how sharing health information with others can benefit the patient will be important for showing the full value of such tools to patients. Previous work has examined how peer support can be enhanced in cancer care [4, 20]. There remains an open opportunity for tools to allow new patients to learn from the experiences of doctors, navigators, and other patients. Particularly, revealing experiences in which health information sharing behaviors benefited the patient can help provide context around the importance of these practices. Such tools may help to eliminate the discrepancies between health information sharing preferences identified in this research.

Challenge: Permanency of Shared Information

In the development of tools that allow patients to learn from others' previous experiences, designers must consider the permanency of the information being shared. The benefit of retaining health information is that such information could be used to help future cancer patients. Several of our participants described a willingness to share information in an effort to help others. Thus, if the health information that patients share with doctors, navigators, and the broader society can be maintained past their cancer treatment, it may provide valuable insight for newly diagnosed patients who are experiencing similar situations. However, sharing personal health information can also have negative lasting consequences.

P3 discussed with us the negative impact sharing health information had on her life. Prior to her own diagnosis, P3's husband had been diagnosed with terminal cancer. P3 shared with us that because everyone in the community knew about her husband's diagnosis and the negative symptoms of his disease, she felt as though his cancer unwillingly became a part of her identity. P3's feeling that people identified her as "the cancer patient's wife," prevented her from sharing with others her own cancer diagnosis, even years after her husband's diagnosis. This story provides one example of how health information permanence negatively influenced one patient's cancer journey. Similar to selecting the types of information shared, patients may need control over the permanency of the information being tracked, and possess the freedom to change the information that is shared over time.

Minimize the Burden of Sharing

One surprising result that emerged from this study was the broad range of health factors all of the doctors and navigators wished to receive from patients. Each of these stakeholders requested at least eleven distinct factors. This desire for extensive health information sharing conflicts with the general desire to reduce the time that patients must spend focused on health tasks. As previously stated, all stakeholders, including patients, doctors, and navigators ought to influence the information that is shared between one another. Once these preferences are set, however, scaffolding sharing processes to minimize the burden may help provide doctors and navigators with rich context while reducing the need for patients to continually think about which information ought to be shared with whom.

Challenge: Respecting Patient Privacy

Previous studies have shown that patients prefer to share different health information with the various people in their lives [14]. Tools may need to provide this level of control to patients in order to encourage continuous use. However, this control over information sharing can also threaten patient care if patients opt not to share important health information with their doctors. Thus, a significant issue with health tracking is respecting patients' sharing decisions even when such decisions may impede on their cancer care. Including explanations within health tracking tools of how and why providers may use shared information to improve the cancer care process for a patient may help alleviate this challenge. Future work should look at how the health information sharing preferences of patients, doctors and navigators can be made more transparent to each other, as this may help to align sharing preferences.

Utilize Healthcare Network Collaboration in Design

Our discussions with doctors, navigators, and patients made apparent the need to include all of these stakeholders in the design process of future health information sharing tools. In our conversations, participants suggested interesting design ideas based on their own experiences. For example, N1 shared a typical discussion about pain:

"I always ask them on a scale of 1 to 10, and can you describe the pain to me. That helps me a lot. Is it throbbing, is it a dull ache, is it over here, is it shooting through the abdomen. The location of it helps a lot. And they are usually pretty descriptive." – N1

Integrating design features that mimic these types of conversations could help health tracking tools provide greater context about a patient's health situation. Further, such features may be easier for doctors and navigators to monitor as they correlate with their existing methods for understanding patient symptoms and side effects. Doctors also brought a unique background, posing a new set of possible future designs. They presented ideas such as combining health-tracking tools with the existing psychosocial distress screening (a 2015 healthcare requirement). The diverse design ideas posed by navigators, patients, and doctors highlight the significant help each can provide to the design of health tracking tools. We strongly encourage researchers to consider their input throughout the design process. Involving these and other stakeholders may also encourage a sense of ownership over tools, helping to remove the ever-present challenge of engaging users over an extended period of time.

Challenge: Developing Standard Measures

In our discussions with these stakeholders, the challenge of measuring many of the health factors in a meaningful way came up frequently. Survey respondents also commented that measuring some of these factors would be difficult. For example, as the radiation oncologist noted, "how do you collect pain?" A Likert scale selection of 7 most likely does not provide enough context around how the patient is feeling. We found our participants held different opinions on how best to measure specific health factors. A challenge for future technologies will be to utilize standard measurements for complex factors such as pain or loneliness that are meaningful for all of the users involved in the design and the use of such tools.

CONCLUSION

Our goal with this study is to support the development of useful health information sharing tools that will allow providers to more easily utilize information shared by patients. Our results indicate a general interest by doctors, navigators and patients to utilize health-tracking tools that include a range of health factors. Both doctors and navigators preferred robust tools despite the potential increase in complexity. The importance of context in understanding cancer patient health issues motivated this need for a broader range of health information.

While patients revealed an overall comfort level in sharing personal information with their doctors and navigators, we identified some discrepancies between health information sharing beliefs. Specifically, emotional issues such as loneliness and satisfaction with care provide challenges, as patients are not always comfortable sharing these issues. Future health-tracking tools may be able to better align the sharing preferences of doctors, navigators, and patients, allowing for health information tracked by patients to be better integrated into the care they receive. To support their development, we identified design implications and challenges to be considered in the design process.

We have focused our efforts for this study in a single cancer care community. Due to the focus on breast cancer, we also experienced gender and age biases (all of our participants were women and the average age was 60). While this scope limits the generalizability of our findings, it also allows us to provide a holistic qualitative account of the issues currently affecting patients' care from multiple perspectives. The findings and challenges we present here may be useful for identifying important questions to address in other cancer care sociotechnical systems. A key challenge with managing longer health journeys is the lack of available ubiquitous care. This study contributes to our understanding of how technologies may help provide more continuous care during people's everyday lives.

ACKNOWLEDGEMENTS

We would like to thank the Georgia Department of Community Health for their funding and support. We would also like to thank our patient and provider participants, the Rome cancer navigators, and all of our partners within the Rome healthcare community. Without these collaborators, none of this work would be possible.

REFERENCES

1. Benjamin, A., Birnholtz, J., Baecker, R., Gromala, D., and Furlan, A. Impression Management Work: How Seniors With Chronic Pain Address Disruptions in Their Interactions. *CSCW '12*, (2012), 799–808.
2. Berry, D.L. Patient-reported symptoms and quality of life integrated into clinical cancer care. *Seminars in oncology nursing 27*, 3 (2011), 203–210.
3. Chen, Y., Hall, B., and Xu, H. Privacy management in dynamic groups: Understanding information privacy in medical practices. *CSCW '13*, (2013), 541–552.
4. Civan, A., Mcdonald, D.W., Unruh, K.T., and Pratt, W. Locating Patient Expertise in Everyday Life. *Group '09*, (2009), 291–300.
5. Consolvo, S., Smith, I.E., Matthews, T., Lamarca, A., and Tabert, J. Location Disclosure to Social Relations: Why, When, & What People Want to Share. *CHI '05*, (2005), 81–90.
6. Ferguson, T. Online patient-helpers and physicians working together: a new partnership for high quality health care. *BMJ (Clinical research ed.) 321*, 7269 (2000), 1129–32.
7. Hayes, G., Abowd, G., Davis, J., Blount, M., Ebling, M., and Mynatt, E.D. Opportunities for pervasive computing in chronic cancer care. *Pervasive Computing*, (2008), 262–279.
8. Jacobs, M., Clawson, J., and Mynatt, E. My Journey Compass: A Preliminary Investigation of a Mobile Tool for Cancer Patients. *CHI '14*, (2014).
9. Jacobs, M., Clawson, J., and Mynatt, E.D. Cancer Navigation: Opportunities and Challenges for Facilitating the Breast Cancer Journey. *CSCW '14*, (2014), 1467–1478.
10. Karlson, A.K., Brush, A.J.B., and Schechter, S. Can I borrow your phone? Understanding concerns when sharing mobile phones. *CHI '09*, (2009), 1647–1650.
11. Klasnja, P., Hartzler, A., Powell, C., and Pratt, W. Supporting cancer patients' unanchored health information management with mobile technology. *AMIA 2011*, (2011), 732–741.
12. Mynatt, E.D., Rowan, J., Jacobs, A., and Craighill, S. Digital Family Portraits: Supporting Peace of Mind for Extended Family Members. *CHI '01*, (2001), 333–340.
13. Ong, L.M., De Haes, J.C., Hoos, a M., and Lammes, F.B. Doctor-patient communication: a review of the literature. *Social science & medicine 40*, 7 (1995), 903–18.
14. O'Kane, A.A., Mentis, H.M., and Thereska, E. Non-Static nature of patient consent: Shifting privacy perspectives in health information sharing. *CSCW '13*, (2013), 553–562.
15. Patel, R. a, Klasnja, P., Hartzler, A., Unruh, K.T., and Pratt, W. Probing the benefits of real-time tracking during cancer care. *AMIA '12*, (2012), 1340–9.
16. Prasad, A., Sorber, J., Stablein, T., Anthony, D., and Kotz, D. Understanding sharing preferences and behavior for mHealth devices. *WPES '12*, (2012), 117–128.
17. Pratt, W., Unruh, K., Civan, A., and Skeels, M. Personal health information management. *Communications of the ACM 49*, 1 (2006), 51–55.
18. Singh, S., Cabraal, A., Demosthenous, C., and Furlong, M. Password Sharing: Implications for Security Design Based on Social Practice. *CHI '07*, (2007), 895–904.
19. Skeels, M.M., Unruh, K.T., Powell, C., and Pratt, W. Catalyzing Social Support for Breast Cancer Patients. *CHI '10*, (2010), 173–182.
20. Skeels, M.M., Unruh, K.T., Powell, C., and Pratt, W. Catalyzing Social Support for Breast Cancer Patients. *CHI '10*, (2010), 173–182.
21. Slevin, M.L., Plant, H., Lynch, D., Drinkwater, J., and Gregory, W.M. Who should measure quality of life, the doctor or the patient? *British journal of cancer 57*, 1 (1988), 109–12.
22. Street, R.L., Makoul, G., Arora, N.K., and Epstein, R.M. How does communication heal? Pathways linking clinician-patient communication to health outcomes. *Patient education and counseling 74*, 3 (2009), 295–301.
23. Tang, P.C., Ash, J.S., Bates, D.W., Overhage, J.M., and Sands, D.Z. Personal health records: Definitions, benefits, and strategies for overcoming barriers to adoption. *JAMIA 13*, 2 (2006), 121–127.
24. Witry, M.J., Doucette, W.R., Daly, J.M., Levy, B.T., and Chrischilles, E. a. Family physician perceptions of personal health records. *American Health Information Management Association (AHIMA) 7*, (2010).

They Said What? Exploring the Relationship Between Language Use and Member Satisfaction in Communities

Tara Matthews*[1], Jalal Mahmud*, Jilin Chen*[1], Michael Muller, Eben Haber*, Hernan Badenes+
*IBM Research - Almaden, {taramatthews, chenjilin}@gmail.com, {jumahmud, ehaber}@us.ibm.com
IBM Research - Cambridge, michael_muller@us.ibm.com
+IBM, Buenos Aires, Argentina, hbadenes@ar.ibm.com

ABSTRACT
In online communities, satisfied members are essential to community success, since they are more likely to contribute and consume content, engage with other members, and feel committed to the community. However, it is difficult for community leaders to know, on an on-going basis, whether members are satisfied. In this paper, we explore the relationship between member satisfaction and language use within content posted in workplace online communities. We hope to find patterns of language use that are associated with satisfied members. We employ linguistic analysis based on LIWC, and a survey to directly measure member satisfaction in 142 workplace communities. We contribute a better understanding of how members interact in effective workplace communities, and show that linguistic analysis could be a useful part of future methods to automatically assess community member satisfaction.

Author Keywords
Online communities; member satisfaction; linguistic analysis, LIWC; workplace.

ACM Classification Keywords
H.5.m. Information interfaces and presentation (e.g., HCI): Miscellaneous.

INTRODUCTION
Scholars, consultants, and practitioners working with online communities have long known that *successful* communities must *meet member needs* [19,31,38]. Satisfied members form the essential core of any successful online community, since they are more likely to contribute and consume content, engage with other members, and feel committed to the community—which are all required for the community to succeed [19,31]. Community development guidelines emphasize that community leaders should frequently assess member satisfaction and work to keep it high, as a prerequisite for achieving any other goals [19,31,38].

Prior work has shown that it is difficult for community leaders to know, on an on-going basis, whether members are satisfied [22]. First, many activities are suggested as potential success factors in prior work, such as setting a clear mission [31], controlling the composition of community membership [20], welcoming new members [19], and encouraging social bonds between members [32]. But it is still unclear what community data can be used to sense the members' degree of satisfaction. Second, the most common method of assessing community member satisfaction is to ask members [31], which is time-consuming, can only be employed periodically, and cannot be employed retrospectively to evaluate past events. Community leaders would benefit from more insight into how satisfied members behave and by research to inform automated methods of assessing satisfaction.

In this paper, we explore whether language use in a community can be used to assess aggregate member satisfaction. Our analysis relies on the LIWC family of dictionaries (Linguistic Inquiry and Word Count) [27]. We study language use in workplace online communities that emphasize sharing information and resources, connecting and building relationships among employees, and collaborating on shared deliverables. We hope to find patterns of language use that are associated with satisfied members. We test those patterns by comparing them with a direct measure of subjective member satisfaction obtained through a survey of members across multiple communities. Our goal is to assess whether and how discourse within a community can signal more or less satisfied members, and what this implies about the types of discussions satisfied members are having. We contribute a better understanding of how members interact in effective communities, and show that linguistic analysis could be a useful part of future methods to automatically predict member satisfaction. We believe that the approach presented in this paper could be used to study communities in other contexts.

RELATED WORK
In this paper, we use linguistic analysis to study member satisfaction within 142 communities. Our analysis focuses on members' language *style* (how they talk) and members' *psychological processes* (how they feel, think about, or perceive their world) [27,29]. Style and psychological process words are more likely than content words to be general across communities in different domains and link to measures of social and psychological phenomena [29,34].

[1] Current affiliation: Google Inc.

CSCW '15, March 14 - 18, 2015, Vancouver, BC, Canada.
Copyright 2015 ACM 978-1-4503-2922-4/15/03…$15.00.
http://dx.doi.org/10.1145/2675133.2675150

A number of researchers have explored what language use in online communities says about community members' behaviors [1,4,5,6,9,13,25,35,37] and sentiment [18,26,40]. Most of these studies have focused on using linguistic analysis to understand *individuals* or *individual contributions* to the community, such as: assessing the effectiveness of new member introductions [9]; describing requests that elicit responses [1,4,35,37]; and studying language patterns of mature members [25] or leaders [5,13].

While the preceding studies addressed individuals and their roles, fewer studies have explored the impact of language use community-wide. Kramer et al. [18] created a tool to characterize different types of discourse in online support groups (specifically, emotion writing, talkative, bipolar chat), so that they could be monitored for changes or compared to other communities. Arguello et al. [1] assessed whether members were likely to post again using linguistic features of their posts. Yu [40] characterized emotional communication in online health communities, overall and by different individual roles. Nguyen et al. [26] created a tool to identify latent groups in social communities based on users' language use. Cassell and Tverky [6] and Vambheim et al. [36] described how language changed in individual communities as they developed over time. However, none of these prior studies have attempted to relate a direct subjective measure of member satisfaction with the community to language use in the community.

Prior literature that describes the behaviors and attributes of successful communities can give us clues about how their members might talk. Two studies of community language showed that the use of first person plural (*we*) words increased and first person singular (*I*) words decreased as communities matured [6,36]. We might expect a similar trend in communities with more satisfied members. Also, members are more committed to communities that are more social and supportive [19,32]. Thus, words indicating social and supportive discussion may be linked to greater member satisfaction. It is noted in prior work that the links between language use and social and psychological phenomena are not always immediately apparent [29]. Thus, we expect that community member satisfaction may be linked to some aspects of language style or psychological processes that we are unable to predict based on prior studies.

METHOD

We study whether and how language style predicts member satisfaction using a survey of members and an analysis of words posted in a set of workplace online communities.

Research Context

This research was conducted in a global enterprise that offers technology products and services to businesses. All communities we studied used the same commercial tool, which was available to all employees and enabled them to easily create and join community spaces with various social tools like forums, blogs, wikis, files, and bookmarks. As a result, there was a proliferation of communities and widespread membership, with 166,000+ communities and 580,000+ distinct members over five years. Communities ranged in size from a few to thousands of members. Many employees were members of multiple communities.

The community tool was used by a variety of community types: including communities of practice, organizational teams, and technical support communities, similar to the community types in [12,24]. These groups used the communities tool primarily to *connect and build relationships among employees* who could *share information and resources* with each other, and sometimes *collaborate* on a shared deliverable. Communities of practice did these activities in the context of a shared interest or practice; teams worked in the context of producing a shared deliverable; and technical support communities shared in the context of a mutually used technology.

Survey

We surveyed workplace community members as part of a larger research project with additional questions [anon]. For this paper, we included a subset of the survey and communities from the larger study, since we ask different research questions here. The survey question we focused on for this study assessed members' satisfaction with a single community by asking them to rate overall "how well this community is meeting your needs," on a scale of 1=very poorly to 5=very well. In prior work, published surveys for online communities focus primarily on outcomes in *learning* communities (e.g., [2,10]). Beyond learning communities, each team of researchers in this space seems to have designed their own unpublished survey (e.g., [11,20]). A rare exception appears to be Ma and Agarwal [21], who asked two questions about satisfaction, based on an earlier survey from an online learning community [10]. With this background, we developed our own question, similar to one of Ma and Agarwal's satisfaction questions [21], and refined it over the course of two prior surveys of enterprise community members. We ran the survey via a web tool that enabled us to name a specific community in recruitment emails and survey questions.

A total of 142 communities were included in this analysis as follows: The company had a total of 166K+

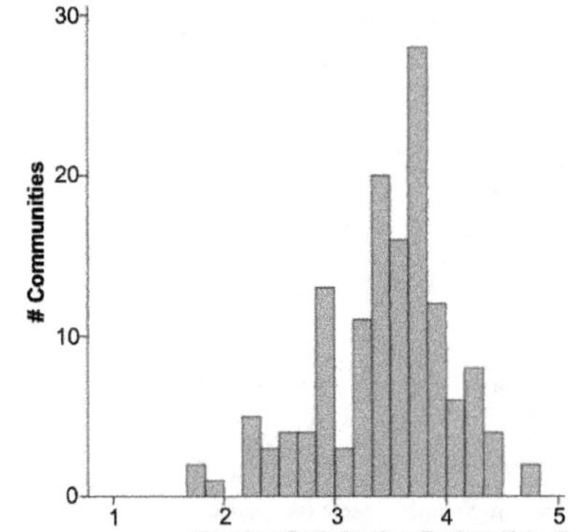

Figure 1. Histogram of average member satisfaction ratings for 142 communities (mean=3.5, std dev=0.57). 1 is low, 5 is high.

communities, but not all of these were actively managed. To sample actively managed communities, we drew from a smaller pool of 666 communities whose leaders participated in an experimental tool to help leaders enhance their community. These communities varied widely in terms of size, longevity, and purpose. The survey was deployed to 478 communities that had enough members (>20) to yield a valid assessment of member satisfaction (see the next section). 378 communities had enough members respond (3+) for analysis. We processed this dataset as follows: (1) removed 8 communities for technical reasons (e.g., the forum, blog, or activity data could not be completely crawled); (2) removed 86 communities with <3000 words[1]; (3) removed 141 communities with >500 members[2].

Figure 1 shows a histogram of average member satisfaction ratings for these 142 communities. In the following two sub-sections, we include details on how members were sampled for the survey, and descriptions of who responded. We will comment on the generality of our findings to other communities in the results section.

Member sampling

We aimed for survey responses from at least 3 members per community and we expected a 15-20% response rate. Thus we sent the survey to 20-26 members per community (depending on community size). We also wanted to survey different types of members. Prior literature distinguishes members who actively post (contributors) and those who only read (consumers, or "lurkers" [30]). We expected contributors (fewer in number) to be more likely to respond to the survey, but we also wanted to poll consumers. Thus we used a stratified sampling method to balance the selection of contributors and consumers to about half and half. Each member received just one survey request.

Survey Response

The response rate was 19% for all participants surveyed. After removing communities with <3 responses, an average of 5.9 members responded per community. We averaged member responses within each community. As a validity check, we ensured that member ratings of the same community generally agreed with each other by computing the intra-class correlation coefficient (ICC) across all respondents per community; the average ICC across communities was 0.69, which is a good level of agreement [7]. Demographically, respondents represented all inhabited world continents (with the biggest populations from North America 30%, Europe 26%, and Asia 25%) and all major business divisions (with the majority from Services 43%, Internal Ops 19%, and Sales 16%). Respondents were 80% non-managers and 15% managers; and 50% contributors and 45% consumers (5% unknown for both).

Linguistic Analysis

Our goal was to analyze how words posted in the communities related to member ratings from the survey. Thus for each of the 142 communities that members rated, we collected all of the words posted to their discussion forum and blog over the community's life, including original posts and comments/replies. We analyzed forum and blog content because these were the two tools within the community space tool that included significant amounts of member-created content; we excluded wikis because they tended to include static resources created by community leaders [23]. An ideal analysis would include only text posted during a limited time period near the survey date. However, activity in the enterprise communities sampled was not high enough to enable this analysis strategy. So that readers may interpret our results, we characterize temporal attributes of the communities analyzed: The average age of communities in our dataset was 2.4 years. Of analyzed communities, 49% had created >50% of their content within 1 year of the survey, and 70% had created >50% of their content within 2 years.

We analyzed these words using the Linguistic Index Word Count (LIWC) 2007 dictionary [27]. LIWC is an important language analysis tool for investigating the relation between word use and social or psychological variables, with nearly 300 citations in the ACM Digital Library [34]. The LIWC dictionary defines 64 word categories, each containing dozens or hundreds of words. Table 1 shows example words from some LIWC categories.

We used 46 out of the 64 categories of words in LIWC, as follows: We removed most categories that focused on what *topics* people talk about, such as Family, Religion, Body, and Ingestion, since these are not general across community topics. We kept two topic categories—Work and Leisure—since they represent a potentially interesting balance of conversation topics for many types of communities. The remaining categories focus on *linguistic style* (how people talk) or *psychological processes* (how people feel, think about, or perceive the world), which are more likely general across domains and link to measures of people's social and psychological worlds [15,34]. Of these, we removed the Fillers and Swear Words categories because a majority of communities in our dataset did not use any words in these categories. The final set of 46 categories analyzed included: Total Function Words, Total Pronouns, Personal Pronouns, I, We, You, She/He, They, Impersonal Pronouns, Articles, Verbs, Auxiliary Verbs, Past Tense, Present Tense, Future Tense, Adverbs, Prepositions, Conjunctions, Negations, Quantifiers, Numbers, Social Processes, Affective

---

[1] A minimum number of words threshold is necessary to lessen sampling error, i.e., the absolute error across LIWC category scores when comparing small and large language samples from the same source. We chose 3000 words as a threshold because, in pilot testing, <3000 words was more likely to result in an unrepresentative sample of text with increased error.

[2] It is problematic to compare communities of very different sizes, since groups of different sizes communicate differently [17]. Our original dataset ranged from 21 to 10K+ members per community (average of 332). A histogram revealed that the bulk of communities had less than 500 members, and above 500 the distribution spread out significantly. We thus included only communities with less than 500 members in our analyses.

LIWC category	Example words from communities	Regression		Collinearity		Descriptive	
		Std. Coef.	Sig.	Tol.	VIF	Mean	Std. Dv.
Anger	critical, cut, argu*, threat	-0.345	.000	.548	1.823	.00105	.00119
Work	team, business, project	-0.198	.001	.692	1.445	.05246	.01605
I	I, I'll, me, mine	-0.208	.002	.412	2.429	.01315	.00825
Article	a, an, the	-0.162	.013	.669	1.496	.05818	.01437
We	let's, our, us, we	0.160	.008	.695	1.438	.01176	.00616
Leisure	blog, book, opera, soccer	0.181	.063	.575	1.738	.01200	.00954
Inhibition	require*, secur*, control	0.110	.056	.749	1.335	.00532	.00245
Anxiety	risk, avoid, confus*	0.144	.107	.583	1.714	.00088	.00081
Assent	agree, yes, OK	0.141	.079	.549	1.823	.00110	.00107

Table 1. For each of the 9 LIWC categories selected by the regression as predictors of *member satisfaction*, lists words from dataset communities and results. See www.liwc.net/descriptiontable1.php for all LIWC categories. * is a wildcard, i.e., a character that will match any character or sequence of characters.

Processes, Positive Emotion, Negative Emotion, Anxiety, Anger, Sadness, Cognitive Processes, Insight, Causation, Discrepancy, Tentative, Certainty, Inhibition, Inclusive, Exclusive, Perceptual Processes, Relativity, Motion, Space, Time, Work, Leisure, Assent, Non-fluencies.

For each of these 46 LIWC categories, we analyzed the proportion of words from that category posted in the community's forum and blog—we call these variables the *category scores*. To explore which of the LIWC categories best predicted member satisfaction, we conducted a regression analysis. We entered the 46 *category scores* as independent variables in an SPSS automatic linear modeling regression, with *member satisfaction* (assessed through the survey) as the dependent variable. We chose automatic linear modeling since it uses feature selection to build a regression model, which helps to avoid correlated predictors in the resultant model [39]. We used "best subsets selection," which checks a large subset of all possible models to choose the best subset of categories to predict the dependent variable, according to the best subsets criterion. This automatic linear modeling procedure first preprocesses the dataset by standardizing variables' ranges and removing outliers [39]. The procedure then applies step-wise linear regression on the dataset, using AICc as the criterion. AICc [14] is a common goodness-of-fit measure for linear regressions and has been routinely used for model selection in step-wise regressions [33]. This regression selected 9 categories, which we discuss in the results.

As part of our exploration, we included in our initial model the most common behavioral "success metrics" proposed in prior work: number of members, contributors, posts, views, and "likes" [16,31]. We collected these data for the 142 communities in our dataset. As in prior work [22], these behavioral data did not improve the prediction power. We also explored various other attributes of the communities—such as geographic dispersion of members, type and goals of the community (collected via survey)—and none of these had any significant impact on the models. Thus, we excluded these measures from the final model.

RESULTS

The linguistic analysis revealed that word choice is a useful indicator of member satisfaction, and highlights some non-obvious dynamics of satisfied members. See Table 1 for the regression results relating word choice to *member satisfaction*. The adjusted R-squared = 22.6%, i.e., our linguistic model fits the member satisfaction data well and explains 22.6% of the variance. Multi-collinearity tests indicate no issues: see Table 1 for VIF values which are all below 2.4 (the traditional red-line for VIF is 5 or greater), and see Table 2 for correlations which ranged from none to moderate. In the following sub-sections, we discuss what the LIWC categories selected as predictors indicate about how people in successful communities use language to communicate with each other.

I vs. We: It's Not About Me, It's About Us

The coefficients in Table 1 show that communities with more satisfied members used significantly fewer *first person singular* words ("I," "me," "mine"), and significantly more *first person plural* words ("we, "our," "us"). These two categories are among the six *pronouns* categories in LIWC. The other LIWC pronoun categories (total first person, total second person, total third person) were not selected by the regression model, indicating that the pronoun effects are due mainly to the singular/plural contrast in self-reference.

Prior work (focusing on individuals) shows that elevated use of *first person singular* correlates with honesty, depression, low status, personal focus, and informality [34]. Elevated use of *first person plural* correlates with high status, and detachedness in some situations or social connectedness to a group in other situations [34]. Interestingly, these two first person pronoun categories each have a mixture of positive and negative potential psychological correlates. Prior studies of health- and education-focused Internet communities may shed some light: they have found that as communities developed, participants increased their use of *we* words and decreased their use of *I* words [6,36]. Similarly, long-term members of another health-focused community used more *we* words and short-term members used more *I* words [25]. Our results in the context of workplace communities suggest that the use of *we* words indicate social connectedness (e.g., "we can do this"), which is one of the more positive correlates noted in prior work [6,34]. Conversely, the use of *I* words may indicate members are more focused on themselves and have not formed strong bonds with other members.

	anger	work	we	I	article	inhib.	leisure	assent	anxiety
anger	1	.030	.268**	-.067	.224**	.319**	.031	-.057	.456**
work		1	.264**	-.188*	.080	.046	-.043	-.334**	.143
we			1	.235**	.404**	-.010	.132	-.165*	.222**
I				1	.252**	-.115	.377**	.224**	.071
article					1	.204**	-.080	.004	.235**
inhib.						1	-.143	-.118	.444**
leisure							1	.056	-.071
assent								1	-.073
anxiety									1

** Correlation is significant at the 0.01 level (2-tailed).
* Correlation is significant at the 0.05 level (2-tailed).

Table 2. Correlation table for the 9 LIWC categories selected by the regression as predictors of *member satisfaction.*

Anger vs. Anxiety: Opening Up

In communities with more satisfied members, the use of *anger* words (like "hate," "argue," "annoyed") was lower and the use of *anxiety* words (like "worried," "confused," "vulnerable") was higher (see Table 1). These are two *affective processes* categories in LIWC, which are broadly split into *positive emotion* and *negative emotion*, and the latter is further split into *anxiety, anger,* and *sadness*. Interpretations should be qualified by the fact that the result for *anxiety* was marginally significant (p=.107).

In general, the use of emotional words indicates that members may be opening up to each other and seeking support [32]. At first look, it is surprising that anger and anxiety have opposite effects. However, prior studies provide evidence that a nuanced balance of negative emotional expression is needed for positive outcomes. Prior work has shown that expressing emotions—including negative emotions—in writing can improve people's quality of life [28]. Pennebaker and Seagal [28] describe that a useful expression of negative emotion requires balance: too few negative words may signal repression (poor ability to identify and label negative emotions) and too many may signal neuroticism (excessive pondering of negative emotions without closure). These past findings were related to the expressions of individuals, but their manifestation in a community setting could be different. Prior work has also noted that the use of emotional words can increase the likelihood of receiving a reply in an online forum [1] and the use of these words between discussants indicates the degree of immersion with each other [34]. Our finding about the positive relationship between anxiety words and satisfaction may indicate that members were opening up to each other and receiving support for their concerns, which are among the known benefits of communities [31].

Work and Leisure: Socializing at Work is Beneficial

Workplace communities are dominated by work-related discussions [24], but we found that the use of *work* words ("team," "project," "customer") was diminished and the use of *leisure* words ("movie," "book," "soccer") was elevated in communities with more satisfied members (see Table 1 for results). It is important to note that the *work* and *leisure* categories in LIWC indicate the topic of discussion rather than the linguistic style of or psychological processes underlying the discussion (these are the only two topical categories from LIWC included in our analysis). So elevated discussion of work as a topic was problematic, whether this was a discussion of how to execute work, what the status of work was, or some other meta-level discussion of work. One possible explanation is that a focus on work at a meta-level indicates the need to resolve issues with the work, rather than being able to focus on doing the work.

Conversely, an increase in discussion of leisure as a topic was positive. Interpretations should be qualified by the fact that this result was marginally significant (p=.063). This result may indicate that when employee members share a bit about their leisure interests, like attending operas or playing soccer, they also like the community more. Discussion of leisure topics may be a sign that members are having fun together and feel comfortable deviating from work-related discussions, which may indicate the presence of positive social relationships with other members [8].

Inhibition & Assent: Working Together

Elevated use of both *inhibition* ("block," "constrain," "stop") and *assent* words ("agree," "yes," "OK") was linked with higher member satisfaction (see Table 1). Interpretations should be qualified by the fact that these results were marginally significant (Table 1). *Inhibition* is one of eight categories in LIWC that represent *cognitive processes*, which attempt to capture words that reflect active thinking. *Inhibition* words, specifically, signal firmness or the author's likeliness to stand behind his/her statements [3]. Prior work has shown that *inhibition* words are used in effective resolutions to online disputes, since they show strength but do not attack others [3]. *Assents* are a type of conversational word that measures agreement and shows that people are responding to each other [34]. The use of words in these two categories implies fairly good social and professional skills, with members being firm when expressing themselves, and agreeable toward others. Some of the major goals of workplace online communities are to collaborate with and to learn from peers [22], which would benefit from such healthy interactions.

Articles: The Little Words that Matter

Communities with more satisfied members use fewer *articles* ("a," "an," "the"). See Table 1 for results. *Articles* are a type of *function word.* One of the premises of Pennebaker's book on linguistic analysis [15,29] is that function words provide considerable insight into people's psychology. Similarly,

Hyland [15] argues that words that are "about" the concepts, rather than the concepts themselves, are important shapers of communication. Increased use of articles is associated with a greater interest in objects, more concrete and complex language, increased formality, and less emotional expression [29]. High article use is a sign of *categorical thinking*, or a focus on objects, things, and categories. Conversely, lower article use is a sign of *dynamic thinking*, or a focus on action, change, and other people [29]. In the context of workplace communities, our results may indicate that a focus on action, change and people over objects and categories is more satisfying.

Limitations

The main limitation of this work is that the language patterns of effective communities may be different in other contexts, such as production-oriented communities on the internet, healthcare support communities, and so on. Also, to develop a homogeneous dataset for statistical analysis, we excluded very large and very small communities. When there is a sufficient number of communities in those two size ranges, our results should be re-tested. Because our study did show there is a relationship between language and member satisfaction, we advocate future studies exploring this relationship in different contexts.

A second limitation relates to the use of LIWC, which uses a simple "bag of words" approach to assess language. This approach assumes that social and psychological meaning can be derived from text, based on the percentage of words that are present from categories representing those concepts. This ignores syntax, punctuation, conversational structure, and other features of text. Despite this, LIWC has been shown in numerous studies to reliably correlate with meaningful psychological and social phenomena [29,34].

Finally, the explanations put forth in this paper for *why* certain language patterns relate to member satisfaction require further study to prove. The results in this paper provide potential hypotheses for a future study.

DISCUSSION & CONCLUSION

Our results show a fairly strong relationship between language use and member satisfaction. In the context of workplace online communities, member satisfaction is higher with increased use of the first person plural ("we"), leisure, inhibition, anxiety, and assent words, and decreased use of anger, work, first person singular ("I"), and article words. Together, these categories explain 22.6% of the variance in member satisfaction ratings. These results provide insight into the dynamics of effective communities, in which members:

- express social connectedness rather than a focus on themselves;
- share their concerns but moderate their anger;
- discuss their leisure interests but moderate meta-discussions about work;
- use firm and agreeable language; and
- exhibit signs of focusing on action, change and people over objects and categories.

Community leaders may want to encourage discussions among members with these attributes.

Only a portion of these results could have been predicted based on prior online communities research. In particular, prior studies have shown elevated use of *we* words and decreased use of *I* words as communities and members matured [6,25,36]; we add that this language trend also occurs when members are more satisfied. Prior work has also shown that members are more committed to communities that are more social and supportive [19,32]. Our findings about *work* vs. *leisure*, *anger* vs. *anxiety*, and *assents* are consistent with these prior studies, and they contribute to our knowledge of exactly how "social" and "supportive" language is enacted by satisfied members—something that was not known prior to this study. Finally, our results about *articles* provide new knowledge about effective online communities, which emphasize dynamic language over categorical language. Dynamic language is story-like and personal—which appears to work better in online communities—while categorical language defines and fits ideas into boxes [29].

While this work has focused on uncovering the relationship between language use and member satisfaction, future work could extend our effort and explore directly how language use, perhaps in combination of other factors, could be used to develop automatic assessments of member satisfaction. Our research suggests new tools for community leaders, enabling them to complement or even replace the more costly survey-based evaluation of member satisfaction. This would provide leaders with quick and easy assessments of satisfaction on an on-going basis. Our results also suggest new tools for researchers to infer member satisfaction retrospectively, at moments-in-time during the history of a community. This would enable new analyses of events that were previously unmeasurable, like past feature changes, leadership changes, and external events.

REFERENCES

1. Arguello, J., Butler, B.S., et al. Talk to me: foundations for successful individual-group interactions in online communities. *Proc. of CHI*, (2006), 959-968.
2. Brady, K.P., et al. The Use of Alternative Social Networking Sites in Higher Educational Settings: A Case Study of the E-Learning Benefits of Ning in Education. *J. of Int. Online Learn. 9*, 2, 2010, 151-170.
3. Brett, J.M., Olekalns, M., et al. Sticks And Stones: Language, Face, And Online Dispute Resolution. *Academy of Management Journal 50*, 1 (2007), 85-99.
4. Burke, M., Joyce, E., Kim, T., et al. Introductions and Requests: Rhetorical Strategies That Elicit Response in Online Communities. In C. Steinfield, et al., eds., *Communities and Technologies*. Springer, 2007, 21-39.

5. Cassell, J., Huffaker, et al. The language of online leadership: Gender and youth engagement on the Internet. *Developmental Psych. 42*, (2006), 436-449.
6. Cassell, J., Tversky, D. The Language of Online Intercultural Community Formation. *Journal of Computer-Mediated Comm. 10*, 2 (2005).
7. Cicchetti, D.V., Sparrow, S.A. Developing criteria for establishing interrater reliability of specific items: applications to assessment of adaptive behavior. *Am. J. of Mental Deficiency 86*, 2 (1981), 127-137.
8. DiMicco, J., Millen, D.R., et al. Motivations for Social Networking at Work. *Proc. of CSCW*, (2008), 711-720.
9. Dove, J.A., Eubanks, D.L., et al. Making an Entrance 2.0: The Linguistics of Introductory Success in Virtual Communities. *Proc. of HICSS*, (2011), 1-10.
10. Duffy, M.K., Shaw, J.D., Stark, E.M. Performance and Satisfaction in Conflicted Interdependent Groups: When and How Does Self-Esteem Make a Difference? *Academy of Mgt. J. 43*, 4 (2000), 772-782.
11. Dutta-Bergman, M.J. The Antecedents of Community-Oriented Internet Use: Community Participation and Community Satisfaction. *J. of CMC 11*, 1, 2005.
12. Holtzblatt, L.J., Damianos, L.E. Measuring the Success of On-line Communities in an Enterprise Networking Tool. In A.A. Ozok, P. Zaphiris, eds., *Online Communities and Social Computing*. Springer, 2011.
13. Huffaker, D.A. Dimensions of leadership and social influence in online communities. 2009.
14. Hurvich, C.M., Tsai, C.L. Regression and time series model selection in small samples. *Biometrika 76*, 2, (1989), 297-307.
15. Hyland, K. *Metadiscourse: Exploring Interaction in Writing*. Bloomsbury, 2005.
16. Iriberri, A., Leroy, G. A life-cycle perspective on online community success. *ACM Comput. Surv. 41*, 2 (2009), 1-29.
17. Kairam, S.R., Wang, D.J., Leskovec, J. The Life and Death of Online Groups: Predicting Group Growth and Longevity. *Proc. of WSDM*, (2012), 673-682.
18. Kramer, A.D.I., Fussell, S.R., Setlock, L.D. Text analysis as a tool for analyzing conversation in online support groups. *CHI Ext. Abstracts*, (2004), 1485-88.
19. Kraut, R.E., Resnick, P. *Building successful online communities: Evidence-based social design*. MIT, '12.
20. Ludford, P., et al. Think different: increasing online community participation using uniqueness and group dissimilarity. *Proc. of CHI*, (2004), 631-638.
21. Ma, M., Agarwal, R. Through a Glass Darkly: Information Technology Design, Identity Verification, and Knowledge Contribution in Online Communities. *Info. Sys. Research 18*, 1 (2007), 42-67.
22. Matthews, T., et al. Goals and Perceived Success of Online Enterprise Communities: What Is Important to Leaders & Members? *Proc. of CHI*, (2014), 291-300.
23. Matthews, T., Whittaker, S., Badenes, H., Smith, B. Beyond End User Content to Collaborative Knowledge Mapping: Interrelations Among Community Social Tools. *Proc. of CSCW*, (2014), 900-910.
24. Muller, M., et al. Diversity among enterprise online communities: collaborating, teaming, and innovating through social media. *Proc. of CHI*, (2012), 2815-24.
25. Nguyen, D., Rosé, C.P. Language use as a reflection of socialization in online communities. *Proc. of Languages in Social Media*, (2011), 76-85.
26. Nguyen, T., Phung, D., Adams, B., Venkatesh, S. A sentiment-aware approach to community formation in social media. *Proc. of ICWSM*, (2012), 527-530.
27. Pennebaker, J.W., et al. *The development and psychometric properties of LIWC2007*. LIWC.net.
28. Pennebaker, J.W., Seagal, J.D. Forming a story: The health benefits of narrative. *Journal of Clinical Psychology 55*, 10 (1999), 1243-1254.
29. Pennebaker, J.W. *The Secret Life of Pronouns: What Our Words Say About Us*. Bloomsbury Press, 2013.
30. Preece, J., et al. The top five reasons for lurking: improving community experiences for everyone. *Computers in Human Behavior 20*, 2 (2004), 201-223.
31. Preece, J. *Online communities: Designing usability and supporting sociability*. Wiley, 2000.
32. Ren, Y., Kraut, R., Kiesler, S. Applying Common Identity and Bond Theory to Design of Online Communities. *Org. Studies 28*, 3 (2007), 377-408.
33. Shtatland, E., et al. Model Building in PROC PHREG with Automatic Variable Selection and Information Criteria. *SUGI 30 Statistics and Data Analysis*, (2005).
34. Tausczik, Y.R., Pennebaker, J.W. The Psychological Meaning of Words: LIWC and Computerized Text Analysis Methods. *Journal of Language and Social Psychology 29*, 1 (2010), 24-54.
35. Tausczik, Y.R., Pennebaker, J.W. Participation in an online mathematics community: differentiating motivations to add. *Proc. of CSCW*, (2012), 207-216.
36. Vambheim, S.M., Wangberg, S.C., et al. Language use in an internet support group for smoking cessation: development of sense of community. *Informatics for Health and Social Care 38*, 1 (2013), 67-78.
37. Wagner, C., Rowe, M., et al. What catches your attention?: An empirical study of attention patterns in community forums. *Proc. of ICWSM*, (2012).
38. Wenger, E., McDermott, R.A., Snyder, W. *Cultivating communities of practice: A guide to managing knowledge*. Harvard Bus., 2002.
39. Yang, H. The Case for Being Automatic: Introducing the Automatic Linear Modeling (LINEAR) Procedure in SPSS Statistics. *Mult. Lin. Regr. View. 39*, 2 (2013).
40. Yu, B. The emotional world of health online communities. *Proc. of iConference*, (2011), 806-807.

Turkers, Scholars, "Arafat" and "Peace": Cultural Communities and Algorithmic Gold Standards

Shilad Sen
Macalester College
St. Paul, Minnesota
ssen@macalester.edu

Macademia Team:[*]
Margaret E. Giesel, Rebecca Gold, Benjamin Hillmann, Matt Lesicko Samuel Naden, Jesse Russell Zixiao "Ken" Wang
Macalester College
St. Paul, Minnesota

Brent Hecht
University of Minnesota
Minneapolis, Minnesota
bhecht@cs.umn.edu

ABSTRACT

In just a few years, crowdsourcing markets like Mechanical Turk have become the dominant mechanism for for building "gold standard" datasets in areas of computer science ranging from natural language processing to audio transcription. The assumption behind this sea change — an assumption that is central to the approaches taken in hundreds of research projects — is that crowdsourced markets can accurately replicate the judgments of the general population for knowledge-oriented tasks. Focusing on the important domain of *semantic relatedness* algorithms and leveraging Clark's theory of common ground as a framework, we demonstrate that this assumption can be highly problematic. Using 7,921 semantic relatedness judgements from 72 scholars and 39 crowdworkers, we show that crowdworkers on Mechanical Turk produce significantly different semantic relatedness gold standard judgements than people from other communities. We also show that algorithms that perform well against Mechanical Turk gold standard datasets do significantly worse when evaluated against other communities' gold standards. Our results call into question the broad use of Mechanical Turk for the development of gold standard datasets and demonstrate the importance of understanding these datasets from a human-centered point-of-view. More generally, our findings problematize the notion that a universal gold standard dataset exists for all knowledge tasks.

Author Keywords

semantic relatedness; gold standard datasets; cultural communities; Amazon Mechanical Turk; user studies; natural language processing

[*] megiesel@gmail.com rebeccagold0@gmail.com bhillmann-@outlook.com mnlesicko@gmail.com samnaden@gmail.com jesse.p.russell@gmail.com zwang@macalester.edu

CSCW '15, March 14 – 18 2015, Vancouver, BC, Canada.

ACM 978-1-4503-2922-4/15/03$15.00.
http://dx.doi.org/10.1145/2675133.2675285

ACM Classification Keywords

H.5.m. Information Interfaces and Presentation (e.g. HCI): Miscellaneous

INTRODUCTION

Less than a decade after their inception, crowdsourcing markets like Amazon's Mechanical Turk[1] have transformed research and practice in computer science. While computer-supported cooperative work researchers have largely focused on understanding crowdsourcing markets, analyzing and developing crowdsourcing mechanisms, and finding new opportunities to apply these mechanisms, other areas of computer science have also embraced crowdsourcing. In natural language processing and many areas of artificial intelligence, crowdsourcing markets — and in particular Mechanical Turk — have become the de facto method of obtaining the critical resource known as *human-annotated "ground truth" datasets.*

Human-annotated ground truth datasets (henceforth referred to by their more common and simpler name: "gold standards") support a large variety of knowledge-oriented tasks. In general, these datasets capture human beings' "right answers" for tasks when no obvious answer for a given problem exists or can be algorithmically created. Gold standard data support algorithms in a wide range of problem spaces ranging from sentiment analysis [40], to audio transcription [8], to machine translation [5].

In 2008, Snow et al. marked a shift to Amazon's Mechanical Turk (AMT) for collecting gold standards [38]. They showed that AMT workers (known as"turkers") closely replicated five well-known gold standard datasets in the domain of natural language processing, but faster and much more cheaply. Out of this paper, a widely-accepted precept has arisen: AMT workers produce gold standard datasets for knowledge-oriented tasks that are more or less the same as those produced by other groups of people (traditionally domain experts, peers, or local undergraduates). We refer to this as the "turkers for all" precept.

Much work in the social sciences, however, would suggest that the "turkers for all" precept will often not hold. For instance, in Clark's definition of common ground, a cultural

[1] https://www.mturk.com

community — whether it is demarcated by professional, religious, ethnic, or other lines — is defined by the (mutually known) shared knowledge it has about a given set of concepts and their relationships [9]. It should follow then that the people who belong to different cultural communities would provide different answers to a variety of knowledge-oriented tasks. For instance, in a text categorization task, we might expect that scientists would categorize a document about Albert Einstein as a biography of a famous scientist, but a group of peace activists may also categorize it as a biography of a public figure against nuclear weapons, a group of Jewish scholars may want to categorize the text as a biography of a famous Jewish person, and so on [23]. We refer to the hypothesis that different communities produce different gold standards as the "communities matter" precept.

This paper analyzes the tension between the Snow et al. "turkers for all" and Clark "communities matter" precepts.

We focus on two broad questions at the core of the tension between these two precepts:

RQ1: Do different cultural communities produce different gold standards?

RQ2: Do algorithms perform differently on gold standards from different cultural communities?

We study these questions within the field of natural language processing, in the domain of semantic relatedness (SR) algorithms. Generally speaking, SR algorithms provide a single numeric estimate of the number and strength of relationships between any two concepts *a* and *b* (typically between 0 and 1) [20]. For instance, if concept *a* is "pyrite" and concept *b* is "iron", we might expect a good SR algorithm to output a high value for $SR(a, b)$. Conversely, if concept *b* is replaced with "socks", we might expect the opposite. SR has a nearly 50 year tradition of evaluation against gold standards, starting with the RG65 dataset collected by Rubenstein and Goodenough [36].

In this paper, we describe an experiment with 111 participants that shows that the "communities matter' hypothesis is supported for both RQ1 and RQ2. Specifically, we show that AMT workers, communities of general academics and subject-area experts each have their own "gold standard" for a series of SR problem instances. Broadly, as the cultural community's depth of knowledge increases, they seem to perceive more connections between concepts (instead of more differences). In addition, we show that SR algorithms determined to be "start-of-the-art" in their ability to replicate a gold standard dataset are indeed only "state-of-the-art" *for a given cultural community*. More specifically SR algorithms have difficulty matching the SR judgements of subject experts (particularly psychologists), even when trained on data from that same group.

We also find support for the "turkers for all" precept in some contexts. Mechanical Turk serves as a tremendously valuable resource offering fast, inexpensive data. Thus, we identify areas where turkers are more likely to provide gold standard judgements that are consistent with other communities. Specifically, for knowledge-oriented tasks for which all or most relevant information is in the common ground of a wide variety of cultural communities, using Mechanical Turk to develop gold standards is likely more appropriate.

To summarize, our work offers three main contributions:

1. We show that AMT-derived gold standards for knowledge-oriented tasks are often not representative of other communities. We explicitly probe when these differences occur.
2. We show that algorithms that perform well against an AMT-derived gold standard do not necessarily perform well against gold standards produced by other populations.
3. Our work problematizes the notion of the gold standard in general, highlighting types of tasks for which gold standards may be problematic and types of tasks for which which they are likely to be appropriate.

These findings have immediate implications for a number of constituencies, for instance researchers who use AMT and other crowdsourcing platforms, SR researchers, and practitioners designing systems that rely on the automatic completion of knowledge tasks, particularly systems for domain experts such as doctors, musicians, scholars, etc. More broadly, by problematizing the gold standard dataset, this work has implications for a methodology employed by researchers in a variety of areas of computer science.

Below, we first cover work related to this research and highlight our methodological approach. Following that, we report the results of our experiment. We then discuss our findings in more detail. Finally, we close by detailing the limitations of our study and highlighting future work in this area.

RELATED WORK

Semantic relatedness

The automatic estimation of the relatedness between two concepts has been an active area of research in artificial intelligence (AI) and natural language processing (NLP) for decades [36, 35, 6, 39, 14].

Semantic relatedness (SR) algorithms — the family of algorithms that perform this estimation – underly an enormous variety of applications. These applications range from low-level tasks like word sense disambiguation (e.g. [28]) and coreference resolution (e.g. [32]) to high-level technologies like search [6, 34] and information visualization systems [4, 37, 3].

SR algorithms are typically trained and evaluated against datasets of "gold standard" relatedness judgements from human participants (e.g. [12, 25]). The literature treats these judgements as by and large universally correct - it does not consider how the population of gold standard contributors (typically university students or AMT crowdworkers) aligns with that of the target application.

The vast majority of work in the semantic relatedness domain is dedicated to developing algorithms that can replicate the human judgements present in a small number of benchmark gold standard datasets. These algorithms are both diverse and numerous, with approaches grounded in areas ranging from network analysis (e.g. [26]) to information theory (e.g. [35]) to information retrieval (e.g. [14, 34]) to the semantic web [13]. SR algorithms rely on a source of world knowledge, which is most commonly derived from Wikipedia (e.g. [14]) or WordNet (e.g. [35]).

WordSim353 [12] is the most widely-used benchmark dataset of SR judgements. The community(ies) from which the annotators of *WordSim353* were selected is not explicitly disclosed. More recently, other SR benchmark datasets have begun to appear in the literature, including *TSA287* [34] and *MTurk771* [18], all of which are made up of judgements from Mechanical Turk. Understanding the effects of this recent trend towards using Mechanical Turk as a source of human relatedness judgements is one of the key motivations behind our consideration of Mechanical Turk in this research.

Some algorithmic SR research has included sub-studies related to our research. For instance, while developing a new semantic relatedness algorithm designed specifically for the bioinformatics domain, Pedersen et al.[30], tangentially noted that SR judgements from doctors and medical coders differed, remarking that "by all means, more experimentation is necessary" in this area. In another primarily algorithmic paper, Pirró and Seco report on the effect of language ability on a small set of concept pairs. They found very high levels of agreement between native and non-native English speakers at the same university after excluding non-native outlier judgements [31]. Snow et al. [38] compared turkers' assessments to traditional SR annotators, also finding very high levels of agreement. Our work is distinguished from that above in scope, depth and, ultimately, outcome. We collect a dataset an order of magnitude larger than these previous datasets. We leverage this data to robustly probe the relationship between community membership and SR ratings. We also reveal divergence in intra- and interrater consistency across communities and demonstrate the effect of domain-related concepts versus general concepts.

In addition to its importance to a large number of research projects and applications in NLP and AI, semantic relatedness has also played a role in the HCI domain. Liesaputra and Witten have leveraged SR algorithms to create electronic books that improve performance on reading tasks [24] and Grieser et al. [17] did the same assess the relatedness of exhibits for museum visitors. Visualization has been a particularly active area of interest, with semantic relatedness being used, for instance, to cluster conversation topics in a system that highlights salient moments in live conversations [4], develop geospatial information that facilitates the development of spatial thinking skills [37], among other applications (e.g. [3]).

Cultural communities and online differences

To situate the results of our gold standard dataset analyses and evaluations of semantic relatedness algorithms, this work adapts Clark's definition of cultural communities from his theory of language as joint action [9]. As part of this theory, Clark defines a cultural community as "a group of people with shared expertise that other people lack." These groups can be delineated by geography, profession, language, hobbies, age, whether or not they are a part of an online community (e.g. AMT) and so on, but what they all share are unique sets of shared knowledge and beliefs. While Clark's theory is typically (and widely) applied in understanding how interlocutors work together to build a shared understanding of a given domain [15, 16], in this work, we are interested in the *pre-existing* shared knowledge that exists in cultural communities. We will show that Clark's formulation can help explain which gold standard datasets are liable to cultural variation and which ones will stay roughly constant across cultural groups (and why).

Cultural differences have been shown to influence annotations on tasks other than SR estimation. Dong and Fu demonstrated that European Americans tag images differently from people with a Chinese background [10] and a similar result has been identified across gender lines [33]. Similarly, Dong et al. found that culture has an effect not only on image tags themselves, but also annotators' reactions to tag suggestions [11]. However, this work has not examined cultural differences on gold standard datasets and has not sought to understand the effect of cultural bias on algorithm performance as we do here. Along the same lines, researchers have looked at the demographics of workers on AMT [22, 29], but have not focused on the effect these demographics have on gold standard datasets.

Crowdsourcing gold standards

A related area of research outside of the SR domain compares the performance of crowdworkers to that of local human annotators. Snow et al. established that "turkers" are able to closely replicate the results of local annotators on many labeling tasks in NLP in addition to SR [38]. Similar results have been seen in studies in psychology [7], translation [5], graphical perception [21], and a number of other areas. Our work adds to the literature that explores the relationship between "the crowd" and other annotators. However, unlike most research in this area, we find that judgements can differ substantially between these two groups of annotators. Importantly, our work also provides insight into the types of tasks for which "the crowd" and others will differ, and those for which this is not the case.

SURVEY METHODOLOGY

To measure the effects of cultural community on gold standards, we collected SR gold standards from different cultural communities[2] using an online survey. Before detailing the survey design and methodology, we provide an overall picture of its experimental and experiential design.

We recruited subjects from two cultural communities related to the "turkers for all" and "communities matter" precepts: AMT crowd workers and scholars. The survey collected *SR assessments* from subjects; a single SR assessment is a relatedness rating between 0 and 4 (inclusive) by a subject for a concept pair (e.g. a rating of 4 by turker number 12413 for the pair "movie", "film"). We followed common practice of SR

[2]The SR datasets in this paper are available online at http://shilad.com/pluraSR200.html

gold standards, which collect assessments from five to twenty subjects for each concept pair and report the mean SR rating for each pair.

To probe the applicability of each precept, we collected assessments for two type of concept pairs: *general knowledge* concept pairs (i.e. "television" and "admission"), and *domain-specific* concept pairs in history, biology, and psychology. With respect to Clark, we hypothesized that general knowledge concepts and their interrelationships would be relatively likely to be in the common ground of a wide variety of cultural groups. We hypothesized that domain-specific concepts in history, biology, and psychology and their interrelationships were *less* likely to be in a broadly-held common ground. In other words, people from different cultural communities (especially professionally delineated ones) would have a different understanding of each concept in these pairs, as well as the relationships between them.

All subjects completed an identically structured online survey. To summarize the survey's experimental design, it collected assessments for the two different types of concept pairs (general and domain-specific). Assessments came from three different cultural communities: AMT workers, scholars, and scholar-experts who were experts for a particular domain-specific assessment (e.g. a psychologist assessing "cognition" and "language"). Membership in each of the three communities is *question-specific* for researchers; a single researcher may be a scholar-expert for some concept pairs (e.g. psychology) and a scholar for others (e.g. history).

After consenting to the study, subjects entered basic demographic information (gender, education level) and indicated whether they conduct scholarly research. Those who did (scholars) provided their primary, secondary, and tertiary fields of study. Next, subjects provided 69 SR assessments spanning 6 pages. Subjects rated each concept pair on a 5 point scale ranging from 0 (not related) to 4 (strongly related) (Figure 1). Subjects could indicate that they "did not know a term" instead of providing an SR rating. After completing the 69 assessments, subjects were asked if they would like to complete a second round of assessments.

Selection of concept pairs for each subject:

Each subject provided 69 assessments of concept pairs. All subjects provided SR judgements for (a) 10 general knowledge assessments, (b) 50 domain-specific assessments chosen from the fields of biology, history, and psychology, (c) 4 validation assessments, and (d) 5 duplicate assessments. Each type of assessment is described in more detail below. The survey randomized the order of all concept pairs and ensured that each page spanned a variety of estimated relatedness values.

General knowledge concepts: General knowledge terms were chosen from *WordSim353*. The concept pairs in *WordSim353* consist of common nouns (e.g. "television", "admission") and a few widely-known named entities (e.g. countries, famous political figures). We randomly sampled 50 concept pairs from the dataset. The sample was stratified to ensure that the concepts captured a diverse set of relatedness values.

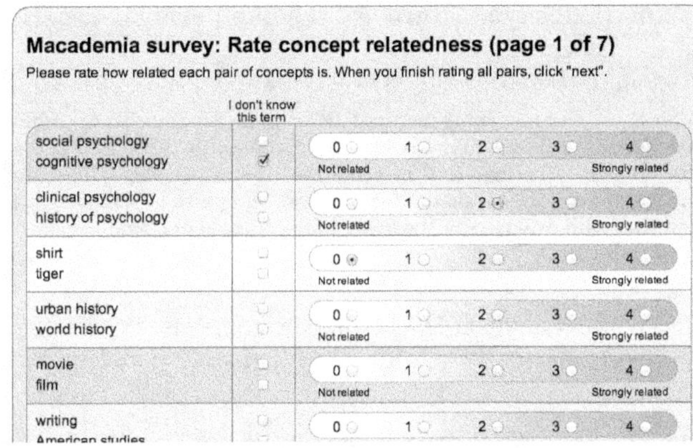

Figure 1. The rating page in the online survey. The subject has indicated that they do not understand the phrase "cognitive psychology.". The assessments on this subject's page include validation concepts ("movie", "film", 5 total), psychology concepts (25 total), and history concepts (25 total).

Domain-specific concepts: We chose 50 candidate concept pairs for each of the fields of biology, history, and psychology. Subjects who were biologists, historians, or psychologists provided 25 domain-expert assessments from their field and 25 assessments from a second target field (history, biology, or psychology). All other subjects provided 25 domain-specific questions from each of two target fields (two of history, biology, or psychology). Further rationale and and our methods for choosing these concept pairs is detailed in the following section.

Validation assessments: We added four validation assessments following the procedure of [18]. These assessments were intended to identify subjects who were not completing the survey in good faith. These concepts pairs contained the two most related ("female", "woman" and "film", "movie") and least related concept pairs ("shirt", "tiger" and "afternoon", "substance") from [18]. Subjects that did not accurately rate these pairs are excluded from our results. This validation test would exclude 94% of subjects who guess randomly.

Duplicate assessments: Subjects also completed five duplicate assessments to measure intra-rater agreement. All duplicate concept pairs were separated by at least one survey page.

Selecting domain-specific concept pairs:

The domain-specific concept pairs were harvested using the Macademia website[3] that visualizes research connections between scholars. Over 2000 users have created profiles on the website, which involves entering one's research interests as free-form text. We selected three diverse and popular fields (history, psychology, biology) as target knowledge areas. For each field, we selected the most common 16 interests, as we hypothesized that these were most likely to be within the common ground of members of each individual field[4] speci-

[3]http://macademia.macalester.edu

[4]We chose this cutoff because at least 16 interests were used three times in all three fields.

knowledge type	turker	scholar	scholar-expert
general	461	861	n/a
domain-specific	2,218	3,086	1,295

Table 1. Experimental manipulations in our study. Rows indicate knowledge type, and columns indicate community. Each cell contains the number of ratings in that condition. For example, 1,295 ratings have been provided for domain-specific concept pairs by scholar-experts (scholars with expertise in the field of the concepts in a pair).

fied by users in the field as candidate concepts. We randomly chose 50 concept pairs from the 16 candidate concepts.[5]

Subject recruitment and basic statistics:

As noted above, we recruited subjects via the Macademia website and Amazon's Mechanical Turk. We emailed invitations to a subset of Macademia users: all psychologists, biologists, and historians and a random sample of other users. We also hired "master" Mechanical Turk workers, who the AMT website describes as "an elite groups of Workers who have demonstrated accuracy on specific types of HITs on the Mechanical Turk marketplace[6]". We chose to recruit 45 turkers to match the number of scholar and scholar-expert subjects. All crowdworkers were paid at an average rate above the United States federal minimum wage.

In total, 145 subjects participated in the study. Twenty subjects did not complete the validation assessments accurately or did not finish the survey and are excluded from our results. To clearly delineate differences between turkers and scholars, we excluded users who were neither turkers nor scholars (10 subjects) and turkers who reported they were scholars (4 subjects).

Of the 111 final valid subjects, 39 were turkers, 42 were scholars in history, psychology, or biology, and the remaining 30 were scholars in some other field. 60% of valid subjects were female and 40% were male. All scholars indicated they held a graduate degree. Of the turkers, 13% had a graduate degree, 59% indicated their highest degree was a two- or four-year degree, and 28% indicated their highest degree was a G.E.D. or high school degree.

Table 1 shows the experimental manipulations we utilized in our study. The rows of the table indicate the knowledge type of the concept pairs (i.e. general or domain-specific). The columns of the table indicate the community of the subject. The numbers in each cell indicate the total number of assessments (not users) for each condition. For example, Table 1 reveals that we collected 861 total assessments of general knowledge concept pairs from all scholars (the *general/scholar* condition) and 1,295 assessments in the *domain-specific/scholar-expert* condition, which contains ratings from scholars who have domain expertise with regard to a given concept pair. Similarly, Table 1 shows that we received 461 assessments from turkers on general knowledge concept pairs (the *general/turker* condition) and 2,218 assessments in the *domain-specific/turker* condition.

Note that all subjects completed assessments that span multiple conditions: turkers assessed both specific and general concept pairs; biologists assessed some concept pairs in their field, some in either psychology or history, some from the general domain; and so on. The upper right column is not studied because the concepts in *WordSim353* are not associated with a specific domain of expertise.

Each concept pair was assessed by an average of 46 subjects. Subjects did not understand at least one concept in 1.6% of assessments. These assessments are not included in our results. Some analyses in later sections compare different groups' responses to each concept pair. To support these analyses, each group from Table 1 must have a reasonable number of responses to each concept pair. The biggest challenge to sample size occurs in the domain-specific/scholar-expert (scholar-expert responses for domain-specific concepts) because only a small subset of our population has domain expertise in a given concept. The mean number of scholar-expert responses per pair was 8.6 (median=9, min=6). Other conditions have more responses. For example, there are 14.8 (median=15, min=7) assessments per concept pair in the domain-specific/turker condition.

RQ1: EFFECTS ON GOLD STANDARDS

In this section, we analyze the judgements collected from the online survey to answer RQ1, which asks whether different cultural communities produce different gold standards. We study two characteristics of the human SR assessments that constitute a gold standard. First, we measure whether different communities coalesce around different numerical estimate values for a particular concept pair.

*RQ1a: Do different communities produce different semantic relatedness **estimates**?*

RQ1a studies whether a gold standard dataset must be matched to the audience of the system it serves. For example, if turkers and historians differ in their mean assessment of the relatedness of"sexuality" and "African history" (looking ahead: they do), a system serving historians may not be able to rely on a gold standard created by turkers.

The second research question measures whether different cultural communities exhibit different levels of agreement within their respective communities.

*RQ1b: Do different communities exhibit different levels of **agreement** in their SR ratings?*

If the answer to this question is yes, some cultural communities will need more contributors than others to obtain a desired level of gold standard sample error [1].

For each of four different analysis (two each for RQ1a and RQ1b), we report differences between the five conditions in

[5]We followed the procedure of Radinksy et al. [34] to ensure that the 50 pairs selected for each field captured a diverse set of relatedness values. Radinksy and colleagues randomly sampled concept pairs stratified by pointwise mutual information calculated using a New York Times corpus. We followed the same procedure, but used a domain-specific corpus for each field, each of which contained 800 scholarly publications in the field chosen by querying the top 50 documents in Google Scholar for each of the 16 interests in the field.

[6]https://www.mturk.com/mturk/help?helpPage=worker

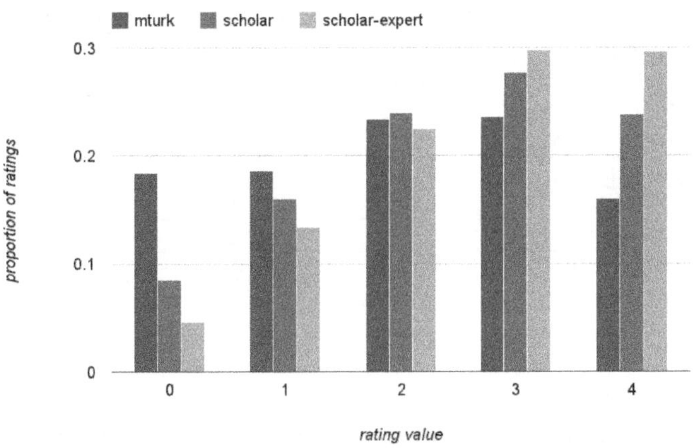

Figure 2. The distribution of ratings for domain-specific knowledge for turkers, scholars, and scholar-experts. In general, turkers judge concepts as less related than scholars and scholar-experts. For example, turkers are four times more likely to rate a domain-specific pair a "0" than scholar-experts.

Table 1 corresponding to the two knowledge types (general, domain-specific) and three cultural contexts (turker, scholar, scholar-expert).

RQ1a: Distribution of assessments

We begin by analyzing the overall distribution of SR ratings for each knowledge type and community. For general knowledge, turkers and scholars generate a similar distribution of ratings. There were no significant differences in mean SR rating between turkers ($\mu = 2.24, \sigma = 1.47, n = 461$) and scholars ($\mu = 3.36, \sigma = 1.4, n = 887$). However, an ANOVA that controls for concept pair means does indeed reveal significant differences between turkers and scholars ($p < 0.05$). We return to this point in the next section (Table 2).

The distribution of ratings for domain-specific knowledge (Figure 2) show marked differences. In aggregate, turkers rate pairs the lowest (mean 2.0), followed by scholars (2.42), and scholar-experts (2.67). Chi-square tests shows these effects to be significant ($\chi^2 = 279, p < 0.0001$). These differences are most apparent at the scale extremes. Turkers assign 18% of judgements a relatedness of 0 compared to 9% of scholars and 4% of scholar-experts. On the opposite end of the spectrum, scholar-experts assign 30% of judgements a 4 compared to 24% and 15% of judgements from scholars and turkers respectively.

In these results, we see our first evidence that both the 'turkers for all' and "communities matter" precepts hold in certain contexts. As Clark's notion of cultural communities suggests, scholar-experts perceive stronger relationships between concepts in their common ground when compared to turkers assessing concepts not in their common ground. The same is true to a lesser degree for scholars (non-experts), although they appear to share more common ground with scholar-experts, which is to be expected given their shared environment and experience.

concept 1	concept 2	turker mean	scholar mean	p-value
Arafat	peace	0.33	2.38	***
hardware	network	1.75	3.15	***
energy	consumer	1.09	2.45	**
plane	car	1.71	2.79	**
dollar	yen	2.89	3.78	**

Table 2. General knowledge concepts with the largest difference between turker and scholar means (* = $p < 0.001$, ** = $p < 0.01$ according to a two-tailed t-test).**

RQ1a: Correlation between community consensus ratings

In this section, we probe differences between average community ratings for both general and domain specific knowledge. For each concept pair, we calculate the mean at the community-level and combine these values to create community-level "consensus lists."

For general knowledge concepts, the Spearman correlation between consensus lists for turkers and scholars ($\rho_s = 0.91, n = 50$) approaches the estimated within-community correlation ($\rho_s = 0.94$).[7] While the between-community correlation for general concepts is high, there are certain concept pairs that are large outliers. Table 2 shows the general knowledge concept pairs that displayed the largest differences between turker and scholar ratings. As a reminder, assessments use a zero to four scale. Most notably, while turkers judge the relatedness between "Arafat" and "peace" to be 0.33 on average, or basically not related at all, the mean scholar rating for the pair is a moderate 2.38. As noted above, the ("Arafat", "peace") pair comes from the *WordSim353* dataset, which has been used to evaluate dozens of SR algorithms. The raters of *WordSim353* also gave the pair a moderate score (mean of 6.73 on a continuous 10-point scale). This suggests that SR algorithms have been evaluated (and trained, in many cases) using a point of view closer to scholars than turkers on this controversial subject. The reasons behind the significant divergence on this pair are unclear, but this result certainly raises the prospect of controversy (i.e. relationship valence) having an effect on semantic relatedness judgements across communities.

For domain-specific concepts, we find broader differences between communities' consensus ratings. While the correlation between turkers and scholars ($\rho_s = 0.88$, $n = 150$ questions) nearly matches the within-condition correlation estimates ($\rho_s = 0.89$, $n = 150$), scholar-experts and turkers are much farther apart in their consensus lists ($\rho_s = 0.76$, $n = 150$). Scholars and scholar-experts are in-between ($\rho_s = 0.82$, $n = 150$). As with the general knowledge analysis, the concept pairs with largest differences provide insight into the dynamics of community disagreement (Table 3). This list appears to favor broad, complex concepts ("sexuality", "African history", "popular religion"). One hypothesis is that scholar-experts' deep domain knowledge includes

[7]The use of Spearman's correlation coefficient is considered to be a best practice in the SR literature because it does not assume interval scales, does not make any assumptions about the distribution of ratings, and for a number of other reasons [42]. Within-condition correlations were estimated using a bootstrap procedure.

group 1	group 2	concept a	concept b	group 1 mean	group 2 mean	p-value
mturk	scholar	psychophysiology	aging	1.30	3.15	***
		introductory biology	statistics	0.80	2.11	***
		research methods	linguistics	1.23	2.51	***
mturk	scholar-expert	sexuality	African history	0.60	2.80	***
		cognition	acculturation	0.73	2.83	***
		modern European history	women	1.56	3.62	***
scholar	scholar-expert	sexuality	historical memory	2.07	3.50	**
		South Asia	popular religion	2.31	3.70	**
		collective memory	women	2.58	3.92	**

Table 3. Domain-specific concepts with the largest difference between turker and scholar means (* indicates $p < 0.001$, ** = $p < 0.01$ according to a two-tailed t-test).**

specific relationships that link concepts that may appear unrelated to non-experts (scholars and turkers). This would also explain scholar-experts' higher absolute SR scores.

These results show that the "communities matter" precept extends beyond individuals in communities to the gold standards that aggregate individuals' assessments. As with the previous analysis, scholars agree more often with scholar-experts than turkers, both in rating distribution and consensus rank order. This may be a sign of interdisciplinarity. Some scholars' specialized knowledge may reach beyond their core field of study. For example, a computer scientist who studies social computing may have some expertise in the SR judgement for the concept pair "personality" and "social psychology". On the other hand, these results may transcend domain knowledge and reflect other cultural commonalities shared by scholars.

RQ1b: Inter-rater agreement

We next examine the inter-rater agreement of judgements in different conditions by measuring the absolute difference between judgments for two raters in the same community.[8]

To calculate absolute differences, for each concept pair we compared responses from all pairs of human raters within a community. We report the mean absolute error (MAE) between the responses and the percentage of responses that disagreed by more than one rating point (e.g. 2 vs 4, or 2 vs 5). We determined confidence intervals for MAE and percentage significant disagreement using a bootstrapping procedure [27] and report 95% confidence intervals.

For general knowledge concepts, we found no meaningful differences in the agreement of within-group ratings. Turkers and scholars exhibited low absolute errors between ratings (turker MAE = 0.92±0.013, scholar MAE = 0.89±0.025) and few significant disagreements (22% ± 1.0 for both). For domain-specific concepts, we found significant differences in inter-rater agreement. Turkers disagreed most often, followed by scholars, followed by scholar-experts. These results held for both MAE (turker = 1.06 ± 0.007, scholar = 0.94 ±0.005, scholar-expert = 0.86±0.007) and percent significant disagreements (turker = 28% ± 0.4, scholar = 23% ± 0.3, scholar-expert = 19% ± 0.6).

[8] We also calculated Pearson correlations between individual raters and found consistent results.

The difference between general knowledge and domain-specific agreement is particularly striking, and begs further study into the mechanisms underlying judgements of domain-specific concepts. The similar levels of agreement in general knowledge judgements suggest that agreement is not simply a function of professional background (scholar vs turker), but is also related to a subject's expertise in the topics of a judgement.

RQ1b: Intra-rater agreement

Finally, we examine the internal agreement within individual subjects. Recall that each subject provided five duplicate ratings for concept pairs, where the duplicating rating was separated from the original rating by at least one page. We report the average difference (MAE) between all subjects' duplicate ratings within a community. Since this represents a paired experimental design (unlike the previous analysis), we can calculate significance using straightforward t-tests.

Overall, the intra-rater agreement of ratings was high (MAE=0.38). Subjects exhibited higher intra-rater agreement for general concepts (MAE=0.237, σ=0.52, n=114) than domain-specific concepts (MAE=0.406, n=554, σ=0.610) These differences are significant (two-sample t-test, $p <= 0.05$).

As with inter-rater agreement, we saw no significant differences in the intra-rater agreement of general knowledge concepts for turkers (MAE=0.24, σ=0.532, n=42) and scholars (mae=0.224, σ=0.517, n=67). We did find significant differences in the intra-rater agreement of domain-specific concepts. Scholar-experts agreed with themselves most (MAE=0.260, σ=0.441, n=96), followed by scholars (MAE=0.382, σ=0.57, n=251), followed by turkers (MAE=0.537, σ=0.738, n=164). These pairwise differences are significant (two-tailed t-test, $p <= 0.05$).

The results for intra-rater agreement parallel the results for inter-rater agreement. We observe no significant community differences in agreement for general knowledge terms, but we do find significant differences for domain-specific knowledge. Scholar-experts agree most strongly, followed by scholars, followed by turkers.

RQ1: Summary

In summary, we find support for the "turkers for all" precept for general knowledge tasks, and "communities matter" for domain-specific concepts. We observe community differences for domain-specific concepts across several measurements: differences in individual ratings, differences in aggregate consensus ratings, and agreement within and between raters.

These finding have direct implications for practitioners and researchers collecting domain-specific gold standards. When collecting a gold standard researchers and practitioners must consider the audience of the gold standard, the system or algorithm that uses it, and the type of knowledge. In addition, to achieve a desired level of sample error in a domain-specific gold standard, more data is needed from people without expert knowledge than with [1]. Because domain expertise is often valued in the marketplace, this finding exposes a monetary tradeoff: more data that is inexpensive from general workers, or less data that is expensive from domain experts.

RQ2: EFFECTS ON ALGORITHMS

We have shown that under some important conditions, different communities do indeed produce different gold standards. Next, we analyze whether the algorithmic "communities matter" precept also holds. That is, we ask:

RQ2: Do algorithms perform differently on gold standards from different cultural communities?

For example, given a particular algorithm and set of problem instances (e.g. concept pairs), do we see different results when the algorithm is trained and evaluated on data from biologists compared to turkers? If the algorithmic "communities matter' precept holds, system designers need to consider the relationship between three entities: the audience they serve, the communities producing their gold standard, and the algorithms that power their system.

We study this question by measuring the performance of SR algorithms on gold standards produced by each cultural community. We evaluate three state-of-the-art algorithms that have been shown to perform well on common gold standards:

1. **MW**, an algorithm developed by Milne and Witten that fist disambiguates each of the two phrases to Wikipedia articles (i.e. the phrase "Apple" → the article "Apple_Inc.") and then measures the overlap in links to and from the two articles [41] (MW).
2. **ESA**, Gabrilovich et al.'s Explicit Semantic Analysis algorithm creates a "concept vector" for each phrase by searching for Wikipedia articles whose text closely match the phrase [14]. The similarity between the phrases is the cosine similarity between the two concept vectors.
3. **ENS**, an ensemble algorithm that linearly combines a variety of SR algorithms as described by Hecht at al. [19].

We developed implementations of each algorithm available in the WikiBrain software framework [9], calibrated to perform similarly to published accuracy measurements [19]. Although SR research typically tunes, trains, and tests algorithms on the same dataset, we employ cross-validation because it is common practice in the CSCW and machine learning communities. Cross-validation results in slightly lower accuracy measurements than described in [19], but constitutes a more realistic measurement.

[9]http://wikibrainapi.org

	MW	ESA	ENS
Spearman's correlation, ρ_s	0.59	0.69	0.76

Table 4. Results for the three algorithms on the WordSim353 dataset. The three algorithms perform relatively similarly on other widely used datasets. Our use of cross-validation leads to slightly lower correlations than reported in the SR literature, but a more robust evaluation.

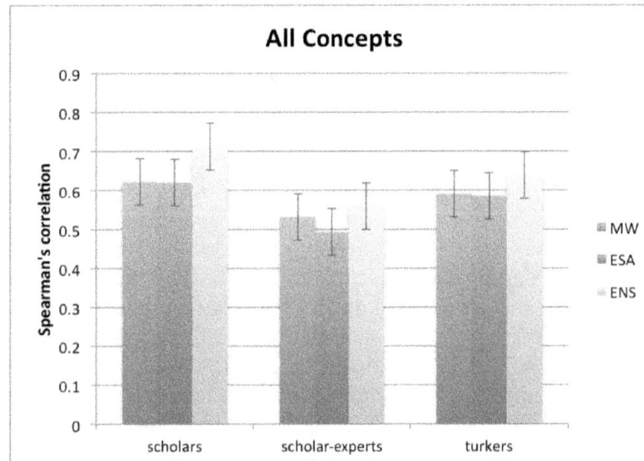

Figure 3. The correlation between algorithmic estimates and gold standard datasets for each of the gold standards and algorithms. The linear ensemble performs best across all groups, followed by MW and ESA. All algorithms are less accurate for scholar-experts than other cultural communities.

As a frame of reference, Table 4 shows the accuracy for the SR three algorithms on the widely used WordSim353 dataset [12]. The table shows Spearman's correlation, ρ_s, between SR estimates and the actual SR values in the gold standard. Spearman's correlation is the most commonly used evaluation measure in the SR community. The linear ensemble ENS performs best, followed by ESA and MW. These algorithmic results (ENS best, ESA second, MW third) generally hold across other reference datasets [19].

We first evaluate each algorithm's performance for each cultural community. Figure 3 shows Spearman's correlation for all three groups' datasets and all three algorithms. As expected, ENS performs best on all three datasets. However, for the domain-specific dataset, MW bests ESA for each group, contradicting years of SR results on datasets such as WordSim353. The differences in performance for ESA and MW may arise from the particular knowledge domains we consider. MW relies on link overlap, and concepts within the same domain likely contain links that overlap more often, creating a stronger signal for MW. In addition, ESA relies on textual search and may perform better for single words than the specific multi-word phrases that commonly appear in our dataset.

The differences in relative SR accuracy between WordSim353, a general knowledge gold standard, and our domain-focused gold standard show that an algorithm that performs well on one gold standard need not perform well on others. They also point to the "community matters" hypothesis for algorithmic performance; MW may be more suitable for an audience of historians, biologists, or psychologists than in other settings.

To provide deeper insight into the algorithmic "community matters" hypothesis, we next focus on algorithmic peformance for domain specific questions, where we saw the largest community differences in previous analyses. As with previous analyses, each algorithm is trained and tested on one community (e.g. historians) by performing cross-validation against that community's gold standard. Figure 4 shows the results for the 150 domain-specific questions, broken out by community. The domain-specific results for the three top-level communities (scholars, scholar-experts, and turkers) show the same trend as all concepts (Figure 3), but with larger effects. The three scholar-expert sub-communities exhibit distinctive SR performance on the 50 concept pairs in their domain. All three algorithms perform roughly the same for historians, while ESA slightly outperforms MW for biologists. Psychologists emerge as a clear outlier, with ENS performing substantially worse than both MW and ENS.

The poor performance of ENS for psychologists is statistically significant, unique, and supports the "community matters' algorithmic hypothesis. The Spearman's correlation for ENS on the 50 psychology pairs is only 0.22 when trained and tested on the psychology dataset, compared to 0.67 for the turker dataset.[10] A standard two-sided confidence interval on this correlation falls just short of significant ($p = 0.06$). However, a non-parametric statistical evaluation that uses the Wilcoxon signed-rank test to leverage the paired structure of the observation finds them to be very significant ($p = 1 \times 10^{-5}$, details described in the Appendix). We next investigate this difference more deeply.

To understand why ENS performed poorly for psychologists, we next consider whether any consistents patterns arise in SR estimates for psychologists. The poor performance primarily arises from highly related concepts that are predicted as moderately related or unrelated. Figure 5 visualizes the five psychology concept pairs most responsible for the decline in algorithmic performance differences between the two communities. The x axis shows actual human relatedness responses (right is more related in the gold standard). The y axis shows algorithmic predicted relatedness (up is predicted to be more related). Arrows and colors visualize the change in actual and predicted relatedness from turkers (blue) to psychologists (red). The green diagonal line x = y shows accurate predictions (predicted rank = actual rank).

To provide intuition for the visualization, we describe the "health psychology", "child development" pair appearing in the upper left. First, consider the blue starting point of the line. The turker gold standard ranked the pair as the 29th most similar (X axis). The turker-trained algorithm predicted

[10]The Spearman's correlation of 0.71 in Figure 4 is calculated on all 150 pairs. When pruning to the 50 psychology pairs the correlation drops slightly to 0.67.

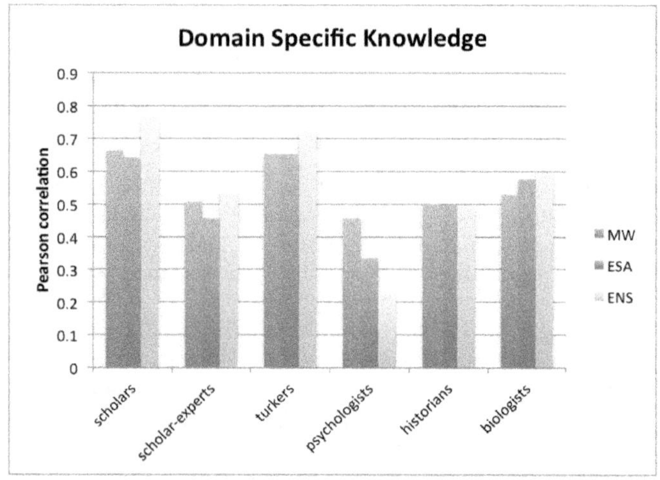

Figure 4. The correlation between algorithmic estimates and gold standard datasets for each of the gold standards and algorithms on the domain-specific questions.

the concept pair would be the 26th most similar pair of the 50 psychology terms (Y axis). Since this is a relatively accurate ranking (26 is close to 29), the blue starting point appears near the green line. The "red shift" to the upper left indicates that performance on the psychology gold standard worsened. Psychologists assessed it as the 37th most related pair (relatively unrelated), while the algorithm trained on the psychology gold standard yielded a predicted rank of 8 (quite related)/

Several patterns emerge from Figure 5. First, all five concept pairs show a decrease in performance for psychologists (i.e. a shift away from the green diagonal line). This is by design; this visualization includes the pairs most responsible for the decline in psychology performance. Second, all shifts except for "health psychology" / "child development" arise from an increase in actual gold standard relatedness coupled with a decrease in predicted relatedness. Third, many of the pairs include a relatively broad psychology concept ("cognition", "language", "neuroscience", "child development", "research methods").

These final two observations — 1) that broad concepts account for the most egregious scholar-expert errors, and 2) that algorithms typically *under*-predict the relatedness of broad concepts for scholar experts — are consistent with our earlier findings. Recall that broad concepts accounted for the largest community differences in human SR estimates (Table 3); scholar experts viewed broad concepts as more related than other cultural communities. Our findings also suggest that the knowledge encoded within Wikipedia, and the algorithms derived from this knowledge, may more closely reflect the perspectives of turkers than domain experts. If true, Wikipedia-based algorithms trained on data from turkers will not only perform differently for domain experts — they will likely perform worse. This may introduce a dangerous scenario in which an algorithm developer targeting domain experts may over-estimate the algorithm's performance if they test (incorrectly) on a turker gold-standard.

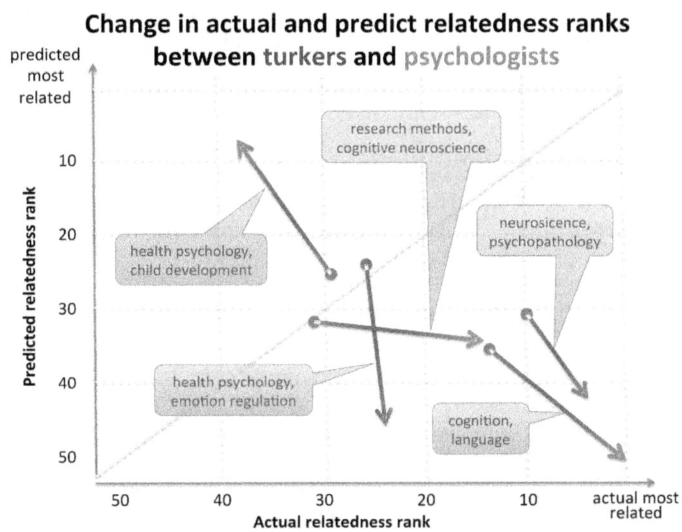

Figure 5. The five biggest shifts in ENS's predicted relatedness (X axis) and actual relatedness (Y axis) between turkers and psychologists. Arrows show change from turkers (blue) to psychologists (red). The green diagonal line shows accurate predictions (predicted rank = actual rank).

To summarize our findings for RQ2, we find support for the algorithmic "communities matters" precept in contexts when domain expertise is relevant. Algorithmic performance differences arise from differences in both community judgements and algorithmic estimates, and performance declines most when these two shifts occur in opposite directions. It seems that as with human assessments, broad abstract concepts lead to the largest community differences in algorithmic SR estimates. Our findings also may suggest that sophisticated algorithms with many tunable parameters (such as ENS) are more susceptible to "community confusion" than relatively simple algorithms with no tunable parameters.

DISCUSSION

This paper investigates the relationship between cultural communities, gold standards, and the algorithms that rely on them. Using 7,921 judgements from 111 subjects, we examine how SR judgements differ across three cultural communities: Mechanical Turk workers, scholars, and scholars who are experts in the field of an SR judgement. We show that different cultural communities can produce different gold standard judgements, and these differences can shape algorithmic accuracy.

The results reported in this paper have important implications for the use of Mechanical Turk in the development of gold standards. Specifically, they show that while workers can produce widely applicable gold standards for some knowledge tasks (i.e. the "turkers for all" precept), there are many others for which this is not the case (i.e. the "community matters" precept).

The work of Clark [9] provides a useful lens to help distinguish these two types of tasks. We saw that the "turkers for all" precept tended to hold when only considering general knowledge concept pairs, but broke down when the concept pairs were more domain-specific. Clark's notion of shared expertise helps explain this difference. For general knowledge concept pairs like those in WordSim353 (e.g. "war" and "troops"), the concepts and their predominant relationships can be understood to be defined similarly in a wide range of cultural communities' shared expertise. Given that SR has been defined as the number and strength of relationships between two concepts [20], broadly shared knowledge may allow communities that have little overlap in member — e.g. turkers and scholars — to provide similar SR ratings of general knowledge concept pairs. In this light, our findings support the use for Mechanical Turk in generating gold standards for knowledge tasks that involve widely-shared and agreed-upon knowledge.

However, our work also suggests that if a knowledge task does not satisfy the above condition — if it requires knowledge that may differ across cultural communities' — the use of AMT in gold standard development is problematic. We saw this occur with domain-specific concept pairs. The concepts included in these pairs are likely understood differently across the shared expertise of different professional cultural communities (i.e. domain experts vs. turkers). As a result, the SR estimates from these two groups differed significantly.

Mechanical Turk has generated gold standards for an enormous variety of knowledge tasks, some of which likely rely exclusively on general knowledge and others of which likely rely heavily on knowledge that varies across cultural communities. For example, simple information extraction tasks — e.g. validating a mailing address that was extracted from a web page — seem to fall in the former category. The knowledge required to validate a mailing address falls in many cultural communities' shared expertise (though certainly not all). On the other hand, other types of tasks like semantic relatedness result in dubious data and unreliable assessments of algorithmic performance. For example, image tagging and sentiment analysis may also represent cultural-specific knowledge tasks; previous research has pointed to cultural differences as a limiting factor in the accuracy of sentiment analysis [2] and it has shown that image tags can vary across national cultures [11].

The implications of this work extend beyond the use of AMT in gold standard development to problematizing the use of gold standards as a whole. While AMT has become the de facto gold standard generation engine in many areas of computer science, our work suggests that many of the same concerns with regard to shared knowledge may apply to the development of gold standards using other means (e.g. undergraduate students). Researchers and practitioners should carefully consider their specific knowledge tasks and the audience of their research and systems when deciding how to develop gold standards. Failing to do so can lead to misunderstandings of algorithmic performance, as we saw when we observed that a single SR algorithm trained on gold standards from two different communities can achieve dramatically different performance. For psychology SR questions, for example, state of the art algorithms are three times better at predicting turker assessments than psychologists for the same concept pairs.

Our findings also have specific implications for the way in which SR algorithms are evaluated and for the entire task of semantic relatedness estimation, a task that has spawned an enormous literature. Namely, our results suggest that SR algorithms should no longer be evaluated in terms of how well they predict contextless SR values, but rather on how well they predict SR values for a given community. In other words, the findings above imply that we need to move from a semantic relatedness defined by $SR(a, b)$ to one that is defined by $SR(a, b, community)$.

To support this change, we are publicly releasing our dataset of 7,921 estimates split across three communities and two types of knowledge (general and domain-specific)[11]. Using this dataset, the many researchers working to develop better SR algorithms can understand the performance of their algorithms according to each of the five conditions we consider in our experiment. Instead of reporting, for instance, "our algorithm's output had an $\rho_s = 0.63$ correlation with human judgements", SR researchers will be able to report "our algorithm's output had an $\rho_s = 0.52$ with turkers' judgements on general knowledge concept pairs, an $\rho_s = 0.65$ with scholar-expert's judgements" (and so on).

Finally, our work also provides insight into the underlying processes by which people make SR estimates. At a high-level, we have seen that differences in SR estimates can be understood through the lens of Clark's definition of cultural communities as the result of one group's shared knowledge that is lacked by other groups. However, Clark's definition is part of a theory of language as joint action, and future work should investigate whether a subject's beliefs about how their judgements will be used affect their responses. For instance, if a participant in our study assumed that her SR judgements would be seen by a very broad audience, there might be a tendency to "regress to the mean" in her assessments (e.g. ignoring a relationship between two concepts well-known in her field, but not widely). On the other hand, if the participant assumed that the judgements were only going to be seen or used by people in her direct academic field, it could have an opposite effect. We are currently working to develop a survey that uses prompts to test this hypothesis.

Our findings suggest a variety of additional new directions. Examining communities beyond turkers and scholars would enrich our understanding of the relationship between community membership and gold standard creation. Would we see the same effects across age groups? National cultures? Personality types? Home towns? Future research should also study whether our findings hold for other knowledge tasks beyond SR (e.g. sentiment analysis, image labeling).

APPENDIX: COMPARING SR ALGORITHMS

When analyzing RQ2, we wanted to know whether the large difference in Spearman's correlation for the ensemble SR algorithm train on turkers ($\rho_s = 0.67$) and psychologists ($\rho_s = 0.22$) was significant. A traditional two-sided confidence interval on the pair of correlations finds them to be just short of significant. However, this statistical test incorrectly assumes that the observations across samples are independent. In fact, the turker and psychology samples have a single observation for each of the 50 concept pairs.

To increase statistical power, we instead use a statistical procedure that leverages the paired structure of the observations. For each concept pair (e.g. "cognition", "language") we computed the rank error for both turkers (for the example, predicted rank = 13, actual rank = 36, rank error = 23) and psychologists (for the example, predicted rank = 1, actual rank = 48, rank error = 47). We then compute the difference in rank errors (23 - 47 = -24). If the errors are negative, the turker prediction was closer. If they are positive, the psychologist prediction was closer Of the 50 concept pairs, the turker-trained SR algorithm performed best on 36 (72%), the psychologist-trained SR aglorithm performed best on 11 (22%), and they tied on the remaining 3 (6%).

Finally, we performed a Wilcoxon signed rank test on the difference in rank errors to determine whether it statistically favored turkers or psychologists. A Wilcoxon test is appropriate because, like Spearman's correlation, it is non-parametric and tells us whether the observed differences differ significantly from zero. The p-value reported by the Wilcoxon test for these differences was $p = 1 \times 10^{-5}$.

[11] http://shilad.com/pluraSR200.html

ACKNOWLEDGMENTS

This research has been generously supported by Macalester College and the National Science Foundation (grants IIS-0964697 and IIS-0808692). We would also like to thank the Macademia users and Mechanical Turk workers who completed our online survey. This research would not be possible without their human SR judgements.

REFERENCES

1. Babbie, E. R., et al. *Survey research methods.* Wadsworth Belmont, CA, 1990.
2. Balahur, A., Steinberger, R., Kabadjov, M., Zavarella, V., Van Der Goot, E., Halkia, M., Pouliquen, B., and Belyaeva, J. Sentiment analysis in the news. *arXiv preprint arXiv:1309.6202* (2013).
3. Bao, P., Hecht, B., Carton, S., Quaderi, M., Horn, M., and Gergle, D. Omnipedia: Bridging the wikipedia language gap. In *CHI '12* (2012).
4. Bergstrom, T., and Karahalios, K. Conversation clusters: grouping conversation topics through human-computer dialog. In *CHI '09* (Boston, MA, 2009), 2349–2352.
5. Bloodgood, M., and Callison-Burch, C. Using mechanical turk to build machine translation evaluation sets. In *Proceedings of the NAACL HLT 2010 Workshop on Creating Speech and Language Data with Amazon's Mechanical Turk* (2010).
6. Budanitsky, A., and Hirst, G. Evaluating WordNet-based measures of lexical semantic relatedness. *Computational Linguistics 32*, 1 (2006), 13–47.
7. Buhrmester, M., Kwang, T., and Gosling, S. D. Amazon's mechanical turk a new source of inexpensive,

yet high-quality, data? *Perspectives on Psychological Science 6*, 1 (Jan. 2011), 3–5.

8. Callison-Burch, C., and Dredze, M. Creating speech and language data with amazon's mechanical turk. In *Proceedings of the NAACL HLT 2010 Workshop on Creating Speech and Language Data with Amazon's Mechanical Turk*, Association for Computational Linguistics (2010), 1–12.
9. Clark, H. H. *Using Language*. Cambridge University Press, May 1996.
10. Dong, W., and Fu, W.-T. Cultural difference in image tagging. In *CHI '10* (Atlanta, Georgia, USA, 2010), 981.
11. Dong, Z., Shi, C., Sen, S., Terveen, L., and Riedl, J. War versus inspirational in forrest gump: Cultural effects in tagging communities. In *ICWSM '12* (May 2012).
12. Finkelstein, L., Gabrilovich, E., Matias, Y., Rivlin, E., Solan, Z., Wolfman, G., and Ruppin, E. Placing search in context: The concept revisited. *ACM Transactions on Information Systems 20*, 1 (2002), 116–131.
13. Freitas, A., Oliveira, J. G., O'Riain, S., da Silva, J. C., and Curry, E. Querying linked data graphs using semantic relatedness: A vocabulary independent approach. *Data & Knowledge Engineering 88*, 0 (2013), 126 – 141.
14. Gabrilovich, E., and Markovitch, S. Computing semantic relatedness using wikipedia-based explicit semantic analysis. In *IJCAI '07* (Hyberabad, India, 2007).
15. Gergle, D., Kraut, R. E., and Fussell, S. R. Action as language in a shared visual space. In *Proceedings of the 2004 ACM Conference on Computer Supported Cooperative Work*, CSCW '04, ACM (New York, NY, USA, 2004), 487–496.
16. Gergle, D., Millen, D. R., Kraut, R. E., and Fussell, S. R. Persistence matters: Making the most of chat in tightly-coupled work. In *Proceedings of the SIGCHI Conference on Human Factors in Computing Systems*, CHI '04, ACM (New York, NY, USA, 2004), 431–438.
17. Grieser, K., Baldwin, T., Bohnert, F., and Sonenberg, L. Using ontological and document similarity to estimate museum exhibit relatedness. 10:110:20. Cited by 0013.
18. Halawi, G., Dror, G., Gabrilovich, E., and Koren, Y. Large-scale learning of word relatedness with constraints. In *KDD '12*, ACM (New York, NY, USA, 2012), 14061414.
19. Hecht, B., Carton, S. H., Quaderi, M., Schöning, J., Raubal, M., Gergle, D., and Downey, D. Explanatory semantic relatedness and explicit spatialization for exploratory search. In *Proceedings of the 35th international ACM SIGIR conference on Research and development in information retrieval*, ACM (2012), 415–424.
20. Hecht, B., and Gergle, D. The tower of babel meets web 2.0: User-generated content and its applications in a multilingual context. In *CHI '10*, ACM (Atlanta, GA, 2010), 291300. ACM ID: 1753370.
21. Heer, J., and Bostock, M. Crowdsourcing graphical perception: using mechanical turk to assess visualization design. In *CHI '10* (2010), 203212.
22. Ipeirotis, P. G. Demographics of mechanical turk.
23. Kittur, A., Chi, E. H., and Suh, B. What's in wikipedia?: Mapping topics and conflict using socially annotated category structure. In *Proceedings of the SIGCHI Conference on Human Factors in Computing Systems*, CHI '09, ACM (New York, NY, USA, 2009), 1509–1512.
24. Liesaputra, V., and Witten, I. H. Realistic electronic books. *International Journal of Human-Computer Studies 70*, 9 (Sept. 2012), 588–610. Cited by 0002.
25. Miller, G. A., and Charles, W. G. Contextual correlates of semantic similarity. 1–28.
26. Milne, D., and Witten, I. H. Learning to link with wikipedia. In *CIKM '08* (Napa Valley, California, USA, 2008), 509518. ACM ID: 1458150.
27. Mooney, C. Z., Duval, R. D., and Duvall, R. *Bootstrapping: A nonparametric approach to statistical inference*. Sage, 1993.
28. Patwardhan, S., Banerjee, S., and Pedersen, T. Using measures of semantic relatedness for word sense disambiguation. In *Computational Linguistics and Intelligent Text Processing*, A. Gelbukh, Ed. Springer Berlin Heidelberg, Jan. 2003, 241–257.
29. Pavlick, E., Post, M., Irvine, A., Kachaev, D., and Callison-Burch, C. The language demographics of amazon mechanical turk. *Transactions of the Association for Computational Linguistics 2* (2014), 79–92.
30. Pedersen, T., Pakhomov, S. V., Patwardhan, S., and Chute, C. G. Measures of semantic similarity and relatedness in the biomedical domain. *Journal of Biomedical Informatics 40*, 3 (2006), 288–299.
31. Pirró, G., and Seco, N. Design, implementation and evaluation of a new semantic similarity metric combining features and intrinsic information content. In *On the Move to Meaningful Internet Systems: OTM 2008*, R. Meersman and Z. Tari, Eds., no. 5332 in Lecture Notes in Computer Science. Springer Berlin Heidelberg, Jan. 2008, 1271–1288.
32. Ponzetto, S. P., and Strube, M. Exploiting semantic role labeling, WordNet and wikipedia for coreference resolution. In *Proceedings of the main conference on Human Language Technology Conference of the North American Chapter of the Association of Computational Linguistics* (2006), 192199.
33. Popescu, A., and Grefenstette, G. Mining user home location and gender from flickr tags. In *ICSWM '10* (2010).

34. Radinsky, K., Agichtein, E., Gabrilovich, E., and Markovitch, S. A word at a time: Computing word relatedness using temporal semantic analysis. In *WWW '11* (Hyberabad, India, 2011), 337–346.

35. Resnick, P. Using information content to evaluate semantic similarity in a taxonomy. In *IJCAI '95* (Montreal, Quebec, Canada, 1995), 448–453.

36. Rubenstein, H., and Goodenough, J. B. Contextual correlates of synonymy. *Communications of the ACM 8*, 10 (Oct. 1965), 627633.

37. Schöning, J., Hecht, B., Raubal, M., Krger, A., Marsh, M., and Rohs, M. Improving interaction with virtual globes through spatial thinking: Helping users ask Why?. In *IUI '08* (Masapalomas, Gran Canaria, Spain, 2008), 129–138.

38. Snow, R., O'Connor, B., Jurafsky, D., and Ng, A. Y. Cheap and fastbut is it good?: evaluating non-expert annotations for natural language tasks. In *EMNLP '08* (2008), 254263.

39. Strube, M., and Ponzetto, S. P. WikiRelate! computing semantic relatedness using wikipedia. In *AAAI '06* (Boston, MA, 2006), 1419–1424.

40. Taboada, M., Brooke, J., Tofiloski, M., Voll, K., and Stede, M. Lexicon-based methods for sentiment analysis. *Computational linguistics 37*, 2 (2011), 267–307.

41. Witten, I., and Milne, D. An effective, low-cost measure of semantic relatedness obtained from wikipedia links. In *Proceeding of AAAI Workshop on Wikipedia and Artificial Intelligence: an Evolving Synergy, AAAI Press, Chicago, USA* (2008), 25–30.

42. Zesch, T., and Gurevych, I. Wisdom of crowds versus wisdom of linguists–measuring the semantic relatedness of words. *Natural Language Engineering 16*, 1 (2010), 25.

Dissecting a Social Botnet: Growth, Content and Influence in Twitter

Norah Abokhodair
The Information School
University of Washington
Seattle, WA, USA
noraha@uw.edu

Daisy Yoo
The Information School
University of Washington
Seattle, WA, USA
dyoo@uw.edu

David W. McDonald
Human Centered Design & Engineering
University of Washington
Seattle, WA, USA
dwmc@uw.edu

ABSTRACT
Social botnets have become an important phenomenon on social media. There are many ways in which social bots can disrupt or influence online discourse, such as, spam hashtags, scam twitter users, and astroturfing. In this paper we considered one specific social botnet in Twitter to understand how it grows over time, how the content of tweets by the social botnet differ from regular users in the same dataset, and lastly, how the social botnet may have influenced the relevant discussions. Our analysis is based on a qualitative coding for approximately 3000 tweets in Arabic and English from the Syrian social bot that was active for 35 weeks on Twitter before it was shutdown. We find that the growth, behavior and content of this particular botnet did not specifically align with common conceptions of botnets. Further we identify interesting aspects of the botnet that distinguish it from regular users.

Author Keywords
Bots; Botnet; Automated Social Actor; Twitter; Social Computing; Arab Spring

ACM Classification Keywords
H5.m. Information interfaces and presentation (e.g., HCI): Miscellaneous.

General Terms
Human Factors.

INTRODUCTION
During the past two years, Laila has been interested in the Syrian uprising. Laila is studying political science and her Arabic is a little rusty, but good enough to search and read tweets. Over time she has observed users who tweet in support of the Syrian government and others who tweet in favor of the Free Syrian Army (FSA). Laila has noticed that users who tweet from a given perspective will share common followers and will retweet each other.

Today, one particular tweet catches Laila's eye. The tweet looks like a news headline favorable to the Syrian government. Laila clicks a shortened URL in the tweet and finds herself on a news website that is known to be backed by the Syrian government. Laila suspects this information might be biased and returns to Twitter to search again. In the results of her search, she notices that the tweet has now been retweeted thousands of times. Laila thinks to herself, "Who are these people?" and wonders why this tweet is so special. She traces the topic to uncover the originator of the tweet. The profile for the account is sparse, with few details about the user.

Online social spaces often challenge users' abilities to understand others, interpret their actions and collaborate. This challenge is not particularly new. However, what is a new and growing challenge is that we can no longer assume that a social space is populated exclusively by people. Bots have become significant players in online social spaces. A recent study estimated that 61.5% of total web traffic comes from bots. One recent study of Twitter revealed that bots make for 32% of the Twitter posts generated by the most active account [5]. In the future, more and more of the social interpretations that we will be challenged to make will be about collections of people interleaved with collections of machines acting like people. In the context of CSCW it is essential for designers and researchers to anticipate and design for the interactions among bots and human participants to improve the potential collaborations.

This study considers one specific social botnet in Twitter to understand how it grows over time, how the content of tweets by the social botnet differ from regular users in the same dataset, and lastly, how the social botnet may have influenced the relevant discussions. Our botnet data comes from a much larger corpus of tweets focused on the Syrian civil war. The botnet emerged from an unrelated set of social network explorations where we were considering the structural properties of tweeting and retweeting around specific events of the Syrian civil war. Our analysis follows the botnet comprised of 130 user accounts, from the earliest evidence we have of its existence through the 35 weeks it was active, up to the day that Twitter suspended the botnet.

In the following we first define a social botnet and cover the prior research related to studies of social bots and botnets. Next, we describe the dataset of tweets in which the Syrian social botnet (SSB) was discovered. We then

CSCW '15, March 14-18, 2015, Vancouver, BC, Canada.

ACM 978-1-4503-2922-4/15/03$15.00
http://dx.doi.org/10.1145/2675133.2675208

describe three analyses we conducted on the data set; (i) growth of the Syrian social botnet over time, (ii) a grounded content analysis of botnet and regular user tweets, and (iii) the potential influence that the botnet had within the context of the data set.

BOTS AS SOCIAL ACTORS

A bot is software designed to automate a task in a computing system. The popularity of bots has risen over the last few years with the rise of web services that simplify programmatic interactions with a wider range of web based resources and a growing corpus of code libraries that implement the onerous, repetitive aspects of accessing a web service.

We characterize a social bot as an *automated social actor* (ASA). This is software designed to act in ways that are similar to how a person might act in the social space. The level of sophistication and the roles that a given ASA will fill in the social space can vary. An ASA could be relatively simple, like bots that aggregate information from web news and re-present it as a set of tweets in Twitter, or quite sophisticated like a conversational bot that is attempting to pass a Turing test. An ASA can be malicious by trying to disrupt a social space, or the ASA can try to augment and support a social space, say by explaining different cultural norms. An ASA becomes more interesting when it attempts to presents itself as an actual person in a social space. That is, when ASAs attempt to pass as an actual person, goals, motivations, and mechanisms behind the bot are interesting to uncover, unpack and understand. One danger of ASAs is passing as a person or organization to promote specific ideologies to create a false sense of consensus.

Our definition draws a subtle distinction between ASAs and the way "botnet" has been predominantly used in the popular press. The popular use of botnet describes a set of physical computers, machines, that have been compromised by malicious software, a virus, that allows remote control of the machine. Often these botnets are used for spamming, phishing, distributed denial of service attacks (DDoS) or other nefarious activities. A relatively recent survey article on botnets covers the research literature that focuses largely on these cyber-security aspects of bots and botnets [14], but also contains some valuable nuggets related to our focus on bots as social actors.

Our definition is closer to the conceptualization of early Internet bots as social entities that would populate IRC (internet relay chat), or MUDs (multi-user domains). Our definition can cover the current botnets involved in astroturfing[1], as well as the range of social and informational uses. We take analytical stance that botnet activities could be deemed good or bad, depending on the social context and the types of actions that the bots take. In our view, ASAs are merely another part of the online social space with which we, as humans, must understand and interact.

In the context of CSCW, understanding bots and the way bots work will directly influence the way we think about the design of collaboration systems and how we analyze the subsequent social activities that occur within those systems. As bots become part of collaborative systems, an effective analysis should be able to differentiate "real" human participation from that of bots, necessitating more sophisticated means of detecting social and collaborative activities of bots and bot networks.

STUDYING SOCIAL BOTS AND BOTNETS

Bots themselves are not a particularly new phenomena. In fact, some of the earliest bots and botnets were social bots; ASAs. In the following section we review related literature on social bots. We structure our review around the social infrastructures in which bots have participated; Internet Relay Chat (IRC), Multi-User Domains (MUDs), Massive Multiplayer Online Games (MMOGs) and ending with contemporary social computing systems.

Bots on Internet Relay Chat (IRC)

Far before ASAs began invading our current social network systems like Facebook or Twitter, they populated IRC. One of the earliest known IRC bots, Eggdrop, emerged as early as 1993 [16]. This bot could be configured to provide a range of triggered actions that helped administer IRC channels. The slightly social aspects of the bot include welcoming and greeting new participants and warnings for some user actions. There have been many bots developed for IRC, with ever increasing social sophistication. One reason that bots were traditionally popular on IRC was due to the simplicity of implementation and ability of scaling IRC [11].

A majority of the studies on IRC bots and botnets have focused on detection techniques, tracking and characterizing botnets. Abu Rajab et al. [1] used a multifaceted approach to track and capture the behavior of IRC based botnets. The study revealed a number of behavioral and structural features of IRC botnets, for example, the authors identified different scanning mechanisms (e.g., uniform, non-uniform, and localized scanning algorithms) botnets used to target its victims. In particular, the authors tracked 192 unique IRC botnets during the three months measurement period and concluded that botnets are generally "long-lived" in reference to the average lifetime of 47 days. In our study, we were able to capture a live botnet and actively track its behavior over more than six months until it was shut down, which adds an interesting case study of an exceptionally long-lived botnet. On botnet size, the authors conclude that it is highly likely that the botnet footprint is greater than the node size, which

1. Astroturfing is a fake "grassroots", populist, campaign in a social media space. This is named after a type of fake field turf (fake grass) that was created in the 1960s.

confirms the need to understand and follow this phenomenon on social networks to reduce potential negative impacts and raise awareness about its implications for the social graph.

Mobs in Multi-User Domains (MUDs & MMOGs)

The advent of Multi-User Dungeons (also Domains) (MUDs) included the need for automated social agents (ASAs) to enrich the playing experience. These mobs (mobiles) were not simply passive monsters that players could kill for experience points. Mobs were towns' people, shopkeepers, bards, and government officials who had their own (programmed) motives and goals. Players could learn about the environment and progress the game through interaction with mobs. But as well, mobs could play key roles regulating the social environment of the game [2,11]. In World of Warcraft (WoW) mobs often shared state and comprised a very simple botnet. Despite solid studies on the social aspects of gaming, little work has focused on the specific social roles played by the mobs (bots) themselves.

With the rapid growth of online gaming market (e.g., MMOGs such as WoW) came an increase in the use of unauthorized game bots [9,19]. These bots provided enhancements and triggering mechanisms for individual players often sitting in between the players' client application and the game server. Some bots could effectively play the game completely in the players' absence. These unauthorized bots were often considered a form of illegitimate play sabotaging game ecologies (i.e., amassing game currency, or experience points).

Yamlolskiy and Govindaraju [19] articulate a typology of these types of game bots reflecting various genres of online games. In this MUD/MMOG space they articulate the idea of a botnet as a collection of bots which share information and coordinate to provide players who employ those bots a competitive advantage.

The concept of federation or collusion among ASAs is important to our study. We leverage this botnet concept to understand how the ASAs in our study work together in their attempt to influence the direction and trending topics in an online social space.

Bots in Contemporary Social Computing Systems

The emergence of social botnets on social network systems (SNS) sparked interest amongst researchers to study this phenomenon and understand it is implications for the social sphere. In 2012, a report by Facebook estimated that 5-6% of all Facebook accounts are fake or bogus, which is considered a high percentage for Facebook as it means that approximately 50 million users are fake [14]. One study by Boshmaf et al. [3] discussed the use, impact, and implication of social bots on Facebook. In their research the authors designed and built a Socialbot Network (SbN) on Facebook to understand the ways in which social bots could threaten SNS by large-scale infiltration. The research focused on social bots that mimic human behavioral patterns to expose private information and destroy trust amongst users rather than bots that raise concerns through spamming. This research showed how vulnerable Facebook is to sophisticated social bots and how they can spread without being flagged by Facebook users and marked by the Facebook Immune System, which is a real-time system embedded in Facebook to protect its users and social graph from malicious spam [18].

The Web Ecology Project [19], called on researchers to participate in a competition to design social bots that have constructive impact on social networks to explore the different ways in which a social bot could influence online discourse. The results of this competition showed that social bots were able to reshape the social graph on Twitter by influencing and initiating some conversations with accounts that were not following each other previously.

Other studies have considered the social implications of bots for the platforms where the bots interact. Geiger [8] elaborates the social roles surrounding bots in Wikipedia, but does not consider how bots interact socially with users within Wikipedia.

While the research projects above explored the potential use cases of SNS based social botnets in general (in both positive and negative manners), we are particularly interested in the political use of social botnets. Recently, following the Arab Spring in 2010, SNS emerged as a political platform for activism. For example the dissemination of news, images and real-time videos from the streets of Egypt in 2011. The simplicity and receptivity of Twitter allows it to be used in many ways creatively by anyone online with good or bad motives. In this regard, a study by Ratkiewicz et al. [15] investigated how Twitter can be exploited through astroturfing campaigns. In their study the authors' analyzed Twitter data that they obtained from an astroturfing detection tool named "Truthy". They concluded that it is vital to detect the astroturfing campaigns before they go viral on Twitter because once they pass the first stages of detection by Twitter's spam detector it is easy to abuse and spread misinformation that can result in a false sense of broad agreement.

THE SYRIAN SOCIAL BOTNET (SSB)

The related work suggests that social botnets have far-reaching implications and they are only getting more sophisticated in terms of scanning for victims and mimicking human behaviors. Much work has focused on automatic detection mechanisms [3, 15] but little has been done to understand the behaviors and characteristics of social botnets in social computing platforms. This paper aims to elaborate our understanding of the latter.

We captured a Twitter based botnet, in the wild, based on hashtags related to the Syrian civil war in April 2012, which we call the Syrian social botnet (SSB). We tracked the SSB for more than six months during the ongoing civil war, from April to December 2012. In this paper we focus on the measurement of influence, structure and growth of the SSB. Additionally, we present the results of our content analysis on a collection of 3000+ English and Arabic tweet samples. To the best of our knowledge this is the first such study on this topic.

Method: Discovering a Social Botnet

We initially started a collection of tweets related to the Syrian civil war in April 2012, approximately one year after the earliest peaceful protests related to the war. We searched for terms related to Syria (the country) and the names of five major Syrian cities (Damascus, Aleppo, Idlib, Hama, Homs) using both the English and Arabic names for each city as well as the country. This initial dataset covers 18 months with between 150K and 500K tweets per day, and approximately equal proportions of English and Arabic tweets. We relied on retweet data to begin a social network analysis because that action is more indicative of attention to content of the tweet [4]. During that analysis we focused on the social structure of specific events during the Syrian civil war (e.g., Houla massacre on May 25, 2012, anniversary of 9/11 attack, Damascus massacre on December 12, 2012). From those events we noticed recurring clusters of users retweeting each other (for an example see Figure 1). Those recurring clusters uncovered the botnet in this study. We examined clustering patterns and identified a set of 20 high-volume twitterers and their social connections based on retweet activity. Next, we traced the profile information and activities of each high-volume Twitterer. We found that 17 accounts had been suspended and had stopped tweeting altogether on the same date and time; around 6:30 AM UTC, November 20, 2012. We examined the content of their last tweets and found that all of the suspended accounts were retweeting a unique news aggregator bot: @GB1.[2] We conducted a preliminary analysis on the social structure around @GB1 and 17 suspended user accounts. Specifically, we snowballed the retweet connections backwards in time to identify 130 usernames, comprising a social botnet, which we named the Syrian social botnet (SSB).

This study focuses principally on the 35 weeks that the botnet was active. We conducted a comprehensive analysis aimed at understanding (i) the growth and structure of the botnet over time, (ii) how the content of the botnet (in Arabic) differs from the content of regular users tweeting in Arabic or English, and lastly, (iii) how the botnet may have influenced the overall discussion.

Growth and Structure of SSB

We wanted to understand how the botnet grew and whether 130 bots all played the same role or whether they behaved differently over time. For each identified bot, we examined (a) the total number of tweets per week, (b) the total number of retweets per week, and (c) the total number of "bot-retweets" per week, which is the portion of retweets of other SSB bots. Upon examining these features, we graphed and analyzed the trend of bot behaviors over the 35 week period (see Figure 2). Each bot was classified into one of five categories based on distinct behavioral patterns: short-lived bots, long-lived bots, generator bots, core bots and peripheral bots.

Core bots are the Twitter user accounts that we consider as primary agents of the SSB (see Figure 2-D). They typically demonstrate the following behavioral patterns: First, core bots tweeted frequently. They normally generated more than 1600 tweets per week (M=1641), which is roughly a tweet every 6 minutes nonstop. Moreover, core bots accelerated their rates of tweeting as the weeks progressed. In particular, on week 28, the median rate of core bot's tweeting reached 5733, which is roughly a tweet every 1.8 minutes (see Figure 1 and Figure 2). Second, roughly half of a core bot's activity focused on retweeting (the ratio of bot-retweets to total tweets: M=0.4691). Particularly, a core bot would only retweet which was created by its fellow core bots in the SSB (the ratio of bot-retweets to total retweets: M=0.9909).

During the 35 week period, the lifespan of core bots varied from 1 to 32 weeks (M=10). In particular, we identified 23 core bots that survived more than 25 weeks (M=28), and we marked them as *long-lived bots* (see Figure 2-C). Conversely, we identified 43 *short-lived bots* that survived less than 6 weeks (M=2) during the first 11 week period (see Figure 2-A). Long-lived bots and short-lived bots are sub types of core bots.

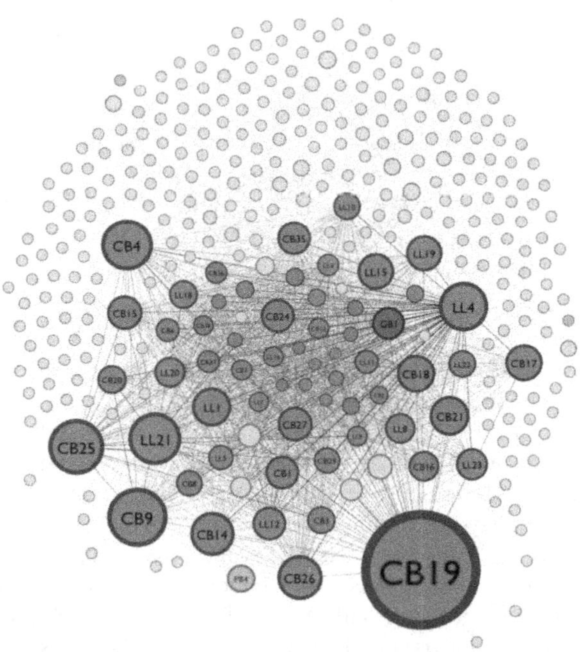

Figure 1. Social network of week 28 (red=core bots and long lived bots; orange=peripheral bots; green=other twitterers).

2. For Twitter data reporting, we are using a pseudonym to reduce searchability and enhance confidentiality.

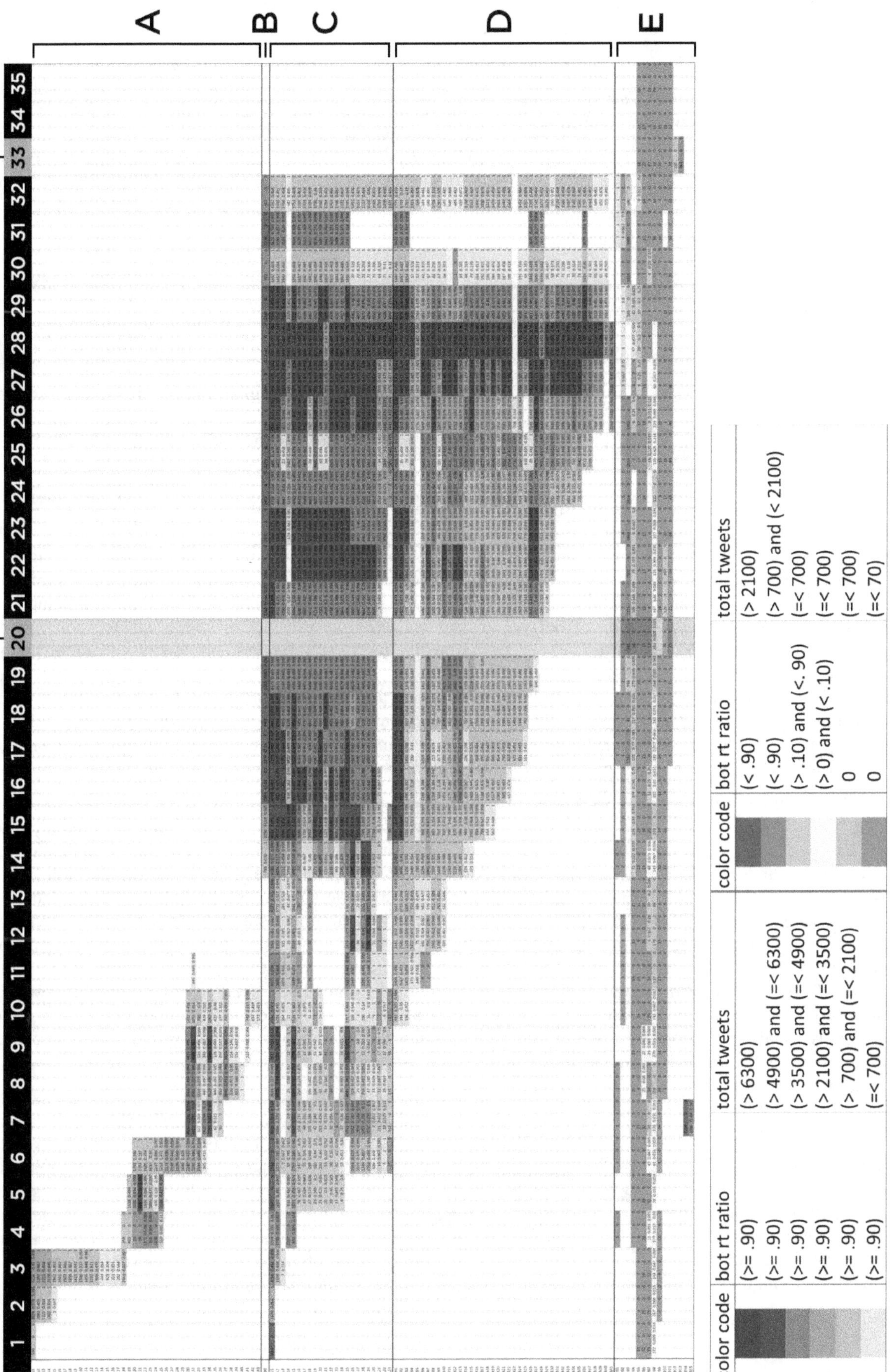

Figure 2. Behavioral pattern analysis of the SSB. We identified five distinct types of the SSB bots: short-lived bot (A), generator bot (B), long-lived bot (C), typical core bot (D), and peripheral bot (E).

Peripheral bots, on the other hand, are potentially legitimate twitterers that we assume to be unwittingly complicit in the SSB by retweeting one or more tweets generated by the core bots. Legitimate users being lured and participating in the network is often observed in astroturfing [15], therefore, we expected that this would also happen in the SSB. Since their pattern of behavior is distinctly different from the core bots and since we cannot unequivocally verify that each of those accounts belong to a "real person," we will call them peripheral bots as opposed to assuming they are actual human users (see Figure 2-E). In contrast to core bots, peripheral bots tweeted occasionally, normally generating no more than 70 tweets per week (M=11). In addition, the ratio of bot-retweets to total retweets was significantly lower for peripheral (M=0) compared to core bots. In other words, peripheral bots seldom retweeted the other bots in the SSB. While core bots temporarily stopped tweeting altogether on week 20 peripheral bots continued to tweet during that void (see Figure 2-F). We identified 15 peripheral bots out of 130 bots total in the SSB.

In addition, we identified one exceptional type of core bot, a *generator bot* (see Figure 2-B). The generator bot typically produced more than 2100 original tweets per week (M=2384.5, that is, constantly posting more than one tweet every 4 minutes). As opposed to typical core bots, the generator bot seldom retweeted anything (the ratio of bot-retweets to total tweets: M=0). However, this bot (@GB1) was heavily retweeted by the other core bots. Despite these atypical traits, we included the generator bot as a subset of core bots based on (a) its high tweeting frequency, and (b) its behavior on ceasing to tweet during the week 20 and after the week 33 shutdown (see Figure 2-G).

Overall, we observed continuous growth of the SSB over the 35 week period. On week 1, we observed only two active core bots. By week 28, however, the number increased to 64 core bots, and the SSB emerged as a predominant cluster shown on the general Syrian retweet network graph (see Figure 1). The SSB's networking activity (including numbers of total tweets, retweets, and bot-retweets) gradually increased over time as well. In particular, the volume of SSB's networking activity spiked on week 28. However, despite this immense volume, the SSB was not immediately shutdown. On week 33, which is five weeks after its peak, the SSB was suspended by Twitter. Unsurprisingly, a close parallel to this growing pattern is found in the SSB's influence on general Twitter community (for details, see the Influence of SSB section).

SSB Content Categories

Another key question for understanding the SSB is how the content of the botnet differs from regular users tweeting about the Syrian civil war. We conducted a grounded content analysis of a random sample of tweets from English twitterers, Arabic twitterers, and the botnet (which tweets in Arabic) and compared the difference between these three types of tweets.

We created a set of grounded categories in several rounds. In the first round we selected a little over 100 tweets at random from the botnet. One coder (a native Arabic speaker), read through the tweets and proposed a draft coding manual. After that the research team met to discuss the codes, leading to a first revision of the initial set of codes. At the outset, two overarching coding categories were identified: Primary Code based on topic and Secondary Code based on geographical context. Initially, we started with a small number of primary codes and two context codes (local and international). The categories and tweet exemplars were then reviewed and discussed with native English speakers to clarify translational, colloquial, and structural issues in the proposed categories to make sure they could fit with English tweets. In a second round, we took a random selection of English and Arabic tweets to test and elaborate the categories from the first round.

Primary codes

Our efforts resulted in 13 primary code categories as follows:

1.1. Opinion. Self-expressive remarks about the ongoing Syrian crisis, including (but not limited to): opinions typically based on personal analysis of the situation, patriotism, critique or criticism, rhetorical questions, jokes that people use to self-express and de-stress from the crisis, prayers for the people of Syria, and poems or similar attempts at artful expression. If the text of the tweet is an excerpt from a news article (i.e., that you can tell by viewing a link and reading the story), then the tweet should be coded "News".

1.2. Testimonial. Testimonial remarks based on personal experience of the Syrian civil war, including references to one's family members, close friends and acquaintances. May link to amateur videos shot during the war (e.g., footage of a battle, funeral or aftermath). If a video link contains any institutional symbols such as a unit name or unit logo, that suggests persistent presentation of information relative to that unit, code as follows: (1) If the video conveys immediacy ("happening now") then code as "Breaking News" instead of Testimonial; (2) If there is no immediacy (i.e., a montage of recorded events) then code as "News" instead of Testimonial.

1.3. Conversation. Conversational remarks that are clearly part of a dialog between two or more people, which cannot otherwise be coded without having access to the whole conversation. One strong indicator is when a @username is first in the post. To test if a tweet falls in the Conversation category, remove the @username and judge whether the tweet could be coded into any other category. If without the @username it could fall into one of the existing categories, then the tweet should be coded as that category. If without

Content Categories	Botnet	Arabic	English
News	538 (52.6%)	359 (35.0%)	376 (37.6%)
Other	325 (31.8%)	29 (2.8%)	39 (3.9%)
Opinion	127 (12.4%)	465 (45.3%)	258 (25.8%)
Spam/Phishing	13 (1.3%)	10 (1.0%)	249 (24.9%)
Testimonial	0 (0.0%)	54 (5.3%)	14 (1.4%)
Conversation	1 (0.1%)	23 (2.2%)	20 (2.0%)
Breaking News	4 (0.4%)	47 (4.6%)	18 (1.8%)
Mobilization of Resistance/Support	3 (0.3%)	9 (0.9%)	7 (0.7%)
Mobilization for Assistance	1 (0.1%)	4 (0.4%)	2 (0.2%)
Solicitation for Information	1 (0.1%)	4 (0.4%)	1 (0.1%)
Information Provisioning	2 (0.2%)	19 (1.9%)	12 (1.2%)
Pop Culture	7 (0.7%)	3 (0.3%)	4 (0.4%)
Total Tweets Coded	1022	1026	1000
Uncodable (removed from analysis)	26	11	207

Table 1. Comparison of tweet content categories between SSB, regular Arabic and English twitter users.

the @username the tweet would be "Uncodeable" then code the tweet as "Conversation".

1.4. Breaking News. Breaking news, information, on the Syrian civil war, typically uses emphasized headings such as "URGENT", "BREAKING NEWS", "IMPORTANT", and "NOTE" to indicate immediacy. Any tweet that is generated by a news aggregator type of user account, where the user account is labeled with some form of "breaking news" is coded here. Headings such as "emergency", "help" or "please help", are not coded here; these terms likely suggest "Mobilization of Resistance/Support" category.

1.5. News. Tweets relating information about the Syrian civil war from an "objective", third party, stance or that are clearly trying to carry an objective tone. Includes tweets from verified news accounts and news aggregator accounts. This category includes reports from NGOs and martyr (obituary) notices. If there is a link in the tweet and that link points to a news article from a reliable source which is either "analysis" of news or "editorial" about news, then the tweet is coded in this category.

1.6. Mobilization of Resistance/Support. Tweets that make calls for organizing, meeting, protesting and gatherings related to the civil war. This includes online petitioning, retweet requests and related forms of slactivism.

1.7. Mobilization for Assistance. Tweets mobilizing people and organizations for social and humanitarian aid such as donations of food, clothing, and money.

1.8. Solicitation for Information. Tweets asking about the situation in Syria. Rhetorical questions about the civil war are coded as "Opinion".

1.9. Information Provisioning. Tweets that provide information that is individually actionable.

1.10. Pop Culture. Tweets that reference celebrities, music, sports and entertainment and related people.

1.11. Other. Tweets related to Syria and other countries, but not clearly associated with the civil war.

1.12. Spam/Phishing. Tweets that look to be some form of spam or phishing.

1.13. Uncodeable. Tweets in languages other than Arabic or English or too short to reasonably interpret and code in another category.

Secondary codes

Additionally, we developed the two code categories based on context. These codes are independent from the primary codes:

2.1. Local Context. Tweets that mention the current situation in (and only in) Syria that is otherwise unspecified. Including: key events in Syria, elections, and military reaction.

2.2. International Context. Tweets with any mentions of foreign countries surrounding Syria and international organizations such as UN and Amnesty International. This category includes mainly: reactions from other countries to the situation in Syria, mobilization in support for Syria in other countries and hashtags listing many foreign countries.

These categories were developed based on an iterative exploration of samples of tweets, assumptions about the way a botnet might work, and what we have observed in the prior literature. One assumption we had was that the botnet would attract attention through use of popular culture references, resulting in the Pop Culture category. Categories like our Information Provisioning category have been reported in crisis informatics research as a way that social media users have of swiftly finding rescue or aid [17]. As well, the Mobilization for Assistance and Mobilization of Resistance/Support categories are similar to content categories from research findings on the role that Internet-based technologies play within social mobilization and political processes [6]. In the case of Opinion and Testimonial categories, we noticed a difference between people commenting about other media, such as a photo, a video or a news article, and video footage or images that were most likely recorded by the twitterer himself. By distinguishing between first-person content and comments on others' content we sought to offer a more nuanced analysis of differences in the botnet, Arabic and English content around this same event.

We used a Cohen's kappa to help measure our coding consistency over primary codes, which are independent from the secondary codes. Cohen's kappa is one measure of inter-coder reliability. Values range from 1.00 to -1.00, with 1.00 indicating perfect agreement and 0.00 indicating agreement that is no better than chance [7,12]. Two commonly referenced benchmarks for interpreting the values of Cohen's kappa are Fleiss, Levin & Paik [7] and Landis & Koch [12]. Cohen's kappa was calculated for the two coders based on a random sample that of 120 English tweets. Our sample was generated from English tweets only due to difficulty in finding a second fluent Arabic speaker. The overall score was k=0.64, indicating "intermediate to good" or "substantial" agreement by the respective benchmarks. We had better agreement in a few categories (News, k=0.74; Spam/Phishing, k=0.75) and poorer agreement in a few categories (Other, k=0.49; Opinion, k=0.50). But overall, the agreement between the two coders for this qualitative coding was relatively high.

Content Analysis: SSB vs. English and Arabic

The coding process considered the content of the tweet, the content at the end of any link or URL in the tweet, and the username of the account as appropriate. In cases where the content at the end of a link had been removed, taken down or made private and unviewable, then the coding decision was based on the content and username alone.

Next, we generated three random samples of tweets; a little over 1000 tweets each from Arabic, English and SSB. Retweets were excluded from these three samples. The random samples were generated in multiple rounds of between 100-200 tweets each. The goal was to have at least 1000 coded tweets from each of the three categories, excluding any tweets from the total which fell into the "Uncodeable" category. A native Arabic speaker coded both the SSB and Arabic tweet samples. The English tweets were coded by a different coder. The team discussed difficult and troublesome tweets in each round to come to a consensus code for the most difficult tweets.

Table 1 illustrates a number of interesting content differences between the tweets by the SSB, regular Arabic twitter users and regular English twitter users. Table 1 also includes the number of tweets that we coded as Uncodeable. This number was quite high in the English sample because in that set there are many tweets that use English terms or hashtags that are names of Syrian cities, but which are actually in another foreign language. For instance, the term "hama" stands out significantly as a Latin character term that often accompanies tweets in Japanese.

One should immediately notice that a little more than half of the tweets by the SSB are News, whereas for regular users (both Arabic and English) News only comprised a little over one third of the total. It is useful to keep in mind that this analysis does not include retweets, so these tweets are often some representations of a news story or an attempt to report or describe events in an objective tone. In the case of the SSB, we noticed that many News tweets led to one of three particular websites all linked to the Syrian Arab news agency (SANA), which is an official reporting source for the Syrian government. Here is an example:

> #Syria http://t.co/fEsxv6wH news reporter in Idlib: armed terrorist groups hijacked four units of the public order brigade at Bab Alhawa checkpoint #Syria
>
> مراسل الإخباريه في ادلب: مجموعات إرهابيه مسلحه تختطف عناصر حفظ النظام على باب الهوى الحدودي #سوريا http://t.co/fEsxv6wH

In contrast, News tweets from regular Arabic and English twitterers included links from a wide range of sources, such as Al-Arabiya, Al-Jazeera, BBC, or Washington Post. Here is an example:

> "Alarabiya.net"published scary pictures of A'zaz massacre in Aleppo http://t.co/zlwkuQ6Q #Al-Arabiya #Syria
>
> "العربيه.نت" تنشر صورا مرعبه لمجزرة اعزاز في حلب http://t.co/zlwkuQ6Q #العربيه #سوريا

Another major difference crosses the Opinion category. This was the most significant category for Arabic twitterers at about 45% of their tweets. In reading the tweets we see that many Arabic twitterers had strong opinions about what was happening on the ground in Syria and they used Twitter to express themselves. Many expressed shock at how the situation evolved toward a civil war. In addition, due to strong religious sentiments across the Middle East, many were sharing prayers and requesting prayers for the victims of the civil war. Here is an example:

> Oh gracious lord.. Whoever is in your charge shall never be humiliated please extend victory to your army in Syria and show us in the near future the end of Bashar … Lord … No one from the Arabs and non-Arabs tyrannize like him…Lord with your ability let him perish #Syria
>
> ياااااارب ياكريم يامن لا يعز عليك نصر جندك ... أرنا فالقريب العاجل نهاية السفاح بشار ... يارب لم يطغ من العرب و العجم مثله يارب بقدرتك اهلكه #سوريا

The frequency of English tweets that we classified as Opinion (25.8%) was lower than that of Arabic tweets, but still the second largest category. This suggests that English twitterers had similarly strong opinions about the civil war. Lastly, Opinion tweets from the SSB were fewer still at 12.4%.

Another standout difference is in the frequency of spam and phishing content. It appears that in the English-speaking world it is common to use major events to attract attention to sales, product marketing, or phishing. About 25% of the English tweet content related to some form of spam/phishing, attempting to leverage interest in the Syrian civil war to gain attention.

Another major difference between the SSB and the Arabic and English tweets was in the category Other. For the SSB this category comprised 31.8% of the content: tweets still associated with Syria, but not clearly related to the conflict. Since the volume was notably high among the SSB, we decided to unpack this category for the SSB tweets only. We checked the distribution of its secondary codes: International context (59%) was somewhat higher than Local context (41%). The sub-category "Other-Local" encompasses the tweets that contain local news about Syria that are not conflict related, for example:

> #Syria Ministry of Education: 13,500 new jobs within the employment program for youth http://t.co/tLAugGrb #vqk
>
> #سوريا وزارة التربية: 13،500 فرصة عمل جديدة ضمن برنامج توظيف الشباب http://t.co/tLAugGrb #vqk

The link in the tweet discusses the plans for an employment program but does not mention the ongoing conflict in the region. This is one of many similar tweets that include news about meetings happening between government officials that do not mention the ongoing war in Syria. The volume of these tweets show how social botnets can influence the online discussion by covering up tweets related to the main event, in other words, by *smoke screening*.

In contrast, the sub-category "Other-International" encompasses tweets that contain news, facts, and any other topic from outside Syria that is not related to the war. An example of this:

> #Syria BBC... Accused of covering up sexual assaults! http://t.co/pvEVLhOq #pil
>
> قناة البي بي سي متهمة في تغطيه الاعتداء الجنسي ... #سوريا http://t.co/pvEVLhOq #pil

The link in the tweet directed to Syria Steps, a Syrian pro-regime website and one of the three frequently linked to websites by the SSB. The article discusses the news of the English DJ and BBC television presenter Jimmy Savile, who committed sexual abuse, which is not related to Syria. In general, the result of our analysis in the SSB's "Other" category shows that one of the SSB goals may have been to flood the hashtag #Syria with irrelevant topics to distract focus from the civil war, in other words, by *misdirecting*. We will return to more details about smoke screening and misdirection in the Discussion section.

Influence of SSB

Our last research question was how the SSB might have influenced the discussion on Twitter regarding the Syrian civil war. We decided to consider the top 100 most retweeted tweets for each week of the dataset. We then considered how many tweets the SSB was able to get into the top 100 and what rank those tweets achieved as a basic measure of the potential influence of the botnet. It is fair to note that the SSB tweets are in Arabic and our analysis here covers the full 35 weeks of botnet dataset, which includes a significant number of English tweets. Thus, the SSB may have had more influence among Arabic Twitter users. Still, given the terms used to collect the dataset our analysis can start to show what it takes for a social botnet to begin to have influence.

Figure 3 illustrates the trend of growing influence of the SSB over the 35 week period. Each week we identified all the tweets in the top 100 most retweeted. We then calculated a botnet influence score based on two metrics: (a) rank influence (the sum of ranked positions of bot retweets in the top 100) and (b) RT influence (a magnitude of retweet cascade represented by the sum of frequencies of bot retweets in the top 100). These graphs reveal a number of interesting characteristics. First, the activity of the botnet is quite "underground" during the first third of its lifespan, apparently having no influence in the top 100 most retweeted content. In the second third it begins to have some influence; but the most significant influence does not occur until the very end, when the total number of bots in the botnet is highest and the frequency of tweeting by each bot is superhumanly high.

We performed a content analysis of all the SSB tweets that made the top 100 for each week using the same content categories developed above. Like the bulk of the human tweets, the top three categories were News, Other, and Opinion, with slight differences in percentage distribution that could simply be a function of the smaller number of tweets that the botnet was able to push up into the top 100 most retweeted tweets each week. That the ratios are similar, suggests the SSB was not discriminating among the tweets that it would attempt to push up through high frequency retweeting.

For example, in week 29, which was one of the intensely active weeks for the SSB (see Figure 3 and Figure 4), a tweet generated by the bot @LL1 shot up to 4th place in the top 100 most retweeted tweet rankings:

> Media Reporter Hosein Mortada: "Who assassinated General Hassan and a few asked questions: http://t.co/OmagQsV4 #Syria
>
> الاعلامي حسين مرتضى:"قاتل الحسن وأسئلة مطروحة": #سوريا http://t.co/OmagQsV4

This tweet got retweeted 1041 times by the SSB user accounts only. Another tweet generated by the bot @CB7 mentions the same journalist and reporter Hosein Mortada. This tweet was retweeted 730 times and ranked 12th in week 28 with only the SSB retweeting it:

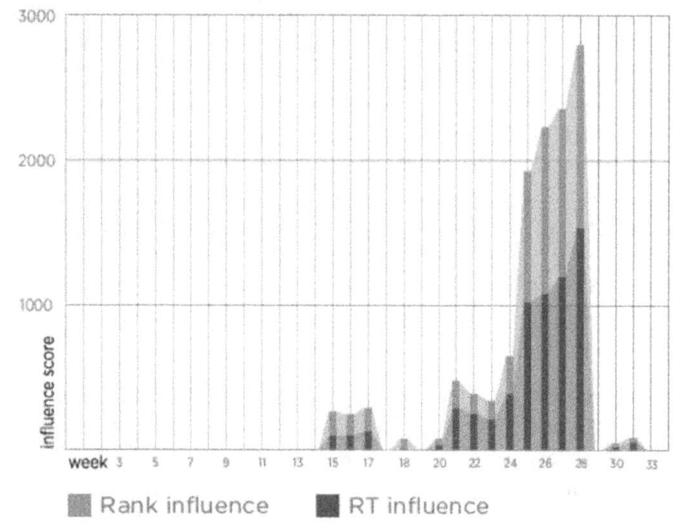

Figure 3. Influence of the SSB on Twitter RT space.

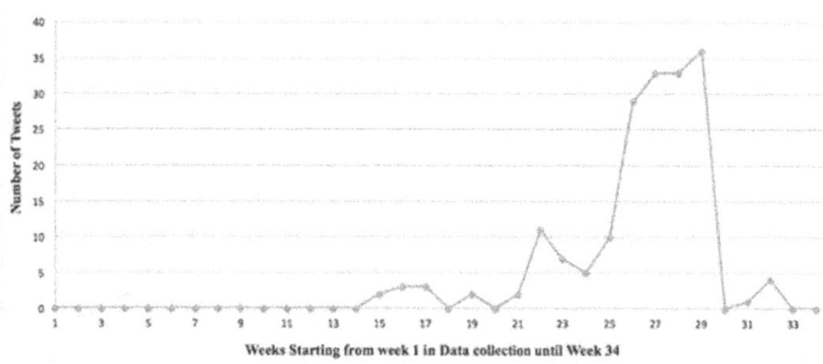

Figure 4. Number of bots entering the weekly top 100 RT chart.

> The Morning Gate news: the #Lebanese reporter Hussein Morteza told "The Morning Gate": Hezbollah has nothing to do with the killing in #Syria.... http://t.co/wW88DdfL #Syria
>
> بوابة الصباح الاخبارية:الإعلامي ال #لبناني حسين مرتضي لـ"الصباح":لا علاقة لحزب الله و #سوريا بمقتل... http://t.co/wW88DdfL #سوريا

Further analysis shows that the link in each tweet directs to a news article from Al-Sabah (which means "The Morning"), which seems to be an Egyptian news portal.

Additionally, as part of understanding how the SSB influence grew over time, we considered who else was retweeting SSB tweets. We computed the ratio of retweeting between SSB accounts and regular accounts for the top 100 most retweeted tweets. This revealed that 15 tweets out of the 181 SSB tweets that made it in to the top 100 were retweeted by accounts likely in control of a real user (in addition to massive retweeting by the SSB). This is an important finding because it confirms that the SSB's intensive activity got attention from regular twitter users.

We looked closely at all 15 tweets that got retweeted by humans and coded them using our coding scheme. Similar to the bulk of human tweets, the 15 tweets were within the top two categories News and Opinion. Interestingly, the ones that received the largest amount of retweeting by human accounts were in the Opinion category, which is a category where the SSB was not very active, but humans were. This shows the SSB was able to garner human attention through topics that mirror or mimic humans interest. An example of an Opinion tweet that was mostly retweeted by humans:

> This image made me laugh a lot as it shows Arabs activists participation in #Syria liberating… And in #Bahrain terrorist http://t.co/UyOlqYzl #Syria
>
> أضحكتني هذه الصوره كثيرا لناشطين عرب توضح أن ما يجري في #سوريا ثوره و في #البحرين إرهاب http://t.co/UyOlqYzl

Although the link attached to this tweet is broken, conducting a simple Google search reveals it used to point to a political cartoon. We then computed the ratio of human to SSB retweets for this specific tweet and found that 237 human accounts retweeted it in comparison to 1043 bot accounts, which is an indicator of some human attention.

DISCUSSION

In this paper we aimed at answering three main questions regarding one specific social bot network on Twitter: to understand how it grows over time, how the content of tweets by the social botnet differ from regular users in the same dataset, and lastly, how the social botnet may have influenced the relevant discussions. Our analysis revealed some interesting findings that sometimes contradict and sometimes support current knowledge on social botnets.

Mimicking human behaviors

The prior literature on social bots suggests that social bots thrive and succeed by mimicking human behavior on social networks. By mimicking human behavior, bots can go unnoticed and improve their chances of impacting the social graph. The results of our qualitative coding showed that the SSB did not work to mimic human behavior whatsoever. Our analysis shows that over half of the SSB tweets (52.6%) were in the News category, while human tweets (in both English and Arabic) are only about one-third News – a large and very detectable difference. Further in the opposite direction, humans are likely to have a large proportion of their content expressing some personal opinion about an event (45% for our Arabic sample and 25% for our English sample). Based on the data, the SSB does not seem to have much in the way of an opinion about what was happening in Syria, especially when compared to other Arabic language twitterers.

This insight raises two problems with regard to the way the prior work has described and presented ASAs. First is the suggestion that ASAs are becoming sophisticated in construction. Our analysis suggests that this ASA did very little to mimic the activity of a human across both the types of content and the frequency of tweeting activity. While there may be some value in mimicking human activity it may not be completely worth the effort depending on the goals of the ASA operators. We point out that the content most similar to human content was a bit more likely to be retweeted by actual people, but the main question remains.

Secondly, there is a notion that an ASA that mimics human behavior is less detectable. The SSB that we studied was live for over six months. The frequency of tweeting and the connectedness of the retweet social network are what allowed us to identify the bots in the network. While we do not actually know when Twitter detected this specific botnet, we know specifically when Twitter disabled the associated accounts. The challenges for botnet detection are multiple. Determining the motives and legitimacy of the botnet are important. If the botnet is supporting the community, disabling it may be a bad idea. Another challenge is determining how wide a net to cast around the botnet. From our data it seems clear that casting a wide net would include a number of real users who probably would not realize they were part of a botnet simply as a function of their retweeting and following behaviors. Bot and botnet detection is not currently conceptualized as an obvious CSCW topic. But as bots and botnets become participants in larger and more complex social computing systems the relevance to CSCW will grow and what CSCW researchers have to contribute will become more important.

Misdirection and Smoke Screening

We observed two distinct tactics that the SSB used to point attention away from relevant information (about the Syrian civil war) and influence perception: *misdirection* and *smoke screening*. Misdirection is a technique that magicians use to get the audience to look somewhere else when completing a trick. Similarly, an ASA network that tries to get the audience to attend to other content is using misdirection. In contrast, a smoke screen serves to hide or provide cover for or obscure some type of activity. When the volume of a botnet campaign is high enough with unrelated content, the unrelated content can effectively hide real content.

In the case of our SSB's tweets, many tweets embedded in the Other category were related to foreign news, in particular, political and natural crises happening worldwide. For example, the SSB was benefiting from the political unrest happening in the Kingdom of Bahrain and tweeting news updates on the Bahraini situation:

> Pan Ki-moon » calls #Bahraini regime to lift the restrictions on public demonstrations http://t.co/UfMEIPzG #glu #Syria
>
> #سوريا #Syria «كي مون» يدعو النظام #البحريني لرفع القيود عن المظاهرات الشعبية #glu http://t.co/UfMEIPzG

Another example is posting photos of New Jersey and New York damaged by Hurricane Sandy on the east coast of the United States.

> Hurricane Sandy Is currently almost 380 miles from New York and is expected to arrive after 5 hours from now http://t.co/mzrexObC #Syria
>
> اعصار_ساندي يبعد حالياً ٣٨٠ ميل تقريباً عن نيويورك ويتوقع وصوله بعد ٥ ساعات من الأن http://t.co/mzrexObC #سوريا

The prevalence of these posts, which were tagged with our collection terms, but seemingly have little to do with the actual events in Syria look to be calculated misdirection, pointing viewers specifically toward other unrelated events. Specifically the SSB was attempting to get people looking for tweets on Syria to pay attention to something major that is happening elsewhere.

This behavior is distinctly different from the way smoke screening is commonly perceived. A few bloggers and news sources such as The Guardian have raised attention to smoke screening on Twitter, describing it as "a cabal of pro-regime accounts, set up for the sole purpose of flooding the #Syria hashtag and overwhelming the pro-revolution narrative" [21].

In the case of the SSB, the remaining tweets embedded in the Other categories were clearly related to events in Syria, just not always related to the civil war. For example:

> #Syria 25 short films will be produced by the General Organization for Cinema as part of the 2013 plan to support youth cinema http://t.co/PN2cCEYN#goq # Syria
>
> #سوريا ٢٥ فيلماً قصيراً ستنتجه المؤسسة العامة للسينما ضمن مشروع دعم سينما الشباب للعام 2013 #goq http://t.co/PN2cCEYN #سوريا

This work and the examples we have provided begin to highlight the shades of difference between misdirection and smoke screening as useful techniques to influence social media attention.

Although a full elaboration is out of the scope of this study, it is worth mentioning that misdirection and smoke screening are distinct from astroturfing. The common description of astroturfing is to use a set of ASAs to tweet or retweet a particular point of view to suggest broad consensus around that view. Misdirection and smoke screening rely on other, potentially irrelevant ideas, as opposed to contesting ideas, and tweets or retweets those ideas suggesting that the audience should find those ideas more interesting.

News reporting

Throughout the coding stage, the Arabic and English coders were comparing notes and discussing differences between the three samples: SSB, Arabic, and English. As expected, there were clear differences in the News category between English and Arabic tweets, which seem related to differences in language and cultural traditions. However, we were not expecting to see the notable difference between Arabic news reporting and the SSB news reporting as they are both in Arabic. In the latter, the main difference was the frequent use of strong language in the SSB tweets about the opposition, the Free Syrian Army (FSA), and countries that support the FSA, by frequently calling them terrorists and posting torture videos. Here are two examples:

> #Syria http://t.co/fEsxv6wH news reporter in Idlib: armed terrorist groups hijacked four units of the public order brigade at Bab Alhawa checkpoint #Syria

> Qaeda member Maen Alrez death moment in Homs #Syria #Bahrain #syria #Homs http://t.co/FhFJBwaU #سوريا

Lifespan model

One of the popular conceptualizations about social media botnets is that they explode onto the social scene and immediately influence social media discussions. However, the lifespan model of the SSB was somewhat different. The botnet was not built in a day: tracking the SSB for 35 weeks, we observed two distinct stages of its growth. In the earlier stage, from Week 1 to 13, the behavioral patterns appear to be fuzzy and irregular (see Figure 1). It is likely that the SSB operators were experimenting with prototypes, in particular, the 43 short-lived bots whose median lifespan was only two weeks. After Week 14, however, the pattern begins to stabilize. After Week 14 the median lifespan increased to 28 weeks and the median total tweets per week increased to 3449. Interestingly, Week 14 is the same week when the generator bot (@GB1) first started to tweet. We suspect that @GB1 played pivotal role in systematizing the SSB. By looking closer at @GB1's tweet contents, we found a peculiar hashtag, which is a combination of three random letters (e.g., #wqz, #hzf, and so on), attached at the end of each tweet generated by @GB1. We assume that these hashtags may be some kind of identification code for the tweets but do not know the exact use. These random letter hashtags require further investigation.

CONCLUSION

This study aimed to understand the behaviors and characteristics of social botnets on social computing and social media platforms. We have presented the results of the three analyses we conducted on the dataset of tweets in which the Syrian social botnet was discovered. The results of the three analyses we conducted on the data set aimed at answering three questions: (i) How did the SSB grew over time, (ii) how the content of the botnet (in Arabic) differs from the content of regular users tweeting in Arabic or English, and lastly, (iii) how the botnet may have influenced the overall Syrian civil war discussion. Our results revealed several new and interesting findings.

As social computing systems grow in sophistication and popularity, bots and collections of bots will take ever more important roles. The collective efforts of individual bots are already critical to supporting Wikipedia [8]. As bots become more social and as they federate in to networks of collective activity, it is essential for designers and researchers to anticipate and design for the interactions between bots and human participants. This work helps set the stage for that by characterizing what is currently happening in the space of social botnets in a specific social media system, Twitter.

Our findings identified a number of differences between what we observed and the way botnets are portrayed in the prior literature. In this paper, we discussed how the SSB in our study was exceptionally long-lived compared to the life span of other reported botnets. This could be due to the fact that the SSB in our study was tweeting in Arabic. This result suggests that there is room for research on the effective detection of social botnets in social media. In addition, from our qualitative coding, it is not clear that the SSB was actually trying to mimic and replicate human behavior. Instead, it seemed mostly interested in flooding Syrian civil war related hashtags with topics that are not war related. That is different from what have been previously discussed in the literature on social bots.

There is an opportunity to continue expanding on this study to answer questions we had during our research. For example, what were the topics the SSB focused on to distract attention from the Syrian civil war? How can the results of this research help increase awareness to this phenomenon and teach SNS users on the dangers of social botnets? In addition, we believe that the results of this work will have a positive impact on the research being conducted on more sophisticated detection software on SNS.

REFERENCES

1. Abu Rajab, M., Zarfoss, J., Monrose, F., and Terzis, A. (2006). A multifaceted approach to understanding the botnet phenomenon. In *Proceedings of the 6th ACM SIGCOMM conference on Internet measurement* (pp. 41-52). ACM.
2. Ackerman, M. S., Muramatsu, J., and McDonald D. W. (2010). Social Regulation in an Online Game: Uncovering the Problematics of Code.In *Proceedings of the ACM 2010 International Conference on Supporting Group Work (GROUP'10).*
3. Boshmaf, Y., Muslukhov, I., Beznosov, K., and Ripeanu, M. (2012). Key challenges in defending against malicious socialbots. In *Proceedings of the 5th USENIX Conference on Large-scale Exploits and Emergent Threats, (LEET 12)* (Vol. 12).
4. Cha, M., Haddadi, H., Benevenutu, F. and Gummadi, K. P. (2010). Measuring User Influence in Twitter: The Million Follower Fallacy.In *Proceedings of the 2010 International AAAI Conference on Weblogs and Social Media (ICWSM'10)*. 10-17.
5. Cheng, A., & Evans, M. (2009, August 1). Twitter Statistics - An In-depth Report At Most Active Twitter Users. *Social media monitoring and analytics solutions*. Retrieved June 3, 2014, from https://www.sysomos.com/insidetwitter/mostactiveusers/
6. El-Nawawy, M., & Khamis, S. (2012). Political activism 2.0: Comparing the role of social media in Egypt's "Facebook Revolution" and Iran's "Twitter

Uprising".CyberOrient. Online Journal of the Virtual Middle East, 6

7. Fleiss, J. L., Levin, B., & Paik, M. C. (2013). Statistical methods for rates and proportions. John Wiley & Sons.
8. Geiger, R. S. (2014). Bots, bespoke, code and the materiality of software platforms. *Information, Communication and Society*, 17, 3, 342-356
9. Gianvecchio, S., Xie, M., Wu, Z., and Wang, H. (2011). Humans and bots in internet chat: measurement, analysis, and automated classification. *IEEE/ACM Transactions on Networking (TON)*, *19*(5), 1557-1571.
10. Halfaker, A., & Riedl, J. (2012). Bots and cyborgs: Wikipedia's immune system. Computer, 45(3), 79–82.
11. Karasaridis, A., Rexroad, B., and Hoeflin, D. (2007, April). Wide-scale botnet detection and characterization. In *Proceedings of the first conference on First Workshop on Hot Topics in Understanding Botnets* (Vol. 7).
12. Landis, J. R., & Koch, G. G. (1977). The measurement of observer agreement for categorical data. biometrics, 159-174.
13. Muramatsu, J. and Ackerman, M. S. (1998). Computing, Social Activity, and Entertainment: A Field Study of a Game MUD. *Computer Supported Cooperative Work: The Journal of Collaborative Computing* 7: 87–122.
14. Protalinski, E. (2012). Facebook: 5-6% of accounts are fake | ZDNet.ZDNet. Retrieved May 27, 2014, from http://www.zdnet.com/blog/facebook/facebook-5-6-of-accounts-are-fake/10167
15. Ratkiewicz, J., Conover, M., Meiss, M., Gonçalves, B., Flammini, A., and Menczer, F. (2011, July). Detecting and Tracking Political Abuse in Social Media. In *ICWSM.*
16. Rodriguez-Gomez, R. A., Macia-Fernandez, G., and Garcia-Teodoro, P. (2013). Survey and Taxonomy of Botnet Research through Life-Cycle. *ACM Computing Survey*. 45, 4 (August 2013).
17. Starbird, K., & Palen, L. (2012, February). (How) will the revolution be retweeted?: Information diffusion and the 2011 Egyptian uprising. In Proceedings of the ACM 2012 Conference on Computer Supported Cooperative Work (pp. 7-16). ACM.
18. Stein, T., Chen, E., and Mangla, K. (2011). Facebook immune system. In *Proceedings of the 4th Workshop on Social Network Systems* (p. 8). ACM.
19. The Web Ecology Project.(2011). The 2011 socialbots competition. http://www.webecologyproject.org/category/competition
20. Yampolskiy, R. V. and Govindaraju, V. (2008). Embedded noninteractive continuous bot detection. *Computers in Entertainment*, 5(4), 7. ACM Press.
21. York, J. C. (2011, April). Syria's Twitter spambots. (T. Guardian, Producer) Retrieved June 2014, from The Guardian: http://www.theguardian.com/commentisfree/2011/apr/21/syria-twitter-spambots-pro-revolution

Two is Better Than One: Improving Multilingual Collaboration by Giving Two Machine Translation Outputs

Ge Gao[1], Bin Xu[2], David Hau[2], Zheng Yao[2], Dan Cosley[2], Susan R. Fussell[1,2]
[1]Department of Communication
[2]Department of Information Science
Cornell University
Ithaca NY 14850 USA
[gg365, bx55, dch229, zy87, drc44, sfussell] @cornell.edu

ABSTRACT
Machine translation (MT) creates both opportunities and challenges for multilingual collaboration: While MT enables collaborators to communicate via their native languages, it can introduce errors that make communication difficult. In the current paper, we examine whether displaying two alternative translations for each message will improve conversational grounding and task performance. We conducted a laboratory experiment in which monolingual native English speakers collaborated with bilingual native Mandarin speakers on a map navigation task. Each dyad performed the task in one of three communication conditions: MT with single output, MT with two outputs, and English as a common language. Dyads given two translations for each message communicated more efficiently, and performed better on the task, than dyads given one translation. Our findings show the value of providing multiple translations in multilingual collaboration, and suggest design features of future MT-based collaboration tools.

Author Keywords
Machine translation; Collaboration; Multilingual communication

ACM Classification Keywords
H.5.3 [Group and Organization Interface]: Computer-supported cooperative work

General Terms
Experimentation; Human Factors

INTRODUCTION
Many modern organizations actively seek opportunities to collaborate across national and language boundaries. As people work together at a global scale, a multilingual context in which collaborators communicate via "a cocktail of languages [17]" arises. Multilingual organizations often require that all members speak English as a common language [9], which puts heavy cognitive load and pressure onto non-native speakers [15, 36, 35]. Non-native speakers report language performance anxiety, status worries, and job insecurity due to lack of fluency in English [29]. Language differences can also make it difficult to establish trust and collaborate effectively in teams consisting of native and non-native speakers [37].

Figure 1. The nature of machine translation mediated communication leads to difficulties in detecting translation errors within each single translation output.

Machine translation (MT) provides an opportunity for multilingual collaborators to interact via their own native languages. Using MT might reduce the cognitive effort and social challenges associated with speaking in a non-native language. At the same time, MT mediated communication can poses new challenges. In particular, the meaning of the original message may be lost or distorted after being processed by MT algorithms [e.g., 43, 44], and it can sometimes be difficult to detect these problematic translations in real time.

In the scenario illustrated by Figure 1, for example, a native English speaker gets a MT translated message from a Chinese speaker, saying "I clear the table, next to my legs kitten asleep". This translated message is different from its original version in Chinese, because the MT algorithm confused "the table legs" with "my legs". Native English speakers, who typically do not know precisely how MT works, would have little chance of detecting this translation error. Such errors can accumulate over the course of a conversation, leading to serious misunderstandings.

CSCW '15, March 14-18, 2015, Vancouver, BC, Canada.

ACM 978-1-4503-2922-4/15/03…$15.00
http://dx.doi.org/10.1145/2675133.2675197

In this paper, we explore the value of one low cost way to help people detect errors and infer the intended meaning of messages: providing multiple translations from multiple MT tools [42]. In the above scenario, for example, the same message is translated differently by Google and Bing:

- Google translation output:
  I clear the table, next to my legs kitten asleep.
- Bing translation output:
  I was cleaning the tables, kittens fell asleep next to my table legs.

Comparing these two translations offers the message recipient additional resources to infer what the original Chinese message means. The consistent parts between the two outputs is information the receiver can be fairly confident about (e.g., that there is a table and a cat), while the inconsistent parts suggest possible translation errors that need to be clarified (e.g., *where* the cat is, whether the table is being "cleared" vs. "cleaned"). In research by Xu and colleagues [42], dyads consisting of English and Mandarin Chinese speakers reported that having two MT outputs rather than one helped them infer the intended meaning of messages in an unstructured chat context.

Building on this work, the current paper presents a laboratory study that explores how giving two MT outputs affects communication efficiency and task performance during multilingual collaboration. We first propose hypotheses based on literature about MT and multilingual collaboration. We test these hypotheses with a laboratory experiment in which monolingual native English speakers collaborated with bilingual native Mandarin speakers in dyads on a map navigation task. Dyads finished the task under one of three communication conditions: MT with a single output for each message, MT with two outputs for each message, and English as a common language. We compared communication efficiency and task performance between these conditions, along with self-evaluations of communication experience and workload.

In general, our data show the value of providing two MT outputs. Dyads given two MT outputs communicated more efficiently and performed better on the task than dyads given a single MT output. Having two MT outputs also did not increase cognitive workload over having a single MT output. This suggests that for areas such as MT where imperfect computer agents sometimes make mistakes, designing systems that explicitly account for these errors is likely to pay dividends.

RELATED WORK AND HYPOTHESES

Although MT was initially used primarily for written documents, [e.g., 19, 26, 33], research has recently begun to explore the use of MT to facilitate real time communication and collaboration among speakers of different native languages. A number of studies [e.g., 16, 22, 25, 41] show that MT has both benefits and costs for communication.

On the positive side, MT allows people communicate with little concern about their language fluency. Previous work on multilingual collaboration suggests that using MT may benefit team collaboration. Lim and Yang [25] found that English-Chinese speaking dyads worked together on a negotiation task performed better using MT vs. English as a common language. Wang and colleagues [41] found that Chinese speaking participants generated more ideas when using MT rather than English as a common language. Hautasaari [16] similarly found that using MT improved the performance of Japanese-English speaking dyads and also increased the use of socio-emotional messages.

On the negative side, however, MT can make it challenging for participants to ground their utterances, that is, to build shared knowledge and beliefs [4]. A key component of conversational grounding is the identification of objects and locations [21]. When a tourist asks directions from a local resident, for example, the two must work together to make sure every landmark is mutually understood. In what Clark and Wilkes-Gibbs [6] call the "basic exchange," a speaker refers to an entity (e.g., "the clock tower") and the listener indicates that he or she has understood (e.g., "got it"). Here, the message recipient provides positive evidence of understanding (e.g., acknowledgement) and no negative evidence of understanding (e.g., questions or requests for confirmation) [5].

Grounding in MT-Mediated Conversation

There is evidence that grounding of referents can be problematic in MT-mediated communication, even more so than when English is used as a common language. For example, very similar names for the identical object or landmark may be translated differently [43, 44]. The following example shows how such inconsistency could induce problems to grounding in MT-mediated communication. In this scenario, an English speaking tourist is looking for the place to rent a bicycle. A Chinese speaker gives direction like this:

> **Chinese message:**
> 图书馆正对着一个钟楼
> [The library faces a clock tower]
> 楼下有一个服务处可以租自行车
> [under the tower there is a service center where you can rent bikes]
>
> **Google translated English:**
> Libraries facing a bell tower
> downstairs there is a place you can rent a bike service

In this example, both "钟楼 (clock tower)" and "楼 (the tower)" refers to the same entity in the original Chinese message. When the message is translated into English, however, the word "楼 (the tower)" is mistranslated into "downstairs", which may impede the grounding of this referent.

Even when a term is translated consistently, it may still be wrong in ways that disrupt grounding, especially when languages are distant both structurally and lexically (e.g., Chinese and English) [3, 39]. The next example shows how grounding could be hurt under this occasion:

> **Chinese message:**
> 向前走直到看见一个卖水果的
> [Go ahead until you see a fruit stand]
> 再右转就到了
> [then turn right you will arrive]

> **Google translated English:**
> Go forward until you see a fruit
> and then turn right on to the

In this example, the word "卖水果的 (fruit stand)" is mistranslated into "fruit", which creates a potential grounding problem. Although similar difficulties of grounding could happen with every message and reference, message recipients have few clues to figure out how different a translated message is from its original version.

Under the assumption that it will be some time until machine translation algorithms are perfected, investigators have turned instead to a consideration of how current MT output can be supplemented to facilitate grounding. We focus on improving grounding in MT rather than grounding when English is used as a second language [e.g., 12, 24] because of the demonstrated value of composing messages in one's native language [41]. Google's translation interface as of mid-2014 allows people to look up alternate translations for individual words. This approach can improve grounding, but requires participants to actively request information. More automated approaches include back-translations to help speakers identify when a translation might be confusing to the recipient [28, 32], keyword highlighting to help people focus on the gist of a translated message [10], and enhancing the verbal message with semantically linked pictures [40].

The Current Study

The solutions outlined above all have additional software requirements beyond the machine translator, such as tools to implement keyword highlighting or picture selection. A simpler approach, the one we investigate in the current study, is to use a chat interface that provides outputs from several established MT algorithms (e.g., Google Translate and Bing) at the same time [42]. With two translation outputs instead of just one, people may be better able to figure out the intended meaning of a message. For example, the Bing translation for the example above,

> **Bing translated message:**
> Go straight until you see a fruit seller, then turn right into the

clarifies that it is a fruit seller not a fruit that is the probable turning point.

Providing participants with two translations may also help them identify otherwise undetectable translation errors. In our example, the shift from "on to" to "into" at the end of the translation flags a potential point of confusion (though neither makes it clear that the traveler has reached the destination). At the same time, when two translations have overlapping content (here, "go forward/straight", "fruit," "turn right"), people may feel more confident about their understanding of the message.

One previous study has compared two vs. one translation(s) in a conversational setting. Xu and colleagues [42] found that two translations increased participants' confidence that they had correctly understood partners' messages. However, they used an informal chat task and did not examine whether the interface affected conversational grounding or task performance. The current study explores these issues in the context of a well-defined collaboration task, the HCRC map task [8], which requires grounding to succeed.

For the reasons outlined above, we expect that providing two MT outputs will improve message comprehension. There are few clues to identify accurate vs. problematic parts of a single MT output, but with two outputs, people can analyze commonalities and differences to better identify the probable meaning of the message.

H1. People will perceive less difficulty in understanding messages with two MT outputs vs. one MT output.

This decreased difficulty in understanding should be reflected in how people ground their messages. When messages are easy to understand, we would expect more positive evidence of understanding, such as basic presentation-acceptance exchanges, and less negative evidence of understanding, such as requests for clarification. Thus, we hypothesize that:

H2a. People will show more positive evidence in grounding (e.g., acknowledgment) with two MT outputs vs. one MT output.

H2b. People will show less negative evidence in grounding (e.g., questions, requests for confirmation) with two MT outputs vs. one MT output.

Because successful grounding of referents is essential for route-giving tasks such as the HCRC map task [e.g., 8, 12], we hypothesize that improvements in grounding from two translations will result in better task performance:

H3. People will achieve better task performance with two MT outputs versus one MT output.

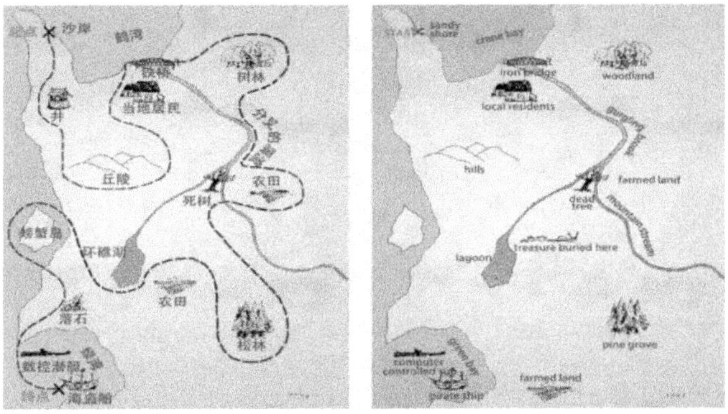

Figure 2. One set of maps used in the navigation task (the left one for the Chinese speaking instructor, the right one for the English speaking follower).

However, processing two translation outputs may require more cognitive effort than processing a single translation. Although Xu and colleagues [42] did not find this for informal chat conversations, we expect that in the context of a longer, more structured task, the overall accumulated reading effort will lead to higher perceived workload:

H4. People will experience higher workload with two MT outputs vs. one MT output.

Finally, given that people often use English as a common language in today's multilingual organizations [9], we want to compare two MT outputs to an English-only condition. While prior work suggests that grounding is more successful with English as a common language vs. MT with one output [43, 44], we wondered if the gap between MT and English as a common language would be reduced or eliminated when two MT outputs are provided,

RQ. How do the perceived difficulty in understanding messages, frequency of positive and negative evidence in grounding, task performance, and perceived workload differ between having two MT outputs versus English as a common language?

METHOD

Overview

We conducted a between-subjects laboratory experiment to examine the effects of two MT translation outputs on conversational grounding and collaborative performance. Dyads consisting of a monolingual native English speaker and a native Mandarin speaker who spoke English as second language performed the HCRC map navigation task [e.g., 1, 7, 38] under one of three communication conditions: MT with a single translation output for each message, MT with two translation outputs for each message, and English as a common language. In the first two conditions, both native English speaking participants and native Mandarin speaking participants typed and received messages in their native languages. In the third condition, participants typed and received messages in English. Post-task surveys, IM logs and task logs were used to measure message understanding, conversational grounding behavior, task performance, and cognitive workload.

Participants

We recruited 96 participants from a U.S. university. Half (N = 48, 22 female) were native English speakers who had grown up in the U.S. and had little or no knowledge of Mandarin. Their mean age was 21.5 years (SD = 2.70). They reported some previous experience with MT (M = 3.88, SD = 1.31 on a 7-point scale ranging from 1= never to 7 = very often). The other half (N = 48, 24 female) were native Mandarin speakers who had grown up in the People's Republic of China and been in the U.S. for two years or less. Their mean age was 26.38 years (SD = 5.66). They spoke English as second language with moderate fluency (M = 4.54, SD = 1.20 on a 7-point scale ranging from 1= not fluent at all to 7 = very fluent) and had some previous experience with MT (M = 3.38, SD = 1.72). Under all conditions, participants were assigned to dyads consisting of one native English speaker and one native Mandarin speaker.

Materials

Task. Dyads completed two HCRC map navigation tasks (Figure 2). Each task consisted of one instructor map and a paired follower map. The instructor map showed a prescribed route around a list of landmarks. The follower map contained similar but not identical landmarks and had no route shown. Each pair of HCRC maps has some differences in the depicted landmarks, adding challenges to the task and increasing the need for grounding work. Both pairs of maps have the same number of landmarks, and require similar steps to complete the navigation. We manually translated the labels on each map into Mandarin Chinese for the Chinese speakers.

Surveys. Participants completed an online pre-experiment questionnaire that collected their demographic information. During the formal experiment, participants were asked to fill out a short online survey after each task. This post-task survey consisted of seven 7-point Likert scale questions. One question is a manipulation check to confirm which communication condition participants were assigned to. Two questions pertained to participants' perceived difficulty of understanding received messages during the task. The other four questions asked about participants' workload while doing the task. Since participants need to work on two sets of maps, they finished two such surveys.

Software and Equipment

We used a custom chat interface with embedded MT that could show one or two MT outputs as appropriate for the experiment condition [42]. The interface consists of an instant messaging (IM) window on the left and a map window on the right, as shown in Figure 3.

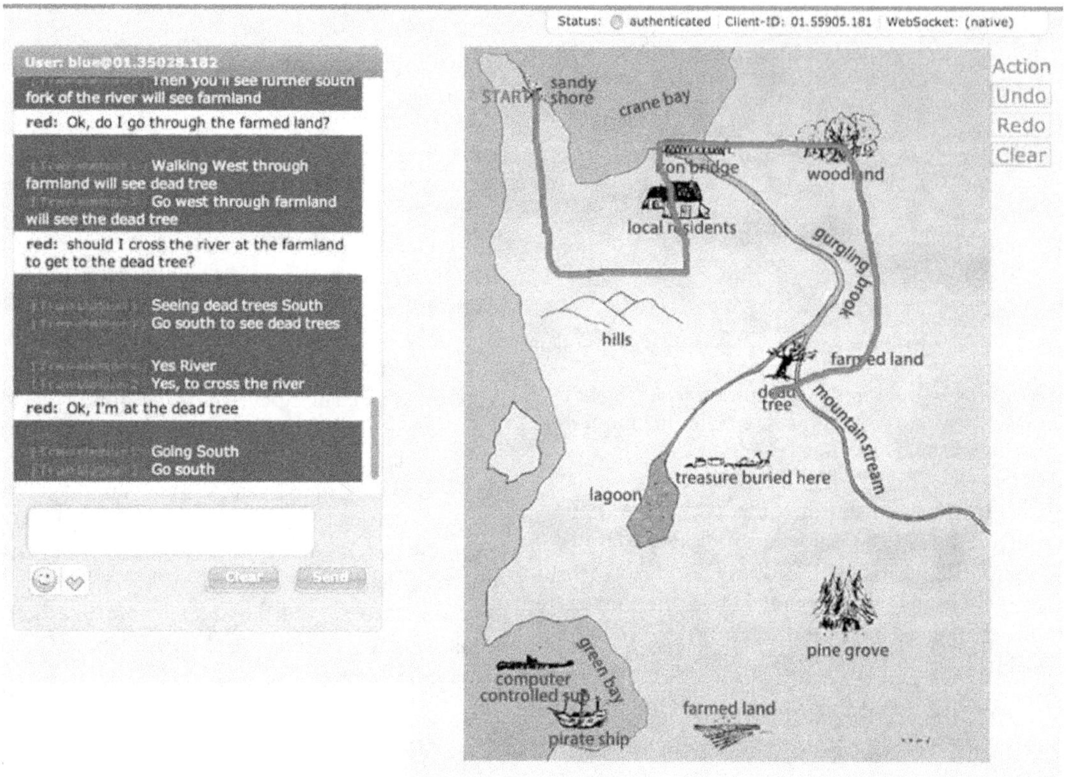

Figure 3. The chat interface as seen by an English speaking follower when getting two MT outputs for each message.

IM window. For the MT mediated conditions, participants typed messages in their native language and received messages translated into their native language. For pairs given two MT outputs, messages were processed by Google and Bing translations, chosen because they are competitive in quality but use distinct algorithms [45]. Pairs in the one MT output condition saw all messages translated by either Google or Bing, counterbalanced between dyads. Translations were always automatically generated and no preview or pre-editing was afforded by this interface. For the English condition, the MT module was absent and participants typed and received messages in English.

Map window. Instructors saw the map with both landmarks and route, while followers saw the map with only landmarks. The interface allowed followers to draw the route on their map following the instructor's guidance, but followers and instructors could only see their own map.

Equipment. Participants used Mac Pro laptops with 13.3 inch monitors and were separated from their partners by a barrier. They wore headphones to reduce distraction from outside noise.

Procedure

Pairs were seated at desks separated by a divider. The experimenter then introduced the study and explained the chat tool, MT module, and map navigation task. After that, the experimenter introduced the detailed procedure. Participants then practiced the chat tool and MT module for 5 minutes before starting the formal task.

In the formal task, dyads were randomly assigned to use one of three communication conditions: MT with one translation output, MT with two translation outputs, or English as a common language. They then performed two map tasks. For the first task, participants were randomly assigned as either an instructor or a follower. In the second task, participants switched roles with their partner and worked on the other map. Each task lasted for 15 minutes. The order of maps and roles were fully counterbalanced using a Latin Square design.

Participants answered a short survey to rate their communication experience and workload after each task. The order of maps and participant roles were fully counterbalanced using a Latin Square design.

Measures

We collected three types of measures of participants' communication and performance: participants' ratings on the post-task survey, coding of evidence in grounding based on the conversation corpus, and navigation performance based on the map route.

Post-Task Survey

Manipulation check. Communication condition was checked by a single choice question asking which language

Coding category	Definition	Example in the current corpus
Positive evidence in grounding		
Acknowledgment	A verbal response that shows a message is understood and accepted.	"Got it."
Negative evidence in grounding		
Align	Queries that check the partner's attention, agreement, or readiness.	"Is everything clear?"
Check	Queries that requests the partner to confirm some unsure information.	"So you want me to go around the bottom of the hills?"
Question-YN	Queries that take a yes or no answer but not counted as a Check or an Align.	"Can you see pelicans?"
Question-W	Any query not covered by the other three types of queries above.	"Where are the stairs?"

Table 1. Evidence of grounding in the current conversation corpus based on the HCRC dialogue structure coding manual.

medium (MT with single output vs. MT with two outputs vs. English as a common language) participants used.

Difficulty of understanding. Participants rated the perceived difficulty of understanding received messages on two 7-point Likert scales ("The unclear information in my partner's messages was distractive", "I had to think harder to understand the unclear information in my partner's messages", 1= strongly disagree, 7 = strongly agree). The questions formed a reliable scale (Cronbach's $\alpha = .86$) and were averaged to create a measure of difficulty of understanding.

Workload. Perceived workload was measured using four 7-point Likert scale adapted from the NASA Task Load Index (TLX [14]) ("Mental demand", "Temporal demand", "Effort", and "Frustration", 1 = low, 7 = high). The questions formed a reliable scale (Cronbach's $\alpha = .82$) and were averaged to create a measure of workload.

Evidence in Grounding

Coding on conversation corpus. We coded the corpus following the HCRC dialogue structure coding manual [2]. This coding scheme differentiates 13 types of conversational moves speakers may generate while doing the map navigation task. We asked two English-Mandarin bilingual speakers, blind to our hypotheses, to work independently and code all IM conversations line by line. Inter-coder agreement was good (Cohen's kappa = .83). The coders then discussed and resolved all disagreements.

Five conversational moves directly pertained to our hypotheses: acknowledgement, check, align, question-YN, and question-W (see Table 1). The first gives positive evidence in grounding, while the other four show negative evidence, i.e., an indication of a lack of understanding [5].

We calculated number of words (as in [13]) used for each type of evidence rather than turns because people use different strategies to break up sentences into turns.

Navigation Performance

Route accuracy. We scored each route the follower drew under the instructor's guidance using the system developed by Diamant and colleagues [7]. Dyads were given one point (1) every time they hit the correct landmark in the right order, but got no score (0) if they hit a wrong landmark or went to the landmark in the wrong order. Route accuracy was calculated as the proportion of correct landmarks.

We did not use time as a measure of task performance, since all groups used the whole session to accomplish the task.

RESULTS

We conducted 3 (communication condition: MT with one output vs. MT with two outputs vs. English as a common language) × 2 (native language: Mandarin vs. English) Mixed Model ANOVAs that took into account the fact that each participant provided two sets of measures. Participants were nested into pairs. The demographic variables (e.g., age and gender) and previous MT experience were set as control variables in all models. The order of trial (first vs. second trial), task (bay map vs. lake map), and role (guider vs. follower) were included as covariates.

Manipulation Check

The manipulation check indicated that all manipulations were successful. All participants identified the language medium they used correctly. The chat logs indicated that all participants used the correct language (English or Mandarin) for their assigned condition.

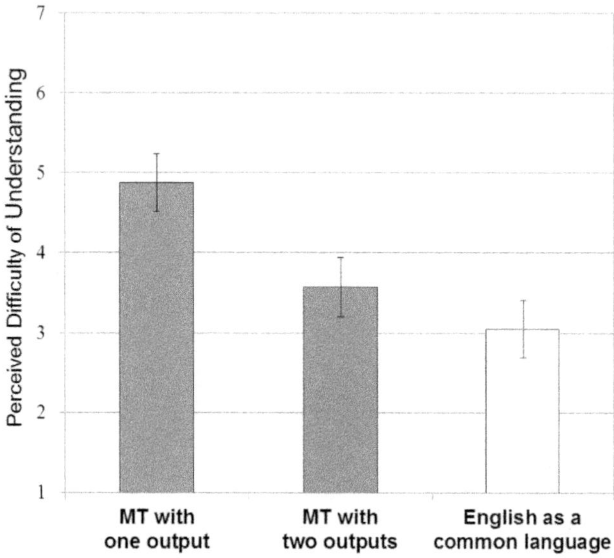

Figure 4. Mean difficulty of understanding by language medium on a scale of 1 (not difficult at all) to 7 (very difficult). (Error bars represent the standard errors of the mean.)

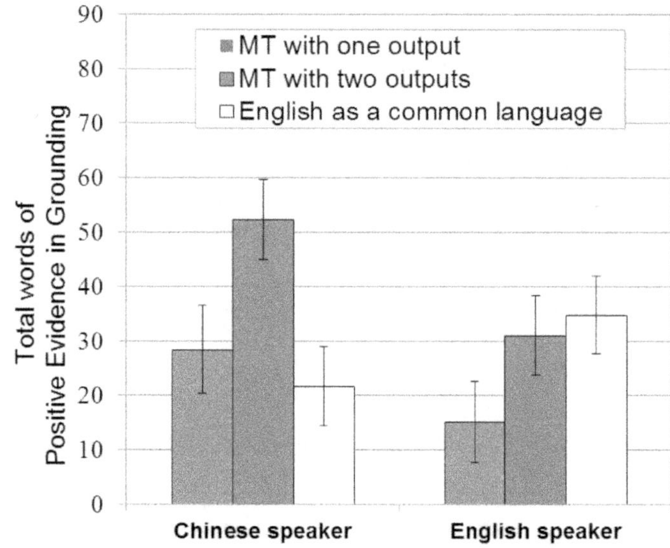

Figure 5. Mean words of positive evidence in grounding by communication condition and native language. (Error bars represent the standard errors of the mean.)

Difficulty of Understanding

H1 predicted that participants would perceive less difficulty in understanding messages when having two MT outputs rather than one. To test this hypothesis, we examined the effect of language medium on participants' rating on the difficulty of understanding.

The results support H1 (Figure 4). There was a significant effect of communication condition on self-reported difficulty of understanding (F [2, 39] = 6.84, p < .01). Pairwise comparisons indicated that participants perceived less difficulty with two MT outputs (M = 3.57, SE = 0.37) vs. one MT output (M = 4.88, SE = 0.36; F [1, 39] = 5.70, *p* = .02). They also perceived less difficulty with English (M = 3.04, SE = 0.36) vs. one MT output (F [1, 39] = 13.16, *p* < .01). However, there was no significant difference between MT with two outputs and English as a common language (F [1, 39] <1). These effects were not qualified by any further interaction effects. For both Chinese and English speaking participants, having two MT outputs helped them understand the received message better.

Evidence in Grounding

H2a and H2b predicted that participants would give more positive evidence (e.g., acknowledgement) and less negative evidence (e.g., questioning and requests for confirmation) of grounding when having two rather than one MT output. To test this hypothesis, we examined the effect of communication condition on the total number of words used for positive and negative evidence of grounding. Given that the map navigation task assigned asymmetric roles to collaborators, this analysis was restricted to messages produced by followers.

Positive Evidence in Grounding

In support of H2a, there was a significant main effect of communication condition on the total words of positive evidence of grounding (F [2, 37] = 3.28, *p* = .05; see Figure 5). Pairwise comparisons indicated that followers gave more acknowledgments when having two MT outputs (M = 41.63, SE = 5.34) vs. only one MT output (M = 21.74, SE = 5.20; F [1, 37] = 6.41, *p* = .01). Further, when participants used MT with two outputs vs. using English as a common language (M = 28.20, SE = 5.06), there was no difference on positive evidence given by followers: F [1, 37] = 3.09, *p* = .09.

We also found a significant interaction between communication condition and the follower's native language (F [2, 37] = 3.38, p = .04; see Figure 5). Native Mandarin speaking followers gave more words of acknowledgement when using MT with two outputs (M = 52.25, SE = 7.34) vs. MT with one output (M = 28.38, SE = 8.27) or English as a common language (M = 21.64, SE = 7.29). Native English speaking followers gave more words of acknowledgment when using MT with two outputs (M = 31.01, SE = 7.26) and English as a common language (M = 34.76, SE = 7.07) than when using MT with one output (M = 15.10, SE = 7.54).

Negative Evidence in Grounding

We examined the effect of communication condition on the total words of all queries (aligns, checks, question-YN, and question-W) given by the follower. As shown in Figure 6, the results partially support H2b. The main effect of communication condition was not significant (F [2, 37] <1). However, there was a significant interaction between communication condition and native language: F [2, 37] =

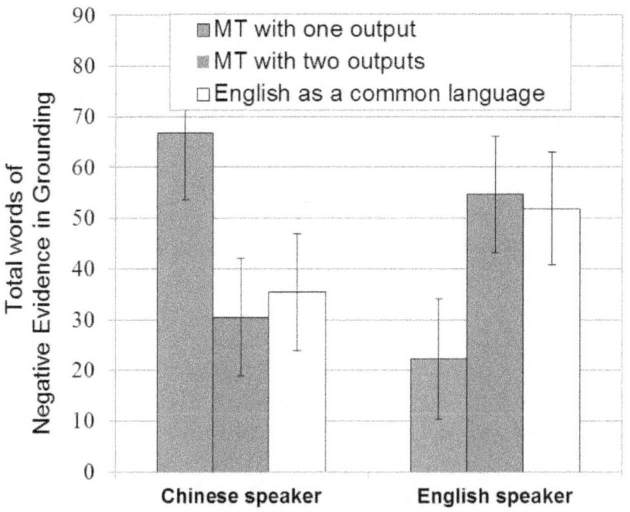

Figure 6. Mean words of negative evidence in grounding by language medium and native language. (Error bars represent the standard errors of the mean.)

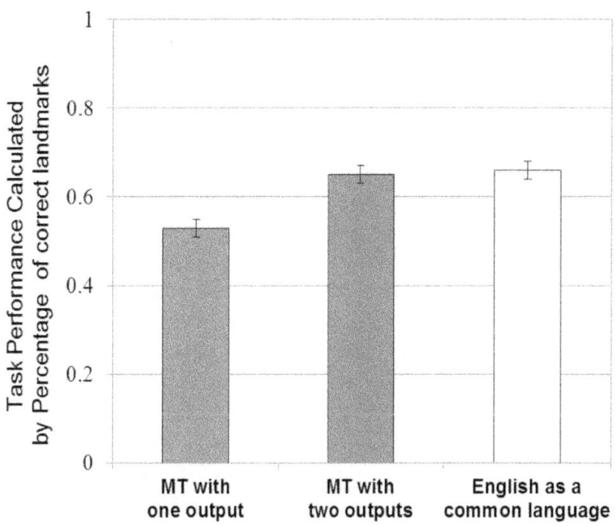

Figure 7. Mean task performance by language medium. (Error bars represent the standard errors of the mean.)

5.07, *p* = .01. The effect of communication condition was opposite for native Mandarin and English speakers. Native Mandarin speaking followers used more query words when using MT with one output (M = 66.70, SE = 13.04) than when using MT with two outputs (M = 30.45, SE = 11.60) or English as a common language (M = 35.42, SE = 11.49). Native English speaking followers used fewer query words when using MT with single outputs (M = 22.28, SE = 11.90) than when using MT with two outputs (M = 54.68, SE = 11.44) or English as a common language (M = 51.87, SE = 11.15).

Task Performance

H3 predicted that participants would perform better with two MT outputs rather than one. As shown in Figure 7, our results support H3. There was a significant effect of communication condition on route accuracy (F [2, 39] = 15.18, p < .01). Pairwise comparisons indicated that dyads having two MT outputs (M = 0.65, SE = 0.02) drew more accurate routes than dyads having only one MT output (M = 0.53, SE = 0.02; F [1, 39] = 19.70, *p* < .01). Dyads using English (M = 0.66, SE = 0.02) also drew more accurate routes than dyads having one MT output (F [1, 39] = 25.07, *p* < .01). Further, when dyads used MT with two outputs vs. using English as a common language, there was no difference in task performance (F [1, 39] <1).

Workload

H4 predicted that participants would experience higher workload when having two rather than one MT output. This hypothesis was not supported (see Figure 8). There was a significant effect of communication condition on workload (F [2, 39] = 4.54, p = .02) but pairwise comparisons indicated no difference in workload with two MT outputs (M = 4.37, SE = 0.30) versus one MT output (M = 4.72, SE = 0.29; F [1, 39] = 0.65, p = .42. Instead, participants using English (M = 3.55, SE = 0.28) reported lower workload than participants given one MT output (F [1, 39] = 8.58, p < .01) or two MT outputs (F [1, 39] = 3.77, p = .05). These effects were not qualified by any further interaction effects.

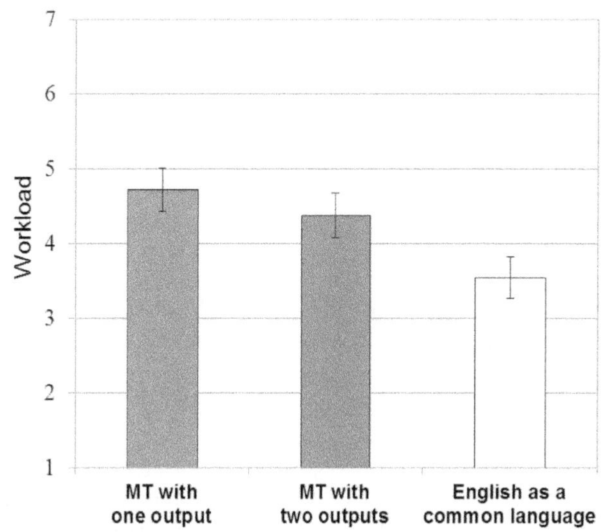

Figure 8. Mean workload by language medium on a scale of 1 (very low) to 7 (very high). (Error bars represent the standard errors of the mean.)

DISCUSSION

We examined conversational grounding, task performance, and cognitive workload as a function of whether participants received two MT outputs, one MT output, or used English as a common language. Our results suggest that two translation outputs improve grounding and performance without increasing cognitive load.[1] We discuss each of these findings below and then suggest some possible implications for the design of tools to support multilingual communication.

Conversational Grounding

Consistent with Yamashita and colleagues [43, 44], our participants had more trouble grounding messages with a single MT output than they did when using English as a common language. Giving people two translations of each message strongly improved grounding. Participants reported that they could understand messages more easily with two rather than one, and this ease of grounding was evidenced in their greater use of acknowledgments. In fact, ease of grounding with two translations did not differ significantly from grounding using English as a common language.

	Original message	Translation output(s) received by an English speaking follower
MT with one output		
Guider	到达一片农田	Reach a field
Follower	Treasure?	Treasure?
Guider	农田	Farmland
MT with two outputs		
Guider	下一个地方是另外一个农田	T1: Next place is another field T2: The next place is another farm
Follower	I am there	I am there

Table 2. Sample dialogues from the one MT output and two MT outputs conditions.

A possible mechanism behind these findings is that message recipients drew on the similarities and differences between the two outputs to infer the meaning of the original message. Table 2 shows an example of how two MT outputs may help people establish grounding efficiently. In each dialogue, a Mandarin speaking instructor is trying to guide an English speaking follower to a farm on the map. When using MT with one output, the word "农田 (farmland)" was translated into "field". The follower had to ask a clarifying question, because a field with hidden treasure was also shown on the map. The dyad with two translations grounded the instructions more easily because the "field" mentioned in T1 was translated as "farm" in T2, and the follower responded with an acknowledgment.

The pattern of results for negative evidence of grounding is more puzzling, especially for native English speakers. Mandarin speaking followers used fewer query words when they had two MT outputs rather than one, consistent with the idea that two translations helped reduce confusion about the meaning of the messages. However, English speaking followers used more queries with two translations. One possibility is that the English speakers were unable to identify when grounding work was required in the one translation case. Chinese bilingual speakers may have been more sensitive to potential translation issues.

For both positive and negative evidence of grounding, English speaking followers use similar amount of words when communicating via two MT outputs vs. English as a common language. This similarity echoes their self-report rating of the difficulty of understanding, and further suggests that ease of grounding is similar in these two conditions. We could not perform a similar comparison for Mandarin speakers because the experimental design required them to speak different languages in these two conditions.

Task Performance

The benefits of having a second translation were also revealed in task performance. As we hypothesized, dyads with two MT outputs performed significantly better than those with one MT output. In fact, their performance did not differ significantly from that of pairs using English as a common language. This suggests that for tasks that require grounding of many different referents (here, the landmarks on the map), the benefits from easy, successful grounding accumulate over the course of a conversation.

As we found no performance differences between using two translations and the use of English as a common language, one might wonder why organizations would chose to use MT at all. We think the justification is that it improves the collaborative experience of non-native speakers. Using a non-native language can be cognitively taxing [35], and non-native speakers brainstorm better using MT than English [41]. There is also evidence that MT improves performance at the group level [16]. Our study suggests that the primary downside of using MT, problematic communication that degrades performance, can be partly overcome by providing two different translations.

Workload

While we had expected that adding a second translation would increase cognitive workload, this was not the case. Self-reported workload using one or two translations was higher than workload using English as a common language.

[1] Although we combined the two translation services in our analyses, the overall pattern of results is similar when comparing each translation service individually with the two translation condition. The two-translation condition improved understanding over Google ($p < .01$) or Bing ($p = .10$) alone and also led to superior performance than Google alone or Bing alone (both $p < .001$). The pattern of results for workload and our speech measures was also similar.

We suspect the similarity in workload between one and two translations can be attributed to subtle variations in workload for two different cognitive tasks: reading a message and figuring out its intended meaning. The second translation may have added to the reading time but reduced the time needed to interpret the message.

The lower workload associated with using English, which was true regardless of the participant's native language, may stem from a different cognitive task, that of message formulation. While it is difficult to produce messages in a non-native language, it is perhaps even more difficult to compose messages that one thinks will be accurately translated by the tool. Since all participants in the MT conditions received as well as produced MT translated messages, they might have been sensitive to the need for careful message construction. These are only speculations and future work will need to use reaction time methods or other more sensitive measures to understand how using MT and English affects cognitive workload.

DESIGN IMPLICATIONS

Apart from the straightforward implication that showing two outputs in MT systems can be helpful, our results suggest some more general ideas for how to make MT systems (and other systems that use error-prone agents) more useful.

Adding channels of communication. While two translations facilitate conversational grounding and task performance, they do not reduce cognitive workload over the one translation case. To make it easier for people to process messages, MT tools might incorporate other channels, for example the rich visual cues that benefit text-based brainstorming [40]. An MT interface might show images that illustrate some part of the original (untranslated) message along with the translations to help with message interpretation. Other channels less explicitly tied to specific messages might also benefit MT. For example, an MT (or other CMC) system might use context sensing features to show aspects of people's physical setting like location, weather, or time. This contextual information might prove useful in interpreting MT output.

Make the presence of computer agency more transparent. Showing two translations rather than one makes the MT system more transparent, exposing seams in the underlying infrastructure. Showing the fact that there are alternatives doesn't just provide a resource for repair; it also foregrounds the fact that translation is happening in the first place and that it is imperfect. Functionally, this has benefits such as encouraging people to attribute problems to the technology rather than to collaborators, in turn improving social outcomes [11]. Philosophically, supporting reflection [30] on the way systems impact our communication is also beneficial, paralleling discussions about how search and recommendation algorithms affect our experience of information [20] and how systems that track our behavior make both correct and incorrect inferences about us [23]. Making alternatives visible is a fundamental way to do this.

Use algorithmic "by-products" as resources to help people make judgments. Systems that do filtering, translation, recommendation, and other tasks for us make choices. Those choices often have data attached to them that could help people decide whether the choices are appropriate. For instance, in recommender systems, the data that supports any given recommended item can be used to help people reason about the quality of the recommendation [e.g., 18, 27, 31, 34]. Similar ideas could be applied to MT systems. When MT algorithms compute translations, they produce information such as confidence levels, word alignment choices, and alternative word translations. Most MT interfaces hide this information and show only a final output—but it might be beneficial to present such information. For example, the interface could visualize the accuracy confidence of translations by putting icons next to the messages telling users whether they should be aware of potential errors, or highlighting the parts of a message where algorithms are not able to find an accurate word alignment.

LIMITATIONS AND FUTURE DIRECTIONS

There were several limitations to this study. First, although our results implied possible effect of participants' English language ability on the grounding process, we were not able to collect any direct measures of language ability. Future studies may want to measure language ability (i.e., TOEFL scores) and include this factor in the data analysis.

Further, a possible side effect of showing two MT outputs that we did not test is that two translations might increase people's awareness of the presence of MT and the possibility of MT errors. Because previous work has shown that beliefs about the presence or absence of MT affect communication and collaboration [11]., more research is needed to separate the effects of having two translations on message understanding vs. attributions about the causes of misunderstandings.

Finally, previous work in related fields has shown other ways to facilitate MT-mediated communication, such as keyword highlighting [10] or adding semantically linked pictures [40]. We can't directly compare our approach relative to these other solutions because of differences in the tasks and procedures of the studies, but this would be a worthwhile goal for future research.

CONCLUSION

Machine translation can allow multilingual collaborators to interact via their own native languages, but MT can introduce translation errors that make communication and collaboration difficult. We examined whether providing two different translations for each message, rather than only one, could improve conversational grounding and task performance. Overall, our results suggest that when people speak different native languages, showing two translations has many benefits and few costs.

ACKNOWLEGEMENTS
This research was funded in part by National Science Foundation grant #1318899 and an unrestricted gift from Google Inc. We thank Leslie Setlock and Huaishu Peng for their assistance and the anonymous reviewers for their valuable comments.

REFERENCES

1. Anderson, A.H. (2006). Achieving understanding in face-to-face and video-mediated multiparty interactions. *Discourse Processes, 41,* 251-287.
2. Carletta, J., Isard, A., Isard, S., Kowtko, J.C., Doherty-Sneddon, G., & Anderson, A.H. (1997). The reliability of a dialogue structure coding scheme. *Computational Linguistics, 23,* 13-31.
3. Chang, P.C. (2009). *Improving Chinese-English Machine Translation through Better Source-Side Linguistic Processing.* Doctoral Dissertation. Stanford University.
4. Clark, H.H. (1996). *Using Language*. Published by Press of Cambridge, Cambridge.
5. Clark, H.H., & Brennan, S.E. (1991). Grounding in communication. *Perspectives on Socially Shared Cognition, 13,* 127-149.
6. Clark, H.H., & Wilkes-Gibbs, D. (1986). Referring as a collaborative process. *Cognition, 22,* 1-39.
7. Diamant, E.I., Fussell, S.R., & Lo, F.L. Where did we turn wrong? Unpacking the effects of culture and technology on attributions of team performance. In *Proc. CSCW 2008*, 383-391.
8. Doherty-Sneddon, G., Anderson, A. H., O'Malley, C., Langton, S., Garrod, S., & Bruce, V. (1997). Face-to-face and video mediated communication: A comparison of dialogue structure and task performance. *Journal of Experimental Psychology: Applied, 3,* 105–125.
9. Feely, A.J., & Harzing, A.W. (2003). Language management in multinational companies. *Cross Cultural Management, 10,* 37–52.
10. Gao, G., Wang, H.C., Cosley, D., & Fussell, S.R. (2013). Same translation but different experience: The effects of highlighting on machine-translated conversations. In *Proc. CHI 2013*, 449-458.
11. Gao, G., Xu, B., Cosley, D., & Fussell, S.R. (2014). How beliefs about the presence of machine translation impact multilingual collaborations. In *Proc. CSCW 2014*, 1549-1560.
12. Gao, G., Yamashita, N., Hautasaari, A.M.J., Echenique, A., & Fussell, S.R. (2014). Effects of public vs. private automated transcripts on multiparty communication between native and non-native English speakers. In *Proc. CHI 2014*, 843-852.
13. Gergle, D., Kraut, R.E., & Fussell, S.R. (2004). Language efficiency and visual technology: Minimizing collaborative effort with visual information. *Journal of Language and Social Psychology, 23,* 1-27.
14. Hart, S.G., & Staveland, L.E. (1998). Development of NASA-TLX: Results of empirical and theoretical research. *Advances in Psychology, 52,* 139-183.
15. Harzing, A. W., & Feely, A. J. (2008). The language barrier and its implications for HQ–subsidiary relationships. *Cross Cultural Management: An International Journal, 15,* 49–60.
16. Hautasaari, A. (2010). Machine translation effects on group interaction: An intercultural collaboration experiment. In *Proc. ICIC 2010*, 70-78.
17. Henderson, J.K. (2005). Language diversity in international management teams. *International Studies of Management and Organization, 35,* 66–82.
18. Herlocker, J.L., Konstan, J.A., & Riedl, J. (2000). Explaining collaborative filtering recommendations. In *Proc. CSCW 2000*, 241-250.
19. Hutchins, W.J. (2005). Machine translation and human translation: In competition or in complementation? *International Journal of Translation, 13,* 5-20.
20. Introna, L.D., & Nissenbaum, H. (2000). Shaping the web: Why the politics of search engines matters. *The information society, 16,* 169-185.
21. Isaacs, E. A., & Clark, H. H. (1987). References in conversation between experts and novices. *Journal of Experimental Psychology: General, 116,* 26-37.
22. Ishata, T. (Eds.). (2011). *The Language Grid.* Published by Press of Springer, Heidelberg.
23. Khovanskaya, V., Baumer, E.P.S., Cosley, D., Voida, S., & Gay, G. (2013). Everybody knows what you're doing: a critical design approach to personal informatics. In *Proc. CHI 2013*, 3403-3412.
24. Li, N., & Rosson, M.B. (2014). Using annotations in online group chats. In *Proc. CHI 2014*, 863-866.
25. Lim, J., & Yang, Y.P. (1998). Exploring computer-based multilingual negotiation support for English-Chinese dyads: Can we negotiate in our native languages? *Behaviour and Information Technology, 27,* 139-151.
26. Locke, W. N., & Booth, A. D. (Eds.). (1995). *Machine Translation of Languages: Fourteen Essays*. Published jointly by Technology Press of the Massachusetts Institute of Technology and Wiley, New York.
27. McNee, S.M., Lam, S.K., Konstan, J.A., & Riedl, J. (2003). Interfaces for eliciting new user preferences in recommender systems. In *Proc. UM 2003*, 178-187.

28. Miyabe, M., & Yoshino, T. (2009). Accuracy evaluation of sentences translated to intermediate language in back translation. In *Proc. IUCS 2009*, 30-35.

29. Neeley, T. B. (2013). Language matters: Status loss and achieved status distinctions in global organizations. *Organization Science, 24,* 476-497.

30. Sengers, P., Boehner, K., David, S., & Kaye, J. (2005). Reflective design. In *Proc. AARHUS 2005*, 49-58.

31. Sharma, A., & Cosley, D. (2013). Do social explanations work?: Studying and modeling the effects of social explanations in recommender systems. In *Proc. WWW 2013*, 1133-1144.

32. Shigenobu, T. (2007). Evaluation and usability of back translation for intercultural communication. Usability and Internationalization. *Global and Local User Interface*. Springer, 259-265.

33. Slocum, J. A. (1985). Survey of machine translation: Its history, current status, and future prospects. *Computational Linguistics, 11,* 1-17.

34. Swearingen, K., & Sinha, R. (2002). Interaction design for recommender systems. *Designing Interactive Systems, 6,* 312-334.

35. Takano, Y. & Noda, A. (1995). Interlanguage dissimilarity enhances the decline of thinking ability during foreign language processing. *Lang. Learning, 45*, 657–681.

36. Tange, H., & Lauring, J. (2009). Language management and social interaction within the multilingual workplace. *Journal of Communication Management, 13,* 218-232.

37. Tenzer, H., Pudelko, M., & Harzing, A. W. (2013). The impact of language barriers on trust formation in multinational teams. *Journal of International Business Studies, 45,* 508-535.

38. Veinott, E.S., Olson, J., Olsen, G.M., & Fu, X. (1999). Video helps remote work: Speakers who need to negotiate common ground benefit from seeing each other. In *Proc. CHI 1999*, 302-309.

39. Vilar, D., Xu, J., D'Haro, L.F., & Ney, H. (2006). Error analysis of statistical machine translation output. In *Proc. LREC 2006*, 697-702.

40. Wang, H.C., Cosley, D., & Fussell, S.R. (2010). Idea expander: supporting group brainstorming with conversationally triggered visual thinking stimuli. In *Proc. CSCW 2010*, 103-106.

41. Wang, H.C., Fussell, S. R., & Cosley, D. (2013). Machine translation vs. common language: Effects on idea exchange in cross-lingual groups. In *Proc. CSCW 2013*, 935-944.

42. Xu, B., Gao, G., Fussell, S.R., & Cosley, D. (2014). Improving machine translation by showing two outputs. In *Proc. CHI 2014*, 3743-3746.

43. Yamashita, N., Inaba, R., Kuzuoka, H., & Ishida, T. (2009). Difficulties in establishing common ground in multiparty groups using machine translation. In *Proc. CHI 2009*, 679-688.

44. Yamashita, N., & Ishida, T. (2006). Effects of machine translation on collaborative work. In *Proc. CSCW 2006*, 515-523.

45. Zhang, R.P., Pan, Y., & Yang, Y. (2006). A comparative case study of Google and Bing translation. In *Proc. ICERI 2012,* 3669-3673.

In the Flow, Being Heard, and Having Opportunities: Sources of Power and Power Dynamics in Global Teams

Pamela Hinds
Management Science &
Engineering, Stanford University
Stanford, CA
phinds@stanford.edu

Daniela Retelny
Management Science &
Engineering, Stanford University
Stanford, CA
dretelny@stanford.edu

Catherine Cramton
School of Management,
George Mason University
Fairfax, VA
ccramton@gmu.edu

ABSTRACT
In our qualitative study of 9 globally distributed software development teams, we found that power and how it was distributed across locations had a significant effect on team dynamics. We describe the sources of power for these teams, which include being in the flow of information, feeling that one's voice is heard by decision makers, and having opportunities for career growth and advancement. We also examine power dynamics across locations by team and show that having more balanced power was typically associated with more power struggles rather than fewer. Four of the 9 teams had ongoing power contests. Each of these teams had some sources of power at one location and other sources of power at the other location. Both sites worried about losing power, felt they should have more, and struggled against losing ground. We conclude with a discussion of the need for CSCW to expand beyond collaboration to address issues of power. We propose ideas for systems to support globally distributed teams in creating more equal access to more sources of power and alleviating unhealthy power dynamics.

Author Keywords
global teams; virtual teams; power; qualitative methods

ACM Classification Keywords
K.4.3 [Information Interfaces and Presentation]: User Interfaces - Interaction styles.

General Terms
Management

INTRODUCTION
Over the last 10-15 years, research on global teams has grown dramatically, including investigations of team dynamics [6, 8, 23, 33], communication structure [10, 19], conflict [20, 21], coordination [16, 18] and leadership [11, 40]. Scholars have also studied the use of technology to support [13, 17, 33, 38] and alleviate many of the challenges encountered by globally distributed teams [3, 27, 28]. Few studies, however, have examined the power dynamics in global teams, particularly the sources of power and how workers respond to power imbalances. This is despite the fact that the distribution of power can have profound and far-reaching effects on individual behavior [9] and team outcomes [2, 41]. In this study, we aim to fill that gap through a qualitative study of 9 teams, each split between two countries and with access to different local resources and thus sources of power.

CSCW '15, March 14–18, 2015, Vancouver, BC, Canada.

http://dx.doi.org/10.1145/2675133.2675199

Power in Organizations
Social power has been defined as "asymmetric control over valued resources in social relations" ([26]: 361). As such, power is both relational and situational [14]. That is, a person has social power relative to another person in a particular situation, but not necessarily in all situations because the "valued resources" are often situation specific. In a software development organization, for example, the ability to access top notch programmers might give a manager power over those who aren't tapped into that network, but her power wouldn't necessarily transfer to a legal firm. Power also implies some type of dependence between parties [12] such that the lower power party or group is dependent upon the higher power party for valued resources. Although related, power is different from status. Both are relational, but power is based on the valued resources that belong to an actor or group vis a vis other actors or groups whereas status is conferred to an individual or group by others based on their assessment that the individual or group has laudable expertise, traits, etc. [2, 14, 24, 26]. In other words, power is more objective whereas status is in the eye of the beholder.

Extensive research has examined what makes people powerful. Over 50 years ago, work by French and Raven [15] reported six sources (bases) of power – legitimate (positional), reward, coercive, informational, expert, and referent. These bases of power continue to be recognized as key sources of power although some (e.g. referent) have been recategorized as status [26]. Emerson [12] and later, Pfeffer and Salancik [34] argued that power comes down to control over valued resources. Those who need resources that are critical and can't be acquired elsewhere are dependent on those who control those resources. Most of French and Raven's sources of power can be seen as valued resources. For example, a supervisor with positional power may control raises, bonuses, and promotions. Research has also shown that position in the network affords power [4]. Ibarra and Andrews [22], for example, show that network centrality regulates access to information, resources, and legitimacy in organizations. In other words, who you know affects access to valued resources.

More recently, research has focused on the effects of power, reporting that "degree and symmetry of power both determine how interpersonal encounters proceed" ([14]: 942). Those with less power tend to be more vigilant, more accommodating, and more envious toward their higher power counterparts [14]. Those with more power, in contrast, tend to be more outspoken, confident, and less aware of others who are not instrumental in helping them to achieve their goals [26]. As a result of these behavioral responses to power imbalances, those in power tend to maintain or increase the power they hold. In their review, Magee and Galinsky [26] conclude that the status quo is challenged infrequently, in part because a power hierarchy meets individual and organizational needs for stability. In the absence of a clear power hierarchy, coordination suffers because roles and activities become ambiguous.

Despite extensive research on how those with power employ strategies to maintain their position, it is clear that power shifts happen. Countries gain and lose power, organizations on the ascendancy give way to newcomers, and leaders are replaced. In particular, as work is sent offshore and global teams span locations, power and how it is held in place or shifts and how teams respond to that is not yet well understood.

Power in Global Teams

Decades of research have explored the relationship between multinational firms and their distant subsidiaries [28]. These macro-level studies have focused on how less powerful subsidiaries gain power in an otherwise imbalanced relationship [30, 31]. Over time, as more critical functions such as R&D have been outsourced, subsidiaries are described as holding the company's "crown jewels" ([30]: 387). This shift of knowledge-based assets away from company headquarters has the effect of granting subsidiaries more power [5]. Despite a large body of research on headquarter-subsidiary power relations, however, little has been said about the experience of the workers themselves when working from different locations that afford different sources of power and as the sources of power are realigned based on the needs of the business.

One exception is work by O'Leary and Mortensen [32] who examined the configurational imbalance (relative numbers of team members) across two sites. They found that locations with (numerical) minority subgroups were at a disadvantage compared to locations with a relatively larger number of team members. Sites with fewer team members were defensive and worried about being overridden or outvoted by their distant colleagues. This early study suggests that a larger relative number of collocated team members may be a source of power in distributed teams, but many questions remain. Because this was a study with student teams and other sources of power were held more or less constant, it isn't possible to infer how other sources of power might come into play in global teams. Additional field research is needed to explore these dynamics.

Metiu [29] reports on such a field study. She found extreme status dynamics on a global team in which work was outsourced from the US to India. In her case, the US team members had higher status (and power) and, in order to maintain their status in the face of an ambitious lower status group (India), the US engineers engaged in "exclusionary acts" such as refusing to interact with the Indian engineers, ignoring their work and, when evaluating the Indian engineers' work, criticizing the quality. Metiu does an excellent job of describing the status closure strategies employed by the high status US-based engineers to maintain the status quo. It was not her goal, however, to examine the sources of power or how the relative sources of power affected the power dynamics on global teams, so these questions remain open. Levina and Vaast [25] also examine status differences in offshore collaborations. They report that separation in time and space accentuated differences in sources of status (social capital), but that the onshore leaders of these teams sometimes shared their resources as a way to renegotiate status differences. Although informative, both of these studies examine outsourcing relationships where the power structure clearly favored the outsourcing location.

Previous CSCW research has also explored how power is affected by geographic and cultural distance as well as by technology. Research has demonstrated, for example, that on globally distributed teams, higher status sites, such as headquarters, or teams with high status individuals have more influence when negotiating times to meet [36]. Similarly, in a study of the use of the Tele-Board system, Gumienny et al. [17] found that individuals with domain expertise who were located at the corporate headquarters in Germany were less motivated and less likely to share knowledge with their counterparts in India and Italy. As a result, the frequency of usage of the Tele-Board system among the German team members was much lower than team members at the remote locations. This nascent research points to the importance of power dynamics in the usage of systems to support distributed and global work.

In our qualitative study of 9 teams in a software development organization, GlobalTech, we found that the sources of power were more complex than simply being located at headquarters and the relative number of team members. We describe the sources of power on these teams, some of which exist by virtue of being geographically distributed and some of which are heightened as a result of being composed of professionals whose work is often ambiguous and highly dependent on expertise. We also describe the power dynamics on these teams, especially how the distribution of sources of power across locations were associated with contested, shifting, or shared power or with an acceptance of an inevitable power imbalance between sites.

METHOD

We conducted a qualitative study of 9 globally distributed teams at GlobalTech, a software development company. In all cases, the teams that we studied were distributed across two and only two locations, India-US, India-Germany, or Germany-US. All locations were well established, having been in place for at least 5 years and with a minimum of several thousand employees in each country. The headquarters of the company was in Germany and Germany also had the largest number of employees. Five of the 6 Germany-based subteams were located at headquarters, but one team (IG2) was at a satellite office elsewhere in Germany. Teams were tasked with providing software development and maintenance, quality management, or product management for the firm's software products. A list of the teams with a description of their projects is provided in Table 1. All of the teams that we studied used a combination of email, audio conferencing, video conferencing (primarily meeting room vs. desktop) and occasional phone calls to communicate across distances. Site visits also took place occasionally.

We spent approximately 18 months collecting data with GlobalTech, starting with ethnographic interviews [35]. We interviewed each team member using a semi-structured protocol in which we explored their experience working in global teams. We asked questions about their daily work, their communication with collocated and distant team members, and any issues or challenges they faced. Our inquiries were open-ended so that what was of importance to the informants guided the conversations. Interviews typically lasted 60-90 minutes and were conducted in meeting rooms and private offices, although sometimes took place in quiet corners of the cafeteria. All interviews were recorded and transcribed.

We also conducted concurrent observations of 6 of the 9 teams. "Concurrent observations" refer to cases in which one member of the research team observed at one location while another observed the same team at the other location. For example, one of the authors was in India observing a team during the same week that another researcher was in Germany observing the same team. Concurrent observations enabled us to get information about topics of conversation, issues, and team dynamics in the same team during the same week. We took copious field notes and shared them with the research team at the end of each day to ensure that we were capturing similar events and ensure that both researchers were aware of key events, meetings, and issues that might affect the other site, thus fine-tuning our observations. The observations took place 3-7 months following our initial interviews.

Finally, we conducted follow up interviews with the project leaders and met with the teams approximately 18 months after the first set of interviews. We used this time to understand what had changed (or not) in the teams and to better understand some of the findings from our initial rounds of analysis.

We analyzed all of our data using NVivo. We started by open-coding, reading through all of the data and identifying themes. Sources of power and power dynamics immediately surfaced as strong and interesting themes. We then iterated with the literature and examined the sources power at the individual level, which enabled us to identify the importance of being in the flow, being heard, and having opportunities. Finally, we conducted a team-level analysis in which we analyzed the data by team by location to better understand each subteam's perception of their sources of power and how the power dynamics were playing out.

FINDINGS

Our analysis suggests that team members at some locations felt that they had less influence and power than those at other locations. Interestingly, it was not only those at headquarters or those collocated with the largest number of team members who felt powerful, although both of these were factors. We found that the sources of power among these globally distributed professionals resided at different locations and fell into three categories; access to information (being in the flow), access to decision makers (being heard), and opportunities for growth. When team members perceived that they had access to these resources, they felt that they could work effectively, influence decisions of importance, and have career opportunities, but if few were present, they expressed frustration and dissatisfaction in their jobs. Some eventually left. Our data also suggest that a relatively even distribution of power across sites was not always optimum. The teams with relatively evenly distributed sources of power were the most likely to experience severe power struggles. We conclude that power struggles were more likely when each site held some sources of power, but not others.

Being in the Flow

A majority of our data regarding power dynamics fell into the category of whether or not workers felt that they had access to strategic information and information critical for doing their jobs. These sources of information included executives, experts, customers, and other GlobalTech workers.

Executives

For the most part, top executives at GlobalTech were located at headquarters. Informants frequently told us about how, as a result, the headquarters location was the source of strategic information and where key meetings took place. As described by a developer from the headquarters location in Germany:

Especially when there was this phase of restructuring, the new department was initiated, then I guess it was not that easy for people in the US to get information, what's going on. I mean these like phases where there's a lot of rumors and there's no official announcement made yet. And, these things are obviously easier to find out when you're over here...

As suggested by this informant, the strategic information, particularly prior to formal announcements, wasn't available to employees who did not have access to top executives. As summarized by one developer in Germany, "The advantage is we are in the headquarters and all the news are going on here." Also, after information was shared, those not at headquarters had less opportunity to make sense of important announcements by participating in formal and informal discussions with top leaders. Even at the day-to-day level, there were high level committees and "standard groups" that were led by key executives located at headquarters. As stated by a developer at headquarters working with US team members, "we have to go to committees and standard groups or whatever because the people from [US location] cannot." Workers from the US and India locations frequently lamented the fact that they were "out of the loop" with regard to this important source of information.

Experts

Even more frequent were complaints about not having access to experts, especially those with know-how on the systems or products on which the developers were working. Some, but not all of this expertise was located at headquarters. One informant from Germany, for example, said "all the base development is sitting here in [headquarters location] and if you have a problem you can go to the colleagues or call them and I think you get better information." On other teams, however, key expertise was at the satellite offices. On one of the India-US teams, for example, the product expertise was located at the US location. As explained one of the Indian developers, "The product was developed in [US location], so any kind of expertise that we need, we have to go to [US location]... then you would need to be interacting with them to get their approval of what you have designed and to give suggestions." As articulated by this informant, having the expertise located elsewhere created a dependency on team members at another location, which reduced local developers' sense of power. On an India-Germany team (at the satellite location in Germany, not headquarters), there was also a clear sense that the German location housed more product expertise, thus giving them an advantage. As one of our Indian developers explained, "In terms of [Product X], it's better to work from [German location] because there are people – I would call them forefathers of [Product X] – they have worked in and out of the product. They know, I mean, they're experts in the modules they are handling." Across locations and informants, being collocated with key product and technical experts was perceived as affording access to critical information needed to successfully accomplish one's work.

Customers

Having direct access to customers was also a critical resource for developers and varied significantly by location. In both Germany and the US, depending on the product, developers often had direct access to customers, which gave them a better sense that they knew how to develop and improve the product. For the most part, developers in India did not have access to customers and it had a profound affect on their sense of power and influence over their work. An Indian developer explained, "their customers are around them in Germany itself... so they are able to talk to them and get all the required information and the business end of it." Similarly, a developer on an India-US team explained how they couldn't get access to customers, which left them unable to understand clients' needs:

So it's very difficult to... you cannot call and talk to them, whereas when you are there in [US city] you tend to pick up the phone, talk to the customer, resolve their issues, understand exactly what they mean... So, sometimes, like, we do not exactly know what is happening. Suppose there is a development plan coming up, there is a huge project coming up. We are not the first people to know... Any person who is going to be close to the customer is going to have more information than you.

Another informant on the same team went on to say that all of their customer contact had to go through members of the team located in the US, which created "total dependence" on those team members. He said that they couldn't even "get clarification" quickly when they needed it. Lack of customer contact affected the ability of workers to act independently and make decisions. They also felt that it inhibited their ability to learn and grow.

It was not just the Indian developers who were frustrated about lack of access to customers. Informants from Germany sometimes felt that customer access was better in the US. As explained by one informant, "obviously that [the US] is seen as a key market for software still, with the big companies coming out of the US directly." Another informant from the same team explained, "In [US city], it is beneficial right now. We have all the customers over there, so that you have the direct experience and the talk with the customers and the implementation." At the same time, there were some teams in the US who were working on products primarily for a European market. One of these team members told us with frustration, "So these questions were on the original agenda for this meeting. They haven't been answered. I have asked for that. I have asked twice for that. But nevertheless, they don't come up. And, I can't answer them because everybody tells me... well, you shouldn't go to the customers, so I can't do the research myself."

The primary customer base for different products varied by location and, as a result, could affect which team members had direct access to customers and customer information. In some cases, especially for India, the barriers were high and many Indian informants reported never having spoken to or met with a customer. US and Germany-based developers, described direct customer contact as inconvenient due to geographic distances, time zones, and absence of customer relationships, but they did not report feeling quite as powerless as the Indian team members for whom there were no major GlobalTech customers in the region and little hope of being any in the near future.

Other GlobalTech Workers

Another major source of valuable information was access to the larger GlobalTech network. This was another case where being at headquarters was a distinct advantage because there were many more employees at headquarters than at the satellite locations. In some cases, however, having access to a relatively larger number of collocated team members counterbalanced this. One team member from the US, for example, described himself as being "close to the center which is here... meaning that most of the team members are here." Across the teams in our study, team members felt more "in the flow" of information when they were collocated with a relatively larger number of team members. For example, in a team with 14 team members in India and 4 in Germany, the Indian team members expressed feeling more "central" in the information flow. Surprisingly, the actual numbers did not seem to matter as much as the relative number. Having "most" of the team members nearby afforded a greater sense of influence.

On the larger stage, however, being tapped into the network of developers at GlobalTech, most of who were at headquarters, also mattered. Numerous informants told us about the power of knowing who to go to, having personal relationships with collocated colleagues, and being able to walk down the hall to ask questions of other developers. An Indian developer visiting headquarters told us that it was better for him to be at the headquarters location because "I need the information about the developments from the developers." One of the German team members, empathizing with his US colleagues, explained:

If you're located here [headquarters], you just walk over to that building, go in there... I've got a question. Okay, thank you. And you leave. So now, you're in the US and you have the same quick questions. You cannot just pop in and ask that question... this person does not know you...

With regard to access to other GlobalTech workers, our analysis suggests that being collocated with larger numbers of other workers was one element that increased the extent to which distributed workers felt that they were "in the flow" of information. Part of it was local to the project itself. That is, people felt more central in the flow of important information if they were located near a larger number of collocated team members, as found by O'Leary and Mortensen [32]. Part of it, however, also had to do with having access to developers across the organization, because through them flowed information that might be useful, in general, to their work at GlobalTech.

Summary

Taken together, access to information surfaced as a critical condition for distributed workers' feeling of power and influence at GlobalTech. When workers were collocated with executives, domain experts, customers, a numerical majority of team members, and/or larger numbers of GlobalTech developers, they felt like they had more access to the information needed to do their jobs, to understand the strategic direction of the organization, and to learn and develop their skills. Although part of this came with being at headquarters, that wasn't always the case. As GlobalTech expanded globally, so did the location of domain experts, relatively larger numbers of team members, and customers. When team members felt that their access was more limited than their distant team members, they expressed frustration and fear that they would not be able to do their jobs well and remain competitive.

Being Heard

Having access to decision makers was also perceived to be a key source of power on these global teams. In particular, team members felt that they were more likely to be seen and "heard" if they were collocated with their managers and with the architect who often made decisions about what contributions were in the next release of the product.

In some cases, especially in India, teams had "local leaders" who were responsible for some of the HR functions locally but, for the most part, the product managers allocated work and were seen as the team leaders. At the time of our study, there were team leaders located in the US and in Germany, but none were yet located in India. In nearly all cases, team members suffered when their leader was located at another site. Those not located with their leaders felt that their leader didn't understand what they did, that their work wasn't visible and that they had little influence over decisions going their way. On one of the US-Germany teams in which the manager was located in the US, a German team member complained that if you want to make a decision, you have to check with the leader in the US and then "you wait until 5:00 to reach him or you cannot reach him so you wait another one or two days until you finally do." A US-based team member also told us about a lack of access as a result of his manager being located in Germany. He said, "if your manager is located here [US], you will definitely... because he's sitting next to you or something nearby... and obviously on a day-to-day basis you tend to interact with him, so he will know... okay, you have done this, you have done this, you have done this..." An Indian developer when asked what it was like having a boss in Germany replied, "Its hard... you do a certain job and its done. If I have a boss here [India], yeah, I know how he feels about it. I can make out from how his emotions are, his expressions."

In addition to lack of visibility and difficulty in decision-making, lack of direct access to one's manager led to fears about what information one's manager might be hearing about them from other sources. In India, for example, a developer reporting to a manager in Germany told us about his concerns that another team member might not like him. He was worried that this team member might provide his manager with a "bad picture" of him, saying "It's a pretty difficult thing, you know, your manager to exactly know what you're doing. And, knowing it, being here and knowing it through someone is different."

In sum, being collocated with decision makers, especially product managers, whose input was essential in decisions related to the product, schedule, future releases, and job assignments, was seen as a pivotal source of power because workers could get their questions answered and continue making progress in their work. They also felt that their work and contributions were understood by their managers and that they had some control over how they were seen.

Having Opportunities

Another strong theme in our data was that workers' felt they had more power when there were opportunities for growth. Some projects were more strategic and perceived as affording more opportunities for skill development and visibility. In addition, some locations, namely India, were growing at a more rapid pace and workers were aware that chances for better assignments and promotions were greater in India than elsewhere. One of the managers in India, for example, explained to us that it was a...

... big advantage to be at the [India location] because the [India location] is growing fast, as compared to the [headquarters location]... which means the growth opportunities here are much faster. So, if you are a fresh guy joining and then, let's say, how long would it take for me to reach a certain level. You are likely to reach that level much faster here in [Indian city] than you would be in [headquarters city].

In the US, in contrast, one of the informants confided, "I think sometimes it worries us because then we don't know where we're going to grow. Because only if in project management, I'm just going to be doing that much, then what's the future?" Some team members explicitly expressed concern that growth would happen in India and the other locations would be reduced in numbers. In fact, during the time of our study, one of the teams split between Germany and India did just that. Several people in Germany were shifted onto less prestigious projects and desirable new development work was transferred to India.

Overall, workers on the global teams saw their sources of power as being in the information flow, being heard, and having opportunities for growth. All of these were seen as pivotal to their ability to get their jobs done well and to their opportunities for job security and career advancement.

Cross-Site Power Dynamics

As mentioned above, the sources of power differed by team and by location. When conducting team-level analysis, it became apparent that some locations had access to more sources of power. It was the distribution of sources of power that seemed to influence the power dynamics between locations. We observed teams with relatively severe power contests, in which both teams had some sources of power, teams in which a shift in power was underway, such as work moving to India, and teams in which the power imbalance was acute, but accepted, at least in the short term. We also observed one team that appeared to share power amicably between sites. Table 1 captures the number of team members at each location, task, relative sources of power, and power dynamics observed on each team. It is important to note that all teams were highly dependent on one another for their success. In most cases, they had a combination of pooled, sequential, and reciprocal interdependence (see [39]) depending on the specific task and issues that arose in a given week. Even teams whose work was highly pooled or sequential found themselves having to jointly solve issues on a regular basis.

Power Contested

In 4 of the 9 teams in our study, power was contested, sometimes fiercely. Surprisingly, in all of these teams, the sources of power were relatively evenly split across locations. Two of these teams were divided between India-US and two divided between Germany-US. The 2 Germany-US teams that displayed a contested power dynamic were split between the US and the headquarters location in Germany. As a result, the team members in Germany were in the flow of information by virtue of being collocated with executives and large numbers of GlobalTech coworkers. This did not, however, necessarily give them access to more resources overall than their US-based counterparts. The team members in Germany had the benefit of being at headquarters, but they lacked access to expertise in user-interface design, which resided at the US location. Leadership resided at both locations, although major decisions were seen as being made in Germany. Still the US team members described themselves as being the "enforcers" of a global UI standard. In addition, a larger customer base for the product was in the US. In this team, neither location dominated and both felt that opportunities for growth were scarce, so a power contest emerged. In our observations, we noticed that the US-based team members frequently remarked about the threat and sense of competition that they felt between themselves and team members in Germany. At the same time, team members in Germany wondered why the work couldn't all be done in Germany. This power contest was present throughout the duration of our study. In GU3, we observed a similar power contest, although the sources of power were somewhat different. Again, the Germany-based team members had the benefit of being at headquarters, but they lacked access to important customers, including the key

	Task Description	**Relative Sources of Power**					**Power Dynamics**
Team Name, Location (# of members)		**In the Flow (Access to Execs)**	**In the Flow (Access to Experts)**	**In the Flow (Access to Customers)**	**Being Heard**	**Having Opportunities**	
IU1 India (6) US (4)	All team members charged with resolving customer problems with respect to implementing, using, or extracting results from a particular system.	No team members at HQ, so relatively equal access to executives.	Access to expertise relatively even.	Primary customer base in US.	Access to decision makers about even.	Most opportunities for growth perceived to be in India.	Contested
IU2 India (7) US (6)	Team develops supply chain management systems. US team involved in front-end design and development; India manages gaps in programming interface.	No team members at HQ, so relatively equal access to executives.	Access to expertise greater in US.	Primary customer base in US.	Decision makers in US decide who gets what work.	Most opportunities for growth perceived to be in India.	Contested
IU3 India (4) US (7)	Development and support of cross-applications. Product management and high-level design in US Second level design, specifications and support in India.	No team members at HQ, so relatively equal access to executives.	Large numbers of experts in US, but high prestige developers in India.	Somewhat better access in the US.	Decision making (including architect) in US, but India reports decisions going their way.	Although growth opportunities were largely in India, team in US grew rapidly. Highly visible project was also seen as a growth opportunity.	Shared
IG1 **India (16)** Germany (8)	Development and support for a set of products. Development support across sites with product management in Germany.	German team members at HQ had more access to executives.	Product expertise in Germany, hard for Indian team members to access.	Customer contact fairly evenly divided.	Relevant decision makers were primarily in Germany.	Most opportunities for growth perceived to be in India.	Imbalance Accepted
IG2 **India (14)** Germany (4)	Support for retail software solution. Ownership for software being transferred from Germany to India.	Although in Germany, the site was not at HQ, so neither had access to executives.	Product expertise in Germany, hard for Indian team members to access.	Customer contact primarily from Germany.	Decision making slowly moving to India, so increasingly balanced.	Most opportunities for growth perceived to be in India.	Shifting
IG3 India (6) Germany (5)	Quality management for a set of products. Test coordination in Germany, but products supported in both locations.	German team members at HQ had more access to executives.	Product and technical expertise in Germany.	Customer contact primarily internal to org and evenly divided.	Local management added, but product management primarily in Germany.	Most opportunities for growth perceived to be in India.	Shifting
GU1 Germany (9) US (7)	US creating user interface. Germany provides back-end functionality and database application.	German team members at HQ had more access to executives.	Germany had access to more expertise in system functionality, but US had more access to expertise in UI design.	Customer base mostly in the US.	Leadership in both locations, so both sides felt they had access to decision makers, but US had lower level access.	Limited opportunities for growth in both locations.	Contested
GU2 Germany (7) US (2)	Software development for a personnel-related functionality. US team works on two and Germany works on another aspect of the functionality.	German team members at HQ had more access to executives.	Key expertise perceived to be in Germany, US access limited.	Key customers in Europe, limited US access.	Decision makers concentrated in Germany.	Limited opportunities for growth in both locations.	Imbalance Accepted

	Task Description	Relative Sources of Power					Power Dynamics
Team Name, Location (# of members)		In the Flow (Access to Execs)	In the Flow (Access to Experts)	In the Flow (Access to Customers)	Being Heard	Having Opportunities	
GU3 Germany (12) US (6)	Product management for related functionalities. Both products handled in both locations.	German team members at HQ had more access to executives.	Germany had access to more expertise in products, but US had more access to expertise in marketing channels.	Market primarily in the US.	Decision makers in both locations, but a key VP in US tilted the balance toward the US.	Limited opportunities for growth in both locations.	Contested

Table 1: Relative Sources of Power and Power Dynamics by Team

market for software and the industry analysts on whom they depended, both of which were primarily in the US. In addition, the VP for this group was located in the US and the Germany-based team members worried about being invisible and not having their voices heard. The power contests on this team were fairly pronounced and showed no signs of diminishing during the course of our study.

In IU1 and IU2, neither the US, nor the India-based team members were at headquarters, so neither had access to executives or relatively larger numbers of experts. Further, although there were more team members in India, numbers were fairly balanced across sites. However, the 2 India-US teams' primary customer bases were in the US. For IU1 and IU2, the products were primarily aimed at the US market and customers were located nearby so the US-based team members interacted regularly with customers. This meant that the India team members were heavily dependent on those in the US to understand and convey customer needs and to ask questions of customers when problems arose. Although the team sizes were relatively similar at each location, the India-based team members complained frequently about lack of access to customers and, as a result, dependence on the US team members to get the information they needed and that was so crucial to do their jobs well. In addition, in IU2, in particular, the Indians were seen to have "very poor" functional expertise compared to those at the US location and their access to expertise was scarce. The US location made 100% of the decisions about how to allocate work. Balancing the scales, team members recognized that growth opportunities were in India. In both of these teams, there were power contests with the US-based team members fearful about losing their jobs to India and the India-based team members frustrated about lack of access to customers and lack of opportunities for more advanced work. In IU2, one junior developer described it as having to resist the "master-slave relationship."

In all of these teams, sources of power were split with some sources held at one location and others held by the other location. Team members at both locations worried about losing ground. They engaged in tactics (or were seen as doing so) to reclaim the power that was slipping away, thus setting up an ongoing power struggle, one that persisted for the duration of our study.

Power Shifting

Two of the 3 teams that were split between Germany and India were in transition, where power had been held predominantly in Germany, but was shifting to India. In IG2, for example, the bulk of the work was in the process of being moved from Germany to India. The Germany-based team members on this team were not at headquarters, but at a satellite location in Germany, so they had only nominally more access to executives and other coworkers than did the Indian team members. They did, however have access to product expertise, which was a critical resource on this team. Customers were located in the US and Europe, so the Germany team members controlled most customer contact. The Indian team members, however, had the benefit of taking on more work while responsibility for this product in Germany was diminishing. On IG3, in contrast, the Germany-based team members were located at headquarters and their extensive interaction with developers and access to customers was seen as a major advantage to their work. At the start of our study, a local manager was added to the India location, but product management remained in Germany. India-based team members reported that important decisions about the design, timeframe, and test coordination were still made in Germany and that their ability to influence these decisions was limited. The number of team members was approximately equal between the sites. India, however, was acquiring more power because increases in headcount were expected in India, but not in Germany. A shift in power was happening in this team, although at a much earlier and slower pace than in IG2. In both cases, there was no power contest evident because the imbalance was seen as transitional.

Power Imbalance Accepted

In 2 teams, there was a clear power imbalance, but it was generally accepted as being unavoidable. IG1, for example, was predominantly located in India (16 vs. 8), providing India with relatively more team members, but decisions flowed from Germany because the product expertise was there. As described by one German team member, "So most of the teams working in that area... are in [headquarters city]... the decision makers are in [headquarters city]... and a lot of good interesting projects are in [headquarters city]... and when someone decides to have a manager for a small... project lead, the its most of the time in [headquarters city]." Both the Germany and the India-based team members seemed to agree that the power on this team resided in Germany and accepted this as unalterable.

Similarly, in GU2 all key sources of power were located in Germany. Most of the team members (7 vs. 2) were located in Germany, the manager was located in Germany, and there was no particular benefit to being in the US for customer access or access to relevant expertise. As a result, the US-based team members on GU2, acknowledged and, to some extent, accepted their limited power on the team, although both of the US-based team members left the team within a year of starting our study. They explained to us that they felt out of the loop and unable to influence decisions important to their jobs.

Our observations suggest that when power was way out of balance, workers didn't fight it. In the case of India, we were told that in the long-term there would be more opportunities so they were, in a sense, biding their time. In the US, however, there was more immediate dissatisfaction and workers in this situation voluntarily left the team.

Power Shared

Only 1 of the 9 teams we studied appeared to share power more or less equally between locations. Unlike the teams with contested power, power was equally distributed because both locations had access to most sources of power rather than splitting the sources of power between locations. In IU3 neither location was at headquarters, there were experts in both locations, and although the project manager was in the US, there was a strong, well-respected leader in India and the US-based project manager went to great lengths to be available to all team members, so team members at both locations felt that they had access to decision makers. Unlike most of the other teams, this was a highly visible and strategic project on which even the US team members felt they could enhance their careers, so this balanced the fact that most growth opportunities were likely located in India. The US had slightly more power in relative numbers of team members (7 vs. 4) and somewhat more access to customers but, overall, both locations had fairly equal access to all of the sources of power, compared with other teams. We also observed that the project manager on this particular team worked hard (and successfully) to convey the importance of everyone on the team to achieving the end goal, thus minimizing the sense of threat seen in other teams.

DISCUSSION

Our ethnography of 9 globally distributed teams suggests that neither a headquarters explanation nor an explanation related to the relative number of collocated team members are sufficient to characterize the complex sources of power and power dynamics in global teams. Although being at headquarters and having more collocated team members certainly mattered to the informants we interviewed, other sources of power came into play. They talked about having the information they needed to do their jobs well, being seen and heard by those who make key decisions, and feeling that opportunities for career growth were available. These were all valued resources to which everyone wanted access and which were more available at some locations than others, depending on the project.

One of the most surprising findings was that 4 of the 9 teams in our study had power contests that were sustained throughout the duration of our study. Looking at the 4 teams with contested power, it is interesting to note that all of these teams included a US location (2 India-US and 2 Germany-US). In the case of the India-US teams, the India team members were trying to claim more power, but the US team members were holding tight and unwilling to relinquish decision-making control or direct customer access. In the German-US teams, the situation was reversed with the US team members struggling to claim power and the German team members fighting to retain the power they had historically. This is consistent with research showing that those with high power attempt to maintain it (see [26]). In our study, when both sites had sources of power, felt entitled to this power, yet felt it slipping away, there were power struggles. Our results are in contrast to what Metiu [29] found in her study of a US-India team. In that team, which also suffered from deep concerns about loss of jobs, status closure attempts were successful. That is, the more powerful (higher status) group succeeded in winning the power contest and bringing the work back to the US from the Indian vendor. We found, however, that in the absence of a powerful organizational boundary (vendor-client), power contests may be less easily and quickly decided. In our study, even over a two-year period, power contests did not dissipate. If anything, they intensified, but did not approach resolution. During that time, team members were frustrated and coordination suffered.

We were also surprised that some of the most severe power contests were in teams where sources of power were more or less equally distributed across locations. Bacharach, et al. [1] report that inconsistencies, for example, when an actor has some sources of status, but not others, can create conflicting expectations and thus tensions. Although Bacharach and colleagues focused on status, we believe this is a plausible explanation for the intense power contests we observed. Team members at each location had valuable sources of power that led them to feel that they *should* have more power and influence than they did. In both the US and India based teams, they reported feeling as though their importance was not recognized by those in the distant location and they worked tirelessly to claim sources of power that would set things right. Previous research would suggest that these power struggles grounded in different sources of power by location were likely exacerbated by distance [33], lack of shared identity [21], lack of visibility and more harsh attributions [7] found on global teams.

In our analysis, power contests seemed to be dominated by concerns over opportunities for capturing work and for growth. Even in GU1 where opportunities for growth were limited in both locations, not being able to influence key executives and decision makers resulted in tensions around job security for the US team members. In the US, they worried that they were misrepresented and misunderstood among the key decision makers in Germany and that this would affect their ability to keep the work they were doing in the US. They believed (and we have evidence to support) that some of the German-based team members were agitating to relocate the work to Germany. In many cases, the resources they were ultimately fighting to keep were their jobs and their ability to advance their careers.

When there was a severe imbalance, however, there appeared to be no hope, so team members in the less powerful location were resigned, at least in the short term, to their fate. In India, they bided their time and worked hard to prove their ability to attract better projects. In the US, they left the team and sought out more balanced situations where they felt their voices could be heard and they would have more opportunities for growth.

We believe that this work adds to understanding globally distributed work, particularly professional workers whose jobs are high in ambiguity and who depend on access to critical expertise. Being globally distributed led to many team members feeling "out of the flow" and, as a result, lacking information they needed to do their jobs. In every team in our study, team members at one or both locations lamented the fact that they did not have ready access to information needed from the distant location. Although limited access to information is not a condition unique to global work, distance and the challenges of building rapport and taking advantage of informal conversations exacerbated these effects to the extent that some team members found it crippling. It was also significantly harder to be *heard* by decision makers when many miles separated them. Not being able to directly influence decision makers contributed to a feeling that it was difficult, if not impossible, to affect decisions important to one's work. Finally, concerns about opportunities for growth were exacerbated by distance. Certainly, within a location, opportunities for growth may vary. At a given time, in a given location, for example, software developers may be in great demand whereas technical writers may not. In this case, however, these were workers in the same profession competing for the same work. It was therefore a direct competition in which one location could win and the other could lose.

There are, of course, many other resources on which power and the distribution of power may rest. Language, for example, has been documented as a critical source of power in global teams. Those with more proficiency in the lingua franca (usually English) tend to be included in more strategic discussions and have more access to decision makers [37]. Although language proficiency was an issue in our study and appeared to magnify power contests, it was not described as a source of power.

Implications for Design

Our work suggests that there may be an opportunity for CSCW research on global teams to move beyond our traditional focus on collaboration support. Our analysis of the sources of power and power dynamics suggest systems supporting team collaboration are crucial, especially by providing access to experts and co-workers, but that global teams might also benefit from systems that create an environment in which collaboration can thrive. Specifically, we found that being "in the flow" was heavily affected by access to executives and "being heard" required access to decision makers. In neither case was this about access to team members. Further, perceiving opportunities for growth diluted power contests. In all three of these cases, the team dynamics were affected by sources of power exogenous to the team, so supporting better team collaboration directly is not the solution.

To date, research has focused on the design and use of technologies that improve important aspects of collaboration, such as social translucence [13], coordination [3, 16, 18], knowledge sharing [38] and conflict [20, 21]. While this research has contributed useful systems and approaches, they do little to address power imbalances. In fact, given that individuals in power are less likely to share knowledge [26, 30], even the introduction of some of these collaboration systems may not alleviate power contests because those in power may resist their use [17]. Based on these insights, we present three opportunities that have the potential to mitigate some of the challenges global teams face when trying to find the right balance of power and, ideally, avoid power contests.

First, we recommend opening a two-way channel between leaders and distant workers that would provide more access to strategic information, more opportunity to contribute to decisions, and more visibility between leaders and distant workers. Visibility, in particular, would need to be bi-directional, e.g. with workers having more visibility into the decisions being considered and leaders having more visibility into the opinions of and effect on distant workers. Such a system would facilitate the flow of information from executives to distant workers. Supporting a two-way channel would help distant workers feel like they are being heard and acknowledged. Even though the manager of the team with shared power was located in the US, he worked hard to solicit input from team members in India, which prevented the detrimental power imbalances experienced in some of the other teams. Although this manager was able to do it, making this process easier for workers and managers could significantly reduce feelings of not being "in the flow" and "being heard," which could then obviate the need to fight for power.

We also noted the critical role of access to opportunities for growth and career development. Our findings suggest that designing systems to improve the transparency of career opportunities may be beneficial to improve collaboration in globally distributed teams. In our teams, job opportunities were primarily local and there was a feeling that others had better opportunities. Unhealthy power dynamics may be diminished by providing more even access to growth opportunities across locations. There are, of course, numerous non-technical challenges to doing this. For example, relocating workers from the US to India may be expensive, infeasible (e.g. visa restrictions), and undesirable for workers. Despite this, we argue that it warrants consideration and research as a means of alleviating a major source of power loss and, as a result, internal competition on these teams. This is another example where going beyond collaboration support could promote an environment in which power imbalances are diminished.

Finally, our findings highlight the need for CSCW systems that provide leaders and supervisors with visibility into existing power dynamics and help them identify the sources of power across teams and locations. When power struggles occur, these tools can help rebalance the distribution of power in global teams by offering recommendations based on the sources of power and the resulting dynamics. For example, the system could remind distant supervisors and leaders to check in with distant workers and highlight the contributions and achievements of distant team members, perhaps with a reminder to acknowledge these achievements. This suggests an opportunity for technology to help leaders and supervisors prevent power contests from occurring and fundamentally change the power dynamics encountered in global teams.

It is important to note that the environment we studied was already well populated with collaboration support technologies such as email, video and teleconferencing tools, aversion control system, telephone, etc. Our informants used these technologies actively in their collaboration. This raises the question of whether or not and how they used existing technologies for power-related activities. Unfortunately, one limitation of our study is that we do not have extensive observational data at a micro level that would allow us to draw conclusions about their use of existing technologies to make claims to or contest power. A future study with more granular observational data could add to our understanding of this interplay and advance our knowledge regarding how power dynamics play out through modern collaboration technologies.

CONCLUSION

In this paper, we present a qualitative study of the power dynamics in 9 globally distributed software teams. Our findings suggest that the sources of power among these teams stem from access to information (being in the flow), access to decision makers (being heard), and opportunities for growth. A closer look at the power dynamics of these teams reveals that power struggles occurred in teams with a more balanced distribution of power across locations. These findings underscore the need for systems that go beyond enabling collaboration, but help to mitigate the source of power contests so that a healthier collaboration environment can emerge.

ACKNOWLEDGMENTS

This material is based on work supported by the National Science Foundation [Grants IIS-0220098 and IIS-0219754] to the first and third authors, respectively. We thank Aditya Johri, Tine Köhler, and Tsedal Neeley for their help with data collection and their insights into the cultures the authors were studying. We also appreciate the generous assistance of the informants and the organization that participated in the study and the helpful comments and recommendations of CSCW reviewing team.

REFERENCES

1. Bacharach, S.B., Bamberger, P., and Mundell, B. Status inconsistency in organizations: From social hierarchy to stress. *Journal of Organizational Behavior 14*, 1 (1993), 21–36.
2. Bendersky, C. and Hays, N.A. Status Conflict in Groups. *Organization Science 23*, 2 (2012), 323–340.
3. Boden, A., Rosswog, F., Stevens, G., and Wulf, V. Articulation Spaces: Bridging the Gap between Formal and Informal Coordination. *Proc. CSCW '14,* ACM Press (2014), 1120–1130.
4. Brass, D.J. Being in the Right Place: A Structural Analysis of Individual Influence in an Organization. *Administrative Science Quarterly 29*, (1984), 518–539.
5. Coff, R.W. When Competitive Advantage Doesn't Lead to Performance: The Resource-Based View and Stakeholder Bargaining Power. *Organization Science 10*, 2 (1999), 119–133.
6. Cramton, C.D. and Hinds, P.J. Subgroup dynamics in internationally distributed teams: Ethnocentrism or cross-national learning? *Research in Organizational Behavior 26*, (2005), 231–263.
7. Cramton, C.D., Orvis, K.L., and Wilson, J.M. Situation Invisibility and Attribution in Distributed Collaborations. *Journal of Management 33*, 4 (2007), 525–546.
8. Cummings, J.N. and Haas, M.R. So many teams, so little time: Time allocation matters in geographically dispersed teams. *Journal of Organizational Behavior 33*, 3 (2012), 316–341.
9. Dansereau, F., Jr., Graen, G., and Haga, W.J. A Vertical Dyad Linkage Approach to Leadership within Formal Organizations: A Longitudinal Investigation of the Role Making Process. *Organizational Behavior and Human Performance 13*, 1 (1975), 46–78.
10. Ehrlich, K. and Cataldo, M. All-for-One and One-for-All? A Multi-Level Analysis of Communication Networks and Individual Performance in Geographically Distributed Software Development. *Proc. CSCW '12*, ACM Press (2012), 945-954.
11. Ehrlich, K. and Cataldo, M. The Communication Patterns

of Technical Leaders: Impact on Product Development Team Performance. *Proc. CSCW '14*, ACM Press (2014), 733-744.
12. Emerson, R.M. Power-dependence Relations. *American Sociological Review 27*, 1 (1962), 31-41.
13. Erickson, T., Smith, D.N., Kellogg, W.A., Laff, M., Richards, J.T., and Bradner, E. Socially Translucent Systems: Social Proxies, Persistent Conversation, and the Design of "Babble." *Proc. CHI '99*, ACM Press (1999), 72–79.
14. Fiske, S.T. Interpersonal Stratification: Status, Power, and Subordination. In *Handbook of Social Psychology*. John Wiley & Sons, Inc. (2010), 941–982.
15. French, J.R.P., Jr. and Raven, B. *The bases of social power.* Ann Arbor, MI: University of Michigan Press, 1959.
16. Grinter, R.E., Herbsleb, J.D., and Perry, D.E. The Geography of Coordination: Dealing with Distance in R&D Work. *Proc. GROUP '99,* ACM Press (1999), 306-315.
17. Gumienny, R., Gericke, L., Wenzel, M., and Meinel, C. Supporting Creative Collaboration in Globally Distributed Companies. *Proc. CSCW '13*, ACM Press (2013), 995-1006
18. Herbsleb, J.D., Mockus, A., Finholt, T.A., and Grinter, R.E. Distance, Dependencies, and Delay in a Global Collaboration. *Proc. CSCW '00*, ACM Press (2000), 319–328.
19. Hinds, P. and McGrath, C. Structures that Work: Social Structure, Work Structure and Coordination Ease in Geographically Distributed Teams. *Proc. CSCW '06*, ACM Press (2006), 343–352.
20. Hinds, P.J. and Bailey, D.E. Out of Sight, Out of Sync: Understanding Conflict in Distributed Teams. *Organization Science 14*, 6 (2003), 615–632.
21. Hinds, P.J. and Mortensen, M. Understanding Conflict in Geographically Distributed Teams: The Moderating Effects of Shared Identity, Shared Context, and Spontaneous Communication. *Organization Science 16*, 3 (2005), 290–307.
22. Ibarra, H. and Andrews, S.B. Power, Social Influence, and Sense Making: Effects of Network Centrality and Proximity on Employee Perceptions. *Administrative Science Quarterly 38*, 2 (1993), 277-303.
23. Jarvenpaa, S.L. and Leidner, D.E. Communication and Trust in Global Virtual Teams. *Organization Science 10*, 6 (1999), 791–815.
24. Keltner, D., Gruenfeld, D.H., and Anderson, C. Power, approach, and inhibition. *Psychological Review 110*, 2 (2003), 265–284.
25. Levina, N. and Vaast, E. Innovating or doing as Told? Status Differences and Overlapping Boundaries in Offshore Collaboration. *MIS Quarterly 32*, 2 (2008), 307–332.
26. Magee, J.C. and Galinsky, A.D. 8 Social Hierarchy: The Self-Reinforcing Nature of Power and Status. *The Academy of Management Annals 2*, 1 (2008), 351–398.
27. Massey, A.P., Hung, Y.-T.C., Montoya-Weiss, M., and Ramesh, V. When Culture and Style Aren't About Clothes: Perceptions of Task-Technology 'Fit' in Global Virtual Teams. *Proc. GROUP '01*, ACM Press (2001), 207–213.
28. Matthiesen, S., Bjørn, P., and Petersen, L.M. "Figure Out How to Code with the Hands of Others": Recognizing Cultural Blind Spots in Global Software Development. *Proc. CSCW '14*, ACM Press (2014), 1107–1119.
29. Metiu, A. Owning the Code: Status Closure in Distributed Groups. *Organization Science 17*, 4 (2006), 418–435.
30. Mudambi, R. and Navarra, P. Is knowledge power? Knowledge flows, subsidiary power and rent-seeking within MNCs. *Journal of International Business Studies 35*, (2004), 385–406.
31. Mudambi, R., Pedersen, T., and Andersson, U. How subsidiaries gain power in multinational corporations. *Journal of World Business 49*, (2014), 101–113.
32. O'Leary, M.B. and Mortensen, M. Go (Con)figure: Subgroups, Imbalance, and Isolates in Geographically Dispersed Teams. *Organization Science 21*, 1 (2010), 115–131.
33. Olson, G. and Olson, J. Distance Matters. *Human–Computer Interaction 15*, 2 (2000), 139–178.
34. Pfeffer, J. and Salancik, G.R. *The external control of organizations: A resource dependence approach.* New York: Harper & Row, 1978.
35. Spradley, J.P. *The ethnographic interview.* New York: Holt, Rinehart and Winston, 1979.
36. Tang, J.C., Zhao, C., Cao, X., and Inkpen, K. Your Time Zone or Mine? A Study of Globally Time Zone-Shifted Collaboration. *Proc. CSCW '11*, ACM Press (2011), 235–244.
37. Vaara, E., Tienari, J., Piekkari, R. & Säntti, R. Language and the Circuits of Power in a Merging Multinational Corporation. *Journal of Management Studies*, 42, 3 (2005), 595–623.
38. Valentine, M., Staats, B., and Edmondson, A. The Rich Get Richer: Enabling Conditions for Knowledge Use in Organizational Work Teams. *Harvard Business School Technology & Operations Mgt. Unit Working Paper*, No. 13-001, (2012), 1–37.
39. Van de Ven, A.H., Delbecq, A.L., and Koenig, R., Jr. Determinants of Coordination Modes within Organizations. *American Sociological Review 41*, 2 (1976), 322–338.
40. Varella, P., Javidan, M., and Waldman, D.A. A Model of Instrumental Networks: The Roles of Socialized Charismatic Leadership and Group Behavior. *Organization Science 23*, 2 (2012), 582–595.
41. Wageman, R., Fisher, C.M., and Hackman, J.R. Leading Teams When the Time is Right: Finding the Best Moments to Act. *Organizational Dynamics 38*, 3 (2009), 192–203.

Why Replacing Legacy Systems is So Hard in Global Software Development: An Information Infrastructure Perspective

Stina Matthiesen
IT University of Copenhagen
Rued Langgaardsvej 7,
2300 Copenhagen,
Denmark
matthiesen@itu.dk

Pernille Bjørn
IT University of Copenhagen,
Rued Langgaardsvej 7, 2300 Copenhagen, Denmark
UCIrvine & Intel Center for Social Computing (ISTC)
Bren Hall, 6th Floor, Irvine, California, USA
pbra@itu.dk

ABSTRACT
We report on an ethnographic study of an outsourcing global software development (GSD) setup between a Danish IT company and an Indian IT vendor developing a system to replace a legacy system for social services administration in Denmark. Physical distance and GSD collaboration issues tend to be obvious explanations for why GSD tasks fail to reach completion; however, we account for the difficulties within the technical nature of the software system task. We use the framework of information infrastructure to show how replacing a legacy system in governmental information infrastructures includes the work of tracing back to knowledge concerning law, technical specifications, as well as how information infrastructures have dynamically evolved over time. Not easily carried out in a GSD setup is the work around technical tasks that requires careful examination of mundane technical aspects, standards, and bureaucratic forms, as well as the excavation work that keeps the information infrastructure afloat.

Author Keywords
Global software development (GSD); outsourcing; ethnographic study; information infrastructure; legacy systems; interface integration; system interfaces; excavation work

ACM Classification Keywords
K.4.3 [Organizational Impacts]: Computer-supported collaborative work; H.5.3 [Group and Organization Interfaces]: Computer-supported cooperative work

INTRODUCTION
Today, working remotely is the norm for how software development is accomplished [25]. In this paper, we study a particular type of software development, namely global software development (GSD), which refers to the development of large-scale software systems organized in globally distributed organizations with IT developers located across different time zones and geographical locations and using IT-enabled collaboration tools [27]. Expanding IT development activities to remote collaborators unquestionably poses additional challenges to collaboration – challenges that are also directly relevant to computer-supported collaborative work (CSCW) research [5]. Previous research has therefore investigated articulation work [9, 35], coordination [8, 13], routine [21], delay [26], knowledge [7], and awareness [16]. Additionally, cross-cultural issues [28, 32], vendor expertise and location [1], and the nature of the collaborative partnership that needs to be established [43] are all considerations to be discussed. Thus, we see research communities and conferences creating a growing a body of literature on GSD [2].

CSCW '15, March 14 - 18 2015, Vancouver, BC, Canada.

ACM 978-1-4503-2922-4/15/03...$15.00
http://dx.doi.org/10.1145/2675133.2675232

Despite the increasing interest in and various studies of GSD in CSCW, there seems to be a tendency to predominantly report on difficulties related to collaborative work, *without* considering the nature and characteristics of software systems involved in the work task. This paper seeks to unfold the nature and characteristics of the software task, determining how it provides certain conditions for the collaborative work in GSD setups.

The software task we investigated is a specific type of task: the replacement of a legacy system. The development of software systems does not emerge from scratch; rather, new systems must be built to replace older systems containing obsolete technologies, also referred to as legacy systems. Legacy systems are systems performing critical business functions essential or useful to an organization. Legacy systems tend to have long lifespans, as they often are too expensive or critical to replace [44]. In this paper, our interest is to focus on the actual work task of replacing a legacy system in order to understand its nature and complexity. We aim to determine why such tasks place constraining and complex challenges on GSD work practices, increasing the risk of failure in collaboration. The work task in GSD is a collaborative task by definition [42] since multiple individuals are required to participate and are thus dependent on each other. Each individual task changes the state of the common field of work, meaning collaborators must act and react accordingly [42].

We report on findings from an ethnographic study on GSD practices conducted between June 2013 and December 2013. The study involves a Danish IT company (MData) engaged in collaboration with an Indian IT vendor (ITech) that won a public tender competition from the Danish government to develop a new system to replace a legacy system that was a core component of the Danish governmental IT infrastructure. In the case of MData and ITech, MData primarily chose to outsource the development of the technical interfaces where no direct users were involved, and it was therefore assumed to be a straightforward task. However, as it turned out, the task was anything but straightforward, and they failed to have it outsourced. In the end, MData had to leave the interface tasks to the Danish developers, who then redid the system development completely. This collaboration failure had less to do with communication, coordination, or cultural complexities – rather, it had to do with the complexity of the task. What made it so difficult to develop the technical interface in the GSD setup? What were the characteristics of the software task replacing technical legacy systems that increased the complexity in solving the task in an outsourcing collaborative setup?

This paper has a three-fold contribution. First, we offer a detailed empirical account of the characteristics of the work task involved in replacing legacy systems that are part of the core IT governmental infrastructure. Second, we point to how replacing legacy systems within governmental setups is *not simply* a technical and pre-defined task, but instead requires a significant amount of work in tracing to the source of information and knowledge concerning both legal and technical specifications, as well as in understanding how the information infrastructure has dynamically evolved over time. Finally, we demonstrate how the framework of information infrastructure can help illuminate the intertwined and complex work involved in replacing legacy systems within governmental IT systems supporting interconnected social services within modern digital societies.

The rest of the paper is outlined as follows: First, we present related work, followed by a description of the research method in presenting the empirical case that accounts for our research approach and data analysis method. Second, as we approach an answer to our research question, we then present the empirical results, highlighting the complex nature of the particular development work we are examining. Third, we zoom out from our findings and discuss how the empirical examples together depict the complexities of GSD when developing an IT system to replace a legacy system, specifically within the governmental IT systems of Denmark. Finally, the paper concludes.

RELATED WORK: LEGACY SYSTEMS & INFORMATION INFRASTRUCTURES

Legacy Systems

Legacy systems are informally known as "large software systems that we don't know how to cope with but that are vital to our organization" [3, p.19]. Legacy systems are socio-technical systems situated within an organization that include people, software, and hardware. These systems have often been around for a long time and are built on now obsolete forms of technology, thus requiring constant maintenance. Legacy systems perform critical business functions that are essential or useful to an organization, which means they often have long lifespans as they are too expensive or critical to replace [44]. Software evolves over time, and in the majority of legacy systems the original structure has disappeared and up-to-date documentation is lacking or non-existent; thus, the most reliable information about the system is the actual source code. In these instances, legacy systems represent years of accumulated experience and knowledge about the organization, and may be the only places were business rules exist [3]. Research on legacy systems is mostly technical in nature, proposing different strategies for how to handle legacy systems in terms of reverse engineering or refactoring [33]. However, the most recent research shows that the challenges of legacy systems are not only technical, but also business-related and organizational [30].

When developing large software systems, there are great challenges in handling and managing dependencies among systems/modules and the developers' work. One of the most influential principles in software engineering is Parnas' idea of modular decomposition and *information hiding* [38]. This involves breaking problems into smaller pieces, allowing people to work on a software module in a more isolated fashion with decreased need for communication and coordination. As an example, this is instatiated through interfaces, which are means of organizing a program as a set of modules that can communicate with one another, with clear specifications of procedures and accessible variables [14, p.179]. Modules are then able to call for and use another module's functions while the actual implementation remains hidden [22]. Interfaces are sometimes called Application Programming Interfaces (APIs), which are pre-defined source code materials with clear documentation of existing programs or sub-systems. These offer a range of services that can be accessed by calling interface procedures in specific ways [44, p.135].

The advantages of Parnas' principle are commonly agreed upon among practitioners and researchers. This principle states that, in facilitating independent IT development work, it is useful to conduct IT development in parallel to separate modules by reducing technical interdependencies among modules, thus creating loose coupling between the tasks. But this principle has been found to be extremely difficult to follow by several CSCW and software engineering scholars. For example, Cataldo and Herbsleb stress "the importance of understanding the dynamic nature of software development" [11, p.8] and propose that the *"right"* set of technical dependencies needs to be identified to determine the relevant work dependencies and to coordinate accordingly. This proposition is based on a conceptual framework of sociotechnical congruence that examines the relationship between a software system's technical dependencies and the task structure of the development work [12]. Moreover, the assumption that interfaces or APIs reduce the need for coordination and communication among software developers has been questioned. For instance, de Souza and his colleagues noticed that working with APIs has side effects on collaborative software development among teams since labour is likewise divided [45]. Furthermore, it is argued that interfaces alone do not induce developers to have less coordination needs [15]. Instead, APIs are enacted in similar ways to contracts, drawing up the boundaries of developers' individual work. APIs also work as devices for communication in the coordination of software developers' work. Therefore, in order for APIs to benefit from their advantages, workarounds are sometimes required. Proper coordination and communication engagement is also required to ensure the alignments of the integration work among the software developers using or implementing the APIs [15].

Nevertheless, the previously mentioned implications have received far less attention than the technical advantages of Parnas' principle. In response to the issues of decomposition and division of labour, Grinter [22] points to recomposition, which refers to all the work necessary to coordinate the dependencies among components. This is the critical body of work that entails reconnecting the software component to a whole system. Through recomposition, aspects of software development work are revealed that include problems caused by waiting for external or internal vendors or development departments to deliver hardware, software, or organizational resources.

Another type of interface, called system interfaces, is a means of organizing communication across various sub-systems. It translates diverse types of inputs from the systems either into outputs that can serve as inputs in other systems or into compared data, producing new types of data for outputs. System interfaces are critical when replacing legacy systems, since new sub-systems have to fit into the existing information infrastructures through these interfaces. The classical software engineering book by Sommerville [44] clearly states that if the "new system and the existing systems must work together, the interfaces of existing systems have to be precisely specified" [44, p.135]. Moreover, it is suggested that such important specifications of system interfaces must be defined early in the process and included in the requirement documentation [44]. However, this is exactly the problem with legacy systems. No formal documentation exists and the years of sprouted source-code, fixes, and add-ons make it impossible to specify the system interfaces in advance.

We join the previously mentioned scholars in investigating the collaborative limitations provided by interfaces and APIs in software development work. But our approach differs from previous software engineering research because we move further into the nature of the concrete development task. We seek to explore how this task materializes within dependencies of a less technical, but more sociocultural, character. Therefore, in this paper we want to investigate the collaborative challenges and complexities involved in replacing legacy system interfaces that are part of a larger governmental information infrastructure.

Information Infrastructures

In unpacking the nature of the IT development task when replacing legacy systems, we turn to the information infrastructures literature, which originated from Star and Ruhleder [47]. Bowker and Star [10] define various characteristics of an infrastructure. For example, an infrastructure is embedded into other structures, technologies, and social arrangements; it transparently supports tasks, within a spatial or temporal scope; and it is shaped by and shapes conventions of practices. Moreover, an infrastructure is also modified by the embodiment of standardized tools and other infrastructures. At the same time, it grows from, inherits strengths and limitations, and wrestles with the inertia of the installed base from which it is built upon. An information infrastructure is large, layered, and complex. It also plays different purposes and means different things to different groups, depending on locations. Finally, it only becomes visible when it is breaking down [46]. Thus, changing infrastructures takes time, requiring negotiations and adjustments with other aspects of the involved systems. Information systems are part of what makes the information infrastructure, and are constructed on the basis of pre-existing work, systems, and practices. The information systems have dynamically evolved over time and are thus part of what shapes the information infrastructure. In this way, pre-exisiting information systems place conditions on the degree of freedom that can be exercised by bringing in new IT systems and practices [37].

In CSCW, information infrastructures literature is mostly known within the area of scientific research exploring distributed collaborative scientific research in terms of cyberinfrastructure (in the United States), e-Science (in the European Union) or eInfrastructure [see e.g. 18, 24, 41]. This type of research seeks to identify what is referred to as scientific information infrastructures, which make up "a specific class of infrastructure that brings together people, information, and technologies to support research" [4, p.245]. Research on scientific information infrastructures investigates how the development of scientific infrastructures seeks to support and benefit from the sharing of resources, knowledge, and data in order to enable new forms of investigations and the emergence of novel science [41].

Information infrastructure research on scientific work has made important contributions to the CSCW community over the last few years [49]. Scholars have focused on various aspects of infrastructural scientific work, such as the design of an infrastructure with long-term resources and where goals of embodying reuse and stability are pursued [40], the role of embeddedness in infrastructure development [4], and the issues of scaling an infrastructure for potential new users [49], to mention a few. While our focus in this paper has little to do with leveraging large-scale distributed practice in the sciences or the challenges of how collaboration is constrained or enabled through the nature of an infrastructure, our use of the information infrastructure approach shares important characteristics. Namely, that information infrastructure is fundamentally a relational concept that only reveals itself through practice, when the ways in which the infrastructure serves certain practices while constraining others become apparent [46]. When investigating larger scale technical systems being developed, it is difficult to point exactly to what the infrastructure consists of; however, it holds that certain dimensions [10, 47] – such as embeddedness, transparency, and embodiment of standards – become visible and fixed in modular increments upon breakdown [46]. Thus, by taking an information infrastructure perspective, as has been used within the studies of scientific work, when exploring the difficulties in replacing a legacy system in the GSD setup, we explore the legacy system as the inertia of the installed base, which is part of structuring the large information infrastructure of the Danish government.

Information infrastructures have been developed as part of a theoretical lens to explore the basic nature and complexities of larger IT systems within healthcare, particularly in Scandinavian countries [6]. Based on the work of Star and others, this set of information infrastructures research seeks to understand the complex IT landscapes that make up healthcare systems in general and, more specifically, hospital systems [19, 23]. The interest is to understand how and why it is so difficult to design and implement large-scale systems supporting governmental healthcare policies that enable the exchange of information across institutions within Scandinavian countries [36]. This has led to discussions between standardization and flexibility [24]. The general lesson from this literature is that IT systems within hospitals are the collective result of patchwork integration of multiple sub-systems [20], each the result of modular incremental changes without any one in particular being "in charge" of the whole.

Interestingly, there are many similarities between governmental hospital systems and social services systems, the latter being the interest in this paper. Thus, in this paper, we apply the theoretical lens of information infrastructures as it has been used in CSCW, as well as in healthcare system research, to study the complexities in replacing legacy technical interface systems in a GSD setup.

METHOD

In order to investigate the complexities of GSD work and the nature of the software development task from a sociocultural angle, we chose to follow a GSD project that was assumed to be both technically complex and highly entangled in sociocultural dependencies. Through an intensive workplace study [34], we investigated the challenges in GSD work and work practices in a particular GSD setup between Denmark and India. Over the course of 2013, we collected ethnographic data [39] at multiple field sites.

The Empirical Case

The field sites included a Danish IT company, here called *MData*, and their global IT supplier in India, here called *ITech*. MData is a large IT and software company with more than 3,200 employees and several branches around Denmark. For more than 40 years, MData has been developing software systems that support the Danish public sector in handling welfare benefits and various administrative systems. MData develops IT solutions for the government and private markets, and one of their core competencies is SAP programming – a standard Enterprise Resource Planning (ERP) system used for managing a business.

From both the Indian and Danish sites, we followed a GSD IT project developing an illness benefit payment system to support Danish municipalities in the administration of public welfare benefits for their citizens. We identify the project as the *SickPay project* developing the *SickPay system*. This new system has to conform to and partly replace some functionality in the current legacy system, a 30-year-old system called *WBenefit*, used by the caseworkers employed in Danish municipalities to administer various citizen welfare benefits, including unemployment benefits, sickness cash payments, and maternity pay. The WBenefit legacy system interlinks with various sub-systems through a range of system interface connections in order to enable communication across the range of Danish government IT systems. The work of replacing some of the functionality from the WBenefit system to the SickPay system therefore entails the implementation of similar system interface connections. Moving forward in this paper, we use *integration* as an emic term for the work of bridging the new development with the legacy code.

MData works on several types of IT projects, including those based on government contracts offered to both the government and the private sector, and MData's own projects developed to extend, change, or maintain current IT solutions or, alternatively, to develop new off-the-shelf products. The WBenefit system is also maintained by a group of MData people – the WBenefit team consisting of eight employees with technical, maintenance, and business-oriented job roles. The WBenefit team knows a lot within the domains of handling welfare benefits, including unemployment benefits, sickness benefits, and maternity allowances in the WBenefit system and other connected IT systems. Similar to the SickPay project, MData is also working on a *MaternityPay* project to develop a *MaternityPay* system to support allowances for parental leave. Since 2006, MData has been engaged in GSD offshore projects with the Indian IT services company ITech to offer customers a reduced time to market and ensure extra resources and growth within the SAP development area. Today, MData employs more than 200 people within five different global suppliers located in Poland and India, with ITech being the largest.

Nearly 60 employees are working on the SickPay project from different sites. This includes three solution teams at MData in Denmark and one partially dispersed team – referred to as the *offshore team* – that consists of six ITech employees in India, five MData employees in Denmark, and one ITech employee and one external application consultant located onsite at MData in Denmark. The project is an agile software development project that progresses in time-limited iterations of five weeks each, or sprints, during which an outline of development tasks is first planned and estimated, then implemented, and finally reviewed/evaluated. Each of the four solution teams has a scrum master and a tester, as well as several IT developers, application consultants, and business specialists who understand the legislation. Business analysts build bridges between the legislation and the system through their knowledge of how the solution could best be implemented within the utilized technology. In addition, the project has a steering group, an end-to-end project manager, a Quality Assurance (QA) test team, a Product Owner & Architecture (POA) team, and a shared service team, all of which are responsible for completing the trajectory between the development and testing phases. The development tasks – the Product Backlog Items (PBI) in the project are initially assigned to the solution teams by the POA team.

The offshore team, consisting of employees from both India and Denmark, "meet" and talk at least once a day at their online daily scrum meetings (booked for 30 minutes each), using shared screens and audio conferencing systems run from the team members' own desktop computers. Across the two sites, business analysts and testers are located in Denmark, while the core team of IT developers are located in India. The collaboration and work on a task would typically flow as described in the following example. The whole offshore team is assigned a number of tasks (PBIs) at the beginning of a sprint and these are kept in a shared document on SharePoint. When assigned a PBI, the business analysts start going through the PBI to acquire knowledge and information in order to create business refinement documents that further detail the development task. These documents are to be handed over to the IT developers. When the refinement documents – which could include drawings of business processes and interface descriptions – are ready, the business analyst schedules an online audio conference meeting with the relevant IT developers and testers, and then hands over as much as s/he knows about the given PBI. The initial meetings can be quite lengthy (lasting up to several hours), depending on the complexity of the task. Following this meeting, the IT developers begin the development and the testers start writing the test cases. At the daily scrum meetings, each team member gives updates on his or her progress and status on current work, which sometimes triggers new meeting sessions to be scheduled, if a given PBI needs further clarifications. At the daily scrum meetings, the scrum master will follow up on how work is flowing and continually assign new PBIs to the team members. At the end of a sprint, work is reviewed and retrospectively PBIs that have not been finalized may be taken into account when the next sprint is planned before launch.

Data Collection and Sources

Field Site / Gathering Technique	DK	IN	Online
Interviews (no./hours)	10/8.8	7 /5	4/2.6
Observation (no./hours)	29/35.6	17/9.1	26/14.3
Field diary entry (no.)	39	9	-
Time spent in field (hours)	137	66	-

Table 1: Data sources of the ethnographic fieldwork conducted in Denmark (DK) and India (IN). Observations and interviews conducted online are also represented in the table.

The data were collected applying ethnography observations in both Denmark and India. Observations entailed shadowing the workers in their daily work and listening in on calls and online meetings, interviews, or document analyses. Various data gathering techniques were used to allow for triangulation of results, including: semi-structured interviews of both a formal and informal nature, observations of various work activities, and retrievals of documentary evidence. The interviews were conducted in face-to-face meetings or in audio meetings through the company's communication platform, Lync. The interview sessions, ranging from 20 minutes to one hour, were all recorded and verbatim transcripts were produced. Notes were taken during the shadowing of team members and non-participant observation of daily scrum meetings, knowledge transfer meetings, and informal conversations in the open-plan office in Denmark. Documentary evidence complemented the primary data and consisted of various company artefacts, such as sourcing governance framework descriptions, strategy documents, newsletters, business case descriptions, sprint backlogs (a detailed list of the tasks that the offshore team must complete in a sprint), and internal email correspondences. In total, we spent around 200 hours in the field and our data sources collected in Denmark and India cover 21 interviews, 59 hours of observations, and a field diary (cf. Table 1). Some interviews were held online, and several hours of observation entailed online meetings, but these were observed from one of the field sites.

Data Analysis

The data analysis started while data were still being collected. In trying to understand the complex whole and the challenges of the work of bridging the new development with the legacy code within GSD practices, our method of analysis was based on an ongoing iterative process of moving between maintaining a close focus on particular situations in the project and keeping a broad perspective of the whole that these situations create [31]. Our aim was to understand – from a close range and a broader perspective – the processes and themes within multiple situations and events in order to illuminate particular challenges within software development in a global setting that involves a legacy system for Danish governmental IT systems. The daily field diary maintained throughout reported on events of the day, as well as questions, thoughts, and reflections on our direction for and inquiry of the research. Thoughts and questions that were noted were sometimes later retrieved when talking with people for verification, or further clarification and elaboration.

We applied approaches from Star [46] for interpretation of our case – understanding the systems and structures involved – to explore information infrastructures that are otherwise difficult to identify. In order to understand the complexities of the SickPay system, we therefore had to investigate the infrastructures in which the the technical system was embedded: in this case, other IT systems, rules, regulations, policies, and sociocultural practices within the Danish welfare system. Thus, the people and systems emergent in our empirical fieldwork data were integral to the information infrastructures that organize and are organized by work practice [10]. In particular, we explored how the existing and inherently embedded rules, regulations, policies, and sociocultural practices affected the GSD work in our case study project.

We read through all the data from observational notes, documentary evidence, and interview transcripts to identify issues and topics that related to the challenges of integrating legacy systems within the Danish welfare system, particularly with global partners involved. In our further work with the data, we compiled several write-ups about the project. By sharing initial findings through informal chats and meetings with those involved in the project, we received helpful comments and clarifications. Working with the write-ups has given us a great opportunity to get an overview of the data, which is central for our analysis [48]. The continuous communication with and reactions of the practitioners have not only served as a form of validation of our interpretations [31], but also helped to drive the themes in our analysis. The insights from the empirical study form a basis from which further investigations can consider the implications of developing a software system within a GSD setting that is to partly replace and conform to other complex IT systems and legacy systems. With our findings, we intend to inform practitioners, as well as research through insights and knowledge that can deepen understanding of the complexities of developing – with legacy systems in complex organizational and infrastructural settings – particularly when both personnel teams and information are distributed across continents. In the next section, we will discuss the details of the case study from which our findings emerged.

RESULTS

In order to answer our research question and understand why the development of technical interfaces within the GSD setup failed to succeed, we here present various examples from our empirical data.

Danish Social Security Benefits

Certain fundamental parts of Danish society are the social security system and its associated benefits that allow Danish citizens to receive cash benefits when sick, unemployed, unfit for work, retired, or on maternity/paternity leave. In Denmark, the labour unions traditionally play important roles in negotiating employer benefits, work environments, policies, and regulations. Moreover, members of labour unions are often entitled to receive unemployment benefits if they are dismissed from their job. In addition, if you live in Denmark, pay taxes on your income, and meet a minimum requirement for employment, you are entitled to cash benefits if you are unable to work due to illness or have been injured. This means that an employee can stay at home during sick leave and receive sickness cash benefits as an economic compensation paid by Danish municipalities. When a citizen – either an applicant or potential beneficiary – applies for sickness benefits, municipal administrators handle the responsibilities of deciding an applicant's eligibility for receiving sickness cash benefits and of calculating and disbursing benefits. The current IT system solution for handling the various types of Danish social benefits – from unemployment benefits to sickness cash benefits – connects to several different systems and solutions within the Danish IT systems supporting the social services and welfare systems.

When a caseworker in a Danish municipality is processing and calculating an applicant's case, multiple systems are invoked and used. For example, there are various categories that a beneficiary will be assessed on, such as whether the beneficiary is unemployed and sick, self-employed and sick, or sick with incoming wages. A beneficiary could, for example, be unemployed and the local service providers could seek to get the beneficiary back into the labour market through employment. This particular task is not handled by the municipalities, but is contracted out to and handled by special job centres distributed all over Denmark.

Thus, when an unemployed beneficiary who is associated to a job centre and receives unemployment benefits becomes sick, the job centres and the municipalities must communicate internally. These entities must share the information that that beneficiary is currently not available to enter the job market, nor entitled to receive unemployment benefits but instead may receive sickness cash benefits.

A New System for the Sickness Cash Benefit

A public tender has been announced for the SickPay system calling for bids on solutions to create a better overview of the benefit case and to make processes more efficient and automated. The goal is to consolidate the multiple information systems for handling the sickness cash benefit into one solution. The public tender provider is *Kombit*, an organization owned by the interest group and a member authority of the Danish municipalities. On behalf of local government authorities, Kombit orders and procures IT solutions and handles the tender competition processes.

The level of multiple information infrastructures that the new system must integrate with is exhaustive. On the extensive loads of data and documents, Kombit writes:

> *the [SickPay] system must integrate with various different solutions and data registers. One of the important integrations is NemRefusion [a common platform for reporting of sickness benefits and maternity leave allowance for companies] where virtually all new cases are born. [...] In addition to the NemRefusion integration, there will be integrations of the different job centre solutions, the self-service module at borger.dk [a Danish common public internet portal], basic data records [social security number](CPR), [the Central Business Register] (CVR), [...], the municipalities' payment and accounting etc.* (Translated from Danish)

As stated in the above function description, the systems supporting the Danish social services involve various systems. The systems are interconnected in various ways and through different connections, and all follow some Danish standards. Moreover, all are systems that must change dynamically in relation to changes in the Danish welfare system, politics, and legislation. In other words, this is an information infrastructure highly integrated within and influenced by Danish society and the technological advancement of, for example, citizens' self-service portals and mandatory social security numbers. These information infrastructures constantly change: information infrastructures change over time; laws are regulated, changed, or repealed; and IT systems are upgraded or replaced with new systems. Therefore, when developing new systems to take part in the information infrastructures of the Danish public sector, replacing or integrating into legacy information systems like WBenefit, stable information infrastructures will have to temporarily be disconnected and thus appear unstable until the new information infrastructures are well reconnected.

GSD Tasks: Interface Integration

In order to further understand the complexities encountered in a GSD setup when integrating into legacy systems for the Danish social services system, we focus on the particular types of tasks addressed by the offshore team. Based on the argument that the tasks are more technically suitable to the competences in the team, the types of tasks that the offshore team receives from the POA team are interface integration tasks, as these are tasks less involved with understanding the Danish welfare system and legislation:

> *[The offshore team] has primarily received integration tasks, because these are technical tasks that are easy or not easy but may be better suited to the skills that lie [in the offshore team], in contrast to the Danish legislation, which can be a bit challenging if you sit in Bangalore and do not have the [Danish] background right.* (Program manager, interview, 7/2/2013, Denmark)

Working on integrating the SickPay system into various external and internal systems through technical interfaces is therefore the main portion of the PBIs for the offshore team. According to the program manager, the technical tasks that he believed to be "*better suited*" for offshore are also the tasks that are less culturally specific. However, this statement prompted us to delve deeper into investigating *what is meant by tasks better suited for offshore.* While the interface integration tasks may not be heavily grounded in knowledge of and the ability to model the Danish welfare system laws, we saw how these tasks are nonetheless highly interdependent on other internal MData systems, as well as external third-party institutions and systems. After five months with the project, there was a realization of the lack of success with the implementation of interfaces. In regards to the type of tasks assigned to the offshore team, a senior project manager in the SickPay project had the following view on this matter:

> *They [the POA team] have given them the hardest tasks of them all, tasks with the most integration to others [institutions and systems]; where we do not have knowledge in the project, and where we need to establish a lot of appointments with WBenefit. With third party and others, you absolutely cannot be offshore while solving these tasks, so I quite simply do not understand it.* (Senior project manager, interview, 12/12/2013, Denmark)

Interestingly, according to a senior project manager, the interface integration tasks that the offshore team had been given could be among the most difficult ones in the project. However, we would argue that it should be of no surprise that there is a broad range of interfaces that the SickPay system must integrate with: The tender provider already stated this. When the senior project manager raised the issues with the assigned GSD tasks we wondered why these were not brought into focus earlier on in the project. The challenges described were that the nature of the system is deeply rooted in the Danish welfare system and thus highly interconnected to various other systems, standards, bureaucratic forms, organizations, and people.

Law-Based Systems and Legacy Systems

To find answers for why the technical interface integration tasks in the SickPay project are described by the senior project manager as the most difficult tasks to solve in a GSD setup, we closely observed some of the systems that the SickPay system must interface with. The WBenefit system that Kombit wants to phase out and eventually replace is also developed and maintained by MData and is one of several systems in MData's law-based social services product portfolio. These law-based systems are part of a greater infrastructure of related systems that together or individually serve different purposes in the Danish welfare systems; however, all conform to Danish society, law, and regulation. The law-based information systems in MData are closely connected to other social services information infrastructures that exist both internally in MData (e.g., MData facilitation systems for handling social services such as *cases*, *pension,* and *income*) and in external systems or institutions (e.g., *The National Labour Market Authority*, *Digital Post, job centres, Statistics Denmark*, *Danish Tax Authorisation*, and *Danish Agency for Governmental Management*). This means that data flows through various systems. For example, the SickPay system must collect data from a range of institutions and their systems in the Danish public sector and welfare system. Thus, the system is required to connect and interact with various interfaces.

The WBenefit team has experience with various peculiarities and inefficiencies within the systems that have become commonplace. To ensure the SickPay project did not overlook certain instances of exceptional cases that could cause grave errors for the beneficiary or the municipality, several clarification meetings were held between, for instance, MData business analysts from the SickPay offshore team and the WBenefit team. To progress on a GSD task, the business analyst located at MData in Denmark must collect information from different systems, people, and organizations in order to produce various business refinement documents. These are then handed over to offshore IT developers in India, enabling them to proceed with the development of the task.

When observing several clarification meetings between the MData business analysts from the SickPay offshore team and members of the WBenefit team, the challenges of developing a system to replace some functionality in a legacy system like WBenefit became evident. For example, in relation to assigning a descriptive case number, explaining how a beneficiary's pay period is calculated in the event of their taking a vacation proved to be more complex than just exchanging technically detailed information. Apparently, WBenefit and the SickPay system had two distinct ways of solving the representation of a beneficiary's case number. In the example provided, a senior developer from the WBenefit team explained how the WBenefit team modelled and handled a sickness beneficiary's case number in regards to the law:

> *One thing is the world and another thing is the model of the world, in this case the sickness benefit. [...] Say I am sick and I have received sickness benefit, now I go on vacation, and I will then receive benefits from another instance, then I am no longer in the sickness benefit arrangement. [...] This means the case number no longer exists; however, what happens in the modelled world to make it programmable is that the case number is still in the system, and when the person returns to be receiving sickness benefits, then there exists some associations to the "old" case number.* (Observation notes, 7/3/13, Denmark)

This specific example demonstrates how the legislation of the Danish welfare system is entangled with the technical implementation and representation of case numbers in the system infrastructure. The rule is: if you are sick and go on vacation, you are basically not allowed to receive sickness benefits. However, the choice of whether or not to keep associations to old case numbers in the system is an implementation decision made by the WBenefit team. As the business analysts from SickPay realize that they have modelled the case numbers differently, it becomes clear that there is a legacy issue in solving the interplay between the system functionality (legislation) and the system implementation in WBenefit. The challenge is to decide how to handle case numbers when communicating with WBenefit:

> *While WBenefit changed the world in the model, to ease the work, the business analysts [from the SickPay system] and the WBenefit team are now discussing whether this makes any sense, and how they should approach the handling of case numbers. In the end they all agree that the SickPay team should discuss it with the people in the MaternityPay project.* (Observation notes, 7/3/13, Denmark)

While the original idea with this clarification meeting was to seek answers from the WBenefit team, additional questions and issues emerged as entanglements in the information infrastructure of the SickPay system became evident. The differing uses of case numbers also added an additional wrinkle to the MaternityPay project, and created an issue the business analysts had to follow up on for supplementary clarification. This situation demonstrated the chain of dependencies is not only technical in nature, but also entails issues of a more sociocultural character, primarily that the business analysts from the SickPay team would have to perform additional work of a more detective nature, which was unforeseen and invisible to anyone before the meeting. Thus, the business analyst had to dig deeper inside the MData project portfolio and inquire with members working on yet another project to track down the relevant people from MaternityPay in order to finish MData's part of the work. Meanwhile, the offshore Indian developers, working on building and integrating the SickPay system's interfaces to other systems inside and outside MData, are highly dependent on the work of their fellow team members in Denmark. The MData business analysts in the SickPay offshore team depend on a range of different people and information infrastructures outside of the SickPay project. For the tasks being outsourced, the meeting between WBenefit and the business analysts demonstrated the difficulties or even impossibilities of being able to specify the integration task all at once. While collecting knowledge on a given task, the need for acquiring additional information from additional resources/people became pertinent and required further excavation work.

Building an AS-IS System

In investigating the challenges of developing technical interfaces for the social services system in Denmark, we demonstrated aspects of the role that the WBenefit system and the embedded information infrastructures play. However, and maybe more importantly, one of the primary obligations that the SickPay system must comply with is that the SickPay system is an "AS-IS system," which means the SickPay system should be "AS-the-WBenefit-IS" in its functionality. When, for example, the WBenefit system disburses money to beneficiaries, the WBenefit system is obligated to deliver specific reports (data extracts) to different stakeholders. These stakeholders include members of external systems, the public sector, and institutions involved in the mechanisms of handling the Danish welfare system, for example: *The National Labour Market Authority*, *Statistics Denmark*, *Danish Tax Authorisation*, *Danish Agency for Governmental Management*, etc. In other words, under an AS-IS system, MData – and now the future SickPay system – are obligated via WBenefit to deliver reports to several institutions in the Danish IT system landscape.

Observing the daily work of the one and only IT developer in the offshore team located in Denmark gave us a great understanding of how various information infrastructures were embedded in the SickPay system. The senior IT developer had previously worked on similar projects in MData, thus he was able to draw on his experiences – in particular, the MaternityPay project that is developing a maternity pay system also highly connected to the old WBenefit system. In discussions, he offered insight into the information infrastructural complexities of developing for a legacy system within the social services sector:

> *In the old days they [the public sector/institutions] got the reports from WBenefit, but in the new solution, they need something from WBenefit and from SickPay, to make the world simpler! [laughs] This was also the case in MaternityPay, only that we just made one report and then WBenefit would merge it and send it out. Now I have 98 reports and then WBenefit said, "I will not merge 98 reports, that we are not able to!"* (Observation, 7/29/13, Denmark)

The senior IT developer had previous experience implementing support for reports (data extracts). However, for the SickPay system, compared to the MaternityPay system, the number of reports that have to be created is more extensive and complex due to distinct rules and regulations for handling maternity leave versus sickness benefits. While sickness benefit is handled locally in each of the 98 municipalities in Denmark, maternity leave is handled at a centralized level:

> *[...] I have agreed with WBenefit that I should send an assembled report, so we have to merge these 98 results before we send it to WBenefit, then they only get one report, and from their side it looks the same as the one they receive from MaternityPay – they get one report they should merge. So we have more PBIs in this sprint that deal with this merge concept.* (Observation, 7/29/13, Denmark)

The implementation then must adhere to the restrictions received from WBenefit. The SickPay system must therefore conform to the WBenefit system when taking over some of WBenefit's functionality, including: gathering data from different systems connecting through a range of interfaces, processing the data, and finally handing over one assembled report to WBenefit. The example of creating reports with data extracts demonstrates how conforming to existing information infrastructures is not a trivial task. First, although there are some similarities between implementing social services benefits for maternity leave and for sickness benefits, the legislation and organizational practices of handling the two social benefits are distinct, as they are embedded in different information infrastructures (sickness and maternity), while being connected through their common connection to the same information infrastructure (Danish Government IT). The different information infrastructures impose different implementation approaches that are still interconnected. Second, the precise way that WBenefit wishes to receive data, due to existing information infrastructures, determines and impacts the software development tasks required to finalize the project. In this case, this means the merge concept. Although the technical tasks are assumed to be more suitable for GSD work compared with tasks requiring more heavy business knowledge, the task of implementing reports is not trivial.

As mentioned earlier, the SickPay project depends on both internal departments in MData and external (third party) organizations in terms of acquiring and collecting sufficient information to develop given interfaces and to integrate with other systems. Due to the many rules in the Danish welfare system, there are various complexities in addition to understanding the business logic and domain when, for example, developing the interface connections for the SickPay system. If a Danish citizen is sick and without job, there are several institutions and systems that need to be connected to the SickPay system. Thus, the SickPay project depends on other institutions, organizations, and system providers to collaborate with them. In particular, during our observations we witnessed how the need to invoke a certain interface (DFDG interface) at a central system at the National Labour Market Authority gave rise to PBIs becoming difficult to complete work on. At first, the National Labour Market Authority was not able to point the offshore team members of the SickPay project in the right direction in terms of whom they should receive information from. In an interview with an IT developer in the offshore team, the effects on the development work were expressed as follows:

> *[...] A part from WBenefit team we faced a huge delay in DFDG interface. [...] I have done full development, initially they have given us... three times I have changed, three to four times I have changed the design.* (Offshore IT developer, interview, 11/29/13, India)

As long as there were uncertainties related to how to access a given interface, these were echoed and reflected in the code design that the IT developer was working on. Yet another challenge emerged when the SickPay project finally managed to track down a third-party company that maintained the central system and had knowledge of the DFDG interface:

> *That DFDG started almost in sprint four or sprint five and went on till sprint twelve. From sprint twelve we got some feedback from them.* (Interview, 11/29/13, India)

As we see in the above quote, the tasks related to the DFDG interface were very difficult to work on – not technically, but due to the inaccessibility of acquiring the right information about the interface. Therefore, work was repeatedly postponed over the course of seven sprints, which resulted in the integration with the DFDG interface requiring an additional seven to eight months of work. The people in the third-party company were very busy and no actual agreement existed about obligations to provide these types of informational instructions. Hence, the company was not particularly interested in spending time informing others about the interface. The DFDG interface obviously has a different meaning or purpose depending on whether a person is part of the company maintaining the interface or part of the SickPay project group seeking knowledge of standards to be followed in order plug into and integrate with the DFDG interface.

Security Information Infrastructures

When investigating what it is that makes it difficult to develop technical interfaces for a social services system in a GSD setup, the role and complexity of additional information infrastructures becomes clear. Due to the nature of the systems involved and their embedded information infrastructures, the SickPay project was subject to follow various standards and security rules in MData, as well as rules of the Danish Act on Processing of Personal Data. This meant that some systems and their data could only be accessed when physically located within the European Union. Moreover, in order to access, develop and integrate, and test other system interfaces or web-services, certain security certificates could be required. In the work of integrating SickPay with another system in MData's own social services portfolio, both a test and development authorization were required. We saw that acquiring such authorization prolonged the development work on the PBIs assigned to the offshore team. This became relevant when a developer from India located onsite in Denmark was to work on an interface and process integration task together with some of the offshore colleagues in India. There were several administrative steps to be followed in order to access the different interfaces that the developing system should integrate with. We observed and followed the process of, first, the discussions of the certificate required at the daily scrum meetings for the offshore team, to the eventual ordering of the certificate, followed by a period of a couple of weeks involving people collaborating across teams.

In this case, Michael, a Danish business analyst on the offshore team located in Denmark, was to order a certificate for Parveen, an Indian IT developer temporarily working onsite in Denmark. As the acquisition process could require Danish language skills when talking to security providers or invoking an internal MData portal, Michael worked on the certificate acquisition for Parveen. It was an urgent matter for the offshore team, and even though it was not the business analyst's area of expertise, he took on the task since no one else had thus far. During the daily scrum meetings, it was reported that the first attempt to order the certificate had, unfortunately, not been done correctly. This incidental delay is one of several that occurred in the following weeks, such as key people that could provide help becoming unavailable due to vacations or illness. The type of certificate required was unfamiliar to the SickPay project and, therefore, took more time to setup. The incidents that slowed down the process connect back to the complexities of the information infrastructures involved, including: obligations to adhere to Danish law, the issuing of authorization certificates by MData, a lack of available staff with knowledge on how to work with the certificates, etc. These connected factors all affect the developers' abilities to start their work on the PBIs. Further, while the certificates were slowly acquired and installed, allowing the

IT developers to access the interface, new issues emerged and another person in the project was now being included:

> *There are some problems on some of the PBIs that others in the team are waiting on me to provide some answers on... for example, there is an interface where we use some certificates, and for some reason the certificate is not working on our system testing, but it works well on our development, and why? Well I don't know [...] the problem is that I cannot say if it will take five minutes or the rest of the day [to solve]* (Observation, 7/29/13, Denmark)

The issues with the certificate were a recurring topic during many of the daily scrum meetings throughout the five-week sprint and resulted in some pending tasks, or "leftovers," that were added on to the following sprint. A challenge to GSD work practice was the embeddedness in information infrastructure that requires locality (meaning physical presence within Denmark or the EU) to acquire a certificate and ensure the data registration laws were followed.

In the previous sections, we have demonstrated some of the challenges that exist with work in a GSD setup in regards to technical interface integration tasks. In the case of GSD, these types of tasks have been initially preferred over development tasks that require more in-depth business knowledge. But we have demonstrated how these technical tasks are inseparable from work that is more sociocultural in character. Not only can we show that system development and integration with legacy systems are socio-technical tasks, but also that the nature of such tasks and their sociocultural embeddedness – in our case, into the whole Danish social service system and information infrastructure – makes them even harder to be completed as part of GSD development. These tasks could include plugging into different systems through technical interfaces and collecting data about the given interfaces from various systems (e.g., legacy systems, internal, external from third party, etc.), or detecting and tracking down the right information, people, systems, and organizations in order to know how to interface with different systems, following security standards and other requests from relational legacy systems.

DISCUSSION

Through our empirical data we investigated what made it so difficult to develop technical interfaces in an outsourcing collaborative setup of GSD. We set out to investigate the characteristics of software development tasks in order to understand how the replacement of and integration with legacy systems increased the complexity of solving related interface tasks.

When viewing the system interface as an information infrastructure, our data clearly demonstrate the ways in which it would have been impossible to create in advance comprehensive requirement specifications for the task being outsourced. Due to the embeddedness, transparency, and incremental development [46] of the system interface, it becomes clear that no such requirement specification could be made in advance. All these factors existed prior to the development of a project relating the interface to a long list of systems and standards created over time without any pre-determined "person in charge." The very task of "specifying" is an unknown entity prior to getting the work done, since the information infrastructure only becomes visible through its breakdown in practice [20, 23]. The idea that you can send a piece or a module of the larger system to be coded elsewhere rests on the assumption that such clear-cut pieces of tasks exist, and that there exists a presumable coherence within IT governmental systems. It presumes a uniformity of the whole IT system that simply does not exist.

The information infrastructure perspective revealed certain complex aspects of legacy systems. We know from earlier work that, while information infrastructures are continuously changing, there is always a certain stable part, or *installed base* [10], that makes the core spine of the information infrastructure. In our case, we can view the legacy system as the "stable" part of the information infrastructure that makes up the "whole" Danish governmental information infrastructure. The legacy system as an information infrastructure is thus embedded into a range of other structures: all existing laws, legislations, policies, together with the complete set of diverse and interlinked IT systems supporting different practices involved in supporting the Danish flexicurity society. This means that when invoking, developing, or integrating with the legacy system the "stable" part of the system constantly needs to be taken into account. In this perspective, we propose the legacy system as the stable part of the information infrastructure, while the unstable parts are all the connecting systems, related rules and regulations, and the sociocultural practices (and at times invisible work) of finding and acquiring the information required to make work flow.

We join others in arguing that it is critical to look across "multiple levels of granularity, various facets of social life, and diverse technological actors" in order to reveal the stories of (cyber)infrastructure [41, p. 241]. For instance, this could imply that all the tweaking of other systems to function together with the legacy system has to be taken into account when replacing the legacy system. Thus, over time, multiple add-ons, new systems, changes in the policies, etc. have to be designed for and appropriated within the legacy system's capabilities. Our contribution in terms of information infrastructures in CSCW points to how legacy systems can be perceived as stable parts of information infrastructures. We argue that the practices of developing, replacing, or integrating new software within legacy systems have to carefully reckon with issues related to dealing with the inertia of the installed base [47] provided by the legacy system. Over time, subtle design and obsolete technology are not necessarily capable of explicitly articulating what those issues are.

At the beginning of the paper, we argued that our focus shares some of the same characteristics as the growing body of research on scientific infrastructures; however, our results point to how these characteristics are highlighted differently. The challenges of designing an infrastructure [40], or growing one [49], for that matter, may have little to do with dealing with the development of sub-components and interfaces that are to conform with the inertia of a 30-year-old legacy system. Thus, in our case the uniqueness of an information infrastructure within governmental IT systems differs from the scientific infrastructures in the way that scientific infrastructures are first and foremost built with the goal supporting cross disciplinary, institutional, and organizational collaboration to leverage scientific research [41]. Governmental information infrastructures were not (necessarily) built on the same premises – facilitating multidimensional collaboration and knowledge sharing. Rather, it is a product and a result of a long history of sub-systems coming to live within the context of supporting the continuously changing Danish welfare system, wherein different stakeholders have different needs and approaches toward building the infrastructure. For instance, the government wants to support different mechanisms in the welfare system based on the current government's policies while saving money on expensive software systems, processes, and labour; the software vendors building these systems are interested in offering the most competitive price to win the tender contracts and position themselves within a continuous flow of new system development jobs; and the caseworker at the municipalities would like to be able to process the case handling in a smooth and timely manner. While we do not argue that building a scientific infrastructure can entail several contradictory agendas, we believe that there is a fundamental difference between the two fields. Scientific infrastructures could be assumed to have a common end-goal in their development and construction; however, the challenges of the already existing information infrastructures in the public sector appear to require a bottom-up analytical approach when trying to understand the requirements, source code, and interlinked systems that have sprouted for many years.

Governmental systems are patchworks, in the same way as hospital systems [20], dynamically put together and evolved over time. The homogeneity and tendency toward centralization and standardization of a unifying governmental system does not exist in practice. Rather, the overall system is patched together by the multiple singular systems that have been developed over time. This means that part of working on the task requires the work of tracing back to information and finding out which information is required to solve the technical task. This work is different from refactoring or reverse engineering [33]. Tracing back to information is about asking questions; however, to ask a question you first need to know which questions to ask. The questions that emerged in our case were both related to technical specifications (such as testing edge-cases) and political specifications; however, in practice, it was not easy for the IT developer in India to determine the differences between these, or even to know if they needed to ask questions on this in the first place. Issues that appeared as technical on the surface could emerge as policy-related in practice, and vice versa. For example, how would the IT developer located in India know to ask – yet even contemplate asking – about how the SickPay interface should be related technically to system modules handling vacation registrations, without knowing that in Danish society people can take vacations during their sick leave.

Understanding governmental IT systems requires reflections on and engagement with the social structures within which they are to be embedded [17]. Often, issues arise in miscommunication caused by the difficulties in interpreting requirement specifications in GSD [29]. However, for legacy systems, the issue is even more complex. In these cases, technical issues and policy issues are closely related and embedded in the information infrastructure of governmental systems and institutions in ways that are completely invisible for people who do not work with such systems on a daily basis, or who are only knowledgeable in the business domain and know less about the technicalities.

Part of the task of replacing legacy systems involves identifying the issues and problems relevant for the development of a new system. This must be done in such a way that allows developers to trace back to information by identifying who has institutional knowledge, where those people are located, and if what they know is relevant for the task. In our case, the delay in tracing to knowledge was not about MData not being prepared in advance for the task. Even though the system interface had been developed on its own by IT developers located in Denmark, the developers would still be required to trace back to information as part of their work. The main issue is not about understanding legacy systems, but that no one has all the required knowledge to solve the problem prior to working on a project. No such coherent and uniform whole exists when we are dealing with legacy systems. It is only through *working in practice* on the task that problems and issues are identified in such a way that developers start gaining the relevant knowledge. Therefore, the accessibility and availability of technical and policy knowledge are critical when designing, developing, and implementing legacy system interfaces.

Our data demonstrate how certain kinds of detective work or excavation work are necessary to locate and acquire the right information about parts of the system when developing system interfaces that are technical and also highly embedded in social practices, third-party/external systems, welfare policies, laws, and regulations. Here it is important to note that excavation work is required because no one knows about all the tweaks made on the legacy system over time. Consequently, there is no such thing as a complete requirement specification existing prior to the project. Thus, identifying or rather excavating the requirement is part of the work of design, since it is only in the very process of designing and constructing the replaced programing code that the excavation work becomes apparent and difficulties arise. In our case, excavation work proved to be highly challenging when business analysts in one location were required to make sense of the system for IT developers located elsewhere. Since excavation work requires both technical and business knowledge, as well as the ability to identify who has the required knowledge for further excavation, one could question the distributed roles of having primarily IT developers in one place and business analysts in another. When managing legacy system replacement projects in GSD, an effort could be made to better balance the technical and business personnel in all locations of the collaborative arrangement, as well as to strengthen the closely coupled work that is required among collaborators [28]. At least in our case, we saw how the business analysts were at times not quite clear on what information was necessary to acquire – for example, on what abstraction level or technical level information was required for the IT developers to start their work.

Part of the work of developing technical system interfaces for legacy systems involves activities of knowledge creation through tracing to, localizing, negotiating, and collecting relevant knowledge. In other words, to obtain the critical information that the developers in our case were bound to participate and interact with involved the whole information infrastructure – including the social organization of work of those who are or have been part of developing the patchwork system (e.g., the WBenefit team, or the DFDG interface provider). These participants could be found within different organizations (since several IT companies in Denmark were developing parts of the patchwork system), as well as the government institutions and systems involved in administrating social services available in Danish society. The work task of developing a technical system interface evolved into a highly complex task revealing an extremely multifaceted information infrastructure without any clear access point for comprehension – a subcomponent of the information infrastructure that could not be logically deconstructed into parts to be sent offshore. Several essential pieces of the task of tracing to relations and associations across institutions, organizations, policies, and technical specifications were opaquely significant, and it was up to the developer to determine which of the connections to follow and which to ignore.

CONCLUSION

Initially, we asked what were the characteristics of the software task of replacing technical legacy systems that increase the complexity in solving the task in an outsourcing collaborative setup. Analyzing our empirical data, we found the framework of information infrastructure very useful in describing and comprehending the complex and intertwined work involved in designing, developing, and implementing governmental IT systems. The conceptual framework of information infrastructures has previously been used to investigate large-scale healthcare information systems and within research aiming toward developing large, distributed, and long-term information infrastructures to support scientific research activities. Our case demonstrates that governmental information infrastructures are not uniform, coherent, or centrally organized. Instead, these comprise a patchwork of embedded systems, which come together in practice to create the fundamental structure of Danish society. These structures cannot easily be understood outside this context.

While our contributions are directed toward the CSCW community, our findings also speak to software engineering by emphasizing the need for a broader focus of a more sociocultural character when examining the nature of software development. This is a need that entails a focus beyond examining relationships between technical dependencies of software systems and the task structure of the development work [12].

We join other software engineering scholars in challenging the idea of reduced communication and coordination due to well-defined interfaces. But we argue through our detailed empirical account that replacing legacy systems within governmental setups is *not simply* a technically pre-defined task. It is a utopic ideal to believe in neat and completely pre-defined software tasks that are easily outsourced. Instead, we argue that software tasks require much excavation work – the work of tracing back to information and knowledge concerning both law and technical specifications, as well as how the information infrastructure has dynamically evolved over time. This work is not easily carried out in a GSD setup.

ACKNOWLEDGMENTS

This study was conducted within the "Next Generation Technologies and Processes for Global Software Development," #10-092313 an interdisciplinary and inter-organizational research project that is financially supported by the National Council for Strategic Research, Ministry of Science, Innovation and Higher Education in Denmark. Please visit www.nexgsd.org for further information. We would like to thank all the anonymous volunteers from ITech and MData who generously offered their time and energy for this research. We also would like to thank Paul Dourish, Lily Nguyen, Morgan Ames, Garnet Hertz, Chris Wolf, and Katherine Lo for their contribution in discussing the argument in this paper. Moreover, we would like to thank Katie Pine and Marisa Cohn for their constructive comments after reading earlier drafts of this paper. Finally, we would like to thank the anonymous reviewers for insightful comments and suggestions.

REFERENCES

[1] Abbott, P. Y. and M. R. Jones (2012). Everywhere and nowhere: nearshore software development in the context of globalisation. *Eur J Inf Syst*. 21(5): 529-551.

[2] Avram, G., et al. (2009). Bridging, Patching and Keeping the Work Flowing: Defect Resolution in Distributed Software Development. *Computer Supported Cooperative Work (CSCW)*. 18(5-6): 477-507.

[3] Bennett, K. (1995). Legacy Systems: Coping with Success. *IEEE Softw*. 12(1): 19-23.

[4] Bietz, M., et al. (2010). Synergizing in Cyberinfrastructure Development. *Computer Supported Cooperative Work (CSCW)*. 19(3-4): 245-281.

[5] Bjorn, P., et al. (2014). Global software development in a CSCW perspective. Proceedings of the companion publication of the 17th ACM conference on Computer supported cooperative work & social computing. ACM: 301-304.

[6] Bjørn, P. and F. Kensing (2013). Special issue on information infrastructures for healthcare: The global and local relation. *International Journal of Medical Informatics*. 82(5): 281-282.

[7] Boden, A., et al. (2009). Knowledge Management in Distributed Software Development Teams - Does Culture Matter? In *Proc. Conference*, IEEE Computer Society: 18-27.

[8] Boden, A., et al. (2007). Coordination Practices in Distributed Software Development of Small Enterprises. In *Proc. ICGSE 2007*. IEEE Computer Society: 235-246.

[9] Boden, A., et al. (2014). Articulation spaces: bridging the gap between formal and informal coordination. In *Proc. CSCW 2014*. ACM: 1120-1130.

[10] Bowker, G. C. and S. L. Star (1999). Sorting Things Out: Classification and Its Consequences, MIT Press.

[11] Cataldo, M., et al. (2008). Socio-technical congruence: a framework for assessing the impact of technical and work dependencies on software development productivity. In *Proc.* of the Second ACM-IEEE international symposium on Empirical software engineering and measurement. ACM: 2-11.

[12] Cataldo, M., et al. (2006). Identification of coordination requirements: implications for the Design of collaboration and awareness tools. In *Proc. CSCW 2006*. ACM Press (2006). 353-362.

[13] Christensen, L. R. and P. Bjorn (2014). Documentscape: intertextuality, sequentiality, & autonomy at work. In. *Proc. CHI 2014*. ACM Press (2014). 2451-2460.

[14] Coulouris, et al. (2005). Distributed Systems: Concepts and Design (4th Edition) (International Computer Science), Addison-Wesley Longman Publishing Co., Inc.

[15] de Souza, C. B. and D. Redmiles (2009). On The Roles of APIs in the Coordination of Collaborative Software Development. *Computer Supported Cooperative Work (CSCW)*. 18(5-6): 445-475.

[16] de Souza, C. R. B. and D. F. Redmiles (2011). The Awareness Network, To Whom Should I Display My Actions? And, Whose Actions Should I Monitor? *Software Engineering, IEEE Transactions on*. 37(3): 325-340.

[17] Dourish, P. (2007). Seeing like an interface. In *Proc. OZCHI 2007*. ACM Press (2007). 1-8.

[18] Edwards, P. N., et al. (2009). Introduction: an agenda for infrastructure studies. *Journal of the Association for Information Systems*. 10(5): 364-374.

[19] Ellingsen, G., and Munkvold, G. (2007). Infrastructural arrangements for integrated care: Implementing an electronic nursing plan in a psychogeriatric ward. *International journal of integrated care* (7): 1-1.

[20] Ellingsen, G. and E. Monteiro (2003). A Patchwork Planet Integration and Cooperation in Hospitals. *Comput. Supported Coop. Work*. 12(1): 71-95.

[21] Esbensen, M., and Bjørn, P. (2014). Routine and standardization in Global software development. GROUP 2014. ACM.

[22] Grinter, R. E. (2003). Recomposition: Coordinating a Web of SoftwareDependencies. *Comput. Supported Coop. Work*. 12(3): 297-327.

[23] Hanseth, O. and N. Lundberg (2001). Designing Work Oriented Infrastructures. *Comput. Supported Coop. Work*. 10(3-4): 347-372.

[24] Hanseth, O., et al. (1996). Developing Information Infrastructure: The Tension Between Standardization and Flexibility. *Science Technology Human Values*. 21(4): 407-426.

[25] Herbsleb, J. D. (2007). Global Software Engineering: The Future of Socio-technical Coordination. 2007 Future of Software Engineering. IEEE Computer Society: 188-198.

[26] Herbsleb, J. D., et al. (2000). Distance, dependencies, and delay in a global collaboration. In *Proc. Conference*, ACM: 319-328.

[27] Hossain, E., et al. (2011). Scrum practices in global software development: a research framework. In *Proc. Conference*, Springer-Verlag: 88-102.

[28] Jensen, R. E. (2014). Why closely coupled work matters in global software development. GROUP 2014. ACM.

[29] Jensen, R. E. and P. Bjørn (2012). Divergence and Convergence in Global Software Development: Cultural Complexities as Social Worlds. From Research to Practice in the Design of Cooperative Systems: Results and Open Challenges. J. Dugdale, C. Masclet, M. A. Grasso, J.-F. Boujut and P. Hassanaly. Published, Springer London: 123-136.

[30] Khadka, R., et al. (2014). How do professionals perceive legacy systems and software modernization? In *Proc. ICSE 2014*. ACM Press (2014). 36-47.

[31] Klein, H. K. and M. D. Myers (1999). A set of principles for conducting and evaluating interpretive field studies in information systems. *MIS Q*. 23(1): 67-93.

[32] Krishna, S., et al. (2004). Managing cross-cultural issues in global software outsourcing. *Commun. ACM*. 47(4): 62-66.

[33] Laguna, M. A. and Y. Crespo (2013). A systematic mapping study on software product line evolution: From legacy system reengineering to product line refactoring. *Sci. Comput. Program.* 78(8): 1010-1034.

[34] Luff, P., et al. (2000). Workplace Studies: Recovering Work Practice and Informing System Design, Cambridge University Press.

[35] Matthiesen, S., et al. (2014). "Figure out how to code with the hands of others": recognizing cultural blind spots in global software development. In *Proc. CSCW 2014*. ACM Press (2014). 1107-1119.

[36] Meum, T. (2013). “Lost in translation”: The challenges of seamless integration in nursing practices. *International Journal of Medical Informatics*. 82(5): e200-e208.

[37] Monteiro, E., et al. (2013). From Artefacts to Infrastructures. *Computer Supported Cooperative Work (CSCW)*. 22(4-6): 575-607.

[38] Parnas, D. L. (1972). On the criteria to be used in decomposing systems into modules. *Commun. ACM*. 15(12): 1053-1058.

[39] Randall, D., et al. (2010). Fieldwork for Design: Theory and Practice, Springer.

[40] Ribes, D. and T. A. Finholt (2009). The long now of technology infrastructure: articulating tensions in development. *Journal of the Association for Information Systems*. 10(5): 375-398.

[41] Ribes, D. and C. P. Lee (2010). Sociotechnical Studies of Cyberinfrastructure and e-Research: Current Themes and Future Trajectories. *Comput. Supported Coop. Work*. 19(3-4): 231-244.

[42] Schmidt, K. and L. Bannon (1992). Taking CSCW seriously. *Computer Supported Cooperative Work (CSCW)*. 1(1-2): 7-40.

[43] Søderberg, A.-M., et al. (2013). Global Software Development: Commitment, Trust and Cultural Sensitivity in Strategic Partnerships. *Journal of International Management*. 19(4): 347-361.

[44] Sommerville, I. (2007). Software Engineering, Addison-Wesley.

[45] Souza, C. R. B. d., et al. (2004). How a good software practice thwarts collaboration: the multiple roles of APIs in software development. In *Proc. SIGSOFT 2004*. ACM: 221-230.

[46] Star, S. L. (1999). The ethnography of infrastructure. *American behavioral scientist*. 43(3): 377-391.

[47] Star, S. L. and K. Ruhleder (1994). Steps towards an ecology of infrastructure: complex problems in design and access for large-scale collaborative systems. In *Proc. CSCW 1994*. ACM Press (1994). 253-264.

[48] Walsham, G. (1995). Interpretive case studies in IS research: nature and method. *European Journal of Information Systems*. 4: 74-81.

[49] Zimmerman, A. and T. A. Finholt (2007). Growing an infrastructure: the role of gateway organizations in cultivating new communities of users. In *Proc. GROUP 2007*. ACM Press (2007). 239-248.

Mood Squeezer: Lightening up the Workplace through Playful and Lightweight Interactions

Sarah Gallacher[1], Jenny O'Connor[2], Jon Bird[3], Yvonne Rogers[1], Licia Capra[1], Daniel Harrison[1], Paul Marshall[1]

[1]University College London, London WC1E 6BT, UK
[2]Imperial College London, London SW7 2AZ, UK
[3]City University London, London EC1V 0HB, UK
{s.gallacher, y.rogers, l.capra, daniel.harrison, paul.marshall}@ucl.ac.uk, j.oconnor@imperial.ac.uk, jon.bird@city.ac.uk

ABSTRACT
Many companies would like to redesign their workspaces to make them more pleasant and even fun places to work in. An assumption is it will result in social and economic benefits. However, it can be difficult to achieve because of cost, level of disruption and regulations. We present an alternative approach that provides an injection of playfulness into 'drab' office buildings. A lightweight technology intervention was designed - Mood Squeezer - that asks people to reflect on their mood by squeezing a colored ball from a box set. The squeezes are mirrored back as an aggregate colorful visualization on a public floor display. An in-the-wild study showed how this intervention was successful at getting people to squeeze their mood, leading to a diversity of conversations throughout the building. We discuss how this lightweight approach to office augmentation can provide new opportunities for opening up a 'closed' workplace.

Author Keywords
Physical computing; Public visualization; Tangible interface; Mood; In the wild; Work; Playful technology

ACM Classification Keywords
H.5.m. Information interfaces and presentation (e.g., HCI): Miscellaneous.

INTRODUCTION
Office buildings are often designed to be utilitarian, with a focus on how to fill them to capacity with people, equipment and furniture. The result can be dull and uniform interiors. However, research shows that drab color schemes, poor lighting and insufficient natural light and ventilation can have a negative impact on employee mood and morale [20, 19]. Many office workers remain seated at their desks for hours on end glued to their computer screens. This can be further exacerbated by a serious and busy work ethic where people tend to eat their lunch and drink their coffee at their desks. The tendency to stay put once at work, however, reduces opportunities for colleagues bumping into each other and having opportunistic conversations. Moreover, the impact of low social connectedness can lead to feelings of isolation and monotony [14].

ACM 978-1-4503-2922-4/15/03…$15.00.
http://dx.doi.org/10.1145/2675133.2675170

Figure 1. The view down a typical corridor in the workplace.

How might these negative aspects of the work environment be reduced and replaced by a more positive work culture? One possibility is to design more imaginative interiors that encourage people to take time out to talk, play and socialize. For example, a few creative and tech industries have begun experimenting with fun, open workplaces where playfulness and interaction are encouraged. The assumed benefits are thought to be social and economic, leading to greater idea cross-pollination, collaboration and productivity. For many established organizations, however, such makeovers can be too costly or difficult to get approval for because of health and safety regulations. How else might existing workspaces be made more open?

Our approach is to capitalize on affordable technology interventions that are designed to be deliberately playful, and that aim to elicit more openness and conversations amongst colleagues who might not normally talk to one another. In this paper we present Mood Squeezer – a technology intervention intended to engage people in a lighthearted and playful way to reflect on their moods throughout the day and to talk to others about them.

Using the principles of playfulness, ambiguity and curiosity, we designed a series of input devices comprising a box of brightly colored, squeezy balls. They are intended to be attractive, luring people to do something lighthearted by literally squeezing the 'color of their mood'. The squeezes are then fed in real time into a corresponding colorful floor display in a public space for all to see. The rationale behind the design was to make people stop in their tracks and do something that would take just a few seconds but which they could reflect upon or talk about subsequently.

To test how an office community approached, reacted and appropriated such a playful technology interventon, an in-the-wild study was conducted over a number of weeks. The findings showed that squeezing balls in this lighthearted way encouraged self-reflection, openness and interaction between many colleagues and engendered more positive attitudes towards the workplace. The research presented here discusses in more detail the rationale for the design of the technology, the findings of the study and the pros and cons of using a lightweight playful approach of opening up office spaces in a lighthearted way.

RELATED WORK

Work and Play

Work has traditionally been viewed as a serious business with economies and livelihoods depending upon it. Playing and having fun in the office is viewed more as a distraction. However, this view is changing. While the "baby boomer" generation (born between 1941 and 1960) often regard fun as counter-productive, the new generation of "millenial" workers (born between 1981 and 2000) tend to view it as an important enabler for building social connections and trust with colleagues [21]. This is particularly the case for the creative and knowledge-based industries where playful office artifacts and engaging spaces are designed to encourage innovation, creativity and collaboration. Fun is viewed as being organic and an asset that can facilitate bonding and the building of harmonious relationships and collaborations amongst employees.

As well as links to increased innovation and productivity [25], academic studies have also linked workplace fun with increased physical wellbeing [12] Organisational Citizenship Behaviour [10], job satisfaction [16] and decreased absenteeism [22]. Management are very aware of the positive benefits and many companies now deliberately introduce fun at work through social practices such as networking/team building events. Although enjoyed by many, for some employees this kind of management-led fun is resented due to the expectation to participate and have social practices imposed upon them [5].

Several tech companies have hired interior design experts in an attempt to create more engaging and conducive office environments. One method has been to place people in open spaces and smaller spaces to make "collisions" between colleagues more inevitable [31]. Another initiative is the Randomised Coffee Trials (RCT) [24] where employees are randomly paired with another staff member each week to sit and have a coffee together. A more persuasive approach at getting people to spend time together is to make it difficult for them to leave. For example, Yahoo!'s ban on telecommuting is intended to encourage people to spend more time physically together working and socializing [30].

While these kinds of incentives and initiatives can have a positive impact on the office environment they can, by the same measure, be perceived negatively by employees if not implemented in a sympathetic way. Top-down approaches to engendering more social working practices can be socially awkward for some. While randomly being paired up with someone for coffee can be a fun way to meet other people in the office, it can also be daunting especially for those who are shy. Moreover, such "packaged fun" can have the opposite effect of what is intended, leading to reservations about obligations to participate. It can also feel artificial, where management are viewed as trying to codify or organize social practices, that people feel should occur more naturally.

Technology Interventions in the Office

Another approach to instilling a sense of togetherness and social cohesion in office settings has been to deploy various technology interventions. A general observation is that such technology interventions have typically taken a more organic or non-intrusive approach to affecting office environments; not requiring employee participation or large amounts of employee time and effort.

Early attempts included using remote video conferencing as a way of promoting a shared space across buildings in different locations. For example, the VideoWindow, developed at Bellcore in 1989, was designed to allow people in different locations to have a conversation as if they were drinking coffee together in the same room. A large video window measuring 3 foot by 5 foot connected the two sites. A study of its use found conversations did take place between people as if they were drinking coffee with each other but that they spoke more loudly and mostly about the video system itself [9]. Since then, a number of other video links have been deployed to promote connectedness and awareness across remote working sites by streaming images between one site and the other [4, 8, 10] onto PCs or large public displays [15, 29]. Nowadays such technology is ubiquitously used for scheduled meetings between colleagues and others but remains a poor facilitator of more informal social events.

Others have argued that technology can have a more playful role in the workplace [28]. For example, the PLEX model of playful experiences explores at a theoretical level the reasons why people play and the benefits of doing so in various contexts including work [18]. Monk [23] notes how blurring the boundaries between tools and toys can be useful in the workplace and highlights successful examples that span both categories, such as the UNIX process manager based on the video game "Doom" [7].

More recently, various physical technology interventions have been introduced in the workplace to elicit more playful and lighthearted experiences. For example, Arnie the talking beer vending machine, was designed to attract employees into communal areas with the promise of free beer and the opportunity to chat with colleagues [1]. Arnie's humorous chatter was found to foster playfulness and to instil a sense of pride and ownership among employees. Vending machines have also been repurposed to encourage people to visit them and in doing so have serendipitously elicited the honey-pot effect [6]. For example, a snack vending machine was reengineered to invite students to grade exam papers whereupon completion they received free chocolate bars [13]. In doing so, it also encouraged them to talk to others while hanging around the vending machine. In contrast, the Break-Time Barometer was designed explicitly to persuade people to come out of their offices and socialise more [17]. The system displays how many people are currently in the staff common room; if there are people there it suggests it would be a good time to join them for a break. Interestingly, however, the opposite often happened. Employees also used the system to gauge when breaks *weren't* happening so that they could take a break without their colleagues being around for company.

Another persuasive technology that triggered much debate amongst colleagues was the Twinkly Lights and Clouds installation that was designed to playfully nudge employees towards taking the stairs instead of the elevator [26]. Two clusters of differently colored balls were hung in the atrium, to appear like clouds, and which moved up and down relative to each other depending on how many people had taken the stairs versus the elevator at a given time. The ambiguous nature of the installation was found to cause people to reflect upon what they meant. There was curiosity and many explanations were generated and exchanged about what the clouds represented with some managing to figure out that they represented something changing in the building. The overall effect was to elicit many conversations throughout the building between people who did not normally talk to each another. Similar to Arnie, it provided the occupants with a sense of ownership and pride when showing it to visitors.

AIMS AND OBJECTIVES

The aim of our research, likewise, was to determine if we could encourage people to be more aware of each other and their place of work by introducing a playful technology that would trigger reflection and conversation. But instead of seeking to promote behavioural change in an organization, the specific goal of our study was to explore the impact of a playful technology on a "serious" work culture. Could it encourage more playfulness, positivity and community pride in the workplace? Or would it be simply ignored or even make people annoyed?

The challenge, therefore, was to create something that could initially attract peoples' attention, was lightweight and fun to interact with while maintaining interest over a period of time. Furthermore, engaging with it should not make people feel socially awkward. To this end, we focused on how to get people to think about how they were feeling at various points during the day and moreover to wonder what others were feeling. While there are various smartphone apps available that allow individuals to track their moods by filling out a short questionnaire at random times each day, they are individually-based and hence privy only to those who choose to use the app. We wanted to design a physical installation that was very much 'out there' for anyone to use throughout the day as they moved through parts of the building. To this end we designed a public installation that required playful input and whose output was projected onto a large floor display for all to walk past and observe. The aim was to provide a lightweight way of cascading conversation throughout the building about people's mood and what others in the building had also expressed.

We were interested in examining people's reactions on first discovering the installation and then subsequently using it, and seeing how others reacted and used it. Would people find it intriguing or silly? Would they reflect on how they were feeling and ask others? Would they talk to each other about it? If so, where and when? Would it engender a sense of connectedness in the building? But to begin, we conducted a preliminary survey in the workplace to get a baseline of how employees viewed their current working environment. The results of the study were used to inform the design and placement of the installation.

THE SETTING

Figure 1 shows a typical view down one of the workplace corridors. Over 200 inhabitants are split across five floors with one communal lift lobby on each floor and one coffee room shared by all floors. Each floor comprises a combination of closed offices on the outside and open plan windowless spaces and corridors on the inside.

PRELIMINARY SURVEY

An online survey was initially conducted on the occupants of the building to elicit their views about the workplace. The survey results showed a number of negative trends. For many, the workplace was not an enticing space to come to each day. From a total of 84 responses, 76% said there was *not* a strong sense of social connectedness in the workplace and 68% felt that management did not do enough to address this. Additionally, only 11% of respondents felt more connected to current colleagues than they had done to colleagues in previous places of work. However, when asked about fun, informal events such as birthday drinks, 67% of respondents agreed that they found them enjoyable. In fact, 92% of respondents indicated that they would like to see more opportunities for informal activities and engagement in the workplace.

To investigate further, we asked 26 of the respondents, who agreed to be interviewed, a further set of questions. To avoid bias, the interviews were carried out by a social scientist from another organization. Each interview consisted of a range of semi-structured questions, partly shaped by the outcomes of the survey. The interviews were transcribed and coded for recurrent themes. These emerged as (i) building discomforts, (ii) social silos, and (iii) serious work ethic.

(i) building discomforts The majority of interviewees highlighted aspects of the building design that were considered depressing. These included a lack of sufficient communal spaces, isolated offices, lack of natural daylight and open plan offices that were either too noisy or resembled a library. For these reasons, working from home was a popular choice among the interviewees.

(ii) social silos The interview results also revealed that there was a strong culture of 'social silos' in the workplace. While all interviewees felt that there was a good level of social connectedness within their own working group, they mentioned that they did not engage with other groups. Even when two separate groups were co-located on the same floor or in the same open plan area, there was little interaction between groups or awareness of what the other group was working on. This was viewed as most problematic when group members were not co-located or where working groups were particularly small. One participant spoke of his isolated experiences, "*what happened to me, for the first year, I was completely alone. My supervisor, me, and no interaction with anyone. And I think my story is similar to a lot of people that are working on something alone.*"

(iii) Serious work ethic Interviewees expressed a desire to get to know and relate to their colleagues but felt that it was almost impossible to speak to someone without an introduction or some other appropriate justification. One respondent noted that, "*occupants of the building with whom I am not personally familiar with are the same as strangers on the street to me*". Another mentioned, "*I have met a number of colleagues, by chance, at conferences overseas, and only realized that they were colleagues when I got talking to them in a bar after a workshop*". Some respondents suggested that the serious nature of the workplace made spontaneous interaction particularly challenging due to the introverted nature of some employees; a working culture of deadlines and solitary endeavor; and living in a large city where attitudes of minding-your-own-business and not talking to strangers are normatively enshrined. These findings suggested that there was a need to 'open' up the building more by providing opportunities throughout the building for people to meet and talk to others. While it is not possible to address the building discomforts identified there is scope for finding ways of breaking down the social silo mentality and the serious work ethic.

DESIGN

To begin, we considered what kind of intervention would be appropriate given the existing culture of the building. We decided to design a technology installation that would give employees and visitors an opportunity to do something fun when moving through the communal spaces on each floor, by the elevators and stairwells, where they might bump into other colleagues from different groups. We wanted them to engage in a lighthearted activity that would allow them to reflect and talk about how they were feeling. It could also provide them with a means of "expressing their emotions", especially if they were having a bad or good moment.

The design we finalized on was a tangible 'SqueezeBox' comprising a row of colored balls (see Figure 2a) that could record people's moods. The design was inspired by how stress balls are used by people. However, instead of being an individual act someone does when stressed, we chose to repurpose the balls as playful, tangible inputs for people to squeeze to express how they are feeling. The addition of color was inspired by previous explorations into mood, color and taste (including a pilot study where we asked people *"what color does your tap water taste like?"*). The mapping of mood to color was deliberately open ended. The intention was to trigger subjective discussions between employees on what mood and color meant to them and to allow people to assign their own rules and appropriate the technology in line with their own views.

The choice of ball colors and the order and placement of the balls on the SqueezeBoxes was aesthetically driven and bright, complimentary colors were chosen from across the spectrum. A poster (see Figure 2a) was designed to be placed above each SqueezeBox, inviting people to "Squeeze the color of your mood".

The output of the squeezes was mirrored in the form of a public floor display visualisation (see Figure 2b) and web-based display (see Figure 2c). When people from different floors squeeze a ball, the color of that ball appears on the digital floor display for everyone to see. To this end, a large digital floor display [3] was repurposed that had previously been set up on one floor of the building. The display was designed to be eye-catching when turned on. It is a large matrix comprising 6 adjacent squares that have glass holes

a) SqueezeBox b) Digital floor display c) Webpage

Figure 2. Images of the input and output devices; a SqueezeBox, the digital floor display and webpage.

in them that are lit up from underneath by a set of LEDs – five of the squares were used to show the mood of five of the floors in the building, respectively. The sixth square was updated every minute to represent the aggregate mood color of the whole building, showing how much each color had been squeezed throughout the entire building that day. For example, if pink was squeezed 30% of the time that day, 30% of the sixth square would turn pink. The digital floor display was labeled with vinyl floor stickers to indicate what each square represented.

The SqueezeBoxes and the digital floor display were controlled by Arduino technology. The SqueezeBoxes used Force Sensitive Resistors (FSRs) inside each ball to detect when a squeeze was happening. All squeeze data was sent via WiFi to a backend server that processed and logged the squeeze data as well as relaying it to the digital floor display and the live webpage. In this way, both output mechanisms were updated in real-time and one could see how a squeeze immediately affected both displays.

The webpage provided an online representation of what was displayed on the floor. This was to enable people also to see what the overall mood of the building was and that of the separate floors from their desks or from home. A Twitter feed and a Facebook page were also created to provide updates about the study as it progressed and to support any online community that could potentially form around it.

METHODOLOGY

An in-the-wild study was conducted to determine how people in the building reacted, interacted and reflected on the Mood Squeezer [26]. It was deployed for four weeks to provide enough time to investigate the initial novelty effect (i.e. the first few days) and then to see how it impacted on the working environment over a longer period of time (a further few weeks). After the official 4-week deployment had ended (and building inhabitants had been notified) we decided to leave the SqueezeBoxes in place for an additional 4 weeks. This follow-up period was to determine the extent to which people continued to squeeze even after they had been informed that the study was finished.

The Mood Squeezer was installed and tested during a weekend so that people entering the building on the Monday morning would find it up and running when first arriving at work. An email was sent to departmental mailing lists to announce its deployment, introduce the digital floor display and provide links to the floor webpage, Twitter feed and Facebook page.

The floor display was activated for 2 hours on each day of the deployment. The reason for this was to encourage staff to come and look at the public visualization display when switched on during a limited period and interact with colleagues rather than being on all the time. During the additional 4 week follow-up period, the floor display was not activated but the website was still available.

Both quantitative and qualitative data were collected during the in-the-wild study. The number, time and location of squeeze data were collected together with observations of what people did at the SqueezeBoxes and the floor display on a daily basis. The observers sat in one of the chairs placed in the communal spaces. Sometimes, when interesting behaviors or conversations materialized, an observer asked the person/s questions – in a way that was not off putting but could have simply been anyone in the building. Observations, discussions and comments were also recorded throughout the building during the four-week deployment.

Building access data was also retrieved from building security. This showed a time-stamped list of all building entry events on the ground floor turnstiles and allowed us to see how busy the building was on each day of the study for comparison against squeeze counts. On the final day of the official deployment period, an exit survey was emailed to all staff within the department to obtain their feedback. In addition, another series of interviews was completed with 25 of the 26 staff members who participated in the preliminary interviews (one member of staff was unavailable due to being on vacation). These interviews focused on their engagement with the Mood Squeezer and asked how/if it had impacted on their daily work life. The interviews were semi-structured and each one was recorded, partially transcribed and coded for recurrent themes.

The quantitative squeeze data is presented and discussed below along with the qualitative results of the in-the-wild observations, exit survey and final interviews.

RESULTS

When arriving in the building in the first week many people stopped to look at the Mood Squeezer and squeezed a ball as indicated by the logged data. A large number of people continued to squeeze the balls, sometimes several times a day, over the course of the study. Their moods changed as reflected by the colors they selected. Many conversations about the installation inside and outside of the building were observed, that included a range of both positive and negative comments. To examine in more detail these findings we first look at the quantitative data collected.

Quantitative Analysis

Squeeze Data

The squeeze data shows that there was a consistent level of interaction with the SqueezeBoxes during the course of the four-week study, with a total of 3,689 squeezes. Figure 3 shows the daily squeeze counts against the building entry figures (based on total entry events where several events may be the same person) across the official four-week deployment. Initial daily squeeze counts were high, averaging around 300 squeezes per day, dropping off to a sustained level of around 130 squeezes per day for the remaining weeks. Squeeze levels peaked at the beginning of each week and declined as the week progressed in line with building entry figures.

The main peak of the squeeze counts over the course of an average day was around 10am (when most people arrived at work) followed by three more peaks at 12pm, 3pm and 5pm, with each peak being slightly less than the previous. Further analysis of the squeeze data did not uncover any other significant patterns. There was no floor that showed significantly more squeezes than the others, and equally there was no ball color that was squeezed significantly more than the others.

To get a better understanding of how many distinct users were interacting with the SqueezeBoxes we also analyzed the data for 'multi-squeeze events'. These are events where 2 or more consecutive squeezes were registered in quick succession of each other (less than 10 seconds) indicating that those squeezes were most likely by the same person. The data shows that 38% of all squeezes were part of a multi-squeeze event suggesting that there were some individuals who seemed to enjoy repeatedly squeezing the balls during a single visit but that most people (62%) squeezed only one ball each interaction.

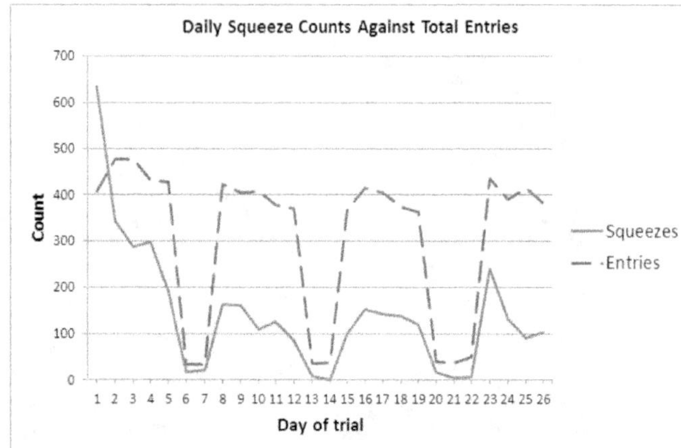

Figure 3. Daily squeezes against building entry figures.

There was little online engagement with Twitter and Facebook. Only twenty-one people liked the Facebook page while eight people followed the Twitter feed. In contrast, there was a much higher level of web page traffic with a total of 725 logins to the floor webpage over the four-week deployment period. This suggests that people were curious to follow the building mood trends but were not motivated enough to engage on the official Facebook page or Twitter feed.

During the four-week follow-up period (when the SqueezeBoxes remained in position after the official deployment ended) the results show that a stable average daily squeeze count of 121 squeezes per day was still maintained despite the fact that users were told the study had ended. This sustained plateau of usage suggests that the novelty effect may have subsided by this time however we cannot know for certain.

Exit Survey

A total of 34 responses were received for the exit survey. Due to the small number of responses we suggest that these results be seen as indicators for impact that should be considered in conjunction with the other quantitative and qualitative results. The exit survey results showed that 96% of respondents stated they had interacted with the SqueezeBoxes during the 4-week deployment period. 41% of the respondents visited the floor display when it was active, and 31% visited the webpage. In terms of interactions between colleagues, over three quarters of respondents (77%) discussed the SqueezeBoxes with others whereas the floor display and the webpage were only discussed by 32% and 7% of respondents, respectively. 26% of respondents stated that they had discussed some element of the study with a colleague who they had not spoken to before – which is higher than expected considering how rarely this was found to be the case in the pre-study survey.

The general attitude towards the study was positive with 71% stating that they found it enjoyable to have the system in the building (with a further 15% as neutral) and 59% stating that they thought similar interventions in the future would be beneficial to the working environment (with a further 22% as neutral).

Qualitative Analysis

In-the-wild Observations

During the four-week deployment phase, observations were made on a daily basis for the two-hour period when the floor display was active. The observations captured some of the diverse ways in which individuals engaged with the SqueezeBox and floor display. Some individuals took a moment to reflect on their mood before selecting a colored ball (figure 4a). For others the engagement was performed very rapidly as they hurried past a SqueezeBox. A number of individuals adopted a more playful approach to engagement by rapidly squeezing many balls in quick succession as if playing a game or musical instrument. It was also observed that other individuals adopted one color and only squeezed this particular color each time they passed by. Others went a stage further by continuously squeezing their chosen color until it monopolized their floor - again as appropriating it like a game or challenge. In one case, the continuous squeezing prompted a staff member from another floor (who was viewing the real-time updates on the webpage) to query if there was a faulty squeeze sensor.

Several occupants brought their friends, guests and children to visit the SqueezeBoxes and the floor display. They were also observed making comments related to a level of identification with, and appropriation of, the installation. For example, one said, "*we have a box on our floor too*". Others commented on the overall state of the selected colors, "*pink is the most popular color at the moment*". Others gave instructions to their visitors on how to interact with a SqueezeBox, "*you have to squeeze the color of your mood and it appears on this floor*". On a few occasions, groups of individuals were observed laughing and having fun around a SqueezeBox and the floor display. While one person squeezed the balls the others watched for a light in the display to change color.

In addition to observing people, overheard comments or discussions were also recorded throughout the building. Staff members were overheard discussing the study in the elevators, while outside smoking and at out-of-hours social events, as well as around the SqueezeBoxes or floor display. In the majority of cases, the discussions related to reflections on their mood or subjective views on the relationship between mood and color. Groups of individuals were observed congregating around a SqueezeBox and collectively deciding on what color to squeeze (figure 4b). Discussions also centered on hypotheses to explain the choice of color or the arrangement of the balls. For

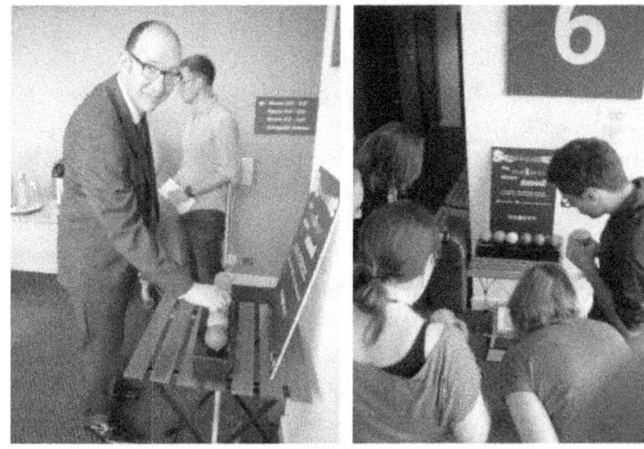

a) Squeezing a yellow mood b) Group interactions at a SqueezeBox

Figure 4. Interactions with the SqueezeBoxes.

example, a common assumption emerged that the balls were arranged from left to right in a scale from most positive color (pink) to least positive color (purple). Indeed, several exit interview respondents confirmed that their color choice was influenced by the comments or assumptions of others. Some individuals had very strong opinions about the mapping; for example, two females were completely adverse to selecting pink as they saw it as a "*Barbie*" color and refused to squeeze it in an act of non-conformity towards the color conventionally associated with girls' toys, clothes, etc. Another member of staff commented that she had associated a different color with each day of the week since she was a young girl and could only squeeze the "*day's color*" no matter what her mood.

On some occasions, a potential squeezer was observed "swerving" away from the SqueezeBox when they realized that someone else was present in the space and might be watching them. When queried further about this behavior, the participants admitted that they felt self-conscious or embarrassed squeezing the balls in front of other unfamiliar colleagues. This suggests that there are two kinds of people: those who are happy to squeeze and those who felt embarrassed in taking part.

Other, discussions were about the technology behind the SqueezeBoxes, such as how they worked or what the study was actually measuring. One individual was even observed with a screwdriver in his hand inspecting the internal electronics of a SqueezeBox!

During the two hours each day when the floor display came on it was observed that few people came to see it. In the first day of deployment only ten people came specifically to view the floor. This dropped off to just a few by the end of the first week. Then in subsequent weeks, it was observed that only passers-by stopped to view it on their usual route on that floor. Discussions about the floor display were rarely captured (however, several people did mention discussing it in the exit interviews). One reason for so few people deviating from their routines to explicitly watch the floor display might have been because walking up or down the stairs or taking the elevator to the 6th floor was a step too far for those who did not normally go there. Another reason might have been that they were not aware of the time of the floor display being lit or they were busy during that period – we only posted the times once in an email that could have been overlooked by many (we did not want to annoy people by sending reminder emails). In contrast, we observed many people interacting with the SqueezeBoxes and then looking afterwards at the results of their squeeze on the website via their phone or tablet. This raises the question of the value of having a separate public floor display as a focal point for all the squeezes from each floor to be shown in this kind of multi-story building.

Exit Interviews

The people who were interviewed after the study were positive about the technology intervention. One respondent for example, commented, "*I enjoyed the project and thought it brought some fun to the building*" while another added, "*the most positive outcome for me is...finally seeing people in this mini 'desert'. I could see colleagues from the floor out of their office for the first time.*" Even those who did not engage with a SqueezeBox commented positively on the visual design of the Mood Squeezer. All agreed that they would like to see more of these interventions appear again in the building.

A number of themes emerged from the interviews about the value and role of such an intervention in an office building where 'serious work' is the norm. These were playfulness, reflection, emergence of social norms, ice-breakers and conversations, openness, groups and honey-pots and showcasing and pride.

Playfulness: The SqueezeBoxes were viewed as playful, fun and innovative. Their presentation was regarded as suitably simple and well-positioned in the communal spaces. The balls were visually and texturally appealing and the interviewees who had squeezed them, commented on the joy of interacting with them: "*They were nice to touch because they were squishable*" (P8). They reminded many respondents of childhood toys and the bright colors of the balls engendered feelings of being light-hearted. It encouraged them to spontaneously be playful around them. One interviewee said, "*... we were like going up and down the floors trying to change the color, but there was a point where the fifth floor was all yellow and then I ran to the fifth floor to try to change the color and there was a person running after me*" (P2). Another commented, "*I went to another floor that was all blue...to change the color or squeeze lots of different colors*" (P6).

Comparisons with stress balls also meant that the SqueezeBoxes were often used as a de-stressing tool. One interviewee commented that they had observed over vigorous squeezing on some occasions prompting them to post on the Facebook page that colleagues should "*squeeze, not bash*".

Reflection: For some, engagement with the squeezy balls became a more personal activity that evoked self-reflection and thought. One interviewee talked about how it made him think more deeply about his mood: "*I tried to do it based on how I felt, which was a bit odd I suppose, because you think what does it mean if I'm feeling yellow or whatever*" (P3). Another gave a detailed description of why he preferred to squeeze pink, "*I kind of squeezed the pink one the most, but it wasn't because it's close to red, meaning I'm angry. So I was instinctively going towards blue because I'm a guy, but then I was like, blue means you're sad. I didn't like the blue. So I was like, I'm not blue. And the yellow means you're ill or something. Orange is like you need to be in the A&E, so pink, like, okay*" (P4). Others suggested they would have liked even more colors to select from to capture their moods, such as black.

Emergence of social norms: Several interviewees expressed their frustration that others were not abiding by "the rules" of squeezing the color of their mood. One mentioned how it made him anxious when he saw others squeezing balls randomly in quick succession. In addition, the open-endedness of the mood-color relationships also made people want an accepted mapping to emerge that everyone would use. For example, one interviewee said, "*I discussed it and realized that my assumption is that it's a scale from happy to sad. I realized that I just randomly made that assumption because so often you do something like that, to represent it in a scale*" (P6). For others, the fact that there was no accepted mapping to begin with was what made it interesting for them to decide what might be appropriate.

Ice-breakers and conversations: The deliberate open-ended mapping between mood and color often acted as a point of discussion between people in the building. It became a conversational ice-breaker in socially awkward situations, such as waiting at the coffee machine or being in the elevator with colleagues who were familiar but not well known. Several interviewees mentioned how the usual mundane small talk about the weather had been replaced with discussions on mood-color and squeezy balls. This sometimes led to more lengthy, in-depth discussions, as described by participant P2: "*It was like extensive discussions and several times...not only one and not only with my colleagues here. Also back home with my family and my friends*". Conversations about the Mood Squeezer also regularly happened outside the workplace. Many interviewees spoke of the discussions they had subsequently with friends and family. Even the interviewee who did not squeeze the balls admitted to discussing the Mood Squeezer at length with colleagues in the pub.

Openness: Being able to talk about one's mood helped many start a conversation. Interviewees talked about how they and their colleagues became more open with each other about how they felt. One interviewee stated, "*and I think also…we have been more open about how we've been feeling during - whilst it's been out there. And that in itself has to be a good thing. So it's had a lot of maybe indirect effects that are actually quite substantial in a way. And the fact that people have been sort of reflecting on their moods has kind of hit a few things home to me, … that the moods can be quite variable*" (P18). Another said, "*it was really good in that people were very mindful of their moods, and kind of talking about it, and I think it created a lot of excitement around the department as a whole*" (P11).

Several other interviewees spoke of the excitement, buzz and a positive department-wide impact on the working environment. One interviewee said, "*well it did sort of liven the place up. I suppose it did. In a bizarre way though, not in a straightforward way. It wasn't like a piece of art*". Another interviewee mentioned, "*so what I liked is the fun, with people and squeezing and talking about colors*" (P18).

Groups and honey-pot effect: Several interviewees commented on how they had noticed or been part of a group activity around the SqueezeBoxes. They talked about squeezing in groups and observing other groups of people squeezing and collectively deciding what colors to choose. One mentioned how the floor display made him and his colleagues stop, view and discuss it, "*[We] went up to the floor display and basically…we were exchanging, so what color do you think you'd squeeze the most and we were theorising how it might be displaying the colors on the floor. What kind of algorithm was being used to choose when they were being shown and what that meant*" (P6). Another said, "*people were hanging [around the floor] and talking about the project so that was great*" (P16).

Showcasing and pride: Some interviewees expressed pleasure at the showcasing of the research work going on within the department. In the preliminary interviews, many interviewees expressed disappointment with the current lack of communication of research activities between various work groups. It was mentioned how the Mood Squeezer provided an example of how this could be better achieved without the need for a more formal forum (such as organized seminars). One interviewee commented, "*I mean here, we've got such a large building and we've got some people doing some great work, but you don't hear about it half the time….this is definitely a way of trying to showcase some of the work that we do" (P4).* Another mentioned how he showed it off to visitors, "*there were a couple of people visiting my lab. They don't work here but they came for one day to present their work and they have a discussion with me and then I was taking them to the balls, like you need to see this" (P2).*

Others talked about feeling proud of the Mood Squeezer. One interviewee referred to it as being like a "*shiny, new water-cooler*", in respect to their attraction and creation of spaces where people could gather for informal activities.

DISCUSSION

The findings from the study suggest that the Mood Squeezer did impact positively on the workplace by encouraging people in the building to be playful, talk more and reflect on various aspects of the organization, the building and their work. The SqueezeBoxes encouraged people to reflect just for brief moments throughout the day without being disruptive or for the most part making people feel socially awkward. Only a few felt the SqueezeBoxes were too childish for such a serious place of work. Most occupants really enjoyed having the SqueezeBoxes become part of the building while some were put out when they were removed after the study. Like the Twinkly Lights and Arnie, they became attached to them and developed a sense of ownership and even pride.

The design of the installation was such that people in the building were free to opt in or out of playing with it as and when they wanted and investments of time and effort were very low. In this way, it was non-intrusive and did not distract from important work matters. However, as observed, people did not often visit the public floor display on the sixth floor. Instead, those who wanted to see the outcome of their squeeze would bring up the webpage on their smartphone, tablet or laptop. It seemed it was too much for people to go to another floor and stand around looking at the visualization. This suggests that the coupling between input and output is context-dependent. The reason we decided to have only one public display rather than one on each floor was that we were able to reuse an existing installation in the building. To have made four more, for each of the other floors, would have been too impractical. Future research could investigate what the effect would be of having other kinds of distributed public displays adjacent to the Squeezeboxes (that are easier and more affordable to make), or have one placed in a central communal space, such as a reception or atrium area, that everyone has to enter through.

Our research inevitably raises the question of whether all we have done is elicit a novelty effect. We would argue that a novelty effect is integral to further sustained engagement. The quantitative data showed sustained usage of this lightweight intervention over eight weeks (four weeks in the official study period and four outside) suggesting it provided people with moments in the day to reflect and something to be shared and talked about with others. We do not suggest that one playful technology intervention will impact on the workplace forever. Rather, that the playful technology implemented in this study showed how it can help towards making a more open and positive work environment for a few months. We suggest that such playful technologies may be used in concert with other kinds of interventions that are changed over time in order to sustain an open, positive atmosphere in the longer term.

Below, we discuss at a more general level how playful interactive installations, that involve constantly changing user input coupled with real-time feedback, can be engaging and uplifting for an office. We also discuss the extent to which such interventions can encourage more social cohesiveness and a sense of well-being – for closed office and open plan buildings that make people tend to stay at their desks. These are discussed in terms of their role on the working environment at three levels: self, inter-personal and organizational.

(i) Self
Results from the in-the-wild observations and the exit interviews showed that the technology intervention provided an opportunity for employees to take time out of their work routines to be playful and lighthearted. Instead of just dashing to get a coffee or going to the toilet, squeezing their mood at one of the Squeezeboxes gave them an opportunity for self-reflection about their mood and feelings. People don't often do this. Equally, it could be argued that a smartphone app could trigger random moments to encourage people to be mindful. However, arguably these are likely to be more disruptive – especially if someone is in the middle of doing something. The squeezy balls were designed simply to catch someone's eye and nudge them to squeeze and reflect if they felt like it rather than having to answer a random set of questions pushed at them via an app. They can simply be overlooked if that person is too busy.

The Mood Squeezer also highlighted social norms in the workplace. For example, some individuals like, and want to stick to rules (such as squeezing their mood color) even getting anxious when others don't follow them. In contrast, others completely disregarded the rules, looking for more playful or personal ways to appropriate the technology. It would be interesting to explore further the extent to which the norms and rules, by which people play, converge over time. The intervention also highlighted the strong relationships that individuals have with colors. For some, certain colors represented stereotypes, conformity or other deeply ingrained associations from childhood and hence squeezing a ball was a statement rather than a frivolous choice related to their mood.

(ii) Inter-personal
The findings all suggested that the technology intervention impacted on interaction and social connectedness between colleagues. Playful interactions and joshing were observed around the installations; some colleagues competed with each other to manipulate the overall mood visualization to be all of one color.

There was much discussion on various aspects of the intervention, mostly driven by the open-ended relationships between mood and color. It provided an interesting icebreaker in socially awkward situations and the survey results showed evidence that the intervention also triggered discussion between previously unknown individuals. People were much more open with each other about their feelings at work and also reflected on how others felt their moods varied during the working day. People also discussed their chosen mood-color mappings and exchanged subjective views with one another. Baker [2] describes such interactions as High Quality Connections (HQCs), defined as having higher emotional capacity, resilience, and openness to new ideas and influences. Discussions about the project and mood-color relationships continued throughout the official deployment phase. At the end of week 3, conversations were still observed in the elevators and between smokers standing outside the building. In week 4 additional comments were still being captured about what specific colors meant to individuals.

(iii) Organizational
The results of the in-the-wild observations and interviews suggest that the technology intervention increased pride and positivity in the workplace. The occupants discussed their workplace and the installations within, at home and while out socializing. The installations acted as a showcase and live demo of current research happening in the department and were proudly presented to friends, family and guests. Some people even brought their children into work to view and interact with them. The installations also gave people a better sense of other work that was going on within the department and was seen as a beneficial way to share work and ideas without the need for a formal forum such as a seminar or a workshop. Indeed, they created a general buzz throughout the department with interviewees talking of excitement, liveliness and fun.

Generalization to Other Workplaces
Our research explored how a public and playful installation that was designed to be lightweight and fun for everyone to interact with, can have an impact on a 'serious' workplace. While a few people found it annoying or it was not for them to be seen playing most people enjoyed the light-heartedness of being able to squeeze and reflect on their mood. Certainly, it would have caused more annoyance, if it had been mandated or we had pestered people more to squeeze their mood. Hence, we argue that for these kinds of playful interventions to be effective they need to be enticing and fun.

One could question if the positive impacts found in our study were specific to the culture of the particular building and the nature of the work carried out there. Informal communication about the study through blogs, tweets and seminar presentations has led to others showing considerable interest in the approach. Since the completion of the study, we have been contacted by a number of external organizations, having quite different cultures, that have cited similar issues in their own offices. In response, a second study is already underway that has repurposed the technology installation at commercial offices in the Canary Wharf area of London. The context of the building and nature of the work is very different to that reported here. Early indications show that the intervention is having even more of an impact at the self, inter-personal and organizational levels. Engagement levels are high; fun and play have already developed around the installations and there is a buzz in the office with much discussion and intrigue around color and mood.

CONCLUSIONS

It is well known how a working environment can affect the wellbeing and productivity of its occupants. While creative and tech industries are designing new offices to meet a variety of needs besides just a place to work, many offices were built to be more utilitarian and maximize space. Here, we have revisited the theme of play in the workplace, putting a fresh spin on previous work by using tangible, playful technologies in a serious working environment. We have shown how a playful technology intervention was introduced into an established serious workplace with a positive impact at the individual, the group and organization levels. As such, we suggest our results merit further investigation into the role of playful technologies in similar serious working environments. In particular, technologies that can provide people with moments to reflect throughout the day by themselves and with others, but most importantly without being annoying, or getting in the way of their work.

ACKNOWLEDGMENTS

This work is funded by ICRI Cities. We would like to thank everyone who participated in the study and for their informative insights, feedback and squeezes. Thanks also to Hans-Christian Jetter for his useful contributions in the early stages of the project.

REFERENCES

1. Arnold Worldwide, Arnie the beer vending machine, online: http://thefurnace.com.au/creative/work/worlds-first-social-beer-vending-machine
2. Baker, W., and Dutton, J.E. Enabling Positive Social Capital in Organizations. (2007)
3. Bird, J., Harrison, D., Marshall, P. The Challenge of Maintaining Interest in a Large-Scale Public Floor Display, *Proc. CHI'13, Workshop on Experiencing Interactivity in Public Spaces(EIPS)*, Paris, France, 2013.
4. Bly, S., Harrison, S., and Irwin, S. Media spaces: Bringin people together in a video, audio and computing environment. *Communications of the ACM 36,* (1993), 28-45.
5. Bolton, S.C., and Houlihan, M. Are we having fun yet? A consideration of workplace fun and engagement. *Employee Relations 31,* 6 (2009), 556-568.
6. Brignull, H., and Rogers, Y. Enticing people to interact with large public displays in public spaces. *Proceedings of INTERACT*. Vol. 3. 2003.
7. Chao, D. Doom as an interface for process management. *Proc. of the SIGCHI conference on Human factors in computing systems*. ACM (2001), 152-157.
8. Dourish, P., and Bly, S. Portholes: Supporting awareness in a distributed work group. *Proc. ACM SIGCHI*, 1992.
9. Fish, R. S., Kraut, R. E., Chalfonte, B. L. The VideoWindow system in informal communication. *Proc. of the 1990 ACM conference on Computer-supported cooperative work,* ACM (1990), 1-11.
10. Fluegge, E. R. *Who put the fun in functional? Fun at work and its effects on job performance*. Doctoral dissertation, University of Florida, 2008.
11. Harrison, S. (ed) *Media space 20+ years of mediated life*. Springer, 2009.
12. Heaphy, E.D., and Dutton, J.E. Positive social interactions and the human body at work: Linking organizations and physiology. *Academy of Management Review 33,* 1 (2008), 137-162.
13. Heimerl, K., Gawalt, B., Chen, K., Parikh, T., Hartmann, B. CommunitySourcing: engaging local crowds to perform expert work via physical kiosks. *Proc. of the 2012 ACM annual conference on Human Factors in Computing Systems,* ACM (2012), 1539-1548.
14. Hofstede, G.H., Hofstede, G.J., Minkov, M. *Cultures and Organizations: Software for the Mind*. McGraw-Hill, USA, 2010.
15. Issacs, E.A., Tang, J.C., Morris, T. Piazza: A Desktop Environment Supporting Impromptu and Planned Interactions. *Proc. of the 1996 ACM Conference on Computer Supported Cooperative Work,* ACM (1996).
16. Karl, K., Peluchette, J. How does workplace fun impact employee perceptions of customer service quality? *Journal of Leadership & Organizational Studies, 13,* 2 (2006), 2-13.
17. Kirkham, R., Mellor, S., Green, D., Lin, J.S., Ladha, K., Ladha, C., Jackson, D., Olivier, P., Wright, P., and Plotz, T. The Break-Time Barometer – An Exploratory System for Workplace Break-time Social Awareness. *Proc. of the 2013 ACM International Joint Conference on Pervasive and Ubiquitous Computing (Ubicomp'13),* ACM (2013).
18. Korhonen, H., Montola, M., Arrasvuori, J. Understanding playful user experience through digital games. *International Conference on Designing Pleasurable Products and Interfaces,* (2009), 274-285.
19. Küller, R., Ballal, S., Laike, T., Mikellides, B., Tonello, G. The impact of light and color on psychological mood: a cross-cultural study of indoor work environments. *Ergonomics 49*, 14 (2006), 1496-1507.
20. Kwallek, N., Lewis, C.M., Lin-Hsiao, J.W.D., Woodson, H. Effects of nine monochromatic office

interior colors on clerical tasks and worker mood. *Color Research & Application 21*, 6 (1996), 448-458.

21. Lamm, E., and Meeks, M.D. Workplace fun: the moderating effects of generational differences. *Employee Relations 31*, 6 (2009), 613-631.

22. Meyer, H. Fun for everyone. *Journal of Business Strategy*, *20*, 2 (1999), 13-17.

23. Monk, A., Hassenzahl, M., Blythe, M., Reed, D. Funology: designing enjoyment. *CHI'02 Extended Abstracts on Human Factors in Computing Systems*. ACM (2002), 924-925.

24. Nesta, Productive Coffee Breaks (PCB), online: http://www.nesta.org.uk/assets/blog_entries/institutionalising_serendipity_via_productive_coffee_breaks

25. Pentland, A. The New Science of Building Great Teams. *Harvard Business Review 90*, 4 (2012).

26. Rogers, Y. Interaction design gone wild: striving for wild theory. *Interactions 18*, 4 (2011), 58-62.

27. Rogers, Y., Hazlewood, W.R., Marshall, P., Dalton, N., and Hertich, S. Ambient Influence: Can Twinkly Lights Lure and Abstract Representations Trigger Behavior Change? *Proc. Ubiquitous Computing (Ubicomp)*, 2010.

28. Väänänen-Vainio-Mattila, K., Palviainen, J. Playful Experiences at Work. *Proc. of the 12th international conference on Human Computer interaction with mobile devices and services (MobileHCI'10)*, 2010.

29. Vyas, D., and Van de Watering, M. Engineering social awareness in work environments. *Proc. Universal Access in Human-Computer Interaction: Ambient Interaction*, (2007), 254-263.

30. Yahoo! telecommuting ban, online: http://articles.latimes.com/2013/feb/26/business/la-fi-yahoo-telecommuting-20130226

31. Zappos employee collisions, online: http://northamerica.mslgroup.com/network/reneeinrealtime/2013/03/13/corporate-luck-and-a-culture-of-collision/

Focused, Aroused, but so Distractible: A Temporal Perspective on Multitasking and Communications

Gloria Mark[1], Shamsi Iqbal[2], Mary Czerwinski[2], Paul Johns[2]

[1]Department of Informatics
University of California, Irvine
Irvine, CA 92697 USA
gmark@uci.edu

[2]Microsoft Research
One Microsoft Way
Redmond, WA 98052 USA
{shamsi,marycz,Paul.Johns}@microsoft.com

ABSTRACT

A common assumption in studies of interruptions is that one is focused in an activity and then distracted by other stimuli. We take the reverse perspective and examine whether one might first be in an attentional state that makes one *susceptible* to communications typically associated with distraction. We explore the confluence of multitasking and workplace communications from three temporal perspectives – prior to an interaction, when tasks and communications are interleaved, and at the end of the day. Using logging techniques and experience sampling, we observed 32 employees *in situ* for five days. We found that certain attentional states lead people to be more susceptible to particular types of interaction. Rote work is followed by more Facebook or face-to-face interaction. Focused and aroused states are followed by more email. The more time in email and face-fo-face interaction, and the more total screen switches, the less productive people feel at the day's end. We present the notion of emotional homeostasis along with new directions for multitasking research.

Author Keywords

Facebook; Email; Face-to-face interaction; multitasking; productivity; interruptions

ACM Classification Keywords

H.5.3 [Information Interfaces and Presentation (e.g., HCI)]: Group and Organization Interfaces; K.4.m [Computers and Society]: Miscellaneous.

General Terms

Human Factors

INTRODUCTION

While studies of multitasking and disruption have long been a focus of the CSCW and CHI communities, the emphasis has mostly been on understanding how disruption occurs from an engaged state, either due to external stimuli such as notifications or visits from colleagues, or self-interruptions. However, there has been little research investigating whether a person's particular mental state at the time could make one more susceptible to being distracted.

Prior work has shown how online interactions, in particular the use of social media and email, can be used to infer what type of attentional state a person is in, such as being focused or bored [22]. However, while such an association was established, the direction of causality was not clear: Does being in a particular attentional state make one more susceptible of switching from their current task to pursue certain online activities? Or rather does switching attention from an ongoing task to certain activities lead one to be in a particular attentional state?

In this paper, we explore the relationship of multitasking and communications in the workplace. As this relationship is a complex phenomenon, we choose to examine this relationship through three temporal perspectives, as multitasking occurs throughout the day: what happens prior to switching activities that may lead to workplace communications, how are communications manifest during task switching, and how do the cumulative effects of multitasking affect people's assessment of work productivity at the end of the day? Understanding the relationship of multitasking and communications is important, as workplace communications comprise a significant portion of the workday [10]. Further, communications such as informal face-to-face interactions or email are noted as a major source of workplace distraction [10, 20, 26]. This study builds on prior work [22], which examined how attentional states in the workplace vary over the day, with digital activities.

We conducted an *in situ* study in a large, U.S. global organization where we tracked online activities of users throughout the workday, and collected self-reports of their engagement and feeling of being challenged using the experience sampling method (ESM) [13]. Leveraging the framework derived in [22], we associated different attentional states with online activities. The results suggest that particular attentional frames of mind lead

CSCW '15, March 14–18, 2015, Vancouver, BC, Canada

ACM 978-1-4503-2922-4/15/03...$15.00
http://dx.doi.org/10.1145/2675133.2675221

people to be susceptible to different types of task switches to varying degrees. We also found a relationship between the amount of task switching and workplace communications. We discuss the impacts of our findings on the current understanding of multitasking and attentional states, and introduce the notion of emotional homeostasis.

RELATED WORK

Multitasking and disruption

Existing work in the domain of multitasking and disruption has primarily focused on how multitasking impacts attention in the workplace, in particular, the effects of an ongoing task being interrupted by another activity. The underlying assumption is that external or internal stimuli cause people to change their focus from their current activity to another task. This may often be characterized as distraction or disruption to the interrupted task, even though the interruption may be beneficial [6, 16, 20]. For example, Czerwinski et al. [4] conducted a diary study to understand how interruptions cause information workers to switch activities in the workplace. Distractions as such can affect focus on ongoing tasks. Mark et al. [20] found that it takes people on average around 23 minutes to resume an interrupted task. Iqbal and Horvitz studied how external interruptions cause information workers to attempt to leave their ongoing task at a stable state and then enter into a 'chain of distraction', comprised of a series of activities including checking email, instant messaging and browsing [10]. O'Conaill and Frohlich [26] showed that 64% of workplace interruptions are beneficial, but the recipient also does not resume work after 40% of the interruptions. More recently, Mark et al. showed in a study of multitasking among Millennials that the amount of multitasking is positively associated with stress, but social media usage coincides with lower stress [24].

Other work has focused on internal interruptions, where a person may interrupt themselves during ongoing work without external stimuli [1, 7, 17]. Jin and Dabbish derived seven categories of self–interruption in the workplace – adjustment, break, routines, waits, inquiry, triggers and collection. However, research has suggested that the organizational environment and individual differences may determine how susceptible one may be to different types of self interruption [7].

Workplace communications such as informal face-to-face (**F2F**) encounters, as well as online interactions with email, comprise a significant chunk of the workday, and have been found to take up over a quarter of people's time in the workplace [10]. Correspondingly, these communications also comprise a significant amount of interruptions. Email and informal F2F interactions alone make up over 40% of interruptions [10]. Facebook (**FB**) users in the workplace on average spend almost nine minutes a day on FB. Typically this involves multiple visits, which also interrupts workflow [23].

While most studies have looked at distraction due to multitasking, no study to our knowledge has attempted to study the phenomenon from the reverse perspective – that people can be in particular frames of mind, or attentional states, that make them more susceptible to being distracted. Linking the attentional state to types of activities can provide a better understanding of the nature of distraction and the subsequent effects on productivity.

Attentional states in the workplace

Attentional states in the workplace are important to study as they appear to be related to mood and possibly job performance. Grandey et al. [11] found that positive affect was related to job satisfaction, whereas negative affect was related to negative emotional reaction, e.g., disappointment, depression and unhappiness. More recently, Mark et al. [23] found that face to face interactions at work were associated with positive mood at the time they occur, whereas more Facebook use was positively correlated with positive mood at the end of the workday. More relevant to our study is that mood has been shown to have an effect on distraction; e.g., Alder and Benbunan-Fich [1] showed that negative feelings trigger more self-interruptions than positive feelings.

We are interested in the relationship of attentional states and people's digital activity. To inform our study we draw from a long legacy of related concepts in psychology, which explain that people's actions are motivated by a desire to achieve a balanced emotional and psychological state. As far back as 460 BC, Hipprocrates proposed that health was related to a harmonious balance of elements in the body. In the early twentieth century, Gestalt theorists were interested in the idea of balance in terms of the perceptual field using the concept of *Pragnanz*: in other words, people try to reduce stress from the stimulus field so as to achieve an internal equilibrium [18]. About the same time, the physiologist Walter Cannon adopted the term homeostasis and expanded its reach to include emotional parameters as well as physical [5]. Kurt Lewin's *field theory* [19] built on the idea of balance and introduced the basic principle of tension reduction as it applies to internal states. According to Lewin, people experience tension when needs are not satisfied, and therefore they strive to attain these needs to reduce tension in order to experience a state of equilibrium. Lewin focuses on a person's momentary needs; any change of state is dependent on the situation and one's particular psychological state at the time. Other related theories that grew out of Lewin's field theory and that similarly discuss notions of achieving a balanced mental state include Heider's *balance theory* [12], which describes that people are motivated to maintain attitudes that are consistent towards other people and objects over time, so as to achieve a psychological balance. *Cognitive dissonance theory* is also related, where discrepancies between attitudes and behaviors introduce dissonance [9]. If a discrepancy exists, a person will aim to reduce the dissonance.

More recently, internal balance, or homeostasis, has been approached in terms of physiological responses. As we are concerned with the reduction of tension, or stress, we are interested in how people maintain *emotional homeostasis* while multitasking. Emotion is typically defined as a mental state that arises spontaneously rather than through conscious effort and is often accompanied by physiological changes [25]. Homeostasis is defined as the ability or tendency of an organism or cell to maintain internal equilibrium by adjusting its physiological processes [25]. Responses to threats of homeostasis from stressors occur by facilitating neural pathways which mediate psychological functions such as arousal, cognition and attention [5]. Stress can thus create an imbalance and influence arousal and attentional state. People are constantly challenged by stressors in the environment and have developed adaptive responses in order to preserve homeostasis. Therefore, emotional homeostasis is a neural and physiological process that maintains the equilibrium of mental states that would enable a human to live and perform at normal levels [4]. It may be that, as workers get more stressed, bored or frustrated in the workplace, they seek out homeostasis by moving to another activity that brings them back to a balanced state.

Thus, these various theories share the basic commonality that people act in a way to seek out and experience a balanced internal state. In the broader context of multitasking in a digital environment, people may switch to activities that will lead them to experience more of a state of equilibrium if the current activity disrupts that balance. Following Lewin [19], Heider [12], and Festinger [9], people may choose actions that will lead them towards reducing inner tension [21]. This is a novel notion in the multitasking literature that we will explore in this work.

INTERACTIONS AND MULTITASKING

As a starting point to examine more broadly how social interactions influence multitasking behavior in the workplace, we investigated the confluence of workplace communications and multitasking in terms of three temporal perspectives: prior to the interaction, throughout the day (how communication acts interleave with multitasking), and the cumulative effects at the end of the day (the effect on assessing productivity). As a first step we chose to focus on three prevalent types of communications that would cover online and offline interactions and work and social purposes. We therefore selected three types of communications common in the workplace: F2F, email, and FB. Our reasoning for

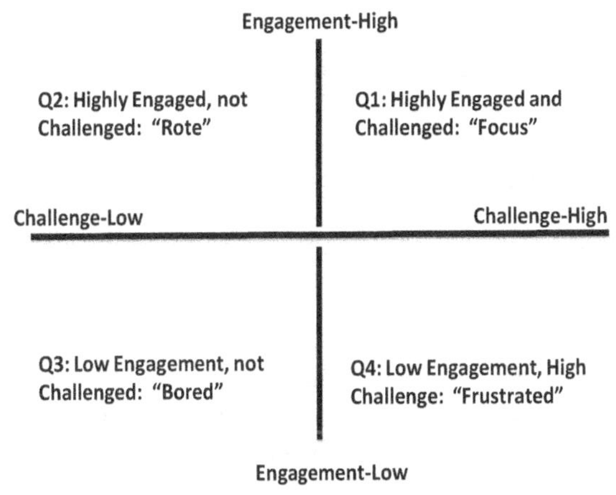

Figure 1. A theoretical framework of different attentional states [22]

selecting these three types of communications is as follows:

F2F: informal F2F interaction is common in the workplace and is a significant source of distractions [8, 10]. F2F encounters are offline and are either work-related or social.

Email: online email communication is also a significant source of distractions, both due to self-interruption as well as external interruption, e.g., due to notifications [10, 16]. Email in the workplace is likely to be mostly work related, although obviously some personal email is also carried out.

FB: Facebook is also online communication and is likely a distraction mostly due to self-interruption. As [23] found, it can function as a quick break when people are engaged in work. FB in the workplace is generally social, though in rare cases it may be work-related.

Thus, we focus on contrasting workplace communications--differing in their online or offline nature and in being social or work-related, to understand the role they play in multitasking. While there are a number of other workplace interactions that also occur with other media (e.g., IM, LinkedIn, phone), as a starting point, we examine these three types (FB, F2F and email).

We emphasize that these types of communications could be work-related or social in nature, but our data does not allow us to make this differentiation. Our approach is to examine how engaging in these types of communications interrupts the *flow* of activity, regardless of whether they are social or work related. Similarly, when we consider a task that involves digital activity, such as Internet switching, we acknowledge that this may also be work-related or not. Our focus is on interruptions of the flow of activity irrespective of whether the communication type or target activity is work-related or not. We next describe the three temporal perspectives that we focus on in our analysis.

Prior to the interaction: attentional states

Studies of multitasking and interruptions assume that people are highly engaged in their work and then the distraction pulls them away from their engagement. In this paper we take the opposite perspective: we examine whether people may first experience a particular attentional state that makes them *susceptible* to distractions such as checking FB, email, or chatting with a colleague. For example, a person may become bored in their current task, which makes them turn to FB as a break. Recent work suggests that FB can be beneficial as a quick break, leading to "grazing behavior", a low cost interaction from a cognitive resources perspective, potentially fun, and which enables the user to maintain some control over the duration of the interaction [23].

To examine this notion of attentional states, we draw on the theoretical framework used by [22], shown in Figure 1. This theoretical framework is based on considering attentional states in terms of two dimensions: engagement and challenge. *Engagement* is important to consider in the workplace as it is a mental state of absorption in an activity [28]. The second dimension that we consider is *challenge* in work. Challenge refers to the amount of mental effort that one exerts to perform a task and has been associated with motivation in work [14].

Figure 1 describes four attentional states, shown in each of the four quadrants. To be focused in work, engagement in an activity is not sufficient. A person can be engaged in an activity but it may not be challenging; a person can be involved in "mindless" activities such as filling out forms. Therefore, it is important to consider how challenging an activity is along with how engaged one is in the activity. Quadrant 1 indicates that when one is highly challenged and highly engaged then the attentional state can be characterized as 'Focus'. Quadrant 2 indicates that an attentional state where one is highly engaged but not challenged describes mechanical type of thinking. This is referred to as 'Rote' to indicate attentional states associated with rote type of work. Quadrant 3 shows that when one is not at all engaged and not challenged, then it indicates a state of being 'Bored'. Quadrant 4 indicates that when one is challenged but not engaged, then one is frustrated. An example of a frustrated attentional state could be when a software developer is working on solving a difficult bug in a program. We stress that these labels are merely referents; what is more important is to consider the underlying dimensions of being challenged and engaged.

Therefore, we apply the framework in Figure 1 to examine a person's attentional state prior to an interaction. Our goal is to examine whether we can find relationships of particular prior attentional states with subsequent initiations of workplace communications. If so, this may suggest that a person may already be in a particular attentional state that makes them susceptible to certain types of interactions (or distractions).

During multitasking: how communications interleave with other activities

A second temporal perspective that we examine concerns how workplace communications interleave with other multitasking behavior. This analysis could shed light on the role workplace communications play in switching between different tasks. Certain communications could serve different functions in multitasking. They can be a break when a person is highly engaged in work, as [23] found with FB. They can also serve to provide information needed to perform tasks, such as when using email or F2F for task completion. They can also be habitual, as when one surfs the Internet, and then one becomes accustomed to also checking FB or email, starting off a chain of distraction [16].

The number of projects a person has can also affect how communications interleave with multitasking. We expect that the more projects one has, the more task switching occurs, which in turn could present more opportunities for initiating further communications. For example, if one switches projects, they may turn to email to retrieve newly pertinent information or they may seek a colleague to consult with for updates. We therefore look at task switches and project count in conjunction with our three main interaction types (FB, F2F and email).

Another common practice of activity switching could be due to switching websites on the Internet. When one switches between projects, email may play a more important role since it is generally work-related; one may need to use email to seek information for projects. On the other hand, when one uses the Internet – even if it is still related to the ongoing task- one may check FB, since it is a relatively low cost switch within the same application. However, if FB is a break from work as [23] suggests, then FB use might be prevalent while one is working and switching between projects. This relates to Lewin's idea of tension reduction. On the other hand, one might also choose to have F2F interaction while switching Internet sites if one is bored.

End of day: cumulative assessment of productivity

Our third temporal perspective focuses on how people feel at the end of the day. A longstanding question about multitasking is the effect that switching tasks has on productivity (cf [2]). It is unclear what effect the relationship of workplace communications and multitasking might have on productivity. We are particularly interested in the effects of FB, F2F and email interactions throughout the day on the cumulative assessment of productivity at the end of the day. The underlying reasoning behind this exploration is that these interactions could have both positive and negative effects on productivity. For example, while FB is generally considered a distraction from ongoing activities, it could also serve as a break during a productive session, and therefore be considered with feeling engaged [23]. Likewise, F2F and email could be both work related and social.

Research foci

In sum, we study three types of workplace communications: FB, email, and F2F, from three different temporal perspectives:

- Attentional states prior to the communication
- Throughout the day: how communications interleave with multitasking
- End of the day: cumulative assessment on feelings of productivity

METHODOLOGY

We conducted an *in situ* study in the fall of 2012 at a large U.S. corporation. We used a mixed-methods approach where we logged people's digital activity along with using experience sampling (ESM). The logging allowed us to track a wide range of digital activities with detailed precision. As stated earlier, ESM was used to collect user perceptions of engagement and challenge, as well as other self-report measures at frequent intervals throughout the day. We also deployed surveys for other subjective and demographic measures. Further details of these, and other, measures not reported in this paper can be found in [23].

Participants were recruited through advertising, convenience sampling and other participants' recommendations. Thirty-two people (17 females, 15 males) participated. Participants included researchers, managers, administrators, an engineer, a department director, a designer, and a consultant.

Methodology. Each participant's digital activity was logged for a period of five work days, typically Monday through Friday. When participants traveled or missed a day, they made up the missed day the following week (in most cases). The computer logging software and ESM software were installed on participants' computers the Friday before the study began. Participants were assured of anonymity in their data and it was protected via encryption.

We logged online interactions with custom-built software that captured all activity in the Windows 7.0 Operating System. This included beginning and end times for the lifespan of every window, and the beginning and end times for each instance of every foreground window. Logging is done only when a window is moved to the foreground, i.e., if an email client is open, its use will not be logged unless it becomes active. Changing tabs in a browser was counted as separate switches. Mouse and keyboard activity were captured, as was computer sleep mode, so that we could ignore periods of time when a window was open but was not being used in the foreground. Capturing what email was being read or any other application interaction was not collected due to privacy and technical limitations. All participants used Outlook for email.

Email and FB interaction were measured through the logging program. F2F interaction was measured through the use of SenseCams [15], a lightweight wearable camera worn around the neck. The camera takes pictures approximately every 15 seconds. The images were then processed with face detection software, a publicly available application (http://research.microsoft.com/en-us/projects/facesdk/). The software does not recognize faces; it only provides information about whether a person was present or not in the photo. The counts in our F2F variable therefore do not measure *distinct* interactions, just the amount of interaction.

We used ESM, in the form of a small pop-up window that appeared on the computer screen to capture the participants' perspective *in situ*. Experience sampling has been shown to have both internal and external validity [13]. Experience sampling has been used extensively in studies to capture the experience of flow, an immersive state in an activity [13]. We used a hybrid interval-contingent and event-contingent sampling approach [13]. The sampling was done: 1) whenever a user left email after uninterrupted active use in that application for at least three consecutive minutes or when in Facebook after a full minute, and 2) whenever a user logged into Windows or unlocked the screen saver (event-contingent). If 15 minutes passed without a sampling, then a probe was triggered (interval-contingent).

Participants were instructed to go about their usual workday activities and were told to answer the ESM probes when the probe windows popped up on their computer screens. We emphasized that they should answer the probe questions as accurately as possible but they could cancel the probe window at any time. Subjects were given the following verbal and written instructions:

"Sometimes the rating scale will pop up and may annoy you, especially if you were in the middle of doing something. If you feel annoyed, do not rate your mood based on the annoyance of the pop-up window. Instead, rate your experience based on the task or interaction you were doing at the time of the pop-up window. If you feel that you cannot rate your mood fairly due to the annoyance of the pop-up window, then hit 'cancel' and the window will disappear."

We used rating scales used in other ESM approaches [21] to measure the following: for Engagement, participants were asked 'In the task/interaction you were just doing: How Engaged Were You?' using a 6-point Likert scale (0=Not at All; 5=Extremely). To measure Challenge, participants were asked the same question as above, but instead: "How Challenged Were You?' using the same Likert scale: (0=Not at All; 5=Extremely). We also measured Valence (positive and negative affect, not

Measure	Description
FB interaction	FB seconds 1, 5, 10 min. prior and after the probe FB counts of unique visits
Email interaction:	Email seconds 1, 5, 10 min. prior and after the probe Email counts of unique visits
F2F interaction:	SenseCam counts 1, 5, 10 min. prior and after the probe
Application Switching	Number of switches between applications (e.g. Word, Excel)
Internet switching	Number of switches on the Internet
Attentional states	Counts of ESM responses that fell into each of the quadrants: Focus, Rote, Bored, Frustrated states.
Arousal	low (-200) to high (+200)
Productivity self-report	daily end of day survey: 7-point Likert scale
Project count	general survey
Positive/negative mood	PANAS mood scale, from daily beginning and end of day survey) [29]

Table 1. Summary of measures used.

reported here) and Arousal, (on a vertical axis that crossed a horizontal Valence axis) using a range of -200 (low arousal) to +200 (high arousal), based on the Circumplex model for Valence/Arousal (for a review, including its validity, see [27]). Subjects were asked to click with their cursor on that point on the scale that best expressed their feeling "right now." The timestamp when participants submitted the probe was recorded. All data from ESM was normalized within participants.

Measures
Table 1 summarizes the measures from our collected data reported in this paper.

RESULTS
Our dataset consisted of 1,509 hours of participant observation (32 participants, five days each). Our experience sampling yielded 2,809 probes, averaging 87.8 responses per participant, and averaging 17.56 probe responses per person per day. Our SenseCam photo capture yielded 204,922 photos. The ESM results were normalized and we used the top and bottom third of responses for the engagement and challenge dimensions (i.e. eliminating the middle responses). Since only seven responses occurred in the 'Frustrated' category, we do not consider this category for the rest of the analysis. The responses fell in the quadrants shown in Fig. 1 as follows: Focused (45.4%), Rote (18.9%), Bored (35.6%).

	FB	Email	F2F
Number visits/day (counts)	20.98 (5.04)	74.05 (10.54)	--
Duration per day (sec.)	583.48 (206.75) (9 min. 43 sec.)	2071.16 (294.46) (34 min. 31 sec.)	86.88 (10.65)[1]
Duration per visit (sec)	17.75 (2.81)	32.06 (2.80)	N/A

Table 2. Average daily values of number of visits, duration, duration per visit, for FB, Email use. For F2F, only counts are available. Mean (SE).

We begin with an overview of our results. Table 2 shows the average daily duration, frequency, and duration per visit for Facebook, email, and F2F interactions. Because the SenseCam does not compute duration, we can only provide counts of faces detected in photos as a proxy for amount of F2F interaction. The average duration per visit for FB is about 18 seconds and for email is about 32 seconds. Participants averaged about 87 SenseCam counts per day (note that SenseCam counts are a proxy for amount of F2F interaction).

We discussed earlier that checking FB and Email might be a frequent and habitual behavior. We found that participants visited FB on average 21 times per day, with a maximum of 264 visits per day. If we examine only those days in our data where people visited FB at least once a day (i.e., of those who used FB on any day), the average visits per day climbs to 38 unique visits per day (SE=4.92). Participants visited email much more daily: averaging 74 times per day, with a maximum of checking 373 times per day.

Based on the work roles participants reported in a survey, work roles were coded into three categories: concerning Administration and technical support (5 people), Research (19 people), and Management (8 people). For Work Role, we found that for average daily duration of FB use, Researchers spend significantly less time on FB (M=309.59, SE=76.06) than Managers (M=952.15, SE=359.62) or Admins (M=669.15, SE=159.14): $F(2, 161)=3.53$, $p<.03$. There is no significant effect of Work Role on Email duration. With F2F, Admins average significantly more F2F time per day (M=101.58, SE=16.37), followed by Managers (M=98.46, SE=13.04), and then Researchers (M=60.47, SE=8.57), $F(2, 161)=4.34$, $p<.02$.

The average Project count per person is 6.7 (sd=3.7), with a range of 1-18. There is a significant difference of Project Count according to Work Role: $F(2,31)=3.68$, $p<.04$. Researchers (M=5.3, SE=.22) have fewer projects on average than Admins (M=8.7, SE=.93) or Managers (M=8.6, SE=.67). The average number of times that a person switches applications daily is 566.0 (SE=41.89), ranging from 183 to 1035 times per day.

Overall, the usage data suggests that both FB and email usage are characterized by short bursts: checking many times per day with a short duration for each visit. Amount of F2F and FB interaction, as well as number of projects, differ by work role.

Attentional state: susceptibility to workplace communications

In our first research question, we are interested to see whether a person's current attentional state is associated with their subsequent workplace communications. Is it possible that a particular attentional state, such as feeling bored or feeling that work is rote, is a precursor to using FB, checking email or having a F2F interaction? Based on the ESM probe data, we can determine what type of attentional state the participant reported experiencing (using the framework in Fig. 1). Our probes asked people to rate how they felt "right now". Since we have timestamps of the logged computer data, we can therefore examine what activity people did *after* reporting their attentional state.

However, it is possible that if the person is already performing a certain workplace communication before the ESM probe, they could continue that communication after the probe. In that case it would be difficult to determine whether it was the attentional state that led to the communication or if it was the prior communication that was simply being continued. For example, if FB causes people to be bored, then a probe after FB use would show a bored state. If a person then subsequently continued FB use, we would not be able to determine if it was the bored state that led to FB use or if rather prior FB use continued after the probe. Therefore, we *controlled* for the same type of communication before the probe as the target communication we are investigating after the probe. By controlling for the same type of communication prior to the attentional state, we can control that this prior behavior is not influencing the analysis of the association of attentional state and behavior *after* the probe. It is important to keep in mind that there could be any number of activities that could influence a person's attentional state.

We used a GLM to examine attentional states prior to the three workplace communication types that we are investigating: FB use, email use, and F2F interaction, to see if there are significant patterns of prior attentional states. As we do not have any a priori knowledge of what window of time to test, we selected the timeframe of a 10-minute window of time prior to, and after, the probe. We also compared 5 and 1-minute windows, with similar results, but as the 10-minute window showed the strongest effects, we will report this analysis throughout the rest of the paper.

Attn'l State	FB (sec.)	Email (sec.)	F2F (SenseCam counts)
Focus	13.26 (3.0)*	86.56 (5.6)*	1.32 (.18)*
Rote	28.62(4.6)*	68.03 (8.7)	1.84 (.28)*
Bored	18.95 (3.5)	64.77 (6.6)*	1.73 (.21)
	$F(2,1070)=3.92$, $p<.02$, $R^2=.13$	$F(2,1070)=3.64$, $p<.03$, $R^2=.20$.	$F(2,1070)=4.30$, $p<.02$, $R^2=.27$

Table 3. Mean (SE) of FB, Email, and F2F durations given each prior attentional state of Focus, Rote, Bored. *Indicates differences based on Bonferroni post hoc test, p<.05. Adjusted R^2 is reported.

Facebook

We found significant differences in FB use duration that followed the different attentional states (see Table 3). FB duration following a Rote state was longer than FB duration following a Bored state, followed by a Focused state; a Bonferroni post-hoc test showed a significant difference between Rote and Focused.

We next checked whether the same results also apply for the number of unique FB visits. In other words, is there a particular attentional state associated with FB checking behavior, as well as FB duration of use? A GLM using the number of FB visits in the next 10 minutes, controlling for FB visits in the prior 10 minutes, shows significant results consistent with the FB duration results in Table 3.

Email

We also found significant differences in email duration that followed the different attentional states (Table 3). Participants were more likely to use email longer after being in a Focused state, followed by a Rote state, followed by a Bored state; a Bonferroni post-hoc test showed a significant difference between Focused and Bored states. Participants are therefore more likely to spend more time in email when they are feeling focused, compared to when they are feeling bored, or doing rote work.

Checking the number of unique Email visits in the next 10 min. controlling for number of Email visits in the prior 10 min. shows no significant effect of Attentional state.

Face-to-face

For F2F, we used the SenseCam photo counts as a proxy for amount of F2F interaction. We used a log transform for F2F to improve normality. We found significant differences in F2F interaction counts following different attentional states (Table 3). Participants were more likely to have more F2F interactions after being in a Rote state, followed by a Bored state, followed by a Focused state. A Bonferroni post-hoc test showed a significant difference between Rote and Focused states. Thus, people are most likely to engage in more F2F interactions when feeling Rote (engaged but not challenged) in their current activity and least when they feel focused (engaged and challenged).

Arousal and workplace communications

The result with email duration was contrary to that of FB and F2F interactions, with the pattern showing that one was first focused before doing email. We decided to explore this more closely. A focused state of attention involves the dimensions of high engagement and high challenge. An underlying mechanism that we expect would correlate with engagement and challenge is arousal. In the ESM probes, we had also asked people to rate their level of arousal. Indeed, we found that Arousal is highly correlated with the dimensions of feeling challenged (r=.42, p<.0001) and engaged (r=.57, p<.0001).

We next looked at whether one's level of arousal is associated with email use. A GLM analysis predicting Email duration in the next 10 minutes, with Arousal and Attentional state as independent variables, controlling for Email duration in the prior 10 minutes, showed a significant effect of Arousal: F(1,1070)=5.30, p<.02, R^2=.20. If Arousal is included in the model then there is a significant Arousal x Attentional State interaction: F(1,1070)=2.92, p<.05, and no main effect of Attentional State. The variance inflation factors (measuring multicollinearity) of Arousal and Attentional state were each 1.4, which is an acceptable level as it is below 5. Thus, Arousal is predictive of subsequent email use, and Arousal and Attentional state (i.e. Focus) interact to predict a higher level of email use.

Since FB and F2F were associated with following Rote work, we did not expect Arousal to be a significant predictor for these social communications (since Rote work should not involve high effort). Indeed, when Arousal was added to the GLM model previously mentioned, and with Attentional state predicting FB use in the next 10 minutes, controlling for FB use in the prior 10 minutes, it shows no significant effect of Arousal. Examining F2F amount in the next 10 minutes, a GLM also showed no significant effect of Arousal, controlling for F2F amount in the prior 10 minutes.

Thus, we had hypothesized that particular attentional states might be associated with particular communication forms that follow. Our results show that when people are in a rote state (feeling engaged but not challenged), they subsequently spend more time on FB and check FB more, as well as having more F2F interaction. However, when people are in a focused state, they are more likely to then spend a longer time on email. Email use is also associated with arousal. Thus, when people are aroused and in a focused state, they then spend a longer period of time doing email.

Throughout the day: Multitasking and communication

We next looked at a second temporal perspective with respect to multitasking: how workplace communications (FB, F2F and email) interleave with multitasking throughout the day. We used the variable of frequency of switching applications and websites as a proxy for multitasking. We also considered project count as we expect that the more projects one is involved in, the more opportunity one has to switch between projects. Activity switches were in turn separated into two categories: application switches and Internet switching. We reasoned that focusing on application switches (App Switches) might involve more different operations than Internet switching, and thus would involve more cognitive shifts, e.g., from a Word document (writing) to Excel

Application Switching						
		App	PC	WR	PC x WR	Adj. R^2
FB (sec.)	F	7.71	17.43	2.73	5.15	0.22
	df	1,161	1,161	2,161	2,161	
	p	0.006	0.0001	0.07	0.007	
Email (sec.)	F	4.36	1.98	2.87	3.99	0.09
	df	1,161	1,161	2,161	2,161	
	p	0.04	0.16	0.06	0.02	
F2F (counts)	F	2.51	1.97	1.9	1.95	N/A
	df	1,161	1,161	2,161	2,161	
	p	0.12	0.16	0.15	0.15	

Table 4. Model showing how average daily application switches (App), project count (PC) and work role (WR) affect average daily duration of FB, Email, and F2F counts.

Internet Switching						
		Int	PC	WR	PC x WR	Adj. R^2
FB (sec.)	F	12.85	19.06	2.51	4.77	0.24
	df	1,161	1,161	2,161	2,161	
	p	0.0001	0.0001	0.08	0.01	
Email (sec)	F	5.71	2.25	3.72	5.99	0.10
	df	1,161	1,161	2,161	2,161	
	p	0.02	0.14	0.03	0.003	
F2F (counts)	F	9.54	2.33	1.88	1.56	0.10
	df	1,161	1,161	2,161	2,161	
	p	0.002	0.13	0.16	0.21	

Table 5. Model showing how average internet switches (Int), project count (PC) and work role (WR) affect average daily duration of FB, Email, and F2F counts.

Application Switching						
		App	PC	WR	PC x WR	Adj. R^2
FB	F	25.1	22.53	0.45	1.06	0.24
	df	1,161	1,161	2,161	2, 161	
	p	0.0001	0.0001	0.64	0.35	
Email	F	56.23	7.21	29.34	20.41	0.49
	df	1,161	1,161	2,161	2, 161	
	p	0.0001	0.008	.0001	.0001	

Table 6. Model showing how average daily application switches (App), project count (PC) and work role (WR) affect frequency of FB and Email visits.

(calculations), to the Internet (search and reading) to email (reading/writing). We also examined Internet switching, as this could reveal insight into whether checking email or FB might be frequent or habitual: when one switches Internet sites one might also check email and FB out of habit. We included Work Role in the model since we found significant differences in FB and F2F behavior with work role.

For all analyses we ran a separate GLM for FB, Email, and F2F, with duration of each communication type as a dependent variable, and with Project Count, App Switches (or Internet switches), and Work Role as independent variables. Since Project Count differs by Work Role, we included an interaction term of Project Count x Work Role.

Duration of FB, Email, F2F.

Table 4 shows a significant relationship of App Switches to both FB and email duration. Thus, the more application switches one does, the longer time one spends in FB and email. There is also a significant Project Count by Work Role interaction for FB and also for email duration. The role of Researcher results in having the fewest projects and spending the least amount of time in FB as well as email, compared to other work roles. F2F showed no significant effects, in contrast to email and FB which did show significant effects.

Table 5 shows a significant relationship of frequency of Internet switching to the duration of time spent in email, FB, and F2F interaction. Thus, the more frequently one switches Internet sites, the more time one spends in the three communication types. A significant Work role by Project count interaction for FB indicates that as Project count increases, FB duration decreases more for Researchers than for Admins and Managers. The significant Work role by Project count interaction for email means that as the number of projects increase, email duration decreases for Admins, whereas for Researchers, email duration increases.

Internet Switching						
		Int	PC	WR	PCx WR	Adj. R^2
FB	F	22.88	24.1	0.05	0.16	0.23
	df	1,161	1,161	2,161	2, 161	
	p	0.0001	0.0001	0.95	0.86	
Email	F	60.32	5.81	38.28	30.39	0.50
	df	1,161	1,161	2,161	2, 161	
	p	0.0001	0.02	.0001	.0001	

Table 7. Model showing how average daily Internet switches (Int), project count (PC) and work role (WR) affect frequency of FB and Email visits.

Frequency of FB, Email

We next ran a separate GLM for FB and Email with number of unique visits of each communication type as a dependent variable, and with Project Count, App Switches (or Internet Switches), and Work Role as independent variables. Tables 6 and 7 show the relationship of FB and email communications with multitasking, from the perspective of number of visits (note that F2F results, as measured by SenseCam counts, are not included here, but rather are shown in Tables 4 and 5).

Table 6 shows that both average daily frequency of visiting FB and email are strongly associated with frequency of App Switches. Also, the more projects one works on, the higher the frequency of checking FB and email. A Project Count x Work role interaction exists only for email: As the number of projects increase, Admins check email more frequently than Researchers or Managers.

Table 7 shows that Internet switching is highly associated with frequency of visiting FB and email. We interpret the significant project count effect for both FB and email as: the more projects one has, the more switching between projects one does, and the more opportunities there are for checking FB and email while switching. Note that both models for email have a very high value of R^2 (.49 and .50) which indicates that project switching and Internet site switching contribute quite a bit to explaining email checking behavior.

In summary, both application switching and Internet site switching are associated with higher FB and email use, in terms of both duration and unique visits. Internet site switching, but not application switching, is associated with more F2F interaction.

End of day: Productivity and interaction.

Finally, we looked at the consequence of interactions and multitasking on the end of the day self-reported productivity. Here we addressed whether the amount of

Model	Parameter estimate	Wald statistic (df=1)	P
Email duration	-.007	4.83	.03
Total switches	-.00001	4.56	.03
F2F	-.009	3.27	.07
Email duration x F2F	.004	4.30	.04
FB duration x F2F	.001	6.18	.01

Table 8. Model of end-of-day self-report of productivity: chi-square (6)=25.61, p<.0001.

different types of workplace communications, along with multitasking, were related to assessing productivity. Remember that productivity self-reports were taken at the end of each day. First, a GLM showed no significant effect of Work Role. Next we looked at mood and productivity. Based on the PANAS scale [29] (see Table 1), people who reported being more productive also scored higher on their rating of positive mood at the end of the day r=.30, p<.001, and scored lower on their rating of negative mood at the end of the day: r=-.19, p<.04. In terms of mood change over the course of the day, (PANAS end of day - PANAS beginning of day), there was a significant correlation of feeling productive and developing a more positive mood over the course of the day: r=.28, p<.004. Thus, the more productive people felt their day was, the higher was their positive affect.

As productivity was measured as a Likert-scale item, we conducted an ordinal regression with productivity as the dependent measure. We created a variable of Total Switches (i.e., all computer screen switches) by combining App switches and Internet switches. We tested a model using the independent variables of FB duration, Email duration, F2F counts, and Total switches, and included all 2-way interactions. We included Project Count as a control variable.

Table 8 shows the significant variables that predict end-of-day feeling of productivity, in the overall model. The Cox and Snell pseudo R^2 is .18. We note that the parameter estimates are not strong. There was a significant negative relationship of email duration and self-reported productivity: the more time spent on email throughout the day, the *less productive* one feels. There was also a negative relation of Total switches and productivity: the more computer screen switches one does over the course of the day, the *lower* the reported productivity. F2F also shows a strong trend of a negative relationship: the more F2F interaction one has over the day, the *less* productive one feels.

We interpret the significant interaction of email and F2F as follows. Though email duration and F2F duration alone each had a negative relation with productivity, perhaps F2F interaction that is work related is a catalyst to sending emails that are work related, leading one to feel more productive. F2F and FB also interact in a positive relationship with productivity. One interpretation is that though F2F alone is negatively related to productivity,

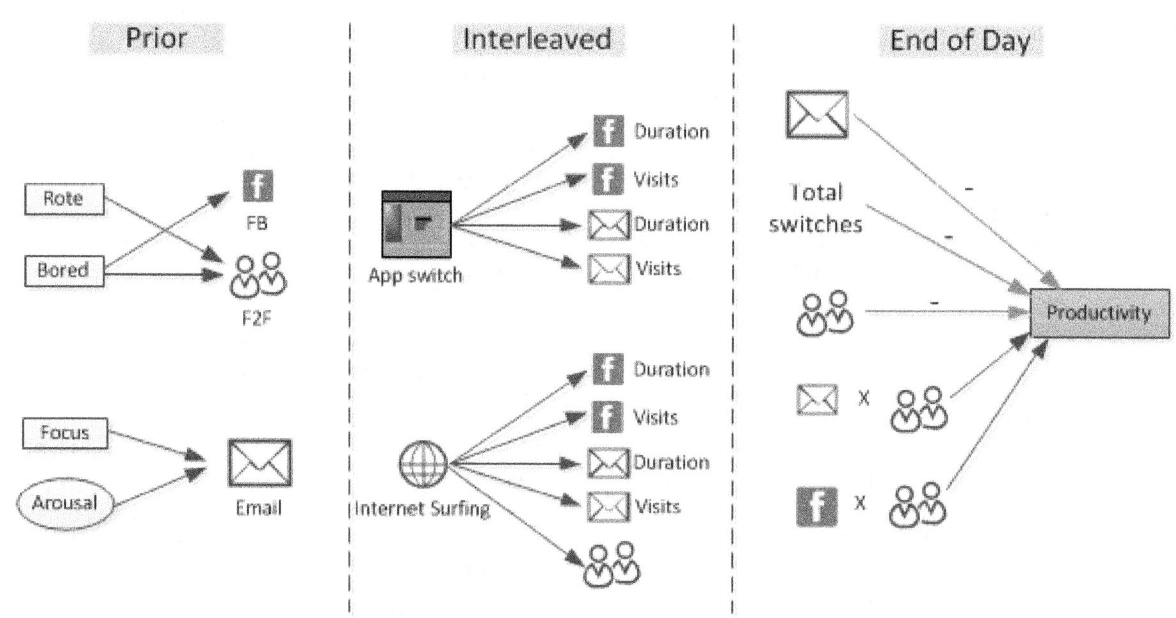

Figure 2. A visual summary of the results of the three temporal perspectives. To simplify, only the results of the interactions are presented. Red arrows indicate a negative association.

when people are engaged in work (along with higher FB use [23]), then perhaps F2F interactions that are work related lead to a higher feeling of productivity. Project count as a control variable showed no significant effect; the results hold irrespective of the number of projects one works on.

Summary of interaction and multitasking

Based on our results, we present a visual summary of our results (Fig. 2) showing the relationship of communication and multitasking according to the three temporal perspectives we examined.

DISCUSSION

In this paper we examined the relationship of multitasking and communication from three different temporal perspectives. First, we examined the attentional state of people *prior* to a communication event. In HCI, it is generally assumed that people work on tasks, are engaged in them, and are then distracted by stimuli, such as email or other people. Our results suggest a reverse perspective for thinking about distractions. People may first be in a certain attentional state which makes them *susceptible* to distractions. We found that when people were in a rote state (high engagement, low challenge), they were more likely to do FB and have more F2F interaction. When they were focused and aroused, they were likely to do more email. We still found these relationships after controlling for the same communication behavior prior to the probe. In other words, our results suggest that distractions could be explained by the current state of one's mind, i.e., one first experiences a particular attentional state and then one is distracted by stimuli.

Our results in particular suggest that certain attentional states are associated with different workplace communication behaviors. FB interactions differ from email interactions in that they are predominantly social and casual. Therefore, when people are not challenged, it makes sense that they might be susceptible to the distractions of FB, which involve low effort. Email, on the other hand, generally involves work, or as Barley [3] claims, email can be regarded as a *symbol* of work (and stress). It also makes sense then that when people are focused and aroused, as we found, they are then in a state where they are prepared to do email. We would like to mention that we cannot claim causality; it is possible that there are other underlying factors that could be associated with activity and subsequent communication behaviors.

When people are in a rote state, as with FB use, they seem to be more susceptible to F2F interactions. F2F interactions can certainly involve either work or social communications. As we did not record the content of F2F meetings, we cannot distinguish the proportions of communications of our participants that involved work. However, the fact that a rote state was likely to precede F2F interactions, and the fact that arousal showed no significant predictive effect (unlike email), suggests that most F2F communications of our sample may have been social.

Our second temporal perspective examined how workplace communications interleaved with multitasking throughout the day. It is also possible that the practice of Application and Internet site switching can also make people susceptible to distractions (in our case, concerning communications). Here we found that our three communication types were involved in multitasking in slightly different ways. Though imperfect, we used the measure of application switching as a proxy for task switching. The fact that both email and FB are associated with application switching suggests that in the course of switching between different applications, people take time to check their email or FB. We expect that when one is engaged in work-related projects, then they might seek email for information or as [23] found, use FB as a work break. It is possible then that application switching also makes people *susceptible* to checking email, or FB; if one is switching anyway, why not check to see if there are recent emails related to work or FB postings that can offer a break?

We offer possible explanations for the relationship of App switching and Internet switching and communications. First, App switching and Internet switching can introduce opportunities for people to self-interrupt. As people are exposed to a variety of different types of information while switching applications, it is likely that some information could trigger reminders that involve communications with people. A second explanation is that this behavior is habitual. People may simply check email, FB and have F2F interaction because they have developed patterns of such behavior over time. Habits can be triggered by context and become deeply ingrained [30]. A third explanation concerns emotional homeostasis which we shall discuss shortly.

Project count was associated with FB use, and with frequency of checking email. We would expect that the more projects one works on, the more social connections and dependencies one would have in the organization, and this could influence email interaction. Also, following the finding that FB might be a break from work [23], the more projects one has, the more one might turn to FB as a short relief from work. The fact that email duration was associated only with application switches and not project count, suggests that time spent on email is compelling irrespective of how many projects one has.

Though our results on productivity are not strong, they do suggest that computer screen switching, and amount of time spent on email and in F2F interaction is detrimental to feeling productive at the end of the day. Opportunity cost could be an explanation: the more time spent in workplace communications, the less time is available for doing other types of work. Also, switching tasks involves a cognitive cost of having to reorient [16] which could result in a lower feeling of productivity. One might feel that they have wasted their time on email or F2F interaction, as people have a limited amount of time during the day. The more time one spends in one activity (e.g., email), the more time it takes away from another activity perhaps more directly associated with feeling productive (e.g., writing a research paper). This result suggests that the time spent on workplace communications via email, and F2F may not be considered by people to necessarily be productive, especially if the time spent on these communications was for social reasons. Such interactions, though, may well be associated with other productivity measures, and this calls for further research.

Though our measure of productivity involved subjective reports, this productivity measure actually can capture many other underlying attitudes. We found, for example, that productivity is highly correlated with positive affect. Thus, subjective productivity could be a barometer for happiness in the workplace.

Multitasking and homeostasis

Our results thus suggest that one's attentional state may make one susceptible to certain kinds of distractions. Further, application switching and Internet site switching are also associated with a higher use of some communication media. Our results lead us to return to our earlier discussion about emotional homeostasis. We put forth the following notion: people might move toward online or offline communications that lead them to be in a state where they are more balanced psychologically [4] [9, 12, 19]. Perhaps people prefer to continue those particular behaviors that will maintain their current psychological state. For example, as we found, if people are switching Internet sites (in a rote state, engaged but not challenged) then perhaps they seek to continue communication behavior in a similar type of attentional state (a casual F2F interaction or FB use). Similarly, it may be possible that, if people are already in a state of focus, they may want to continue doing work that requires a degree of focus. By continuing to experience this same attentional state, they are trying to attain a psychological balance, or emotional homeostasis. As claimed in prior work [9, 12, 19], people desire to reduce tension and maintain equilibrium.

However, switching activities could have varying consequences. In some cases, people may switch tasks and communication in order to try to attain emotional homeostasis. On the other hand, there may also be a cognitive cost to switching, as it may increase tension. The cognitive cost may not only be in switching contexts but also in switching attentional states. These different potential outcomes lead us to distinguish between external and internal interruptions and activity switching. External switches are triggered by sources outside of a person, e.g., another person, an email notification, or a telephone ringing. Internal switches are triggered by oneself, i.e., a person chooses to switch their activity due to their current needs and motivations. Some research suggests that external interruptions are associated with stress [21]. We propose that it is the internal switches due to one's own volition that could be explained by emotional homeostasis.

Internal switches could be geared toward achieving equilibrium. We see two ways that the notion of homeostasis applies. First, perhaps people self-interrupt to reduce tension from their current activity, as reducing tension is geared towards achieving a balance, per Lewin's field theory notion [19]. Some support for this is suggested by [23] which found that Facebook use is associated with a more positive mood. People may turn to social media such as Facebook as a social break to thus reduce current tension that is experienced. A second way that emotional homeostasis could apply is that people may self-interrupt to a particular activity that enables them to continue their current attentional state. For example, if people are already in a focused state, then they are already in a state conducive to email use (see [23]). It may require effort to move from a state of low challenge to one of high challenge (a characteristic of focus, see Table 1). Thus, if people are already in a state of high challenge and high engagement, it is less effort to simply continue to do activities that maintain this attentional state. This would enable one to maintain a balanced emotional state.

We did not collect contextual information to enable us to distinguish self-interruptions from external interruptions. However, we believe that most FB use was due to self-interruption. We also polled our participants on their email behavior, and of the 15 who replied, 67% reported that they self-interrupt half or more of the time to check email, as opposed to being externally interrupted by an email notification. F2F interaction could be due to either a self-interruption or external interruption. Therefore, we believe that our results could be consistent with the idea that people self-interrupt to try to move towards a state of equilibrium.

We therefore propose the following hypothesis: people switch tasks (and consequently, attentional states) so as to attain an emotional equilibrium. Perhaps people seek out those communication media and those communication partners to attain a balanced state. Thus, perhaps we turn to our colleagues and friends for emotional homeostasis? This is a hypothesis that can be empirically tested in future research.

Implications for multitasking research

Our study can be used to inform other multitasking research. Our results could lead to further investigations about what other subsequent behaviors could be associated with attentional states, including the use of other types of digital and communication media. Moreover, an understanding of how state transitions occur and what the associated activities are could be an interesting avenue to explore. Also, a wider range of attentional, as well as emotional states could also be examined. The idea of emotional homeostasis, a new idea in multitasking research, should be further studied as well.

Our results contrasting application switching and Internet switching could lead to other investigations around why Internet switching might lead people to check and spend more time on FB and Email, as well as engage in more F2F interactions. Is this behavior habitual or are there perhaps other factors involved, such as that Internet switching provides cues which lead one to switch more to these tasks? All of these questions invite further scrutiny.

Our goal is to understand the workplace experience so as to provide insight on how people can improve their experiences. Our results on productivity self-reports, coupled with our multitasking results, suggest that people could feel more productive (and consequently, happier) in the workplace if they could have a better understanding of their own workplace communication behavior. We feel that our results can be used to inform the design of workplace tools that could provide people with better feedback on their communication patterns and activity switching behaviors.

Limitations

Our participants all had at least a Bachelor's degree and half were researchers. Therefore, we can only generalize our results to highly educated information workers. It is very possible that the ESM probes could have led to switching behaviors, as they interrupted participants. Interruptions have been recognized as an issue with ESM [13]. However, the probe could be answered in a few seconds and the participants were instructed to cancel any probe that they could not answer due to it interrupting them. When asked after the study, some participants reported that this interruption side effect was a hindrance.

We used SenseCam photos as a proxy for face-to-face interaction. Our software could not distinguish unique faces--we can only use the counts as an estimate of amount of F2F interaction, not number of different interactants. Therefore, the F2F interaction measure should be regarded as a rough proxy of how much F2F interaction one had, not number of people. The SenseCam likely underestimated interaction counts since a photo was taken about every 15 seconds; an interaction that occurred between shots would not have been captured.

CONCLUSIONS

Our study raises new issues concerning multitasking and distractions. Our results suggest that, contrary to what has been assumed for some time in multitasking research, people may first be in a particular attentional state that makes them susceptible to being distracted. Our results of window switching due to attentional and interaction baselines also suggest that this type of multitasking behavior could encourage further communication behavior, some of which could be distractions from work. The relationship of multitasking and communications (as potential distractors or attractors) is very complex and we hope that our study can lead to new research directions to gain a deeper understanding of the topic.

ACKNOWLEDGMENTS

This material is based upon work supported by the NSF under grant #1218705.

REFERENCES

1. Adler, R.F. and Benbunan-Fich, R. Self-interruptions in discretionary multitasking. *Computers in Human Behavior*, 2013, *29* (4). 1441-1449.
2. Aral, S., Brynjolfsson, E. and Alstyne, M.W.V. Information Technology and Information Worker Productivity. *Information Systems Research*, 2011.
3. Barley, S., Meyerson, D. and Grodal, S. Email as a Source and Symbol of Stress. *Organization Science*, 2011, *22* (4). 887-906.
4. Buck, R. Social and emotional functions in facial expression and communication: The readout hypothesis. *Biological Psychology*, 1994, *38*. 95-115.
5. Chrousos, G. and Gold, P. The concepts of stress and stress symptom disorders: Overview of physical and behavioral homeostatis. *JAMA*, 1992, *267* (9). 1244-1252
6. Czerwinski, M., Horvitz, E. and Wilhite, S., A diary study of task switching and interruptions. in *Proceedings of the ACM Conference on Human Factors in Computing Systems*, (2004), 175-182.
7. Dabbish, L., Mark, G., #237, Gonz, c.M., #225 and lez. Why do i keep interrupting myself?: environment, habit and self-interruption *Proceedings of the SIGCHI Conference on Human Factors in Computing Systems*, ACM, Vancouver, BC, Canada, 2011, 3127-3130.
8. Ean, L.C. Face-to-face Versus Computer-mediated Communicaton: Exploring Employee's Preference of Effective Employee Communication Channel. *International Journal for the Advancement of Science and Arts*, 2010, *1* (2). 38-47.
9. Festinger, L. *A Theory of Cognitive Dissonance*. Stanford University Press, Stanford, CA, 1957.
10. Gonzalez, V.M. and Mark, G., "Constant, Constant, Multi-tasking Craziness": Managing Multiple Working Spheres. in *Proceedings of the ACM Conference on Human Factors in Computing Systems*, (Vienna, Austria, 2004), 113-120.
11. Grandey, A.A., Tam, A.P. and Brauburger, A.L. Affective States and Traits in the Workplace: Diary and Survey Data from Young Workers. *Motivation and Emotion*, 2002, *26* (1). 31-55.

12. Heider, F. Social perception and phenomenal causality. *Psychological Review*, 1944, *51* (6). 358-374.
13. Hektner, J., Schmidt, J. and Csikszentmihalyi, M. *Experience Sampling Method: Measuring the quality of everyday life*. Sage, Thousand Oaks, CA, 2007.
14. Herzberg, F. *The Motivation to Work*. Transaction Publishers, 1993.
15. Hodges, S., Williams, L., Berry, E., Izadi, S., Srinivasan, J., Butler, A., Smyth, G., Kapur, N. and Wood, K. SenseCam: A Retrospective Memory Aid *Ubicomp*, 2006, 177-193.
16. Iqbal, S.T. and Horvitz, E., Disruption and Recovery of Computing Tasks: Field Study, Analysis and Directions. in *Proceedings of the ACM Conference on Human Factors in Computing Systems*, (San Jose, California, USA, 2007), 677-686.
17. Jin, J. and Dabbish, L.A. Self-interruption on the computer: a typology of discretionary task interleaving *Proceedings of the SIGCHI Conference on Human Factors in Computing Systems*, ACM, Boston, MA, USA, 2009, 1799-1808.
18. Kohler, W. *Dynamics in Psychology*. Liverright, New York, 1942.
19. Lewin, K. Defining the "Field at a Given Time.". *Psychological Review*, 1943, *50*. 292-310.
20. Mark, G., Gonzalez, V.M. and Harris, J. No task left behind?: examining the nature of fragmented work in *Proceeding of the SIGCHI conference on Human factors in computing systems* ACM Press, Portland, Oregon, USA 2005, 321-330
21. Mark, G., Hausstein, D. and Klocke, U. The cost of interrupted work: more speed and stress *Proceedings of the SIGCHI Conference on Human Factors in Computing Systems*, ACM, Florence, Italy, 2008, 107-110.
22. Mark, G., Iqbal, S.T., Czerwinski, M. and Johns, P. Bored mondays and focused afternoons: the rhythm of attention and online activity in the workplace *Proceedings of the 32nd annual ACM conference on Human factors in computing systems*, ACM, Toronto, Ontario, Canada, 2014, 3025-3034.
23. Mark, G., Iqbal, S.T., Czerwinski, M. and Johns, P. Capturing the Mood: Facebook and Face-to-Face Encounters in the Workplace *ACM Conference on Computer Supported Cooperative Work*, 2014, (to appear).
24. Mark, G., Wang, Y. and Niiya, M. Stress and multitasking in everyday college life: an empirical study of online activity *Proceedings of the SIGCHI Conference on Human Factors in Computing Systems*, ACM, Toronto, Ontario, Canada, 2014, 41-50.
25. Neuberg, S.L., Kenrick, D.T. and Schaller, M. Human Threat Management Systems: Self-Protection and Disease Avoidance. *Neuroscience and Biobehavioral Reviews*, 2011, *35*. 1042-1051.
26. O'Conaill, B. and Frohlich, D., Timespace in the workplace: dealing with interruptions. in *CHI*, (1995), 262-263.
27. Posner, J., Russell, J.A. and Peterson, B.S. The circumplex model of affect: An integrative approach to affective neuroscience, cognitive development, and psychopathology. *Development and Psychopathology*, 2005, *17*. 715-734.
28. Schaufeli, W., Salanova, M., Gonzalez-Rom, V. and Bakker, A. The measurement of engagement and burnout: A two sample confirmatory factor analytic approach. *Journal of Happiness studies*, 2002, *3*. 71-92.
29. Watson, D., Clark, A.L. and Tellegen, A. Development and validation of brief measures of positive and negative affect: The PANAS scales. *Journal of Personality and Social Psychology*, 1988, *56* (6). 1063-1070.
30. Wood, W. and Neal, D.T. A new look at habits and the habit-goal interface. *Psychological Review*, 2007, *114* (4). 843-863.

The Importance of Publicly Available Social Networking Sites (SNSs) to Entrepreneurs

Toni Ferro
Human Centered Design and Engineering
University of Washington
tdferro@uw.edu

ABSTRACT
This study examines the use of social networking sites (SNSs) such as Facebook and LinkedIn by entrepreneurs. The results contribute to the growing body of research on the uses of SNSs in the workplace. The findings show that entrepreneurs use SNSs in some of the same ways workers at large companies do (e.g. to cultivate business relationships and find job candidates) as well as some unique ways (e.g. to find credible subcontractors and to develop fundamental business relationships). Understanding the potential of SNSs to support work suggests implications for SNS design and theory development.

Author Keywords
Social networking sites; SNS; publicly available online service; PAOS; coworking.

ACM Classification Keywords
H.5.3 [Information Interfaces and Presentation]: Group and Organization Interfaces – Computer Supported Cooperative Work.

General Terms
Management; Design.

INTRODUCTION
In 2008, Skeels and Grudin predicted that social networking sites (SNSs) would eventually become as important in the workplace as email and instant messaging [25]. And recent research has indicated that SNSs have the potential to provide important workplace benefits such as supporting relationship development and socializing new members in an organization [13, 26].

However, to date, SNSs have not been broadly adopted in the workplace. Studies have shown that some employers have guidelines prohibiting the use of SNSs in the workplace and other employers restrict access to SNSs on their networks altogether [13, 15]. The reluctance of workplaces to adopt SNSs is not surprising given the difficulty of envisioning the workplace benefits of SNSs. Unlike other workplace software that supports specific tasks such as submitting expense sheets, tracking budgets, or storing documents, SNSs such as Facebook are perceived to have primarily social uses and to be "productivity killers" [2, 25]. SNSs exhibit what Richter and Reimer call nutzungsoffenheit, "a type of openness whereby the artefact does not lend itself to or even determine a particular form of usage" [24]. Perceptions of SNSs as counter-productive in the workplace combined with their openness complicates the definition of specific user goals and makes predictions about the value of deploying SNSs within the workplace difficult, just as it was for email and IM [25].

Difficulty predicting the value of SNSs in the workplace is at odds with the reality that business owners need clear information to make good investment, policy, and design decisions. Studies examining SNSs in the workplace are needed to provide information about what large companies can hope to achieve by deploying them, what entrepreneurs can hope to achieve by using them, as well as the true disadvantages of SNS use in the workplace.

Theory development in particular is needed to bring clarity to our currently limited understanding of social networking in the workplace. SNSs encourage individual and collective creativity; therefore the advantages and disadvantages of SNSs in the workplace are more feasibly articulated through low-level theories as opposed to findings about specific systems.

Developing theory requires a broad array of SNS studies in a variety of work contexts. To date many studies of social networking at work have focused on workers in large corporations [2, 7, 8, 25, 26, 28, 29, 30]. These studies have surfaced important findings about the potential of SNSs in the workplace and more studies like these are needed.

The study presented here contributes to the existing body of research by examining how entrepreneurs use publicly available SNSs such as Facebook and LinkedIn to support their work. This study's focus on entrepreneurs broadens the base of findings about SNSs in the workplace, contributing to our understanding of the advantages and disadvantages of SNSs in the workplace. In addition, this study supports theory development about the design and use of SNSs in the workplace. The next section reviews relevant previous research.

CSCW 2015, March 14–18, 2015, Vancouver, BC, Canada.
Copyright 2015 © ACM 978-1-4503-2922-4/15/03...$15.00.
http://dx.doi.org/10.1145/2675133.2675300.

SOCIAL NETWORKING SITES (SNSS) IN THE WORKPLACE

Nardi et. al. argue that "the assemblage of people found through personal networks" are more important to a worker's success than their organization or team [20]. Recent studies into the value of SNSs in the workplace support this argument.

Arguably, the most well understood use of SNSs in the workplace is for business marketing. At the time of this writing a Google Books search for "social media marketing" results in more than 1.4 million results and includes titles such as "Social Media Marketing for Dummies" and "Maximizing LinkedIn for Sales and Social Media Marketing." Academic papers about the impact of social media on marketing are common as well [16, 18].

Recently, many studies have examined the practices workers undertake through SNSs apart from marketing and sales. Log analyses, survey studies, and interview studies have resulted in both high-level quantitative results and detailed qualitative results about how workers are using SNSs in the workplace.

When reviewing the previous studies of SNSs in the workplace some usage patterns emerge. Categorizing the previous findings supports the development of hypotheses about the use of SNSs in the workplace and creates a framework for analyzing the findings presented here.

Five high-level categories of SNS use emerged from the previous research: Relationship development, building, and maintenance; Information seeking; Self presentation; Status awareness; and Organization socialization. A detailed summary of findings are presented in Table 1 by category along with the problems relating to SNSs in the workplace reported in previous studies.

User base is an important dimension of SNS use in the workplace and is also accounted for in Table 1. Some previous studies examined enterprise proprietary SNSs used only by employees of a specific company. Other studies examined publicly available SNSs (for example, Facebook). The following sections discuss previous studies that examined the uses of enterprise proprietary and publicly available SNSs in the workplace.

Enterprise Proprietary SNSs

The most notable study of enterprise proprietary SNSs was conducted at IBM. Researchers studied the use of Beehive, an IBM-developed, Facebook-like application. IBM researchers reported Beehive uses in all five of the usage categories presented in Table 1 [7, 8, 26]. Another study looked at the use of an enterprise proprietary SNS by the Rat City Rollergirls (RCRG), a Roller Derby League of about 100 people located in Seattle, Washington [11]. And researchers investigated the use of Yammer, an enterprise-proprietary, Twitter-like application, deployed within a large (~30,000 employees) Fortune 500 company [29].

Enterprise Proprietary SNSs: Relationship development, building, and maintenance

Findings related to relationship development, building, and maintenance appeared frequently in the studies of enterprise proprietary SNSs in the workplace. Importantly, researchers report a number of different ways that participants use SNSs to make new contacts. This is in contrast to previous SNS research conducted in non-work contexts, which shows that individuals do not frequently use SNSs to initiate new connections [2, 19].

IBM employees use Beehive to perform "people sensemaking" by examining "profiles of people they do not know" and gleaning information about them that helps them in future online or in-person interactions. Sometimes connecting to new people through Beehive lead to "significant business and personal interactions outside the site." IBM employees expect that forming relationships on Beehive with others doing work they are interested in will help them achieve their long-term goals. And IBM employees use Beehive specifically to promote their projects and draw the attention of company executives [7]. Similarly, in a study of a Fortune 500 company more than 40% of participants Agree or Strongly Agree that Yammer helps them "Find people who share similar interests" [29].

In addition to meeting new people through SNSs, enterprise workers frequently use SNSs to maintain existing relationships. IBM employees connect with close colleagues as well as acquaintances on Beehive in order to "maintain relationships with others on the site" [7, 8].

The Rat City Rollergirls have no physical space of their own. Their SNS serves as a place where league members build and maintain relationships with each other. League members use their SNS to conduct such activities as planning happy hours and craft nights, sharing photos and YouTube clips, and asking for help with house sitting [11].

Enterprise Proprietary SNSs: Information seeking

Information seeking using enterprise proprietary SNSs was only reported in the study of Yammer in a Fortune 500 Company. Yammer was used for reaching out to ask questions of others [29]. Unsurprisingly, enterprise proprietary SNSs are not used for a wide variety of information seeking activities given that they primarily contain information that is generated within the company.

Enterprise Proprietary SNSs: Self presentation

Self-presentation using enterprise proprietary SNSs was only reported in the study of IBM employees using Beehive. IBM employees present themselves on Beehive by posting personal photos, discussing hobbies, highlighting

Table 1. A summary of previous research findings about the uses of enterprise proprietary and publicly available SNSs to support work

Enterprise Proprietary SNSs	Publicly Available SNSs
Relationship Development, Building, and Maintenance	
Finding people who share similar interests [7, 29]	Participating in professional groups [28]
People sensemaking [7]	Learning about colleagues to prepare for an initial conversation [25]
Keeping in contact with others [7, 8], media sharing (photos and videos) [11]	Finding business partners [23], recruiting employees [28]
Planning offline activities [11]	Developing associations [13], strengthening relationships through information exchange [25], Increasing feelings of connectedness [30]
Soliciting help [11]	Managing contact information [23], keeping a relationship alive after meeting someone in person [25]
Promoting projects to executives (potential supporters) [7]	Building social capital by connecting contacts to each other [25]
	Staying in touch with past colleagues and alumni [23, 25, 28]
Information Seeking	
Reaching out to ask questions [29]	Following technical news [28], keeping up on industry trends [25, 30], learning about a topic [13]
	Searching for experts [23]
	Finding current product reviews [30]
Self Presentation	
Presenting oneself [7]	Presenting oneself [23], sharing personal information [13]
	Boundary regulation (negotiating the professional and personal online) [25, 28]
Status Awareness	
Finding out what other individuals are working on [7, 29]	Finding out what other individuals are working on [25], awareness of what other groups are working on [30], awareness of others' job statuses [25]
Awareness of others' moods and personal lives [7]	Awareness of others' moods and personal lives [25]
Awareness of others' physical location and travel plans [7]	Awareness of others' physical location and travel plans [25]
Awareness of specific project and task statuses [11]	
Awareness about the company and the industry [29]	
Organization Socialization	
Integration of new and off-site organization members [11, 26]	
Increased group cohesion [7]	
Problems with SNSs in the workplace	
Managing multiple profiles [7]	Boundary regulation [25, 28]
Noise-to-value problems [29]	Targeted advertising and location tracking [28]

their professional experience, and describing their goals. IBM researchers note that "identity management and people sensemaking are tightly coupled" and that technology design plays a role in how identities are crafted and interpreted online [7].

Enterprise Proprietary SNSs: Status awareness

The IBM study and the RCRG study included findings related to status awareness. Log data showed that Beehive status messages most frequently contained "a description of the user's current work activity, a reference to the user's mood or state of mind, or a statement about his/her physical location." Beehive users find this information valuable for people sensemaking and maintaining awareness of the locations and moods of others [7].

RCRG members post personal status messages as well as project statuses to their SNS. One participant requests project updates through the SNS by posting questions such as "Who is responsible for this project and where are you at?" In addition, the teams in the league use their SNS to track participation at practice, which determines whether or not a member can participate in the next bout [11].

Nearly 60% of participants in the Yammer study Agree or Strongly Agree that Yammer helps them "Find out what others are working on" [29]. And nearly 40% of participants Agree or Strongly Agree that Yammer helps them learn more about their company (for example, events and product releases) and their industry [29].

Enterprise Proprietary SNSs: Organization socialization

Findings related to organization socialization were unique to enterprise proprietary SNSs. Members of the RCRG are added to SNS groups for their team and committees as soon as they join the league. New members have built-in associations and are able to interact with other members and get information about what is going on in the league right away [11].

Researchers at IBM found that newer employees and employees outside the US realized "greater social capital benefits" from using Beehive than other users suggesting that Beehive contributes to organization socialization. New and distributed employees were able to create large contact networks in the organization through Beehive without having to meet and interact with people face to face [26]. In addition an IBM manager reported that online interaction through Beehive increased "group cohesion amongst his employees" [7].

Publicly Available SNSs

The most notable study of the use of publicly available SNSs in the workplace was conducted at Microsoft where researchers examined the use of publicly available SNSs such as Facebook, Linked In, and Twitter over the course of five years [2, 25, 28]. In another study, researchers surveyed workers in technically oriented online groups (e.g. meetup groups and Google groups) about their work-related use of publicly available online services (PAOSs) such as Twitter, Linked In, Basecamp, and Google Docs [13]. German researchers asked workers and students about the activities they conduct using publicly available SNSs [23]. And finally, researchers studied Twitter use at a large IT company [30].

Publicly Available SNSs: Relationship development, building, and maintenance

As in studies of enterprise proprietary SNSs, all of the previous studies of publicly available SNSs in the workplace included findings about relationship development, building, and maintenance. Most commonly, study participants use SNSs to build and maintain existing relationships.

Microsoft employees use Facebook for reconnecting to former classmates and colleagues" and for strengthening their existing relationships through information sharing on Facebook [25, 28]. Microsoft employees use LinkedIn to keep track of business contacts and to "keep a relationship alive" after meeting someone "at a trade show, conference, or professional meeting" [25]. One Microsoft employee connects members of her LinkedIn network to each other as a way to "build social capital" [25].

German workers and students also use SNSs to stay in touch with people they already know (87.1%) and to manage their contacts (67.3%) [23]. And Twitter users at a large IT company feel more connected to coworkers they already know when they see their personal life updates on Twitter [30]. Finally, more participants in a survey of members of online groups use publicly available SNSs for Developing Associations (62%) than other types of activities such as information sharing (50%) [13].

Publicly available SNSs are also used for making new business connections and for learning more about people before meeting them. German participants use SNSs to find business partners (17%) [23] and Microsoft sales and marketing employees use LinkedIn for recruiting and participating in online groups [28]. Like workers at IBM who use Beehive for people sensemaking, Microsoft employees and employees at a large IT company use SNSs to prepare for their first interaction with someone they will soon meet [25, 30].

Publicly Available SNSs: Information seeking

Unsurprisingly, information seeking through publicly available SNSs is more common than information seeking through enterprise proprietary SNSs. Employees at large companies use Facebook and Twitter status updates from colleagues to learn about new technology as well as broader industry trends such as career evolutions [25, 28, 30]. An employee at a large IT company uses Twitter to find current information about products, explaining that Amazon reviews are not as up to date as the information on Twitter

[30]. German workers and students use SNSs to search for experts (49.8%) [23] and members of online groups use SNSs to learn about specific topics (60%) [13].

Publicly Available SNSs: Self presentation

Findings related to self-presentation came up in the Microsoft studies of SNSs in the workplace very differently than they did for employees in the IBM study. Microsoft employees experienced issues with "boundary regulation," in that they had trouble keeping the boundary between their personal and professional lives in place while using a single profile on Facebook. Some Microsoft participants noted that it is difficult to maintain an online identity that makes sense to their entire network [25, 28].

Many German workers and students reported using SNSs specifically for "presenting myself" (44.6%), sharing pictures (62.6%), and sharing information (80.2%) [23]. Members of online groups reported using SNSs for work related sharing of their personal information (46%) [13].

Publicly Available SNSs: Status awareness

Somewhat surprisingly, publicly available SNSs are used for status awareness in some of the same ways enterprise proprietary SNSs are used. Microsoft participants use Facebook to stay aware of the "mood, personal life, travel plans, projects, and job status" of people in their network. And some participants specifically use Facebook to determine when a coworker will return from a trip [25]. Employees in a large IT company use Twitter to keep up with what is going on with their coworkers (are they working late a lot, are they dealing with something important at home, etc.), and to stay aware of what other groups are working on [30].

SNSs are open systems that do not predetermine specific uses and therefore the studies discussed here have surfaced important information about how workers are leveraging SNSs to support their business goals.

Other studies of SNSs in the workplace

Other studies of SNSs in the workplace focus on such things as security concerns with social media in the workplace [21], motivating workers to contribute to social media in the workplace [5], methods of SNS implementation in the enterprise [24], and the communication affordances of SNSs [27]. These studies do not focus specifically on the activities workers conduct through SNSs and so are not discussed in detail here.

RESEARCH QUESTIONS

This study broadens the base of findings from which to develop design guidelines and theoretical understandings of the value of SNSs to support work. This study focuses on how entrepreneurs use SNSs and addresses the following research questions.

R1: How do entrepreneurs use SNSs to support their work?

R2: How are the uses of SNSs different for entrepreneurs than for workers in large companies?

R3: How do previous findings and findings about entrepreneurs effect workplace systems design and design theory?

METHODS

This study consists of semi-structured interviews with 14 entrepreneurs. Seven are sole proprietors (or independent contractors), six are cofounders of companies with between two and six employees, and one is retired and works on personal projects. Seven of the participants are men and seven are women. The participants, their professions and their company sizes are listed in Table 2. Participant names have been anonymized.

Participants were recruited through coworking location email lists and proprietors, and through others who work at coworking locations. Coworking locations provide office space (usually for a fee) to workers such as independent contractors, sole proprietors, and employees of startups.

The interviews were semi-structured and were roughly one hour long. The interviews included questions about the participant's work, their company, their coworkers, and their use of publicly available SNSs and other services to support their work. If participants did not bring up Facebook, LinkedIn, or Twitter, they were asked about their

Table 2. Study participants

Name	Profession	Employees
Alex	Software developer – independent contractor (IC)	1
Bob	Cofounder of a tech startup	4
Cameron	Cofounder of a tech startup	2
David	Software developer – IC	1
Eric	Technical director for corporate events – IC	2
Felicia	Lawyer – sole entrepreneur	1
Georgia	Cofounder of a non-tech startup	2
Kelly	Lawyer – sole entrepreneur	1
Larry	Cofounder of a non-tech startup	6
Mary	Cofounder of a tech startup	2
Nancy	Online magazine writer, editor, and book author	4
Oliver	Marketing specialist – IC	1
Patsy	Performer – sole entrepreneur	1
Rachel	Author and writing coach	1

business use of these systems. The interviews were transcribed and coded using Dedoose for mentions of Facebook, LinkedIn, and Twitter, as well as other types of publicly available systems.

Like previous studies of SNSs in the workplace, this study is not intended to be generalized broadly. As Table 2 shows, roughly half of the participants in this study have technology-related jobs and therefore it is reasonable to expect that they use technology to support their work more regularly than other types of entrepreneurs. The findings presented here are intended only to contribute to and complement the growing body of findings about the uses of SNSs in the workplace not to suggest that the uses presented here apply to all entrepreneurs. These results expand the kinds of workers and contexts represented in the body of research about SNSs in the workplace.

RESULTS

The participants in this study use publicly available SNSs to support their work in a variety of ways. To relate this work to previous studies about SNSs in the workplace, the results are presented using the same high-level categories that emerged out of previous studies (see Table 1) and the relevant previous studies are referenced in each subsection.

Relationship development, building, and maintenance

As in previous studies, relationship development, building, and maintenance are the most frequent interactions participants report conducting through SNSs. Participants use SNSs to develop new relationships with potential funders, clients, mentors, and visionaries and to find candidates for job openings. Participants also use SNSs for building and cultivating relationships that were started elsewhere and for participating in business communities.

Relationship development: Connecting to potential funders, clients, mentors, and visionaries

This study shows that like workers in the enterprise, entrepreneurs use SNSs for making new contacts with people they have not met. Entrepreneurs in particular use SNSs to connect to people outside their companies such as potential funders and mentors.

Entrepreneurs value SNSs as a way to connect with people who can provide them support such as funding or mentorship. For example, Mary, the co-founder of a two-person startup, uses SNSs to create and cultivate relationships with potential funders and mentors. At the time of the study Mary's company was taking part in a business accelerator. (Business accelerators provide funding and mentorship for startups to reduce the time it takes them to get their product to market. In exchange the partners in the business accelerator get a partial share in the businesses they fund [6].) Because Mary is in the very early stages of getting her startup off of the ground, making new business contacts is critical. When she joined her business accelerator some of the partners in the accelerator suggested she "go out there on my LinkedIn and see who you want to meet and I can connect you to whoever." She feels that making connections through the LinkedIn accounts of her accelerator's partners is a "powerful thing."

Connecting with new people through SNSs is also important for Felicia and Kelly, who are both lawyers and sole entrepreneurs in the early stages of establishing their businesses. They value SNSs such as LinkedIn as well as online groups not just to reconnect with previous business contacts, but also to connect to new people who are doing similar work and can provide tips about getting their businesses off the ground.

In addition to using Linked In, entrepreneurs use Facebook to connect to leaders in their fields. Rachel writes books relating to "consciousness and the human potential movement," and helps others with their writing through workshops and coaching. She characterizes making new connections on Facebook and LinkedIn as "meeting people." She recently started an online friendship with a "visionary" artist. When asked if this type of activity affected her work Rachel said "absolutely," explaining that it makes a difference in her writing and the workshops she conducts. She said connecting to people "expands my inner world and expands my view of the world," and that many of her connections reflect "the latest in thought" in her field.

These findings show that entrepreneurs use publicly available SNSs to connect to potential supporters and people with similar interests in much the way employees at IBM use Beehive. IBM employees use Beehive to "campaign" for their projects and to get their "ideas in front of senior management" [8]. Entrepreneurs value publicly available SNSs as a way of making contacts with people who have the potential to support their projects, such as funders and mentors. Previous research also found that employees at large corporations use SNSs to find people with similar interests in much the same way that Rachel did when connecting to an artist she was interested in on Facebook [7, 29].

Relationship development: "Prospecting" for employees

Finding potential employees through SNSs was a common activity reported by participants. Bob and Larry are both founders of small startups that use SNSs to find candidates to fill positions at their companies. Bob uses LinkedIn "for prospecting potential candidates" and posting job openings. And employees at Larry's company use LinkedIn when they are "looking for certain talent." Using LinkedIn is one of the ways they "shake the trees to see if [they] can find people that want to jump in." In addition, if a candidate is recommended to Larry's company, they use LinkedIn to "scope them out."

Facebook is also used to find reliable subcontractors. Oliver, a sole entrepreneur who helps startups design and develop their brands, used his Facebook network to find a graphic artist to help with a project. He posted to Facebook that he was "looking for a cartoonist." He got 25 responses to his post, asked for a sketch from each artist, and selected one that he still works with. Oliver's Facebook network gave him quick access to a broad range of potential subcontractors that had the credibility of being recommended to him by people he already knows.

Bob and Larry's activity is similar to Microsoft recruiters who rely so heavily on LinkedIn for recruiting new employees that one participant reported "I can't recall how I did this job before LinkedIn" [2]. Oliver's activity in finding a credible subcontractor by using his network on an SNS appears to be unique to entrepreneurs.

Larry reported using LinkedIn for "scoping people out" while considering them for future employment. This type of activity is related to the people sensemaking IBM researchers identified [7] and could be considered a specific type of people sensemaking activity.

Relationship building: Cultivating business relationships

Cultivating existing business relationships through SNSs was commonly reported by entrepreneurs. Nancy, a full-time writer, reported that sharing information on Facebook was important to building a rapport with her eventual business partner, Adam, who lives overseas. Nancy and Adam built their partnership through repeated interactions over time on publicly available SNSs.

Nancy met Adam when he put a link to her blog on his blog and she contacted him to thank him. They started communicating frequently through email and became Facebook friends as a way of getting to know each other better. She said their relationship grew like any other; they started "spending more and more time together." They had "long discussions on Facebook" and through their discussions they decided to work together.

> *"...by September we had decided to work together, by October we had decided what we were doing and by December we were story gathering and we finished that book in May of last year."*

Nancy's experience getting to know her co-founder through information sharing on an SNS is similar to activity reported in the IBM studies where 1) participants met people with similar interests on Beehive and 2) new and distributed team members were more quickly socialized into their organization [26]. However, the types of relationships that the IBM participants formed were not as fundamental to their professional lives as the connection that Nancy reported making with Adam. For example, IBM workers did not report engaging in activities with colleagues they met on Beehive that compared to starting small businesses or co-writing books. Forming this type of fundamental working relationship through SNSs appears to be unique to entrepreneurs.

Relationship building: Participating in business communities

Entrepreneurs use SNSs as a way to enjoy the camaraderie of a business community. Oliver, a marketing contractor, takes part in a Facebook group that was formed by a marketing professional he admires. He actively takes part in the group by posting and responding to other people's posts. When asked if he expects that his participation in this group will bring him work at some point, he responded no,

> *"there are communities that you choose to be a part of and being a part of that community means participating in it ..."*

Oliver participates in this group to feel like he is part of a professional community, something employees of large companies may inherently feel because there are so many other employees working at their company.

Kelly and Felicia, lawyers starting their own businesses, also participate in groups as a way to take part in their business community. They both belong to online groups through the state and local bar associations as well as to an online group for moms who are also attorneys.

Kelly said of her online groups "it feels good to have them there." Being a member of professional communities is a security blanket for Kelly as she anticipates needing help or having questions as her business becomes more established.

Using publicly available online groups as a way to belong to business communities is certainly not unique to entrepreneurs, however this study suggests that business community membership may be more important for at least some entrepreneurs than for workers in large companies. Joining groups as a way to feel a part of a community is not something that came up in previous research. Researchers at Microsoft found that participants joined LinkedIn and Facebook groups, but primarily as a method of "boundary regulation" – as a way of segmenting their connection populations [29].

Relationship maintenance: Keeping business relationships alive

Once business contacts are made, SNSs are an important resource for entrepreneurs, making it possible for them to build on those business relationships in a low-key way with very little effort. Just as was described in the Microsoft study, entrepreneurs do such things as connect to business contacts they have met in person through SNSs as well as connect the people in their networks to each other in order to build social capital [25].

After Mary, a startup founder, meets someone at a conference she will "shoot a LinkedIn to them." This reminds the contact of their meeting and creates a communication pathway for her to contact them in the future either online or through her newsletter. And Rachel, a writer, also stays connected to people she met at a workshop by connecting to them through a Facebook group that was created specifically for workshop attendees.

Both Mary and Rachel like connecting their contacts to each other. Mary has nearly 400 business contacts on LinkedIn and builds social capital by connecting them.

> *"When somebody wants to meet somebody in my network, I can usually get something in return."*

Rachel also benefits from connecting other people to each other. She explained,

> *"On LinkedIn I call myself The Connectrix, because I love to connect people. Not only people, but you know people and information, people and opportunities, etc."*

Overall, relationship development, building, and maintenance are important to entrepreneurs who do such things as find new collaborators or employees, learn more about potential collaborators or employees, create contacts with potential clients and funders, meet mentors, and cultivate business relationships through publicly available SNSs.

Self presentation

For entrepreneurs, self-presentation is critical, particularly for sole entrepreneurs. For some entrepreneurs, their SNS presence is necessarily a blend of work and personal information, because their business identity is tightly coupled with their professional identity.

Demonstrating "thought leadership" is particularly important to Oliver, a sole entrepreneur, who works as a marketing consultant for small businesses. He participates in groups on Google+ specifically to present himself as capable of providing valuable services to small businesses. He describes his participation as,

> *"...connecting with communities that are dealing with small business issues and trying to be helpful there, trying to raise my profile within those communities as someone who is always there and always helpful, building social capital so that people look to me for answers."*

Self-presentation through interaction is also important to Nancy and her collaborator, Adam. Nancy and Adam write an online magazine and online books about "self-organizing workgroups" and "soul-satisfying work." They have a Facebook page where they post links to their articles and information about their books. However, they also interact with each other, conducting online conversations on their Facebook page, as a way of demonstrating self-organized work.

For other entrepreneurs, Facebook allows them to market themselves as individuals. Patsy, a performer, explained that Facebook is a required part of the business, because

> *"...often as part of my contract with the producer of the show, I have to promote on social media."*

Presenting herself on Facebook in a way that consists of more than just advertising is important for Patsy to be successful,

> *"[I] also just try to be a human on there ... so people don't feel like they are constantly being marketed to."*

For Patsy it is required to advertise her upcoming performances and for her it is important to interact and engage with her professional followers in a personal way.

Self presentation through SNSs is uniquely important to entrepreneurs, who use interactions on SNSs to establish themselves as thought leaders and engage directly with their potential clients.

IBM researchers found that users presented themselves on Beehive by posting "about you" information, status messages, photos, and lists [7]. In contrast, some entrepreneurs establish themselves primarily through their interactions with groups and individuals instead of only through profile information and status posts.

Status awareness

No entrepreneurs mentioned using SNSs to keep up with another's work, travel plans, or moods. The entrepreneurs in this study were either sole entrepreneurs or had only a few coworkers that they worked with closely and kept up with in other ways. Only Patsy, a performer, reported relying on Facebook for status awareness.

Patsy performs in about 50 shows a year and uses Facebook as a way to find "gigs." "Calls for auditions" are posted on Facebook, which makes it the "best way to stay abreast" of which shows are happening and where applications are open. She follows a Facebook group dedicated to performers that lets her know "if somebody is looking for acts." Patsy is on Facebook all day, because "messages and notifications" come up there and it is the best way for her to track what performances are happening when.

In general, entrepreneurs did not report using SNSs to monitor the status of their projects or coworkers as workers in large companies did. However, uniquely to entrepreneurs like Patsy, using Facebook all day to monitor the day-to-day status of work opportunities is critical.

Problems with SNSs in the workplace

Overall, publicly available SNSs are important to entrepreneurs, however some participants discussed shortcomings and weaknesses in the SNSs they use and other participants reported not using specific SNSs at all.

Patsy and Oliver have problems with "boundary regulation" on Facebook as Microsoft employees reported in [25]. As a result Patsy, a performer, has two profiles, one for herself and one for her performer persona and Oliver keeps his personal profile and his business page entirely separate.

Patsy is frustrated by Facebook's policy that does not allow multiple personal profiles and does not allow profiles to be under performer names. Instead Facebook wants performers to use business pages. The problem with business pages is that "everyone who likes your [business] page doesn't automatically see your posts anymore." Instead "you have to pay for people to see your promoted posts." She says for performers this is especially unfair, because "I shouldn't have to pay for my friends to see my posts."

Patsy has additional concerns with Facebook in that she does not like the "quality of the interaction," it offers and resents "the demands that it makes on you." In her profession she has to use Facebook to be successful because of its "ubiquity," and therefore Facebook has taken away some of her agency as a performer. This is a particular problem, because she feels that with Facebook she is not a technology consumer and instead is being consumed. She does not feel like Facebook is providing a service that helps her with her business and instead she feels like Facebook is taking any information it can from her.

Oliver also uses Facebook for business begrudgingly. He echoed Patsy's concerns and said that he does not have business conversations on Facebook, because "their [Facebook's] motivation is to sell you and everything they can get about you," which makes it a bad place for business communication. In addition Oliver has had trouble getting support from Facebook when he has had problems with his business page. He had so much trouble that he abandoned a business page that he was having problems with and started his current one under a slightly different name.

Other participants expressed no desire to use Facebook for business. Larry does not use Facebook for business simply because "It's not a business tool." And Mary, who uses LinkedIn for business activities, said Facebook is a "silly way to communicate" and that she would prefer that people pick up the phone and call her. Bob thinks Facebook is a good tool for Business-to-Consumer (B2C) marketing, but that it does not help much for his company, which is Business-to-Business (B2B).

Facebook was not the only SNS that participants had complaints about. Many participants reported not understanding what LinkedIn was for, saying they had profiles and had accepted connections, but were not sure how else to use it.

These results illustrate a lack of consensus about the value of publicly available SNSs for business. Many participants reported using and valuing SNSs for work, however, some of the same participants reported finding the SNSs they use or other SNSs to be frustrating to use for business or to have no business value at all.

These results show very little discussion of Twitter, even though Twitter was specifically discussed with each participant. Some participants used Twitter for a while, but then stopped and others openly said they felt it had little value. The participants that use Twitter use it primarily to disseminate information, often in sync with their Facebook accounts. No participants reported connecting to new people through Twitter as was found of Yammer in [29] and only one participant said that he had used Twitter to keep up with colleagues as was discussed in [30], and he no longer used Twitter at the time of the interview.

DISCUSSION

Studies of SNSs in the workplace have previously focused on enterprise-proprietary and publicly available SNSs in large corporations. Five categories of work activities emerged from previous research. The research presented here contributes to the existing findings by focusing on entrepreneurs and their use of SNSs to support their work. What is interesting about these findings is not that some activities are unique to entrepreneurs and instead that the business uses of SNSs are broader than previously reported. Together with previous studies this study contributes to the overall picture of the emerging role SNSs are playing in the workplace.

Entrepreneurs use SNSs in many of the same ways as workers in large companies. That such vastly different populations of workers use SNSs in similar ways points to the potential of SNSs to more broadly support workers in the future. Like workers in large companies, entrepreneurs use publicly available SNSs to connect with potential funders and mentors, to connect to people with similar interests, to find job candidates, to cultivate business relationships, to keep business relationships alive, to build social capital by connecting others, and to present themselves.

In addition, entrepreneurs use publicly available SNSs in unique ways. Participants used SNSs to find credible subcontractors, to develop fundamental business relationships, to participate in business communities, to establish their business identity by demonstrating thought leadership and through interaction with others, and to maintain awareness of job opportunities. A summary list of the activities participants reported conducting through SNSs is listed in Table 3.

These findings have implications both on the design of SNSs that support work and research programs that investigate social media in the workplace.

Designing Social Networking Sites to Support Work

The prospect of designing SNSs specifically to support work requires new ways of thinking about workplace systems design. Designing information systems typically requires what Gerson and Star referred to as "due process" where the varying needs of the system's users are articulated. Difficulties ultimately arise because systems requirements must align with implementation conditions that are impossible to perfectly document ahead of time [14]. Hughes et. al. similarly argue that design teams need a requirements document that distills the "rich, highly

Table 3. The activities entrepreneurs conduct through publicly available SNSs

SNS	Activity
Facebook	
Relationship development, building, and maintenance	Meeting thought leaders in your field
	Using a social network to find credible job candidates
	Spending time with potential business partners to get to know them better
	Building social capital by connecting others
	Keeping communication pathways open to business contacts
Self presentation	Exhibiting "thought leadership"
	Interacting with professional followers
Status awareness	Staying aware of job opportunities
LinkedIn	
Relationship development, building, and maintenance	Looking for and learning about job candidates
	Receiving introductions to potential funders and clients
	Building social capital by connecting others
	Keeping communication pathways open to business contacts
Online Groups	
Relationship Development, Building and Maintenance	Finding advisors and mentors
	Participating in a professional community
	Keeping communication pathways open to business contacts
Self presentation	Building social capital by participating in groups with potential customers
Status Awareness	Staying aware of job opportunities
Twitter	
Self presentation	Exhibiting "thought leadership"

detailed, highly textured" description that is the result of user research into a "resulting set of compromises" [17].

Designing SNSs requires a different kind of due process and comes with a different set of difficulties. Requirements documents that attempt to identify SNS use cases and user scenarios have little value. User scenarios that are developed and evaluated before an SNS is launched are likely to have very little (if any) relationship to the actual practices enacted by users once the SNS is deployed.

The value of SNSs lies in their ability to invite and compel creative, purpose-driven, opportunistic appropriations. Creative uses for SNSs such as building social capital by connecting others and attracting the attention of potential funders are unlikely to be identified and documented through requirements gathering. The tensions that exist in the design of traditional workplace systems (requirements documents and codified systems vs. complex realities) are altered when designing open systems such as SNSs.

Another tension in systems design is illustrated by Ackerman's social-technical gap. He notes that there is a gap between how people live their lives and what technical systems can realistically support. People are nuanced and make complex decisions where technology lacks nuance and makes decisions based on predefined models. People are able to recontextualize information for different people, whereas technologies cannot. People are good at communicating, dealing with conflict, actively negotiating and renegotiating norms, whereas systems are not [1].

The openness of SNSs provides some relief from the difficulties that arise from the fundamental divide between human and machine. The potential for SNSs to change the nature of the socio-technical gap is evidenced by their current workplace uses. Workers and entrepreneurs use SNSs for self-presentation, awareness, people sensemaking, relationship development and maintenance, among other activities that require nuance and active negotiation and renegotiation of norms. The specifically human ways in which workers are appropriating SNSs to support their work goals suggests that SNSs can ameliorate some of the difficulties of the socio-technical gap (for example, organization socialization) as well as provide new opportunities for engagement with others (for example, attracting the attention of potential supporters).

The challenge then for workplace SNS designers is to create open systems that invite creative, opportunistic appropriations that support business goals. While it may seem that building an open system that supports a variety of uses is easier than building a system for specific purposes, in reality designing workplace SNSs that are adopted broadly may require in depth research that goes beyond specific work practices and use cases.

Orlikowski highlights important elements of a worker's social practice that may help designers assess the needs of their users. She suggests that technology use is determined by the "facilities," "norms," "interpretive schemes," and other structures inherent to the user. Orlikowski examined the deployment of Lotus Notes into different companies. Different groups adopted the system in different ways based on the facilities (e.g. email, database), norms (e.g. learning through doing, being a team player), interpretive schemes (e.g. technology is good, technology is bad), and other structures in the organization (e.g. cooperative culture, team incentive structure). Orlikowski suggests that understanding more about these elements of the users and groups can help designers better understand how to design systems that support users [22].

Bradner et. al. develop a similar concept of "social affordances" that foregrounds the complexity of the interaction between users within groups. The authors conducted a study of Babble (an early type of IM) and found again that different groups had adopted the system differently. In one group the manager used the system to "waylay" employees by waiting for them to sign into Babble and then instant messaging them some work that needed done. And in another group Babble was used as a way to unobtrusively ask questions of more senior people. Therefore, similar to Orlikowski's argument, Bradner et. al. argue that the relationship between the social characteristics of a group and the properties of the technology result in social affordances that have an impact on the systems adoption and use [4].

Both the Orlikowski and the Bradner study were conducted on systems that were already deployed in the workplace making it possible to assess the structures and social affordances affecting system adoption. Because of the difficulties in predicting the uses of SNSs in the workplace, implementation, research, and iteration cycles may be required before a successful SNS design is reached. SNSs have the potential to support business goals, however, new ways of thinking about workplace systems design and iteration cycles are required to realize their potential.

Redefining Social Networking Sites (SNSs)

In 2013, Ellison and boyd defined SNSs as systems where a user can 1) create a profile, 2) create and share a list of other users they are connected to, and 3) read and contribute to streams of content. In addition, they argued that SNSs are fundamentally different from earlier types of online services because they are centered on individuals' profiles instead of on topics [3, 10]. However, as has been discussed in previous research, this feature-based definition has become increasingly problematic. A growing number of sites such as YouTube and Flickr have incorporated the features Ellison and boyd use to define SNSs even though their primary purposes are quite different [9].

The results of this study also illustrate the potential problems with this definition. Using Ellison and boyd's definition, Facebook, Linked In, and Twitter are all SNSs. However, participants in this study do not use Twitter in the same ways that they use Facebook and LinkedIn. For example, no participants in this study use Twitter to meet new business contacts or review information about a potential collaborator.

That participants use Twitter in fundamentally different ways than they use Facebook and LinkedIn and sometimes use online groups to conduct similar activities as those they conduct on Facebook and LinkedIn, affirms the notion discussed in previous research that feature-based understandings of publicly available online services are not sufficient and that new non-feature based ways of differentiating online services are needed [9, 12].

Classifying online services in terms of the work practices that take place through them has important implications for the design and implementation of systems and for future research programs. For example, knowing that for some entrepreneurs groups are used to conduct similar activities to those that are conducted through SNSs could affect the development and deployment of enterprise systems. And future studies like the Microsoft study that examined the use of Facebook, LinkedIn, and Twitter could change with the realization that online groups (even those not attached to systems with people networks) are used to conduct activities that are similar to those conducted through SNSs. Further research that examines the activities entrepreneurs are conducting through various social media systems could help businesses more intelligently determine what types of systems they need to deploy to achieve certain goals.

CONCLUSIONS

Patsy's use of Facebook all day to support her business indicates that Skeels' and Grudin's prediction that SNSs will become as important for work as email and IM [25] is here, at least for some entrepreneurs. Patsy's constant connection to Facebook speaks to the potential for enterprise systems that incorporate status posts (where Patsy communicates like "a human") and group membership (where Patsy connects to others in her field and sees job postings).

The notion of incorporating an enterprise system where workers spend time "acting like a human" and posting social posts remains controversial. The findings presented here as well as the findings presented in previous studies illustrate the potential value of overtly incorporating social interaction into workplace systems. New ways of thinking about the design and assessment of workplace systems will be needed to realize the potential of SNSs in the workplace.

ACKNOWLEDGMENTS

Thanks to the coworking location proprietors and participants for theis input on this study. And thanks to Dr. Mark Zachry for his feedback on this paper.

REFERENCES

1. Ackerman, M. S. The Intellectual Challenge of CSCW: The Gap Between Social Requirements and Technical

Feasibility. *Human-Computer Interaction 15*, (2), 179–203.

2. Archambault, A. and Grudin, J. A longitudinal study of Facebook, Linkedin, & Twitter use. *CHI 2012*.
3. boyd, d. m. and Ellison, N.B. Social Network Sites: Definition, History, and Scholarship. *Journal of Computer Mediated Communication*, *13*, (1), 210–230.
4. Bradner, E., Kellogg, W. A., and Erickson, T. The Adoption and Use of 'BABBLE': A Field Study of Chat in the Workplace. *ECSCW* 1999.
5. Brzozowski, M. J., Sandholm, T. and Hogg, T. Effects of Feedback and Peer Pressure on Contributions to Enterprise Social Media Categories and Subject Descriptors. *GROUP* 2009.
6. Cohen, S. What Do Accelerators Do? Insights from Incubators and Angels. *Innovations*, *8*, (3/4), 19–25.
7. DiMicco, J. M., Geyer, W., Millen, D.R., Dugan, C. and Brownholtz, B. People sensemaking and relationship building on an enterprise social networking site. *HICSS* 2009.
8. Dimicco, J. M., Millen, D. R., Geyer, W., Dugan, C., Brownholtz, B., Muller, M. and Street, R. Motivations for Social Networking at Work. *CSCW* 2008.
9. Divine, D., Ferro, T., and Zachry, M. Work through the Web: A Typology of Web 2.0 Services. *SIGDOC* 2011.
10. Ellison, N. B and boyd, d. Sociality through Social Network Sites. in Dutton, W. H. ed. *The Oxford Handbook of Internet Studies.* Oxford University Press, Oxford, 2013, 151-172.
11. Ferro, T. The Rat City Rollergirls and the Potential of Social Networking Sites to Support Work. *SIGDOC* 2012.
12. Ferro, T. and Zachry, M. Networked knowledge workers on the web: An examination of trends 2008 – 2010. in Cruz-Cunha, M. M. ed. *The Handbook of Research on Business Social Networking: Organizational, Managerial, and Technological Dimensions*. Business Science Reference, Hershey, PA, 2011, 942–963.
13. Ferro, T. and Zachry, M. Technical Communication Unbound: Knowledge Work, Social Media, and Emergent Communicative Practices. *Technical Communication Quarterly*, *23*, (1), 6–21.
14. Gerson, E. M. and Star, S. L. Analyzing Due Process in the Workplace. *ACM Transactions on Office Information Systems, 4*, (3), 257 – 270.
15. Half, R. Whistle-but don't tweet- while you work. Robert Half Technology, 2009.
16. Hoffman, D. L. and Fodor, M. Can You Measure the ROI of Your Social Media Marketing? *Sloan Management Review*, *52*, (1).
17. Hughes, J. A., Randall D., and Shapiro, D. From Ethnographic Record to System Design: Some Experiences from the Field. *Computer Supported Cooperative Work* 1993.
18. Kotler, P. Reinventing Marketing to Manage the Environmental Imperative. *Journal of Marketing*, *75*, (4), 132-135.
19. Lampe, C., Ellison, N. and Steinfield, C. A Face(book) in the Crowd: Social Searching vs. Social Browsing. *CSCW* 2006.
20. Nardi, B. A., Whittaker, S. and Schwarz, H. NetWORKers and Their Activity in Intensional Networks. *CSCW* 2002.
21. Nuha, N., Molok, A., Islamic, I., Lumpur, K., Chang, S. and Ahmad, A. Disclosure of organizational information on social media: perspectives from security managers. *PACIS* 2013.
22. Orlikowski, W. J. Using Technology and Constituting Structures : A Practice Lens for Studying Technology in Organizations. in Ackerman, M. S., Halverson, C. A., and et. al. ed. *Resources, Co-Evolution and Artifacts*. Springer, London, 2008. 255–305.
23. Richter, A. and Koch, M. Functions of Social Networking Services. *International Conference on the Design of Cooperative Systems*, 2008.
24. Richter, A. and Riemer, K. Corporate Social Networking Sites – Modes of Use and Appropriation through Co-Evolution. *ACIS* 2009.
25. Skeels, M. and Grudin, J. When social networks cross boundaries: a case study of workplace use of Facebook and Linkedin. *GROUP* 2009.
26. Steinfield, C., DiMicco, J. M., Ellison, N. B. and Lampe, C. Bowling online: Social networking and social capital within the organization. *Communities and Technology*, 2009.
27. Treem, J. W. and Leonardi, P. M. Social Media Use in Organizations: Exploring the Affordances of Visibility, Editability, Persistence, and Association. *Communication Yearbook*, *36*, 143–189.
28. Zhang, H., De Choudhury, M., and Grudin, J. Creepy but Inevitable? The Evolution of Social Networking. *CSCW* 2014.
29. Zhang, J., Qu, Y., Cody, J. and Wu, Y. A case study of micro-blogging in the enterprise: use, value, and related issues. *CHI* 2010.
30. Zhao, D. and Rosson, M. B. How and Why People Twitter: The Role that Micro-blogging Plays in Informal Communication at Work. *GROUP* 2004.

Author Index

www.ingramcontent.com/pod-product-compliance
Lightning Source LLC
LaVergne TN
LVHW080101011026
849160LV00013B/1012
* 9 7 8 1 4 5 0 3 3 7 6 6 3 *